The Rough Guide

W9-APH-880

Spain

written and researched by

Simon Baskett, Jules Brown, Marc Dubin, Mark Ellingham, John Fisher, Geoff Garvey, Graham Kenyon, Phil Lee, Chris Lloyd and Iain Stewart

with additional updating by

Robert Alcock, Bethan Davies, Sarah Lazarus,
Holly Pelham and Paul Smith

ROUGH GUIDES

NEW YORK • LONDON • DELHI
www.roughguides.com

Rias Altas

Rias Bajas

Gijón
Santander
A Coruña
Oviedo
Cangas
de Onis
Bilbao
Santiago de
Compostela
Lugo
ASTURIAS
PICOS DE
EUROPA
PAIS
GALICIA
Rio Ebro
CANTABRIA
LA
Ponferrada
León
Pontevedra
Ourense
Astorga
Burgos
Vigo
Tui
Palencia
Rio Miño
A Guarda
Valença
Verin
Zamora
Valladolid
Rio Duero
Caminha
Chaves
CASTILLA-LEÓN
Braga
Bragança
Porto
Vila Real
Salamanca
Segovia
Guadalajara
Viseu
Ávila
Ciudad
Rodrigo
MADRID
SIERRA DE GREDOS
COMUNIDAD
DE
Coimbra
MADRID
P O R T U G A L
Plasencia
Aranjuez
Castelo
Branco
Rio Tajo
Toledo
EXTREMADURA
Rio Tajo
Cáceres
Trujillo
Santarem
Mérida
Ciudad
Real
LISBON
Badajoz
Rio Guadiana
Evora
Jerez de los
Caballeros
Zafra
Valdepeñas
CASTILLA-LA MANCHA
Beja
Úbeda
Aracena
Córdoba
Jaén
Baeza
Vila Real
de Santo
Antonio
Sevilla
Ecija
ANDALUCÍA
Rio Guadalquivir
Faro
Ayamonte
Huelva
Granada
Coto
Doñana
Antequera
SIERRA NEVADA
LAS
ALPUJARRAS
Ronda
Málaga
Cádiz
Arcos de
la Frontera
Costa de la Luz
Marbella
Costa del Sol
Algeciras
Gibraltar
Ceuta
Tangier
Tétouan
N
Melilla
Standard motorway
Toll motorway
0   150 km
MOROCCO
▽ *Canary Islands*

ii

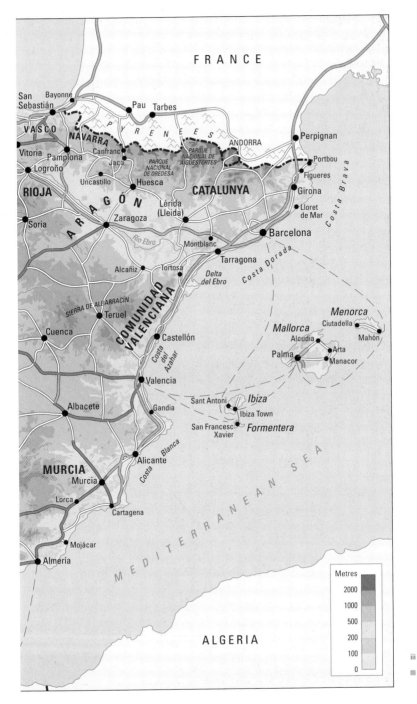

FRANCE

San Sebastián Bayonne Pau Tarbes

VASCO NAVARRA P Y R E N E E S ANDORRA Perpignan

Vitoria Canfranc PARQUE NACIONAL DE AIGÜESTORTES Portbou

Pamplona Jaca PARQUE NACIONAL DE OREDESA Figueres

Logroño Uncastillo Huesca CATALUNYA Girona Costa Brava

RIOJA A R A G Ó N Lérida (Lleida) Lloret de Mar

Soria Zaragoza Barcelona

Río Ebro Montblanc

Alcañiz Tortosa Tarragona Costa Dorada

SIERRA DE ALBARRACÍN Delta del Ebro

Cuenca Teruel Menorca

COMUNIDAD VALENCIANA Mallorca Ciutadella Mahón

Castellón Alcudia Arta

Costa del Azahar Palma Manacor

Albacete Valencia

Gandia Sant Antoni Ibiza

Costa Blanca Ibiza Town

San Francesc Xavier Formentera

MURCIA Alicante

Murcia

Lorca

Cartagena M E D I T E R R A N E A N   S E A

Mojácar

Almería

ALGERIA

Metres	
2000	
1000	
500	
200	
100	
0	

iii

Introduction to

Spain

If you are coming to Spain for the first time, be warned: this is a country that fast becomes an addiction. You might intend to come just for a beach holiday, or a tour of the major cities, but before you know it you'll find yourself hooked by something quite different – by the celebration of some local fiesta, perhaps, or the amazing nightlife in Madrid, by the Moorish monuments of Andalucía, by Basque cooking, or the wild landscapes and birds of prey of Extremadura. And by then, of course, you will have noticed that there is not just one Spain but many. Indeed, Spaniards often speak of Las Españas (the Spains) and they even talk of the capital in the plural – Los Madriles, the Madrids.

This regionalism is an obsession, and perhaps the most significant change to the country over recent decades has been the creation of seventeen *autonomías* – autonomous regions – with their own governments, budgets and cultural ministries. The old days of a unified nation, governed with a firm hand from Madrid, seem to have gone forever, as the separate kingdoms which made up the original Spanish state reassert themselves. And the differences are evident wherever you look: in language, culture and artistic traditions, in landscapes and cityscapes, and attitudes and politics.

The cities – above all – are compellingly individual. Barcelona, for many, has the edge: for Gaudí's splendid *modernista* architecture, the lively promenades of Las Ramblas, 4km of beach, and designer clubs *par excellence*. But Madrid,

Fact file

• Spain's land area is around half a million square kilometres – about twice the size of the UK or Oregon. Of its 40 million-strong population some 99 percent declare themselves Catholic.

• Politically, Spain is a parliamentary monarchy – democracy and the monarchy having been restored in 1977, after the death of General Franco, the dictator who seized power in the Civil War of 1936–39.

• Regionalism is a major force in Spanish politics, with the country divided into seventeen autonomous regions. The most powerful are Catalunya and the Basque Country, where nationalism is a potent force. In the Basque country, the paramilitary organization, ETA, conducts an ongoing campaign of terrorism targeted at "the Spanish state".

• Spanish (Castilian) is spoken as a first language by 74 percent of the population, while seventeen percent speak variants of Catalan (in Catalunya, parts of Valencia and Alicante provinces, and the Balearic islands), seven percent speak Galician, and two percent Basque. As the regional languages were banned under Franco, the vast majority of the people who speak them are also fluent in Castilian.

• The most important newspapers are *El País* and *El Mundo*, both of which are liberal in outlook. But Spaniards read fewer papers than almost all other Europeans – and the bestseller is *Marca*, a daily devoted purely to football.

• A minority of Spaniards attend bullfights; it doesn't rain much on the plains; and they only dance flamenco in the southern region of Andalucía.

although not as pretty, claims as many devotees – most recently, of course, one David Beckham. The city and its people, immortalized in the movies of Pedro Almodóvar, have a vibrancy and style that is revealed in a thousand bars and summer terrazas. Not to mention three of the world's finest art museums and Real Madrid. Then there's Sevilla, home of flamenco and all the clichés of southern Spain; Valencia, the vibrant Levantine city with an arts scene and nightlife to equal any European rival; and Bilbao, a recent entry on Spain's cultural circuit, due to Frank Gehry's astonishing Guggenheim museum.

Monuments range just as widely from one region to another, dependent on their history of control and occupation by Romans and Moors, their role in the "golden age" of Imperial Renaissance Spain, or their twentieth-century fortunes. Touring

△ Aigües Torres Sant Maurici National Park

Castile and León, you confront the classic Spanish images of vast cathedrals and *reconquista* castles – literally hundreds of the latter; in the northern mountains of Asturias and the Pyrenees, tiny, almost organic Romanesque churches dot the hillsides and villages; Andalucía has the great mosques and Moorish palaces of Granada, Sevilla and Córdoba; Castile has the superbly preserved medieval capital, Toledo, and the gorgeous Renaissance university city of Salamanca; while the harsh landscape of Extremadura cradles the ornate *conquistador* towns built with riches from the "New World".

Not that Spain is predominantly about buildings. The landscape holds just as much fascination – and variety. The evergreen estuaries of Galicia could hardly be more different from the high, arid plains of Castile, or the gulch-like desert landscapes of Almería. Agriculture makes its mark in the patterned hillsides of the wine- and olive-growing regions and the rice fields of the Levante. Spain is also one of the most mountainous countries in Europe, and there is superb walking and wildlife in a dozen or more sierras – above all in the Picos de Europa and Pyrenees. Spain's unique

△ Pilgrims' shells and staffs on the Camino de Santiago

fauna boasts protected species like brown bears, the Spanish lynx and Mediterranean monk seals as well as more common wild boar, white storks and birds of prey.

One of Spain's greatest draws is undeniably its beaches – and here too there is a lot more variety than the holiday brochure image. Sure, long tracts of coastline – along the Costa del Sol, in particular – have been developed into concrete hotel and villa complexes, but delightful pockets remain even on the big tourist costas. On the Costa Brava, the string of coves between Palamos and Begur is often overlooked, while in the south there are superb wind-surfing waters around Tarifa and some decidedly low-key resorts along the Costa de la Luz. In the north, the cooler Atlantic coastline boasts the surfing sands of Cantabria and the unspoilt coves of Galicia's estuaries. Offshore, the Balearic islands have some superb sands and, if you're up for it, Ibiza also offers one of the most hedonistic backdrops to beachlife in the Mediterranean.

Hedonism, actually, is pretty much

Spanish time

Spanish time is notionally one hour ahead of the UK – but conceptually Spain might as well be on a different planet. Nowhere in Europe keeps such late hours. Spaniards may not take a traditional midday siesta so much as they used to, but their life cycles remain committedly nocturnal. They'll saunter out around 8pm or 9pm in the evening for a paseo, to greet friends and maybe have a drink and tapas, and if they're eating out, they'll commonly start at 10 or 11pm, often later in Madrid, where it's not unusual for someone to phone around midnight to see if you're going out for the evening.

Like everything else, practices differ somewhat by region. Madrid is famed for staying up the latest, with Andalucía a close second. In the north, particularly in Catalunya, they keep more northern European hours. And, of course, summer nights are the real late, late shows.

△ Plaza Callao at night, Madrid

△ Galician coastline

unavoidable. Wherever you are in Spain, you can't help but notice the Spaniards' infectious enthusiasm for life. In the cities there is always something happening – in bars and clubs, on the streets, and especially at fiesta times. And even in out-of-the-way places there's a surprising range of nightlife and entertainment, not to mention the daily pleasures of a round of tapas, moving from bar to bar, having a beer, a glass of wine or a *fino* (dry sherry) and a bite of the house speciality.

The identity and appeal of each of the regions is explored in the chapter introductions, where you'll find a rundown on their highlights, while in the following pages you'll find a selection of the very best of Spain.

Tapas

Tapas have become international fare in recent years – yet nothing can prepare you for the variety on offer on their home soil. That is, if you're prepared to do things properly, wandering from one bar to another to sample a particular speciality. Although many bars will have a range of tapas on display or on their menu board, most tend to be known for just one or two dishes ... and the locals would not think of ordering anything else. So you might go to one place for a slice or two of *jamón serrano* (cured ham), another for *pulpo Gallego* (deliciously tender pot-cooked octopus), a third for the bizarre *pimientos de Padron* (strange small peppers – about one in ten of which are chilli-hot), and then maybe on to a smoky old bar that serves just *fino* (dry sherry) from the barrel along with slices of *mojama* (dried, pressed roe).

Fiestas

It's hard to beat the experience of arriving in some small Spanish village, expecting no more than a bed for the night, to discover the streets decked out with flags and streamers, a band playing in the plaza and the entire population out celebrating the local fiesta. Everywhere in Spain, from the tiniest hamlet to the great cities, devotes at least a couple of days a year to its festivals. Usually it's the local saint's day, but there are celebrations of harvests, of deliverance from the Moors, of safe return from the sea – any excuse will do. There are also the events of the Catholic calendar, most notably Semana Santa (Holy Week), which in Andalucía sees theatrical religious floats carried through the streets, accompanied by hooded penitents atoning for the year's misdeeds.

Each festival is different. In the Basque country there will often be bulls running through the streets (most famously at Pamplona in July); in Andalucía, horses, flamenco and the guitar are an essential part of any celebration; in Valencia they specialize in huge bonfires and deranged firework displays (climaxing in Las Fallas in March). But this is just the mainstream. Fiestas can be very strange indeed, ranging from parades of devils to full-blown battles with water or even tomatoes.

For more on fiestas, see p.51, and for a calendar of local events, see the listings at the beginning of each chapter.

When to go

Overall, spring, early summer and autumn are ideal times for a Spanish trip – though the weather varies enormously from region to region. The high central plains suffer from fierce extremes, stiflingly hot in summer, bitterly cold and swept by freezing winds in winter. The Atlantic coast, in contrast, has a tendency to damp and mist, and a relatively brief, humid summer. The Mediterranean south is warm virtually all year round, and in parts of Andalucía positively subtropical, warm enough to wear a T-shirt by day even in the winter months.

In high summer the other factor worth considering is tourism itself. Spain plays host to some thirty million tourists a year – almost one for every resident – and all the main beach and mountain resorts are packed in July and August, as are the major sights. August, Spain's own holiday month, sees the coast at its most crowded and the cities, by contrast, pretty sleepy.

Note that these are all **average temperatures** – and whilst Sevilla, the hottest city in Spain, can soar into the nineties at midday in summer, it is a fairly comfortable 23–27°C (75–80°F) through much of the morning

and late afternoon. Equally, bear in mind that temperatures in the north, in Galicia for example, can approach freezing point at night in winter, whilst mountainous regions can get extremely cold at any time of year.

Average temperatures

		Jan	Mar	May	Jul	Sep	Nov
Madrid, Castile	(°C)	9	15	21	31	25	13
	(°F)	49	59	70	88	77	56
Málaga, Costa del Sol	(°C)	17	19	23	29	29	20
	(°F)	63	67	74	84	84	68
Sevilla, Andalucía	(°C)	15	21	26	35	32	20
	(°F)	59	70	78	95	90	68
Pontevedra, Galicia	(°C)	14	16	20	25	24	16
	(°F)	58	61	68	77	75	61
Santander, Cantabria	(°C)	12	15	17	22	21	15
	(°F)	54	59	63	72	70	59
Barcelona, Catalunya	(°C)	13	16	21	28	25	16
	(°F)	56	61	70	83	77	61
Cap Bagur, Costa Brava	(°C)	14	16	20	27	25	16
	(°F)	58	61	68	80	77	61
Alicante, Costa Blanca	(°C)	16	20	26	32	30	21
	(°F)	61	68	78	90	86	70
Mallorca, Balearics	(°C)	14	17	22	29	27	18
	(°F)	58	63	72	84	80	65

things not to miss

It's not possible to see everything that Spain has to offer in one trip – and we don't suggest you try. What follows is a selective taste of the country's highlights: outstanding buildings, natural wonders, spectacular festivals and unforgettable journeys. They're arranged in five colour-coded categories, which you can browse through to find the very best things to see and experience. All highlights have a page reference to take you straight into the guide, where you can find out more.

01 Guggenheim Museum, Bilbao Page **515** • The undulating titanium of Gehry's flagpiece has become one of the iconic buildings of our age.

02 Skiing Pages **385, 699 & 841** • Spain's mountian ranges – from the Pyrenees to the Sierra Nevada – offer some wonderful skiing right through to late spring.

04 Goya Page **102** • The genius of this artist ranges through his light court scenes to the haunting black paintings he created near the end of his life.

03 Jamón serrano Page **237** • A few thin slices of the best cured *jamón* are a must for any carnivore.

05 Las Alpujarras Page **386** • Drive over lemons and walk old mulepaths in this picturesque region of mountain villages nestling in the southern folds of the Sierra Nevada.

06 Picasso Page **106** • Picasso's portrayal of the agony of Spain's struggle and suffering against fascism in *Guernica* is the centrepiece of Madrid's Reina Sofia gallery.

07 Salamanca Page **415** • Wander the narrow streets of this ancient university town with its untouched Gothic and Renaissance buildings.

08 Modernisme Page **754** • The sculptural forms of Barcelona's *modernista* architects – most famously Gaudí – define the city's exuberant architectural heritage.

09 Las Fallas Page **921** • In March, Valencia erupts in festivities as giant models are burnt and fireworks crackle across town to celebrate San José.

11 Parque Natural de Monfragüe Page **225** ● Birds of prey, especially eagles and vultures, abound in this protected area of Extremadura.

10 Semana Santa Page **302** ● Easter Week sees processions of masked penitents parade around villages and towns across Spain, with the biggest events in Sevilla and Málaga.

12 Paella Page **926** ● The subtle saffron taste of this rice-based dish is best enjoyed with a sea view in its home province of Valencia.

13 Port Aventura Page **898** ● Travel through time and around the globe in a day of rides and fun at Spain's premier theme park.

14 **Carnaval** Page **51** • Take to the streets with fancy dress and floats; Cádiz and Sitges throw two of the most spectacular carnival parties.

15 **Picos de Europa** Page **567** • This stunning northern area of mountain peaks and gorges has superb walking, canoeing and rock-climbing.

16 **Seafood** Page **46** • From Galicia's *pulpo* (octopus) and *veiras* (scallops) to Andalucía's fried *boquerones* and tiny *chanquetes*, Spain's seafood is unbeatable for quality and variety.

17 **Velázquez** Page **101** • The greatest Spanish artist? Decide for yourself in the salons of the Prado gallery in Madrid.

18 **San Fermín, Pamplona** Page **528** • There's no festival quite like San Fermín – but leave the Running of the Bulls to the locals.

19 **Ibiza and Formentera's beaches** Page **967** • The islands' little-developed beaches vary from gem-like coves to sweeps of white sand.

20 **Sherry** Page **48** • There are few greater pleasures than a chilled glass of *fino* or *manzanilla* accompanied by a bite of the local speciality.

21 **Miró** Page **752** • The bold paintings and abstract forms of the artist's work are housed in the wonderfully sympathetic building of the Fundació.

22 The Pyrenees Page **708** • This spectacular range separating France from Spain rises to over 3000m near Benasque; here wild ponies graze at the Puerto de Escaleta.

23 Aqueduct, Segovia Page **186** • Eight hundred metres long, this solid piece of Roman engineering has been spanning the Castilian town for nearly 2000 years.

24 Clubbing Page **977** • Forget sleep, experience everything else to excess, on Ibiza – the ultimate party island.

25 La Liga Page **55** • Spanish football is arguably the best in Europe right now. Get to a match (or just watch in a bar) and see for yourself what tempted the boy Beckham.

26 A night on the tiles, Madrid Page **127** • Delight in the capital's most traditional of rituals – a night of bar hopping and clubbing rounded off by a dawn reviver of hot chocolate and *churros*.

27 Cota de Doñana Page **339** • Doñana's unique habitats enable this vast national park to host a myriad birds and other wildlife, including the Iberian lynx.

28 Wine Page **47** • Spain has a formidable range of quality wines – as well as the famed Riojas, try the Albariño whites from Galicia, or the Ribeira del Duero reds.

29 **Mini Hollywood, Almería** Page **402** • Ride into town for a shoot-out or a drink at the saloon on the set of *The Good, the Bad and the Ugly*, deep in Almerían desert.

30 **Pavelló Mies van der Rohe**
Page **750** • Visit Barcelona for the perfect lines of this exquisite building by the father of Modernism.

31 **Mezquita, Córdoba** Page **349**• Nothing can prepare you for the breathtaking Grand Mosque of Córdoba – one of the world's most beautiful buildings.

32 The Rastro, Madrid Page 94 • Join the locals and spend the morning rooting for bargains and meeting friends at the capital's flea market.

33 Fería de Abril Page 303 • Sevilla's week-long fiesta is Andalucía at its celebratory best, with a vast fair of flamenco dance tents, and horsemen and women dressed to kill.

34 Paradores Page 42 • Converted castles and monasteries provide the atmospheric setting for many of these luxurious hotels.

35 **Sevilla** Page **297** • The quintessential Andalucian city with sun-drenched plazas, Moorish monuments and more bars than seems remotely feasible.

36 Dalí Museum, Figueres
Page **830** • The egg-capped museum is as surreal as its creator – who lies in a mausoleum within.

37 Deià old town, Mallorca
Page **1001** • Explore the labyrinthine alleys overlooking terraced fields tumbling down to the sea.

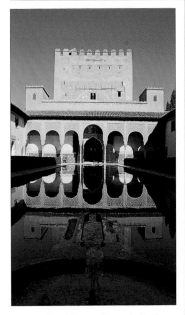

38 Alhambra, Granada
Page **371** • The legendary Moorish palace complex is a monument to sensuality and contemplative decoration.

39 Flamenco
Page **1083** • The stamp of heels and heart-rending lament of a *cante jondo* encapsulate the soul of the Spanish South.

40 Windsurfing Page **325** • Catch the wind in Tarifa at one of the world's top windsurfing spots.

41 Toledo Page **151** • The capital of medieval Spain, Toledo has changed little since its depiction in El Greco's paintings.

42 El Camino de Santiago Pages **610 & 618** • The medieval pilgrim route to the shrine of Santiago left a swath of Renaissance and Gothic buildings, not least the great cathedral of Santiago de Compostela at the end of the road.

Using this Rough Guide

We've tried to make this Rough Guide a good read and easy to use. The book is divided into six main sections, and you should be able to find whatever you want in one of them.

Colour section

The front colour section offers a quick tour of Spain The **introduction** aims to give you a feel for the place, with suggestions on where to go. We also tell you what the weather is like and include a basic country fact file. Next, our authors round up their favourite aspects of Spain in the **things not to miss** section – whether it's great food, amazing sights or a special hotel. Right after this comes a full **contents** list.

Basics

The Basics section covers all the **pre-departure** nitty-gritty to help you plan your trip. This is where to find out which airlines fly to your destination, what paperwork you'll need, what to do about money and insurance, about Internet access, food, security, public transport, car rental – in fact, just about every piece of **general practical information** you might need.

Guide

This is the heart of the Rough Guide, divided into user-friendly chapters, each of which covers a specific region. Every chapter starts with a list of **highlights** and an **introduction** that helps you to decide where to go, depending on your time and budget. Likewise, introductions to the various towns and smaller regions within each chapter should help you plan your itinerary. We start most town accounts with information on arrival and accommodation, followed by a tour of the sights, and finally reviews of places to eat and drink, and details of nightlife. Longer accounts also have a directory of practical listings. Each chapter concludes with **public transport** details for that region.

Contexts

Read Contexts to get a deeper understanding of what makes Spain tick. We include a brief history, articles about **architecture**, **wildlife** and **music**, and a detailed further reading section that reviews dozens of **books** relating to the country.

Language

The **language** section gives useful guidance for speaking Spanish and pulls together all the vocabulary you might need on your trip, including a comprehensive menu reader. Here you'll also find a glossary of words and terms peculiar to the country.

Index + small print

Apart from a **full index**, which includes maps as well as places, this section covers publishing information, credits and acknowledgements, and also has our contact details in case you want to send in updates and corrections to the book – or suggestions as to how we might improve it.

Contents

Map and chapter list

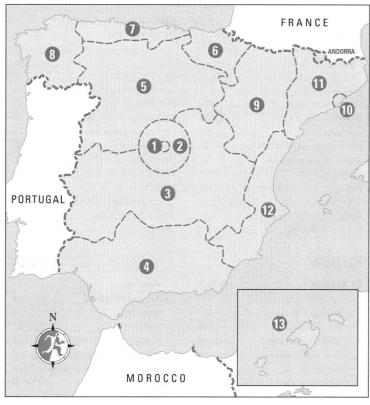

Contents

Contexts

1027–1124

Language

1115

Index and small print

1137–1152

Basics

Basics

Getting there

The most convenient way of getting to Spain from the UK and Ireland is to fly – flights from London take around two hours to Madrid and Barcelona and two and a half hours to Málaga, and the lowest-priced air fares are cheaper than tickets for the long train or bus journey. There are also direct ferry services from Plymouth to Santander and from Portsmouth to Bilbao. From North America a number of airlines fly direct to Madrid, many with onward connections to Barcelona. Occasionally, however – and especially if you're coming from Canada – you may find it cheaper to route via London, picking up an inexpensive onward flight from there. There are no direct flights to Spain from Australia or New Zealand; the quickest route is via Asia.

Air fares always depend on the **season**, with the highest being around Easter and June to the end of September, when the weather is best; fares drop during the "shoulder" seasons – October and March to mid-May – and you'll get the best prices during the low season, November to March (excluding Christmas and New Year when prices are hiked up and seats are at a premium). Note also that flying at weekends ordinarily adds £35/$50 to the round-trip fare; price ranges quoted below assume midweek travel.

You can often cut costs by going through a **specialist flight agent** – either a consolidator, who buys up blocks of tickets from the airlines and sells them at a discount, or a **discount agent**, who in addition to dealing with discounted flights may also offer special student and youth fares and a range of other travel-related services such as travel insurance, rail passes, car rentals, tours and the like. Some agents specialize in **charter flights**, which may be cheaper than anything available on a scheduled flight, but again departure dates are fixed and withdrawal penalties are high. For some of the popular holiday destinations, such as the Costa del Sol or the Balearics, you may even find it cheaper to pick up a bargain **package deal** from one of the tour operators listed below and then find your own accommodation when you get there.

If Spain is only one stop on a longer journey, you might want to consider buying a **Round-the-World (RTW) ticket**. Some travel agents can sell you an "off-the-shelf" RTW ticket that will have you touching down in about half a dozen cities; others will have to assemble one for you, which can be tailored to your needs but is apt to be more expensive. Figure on £1100/$1800 for an RTW ticket including Spain.

Booking flights online

Many airlines and discount travel websites offer you the opportunity to book your tickets online, cutting out the costs of agents and middlemen. Good deals can often be found through discount or auction sites, as well as through the airlines' own websites.

Online booking agents and general travel sites

ⓦ **travel.yahoo.com** Incorporates a lot of Rough Guide material in its coverage of destination countries and cities across the world, with information about places to eat, and sleep etc.
ⓦ **www.etn.nl/discount.htm** A hub of consolidator and discount agent Web links, maintained by the non-profit European Travel Network.
ⓦ **www.expedia.com** Discount airfares, all-airline search engine and daily deals (US only; for the UK,
ⓦ www.expedia.co.uk; for Canada,
ⓦ www.expedia.ca).
ⓦ **www.flyaow.com** Online air travel info and reservations site.
ⓦ **www.gaytravel.com** Gay online travel agent, offering accommodation, cruises, tours and more.
ⓦ **www.hotwire.com** Bookings from the US only.

11

Last-minute savings of up to forty percent on regular published fares. Travellers must be at least 18 and there are no refunds, transfers or changes allowed. Log-in required.

ⓦ**www.lastminute.com** Offers good last-minute holiday package and flight-only deals (UK only; for Australia, ⓦwww.lastminute.com.au).

ⓦ**www.priceline.com** Name-your-own-price website that has deals at around forty percent off standard fares. You cannot specify flight times (although you do specify dates) and the tickets are non-refundable, non-transferable and non-changeable (US only; for the UK, ⓦwww.priceline.co.uk).

ⓦ**www.skyauction.com** Bookings from the US only. Auctions tickets and travel packages using a "second bid" scheme. The best strategy is to bid the maximum you're willing to pay, since if you win you'll pay just enough to beat the runner-up regardless of your maximum bid.

ⓦ**www.travelocity.com** Destination guides and best deals for car hire, accommodation and lodging as well as fares. Provides access to the travel agent system SABRE, the most comprehensive central reservations system in the US.

ⓦ**www.travelshop.com.au** Australian website offering discounted flights, packages, insurance and online bookings.

From the UK and Ireland

There are numerous flights from the UK and Ireland to Spain throughout the year, with charters and cut-price no-frills airlines generally being the least expensive. **Charters** are usually block-booked by package holiday firms, but even in the middle of August they're rarely completely full and spare seats are often sold off at discounts.

Cut-price airlines – such as easyJet, bmibaby and Ryanair – are just as inexpensive, offering mostly single fares, sold direct, on **no-frills flights**. It is advisable to book as far ahead as possible, as these airlines have limited cheap seats on each flight and regular seats are more than twice as expensive. Tickets can be bought over the phone or slightly discounted on the Internet.

Iberia, Spain's national airline, and British Airways have the widest range of **scheduled flights**, including regular services from London to Santiago, Bilbao, Valencia and Sevilla, as well as to the main Spanish destinations. Iberia also offers direct flights from Manchester to Barcelona, while British

Airways flies direct from both Manchester and Birmingham to Madrid and Barcelona. From Dublin you can fly direct with Iberia to Madrid and Barcelona. Aer Lingus also operates direct services from Dublin, but only from April to late October. There are no direct scheduled flights from Belfast to Spain: most routeings are via London or Birmingham.

A typical high-season scheduled **fare** from London to Madrid costs around £180, not including airport tax, though special offers can take the price as low as £55. In low season, reckon on paying around £135, but again, discounts can take this as low as £35. Fares from Dublin to Madrid in high season are around €360, including tax, and €300 in low season. For non-direct flights via London, fares on Aer Lingus, BA and Iberia are basically the same. There is also a scheduled service with Air Europa which only flies from Gatwick to Madrid and Palma, but whose six weekly services tend to be rather cheaper than either BA or Iberia.

Package holiday deals can be worth looking at, especially if you book early, late or out of season. While the cheaper, mass-market packages may seem to restrict you to some of the worst parts of the coast, remember that there's no compulsion to stick around your hotel. Get a good enough deal and it can be worth it simply for the flight – with transfer to a reasonably comfortable hotel laid on for a night or two at each end. Bargains can be found at virtually any high-street travel agent.

City breaks are often available at excellent package rates and destinations on offer include Barcelona, Madrid, Sevilla and Granada, flying from London or Manchester. Prices **from London** vary between around £200 (Madrid) and £240 (Barcelona) for three days (two nights). Prices **from Belfast** run from £300 to £350; city breaks **from Dublin** will cost around €340 (Madrid) and €450 (Barcelona). Adding extra nights or upgrading your hotel is possible, too, usually at a fairly reasonable cost. The prices normally include return flights, airport transfer and bed and breakfast in a centrally located one-, two- or three-star hotel. Again, ask your travel agent for the best deal – especially for those under 26 – and check the addresses on p.12.

Fly-drive deals are well worth considering, too, as a combined air ticket and car rental arrangement can be excellent value. There are also some very good (and very attractive) deals available in **villas and apartments**, especially from companies who specialize in off-the-beaten-track farmhouses and the like. Several companies offer a range of *casas rurales*, on a similar basis to French *gîtes*. Other specialist companies offer an enticing range of **activity or cultural holidays**, ranging from trekking and kayaking to wine and yoga, or more upmarket tours based around the country's historic *paradores*.

Airlines

Aer Lingus UK ☎0845/084 4444, Republic of Ireland ☎0818/365 000, ⓦwww.aerlingus.ie. Direct flights from Dublin to Barcelona and Madrid.

Air Europa ☎0870/240 1501, ⓦwww.aireuropa.com. From Gatwick to Madrid and in summer (May–Sept) to Palma.

Britannia Airways ☎01582/424 155, ⓦwww.britanniaairways.com. Charter flights from twenty UK airports to fourteen destinations in mainland Spain, the Balearics and the Canaries.

bmibaby UK ☎0870/264 2229, Republic of Ireland ☎01/236 6130, ⓦwww.bmibaby.com. British Midland's budget airline, running flights from Cardiff, East Midlands and Manchester to Alicante, Palma and Málaga; East Midlands and Manchester to Barcelona and Murcia; East Midlands to Ibiza; and Teesside to Málaga.

British Airways UK ☎0870/850 9850, Republic of Ireland ☎0141/2222345, ⓦwww.britishairways.com. From Heathrow or Gatwick to Madrid, Sevilla, Bilbao, Palma, Murcia, Barcelona, Málaga, Alicante, Valencia and Gibraltar. Also has direct flights from Glasgow and Birmingham to Madrid and Barcelona, with Madrid also served direct from Manchester and Edinburgh.

British Midland UK ☎0870/607 0555, Republic of Ireland ☎01/407 3036, ⓦwww.flybmi.com. Regular scheduled flights from London Heathrow to Madrid, Palma and Alicante, and to Tenerife in the winter. The online booking service includes both British Midland and bmibaby flights.

easyJet ☎0870/600 0000, ⓦwww.easyjet.com. Budget scheduled flights from London Gatwick, Stansted, Luton, Bristol and Liverpool to Alicante, Barcelona, Málaga and Palma; Luton also flies to Madrid, and Stansted offers routes to Bilbao and Ibiza; East Midlands to Alicante, Barcelona and Málaga; Newcastle to Alicante and Barcelona.

Iberia Airlines UK ☎0845/601 2854, Republic of Ireland ☎01/677 9846, ⓦwww.iberia.com. From Heathrow and Gatwick direct to Madrid, Barcelona, Bilbao, Santiago, Sevilla, Málaga, Alicante, Valencia and Oviedo with internal connections to most other airports in Spain. Also has direct flights from Manchester to Barcelona and from Dublin to Madrid and Barcelona.

Ryanair UK ☎0870/156 9569, Republic of Ireland ☎01/609 7800, ⓦwww.ryanair.com. Seasonal flights from Dublin to Girona and Málaga, and from Stansted to Girona, Reus, Jerez and Murcia.

Virgin Express ☎0800/891199, ⓦwww.virgin-express.com. From Heathrow to Madrid, Barcelona and Málaga. Note that all flights involve changing planes at Brussels.

Flight and travel agents

Air 2000 ☎0870/750 0001, ⓦwww.air2000.com. Charter arm of First Choice Holidays.

Aran Travel International Republic of Ireland ☎091/562 595, ⓦhomepages.iol.ie/~arantvl/aranmain.htm. Good-value flights.

AVRO plc ☎020/8715 4440, ⓦwww.avro-flights.co.uk. UK specialists in charter and scheduled flights.

Bridge the World ☎0870/444 7474, ⓦwww.bridgetheworld.com. Specializing in round-the-world tickets, with good deals aimed at the backpacker market.

CIE Tours International Republic of Ireland ☎01/703 1888, ⓦwww.cietours.ie. General flight and tour agent.

Co-op Travel Care ☎0870/112 0099, ⓦwww.travelcareonline.com. Flights and holidays to the whole of Spain.

Flightbookers ☎0870/010 7000, ⓦwww.ebookers.com. Low fares on an extensive selection of scheduled flights.

Flying Visits Republic of Ireland ☎062/51019, ⓦwww.flyingvisits.ie. City breaks from Dublin to Barcelona and Madrid, and from Cork to Barcelona and Alicante.

Hotel Connect ☎0845/230 888, ⓦwww.hotel.connect.co.uk. London-based accommodation-booking service covering most of the country.

Joe Walsh Tours Republic of Ireland ☎01/676 0991, ⓦwww.joewalshtours.ie. General budget fares agent.

Lee Travel Republic of Ireland ☎021/277 111, ⓦwww.leetravel.ie. Flights and holidays worldwide.

McCarthy's Travel Republic of Ireland ☎021/427 0127, ⓦwww.mccarthystravel.ie. General flight agent.

North South ☎ & ℱ 01245/608 291,
ⓦ www.northsouthtravel.co.uk. Friendly,
competitive travel agency – profits are used to
support projects in the developing world, especially
the promotion of sustainable tourism.
Rosetta Travel Northern Ireland ☎ 028/9064 4996,
ⓦ www.rosettatravel.com. Flight and holiday agent.
STA Travel ☎ 0870/1600 599,
ⓦ www.statravel.co.uk. Worldwide specialists in
low-cost flights and tours for students and under-
26s, though other customers welcome.
Student & Group Travel Republic of Ireland
☎ 01/677 7834. Student and group specialists.
Trailfinders UK ☎ 020/7628 7628,
ⓦ www.trailfinders.co.uk, Republic of Ireland
☎ 01/677 7888, ⓦ www.trailfinders.ie. One of the
best-informed and most efficient agents for
independent travellers.
usit NOW Republic of Ireland ☎ 01/602 1600,
Northern Ireland ☎ 028/9032 7111,
ⓦ www.usitnow.ie. Student and youth specialists for
flights and trains.

Tour operators

www.pride-holidays.com Netherlands-based
online gay and lesbian travel agent, offering good
deals on all types of holiday.
Accessible City Breaks ☎ 01452/729739,
ⓦ www.accessiblecitybreaks.co.uk. City breaks to
Barcelona and Madrid for wheelchair users, sensory
impaired and slow walkers.
Adventure Holidays in Spain
ⓦ www.holidayjunction.co.uk. Activity holidays
including trekking, mountain biking, canoeing and
sea kayaking in northern Spain, Andalucía and
Mallorca.
Alto-Aragon ☎ 01869/337339,
ⓦ www.altoaragon.co.uk. Established English-run
company based in the Valle de Echo organizing
summer hiking and winter cross-country skiing
programmes in the high Pyrenees.
A Taste of Spain ⓦ www.atasteofspain.com.
Organizes cooking holidays in farmhouses throughout
Spain. Prices include accommodation, classes,
excursions and return flights.
Bravobike ☎ 914 139 503, ⓦ www.bravobike.com.
Personalized and guided cycling tours of Madrid, La
Rioja, Extremadura and the Camino de Santiago; also
trekking, horse riding and golf.
Cox & Kings ☎ 020/7873 5018,
ⓦ www.coxandkings.co.uk. Nature tours of the
Aragonese Pyrenees, Andalucía, Extremadura and the
Camino de Santiago, staying in farmhouses.
Discover Andalucía ☎ 956 447 577,
ⓦ www.discoverandalucia.com. Activity holidays

including guided bird-watching, painting and
archeology breaks. Also offers multi-adventure,
mountain biking, cycling and canyoning trips.
Euroadventures ☎ 986 221 399,
ⓦ www.euroadventures.net. Spain-based company
offering sailing, walking, culinary, wine and culture
holidays throughout Spain.
European Cultural and Activity Tours
☎ 01786/812 302, ⓦ www.europe-culture
-activity-tours.com. Links to small, specific-interest
tour operators.
Exodus Travels ☎ 020/8675 5550,
ⓦ www.exodus.co.uk. Walking and cycling in
Andalucía, Mallorca, the Picos de Europa and the
Pyrenees (and most of the other minor mountain
ranges), as well as multi-adventure (climbing, caving,
rafting, etc) cultural and sightseeing trips.
Explore Worldwide Ltd ☎ 01252/760 000,
ⓦ www.exploreworldwide.co.uk. Walking in
Andalucía, Sierra Nevada and the Picos de Europa.
Fantasia Adventure Holidays
ⓦ www.fantasiaadventureholidays.com. Spain-
based British company offering horse-riding,
photography and bird-watching holidays on the Costa
de la Luz.
Golf in the Sun ☎ 01327/350394,
ⓦ www.golfinthesun.co.uk. Golfing holidays and
accommodation in three- and four-star hotels in
Catalunya and Andalucía.
Hotels Abroad ☎ 01689/882500,
ⓦ www.hotelsabroad.co.uk. Specialist operator with
a wide range of accommodation, from rustic
farmhouses to luxurious country manors. Can also
arrange ferries and car rental at discount rates.
Iberocycle ⓦ www.iberocycle.com. Spain-based
company specializing in cycling tours of northern
Spain, La Rioja and Andalucía.
Individual Travellers ☎ 08700/780 194,
ⓦ www.indiv-travellers.com. Farmhouses, cottages
and village houses all over Spain. Can also arrange
flights and ferries.
Inn Travel ☎ 01653/629 000,
ⓦ www.inntravel.co.uk. Graded walking holidays in
Catalunya, Andalucía and the Pyrenees. Independent
walking (not in a group) from inn to inn, while your
luggage is carried on ahead.
Keytel International ☎ 020/7616 0300,
ⓦ www.keytel.co.uk. Official UK agents for Spain's
paradores; occasionally has special offers.
Madrid and Beyond ☎ 917 580 063,
ⓦ www.madridandbeyond.com. Madrid-based
British specialist operator offering anything from
accommodation reservations to city breaks or tailor-
made itineraries throughout Spain.
Martin Randall Travel ☎ 020/8742 3355,
ⓦ www.martinrandall.com. Small-group cultural

tours to Catalunya, Madrid, Toledo and Sevilla, among others; led by experts on art, archeology and music.

Mountain Bike España UK ☎01494/870486 or Spain ☎952 491 137, ⓦwww.mountbik -espana.co.uk. Small company organizing guided mountain-bike tours around the mountains and national parks above Málaga.

Ramblers Holidays ☎01707/331133, ⒺInfo@ramblersholidays.co.uk. Walking, hiking and sightseeing holidays throughout Spain.

Rusticae Hotels ⓦwww.rusticae.es. Association of charming rustic hotels throughout Spain with online reservations.

Rustic Blue ☎958 763 381, ⓦwww.rusticblue.com. Spain-based company specializing in rural holidays, from traditional villages to furnished cave dwellings in the Sacromonte area of Granada. Also organizes specialized and adventure tours.

Sherpa Expeditions ☎020/8577 2717, ⓦwww.sherpa-walking-holidays.co.uk. Trekking in the Sierra Nevada, the Alpujarras, the Pyrenees, the Picos de Europa, Mallorca and the Canaries.

Spain Yoga ☎958 785 834, ⓦwww.spainyoga.com. Yoga holidays run by an experienced British teacher for all levels in a farmhouse in Andalucía.

Spanish Travel Services ☎020/7874 0990, ⓦwww.apatraveluk.com. Spanish flight, city-break and package specialists.

Spanish Yoga Holidays ☎01395/519 628, ⓦwww.spanishyogaholidays.com. Yoga holidays run by an experienced British couple.

Spirit of Adventure ☎01822/880 277, ⓦwww.spirit-of-adventure.com. Activity holidays including climbing, trekking and sea kayaking in Catalunya, Andalucía, Galicia and the Picos de Europa.

Travellers Way ☎01527/559 000, ⓦwww.travellersway.co.uk. Tailor-made holidays and city breaks all over Spain.

Vintage Spain ☎699 246 534, ⓦwww.vintagespain.com. Wine tasting tours of La Rioja, Ribera de Duero and La Mancha by Spain-based operator.

Waymark Holidays ☎01753/516 477, ⓦwww.waymarkholidays.co.uk. Walking holidays in Andalucía, the Pyrenees, the Picos de Europa and along the Camino de Santiago.

Winetrails ☎01306/712111, ⓦwww.winetrails.co.uk. Walking and cycling wine tours of La Rioja, Jerez and Andalucía, staying in small country hotels.

www.yogamallorca.com ☎01386/870 359. Yoga retreats and holidays in Mallorca.

By rail

With the **Channel Tunnel**, you have the choice between crossing over to the continent by boat or taking the Eurostar from Waterloo International in London. Both options involve changing trains in **Paris** (from Nord to Austerlitz via Metro line 5), and again at the **Spanish border**. The standard rail and boat journey is around 27 to 29 hours from London to Barcelona, another five hours to Madrid; with the Eurostar, it's around 17 hours to Barcelona. If you're prepared to pay a good deal extra, you can take the Trenhotel from Paris to Madrid or Barcelona direct, which reduces these journeys by two to three hours.

Two exciting (but more expensive) **alternatives** are the minor routes which cross the central Pyrenees to enter Aragón at Canfranc, or Catalunya at Puigcerdà. On the first of these, Rail Europe will issue a ticket only as far as Oloron in France, from where you have to cross the border by bus. Similarly, on the Catalan route, Rail Europe fares are sold only as far as the French station at Bourg-Madame, just over the frontier from Puigcerdà, where you must change trains. Tickets bought from Connex, however, will take you through to your final destination in Spain. On both routes you may have to spend the night at either of the border towns if you want to see the mountains in daylight.

A **standard rail ticket** currently costs £225 return from London to Madrid and £165 to Barcelona, is valid for two months and allows you to stop anywhere along the way. There is a slight discount for students. If you're travelling by **Eurostar**, it's £160–275 for a return to Madrid or Barcelona (depending on age, season and time of day). Reservation charges from Paris are £3–4 for a seat or around £16 for a couchette (included in the price if you're taking the Eurostar).

Tickets are bookable through some travel agents, main Connex stations and Usit Campus; note that Rail Europe will only sell tickets using the Eurostar. It's also currently cheaper – especially if you're under-26 or a student – to buy your Eurostar tickets from an agent.

If you plan to travel extensively in Europe by train, you might consider buying a rail pass. Details of these are given on p.31.

Eurotunnel, cross-Channel and motorail services

The fastest way to get your car across to the continent is the Eurotunnel service via the Channel Tunnel. The alternative is one of the time-honoured ferry crossings. Once across, if you don't fancy the long drive through France, you could consider putting your car on the Motorail service from Calais to Biarritz or Narbonne, both near the border.

Eurotunnel operates shuttle trains via the Channel Tunnel for vehicles and their passengers only. The service runs continuously between Folkestone and Coquelles, near Calais, with up to four departures per hour (only 1 per hour midnight–6am) and takes 35min (45min for some night departure times), though you must arrive at least 30min before departure. It is possible to turn up and buy your ticket at the toll booths (after exiting the M20 at junction 11a), though at busy times booking is advisable. Rates depend on the time of year, time of day and length of stay (the cheapest ticket is for a day-trip, followed by a five-day return); it's cheaper to travel between 10pm and 6am, while the highest fares are reserved for weekend departures and returns in July and August.

The more traditional cross-Channel options are the **ferry** links between Dover or Folkestone and Calais or Boulogne, or ferries to Caen, Le Havre, Cherbourg and St Malo (from Portsmouth or Poole), or even Roscoff (from Plymouth). Any of these cuts out the trek round or through Paris, and opens up some interesting detours around Brittany and the French Atlantic coast.

Ferry **prices** vary according to the time of year and, for motorists, the size of your car. The Dover–Calais/Boulogne runs, for example, start at about £275–290 open return for a car, two adults and two kids, but these figures can nearly double in high season. Foot passengers should be able to cross for about £17 one-way, or £34 open return. For both ferries and tunnel, fares are lower if you travel during the off-peak time – generally between 10pm and 6am.

Once you're across the Channel you can significantly reduce your driving time by taking the SNCF-operated **Motorail** service, which runs between April and September. Cars and motorbikes are loaded onto the train at Calais – there's one train a week to Biarritz, on the Atlantic coast, and four to Narbonne, on the Mediterranean side of the Pyrenees. The single fare for the Biarritz run costs £465, while the Narbonne route will set you back £505; the price includes a sleeper cabin.

Rail contacts

Eurostar ☎0870/160 6600,
ⓦwww.eurostar.com.
Eurotunnel ☎0870/535 3535,
ⓦwww.eurotunnel.com.
Northern Ireland Railways ☎028/9089 9411,
ⓦwww.nirailways.co.uk. Also sells Interail passes.
Rail Europe ☎0870/584 8848,
ⓦwww.raileurope.co.uk.
SNCF (Motorail service) ☎(+33) 836.35.35.39,
ⓦwww.sncf.fr.
Trainseurope ☎0900/195 0101,
ⓦwww.trainseurope.co.uk.

The ferry to Bilbao and Santander

There are two direct ferry sailings to Bilbao and Santander from Britain. See p.17 for ferry company addresses, or contact your local travel agent for the latest ticket and sailing details; alternatively, you can check out the ferries' website at ⓦwww.seaview.co.uk.

The ferry to **Santander** leaves from Plymouth and is operated by Brittany Ferries. It takes 24 hours and runs on Mondays and Wednesdays during the summer (April to mid-Sept) and Wednesdays and Sundays in March, October and November. Ticket prices vary enormously according to the season, the number of passengers carried and the length of time you want the ticket to be valid for; for example, a return ticket for a car and two adults can cost anything from £485 in low season to £790 in high season. Foot passengers pay around £45–95 one-way (depending on season), and everyone has to book some form of accommodation; a Pullman seat is cheapest at £6 and two-berth cabins are available for £65–85. Tickets are best booked in advance, through any major travel agent.

P&O operates a twice-weekly ferry service from **Portsmouth to Bilbao**. The journey takes approximately 35 hours and leaves Portsmouth on Saturdays and Tuesdays. Return fares for a car and two people work out at between £540 and £935 (according to season), with foot passengers paying £198–325. Cabins are included in these prices. Note that this sailing is significantly cheaper for motorcyclists than for cars, especially if you can find one of the frequent discounts offered by motorcycling publications. Note that this route is often closed for a couple of weeks in January for maintenance.

Ferry companies

Brittany Ferries UK ☎0870/901 2400, **Republic of Ireland** ☎021/4277 801,
ⓦwww.brittanyferries.co.uk. Poole to Cherbourg; Portsmouth to Caen and St Malo; Plymouth to Roscoff and Santander (March–Nov/Dec); Cork to Roscoff (March–Oct only).
Hoverspeed ☎0870/240 8070,
ⓦwww.hoverspeed.co.uk. Twenty-four daily departures. Dover to Calais and Ostend; Newhaven to Dieppe.
Irish Ferries GB ☎0870/517 1717, **Northern Ireland** ☎0800/0182 211, **Republic of Ireland** ☎1890/313 131, ⓦwww.irishferries.com. Dublin to Holyhead; Rosslare to Pembroke, Cherbourg and Roscoff. Continental services March to end Sept.
P&O Portsmouth ☎0870/242 4999,
ⓦwww.poportsmouth.com. Portsmouth to Cherbourg, Le Havre and Bilbao.
Sea Cat UK ☎0870/5523 523, **Republic of Ireland** ☎1800/805055, ⓦwww.seacat.co.uk. Belfast to Stranraer, to Heysham, to Troon; Dublin to Liverpool.
Sea France ☎0870/571 1711,
ⓦwww.seafrance.com. Dover to Calais.

By bus

The main bus routes from Britain to Spain are from London to Barcelona (5 weekly in summer, 3 weekly out of season; 25hr), and Alicante (3 weekly; 32hr) via San Sebastián (21hr). There are also two buses a week to Algeciras (39hr), via Paris, Madrid (27hr), Málaga (36hr) and the Costa del Sol; at least one a week to Pamplona (23hr); and one to Santiago (32hr) along the north coast. Fares start at around £97 single, £132 return (to Madrid), rising to £104 single, £142 return to Alicante.

All these routes are operated by **Eurolines** in Britain and by Iberbus/Linebus and Julia in Spain. In both Britain and Spain tickets are bookable through most major travel agents and on the Internet at ⓦwww.eurolines.co.uk; Eurolines also sells tickets and through-transport to London at all British National Express bus terminals.

Also worth looking at is the **Eurolines Pass**, which allows unlimited travel on all of Eurolines' routes and is available in fifteen-, thirty- and sixty-day versions. The price is seasonal with an under-26s and senior citizens' thirty-day pass costing £153 in low season, rising to £209 during the high season; over-26s will pay £189 and £259 for low/high season. The sixty-day version will cost an additional 15 percent or so, while the fifteen-day one is around thirty percent less. The pass is ideal if you're planning a lot of travel to the major cities, though you'll have to plan your route carefully and be prepared to see a lot of Madrid.

Bus information

Busabout ☎020/7950 1661,
ⓦwww.busabout.com. Busabout runs every 2–3 days on 5 circuits in summer, fewer in winter, taking in 70 European cities, with add-on connections to 5 more, plus a link to London and through tickets from elsewhere in Britain and Ireland. Tickets are available in increments of 15 days, 21 days, 1 month, 2 months or 3 months; there are also special deals on set itineraries. Also sells Flexipasses, allowing 10 or 15 days' travel within 2 months, 21 days' travel within 3 months, or 30 days out of 4 months. The passes are available from STA Travel in the US.
Eurolines UK ☎0870/514 3219, **Republic of Ireland** ☎01/836 6111, ⓦwww.eurolines.co.uk. Tickets can also be purchased from any Eurolines or National Express agent (☎0870/580 8080, ⓦwww.nationalexpress.co.uk or ⓦwww.gobycoach.com). As well as ordinary tickets on its scheduled coach services to an extensive list of over 460 European cities, Eurolines offers a pass for Europe-wide travel, for either 15, 30 or 60 days between 46 European cities, including London, Barcelona and Madrid. Eurolines services to and from Ireland include Dublin–London (via Birmingham and Holyhead); Cork and Killarney–London (via Bristol and Fishguard), Limerick and Tralee–London (via Bristol and Fishguard) and Belfast–London (via Birmingham, Manchester and Stranraer).

Ulsterbus Northern Ireland ☎ 028/9033 7003, ⓦ www.ulsterbus.co.uk. Runs services from Belfast using the Larne–Stranraer crossing to London, Birmingham (via Manchester) and Edinburgh (via Glasgow). Also sells bus passes.

Flights from the US and Canada

There is a fair variety of scheduled and charter flights from most parts of North America to Madrid, often with connections on to Barcelona. Occasionally, however – and especially if you're coming from Canada – you'll find it cheaper to route via London, picking up an inexpensive onward flight from there (see "Flights from the UK and Ireland" for all the details). If Spain is part of a longer European trip, you'll also want to check out details of the Eurail pass, which must be purchased in advance of your arrival and can get you by train from anywhere in Europe to Spain. Price ranges quoted in the following sections assume midweek travel and include tax (around $50 or CAN$40–55).

Iberia flies nonstop to Madrid from New York, Miami and Chicago, and has the advantage that it offers connecting flights to almost anywhere in Spain, often very good value if booked with your transatlantic flight. Several **US airlines** fly direct from the East Coast to Madrid; Delta Airlines also operates a nonstop flight to Barcelona. Finally, you might check out **Air Europa**'s New York–Madrid flights, which are less frequent, but very competitively priced.

You may also find good deals on **routeings via other major European cities** with the airlines of those countries: KLM via Amsterdam, Lufthansa via Frankfurt, TAP via Lisbon, or British Airways via London, for example. Remember, though, that you may be better off continuing with a locally bought flight, or overland (especially if you plan to buy a rail pass). The widest range of deals is on the New York–London route, served by dozens of airlines. Competition is intense, so look for bargains, especially out of season.

At the time of writing, the major carriers were offering the following round-trip **fares** to Madrid: from New York $615/925 (low/high season respectively); from Chicago $720/1100; from LA $855/1520; and from Miami $695/990. With special promotional offers, round-trip fares can drop as low as $300 from New York and $500 from LA. Flying time is around seven hours from New York to Madrid.

There are no nonstop flights **from Canada** to Spain. However, you should be able to find a fairly convenient routeing using a combination of airlines – most likely via another European capital – from any of the major cities. West of the Rockies you're probably best off either flying Vancouver–London and continuing on to Madrid or another Spanish city from there, or alternatively getting a flight from Seattle.

At the time of writing, APEX round-trip **fares** to Madrid start at around CAN$1200 in the low season or CAN$1695 in the high season from Toronto or Montréal, and CAN$1590/2250 from Vancouver.

Package tours may not sound like your kind of travel, but don't dismiss the idea out of hand. In addition to the fully escorted variety, many agents can put together very flexible deals, sometimes amounting to no more than a flight plus car or rail pass and accommodation; if you're planning to travel in moderate or luxury style, and especially if your trip is geared around special interests, such packages can work out cheaper than the same arrangements made on arrival. A package can also be great for your peace of mind, if only to ensure a worry-free first week while you're finding your feet on a longer tour (of course, you can jump off the itinerary any time you like). Most companies will expect you to book through a local travel agent, and since it costs the same you might as well.

Plenty of tour companies offer whirlwind itineraries around Spain. Most of these also offer independent **city breaks** or more structured **escorted tours** based around cultural, gastronomic or outdoor activities. Other options include **trekking** (backpacking) in the Basque Pyrenees or basking on the **beaches** of the Costa del Sol.

Airlines

Air France ☎ 1-800/237-2747, Canada ☎ 1-800/667-2747, ⓦ www.airfrance.com. From New York, Chicago, Atlanta, Miami, San Francisco, Los Angeles, Washington DC, Toronto and Montréal to Madrid, Barcelona, Málaga and Sevilla, all via Paris.

American Airlines ☎1-800/433-7300,
🕸www.aa.com. Daily nonstop flights from Miami
and Chicago to Madrid.
British Airways ☎1-800/247-9297,
🕸www.british-airways.com. From Montréal,
Toronto and Vancouver plus 21 gateway cities in the
US to Madrid, Barcelona and other major cities, all
via London.
Continental Airlines domestic ☎1-800/523-
3273, international ☎1-800/231-0856,
🕸www.continental.com. Daily nonstop flights from
Newark to Madrid.
Delta Airlines domestic ☎1-800/221-1212,
international ☎1-800/241-4141,
🕸www.delta.com. Daily nonstop flights from New
York and Atlanta to Madrid and Barcelona with
connections from most other major North American
cities.
Iberia ☎1-800/772-4642, 🕸www.iberia.com,
From New York, Miami and Chicago nonstop to
Madrid with connections to many other Spanish
cities.
Lufthansa US ☎1-800/645-3880, Canada ☎1-
800/563-5954, 🕸www.lufthansa-usa.com. From
major US cities to Madrid, Barcelona, Valencia,
Málaga, Bilbao and Palma, Mallorca, all via Frankfurt.
Northwest/KLM ☎1-800/447-4747 or 1-
800/374-7747, 🕸www.nwa.com. From major US
and Canadian cities to Madrid and Barcelona via
Amsterdam.
TAP Air Portugal ☎1-800/221-7370,
🕸www.tap-airportugal.pt. Flights to Madrid and
Barcelona via Lisbon, daily from New York.
United Airlines domestic ☎1-800/241-6522,
international ☎1-800/538-2929, 🕸www.ual.com.
Daily nonstop flights from Philadelphia to Madrid.

Courier flights

Air Courier Association ☎1-800/282-1202,
🕸www.aircourier.org. Courier flight broker.
Membership (3 months/$19, 1yr/$29, 3yr/$58,
5yr/$87) also entitles you to twenty percent discount
on travel insurance and name-your-own-price non-
courier flights.
International Association of Air Travel
Couriers ☎308/632-3273, 🕸www.courier.org.
Courier flight broker with membership fee of $45/yr
or $80 for two years.

Discount travel companies

Air Brokers International ☎1-800/883-3273 or
415/397-1383, 🕸www.airbrokers.com.
Consolidator and specialist in round-the-world
tickets.

Airtech ☎212/219-7000, 🕸www.airtech.com.
Standby seat broker; also deals in consolidator fares
and courier flights.
Airtreks.com ☎1-877-AIRTREKS or 415/912-
5600, 🕸www.airtreks.com. Round-the-world
tickets. The website features an interactive database
that lets you build and price your own round-the-
world itinerary.
Council Travel ☎1-800/2COUNCIL,
🕸www.counciltravel.com. Nationwide organization
that mostly specializes in student/budget travel.
Flights from the US only. Owned by STA Travel.
Educational Travel Center ☎1-800/747-5551
or 608/256-5551, 🕸www.edtrav.com.
Student/youth discount agent.
New Frontiers ☎1-800/677-0720 or 310/670-
7318, 🕸www.newfrontiers.com. French discount-
travel firm based in Los Angeles.
SkyLink US ☎1-800/AIR-ONLY or 212/573-8980,
Canada ☎1-800/SKY-LINK,
🕸www.skylinkus.com. Consolidator.
STA Travel US ☎1-800/781-4040, Canada 1-
888/427-5639, 🕸www.sta-travel.com. Worldwide
specialists in independent travel; also student IDs,
travel insurance, car rental, rail passes, etc.
Student Flights ☎1-800/255-8000 or 480/951-
1177, 🕸www.isecard.com. Student/youth fares,
student IDs.
TFI Tours ☎1-800/745-8000 or 212/736-1140,
🕸www.lowestairprice.com. Consolidator.
Travac ☎1-800/TRAV-800,
🕸www.thetravelsite.com. Consolidator and charter
broker with offices in New York City and Orlando.
Travelers Advantage ☎1-877/259-2691,
🕸www.travelersadvantage.com. Discount travel
club; annual membership fee required (currently $1
for 3 months' trial).
Travel Avenue ☎1-800/333-3335,
🕸www.travelavenue.com. Full-service travel agent
that offers discounts in the form of rebates.
Travel Cuts Canada ☎1-800/667-2887, US ☎1-
866/246-9762, 🕸www.travelcuts.com. Canadian
student-travel organization.
Worldtek Travel ☎1-800/243-1723,
🕸www.worldtek.com. Discount travel agency for
worldwide travel.

Tour operators

Abercrombie and Kent ☎1-800/323-7308 or
630/954-2944, 🕸www.abercrombiekent.com.
Upmarket independent and fully escorted holidays,
including walking tours in Andalucía.
Adventure Center ☎1-800/228-8747 or 510/654-
1879, 🕸www.adventure-center.com. Active vacations
in the Picos, Andalucía and the Sierra Nevada.

Delta Vacations ☎1-800/654-6559,
ⓦwww.deltavacations.com. City breaks with
optional car rental and city tours.
Easy Rider Tours ☎1-800/488-8332 or
978/463-6955, ⓦwww.easyridertours.com.
Cycling/hiking tours in Andalucía and along the
pilgrim's way to Santiago de Compostela.
EC Tours ☎1-800/388-0877,
ⓦwww.ectours.com. Pilgrimages, historic city
tours, wine and gourmet tours.
Escapade Tours ☎1-800/356-2405,
ⓦwww.isram.com. City breaks and multi-city
packages.
Far & Wide ☎1-866/327-9433,
ⓦwww.farandwide.com. Independent, customized
and escorted tours of Catalunya and Andalucía.
Hidden Trails ☎604/323 1141,
ⓦwww.hiddentrails.com. A Canadian site which
organizes horse-riding holidays throughout Spain
following themed trips.
M.I. Travel Inc ☎1-800/848-2314 or 212/967-
6565, ⓦwww.mitravel-melia.com. City packages
and motorcoach tours.
Mountain Travel/Sobek ☎1-888/687-6235,
ⓦwww.mtsobek.com. Hiking in the Picos de
Europa and Basque Pyrenees.
Olé Spain ☎1-888/869-7156,
ⓦwww.olespain.com. Cultural walking tours in
Catalunya, Andalucía and Extremadura.
Petrabax Tours ☎1-800/634-1188,
ⓦwww.petrabax.com. Motorcoach tours, *parador*
bookings, plus a variety of set packages.

Flights from Australia and New Zealand

There are no direct flights to Spain from
Australia or New Zealand, but changing
planes once or twice can get you there within
24 hours via Asia or 30 hours via the US –
not counting time spent on stopovers. Flights
via Asia are generally the cheaper option.

Most regular return economy **fares** to
Spain cost between A$2100 in the low sea-
son and A$3300 in the high season from
eastern Australian gateways. From Perth
and Darwin expect to pay A$100–200 less
than this if you're travelling via Asia, or
A$400 more if routeing via the US. Fares
from Auckland cost between NZ$2500 in
the low season and NZ$3100 in the high
season. Fares rise by about A$300/NZ$300
in the shoulder season and then by about
this much again in high season.

Alternatively, you can find a **rock-bottom
return fare** to a European hub city with the

likes of Garuda or Sri Lanka Airlines for
around A$1600/NZ$1850 low season, and
then either pick up a cheap charter flight
(see p.13) or travel overland by road (see
p.16) or rail (see "Rail Passes" on p.31).
However, with the high living and transport
costs in northwestern Europe, this rarely
works out any cheaper in practice.

The cheapest **scheduled** flights **from
Australia** are via Asia and there are several
airlines that fly into both Barcelona and
Madrid. The lowest fares are offered by Japan
Airlines (to Madrid, with an overnight stop in
either Tokyo or Osaka included in the fare) –
from A$1800 in the low season to A$2900 in
the high season. Mid-range fares are with
Thai Airways, Air France and Lauda Air via
their respective gateway cities of Bangkok,
Paris and Vienna for A$2000–3000. A little
more expensive, at A$2200–3200, but faster
– with only a short refuelling stop or quick
change of planes in Singapore – are
Singapore Airlines' flights to Madrid.

Travelling **from New Zealand** to Spain via
Asia, Thai Airways (via Sydney) has through
fares from Auckland to both Madrid and
Barcelona, and Japan Airlines (JAL) has
flights to Madrid – all with either a transfer or
overnight stop in their carrier's home city –
for between NZ$2500–3100 (low/high sea-
son). Qantas (via Sydney and Bangkok) and
Singapore Airlines (via Singapore) both also
fly to Madrid, but are more expensive at
NZ$2700–3300.

Organized tours may seem a little expensive but are well worth it, especially if your
time is limited, if you're unfamiliar with the
country's customs and language, have special interests or you just don't like travelling
alone. Adventure tours are also worth considering, especially if you want to cover a lot
of ground or get to places that could be difficult to reach independently.

Airlines

Air France Australia ☎02/9244 2100, New
Zealand ☎09/308 3352, ⓦwww.airfrance.fr. Daily
flights to Madrid and Barcelona from major
Australian gateway cities, with transfers in Paris and
either Singapore or Bangkok. Code-shares with
Qantas for the first leg.
Garuda Indonesia Australia ☎02/9334 9970,
New Zealand ☎09/366 1862, ⓦwww.garuda

-indonesia.com. Several flights weekly from major cities in Australia and New Zealand to London, Frankfurt and Amsterdam, with either a transfer or an overnight stop in Denpasar or Jakarta: connections to destinations in Spain.

Japan Airlines Australia ☎02/9272 1111, New Zealand ☎09/379 9906, ⓦwww.japanair.com. Daily flights to Madrid from Brisbane and Sydney, and several flights a week from Cairns and Auckland, with either a transfer or overnight stop in Tokyo or Osaka. Code-shares with Iberia and Air New Zealand.

Lauda Air Australia ☎1800/642 438 or 02/9251 6155, New Zealand ☎09/522 5948, ⓦwww.aua.com. Bookings through Austrian Airlines. Four flights weekly to Barcelona from Sydney with transfers in Munich and Vienna.

Qantas Australia ☎13 13 13, ⓦwww.qantas.com.au; New Zealand ☎0800/808 767, ⓦwww.qantas.co.nz. Daily flights to Madrid from major cities in Australia and New Zealand with a transfer in either Singapore or Bangkok and London.

Singapore Airlines Australia ☎13 10 11, New Zealand ☎0800/808 909, ⓦwww.singaporeair.com. Daily flights to Madrid from Brisbane, Sydney, Melbourne, Perth and Auckland with either a transfer or overnight stop in Singapore, and on some flights a transfer in Zurich.

Sri Lankan Airlines Australia ☎02/9244 2234, New Zealand ☎09/308 3353, ⓦwww.srilankan.lk. Three flights a week to London, Paris and Rome from Sydney with a transfer or overnight stop in Colombo: connections to destinations in Spain.

Thai Airways Australia ☎1300/651 960, New Zealand ☎09/377 0268, ⓦwww.thaiair.com. Several flights weekly to Madrid and Barcelona from Sydney, Melbourne, Brisbane and Auckland with a transfer in either Rome or Frankfurt and another transfer or overnight stop in Bangkok.

Travel agents

All the agents listed below offer competitive discounts on air fares as well as a good selection of package holidays and tours, and can also arrange car rental and bus and rail passes.

Flight Centre Australia ☎13 31 33 or 02/9235 3522, ⓦwww.flightcentre.com.au, New Zealand ☎0800 243 544 or 09/358 4310, ⓦwww.flightcentre.co.nz.

Holiday Shoppe New Zealand ☎0800/808 480, ⓦwww.holidayshoppe.co.nz.

New Zealand Destinations Unlimited New Zealand ☎09/414 1685, ⓦwww.holiday.co.nz.

Northern Gateway Australia ☎1800/174 800, ⓦwww.northerngateway.com.au.

STA Travel Australia ☎1300/733 035, ⓦwww.statravel.com.au, New Zealand

☎0508/782 872, ⓦwww.statravel.co.nz.

Student Uni Travel Australia ☎02/9232 8444, ⓦwww.sut.com.au, New Zealand ☎09/379 4224, ⓦwww.sut.co.nz.

Trailfinders Australia ☎02/9247 7666, ⓦwww.trailfinders.com.au.

Specialist agents

Adventure World Australia ☎02/8913 0755, ⓦwww.adventureworld.com.au, New Zealand ☎09/524 5118, ⓦwww.adventureworld.co.nz. Agents for a vast array of international adventure travel companies that offer small-group tours, including Explore's 15-day trek through the High Alpujarras, staying in *hostales* and *pensiones* along the way.

Australian Pacific Touring Australia ☎1800/675 222 or 03/9277 8555, New Zealand ☎09/279 6077, ⓦwww.aptours.com. Escorted tours and independent travel.

Australians Studying Abroad Australia ☎1800/645 755 or 03/9509 1955, ⓦwww.asatravinfo.com.au. Offers guided study tours, focusing on Spain's art and culture; some courses can be credited towards Australian tertiary awards.

CIT Australia ☎02/9267 1255, ⓦwww.cittravel.com.au. Specializes in city tours and accommodation packages, plus bus and rail passes and car rental.

IB Tours Australia ☎02/9560 6722, ⓦwww.ib -tours.com.au. Villas in Spain, Portugal and Morocco, as well as car rentals and city stays.

Ibertours Australia ☎03/9670 8388 or 1800/500 016, ⓦwww.ibertours.com.au. Escorted and solo tours to rural and urban areas of Spain, Portugal and Morocco, plus help organizing study trips.

Tour operators

Contiki Australia ☎02/9511 2200, New Zealand ☎09/309 8824, ⓦwww.contiki.com. Frenetic tours for 18- to 35-year-old party animals.

Explore Holidays Australia ☎02/9423 8080, ⓦwww.exploreholidays.com.au. Accommodation and package tours.

Tempo Holidays Australia ☎1300/362 844, ⓦwww.yallatours.com.au. Mediterranean specialists offering city stays, packages, car rental, tours, and all transport arrangements.

Viator Australia ☎02/8219 5400, ⓦwww.viator.com. Bookings for hundreds of travel suppliers worldwide, including Spain.

Walkabout Gourmet Adventures Australia ☎03/5159 6556, ⓦwww.walkaboutgourmet.com. Classy food, wine and walking tours in Spain.

Red tape and visas

Citizens of EU countries (and of Norway, Iceland, Liechtenstein and Switzerland) need only a valid passport or national identity card to enter Spain. US, Canadian, Australian and New Zealand citizens do not need a visa for stays of up to ninety days, but this must be for tourism or study purposes only and not for work. Visa requirements do change and it is always advisable to check the current situation before leaving home.

As of March 1 2003, EU nationals (and citizens of Norway, Iceland, Liechtenstein and Switzerland) no longer need apply for a residence permit to **stay longer**, as a valid passport or identity document now acts as a permit. This now entitles EU citizens to reside as employees, self-employed or students; retired people or those of independent means will still have to apply for a residence permit. The British Embassy in Spain (Ⓦwww.ukinspain.com) has useful general information for EU citizens.

US citizens can apply for one ninety-day extension, showing proof of funds, but this must be done from outside Spain. Other nationalities will need to get a special visa from a Spanish consulate before departure (see below for addresses).

Spanish embassies and consulates abroad

Australia 15 Arkana St, Yarralumla, ACT 2600 ☏02/6273 3555; 24th Floor, St Martin's Tower, 31 Market St, Sydney, NSW 2000 ☏02/9261 2433, Ⓔconsulspain@smartchat.net.au; 4th Floor, 540 Elizabeth St, Melbourne, VIC 3000 ☏03/9347 1966, Ⓔconspainmelb@primus.com.au.
Britain 20 Draycott Place, London SW3 2RZ ☏020/7589 8989; Suite 1a, Brook House, 70 Spring Gardens, Manchester M2 2BQ ☏0161/236 1262; 63 North Castle St, Edinburgh EH2 3LJ ☏0131/220 1843.
Canada 350 Sparks St #802, Ottawa, Ontario K1R 7S8 ☏613/237-2193, Ⓦwww.docuweb.ca/SpainInCanada; 1 Westmount Sq #1456, Ave Wood, Montréal, Quebec H3Z 2P9 ☏514/935-5235, Ⓦwww.total.net/~consular; 1200 Bay St #400, Toronto, Ontario M5P 2A5 ☏416/967-4949.

Ireland 17a Merlyn Park, Ballsbridge, Dublin 4 ☏01/269 1640.
New Zealand contact the consulate in Sydney.
US 2375 Pennsylvania Ave NW, Washington DC 20037 ☏202/452-0100, Ⓦwww.spainemb.org/ingles/indexing.htm; 150 E 58th St, New York, NY 10155 ☏212/355-4090, Ⓦwww.spainconsul-ny.org; 545 Boylston St #803, Boston, MA 02116 ☏617/536-2506, Ⓦwww.spainconsul-ny.org/boston.html; 180 N Michigan Ave #1500, Chicago, IL 60601 ☏312/782-4588, Ⓔcgspain.chicago@mail.mae.es; 1800 Bering Drive #660, Houston, TX 77057 ☏713/783-6200, Ⓔspainconsulatehoust@prodigy.net; 5055 Wilshire Blvd #960, Los Angeles, CA 90036 ☏323/938-0158, Ⓔconsplax@mail.mae.es; 2655 Le Jeune Rd #203, Coral Gables, Miami, FL 33134 ☏305/446-5511, Ⓔcgspain.miami@mail.mae.es; 2102 World Trade Center, 2 Canal St, New Orleans, LA 70130 ☏504/525-4951, Ⓔconspneworleans@mail.mae.es; 1405 Sutter St, San Francisco, CA 94109 ☏415/922-2995, Ⓔconspsfo@mail.mae.es.

Embassies and consulates in Spain

Australia Pl Descubridor Diego de Ordas 3, 28003 Madrid ☏914 419 300, Ⓦwww.embaustralia.es.
Canada c/Núñez de Balboa 35, 28001 Madrid ☏914 233 250, Ⓦwww.canada-es.org.
Ireland Paseo de la Castellana 46-4, 28046 Madrid ☏915 763 500.
New Zealand Pl de la Lealtad 2-3, 28014 Madrid ☏915 310 997.
UK c/Fernando el Santo 16, 28010 Madrid ☏914 233 250, Ⓦwww.ukinspain.com.
US c/Serrano 75, 28006 Madrid ☏915 872 200, Ⓦwww.embusa.es.

Health

As an EU country, Spain has free reciprocal health agreements with other member states (you should carry form E111, available from main post offices). Even so, some form of travel insurance is still all but essential; with it, you should be able to claim back the cost of any drugs prescribed by pharmacies.

No **inoculations** are required for Spain, though if you plan on continuing to North Africa, typhoid and polio boosters are highly recommended. The worst that's likely to happen to you is that you might fall victim to an upset stomach. To be safe, wash fruit and avoid tapas dishes that look as if they were cooked last week.

For minor complaints go to a **farmacia** – they're listed in the Yellow Pages (*Paginas Amarillas*) in major towns and you'll find one in virtually every village. Pharmacists are highly trained, willing to give advice (often in English), and able to dispense many drugs which would be available only on prescription in other countries. They keep usual shop hours (Mon–Fri 9am–1.30pm & 5–8pm), but some open late and at weekends, while a rota system keeps at least one open 24 hours. The rota is displayed in the window of every pharmacy, or you can check in one of the local newspapers under *Farmacias de guardia*.

In more serious cases you can get the address of an English-speaking doctor from the nearest relevant consulate, or with luck from a *farmacia*, the local police or turismo. If you have special medical or dietary requirements, it is advisable to carry a letter from your doctor, translated into Spanish, indicating the nature of your condition and necessary treatments.

In **emergencies** dial ☎091 for the *Servicios de Urgencia*, or look up the *Cruz Roja Española* (Red Cross) which runs a national ambulance service. Treatment at hospitals for EU citizens in possession of form E111 is free; otherwise you'll be charged at private hospital rates, which can be very expensive. **Dentists** are all private, and you should expect to pay around € 55 for a filling. The local phone book will have a list, or you could ask at your hotel or local tourist office.

Insurance

Even though EU health care privileges apply in Spain, you'd do well to take out an insurance policy before travelling to cover against theft, loss and illness or injury. Before paying for a new policy, however, it's worth checking whether you are already covered: some all-risks home insurance policies may cover your possessions when overseas, and many private medical schemes include cover when abroad.

In Canada, provincial health plans usually provide partial cover for medical mishaps overseas, while holders of official student/teacher/youth cards in Canada and the US are entitled to meagre accident cov-

erage and hospital inpatient benefits. Students will often find that their student health coverage extends during the vacations and for one term beyond the date of last enrolment.

Rough Guide travel insurance

Rough Guides Ltd offers a low-cost **travel insurance** policy, especially customized for our statistically low-risk readers by a leading British broker, provided by the American International Group (AIG) and registered with the British regulatory body, GISC (the General Insurance Standards Council). There are five main Rough Guides insurance plans: No Frills for the bare minimum for secure travel; Essential, which provides decent all-round cover; Premier for comprehensive cover with a wide range of benefits; Extended Stay for cover lasting four months to a year; and Annual multi-trip, a cost-effective way of getting Premier cover if you travel more than once a year. Premier, Annual Multi-Trip and Extended Stay policies can be supplemented by a "Hazardous Pursuits Extension" if you plan to indulge in sports considered dangerous, such as scuba-diving or trekking. For a policy quote, call the Rough Guide Insurance Line: toll-free in the UK ℡0800/015 09 06 or ℡+44 1392 314 665 from elsewhere. Alternatively, get an online quote at ⓦwww.roughguides.com/insurance.

After exhausting the possibilities above, you might want to contact a specialist travel insurance company, or consider the travel insurance deal we offer (see above). A typical travel insurance policy usually provides cover for the loss of baggage, tickets and – up to a certain limit – cash or cheques, as well as cancellation or curtailment of your journey. Most of them exclude so-called dangerous sports unless an extra premium is paid: in Spain this can mean scuba diving, windsurfing, skiing and trekking. Many policies can be chopped and changed to exclude coverage you don't need – for example, sickness and accident benefits can often be excluded or included at will. If you do take medical coverage, ascertain whether benefits will be paid as treatment proceeds or only after your return home, and whether there is a 24-hour medical emergency number. When securing baggage cover, make sure that the per-article limit – typically under £500 – will cover your most valuable possession. If you need to make a claim, you should keep receipts for medicines and medical treatment, and in the event you have anything stolen, you must obtain an official statement from the police, called a *parte*.

ⓘ Information, maps and websites

The Spanish National Tourist Office (SNTO; ⓦwww.tourspain.es) produces and gives away an impressive variety of maps, pamphlets and special-interest leaflets. If you can, visit one of their offices before you head off.

Information offices

In Spain itself you'll find SNTO turismos (tourist offices) in virtually every major town, and from these you can usually get more specific local information. SNTO offices are often supplemented by separately administered provincial or municipal bureaus. These vary enormously in quality, but while they are generally extremely useful for regional information, and local maps, they are not always as helpful about what goes on outside their patch.

Spanish turismo **hours** are usually Mon–Fri 9am–1pm and 3.30–6pm, Sat 9am–1pm, but you can't always rely on the official hours, especially in the more out-of-the-way places. In many major cities and coastal resorts the offices tend to remain open all day Saturday and on Sunday morning between April and September.

In the main cities, branches of the department store **El Corte Inglés** also provide information services and useful free maps.

SNTO offices abroad

Australia The Spanish National Tourist Office (SNTO), 1st Floor, 178 Collins St, Melbourne, VIC ☎03/9650 7377 or 1/800 817 855.
Britain 22–23 Manchester Square, London W1U 3PX ☎020/7486 8077, ⓦwww.tourspain.co.uk.
Canada 2 Bloor St West, 34th Floor, Toronto, Ontario M4W 3E2 ☎416/961-3131, ⓦwww.tourspain.toronto.on.ca.
New Zealand contact the office in Australia.
US 666 Fifth Ave, 35th Floor, New York, NY 10103 ☎212/265-8822; San Vincente Plaza Bldg, 8383 Wilshire Blvd, Suite 956, Beverly Hills, CA 90211 ☎323/658-7188; 845 North Michigan Ave, Suite 915-E, Chicago, IL 60611 ☎312/642-1992; 1221 Brickell Ave, Suite 1850, Miami, FL 33131 ☎305/358-1992, ⓦwww.okspain.org.

Maps

In addition to the maps in this book and the various free leaflets available, the one extra you'll want is a reasonable **road map**. This is best bought in Spain, where you'll find a good selection in most bookshops (*librerías*) and at street kiosks or petrol stations. Among the best are those published by Editorial Almax and Distrimapas Telstar, which also produces reliable indexed **street plans** of the main cities. Good alternatives, especially if you're shopping before arrival, are the 1:300,000 *Euro Road Atlas* put out by RV (Reise und Verkehrsverlag, Stuttgart; packaged in Spain by Plaza & Janes), or the slightly larger-scale but generally excellent and accurate Michelin, covering the country in six 1:400, 000 regional maps sold in atlas format. Less detailed offerings from Firestone or Rand McNally are another option.

Serious **trekkers** can get more detailed maps from La Tienda Verde at c/Maudes 38, Madrid (☎915 343 257; ⓜPlaza de Castilla), and in Barcelona at Librería Quera at c/Petritxol 2, Barcelona (☎933 180 743,

ⓦwww.llibreriaquera.com; ⓜLiceu) or the Institut Cartogràfic de Catalunya, c/Balmes 209–211 (☎932 188 758). These outlets – and many other bookshops in Spain, plus a few specialists overseas – stock the full range of **topographical maps** issued by two government agencies: the IGN (Instituto Geográfico Nacional) and the SGE (Servicio Geográfico del Ejército). They are available at scales of 1:200,000, 1:100,000, 1:50,000 and even occasionally 1:25,000. The various SGE series are considered to be more up to date, although neither agency is hugely reliable. A Catalunya-based company, Editorial Alpina (ⓦwww.editorialalpina.com), produces useful 1:40,000 or 1:25,000 **map/booklet** sets for most of the Spanish mountain and foothill areas of interest, and these are also on sale in many bookshops; the relevant editions are noted in the text where appropriate.

Internet sources for maps include In Internet, a Barcelona-based firm which has a website (ⓦwww.netmaps.es, with a page in English) where you can buy a wide selection of different types of maps. Another (in Spanish only) web-based source is at ⓦwww.verdinet.com/mapas/; here you can purchase detailed maps (including SGE maps) with postal costs included.

Map outlets

In the UK and Ireland

Blackwell's Map and Travel Shop 50 Broad St, Oxford OX1 3BQ ☎01865/793 550, ⓦmaps.blackwell.co.uk.
Easons Bookshop 40 O'Connell St, Dublin 1 ☎01/858 3881, ⓦwww.eason.ie.
Heffers Map and Travel 20 Trinity St, Cambridge CB2 1TJ ☎01865/333 536, ⓦwww.heffers.co.uk.
Hodges Figgis Bookshop 56–58 Dawson St, Dublin 2 ☎01/677 4754.
The Map Shop 30a Belvoir St, Leicester LE1 6QH ☎0116/247 1400, ⓦwww.mapshopleicester.co.uk.
National Map Centre 22–24 Caxton St, London SW1H 0QU ☎020/7222 2466, ⓦwww.mapsnmc.co.uk.
Newcastle Map Centre 55 Grey St, Newcastle-upon-Tyne, NE1 6EF ☎0191/261 5622.
Ordnance Survey Ireland Phoenix Park, Dublin 8 ☎01/802 5300, ⓦwww.osi.ie.

Ordnance Survey of Northern Ireland Colby House, Stranmillis Ct, Belfast BT9 5BJ ☎028/9025 5755, ⓦwww.osni.gov.uk.
Stanfords 12–14 Long Acre, WC2E 9LP ☎020/7836 1321, ⓦwww.stanfords.co.uk.
The Travel Bookshop 13–15 Blenheim Crescent, W11 2EE ☎020/7229 5260, ⓦwww.thetravelbookshop.co.uk.

In the US and Canada

Adventurous Traveler.com ☎1-800/282-3963, ⓦadventuroustraveler.com.
Book Passage 51 Tamal Vista Blvd, Corte Madera, CA 94925 ☎1-800/999-7909, ⓦwww.bookpassage.com.
Distant Lands 56 S Raymond Ave, Pasadena, CA 91105 ☎1-800/310-3220, ⓦwww.distantlands.com.
Elliot Bay Book Company 101 S Main St, Seattle, WA 98104 ☎1-800/962-5311, ⓦwww.elliotbaybook.com.
Globe Corner Bookstore 28 Church St, Cambridge, MA 02138 ☎1-800/358-6013, ⓦwww.globecorner.com.
Map Link 30 S La Patera Lane, Unit 5, Santa Barbara, CA 93117 ☎1-800/962-1394, ⓦwww.maplink.com.
Rand McNally US ☎1-800/333-0136, ⓦwww.randmcnally.com. Around thirty stores across the US; dial ext 2111 or check the website for the nearest location.
The Travel Bug Bookstore 2667 W Broadway, Vancouver V6K 2G2 ☎604/737-1122, ⓦwww.swifty.com/tbug.
World of Maps 1235 Wellington St, Ottawa, Ontario K1Y 3A3 ☎1-800/214-8524, ⓦwww.worldofmaps.com.

In Australia and New Zealand

The Map Shop 6–10 Peel St, Adelaide, SA 5000 ☎08/8231 2033, ⓦwww.mapshop.net.au.
Specialty Maps 46 Albert St, Auckland 1001 ☎09/307 2217, ⓦwww.specialtymaps.co.nz.
MapWorld 173 Gloucester St, Christchurch ☎0800/627 967 or 03/374 5399, ⓦwww.mapworld.co.nz.
Mapland 372 Little Bourke St, Melbourne, Victoria 3000 ☎03/9670 4383, ⓦwww.mapland.com.au.
Perth Map Centre 900 Hay St, Perth, WA 6000 ☎08/9322 5733, ⓦwww.perthmap.com.au.

Spain on the Internet

Spain is represented pretty strongly on the Internet, with websites in both English and Spanish offering information on most conceivable subjects. The websites detailed below are useful starting points and most contain numerous links on to more detailed areas.

ⓦ**www.red2000.com** Regional information on the country and culture, with a database of hotels, car rental, language courses and more.
Go Spain ⓦwww.gospain.org. Almost every Spain-related link; especially good for fiesta listings.
Hotel Search ⓦwww.hotelsearch.com. Extensive, though not exhaustive, list of Spanish accommodation, in English.
Museums in Spain ⓦwww.icom-ce.org. A comprehensive list of all Spain's museums and art galleries.
Paginas Amarillas ⓦwww.paginas-amarillas.es. Spain's Yellow Pages online, with dedicated eating and accommodation sections. Very useful, though unfortunately only available in Spanish.
El País Digital ⓦwww.elpais.es/. Impressive digital version of Spain's major newspaper. To access the stories behind the headlines, you'll need a subscription, currently €80/£56/$94 a year.
Restaurant Menus ⓦwww.webarcelona.com. City guide to Barcelona with excellent link to a five-page list of translations of dishes and food – handy to print out and take along.
Sí Spain ⓦwww.sispain.org. Cultural affairs site of the Spanish Foreign Ministry, with the latest on the cultural scene plus very good links to other sites.
Soccer Spain ⓦwww.soccer-spain.com. English-language news, views, fixtures and results from La Liga. Marca, the leading Spanish sports paper, also has a good and comprehensive site (ⓦwww.marca.com) which allows you to delve into the lower league stats, too.
Spanish Search Engines ⓦwww.searchenginecolossus.com. Choose the Spain entry on this site for a comprehensive list of Spanish search engines including many regional and local ones.
Turespaña ⓦwww.tourspain.es. Generic website of the Spanish Tourist Board with complete information on themed routes, events and curiosities.
Travlang – Learn Spanish ⓦwww.travlang.com/languages/. Select "Spanish". Good site for picking up a bit of the lingo before you set off (including a neat pronunciation tool).
Yahoo España ⓦwww.//es.yahoo.com/. The Spanish cousin of Yahoo's main search engine which is excellent for digging out things Hispanic.

Costs, money and banks

Although still thought of as a budget destination, prices in Spain have increased considerably over the last ten years, and if you're spending a lot of your time in the cities, you can expect to spend almost as much as you would at home. However, there are still few places in Europe where you'll get a better deal on the cost of simple meals and drinks.

Spanish **bancos** (banks) and **cajas de ahorros** (savings banks) have branches in all but the smallest villages, and most of them are prepared to change travellers' cheques (albeit often with hefty commissions). The Banco Santander Central Hispano (BSCH) and Banco Bilbao Vizcaya Argentaria (BBVA) are two of the most efficient and widespread; both can change most brands of travellers' cheques, and give cash advances on credit cards; commissions at the Banco Santander Central Hispano are generally the lowest.

ATM cash machines (*cajeros automaticos*) are now widespread throughout the country in cities, towns and even many villages, and you only need a valid card with PIN number to use them. This is probably the most convenient way to get cash when you need it, although you would be wise not to rely on this method exclusively – it's not uncommon for cards to be swallowed up or, indeed, lost or stolen. **Money-changing machines** now feature in many larger cities, and feeding in pounds or dollars will give you instant cash.

Banking hours are generally Mon–Fri 8.30am–2pm, with some city branches open Sat 8.30am–1pm (except from June to September when all banks close on Saturday), although times can vary from bank to bank. Outside these times, it's usually possible to change cash at larger hotels (generally with bad rates and low commission) or with travel agents, who may initially grumble but will eventually give a rate with the commission built in – useful for small amounts in a hurry.

In tourist areas you'll also find specialist **casas de cambio**, with more convenient hours (though rates vary), and most branches of El Corte Inglés, a major department store found throughout Spain, have efficient exchange facilities open throughout store hours, offering competitive rates and generally a much lower commission than the banks (though they're worse for cash).

Currency

On January 1, 2002, Spain was one of twelve European Union countries to change over to a single currency, the euro (€). The euro is split into 100 cents. There are seven euro notes – in denominations of 500, 200, 100, 50, 20, 10, and 5 euros, each a different colour and size – and eight different coin denominations, including 2 and 1 euros, then 50, 20, 10, 5, 2, and 1 cents. Euro coins feature a common EU design on one face, but different country-specific designs on the other. No matter what the design, all euro coins and notes can be used in any of the twelve member states (Austria, Belgium, Finland, France, Germany, Greece, Ireland, Italy, Luxembourg, Portugal, Spain and the Netherlands).

At the time of writing, the **exchange rate** for the euro was around €1.40 to the pound sterling (or £0.70 to one euro) and €1.15 to the dollar (or $0.87 to one euro). You can take into Spain as much money as you want (in any form), although amounts over €6000 must be declared, and you may only take amounts over €6000 out if you can prove that you brought more with you in the first place. Not, perhaps, a major holiday worry.

Average costs

On average, if you're prepared to buy your own picnic lunch, stay in inexpensive *pensiones*, and stick to local restaurants and bars, you could get by on £20–25/$30–35 a day. If you intend to upgrade your accommodation, experience the city nightlife and eat fancier meals, then you'll need more like

£35/$60 a day. On £45–50/$70–80 a day and upwards you'll be limited only by your energy reserves – though of course if you're planning to stay in four- and five-star hotels or Spain's magnificent *paradores*, this figure often won't even cover your room.

Room prices vary considerably according to season. In the summer you'll find little below £15/$24 single, £20/$30 double, and £25–30/$35–40 might be a more realistic average. Campsites start at around £2/$3.50 a night per person (£2.50–3/$4–5 in some of the major resorts), plus a similar charge for a tent and a car respectively.

The cost of **eating** can vary wildly, but in most towns there'll be restaurants offering a basic three-course meal for somewhere between £4.50–7/$7–12. As often as not, though, you'll end up wandering from one bar to the next sampling tapas without getting round to a real sit-down meal – this is certainly tastier, though rarely any cheaper (see "Eating and Drinking", p.44). Drink, and wine in particular, costs ridiculously little: £7–$12 will see you through a night's very substantial intake of the local vintage.

Long-distance **transport**, if used extensively, may prove a major expense; although prices compare well with the rest of Europe, Spain is a very large country. Madrid to Sevilla, for example – a journey of over 500km – costs around £35/$60 by bus or train. Urban transport almost always operates on a flat fare of £0.70–1/$1.20–1.75.

All of the above, inevitably, are affected by where you are and when. The big cities and tourist resorts are invariably more expensive than remoter areas, and certain regions tend also to have higher prices – notably the industrialized north, Euskal Herria, Catalunya and Aragón, and the Balearic Islands. Prices are hiked up, too, to take advantage of special events. Despite official controls, you'd be lucky to find a room in Sevilla during its April *feria*, or in Pamplona for the running of the bulls, at less than double the usual rate. As always, if you're travelling alone you'll end up spending much more than you would in a group of two or more – sharing rooms saves greatly.

One thing to look out for on prices generally is the addition of sales tax – **IVA** (pronounced "iba") – which may come as an unexpected extra (currently seven percent for hotels and restaurants, sixteen percent for other goods and services) when you pay the bill for food or accommodation, especially in more expensive establishments.

Youth and student discounts

Once obtained, various official and quasi-official **youth/student ID cards** soon pay for themselves in savings. Full-time students are eligible for the International Student ID Card (ISIC, ⓦwww.isiccard.com), which entitles the bearer to special air, rail and bus fares and discounts at museums, theatres and other attractions. For Americans there's also a health benefit, providing up to $3000 in emergency medical coverage and $100 a day for 60 days in the hospital, plus a 24-hour hotline to call in the event of a medical, legal or financial emergency. The card costs $22 in the US; Can$16 in Canada; AUS$16.50 in Australia; NZ$21 in New Zealand; £6 in the UK; and €12.70 in the Republic of Ireland.

You only have to be 26 or younger to qualify for the **International Youth Travel Card**, which costs £7/US$22 and carries the same benefits. Teachers qualify for the **International Teacher Card**, offering similar discounts and costing US$22, Can$16, AUS$16.50 and NZ$21. All these cards are available in the US from Council Travel, STA, Travel CUTS and, in Canada, Hostelling International (see p.19 for addresses); in Australia and New Zealand from STA or Campus Travel; and in the UK from STA.

Several other travel organizations and accommodation groups also sell their own cards, good for various discounts. A university photo ID might open some doors, but is not easily recognizable, as are the ISIC cards. However, the latter are often not accepted as valid proof of age, for example in bars or clubs.

Cash and travellers' cheques

A safe and easy way to carry funds is in **travellers' cheques** issued by any recognized bank. Both sterling and dollar cheques are widely accepted, but it's advisable to bring them in euros if you can, primarily because their acceptance will be even more widespread and especially as they won't be liable to fluctuations in value as you're travelling.

The usual fee for travellers' cheque sales is one or two percent, though this fee may be waived if you buy the cheques through a bank where you have an account. It pays to get a selection of denominations. Make sure to keep the purchase agreement and a record of cheque serial numbers safe and separate from the cheques themselves. In the event that cheques are lost or stolen, the issuing company will expect you to report the loss to their office in Spain; most companies claim to replace lost or stolen cheques within 24 hours.

Credit and debit cards

Credit cards are a very handy back-up source of funds, and can be used either in ATMs or over the counter. Mastercard, Visa and American Express are accepted just about everywhere, but other cards may not be recognized. Remember that all cash advances are treated as loans, with interest accruing daily from the date of withdrawal; there may be a transaction fee on top of this. However, you may be able to make withdrawals from ATMs using your debit card, which is not liable to interest payments, and the flat transaction fee is usually quite small – your bank will be able to advise on this. Make sure you have a personal identification number (PIN) that's designed to work overseas. Visa, Mastercard (Access) or British automatic bank cards, and US cards in the Cirrus or Plus systems, can be used for **withdrawing cash** from ATMs in Spain: check with your bank to find out about these reciprocal arrangements – the system is highly sophisticated and can usually give instructions in a variety of languages.

Lost or stolen cards

To cancel lost or stolen credit cards, call the following numbers:
American Express ☎915 720 303
Diners Club ☎915 474 000
Mastercard ☎900 971 231
Visa ☎900 974 445

A compromise between travellers' cheques and plastic is Visa TravelMoney, a disposable pre-paid debit card with a PIN which works in all ATMs that take Visa cards. You load up your account with funds before leaving home, and when they run out, you simply throw the card away. You can buy up to nine cards to access the same funds – useful for couples or families travelling together – and it's a good idea to buy at least one extra as a back-up in case of loss or theft. There is also a 24-hour toll-free customer assistance number (☎900 951 125). The card is available in most countries from branches of Citicorp. For more information, check the Visa TravelMoney website at ⓦusa.visa.com/personal/cards/visa_travel_money.html.

Wiring money

Having money wired from home using one of the companies listed below is never convenient or cheap, and should be considered a last resort. It's also possible to have money wired directly from a bank in your home country to a bank in Spain, although this is somewhat less reliable because it involves two separate institutions. If you go down this route, your home bank will need the address of the branch bank where you want to pick up the money and the address and telex number of the Madrid head office, which will act as the clearing house; money wired this way normally takes two working days to arrive, and costs around £25/$40 per transaction.

Money-wiring companies

Thomas Cook US ☎1-800/287-7362, Canada ☎1-888/823-4732, GB ☎01733/318 922, Northern Ireland ☎028/9055 0030, Republic of Ireland ☎01/677 1721, ⓦwww.thomascook.com.
Travelers Express MoneyGram US ☎1-800/955-7777, Canada ☎1-800/933-3278, UK ☎0800/018 0104, Republic of Ireland ☎1850/205 800, Australia ☎1800/230 100, New Zealand ☎0800/262 263, ⓦwww.moneygram.com.
Western Union US and Canada ☎1-800/325-6000, Australia ☎1800/501 500, New Zealand ☎0800/270 000, UK ☎0800/833 833, Republic of Ireland ☎1800/395 395, ⓦwww.westernunion.com.

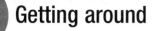

Getting around

Most of Spain is well covered by public transport. The rail network reaches all the provincial capitals and the main towns along the inter-city lines, although a good alternative is the extensive bus service, which is often more direct, more frequent and cheaper. On shorter or less obvious routes, especially, buses tend to be quicker and will also normally take you closer to your destination; some train stations are several kilometres from the town or village they serve and you've no guarantee of a connecting bus. Approximate journey times and frequencies can be found in the "Travel details" at the end of each chapter, and local peculiarities are also pointed out in the text of the Guide. Car rental may also be worth considering, with costs among the lowest in Europe. If your trip to Spain is part of a wider European tour and if you're only really visiting the larger cities, then it may be worth investing in a rail pass, such as the InterRail ticket.

By bus

Buses will probably meet most of your transport needs, especially if you're venturing away from the larger towns. Many smaller villages are accessible only by bus, almost always leaving from the capital of their province. Service varies in quality, but buses are generally reliable and comfortable enough – especially for long distances – with prices pretty standard at around £3.50/$5.85 per 100km. The only real problem involved is that many towns still have no main bus station, and buses may leave from a variety of places (even if they're heading in the same direction, since some destinations are served by more than one company); even in larger cities, you may find some routes don't run from the main station. Where a new terminal has been built, it's often on the outer fringes of town. As far as possible, departure points are detailed in the text.

One important point to remember is that all public transport, and the bus service especially, is drastically reduced on **Sundays and holidays** – it's best not even to consider travelling to out-of-the-way places on these days. The words to look out for on timetables are *diario* (daily), *laborables* (workdays, including Saturday), and *domingos y festivos* (Sundays and holidays).

By train

RENFE, the Spanish rail company, operates a horrendously complicated variety of train services, divided into three main sections. **Cercanías** are local commuter trains in and around the major cities. **Regionales** are equivalent to buses in speed and cost, and run between cities – Regional exprés and Delta trains can cover longer distances. **Largo recorrido** (long-distance) express trains have a bewildering number of names: in ascending order of speed and luxury, they are known as Diurno, Intercity (IC), Estrella (often just signified by a star *), Talgo, Talgo P(endular), Talgo 200 (T200), and Trenhotel. Anything above Intercity can cost upwards of twice as much as standard second class. There is also a growing number of super-high-speed trains from Madrid, such as AVE to Sevilla and EuroMed to Alicante; for those who can afford it, these have cut travelling times dramatically, with Madrid to Sevilla, for example, taking 2hr 30min compared with 6–9 hours on the slower trains. The long overdue AVE connection between Madrid and Barcelona has been bogged down in funding squabbles for some years, and despite contracts being awarded and work starting on some sections, it still looks no nearer a reality. What all these options mean for budget travellers, however, is that you often have to switch between *regional* trains to find an alternative route, and rail staff can be reluctant to work these out for you. However, you can ring the centralized RENFE information and reservation number on ☎902 240 202 – though you'll need to speak Spanish – or look on the Internet at Ⓦ www.renfe.es (English version available).

In recent years many bona fide train services have been phased out in favour of buses operated jointly by RENFE and a private bus company. This is particularly the case when the connection with outlying towns is either indirect or the daily train or trains leave at inconvenient times. On some routes the **rail buses** outnumber the conventional departures by a ratio of four to one. Prices are the same as on the trains, and these services usually leave and arrive from the bus stations of the towns concerned.

The Spanish tend to use *largo recorrido* trains in much the same way as aeroplanes, with **advance booking** essential for both the outward and return journey. Most RENFE train tickets can be booked in advance from **Britain** through Spanish Rail Service (Ⓣ 0207/629 4543), or **North America** through V.E. Tours (Ⓣ 1-800/222-8383, Ⓕ 305/477-4220); there's no RENFE representation in Ireland or Australasia.

Be aware that the different train types produce their own separate timetables; looking at just one can give the false impression that the overall service is dramatically less than it is.

Tickets and fares

RENFE offers a whole range of **discount fares** of between 25 and 40 percent for those over sixty, the disabled, children aged four to eleven years and groups of more than ten. Return fares are also discounted by ten percent on *regionales* (valid for fifteen days) and twenty percent on *largo recorridos* (valid for sixty days) – you can buy a single, and so long as you show it when you buy the return, you'll still get the discount.

Tickets can be bought at the stations between sixty days and ten minutes before departure from the *venta anticipada* window, or in the final two hours from the *venta inmediata* window. Don't leave it to the last minute, though, as there are usually long queues. There may also be separate windows for *largo recorrido* (long-distance) trains and *regionales* or *cercanías* (locals). If you board the train without a ticket the conductor may charge you up to double the normal fare; if you don't have the cash, they'll call the police. If you do get on a train

without a ticket it's always best to find the conductor first and explain, rather than wait to have them find you.

A good way to avoid the queues is to buy tickets at **travel agents** which display the RENFE sign – they have a sophisticated computer system which can also make seat reservations (£2.50/$3.50: obligatory on *largo recorrido* trains): the cost is the same as at the station. Most larger towns also have a **RENFE office** in the centre, or you can use the centralized 24-hour **telephone reservation service** – Ⓣ 902 240 202.

You can change the departure date of an electronically issued, reserved-seat, *largo recorrido* ticket up to one hour before your originally scheduled departure with a penalty of £1.25/$2.10. If you want to cancel the same sort of ticket, as long as you do so at least half an hour before departure, you'll be entitled to an 85 percent refund of the ticket price.

Rail passes

Rail passes are only worth considering if you plan to travel very extensively around Spain or are visiting the country as part of a wider tour of Europe. Otherwise, it often works out more economical to buy individual tickets as you need them and certainly more convenient to be free to choose long-distance buses on some routes. There are a number of different passes available. Some, such as the Eurail pass, have to be bought before leaving home, others can only be bought in the country itself. RENFE also offers its own passes, available in advance from selected agents or from RENFE offices in Spain. One thing to be aware of is that even with a pass, you'll sometimes be charged a supplement that is often almost the same price as the ordinary ticket, which is galling after you've splashed out on the pass in the first place.

Note that **InterRail** and **Eurail passes** are valid on all RENFE trains except EuroMed, but that there is a supplement payable for travelling on the fastest trains. The apparently random nature of these **surcharges** can be a source of considerable irritation. It's better to know what you're letting yourself in for by reserving a seat in advance, something you'll be obliged to do in any case on some trains; for £2.80/$4.75 you'll get a large, computer-printed ticket.

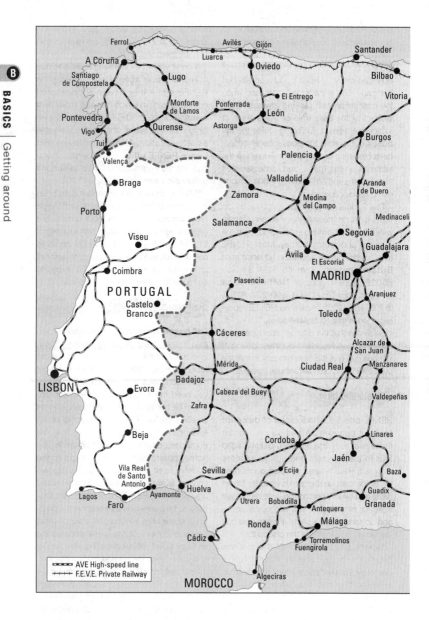

```
▭▭▭▭  AVE High-speed line
++++  F.E.V.E. Private Railway
```

Euro Domino pass

British and Irish citizens might also consider purchasing the **Spanish Euro Domino Pass** from Rail Europe (see p.34) or some travel agents before arrival. The passes are available for between three and eight days' unlimited travel within a one-month period. There is a discounted youth price for those

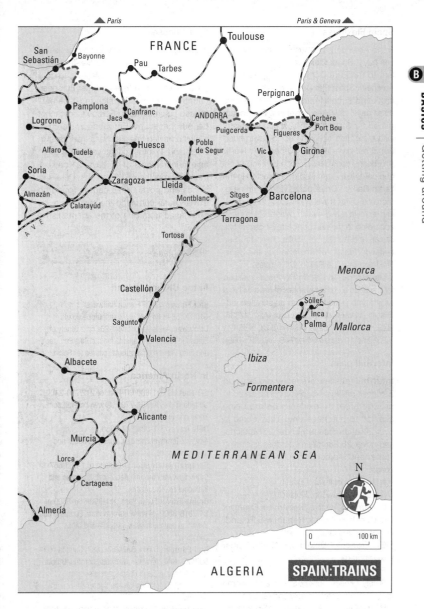

under 26, and a half-price child (age 4–11) fare. Prices for under/over 26s are three days (£52/69), five days (£80/105) and eight days (£122/159). Most high-speed train supplements are also included in the price.

Individual passes can be bought for any of 28 European and North African countries, and you can buy as many separate country passes as you want.

Spain Flexipass

North American and Australasian travellers can buy a **Spain Flexipass**, roughly equivalent to the Euro Domino pass. The North American Spain Flexipass, available in both first- and second-class versions, allows three days' unlimited travel in a two-month period for $215/165 (first-/second-class), with the option of buying up to seven additional rail days at $35/30 per day. North Americans considering a combination of rail and car travel might also be interested in the Spain **Rail 'n' Drive pass**, valid for three or more days' rail travel and two or more days' car rental in a two-month period. Prices vary according to the number of travel days, style of car, and number of adults sharing it. See below for details of where to buy the Spain Flexipass and the Rail 'n' Drive pass.

The Australasian Spain Flexipass is issued for travel on a certain number of days within a two-month period and available in second-/first-class versions: 3 days cost (A$261/336, NZ$327/419); 5 days (A$454/513, NZ$471/583); and 10 days (A$613/748, NZ$831/993).

InterRail pass

InterRail passes are only available to European residents, and you will be asked to provide proof of residency before being allowed to purchase one. They come in over-26 and (cheaper) under-26 versions, and cover 28 European countries (including Turkey and Morocco) grouped together in zones:

A Republic of Ireland/Britain
B Norway, Sweden, Finland
C Germany, Austria, Switzerland, Denmark
D Czech & Slovak Republics, Poland, Hungary, Croatia
E France, Belgium, Netherlands, Luxembourg
F Spain, Portugal, Morocco
G Italy, Greece, Turkey, Slovenia plus some ferry services between Italy and Greece
H Bulgaria, Romania, Yugoslavia, Macedonia

The passes are available for 22 days (one zone only) or 1 month and you can purchase up to 3 zones or a global pass covering all zones. You can save £5 by booking via the InterRail website (ⓦ www.inter-rail.co.uk).

Eurail passes

A **Eurail pass** is not likely to pay for itself if you're planning to stick to Spain, but is worth considering if you're planning to do a fair amount of train travel in other European countries. The pass, which must be purchased before arrival in Europe (and cannot be purchased by European residents), allows unlimited free first-class train travel in Spain and 17 other countries, and is available in increments of 15 days, 21 days, 1 month, 2 months and 3 months. Details of prices and possibilities can be found on ⓦ www.eurail.com, and the passes can be purchased from one of the agents listed below.

Rail contacts

In the UK and Ireland

Rail Europe (SNCF French Railways) ☏ 0870/5848 848, ⓦ www.raileurope.co.uk. Discounted rail fares for under-26s on a variety of European routes; also agents for InterRail, Eurostar and Euro Domino, and sells rail passes for Spain.

In North America

CIT Rail US ☏ 1-800/CIT-RAIL or 212/730-2400, Canada ☏ 1-800/361-7799, ⓦ www.cit-rail.com. Eurail and Europass.
DER Travel ☏ 1-888/337-7350, ⓦ www.dertravel.com/rail. Eurail, Europass and individual country passes.
Europrail International Canada ☏ 1-888/667-9734, ⓦ www.europrail.net. Eurail, Europass and individual country passes.
Online Travel Eurail Pass ☏ 1-800/660-5300 or 847/318-8890, ⓦ www.eurorail.com. Europass and individual country passes for Spain and other countries.
Rail Europe US ☏ 1-877/257-2887, Canada ☏ 1-800/361-RAIL, ⓦ www.raileurope.com/us. Official North American Eurail Pass agent; also sells Europass, multinational passes and single-country passes.
ScanTours ☏ 1-800/223-7226 or 310/636-4656, ⓦ www.scantours.com. Eurail and other European country passes.

In Australia and New Zealand

CIT World Travel Australia ☏ 02/9267 1255 or 03/9650 5510, ⓦ www.cittravel.com.au. Eurail and Europass.

Rail Plus Australia ☏1300/555 003 or 03/9642
8644, ⓦwww.railplus.com.au. Sells Eurail and
Europass.
Trailfinders Australia ☏02/9247 7666,
ⓦwww.trailfinder.com.au. All Europe passes.

By car

Whilst getting around on public transport is
easy enough, you'll obviously have a great
deal more freedom if you have your **own car**.
Major roads throughout the country are good,
although some of the minor roads can be
rather hairy and are little more than dirt tracks
in the more remote regions. Driving in cities
can often seem a free-for-all, with traffic lights
providing a challenge and most drivers barrelling over pedestrian crossings. The open
road also has its dangers – Spain has one of
the highest incidences of traffic accidents in
Europe – and it pays to keep a weather eye
open for racers. A major plus is that Spain
has some of the lowest fuel prices on the
continent (but still almost double US prices).

Most foreign **driver's licences** are honoured in Spain – including all EU, US and
Canadian ones – but an International Driver's
Licence (available from motoring organizations, like the AA or RAC, in your home
country) is an easy way to set your mind at
rest. If you're bringing your own car, while it
is no longer compulsory to have a green card
and a bail bond, many insurers still advise
travellers to bring one. A green card will
prove to the Spanish authorities the extent of
your insurance cover. Always check current
requirements with your insurer in plenty of
time before leaving home. You must also
always carry two hazard triangles, an official
first-aid kit and a set of spare bulbs.

Away from main roads and on city side
streets you yield to vehicles approaching
from the right. **Speed limits** are posted –
maximum on urban roads is 60kph, on other
roads 90kph or 100kph where there is an
arcén, or hard shoulder; the limit on *autopis-
tas* or motorways is 120kph. On the main
highways speed traps are common, especially in the morning. If you're stopped for
any violation, the Spanish police can and
usually will levy a stiff, on-the-spot fine
(which can range from £210–420/$350–700
before letting you go on your way, especially
since as a foreigner you're unlikely to want,

or be able, to appear in court. Should you
not have the cash on you they will obligingly
escort you to the nearest cash machine and
issue you with a receipt there and then;
should you lack the ability to pay up immediately they can impound the vehicle and take
your passport as security.

In the big cities at least you'll probably
want to pay extra for a hotel with parking,
use a guarded pay car park, or be prepared
to strip the car of all its contents should you
park on the street (see "Vehicle crime" on
p.36). **Parking laws** are rigorously enforced
in cities, and any illegally parked vehicle will
be removed promptly – the authorities
sometimes (but don't count on this) leave a
sticker on the road telling you where to pay
the hefty fine (£65/$105 upwards) to retrieve
it. If your car disappears off the street it is
best to assume that it has been towed to
the local pound, and enquiries in any hotel,
government office or police station should
produce the address. You will be required to
pay the fine in cash. It's worth noting that it
is also a towable offence to park, on a taxi-
rank, so study any street signs carefully
wherever you park, and if in doubt ask locals
to be absolutely sure. The EU's new disabled
parking badges will satisfy even the most
pedantic of police.

Motoring organizations

In the UK and Ireland

AA ☏0870/600 0371, ⓦwww.theaa.com.
AA Ireland Dublin ☏01/617 9988,
ⓦwww.aaireland.ie.
RAC ☏0800/550 055, ⓦwww.rac.co.uk.
RAC Ireland ☏1890/483 483, ⓦwww.rac.ie.

In North America

AAA ☏1-800/AAA-HELP, ⓦwww.aaa.com. Each
state has its own club – check the phone book for
local address and phone number.
CAA ☏613/247-0117, ⓦwww.caa.ca. Each region
has its own club – check the phone book for local
address and phone number.

In Australia and New Zealand

AAA Australia ☏02/6247 7311,
ⓦwww.aaa.asn.au.
New Zealand AA New Zealand ☏09/377 4660,
ⓦwww.nzaa.co.nz.

Vehicle rental

Renting a car lets you out of many of the hassles, and Spain is one of the cheapest countries in Europe for this. You'll find a choice of companies in any major town, with the biggest ones – Hertz, Avis and Europcar – represented at the airports as well as in town centres. Local companies can often offer excellent value for money. You'll need to be 21 or over (and have been driving for at least a year), and you're looking at from €40 per day for a small car (less for the week, special rates at the weekend).

Fly-drive deals with Iberia and other operators can be good value if you know in advance that you'll want to rent a car; expect to pay around £120–180/$200–300 a week for low/high season. The big companies all offer schemes, but you'll often get a better deal through someone who deals with local agents. On the Internet, **easyRentacar.com** (ⓦwww.easyRentacar.com) offers car rental from Barcelona, Málaga and Madrid from as little as £8.75/$14.65 up to £24/$40 per day but with mileage restrictions and glaring company advertising on the exterior (see below). If you're going in high season try and book well in advance.

Vehicle crime is rampant in Spain, particularly in the major cities – never leave anything visible in the car, empty it if the vehicle is to be left on a city street overnight and check that all locks are fully functioning when you take delivery. It's a good idea to establish whether you have to pay extra if you remove any stickers bearing the rental company's name or logo. Many people are uncomfortable with these and regard them as a magnet for thieves, but there are often significant financial penalties written into the small print of your car rental document. When renting a car, it's worth paying the extra fee for insurance (around €6) to cover any damage from petty theft.

Renting **motorcycles** and **scooters** is also possible and prices start from around £16.80/$28 for 4 hours or £35/$58.50 a day; it's proportionately cheaper by the week. You have to be fourteen or over to ride a machine under 75cc, eighteen for one over 75cc, and crash helmets are compulsory. Note that mopeds and motorcycles are often rented out with insurance that doesn't include theft – always check with the company first.

Car rental agencies

In Britain

Avis ☎0870/606 0100, ⓦwww.avis.co.uk.
Budget ☎0800/181 181, ⓦwww.budget.co.uk.
Europcar ☎0845/722 2525,
ⓦwww.europcar.co.uk.
National ☎0870/536 5365,
ⓦwww.nationalcar.co.uk.
Hertz ☎0870/844 8844, ⓦwww.hertz.co.uk.
Suncars ☎0870/500 5566, ⓦwww.suncars.com.
Thrifty ☎01494/751 600, ⓦwww.thrifty.co.uk.
Transhire ☎0870/789/8000,
ⓦwww.transhire.com.

In Ireland

Argus Republic of Ireland ☎01/490 4444,
ⓦwww.argus-rentacar.com.
Atlas Republic of Ireland ☎01/844 4859,
ⓦwww.atlascarhire.com.
Avis Northern Ireland ☎028/9024 0404, Republic of Ireland ☎01/605 7500, ⓦwww.avis.ie.
Budget Republic of Ireland ☎0903/277 11,
ⓦwww.budget.ie.
Cosmo Thrifty Northern Ireland ☎028/9445 2565, ⓦwww.thrifty.co.uk.
Dan Dooley Republic of Ireland ☎06/253 103,
ⓦwww.dan-dooley.ie.
Europcar Northern Ireland ☎028/9442 3444, Republic of Ireland ☎01/614 2888,
ⓦwww.europcar.ie.
Hertz Republic of Ireland ☎01/676 7476,
ⓦwww.hertz.ie.
Holiday Autos Republic of Ireland ☎01/872 9366, ⓦwww.holidayautos.ie.
McCausland Northern Ireland ☎028/9033 3777,
ⓦwww.mccausland.co.uk.
SIXT Republic of Ireland ☎1850/206 088,
ⓦwww.irishcarrentals.ie.
Thrifty Republic of Ireland ☎1800/515 800,
ⓦwww.thrifty.ie.

In North America

Alamo US ☎1-800-522-9696,
ⓦwww.alamo.com.
Auto Europe US ☎1-800/223-5555, Canada ☎1-888/223-5555, ⓦwww.autoeurope.com.
Avis US ☎1-800/331-1084, Canada ☎1-800/272-5871, ⓦwww.avis.com.
Budget US ☎1-800/527-0700,

www.budgetrentacar.com.
Dollar US ☎1-800/800-4000, ⓦwww.dollar.com.
Enterprise Rent-a-Car US ☎1-800/325-8007,
ⓦwww.enterprise.com.
Europcar US & Canada ☎1-877/940 6900,
ⓦwww.europcar.com.
Europe by Car US ☎1-800/223-1516,
ⓦwww.europebycar.com.
Hertz US ☎1-800/654-3001, Canada ☎1-
800/263-0600, ⓦwww.hertz.com.
Holiday Autos US ☎1-800/422-7737,
ⓦwww.holidayautos.com.
National ☎1-800/227-7368,
ⓦwww.nationalcar.com.
Thrifty ☎1-800/367-2277, ⓦwww.thrifty.com.

In Australia

Avis ☎13 63 33 or 02/9353 9000,
ⓦwww.avis.com.au.
Budget ☎1300/362 848, ⓦwww.budget.com.au.
Dollar ☎02/9223 1444, ⓦwww.dollarcar.com.au.
Europcar ☎1300/131 390,
ⓦwww.deltaeuropcar.com.au.
Hertz ☎13 30 39 or 03/9698 2555,
ⓦwww.hertz.com.au.
Holiday Autos ☎1300/554 432,
ⓦwww.holidayautos.com.au.
National ☎13 10 45, ⓦwww.nationalcar.com.au.
Thrifty ☎1300/367 227, ⓦwww.thrifty.com.au.

In New Zealand

Apex ☎0800/93 95 97 or 03/379 6897,
ⓦwww.apexrentals.co.nz.
Avis ☎09/526 2847 or 0800/655 111,
ⓦwww.avis.co.nz.
Budget ☎09/976 2222, ⓦwww.budget.co.nz.
Hertz ☎0800/654 321, ⓦwww.hertz.co.nz.
Holiday Autos ☎0800/144 040,
ⓦwww.holidayautos.co.nz.
National ☎0800/800 115,
ⓦwww.nationalcar.co.nz.
Thrifty ☎09/309 0111, ⓦwww.thrifty.co.nz.

Hitching

As in most other countries these days, we do not recommend **hitching** in Spain as a safe method of getting around.

If you are determined to hitch, be warned that the road down the east coast (Barcelona–Valencia–Murcia) is notoriously difficult, and trying to get out of either Madrid or Barcelona can prove to be a nightmare (you're best off taking a bus out to a smaller place on the relevant road). Thumbing on back roads is, however, often surprisingly productive; the fewer cars there are, the more likely they are to stop.

Regionally there's considerable variation as well: the Basque country, and the north in general, often prove quite easy, whereas Andalucía tends to involve long (and very hot) waits.

By bicycle

Taking your own bike can be an inexpensive and flexible way of getting around, and of seeing a great deal of the country that would otherwise pass you by. Do remember, though, that Spain is one of the most mountainous countries in Europe and in the searing high summer temperatures, attempting to scale hills becomes an endurance test. Seasoned cycle tourists start out at dawn, covering the main part of the day's schedule by mid-morning, before the temperature peaks. That leaves the rest of the day for sightseeing, picnicking around riverbanks or dipping into the often pleasant village swimming pools, before covering a few more kilometres in the cooler hours before sunset.

The Spanish are keen cycle fans – both on and off-road – which means that you'll be well received and find reasonable facilities. There are **bike shops** in the larger towns and parts can often be found at auto repair shops or garages – look for Michelin signs. On the road, cars tend to hoot before they pass, which can be alarming at first but is useful once you're used to it. When cycling on major roads in a group always go in single file – never side by side – as this is dangerous and has resulted in several deaths in recent years. Cycle-touring guides to the better areas can be found in good bookshops – in Spanish, of course.

Getting your bike there should present few problems. Most **airlines** are happy to take them as ordinary baggage provided they come within your allowance (though it's sensible to check first and get an agreement in writing from the agent or airline as they may try to charge you up to £60/$80 at the airport); crowded charters may be less obliging. Deflate the tyres to avoid explosions in the unpressurized hold. Spanish **trains** are also reasonably accessible, though bikes can only go on a train with a guard's van (*furgón*) and must be registered – go to the *Equipajes* or *Paquexpres* desk at the station. If you are not travelling with the bike you can either send it as a package or buy an undated ticket and use the method above.

When staying in major towns and cities try not to leave your bike on the street overnight, even with a secure lock, as thieves view them as easy pickings. Most *hostales* seem able to find somewhere safe for overnight storage.

By plane

Iberia and the smaller, slightly cheaper subsidiary Aviaco, as well as the independent companies Spanair and AirEurope, operate an extensive network of internal flights. While these are quite reasonable by international standards, they still work out very pricey, and are only really worth considering if you're in a hurry and need to cross the entire peninsula. The main exceptions are the route between Madrid and Barcelona, which is very poorly serviced by public transport, or getting to, and between, the Balearic Islands, for which flights are only marginally more expensive than the ferries. In peak season you may well have to reserve long in advance for these (see "The Balearic Islands" for more details).

From North America, Central Holidays/ Discover Spain Vacations sell the **Spain Airpass** for $206 for three flights on Iberia or Aviaco within Spain (in conjunction with an Iberia transatlantic flight). Air Europa (see p.13) is a carrier offering internal flights which can be booked from North America. In Australia, the Spain Airpass is available from Spanish Tourism Promotions in Melbourne (see p.25). The Spain Airpass isn't available in Britain and Ireland.

Post, phones and the Internet

Post offices (*Correos*) are generally found near the centre of towns and are normally open from 8am to noon and again from 5 to 7.30pm, though big branches in large cities may have considerably longer hours and usually do not close at midday. Except in the cities there's only one post office in each town, and queues can be long: stamps are also sold at tobacconists (look for the brown and yellow *Tabac* sign).

You can have letters sent **poste restante** (*Lista de Correos*) to any Spanish post office: they should be addressed (preferably with the surname underlined and in capitals) to *Lista de Correos* followed by the name of the town and province. To collect, take along your passport and, if you're expecting mail, ask the clerk to check under all of your names – letters are often to be found filed under first or middle names.

Outbound mail is reasonably reliable, with letters or cards taking around three days to a week to the UK and Europe, a week to ten days to North America, New Zealand and Australia, although it can be more erratic in the summer.

Phones

Spanish public **phones** work well and have instructions in English. If you can't find one, many bars also have pay phones you can use. Cabins and other phones take euros but you're best off buying a phone card (from a *kiosko* or *tabac*) of €10 or €15, which avoids hassles finding the right change. All cabins should display instructions in a variety of languages. Spanish provincial (and some overseas) dialling codes are displayed in the cabins. The **ringing tone** is long, **engaged** is shorter and rapid; the standard Spanish response is *digáme* ("speak to me"), often abbreviated to *diga*, or the even more laconic *sí*.

Useful telephone numbers

Directory Enquiries ☎1003
International Operator ☎1008
(Europe)
International Operator ☎1005 (rest
of the world)
Alarm call ☎096
Time ☎093
Weather ☎906 365 365

For **international calls**, you can use any street cabin or go to a **locutorio**, an office where you pay afterwards. Phoning within Spain is cheaper after 8pm and all weekend for metropolitan and inter-provincial calls. International rates are slightly cheaper between 8pm and 8am; the reduced rates apply all day on Saturday and Sunday. If you're using a cabin to call abroad and don't use a phone card, you're best off putting at least €2 in to ensure a connection.

Calling home from Spain

One of the most convenient ways of phoning home from abroad is via a **telephone charge card** from your phone company back home. Using a PIN number, you can make calls from most hotel, public and private phones that will be charged to your account. Since most major charge cards are free to obtain, it's certainly worth getting one at least for emergencies; enquire first, though, whether your destination is covered, and bear in mind that rates aren't necessarily cheaper than calling from a public phone.

In **the UK and Ireland**, British Telecom (☎0800/345 144, ◉www.payphones.bt .com) will issue free to all BT customers the BT Charge Card, which can be used in 116 countries; AT&T (dial ☎0800/890 011, then 888/641-6123 when you hear the AT&T prompt to be transferred to the Florida Call Centre; free 24 hours) has the Global Calling Card; while NTL (☎0500/100 505) issues its own Global Calling Card, which can be used in more than sixty countries, though the fees cannot be charged to a normal phone bill.

In the **US and Canada**, AT&T, MCI, Sprint, Canada Direct and other North American long-distance companies all enable their customers to make credit-card calls while overseas, billed to your home number. Call your company's customer service line to find out if they provide service from Spain, and if so, what the toll-free access code is.

To call **Australia and New Zealand** from overseas, telephone charge cards such as Telstra Telecard or Optus Calling Card in Australia, and Telecom NZ's Calling Card can be used to make calls abroad, which are charged back to a domestic account or credit card. Apply to Telstra (☎1800/038 000), Optus (☎1300/300 937), or Telecom NZ (☎04/801 9000).

Once in Spain, you can buy the **España Mundo** card from tobacconists for €30 (details on ☎900 902 902), which will let you call Europe or North America at discount rates.

To Britain: dial ☎00 then 44 + area code minus first 0 + number.
To Ireland: dial ☎00 then 353 + area code minus first 0 + number.
To North America: dial ☎00 then 1 + area code + number.
To Australia: dial ☎00 then 61 + area code minus first 0 + number.

Calling Spain from abroad

From Britain: dial ☎00 + 34 + number.
From North America: dial ☎011 + 34 + number.
From Australia: dial ☎0011 + 34 + number.
From New Zealand: dial ☎00 + 34 + number.

Mobile phones

If you want to use your mobile phone abroad, you'll need to check with your phone provider whether it will work abroad, and what the call charges are. In the UK, for all but the very top-of-the-range packages, you'll have to inform your phone provider before going abroad to get international access switched on. You may get charged extra for this depending on your existing package and where you are travelling to. You are also likely to be charged extra for incoming calls when abroad, as the people calling you will be paying the usual rate. If you want to retrieve messages while you're away, you'll have to ask your provider for a new access code, as your home one is unlikely to work abroad. For further information about using your phone abroad, check out ⓦwww.telecomsadvice.org.uk/features /using_your_mobile_abroad.htm.

Unless you have a tri-band phone, it is unlikely that a mobile bought for use in the US will work outside the States. For details of which mobiles will work outside the US, contact your mobile service provider. Most mobiles in Australia and New Zealand use GSM, which works well in Europe.

The Internet

The **Internet** has made great inroads into Spanish life and access is widely available at cafés (more commonly referred to as *ciber-cafés* in Spanish), some computer shops and many *locutorios*. Prices vary; in cities hourly

rates can be as little as €2, rising to around €6–8 in some smaller towns. For details of useful websites on Spain, see p.26.

One of the best ways to keep in touch while travelling is to sign up for a free Internet email address that can be accessed from anywhere, for example YahooMail or Hotmail – accessible through ⓦwww.yahoo.com and ⓦwww.hotmail.com. Once you've set up an account, you can use these sites to pick up and send mail from any Internet café, or hotel with Internet access.

ⓦwww.kropla.com is a useful website giving details of how to plug your laptop in when abroad, phone country codes around the world, and information about electrical systems in different countries.

The media

Your exposure to the local media is mostly going to be in bars or your hotel, where local and national newspapers are usually available for customers, although in many cases these will be one of the several devoted to football. Otherwise, you're rarely far from a kiosk, the larger of which stock all Spanish and some foreign papers. In the major towns and on the coast, English-language newspapers are generally available on the day of issue, some of which are published in continental Europe. In bars or in some of the more down-to-earth restaurants, you'll also see as much of the dreadful TV service as you're ever likely to want, while the usual satellite channels are commonly available in sports-orientated bars.

The press

Of the **Spanish newspapers** the best are the centre-left *El País* and the centre-right *El Mundo*, both of which have good arts and foreign news coverage, including comprehensive regional "what's on" listings and supplements every weekend. Other national papers include the solidly elitist *ABC* and Barcelona's *La Vanguardia*. The regional press is generally run by local magnates and is predominantly right of centre, though often supporting local autonomy movements. Nationalist press includes *Avui* in Catalunya, printed largely in Catalan, and the Basque papers *El Correo Español del Pueblo Vasco*, *Deia* and *Gara*, the last a supporter of ETA.

British newspapers and the *International Herald Tribune* are on sale in most large cities and resorts. There are also various English-language magazines produced by and for the expatriate communities in the main cities and on the *costas*; all are of limited interest, though occasionally they carry details of local events and entertainment.

TV and radio

You'll inadvertently catch more **TV** than you expect sitting in bars and restaurants where the set often blares away on a shelf in one corner. It's improved a lot since the days when the news regularly came on over an hour late and the highlight one Christmas

Eve, not so long ago, was a documentary on hemorrhoids, but it's still irredeemably awful. The most thoroughly appalling concoction of asinine game shows, wooden soaps, cheesy time-warp gala shows and what can most politely be described as endless bouts of televised radio will soon send you out in search of other more gainful activities. Sports fans are better served – particularly **football** and basketball followers – and despite many of the best games now being on pay-per-view, most bars subscribe and are a fun place to enjoy the atmosphere of a match. Films – usually dubbed – are often played back-to-back at weekends and on holidays, but the practice of frequent ten-minute ad breaks means a two-hour film will fill a three-hour slot and become unwatchable.

Things are generally a little better on the **radio** with hundreds of local channels alongside a handful of national ones; twiddle the dial a little and stop when you hear something that takes your fancy. If you have a radio which picks up short wave you can tune in to the BBC World Service, broadcasting in English for most of the day on frequencies between 12MHz (24m) and 4MHz (75m). You can also listen to Voice of America through their website (Ⓦwww.voa.gov), where you'll find the range of frequencies on which they broadcast.

Accommodation

Ranging from the humblest of *pensiones* to superb five-star luxury, accommodation in Spain is still reasonably priced compared with other European countries and offers a broad range of styles and facilities. In almost any town you'll be able to get a no-frills double for under €30 and a single for €12–20, while you should expect to pay upwards of €90 for a three-star hotel; for four- and five-star establishments, services and prices go through the roof.

We've detailed where to find places to stay in most of the destinations listed in the Guide, and given a price range for each (see below), from the most basic rooms to luxury hotels. As a general rule, all you have to do is head for the cathedral or main square of any town, invariably surrounded by an old quarter full of accommodation possibilities. In Spain, unlike most countries, you don't always have to pay more for a central

Accommodation price codes

All the establishments listed in this book have been categorized according to the price codes outlined below. They represent the price for the **cheapest available double room in high season**; effectively, this means that anything in the ❶ and most places in the ❷ range will be without private bath, though there's usually a washbasin in the room. In the ❹ category and above you will probably be getting private facilities. Remember, though, that many of the budget places will also have more expensive rooms including en-suite facilities. We've used price codes for double rooms in youth hostels but have given the euro rate for dorm beds.

❶ Under €30	❷ €31–45	❸ €46–60
❹ €61–80	❺ €81–100	❻ €101–120
❼ €121–160	❽ €161–200	❾ Over €200

location (this goes for bars and cafés, too), though you do tend to get a comparatively bad deal if you're travelling on your own as there are relatively few single rooms. If there are more than two of you, most places have rooms with three or four beds at not a great deal more than the double-room price – a bargain, especially if you have children in tow. If you're making your own reservation in high season on the *costas*, many hotels only take bookings for a minimum of a week, while some also require that you reserve at least half board; having said that, there are still plenty of places that are more flexible, although you will need to book well in advance.

Hotel vouchers (*bonos*), available from local travel agents, often give substantial discounts at medium to upmarket hotels; simply present the voucher at the hotel instead of payment.

Fondas, pensiones, hostales, hotels and casas rurales

The variety of types and places to stay is fiendishly complicated and it is further exacerbated by the various regions often using their own distinctions or by establishments continuing to use older denominations after new ones have been introduced. As a rule, the least expensive of all are **fondas** (identifiable by a square blue sign with a white **F** on it, and often positioned above a bar), closely followed by **casas de huéspedes** (**CH** on a similar sign), the more common **pensiones** (**P**) and less frequent **hospedajes**. Distinctions between all of these are rather blurred, but in general you'll sometimes find food served at both *fondas* and *pensiones* while *casas de huéspedes* (literally "guest houses") were traditionally for longer stays. However, as Spain upgrades its tourist facilities, both *fondas* and *casas de huéspedes* are gradually disappearing and, along the *costas* particularly, they are very rare.

Slightly more expensive but far more common are **hostales** (marked **Hs**) and **hostal-residencias** (**HsR**). These are categorized from one star to three stars, but even so prices vary enormously according to location – in general the more remote, the less expensive. Most *hostales* offer good functional rooms, usually with private shower, and, for doubles at least, they can be excellent value.

Moving up the scale you finally reach fully-fledged **hotels** (**H**), again star-graded by the authorities (from one to five). One-star hotels cost no more than three-star *hostales* – sometimes they're actually less expensive – but at three stars you pay a lot more, and at four or five you're in the luxury class with prices to match.

Near the top end of this scale there are also state-run **paradores** (W www.parador .es): usually beautiful places, often converted from castles, monasteries and other minor Spanish monuments, although the ones on the coasts are more commonly purpose-built in the 1960s. Even if you can't afford to stay, the buildings are often worth a look in their own right, and usually have pleasantly classy bars and restaurants.

Outside all of these categories you will sometimes see **camas** (beds) and **habitaciones** (rooms) advertised in private houses or above bars, often with the phrase *camas y comidas* ("beds and meals"). If you're travelling on a very tight budget these can be worth looking out for – particularly if you're offered one at a bus station and the owner is prepared to bargain with you.

Finally, **casas rurales** (rural houses) or casas de pagès in Catalunya, a scheme established along the lines of French *gîtes*, have gone from strength to strength in Spain and can offer excellent value – they are where many Spanish holiday-makers stay if they have the choice. Accommodation at these can vary from bed and breakfast at a farmhouse to self-catering in a restored manor. Local *turismos* have details.

If you have any **problems** with Spanish rooms – overcharging, most obviously – you can usually produce an immediate resolution by asking for the *libro de reclamaciones* (complaints book). By law all establishments must keep one and bring it out for regular inspection by the authorities. Although little is ever written in them they are worth using and, as the pages are numbered, difficult to tamper with. If you do make an entry, English is acceptable but write clearly and simply; add your home address, too, as you are entitled to be informed of any action, including – but don't count on it – compensation. Most establishments prefer to keep them empty, thus attracting no unwelcome attention from officialdom which, of course, works in your favour. You can also take your complaint to any local turismo, who will, if possible, attempt to resolve the matter while you wait.

Youth hostels, mountain refuges and monasteries

Albergues Juveniles (youth hostels) are rarely very practical, except in northern Spain (especially the Pyrenees) where it can be difficult for solo, short-term travellers to find any other bed in summer. Outside Andalucía, which has upgraded its nineteen hostels, only about twenty Spanish *albergues* stay open all year – the rest operate just for the summer (or spring and summer) in temporary premises – and in cities they tend to be inconveniently located. The most useful are detailed in the Guide, or you can get a complete list with opening times and phone numbers from the YHA (see below). Be warned that they tend to have curfews, are often block-reserved by school groups and demand production of a YHA card (though this is generally available on the spot if you haven't already bought one from your national organization). At around €12 for under-26s and €18 for over-26s in high season per person, you can quite easily pay the same as for sharing a cheap double room in a *hostal* or *pensión*.

In isolated mountain areas the Federación Madrileña de Montañismo, Apodaca 18, 1° Dcha, Madrid 28004 (☎915 038 074), and two Catalunya-based clubs – the Federació d'Entitats Excursionistes de Catalunya (Rambla 41 1r Pral., 08002 Barcelona; ☎934 120 777, ⊛www.feec.es), and the Unió Excursionista de Catalunya de Gràcia (Santa Agata 30, 08012 Barcelona; ☎932 175 650, ⊛www.gencat.es/entitats/ unexcag.htm) – run a number of **refugios**: simple, cheap dormitory huts for climbers and trekkers, generally equipped only with bunks and a very basic kitchen, and costing around €3 per person. Again off the beaten track, it is sometimes possible to stay at Spanish **monasterios** or **conventos**. Often severely underpopulated, these may let empty cells for a small charge. You can just turn up and ask – many will take visitors regardless of sex – but if you want to be sure of a reception it's best to approach the local turismo first, and phone ahead. There are some particularly wonderful monastic locations in Galicia, Catalunya and Mallorca.

Those following the **Camino de Santiago** can also take advantage of monastic accommodation specifically reserved for pilgrims along the route; see p.618 for more information.

Youth hostel associations

In UK and Ireland

Irish Youth Hostel Association ☎01/830 4555, ⊛www.irelandyha.org. Annual membership €15; under-18s €7.50; family €31.50; lifetime €75.
Hostelling International Northern Ireland ☎028/9032 4733, ⊛www.hini.org.uk. Adult membership £10; under-18s £6; family £20; lifetime £75.
Scottish Youth Hostel Association ☎0870/155 3255, ⊛www.syha.org.uk. Annual membership £6, for under-18s £2.50.
Youth Hostel Association (YHA) ☎0870/770 8868, ⊛www.yha.org.uk. Annual membership for residents of England and Wales £13; under-18s £6.50; lifetime £190 (or five annual payments of £40).

In North America

Hostelling International-American Youth Hostels ☎202/783-6161, ⊛www.hiayh.org. Annual membership for adults (18–55) is $25, for seniors (55 or over) is $15, and for under-18s and groups of ten or more, is free. Lifetime memberships are $250.
Hostelling International Canada ☎1-800/663 5777 or 613/237 7884, ⊛www.hostellingintl.ca. Rather than sell the traditional 1- or 2-year memberships, the association now sells one Individual Adult membership with a 28- to 16-month term. The length of the term depends on when the membership is sold, but a member can receive up to 28 months of membership for just $35. Membership is free for under-18s and you can become a lifetime member for $175.

In Australia and New Zealand

Australia Youth Hostels Association ☎02/9261 1111, ⊛www.yha.com.au. Adult membership rate US$52 (under-18s, US$16) for the first twelve months, and then US$32 each year after.
Youth Hostelling Association New Zealand ☎0800/278 299 or 03/379 9970, ⊛www.yha.co.nz. Adult membership NZ$40 for one year, NZ$60 for two and NZ$80 for three; under-18s free; lifetime NZ$300.

Camping

There are literally hundreds of authorized campsites in Spain, mostly on the coast and in holiday areas. They work out at about £2.10/$3.50 per person plus the same again for a tent, and a similar amount for each car or caravan, perhaps twice as much for a van. Some of the best located sites or the ones with top-range facilities can work out significantly more expensive. Again, we've detailed the most useful in the text, but if you plan to camp extensively, pick up the free *Mapa de Campings* from the National Tourist Board, the more complete *Guía de Campings* (€6), which you can find in larger or specialist bookshops, or see ⓦ www.vay-acamping.net.

In most cases, **camping outside campsites** is legal – but there are certain restrictions. There must be fewer than ten people in your group, and you're not allowed to camp "in urban areas, areas prohibited for military or touristic reasons, or within 1km of an official campsite". What this means in practice is that you can't camp on the beach (though you can, discreetly, nearby) but with a little sensitivity you can set up a tent for a short period almost anywhere in the countryside. Whenever possible, ask locally first.

If you're planning to do a lot of camping, an **international camping carnet** is a good investment. The carnet gives discounts at member sites and serves as useful identification. Many campsites will take it instead of making you surrender your passport during your stay, and it covers you for third-party insurance when camping. In the **UK and Ireland**, the carnet costs £4.50, and is available to members of the AA or the RAC (see above), or for members only from either of the following: the **Camping and Caravanning Club** (☎024/7669 4995, ⓦ www.campingandcaravanningclub.co.uk; annual membership £27.50), or the foreign touring arm of the same company, the **Carefree Travel Service** (☎024/7642 2024), which provides the international camping carnet free if you take out insurance with them; they also book ferry crossings and inspect camping sites in Europe.

In the **US and Canada**, the carnet is available from home motoring organizations, or from **Family Campers and RVers** (FCRV; ☎1-800/245-9755, ⓦ www.fcrv.org). FCRV annual membership costs $25, and the carnet an additional $10. In **Australia and New Zealand**, the carnet can be bought through home motoring organizations for around A$10.

Eating and drinking

There are two ways to eat out in Spain: you can go to a *restaurante* or *comedor* (dining room) and have a full meal, or you can have a succession of tapas (small snacks) or *raciones* (larger ones) at one or more bars. At the bottom line a *comedor* – where you'll get a basic, filling, three-course meal with a drink, the *menú del día* – is the cheapest option, but they're often tricky to find, and drab places when you do. Bars tend to work out pricier but a lot more interesting, allowing you to do the rounds and sample local or house specialities. Restaurants range from the very ordinary to the superb, with prices to match, although eating out is still much cheaper than in northern Europe; most offer a *menú del día* at lunchtime from Monday to Friday, which works out much cheaper than eating *a la carta*.

Breakfast, snacks and sandwiches

For **breakfast** you're best off in a bar or café, though some *hostales* and *fondas* will serve the "Continental" basics, while three-star hotels and upwards often provide a sizeable buffet The traditional Spanish breakfast is *chocolate con churros* – long tubular doughnuts (not for the weak of stomach) with thick drinking chocolate. But most places also serve *tostadas* (toast) with oil (*con aceite*) or butter (*con mantequilla*) – and jam (*y mermelada*), or more substantial egg dishes such as *huevos fritos* (fried eggs), which are not a typical Spanish breakfast but do tend to be on offer in tourist areas. *Tortilla* (potato omelette) also makes an excellent breakfast.

Coffee and pastries (*pasteles* or *bollos*) or doughnuts are available at most cafés, too, though for a wider selection of cakes you should head for one of the many excellent *pastelerías* or *confiterías*. In larger towns there will often be a *panadería* or *croissantería* serving quite an array of appetizing baked goods besides the obvious bread, croissants and pizza. For ordering coffee see p.49.

Some bars specialize in **bocadillos** – hearty French bread-style sandwiches with a choice of fillings. If you want them wrapped to take away with you, ask for them *para llevar*. Incidentally, don't confuse it with the word "sandwich" when you order a *bocadillo*, as, in Spain, this is usually on sad, processed white bread – often with ham and cheese or something with a lot of mayonnaise.

Tapas and raciones

One of the advantages of eating in **bars** is that you are able to experiment. Many places have food laid out on the counter, so you can see what's available and order by pointing without necessarily knowing the names; others have blackboards or *"lista de las tapas"* (see p.1122). **Tapas** (often called **pinchos** or **pintxos** in northern Spain) are small portions, three or four small chunks of fish or meat, or a dollop of salad, which traditionally used to be served up free with a drink. These days you often have to pay for anything more than a few olives, but a single helping rarely costs more than €2.50 unless you're somewhere flashy. **Raciones** (costing around €6–10) are simply bigger plates of the same, intended for sharing among a couple of people, and can be enough in themselves for a light meal. The more people you're with, of course, the better; half a dozen *tapas* or *pinchos* and three *raciones* can make a varied and quite filling meal for three or four people.

Tascas, **bodegas**, **cervecerías** and **tabernas** are all types of bar where you'll find tapas and *raciones*. Most of them have different sets of prices depending on whether you stand at the bar to eat (the basic charge) or sit at tables (up to fifty percent more expensive – and even more if you sit out on a terrace).

Wherever you have tapas, it is important to find out what the local **special** is and order it. Spaniards will commonly move from bar to bar, having just the one dish that they consider each bar does well. A bar's "non-standard" dishes, these days, can all too often be microwaved – which is not a good way to cook squid.

Meals and restaurants

Once again, there's a multitude of distinctions. You can sit down and have a full meal in a *comedor*, a *cafetería*, a *restaurante* or a *marisquería* – all in addition to the more food-oriented bars.

Comedores are the places to seek out if your main criteria are price and quantity. Sometimes you will see them attached to a bar (often in a room behind), or as the dining room of a *hostal* or *pensión*, but as often as not they're virtually unmarked and discovered only if you pass an open door. Since they're essentially workers' cafés they tend to serve more substantial meals at lunchtime than in the evenings (when they may be closed altogether). When you can find them – the tradition, with its family-run business and marginal wages, is on the way out – you'll probably pay around €6–8 for a **menú del día**, **cubierto** or **menú de la casa**, all of which mean the same – a complete meal of three courses, usually with bread, wine and dessert included.

The highway equivalent of *comedores* are **ventas**, which you'll be extremely glad of if you're doing much travelling by road. These roadside inns dotted along the main roads between towns and cities have been serving

Spanish wayfarers for hundreds of years – many of them quite literally – and the best *ventas* are wonderful places to get tasty country cooking at bargain prices. Again, the *menú del día* is the one to go for, and the best places usually have quite a gathering of lorries in their car park, shrewd long-distance truck drivers being among the best customers.

Replacing *comedores* to some extent are **cafeterías**, which the local authorities grade from one to three cups (the ratings, as with restaurants, seem to be based on facilities offered rather than the quality of the food). These can be good value, too, especially the self-service places, but their emphasis is more northern European and the light snack-meals served tend to be dull. Food here often comes in the form of a **plato combinado** – literally a combined dish – which will be something like egg and chips or *calamares* and salad (or occasionally a weird combination like steak and a piece of fish), often with bread and a drink included. This will generally cost in the region of €6–9. *Cafeterías* often serve some kind of *menú del día* as well. You may prefer to get your *plato combinado* at a bar, which in small towns with no *comedores* may be the only way to eat inexpensively.

Moving up the scale, there are **restaurantes** (designated by one to five forks) and **marisquerías**, the latter serving exclusively fish and seafood. *Restaurantes* at the bottom of the scale are often not much different in price from *comedores*, and will also generally have *platos combinados* available. A fixed-price *menú del día* is often better value, though: generally three courses plus wine and bread for around €7–12. Move above two forks, however, or find yourself in one of the more fancy *marisquerías* (as opposed to a basic seafront fish-fry place), and prices can escalate rapidly. However, even here most of the top restaurants offer an upmarket *menú* called a **menú de degustación** (a sampler meal, usually including wine) which is often excellent value and allows you to try out some of the country's finest cooking for €25–35.

To avoid receiving confused stares from waiters in restaurants, you should always ask for **la carta** when you want a menu; *menú* in Spanish refers only to a fixed-price meal. In addition, in all but the most rock-bottom establishments it is customary to leave a small **tip** (*propina*): Spaniards are judicious tippers, so only do so if the service merits it. The amount is up to you, though five percent of the bill in a restaurant is quite sufficient. Service is normally included in a *menú del día*. The other thing to take account of in medium- and top-price restaurants is the addition of **IVA**, a seven percent tax on your bill. It should say on the menu if this is not included in the price.

Spaniards generally eat very late, so most of these places serve food from around 1pm until 4pm and from 8pm to midnight. Many restaurants **close on Sunday or Monday evening**. Outside these times, generally the only places open are the **fast-food** joints; *Pans & Co* and *Bocatta* serve surprisingly good *bocadillos* and often have special offers.

What to eat

It's possible to make a few generalizations about Spanish food. If you like **fish and seafood** you'll be in heaven in Spain, as this forms the basis of a vast array of tapas and is fresh and excellent even hundreds of miles from the sea. It's not cheap, unfortunately, so rarely forms part of the lowest priced menus (though you may get the most common fish – cod, often salted, and hake – or squid) but you really should make the most of what's on offer. Fish stews (*zarzuelas*) and rice-based paellas (which also contain meat, usually rabbit or chicken) are often memorable in seafood restaurants. Paella comes originally from Valencia and is still best there, but you'll find versions of it all over Spain.

Meat is most often grilled and served with a few fried potatoes and a couple of salad leaves, or cured or dried and served as a starter or in sandwiches. *Jamón serrano*, the Spanish version of Parma ham, is superb, though the best varieties, from Extremadura and Huelva in the southwest, are extremely expensive. In country areas game is very much on the menu, too – you may find the baby animal specialities of central Spain, such as *cochinillo* (suckling pig) or *lechal* (suckling lamb), less appetizing.

Vegetables rarely amount to more than a few fries or boiled potatoes with the main dish (though you can often order a side dish à la carte). It's more usual to start your meal with a **salad** or, in the north especially, you may get hearty vegetable soups or a plate of boiled potatoes and greens as a starter.

Dessert in the cheaper places is nearly always fresh fruit or flan, the Spanish crème caramel, with the regions often having their own versions such as *crema catalana* in Catalunya and the Andalucian *tocino de cielo*. There are also various varieties of *pudín* – rice pudding or assorted blancmange mixtures – and a range of commercial ice-cream dishes. In some fancier restaurants you may discover a chef who has a flair for desserts, but they are not generally a high point of Spanish cuisine.

Vegetarians

Vegetarians have a fairly hard time of it in Spain: there's usually something to eat, but you may get weary of eggs and omelettes (*tortilla francesa* is a plain omelette, *tortilla de patatas* comes with potatoes). In the big cities you'll find vegetarian restaurants and ethnic places which serve vegetable dishes. Otherwise, superb fresh produce is always available in the markets and shops, and cheese, fruit and eggs are available everywhere.

In restaurants you're faced with the extra problem that pieces of meat – especially ham, which the Spanish don't seem to regard as real meat – and tuna are often added to vegetable dishes and salads to "spice them up". The phrases to get to know are *Soy vegetariano/a. Como sólo verduras. Hay algo sin carne?* ("I'm a vegetarian. I only eat vegetables. Is there anything without meat?"); you may have to add *y sin mariscos* ("and without seafood") and *y sin jamón* ("and without ham") to be really safe.

If you're a **vegan**, you're either going to have to be not too fussy or accept weight loss if you're away for any length of time. Some salads and vegetable dishes are strictly vegan, but they're few and far between. Fruit and nuts are widely available, nuts being sold by street vendors everywhere.

A good resource for those with Internet access is a new **website** – ⓦwww.veg.org – which hopes to compile, with a little help from users, a guide to vegetarian restaurants in Spain. There are also plenty of places recommended in the Guide.

Alcoholic drinks

In recent years, Spanish **wine** has enjoyed a huge upturn in quality and clout, led largely by Rioja, which has some of the most stringent standards of any Designation of Origin anywhere. No less prestigious is **sherry**, produced around Andalucía in the "Sherry Triangle" around Jerez, and some of the locally produced **brandies**. Foreign brands of **beer** are increasingly common, but local breweries produce some very good lagers that are often a cheaper option.

Wine

Over fifty percent of the European Union's vineyards lie in Spain and **vino** (wine), either *tinto* (red), *blanco* (white) or *rosado/clarete* (rosé), is the invariable accompaniment to every meal. As a rule, wine is inexpensive and generally ranges from drinkable to superb, with price offering a fair indication of quality. The wines to look out for are whites from Galicia and reds from Rioja, Navarra and Ribera del Duero. *Cava* (Spain's champagne) generally comes from Catalunya and is a real bargain, whilst Andalucía is noted for its sherries and brandies. One thing worth knowing about Spanish wine is the terms related to the ageing process which defines the best wines; *crianza* wines must have a minimum of two years' ageing before sale; red *reserva* wines at least two years (of which one must be in oak barrels); red *gran reserva* at least two years in oak and three in the bottle. White *gran reserva* guarantees five years' ageing (of which six months must be in oak). One thing to look for is a **Designation of Origin** (DO) label on the back of the bottle, denoting that the wine has satisfied the demanding quality assessment carried out by the relevant regional wine control board.

Spain's most famous red wine, and deservedly so, is Rioja, from the area round Logroño on the edge of the Basque country, which is unbeatable for the stringent quality standards it has to pass to earn the DO label, and for its finesse; it is widely available everywhere (Cune, López Heredia, Marques de Caceres, Paternina and La Rioja Alta are brands to try). Another top-drawer and currently fashionable region is Ribera del Duero in Castilla-León which makes Spain's most expensive wine, Vega Sicilia, besides other outstanding reds (Pesquera, Viña Pedrosa and Senorio de Nava are names to look out for). The new kid on the block is Priorat, from the Tarragona area in Catalunya, a rather high-alcohol content wine that is rapidly gaining in reputation, borne out by the exorbitant prices; if you want to try it but balk at the cost, try the neighbouring Montsant DO, which is similar but a fraction of the price. There are also scores of local wines – some of the best are Navarra (Chivite, Palacio de la Vega), Somontano, from Aragón (Enate, Viñas del Vero), and other areas of Catalunya (most notably Raimat and Alella), a region which also produces the champagne-like **cava** (the best labels to sample are Recaredo and Juve i Camps). Galicia, too, in the temperate northwest, produces some notable white wines (Ribeiro, Fefiñanes and Albariño are prominent producers). Reasonable-quality wines and Riojas are available in most restaurants and bars, although in many low-budget eating places you'll rarely be offered a wide choice. A popular way of drinking table wine served with a *menú del día* or cheap red wine on a hot day is to mix it with *gaseosa*, a lemon-flavoured fizzy drink called *Tinto de Verano*. In a bar, a small glass of wine will generally cost around €0.50–0.70; in a restaurant, if wine is not included in the menu, prices start at around €5 a bottle, although you'll be paying at least double this and more for quality wine. If it is included, you'll usually get a whole bottle for two people, a *media botella* (a third to a half of a litre) for one.

Sherry

The classic Andalucian wine is **sherry** – *vino de Jerez,* which refers to the wines produced in a triangular-shaped area to the west of the town of Jerez de la Frontera. Served chilled or at *bodega* temperature – *fino* (the Spanish name for dry sherry) is a perfect drink to wash down tapas – and, like everything Spanish, it comes in a perplexing variety of forms. The main distinctions are between *fino* or *jerez seco* (dry sherry), *amontillado* (medium dry), and *oloroso* or *jerez dulce* (sweet), and these are the terms you should use to order. *Manzanilla* is another member of the sherry family produced in the seaside town of Sanlúcar de Barrameda; the vineyard's proximity to the sea gives it a delicate, briny tang. Similar – though not identical – is *montilla*, an excellent dry sherry-like wine from the province of Córdoba. The main distinction between this and the other *finos* is that no alcohol is added at the production stage, prompting the *cordobeses* to claim that theirs is the more natural product, but sales and popularity still lag way behind those of its rival.

Beer and sangría

Cerveza, lager-type beer, is generally pretty good, though more expensive than wine. It comes in 300-ml bottles (*botellines*) or, for about the same price, on tap – a *caña* of draught beer is a small glass, a *caña doble* larger, and asking for *un tubo* (a tubular glass) gets you about half a pint. Many bartenders will assume you want a *doble* or *un tubo*, so if you don't, say so. Mahou, Cruz Campo, San Miguel, Estrella Dorada and Victoria are all decent beers, and local brands too are worth trying, such as Estrella de Galicia or Alhambra. If you would prefer a shandy, ask for a *clara*.

Equally refreshing, though often deceptively strong, is **sangría**, a wine-and-fruit punch which you'll come across at fiestas and in tourist bars; a variation in Catalunya is sangría de cava. *Tinto de verano* is a similar red wine and soda or lemonade combination which is a great refresher in high temperatures; variations on this include *tinto de verano con naranja* (red wine with orangeade) or *con limón* (mixed with a Fanta lemon juice).

Liqueurs and spirits

In mid-afternoon – or even at breakfast – Spaniards take a *copa* of **liqueur** with their coffee. The best are *anís* (like Pernod) or *coñac*, excellent local brandy with a distinct vanilla flavour; try Magno, Soberano, or Carlos III ("tercero") to get an idea of the variety, or Carlos I ("primero"), Lepanto, or Gran Duque de Alba for a measure of the quality. Most brandies are produced by the great sherry houses in Jerez, but two equally good ones that aren't are the Armagnac-like Mascaró and Torres, both produced in Catalunya. As an alternative to brandy at the end of a meal, many restaurants and bars serve *chupitos* – little shot glasses full of a variety of flavours of schnapps or local fire water such as Patxarán in Navarra and the Basque Country, Ratafía in Catalunya or Orujo in Galicia.

In bars **spirits** are ordered by brand name, since there are generally less expensive Spanish equivalents for standard imports. Larios gin from Málaga, for instance, is about half the price of Gordon's. Specify *nacional* to avoid getting an expensive foreign brand. Spirits can be pricey at the trendier bars; however, wherever they are served, they tend to be staggeringly generous – the bar staff pouring from the bottle until you suggest they stop. Given their relatively low price for the size of the measures, long drinks are very popular, especially the universal *Gin-Tónic* and the even more common *Cuba Libre*, or rum and Coke – as a change from the ubiquitous Bacardi, try the Spanish Caribbean rums (*ron*) such as Cacique from Venezuela or Havana Club from Cuba. Juice is *zumo*; orange, *naranja*; lemon, *limón*; and tonic *tónica*.

Soft drinks and hot drinks

Soft drinks are much the same as anywhere in the world, but try in particular *granizado* (slush) or *horchata* (a milky drink made from tiger nuts or almonds) from one of the street stalls that spring up everywhere in summer.

You can also get these drinks from *horchaterías* and from *heladerías* (ice cream – *helados* – parlours), or in Catalunya from the wonderful milk bars known as *granjas*. Although you can drink the **water** almost everywhere, it usually tastes better out of the bottle – inexpensive *agua mineral* comes either sparkling (*con gas*) or still (*sin gas*).

Café (coffee) – served in cafés, *heladerías* and bars – is invariably espresso and, unless you specify otherwise, served black (*café solo*). If you want it white, ask for *café cortado* (small cup with a drop of milk) or *café con leche* (made with lots of hot milk). For a large cup of weaker coffee ask for an *americano*. Coffee is also frequently mixed with brandy, cognac or whisky, all such concoctions being called *carajillo*. Iced coffee is *café con hielo*, another great high-summer refresher: a *café solo* is served with a glass of ice cubes. Pour the coffee onto the cubes – it cools instantly.

Té (tea) is also available at most bars, although bear in mind that Spaniards usually drink it black. If you want milk it's safest to ask for it afterwards, since ordering *té con leche* might well get you a glass of milk with a tea bag floating on top. Perhaps a better bet would be **herbal teas** (*infusions*): *manzanilla* (camomile, not to be confused with the sherry of the same name), *poleomenta* (mint tea) and *hierba luisa* (lemon verbena) are all popular herbal infusions.

Chocolate (hot chocolate) is incredibly thick and sweet, and is a popular early-morning drink after a long night on the town. If you'd prefer a thinner cocoa-style drink ask for a brand name, like Cola Cao.

Opening hours and public holidays

Almost everything in Spain – shops, museums, churches, tourist offices – closes for a siesta of at least two hours in the hottest part of the day. There's a lot of variation (and the siesta tends to be longer in the south) but basic summer working hours are 9.30am–1.30pm and 4.30–8pm. Certain shops (mainly big chains and department stores) do now stay open all day, and there is a move towards "European" working hours. Nevertheless, you'll get far less aggravated if you accept that the early afternoon is best spent asleep, or in a bar, or both.

Museums, with very few exceptions, follow the rule above, with a break between 1pm and 4pm; watch out for Sundays (most open mornings only) and Mondays (most close all day). Admission charges vary, but there's usually a big reduction or free entrance if you show a student or pension card. Anywhere run by the Patrimonio Nacional (such as El Escorial and the Royal Palace in Madrid) is free to EU citizens on Wednesdays – you'll need to show your passport.

Note that the official beginning of **summer opening hours** for Patrimonio Nacional monuments – and some privately owned ones – varies from year to year, and is generally not announced until April/May. Where this is the case, we have given opening hours for "summer" and "winter"; contact the local turismo for more up-to-date information.

Getting into **churches** can be a problem. The really important ones, including most cathedrals, operate in much the same way as museums and almost always have some entry charge to view valued treasures and paintings, or their cloisters. Other churches, though, are kept locked, opening only for worship in the early morning and/or the evening (between around 6–9pm), so you'll either have to try at these times, or find someone with a key. A sacristan or custodian almost always lives nearby, and most people will know where to direct you. You're expected to give a small tip, or donation.

For all churches "decorous" dress is required, ie no shorts, bare shoulders, etc.

Spanish national holidays

January 1 *Año Nuevo*, New Year's Day
January 6 *Epifanía*, Epiphany
Easter Thursday *Jueves Santo* (except Cantabria, Catalunya and Comunitat Valenciana)
Good Friday *Viernes Santo*
Easter Sunday *Domingo de la Resureccion*
Easter Monday *Lunes de Pascua* (Catalunya and Comunitat Valenciana)
March 19 *San José* (Cantabria, Castilla-La Mancha, Castilla-León, Comunitat Valenciana, Madrid and Murcia)
May 1 *Fiesta del Trabajo*, May Day
August 15 *La Asunción*, Assumption of the Virgin
October 12 *Día de la Hispanidad*, National Day
November 1 *Todos los Santos*, All Saints
December 6 *Día de la Constitución*, Constitution Day
December 8 *Inmaculada Concepción*
December 24 *Navidad*, Christmas Day
December 26 *Sant Esteve* (Baleareas and Catalunya), Boxing Day

Public holidays

Public holidays can (and will) disrupt your plans at some stage. Alongside the national holidays (see opposite) there are scores of local fiestas (different in every town and village, usually marking the local saint's day); any of them will mean that everything except bars (and *hostales*, etc) locks its doors.

In addition, **August** is traditionally Spain's own holiday month, when the big cities – especially Madrid – are semi-deserted, and many of the shops and restaurants closed for the duration of the month. However, more widespread adoption of European working practices and the advent of air conditioning mean this is slowly but surely changing. In contrast, it can prove nearly impossible to find a room in the more popular coastal and mountain resorts at these times; similarly, seats on planes, trains and buses in August should if possible be booked in advance.

Fiestas

Fiestas are an absolutely crucial part of Spanish life. Even the smallest village and most modern suburb of a city give at least a couple of days a year over to partying, and happening across a local event can be huge fun, propelling you right into the heart of its culture. But as well as such community celebrations, Spain has some really major events: most famously, the Running of the Bulls at Pamplona, the April Feria of Sevilla, and the great religious processions of Semana Santa, leading up to Easter. Also huge fun is carnival, in February, which was banned under Franco and has been restored with a vengeance; the best on the mainland are in Cádiz and Sitges. Any of these can be worth planning your whole trip around. One thing they all tend to have in common is a curious blend of religious ceremony with surprisingly large doses of pagan ritual – sombre processions of statuary followed by exuberant merrymaking – in which fire plays a prominent part. This is especially the case of San Juan, celebrated along the Mediterranean coast with young men jumping over bonfires, and extravagant firework displays and competitions.

Many local festivals hark back to the region's industry, such as the wine harvest in La Rioja or the fishermen's maritime processions on the coast. Increasingly popular throughout the country are music festivals, especially in the north and Catalunya, which attract some big names from jazz, opera and classical music, and which are often accompanied by street markets and festivities.

Following is a very basic **calendar of fiesta highlights**. For more detailed listings, see the boxes at the beginning of each chapter, which cover each region's best events, and consult local tourist offices. Outsiders are always welcome at fiestas, the one problem being that it can be hard to find a hotel, unless you book well in advance.

January
5: Cabalgata de Reyes when the three Magi arrive to bring the children their presents for Epiphany. Any medium to large city will stage a spectacular and colourful procession as the three kings are driven through the streets throwing sweets to the crowds.
16–17: San Antoni's day is preceded by bonfires and processions, especially on the Balearic Islands.

February
Carnaval (the week preceding Ash Wednesday and Lent) is an excuse for wild partying and masques, most riotous in Cádiz (Andalucía), Sitges (Catalunya) and Águilas (Valencia).

March
12–19: Las Fallas in Valencia is the biggest of the bonfire festivals held for San José, climaxing on the Night of Fire when enormous caricatures are burnt and firecrackers take over the streets. See p.921.

Easter (March/April)
Semana Santa (Holy Week) is celebrated across Spain with religious processions, at their most theatrical in the cities of Sevilla, Málaga, Murcia and Valladolid, where *pasos* – huge floats of religious scenes – are carried down the streets, accompanied by hooded penitents atoning for the year's misdeeds. Good Friday sees the biggest processions.

April
22–24: Moros y Cristianos – mock battle between Moors and Christians – in Alcoy, Valencia. (Similar events take place throughout the year all around Spain).

23: San Jordi – Catalunya's patron saint's day is a big party across the region and is also celebrated as National Book Day throughout Spain.
Last week: Feria de Abril – spectacular week-long fair in Sevilla.

May
Early May: Horse Fair at Jerez (Andalucía).
7–22: San Isidro – Madrid's patron saint (15th) – is a signal for parades, free concerts, and the start of the bullfight season.
Pentecost (Whitsun: 7th Sunday after Easter): the great pilgrimage to El Rocío (p.340), near Huelva (Andalucía).
Corpus Christi (Thursday after Trinity; May/June) is a focus for religious processions, accompanied by floats and penitents, notably in Toledo, Granada and Valencia. Many town fiestas also take place, including the spectacular costumed events of the Festa de la Patum (Catalunya, p.850).
Last week: Feria de la Manzanilla in Sanlúcar de Barrameda (Andalucía) to celebrate the town's famous sherry.

June
23–24: San Juan and midsummer's eve is celebrated with bonfires all over Spain – particularly in San Juan de Alicante, where a local version of Las Fallas takes place.
29: San Pedro – patron of fishermen – is honoured by flotillas of boats, and partying all along the coast.

July
7–14: San Fermin – the famed running of the bulls at Pamplona (p.526).
25: Santiago – Spain's patron saint, St James – is honoured at Santiago de Compostela, with fireworks and bonfires (p.605–6).
26: Blanes – Spectacular week-long fireworks competition on the beach, with teams from all around the world.
Last three weeks: Pirineos Sur – World music

festival on a floating stage at Lanuza, near Sallent de Gállego, in the Pyrenees.

August
10–11: Elche (Valencia) hosts mock battles between Christians and Moors, ending with a centuries-old mystery play.
First/second week: Mass canoe races down the Río Sella in Asturias.
Third week: Toledo's main fiesta, climaxing in amazing fireworks at the weekend.
Last week: Gigantones (giant puppets) are paraded in Alcalá de Henares (Castile).
Last Wed (usually): La Tomatina in Buñol, near Valencia: the country's craziest fiesta, a two-hour tomato fight (p.930).

September
First week: Vendimia (grape harvest) celebrations in Valdepeñas (New Castile), Jerez (Andalucía) and other wine towns.
11: Diada Nacional de Catalunya Catalan public holiday commemorating its loss of independence. Various cultural and sporting events over the weekends before and after.
21: Rioja wine harvest celebrated in Logroño (Old Castile).

October
1: San Miguel Villages across the country celebrate their patron saint's day.
12: La Virgen del Pilar – the patron saint of Aragón – is an excuse for bullfights and *jota* dancing at Zaragoza and elsewhere.

December
24: Nochebuena Christmas Eve is particularly exuberant, with parties and carousing early in the evening before it all suddenly stops in time for family dinner or mass.
31: Nochevieja New year is celebrated by eating a grape for every stroke of the clock in Plaza del Sol in Madrid and main squares and bars throughout the country.

Bullfights

Bullfights are an integral part of many fiestas. In the south, especially, any village that can afford it will put on a *corrida* for an afternoon, while in big cities like Madrid or Sevilla, the main festival times are accompanied by a week-long (or more) season of prestige fights. With the clamorous exception of Pamplona, bull-fighting is far more popular in Madrid and all points south than it is in the north or on the islands. Some northern cities don't have bullrings, while the Canary Islands' regional government has gone so far as to ban bullfighting.

Los Toros, as Spaniards refer to bullfighting, is big business. It is said that 150,000 people are involved, in some way, in the industry, and the top performers, the **matadores**, are major earners, on a par with the country's biggest pop stars. There is some **opposition** to the activity from animal welfare groups but it is not widespread: if Spaniards tell you that bullfighting is controversial, they are likely to be referring to practices in the trade. In recent years, bullfighting critics (who you will find on the arts and not the sports pages of the newspapers) have been expressing their perennial outrage at the widespread but illegal shaving of bulls' horns prior to the *corrida*. Bulls' horns are as sensitive as fingernails, and filing them a few millimetres deters the animal from charging; they affect the bull's balance, too, further reducing the danger for the *matador*.

Notwithstanding such abuse (and there is plenty more), *Los Toros* remain popular throughout the country. To *aficionados* (a word that implies more knowledge and appreciation than "fan"), the bulls are a culture and a ritual – one in which the emphasis is on the way man and bull "perform" together – in which the *arte* is at issue rather than the cruelty. If pressed on the issue of the slaughter of an animal, they generally fail to understand. Fighting bulls are, they will tell you, bred for the industry; they live a reasonable life before they are killed, and, if the bull-fight went, so too would the bulls.

If you spend any time at all in Spain during the **season** (which runs from March to October), you will encounter *Los Toros* on a bar TV – and that will probably make up your mind whether to attend a *corrida*. If you decide to go, try to see a big, prestigious event, where star performers are likely to despatch the bulls with "art" and a successful, "clean" kill. There are few sights worse than a *matador* making a prolonged and messy kill, while the audience whistles and chucks cushions over the *barrera*. If you have the chance to see one, the most exciting and skilful events are those featuring **mounted matadores**, or *rejoneadores*; this is the oldest form of *corrida*, developed in Andalucía in the seventeenth century.

Established and popular *matadores* include the veteran Enrique Ponce, César Rincón, Victor Mendes, Joselito, Litri, David "El Rey" Silveti and José María Manzanares. Two newer stars are erstwhile prodigy Julián "El Juli" López, and Granada's emerging David "El Fandi" Fandila. Cristina Sánchez, the first woman to make it into the top flight for many decades, retired in 1999, blaming sexist organizers, crowds and fellow *matadores* – many of whom refused to appear on the same bill as a woman. A complete guide to bullfighting with exhaustive links can be found at ⓦ www.mundo-taurino.org.

The corrida

The **corrida** begins with a procession, to the accompaniment of a *paso doble* by the band. Leading the procession are two *algauziles* or "constables", on horseback and in traditional costume, followed by the three *matadores*, who will each fight two bulls, and their *cuadrillas*, their personal "team", each comprising two mounted *picadores* and three *banderilleros*. At the back are the mule teams who will drag off the dead bulls.

Once the ring is empty, the *algauzil* opens the *toril* (the bulls' enclosure) and the first

53

bull appears – a moment of great physical beauty – to be "tested" by the *matador* or his *banderilleros* using pink and gold capes. These preliminaries conducted (and they can be short, if the bull is ferocious), the **suerte de picar** ensues, in which the *picadores* ride out and take up position at opposite sides of the ring, while the bull is distracted by other *toreros*. Once they are in place, the bull is made to charge one of the horses; the *picador* drives his short-pointed lance into the bull's neck, while it tries to toss his padded, blindfolded horse, thus tiring the bull's powerful neck and back muscles. This is repeated up to three times, until the horn sounds for the *picadores* to leave. Cries of "*fuera!*" (out) often greet the overzealous use of the lance, for by weakening the bull too much they fear the beast will not be able to put up a decent fight. For many, this is the least acceptable stage of the *corrida*, and it is clearly not a pleasant experience for the horses, who have their ears stuffed with oil-soaked rags to shut out the noise, and their vocal cords cut out to render them mute.

The next stage, the *suerte de banderillas*, involves the placing of three sets of *banderillas* (coloured sticks with barbed ends) into the bull's shoulders. Each of the three *banderilleros* delivers these in turn, attracting the bull's attention with the movement of his own body rather than a cape, and placing the *banderillas* whilst both he and the bull are running towards each other. He then runs to safety out of the bull's vision, sometimes with the assistance of his colleagues.

Once the *banderillas* have been placed, the *suerte de matar* begins, and the *matador* enters the ring alone, having exchanged his pink and gold cape for the red one. He (or she) salutes the president and then dedicates the bull either to an individual, to whom he gives his hat, or to the audience by placing his hat in the centre of the ring. It is in this part of the *corrida* that judgements are made and the performance is focused, as the *matador* displays his skills on the (by now exhausted) bull. He uses the movements of the cape to attract the bull, while his body remains still. If he does well, the band will start to play, while the crowd *olé* each pass. This stage lasts around ten minutes and ends with the kill. The *matador*

attempts to get the bull into a position where he can drive a sword between its shoulders and through to the heart for a *coup de grâce*. In practice, they rarely succeed in this, instead taking a second sword, crossed at the end, to cut the bull's spinal cord; this causes instant death.

If the audience are impressed by the *matador*'s performance, they will wave their handkerchiefs and shout for an award to be made by the president. He can award one or both ears, and a tail – the better the display, the more pieces he gets – while if the *matador* has excelled himself, he will be carried out of the ring by the crowd, through the *puerta grande*, the main door, which is normally kept locked. The bull, too, may be applauded for its performance, as it is dragged out by the mule team.

Tickets for *corridas* are €18 and up – much more for the prime seats and prestigious fights. The cheapest seats are *gradas*, the highest rows at the back, from where you can see everything that happens without too much of the detail; the front rows are known as the *barreras*. Seats are also divided into *sol* (sun), *sombra* (shade), and *sol y sombra* (shaded after a while), though these distinctions have become less crucial as more and more bullfights start later in the day, at 6pm or 7pm, rather than the traditional 5pm. The *sombra* seats are more expensive, not so much for the spectators' personal comfort as the fact that most of the action takes place in the shade. On the way in, you can rent **cushions** – two hours sitting on concrete is not much fun. Beer and soft drinks are sold inside.

Anti-bullfight organizations

Spain's main opposition to bullfighting is organized by ADDA (Asociación para la defensa del animal). They coordinate the Anti-Bullfight Campaign (ABC) International and also produce a quarterly newsletter in Spanish and English. Their bilingual website – ⓦ www.addaong.org – has information about international campaigns and current actions. For an eloquent argument in English against bullfighting, try ⓦ www.canaryforum.com /gc/bull where you'll find a stark description of everything surrounding the spectacle.

Football

To foreigners, the bullfight is easily the most celebrated of Spain's spectacles. In terms of popular support in modern Spain, however, it ranks far below *fútbol* (soccer). If you want the excitement of a genuinely Spanish event, watching a Sunday-evening game in *La Liga* usually produces as much passion as anything you'll find in the Plaza de Toros. ⓦwww.soccer-spain.com is a very good website in English, where you'll find comprehensive news and articles.

For many years, the country's two dominant teams have been big-spending **Real Madrid** and **F.C. Barcelona,** and these two have shared the League and Cup honours more often than is healthy. Recently, however, both teams have faced a bit more opposition, notably from the brief stardom of **Deportivo La Coruña** (winners of La Liga in 2000), **Valencia** and **Celta de Vigo** (from Galicia). Other significant teams include **Athletic Bilbao** (who have never fielded a non-Basque), **Real Sociedad** (from San Sebastián), **Real Zaragoza, Deportivo Alavès** (from Vitoria in the Basque country), and the Sevilla teams **Sevilla** and **Real Betis**. Real Madrid and Barcelona's respective local rivals, **Atlético de Madrid** and **Espanyol**, have lately earned the reputation as *ascensor* (elevator) teams by successive promotions and relegations into and out of the first division.

The league **season** runs from early-September until mid-June, with a short break for Christmas and the New Year. Most of the league games kick off at 5pm or 7pm on Sundays, though live TV demands that one key game kicks off at 9pm on Saturday and Sunday.

With the exception of a few big games – mainly those involving Real Madrid and Barcelona – **tickets** are not too hard to get. They start at around €15 for First Division games, with the cheapest in the *fondo* (behind the goals); *tribuna* (pitchside stand) seats are very much pricier. Trouble is very rare: English fans, in particular, will be amazed at the easy-going family atmosphere and mixed-sex crowds.

If you don't go to a game, the atmosphere can be pretty good **watching on TV** in a local bar, especially in a city whose team is playing away. Many bars advertise the matches they screen, and they will often feature Sunday-afternoon **English league and cup games**, if they have satellite.

Two essential phrases: "¿Como va el partido?" (What's the score), and "Fuera de juego" (offside).

Trouble, the police and sexual harassment

While you're unlikely to encounter any trouble during the course of a normal visit, it's worth remembering that the Spanish police, polite enough in the usual course of events, can be extremely unpleasant if you get on the wrong side of them. At a national level there are three basic types: the Guardia Civil, the Policía Municipal, and the Policía Nacional, all of them armed. Regional police forces are found in Catalunya (Mossos d'Esquadra) and Euskal Herria (Ertzaintza), which are locally-recruited forces that are gradually phasing out the Guardia Civil in rural areas and taking over some of the responsibilities of the Policía Nacional.

Avoiding trouble

Almost all the problems tourists encounter are to do with **petty crime** – pickpocketing and bag-snatching – rather than more serious physical confrontations, so it's as well to be on your guard and know where your possessions are at all times. Sensible **precautions** include: carrying bags slung across your neck, not over your shoulder (although obviously no bag at all is preferable); not carrying anything in zipped pockets facing the street; having photocopies of your passport, and leaving passport and tickets in the hotel safe; and noting down travellers' cheque and credit card numbers. There are also several ploys to be aware of and situations to avoid as you do the rounds of the city:

• Thieves often work in pairs, so watch out for people standing unusually close if you're studying postcards or papers at stalls; keep an eye on your wallet if it appears you're being distracted. **Ploys** (by some very sophisticated operators) include: the "helpful" person pointing out birdshit (shaving cream or something similar) on your jacket while someone relieves you of your money; the card or paper you're invited to read on the street to distract your attention; the move by someone in a café for your drink with one hand (the other hand's in your bag as you react to save your drink); and the beggars who place trays under your face while rifling your bag unseen below. Keep an eye out also for anyone suspicious clutching a tatty rolled-up newspaper; pickpockets use newspapers to hide lifted wallets before finding a quiet place to go through them.

• If you have a **car** don't leave anything in view when you park it, especially in major cities; take the radio with you. Vehicles are rarely stolen, but luggage and valuables left in cars do make a tempting target and rental cars are easy to spot. At beauty spots, beaches and out-of-the-way attractions, peruse the ground carefully when you park; if it's strewn with broken window glass it's a sure sign that thieves are frequent visitors and you'll need to park elsewhere or take appropriate action.

• **Looking for hotel rooms**, don't leave any bags unattended anywhere. This applies especially to blocks where the hotel or *hostal* is on the higher floors and you're tempted to leave baggage in the hallway or ground-floor lobby.

• A fairly frequent crime is from **roadside thieves** posing as "good Samaritans" to persons experiencing car and tyre problems. The thieves typically attempt to divert the driver's attention by pointing out a mechanical problem and then steal items from the vehicle while the driver is looking elsewhere. The problem is particularly acute with vehicles rented at Madrid's Barajas airport and at rest stops (rather than services) on motorways. Be cautious about accepting help from anyone other than a uniformed Spanish police officer and, if you do break down, keep your valuables in sight or lock them in the vehicle.

The police

The **Guardia Civil**, in green uniforms, are the most officious and the ones to avoid. Though their role has been cut back since they operated as Franco's right hand, they remain a reactionary force.

If you do need the police – and above all if

you're reporting a serious crime such as rape – you should always go to the more sympathetic **Policía Municipal**, who wear blue-and-white uniforms. In the countryside there may be only the Guardia Civil; though they're usually helpful, they are inclined to resent the suggestion that any crime exists on their turf and you may end up feeling as if you are the one who stands accused.

The blue-uniformed **Policía Nacional** are mainly seen in cities, armed with submachine guns and guarding key installations such as embassies, stations, post offices and their own barracks. They are also the force used to control crowds and demonstrations.

The **Mossos d'Esquadra** in Catalunya wear blue uniforms with red and white trim, while the Basque **Ertzaintza** are kitted out in blue and red, with red berets. You are most likely to come into contact with them if you're driving, as they have taken over a great deal of traffic responsibilities. To report crimes in these two areas, your best bet is still to go to the Policía Municipal; in small towns, there is a certain overlap between the regional and municipal forces, occasionally to the point of sharing buildings.

What to do if you're robbed

If you're robbed, you need to **go to the police** to report it, not least because your insurance company will require a police report. Don't expect a great deal of concern if your loss is relatively small – and expect the process of completing forms and formalities to take ages. In the unlikely event that you're **mugged**, or otherwise threatened, never resist; hand over what's wanted and go straight to the police, who on these occasions will be more sympathetic.

If you have your passport stolen or lose all your money, you can contact your **consulate** (see "Listings" in the Guide for individual cities), which is required to assist you to some degree.

Offences

There are a few **offences** you might commit unwittingly that it's as well to be aware of:

• In theory you're supposed to carry some kind of **identification** at all times, and the police can stop you in the streets and demand it. In practice they're rarely bothered if you're clearly a foreigner, but given the occasional terrorist and illegal-immigrant clampdowns it would be wise to carry some means of identification even if it's only a photocopy of your passport details.

• **Unauthorized camping** might bring you into contact with officialdom, though these days a warning to move on is more likely than any real confrontation; it's best to check with the local tourist office or Policía Municipal before camping outside a recognized site. It's illegal to camp on a beach and some towns don't allow sleeping on a beach between certain times of the night; in the main resorts, the police will move you on.

• There are now **nudist** beaches and mixed beaches (both nudist and clothed) on all the major *costas* and **topless** tanning is commonplace; however, in country areas where attitudes are still very traditional, you should take care not to upset local sensibilities.

• Spanish **drug laws** are in a somewhat bizarre state at present. After the socialists came to power in 1983, cannabis use (possession of up to 8g of what the Spanish call *chocolate*) was decriminalized. Subsequent pressures, an influx of harder drugs and a more right-wing government changed that policy and – in theory at least – any drug use is now forbidden. You'll see signs in some bars saying *no porros* ("no joints"), which you should heed. However, the police are in practice little worried about personal use. Larger quantities (and any other drugs) are a very different matter.

Should you be **arrested** on any charge, you have the right to contact your **consulate**, although they're notoriously reluctant to get involved. If you've been detained for a drugs offence, don't expect any sympathy or help from your consulate.

Sexual harassment

Spain's macho image has faded dramatically and these days there are relatively few parts of the country where foreign women travelling alone are likely to feel threatened, intimidated, or to attract unwanted attention.

Inevitably, the **big cities** – like any others in Europe – have their no-go areas, where street crime and especially drug-related hassles are on the rise, but there is little of the pestering and propositions that you have to contend with in, say, the larger French or Italian cities. The outdoor culture of *terrazas* (terrace bars) and the tendency of Spaniards to move around in large, mixed crowds, filling central bars, clubs and streets late into the night, help to make you feel less exposed. If you are in any doubt, there are always **taxis** – plentiful, reasonably priced, well-marked and certainly the safest way to travel late at night. Make full use of them, particularly in Madrid and Barcelona.

The major **resorts** of the *costas* have their own artificial holiday culture. The Spaniards who hang around in discos here or at fiesta fairgrounds pose no greater or lesser threat than similar operators at home; in fact, most

problems are more likely to arise from other alcohol-fuelled holidaymakers. The language barrier simply makes it harder to know who to trust. *Déjame en paz* ("leave me in peace") is a fairly standard rebuff.

Predictably, it is in **more isolated regions**, separated by less than a generation from desperate poverty (or still starkly poor), that most serious problems can occur. You do need to know a bit about the land you're travelling around. In some areas you can walk for hours without coming across an inhabited farm or house. It's rare that this poses a threat – help and hospitality are much more the norm – but you are certainly more vulnerable. That said, **trekking** is becoming more popular in Spain as a whole and many women happily tramp the footpaths, from Galicia to the Sierra Nevada. In the south, especially, though, it is worth finding rooms in the larger villages, or, if you camp out, asking permission to do so on private land, rather than striking out alone.

Work

Residents of EU countries no longer need either a residence or work permit to work in Spain; your passport is now sufficient. However, although it is theoretically possible for EU nationals to seek employment in Spain, realistically, unless you have a particular skill and have applied for a job advertised in your home country, the only real chance of long-term work in Spain is in language schools. Non-EU residents intending to stay in Spain longer than three months will need a *permiso de residencia* – see "Red Tape and Visas" (p.22). European Union citizens may find the EU's website for those planning to live or work abroad within the EU a useful resource; it can be found at ⓦ http://citizens.EU.int/.

Teaching and office work

Finding a teaching job was once a question of pacing the streets, stopping in at every language school around and asking about vacancies, although nowadays you should be aware that schools that recruit this way

are less likely to take the work – and paying you – as seriously as you'd like. Numbers of students at language schools have dropped drastically in recent years, and jobs are consequently harder to come by unless you have some sort of teaching qualification; a TEFL (Teaching English as a Foreign

Language) or ESL (English as a Second Language) certificate gives you a much better chance of success and will almost certainly be required by the more reputable institutions. For the addresses of schools look in the Yellow Pages (*Páginas Amarillas*) under *Idiomas enseñanza* or *Academias de Idiomas*. Other options are to try advertising **private lessons** (better paid at €10–15 an hour, but harder to make a living at) on the *Philología* noticeboards of university faculties or in local bookshops.

Another possibility, if your Spanish is excellent, is **translation work**, most of which will be business correspondence – look in the Yellow Pages under *Traductores*. If you intend doing agency work, you'll need access to a PC and either email or fax.

Temporary work

If you're looking for **temporary work** the best chances are in the **bars and restaurants** of the big Mediterranean resorts. This may help you have a good time but it's unlikely to bring in much money. If you turn up in spring and are willing to stay through the season you might get a better deal – also true if you're offering some special skill such as windsurfing (there are schools sprouting up all along the coast). Quite often there are jobs at **yacht marinas**, too, scrubbing down and repainting the boats of the rich; just turn up and ask around, especially from March until June. As an inexperienced foreigner you've no hope at all of work on harvests as most agricultural work goes to North African immigrants prepared to work for around €25 per day.

Travellers with disabilities

Spain is not exactly at the forefront of providing facilities for travellers with disabilities. That said, there are accessible hotels in the major cities and resorts and, by law, all new public buildings are required to be fully accessible. There are also a number of active groups of disabled people: ONCE, the Spanish organization for the blind, is particularly weighty, its huge lottery bringing with it considerable power.

Transport is still the main problem, since buses (outside the main cities, at least) are virtually impossible for wheelchairs and trains only slightly better (though there are wheelchairs at major stations and wheelchair spaces in some carriages – especially on the more modern trains such as the AVE between Madrid and Sevilla). Hertz has cars with hand controls available in Madrid and Barcelona (with advance notice), and taxi drivers are usually helpful. The Brittany Ferries crossing from Plymouth to Santander offers good facilities if you're **driving to Spain** (as do most cross-Channel ferries).

Once out of the cities and away from the coast, the difficulties increase. Road surfaces in the mountain regions can be rough

and toilet facilities for disabled motorists are a rare sight. If you've got the money, *paradores* are one answer to the problem of unsuitable **accommodation**. Many are converted from castles and monasteries and although not built with the disabled guest in mind, their grand scale – with plenty of room to manoeuvre a wheelchair inside – tends to compensate.

Here are several websites which may prove useful when planning your holiday:

🌐 **www.everybody.co.uk** – a database of wheelchair-accessible hotels and airlines.

🌐 **www.disabilityresources.org** – a comprehensive interactive database with lots of information on travel and other topics.

🌐 **www.access–able.com** – a site specifically

geared to journey planning for elderly and disabled travellers, and a section on Spain can be researched by province or city or subject (eg hotels, tours and trips, medical services, etc).

Contacts for travellers with disabilities

In Spain

Spanish National Tourist Office (see p.25 for addresses). Publishes a fact sheet listing a variety of useful addresses and some accessible accommodation.

ECOM (Federation of Spanish private organizations for the disabled) Gran Vía de les Corts Catalanes 562 principal, 2ª, 08011 Barcelona ⊕934 515 550; c/Germán Pérez Carrasco, 65, Madrid ⊕914 060 270. Produces an access city guide for Barcelona and Madrid.

Organización Nacional de Ciegos de España (ONCE) c/Prado 24, 28014 Madrid ⊕915 974 727; c/Calabria 66–76, Barcelona 08015 ⊕933 259 200, ⓦwww.once.es. The national and extremely influential organization for the blind.

Comité de Representantes de Minusválidos (CERMI) c/Prim 3, Madrid (ⓜBanco de España), ⓦwww.cermi.es. Provides information and sells Braille maps and a wide range of aids for the blind.

Rompiendo Barreras Travel c/Roncevalles 3, 28007 Madrid ⊕915 513 622, ⓦwww.rbtravel.es. Spanish travel agency dedicated to disabled travel. Provides a wide range of information (in Spanish) and organizes hotels, tours, rural tourism and lots more all over Spain. Although operating in Spanish, they will respond to communications in English.

In the UK and Ireland

Access Travel 6 The Hillock, Astley, Lancashire M29 7GW ⊕01942/888 844, ⓦwww.access -travel.co.uk. Tour operator that can arrange flights, transfer and accommodation. This is a small business, personally checking out places before recommendation.

Accessible City Breaks ⊕01452/729739, ⓦwww.accessiblecitybreaks.co.uk. City breaks to Barcelona and Madrid for wheelchair users, sensory impaired and slow walkers.

Holiday Care 2nd floor, Imperial Building, Victoria Rd, Horley, Surrey RH6 7PZ ⊕0845/124 9971, minicom ⊕0845/124 9976,

ⓦwww.holidaycare.org.uk. Provides a free comprehensive travel pack on Spain with details of facilities in hotels, resorts etc. Information on financial help for holidays available.

Irish Wheelchair Association Blackheath Drive, Clontarf, Dublin 3 ⊕01/818 6400, ⓦwww.iwa.ie. Useful information provided about travelling abroad with a wheelchair.

Tripscope Alexandra House, Albany Rd, Brentford, Middlesex TW8 0NE ⊕0845/7585 641, ⓦwww.tripscope.org.uk. This registered charity provides a national telephone information service offering free advice on UK and international transport for those with a mobility problem.

In the US and Canada

Access-Able ⓦwww.access-able.com. Online resource for travellers with disabilities.

Directions Unlimited 123 Green Lane, Bedford Hills, NY 10507 ⊕1-800/533-5343 or 914/241-1700. Travel agency specializing in bookings for people with disabilities.

Mobility International USA 451 Broadway, Eugene, OR 97401 ⊕541/343-1284, ⓦwww.miusa.org. Information and referral services, access guides, tours and exchange programmes. Annual membership $35 (includes quarterly newsletter).

Society for the Advancement of Travelers with Handicaps (SATH) 347 5th Ave, New York, NY 10016 ⊕212/447-7284, ⓦwww.sath.org. Non-profit educational organization that has actively represented travellers with disabilities since 1976.

Wheels Up! ⊕1-888/38-WHEELS, ⓦwww.wheelsup.com. Provides discounted airfare, tour and cruise prices for disabled travellers; also publishes a free monthly newsletter and has a comprehensive website.

In Australia and New Zealand

ACROD (Australian Council for Rehabilitation of the Disabled) PO Box 60, Curtin ACT floor, 1–5 Commercial Rd, Kings Grove 2208; ⊕02/6282 4333, TTY ⊕02/6282 4333, ⓦwww.acrod.org.au. Provides lists of travel agencies and tour operators for people with disabilities.

Disabled Persons Assembly 4/173–175 Victoria St, Wellington, New Zealand ⊕04/801 9100 (also TTY), ⓦwww.dpa.org.nz. Resource centre with lists of travel agencies and tour operators for people with disabilities.

Senior travellers

The senior traveller market is well catered for in Spain, especially in the south, where the long summer and mild winters can mean real out-of-season bargains for older visitors who tend to be more flexible in their travel arrangements. Most public museums, galleries and archeological sites offer discounts to senior visitors (usually the same as a student discount) and it is always worth enquiring when purchasing your ticket. Similarly, there are deals to be had for the over-60s on the extensive train network (see p.30).

Contacts for senior travellers

In the UK

Saga Holidays ☎ 0130/377 1111, ⓦ holidays.saga.co.uk. The country's biggest and most established specialist in tours and holidays aimed at older people.

In the US

American Association of Retired Persons ☎ 1-800/424-3410 or 202/434-2277, ⓦ www.aarp.org. Can provide discounts on accommodation and vehicle rental. Membership open to US and Canadian residents aged 50 or over for an annual fee of US $12.50.

Elderhostel ☎ 1/877-426-8056, ⓦ www.elderhostel.org. Runs an extensive worldwide network of educational and activity programmes, cruises and homestays for people over 60 (companions may be younger). Programmes generally last a week or more and costs are in line with those of commercial tours.

Saga Holidays ☎ 1-800/343-0273, ⓦ www.sagaholidays.com. Specializes in worldwide group travel for seniors. Saga's Road Scholar coach tours and their Smithsonian Odyssey Tours have a more educational slant.

Vantage Deluxe World Travel ☎ 1-800/322-6677, ⓦ www.vantagetravel.com. Specializes in worldwide group travel for seniors.

Gay and lesbian travellers

Gay and lesbian life in Spain has come a long way in the twenty-five years or so since Franco's death, and Spanish attitudes have changed dramatically. There are strong lobbying movements for same-sex marriages and for same-sex couples to have equal rights; these movements are given greater strength by the support of some autonomous governments. The age of consent is 16 – the same as for heterosexual couples.

Today, almost every town in Spain has its gay bars and associations, while gay magazines, newspapers and radio programmes are widespread. Most major cities, including Madrid, Barcelona, Valencia and Vitoria, have passed partnership laws, giving same-sex couples almost the same rights as heterosexual couples. In 1995 Spain included a clause in its criminal code making it an offence to discriminate in housing and employment based on sexual orientation, and imposing tougher sentences on hate crimes against the gay community. A bill is currently going through the Spanish Parliament, which, if passed, would establish partnership rights for same-sex couples throughout Spain.

There are thriving gay communities in most of Spain's main cities, notably, of course, Madrid (particularly the Chueca quarter) and Barcelona, famous for its Gay Pride festival at the end of June and the International Gay and Lesbian Film Festival from September to November. For gay resorts Sitges is unbeatable, and, as in Cádiz, *carnaval* is a wonderfully hedonistic time to visit. Ibiza and Torremolinos are two other popular holiday destinations.

The Spanish term for the gay scene is "el ambiente" (literally, the atmosphere), while another useful expression is "entiendo", literally "I understand", but meaning "I'm gay".

Contacts for gay and lesbian travellers

In Spain

Ⓦ **www.cogailes.org/english** Website of a Barcelona-based organization that is part of the International Gay and Lesbian Association, giving a good general view of the scene in Spain and links to other sites.

Ⓦ **www.gayinspain.com** Comprehensive region-by-region guide in English and Spanish with details of gay nightlife, hotels, shops and beaches.

Ⓦ **www.geocities.com/WestHollywood/1007/ #links** Curious site showing the now infamous Gay Spain: Feel the Passion site, created by the Spanish Tourist Board and distributed in the US through the SNTO. Withdrawn by the right-wing Partido Popular government in 1997, as it supposedly did not match the image of Spain that the government wished to project, it's not entirely up to date but is nonetheless interesting for its content and history.

In the UK

Ⓦ **www.gaytravel.co.uk** Online gay and lesbian travel agent, offering good deals on all types of holiday. Also lists gay- and lesbian-friendly hotels around the world.

Dreamwaves Holidays ☎0870/042 2475, Ⓦ www.gayholidaysdirect.com. Specializes in exclusively gay holidays, including skiing trips and summer sun packages.

MadisonTravel ☎01273/202 532, Ⓦ www.madisontravel.co.uk. Established travel agents specializing in packages to gay- and lesbian-friendly mainstream destinations, and also to gay/lesbian destinations.

Respect Holidays ☎0870/770 0169, Ⓦ www.respect-holidays.co.uk. Offers exclusively gay packages to all popular European resorts.

In North America

Damron ☎1-800/462-6654 or 415/255-0404, Ⓦ www.damron.com. Publisher of the *Men's Travel Guide*, a pocket-sized yearbook full of listings of hotels, bars, clubs and resources for gay men; the *Women's Traveler*, which provides similar listings for lesbians; the *Road Atlas*; and *Damron Accommodations*, which provides detailed listings of over 1000 accommodations for gays and lesbians worldwide. All of these titles are offered at a discount on the website.

gaytravel.com ☎1-800/GAY-TRAVEL, Ⓦ www.gaytravel.com. The premier site for trip planning, bookings, and general information about international gay and lesbian travel.

Gay & Lesbian Travel Association ☎1-800/448-8550 or 954/776-2626, Ⓦ www.iglta.org. Trade group that can provide a list of gay- and lesbian-owned or -friendly travel agents, accommodation and other travel businesses.

In Australia and New Zealand

Tourism Australia Ⓦ www.galta.com.au. Directory and links for gay and lesbian travel in Australia and worldwide.

Travel ☎08/8274 1222, Ⓔ parkside@herveyworld.com.au. Gay travel agent associated with local branch of Hervey World Travel; all aspects of gay and lesbian travel worldwide.

Silke's Travel ☎1800/807 860 or 02/8347 2000, Ⓦ www.silkes.com.au. Long-established gay and lesbian specialist, with the emphasis on women's travel.

Tearaway Travel ☎1800/664 440 or 03/9510 6644, Ⓦ www.tearaway.com. Gay-specific business dealing with international and domestic travel.

Travelling with children

Spain is a good country to travel with children of any age; they will be well received everywhere and babies and toddlers, in particular, will be made a real fuss of. If you're travelling independently there are numerous theme parks and leisure activities specifically aimed at kids mentioned throughout the Guide; in particular, see p.147 for Madrid, Port Aventura in Catalunya (see p.898) and Mini Hollywood in Almería (see p.402); and the many popular water parks dotted about the coast. Many tourist attractions and sights have discounts or free entry for children, and some cities and resorts produce pamphlets of attractions aimed at kids; Barcelona is especially well organized.

RENFE allows children under four to travel free on trains, with forty-percent discount for those between four and twelve years.

Accommodation shouldn't be a problem as *hostales* and *pensiones* generally welcome accompanied children and offer rooms with three or four beds. If you're travelling in the north, or out of season, however, bear in mind that many *hostales* (as opposed to more expensive hotels) don't have heating systems – and it can get very cold. The wide availability of self-catering options can be appealing for a family holiday and Spain has a good choice of accommodation from seaside apartments to country *casas rurales*. There are also myriad package-tour companies that cater specifically for holidays with children (see below) and arrange activities for kids of all ages throughout the holiday. Some of the larger hotels and campsites on the *costas* have children's clubs and offer a babysitting (*canguro*) service.

As in other Mediterranean countries, children stay up late in Spain, especially in the summer. It's very common for them to be running around pavement cafés or restaurants and your kids will no doubt enjoy joining in. It's expected that families dine out with their children – it's not unusual to see up to four generations of the same family eating tapas in a bar – so young ones will be welcomed in restaurants, although you'll rarely find high chairs or specific children's menus.

As far as **babies** go, food seems to work out quite well (*hostales* sometimes prepare food specially, or will let you use the kitchen to do so). Disposable nappies (*panuelos,* or more colloquially, *Dodots*) and other standard needs are very widely available. Many *hostales* will be prepared to babysit, or at least to listen out for trouble. This is obviously more likely if you're staying in an old-fashioned family-run place than in the fancier hotels.

A very good service that is just beginning to emerge is rental of equipment for children, such as cots, car safety seats or pushchairs. Kidztogo (Ⓦwww.kidztogo.com) offers an excellent service throughout the Costa del Sol, delivering and collecting such items to your hotel or apartment.

Contacts for travellers with children

In the UK and Ireland

Club Med ⓉO700/2582 932, Ⓦwww.clubmed.co.uk. Specializes in purpose-built holiday resorts, with kids' club, entertainment and sports facilities on site.

Mark Warner Holidays ⓉO870/770 4222, Ⓦwww.markwarner.co.uk. Holiday villages with children's entertainment and childcare included.

Simply Travel ⓉO20/8541 2200, Ⓦwww.simply -travel.com. Upmarket tour company offering villas and hotels in the less touristy parts of Portugal, Greece, Turkey, Italy and Spain. In some destinations, they can provide qualified, English-speaking nannies to come to your villa and look after the children.

In the US

Rascals in Paradise Ⓣ415/921-7000, Ⓦwww.rascalsinparadise.com. Can arrange scheduled and customized itineraries built around activities for kids in Spain and other countries.

Travel With Your Children Ⓣ1-888/822-4388 or 212/477-5524 Publishes a regular newsletter, *Family Travel Times* (Ⓦwww.familytraveltimes .com), as well as a series of books on travel with children including *Great Adventure Vacations With Your Kids.*

Directory

Addresses are written as: c/Picasso 2, 4° izda. – which means Picasso street (*calle*) no. 2, fourth floor, left- (*izquierda*) hand flat or office; dcha. (*derecha*) is right; cto. (*centro*) centre. Other confusions in Spanish addresses result from the different spellings, and sometimes words, used in Catalan, Basque and Galician – all of which are replacing their Castilian counterparts – and from the gradual removal of Franco and other fascist heroes from the main *avenidas* and plazas. Note that some maps – including the official ones – haven't yet caught up. In some towns dual numbering systems are also in effect, and looking at the plates it's difficult to tell which is the old and which the new scheme.

Airport tax You can happily spend your last euro – there's no departure tax.

Contraceptives Widely available in pharmacies, supermarkets and bars, and *condones* (condoms) often from machines outside pharmacies.

Electricity Current in most of Spain is 220 or 225 volts AC (just occasionally it's still 110 or 125V); most European appliances should work as long as you have an adaptor for European-style two-pin plugs. North Americans will need this plus a transformer.

Feminism The Spanish women's movement, despite having to deal with incredibly basic issues (such as trying to get contraception available on social security), is radical, vibrant and growing fast. Few groups, however, have permanent offices, and if you want to make contact it's best to do so through the network of feminist bookshops in the major cities. Some of the more established are: Madrid – Librería de Mujeres, c/San Cristóbal 17, near Plaza Mayor (☏915 217 043); Valencia – Ideas, c/Gravador Esteve 33 (☏963 348 318); Sevilla – Librería Fulmen, c/Zaragoza 36. In Barcelona, the most useful contact address is Ca la Dona, c/Caspe 38 (☏934 127 161), a women's centre used for meetings of over twenty feminist and lesbian organizations.

Fishing Fortnightly permits are easily and cheaply obtained from any ICONA office – there's one in every big town (addresses from the local turismo).

Language courses are offered at most Spanish universities, and in a growing number of special language schools for foreigners. For details overseas and a complete list write to a branch of the Instituto Cervantes: the London one is at 102 Eaton Square, London SW1W (☏020/7235 0353), or check other centres on their website ⓦwww.cervantes.es. Many American universities also have their own courses based in Spain.

Laundries You'll find a few self-service laundries (*lavanderías automáticas*) in the major cities, but they're rare – you normally have to leave your clothes for the full (and somewhat expensive) works at a *lavandería*. Note that you're not allowed by law to leave laundry hanging out of windows over a street. A dry cleaner is a *tintorería*.

Left luggage You'll find self-service *consignas* at most important Spanish train stations. Lockers are large enough to hold most backpacks, plus a smaller bag, and cost about €2.40–3.60 a day; put the coins in to free the key or key-card. These are not a viable alternative for long-term storage, however, as they're periodically emptied out by station staff. Bus terminals have staffed *consignas* where you present a claim stub to get your gear back; the cost is about the same.

Skiing There are resorts in the Pyrenees, Sierra Nevada, and outside Madrid and Santander, all detailed in the relevant chapters. The SNTO's *Skiing in Spain* pamphlet is also useful. If you want to arrange a weekend or more while you're in Spain, Viajes Ecuador (the biggest travel firm in the country, with branches in most cities) is good for arranging cheap all-inclusive trips.

Swimming pools Even quite small Spanish towns and villages have a public swimming pool, or *piscina municipal* – a lifesaver in the summer and yet another reason not to keep exclusively to the coast.

Time Spain is one hour ahead of the UK, six hours ahead of Eastern Standard Time, nine hours ahead of Pacific Standard Time. In Spain the clocks go forward in the last week in March and back again in the last week in October. It's worth noting, if you're planning to cross the border, that Portugal is an hour behind Spain throughout the year.

Toilets Public ones are generally reasonably clean but very rarely have any paper (best to carry your own). They can very occasionally be squat-style. They are most commonly referred to and labelled *Los Servicios*, though signs may point you to *baños*, *aseos*, *retretes* or *sanitarios*. *Damas* (Ladies) and *Caballeros* (Gentlemen) are the usual distinguishing signs for sex, though you may also see the confusing *Señoras* (Women) and *Señores* (Men).

Guide

Guide

Madrid

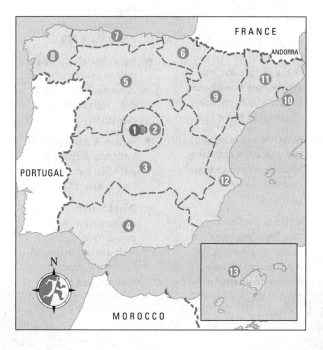

CHAPTER 1 Highlights

✳ **Monasterio de las Descalzas Reales** A fascinating hoard of art treasures hidden away in the centre of Madrid. See p.90

✳ **El Palacio Real** Over-the-top royal opulence in this former residence of the Spanish monarchs. See p.92

✳ **A night on the tiles** Start late at a bar, then on to a club and try to make it into the early hours before collapsing over *chocolate con churros*. See p.128

✳ **El Rastro** A Sunday stroll from Plaza Mayor through Madrid's shambolic flea market, El Rastro. See p.94

✳ **A visit to the Prado** The Goya, Velázquez and Bosch collections alone make the trip to one of the world's greatest art

museums worthwhile. See p.99

✳ **Guernica** See this icon of twentieth-century art at the Reina Sofía museum. See p.106

✳ **Urban oases** Escape from the bustle of the city to the Retiro or the shady oasis of the nearby Jardines Botánicos. See p.107 & 109

✳ **Tapas** Sample the specialities as you hop from bar to bar in the Huertas or La Latina districts. See p.118

✳ **Verbenas** Join in with the traditional August *verbenas* in the *barrio* of La Latina. See p.73

✳ **Real Madrid** Watch Real's dazzling array of stars parade their footballing skills at the spectacular Santiago Bernabéu stadium. See p.115

△ Palacio Real, Madrid

Madrid

M adrid became Spain's capital simply through its geographical position at the centre of Iberia. When Felipe II moved the seat of government here in 1561 his aim was to create a symbol of the unification and centralization of the country, and a capital from which he could receive the fastest post and communications from each corner of the nation. The site itself had few natural advantages – it is 300km from the sea on a 650-metre-high plateau, freezing in winter, burning in summer – and it was only the determination of successive rulers to promote a strong central capital that ensured Madrid's survival and development.

Nonetheless, it was a success, and today Madrid is a vast, predominantly modern city, with a population of some four million and growing. The journey in – through a stream of soulless suburbs – isn't pretty, but the streets at the heart of the city are a pleasant surprise, with pockets of medieval buildings and narrow, atmospheric alleys, dotted with the oddest of shops and bars, and interspersed with eighteenth-century Bourbon squares. By comparison with the historic cities of Spain – Toledo, Salamanca, Sevilla, Granada – there may be few sights of great architectural interest, but the monarchs did acquire outstanding picture collections, which formed the basis of the **Prado** museum. This has long ensured Madrid a place on the European art tour, and the more so since the 1990s arrival – literally down the street – of the **Reina Sofía** and **Thyssen-Bornemisza** galleries, state-of-the-art homes to fabulous arrays of modern Spanish painting (including Picasso's *Guernica*) and European and American masters.

As you get to grips with the place you soon realize that it's the inhabitants – the **madrileños** – that are the capital's key attraction: hanging out in the traditional cafés or the summer terrazas, packing the lanes of the Sunday Rastro flea market, or playing hard and very, very late in a thousand **bars**, clubs, discos and *tascas*. Whatever Barcelona or San Sebastián might claim, the Madrid scene, immortalized in the movies of Pedro Almodóvar, remains the most vibrant and fun in the country. The city centre is also in better shape than for many years as a result of the ongoing impact of a series of urban rehabilitation schemes – funded jointly by the European Union and local government – in the older *barrios* (districts) of the city. Improvements have been made to the transport network, with extensions to the metro, the construction of new ring roads and the excavation of a series of road tunnels designed to bring relief to the city's overcrowded streets. Preparations are already underway to implement an ambitious plan to extend the city northwards beyond Plaza Castilla and to construct a series of state-of-the-art sports facilities to support a bid for the 2012 Olympics.

Madrid's fiestas

Look out for **fiestas** whenever you're in Madrid: there are dozens, some of which involve the whole city, others just an individual *barrio*. The more important dates celebrated in the capital are listed below; for national holidays see p.50.

Also well worth checking out are cultural festivals organized by the city council, in particular the **Veranos de la Villa** (July–Sept) and **Festival de Otoño** (Sept–Nov) concerts (classical, rock, flamenco), theatre and cinema. Many events are free and, in the summer, often open-air, taking place in the city's parks and squares. Annual festivals for alternative theatre (Feb), flamenco (Feb), books (end of May), dance (mid-May to mid-June), photography (mid-June to mid-July) and jazz (Nov) are also firmly established on the cultural agenda. Full programmes are published in the monthly *En Madrid* tourist handout, free from any of the tourist offices listed on p.77.

January

5 *Cabalgata de los Reyes* (Cavalcade of the Three Kings); an evening procession through the city centre in which children are showered with sweets.

February

Week before Lent *Carnaval* – the excuse for a lot of partying and fancy-dress parades, especially in the gay zone around Chueca. The end of *Carnaval* is marked by the bizarre and entertaining parade, *El Entierro de la Sardina* (The Burial of the Sardine), on the Paseo de la Florida.

March/April

Easter Week *Semana Santa* is celebrated with a series of solemn processions around Madrid, although for a more impressive backdrop head for Toledo (routes and times of processions are available from tourist offices).

May

2 *Fiesta del Dos de Mayo* in Malasaña and elsewhere in Madrid. Bands and party-

The city's development

Modern Madrid is enclosed by dreary suburbs: acres of high-rise concrete seemingly dumped without thought onto the dustiest parts of the plain. The great spread to suburbia began under Franco, but it has continued unabated ever since and in recent years unchecked property speculation has taken its toll on the green spaces that surround the capital. Franco also extended the city northwards along the spinal route of the Paseo de la Castellana, to accommodate his ministers and minions during development extravaganzas of the 1950s and 1960s. Large, impressive, and unappealingly sterile, these constructions leave little to the imagination; but then, you're unlikely to spend much time in these parts of town.

In the centre, things are very different. The oldest streets at the very heart of Madrid are crowded with ancient buildings, spreading out in concentric circles which reveal the development of the city over the centuries. Only the cramped street plan gives much clue as to what was here before Madrid became the **Habsburg** capital (in 1561), but the narrow alleys around the Plaza Mayor are still among the city's liveliest and most atmospheric. Later growth owed much to the French tastes of the **Bourbon** dynasty in the eighteenth century, when for the first time Madrid began to develop a style and flavour of its own.

The early **nineteenth-century** brought invasion and turmoil to Spain as Napoleon established his brother Joseph on the throne. Madrid, however, con

ing around the Plaza Dos de Mayo – a bit low-key in recent years, having been the funkiest festival in the city during the 1980s.

15 *Fiestas de San Isidro* – Madrid's patron saint – spread for a week either side of this date, and among the country's biggest festivals. A nonstop round of carnival events: bands, parades and loads of free entertainment, usually centred around Plaza Mayor. There's a band each night in the Jardines de las Vistillas (south of the Palacio Real), and the evenings there start out with *chotis* (a dance typical of Madrid) music and dancing. The fiestas also herald the start of the bullfighting season.

June

13 *Fiesta de la Ermita de San Antonio de la Florida*; events around the church and in the adjacent Parque de la Bombilla.

17–24 *Fiestas de San Juan*; bonfires and fireworks in El Retiro.

July

9–16 *La Virgen del Carmen*; local fiesta in Chamberí *barrio*, north of the city centre.

August

6–15 *Castizo fiestas.* Traditional *fiestas* of *San Cayetano, San Lorenzo* and *La Virgen de la Paloma* in La Latina and Lavapiés *barrios*. Much of the activity takes place around Calle Toledo, the Plaza de la Paja and the Jardines de las Vistillas.

December

25 *Navidad.* During Christmas, Plaza Mayor is filled with stalls selling decorations and displaying a large model of a crib. El Corte Inglés, at the bottom of c/Preciados, has an all-singing, all-dancing clockwork Christmas scene, which plays at certain times of the day to the delight of assembled children.

31 New Year's Eve (*nochevieja*) is celebrated at bars, restaurants and parties all over the city, and there are bands in some of the squares. Puerta del Sol is the customary place to gather, waiting for the strokes of the clock – it is traditional to swallow a grape on each strike.

tinued to flourish, gaining some very attractive buildings and squares. With the onset of the twentieth century, the capital became the hotbed of the political and intellectual discussions which divided the country; *tertulias* (political/ philosophical discussion circles) sprang up in cafés across the city (some of them are still going) as the country entered the turbulent years of the end of the monarchy and the foundation of the Second Republic.

The **Civil War**, of course, caused untold damage, and led to forty years of isolation, which you can still sense in Madrid's idiosyncratic style. The Spanish capital has changed immeasurably, however, in the three decades since Franco's death, initially guided by a poet-mayor, the late and much lamented Tierno Galván. His efforts – the creation of parks and renovation of public spaces and public life – have left an enduring legacy, and were a vital ingredient of the *movida madrileña*, the "happening Madrid", with which the city broke through in the 1980s. Since the early 1990s the centre-right *Partido Popular* has been in control of the local council, bringing with it a more restrictive attitude towards bar and club licensing. Unfortunately there has also been a simultaneous tendency towards homogenization with the rest of Europe as franchised fast-food joints and coffee bars spring up all over the place. Nevertheless, in making the transition from provincial backwater to major European capital, Madrid has still managed to preserve its own stylish and quirky identity.

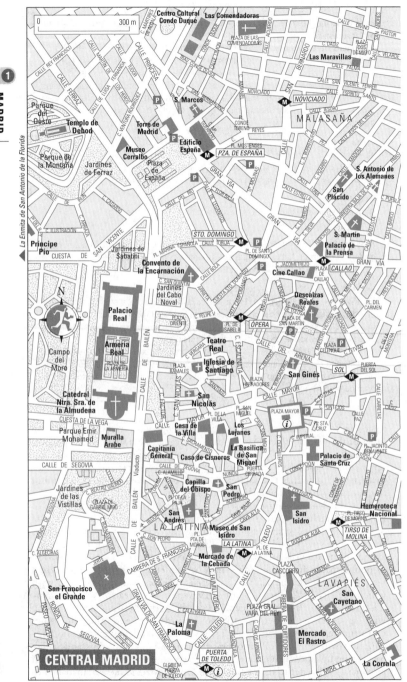

La Ermita de San Antonio de la Florida

0   300 m

Centro Cultural
Conde Duque

Las Comendadoras

PLAZA DE LAS
COMENDADORAS

Las Maravillas

S. Marcos

NOVICIADO

MALASAÑA

Parque
del
Oeste

Templo de
Debod

Torre de
Madrid

Edificio
España

PZA. DE ESPAÑA

S. Antonio de
los Alemanes

Parque
de la Montaña

Museo
Cerralbo

Jardines
de Ferraz

Plaza
de
España

San
Plácido

GRAN VIA

Príncipe
Pío

CUESTA DE SAN VICENTE

Jardines de
Sabatini

STO. DOMINGO

S. Martín

Palacio de
la Prensa

Convento de
la Encarnación

Cine Callao

GRAN VIA

CALLAO

Jardines
del Cabo
Noval

PL DE SANTO
DOMINGO

PLAZA DE
CALLAO

Descalzas
Reales

PL. DEL
CARMEN

Campo
del
Moro

Palacio
Real

PLAZA
ORIENTE

PL. DE
ISABEL II

ÓPERA

PLAZA DE
SAN MARTÍN

Teatro
Real

Armería
Real

PLAZA DE
LA ARMERÍA

Iglesia de
Santiago

PUERTA
DEL SOL

SOL

Catedral
Ntra. Sra. de
la Almudena

CUESTA DE LA VEGA

San
Nicolás

San Ginés

CALLE MAYOR

PLAZA MAYOR

Parque Emir
Mohamed

Muralla
Árabe

Casa de
la Villa

Los
Lujanes

PL. DE LA
VILLA

CALLE DE SEGOVIA

Jardines
de las
Vistillas

PLAZA DE
GABRIEL MIRÓ

Capitanía
General

Casa de Cisneros

La Basílica
de San
Miguel

Palacio de
Santa Cruz

Capilla
del Obispo

San
Pedro

Hemeroteca
Nacional

San
Andrés

Museo de San
Isidro

San
Isidro

TIRSO DE
MOLINA

LA LATINA

LA LATINA

San Francisco
el Grande

Mercado de
la Cebada

PLAZA
CASCORRO

LAVAPIÉS

San
Cayetano

La
Paloma

CALLE TOLEDO

Mercado
El Rastro

PUERTA
DE TOLEDO

CENTRAL MADRID

GLORIETA
PUERTA
DE TOLEDO

La Corrala

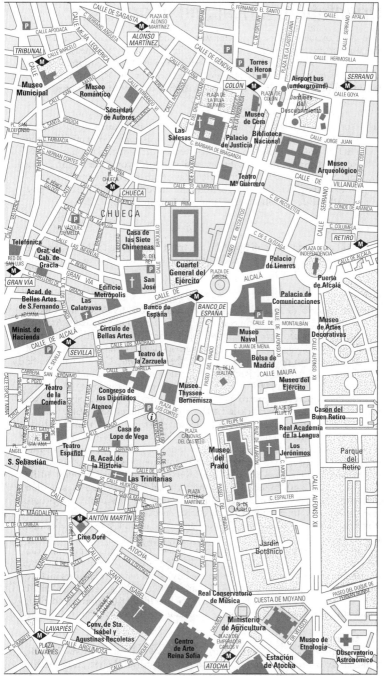

▼ Estación Sur de Autobuses

Orientation, arrival and information

The city's layout is pretty straightforward. At the heart of Madrid – indeed at the very heart of Spain since all distances in the country are measured from here – is the **Puerta del Sol** (often referred to as just "Sol"). Around it lie the oldest parts of Madrid, neatly bordered to the west by the **Río Manzanares**, to the east by the park of **El Retiro**, and to the north by the city's great thoroughfare, the **Gran Vía**.

Within this very compact area, you're likely to spend most of your time. The city's three big museums – the **Prado, Thyssen-Bornemisza** and **Reina Sofía** – lie in a "golden triangle" just west of El Retiro and centred around Paseo del Prado, while over towards the river are the oldest, Habsburg parts of town, centred around the beautiful arcaded **Plaza Mayor**. After Gran Vía, the most important streets (*calles* – abbreviated as c/) are **c/Alcalá** and its continuation, **c/Mayor**, which cut right through the centre from the main post office at **Plaza de Cibeles** to the Bourbon **Palacio Real**.

Arrival

If Madrid is your first stop in Spain, by **air, train** or **bus**, you are likely to arrive a little way from the centre. Transport into the centre, however, is relatively cheap, easy and efficient.

By air

The **Aeropuerto de Barajas** (general information ☎913 936 000; flight information ☎902 353 570) is 16km east of the city, at the end of Avenida de América (the NII road). It has three interconnecting terminals: T1 for nearly all international flights (*vuelos internacionales*); T2 for domestic flights (*nacionales*) plus some of Iberia's flights from continental Europe; T3 for the *Puente Aéreo* (the air shuttle with Barcelona). A vast new Richard Rogers-designed terminal building, which is scheduled to open in 2004, will help double the present capacity.

From the airport, the **metro** link takes you from T2 to the city's Nuevos Ministerios station, where check-in facilities for some airlines are available for your return journey, in just twelve minutes (daily 6am–1.30am, Fri & Sat until 2.30am; €1.10). From there it's a fifteen-minute metro ride to most city-centre locations.

The route by road to central Madrid is more variable, depending on rush-hour traffic, and can take anything from twenty minutes to an hour. Outside the terminal, there is a **shuttle bus** every ten to fifteen minutes (daily 4.45am–2am; €2.40) to an underground terminal in the central Plaza Colón (Metro Serrano; pedestrian entrance from c/Goya). If your plane arrives outside these times, there should be additional special connecting bus services. **Taxis** are always available outside, too, and cost around €18 to the centre, unless you get stuck in traffic.

Half a dozen or so **car rental** companies have stands at the airport and can generally supply clients with maps and directions (see p.143 for addresses and phone numbers of car rental offices in the city). Other airport facilities include 24-hour currency exchange, an ATM, a post office, left luggage lockers in T1 and T2, a RENFE office for booking train tickets (daily 8am–9pm), a chemist, a tourist office (see p.77 for opening hours) and hotel reservations desk.

By train

Trains from France and north/northeast Spain arrive at the **Estación de Chamartín**, a modern terminal isolated in the north of the city; it has all the usual big station facilities, including currency exchange. A metro line connects

Chamartín with the centre, and there are also regular connections by the commuter *trenes de cercanías* with the much more central Estación de Atocha; just take any *cercanía* headed in that direction.

The **Estación de Atocha**, expanded and imaginatively remodelled back in the early 1990s, has two separate terminals: one for **Toledo** and other local services, the other for all points in **south and eastern Spain**, including the high-speed AVE trains to Sevilla and the soon-to-be-inaugurated route to Barcelona.

If you're coming from local towns around Madrid, you may arrive at **Príncipe Pío** (aka Estación del Norte), fairly close to the centre below the Palacio Real, which is also connected to the metro network.

For train **information and reservations** call ☎902 240 202. Tickets can be bought at the individual stations, at Aeropuerto de Barajas arrivals, registered travel agents and at the city centre RENFE office, c/Alcalá 44 (ⓂBanco de España; Mon–Fri 9.30am–8pm). Bear in mind that you'll need to book in advance for most long-distance trains, especially at weekends or holiday time.

By bus

Bus terminals are scattered throughout the city, but the largest – used by all of the international bus services – is the Estación Sur de Autobuses on c/Méndez Álvaro on the corner of c/Retama, 1.5km south of the Atocha train station (☎914 684 200, Ⓦwww.estaciondeautobuses.com; ⓂMéndez Álvaro). For details of others, see the "Travel details" section at the end of this chapter (p.145).

By car

All the main roads into Madrid bring you right into the city centre, although eccentric signposting and even more eccentric driving can be very unnerving. The inner ring road, the M30, and the Paseo de la Castellana are all notorious bottlenecks, although virtually the whole city centre can be close to gridlock during the peak **rush-hour periods** (Mon–Fri 7.30–9.30am & 6–8.30pm). Be prepared for a long trawl around the streets to find **parking**, and even then in most central areas you'll have to buy a ticket in one of the roadside metres (€1.50 for a maximum stay of two hours in the blue-coloured bays; €1.20 for a maximum stay of an hour in the green-coloured bays). A better, and safer, option is to put your car in one of the many signposted *parkings* (€1.65 for the first hour, then €1.45 for subsequent hours). Your own transport is really only of use for out-of-town excursions, so it's advisable to find a hotel with or near a car park and keep your car there during your stay in the city. If you are staying more than a couple of weeks, you can get long-term parking rates at neighbourhood garages.

Information and maps

There are year-round **turismo** offices at the following locations: Aeropuerto de Barajas (Mon–Fri 8am–8pm, Sat & Sun 8am–2pm; ☎913 058 656); Estación de Atocha (Mon–Fri 9am–9pm, Sat & Sun 9am–1pm; ☎915 284 630); Estación de Chamartín (Mon–Fri 8am–8pm, Sat 9am–2pm; ☎913 159 976); Plaza Mayor 3 (Mon–Sat 10am–8pm, Sun 10am–3pm; ☎915 881 636; ⓂSol); Mercado Puerta de Toledo, Ronda de Toledo 1 (Mon–Sat 9am–7pm, Sun 9.30am–2.30pm; ☎913 641 876; ⓂPuerta de Toledo); c/Duque de Medinaceli 2 (Mon–Fri 9am–7pm, Sat 9am–3pm; ☎914 294 951; ⓂBanco de España). The Madrid tourist board has a website at Ⓦwww.munimadrid .es/turismo, and the regional authority has one at Ⓦwww.madrid.org/turismo. In the **summer**, turismo posts operate at popular tourist spots such as the

Puerta del Sol and the Prado, and there are staff (in blue and yellow uniforms) on call outside the Palacio Real, *ayuntamiento* (town hall) and the Prado, and in the Plaza Mayor and Plaza del Callao. You can **phone for information** in English on ☎010 within the city and ☎915 404 010 and ☎915 404 040 from outside (Mon–Fri 8am–9pm, Sat 9am–2pm; not operational on Sat in Aug). There is also a tourist information line on ☎901 300 600 and a general number ☎902 100 007 that links all the regional turismo offices mentioned above.

Free **maps** of the whole central area of **Madrid** are available from any of the turismos detailed above. However, if you intend to do more than just a day's sightseeing, you would be well advised to invest in the Almax *Madrid Centro* map (€2), available from just about any kiosk in the city; this is very clear, 1:10,000 in scale, fully street-indexed, and has a colour plan of the metro on the reverse. The area covered on this represents just about everything of interest; if you want more, Almax also produces a rather less clear, 1:12,000-scale *Madrid Ciudad* (€4.94) that goes right out into the suburbs. Again, it's widely available.

Safety and crime

As far as safety goes, there's little cause for concern. Central Madrid is so populated – and so busy at just about every hour of the day and night – that it never seems to carry any "big city" threat. Which is not to say that **crime** is not a problem, nor that there aren't sleazy pockets to be avoided. Madrid has a big drug problem, all too evident around the Plaza de España and some of the streets just north of Gran Vía. Drugs, it is reckoned, account for ninety percent of crimes in Madrid, and if you are unlucky enough to be threatened for money, it's unwise to resist.

In recent years parts of the *barrio* of Lavapiés have also been a focus of night-time criminal activity so it is best to stick to the busier streets here. Be aware also that although the city council is now trying to combat the problem, the main routes through the Casa de Campo and the Parque del Oeste are still frequented by prostitutes and their clients and are best steered clear of at night. Calle Montera, which runs between Puerta del Sol and Gran Vía, and the streets just to the north are also affected by the problem, and so it is worth taking a little extra care around here.

Tourists in Madrid, as everywhere, are prime targets for pickpockets and petty thieves. The main shopping areas, parks, the metro and anywhere with crowds, are their favourite haunts; burger bars and the Rastro market seem especially popular. Be aware that they often work in groups, and associates will try to distract your attention while your pocket is being picked. Tourists are also obvious targets for muggers, and in all areas it is advisable to keep jewellery, watches and cameras hidden, and to stay away from dark, empty streets at night. Remember that if you're parking a car overnight it would be a wise investment to pay for a covered garage space rather than just leaving it on the street, especially if you cannot remove the radio.

To report a crime you have to make an official statement to the police known as a *denuncia* – often a time-consuming and laborious business, but a necessary procedure for any insurance claim. If you have something stolen call ☎900 100 333 (English spoken). In an emergency, call ☎112.

Transport and tours

Madrid is a pretty easy city to get around. The central areas are walkable, the metro is modern and efficient, buses serve out-of-the-way districts, and taxis are always available.

If you're using public transport extensively and staying long-term, **passes** (*abonos*) covering the metro, train and bus, and available for each calendar month, are worthwhile. If you have an InterRail or Eurail pass, you can use the RENFE urban and suburban trains (*cercanías*) free of charge – they're an alternative to the metro for some longer city journeys.

The metro

The clean and highly efficient **metro** (⊛www.metromadrid.es) is by far the quickest way of getting around Madrid, serving most places you're likely to want to get to. It runs from 6am until 2am (Fri & Sat until 2.30am); the flat fare is €1.10 for nearly all journeys, or €5.20 for a ten-trip ticket (*bono de diez viajes*), which can be used on buses, too. Lines are colour-coded, and the direction of travel is indicated by the name of the terminus station. Note that there are surcharges for the new MetroSur extension serving the southern commuter towns and for Line 9 beyond Puerta de Arganda. You can pick up a free colour map of the system (*plano del metro*) at any station.

Buses

The urban **bus network** (⊛www.emtmadrid.es) is comprehensive but a little more complicated: in the text, where there's no metro stop, we've indicated which bus to take. There are information booths in the Plaza de Cibeles and Puerta del Sol, which dispense a huge route map (*plano de los transportes de Madrid*), and – along with other outlets – sell bus passes. Fares are the same as for the metro, at €1.10 a journey, or €5.20 for a ten-trip ticket (*bono de diez viajes*) which can be used on both forms of transport. When you get on a bus, you punch your ticket in a machine by the driver.

Buses run from 6am to midnight. In addition, there are *búho* (owl) night buses that operate on twenty routes around the central area and out to the suburbs: departures are half-hourly midnight–5.30am, from Plaza de Cibeles and Puerta del Sol.

Taxis

One of the best things about Madrid is that there are thousands of **taxis** – white cars with a diagonal red stripe on the side – which are reasonably cheap; €5 will get you most places within the centre and, although it's common to round up the fare, you're not expected to tip. The minimum fare is €1.45 and supplements are charged for baggage, for going to the train and bus stations or outside the city limits (which includes going to the airport) and for night trips (11pm–7am). In any area in the centre, day and night, you should be able to wave down a taxi (available ones have a green light on top of the cab) in a couple of minutes. To phone for a taxi, call ☎915 478 200, 915 478 500, 914 051 213 or 914 459 008.

Local trains

The **local train** network, or *cercanías*, is the most efficient way of connecting between the main railway stations and provides the best route out to many of

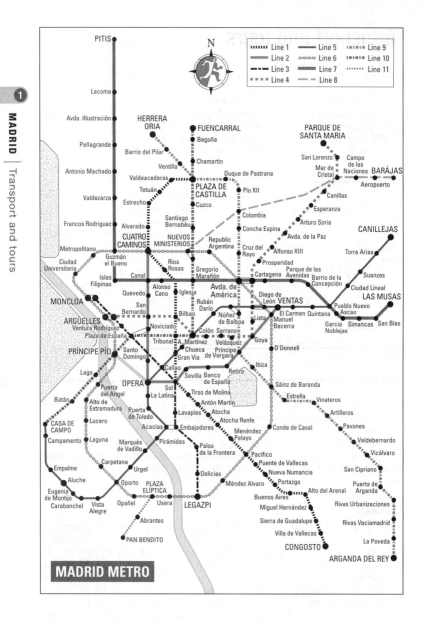

MADRID METRO

the suburbs and to nearby towns such as Alcalá de Henares. Most trains are air-conditioned, fares are cheap and there are good connections with the metro. Trains generally run every fifteen to thirty minutes from 6am to midnight/1am. For more information go to the RENFE website at Ⓦwww.renfe.es and click on the *cercanías* section for Madrid.

Madrid card

The local authority has recently introduced a new Madrid tourist card (ⓦwww.madridcard.com) which gives the holder the right of admission to 40 major museums, the use of public transport, an open-top bus tour and a guided walking tour of the old city, as well as discounts at a number of shops and restaurants. It costs €28 for one day (€42 for two and €55 for three) and is on sale at the Plaza Mayor and c/Duque de Medinaceli tourist offices. Do your sums before you splash out, though, as you would need to cram a lot in to a day's sightseeing to get your money's worth.

City tours

The turismo in Plaza Mayor (see p.77) can supply details of guided English-language **walking tours** around the city. A tour of *Madrid de los Austrias* departs at 10am on Saturdays from the Plaza Mayor tourist office and costs €6 (for more information on this and other walks see ⓦwww.munimadrid.es /turismo; info ☎915 882 900, reservations ☎902 221 622). For a **bus tour** of all the major city sights try Madrid Vision, c/San Bernardo 23 (☎917 651 016, ⓦwww.madridvision.es; ⓂNoviciado); tickets cost €9.62 (children €4.81, under-7s free), allowing you to jump on and off at various places throughout the city. Pick-up points include Puerta del Sol, Plaza de España and the Prado.

Accommodation

Madrid has lots of accommodation, and – business hotels apart – most of it is pretty central. It is, on the whole, pretty functional, although with increasing competition in the sector many *hostales* and hotels have been busy **upgrading** their facilities in recent years. At the lower end of the range, there are bargains to be had, with double rooms as low as €30 a night – and less if you are look-ing for an extended stay. Move up a few notches and you can find plenty of places at around €50–70 a night, offering a comfortable room with a private bath or (more often) shower. For extra comfort and improved facilities you will need to be prepared to pay around €100, while for a step up in class and accompanying luxury be prepared to stump up at least €150 a night. Many of the more expensive category hotels serving business travellers offer special weekend offers, and a great way to get the **best rates** at the more upmarket places in town is to book using the voucher schemes run by nearly all Spanish travel agents in the city. Ask for **talones de hoteles** or *bancotel* vouchers and you will be shown a brochure listing all the hotels participating in the scheme (see "Travel Agencies" on p.44).

If you prefer to have others find you a room, there are accommodation servic-es at the airport, the Estación Sur de Autobuses, and Atocha and Chamartín train stations. Brújula is particularly helpful, with offices at Atocha station (open daily 8am–10pm; ☎915 391 173) and Chamartín (daily 7.30am–9.30pm; ☎913 257 894). The service covers the whole of Spain and there is a €2.50 booking fee.

Pensiones, hostales and hotels

The main factor to consider in choosing a hotel is location. If you want to be at the heart of the old town, you'll probably choose the areas around **Puerta**

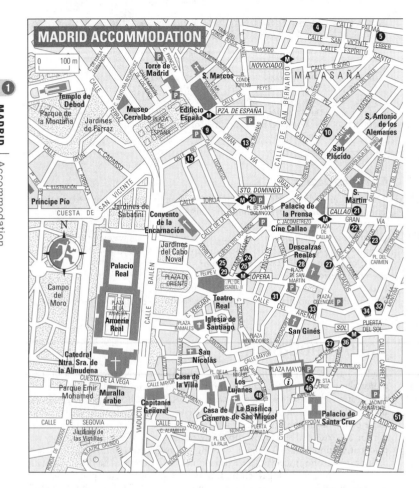

MADRID ACCOMMODATION

del Sol, **Plaza de Santa Ana** or **Plaza Mayor**; if you're into nightlife, **Malasaña** or **Chueca** may appeal; if you want a quieter location and a bit of class, there are the **Paseo del Prado**, **Recoletos** or **Salamanca** areas. You'll notice that buildings in the more popular hotel/*hostal* areas often house two or three separate establishments, each on separate **floors**; these are generally independent of each other. Floors (*pisos*) are written as 1° (first floor in British parlance, second in American), 2° and so on, and often specify *izquierda* (*izq* or *izda*) or *derecha* (*dcha*), meaning to the left or to the right of the staircase. A problem with some of the *hostales* in larger buildings – on Gran Vía, for example – is that they are often inaccessible at night, unless you've been given a front-door key, as there's not always an entryphone or doorbell at street level. If you book a room and intend to arrive after, say, 9pm, check that you will be able to get in. Another thing to bear in mind is **noise**; bars, clubs, traffic and roadworks all contribute to making Madrid a high-decibel city, so avoid rooms

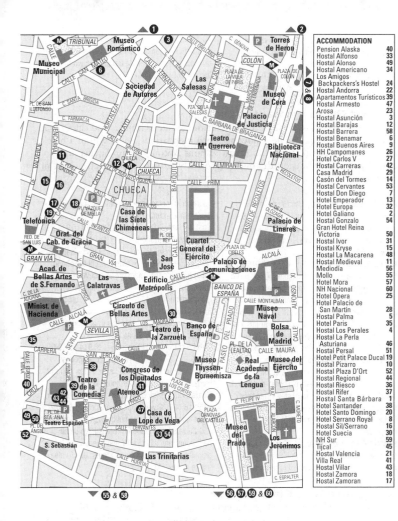

on the lower floors or choose a place away from the main centre of nightlife if you want a bit of peace and quiet. As for facilities, air conditioning is a welcome extra in summer when temperatures can soar towards 40°C.

Around Estación de Atocha

Much of the cheapest accommodation in Madrid is to be found in the area immediately around the Estación de Atocha. However, the *pensiones* closest to the station are a little grim. The places below, however, are good, safe choices.

Hostal Barrera c/Atocha 96, 2ª ☏915 275 381, ⓦwww.hostalbarrera.com; ⓜAntón Martín. Friendly, good-value fourteen-room *hostal* with an English-speaking owner. Rooms have bath or shower, a/c and TV. Internet access available. ❸
Hotel Mediodía Plaza del Emperador Carlos V 8

☏915 273 060, ⓕ915 307 008; ⓜAtocha. Huge, slightly fading 165-roomed hotel right next to the Reina Sofía and the Estación de Atocha. The simple but comfortable rooms, all with bathroom and TV, are excellent value. ❹
Pensión Mollo c/Atocha 104, 3º & 4º ☏915 287

176; ⓂAtocha/Antón Martín. Recently refurbished good-value *hostal* close to the station. Doubles have en-suite showers. ❷

NH Sur Paseo de la Infanta Isabel 9 ☎915 399 499, Ⓦwww.nh-hoteles.com; ⓂAtocha. Part of the NH chain, this smart 68-room hotel is right next to the station and close to the Retiro. Special promotion rates can bring the price down to as low as €60 a night. ❽

Around Plaza de Santa Ana

Plaza de Santa Ana is at the heart of Madrid nightlife, with bars and cafés open until very late at night. The following recommendations are all within a block or two of the square, with the metro stations Antón Martín, Sevilla and Sol close by. Go for rooms on the higher floors if you want to avoid the worst of the noise.

Pensión Alaska c/Espoz y Mina 7, 4º ☎915 211 845, Ⓔpensionalaska@hotmail.com; ⓂSol. Six large doubles, all with bathroom and TV, in this seven-room *pensión* formerly known as the *Hostal Valencia*. ❸

Hostal Alonso c/Espoz y Mina 17, 3º ☎915 315 679, Ⓔhostal-alonso@hotmail.com; ⓂSol. Basic but very good-value and friendly *hostal* popular for its location. Book ahead if you can. ❷

Hostal Carreras c/Príncipe 18, 3º ☎ & Ⓕ915 220 036; ⓂSevilla. Large light rooms in this very pleasant 14-room *hostal*. Cheaper rooms have handbasins only, others have showers or baths. ❸

Gran Hotel Reina Victoria Plaza de Santa Ana 14 ☎915 314 500, Ⓦwww.trypreinavictoria .solmelia.com; ⓂSol. Lovely old hotel in a historic building, where the bullfighters stay when they're in town. Rooms are a hefty €217 a night, but this is the pick of Madrid's class hotels in this price range. ❾

Hostal Persal Plaza del Ángel 12 ☎913 694 643, Ⓦwww.hostalpersal.com; ⓂSol. Friendly and excellent-value 80-room hotel. All the recently-refurbished rooms have a/c, bathroom and TV. Breakfast is included. ❹

Hostal Plaza D'Ort Plaza del Ángel 13 ☎914 299 041, Ⓦwww.plazadort.com; ⓂSol. Next door to the *Hostal Persal*, all rooms in this very clean *hostal* have a shower or bath, TV and telephone, some have a/c too. There are also several self-catering apartments, making it a good family or group option. ❸

Hostal Regional c/Príncipe 18, 4º ☎915 223 373; ⓂSol. Small, basic rooms in an elegant old building off Plaza de Santa Ana. ❷

Hotel Santander c/Echegaray 1 ☎914 296 644, Ⓕ913 691 078; ⓂSevilla. Spacious, spotless rooms – many have a small seating area – in this pleasant 35-room two-star hotel. ❹

Hostal Villar c/Príncipe 18, 1º ☎915 316 600 or 915 316 609, Ⓦwww.villar.arrakis.es; ⓂSevilla. Large *hostal* in the same building as the *Regional* and *Carreras*. The standard rooms have small bathrooms, and all have TV and telephone. Air conditioning is available in some rooms. Good-value triples at €56. ❷

Sol, Ópera and Plaza Mayor

This really is the heart of Madrid and prices, not surprisingly, are a bit higher, though you can still find bargains in the streets around the Plaza Mayor. Be aware that Sol itself is likely to be disrupted by building works in the next few years due to the construction of a new underground *cercanías* railway station.

Hostal Alfonso Plaza Celenque 1, 2º ☎915 319 840, Ⓕ915 329 225; ⓂSol/Ópera. Nicely located just off c/Arenal, this clean *hostal* has fourteen doubles, two triples and a handful of singles at a competitive price, all with bathrooms and TV. ❸

Hostal Americano Puerta del Sol 11, 3º & 4º ☎915 222 822, Ⓕ915 221 192; ⓂSol. Nicely furnished 44-room *hostal*, with recently improved bathrooms and a pleasant communal living room. ❷–❸

Hotel Carlos V c/Maestro Vitoria 5 ☎915 314 100, Ⓦwww. bestwestern.com/prop_92119; ⓂSol. Large, comfy rooms at this century-old hotel, in a pedestrianized part of town, just off c/Preciados behind the Descalzas Reales monastery. Some rooms have balconies. Price includes breakfast. ❼

Casa Madrid c/Arrieta 2, 2º ☎915 595 791, wwww.casademadrid.com; ⓂÓpera. This exclusive boutique-style hotel opposite the Teatro Real offers seven stunning rooms decorated with a range of hand-painted frescoes. Ideal for a romantic escape, but not really the place to take children. Individual attention guaranteed. ❽

Hotel Europa c/Carmen 4 ☎915 212 900, Ⓦwww.hoteleuropa.net; ⓂSol. Well-established, family-run hotel with recently refurbished rooms and a newish restaurant. ❹

HH Campomanes c/Campomanes 4° ⊤915 488 548, ⓦwww.hhcampomanes.com; ⓂÓpera. Chic designer hotel with a perfect location in a quiet street close to the opera house. Compact rooms, neat bathrooms and friendly staff. Buffet breakfast included in the price. ❺

Hostal Ivor c/Arenal 24, 2° ⊤915 471 054, ⓕ915 418 897; ⓂÓpera. Good standard *hostal* with comfortable en-suite rooms, all with TV. ❸

Hostal La Macarena Cava de San Miguel 8, 2° ⊤913 659 221, ⓕ913 642 757; ⓂSol. Fine, refurbished, family-run *hostal* in a characterful alley just off the Plaza Mayor. The well-kept rooms are a little on the small side. ❹

Hotel Ópera c/Cuesta de Santo Domingo 2 ⊤ 915 412 800, ⓦwww.hotelopera.com; ⓂÓpera. With a very pleasant location near the Plaza de Oriente, this modern hotel has 79 comfortable, large rooms at a pretty reasonable price. The café downstairs, appropriately enough, offers dinner served by singing waiters. ❼

Hotel Palacio de San Martín c/Plaza de San Martín 5 ⊤ 917 015 000, ⓦwww.intur.com/san-martin/fsanmartin.html; ⓂÓpera/Sol. Newly opened hotel in a historic building in this attractive square alongside the Descalzas Reales monastery. Fine rooftop restaurant. ❼

Hotel Paris c/Alcalá 2 ⊤915 216 496, ⓕ915 310 188; ⓂSol. Old-fashioned hotel whose hey-day was back in the nineteenth century. Half the rooms have a/c. Very good value for so central a position. Price includes breakfast. ❺

Hostal La Perla Asturiana Plaza de Santa Cruz 3 ⊤913 664 600, ⓦwww.perlaasturiana.com; ⓂSol. Small, basic rooms in this nicely located *hostal*, overlooking a pleasant square. ❷–❸

Hostal Riesco c/Correo 2–3 ⊤915 222 692, ⓕ915 329 088; ⓂSol. Old-style, characterful place in a street just off Sol. All rooms in this friendly family-run *hostal* are en suite and have a/c. ❷

Hostal Rifer c/Mayor 5, 4° ⊤915 323 197, ⓕ915 323 197; ⓂSol. Clean, bright rooms in the highest – and therefore quietest – of three options in this block, with a friendly owner. ❷

Hostal Tijcal c/Zaragoza 6, 3° ⊤913 655 910, ⓦwww.hostaltijcal.com; ⓂSol. Situated between Plaza Santa Cruz and Plaza Mayor, this quirky, but extremely friendly, *hostal* offers rooms with a/c (€6 supplement), bathroom and TV (some also have good views). There is a sister *hostal*, the *Tijcal 2*, at c/Cruz 26 ⊤913 604 628, ⓕ915 211 477. ❸–❹

Around Paseo del Prado

This is a quieter area, though still very central, which hosts some of the city's most expensive hotels – as well as some more modest options.

Hostal Armesto c/San Agustín 6, 1° ⊤& ⓕ914 299 031; ⓂAntón Martín. A clean and friendly option, in a quiet street near the tourist office. The best rooms overlook the pleasant little garden in the Casa de Lope de Vega next door. ❸

Hostal Cervantes c/Cervantes 34, 2° ⊤914 298 365, ⓦwww.hostal-cervantes.com; ⓂAntón Martín. If you can't get in to the *Gonzalo* on the floor above, this is another friendly option, although slightly more expensive. All rooms have their own bathroom, TV and ventilator and are pleasantly furnished. ❸

Hostal Gonzalo c/Cervantes 34, 3° ⊤914 292 714, ⓕ914 202 007; ⓂAntón Martín. Has to be one of the most welcoming *hostales* in the city. Twelve bright, en-suite rooms, a charming owner and a great price. Highly recommended. ❸

Hotel Mora Paseo del Prado 32 ⊤914 201 569, ⓕ914 200 564; ⓂAtocha. Friendly, recently refur-bished, 62-room hotel. All rooms have a/c and some have pleasant views along the Paseo del Prado. Perfectly positioned for all the galleries on the Paseo

del Arte and very good value. ❹

NH Nacional Paseo del Prado 48 ⊤914 296 629, ⓦwww.nh-hoteles.com; ⓂAtocha. Large, plush hotel, part of the NH chain, attractively situated opposite the Jardines Botánicos. Special offers can reduce the price substantially. ❾

Hotel Suecia c/Marqués de Casa Riera 4 ⊤915 316 900, ⓦwww.hotelsuecia.com; ⓂBanco de España. Tucked away in a quiet street behind the Círculo de Bellas Artes, the recently refurbished *Suecia* is a cut above the other options in this price range. Brightly decorated rooms and slick service. ❽

Villa Real Plaza de las Cortes 10 ⊤914 203 767, ⓦwww.derbyhotels.es/hoteles/villareal.htm; ⓂSevilla. High-class hotel with its own art collec-tion owned by Catalan archeologist Jordi Clos. Each of the 96 elegant double rooms has a spa-cious sitting area. The rooftop restaurant has fine views over the Congresos de Diputados and down towards the Paseo del Prado. ❾

Plaza de España and Gran Vía

The huge old buildings along the Gran Vía – which stretches all the way from Plaza de España to c/Alcalá – hide a vast array of hotels and *hostales* at every price, often with a delightfully decayed elegance, though also noisy from outside traffic. After dark, the area can feel somewhat seedy.

Hostal Andorra Gran Vía 33, 7º ☎ 915 323 116, ⓔ andorra@arrakis.es; Ⓜ Callao. Smart, clean and quiet, with bathrooms in all the rooms. ❸

Hotel Arosa c/Salud 21 ☎ 915 321 600, ⓦ www.bestwestern.com/es/arosa; Ⓜ Gran Vía/Sol. Friendly, well-equipped hotel right in the heart of town between Sol and Gran Vía. Spacious, air-conditioned rooms. Some of the surrounding streets are a bit down at heel but don't let this put you off. ❽

Hostal Buenos Aires Gran Vía 61, 2º ☎ 915 420 102, ⓕ 915 422 869; Ⓜ Plaza de España. Well-appointed *hostal*, at the Plaza de España end of this street. Rooms have a/c, TV and en-suite bathroom. ❸–❹

Casón del Tormes c/Río 7 ☎ 915 419 746, ⓦ www.bestwestern.com/prop_92198; Ⓜ Plaza de España. Plush 63-room hotel in a surprisingly quiet street off Plaza de España. Rooms are comfortable, en suite and air-conditioned, and

the English-speaking staff are helpful. A very good option in this price range. Breakfast included. ❻

Hotel Emperador Gran Vía 53 ☎ 915 472 800, ⓦ www.emperadorhotel.com; Ⓜ Santo Domingo/Plaza de España. The only real reason to come here is the rooftop swimming pool with its magnificent views. Otherwise it is rather impersonal, though rooms are large and well decorated. ❾

Hotel Santo Domingo Plaza de Santo Domingo 13 Vía 53 ☎ 915 479 800, ⓦ www.bestwestern.com/prop_92194; Ⓜ Santo Domingo. Modern, attractively decorated rooms in this well-run and friendly hotel. There are reductions at the weekend. ❼–❽

Hostal Valencia Gran Vía 44, 5º & 6º ☎ 915 221 115, ⓦ www.hostal-valencia.com; Ⓜ Callao. Best of a whole block of *hostales*, though rooms at the front can be noisy. Good-value triples and quadruples available, too. ❸

North of Gran Vía

North of Gran Vía, there are further wedges of *hostales* on and around c/Fuencarral and c/Hortaleza, near Metro Gran Vía. Fuencarral itself can be noisy, so for a room facing away from the street; the streets around its southern end form a red-light district, so take care after dark. The higher the street numbers, the further these streets are from Gran Vía – and the nearer to Malasaña (see below).

Hotel Petit Palace Ducal c/Hortaleza 3, 3º ☎ 915 211 045, ⓦ www.hthoteles.com; Ⓜ Gran Vía. A major upgrading from the old *hostal* that used to occupy this property. One of a series of self-styled high-tech hotels with 60 all-new rooms with high-speed Internet connections and other mod cons. ❻

Hostal Kryse c/Fuencarral 25, 1º ☎ 915 311 512, ⓕ 915 228 153; Ⓜ Gran Vía. One of a trio of clean, friendly bars run by the same management. Small bathroom, TV and ceiling fans in all 25 rooms. ❷

Hostal Medieval c/Fuencarral 46, 2º ☎ 915 222 549; Ⓜ Chueca. Well-run, friendly place with a range of rooms, in an old building overlooking a square. All of the airy rooms have showers, but toilets are shared. Triples available. ❷

Hostal Pizarro c/Pizarro 14, 1º ☎ 915 319 158, ⓦ www.hostalpizarro.com; Ⓜ Plaza de España. Comfortable, fairly upmarket *hostal* on a street just off c/Luna. ❷

Hostal Zamora Plaza Vázquez de Mella 1, 4º Izda. ☎ 915 217 031; Ⓜ Gran Vía. Seventeen rooms in this pleasant *hostal*, most of which overlook the recently spruced-up plaza. All of the simple rooms have bathrooms and TV and some have a/c. There are good-value family rooms, too. ❸

Hostal Zamoran c/Fuencarral 18, 2º Izda ☎ 915 322 060; Ⓜ Gran Vía. Good-value *hostal*, with large, clean, en-suite rooms (all with TV). ❷

Malasaña

Malasaña, west of c/Fuencarral and centred around Plaza Dos de Mayo, is an old working-class district, and one of the main nightlife areas of Madrid. The *hostales* here tend towards the basic, but if you stay you'll get a feel for what the city is really like – and you'll still be within walking distance of the sights.

Hostal Barajas c/Augusto Figueroa 17 ☎ 915 324 078, ⓦ www.hostalbarajas.com;

Ⓜ Tribunal/Chueca. An unusually well appointed *hostal* for this area, offering simply decorated en-

suite rooms, all with a/c and TV. **❷**
Hostal Palma c/Palma 17, 1° ☎914 475 488; ⓜTribunal. Basic but clean rooms (some with balcony) at a budget price, behind the metro station. **❶**
Hostal Los Perales c/Palma 61, 1° ☎915 227 191; ⓜNoviciado. Best budget option in a building

with several *hostales*. Can be a little noisy. **❶–❷**
Hostal Sil/Serrano c/Fuencarral 95, 2° & 3° ☎914 488 972, ⓕ914 474 829; ⓜTribunal. Two *hostales* at the quieter end of c/Fuencarral with a/c, new bathrooms and TV. **❹**

Chueca and Santa Bárbara

Chueca, east of c/Fuencarral, is another nightlife centre and the city's *zona gay*. After some years of neglect, the *barrio* has been given a new lease of life with the opening of numerous new bars, clubs and restaurants. The northern reaches of Chueca, around Plaza Santa Bárbara (ⓜAlonso Martínez), are rather more spacious and still full of nightlife.

Hostal Asunción Plaza Santa Bárbara 8, 2° ☎913 082 348, ⓕ913911 306; ⓜAlonso Martínez. Small but well-furnished rooms with bath, TV and minibar (some are air-conditioned, too). Free Internet use for guests. Pretty position overlooking the square. **❷**
Hostal Benamar c/San Mateo 20, 2° ☎913 080 092, ⓦwww.geocities.com/benamar_es/;

ⓜTribunal. A good budget option. Some of the 22 clean rooms have a/c and all have washbasins. **❷**
Hostal Santa Bárbara Plaza Santa Bárbara 4, 3° ☎914 457 334 or 914 469 308, ⓕ914 462 345; ⓜAlonso Martínez. Nice, air-conditioned *hostal* in a good location, with English-speaking Italian *dueño*. **❸**

Recoletos and Salamanca

This is Madrid at its most chic: the Bond Street/Rue de Rivoli region of smart shops and equally well-heeled apartment blocks. It's a safe, pleasant area, just north of the Parque del Retiro, but a good walk from the main sights.

Hostal Don Diego c/Velázquez 45, 5° ☎914 350 760, ⓔhostaldondiego@hotmail.com; ⓜVelázquez. Very comfortable, recently refurbished little hotel – rooms are air-conditioned and have satellite TV. Quite reasonably priced for the area. Some English-speaking staff. **❹**
Hotel Galiano c/Alcalá Galiano 6 ☎913 192 000, ⓦwww.hotelgaliano.com; ⓜColón. Hidden away in a quiet street off the Paseo de la Castellana, this

small hotel has a sophisticated feel and friendly service. Car parking facilities. **❻–❼**
Hotel Serrano Royal c/Marqués de Villamejor 8 ☎915 769 626, ⓦwww.husa.es; ⓜRubén Darío. Modern four-star hotel, handily sited between c/Serrano and Paseo de la Castellana. Standard priced doubles are around €170, but enquire for special offers – especially in summer – that can bring the price down to as low as €60. **❽**

Apartments

Apartamentos Turísticos c/Príncipe 11 ☎902 113 311, ⓦwww.atprincipe11.com; ⓜSevilla. Good option for families or groups. The 36 apartments in this centrally located block range from

small studios to family suites for up to six. All are air-conditioned and have kitchenettes. Prices range from €92 for a four-person to €140 for a family one. **❼**

Youth hostels and campsites

Madrid has just one campsite located well out of the centre, and a very handy backpackers' hostel right in the heart of the city.

Camping Osuna Avda. de Logroño s/n, out near the airport, just north of the NII road to Barcelona ☎917 410 510, ⓕ913 206 365; ⓜCanillejas/Campo de las Naciones, then bus #105. Friendly, with good facilities, including a popular bar, reasonable prices and plenty of shade, but the ground is rock hard and, with planes landing and taking off overhead, it's extremely noisy. Around €8 a night per person plus tent.

Los Amigos Backpackers's Hostel ☎ & ⓕ915 471 707, ⓦwww.losamigoshostel.com; ⓜÓpera. Great backpacking option in a quiet side street by the Opera house. Dormitories cater for 4–6 people, and there are a couple of communal rooms, plus access to the Internet. Friendly staff all speak English. Bed linen and use of kitchen included in €17 price.

The City

Madrid's main sights occupy a compact area between the **Palacio Real** (Royal Palace) and the gardens of **El Retiro**. The great trio of museums – the **Prado**, **Thyssen-Bornemisza** and **Reina Sofía** – are ranged along the Paseo del Prado, over towards the Retiro. The oldest part of the city, an area known as **Madrid de los Austrias** after the Habsburg monarchs who built it, is centred on the gorgeous, arcaded **Plaza Mayor**, just to the east of the Palacio Real.

If you have very limited time, you might well do no more sightseeing than this. However, monuments are not really what Madrid is about, and to get a feel for the city you need to branch out a little, and experience the contrasting character and life of the various *barrios*. The most central and rewarding of these are the areas **around Plaza de Santa Ana and c/Huertas**, east of Puerta del Sol; **La Latina and Lavapiés**, south of Plaza Mayor, where the Sunday market, **El Rastro**, takes place; and **Malasaña and Chueca**, north of Gran Vía. By happy circumstance, these *barrios* have some of Madrid's finest concentrations of tapas bars and restaurants (see p.116).

Sol, Plaza Mayor and Ópera: Madrid de los Austrias

Madrid de los Austrias – Habsburg Madrid – was a mix of formal planning, at its most impressive in the expansive and theatrical Plaza Mayor, and areas of shanty-town development, knocked up as the new capital gained an urban population. The central area of old Madrid still reflects both characteristics, with its twisting grid of streets, alleyways and steps, and its Flemish-inspired architecture of red brick and grey stone, slate-tiled towers, and Renaissance doorways.

Puerta del Sol

The obvious starting point for exploring Habsburg Madrid (and most other areas of the centre) is the **Puerta del Sol** (Ⓜ Sol). This square marks the epicentre of the city – and, indeed, of Spain. It is from this point that all distances are measured, and here that six of Spain's *Rutas Nacionales* (the roads known as the NI, to Burgos, the NII, to Zaragoza, and so on) officially begin. On the pavement outside the clock-tower building on the south side of the square, a stone slab shows Kilometre Zero.

Summer in Madrid

Madrid virtually shuts down **in the summer**; from around July 20 you'll suddenly find that many of the bars, restaurants and offices are closed, and their inhabitants gone to the coast and countryside. Only in September does the city open properly for business again.

Luckily for visitors, and those *madrileños* who choose to remain, the main sights and museums stay open, and a summer nightlife takes on a momentum of its own in outdoor terrace bars, or *terrazas*. In addition, the city council has in recent years initiated a major programme of summer entertainment, *Los Veranos de la Villa*. It's not a bad time to be in town at all, so long as you can cope with the soaring temperatures and you're not trying to get anything done.

Note that, throughout the year, most museums (and many bars and restaurants) **close on Monday**. Major attractions that stay open on Mondays include the Reina Sofía and the Palacio Real.

Madrid's freebies

Free entrance can be gained to many of Madrid's premier attractions. Sites classed as *Patrimonio Nacional* such as the Palacio Real, the Convento de la Encarnación, El Pardo (see p.115) and the Monasterio de las Descalzas are free to EU citizens on Wednesdays (bring your passport). Seven museums run by Madrid City Council including the Museo Municipal, the Museo de San Isidro, La Ermita de San Antonio, the Templo de Debod and the Museo de Arte Contemporaneo no longer charge admission. Most museums are free for under 18s and give substantial discounts to the retired and students (bring ID in all cases). In addition, many museums and sights that normally charge entry set aside certain times when entrance is free, and nearly all are free on International Museum Day on May 18. These include the following:

Centro de Arte Reina Sofía: Sat after 2.30pm & Sun 10am–2.30pm.
Museo de América: Sun 10am–2.30pm.
Museo Arqueológico: Sat 2.30–8.30pm & Sun 9.30am–2.30pm.
Museo de Artes Decorativas: Sun 10am–2pm.
Museo Cerralbo: Wed 9.30am–2.30pm & Sun 10am–2pm.
Museo del Ejército: Sat 10am–2pm.
Museo Lázaro Galdiano: Sat 10am–2pm.
Museo del Prado: Sun 9am–2pm.
Museo Romántico: Sun 10am–2pm.
Real Academia de Bellas Artes: Wed 9am–6.30pm.

The square is a popular meeting place, especially by the fountain, or at the corner of c/Carmen, with its statue of a bear pawing a *madroño* (strawberry tree) – the city's emblem. These apart, there's little of note, though the square fulfils something of a public role when there's a demonstration or celebration. At New Year, for example, it is packed with people waiting for the clock to chime midnight. The square's main business, however, is shopping, with giant branches of the **department stores** El Corte Inglés and the French chain FNAC in c/Preciados, at the top end of the square. It is worth noting that in the course of the next few years the area is likely to be heavily disrupted by the construction of a subterranean train station beneath c/Montera.

Plaza Mayor

Follow c/Mayor (the "Main Street" of the medieval city) west from the Puerta del Sol and you could easily walk right past Madrid's most important landmark: **Plaza Mayor**. This is set back from the street and, entered by stepped passageways, appears all the more grand in its continuous sweep of arcaded buildings. It was planned by Felipe II – the monarch who made Madrid the capital – as the public meeting place of the city, and was finished thirty years later in 1619 during the reign of Felipe III, who sits astride the stallion in the central statue. The architect was Juan Gómez de Mora, who was responsible for many of the civic and royal buildings in this quarter.

The square, with its hundreds of balconies, was designed as a theatre for public events, and it has served this function throughout its history. It was the scene of the Inquisition's *autos-da-fé* (trials of faith) and the executions which followed; kings were crowned here; festivals and demonstrations passed through; plays by Lope de Vega and others received their first performances; bulls were fought; and gossip was spread. The more important of the events would be watched by royalty from their apartments in the central **Casa Panadería**, a palace named after the bakery which it replaced. It was rebuilt after a fire in

1692 and subsequently decorated with frescoes. However, the present delightful, and highly kitsch, array of allegorical figures that adorn the facade was only added in 1992. Today the palace houses municipal offices and an exhibition centre displaying temporary exhibits on the history of Madrid (Mon–Fri 11am–2pm & 5–8pm, Sat, Sun & holidays 11am–2pm; free).

Nowadays, Plaza Mayor is primarily a tourist haunt, full of expensive outdoor cafés and restaurants (best stick to a drink). However, an air of grandeur clings to the plaza, which still performs public functions. In the summer months and during the major *madrileño* fiestas (see pp.72–3) it becomes an outdoor **theatre** and **music stage**; in the autumn there's a **book fair**; and in the winter, just before Christmas, it becomes a **bazaar** for festive decorations and religious regalia. Every Sunday, too, stamp and coin sellers set up their stalls.

In the alleys just below the square, such as c/Cuchilleros and c/Cava de San Miguel, are some of the city's oldest *mesones*, or taverns. Have a drink in these in the early evening and you are likely to be serenaded by passing *tunas* – musicians and singers dressed in traditional costume of knickerbockers and waistcoats who wander around town playing and passing the hat. These men-only troupes are attached to various faculties of the university and are usually students supplementing their grants.

Plaza de la Villa, San Miguel and San Ginés

West along c/Mayor, towards the Royal Palace, is **Plaza de la Villa**, an example of three centuries of Spanish architectural development. Its oldest surviving building is the recently renovated fifteenth-century **Torre de los Lujanes**, a fine Mudéjar (Moors working under Christian rule) tower, where Francis I of France is said to have been imprisoned in 1525 after his capture at the Battle of Pavia in Italy. Opposite is the old town hall, the **ayuntamiento**, begun in the seventeenth century, but remodelled in a Baroque style (tours in Spanish only at 5pm every Monday; free). Finally, fronting the square is the **Casa de Cisneros**, built by a nephew of Cardinal Cisneros in the sixteenth-century Plateresque ("silversmith") style. Baroque is also seen round the corner in c/San Justo, where the parish church of **San Miguel** (Mon–Sat 11am–12.15pm & 5.30–7pm) shows the imagination of the eighteenth-century Italian architects who designed it.

Another fine – but much more ancient – church is San Ginés, north of Plaza Mayor on c/Arenal. This is of Mozarabic origin (built by Christians under Moorish rule) and has an El Greco canvas of the moneychangers being chased from the temple on show in the Capilla del Cristo. The church is open only during services. Alongside the church, in somewhat uneasy juxtaposition, stands a cult temple of the twentieth century, the *Joy Madrid* disco, and, behind it, the **Chocolatería San Ginés**, a Madrid institution, which at one time catered for the early-rising worker but now churns out *churros* and hot chocolate for the late nightclub crowd (see p.133).

Descalzas Reales and Encarnación convents

A couple of blocks north of San Ginés is one of the hidden treasures of Madrid, the **Monasterio de las Descalzas Reales** (ⓦwww.patrimonio nacional.es; ⓂSol/Callao) at Plaza de las Descalzas Reales 3. This was founded by Juana de Austria, daughter of the Emperor Carlos V, sister of Felipe II, and, at age nineteen, already the widow of Prince Don Juan of Portugal. In her wake came a succession of titled ladies (*Descalzas Reales* means "Barefoot Royals"), who brought fame and, above all, fortune to the convent, which is unbelievably rich, though beautiful and tranquil, too. It is still in use, with shoeless nuns tending patches of vegetable garden.

Whistle-stop guided tours (Tues–Thurs & Sat 10.30am–12.45pm & 4–5.45pm, Fri 10.30am–12.45pm, Sun & some holidays 11am–1.45pm; €5, free on Wed for EU citizens, joint ticket with Convento de la Encarnación €6) conduct visitors (usually in Spanish only) through the cloisters and up an incredibly fancy stairway to a series of chambers packed with art and treasures of every kind. The former dormitories are perhaps the most outstanding feature, decorated with a series of Flemish tapestries based on designs by Rubens and a striking portrait of St Francis by Zurbarán. These were the sleeping quarters for all the nuns including St Teresa of Ávila for a time, although the empress María of Germany preferred a little more privacy and endowed the convent with her own luxurious private chambers. The other highlight of the tour is the Joyería (Treasury), piled high with jewels and relics of uncertain provenance. The nuns kept no records of their gifts, so no one is quite sure what many of the things are – there is a bizarre cross-sectional model of Christ – nor which bones came from which saint. Whatever the case, it's an exceptional hoard.

Over towards the Palacio Real in Plaza de la Encarnación is the **Convento de la Encarnación** (Tues–Thurs & Sat 10.30am–12.45pm & 4–5.45pm, Fri 10.30am–12.45pm, Sun & some holidays 11am–1.45pm; €3.60, free on Wed for EU citizens, joint ticket with Monasterio de las Descalzas Reales €6; Ⓦwww.patrimonionacional.es; ⓂÓpera). This was founded a few years after Juana's convent, by Margarita, wife of Felipe III, though it was substantially rebuilt towards the end of the eighteenth century. It houses an extensive but disappointing collection of seventeenth-century Spanish art, and a bizarre library-like reliquary which is reputed to be one of the most important in the Catholic world. The most famous relic housed here is a small glass bulb said to contain the blood of the fourth-century doctor martyr, St Pantaleon, whose blood supposedly liquefies at midnight on the eve of his feast day (July 26).

Ópera: Plaza de Oriente and the cathedral

West of Sol, c/Arenal leads to the **Teatro Real** or Ópera (tours Tues–Sun 10.30am–1.30pm; €3; tickets on sale from 10am, info ☎915 160 996, Ⓦwww.teatro-real.com; ⓂÓpera), which gives this area its name. Built in the mid-nineteenth century, it almost sank a few decades later as a result of subsidence caused by underground canals and was forced to close in 1925; it finally reopened in 1997 after an epic ten-year refurbishment which ended up costing a mind-boggling 150 million euros (for details of tickets for performances, see p.137).

Around the back, the opera house is separated from the Palacio Real by the **Plaza de Oriente**, one of the most elegant and agreeable open spaces in Madrid and used in the bad old days by Franco as the venue for his public addresses; small groups of neo-Fascists still gather here on the anniversary of his death on November 21. One of the square's main attractions – and the focus of its life – is the elegant *Café del Oriente*, whose summer terraza is one of the stations of Madrid nightlife. The café (which is also a prestigious restaurant) looks as traditional as any in the city but was in fact opened in the 1980s by a priest, Padre Lezama, who ploughs his profits into various charitable schemes.

The café apart, the dominant features of Plaza de Oriente are statues: 44 of them, depicting Spanish kings and queens, which were originally designed to go on the palace facade but found to be too heavy (some say too ugly) for the roof to support. The **statue of Felipe IV** on horseback, in the centre of the square, clearly belongs on a different plane; it was based on designs by Velázquez, and Galileo is said to have helped with the calculations to make it balance.

Facing the Palacio Real to the south, across the shadeless Plaza de la Armería, is Madrid's cathedral, **Nuestra Señora de la Almudena** (winter daily 9am–9pm; summer daily 10am–2pm & 5–9pm; ⓜ Ópera), its Neoclassical bulk as undistinguished inside as out. The cathedral was planned centuries ago, bombed out in the Civil War, worked upon at intervals since, plagued by lack of funds and eventually opened for business in 1993 by Pope John Paul II.

South again from here, c/Bailén crosses c/Segovia on a high **viaduct** (now lined with panes of reinforced glass to prevent once-common suicide attempts), which was constructed as a royal route from the palace to the church of San Francisco el Grande, avoiding the rabble and river which flowed below. Close by is a patch of **Moorish wall** from the medieval fortress here, which the original royal palace replaced. Across the aqueduct, the **gardens** of Las Vistillas ("the views") beckon, with their summer terrazas looking out across the river and towards the distant Sierra.

El Palacio Real

The **Palacio Real** or Royal Palace (April–Sept Mon–Sat 9am–6pm, Sun & holidays 9am–2.30pm; Oct–March Mon–Sat 9.30am–5pm, Sun & holidays 9am–2pm; closed occasionally for state visits; free on Wed for EU citizens; ⓦ www.patrimonionacional.es) scores high on statistics. It claims more rooms than any other European palace; a library with one of the biggest collections of books, manuscripts, maps and musical scores in the world; and an armoury with an unrivalled collection of weapons dating back to the fifteenth century. If you are around on the first Wednesday of the month (except July & Aug) at noon–1pm, look out for the changing of the guard outside the palace, a tradition which has recently been revived.

Optional **guided tours** in various languages (€8; usually with a wait for a group to form) have been abbreviated in recent years, now taking in around 25 (rather than 90) rooms and apartments, including the Royal Armoury Museum and Royal Pharmacy. Nevertheless, they're still a pretty hard slog, rarely allowing much time to contemplate the extraordinary opulence: acres of Flemish and Spanish tapestries, endless Rococo decoration, bejewelled clocks and pompous portraits of the monarchs, as well as a permanent display of Goya's cartoons and tapestries. You're probably better off going **without a guide** (€7), as each room is clearly signed and described in English anyway, the main disadvantage being trying to fight your way past the guided groups. The palace also houses an impressive exhibition space, the *Galería de Pinturas* (same opening hours; €3.40), which houses work by Velázquez, Caravaggio and Goya amongst others and is also used for temporary exhibitions.

The palace and outhouses

The Habsburgs' original palace burned down on Christmas Day 1734. Its replacement, the current building, was based on drawings made by Bernini for the Louvre. It was constructed in the mid-eighteenth century and was the principal royal residence from then until Alfonso XIII went into exile in 1931; both Joseph Bonaparte and the Duke of Wellington also lived here briefly. The present royal family inhabits a considerably more modest residence in the western outskirts of the city, using the Palacio Real on state occasions only.

The **Salón del Trono** (Throne Room) is the highlight for most visitors, containing the thrones installed for Juan Carlos and Sofía, the current monarchs, as well as the splendid ceiling by Tiepolo, a giant fresco representing the glory of Spain – an extraordinary achievement for an artist by then in his seventies.

1

PALACIO REAL

1 Escalera Principal
2 Antecámara de Gasparini
3 Salón de Gasparini
4 Tranvía
5 Salón de Carlos III
6 Sala de Porcelana
7 Sala Amarilla
8 Salas de Exposición
9 Cámara Fuerte
10 Relicario
11 Anterrelicario

12 Antecámara de la Reina Cristina
13 Saleta Reina Cristina
14 Salón de Espejos
15 Salón de Armas
16 Tranvía
17 Antecámara Oficial
18 Salón de Grandes
19 Salón de Billar
20 Salón Chino-Japonés
21 Saleta de Estucos
22 Maderas Finas

The palace outbuildings and annexes include the recently refurbished **Armería Real** (Royal Armoury), a huge room full of guns, swords and armour, with such curiosities as the suit of armour worn by Carlos V in his equestrian portrait by Titian in the Prado. Especially fascinating are the complete sets of armour, with all the original spare parts and gadgets for making adjustments. There is also an eighteenth-century **Farmacia**, a curious mixture of alchemist's den and laboratory, whose walls are lined with jars labelled for various remedies. The **Biblioteca Real** (Royal Library) can now only be visited by prior arrangement for research purposes.

The gardens

Immediately north of the palace, the **Jardines Sabatini** provide a shady retreat and venue for summer concerts, while to the rear the larger, and far more beautiful, park of the **Campo del Moro** (April–Sept Mon–Sat 10am–8pm, Sun 9am–8pm; Oct–March Mon–Sat 10am–6pm, Sun 9am–6pm; occasionally closed for state visits; access only from the far west side off the Paseo de la Virgen del Puerto) affords shady walks and a splendid view of the western facade of the palace.

South of Plaza Mayor: La Latina, Lavapiés and El Rastro

The areas south of Plaza Mayor have traditionally been tough, working-class districts, with tenement buildings thrown up to accommodate the expansion of the population in the eighteenth and nineteenth centuries. In many places these old houses survive, huddled together in narrow streets, but the character of **La Latina** and **Lavapiés** has changed as their inhabitants, and the districts themselves, have become younger and more fashionable. The streets of Cava Baja and Cava Alta, for example, in La Latina, include some of the city's most fashionable bars and restaurants. These are attractive *barrios* to explore, particularly for bar-hopping or during the Sunday-morning flea market, **El Rastro**, which takes place along and around the Ribera de Curtidores (Ⓜ La Latina or Tirso de Molina).

Around La Latina

La Latina is a short walk south from Plaza de la Villa (see p.90) and, if you're exploring Madrid de los Austrias, it's a natural continuation, as some of the squares, streets and churches here date back to the early Habsburg period. One of the most attractive pockets is around **Plaza de la Paja**, a delightful square behind the large church of San Andrés, and once home to one of the city's medieval markets. In summer, there are a couple of terrazas here, tucked well

---

The Rastro

Madrid's flea market, **El Rastro**, is as much part of the city's weekend ritual as a Mass or a *paseo*. This gargantuan, thriving, thieving shambles of a street market sprawls south from Metro Latina to the Ronda de Toledo, especially along Ribera de Curtidores. Through it, crowds flood between 10am and 3pm every Sunday and increasingly on Fridays, Saturdays and public holidays, too. On offer are second-hand clothes, military surplus items, budgies and canaries, sunshades, razor blades, fine antiques and Taiwanese transistors, cutlery and coke spoons – in fact just about anything you might (or more likely, might not) need.

Some of the goods – broken telephone dials, plastic shampoo bottles half-full of something which may or may not be the original contents – are so far gone that you can't imagine any of them ever selling. Other items may be quite valuable, but on the whole it's the stuff of markets around the world you'll find here: pseudo-designer clothes, bags and T-shirts. Don't expect to find fabulous bargains, or the hidden Old Masters of popular myth; the serious antique trade has mostly moved off the streets and into the shops along the street, while the real junk is now found only on the fringes. Nonetheless, the atmosphere of the Rastro is always enjoyable and the bars around these streets are as good as any in the city.

One warning: keep a close eye on your bags, pockets, cameras (best left at the hotel) and jewellery. The Rastro rings up a fair percentage of Madrid's tourist thefts.

away from the traffic. The church was badly damaged by an anarchist attack in 1936 and the adjoining **Capilla del Obispo** is undergoing a long-running restoration programme. However, the main church, whose brick cupola has been restored to its former glory, and the richly decorated interior of the Baroque **Capilla de San Isidro** (Mon–Sat 8.30am–11.30pm & 6–8pm, Sun 9am–2pm) are open to visitors.

A couple of minutes' walk southwest of here is one of Madrid's grandest, richest and most elaborate churches, **San Francisco el Grande** (ⓂPuerta de Toledo/La Latina). Built towards the end of the eighteenth century as part of Carlos III's renovations of the city, it has a dome even larger than that of St Paul's in London. Inside (Tues–Sat: June–Sept 11am–12.30pm & 5–7pm; Oct–May 11am–1pm & 4–7pm; €3 with guided tour) are paintings by, among others, Goya and Zurbarán, and frescoes by Bayeu. After a painfully slow twenty-year restoration programme it is now possible to appreciate this magnificent church in something close to its original glory.

A short walk up the Carrera de San Francisco opposite the entrance to the church brings you to the lively series of plazas close to the Mercado de la Cebada. The Plaza de San Andrés is now home to one of the city's newest museums, the **Museo de San Isidro** (Sept–July Tues–Fri 9.30am–8pm, Sat & Sun 10am–2pm; Aug Tues–Sat 9.30am–2.30pm, Sat & Sun 10am–2pm; free; Ⓦwww.munimadrid.es/museosanisidro), housed in a sixteenth-century mansion owned by the counts of Paredes and supposedly once the home to the city's patron saint. The archeological collection, which consists of relics from the earliest settlements along the Manzanares river, has been transferred here to the basement, while the rest of the museum has been given over to the patron saint and his miraculous activities. The museum is still in the process of building up its collections, but there are plans afoot to extend its exhibits on the early history of Madrid.

The Ribera de Curtidores, heart of the Rastro, begins just behind another vast church, **San Isidro** (Mon–Sat 8am–12.30pm & 6–8.30pm; Sun & holidays 9am–2pm & 6–8.30pm). The patron saint's remains are entombed within, and his church acted as the city's cathedral prior to the completion of the Almudena by the Palacio Real. Relics apart, its chief attribute is size – it's as bleak as it is big. Next door is the **Instituto Real**, a school which has been in existence considerably longer than the church and counts among its former pupils such literary notables as Calderón de la Barca, Lope de Vega, Quevedo and Jacinto Benavente.

If you continue to the end of Ribera de Curtidores, whose antique shops (some, these days, extremely upmarket) stay open all week, you'll see a large arch, the **Puerta de Toledo**, at one end of the Ronda de Toledo. The only surviving relation to the Puerta de Alcalá in the Plaza de la Independencia, this was built originally as a triumphal arch to honour the conquering Napoleon. After his defeat in the Peninsular Wars, it became a symbol of the city's freedom. Just in front of the arch, the Mercado Puerta de Toledo, once the site of the city's fish market, has pretensions to be a stylish arts and crafts centre, but in reality it stands largely empty, apart from the underused tourist office that lies within.

Lavapiés and the Cine Doré

A good point to start exploring Lavapiés is the Plaza Tirso de Molina (ⓂTirso de Molina). From here, you can follow c/Mesón de Paredes, stopping for a drink at *Taberna Antonio Sánchez* at no. 13, down past rows of wholesale shops to **La Corrala**, on the corner of c/Sombrerete. This is one of many traditional *corrales* – tenement blocks – in the quarter, built with balconied apartments

△ Cafe con leche, Piazza Santa Ana

opening onto a central patio. Plays – especially farces and *zarzuelas* (a kind of operetta) – used to be performed regularly in Spanish *corrales*, and the open space here usually hosts a few performances in the summer. It has been well renovated and declared a national monument.

From Lavapiés, you can take c/Argumosa towards the Centro de Arte Reina Sofía (see p.106). Don't miss out on the opportunity to sample some of the excellent local bars on this pleasant tree-lined street while you are here. To the north of the quarter, near Metro Antón Martín, is the **Cine Doré**, the oldest cinema in Madrid, dating from 1922, with a late *modernista*/Art Nouveau facade. It has been converted to house the Filmoteca Nacional, an art-film centre (see p.138), and it has a pleasant and inexpensive café/restaurant (Tues–Sun 1.30pm– 12.30am).

East of Sol: Plaza de Santa Ana to Cibeles

The **Plaza de Santa Ana/Huertas** area forms a triangle, bordered to the east by the Paseo del Prado, to the north by c/Alcalá, and along the south by c/Atocha, with the Puerta del Sol at the western tip. The city reached this district after extending beyond the Royal Palace and the Plaza Mayor, so the buildings date predominantly from the nineteenth century. Many of them have literary associations: there are streets named after Cervantes and Lope de Vega (where one lived and the other died), and the *barrio* is host to the Atheneum club, Círculo de Bellas Artes (Fine Arts Institute), Teatro Español, and the Congreso de los Diputados (parliament). Just to the north, there is also an important museum, the **Real Academia de Bellas Artes de San Fernando**.

For most visitors, though, the major attraction is that in this district are some of the best and most beautiful bars and *tascas* in the city. They are concentrated particularly around Plaza de Santa Ana, which – following a rather seedy period – has been smartened up by the council.

Santa Ana and around

The bars around **Plaza de Santa Ana** (Ⓜ Sol/Sevilla) really are sights in themselves. On the square itself, the dark-panelled **Cervecería Alemana** was a firm favourite of Hemingway and has hardly changed since the turn of the twentieth century. It's a place to drink beer, and go easy on tapas (the *empanadillas* are good) if you don't want to run up a significant bill. Another notable place is the *Bar Torero* of the **Gran Hotel Reina Victoria**, the smart hotel flanking Plaza de Santa Ana; this is where bullfighters stay when in town, and the bar is packed with taurine memorabilia.

Viva Madrid, on the northeast corner at c/Manuel Fernández y González 7, should be another port of call, if only to admire the fabulous tilework, original zinc bar and a ceiling supported by wooden caryatids. One block east from here is **c/Echegaray**, where one of the highlights is **Los Gabrieles** at no. 17. This is a bar with museum-piece *azulejos* (tiles), endowed by sherry companies in the late nineteenth century and fabulously inventive: there are skeletons climbing over barrels, Goya-esque idylls with sherry and bulls, and a superb co-opting of Velázquez's *Los Borrachos*.

Huertas, the Cortes and the Círculo de Bellas Artes

The area around the recently pedestrianized c/Huertas itself is workaday enough – sleepy by day but buzzing by night – and again packed with bars. North of the street, and parallel, are two streets named after the greatest figures of Spain's seventeenth-century literary golden age, Cervantes and Lope de Vega. Bitter rivals in life, both are probably spinning in their graves now, since

Cervantes is interred in the Convento de las Trinitarias on the street named after Lope de Vega, while the latter's house, the **Casa de Lope de Vega** (Tues–Fri 9.30am–2pm, Sat 10am–1.30pm, closed mid-July to mid-Aug; €1.50; ⓜAntón Martín), finds itself at c/Cervantes 11. The delightful little museum provides a fascinating reconstruction of life in seventeenth-century Madrid; ring the bell and someone will take you on a short tour (usually English is spoken).

A block to the north is **El Congreso de Los Diputados** (ⓜSevilla), an unprepossessing nineteenth-century building where the congress (the lower house) meets. Sessions can be visited by appointment only, though anyone can turn up (with a passport) for a tour on Saturday mornings (tours every 30 mins, 10.30am–12.30pm; closed Aug). You're shown, amongst other things, the bullet holes left by Colonel Tejero and his Guardia Civil associates in the abortive coup attempt of 1981.

Cut across to c/Alcalá from the Plaza de las Cortes and you will emerge close to the **Círculo de Bellas Artes** at Marqués de Casa Riera 2 (ⓜSevilla), a strange-looking 1920s building crowned by a statue of Pallas Athene. This is Madrid's best arts centre, and includes a theatre, music hall, cinema, exhibition galleries (Tues–Fri 5–9pm, Sat 11am–2pm & 5–9pm, Sun 11am–2pm) and a very pleasant bar (daily 8am–2am) – all marble and leather decor, with a nude statue reclining in the middle of the floor. It attracts Madrid's arts and media crowd but is not in the least exclusive, nor expensive, and there's an adjoining terraza, too. The Círculo is theoretically a members-only club, but it issues €0.60 (€1 after 4pm) day membership on the door, for which you get access to all areas.

Calle Alcalá to Cibeles

At the Círculo, you are on the corner of Gran Vía (see p.110), and, only a couple of hundred metres to the east, c/Alcalá meets the Paseo del Prado at the **Plaza de la Cibeles**. The wedding-cake building on the far side of this square is Madrid's main post office, the aptly entitled **Palacio de Comunicaciones**. Constructed from 1904 to 1917, it is vastly more imposing than the parliament and runs the Palacio Real pretty close. It's a fabulous place, flanked by polished brass postboxes for each province and preserving a totally Byzantine system within, where scores of counters each offer just one specific service, from telegrams to string, and, until quite recently, scribes.

Awash in a sea of traffic in the centre of the square is a **fountain** and statue of the goddess Cibeles, which survived the bombardments of the Civil War by being swaddled from helmet to hoof in sandbags. It was designed, as were the two other fountains gushing magnificently along the Paseo del Prado, by Ventura Rodríguez, who is honoured in modern Madrid by having a metro station and a street named after him. The fountain is the scene of celebrations for victorious Real Madrid fans (Atlético fans bathe in the fountain of Neptune just down the road).

Madrid's three principal art museums, the Prado (see p.99), Thyssen-Bornemisza (see p.104) and Centro de Arte Reina Sofía (see p.106), all lie to the south of here, along the Paseo del Prado. To the north, on Paseo de Recoletos, are a couple of the city's most lavish **traditional cafés**, the *Café Gijón* at no. 21 and *Café del Espejo* at no. 31 (see box on p.117).

Real Academia de Bellas Artes de San Fernando

Art buffs who have some appetite left after the Prado, Thyssen-Bornemisza and Reina Sofía, will find the **Real Academia de Bellas Artes de San**

Fernando (Tues–Fri 9am–6.30pm, Mon, Sat, Sun & holidays 9am–2pm; €2.50, free Wed; ⓂSevilla) next on their list. Located two hundred metres east of Sol at c/Alcalá 13, it has traditionally been viewed as one of the most important art galleries in Spain. Admittedly, you have to plough through a fair number of dull academic canvases, but there are hidden gems. These include a group of small panels by **Goya**, in particular *The Burial of the Sardine*; portraits of the monks of the Merced order by Zurbarán and others; and a curious *Family of El Greco*, which may be by the great man or his son. Two other rooms are devoted to foreign artists, especially Rubens. Upstairs, there is a series of engravings by Picasso, and a brutally graphic series of sculptures depicting the *Massacre of the Innocents* by José Ginés. Twenty-two rooms have recently been added to the gallery, but staff shortages mean that not all of the rooms are open on any one day and there are frequent changes to the opening hours. It is also home to the national chalcography (copper or brass engraving) collection (Mon–Fri 10am–2pm, Sat 10am–1.30pm; free) which includes a number of Goya etchings.

Museo del Prado

The **Museo del Prado** (Tues–Sun 9am–7pm, holidays usually 9am–2pm but closed New Year's Day, Good Friday, May 1 & Christmas Day; €3, free on Sun; Ⓦmuseoprado.mcu.es; ⓂBanco de España/Atocha) is Madrid's premier tourist attraction, and one of the oldest and greatest collections of art in the world. Built as a natural science museum in 1775, the Prado opened to the public in 1819, and houses the finest works collected by Spanish royalty – for the most part avid, discerning, and wealthy buyers – as well as Spanish paintings gathered from other sources over the past two centuries. There are 7000 paintings in all, of which around 1500 (still a pretty daunting tally) are on permanent display. A controversial 43 million-euro plan to modernize and extend the museum (adding three nearby buildings) is due to be completed by 2005 and will enable the Prado to double the number of works currently on show. Local residents, however, are opposing the proposed plan – designed by Spain's leading architect Rafael Moneo – to construct a new glass-fronted building to house the museum's offices in the cloisters of the church of San Jerónimo el Real, and it is already running behind schedule.

The museum's highlights are its Flemish collection – including almost all of **Bosch**'s best work – and of course its incomparable display of Spanish art, in particular that of **Velázquez** (including *Las Meninas*), **Goya** (including the *Majas* and the *Black Paintings*), and **El Greco**. There's also a huge section of Italian painters (**Titian**, notably) collected by Carlos V and Felipe II, both great patrons of the Renaissance, and an excellent collection of seventeenth-century Flemish and Dutch pictures gathered by Felipe IV. The museum has also hosted an increasing number of critically acclaimed temporary displays in recent years. Even in a full day you couldn't hope to do justice to everything here, and it's perhaps best to make a couple of more focused visits. If you are tempted to take advantage of the long opening hours, however, there's a decent cafeteria and restaurant in the basement.

Combined entry ticket

If you plan to visit all three art museums on the Paseo del Prado during your stay, it's well worth buying the under-advertised **Paseo del Arte ticket** (€7.66) which is valid for a year and allows one visit to each museum at a substantial saving.

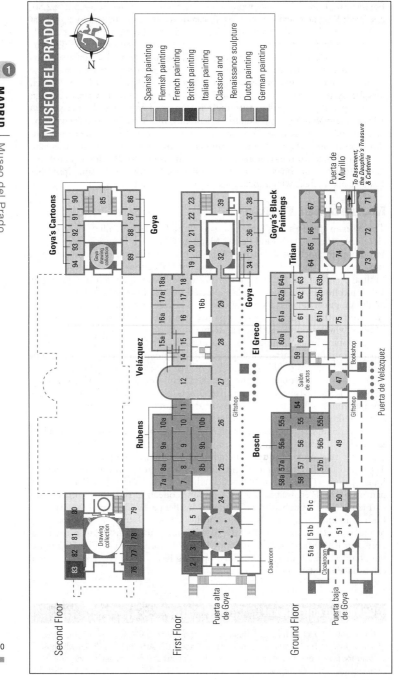

MUSEO DEL PRADO

N

Spanish painting
Flemish painting
French painting
British painting
Italian painting
Classical and
Renaissance sculpture
Dutch painting
German painting

Second Floor

80
81
82
83
79
78
77
76
Drawing collection

First Floor

Goya's Cartoons

90
91
92
93
94
85
Goya drawing collection
86
87
88
89
Goya

19 20 21 22 23
39
32
34 35 36 37 38
Goya's Black Paintings

Velázquez

15a 16a 17a 18a
14 15 16 17 18
16b
12
27 28 29
26
25
El Greco
Goya

Rubens

7a 8a 9a 10a
7 8 9 10 11
8b 9b 10b
24
Bosch

2 3 4 5 6
1
Giftshop
Cloakroom

Puerta alta de Goya

Ground Floor

Titian

60a 61a 62a 64a
60 61 62 63
61b 62b 63b
59
64 65 66 67
74
72 73
71
75
Puerta de Murillo
To Basement, the Dauphin's Treasure & Cafeteria

Salón de actos
Bookshop
47
54
55a 55
55b
56a 56
56b
57a 57
57b
58a
58
49
Giftshop
Puerta de Velázquez

51a 51b
51c
51
50
Cloakroom

Puerta baja de Goya

Organization, catalogues and entrances

After recent major work at the museum, including the installation of air conditioning and the remodelling of the roof to let in more light, most of the national schools now seem to have found a permanent home, although it is worth bearing in mind that paintings are sometimes moved around to make way for temporary shows; any changes will usually be shown on the **free maps** available on your way into the museum.

What follows is, by necessity, only a brief guide to the museum contents. A range of illustrated **guides and catalogues** (€9, 15 & 24) describing and explaining the paintings, is on sale in the museum shop, and there are useful **colour booklets** (€1) on Velázquez, Goya, El Greco, Titian and Bosch available in their respective galleries.

There are two main **entrances** to the museum: the **Puerta de Goya**, which has an upper and a lower entrance opposite the Hotel Ritz on c/Felipe IV, and the **Puerta de Murillo** on Plaza de Murillo, opposite the botanical gardens. The Puerta de Goya upper entrance takes you up to the first floor (US second floor), with the seventeenth-century Flemish and Dutch art giving way to the main Spanish collections; its ground-floor entrance is the one to take if you want to embark on a chronological tour. The Puerta de Murillo entrance at the other end of the building opposite the botanical gardens usually has shorter queues, and steers you past the impressive classical sculpture and on to the Italian Renaissance galleries. A very early start or a lunchtime visit are advisable if you want to avoid the worst of the crowds and tour groups.

Spanish painting

The Prado's collections of Spanish painting begin with the cycles of twelfth-century **Romanesque frescoes** (Room 51c), reconstructed from a pair of churches from the Mozarabic (Muslim rule) era in Soria and Segovia. **Early panel paintings** – exclusively religious fourteenth- and fifteenth-century works – include a huge *retablo* (altarpiece) by Nicolás Francés; the anonymous *Virgin of the Catholic Monarchs*; Bermejo's *Santo Domingo de Silos*; and Pedro Berruguete's *Auto-da-Fé*.

The Golden Age: Velázquez and El Greco

Collections from Spain's Golden Age – the late sixteenth and seventeenth centuries under Habsburg rule – are prefigured by a collection of paintings (rooms 60a, 61a and 62a) by **El Greco** (1540–1614), the Cretan-born artist who worked in Toledo from the 1570s. You really need to have taken in the works in Toledo to appreciate fully his extraordinary genius, but the portraits and religious works here, ranging from the Italianate *Trinity* to the visionary late *Adoration of the Shepherds*, are a good introduction.

Upstairs, in rooms 12, 14, 15, 15a and 16, you confront the greatest painter of Habsburg Spain, **Diego Velázquez** (1599–1660). Born in Portugal, Velázquez became court painter to Felipe IV, whose family is represented in many of the works: "I have found my Titian," Felipe is said to have remarked on his appointment. Velázquez's masterpiece, *Las Meninas* (room 12), is displayed alongside studies for the painting: Manet remarked of it, "After this I don't know why the rest of us paint," and the French poet Théophile Gautier asked "But where is the picture?" when he saw it, because it seemed to him a continuation of the room. *Las Hilanderas*, showing the royal tapestry factory at work, *Christ Crucified*, *Los Borrachos* (The Drunkards) and *The Surrender of Breda* (note the compositional device of the lances) are further magnificent works. In fact, almost all of the fifty works on display (around half of the artist's surviving output) warrant close attention. Don't overlook the two small panels of the *Villa Medici*, painted in Rome in 1650, in virtually Impressionist style.

In the adjacent rooms are examples of just about every significant Spanish painter of the seventeenth century, including many of the best works of **Francisco Zurbarán** (1598–1664), **Bartolomé Esteban Murillo** (1618–82), **Alonso Cano** (1601–67), **Juan de Valdes Leal** (1622–60), and **Juan Carreño** (1614–85). Note, in particular, Carreño's portrait of the last Habsburg monarch, the drastically inbred and mentally retarded Carlos II, rendered with terrible realism. There's also a fine selection of works by **José Ribera** (1591–1625), who worked mainly in Naples, and was influenced there by Caravaggio. His masterpieces are considered *The Martyrdom of St Philip* and the dark, realist portrait of *Saint Andrew*.

Goya

The final suite of Spanish rooms (rooms 32–39 and 85–94) provides an awesome and fabulously complete overview of the works of **Francisco de Goya** (1746–1828), the largest and most valuable collection of his works in the world, with some 140 paintings and 500 drawings and engravings. Goya was the greatest painter of Bourbon Spain, a chronicler of Spain in his time and an artist whom many see as the inspiration and forerunner of Impressionism and modern art. He was an enormously versatile artist: contrast the voluptuous *Maja Vestida* and *Maja Desnuda* (The Clothed and Naked Belles) with the horrors depicted in *Dos de Mayo* and *Tres de Mayo* (on-the-spot portrayals of the rebellion against Napoleon in the streets of Madrid and the subsequent reprisals). Then there are the series of pastoral cartoons – designs for tapestries – and the extraordinary *Black Paintings*, a series of disconcerting murals painted on the walls of his home by the deaf and embittered painter in his old age. His many portraits of his patron, Carlos IV, are remarkable for their lack of any attempt at flattery, while those of Queen María Luisa, whom he despised, are downright ugly.

Italian painting

The Prado's early Italian galleries (49, 56b, 60–63b and 75) are distinguished principally by **Fra Angelico**'s *Annunciation* (c. 1445) and by a trio of panels by **Botticelli** (1445–1510). The latter illustrate a deeply unpleasant story from the *Decameron* about a woman hunted by hounds; the fourth panel (in a private collection in the US) gives a happier conclusion.

With the sixteenth-century Renaissance, and especially its Venetian exponents, the collection really comes into its own. The Prado is said to have the most complete collection of Titians and painters from the Venice school in any single museum. There are major works by **Raphael** (1483–1520), including a fabulous *Portrait of a Cardinal*, and epic masterpieces from the Venetians **Tintoretto** (1518–94), including the beautifully composed *Lavatorio*, bought by Felipe IV when Charles I of England was beheaded and his art collection was auctioned off, and **Veronese** (1528–88), as well as **Caravaggio** (1573–1610). The most important works, however, are by **Titian** (1487–1576). These include portraits of the Spanish emperors *Carlos V* and *Felipe II* (Charles's suit of armour is preserved in the Palacio Real), and a famous, much-reproduced piece of erotica, *Venus, Cupid and the Organist* (two versions are displayed here), a painting originally owned by a bishop.

Flemish, Dutch and German painting

The biggest name in the **early Flemish collection** (rooms 55–58a) is **Hieronymus Bosch** (1450–1516), known in Spain as "El Bosco". The Prado has several of his greatest triptychs: the early-period *Hay Wain*, the middle-period *Garden of Earthly Delights* and the late *Adoration of the Magi* – all familiar from countless reproductions but infinitely more chilling in the original. Bosch's hallucinatory genius for the macabre is at its most extreme in these triptychs, but is reflected here in many more of his works, including three versions of *The Temptations of Saint Anthony* (though only the smallest of these is definitely an original). Don't miss, either, the amazing table top of *The Seven Deadly Sins*.

Bosch's visions find an echo in the works of **Pieter Brueghel the Elder** (1525–69), whose *Triumph of Death* must be one of the most frightening canvases ever painted. Another elusive painter, **Joachim Patinir**, is represented by four of his finest works. From an earlier generation, **Rogier van der Weyden**'s *Descent from the Cross* is outstanding; its monumental forms make a fascinating contrast with his miniature-like *Pietà*. There are also important works by Memling, Bouts, Gerard David and Massys.

The collection of over 160 works of **later Flemish and Dutch** art has been imaginatively rehoused in a new suite of twelve rooms on the first floor (rooms 7–11). Grouped by themes, such as religion, daily life, mythology, and landscape, the rooms have been tastefully decorated, while many of the paintings have been given a new lease of life by their restoration to their startling original colours. There are enough works here to make an excellent comparison between the flamboyant Counter-Reformation propaganda of Flanders and the more austere bourgeois tastes of Holland.

Rubens (1577–1640) is extensively represented with the beautifully restored *Three Graces*, *The Judgement of Paris* and by a series of eighteen mythological subjects designed for Felipe IV's hunting lodge in El Pardo (though he supervised rather than executed these). There is, too, a fine collection of works by his contemporaries, including **Van Dyck**'s dramatic *Piedad* and his magnificent portrait of himself and Sir Endymion Porter. **Jan Brueghel**'s representations of the five senses and **David Teniers**' scenes of peasant lowlife also merit a closer look. For political reasons, Spanish monarchs collected few works painted from seventeenth-century Protestant Holland; an early **Rembrandt**, *Artemesia*, in which the artist's pregnant wife served as the model, is, however, an important exception.

The **German room** (54) on the ground floor is dominated by **Dürer** (1471–1528) and **Lucas Cranach the Elder** (1472–1553). Dürer's magnificent *Adam and Eve* was saved from destruction at the hands of the prudish Carlos III only by the intervention of his court painter, Mengs. The most interesting of Cranach's works is a pair of paintings depicting Carlos V hunting with Ferdinand I of Austria.

French and British painting

Most of the **French** work held by the Prado is from the seventeenth and eighteenth centuries (rooms 2–4 on the first floor and rooms 76–78 and 80 on the second). Among the outstanding painters represented is **Nicolas Poussin** (1594–1665), with his Baroque work shown to best effect in *Triumph of David*, *Landscape with St Jerome* and *Mount Parnassus*. The romantic landscapes and sunsets of **Claude Lorraine** (1600–82) are well represented, and look out for **Hyacinthe Rigaud**'s (1659–1743) portrayal of the imperious *Louis XIV*.

British painting is thin on the ground – a product of the hostile relations between the Spanish and English from the sixteenth to nineteenth centuries. There is, however, a small sample of eighteenth-century portraiture from Joshua Reynolds (1723–92) and Thomas Gainsborough (1727–88) in Room 83.

The Tesoro del Dauphin and the Casón del Buen Retiro

The museum's basement houses the **Tesoro del Dauphin** (Treasure of the Dauphin), a display of part of the collection of jewels that belonged to the Grand Dauphin Louis, son of Louis XIV and father of Felipe V, Spain's first Bourbon king. The collection includes goblets, cups, trays, glasses and other pieces richly decorated with rubies, emeralds, diamonds, lapis lazuli and other precious stones.

Just east of the Prado is the **Casón del Buen Retiro** (undergoing restoration until at least 2004) which used to be a dance hall for the palace of Felipe IV, but is now devoted to nineteenth-century Spanish art. It is included in the entrance ticket to the main museum but, considering the riches which have gone before, is not of compelling interest.

Museo Thyssen-Bornemisza

The **Museo Thyssen-Bornemisza** (Tues–Sun 10am–7pm; the museum has experimented with opening until 10pm in the evenings during July & Aug, but check beforehand; €4.80 or see p.99 for combined ticket; Ⓦ www.museothyssen.org; Ⓜ Banco de España) occupies the old Palacio de Villahermosa, diagonally opposite the Prado, at the end of the Carrera de San Jerónimo. This prestigious site played a large part in Spain's acquisition – for a knock-down $350 million in June 1993 – of what many argue was the world's greatest private art trove after that of the British royals: 700-odd paintings accumulated by father-and-son German-Hungarian industrial magnates. The son, Baron Hans Heinrich Thyssen, died in April 2002 aged 81. Another trump card was the late baron's fifth wife, "Tita" Cervera, a former Miss Spain, who steered the works to Spain against the efforts of Britain's Prince Charles, the Swiss and German governments, the Getty foundation, and other suitors. The museum is in the throes of an extension plan – due to be completed in mid-2004 – which will take in two neighbouring buildings and accommodate much of Tita's own personal collection as well as provide the site for a new temporary exhibition space and an enlarged café.

A terribly kitsch portrait of Tita with a lapdog hangs in the great hall of the museum, alongside those of her husband and King Juan Carlos and Queen Sofía. Pass beyond, however, and you are into seriously premier-league art: **medieval to eighteenth-century** on the top floor, **seventeenth-century Dutch** and **Rococo and Neoclassicism to Fauves and Expressionists** on the first floor, and **Surrealists**, **Pop Art** and the **avant-garde** on ground level. Highlights are legion in a collection that displays an almost stamp-collecting mentality in its examples of nearly every major artist and movement: how the Thyssens got hold of classic works by everyone from Duccio and Holbein, through El Greco and Caravaggio, to Schiele and Rothko, takes your breath away.

The museum had no expense spared on its design – again in the hands of the ubiquitous Rafael Moneo, responsible for the remodelling of Atocha and the current extension at the Prado – with stucco walls (Tita insisted on salmon pink) and marble floors. There's a handy cafeteria and restaurant in the basement which allows re-entry, so long as you get your hand stamped at the exit desk. The basement is also home to a temporary exhibition space, which has staged a number of interesting and highly successful shows (separate entry fee of €3.60 or €6 for a combined ticket with the main museum). There's also a shop, where you can buy the first instalments of the fifteen-volume catalogue of the baron's collection as well as the more modest, but informative, illustrated **guide** to the museum (€10.90). Audio guides (€3) are available at the desk in the main hall. The Monestir de Pedralbes in Barcelona (see p.761) houses around eighty works of sacred art that are also part of the collection.

European old masters: the second floor

Take a lift to the second floor and you will find yourself at the chronological start of the museum's collections: European painting (and some sculpture) from the fourteenth to the eighteenth century. The core of these collections was accumulated in the 1920s and 1930s by the late baron's father, Heinrich, who was a friend of the art critics Bernard Berenson and Max Friedländer.

He was clearly well advised. The early paintings include incredibly good (and rare) devotional panels by the Sienese painter **Duccio di Buoninsegna**, and the Flemish artists **Jan van Eyck** and **Rogier van der Weyden**. You then move into a fabulous array of Renaissance portraits (Room 5), which include three of the very greatest of the period: **Ghirlandaio**'s *Portrait of Giovanna Tornabuoni*, **Hans Holbein**'s *Portrait of Henry VIII* (the only one of many variants in existence which is definitely genuine), and **Raphael**'s *Portrait of a Young Man*. *A Spanish Infanta* by **Juan de Flandes** may represent the first of Henry VIII's wives, Catherine of Aragón, while the *Young Knight* by **Carpaccio** is one of the earliest known full-length portraits. Beyond these is a collection of **Dürers** and **Cranachs** to rival that in the Prado, and as you progress through this extraordinary panoply, display cases along the corridor contain scarcely less spectacular works of sculpture, ceramics and gold- and silverwork.

Next in line, in Room 11, are **Titian** and **Tintoretto**, and three paintings by **El Greco**, one early, two late, which make an interesting comparison with each other and with those in the Prado. **Caravaggio**'s monumental *St Catherine of Alexandria* is the centrepiece of an important display of works by followers of this innovator of chiaroscuro. And finally, as you reach the eighteenth century, there is a room containing three flawless **Canaletto** views of Venice.

Americans, Impressionists and Expressionists: the first floor

Hans Heinrich Thyssen began collecting, according to his own account, to fill the gaps in his late father's collection, after it was split among his siblings. He, too, started with old masters – his father thought nineteenth- and twentieth-century art was worthless – but in the 1960s started on German Expressionists, closely followed by Cubists, Futurists, Vorticists and De Stijl, and also American art of the nineteenth century. The first floor, then, is largely down to him.

After a comprehensive round of seventeenth-century Dutch painting of various genres, Rococo and Neoclassicism, you reach the **American painting** in rooms 29 and 30. The collection, one of the best outside the US, concentrates on landscapes and includes James Goodwyn Clonney's wonderful *Fishing Party on Long Island Sound*, and works by James Whistler, Winslow Homer and John Singer Sargent. It is followed by a group of European **Romantics** and **Realists**, including Constable's *The Lock*, bought not so long ago for £10.8 million, forming one of a group of British representatives at the museum, along with a Henry Moore (Room 45) and a Sisley (Room 32).

Impressionism and **post-Impressionism** are another strong point of the collection – with works by Manet, Monet and Renoir from the former and Gauguin, Degas, Lautrec and Cézanne from the latter (Room 33) – and it is especially strong in the choice of paintings by Vincent van Gogh, which include one of his last and most gorgeous works, *Les Vessenots*. **Expressionist** representatives, meanwhile, include an unusually pastoral Edvard Munch, *Evening* (Room 35), Egon Schiele's Mondrian-like *Houses on the River*, and some stunning work by Ernst Ludwig Kirchner, Wassily Kandinsky and Max Beckmann.

Avant-gardes: the ground floor

Works on the ground floor run from the beginning of the twentieth century through to around 1970. The good baron didn't, apparently, like contemporary art: "If they can throw colours, I can be free to duck," he explained, following the gallery's opening.

The most interesting work in his "experimental avant-garde" sections is from the **Cubists**. There is an inspired, side-by-side hanging of parallel studies by Picasso (*Man with a Clarinet*), Braque and Mondrian (Room 41). Later choices – a scattering of Joan Miró, Jackson Pollock, Magritte and Dalí, Rauschenberg and Lichtenstein – do less justice to their artists and movements, though there is a great work by Edward Hopper, *Hotel Room*, and a fascinating **Lucian Freud**, *Portrait of Baron Thyssen*, posed in front of the Watteau *Pierrot* hanging upstairs.

Centro de Arte Reina Sofía

It is fortunate that the **Centro de Arte Reina Sofía** (Mon & Wed–Sat 10am–9pm, Sun 10am–2.30pm; €3, free on Sat after 2.30pm & Sun, or see p.99 for information on combined ticket; closed Jan 1 & Dec 25; ⓦmuseo reinasofia.mcu.es; ⓂAtocha), facing Atocha station at the end of Paseo del Prado, keeps slightly different opening hours and days to its neighbours. For this leading exhibition space and permanent gallery of modern Spanish art – its centrepiece is Picasso's greatest picture, *Guernica* – is another essential stop on the Madrid art circuit, and one that really mustn't be seen after a Prado-Thyssen overdose.

The museum, a vast former hospital, is a kind of Madrid response to the Pompidou centre in Paris. Transparent lifts shuttle visitors up the outside of the building, whose levels feature a cinema, excellent art book and design shops, a print, music and photographic library, a restaurant, bar and café in the basement and a peaceful inner courtyard garden, as well as the exhibition halls and the permanent collection of twentieth-century art (second and fourth floors). Like the other two great art museums, it too is in the midst of a major extension programme – here the French architect Jean Nouvel is supervising a scheme which will add three state-of-the-art buildings behind the main block which will house temporary exhibitions, an auditorium and a library. Temporary exhibitions on Salvador Dalí and Roy Lichtenstein are planned to coincide with its inauguration in mid-2004. In the meantime, the first and third floors of the main building host the museum's impressive array of temporary exhibitions.

The permanent collection

It is for **Picasso's Guernica** that most visitors come to the Reina Sofía, and rightly so. Superbly displayed, this icon of twentieth-century Spanish art and politics carries a shock that defies all familiarity. Picasso painted it in response to the bombing of the Basque town of Gernika by the German Luftwaffe, acting in concert with Franco, in the Spanish Civil War. In the preliminary studies, displayed around the room, you can see how he developed its symbols – the dying horse, the woman mourning her dead, the bull, the sun, the flower, the light bulb – and then return to the painting to marvel at how he made it all work.

The work was first exhibited in Paris in 1937, as part of a Spanish Republican Pavilion in the Expo there, and was then loaned to the Museum of Modern Art in New York, until, as Picasso put it, Spain had rid itself of fascist rule. The artist never lived to see that time, but in 1981, following the restoration of democracy, the painting was, amid much controversy, moved to Madrid to hang (as Picasso had stipulated) in the Prado. Its transfer to the Reina Sofía in 1992 again prompted much soul-searching and protest, though for anyone who saw it in the old Prado annexe, it looks truly liberated in its present setting.

Guernica hangs midway around the permanent collection on the second floor. It is preceded by an intriguing introductory room entitled *The turn of the twentieth century* which examines the ground-breaking Basque and Catalan schools. Strong sections on **Cubism** and the **Paris School** follow, in the first of which Picasso is again well represented, alongside an intriguing straight Cubist work by Salvador Dalí (*Cadaqués Countryside*). There are also good collections of other avant-garde Spaniards of the 1920s and 1930s, including Juan Gris.

Dalí and **Miró** make heavyweight contributions to the post-*Guernica* halls, while an impressive collection of Spanish sculpture is to be found in the final rooms.

The fourth floor covers Spain's postwar years up to the present day and includes Spanish and international examples of **abstract** and **avant-garde** movements. Outstanding pieces from **Francis Bacon** (*Reclining Figure*), **Henry Moore** and **Graham Sutherland** provide a British context, while challenging work from **Antoni Tapiès**, **Antonio Saura** and **Eduardo Chillida** provide the Spanish perspective.

Parque del Retiro and around

When you get tired of sightseeing, Madrid's many parks are great places to escape for a few hours. The most central and most popular of them is **El Retiro**, a delightful mix of formal gardens and wider open spaces. Nearby, in addition to the Prado, Thyssen-Bornemisza and Reina Sofía galleries, are a number of the city's **smaller museums**, plus the startlingly peaceful **Jardines Botánicos**.

Parque del Retiro

Originally the grounds of a royal retreat (*retiro*) and designed in the French style, the **Parque del Retiro** (Ⓜ Retiro) has been public property for more than a hundred years. In its 330 acres you can jog, row in the lake (you can rent boats by the Monumento a Alfonso XII), picnic (though officially not on the grass), have your fortune told, and – above all – promenade. The busiest day is Sunday, when half of Madrid, spouses, in-laws and kids, turn out for the *paseo*. Dressed for show, the families stroll around among the various activities, nodding at neighbours and building up an appetite for a long Sunday lunch.

Strolling aside, there's almost always something going on in the park, including a good programme of **concerts** and **ferias** organized by the city council. Concerts tend to be held in the Quiosco de Música in the north of the park. The most popular of the fairs is the *Feria del Libro* (Book Fair), held in early June, when every publisher and half the country's bookshops set up stalls and offer a 25-percent discount on their wares. At weekends there are **puppet shows** by the Puerta de Alcalá entrance, and on Sundays you can often watch groups of South American musicians performing by the lake.

Travelling art exhibitions are frequently housed in the beautiful **Palacio de Velázquez** (May–Sept Mon & Wed–Sat 11am–8pm, Sun 11am–4pm; Oct–April Mon & Wed–Sat 10am–6pm, Sun 10am–4pm; free) and the nearby **Palacio de Cristal** (during exhibitions same hours; ☎915 746 614 for

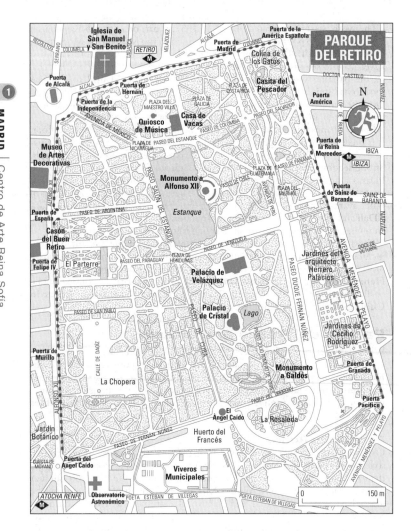

information) and **Casa de Vacas** (daily 10.30am–2.30pm & 4–8pm, closed Aug; free). Look out, too, for **El Ángel Caído** (Fallen Angel), the world's only public statue to Lucifer, in the south of the park. A number of **stalls and cafés** along the Paseo Salón del Estanque sell drinks, *bocadillos* and *pipas* (sunflower seeds), and there are terrazas, too, for *horchata* and *granizados*. The park has a safe reputation, at least by day; in the late evening it's best not to wander alone, and there are plans to close the park completely at night because of an increase in petty vandalism. Note also that the area east of La Chopera is known as a cruising ground for gay prostitutes.

Puerta de Alcalá to San Jerónimo: some minor museums

Leaving the park at the northwest corner takes you to the Plaza de la Independencia, in the centre of which is one of the two remaining gates from the old city walls. Built in the late eighteenth century, the **Puerta de Alcalá** was the biggest in Europe at that time and, like the bear and bush, has become one of the city's monumental emblems.

South from here, you pass the **Museo de Artes Decorativas** (Tues–Fri 9.30am–3pm, Sat & Sun 10am–2pm; €2.40, free on Sun; ⓜBanco de España/Retiro), which has its entrance at c/Montalbán 12. The furniture and decorations here are not very thrilling but there are some superb *azulejos* and other decorative ceramics.

A couple of blocks west, in a corner of the Naval Ministry at c/Montalbán 2, is a **Museo Naval** (Tues–Sun 10.30am–1.30pm, closed mid-July to end of Aug; free; ⓜBanco de España), strong, as you might expect, on models, charts and navigational aids from or relating to the Spanish voyages of discovery. The army has its museum, the **Museo del Ejército**, just to the south of here at c/Méndez Núñez 1 (Tues–Sun 10am–2pm; €0.60, free on Sat; ⓜRetiro). It is a traditional display, packed with arms, armour, models and memorabilia of various battles, from earliest times to the Civil War – in which Franco, here, remains the good guy. The museum is being moved to the Alcázar at Toledo (see p.160) as the building (once part of Felipe IV's Palacio de Buen Retiro) features as part of the Prado extension plans, so the displays will be gradually transferred to the new site over the next few years.

South again, past the Prado's Casón del Buen Retiro annexe (also part of the original Retiro palace), is **San Jerónimo el Real** (Mon–Fri 8am–1.30pm & 6–8pm, Sat & Sun 9am–1.30pm & 6.30–8pm, Oct–July opens one hour earlier in the afternoon), Madrid's society church, where in 1975 Juan Carlos (like his predecessors) was crowned. Opposite is the **Real Academía Española de la Lengua** (Royal Language Academy), whose job it is to make sure that the Spanish language is not corrupted by foreign or otherwise unsuitable words; the results are entrusted to their official dictionary – a work that bears virtually no relation to the Spanish you'll hear spoken on the streets.

The botanical gardens and Atocha

Immediately south of the Prado are the delightful, shaded **Jardines Botánicos** (daily 10am–dusk; €1.50; ⓜAtocha). Opened in 1781 by Carlos III (known as *El Alcalde* – "the mayor" – for his urban improvement programmes), they once contained over 30,000 plants. The numbers are down these days, though the gardens were well renovated in the 1980s, after years of neglect, and the worldwide collection of flora is fascinating for any amateur botanist; don't miss the hothouse with its tropical collection and amazing cacti.

On the other side of the botanical gardens is the sloping Cuesta de Moyano, lined with **bookstalls**; though it's at its busiest on Sundays, some of the stalls are open every day. Across the way, the **Estación de Atocha** is worth a look even if you're not travelling out of Madrid. It's actually two stations, old and new: the former, a glorious 1880s glasshouse, was revamped in the early 1990s with a spectacular tropical garden centrepiece. It's a wonderful sight from the walkways above, and train buffs and architects will want to take a look at the high-speed AVE trains (Sevilla in two and a half hours) and the station beyond.

Also in this area, at c/Alfonso XII, is the **Museo Nacional de Antropología/Etnología** (Tues–Sat 10am–7.30pm, Sun 10am–2pm; €2.40, free Sat after 2.30pm & Sun; ⓜAtocha), designed to give an overview of different cultures of the world, in particular those intertwined with Spanish history. The most unusual exhibits are to be found in a side room on the ground floor – a macabre collection of deformed skulls, a Guanche (the original inhabitants of the Canary Islands) mummy and the skeleton of a circus giant (2.35m tall). A little further to the east, the **Real Fábrica de Tapices** at c/Fuenterrabia 2 (Mon–Fri 10am–2pm, closed Aug; €2.50; ⓦwww.real fatapices.com; ⓜAtoche Renfe/Menéndez Pelayo) still turns out handmade tapestries, many of them based on the Goya cartoons in the Prado. They are fabulously expensive, but the entrance fee is a bargain if you ask for a tour of the fascinating manufacturing process.

The Gran Vía, Chueca and Malasaña

The **Gran Vía**, Madrid's great thoroughfare, runs from Plaza de Cibeles to Plaza de España, effectively dividing the old city to the south from the newer parts northwards. Permanently jammed with traffic and crowded with shoppers and sightseers, it's the commercial heart of the city, and – if you spare the time to look up – quite a monument in its own right, with its early twentieth-century, palace-like banks and offices, and the huge hand-painted posters of the cinemas. Look out, too, for the towering **Telefónica** building, which was the chief observation post for the Republican artillery during the Civil War, when the Nationalist front line stretched across the Casa de Campo to the west.

North of the Telefónica, c/Fuencarral heads north to the Glorieta de Bilbao. To either side of this street are two of Madrid's most characterful *barrios*: **Chueca**, to the east, and **Malasaña**, to the west. Their chief appeal lies in an amazing concentration of bars, restaurants and, especially, nightlife. However, there are a few reasons – cafés included – to wander around here by day.

Chueca

Plaza de Chueca (ⓜChueca) once teetered on the verge of infamy, owing to its popularity with drug dealers and prostitutes. However, most of the addicts have been moved on and there is now a strong neighbourhood feel, with kids and grannies giving a semblance of innocence by day, and a lively gay scene springing into action at night. It is also fronted by one of the best old-style *vermut* bars in the city, *Bodega Ángel Sierra*, on c/Gravina at the northwest corner. The whole area has become somewhat gentrified in recent years with the rise of a host of stylish bars, cafés and restaurants, many of which have been established by the local gay community.

From Plaza de Chueca east to **Paseo Recoletos** (the beginning of the long Paseo de la Castellana) are some of the city's most enticing streets. Offbeat restaurants, small private art galleries, and odd corner shops are to be found here in abundance, and the **c/Almirante** has some of the city's most fashionable clothes shops, too. On the parallel c/Prim, **ONCE**, the national association for the blind, has its headquarters. ONCE is financed by a lottery, for which the blind work as ticket sellers, and many come here to collect their allocation of tickets. The lottery has become such a major money-spinner that the organization is now one of the wealthiest businesses in Spain.

To the south, the Ministry of Culture fronts the **Plaza del Rey**, which is also worth a look for the other odd buildings surrounding it, especially the **Casa de las Siete Chimeneas** (House of Seven Chimneys), which is supposedly haunted by a mistress of Felipe II who disappeared in mysterious circumstances.

To the north, on the edge of the Santa Bárbara *barrio*, on c/Fernando VI, is the **Sociedad de Autores** (Society of Authors), housed in the only significant *modernista* building in Madrid, designed by José Grasés Riera, part of the Gaudí school. Nearby, the **Museo Romántico**, at c/San Mateo 13 (closed for refurbishment until mid-2004; Tues–Sat 9am–2.45pm, Sun 10am–1.15pm, closed Aug; €2.40, free on Sun; ⓜTribunal), has its admirers for its late-Romantic-era furnishings, though casual visitors are unlikely to be impressed. The **Museo Municipal** at c/Fuencarral 78 (Tues–Fri 9.30am–8pm, mid-July to mid-Sept 9.30am–2.30pm, Sat & Sun 10am–2pm; free; ⓜTribunal) is more interesting for its models and maps of old Madrid, which show the incredible expansion of the city in the last century. It, too, is undergoing refurbishment (until 2005), but there is an abbreviated exhibition in the chapel of this former city almshouse. The building itself has a superb Churrigueresque facade by Pedro de Ribera.

Malasaña

The heart, in all senses, of Malasaña is the **Plaza Dos de Mayo**, named after the insurrection against Napoleonic forces on May 2, 1808; the rebellion and its aftermath are depicted in a series of Goyas at the Prado (see p.102). The surrounding district bears the name of one of the martyrs of the uprising, fifteen-year-old Manuela Malasaña, who is also commemorated in a street (as are several other heroes of the time). On the night of May 1 all of Madrid shuts down to honour its heroes, and the plaza is the scene of festivities lasting well into the night.

More recently, the quarter was the focus of the *movida madrileña*, the "happening scene" of the late 1970s and early 1980s. As the country relaxed after the death of Franco and the city developed into a thoroughly modern capital under the leadership of the late mayor, Galván, Malasaña became the mecca of the young. Bars appeared behind every doorway, drugs were sold openly in the streets, and there was an extraordinary atmosphere of new-found freedom. Times have changed – and *chocolate* (dope) sellers are less tolerated by residents and police alike. A good deal of renovation has been going on in recent years, but the *barrio* retains a somewhat alternative – nowadays rather grungy – feel, with its bar custom spilling onto the streets, and an ever-lively scene in the Plaza Dos de Mayo terrazas.

There are no regular sights in this quarter but the streets have an interest of their own and some fine traditional bars – *Casa Camacho* at c/San Andrés 2 is a great place for *vermut*, and strolling along c/Manuela Malasaña you can take your pick from some of the trendiest cafés in town. There are also some wonderful old shop signs and architectural details, best of all the **old pharmacy** on the corner of c/San Andrés and c/San Vicente Ferrer, with its irresistible 1920s *azulejo* scenes depicting cures for diarrhoea, headaches and suchlike.

Plaza de España, Parque del Oeste and Casa de Campo

The **Plaza de España** (ⓜPlaza de España), at the west end of Gran Vía, was home, until the flurry of corporate building in the north of Madrid, to two of the city's tallest buildings – the **Torre de Madrid** and the **Edificio de España**. These rather stylish 1950s buildings look over an elaborate monument to Cervantes in the middle of the square, which in turn overlooks the bewildered-looking bronze figures of Don Quixote and Sancho Panza.

The plaza itself is a little on the seedy side, especially at night. However, to its north, **c/Martín de los Heros** is a lively place, day and night, with a couple of the city's best cinemas, and behind them the **Centro Princesa**, with shops, clubs, bars and a 24-hour branch of the ubiquitous VIPS – just the place to have your film developed at 4am, or a bite to eat before heading on to a small-hours club. Up the steps opposite the Centro Princesa is c/Conde Duque, dominated by the massive former barracks of the royal guard, constructed in the early eighteenth century by Pedro de Ribera. The barracks have been turned into a dynamic cultural centre, **El Centro Cultural de Conde Duque** (Tues–Sat 10am–2pm & 5.30–9pm, Sun & holidays 10.30am–2.30pm; free), which is home to the city's collection of contemporary art; it also hosts a variety of temporary exhibitions, and stages concerts, plays and dance as part of the *Veranos de la Villa* season. Just to the east of this, the **Plaza de las Comendadoras** – named after the convent that occupies one side of the square – is a tranquil space bordered by a variety of interesting craft shops, bars and cafés.

A block to the west is the **Museo Cerralbo**, c/Ventura Rodríguez 17 (Tues–Sat 9.30am–2.30pm, July closes 2pm, Sun 10am–2pm; closed Aug; €2.40, free on Wed & Sun; Ⓦwww.mcu.es/bbaa/index.html; ⓂVentura Rodríguez), an elegant mansion endowed with its collections by the Marqués de Cerralbo. The rooms, stuffed with paintings, furniture, armour and artefacts, provide a fascinating insight into the lifestyle of the nineteenth-century aristocracy, though there is little of individual note.

Beyond lies the leafy suburb of Moncloa and two of the most pleasant green spaces in the city, the tranquil **Parque del Oeste** and the semi-wild **Casa de Campo**.

Parque del Oeste – and Goya's Ermita frescoes

The **Parque del Oeste** stretches northwest from the Plaza de España, following the railway tracks of Príncipe Pío up to the suburbs of Moncloa and Ciudad Universitaria (see p.113). On its south side, five minutes' walk from the square, is the **Templo de Debod** (April–Sept Tues–Fri 10am–2pm & 6–8pm, Sat & Sun 10am–2pm; Oct–March Tues–Fri 9.45am–1.45pm & 4.15–6.15pm, Sat & Sun 10am–2pm; free; ⓂPlaza de España), a fourth-century BC Egyptian temple given to Spain in recognition of the work done by Spanish engineers on the Aswan High Dam (which inundated its original site). Reconstructed here stone by stone, it seems comically incongruous, and even more so with a new multimedia exhibition on the culture of Ancient Egypt housed inside. In summer, there are numerous terrazas in the park, while, year-round, a **teleférico** (April–Sept daily 11am–2.30pm & 4.30pm–dusk; Oct–March Sat, Sun & holidays noon–2.30pm & 4.30pm–dusk; €2.80 single, €4 return; ⓂArgüelles/Ventura Rodríguez) shuttles its passengers high over the river from Paseo del Pintor Rosales to the middle of the Casa de Campo (see p.113), where there's a bar/restaurant with pleasant views back towards the city. Just below the starting point of the teleférico is the beautiful Rosaleda, a vast **rose garden** at its best in May and June.

Rail lines from commuter towns to the north of Madrid terminate at the **Príncipe Pío** (aka Estación del Norte), a quietly spectacular construction of white enamel, steel and glass which is also set to house a shopping and leisure complex. About 300m from the station along the Paseo de la Florida is the *Casa Mingo* (see "Restaurants" on p.127), an institution for roast chicken washed down by cider – ideal for take-outs to the Casa de Campo. Almost alongside it, at Glorieta de la Florida 5, the **Ermita de San Antonio de la Florida** (Tues–Fri 10am–2pm & 4–8pm, July 13–23 closed afternoons; Sat & Sun 10am–2pm; free; ⓂPríncipe Pío). If you can, go on Saturdays, when there are guided tours in English three times a day. This little church on a Greek cross plan was built by an Italian, Felipe Fontana, between 1792 and 1798, and decorated by **Goya**, whose frescoes are the only reason to visit. In the dome is a depiction of a miracle performed by St Anthony of Padua. Around it, heavenly bodies of angels and cherubs hold back curtains to reveal the main scene: the saint resurrecting a dead man to give evidence in favour of a prisoner falsely accused of murder (the saint's father). Beyond this central group, Goya created a gallery of highly realist characters – their models were court and society figures – while for a lesser fresco of the angels adoring the Trinity in the apse, he took prostitutes as his models. The *ermita* also houses the artist's mausoleum.

Moncloa

The wealthy suburb of **Moncloa** contains the Spanish prime ministerial home and merits a visit even if you are not using the bus terminal for El Pardo and El Escorial (see p.167). The metro will bring you out next to the mammoth building housing the Air Ministry and the giant Arco de la Victoria, built by Franco in 1956 to commemorate the Nationalist victory in the Civil War. Beyond this lies the leafy expanses of the Parque del Oeste and the campuses of the **Ciudad Universitaria**. During term time, the end of each day sees the area become one big student party, with huddles of picnickers and singing groups under the trees. Take the Plaza de Moncloa metro exit and the path on your right through the trees will lead you to the **Mirador del Faro** (Tues–Sun: June–Aug 11am–1.45pm & 5.30–8.45pm; Sept–May 10.30am–2pm & 5.30–8pm; €1.25), a futuristic 92-metre-high tower with stunning views over the city and to the mountains beyond. Just past this, with its main entrance on Avda. Reyes Católicos 6, the **Museo de América** (Tues–Sat 9.30am–3pm, Sun 10am–2.30pm; €3, free on Sat after 2pm and Sun) contains a fine collection of artefacts, ceramics and silverware from Spain's former colonies in Latin America. The highlight is the fabulous Quimbayas treasure – a breathtaking collection of gold objects and figures from the Quimbaya culture of Colombia.

Casa de Campo

If you want to jog, play tennis, swim, picnic, go to the fairground or see pandas, then the **Casa de Campo** is the place to head. This enormous expanse of heath and scrub is in parts surprisingly wild for a place so easily accessible from the city; other sections have been tamed for more conventional pastimes. Far larger and more natural than the city parks, the Casa de Campo can be reached by metro (Ⓜ Batán/Lago), various buses (#33 from Príncipe Pío is the easiest), or the cable car mentioned above. The walk from the Príncipe Pío station via the Puente del Rey isn't too strenuous, either.

Picnic tables and café-bars are dotted throughout the park and there's a **jogging track** with exercise posts, a municipal open-air **swimming pool** (daily June–Sept 10.30am–8pm; €3.40) close to Metro Lago, tennis courts, and rowing boats to hire on the **lake** (again near Metro Lago).

Sightseeing attractions include a **Zoo** and the recently modernized amusement park, the **Parque de Atracciones** (see p.139). Although some of the **main access roads** through the park are frequented by prostitutes, the city council are taking measures to clamp down on the trade and there are few problems during daylight hours.

Salamanca and the Paseo de la Castellana

Salamanca, the area north of the Parque del Retiro, is a smart address for apartments and, even more so, for shops. The *barrio* is the haunt of *pijos* – universally denigrated rich kids – and the grid of streets between c/Goya and c/José Ortega y Gasset contains most of the city's designer emporiums. The buildings are largely modern and undistinguished, though there is a scattering of museums and galleries that might tempt you up here, in particular the Sorolla and the Lázaro Galdiano, the pick of Madrid's smaller museums.

Plaza de Colón

Taking the area from south to north, the first point of interest is **Plaza de Colón** (ⓜColón), endowed at street level with a statue of Columbus (Cristóbal Colón), and some huge stone blocks arranged as a megalithic monument to the discovery of the Americas. Below the plaza and underneath the cascading waterfall facing the Castellana is the 1970s **Centro Cultural Villa de Madrid**, which is still a good place for film and theatre and occasional exhibitions (Tues–Sat 10am–9pm Sat & Sun 10am–2pm).

Off the square, too, with its entrance at c/Serrano 13, is the **Museo Arqueológico Nacional** (Tues–Sat 9.30am–8.30pm, closes 6.30pm in July & Aug; Sun 9.30am–2.30pm; €3, free Sat 2.30–8.30pm & Sun; ⓦwww.man.es; ⓜColón/Serrano). As the national collection, this has some impressive pieces, among them the celebrated Celto-Iberian busts known as *La Dama de Elche* and *La Dama de Baza*, and a wonderfully rich hoard of Visigothic treasures found at Toledo. The exhibition, however, is very old-fashioned and rooms are often closed for somnolent rearrangement, sometimes at very short notice. In the gardens, downstairs to the left of the main entrance, is a reconstruction of the Altamira Caves, with their prehistoric wall paintings.

North of Colón

North of Colón is the **Museo de Escultura al Aire Libre** (ⓜRubén Darío; free), an innovative use of the space underneath the Juan Bravo flyover, with its haphazard collection of sculptures, including the six-tonne suspended block titled *The Meeting* by the late Eduardo Chillada.

The **Museo Lázaro Galdiano** (Tues–Sun 10am–2pm, July & Sept guided tours in the evenings 7–11pm, closed Aug; €3, free Sat; ⓦwww.flg.es; ⓜGregorio Marañon/Rubén Darío; closed until early 2004 for extension and refurbishment) is a little further north at c/Serrano 122. This former private collection was given to the state by José Galdiano in 1948 and spreads over the four floors and 37 rooms of his former home. It is a vast jumble of art works, with some very dodgy attributions, but includes some really exquisite and valuable pieces. Among painters represented are El Greco, Bosch, Gerard David, Dürer and Rembrandt, as well as a host of Spanish artists, including Berruguete, Murillo, Zurbarán, Velázquez and Goya. Other exhibits include a collection of clocks and watches, many of them once owned by Carlos V.

Not far to the west of here, across the Paseo de la Castellana, is another little jewel of a gallery, the **Museo Sorolla**, c/General Martínez Campos 37 (Tues–Sat 10am–3pm, July & Aug closes 2.30pm, Sun 10am–2pm; €3, free Sun; ⓦwww.mcu.es/nmuseos/sorolla; ⓜGregorio Marañón/Iglesia). Here there is a large collection of work by the painter Joaquín Sorolla (1863–1923), tastefully displayed in his old home and studio; the best paintings are striking, impressionistic plays on light and texture. The house itself, with its cool and

Los Galacticos

With the signing of England captain David Beckham in 2003, **Real Madrid** further cemented their position as the most glamorous team in club football. The former Manchester United midfielder joins an all-star cast – known by the Spanish sports press as "Los Galictos" (the "Galactic team") – that includes Ronaldo, Zinedine Zidane, Luis Figo, Roberto Carlos and Raul to complete what must rank as one of the most exciting line-ups in the history of the game. The nine-times winners of the **European Cup** and 29-times Spanish champions play in the imposing Bernabéu stadium, venue of the 1982 World Cup final and a ground that ranks as one of the world's great sporting arenas. Since the club's recent spate of superstar recruits, tickets to games have become increasingly difficult to get hold of, but Real do run a telephone booking service and there are several agencies that specialize in tickets (see below). If you don't get lucky you can still catch a glimpse of the hallowed turf by visiting the permanent **trophy exhibition** (Tues–Sun 10.30am–7.15pm; closes two hours before kickoff on match days; entry at gate 3 of the stadium; €4; Ⓜ Santiago Bernabéu), complete with endless cabinets of gleaming silverware and video footage of the team's greatest triumphs. If you want to go the whole hog and visit the changing rooms, walk round the pitch and sit in the VIP box, the full tour is a costly €12 (entry at gate 3; information ☎902 281 709).

The city is also home to another of the country's biggest teams, Atlético Madrid, who play at the Vicente Calderón in the south of the city (Ⓜ Pirámides), and the more modest Rayo Vallecano who are based at the Teresa Rivero stadium in the working -class suburb of Vallecas (Ⓜ Portazgo).

Real Madrid ☎913 984 300, information line ☎902 271 708, tickets ☎902 324 324, Ⓦ www.realmadrid.com; tickets cost from around €15 to €80 and usually go on sale in the week before a match and can be purchased by credit card on the ticket line (best to ignore the options you're given on the line and wait to speak to an operator). Pick them up from the automatic tills on C/Rafael Salgado. Ⓦ www.sports emotions.com offer tickets for Real Madrid matches, but the prices are very steep and it is better to go through the club.

Atlético Madrid ☎913 664 707, Ⓦ www.clubatleticodemadrid.com; tickets from around €20.

Rayo Vallecano ☎914 782 253, Ⓦ www.rayovallecano.es; tickets from €12.

---

shady Andalucian-style courtyard and gardens, is worth the visit alone and a wonderful escape from the traffic-choked streets.

A little to the north just off the Paseo de la Castellana on c/José Gutiérrez Abascal is the **Museo de Ciencias Naturales**, or Natural History Museum (Tues–Fri 10am–6pm, Sat 10am–8pm, Sun 10am–2.30pm; €3; Ⓜ Nuevos Ministerios), with a rather dull collection of stuffed animals and audiovisual displays on the evolution of life on earth. Further north along the Paseo de la Castellana, you reach the **Zona Azca** (Ⓜ Nuevos Ministerios/Santiago Bernabéu), a business quarter, with the city's tallest skyscraper and corporate headquarters – the 43-storey Torre Picasso designed by Minori Yamasaki (also the architect of New York's infamous Twin Towers). Just beyond it, and easily the most famous sight up here, is the magnificent **Santiago Bernabéu** football stadium, home of Real Madrid (see above for booking match tickets).

El Pardo

Franco had his principal residence at **EL PARDO**, a former royal hunting ground, 9km northwest of central Madrid. A garrison still remains at the town – where most of the Generalísmo's staff were based – but the stigma of the place has lessened over the years, and it is now a popular weekend excursion for *madrileños*, who come here for long lunches in the terraza restaurants, or to play tennis or swim at one of the nearby sports centres.

The tourist focus is the **Palacio del Pardo** (April–Sept Mon–Sat 10.30am–6pm, Sun 9.30am–1.30pm; Oct–March Mon–Sat 10.30am–5pm, Sun 10am–1.30pm; closed occasionally for official visits; guided tours €3 while restoration work continues and thereafter €5, free Wed for EU citizens; ⓦwww.patrimonionacional.es), rebuilt by the Bourbons on the site of a hunting lodge of Carlos V. The interior is pleasant enough, with its chapel and theatre, a portrait of Isabel la Católica by her court painter Juan de Flandes, and an excellent collection of tapestries, many after the Goya cartoons in the Prado. Guides detail the uses Franco made of the *palacio*, but pass over some of his stranger habits. He kept by his bed, for instance, the mummified hand of Santa Teresa of Ávila. Tickets to the palace are also valid for the **Casita del Príncipe** (closed for refurbishment until mid-2004), though this cannot be entered from the gardens and you will need to return to the main road. Like the *casitas* (pavilions) at El Escorial, this was built by Juan de Villanueva, and is highly ornate.

You can reach El Pardo by local **bus** (every fifteen minutes until midnight from the bus terminal at Metro Moncloa), or by any city **taxi** (€10–12).

Restaurants and tapas bars

The sections below review Madrid's best places for **eating and drinking** and include bars, cafés, cervecerías (beer halls), *marisquerías* (seafood bars) and *restaurantes*. They have been divided simply between "**tapas bars**" and "**restaurants**", depending on whether they concentrate more on bar food or sit-down meals. Sometimes this division is arbitrary, as many places have a bar area, where you can get tapas, together with a more formal *comedor* (canteen) or restaurant out the back or upstairs. At almost any of our recommendations you could happily eat your fill – money permitting – though at bars, *madrileños* usually eat just a tapa or share a *ración* of the house speciality then move on to repeat the procedure down the road.

Hours

The hours for having **cañas y tapas** (drinks and tapas) are from around noon to 2pm, and 8pm to 10pm, though most bars will do you a snack at any hour of the day, and they generally stay open till midnight or beyond. Summer hours are generally later than winter, and Sundays are early to bed.

Restaurant prices in Madrid

As a rough guide, you'll be able to get a three-course meal with drinks in Madrid for:
Inexpensive Under €15 a head
Moderate €15–30 a head
Expensive €30–40
Very expensive Over €40
But bear in mind that the lunchtime *menú del día* often allows you to eat for much less than the price category might lead you to expect; check the listings for details. Most – but by no means all – of the restaurants listed in the "moderate" category or above will accept **credit/charge cards** (*tarjetas*). If in doubt, phone ahead to check.

Café life

Madrid has a number of cafés that are institutions. They serve food but are much more places to drink coffee, have a *copa* or *caña*, or read the papers. Some also act as a meeting place for the semi-formal *tertulia* – a kind of discussion/drinking group, popular among Madrid intellectuals of the past and revived in the 1980s. Many cafés also have summer – or all-year – terrazas (outside terraces), though be aware that sitting outside puts up the prices. Other cafés and *pastelerias* are simpler affairs, good places to grab a breakfast croissant or a teatime snack. Good choices include:

Café los Austrias Plaza de Ramales; ⓂOpera. Relaxing café with marble table-tops and dark-wood interior; a good stop after a visit to the Palacio Real.

Café Barbieri c/Ave María 45; ⓂLavapiés. A relaxed place with inobtrusive music, old-style decor, newspapers, and a wide selection of coffees.

Café El Botánico c/Espalter/Plaza Murillo; ⓂAtocha. A quiet place to sit with a drink, close to the south entrance (Puerta de Murillo) of the Prado.

Café Central Plaza del Ángel 10; ⓂSol. A jazz club by night but a regular café by day, again with newspapers supplied.

Café Comercial Glorieta de Bilbao; ⓂBilbao. One of the city's most popular meeting points – a lovely traditional café, well poised for the Chueca/Santa Bárbara area.

Café del Espejo Paseo de Recoletos 31 ⓂColón. Opened in 1991 but you wouldn't guess it – mirrors, gilt, and a wonderful glass pavilion, plus a leafy outside terraza.

Café Gijón Paseo de Recoletos 21; ⓂBanco de España. Famous literary café – and a centre of the intellectual/arty *movida* in the 1980s – decked out in Cuban mahogany and mirrors. Has a summer terraza.

Café de Oriente Plaza de Oriente 2; ⓂÓpera. Elegant, Parisian-style café with a popular terraza looking out towards the Royal Palace.

Círculo de Bellas Artes c/Alcalá 42; ⓂBanco de España. Day membership to the Círculo is €0.60 (€1 after 4pm), which gives you access to exhibitions, and to a stylish bar, where you can loll on sofas and have drinks at normal prices. Outside, in summer, there's a comfortable terraza.

La Mallorquina Puerta del Sol 2; ⓂSol. Good for breakfast or snacks – try one of their *napolitanas* (cream slices) in the sunny upstairs salon.

Yenes c/Mayor 1; ⓂSol. Wedge yourself on to a bar stool and enjoy a fine array of cakes and croissants; less bustling than *La Mallorquina* opposite.

Restaurant meals (*comidas*) are taken late: few *madrileños* will start lunch before 2pm or dinner much before 9pm, and if you turn up much earlier you may find yourself alone, or the restaurant (in the evening) not yet open. On the other hand, most people do arrive for dinner by 10pm; Madrid being Madrid, though, there are quite a number of late-night options and the listings magazines all have sections for restaurants open past midnight (*después de media noche/de madrugada*). Many restaurants close on Sundays and/or Mondays and for all or part of July and August.

Cuisines

Madrid's restaurants and bars offer every regional style of **Spanish cooking**: Castilian for roasts (*horno de asar* is a wood-burning oven) and stews (such as the meat and chickpea *cocido*), *gallego* for seafood, *andaluz* for fried fish, Levantine (Valencia/Alicante) for paella and other rice (*arroz*)-based dishes, Asturian for winter stews like *fabada*, and Basque for the ultimate gastronomy (and correspondingly high prices).

①

Madrid's vegetarian restaurants

Madrid can be an intimidating city for veggies, given the mass of ham, fish and seafood on display in bar and restaurant windows and on counters. However, you can order vegetables separately at just about any restaurant in the city – Argentine steakhouses, perhaps, excepted – and there is good pizza and pasta to be had at a number of Italian places. You can even find the odd vegetarian paella.

More crucially, the capital now has a growing number of good-value **vegetarian restaurants**, scattered about the centre. These include:

Al Natural c/Zorilla 11 ☎913 694 709; ⓜ Banco de España. Veggie and non-veggie food, including a very good mushroom and spinach pie. Excellent wines and a good-value *menú del día* at €9. Closed Sun night. Inexpensive to moderate.

Artemisa c/Ventura de la Vega 4 ☎914 295 092, ⓜ Sevilla; c/Tres Cruces 4 ☎915 218 721, ⓜ Gran Vía. A popular place (you may have to wait for a table), best for its veggie pizzas and an imaginative range of salads. No smoking – even more of a novelty than veggie food in Madrid. Closed Sun night. Moderate.

Elqui c/Buenavista 18 ☎914 680 462; ⓜ Lavapiés/Antón Martín. Excellent vegetarian venue in the heart of Lavapíes. Light and very tasty main courses, imaginative soups and some great fruit-based drinks. There's a self-service lunchtime *menú* for €7.50. No smoking. Open Tues–Fri for lunch and Fri and Sat evenings.

El Estragón Plaza de la Paja 10 ☎913 658 982; ⓜ La Latina. Creative vegetarian cuisine and great desserts in a fine setting on the edge of this ancient plaza. *Menú del día* at €10 (dinner *menú* is €18). Inexpensive to moderate.

La Isla del Tesoro c/Manuela Malasaña 3 ☎915 931 440; ⓜ Bilbao. Tropical beach decor serves as the backdrop for some cosmopolitan vegetarian food at this great-value place on one of the most interesting streets in Malasaña. *Constantly* changing

Over the last few years, dozens of **foreign cuisines** have appeared. There are some good Peruvian, Argentinian, Middle Eastern and Italian places, a growing number of oriental-influenced restaurants with some inventive fusion-style cuisine and a recent explosion of Turkish kebab houses in the centre of town. There has also been an unfortunate rise of franchised restaurant chains and coffee bars.

Sol, Plaza Mayor and Ópera

The central area is the most varied in Madrid in terms of price and choice of food. Indeed, there can be few places in the world which rival the streets around Puerta del **Sol** for sheer number of places to eat and drink. Around the smarter **Ópera** district, you need to be more selective, while on **Plaza Mayor** itself, stick to drinks. Unless we indicate otherwise, all these places are easily reached from **Metro Sol**.

Tapas bars

Las Bravas c/Alvarez Gato 3. As the name suggests, *patatas bravas* (spicy potatoes) are the tapa to try at this bar, just south of Puerta del Sol; the *tortilla* is tasty, too. On the outside of the bar are novelty mirrors, a hangover from the days when this was a barber's and the subject of a story by Valle Inclán. Standing room only, but if it's too crowded you'll find other branches nearby at c/Espoz y Mina 13, c/Cruz 15 and Pasaje Mathéu 5.
Casa del Abuelo c/Victoria 12. Tiny, highly atmos-

pheric bar serving just their sweet, rich red house wine and cooked prawns – try them *al ajilo* (in garlic) or *a la plancha* (fried). You'll be given a voucher for a free glass of wine at the sister bar round the corner in c/Nuñez de Arce (see also "Restaurants" opposite).
Casa del Labra c/Tetuán 12 ☎915 310 081 – opposite El Corte Inglés. A great, traditional place where the Spanish Socialist Party was founded. Order a drink at the bar and a *ración* of cod fried in batter (*bacalao*) or some of the best *croquetas* in

town at the counter to the right of the door. There is a fairly expensive restaurant at the back with classic *madrileño* food on offer.

Lhardy Carrera de San Jerónimo 8 ☏915 213 385. *Lhardy* is one of Madrid's most famous and expensive restaurants. Once the haunt of royalty, it's a beautiful place but greatly overpriced. Downstairs, however, there's a wonderful bar, where you can snack on canapés, *fino* (dry sherry) and *consommé*, without breaking the bank.

Mejillonera El Rocío Pasaje Matheu. Mussels (*mejillones*) served in every way conceivable at one of many bars on this pedestrian-only alleyway between c/Espoz y Mina and c/Victoria, south of Puerta del Sol.

Mesón del Champiñones & Mesón de la Tortilla Cava de San Miguel 17 & 15. These are two of the oldest *tabernas* in Madrid, just down the steps at the southwest corner of Plaza Mayor. They specialize, as you'd imagine, in mushrooms and *tortilla* respectively, although the quality is not what it was. At weekends, both places come alive as people gather to sample the excellent wines and *sangría*.

Museo del Jamón Carrera de San Jerónimo 6. The largest branch of this Madrid chain, from whose ceilings are suspended hundreds of *jamones* (hams). The best – and they are not cheap – are the *jabugos* from the Sierra Morena, though a ham croissant will set you back under €2.

La Oreja de Oro c/Victoria 9. Standing room only in this down-to-earth bar just opposite *La Casa del Abuelo*. Try the *pulpo a la Gallega* (sliced octopus served on a bed of potatoes seasoned with cayenne pepper) washed down with Ribeiro wine served in terracotta bowls. Plenty of other seafood tapas on offer, too. Closed Aug.

El Oso y El Madroño c/Bolsa 4. A tiny *castizo* (traditional *madrileño*) bar where you can have a drink to the accompaniment of the *madrileño chotis* and chat to the barmen who seem to have been there forever. Specialities are *cocido*, snails, *sangría* and *jerez* (sherry).

La Zapatería c/Victoria 8. A relative newcomer on the scene which has carved out a niche of its own with its excellent *patatas a lo pobre* (pan-fried potatoes) mixed with either *chorizo* or *morcilla*

(blood sausage). Does a nice line in *caracoles* (snails) too.

Restaurants

El Abuelo c/Núñez de Arce 3. There's a *comedor* at the back of this spit-and-sawdust bar, where you can order a selection of delicious *raciones* – the *croquetas* are especially good – and a jug of house wine. Inexpensive.

El Botín c/Cuchilleros 17 ☏913 664 217; ⓂSol/Tirso de Molina. One of the city's oldest restaurants, established in 1725, highly picturesque, and favoured by Hemingway. Inevitably, it's a tourist haunt but not such a bad one, with quality Castilian roasts – especially suckling pig (*cochinillo*) and lamb (*lecha*). The set menu is around €30. Expensive.

Casa Ciriaco c/Mayor 84 ☏915 480 620; Ⓜ Ópera. Attractive, old-style *taberna* – trout, chicken and so on, served up in old-style portions. The *menú* is €17; main *carta* dishes a bit less. Closed Wed & Aug. Moderate.

Casa Gallega c/Bordadores 11 ☏915 419 055; ⓂÓpera/Sol. An airy and welcoming *marisquería* that has been importing seafood on overnight trains from Galicia since it opened in 1915. Costs vary greatly according to the rarity of the fish or shellfish that you order. *Gallego* staples such as *pulpo* (octopus) and *pimientos de Padrón* (tiny, randomly piquant peppers) are brilliantly done and inexpensive, but the more exotic seasonal delights will raise a bill for two to around the €65 mark. Another branch at Plaza San Miguel ☏915 473 055. Expensive.

Casa Santa Cruz c/Bolsa 12 ☏915 218 623; Formerly a hermitage and later the Stock Exchange, this beautiful place is not remotely cheap but the food – a mixture of *nueva cocina* and Castilian staples – has the same top quality as the decor. A rather restrained atmosphere compared to some of its more lively neighbours. Expensive.

La Finca de Susana c/Arlabán 4; Ⓜ Sevilla. One of two great-value restaurants set up by a group of Catalan friends (the other is *La Gloria de Montera* just off Gran Vía, see p.123). Tasty *menú del día* for around €8, consisting of simple dishes served with imagination. Arrive early to avoid queuing as you can't book (opens 8.30pm). Inexpensive.

Around Santa Ana and Huertas

You should spend at least an evening eating and drinking at the historic, tiled bars in this central area. Restaurants are good, too, and frequented as much by locals as tourists.

Tapas bars

La Costa de Vejer corner of c/Núñez de Arce and c/Alvarez del Gato; Ⓜ Sol. The speciality here is

prawns (*gambas*), grilled with garlic, which are an absolute must, but you can't go wrong with the rest of the tapas either.

◀ La Ermita de San Antonio de la Florida

RESTAURANTS

El 26 de Libertad	17
El Abuelo	49
Al Natural	30
Alquezar	77
Ancha	31
Annapurna	2
Artemisa	37
El Asador Frontón	74
La Bardemcilla	13
La Barraca	26
Bazaar	18
Bluefish	1
La Bola	25
El Botín	54
El Buey	21
Carmencita	20
La Carreta	22
Casa Alberto	58
Casa Ciriaco	42
Casa Gades	11
Casa Gallega	33
Casa Lastra Sidrería	82
Casa Lucio	70
Casa Santa Cruz	47
El Cenador del Prado	55
Champagnería Gala	76
El Comunista (Tienda de Vinos)	15
Da Nicola	9
Domine Cabra	61
Dorna	86
El Economico/ Soidermersol	87
Elqui	84
El Estragón	59
La Farfala	60
La Finca de Susana	32
La Gloria de Montera	27
El Inti de Oro	43
Las Letras	44
Momo	12
La Musa Latina	65
Nova Galicia	24
Paradis	48
Posada de la Villa	69
Prada A Tope	41
Salvador	16
La Sanabresa	63
Taberna Griega	7
La Tasca Suprema	6
Teatriz	3
La Vaca Verónica	72
Viridiana	29
Viuda de Vacas	75

TAPAS BARS

Alkalde	8
El Almendro	73
Almendro 13	66
El Bocaito	23
Las Bravas	45
Los Caracoles	83
La Carpanta	62
Casa del Abuelo	40
Casa Camacho	5
Casa del Labra	28

0   300 m

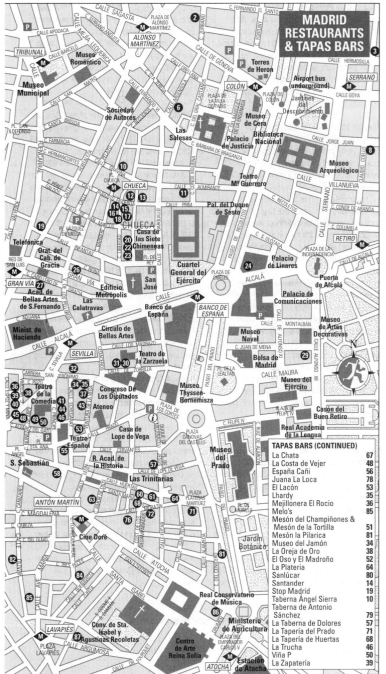

MADRID RESTAURANTS & TAPAS BARS

TAPAS BARS (CONTINUED)

La Chata	67
La Costa de Vejer	48
España Cañi	56
Juana La Loca	78
El Lacón	53
Lhardy	35
Mejillonera El Rocio	36
Melo's	85
Mesón del Champiñones & Mesón de la Tortilla	51
Mesón la Pilarica	81
Museo del Jamón	34
La Oreja de Oro	38
El Oso y El Madroño	52
La Plateria	64
Sanlúcar	80
Santander	14
Stop Madrid	19
Taberna Ángel Sierra	10
Taberna de Antonio Sánchez	79
La Taberna de Dolores	57
La Tapería del Prado	71
La Tapería de Huertas	68
La Trucha	46
Viña P	50
La Zapatería	39

Estación Sur de Autobuses

España Cañí Plaza del Ángel 14; Ⓜ Sol. An attractive tiled exterior fronts this attractive bar with a fine selection of tapas; a great place to soak up flamenco sounds and the house *sangría*.

El Lacón c/Manuel Fernández y González 8; Ⓜ Sol. Large Galician bar-restaurant with plenty of seats upstairs. Great *pulpo, caldo gallego* (meat and vegetable broth) and *empanadas* (pastry slices filled with tuna and vegetables). Closed Aug.

La Taberna de Dolores Plaza de Jesús 4; Ⓜ Antón Martín. Splendid canapés at this popular and friendly tiled bar at the bottom of Huertas. The beer is really good, and the food specialities include Roquefort and anchovy, and smoked-salmon canapés. Get here early if you want a space at the bar.

La Tapería de Huertas c/Santa María 28; Ⓜ Antón Martín. An ideal place to go if you want to try a wide variety of tapas without having to eat a *ración* of each dish: the neat little *cazuelitas* are just the right size for two. A good selection of wines and plenty of tapas that will suit vegetarians.

La Trucha c/Manuel Fernández y González 3 ☎ 914 295 833; Ⓜ Antón Martín. Ever-popular tapas bar and moderately priced restaurant sandwiched between Santa Ana and c/Echegaray. Smoked fish and *pimientos de Padrón* are specialities. Usually very crowded. Closed Sun.

Viña P Plaza de Santa Ana 3; Ⓜ Sol. Very friendly staff serving a great range of tapas in a bar decked out with bullfighting mementos and posters. Try the asparagus, stuffed mussels and the mouthwatering *almejas a la marinera* (clams in a garlic and white wine sauce).

Restaurants

Casa Alberto c/Huertas 18 ☎ 914 299 356; Ⓜ Antón Martín. Traditional *taberna* with a zinc bar and a small dining room at the back. Specialities include *albondigas* (meatballs) and *rabo de toro* (oxtail). Closed Sun night & Mon. Moderate to expensive.

El Cenador del Prado c/Prado 4 ☎ 914 291 561; Ⓜ Sevilla. Relaxing and stylish decor serve as the backdrop to imaginative cuisine combining Spanish, Mediterranean and Far Eastern influences. There's a *menú de degustación* at €17.50 and some spectacular desserts. Closed Sat lunch & Sun. Moderate to expensive.

Champagnería Gala c/Moratín 22 ☎ 914 292 562; Ⓜ Antón Martín. Fantastic-value restaurant specializing in paellas and *fideuás* (like paella only made with noodles instead of rice). Book ahead and try and get a table in the indoor patio at the back, but avoid the weekends when the crowds mean that the food isn't always quite up to standard. Inexpensive to moderate.

Domine Cabra c/Huertas 54 ☎ 914 294 365; Ⓜ Antón Martín. Interesting mix of traditional and modern, with *madrileña* standards given the *nueva cocina* treatment. Very good-value *menús* at €15 & €24. Closed Sun night. Moderate.

La Farfala c/Santa María 17 ☎ 913 694 691; Ⓜ Antón Martín. The place to go for late-night food and a lively party atmosphere in the Huertas area. Good range of tasty pizzas and Argentinian-style meat. Open till 4am at weekends. Inexpensive.

El Inti de Oro c/Ventura de la Vega 12 ☎ 914 296 703; Ⓜ Sevilla. An ideal introduction to Peruvian cuisine. Try the *cebiche de merluza* (a refreshing raw fish salad) and the *aji de gallina* (chicken in walnut sauce); the local liqueurs are worth sampling, too. Another branch at the nearby c/Ventura de la Vega 12 (☎ 914 296 703). Moderate.

Las Letras c/Echegaray 26 ☎ 914 291 206; Ⓜ Sevilla. Designerish touches to the decor and the food in this small bar-restaurant which picks up where its predecessor *Lerranz* left off; the set menu is €8.50. Moderate. Closed Sun & second half of Aug.

Prada A Tope c/Príncipe 11 ☎ 914 295 221; Ⓜ Sevilla. Excellent quality produce from El Bierzo in León; the *pimientos asados*, *morcilla* and *tortilla* are extremely tasty. Closed Mon. Moderate.

La Sanabresa c/Amor de Diós 12 ☎ 914 290 338; Ⓜ Antón Martín. A real local with a TV in one corner and an endless supply of customers who come for its excellent and reasonably priced dishes. Don't miss the grilled aubergines. Closed Sun. Inexpensive.

La Vaca Verónica c/Moratín 38 ☎ 914 297 827; Ⓜ Antón Martín. Excellent Argentinian-style meat, really good fresh pasta in imaginative sauces, quality fish dishes and tasty vegetables. Try the *Filet Verónica* and the *carabinero con pasta*. The *menú del día* is a good deal at €11.50, and the service is friendly. Closed Sat lunch & Sun. Moderate.

Gran Vía and Plaza de España

On the **Gran Vía**, burger bars fill most of the gaps between shops and cinemas. However, head a few blocks in and there's plenty on offer.

Tapas bars

Stop Madrid c/Hortaleza 11; (M) Gran Vía. An old-time spit-and-sawdust bar specializing in products from Extremadura, revitalized with Belgian, Mexican and German beers as well as *vermut* on tap. Tapas are largely *jamón* and *chorizo*, with the *Canapé Stop* of ham and tomato doused in olive oil well worth a try.

Restaurants

La Barraca c/Reina 29 ☎915 327 154; (M)Gran Vía/Banco de España. Step off the dingy street into this little slice of Valencia for some of the best paellas in town. Service is attentive but not overfussy, the starters are excellent and there's a great lemon sorbet for dessert. A three-course meal with wine will set you back somewhere around €35 a head. Expensive.

La Bola c/Bola 5 ☎915 476 930; (M) Santo Domingo. Established back in 1870, this is the place to go for *cocido madrileño* (soup followed by chickpeas and other vegetables and then a selection of meats), which is only served at lunchtime. Don't plan on doing anything energetic afterwards as it is incredibly filling. No cards. Closed Sun

night. Moderate.

El Buey Plaza de la Marina Española 1 ☎915 413 041; (M) Santo Domingo. A meat-eaters' paradise specializing in steak which you fry up yourself on a hotplate. Very good side dishes, including a great leek and seafood pie and excellent homemade desserts. Moderate.

Da Nicola Plaza Los Mostenses ☎915 422 574; (M)Santo Domingo. Extremely popular (so book ahead) Italian restaurant just to the north of Gran Vía.

La Gloria de Montera c/Caballero de Gracia 10; (M)Gran Vía. Sister restaurant to *La Finca de Susana* (see p. 119) with the same successful formula. Excellent-value *menú* with imaginative, well-presented dishes on offer in a cool setting in a gloomy street just off Gran Vía. Inexpensive to moderate.

Nova Galicia c/Conde Duque 3 ☎915 594 260; (M)Plaza de España. Excellent-value Galician restaurant specializing in seafood tapas and *arroz con bogavante* (rice with lobster). Pass through the ordinary-looking front bar and into the dining room hidden behind. Closed second half of Aug. Moderate.

La Latina and Lavapiés: the Rastro area

South from Sol and Huertas are the quarters of La Latina and Lavapiés whose tiny streets retain an appealing neighbourhood feel, and have a great selection of bars and restaurants.

Tapas bars

El Almendro c/Almendro 27; (M) La Latina. On the corner of the Plaza de San Andrés, this is just the place for highly original seated tapas. Imaginatively presented and very tasty.

Almendro 13 c/Almendro 13; (M) La Latina. Fashionable wooden-panelled bar that serves great *fino* from chilled black bottles. Tuck into the original tapas of *huevos rotos* (fried eggs on a bed of crisps) and *roscas rellenas* (rings of bread stuffed with various meats).

Juana La Loca c/Plaza Puerta de Moros 4; (M) La Latina. Trendy Basque *pintxos* bar serving original – *solomillo de avestruz* (ostrich steak) is one of the most popular choices – and very tasty, but fairly pricey canapés.

Los Caracoles Plaza Cascorro 18; (M)La Latina. A favourite since the 1940s, this does a good range of tapas as well as its namesake *caracoles* (snails). The place to come after a trek around the Rastro.

La Carpanta c/Almendro 22; (M)La Latina. Lively bar just off the Plaza de San Andrés with a good range of tapas and a cosy brick-lined dining area at the back.

La Chata c/Cava Baja 24; (M) La Latina. One of the

most traditional, and popular, tiled tapas bars in Madrid, with hams hanging from the ceiling, taurine and football mementos on the walls, and a good selection of *raciones*, including *cebolla rellena* and *pimientos del piquillo rellenos* (stuffed onions and peppers). Closed Sun night.

Melo's c/Avemaría 44; (M) Lavapiés. Standing room only at this very popular Galician bar serving huge *zapatillas* (hunks of Galician country bread filled with *lacón* and *queso*) and great *pimientos de Padrón*. Usually closed Aug.

Sanlúcar c/San Isidro Labrador 14; (M) La Latina. A little slice of Andalucía in this La Latina bar. Chilled *fino*, prawns and excellent *salmorejo* (a thick gazpacho-style dish with pieces of ham) are all on offer. Closed Sun night & Mon.

Taberna de Antonio Sánchez c/Mesón de Paredes 13 ☎915 397 826; (M)Tirso de Molina. Seventeenth-century bar – said to be the oldest *taberna* in Madrid – decorated with a wooden interior and a stuffed bull's head (one of which killed Antonio Sánchez, the son of the founder). Lots of *finos* on offer, plus *jamón* and *queso* tapas or *tortilla de San Isidro* (with salted cod). Closed Sun night.

Restaurants

Alquezar c/Lavapiés 53 ☎915 277 261; Ⓜ Tirso de Molina. Authentic and good-value Middle Eastern food in the heart of the cosmopolitan Lavapíes *barrio*. Moderate.

El Asador Frontón Plaza Tirso de Molina 7, 1º – entrance just off the square ☎913 691 617; Ⓜ Tirso de Molina. Old, charming neighbourhood restaurant, where publishers and the like settle down for a long afternoon's lunch. Wide range of classic Castilian dishes – all delicious. Moderate.

El Economico/Soidermersol c/Argumosa; Ⓜ Lavapiés. Traditional workmen's *comedor*. It may not be quite as atmospheric as it was, but it still serves a great-value €7 lunchtime *menú*. Inexpensive.

Casa Lastra Sidrería c/Olivar 3 ☎913 690 837; Ⓜ Antón Martín/Tirso de Molina. Very popular restaurant serving classic Asturian fare: *chorizo a la sidra* (chorizo in cider), *entrecot al cabrales* (steak in a strong blue-cheese sauce), *fabada* (a warming winter stew of beans, *chorizo* and *morcilla*) and, of course, *sidra natural* (cider). Closed July. Moderate.

Casa Lucio c/Cava Baja 35 ☎913 653 252; Ⓜ La Latina. *Madrileños* come here for the expected:

classic Castilian dishes such as *cocido*, *callos* (tripe) and roasts, cooked to perfection. It is where Queen Sofía took George Bush's wife, Laura, when the first family visited a few years back. Booking is essential. Closed Sat lunch & Aug. Expensive.

La Musa Latina c/Costanilla de San Andrés 12 ☎913 540 255; Ⓜ La Latina. Stylish restaurant/bar with a frontage on the pleasant Plaza de la Paja. Great salads, imaginatively presented tapas and an excellent wine list. Excellent *menú del día* at just €8. Inexpensive to moderate.

Posada de la Villa c/Cava Baja 9 ☎913 661 860; Ⓜ La Latina. The most attractive-looking restaurant in Latina, spread over three floors of a seventeenth-century mansion. Cooking is typically *madrileña*, including superb roast lamb. Reckon on a good €45 per person for the works – though you could get away with less. Closed Sun night & Aug. Very expensive.

Viuda de Vacas c/Cava Alta 23 ☎913 665 847; Ⓜ La Latina. Highly traditional, family-run restaurant. The place looks rather down-at-heel but the good-quality Castilian fare certainly isn't. Closed Thurs & Sun nights. Inexpensive to moderate.

Chueca and Santa Bárbara

Chueca – and **Santa Bárbara** to its north – have a combination of some superb traditional old bars and stylish new restaurants, as well as a vast amount of nightlife. The southern part of Chueca, however, around the edges of Gran Vía, is quite a big drug area, which can leave you feeling a little uneasy after dark.

Tapas bars

El Bocaito c/Libertad 4–6; Ⓜ Chueca. Munch away on a variety of delicious canapés and tapas, washed down by a cold beer, at this busy bar; watch out for the *Luisito*, the hottest canapé your taste buds are ever likely to encounter. Closed Sat lunch, Sun & two weeks in Aug.

Cervecería Santa Bárbara Plaza Santa Bárbara 8; Ⓜ Alonso Martínez. Popular, but pricey, meeting place in this part of town, with *cañas* and prawns to keep you going.

Santander c/Augusto Figueroa 25; Ⓜ Chueca. It's worth a visit to this bar in the heart of Chueca for the good range of tapas, including *empanadas*, *tortillas* and quiche lorraine, as well as a huge variety of fresh home-made canapés at reasonable prices. Closed Aug.

Taberna Ángel Sierra c/Gravina 11, on Plaza Chueca; Ⓜ Chueca. One of the great bars of Madrid, with a traditional zinc counter, constantly washed down. Everyone drinks *vermut*, which is on tap and delicious, and free tapas of the most exquisite *boquerones en vinagre* are despatched (*raciones*, too,

for the greedy – though they are pricey).

Restaurants

El 26 de Libertad c/Libertad 26 ☎915 222 522; Ⓜ Chueca. Imaginative cuisine served up in an attentive but unfussy manner in this brightly decorated restaurant popular with the Chueca locals. Closed Sun night in July & Aug. Moderate.

Annapurna c/Zurbano 5 ☎913 198 716; Ⓜ Colón. One of the best Indian restaurants in Madrid, *Annapurna* could hold its own in London, especially if you go for the tandoori dishes or thali. Closed Sat lunch & Sun. Moderate to expensive.

La Bardemcilla c/Augusto Figueroa 47 ☎915 214 256; Ⓜ Chueca. A popular spot owned by actor Javier Bardem's family. A tasty *menú del día* at around €9. Closed Sat lunch & Sun.

Bazaar c/Libertad 21; Ⓜ Chueca. Quality fusion-style cuisine with Mediterranean and Asian influences from a new arrival that has already become a big hit on the Chueca scene. No reservations, so arrive early to avoid a long wait.

Carmencita c/Libertad 16 ☎915 316 612;

Ⓜ Chueca. Beautiful old restaurant, dating back to 1830, with panelling, brass, marble tables – and a new Basque-influenced chef. Lunch *menú* is a bargain at €9 but eating à la carte is expensive. *Gallina en pepitoria* (chicken in almond sauce) is the speciality. Closed Sat night, Sun & holidays. Moderate to expensive.

La Carreta c/Barbieri 10 ☎915 327 042; Ⓜ Chueca/Banco de España. A fun atmosphere at this Argentinian restaurant, heavy on steaks and red meat. At weekends you can listen to tangos from the resident pianist. A good late-night option in this area, as it's open daily well into the early hours. Closed Tues eve. Moderate to expensive.

Casa Gades c/Conde de Xiquena 4 ☎915 312 637; Ⓜ Chueca/Banco de España. Very attractive restaurant in a fashionable area on the edge of Chueca, owned by the flamenco dancer Antonio Gades. Food is a mix of Spanish and Italian. Closed Mon. Expensive.

El Comunista (Tienda de Vinos) c/Augusto Figueroa 35 – between Libertad and Barbieri;

Ⓜ Chueca. Long-established *comedor*; its unofficial (but always used) name dates back to its time as a student haunt under Franco. The garlic soup is recommended. Inexpensive to moderate.

Momo c/Augusto Figueroa 41 ☎915 327 162; Ⓜ Chueca. Kitsch decor and creative cuisine at very reasonable prices – around €8–9 for the *menú del día* – in this very popular restaurant in the heart of Chueca. Inexpensive.

Salvador c/Barbieri 12 ☎915 214 524; Ⓜ Chueca. Bullfighting decor and traditional specialities such as *rabo de toro* (bull's tail), *gallina en pepitoria* (chicken fricassee), fried *merluza* (hake) and *arroz con leche* (rice pudding) – all excellent. Closed Sun night & Aug. Moderate to expensive.

La Tasca Suprema c/Argensola 7 ☎913 080 347; Ⓜ Alonso Martínez. Very popular neighbourhood local, worth booking ahead. Castilian home cooking to perfection, including *cocido* on Mon & Thurs and excellent *pimientos de piquillo* (piquant red peppers). Open for lunch only; closed Sun & Aug. Inexpensive.

Malasaña and Bilbao

Malasaña is another characterful area, with a big nightlife scene and dozens of bars. Further north, the area around Plaza de Olavide – a real neighbourhood square – offers some good-value places, well off any tourist trails.

Tapas bars

Albur c/Manuela Malasaña 15; Ⓜ Bilbao. Wooden tables, rustic decor and excellent food, although the service can be a little slow. The *champiñones en salsa verde* and the *patatas albur* are both worth sampling; the well-kept wines are the ideal accompaniment.

La Camocha c/Fuencarral 95; Ⓜ Bilbao. Asturian cider bar serving splendid *pulpo* and *almejas a la sidra*. You can use the special cider-pouring instruments on the wall to make sure it is properly aerated.

Casa Camacho c/San Andrés 2 – just off Plaza Dos de Mayo; Ⓜ Tribunal. Irresistible old *bodega*, with a traditional bar counter, *vermut* on tap, and basic tapas. An ideal place to start the evening. Packed out at weekends.

Casa Vila c/Santa Engracia 87☎914 469 757; Ⓜ Iglesia. Quality tapas bar with a very popular summer terrace. Don't miss the excellent *huevos rotos con jamón* (fried eggs served with chunks of serrano ham). Closed Sun.

La Musa c/ Manuel Malasaña 18 ☎914 487 558; Ⓜ Bilbao. It's easy to see why *La Musa* has become such a firm favourite on the Malasaña scene. A variety of imaginative – and very tasty – tapas, generous helpings, a strong wine list

and chic decor are all part of the recipe for success.

Restaurants

Balear c/Sagunto 18 ☎914 479 115; Ⓜ Iglesia. This Levantine restaurant serves only rice-based dishes, but they're superb. There's an inexpensive house *cava*, and you can turn up any time before midnight. Closed Sun & Mon night. Moderate.

Bluefish c/ San Andrés 26 ☎914 486 765; Ⓜ Bilbao. Imaginative food and a very good *menú del día* at this trendy Malasaña restaurant-barcocktail joint. They do a great Sunday brunch, too. Closed Mon. Moderate.

La Despensa c/Cardinal Cisneros 6 ☎ 914 461 794; Ⓜ Bilbao. Good standard, no-nonsense lunchtime fare with an inexpensive *menú del día*. Inexpensive.

La Giralda c/Hartzenbush 12 ☎914 457 779; Ⓜ Bilbao. An *andaluz* fish and seafood restaurant of very high quality: perfectly cooked *chipirones*, *calamares*, and all the standards, plus wonderful *mero* (grouper). A second branch, across the road at no. 15, does a similarly accomplished job on *pescados fritos*. Closed Sun & holidays. Moderate to expensive.

Mesón Do Anxó c/Cardenal Cisneros 6; ⓜBilbao. A *gallego* café-restaurant with Formica tables – as unpretentious as they come – but serving superb *pulpo*, *pimientos de Padrón* and other staples of the region. Closed Sun. Moderate.

Taberna Griega c/Tesoro 6 ☎915 321 892; ⓜTribunal. Enjoyable Greek restaurant, with live bouzouki music most weekends. Open until well after midnight. Inexpensive.

Paseo del Prado, Recoletos and Retiro

This is a fancier area with few bars of note but some extremely good, if expensive, restaurants, well worth considering, even if you're not staying at the *Ritz*.

Tapas bars

La Tapería del Prado Plaza Platerías de Martínez 1; ⓜAtocha/Banco de España. Modern and slightly pricey bar opposite the Prado serving up an inventive range of tapas and *raciones*.
Mesón la Pilarica Paseo del Prado 39; ⓜAtocha. One of the nearest decent places to the Prado on this road, this is a good place to sample *serrano* ham.
La Platerría c/Moratín 49; ⓜAtocha/Banco de España. Just across the square from the *Tapería*, this bar has an enormously popular summer terraza and a good selection of tasty tapas.

Restaurants

Ancha c/Zorrilla 7 ☎914 298 186; ⓜSevilla/Banco de España. Highly regarded restaurant in a rather gloomy street behind the Cortes – hence popular with politicians. Mahogany-panelled decor, and imaginative variations on traditional Castilian dishes. Good-value lunchtime *menú*. Closed Sun & holidays. Expensive.
Dorna c/Atocha 118 ☎915 275 299; ⓜAtocha.

Bustling place with somewhat brusque waiters, but a decent stop before (or after) a visit to the Reina Sofía. Inexpensive to moderate.
Paradis Casa de América c/Paseo de Recoletos 2 ☎915 754 540; ⓜBanco de España. Wonderful setting with a great summer terrace in the Palacio de Linares close to Cibeles. There are other Paradises in Barcelona and New York – the chain is run by a Catalan duo – and the American influence is apparent in designerish details like a *carta* for olive oils. Nonetheless, the cooking is light, Mediterranean and tasty; try the wonderful *arroz negro* with seafood. Closed Sat lunch, Sun & Aug. Expensive. Branch c/Marqués de Cubas 14 ☎914 297 303; ⓜBanco de España.
Viridiana c/Juan de Mena 14 ☎915 315 222; ⓜRetiro/Banco de España. Bizarre temple of Madrid *nueva cocina*, offering mouthwatering creations like *solomillo* (sirloin) with black truffles, and herrings with avocado and mango. Dishes often arrive with sparklers or other pyrotechnic devices attached. Main courses are around €20; no cards accepted. Closed Sun & Aug. Very expensive.

Salamanca

Salamanca is Madrid's equivalent of Bond Street or Fifth Avenue, full of designer shops and expensive-looking natives. Recommendations below are correspondingly pricey but high quality.

Tapas bars

Alkalde c/Jorge Juan 10 ☎915 673 359; ⓜSerrano. This serves up pricey Basque tapas, a treat which you could turn into a tasty meal.
Hevia c/Serrano 118; ⓜNúñez de Balboa. Plush venue and clientele for pricey, but excellent tapas and canapés – the hot Camembert is a must. Closed part of Aug.
José Luís c/Serrano 89 ☎915 630 958; ⓜSerrano. Upmarket tapas bar with dainty and delicious sandwiches laid out along the bar. You take what you fancy, in the safe knowledge that the barman will have notched up another few hundred euro to expand his chain of bars in the Americas.

Restaurants

El Amparo Callejón Puigcerdá 8 ☎914 316 456; ⓜSerrano. Most critics rate this designer restaurant among the top five in Madrid – and you'll need to book a couple of weeks ahead to get a table. If you strike lucky, the rewards are faultless Basque cooking from a woman chef, Carmen Guasp – "Guaspi" to the Spanish media. Main dishes are €20–25 so expect a bill of at least €45 a head. Closed Sat lunch & Sun. Very expensive.
Casa Portal c/Dr Castelo 26 ☎915 742 026; ⓜRetiro. Superlative Asturian cooking – go for the *fabada* (beans and sausage stew) or *besugo* (bream). Closed Sun & Mon night, holidays & Aug. Moderate to expensive.

El Pescador c/José Ortega y Gasset 75 ☎914 021 290; Ⓜ Lista. One of the city's top seafood restaurants, run by *gallegos* and with specials flown in from the Atlantic each morning. The clientele can be a bit intimidating – it is reputedly one of Felipe González's favourites – but you'll rarely experience better seafood cooking. Closed Sun & Aug. Expensive.

Suntory Paseo de la Castellana 36 ☎915 773 733; Ⓜ Rubén Darío. Authentic and upmarket Japanese restaurant, where a mixed sushi will set you back around €30. The best bet is to go for the lunchtime set menu. Closed Sun & holidays. Very expensive.

Teatriz c/Hermosilla 15 ☎915 775 379; Ⓜ Serrano. As the name suggests, this was once a theatre, and the layout has been maintained by designers Philippe Starck and Mariscal – as trendy a European combination as could be conceived. Although primarily a nightspot (see p.133), there's a fine restaurant in the old stalls with light, *nouvelle cuisine*-influenced dishes. (Surprisingly) moderate.

Zalacaín c/Alvarez de Baena 4 ☎915 614 840; Ⓜ Gregorio Marañon. Luxurious setting for the best restaurant in town and the only one with three Michelin stars. Basque-style cooking from master chef Benjamín Urdaín, but you pay very heavily for the pleasure, with a meal setting you back around €70 per person. Closed Sat lunch, Sun & Aug. Very expensive.

The west

Picnicking in the Casa de Campo aside, the west doesn't hold much in the way of culinary interest. However, two excellent restaurants deserve a mention.

Casa Mingo Paseo de la Florida 2 – next to the chapel of San Antonio de la Florida ☎915 477 918; Ⓜ Príncipe Pío. Famous Asturian café-restaurant where you eat roast chicken – which is basically all they serve – washed down with *sidra* (cider), and followed up by *yemas* (candied egg yolk) or aged Roquefort-like cheese (*cabrales*). Good value and great fun. You can also buy a takeout (chicken and cider) for a picnic in the Casa de Campo, if you prefer. Moderate.

La Vaca Argentina Paseo del Pintor Rosales 52 ☎915 596 605; Ⓜ Argüelles. Good views and great grilled steaks (*churrasco*) at this Argentinian restaurant overlooking the Parque del Oeste. Its terrace is a very pleasant place to eat in summer. Other branches at c/Bailén 20 ☎913 656 654; Ⓜ La Latina; c/Caños del Peral ☎915 413 318; Ⓜ Ópera; and Ribera del Manzanares 123 ☎915 593 780; Ⓜ Príncipe Pío with a fine riverside terrace. Moderate.

Nightlife

Madrid **nightlife** is a pretty serious phenomenon. This is one of the few cities in Europe where you can get caught in traffic jams at 4am, when the clubbers are either going home or moving on to the dance-past-dawn discos.

As with everything *madrileño*, there is a bewildering variety of nightlife venues – all of which are covered, to some degree, in the area reviews following. Most common are the **discobares** – bars of all musical and sexual persuasion, whose unifying feature is background (occasionally live) pop, rock, dance or salsa music. These get going from around 11pm and will stay open routinely to 2am or 3am, as will the few quieter **cocktail bars** and **pubs**.

Discotecas – which we've separated in the listings – are rarely worth investigating until around 1am (the *madrugada* – early morning). Most of them pick their clientele through a dress code exclusivity and you may at times need to ingratiate yourself with the doorman. Being foreign, oddly enough, seems to make it easier to get in. Entry charges are quite common and quite hefty (€3.50–18) at *discotecas* (and some of the more disco-like *discobares*) but tend to cover you for a first drink. Free entries can sometimes be picked up from touts in the streets, in tourist offices or bars. Be aware that many *discotecas* in Spain are fairly ephemeral institutions and frequently only last a season before opening up somewhere else under a different name, so it's a good idea to consult *La Guía del Ocio* or *Metrópoli* (see p.135) or the website ⓦ www.clubbing spain.com for the very latest information.

Terrazas and chiringuitos

Madrid is a different city during summer, as temperatures soar, and life moves outside, becoming even more late-night. In July and August, those *madrileños* who haven't headed for the coast meet up with each other, from 10pm onwards, at one or other of the city's immensely popular **terrazas**. These can range from a few tables set up outside a café or alongside a **chiringuito** – a makeshift bar – in one of the squares, to extremely trendy (and very expensive) designer bars, which form the summer annexe of one or other of the major clubs or *discotecas*. Most places offer cocktails, in addition to regular drinks, and the better or more traditional ones also serve *horchata* (an almond-ish milkshake) and *granizado* (crushed-ice lemon). A few of the terrazas operate year-round.

Be aware that many of the terrazas run by the **clubs** vary their sites year by year as they fall foul of licensing and noise regulations.

Paseo de Recoletos and Paseo de la Castellana

The biggest concentration of terrazas is to be found up and down the grass strip in the middle of the Paseo de Recoletos and its continuation, Paseo de la Castellana. On the nearer reaches of Paseo de Recoletos are terrazas of the **old-style cafés** *Gran* (no. 8), *Gijón* (no. 21) and *Espejo* (no. 31), which are popular meeting points for *madrileños* of all kinds.

Past Plaza de Colón, the **trendier terrazas** begin, most pumping out music, and some offering entertainment – especially midweek, when they need to attract custom. They are extremely posey places, with clubbers dressing up for a night's cruise along the length – an expensive operation, with cocktails at €8 a shot, and even a *caña* costing €4. If you want to take in a good selection, walk up from Plaza de Colón for around 500m or take the metro up to Santiago Bernabéu and you'll find *Castellana 99* and *Boulevard* – two of the most fashionable terrazas.

Bars

Madrid's bar scene has something to offer every conceivable taste in terms of drinks, music and atmosphere. In recent years the notoriously late opening hours have been somewhat curtailed by the local authorities who are attempting to close bars by 3am, but there are still plenty of opportunities to dance the night away if you head for a disco afterwards. In *discobares* and *discotecas*, *bakalao*, a Spanish (originally Ibizan) version of house music, is still horribly popular. Perhaps in reaction to it, the more traditional bar scene has revived and expanded, and in the listings below you'll find a fair number of *bares de copas* (drinking bars) where the music is restrained – and even a couple with chamber orchestras.

Sol, Plaza de Santa Ana and Huertas

Alhambra c/Victoria 5; Ⓜ Sol. A friendly tapas bar by day, *Alhambra* transforms itself into a fun discobar by night with the crowds spilling over into the *El Buscón* bar next door.

Cervecería Alemana Plaza de Santa Ana; Ⓜ Sol. Recently refurbished but still stylish old beer house, frequented by Hemingway and, these days, seemingly every other American tourist. Order a *caña* and go easy on the tapas, as the bill can mount up fast. Daily except Tues 10am–12.30am, Fri & Sat until 2am.

Cervecería Santa Ana Plaza de Santa Ana; Ⓜ Sol. Cheaper than the *Alemana*, with tables outside, friendly service, and a good selection of tapas. Daily 11am–1.30am.

La Fídula c/Huertas 57; Ⓜ Antón Martín. A fine bar where you can sip *fino* to the accompaniment of classical tunes, performed from the tiny stage. Daily 8pm–3am.

Elsewhere in Madrid

Jardines Las Vistillas c/Bailén – on the south side of the viaduct (Ⓜ La Latina – though it's not very close). This popular terraza is good for a relaxing drink while enjoying the vistillas ("little vistas") over towards the Almudena cathedral and the Guadarrama mountains to the northwest.

Paseo del Pintor Rosales Ⓜ Argüelles. There is a clutch of late-night terrazas catering for all tastes around the base of the *teleférico*, with views across the river to the Casa de Campo.

Plaza de Comendadoras Ⓜ Ventura Rodríguez. One of the city's nicest squares, this has a couple of very popular terrazas – attached to the *Café Moderno* and to the Mexican restaurant.

Plaza Dos de Mayo Ⓜ Tribunal. The *chiringuito* on Malasaña's main square is always a lively affair, though the square has something of a reputation for drug addicts.

Plaza de Olavide Ⓜ Quevedo. An attractive neighbourhood square, with more or less year-round terrazas belonging to four or five cafés and tapas bars.

Plaza de Oriente Ⓜ Ópera. The *Café de Oriente* terraza is a station of Madrid nightlife and enjoys a marvellous location next to the opera house, gazing across the plaza to the Palacio Real.

Plaza de la Paja Ⓜ La Latina. One off the most pleasant terrazas in the heart of old Madrid in this former market square in La Latina.

Plaza San Andrés Ⓜ La Latina. Just the other side of the church of San Andrés a host of bars spill out onto this atmospheric plaza. The place is buzzing in the summer and makes a great meeting place before a bar crawl around the area.

Plaza de Santa Ana Ⓜ Sol. Several of the *cervecerías* here have seats outside and there's a *chiringuito* in the middle of the square from June to September.

La Vieja Estación Glorieta de Carlos V Ⓜ Atocha. Above the main entrance to Atocha station, this attracts a glamorous clientele ranging from football stars to TV personalities. If you don't fancy people-watching, there are concerts, talent contests and exhibitions laid on for good measure.

Los Gabrieles c/Echegaray 17; Ⓜ Sol. This tiled bar is a Madrid monument and it's worth going earlier than is cool to appreciate the fabulous tableaux, created by sherry companies in the 1880s. Drinks are reasonable, considering the venue; tapas don't go much beyond olives and crisps. Very crowded after 10pm, especially at weekends. Daily 2.30pm–2.30am.

Naturbier Plaza de Santa Ana 9; Ⓜ Sol. Next door to the *cervecerías Alemana* and *Santa Ana*, the *Naturbier* brews its own tasty, cloudy beer and serves a variety of German sausages to accompany it. Daily 8pm–3am.

No se lo digas a nadie c/Ventura de la Vega 7; Ⓜ Sol. This is run by a women's co-op, though it has mellowed a bit in recent years (the toilets no longer proclaim *nosotras* and *ellos* – "us" and "them"). Nonetheless, it retains a political edge, hosting benefit events from time to time, and has a different atmosphere from other bars in this area. There is no door policy or dress code and the drinks are reasonably priced. Upstairs there's a pool table and plenty of places to sit; downstairs is a disco playing mainly dance music. Mon–Thurs 9pm–3am, Fri & Sat 9pm–5am.

Reporter c/Fúcar 6; Ⓜ Anton Martín. The cool terrace garden in this neat bar just off Huertas makes a great place for a relaxing cocktail. Also does tapas and a *menú del día* during the day. Tues–Sun noon–2.30am.

Salón del Prado c/Prado 4; Ⓜ Sol. Elegant café-bar which hosts classical concerts on Thursday nights at 11pm. Turn up early if you want a table. Daily 2pm–2am.

Suite c/Virgen de los Peligros; Ⓜ Sevilla. Stylish cocktail bar that doubles up as a restaurant by day and a club by night. A great place to start off a night on the tiles. Mon–Thurs 9.30pm–3am, Fri & Sat 9.30pm–4.30am.

La Taberna de Dolores Plaza de Jesús 4; Ⓜ Antón Martín. Splendid canapés at this popular and friendly tiled bar at the bottom of Huertas. Decorated with beer bottles from around the world, the beer is really good, and the food specialities include Roquefort and anchovy, and smoked-salmon canapés. Get here early if you want a space at the bar. Daily 11am–midnight.

La Venencia c/Echegaray Ⓜ Sol. For a real taste of old Madrid, this is a must: a long, narrow bar,

Gay and lesbian Madrid

Much of Madrid's nightlife has a big gay input and gay men especially will feel at home in most of the listings in our clubs/*discotecas* section (see p.133). However, around Plaza Chueca, graffiti-plastered walls proclaim the existence of a *zona gay*, and the surrounding streets, especially c/Pelayo, harbour at least a dozen exclusively gay bars and clubs, as well as a café that's traditionally gay – the *Café Figueroa* at c/Augusto Figueroa 17. Wandering about, be aware that the area just north of Gran Vía is a red-ight and drug centre, so taxis are best late at night. The lesbian scene, which is rather less developed, has a current focus in Lavapiés.

The main gay organization in Madrid is Coordinadora Gay de Madrid, c/Fuencarral 37 (Mon–Fri 5–9pm, Aug from 7pm; ☎915 224 517, ⓦ www.cogam.org; ⓜ Chueca), which can give information on health, leisure and gay rights. Feminist and lesbian groups are based at the Centro de la Mujer, c/Barquillo 44, 1°izda; ☎913 193 689. The Chueca website ⓦ www.chueca.com is full of information about everything going on in the area.

Gay and lesbian bars and discotecas

Café Acuarela c/Gravina 10; ⓜ Chueca. Very comfortable café, stylish decor and the perfect place for a quiet drink. Popular with a mixed crowd.

Ambient c/San Mateo 21; ⓜ Alonso Martínez. Thriving lesbian bar with pool, table football, occasional live acts and a market on Sunday.

Liquid c/Barquillo 8; ⓜ Chueca. Smart and stylish new arrival on the gay scene. The two bars are lined with video screens playing a selection of modish music.

La Lupe c/Torrecilla del Leal 12; ⓜ Antón Martín. Mixed gay, lesbian and alternative bar that has received a recent makeover. Good music, cheap drinks and occasional cabaret.

Medea c/Cabeza 33; ⓜ Tirso de Molina/Antón Martín. Women-only disco which has a huge dance floor and wide-ranging selection of danceable music. Gets going from about 1am.

New Leather Bar c/Pelayo 42; ⓜ Chueca. The name implies a leather scene but this bar has a mixed gay crowd.

Ricks c/Infantas 26; ⓜ Banco de España. Mixed straight/gay *discobar* which gets wild at weekends when every available space is used for dancing. Open and light, with a friendly atmosphere. Pricey drinks.

La Sastrería c/Hortaleza 74; ⓜ Chueca. This popular two-floored café-bar is a great place for an afternoon coffee, tea or fruit juice as well as an evening drink.

Shangay Tea Dance at the *Flamingo Club*, c/Mesonero Romanos 13; ⓜ Callao. A compulsory Sunday-night stop, featuring live shows and 70s disco hits. €6 entry including first drink. Open Sun 9pm–2am.

Stars Dance Café c/Marqués de Valdeiglesias 5; ⓜ Gran Vía. Quiet and low-key during the day and gradually livens up as the night goes on. Popular meeting point for the gay community but clientele is mixed.

Truco c/Gravina 10; ⓜ Chueca. Long-established women's bar with a popular summer *terraza* that spills out on to the main plaza in Chueca.

---

serving just sherry – try the extra-dry *fino* – cheese, and delicious cured tuna (*mojama*) and olives. Decoration is unchanged for decades, with ancient barrels and posters. Daily 7.30pm–1.30am. Closed Aug.

Viva Madrid c/Manuel Fernández y González 7 ⓜ Antón Martín. Another fabulous tiled bar – both outside and in – with wines and sherry, plus basic tapas. Open to 2.30am and always crowded.

Gran Vía

El Cock c/Reina 16 – just behind *Museo Chicote*; ⓜ Gran Vía. A smart wooden-panelled bar, styled like a gentlemen's club, and very *de moda*. The music is good, although there's no dancing. *Cañas* or wine cost around €4. Daily 7pm–3am; July–Aug, Mon–Sat 9pm–4am.

Del Diego c/Reina 12; ⓜ Gran Vía. Stylish cocktail bar set up by a former *Museu Chicote* waiter who

△ Tiled bar, Madrid

personally mixes all the excellent cocktails. Friendly, unhurried atmosphere and open until the early hours. The house special, vodka-based *Del Diego*, is the one to go for. Mon–Sat 9pm–3am. Closed Aug.

Larios Café c/Silva 4; Ⓜ Santo Domingo/Callao. Salsa and flamenco on the dance floor, Cuban food in the restaurant at this stylish multipurpose venue just north of Gran Vía. Daily 9pm–4am.

Museo Chicote Gran Vía 12; Ⓜ Gran Vía. *Chicote* is a piece of design history, virtually unaltered since it opened in 1931, full of Art Deco lines and booths. Once a haunt of Buñuel and Hemingway, these days it's not uncommon to bump into Pedro Almodóvar and his entourage. Busiest after midnight. Open Mon–Sat 5pm–1.30am.

La Latina and Lavapiés

Aloque c/Torrecilla del Real 20; Ⓜ Antón Martín. Relaxed wine bar where you can try top-quality wine by the glass; the innovative tapas are excellent, too. Daily 7.30am–1pm. Closed Aug.

Kappa c/Olmo 26; Ⓜ Antón Martín. Relaxing chill-out bar, with comfy seats, good music and a mixed gay and straight crowd. DJs get the party going at the weekend. Tues–Thurs & Sun 8.30pm–2am, Fri & Sat 8.30pm–3.30am.

Montes c/Lavapiés 40; Ⓜ Lavapiés/ Tirso de Molina. A Lavapiés favourite for those in search of a decent glass of wine. Ask owner César for advice and he'll help you find one to suit. A great place to start the evening. Tues–Sat noon–4pm & 7.30pm–midnight. Closed Aug.

El Tempranillo Cava Baja 38; Ⓜ La Latina. Excellent little bar serving tasty tapas and a vast range of Spanish wines by the glass – a great place to discover your favourite variety. Daily noon–4pm & 9pm–2am.

El Viajero Plaza de la Cebada; Ⓜ La Latina. Bar, disco, restaurant and summer terraza on different floors of this fashionable La Latina nightspot. Great views of San Francisco El Grande from the terraza at the top. The food (meat, pizzas and pastas) is good, too. Tues–Sun 2pm–2.30am, Fri & Sat till 3am.

Chueca and Santa Bárbara

Big Bamboo c/Barquillo 42; Ⓜ Alonso Martínez. Reggae music and great cocktails, including an upside-down margarita poured directly down the throat – mixing takes place by vigorous shaking of the head before you swallow. Plenty of room for dancing. Open daily 10.30pm–5am, Fri & Sat till 6am.

Pan c/San Bartolomé 21; Ⓜ Chueca. Deep in the heart of Chueca, this has a relaxed atmosphere

and good music. On any day of the week you'll find people drinking till 4am, or playing board games in the room at the back. Perhaps best enjoyed during the week, as it's a small place and gets packed at weekends.

Finnegans Plaza de las Salesas 9; Ⓜ Colón. Large Irish bar with several rooms, complete with bar fittings and wooden floors brought over from the Emerald Isle. English-speaking staff and TV sports and a pub quiz on Mon nights. Daily 1pm–2am.

Kingston's c/Barquillo 29; Ⓜ Chueca. Relaxed multicultural *discobar*. Music ranges from soul and funk to reggae and rap. At the weekend professional dancers get things going. Open Mon–Thurs 11pm–5am, Fri, Sat & Sun 11pm–6am.

The Quiet Man c/Valverde 44; Ⓜ Tribunal. One of the first Irish bars on the scene, designed in the style of a turn-of-the-twentieth-century Dublin pub. Mon–Thurs 5.30pm–2am, Fri & Sat 1pm–3.30am.

Malasaña and north

Bar Plaza Dos de Mayo Plaza Dos de Mayo; Ⓜ Tribunal. Old-style wood and tiles bar, which gets packed at weekends. Good music, regular prices, and it opens up in the summer so you can watch the goings-on in the square. Daily 1pm–2am, Sat & Sun closes 3am.

Café del Foro c/San Andrés 38; Ⓜ Tribunal. Expensive but enjoyable bar with live music or some form of entertainment most nights. Attracts a slightly older, fairly smart crowd. The decor is designed by Costus, who was Almodóvar's sidekick. Open daily 7pm till 3am or 4am.

Café Libertad 8 c/Libertad 8; Ⓜ Chueca. The place to go to listen to budding *cantautores* (singer-songwriters). Some big names – including Rosana and Pedro Guerra – started off in this café, which has been going for more than 25 years. Open Mon–Thurs 5pm–2am, Fri 5pm–3am, Sat 7pm–3am & Sun 6pm–1am.

Pepe Botella c/San Andrés 12 – on Plaza Dos de Mayo; Ⓜ Tribunal. Formerly a restaurant, now a relaxed wine bar, with friendly staff, decent music and no fruit machine. Daily 11am–3am, Aug opens at 3pm.

Tupperware c/Corredera Alta de San Pablo 26; Ⓜ Tribunal. *The* place to go for the latest on the indie scene, with a mixture of grunge, Brit pop and old classics from the punk era. Daily 9pm–3.30am.

La Vaca Austera c/Palma 20; Ⓜ Tribunal. American-style rock bar playing punk/indie classics, with pool tables, mixed clientele and friendly atmosphere. Mon–Sat 10pm–3.30am.

Vía Lactea c/Velarde 18; Ⓜ Tribunal. Call in here to see where the *movida* began. *Vía Lactea* was a key meeting place for Spain's designers, directors, pop stars and painters in the 1980s, and it retains its original decor from the time, billiard tables included. Stage downstairs. Young studenty clientele. Daily 8pm–3am.

Salamanca

Alquimia c/Villanueva; Ⓜ Retiro. Lavish Baroque decor in this restaurant-bar-club modelled on an English gentlemen's club. A popular backdrop for media presentations and pop videos.

Teatriz c/Hermosilla 15; Ⓜ Serrano. This former theatre, redesigned by the Catalan, Mariscal, together with Philippe Starck, is as elegant a club/bar as any in Europe. There are bars on the main theatre levels, a restaurant in the stalls and a tapas bar in the circle. Down in the basement there's a library-like area and small disco. Drinks are fairly pricey (€9 for spirits) but there's no entrance charge. Bar 9pm–3am; restaurant 1.30–4.30pm & 9pm–1am; closed Sat lunch, Sun & Aug.

Discotecas

Discotecas – or clubs – aren't always that different from *discobares*, though they tend to be bigger and flashier, with a lot of attention to the lights, sound system and decor, and stay open very late – most until 4am, some till 6am, and a couple till noon. In summer, many of the trendier clubs suspend operations and set up outdoor *terrazas* (see pp.128 & 129).

Sol, Ópera and Plaza de Santa Ana

Joy Madrid c/Arenal 11; Ⓜ Sol. This big-name disco is frequented by musicians, models and media folk, for whom the €15 entry and rigorous door policy hold no fear. If you can't get in – and 3–5am is the hippest time here – console yourself with the *Chocolatería San Ginés* (see below), on the street behind. Open 11.30pm–5.30am, Fri & Sat till 6am.

Kapital c/Atocha 125; Ⓜ Atocha. Seven floors to cater for most tastes in this macro-disco, with two dance floors, a cinema and a top-floor terrace. Open Thurs–Sat midnight–6am.

Palacio de Gaviria c/Arenal 9, Ⓦ www.palacio gaviria.com; Ⓜ Ópera/Sol. Aristocratic, nineteenth-century palace where you can wander through a sequence of extravagant Baroque salons, listen to a chamber concert in the ballroom, watch a live show or simply dance the night away. Entrance is between €9–15 depending on the night of the week and includes a first drink. After this, expect to pay €9 a drink. Daily 11pm–late.

The Room/Mondo at Stella c/Arlabán 7; Ⓜ Sevilla. Stella has undergone a complete makeover but remains a big favourite with the city's serious party goers especially for the *Room* sessions on Fri and Sat. Entrance €9–11 including first drink.

Torero c/Cruz 26; Ⓜ Sol/Sevilla. Very popular and enjoyable two-floored disco right in the heart of the Santa Ana area. Strict door policy. Open Tues–Sat.

Gran Vía

Arena c/Princesa 1; Ⓜ Plaza de España. Big, modern and very popular former cinema. Reggae and funk progresses to house music during the night. Occasional live concerts, too – David Gray and Supergrass are among the artists that have performed here recently. Open Fri & Sat from midnight.

Bash Line Plaza de Callao 4; Ⓜ Callao. There's funk on Wed, disco on Thurs and the OHM club on Fri & Sat, which is popular with a gay crowd. For those with real stamina there's also a Sun night session called "Weekend". Entry around €9.

Chocolate before bed

If you stay up through a Madrid night, then you must try one of the city's great institutions – the **Chocolatería San Ginés** (Tues–Sun 6pm–7.30am) on Pasadizo de San Ginés, off c/del Arenal between the Puerta del Sol and Teatro Real. Established in 1894, this serves *chocolate con churros* to perfection – just the thing after a night's excess. There's an almost mythical *madrileño* custom of winding up at San Ginés after the clubs close (not that they do any longer), before heading home for a shower and then off to work. And why not?

①

Davai c/Flor Baja 1, esq. Gran Vía 59; Ⓜ Santo Domingo/Plaza de España. A two-floor multi-club operating under several different names during the week and catering for a wide range of musical tastes with everything from house to 1970s disco. Open daily 11pm–5am.

El Sol c/Jardines 3; Ⓜ Gran Vía. Hosts around twenty live concerts a month, but continues afterwards (usually from about 1.30am) as a disco playing house, soul and acid jazz. Entry €6–12. Open daily 11.30pm–5am, Fri & Sat till 5.30am.

Chueca and Santa Bárbara

Barnon c/Santa Engracia 17; Ⓜ Alonso Martínez. Posey bar and club popular with *pijas* and *pijos* and at one time a favourite hang-out of Real Madrid footballers. Daily 11pm–late.

Milenio c/Pelayo 59 Ⓦ www.webmilenio.com; Ⓜ Alonso Martínez /Tribunal. Two-floored disco popular with the international crowd. Thurs for pop and dance, with a funky session in the basement, Fri and Sat for Latin and English sounds.

Pachá c/Barceló 11; Ⓜ Tribunal. An eternal survivor on the Madrid disco scene. Once a theatre and still very theatrical, it is exceptionally cool during the week, less so at the weekend when the out-of-towners take over. Good if you like techno and house. Entry €12 with drink. Thurs–Sat midnight–5am.

Out of the centre

Divino Aqualung Paseo del Ermita Santo 48; Ⓜ Puerta del Angel. New disco which promises to "bring the spirit of Ibiza back to Madrid". Six bars, light shows, go-go dancers and a capacity for 2500 people. Entry €9 with drink. Open Fri & Sat midnight–6am, Sun 5pm–midnight.

Macumba Clubbing Estación de Chamartín s/n Ⓦ www.spaceofsound.net; Ⓜ Chamartín. Guest DJs from the Ministry of Sound come for the Saturday *Elite Noche* session at this club on top of the Chamartín train station. If you've still got energy left, the *Space of Sound* "after hours" club will allow you to strut your stuff from 9am on a Sunday. Entry €15.

Performance: music, film and theatre

Most nights in Madrid, you can take in performances of **flamenco**, **salsa**, **rock** (local and imported), **jazz**, **classical music** and **opera** at one or other of the city's venues. Often, it's the smaller, offbeat clubs that are the more enjoyable, though there are plenty of big auditoria – including the football stadiums and bullring – for big-name concerts. In summer, events are supplemented by the council's **Veranos de la Villa** cultural programme and in autumn by the **Festival de Otoño.** These also encompass **theatre** and **film**, both of which have fairly healthy year-round scenes.

Flamenco

Flamenco underwent something of a revival in Madrid in the 1990s, in large part due to the "new flamenco" artists, like Ketama and Joaquín Cortes, who are unafraid to mix it with a bit of blues, jazz, even rock. The city has its own flamenco festival in May, when you can stand a chance of catching some of the bigger names. The club listings below span the range between purist flamenco and crossover experiments and most artists – even major stars – appear in them. Although the following clubs and cafés may open earlier, be aware that in many cases performances won't really get going until around midnight.

Café de Chinitas c/Torija 7 ☎ 915 595 135; Ⓜ Santo Domingo. One of the oldest flamenco clubs in Madrid, with a dinner-dance spectacular. It's expensive but the music is authentic. Reservations are essential, though you may get in late when people start to leave (at this time you

don't have to eat and the steep entrance fee of €27 does at least include your first drink). Open Mon–Sat 9pm–2am.

Candela c/Olmo 2 ☎ 914 673 382; Ⓜ Antón Martín. A legendary bar frequented by musicians – the late, great Camarón de la Isla is reputed to

Listings information is in plentiful supply in Madrid. The newspapers *El País* and *El Mundo* have excellent daily listings, and on Fridays both publish sections devoted to events, bars and restaurants in the capital. Of the two, *El Mundo*'s **Metrópoli** (ⓦ www.metropoli.com) is the better – a separate colour magazine, full of previews and details of the week's exhibitions, films, theatre and concerts, and with extensive listings of clubs, bars and restaurants (including opening hours and average prices – usually on the high side of what you'll spend).

If your time in Madrid doesn't coincide with the Friday *Metrópoli* supplement, or you want maximum info, pick up the weekly listings magazine **Guía del Ocio** (ⓦ www.guiadelocio.com; €1) at any kiosk. The *ayuntamiento* publishes a monthly "What's On" pamphlet, **En Madrid**, which is free from any of the tourist offices and lists forthcoming events in the city, and a useful monthly review magazine, **La Netro**, is available free at most kiosks. *In Madrid* (ⓦ www.in-madrid.com), meanwhile, is a free monthly magazine – available in many bars – which bills itself as "Madrid's English monthly for the Hip, Cool and Transient" and features useful reviews of clubs and bars.

One word that might perplex first-timers in Madrid – and which crops up in all the listings magazines – is **madrugada**. This refers to the hours between midnight and dawn and, in this supremely late-night/early-morning city, is a necessary adjunct to announcements of important events. *Tres de la madrugada* means an event is due to start at 3am.

have sung here until 11am on one occasion. Open Tues–Sun.

Caracol c/Bernadino Obregón 18 ⓣ915 273 594; ⓜEmbajadores. Regular flamenco shows especially in summer, but this venue also hosts a wide range of Latin, African and rock music, so check beforehand. €15 entry which includes a drink.

Cardamomo c/Echegaray 15; ⓜSevilla/Sol. Noisy and fun flamenco bar close to Santa Ana with live acts every Wed and Sun. An unpretentious atmosphere that couldn't be more different from the formal *tablaos*. No entry charge and drinks are standard prices.

Las Carboneras Plaza Conde de Miranda ⓣ915 428 677; ⓜSol. A relative newcomer to the restaurant/*tablao* scene, geared to the tourist market and slightly cheaper than its rivals, but a good alternative if you want to get a taste of flamenco. Open Mon–Sat, shows 9pm & 10.30pm.

Corral de la Morería c/Morería 17 ⓣ 913 658 446, ⓦwww.corraldelamoreria.com; ⓜLa Latina. This is a good venue for some serious acts off the tourist circuit, but again expensive at about €27 for the show plus a drink. Open daily 9pm–2am, Sat opens 10.45pm.

Casa Patas c/Cañizares 10 ⓣ913 690 496; ⓜAntón Martín. Small, but very popular flamenco *tablao* that gets its share of big names. The best nights are Thurs and Fri. Entry €12. Open Mon–Sat 9pm–2am.

La Soleá c/Cava Baja 34 ⓣ913 653 308; ⓜLa Latina. This brilliant, long-established flamenco bar is the genuine article. People sit around in the salon, pick up a guitar or start to sing and gradually the atmosphere builds up until everyone else is clapping or dancing. Has to be seen to be believed. Open Mon–Sat 8.30pm–3am. Closed Aug.

Pop, rock and blues

Madrid is very much on the international rock tour circuit and you can catch big (and small) American and British acts in front of enthusiastic audiences. One of the more endearing Spanish habits is to translate foreign names – including some bands: thus, just as Prince Charles is always known as Príncipe Carlos, U2 are, of course, U-Dos. **Tickets** for most big rock concerts are sold by Madrid Rock, Gran Vía 25 (ⓜCallao), FNAC, c/Preciados 28 (ⓜCallao) and El Corte Inglés, c/ Preciados 1–4 (ⓜSol). For telephone bookings, see ticket agencies in the "Listings" section (p.144).

In the smaller clubs, you have a chance of seeing a very wide range of local bands. Madrid has long been the heart of the Spanish music scene (see "Music" on p.1044).

Clubs

Al Lab'Oratorio c/Colón 14; Ⓜ Tribunal. Famous 1980s bar with very loud rock music on the sound system, and a little stage downstairs where local bands play on Thur and Sat. No entry charge but the drinks are expensive. Open Tues–Sat 9pm–3am.

Chesterfield Café c/Serrano Jover 5 ☎915 422 817; Ⓜ Argüelles. As well as offering Tex-Mex-style food, this club is a live venue (Wed–Sun). Sets begin at midnight (1am on Fri and Sat).

La Coquette c/Arenal 22, entrance at c/Hileras 14; Ⓜ Ópera. Small, smoky blues bar, where people sit around in the near dark watching the band perform on a tiny stage. Live music most nights. Open daily 8pm–2.30am.

Honky Tonk c/Covarrubias 24 ☎914 456 886; Ⓜ Alonso Martínez. Nightly blues and rock sets in this late-opening bar just north of Alonso Martínez.

Maravillas c/San Vicente Ferrer 33 ☎915 233 071; Ⓜ Tribunal. Small but usually uncrowded indie venue where bands play anything from jazz to funk to reggae, often till around 4am.

Siroco c/San Dimás 3 ☎915 933 070; Ⓜ San Bernardo. Live bands most nights at this popular little soul club, not far north of Gran Vía. Closed Sun.

El Sol c/Jardines 3 ☎913 611 184; Ⓜ Sol/Gran Vía. Hosts around twenty live concerts a month; afterwards it continues as a disco. Very good acoustics. Open daily 11.30pm–5am.

Major concert venues

The city's main indoor arena, the **Palacio de Deportes**, was burned down recently so the following venues are likely to feature more frequently when bigger groups complete the Spanish leg of their European tours.

La Cubierta Plaza de Toros de Leganés ☎917 651890; Ⓜ Casa del Reloj. Bullring in the southern industrial suburb of Leganés, often used as a venue for heavy rock artists of the Iron Maiden and Megadeth variety, although for a complete contrast a re-formed Soft Cell also made an appearance not that long ago.

Palacio de Vistalegre Avda. Plaza de Toros Ⓦ www.palaciovistalegre.com; Ⓜ Oporto/Vista Alegre. This covered bullring in the south of the city has become one of the favoured venues of touring groups since the demise of the Palacio de Deportes.

Estadio de la Comunidad de Madrid Avda. de Arcentales s/n ☎917 202 400; Ⓜ Las Musas. Huge sports stadium – known as "La Peineta"

because of the main stand's resemblance to a flamenco dancer's ornamental comb – on the outskirts of the city which has played host to major rock acts like Bon Jovi and Bruce Springsteen.

Plaza de Toros de las Ventas Las Ventas ☎913 562 200 or 917 264 800, Ⓦ www.las-ventas.com; Ⓜ Ventas. The bullring is a pretty good concert venue, put to use in the summer festival. Tickets are usually one price, though you can pay more for a (good) reserved seat (*asiento reservado*).

La Riviera Paseo Bajo Virgen del Puerto s/n, Puente de Segovia ☎913 652 415; Ⓜ Puerta del Ángel. Fun disco and concert venue right next to the river that has hosted Coldplay and Placebo amongst other recent visitors.

Latin music

Madrid attracts big-name Latin artists and if you happen to coincide with the summer festival you'll stand a good chance of catching someone of the stature of Juan Luís Guerra from the Dominican Republic – a huge star in Spain. Gigs by top artists tend to take place at the venues listed above. The local scene is a good deal more low-key but there's enjoyable salsa, nonetheless, in a handful of clubs.

Café del Mercado Ronda de Toledo 1, in the Centro Artesano Puerta de Toledo ☎913 653 786; Ⓜ Puerta de Toledo. Live music every day in a spacious, comfortable club and a *Gran Baile de Salsa* every Fri and Sat at 2am.

Galileo Galilei c/Galileo 100; Ⓜ Islas Filipinas. Bar, concert venue and disco all rolled into one. Latin music is regularly on offer, but you'll need to check the *Guía del Ocio* to find out which night, as it also hosts cabaret, flamenco and singer-songwriters.

Oba-Oba c/Jacometrezo 4; Ⓜ Callao. Samba and lambada with lethal *caiprinhas* from the bar. Daily 11pm–5.30am.

El Son c/ Victoria 6; Ⓜ Sol. Live Cuban music Mon to Thurs at this small Latin club which has picked up where its predecessor Massai left off. There's no space to stand and watch, so make sure you bring your dancing shoes. Open daily 7pm onwards.

Jazz

Madrid doesn't rank with London, Paris or New York on the jazz front but the clubs are friendly, unpretentious places. Look out for the annual jazz festival staged at a variety of venues in November.

Clamores c/Alburquerque 14 ☎914 457 938, Ⓦ www.salaclamores.com; Ⓜ Bilbao. Large, low-key and enjoyable jazz bar with accomplished (if not very famous) artists, not too exorbitant drinks and a nice range of snacks. Sets start at around 10.30pm and the bar stays open to 4am. €3–6 for gigs, otherwise free.

Café Central Plaza del Ángel 10 ☎913 694 143; Ⓜ Sol. Once voted no. 6 in a "Best Jazz Clubs of the World" poll in *Wire* magazine, this is an attractive venue – small and relaxed – and it gets the odd big name, plus strong local talent. The Art Deco café is worth a visit in its own right. €8.50–10.25 for gigs, otherwise free.

Café Jazz Populart c/Huertas 22 ☎914 298 407; Ⓜ Antón Martín. Nightly sets from jazz and blues bands. It's open from 6pm, gets cooking around 11pm and stays open till 2am or so. €6 for gigs, otherwise free.

Segundo Jazz c/Comandante Zorita 8 ☎915 549 437; Ⓜ Nuevos Ministerios. Typical atmospheric basement club with live music during the week only. Last set at 2.15am.

Classical music and opera

The **Teatro Real** is the city's prestigious opera house and, along with the **Auditorio Nacional de Musica**, is home to the Orquesta Nacional de España. Equally enjoyable are the salons and small auditoria for chamber orchestras and groups.

Auditorio Nacional de Música c/Príncipe de Vergara 146 ☎913 370 100, Ⓦ www.auditorio nacional.mcu.es; Ⓜ Cruz del Rayo. This is the home of the Spanish National Orchestra and host to most international visiting orchestras.

Centro de Arte Reina Sofía c/Santa Isabel ☎914 675 062, Ⓦ museoreinasofia.mcu.es; Ⓜ Atocha. This arts centre often has programmes of contemporary music.

La Corrala c/Mesón de Paredes ☎915 309 600; Ⓜ Lavapiés. A surviving tenement block, once typical of working-class Madrid, which stages *zarzuelas* during the *Veranos de la Villa* summer season.

La Fídula c/Huertas 57; Ⓜ Antón Martín. A chamber orchestra plays Wed to Sun nights in this café.

Fundación Juan March c/Castelló 77 ☎914 354 240; Ⓜ Núñez de Balboa. Small auditorium used for recitals two or three times a week.

Teatro Calderón c/Atocha 18 ☎916 320 114; Ⓜ Sol. Venue for a very popular annual opera season – a lot easier to get tickets here than at the Teatro Real.

Teatro Monumental c/Atocha 65 ☎914 298 119; Ⓜ Atocha. A large theatre, offering orchestral concerts, opera, *zarzuela* and flamenco recitals. Tickets are sold for stalls (*butaca de patio*) or a series of dizzying circles (*entresuelo*).

Teatro Real Plaza Isabel II info: ☎915 160 660, box office ☎915 160 606, ticket line ☎903 244 848, Ⓦ www.teatro-real.com; Ⓜ Ópera. Madrid's opulent opera house. Ticket prices range from €12–€150, but you'll need to book well in advance for the best seats.

La Zarzuela c/Jovellanos 4 ☎915 245 400; Ⓜ Sevilla. The main venue for Spanish operetta.

Film

Cines – cinemas – can be found all over the central area and there is a handful of grand old picture houses strung out along the length of the Gran Vía, which still advertise their offerings with the traditional hand-painted posters. These cinemas offer major releases (which often make it here well before London) dubbed into Spanish, though a number of cinemas have regular **original language** screenings, with subtitles; these are listed in a separate *versión original/subtitulada (v.o.)* section in the newspapers. **Tickets** for films cost €5.50–5.75 but most cinemas have a *día del espectador* (usually Mon or Wed) with €4–4.25 admission. Be warned that on Sunday night half of Madrid goes to a movie and queues can be long.

Alphaville, Renoir and **Princesa** c/Martín de los Heros and c/Princesa 3; Ⓜ Plaza de España. This trio of multiscreen cinemas, within 200m of each other, show regular *v.o.* films.

Ideal Yelmo Complex c/Doctor Cortezo 6; Ⓜ Sol/Tirso de Molina. Nine-screen complex which shows a good selection of *v.o.* films.

Filmoteca/Cine Doré c/Santa Isabel 3; Ⓜ Antón Martín. Beautiful old cinema, now home to an art-film centre, with imaginative programmes of classic and contemporary films, all shown in *v.o.* at an

admission price of just €1.35. In summer, there are open-air screenings on a little terraza – they're very popular, so buy tickets in advance.

Luna c/Luna 2; Ⓜ Callao. Four-screen cinema showing some of the latest releases (often in *v.o.*) located in a grim-looking square just north of the Gran Vía.

Pequeño Cine Estudio c/Magellanes 2; Ⓜ Quevedo/San Bernardo. Small independent cinema that specializes in screening classic films in *v.o.*

Theatre and cabaret

Madrid is enjoying a renaissance in theatre; you can catch anything from Lope de Vega to contemporary and experimental productions, and there's also a new wave of cabaret and comedy acts. Look out, too, for the annual *Festival de Otoño* running from September to November, and the alternative theatre festival in February.

Berlin Cabaret Costanilla de San Pedro 11 ☎ 913 662 034; Ⓜ La Latina. Varied cabaret and comedy in a traditional, slightly seedy club setting. Admission is normally free, but drinks are expensive. Open Mon–Sat 11pm–5am, Fri & Sat till 6am.

Centro Cultural de la Villa Plaza de Colón ☎ 914 800 300; Ⓜ Colón. Arts centre where you're likely to see some of the more experimental companies on tour as well as popular works and *zarzuela* performances.

Teatro de la Abadía c/Fernández de los Ríos 42 ☎ 914 481 181, 🌐 www.teatroabadia.com; Ⓜ Quevedo/Argüelles. Beautifully decorated theatre set in pleasant grounds just off the main street. It has staged some very successful productions and is especially popular in the *Festival de Otoño*.

Teatro de Bellas Artes and Círculo de Bellas Artes c/Marqués de Riera 2 ☎ 915 324 437, Círculo 913 605 400; Ⓜ Banco de España. A beautiful old theatre with a reputation for quality, while

the Círculo has a theatre staging more adventurous productions.

Teatro de la Comedia c/Príncipe 14 ☎ 915 214 931; Ⓜ Sol/Sevilla. Grand old theatre hosting classical productions.

Teatro Español c/Príncipe 25 ☎ 913 601 480; Ⓜ Sol/Sevilla. Classic Spanish theatre on the site of one of the city's old corrales.

Teatro de Madrid Avda. de la Ilustración s/n ☎ 917 301 750; Ⓜ Barrio del Pilar. Large, modern theatre next to the large La Vaguada shopping centre in the north of the city, presenting some excellent ballet, drama and touring cultural shows.

Teatro María Guerrero c/Tamayo y Baus 4 ☎ 913 194 769/913 101 500; Ⓜ Colón. This is the headquarters of the Centro Dramático Nacional which stages high-quality Spanish and international productions in a beautiful neo-Mudéjar interior.

Teatro Nuevo Apolo Plaza Tirso de Molina 1 ☎ 913 690 637; Ⓜ Tirso de Molina. Madrid's principal venue for major musicals.

Children

Many of the main sights may lack children-specific services or activities, but there's plenty to keep children occupied for a short stay. There are various parks – the Retiro being a particular favourite – and a host of well-attended public swimming pools (see Directory, p.144). Children are, in general, doted on in Spain and welcome in nearly all cafés and restaurants. Below are just a few places that might appeal.

Imax Madrid Parque Tierno Galván ⓦ www.imax madrid.com; Ⓜ Méndez Alvaro. Three different types of screen showing natural history-style features in Spanish at this futuristic cinema. Entrance prices vary €5.90–7. Continuous shows: Mon–Fri 11.20am–1pm & 3.45pm–1am, Sat & Sun 11.20am–2.15pm & 3.45pm–1am.

Planetario Parque Tierno Galván ☎ 914 673 461, ⓦ www.planetmad.es; Ⓜ éndez Álvaro. Exhibition halls, audiovisual displays and projections on a variety of astronomical themes (all in Spanish). €3, under-14s €1.20. Tues–Sun 11am–1.45pm & 5–7.45pm.

Museo de Cera (Wax Museum) Paseo de Recoletos 41 ☎ 913 080 825, ⓦ www.museocera-madrid.com; Ⓜ Colón. Expensive and tacky, but nevertheless popular with children. There's also a chamber of horrors and a film history of Spain, for which you pay a supplement. €9, under-10s & over-65s €6, under-4s free. Mon–Fri 10am–2.30pm & 4.30–8.30pm, Sat, Sun & holidays 10am–8.30pm.

Museo del Ferrocarril Paseo de las Delicias 61 ☎ 902 228 822, ⓦ www.museodelferrocarril.org; Ⓜ Delicias. An impressive collection of engines, carriages and wagons that once graced the railway lines of Spain. Also home to a fascinating collection of model railways and there's an atmospheric little cafeteria housed in one of the more elegant carriages. €3.50, under-12s €2, under-4s free. Tues–Thurs 10am–5pm, Fri–Sun 10am–3pm.

Zoo–Aquarium Casa de Campo ☎ 917 119 950, ⓦ www.zoomadrid.com; Ⓜ Casa de Campo/Batán/bus #33. There are over 2000 different species, including a new pair of koalas and venomous snakes, plus an impressive aquarium, a children's zoo and parrot show. €12.15, under-7s €9.80, under-3s free. Daily 10am–dusk.

Faunia Avda. de las Comunidades 28 ☎ 913 016 210, ⓦ www.faunia.es; Ⓜ Valdebernardo, bus #130, 8, 71; special buses from Ⓜ Pavones on Sat, Sun & hols. An innovative nature park providing an entertaining and educational experience for children of all ages, recreating a series of ecosystems to provide a home to 720 different animal species. Highlights are the Arctic dome with its penguins and the storms in the indoor tropical rainforest. €17.50, Under-10s €12, under-3s free. Daily 10.30am–9pm.

Parque de Atracciones Casa de Campo ☎ 915 268 030 or 914 632 900, ⓦ www.parquede atracciones.es; Ⓜ Batán/bus #33 & #65. A theme park packed full of rides, whose attractions include the 63-metre vertical drop (*la lanzadera*), the whitewater raft ride, *los rápidos*, and the haunted mansion, *el viejo caserón*. Access only €5, €20.90 for a day ticket, which includes most rides, children €11.80. July & Aug daily noon–midnight, Fri & Sat till 2am; Sept–June daily noon–11pm, Sat till 1am.

Warner Brothers Movie World San Martín de la Vega. Carretera Andalucía (N-IV) km 22. ☎ 918 211 234, ⓦ www.warnerbrospark.com. Trains from Atocha every half hour, change at Pinto. All-American amusement park divided into five different themed areas, each with its own set of rides and Warner Bros characters. The rollercoasters, raft rides and the 40-metre-high free-fall tower are undeniably impressive, but queues are lengthy, the entrance fee hefty and it's a long way out of town. €32, under-12s €24, under-3s free. Open April–May Thurs–Sun, June–Sept daily, Oct–Nov Fri–Sun: weekdays 10am–8pm, weekends & hols 10am–midnight, but subject to variations.

Shopping

Shopping districts in Madrid are pretty defined. The biggest range of stores is along Gran Vía and around Puerta del Sol, which is where the **department stores** – such as El Corte Inglés – have their main branches. For **fashion** (*moda*), the smartest addresses are calles Serrano, Goya, Ortega y Gasset and Velázquez in the Salamanca *barrio*, while more alternative designers are to be found in Malasaña and Chueca (c/Almirante, especially). For street fashion there's plenty on offer in and around c/Fuencarral. The **antiques** trade is centred down towards the Rastro, on and around c/Ribera de Curtidores, or in the Puerta de Toledo shopping centre, while for **general weirdness**, it's hard to beat the shops just off Plaza Mayor, where luminous saints rub shoulders with surgical supports and fascist memorabilia. The cheapest, trashiest **souvenirs** can be collected at the Todo a un euro ("Everything for a euro") shops scattered all over the city. If you want international shops or some of the more

Opening hours and late-night shopping

Usual **opening hours** are Monday–Friday 9.30am–2pm & 5–8pm, Saturday 10am–2pm. Most shops are closed on Sunday, but the larger stores do open on the first Sunday of each month (not in Aug) and those selling "cultural" goods such as books, CDs and videos are allowed to open every day. There are, however, two chains of late-night shops – Vip's and 7 Eleven – that stay open into the small hours and on Sundays. Branches sell newspapers, cigarettes, booze, groceries, books, CDs – all the things you need to pop in for at 3am. Larger branches also have café-restaurants, one-hour photo developing and other services.

popular chain stores head for Madrid 2, a large shopping centre next to ⓜBarrio de Pilar. There is a smaller, more upmarket (and more expensive) mall at ABC Serrano at c/Serrano 61 and Paseo de la Castellana 34 (ⓜRubén Darío).

Most areas of the city have their own *mercados del barrio* – indoor **markets**, devoted mainly to food. Among the best and most central are those in Plaza San Miguel (just west of Plaza Mayor); La Cebada in Plaza de la Cebada (ⓜLa Latina); and Antón Martín in c/Santa Isabel (ⓜAntón Martín). The city's biggest market is, of course, **El Rastro** – the flea market – which takes place on Sundays in La Latina, south of Plaza Mayor. For details of this great Madrid institution, see the box on p.94.

Other specialized markets include a second-hand **book market** on the Cuesta de Moyano, near Atocha station (see p.107), and the stamp and coin markets in Plaza Mayor on Sundays.

Crafts and miscellaneous

Alvarez Gómez c/Serrano 14 ⓦwww.alvarez-gomez.com; ⓜSerrano. Gómez has been making the same perfumes in the same bottles for the past century. The scents – carnations, roses, violets – are as simple and straight as they come. Mon–Sat 10am–2pm & 5–8.30pm. There is a more central branch at c/Sevilla 2 (Mon–Sat 10am–8.30pm).

El Arco de los Cuchilleros Plaza Mayor 9; ⓜSol. The location of this shop may be at the heart of tourist Madrid but the goods are a far cry from the swords, lace and castanets that fill most shops in the area. El Arco handles thirty or so workshops and artisans, who reflect Spanish *artesanía* at its most innovative and contemporary. They encompass ceramics (six of Madrid's top potters), leather (from Oviedo), wood (including some fine games), jewellery and textiles. Mon–Sat 11am–8pm, Sun 11am–2.30pm.

Area Real Madrid c/Carmen 3; ⓜSol. Newly opened club store just off Sol where you can pick up replica shirts and all manner of – expensive – souvenirs related to the club's history. There are smaller branches in the shopping centre on the corner of Real's Bernabéu stadium at c/Concha Espina 1 and at Gate 3 of the stadium itself (ⓜSantiago Bernabéu).

Conde Hermanos c/Felipe II 2; ⓜÓpera (Mon–Fri 9.30am–1.30pm & 4.30–8pm) & **José Ramírez**, c/Concepción Jerónima ⓜSol/Tirso de Molina (Mon–Fri 9.30am–2pm & 5–8pm, Sat 10am–2pm). Two of the most renowned guitar workshops in Spain; the latter even has a museum of antique instruments. Prices start at around €110 and head skywards for the quality models and fancy woods.

El Flamenco Vive c/Unión 4; ⓜÓpera. Specializes in all things Andalucian; flamenco music, guitars, percussion, dance accessories, books etc. Mon–Sat 10.30am–2pm & 5–9pm.

Fútbol Total c/Eloy Gonzalo 7; ⓜQuevedo & Estación de Trenes Charmartín. Just the place to get your Real, Atlético or even Rayo shirt. In fact the strip of practically every Spanish team is available, for around €50. Mon–Sat: July–Sept 10.30am–2pm & 5.30–8.30pm; Oct–June 10.30am–2pm & 5–9pm.

Intermon c/Alberto Aguilera 15; ⓜArgüelles. Arts and crafts from Asia, Africa and South America. Some of the profits are invested in development programmes. Mon–Sat 10am–2pm & 5–8pm.

Casa Jiménez c/Preciados 42; ⓜCallao. If you want to buy a fan that's a work of art, this is the place to come. Mon–Sat 10am–1.30pm & 5–8pm, closed Sat pm in July and all day Sat in Aug.

Palomeque c/Hileras 12; Ⓜ Ópera. A religious department store stocking everything from rosary beads and habits to your very own plastic baby Jesus. If you want to complete your postcard collection of Spanish saints and virgins, this is the place for you. Mon–Fri 10am–2pm & 5–8pm, Sat 10am–2pm.

Puck c/Duque de Sesto 30; Ⓜ Goya. This is the best – indeed, about the only really decent – toyshop in central Madrid. Mon–Sat 10am–1.30pm & 4.30–8pm.

Puerta de Toledo shopping centre Ⓜ Puerta de Toledo. This centre has several shops specializing in antiques, jewellery and crafts. Closed Mon.

Seseña c/Cruz 23; Ⓜ Sol. Tailor specializing in traditional *madrileño* capes for royalty and celebrities. Clients have included Luis Buñuel and Gary Cooper. Mon–Sat 10am–1.30pm & 4.30–8pm.

Casa Yustas Plaza Mayor 30 Ⓦ www.casa yustas.com; Ⓜ Sol. Madrid's oldest hat shop, established in 1894. Pick from traditional designs for men's and women's hats (*sombreros*), caps (*gorras*) and berets (*boinas*). No cards. Mon–Sat 9.30am–9.30pm, Sun & holidays 11am–9.30pm.

Books, comics and maps

Casa del Libro Gran Vía 29 & Maestro Victoria 3; Ⓜ Callao. The city's biggest bookstore, with three floors covering just about everything, including a wide range of fiction in English. Mon–Sat 9.30am–9.30pm.

Desnivel Plaza Matute 6 Ⓦ www.libreriadesnivel.com; Ⓜ Antón Martín. This centrally located bookshop stocks a good range of guides and maps covering mountaineering in all parts of Spain.

FNAC c/Preciados 28; Ⓜ Callao. The book department of this huge store is a good place to sit and peruse books and magazines in all languages.

Librería Antonio Machado c/Fernando VI 17; Ⓜ Alonso Martínez. The city's best literary bookshop. Mon–Sat 10am–2pm & 5–8pm.

Pasajes c/Genova 3 Ⓔ pasajes@infornet.es; Ⓜ Alonso Martínez/Colón. Specializes in English and foreign-language books. Also has a useful noticeboard service for flat-sharing and Spanish classes. Mon–Fri 10am–2pm & 5–8pm, Sat 10am–2pm.

La Tienda Verde c/Maudes 23 & 38; Ⓜ Cuatro Caminos. Trekking and mountain books, guides and survey (*topográfico*) maps. Mon–Sat 9.30am–2pm & 4.30–8pm.

Fashion: clothes and shoes

Branches of chain stores such as Mango, Zara, Cortefiel and Springfield are scattered all over the city and at sale times in January and July there are often some great bargains to be picked up. If your tastes run to the more select in the fashion stakes try some of the shops listed below.

Adolfo Domínguez c/José Ortega y Gasset 4 & c/Serrano 96; Ⓜ Serrano. The classic modern Spanish look – subdued colours, free lines. Domínguez's designs are quite pricey but he has a cheaper *Basico* range. Both branches have men's clothes; women's are only available at the Ortega y Gasset branch. Mon–Sat 10am–2pm & 5–8.30pm (Serrano branch open at lunchtime).

Agatha Ruiz de la Prada c/Marqués de Riscal 8; Ⓜ Rubén Darío. Outlet for the striking clothes and accessories of this *movida* designer. Mon–Fri 10am–2pm & 5–8pm, Sat 10am–2pm.

Ararat c/Conde Xiquena 13 & c/Almirante 10 & 11; Ⓜ Chueca. A trio of shops with clubby Spanish and foreign designs at reasonably modest prices. Men's clothes in c/Conde Xiquena, women's in c/Almirante. Mon–Sat 11am–2pm & 5–8.30pm.

Berlín c/Almirante 10; Ⓜ Chueca. Women's clothes from vanguard European designers. Mon–Sat 11am–2pm & 5–8.30pm.

Blackmarket c/Colón 3; Ⓜ Chueca. Adventurous clothes for women. Mon–Sat 10.30am–2pm & 5–8.30pm.

Camper c/Gran Vía 54; Ⓜ Callao. Spain's best shoe-shop chain, with covetable designs at modest prices. There are lots of other branches around the city. Mon–Sat 10am–2pm & 5–8.30pm.

Caracol Cuadrado c/Justiniano 6; Ⓜ Serrano. Bargain store selling last season's designs from big names, including Sybilla – Spain's trendiest designer. Men and women. Mon–Sat 10.30am–2.30pm & 5–8.30pm.

Ekseptión c/Velázquez 28; Ⓜ Velázquez. A dramatic walkway gives onto some of the most *moderno* clothes in Madrid, from Sybilla and Antoni Miró, among others. Expensive. Men and women. Mon–Sat 10.30am–2.30pm & 5–8.30pm.

Excrupulus Net c/Almirante 7; Ⓜ Chueca. Groovy shoes from Spanish designers, Muxart and Looky. Men and women. Mon–Sat 11am–2pm & 5–8.30pm.

Glam c/Fuencarral 35; Ⓜ Gran Vía/Chueca & c/Hortaleza 62 Ⓜ Chueca. The clientele and the clothes wouldn't look out of place in an Almodóvar film. Mon–Sat 10am–2pm & 5–9pm.

Hernanz c/Toledo 18; ⓜTirso de Molina. This shoe shop stocks *alpargatas* – espadrilles – in just about every imaginable colour. No cards. Mon–Fri 9.30am–1.30pm & 5–8.30pm, Sat 9.30am–1.30pm.

Josep Font-Luz D'az c/Serrano 58 – patio; ⓜSerrano. Beautiful, minimalist shop, selling original and expensive women's designs by this young and *muy de moda* Catalan duo. Women only. Mon–Sat 10am–2pm & 5–8.30pm.

Manuel Herrero c/Preciados 7; ⓜSol. Traditional shop specializing in leather; particularly good for coats and jackets.

Sybilla c/Jorge Juan 12; ⓜRetiro. Sybilla was Spain's top designer of the 1980s – a Vivienne Westwood of Madrid, if you will. She remains at the forefront of the scene, and her prices show it. Women only. All cards. Mon–Sat 10am–2pm & 4.30–8.30pm.

Food and drink

Casa Mira Carrera de San Jerónimo 30; ⓜSol. Old, established *pasteleria*, selling delicious *turrón*, *mazapán*, *frutas glaseadas*, and the like. Daily 10am–2pm & 5–9pm.

Lhardy Carrera de San Jerónimo 8; ⓜSol. This bar and deli is attached to one of Madrid's top restaurants – and is a lot more affordable. You can put together wonderful and elaborate picnics (the *croquetas* and *empanadillas* are legendary), assuming you can resist consuming them on the spot. Mon–Sat 9.30am–3pm & 5–9pm, Sun 9am–2pm.

Mallorca c/Serrano 6; ⓜSerrano. The main branch of Madrid's best deli chain – like *Lhardy*, a pricey but fabulous treasure trove for picnics, or cakes or chocs for presents. All branches have small bars for drinks and canapés. Daily 9.30am–9pm.

La Mallorquina Puerta del Sol 2; ⓜSol. Wonderful-smelling pastry shop and café selling everything you've always been told not to eat. Mon–Sat 9am–9.45pm.

Mariano Aguado c/Echegaray 19; ⓜSevilla. Fine selection of Spanish wines and, especially, sherries (*vinos de Jerez*). Mon–Sat 9.30am–2pm & 5.30–8.30pm.

Mariano Madrueño c/Postigo San Martín 3; ⓜCallao. The place to get wines and liqueurs such as *Pacharán* sloe gin. Mon–Fri 9.30am–2pm & 5–8pm, Sat 9.30am–2pm.

Reserva y Cata c/Conde de Xiquena 13 ⓦwww.reservaycata.com; ⓜColón/Chueca. Well-informed staff at this friendly specialist shop will help you select from some of the best new wines in the Iberian peninsula. Mon–Fri 11am–2.30pm, Sat 11am–2.30pm. Also branch at c/Ramiro II 7; ⓜRíos Rosas.

Tienda Olivarero c/Mejia Lequerica 1; ⓜAlonso Martínez. Outlet for olive growers' cooperative, with information sheets to guide you towards purchasing the best olive oils. Mon–Sat 9.30am–2pm & 5.30–7.30pm.

Records and CDs

FNAC c/Preciados 28; ⓜCallao. Large French store with a huge collection of cassettes and CDs.

Madrid Rock Gran Vía 25; ⓜGran Vía. A big, slightly chaotic store, good for rock CDs and concert tickets. Daily 10am–10pm.

La Metralleta Plaza de San Martín; ⓜÓpera. Down the steps on the edge of the plaza, *La Metralleta* buys and sells CDs, records, film posters, calendars and anything connected with the entertainment industry. Lots of bargains and a good place to find the more obscure stuff. Mon–Sat 10am–2.30pm & 4.30–8.30pm.

Children

Bazar Mila Gran Vía 33; ⓜGran Vía. Packed toy shop that is just the place to get your Spanish set of Monopoly or plastic models of Real and Atlético players.

Mothercare Madrid 2, La Vaguada, Avda. Monforte de Lemos; ⓜBarrio del Pilar. As you would expect, you'll find a wide range of clothes and every accessory you might conceivably require for a young child. Branch c/Claudio Coello 44 (ⓜSerrano).

Prénatal c/ Fuencarral 17; ⓜQuevedo, c/San Bernardo 97–99; ⓜSan Bernardo & Madrid 2, La Vaguada; Avda. Monforte de Lemos; ⓜBarrio del Pilar. Spanish equivalent of Mothercare with more branches around the city and often a little cheaper.

Listings

Airlines Aer Lingus ℡915 414 216, ⓦwww
.aerlingus.ie; Air Europa ℡902 401 501,
ⓦwww.air-europa.com; Air France ℡901 112
266, 913 300 440, ⓦwww.airfrance.com;
American Airlines ℡901 100 000, 914 531 400,
ⓦwww.aa.com; British Airways ℡902 111 333,
913 769 666, ⓦwww.britishairways.com; British
Midland ⓦwww.flybmi.com; Easyjet ℡902 299
992, ⓦwww.easyjet.com; Iberia ℡915 878 156 or
902 400 500, ⓦwww.iberia.com; KLM ℡902 222
747, 912 478 100, ⓦwww.klm.com. The Iberojet
counter at the airport sells discounted seats on all
scheduled flights, if you're prepared to queue up
and take the risk of not getting on. Tickets for the
Puente Aéreo to Barcelona are available in
Terminal 2.

Banks and exchange The main Spanish banks
are concentrated on c/Alcalá and Gran Vía.
Opening hours are normally Mon–Fri 9am–2pm,
but they're also often open on Sat 9am–1pm from
Oct to May. International banks include: Bank of
America, c/Capitán Haya 1 ℡915 555 000,
ⓜSantiago Bernabéu; Barclays, Plaza de Colón 1
℡914 102 800, ⓜColón; Citibank, c/José Ortega
y Gasset 29 ℡914 355 190, ⓜNúñez de Balboa;
and Lloyds, c/Serrano 90 ℡915 767 000,
ⓜNúñez de Balboa. In addition to the banks,
branches of El Corte Inglés department store all
have exchange offices with long hours and highly
competitive rates; the most central is on Puerta del
Sol. Barajas airport has a 24-hr currency exchange
office. Although they don't usually charge commission, the rates at the exchange bureaux scattered
throughout the city are often very poor. Western
Union, Gran Vía (℡ 914 428 180 or 900 633 633;
ⓜ Gran Vía) provides money transfer services.

Bicycles Madrid is a bike-unfriendly city, but
determined cyclists should try Calmera, c/Atocha
98 ℡915 277 574 (Mon–Sat 9.30am–1.30pm &
4.30–8pm; ⓜAntón Martín) and Karacol at
c/Tortosa 8, nr Atocha ℡915 399 633 (Mon–Fri
10.30am–2pm & 5.30–8pm, Sat 10.30am–2pm;
ⓜAtocha). For bike tours outside Madrid get in
touch with ⓦwww.bravobike.com.

Bullfights Madrid's main Plaza de Toros, the monumental Las Ventas (c/Alcalá 237; ⓜVentas),
hosts some of the year's most prestigious events,
especially during the May San Isidro festivities,
though the main season runs from March to
October. Tickets (prices range from about
€3.50–110) are available at the box office at
Ventas (℡917 264 800 or 913 562 200,
ⓦwww.las-ventas.com; March–Oct Fri & Sat

10am–2pm & 5–8pm, from 10am on day of fight),
the Caja Madrid ticket line ℡902 488 488 or at
Localidades de Galicia (℡915 312 732 or 915
319131, ⓦwww.eol.es/lgalicia); at the latter you
pay around fifty percent more than the printed
prices, which are for season tickets sold en bloc.
There is a second bullring in the suburb of
Carabanchel (c/Utebo 1; ℡914 220 780/1; ⓜVista
Alegre), about 4km to the southwest of the centre.

Car rental Major operators have branches at the
airport and train stations. Central offices include:
Atesa, Atocha ℡915 061 846/47,
ⓦwww.atesa.com, ⓜAtocha Renfe; Avis, Gran Vía
60 ℡915 472 048, reservations ℡902 135 531,
ⓦwww.avisworld.com, ⓜPlaza de España;
Europcar, c/San Leonardo 8 ℡917 211 222, 901
102 020, ⓦwww.europcar.com, ⓜPlaza de
España – also an office in Atocha station; and
Hertz, Atocha station ℡914 681 318, 917 330
400, ⓦwww.hertz.com, ⓜAtocha. Easy-Rent-a-
Car, c/Agustín de Foxa 27, Parking Centro Norte
and Parking Garage Ruiz (1st floor), Ronda de
Atocha 12, ℡0906 586 0586 (telephone bookings
available from Britain only), ⓦwww.easycar.com,
ⓜChamartín.

Disabled access Madrid is not particularly well
geared up for the disabled (minusválidos), although
the situation is gradually improving. The
Organizacíon Nacional de Ciegos de España (ONCE)
at c/Prado 24 (℡915 894 600 or 915 773 756,
ⓦwww.once.es) provides good specialist advice,
as does the Federación de Asociaciones de
Minusválidos Físicos de la Comunidad de Madrid
(FAMMA) c/Galileo 69 (℡915 933 550,
ⓦwww.famma.org; ⓜ Quevedo).Wheelchair-
adapted taxis can be ordered from Radio Taxi
(℡915 478 200).

Embassies Australia, Plaza Descubridor Diego
Ordás 3 ℡914 419 300, ⓦwww.embaustralia.es,
ⓜRíos Rosas; Britain, c/Fernando el Santo 16
℡913 190 200, ⓦwww.ukinspain.com, ⓜAlonso
Martínez; British Consulate c/Marqués Ensenada
16 ℡915 085 300; Canada, c/Núñez de Balboa 35
℡914 314 300, ⓦwww.canada-es.org, ⓜNúñez
de Balboa; Ireland, Paseo de la Castellana 46
℡913 190 200, ⓜRubén Dario; New Zealand,
Plaza Lealtad 2 ℡915 230 226, ⓜBanco de
España; US, c/Serrano 75 ℡915 774 000,
ⓦwww.embusa.es, ⓜRubén Darío.

Emergencies For police, medical services and the
fire brigade call ℡112.

Hospitals The most central hospitals are: El
Clínico, Plaza de Cristo Rey ℡913 303 747,

Moncloa; Hospital Gregorio Marañon, c/Dr Esquerdo 46 ℡915 868 000, Ⓜ O'Donnell; and Ciudad Sanitaria La Paz, Paseo de la Castellana 261 ℡913 582 831, Ⓜ Diego de León. First aid stations are scattered throughout the city and open 24hr a day: one of the most central is at c/Navas de Tolosa 10 ℡915 210 025, Ⓜ Callao. English-speaking doctors are available at the Anglo-American Medical Unit, c/Conde de Aranda 1 ℡914 351 823, Ⓜ Retiro; Mon–Fri 9am–8pm, Sat 10am–3pm.

Internet access The best equipped and most central Internet cafés are: *Bbigg*, c/Alcalá 21 ℡916 647 700, ⓦwww.BBIGG.com; Ⓜ Sevilla; *Easy Everything*, c/Montera 10–12 ⓦwww.easyeverything.com; Ⓜ Sol; open 24 hrs; and *Ono.com*, Gran Vía 59 24 hrs; ℡915 474 930; Ⓜ Plaza de España. Prices range from €1.20–3.50 per hour.

Language schools Madrid has numerous language schools, offering intensive courses in Spanish language (and culture). One of the most established is International House, c/Zurbano 8 ℡913 101 314, ⓦwww.lhmadrid.es; Ⓜ Alonso Martínez.

Laundry Central *lavanderías* include: c/Barco 26 (Ⓜ Gran Vía); c/Cervantes 1–3 (Ⓜ Sol); c/Donoso Cortés 17 (Ⓜ Quevedo); c/Hermosilla 121 (Ⓜ Goya); and c/Palma 2 (Ⓜ Tribunal).

Left luggage If you want to leave your bags there are *consignas* at Barajas airport between terminals 1 and 2, the Estación Sur, the Conde de Casal bus station, and lockers at Atocha and Chamartín train stations.

Pharmacies *Farmácias* are distinguished by a green cross; each district has a rota with one staying open through the night – for details ℡098 (Spanish only) or check the notice on the door of your nearest pharmacy or the listings magazines. Madrid also has quite a number of traditional herbalists, best known of which is Maurice Mességue, c/Goya 64 (Ⓜ Goya; Mon–Fri 10am–2pm & 5–8pm, Sat 10am–2pm).

Police If you've had something stolen call ℡900 100 333 (English spoken). In an emergency call ℡112. For reporting crimes see p.57 on "Safety and Crime". Centrally located police stations (*comisarías*) are at c/Luna 29 (℡915 211 236, Ⓜ Callao) and c/Huertas 76 (℡912 490 994; Ⓜ Antón Martín).

Post office The main one is the Palacio de Comunicaciones in the Plaza de las Cibeles (Mon–Sat 8am–midnight, 8.30am–9.30pm, Sun 8am–2.30pm; Mon–Fri 9am–8pm, Sat 9am–2pm for *Lista de Correos* – poste restante). The easiest places to buy stamps are the *estancos*, recogniza-

ble by their brown and yellow signs bearing the word *Tabacos*.

Skiing There is skiing in the Sierra Guadarrama at Valdesqui (℡918 523 94, ⓦwww.valdesqui.es) and Navacerrada (℡918 523 302, 918 521 435, ⓦwww.puertonavacerrada.com). Reckon on between €22–30 for a day lift pass. There is also a huge dry ski slope at the Xanadú entertainment and shopping complex at Arroyomolinos, ctra NV, km 23.5; ℡902 263 026, ⓦwww.madridxanadu.com.

Swimming pools and aquaparks The Piscina Canal Isabel II, Avda. de Filipinas 54 (daily 10am–8.30pm; Ⓜ Ríos Rosas), is a large and well-maintained outdoor swimming pool, and the best central option. Alternatively, try the open-air *piscina* in the Casa de Campo (daily 10am–8.30pm; Ⓜ El Lago). Both these pools have café-bars attached. Also worth trying are the pools at Barrio del Pilar, Avda. Monforte de Lemos (Ⓜ Barrio del Pilar/Begoña), and La Elipa, Parque de la Elipa, c/O'Donnell s/n (Ⓜ Estrella). There are also a number of aquaparks around Madrid. The closest is Aquamadrid 16km out on the N2 Barcelona road (Bus Continental Auto #281, #282, #282, or #385 from Avda. de América). Note that the "swimming season" is from May to September, so outside these months most outdoor pools are closed.

Telephones International calls can be made from any phone box or from any *locutorio*. The main *telefónica* office at Gran Vía 30 (Ⓜ Gran Vía) has ranks of phones and is open until midnight. Phone cards cost €5 or €10, €15 and €20 and can be bought at post offices or *estancos*.

Ticket agencies For theatre and concert tickets try: Tele-Entradas, a telephone booking service run by BBVA ℡902 150 025, ⓦwww.bbvaticket.com; Caja de Cataluña ℡902 101 212; Caja de Madrid ℡902 488 488; Caixa Catalunya/Tele Entrada ℡902 101 212; El Corte Inglés ℡902 400 222, ⓦwww.elcorteingles.es; FNAC, c/Preciados 28 ℡915 956 100; Ⓜ Callao; Madrid Rock, Gran Vía 25 ℡915 236 652; Ⓜ Gran Vía; and Servi-Caixa ℡902 332 211. Localidades Galicia, Plaza del Carmen 1 ℡915 312 732 or 915 319131, ⓦwww.eol.es/lgalicia; Ⓜ Sol, sells tickets for football games, bullfights, theatres and concerts.

Travel agencies Víajes Zeppelin, Plaza Santo Domingo 2 (℡915 477 904; Ⓜ Santo Domingo), are English-speaking, very efficient and offer some excellent deals on flights and holidays. Nuevas Fronteras, c/Luisa Fernanda 2 (℡915 423 990; Ⓜ Ventura Rodríguez), and in the Torre de Madrid, Plaza de España (℡912 474 200) can be good for flights, or try Top Tours, c/Capitán Haja 20 (℡915

550 604; Ⓜ Cuzco). The popular high-street agencies Halcón Viajes and Viajes Marsans have branches scattered all over the city. For student and youth travel try TIVE, c/Fernando el Católico 88 (Ⓣ 915 430 208; Ⓜ Moncloa) or Asatej at c/Fernando el Católico 60; Ⓜ Moncloa). Many other travel agents are concentrated on and around the Gran Vía and c/Princesa.

Women's groups The best places to make contact are at the Centro de La Mujer, c/del Barquillo 44, 1º (Ⓣ 913 193 689; Ⓜ Chueca), and at Madrid's feminist bookshop, the Librería de Mujeres, c/San Cristóbal 17, just east of Plaza Mayor (Ⓣ 915 217 043; Ⓜ Sol).

Travel details

Trains

For information on booking tickets see p.30.

Atocha Station (Ⓜ Atocha): Alcalá de Henares (every 20 mins; 30min); Algeciras (2 daily; 6–10hr); Almería (1–2 daily; 6hr 45min); Aranjuez (every 15/30min; 40min); Badajoz (4 daily; 5hr 40min–7hr); Cáceres (6 daily; 3hr 20min–5hr); Cádiz (2 daily; 5hr); Ciudad Real (20 daily; 50min–1hr); Córdoba (23–29 daily; 2hr 20min; 1hr 40min AVE); Cuenca (4 daily; 2hr 30min); Granada (2 daily; 6hr); Huelva (1 daily; 4hr 50min); Jaén (3 daily; 4hr 10min); Jerez (2 daily; 4hr 10min); Málaga (7 daily; 4hr 10min); Mérida (5 daily; 4hr 10min–4hr 50min); Sevilla (15 daily; 3hr 25min; 2hr 30min AVE); Toledo (9 daily, 1hr 15min); Valencia (12 daily; 3hr 30min). Plus most destinations in the south and west.

Chamartín (Ⓜ Chamartín): A Coruña (2 daily; 8hr 30min–10hr); Albacete (22 daily; 2hr–2hr 20min); Alicante (7 daily; 4hr); Ávila (20 daily; 1hr 20min–2hr 10min); Barcelona (7 daily; 7–9hr); Bilbao (2–3 daily; 6hr–8hr 45min); Burgos (6 daily; 3hr 10min–4hr); Cartagena (4 daily; 5hr); Ferrol (1 daily; 11hr); Gijón (3 daily, 6hr 15min–9hr); Guadalajara (every 30min; 1hr); Huesca (1 daily; 5hr); León (7 daily; 4hr–4hr 30min); Lisbon (1 daily; 9hr 30min); Lleida (4 daily; 5hr); Lugo (1 daily; 8hr 30min); Oviedo (3 daily; 6–8hr); Pamplona (2 daily; 4hr 30min); Paris (1 daily; 13hr 30min); Pontevedra (2 daily; 8hr 30min–10hr); Salamanca (5 daily; 2hr 30min); San Sebastián (3 daily; 6hr 30min); Santander (3 daily; 5hr 30min); Santiago (2 daily; 7hr 15min–9hr 30min); Segovia (9 daily; 1hr 50min–2hr); Valladolid (3 daily; 2hr 30min); Vigo (2 daily; 7hr 50min–10hr); Vitoria (7 daily, 4hr 30min–6hr); Zamora (2 daily; 3hr–3hr 20min); Zaragoza (10 daily; 3hr–3hr 40min). Plus most other destinations in the northeast and northwest.

Buses

Estación Sur de Autobuses c/Méndez Álvaro s/n, Ⓣ 914 684 200, Ⓦ www.estaciondeautobuses.com, Ⓦ www.alsa.es; Ⓜ Méndez Álvaro: Albacete (11 daily; 3hr); Alicante (8 daily; 5hr);

Almería (3 daily; 6hr 30min); Aranda (4 daily; 2hr); Aranjuez (35 mins, Mon–Fri every 15–30 mins, Sat & Sun hourly); Ávila (8 daily, 1hr 30min); Barcelona (15 daily; 7hr 30min–8hr); Ciudad Real (2–4 daily; 3hr); Córdoba (7 daily; 4hr 30min); Gijón (15 daily; 5hr); Granada (12 daily; 5hr); Jaén (2–6 daily; 5hr); León (11 daily; 4hr 15min); Málaga (10 daily; 6hr); Marbella (10 daily; 6hr); Oviedo (15 daily; 5hr); Palencia (5 daily; 3hr); Pontevedra (3 daily; 7hr); Santiago (4 daily; 9hr); Sevilla (11 daily; 6hr); Toledo (every 15min; 1hr 15min); Valencia (12 daily; 4hr); Valladolid (18 daily; 2hr 15min); Zaragoza (17 daily; 4hr); and international services to France and Portugal.

Auto-Res Fernández Shaw 1 Ⓣ 915 517 200 or 902 022 999, Ⓦ www.auto-res.es; Ⓜ Conde Casal: Badajoz (9 daily; 4hr 30min–5hr); Cáceres (7–10 daily; 3hr 50min–4hr 30min); Ciudad Rodrigo (1–2 daily; 3hr 40 min–4hr); Cuenca (10 daily; 2hr–2hr 30min); Mérida (10 daily; 4–5hr); Salamanca (24 daily; 2hr 15min–2hr 30min); Trujillo (10 daily; 4–5hr); Zamora (9 daily, 2hr 45min–3hr 15min).

Continental Auto Avda. de América 9 Ⓣ 917 456 300, Ⓦ www.continental-auto.es; Ⓜ Avda. de América: Alcalá (every 15 min; 40min); Bilbao (10 daily; 4hr 30min); Burgos (9 daily; 2hr 45min); El Burgo de Osma (2 daily; 4hr); Guadalajara (15 daily; 1hr); Logroño (5 daily; 4hr 30min–5hr 30min); Pamplona (4 daily; 5–6hr); San Sebastián (9 daily; 6–8hr); Santander (7 daily; 5hr 45min); Soria (5 daily; 2hr 30min–3hr); Vitoria (8 daily; 5hr).

Herranz Intercambiador de Autobuses de Moncloa Ⓣ 918 904 100, an underground terminal just above Metro Moncloa: El Escorial (approx. every 30min; 55min–1hr). Onward connections to El Valle de los Caídos.

La Sepulvedana Paseo de la Florida 11 Ⓣ 915 304 800, Ⓦ www.lasepulvedana.es; Ⓜ Pío: Ávila (8 daily; 1hr 30min); Segovia (31 daily; 1hr 15min).

La Veloz Avda. Mediterraneo Ⓣ 914 097 602; Ⓜ Conde Casal: Chinchón (Daily every 30min–hr; 45 mins).

Around Madrid

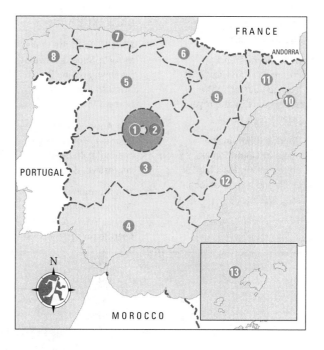

CHAPTER 2

Highlights

✳ **A view of El Greco's Toledo** The terrace bar of the *parador* provides the perfect viewing point of the ancient city. See p.151

✳ **The Cathedral in Toledo** A splendid mixture of decorations and styles befitting a former capital. See p.156

✳ **Strawberries and cream at Aranjuez** Indulge yourself in the street cafés by the royal palace. See p.164

✳ **Sunday lunch in the plaza at Chinchón** No better setting for a big lunch and a drop of local *anís*. See p.166

✳ **El Escorial** A window on the mind of Philip II, perched spectacularly in the foothills of the Sierra Guadarrama. See p.167

✳ **A hike in the sierra** Head out to Gredos or Guadarrama for a break from the city heat. See p.171 & p.180

✳ **A walk along the walls at Ávila** Superb views of the town and the harsh Castilian landscape. See p.175

✳ **The Aqueduct at Segovia** Roman engineering at its most impressive. See p.186

✳ **The fountains at La Granja** A beautiful display at the royal retreat near Segovia. See p.190

△ Avila city walls

Around Madrid

T he lack of historic monuments in Madrid is more than compensated for by the region around the capital. Within a radius of 100km – and within an hour's travel by bus or train – are some of the greatest cities of Spain. Above all, there is **Toledo**, which preceded Madrid as the Spanish capital. Immortalized by El Greco, who lived and worked there for

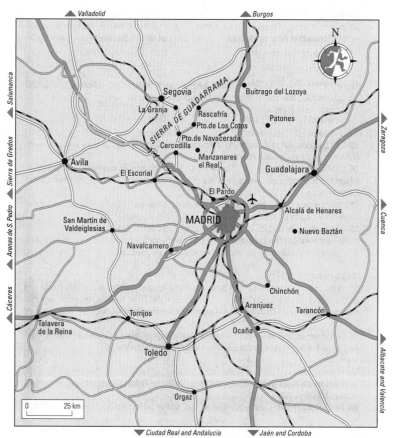

February

First Sunday in the month *Santa Agueda* women's festival in Segovia, when married women take over city administration and parade and celebrate in traditional costume. Occurs to an extent throughout the province, especially in Zamarramala just outside the city.

Week before Lent *Carnaval* is the excuse for lively fiestas all over the place.

March/April

Holy Week *Semana Santa* is celebrated everywhere, but with great formality and processions in Toledo and an impressive Passion play on Saturday in the Plaza Mayor at Chinchón.

Mid-April *Fiesta del Anís y del Vino* in Chinchón.

May

Corpus Cristi (variable – the Thursday after Trinity, which sometimes falls in June) sees a very solemn, costumed religious procession in Toledo.

June

24–29 *San Juan y San Pedro*. A lively procession with floats and music in Segovia.
30 In Hita (north of Guadalajara) the fiesta has a medieval theme, with performances of old theatre, feasts, dances, and sporting events including falcony and bull-lancing.

July

There's a big festival in Ávila in **mid-July**; a rowdy affair with bullfights, music and dances. In Segovia the festival runs throughout **July and August**, with music, folk and dance festivities.

August

15 Celebrations for the *Virgen de la Asunción* in Chinchón include an *encierro*, with bulls running through the street.
25 Entertaining fiestas in La Granja (near Segovia; one of the rare occasions on which the monumental fountains in the palace gardens are switched on) and Orgaz (near Toledo).
The **third week of the month** marks the August fiestas in Toledo, in honour of the *Virgen del Sagrario*; amazing fireworks on the final weekend.
28 Bull-running in Cuéllar (north of Segovia) – one of the oldest in Spain.
In the **last week in the month** there are some spectacular parades of giant puppets, and plenty of theatre, music and dance in Alcalá de Henares.

September

Aranjuez holds a fiesta over the **first weekend of the month**, and a re-enactment of the *Motín de Aranjuez* (Mutiny of Aranjuez) – the 1808 popular rebellion against the royal favourite Godoy, which forced the abdication of Carlos IV in favour of Fernando VII.
27 *La Virgen de la Fuencisla* in Segovia. The image of the city's patron saint is carried from the sanctuary in the Eresma valley to the cathedral.

October

Second week Ávila goes wild for the *Feria de Santa Teresa*. There are organ recitals in the churches, too.
25 *San Frutos*. Fiestas in Segovia in honour of the patron saint of the city.

most of his later career, the city is a living museum to the many cultures – Visigothic, Moorish, Jewish and Christian – which have shaped the destiny of Spain. If you have time for just one trip from Madrid, there is really no other choice.

That said, **Segovia**, with its stunning Roman aqueduct and irresistible Disney-prototype castle, puts up strong competition, while Felipe II's vast palace-mausoleum of **El Escorial** is a monument to out-monument all others. And there are smaller places, too, less known to foreign tourists: **Aranjuez**, an oasis in the parched Castilian plain, famed for its asparagus, strawberries and lavish Baroque palace; the beautiful walled city of **Ávila**, birthplace of St Teresa; and Cervantes's home town, **Alcalá de Henares**, with its sixteenth-century university. For walkers, too, trails amid the sierras of **Gredos** and **Guadarrama** provide enticing escapes from the midsummer heat.

All of the towns in this chapter can be visited as an easy day-trip from Madrid, but they also offer interesting jumping-off points into Castile and beyond; details of onward travel follow each main entry. Wherever you're going, it's a good idea to pick up leaflets in advance from one of the tourist offices in Madrid.

Toledo

Despite its reputation as one of Spain's greatest cities, **TOLEDO** can, in some ways, be a bit of a disappointment. Certainly, it's a city redolent of past glories, and is packed with sights – hence the whole city's status as a National Monument and UNESCO Patrimony of Mankind – but the extraordinary number of day-trippers has taken the edge off what was once the most extravagant of Spanish experiences. Still, the setting is breathtaking, and if you're an **El Greco** fan, you'd be mad to miss this city.

In a landscape of abrasive desolation, Toledo sits on a rocky mound isolated on three sides by a looping gorge of the Río Tajo. Every available inch of this outcrop has been built upon: churches, synagogues, mosques and houses are heaped upon one another in a haphazard spiral which the cobbled lanes infiltrate as best they can. To see Toledo at its best, you'll need to stay at least a night: a day-trip will leave you hard pressed to see everything. More importantly, in the evening with the crowds gone and the city lit up by floodlights – resembling one of El Greco's moonlit paintings – Toledo is a different place entirely.

Toledo also hosts one of the most extravagant celebrations of **Corpus Christi** in the country, with street processions and all the works. Other local festivals take place on May 25 and August 15 and 20.

Some history

Toledo was known to the Romans, who captured it in 192 BC, as *Toletum*, a small but well-defended town. Taken by the Visigoths, who made it their capital, it was already an important cultural and trading centre by the time the **Moors** arrived in 712. The period which followed, with Moors, Jews and Mozárabes (Christians subject to Moorish rule) living together in relative equality, was one of rapid growth and prosperity and Toledo became the most important northern outpost of the Muslim emirates. Though there are few physical remains of this period, except the miniature mosque of **Cristo de la Luz**, the long domination has left a clear mark on the atmosphere and shape of the whole city.

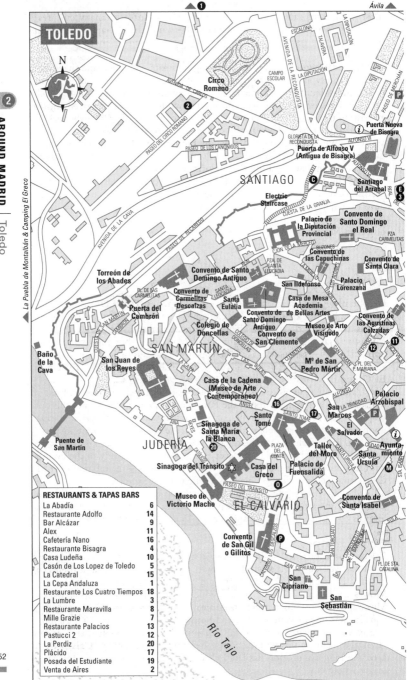

TOLEDO

N

Ávila

Circo Romano

CAMPO ESCOLAR

Puerta Nueva de Bisagra

Puerta de Alfonso V (Antigua de Bisagra)

SANTIAGO

Santiago del Arrabal

Electric Staircase

Palacio de la Diputación Provincial

Convento de Santo Domingo el Real

Convento de las Capuchinas

Convento de Santa Clara

Torreón de los Abades

Convento de Santo Domingo Antiguo

San Ildefonso

Palacio Lorenzana

Convento de Carmelitas Descalzas

Santa Eulalia

Casa de Mesa Academia

Puerta del Cambrón

Convento de Bellas Artes

Convento de las Agustinas Calzadas

Colegio de Doncellas

Convento de Santo Domingo Antiguo

Museo de Arte Visigodo

Baño de la Cava

San Juan de los Reyes

Convento de San Clemente

Mª de San Pedro Mártir

SAN MARTÍN

Casa de la Cadena (Museo de Arte Contemporáneo)

San Marcos

Palacio Arzobispal

Puente de San Martín

Sinagoga de Santa María la Blanca

Santo Tomé

El Salvador

JUDERÍA

Taller del Moro

Ayunta-miento

Santa Úrsula

Sinagoga del Tránsito

Casa del Greco

Palacio de Fuensalida

Museo de Victorio Macho

EL CALVARIO

Convento de Santa Isabel

Convento de San Gil o Gilitos

San Cipriano

San Sebastián

Río Tajo

La Puebla de Montalbán & Camping El Greco

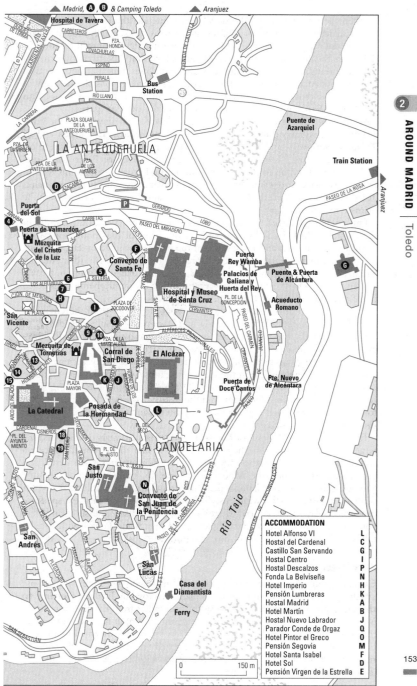

▲ *Madrid,* **A** , **B** *& Camping Toledo* ▲ *Aranjuez*

Hospital de Tavera

Bus Station

Puente de Azarquiel

Train Station

LA ANTEQUERUELA

Puerta del Sol

4

Puerta de Valmardón

Mezquita del Cristo de la Luz

5 Convento de Santa Fe

Puerta Rey Wamba

Palacios de Galiana y Huerta del Rey

Puente & Puerta de Alcántara

6
7

H

Hospital y Museo de Santa Cruz

Acueducto Romano

San Vicente

I

8

9
10

13
14
15

Mezquita de Tornerías

Corral de San Diego

El Alcázar

Puerta de Doce Cantos

Pte. Nuevo de Alcántara

Plaza Mayor

K **J**

La Catedral

Posada de la Hermandad

L

18
19

San Justo

LA CANDELARIA

Río Tajo

San Andrés

N

Convento de San Juan de la Penitencia

San Lucas

Casa del Diamantista

Ferry

ACCOMMODATION	
Hotel Alfonso VI	L
Hostal del Cardenal	C
Castillo San Servando	G
Hostal Centro	I
Hostal Descalzos	P
Fonda La Belviseña	N
Hotel Imperio	H
Pensión Lumbreras	K
Hostal Madrid	A
Hotel Martín	B
Hostal Nuevo Labrador	J
Parador Conde de Orgaz	Q
Hotel Pintor el Greco	O
Pensión Segovia	M
Hotel Santa Isabel	F
Hotel Sol	D
Pensión Virgen de la Estrella	E

0   150 m

153

When the Christian king Alfonso VI "reconquered" the town in 1085, with the assistance of El Cid, Moorish influence scarcely weakened. Although Toledo became the capital of Castile and the base for campaigns against the Moors in the south, the city itself was a haven of cultural tolerance. Not only was there a school of translators revealing the scientific and philosophical achievements of the East, but Arab craftsmen and techniques remained responsible for many of the finest buildings of the period: look, for example, at the churches of **San Román** or **Santiago del Arrabal** or at any of the old **city gates**.

At the same time Jewish culture remained powerful. There were, at one time, at least seven **synagogues** – of which two, **Santa María la Blanca** and **El Tránsito**, survive – and Jews occupied many positions of power. The most famous was Samuel Levi, treasurer and right-hand man of Pedro the Cruel until the king lived up to his name by murdering him and stealing his wealth. From this period, too, dates the most important purely Christian monument, Toledo's awesome **Catedral** (the city has remained the seat of the Catholic primate to this day).

This golden age ended abruptly in the sixteenth century with the transfer of the capital to Madrid, following hard on the heels of the Inquisition's mass expulsion of Muslims and Jews; some of the latter responded by taking refuge in Catholicism, becoming known as *Conversos*. Few Jews remain today, though Samuel Toledano, late president of the Spanish Israelite Community, was descended from a fifteenth-century grand rabbi, his family name considered proof of his descent from *Conversos*.

The city played little part in subsequent Spanish history until the Civil War (see the box on the **Alcázar**, p.161) and it remains, despite the droves of tourists, essentially the medieval city so often painted by El Greco. Sadly, however, the Tajo, the city's old lifeblood, is now highly polluted, and its waters greatly depleted by industry and agriculture. And, as in so many ancient towns, fewer and fewer people live in the city centre; most who work there prefer to commute from the expanding suburbs. That said, many of the leading sights have undergone recent renovation and the historic core is in better shape than for many years, although traffic remains a problem and cars roar along even the tiniest alleyways in the centre.

Toledo has been a byword for fine **steel** for a thousand years or more and the glint of knives in souvenir shops is one of the first things you'll notice on arrival. Some have traced the craft back to the Romans and it was certainly a growth industry when the Moors were here. By the seventeenth century, Samuel Butler was complaining that "the trenchant blade, Toledo trusty, for want of fighting was growing rusty". Today it's surprising that, except for a modern display in the Alcázar, there's little to see outside the shops; in these you can still admire attractive damascene steel swords and knives, with handles inlaid with decorative gold and silver filigree.

Arrival

General orientation is pretty straightforward in Toledo, with the compact old city looped by the Tajo, and the new quarters across the bridges. **Getting to the city**, too, is easy, with buses every thirty minutes from the Estación Sur in Madrid (every 30 min; daily 6.45am–10pm; 1hr 15min). It is worth noting that the **train** service (from Atocha) will undergo temporary **disruption** in 2004 because of the construction of a new high-speed line that will cut the journey time in half, so it is best to check the times with Renfe (℡902 240 202, ⓦ www.renfe.es) before you travel.

Toledo's **train station**, a marvellous 1919 mock-Mudéjar creation, is some way out on the Paseo de la Rosa, a twenty-minute walk – take the left-hand fork off the dual carriageway and cross the Puente de Alcántara – or a bus ride (#5 or #6) to the heart of town. The **bus station** is on Avenida de Castilla la Mancha in the modern, lower part of the city; bus #5 runs to Plaza de Zocódover, though if you take short cuts through the *barrio* at the bottom of the hill just inside the walls, it's a mere ten minutes to the Puerta Nueva de Bisagra.

If you're **driving** – and from Madrid there's little point if you're not going on elsewhere – the best places to park are in the streets around the Circo Romano in the new town or in the underground car park close to the new mechanical staircase (Mon–Fri 7am–10pm, Sat, Sun & holidays 8am–10pm) that leads up into the old city.

Information

Toledo's main **turismo** (Mon–Sat 9am–7pm, winter Mon–Fri closes 6pm, Sun & holidays 9am–3pm; ☎925 220 843, ⓦwww.castillalamancha.es/clmturiocio) is outside the city walls opposite the Puerta Nueva de Bisagra and next to a convenient taxi rank; it has full lists of places to stay, maps showing the monuments, walking tours, admission times and charges. There's another office in the *Zococentro* shop at c/Sillería 16 in the centre and a small turismo run by the local *ayuntamiento* in the plaza opposite the cathedral (Mon 10.30am–2.30pm, Tues–Sun 10.30am–2.30pm & 4.30–7pm; ☎925 254 030, ⓦwww.diputoledo .es/turismo). For **Internet** access try Discad Multimedia at c/Cervantes 17 just off Plaza de Zocódover and the Locutorio at Plaza de la Magdalena 7.

Accommodation

Booking a **room** in advance is important in Toledo, especially at weekends, or during the summer. If you're on a limited budget, hotel choice is complemented by private rooms, but you'll need to arrive early in the day. The turismo provides a helpful list of all the accommodation available in town. Be aware that prices in many places almost double at Easter, bank holidays and at Corpus Christi.

Budget options

Fonda La Belviseña Cuesta del Can 5 ☎925 220 067. South of the Alcázar; cheap and basic *fonda* with shared bathrooms; popular, so the dozen rooms fill up quickly. 1am curfew. ❶

Castillo San Servando Across the Puente de Alcántara and just off Paseo de la Rosa on Cuesta de San Servando ☎925 224 554, Ⓔcastillosanser@terra.es. Toledo's youth hostel and student residence is on the outskirts of town in a wing of the fourteenth-century Castillo San Servando; a fifteen-minute walk (signposted) from the train station. It's a good option, with a fine view of the city, and booking is advised. YH card required. Closed mid-Aug to mid-Sept. Under 30s €8.41, over 30s €11 in two- or four-room dormitories.

Hostal Centro c/Nueva 13 ☎925 257 091, ⓦwww.hostalcentro.com. New and very pleasant air-conditioned 23-room *hostal* situated close to Plaza de Zocódover. Good value. ❷

Hotel Imperio c/Cadenas 5–7 ☎925 227 650, ⓦwww.terra.es/personal/himperio. Modern and decently furnished with an in-house coffee shop and reasonable restaurant next door. Air-conditioned rooms. ❷

Pensión Lumbreras c/Juan Labrador 9 ☎925 221 571. Twelve simple rooms around a neat little courtyard; those on top floor have fine rooftop views and some have a/c. Rooms with bath available. The *pensión* shares a reception with the nearby *Carlos V* hotel. ❷

Hostal Madrid c/Marqués de Mendigorría 7 & 14 ☎925 221 114, Ⓕ925 228 113. Comfortable *hostal* with a/c in some rooms, but a bit of a way from the old town. ❷

Hostal Nuevo Labrador c/Juan Labrador 10 ☎925 222 620, Ⓕ925 229 399. Well-placed in a shady street near to the Alcazar, this friendly and modern *hostal* has 12 good-value rooms. ❷

Pensión Segovia c/Recoletos 2 ☎925 211 124.

On a narrow street off c/Armas. Well maintained and very cheap; the rooms have washbasins – you pay extra for showers. ❶

Pensión Virgen de la Estrella c/Real del Arrabal 18, 1º ⓣ925 253 134. Small, with shared facilities, but decent enough, on the main road up to the old town, near Puerta de Bisagra – ask at the bar of the same name across the road. One of the cheapest options in town. ❶

Moderate and expensive options

Hotel Alfonso VI c/General Moscardó 2 ⓣ925 222 600, ⓦ www.hotelalfonsovi.com. Very pleasant four-star hotel facing the Alcázar; some of the 83 rooms with balconies have views of the Río Tajo. Discounts for online reservations. ❼

Hostal del Cardenal Paseo de Recaredo 24 ⓣ925 224 900, ⓔ cardenal@macom.es. Splendid old palace with famous restaurant and delightful gardens, located outside the city wall, near Puerta Nueva de Bisagra. ❻

Hostal Descalzos c/Descalzos 30 ⓣ925 227 114, ⓦ www.hostaldescalzos.com. Very good-value, centrally located *hostal*, handy for the main sights. Some of the modern air-conditioned en-suite rooms have good views, plus there's a small open-air pool, too. ❸

Martín c/Espino 6 ⓣ & ⓕ925 221 733, ⓦ www.hotelesmartin.com. Relatively new and good value for money, in a residential area close to the bus station and Museo Hospital Tavera. ❸

Parador Conde de Orgaz Cerro del Emperador s/n ⓣ925 221 850, ⓦ www.parador.es. Superb views of the city from the terrace of Toledo's top

hotel, but it's a fair walk from the centre. ❼

Hotel Pintor el Greco c/Alamillos de Transito 13 ⓣ925 285 191, ⓦ www.hotelpintorelgreco.com. Well-equipped and nicely furnished hotel in a refurbished seventeenth-century bakery situated in the old Jewish quarter. It has 33 rooms, many with fine views across the Tajo. The hotel has its own parking. ❻

Hotel Santa Isabel c/Santa Isabel 24 ⓣ925 253 120, ⓦ www.santa-isabel.com. Best of the mid-range hotels is housed in a converted nobleman's house right in the centre, with airy wooden-panelled floors and safe parking. Recommended. ❸

Hotel Sol c/Azacanes 15 ⓣ925 213 650, ⓦ www.fedeto.es/hotel-sol. Good-value family hotel, on a quiet side street just off the main road up to the Plaza de Zocódover before the Puerta del Sol. The owners also run the cheaper *hostal* across the street at no.40 – ask at reception. ❸

Camping

Camping El Greco Ctra. De Toledo-Puebla de Montalbán km 0.7 ⓣ & ⓕ925 220 090, ⓔ elgreco@retemail.es. Much the best campsite in the area and a thirty-minute walk from the Puerta de Bisagra: cross the Puente de la Cava towards Puebla de Montalbán, then follow the signs. There are great views of the city from here – and a bar to enjoy them from – plus a swimming pool to cool off in after a hard day's sightseeing. Open all year.

Camping Toledo Autovía Madrid–Toledo, km 63 ⓣ & ⓕ925 353 013. Nine kilometres northeast of Toledo, off the Madrid road by the village of Olias del Rey. This is a handy site if you have your own vehicle. Open April–Sept.

The City

The street layout and labelling in Toledo can be confusing, but the old core is so small that it should never take too long to get back on track; part of the city's charm is that it's a place to wander and absorb, so don't overdose on "sights" if you can avoid it. You shouldn't leave without seeing at least the El Grecos, the cathedral, the synagogues and Alcázar, but give it all time and you may stumble upon things not listed in this or any other guidebook. Enter any inviting doorway and you'll find stunning patios, rooms and ceilings, often of Mudéjar workmanship.

The cathedral

In a country so overflowing with massive religious institutions, the metropolitan **Catedral** has to be something special – and it is. A robust Gothic construction which took over 250 years (1227–1493) to complete, it has a richness of internal decoration in almost every conceivable style, with masterpieces of the Gothic, Renaissance and Baroque periods. The exterior is best appreciated from outside the city, where the 100-metre spire and the weighty buttressing can be seen to greatest advantage. From the street it's less impressive, so hemmed in by surrounding houses that you can't really sense the scale or grandeur of the whole.

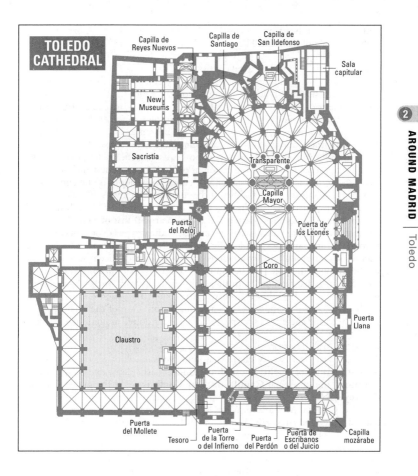

There are eight doorways, but the main entrance is at present through the **Puerta Llana** on the southern side of the main body of the cathedral. Tickets (€4.95, free Wed pm for EU citizens; audio guides €3) for the various chapels, chapter houses and treasuries that require them are sold in the cathedral shop opposite. The main body of the cathedral is closed from noon to 3.30pm; the parts which need **tickets** can be visited daily from Monday to Saturday 10.30am to 6pm and Sunday 2 to 6pm (in September through to April, open to 7pm). The *coro* is closed on Sunday morning, and the New Museums on Monday.

The Coro and Capilla Mayor

Inside the cathedral, the central nave is divided from four aisles by a series of clustered pillars supporting the vaults, 88 in all, the aisles continuing around behind the main altar to form an apse. There is magnificent **stained glass** throughout, mostly dating from the fifteenth and sixteenth centuries, particularly beautiful in two rose windows above the north and south doors. Beside the south door (Puerto de los Leones) is a huge, ancient **fresco of St Christopher**.

At the physical heart of the church, blocking the nave, is the **Coro** (Choir), itself a panoply of sculpture. The carved wooden stalls are in two tiers. The lower level, by Rodrigo Alemán, depicts the conquest of Granada, with each seat showing a different village being taken by the Christians. The portraits of Old Testament characters on the stalls above were executed in the following century, on the north side by Philippe Vigarni and on the south by Alonso Berruguete, whose superior technique is evident. He also carved the large **Transfiguration** here from a single block of alabaster. The *reja* (grille) which encloses the *coro* is said to be plated with gold, but it was covered in iron to disguise its value from Napoleon's troops and has since proved impossible to renovate.

The **Capilla Mayor** stands directly opposite. Its gargantuan altarpiece, stretching clear to the roof, is one of the triumphs of Gothic art, overflowing with intricate detail and fanciful embellishments. It contains a synopsis of the entire New Testament, culminating in a Calvary at the summit. On either side are the tombs of the mighty, including (on the left) those of kings Alfonso VII and Sancho III and the powerful Cardinal Mendoza and (on the right) that of Sancho II.

Directly behind the main altar is an extraordinary piece of fantasy – the Baroque **Transparente**. Wonderfully and wildly extravagant, with its marble cherubs sitting on fluffy marble clouds, it's especially magnificent when the sun reaches through the hole punched in the roof for just that purpose. You'll notice a red cardinal's hat hanging from the vaulting just in front of this. Spanish primates are buried where they choose, with the epitaph they choose, and with their hat hanging above them, where it stays until it rots. One of them chose to be buried here, and there are other pieces of headgear dotted around the cathedral.

Chapels and treasures

There are well over twenty **chapels** around the walls, all of which are of some interest. Many of them house fine tombs, particularly the **Capilla de Santiago**, the octagonal **Capilla de San Ildefonso** and the gilded **Capilla de Reyes Nuevos**.

In the **Capilla Mozárabe**, Mass is still celebrated daily according to the ancient Visigothic rites. When the Church tried to ban the old ritual in 1086 the people of Toledo were outraged. The dispute was put to a combat, which the Mozárabe champion won, but the Church demanded further proof: trial by fire. The Roman prayer book was blown to safety, while the Mozárabe version remained, unburned, in the flames. Both sides claimed victory, and in the end the two rituals were allowed to coexist. If you want to attend Mass, be there at 9.30am and look out for the priest – you may well be the only celebrant.

The Capilla de San Juan houses the riches of the cathedral **Tesoro** (Treasury), most notably a solid silver *custodia* (repository for Eucharist wafers) ten foot high and weighing over two hundred kilos. It was made by German-born silversmith Enrique de Arfe in the sixteenth century, and gilded seventy years later. An even more impressive accumulation of wealth is displayed in the **Sacristía** (Sacristy), where paintings include a *Disrobing of Christ* and portraits of the Apostles by El Greco, Velázquez's portrait of Cardinal Borja and Goya's *Christ Taken by the Soldiers*.

In the adjoining rooms, the so-called **New Museums** house works of art that were previously locked away or poorly displayed. Among them are paintings by Caravaggio, Gerard David and Morales, and El Greco's most important piece of sculpture (only a few pieces survive), a polychromed wooden group of San Ildefonso and the Virgin. The **Sala Capitular** (Chapter House) has a magnificent sixteenth-century *artesonado* ceiling and portraits of all Spain's archbishops to the present day.

Santo Tomé and the Casa del Greco

The outstanding attraction of Toledo is El Greco's masterpiece, *The Burial of the Count of Orgaz*. It's housed, alone, in a small annexe to the church of **Santo Tomé** (daily 10am–6.45pm, winter closes 5.45pm; €1.50, free Wed after 2.30pm for EU citizens; ⓦ www.santotome.org) and depicts the count's funeral, at which St Stephen and St Augustine appeared in order to lower him into the tomb. It combines El Greco's genius for the mystic, exemplified in the upper half of the picture where the count's soul is being received into heaven, with his great powers as a portrait painter and master of colour. The identity of the sombre-faced figures watching the burial has been a source of endless speculation. On two identities, however, there is universal agreement; El Greco painted himself seventh from the left looking out at the viewer and his son in the foreground. Less certain are the identities of the rest of the mourners; Cervantes and Lope de Vega are unlikely to have been included as neither had achieved fame by 1586, but the odds are on for Felipe II's presence among the heavenly onlookers, even though he was still alive when it was painted. A search for the count's bones came to an end in early 2001 when they were unearthed from a tomb located, appropriately enough, directly below the painting.

From Santo Tomé the c/de los Amarillos leads down to the old **Judería** (Jewish quarter) and to the **Casa y Museo del Greco** (Tues–Sat 10am–2pm & 4–6pm, Sun 10am–2pm; €1.20 while the casa is closed, thereafter €3, free Sat pm & Sun), which despite its name wasn't the artist's actual home. The building in fact dates from the beginning of the twentieth century and the evidence suggests that he lived nearby. The living quarters, furnished in sixteenth-century style, are closed for restoration, but the museum part of the house displays many classic El Grecos, among them his famous *View and Map of Toledo* and another complete series of the Twelve Apostles, completed later than the set in the cathedral and subtly different.

The Taller del Moro, two synagogues and San Juan de los Reyes

Between Santo Tomé and the Casa del Greco you pass the entrance to the **Palacio de Fuensalida** (Palace of the Counts of Fuensalida; closed to the public), a beautiful fifteenth-century mansion where Carlos V's Portuguese wife Isabel died. A garden separates it from the **Taller del Moro** (Tues–Sat 10am–2pm & 4–6.30pm, Sun 10am–2pm; €0.60, Sat pm & Sun free; closed for restoration), three fourteenth-century rooms of a Mudéjar palace which were later used by masons working on the cathedral, with magnificent Mudéjar decoration and doorways intact. It is approached through its own entrance in the c/Taller del Moro.

Almost next door to the Casa del Greco, on c/Reyes Católicos, is the **Sinagoga del Tránsito**, built along Moorish lines by Samuel Levi in 1366. It became a church after the expulsion of the Jews, but is currently being restored to its original form. The interior is a simple galleried hall, brilliantly decorated with polychromed stuccowork and superb filigree windows. Hebrew inscriptions praising God, King Pedro and Samuel Levi adorn the walls. Nowadays it houses a small **Sephardic Museum** (Tues–Sat 10am–2pm & 4–6pm, Sun 10am–2pm; €2.40, free Sat pm & Sun), tracing the distinct traditions and development of Jewish culture in Spain.

The only other surviving synagogue, **Santa María la Blanca** (daily 10am–2pm & 3.30–7pm, winter closes 6pm; €1.50), is a short way down the same street. Like El Tránsito, which it predates by over a century, it has been both church and synagogue, though as it was built by Mudéjar craftsmen it actually looks more like a mosque. Four rows of octagonal pillars each support seven horseshoe arches, all of them with elaborate and individual designs moulded in plaster, while a fine sixteenth-century *retablo* has been preserved from its time as a church. The whole effect is quite stunning, accentuated by a deep-red floor tiled with decorative *azulejos*.

Continuing down c/Reyes Católicos, you come to the superb church of **San Juan de los Reyes** (daily 10am–6.45pm, winter closes 5.45pm; €1.50, free Wed pm), its exterior bizarrely festooned with the chains worn by the Christian prisoners from Granada released on the reconquest of their city. It was originally a Franciscan convent founded by the "Catholic Kings", Fernando and Isabel, to celebrate their victory at the Battle of Toro, and in which, until the fall of Granada, they had planned to be buried. Designed by Juan Guas in the decorative late-Gothic style known as Isabelline (after the queen), its double-storeyed cloister is quite outstanding: the upper floor has an elaborate Mudéjar ceiling, and the crests of Castile and Aragón – seven arrows and a yoke – are carved everywhere in assertion of the new unity brought by the royal marriage. This theme is continued in the airy church where imperious eagles support the royal shields.

A few hundred metres south of here, splendidly situated on a spur overlooking the Tajo, is the **Museo de Victorio Macho**, Plaza de Victorio Macho 2 (Mon–Sat 10am–7pm, Sun 10am–3pm; €3), which contains the sculptures, paintings and sketches of the Spanish artist Victorio Macho (1887–1966) set in a delightfully tranquil garden. The auditorium on the ground floor shows a documentary film (available in English) about the city and its history.

The Alcázar

At the heart of modern Toledo is the **Plaza de Zocódover** (its name derives from the Arabic word *souk*), where everyone converges for an afternoon drink. Dominating this square, indeed all Toledo, is the bluff, imposing **Alcázar** (Tues–Sun 9.30am–2.30pm; €2, free Wed for EU citizens, entrance off Cuesta del Alcázar). There has probably always been a fortress at this commanding location, but the present building was originated by Carlos V, though it has been burned and bombarded so often that almost nothing remaining is original. The most recent destruction was in 1936 during one of the most symbolic and extraordinary episodes of the Civil War, involving a two-month siege of the Nationalist-occupied Alcázar by the Republican town (see box, opposite).

After the war, Franco's regime completely rebuilt the fortress as a monument to the glorification of its defenders – the fascist newspaper *El Alcázar* also commemorates the siege – and their propaganda models and photos are still displayed, as well as the cellars where the besieged families hid. The rest of the building houses an Army Museum which will eventually provide a home for all the exhibits once housed in the Madrid branch (see p.109; full opening scheduled for 2004).

The Alcázar also offers the best views of the town, its upper windows level with the top of the cathedral spire (though in recent years access has been restricted, as part of the building is still occupied by the military). Across the river, next to a modern military academy, stands the ancient **Castillo de San Servando**, Arabic in origin and remodelled in Mudéjar style in the fourteenth century; one wing of the castle now serves as a youth hostel.

A couple of blocks to the west of the Alcázar in the Mezquita de las Tornerías on c/Tornerías, the **Centro de Promoción de la Artesanía** (Tues–Sat 10am–2pm & 5–8pm, Sun 10am–2pm; free) houses good displays of beautiful local crafts, mainly pottery. The renovated eleventh-century mosque, deconsecrated by the Reyes Católicos around 1500, is worth a visit in itself.

The siege of the Alcázar

At the outset of the Spanish Civil War, on July 20, 1936, Colonel José Moscardó – a leading Nationalist rebel – and the cadets of the military academy under his command were driven into the Alcázar. They barricaded themselves in with a large group that included six hundred women and children, and up to a hundred left-wing hostages (who were never seen again).

After many phone calls from Madrid to persuade them to surrender, a Toledo attorney phoned Moscardó with an ultimatum: within ten minutes the Republicans would shoot his son, captured that morning. Moscardó declared that he would never surrender and told his son, "If it be true, commend your soul to God, shout *Viva España*, and die like a hero." (His son was actually shot with others a month later in reprisal for an air raid.) Inside, though not short of ammunition, the defenders had so little food they had to eat their horses.

The number of Republican attackers varied from 1000 to 5000, with people coming from Madrid to take pot shots from below. Two of the three mines they planted under the towers exploded but nothing could disturb the solid rock foundations. The besiegers tried spraying petrol all over the walls and setting fire to it, but with no effect. Finally, General Franco decided to relieve Moscardó and diverted an army that was heading for Madrid. On September 27, General José Varela commanded the successful attack on the town, which was followed by the usual bloodbath – not one prisoner being taken.

As the historian Raymond Carr put it, "in civil war, symbols count". The day after Franco entered Toledo to consolidate his victory, he was declared head of state and spoke to the nation – according to Radio Castillo, he was "the authentic voice of Spain in the plenitude of its power".

From the Museo de Santa Cruz to the Hospital de Tavera

Just north of the Plaza de Zocódover is the **Hospital y Museo de Santa Cruz** (Mon 10am–2pm & 4–6.30pm, Tues–Sat 10am–6.30pm, Sun 10am–2pm; €1.25, free Sat pm & Sun while being renovated), a superlative Renaissance building with a fine Plateresque facade, housing some of the greatest El Grecos in Toledo, including *The Assumption*, a daringly unorthodox work of feverish spiritual intensity, and a *Crucifixion* with the town as a backdrop. As well as outstanding works by Goya and Ribera, the museum also contains a huge collection of ancient carpets and faded tapestries (including a magnificent fifteenth-century Flemish tapestry called *The Astrolabe*), a military display (note the flags borne by Don Juan of Austria at the Battle of Lepanto), sculpture and a small archeological collection. Don't miss the patio with its ornate staircase – the entrance is beside the ticket office.

If you leave the city by the Cuesta de Armas which runs out of the Plaza de Zocódover and down the hill you will come to Toledo's main gate, the sixteenth-century **Puerta Nueva de Bisagra**, marooned in a constant swirl of traffic. Its patterned-tile roofs bear the coat of arms of Carlos V. Alongside is the gateway that it replaced, the ninth-century Moorish portal through which Alfonso VI and El Cid led their triumphant armies in 1085. On your way down look out for the intriguing exterior of the Mudéjar church of **Santiago del Arrabal**. The Cuesta del Cristo de la Luz leads up here past the tiny mosque of **Mezquita del Cristo de la Luz** (summer Mon & Thurs–Sat 10am–2.30pm & 3.30–7pm; winter Mon & Thurs–Sat 10am–6pm; ☎925 254 191, ✉cristodelaluz@terra.es; €1.50). Although this is one of the oldest Moorish monuments in Spain (it was built by Musa Ibn Ali in the tenth century on the foundations of a Visigothic church), only the nave, with its nine different cupolas, is the original Arab construction. The apse was added when the building was converted into a church, and is claimed to be the first product of the Mudéjar style. According to legend, as King Alfonso rode into the town in triumph, his horse stopped and knelt before the mosque. Excavations revealed a figure of Christ, still illuminated by a lamp which had burned throughout three and a half centuries of Muslim rule -- hence the name *Cristo de la Luz*.

The mosque itself, set in a small park and open on all sides to the elements, is so small that it seems more like a miniature summer pavilion, but it has an elegant simplicity of design that few of the great monuments can match. Below are the battlements of the **Puerta del Sol**, a great fourteenth-century Mudéjar gateway. Occasionally you'll see the mosque used for prayer by visiting Muslims.

Beyond and directly in front along the Paseo de Merchán is the **Hospital de Tavera** (daily 10.30am–1.30pm & 3.30–6pm; €3). This, a Renaissance palace with beautiful twin patios, houses the private collection of the Duke of Lerma. The gloomy interior is a reconstruction of a sixteenth-century mansion dotted with fine paintings, including a *Day of Judgement* by Bassano; the portrait of Carlos V by Titian is a copy of the original in the Prado. The hospital's archives are kept here, too: thousands of densely handwritten pages chronicling the illnesses treated. The museum contains several works by El Greco, and Ribera's gruesome portrait of a freak "bearded woman". Also here is the death mask of Cardinal Tavera, the hospital's founder, and in the church of the hospital is his ornate marble tomb – the last work of Alonso de Berruguete.

The Museo de Arte Visigótico and the Convento de Santo Domingo de Antiguo

The **Museo de Arte Visigótico** (Tues–Sat 10am–2pm & 4–6.30pm, Sun 10am–2pm; €0.60, free Sat pm & Sun) can be found in a very different, though equally impressive, building, the church of **San Román**, a short way to the northeast of the cathedral. Moorish and Christian elements – horseshoe arches, early murals and a splendid Renaissance dome – combine to make it the most interesting church in Toledo. Its twelfth-century Mudéjar tower originally stood apart from the main body of the church, in the manner of Muslim minarets. Visigothic jewellery, documents and archeological fragments make up the bulk of the collection.

A little way to the north of here and close to the mechanical staircase leading out of the old city is the **Convento de Santo Domingo Antiguo**, whose chief claim to fame is that El Greco's remains lie in the crypt, which can be glimpsed through a peephole in the floor. The nuns display their art treasures in the old choir (Mon–Sat 11am–1pm & 4–7pm, Sun 4–7pm; winter open Sat, Sun & holidays only; €1.50, free Tues), but more interesting is the high altarpiece of the church, El Greco's first major commission in Toledo. Unfortunately, most of the canvases have gone to museums and are here replaced by copies, leaving only two *St Johns* and a *Resurrection*.

Eating, drinking and nightlife

Toledo is a major tourist centre and inevitably many of its cafés, bars and restaurants are geared to passing trade. However, the city is also popular with Spanish visitors, so decent, authentic places do exist – and there's a bit of nightlife, too, for the local population.

Most **restaurants** in town do a good-value lunchtime *menú*, with game such as partridge (*perdiz*), pheasant (*faisán*) or quail (*cordoniz*) appearing in the more upmarket places, and everyone offering a tasty local speciality, *carcamusa* – a meat stew in a spicy tomato sauce. In the evenings, on a budget, you need to be selective: this can be an expensive town. As a rule, the nearer you get to the centre, the more you'll pay.

Inexpensive restaurants

Alex Plaza de Amador de los Ríos 10, at the top end of c/Nuncio Viejo. Reasonable-value restaurant with a much cheaper café at the side. *Conejo* and *perdiz* are the specialities here. Nice location and a shady summer terrace.

Bar Alcázar aka *Champi* c/Sierpe 5. A fairly standard bar, but it serves a good range of tapas and *raciones*.

Cafetería Nano c/Santo Tomé 10. Good-value chain where you can eat well for €9. You'll find it under the trees, near the church entrance.

Casa Ludeña Plaza Magdalena 13. One of many places around this square, offering a cheap *menú* and the best *carcamusa* in town.

La Catedral c/Nuncio Viejo 1. Wide range of tapas and wines at this modern bar in the heart of the city.

La Cepa Andaluza Avda. Méjico 11. Bar with dependable Andalucian cooking – fried fish and the like.

Pastucci 2 c/Sinagoga 10. Very reasonable pizzeria with Italian staples and a pleasant atmosphere.

Posada del Estudiante Callejón de San Pedro 2. Secluded workers' café near the cathedral, open only for very cheap lunchtime *menú* – well worth hunting out.

Restaurante Bisagra c/Real del Arrabal 14. Reasonably priced *menú* in elegantly refurbished surroundings.

Restaurante Palacios c/Alfonso X El Sabio 3. Friendly and popular local restaurant, with good roasted *perdiz*.

Moderate and expensive restaurants

La Abadía c/Nuñez de Arce 3. Popular restaurant-bar that does breakfasts, a good-value *menú del día* and tapas.

Restaurante Adolfo c/Granada 6. One of the best restaurants in town, tucked behind a marzipan café, in an old Jewish town house (ask to see the painted ceiling downstairs), and serving very imaginative food. Allow €35 a head. Closed Sun evening.

Casón de Los Lopez de Toledo c/Sillería 3. Upmarket restaurant in a quiet street close to Plaza Zocódover with a tasty *menú* at €18.

Restaurante Los Cuatro Tiempos c/Sixto Ramón Parro 5 at southeast corner of the cathedral. Excellent mid-price restaurant with local specialities and good tapas, including very good *caracoles*. The *menú del día* is €18.

La Lumbre c/Real de Arrabal 3. Well-regarded restaurant, just above the Puerta de Bisagra, specializing in meat dishes and local cuisine.

Restaurante Maravilla c/Barrio Rey 7. In the *hostal* of the same name, and offering an excellent *menú*, which includes traditionally prepared *perdiz*.

Mille Grazie c/Cadenas 2. Popular restaurant with a wide variety of Italian dishes. The tortellini with walnut and cream sauce is particularly good. Closed Mon & Sun evening.

La Perdiz c/Reyes Católicos 7. Quality restaurant which does a very good *menú de degustación* for €21. A good selection of local wines.

Plácido c/Santo Tomé 2. Good standard Toledan cuisine with a cool terrace and patio for the summer. Two different *menús* at €11.50 and €16.

Venta de Aires c/Circo Romano 35. Popular restaurant housed in a famous old inn, a little way out of the centre, with outdoor eating in the summer. Allow €20 a head.

Late bars and entertainment

By Spanish standards, Toledo's **nightlife** is rather tame. You'll find most late-night bars running along c/Sillería and its extension c/Alfileritos, west of Plaza de Zocódover. *Art-Café* is a very pleasant early stop with good tapas, German beer and art exhibitions. *TBO* on c/Sillería is a popular place later in the evening, while *La Abadía*, c/Nuñez de Arce 3, is a fashionable but civilized bar which serves a large range of foreign beer and attracts an older crowd than most along here.

Alternative places that frequently offer live music are *Broadway Jazz Club*, on c/Alfonso XII, *El Último* at Plaza Colegio Infantes 4 and *La Taberna de Garcilaso* at nearby c/Rojas 5.

Out of the tourist season, between September and March, **classical concerts** are held in the cathedral and other churches; details can be obtained from the turismo.

On from Toledo

The train line comes to a halt at Toledo but there are **bus** connections south to **Ciudad Real** (see p.210), west to **La Puebla de Montalbán** (see p.215) and **Talavera de la Reina** (see p.215) on the way to Extremadura, and east to **Cuenca** (see p.203). If you have transport of your own, or fancy slow progress by bus and on foot, the **Montes de Toledo** (see p.214), southwest of the city, is an interesting rural backwater.

More local excursions, by bus, to the south of Toledo, could include **Guadamur** (14km from Toledo), whose outstanding castle stands on a nearby hilltop, and **Orgaz**, once home to the count of El Greco's masterpiece *The Burial of the Count of Orgaz*, now a quiet village with a beautiful plaza, a magnificent Baroque church and a small fifteenth-century castle overlooking the main road to Ciudad Real.

Aranjuez and Chinchón

The frequent Madrid–Toledo trains run via **Aranjuez**, a little oasis in the beginnings of New Castile, where the eighteenth-century Bourbon rulers set up a spring and autumn retreat. Their palaces and luxuriant gardens, which inspired the composer Joaquín Rodrigo to write the famous *Concierto de Aranjuez*, and the summer strawberries (served with cream – *fresas con nata* – at roadside stalls), combine to make it an enjoyable stop. In summer (end of April to July & Sept to mid-Oct Sat & Sun), an old wooden **steam train**, the Tren de la Fresa, makes runs between Madrid and Aranjuez; it leaves Atocha station at 10.05am and returns from Aranjuez at 6pm, arriving back at Atocha at 7pm. Train enthusiasts won't begrudge the extra cost (€22; information ☏902 228 822), which includes a guided bus tour in Aranjuez, entry to the monuments and *fresas con nata* on the train. The less romantic, but highly efficient, standard trains leave every 15–30 minutes from Atocha, with the last train returning from Aranjuez at about 11.30pm. Buses run every half hour during the week and every hour at weekends from Estación Sur.

Nearby, too, connected by sporadic buses from Aranjuez at c/Almíbar 138 (Mon–Fri 4 daily, Sat 2 daily) and hourly services from the bus station at Avda. Mediterraneo 49 (ⓜConde Casal) in Madrid, is **Chinchón**, a picturesque village that is home to Spain's best-known *anís* – a mainstay of breakfast drinkers across Spain.

Aranjuez

The beauty of **ARANJUEZ** is its greenery – it's easy to forget just how dry and dusty most of central Spain is until you come upon this town, with its lavish palaces and luxuriant gardens at the confluence of the Tajo and Jarama rivers. In summer, Aranjuez functions principally as a weekend escape from Madrid and most people come out for the day, or stop en route to or from Toledo. If you wanted to break your journey, you'd need to camp or reserve a room in advance, as there's very little accommodation available.

The eighteenth-century **Palacio Real** (Tues–Sun: April–Sept 10am–6.15pm; Oct–March 10am–5.30pm; €5, free Wed for EU citizens) and its **gardens** (daily: April–Sept 8am–8.30pm; Oct–March 8am–6.30pm; free) were an attempt by the Spanish Bourbon monarchs to create a Versailles in Spain; Aranjuez clearly isn't in the same league but it's a very pleasant place to while away a few hours.

The palace is more remarkable for the ornamental fantasies inside than for any virtues of architecture. There seem to be hundreds of rooms, all exotically furnished, most amazingly so the **Porcelain Room**, entirely covered in decorative ware from the factory which used to stand in Madrid's Retiro park. The **Smoking Room** is a copy of one of the finest halls of the Alhambra in Granada, though executed with less subtlety. Most of the palace dates from the reign of the "nymphomaniac" Queen Isabel II, and many of the scandals and intrigues which led to her eventual abdication were played out here.

Outside, on a small island, are the fountains and neatly tended gardens of the **Jardín de la Isla**. The **Jardín del Príncipe**, on the other side of the main road, is more attractive, with shaded walks along the river and plenty of spots for a siesta. At its far end is the **Casa del Labrador** (June–Sept Tues–Sun 10am–6.15pm; Oct–March Tues–Sun 10am–5.15pm; visits by appointment only ☎918 910 305; €5, free Wed for EU citizens), which is anything but what its name (Labourer's House) implies. In a hotchpotch of styles, ranging from Neoclassical to Rococo, it was described by Richard Ford well over a century ago as "another plaything of that silly Charles IV, a foolish toy for the spoiled children of fortune, in which great expense and little taste are combined to produce a thing which is perfectly useless". Great expense is right, for the house contains more silk, marble, crystal and gold than would seem possible in so small a place, as well as a huge collection of fancy clocks. The guided tour goes into great detail about the weight and value of every item.

Also in the gardens, by the river, is the small **Casa de los Marinos** or **Museo de Faluas** (Tues–Sun: April–Sept 10am–6.15pm; Oct–March 10am–5.15pm; €3.40, free Wed for EU citizens), a museum containing the brightly coloured launches in which royalty would take to the river. You can do the modern equivalent and take a boat trip through the royal parks from the jetty by the bridge next to the palace (Tues–Sun 11am–sunset; €7).

A bus service occasionally connects the various sights, but all are within easy walking distance of each other, and the town's a very pleasant place to stroll around. Look out for the suitably regal eighteenth-century **Plaza de Toros** and the exhibition space entitled *Aranjuez – una gran fiesta* (summer Tues–Sun 10am–6.30pm; winter Tues–Sun 10am–5.30pm; €3, free Wed for EU citizens), part of which is a **museo taurino** with its *trajes de luces*, swords and associated taurine memorabilia, and part of which traces the town's history and royal heritage. Nearby in c/Naranja and c/Rosa are a number of **corralas**, traditional-style wooden-balconied tenement blocks.

Practicalities

You'll find a helpful **turismo** in the Casa de Infantes, facing the Plaza de San Antonio (daily 10am–7.30pm, Oct–May closes 6pm; ☎918 910 427, ⓦwww.aranjuez.com & ⓦwww.aranjuez.net). The best **hostal** choices are the air-conditioned *Rusiñol*, c/San Antonio 76 (☎918 910 155, ⒡918 925 345; ❷), in the centre of town, and the *Castilla*, Carrera de Andalucía 98 (☎918 912 627, ⓦwww.aranjuez.com/hostalcastilla; ❷–❸). For more luxury try the *Hotel Don Manuel* at c/Príncipe 71 (☎918 754 086, ⓦwww.egidohoteles.com; ❹), a sleek business-style hotel. The **campsite**, *Soto del Castillo*, Soto del Rebollo (☎918 911 395, ⒡918 914 197), is on a far bend of the Río Tajo; it's equipped with a swimming pool, and hires out bicycles and rowing boats.

With plenty of fresh produce around (including the famous strawberries and asparagus in season), the splendid nineteenth-century **Mercado de Abastos** on c/Stuart is a good place to buy your own food for a picnic. If you're after a memorable **restaurant** meal, *Casa José*, c/Abastos 32 (closed Sun eve &

Mon), offers good, but expensive, *nouvelle cuisine*, while *Casa Pablo*, c/Almíbar 42 (closed Aug), is more traditional, with walls covered with pictures of local dignitaries and bullfighters; its nearby offshoot, *Casa Pablete*, c/Stuart 108 (closed Tues & Aug), is good for tapas. Probably the best-known restaurant is the pleasant riverside *El Rana Verde*, c/Reina 1, which dates back to the late nineteenth century and serves a wide-ranging *menú* at €12.

Chinchón

CHINCHÓN, 45km southeast of Madrid, is an elegant little town, with a fifteenth-century castle and a fine Plaza Mayor, next to which stands the **Iglesia de la Asunción**, with a panel by Goya of *The Assumption of the Virgin*. It is as the home of *anís*, however, that the town is best known; your best bet for a sample of the local spirit is one of the local bars or the Alcoholera de Chinchón, a shop on the Plaza Mayor. Most visitors come for a tasting and then eat out at one of the town's traditional *mesones*: try the *Mesón del Comendador*, one of a cluster of good restaurants serving classic Castilian fare on the Plaza Mayor, or the *Mesón del Duende* – both are modestly priced. More expensive is the *Mesón Cuevas del Vino*, in an old olive oil mill at c/Benito Hortelano 13 which today has its own *bodega* (wine cellar), while the *Casa de Pregonero*, again on the Plaza Mayor, adds modern touches to the traditional dishes and has some great starters and desserts, but will set you back between €35–40 a head. If you fancy an overnight **stay** you could splash out on the *Parador de Chinchón* (☎918 940 836, Ⓦ www.parador.es; ⑥), which has been established in the former Augustinian monastery just off the Plaza Mayor. A more modest option but still very pleasant is the *Hostal Chinchón* (☎918 935 398, Ⓦ www.hostalchinchon.com; ②–③), which is also close to the Plaza Mayor at c/José Antonio 12 and comes complete with air-conditioning and a pool.

If you're visiting over Easter, you'll be treated to the townsfolk's own enactment of the *Passion of Christ*, though be aware that the small town becomes packed with visitors at this time. In April 1995 the town launched its *Fiesta del Anís y del Vino*, an orgy of *anís* and wine tasting; understandably, it was an immediate success and is now held every mid-April. An older annual tradition takes place on July 25, when the feast of St James (*Santiago* in Spanish) is celebrated with a bullfight in the Plaza Mayor. There is a small **turismo** in the Plaza Mayor (Mon–Fri 10am–8pm, Sat & Sun 11.30am–8pm; ☎918 935 323, Ⓦ www.ciudad-chinchon.com).

El Escorial, El Valle de los Caídos and the Sierra de Guadarrama

Northwest of Madrid, in the foothills of the Sierra de Guadarrama, is one of Spain's best-known and most visited sights – Felipe II's vast monastery-palace complex of **El Escorial**. Travel writers tend to go into frenzies about the symbolism of this building – "a stone image of the mind of its founder" was how the nineteenth-century writer Augustus Hare described it. The vast granite building, which contains a royal palace, a monastery, a mausoleum and one of the finest libraries of the Renaissance, embodies all that was important to one of the most powerful rulers in European history, The town around the monastery, **San Lorenzo del Escorial**, is an easy day-trip from Madrid, or if you plan to travel on, rail and road routes continue to Ávila (see p.175) and

Segovia (see p.182). The heart of the **Sierra de Guadarrama**, too, lies just to the north, offering Madrid's easiest mountain escape.

Tours from Madrid to El Escorial often take in **El Valle de los Caídos** (The Valley of the Fallen), 9km north. This is an equally megalomaniac yet far more chilling monument: an underground basilica hewn under Franco's orders, allegedly as a monument to the Civil War dead of both sides, though in reality as a memorial to the Generalísmo and his regime.

El Escorial

The monastery of **EL ESCORIAL** was the largest Spanish building of the Renaissance: rectangular, overbearing and severe, from the outside it more resembles a prison than a palace. Built between 1563 and 1584, it was originally the creation of Juan Bautista de Toledo, though his one-time assistant, **Juan de Herrera**, took over and is normally given credit for the design. **Felipe II** planned the complex as both monastery and mausoleum, where he would live the life of a monk and "rule the world with two inches of paper". Later monarchs had less ascetic lifestyles, enlarging and richly decorating the palace quarters, but Felipe's simple rooms, with the chair that supported his gouty leg and the deathbed from which he could look across into the church where Mass was constantly celebrated, remain the most fascinating.

There's so much to see that you will need to set out early to do the sight real justice, but despite the size of the task it is still a highly rewarding visit.

Arrival and information

From **Madrid** there are up to 31 **trains** a day (5.45am–11.30pm from Atocha, calling at Chamartín, and up to twelve every weekday going on to Ávila), with **buses** (from the *intercambiador* at Moncloa) running every fifteeen minutes on weekdays and hourly at weekends. If you arrive by train, get straight on the local bus which shuttles you up to the centre of town – they leave promptly and it's a long uphill walk. If you're travelling by bus, stay on it and it will take you right up to the monastery. The **turismo** (Mon–Thurs 11am–6pm, Fri–Sun 10am–7pm; ☎918 905 313, ⓦwww.sanlorenzodeelescorial.org) is at c/Grimaldi 2, the small street to the north of the visitors' entrance to the monastery and running into c/Floridablanca.

El Escorial is an agreeable place to spend the night and has a number of friendly bars, good restaurants and a laid-back night-time scene centred around the Plaza de San Lorenzo. It is also possible to continue on to Ávila in the evening or to just make it a day-trip from Madrid. **Moving on** to Segovia by train is a bit trickier as it involves backtracking to Villalba (15min) and hooking up with a Madrid–Segovia train from there.

Accommodation

If you want to stay in the town, San Lorenzo del Escorial, there's a range of **accommodation**. Everything is close to the monastery, but in summer it's a favourite retreat from the heat of Madrid so make sure you book in advance.

Budget options

El Escorial c/Residencia 14 ☎918 905 924, ⓕ918 900 620. A large 45-room youth hostel situated up on the hill above the monastery. Bed and breakfast €11.56 for over 26's, €7.80 for under 26's. Only open to YHA members. There is another smaller hostel down in the park beside the monastery, the *Santa María del Buen Aire* (☎918 903 640, ⓕ918 903 792; closed temporarily for refurbishment), which has a pool and camping space, but it is usually packed with school groups.

Hotel Tres Arcos c/Juan de Toledo 42 ☎918 906 897, ⓦwww.terra.es/personal3/3arcos. Twenty-nine neat and simple rooms all with en-suite bathrooms at this family-run hotel located on one of the town's main streets. ❷

Moderate and expensive options

Hotel Botánico c/Timoteo Padrós 16 ☎918 907 879, ⊛www.valdesimonte.com. Twenty individually decorated rooms in this plush hotel set in the verdant grounds of a former palace. ❻

Hostal Cristina c/Juan de Toledo 6 ☎918 901 961, ⊜hcristina@jazzviajeros.com. A little old-fashioned and tends to be overshadowed by the plush *Hotel Victoria Palace* next door, but the 16-room *Hotel Cristina* is a very good value option. ❸

Hotel Florida c/Floridablanca 12 ☎918 901 721, ⊛www.hflorida.com. If you've got a little more cash to splash out, this is a well-appointed mid-range place which is now part of the Best Western chain. Fifty air-conditioned rooms at €71, while for an extra €20 you get a superior room with views of the monastery. ❹

Hotel Miranda Suizo c/Floridablanca 18 ☎918 904 711, ⊛www.hotelmirandasuizo.com. A few doors up from the *Florida*, this is a traditional but very comfortable option, with a lively bar and café. ❺

Hotel Victoria Palace c/Juan de Toledo 4 ☎918 969 890, ⊛www.hotelvictoriapalace.com. El Escorial's top hotel with its own pool, views of the monastery and all the facilities you would expect in this category. ❼

Camping

Caravaning El Escorial Carretera de Guadarrama a El Escorial km 3.5 ☎918 902 412, ⊛www.campingelescorial.com. A well-equipped campsite with several swimming pools and three tennis courts situated 6km out on the road back towards Guadarrama.

The monastery

Visits to the **Real Monasterio del Escorial** (Tues–Sun: April–Sept 10am–7pm; Oct–March 10am–6pm; €7 non-guided, €8 guided, combined ticket for monastery & El Valle de los Caídos €8.50 non-guided, €9.50 guided, free Wed for EU citizens; ⊛www.patrimonionacional.es) used to be deeply regulated, with compulsory guided tours to each section. Recently, they've become more relaxed and you can use your ticket (purchased in the **visitors' entrance**) to enter, in whatever sequence you like, the basilica, sacristy, chapter houses, library and royal apartments. The outlying **Casita del Príncipe** (aka **de Abajo**) and **Casita del Infante** (aka **de Arriba**) have separate opening hours and admission fees. To escape the worst of the crowds avoid Wednesdays and try visiting just before lunch, or pick that time for the royal apartments, which are the focus of all the bus tours. At present the Casita del Príncipe is closed as part of the programme of ongoing restoration.

For sustenance, you'll find a **cafetería** near the ticket office; drinks are OK but meals a bit of a rip-off.

The Biblioteca, Patio de los Reyes, Basilica and courtyards

A good starting point is to head for the west gateway, facing the mountains, and go through the traditional **main entrance**. Above it is a gargantuan statue of San Lorenzo holding a gridiron, the emblem of his martyrdom. Within is the **Biblioteca**, a splendid hall, with shelves designed by Herrera to harmonize with the architecture, and frescoes by Tibaldi and his assistants, showing the seven Liberal Arts. Its collections include the tenth-century *Codex Albeldensis*, St Teresa's personal diary, some gorgeously executed Arabic manuscripts, and a Florentine planetarium of 1572 demonstrating the movement of the planets according to the Ptolemaic and Copernican systems. Beyond is the **Patio de los Reyes**, named after the six statues of the kings of Israel on the facade of the basilica straight ahead. Off to the left is a school, to the right the monastery, both of them still in use.

In the **Basilica**, notice the flat vault of the *coro* above your head as you enter, which is apparently entirely without support, and the white marble Christ carved by Benvenuto Cellini, and carried here from Barcelona on workmen's shoulders. This is one of the few things permanently illuminated in the cold,

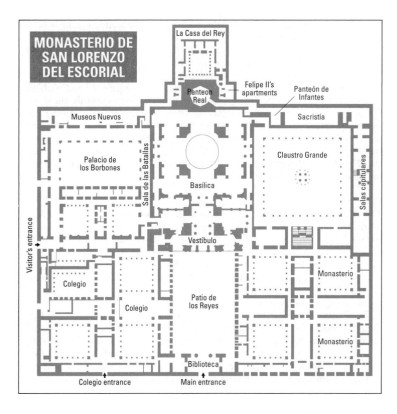

dark interior, but put some money in the slot to light up the main altarpiece and the whole aspect of the church is brightened. The east end is decorated by Italian artists: the sculptures are by the father-and-son team of Leone and Pompeo Leoni, who also carved the two facing groups of Carlos V with his family and Felipe II with three of his wives; Mary Tudor is excluded.

You can also wander at will in some of the Escorial's courtyards; most notable is the **Claustro Grande**, with frescoes of the life of the Virgin by Tibaldi, and the secluded gardens of the **Patio de los Evangelistas** which lie within.

The treasuries, Mausoleum and royal apartments

The **Sacristía** and **Salas Capitulares** (Chapter Houses) contain many of the monastery's religious treasures, including paintings by Titian, Velázquez and José Ribera. Beside the sacristy a staircase leads down to the **Panteón Real**, the final resting place of all Spanish monarchs since Carlos V, with the exception of Felipe V and Fernando VI. Alfonso XIII, who died in exile in Rome, was recently brought to join his ancestors.

The deceased monarchs lie in exquisite gilded marble tombs: kings (and Isabel II) on one side, their spouses on the other. Just above the entry is the Pudridero Real, a separate room in which the bodies rot for twenty years or so before the cleaned-up skeletons are moved here. The royal children are laid in the **Panteón de los Infantes**; the tomb of Don Juan, Felipe II's bastard half-brother, is grander than any of the kings', while the wedding-cake babies' tomb with room for sixty infants is more than half full.

What remains of the Escorial's art collection – works by Bosch, Gerard David, Dürer, Titian, Zurbarán and many others, which escaped transfer to the Prado – is kept in the elegant suite of rooms known as the **New Museums**. Don't miss the newly restored **Sala de Batallas**, a long gallery lined with an epic series of paintings depicting important imperial battles. Finally, there are the surprisingly modest **Salones Reales** (Royal Apartments) containing the austere **quarters of Felipe II**, with the chair that supported his gouty leg and the deathbed from which he was able to contemplate the high altar of the Basílica. If you make a reservation (☎918 905 903) you can also visit the **Palacio de los Borbones**, the more lavish royal quarters of Felipe's successors that take up the northeastern corner of the complex.

Outlying lodges

The **Casita del Príncipe** (aka Casita de Abajo; June–Sept Sat & Sun 10am–1pm & 4–6.30pm; €3.60; compulsory tours every 30min for a maximum of 10 people; reservations ☎918 905 903; closed for refurbishment until mid-2004) and the **Casita del Infante** (aka Casita de Arriba; Easter & mid-July to mid-Sept Tues–Sun 10am–6.45pm; €3.40, free Wed for EU citizens) are two eighteenth-century royal lodges, both full of decorative riches, and built by Juan de Villanueva, Spain's most accomplished Neoclassical architect – so worth seeing in themselves as well as for their formal gardens.

The Casita del Infante, which served as present King Juan Carlos's student digs, is a short way up into the hills and affords a good view of the Escorial complex; follow the road to the left from the main entrance and then stick to the contours of the mountain around to the right – it's well signposted. The Casita del Príncipe, in the Jardines del Príncipe below the monastery, is larger and more worthwhile, with an important collection of Giordano paintings and four pictures made from rice paste.

The Silla de Felipe

Around 3km out of town is the **Silla de Felipe** – "Felipe's Seat" – a chair carved into a rocky outcrop with a great view out towards the palace. His majesty is supposed to have sat here to watch the construction going on. You can reach it on foot by following the path through the arches beyond the main entrance to the monastery by the biblioteca; keep to the left as you go down the hill and then cross the main road and follow the signs. If you have a car, take the M-505 Ávila road and turn off at the sign after about 3km.

Eating and entertainment

The *Hotel Parilla Príncipe* at c/Floridablanca 6 has a good **restaurant**, while round the corner at c/San Antón 4, *La Cueva* is a good bet for both **tapas** and a larger meal. At the top end of the scale, *El Charolés*, c/Floridablanca 24, is renowned for its fish and stews, while *Los Pilares* (☎918 961 972) at c/Juan de Toledo 58 near the bus station specializes in recreating dishes from the era of Felipe II such as capon and bean stew, and will set you back €33 per person. A more low-key, but highly enjoyable, place is *La Fonda Genara* on the lively Plaza de San Lorenzo 2, inside the *centro coliseo*, which is filled with theatrical mementos and has a wide-ranging menu of good-quality Castilian fare; expect to pay around €30 per person. The *Cervecería Los Pescaítos*, two blocks west at c/Joaquín Costa 8, is a friendly bar serving fish dishes. Alternatively, grab a **bocadillo** from a drinks stand on c/Floridablanca and save your appetite for later. For purely liquid refreshment *Bar Erriuga*, on c/Ventura Rodríguez 7, is one of the best bets.

If by design or default you end up staying the night in El Escorial, there are several **cinemas**, along with the eighteenth-century **Coliseo** where you'll find jazz and classical **concerts** and theatrical productions year-round. Details of shows can be picked up from the turismo, or check out the free weekly *La Semana del Escorial*.

El Valle de los Caídos

The entrance to the **Valle de los Caídos** (Valley of the Fallen) lies 9km north of El Escorial: from here a road (along which you are not allowed to stop) runs 6km to the underground basilica. Above it is a vast cross, reputedly the largest in the world, and visible for miles along the road to Segovia. To visit El Valle de los Caídos from El Escorial, there is a local bus run by Herranz, which starts from the office in Plaza de la Virgen de Gracía, just north of the visitors' entrance to the monastery. The bus runs from El Escorial at 3.15pm, returning at 5.30pm (Tues–Sun; €7.80 return including entrance to the monument).

The **basilica complex** (Tues–Sun: April–Sept 10am–6.30pm; Oct–March 10am–5pm; €5, combined ticket with El Escorial €8.50 unguided, €9.50 guided, free Wed for EU citizens) denies its claims of memorial "to the Civil War dead of both sides" almost at a glance. The debased and grandiose architectural forms employed, the grim martial statuary, the constant inscriptions "Fallen for God and for Spain", and the proximity to El Escorial clue you in to its true function: the glorification of General Franco and his regime. The dictator himself lies buried behind the high altar, while the only other named tomb, marked simply "José Antonio", is that of his guru, the Falangist leader José Antonio Primo de Rivera, who was shot dead by Republicans at the beginning of the war. The "other side" is present only in the fact that the complex was built by the Republican army's survivors – political prisoners on quarrying duty.

From the entrance, a shaky funicular (Tues–Sun: April–Sept 11am–1.30pm & 4–6.30pm; Oct–Mar 11am–1.30pm & 3–5.30pm; €3) ascends to the base of the **cross**, offering, as you can imagine, a superlative view over the Sierra de Guadarrama and a closer look at the giant figures propping up the base of the cross.

The Sierra de Guadarrama

The routes from Madrid and El Escorial to Segovia strike through the heart of the **Sierra de Guadarrama** – a beautiful journey, worth taking for its own sake. The road is occasionally marred by suburban development, especially around **Navacerrada**, Madrid's main ski station, but from the train it's almost entirely unspoiled. There are plenty of opportunities for walking, but make sure you buy the appropriate maps in Madrid.

If you want to base yourself in the mountains for a while you'd do best to head for **Cercedilla**, 75 minutes by train on the Madrid–Segovia line – and a little way off the main road. Alternatively, over to the east, there is **Manzanares el Real**, with an odd medieval castle and a reservoir-side setting.

In the shadow of the mountains to the north is the Valle de Lozoya. At the western end is the village of **Rascafría** and the nearby Benedictine monastery of El Paular, and to the east the old fortified town of **Buitrago** with a medieval core and small Picasso museum.

Cercedilla and the Puerto de Navacerrada

CERCEDILLA is an alpine-looking village perched at the foot of the valley leading up to the Puerto de Fuenfría and makes an excellent base for summer walking. Like Manzanares el Real, it is much frequented by *madrileños* at weekends, but has the advantage of being accessible by **train** from Madrid (over twenty a day, 6am–11pm from Atocha, calling at Chamartín, and nine daily going on to Segovia) and buses leaving every half hour from the Intercambiador de Autobuses de Moncloa. **Accommodation** is limited to the recently refurbished *Hostal El Aribel*, near the station (☎918 521 511, ⒲www.elaribel.es.vg; ❷) at c/Emilio Serrano 71, and two **youth hostels** up on the Dehesas road: *Villa Castora* (☎918 520 334, Ⓕ918 522 411) which is close to the town, and, 2km up the road in the meadows leading up to Fuenfría, *Las Dehesas* (☎918 520 135, Ⓕ918 521 836). At both a YH card is needed and bed and breakfast costs €10.80 for over 26's, €7.80 for under 26's. Further up still, you'll find a helpful **information booth** (daily 10am–6pm; ☎918 522 213). There are several **eating** places in town: *Los Frutales* on the Carretera de las Dehesas does good *croquetas, judías con perdiz* (partridge and beans) and *trucha* (trout), the train station has a restaurant on the first floor or you could try the restaurant at *Hostal El Aribel*. For the more energetic the village is the starting point for a very pleasant five-hour round-trip **walk** along the pine-fringed Calzada Romana (old Roman road) up to the Puerto de la Fuenfría (1796m) with its striking views down into Segovia province. Follow the signs up to Las Dehesas where there is an information centre (daily 9am–6pm; ☎918 522 213) which provides maps and advice. Then head past the meadows and follow the clearly indicated path up to the Puerto.

From Cercedilla, you can embark on a wonderful little train ride to the **Puerto de Navacerrada** (information ☎918 539 978, ⒲www.puerto navacerrada.com), the most important pass in the mountains and the heart of the ski area, or a little further on to **Cotos** where a number of well-maintained walks around the **Parque Natural de Peñalara** (⒲www.parquedeguadarra-ma.com) begin. The train runs hourly over weekends and holidays and passes through the *parque natural*, an extension of the upper Manzanares basin: watch out for roe deer and wild boar. In winter it is possible to ski in both Navacerrada and Cotos, but be prepared for long queues and traffic jams at weekends.

Navacerrada is also the starting point for a number of impressive walks along the **high peaks**, while Cotos is the gateway to the highest peak in the Sierra, Peñalara (2430m). It can be reached in about four hours, but is a tough ascent. Less challenging but very enjoyable is the easy hike to the Laguna Grande. There is a small **information booth** just above the small café close to the Cotos train station that will give advice on all routes (summer Mon–Fri 10am-6pm, Sat, Sun & holidays 10am–8pm; winter daily 10am–6pm; ☎918 691 757).

El Paular and Rascafría

Some 10km below Cotos in the beautiful Valle de Lozoya is the **Monasterio de Santa María de El Paular**, originally a Carthusian monastery founded at the end of the fourteenth century, and now home to a handful of Benedictine monks who provide guided tours (Spanish only; daily noon, 1pm and 5pm; closed Thurs pm; free) of the slient cloisters and the main church. Part of the monastery has been turned into a *parador*-style hotel *Santa María de El Paular* (☎918 691 011, Ⓕ918 691 006; ❼), with a delightful courtyard bar, ideal for cool summer refreshments. Nearby is the pleasant little mountain village of **Rascafría**, where there is plenty of **accommodation** and a bus link back to Madrid (twice a day, 2 hrs 15min). The 12-room *Los Calizos* (☎918 691 112;

△ Manzanares el Real castle

❻) is a tranquil upmarket hotel with a fine restaurant and extensive grounds a little way out on the road to Miraflores. The *Hostal Rosali* (☎918 691 213; ❷) is much cheaper, but still a very cosy option closer to town.

Manzanares el Real and La Pedriza

Some 50km north of Madrid, on the shores of the Santillana *embalse* (reservoir), lies **MANZANARES EL REAL**, a town which in former times was disputed between the capital and Segovia. Nowadays it's geared to Madrid weekenders, whose villas dot the landscape for miles around. Nearby, however, the ruggedly beautiful **La Pedriza**, a spur of the Sierra de Guadarrama, has been declared a regional park (access limited to 350 cars a day at weekends; free; information centre open daily 10am–6pm; ☎918 539 978), and has some enjoyable walks, as well as some much-revered technical climbs, notably the ascent to the jagged Peña del Diezmo. It is also home to a very large colony of griffon vultures.

In Manzanares itself, the one attraction is the **castle** (daily 10am–1pm & 3–5.30pm; free), which despite its eccentric appearance is a perfectly genuine fifteenth-century construction, built around an earlier chapel. It was soon modified into a palace by the architect Juan Guas, who built an elegant gallery on the south side, false machicolations on the other, and studded the tower with stones resembling cannonballs. The interior has been heavily restored, but it makes for an interesting visit.

As befits Manzanares, **accommodation** is expensive and limited to the small *Hostal Tranco* (☎918 530 423; ❸) and the more upmarket *Hotel Parque Real* (☎918 539 912, ✆918 539 960; ❸–❹). However, there is usually space at one of the two **campsites**, *El Ortigal* (☎918 530 120) at the foot of La Pedriza and close to the park on c/Montañeros, or the well-equipped *La Fresneda* (☎ & ✆918 476 523) on the Carretera M608 towards Soto del Real. **Food** is not cheap either, but good meals can be had at *Los Arcos* in c/Real, the *Restaurante Parra* in c/Panaderos and the newly opened *Asador del Carmen* in the urbanización Lago Santillana. **Buses** from Madrid run hourly (daily 7.30am–9.30pm) from Plaza de Castilla (ⓂPlaza de Castilla).

Buitrago de Lozoya and Patones

Further east beyond the road to Burgos is the attractive little town of **Buitrago de Lozoya** (13 buses a day from Plaza de Castilla in Madrid), a fortified settlement with defensive walls that date from the twelfth century, a fine Mudéjar church and, more surprisingly, a small **Picasso museum** (Tues–Fri 11am–2pm & 4–6pm, Sat 10am–1.30pm & 3.30–6.30pm, Sun 10am–2.30pm; free). The collection, based on work donated by the artist to his friend and local barber Eugenio Arias, features an interesting selection of 60 minor pieces dated from between 1948 and 1972.

Nearby on the southern edge of the so-called Sierra Pobre is the picturesque mountain village of **Patones de Arriba** (three buses a day to nearby Patones Abajo from Plaza de Castilla), abandoned in the 1930s but since restored and now a fashionable weekend destination for many *madrileños* who head for a Castilian roast lunch at one of the *mesones* or even stay the night at the luxury boutique hotel *El Tiempo Perdido* (☎918 432 152, ✆918 432 148; ❽). The black slate architecture of the village is undeniably beautiful, the views are good, and you can be assured of a good meal, but there is little else to detain the casual visitor. For information about the region as a whole consult the **website** Ⓦwww.sierranorte.com.

Ávila

Two things distinguish **ÁVILA**: its eleventh-century **walls**, two perfectly pre-served kilometres of which surround the old town, and the mystic writer **Santa Teresa**, who was born here and whose shrines are a major focus of religious pilgrimage. Set on a high plain, with the peaks of the Sierra de Gredos behind, the town is quite a sight, especially if you time it right and approach with the evening sun highlighting the golden tone of the walls and the details of the 88 towers.

The walls were ordered by Alfonso VI, after his capture of the city from the Moors in 1090; they took his Muslim prisoners nine years to construct. At closer quarters, they prove a bit of a facade, as the old city within is sparsely populated and a little dishevelled, most of modern life having moved into the new developments outside the fortifications. However, the fine **Romanesque churches** dotted in and about the old city, plus good walks around the walls, make the town a worthwhile stopover, either combined with El Escorial, or en route to Salamanca.

Arrival and information

From **Madrid** (Chamartín station) there are up to 24 **trains** a day to Ávila; **buses** are less frequent (Estación del Sur; eight on weekdays, three at weekends). The train station is a fifteen-minute walk to the east of the old town, or a local bus into Plaza de la Victoria. On foot, follow the broad Avenida José Antonio to its end, by the large church of Santa Ana, and bear left up c/Duque de Alba to reach Plaza Santa Teresa. Buses use a terminal on the Avenida de Madrid, a little closer in: walking from here, cross the small park opposite, then turn right up c/Duque de Alba, or take a local bus to Plaza de la Victoria near the cathedral. **Driving**, follow signs for the walls (*murallas*) or the *parador* and you should be able to park just outside the old town.

Ávila's walls make orientation straightforward, with the **cathedral** and most other sights contained within. Just outside the southeast corner of the walls is the city's main square, **Plaza Santa Teresa**, and the most imposing of the old gates, the **Puerta del Alcázar**. Within the walls, the old market square, **Plaza de la Victoria**, fronts the *ayuntamiento* at the heart of the old city.

The main **turismo** (Mon–Fri 9am–2pm & 5–7pm, Sat & Sun 10am–2pm & 5–8pm; ☎920 211 387, ⓦwww.jcyl.es/turismo) is in the Plaza de la Catedral, and there's another, smaller office next to the Basílica de San Vicente (July–Sept only; same hours; ⓦwww.avilaturismo.com).

Accommodation

There are numerous cheap *hostales* around the train station and along Avenida José Antonio, but you should be able to find something nearer the walled centre of town. You'll find a well-maintained **campsite**, *Camping Sonsoles* (☎920 256 336; open June–Sept), 2km out on the Toledo road, near the football stadium.

Budget options

Hostal Bellas c/Caballeros 19 ☎ 920 212 910, ⓕ 920 352 449, ⓦwww.hostalbellas.com. Eager-to-please owners in this recently refurbished centrally located *hostal*. Most rooms have showers and there are discounts out of season. ❷

Hostal Casa Felipe Plaza del Mercado Chico 12

☎920 213 924. Reasonable and centrally located; some rooms have showers and overlook the square. ❷

Hostal Continental Plaza de la Catedral 4 ☎920 211 502, ⓕ 920 211 563. An attractive old hotel, opposite the cathedral; its charms are fading fast, but the rooms are large and en suite and some

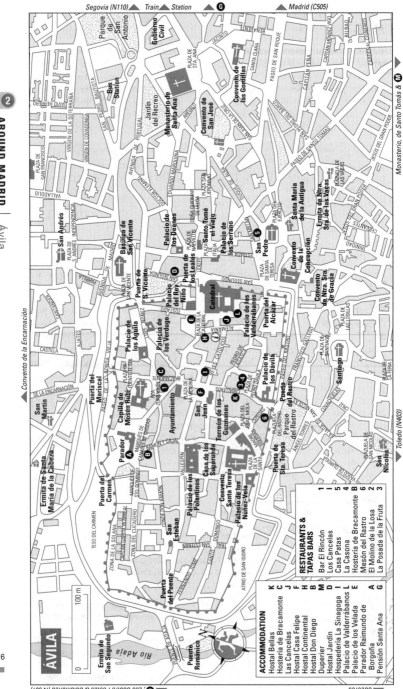

Segovia (N110) ▲   Train ▲ Station   ▲ **G**   ▲ Madrid (C505)

◀ Convento de la Encarnación

ÁVILA

0   100 m

Ermita de Santa María de la Cabeza

Ermita de San Segundo

Río Adaja

Puente Románico

Monasterio, de Santo Tomás & **M** ▶

Toledo (N403) ▶

Cáceres ▶

Los Cuatro Postes & Salamanca (N 501) ▲

RESTAURANTS & TAPAS BARS

Bar El Rincón	1
Los Cancelas	I
Casa Patas	5
La Casona	4
Hostería de Bracamonte	B
Mesón del Rastro	6
El Molino de la Losa	2
La Posada de la Fruta	3

ACCOMMODATION

Hostal Bellas	K
Hostería de Bracamonte	C
Las Cancelas	J
Hostal Casa Felipe	F
Hostal Continental	H
Hostal Don Diego	B
Duperier	M
Hostal Jardín	D
Hospedería La Sinagoga	I
Palacio de Valderrábanos	L
Palacio de los Velada	E
Parador Raimundo de Borgoña	A
Pensión Santa Ana	G

have great views onto the square. **❷**

Hostal Don Diego c/Marqués de Canales y Chozas 5 ☎920 255 475, ⓕ920 254 549. Friendly, very good-value *hostal* just opposite the *Parador*. All thirteen rooms have bath or shower. **❷**

Duperier Avda. de Juventud s/n ☎ & ⓕ920 221 716. Small youth hostel (with 11pm curfew) out past the monastery, near the local swimming pool. Rooms with bath and meals available. Open July to mid-Sept. YH card needed; €6.61, €9.36 for over 26's.

Hostal Jardín c/San Segundo 38 ☎920 211 074. Large *hostal* near Puerta de los Leales, which often has rooms when other places are full. **❷–❸**

Pensión Santa Ana c/Alfonso de Montalvo 2 ☎ & ⓕ920 220 063. Fail-safe option between the train station and city centre. Eight rooms with shared facilities. **❶**

Moderate and expensive options

Hostería de Bracamonte c/Bracamonte 6 ☎920 251 280, ⓕ920 253 838, ⓦwww.hospederia bracamonte.com. Atmospheric and elegant hotel, between the city walls and the Plaza de la Victoria, created from a number of converted Renaissance mansions. No a/c. **❹–❺**

Las Cancelas c/Cruz Veija 6 ☎920 212 249.

Another converted fifteenth-century building. Some of the fourteen rooms have good views of the cathedral and walls. There's a good bar and restaurant, too. **❸**

Palacio de Valderrábanos Plaza de la Catedral 9 ☎920 211 023, ⓦwww.palaciovalderrabanos hotel.com. This former bishop's palace beats the *parador* for ambience and its rooms are just as good. **❻**

Palacio de los Velada Plaza de la Catedral 10 ☎920 255 100, ⓦwww.veladahoteles.com. Beautifully converted sixteenth-century palace and the priciest hotel in town at €125 a room, but look out for some good weekend deals that can bring the price down substantially. **❼**

Parador Raimundo de Borgoña c/Marqués de Canales y Chozas 2 ☎920 211 340, ⓦwww.paradores.es. A converted fifteenth-century mansion – not the most exciting *parador* in Spain, but pleasant enough, with the usual comforts. It's the cheapest of Ávila's top hotels, with doubles at €95. **❻**

Hospedería La Sinagoga c/Reyes Católicos 22 ☎920 352 321, ⓦwww.lasinagoga.com. As the name suggests, this marvellous little hotel was a synagogue in the fifteenth century. Modern, comfortable and good-value rooms in a tastefully restored and atmospheric building. **❹**

The Town

The focus of Ávila's sights is, inevitably, **Santa Teresa**, with whom most of the numerous convents and churches claim some connection. On the secular front, a circuit outside the **walls** makes a fine walk, and from the Puerta del Alcázar you can climb up and stroll around a section.

Santa Teresa de Ávila

Santa Teresa (1515–82) was born to a noble family in Ávila and from childhood began to experience visions and religious raptures. At the age of seven she attempted to run away with her brother to be martyred by the Moors: the spot where they were recaptured and brought back, **Los Cuatro Postes**, is a fine vantage point from which to admire the walls of the town.

Teresa's religious career began at the Carmelite convent of La Encarnación, where she was a nun for 27 years. From this base, she went on to reform the movement and found convents throughout Spain. She was an ascetic, but her appeal – and her importance to the Counter-Reformation – lay in the mystic sensuality of her experience of Christ, as revealed in her autobiography, for centuries a bestseller in Spain. As joint patron saint of Spain (together with Santiago – or St James), she remains a central pillar in Spanish Catholicism and schoolgirls are brought into Ávila by the busload to experience first-hand the life of the woman they are supposed to emulate.

On a more bizarre note, one of Santa Teresa's mummified hands has now been returned to Ávila after spending the Franco years by the bedside of the great dictator.

Santa Teresa in Ávila

The obvious place to start a tour of Teresa's Ávila is the **Convento de Santa Teresa** (daily 8.30am–1.30pm & 3.30–8pm; free), built over the saint's birth-place just inside the south gate of the old town – entered off the Paseo del Rastro. Most of the convent remains *de clausura* but you can see the very spot where she was born, now an elaborate chapel in the Baroque church, which is decorated with scenes of the saint demonstrating her powers of levitation to various august bodies. In a small reliquary (daily: 9.30am–1.30pm & 3.30–7pm, summer 9.30am–1.30pm & 3.30–8pm; free), beside the gift shop, is a **museum** (summer daily 10am–2pm & 4–7pm, winter 10am–1.30pm & 3.30–5.30pm; €2) containing memorials of Teresa's life, including not only her rosary beads, but also one of the fingers she used to count them with.

Heading through the old town, and leaving by the Puerta del Carmen, you can follow a lane, c/Encarnación, to the **Convento de la Encarnación** (Mon–Fri 9.30am–1.30pm & 3.30–6pm, Sat & Sun 9.30am–2pm & 3.30–6pm; €1.20). Each of the rooms here is labelled with the act Teresa performed, while everything she might have touched or looked at is on display. A small museum section also provides a reasonable introduction to the saint's life, with maps showing the convents, and a selection of her sayings – the pithiest, perhaps, "Life is a night in a bad hotel."

A third Teresan sight lies a couple of blocks east of the Plaza de Santa Teresa. This is the **Convento de San José** (daily: summer 10am–1pm & 4–7pm; winter 10am–12.30pm & 3–6pm; €1), the first monastery that the saint founded, in 1562. Its museum contains relics and memorabilia, including the coffin in which Teresa once slept, and assorted personal possessions. The tomb of her brother Lorenzo is in the larger of the two churches.

Lastly, you might want to make your way up to **Los Cuatro Postes**, a little four-posted shrine, 1.5km along the Salamanca road west of town. It was here, aged seven, that the infant Teresa was recaptured by her uncle, running away with her brother to seek Christian martyrdom fighting the Moors.

The cathedral and other sights

The three most beautiful churches in Ávila – the cathedral, San Vicente, and the Monasterio de Santo Tomás – are less directly associated with its most famous resident. Around the cathedral and Santo Tomé el Viejo (just outside the northeast corner of the walls), there is also a scattering of impressive **Renaissance mansions** – none of them is open to visitors but they give a glimpse of old Castilian wealth in their coats of arms and decorative facades.

Ávila's **Catedral** (summer Mon–Sat 10am–8pm, Sun noon–7pm; winter Mon–Fri 10am–5pm, Sat 10am–6pm, Sun noon–6pm; closed Jan 1 & 6, Oct 15 & Dec 25; €3) was started in the twelfth century but has never been finished, as evidenced by the missing tower above the main entrance. The earliest Romanesque parts were as much fortress as church, and the apse actually forms an integral part of the city walls. Their defensive function was real, with the twelfth-century Bishop Sancho providing sanctuary here for the young Alfonso IX, prior to his accession.

Inside, the succeeding changes of style are immediately apparent; the **Romanesque** parts are made of a strange red-and-white mottled stone, then there's an abrupt break and the rest of the main structure is pure white stone and **Gothic** forms. Although the proportions are exactly the same, this newer half of the cathedral seems infinitely more spacious. The *coro*, whose elaborate carved back you see as you come in, and two chapels in the left aisle, are **Renaissance** additions. Here you can admire the carved stalls in the *coro* (the work of a Dutch sculptor, Cornelius) and the elaborate marble tomb of a fif-teenth-century bishop known as El Tostado (the "toasted" or "swarthy"). The thirteenth-century *sacristia* with its star-shaped cupola and gold inlay decor, and the treasury-museum with its monstrous silver *custodia* and ancient religious images are also worth a visit.

The **Basílica de San Vicente** (daily: summer 10am–2pm & 4–7pm; winter 10am–1.30pm & 4–6pm; €1.40), like the cathedral, is a mixture of architec-tural styles. Its twelfth-century doorways and the portico which protects them are magnificent examples of Romanesque art, while the church itself shows the influence of later trends. San Vicente was martyred on this site, and his tomb narrates the gruesome story of torture and execution by the Romans. Legend has it that following the martyrdom a rich Jew who had been poking fun at them was enveloped and suffocated by a great serpent that miraculously emerged from the rocks. On the verge of asphyxiation he repented and con-verted to Christianity, later building the church on the very same site, and he, too, is said to be buried here. In the crypt you can see part of the rocky crag where San Vicente and his sisters were executed and from which the serpent later supposedly appeared. The warm pink glow of the sandstone of the church is a characteristic feature of Ávila, also notable in the church of **San Pedro**, on Plaza de Santa Teresa.

Just outside the city walls, through the Puerta del Peso de la Harina, is the small **Museo Provincial**, housed in the sixteenth-century Palacio de los Deanes (summer Tues–Sat 10am–2pm & 4–7pm, Sun 10am–2pm; winter Tues–Sat 10am–2pm & 4.30–7.30pm, Sun 10.30am–2pm; €1.20, free Sat & Sun) where the cathedral's deans once lived. Today, its eclectic exhibits include collections of archeological remains, ceramics, agricultural implements, tradi-tional costumes and furnishings from around the Ávila province, as well as some fine Romanesque statues and a wonderful fifteenth-century triptych depicting the life of Christ. The ticket also allows you entry to the museum storeroom in the church of Santo Tomé El Viejo just opposite.

It's possible to walk along the **city walls** from Puerta del Alcázar to Puerta del Rastro (summer daily 11am–8pm; winter Tues–Sat 11am–6pm; €3.50); the view of the town is stunning. There have been some experiments with late opening in the summer, but check with the turismo. Tickets are available from the green kiosk by the Puerta del Alcázar.

Eating and drinking

Ávila has a decent if unexceptional array of **bars** and **restaurants**, some of them sited just outside the walls. Within the walls, a stroll from Plaza de la Victoria along c/Vallespin will allow you to compare *menús* and prices. **Local specialities** include the Castilian standby *cordero asado* (roast lamb), *judias del barco con chorizo* (haricot beans with sausage), *mollejas* (cow's stomach) and *yemas de Santa Teresa* (candied egg-yolk) – the last of these sold in confectioners all over town. For **nightlife** head outside the city walls to c/Capitán Peña where the strip of four *discobares* next to each other keeps the walking to a minimum.

Bar El Rincón Plaza Zurraquín 6. To the north of Plaza de la Victoria, this bar serves a generous three-course *menú* for €10.

Los Cancelas c/Cruz Vieja 6. Next to the cathedral and in the hotel of the same name, this friendly restau-rant is popular with locals and it serves some great *cordero asado* (roast lamb); the *menú* is €10.80.

Casa Patas c/San Millán 4. Pleasant bar, with good tapas, and a little *comedor* (evenings only), near the church of San Pedro. Closed Wed & Sept.

La Casona Plaza de Pedro Dávila 6. Popular restaurant specializing in lamb, with *menús* start-ing at €9.60.

Hostería de Bracamonte c/Bracamonte 6.
Comfy, rustic atmosphere in this restaurant housed within the walls of a converted Renaissance mansion. Speciality is *codero asado* for €13.20. Closed Tues.

Mesón del Rastro Plaza del Rastro 1. Excellent bar, attached to the *hostal* of the same name, with a range of tapas. Behind it is a modest-priced restaurant, an old-fashioned place with solid, traditional food.

El Molino de la Losa c/Bajada de la Losa 12 ☎920 211 101. Converted fifteenth-century mill out by Los Cuatro Postes, with a deserved reputation and handy if you're with kids (there's a play area in the garden). The *menú* is €20. Closed Mon & mid-Oct to mid-March.

La Posada de la Fruta Plaza de Pedro Dávila 8. With an attractive, sunny, covered courtyard, this is a nice place for a drink, and also serves some good standard Castilian fare.

On from Ávila

Ávila is quite a nexus with road and rail routes to Salamanca and Valladolid, from where you can get to just about anywhere in northern Spain, while to the east Segovia (see p.182) is less than two hours away by bus. Within striking distance, too, to the south, is the beautiful Sierra de Gredos (see below).

On the **Salamanca route**, both road and rail routes pass through **Peñaranda de Bracamonte**, a crumbling old town with a couple of large plazas and ancient churches. From here, if you have your own vehicle, you can continue to Salamanca on a slightly longer route through **Alba de Tormes**. Santa Teresa died here, and the Carmelite convent which contains the remains of her body (not much of it, to judge by the number of relics scattered around Spain) is another major target of pilgrimage. There are the remains of a castle here, too, and several other interesting churches.

Heading north **towards Valladolid**, road and rail both pass through **Medina del Campo** with its beautiful castle (see p.434).

The Sierra de Gredos

The **Sierra de Gredos** continues the line of the Sierra de Guadarrama, enclosing Madrid to the north and west. A major mountain range, with peaks in excess of 2500m, Gredos offers the best trekking in central Spain, including high-level routes across the passes as well as more casual walks around the villages.

By bus, the easiest access is from Madrid to **Arenas de San Pedro**, from where you can explore the range, and then move on west into the valley of La Vera in Extremadura (see p.217). If you have your own transport, you could head into the range south from Ávila along the C502, and you might prefer to base yourself in one of the villages on the north side of the range, along the **Tormes valley**, and do circular walks from there. The *casas rurales* that are scattered throughout the villages often make a good base, especially if you are travelling in a group (information line ☎902 424 141, ⓦ www.casasgredos.com & ⓦ www.gredos.com).

Arenas de San Pedro and Mombeltrán

ARENAS DE SAN PEDRO is a sizeable town with a somewhat prettified fifteenth-century castle and a Gothic church. It has a good range of **accommodation**: pleasant options include the *Hostería Los Galayos* (☎ & ⓕ920 371 379, ⓦ www.losgalayos.com; ❸), which also has a reliable restaurant, the roomy *Posada de la Triste Condesa* (☎920 372 567; ❸), *Hostal Castillo* (☎920 370 091;

❷) and the cosily furnished *El Canchal* (☎920 370 958, ⓕ920 370 914; ❸). If you haven't already obtained **maps** of Gredos, you can pick up a functional pamphlet from the **turismo** (Mon–Fri 9.30am–1.30pm & 4.30–7.30pm, Sat 9.30am–1.30pm; ☎920 372 368, ⓦwww.ayto-arenas.com) on the main street c/Triste Condesa or buy more detailed sheets from the bookshop Librería Nava on the same road.

MOMBELTRÁN, 12km north (an enjoyable, mainly downhill, walk from Arenas), is an attractive alternative stop, with its fifteenth-century **castle** of the Dukes of Albuquerque set against a stunning mountain backdrop. The village has two **hostales**, the *Albuquerque* (☎920 386 032; ❷) and *Marji* (☎920 386 031; ❸), and a summer-only **campsite**, *Prados Abiertos* (☎920 386 061), 4km south of the centre towards Arenas de San Pedro.

El Arenal and El Hornillo

The main reason to stop in Arenas de San Pedro is to make your way up to the villages of El Hornillo and El Arenal, respectively 6km and 9km to the north, the trail heads for some excellent **mountain walks**. There are no buses but it's a pleasant walk up from Arenas to El Arenal on a track running between the road and the river – start out past the sports centre and swimming pool in Arenas.

You can walk over the top of Gredos from **EL ARENAL** – the path via the pass at Puerto de la Cabrilla is in reasonable shape – and strike out along the ridge in either direction, to the main road at Puerto del Pico or back to El Arenal. **EL HORNILLO**, however, is the more common trail, and the beginning of the Circo de Gredos, one of the main recognized trekking routes over the Gredos watershed.

An alternative trek is to head due south from El Arenal, along a well-defined path over a broad pass to Candeleda (see p.182); this is a long day's walk but it's more or less all downhill.

The Circo de Gredos

The walk from El Hornillo over the **Gredos watershed** takes most of a day to accomplish, exchanging the pine and granite of the steep south slopes for the *matorral* (scrub thickets), cow pastures and wide horizons on the northern side. Over the top, you'll emerge on a twelve-kilometre stretch of paved road linking **Hoyos del Espino**, a village in the Tormes valley, and the so-called **Plataforma**, jumping-off point to the highest peaks of the Gredos. It's best to call it a day just above the Plataforma, where there's a *refugio* (mountain refuge) on the high Pozas meadows. From here, you can proceed up to the Circo de Laguna Grande, a spectacular two-hour walk beyond Pozas on a well-defined path.

Hoyos makes a good base as there are several places to stay, a good few bars and shops. *Aparthotel Gredos* (☎920 349 252 or 653 161 069; ❷) offers thirteen studio apartments for two or three at €40. Just outside the village, and if you want some real comfort, is the wonderful *Hotel Milano Real* (☎920 349 108, ⓦwww.elmilanoreal.com; ❹), which has thirteen comfortable doubles and eight suites (€125), each one decorated according to a different theme. It also has a high-quality restaurant with a good-value *menú de degustación* at €30. There is a well-established **campsite** on the road towards the Plataforma (Camping Gredos ☎920 207 585; Easter to mid-Oct).

Circo de Laguna Grande and Circo de las Cinco Lagunas

The **Circo de Laguna Grande** is the centrepiece of the Gredos range, with its highest peak, **Almanzor** (2593m), looming above, surrounded by pinnacles sculpted into utterly improbable shapes. The valley with its huge lake is popular with day-trippers and weekenders, as you can drive up here from Hoyos del Espino, and its **refugio** is often full, especially at weekends, so it is best to reserve (☎920 207 576); camping out by the refugio is, however, an accepted alternative.

The valley path, actually Alfonso XIII's old hunting route, continues west for a couple of hours before ending abruptly at the edge of a sharp, scree-laden descent into the **Circo de las Cinco Lagunas**. The drop is amply rewarded by virtual solitude, even in midsummer, and sightings of *Capra pyrenaica gloriae*, the graceful (and almost tame) Gredos mountain goat. Protected by law since the 1920s, they now number several thousand and frequent the north slopes of Gredos in the warmer months.

The Tormes valley: Navarredonda

On the north side of Gredos is the Tormes valley, trailed by the C500 to the main N110 at El Barco de Ávila. There is accommodation at **NAVARREDONDA**, including a **youth hostel** (☎920 348 005; YHA card needed; €9.32, €6.61 for under 26's), a **campsite**, *Camping Navagredos* (☎920 207 476; May–Sept), a beautifully furnished **casa rural**, the *Casa de Arriba* (☎920 348 024, 🖳 www.casaadearriba.com; ❹), and Spain's first ever **parador** (☎920 348 048, 🖳 www.parador.es; ❺) at km 43 on the C500.

Candeleda and Madrigal de la Vera

The village of **CANDELEDA**, on the Arenas–Jarandilla road, is nothing special but it's amazingly popular with Spanish summer holidaymakers, who book its *hostales* weeks in advance. The **turismo** is in the Casa Cultura, close to the Plaza Mayor (daily 10am–1.30pm & 5–8pm; ☎920 380 396), and can provide helpful information on walking and hiking in the area. If you're planning ahead, the best-value **place to stay** is *Hostal La Pastora* (☎920 382 127; ❷) and the fanciest the *Hostal Pedrós* (☎920 380 951; ❷). Campers sometimes set up their tents alongside the river, west of town.

At **MADRIGAL DE LA VERA**, a more attractive village 12km to the west of Candeleda, there's an official campsite, *Alardos* (☎927 565 066; March–Sept), and yet another route across the Gredos, this time leading to **Bohoyo**, a hamlet 4km southwest of El Barco de Ávila.

Segovia and around

After Toledo, **SEGOVIA** is the outstanding trip from Madrid. A relatively small city, strategically sited on a rocky ridge, it is deeply and haughtily Castilian, with a panoply of squares and mansions from its days of Golden Age grandeur, when it was a royal resort and a base for the Cortes (parliament). It was in Segovia that Isabel la Católica was proclaimed queen of Castille in 1474.

For a city of its size, there are a stunning number of outstanding architectural monuments. Most celebrated are the **Roman aqueduct**, the **cathedral** and the fairy-tale **Alcázar**, but the less obvious attractions – the cluster of ancient churches and the many mansions found in the lanes of the old town, all in a warm, honey-coloured stone – are what really make it worth a visit. Just a few kilometres outside the city and reasonably accessible from Segovia are two Bourbon palaces, **La Granja** and **Riofrío**.

Arrival and information

Well connected by road and rail, Segovia is an easy trip from Madrid with nine trains daily (1hr 50min–2hrs) from Chamartín and Atocha, as well as up to 31 buses (operated by La Sepulvedana, Paseo de la Florida 11; Ⓜ Príncipe Pío). The city's own **train station** is some distance out of town – take bus #3 to the central Plaza Mayor; the **bus station** is on the same route.

The **turismo** (daily 9am–8pm, Fri & Sat closes an hour later; ☎902 203 030, Ⓦ www.jcyl.es/turismo & Ⓦ www.infosegovia.com), in the **Plaza Mayor**, offers a list of local accommodation plus a *Guía Semanal* with transport timetables and current events; most significant facts are displayed in the window if it's closed. You'll find a second tourist office in the busy **Plaza de Azoguejo** (daily 10am–8pm; ☎921 462 914, Ⓔsegoviaturism@vianwe.com) by the aqueduct which has a detailed map of the city on sale for €0.30. There is an **Internet café** close by at c/Tedosio el Grande 10 (Mon–Sat 9am–1am).

Accommodation

Most of the **accommodation** is to be found in the streets around the Plaza Mayor and Plaza de Azoguejo, but rooms can be hard to come by even out of season, so it's worth booking ahead if you're considering more than a day-trip. Be warned that in winter, at over 1000m, the nights can be very cold and sometimes snowy, and the more basic rooms aren't generally heated.

Budget options

Hostal Don Jaime c/Ochoa Ondategui 8 ☎921 444 787, Ⓕ921 444 790. Excellent sixteen-room *hostal* near Plaza de Azoguejo. All doubles have their own bathroom. ❷

Emperador Teodosio Paseo Conde de Sepúlveda 4 ☎921 441 111, Ⓕ921 441 047. Pleasant, spacious student residence which becomes a youth hostel for July and Aug. Located between the train and bus stations. €9.32 for over-26, €6.61 under-26. ❶

Pensión Ferri c/Escuderos 10 ☎921 460 957. On a street off Plaza Mayor, quiet, clean and with a small garden. ❶

Hospedaje El Gato Plaza del Salvador 10 ☎921 423 244, Ⓕ921 438 047. Recently refurbished *hostal* situated just below the aqueduct. Ten quiet rooms, all with a/c, en-suite bathrooms and satellite TV. ❷

Hostal Juan Bravo c/Juan Bravo 12 ☎921 463 413. Lots of big, comfortable rooms and plant-festooned bathrooms. A good budget option. ❷

Hostal Plaza c/Cronista Lecea 11 ☎921 460 303, Ⓕ921 460 305. Clean *hostal*, centrally located just off the Plaza Mayor. A/c in some rooms. Also has a garage. ❷

Moderate and expensive options

Hotel Acueducto Avda. Padre Claret 10 ☎902 250 550, Ⓦ www.hotelacueducto.com. Pleasant hotel outside the city walls and overlooking the aqueduct. The restaurant gets busy with bus parties during the day, but is quiet most evenings. ❹–❺

Hotel Alcázar c/San Marcos 5 ☎921 438 568, Ⓦ www.alcazar-hotel.com. Tranquil eight-room hotel situated next to the River Eresma with a relaxing garden with views of the Alcázar. Look out for the special offers on the website. ❻

Hostal Hidalgo c/José Canalejas 3 & 5 ☎921 463 529, Ⓕ921 463 531. Small, beautiful old building overlooking the church of San Martín, with a good restaurant. *El Hidalgo 2*, the sister *hostal* nearby at c/Juan Bravo 21 (☎921 463 529), is cheaper and also worth a try. Both ❸

Hotel Infanta Isabel Plaza Mayor 12 ☎921 461 300, Ⓦ www.hotelinfantaisabel.com. Comfortable new hotel – better value than the *parador* – ideally positioned on Plaza Mayor. ❺

Hotel Los Linajes c/Dr Velasco 9 ☎921 460 475, Ⓔhotelloslinajes@terra.es. Good-value cosy hotel set in part of an old palace in a quiet corner of the walled city. It has a fine garden overlooking the river valley, and all rooms are air-conditioned. ❺

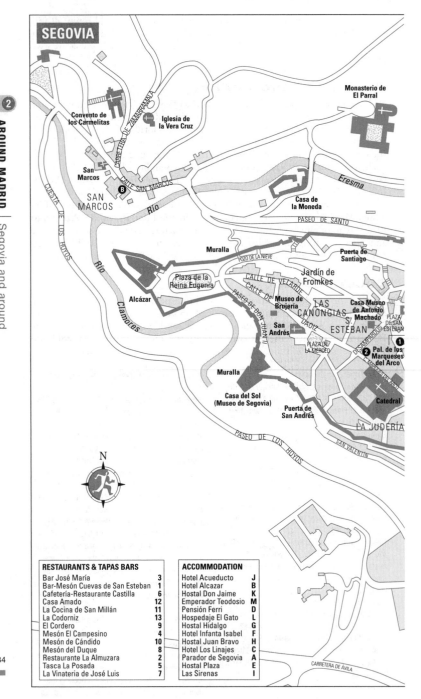

SEGOVIA

Monasterio de
El Parral

Convento de
los Carmelitas

Iglesia de
la Vera Cruz

San
Marcos

SAN
MARCOS

Río

Eresma

Casa de
la Moneda

PASEO DE SANTO

Muralla

POZO DE LA NIEVE

Puerta de
Santiago

Plaza de la
Reina Eugenia

CALLE DE VEZARDE

Jardín de
Fromkes

CALLE DE

Alcázar

PASEO DE DON JUAN II

Museo de
Brujería

LAS
CANONGIAS

Casa Museo
de Antonio
Machado

PLAZA
DE SAN
ESTEBAN

San
Andrés

DAOIZ

S. ESTEBAN

PLAZA DE
LA MERCED

2

Pal. de los
Marqueses
del Arco

1

C. MARQUES DEL ARCO

Muralla

Casa del Sol
(Museo de Segovia)

Puerta de
San Andrés

Catedral

LA JUDERÍA

SAN VALENTÍN

PASEO DE LOS HOYOS

N

CARRETERA DE ÁVILA

RESTAURANTS & TAPAS BARS

Bar José María	3
Bar-Mesón Cuevas de San Esteban	1
Cafetería-Restaurante Castilla	6
Casa Amado	12
La Cocina de San Millán	11
La Codorniz	13
El Cordero	9
Mesón El Campesino	4
Mesón de Cándido	10
Mesón del Duque	8
Restaurante La Almuzara	2
Tasca La Posada	5
La Vinatería de José Luis	7

ACCOMMODATION

Hotel Acueducto	J
Hotel Alcazar	B
Hostal Don Jaime	K
Emperador Teodosio	M
Pensión Ferri	D
Hospedaje El Gato	L
Hostal Hidalgo	G
Hotel Infanta Isabel	F
Hostal Juan Bravo	H
Hotel Los Linajes	C
Parador de Segovia	A
Hostal Plaza	E
Las Sirenas	I

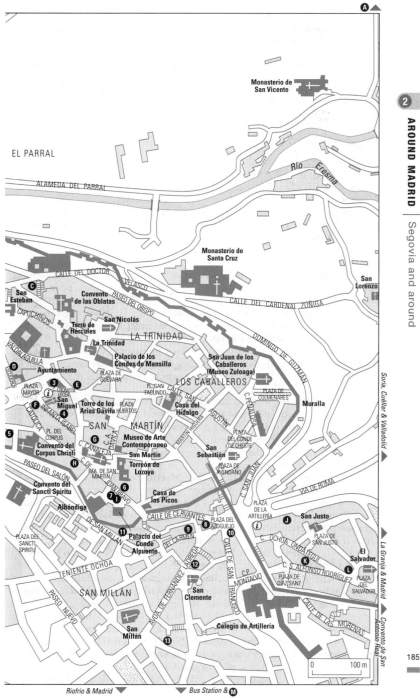

EL PARRAL

Monasterio de
San Vicente

Río Eresma

ALAMEDA DEL PARRAL

Monasterio de
Santa Cruz

San
Lorenzo

CALLE DEL DOCTOR VELASCO

PASEO DEL OBISPO

CALLE DEL CARDENAL ZÚÑIGA

C San
Esteban

Convento
de las Oblatas

CAPUCHINOS

San Nicolás

Torre de
Hércules

LA TRINIDAD

DOMINGO DE GUZMÁN

VALDELAGUILLA

La Trinidad

Palacio de los
Condes de Mansilla

San Juan de los
Caballeros
(Museo Zuloaga)

D Ayuntamiento

PLAZA DE
GUEVARA

LOS CABALLEROS

PLAZA DE
COLMENARES

PLAZA
MAYOR

3 CRONISTA
LECEA

PL. SAN
FACUNDO

CALLE SAN

Muralla

i

San
Miguel

E

Torre de los
Arias Dávila

Casa del
Hidalgo

C. PEROCOTA

LATIVICA

INFANTA ISABEL

4

PLAZA
HUERTOS

AGUSTÍN

PLAZA
DEL CONDE
DE CHESTE

F

SAN

MARTÍN

5

PL. DEL
CORPUS

G

Museo de Arte
Contemporáneo

C. MARTÍN HIGUERA

Convento del
Corpus Christi

C. CANALEJA

C. DÁVILA

San Martín

San
Sebastián

H

C. DE

PZA. DE SAN
MARTÍN

Torreón de
Lozoya

PLAZA DE
AVENDAÑO

PASEO DEL SALÓN

Convento del
Sancti Spiritu

JUAN BRAVO

6

Casa de
los Picos

C. SAN JUAN

VÍA DE ROMA

7

J

San Justo

Alhóndiga

CALLE DE CERVANTES

PLAZA DEL
AZOGUEJO

PLAZA
DE LA
ARTILLERÍA

i

PLAZA DE
SAN JUSTO

PLAZA DEL
SANCTI
SPIRITU

DE SAN MILLÁN

11

Palacio del
Conde
Alpuente

9

DEL CARMEN

8

10

C. OCHOA ONDÁTEGUI

El
Salvador

TENIENTE OCHOA

SAN MILLÁN

12

CALLE DE SAN FRANCISCO

CALLE DE LAS MORENAS

K

C. S. ALFONSO RODRÍGUEZ

L

PLAZA DE
DÍAZ SANZ

PLAZA
DEL
SALVADOR

PASEO NUEVO

AVDA. DE FERNÁNDEZ LADREDA

San
Clemente

C.P.
MONTALVO

CALLE DE ROMA

San
Millán

13

Colegio de Artillería

0   100 m

Riofrío & Madrid   Bus Station & **M**

Parador de Segovia Carretera de Valladolid s/n
🕾 921 443 737, 🕸 www.parador.es. Not very convenient for visiting the sights (you'll need a car),
but for facilities and fantastic views of the city –
especially beautiful when illuminated at night – it
can't be beaten. ❼
Las Sirenas c/Juan Bravo 30 🕾 921 462 663, ✉
hotelsirenas@terra.es. Classic decor, big rooms, a neat
garden and terrace all at a very reasonable price. ❸

Camping

Camping Acueducto Avda. Don Juan de Borbón
49 🕾 & 🖷 921 425 000, ✉ acueducto@
mmteam.interbook.net; open Easter–Sept. The
nearest campsite, several kilometres out on the
road to La Granja; take a #6 "Nueva Segovia" bus
from the Plaza Mayor. A quiet site with a swimming pool and plenty of shade.

The City

Segovia has more than a full day's worth of sights. If you're on a flying visit
from Madrid, obvious priorities are the Roman **aqueduct** which makes a
breathtaking landmark at the entrance to the city, the Gothic **cathedral** and
Alcázar in the old town, and the church of **Vera Cruz**, that lies just to the
north in the valley beyond the city walls. Given more time, take a walk out of
the city for the **views**, or just wander at will through the **old quarters** of the
city, away from the centre: each has a village atmosphere of its own.

The aqueduct

The most photographed sight in Segovia is the stunning **aqueduct**. Over 800m
of granite, supported by 166 arches and 120 pillars and at its highest point towering some 30m above the Plaza de Azoguejo, it stands up without a drop of
mortar or cement. No one knows exactly when it was built, but it was probably around the end of the first century BC under either Emperor Domitian or
Trajan. It no longer carries water from the Río Frío to the city, and in recent
years traffic vibration and pollution have been threatening to undermine the
entire structure. If you climb the stairs beside the aqueduct you can get a view
looking down over it from a surviving fragment of the city walls.

The synagogue, Plaza de San Martín and La Trinidad

Passing under the aqueduct and up the hill along c/Cervantes you will be
directed towards the old city past the curious fifteenth-century Casa de los
Picos (House of Spikes) with its waffle-like facade made up of pyramid-shaped
stones to your right and the former corn exchange, the **Alhondiga** down a
few steps on your left.

A little further on is the **Plaza de San Martín**, one of the city's grandest
squares, whose ensemble of buildings includes the fourteenth-century
Torreón de Lozoya (open for exhibitions Mon–Sat 7–9pm & Sun
noon–2pm & 7–9pm), and the twelfth-century church of **San Martín**, which
demonstrates all the local stylistic peculiarities, though the best of none of
them. It has the characteristic covered portico, a fine arched tower, and a typically Romanesque aspect; also, like most of Segovia's churches, it can be visited only when it's open for business, during early morning or evening services.
In the middle of the plaza is a **statue of Juan Bravo**, a local folk hero who
led the *comuneros* rebellion against Carlos V in protest against tax increases, the
undermining of local power and the influence of foreign advisers. On the
northern side of the square is the **Museo de Arte Contemporáneo**
(Tues–Fri 11am–2pm & 4–7pm, Sat 11am–7pm, Sun 11am–2pm; €2.40, free
Thurs), dedicated to local artist Esteban Vicente (1903–2000).

One of the lesser-known sights of Segovia is the **Synagogue**, which now
serves as the convent church of **Corpus Cristi** (daily 9.30am–1.30pm &
4.30–6pm; due to re-open after renovation in 2004), in a little courtyard at the

end of c/Juan Bravo near the east end of the cathedral. You can see part of its exterior from the Paseo del Salón, near which are the streets of the old *Judería*. It's very similar in style to Santa María la Blanca in Toledo, though less refined. During the nineteenth century it was badly damaged by fire, so what you see now is a reconstruction, but historic synagogues are so rare in Spain that this is still of interest.

North of here, the church of **La Trinidad** (daily 10am–2pm & 4.30–7.30pm) preserves the purest Romanesque style in Segovia: each span of its double-arched apse has intricately carved capitals, every one of them unique. Nearby – and making a good loop to or from the Alcázar – is the **Plaza San Esteban**, recently restored and worth seeing for its superb, five-storeyed, twelfth-century church tower.

From the Plaza Mayor to the Alcázar

Calle Juan Bravo eventually leads on to the bar-filled **Plaza Mayor**. Dominating one corner of the plaza are the exuberant lines of the **Catedral** (daily: April–Oct 9am–6.30pm; Nov–March 9.30am–5.30pm). Construction began in 1525, on the orders of Carlos V, to make amends for the damage done to the city during the *comuneros* revolt. However, it was not completed for another 200 years, making it the last major Gothic building in Spain, and arguably the last in Europe. Accordingly it takes the style to its logical – or perhaps illogical – extreme, with pinnacles and flying buttresses tacked on at every conceivable point. Though impressive for its size alone, the interior is surprisingly bare for so florid a construction and its space cramped by a great green marble *coro* at its very centre. The treasures are almost all confined to the museum (same hours as cathedral, except Sun opens at 2.30pm; €1.80) which opens off the cloisters.

Down beside the cathedral, c/Daoiz leads past a line of souvenir shops to the twelfth-century Romanesque church of San Andrés. Off to the right at c/Desamparados 5 is the **Casa-Museo de Antonio Machado**, (summer Tues 11am–2pm & Wed–Sun 11am–2pm & 4.30–7.30pm; winter Tues 11am–2pm & Wed–Sun 11am–2pm & 4–6pm; €1.50, free Wed). This little house displays the spartan accommodation and furnishings of one of Spain's greatest poets of the early twentieth century; he is generally more associated with Soria but spent the last years of his life teaching here.

Back on c/Daoiz is the newly inaugurated **Museo de Brujería** (daily 10.30am–2.30pm & 4.30–8.30pm; €4), of passing interest for most visitors, but a compulsory stop if you are a devotee of the dark arts. Some 300 ghoulish exhibits related to the history of witchcraft and related practices are on display in this suitably atmospheric house. A dried vampire's head, instruments of torture used by the Inquisition and a variety of witches' potions and brews all form part of the Italian owner's eclectic collection.

A couple of hundred metres further on, the street opens out on to a small park in front of the **Alcázar** (daily: April–Sept 10am–7pm; Oct–March 10am–6pm; €3, free Tues for EU citizens). An extraordinary fantasy of a castle, with its narrow towers and flurry of turrets, it will seem eerily familiar to just about every visitor, having served as the model for the original Disneyland castle in California. It is itself a bit of a sham; although it dates from the fourteenth and fifteenth centuries, it was almost completely destroyed by a fire in 1862 and rebuilt as a deliberately hyperbolic version of the original. Still, it should be visited if only for the splendid *artesonado* ceilings and the magnificent panoramas from the tower.

Walks around Segovia and the Monasterio del Parral

Segovia is an excellent city for **walks**. Follow the signposted bypass road outside the city on the south side, and you'll get ever-changing views of the cathedral and the Alcázar from across the valley. The road then doubles back along the other side of the Alcázar, passing near the Convento de los Carmelitas and Vera Cruz.

From there you could continue to the **Monasterio del Parral** (Mon–Sat 10am–12.30pm & 4.30–6.30pm, Sun 10–11.30am & 4.30–6.30pm; free); or better still, follow the track which circles behind Vera Cruz to the monastery. El Parral is a sizeable and partly ruined complex occupied by Hieronymites, an order found only in Spain. Ring the bell for admission and you will be shown the cloister and church; the latter is a late-Gothic building with rich sculpture at the east end. Gregorian Masses can be heard during the week at 1pm and on Sundays at noon. For a relaxing stroll, follow the beautiful tree-lined path alongside the Río Eresma. You can then wind your way back up the hill to the old town in a round-trip of a little over an hour. For the **best view** of all of Segovia, however, take the main road north for 2km or so towards Cuéllar. A panorama of the whole city, including the aqueduct, gradually unfolds.

Vera Cruz

The best of Segovia's ancient churches is undoubtedly **Vera Cruz** (Tues–Sun 10.30am–1.30pm & 3.30–7pm, winter closes 6pm; closed Nov; €1.50), a remarkable twelve-sided building outside town in the valley facing the Alcázar, which can be reached by taking the path down to Paseo San Juan de La Cruz. It was built by the Knights Templar in the early thirteenth century on the pattern of the church of the Holy Sepulchre in Jerusalem, and once housed part of the True Cross (hence its name; the sliver of wood itself is now in the nearby village church at Zamarramala). Inside, the nave is circular, and its heart is occupied by a strange two-storeyed chamber – again twelve-sided – in which the knights, as part of their initiation, stood vigil over the cross. Climb the tower for a highly photogenic vista of the city.

While you're over here you could take in the prodigiously walled **Convento de las Carmelitas** (daily summer: 10am–1.30pm & 4–8pm, winter closes an hour earlier, closed Mon 10am–1.30pm; free), which is also referred to as the monastery of San Juan de la Cruz, and contains the gaudy mausoleum of its founder-saint.

Beyond the Aqueduct – the Convento de San Antonio el Real, San Millán and San Justo

If you follow the line of the aqueduct away from the old city you will come to the **Convento de San Antonio Real** (Tues–Sat 10am–2.30pm & 4–7.30pm, Sun 11am–2pm; €2), a little gem of a palace originally founded by Enrique IV in 1455 and containing an intriguing collection of Mudéjar and Hispano-Flemish art.

Back toward the city but still outside the old walls are two fine Romanesque churches. Between the bus station and the aqueduct is the church of **San Millán** (daily 10am–2pm & 4.30–7.30pm) with a fine *mozárabe* tower and open porticoes. Its interior has been restored to its original form. Facing the aqueduct is **San Justo** (Tues–Sat: summer noon–2pm & 5–7pm; winter 11am–1.45pm & 4–7pm) which has a wonderful Romanesque wall painting in the apse and a twelfth-century sculpture of Christ complete with hinged arms.

Eating and drinking

Segovia takes its cooking seriously, with restaurants of Madrid quality – and prices. **Culinary specialities** include roast suckling pig (*cochinillo asado*), displayed in the raw in the windows of many restaurants, and the rather healthier *judiones*, large white beans from La Granja. There is a concentration of cheaper **bar-restaurants** on c/Infanta Isabella, off the Plaza Mayor, and late-night bars on c/Escuderos and c/Judería Vieja, and along Avenida Fernández Ladreda.

Inexpensive restaurants and bars

Bar José María c/Cronista Lecea 11, just off Plaza Mayor. Bar-annexe to one of Segovia's best restaurants (see below), serving delicious and modest-priced tapas.

Bar-Mesón Cuevas de San Esteban c/Valdelaguila 15, off the top end of Plaza San Esteban. A cavern-restaurant and bar (serving draught beer), popular with locals and excellent value. The *menú del día* is €9.81.

Cafetería-Restaurante Castilla c/Juan Bravo 58. Generous helpings and friendly service in this unpretentious bar – and you can eat out on a terrace.

La Codorniz c/Ancieto Marinas 1, opposite San Millán church. Inexpensive *menús* and lots of *combinados* involving *cordoniz* (quail).

El Cordero c/Carmen 4 & 6. Plenty of variety here, with no less than seven different *menús* to choose from, ranging in price from €8–15.

Mesón El Campesino c/Infanta Isabella 12. One of the best budget restaurants in town, serving decent-value *menús* and *combinados* to a young crowd. Closed Aug.

Restaurante La Almuzara c/Marqués del Arco 3. Just behind the cathedral, this is a good-value, genuine vegetarian restaurant, with some non-veggie dishes on offer, too. Closed Aug.

Tasca La Posada c/Judería Vieja 19. A fine *bar-mesón* for tapas, *raciones*, or a *menú*.

La Vinatería de José Luis c/Herreria 3. Imaginative tapas and good selection of wines in this friendly bar off c/Juan Bravo.

Moderate and expensive restaurants

Casa Amado Avda. Fernández Ladreda 9 ☎921 432 077. Small but popular local restaurant serving traditional dishes, near the Plaza Azoguejo. Allow €25 per head, although there are also *menús* at €12 and €17. Closed Wed & the second fortnight in Oct.

La Cocina de San Millán c/San Millán 3 ☎921 460 233. Nestling below the steps which lead up to the old town, this cosy restaurant serves up imaginative cooking at reasonable prices. Closed Sun night & Jan 7–31.

Mesón de Cándido Plaza Azoguejo 5 ☎921 428 103. In the shadow of the aqueduct you will find the city's most famous restaurant, reopened in 1992 by the founder's son and still the place for *cochinillo* and other roasts. Expect to top €27 if you have the *cochinillo*.

Mesón del Duque c/Cervantes 12 ☎921 462 487. Rival to the nearby *Cándido*, and also specializing in Castilian roasts. The *menú* is €25.50 and includes *cochinillo*.

Mesón José María c/Cronista Lecea 11, just off Plaza Mayor ☎921 461 111. Currently reckoned to be the city's best and most imaginative restaurant, run by a former Cándido protégé, with modern variations on Castilian classics. The *menú* is around €25.

Out of town

La Posada de Javier In the village of Torrecaballeros, 8km northeast on the N110 ☎921 401 136. Serious *madrileño* – and *segoviano* – gourmands eat out in the neighbouring villages, and this lovely old farmhouse is one of the most popular choices. It isn't cheap, however, with a *menú* costing at least €25. Booking is essential at weekends. Closed Sun night, Mon & July.

La Granja and Riofrío

Segovia has a major outlying attraction in the Bourbon summer palace and gardens of **La Granja**, 10km southeast of the town on the N601 Madrid road, and connected by regular bus services. True Bourbon aficionados, with time and transport, might also want to visit a second palace and hunting museum 12km west of La Granja at **Riofrío**.

La Granja

LA GRANJA (or San Ildefonso de la Granja, to give it its full title) was built by the reluctant first Bourbon king of Spain, Felipe V, no doubt homesick for the luxuries of Versailles. Its glories are the mountain setting and the extravagant wooded grounds and gardens, but it's also worth casting an eye over the **palace** (April–Sept Tues–Sun 10am–6pm; Oct–March Tues–Sat 10am–1.30pm & 3–5pm, Sun 10am–2pm; compulsory guided tour €5, free Wed for EU citizens; Ⓦwww.patrimonionacional.es). Though destroyed in parts and damaged throughout by a fire in 1918, much has been well restored. Everything is furnished in plush French imperial style but it's almost all of Spanish origin; the majority of the huge chandeliers, for example, were made in the **glass factory** still operating in the village of San Ildefonso (mid-June to mid-Sept Tues–Fri 10am–6pm, Sat, Sun & holidays 10am–7pm; mid-Sept to mid-June Tues–Sat 10am–6pm, Sun 10am–3pm; €3.40; Ⓦwww.fcnv.es). Here you can visit an exhibition on the history of the craft and still see the glass being blown and decorated in the traditional manner in the old workshops alongside the ovens. The palace is also home to a superlative collection of sixteenth-century tapestries, one of the most valuable in the world.

The highlight of the **gardens** (daily: summer 10am–9pm; winter 10am–6pm; €3.40, free Wed for EU citizens) is its series of fountains, which culminate in the 15-metre-high jet of La Fama. They're fantastic and really not to be missed, which means timing your visit from 5.30pm on Wednesdays or weekends, when some are switched on. Only on three saints' days in the year – normally May 30 (San Fernando), July 25 (Santiago) and August 25 (San Luis) – are all of the fountains set to work, with accompanying crowds to watch.

The **village** of San Ildefonso de la Granja is a pleasant place to while away any spare time, with several decent **bars** and **restaurants**: try the *Bar La Villa* off the main square for tapas, *Casa Zaca*, also off the square, for lunch, or *Bar Madrid*, near the palace. There's a range of **accommodation**, too, if you prefer to stay here rather than Segovia: try the friendly *Hotel Roma* at c/Guardas 2 (☏921 470 752, Ⓦwww.hotelroma.org; ❹), right outside the palace gates, or the cheaper, but less welcoming, *Pensión Pozo de la Nieve*, c/Baños 4 (☏921 470 598; ❶).

Riofrío

The palace at **RIOFRÍO** (April–Sept Tues–Sun 10am–6pm; Oct–March Tues–Sat 10am–1.30pm & 3–5pm, Sun 10am–2pm; €5, €2.25 toll for cars, free Wed for EU citizens; Ⓦwww.patrimonionacional.es) was built by Isabel, the widow of Felipe V, who feared she would be banished from La Granja itself by her stepson Fernando VI. He died, however, leaving the throne for Isabel's own son, Carlos III, and Riofrío was not occupied until the nineteenth century when Alfonso XII moved in to mourn the death of his young queen Mercedes. He, too, died pretty soon after, which is perhaps why the palace has a spartan and slightly tatty feel.

The complex, painted in dusty pink with green shutters, is surrounded not by manicured gardens but by a **deer park**, which you can drive but not wander into. Inside the palace, you have to join a guided tour, which winds through an endless sequence of rooms, none stunningly furnished. About half the tour is devoted to a **museum of hunting**; the most interesting items here are reconstructions of cave paintings, including the famous Altamira drawings.

North from Segovia

Heading **north from Segovia**, you're faced with quite a variety of routes. The train line heads northwest towards Valladolid and León, past the castles of **Coca** and **Medina del Campo** – two of the very finest in Spain. If you have transport of your own, or time for convoluted local bus routes, you can take in further impressive castles in Segovia province at **Pedraza**, **Turégano** and **Cuéllar**, and still more by striking north again to **Peñafiel** and the chain of castles along the River Duero. If you are looking for a night's stop in a small town, Pedraza or Turégano, around 40km from Segovia, would fit the bill nicely.

For details on this area, see the "Old Castile and León" chapter, p.409.

East of Madrid

East of the capital there's considerably less to detain you. The only tempting day-trip is to the old university town of **Alcalá de Henares**, Cervantes's birthplace. Further afield, the largely modern city of **Guadalajara** has little to recommend it, although the region southwest of here, the **Alcarria**, has its charms, especially if you want to follow the footsteps of Spain's Nobel prizewinner, Camilo José Cela, who described his wanderings here in the 1940s in his book, *Viaje a la Alcarria*.

Alcalá de Henares

ALCALÁ DE HENARES, a little over 30km from Madrid, is one of Europe's most ancient university towns, and renowned as the birthplace of Miguel de **Cervantes**. In the sixteenth century the university was a rival to Salamanca's, but in 1836 the faculties moved to Madrid and the town went into decline. Almost all the artistic heritage was lost in the Civil War and nowadays it's virtually a suburb of Madrid. It is not somewhere you'd want to stay longer than it takes to see the sights, but that's no problem with regular trains (Chamartín or Atocha; daily every 15–30min from 5.30am–11.45pm) and buses (daily every 15min, operated by Continental Auto) from Madrid throughout the day. If you like everything organized for you, the **Tren de Cervantes** leaves Atocha at 11am on Saturday and Sunday (mid-April to late June & late Sept to early Dec; €14; info ☎918 892 694) complete with staff in period costume, and includes a guided tour of the main sights, before returning to Madrid at 7pm.

The **Universidad Antigua** (45min guided tours usually in Spanish Mon–Fri 11.30am, 12.30pm, 1.30pm, 5pm, 6pm & 7pm, Sat, Sun & holidays 11am, 11.45am, 12.30pm, 1.15pm, 2pm, 5pm, 5.45pm, 6.30pm, 7.15pm & 8pm; €2.50) stands at the heart of the old town in Plaza San Diego. It was endowed by Cardinal Cisneros (also known as Cardinal Jiménez) at the beginning of the sixteenth century and features a fabulous Plateresque facade and a Great Hall, the **Paraninfo**, with a gloriously decorated Mudéjar *artesonado* ceiling. Next door, the **Capilla de San Ildefonso** has another superb ceiling, intricately stuccoed walls, and the Italian marble tomb of Cardinal Cisneros, although his actual remains are buried in the cathedral in Plaza de los Santos Niños.

The **Museo Casa Natal de Cervantes** at c/Mayor (Tues–Sun 10am–2pm & 4–7pm; free) claims to be the birthplace of Cervantes in 1547: though the house itself is hardly thirty years old, it's authentic in style, furnished with genuine sixteenth-century objects, and contains a small museum with a few early editions of *Don Quixote* and other curiosities related to the author.

To the west of the university, the **Monasterio de San Bernardo**, Via Complutense (guided tours Mon–Fri 11.30am, 12.30pm, 1.30pm, 5pm, 6pm & 7pm, Sat & Sun 11am, 11.45am, 12.30pm, 1.15pm, 2pm, 5pm, 5.45pm, 6.30pm, 7.15pm & 8pm; €2.50), was founded by the Cistercians in 1617 and has recently opened its doors as a museum of religious art, recreating the atmosphere of a monastery of that era, complete with cells and kitchen.

Just off the central Plaza Cervantes is the oldest surviving public theatre in Europe, the **Corral de Comedias** (guided tours with English usually spoken Tues–Sat 11.15am, noon, 12.45pm, 1.30pm, 2.15pm, 4pm, 4.40pm & 5.20pm, Sun 11am, 11.45am, 12.30pm & 1.15pm; free; reservations ☎918 822 964), which has been brought to life once more after a twenty-year restoration programme. Originally dating from 1601, the theatre was discovered beneath a crumbling old cinema by three drama students in 1980. Like Shakespeare's Globe, it was a hub of rowdy heckling and lively dramatics throughout the first half of the seventeenth century. The 25-minute guided tour gives a fascinating glimpse into the history of the place.

Practicalities

The local **turismo** (daily: summer 10am–2pm & 5–7.30pm, closed Mon in July & Sept; winter 10am–2pm & 5–6.30pm; ☎918 892 694, Ⓦwww.alcala dehenares-turismo.com), just off the central Plaza de Cervantes, can arrange guided tours for €5, and has maps and other handy information. There is another office in Plaza de los Santos Niños (same hours, but closed Tues in July & Aug; ☎918 810 634). You'll find no shortage of **places to eat** centrally; the friendly *El Bierzo en Alcalá* at c/Mayor 40 does a good-value *menú del día*, but if you want to splash out, the best restaurant in town is the *Hostería del Estudiante* (☎918 880 527; closed Aug) which is run by the Parador chain and is situated in part of the old university. If you decide you want to **stay** there are plenty of *hostales* in and around the Plaza Cervantes, while conveniently located by the train station is the *Hostal Jacinto* (☎ & Ⓕ918 891 432; ❷). More upmarket are the *Hotel Bedel* which looks out over the old university in Plaza San Diego (☎918 893 700, reductions if you book ahead; ❺–❻) and the *Hostal Cervantes* (☎918 831 217, Ⓦwww.hostalcervantes.com; ❹), located in a renovated sixteenth-century building at c/Imagen 12.

Guadalajara

GUADALAJARA, twenty kilometres north from Alcalá de Henares, is not terribly exciting despite its famous name. Severely battered during the Civil War, it's now a small industrial city, provincial and scruffy. There are, however, a few worthwhile buildings which survived bombardment, notably the **Palacio del Infantado** (Mon–Fri 9am–9pm, Sat 10am–2pm & 4.30–7pm, Sun 10am–2pm; free) and an assortment of medieval churches in the old historical core. The *palacio*, the former home of the Duke of Mendoza, boasts a wonderful decorative facade and cloister-like patio, and now houses a fairly average **local art museum** (Tues–Sat 10.30am–2pm & 4.15–7pm, Sun & hols 10.30am–2pm; €1.20, free Sat & Sun). It is to be found a few blocks to the northwest of the town's large, park-like central square, Plaza Capitán Beixareu Rivera.

There's a friendly **turismo** opposite the palace (Mon–Sat 10am–2pm & 4–7.30pm, Sun 10am–2pm; ☎949 211 626, Ⓦwww.dguadalajara.es) in Plaza de Caídos. If you needed, or wanted, **to stay**, the recently refurbished *Hotel España*, c/Teniente Figueroa 3 (☎949 211 303, Ⓕ949 211 305; ❷), is a decent option close to the Palacio del Infantado; even cheaper is *Pensión Galicia*, c/San Roque 16 (☎949 220 059, Ⓕ949 214 807; ❶), just outside the old core, while for more comfort try the *Hotel Husa Pax* (☎949 248 060, Ⓕ949 226 955; ❺), at nearby Avda. Venezuela 15, which has a swimming pool. **Bars** and **restaurants** are plentiful, too. *Can Vic* on Plaza Fernando Beládiez is a good, low-priced place, or for a seafood and fish blowout there's *Casa Victor* at c/Bardales 6. Late-night and music bars are mostly to be found along c/Sigüenza. There is a regular **train service** from Madrid running every 15–30 minutes from Atocha from 5.30am–11.45pm with a journey time of about 50 minutes.

Moving on

The main road and rail lines from Madrid to Zaragoza and Barcelona both pass through Alcalá and Guadalajara, and continue more or less parallel throughout their journeys. Sigüenza (see p.201) and Medinaceli (see p.446) each make excellent resting points on your way. From Guadalajara you can also cut down to Cuenca, and from there continue towards Valencia and the coast. This is a very beautiful drive, past the great dams of the Embalse de Entrepeñas and Embalse de Buendía, and takes you through the heart of the Alcarria region.

The Alcarria

The **Alcarria** has few particular monuments, but the wild scenery and sporadic settlements are eerily impressive, especially coming upon them so close to Madrid. Many of the high sierra villages, north of the N320, were deserted during the Nationalist advance on Madrid in the Civil War and today have only a handful of permanent inhabitants, plus a few *madrileño* weekenders who are restoring the old cottages.

The largest town of the region, **PASTRANA**, 15km south of the N320, merits a diversion. The museum of its vast **Colegiata** church (daily 11am–2pm & 4.30–6.30pm; €3) contains some wonderful fifteenth-century tapestries depicting the conquest of Tangier and Asilah by Alfonso V of Portugal, as well as richly decorated ebony and bronze altarpieces from the Philippines. These were brought to Pastrana by the princess of Eboli, duchess of the town, who after a court scandal was imprisoned in the and allowed to sit out on the balcony (now known as Plaza de la Hora), for one hour a day. Also of interest is the **Convento del Carmen**, a ten-minute walk out of town. This Carmelite convent was founded by St Teresa and within you'll find a small museum of assorted religious art and yet more relics of the saint (Tues–Sun 11am–1.30pm & 3.30–6pm; €3). Part of this convent has recently become a *parador*-style **hotel**, the *Hospedería Real de Pastrana* (☎ & Ⓕ949 371 060, ⓦwww.hosterias-reales.es; ❺), which has its own upmarket restaurant, too. The only other place to stay is back in town at *Hostal Moratín*, c/Moratín 3 (☎949 370 116, ⓦwww.hostalmoratin.com; ❷), a clean and comfortable place on the main road. Meanwhile, Pastrana's twisting streets, including its former **Jewish and Arab quarters**, offer endless rambling, and there's a modest **turismo** (Sat 10am–2pm & 4–8pm, Sun 10am–2pm; ☎949 370 672, ⓦwww.pastrana.org) on the edge of town, but there's little diversion to be had in the evening. For good-value local **food** try the *Princesa de Éboli* on c/Monjas (Sat, Sun & holidays only) or the *Convento de San Francisco* next to the turismo in the Plaza del Deán which offers a varied *menú* in atmospheric surroundings.

Travel Details

Trains

Atocha, Madrid (Ⓜ Atocha) to: Alcalá (every 15–30min; 30min); Aranjuez (every 15–30min; 45min); Cuenca (4 daily; 2hr 20–2hr 45min); El Escorial via Chamartín (25 daily; 1hr); Guadalajara via Chamartín (every 15–30min; 55min); Segovia via Chamartín (9 daily; 2hr); Toledo via Aranjuez (3 daily; 1hr 15min; check with Renfe because of installation of new line).

Chamartín, Madrid (Ⓜ Chamartín) to: Ávila (24 daily; 1hr 20min–2hr 10min); Cercedilla (23 daily; 1hr 15min).

Aranjuez to: Cuenca (5 daily; 1hr 50min–2hr 10min); Madrid (every 15–30min; 45min); Toledo (10 daily; 30min).

Ávila to: Madrid (35 daily; 1hr 20min–2hr 10min); El Escorial (9 daily; 1hr); Medina del Campo (15 daily; 20–40min); Salamanca (6 daily; 1hr 30min); Valladolid (15 daily; 1hr–1hr 10min).

Cercedilla to: Madrid (21 daily; 1hr 15min); Puerto de Navacerrada (6 daily; 25min); Cotos (6 daily; 40 min); Segovia (9 daily; 40–50min).

El Escorial to: Ávila (9 daily; 1hr); Madrid (21 daily; 1hr).

Segovia to: Cercedilla (9 daily; 40min); Madrid (9 daily; 1hr 55min–2hr).

Toledo to: Aranjuez (8–9 daily; 30min); Madrid (7 daily; 1hr 15min–1hr 30min; check with Renfe because of installation of new line).

Buses

Estación Sur de Autobuses, Madrid c/Méndez Álvaro s/n ☎ 914 684 200 (Ⓜ Méndez Álvaro) to: Aranjuez (Mon–Fri every 30min, Sat & Sun hourly; 45min); Ávila 5–10 daily; 1hr 20min–1hr 40min); Toledo (every 15–30min; 1hr 15min); Arenas de San Pedro (9–14 daily; 2hr 15min).

Auto-Res, Madrid Plaza Conde de Casal ☎ 902 020 999 (Ⓜ Conde de Casal) to: Cuenca (4–9 daily; 2hr–2hr 30 min); Salamanca (8–20 daily; 2hr30 min–3hr)

La Veloz, Madrid Avda. del Mediterráneo 49 ☎ 914 097 602 (Ⓜ Conde de Casal) to: Chinchón (10–15 daily; 45min).

Herranz, Madrid Intercambiador de Autobuses, Moncloa (Ⓜ Moncloa) to: El Escorial (every 15–30min; 1hr).

La Sepulvedana, Madrid Intercambiador de Autobuses, Moncloa Ⓦ www.lasepulvedana.es (Ⓜ Moncloa) to: Cercedilla (every 30min; 50min–1hr 10min).

La Sepulvedana, Madrid Paseo de la Florida 11 ☎ 915 304 800, Ⓦ www.lasepulvedana.es (Ⓜ Príncipe Pío) to: Segovia (every 15min–1hr; 1hr 15min).

Continental Auto, Madrid Avda. de América 9 ☎ 917 456 300, Ⓦ www.continental-auto.es (Ⓜ Avda. de América;) to: Alcalá (every 15min; 40min); Guadalajara (every 30min; 45min).

Intercambiador de Autobuses, Madrid Plaza de Castilla (Ⓜ Plaza de Castilla) to: Manzanares del Real (hourly; 40min).

Ávila to: Arenas de San Pedro (1 daily Mon–Fri; 1hr 30min); Madrid (8 daily; 1hr 30min); Salamanca (2–3 daily; 1hr 30min); Segovia (2–7 daily; 1hr).

El Escorial to: Guadarrama (every 30min–1hr; 15min); Madrid (every 15–30min; 1hr); Valle de los Caídos (1 daily; 15min).

Segovia to: Ávila (2–3 daily; 1hr); La Granja (12 daily; 20min); Madrid (every 30min; 1hr 15min); Salamanca (1–3 daily; 2–3hr); Valladolid (5–9 daily; 2hr 30min).

Toledo to: Ciudad Real, for the south (1 daily; 2hr); Cuenca (Mon–Fri 1 daily; 2hr 30min); Guadamur (7 daily; 20min); Madrid (every 30min; 1hr 15min); Orgaz (3–10 daily; 30min); La Puebla de Montelbán (5 daily Mon–Fri, 1 daily Sat; 40min); Talavera de la Reina, for Extremadura (10 daily; 1hr).

New Castile and Extremadura

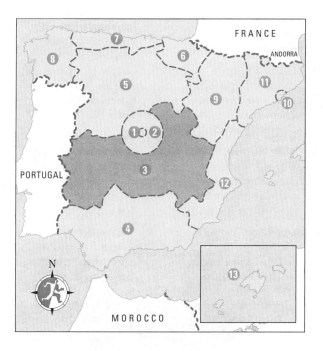

CHAPTER 3

Highlights

✻ **Museo de Arte Abstracto, Cuenca** One of the famous hanging houses is the wonderful setting for this great little museum.
See p.206

✻ **La Ciudad Encantada** Weird and wonderful limestone formations near Cuenca. See p.207

✻ **Jarandilla to Yuste** Trace the last journey of Carlos V from the castle-*parador* to the monastery. See p.217

✻ **Cherry blossom, Valle de Jerte** A spectacular display when the trees burst into bloom for ten days in spring. See p.220

✻ **Jamón** Treat yourself to a *ración* of the finest dried ham washed down with *pitarra* wine. See p.237

✻ **The Roman ruins in Mérida** A fantastic array of Roman buildings and artefacts. See p.238

✻ **Cáceres** Wander around the atmospheric historic core at night. See p.232

✻ **Vulture spotting, Monfragüe Natural Park** You don't have to be a dedicated ornithologist to be impressed by these prehistoric-looking creatures.
See p.225

✻ **Trujillo** A visit to the birthplace of Pizarro is worthwhile for the view of the town from the Cáceres road alone.
See p.226

✻ **The monastery at Guadalupe** Stay the night at the impressive monastery-shrine.
See p.230

△ La Mancha windmills

3

New Castile and Extremadura

The vast area covered by this chapter is some of the most travelled, yet least visited, country in Spain. Once south of Toledo (covered in the previous chapter, "Around Madrid"), most tourists thunder nonstop across the plains of New Castile to Valencia and Andalucía, or follow the great rivers through Extremadura into Portugal. At first sight this is understandable. **New Castile** in particular is Spain at its least welcoming: a vast, bare plain, burning hot in summer, chillingly exposed in winter. But the first impression is not an entirely fair one – away from the main highways the villages of the plain are as welcoming as any in the country, and in the northeast, where the mountains start, are the extraordinary cliff-hanging city of **Cuenca** and the historic cathedral town of **Sigüenza**. New Castile is also the agricultural and wine-growing heartland of Spain and the country through which Don Quixote cut his despairing swathe.

It is in **Extremadura**, though, that there is most to be missed. This harsh environment was the cradle of the *conquistadores*, men who opened up a new world for the Spanish empire. Remote before and forgotten since, Extremadura enjoyed a brief golden age when its heroes returned with their gold to live in a flourish of splendour. **Trujillo**, the birthplace of Pizarro, and **Cáceres** both preserve entire towns built with *conquistador* wealth, the streets crowded with the ornate mansions of returning empire builders. Then there is **Mérida**, the most completely preserved Roman city in Spain, and the monasteries of **Guadalupe** and **Yuste**, the one fabulously wealthy, the other rich in imperial memories. Finally, for little-visited wild scenery and superb fauna, northern Extremadura has the **Parque Natural de Monfragüe**, where even the most casual birdwatcher can look up to see eagles and vultures circling the cliffs.

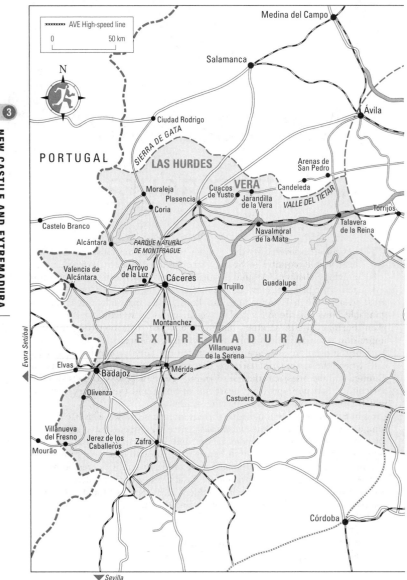

New Castile

The region that was for so long called **New Castile** – and that until the 1980s held Madrid in its domain – is now officially known as **Castilla-La Mancha**.

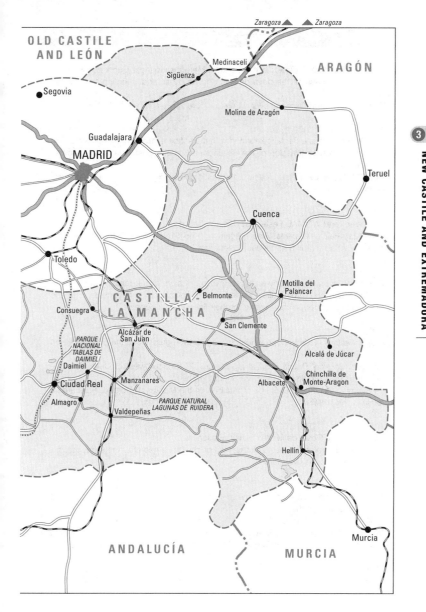

Although the heavily cultivated plains that cover much of the terrain are less bleak than they once were – the name La Mancha comes from the Arab *manxa*, meaning steppe – the main points of interest are widely spaced on an arc drawn from Madrid, with little between that rewards exploration. If you are travelling east on **trains and buses** towards Aragón, there's little to justify a stop other than Sigüenza (en route to Zaragoza) or Cuenca (en route to Teruel). To the south, Toledo has bus links within its own province, but heading for Andalucía

Fiestas

February
First weekend *La Endiablada* at Almonacid Marquesado (near Cuenca), a very old festival which sees all the boys dressing up as devils and parading through the streets.
Week before Lent *Carnaval* everywhere.

March/April
Holy Week (*Semana Santa*) celebrated with magnificent ritual (floats, penitents, etc) in Cuenca. *Pascua* (Passion of the Resurrection). Major Easter fiestas in Cáceres and Trujillo.
April 23 *San Jorge*. Tremendously enthusiastic celebrations that continue for several days in Cáceres.

May
First weekend WOMAD Festival at Cáceres (see p.232).
Late May Fair at Cáceres. Also – again with no fixed date – *Cabalata*, muleteer races, at Atienza (30km northeast of Sigüenza).

June
23–27 *San Juan*. Particularly manic festival in the picturesque town of Coria (50km west of Plasencia) with a bull let loose for a few hours a day, everyone dancing and drinking in the streets, and running for their lives when it appears.

July
Drama Festival in Mérida throughout July and into August, when the plays move on to Alcántara.
Spanish Classical Drama Festival at Almagro (25km southwest of Ciudad Real) – from the first Thursday until the last Sunday of the month.
14 Fiestas start in La Puebla de Montalbán, in the Montes de Toledo. Bulls are let loose in the streets.

August
First Tuesday *Fiesta de Martes Mayor*, Plasencia.
24–25 *San Bartolomé*. Fiestas at any town or church named after the saint, particularly at Jerez de los Caballeros.

September
First week *Vendimia* – grape harvest – celebrations at Valdepeñas. Major fair at Trujillo also early in the month.
7–17 *Virgin of Los Llanos*, Plasencia.
Week leading up to third Sunday Festivals in Jarandilla and Madrigal de la Vera with bulls running in front of cows – which are served up on the final day's feast.

October
1 *San Miguel*. Fiestas at any town or church named after the saint, particularly at Badajoz.

or Extremadura you'd do better returning to Madrid and starting out again; the Toledo rail line stops at the town.

If you do have a **car**, and are **heading south**, the Toledo–Ciudad Real road, the Montes de Toledo and the marshy Parque Nacional de las Tablas de Daimiel all provide good alternatives to the sweltering NIV *autovía*. **Heading east**, through Cuenca to Teruel, the best route is to follow the Río Júcar out of the province, by way of the weird rock formations in the Ciudad Encantada and the source of the Río Tajo. **Heading west**, into Extremadura, the NV is one of the dullest and hottest roads in Spain and can be avoided by following the C501 through the Sierra de Gredos (see previous chapter, "Around Madrid") or by cutting onto it from Talavera de la Reina; this would bring you to the Monastery of Yuste by way of the lush valley of La Vera.

The sections following cover the main sights and routes of New Castile in a clockwise direction, from northeast to southwest of Madrid.

Sigüenza

SIGÜENZA, 120km northeast of Madrid, is a sleepy little town with a beautiful cathedral. At first sight it seems quite untouched by contemporary life, though appearances are deceptive: taken by Franco's troops in 1936, the town was on the Nationalist front line for most of the Civil War, and its people and buildings paid a heavy toll. However, the postwar years saw the cathedral restored, the Plaza Mayor recobbled and the bishop's castle rebuilt, so that the only evidence of its troubled history is in the facades of a few buildings, including the pencil-thin cathedral bell tower, pockmarked by bullets and shrapnel.

Sigüenza's main streets lead you towards the hilltop **Catedral** (daily 9.30am–1.30pm & 4.30–7.30pm; guided tours of chapels Tues–Sat 11am, noon, 4.30pm & 5.30pm, Sun noon & 5.30pm; €3; note hours can change on Sun because of Mass), built in the pinkish stone which characterizes the town. Begun in 1150 by the town's first bishop, Bernardo de Toledo, it is essentially Gothic, with three rose windows, though it has been much altered over the years. Facing the main entrance is a huge marble *coro* with an altar to a thirteenth-century figure of the Virgin. To the right of the *coro* is the cathedral's principal treasure, the alabaster tomb of Martín Vázquez de Arce, known as *El Doncel* (the page boy); a favourite of Isabel la Católica, he was killed fighting the Moors in Granada. On the other side of the building is an extraordinary doorway: Plateresque at the bottom, Mudéjar in the middle and Gothic at the top – an amazing amalgam, built by a confused sixteenth-century architect. Take a look, too, at the sacristy, whose superb Renaissance ceiling has 304 heads carved by Covarrubias. In a chapel opening off this (with an unusual cupola, best seen in the mirror provided) is an El Greco *Annunciation*.

More treasures are displayed in the **cloister**, while further art works from local churches and convents, including a saccharine Zurbarán of *Mary as a Child*, are displayed in the nearby **Museo Diocesano del Arte** (Tues–Sun 11am–2pm & 4–7pm; €2; closed for refurbishment).

The cathedral looks out over the **Plaza Mayor** from where c/Mayor leads up to the castle, passing close by the church of **San Vicente**. This is much the same age as the cathedral and is interesting mainly as a chance to see just how many layers of remodelling had to be peeled off by the restorers; an ancient figure of Christ above the altar is the only thing to detain you inside.

The **castle** started life as a Roman fortress, was adapted by the Visigoths and further improved by the Moors as their Alcazaba. Reconquered in 1124, it became the official residence of the warlike Bishop Bernardo and his successors. The Civil War virtually reduced the castle to rubble, but it was almost completely rebuilt in the 1970s and converted into a *parador*. You can still visit the central patio even if you are not staying at the hotel.

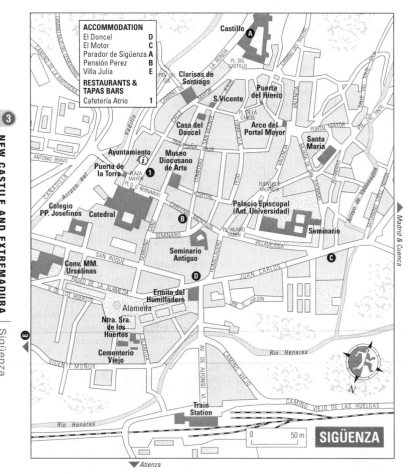

ACCOMMODATION
El Doncel   D
El Motor   C
Parador de Sigüenza   A
Pensión Perez   B
Villa Julia   E

RESTAURANTS &
TAPAS BARS
Cafetería Atrio   1

Madrid & Cuenca

Atienza

Practicalities

There's a rather lacklustre **turismo** in the town hall, at the top end of the Plaza Mayor (summer Mon–Fri 10am–2.30pm & 4–6.30pm, Sat 9.30am–3pm & 4–7pm, Sun 9.30am–3.30pm; winter as summer except closed Mon; ℡949 347 007). The town makes for a relaxing stopover en route to Soria and the north or as a base to explore the rest of the region, and accommodation is not usually a problem. Central places include the *Pensión Perez*, c/García Atance 13 (℡949 391 269; ●), *Hostal El Doncel*, Paseo de la Alameda 1 (℡949 390 001, Ⓦwww.eldoncel.com; ●), and the slightly more upmarket *El Motor*, Avda. Juan Carlos I 2 (℡949 390 827, Ⓦwww.hostalelmotor.com; ●). The *Villa Julia*, Paseo de las Cruces 27 (℡949 393 339; ●), is a more expensive but extremely comfortable *casa rural* (private house) with just five double en-suite rooms, while the hilltop *Parador de Sigüenza* (℡949 390 100, Ⓔsiguenza@parador.es; ●), situated in the castle, has fine views from the upper floors. For **meals**, try the hotel restaurants at *El Motor* and *El Doncel*, or settle for excellent tapas at the *Cafetería Atrio* on the Plaza Mayor.

Heading northeast from Sigüenza, **Medinaceli** (see p.446) is just over the border in Old Castile, a couple of stops on the Zaragoza line (only slow trains call at Sigüenza and Medinaceli). To the northwest is Atienza, a former fortress town with five Romanesque churches and an almost impregnable castle perched high on the hill above. Heading south, a good route for drivers leads **towards Cuenca**, past great reservoirs watered by the Tajo and Guadiela rivers, and skirting around the **Alcarria** region.

Cuenca and around

The mountainous, craggy countryside around **CUENCA** is as dramatic as any in Spain, and all the more so in the context of New Castile. The city itself, too, the capital of a sparsely populated province, is an extraordinary-looking place, enclosed on three sides by the deep gorges of the Huécar and Júcar rivers, with balconied houses hanging over the cliff top – the finest of them converted to a museum of abstract art. No surprise, then, that this is a popular weekend outing from Madrid; to get the most from a visit, try to come on a weekday, and take the time to stay a night and absorb the atmosphere. An overnight stay will also allow enough time to make the short trip to the see the extraordinary limestone formations of the **Ciudad Encantada** and to visit the picturesque source of the Río Cuervo. The rather less impressive source of the Río Tajo can be found to the south.

Arrival and information

The old town of Cuenca – the **Ciudad Antigua** – stands on a high ridge, looped to the south by the Río Huécar and the **modern town** and its suburbs. If you're driving in, follow signs for the Catedral and try one of the car parks up at the top of the old town. The **train and bus stations** are next to each other at the southern edge of the modern part of town. To get to the old town from here, head to the Puerta de Valencia, from where it's a steep climb; bus #1 or #2 will save you the twenty-minute walk.

Cuenca's helpful **turismo** is in the Plaza Mayor (winter Mon–Sat 9am–2pm & 5–8pm, Sun 9am–2pm; summer Mon–Sat 9am–9pm, Sun 9am–2.30pm; ☏969 323 119, ⓦwww.aytocuenca.org & www.cuenca.org) and provides information and maps on the town and the whole province. There is another office in the new town at Plaza Hispanidad (Mon–Thurs 10am–2pm & 5–8pm, Fri & Sat 10am–8pm, Sun 10am–2pm). **Internet access** is available in the new town at *Cyber Viajero* at Avda. República Argentina 3 (ⓦwww.cyberviajero.com; €2 per hour).

Accommodation

You'll find most **places to stay** in the new town, with a concentration of *hostales* along c/Ramón y Cajal, but there are several reasonably priced options in the old town.

Budget options

Pensión Central c/Dr Chirino 7 ☏969 211 511. Good-value *pensión* offering fifteen large rooms with separate bath. ❶

Pensión Cuenca Avda. República Argentina 8 ☏969 212 574. Modern *pensión* located near the train and bus stations offering some rooms with showers. ❶

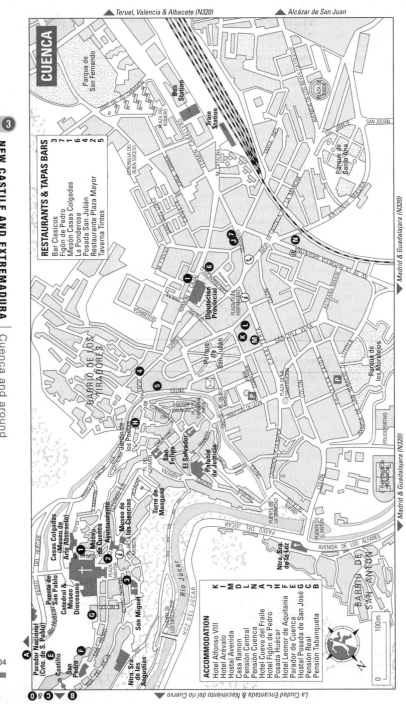

CUENCA

RESTAURANTS & TAPAS BARS

Bar Clasicos   3
Figón de Pedro   7
Mesón Casas Colgadas   1
La Ponderosa   6
Posada San Julián   4
Restaurante Plaza Mayor   2
Taverna Tintes   5

ACCOMMODATION

Hotel Alfonso VIII   K
Hotel Arévalo   I
Hostal Avenida   M
Casa Ramon   D
Pensión Central   N
Pensión Cuenca   L
Hotel Cueva del Fraile   A
Hotel Figón de Pedro   J
Posada Huécar   H
Hotel Leonor de Aquitania   F
Parador de Cuenca   E
Hostal Posada de San José   G
Pensión Real   C
Pensión Tabanqueta   B

Posada Huécar c/Paseo del Huécar 3 ☏ & ⒻⒻ969
214 201, Ⓦwww.posadahuecar.com. A characterful
inn on the banks of the Río Huécar with pleasantly
furnished rooms, all with en-suite bathrooms. ❷–❸
Pensión Real c/Larga 41 ☏969 229 977. The
last building in the old town, with commanding
views of Cuenca. Four rooms, with shared bath-
room/shower. ❶
Pensión Tabanqueta c/Trabuco 13 ☏969 211
290. Clean and cheap, some rooms have great
views of the Júcar gorge. There's a lively bar
which serves good food at affordable prices.
Shared bathrooms. ❶

Moderate and expensive options

Hotel Alfonso VIII c/Parque de San Julián 3
☏969 212 512, Ⓦwww.hotel-alfonsoviii. com.
Nicely located – but pricey – hotel in the new
town, facing the park. They also offer two-room
apartments for just over €100. ❺
Hotel Arévalo c/Ramón y Cajal 29 ☏ & Ⓕ969
223 979. Centrally located 35-room hotel with
secure parking. The top-floor rooms have fine
views of the old city. ❸
Hostal Avenida Avda. Carretería 25 ☏969 214
343, Ⓕ969 212 335. Near the park, and well
located for the old town, this *hostal* is functional
but comfortable. All rooms have TV and bath and
some are air-conditioned. ❸
Casa Ramon c/Paz s/n ☏659 066 204,
Ⓦwww.casa-ramon.com. Two modern apartments
that can accommodate up to five people up at the
top of the old town by the castle. €130 for five
people, €80 for two, but rates are cheaper outside
the peak holiday periods.

Hotel Cueva del Fraile Ctra. Cuenca-
Buenache km 7 ☏969 211 571, Ⓦwww.hotel
cuevadelfraile.com. A sixteenth-century former
monastery 5km out from Cuenca. The rooms
are pleasantly furnished in antique style and
the extensive grounds include a pool. It also has
its own restaurant serving local specialities.
❺–❻
Hotel Figón de Pedro c/Cervantes 13 ☏&
Ⓕ969 224 511. Well-run hotel at the heart of the
modern town, with an excellent restaurant. ❸
Hotel Leonor de Aquitania c/San Pedro 58–60
☏969 231 000, Ⓦwww.hotelleonordeaqui-
tania.com. Cuenca's prime hotel, beautifully situated in an eighteenth-century nobleman's house
in the old town. Tastefully decorated rooms with
superb views and prices to match. A great spot
for a meal, too. ❺–❻
Parador de Cuenca Convento de San Pablo
☏969 232 320, Ⓦwww.parador.es. Expensive,
but not that special, although it does have a pool
and good views across the gorge to the *casas colgadas*. ❻
Hostal Posada de San José c/Julián Romero 4
☏969 211 300, Ⓦwww.posadasanjose.com.
Lovely old building with a tranquil garden in the
old town near the cathedral. Only 30 stylishly decorated rooms (21 with bath), so be sure to book
ahead. A good-quality restaurant, too. ❹

Camping

Carvanning Cuenca 6km north of the city on the
CM 2105 ☏969 231 656. A riverside location for
this well-appointed campsite with a pool.
Surrounded by shady pines and open from mid-
March to December. No bus.

The Ciudad Antigua

Cross one of the many bridges over the River Huécar and you start to climb
steeply (most of the streets are stepped) towards the **Ciudad Antigua**, a narrow wedge of lanes, petering out in superb views to west and east.

More or less at the centre of the quarter is the Plaza Mayor, a fine space,
entered through the arches of the Baroque *ayuntamiento* and ringed by cafés
and ceramic shops. Occupying most of its east side is the **Catedral** (daily
9am–2pm & 4–6pm, summer closes 7pm; free), whose incongruous, unfinished
facade betrays a misguided attempt to beautify a simple Gothic building. The
interior is much more attractive, especially the carved Plateresque arch at the
end of the north aisle, and the chapel next to it, with distinctly un-Christian
carvings round its entrance. The east chapel, directly behind the high altar, has
a superb *artesonado* ceiling, which can just about be glimpsed through the
locked door.

Alongside is a small **Tesoro Catedralicio** (Tues–Sat 11am–2pm & 4–6pm,
summer closes 7pm, Sun 11am–2pm; €1.50) which contains some beautiful
gold and silver work as well as wooden doors by Alonso Berruguete. The

ceiling here, now a sea of Baroque icing-sugar shades, was originally a beautiful Mudéjar work like the one in the east chapel. Further religious treasures are to be found down c/Obispo Valero in the **Museo Diocesano** (Tues–Sat 11am–2pm & 4–6pm, summer closes an hour later, Sun 11am–2pm; €1.80), including two canvases by El Greco, a magnificent *Crucifixion* by Gerard David, and a Byzantine diptych unique in Spain. Right opposite is an excellent **Museo de Cuenca** (winter Tues–Sat 10am–2pm & 4–7pm, Sun 10am–2pm; summer Tues–Sat 10am–2pm & 5–7pm, Sun 11am–2pm; €1.20), which traces the city's history from prehistoric times and showcases a good local Roman collection from local finds.

The artistic highlight of Cuenca, however, has to be the **Museo de Arte Abstracto** (Oct–June Tues–Fri 11am–2pm & 4–6pm, Sat 11am–2pm & 4–8pm, Sun 11am–2.30pm; July–Sept Tues–Fri 11am–2pm & 5–7pm, Sat 11am–2pm & 4–8pm, Sun 11am–2.30pm; €3; ⓦwww.march.es/cuenca), a gallery established in the 1960s by Fernando Zóbel, one of the leading artists in Spain's "abstract generation". It is now run by the prestigious Fundación Juan March, which displays works from a core collection of abstract painting and sculpture by, among many others, Eduardo Chillida, José Guerrero, Lucio Muñoz, Antonio Saura, Antonio Tàpies and Fernando Zóbel, and hosts some of the best exhibitions to be found in provincial Spain. The museum itself is a stunning conversion from the extraordinary *Casas Colgadas* ("hanging houses"), a pair of fifteenth-century houses, with cantilevered balconies, literally hanging from the cliff face.

Not far away in the small Plaza de la Merced is the **Museo del las Ciencias** (Tues–Sat 10am–2pm & 4–7pm, Sun 10am–2pm; €1.20 for museum, €1.20 for the planetarium). Housed in an old convent and an adjoining modern extension, it is an ambitious, and largely successful, attempt to explain the origins of the universe and the history of the earth in the context of the local region. There are other monuments signposted in Cuenca, but the greatest attraction is the place itself. Have a drink in one of the bars opposite the cathedral in the Plaza Mayor, or walk along the gorge of the Huécar and look up at the *Casas Colgadas* and the other less secure-looking buildings high above the river. At night the effect is even more dramatic. There are also excellent **views** to be had from the top of the old city; just follow the road out of the Plaza Mayor or take bus #1 or #2 until you reach the castle. If you have a car you can also do the 14km round-trip known as the *ruta turística* which starts here and loops round the gorge back to the city.

Eating, drinking and nightlife

There are plenty of **places to eat** around the Plaza Mayor, though the food is probably better down at the bars and restaurants of the modern town. Some of the best places are reviewed below – note that almost all shut at around 11pm.

The Plaza Mayor is the place to head for evening *copas*, with its vibrant and diverse range of **bars**. The liveliest places are along c/Seuro Catalina and in the little alleyways overlooking the Río Júcar, where you'll find *La Repos*, a good stand-up drinking bar, and the *Taberna-Artística Los Elefantes*, a long-time artists' hangout playing a good range of alternative music. Also try out the excellent *Las Tortugas* at no. 39, a great place for a later drink. Another popular area is on and around c/Parque del Huécar, where the crowds start off around midnight, moving on later to c/Alferez Rubianes. If this isn't to your taste, there is a host of bars around the stations and c/Fermin Caballero which play salsa.

Bar Clasicos c/Severo Catalina s/n. Cosy little place in the street below the Plaza Mayor. It does a good-value €9 *menú del día* and has a small terrace that overlooks the Río Júcar.

Figón de Pedro c/Cervantes 13 ☎969 226 821. Renowned restaurant, serving classic Castilian roasts and superb fish dishes. Closed Sun evening. Expensive – even the *menú* is over €19.

Mesón Casas Colgadas c/Canónigos 3 ☎969 223 509. A good restaurant up in the old town, housed in a fine hanging house. Features suckling pig and other Castilian specialities. Closed Mon evening. Expect to pay at least €25.

La Ponderosa c/San Francisco 20. The best tapas selection in a street full of worthwhile *mesónes*. Closed Sun & July.

Posada San Julián c/Torres 1. Housed in a sixteenth-century town house, with a decent, inexpensive *menú* (not served Sun).

Restaurante Plaza Mayor Local specialities and liquor (*resoli*) served in this restaurant on the main plaza. Menus at €12.62 and €16.23.

Taverna Tintes c/Tintes 7. This popular and atmospheric local serves up a wide range of moderately priced dishes. Closed Mon.

La Ciudad Encantada – and on towards Albarracín

The classic excursion from Cuenca is to the **Ciudad Encantada**, a twenty-square-kilometre "park" of karst limestone outcrops, sculpted by erosion into a bizarre series of abstract, natural and animal-like forms. A few of the names – "fight between an elephant and a crocodile", for example – stretch the imagination a little, but the rocks are certainly amazing, and many of the creations really do look knocked into shape by human hands. The fantasy landscape was used as a backdrop for Arnold Schwarzenegger's first major film *Conan the Barbarian*.

The most interesting area of sculptures is enclosed (daily 9am–dusk; €3), and the extensive car park and restaurants outside testify to its popularity with weekending *madrileños*. However, off season, or during the week, you can have the place almost to yourself. You will need transport to get to the park, which is around 20km northeast of Cuenca, on signed backroads towards Albarracín. If you get stuck, there is a **hostal**, the *Ciudad Encantada* (☎969 288 194; ❸), opposite the entrance gate. Another 30km further north on the CM 2106 past Tragacete is the picturesque **source of the Río Cuervo**, a moss-covered crag covered in waterfalls.

To the source of the Tajo

If you have transport, the route east from the Ciudad Encantada towards Albarracín (see chapter 9, p.659) is a delight, edging through the verdant **Júcar Gorge** and across the wild, scarcely populated Serranía de Cuenca. En route, still in Cuenca Province, you might stop at **UÑA**, a village sited between a lagoon and barrage, where the *Hotel Agua Riscas* (☎969 282 852; ❷) at c/Egido 23 has decent rooms, a panoramic restaurant and a garden bar.

Just over the provincial border, in Teruel Province, the road between Uña and Frías de Albarracín runs past a point known as García, where a signpost directs you to the **source of the Río Tajo**. Below a hideous 1960s sculpture a trickle of muddy water seeps out, setting the course of one of Iberia's great rivers on its way to the Atlantic Ocean at Lisbon.

Belmonte, El Toboso and Alarcón

Travelling south from Cuenca – or east from Toledo – Cuenca Province has a few more places where you might consider breaking your journey if you have your own transport: the castle villages of **Belmonte** (on the N420) and **Alarcón** (just off the NIII to Valencia), while the Roman ruins at **Segóbriga** (again just off the NIII, but this time back towards Madrid, near Saelices) are an impressive sight.

Segóbriga

Just south of the NIII, near the village of Saelices, **SEGÓBRIGA** (mid-April to mid Sept Tues–Sun: 9am–9pm, mid-Sept to mid-April 10am–6pm; €2) makes a worthy detour for anyone interested in Roman ruins. References to the town date back to the second century BC and it developed into a prosperous settlement largely thanks to the presence of nearby gypsum mines. The town reached its peak about four hundred years later, but declined under the Visigoths and was effectively abandoned during the Arab occupation. The best preserved structures are the theatre and amphitheatre – which had a capacity for 5500 people – but there are also some interesting additions made by the Visigoths. There is a small museum on the site that recounts the history of what was a fairly important settlement.

Belmonte and El Toboso

The village of **BELMONTE** is partly encircled by a vast curtain wall, at the corner of which is a magnificent fourteenth-century castle (daily 10.30am–2pm & 5.30–8pm; €2). Partially rebuilt in the last century, it is really little more than a shell, although belated restoration is revealing what must once have been stunning Mudéjar *artesonado* ceilings. The village, too, has seen better days, though it has a fine collegiate church, and a pleasant little hotel, *La Muralla* (☎967 171 045; ❶), on c/Isabel I de Castilla.

Continuing west from Belmonte, Cervantes enthusiasts might consider a detour to the attractive village of **EL TOBOSO** (🌐www.eltoboso.org), on a minor road south of the N301. This was the home of Don Quixote's mistress, Dulcinea, whose "house" has of course been identified and turned into a **small museum** (Tues–Fri 9.45am–2pm & 4–6.45pm, Sat & Sun 10am–2pm & 4–6.30pm; €0.60, free Sat & Sun), with an adjoining restaurant. West again from here, you could cut across country – and past the NIV – to **Consuegra** (see p.210), with its eleven windmills.

Alarcón

ALARCÓN occupies an impressive defensive site sculpted by the burrowing of the Río Júcar. Almost completely encircled and walled, the village is accessible by a spit of land just wide enough to take a road which passes through a succession of **fortified gateways**. Unlike Belmonte, Alarcón has a bit of life about it, at least at weekends, as many of the old escutcheoned houses have been restored as retreats by *madrileños*.

At the top of the village is an exquisite **castle**, eighth-century in origin and captured from the Moors in 1184 after a nine-month siege. This has been converted to house an expensive **parador**, the *Parador Marqués de Villena* (☎969 330 315, 🌐www.parador.es; ❼), one of the country's smallest and most characterful. More affordable accommodation is provided in the four bright and clean rooms at the *Pensión El Infante*, c/Dr Tortosa 6 (☎969 330 323, 🌐www.posadaelinfante.com; ❷). Either option should be booked ahead in summer or at weekends. The *parador*, with its atmospheric castle dining hall, is the best place to eat, but there is cheaper fare to be found in bars on the main Plaza de Don Juan Manuel.

Albacete Province

Travelling between Madrid or Cuenca and Alicante or Murcia, you'll pass through **Albacete Province**, one of Spain's more forgettable corners. Hot, arid plains for the most part, this is very much the Spain of Castilla–La Mancha, with a dull provincial capital, **Albacete**, to match. Scenically, the only relief is in the hyperactive **Río Júcar**, which, in the north of the province, sinks almost without warning into the plain.

The Río Júcar: Alcalá del Júcar

If you are driving, it is certainly worth taking a detour off the main roads east to take the scenic route along the banks of the Río Júcar, between Valdeganga and the stunning village of **ALCALÁ DEL JÚCAR**. Almost encircled by the river, the village is an amazing sight, with its houses built one on top of the other and burrowed into the white cliff face. Several of these **cuevas** (caves) have been converted into bars and restaurants and make a great place for a drink, with rooms carved up to 170m through the cliff and windows over-looking the river on each side of the loop. They're open daily in summer but otherwise only at weekends. Alcalá also boasts a **castle** – adapted at intervals over the past 1500 years, though today just a shell – with great views. If you want **to stay**, there are two simple **hostales** on the main road at the bottom of the village – *Hermanos Plaza* (☎967 473 029; **②**) and the *Júcar* (☎967 473 055; **②**) – and the rather nicer *Hostal Rambla* (☎967 474 064; **③**) up on Avda. de los Robles. There is also a popular campsite, *El Berrocal*, with a swimming pool on the banks of the river on the outskirts of town (☎967 473 212).

Albacete

ALBACETE was named *Al-Basit* – the plain – by the Moors, but save for a few old backstreets, it is basically a modern city. The underworked **turismo** is at c/Tinte 2 (Mon–Fri: summer 10am–2pm & 6–8pm; winter 10am–2pm & 4.30–6.30pm, Sat 10am–6pm, Sun 10am–3pm; ☎967 580 522). The **Catedral** is not of any great interest and is noteworthy only for the presence of Ionic columns instead of normal pillars astride its nave. The **Museo de Albacete** (Tues–Fri 10am–2pm & 4.30–7pm, Sat 9am–7pm, Sun 9am–2pm, open mornings only in summer; €1.20, free Sat & Sun), however, has a more than respectable archeological and ethnographical collection, whose prize exhibits are five small Roman dolls, perfectly sculpted and jointed, and an array of local Roman mosaics. For Spaniards, Albacete is synonymous with high-quality knives, a speciality which, as with Toledo, can be traced back to the Moors: if you're after some top cutlery, now's your chance.

Albacete has plenty of **accommodation**, but there's no real reason to stay unless you want to break a longer journey. One of the best medium category places to stay is the modern *Hotel San José* (☎967 507 402, ⓦwww.hotels anjose-albacete.es; **④**) in c/San José de Calasanz 12, close to the pleasant city-centre park. Don't be tempted, however, by signs to Albacete's *parador*, a modern creation southeast of the town, right on the flight path of a military airfield.

Chinchilla de Monte Aragón and Almansa

Thirteen kilometres southeast of Albacete, **CHINCHILLA DE MONTE ARAGÓN** is a breezy hilltop village worth a look if you're passing by, though most of its grand mansions and churches are either decayed or locked up for restoration. The hilltop **fortress**, so impressive from the road below, is a windy ruin not really deserving of the climb, but the **Convento de Santo Domingo**, in the lower part of the village, has interesting fourteenth-century Mudéjar work. There is also a small but nationally representative **Museo de Cerámica** at c/Penuela (Sat 5–7pm, Sun 1–2pm & 5–7pm; €0.70). Further along the A430 and just before the border with Valencia is **ALMANSA**, with its spectacular Arab **castle** constructed on a great rock above the town.

Ciudad Real and the heartland of La Mancha

There is a huge gap in the middle of the tourist map of Spain between Toledo and the borders of Andalucía, and from Extremadura almost to the east coast. This, the province of **Ciudad Real**, comprises the heartland of **La Mancha**. The tourist authorities try hard to push their *Ruta de Don Quixote* across the plains, highlighting the windmills and other Quixotic sights: the signposted route, which starts at Belmonte and finishes at Consuegra, can be done in a day, but much of it is fanciful and, unless you're enamoured of the book, it's only of passing interest.

Nonetheless, there are a few places which merit a visit if you've got time to spare, most notably **Consuegra**, for the best windmills, **Almagro**, for its arcaded square and medieval theatre, and **Calatrava**, for the castle ruins of its order of knights. It is also the heart of wine-producing country, and many of the *bodegas* in **Valdepeñas** offer free tastings. The **websites** Ⓦ www.elquijote.com, Ⓦ www.viajealamancha.es, Ⓦ www.castillalamancha.es and Ⓦ www.jccm.es all give more information about the area.

Consuegra

CONSUEGRA lies just to the west of the NIV *autovía*, roughly midway from Madrid to Andalucía, and has the most picturesque and typical of Manchegan settings, below a ridge of twelve restored (and highly photogenic) windmills. The first of these is occupied by the town's **turismo**, with uncertain – indeed, truly Quixotic – opening hours, but good for information on the *Ruta de Don Quixote*, while others house shops and workshops. They share their plateau with a ruined **castle**, once the headquarters of the order of St John in the twelfth century, which offers splendid views of the plain from its windswept ridge. The town below is also attractive, with a lively Plaza Mayor and many Mudéjar churches.

Places to stay are limited to two friendly places, the *Hostal-Restaurant San Poul* (Ⓣ 925 481 315 or 925 475 163; ❸) in the centre and the busy and comfortable *Hotel Las Provincias* (Ⓣ 925 480 300, Ⓕ 925 467 608; ❷), within walking distance on the main road north of town.

Ciudad Real

CIUDAD REAL, capital of the province at the heart of this flat country, makes a good base for excursions and has connections by bus with most villages in the area. It has a few sights of its own, too, including a Mudéjar gateway, the **Puerta de Toledo**, which fronts the only surviving fragment of its medieval walls, at the northern edge of the city on the Toledo road. Further in, take a look at fourteenth-century **San Pedro**, an airy, Gothic edifice, housing the alabaster tomb of its founder and a good Baroque *retablo*, and the **Museo Provincial** (Sept 1 to July 15 Tues–Sat 10am–2pm & 5–8pm, Sun 10am–2pm; July 15 to Aug 31 Tues–Sat 10am–2pm; free), a modern building opposite the cathedral, with two floors of local archeology (the second also has some stuffed local wildlife) and a third devoted to artists of the region. The newest attraction is the entertaining **Museo de Don Quijote** (Mon–Sat 10am–2pm & 6–9pm, Sun 10am–2pm; free), where personalities from the story guide you round the exhibits which include some neat audiovisuals that bring the tale to life.

The romantic adventures of **Don Quixote**, set against the backdrop of La Mancha, with its castles, windmills, cornfields and vineyards, have captivated readers ever since *Don Quijote de La Mancha* was first published in 1604.

Not a novel in the modern sense, **Miguel Cervantes'** book is a sequence of episodes following the adventures of a country gentleman in his fifties, whose mind has been addled by romantic tales of chivalry. In a noble gesture, he changes his name to Don Quixote de La Mancha, and sets out on horseback, in rusty armour, to right the wrongs of the world. At his side throughout is **Sancho Panza**, a shrewd, pot-bellied rustic given to quoting proverbs at every opportunity. During the course of the book, Quixote, an instantly sympathetic hero, charges at windmills and sheep (mistaking them for giants and armies), makes ill-judged attempts to help others, and is mocked by all for his efforts. Broken-hearted but wiser, he returns home and, on his deathbed, pronounces: "Let everyone learn from my example... look at the world with common sense and learn to see what is really there."

Cervantes' life was almost as colourful as his hero's. The son of a poor doctor, he fought as a soldier in the sea battle of **Lepanto**, where he permanently maimed his left hand and was captured by pirates and put to work as a slave in Algiers. Ransomed and sent back to Spain, he spent the rest of his days writing novels and plays in relative poverty, dying ten years after the publication of *Don Quixote*, "old, a soldier, a gentleman and poor".

Spanish academics have spent as much time dissecting the work of Cervantes as their English counterparts have Shakespeare's. Most see the story as a satire on the popular romances of the day, with the central characters representing two forces in Spain; Quixote the dreaming, impractical nobility, and Sancho the wise and down-to-earth peasantry. There are also those who read in it an ironic tale of a visionary or martyr frustrated in a materialistic world, while yet others see it as an attack on the Church and establishment. Debates aside, this highly entertaining adventure story, rich in characters, and with an eminently lovable hero, is said to have been reprinted so often that, worldwide, it is second only to the Bible in the printing stakes.

Out of the wealth of artistic interpretations inspired by Cervantes' holy fool (including a bizarre and original short story by Jorge Luís Borges), perhaps the most enduring are **Jules Massenet's** folksy opera and **Strauss's** symphonic poem, in which the hero is portrayed by a lofty cello.

The local **turismo** (Mon–Sat 10am–2pm & 4–7pm, Sun 10am–2pm; ☎ & ℱ926 200 037) is at c/Alarcos 21 in the centre of town, a ten-minute walk from the **bus station** on the Ronda de Ciruela. Ciudad Real's new **train station**, with high-speed AVE connections to Madrid and south to Sevilla and Córdoba, lies out of town at the end of Avenida de Europa; bus #5 connects with the central Plaza de Pilar.

Accommodation is not always easy to find, particularly at the lower end of the scale, so it's worth booking ahead. Decent options include *Pensión Esteban*, c/Reyes 15 (☎926 224 578; ❷), *Pensión Escudero*, c/Galicia 48 (☎926 252 309; ❷), and the very reasonably priced four-star *Hotel Santa Cecilia*, c/Tinte 3 (☎926 228 545, ⓦwww.santacecilia.com; ❹-❺). An impressive range of **tapas bars** includes *Casa Lucio*, off c/Montesa at Pasaje Dulcinea del Toboso, and *Gran Mesón*, Ronda Ciruela 34, which also has a swankier restaurant, *Miami Park*, down the road at no. 48. The town's **nightlife** at the weekend generally starts off with tapas on c/Palma, carrying on to the bars along Avenida Torreón del Alcázar and around. For those with the energy, it then moves off under the train tracks to the *Playa Park* complex, where there's *makina* at *Isla Tortuga* and salsa at *La Ribera*.

Wet La Mancha and two parks

A respite from the arid monotony of the Castilian landscape, and a treat for bird-watchers, is provided by the oasis of **La Mancha Húmeda** ("Wet La Mancha"). This is an area of lagoons and marshes, both brackish and fresh, along the high-level basin of the **Río Cigüela** and **Río Guadiana**. Although drainage for agriculture has severely reduced the amount of water, so that lakes almost dry up in the summer, there is still a good variety of interesting plant and bird life to be found here. You're best off visiting from April to July when the water birds are breeding, or from September to midwinter when migrating birds pass through.

Major parks between Ciudad Real and Albacete include the **Parque Nacional de las Tablas de Daimiel**, 11km north of Daimiel itself, which is renowned for its bird life. There's an **information centre** (daily: winter 8am–6.30pm; summer 8.30am–8pm; ☏926 693 118) alongside the marshes, but the park is accessible only by car or taxi, while Daimiel has little **accommodation** on offer outside the upmarket *Hotel Las Tablas* (☏926 852 107, ⊛www.Domus-hoteles.es; ❹).

Rather more traveller-friendly, but more crowded in the summer months, is the **Parque Natural de las Lagunas de Ruidera**, which lies northeast of Valdepeñas (with frequent buses from Albacete). You'll find an **information centre** (July & Aug daily 10am–9pm; Sept–June Wed–Sun 10am–2pm & 4–6pm; ☏926 528 116) on the roadside, as you enter Ruidera from Manzanares, and several nature trails inside the park, as well as swimming and boating opportunities. You can also stay overnight; **accommodation** ranges from a campsite, *Los Molinos* (☏926 528 089; Easter & July to mid-Sept), with a pool, and the *Hostal La Noria* (☏926 528 032; ❷), to the good-value *Don Quijote Aparthotel* (☏625 406 772/926 504 280; ❸) and the comfortable *Hotel Entrelagos* (☏ & ⨏926 528 022; ❸).

Almagro

Twenty kilometres east of Ciudad Real is **ALMAGRO**, an elegant little town, which for a period in the fifteenth and sixteenth centuries was quite a metropolis in southern Castile. Today, its main claim to fame is the **Corral de las Comedias**, in the Plaza Mayor, a perfectly preserved sixteenth-century open-air theatre, unique in Spain. Plays from its sixteenth- and seventeenth-century heyday – the golden age of Spanish theatre – are performed regularly in the tiny auditorium, and in July it hosts a fully fledged theatre festival. By day the theatre is open to visitors (April–June & Sept Tues–Fri 10am–2pm & 5–8pm, Sat 10am–2pm & 5–8pm, Sun 11am–2pm; July & Aug Tues–Fri 10am–2pm & 6–9pm, Sat 11am–2pm & 6–8pm, Sun 11am–2pm; Oct–March Tues–Sat 10am–2pm & 4–7pm, Sat 10am–2pm & 4–6pm, Sun 11am–2pm; €2.40). Across the square on Callejon de Villar the **Museo del Teatro** (same hours as theatre except July & Aug open on Saturday until 9pm; €1.20) houses photos, posters, model theatres and other paraphernalia, but is probably only of passing interest to anyone other than theatre buffs.

The **Plaza Mayor** itself is magnificent: more of a wide street than a square, it is arcaded along its length, and lined with rows of green-framed windows – a north European influence brought by the Fugger family, Carlos V's bankers, who settled here. Also resident in Almagro for a while were the Knights of Calatrava (see opposite), though their power was on the wane by the time the **Convento de la Asunción de Calatrava** was built in the early sixteenth century. Further traces of Almagro's former importance are dotted throughout the town in the grandeur of numerous **Renaissance mansions**.

Back in the Plaza Mayor, you can have an open-air snack or browse among the shops in the arcades, where **lacemakers** at work with bobbins and needles are the main attraction. On Wednesday mornings there's a lively **market** in c/Ejido de San Juan.

Practicalities

There's a small **turismo** just south of Plaza Mayor on c/Bernadas 2 (April–June & Sept Tues–Fri 10am–2pm & 5–8pm, Sat 11am–2pm & 5–8pm, Sun 11am–2pm; July & Aug Tues–Fri 10am–2pm & 6–9pm, Sat 11am–2pm & 6–8pm, Sun 11am–2pm; Oct–March Tues–Fri 10am–2pm & 4–7pm, Sat 10am–2pm & 4–6pm, Sun 11am–2pm; ☎926 860 717, ⓦwww.ciudad -almagro.com). Almagro invites a stay more than anywhere in this region, although **accommodation** can be fairly limited during the theatre festival and at holiday weekends. Cheapest options are the *Hostal Los Escudos*, c/Bolaños 55 (☎ & ⒻGS926 861 574; ❺), and, next to the convent, the *Hospedería Almagro*, Ejido de Calatrava s/n (☎926 882 087, Ⓕ926 882 122; ❷). The *Hotel Don Diego*, on the Ronda de Calatrava (☎926 861 287, Ⓕ926 860 574; ❹), due east of the plaza, is a good mid-range hotel. The recently refurbished *Casa del Rector* (☎926 261 259; ❹), at c/Pedro Oviedo 8, is another good-value mid-range place, and at the top of the range there is a very good *parador* (☎926 860 100, ⓦwww.parador.es; ❼) in a former Franciscan convent on c/Gran Maestre.

A number of **bars**, good for tapas, are to be found around the Plaza Mayor, and the *bodega* at the *parador* is worth a stop for a drink, too. The best **restaurant** in town is the *Mesón El Corregidor* at Jerónimo Ceballos 2 (closed Mon & first week in Aug); it's moderately expensive at around €25 per head. A cheaper option is *La Cuerda*, in front of the train station at Plaza del General Jorreto 6, which has a good *menú* specializing in fish and *arroz* for around €8 (closed Mon evening and first fortnight in Sept).

Moving on, Almagro has two direct **trains** a day to Madrid, and five trains and **buses** daily to Ciudad Real; buses stop near the *Hotel Don Diego* on the Ronda de Calatrava.

Calatrava La Nueva

The area known as the **Campo de Calatrava**, south of Almagro and Ciudad Real, was the domain of the **Knights of Calatrava**, a Cistercian order of soldier-monks at the forefront of the reconquest of Spain from the Moors. So influential were they in these parts that Alfonso X created Ciudad Real as a royal check on their power. Even today, dozens of villages for miles around are suffixed with their name.

In the opening decades of the thirteenth century, the knights pushed their headquarters south, as land was won back, from Calatrava La Vieja, near Daimiel, to a commanding hilltop 25km south of Almagro, protecting an important pass – the Puerto de Calatrava – into Andalucía. Here, in 1216, they founded **Calatrava La Nueva**, a settlement that was part monastery and part castle, and whose main glory was a great Cistercian church. The site (Tues–Sun: summer 10am–2pm & 5–8pm; winter 10am–2pm & 4–7pm; free) is reached by turning west off the main road (C410) and following the signposts uphill. Once there, you will get a good idea of what must have been an enormously rich and well-protected fortress. The church itself is now completely bare but preserves the outline of a striking rose window and has an amazing stone-vaulted entrance hall.

On the hill opposite is a further castle ruin, known as **Salvatierra**, which the knights took over from the Moors.

Valdepeñas and beyond

The road from Ciudad Real through Almagro continues to **VALDEPEÑAS**, centre of the most prolific wine region in Spain and handily situated just off the main Madrid–Andalucía motorway. You pass many of the largest **bodegas** on the slip road into town coming from the north and Madrid; most of them offer free tastings – ask at the **turismo** on the Plaza España (Tues–Sat 10am–2pm & 5–7pm, Sun 10am–2pm; ☎926 312 552, ⓦwww.ayto-valdepenas.org). Another option is the hi-tech **museo del vino** at c/Princesa 39 close to Plaza de España (winter Tues–Sat 10am–2pm & 5–7pm, Sun noon–2pm; summer Tues–Sat 10am–2pm & 6–8pm; free). The town holds a popular wine **festival** at the beginning of September. Wine aside, there are few other sights. There is a **windmill**, again on the Madrid road, which the tourist office says "could be the biggest in Europe", and a museum dedicated to the abstract drawings and other work of local artist Gregorio Prieto (winter Tues–Sat 10am–2pm & 5–8pm, Sun 11am–2pm; summer Tues–Sat 10am–2pm & 6–9pm, Sun 11am–2pm; free). If you choose to make a stopover here try the cosy *Hostal Valdepeñas* (☎926 322 328; ❷–❸) at Avda. Gregorio Prieto 47 or the more upmarket *Hospedería Museo Valdepeñas* (☎926 310 795, ⓕ926 310 882; ❹) at c/Unión 98.

Heading south beyond Valdepeñas you enter Andalucía through the **Gorge of Despeñaperros** (literally, "throwing over of the dogs"), a narrow mountain gorge once notorious for bandits and still a dramatic natural gateway which signals a change in both climate and vegetation, or as Richard Ford put it (travelling south to north), "exchanges an Eden for a desert".

The first towns of interest across the regional border, and more tempting places to break your journey than anywhere in this part of La Mancha, are **Úbeda** and **Baeza** (see p.360–1). Both towns are connected by bus with the train station of **Linares-Baeza**, which is also where you'll change trains if you're heading for Córdoba. The provincial capital of **Jaén** (see p.358), the first city on the main bus and train routes, is comparatively dull.

The Montes de Toledo and west into Extremadura

The **Montes de Toledo** cut a swathe through the upper reaches of La Mancha, between Toledo, Ciudad Real and Guadalupe. If you're heading into Extremadura, and have time and transport, the deserted little roads across these hills (they rise to just over 1400m) provide an interesting alternative to the main routes. This is an amazingly remote region to find so close to the centre of Spain: its people are so unused to visitors that in the smaller villages you'll certainly get a few odd looks. Covered below, too, is the **main route west** from Toledo into Extremadura, which runs just north of the hills.

Toledo to Navalmoral

The CM4, west of Toledo, provides a direct approach into **Extremadura**, linking with the NV from Madrid to Trujillo, and with roads north into the valley of **La Vera** (see p.217). It follows the course of the Río Tajo virtually all the way to **Talavera de la Reina**, beyond which an attractive minor road, from **Oropesa**, with its castle *parador*, runs to **El Puente del Arzobispo** and south of the river to the Roman site of **Los Vascos**.

La Puebla de Montalbán – and Montalbán Castle

LA PUEBLA DE MONTALBÁN, the first town west of Toledo, offers one of the best approaches into the Montes de Toledo. In itself, it is an unexceptional little place, but it has a claim to fame as the birthplace of **Fernando de Rojas**, a precursor of the golden age dramatists, whose play *La Celestina* was first published in 1500 and is still performed in Spain. He is remembered by a plaque in the Plaza Mayor on the *ayuntamiento*, a building, like those surrounding it, endowed with an attractive facade of pillars and balconies. Across the square, the sixteenth-century **Palacio de los Condes de Montalbán** is an impressive, rambling affair, brooding behind small, barred windows.

There's a **hostal** on the Toledo side of town, the *Legázpiz* (☎ 925 750 032; ①), at Avda. de Madrid 55, though there's little reason to stay unless you happen to coincide with the July fiestas, which include bull-running through the streets.

South of La Puebla de Montalbán, the CM4009 leads into the foothills of the Montes de Toledo. At kilometre stone 31 (15km south of La Puebla), a track leads 2km west to the **Castillo de Montalbán**. This is clearly visible from the road – a low, golden-brown edifice with central turrets – though close up you discover that only the walls actually survive. The interior is open for visits on Saturday mornings.

Talavera de la Reina, Oropesa and Navalmoral de la Mata

Continuing west from La Puebla de Montalbán, you reach **TALAVERA DE LA REINA**, an unremarkable town at the junction of major road and rail routes. The town has long been one of the most important centres of ceramic manufacture in Spain, and there are thirty functioning porcelain factories still here. If you decide to stop, take a look round the many shops down the main street displaying the local products: much is the usual mass-produced tourist trash, but there are still a few genuine craftsmen working here. The most attractive part of town is the park on the banks of the Río Tajo, where you'll find a friendly **turismo**, a *hostal* and a few places to eat.

Far more promising for a night's stop is **OROPESA**, which lies 33km further west, overlooking the busy NV. The *Parador Virrey de Toledo* (☎ 925 430 000, ⓦ www.parador.es; ⑥) is installed in part of the village **castle**, a warm, stone building on a Roman site, rebuilt from Moorish foundations in the fifteenth century by Don García Álvarez de Toledo. Below it, stretches of the old town walls survive, along with a few noble mansions and a pair of Renaissance churches. There are great views from the neatly manicured gardens across to the hulking silhouettes of the Gredos mountain range on the horizon.

West again, **NAVALMORAL DE LA MATA** has nothing to offer other than its road, rail and bus connections to more engrossing places such as the **Monastery of Yuste** across the rich tobacco-growing area to the north, **Plasencia** to the west, and **Trujillo** and **Guadalupe** to the south.

El Puente del Arzobispo and Los Vascos

EL PUENTE DEL ARZOBISPO, astride the Río Tajo 14km south of Oropesa, is, like Talavera, famed for the production of pottery and decorated tiles. Approaching from the south, you drive in across the ancient **bridge** over the river which gives the place its name. According to legend, this was built after the villagers appealed to a fourteenth-century archbishop to build them a bridge across the river. At first he refused, and when pressed pulled a ring from his finger and flung it into the Tajo, saying that he would build the bridge when the ring came back to him. Three days later he cut open his dinner of fish from the river, only to find the ring inside.

Today the ceramics industry dominates, with small factories and shops selling their products everywhere. The wares are not terribly exciting but the tiles do brighten up the Plaza Mayor, with its tile-covered benches, and the exuberantly ornate archbishop's house.

The other local attraction is the ruined **Roman city of Los Vascos**, in beautiful country some 10km southeast of town, near the village of Navalmoralejo. There's little to see beyond a few walls, but it's an enjoyable excursion.

Into the hills

The most accessible route into the Montes de Toledo is to follow the CM4009 and then the CM403 south of La Puebla de Montalbán, which runs through the backwater village of **Las Ventas Con Peña Aguilera**, overlooked by rock-studded hills, including a curious outcrop shaped like three fat fingers – the name Peña Aguilera means "Crag of Eagles". Southwest of Las Ventas, a tiny road leads to **San Pablo de los Montes**, a delightful village of fine stone houses nestling against the mountains. Beyond here, you can walk over the hills to the spa of **Baños del Robledillo**, a spectacular five- to six-hour trek (get directions locally or at the turismo in Puebla de Montalbán at Avda. de Madrid 1 (℡925 776 542).

If you keep to the CM403 south of Las Ventas, you will come to the main pass over the Montes de Toledo, the **Puerto del Milagro**, with great views of the hills dipping down on either side to meet the plain. Past the Puerto del Milagro, you can drive through lovely scenery towards Ciudad Real, or turn right along the CM4017 at the El Molinillo junction to follow a road through the hills via Retuerta del Bullaque to **Navas de Estena**. Here the road curves round to the north, passing a large crag with caves 5km beyond Navas, allowing you to loop round to Navahermosa and on to the CM401 to Guadalupe.

The western villages

If isolated villages and obscure roads appeal, you could strike south from the CM401, or west from the CM403 (just south of the Puerto del Milagro), into the most remote part of the Montes de Toledo. The latter approach would take you some 54km, without a village, before you reached **Valdeazores**, itself scarcely inhabited with a population of just 35. You could bypass this, if you wanted, following a road past the Cijara reservoir, and on to the N502 at Puerto Rey, passing nothing save the odd *finca*.

Coming from the CM401, the first place you reach is **Roblado del Buey**, where there's a single bar. From here, a pine forest extends south to Los Alares. To the west, and the only place in these parts that gets any visitors, is **Piedraescrita**, a well-kept village with an incredibly spruce bar, and a miraculous image of the Virgin that pulls in the odd Spanish pilgrim. West again is the area's main administrative centre, **Robledo del Mazo**, with a doctor, pharmacy and bar.

Extremadura

Extremadura is slowly getting on the tourist trail – and deservedly so. The grand old *conquistador* towns of **Trujillo** and **Cáceres** are excellent staging posts en route south from Madrid or from Salamanca to Andalucía; **Mérida** has numerous Roman remains and an exemplary museum of local finds; and there is superb bird life in the **Parque Natural de Monfragüe**. Almost inaccessible by public transport, but well worth visiting, is the great **Monastery of Guadalupe**, whose revered icon of the Virgin has attracted pilgrims for the past five hundred years.

This section of the chapter is arranged north to south, starting with the lush hills and valley of **La Vera**, the first real patch of green you'll come to if you've driven along the NV west from Madrid.

La Vera and the Monasterio de Yuste

La Vera lies just south of the Sierra de Gredos (see p.180), a range of hills tucked above the **Río Tiétar** valley. It is characterized by the streams – or *gargantas* – which descend from the mountains and in spring and summer attract increasing bands of weekenders from Madrid to the picturesque villages of **Candeleda** and **Jarandilla**. At the heart of the region is the **Monasterio de Yuste**, the retreat chosen by Carlos V to cast off the cares of empire.

Jarandilla and around

La Vera really comes into its element between Candeleda and Jarandilla de la Vera, along the C501, as the *gargantas* flow down from the hills. They are flanked in summer by some superb seasonal **campsites**: *Minchones* (☎927 565 403; Easter & June to mid-Sept) is just outside **Villanueva de la Vera**, a village which gained British media notoriety in the 1980s with its *Pero Palo* fiesta, in which donkeys are horribly mistreated. It seems strange to imagine any cruelty, given the rural idyll hereabouts and the incredibly house-proud appearance of the villages, especially **Losar**, which has an almost surreal display of topiary.

The main village in these parts is **JARANDILLA DE LA VERA**, a good target if you want a roof over your head, with a choice of three medium-range places to stay: the *Marbella* (☎927 560 218; ❷), the *Hotel Jaranda* (☎927 560 206, Ⓦ www.hoteljaranda.com; ❸-❹) and the highly original *Posada de Pizarro* (☎927 560 727, Ⓦ www.laposadadepizarro.com; ❸-❹), with its frescoes on the bedroom walls. There is also a wonderful fifteenth-century **parador**, the *Parador Carlos V* (☎927 560 117, Ⓦ www.parador.es; ❼), in the castle where the emperor stayed during the construction of Yuste. If you've got a tent to pitch, head for the attractive *Camping Jaranda* (☎927 560 454; mid-March to Sept). In the village there is a scattering of bars and a Roman bridge. Buses run through here, en route between Madrid and Plasencia; the stop is outside *Bar Charly* on the main road.

There is good walking around Jarandilla. A track into the hills leads to the village of **El Guijo de Santa Barbara** (4.5km) and then ends, leaving the ascent of the rocky valley beyond to walkers. An hour's trek away is a pool known as *El Trabuquete* and a high meadow with shepherds' huts known as *Pimesaíllo*. On the other side of the valley – a serious trek needing a night's camping and good area maps – is the *Garganta de Infierno* (Stream of Hell) and natural swimming pools known as *Los Pilones*.

△ Storks' nest, Extremadura

The Monasterio de Yuste

There is nothing especially dramatic about the **Monasterio de Yuste** (Mon–Sat 9.30am–12.30pm & 3.30–6.30pm, Sun 9.30–11.30am & 3.30–6.30pm; compulsory guided tour in Spanish €2.50, free Wed am; Ⓦ www.yuste.org/monasterio), the retreat created by Carlos V after renouncing his empire: just a simple beauty and the rather gloomy accoutrements of the emperor's last years. The monastery had existed here for over a century before Carlos's retirement and he had earmarked the site for some years, planning his modest additions – which included a pleasure garden – while still ruling his empire from Flanders. He retired here with a retinue that included an Italian clockmaker, Juanuelo Turriano, whose inventions were his last passion.

The imperial apartments are draped throughout in black, and exhibits include the little sedan chair in which he was brought here, and another designed to support the old man's gouty legs. If you believe the guide, the bed and even the sheets are the very ones in which Carlos died, though since the place was sacked during the Peninsular War and deserted for years after the suppression of the monasteries, this seems unlikely. A door by the emperor's bed opens out over the church and altar so that even in his final illness he never missed a service.

Outside, there's a snack bar and picnic spots, and you'll find a track signposted through the woods to Garganta La Olla (see below).

Cuacos de Yuste

The monastery is 2km into the wooded hills from **CUACOS DE YUSTE**, an attractive village with a couple of squares, including the tiny Plaza de Don Juan de Austria, named after the house (its upper floor reconstructed) where Carlos's illegitimate son Don Juan lived when visiting his father. The surrounding houses, their overhanging upper floors supported on gnarled wooden pillars, are sixteenth-century originals, and from the beams underneath the overhang tobacco is hung out to dry after the harvest. There are several **bars**, a good family-run **hotel**, *La Vera* (Ⓣ 927 172 178, Ⓦ www.verahotel.com; ❸), with a swimming pool, and a shady **campsite**, *Carlos I* (Ⓣ 927 172 092; late-March to mid-Sept).

Jaraíz de la Vera and Garganta La Olla

West towards Plasencia, one last place you might be tempted to stop is **JARAÍZ DE LA VERA**. This has pleasant walking and a couple of reasonable **places to stay**: the friendly *Hostal Dacosta* (Ⓣ 927 460 219, Ⓕ 927 460 900; ❷) and the comfortable *Hotel Jefi* (Ⓣ 927 461 363, Ⓕ 927 170 564; ❸), both of which have good restaurants.

Just outside Jaraíz, a left turning leads for around 5km to **GARGANTA LA OLLA**, a beautiful, ramshackle mountain village set among cherry orchards. There are several things to look out for: the **Casa de Putas** (a brothel for the soldiers of Carlos V's army, now a butcher's but still painted the traditional blue) and the **Casa de la Piedra** (House of Stone), a house whose balcony is secured by a three-pronged wooden support resting on a rock. The latter is hard to find; begin by taking the left-hand street up from the square and then ask. If you want to spend the night here, it's Hobson's choice of the tiny *Hostal Yuste* (Ⓣ & Ⓕ 927 179 604; ❷).

From Garganta, there is a signposted short-cut track to the Monasterio de Yuste (see above).

El Valle de Jerte

Immediately north of La Vera, the main Plasencia–Avila road follows the valley of the **Río Jerte** (from the Greek *Xerte*, meaning "joyful") to the pass of Puerto de Tornavacas, the boundary with Ávila Province. The villages here are more developed than those of La Vera but the valley itself is renowned for its cherry trees, which for a ten-day period in spring cover the slopes with white blossom. If you're anywhere in the area at this time, it's a beautiful spectacle.

If you have transport, you can follow a minor road across the sierra to the north of the valley from **Cabezuela del Valle** to **Hervás**, where there's a fascinating former Jewish quarter. This is the highest road in Extremadura, rising to 1430m.

On the **southern side** of the valley, the main point of interest is the **Puerto del Piornal** pass, just behind the village of the same name. The best approach is via the villages of **Casas del Castañar** and **Cabrero**. Once at the pass you can continue over to Garganta La Olla in La Vera.

Plasencia

Set in the shadow of the Sierra de Gredos, and surrounded on three sides by the Río Jerte, **PLASENCIA** looks more impressive from afar than it actually is. Once you get up into the old city the walls are hard to find – for the most part they're propping up the backs of houses – and the cathedral is barely half-built, but it still merits a visit. Plasencia has some lively bars, delightful cafés and a fine, arcaded **Plaza Mayor**, the scene of a farmers' **market** every Tuesday morning, held here since the twelfth century.

Arrival and information

Plasencia's **turismo** is at c/Santa Clara 2 (Mon–Fri 9am–2pm & 5–9pm, Sat & Sun 9am–2pm & 4–7.30pm; ☎927 423 843, ⓦwww.aytoplasencia.es) just off the Plaza de la Catedral, and there's a **provincial office**, which also provides information on the surrounding area, on c/Rey 8, off the Plaza Mayor (summer Tues–Fri 9am–2pm & 5–7pm, Sat & Sun 9.30am–2pm; winter Tues–Fri 9am–2pm & 4–7pm, Sat & Sun 9.30am–2pm; ☎927 017 840, ⓦwww.turismodeextremadura.com). If you arrive by **bus**, you'll be about fifteen minutes' walk from the centre, along the gently inclining Avenida del Valle to the west; the **train station** is much further out – take a taxi (around €3.50) unless you fancy the hike. There are up to five trains a day to and from Madrid, and many more buses. If you're driving, be warned that navigation in and around town is notoriously difficult.

Accommodation

Good **places to stay** include two reasonably priced options near the Plaza Mayor: the *Hostal La Muralla*, c/Berrozana 6 (☎927 413 874; ❷), and *Hotel Rincón Extremeño*, c/Vidrieras 6 (☎927 411 150, ⓕ927 420 627; ❷), which has twelve en-suite rooms with TV and air conditioning, as well as cheaper rooms without. For more comfort, there's *Hotel Los Álamos* on the Cáceres road facing the tobacco factory (☎ & ⓕ927 411 550; ❷), and *Hotel Alfonso VIII*, c/Alfonso VIII 32 (☎927 410 250, ⓦwww.hotelalfonsoviii.com; ❸), on the main road near the post office. Both of these have good, but pricey, restaurants, as does the new *parador* (☎927 425 870, ⓦwww.parador.es; ❼), housed in a beautiful restored fifteenth-century Gothic convent and centrally located on Plaza de San Vincente Ferrer. There's also a **campsite** with a swimming pool 2.5km out on the Ávila road, *La Chopera* (☎927 416 660; ⓕ927 416 660; March–Sept).

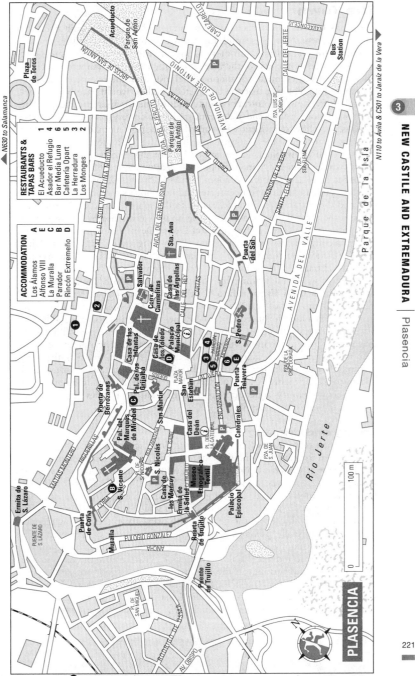

PLASENCIA

ACCOMMODATION

Los Álamos	A
Alfonso VIII	E
La Muralla	C
Parador	B
Rincón Extremeño	D

RESTAURANTS & TAPAS BARS

El Acueducto	1
Asador el Refugio	4
Bar Media Luna	6
Cafetería Opart	5
La Herradura	3
Los Monges	2

N630 to Salamanca

N110 to Ávila & C501 to Jaraíz de la Vera

Train Station, N630 to Cáceres & A

Parque de la Isla

Rio Jerte

100 m

The Town

Plasencia's **Catedral** is in fact two churches – old and new – built back-to-back. Work began on the second, **La Nueva** (winter Mon–Sat 9am–1pm & 4–6pm, Sun 9am–1pm; summer Mon–Sat 9am–1pm & 5–7pm, Sun 9am–1pm; free) at the end of the fifteenth century, but after numerous technical hitches it was eventually abandoned in 1760 when the open end was simply bricked up. The fact that the completed building would have been a particularly lofty Gothic construction only adds to the foreshortened feel of the interior. It does have some redeeming features, however, most notably the Renaissance choir stalls intricately carved by Rodrigo Alemán and described with some justice by the National Tourist Board as "the most Rabelaisian in Christendom". The older, Romanesque part of the cathedral, known as **La Vieja** (winter Mon–Sat 9am–12.30pm & 4–5.30pm, Sun 9–11.30am; summer Mon–Sat 9am–12.30pm & 5–6.30pm, Sun 9–11.30am; €2) was built between the thirteenth and fourteenth centuries and now houses the obligatory **museum**, and the entrance fee includes access to the similarly aged **cloisters**. Free tours of the cathedral (in Spanish) can be booked at the nearby tourist office.

Opposite the cathedral is the **Casa del Deán** (Dean's House), with an interesting balcony like the prow of a ship. Continuing away from the cathedral along c/Blanca you come out at the **Plaza de San Nicolás**, where, according to local tradition, the church was built to prevent two local families from shooting arrows at each other from adjacent houses. On c/Trujillo, near the hospital, the **Museo Etnográfico Textil Provincial** (July & Aug Mon–Sat 9.30am–2.30pm; rest of year Wed–Sat 11am–2pm & 5–8pm, Sun 11am–2pm; free) is worth a look for its colourful costumes and local crafts, excellently displayed in a fourteenth-century hospital. Many of the exhibits are still much in evidence in the more remote villages in the north of Plasencia province.

At the entrance to the city on the main road in from Ávila is the very pleasant **Parque de la Isla** on the banks of the Río Jerte, a good place for a relaxing walk or picnic. A little north of here are the remaining 55 arches of the sixteenth-century aqueduct, designed by Juan de Flandes, that used to bring in the city's water supply.

Eating and drinking

Finding good **restaurants** is not as easy as finding bars in Plasencia, but try the area between the cathedral and the Plaza Mayor. Easily the best budget options are the *platos* at *Cafeteria Opart*, c/Bravo 7, off c/Talavera, and the €6 *menú* at *Restaurante Los Monges*, c/Sor Valentina Mirón 24, just up from Puerta Berronzana. Another good, and rather fancier, place is *El Acueducto*, at c/Sol Valentina Mirón 13, near the monument from which it takes its name.

Bars are much thicker on the ground, with over fifty in the old town alone. This is the land of the *pincho*, a little sample of food provided free with your beer or wine – among which is the local *pitarra* wine. A high tally of promising bars is to be found in c/Patalón (go down c/Talavera from the main square and it's the second turning on the left); *La Herradura* is good for *pinchos* and *pitarra*, and the *Asador el Refugio* for fish, squid and octopus *pinchos*. In the next street down, the atmospheric *Bar Media Luna* is famous for its ham (*jamón Iberico*) – it's expensive, but if you're lucky you'll get a taste as a *pincho*.

Las Hurdes and the Sierra de Gata

Las Hurdes, the abrupt rocky lands north of Plasencia, have always been set apart and are a rich source of mysterious tales. According to legend, the region was unknown to the outside world until the time of Columbus, when two lovers fleeing from the Court of the Duke of Alba chanced upon it. The people who welcomed them were supposedly unaware of the existence of other people or other lands. Shields and other remnants belonging to the Goth Rodrigo and his court of seven centuries earlier were discovered by the couple, giving rise to the saying that the *Hurdanos* are descendants of kings.

Fifty years ago, the inhabitants of the remoter areas were still so unused to outsiders that they hid in their houses if anyone appeared. **Luis Buñuel** filmed an unflatteringly grotesque documentary, *Las Hurdes: Tierra Sin Pan* ("Land Without Bread"), here in 1932, in which it was hard to discern any royal descent in his subjects. Modernity has crept up on the villages these days, though they can still feel very remote, and the soil is so barren that tiny terraces have been constructed on the riverbeds as the only way of getting the stubborn land to produce anything. To explore the region, you really need transport of some kind and certainly a detailed local **map** – regular Spanish road maps tend to be pretty sketchy.

Las Hurdes villages

You could approach Las Hurdes from Plasencia, Salamanca or Ciudad Rodrigo (the region borders the Sierra Peña de Francia – see p.428). From Plasencia the approach is along the EX370 and then the EX204. The village of **PINOFRANQUEADO** marks the start of the region and has a campsite, *hostales* and a natural swimming pool. Fifteen kilometres further along on the road at Vegas de Coria you can turn off to reach **NUÑOMORAL**, a good base for excursions, with an excellent and inexpensive **hostal**, *El Hurdano* (☎927 433 012; ❷); this does big dinners, and there is a bank alongside – not a common sight in these parts. For hire of mules, donkeys and horses at reasonable prices, ask at the *Bar Emiliano* at the top of the town opposite the medical centre. Nuñomoral is also the village best connected to the outside world, with early-morning buses to both Ciudad Rodrigo and Plasencia.

A few kilometres to the north of Nuñomoral, the tiny village of **LA HUETRE** is worth a visit; take a left fork just before the village of Casares de las Hurdes. The typical slate-roofed houses are in better-than-usual condition and have an impressive setting, surrounded by steep rocky hills. Walkers might also head for the remote and disarmingly primitive settlement of **EL GASCO**, at the top of Valle de Malvellido, the next valley to the south, where there is a huge waterfall beneath the Meancera Gorge.

The Sierra de Gata

The **Sierra de Gata** creates a westerly border to Las Hurdes, in a series of wooded hills and odd outcrops of higher ground. It is almost equally isolated – in some of the villages the old people still speak *maniego*, a mix of Castilian Spanish and Portuguese – and its wooded valleys are in parts stunningly beautiful. Unfortunately, much has been damaged in recent summers by forest fires, which, like similar fires in Las Hurdes, are said to have been deliberately started to claim insurance money.

For a trip into the heart of the region, take the EX204 south from Las Hurdes to **Villanueva de la Sierra** and follow the EX205 west. A couple of kilometres past the Río Arrago, a very minor road veers north towards **Robledillo de Gata**, a village of old houses packed tightly together. A shorter, easier detour, south of the EX205, around 5km on, is provided by the hilltop village of **Santibáñez el Alto**, whose oldest houses are built entirely of stone, without windows. At the top of town, look out for a tiny bullring, castle remains and the old cemetery – there's a wonderful view over the Borbollón reservoir from here. Another 3km along the EX205, a turn-off to the north takes you on a winding road up to **GATA**, a pretty village with rooms at the *Pensión Avenida* (☎927 642 271; ❶).

On to the west, keeping to the EX205, is **HOYOS**, the largest village of the region, with some impressive mansions. There's only one *hostal* in the village, *Pensión El Redoble*, c/La Paz 14 (☎927 514 665; ❷), but there's a pleasant **campsite** 3km below the village by a natural swimming pool, created by the damming of the river. Lastly, further along the EX205, another turning leads north to **SAN MARTÍN DE TREVEJO**, one of the nicest of the many lonely villages around; if you're here at mealtime there's good, cheap village fare in great abundance at the *Bar Avenida del 82* (aka *Casa de Julia*). If you need to stay, there are comfortable rooms at the recently refurbished *Hostal San Martín* (☎927 144 201; ❷).

South to Cáceres: Coria and the Convento del Palancar

Heading south from the Sierra de Gata towards Cáceres along the C526, **CORIA** makes an interesting stop. It looks nothing much from the main road, but a visit reveals a cool and quiet old town with lots of stately whitewashed houses, enclosed within third- and fourth-century **Roman walls**. For the most part the walls are built into and around the houses, but a good stretch is visible between the deserted tower of the fifteenth-century castle, built by the Dukes of Alba, and the cathedral.

The **Catedral** (Mon–Sat 10am–1pm & 5–7pm, Sun 10am–1pm; museum €2) has beautifully carved west and north portals in the Plateresque style of Salamanca and, inside, the choir stalls and *retablo* are worth seeing. The building overlooks a striking medieval bridge across fields, the river having changed course three hundred years ago.

Coria has a small **turismo** (☎927 501 351; ⓦwww.coria.org) of uncertain hours inside the *ayuntamiento* on Avenida de Extremadura, as well as plenty of **accommodation**. The *Pensión Casa Piro*, Plaza del Rollo 6 (☎927 500 027; ❶), is cheap and well placed, facing a gate in the walls; *Hotel Los Kekes*, Avda. Sierra de Gata 49 (☎ & ⓕ927 504 080; ❸), has more comforts and a decent restaurant; and *Pensión Bravatas* (☎927 500 401; ❶) is a budget place on the other side of the Avenida Sierra de Gata at no. 32.

Convento del Palancar

A detour off the EX109, south of Coria, will take you to the **Convento del Palancar** (daily except Wed 10am–1pm & 4.30–7pm; voluntary contribution), a monastery founded by San Pedro de Alcántara in the sixteenth century and said to be the smallest in the world at only seventy square metres. It's hard to imagine how a community of ten monks could have lived in these cubbyholes, though San Pedro himself set the example, sleeping upright in his cubicle. A small monastic community today occupies a more modern monastery alongside; ring the bell (daily except Wed 10am–1pm & 4–6.45pm; voluntary contribution) and a monk will come and show you around.

To reach Palancar, turn left off the EX109 just after Torrejoncillo and follow the road to **Pedroso de Acim**; a left turn just before the village leads to the monastery.

The Parque Natural de Monfragüe

South of Plasencia a pair of dams, built in the 1960s, has turned the **Ríos Tajo and Tiétar** into a sequence of vast reservoirs. It's an impressive sight, driving across one of the half-dozen bridges, and it's a tremendous area for wildlife. Almost at random here, you can look up to see storks, vultures and even eagles circling the skies.

The best area for concerted wildlife viewing – and some very enjoyable walks – is the **PARQUE NATURAL DE MONFRAGÜE**, Extremadura's only protected area, which extends over 17,850 hectares to either side of the Plasencia-Trujillo road, with its headquarters at **Villareal de San Carlos**. The landscape is a wonderful diversity of rivers, woods, scrubland and pasture, and attracts an incredible range of flora and fauna. It has been spared the blights of much of the region hereabouts, which, after the completion of the dams, saw the widespread destruction of wildlife habitats and the indiscriminate planting of inflammable eucalyptus by the rapidly expanding paper industry, despite the fire risk involved.

There are over two hundred **species of animals** in the park, including reptiles, deer, wild boar and the ultra-rare Spanish lynx (which you are most unlikely to see). Most important is the **bird population**, especially the black stork – this is the only breeding population in western Europe – and birds of prey such as the black vulture (not averse to eating tortoises), the griffon vulture (partial to carrion intestine), the Egyptian vulture (not above eating human excrement), the rare Spanish imperial eagle (identifiable by its very obvious white shoulder patches), the golden eagle and the eagle owl (the largest owl in Europe).

Ornithologists should visit Monfragüe in May and June, botanists in March and April, and everybody should avoid July to September, when the heat is stifling.

Park practicalities

The easiest **approach to the park** is along the EX208 from Plasencia to Trujillo, which runs past the park headquarters at Villareal de San Carlos. Transport of your own is an advantage unless you are prepared to do some walking. There is just one **bus** along the road, which runs daily between Plasencia and Torrejón El Rubio, 16km south of Villarreal de San Carlos, and on Mondays and Fridays covers the whole distance to Trujillo. It's not a promising hitching route, though at weekends you should get a lift with Spanish birdwatchers. The nearest **train station** is Monfragüe, 18km from Villareal de San Carlos and a stop for slow trains on the Madrid–Cáceres line.

VILLARREAL DE SAN CARLOS has a couple of bars and a restaurant, plus an **information centre** (daily: summer 9am–2.30pm & 4.30–7.30pm; winter 9am–2.30pm & 4–6pm; ☎927 199 134), where you can pick up a colourful leaflet with a map detailing three colour-coded walks from the village. There is also a seasonal shop, selling wildlife T-shirts and the like, and a useful guide to the park (in Spanish) by José Luís Rodríguez.

There's no **accommodation** in Villarreal, and camping is prohibited in the park, but there are some places to stay in **TORREJÓN EL RUBIO**: the *Pensión Monfragüe* (☎927 455 026; ❶) and the nearby *Posada El Arriero* (☎927 455 050; ❶-❷), which is the more friendly option. More expensive, but good value for money, is the *Hotel Carvajal*, Plaza de Pizarro 54 (☎927 455 254, ⓦwww.bme.es/ctrmonfrague; ❷). The nearest **campsite** is *Camping Monfragüe* (☎927 459 233), a well-equipped, year-round site with a swimming pool and restaurant, 12km north of Villarreal on the Plasencia road. It is near the turning to the Monfragüe train station and it also has **bikes for rent** to get to Monfragüe.

Into the park

Walking in Monfragüe, it is best to stick to the colour-coded paths leading from Villarreal de San Carlos. Each of them is well paint-blobbed and leads to rewarding birdwatching locations. Elsewhere, it is not easy to tell where you are permitted to wander, and all too easy to find yourself out of the park area in a private hunting reserve.

The **Green Route**, to the Cerro Gimio, is especially good, a two and a half-hour stroll looping through woods and across streams, in a landscape unimaginable from Villarreal, to a dramatic cliff-top viewing station. The longer **Red Route** heads south of Villarreal, over a bridge across the Río Tajo, and past a fountain known as the *Fuente del Francés* after a young Frenchman who died there trying to save an eagle. Two kilometres further is a great crag known as the *Peñafalcón*, which houses a large colony of griffon vultures, and the Castillo de Monfragüe, a castle ruin high up on a rock, with a chapel next to it; there is an observation post nearby. All these places are accessible from the EX208 and if you're coming in on the bus, you could ask to get off here. There are also two routes of 8km and 12km respectively that have been designed for **cars** and include a number of viewing points.

On the south side of the park, towards Trujillo, you pass through the **dehesas**, strange Africa-like plains which are among the oldest woodlands in Europe. The economy of the *dehesas* is based on grazing, and the casualties among the domestic animals provide the vultures of Monfragüe with their daily bread. The information centre in Villarreal also provides details of routes that can be done on horseback or bicycle.

Trujillo

TRUJILLO is the most attractive town in Extremadura: a classic *conquistador* stage set of escutcheoned mansions, stork-topped towers and castle walls. Much of it looks virtually untouched since the sixteenth century, and is redolent above all of the exploits of the conquerors of the Americas; Francisco Pizarro, the conqueror of Peru, was born here, as were many of the tiny band who with such extraordinary cruelty aided him in defeating the Incas.

Arrival and information

Trujillo could be visited easily enough as a day-trip from Cáceres, but if you can book, it is worth staying the night. There is no train station, but the town is well served by **buses**, with up to eight a day to and from Madrid. Coming in by bus, you'll arrive in the lower town, just five minutes' walk from the Plaza Mayor, where there is a **turismo** (Mon–Sat 9.30am–2pm & 4.30–7pm, Sun 10am–2pm & 4.30–7pm; ☎927 322 677, ⓦwww.ayto-trujillo.com) which gives discount tickets for combined visits to some of the main sites and pro-

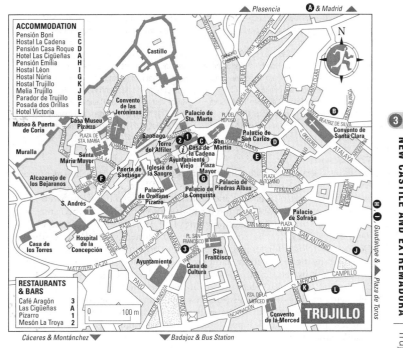

vides information on guided tours (11.30am & 6pm; €6.50). If you're driving, follow the signs to the Plaza Mayor, and with luck you can park beyond the square and further along c/García de Paredes.

Accommodation

Places to stay are in high demand – so book ahead if you can. The turismo can provide accommodation lists. The nicest rooms are around the Plaza Mayor, or, if money is no object, at the *parador*.

Budget options

Pensión Boni c/Domingo de Ramos 11 ☏ 927 321 604. Cheap and meticulously run, just off the northeast corner of the Plaza Mayor. Good-value triples available at €35. **❶**

Hostal La Cadena Plaza Mayor 8 ☏ 927 321 463. Attractive *hostal*, with rooms overlooking all the action and a decent restaurant. **❷**

Pensión Casa Roque c/Domingo de Ramos 30 ☏ 927 322 313. Excellent and well-located *pensión*. The owner runs the Margarita gift shop on the Plaza Mayor. **❶**

Pensión Emilia c/General Mola 28 ☏ 927 320 083. Clean and comfortable *pensión* with an economical restaurant and bar downstairs. **❶**

Hostal Núria Plaza Mayor 27 ☏ 927 320 907. Comfortable *hostal* with good views over the Plaza Mayor. **❷**

Hostal Trujillo c/Francisco Pizarro 4 ☏ 927 322 274, ⓦ www.hostaltrujillo.com. A pleasant *pensión* situated in a fifteenth-century building between the Plaza Mayor and the bus station. Eighteen air-conditioned rooms and a good restaurant. **❷**

Moderate and expensive options

Hotel Las Cigüeñas Avda. Madrid ☏ 927 321 250, ⓦ www.hotelasciguenas.com. Pleasant, modern accommodation down on the main road, but a bit inconvenient for the major sights. **❹**

Hostal León General Mola 23–25 ☎927 321 792, ℱ927 322 981. Decent *pensión* with the advantage of secure parking. ❸

Melia Trujillo Plaza del Campillo 1 ☎927 458 900, ⓦwww.solmelia.com. Swish hotel situated in the recently converted *convento* de San Antonio. 72 double rooms and a swimming pool. ❻

Parador de Trujillo Plaza Santa Beatriz de Silva ☎927 321 350, ⓦwww.parador.es. Upmarket accommodation in a sixteenth-century former *convento* north of the Plaza Mayor. ❻

Posada dos Orillas c/Cambrones 6 ☎927 659 079, ⓦwww.dosorillas.com. Seven individually designed and decorated rooms in this converted inn in the heart of the old quarter. It has a delightful patio area where you can take breakfast and a pricey restaurant serving up some imaginative, well-presented salads and local specialities. ❺

Hotel Victoria Plaza de Campillo 22 ☎927 321 819, ℱ927 323 084. Modern and friendly hotel, with a pool, good restaurant and comfortable en-suite rooms with TV. ❹

The Town

Trujillo is a very small place, still little larger than its extent in *conquistador* times. At the centre of a dense web of streets is the **Plaza Mayor**, a grand square overlooked by a trio of palaces and churches, and ringed by a half-dozen cafés and restaurants, around which life for most visitors revolves. In the centre is a bronze statue of Pizarro – oddly, the gift of an American sculptor, one Carlos Rumsey, in 1929. In the square's southwest corner is the **Palacio de la Conquista** (closed for long-term restoration), the grandest of Trujillo's mansions with its roof adorned by statues representing the twelve months. Just one of many built by the Pizarro clan, it was originally inhabited by Pizarro's half-brother and son-in-law Hernando, who returned from the conquests to live here with his half-Inca bride (Pizarro's daughter). Diagonally opposite, and with a skyline of storks, is the bulky church of **San Martín** (Mon–Sat 9.30am–2pm & 4.30–7.30pm, Sun 9.30am–12.30pm; €1.25). Its tombs include, among others, that of the family of Francisco de Orellana, the first explorer of the Amazon. Adjacent is the **Palacio de los Duques de San Carlos** (Mon–Sat 9.30am–1pm & 4.30–6.30pm, Sun 10am–12.30pm; €1.20), home to a group of nuns who moved out of their dilapidated convent up the hill and restored this palace in return for the lodgings. The chimneys on the roof boast aggressively of cultures conquered by Catholicism in the New World – they are shaped like the pyramids of Aztecs, Incas and others subjected to Spanish rule.

From the plaza, c/Ballesteros leads up to the walled upper town, past the domed **Torre del Alfiler** with its coats of arms and storks' nests, and through the fifteenth-century gateway known as the Arco de Santiago. Built up against the walls is the **Iglesia de Santiago** (daily: summer 10am–2pm & 5–8.30pm; winter 10am–2pm & 4–7pm; €1.20) which dates from the thirteenth century and was sometimes used as a venue for council meetings in the Middle Ages, while opposite it is the Palacio de los Chaves which was where the *Reyes Católicos*, Fernando and Isabel, stayed when they were in town. A short way up the hill is **Santa María Mayor** (daily 10am–2pm & 4.30–7pm, summer closes 8pm; €1.25), the most interesting and important of the town's many churches. The building is basically Gothic but contains a beautiful raised Renaissance *coro* noted for the technical mastery of its almost flat vaults. There is a fine Hispano-Flemish reredos by Fernando Gallego, and tombs including those of the Pizarros – Francisco was baptized here – and Diego García de Paredes, a man known as the "Sansón Extremeño" (Extremaduran Samson). Among other exploits, this giant of a man, armed only with his gargantuan sword, is said to have defended a bridge against an entire French army and to have picked up the font, now underneath the *coro*, to carry holy water to his mother. You are now allowed to clamber up the **tower** which provides magnificent views of the town, the parched plains over towards Cáceres and the Sierra de Gredos.

Further up the hill, in the Pizarros' former residence, the **Casa Museo Pizarro** (daily 10am–2pm & 4–7pm, summer closes 8.30pm; €1.25) is a small, dull and overpriced affair, with little beyond period furniture and a few panels on the conquest of Peru. More detailed exhibits on the conquest are to be found in the nearby **Museo de la Coria** (Sat, Sun & public holidays 11.30am–2pm; free), which is housed in an old Franciscan convent.

The **castle** (daily 10am–2pm & 5–7pm, summer closes 8.30pm; €1.25) is now virtually in open countryside; for the last hundred metres of the climb you see nothing but the occasional broken-down remnant of a wall clambered over by sheep and dogs. The **fortress** itself, Moorish in origin but much reinforced by later defenders, has recently been restored, and its main attraction is the panoramic view of the town and its environs from the battlements. Looking out over the barren heath which rings Trujillo, the extent to which the old quarter has fallen into disrepair is abundantly evident, as is the castle's superb defensive position.

Of the many other town mansions, or *solares*, the most interesting is the **Palacio de Orellana-Pizarro**, just west of the main square (Mon–Sat 10am–1pm & 4–6pm, Sat & Sun 11am–2pm & 4.30–7pm; free). Go in through the superb Renaissance arched doorway to admire the courtyard, an elegant patio decorated with the alternating coats of arms of the Pizarros – two bears with a pine tree – and the Orellanas.

Eating, drinking and nightlife

There are plenty of **bar-restaurants** right in the Plaza Mayor, the best known of which is probably *Mesón La Troya*, which offers a huge *menú* for €15 – you'll find a giant salad and omelette on your plate before they've even asked what you want to order – although it is a case of quantity over quality. The *Pizarro*, next door, has much better food, costing €12 for the *menú* or around €20 a head à la carte. There are excellent *raciones* and tapas at the *Bar Las Cigüeñas* (in the hotel of the same name) and – more cheaply – in the old town at *Café Aragón*, c/Plazuela de Aragón 5. Otherwise, for budget eating, all the *pensiones* along c/General Mola have reasonably priced *menús* on offer – the cheapest being the *Emilia*. If you're driving, you could try out *La Majada*, 4km south of town on the road to Mérida, for good fish, local sausages and partridge. At the weekend Trujillo's **nightlife** revolves around c/Ballesteros, north of Plaza Mayor, where you'll find most of its youth at the new *Bar Sotana*.

Guadalupe

The small town of **GUADALUPE**, perched up in the sierra to the west of Trujillo, is dominated in every way by the great **Monasterio de Nuestra Señora de Guadalupe**, which for five centuries has brought fame and pilgrims to the area. It was established in 1340, on the spot where an ancient image of the Virgin, said to have been carved by St Luke, was discovered by a shepherd fifty or so years earlier. The delay was simply a question of waiting for the Reconquest to arrive in this remote sierra, with its lush countryside of forests and streams.

Arrival and information

Guadalupe's generally helpful **turismo** is in the arcaded Plaza Mayor (summer Tues–Fri 10am–2.30pm & 5–7pm, Sat & Sun 10am–2.30pm; winter Tues–Fri

10am–2.30pm & 4–6pm, Sat & Sun 10am–2.30pm; ☎927 154 128, ⓦwww.puebladeguadalupe.net). **Banks** and a **post office** are to be found close by this central square, near the steps of the monastery church. **Buses** leave from either side of Avenida de Barcelona uphill from the *ayuntamiento*, 200m from the Plaza Mayor: Mirat operates services to Trujillo and Cáceres, Doalde runs buses to Madrid (though you might have to change at Talavera de Reina).

Accommodation

There are plenty of **places to stay** in Guadalupe and the only times you're likely to have difficulty finding a room are during Easter Week or around September 8, the Virgin's festival day. The **campsite**, *Las Villuercas* (☎927 367 139; open all year), is 2km out of town towards Trujillo, close to the main road.

Hospedaría del Real Monasterio Plaza Juan Carlos s/n ☎927 367, ⓦ www.monasterio guadalupe.com. Housed in a wing of the monastery and popular with Spanish pilgrims, it's better value than the *parador*, very atmospheric and serves excellent food, too. ❸
Hostal Alfonso XI c/Alfonso Onceno 21 ☎ & Ⓕ927 154 184. Comfortable, nicely furnished *hostal* with a/c in most rooms. ❸
Hostal Isabel Plaza Santa María 13 ☎927 367 126. Modern *hostal* offering rooms with bath, and a bar downstairs. They have recently opened another branch with the same name next to the *parador* with antique furnished rooms and a/c for the same price. ❷

Hostal Lujuan c/Gregorio López 19 ☎& Ⓕ927 367 170. Decent, mid-priced rooms, reasonably central and with a reliable restaurant (the *menú* costs around €7.50). ❷–❸
Parador de Guadalupe c/Marqués de la Romana 12 ☎927 367 075, Ⓔguadalupe@parador.es. Beautiful *parador*, housed in a fifteenth-century hospital, with a swimming pool and immaculate patio gardens. ❻
Hostal Taruta c/Alfonso Onceno 16 ☎927 367 151. This *hostal* can arrange rooms in private houses if its own are fully booked, and offers discounts for full board, with meals in a *comedor* downstairs, which also serves an inexpensive range of *platos*. ❷

The Town

In the fifteenth and sixteenth centuries, Guadalupe was among the most important pilgrimage centres in Spain: Columbus named the Caribbean island in honour of the Virgin here, and a local version was adopted as the patron saint of Mexico. Much of the monastic wealth, in fact, came from returning *conquistadores*, whose successive endowments led to a fascinating mix of styles. The **monastery** was abandoned in the nineteenth-century dissolution, but early this century was reoccupied by Franciscans, who continue to maintain it.

The town itself is a fitting complement to the monastery and countryside: a net of narrow cobbled streets and overhanging houses constructed around the Plaza Mayor, the whole overshadowed by the monastery's bluff ramparts. There's a timeless feel, only slightly diminished by modern development on the outskirts, and a brisk trade in plastic copies of religious treasures.

The church and monastery

The **monastery church** (daily 9am–8.30pm; free) opens onto the Plaza Mayor (aka Plaza de Santa María). Its gloomy Gothic interior is, like the rest of the monastery, packed with treasures from generations of wealthy patrons. Note especially the incredibly ornate *rejas* (grilles).

The entrance to the **monastery** proper (daily 9.30am–1pm & 3.30–6.30pm; ⓦwww.monasterioguadalupe.com; €3) is to the left of the church. The (compulsory) guided tour begins with a Mudéjar **cloister** – two brick storeys of horseshoe arches with a strange pavilion or tabernacle in the middle – and moves on to the **museum**, with an apparently endless collection of rich vestments, early illuminated manuscripts and religious paraphernalia, along with some fine art works including a triptych by Isenbrandt and a small Goya. The **Sacristía**, beyond, is the finest room in the monastery. Unaltered since it was built in the seventeenth century, it contains eight paintings by Zurbarán, which, uniquely, can be seen in their original context – the frames match the window frames and the pictures themselves are a planned part of the decoration of the room.

Climbing higher into the heart of the monastery, you pass through various rooms filled with jewels and relics before the final ascent to the Holy of Holies. From a tiny room high above the main altar you can look down over the church while a panel is spun away to reveal the climax of the tour – the bejewelled and richly dressed **image of the Virgin**. The Virgin is one of the few black icons ever made – originally carved out of dark cedarwood, its colour has further deepened over the centuries under innumerable coats of varnish. The story goes that the image was originally carved by Saint Luke, made its way to Spain and was then hidden during the Arab occupation for over 500 years. It was eventually rediscovered by a local cowherd on the banks of the Río Guadalupe at the beginning of the thirteenth century.

On the way out, drop in at the **Hospedaría del Real Monasterio**, around to the right. The bar, in its Gothic cloister, with lovely gardens outside, is one of the world's more unusual places to enjoy a *Cuba libre*.

Eating and drinking

You can **eat** at most *hostales* and *pensiones*, with just about everywhere – including the restaurants on Plaza Mayor – serving €8 *menús*. The one at *Hostal Lujuan* is particularly good value, while the *Hospedaria del Real Monasterio* has a courtyard setting. Perhaps the best restaurant in town is the *Mesón del Cordero* at c/Alfonso Onceno 27, a more expensive place with home cooking and grand views from the dining room. What there is of Guadalupe's **nightlife** takes place at the bottom of c/Alfonso Onceno, where *Casamalia*, at no. 14, is a young and lively bar.

The Sierra de Guadalupe: routes to Trujillo

A truly superb view of Guadalupe set in its sierra can also be enjoyed from the road (EX118) north to Navalmoral. Five kilometres out of town, the **Ermita del Humilladero** marks the spot where pilgrims to the shrine traditionally caught their first glimpse of the monastery.

The surrounding **Sierra de Guadalupe** is a wild and beautiful region, with steep, rocky crags abutting the valley sides. If you have your own transport, a good route is to strike northwest of the EX102 at Cañamero, up to the village of **Cabañas del Castillo**, a handful of houses, most of them empty as only twelve inhabitants remain, nestling against a massive crag and ruined castle. Beyond here, you can reach the main **Navalmoral–Trujillo road** close to the **Puerto de Miravete**, a fabulous viewpoint, with vistas of Trujillo in the far distance. Another great drivers' route, again leaving the EX102 at Cañamero, is to follow the narrow road **through Berzocana** to Trujillo.

Cáceres

CÁCERES is in many ways remarkably like Trujillo. It features an almost perfectly preserved walled town, the Ciudad Monumental, packed with *solares* built on the proceeds of American exploration, while even more than in Trujillo every available tower and spire is crowned by a clutch of storks' nests. As a provincial capital, however, Cáceres is a much larger and livelier place, especially in term time, when the students of the University of Extremadura are in residence. With its Roman, Moorish and *conquistador* sights, and a lively bar and restaurant scene, it is an absorbing and highly enjoyable city. It also provides a dramatic backdrop for an annual **WOMAD** festival, held over the second weekend in May and attracting up to 70,000 spectators.

The walled **old town** stands at the heart of Cáceres, with a picturesque **Plaza Mayor** just outside its walls. Almost everything of interest is contained within – or a short walk from – this area, and you would do well to base yourself as close to it as possible.

Arrival and information

If you arrive by **train or bus**, you'll find yourself around 3km out from the old town, at the far end of the Avenida de Alemania. It's not an enjoyable walk, so take bus #1, which runs down the *avenida* to Plaza de San Juan, a square adjoining the Plaza Mayor; an irregular shuttle bus from the train station (free if you show a rail ticket) also runs into town, to the Plaza de América, a major traffic junction west of the old town. If you're driving, be warned that increasing pedestrianization is making access to some streets impossible by car; your best bet is to try the car park on Avenida de España, on the main road in from Madrid, or park well outside the old town.

Cáceres has a helpful regional **turismo** (Mon–Fri 9am–2pm & 5–7pm, winter closes 6.30pm, Sat 9.45am–2pm; ☎927 246 347, ⒲www.turismo extremadura.com) in the Plaza Mayor, with a smaller municipal office (daily 10am–1pm & 4–6pm) nearby that organizes hourly guided tours of the main sites (1hr 30min; €5). The main **post office** is at c/Miguel Primo Rivera 2, near the Plaza de América, and **Internet access** is available at *Mir@zur* on Plaza Mayor and at *Ciber Cáceres* at c/Leon Leal 1.

Accommodation

There is usually plenty of **accommodation** to go round (much of it overpriced), but it's a good idea to book ahead if you're visiting during Easter. It is also worth noting that the places right on the Plaza Mayor can get rather noisy at night.

Budget options

Pensión Carretero Plaza Mayor 22–23 ☎927 247 882. Best value in town – very basic, large rooms, spotless bathrooms and a TV lounge – though some rooms can be noisy at the weekend. ❶

Pensión Castilla c/Ríos Verdes 3 ☎927 244 404. Just off the Plaza Mayor, with small, clean rooms, and separate bath. ❷

Pensión Márquez c/Gabriel y Galán 2 ☎927 244 960. Just off the Plaza Mayor, the cheapest place in town and fairly decent; it's popular, so check in early. ❶

Hostal Plaza de Italia c/Constancia 12 ☎927 627 294. Very friendly and clean option, a 5min walk from the Plaza Mayor. ❷–❸

Moderate and expensive options

Hotel Alfonso IX c/Moret 20 ☎927 246 400, ⒲www.hotelalfonsoix.com. Nicely located on a pedestrianized street off c/Pintores, this slightly aged hotel offers en-suite rooms with a/c and satellite TV. ❹

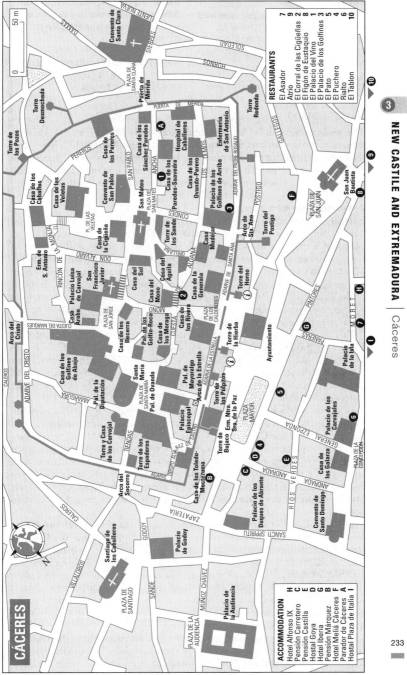

CÁCERES

50 m

0

ACCOMMODATION

Hotel Alfonso IX	H
Pensión Carretero	C
Pensión Castilla	E
Hostal Goya	D
Hotel Iberia	G
Pensión Márquez	B
Hotel Meliá Cáceres	F
Parador de Cáceres	A
Hostal Plaza de Italia	I

RESTAURANTS

El Asador	7
Atrio	9
El Corral de las Cigüeñas	2
El Figón de Eustaquio	8
El Palacio del Vino	1
El Palacio de los Golfines	3
El Pato	5
El Puchero	4
Rialto	6
El Tablón	10

Hostal Goya Plaza Mayor 11 ☎927 249 950, ⓕ927 213 758. Upmarket (and good-value) *hostal* on the Plaza Mayor, with en-suite rooms. ❸
Hotel Iberia c/Pintores 2 ☎927 247 634, ⓕ927 248 200. Tastefully restored building in a corner of the Plaza Mayor. ❹
Hotel Meliá Cáceres Plaza de San Juan 11 ☎927 215 800, ⓦwww.solmelia.es. Part of the growing Meliá chain, this hotel is in a sixteenth-century palace, just outside the walls of the old town, and is in many ways a nicer place than the *parador*. ❽
Parador de Cáceres c/Ancha 6 ☎927 211 759, ⓦwww.parador.es. The *parador* occupies a *conquistador* mansion in the Ciudad Monumental – the only hotel within the walls. ❼

The Town

The **walls** of the Ciudad Monumental are basically Moorish in construction, though parts date back to the Romans – notably the **Arco del Cristo** – and they have been added to, refortified and built against pretty much throughout the centuries. The most intact section, with several original adobe Moorish towers, runs in a clockwise direction, facing the walls from the Plaza Mayor.

Around the old town

Entering the old town – the **Parte Vieja**, as it's also known – from the Plaza Mayor, you pass through the low **Arco de la Estrella**, an entrance built by Manuel Churriguera in the eighteenth century. To your left, at the corner of the walls, is one of the most imposing *conquistador solares*, the **Casa de Toledo-Moctezuma** with its domed tower. It was to this house that a follower of Cortés brought back one of the New World's more exotic prizes, a daughter of the Aztec emperor, as his bride. The building has recently been restored – it was in imminent danger of collapse – to house the provincial historical archives, and it also stages occasional exhibitions.

Walking straight ahead through the Arco de la Estrella brings you into the **Plaza de Santa María**, flanked by another major *solar*, the Casa de los Golfines de Abajo, the Palacio Episcopal, and the Gothic church of Santa María – Cáceres's finest. Inside, you can illuminate a fine sixteenth-century carved wooden *retablo*, while in the surrounding gloom are the tombs of many of the town's great families.

A couple of blocks west, at the town's highest point, is the Plaza de San Mateo, flanked by the church of **San Mateo**, another Gothic structure with fine chapels, and the **Casa de la Cigüeña** (House of the Stork), whose narrow tower was the only one allowed to preserve its original battlements when the rest were shorn by royal decree. It is now a military installation and, although the tower features on half the postcards in Cáceres, soldiers discourage the taking of further snapshots. On the other side of the square, notice the **family crests** on the **Casa del Sol**, and indeed many of the other buildings within the walls.

Just behind, in the Plaza de las Veletas, is the **Casa de las Veletas**, which houses the archeology and ethnology sections of the **Museo de Cáceres** (mid-April to end Sept Tues–Sat 9am–2.30pm & 5–8.15pm, Sun 10.15am–2.30pm; Oct to mid-April Tues–Sat 9am–2.30pm & 4–7.15pm, Sun 10.15–2.30pm; €1.20, EU citizens free). The collections here take second place to the building itself. Typical of the local style, its beautifully proportioned rooms are arrayed around a small patio and preserve the *aljibe* (cistern) of the original Moorish Alcázar with its horseshoe arches. It also has an extraordinary balustrade, created from Talavera ceramic jugs.

From here, a footbridge leads to the museum's art collection in the **Casa de los Caballos** (House of Horses), open mornings only. The modern art and sculpture includes works by Miró, Picasso and Eduardo Arroyo, while the highlight of the medieval section is El Greco's *Jesús Salvador*. There is also a temporary exhibition space for up-and-coming contemporary artists.

Something could be said about almost every other building but look out, too, for the **Casa de los Golfines de Arriba** on c/Adarve Padre Rosalío, the alleyway that runs alongside the walls parallel to the Plaza Mayor. It was in this latter *conquistador* mansion that Franco had himself proclaimed *Generalísimo* and head of state in October 1936. Near the Casa del Sol is another *solar*, the **Casa del Mono** (House of the Monkey), which is now a public library; the facade is adorned with grotesque gargoyles and a stone monkey is chained to the staircase in the courtyard.

You might take time, too, for a visit to the **Casa Árabe** (daily 10.30am–1.30pm & 4.30–7.30pm; €1.50), off Plaza San Jorge at Cuesta del Marqués 4. The owner of this Moorish house has had the bright idea of decorating it more or less as it would have been when occupied by its original owner. The Alhambra it's not, but it at least provides a context for all the horseshoe arches and curving brick ceilings and it still possesses the original cistern supplied by water from the roof.

Outside the walls

Outside the walls, it's worth wandering up to the sixteenth-century church of **Santiago de los Caballeros**, which fronts the plaza of the same name, opposite a more or less contemporary mansion, **Palacio de Godoy**, with its corner balcony. The church, open only for Masses, has a fine *retablo* by Alonso Berruguete.

If you want to enjoy a good view of the old town, exit the walls through the Arco del Cristo down to the main road and turn right onto c/Fuente Concejo, following the signs for about five minutes or so, and you will have the whole town set out below you.

Eating, drinking and nightlife

There is a good range of **bars, restaurants and bodegas** in and around the Plaza Mayor, while the old town offers a bit more style at not too inflated a price.

Cáceres has the best **nightlife** in the region – especially during term time – with the night starting off in the bars along c/Pizarro, south of Plaza de San Juan, moving on to c/Dr Fleming and the discos in the nearby Plaza de Albatros. There are also several late-night bars around Plaza Mayor, and live music can be heard in many places along the nearby c/General Ezpondaz.

Restaurants

El Asador c/Moret 34. Reasonably priced restaurant, off c/Pintores, serving local dishes and fronted by a popular tapas bar.

Atrio Avda. de España 30, block B. High-class restaurant, southwest of Plaza Mayor, with an extensive menu, but it'll cost you. Allow at least €35 per head. Closed Sun evening.

El Corral de las Cigüeñas Cuesta de Aldana 6. A beautiful spot to enjoy a meal in the old town, with tables in a large, palm-shaded courtyard; reasonably priced *platos combinados*.

El Figón de Eustaquio Plaza de San Juan 12. This features an extensive list of regional dishes, cooked with care and flair. Allow €25–30 a head,

or try the cheaper lunchtime *menú* at €17.50.

El Palacio del Vino c/Ancha 4. Pleasant, traditional *mesón* near the *parador* in the old town; allow around €18 a head.

El Palacio de los Golfines c/Adarve Padre Rosalío 2. Stylishly presented food in a magnificent setting in an old palace just inside the city walls. An extensive wine list, too. Expect to pay around €30–35. Closed Sun evening.

El Pato Plaza Mayor 24. Popular restaurant fronting the square – slightly more expensive than its neighbours but probably worth the extra.

El Puchero Plaza Mayor 10. The cheapest restaurant on the plaza, with an ever-popular *terraza*, but as you would expect the food is not outstanding.

Rialto Plaza de la Concepción 29. No frills but good-value restaurant popular with young locals.

El Tablon c/Donoso Cortés 13–15. A very good quality €9 *menú* at this little place close to the Plaza de San Juan.

Bars

Bar del Jamón Plaza de San Juan 10. Small place to enjoy *pitarra* and a *pincho*.

El Extremeño Plaza del Duque 10, off the Plaza Mayor. A student favourite, with Guinness on tap and beer sold by the metre.

Lancelot Rincon de la Monja 2. Opposite the Casa Arabé, a relaxed English-run bar.

La Machacona c/Andrada 8. Down an alley under the arcades off the Plaza Mayor, this is a good place to hear Latin sounds and occasional live music.

El Torre de Babel c/Pizarro 8. Laid-back café with occasional live music, plus clothes and jewellery stalls downstairs.

Northwest of Cáceres: Arroyo and Alcántara

Northwest of Cáceres is the vast **Embalse de Alcántara**, one of a series of reservoirs harnessing the power of the Río Tajo in the last few kilometres before it enters Portugal. The scheme swallowed up large tracts of land and you can see the old road and railway to Plasencia disappearing into the depths of the reservoir (their replacements cross the many inlets on double-decker bridges), along with the tower of a castle.

The EX207 loops away to the south of the reservoir, through **Arroyo de la Luz** and **Brozas**, each with fine churches, before reaching **Alcántara**, with its superb Roman bridge across the Tajo. The Portuguese border – and the road to Costelo Branco and Coimbra – is just a dozen kilometres beyond.

Arroyo de la Luz and Brozas

ARROYO DE LA LUZ (Stream of Light), despite its romantic name, is one of the least memorable Extremaduran towns. However, it does have one sight of note: the gaunt, late-Gothic church of **La Asunción**, which houses a huge *retablo* of twenty panels by Luís Morales. This Extremaduran artist (1509–86) is known to the Spanish as "El Divino", though his heart-on-sleeve style has never found much favour with art historians. His work is certainly a lot more impressive seen, *in situ*, than in a museum. To view it, ask for the keys from the local police at the side door of the *ayuntamiento*, which faces the south side of the church, and bring some coins for the meter.

Arroyo has a single **hostal**, inevitably called the *Divino Morales* (☎ 927 270 257; ❷), at the edge of town where the buses stop, and a couple of basic restaurants. A more pleasant place to eat, drink, or stay, however, is the old *Hostal La Posada* (☎ 927 395 019; ❸) at **BROZAS**, 35km on towards Alcántara. Brozas itself is an old *conquistador* town, centred on a seventeenth-century castle. Its Gothic church of Santa María La Mayor has a spectacular Baroque *retablo*. More impressive still are the fantastic views over the plain and the low hills to the south.

Alcántara

The name **ALCÁNTARA** comes from the Arabic for "bridge" – in this case a beautiful six-arched **Puente Romano** spanning a gorge of the Río Tajo. Completed in 105 AD, and held together without mortar, it was reputed to be the loftiest bridge ever built in the Roman empire, although it's far from certain which bits, if any, remain genuinely Roman.

The bridge is quite a distance from the town itself, which is built high above the river; if you're on foot, don't follow the signs via the road – instead, head to the far side of the town and down the steep cobbled path.

Further Roman remains include a **triumphal arch** dedicated to Trajan and a tiny **classical temple**. The dominating landmark, however, is the recently restored **Convento San Benito**, erstwhile headquarters of the Knights of Alcántara, one of the great orders of the Reconquest. For all its enormous bulk, the convent and its church are only a fragment; the nave of the church was never built. Outside, the main feature is the double-arcaded Renaissance gallery at the back; it serves as the backdrop for a season of classical plays which moves here from Mérida in August. Entry to the convent (guided tours Tues–Sat 10.15am, 11.15am, 12.15pm, 1.15pm, 5pm, 6pm & 7pm; Sun 10.15am, 11.15am, 12.15pm & 1.15pm; free) is through the adjacent *Fundación de San Benito*, who have been making attempts to restore the cloister and the Plateresque east end with its elaborate wall tombs.

Alcántara also contains the scanty remains of a **castle**, numerous **mansions** and street after street of humbler whitewashed houses. The place is marvellous for scenic walks, whether in the town, along the banks of the Tajo, or – best of all – in the hills on the opposite bank.

Practicalities

The **turismo**, Avda. de Mérida 21 (May–Sept Tues–Fri 10am–2pm & 5–7pm, Sat & Sun 10.30am–12.30pm; Oct–April Tues–Fri 10am–2pm & 4.30–6.30pm, Sat & Sun 10.30am–12.30pm; ☎927 390 863, ⓔofici turismo@inicia.es), is very helpful and can provide a town map.

The town has one **hostal**, the *Kantara Al Saif*, just out of town on the Avenida de Mérida (☎927 390 246, ⓔal-saif@teleline.es; ❷), with an adjoining restaurant and café. There is also a very well kept *Casa Rural*, the *Casa La Cañada* (☎927 390 298; ❸), and a campsite, *the Puente de Alcántara* (☎927 390 934; open all year), which can help organize birdwatching trips, hikes and excursions on bikes and horseback. **Buses**, which run twice a day to and from Cáceres, stop at a little square ringed by cafés at the entrance to the historic part of the town. Here you can **eat** cheaply at *Restaurante El Gorrón* and at *Restaurante Antonio*, near the turismo building.

Jamón serrano: a gastronomic note

Extremadura, to many Spaniards, means ham. Together with the Sierra Morena in Andalucía, the Extremaduran sierra is the only place in the country which supports the pure-bred Iberian pig, source of the best *jamón serrano*. For its ham to be as highly flavoured as possible, the pig, a subspecies of the European wild boar exclusive to the Iberian peninsula, is allowed to roam wild and eat acorns for several months of the year. The undisputed kings of hams in this area, praised at length by Richard Ford in his *Handbook for Travellers*, are those that come from Montánchez, in the south of the region. The village is midway between Cáceres and Mérida, so if you're in the area try some in a bar, washed down with local red wine – but be warned that the authentic product is extremely expensive, a few thinly cut slices often costing as much as an entire meal. The local wine *pitarra* is an ideal accompaniment.

Mérida

The former capital of the Roman province of Lusitania, **MÉRIDA** (the name is a corruption of *Augusta Emerita*) contains more **Roman remains** than any other city in Spain. Even for the most casually interested, the extent and variety of the remains here are compelling, with everything from engineering works to domestic villas, by way of cemeteries and places of worship, entertainment and culture. With a little imagination, and a trip to the wonderful modern museum, the Roman city is not difficult to evoke – which is just as well, for the modern city, in which the sites are scattered, is no great shakes.

Each July and August, the Roman theatre in Mérida hosts a **theatre festival** (ⓦwww.festivaldemerida.com), including performances of classical Greek plays and Shakespeare's Roman tragedies.

Arrival and information

Mérida sees a lot of visitors and has plenty of facilities to cater for them. If you want maps, guidebooks or information on the region, look in at the helpful **turismo** (summer Mon–Fri 9am–1.45pm & 5–7.15pm, Sat & Sun 9.30am–2pm; winter Mon–Fri 9am–1.45pm & 4–6.30pm, Sat & Sun 9am–1.45pm; ☎924 315 353, ⓦwww.turismoextremadura.com), just outside the gates to the theatre and amphitheatre site. There is another office run by the local *ayuntamiento* which has longer opening hours (daily 9.30am–2pm & 5–9pm; ⓦwww.merida.es) just off Plaza Puerts de la Villa.

The **train station** is pretty central, with the theatre site and Plaza de España no more than ten minutes' walk away. The **bus station** is on the other side of the river and is a grittier twenty minutes' walk from the town centre, along Avenida de Libertad, which extends from the new single-arch bridge. For inexpensive time online try *Ware Nostrum*, c/Baños 24, a friendly **Internet café** (daily 4pm–1am; €1.80 per hour) or the *Escuela de Idiomas* at c/Santa Eulalia 19, 1° (Mon–Fri 11am–1.30pm & 5.30–10pm; €1.50 per hour).

Accommodation

There is no shortage of **places to stay**, but prices tend to be high; if you're on a tight budget, be prepared to do some searching.

Budget options

Hostal El Alfarero c/Sagasta 40 ☎ & ⒻEE 924 303 183, Ⓔlalfarero@telefonica.net. Very cosy and nicely decorated *hostal* with nine air-conditioned doubles all with their own bathroom. On the way up from the Plaza de la Villa up to the Teatro Romano. ❷

Hostal Bueno c/Calvario 9 ☎924 302 977. Basic but clean *hostal* – all the rooms have (tiny) bathrooms. ❶–❷

Hostal Nueva España Avda. de Extremadura 6 ☎924 313 356. Good-value *hostal* with large rooms, out towards the train station. They don't do telephone reservations. ❷

Hostal La Salud c/Vespasiano 41 ☎ & ⒻEE 924 312 259, Ⓔhsalud@blunet.com. Small, simple rooms in this good-value *hostal* near the Acueducto de los Milagros. ❷

Hotel Vetonia c/Calderón de la Barca 26 ☎924 311 462/3. Comfortable, small hotel with easy parking right outside and wheelchair access. ❷

Moderate and expensive options

Hotel Cervantes c/Camilo José Cela 8 ☎924 314 961, ⓦwww.hotelcervantes.com. Comfortable hotel, off c/Cervantes, with secure parking and its own café. ❹

Hotel Lusitania c/Oviedo 12 ☎924 316 112, ⒻEE924 316 109. Reliable but unremarkable hotel, best kept in reserve if everywhere else is full. ❸

Hotel Meliá Mérida Plaza de España 19 ☎924 383 800, ⓦwww.solmelia.es. An upmarket newcomer on the scene in a former palace bang on the city's main plaza. It used to be the site of the *Hotel*

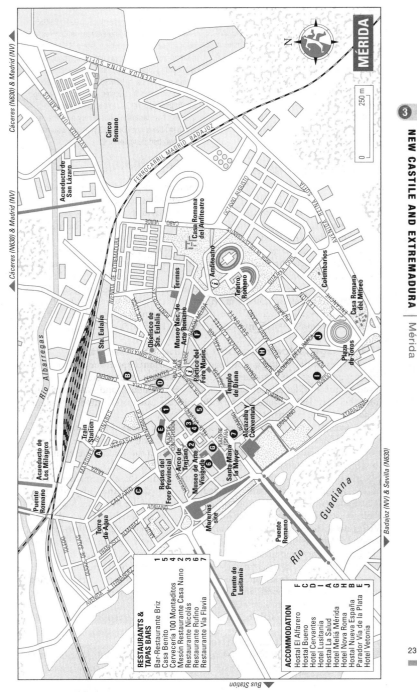

MÉRIDA

N

0   250 m

Cáceres (N630) & Madrid (NV)
Cáceres (N630) & Madrid (NV)
Cáceres (N630) & Madrid (NV)

AVENIDA REINA SOFIA

AVENIDA JUAN CARLOS

Circo Romano

FERROCARRIL MADRID BADAJOZ

Acueducto de San Lázaro

Casa Romana del Anfiteatro

Anfiteatro

Termas

Teatro Romano

Columbarios

Casa Romana del Mitreo

Plaza de Toros

Sta. Eulalia

Obelisco de Sta. Eulalia

Museo Nac. de Arte Romano

Pórtico del Foro Munic.

Templo de Diana

Alcazaba y Conventual

Santa María la Mayor

Arco de Trajano

Restos del Foro Provincial

Museo de Arte Visigodo

Morerías site

Río Albarregas

Acueducto de Los Milagros

Puente Romano

Torre de Agua

Train Station

Río Guadiana

Puente Romano

Puente de Lusitania

Río Guadiana

Badajoz (NV) & Sevilla (N630)

▲ Bus Station

RESTAURANTS & TAPAS BARS

Bar-Restaurante Briz	1
Casa Benito	5
Cervecería 100 Montaditos	4
Mesón Restaurante Casa Nano	2
Restaurante Nicolás	3
Restaurante Rufino	6
Restaurante Vía Flavia	7

ACCOMMODATION

Hostal El Alfarero	F
Hostal Bueno	C
Hotel Cervantes	D
Hotel Lusitania	I
Hostal La Salud	A
Hotel Meliá Mérida	G
Hotel Nova Roma	H
Hostal Nueva España	B
Parador Vía de la Plata	E
Hotel Vetonia	J

Emperatriz but is now part of the Meliá chain's range of self-styled boutique hotels. **❼**

Hotel Nova Roma c/Suavez Somontes 42 ☎924 311 261, ℉924 300 160. Large, modern hotel in central location. Book ahead if you're coming during the theatre festival. **❺**

Parador Vía de la Plata Plaza Constitución 3 ☎924 313 800, ✉merida@parador.es. Well-run and friendly *parador* in an eighteenth-century Baroque convent, near the Arco de Trajano. **❼**

Camping

Camping Lago de Proserpina ☎924 123 055. Signposted off the NV and the road to Cáceres, a pleasant site by the reservoir (see p.236) 5km north of town, offering swimming, fishing and windsurfing. Open April to mid-Sept.

Camping Mérida ☎924 303 453, 🖥www.pagina .de/campingmerida. Located 4km out of town on the Trujillo road (N430), this is the closer of Mérida's two campsites, but is very near the road and has little shade. Open all year and also has three two-bed bungalows. **❸**

The Roman sites

Built on the site of a Celto-Iberian settlement and founded by the Emperor Octavius Augustus in 25 BC as a home for retired legionaries, Mérida became the tenth city of the Roman Empire and the final stop on the *Vía de la Plata*, the Roman road which began in Astorga in northern Castile. The old city stretched as far as the modern bullring and Roman circus, covering only marginally less than the triangular area occupied by the modern town. Visiting the sites, a single €7.20 **combined ticket**, which can be bought at any of the sites, covers the Roman theatre and amphitheatre, the Roman villas Casa del Anfiteatro and Casa del Mitreo, the Columbarios burial ground, the Circo Romano, the archeological site at Morerías, the Alcazaba and the Basílica de Santa Eulalia – all of which have the same opening hours (daily: summer 9.30am–1.45pm & 5–6.15pm; winter 9.30am–1.45pm & 4–6.15pm).

The bridge, Alcazaba and around the centre

The obvious point to begin your tour is the magnificent **Puente Romano**, the bridge across the islet-strewn Río Guadiana. It is sixty arches long (the seven in the middle are fifteenth-century replacements) and was still in use until the early 1990s, when the new **Puente de Lusitania** – itself a structure to admire – was constructed.

Defence of the old bridge was provided by a vast **Alcazaba** (combined ticket or €2.55), built by the Moors to replace a Roman construction. The interior is a rather barren archeological site, although in the middle there's an *aljibe* to which you can descend by either of a pair of staircases.

North of the Alcazaba, past the airy sixteenth-century Plaza de España, the heart of the modern town, is the so-called **Templo de Diana**, adapted into a Renaissance mansion, and further along are remains of the **Foro**, the heart of the Roman city. To the west of the plaza, a convent houses the **Museo de Arte Visigodo** (Tues–Sun: summer 10am–2pm & 5–7pm; winter 10am–2pm & 4–6pm; €2.40), with an unexciting collection of about a hundred lapidary items. Just behind here is the great **Arco Trajano**, once wrongly believed to be a triumphal arch; it was, in fact, a marble-clad granite monumental gate to the forum. Heading to the river from here you'll also discover the **Morerías archeological site** (combined ticket or €2.55) along c/Morerías, where you can watch the digging and preservation of houses and factories from Roman through Visigoth to Moorish times – particularly of interest are the well-preserved Roman mosaics.

The theatre and amphitheatre

A ten-minute walk east of the Plaza de España will take you to Mérida's main archeological site (combined ticket or €5.10), containing the theatre and amphitheatre. Immediately adjacent are a Roman villa and the museum of Roman art.

The elaborate and beautiful **Teatro Romano** is one of the best preserved anywhere in the Roman Empire. Constructed around 15 BC, it was a present to the city from Agrippa, as indicated by the large inscription above the passageway to the left of the stage. The stage itself, a two-tier colonnaded affair, is in a particularly good state of repair, while many of the seats have been entirely rebuilt to offer more comfort to the audiences of the annual July and August season of classical plays.

Adjoining the theatre is the **Anfiteatro**, a slightly later and very much plainer construction. As many as 15,000 people – almost half the current population of Mérida – could be seated to watch gladiatorial combats and fights with wild animals.

The **Casa del Anfiteatro** (combined ticket or €2.55) lies immediately below the museum, and offers an approach to it from the site. It has wonderful mosaics, including a vigorous depiction of grape-treading.

The Museo Nacional de Arte Romano

The **Museo Nacional de Arte Romano** (June–Sept Tues–Sun 10am–2pm & 5–7pm; Oct–May Tues–Sun 10am–2pm & 4–6pm; €2.40, free Sat afternoons & Sun mornings; ⓦwww.mnar.es), constructed in 1986 above the Roman walls, is a wonderfully light, accessible building, using a free interpretation of classical forms to present the mosaics and sculpture as if emerging from the ruins. Spain's leading architect, Rafael Moneo, achieved perfectly his aim here to allow visitors "to see the entire collection almost in a glance".

The exhibits, displayed on three levels of the basilica-like hall, live up to their showcase. They include statues from the theatre, the Roman villa of **Mithraeus** (Mitreo; see below) and the vanished forum, and a number of mosaics – the largest being hung on the walls so that they can be examined at each level. Individually, the finest exhibits are probably the three statues, displayed together, depicting Augustus, the first Roman emperor; his son Tiberius, the second emperor; and Drusus, Augustus's heir apparent until (it is alleged) he was murdered by Livia, Tiberius's mother.

Further out: the hippodrome, aqueducts and Mitreo villa

The remaining monuments are further out from the centre, on the other side of the railway tracks. From the museum, it's a fifteen-minute walk if you cut down the streets towards Avenida de Extremadura and then head east out of the city to the **Circo Romano**, essentially an outline, where up to 30,000 spectators could watch horse and chariot races. Across the road from here, a stretch of the **Acueducto de San Lázaro** leads off towards the Río Albarregas.

The more impressive aqueduct, however, is the **Acueducto de los Milagros**, of which a satisfying portion survives in the midst of vegetable gardens, west of the train station. Its tall arches of granite, with brick courses, brought water to the city in its earliest days from the reservoir at Proserpina, 5km away (see p.242). The best view of the aqueduct is from a low and inconspicuous **Puente Romano** across the Río Albarregas; it was over this span that the *Vía de la Plata* entered the city.

Two further sights are the church of **Santa Eulalia** (combined ticket or €2.55), by the train station, which has a porch made from fragments of a former Temple of Mars, and a second Roman villa, the **Mitreo** (combined ticket or €3.20), in the shadow of the Plaza de Toros, south of the museum and theatres. The villa has a magnificent but damaged mosaic depicting the cosmos. A short walk away is the Columbarios burial ground with two family sepulchres and an interesting series of exhibits on Roman death rites.

Proserpina and Cornalvo reservoirs

You can swim in the **Embalse de Proserpina**, a Roman-constructed reservoir 5km north of town, and a popular summer escape, with a line of holiday homes. Alternatively, if you have transport, head to the **Embalse de Cornalvo**, 18km east of Mérida (turn left after the village of Trujillanos). There's a Roman dyke here, and a small national park has recently been created in the area.

Eating and drinking

The whole area between the train station and the Plaza de España is full of **bars and cheap restaurants** – fliers for many of which will be stuffed into your hands outside the theatre site entrance. Alternatively, search out one of the following:

Bar-Restaurante Briz c/Félix Valverde Lillo 7, just off Plaza de España. Reliable restaurant offering local speciality *raciones* and a €9.60 *menú*. Closed Sun evening.

Casa Benito c/San Francisco 3. Bullfighters' ephemera line the walls of this bar, which serves the local speciality tapas and *pitarra* wine. Closed Sun.

Cervecería 100 Montaditos c/Félix Valverde Lillo 5. A lively bar serving good beer, decent snacks and good breakfasts.

Mesón Restaurante Casa Nano c/Casterlar 3. Nice restaurant with a *menú* at around €18.

Restaurante Nicolás c/Félix Valverde Lillo 13. Good range of Extremaduran dishes and *menú* at €12, otherwise allow €20 a head. Located close to the Mercado Municipal. Closed Sun evenings.

Restaurante Rufino Plaza de Santa Clara 2. Traditional dishes in pleasant surroundings at this centrally located restaurant, opposite the Museo Visigodo. Allow €12–18 a head or try the enormous €16.20 *menú*.

Restaurante Vía Flavia Plaza de España 9. Friendly place right on the central plaza serving a good range of local dishes. The *menú* is a very good-value €8.20.

Badajoz

The valley of the Río Guadiana, followed by road and rail, waters rich farmland between Mérida and **BADAJOZ**. The main reason for visiting this provincial capital, traditional gateway to Portugal and the scene of innumerable sieges, is still to get across the border – it's not somewhere you'd want to stay long. Crude modern development has largely overrun what must once have been an attractive old centre, and few of the monuments have survived. The troubled history of Badajoz, springing from its strategically important position on the Río Guadiana, is in many ways more interesting than its present day. Founded by the Moors in 1009, the city was taken by the Christian armies of Alfonso IX in 1230, used as a base by Felipe II against the Portuguese in 1580, stormed by British forces under the Duke of Wellington in 1812, and taken by Franco's Nationalist troops in 1936.

Arrival and information

If you're arriving by **bus**, you'll have a fifteen-minute-plus walk to the centre, as the station is awkwardly located in wasteland beyond the ring road at the southern edge of the city. Your best bet is to hop on city bus #3 or #4 to

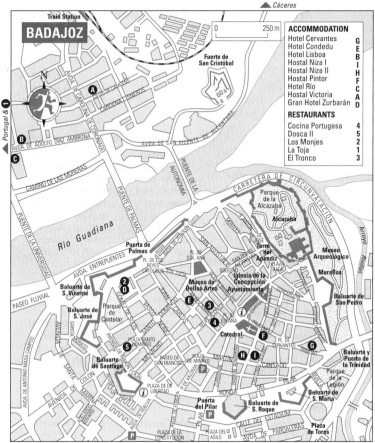

Cáceres

BADAJOZ

Train Station

Fuerte de
San Cristóbal

ACCOMMODATION	
Hotel Cervantes	G
Hotel Condedu	E
Hotel Lisboa	B
Hostal Niza I	I
Hostal Niza II	H
Hostal Pintor	F
Hotel Río	C
Hostal Victoria	A
Gran Hotel Zurbarán	D
RESTAURANTS	
Cocina Portugesa	4
Dosca II	5
Los Monjes	2
La Toja	1
El Tronco	3

Río Guadiana

Puerta de
Palmas

Parque
de la
Alcazaba

Alcazaba

Museo
Arqueológico

Murallas

Baluarte de
S. Vicente

Museo de
Bellas Artes

Iglesia de la
Concepción
Ayuntamiento

Baluarte de
San Pedro

Baluarte de
S. José

Parque
de
Castelar

Catedral

Baluarte y
Puerta de
la Trinidad

Baluarte
de Santiago

Parque
de la
Legión

Baluarte de
S. María

PLAZA DE LA
LIBERTAD

Puerta
del Pilar

Baluarte de
S. Roque

Plaza
de Toros

Museo de Arte Contemporáneo & Bus station

Avenida de Europa or #6 to the Plaza de la Libertad. The **train station** is still further from the action, on the far side of the river, up the road which crosses the Puente de Palmas. Buses #1 and #2 go to the Plaza de la Libertad, or it's around €3 in a taxi. If you're looking for **parking**, follow the signs to Plaza de Minayo where you'll find an attended underground car park.

The town has two tourist offices. The efficient municipal **turismo** (June–Sept Mon–Fri 10am–2pm & 6–8pm, Sat 10am–2pm; Oct–May Mon–Fri 10am–2pm & 4–6pm, Sat 10am–2pm; ☎924 224 981, ⓦwww .aytobadajoz.es) is in c/San Juan, just off Plaza de España, while the **Junta de Extremadura** office (Mon–Fri 10am–2pm & 5–7pm, Sat & Sun 10am–2pm; ☎924 013 659; ⓦwww.turismoextremadura.com), good for information on the whole region, is down the hill on Plaza de la Libertad – follow the signs from any approach to the town. For **Internet access**, go to Locutorio Público Extremeño, opposite the *Burger King* at Avda. Fernando Calzadilla 2 (7am–11pm; €3 per hour).

The **Portuguese frontier** is 4km west of Badajoz. You can get to the border by local bus, from where you can catch local Portuguese buses to Elvas, the first sizeable town on the Portuguese side of the border. There are two long-distance buses and one train to Lisbon daily, all via Elvas – the bus is by far the cheaper, faster and more hassle-free option.

Accommodation

There's plenty of **accommodation** available in Badajoz, much of it inexpensive, if not terribly desirable. The best location is around the Plaza de España, particularly on c/Arco Agüero.

Budget options

Hotel Cervantes c/Trinidad 2 ☎ 924 223 710, ⓕ 924 222 935. On the Plaza Cervantes, by the cathedral, this hotel has impressive common areas but rather ordinary rooms. ❷

Hostal Niza I and II c/Arco Agüero 34 & 45 ☎ 924 223 881, ⓦ www.coeba.es/hostalniza. Comfortable rooms in these two *hostales*. The *Niza I* used to be cheaper and less well-equipped but has been upgraded recently and both now cost around €40 for a double room with en-suite bathroom. ❷

Hostal Pintor c/Arco Agüero 26 ☎ 924 224 228. Cheap but charming *pensión* on the first floor of this building, offering good value for money. ❷

Hostal Victoria c/Luís de Camōens 3 ☎ 924 271 662, ⓕ 924 267 551. Good-value *hostal* near the train station, but a fair distance from the centre. Double rooms have bath and TV. ❷

Moderate and expensive options

Hotel Condedu c/Muñoz Torrero 27 ☎ 924 207 247, ⓦ www.alextur.net/hotel/condedu/index.htm. Comfortable and well-located hotel (aka *Hotel Conde Duque*), handy for the museum and cathedral. ❸

Gran Hotel Zurbarán Paseo Castelar ☎ 924 001 400, ⓦ www.barcelo.com. Priciest hotel in town, with swimming pool and renowned restaurant. Look out for weekend deals that can bring the price down substantially. ❻

Hotel Lisboa Avda. Díaz Ambrona 13 ☎ 924 272 900, ⓕ 924 272 250. Large, comfortable hotel with en-suite rooms and a very reasonably priced restaurant. ❸

Hotel Río Avda. Adolfo Díaz Ambrona s/n ☎ 924 272 600, ⓦ www.sercotel.es. At the far end of Puente de la Universidad, with swimming pool, parking and a good restaurant (which is closed at weekends & Aug). ❺

The Town

At the heart of old Badajoz is the **Plaza de España** and the squat thirteenth-century **Catedral** (Tues–Sat: summer 11am–1pm & 6–8pm; winter Tues–Sat 11am–1pm & 5–7pm; free), a fortress-like building, prettified a little during the Renaissance by the addition of a portal and embellishment of the tower. The *museo* (same hours; €2) contains work by local-born artist Luis de Morales (1520–1586).

Northeast of the square, c/de San Juan leads to **Plaza Alta**, once an elegant arcaded concourse – now rather seedy – and what remains of the town's fortress, the **Alcazaba**. This is largely in ruins but preserves Moorish entrance gates and fragments of a Renaissance palace inside. Part of it houses a **Museo Arqueológico** (Tues–Sun 10am–3pm; free), with local Roman and Visigothic finds. Defending the townward side is the octagonal Moorish **Torre del Aprendiz**, or *Torre Espantaperros* ("dog-scarer" – the dogs in question being Christians).

Nearby in the Plaza de Santa María is the brand new **Museo de la Ciudad** (April–Sept: Tues–Sat 10am–2pm & 4–9pm, Sun 10am–2pm; Oct–May Tues–Sat 10am–2pm & 4.30–7.30pm, Sun 10am–2pm; free) which gives an interesting and well thought-out survey of the city's chequered history from prehistoric times through to the present day.

The Río Guadiana is the city's only other distinguished feature, and in particular the graceful **Puente de Palmas**, or Puente Viejo, spanning its course.

The bridge was designed by Herrera (architect of El Escorial) as a fitting first impression of Spain, and leads into the city through the **Puerta de Palmas**, once a gate in the walls, now standing alone as a sort of triumphal arch.

From the plaza behind this arch, c/Santa Lucía leads to c/Duque de San Germán where you'll find the **Museo de Bellas Artes** (Tues–Fri 10am–2pm & 4–6pm, summer till 8pm, Sat & Sun 10am–2pm; free), which includes works by Morales, and a couple of good panels by Zurbarán. Near Plaza de la Constitución and off Avenida Calzadillas Maestre is the **Museo de Arte Contemporáneo** (summer Tues–Sat 10.30am–1.30pm & 6–9pm, Sun 10.30am–1.30pm; winter Tues–Sat 10.30am–1.30pm & 5–8pm, Sun 10.30am–1.30pm; free). This striking building houses a wealth of modern paintings, installations and sculpture, by artists from Spain, Portugal and Latin America.

Eating, drinking and nightlife

The area around c/Muñoz Torrero, a couple of blocks below the Plaza de España, is the most promising site for reasonably priced food and tapas bars. For **nightlife**, *Mercantil* (daily 4.30pm–2/5am), off Plaza España at c/Zurbarán 10, is a stylish bar which also has live guitar-based music at the weekend.

Cocina Portuguesa c/Muñoz Torrero 7. Best budget bet in Badajoz with tasty, reasonably priced Portuguese cooking and a cheap *menú*.

Dosca II Avda. de Colón 3. Just off Plaza Santo Domingo, this well-priced place is very popular with locals, serving a wide range of generous, well-cooked specialities in the nautically themed restaurant. Under €15 a head.

Los Monjes *Gran Hotel Zurbarán*, Paseo Castelar ☏924 223 741. Probably the best food in town, with a pricey range of Spanish dishes, but a slightly characterless place. À la carte will probably set

you back around €35, though there's also a lunchtime buffet at half the price. Reservation recommended.

La Toja Avda. Elvas 22 – the Portugal road. An excellent restaurant, run by a *gallego*, so serving food from Extremadura and Galicia. A bit of a trek from the centre, though if you drive it has its own parking. Allow around €30 a head. Closed Sun pm.

El Tronco c/Muñoz Torrero 16. Perhaps the best reason to stay in town – this has a vast range of superb-value bar snacks and excellent regional food and wine in the restaurant.

Southern Extremadura

The routes **south from Mérida or Badajoz** cross territory that is mostly harsh and unrewarding, fit only for sheep and the odd cork or olive tree, until you come upon the foothills of the Sierra Morena, on the borders of Andalucía. En route, **Olivenza**, a town that has spent more time in Portugal than Spain, is perhaps the most attractive stop, and offers a road approach to Évora, the most interesting city of southern Portugal.

Olivenza

Twenty-five kilometres southwest of Badajoz, whitewashed **OLIVENZA** seems to have landed in the wrong country; long disputed between Spain and Portugal, it has been Spanish since 1801. Yet not only are the buildings and the town's character clearly Portuguese, the oldest inhabitants still cling to this language – you may overhear them chatting as they relax in the main square, the Plaza de España, where the buses stop. There's a local saying here: "the women from Olivenza are not like the rest, for they are the daughters of Spain and the granddaughters of Portugal."

The town has long been strongly fortified, and traces of the **walls and gates** can still be seen, even though houses have been built up against them. They extend up to the **castle**, which has three surviving towers, and an ethnographic **museum** (Tues–Fri 11am–2pm & 5–8pm, Sat 10am–2pm & 5–8pm, winter afternoons 4–7pm, Sun 10am–2pm) within. Right beside the castle is the seventeenth-century church of **Santa María del Castillo** (Tues–Sat 11am–2pm & 5–8pm, winter afternoons 4–7pm, Sun 11am–2pm), and around the corner, **Santa María Magdalena** (same hours), built a century later. The latter is in the distinctive Portuguese Manueline style, with arcades of twisted columns; the former is a more sober Renaissance affair with three aisles of equal height and a notable work of art in the huge "Tree of Jesse" *retablo*. Both have sturdy bell towers and light, airy interiors adorned with *azulejo* and ornate Baroque altars. Just across the street from Santa María Magdalena is a former **palace**, now the public library, with a spectacular Manueline doorway. Continuing down this street, then taking the first turning on the left onto c/Coridad, you come to the early sixteenth-century **Hospital**, which still serves its original purpose. Its chapel (Tues–Sun 10am–2pm) is covered with early-eighteenth-century *azulejos*.

There's a **turismo** kiosk on the Plaza de España (summer Tues–Fri 10am–2pm & 5–7pm, Sat & Sun 10am–2pm; winter Tues–Fri 10am–2.30pm & 4–7pm, Sat & Sun 10am–2pm). Should you want to stay in Olivenza, there's a **hotel** on the fringes of town, at the exit to Badajoz, the *Heredero* (T 924 490 835, F 924 491 261; ❸), which has a restaurant. You'll find a public **swimming pool** by the football ground, on Avenida Portugal, near the Badajoz exit.

Towards Portugal

Twelve kilometres northwest of Olivenza, a road heading towards Portugal stops abruptly at the ruined bridge of **Puente Ayuda**, where the Río Guadiana forms the border between the two countries. There's no way on other than to swim, but it's a picturesque picnic spot; the river runs across many exposed rock beds giving good fishing, and it's also an ideal spot for some discreet camping. To **enter Portugal**, you need to follow the EX107 south from Olivenza for 39km to the Spanish border at **Villanueva del Fresno**. From here it's 16km to **Mourao**, the first Portuguese town on this approach, which is on the main road (and bus route) to Évora.

South to Jerez de los Caballeros

The road from Badajoz to Jerez de los Caballeros is typical of southern Extremadura, striking across a parched landscape whose hamlets – low huts and a whitewashed church strung out along the road – look as if they have been dumped from some low-budget Western set of a Mexican frontier town. It's a cruel country which bred cruel people, if we are to believe the names of places like Valle de Matamoros (Valley of the Moorslayers), and one can easily understand the attraction which the New World and the promise of the lush Indies must have held for its inhabitants.

It is hardly surprising, then, that **JEREZ DE LOS CABALLEROS** produced a whole crop of *conquistadores*. The two most celebrated are Vasco Núñez de Balboa, discoverer of the Pacific, and Hernando de Soto (also known as the Conqueror of Florida), who in exploring the Mississippi became one of the first Europeans to set foot in North America. You're not allowed to forget it either – the bus station is in the Plaza de Vasco Núñez de Balboa, complete with a statue of Vasco in the very act of discovery, and from it the Calle Hernando de Soto leads up into the middle of town.

It's a quiet, friendly place, through which many tourists pass but few stay. Grass grows up through many of the cobbled streets and life goes on unhurriedly. From a distance it is the church towers that dominate the walled old town: a passion for building spires gripped the place in the eighteenth century, when three churches had new ones erected. The silhouette of each is clearly based on that of the Giralda at Sevilla, but they are all distinctively decorated: the first is **San Miguel**, in the central Plaza de España, made of carved brick; the second is the unmistakeable red-, blue- and ochre-glazed tower of **San Bartolomé**, on the hill above it, with a striking tiled facade; and the third, rather dilapidated, belongs to **Santa Catalina**, outside the walls.

Above the Plaza de España the streets climb up to the restored remains of a **castle** of the Knights Templar (this was once an embattled frontier town), mostly late thirteenth century but with obvious Moorish influences. Adjoining the castle, and predating it by over a century (as do the town walls), is the church of **Santa María**. Built on a Visigothic site, it's more interesting seen from the battlements above than from the inside. In the small park below the castle walls, a café commands fine views of the surrounding countryside and the magnificent sunsets.

There's a small **turismo** in the *ayuntamiento* on Plaza de San Agustín (daily 9.30am–2.30pm & 4.30–6.30pm; ☎924 730 372). **Places to stay** are few. By far the cheapest is the *Pensión El Gordito*, Avda. de Portugal 104 (☎924 731 452; ❶), which is good for the price. The more upmarket alternative is the *Hotel Oasis*, c/El Campo 18 (☎924 731 836, ✉doasis@interbook.net; ❷). The *Oasis* has the only real **restaurant** in town; for tapas and *pitarra* wine, try *La Ermita*, an old chapel on c/Dr Benitez.

Zafra

If you plan to stick to the main routes or are heading south from Mérida, **ZAFRA** is rather less of a detour, though it's also much more frequented by tourists. It's famed mainly for its **castle** – now converted into a *parador* – which is remarkable for the white marble Renaissance patio designed by Juan de Herrera.

Two beautiful arcaded plazas, the Plaza Grande and the Plaza Chica, adjoin each other in the town centre. The most attractive of several interesting churches is **Nuestra Señora de la Candelaria** (summer: Mon, Tues, Thurs, Fri 10.30am–1.30pm & 6.30–8.30pm, Sat & Sun 11am–1pm; winter opens and closes an hour earlier), with nine panels by Zurbarán in the *retablo* and a chapel by Churriguera; the entrance is on c/José through a small gateway, around the side of the church. Also worth a look are the tombs of the Figueroa family (the original inhabitants of the castle) in the **Convento de Santa Clara** (closed until mid-2004, but usually open daily: summer 6–8pm; winter 5–7pm), just off the main shopping street, c/Sevilla; ring the bell to get in.

This region is famous for its wines, and you can visit the **Bodega Medina**, c/Cestria (Mon–Fri 10.30am–2pm & 4–7pm); call in at the **turismo** in the Plaza de España (Mon–Fri 9.30am–4.30pm, Sat & Sun 10.30am–2.30pm; ☎924 551 036, ⊛www.zafraturismo.com) to make an appointment.

Accommodation options include the splendid *parador* (☎924 554 540, ⊛www.parador.es; ❻), housed in a fifteenth-century castle in the centre, the newly refurbished *Hotel Victoria*, Plaza de España 8 (☎924 554 382; ❷), the well-appointed *Hotel Las Palmeras*, Plaza Grande 14 (☎924 552 208, ☎924 555 385; ❷), and the small but very tidy *Hostal Carmen*, Avda. Estación 9 (☎924 551 439, ☎924 551 439; ❷), which also boasts an excellent medium-priced restaurant. The cheapest and best-value place, however, is the friendly *Hostal Arias* (☎924 554 855, ☎924 554 888; ❶-❷), 200m out of town on the Carretera Badajoz–Granada, which has en-suite rooms and a good restaurant with an €8 *menú*.

South of Zafra: the Sierra Morena

Beyond Zafra the main road and the railway head straight down through the **Sierra Morena** (see p.319) towards **Sevilla**. By **road** it's more interesting – though bus services are less frequent – to go through **Fregenal de La Sierra** (where the road from Jerez de los Caballeros joins up) into the heart of the sierra around Aracena. On the **train** you can reach another interesting region by getting off at the station of Cazalla-Constantina, while if you're heading for **Córdoba** and eastern Andalucía, you should change at Los Rosales before reaching Sevilla.

Travel details

Trains

Albacete to: Alicante (10 daily; 1hr 30min); Madrid (23 daily; 2hr 10min–3hr); Valencia (15 daily; 1hr 30min–2hr 25min).

Badajoz to: Cáceres (2 daily; 1hr 55min); Lisbon via Elvas (1 daily; 5hr); Madrid (3 daily; 5hr 15 min–6hr 15min); Mérida (7 daily; 40min–1hr).

Cáceres to: Badajoz (3 daily; 2hr); Lisbon (1 daily; 5hr 15min); Madrid (5 daily; 2hr 20min–3hr 55min); Mérida (5 daily; 50min–1hr); Plasencia (2 daily; 1hr 20min); Sevilla (1 daily; 5hr 40min); Zafra (2 daily; 2hr 10min).

Ciudad Real to: Almagro (5 daily; 1hr 15min); Madrid (25 daily; 50min–1hr).

Cuenca to: Madrid (5 daily; 2hr 30min–2hr 55min); Valencia (4 daily; 2hr 45min–3hr 10min).

Madrid to: Albacete (22 daily; 2hr–2hr 20min); Almagro (1 daily; 2hr 40min); Badajoz (4 daily; 5hr 40min–7hr); Cáceres (6 daily; 3hr 20min–5hr); Ciudad Real (2 daily; 3hr; 20 daily AVE; 55min); Cuenca (4 daily; 2hr 30min); Mérida (5 daily; 4hr 10min–4hr 50min); Navalmoral (7 daily; 2hr–2hr 20min); Plasencia (4 daily; 3hr 10min–3hr 30min); Sigüenza (6 daily; 1hr 40min); Talavera de la Reina (7 daily; 1hr 30min).

Mérida to: Badajoz (7 daily; 45min); Cáceres (4 daily; 1hr); Madrid (4 daily; 4hr 30min–5hr 50min); Plasencia (2 daily; 2hr 25min); Sevilla (1 daily; 4hr 35min).

Plasencia to: Badajoz (1 daily; 3hr 30min); Cáceres (3 daily; 1hr 20min); Madrid (2 daily; 3hr 20min); Mérida (3 daily; 2hr 20min).

Sigüenza to: Barcelona (1 daily; at least 6hr 30min), via Zaragoza (3–4hr); Madrid (7 daily; 1 hr 40min); Medinaceli (4 daily; 15–20min).

Buses

Albacete to: Alicante (7 daily; 1hr 50min–2hr 25min); Cuenca (2–3 daily; 2hr 45min); Madrid (19 daily; 3hr 10min–3hr 30min); Murcia (11 daily; 1hr 45min–2hr 30min); Parque Natural de las Lagunes de Ruidera (Mon–Sat 1 daily; 2hr); Valencia (6 daily; 2hr 5min–3hr 15min).

Badajoz to: Cáceres (7 daily; 2hr); Caia (Portuguese frontier; 4 daily; 30min); Córdoba (3 daily; 5hr); Lisbon (2 daily; 7hr); Madrid (7 daily; 4hr 30min–5hr); Mérida (8 daily; 45min); Murcia (1 daily; 9hr 20min); Olivenza (12 daily; 30min); Sevilla (2–5 daily; 4hr 30min); Zafra (8 daily; 1hr 30min).

Cáceres to: Alcántara (2 daily; 1hr 30min); Arroyo de la Luz (8–15 daily; 30min); Badajoz (4 daily; 1hr 15min–1hr 45min); Coria (4 daily; 1hr 15min); Guadalupe (2 daily; 2hr 30min); Madrid (8 daily; 4hr); Mérida (4 daily; 1hr); Plasencia (4–5 daily; 1hr 20min); Salamanca (4 daily; 3hr 30min); Sevilla (8 daily; 4hr); Trujillo (8 daily; 45min).

Ciudad Real to: Almagro (6 daily; 1hr); Córdoba (1 daily; 4hr 30min); Jaén (2 daily; 4hr); Madrid (4 daily; 4hr); Toledo (1 daily; 3hr), Valdepeñas (3 daily; 2hr).

Cuenca to: Albacete (2–3 daily; 2hr 45min); Barcelona (1 daily; 9hr); Madrid (9 daily; 2hr–2hr 30min); Teruel (1 daily; 2hr 30min); Valencia (2–3 daily; 2hr 30min–3hr 30min).

Guadalupe to: Cáceres (2 daily; 2hr 30min); Madrid (2 daily; 4hr); Trujillo (2 daily; 2hr–2hr 30min).

Madrid to: Albacete (11 daily; 3hr); Badajoz (9 daily; 4hr 30min–5hr); Cáceres (7–10 daily; 3hr 50min–4hr 30min); Cuenca (10 daily; 2hr–2hr 30min); Jarandilla (1 daily; 3hr 30min); Mérida (10 daily; 4–5hr); Plasencia (2 daily; 4hr); Talavera de la Reina (15 daily; 1hr 30min); Trujillo (10 daily; 4–5hr).

Mérida to: Badajoz (8 daily; 45min); Cáceres (7 daily; 1hr); Guadalupe (4 daily; 2hr); Jerez de los Caballeros (1–3 daily; 2hr); Madrid (8–9 daily; 4hr

3

20min); Murcia (1 daily; 9hr); Salamanca (5 daily; 4hr); Sevilla (6–8 daily; 3hr 15min, some stopping in Zafra); Trujillo (4 daily; 2hr); Zafra (1–3 daily; 1hr 10min).

Navalmoral to: Jarandilla (2 daily; 3hr); Plasencia (2 daily; 2–4hr); Trujillo (6 daily; 1hr).

Plasencia to: Cáceres (4–5 daily; 1hr 20min); Jarandilla (2 daily; 2hr); Madrid (2 daily; 4hr);

Salamanca (4 daily; 2hr).

Talavera de la Reina to: Guadalupe (2 daily; 2hr 30min); Madrid (15 daily; 1hr 30min); Toledo (10 daily; 1hr 30min).

Trujillo to: Cáceres (8 daily; 45min); Guadalupe (2 daily; 2hr); Madrid (13–16 daily; 3hr–3hr 30min); Mérida (4 daily; 2hr).

Andalucía

CHAPTER 4

Highlights

✻ **Seafood** Thousands of restaurants and bars serving the freshest fish and crustaceans in Spain. See p.46

✻ **Semana Santa** Andalucía's major Holy Week festival is memorably celebrated in Sevilla, Málaga, Córdoba and Granada. See p.302

✻ **Flamenco** The passionate dance, song and music of the Spanish South. See p.1083

✻ **Sevilla** Andalucía's pulsating capital city is a treasurehouse of churches, palaces and museums. See p.296

✻ **Sherry** Andalucía's classic wine makes the perfect partner for tapas. See p.48

✻ **Coto de Doñana** Europe's largest and most important wildlife sanctuary. See p.339

✻ **Mezquita, Córdoba** This 1200-year-old Moorish mosque is one of the most beautiful ever built. See p.349

✻ **Bars** Spain has more bars than any other European country and Andalucía has some of the best: *El Pisto* in Córdoba is one not to miss. See p.355

✻ **Alhambra** Granada's Moorish palace is one of the world's most sensual buildings. See p.371

✻ **The Alpujarras** A wildly picturesque region dotted with traditional mountain villages. See p.386

△ Señoritas, Feria de Abril, Feria

Andalucía

A ndalucía is the southernmost territory of the country and the most quintessentially Spanish part of the Iberian peninsula. The popular image of Spain as a land of bullfights, flamenco, sherry and ruined castles derives from this beguiling region. Above all, it's the great **Moorish monuments** that compete for your attention in this part of Spain. The Moors, a mixed race of Berbers and Arabs who crossed into Spain from Morocco and North Africa, occupied *al-Andalus* for over seven centuries. Their first forces landed at Tarifa in 710 AD and within four years they had conquered virtually the entire country; their last kingdom, Granada, fell to the Christian Reconquest in 1492. Between these dates they developed the most sophisticated civilization of the Middle Ages, centred in turn on the three major cities of **Córdoba**, **Sevilla** and **Granada**. Each one preserves extraordinarily brilliant and beautiful monuments, of which the most perfect is Granada's **Alhambra palace**, arguably the most sensual building in all of Europe. **Sevilla**, not to be outdone, has a fabulously ornamented Alcázar and the grandest of all Gothic cathedrals. Today, Andalucía's capital and seat of the region's autonomous parliament is a vibrant contemporary metropolis that's impossible to resist. Córdoba's exquisite **Mezquita**, the grandest and most beautiful mosque constructed by the Moors, is a landmark building in world architecture and also not to be missed.

These three cities have, of course, become major tourist destinations, but it's also worth leaving the tourist trail and visting some of the smaller **inland towns** of Andalucía. Renaissance towns such as **Úbeda**, **Baeza** and **Osuna**, **Guadix** with its cave suburb, Moorish **Carmona**, and the stark white hill towns around **Ronda**, are all easily accessible by local buses. Travelling for some time here, you'll get a feel for the landscape of Andalucía: occasionally spectacularly beautiful but more often impressive on a huge, unyielding scale.

Finding accommodation at Easter

Andalucía's major festival is the celebration of **Easter**, and you should be aware that during the whole of Easter week (Semana Santa) it is almost impossible to find accommodation in the cities of Málaga, Sevilla, Córdoba and Granada plus the other provincial capitals without booking well in advance. However, the smaller towns and villages surrounding them remain largely unaffected, should still have vacancies and are easy enough to reach with your own transport or by bus. Still, it would be wise to ring ahead first. Following Easter Sunday, things revert to normal.

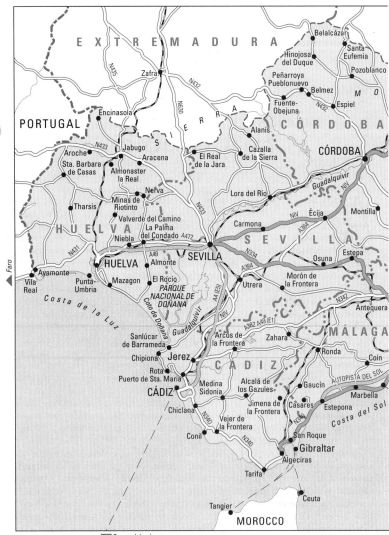

Canary Islands

The province also takes in mountains – including the **Sierra Nevada**, Spain's highest range. You can often ski here in March, and then drive down to the coast to swim the same day. Perhaps more compelling, though, are the opportunities for walking in the lower slopes, **Las Alpujarras**. Alternatively, there's good trekking amongst the gentler (and much less-known) hills of the **Sierra Morena**, north of Sevilla.

On the **coast** it's easy to despair. Extending to either side of **Málaga** is the **Costa del Sol**, Europe's most heavily developed resort area, with its poor beaches hidden behind a remorseless density of concrete hotels and apartment

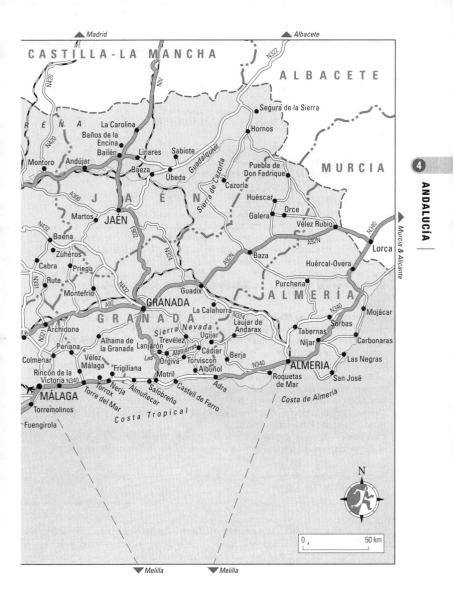

complexes. However, the province offers two alternatives, much less developed and with some of the best beaches in all Spain. These are the villages **between Tarifa and Cádiz** on the Atlantic, and those **around Almería** on the southeast corner of the Mediterranean. The Almerian beaches allow warm swimming through all but the winter months; those near Cádiz, more easily accessible, are fine from about June to September. Near Cádiz, too, is the **Coto de Doñana** national park, Spain's largest and most important nature reserve, which is home to a spectacular range of flora and fauna.

Fiestas

January
1–2 *La Toma* Celebration of the entry of the Reyes Católicos into the city – at Granada.
6 *Romería de la Virgen del Mar* Pilgrimage procession from Almería.
17 *Romería del Ermita del Santo* Similar event at Guadix.

February
1 *San Cecilio* fiesta in Granada's traditionally gypsy quarter of Sacromonte.
Week before Lent *Carnaval* is an extravagant week-long event in all the Andalucían cities. Cádiz, above all, celebrates, with uproarious street parades, fancy dress and satirical music competitions.

March and April
Holy Week (*Semana Santa*) has its most elaborate and dramatic celebrations in Andalucía. You'll find memorable processions of floats and penitents at Sevilla, Málaga, Granada and Córdoba, and to a lesser extent in smaller towns such as Jerez, Arcos, Baeza and Úbeda. All culminate with dramatic candlelight processions at dawn on Good Friday, with Easter Day itself more of a family occasion.
Last week of April (approximately 2 weeks after Easter) Week-long *Feria de Abril* at Sevilla: the largest fair in Spain. A small April fair – featuring bull running – is held in Vejer.

May
First week *Cruces de Mayo* in Córdoba celebrates the Holy Cross and includes a "prettiest patio" competition in a town full of prize examples.
Early May (usually the week after Sevilla's fair). Somewhat aristocratic *Horse Fair* at Jerez de la Frontera.
3 *Moros y Cristianos* ("Moors and Christians") carnival at Pampaneira (Alpujarras).
17 *San Isidro Romería* at Setenil (Cádiz).
Pentecost (7 weeks after Easter) *Romería del Rocío*, when horse-drawn carriages and processions converge from all over the south on El Rocío (Huelva).
Corpus Christi (Thursday after Trinity) Bullfights and festivities at Granada, Sevilla, Ronda, Vejer and Zahara de la Sierra.
Last week *Feria de la Manzanilla*, Sanlúcar de Barrameda. Prolonged binge to celebrate the town's major product, with flamenco and sporting events on the river beach.

June
Second week *Feria de San Bernabé* at Marbella, often spectacular since this is the richest town in Andalucía.

The realities of life in **contemporary Andalucía** can be stark. **Unemployment** in the region is the highest in Spain – over twenty percent in some areas – and a large proportion of the population still scrapes a living from seasonal agricultural work. The *andaluz* villages, bastions of anarchist and socialist groups before and during the Civil War, saw little economic aid or change during the Franco years, and although much government spending – particularly by the autonomous regional government in Sevilla using substantial EU funding – has been channelled into improving infrastructure such as hospitals, road and rail links, the lack of employment opportunities away from

13 *San Antonio* fiesta at Trevélez (Alpujarras) with mock battles between Moors and Christians.

Third week The Algeciras fair and fiesta, another major event of the south.

23–24 *Candelas de San Juan* – bonfires and effigies at Vejer and elsewhere.

30 Conil *feria*.

End June/early July *International Festival of Music and Dance* – major dance/flamenco groups and chamber orchestras perform in Granada's Alhambra palace, Generalife and Carlos V palace.

July

Early July The *International Guitar Festival* at Córdoba brings together top international acts from classical, flamenco and Latin American music.

End of month *Virgen del Mar* – Almería's major annual shindig, with parades, horse-riding events, concerts and lots of drinking.

August

5 Trevélez observes a midnight *romería* to Mulhacén.

13–21 *Feria de Málaga* – one of Andalucía's most enjoyable fiestas for visitors, who are heartily welcomed by the ebullient *malagueños*.

15 *Ascension of the Virgin Fair* with *casetas* (dance tents) at Vejer and elsewhere. Riotous *Noche del Vino* wine festival at Competa (Málaga).

Third week The first cycle of horse races along Sanlúcar de Barrameda's beach, with heavy official and unofficial betting; the second tournament takes place a week later.

23–25 *Guadalquivir festival* at Sanlúcar de Barrameda, with bullfights and an important flamenco competition.

September

First two weeks Ronda's annual *feria*, with flamenco contests and *Corrida Goyesca* – bullfights in eighteenth-century dress.

1–3 Celebration of the *Virgen de la Luz* in Tarifa: processions and horseback riding.

First/second week *Vendimia* (celebration of the vintage) at Jerez.

29–Oct 2 *Feria* in Órgiva (Alpujarras).

October

1 *San Miguel* fiesta in Granada's Albaicín quarter and elsewhere, including Torremolinos.

15–23 *Feria de San Lucas* – Jaén's major fiesta, dating back to the fifteenth century.

the coastal tourist zones persists. For all its poverty, however, Andalucía is also Spain at its most exuberant: the home of flamenco and the bullfight, and those wild and extravagant clichés of the Spanish South. These really do exist and can be absorbed at one of the hundreds of annual **fiestas**, **ferias** and **romerías**. The best of them include the giant April Feria in Sevilla, the ageless pilgrimage to El Rocío near Huelva in late May, and the dramatically moving Semana Santa (Easter) celebrations at Málaga, Granada, Sevilla, Córdoba and Jerez, as well as in countless small villages.

The Costa del Sol

The outstanding feature of the **Costa del Sol** is its ease of access. Hundreds of flights arrive here every week and **Málaga airport** is positioned midway between **Málaga**, the main city on the coast, and Torremolinos, its most grotesque resort. You can easily reach either town by taking the electric train which runs every thirty minutes (daily 7am–11.45pm) along the coast between Málaga and **Fuengirola**, 20km to the southwest. Frequent bus connections also link all the major coastal resorts, while a new toll *autopista* or motorway between Málaga and Estepona has taken the strain off the often-overloaded coastal highways. Inland, Granada, Córdoba and Sevilla are all within easy reach of Málaga; so, too, are **Ronda** and the "White Towns" to the west, and a handful of relatively restrained coastal resorts such as **Nerja** and **Almuñecar** to the east. **Beaches** along the Costa del Sol are generally grit-grey rather than golden, but the sea is reliably clean.

Economically, the coastal hinterland is undergoing a resurgence, far outstripping the more sluggish progress in the rest of Andalucía. Over the last decade cultivation of subtropical fruits such as mangos, papayas, guavas, lychees and avocados has replaced the traditional orange, lemon and almond trees, whilst in the province of Almería a plastic-greenhouse revolution has turned this zone into one of northern Europe's main vegetable and fruit suppliers. Most farm labourers, however, can't afford coastal land; those who buy are often former migrants to France and Germany who have been forced to return because of the unemployment situation there.

The carretera nacional N340

A special note of warning has to be made about the **Costa del Sol's main highway**, which is one of the most dangerous roads in Europe. Nominally a national highway, it's really a 100-kilometre-long city street, passing through the middle of towns and *urbanizaciones*. Drivers treat it like a motorway, yet pedestrians have to get across, and cars are constantly turning off or into the road – hence the terrifying number of accidents, including, on average, over a hundred fatalities a year. A large number of casualties are inebriated British package tourists unfamiliar with left-hand-drive vehicles and traffic patterns. The first few kilometres, between the airport, with its various car rental offices, and Torremolinos, are among the most treacherous, but worse still is the stretch heading west from Marbella: around thirty accidents a year occur on each kilometre between Marbella and San Pedro.

A new four-lane toll motorway to relieve this road of traffic – the Autopista del Sol (A7-E15) linking Málaga with Estepona in the west – has recently been completed, with an extension planned to reach Almería in the east in the next few years. Due to misleading road signs, it is easy to end up on the motorway without intending to, forcing you to pay the toll to get off.

If you do use the N340 don't make dangerous (and illegal) left turns from the fast lane – use the "Cambio de Sentido" junctions which also allow you to reverse direction. Also be particularly careful after heavy rain, when the hot, oily road surface can easily send you into a skid. Pedestrians should only cross at traffic lights, a bridge or an underpass.

Málaga

MÁLAGA seems at first an uninviting place. It's the second city of the south (after Sevilla), with a population of half a million, and is also one of the poorest: official unemployment figures for the area estimate the jobless at one in four of the workforce. Yet though many people get no further than the train or bus stations, and though the clusters of high-rises look pretty grim as you approach, the city does have its attractions. The recently renovated and elegant central zone has a number of interesting churches and museums, not to mention the **birthplace of Picasso** and the new **Picasso Museum**, housing an important collection of works by Málaga's most famous son. Around the old fishing villages of **El Palo** and **Pedregalejo**, now absorbed into the suburbs, are a series of small beaches and a *paseo* lined with some of the best **fish and seafood cafés** in the province. Overlooking the town and port are the formidable Moorish citadels of the **Alcazaba** and **Gibralfaro** – excellent introductions to Islamic architecture, before pressing on to the main sites at Córdoba and Granada.

Arrival

From the **airport**, the **electric train** provides the easiest approach to Málaga (every 30min, 7am–11.45pm; €1). From the Arrivals hall (*Llegadas*), go up one floor to the *Salidas* or Departures hall, take any exit and then turn right to reach a pedestrian overpass at the end of the airport building. Follow the *Ferrocarril* signs and cross the overpass (trolleys allowed) to the unmanned station; you can buy tickets from a ticket machine just next to it or on the train. Make sure that you're on the Málaga platform (the furthest away from you, reached by an underpass) and stay on the train right to the end of the line, the **Centro–Alameda** stop (about a 12min ride). The stop before this is RENFE, the main **train station**, a slightly longer walk into the heart of town (bus #3 runs from here to the centre every 10min or so). Alternatively, city **bus** #19 leaves from a stop outside the Arrivals hall (every 30min until midnight; €1), stopping at the train and bus stations en route to the centre and the Paseo del Parque near the port, from where you can also pick it up in the opposite direction when you're returning to the airport. A **taxi** into town from the rank outside the Arrivals terminal will cost between €9–12 depending on traffic and quantity of baggage.

The **bus station** is just behind the RENFE station, from where all buses (run by a number of different companies) operate. In summer it's best to arrive an hour or so early for the bus to Granada, since tickets can sell out.

Arriving in Málaga by **car**, you'll face the serious problem of parking; using one of the many well-signed car parks around the city centre (see map on p.260; about €1.50 per hour) will save you a tedious search for an on-street parking place. As **theft from cars** is rampant in Málaga, you should strip your vehicle of all valuables before leaving it on the street overnight, or use a hotel with a garage or one of the pay car parks mentioned above. You should also remove any visible stickers bearing a car rental company's name or logo, as these are a magnet for thieves.

Málaga also has the remnants of a **passenger ferry port**, though these days there's a service only to the Spanish enclave of Melilla in Morocco (see "Listings" on p.267). If you're heading for Fes and eastern Morocco, this is a useful connection – particularly so for taking a car over – though most people go for the quicker services at Algeciras (see p.284) and Tarifa (see p.325) to the west.

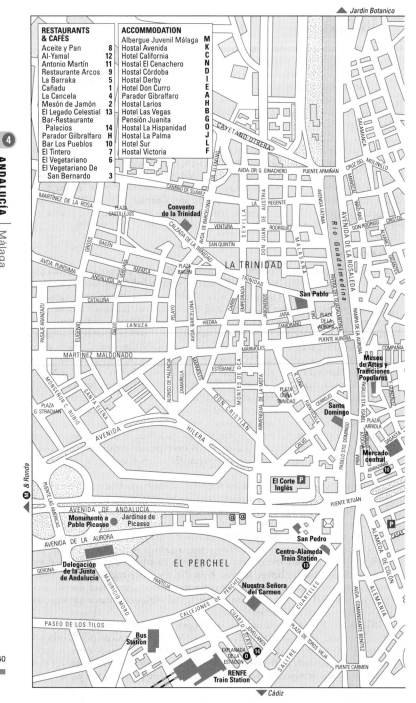

RESTAURANTS & CAFÉS

Aceite y Pan	8
Al-Yamal	12
Antonio Martín	11
Restaurante Arcos	9
La Barraka	5
Cañadu	1
La Cancela	4
Mesón de Jamón	2
El Legado Celestial	13
Bar-Restaurante Palacios	14
Parador Gilbralfaro	H
Bar Los Pueblos	10
El Tintero	7
El Vegetariano	6
El Vegetariano De San Bernardo	3

ACCOMMODATION

Albergue Juvenil Málaga	M
Hostal Avenida	K
Hotel California	C
Hostal El Cenachero	N
Hostal Córdoba	D
Hostal Derby	I
Hotel Don Curro	E
Parador Gibralfaro	A
Hostal Larios	H
Hotel Las Vegas	B
Pensión Juanita	G
Hostal La Hispanidad	O
Hostal La Palma	J
Hotel Sur	L
Hostal Victoria	F

▼ Cádiz

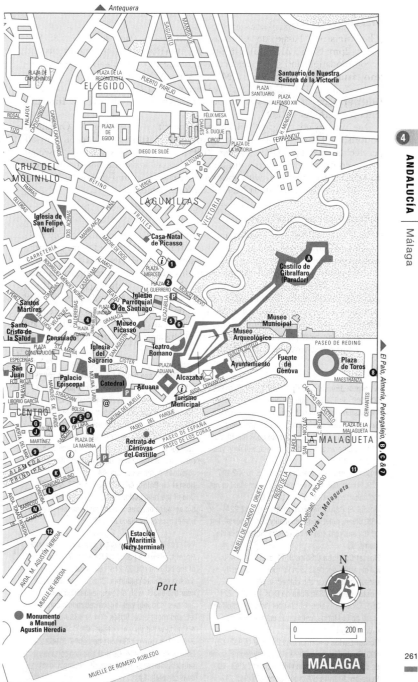

▲ Antequera

PLAZA DE CAPUCHINOS
EL EGIDO
PLAZA DE LA RECONQUISTA
PUERTO PAREJO

Santuario de Nuestra Señora de la Victoria
PLAZA SANTUARIO
PLAZA ALFONSO XIII

ROSAL
TIZO
PALAFOX
CAPUCHINOS
CARRERA CAPUCHINOS
PLAZA DE EGIDO
FÉLIX MESA
CHAVES
S. DUQUE
PLAZA DE LA VICTORIA
FERRANDIZ

DIEGO DE SILOÉ

CRUZ DEL MOLINILLO
REFINO
C. VERDE
ALTOZANO

PARRAS
OLLERIAS
Iglesia de San Felipe Neri
DOS ACERAS
PIÑA
FRAILES
LAGUNILLAS
LA VICTORIA

CARRETERIA
MARIBLANCA
MADRE DE DIOS
ÁLAMOS
Casa Natal de Picasso
Castillo de Gibralfaro (Parador)
A

RODRIGUEZ MENDEZ NÚÑEZ
COMEDIAS
CASAPALMA
PLAZA MERCED
(i) 1
PLAZA M. GUERRERO 2
MÉNDEZ NUÑEZ
P

A PEREZ
Santos Mártires
VELAZQUEZ
STA. LUCIA
CARBÓN
CALDERERIAS
GRANADA
Iglesia Parroquial de Santiago
PLAZA UNCIBAY
3
ALCAZABILLA
5 6

Santo Cristo de la Salud
Consulado
Museo Picasso
4
SAN AGUSTIN

Museo Municipal

PLAZA CONSTITUCIÓN
STA. MARIA
Iglesia del Sagrario
MOLINA LARIO
CISTER
Teatro Romano
Museo Arqueológico
PASEO DE REDING

ESPECERIAS
San Juan (i)
FCO. RIOJA
Palacio Episcopal
Catedral
Aduana
Alcazaba
Ayuntamiento
Fuente de Génova
Plaza de Toros
8

LIBORIO GARCIA
MARQUES DE LARIOS
STRACHAN
BOLSA
@
Turismo Municipal
AVDA. CERVANTES
(i)
MAESTRANZA
CÁNOVAS DEL CASTILLO
CERVANTES

CENTRO
PUERTA DEL MAR
F E D
DE LARA
I
CORTINA DEL MUELLE
PASEO DEL MUELLE
PASEO DEL PARQUE
PLAZA DE LA MALAGUETA

G J
H
SÁNCHEZ
MARTÍNEZ
9
PLAZA DE LA MARINA
(i)
Retrato de Cánovas del Castillo
PASEO DE ESPAÑA
PASEO DE LOS CURAS
LA MALAGUETA
FARO

ALAMEDA
PRINCIPAL
K
P
MUELLE DE RICARDO G. ORUETA
PASEO DE LA FAROLA
SAN

AVDA. TOMAS HEREDIA
BARROSO
TRINIDAD GRUND
L
N
CAMPO
12
PASEO DE LA MALAGUETA
P. MARÍTIMO
11
P. PICASSO

AVDA. M. AGUSTÍN HEREDIA
MUELLE DE HEREDIA
Estación Marítima (ferry terminal)
Playa La Malagueta

Monumento a Manuel Agustín Heredia

Port

N

MUELLE DE ROMERO ROBLEDO

0   200 m

MÁLAGA

▶ El Palo, Almería, Pedregalejo, B, C & I

Information

The **turismo**, Pasaje de Chinitas 4 (Mon–Fri 9am–7pm, Sat & Sun 10am–2pm; ☎952 213 445), can provide information on cultural events and accommodation, and sells a detailed map of the city. There's also a new **turismo municipal**, Plaza de la Marina s/n (Mon–Fri 9am–7pm, Sat–Sun 10am–7pm; ☎952 122 020), at the eastern end of the Alameda Principal, with other branches at the bus station and in the airport arrivals hall. For **Internet** cafés see "Listings" (p.268).

One way to get to grips quickly with the city – including the Gibralfaro Moorish hill fort – is on an **open-topped bus tour**. This hop-on hop-off service is operated by *Malagatour* (☎952 363 133, ⓦwww.citysightseeing -spain.com; €11.50, tickets valid 24hr) and buses leave the bus station every half-hour (9.15am–7pm) with about a dozen stops around the centre, including the cathedral, Plaza de la Merced and the Alameda.

Accommodation

Málaga boasts dozens of **fondas** and **hostales**, so budget rooms are only really hard to come by around Easter and *feria* time in August, and there are some real bargains available in winter. Further upmarket, the town has a large number of central **hotels** of all categories, with some of the more luxurious sited to the east of the bullring, close to the sea. Numerous budget accommodation possibilities are to be found in the area just south of the Alameda Principal and in the streets east and west of c/Marques de Larios, which cuts between the Alameda and Málaga's main square, the Plaza de la Constitución; these are probably the best places to start looking. The nearest **campsite** lies 10km west along the coast towards Torremolinos (see p.273).

Budget

Albergue Juvenil Málaga Plaza de Pio XII ☎952 308 500, ⓕ952 308 500. Modern youth hostel on the western outskirts of town, with double and single rooms, disabled facilities and its own sun terrace. Tends to fill up in season so book ahead. Bus #18 heading west from the Alameda will drop you nearby. €13.35

Hostal Avenida Alameda Principal 5 ☎952 217 729. Functional place right on the Alameda, but not too noisy; some rooms with bath. ➊

Hostal El Cenachero c/Barroso 5 ☎952 224 088. Clean, quiet and reasonably priced *hostal*; left off the seafront end of c/Córdoba. Some en-suite rooms. ➋

Hostal Córdoba c/Bolsa 9–11 ☎952 214 469. Inexpensive, spotless, simple rooms in a family-run establishment near the cathedral. ➊

Hostal Derby c/San Juan de Dios 1 ☎952 221 301. Excellent-value fourth-floor *hostal*, just off the Plaza de la Marina, with some en-suite rooms overlooking the harbour. ➋

Hostal Larios c/Marqués de Larios 9 ☎952 225 490. Central hostel with neat and tidy rooms, some en suite. All rooms come with a/c and TV. ➋–➌

Pensión Juanita c/Alarcón Luján 8 ☎952 213 586. Central and friendly *pensión* offering rooms with and without bath on the fourth floor (with a lift). Large family rooms also available. ➋

Hostal La Hispanidad Explanada de la Estación 5 ☎952 311 135. Facing the train station, this makes a useful sleepover if you've got an early train (or bus) to catch. Labyrinthine place with clean rooms (some with bath) named after different countries of the Americas. ➊

Hostal La Palma c/Martínez 7 ☎952 226 772. One of the best budget places in town with new a/c en-suite doubles in addition to simpler rooms; sometimes gives discounts. ➊

Moderate and expensive

Hotel California Paseo de Sancha 17, 500m east of the bullring ☎952 215 164, ⓦwww.costadel sol.spa.es/hotel/california. Charming small hotel near the beach with a flower-bedecked entrance and safe parking; well-appointed rooms come with a/c and room-safe. Buses #34 or #35 from the Alameda will drop you outside. ➍

Hotel Don Curro c/Sancha de Lara 7 ☎952 227 200, ⓕ952 215 946. Central and comfortable, if rather featureless, hotel with a/c rooms and its own car park. ➎

Parador Gibralfaro Monte de Gibralfaro ☎952 221 902, ⓦwww.parador.es. You won't get a better panoramic view of the coast than from this eagle's nest on top of the Gibralfaro hill; it's quite small as *paradores* go, but has recently been refurbished and has a pool. Own garage. **❼**

Hotel Sur c/Trinidad Grund 13 ☎952 224 803, ⓕ952 212 416. Quiet, efficient and central hotel with secure garage; all rooms have bath and TV. **❸**

Hotel Las Vegas Paseo de Sancha 22 ☎952 217 712, ⓕ952 224 889. Smart hotel, reasonably close to the beach, with its own swimming pool and indoor parking. **❺**

Hostal Victoria c/Sancha de Lara 3 ☎952 224 223. Pleasant, upmarket *hostal* with good-value double and single rooms, just north of the Alameda. **❸**

The City

The city's position, well inside the ring road and east of the airport, means that most visitors to the Costa del Sol rarely visit the heart of Málaga itself. However, a costly facelift centred on an elegant marble-paved and pedestrianized **Calle Marqués de Larios** leading into a revamped Plaza de la Constitución, and the newly created **Museo Picasso**, is aimed at boosting the city's image. Along the coast, plans to create hotel-lined promenades along the beaches to the east and west of the centre are well advanced. Away from the seafront glitz, however, it's to be hoped that the city's unique and vibrant character will survive the development unscathed.

The Alcazaba and Gibralfaro

The impressive **Alcazaba** (Tues–Sun 9.30am–7.30pm; €1.80) is the place to make for if you're killing time between connections, just fifteen minutes' walk from the train or bus stations, and can be clearly seen from most central points. To the left of its entrance stands a recently refurbished **Roman theatre**, accidentally unearthed in 1951 and now a venue for various outdoor entertainments. The citadel, too, is Roman in origin with blocks and columns of marble, interspersed among the Moorish brick of the double- and triple-arched gateways. The main structures, reopened in 2002 following a costly three-year restoration, were begun by the Moors in the eighth century, probably soon after their conquest, but the palace higher up the hill dates from the early decades of the eleventh century. It was the residence of the Arab emirs of Málaga, who carved out an independent kingdom for themselves upon the break-up of the western caliphate. Their independence lasted a mere thirty years, but for a while their kingdom included Granada, Carmona and Jaén. The complex's **palace** was heavily restored in the 1930s, but some fine stuccowork, the ceilings and elegant patios give a flavour of what the palace must once have been. As well as climbing to the palace from the main entrance on c/Acazabilla, it can also be reached by a new lift constructed inside the hill itself. With its entrance on c/Guillen Sotelo, directly behind the *Ayuntamiento*, it transports you effortlessly upwards to emerge in the heart of the structure.

Above the Alcazaba, and connected to it by a long double wall, is the **Gibralfaro castle** (daily 9.30am–7.30pm; €1.80), reached either by climbing a path 250m uphill from the rear of the palace or by taking the road to the right of the Alcazaba, then following a path up through gardens, a ramble of towers, bougainvillea-draped ramparts and sentry-box-shaped Moorish wells. You can also approach from the town side, as the tourist coaches do, but it's not advisable, particularly around dusk after dark. If you want to avoid the climb altogether, bus #35 goes east from the Paseo del Parque to drop you off just outside the entrance to the Gibralfaro. Last used in 1936 during the Civil War, the castle, like the Alcazaba, has been wonderfully restored and now houses an interesting **museum** devoted to its history – a scale model lets you see how the city would have looked in Moorish times. A walk around the battlements affords terrific **views** over the city, while the nearby *parador* (reached by following the road leading out of the castle's car park for 500m) has a pleasant terrace café and restaurant with more fine views.

The cathedral

The city's most conspicuous edifice seen from the heights of the Gibralfaro castle is Málaga's peculiar, unfinished **Catedral** (April–Sept 10am–6.45pm; Oct–March 10am–12.45pm & 4–6.45pm; closed Sun except for services; €2). Constructed between the sixteenth and eighteenth centuries, it is still lacking a tower on the west front because a radical *malagueño* bishop donated the earmarked money to the American War of Independence against the British. Unfortunately – and despite its huge scale – it also lacks any real inspiration and is distinguished only by an intricately carved seventeenth-century *sillería* (choir stall) by noted sculptor Pedro de Mena. However, **Iglesia del Sagrario** (same ticket and hours as cathedral), on the cathedral's northern flank, is worth a look if only for its fine Gothic portal, dating from an earlier, uncompleted Isabelline church. Inside, a restored and magnificent gilded Plateresque retablo, which is brilliantly illuminated during services, is the work of Juan Balmaseda.

Museo Picasso and other museums

Just around the corner from the cathedral on c/San Agustín is the new **Museo Picasso Málaga** (Tues–Thurs 10am–8pm, Fri & Sat 10am–9pm, Sun 10am–8pm; permanent collection €6, temporary collection €4.50, combined ticket for both €8; Ⓦ www.museopicassomalaga.org), housed in the elegant sixteenth-century mansion of the Counts of Buenavista. A source of enormous pride for the city, it opened in 2003, just over one hundred years since Picasso left Málaga at the age of ten and to where he only returned once for an unhappy, fleeting visit in 1901. In later life he toyed with the idea of "sending two lorries full of paintings" to set up a museum in Málaga but vowed never to visit Spain while the ruling General Franco was still alive. Picasso died in 1973 and was outlived by the dictator by two years.

The museum displays 204 works donated by Christine and Bernard Ruiz-Picasso, the artist's daughter-in-law and grandson respectively (the **permanent collection**), while a significant number of limited-period loans from the Ruiz-Picassos and major museums make up the **temporary collection**. Whilst not on a par with the Picasso museums in Paris and Barcelona, the museum does allow you to see some of the lesser known works that Picasso kept for himself or gave away to his lovers, family and friends – rather harshly described as the "less saleable stuff" by one critic.

Among the highlights are, in Room 2, *Olga Koklova con Mantilla* (a portrait of his first wife, draped in a hotel tablecloth) and a moving portrait of his close-cropped son Paul, painted in 1923. Other rooms have canvases from the breadth of Picasso's career including his Blue, Pink and Cubist periods, as well as sculptures in wood, metal and stone and a few ceramics. Two other influential women who figured prominently in the artist's long and turbulent love life are also the subject of powerful images: in the temporary collection *Mujer Sentada en un Sillón (Dora)* is a portrait of the beguiling yet tragic Dora Maar, and in Room 8, *Jacqueline Sentada* is a seated representation of his second wife, Jacqueline Roque.

The museum's basement has the unexpected surprise of **archeological remains** revealed during the construction of the museum. Substantial chunks of a Phoenican city wall and tower dating from the seventh century BC protected these early colonists from attacks by the Iberian tribes. From later periods you can view the remains of a Roman *salazones* factory used to produce the famous *garum*, a fish-based sauce and Roman delicacy, and also the remains of the cellar of the sixteenth-century Palacio de Buenavista. A case nearby displays some of the finds unearthed in the excavations including Phoenician, Greek and Roman pottery fragments and a sixth-century BC Egyptian scarab.

The museum also has a good, if cramped, **bookshop** and an equally cramped **café**, although this spills out onto a pleasant garden terrace in fine weather.

The **Museo de las Bellas Artes** has been made homeless by the new museum and works – including some by Murillo and Zurbarán – are temporarily on display in the Aduana (Tues 3–8pm, Wed–Fri 9am–8pm, Sat & Sun 9am–3pm; free). When refurbishment of the building begins (possibly in 2004) it is likely to be closed for some time; consult the turismo or Ⓦwww .andalucia.org for the latest news.

Picasso was born a couple of hundred metres away from the new museum in the Plaza de la Merced, where the **Casa Natal de Picasso** (Mon–Sat 10am–2pm & 5–8pm, Sun 10am–2pm; free) is home to the Fundación Picasso, a centre for scholars researching the painter's life and work. There's a photo display of Picasso's life here, as well as occasional exhibitions, but despite welcoming staff there's not an awful lot to see. One of the rooms of the house has been restored to resemble how it might have looked when the artist's family lived here: among a number of personal belongings of the Ruiz-Picasso family on view is Picasso's christening gown used for his baptism in the nearby Iglesia de Santiago.

Another recent addition to the city's museums is the **Museo Municipal**, Paseo de Reding 1 (Mon–Sat 10am–8pm; free), which is used to house visiting exhibitions from abroad. It's always worth checking out what's on here, as recent offerings have included major exhibitions of Flemish, Egyptian and Italian art.

The Jardín Botánico La Concepción

A pleasant trip out of town is to the **Jardín Botánico La Concepción** (guided visits Tues–Sun: June–Sept 10am–6.30pm; Oct–May 10am–4.30pm; €2.85), 5km north of the city and signposted off the N331 *autovía*. A spectacular tropical garden, much of which was planted in the nineteenth century, this formerly private estate was founded in the 1850s by Amelia Loring, granddaughter of the British consul, and purchased in 1990 by the Málaga city council, since when it has been open to the public. Specimens on view include exotic blooms, thirty species of palm plus other trees of all shapes and continents such as the Australian banyan with its serpentine aerial roots. To get there, **bus** #2 from the north side of the Alameda will drop you at the gates on Saturday and Sunday, and on weekdays at its terminus 700m short, leaving a ten-minute walk to the entrance. Another way of visiting the garden by bus is to use the Málagatour sightseeing bus (see "Arrival and information" p.262) which has a stop here. A **taxi** ride to La Concepción will cost about €5 one-way from the centre.

Eating and drinking

Málaga has no shortage of **places to eat and drink**, and, though it's hardly a gourmet paradise, the city has a justified reputation for its seafood. It's greatest claim to fame is undoubtedly its **fried fish**, acknowledged as the best in Spain. You'll find many fish restaurants grouped around the Alameda, although for some of the very best you need to head out to the suburbs of Pedregalejo and El Palo, served by bus #11 (from the Paseo del Parque). On the seafront *paseo* at **Pedregalejo**, almost any of the cafés and restaurants will also serve you up terrific seafood. Further on, after the *paseo* disappears, you find yourself amid fishing shacks and smaller, sometimes quite ramshackle, cafés in **El Palo**, an earthier sort of area for the most part, with a beach and huts, and in summer or at weekends an even better place to eat.

Inexpensive restaurants

Aceite y Pan c/Cervantes 5. Facing the eastern wall of the Plaza de Toros, this place serves up a wide variety of seafood. When you've chosen your fish from the chilled display you can eat inside or, more atmospherically, at tables on the pavement. Closed Mon.

Restaurante Arcos Alameda 31. Efficient central place serving all-day *platos combinados* and late-night meals, with a *menú* for €6; for breakfast they also serve *pan tostada* using wholemeal bread.

La Barraka c/Alcazabilla, just north of the Roman Theatre. Good dining place serving up the cheapest three-course *menú* in town for a remarkable €5.50 including wine. There are a few terrace tables on the newly pedestrianized street.

Cañadu Plaza de la Merced 21. Vegetarian place serving a good selection of salad- and pasta-based dishes accompanied by organic wines and beers.

La Cancela c/Denis Belgrano 3, off c/Granada. A *malagueño* institution – *ajo blanco* (chilled almond soup) is a must here – with an economical *menú* and outdoor tables in a pleasant, pedestrianized street.

Mesón de Jamón Plaza María Guerrero 5, just off the Plaza Merced. Good-value *menú* and a selection of ham and cheese tapas.

El Legado Celestial c/Peregrino 2, at the back of the *Correo*. Delightful vegetarian and vegan self-service restaurant with an Asian slant. Standard charge of €6 and the menu includes a large selection of salads and a dozen or so hot dishes as well as some tempting desserts. Drinks are squeezed juices (the lemon, orange, apple & carrot cocktail is recommended) and teas, but no alcohol.

Bar-Restaurante Palacios c/Eslava 4, near the train station. Plain, honest food at bargain prices in a vibrant *comedor popular*, with friendly waiters; specialities include *jamón iberico*, fish *surtido* and a mean *paella*.

Bar Los Pueblos c/Ataranzas, almost opposite the market. Serves satisfying, inexpensive food all day

– bean soups and *estofados* are its specialities; *gazpacho* is served in half-pint glasses.

El Tintero El Palo. Right at the far east end of the seafront, just before the *Club Náutico* (bus #11; ask for "Tintero"), this is a huge beach restaurant where the waiters charge round with plates of fish (all costing the same for a plate – around €5) and you shout for, or grab, anything you like. The fish to go for are, above all, *mero* (a kind of gastronomically evolved cod) and *rosada* (dogfish and catfish), along with Andalucian regulars such as *boquerones* (fresh anchovies), *gambas* (prawns) and *sepia* (cuttlefish). Haute cuisine it certainly isn't, but for sheer entertainment it's a must.

El Vegetariano Pozo del Rey 5, Just north of the Roman Theatre. Atmospheric little veggie place offering a variety of imaginative pasta-, cheese- and salad-based dishes. They have a twin restaurant, *El Vegetariano de San Bernardo* – which despite its name also serves meat dishes – at the junction of c/Niño de Guevara and c/Cañuelos de San Bernardo, a couple of blocks west of Plaza de la Merced. Both closed Sun.

Moderate to expensive restaurants

Al-Yamal c/Blasco de Garay 3, near *Hostal El Cenachero*. Good North African restaurant serving up meat in spicy sauces, couscous and other Arabic dishes.

Antonio Martín Paseo Maritimo ☎952 227 398. One of Málaga's renowned fish restaurants and the traditional haunt of *matadores* celebrating their successes in the nearby bullring. It's fairly pricey and a signature dish such as *rape a la marinera* will set you back around €12.

Parador Gilbralfaro Monte Gilbralfaro ☎952 221 902. Superior dining on the terrace with spectacular views over the coast and town. The *menú* is excellent value at around €24. Ring to book a front line table. If you can't face the climb, a taxi or bus #35 heading east along the Paseo del Parque will take you there.

Bars and cafés

A number of **traditional bars** serve the sweet **Málaga wine** (Falstaff's "sack"), made from muscatel grapes and dispensed from huge barrels; try it with shellfish at *Antigua Casa Guardia*, a great old nineteenth-century bar at the corner of c/Pastora, on the Alameda's north side. The new-season wine, Pedriot, is incredibly sweet; much more palatable is Seco Añejo, which has matured for a year.

Málaga has plenty of good **tapas bars**: *Gorki*, in c/Strachan near the turismo, is a popular place at *aperitivo* time, whilst the diminutive size of the bustling *Orellana* at c/Moreno Monroy 5, slightly north, is in inverse proportion to its reputation as one of the best in town. Other good options include *Bodegas Quitapeñas* (aka *La Manchega*), c/Marín García 4, off the west side of c/Marqués de Larios, the nearby *Bar la Tasca* in the same street and the *Antigua Reja* on Plaza de Uncibay off c/de Méndez Núñez.

Nightlife

You'll find most of Málaga's **nightlife** northeast of the cathedral along and around calles Granada and Beatas and the streets circling the nearby **Plaza de Uncibay** and c/Alamos, as well as in **Malagueta**, south of the bullring. Liveliest at weekends and holidays, dozens of youthful and rather similar disco-bars fill the crowded streets in these areas with a cacophony of sound, and over the summer – it's often dead out of season – the scene spreads out along the seafront to the suburb of **Pedregalejo**. Here, the streets just behind the beach host most of the action, and lots of **discos** and smaller **bars** lie along and off the main street, Juan Sebastián Elcano. Málaga's daily paper, *Sur*, is good for local entertainment **listings** – there's also a weekly English edition *Sur in English* which appears on Fridays and is available from tourist offices and hotels.

Abisinia c/Beatas 39. Lively music bar which gets crowded after midnight.

Anden Plaza de Uncibay. Disco-bar open till very late with a wild crowd.

La Botellita Pasaje Mitjana, slightly west of Plaza de Uncibay, adjacent to *Luna Rubia*. Spanish music, youthful crowd and a wide range of drinks at non-club prices; open till late.

La Chancla on the beach in Pedregalejo. One of a recent rash of bars on the beach; this one bursts forth at midnight and continues until 3am or later.

Cosa Nostra c/Lazcano 5, slightly west of Plaza de Uncibay. Music bar with a mafia theme, which regularly stages live bands (Thurs–Sun 11pm–6am).

Luna Rubia Pasaje Mitjana 4, slightly west of Plaza de Uncibay. Wide range of international sounds and open till dawn.

O'Neill's c/Luis de Velázquez 3, just north of Plaza de la Constitución. Raucous and bustling Irish-style

music bar popular with Málaga's clubbing set.

El Pimpi c/Granada 62. Cavernous multi-roomed nightspot with traditional decor and a wide selection of sounds.

Psicodelia c/Madre de Dios 11, off the north end of Plaza de la Merced. Gay bar with eclectic music background.

Ragtime c/Reding 12, Malagueta. Specializing in jazz, blues and rock, often with live performers.

Siempre Asi c/Convalecientes, north of Plaza Uncibay. Another late-opening bar specializing in Spanish rock and techno. Thurs–Sat 11pm–3.30am.

Vankuver Pasaje Mitjana, just off Plaza de Uncibay. Wide range of international sounds and open until dawn.

ZZ Pub c/Tejón y Rodríguez 6, northwest of Plaza de Uncibay. Predominantly rock sounds on the sound system and often hosts live bands (try Mon & Thurs). Open till dawn at weekends.

Listings

Banks Numerous banks all over town have ATMs, especially along c/Marqués de Larios and on the Plaza de la Constitución. El Corte Inglés (see shopping) will also change currency free of charge.

Car, scooter and motorbike rental Reliable and inexpensive deals are available from Larios Car Hire, c/Roger de Flor 1, at the side of the bus sta-

tion (℡951 092 069, ⊛www.larioscarhire.com). The same company also rents out mountain bikes and a variety of outboard dinghies, boats and trailer-tents.

Consulates Britain, Edificio Eurocom, c/Mauricio Moro Pareto 2 (℡95 235 23 00); Ireland, Avda. Los Boliches s/n, Fuengirola (℡952 475 108); USA,

Apartment 1C, Avda. Juan Gómez 8, Fuengirola (℡ 952 474 891).

Ferries Daily sailings to Melilla in North Africa (Tues–Sat 1pm, Sun & Mon 11pm; 7hr). Tickets from Trasmediterranea, Estación Maritima (℡ 952 061 206, ⓦ www.trasmediterranea.es), south of Plaza de la Marina. Tickets start at around €27 one-way.

Hiking maps A wide range of hiking maps (including CNIG and IGN series) at various scales is available from *Índice*, c/Panaderos 2 (℡ 952 060 503, ⓦ www.ine.es), just north of the Alameda Principal.

Hospital Cruz Roja, Avda. José Silvela 64 ℡ 952 250 450.

Internet Two handy Internet cafés lie close to each other on the south side of Avda. Andalucía, near El Corte Inglés: *Cyber@lameda* (℡ 952 354 222; €2 per hr) at no. 13, a good bar which serves meals, and nearby, at no.11, *Ciber Málaga Café* (℡ 952 040 303; €2.40 per hr). *Navegaweb*, c/Molino Lario 11 beneath the cathedral's shorter tower, is also central (€2.10 per hr).

Laundry The friendly Lavandería Pizarro, Alameda de Colón 18 (℡ 952 222 868), to the south of the Puente Tetuán bridging the Guadalmedina, will wash, dry and fold 5kg of laundry the same day for €10.

Left luggage There are lockers at the train station (daily 7am–10.45pm), and also at the bus station (daily 6.30am–11pm).

Pharmacy A useful pharmacy, Farmacia Caffarena, in Alameda Principal 2 just off the southern end of c/Marqués de Larios (℡ 952 212 858), is open 24hr.

Police The Policía Local are at Avda. La Rosaleda 19 (℡ 952 126 500); in emergencies dial ℡ 092 (local police) or ℡ 091(national).

Post office Avda. de Andalucía 1, on the left across the bridge at the end of the Alameda (Mon–Fri 8.30am–8pm, Sat 8.30am–2pm).

Shopping El Corte Inglés, Avda. de Andalucía, is a great department store and their wine cellar in the basement supermarket has a terrific selection of the nation's wines and spirits. La Mallorquina, Plaza Felix Saenz, is a good place to pick up *malagueño* cheeses, wines, almonds and dried fruit to take home. A useful shopping mall 3 mins' walk from El Corte Inglés is Larios Centro Comercial, Avda. de la Aurora 25, which houses over a hundred shops and stores selling everything from clothes to cosmetics.

Telephones Locutorio at c/Molina Lario 11, near the cathedral (Mon–Sat 9am–9pm, Sun 10am–1pm). However, international calls are more easily made from cardphones in the street. Cards can be purchased from any *estanco* (state tobacco outlet).

El Chorro, Antequera and El Torcal

North of Málaga are two impressive sights: the magnificent limestone **gorge** near **El Chorro** and the prehistoric **dolmen caves** at **Antequera**. Located close to the junction of roads inland to Sevilla, Córdoba and Granada and on direct train lines, both are possible as day-trips from Málaga but also offer overnight accommodation for a more relaxed stay. Approaching Antequera along the old road from Málaga (MA423) via Almogía and Villenueva de la Concepción, you also pass the entrance to the popular natural park famed for its haunting rock sculptures, **El Torcal**.

El Chorro Gorge

Fifty kilometres north of Málaga, **Garganta del Chorro** is an amazing place – an immense five-kilometre-long cleft in a vast limestone massif – which has become andalucía's major centre for rock climbers. The gorge's most stunning feature, however, is a concrete catwalk, *El Camino del Rey*, which threads the length of the gorge, hanging precipitously halfway up its side. Built in the 1920s as part of a hydroelectric scheme, it was one of the wonders of Spain but has fallen into disrepair, and access to the catwalk has finally been cut at each end of the gorge, making it impossible to gain access without a guide and climbing gear (see p.269). It's still possible to explore the rest of the gorge, however, and get a view of the *Camino* by doing the walk described below. A glimpse of both gorge and *Camino* can also be had from any of the trains going north from Málaga – the line, slipping in and out of tunnels, follows the river for a considerable distance along the gorge, before plunging into a last long tunnel just before its head.

Now that easy access to the *Camino* is no longer possible, one of the best ways of viewing the gorge is to follow a twelve-kilometre **walk** out from the village. Follow the road from the train station, signposted *Pantano de Guadalhorce*, reached by crossing over the dam and turning right, then following the road north along the lake towards the hydroelectric plant. After 8km turn right at a junction to reach – after 2km – the bar-restaurant *El Mirador*, poised above a road tunnel and overlooking the various lakes and reservoirs of the Guadalhorce scheme. From the bar (where you should leave any transport) a dirt track on the right heads towards the gorge. Follow this and take the first track on the right after about 700m. This climbs for some 2km to where it splits into two small trails. The trail to the left leads after 300m to a magnificent **viewpoint** over the gorge from where you can see the *Camino del Rey* clinging to the rock face. The right-hand track climbs swiftly to an obvious peak, the Pico de Almochon, with more spectacular views, this time over the lakes of the Embalse de Guadalhorce.

Practicalities

EL CHORRO is served by a couple of daily direct trains (45min), but no buses, from Málaga. Getting there with your own transport, take the MA402 heading east from Málaga towards Álora and turn east at Valle de Abdalajís along the minor MA226, a journey of around 70km. In the village there's an excellent **campsite** (☎952 495 197) with a pool and restaurant, reached by heading downhill to your right for 400m after getting off the train. The campsite also offers bunk beds in an *albergue* (€10 including breakfast) and rents out mountain bikes for €2 per hour. A new hostel, *Refugio La Garganta* (☎952 495 101; €9), passed on the way to the campsite, has slightly cheaper dorm beds and there's a communal kitchen. Near the station, *Bar-Restaurante Garganta del Chorro* (☎952 497 219, Ⓦwww.lagarganta.com; ❺) has pleasant **rooms** inside a converted mill and overlooking a pool. Signs from the station will also direct you 2km to the *Finca La Campana* (mobile ☎626 963 942, Ⓦwww.el -chorro.com), with an economical bunkhouse (€10 per bunk) and a couple of pleasant cottages (❷). Run by Swiss climbers Jean Hofer and his wife Christine, the place also offers courses in rock climbing and caving, rents out mountain bikes (around €10 per day), and can arrange horse-riding and hiking excursions, as well as **guided trips** along the *Camino del Rey* using ropes. For **food**, besides the campsite and the *Garganta*'s decent restaurant, *Bar Isabel* on the station platform does tapas, where there's also a **shop** selling provisions.

Antequera and around

ANTEQUERA, some 55km north of Málaga on the main rail line to Granada, is an ordinary, modern town, but it does have peripheral attractions in a Baroque church, **El Carmen** (Mon & Tues 10.30am–2pm & 5–8pm, Wed–Fri 10am–2pm & 5–11pm, Sat 10am–2pm & 5–8pm, Sun 10am–2pm; €1.30), which houses one of the finest *retablos* in Andalucía, and a group of three prehistoric **dolmen caves**. The most impressive and famous of these is the **Cueva de Menga** (Tues 9am–3pm, Wed–Sat 9am–5.30pm, Sun 9.30am–2.30pm; free), its roof formed by an immense 180-tonne monolith. To reach this, and the nearby **Cueva de Viera** (same hours), take the Granada road out of town – the turning, rather insignificantly signposted, is after about 1km on the left. A third cave, **El Romeral** (same hours), is rather different (and later) in its structure, with a domed ceiling of flat stones; it also lies to the left of the Granada road, 2km further on, behind a sugar factory with a chimney.

If you want to **stay** in Antequera there's a good *pensión, Madrona*, c/Calzada 25 (☎952 840 014; ❶), near the market, which serves excellent food. Alternatively, the new *Hotel Plaza San Sebastián* (☎952 844 239; ❷), with air-conditioned en-suite rooms facing the church of San Sebastián, is a slightly plusher option. Camping is no longer allowed inside the park but there is a **campsite**, *Camping Torcal* (April–Sept), just off the A3310, 6km south of Antequera. Town maps and information on El Torcal are available from a helpful **tourist office** (Mon–Sat 10am–2pm & 5–8pm, Sun 10am–2pm; ☎952 702 505, ⓦwww.turismoantequera.com) on Plaza San Sebastián, alongside the church of the same name.

El Torcal, 13km south of Antequera, is one of the most geologically arresting of Spain's natural parks. A massive high plateau of glaciated limestone tempered by a lush growth of hawthorn, ivy and wild rose, it can be painlessly explored using the **walking routes** that radiate from the centre of the park – trails are outlined in a leaflet available from the **Centro de Recepción** (daily 10am–5pm; ☎952 031 389). The only **waymarked route** (in green) is also the shortest (1.5km) and most popular, and in summer you may find yourself surrounded by gangs of schoolkids who arrive en masse for vaguely educational trips. The best way to see the most surreal sculptures of the limestone formations is on the more peaceful five-kilometre trail, which can only be done with a guide (arrange by phone or on arrival; free). **Buses** run from Málaga (Mon–Fri 5 daily, Sat & Sun 1); ask the driver to drop you at the road for El Torcal from where it's a four-kilometre uphill slog to the visitor centre. If you can afford it, the most convenient way to visit the park, however, is to take the **taxi turistico**, which can be arranged through the tourist office at Antequera; for €18 a taxi will drop you off at the Centro de Recepción and wait until you have completed the green route before returning you to Antequera.

East from Málaga: the coast to Almería

The eastern section of the **Costa del Sol**, from Málaga to Almería, is uninspiring. Though far less developed than the stretch of wall-to-wall concrete from Torremolinos to Marbella in the west, it's not exactly unspoiled. If you're looking for a village and a beach and not much else, then you'll probably want to keep going at least to Almería.

Nerja and around

There's certainly little to tempt anyone to stop before **NERJA**. Nestling in the foothills of the Almijara range, this was a village before it was a resort, so it has some character, and villa development has been shaped around it. The focus of the whitewashed old quarter is the **Bálcon de Europa**, a striking palm-fringed belvedere overlooking the sea. The beaches flanking this are also reasonably attractive, with a series of coves within walking distance if you want to escape the crowds. There are plenty of other great **walks** around Nerja, too, well documented in a locally available guide, *Twelve Walks Around Nerja*, by local resident and hiker Elma Thompson, available from Librería Idiomas, almost opposite the turismo (which also produces its own leaflet on walks).

Nerja's chief tourist attraction, the **Cuevas de Nerja** (daily: July–Aug 10am–2pm & 4–8pm; rest of year closes 6.30pm; Ⓦwww.cuevanerja.com; €5), 3km from the town, are a heavily commercialized series of caverns, impressive in size – and home to the world's longest known **stalactite** at 63m – though otherwise not tremendously interesting. They also contain a number of prehistoric paintings, but these are not presently on public view.

Practicalities

The main **bus station** (actually a stand) is on c/San Miguel at the north end of the town close to Plaza Cantarero; from here hourly buses leave for the *cuevas*. It's a five-minute walk south from the station to the beach and centre – or old town – where you'll find the helpful **turismo**, c/Puerta del Mar 2 (April–Sept daily 10am–2pm & 5.30–8.30pm; Ⓣ952 521 531, Ⓦwww .nerja.org), just to the east of the Balcón de Europa, an attractive, palm-lined belvedere. If you want to explore the area, Club Nautico de Nerja, Avda. Castilla Pérez 2 (Ⓣ952 524 654), west of the centre, rents out **mopeds** and **bikes**, as well as offering horse-riding and diving tuition.

Nerja's main drawback, and a thorny problem through most of the summer, is the scarcity of **accommodation**. There are a dozen or so *hostales*, most reserved well in advance, although some have arrangements with *casas particulares* who mop up the overflow; the turismo can provide a full accommodation list. Central budget choices include the friendly *Hostal Montesol*, c/Pintada 130, just off Plaza Cantarero near the bus station (Ⓣ952 520 014; ❷), and, west of the turismo, the tidy *Hostal Atenbeni*, c/Diputación 12 (Ⓣ952 521 341; ❷), and the very pleasant *Hostal Mena*, c/El Barrio 15 (Ⓣ952 520 541; ❷), with a garden. Overlooking one of Nerja's most popular beaches, Playa de Burriana, are the *Parador Nacional*, c/Almuñécar 8 (Ⓣ952 520 050, Ⓦwww.parador.es; ❻), with a pool set in attractive gardens and a lift to the beach, and the nearby *Hotel Paraiso del Mar* c/Carabeo 22 (Ⓣ952 521 621, Ⓦwww.hotelparaisodelmar.es; ❺), with similar facilities plus a sauna dug out of the cliff face. The **campsite**, *Nerja Camping* (Ⓣ952 529 714; open all year), with pool, bar and restaurant, is 4km east of town along the N340.

Almuñécar

Beyond Nerja the road climbs inland, running high above the coast until it surfaces 11km further on at **LA HERRADURA**, a fishing village-resort suburb of Almuñécar, which is a good place to stop off and swim. If you don't fancy staying in Almuñécar there are also three seafront summer **campsites** here, the best of which is the westernmost *La Herradura* (Ⓣ958 640 056).

ALMUÑÉCAR itself is marred by a number of towering holiday apartments, though if you've been unable to find a room in Nerja you might want to stay here for a night. The rocky grey-sand beaches are rather cramped but the esplanade behind them, with palm-roofed bars (many serving free tapas with each drink) and restaurants, is fun, and the old quarter – clustered around a sixteenth-century castle – attractive.

Half a dozen good-value **fondas** and **hostales** ring the central Plaza de la Rosa in the old part of town; the cosy *Hostal Plaza Damasco*, c/Cerrajos 8 (Ⓣ958 630 165; ❷), and the functional but economical *Hostal Victoria*, Plaza de la Victoria (Ⓣ958 630 022; ❶), are two of the best. If you want to be right by the beach, try *Hotel Epsylon*, Paseo de la China 5 (Ⓣ & Ⓕ958 634 202; ❷), at the extreme western end of the seafront, a giant place with good-value seaview rooms with en-suite facilities.

The **bus station**, which has frequent connections to Málaga and Granada, is located at the junction of Avenida Juan Carlos I and Avenida Fenicia, northeast of the centre, while the **turismo** (Mon–Sat 10am–2pm & 6–9pm; ☎958 631 125, ⓦwww.almunecar-ctropical.org) can be found in an imposing neo-Moorish mansion on Avenida de Europa, behind the Playa San Cristóbal beach at the west end of the town.

A couple of places worth seeking out for **eating and drinking** include *La Tasca*, c/Alta del Mar 10, near Plaza de la Rosa, a small, friendly restaurant serving up tapas, paellas and a wide range of regional dishes; there's a *menú* for €9. For tapas and *platos combinados*, *Bodega Francisco*, c/Real 15, north of Plaza de la Rosa, is a wonderful old bar with barrels stacked up to the ceiling behind the counter and walls covered with ageing *corrida* posters and mounted boars' heads. More upmarket, the excellent *Horno de Candida*, c/Orovia 3, close to the *ayuntamiento*, is the restaurant of the town's hotel and catering school, with a delightful roof terrace.

Salobreña and beyond

SALOBREÑA, 10km further east on the coast road, is a compact and more laid-back version of its neighbour Almuñécar. A white hilltop town gathered beneath the shell of a Moorish castle and surrounded by sugar-cane fields, it's set back 2km from the sea and is thus comparatively little developed. Its beach – a black sandy strip, only partially flanked by hotels and seafront *chiringuitos* – is a far more relaxed affair than that at Almuñécar.

Buses arrive and leave from Plaza de Goya, close to the **turismo** (Mon–Fri 10am–1.30pm & 5–7.30pm, Sat 10am–1.30pm; ☎958 610 314), who can supply a town map to help you find your way around. Along and off Avda. García Lorca, the main avenue that winds down from the town to the beach, are a few **pensiones** and **hostales**: *Pensión Castellmar*, c/Nueva 21 (☎958 610 227; ❶), has the best views, while the slightly cheaper *Pensión Mari Carmen* (☎958 610 906; ❶), over the road, is equally good, with fans in the rooms; both have some en-suite rooms. The most atmospheric **places to eat** are the restaurants and *chiringuitos* lining the seafront, notably *El Peñon*, on the promontory from which it takes its name, serving up great paella, and the nearby – and more reasonably priced – *La Bahía*.

Just before **Motril**, the N323 heads north to Granada, a great route with spectacular views of the Sierra Nevada. The coast road continues towards Almería through an unremarkable sprawl of resorts, of which the most worthwhile for a stopover is **CASTELL DE FERRO**. It's quite sheltered, still preserving remnants of its former existence as a small fishing village, with good, wide beaches to the east and west. Avoid the small town beach fronting a cluster of *hostales* and restaurants, which is litter-strewn and uninspiring. If you want to stay, head for the seafront where there are numerous possibilities: the friendly *Hostal Bahía*, Plaza de España 12 (☎958 656 060; ❶), is worth trying. The closest **campsite** to town is *El Sotillo* (☎958 656 078; June–Sept), near the beach. For the coast further east, see p.403.

The Costa del Sol resorts

West of Málaga – or more correctly, west of Málaga airport – the real **Costa del Sol** gets going, and if you've never seen this level of touristic development it's quite a shock. These are certainly not the kind of resorts you could envisage anywhere else in Europe. The 1960s and 1970s hotel and apartment tower blocks were followed by a second wave of property development in the 80s and 90s, this time villa homes and leisure complexes, funded by massive international investment. It's estimated that 300,000 foreigners now live on the Costa del Sol, the majority of them British and other northern Europeans, though marina developments such as Puerto Banús have also attracted Arab and Russian money.

Approached in the right kind of spirit, it is possible to have fun in **Torremolinos**, nearby **Fuengirola** and, at a price, in **Marbella**. But if you've come to Spain to be in Spain, put on the shades and keep going at least until you reach Estepona.

Torremolinos

The approach to Torremolinos – an easy thirty-minute ride on the electric train from Málaga – is a rather depressing business. There are half-a-dozen beaches, but it's a drab, soulless landscape of kitchenette apartments, new *urbanizaciones* and half-finished developments. In recent years the local council has been trying to give the resort a facelift, the main feature of which has been the construction of a new seafront promenade and the renovation of the old town, the narrow alleyways of which are not without charm.

TORREMOLINOS, to its enduring credit, is certainly different: a vast, grotesque parody of a seaside resort, which in its own kitschy way is fascinating. This bizarre place, lined with sweeping (but crowded) beaches and infinite shopping arcades, crammed with (genuine) Irish pubs and (probably less genuine) real-estate agents, has a large permanent expatriate population of British, Germans and Scandinavians. It's a weird mix, which, in addition to thousands of retired people, has attracted – due to a previous lack of extradition arrangements between Britain and Spain – an extraordinary concentration of British crooks and more recently Russian mafia bosses.

Practicalities

If any of these attracts you – or you're simply curious about the awfulness of the place – it's easy enough to find a place to **stay**. There are plenty of cheap *hostales* sandwiched between the high-rise horrors: *Pensión Beatriz*, c/Peligro 4 (☏952 385 110; ❶), and *Hostal Micaela*, c/Bajondillo 4 (☏952 383 310; ❷), are both near the beach and fairly cheap. The resort's **campsite** (☏952 382 602) lies 3km east of the centre on the main Málaga–Cádiz highway, 500m from the sea; get there by taking the *cercanía* train to the Los Alamos stop or bus "Línea B" from the central Plaza Costa del Sol. The **turismo** in Plaza Pablo Picasso, a little to the north of Plaza Costa del Sol (Mon–Fri 9.30am–1.30pm; ☏952 379 512, ⓦwww.ayto-torremolinos.org), can provide more information on accommodation availability.

The sheer competition between Torremolinos's **restaurants**, **clubs** and **bars** is so intense that if you're prepared to walk round and check a few prices you can have a pretty good night out on remarkably little. The more elegant part of the resort lies to the east at **La Carihuela**, where there's a decent beach, a clutch of good seafood restaurants – the outstanding *El Roqueo* on the seafront is a place to try – and for a bed the pleasant *Hostal Flor Blanco*, Paseo de la Carihuela 41 (☏952 382 071; ❺), lies 50m from the strand with some seaview rooms.

Fuengirola

FUENGIROLA, 14km further west or a fifteen-minute train ride from Torremolinos, is very slightly less developed and infinitely more staid. It's not so conspicuously ugly, but it is distinctly middle-aged and family-oriented. The huge, long beach has been divided up into restaurant-beach strips, each renting out lounge chairs and pedal-boats. At the far end is a windsurfing school.

An efficient **turismo** (Mon–Fri 9.30am–2pm & 4.30–7pm, Sat 10am–1pm; ℡952 467 457, ⓦwww.fuengirola.org) is located at Avda. Jesús S. Rein 6, close to the **train** (℡952 478 540) and **bus** (℡952 475 066) stations. **Rooms** are difficult to find in August, but you could try *Hostal Italia* (℡952 474 193; ❸), off the east side of the focal Plaza de la Constitución, which has en-suite rooms with balcony and room-safe, or the slightly cheaper *Hostal Marbella*, c/Marbella 34, off the west side of the same square (℡952 475 802; ❸). Fuengirola's nearest **campsite** (℡952 474 108; open all year) lies 2km to the east of the centre and is reached by a turn-off near the junction of the N340 and the road to Mijas; bus "Línea Roja" from Avenida Ramón y Cajal on the main Marbella road will take you there. For excellent **seafood**, try the mid-priced *Bar La Paz Garrido* on Avenida de Mijas just north of the Plaza de la Constitución; alternatively, there are two central seafront "eat-as-much-as-you-can for €6" places, *Versalles*, Paseo Maritimo 3, and the nearby *Las Palmeras*, closer to the harbour.

Marbella and around

Sheltered by the hills of the Sierra Blanca, **MARBELLA**, 25km further west, stands in considerable contrast to most of what's come before. Since it attracted the attentions of the smart set in the 1960s the town has zealously polished its reputation as the Costa del Sol's most stylish resort. Glitz comes at a price, of course, and many of the chic restaurants, bars and cafés cash in on the hype and everything costs considerably more. Marbella has the highest per capita income in Europe and more Rolls Royces than any European city apart from London (although many of the classy cars here are rumoured to have been stolen elsewhere and re-registered in Spain). Recently the Spanish government and local police have been exercised by the arrival in Marbella of Russian and Italian mafia bosses who have been buying up property and using Marbella as a base to control their criminal empires, while in an ironic twist of history, there's been a massive return of Arabs to the area, especially since King Fahd of Saudi Arabia built a White House lookalike, complete with adjacent mosque, on the town's outskirts, where he and a veritable army of courtiers and servants spend the summer months.

To be fair, the town has been spared the worst excesses of concrete architecture and also retains the greater part of its **old town** – set back a little from the sea and the new development. Centred on the attractive Plaza de los Naranjos and still partially walled, the old town is hidden from the main road and easy to miss. Slowly, this original quarter is being bought up and turned into clothes boutiques and restaurants, but the process isn't that far advanced. You can still sit in an ordinary bar in a small old square and look up beyond the whitewashed alleyways to the mountains of Ronda.

The seriously rich don't stay in Marbella itself. They secrete themselves away in villas in the surrounding hills or laze around on phenomenally large and luxurious yachts at the marina and casino complex of **Puerto Banús**, 6km out of town to the west. If you're impoverished, this fact is worth noting as it's sometimes possible to find work scrubbing and repairing said yachts – and the pay can be very reasonable. As you'd expect, Puerto Banús has more than its complement of cocktail bars and seafood restaurants, most of them very pricey.

Practicalities

From the new **bus station** (☎952 764 400) in the north of the town, buses #2 or #7 will drop you close by the old town; otherwise it's a twenty-minute walk south along c/Trapiche. Rooms fill up fast here in July and August, when you'll really need to ring ahead to be sure of getting a bed for the night. Marbella's only budget **pensiones** are on the eastern flank of the old town. The lowest priced are the friendly *Hostal Juan*, c/Luna 18 (☎952 779 475; ❶), with some en-suite rooms, and *Hostal Guerra*, Llanos de San Ramón 2 (☎952 774 220; ❷), on opposite sides of the main road as you come into town from the east. At c/Trapiche 2 to the north of the old town, the *Albergue Juvenil-Campamento* (☎952 771 491; €13.35) has even cheaper beds in smart double and four-person en-suite rooms; there's also a **campsite** with a pool. There are plenty of more expensive places, too: *Hostal Enriqueta*, c/los Caballeros 18 (☎952 827 552; ❸), is comfortable and quiet, as is the charming *Hostal La Pilarica*, c/San Cristóbal 31 (☎952 774 252; ❸), in a street lined with potted plants – the work of the enthusiastic residents. The most central upmarket option is *Hotel El Fuerte*, Avda. Severo Ochoa 10 (☎952 861 500, ⓦwww.hotel-elfuerte.es; ❻), with beach access, gardens and a pool. If you need help in finding a room, call in at the **turismo** in Plaza de los Naranjos (Mon–Fri 9am–9pm, Sat 10am–2pm; ☎952 823 550), which provides a street-indexed town map and list of addresses.

Food is available everywhere, although it's worth avoiding the overpriced restaurants on the Plaza de los Naranjos, which turn the whole square into their dining terrace after dark. You're better off seeking out some of Marbella's excellent **tapas bars** such as *Bar Altamarino*, Plaza de Altamarino 4, just west of Plaza de los Naranjos, the nearby *Marisquería La Pesquera*, Plaza de la Victoria s/n, or *El Estrecho*, c/San Lazaro 12, a narrow alley to the southeast of the Plaza de Naranjos where a clutch of other bars is also to be found.

Estepona and around

The coast continues to be upmarket (or "money-raddled", as Laurie Lee put it) until you reach **ESTEPONA**, about 30km west, which is about as Spanish as the resorts round here get. It lacks the enclosed hills that give Marbella character, but the hotel and apartment blocks which sprawl along the front are restrained in size, and there's space to breathe. The fine sand beach has been enlivened a little by a promenade studded with flowers and palms, and, away from the seafront, the old town is very pretty, with cobbled alleyways and two delightful plazas.

The **fish market** is definitely worth seeing: Estepona has one of the biggest fishing fleets on this coast, and the daily dawn ritual in the port, where the returning fleets auction off the fish they've just caught, is worth getting up early for – be there at 6am, since it's all over by 7am.

From May onward, Estepona's **bullfighting** season gets under way in a modern bullring reminiscent of a Henry Moore sculpture. This building has now taken on an additional role as the location for no fewer than four new museums (same hours Mon–Fri 9am–3pm, Sat 10am–2pm; free): the **Museo Etnográfico** (folk museum), the **Museo Arqueológico**, the **Museo Paleontológico** (paleontology) and, perhaps the most interesting, the **Museo Taurino** (bullfighting), with fascinating exhibits and photos underlining the importance of *taurinismo* in Andalucian culture. At the beginning of July, the *Fiesta y Feria* week transforms the place, bringing out whole families in flamenco-style garb.

△ Casares

Beyond Estepona, 8km along the coast, a minor road (the MA546) climbs a further 13km into the hills to **CASARES**, one of the classic *andaluz* White Towns (see p.286). In keeping with the genre, it clings tenaciously to a steep hillside below a castle, and has attracted its fair share of arty types and expatriates. But it remains comparatively little known; bus connections are just about feasible for a day-trip (currently leaving at 11am with a return at 4pm; further details from the turismo).

Further west, 3km inland from the village of Manilva, are some remarkably well-preserved **Roman sulphur baths**. If you want to partake of these health-giving waters you'll have to be prepared to dive into a subterranean cavern, and to put up with the overpowering stench of sulphur, which clings to your swimwear for weeks.

The beaches beyond Estepona have greyish sands (a trademark of the Costa del Sol that always seems surprising – you have to round the corner to the Atlantic coast at Tarifa before you meet yellow sand), and there are more greyish developments before the road turns inland towards San Roque and Gibraltar.

Practicalities

Estepona's **bus station** is on Avenida de España, to the west of the centre behind the seafront. The efficient and centrally located **turismo** (Mon–Fri 9am–6pm, Sat 9.30am–1.30pm; ☎952 800 913) at Avda. San Lorenzo 1, west of the centre near the seafront, will supply town maps and can help you find a **room**. Otherwise, *Hostal El Pilar* (☎952 800 018, ✉pilarhos@anit.es; ❷), on the pretty Plaza Las Flores, and the friendly *Pensión San Miguel*, c/Terraza 16 (☎952 802 616; ❶), with its own bar, are both good bets. Estepona's nearest **campsite** is the seafront *La Chullera III* (☎952 890 320; open all year), 8km south of town, just beyond the village of San Luís de Sabanillas. The town is well provided with **places to eat**, among them a bunch of excellent *freidurías* and *marisquerías* along c/Terraza, the main street which cuts through the centre – try *La Gamba* at no. 25 or *El Chanquete* at no. 86. There's also an excellent *churrería*, *Churrería Parrado*, c/Real 116, to the west of c/Terraza (one block back from, and parallel to, the promenade) – get there before 11am, as they sell out early. Another good place for buying food is the covered **market** on c/Castillo, open in the mornings. Estepona's **nightlife** centres on the pedestrianized c/Real, running behind and parallel to the seafront, whose **clubs** and **music bars** – with plenty of terrace tables on hot summer nights – compete for the custom of a mainly local clientele.

San Roque and La Línea de la Concepción

Situated 35km beyond Estepona in Cádiz province, **SAN ROQUE** was founded by the people of Gibraltar fleeing the British, who had captured the Rock and looted their homes and churches in 1704. They expected to return within months, since the troops had taken the garrison in the name of the Archduke Carlos of Austria, whose rights Britain had been promoting in the War of the Spanish Succession. But it was the British flag that was raised on the conquered territory – and so it has remained. There are few sights, but c/San Felipe leads up from the main square to a **mirador** with views of the Rock of Gibraltar and the hazy coast of Africa beyond.

The **"Spanish-British frontier"** is 8km away at **LA LÍNEA DE LA CONCEPCIÓN**, obscured by San Roque's huge oil refinery. In February 1985 the gates were reopened after a sixteen-year period of Spanish-imposed isolation, and since then crossing has been a routine affair of passport stamping, except for the odd diplomatic flare-up when the Spanish authorities decide to operate a go-slow to annoy the Rock's inhabitants. If you're planning a stay in Gibraltar, be warned that accommodation there is very expensive and in summer the few budget places available are in tremendous demand; La Línea is more realistic, although even here prices have risen and it's now more expensive than neighbouring towns. There are no sights as such; it's just a fishing village that has exploded in size due to the job opportunities in Gibraltar and Algeciras.

Practicalities

At the heart of La Línea is the large, modern and undistinguished Plaza de la Constitución, where you'll find the post office. The **turismo** (Mon–Fri 8am–3pm, Sat 9am–1pm; ☎956 769 950), which provides a useful town map labelling *hostales*, and **bus station** are both on Avda. 20 Abril, to the south of the square. The closest main-line **train station** is San Roque-La Línea, 12km away, from where you can pick up a train to Ronda and beyond. Buses link La Línea with Sevilla (daily; 4hr), Málaga (daily; 2hr 30min), Cádiz via Tarifa (daily; 2hr 30min), and as far as Ayamonte on the Portuguese border (daily; 7hr). Local **buses** from La Línea to Algeciras take thirty minutes, with departures every hour.

Most of the budget **hostales** are also around Plaza de la Constitución. The friendly *La Campana*, c/Carboneras 3, just off the square (☎956 173 059; ❷), is clean and has rooms with baths and TVs; if this is full, try *Hotel-Restaurante Carlos* (☎956 762 135; ❷) almost opposite. Slightly further north, *Hostal Florida*, c/Sol 37 (☎956 171 300; ❷), is another possibility, with a good-value restaurant downstairs, and cheaper rooms are on offer at the basic but clean *Pensión La Perla*, c/Clavel 10 (☎956 769 513; ❶), off the north side of the square.

For **eating and drinking**, the *hostales Campana* and *Carlos* (see above) both have good and economical restaurants. Off the east side of Plaza de la Constitución an archway leads to the smaller, pedestrianized Plaza Cruz de Herrera, which is packed with lots of reasonably priced bars and restaurants, among which *La Nueva Mesón Jerezana* does good *fino* and *jamón*. Slightly north lies c/Real, the main pedestrianized shopping street and another area with plenty of bars and cafés: just off the north side is *La Venta*, c/Dr Villar 19, which does a good-value *menú* and an excellent paella, while to the south at Avda. de España 22 is an excellent *marisquería*, *Bar Aquarium*. C/Clavel, signposted from the main plaza to the Plaza de Toros, has more options: *Bar Alhambra* halfway down is basic and excellent value.

Gibraltar

GIBRALTAR's interest is essentially its novelty: the genuine appeal of the strange, looming physical presence of its rock, and the dubious one of its preservation as one of Britain's last remaining colonies. For most of its history it has existed in a limbo between two worlds without being fully part of either. It's a curious place to visit, not least to witness the bizarre process of its opening to mass tourism from the Costa del Sol. Ironically, this threatens both to destroy Gibraltar's highly individual hybrid society and at the same time to make it much more British, after the fashion of the expatriate communities and huge resorts of the Costa. In recent years the economic boom Gibraltar enjoyed throughout the 1980s, following the reopening of the border with Spain, has started to wane, and the future of the colony – whether its population agrees to it or not – is almost certain to involve closer ties with Spain.

Phoning Gibraltar

From Spain (except Cádiz province): dial 9567 + number.
From Cádiz province: dial 7 + number.
From UK: dial 00 + 350 + number.
From North America: dial 011 + 350 + number.

Arrival, information and orientation

Owing to the relatively scarce and pricey accommodation, you're far better off visiting the Rock on a day-trip from La Línea or Algeciras (see p.284), from where there are buses on the hour and half-hour – a 30min journey. If you have a **car**, don't attempt to bring it to Gibraltar – the queues at the border are always atrocious and parking is a nightmare due to lack of space. Use the underground car parks in La Línea – there's one beneath the central Plaza de la Constitución – and either catch the **bus** (10min past or 20min to the hour; 60p) from the border, or take an easy ten-minute **walk** across part of the airport runway to the town centre.

When you reach it, the town has a necessarily simple layout as it's shoe-horned into the narrow stretch of land on the peninsula's western edge in the shadow of the towering Rock. **Main Street** (La Calle Real) runs for most of the town's length, a couple of blocks back from the port. In and around Main Street are most of the shops, together with many of the British-style pubs and hotels. For information, the main **tourist office** (Mon–Fri 9am–5.30pm; ☎74950, ⓦ www.gibraltar.gi/tourism) is in Duke of Kent House on Cathedral Square, and there are also sub-offices open daily in Casemates Square (Mon–Fri 9am–5.30pm, Sat & Sun 10am–3pm; ☎74982), and in the customs and immigration building at the border (Mon–Fri 9am–4.30pm, Sat 10am–3pm, Sun 10am–1pm; ☎50762). Much of Gibraltar – with the exception of the cut-price booze shops – closes down at the weekend, but the tourist sights remain open, and this can be a quiet time to visit.

The **currency** used here is the **Gibraltar pound** (the same value as the British pound, but different notes and coins); if you pay in euros while in Gibraltar, you generally fork out about five percent more. It's best to change your money once you arrive in Gibraltar, since the exchange rate is slightly higher than in Spain and there's no commission charged. Gibraltar pounds can be hard to change in Spain.

Working in Gibraltar

If you're staying around for a while, Gibraltar is not a bad place to **look for work**, although you'll need to be persistent as competition abounds, and if you're working officially, taxes are high. Gibraltar Radio broadcasts vacancies on Tuesday at about noon, but door-to-door (or site-to-site) footslogging is vital. One possibility is crewing work on a yacht – look at the noticeboard in the chandler's store on Marina Bay, or put an ad there yourself; at the end of summer the yacht marina fills up with boats heading for the **Canaries**, **Madeira** and the **West Indies**, and many take on crew to work in exchange for passage.

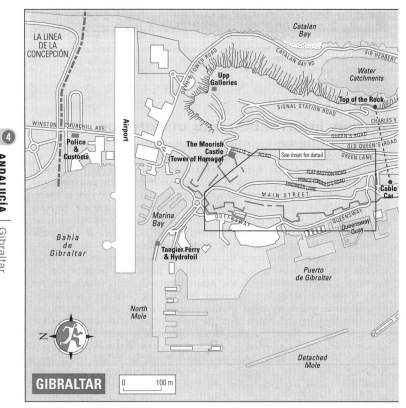

Accommodation

Shortage of space on the rock means that **places to stay** are at a premium. The only remotely budget beds are at the friendly *Toc H Hostel* on Line Wall Rd (☎73431; about £6.50 a person) – and these are none too comfortable and almost always occupied by long-term residents – or at the basic *Emile Youth Hostel* at the Montagu Bastion, Line Wall Rd (☎51106; about £12 for a dorm bed or £25 for a double room without bath; prices include breakfast). Otherwise, you're going to have to pay normal British hotel prices: the next step up includes the *Queen's Hotel* on Boyd St (☎74000, Ⓦwww.queenshotel.gi), the *Bristol* in Cathedral Square (☎76800, Ⓦwww.Gibraltar.gi/bristolhotel), or the slightly cheaper *Cannon Hotel*, 9 Cannon Lane, near the cathedral (☎51711, Ⓦwww.cannonhotel.gi), all charging £35–65 for a double room.

If this tempts you to find a bit of sand to bed down on, forget it: no **camping** is allowed and if you're caught sleeping rough or inhabiting abandoned bunkers, you are more than likely to be arrested and fined. This law is enforced by Gibraltar and Ministry of Defence police, and raids of the beaches are frequent.

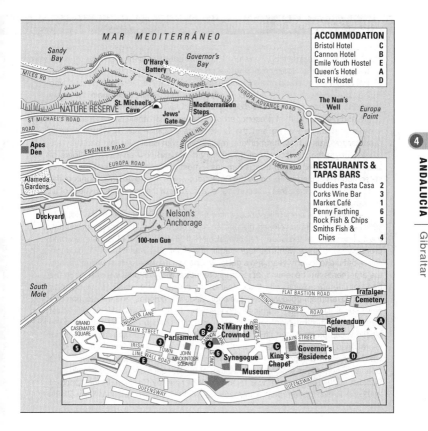

Around the Rock

From near the end of Main Street you can hop on a **cable car** (daily 10am–6pm, last trip down 5.45pm; £6.50 return) which will carry you up to the summit – **The Top of the Rock** as it's logically known – via **Apes' Den** halfway up, a fairly reliable viewing point to see the tailless monkeys and hear the guides explain their legend. To enter the Nature Reserve (as the area at the top of the Rock, containing the Apes' Den, St Michael's Cave and other sights, is designated) you should buy an inclusive ticket for £9, which includes entry to the reserve plus return cable-car ride; if you walk up or get a taxi, entrance to the reserve will cost £7. From The Top of the Rock you can look over the Strait of Gibraltar to the Atlas Mountains of Morocco and down to the town, the elaborate water catchment system cut into the side of the rock, and ponder whether it's worth heading for one of the beaches.

The cable car makes a stop at the Apes' Den en route to The Top of the Rock, from where it's an easy walk south along St Michael's Road through the Nature Reserve – so titled because of the 600-plus plant and tree species which are to be found in this zone – to **Saint Michael's Cave**, an immense natural cavern which led ancient people to believe the rock was hollow and gave rise to its old name of *Mons Calpe* (Hollow Mountain). The cave was used

British sovereignty in Gibraltar

Sovereignty of the Rock (a land area smaller than the city of Algeciras across the water) will doubtless eventually return to Spain, but at present a stalemate exists between Britain and Spain regarding the colony's future. For Britain it's a question of divesting itself of the colony without incurring the wrath of Gibraltar's citizens who are rabidly opposed to any further involvement with Spain. For Spain there are unsettling parallels with the *presidios* (Spanish enclaves) on the Moroccan coast at Ceuta and Melilla – both at present part of Andalucía. Nonetheless, the British presence is in practice waning and the British Foreign Office clearly wants to steer Gibraltar towards a new, harmonious relationship with Spain. To this end they are running down the significance of the military base, and now only a token force of less than a hundred British troops remains – most of these working in a top-secret hi-tech bunker buried deep inside the Rock from where the Royal Navy monitors the sea traffic through the Strait (accounting for a quarter of the world's movement of all shipping).

The Gibraltarians are firmly opposed to a return to Spanish control of the Rock. In 1967, just before Franco closed the border in the hope of forcing a quick agreement, the colony voted on the issue – rejecting it by 12,138 votes to 44. Most people would probably sympathize with that vote – against a Spain that was then still a dictatorship – but close to forty years have gone by, Spanish democracy is now secure, and the arguments are becoming increasingly tenuous. May 1996 saw a change in the trend of internal politics, with the defeat of the colony's pugnaciously anti-Spanish Labour government (following two previous landslide victories) and the election of a new Social Democratic administration led by Peter Caruana. However, whilst Caruana talked of opening up a more constructive dialogue with Spain during the election campaign, once in control he soon began to voice the traditional Gibraltarian paranoia. His stance has caused some dismay in Madrid and London, who were both behind Spain's offer in 1997 to give the colony the status of a Spanish autonomous region (similar to that of the Basques and Catalans) inside the Spanish state. The proposal was rejected out of hand by Caruana. In the spring of 2002 the British government – perhaps partly due to British premier Tony Blair's

during the last war as a bomb-proof military hospital and nowadays hosts occasional concerts. If you're adventurous you can arrange at the tourist office for a guided visit to Lower Saint Michael's Cave, a series of chambers going deeper down and ending in an underground lake.

Although you can take the cable car both ways, it's an interesting walk up from the town via Willis's Road to visit the **Tower of Homage**. Dating from the fourteenth century, this is the most visible surviving remnant of the old **Moorish Castle**. Further up you'll find the **Upper Galleries** (aka the Great Siege Tunnels), blasted out of the rock during the Great Siege of 1779–82, in order to point guns down at the Spanish lines.

To walk down, a twenty-minute descent, follow Signal Station Road and St Michael's Road to O'Hara's Road and the **Mediterranean Steps** – a very steep descent most of the way down the east side, turning the southern corner of the Rock. You'll pass through the Jews' Gate and into Engineer Road, from where the return to town is through the Alameda Gardens and past the **Trafalgar Cemetery**, overgrown and evocative, with a good line in imperial epitaphs. A grand tour of the Rock takes a half to a full day, and all sites on it are open from 9.30am to 7pm in summer, 10am to 5.30pm in winter.

Back **in town**, incorporated into the **Gibraltar Museum**, in Bomb House Lane (Mon–Fri 10am–6pm, Sat 10am–2pm; £2), are two well-preserved and

close relationship with Spanish leader José María Aznar – moved Gibraltar up the political agenda and it was suggested that a referendum on a new power-sharing agreement with Spain could be put to the Gibraltar voters within a year. Scenting what it saw as a sell-out, the Gibraltar governing council, led by Caruana, began a campaign to kill any idea of a deal with Spain, and, against the British government's wishes, announced that the Gibraltar administration would hold its own referendum on the issue. The predictable result turned out to be a 99 percent vote against any sharing of sovereignty with Spain. This left the Blair government with no real hope of making progress, given that the Gibraltarians must approve any deal. It now seems that the issue has resumed its traditional place on the political back burner, with the British government attempting to persuade the Rock's inhabitants that any future developments must involve Spain.

What most outsiders don't realize about the political situation is that the Gibraltarians feel very vulnerable, caught between the interests of two big states; they are well aware that both governments' concerns are primarily strategic and political rather than with the wishes of the people of Gibraltar. Until very recently people were sent over from Britain to fill all the top civil service and Ministry of Defence jobs, a practice which, to a lesser degree, still continues – the present governor is David Durie, a senior Whitehall civil servant. Large parts of the Rock are no-go areas for "natives"; the South District in particular being taken up by military facilities. Local people also protest about the Royal Navy nuclear-powered submarines which dock regularly at the naval base, and secrecy surrounds the issue of whether nuclear warheads and/or chemical and biological weapons are stored in the arsenal, probably deep inside the Rock itself. This whole issue came to a head in the late summer of 2000 when the Royal Navy submarine *Tireless* limped into Gibraltar with a problem in its nuclear reactor. Tension mounted over the following months as the populations of the towns surrounding the Bay of Algeciras staged angry demonstrations sparked by the British government's refusal to give any information about the potential dangers or when the sub would be leaving. It finally departed in May 2001, but the affair was a public relations disaster for Britain and Gibraltar and caused serious diplomatic strains between Madrid and London.

beautiful fourteenth-century **Moorish Baths**. The museum, along with **Nelson's Anchorage** on Rosia Road – where the body of the naval commander was brought ashore following the Battle of Trafalgar – the **casino** and the **miniature golf**, is about the extent of the sightseeing, though you may also be interested in daily dolphin-spotting **boat trips**, run by companies operating from Marina Bay (Nautilus ☎73400, Dolphin World mobile ☎54481000) and Queensway Quay (Nimo ☎73719). Trips cost a steep £15–20 depending on the company; the cheaper Nimo charges £7 for kids, whilst the other two allow one under-12 to travel free with each adult. You should ring first to book places or ask the tourist office to do it for you.

Gibraltar has plans to reclaim an area equivalent to that of the present town from the sea, and is currently doing feasibility surveys on pumping up sand from the seabed. But at present there is just the one tiny fishing village at **Catalan Bay**, which is where you'll find the **beach** with most character. It's easily reached by following Devil's Tower Road from near the airport (a 20min walk) or bus #4 from the centre. The inhabitants of the village like to think of themselves as very distinct from the townies on the other side of the Rock. About 48km of recent tunnels, or **galleries**, have been bored through the Rock for military purposes – these are now being adapted to help solve the territory's traffic-flow crisis brought on by the extraordinary surplus of cars.

Eating and drinking

Restaurants are far more plentiful than places to stay, though by Spanish standards they are still relatively expensive: pub snacks or fish and chips are reliable standbys. Main Street is crowded with touristy places, among which *Smiths Fish and Chip Shop*, at no. 295 near the Convent, is worth a try. Other good choices are the *Penny Farthing* on King Street, always busy for home-cooked food at reasonable prices, and *Buddies Pasta Casa* on Cannon Lane, serving up decent pasta in all its varieties. *Corks Wine Bar*, 79 Irish Town, is a pleasant place for light meals, and the *Market Café* in the public market (off Casemates Square) serves up traditional English breakfasts all day long. Nearby, on Casemates Square itself, *Rock Fish & Chips*, a friendly Moroccan-run chip shop, makes an excellent job of the British national dish (eat-in or take away).

Pubs all tend to mimic traditional English styles (and prices), the difference being that they are often open into the wee hours; another drawback is that few of them have terraces and many resemble saunas in high summer. For pub food, the *Royal Calpe*, 176 Main Street, *Calpe Hounds*, Cornwall's Lane, and *Clipper*, 78 Irish Town, are among the best. The more obvious pubs grouped together on Main Street, however, tend to be rowdy and are often full of squaddies and visiting UK or US sailors at night. For a quieter alternative, try the *Cannon Bar* in Cannon Lane beside the cathedral, or the *Piccadilly Gardens Bar*, 3 Rosia Rd, just beyond the Referendum Gates. The *Star Bar*, 12 Parliament Lane, off the west side of Main Street near the Post Office, is reputedly Gibraltar's oldest and was a favourite hang-out of Lord Nelson when it traded under its original name, *La Estrella*.

Onward travel

One decidedly functional attraction of Gibraltar is its role as a port for **Morocco**. A catamaran service, the *Tanger Jet*, sails to Tangier on Fridays at 6pm, taking one hour. The return trip from Tangier is on Sundays at 5.30pm (local time). The number of sailings may increase in future and you should check with the agent (see below) for the current timetable. Tickets cost £18 one way and £30 return for a foot passenger, and £46 single and £92 return for a car. Tickets and updated timetables are available from the agent Turner, 65/67 Irish Town (☎78305, ✉ turner@gibnynex.gi). Turner also act as agents for one- and two-day excursions to Tangier (sailing from Algeciras or Tarifa) by catamaran operated by FRS (ⓦ www.frs.es), including a sightseeing tour, lunch and hotel (for the two-day option) costing around €48 for the one day, and €84 for the two-day package.

Bland Travel, Cloister Building, Irish Town (☎79200, ✉ henry@bland.gi; closed Sat & Sun) is the leading travel agent in Gibraltar and can assist with British Airways (two daily) and Monarch Airlines (one daily) flights to London. There are currently no flights between Gibraltar and Morocco.

Algeciras

ALGECIRAS occupies the far side of the bay from Gibraltar, spewing out smoke and pollution in the direction of the Rock. The last town of the Spanish Mediterranean, it must once have been an elegant resort; today it's unabashedly a port and industrial centre, its suburbs extending on all sides. When Franco closed the border with Gibraltar at La Línea it was Algeciras that he decided to develop to absorb the Spanish workers formerly employed in the British naval dockyards, thus breaking the area's dependence on the Rock.

Moroccans in Algeciras

It's easy to take a romantic view of the exotic hustle and bustle in the port area, but there's a miserable story behind some of it. Algeciras is the main port for Moroccan migrant workers, who drive home every year during their holidays from the factories, farms and mines of northern Europe and the new intensive fruit and vegetable plantations of Almería. Half a million cross Spain from the end of June to the beginning of August in perilously overloaded vehicles, frequently becoming victims of all levels of racial discrimination (they are still referred to as *los Moros*), from being ripped off to being violently attacked and robbed.

Most travellers are scathing about the city's ugliness, and unless you're waiting for a bus or train, or heading for Morocco, there's admittedly little reason to stop. Yet some touch of colour is added by the groups of Moroccans in transit, dressed in flowing *jallabahs* and slippers, and lugging unbelievable amounts of possessions (see box above). Algeciras has a real port atmosphere, and even passing through it's hard to resist the urge to get on a boat south, if only for a couple of days in Tangier. Once you start to explore, you'll also discover that the old town has some very attractive corners which seem barely to have changed in fifty years, especially around the Plaza Alta.

Practicalities

If you're heading for a morning ferry, or want to stay awhile, Algeciras has plenty of budget **hostales** and **pensiones** in the grid of streets to the north of the railway line between the port and the train station. There are several in c/Duque de Almodóvar, c/José Santacana and c/Rafael de Muro. Try the basic but clean *Levante*, c/Duque de Almodóvar 21 (T956 651 505; ❶), or the more comfortable *González*, c/José Santacana 7 (T956 652 843; ❶), which has some rooms with bath. On Plaza Palma, the market square slightly in from the port, the surprisingly spruce *Hostal Nuestra Señora de la Palma* (T956 632 481; ❶) is another good option with en-suite rooms. Algeciras's luxurious **youth hostel**, Ctra. Nacional 340 (T956 679 060; €13.35), has a pool, tennis courts and double rooms with bath, but lies 8km west of town on the Tarifa road; buses heading for Tarifa will drop you there if you ask. Should you have trouble finding a place to stay, pick up a town plan and check out the full accommodation list in the **turismo**, c/Juan de la Cierva (official hours Mon–Fri 9am–2pm, but frequently fails to open; T956 572 636; English spoken), on the south side of the train track near the port. Prices tend to go up dramatically in high season, but lots of simple *casas de huéspedes* are clustered round the market.

The port area also has plenty of **places to eat**. Across the train line from the turismo and invariably crowded is the good-value *Casa Gil* at c/Sigismundo Moret 2. Fifty metres further along the same street, *Casa Sánchez*, at the corner of c/Río, is another good place with a *menú*, and they also have a few **rooms** (❶). The bustling and colourful daily **market** in the nearby Plaza Palma is a useful place to buy food for travelling or picnics. Good **tapas** are on offer at *Bar Castro*, c/Castillo 14, just north of the market and en route uphill to the elegant main square, **Plaza Alta**, where there are more bars, cafés and *heladerías*.

Onward travel

Morocco is easily visited from Algeciras: in summer there are hourly ferry **crossings to Tangier** daily; 1hr 10min), and at least ten to the Spanish *presidio* of **Ceuta** (daily; 1hr 30min), little more than a Spanish Gibraltar with a brisk business in duty-free goods, but a relatively painless way to enter Morocco. For up-to-date information on hydrofoils and fast-ferries check on the Transafric website below or Ⓦwww.euroferrys.com and Ⓦwww.frs.es. **Tickets** cost €23.30 one-way to Tangier and €21.05 to Ceuta, and are sold at the scores of travel agents along the waterfront and on most approach roads; they all cost the same, though some places may give you a better rate of exchange than others if you want to pay in foreign currency. On the harbourfront, Transmediterranea (Ⓣ956 583 400, Ⓦwww.transmediterranea.es) and the turismo (see p.285) can provide up-to-date information on **timetable** changes. The same information is also available from Viajes Transafric, Avda. Marina 4 (Ⓣ956 654 311; Ⓦwww.transafric.com), near the port, who are reliable and also do a daily all-inclusive **day-trip to Tangier** by fast-ferry which includes a guided tour, lunch and time for shopping for €45.

Wait till Tangier – or if you're going via Ceuta, Tetouan – before buying any **Moroccan currency**; rates in the embarkation building kiosks are very poor. Make sure that your ticket is for the next ferry, and beware the ticket sellers who congregate near the dock entrance wearing official Ceuta/Tangier badges: they add a whopping "commission" to the normal price of a ticket.

At Algeciras the **train line** begins again, heading north to Ronda, Córdoba and Madrid. The route to Ronda – one of the best rail journeys in Andalucía – is detailed below; there are four departures a day. For Madrid (and Paris) there's a night express, currently leaving at 11pm, and also Linebus/Iberbus coaches to Paris and London. For Málaga, six daily **buses** leave from the *Empresa Portillo*, Avenida Virgen del Carmen on the waterfront (Ⓣ956 651 055); from here, too, there are less frequent, direct connections to Granada and Almería. Buses to Barcelona via Alicante and Valencia are operated by Bacoma (Ⓣ902 422 242) and leave from outside the harbour offices, but the journey is appallingly slow at 21 hours, with a change in Málaga. For buses to Tarifa, Cádiz, Sevilla, Madrid and most other destinations you'll need the **main bus station** (Ⓣ956 653 456), in c/San Bernardo, behind the port, next to *Hotel Octavio* and just short of the **train station**: to get there follow the train tracks. The bus to La Línea also goes every half-hour from here.

Ronda and the White Towns

Andalucía is dotted with small, brilliantly whitewashed settlements – the **Pueblos Blancos** or "White Towns" – most often straggling up hillsides towards a castle or towered church. Places like **Mijas**, up behind Fuengirola, are solidly on the tourist trail, but even here the natural beauty is undeniable. All of them look great from a distance, though many are rather less interesting on arrival. Arguably the best lie in a roughly triangular area between Málaga, Algeciras and Sevilla; at its centre, in a region of wild, mountainous beauty, is the spectacular town of **Ronda**.

To Ronda from the coast

Of several possible approaches to Ronda from the coast, the stunningly scenic route up from Algeciras is the most rewarding – and worth going out of your way to experience. From Málaga, most of the buses to Ronda follow the coastal highway to San Pedro before turning into the mountains via the modern A376 *autovía*: dramatic enough, but rather a bleak route, with no villages and only limited views of the sombre rock face of the Serranía – an alternative route, via Álora and Ardales, is far more attractive and is taken by a couple of daily buses from Málaga. The train ride up from Málaga is better, with three connecting services daily, including a convenient 6.05pm departure after the last bus leaves.

The **Algeciras route** – via Gaucín – is possible by either bus or train (a spectacularly scenic option), or, if you've time and energy, can be walked in four or five days. En route, you're always within reach of a river and there's a series of hill towns, each one visible from the next, to provide targets for the day. Casares is almost on the route, but more easily reached from Estepona (see p.275).

Castellar de la Frontera

The first White Town on the route proper is **CASTELLAR DE LA FRONTERA**, 27km north from Algeciras, a bizarre village within a thirteenth-century castle, whose population, in accord with some grandiose scheme, was moved downriver in 1971 to the "new" town of Nuevo Castellar, whose modern square frames an image of their former castle home on the hill behind. The relocation was subsequently dropped and a few villagers moved back to their old houses, but most of them were taken over by retired hippies (mainly affluent Germans). The result didn't entirely work, with suspicion from the locals and hostile exclusivity from some of the new arrivals fuelling tensions which remain today. The only **place to stay** inside the castle walls is *Casas Rurales Castillo* (☎956 236 620, ⓦ www.cadiz.org/tugasa; ❹), which consists of a number of restored village houses, or there's the more economical *Hostal El Pilar* c/León Esquivel 4 (☎956 693 022; ❷), below in the dull new town. There's a **bar** near the entrance to the castle and, within the walls, *El Aljibe* is a decent traditional **restaurant** attached to the *Casas Rurales* accommodation (see above); an average *venta* at the start of the climb to the village on the main A369 is the only other food option, otherwise there's not a lot more to detain you.

Jimena de la Frontera and Gaucín

JIMENA DE LA FRONTERA, 20km further north along the A369, is a far larger and more open hill town, rising to a grand Moorish castle with a triple-gateway entrance. There are several **bars** and, among a number of **places to stay**, a beautiful old *fonda* (which has no sign – ask for the *Casa María*, c/Sevilla 36; ❶). More upmarket places include the charming and friendly *Posada La Casa Grande*, c/Fuentenueva 42, a street off the top of c/Sevilla (☎956 640 578, ⓦ www.posadalacasagrande.com; ❷), where rooms with and without bath are located in three knocked-together and tastefully restored village houses. They also rent out fully-equipped apartments (❸) and will accept a one-night stay; keep an eye out for their pet iguana who lives in the hotel's library. The more expensive *Hostal El Anon* (☎956 640 113, ⓔ elanon@mx3redistb.es; ❸), with restaurant and rooftop pool at c/Consuelo 32, is another possibility, and a little way out of town near the train station, *Hostal Los Arcos* (☎956 640 328; ❷) also has en-suite rooms. Jimena's new **campsite** *Camping Los Alcornocales* (☎956 640 060, ⓦ www.arrakis.es/-camping) occupies a suberb location with great views on the north side of town (reached by following c/Sevilla to its end), and has its own restaurant. Other **places to eat** include *Bar Ventorillo*, at the foot of c/Sevilla, with a *menú* for €7, and the equally good *Restaurante Bar Cuenca*, de los Deportes, on the way into town, which also serves tapas and has a pretty terrace patio at the rear. *Café Lorca*, c/Sevilla 18 and a little further up from *Bar Ventorillo*, is a relaxing, modern English-run wine bar, with soothing sounds, and shepherd's pie and lasagne-type home cooking.

Beyond Jimena, it's 23km further along the A369 – or on foot a sixteen -kilometre climb – through woods of cork oak and olive groves to reach **GAUCÍN**; along the way there are bars at San Pablo de Buceite, a hamlet about 7km out. Gaucín, almost a mountain village, commands tremendous views (to Gibraltar and the Moroccan coast on a very clear day), and makes a great place to stop over. There are **rooms** and food to be had at *Hostal Moncada*, c/Luís Armiñian (☎952 151 324; ❶), next to the *gasolinera* as you enter the village from Jimena (get a room at the back for a view). Gaucín's charming *fonda*, the *Nacional*, c/San Juan de Dios 8, closed its doors a few years back after 125 years in business, but is steeped in history and still serves **meals**.

You can reach the village by bus, but far more rewarding is the thirteen -kilometre, mostly uphill, walk from its **train station**. Though it's now known as Gaucín, this station is actually at El Colmenar, on the fringes of the Cortés nature reserve: if you need to rest up before the hike (getting on for 3hr) there's a **hostal**, *Bar-Restaurante Flores* (☎952 153 026; ❶), and several bars here. Should you chicken out, the *hostal* can arrange a taxi ride (about €12 one-way).

The train line between Gaucín and Ronda passes through a handful of tiny villages. En route, you can stop off at the station of Benaoján-Montejaque: from here it's an hour's trek to the prehistoric **Cueva de la Pileta** (see p.292). From Benaoján, Ronda is just three stops (and thirty minutes) down the line.

Ronda

Rising amid a ring of dark, angular mountains, the full natural drama of **RONDA** is best appreciated as you enter the town. Built on an isolated ridge of the sierra, it's split in half by a gaping river gorge, **El Tajo**, which drops sheer for 130m on three sides. Still more spectacular, the gorge is spanned by a stupendous eighteenth-century arched bridge, the **Puente Nuevo**, while tall whitewashed houses lean from its precipitous edges.

Much of the attraction of Ronda lies in this extraordinary view, or in walking down by the Río Guadalévin, following one of the donkey tracks through the rich green valley. Birdwatchers should look out for the lesser kestrels nesting in and launching themselves from the cliffs beneath the Alameda park; lower down you can spot crag martins. The town itself is also of interest with a number of museums and, surprisingly, has sacrificed little of its character to the flow of day-trippers from the Costa del Sol.

Arrival, information and accommodation

Ronda's **train** and **bus stations** are both in the Mercadillo quarter to the northeast of the bullring. Trains arrive on Avenida Andalucía, a ten-minute walk or easy bus ride from the centre, and all the bus companies use the terminal close by on Plaza Redondo. The **turismo** (Mon–Fri 9am–8pm, Sat & Sun 10am–2pm; ☎952 871 272) is at the northern end of the focal Plaza de España, and can help with accommodation and provide a map. A useful **municipal tourist office** (Mon–Fri 9.30am–8pm, Sat & Sun 10am–2pm & 3.30–7.30pm; ☎952 187 119) has opened nearby, opposite the south side of the bullring. Ronda's official **website** ⓦwww.turismoderonda.es is a useful source of information on all aspects of the town.

Most of the **places to stay** are also in the Mercadillo quarter, within easy walking distance of the focal Plaza de España. Ronda's **campsite**, *Camping El Sur* (☎952 875 939), with pool, bar and restaurant, lies 2km out of town along the road to Algeciras.

Hostal Águilar c/Naranja 28 ☎952 871 994. Clean, welcoming, family-run *hostal* for rooms with and without bath, off c/Cristo. ❶

Alavera de los Baños c/San Miguel s/n, next door to the Baños Arabes ☎ & ℻952 879 143, ⓦwww.andalucia.com/alavera. Enchanting small hotel with stylish rooms, garden, pool, restaurant and views from rear rooms to grazing sheep on the hill across the river. Breakfast included. ❸

Hostal Andalucía c/Martínez Astein 19 ☎952 875 450. Pleasant en-suite rooms in leafy surroundings opposite the train station. ❷

Hotel Colón, c/Pozo 1, on the Plaza de la Merced. Charming small hotel with en-suite facilities and – in rooms 301 & 302 – your own spacious roof terrace. ❷

En Frente Arte c/Real 40 ☎952 879 088, ⓦwww.enfrentearte.com. Stylish new hotel inside a restored mansion with distinctive and elegant rooms. Breakfast is included in the price, as are soft drinks and draught beer. Additional luxuries include a delightful garden pool, games room, free sauna and Internet access. Reductions for longer stays ❹

Hostal González c/San Vincente de Paúl 3, west of the centre ☎952 871 445. Friendly family *hostal* with impeccable budget rooms (singles

€10, doubles around €16) sharing bath. When not too busy they may even collect you from the train or bus stations. ❶

Hotel La Española c/José Aparicio 3 ☎952 871 052, ⓦwww.ronda.net/usuar/laespanola. Cosy rooms with bath in the alley behind the turismo, some with amazing views, plus a terrace restaurant. ❹

Parador de Ronda Plaza de España ☎952 877 500, ⓦwww.parador.es. Ronda's imposing *parador* has spectacular views overlooking El Tajo, plus a pool, terrace bar and restaurant. ❻

Los Pastores 3km outside town along the Algeciras road (A369), on the right with a red sign ☎952 114 464, ⓦwww.lospastores.com. Very pleasant rural option in a Dutch-owned former farmhouse surrounded by fine walking country. Three en-suite doubles; breakfast available. ❷

Hostal Ronda Sol c/Cristo 11, near the intersection with c/Sevilla ☎952 874 497. Good-value budget *hostal* for rooms with shared bath, but check what you're offered as two interior rooms (lacking windows) are a bit claustrophobic. ❶

Hotel San Francisco c/Cabrera-Prim 18 ☎952 873 299, ℻952 873 299. Former *hostal* upgraded to a pleasant small hotel with attractive a/c rooms and own *cafetería*. Breakfast included. ❷

The Town

Ronda divides into three parts: on the south side of the bridge is the old Moorish town, **La Ciudad**, and further south still, its **San Francisco** suburb. On the near north side of the gorge, and where you'll arrive by public transport, is the largely modern **Mercadillo** quarter.

La Ciudad

The **Ciudad** retains intact its Moorish plan and a great many of its houses, interspersed with a number of fine Renaissance mansions. It is so intricate a maze that you can do little else but wander at random. However, at some stage, make your way across the eighteenth-century **Puente Nuevo** bridge, peering down the walls of limestone rock into the yawning *Tajo* and the Río Guadalvín, far below. The bridge itself is a remarkable construction and now has its own **Centro de Información** (April–Sept Mon–Fri 10am–7pm, Sat–Sun 10am–3pm; Oct–March same hours but closes Mon–Fri 6pm; €2) housed in a former prison above the central arch; entry is to the side of the Parador in Plaza de España. Once across the bridge, veering left along c/Santo Domingo, also known as c/Marqués de Parada, will bring you, at no. 17, to the somewhat arbitrarily named **Casa del Rey Moro** (House of the Moorish King), an early eighteenth-century mansion built on Moorish foundations. The gardens (but not the house itself) have recently been opened to the public (daily 10am–8pm; €4), and from here a remarkable underground stairway, the *Mina*, descends to the river; these 365 steps (which can be slippery after rain), guaranteeing a water supply in times of siege, were cut by Christian slaves in the fourteenth century. There's a viewing balcony at the bottom where you can admire the Tajo's towering walls of rock and its bird life.

Further down the same street is the **Palacio del Marqués de Salvatierra**, a splendid Renaissance mansion with an oddly primitive, half-grotesque frieze of Adam and Eve on its portal. Just down the hill you reach the two old town bridges – the **Puente Viejo** of 1616 and the single-span Moorish **Puente de San Miguel**; nearby, on the southeast bank of the river, are the distinctive hump-shaped cupolas and glass roof-windows of the old **Baños Árabes** (Tues 9am–1.30pm & 4–6pm, Wed–Sat 9.30am–3.30pm; Oct–March also open Sun 10am–2pm; free). Dating from the thirteenth century and recently restored, the complex is based on the Roman system of cold, tepid and hot baths and is wonderfully preserved; note the sophisticated barrel-vaulted ceiling and brickwork octagonal pillars supporting horseshoe arches.

At the centre of the Ciudad quarter on Ronda's most picturesque square, the Plaza Duquesa de Parcent, stands the cathedral church of **Santa María La Mayor** (daily 10am–7pm; Oct–March closes 6pm; €2), originally the Arab town's Friday mosque. Externally it's a graceful combination of Moorish, Gothic and Renaissance styles with the belfry built on top of the old minaret. The interior is decidedly less interesting, but you can see an arch covered with Arabic calligraphy, and just in front of the street door, a part of the old Arab *mihrab*, or prayer niche, has been exposed. Slightly west of the square on c/Montero lies the fourteenth-century **Casa de Mondragón**, probably the real palace of the Moorish kings (Mon–Fri 10am–7pm, Sat & Sun 10am–3pm; Oct–March closes 6pm; €2). Inside, three of the patios preserve original stuccowork and there's a magnificent carved ceiling, as well as a small museum covering local archeology and aspects of Moorish Ronda.

To the northeast of the Plaza Duquesa de Parcent on c/Armiñan, which bisects La Ciudad, at no. 29 you'll find the new **Museo Lara** (daily 11am–8.30pm; Oct–March closes 7pm; €2.50), containing the collection of *rondeño* Juan Antonio Lara, a member of the family which owns and runs the local bus company of the same name. An avid collector since childhood, Señor Lara has filled the spacious museum with a fascinating collection of antique clocks, pistols and armaments, musical instruments and archeological finds, as well as early cameras and cinematographic equipment.

Near the end of the Ciudad are the ruins of the **Alcázar**, destroyed by the French in 1809 ("from sheer love of destruction", according to Richard Ford), and now partially occupied by a school. Once it was virtually impregnable – as indeed was this whole fortress capital, which ruled an independent and isolated Moorish kingdom until 1485, just seven years before the fall of Granada.

The principal gates of the town, the magnificent Moorish **Puerto de Almocabar**, through which passed the Christian conquerors (led personally by Fernando), and the triumphal **Puerta de Carlos V**, erected later during the reign of the Hapsburg emperor, stand side by side to the southeast of the Alcázar at the entrance to the suburb of San Francisco.

Mercadillo

The **Mercadillo** quarter, which grew up in the wake of the Christian conquest, is of comparatively little interest, with just a couple of buildings worth a quick look. The first is a remarkably preserved inn where Miguel Cervantes once slept, the sixteenth-century **Posada de las Ánimas** (also known as the Hogar del Pensionista) in c/Cecilia, the oldest building in the quarter. The other is the eighteenth-century **Plaza de Toros** (daily 10am–8pm; Oct–March closes 6pm; €5), close by the Plaza de España and the beautiful cliff-top *paseo* – with stretches now named after Rondaphiles and bullfighting fans Hemingway and Orson Welles – from which you get good views of the old and new bridges. Ronda played a leading part in the development of bull-fighting and was the birthplace of the modern *corrida* (bullfight). The ring, built in 1781, is one of the earliest in Spain and the fight season here is one of the country's most important. At its September *feria* the *corrida goyesca*, honouring Spain's great artist Goya, who made a number of paintings of the fights at Ronda, takes place in eighteenth-century costume. You can visit the bullring to wander around the arena, and there's a museum inside stuffed with memorabilia such as famous bullfighters' *trajes de luces* (suits) and photos of the ubiquitous Hemingway and Welles visiting the ring.

The Puente Nuevo bridge was originally the town prison (now housing an information centre: see p.289) which last saw use during the Civil War, when Ronda was the site of some of the south's most vicious massacres. Hemingway, in *For Whom the Bell Tolls*, recorded how prisoners were thrown alive into the gorge. These days, Ronda remains a major military garrison post and houses much of the Spanish Africa Legion, Franco's old crack regiment, who can be seen wandering around town in their tropical green coats and tasselled fezzes. They have a mean reputation.

Eating and drinking
Most of the bargain **restaurants** are grouped round the far end of the Plaza del Socorro, though there are also some to be found near the Plaza de España.

Bar-Galeria Enfrente Arte c/Espiritu Santo 9, close to the Puerta de Almocabar in La Ciudad. The bar of the hotel of the same name (see p.289) stages art exhibitions plus frequent musical and literary events. The views towards the Serranía de Ronda through panoramic windows are wonderful. Open till late.

Bar Luciano c/Armiñan 42, La Ciudad. Pleasant bar-restaurant with a good-value *menú* for around €8.

Bar Valencia c/Naranja 6, a couple of blocks east of Plaza del Socorro. Good *platos combinados* served up in an earthy atmosphere with an unbelievably cheap *menú* for around €3.50.

Bodega La Giralda c/Nueva 19. Traditional and excellent tapas in a great setting.

Café Alba c/Espinel 44. Piping hot *churros* and delicious breakfast coffee.

Don Miguel Plaza de España ☎ 952 871 090. High-quality restaurant offering *rondeño* specialities such as *perdiz estofado* (partridge stew) along with a *menú* for around €15 and a terrace with a marvellous view of the Tajo.

Doña Pepa Plaza del Socorro. Family-run and reliable restaurant with some vegetarian possibilities

and a separate cafeteria-bar serving *bocadillos* and freshly squeezed orange juice.

Bar Relax c/Los Remedios 27, south of Plaza del Socorro. Pleasant English-run vegetarian oasis serving up salads, juices, fresh soups and a range of other dishes. Cocktails served in the evening.

La Farola Plaza Carmen Abela 9. Friendly and economical *raciones* and *platos combinados* place; open till late.

Parador de Ronda Plaza de España ☎ 952 877 500. The *parador's* elegant restaurant has a menu offering an excellent choice of local and regional dishes, many of them appearing on a bargain *menú gastronomico* for around €25.

Restaurante del Escudero Paseo de Blas Infante 1, near the Plaza de Toros ☎ 952 871 367. Superb stylish new restaurant housed in an elegant mansion with Ronda's best garden terrace (when the wind's not up) offering views towards the Serranía de Ronda. There's a *menú* for around €12. Closed Sun eve.

Restaurante La Merced Plaza de la Merced s/n. Good place for well-prepared *platos combinados*, and has a *menú* for around €7.

Around Ronda
Ronda makes an excellent base for exploring the superb countryside in the immediate vicinity or for visiting more of the White Towns. Fifteen kilometres away, **Setenil**, dug into the cliffs and with cave dwellings, is one of the most unusual – nearby **Olvera** and **Teba** are worth a visit, too. Other possible excursions are to the remarkable **Cueva de la Pileta**, with prehistoric cave paintings, and the Roman ruins of **Ronda la Vieja**.

Walks around Ronda

Good walking routes from Ronda are pretty limitless. One of the best, and a good way to get a sense of the town as a rural market centre set among farmland, is to take the path down to the gorge from the Mondragón palace terrace. In the fields below there's a network of paths and some stupendous views. A couple of hours' walk will bring you to the main road to the northwest where you can hitch or walk back the 4–5km into Mercadillo. Another excursion is to an old, unused **aqueduct** set in rocky pasture – from the market square just outside the Ciudad in the San Francisco area, take the straight residential street which leads up and out of town. After about an hour this ends in olive groves, by a stream and a large water trough. A path through the groves leads to the aqueduct.

Further afield, if you're mobile or energetic, are the ruins of a town and **Roman theatre** at a site known as **Ronda la Vieja**, 12km from Ronda and reached by turning right 6km down the main A376 road to Arcos/Sevilla. At the site (Tues–Sat 9am–3.30pm, Sun 10am–4.30pm; free) a friendly farmer, who is also the guardian, will present you with a plan (in Spanish) and record your nationality for statistical purposes.

Based on Neolithic foundations – note the recently discovered prehistoric stone huts beside the entrance – it was as a Roman town in the first century AD that Acinipo (the town's Roman name), reached its zenith. Immediately west of the theatre, the ground falls away in a startlingly steep escarpment offering fine views all around, taking in the hill village of Olvera to the north. From here a track leads off towards the strange "cave village" of Setenil (see below).

The Cueva de la Pileta

West from Ronda is the prehistoric **Cueva de la Pileta** (daily guided visits on the hour 10am–1pm & 4–6pm; €6.50; limit of 25 persons per tour, booking essential at peak times ☎952 167 343), a fabulous series of caverns with some remarkable paintings of animals (mainly bison), fish and what are apparently magic symbols. These etchings and the occupation of the cave date from about 25,000 BC – hence predating the more famous caves at Altamira in northern Spain – to the end of the Bronze Age. The tour lasts one hour on average, but can be longer, and is in Spanish – though the guide does speak a little English. There are hundreds of bats in the cave, and no artificial lighting, so visitors carry lanterns; you may also want to take a jumper, as the caves can be extremely chilly. Be aware if you leave a car in the car park that thieves are active here.

To reach the caves from Ronda take either an Algeciras-bound local train (4 daily; 35min) to the Estación Benaoján-Montejaque, or a bus, which drops you a little closer in Benaoján. There's a bar at the train station if you want to stock up on drink before the hour-long walk (6km) to the caves. Follow the farm track from the right bank of the river until you reach the farmhouse (approximately 30min). From here, a track goes straight uphill to the main road just before the signposted turning for the caves. If you're driving, follow the road to Benaoján and take the turn-off, from where it is about 4km.

Setenil, Olvera and Teba

North of Ronda, and feasible as a day-trip from the town, are Setenil and Olvera. **SETENIL**, on a very minor road to Olvera, is the strangest of all the White Towns, its cave-like streets formed from the overhanging ledge of a gorge. Many of the houses – sometimes two or three storeys high – have natural roofs in the rock. There are a couple of bars, and a reasonably priced **hotel** with a good restaurant, *El Almendral* (☎956 134 029, ❽ www.cadiz.org/tugasa;

❷), on the road just outside town. Four buses a day run from Ronda, or it's a possible walk from Ronda la Vieja. The train station is a good 8km from the village itself.

OLVERA, 15km beyond, tumbles down a hill topped by its church and a fine Moorish castle. There's just one bus a day from Ronda, but there are a couple of **pensiones** if you want to stay and explore the region: the good-value *Maqueda*, c/Calvario 35 (☏956 130 733; ❶), and the nearby and slightly more expensive *Medina*, c/Sepulveda 6 (☏956 130 173; ❶), with en-suite rooms. For **food**, superb *fino*, tapas and a budget *menú* are to be had at the friendly *Bar Manolo* in Plaza Andalucía, at the foot of the main street.

An imaginitive new development in Olvera is the transformation of the disused rail line – running 34km east to Puerto Serrano through rolling, wooded hill country – into a track for cyclists and walkers with stations along the route transformed into hotels. Known as the **Via Verde** (Ⓦwww.fundacionvia verdedelasierra.com), you can hire a mountain bike for €9 per day from Olvera's dapper station-hotel (mobile ☏661 463 207, Ⓔestacionverde @hotmail.com; ❸) which has very comfortable en-suite rooms and its own restaurant. They will give you a route map and ring ahead to book rooms at your next stop. If you don't want to do the return journey you may deposit the bike in Puerto Serrano.

TEBA is a small community with a calm and prosperous air situated in the mountains five or six kilometres south of the A382 between Campillos and Olvera, or straight up on the A367 from Ronda. It's easily seen from the A382 and is approached by way of a single, clearly marked road which winds its way up to the town. The lower square, Plaza de la Constitución, has all the **accommodation**: three clean, friendly and relatively inexpensive places, of which the best is *Hostal Sevillano*, c/San Francisco 26 (☏952 748 011; ❶), just off the plaza; it also serves food in its bar/restaurant below and has a good-value *menú*. Sights around the village include the enormous Baroque church of **Santa Cruz** (daily 5–6pm; if closed at this time knock at the adjoining house of the *cura*), which is stuffed full of treasures, and the Plaza de España where there's a **monument** in Scottish granite to Robert the Bruce. Bruce's recently rediscovered heart (at Melrose Abbey in Scotland) played a part in the battle against the Moors here in 1331; one of his knights carried the organ as a talisman and threw it into the Moorish ranks to encourage his timid soldiers to charge. On the hill above the town are the remains of a **Moorish castle**, constructed on Roman ruins, which has a superb keep. The views from here over the surrounding countryside are spectacular.

Towards Cádiz and Sevilla

Ronda has good transport connections in most directions (see "Travel details" at the end of this chapter). Almost any route to the north or west is rewarding, taking you past a whole series of White Towns, many of them fortified since the days of the Reconquest from the Moors – hence the mass of "de la Frontera" suffixes.

Grazalema, Ubrique and Medina Sidonia

Perhaps the best of all the routes, though a roundabout one, and tricky without your own transport, is to **Cádiz** via Grazalema, Ubrique, and Medina Sidonia. This passes through the **Sierra de Grazalema Natural Park** before skirting the nature reserve of **Cortes de la Frontera** (which you can drive through by following the road beyond Benaoján) and, towards Alcalá de los Gazules, running through the northern fringe of the **Parque Natural de los**

Alcornocales, which derives its name from the forests of cork oaks, one of its main attractions.

Twenty-three kilometres from Ronda, **GRAZALEMA** is a striking village at the centre of the Sierra de Grazalema Natural Park, with the **Puerto de las Palomas** (Pass of the Doves – at 1350m the second highest pass in Andalucía) rearing up behind. Cross this, and you descend to Zahara and the main road west (see below).

UBRIQUE, 20km southwest, is a natural mountain fortress which was a Republican stronghold in the Civil War. According to Nicholas Luard's book, *Andalucía*: "It proved so difficult for the besieging nationalists to take, they eventually called up a plane from Sevilla to fly over the town and drop leaflets carrying the message: "Ubrique, if in five minutes from now all your arms are not piled in front of the Guardia Civil post and the roofs and terraces of your houses are not covered in white sheets, the town will be devastated by the bombs in this plane." The threat was effective, although not quite in the way the nationalists had intended. Without spreading a single white sheet or leaving a gun behind them, Ubrique's citizens promptly abandoned the town and took to the hills behind. This is a Civil War story typical of these parts. More unusual, however, is that the town today is relatively prosperous, surviving very largely on its medieval guild craft of **leather-making**. The products (footwear, bags and accessories, often at bargain prices) of the town's numerous workshops are sold at shops along the main street, Avenida Dr Solis Pascual.

Zahara de la Sierra

Heading directly to Jerez or Sevilla from Ronda, a beautiful rural drive, you pass below **ZAHARA DE LA SIERRA** (or *de los Membrillos* – "of the Quinces"), perhaps the most perfect example of these fortified hill towns. Set in beautiful country, a landmark for miles around, its red-tiled houses huddle round a church and castle on a stark outcrop of rock. The creation of a new *embalse* (reservoir) below Zahara's walls has dramatically changed the landscape to the north and east of the town, which now overlooks a huge expanse of water. Once an important Moorish citadel, Zahara's capture by the Christians in 1483 opened the way for the conquest of Ronda – and ultimately Granada. There's a clutch of **places to stay**: the homely and simple *Pensión Gonzalo*, c/San Juan 9, with no sign, opposite the church (❶), *Los Estribos*, c/Fuerte 3 (☎956 137 445; ❶), near the swimming pool, and the excellent *Hotel Marqués de Zahara*, c/San Juan 3 (☎956 123 061; ❸), with a good **restaurant**.

Arcos de la Frontera

Of more substantial interest, and a better place to break the journey, is **ARCOS DE LA FRONTERA**. This was taken from the Moors in 1264, over two centuries before Zahara fell – an impressive feat, for it stands high above the Río Guadalete on a double crag and must have been a wretchedly impregnable fortress. This dramatic location, enhanced by low, white houses and fine sandstone churches, gives the town a similar feel and appearance to Ronda – only Arcos is poorer and, quite unjustifiably, far less visited. The streets of the town, despite particularly manic packs of local bikers, are if anything more interesting, with their mix of Moorish and Renaissance buildings. At the heart is the Plaza del Cabildo, easily reached by following the signs for the *parador*, which occupies one side of it. Flanking another two sides are the castle walls and the large Gothic-Mudéjar church of **Santa María de la Asunción**; the last side is left open, offering plunging views to the river valley.

Practicalities

A **turismo** on the west side of Plaza del Cabildo (Mon–Sat 10am–2pm & 4–8pm; ☎956 702 264, ⊚www.ayuntamientoarcos.org) can provide a town map and also does daily guided tours of the old town (except Sun). Budget **accommodation** in the **old town** is confined to the *Pensión de Callejón de las Monjas* (☎956 702 302; ❶), immediately behind the church of Santa María, and the very friendly *Hostal San Marcos*, c/Marquéz de Torresoto 6 (☎956 700 721; ❶), the better alternative, with its own restaurant. More upmarket options are the elegant *Parador de Arcos de la Frontera* (☎956 700 500, ⊚www.parador.es; ❻), perched on a rock pedestal with stunning views, the *Hotel Marqués de Torresoto*, c/Marqués de Torresoto 4 (☎956 700 717, ℻956 704 205; ❹), housed in a converted seventeenth-century mansion with colonnaded patio and Baroque chapel, and a new hotel, *La Casa Grande*, c/Maldonado 10 (☎ & ℻956 703 930, ⊚www.lacasagrande.net; ❺), with beautiful rooms inside an eighteenth-century mansion and a stunning terrace view across the river valley. In the **new town** you'll find a couple of places on either side of the main street, c/Corredera, including the excellent *Hotel Fonda Comercio* (☎956 700 057; ❸), Arcos's oldest inn, welcoming visitors for well over a century, and recently refurbished.

Eating and drinking tends to be expensive in the old quarter, where most of the hotels have their own restaurants. A more modest good-value option is *La Terraza* in the gardens of the Paseo de Andalucía to the southwest of the Plaza del Cabildo, which serves a wide variety of *platos combinados* at outdoor tables, while *Alcaraván*, c/Nueva 1, close to the castle walls, is an interesting cave restaurant which does tapas and *platos asados* (roasts). Nearby, *Mesón de Ana*, c/Dean Espinosa 10, is a pleasant little café-bar serving *platos combinados* and lots of snacks. The small and economical restaurant of the *Hostal San Marcos* is also recommended. In the new town *Los Faraones*, c/Debajo del Corral 14, is a well-established North African restaurant with a couple of €9 *menús*, one meat, one vegetarian. If you're looking to push the boat out, Arcos's best restaurants – both in the old town – are *El Convento*, c/Marqués de Torresoto 7, located in the patio of an old *casa señorial*, and the elegant restaurant of the *parador* (see above), serving regional specialities on a *menú* for around €25.

Just out of town, towards Ronda, a road leads down to a couple of sandy **beaches** on the riverbank (hourly buses from the bus station), where there's a pleasant two-star waterfront *hostal*, *La Molinera* (☎956 708 002, ✉rumave@teleline.es; ❸), and a **campsite**, *Arcos de la Frontera* (☎956 708 333), close to the Bornos reservoir (aka Lago de Argos); bring mosquito protection if you stay at either, and if you swim here, or further along towards the namesake village, take care – there are said to be whirlpools in some parts.

Sevilla, the west and Córdoba

With the major exception of **Sevilla** – and to a lesser extent **Córdoba** – the west and centre of Andalucía are not greatly visited. The coast here, certainly the Atlantic **Costa de la Luz**, is a world apart from the Mediterranean resorts, with the entire stretch between Algeciras and Tarifa designated a "potential military zone". This probably sounds grim – and in parts, marked off by *Paso Prohibido* signs, it is – but the ruling has also had happier effects, preventing foreigners from buying up land and placing strict controls even on Spanish developments. So, for a hundred or more kilometres, there are scarcely any villa developments and only a modest number of hotels and campsites – small, easygoing and low-key even at the growing resorts of breezy **Tarifa**, one of Europe's prime windsurfing locations, and **Conil**. On the coast, too, there is the attraction of **Cádiz**, one of the oldest and, though it's now in decline, most elegant seaport towns in Europe.

Inland rewards include the smaller towns between Sevilla and Córdoba, Moorish **Carmona** particularly, and in the sherry zone of Cádiz province where **Jerez** and its neighbours have plenty of bodegas to visit. But the most

Moorish Sevilla

Sevilla was one of the earliest Moorish conquests (in 712) and, as part of the caliphate of Córdoba, became the second city of *al-Andalus*. When the caliphate broke up in the early eleventh century it was by far the most powerful of the independent states (or *taifas*) to emerge, extending its power over the Algarve and eventually over Jaén, Murcia and Córdoba itself. This period, under a series of three Arabic rulers from the Abbadid dynasty (1023–91), was something of a golden age. The city's court was unrivalled in wealth and luxury and was sophisticated, too, developing a strong chivalric element and a flair for poetry – one of the most skilled exponents being the last ruler, al-Mu'tamid, the "poet-king". But with sophistication came decadence and in 1091 Abbadid rule was usurped by a new force, the Almoravids, a tribe of fanatical Berber Muslims from North Africa, to whom the Andalucians had appealed for help against the rising threat from the northern Christian kingdoms.

Despite initial military successes, the Almoravids failed to consolidate their gains in *al-Andalus* and attempted to rule through military governors from Marrakesh. In the middle of the twelfth century they were in turn supplanted by a new Berber incursion, the Almohads, who by about 1170 had recaptured virtually all the former territories. Sevilla had accepted Almohad rule in 1147 and became the capital of this last real empire of the Moors in Spain. Almohad power was sustained until their disastrous defeat in 1212 by the combined Christian armies of the north, at Las Navas de Tolosa. In this brief and precarious period Sevilla underwent a renaissance of public building, characterized by a new vigour and fluidity of style. The Almohads rebuilt the Alcázar, enlarged the principal mosque – later demolished to make room for the Christian cathedral – and erected a new and brilliant minaret, a tower over 100m tall, topped with four copper spheres that could be seen for miles round: the Giralda.

beautiful, and neglected, parts of this region are the dark, ilex-covered hills and poor rural villages of the **Sierra Morena** to the north and northwest of Sevilla. Perfect walking country with its network of streams and reservoirs between modest peaks, this is also a botanist's dream, brilliant with a mass of spring flowers.

On a more organized level, though equally compelling if you're into bird-watching or wildlife, is the huge nature reserve of the **Coto de Doñana National Park**, spreading back from Huelva in vast expanses of *marismas* – sand dunes, salt flats and marshes. The most important of the Spanish reserves, Doñana is vital to scores of migratory birds and to endangered mammals such as the Iberian lynx.

Sevilla

"Seville," wrote Byron, "is a pleasant city, famous for oranges and women." And for its heat, he might perhaps have added, since **SEVILLA**'s summers are intense and start early, in May. But the spirit, for all its nineteenth-century chauvinism, is about right. Sevilla has three important monuments and an illustrious history, but what it's essentially famous for is its own living self – the greatest city of the Spanish south, of Carmen, Don Juan and Figaro, and the archetype of Andalucian promise. This reputation for gaiety and brilliance, for theatricality and intensity of life, does seem deserved. It's expressed on a phenomenally grand scale at the city's two great festivals – **Semana Santa** (in the week before Easter) and the **Feria de Abril** (which starts two weeks after Easter Sunday and lasts a week). Either is worth considerable effort to get to. Sevilla is also Spain's second most important centre for **bullfighting**, after Madrid.

Despite its elegance and charm, and its wealth, based on food processing, shipbuilding, aircraft construction and a thriving tourist industry, Sevilla lies at the centre of a depressed agricultural area and has an unemployment rate of nearly twenty percent – one of the highest in Spain. The total refurbishment of the infrastructure boosted by the 1992 Expo – including impressive new roads, seven bridges, a high-speed rail link and a revamped airport – was intended to regenerate the city's (and the region's) economic fortunes but has hardly turned out to be the catalyst for growth and prosperity promised at the time. Indeed, some of the colossal debts are still unpaid over a decade later.

Meantime, **petty crime** is a big problem, and the motive for stealing is usually cash to feed drug addiction. Bag-snatching is common (often Italian-style, from passing *motos*), as is breaking into cars. There's even a special breed called *semaforazos* who break the windows of cars stopped at traffic lights and grab what they can. Be careful, but don't be put off. Despite a worrying rise in the number of muggings in recent years, when compared with cities of similar size in northern Europe, violent crime is still relatively rare.

Arrival, orientation and information

Bisected by the Río Guadalquivir, Sevilla is fairly easy to find your way about (though hell if you're driving). The **old city** – where you'll want to spend most of your time – takes up the east bank. At its heart, side by side, stand the three great monuments: the **Giralda tower**, the **Cathedral** and the **Alcázar**, with the cramped alleyways of the **Barrio Santa Cruz**, the medieval Jewish quarter and now the heart of tourist life, extending east of them. North of here is

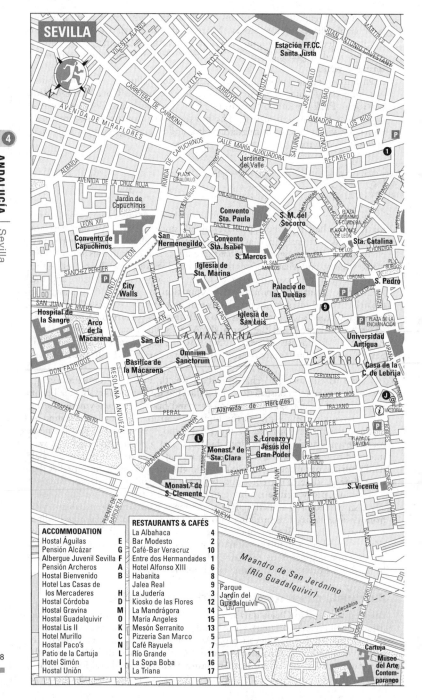

SEVILLA

Estación FF.CC.
Santa Justa

Jardines
del Valle

Convento
Sta. Paula

S. M. del
Socorro

Convento de
Capuchinos

San
Hermenegildo

Convento
Sta. Isabel

Sta. Catalina

S. Marcos

Iglesia de
Sta. Marina

S. Pedro

Palacio de
las Dueñas

City
Walls

Hospital de
la Sangre

Arco
de la
Macarena

Iglesia de
San Luis

San Gil   LA MACARENA

Universidad
Antigua

Omnium
Sanctorum

CENTRO

Basílica de
la Macarena

Casa de la
C. de Lebrija

Alameda de Hércules

JESÚS DEL GRAN PODER

S. Lorenzo y
Jesús del
Gran Poder

Monast.º de
Sta. Clara

Monast.º de
S. Clemente

Meandro de San Jerónimo
(Río Guadalquivir)

S. Vicente

Parque
Jardín del
Guadalquivir

Cartuja

Museo
del Arte
Contem-
poraneo

ACCOMMODATION	
Hostal Águilas	E
Pensión Alcázar	G
Albergue Juvenil Sevilla	F
Pensión Archeros	A
Hostal Bienvenido	B
Hotel Las Casas de los Mercaderes	H
Hostal Córdoba	D
Hostal Gravina	M
Hostal Guadalquivir	O
Hostal Lis II	K
Hotel Murillo	C
Hostal Paco's	N
Patio de la Cartuja	L
Hotel Simón	I
Hostal Unión	J

RESTAURANTS & CAFÉS	
La Albahaca	4
Bar Modesto	2
Café-Bar Veracruz	10
Entre dos Hermandades	1
Hotel Alfonso XIII	6
Habanita	8
Jalea Real	9
La Judería	3
Kiosko de las Flores	12
La Mandrágora	14
María Angeles	15
Mesón Serranito	13
Pizzeria San Marco	5
Café Rayuela	7
Río Grande	11
La Sopa Boba	16
La Triana	17

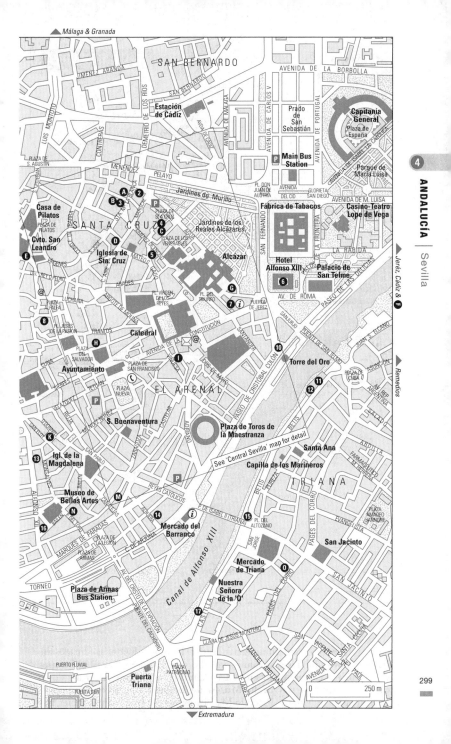

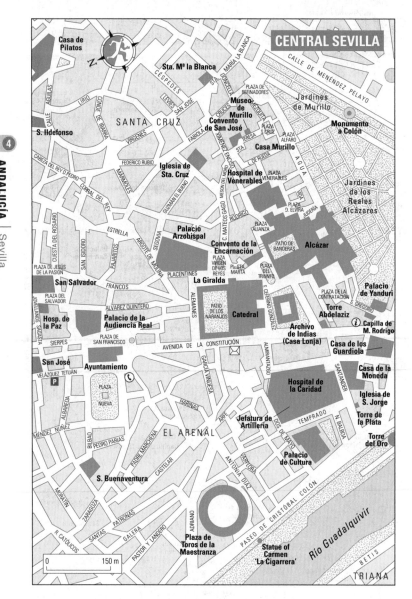

the main shopping and commercial district, its most obvious landmarks the **Plaza Nueva** and **La Campana**, and the smart, pedestrianized c/**Sierpes** which runs between them. From La Campana, c/Alfonso XII runs down towards the river by way of the **Museo de Bellas Artes**, second in importance in Spain only to the Prado in Madrid. Across the river is the earthier, traditionally working-class district of **Triana**, flanked to the south by the **Los Remedios** *barrio*, the city's wealthier residential zone where the great April *feria* takes place.

Points of arrival, too, are straightforward, though the **train station**, Santa Justa, is a fair way out on Avenida Kansas City, the airport road. Buses #27 and #32 will take you from outside here to the Plaza de la Encarnación (roughly dead centre of our city map), from where all sights are within easy walking distance; alternatively, buses #70 and #C1 will take you to the Prado de San Sebastián bus station (see below). A bus map detailing all routes is available from the turismo. The **airport** bus, operated by Amarillos (hourly; €2.10), takes 30min to the centre and terminates at the Puerta de Jerez, at the top of Avenida Roma between the turismo and the Fábrica de Tabacos. To take the same trip by taxi costs around €15.

The **main bus station** is at the Prado de San Sebastián. Most companies and destinations go from here: exceptions include buses for Badajoz, Extremadura (the provinces of Cáceres and Badajoz), Huelva, Madrid and international destinations which arrive and depart from the station at Plaza de Armas by the Puente del Cachorro on the river.

The main **turismo** is at Avda. de la Constitución 21 (Mon–Sat 9am–7pm, Sun 10am–2pm; ☏954 221 404, Ⓦwww.turismosevilla.org); they have accommodation lists and you can get a copy of the very useful free listings magazine *El Giraldillo* here, too. There's also a less chaotic **municipal tourist office** at c/Arjona 28, near the river just north of the bullring (Mon–Fri 8.30am–9pm, Sat 8.30am–2.45pm; ☏954 221 714) by the Puente de Triana, with a sub-office at the Santa Justa train station.

One way to get to grips with the city is to take an **open-top bus tour** – especially good if you're pressed for time. This hop-on hop-off service is operated by Sevirama (☏954 560 693) and the buses leave half-hourly from the riverside Torre del Oro, stopping at or near the main sites (all-day tickets cost €11).

Accommodation

The most attractive **area to stay** is undoubtedly the **Barrio Santa Cruz**, though this is reflected in the prices. In mid-season or during the big festivals you can find yourself paying ridiculous amounts for what is little more than a cell; rooms are relatively expensive everywhere, in fact. Nonetheless, there are reasonable places to be found in the *barrio* and on its periphery (especially immediately north, and south towards the bus station) and they're at least worth a try before heading elsewhere. Slightly further out, another promising area is to the north of the Plaza Nueva, and especially over towards the river and the Plaza de Armas bus station. It's always worth trying to bargain the price down a little, though you may not always succeed.

At peak times you may face quite a walk, and if you're planning to arrive during any of the major festivals you'd be advised to book ahead. The list below is no more than a start, and it's worth checking at the places you'll pass between all these. If you're still unable to find anything (which can happen at busy periods) the turismo has complete lists and should be able to help.

Budget options

Hostal Águilas c/Águilas 15 ☏954 213 177. Small, comfortable and quiet *hostal* with some en-suite rooms, near the Casa de Pilatos. ❷

Pensión Alcázar c/Deán Miranda 12 ☏954 228 457. Cosy, friendly and fair-priced *pensión* with ensuite a/c rooms or *ventiladores* (ceiling fans) in a tiny street off the Plaza de la Contratación next to the Alcázar. ❷

Sevilla boasts two of the largest festival celebrations in Spain. The first, **Semana Santa** (Holy Week at Easter), always spectacular in Andalucía, is here at its peak with extraordinary processions of hooded penitents and impressive *pasos* or floats decorated with large-as-life scenes from the Passion carried through the streets. The second, the **Feria de Abril**, is unique to the city: a one-time market festival, long converted to a week-long party of drink, food and flamenco. The *feria* follows close on the heels of *Semana Santa*. If you have the energy and time, experience both.

Semana Santa

Semana Santa may be a religious festival, but for most of the week solemnity isn't the keynote – there's lots of carousing and frivolity, and bars are full day and night. In essence, it involves the marching in procession of fifty-odd brotherhoods (*cofradías*) of the church and penitents (*nazarenos*), followed by *pasos*, elaborate platforms or floats on which sit precious seventeenth-century images of the Virgin or Christ in tableaux from the Passion. For weeks beforehand the *cofradías* painstakingly adorn the hundred or so *pasos*, spending vast amounts on costumes and precious stones. The bearers (*costaleros*) walk in time to stirring, traditional dirges and drumbeats from the bands, which are often punctuated by impromptu and moving street-corner *saetas* from the citizenry – short, fervent, flamenco-style hymns about the Passion and the Virgin's sorrows.

The last lap of the official route for every *paso* goes from La Campana south along c/Sierpes, through the cathedral, and around the Giralda and the Bishop's Palace. Throughout the week *pasos* leave churches all over town from early afternoon onward, snaking through the city and back to their resting place many hours later. Good Friday morning is the climax, when the *pasos* leave the churches at midnight and move through the town for much of the night, watched by large crowds. The highlight is the arrival at the cathedral of the *paso* bearing *La Macarena*, an image of the patroness of bullfighters, and, by extension, of Sevilla itself.

The pattern of events changes every day; banks, hotels and businesses produce free skeleton timetables, and route maps are also issued with local papers, which are essential if you want to know which events are where – the ultra-Catholic *ABC*

Albergue Juvenil Sevilla c/Isaac Peral 2 ☎954 613 150 (they tend not to answer). Leafy if often crowded youth hostel some way out in the university district; take bus #34 from the Puerta de Jerez by the turismo or Plaza Nueva. €13.35

Pensión Archeros c/Archeros 23, near church of Santa María la Blanca ☎954 418 465. Pleasant and economical little rooms with a charming plant-filled patio, tucked away in quiet street on the northern edge of the Barrio Santa Cruz. Has a few more expensive en-suite rooms. ❶

Hostal Bienvenido c/Archeros 14 ☎954 413 655. East of c/Santa María la Blanca, this *hostal* offers small rooms (some en suite) but has a nice roof terrace. ❷–❸

Hostal Gravina c/Gravina 46 ☎954 216 414. Pleasant, simple family-run *hostal* close to the Museo de Bellas Artes. ❶

Hostal Lis II c/Olavide 5, a couple of blocks east of the Museo de las Bellas Artes ☎954 560 228, ⓦwww.sol.com/hostalisii. A clean, pleasant and

simple place for rooms with and without bath and offering Internet access (extra charge) to guests. ❷

Hostal Paco's c/Pedro del Toro 7, off c/Gravina ☎954 217 183, ⓕ954 219 645. Friendly offshoot of the *Hostal Gravina* (above), this has small rooms among the cheapest in town, including some en-suite. ❷

Moderate and expensive options

Hotel Las Casas de los Mercaderes c/Álvarez Quintero 12 ☎954 225 858, ⓦwww.casas ypalacios.com. Near the cathedral, this converted former *bodega* has been transformed into a very comfortable hotel with a delightful seventeenth-century patio, a roof terrace and great views from some rooms (especially nos. 201–206). ❺

Hostal Córdoba c/Farnesio 12 ☎954 227 498. Good standard (if slightly overpriced) *hostal*, offering a/c rooms (some more expensive ones with bath), close to the church of Santa Cruz. ❸

paper has the best listings, with piles of background and historical info on each brotherhood. On Maundy Thursday women dress in black and it's considered respectful for tourists not to dress in shorts or T-shirts. Triana is a good location on this day, and there's always a crush of spectators outside the cathedral and on the ancient c/Sierpes, the most awe-inspiring venue. Plaza de la Virgen de los Reyes under the Giralda is a good viewing point, but even here it gets chaotic. The best way of all to see the processions is to pick them up near their starting and finishing points in their respective *barrios*; here you'll see the true *teatro de la calle* – theatre of the streets.

Feria de Abril
The Feria de Abril is staged a fortnight after Semana Santa ends and lasts nonstop for a week. For its duration a vast area on the far bank of the river in the *barrio* of Los Remedios, the *Real de la Feria*, is totally covered in rows of *casetas*, canvas pavilions or tents of varying sizes. Some of these belong to eminent *sevillano* families, some to groups of friends, others to clubs, trade associations or political parties. In each one – from around nine at night until perhaps six or seven the following morning – there is flamenco (more correctly, *sevillanas*) singing and dancing. Many of the men and virtually all the women wear traditional costume, the latter in an astonishing array of brilliantly coloured, flounced gypsy dresses.

The sheer size of this spectacle is extraordinary, and the dancing, with its intense and knowing sexuality, a revelation. But most infectious of all is the universal spontaneity of enjoyment; after wandering around staring with the crowds you wind up a part of it, drinking and dancing in one of the "open" *casetas* which have commercial bars. Among these you'll usually find lively *casetas* erected by the anarchist trade union CNT and various leftist groups.

Earlier in the day, from 1pm until around 8pm, Sevillana society parades around the fairground in carriages or on horseback. An incredible extravaganza of display and voyeurism, this has subtle but distinct gradations of dress and style; catch it at least once. Each day, too, there are bullfights (at around 5.30pm; very expensive tickets are available in advance from the ring) with big name *matadores* performing in some of the best line-ups of the season.

Hostal Guadalquivir c/Pagés del Corro 53 ☏954 332 100, ℻954 332 104. The Triana *barrio*'s only *hostal* is atmospheric and friendly; some rooms en suite. ❷
Hotel Murillo c/Lope de Rueda 7 ☏954 216 095, ⓦwww.sol.com/hotel.murillo. Traditional hotel in restored mansion with all facilities plus amusingly kitsch features such as suits of armour and paint-palette key rings. Close to the Plaza Santa Cruz. ❸
Patio de la Cartuja c/Lumbreras 8, off west side of Alameda's northern end ☏954 900 200, ⓦwww.patiosdesevilla.com. Stylish and excellent-value apart-hotel created from an old *sevillano corral*; en-suite apartments with balconies, kitchen and lounge are set around a tiled patio. Own garage. ❺
Hotel Simón c/García de Vinuesa 19 ☏954 226 660, ℻954 562 241. Well-restored mansion in an excellent position across from the cathedral. All rooms are en suite and air-conditioned and this can be a bargain out of high season. ❹

Hostal Unión c/Tarifa 4 ☏954 229 294. Slightly east of the Plaza Duque de la Victoria and one of the best-value places in this area. Clean, economical rooms with bath. ❶–❷

Camping
Camping Sevilla ☏954 514 379. Right by the airport, so some noise but otherwise not a bad site; has a pool. The airport bus will get you there, or take bus #70 from outside the main Prado de San Sebastián bus station and ask to be dropped at "Parque Alcosa". The site has its own thrice-daily minibus service ferrying clients to and from central Sevilla with a terminus on Avda. de Portugal near the Prado bus station (services to the campsite at 6.30pm and 10pm).
Club de Campo ☏954 720 250. About 12km south of the centre in Dos Hermanas, with a pool. Half-hourly Amarillos buses from the main bus station or c/Palos de la Frontera, south of the cathedral.

The Cathedral

Sevilla's **Catedral** (July–Sept Mon–Sat 9.30am–4.30pm, Sun 2.30–6pm; Oct–June Mon–Sat 11am–5pm, Sun 2–6pm; €6 including admission to the Giralda, free Sun) was conceived in 1402 as an unrivalled monument to Christian glory: "a building on so magnificent a scale that posterity will believe we were mad". To make way for this new monument, the Almohad mosque (see box on p.296) that stood on the proposed site was almost entirely demolished. Meanwhile, the canons, inspired by their vision of future repute, renounced all but a subsistence level of their incomes to further the building.

The cathedral was completed in just over a century (1402–1506), an extraordinary achievement as it's the largest Gothic church in the world. As Norman Lewis says, "It expresses conquest and domination in architectural terms of sheer mass." Though it is built upon the huge, rectangular base-plan of the old mosque, the Christian architects (probably under the direction of the French master architect of Rouen Cathedral) added the extra dimension of height. Its central nave rises to 42 metres, and even the side chapels seem tall enough to contain an ordinary church. The total area covers 11,520 square metres, and new calculations, based on cubic measurement, have now pushed it in front of St Paul's in London and St Peter's in Rome as the largest church in the world.

From the old mosque, the magnificent **Giralda** and the Moorish entrance court, the **Patio de los Naranjos**, were spared, though the patio is somewhat marred by Renaissance embellishments. The patio was originally entered from c/Alemanes, through the **Puerta del Perdón**, the original main gateway and now the **visitor** exit – the **main visitor entrance** is on the cathedral's south side, through the Puerta de San Cristóbal.

Sevilla's parish churches

Sevilla's parish churches display a fascinating variety of architectural styles. Several are converted mosques with belfries built over their minarets, others range through Mudéjar and Gothic (sometimes in combination), Renaissance and Baroque. Most are kept locked except early in the morning, or in the evenings from about 7 until 10pm – a promising time for a church crawl, especially as they're regularly interspersed with bars.

For a good circuit, make first towards Gothic San Pedro, where a marble tablet records Velázquez's baptism, and San Marcos, with a fine minaret tower. Nearby, in this old cobbled part of town, is the fifteenth-century Convento de Santa Paula (Tues–Sun 10.30am–12.30pm & 4.30–6.30pm; free, but donations welcome), its church decorated with a vivid ceramic facade and superb *azulejos*, with an excellent museum containing fine artworks by Zurbarán and Ribera among others. Further on, you meet the last remaining stretch of Moorish city walls – remains of the Almoravid fortifications which once spanned 12 gates and 166 towers. Now there's only one gate, the Puerta Macarena; beside it a basilica houses the city's cult image and patroness of matadors, *La Esperanza Macarena*, a tearful Virgin seated in the midst of gaudy magnificence.

Looping down towards the river, you reach the Monasterio de Santa Clara (entered from c/Santa Clara no. 40) – once part of the palace of Don Fadrique, brother of Alfonso X, and with a Romanesque-Gothic tower dating from 1252 (tower currently visitable only by appointment ☎954 224 808). A couple of blocks away are the distinctive columns (two at the far end are Roman) of the Alameda de Hércules. This leads back towards the town centre, with two more churches worth a look on the way: the Renaissance chapel of the Universidad Antigua and Baroque San Salvador, the latter built on the site of Sevilla's first Friday mosque (part of whose minaret is incorporated in its tower).

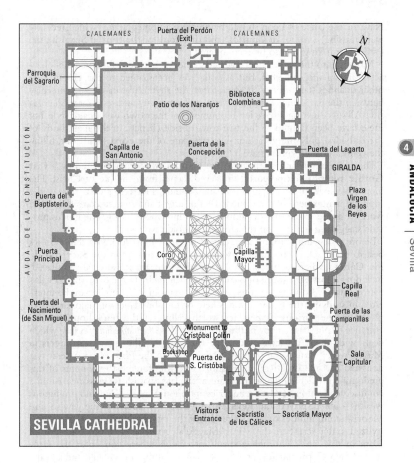

SEVILLA CATHEDRAL

The interior

Entering the cathedral by the Puerta de San Cristóbal, you are guided through a reception area which brings you into the church to the west of the portal itself. Turn right once inside to head east, where you will soon be confronted by the **Monument to Christopher Columbus** (*Cristóbal Colón* in Spanish), actually the explorer's tomb, and located before the doorway dedicated to the saint he was named after. Columbus's remains were originally interred in the cathedral of Havana, on the island that he had discovered on his first voyage in 1492. But during the upheavals surrounding the declaration of Cuban independence in 1902, Spain transferred the remains to Sevilla and the monumental tomb – in the late Romantic style by Arturo Mélida – was created to house them. However, doubts have always been voiced concerning the authenticity of the remains in the tomb, and at the time of writing scientists from the University of Granada are carrying out DNA tests in an attempt to confirm that they are those of Columbus. The mariner's coffin is held aloft by four huge allegorical figures, representing the kingdoms of León, Castile, Aragón and

Navarra; the lance of León should be piercing a pomegranate (which recently went missing), symbol of Granada (and the word for the fruit in Spanish), the last Moorish kingdom to be reconquered.

Moving into the **nave**, sheer size and grandeur are, inevitably, the chief characteristics of the cathedral. But as you grow accustomed to the gloom, two other qualities stand out with equal force: the rhythmic balance and interplay between the parts, and an impressive overall simplicity and restraint in decoration. All successive ages have left monuments of their own wealth and style, but these have been limited to the two rows of side chapels. In the main body of the cathedral only the great box-like structure of the **coro** stands out, filling the central portion of the nave.

The *coro* extends and opens onto the **Capilla Mayor**, dominated by a **vast Gothic retablo** composed of 45 carved scenes from the life of Christ. The lifetime's work of a single craftsman, Fleming Pieter Dancart, this is the supreme masterpiece of the cathedral – the largest and richest altarpiece in the world and one of the finest examples of Gothic woodcarving. The guides provide staggering statistics on the amount of gold involved.

Before proceeding around the edge of the nave in a clockwise direction it's best to backtrack to the church's southeast corner to take in the **Sacristía de los Cálices** where many of the cathedral's main art treasures are displayed, including a masterly image of *Santas Justa y Rufina* by Goya, depicting Sevilla's patron saints, who were executed by the Romans in 287. Should you be interested in studying the many canvases here or the abundance of major artworks placed in the various chapels, it's worth calling at the bookshop near the entrance to purchase a copy of the official *Guide to the Cathedral of Seville* which deals with them in detail. Alongside this room is the grandiose **Sacristía Mayor** which houses the treasury. Embellished in the Plateresque style, it was designed in 1528 by Diego de Riaño, one of the foremost exponents of this predominantly decorative architecture of the late Spanish Renaissance. Amid a confused collection of silver reliquaries and monstrances – dull and prodigious wealth – are displayed the **keys** presented to Fernando by the Jewish and Moorish communities on the surrender of the city; sculpted into the metal in stylized Arabic script are the words "May Allah render eternal the dominion of Islam in this city." Through a small antechamber here you enter the oval-shaped **Sala Capitular** (chapter house), with paintings by Murillo and an outstanding **marble floor** with geometric design.

The route continues by proceeding to the southwest corner and the Puerta del Nacimiento and then turning right (or north) along the west wall, passing the Puerta Principal. In the northwest corner the **Capilla de San Antonio** has Murillo's *Vision of St Anthony* depicting the saint in ecstatic pose before an infant Christ. The nave's north side leads to the Puerta de la Concepción, through which you will exit – but before doing so, continue to the northeast corner to view the domed Renaissance **Capilla Real** (which is not always open), built on the site of the original royal burial chapel and containing the body of Fernando III (*El Santo*) in a suitably rich, silver shrine before the altar. The large tombs on either side of the chapel are those of Fernando's wife, Beatrice of Swabia, and his son, Alfonso the Wise. You are now close to the entry to the Giralda tower.

The Giralda

The **entrance to the Giralda** (same ticket as cathedral) lies to the left of the Capilla Real in the cathedral's northeast corner. Unquestionably the most beautiful building in Sevilla, the **Giralda**, named after the sixteenth-century *giraldillo* or weather vane on its summit, dominates the city skyline. From the entrance you can ascend to the **bell chamber** for a remarkable **view** of the city – and, equally remarkable, a glimpse of the Gothic details of the cathedral's buttresses and statuary. But most impressive of all is the tower's inner construction, a series of 35 gently inclined ramps wide enough to allow two mounted guards to pass.

The **minaret** was the culmination of Almohad architecture, and served as a model for those at their imperial capitals of Rabat and Marrakesh. It was used by the Moors both for calling the faithful to prayer (the traditional function of a minaret) and as an observatory, and was so venerated that they wanted to destroy it before the Christian conquest of the city. This they were prevented from doing by the threat of Alfonso (later King Alfonso X) that "if they removed a single stone, they would all be put to the sword". Instead it became the bell tower of the Christian cathedral.

The Moorish structure took twelve years to build (1184–96) and derives its firm, simple beauty from the shadows formed by blocks of brick trelliswork, different on each side, and relieved by a succession of arched niches and windows. The original harmony has been somewhat spoiled by the Renaissance-era addition of balconies and, to a still greater extent, by the four diminishing storeys of the belfry – added, along with the Italian-sculpted bronze figure of "Faith" which surmounts them, in 1560–68, following the demolition by an earthquake of the original copper spheres. Even so, it remains in its perfect synthesis of form and decoration one of the most important and beautiful monuments of the Islamic world.

To reach the cathedral's **exit**, retrace your steps to the Puerta de la Concepción (see p.306) and beyond this cross the **Patio de los Naranjos** to the Puerta del Perdón, the former main entrance. In the centre of the patio remains a **Moorish fountain** used for the ritual ablutions before entering the mosque. Interestingly, it incorporates a sixth-century font from an earlier Visigothic cathedral, which was in its turn levelled to make way for the mosque.

Archive of the Indies and Ayuntamiento

If the Columbus monument has inspired you, or you have a fervent interest in the navigator's travels, visit **La Casa Lonja**, an austerely impressive sixteenth-century edifice and the city's old stock exchange (*lonja*), opposite the cathedral. This now houses the remarkable **Archivo de las Indias** (Mon–Fri 10am–1pm; free), a monumental storehouse of the archives of the Spanish empire. Among the selection of documents on display are Columbus's log and a changing exhibition of ancient maps and curiosities. At the time of writing the building is undergoing an extensive **refurbishment** with no reopening date scheduled; consult the turismo for the current situation. Another building worth a look and sited slightly to the north of the cathedral is the sixteenth-century **Ayuntamiento** on Plaza de San Francisco, with a richly ornamented Plateresque facade by Diego de Riaño. The interior is open for infrequent guided visits (Tues, Wed & Thurs 5.30–6.30pm; free).

The Alcázar

Rulers of Sevilla have occupied the site of the **Alcázar** (April–Sept Tues–Sat 9.30am–7pm, Sun 9.30am–5pm; Oct–March Tues–Sat 9.30am–6pm, Sun 9.30am–1.30pm; €5) from the time of the Romans. Here was built the great court of the Abbadids, which reached a peak of sophistication and

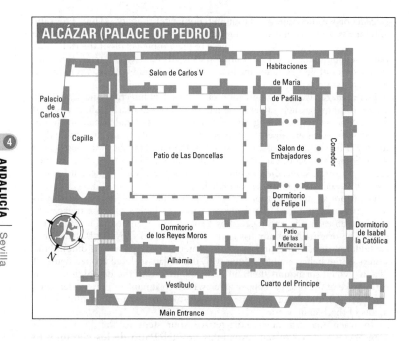

ALCÁZAR (PALACE OF PEDRO I)

- Palacio de Carlos V
- Salon de Carlos V
- Habitaciones de Maria de Padilla
- Capilla
- Patio de Las Doncellas
- Salon de Embajadores
- Comedor
- Dormitorio de Felipe II
- Dormitorio de los Reyes Moros
- Patio de las Muñecas
- Dormitorio de Isabel la Católica
- Alhamia
- Vestibulo
- Cuarto del Principe
- Main Entrance

exaggerated sensuality under the cruel and ruthless al-Mu'tadid – a ruler who enlarged the palace in order to house a harem of eight hundred women, and who decorated the terraces with flowers planted in the skulls of his decapitated enemies. Later, under the **Almohads**, the complex was turned into a citadel, forming the heart of the town's fortifications. Its extent was enormous, stretching to the Torre del Oro on the bank of the Guadalquivir.

Parts of the Almohad walls survive, but the present structure of the palace dates almost entirely from the Christian period. Sevilla was a favoured residence of the Spanish kings for some four centuries after the Reconquest – most particularly of **Pedro the Cruel** (Pedro I; 1350–69) who, with his mistress María de Padilla, lived in and ruled from the Alcázar. Pedro embarked upon a complete rebuilding of the palace, employing workmen from Granada and utilizing fragments of earlier Moorish buildings in Sevilla, Córdoba and Valencia. Pedro's works form the nucleus of the Alcázar as it is today and, despite numerous restorations necessitated by fires and earth tremors, it offers some of the best surviving examples of **Mudéjar architecture** – the style developed by Moors working under Christian rule. Later monarchs, however, have left all too many traces and additions. Isabel built a new wing in which to organize expeditions to the Americas and control the new territories; Carlos V married a Portuguese princess in the palace, adding huge apartments for the occasion; and under Felipe IV (c. 1624) extensive renovations were carried out to the existing rooms. On a more mundane level, kitchens were installed to provide for General Franco, who stayed in the royal apartments (see opposite) whenever he visited Sevilla.

Entry - the Salón del Almirante

The Alcázar is entered from the Plaza del Triunfo, adjacent to the cathedral. The gateway, flanked by original Almohad walls, opens onto a courtyard where Pedro I (who was known as "the Just" as well as "the Cruel", depending on one's fortunes) used to give judgement; to the left is his **Sala de Justicia** and beyond this the **Patio del Yeso**, the only surviving remnant of the Almohads' Alcázar. The main façade of the palace stands at the end of an inner court, the **Patio de la Montería**; on either side are galleried buildings erected by Isabel. This principal façade is pure fourteenth-century Mudéjar and, with its delicate, marble-columned windows, stalactite frieze and overhanging roof, is one of the finest things in the whole Alcázar. But it's probably better to look round the **Salón del Almirante** (or *Casa de Contración de Indias*), the sixteenth-century building on the right, before entering the main palace. Founded by Isabel in 1503, this gives you a standard against which to assess the Moorish forms. Here most of the rooms seem too heavy, their decoration ceasing to be an integral part of the design. The only notable exception is the **Sala de Audiencias** (or Capilla de los Navigantes, Chapel of the Navigators) with its magnificent *artesonado* ceiling inlaid with golden rosettes; within is a fine sixteenth-century **retablo** by Alejo Fernández depicting Columbus (in gold) and Carlos V (in a red cloak) sheltering beneath the Virgin. In the rear, to the left, are portrayed the kneeling figures of the Indians to whom the dubious blessings of Christianity had been brought by the Spanish conquest.

The **royal apartments**, known as the **Palacio Real Alto**, have now been opened for visits when not in use, and a temporary desk located in front of the Salón del Almirante sells tickets (an additional €3) for a guided tour lasting about thirty minutes. This takes in the **royal chapel** with a fine early sixteenth-century **retablo** by Nicola Pisano, the so-called **bedroom of Pedro I**, with fine early Mudéjar plasterwork, and the equally splendid **Sala de Audiencias** – with more stunning plaster and tile decoration – which is still used by the royal family when receiving visitors in Sevilla.

The Palace of Pedro I

As you enter the **Main Palace** the "domestic" nature of Moorish and Mudéjar architecture is immediately striking. This involves no loss of grandeur but simply a shift in scale: the apartments are remarkably small, shaped to human needs, and take their beauty from the exuberance of the decoration and the imaginative use of space and light. There is, too, a deliberate disorientation in the layout of the rooms which makes the palace seem infinitely larger and more open than it really is. From the entrance court a narrow passage leads straight into the central courtyard, the **Patio de las Doncellas** (Patio of the Maidens), its name recalling the Christians' tribute of one hundred virgins presented annually to the Moorish kings. The court's stuccowork, *azulejos* and doors are all of the finest Granada craftsmanship. Interestingly, it's also the only part of the palace where Renaissance restorations are successfully fused – the double columns and upper storey were built by Carlos V, whose *Plus Ultra* ("yet still further") motto recurs in the decorations here and elsewhere.

Past the **Salón de Carlos V**, distinguished by a superb ceiling, are three rooms from the original fourteenth-century design built for María de Padilla (who was popularly thought to use magic in order to maintain her hold over Pedro – and perhaps over other gallants at court, too, who used to drink her bath water). These open onto the **Salón de Embajadores** (Salon of the Ambassadors), the most brilliant room of the Alcázar, with a stupendous *media naranja* (half-orange) wooden dome of red, green and gold cells, and horseshoe arcades inspired by the great palace of Medina Azahara outside Córdoba (see p.356). Although restored, for the worse, by Carlos V – who added balconies and an incongruous frieze of royal portraits to commemorate his marriage to Isabel of Portugal here – the salon stands comparison with the great rooms of Granada's Alhambra. Adjoining are a long dining hall (*comedor*) and a small apartment installed in the late sixteenth century for Felipe II.

Beyond is the last great room of the palace – the **Patio de las Muñecas** (Patio of the Dolls), which takes its curious name from two tiny faces decorating the inner side of one of the smaller arches. It's thought to be the site of the harem in the original palace. In this room Pedro is reputed to have murdered his brother Don Fadrique in 1358; another of his royal guests, Abu Said of Granada, was murdered here for his jewels (one of which, an immense ruby which King Pedro later gave to Edward, the "Black Prince", now figures in the British crown jewels). The upper storey of the court is a much later, nineteenth-century restoration. On the other sides of the patio are the **bedrooms** of Isabel and of her son Don Juan, and the arbitrarily named Dormitorio del los Reyes Moros (Bedroom of the Moorish Kings).

Palacio de Carlos V and the gardens

To the left of the main palace loom the large and soulless apartments of the **Palacio de Carlos V** – something of an endurance test, with endless tapestries and pink-orange or yellow paintwork. Their classical style asserts a different and inferior mood. Best to hurry through to the beautiful and rambling **Alcázar gardens**, the confused but enticing product of several eras, where you can take a well-earned rest from your exertions. Here you'll find the vaulted baths in which María de Padilla is supposed to have bathed (in reality, an auxiliary water supply for the palace) and the **Estanque de Mercurio** with a bronze figure of the messenger of the gods at its centre. This pool was specially constructed for Felipe V in 1733, who whiled away two solitary years at the Alcázar fishing here and preparing himself for death through religious flagellation. Just to the left of the pool a path beyond the Puerta de Marchena leads to a pleasant **cafetería** with a terrace overlooking the gardens. South of here towards the centre of the gardens there's an unusual and entertaining **maze** of myrtle bushes and, nearby, the **pavilion of Carlos V**, the only survivor of several he built for relaxation.

The Plaza de España and María Luisa Park

Ten minutes' walk to the south of the Alcázar, the Plaza de España was laid out in 1929 for an ill-fated "Fair of the Americas". Both this and the adjoining María Luisa Park are among the most pleasant – and impressive – public spaces in Spain.

En route you pass by the **Fábrica de Tabacos**, the city's old tobacco factory and the setting for Bizet's *Carmen*. Now part of the university, this massive structure was built in the 1750s and for a time was the largest building in Spain after El Escorial. At its peak in the following century it was also the country's largest single employer, with a workforce of some 4000 women *cigarreras* – "a class in themselves," according to Richard Ford, who were forced to undergo "an ingeniously minute search on leaving their work, for they sometimes carry off the filthy weed in a manner her most Catholic majesty never dreamt of."

The **Plaza de España**, beyond, was designed as the centrepiece of the Spanish Americas Fair, which was somewhat scuppered by the Wall Street crash. A vast semicircular complex, with its fountains, monumental stairways and mass of tile work, it would seem strange in most Spanish cities but here it looks entirely natural, carrying on the tradition of civic display. At the fair, the Plaza de España was used for the Spanish exhibit of industry and crafts, and around the crescent are *azulejo* scenes representing each of the provinces – an interesting record of the country at the tail end of a moneyed era.

Spaniards and tourists alike come out to the plaza to potter about in the little boats hired out on its tiny strip of canal, or to hide from the sun and crowds amid the ornamental pools and walkways of the **Parque de María Luisa**. The park is designed like the plaza in a mix of 1920s Art Deco and mock-Mudéjar. Scattered about, and round its edge, are more buildings from the fair, some of them amazingly opulent.

Towards the end of the park, the grandest mansions from the fair have been adapted as **museums**. The furthest now houses the city's **Museo Arqueológico** (Tues 3–8pm, Wed–Sat 9am–8pm, Sun 9am–2pm; €1.50, free to EU citizens), the most important archeology collection in Andalucía. The main exhibits include a hoard of prehistoric treasure found in the Sevilla suburb of Camas in 1958, as well as Roman mosaics and artefacts from nearby Italica and a unique Phoenician statuette of Astarte-Tanit, the virgin goddess once worshipped throughout the Mediterranean. Opposite, the fabulous-looking **Popular Arts Museum** (Tues 3–8pm, Wed–Sat 9am–8pm, Sun 9am–2pm; €1.50, free to EU citizens) is often besieged by schoolkids but has interesting displays relating to traditional arts and crafts and the April *feria*.

Barrio Santa Cruz, the river and Triana

Santa Cruz is very much in character with the city's romantic image, its streets narrow and tortuous to keep out the sun, the houses brilliantly whitewashed and barricaded with *rejas* (iron grilles), behind which girls once kept chaste evening rendezvous with their *novios*. Of numerous mansions, by far the finest is the so-called **Casa de Pilatos** (daily 9am–7pm, Oct–June closes 6pm; €5; free on Tues 1–5pm), built by the Marqués de Tarifa on his return from a pilgrimage to Jerusalem in 1519 and popularly thought to have been in imitation of the house of Pontius Pilate. In fact it's an interesting and harmonious mixture of Mudéjar, Gothic and Renaissance styles, featuring brilliant *azulejos*, a tremendous sixteenth-century stairway and one of the most elegant domestic patios in the city.

Patios are a feature of almost all the houses in Santa Cruz: they are often surprisingly large and in summer they become the principal family living room. One of the most beautiful is within the Baroque **Hospicio de los Venerables Sacerdotes** (daily 10am–2pm & 4–8pm; guided visits every 30min; €4.75), near the centre in a plaza of the same name – one of the few buildings in the *barrio* worth actively seeking out. A couple of blocks east of the Hospicio is the **Museo de Murillo**, c/Santa Teresa 8 (currently closed for refurbishment, enquire at turismo for latest information), the seventeenth-century *sevillano* artist's former home; it's furnished with contemporaneous artworks, craftsmanship and furniture – though no original artworks of his own.

Down by the **Guadalquivir** are pedal-boats for idling away the afternoons, and at night a surprising density of local couples. The main riverside landmark here is the twelve-sided **Torre del Oro**, built by the Almohads in 1220 as part of the Alcázar fortifications. It was connected to another small fort across the river by a chain which had to be broken by the Castilian fleet before their conquest of the city in 1248. The tower was later used as a repository for the gold brought back to Sevilla from the Americas – hence its name. It now houses a small **naval museum** (Tues–Fri 10am–2pm, Sat & Sun 11am–2pm; closed Aug; €1). A couple of hundred metres upriver from the Torre del Oro lies the

△ Semana Santa outfitters

Maestranza bullring (daily 9am–2pm & 3–7pm; €4), one of the top three rings in Spain and the setting for the tragic finale of Bizet's opera *Carmen*. Guided visits (in English) allow you to see the impressive interior and a museum documenting its history.

One block away, with its entry on c/Temprado, is the **Hospital de la Caridad** (Mon–Sat 9am–1.30pm & 3.30–6.30pm, Sun 9am–1pm; €3), founded in 1676 by Don Miguel de Mañara, the inspiration for Byron's Don Juan. According to the testimony of one of Don Miguel's friends, "there was no folly which he did not commit, no youthful indulgence into which he did not plunge . . . (until) what occurred to him in the street of the coffin." What occurred was that Don Miguel, returning from a reckless orgy, had a vision in which he was confronted by a funeral procession carrying his own corpse. He repented his past life, joined the Brotherhood of Charity (whose task was to bury the bodies of vagrants and criminals), and later set up this hospital for the relief of the dying and destitute, for which purpose it is still used. Don Miguel commissioned a series of eleven paintings by Murillo for the chapel, six of which remain. Alongside them hang two *Triumph of Death* pictures by Valdés Leal. One, depicting a decomposing bishop being eaten by worms (beneath the scales of justice labelled *Ni más, Ni menos* – No More, No Less), is so powerfully repulsive that Murillo declared that "you have to hold your nose to look at it".

Museo de Bellas Artes

North of the hospital, near the Plaza de Armas bus station, lies one of Spain's most impressive art galleries, the **Museo de Bellas Artes** (Tues 3–8pm, Wed–Sat 9am–8pm, Sun 9am–2pm; €1.50, free to EU citizens), housed in recently modernized premises in a beautiful former convent. You should be aware that the museum has a policy of rotating its collection and not all the works mentioned here may be exhibited.

Among the highlights of an outstanding collection is a wonderful late-fifteenth-century sculpture in painted terracotta in Room 1, *Lamentation over the Dead Christ*, by the Andalucian Pedro **Millán**, the founding father of the Sevilla school of sculpture. A marriage of Gothic and expressive naturalism, this style was the starting point for the outstanding seventeenth-century period of religious iconography in Sevilla. Room 3 has a *retablo* of the Redemption, c.1562, with fine woodcarving by Juan Giralte, while a monumental *Last Supper* by Alonso Vázquez covers an end wall of Room 4.

Beyond a serene patio and cloister, Room 5 is located in the monastery's former church, where the recently restored paintings on the vault and dome by the eighteenth-century *sevillano*, Domingo Martínez, are spectacular. Here also is the nucleus of the collection: **Zurbarán**'s *Apotheosis of St Thomas Aquinas*, as well as a clutch of works by **Murillo** in the apse, crowned by the great *Immaculate Conception* – known as "*la colosal*" to distinguish it from the other work here with the same name. In an alcove nearby you'll see the same artist's *Virgin and Child*: popularly known as *La Servilleta* because it was said to have been painted on a dinner napkin, the work is one of Murillo's greatest.

Upstairs, Room 6 (quadrated around the patio) displays works from the Baroque period, among which a moving *Santa Teresa* by **Ribera** – Spain's master of *tenebrismo* (darkness penetrated by light) – and a stark *Crucifixion* by Zurbarán stand out. Room 10 contains more imposing canvases by Zurbarán, including *St Hugo visiting the Carthusian monks at supper* and another almost sculptural *Crucifixion* to compare with the one in Room 6.

The collection ends with works from the Romantic and Modern eras, where an austere late work by **Goya**, in Room 11, of the octogenarian *Don José Duaso* compensates for some not terribly inspiring works accompanying it. Room 14 contains *Juan Centeno y su cuadrilla* by Huelvan artist (and friend of Picasso) Daniel Vázquez Díaz: this monumental image of the *torero* and his team provides an appropriately *andaluz* conclusion to a memorable museum.

Triana and La Cartuja

Over the river is the **Triana** *barrio*, scruffy, lively and well away from the tourist trails. This was once the heart of the city's *gitano* community and, more specifically, home of the great flamenco dynasties of Sevilla who were kicked out by developers early last century and are now scattered throughout the city. The *gitanos* lived in extended families in tiny, immaculate communal houses called *corrales* around courtyards glutted with flowers; today only a handful remain intact. Triana is still, however, the starting point for the annual pilgrimage to El Rocío (at the end of May), when a myriad painted wagons leave town, drawn by oxen. It houses, too, the city's oldest working **ceramics factory**, Santa Ana, where the tiles, many still in the traditional, geometric Arabic designs, are hand-painted in the adjoining shop.

At Triana's northern edge lies **La Cartuja** (Tues–Fri 10am–8pm, Sat 11am–8pm, Sun 10am–2.30pm; Oct–March closes Tues–Sat at 7.30pm; €3, free Tues for EU citizens), a fourteenth-century former Carthusian monastery expensively restored as part of the Expo '92 world fair. Part of the complex is now given over to the **Centro Andaluz de Arte Contemporáneo** (same hours and ticket as La Cartuja), which, in addition to displaying some important works by contemporary *andaluz* artists, frequently stages exhibitions of work by international painters and sculptors.

The remnants of much of the **Expo '92 site** itself have been incorporated into the **Isla Mágica** (April–Sept Tues–Thurs 11am–7pm, Fri–Sun 11am–10pm; July–Aug Fri–Sun closes midnight; €19, half-day after 4pm €13), an amusement park based on the theme of sixteenth-century Spain, with water and rollercoaster rides, shows and period street animations.

Outside the city: Roman Italica

The Roman ruins and remarkable mosaics of **ITALICA** (April–Sept Tues–Sat 8.30am–8.30pm, Sun 9am–3pm; Oct–March Tues–Sat 9am–5.30pm, Sun 10am–4pm; €1.50, free to EU citizens) lie some 9km to the north of Sevilla, just outside the village of Santiponce. There's also a well-preserved **Roman theatre** in Santiponce itself, signposted from the main road.

Italica was the birthplace of two emperors (Trajan and Hadrian) and one of the earliest Roman settlements in Spain, founded in 206 BC by Scipio Africanus as a home for his veterans. It rose to considerable military importance in the second and third centuries AD, was richly endowed during the reign of Hadrian (117–138), and declined as an urban centre only under the Visigoths, who preferred Sevilla, then known as *Hispalis*. Eventually the city was deserted by the Moors after the river changed its course, disrupting the surrounding terrain.

Throughout the Middle Ages the ruins were used as a source of stone for Sevilla, but somehow the shell of its enormous **amphitheatre** – the third largest in the Roman world – has survived. Today it's crumbling perilously, but you can clearly detect the rows of seats, the corridors and the dens for wild beasts. Beyond, within a rambling and unkempt grid of **streets** and **villas**, about twenty **mosaics** have been uncovered. Most are complete, including excellent coloured floors depicting birds, Neptune and the seasons, and several fine black-and-white geometric patterns.

Getting to Italica, buses depart every half-hour from the Plaza de Armas station for the twenty-minute journey; you need the Empresa Casal service to Santiponce, which departs from Bay 33. Santiponce is not well endowed with facilities, but the *Ventarillo Canario* **restaurant** almost opposite the Italica site entrance does good and economical *platos combinados* and is famous for its grilled steaks served on wooden slabs with *papas arrugadas* – small baked potatoes in *mojo* spicy sauce.

Eating and drinking

Sevilla is packed with lively and enjoyable bars and restaurants, and you'll find somewhere to eat and drink at just about any hour. With few exceptions, anywhere around the sights and the **Barrio Santa Cruz** will be expensive. The two most promising central areas are down **towards the bullring** and north of here towards the Plaza de Armas bus station. The **Plaza de Armas** area is slightly seedier but has the cheapest *comidas* this side of the river. Wander down c/Marqués de Paradas, and up c/Canalejas and c/San Eloy, and find out what's available. Across the river in **Triana**, c/Betis and c/Pureza are also good hunting grounds.

Barrio Santa Cruz and Cathedral area

La Albahaca Plaza Santa Cruz 29. Charming, traditional and expensive restaurant with outdoor tables in one of the Barrio Santa Cruz's prettiest squares. Closed Sun.

Bar Modesto c/Cano y Cueto. At the north end of Santa Cruz, this mid-priced bar-restaurant offers a tempting *menú* (€12) and great tapas. House specials include *punta de solomillo* (pork tenderloin), *coquinas* (clams) and *cañaillas* (murex shellfish).

Hotel Alfonso XIII c/San Fernando 2 ☎954 222 850. Swankiest place in town constructed to house guests visiting the 1929 exhibition; worth a look at this beautiful building and its stunning patio even if you don't sit down in the pricey restaurant. Has recently opened a Japanese restaurant (☎954 220 988) in its grounds with a *menú* for €17.

La Judería c/Cano y Cueto 13, near the Iglesia de Santa María la Blanca. Solid mid-priced restaurant with a tempting *menú* for around €15. *Revueltos* are a speciality here.

Pizzeria San Marco c/Meson del Moro 4, Santa Cruz. Good, economical Italian pasta and pizzas served inside a remarkable twelfth-century Moorish bathhouse.

Café Rayuela c/Miguel de Mañara 9. Pleasant lunch-time venue serving value-for-money *raciones* and salads at outdoor tables in a pedestrianized street behind the turismo.

Triana and the Río Guadalquivir

Café-Bar Veracruz Paseo de Cristóbal Colón s/n, opposite the Torre del Oro near the river. Simple no-frills roadside place offering a bargain €6 *menú*, makes a good lunch stop.

Habanita c/Golfo s/n, a small street off c/Pérez Galdos close to Plaza de la Encarnación. Vegetarian dishes with a Cuban slant are served up at this economical diner; try their *yuca con salsa mojito* (sweet potato with spicy sauce) and *berenjenas Habanita* (aubergine house-style).

Jalea Real c/Sor Ángela de la Cruz 37, near the church of San Pedro. Excellent, moderately priced vegetarian restaurant run by a friendly and enthusiastic *sevillana*. Closed Mon.

Río Grande c/Betis 70. This Triana restaurant has the best view in town from its terrace on the river's west bank, and a medium-priced *menú*. Its tapas bar is also worth a visit.

La Sopa Boba, c/Bailén 34, just off the Plaza del Museo on the Museo de Bellas Artes' doorstep. Tasty experimental home cooking, with a good-value *menú*.

La Triana c/Castilla 36 in Triana ☎954 333 819. Excellent new upmarket restaurant with a wonderful terrace overlooking the river. Superb service and a *menú* for €18. House specials include *lomo con salsa de castañas y ciruelas* (pork with chestnut and plum sauce) and *rollitos de pavo* (turkey). They also have tapas and *raciones*.

Centro, La Macarena, Almeda and Santa Justa

Entre dos Hermandades c/Recaredo 13, near the Casa de Pilatos. Friendly restaurant and bar with perhaps the best value *menú* in town; €5 gets you three courses with wine and bread.

Kiosko de las Flores c/Betis next door to the *Río Grande* (above). One of Sevilla's best-loved fried fish emporia on the riverside with a delightful terrace; economical tapas served in the bar and moderately priced *raciones* on the terrace – just the place on a summer night. Closed Mon.

La Mandrágora c/Albuera 11, just north of the Maestranza bullring, across c/Reyes Católicos.

Sevilla's second vegetarian restaurant, with a wide range of dishes and a *menú*.

María Angeles Puente de Triana ☎954 331 251. Sitting atop the western end of the Puente de Triana (aka Puente de Isabel II) the dining room gives amazing river views. The kitchen here is Basque and the fish and meat is imported from their northern homeland. Dishes are mid-priced but there's a *menú* for €12 and a decent tapas bar (with more great views) that also opens for breakfast.

Mesón Serranito Alfonso XII 9, behind the El Corte Inglés department store. Cosy little restaurant beyond the tapas bar out front, with excellent fish and meat dishes and an economical *menú*.

Bars

For casual eating and drinking and taking tapas – Sevilla's great speciality – there are **bars** all over town. The tapas venues all serve barrelled sherries from nearby Jerez and Sanlúcar (the locals drink the cold, dry *fino* with their tapas, especially *camarones* or shrimps); a *tinto de verano* is the local version of *sangría* – wine with lemonade, a great summer drink. Outside the centre, you'll find lively bars in the **Plaza Alfafa** area, and across the river in **Triana** – particularly in c/Castilla, c/Betis, and in and around c/Salado. Over recent years a zone that has emerged as a focus for artistic, student and gay barhoppers is the **Alameda** (de Hércules). In summer much of the action emigrates to the bars along the **river's east bank** to the north of the Triana bridge as far as the spectacular Puente de la Barqueta, built for Expo '92. Many of these open for a season only, springing up the following year under a new name and ownership. Tapas bars tend to close around nine in the evening but many drinking bars keep going until well beyond midnight.

Barrio Santa Cruz and Cathedral area

Bar Giralda c/Mateus Gagos 1. Excellent and popular bar in converted ancient Moorish bathhouse, with a wide selection of tapas.

Casa Morales c/García de Vinuesa 11. Atmospheric traditional bar (founded 1850) with barrelled wine.

La Gitanilla c/Ximénez de Enciso s/n. One of the liveliest places in Santa Cruz, with inexpensive drinks, but pricey tapas.

Las Teresas c/Santa Teresa 2, to the north of Plaza Santa Cruz. Good beer and sherry served in this atmospheric bar with hanging cured hams and tiled walls lined with faded *corrida* photos. It's also worth stopping here for breakfast the morning after.

Triana and the Río Guadalquivir

Anima c/Miguel Cid 80, north of the Museo de Bellas Artes. Lovely old tiled bar which mounts periodic art and photo exhibitions.

La Barqueta just south of the spectacular bridge of the same name. Stylish open-air bar which puts on music, concerts, theatre and shows throughout the summer.

El Capote c/Radio Sevilla off c/Arjona, close to the Puente de Triana. Popular summer terrace bar with a varied clientele which gets younger as the night wears on.

La Otra Orilla Paseo de Nuestra Señora de la "O" s/n, near the Puente de Triana. Riverside open-air bar owned by the proprietors of *La Barqueta* (above), with a similar ambience.

Centro, La Macarena, Almeda and Santa Justa

Bulebar Alameda de Hercules 83. Lively *copas* bar that stays open late with an outdoor plant-filled terrace looking onto the Alameda. They often stage theatre or other music shows, usually on Wed. Also do good tapas.

Bar Eslava c/Eslava 3–5, near the church of San Lorenzo. Very good and extremely popular – which often means you can't get through the door – tapas bar with restaurant attached.

El Refugio c/Huelva 5. Slightly west of Plaza del Salvador, this serves a wide variety of snacks, including vegetarian tapas.

El Rinconcillo c/Gerona 32, by the church of Santa Catalina. Sevilla's oldest bar (founded in 1670) does a fair tapas selection as well as pro-viding a hangout for the city's literati.

Sopa de Ganso c/Pérez Galdos 8, close to Plaza Alfalfa. Young, lively bar in one of the city's main nightlife zones. Until midnight it operates as a tapas bar and – on the stroke of twelve – the illumination changes from orange to blue, the food stops and it becomes a late-night *copas* bar with cool sounds.

Nightlife

Sevilla is a wonderfully late-night city, and in summer and during fiestas, the streets around the central areas – particularly the Plaza de Alfalfa, the Alameda de Hercules and Triana riverfront zones – are often packed out until the small hours.

Flamenco

Flamenco music and dance is on offer at dozens of places in the city, some of them extremely tacky and expensive. Unless you've heard otherwise, avoid the fixed "shows" or *tablaos* (many of which are a travesty, even using recorded music). The spontaneous nature of flamenco makes it almost impossible to timetable into the two-shows-a-night cabaret demanded by impresarios. The nearest you'll get to the real thing is at *Los Gallos*, in the Plaza Santa Cruz (Ⓦ www.tablaolosgallos.com), which has a professional cast. However, it is pricey (€27 incl. one drink), and you'd probably do just as well at *El Tamboril*, a renowned flamenco bar in the opposite corner of the same square. Singers and dancers aren't guaranteed to drop in (around midnight is best), but when they do, you're in for an unforgettable night.

Another excellent bar which often has spontaneous flamenco (try Mon or Thurs after 10pm) is *La Carbonería*, c/Levies 18, just to the northeast of the church of Santa Cruz. It used to be the coal merchant's building (hence the name) and is a large, simple and welcoming place. *Quita Pesares*, in the Plaza Jerónimo de Córdoba near the church of Santa Catalina, is run by a flamenco singer, and is a chaotic place where there's often impromptu music (especially at weekends) when things get lively around midnight. Other places to try are *Casa de la Memoria de Al-Andalus*, c/Jiménez de Enciso 28 in Barrio Santa Cruz (☎954 560 670), which has concerts most nights and charges €11 for entry, and *Sol Café Cantante*, c/Sol 5, in *barrio* La Macarena, a very good and serious flamenco theatre dedicated to discovering new talent, which also stages big-name artists from all over Andalucía; shows here start at 10pm (Thurs–Sat only) and cost €12, including one free drink.

Live music and clubs

For **rock and pop music** the bars around Plaza Alfalfa and the Alameda de Hércules have most of the best action. Recommended music bars on the Alameda include *Bulebar* and *La Habanilla* at the northern end, *El Baron Rampante* in c/Arias Montano about halfway along, and *Fun Club* – which stages frequent live gigs – on the Alameda proper. At c/Adriano 10, on the north side of the bullring, *Arena* is another popular music bar specializing in rock, jazz and funk. **Live jazz** can be found at the popular *Naima*, just off the Alameda at c/Trajano 47 (closed Aug). The vibrant café-bar *La Imperdible*, Plaza

San Antonio de Padua, between the Alameda de Hércules and the river (closed July & Aug), stages live music, with various other entertainments (including multilingual poetry evenings) throughout the week.

Major **concerts**, whether touring British and American bands or big Spanish acts like Paco de Lucía, Alejandro Sanz or Ketama, often take place in the old Expo site across the river in Cartuja or in one or other of the football stadiums. Check *El Giraldillo* (the turismo's free listings magazine), the local paper *El Correo* or street posters for possibilities. La Teatral, c/Velázquez 12 near the Plaza del Duque de la Victoria (☎954 228 229), is the official ticket agent for many concerts, and tickets are also sold by the El Corte Inglés department store.

A strong night-time **club and disco** scene in Triana livens up c/Betis and its northern extension c/Castilla where the disco-club *Boss*, c/Betis 67, is a popular venue, as is *La Otra Orilla* (on the river behind the church of Nuestra Señora de la O) with a great terrace overlooking the river. Another popular hot spot for late-night clubbing is *Luna Park*, facing the Teatro Lope de Vega, Avda. de María Luisa s/n, near the Plaza de España (top right-hand corner of our city map) with dance spaces offering salsa, house, garage and more – weekends are best, and not before midnight.

Listings

Airport For flight information, call ☎954 449 000. For international and domestic flights run by Iberia ring ☎902 400 500.

Banks and currency exchange ATMs are located throughout the centre of town, for example around the Avda. de la Constitución and around Plaza Duque de la Victoria. *Bureaux de change* can be found on Plaza Nueva but banks are a cheaper option. American Express, Plaza Nueva 7 ☎954 211 617 (Mon–Fri 9.30am–1.30pm & 4.30–8pm, Sat 9.30am–1pm), and the El Corte Inglés department store on Plaza Duque de la Victoria (Mon–Sat 10am–10pm), offer good exchange rates, and most large hotels change notes (although rates tend to be poor).

Bike and scooter rental Human Cycles, c/San Esteban 24 near the Casa de Pilatos (☎954 531 411) rents out cycles for €15 per day (no half days) and El Ciclismo, Paseo Catalina de Ribera 2, at the north end of the Jardines de Murillo (closed Aug; ☎954 411 959), is another possibility, with similar prices. Motorcycles, scooters and cycles can be rented from Alkimoto, c/Fernando Tirado 5 (☎954 584 927), slightly south of the Santa Justa train station; prices for cycles are €6 per day and prices start at €21 per day for scooters and motorcycles.

Books and newspapers A wide range of books in English is stocked by Vértice, c/San Fernando 33, near the Alcázar. The Beta chain is good for guides and maps; central branches include Avda. de la Constitución 9 and 27 and Plaza de la Gavidia 7. El Corte Inglés on Plaza Duque de la Victoria stocks English titles and international press. A more comprehensive range of international newspapers is stocked by Esteban, c/Alemanes 15, next to the cathedral. Sevilla's best all-round daily paper is currently *El Diario de Sevilla*, although the older *El Correo* and *Sevilla Información* also sell well; all are good for entertainment listings and local news.

Bullfights The main *corridas* are staged during the April *feria*, but not regularly outside this month. Details and tickets from the Plaza de Toros (☎954 210 315) on fight days from 4.30pm or in advance (with commission) from a *taquilla* (ticket window) at c/Adriano 24.

Car rental Avis (☎954 537 861) and Europcar (☎954 533 914) are located on the main concourse of the Santa Justa train station. Good local deals are to be had from Atlantic, c/Almirante Lobo 2 (☎954 227 893), just off the Puerta de Jerez, and Ata S.A. (☎954 216 549) in the same building.

Cinema Most movies showing are listed in *El Giraldillo*, the listings mag available from the turismo; "*V.O.*" indicates a screening in the original-language; Cine Avenida, c/Marqués de Paradas 15, specializes in *V.O.* films. Open-air *cines de verano* (July–Sept) are great places for a beer and a tapa while watching a movie – one of the best, showing many "*V.O.*" movies, is at the Diputación de Sevilla (opposite the Jardines de Murillo); you should consult the turismo for the latest locations of others, as they tend to change yearly.

Consulates Australia, c/Federico Rubio 14 ☎954 220 971; Canada, Avda. de los Pinos 34, Casa 4, Mairena del Aljarafe ☎954 229 413; Ireland, Plaza

Santa Cruz 6, Bajo A ☏954 216 361; UK, nearest in Málaga: ☏952 352 300; USA, Paseo de las Delicias 7 ☏954 231 885.

Football Sevilla has two major first division teams: Sevilla CF play at the Sánchez Pizjuan stadium (☏954 535 353) and Real Betis (currently the more successful outfit) use the Estadio Benito Villamarín (☏954 610 340). Match schedules are in the local or national press and tickets are surprisingly easy to get hold of for many matches (check the stadium or tourist offices).

Hiking maps 1:50,000, 1:100,000 and 1:200,000 maps can be purchased from Cartolap, Edificio Sevilla, c/San Francisco Javier 9, Local 4 (☏954 656 612), south of the Santa Justa train station. A "made-to-measure" map service will make up maps in the above scales for a defined area; ring Cartofoto del Sur, c/Las Cruzadas 7, immediately behind the Plaza de España (☏954 423 063). Risko, Avda. Kansas City 26, close to Santa Justa train station (☏954 570 849), also stocks maps as well as a wide range of outdoor equipment.

Hospital English-speaking doctors available at the Hospital Universitario Virgen Macarena, c/Dr Marañon s/n (☏955 614 140) behind the Andalucía parliament building to the north of the centre. For emergencies, dial ☏061.

Internet access There are numerous Internet cafés all around the centre of town and several bars now have screens for online access. Almost opposite the cathedral's main entrance, *Seville Internet Center*, c/Almirantazgo 2 on the first floor (daily 9am–10pm; €3 per hr, minimum €0.50 per minute; ☏954 500 275) is probably the most central location. Much cheaper is *Ciberducke*, Plaza del Duque de la Victoria 11 near El Corte Inglés (daily 10am–11pm; €1.50 per hr, minimum €0.15 for 10 min; ☏954 563 417). *Alfalfa 10*, Plaza de Alfalfa 10 (daily noon–1am; €2.70 per hr, minimum €0.75 for 15min; ☏954 213 841) is another possibility.

Markets Entertaining Sunday *mercadillos* (roughly 10am–2pm depending on weather) take place on the Plaza del Cabildo opposite the Cathedral (stamps, coins, pins, ancient artefacts), Plaza de Bellas Artes in front of the museum (various art, tiles and woodcarvings) and Plaza Alfalfa (pets). Calle Feria's longstanding *El Hueves* (Thursday market) with second-hand articles and antiques, near the Alameda de Hercules, is another good one. The enormously popular main Sunday market which used to take place along the Alameda de Hercules has been moved following the revamping of this landmark and now takes place in the Parque del Alamillo, reached by crossing the spectacular Puente del Alamillo (off the left side of our city map beyond the Puente de la Barqueta) to the river's west bank and veering right; items on sale here cover the whole gamut including antique furniture, clothes, books, broken toys, household appliances, as well as piles of fascinating junk.

Police Bag-snatching is big business. If you lose something, get the theft documented ("quiero hacer una denuncia" are the words you should use) at the Plaza de la Gavidia station ☏954 289 300, near Plaza de la Victoria. Dial ☏092 (local police) or ☏091 (national) in an emergency.

Post office Avda. de la Constitución 32, by the cathedral; *Lista de Correos* (poste restante) Mon–Fri 8.30am–8.30pm, Sat 9.30am–2pm.

Taxis The main central taxi ranks are in Plaza Nueva, the Alameda de Hércules and the Plaza de Armas and Prado de San Sebastián bus stations. The basic charge for a short journey is €3.50. A reliable taxi service, Radio Taxi, will come and collect you if you ring them on ☏954 580 000.

Telephones c/Sierpes 11, down a passageway (Mon–Fri 10am–2pm & 5–8.30pm, Sat 10am–2pm). However, it's much more convenient to make local and international calls with a *tarjeta telefónica* (phonecard) which can be purchased at *kioskos* and *estancos* (state tobacco shops).

Train information For tickets/info go to the RENFE office, off the Plaza Nueva at c/Zaragoza 29; Mon–Fri 9.15am–1.30pm & 4–7pm for information and reservations. The central number for all train and timetable enquiries, plus reservations, is ☏902 240 202.

The Sierra Morena

The longest of Spain's mountain ranges, the **Sierra Morena** extends almost the whole way across Andalucía – from Rosal on the Portuguese frontier to the dramatic pass of Despeñaperros, north of Linares. Its hill towns marked the northern boundary of the old Moorish caliphate of Córdoba and in many ways the region still signals a break, with a shift from the climate and mentality of the south to the bleak plains and villages of Extremadura and New Castile. The range is not widely known – with its highest point a mere 1110m, it's not a dramatic sierra – and even Andalucians can have trouble placing it.

Climate, flora and fauna

The Morena's climate is mild – sunny in spring, hot but fresh in summer – but it can be very cold in the evenings and mornings. Tracks are still more common than roads, and tourism, which the government of Andalucía is keen to encourage, has so far meant little more than a handful of new signs indicating areas of special interest.

A good **time to visit** is between March and June, when the flowers, perhaps the most varied in the country, are at their best. You may get caught in the odd thunderstorm but it's usually bright and hot enough to swim in the reservoirs or splash about in the clear springs and streams, all of which are good to drink. If your way takes you along a river, you'll be entertained by armies of frogs and turtles plopping into the water as you approach, by lizards, dragonflies, bees, hares and foxes peering discreetly from their holes – and, usually, no humans present for miles round.

The locals maintain that, while the last bears disappeared only a short time ago, there are still a few wolves in remoter parts. Of more concern to anyone trekking in the Sierra Morena, however, are the **toros bravos** (fighting bulls), since you are quite likely to come across them. They should always be in fenced-off pastures with explicit signs warning you to keep out (*toros peligros* are the words to look out for), but these often disappear or are not put up in the first place. Apparently, a group of bulls is less to be feared than a single one, and a single one only if he directly bars your way and looks mean. The thing to do, according to expert advice, is to stay calm, and without attracting the bull's attention, go round. If you even get a whiff of a fighting bull, though, it might well be best to adopt the time-honoured technique – drop everything and run.

Getting around the sierra

East–west **transport** in the sierra is very limited. Most of the bus services are radial and north–south, with Sevilla as the hub, and this leads to ridiculous situations where, for instance, to travel from Santa Olalla to Cazalla, a distance of some 53km, you must take a bus to Sevilla, 70km away, and then another up to Cazalla – a full day's journey of nearly 150km just to get from one town to the next. The best solution if you want to spend any amount of time in Morena is to organize your routes round **treks**. A bicycle, too, could be useful, but your own car much less so – this is not Michelin car-window-view territory. If you have a **bike**, you'll need plenty of gears, especially for the road between El Real de la Jara and El Pintado (Santa Olalla–Cazalla), while the roads round Almonaster, and between Cazalla and Constantina, are very bad for cycling.

Buses from Sevilla to the sierra leave from the Plaza de Armas station. If you just want to make a quick foray into the hills, **Aracena** is probably the best target (and the most regularly served town). If you're planning on some walking it's also a good starting point: before you leave Sevilla, however, be sure to get yourself a decent **map** (see Sevilla "Listings" on p.318) which, though it will probably be crammed with misleading information, should point you in the right direction to get lost somewhere interesting.

Aracena – and its sierra

Some 90km northwest of Sevilla, **ARACENA** is the highest town in the Sierra Morena with a sharp, clear air, all the more noticeable after the heat of the city. A substantial but pretty place, it rambles partly up the side of a hill topped by the **Iglesia del Castillo**, a Gothic-Mudéjar church built by the Knights Templar around the remains of a Moorish castle. The town is flanked to the south and west by a small offshoot of the Sierra Morena – the **Sierra de Aracena** – a wonderfully verdant corner of Andalucía with wooded hills and cobble-streeted villages.

Although the church is certainly worth the climb, Aracena's principal attraction is the **Gruta de las Maravillas** (daily 10.30am–1.30pm & 3–6pm; guided hourly visits, half-hourly at weekends; €6), the largest and arguably the most impressive cave in Spain. Supposedly discovered by a local boy in search of a lost pig, the cave is now illuminated and there are guided tours as soon as two dozen or so people have assembled. To protect the cave there is now a strict limit of **35 persons per visit**, and at weekends and holiday periods you would be advised to try to visit the cave before noon; coach parties with advance bookings tend to fill up the afternoon allocation. On Sunday there is a constant procession, but usually plenty of time to gaze and wonder. The cave is astonishingly beautiful, and funny too – the last chamber of the tour is known as the Sala de los Culos (Room of the Buttocks), its walls and ceiling an outrageous, naturally sculpted exhibition, tinged in a pinkish orange light. Close by the cave's entrance are a couple of excellent restaurants, open lunchtime only. Aracena is at the heart of a prestigious *jamón*-producing area, so try to sample some, and, when they're available, the delicious wild asparagus and local snails – in the fields in spring and summer respectively.

Practicalities

Aracena has a **turismo**, located at the Gruta (daily 10am–2pm & 4–6.30pm; ☎959 128 206). There are limited **places to stay**, the best of which, at the bottom end of the scale, is *Casa Manolo*, below the main square at c/Barberos 6 (☎959 128 014; ❶). Alternatively, the *Hotel Sierra de Aracena*, Gran Vía 21 (☎955 126 175; ❸), offers relative luxury. There's also a **campsite** with pool (☎959 501 005; April–Sept) about 3km out along the Sevilla road, then left for 500m on the road towards Corteconcepción. For **meals**, the medium-priced *Restaurante José Vicente*, Avda. Andalucía 51 (☎959 128 455), opposite the park, specializes in *jamón* and pork dishes, including a mouthwatering *solomillo* (pork loin); a recent addition here is an outstanding tapas bar. Good tapas and *platos combinados* are on offer at the more basic *Café-Bar Manzano*, at the southern end of the main square, Plaza Marqués de Aracena. If you intend to do some **walking in the sierra**, useful information (including maps and leaflets on flora and fauna) on the surrounding Parque Natural Sierra de Aracena y Picos de Aroche is obtainable from an **information centre** in the ancient *cabildo* (town hall), Plaza Alta 5 (daily 10am–2pm & 4–6pm). You should also ask at the turismo for a pamphlet entitled *Senderismo* (paths), which details waymarked trails between the local villages.

Villages around Aracena

Surrounding Aracena you'll find a scattering of attractive but economically depressed villages, most of them dependent on the **jamón industry** and its curing factory at Jabugo. *Jamón serrano* (mountain ham) is a *bocadillo* standard throughout Spain and some of the best, *jamón de bellota* (acorn-fed ham), comes from the Morena, where herds of sleek grey pigs grazing beneath the trees are a constant feature. In October the acorns drop and the pigs, waiting patiently below, gorge themselves, become fat and are promptly whisked off to be slaughtered and then cured in the dry mountain air.

The **sierra villages** – Jabugo, Aguafría, Almonaster La Real – all make rewarding bases for walks, though all are equally ill-served by public transport (details from the Aracena turismo). The most interesting is **ALMONASTER**

LA REAL, whose castle encloses a tiny ninth-century mosque, **La Mezquita** (daily 9.30am–sunset), with what is said to be the oldest **mihrab** in Spain. Tacked onto the mosque is the village bullring which sees action once a year in August during the annual fiesta. The village also has a couple of **places to eat and stay**: the very hospitable *Pensión La Cruz*, Plaza El Llano 8 (☎959 143 135; ❶), in the centre with a good restaurant, and *Hotel Casa García* (☎955 143 109; ❷), at the entrance to the village, which also has a fine restaurant, with great *jamón* and *ensaladilla*. There are some superb paint-splashed waymarked walks northwest of the village, off the Cortegana road; a leaflet detailing these and other walks in the area can be found at the *ayuntamiento* on Plaza de la Constitución.

Zufre and east to Cazalla and Constantina

From Aracena a single daily **bus** (except Sun) – currently at 5.30pm, connecting with the bus from Sevilla – covers the 25km southeast to Zufre. Timetables and frequency of service change, so check with the turismo in Aracena for the latest information. Ten kilometres out of Aracena you come upon the **Embalse de Aracena**, one of the huge reservoirs that supply Sevilla, and from here a lovely but circuitous route will take you down towards **Zufre** along the **Rivera de Huelva**. From Zufre east there are no buses directly linking the villages en route to Cazalla.

Zufre

ZUFRE must rank as one of the most spectacular villages in Spain, hanging like a miniature Ronda on a high palisade at the edge of a ridge. Below the crumbling Moorish walls, the cliff falls away hundreds of metres, terraced into deep green gardens of orange trees and vegetables. Within the town the **ayuntamiento** and **church** are both interesting examples of Mudéjar style, the latter built in the sixteenth century on the foundations of a mosque. In the basement of the *ayuntamiento* too, is a gloomy line of stone seats, said to have been used by the Inquisition. The focus of town, however, is the **Paseo**, a little park with rose gardens, a balcony, a bar at one end and a *Casino* (bar-club) at the other. Here the villagers gather for much of the day: there is little work either in Zufre or its surrounding countryside. For **accommodation** Zufre has a new *hostal, La Posa*, c/Cibarranco 5 (☎959 198 110; ❶), with en-suite rooms, while for **food and drink** a couple of bars – *Aleman* and *Benito* on the Plaza La Quebrada in the warren of Moorish streets above the park – serve tapas.

Santa Olalla

SANTA OLALLA DEL CALA, the next village to the east, is a walkable 16km from Zufre, which – without transport of your own – may be your only option as there is no bus link, although locals are often willing to give lifts. It's a flattish route through open country with pigs and fields of wheat and barley, and then a sudden view of the Moorish **castillo** above the town. There have been several half-hearted attempts to reconstruct the castle, but they haven't been helped by its adaptation in the last century as the local cemetery – the holes for coffins in the walls rather spoil the effect. Below its walls is the fifteenth-century parish **church**, with a fine Renaissance interior.

Coming from Zufre, it's a surprise to find several **hostales** to choose from in Santa Olalla, and this is due to the town's location astride the main Sevilla–Badajoz road which sees a fair amount of traffic between the two cities including regular buses, which stop outside the friendly *Bar Primitivo*, c/Marina 3. Nearby, rooms are to be had at the comfortable *Casa Carmelo*, c/Marina 23

(☎959 190 169; ❶), some with bath. For **food** both places serve economical *menús*, with the latter specializing in the excellent *jamones* and *salchichas* from the pig farms hereabouts.

Real de la Jara

After 4km of winding through stone-walled olive groves, the road flattens out into a grassy little valley above the **Río Cala** – a spot where the villages of Real and Olalla hold their joint *romería* at the end of April. These country *romerías* are always good to stumble upon, and if you happen on one in the Sierra Morena you should be well looked after. Proceedings start with a formal parade to the local *ermita*, but they're very soon given over to feasting and dancing, the young men wobbling about on donkeys and mules in a wonderful parody of the grand *hidalgo* doings of Jerez and Sevilla, children shrieking and splashing in the river, and everyone dancing *sevillanas* to scratchy cassettes.

REAL DE LA JARA, 8km east of Santa Olalla, is in much the same mould, with two impressive, ruined Moorish *castillos*. For **rooms** there's a friendly *casa de huéspedes* at c/Real 70 (❶); there are also a few bars serving food and a very welcome public swimming pool. Cazalla de la Sierra, the next village, is some 45km along a mountainous route which sees few cars.

Cazalla and the central sierra

Another regional sierra "capital", **CAZALLA DE LA SIERRA** seems quite a metropolis with its comparative abundance of facilities, and in fact the town dates back to the times of the Romans – its original name of *Callentum* was later changed to *Kazalla* ("fortified city") by the Moors.

The main sight is the church of **Nuestra Señora de la Consolación** at the southern end of town, an outstanding example of *andaluz* "mix and match" architecture – begun in the fourteenth century, continued with some nice Renaissance touches and finally completed in the eighteenth century.

There are also some fine spots within easy wandering distance of the town: a walk of just 5km will take you east to the **Ermita del Monte**, a little eighteenth-century church on a wooded hill above the Ribera de Huéznar. To begin the walk head south from the centre along the road to El Pedroso – the way leading to the *ermita* is signed on the left after 200m.

A rather sleepy **tourist office** at Paseo del Moro 2 (Wed–Fri 10am–2pm, Sat & Sun 10.30am–2.30pm; closed Mon & Tues; ☎954 884 560) has information on the region but not a town map; this is available from the *ayuntamiento* (same hours) a five-minute walk away at Plaza Dr. Narcea 1. Among a number of **hostales** in Cazalla the best is perhaps *La Milagrosa*, c/Llana 29, on the main street (☎954 884 260; ❶). There are also several upmarket hotels, including the charming *Posada del Moro*, c/Paseo del Moro s/n (☎954 884 326, ©954 884 858; ❸), with its own good restaurant and delightful rooms overlooking a garden and pool. There are numerous bars around the centre of town and plenty of **places to eat** – *Bar Gonzalo*, c/Caridad 3, in the centre, serves a good-value *menú*, and the *casino* on the central La Plazuela serves simple and hearty meals. The *casino* is essentially a place to drink and relax – quieter and more comfortable than most of the bars – and serves as a kind of club, with locals paying a nominal monthly membership charge. Most towns of Cazalla's size have one, and tourists and visitors are always welcome to use the facilities free of charge – worth doing, since the membership rule means everybody drinks at reduced prices. For more upmarket fare, the restaurant of the *Posada del Moro* (see above) is a cut above the rest, and the economical *Mesón del Moro* nearby, in the same street, is a reliable place for regional meat and game dishes.

Cazalla is well served by public transport, with daily **buses** connecting it with Sevilla. Buses also run at 7am and 11.45am to the Estación de Cazalla y Constantina, twenty minutes to the east, from where there are three or four **trains** a day northwest to Zafra and Extremadura, and a similar number that follow the river down towards El Pedroso and ultimately Sevilla. If you're making for El Pedroso, though, you might consider walking from the station – a lovely route, with great river swimming and a fabulous variety of valley flora and fauna; it takes about five hours. A kilometre south of the station there's also an excellent place to stay, the *Molino del Corcho* with rooms and food (☎955 954 249; ❶) in a restored old watermill.

El Pedroso and Constantina

EL PEDROSO, 15km south of Cazalla, is a pretty little town with a notable Mudéjar church, Nuestra Señora de la Consolación. **Accommodation** is limited, though the town now boasts a sparkling new hotel, the *Casa Montehuéznar*, Avda. de la Estación 15 (☎954 889 000, ⓦwww.monte hueznar.com; ❸), up the street opposite the station in a restored mansion with its own good restaurant. For more simple rooms enquire at the train station *cantina* (bar) or *Bar Serranía*, an excellent **tapas bar**, across the road from the station, which serves up local specialities such as venison, hare, pheasant and partridge. Eighteen kilometres further to the east – and perhaps as good a place as any to cut back to Sevilla if you're not counting on trekking the whole length of the range – lies **CONSTANTINA**, a lively and beautiful mountain town with a population of almost 15,000, founded in the fourth century by the Romans during the reign of the Emperor Constantine, and named after his son. High above the town is the impressive **Castillo de la Armada**, surrounded by shady gardens descending in terraces to the old quarters. At the base is the sixteenth-century parish church of **La Encarnación**, once again with a Mudéjar tower, Moorish influence having died hard in these parts.

Constantina has a **turismo** inside the *ayuntamiento*, c/Eduardo Dato 7 (Mon–Fri 8am–3pm; ☎954 880 000), which can provide a useful town map. The cheapest of the **places to stay** is the modern youth hostel on c/Cuesta Blanca s/n (☎955 881 589; €13.35), uphill behind a pump station at the south end of the town, with single and twin rooms. Everything else is priced above the budget category, including the delightful *Casa Mari Pepa*, c/José de la Bastida 25 (☎955 880 158; ❸), with distinctively decorated en-suite rooms in a refurbished mansion. There are plenty of places for **eating and drinking** along and around c/Mesones, the main street. North of here the town's best eatery, *Cambio de Tercio*, Virgen del Robledo 53, near the Plaza de Toros, is well worth a visit and serves up meat and game dishes of the region in an economical bar or a more upmarket restaurant behind. Constantina even runs to a bit of **nightlife** with a clutch of discos – *Bonny Dog* is the most central – drawing the younger set in from miles around at weekends. Travelling on to Sevilla, there are two buses a day currently running at 6.45am and 3pm, but check with the turismo or the operator Linesur (☎954 902 368) for the latest information.

The Costa de la Luz

Stumbling on the villages along the **Costa de la Luz**, between Algeciras and Cádiz, is like entering a new land after the dreadfulness of the Costa del Sol.

The journey west from Algeciras seems in itself a relief, the road climbing almost immediately into rolling green hills, offering fantastic views down to Gibraltar and across the Strait to the just-discernible white houses and tapering mosques of Moroccan villages. Beyond, the Rif Mountains hover mysteriously in the background and on a clear day, as you approach **Tarifa**, you can distinguish Tangier on the edge of its crescent-shaped bay. Beyond Tarifa lies a string of excellent golden sand beaches washed by Atlantic breakers and backed by a clutch of low-key resorts such as **Zahara de los Atunes** and **Conil**. Inland the haunting Moorish hill town of **Vejer** beckons, whilst set back from the sea at Bolonia is the ancient Roman settlement of **Baelo Claudia**.

Tarifa and around

TARIFA, spreading out beyond its Moorish walls, was until the mid-1980s a quiet village, known in Spain, if at all, for its abnormally high suicide rate – a result of the unremitting winds that blow across the town and its environs. Today it's a prosperous, popular and, at times, very crowded resort, following its discovery as Europe's prime **windsurfing** spot. There are equipment rental shops along the length of the main street, and regular competitions held year-round. Development is moving ahead fast as a result of this new-found popularity, but for the time being it remains a fairly attractive place.

If windsurfing is not your motive, there can still be an appeal in wandering the crumbling ramparts, gazing out to sea or down into the network of lanes that surround the fifteenth-century, Baroque-fronted church of **San Mateo** (daily 9am–1pm & 5.30–9pm; free), which has a beautiful late Gothic interior. Also worth a look is the **Castillo de Guzman** (Tues–Sun 11am–2pm & 6–8pm; €1.80), the site of many a struggle for this strategic foothold into Spain. It is named after Guzmán el Bueno (the Good), Tarifa's infamous commander during the Moorish siege of 1292, who earned his tag for a superlative piece of tragic drama. Guzmán's nine-year-old son had been taken hostage by a Spanish traitor and surrender of the garrison was demanded as the price of the boy's life. Choosing "honour without a son, to a son with dishonour", Guzmán threw down his own dagger for the execution. The story – a famous piece of heroic resistance in Spain – had echoes in the Civil War siege of the Alcázar at Toledo, when the Nationalist commander refused similar threats, an echo much exploited for propaganda purposes.

A recent innovation in Tarifa is **whale and dolphin spotting** excursions to the Strait of Gibraltar which leave daily from the harbour. The trip is a fairly steep €27 (reductions for under-14s), but this includes another trip free of charge if there are no sightings. Places must be booked in advance from either of two non-profit-making organizations: Whale Watch, Avda. de la Constitución 6, close to the turismo (☎56 627 013, reservations ☎639 476 544, ⓦwww.whalewatchtarifa.com) and FIRMM (Foundation for Information and Research on Marine Mammals), c/Pedro Cortés 3, slightly west of the church of San Mateo (☎956 62 70 08, ⓦwww.firmm.org). A more commercial operation, Turmares, with a kiosk on the Paseo de la Alameda near the turismo mobile ☎606 652 970, ⓦwww.turmares.com), also runs whale-spotting trips (€24, kids €15) with a glass-bottomed boat.

Practicalities

The **turismo** (April–Sept daily 10am–2pm & 6–8pm; Nov–March Mon–Fri only; ☎956 680 993, ⓦwww.aytotarifa.com; the private ⓦwww.tarifainfo .com is also useful) on the central Paseo la Alameda can help with maps and accommodation. Tarifa has plenty of **places to stay**, though finding a bed in summer can often be a struggle, with crowds of windsurfers packing out every available *hostal*. The *Hostal-Restaurante Villanueva*, Avda. Andalucía 11 (☎956 684 149; ②), is very clean and has a good restaurant, while the excellent *Hostal La Calzada*, c/Justina Pertíñez 7 (☎956 680 366; ③), near San Mateo church, and the charming *Pensión Correo*, c/Coronel Móscardo 8 (☎956 680 206; ②), located in the old post office, just south of the church entrance, are also recommended. On the main road into town just outside the walls, *Casa Facundo*, c/Batalla del Salado 47 (☎956 684 298, ✉h.facundo@terra.es; ③) is a reliable *hostal* for en-suite rooms with TV.

On the main Algeciras–Cádiz road (c/Batalla del Salado) you'll find the **bus station** (frequent services to Sevilla, Málaga, Cádiz and points in between), a supermarket, many of the larger hotels and, further out of town, plenty of **campsites** (see below). The same street also has the enterprising Aky Oaky at no. 37,(☎956 685 356) who hire out **mountain bikes**, organize horse treks and run visits to local *ganaderías* (breeding ranches) to see *toros bravos* (fighting bulls); they also offer organized walking, rock-climbing and caving activities.

For **meals**, the restaurant of the *Hostal Villanueva* (see below) specializing in *urta* (Cádiz sea bream) is a good bet, as is the pricier *Restaurante Alameda*, Paseo Alameda 4, near the turismo, which does a variety of *platos combinados* and has a pleasant terrace. One newcomer worth a try is the atmospheric *Mandragora*, c/Independencía 3, behind the Iglesia de San Mateo, offering dishes from both sides of the straits: as well as Moroccan *couscous*, it does excellent tapas (*raciones* only in the evenings), including *boquerones rellenos* (stuffed anchovies). Of the dozen or so **bars** dotted around the centre, the German-run *Bistro Point* is a windsurfers' hang-out and a good place for finding long-term accommodation as well as secondhand windsurfing gear. *Bar Morilla*, c/Sancho IV El Bravo 2, facing San Mateo's main entrance, is a favourite meeting place with locals and a good tapas stop. *Bar El Trato*, c/Sancho El Bravo IV 28, doubles as Tarifa's **Internet centre** where you can pick up your emails over a beer (€0.90 for 10min); *Ciber Pandor@*, Sancho IV El Bravo, 5 almost fronting San Mateo, is another possibility.

There are plenty of **nightlife** possibilities in the summer months, with many bars staging live music to keep the windsurfers happy. The local council does its bit by erecting a huge marquee, La Jaima, on the Playa de los Lances, the main beach on the Atlantic (or western) side of town, which becomes a raucous disco from midnight on.

Tarifa Beach

Heading northwest from Tarifa, you find the most spectacular **beaches** of the whole Costa de la Luz – wide stretches of yellow or silvery-white sand, washed by some magical rollers. The same winds that have created such perfect conditions for windsurfing can, however, sometimes be a problem for more casual enjoyment, sandblasting those attempting to relax on towels or mats and whipping the water into whitecaps.

The beaches lie immediately west of the town. They get better as you move past the tidal flats and the mosquito-ridden estuary – until the dunes start and the first camper vans lurk among the bushes. At **TARIFA BEACH**, a little bay 9km from town, there are restaurants, a windsurfing school, campsites and a pricey *hostal*, *Millon* (☎956 685 246; ⑤), at the base of a tree-tufted bluff. For more seclusion head for one of the numerous **beach campsites** on either side, signposted from the main road or accessible by walking along the coast. All of these – the main ones are *Río Jara* (☎956 680 570), *Tarifa* (☎956 684 778),

Torre de la Peña (☎956 684 903) and *Paloma* (☎956 684 203) – are well equipped, inexpensive and open all year. Also on this stretch, 7km west of Tarifa, is the luxurious *Hurricane Hotel* (☎956 684 919, ⓦwww.hotel hurricane.com; ❼), set in dense gardens with a gym, two pools, windsurfing school and its own restaurant.

On to Morocco

Tarifa offers the tempting opportunity of a quick approach **to Morocco** – Tangier is feasible as a day-trip on a daily catamaran ferry. Normally this leaves at 11.30am and 6pm (Fri 7pm), returning at 8.15am or 5.30pm (local time – which is 2hr behind Spanish time in summer, 1hr in winter); check current times with Viajes Marruecotur (see below) or the turismo. The trip takes 35 minutes; tickets are available from the FRS (Ferrys Rápido del Sur office (☎956 681 830, ⓦwww.frs.es) at the port entrance, Viajes Marruecotur or travel agents along c/Batalla del Salado. If you're planning to do a day-trip you'd be wise to book a few days in advance or you may find that a tour company has taken over the whole boat. A day-trip would only allow you time for a brief look around, and an overnight stay might be a better way of justifying the €45 round-trip ticket. Catamaran-based one- or two-day **excursions** to Tangier are also available, starting at €48 for the one-day package which includes a sightseeing tour, lunch and all transport. Details of these and all other ferry information are available from the helpful Viajes Marruecotur, Avda. Constitución 5, near the turismo (☎956 681 821, ⓔmcotur@e-savia.net; English spoken). This crossing is a lot more expensive than going from Algeciras (see p.284), but might be a better bet if the latter is chock-a-block, which usually happens in summer or when Moroccans are returning home for the two major Islamic festivals (which rotate between January, February and March).

The coast west of Tarifa

Around the coast from *Paloma* campsite are extensive ruins of the Roman town of **BOLONIA**, or *Baelo Claudia* as the Romans knew it, where you can make out the remains of three temples and a theatre, as well as a forum and numerous houses (June–Sept Tues–Sat 10am–7.30pm, Sun 10am–1.30pm; rest of year Tues–Sat 10am–5.30pm, Sun 10am–1.30pm; free with EU passport, otherwise €1.50). The site can be reached down a small side road which turns off the main Cádiz road 15km after Tarifa. There's also a fine **beach** here with bars and eating places and a pleasant **place to stay**, *Hostal Baelo*, c/El Lentiscal 15 (☎956 688 562; ❸). Alternatively, it's a good walk along the coast from either *Paloma* or, from the west, Zahara de los Atunes (3–4hr).

Tuna fishing

The catch of the bluefin tuna is a ritual which has gone on along the Costa de la Luz for a thousand years and, today, still employs many of the age-old methods. The bluefin is the largest of the tuna family, weighing in at around 200 kilos each, and the season lasts from April to June as the fish migrate south towards the Mediterranean, and from early July to mid-August when they return, to be herded and caught by huge nets. The biggest market is Japan, where tuna is eaten raw as sushi. Tuna numbers, however, are declining and the season shortening – probably the result of overfishing – much to the concern of the people of Conil de la Frontera and Zahara de los Atunes, for whom the catch represents an important source of income.

Twenty-eight kilometres along the N340 **ZAHARA DE LOS ATUNES** is a former fishing village rapidly transforming itself into a modest resort. It has an eight-kilometre-long strand, soon to be backed by the almost obligatory *paseo marítimo* (promenade), currently under construction. Best of a number of **places to stay** is the *Hostal Monte Mar*, c/Peñon 12 (☎956 439 047; ❷), bang on the beach, with sea-view balcony rooms. A pleasant upmarket option is the seafront *Hotel Gran Sol*, at Avda. de la Playa 20 (☎956 439 301, ⓦwww.gransolhotel.com; ❹), where a new extension has rooms overlooking a garden pool. **Camping** is also feasible at *Bahía de la Plata* (☎956 439 040), at the south end of the beach, but don't forget the insect repellent.

Vejer de la Frontera

While you're on the Costa de la Luz, be sure to take time to visit **VEJER DE LA FRONTERA**, a classically white, Moorish-looking hill town set in a cleft between great protective hills that rear high above the road from Tarifa to Cádiz. If you arrive by bus, it usually makes a stop at two *hostal-restaurantes* on the major road at the foot of the hill – *La Barca de Vejer* (☎956 450 083, ⓕ956 451 083; ❹) does superb *bocadillos de lomo* – before toiling up to the *pueblo* proper. The road winds up for another 4km, but just by one of the bus-stop cafés there's a donkey path that takes only about twenty minutes to reach the town. This is a perfect approach – for the drama of Vejer is in its isolation and its position, which gradually unfold before you. Less adventurously, should you decide to let the bus do the work it will drop you at the Parque de Los Remedios terminal from where you'll need to ascend a further 300m along c/Los Remedios to reach La Plazuela, the effective centre of town. Arriving **by car**, by the Parque de Los Remedios bus halt is the town's **car park** which, given Vejer's tortuously narrow streets, one-way system and traffic congestion, you'd be strongly advised to make use of.

Until the end of the twentieth century the women of Vejer wore long, dark cloaks that veiled their faces like nuns' habits; despite being adopted as the town's tourist icon, this custom seems now to be virtually extinct, but the place has a remoteness and Moorish feel as explicit as anywhere in Spain. There's a castle and a church of curiously mixed styles (mainly Gothic and Mudéjar), but the main fascination lies in exploring the brilliant white and labyrinthine alleyways, wandering past iron-grilled windows, balconies and patios, and slipping into a succession of bars.

Practicalities

There's a **turismo** in the Parque de Los Remedios, Avda. de los Remedios 2, close to where the bus drops you (Mon–Sat 10am–3pm & 6–10pm; ☎956 451 376, ⓦwww.aytovejer.org), which can provide a good town map, accommodation list and information on the budget *casas particulares* nearby. Should you be interested in exploring the area around Vejer, Naturalsur, Avda. Los Remedios 95 (☎956 451 564, ⓦwww.naturalsur.com), near the same bus halt, organizes guided treks and mountain-bike trips through the gorges and natural parks of the area; the same company also does kayak trips along the rivers of the nearby Alcornocales natural park.

Outside August, finding **accommodation** shouldn't be a problem. A good place to start looking is at the welcoming and well-run *Hostal la Janda*, c/Cerro Clarisas s/n (☎956 450 142; ❷), or the delightful, upmarket *Hotel Convento de San Francisco* (☎956 643 570; ❸) on La Plazuela, which also stocks town maps if the turismo is closed. Both are rather hidden away, so ask for directions. A welcome addition to Vejer's hotel range is *La Casa del Califa*, Plaza de España

16 (⏃956 447 730, ⓦ www.vejer.com/califa; ❸), in a refurbished ancient town house, where stylish rooms are decorated with Moroccan fittings and guests have use of two patios and a library. The price includes buffet breakfast and readers with this guide can claim a ten-percent reduction. Not far away, *Casa Rural Leonor*, c/Rosario 25 (⏃956 451 085, ⓦ www.casaleonor.es; ❷), is another budget possibility with pleasant en-suite rooms. More economical options are available at nos. 7 or 16 c/Filmo, around the corner from the turismo, where families let out rooms during the summer. Vejer's **campsite** (⏃956 450 098; June–Sept) lies below the town on the main N340 Málaga to Cádiz road.

There are budget **places to eat** scattered all around the old town, and two places, which are slightly more upmarket but worth the extra, are the restaurant of the *Hotel Convento de San Francisco* and the restaurant of the *La Casa del Califa* hotel (see p.328 for both), where – in keeping with the house style, the kitchen offers a cuisine with a Spanish-North African slant. A couple of the best **tapas bars** are *Mesón Pepe Julián*, c/Juan Relinque 7, just off La Plazuela, or, at the other end of town, *Bar Peneque* on Plaza de España, almost opposite the *Casa del Califa* hotel.

Conil

Back on the coast, a dozen or so kilometres on, **CONIL** is an increasingly popular resort. Outside July and August, though, it's still a good place to relax, and in mid-season the only real drawback is trying to find a room. Conil town, once a poor fishing village, now seems entirely modern as you look back from the beach, though when you're actually in the streets you find many older buildings, too. The majority of the tourists are Spanish (with a lesser number of Germans), so there's an enjoyable atmosphere, and, if you are here in mid-season, a very lively nightlife.

The **beach**, Conil's *raison d'être*, is a wide bay of brilliant yellow stretching for miles to either side of town and lapped by an amazingly, not to say disarmingly, gentle Atlantic – you have to walk halfway to Panama before it reaches waist height. The area immediately in front of town is the family beach; up to the northwest you can walk to some more sheltered coves, while across the river to the southeast is a topless and nudist area. Walking along the coast in this direction the beach is virtually unbroken until it reaches the cape, the familiar-sounding **Cabo de Trafalgar**, off which Lord Nelson achieved victory and met his death on October 21, 1805. If the winds are blowing, this is one of the most sheltered beaches in the area. It can be reached by road, save for the last 400m across the sands to the rock.

Practicalities

Most **buses** use the Transportes Comes station on c/Carretera; walk towards the sea and you'll find yourself in the centre of town. There's a helpful **turismo** (July & Aug daily Mon–Sat 9.30am–2pm & 6.30–9.30pm; Sept–June Mon–Sat 9.30–2pm; ⏃956 440 501, ⓦ www.conil.org) along the way at the junction of c/Carretera and c/Menéndez Pidal – it's worth picking up a copy of their useful free booklet *Conil en su Bolsillo*, which details all the town's tapas bars, restaurants, and much more. **Accommodation** needs are served by numerous hotels and *hostales*. The central *Hostal La Villa*, Plaza de España 6 (⏃956 441 053; ❷), is one of the most reasonable, and nearby is the even cheaper and more atmospheric *Pensión Los Hermanos*, c/Virgen 2 (⏃956 440 196; ❶), Conil's oldest *fonda*. Near the Torre del Guzmán in the old quarter, *Hostal Santa Catalina*, c/Carcel 2, just off Plaza Santa Catalina (⏃956 441 583; ❸), is another decent place for air-conditioned rooms with TV. Conil also has a number of luxury hotels and, at the opposite end of the scale, a multitude of private rooms for rent; details of both are available from the turismo. **Campsites** include *Fuente del Gallo* in the nearby *urbanización*, Fuente del Gallo (☎956 440 137; March–Oct), a three-kilometre walk despite all signs to the contrary.

Seafood is king here and Conil has lots of good **restaurants** along the front; try the *ortiguillas* – deep-fried sea anemones – which you see only in the Cádiz area. Two of the best restaurants, *Francisco* and *La Fontanilla*, are to be found side by side on the Playa de la Fontanilla, the town's northernmost beach. During the summer, Conil's great **nightlife** attraction is *Las Carpas* ("the tents"), a huge triple entertainment complex on the beach which caters for all ages and features techno, salsa, dance bands and flamenco shows, often all in action at the same time in the separate venues. It's all provided by the town council and, best of all, it's absolutely free.

Cádiz

CÁDIZ is among the oldest settlements in Spain, founded about 1100 BC by the Phoenicians and one of the country's principal ports ever since. Its greatest period, however, and the era from which the central part of town takes most of its present appearance, was the eighteenth century. Then, with the silting up of the river to Sevilla, the port enjoyed a virtual monopoly on the Spanish-American trade in gold and silver, and on its proceeds were built the cathedral – itself golden-domed (in colour at least) and almost Oriental when seen from the sea – the public halls and offices, and the smaller churches.

Inner Cádiz, built on a peninsula-island, remains much as it must have looked in those days, with its grand open squares, sailors' alleyways and high, turreted houses. Literally crumbling from the effect of the sea air on its soft limestone, it has a tremendous atmosphere – slightly seedy, definitely in decline, but still full of mystique.

Arrival, information and accommodation

Arriving by **train**, you'll find yourself on the periphery of the old town, close to the Plaza de San Juan de Dios, busiest of the city's many squares. By **bus**, you'll arrive either at the Los Amarillos terminal between Plaza San Juan de Dios and the port (serving Rota, Chipiona and the resorts west of Cádiz) or on the north side of the port at the Autobuses Comes station on Plaza de la Hispanidad (used by buses from Sevilla, Tarifa and most other destinations toward Algeciras). There's a **turismo** on Avda. Ramón de Carranza s/n (Mon 9am–2pm, Tues–Fri 9am–7pm, Sat 9am–2pm; ☎956 258 646) near to Plaza de San Juan de Dios; there's also a useful **turismo municipal** on the Plaza San Juan de Dios (Mon–Fri 9am–2pm & 5–8pm, Sat & Sun 10am–1.30pm & 5–7.30pm; ☎956 241 001). **Internet access** is available at *Ciber La Sal*, c/Dr Marañon 14 (☎956 211 539; €1.20 per 30min), a stone's throw from the *Hotel Atlántico parador* (see p.331). *Novap Computers*, Cuesta de las Calesas 45, near the train station, is a computer shop with Internet access (☎956 264 468; €1.80 per hr, min €0.45 for 15min).

One way to get to grips with the city is to do an **open-top bus tour** – especially good if you're pressed for time; two competing companies do the same hop-on, hop-off clockwise route around the peninsula. Tour por Cádiz (daily 10am–7pm; €8) and Cádiz Tour (daily 9.30am–6.30pm; €8) both have stops at or near Plaza San Juan de Dios, the cathedral, the Parque Genoves, the Playa de la Victoria and places in between. With Cádiz Tour your ticket is valid for 24 hours from the time you board; Tour por Cádiz tickets are valid only on the day of purchase.

Accommodation

Radiating around the Plaza de San Juan de Dios is a dense network of alley-ways crammed with **hostales** and **fondas** and a few less inviting options. More salubrious places to stay are to be found a couple of blocks away, towards the cathedral or Plaza de Candelaria.

Pensión La Argentina c/Conde O'Reilly 1 ☎956 223 310. Simple, cheap and spotless rooms close to the Plaza de España. ❶

Hotel Atlántico Parque Genovés 9 ☎956 226 905, ℱ956 214 582. Functional, if somewhat charmless, modern *parador* with Atlantic views and an outdoor pool. ❻

Hostal Bahía c/Plocia 5 ☎956 259 061. Good-value *hostal*, conveniently located, offering rooms with bath. Request their more attractive balcony rooms. ❸

Hostal Colón c/Marqués de Cádiz 6 ☎956 285 351. Good option for simple but spacious rooms sharing a bathroom. ❶

Las Cuatro Naciones c/Plocia 3 ☎956 255 539. Clean, unpretentious place with low-priced rooms, close to Plaza San Juan de Dios. ❶

Hostal España Marqués de Cádiz 9 ☎956 285 500. Pleasant *hostal* with reasonable rooms (some en suite) ranged around a patio. ❷

Hostal Fantoni c/Flamenco 5 ☎956 282 704. Good-value *hostal* in renovated town house with lots of *azulejos*, cool marble and some en-suite rooms. ❶–❷

Hotel Regio II Avda. Andalucía 79 ☎956 253 008, ℱ956 253 009. Good-quality out-of-the-centre hotel behind the main Playa de la Victoria beach. Rooms come with a/c and there's a garage. ❹

Quo Qádis Youth Hostel c/Diego Arias 1, close to Plaza Manuel de Falla ☎ & ℱ956 221 939. Privately owned and somewhat eccentrically run hostel in a restored mansion with dormitory, single and double rooms. Hires out bicycles to residents, as well as offering courses in flamenco and trips around the city and to surrounding beauty spots. Prices include breakfast and there's a restaurant with vegetarian options. €12.50

The Town

Unlike most other ports of its size, Cádiz seems immediately relaxed, easy-going, and not at all threatening, even at night. Perhaps this is due to its reassuring shape and compactness, the presence of the sea and the striking **sea fortifications** and waterside **alamedas** making it impossible to get lost for more than a few blocks. But it probably owes this tone as much to the town's tradition of liberalism and tolerance – one maintained all through the years of Franco's dictatorship even though this was one of the first towns to fall to his forces, and was the port through which the Nationalist armies launched their invasion. In particular, Cádiz has always accepted its substantial gay community, who are much in evidence at the city's brilliant *carnaval* celebrations.

Cádiz is more interesting in its general ambience – its blind alleys, cafés and backstreets – than for any particular buildings. As you wander, you'll find the **Museo de Bellas Artes y Arqueológico**, at Plaza de Mina 5 (April–Sept Tues 2.30–8pm, Wed–Sat 9am–8pm, Sun 9.30am–2.30pm; Oct–March Tues–Sat closes 6pm; €1.80, free to EU citizens), incorporating the **archeological museum** on the ground floor with many important finds and artefacts from the city's lengthy history including two remarkable fifth-century BC **Phoenician carved sarcophagi** in white marble (one male, the other female), unique to the western Mediterranean. The upper floor houses the **Museo de Bellas Artes**. This contains a quite exceptional series of saints painted by **Francisco Zurbarán**, brought here from the Carthusian monastery at Jerez and one of only three such sets in the country (the others

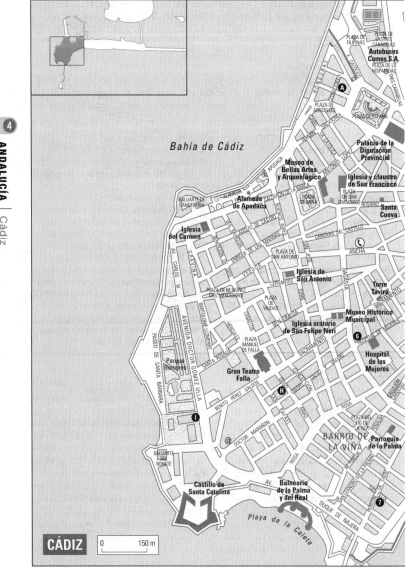

Bahía de Cádiz

Castillo de San Sebastián ▼

are at Sevilla and Guadalupe) preserved intact, or nearly so. With their sharply defined shadows and intense, introspective air, Zurbarán's saints are at once powerful and very Spanish – even the English figures such as Hugh of Lincoln, or the Carthusian John Houghton, martyred by Henry VIII when he refused to accept him as head of the English Church. Perhaps this is not surprising, for

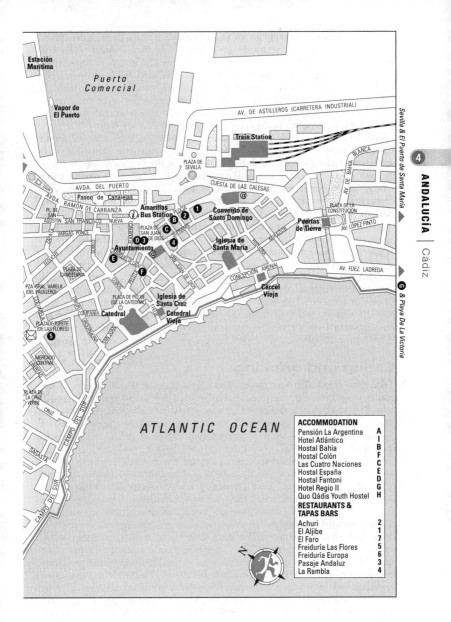

ACCOMMODATION

Pensión La Argentina	A
Hotel Atlántico	I
Hostal Bahía	B
Hostal Colón	F
Las Cuatro Naciones	C
Hostal España	E
Hostal Fantoni	D
Hotel Regio II	G
Quo Qádis Youth Hostel	H

RESTAURANTS & TAPAS BARS

Achuri	2
El Aljibe	1
El Faro	7
Freiduría Las Flores	5
Freiduría Europa	6
Pasaje Andaluz	3
La Rambla	4

the artist spent much of his life travelling round the Carthusian monasteries of Spain and many of his saints are in fact portraits of the monks whom he met. Other important artists displayed here include Murillo, Rubens and Alonso Cano.

Even if you don't normally go for High Baroque, it's hard to resist the attraction of the huge and seriously crumbling eighteenth-century **Catedral Nueva** (visits, including museum: Tues–Fri 10am–12.45pm & 4.30–6.45pm, Sat 10am–12.45pm; €3), now undergoing a belated (and astronomically expensive) restoration. The cathedral is decorated entirely in stone, with no gold in sight, and in absolutely perfect proportions. In the crypt you can see the tomb of Manuel de Falla, the great *gaditano* composer of such Andalucía-inspired works as *Nights in the Gardens of Spain* and *El Amor Brujo*.

Over on the seaward side of the mammoth complex, the "old" cathedral, **Santa Cruz** (Tues–Sun 10am–1pm & 5.30–8.30pm; free), was one of the buildings severely knocked about by the Earl of Essex during the English assault on Cádiz in 1596, causing the thirteenth-century church to be substantially rebuilt. A fine Gothic entry portal survived and inside there's a magnificent seventeenth-century *retablo* with sculptures by Martínez Montañés. A first-century BC **Roman theatre** (Tues–Sun 9am–2pm; free) has been excavated behind. To the north of the cathedral along c/Sacramento, the **Torre Tavira** (daily: June–Sept 10am–8pm; Oct–May 10am–6pm; €3.50), c/Marqués del Real Tesoro 10, is an eighteenth-century mansion with the tallest tower in the city, from where there are great **views** over the rooftops to the sea beyond; it also houses an entertaining **camera obscura**. Lastly, there are two churches of note for the paintings they contain. Foremost of these is the chapel of the **Hospital de las Mujeres** (Mon–Sat 10am–1.30pm; €0.60; ask the porter for admission), which has a brilliant **El Greco**, *St Francis in Ecstasy*. The other, an oval, eighteenth-century chapel, **Santa Cueva** (Tues–Fri 10am–1pm & 4.30–8pm, Sat–Sun 10am–1pm; €1.50), on c/Rosario, has three fine frescoes on Eucharistic themes by **Goya**.

Eating and drinking

Take-away **fried fish** was invented in Cádiz (despite English claims to the contrary), and there are numerous *freidurías* (fried-fish shops) around the town, as well as stands along the beach in season; few eating experiences here can beat strolling the city streets while dipping into a *cartucho* (paper funnel) of *pescado frito*. In the bars, *tortilla de camarones* (shrimp omelette) is another superb local speciality.

A couple of *freidurías* worth seeking out are the *Freiduría Las Flores* on the square of the same name and the nearby and equally good *Freiduría Europa*, c/Hospital de Mujeres 21 (at the junction with c/Sagasta). The Plaza de San Juan de Dios, protruding across the neck of the peninsula from the port and the first long stretch of Cádiz's naval dockyards, has several cafés and inexpensive **restaurants**. In the square's southwest corner, *Pasaje Andaluz* is a friendly diner with outdoor terrace and a *menú* offering meat and fish dishes, while nearby *La Rambla*, c/Sopranis 11, is an efficient little tapas and *raciones* place specializing in seafood and also makes a good breakfast stop. Superior quality fare is to be had at the popular *Restaurante Achuri*, c/Plocia 15 off the square's northern end (☎956 253 613; closed Sun–Wed evenings), serving up some excellent Basque and *andaluz*-inspired dishes in a pleasant setting. When closed, the nearby *El Aljibe*, c/Plocia 25 (☎956 266 656; closed Sun eve), is a good substitute.

For fish you must also visit the tiny **Plaza Tío de la Tiza**, in the old fishing quarter near the Playa de la Caleta beach, which has dozens of good seafood places, with outdoor tables filling the surrounding streets in summer. The more upmarket *El Faro*, c/San Félix 15, nearby, is one of the best fish restaurants in Andalucía – their €18 *menú* is good value – with an equally outstanding tapas bar attached.

The Cádiz coast

Cádiz has two main beaches – the excellent **Playa de la Victoria**, to the left of the promontory approaching the town (reached from the centre on bus #1 from Plaza de España), and the none-too-clean **Playa de la Caleta** on the peninsula's western tip – but for clearer waters it's best to cross the bay to **El Puerto de Santa María**. Further north along the coast towards Sanlúcar de Barrameda, beaches are more or less continuous, with two of the best flanking the resorts of **Rota** and **Chipiona**. These are both popular weekend retreats from Cádiz, and during July and August pretty much packed.

El Puerto de Santa María

EL PUERTO DE SANTA MARÍA is the obvious choice, a traditional family resort for both *gaditanos* (as inhabitants of Cádiz are known) and *sevillanos* – many of whom have built villas and chalets along the fine **Playa Puntillo**. This strand is a little way out from the town (a ten- to fifteen-minute walk or a local bus ride), a pleasant place to while away an afternoon; there are friendly beach bars where for ridiculously little you can nurse a litre of *sangría* (bring your own food). In the town itself the principal attraction is a series of **sherry bodegas** – long, whitewashed warehouses flanking the streets and the banks of the river. Until the train was extended to Cádiz, all shipments of sherry from Jerez came through Santa María, and its port is still used to some extent. Many of the firms offer free tours and tastings to visitors (Mon–Fri from around 10am till noon), though this is not a regular process and you need to phone the day before or organize a visit through the turismo, either in Cádiz or Puerto de Santa María itself. The most worthwhile tours are offered by two of the town's major producers, Osborne & Duff Gordon, c/Los Moros s/n (Mon–Fri visits at 10.30am in English, 11am & noon in Spanish; ☎956 869 100; €3), and Fernando de Terry, c/Santísima Trinidad 2 (Mon, Tues & Thurs 10am–1.30pm, €3; Wed, Fri & Sat single guided visit, including stables, at 11am, €8; ☎956 857 700), situated in a beautiful, converted, seventeenth-century convent. The turismo can provide details of visits to smaller bodegas who do not require advance booking.

The **ferry** (known locally as *El Vapor*, alluding to the earlier steamboats) from Cádiz is quicker and cheaper than the bus at €2 one-way; the forty-minute trip across the bay departs from the Estación Marítima at 10am, noon, 2pm, 6.30pm and 8.30pm (summer only), returning to Cádiz at 9am, 11am, 1pm, 3.30pm and 7.30pm, with extra sailings in season according to demand (especially in the evening). A **catamaran** service operated by the MareSur 2000 company (mobile ☎670 697 905) leaves from the same quay seven times daily between 7.25am and 5.30pm, and does the trip in half the time of the *vapor*; tickets cost €2.50 one-way or €4.50 return. El Puerto's **turismo** is situated at c/Luna 22 (daily 10am–2pm & 6–8pm; ☎956 542 413, ⓦwww.elpuertosm.es). There are plenty of **places to stay** – good budget options include the very pleasant *Hostal Loreto*, c/Ganado 17 (☎956 542 410; ❷), and the serviceable *Pensión Santa María*, c/Pedro Muñoz Seco 38 (☎956 857 525; ❶), both close to the turismo. A good upmarket choice is Hotel Santa María, Avda. Bajamar s/n (☎956 873 211, ⓦwww.hotelsantamaria.es; ❺), with air-conditioned rooms fronting the river and a rooftop pool. Bus #2 from the Plaza de las Galeras Reales goes to the **campsite** at Playa Las Dunas (☎956 872 210; open all year), near the beach with plenty of shade. Close by and a little upstream from the centre you'll also find some excellent seafood **restaurants**, including the justly famous and great fun *Romerijo*, c/Ribera del

Marisco, one of the most popular *marisquerías* in town, where you can buy your choice of shellfish in a *cartucho* (paper funnel) and eat on their terrace with a beer. The same outfit has a *freiduría* bar-restaurant over the road from here where a generous *frito variado* (assorted fried fish) easily serves two.

Rota and Chipiona

ROTA, 16km along the coast, is marred by its proximity to one of the three major **US bases** in Spain – installed in the 1950s as part of a deal in which Franco exchanged strips of Spanish sovereign territory for economic aid and international "respectability". As a resort, it's no great shakes, but does boast two splendid beaches, and enough discos, bars and fish restaurants to satisfy your needs should you decide to visit.

CHIPIONA, at the edge of the next point, is simpler: a small, straightforward seaside resort crammed with family *pensiones*. Older tourists come here for the **spa waters**, channelled into a fountain at the church of Nuestra Señora de Regla, but for most it's the **beaches** that are the lure. South of the town and lighthouse is the long **Playa de Regla**, where, outside July and August, it's easy enough to leave the crowds behind; northeast, towards Sanlúcar, are sand bars and rocks. If you're planning on staying in the town, the **hostales** along the beach are the most attractive – try the seafront *Hostal Rompeolas*, Avda. de Jerez 28 (✆956 373 358; ❹), which has two similar places nearby, and all cut prices by half outside July and August; in high season you'll probably need help getting a room from the women who meet new arrivals at the bus station; failing this, a **turismo** inside the Casa de Cultura on the central Plaza de Andalucía (Mon–Fri 10am–1.30pm & 7–9pm; ✆956 372 828) should be able to advise. The combined **campsite and youth hostel**, *Pinar de Chipiona* (✆956 371 480; open all year; €13.35), is 3km out of town towards Rota – any Rota-bound bus will drop you off.

Sanlúcar de Barrameda

Like Puerto Santa María, **SANLÚCAR DE BARRAMEDA** also has its sherry connections. Nine kilometres east of Chipiona and set at the mouth of the Guadalquivir, it's the main depot for **Manzanilla** wine, a pale, dry variety much in evidence in the bars, which you can also sample during visits (booked in advance by phone) to the town's **bodegas**. *Bodega Antonio Barbadillo*, c/Eguilaz 11 (Mon–Sat visits noon & 1pm; €3; ✆956 38 55 00), the town's major producer, has the most interesting visits, and a list of other *bodegas* offering visits is available from the turismo (see p.337). Sanlúcar is also the setting for some exciting horse races along the beach in the last two weeks of August, the best time to be here.

There's not a great deal to see, although the attractive old quarter in the upper town, or Barrio Alto, is worth taking time to explore. The town's port was the scene of a number of important maritime exploits: Magellan set out from here to circumnavigate the globe, Pizarro embarked to conquer Peru, and 4km upriver, from the fishing harbour of Bonanza, Columbus sailed on his third voyage to the Americas. The few buildings of interest – the ducal palace of **Medina Sidonia**, the **Palacio de Orleáns y Borbón** (Mon–Fri 10am–1.30pm; free) built by the dukes of Montpensier and decorated in a wild neo-Mudéjar style, the thirteenth-century church of **Nuestro Señora de la O** with its fine Gothic-Mudéjar portal, and the substantial remains of the Moorish **Castillo de Santiago** – are all perched above the main part of town on the Cuesta de Belén in the Barrio Alto.

One of the best things about Sanlúcar is its shell-encrusted **river beach** and warm waters, a couple of kilometres' walk from the town centre and usually quite deserted. This is flanked, on the opposite shore, by the beginnings of the **Coto Doñana National Park** (see p.339), whose vast marshy expanses (strictly regulated access) signal the end of the coast road to the west. Visits to the park from Sanlúcar are now possible with a recently introduced boat cruise which, while it doesn't allow for serious exploration, is nevertheless a wonderful introduction to this remarkable area. The trip lasts approximately four hours and allows two short guided walks on board the park to spot wildlife. The *Real Fernando* – which has a *cafetería* on board – leaves daily from the Bajo de Guía quay (June–Sept at 10am & 5pm; April, May & Oct 10am & 4pm; Nov–March 10am only; €14.50; advance booking essential; ☎956 363 813, ⓔreal_fdo@teleline.es). Tickets should be collected (at least 30min before sailing) from the Fábrica de Hielo, Bajo de Guía s/n, the national park's **exhibition centre** (daily 9am–8pm) opposite the *Real Fernando*'s jetty. Also note that binoculars are pretty essential, and, whilst they can be hired on board, having your own is a distinct advantage.

    Accommodation is limited, especially in August when you may struggle to find anything at all. For a central position try the basic but clean *Pensión Blanca Paloma*, Plaza San Roque 9 (☎956 363 644; ❶), or, moving upmarket, in the Barrio Alto the charming *Posada de Palacio*, c/Caballeros 11 (☎956 364 840, ⓦwww.posadadepalacio.com; ❹), housed in an elegantly converted eighteenth-century *casa palacio*, with pool. Alternatively, seek assistance from the **turismo** at Calzada del Ejército (April–Sept daily 10am–2pm & 6–8pm; rest of year Mon–Fri only; ☎956 366 110, ⓦwww.aytosanlucar.org), on the avenue leading to the estuary, which can also provide a good town map. For **food**, head to the Bajo de Guía – a river beach backed by a line of great seafood restaurants. You can walk there by continuing past the turismo to the end of the Calzada del Ejército and turning right (or east) when you hit the river, about a kilometre from the town centre. *El Bigote* and *Mirador de Doñana* are outstanding – serving up some of the finest seafood in Andalucía.

Jerez de la Frontera

JEREZ DE LA FRONTERA, inland towards Sevilla, is the home and heartland of sherry (itself an English corruption of the town's Moorish name – *Xerez*) and also, less known but equally important, of Spanish brandy. An elegant and prosperous town, it's a tempting place to stop, arrayed as it is round the scores of wine *bodegas*, with plenty of sights to visit in between. Life is lived at a fairly sedate pace for most of the year here, although things liven up considerably when Jerez launches into one or other of its two big **festivals** – the May Horse Fair (perhaps the most snooty of the Andalucian *ferias*), or the celebration of the vintage towards the end of September. Jerez is also famous throughout Spain for a long and distinguished **flamenco** tradition, and if you're interested in finding out more about Andalucía's great folk art then a visit to the **Centro Andaluz de Flamenco**, Plaza de San Juan (Mon–Fri 9am–2pm; ⓦwww.caf.cica.es; free), in the atmospheric *gitano* quarter, the Barrio de Santiago, is a must. There is an audiovisual introduction to *El Arte Flamenco* (hourly on the half hour), plus videos of past greats, and information on flamenco venues in the town.

    The **tours of the sherry and brandy processes** can be interesting – almost as much as the sampling that follows – and, provided you don't arrive in August when much of the industry closes down, there are a great many firms and *bodegas* to choose from. The visits are conducted either in English (very much the second language of the sherry world) or a combination of English and Spanish and last for about an hour. Jerez's "big two" are **González Byass**, c/Manuel González s/n (tours: July–Sept Mon–Sat hourly visits 11.30am–2pm, the final visit includes free tapas; Sun hourly 11.30am–1.30pm; Aug also Tues & Thurs 8pm, this visit includes free tapas and flamenco; call or consult website for other periods; €7, includes a visit to their brandy *bodega*; book in advance ☎956 35 70 16, ⓦwww.gonzalezbyass.es), makers of the famous *Tio Pepe* brand, and the more central **Pedro Domecq**, c/San Ildefonso 3 (tours: Mon–Fri 9am–1pm; €3.75 book in advance; ☎956 151 516, ⓦwww.domecq.es), producers of *La Ina*; besides manufacturing sherry both *bodegas* are major brandy producers, too. Many of these firms were founded by British Catholic refugees, barred from careers at home by the sixteenth-century Supremacy Act, and even now they form a kind of Anglo-Andalucian tweed-wearing and polo-playing aristocracy (on display, most conspicuously, at the Horse Fair). The González cellars – the *soleras* – are perhaps the oldest in Jerez and, though it's no longer used, preserve an old circular chamber designed by Eiffel (of the tower fame). If you feel you need comparisons, you can pick up a list of locations and opening times of the other *bodegas* from the turismo (see below) or from any travel agent in the centre.

The most attractive of the town's buildings – including the imposing Gothic-Renaissance **Catedral de San Salvador** (Mon–Fri 11am–1pm & 6–8pm, Sat 11am–2pm & 6–8pm, Sun 11am–2pm 5.30–8pm; free) and the impressive eleventh-century Moorish **Alcázar** (May–Sept Mon–Sat 10am–8pm, Sun 10am–3pm; Oct–April daily 10am–6pm; €1.50 or €3.25, including camera obscura) next to the González *bodega* – are within a couple of minutes' walk of the central Plaza del Arenal. An excellent **Archeological Museum** (June–Aug Tues–Sun 10am–2.30pm; Sept–May Tues–Fri 10am–2pm & 4–7pm, Sat & Sun 10am–2.30pm; €1.50) lies five minutes north of the centre in the Plaza del Mercado on the edge of the Barrio de Santiago; star exhibits include a seventh-century BC Greek military helmet, a Visigothic sarcophagus and a fine Caliphal bottle vase. Evidence of Jerez's great enthusiasm for horses can be seen at the **Royal Andalucian School of Equestrian Art**, Avda. Duque de Abrantes s/n, which offers the chance to watch them performing to music (Tues & Thurs at noon; July 15 to Oct 15 also Fri at noon; €12–18; information ☎956 319 635, reservations ☎902 101 212, ⓦwww.realescuela.org). Training, rehearsals (without music) and visits to the stables take place on other weekdays between 11am and 1pm, when admission is a more affordable €6.

Practicalities

The **turismo** is located in the southwest corner of the town's main square, the elegant palm-fringed **Plaza del Arenal** (April–Sept Mon–Fri 10am–2pm & 5–7pm, Sat & Sun 10am–3pm; Oct–March Mon–Fri 9.30am–2.30pm & 4.30–6.30pm, Sat & Sun 9.30am–3.30pm; ☎956 359 654, ⓦwww.webjerez.com). The **train** and **bus** stations are more or less next door to each other, eight blocks east of the Plaza. **Internet** access is available a little to the northwest of here at *Ciber Jerez*, c/Santa María 3, near the market (Mon–Sat 10am–11pm; ☎956 334 016; €1.50 per hr).

For **accommodation**, the most central budget rooms are at *Hostal Las Palomas*, c/Higueras 17 (☎956 343 773; ➊), with clean and simple rooms (some en suite), while a bit further out in the suburbs is the good-value *Albergue Juvenil*, Avda. Carrero Blanco 30 (☎956 143 901; ➊), with a pool; bus #9 from outside the bus station will take you there. Moving slightly upmarket,

4

there's the excellent *Hostal San Andrés*, c/Morenos 12 (☎956 340 983, ⓕ956 343 196; ❶–❷), which has rooms with and without bath, and the friendly *Hotel Torres*, c/Arcos 29 (☎956 323 400, ⓕ956 321 816; ❷), both northeast of the bus station, with similar facilities and charming patios.

For **food** there are tapas bars and eating places all over the central zone; one of the best tapas venues is *Juanito*, c/Pescadería Vieja 4 (off the west side of Plaza del Arenal), and, not far away to the northeast of here, *Mesón Alcazaba*, c/Medina 19, is a decent place to eat with a nice patio and a filling low-priced *menú*. One restaurant with a difference is *La Carbona*, c/San Francisco de Paula 2, slightly northwest of the bus station, where in a wonderfully cavernous room (actually an old *bodega*), they serve up charcoal-grilled fish and meat dishes, with the bonus on Thursday to Saturday evenings of live piano, opera or flamenco performances to accompany your meal.

Huelva Province

The **province of Huelva** stretches between Sevilla and Portugal, but aside from its scenic section of the Sierra Morena (see p.319) to the north and a chain of fine **beaches** to the west of the provincial capital it's a pretty dull part of Andalucía, laced with large areas of swamp – the *marismas* – and notorious for mosquitoes. This distinctive habitat is, however, particularly suited to a great variety of wildlife, especially birds, and over 60,000 acres of the delta of the Río Guadalquivir (the largest roadless area in western Europe) have been fenced off to form the **Coto de Doñana National Park**. Here, amid sand dunes, pine woods, marshes and freshwater lagoons, live scores of flamingos, along with rare birds of prey, 30 pairs of lynx, mongooses and a startling variety of migratory birds.

Coto de Doñana National Park

The seasonal pattern of its delta waters, which flood in winter and then drop in the spring, leaving rich deposits of silt, raised sandbanks and islands, gives **Coto Doñana** its uniqueness. Conditions are perfect in winter for ducks and geese, but spring is more exciting: the exposed mud draws hundreds of flocks of breeding birds. In the marshes and amid the cork-oak forests behind, you've a good chance of seeing squacco herons, black-winged stilt, whiskered tern, pratincole and sand grouse, as well as flamingos, egrets and vultures. There are, too, occasional sightings of the Spanish imperial eagle, now reduced to fourteen breeding pairs. Conditions are not so good in late summer and early autumn, when the *marismas* dry out and support far less bird life.

The park, however, is under threat from development. Even at current levels the drain on the water supply is severe, and made worse by **pollution** of the Guadalquivir by farming pesticides, Sevilla's industry and Huelva's mines. The seemingly inevitable disaster finally occurred in 1998 when an upriver mining dam used for storing toxic waste burst, unleashing millions of litres of pollutants into the Guadiamar river which flows through the park. The noxious tide was stopped just 2km from the park's boundary, but catastrophic damage was done to surrounding farmland, with nesting birds decimated and fish poisoned.

Equally disturbing are the proposals for a huge new tourist centre to be known as the **Costa Doñana**, on the very fringes of the park. Campaigning by national and international environmental bodies resulted in this project being shelved, but the threat remains, much of the pressure stemming from local people who see much-needed jobs in the venture.

Visiting the park

Visiting the Doñana involves (perhaps understandably) a certain amount of frustration. At present it's open only to a boat cruise from Sanlúcar (see p.336) and to brief, organized **tours** (April–Sept daily 8.30am & 5pm; Oct–April Tues–Sun 8.30am & 3pm; €19.50) by all-terrain 24-seater buses – four hours at a time along one of five charted, eighty-kilometre routes. The starting point for these, and the place to book them (essential and as far ahead as possible in high season), is at the Centro de Recepción de Acebuche (English spoken; ☏959 448 711, ✉donana@mma.es), 4km north of Matalascañas towards El Rocío and Almonte, or at the Cooperativa Marismas del Rocío, Plaza del Acebuchal 16, El Rocío (☏959 430 432, ⊕959 430 451). The tours are quite tourist-oriented and point out only spectacular species like flamingos, imperial eagles, deer and wild boar (binoculars are pretty essential). If you're a serious ornithologist, the tour isn't for you; instead, enquire at the Centro about organizing a private group tour. There are excellent birdwatching **hides** (daily 8am–8pm) at the El Acebuche, La Rocina and El Acebron reception centres, as well as a 1500-metre footpath from El Acebuche, which creates a mini-trek through typical *cotos* or terrains to be found in the reserve. Although binoculars are on hire, they sometimes run out, and you'd be advised to bring your own. The natural history exhibition at the Centro is worthy of a visit in itself.

Matalascañas

Birds and other wildlife apart, the resort settlement of **MATALASCAÑAS** on the park's coastal edge is utterly characterless with its large hotel complexes and a concrete shopping centre. In summer, the few *hostal* rooms are generally booked solid and you'll probably end up camping – either unofficially at the resort itself, or at the vast *Camping Rocío Playa* (☏959 430 238; open all year), 1.5km down the road towards Huelva. This site is a little inconvenient without your own transport if you're planning to take regular trips into the Doñana, but if you just want a **beach**, it's not a bad option. Playa Doñana and its continuation Playa Mazagón (with another campsite, *Doñana Playa*; ☏959 536 281; open all year) are fine strands stretching the whole distance to Huelva, and with hardly another foreign tourist in sight. This route is covered by three daily buses in both directions.

El Rocío

Set on the northwestern tip of the *marismas*, **EL ROCÍO** is a tiny village of white cottages and a church stockade where perhaps the most famous pilgrimage-fair of the south takes place annually at Pentecost. This, the **Romería del Rocío**, is an extraordinary spectacle, with whole village communities and local "brotherhoods" from Huelva, Sevilla and even Málaga converging in lavishly decorated ox carts and on horseback. Throughout the procession, which climaxes on the Saturday evening, there is dancing and partying, while by the time the carts arrive at El Rocío they've been joined by busloads of pilgrims. The fair commemorates the miracle of Nuestra Señora del Rocío (Our Lady of the Dew), a statue found – so it is said – on this spot and resistant to all attempts to move it elsewhere. The image, credited with all kinds of magic and fertility powers, is paraded before the faithful early on the Sunday morning.

El Rocío is a nice place to stay, with wide, sandy streets, cowboy-hatted horse-riding farmers and a frontier-like feeling. **Accommodation** prices, however, tend to be on the high side; do not even think about getting a room during the *romería* as they not only cost over ten times normal prices, but are booked up years ahead. Worth a try in quieter times are the pleasant *Hostal Isidro*, Avda. los Ansares 59 (☏959 442 242; ❷), and the more central *Hostal*

Cristina, c/Real 32 (☎959 406 513; ❷), with en-suite rooms and its own economical restaurant. Moving upmarket, there's a choice between the inviting *Hotel Toruño*, Plaza Acebuchal 22 (☎959 442 323, ℱ959 442 338; ❹), with *marismas* views, and the mammoth complex of apartments and rooms at *Puente del Rey*, Avda. Canaliega 1 (☎959 442 575, ℱ959 442 070; ❺), at the entrance to the town. In the spring, as far as **birdwatching** goes, the town is probably the best base in the area. The adjacent *marismas* and pine woods are teeming with birds, and following tracks east and southeast of El Rocío, along the edge of the reserve itself, you'll see many species (up to a hundred if you're lucky).

Huelva and the coast down to Portugal

Large, sprawling and industrialized, **HUELVA** is the least attractive and least interesting of Andalucía's provincial capitals. It has claims as a "flamenco capital", but unless you're really devoted it's unlikely you'll want to stop long enough to verify this. By day – and in the evening as well – the most enticing thing to do is to head 21km south via an impressive road bridge spanning the marshlands of the Río Odiel estuary, now designated the Paraje Natural Marismas del Odiel, an important wildlife sanctuary, to **Punta Umbría**, the local resort. This is hardly an over-inspiring place either, but it does at least have some life, a fair beach, numerous *hostales* and seafood restaurants and a campsite. One trip well worth doing by bus or with your own transport is along the Columbus trail: a clutch of locations associated with the fifteenth-century **voyages of Christopher Columbus**.

The Columbus Trail

Across the Río Tinto estuary from Huelva, the monastery of La Rábida and the villages of Palos and Moguer are all places connected with the voyages of Columbus to the New World. Frequent buses from Huelva's main bus station at Avda. de Portugal 9 (☎959 256 900) link all three places, and both Palos and Moguer have accommodation. **La Rábida** (Tues–Sat guided tours hourly 10am–1pm & 4–7pm, Sun 10.45am–1pm & 4.45–7pm; €2.50), 8km from Huelva and easily reached by bus, is a charming and tranquil fourteenth-century Franciscan monastery whose fifteenth-century abbot was instrumental in securing funds for the voyage from the monarchs Fernando and Isabel. Nearby, on the estuary, the **Harbour of the Caravels** (April–Sept Tues–Fri 10am–2pm & 5–9pm, Sat & Sun 11am–8pm; €3) has impressive full-size replicas of the three caravels which made the epic voyage to the New World, and an adjoining museum features a replica geography book annotated in Columbus's own surprisingly delicate hand among its displays. At **PALOS**, 4km to the north, is the church of **San Jorge** where, in August 1492, Columbus and his crew heard Mass before setting sail from the now silted-up harbour. Should you want **to stay**, the welcoming *Cafetería Pensión Rábida*, c/Rábida 9 (☎959 350 163; ❶), is a good bet for some of the cheapest en-suite rooms in Andalucía and serves equally economical tapas and *platos combinados* in its *cafetería*. A further 8km north, at the whitewashed town of **MOGUER**, is the fourteenth-century **Convent of Santa Clara** in whose church Columbus spent a whole night in prayer as thanksgiving for his safe return. The small town is a beautiful place, the birthplace of the Nobel prize-winning poet Juan Ramón Jiménez, and boasts a scaled-down, whiter version of Sevilla's Giralda attached to the church of **Nuestra Señora de la Granada**. If you want to stay overnight, *Hostal Pedro Alonso Niño*, c/Pedro Alonso Niño 13 (☎959 372 392; ❶), is delightful and has excellent-value en-suite rooms. One **bar** worth seeking out is *Mesón El Lobito* at c/La Rabida 31, which is in a bizarre league of its own when it comes to decor; it also sells wine at crazy prices (€0.15 per glass) and does decent fish and meat dishes *a la brasa*.

From Huelva it's best either to press on inland to the Sierra Morena or straight **along the coast to Portugal**. There are a number of good beaches and some low-key resorts noted for their seafood, such as **Isla Cristina**, along the stretch of coastline between Huelva and the frontier town of **Ayamonte**, but not much more to detain you. A good bus service along this route and a new road suspension bridge across the Rio Guadiana estuary and border, linking Ayamonte and **Villa Real de Santo Antonio** in Portugal, make for a relatively painless crossing of the country border. From this approach, a good first night's target in Portugal is Tavira, on the Algarve train line. Note that Portugal is an hour behind Spain throughout the year.

Sevilla to Córdoba

The direct route from **Sevilla to Córdoba**, 135km along the valley of Guadalquivir, followed by the train and some of the buses, is a flat and rather unexciting journey. There's far more to see following the route just to the south of this, via **Carmona** and **Écija**, both interesting towns, and more still if you detour further south to take in **Osuna** as well. There are plenty of buses along these roads, making travel between the villages easy. Overnighting too is possible with plenty of places to stay – although **Carmona** is an easy day-trip from Sevilla.

Carmona

Set on a low hill overlooking a fertile plain, **CARMONA** is a small, picturesque town made recognizable by the fifteenth-century tower of the Iglesia de San Pedro, built in imitation of the Giralda. The tower is the first thing you catch sight of and it sets a tone for the place – an appropriate one, since the town shares a similar history to Sevilla, less than 30km distant. It was an important Roman city (from which era it preserves a fascinating subterranean necropolis) and under the Moors was often governed by a brother of the Sevillan ruler. Later, Pedro the Cruel built a palace within its castle, which he used as a "provincial" royal residence.

The **Iglesia de San Pedro** (Sept–June Mon & Thurs–Sun 11am–2pm, also Mon & Thurs 4–6pm; July–Aug Thurs–Mon 11am–2pm; €3.60) is a good place to start exploring the town; it dominates Carmona's main thoroughfare, c/San Pedro, and has a splendid Baroque *sagrario* (sacristy) within. Buses stop just short of the church in the Paseo del Estatuto, from where, looking east, you get a view of the magnificent Moorish **Puerta de Sevilla**, a grand and fortified Roman gateway (with substantial Carthaginian and Moorish elements) to the old town which now houses the turismo (see "Practicalities" opposite). The gate's upper ramparts can now be visited (Mon–Sat 10am–6pm, Sun 10am–3pm; €2) on guided tours organized by the turismo. The **old town** is circled by 4km of ancient walls, inside which narrow streets wind up past Mudéjar churches and Renaissance mansions. Follow c/Prim uphill to the **Plaza San Fernando** (or Plaza Mayor), modest in size but dominated by splendid Moorish-style buildings. Behind it there's a bustling fruit and vegetable market most mornings.

Close by to the east is **Santa María la Mayor** (Mon–Fri 9am–2pm & 6–7.30pm, Sat 9am–2pm; closed Aug; €2), a fine Gothic church built over the former main mosque, whose elegant patio it retains; like many of Carmona's churches, it is capped by a Mudéjar tower, possibly utilizing part of the old minaret. Slightly east of here and housed in the elegant eighteenth-century Casa del Marqués de las Torres is the new **Museo de la Ciudad** (daily: June–Sept 10am–2pm & 6.30–9.30pm; Oct–May 11am–7pm; closed Tues afternoon; €2), documenting the history of the town with mildly interesting displays of artefacts from the prehistoric, Iberian, Carthaginian, Roman, Moorish and Christian epochs. The most entertaining feature is a series of interactive screens in a section dedicated to the role of flamenco in Andalucian culture – enabling you to call up an artiste of your choice and fill the museum with his or her spirited rendition. Dominating the ridge of the town are the massive ruins of **Pedro's Alcázar**, destroyed by an earthquake in 1504 and now taken over by a remarkably tasteful but expensive *parador* (see below). To the left, beyond and below, the town comes to an abrupt and romantic halt at the Roman **Puerta de Córdoba**, from where the ancient Córdoba road (once the mighty Via Augusta heading north to Zaragoza and Gaul, now a dirt track) drops down to a vast plain.

The extraordinary **Roman necropolis** (guided tours: June–Sept Tues–Fri 8.30am–2pm, Sat 10am–2pm; Oct–May Tues–Fri 9am–5pm, Sat & Sun 10am–2pm; €2, free with EU passport) lies on a low hill at the opposite end of Carmona; walking out of town from San Pedro take c/Enmedio, the middle street (parallel to the main Sevilla road) of three that leave the western end of the Paseo del Estatuto; follow this for about 450m. Here, amid the cypress trees, more than nine hundred family tombs dating from the second century BC to the fourth century AD can be found. Enclosed in subterranean chambers hewn from the rock, the tombs are often frescoed and contain a series of niches in which many of the funeral urns remain intact. Some of the larger tombs have vestibules with stone benches for funeral banquets, and several retain carved family emblems (one is of an elephant, perhaps symbolic of long life). Most spectacular is the **Tumba de Servilia** – a huge colonnaded temple with vaulted side chambers. Opposite is a partly excavated **amphitheatre**, though as yet it isn't included in the tour.

Practicalities

The **turismo** (Mon–Sat 10am–6pm, Sun 10am–3pm; ☏954 190 955, Ⓦwww.turismo.carmona.org), in the arch of the Puerta de Sevilla, is well stocked with information and can provide a town map and guide to Carmona's tapas bars. Budget **accommodation** is limited: the best bets are *Pensión El Comercio* (☏954 140 018; ❷–❸), built into the town's gateway with some rooms en-suite, or the nearby *Hotel San Pedro*, c/San Pedro 17 (☏954 190 087; ❸), close to the church of the same name. If you're on a tight budget you could try the uninspiring, but clean, *El Potro*, c/Sevilla 78 (☏954 141 465; ❶), some 100m back along the Sevilla road. The *Parador Alcázar del Rey Don Pedro* (☏954 141 010, Ⓔcarmona@parador.es; ❻), in the ruins of the palace, is Carmona's most atmospheric upmarket hotel, and even if you don't stay it's worth calling at the bar for a drink to enjoy the fabulous views from its terrace.

The old town is an expensive place for **food**; cheapest places are the tapas bars on c/Prim, off the west side of Plaza de San Fernando – *Bar Goya* and *El Tapeo* are two worth seeking out (the latter also offers a good-value *menú del día*) – while *El Potro* (see above) has a decent and economical, if rather soulless, restaurant. For more elaborate fare, *Molino de la Romera*, c/Pedro s/n, near the *parador*, has a great terrace view across the plain and serves a reasonably priced *menú*.

Écija

Lying midway between Sevilla and Córdoba in a basin of low sandy hills, ÉCIJA is known, with no hint of exaggeration, as *la sartenilla de Andalucía* ("the frying pan of Andalucía"). In mid-August it's so hot that the only possible strategy is to slink from one tiny shaded plaza to another, or with a burst of energy to make for the riverbank.

The heat is worth enduring, since this is one of the most distinctive and individual towns of the south, with eleven superb, decaying church towers, each glistening with brilliantly coloured tiles. It has a unique domestic architecture, too – a flamboyant style of twisted and florid forms, best displayed on c/Castellar where the magnificent painted and curved frontage of the huge **Palacio de Peñaflor** (Mon–Fri: March–Sept 9am–1.30pm; Oct–Apr 10am–1pm & 4.30–7.30pm, Sat & Sun 11am–1pm; free) runs along the length of the street; the building has a fine patio and now houses Écija's public library. Other sights not to be missed are the beautiful polychromatic tower of the church of **Santa María**, overshadowing the main Plaza de España, and the **Palacio de Benamejí**, a stunning eighteenth-century palace on c/Castillo, south of Plaza de España, with a beautiful interior patio, now declared a national monument. This building houses the town **museum** Tues–Fri 9.30am–1.30pm & 4.30–6.30pm, Sat & Sun 9am–2pm; free), displaying archeological finds from all periods, with a particularly interesting section on *Astigi*'s (the town's Roman name) role in the olive-oil trade. One sensational recent addition here is the **Amazona de Écija**, a stunning, life-size, almost totally intact first-century AD Roman statue discovered in the 2002 excavations in the Plaza de España (see below), depicting an Amazon resting against a pillar.

The central **Plaza de España** is now an archeological site and has been so since the town council decided it would solve its traffic congestion problem by building an underground car park. Digging had hardly broken the surface before a Roman temple and bath complex, followed by a Moorish cemetery complete with thousands of burials, were discovered, and it now seems clear that the car park plans will need to be reconsidered. In the meantime, the politicians and archeologists are trying to decide what happens next.

Overlooking the Plaza de España, the Ayuntamiento houses the **turismo** (Mon–Fri 9.30am–3pm, Sat–Sun 10.30am–2pm; ⓦwww.ecija.org) who can provide maps and information to help you find the thirty-plus notable buildings throughout the town; an additional feature here is a **camera obscura** (same hours; €1.80), which is an effortless way to appreciate Éjica's marvellous collection of church towers.

Places to stay are limited; the only budget option is the friendly *Pensión Santa Cruz*, c/Romero Gordillo 8 (☎954 830 222; ❶), off the eastern end of Plaza de España. The *Hotel Platería*, c/Garcilópez 1 (☎955 902 752, ⓔhotel@plateria.com; ❸) just around the corner, is a step upmarket with excellent modern rooms around a central patio, while the *Hotel Sol Pirula* (☎954 830 300, ⓕ954 835 879; ❸), south of the centre at c/Cervantes 50, has comfortable air-conditioned rooms and a restaurant. The town has plenty of **places to eat** and one of the nicest is *Las Ninfas*, using the Palacio de Benamejí's patio (see above) as its terrace. Other places are to be found along the streets surrounding the Plaza de España. On the square itself, the *Bar El Bisturi* does tapas and *platos combinados*, or there's more choice at *La Reja*, c/Garcilopez 1, close to the *Hotel Platería* (see above).

Osuna

OSUNA (like Carmona and Écija) is one of those small Andalucian towns which are great to explore in the early evening: slow in pace and quietly enjoyable, with elegant streets of tiled, whitewashed houses interspersed by fine **Renaissance mansions**. The best of these are off the main street, c/Carrera, which runs down from the central Plaza Mayor, and in particular on c/San Pedro which intersects it; at no. 16 the **Cilla del Cabildo** has a superb geometric relief round a carving of the Giralda, and further along the eighteenth-century **Palacio de los Marqueses de Gomera** – now a hotel and restaurant (see below) – is a stunning Baroque extravaganza. There's also a marvellous **casino** on Plaza Mayor, with 1920s Mudéjar-style decor and a grandly bizarre ceiling, which is open to all visitors and makes an ideal place for a cool drink.

Two huge stone buildings stand on the hilltop: the old university (suppressed by reactionary Fernando VII in 1820) and the lavish sixteenth-century **Colegiata** (guided tours Mon–Sat 10am–1.30pm & 4–7pm, Sun 10am–1.30pm; Sept–June afternoon hours 3.30–6.30pm; €2), which contains the gloomy but impressive **pantheon and chapel** of the dukes of Osuna, descendants of the kings of León and once "the lords of Andalucía", as well as a **museum** displaying some fine artworks, including imposing canvases by Ribera. Opposite the entrance to the Colegiata is the Baroque convent of **La Encarnación** (same hours as Colegiata; €2), which has a fine plinth of ninth-century Sevillan *azulejos* round its cloister and gallery.

Osuna has plenty of **accommodation** but not a lot of budget options. Lowest priced is *Hostal Cinco Puertas*, c/Carrera 79 (☎ & ℱ954 811 243; ❷), with some en-suite rooms, while the slightly pricier *Hostal Caballo Blanco*, in a restored coaching inn opposite (☎954 810 184; ❸), is friendly, with en-suite rooms plus a decent restaurant, and is worth the extra. The outstanding upmarket option is the *Hotel Palacio Marqués de la Gomera*, c/San Pedro 20 (☎954 812 223, ⓦwww.hotelpalaciodelmarques.com; ❹), housed inside one of the most beautiful *casa palacios* in the country (see above). The **turismo** on the Plaza Mayor (Mon–Fri 9am–2pm & 4–6pm; ☎954 815 732, ⓦwww.ayto.osuna.es) can also help with finding accommodation. There are plenty of **food and drink** possibilities along c/Carrera and around the Plaza Mayor – one restaurant worth seeking out is the *Mesón del Duque*, Plaza de la Duquesa 2, uphill behind the casino, offering an economical *menú* you can eat out on a jasmine-fringed terrace.

Córdoba

CÓRDOBA lies upstream from Sevilla beside a loop of the Guadalquivir, which was once navigable as far as here. It is today a minor provincial capital, prosperous in a modest sort of way. Once, however, it was the largest city of Roman Spain, and for three centuries it formed the heart of the western Islamic empire, the great medieval caliphate of the Moors.

It is from this era that the city's major monument dates: the **Mezquita**, the grandest and most beautiful mosque ever constructed by the Moors in Spain. It stands right in the centre of the city, surrounded by the old Jewish and Moorish quarters, and is a building of extraordinary mystical and aesthetic power. Make for it on arrival and keep returning as long as you stay; you'll find

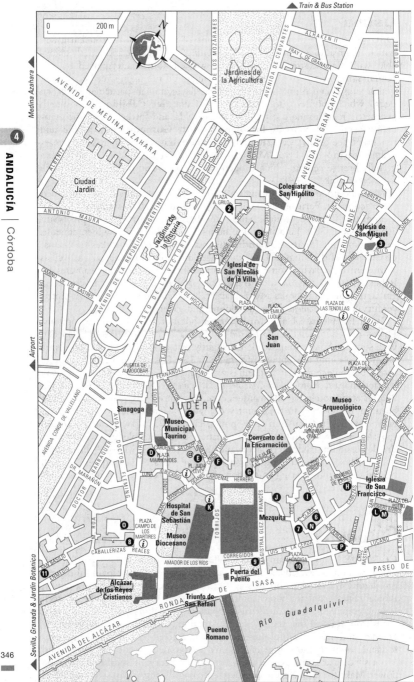

Train & Bus Station

Medina Azahara

Airport

Sevilla, Granada & Jardín Botanico

Jardines de
la Agricultura

Ciudad
Jardín

Jardines de
la Victoria

Colegiata de
San Hipólito

Iglesia de
San Miguel

Iglesia de
San Nicolás
de la Villa

San
Juan

Museo
Arqueológico

Sinagoga

LA
JUDERÍA

Museo
Municipal
Taurino

Convento de
la Encarnación

Iglesia de San
Francisco

Hospital
de San
Sebastián

Museo
Diocesano

Mezquita

Alcázar
de los Reyes
Cristianos

Puerta del
Puente

Triunfo de
San Rafael

Puente
Romano

Río Guadalquivir

PASEO DE

Torre de la Calahorra

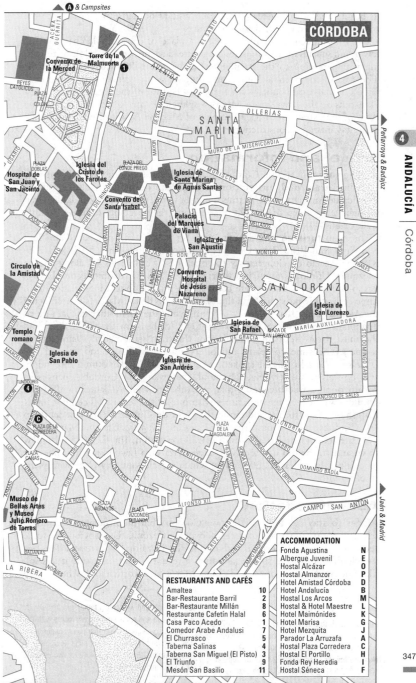

CÓRDOBA

ACCOMMODATION

Fonda Agustina	N
Albergue Juvenil	E
Hostal Alcázar	O
Hostal Almanzor	P
Hotel Amistad Córdoba	D
Hotel Andalucía	B
Hostal Los Arcos	M
Hostal & Hotel Maestre	L
Hotel Maimónides	K
Hotel Marisa	G
Hotel Mezquita	J
Parador La Arruzafa	A
Hostal Plaza Corredera	C
Hostal El Portillo	H
Fonda Rey Heredia	I
Hostal Séneca	F

RESTAURANTS AND CAFÉS

Amaltea	10
Bar-Restaurante Barril	2
Bar-Restaurante Millán	8
Restaurante Cafetín Halal	6
Casa Paco Acedo	1
Comedor Arabe Andalusi	7
El Churrasco	5
Taberna Salinas	4
Taberna San Miguel (El Pisto)	3
El Triunfo	9
Mesón San Basilio	11

its beauty and power increase with each visit, as of course is proper, since the mosque was intended for daily attendance.

The Mezquita apart, Córdoba itself is a place of considerable charm. It has few grand squares or mansions, tending instead to introverted architecture, calling your attention to the tremendous and often wildly extravagant **patios**. These have long been acclaimed, and they are actively encouraged and maintained by the local council, which runs a "Festival of the Patios" in May. Just 7km outside the town more Moorish splendours are to be seen among the ruins of the extravagant palace complex of **Medina Azahara** which is undergoing fascinating reconstruction.

Arrival and information

Finding your way around Córdoba is no problem. From the magnificent new combined **train and bus station** on the Plaza de las Tres Culturas, off the Avenida de America at the northern end of town, the broad Avenida del Gran Capitán leads down to the old quarters and the Mezquita (a fifteen-minute walk or bus #3).

The main **turismo** (April–Sept Mon–Fri 9.30am–6.30pm, Sat 10am–2pm & 5–7pm, Sun 10am–2pm; Oct–March Mon–Sat closes 6pm; ☎957 471 235) is at the Palacio de Congresos y Exposiciones at c/Torrijos 10, alongside the Mezquita. Córdoba's municipal tourist office (𝕎 www.turismodecordoba.org) has joined forces with a private company to provide tourist information from three central **kioskos**; one is in the Plaza Campo de los Martires almost facing the Alcázar (daily 10am–2pm & 6–9pm), while there's another in Plaza de las Tendillas in the centre of the modern town (daily 10am–2pm & 5–8pm) and the third is on the main concourse of the train station (daily 9am–2pm & 5–9pm). The same company also offers guided **walks** around the old city (*Paseos por Córdoba*; English spoken; €12); the walks last 1hr 30min and end up at a typical *cordobés* taverna. You should be aware that Córdoba changes its **monument timetables** more than any other town in Andalucía, and so you should always check opening times with one of the tourist offices. For information on fringe theatre and music, the **Casa de Cultura** is at Plaza del Potro 10. Córdoba's most central Internet cafés are *Ch@t*, c/Claudio Marcelo 15, near the focal Plaza Tendillas (min €1.20 for 30min, 1hr €1.80) in the new town and, in the old quarter, *Navegaweb*, Plaza Juda Levi, inside the Albergue Juvenil building (min €1.20 for 1hr) which is a pleasant, airy place with plenty of monitors.

Accommodation

Places to stay can be found all over Córdoba, but the majority are concentrated in the narrow maze of streets above the Mezquita. Less obvious are some recently refurbished *fondas* in and around the Plaza de la Corredera. This is a wonderful, ramshackle square (although a recent facelift has made it less so), like a decayed version of Madrid's Plaza Mayor, and worth a look whether you stay or not.

Budget options

Fonda Agustina c/Zapatería Vieja 5 ☎957 470 872. Charming and spotlessly clean little *fonda*, with basic rooms in a tranquil location. ❶

Hostal Alcázar c/San Basilio 2, near the Alcázar ☎957 202 561, 𝕎 www.hostalalcazar.com.

Comfortable and welcoming family-run *hostal* with a nice patio and some en-suite a/c rooms with TV. Also has some good-value apartments opposite (sleeping up to four) priced per night (2 nights minimum) at €60 for four or €42 for two persons. Breakfast included. ❶–❷

Albergue Juvenil Plaza Judá Leví ℡957 290 166, ℻957 290 500. Excellent modern youth hostel (with twin, triple and four-person en-suite rooms), which also serves meals. €13.35

Hostal Almanzor Corregidor Luís de la Cerda 10 ℡957 485 400. East of the Mezquita, this small but charming *hostal* has rooms with or without bath. ❶–❷

Hostal Los Arcos c/Romero Barros 14 ℡957 485 643, ℻957 486 011. Excellent *hostal* with simple rooms around a delightful patio. ❶–❷

Hostal Plaza Corredera c/Rodríguez Marín 15, at the corner of Plaza Corredera ℡957 484 570. Clean, friendly and recently refurbished place with simple rooms and great views over the plaza from some. ❶

Hostal El Portillo c/Cabezas 2 ℡ & ℻957 472 091. Beautiful old *hostal* with elegant patio, offering both singles and doubles with shared bath. ❶

Fonda Rey Heredia c/Rey Heredia 26 ℡957 474 182. Clean and airy simple rooms (some en suite) in one of three very reasonable *fondas* on this street. ❶

Hostal Séneca c/Conde y Luque 7 ℡ & ℻957 473 234, just north of the Mezquita. Wonderful place to stay with simple rooms around a stunning patio where you can take breakfast. Very popular, so booking ahead advised. ❷

Moderate and expensive options

Hotel Amistad Córdoba Plaza de Maimónides 3 ℡957 420 335, ℻957 420 365. Stylish hotel with comfortable rooms incorporating two eighteenth-century mansions, near the old wall in the Judería. ❺

Hotel Andalucía c/José Zorilla 3, near the church of San Hipolito ℡957 476 000, ℻957 478 143. Handy hotel for drivers who want to avoid the Mezquita maze, offering pleasant rooms with bath, and relatively easy parking. ❸

Hostal & Hotel Maestre c/Romero Barros 4 & 16 ℡ & ℻957 475 395. Excellent *hostal* between c/San Fernando and the Plaza del Potro; their neighbouring hotel has a/c rooms with TV. If you're carrying this *Rough Guide*, they'll offer you free parking in their garage. ❷–❸

Hotel Maimónides c/Torrijos 4 ℡957 471 500, ℻957 483 803. This upmarket hotel has a particularly central and attractive location, near to the turismo – it also has a garage. ❺

Hotel Marisa c/Cardenal Herrero 6 ℡957 473 142, ℻957 474 144. Two-star hotel with a superb position immediately outside the Mezquita. Rooms come with a/c but not TV. Own garage. ❹

Hotel Mezquita Plaza Santa Catalina 1, by the Mezquita's east wall ℡957 475 585, ℮hotelmezquita@wanadoo.es. Atmospheric and central new hotel in a converted sixteenth-century mansion with excellent a/c rooms. ❹

Parador La Arruzafa Avda. de la Arruzafa s/n, off the Avda. El Brillante ℡957 275 900, ℗www.parador.es. Córdoba's modern *parador* is located on the outskirts of the city 5km to the north of the Mezquita, but compensates with pleasant gardens, a pool and every other amenity (including a shooting range). ❻

Camping

Campamento Municipal Avda. El Brillante 50 ℡957 278 481. Córdoba's local campsite (with restaurant and pool) is 2km north of the centre in the *barrio* El Brillante, and served by bus #10 from the bus station. Tents and equipment for hire. Open all year.

Camping Los Villares ℡957 330 145. If you have your own transport, this site (7km north of the city along a minor road to Santo Domingo; the campsite lies just beyond this) is a better option, set in woodland with nature trails and a restaurant. Open all year.

Moorish Córdoba and the Mezquita

Córdoba's **domination of Moorish Spain** began thirty years after its conquest – in 756, when the city was placed under the control of **Abd ar-Rahman I**, the sole survivor of the Umayyad dynasty which had been bloodily expelled from the eastern caliphate of Damascus. He proved a firm but moderate ruler, and a remarkable military campaigner, establishing control over all but the north of Spain and proclaiming himself emir, a title meaning both "king" and "son of the caliph". It was Abd ar-Rahman who commenced the building of the Great Mosque (*La Mezquita*, in Spanish), purchasing from the Christians the site of the cathedral of St Vincent (which, divided by a partition wall, had previously served both communities). This original mosque was completed by his son **Hisham** in 796 and comprises about one-fifth of the present building, the first dozen aisles adjacent to the Patio de los Naranjos.

The **Cordoban emirate**, maintaining independence from the eastern caliphate, soon began to rival Damascus both in power and in the brilliance of its civilization. **Abd ar-Rahman II** (822–52) initiated sophisticated irrigation programmes, minted his own coinage and received embassies from Byzantium. He in turn substantially enlarged the mosque. A focal point within the culture of *al-Andalus*, this was by now being consciously directed and enriched as an alternative to Mecca; it possessed an original script of the Koran and a bone from the arm of Muhammad and, for the Spanish Muslim who could not go to Mecca, it became the most sacred place of **pilgrimage**. In the broader Islamic world it ranked third in sanctity after the Kaaba of Mecca and the Al Aksa mosque of Jerusalem.

In the tenth century, Córdoba reached its zenith under a new emir, **Abd ar-Rahman III** (912–61), one of the great rulers of Islamic history. He assumed power after a period of internal strife and, according to a contemporary historian, "subdued rebels, built palaces, gave impetus to agriculture, immortalized ancient deeds and monuments, and inflicted great damage on infidels to a point where no opponent or contender remained in *al-Andalus*. People obeyed en masse and wished to live with him in peace." In 929, with Muslim Spain and part of North Africa firmly under his control, Abd ar-Rahman III adopted the title of "caliph". It was a supremely confident move and was reflected in the growing splendour of Córdoba, which had become the largest, most prosperous city of Europe, outshining Byzantium and Baghdad (the new capital of the eastern caliphate) in science, culture and scholarship. At the turn of the tenth century, Moorish sources boast of the city's 27 schools, 50 hospitals (with the first separate clinics for the leprous and insane), 900 public baths, 60,300 noble mansions, 213,077 houses and 80,455 shops.

The **development of the Great Mosque** paralleled these new heights of confidence and splendour. Abd ar-Rahman III provided it with a new minaret (which has not survived and provided the core for the later belfry), 80m high, topped by three pomegranate-shaped spheres, two of silver and one of gold and each weighing a ton. But it was his son **al-Hakam II** (961–76), to whom he passed on a peaceful and stable empire, who was responsible for the most brilliant expansion. He virtually doubled its extent, demolishing the south wall to add fourteen extra rows of columns, and employed Byzantine craftsmen to construct a new *mihrab* or prayer niche; this remains complete and is perhaps the most beautiful example of all Moorish religious architecture.

Al-Hakam had extended the mosque as far to the south as was possible. The final enlargement of the building, under the chamberlain-usurper **al-Mansur** (977–1002), involved adding seven rows of columns to the whole east side. This spoiled the symmetry of the mosque, depriving the *mihrab* of its central position, but Arab historians observed that it meant there were now "as many bays as there are days of the year". They also delighted in describing the rich interior, with its 1293 marble columns, 280 chandeliers and 1445 lamps. Hanging inverted among the lamps were the bells of the pilgrimage cathedral of Santiago de Compostela. Al-Mansur made his Christian captives carry them on their shoulders from Galicia – a process which was to be observed in reverse after Córdoba was captured by Fernando el Santo (the Saint) in 1236.

Entering the Mezquita

As in Moorish times, the **Mezquita** (April–Sept Mon–Sat 10am–7.30pm, Sun 2–7.30pm; Oct–March Mon–Sat 10am–5.30pm, Sun 2–6.30pm; €6.50; free entrance at side doors 8.30am–10am for services but without lighting) is approached through the **Patio de los Naranjos**, a classic Islamic ablutions

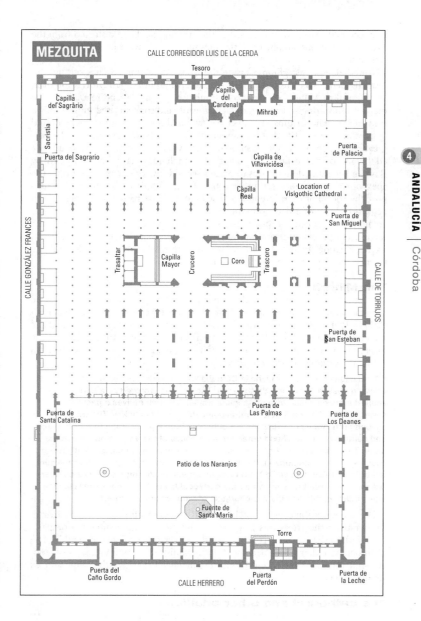

MEZQUITA

CALLE CORREGIDOR LUIS DE LA CERDA

Tesoro

Capilla del Sagrario

Capilla del Cardenal

Mihrab

Sacristia

Puerta del Sagrario

Puerta de Palacio

Capilla de Villaviciósa

Capilla Real

Location of Visigothic Cathedral

Puerta de San Miguel

CALLE GONZÁLEZ FRANCES

Trasaltar

Capilla Mayor

Crucero

Coro

Trascoro

CALLE DE TORRIJOS

Puerta de San Esteban

Puerta de Santa Catalina

Puerta de Las Palmas

Puerta de Los Deanes

Patio de los Naranjos

Fuente de Santa Maria

Torre

Puerta del Caño Gordo

CALLE HERRERO

Puerta del Perdón

Puerta de la Leche

court which preserves its orange trees, although the fountains for ritual purification before prayer are now purely decorative. Originally, when in use for the Friday prayers, all nineteen naves of the mosque were open to this court, allowing the rows of interior columns to appear an extension of the trees with brilliant shafts of sunlight filtering through. Today, all but one of the entrance gates is locked and sealed and the mood of the building has been distorted from the open and vigorous simplicity of the mosque, to the mysterious half-light of a cathedral.

Nonetheless, a first glimpse inside the Mezquita is immensely exciting. "So near the desert in its tentlike forest of supporting pillars," Jan Morris found it, "so faithful to Mahomet's tenets of cleanliness, abstinence and regularity." The mass of supporting pillars was, in fact, an early and sophisticated innovation to gain height. The original architect had at his disposal columns from the old Visigothic cathedral and from numerous Roman buildings; they could bear great weight but were not tall enough, even when arched, to reach the intended height of the ceiling. His solution (which may have been inspired by Roman aqueduct designs) was to place a second row of square columns on the apex of the lower ones, serving as a base for the semicircular arches that support the roof. For extra strength and stability (and perhaps also deliberately to echo the shape of a date palm, much revered by the early Spanish Arabs) the architect introduced another, horseshoe-shaped arch above the lower pillars. A second and purely aesthetic innovation was to alternate brick and stone in the arches, creating the red-and-white striped pattern which gives a unity and distinctive character to the whole design.

The Mihrab

This uniformity was broken only at the culminating point of the mosque – the domed cluster of pillars surrounding the sacred **Mihrab**, erected under al-Hakam II. The *mihrab* had two functions in Islamic worship: it indicated the direction of Mecca (and hence of prayer) and it amplified the words of the *imam*, or prayer leader. At Córdoba it was also of supreme beauty. As Titus Burckhardt wrote, in *Moorish Art in Spain*:

"The design of the prayer niche in Córdoba was used as a model for countless prayer niches in Spain and North Africa. The niche is crowned by a horseshoe-shaped arch, enclosed by a rectangular frame. The arch derives a peculiar strength from the fact that its central point shifts up from below. The wedge-shaped arch stones or *voussoirs* fan outwards from a point at the foot of the arch and centres of the inner and outer circumferences of the arch lie one above the other. The entire arch seems to radiate, like the sun or the moon gradually rising over the edge of the horizon. It is not rigid; it breathes as if expanding with a surfeit of inner beatitude, while the rectangular frame enclosing it acts as a counterbalance. The radiating energy and the perfect stillness form an unsurpassable equilibrium. Herein lies the basic formula of Moorish architecture."

The inner vestibule of the niche (which is fenced off – forcing you to risk the wrath of the attendants in getting a glimpse) is quite simple in comparison, with a shell-shaped ceiling carved from a single block of marble. The chambers to either side – decorated with exquisite Byzantine mosaics of gold, rust-red, turquoise and green – constitute the *maksura*, where the caliph and his retinue would pray.

The cathedral and other additions

Originally the whole design of the mosque would have directed worshippers naturally towards the *mihrab*. Today, though, you almost stumble upon it, for in the centre of the mosque squats a Renaissance **cathedral coro**. This was built in 1523 – nearly three centuries of enlightened restraint after the Christian conquest – and in spite of fierce opposition from the town council. The erection of a *coro* and *capilla mayor*, however, had long been the "Christianizing" dream of the cathedral chapter and at last they had found a monarch – predictably Carlos V – who was willing to sanction the work. Carlos, to his credit, realized the mistake (though it did not stop him from destroying parts of the Alhambra and Sevilla's Alcázar); on seeing the work completed, he told the chapter, "You have built what you or others might have built anywhere, but you have destroyed something that was unique in the world." To the left of the *coro* stands an earlier and happier Christian addition – the Mudéjar **Capilla de Villaviciosa**, built by Moorish craftsmen in 1371 (and now partly sealed up). Beside it are the dome and pillars of the **earlier mihrab**, constructed under Abd ar-Rahman II.

The **belfry**, at the corner of the Patio de los Naranjos, is contemporary with the cathedral addition. If it's open after restoration, the climb is a dizzying experience and the views over the Mezquita and town are tremendous. Close by, the **Puerta del Perdón**, the main entrance to the patio, was rebuilt in Moorish style in 1377. Original "caliphal" decoration (in particular, some superb latticework), however, can still be made out in the gates along the east and west sides of the mosque.

The rest of town

After the Mezquita, Córdoba's other remnants of Moorish – and indeed Christian – rule are not individually very striking. The river, though, with its great **Arab waterwheels** and **Roman bridge** (the Puente Romano), is an attractive area in which to wander. At the bridge's eastern end the medieval **Torre de la Calahorra** (daily 10am–2pm & 4.30–8.30pm; €4) houses a gimmicky, hi-tech museum containing models of the pre-cathedral Mezquita, weird talking tableaux and a rather incongruous multimedia presentation on the history of man; there's a great panoramic view, though, from the top of the tower towards the city. On the western riverbank the wheels, and the ruined mills, were in use for several centuries after the fall of the Muslim city, grinding flour and pumping water up to the fountains of the Alcázar, or Palace Fortress. This originally stood beside the Mezquita – on the site now occupied by the **Museo Diocesano** (Mon–Fri 9.30am–1.30pm & 4–6pm, Sat 9.30am–1.30pm; last entry 30min before closing; €1.50, or free with Mezquita ticket), now a museum of religious art with some fine examples of medieval wood sculpture. After the Christian conquest the Alcázar was rebuilt a little to the west by Fernando and Isabel, hence its name, **Alcázar de los Reyes Cristianos**. The buildings (Tues–Sat 10am–2pm & 5.30–7.30pm, Sun 9.30am–2.30pm; last entry 30min before closing; €2, free Fri) are a bit dreary, having served as the residence of the Inquisition from 1428 to 1821. However, they display some fine mosaics from Roman Córdoba, among which is one of the largest complete Roman mosaics in existence, and the wonderful **gardens** are a great place to get your breath back. Three hundred metres down river from the Alcázar on the opposite bank lies a new **Jardín Botánico** (April–Sept Tues–Sun 10.30am–9pm; Oct–March Tues–Sun 10.30am–6pm; €2), displaying exotic trees, shrubs and plants from all over the world including Andalucía's very own arboreal rarity, the **pinsapo Spanish fir**, a pre-Ice Age survivor transplanted from its only European habitat in the Sierra de Grazalema. The garden has a pleasant **cafetería**.

Judería

Between the Mezquita and the beginning of the Avenida del Gran Capitán lies the **Judería**, Córdoba's old Jewish quarter, and a fascinating network of lanes – more atmospheric and less commercialized than Sevilla's Barrio Santa Cruz, though souvenir shops are beginning to gain ground. Near the heart of the quarter, at c/Maimónides 18, is a **synagogue** (Tues–Sat 9.30am–2pm &

3.30–5.30pm, Sun 9.30am–1.30pm; last entry 30min before closing; €0.30, free to EU citizens), one of only three in Spain – the other two are in Toledo – that survived the Jewish expulsion of 1492. This one, built in 1316, is minute, particularly in comparison with the great Santa María in Toledo, but it has some fine stuccowork elaborating on a Solomon's-seal motif and retains its women's gallery. Outside is a statue of Maimónides, the Jewish philosopher, physician and Talmudic jurist, born in Córdoba in 1135. Just along from the synagogue in the same street, c/Judíos, at no. 12 there's a restored twelfth-century mansion **La Casa Andalusí** (daily 10.30am–7.30pm; €2.50), which attempts to recreate the atmosphere of the Moorish period with furniture and a variety of exhibits.

Nearby is a rather bogus **Zoco** – an Arab *souk* turned into a crafts arcade – and, adjoining this, a small **Museo Taurino** (Tues–Sat 10am–2pm & 5.30–7.30pm, Sun 9.30am–2.30pm; €3, free Fri). The latter warrants a look, if only for the kitschy nature of its exhibits: row upon row of bulls' heads, two of them given this "honour" for having killed matadors. Beside a copy of the tomb of Manolete – most famous of the city's fighters – is exhibited the hide of his taurine nemesis, Islero.

Other museums and mansions

More interesting, perhaps, and more rewarding, is the **Museo Arqueológico** (Tues 3–8pm, Wed–Sat 9am–8pm, Sun 9am–3pm; last entry 30min before closing; €1.50, free to EU citizens). During its original conversion, this small Renaissance mansion was revealed as the unlikely site of an original Roman patio. As a result, it is one of the most imaginative and enjoyable small museums in the country, with good local collections from the Iberian, Roman and Moorish periods. Outstanding is an inlaid tenth-century bronze stag found at the Moorish palace of Medina Azahara (see p.356) where it was used as the spout of a fountain.

A couple of blocks below the Archeological Museum, back towards the river, you'll come upon the **Plaza del Potro**, a fine old square named after the colt (*potro*) which adorns its fountain. This, as local guides proudly point out, is mentioned in *Don Quixote*, and indeed Cervantes himself is reputed to have stayed at the inn opposite, the **Mesón del Potro**, which now houses the Casa de Cultura and is used for *artesanía* displays and art exhibitions. On the other side of the square is the **Museo de Bellas Artes** (Tues 3–8pm, Wed–Sat 9am–8pm, Sun 9am–3pm; last entry 30min before closing; €1.50, free to EU citizens), with paintings by Ribera, Valdés Leal and Zurbarán, and across its courtyard is the small **Museo Julio Romero de Torres** (Tues–Sat 10am–2pm & 5.30–7.30pm, Sun 9.30am–2.30pm; last entry 30min before closing; €2.95, free Fri), devoted to the Córdoban artist **Romero de Torres** (1885–1930), a painter of some sublimely dreadful canvases, many of which depict reclining female nudes with furtive male guitar players.

In the north of town, towards the train station, are numerous Renaissance churches – some converted from mosques, others showing obvious influence in their minarets – and a handful of convents and palaces. The best of these, still privately owned, is the **Palacio del Marqués de Viana** (guided tours: Mon–Sat 10am–2pm & 4–6pm, 10am–1pm; patios €3, house additional €3), whose main attraction for many visitors is its twelve flower-filled patios.

Eating, drinking and nightlife

Bars and **restaurants** are on the whole reasonably priced – you need only to avoid the touristy places round the Mezquita. There are lots of good places to eat not too far away in the Judería and in the old quarters off to the east, above the Paseo de la Ribera. Two celebrated specialities worth trying here are *rabo de toro* (slow-stewed bull's tail) and *salmorejo*, the delicious *cordobés* variant of gazpacho, made with bread, tomatoes, oil and chopped *jamón* often topped off with sliced hard-boiled eggs.

Restaurants

Amaltea c/Ronda de Isasa 10 ☎957 491 968. Excellent organic restaurant with lots of veggie options, run by a charming Wolverhampton-educated *cordobésa*. Specialities of the house include *tabulé de cous-cous* and *calabacín con cabrales* (courgettes with strong cheese). Plenty of organic wines and a few special beers, too – try the *Alhambra 1925*. Some dishes are pricier, but it's possible to eat here for under €10.

Bar-Restaurante Barril c/Concepción 16. Super-efficient tapas and breakfast bar with a small terrace and serving all-day *platos combinados*.

Bar-Restaurante Millán Avda. Dr. Fleming 14, just northwest of the Alcázar. Tranquil, economical restaurant with a charming *azulejo*-lined room. The *rabo de toro* (Córdoba's traditional dish – a very superior oxtail stew) and *salmorejo* are excellent here.

Casa Paco Acedo beneath the ancient Torre de Malmuerta at the northern end of town. The house specialities at this celebrated and economical *cordobés* institution include *salmorejo* and a memorable *rabo de toro*.

Comedor Arabe Andalusi Plaza Abades 4, west of the Mezquita. Wonderful, welcoming little Arab halal restaurant serving up meat and fish kebabs (*chawarma*), falafel and many other Middle Eastern dishes; economically priced, with a pleasant terrace on the square.

El Churrasco c/Romero 16 (not c/Romero Barros) ☎957 290 819. Expensive and renowned restaurant, famous for its *churrasco* (a grilled pork dish, served with pepper sauces) and *salmorejo* (a thick Córdoban version of *gazpacho* with hunks of ham and egg).

Mesón San Basilio c/San Basilio 19, west of the Alcázar. Good and unpretentious busy local restaurant offering well-prepared fish and meat *raciones* and *platos combinados* plus a *menú* for €6 (€9 at weekends).

Restaurante Cafetín Halal c/Rey Heredia 28. Islamic cultural centre serving excellent, inexpensive food with vegetarian options. No alcohol.

Restaurante El Triunfo c/Corregidor Luís de la Cerda 79, facing the Mezquita. One of the few worthwhile places near the Mezquita, with plenty of cool marble and offering a wide range of mid-priced meat and fish dishes.

Taberna Salinas c/Tundidores 3, just off the Plaza Corredera. Century-old, reasonably priced *taberna* with dining rooms around a charming patio. Good *raciones* place – try their *naranjas con bacalao* (cod with oranges) – and serves a great *salmorejo*.

Taberna San Miguel (El Pisto) Plaza San Miguel 1, behind the church. Known to all as *El Pisto* (the barrel), this is one of the city's legendary bars – over a century old – and not to be missed. Wonderful *montilla* and tapas; *rabo de toro* and *callos en salsa picante* (tripe in spicy sauce) are house specials.

Bars, nightlife and flamenco

The local barrelled **wine** is predominantly Montilla-Moriles – brewed in the towns of the same name just to the south – which vaguely resembles mellow, dry sherry and is magnificent here on its own turf. The *Bar Plateros*, c/San Francisco 6, opposite the *Hostal Maestre*, specializes in *montilla* and also turns out great tapas. There is a chain of similar places throughout the town, all good places to try their *fiti-fiti* ("fifty-fifty"), comprising a half-and-half combo of white and sweet wine. One bar not to be missed is the century-old *Taberna San Miguel* (aka *El Pisto*) behind the church of the same name to the north of Plaza Tendillas, which is hung with guitars and faded *corrida* posters and has excellent tapas, especially *callos* (tripe) and *manitas* (trotters) in sauce. A lively beer bar serving beers from all over the world is *El Borracho de Oro*, c/San Felipe 15, off the south end of Avenida del Gran Capitán.

Córdoba takes its tranquillity seriously, especially after dark, when the old quarter turns very quiet. The in-town **nightlife** scene happens to the north of Plaza Tendillas and in and around c/Alfaros and c/Alfonso XIII, near the Roman temple (roughly dead centre of our city map). In the first group, *Seven* at c/Cruz Conde 32 (down a passage) is a popular club full of smoke, the occasional drag queen and techno sounds which closes at 7am, whilst the near-by *Golden*, c/H. Diaz del Moral 3, and *Qu*, c/Gongora 10, are equally frenzied at weekends. Near the Roman temple, at c/Alfonso XIII 3, *Soul* is a popular bar with students and often stages live gigs, while *Velvet Café* and *Millenium* (sic) are similar places along c/Alfaros, slightly north. To really let their hair down well away from any restraints, Córdoba's younger set migrates in summer to the **El Brillante** suburb (just off our map, to the northwest of the Plaza de Colón). Here a whole *barrio* of **disco-bars** and music venues line the main road and are jammed to capacity with a heaving mass of bodies at weekends. For the heart of the action, head for **El Tablero**, a lively plaza surrounded by bars, restaurants and disco-bars (bus #10 from the bus station or a taxi for around €3.50 will get you there). You'll find the best, and most authentic, **flamenco** in town at *Tablao Cardenal*, c/Torrijos 10 (next to the turismo), though it doesn't come cheap at around €18 a ticket (includes one drink). Performances begin at 10.30pm and you can book a good table by phone (☎957 483 320; closed Sun).

Medina Azahara

Seven kilometres to the northwest of Córdoba lie the vast and rambling ruins of **Medina Azahara**, a palace complex built on a dream scale by **Caliph Abd ar-Rahman III**. Naming it after a favourite, az-Zahra (the Radiant), he spent one-third of the annual state budget on its construction each year from 936 until his death in 961. Ten thousand workers and 1500 mules and camels were employed on the project, and the site, almost 2000m long by 900m wide, stretched over three descending terraces. In addition to the palace buildings, it contained a zoo, an aviary, four fish ponds, 300 baths, 400 houses, weapons factories and two barracks for the royal guard. Visitors, so the chronicles record, were stunned by its wealth and brilliance: one conference room was provided with pure crystals, creating a rainbow when lit by the sun; another was built round a huge pool of mercury.

Medina Azahara was a perfect symbol of the western caliphate's extent and greatness, but it was to last for less than a century. **Al-Hakam II**, who succeeded Abd ar-Rahman, lived in the palace, continued to endow it, and enjoyed a stable reign. However, distanced from the city, he delegated more and more authority, particularly to his vizier Ibn Abi Amir, later known as **al-Mansur** (the Victor). In 976 al-Hakam was succeeded by his eleven-year-old son Hisham II and, after a series of sharp moves, al-Mansur assumed the full powers of government, keeping Hisham virtually imprisoned at Medina Azahara, to the extent of blocking up connecting passageways between the palace buildings.

Al-Mansur was equally skilful and manipulative in his wider dealings as a dictator, retaking large tracts of central Spain and raiding as far afield as Galicia and Catalunya; consequently, Córdoba rose to new heights of prosperity. But with his death in 1002 came swift decline as his role and function were assumed in turn by his two sons. The first died in 1008; the second, Sanchol, showed open disrespect for the caliphate by forcing Hisham to appoint him as his successor. At this a popular revolt broke out and the caliphate disintegrated into civil war and a series of feudal kingdoms. Medina Azahara was looted by a mob at the outset, and in 1010 was plundered and burned by retreating Berber mercenaries.

The site

For centuries **the site** (May–Oct daily 10am–8.30pm; call ☎957 329 130 for rest of year; €1.50, free to EU citizens) continued to be looted for building materials; parts, for instance, were used in the Sevilla Alcázar. But in 1944 excavations unearthed the remains of a crucial part of the palace – the **Royal House**, where guests were received and meetings of ministers held. This has been meticulously reconstructed and, though still fragmentary, its main hall must rank among the greatest of all Moorish rooms. It has a different kind of stuccowork from that at Granada or Sevilla – closer to natural and animal forms in its intricate Syrian *Hom* (Tree of Life) motifs. Unlike the later Spanish Arab dynasties, the Berber Almoravids and the Almohads of Sevilla, the caliphal Andalucians were little worried by Islamic strictures on the portrayal of nature, animals or even men – the beautiful hind in the Córdoba museum is a good example – and it may well have been this aspect of the palace that led to such zealous destruction during the civil war.

The reconstruction of the palace gives a scale and focus to the site. Elsewhere you have little more than foundations to fuel your imaginings, amid an awesome area of ruins, hidden beneath bougainvillea and rustling with cicadas. Perhaps the most obvious of the outbuildings yet excavated is the **mosque**, just beyond the Royal House, which sits at an angle to the rest of the buildings in order to face Mecca.

Biologists from the University of Córdoba recently finished a study of soil samples from the site which has enabled them to determine exactly which plants and flowers were planted in the extensive gardens; plans are now being drawn up to reconstruct these as accurately as possible.

To reach Medina Azahara, follow the Avenida de Medina Azahara west out of town, onto the road to Villarubia and Posadas. About 4km down this road, make a right turn, after which it's another two or three kilometres. City **bus** #0–1 from a stop on the Avenida de la Republica Argentina (at the northern end near a petrol station) will drop you off at the intersection for the final three-kilometre walk to the site – ask the driver for the "Cruz de Medina Azahara". A **taxi** will cost you about €15 one-way for up to five people, or there's a special round-trip deal ("Taxi-Tour Córdoba") for €30 which includes a one-hour wait at the site while you visit. A convenient taxi rank is located outside the turismo on the west side of the Mezquita. Alternatively, Córdoba Vision runs daily **guided trips** (except Mon) to the site at 10.30am (plus May–Sept Tues–Sat 6pm & Oct–April Tues–Sat 4pm; ☎957 76 02 41, English spoken; €18); buses leave from the Triunfo de San Rafael monument close to the turismo, which can also assist with booking.

Eastern Andalucía

There is no more convincing proof of the diversity of Andalucía than its eastern provinces: **Jaén**, with its rolling, olive-covered hills; **Granada**, dominated by Spain's highest peaks, the Sierra Nevada; and **Almería**, waterless and in part semi-desert.

Jaén is slightly isolated from the main routes around Andalucía, but if you're coming down to Granada from Madrid you might want to consider stopping over in the small towns of **Úbeda** or **Baeza**, both crammed with Renaissance architectural jewels and served on the main train line by their shared station of

Linares-Baeza. Úbeda also serves as the gateway to **Cazorla** and its neighbouring natural park, Andalucía's largest.

Granada, a prime target of any Spanish travels, is easily reached from Sevilla, Córdoba, Ronda, Málaga or Madrid. When you've exhausted the city, there are dozens of nearby possibilities, perhaps the most enticing being the walks in the newly created **national park of the Sierra Nevada** and its lower southern slopes, **Las Alpujarras**. The **Almería beaches**, least developed of the Spanish Mediterranean, are also within striking distance.

Jaén Province

There are said to be over 150 million olive trees in the province of Jaén. They dominate the landscape as infinite rows of green against the orange-red earth, occasionally interspersed with stark white farm buildings. It's beautiful on a grand, sweeping scale, though concealing a bitter and entrenched economic reality. The majority of the olive groves are owned by a mere handful of families, and for most residents this is a very poor area.

Sights may not be as plentiful in this zone as in other parts of Andalucía, but there are a few gems worth going out of your way to take in. Fairly dull in itself, the provincial capital of **Jaén** is worth a visit to see a fine cathedral and Moorish baths, whilst further to the northwest **Baeza** and **Úbeda** are two remarkable Renaissance towns. Extending northeast from the town of Cazorla, the **Parque Natural de Cazorla** is a vast expanse of dense woodlands, lakes and spectacular crags.

Jaén

JAÉN, the provincial capital and by far the largest town, is an uneventful sort of place with traces of its Moorish past in the winding, narrow streets of the old quarter and in the largest surviving Moorish baths in Spain. Activity is centred around the Plaza de la Constitución and its two arterial streets, Paseo de la Estación and Avenida de Madrid. The town is overlooked by the Cerro de Santa Catalina, a wooded hill topped by a recently restored Moorish fort, now partly transformed into a spectacular *parador* (see p.360).

West of the main plaza is the imposing seventeenth-century Renaissance **Catedral** (Mon–Sat 8.30am–1pm & 5–8pm, Sun 9am–1pm; museum daily 10am–1pm; church free, museum €1.80), by the great local architect Andrés de Vandelvira, with a dramatic west facade flanked by twin towers. To the north of the cathedral, between the churches of San Andrés and Santo Domingo, you'll find the painstakingly restored Moorish *hammam* in the **Baños Arabes** (Tues–Fri 9am–8pm, Sat & Sun 9.30am–2.30pm; free). Among the finest of their kind in Spain, the baths were originally part of an eleventh-century Moorish palace, and are now located inside the sixteenth-century Palacio de Villardompardo, which was constructed over it. On view are the various rooms (containing hot, tepid and cold baths), with pillars supporting elegant horseshoe arches and brickwork ceilings pierced with distinctive star-shaped windows. Jaén's **Museo Provincial**, Paseo de la Estación 29 (Tues 3–8pm, Wed–Sat 9am–8pm, Sun 9am–3pm; free), has a large archeological collection including some remarkable fifth-century BC Iberian sculptures, now set to become the centrepiece of a major new museum of Iberian art.

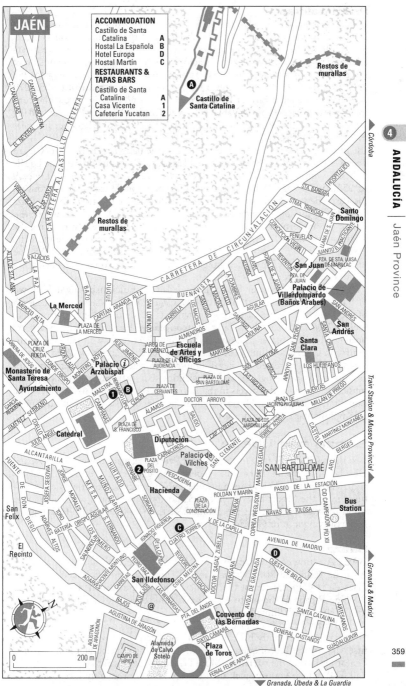

JAÉN

ACCOMMODATION
Castillo de Santa
Catalina **A**
Hostal La Española **B**
Hotel Europa **D**
Hostal Martín **C**
**RESTAURANTS &
TAPAS BARS**
Castillo de Santa
Catalina **A**
Casa Vicente **1**
Cafetería Yucatan **2**

Restos de
murallas

Castillo de
Santa Catalina

Restos de
murallas

Santo
Domingo

San Juan

Palacio de
Villardompardo
(Baños Árabes)

San
Andrés

Santa
Clara

La Merced

Escuela
de Artes y
Oficios

Monasterio de
Santa Teresa

Palacio
Arzobispal

Ayuntamiento

Catedral

Diputación

Palacio de
Vilches

SAN BARTOLOMÉ

Hacienda

San
Felix

Bus
Station

El
Recinto

San Ildefonso

Convento de
las Bernardas

Alameda
de Calvo
Sotelo

Plaza
de Toros

0   200 m

▼ Granada, Úbeda & La Guardia

Practicalities

Jaén's **turismo**, c/Maestra 13 (Mon–Fri 8.30am–2.30pm, Sat 10am–12.30pm; ☎953 19 04 55), with plenty of town information, is located slightly to the north of the cathedral. The train and bus stations are located along the central Paseo de la Estación which exits from the north side of Plaza de la Constitución; the **bus station**, Plaza Coca de la Pinera (☎953 250 106), is off to the right after 300m, while the **train station** (☎953 270 202) lies to the left a further kilometre or so beyond (bus #10 from the centre). **Internet** access is available at *Cyber Cu@k*, Adarves Bajos 24 (daily 10.30am–12.30pm & 5.30pm–midnight; ☎953 190 616; €1.50 per hr), near the Plaza de Toros.

If you want to **stay**, budget options include the basic *Hostal Martín*, c/Cuatro Torres 5 (☎953 243 678; ❶), near the Plaza de la Constitución, and the equally basic (with some rooms en suite) *Hostal La Española*, c/Bernardo López 9 (☎953 230 254; ❷–❸), by the cathedral. There are more expensive options on the Paseo de la Estación and Avenida de Madrid, including *Hotel Europa*, Plaza de Belén 1, just off Avenida de Madrid (☎953 222 700, ⓦwww.husa.es; ❸), which has modern air-conditioned rooms and its own garage. Overlooking the town, and built in the shell of a Moorish castle with stunning views, is the *Parador Castillo de Santa Catalina* (☎953 230 000, ⓦwww.parador.es; ❻), one of the most spectacularly sited hotels in Spain; even if you're not staying, it's worth calling in for a drink at the bar.

Calle Nueva, immediately east of Plaza de la Constitución, has a whole crowd of **bars** and **places to eat**. Alternatively, *Casa Vicente*, c/Maestre 8, just north of the cathedral, is one of the best restaurants in town with prices to match, while *Cafetería Yucatan*, up a flight of steps off the Plaza del Posito, is a good breakfast bar and serves *platos combinados* until late. To feast in baronial splendour you'll need to climb – or take a taxi – to the *Castillo de Santa Catalina parador*, whose recreated medieval dining room offers a good-value *menú* for around €23 including *jiennense* specialities. For **late-night drinking** and music bars head for the streets in the Barrio de San Ildefonso to the east of the cathedral, focusing on c/Hurtado, where the friendly *Bar Azulejo* at no. 8 gives a complimentary tapa with every drink.

Baeza and Úbeda

Less than an hour from Jaén are the rarely visited, elegant towns of **Baeza** and **Úbeda**. Each has an extraordinary density of exuberant Renaissance palaces and richly endowed churches, plus fine public squares. Both towns were captured from the Moors by Fernando el Santo and, repopulated with his knights, stood for two centuries at the frontiers of the reconquered lands facing the Moorish kingdom of Granada.

Baeza

BAEZA is tiny, compact and provincial, with a perpetual Sunday air about it. At its heart are the Plaza Mayor – in fact comprised of two linked plazas, the Plaza de la Constitucíon at the southern end with a garden, and the smaller Plaza de España to the north – and *paseo*, flanked by cafés and very much the hub of the town's limited animation.

The **Plaza de Leones**, an appealing cobbled square enclosed by Renaissance buildings, stands slightly back at the far end. Here, on a rounded balcony, the first Mass of the Reconquest is reputed to have been celebrated; the mansion beneath it houses the **turismo** (Mon–Fri 9am–2.30pm, Sat 10am–1pm; ☎953 740 444), where you can pick up a map (which conveniently incorporates an

Úbeda town map as well) and English-language walking-tour brochure of the town. There are no charges to enter any of Baeza's monuments, but you may offer the guardian a small *propina* (tip).

Finest of Baeza's mansions is the **Palacio de Jabalquinto** (patio open Tues–Sun 10am–1pm & 4–6pm), now a seminary, with an elaborate "Isabelline" front (showing marked Moorish influence in its stalactite decoration). Close by, the sixteenth-century **Catedral** (daily 10.30am–1pm & 4–6pm, April–Sept closes 7pm), like many of Baeza and Úbeda's churches, has brilliant painted *rejas* (iron screens) created in the sixteenth century by Maestro Bartolomé, the Spanish master of this craft. In the cloister, part of the old mosque has been uncovered, but the cathedral's real novelty is a huge silver *custodia* – cunningly hidden behind a painting of St Peter which whirls aside for a €1 coin.

There are some good walks around town: wandering up through the Puerta de Jaén on the Plaza de los Leones and along the Paseo Murallas/Paseo de Don Antonio Machado takes you round the edge of Baeza with good views over the surrounding plains. You can cut back to the Plaza Mayor via the network of narrow stone-walled alleys – with the occasional arch – that lie behind the cathedral.

Accommodation is adequate but mostly upmarket: for budget options try the *Hostal El Patio*, c/Conde Ramones 13, near the Plaza de Leones (☎953 740 200; ●), an old Renaissance mansion set around an enclosed courtyard with a wood-beamed dining hall; or the *Hostal Comercio* (☎953 740 100; ●) on c/San Pablo, a main road at the end of the central square, at no. 21 – both have some rooms with bath. Best of the central pricier places is *Hotel Baeza*, c/Concepción 3, near the Plaza de España (☎953 748 130, ℻953 742 519; ●), partly set inside a former Renaissance palace. Good bets for **food** and **drink** include the ancient *Cafetería Mercantil*, on the Plaza de España, which, besides being the best place for a lazy terrace breakfast, offers decent tapas and *raciones* later in the day. Nearby, *Casa Lucas*, Plaza España 13, is a local favourite for more tapas and economical *platos combinados*. For a bit more style try the pleasant terrace of the mid-priced *Restaurante Sali* around the corner at c/Benavides 9, with a view of Baeza's magnificent sixteenth-century *ayuntamiento*. *El Pasaje* at no. 3 on the same street is another possibility, with a *menú* for around €9.

The nearest **train station** is Linares-Baeza 14km from Baeza and served by frequent trains from Sevilla, Córdoba and Granada (there is a connecting bus for most trains, except on Sun; €12 taxi ride). Most bus connections are via Úbeda.

Úbeda

ÚBEDA, 9km east of Baeza, is a larger town with modern suburbs. Follow the signs to the *Zona Monumental* and you'll eventually reach the **Plaza de Vázquez de Molina**, a tremendous Renaissance square which is one of the most impressive of its kind in Spain.

Most of the buildings round the square were the late sixteenth-century work of Andrés de Vandelvira, the architect of Baeza's cathedral and numerous churches in both towns. One of these buildings, the **Palacio de las Cadenas**, originally a palace for Felipe II's secretary, houses Úbeda's *ayuntamiento* and features a magnificent facade fronted by monumental lions. In another part of the same building the **Museo de Alfarería** (daily 10.30am–2pm & 5–7pm; closed for renovation at time of writing) displays pottery of varying ages and types from all over Spain as well as Úbeda itself, still an important centre of ceramic craftsmanship. At the opposite end of the square, the **Capilla del Salvador**

(Mon–Sat 10am–2pm & 5–7.30pm, Sun 10.45am–2pm & 4.30–7.30pm; €2.25), erected by Vandelvira, though actually designed by Diego de Siloé, architect of the Málaga and Granada cathedrals, is the finest church in Úbeda. It's a masterpiece of Spanish Renaissance architecture with a dazzling Plateresque facade, its highlight a carving of the Transfiguration of Christ flanked by statues of St Peter and St Paul. Inside, the Transfiguration theme is repeated in a brilliantly animated *retablo* by Alonso de Berruguete, who studied under Michelangelo.

Following c/Horno Contado out of the Plaza de Vázquez de Molina leads to yet another delightful square, the Plaza del Primero de Mayo, and the idiosyncratic church of **San Pablo**, with a thirteenth-century balcony and various Renaissance additions.

The **turismo** (Mon–Fri 9am–8pm, Sat–Sun 10am–2pm; ☎953 750 897) is housed in its own Renaissance mansion, the Palacio del Marqués de Contadero, c/Baja Marqués 4, just to the west of the Plaza de Vázquez de Molina, and can provide a town map. Most of the budget **accommodation** options are grouped around the main **bus station** on Avenida de Ramón y Cajal, in the modern part of town – the *Hostal Castillo* at no. 16 (☎953 750 430; ❶–❷) and *Hostal Sevilla* at no. 9 (☎953 750 612; ❷) are both reasonable, and have some rooms with bath. For some of the least expensive (en-suite) rooms in town, try *Hostal San Miguel*, Avda. Libertad 69 (☎953 752 049; ❶), a fifteen-minute walk north from the bus station along Avenida de Ramón y Cajal, with a decent restaurant below. In the monumental quarter, among a number of upmarket options the *Parador Condestable Dávalos*, Plaza de Vázquez de Molina 1 (☎953 750 345, ☏953 751 259; ❻), housed in yet another fabulous sixteenth-century Renaissance mansion, is outstanding.

There are plenty of **places to eat** around Avenida Ramón y Cajal: *El Gallo Rojo*, c/Torrenueva 3, has outdoor tables in the evening; *El Olivo*, Avda. Ramón y Cajal 6, serves good *platos combinados*; and *Hostal Castillo* has its own excellent-value restaurant with an economical *menú*. For a treat, the elegant restaurant of the *parador* offers a great-value *menú* – with regional specialities – for about €25.

Cazorla and the Parque Natural

During the reconquest of Andalucía, **CAZORLA** acted as an outpost for Christian troops, and the two castles which still dominate the town testify to its turbulent past – both were originally Moorish but later altered and restored by their Christian conquerors. Today it's the main base for visits to the **Parque Natural de las Sierras de Segura y Cazorla**, a vast protected area of magnificent river gorges and forests. Cazorla also hosts the **fiesta de Cristo del Consuelo**, with fairgrounds, fireworks and religious processions on September 16–21.

Cazorla itself is constructed around three main squares. Buses arrive in the busy, commercial **Plaza de la Constitución**, linked by the main c/de Muñoz to the second square, the **Plaza de la Corredera** (or *del Huevo*, "of the Egg", because of its shape). The seat of the administration, the *ayuntamiento*, is here, a fine Moorish-style palace at the far end of the plaza. Beyond, a labyrinth of narrow, twisting streets leads to Cazorla's liveliest square, the **Plaza Santa María**. This takes its name from the old cathedral which, damaged by floods in the seventeenth century, was later torched by Napoleonic troops. Its ruins, now preserved, and the fine open square form a natural amphitheatre for concerts and local events as well as being a popular meeting place. The square is dominated by **La Yedra**, an austere, reconstructed castle tower, which houses the **Museo de Artes y Costumbres** (Mon–Sat 9.30am–2.30pm; free), an interesting folklore museum displaying domestic utensils and furniture.

Cazorla practicalities

Cazorla's official **turismo** (April–Sept Wed–Sun 10am–2pm; ☎953 710 102, ⓦwww.sierracazorla.com) is at Paseo del Santo Cristo 17, 100m north of Plaza de la Constitución, and can provide a useful town map. Alternatively, Quercus, in the Plaza de la Constitución (Mon–Fri 10am–2pm, Sat & Sun 10am–2pm & 5–8pm; ☎953 720 115, ⓦwww.excursionesquercus.com), is a privately run tourist office; the staff are friendly but their information, especially that pertaining to independent ramblings, is none too reliable as the office ostensibly exists to promote Land Rover excursions, photo safaris and the like. Their horse-riding treks into the park are popular – horses can be rented hourly, or by the day or half-day.

There is a surprising range of **accommodation** in Cazorla. *Pensión Taxi*, Travesía de San Antón 7 (☎953 720 525; ❷), off Plaza de la Constitución, is at the bottom end; as a resident, you can also eat for very little in their *comedor*. Better facilities (all rooms en suite) are available at the very friendly *Hotel Guadalquivir*, c/Nueva 6 (☎953 720 268, ⓦwww.hguadalquivir.com; ❷), off Plaza de la Corredera, while in the square itself, the equally friendly *Hostal Betis* (☎953 720 540; ❶) has rooms with and without bath, some overlooking the plaza. There is also a clutch of more upmarket places, of which the *Villa Turística de Cazorla*, Ladera de San Isidro s/n (☎953 710 100, ⓦwww.villacazorla.com; ❹), is the best; it's a five-minute walk from Plaza de la Constitución and reached by crossing the bridge over the river below the square. If you have a car there are some very attractive alternatives out in the sierra, including the *Hotel Sierra de Cazorla* (☎953 720 015, ⓕ953 720 017; ❸), 2km outside the town, with a pool, and the *Parador El Adelantado* (☎953 727 075, ⓕ953 727 077; ❻), a well-designed modern building with pool in a wonderful setting 25km away in the park. Cazorla also has an efficient **youth hostel**, at Mauricio Martínez 2 (☎953 710 329; €13.35; April–Oct, Christmas and Easter), reached by walking along c/Juan Domingo from Plaza de la Constitución for five minutes. Ask at the *Mesón la Cueva* (see below) if you want to **rent an apartment** for a longer stay.

For **eating** and **drinking** there are several spit-and-sawdust **bars** with good tapas clustered round the Plaza Santa María, along with the rustic *Mesón la Cueva*, which offers authentic local food cooked on a wood-fired range – the *conejo* (rabbit) is recommended – though when they are overrun in high season things can tend to deteriorate. Other places where you can **eat** well are *Mesón Don Chema*, down some steps off c/Muñoz, serving *platos combinados* and an economical *menú*, or the more expensive *La Sarga*, Plaza del Mercado, at the bottom of the same steps, where regional dishes are prepared with flair and there's a *menú* for €11.

The Parque Natural

Even casual visitors to the park are likely to see a good variety of wildlife, including *Capra hispanica* (Spanish mountain goat), deer, wild pig, birds and butterflies. Ironically, though, much of the best viewing will be at the periphery, or even outside the park, since the wildlife is most successfully stalked on foot and walking opportunities within the park itself are surprisingly limited.

Information

The main **information centre** inside the park is the Torre del Vinagre Centro de Interpretación (daily 11am–2pm & 5–8pm, Oct–March closes 7pm; ☎953 713 040; see box on p.364). It's worth getting a good **map** (also available from the options in town): the 1:100,000 map, *Parque Natural de las Sierras de Cazorla y Segura*, and the 1:50,000 version, *Cazorla*, are recommended, but best of all is

The Río Borosa walk

The classic walk along the Río Borosa can currently be done as a day-trek even if you are relying on public transport – though you should check the bus timetables before setting out. The early-morning bus to Coto Ríos can drop you at the visitors' centre at Torre del Vinagre where the route begins. Cross the road and take the path to the side of the Jardín Botanico. When you reach an electricity pylon turn left onto a downhill track. After passing a campsite and sports field to the left, cross a footbridge over the river and turn right, aiming for a white building peeping above the trees. Soon you'll pass a small campsite (with an open-air bar in summer) and about a kilometre from the footbridge you'll come to a car park at a trout hatchery (*piscifactoría*).

From here follow the rough track along the northwest (right) bank of the Borosa, swift and cold even in summer. Within a few minutes a signposted footpath diverges to the right; this also marks the beginning of the gorge. Two or three wooden bridges now take the path back and forth across the river, which is increasingly confined by sheer rock walls. At the narrowest points the path is routed along planked catwalks secured to the limestone cliff. The walk from Torre del Vinagre to the end of the narrows takes about two hours.

There the footpath rejoins the track; after another half-hour's walk you'll see a turbine and a long metal pipe bringing water from two lakes – one natural, one a small dam – up the mountain. The road crosses one last bridge over the Borosa and stops at the turbine house. When you get to a gate, beyond which there's a steeply rising gully, count on another full hour up to the lakes. Cross a footbridge and start the steep climb up a narrow track over the rocks below the cliff (at one point the path passes close to the base of the palisade – beware falling stones). At the top of the path is a cavernous amphitheatre, with a waterfall in winter. The path ends about halfway up the cliff, where an artificial tunnel has been bored through rock; walk through it to get to the lake.

Allow three and a half hours' walking time from Torre del Vinagre, slightly less going down. It's a full day's excursion but you should have plenty of time to catch the afternoon bus back – it currently passes the visitors' centre at 4.40pm, but it would be a good idea to confirm this before starting out. This walk is clearly detailed on the relevant Editorial Alpina map (see information on p.363).

the new 1:40,000 set of map and guide packs to the Sierras de Cazorla and Segura (divided into three zones), published by Editorial Alpina, which are now the most accurate maps available, detailing *senderos* (footpaths), mountain-bike routes, refuges, campsites and hotels.

Transport and accommodation

Public transport into the park is sparse. Two daily **buses** (except Sun) link Cazorla with **Coto Ríos** (a 1hr 15min journey) in the middle of the park: one currently running at 6.30am, the other at 2.40pm; there's also a 6.30pm bus on Saturday. Return buses from Coto (not Sun) leave at 8am and 4.30pm. Distances between points are enormous, so to explore the park well you'll need a car or to be prepared for long treks. There are ten official campsites throughout the park, which are accurately marked on the Alpina map (see above). There is more accommodation at Coto Ríos, with three privately run **campsites** and a succession of *hostales*. Before setting out you should get the latest update on transport and accommodation from the turismo in Cazorla.

Walks

There are only three signposted **tracks** in the park, all pitifully short. One leads from the Empalme de Vadillo to the Puente de la Herrera via the Fuente del

Oso (2km each way); another of about 1700m curls round the Cerrada (narrows) de Utrero near Vadillo-Castril village; and the best marked segment, through the lower Borosa gorge (see box opposite), is also a mere 1700m long. With the aid of a good map (see p.364) you can follow your own trails, but as there are very few settlements of any kind in many areas of the park it would be wise to travel prepared for all eventualities (food and sleeping gear are a must) and take a compass.

Granada

If you see only one town in Spain it should be **GRANADA**. For here, extraordinarily well preserved and in a tremendous natural setting, stands the **Alhambra** – the most exciting, sensual and romantic of all European monuments. It was the palace-fortress of the Nasrid sultans, rulers of the last Spanish Moorish kingdom, and in its construction Moorish art reached a spectacular and serene climax. But the building seems to go further than this, revealing something of the whole brilliance and spirit of Moorish life and culture. There's a haunting passage in Jan Morris's book, *Spain*, which the palace embodies:

"Life itself, which was seen elsewhere in Europe as a kind of probationary preparation for death, was interpreted [by the Moors] as something glorious in itself, to be ennobled by learning and enlivened by every kind of pleasure."

Built on the slopes of three hills, the rest of the city basks in the Alhambra's reflected glory. Because the Moorish influence here was so ruthlessly extinguished following capitulation to Fernando and Isabel (see p.368), Granada tends to be more sober in character and austere in its architecture than Andalucía's other provincial capitals. Many visitors, once they've viewed the Alhambra, are too jaded or can't be fussed to take in the city's other sights, which is a pity, for Granada has much to offer. The hilltop **Albaicín**, the former Moorish town, is a fascinating quarter full of narrow alleyways and small squares, and a great place for an hour's stroll. Not far away, too, is the cathedral with the gem of the **Capilla Real** attached to it, the final resting place of the Catholic monarchs who ended Moorish rule in Spain. Add in an **Archeological Museum**, **Moorish baths** and some fine churches, including

The Bono Turistico

One money-saving offer worth thinking about is a **Bono Turistico** (City Pass) which gives you access to eight of the city's monuments including the Alhambra, Capilla Real, Catedral and La Cartuja for €18. The *Bono* is valid for a week and comes in the form of a plastic card which you swipe through the gates at any of the monuments listed. You can enter once only and will have a specified time for visiting the Palacios Nazaríes (royal palaces) of the Alhambra. The *Bono* also includes ten bus journeys on public transport. The cards can be purchased from the ticket offices of the Alhambra or the Capilla Real, not from the tourist offices. They can also be purchased at the Caja General de Ahorros bank at Plaza Isabel la Católica 6 during business hours, but here you will incur a commission charge of €2. The cards can also be ordered online (ⓦwww.granadatur.com or ⓦwww.caja.caja -granada.es/bono), but you will need to collect them when you arrive in Granada.

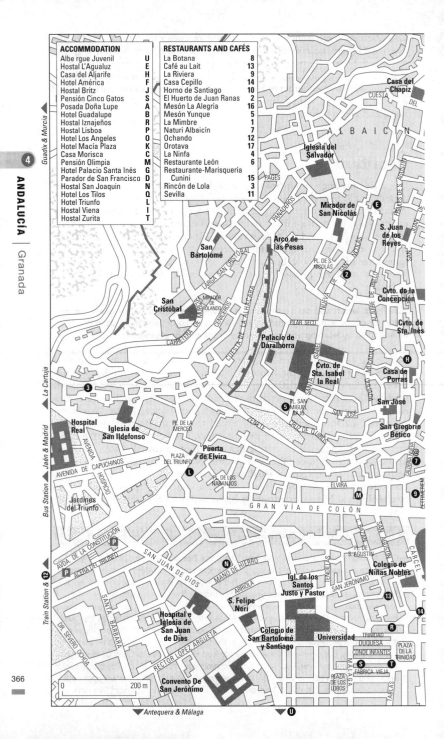

ACCOMMODATION

Albe rgue Juvenil	U
Hostal L'Agualuz	E
Casa del Aljarife	H
Hotel América	F
Hostal Britz	J
Pensión Cinco Gatos	S
Posada Doña Lupe	A
Hotel Guadalupe	B
Hostal Iznajeños	R
Hostal Lisboa	P
Hotel Los Angeles	O
Hotel Macía Plaza	K
Casa Morisca	C
Pensión Olimpia	M
Hotel Palacio Santa Inés	G
Parador de San Francisco	D
Hostal San Joaquin	N
Hotel Los Tilos	Q
Hotel Triunfo	L
Hostal Viena	I
Hostal Zurita	T

RESTAURANTS AND CAFÉS

La Botana	8
Café au Lait	13
La Riviera	9
Casa Cepillo	14
Horno de Santiago	10
El Huerto de Juan Ranas	2
Mesón La Alegría	16
Mesón Yunque	5
La Mimbre	1
Naturi Albaicín	7
Ochando	12
Orotava	17
La Ninfa	4
Restaurante León	6
Restaurante-Marisquería Cunini	15
Rincón de Lola	3
Sevilla	11

0 — 200 m

▼ Antequera & Málaga   ▼ U

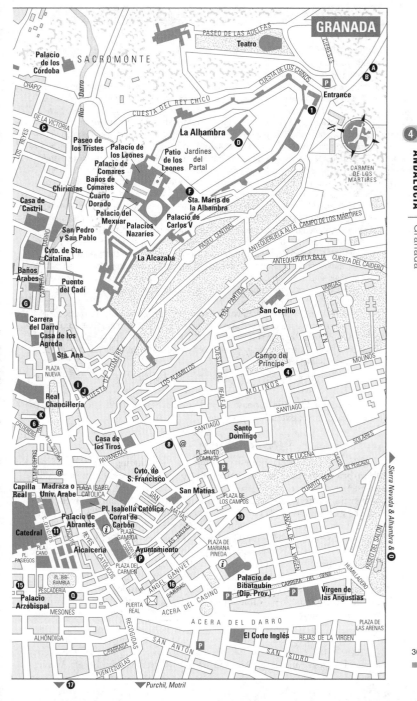

GRANADA

Teatro

PASEO DE LAS ADELFAS

Palacio de los Córdoba

SACROMONTE

CUESTA DE LOS CHINOS

Entrance

A
B

P

Ⓐ

❶

CHAPIZ

Darro

CUESTA DEL REY CHICO

DE LA VICTORIA

C

La Alhambra

D

N

🏃

④

Paseo de los Tristes

Palacio de los Leones

Patio de los Leones

Jardínes del Partal

CARMEN DE LOS MÁRTIRES

Palacio de Comares

Baños de Comares

Chirimías

Cuarto Dorado

F

Sta. María de la Alhambra

Casa de Castril

Palacio del Mexuar

Palacios Nazaríes

Palacio de Carlos V

CAMPO DE LOS MÁRTIRES

San Pedro y San Pablo

Cvto. de Sta. Catalina

La Alcazaba

PASEO CENTRAL

ANTEQUERUELA ALTA

Baños Arabes

Puente del Cadí

ANTEQUERUELA BAJA

CUESTA DEL CAIDERO

G

VARGAS

San Cecilio

MOLINOS

Carrera del Darro

Casa de los Ágreda

Sta. Ana

BELÉN

PEÑA PARTIDA

PLAZA NUEVA

I J

CUESTA DE GOMÉREZ

LOS ALAMILLOS

CUESTA DEL REALEJO

Campo del Príncipe

④

Real Chancillería

MOLINOS

SANTIAGO

K

❻

CALDERERÍA

FUSTERA

SANTIAGO

Santo Domingo

SOLARES

Casa de los Tiros

❽

@

PL. SANTO DOMINGO

P.S. DE LUCENA

ALMIREHIRAS

PAVANERAS

P

DEL PESCADO

@

CUARTO REAL

Cvto. de S. Francisco

San Matías

Capilla Real

Madraza o Univ. Arabe

PLAZA ISABEL CATÓLICA

PLAZA DE LOS CAMPOS

SAN MATÍAS

Pl. Isabella Católica

Corral de Carbón

ANCHA DE LA VIRGEN

Catedral

Palacio de Abrantes

i

PLAZA GAMBOA

❿

REYES CATÓLICOS

C. OFICIOS

⓫

PL. CANO

LAS NAVAS

Alcaicería

Ayuntamiento

P

CÁRCEL

PLAZA DE MARIANA PINEDA

PLAZA DEL CARMEN

i

HUMILLADERO

PL. PASIEGOS

Q

PL. BIB-RAMBLA

PESCADERÍA

CÁRCEL

ANGEL GANIVET

GAMBRAS

Palacio de Bibataubín (Dip. Prov.)

CARRERA DEL GENIL

Virgen de las Angustias

⓯

Palacio Arzobispal

PUERTA REAL

CASINO

P

P

ALHÓNDIGA

MESONES

⓰

ACERA DEL CASINO

ACERA DEL DARRO

PLAZA DE LAS ARENAS

RECOGIDAS

C/PARRAGA

SAN ANTÓN

P

El Corte Inglés

REJAS DE LA VIRGEN

PUENTEZUELAS

SAN ISIDRO

⓱

Purchil, Motril

▶ Sierra Nevada & Alhambra & ⑩

Moorish Granada

Granada's glory was always precarious. It was established as an independent kingdom in 1238 by Ibn Ahmar, a prince of the Arab Nasrid tribe which had been driven south from Zaragoza. He proved a just and capable ruler, but all over Spain the Christian kingdoms were in the ascendant. The Moors of Granada survived only through paying tribute and allegiance to Fernando III of Castile – whom they were forced to assist in the conquest of Muslim Sevilla – and by the time of Ibn Ahmar's death in 1275 theirs was the only surviving Spanish Muslim kingdom. It had, however, consolidated its territory (stretching from just north of the city down to a coastal strip between Tarifa and Almería) and, stimulated by refugees, developed a flourishing commerce, industry and culture.

By a series of shrewd manoeuvres Granada maintained its autonomy for two and a half centuries, its rulers turning for protection, in turn as it suited them, to the Christian kingdoms of Aragón and Castile and to the Merinid Muslims of Morocco. The city-state enjoyed a particularly confident and prosperous period under Yusuf I (1334–54) and Mohammed V (1354–91), the sultans responsible for much of the existing Alhambra palace. But by the mid-fifteenth century a pattern of coups and internal strife became established and a rapid succession of rulers did little to stem Christian inroads. In 1479 the kingdoms of Aragón and Castile were united by the marriage of Fernando and Isabel and within ten years had conquered Ronda, Málaga and Almería. The city of Granada now stood completely alone, tragically preoccupied in a civil war between supporters of the sultan's two favourite wives. The Reyes Católicos made escalating and finally untenable demands upon it, and in 1490 war broke out. Boabdil, the last Moorish king, appealed in vain for help from his fellow Muslims in Morocco, Egypt and Ottoman Turkey, and in the following year Fernando and Isabel marched on Granada with an army said to total 150,000 troops. For seven months, through the winter of 1491, they laid siege to the city, and on January 2, 1492, Boabdil formally surrendered its keys. The Christian Reconquest of Spain was complete.

a spectacular **La Cartuja** monastery, and you have more than enough to start you thinking about extending your stay.

Arrival and information

Virtually everything of interest in Granada – including the hills of the **Alhambra** (to the east) and **Sacromonte** (to the north) – is within easy walking distance of the centre.

The **train station** (☎958 204 000) is a kilometre or so out on Avenida de Andaluces, off Avenida de la Constitución; to get into town, buses #3, #4, #6 and #9 run direct to Gran Vía de Colón and the centre of town, and bus #11 takes a circular route – inbound on the Gran Vía and back out via the Puerta Real and Camino de Ronda. The most central stop is by the cathedral on the Gran Vía.

The city's main **bus station**, Carretera de Jaén s/n, is some way out of the centre in the northern suburbs, and handles all services except those to the Sierra Nevada, Valencia and Barcelona. Bus #3 leaves from outside and will drop you near the cathedral (a fifteen-minute journey). For information on bus departures check with the individual companies: Alsina Graells (☎958 185 480) at the main bus station runs services to and from Madrid, Jaén, Úbeda, Córdoba, Sevilla, Málaga, Alpujarras, Motril, Guadix, Almería and the coast; Empresa Bonal (☎958 273 100), Avda. Constitución 34, has buses to the north side of the Sierra Nevada; Empresa Autedía (☎958 153 636), c/Rector Martín 10, off Avenida

Constitución, runs more services to Guadix; and Empresa Bacoma (☎958 284 251), Avda. Andalucía 12, near the train station, has buses to Valencia/Alicante and Barcelona. All terminals are on bus routes #3, #4 and #11.

Arriving **by air**, there's a bus (7 daily; 30min; €2.55 one way) connecting the airport, 17km west of the city on the A92 *autovía*, with Plaza Isabel La Católica; alternatively, a taxi should cost about €18.

Full details and bus timetables – and much else besides – should be posted on the walls of the **turismo** (Mon–Sat 9am–7pm, Sun 10am–2pm; ☎958 221 022), in the Corral del Carbón near the cathedral, just off the eastern side of c/Reyes Católicos. There's also a very helpful (and less frenetic) **municipal tourist office** (Mon–Fri 9am–8pm, Sat 10am–4pm; ☎958 247 128, ⓦwww.granadatur.com) at Plaza Mariana Pineda 10. For listings, the monthly *Guía del Ocio* (available from newspaper *kioscos*) details most of what's happening on the cultural and entertainment front, though it tends to be less up-to-date than the city's daily paper, *Ideal*, which is particularly good in its weekend editions. One way to get to grips with the city – particularly if it's your first visit – is with a **guided walk**; The Walk (mobile ☎600 744 395; €8) does two-and-a-half-hour English-speaking tours of the city throughout the year, starting out daily at noon from the fountain in Plaza Nueva and taking in the Albaicín and other central locations.

Accommodation

As Granada's popularity as a tourist destination has grown the city often finds that it has problems finding beds for all its visitors. Semana Santa (Easter week) is always impossible without booking well in advance, and many of the spring and summer months can be difficult, too. Booking accommodation as far ahead as you can is the best way to avoid a long and frustrating trek to find a room. Likely areas with **places to stay** in the centre of town include along the Gran Vía (de Cólon), c/Reyes Católicos, in and around the Plaza Nueva and Puerta Real and off the Plaza del Carmen (particularly c/Las Navas). In the university zone, the Plaza de la Trinidad (and east of here) is another good place to look, along with the Cuesta de Gomérez, which leads up from the Plaza Nueva towards the Alhambra. The main problem, almost anywhere, is **noise**, though the new road to the Alhambra, diverting traffic away from the centre, has transformed the once-deafening Cuesta de Gomérez, the main route to the monument, now a semi-pedestrianized street (taxis and buses only). The atmospheric Albaicín now has a couple of decent *hostales*, in addition to a number of upmarket hotels, some definitely worth trying if you can afford to splash out.

Budget options

Albergue Juvenil Camino de Ronda 171, at the junction with Avda. Ramón y Cajal ☎958 002 900, ⓕ958 002 908. If you arrive late in the day, Granada's youth hostel is conveniently close to the train station: turn left onto Avda. de la Constitución and left again onto Camino de Ronda. From the bus station, take bus #3 to the cathedral and then the circular #11, which will drop you outside. Efficiently run with lots of facilities, all rooms are en-suite doubles, the staff is friendly but the food is institutional; it can also be booked up for days ahead in summer. €13.35
Hostal Britz Cuesta de Gomérez 1 ☎958 223

652. Very comfortable and well-placed *hostal*, en route to the Alhambra. Some rooms with bath. ❶–❷
Pensión Cinco Gatos c/Fabrica Vieja 4 ☎958 203 680. Homely *pensión* with clean, inexpensive rooms – some with bath – and an ebullient (feline-fancying) *dueña*. ❶–❷
Posada Doña Lupe Avda. del Generalife s/n ☎958 221 473, ⓕ958 221 474. A stone's throw from the entrance to the Alhambra, with economically priced rooms (some en suite) and a rooftop pool, but blighted by a rule-ridden student hostel ambience. ❶–❷
Hostal Iznajeños c/Lucena 1, a tiny street just off

Plaza de la Trinidad ☎958 278 255. Very friendly family *pensión* with spotless, economical rooms. **①**

Hostal Lisboa Plaza del Carmen 27 ☎958 221 413. Clean and comfortable central *hostal*, offering rooms with and without bath. **①–②**

Pensión Olimpia c/Alvaro de Bazán 6, off Gran Vía de Colón opposite Banco de Jeréz building ☎958 278 238. Welcoming, central *pensión* offering good-value basic accommodation. **①**

Hostal San Joaquin c/Mano de Hierro 14, close to the church of San Juan ☎958 282 879, @informacion@hostalsanjoaquin.com. Great, rambling old *hostal*, with simple rooms (some en suite) and charming patios. **①**

Hostal Viena c/Hospital de Santa Ana 2 ☎958 221 859, @austria@arrakis.es. In a quiet street (first left off the Cuesta de Gomérez), this is a pleasant, efficient Austrian-run *hostal* offering some rooms with bath. If full, they have other places nearby. **①**

Hostal Zurita Plaza de la Trinidad 7, west of the cathedral ☎958 275 020. Friendly place where immaculate rooms come with and without bath, and all have TV and a/c. Has own garage. **②**

Moderate and expensive options

Hostal L'agualuz Placeta del Comino, near the Mirador San Nicolas, in the Albaicín ☎958 226 827. New bed and breakfast place with en-suite rooms above a restaurant. Significant price reductions in late July and Aug. Breakfast included. **③**

Casa del Aljarife Placeta de la Cruz Verde 2 ☎ & @958 222 425, @www.granadainfo.com/most. This Albaicín upmarket *hostal* occupies a restored sixteenth-century mansion near the heart of the *barrio*, has attractive en-suite a/c rooms and allows use of email and fax. **⑤**

Hotel América Real de la Alhambra 53 ☎958 227 471, @www.hamerica.com. Simple, one-star hotel, in the Alhambra grounds; you're paying for location rather than creature comforts (no TV), but repeated price hikes call into question whether it's any longer worth it. Booking essential. **⑥**

Hotel Guadalupe Paseo de la Sabica s/n ☎958 223 423, @www.hotelguadslupe.es. Recently refurbished hotel a stone's throw from the Alhambra's entrance. Many of the well-equipped a/c rooms have Alhambra views. June–Aug room rates cut by thirty percent. Clients get reduced-price parking in Alhambra car park, or the Alhambra bus from Plaza Nueva drops you nearby. **⑥**

Hotel Macía Plaza Plaza Nueva 4 ☎958 227 536, @www.maciahoteles.com. Centrally located hotel, with comfortable rooms overlooking this atmospheric square. Weekend discounts in July & August. They have a couple of other hotels of the same standard nearby if this one is full. **④**

Hotel Los Angeles Cuesta Escoriaza 17 ☎958 221 423, @www.hotellosangeles.net. Pleasant modern hotel on leafy, quiet avenue within easy walking distance of the Alhambra. All rooms come with balcony and there's a garden, pool and car park. **⑤**

Casa Morisca Cuesta de la Victoria 9 ☎958 215 796, @www.hotelcasamorisca.com. Romantic, small new hotel inside an immaculately renovated fifteenth-century Moorish mansion with exquisite patio in the Albaicín; there are recreated Moorish furnishings throughout, and Room 15 (with Alhambra views) is the one to go for. **⑥**

Hotel Palacio Santa Inés Cuesta de Santa Inés 9 ☎958 222 362, @www.lugaresdivinos.com. Sumptuous six-room hotel in a restored sixteenth-century mansion on the edge of the Albaicín, with views of the Alhambra. The nearby and equally attractive *Carmen de Santa Inés* (same phone no.) is owned by the same proprietors and occupies a restored Moorish *carmen* (garden villa). **⑥**

Parador de San Francisco Real de la Alhambra ☎958 221 440, @www.parador.es. Without question the best – and most expensive – place to stay in Granada; a fifteenth-century converted monastery in the Alhambra grounds. High-season double room rates start at €220. Advance booking (at least three months ahead) essential. Call in for a drink at the attractive terrace bar. **⑨**

Hotel Los Tilos Plaza de Bib-Rambla 4 ☎958 266 712, @www.hotellostilos.com. Plain, two-star hotel well located near the cathedral on a pleasant square; make sure to request an exterior room if you don't want to overlook a gloomy light well. Some higher rooms (try 301 & 302 or 401 & 402) have great Alhambra views. **③**

Hotel Triunfo Plaza del Triunfo 19 ☎958 207 444, @www.h-triunfo-granada.com. Well-appointed upmarket hotel on the edge of the Albaicín, flanked by an imposing Moorish arch, the Puerta de Elvira. Own garage. **⑤**

Camping

Camping Sierra Nevada Avda. de Madrid 107 ☎958 150 062 (March–Oct). Closest site to the centre (bus #3 from the centre or a 3min walk south from the bus station), and with a welcome pool.

Camping Reina Isabel 4km along the Zubia road to the southwest of the city ☎958 590 041. With a pool, this is a less noisy and shadier site than the one above, making a pleasant rural alternative; can be reached by the Zubia-bound bus from the bus station, but with your own transport the city is still in easy reach.

The Alhambra

There are three distinct groups of buildings on the Alhambra hill: the **Palacios Nazaríes** (Royal Palace, or Nasrid Palaces), the palace gardens of the **Generalife**, and the **Alcazaba**. This last, the fortress of the eleventh-century Ziridian rulers, was all that existed when the Nasrid ruler Ibn al-Ahmar made Granada his capital, but from its reddish walls the hilltop had already taken its name: *Al Qal'a al-Hamra* in Arabic means literally "the red fort". Ibn al-Ahmar rebuilt the Alcazaba and added to it the huge circuit of walls and towers which

Admission to the Alhambra

To protect the Alhambra only 6300 daily admissions are allowed (daily: March–Oct 8.30am–8pm; Nov–Feb 8.30am–6pm; €8). If you are buying your tickets in person you have two options: they can be purchased at the entrance (ticket office opens at 8am and shuts one hour before the closing time above) but the overwhelming number of visitors to the monument has made it imperative to turn up as early in the day as possible to be sure of getting in, and you should be prepared for queues of one to two hours in high season. Alternatively, they can be bought on the day from the main Granada branch of the Banco de Bilbao Vizcaya Argentaria (BBVA; Mon–Fri 9am–2pm; €0.75 commission per ticket), Plaza Isabel la Católica 1, in the centre.

However, the best way to avoid the queues is to use the reservation system (English spoken), also operated by the BBVA, which enables you to book your tickets in advance from anywhere in Spain or abroad (inside Spain ☎902 224 460; outside Spain ☎+34 913 465 936, ⊕www.alhambratickets.com) a minimum of one day, or a maximum of one year, ahead. This scheme accounts for 75 percent of tickets sold and you are strongly advised to use it to avoid tedious queuing or disappointment if your time in Granada is limited. You can usually choose your time slot for the Palacios Nazaríes (see below) but at peak periods a time will be allocated to you. You are required to pay for the tickets with a credit card (Visa or Mastercard only) and a commission of €0.88 is levied for each ticket. Once your booking is confirmed you are given a code number which allows you to collect your tickets from any of the 2800 BBVA branches in Spain (at least one day before the visit takes place) or the Alhambra ticket office (at least thirty minutes before your allotted visit time). For both points of collection you will need to provide the code number and your passport. Tickets can also be reserved on the Alhambra's Spanish website ⊕www.alhambratickets.com, which is easy to get the gist of and can be accessed from abroad; the same collection conditions apply. Finally, you can also book advance tickets in person from any branch in Spain of the BBVA who will charge €1 commission on each ticket.

The tickets have sections for each part of the complex – Alcazaba, Palacios Nazaríes (royal palace), Generalife – which must be used on the same day. Note that you will not be allowed to enter the complex (even with pre-booked tickets) less than an hour before closing time. To alleviate the severe overcrowding of recent years, tickets are stamped with a half-hour time slot during which you must enter the Palacios Nazaríes. You will not be allowed to enter before or after this time, but once inside you can stay as long as you like.

The Alhambra is also open for floodlit visits (limited to the Palacios Nazaríes; €8) on Tuesday to Saturday nights from March to October (10–11.30pm; ticket office open 9.45–10.15pm only) and on Friday and Saturday nights from November to February (8–9.30pm; ticket office open 7.45–8.15pm only) and occasional concerts are held in its courts (details from the turismo). The two museums in the Palace of Carlos V have separate admission fees and hours (see p.377).

To check any changes to opening times, admission charges or booking procedures, visit the Alhambra's website ⊕www.alhambra-patronato.es where the latest information is posted.

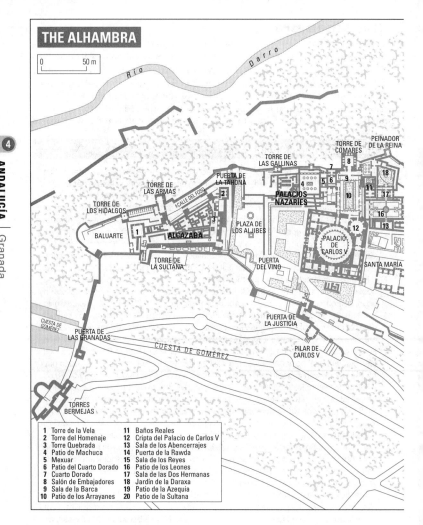

THE ALHAMBRA

0   50 m

Río   Darro

PEINADOR DE LA REINA
TORRE DE COMARES
TORRE DE LAS GALLINAS
PUERTA DE LA TAHONA
TORRE DE LAS ARMAS
#CALLE DEL FOSO
TORRE DE LOS HIDALGOS
PALACIOS NAZARÍES
BALUARTE
ALCAZABA
PLAZA DE LOS ALJIBES
PALACIO DE CARLOS V
TORRE DE LA SULTANA
PUERTA DEL VINO
SANTA MARÍA
CUESTA DE GOMÉREZ
PUERTA DE LAS GRANADAS
PUERTA DE LA JUSTICIA
CUESTA DE GOMÉREZ
PILAR DE CARLOS V
TORRES BERMEJAS

1	Torre de la Vela	**11**	Baños Reales
2	Torre del Homenaje	**12**	Cripta del Palacio de Carlos V
3	Torre Quebrada	**13**	Sala de los Abencerrajes
4	Patio de Machuca	**14**	Puerta de la Rawda
5	Mexuar	**15**	Sala de los Reyes
6	Patio del Cuarto Dorado	**16**	Patio de los Leones
7	Cuarto Dorado	**17**	Sala de las Dos Hermanas
8	Salón de Embajadores	**18**	Jardín de la Daraxa
9	Sala de la Barca	**19**	Patio de la Azequia
10	Patio de los Arrayanes	**20**	Patio de la Sultana

forms your first view of the castle. Within the walls he began a palace, which he supplied with running water by diverting the River Darro nearly 8km to the foot of the hill; water is an integral part of the Alhambra and this engineering feat was Ibn al-Ahmar's greatest contribution. The Palacios Nazaríes was essentially the product of his fourteenth-century successors, particularly Yusuf I and Mohammed V, who built and redecorated many of its rooms in celebration of his accession to the throne (in 1354) and the taking of Algeciras (in 1369).

After their conquest of the city, **Fernando and Isabel** lived for a while in the Alhambra. They restored some rooms and converted the mosque but left the palace structure unaltered. As at Córdoba and Sevilla, it was **Emperor Carlos V**, their grandson, who wreaked the most insensitive destruction,

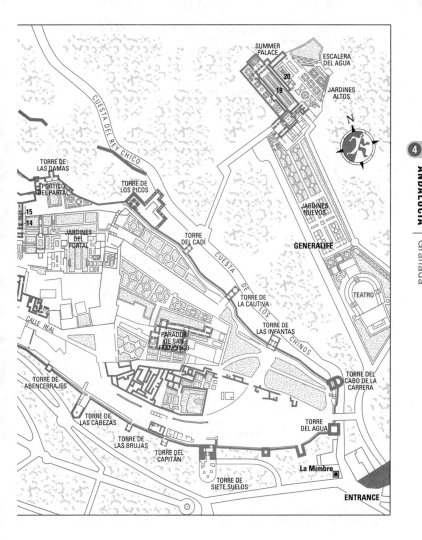

demolishing a whole wing of rooms in order to build a Renaissance palace. This and the Alhambra itself were simply ignored by his successors, and by the eighteenth century the Palacios Nazaríes was in use as a prison. In 1812 it was taken and occupied by **Napoleon's forces**, who looted and damaged whole sections of the palace, and on their retreat from the city tried to blow up the entire complex. Their attempt was thwarted only by the action of a crippled soldier who remained behind and removed the fuses.

Two decades later the Alhambra's "rediscovery" began, given impetus by the American writer **Washington Irving**, who set up his study in the empty palace rooms and began to write his marvellously romantic *Tales of the Alhambra* (on sale all over Granada – and good reading amid the gardens and courts). Shortly after its publication, the Spaniards made the Alhambra a **national monument** and set aside funds for its restoration. This continues to the present day and is now a highly sophisticated project, scientifically removing the accretions of later ages in order to expose and meticulously restore the Moorish creations.

Approaches and orientation

The standard **approach** to the Alhambra is along the Cuesta de Gomérez, the semi-pedestrianized road which climbs uphill from Granada's central Plaza Nueva. The only vehicles allowed to use this road in daytime are taxis and the **Alhambrabus** (line #30), a dedicated minibus service (daily 7am–10pm, every 10min; €0.85) linking Plaza Nueva with the Alhambra palace. To get there **by car** you will need to use the route which is signed from the Puerta Real, to the south of the cathedral; this guides you along the Paseo del Salón and the Paseo de la Bomba, eventually bringing you to the Alhambra's car park, close to the new entrance on the eastern edge of the complex.

Should you decide to **walk** up the hill along the Cuesta de Gomérez (a pleasant twenty-minute stroll from the Plaza Nueva), after a few hundred metres you reach the **Puerta de las Granadas**, a massive Renaissance gateway erected by Carlos V. Here two paths diverge to either side of the road: the one on the right climbs up towards a group of fortified towers, the **Torres Bermejas**, which may date from as early as the eighth century. The left-hand path leads through the woods past a huge terrace-fountain (again courtesy of Carlos V) to the main gateway – and former entrance – of the Alhambra. This is the **Puerta de la Justicia**, a magnificent tower which forced three changes of direction, making intruders hopelessly vulnerable. It was built by Yusuf I in 1340 and preserves above its outer arch the Koranic symbol of a key (for Allah the Opener) and an outstretched hand, whose five fingers represent the five Islamic precepts: prayer, fasting, alms-giving, pilgrimage to Mecca and the oneness of God. The **entrance** to the Alhambra – at the eastern end, near to the Generalife gardens – lies a further five-minute walk uphill, reached by following the wall to your left.

Within the citadel stood a complete "government city" of mansions, smaller houses, baths, schools, mosques, barracks and gardens. Of this only the **Alcazaba fortress** and the **Palacios Nazaríes** remain; they face each other across a broad terrace (constructed in the sixteenth century over a dividing gully), flanked by the majestic though incongruous **Palace of Carlos V**.

Within the walls of the citadel, too, are the beautiful *Parador San Francisco* (a converted monastery, where Isabel was originally buried – terrace bar open to non-guests, see p.370), and the *Hotel América* (see p.370). There are a handful of **drinks stalls** around as well, including one, very welcome, in the Portal gardens (towards the Carlos V Palace after you leave the Palacios Nazaríes).

The Alcazaba

The entrance to the Alhambra now brings you into the complex at the eastern end, near to the Generalife gardens. However, as you will have a time slot for entering the Palacios Nazaríes (usually up to an hour ahead), it makes sense chronologically and practically to start your visit with the **Alcazaba** at the Alhambra's opposite, or western, end. To get there from the entrance, walk up the short avenue lined with cypresses to a three-way fork, taking the signed path to the Alhambra. Cross the bridge over the "moat", following signs to the Alcazaba and Palacios Nazaríes, and you will eventually pass the gates of the *Parador de San Francisco* (on your right) and the *Hotel América* to enter the Calle Real. Continue alongside the Palace of Carlos V to pass through the **Puerto del Vino** – named from its use in the sixteenth century as a wine cellar – into the Alcazaba.

The Alcazaba is the earliest and most ruined part of the fortress. At its summit is the **Torre de la Vela**, named after a huge bell on its turret which until recent years was rung to mark the irrigation hours for workers in the *vega*, Granada's vast and fertile plain. It was here, at 3pm on January 2, 1492, that the Cross was first displayed above the city, alongside the royal standards of Aragón and Castile and the banner of St James. Boabdil, leaving Granada for exile in the Alpujarras, turned and wept at the sight, earning from his mother Aisha the famous rebuke: "Do not weep like a woman for what you could not defend like a man." The **Aljibe**, a cistern beneath the area between the Alcazaba and Palacios Nazaríes, is open for viewing on Monday, Wednesday and Friday from 9.30am to 1.30pm.

The Palacios Nazaríes

It is amazing that the **Palacios Nazaríes** has survived, for it stands in utter contrast to the strength of the Alcazaba and the encircling walls and towers. It was built lightly and often crudely from wood, brick and adobe, and was designed not to last but to be renewed and redecorated by succeeding rulers. Its buildings show a brilliant use of light and space but they are principally a vehicle for ornamental stucco decoration. This, as Titus Burckhardt explains in *Moorish Culture in Spain*, was both an intricate science and a philosophy of abstract art in direct contrast to pictorial representation:

With its rhythmic repetition, [it] does not seek to capture the eye to lead it into an imagined world, but, on the contrary, liberates it from all pre-occupations of the mind. It does not transmit any specific ideas, but a state of being, which is at once repose and inner rhythm.

Burckhardt adds that the way in which patterns are woven from a single band, or radiate from many identical centres, served as a pure simile for Islamic belief in the oneness of God, manifested at the centre of every form and being. Arabic inscriptions feature prominently in the ornamentation. Some are poetic eulogies to the buildings and builders, others to various sultans (notably Mohammed V). Most, however, are taken from the Koran, and among them the phrase *Wa-la ghaliba illa-Llah* (There is no Conqueror but God) is tirelessly repeated. This became the battle cry (and family motto) of the Nasrids upon Ibn al-Ahmar's return in 1248 from aiding the Castilian war of Fernando III against Muslim Sevilla; it was his reply to the customary, though bitterly ironic, greetings of *Mansur* (Victor), ridiculing his role as a feudal puppet of the Christian enemy.

Wa-la-ghaliba illa-Llah stylized inscription from the Alhambra

The palace is structured in three parts, each arrayed round an interior court and with a specific function. The sultans used the **Mexuar**, the first series of rooms, for business and judicial purposes. In the **Serallo**, beyond, they received embassies and distinguished guests. The last section, the **Harem**, formed their private living quarters and would have been entered by no one but their family or servants.

The Mexuar

The council chamber, the main **reception hall** of the Mexuar, is the first room you enter. It was completed in 1365 and hailed (perhaps formulaically) by the court poet and vizier Ibn Zamrak as a "haven of counsel, mercy, and favour". Here the sultan heard the pleas and petitions of the people and held meetings with his ministers. At the room's far end is a small oratory, one of a number of prayer niches scattered round the palace and immediately identifiable by their distinctive alignment (to face Mecca). This "public" section of the palace, beyond which few would have penetrated, is completed by the Mudéjar **Cuarto Dorado** (Golden Room), decorated under Carlos V, whose *Plus Ultra* motif appears throughout the palace, and the **Patio del Cuarto Dorado**. This has perhaps the grandest facade of the whole palace, for it admits you to the formal splendour of the Serallo.

The Serallo

The Serallo – the part of the complex where important guests were received – was built largely to the design of Yusuf I, a romantic and enlightened sultan who was stabbed to death by a madman while worshipping in the Alhambra mosque. Its rooms open out from delicate marble-columned arcades at each end of the long **Patio de los Arrayanes** (Patio of the Myrtles).

At the court's north end, occupying two floors of a fortified tower, is the royal throne room, known as the **Salón de Embajadores** (Hall of the Ambassadors). As the sultan could be approached only indirectly, it stands at an angle to the entrance from the Mexuar. It is the largest room of the palace, perfectly square and completely covered in tile and stucco decoration. Among the web of inscriptions is one that states simply "I am the Heart of the Palace." Here Boabdil signed the terms of his city's surrender to the Catholic kings, whose motifs (the arms of Aragón and Castile) were later worked into the room's stunning wooden dome, a superb example of *lacería*, the rigidly geometric "carpentry of knots". Here too, so it is said, Fernando met Columbus to discuss his plans for finding a new sea route to India – which led to the discovery of the Americas. The dome itself, in line with the mystical-mathematical pursuit of medieval Moorish architecture, has a complex symbolism representing the seven heavens. Carlos V tore down the rooms at the southern end of the court; from the arcade there is access to the gloomy **Chapel Crypt** of his palace which has a curious "whispering gallery" effect.

The Harem

The **Patio de los Leones** (Court of the Lions), which has become the archetypal image of Granada, constitutes the heart of the harem section of the palace. The stylized and archaic-looking lions beneath its fountain probably date, like the patio itself, from the reign of Mohammed V, Yusuf's successor; a poem inscribed on the bowl tells how much fiercer they would look if they weren't so restrained by respect for the sultan. The court was designed as an interior garden and planted with shrubs and aromatic herbs; it opens onto three of the palace's finest rooms, each of which looks onto the fountain.

The most sophisticated rooms in this part of the complex, apparently designed to give a sense of the rotary movement of the stars, are the two facing each other across the court. The largest of these, the **Sala de los Abencerrajes**, has the most startlingly beautiful ceiling in the Alhambra: sixteen-sided, supported by niches of stalactite vaulting, lit by windows in the dome and reflected in a fountain on the floor. This light and airy quality stands at odds with its name and history, for here Abu'l-Hasan (Boabdil's father) murdered sixteen princes of the Abencerraje family, whose chief had fallen in love with his favourite, Zoraya; the rust stains in the fountain are popularly supposed to be the indelible traces of their blood.

At the far end is the **Sala de los Reyes** (Hall of the Kings), whose dormitory alcoves preserve a series of unique paintings on leather. These, in defiance of Koranic law, represent human scenes; it's believed that they were painted by a Christian artist in the last decades of Moorish rule. The second of the two facing chambers on the court's north side, the **Sala de las Dos Hermanas** (Hall of the Two Sisters), is more mundanely named – from two huge slabs of marble in its floor – but just as spectacularly decorated, with a dome of over five thousand "honeycomb cells". It was the principal room of the sultan's favourite, opening onto an inner apartment and balcony, the **Mirador de Daraxa** (known in English as the "Eyes of the Sultana"); the romantic garden patio below was added after the Reconquest.

Beyond, you are directed along a circuitous route through **apartments** redecorated by Carlos V (as at Sevilla, the northern-reared emperor installed fireplaces) and later used by Washington Irving. Eventually you emerge at the **Peinador**, or Queen's Tower, a pavilion that served as an oratory for the sultanas and as a dressing room for the wife of Carlos V; perfumes were burned beneath its floor and wafted up through a marble slab in one corner.

From there, passing the **Patio de la Reja** (Patio of the Grille) added in the seventeenth century, you reach the **Baños Reales** (Royal Baths). These are tremendous, decorated in rich tile mosaics and lit by pierced stars and rosettes once covered by coloured glass. The central chamber was used for reclining and retains the balconies where singers and musicians – reputedly blind to keep the royal women from being seen – would entertain the bathers. The visit route exits via the exquisite **Portico del Partal** with the **Torre de las Damas** (Ladies' Tower) and elegant portico overlooking a serene pool. What appears no more than a garden pavilion today is in fact the surviving remnant of the early fourteenth-century Palace of the Partal, a four-winged structure originally surrounding the pool, the Alhambra's largest expanse of water. The **Jardines del Partal** lie beyond this and the nearby turnstile brings you out close to the entrance to the Palace of Carlos V.

Palacio de Carlos V

The grandiose **Palacio de Carlos V** seems totally out of place here, its austere stone-built architecture jarring with the delicate oriental style and materials of the Moorish palace. Begun in 1526 but never finished, it is in fact a distinguished piece of Renaissance design in its own right – the only surviving work of Pedro Machuca, a former pupil of Michelangelo. On its upper floors – reached by steps from a circular central courtyard where bullfights were once held – is a mildly interesting **Museo de Bellas Artes** (Tues 2.30–8pm, Wed–Sat 9am–8pm, Sun 9am–2.30pm; Nov–March Tues–Sat closes 6pm; €1.50, free for EU citizens) with some notable examples of *andaluz* wood sculpture. The lower floor holds the **Museo de la Alhambra** (aka Museo Hispano-Musulman; Tues–Sat 9am–2pm; free), a small but fascinating collection of Hispano-Moorish art, displaying many items discovered during the Alhambra restoration; the star exhibit is a beautiful fifteenth-century metre-and-a-half-high **Alhambra vase** (Jarrón de las Gacelas), made from local red clay enamelled in blue and gold and decorated with leaping gazelles. Note, however, that both museums frequently fail to open on their advertised days and are liable to close early in slack periods.

The Generalife

Paradise is described in the Koran as a shaded, leafy garden refreshed by running water where the "fortunate ones" may take their rest. It is an image which perfectly describes the **Generalife**, the gardens and summer palace of the sultans. Its name means literally "garden of the architect" and the grounds consist of a luxuriantly imaginative series of patios, enclosed gardens and walkways.

By chance, an account of the gardens during Moorish times, written rather poetically by the fourteenth-century court vizier and historian Ibn Zamrak, survives. The descriptions that he gives aren't all entirely believable, but they are a wonderful basis for musing as you lie around by the patios and fountains. There were, he wrote, celebrations with horses darting about in the dusk at speeds that made the spectators rub their eyes (a form of festival still indulged in at Moroccan *fantasías*); rockets shot into the air to be attacked by the stars for their audacity; tightrope walkers flying through the air like birds; and men bowled along in a great wooden hoop, shaped like an astronomical sphere.

Today, devoid of such amusements, the gardens are still evocative – above all, perhaps, the **Patio de los Cipreses** (aka Patio de la Sultana), a dark and secretive walled garden of sculpted junipers where the Sultana Zoraya was suspected of meeting her lover Hamet, chief of the unfortunate Abencerrajes. Nearby, too, is the inspired flight of fantasy of the **Escalera del Agua**, a staircase with water flowing down its stone balustrades. From here you can look down on the wonderful old Arab quarter of the Albaicín (see below).

The Albaicín and Sacromonte

If you're spending just a couple of days in Granada it's hard to resist spending both of them in the Alhambra. You shouldn't miss, however, the run-down medieval streets of the **Albaicín**, Spain's largest and most characteristic surviving Moorish *barrio*, or the cave-quarter of the **Sacromonte** extending up from the Río Darro.

The Albaicín

The Albaicín stretches across a fist-shaped area bordered by the river, the Sacromonte hill, the old town walls and the winding Calle de Elvira (parallel to the Gran Vía de Colón, the main avenue which bisects central Granada). The best approach is along the Carrera del Darro, beside the river. At no. 31 on this street are the remains of the **Baños Árabes** (Tues–Sat 10am–2pm; free), marvellous and little-visited Moorish public baths. Nearby, and just to the east of Plaza Nueva behind the church of Santa Ana, the Baños Arabes Al Andalus, c/Santa Ana 16 (reservation required ☏958 229 978; bath €11), gives you some idea of what a **Moorish bathhouse** would have been like when functioning. Here you can wallow in the graded temperatures of the recreated traditional baths – decorated with mosaics and plaster arabesques – or take tea in the peaceful *tetería* (tea room) upstairs.

Continuing along the Carrera del Darro, at no. 43 is the **Casa de Castril** (Tues 3–8pm, Wed–Sat 9am–8pm, Sun 9am–2pm; €1.50, free to EU citizens), a Renaissance mansion which houses the town's **Archeological Museum**.

Of particular note here are some remarkable finds from the Neolithic Cueva de los Murciélagos (Cave of the Bats) in the Alpujarras; there are also exhibits from Granada's Phoenician, Roman, Visigothic and Moorish periods. Beside the museum a road ascends to the churches of San Juan (with an intact thirteenth-century minaret) and to **San Nicolás**, whose square offers a stunning **view of the Alhambra** considered the best in town.

Sacromonte

Continuing parallel with the river takes you up into the gypsy cave-quarter of Sacromonte. Like many cities in Andalucía, Granada has an ancient and still considerable *gitano* population, from whose clans many of Spain's best flamenco guitarists, dancers and singers have emerged. They have traditionally lived in caves in this area, although these days the *barrio* is better known for its nightlife (see p.383). If you wander up here in the daytime, take a look at the old **caves** on the far side of the old Moorish wall – most of them deserted after severe floods in 1962. There are fantastic views from the top. Sacromonte now has its own museum, the **Centro Interpretación del Sacromonte**, Barranco de los Negros s/n (Tues–Sun 10am–8pm; €3), depicting the life and times of the *barrio*.

The Capilla Real, cathedral and churches

In addition to the city's Moorish legacy it's worth the distinct readjustment and effort of will to appreciate the city's later Christian monuments.

The **Capilla Real** (April–Sept Mon–Sat 10.30am–1pm & 4–7pm, Sun 11am–1pm & 4–7pm; Oct–March daily 10.30am–1pm & 3.30–6.30pm; €2.50), in the centre of town at the southern end of Gran Vía de Colón, is an impressive building, flamboyant late-Gothic in style and built ad hoc in the first decades of Christian rule as a mausoleum for Los Reyes Católicos, the city's "liberators". The actual **tombs** are as simple as could be imagined: Fernando (marked with an "F") and Isabel, flanked by their daughter Joana ("the Mad") and her husband Felipe ("the Handsome"), resting in lead coffins placed in a plain crypt. But above them – the response of their grandson Carlos V to what he found "too small a room for so great a glory" – is a fabulously elaborate **monument** carved in Carrara marble by Florentine Domenico Fancelli in 1517, with sculpted Renaissance effigies of the two monarchs; the tomb of Joana and Felipe alongside is a much inferior work by Ordoñez. In front of the monument is an equally magnificent **reja**, the work of Maestro Bartolomé of Baeza, and a splendid **retablo** behind depicts Boabdil surrendering the keys of Granada.

Isabel, in accordance with her will, was originally buried on the Alhambra hill (in the church of San Francisco, now part of the *parador*), but her wealth and power proved no safeguard of her wishes. The queen's final indignity occurred during the 1980s when the candle that she asked should perpetually illuminate her tomb was replaced by an electric bulb – it was restored in 1999 following numerous protests. In the Capilla's **Sacristy** is displayed the sword of Fernando, the crown of Isabel and her outstanding personal collection of **medieval Flemish paintings** – including important works by Memling, Bouts and van der Weyden – and various Italian paintings, including panels by Botticelli and Pedro Berruguete.

For all its stark Renaissance bulk, Granada's **Catedral**, adjoining the Capilla Real and entered from the door beside it (April–Sept Mon–Sat 10.45am–1.30pm & 4–8pm, Sun 4–8pm; Oct–March Mon–Sat 10.45am–1.30pm & 4–7pm, Sun 4–7pm; €2.50), is a disappointment. It was begun in 1521, just as the chapel was finished, but was then left incomplete well into the eighteenth century. At least it's light and airy inside, though, and it's fun to go round putting coins in the slots to light up the chapels, where an El Greco *St Francis* and sculptures by Pedro de Mena and Montañes will be revealed.

Other churches have more to offer, and with sufficient interest you could easily fill a day of visits. Northwest of the cathedral, ten minutes' walk along c/San Jerónimo, the Baroque **San Juan de Dios**, with a spectacular *retablo*, is attached to a majestically portalled hospital (still in use; porter will allow a brief look). Close by is the elegant Renaissance **Convento de San Jerónimo** (April–Sept Mon–Sat 10am–1.30pm & 4–7.30pm, Sun 11am–1.30pm & 4–7.30pm; Oct–March daily 10am–1.30pm & 3–6.30pm; €2.10), founded by the Catholic kings, though built after their death, with two imposing patios and a wonderful frescoed church.

Lastly, on the northern outskirts of town, is **La Cartuja** (April–Sept Mon–Sat 10am–1pm & 4–8pm, Sun 10am–12pm & 4–8pm; Oct–March Mon–Sat 10am–1pm & 3.30–6pm, Sun 3.30–6pm; €2.50), perhaps the grandest and most outrageously decorated of all the country's lavish Carthusian monasteries. It was constructed at the height of Baroque extravagance – some say to rival the Alhambra – and has a chapel of staggering wealth, surmounted by an altar of twisted and coloured marble. It's a further ten- to fifteen-minute walk beyond San Juan de Dios (or take bus #8 or #C from the centre going north along Gran Vía).

Fuente Vaqueros Lorca museum

To the west of the city, in the pleasant *vega* village of Fuente Vaqueros, the birthplace of Federico García Lorca, Andalucía's greatest poet and dramatist, has been transformed into a **museum** (Tues–Sun: April–Sept 10am–1pm & 5–7pm; July–Aug closed afternoons; guided visits on the hour; ring to confirm winter timetable ☎958 516 453; €1.20; ⓦwww.museogarcialorca.org), and contains a highly evocative collection of Lorca memorabilia. Buses operated by Ureña (hourly from 8am; 20min) leave from Granada's Avenida de Andaluces, fronting the train station. Economical rooms are available in the village at *Hostal-Restaurante Moli-Lorc*, c/Ancha Escuelas 11 (☎958 516 348; ❶), next to the church, which incidentally holds the font where Lorca was baptized.

Eating

When it comes to **restaurants** Granada certainly isn't one of the gastronomic centres of Spain, possibly due in part to the *granadino* **tapas bars** which tempt away potential diners by giving out some of the most generous tapas in

Andalucía – one comes free with every drink. We have recommended a few of the best of these below, and the municipal tourist office gives out a handy tapas bar leaflet to help you locate more (see p.369). A flavour of North Africa is to be found along c/Calderería Nueva and its surrounds in "Little Morocco", where you'll find health-food stores as well as numerous Moroccan tearooms and eating places. This street is useful for assembling **picnics** for Alhambra visits, as is the revamped ultramodern Mercado Municipal in Plaza San Agustín just north of the cathedral (Mon–Sat early until 1.30pm). The warren of streets between **Plaza Nueva** and **Gran Vía** has plenty of good-value places, particularly tapas bars, as does the area around **Plaza del Carmen** (near the *ayuntamiento*) and along c/Navas leading away from it. Another good location is the **Campo del Príncipe**, a pleasant square below the south side of the Alhambra hill, with a line of open-air restaurant terraces, highly popular on summer nights.

City centre and Albaicín

Bar-Restaurante Sevilla c/Oficios 12, opposite the entrance to the Capilla Real ☎958 221 223. One of the few surviving pre-war restaurants, and a haunt of Lorca, this is a pleasant restaurant with a good-value *menú* and an outdoor terrace – beneath the walls of the Capilla Real – in the evenings. Closed Mon.

Café au Lait Callejón de los Franceses 31, near the cathedral. New and laid-back French-style café-bar with pleasant palm-shaded terrace; serves a good-value breakfast (€1.50 complete with domestic or foreign newspapers) and later does tapas and *menús del día* from €6–12.

Cafetería-Restaurante La Riviera c/Cettimeriem 5. Popular café with a good *menú económico*, including a vegetarian option.

Casa Cepillo c/Pescadería 8, off c/Príncipe behind the Alcaicería. Cheap *comedor* that's very popular with locals for its great-value *menús* – fish and squid are the specialities.

Horno de Santiago Plaza de Los Campos 8 ☎958 223 476. Probably the city's best restaurant, offering classic *granadino* meat, fish and game dishes in a pleasant setting. There's a *menú de degustación* for €21. Closed Aug & Sun eve.

El Huerto de Juan Ranas c/Atarazana Vieja 6, near the Mirador de San Nicolás ☎958 286 925. Mid-priced restaurant with a stunning view of the Alhambra from its garden terrace. Wide range of meat and fish dishes, and some interesting desserts such as *cielo lindo* (*tocino de cielo* variation) and *pastel de chocolate*. You can enjoy the same view for the price of a drink from their terrace bar.

Mesón La Alegría c/Moras 4, east of Puerta Real. This economical *mesón* is a favourite of *granadinos* working nearby and specializes in *carnes asados* (roasted meats).

Mesón Yunque Plaza San Miguel Bajo in the Albaicín. Owned by flamenco singer, Antonio, this mid-priced place has a great atmosphere, with tasty meat and fish dishes served at indoor and outdoor tables on this delightful square.

Naturi Albaicín c/Calderería Nueva 10. Imaginative vegetarian cooking at reasonable prices, serving up fine salads, stuffed mushrooms, and the like.

Restaurante León c/Pan 3. Long-established *cordobés* restaurant serving many *carne de monte* (game) dishes with a good-value *menú del día*, for €6.

Restaurante-Marisquería Cunini c/Pescadería 9 ☎958 267 587. One of Granada's established upmarket restaurants, serving mainly fish, with an outstanding (and cheaper) tapas bar attached. There's a *menú* for around €15.

Around town

Bar-Restaurante Orotava Junction of c/Pedro Antonio de Alarcón and c/Sol. This no-frills diner serves up what has to be Granada's cheapest *menú del día* at €3.75 for three courses including bread and wine.

La Botana Santa Escolástica s/n, near the Casa de los Tiros. Stylish restaurant and bar with raucous musical background and an eclectic cuisine, including some vegetarian options.

La Mimbre Paseo del Generalife s/n, near the Alhambra's entrance. With a delightful terrace shaded by willows (*mimbres*), this is one of the best restaurants on the Alhambra hill. The food is good but they are sometimes overwhelmed in high season. There's a *menú* for €17.50 which you may need to ask for.

La Ninfa Campo del Príncipe. Popular Italian restaurant that puts out tables on this pleasant plaza, and is often full to bursting at weekends. The *ensalada primavera* is a must for your first course and the desserts are diet-bustingly delicious. When full, the *Lago de Como* (on the opposite side of the square) is a reasonable alternative.

Café-bar Ochando Avda. de los Andaluces. Situated right by the train station and open 24 hours, this café is handy for late or early travellers, and serves a good breakfast.

Rincón de Lola Plazita Rosales near the Hospital Real. Good little economical vegetarian restaurant with well-prepared dishes and tasty home-made desserts.

Bars and nightlife

Enjoyable central **bars** include *Bodegas Castañeda* on the corner of c/Elvira and c/Almireceros, near the top of the Gran Vía, a traditional, though modernized, *bodega*, the lively *Bodegas La Mancha*, c/Joaquín Costa 10 around the corner, and the earthy *Bar Sabanilla*, c/San Sebastián 14, up an alley off the southeast corner of Plaza Bib Rambla, which claims to be the oldest bar in Granada, and serves a free tapa with every drink. The bar of the *Hotel Reina Cristina*, c/Tablas 4 off the Plaza de la Trinidad – the building in which Lorca spent his last days before being seized by the fascists – is also an excellent place for a tapa and a glass of *fino*. All these stay open until around midnight.

If you want to go on **drinking through the early hours,** head out to the student areas round the university. Calle San Juan de Dios (and its continuations c/Gran Capitán and Plaza Gran Capitán), Carril del Picón and particularly c/Pedro Antonio de Alarcón – the stretch between Plaza Albert Einstein and c/Obispo Hurtado is the main focus – are all extremely lively. The streets to the east of c/Pedro Antonio – c/Casillas de Prats, c/Trajano and Plaza Menorca – have most of the **pubs** and **disco-bars**; current vogue places include *Biblioteca, Gente Guapa, Morgan, Pub M, Babel* and *Chueka* (a popular **gay bar** in nearby c/Goya), though new places open almost weekly in summer. Other places to try are *Granada 10,* near the cathedral at c/Carcel Baja 10, a beautifully restored retro cinema that reopens as a disco when the films finish; *Dar Ziryab,* nearby at c/Calderería Nueva 11, an Arabic cultural centre that often stages live traditional music; and, just south of Plaza de la Trinidad, *Salsero Mayor,* c/La Paz 20, which specializes in salsa, *merengue* and Latin jazz. The Campo del Príncipe, a square on the eastern slopes of the Alhambra, is another popular drinking haunt, as are the areas around Plaza Nueva, where on weekend evenings throngs of drinkers jam the narrow streets solid. Also worth seeking out are *La Sal,* c/Marqués de Falces, *Pie de la Vela,* a gay and lesbian (but not exclusively so) bar, just off Plaza Nueva on Paseo de los Tristes, and *Rincon de San Pedro,* Carrera del Darro, a mixed-music gay bar. Another place worth a try a stone's throw from the cathedral is *Echevaria,* c/Postigo de la Cuna 2, a tiny alley off c/Azacayas which is off the east side of Gran Vía, a lively bar where jazz and flamenco are the favourite sounds.

When it comes to **flamenco**, finding anything near the real thing in Granada is not as easy as you might think. One place to try in the Albaicín is *El Niño de los Almendras,* a signless place in c/Muladar de Doña Sancha at the junction with c/La Tiña and southeast of Plaza San Miguel Bajo. This tiny bar – done up inside to resemble a cave – is owned by the flamenco singer of the same name. It's only open Friday nights (starts around midnight) but *inolvidable* flamenco often happens here. In nearby Sacromonte (see opposite), *Los Faroles,* almost at the very end of the line of "caves" – ask anyone for directions as it's well known – is another good place owned by the genial Quiqui, another flamenco singer. If the mood is favourable, impromptu flamenco often happens here after dark, but not always. This place is also good for a lunchtime or evening drink with a view of the Alhambra from its terrace.

Sacromonte

Sacromonte is traditionally the home of Granada's gypsy population and, therefore, also the city's flamenco performers. These days, however, although there are occasionally good shows to be had, more often they're straight-faced and fabulously shameless rip-offs: you're hauled into a cave, leered at if you're female, and systematically extorted of all the money you've brought along (for the dance, the music, the castanets, the watered-down sherry...). The simple solution is to take only as much money as you want to part with. Turn up mid-evening; the lines of caves begin off the Camino de Sacromonte, just above the Casa del Chapiz. When the university is in session, several of the cave dwellings are turned into **discos**, packed with students at weekends.

Listings

Airport Granada airport (⊕958 245 223) handles domestic flights to Madrid and Barcelona; details from Iberia (⊕958 229 971).

Books, newspapers and maps Metro, c/Gracia 31, off c/Alhóndiga, to the southwest of Plaza de la Trinidad, is the best international bookshop with a wide selection of books on Granada, Lorca etc, plus walking maps. For maps, try also the Librería Dauro at c/Zacatín 3 (a pedestrian street between the cathedral and c/Reyes Católicos), or for a more specialist selection Cartografica del Sur, c/Valle Inclán 2, southwest of the train station. Foreign press is sold by the *kioscos* in Plaza Nueva and Puerta Real.

Bullfights are held in season at the Plaza de Toros, Avda. del Doctor Olóriz 25. The bullring's ticket office (⊕958 272 451) or any of the tourist offices has details of upcoming *corridas*.

Car rental Autos Fortuna, c/Infanta Beatriz 2 ⊕958 260 254, are a reliable local outfit who undercut the big boys. Atesa, Avda. Andaluces near the train station (⊕958 28 87 55, ⦿www.atesa.es), has reasonable deals with national back-up.

Football C.F. Granada play in Spain's lower leagues, and are currently trying to regain Segunda División "B" status; tickets are easy to come by in season. The stadium, Nuevo los Cármenes ⊕958 25 33 00, ⦿www.granadacf.com, lies northwest of the Hospital Real.

Hospital Cruz Roja (Red Cross), c/Escoriaza 8 ⊕958 222 222, or Hospital Clinico San Cecilio, Avda. Dr Olóriz, near the Plaza de Toros ⊕958 270 200. For advice on emergency treatment phone ⊕061.

Internet access The most central Internet location with plenty of screens is *Navegaweb*, c/Reyes Catolicos 55, slightly north of Plaza Isabel la Catolica (⊕958 210 528; €1.50 per hr). *Net*, Plaza de los Girones 3, near the Casa de Los Tiros (Mon–Fri 9am–midnight, Sat–Sun 10.30am–midnight; min €0.40 for 15min; ⊕958 226 919), is another efficient online operation. They have another branch at c/Buen Suceso 22 ⊕958 226

919 (same hours) just off Plaza de la Trinidad. Slightly west of Plaza Nueva *Madar Internet*, c/Calderería Nueva 12 (Mon–Fri 10am–midnight, Sat–Sun noon–midnight; €1 per hr, €0.40 for 15min; ⊕958 22 94 29), is another reliable place.

Laundry Lavandería Duquesa, c/Duquesa 24 near the church of San Jerónimo (Mon–Fri 9.30am–2pm & 4.30–9pm, Sat 9.30–2pm; ⊕958 28 06 85) is very efficient and will wash, fold and dry 4kg the same day for €8.50. Lavandería La Paz, c/La Paz 19 just west of Plaza de la Trinidad, has similar hours and prices.

Police For emergencies dial ⊕091 (national) or ⊕092 (local). The Policía Nacional are located at c/Duquesa 15 off Plaza Trinidad ⊕958 278 300. The Policía Local station is in the *ayuntamiento* building on Plaza del Carmen ⊕958 209 461. There is also a property lost-and-found section in the same building (⊕958 248 103).

Post office Puerta Real; Mon–Fri 9am–8pm, Sat 9am–2pm.

Shopping Artesanía El Suspiro, Plaza Santa Ana 1 at the northeast end of Plaza Nueva, has a selection of ceramics from surrounding *granadino* villages, as well as Moroccan pottery and jewellery. Castellano, c/Almireceros 6, between c/Elvira and Gran Vía, is the best place to buy *jamón serrano* and also stocks regional wines and brandies. La Alcena, c/San Jerónimo 3, on the cathedral's north side, is a great place to find the special products of Andalucía, including olive oil, wines, cheeses, *embutidos* and lots more; the friendly proprietor speaks good English. Handmade (on the premises) guitars can be tried out and purchased at a number of shops along the Cuesta de Gomérez, leading to the Alhambra; Casa Morales at no. 9 is reputed. Granada's branch of the El Corte Inglés department store is on the Acera del Darro, to the south of Puerta Real.

Swimming pool Piscina Miami ⊕958 250 031, junction c/Arabial and c/Virgen Blanca (west of the centre), has an Olympic-size pool, kids' pool, sunbeds and a good restaurant.

The Sierra Nevada National Park

The mountains of the **Sierra Nevada**, designated Andalucía's second **national park** in 1999, rise to the south of Granada, a startling backdrop to the city, snow-capped for much of the year and offering good trekking and also skiing from late November until late May. The ski slopes are at **Solynieve** ("Sun and Snow", aka Pradollano), an unimaginative, developed resort just 28km away from the city centre. From here, you can make the two- to three-hour trek up to **Veleta** (3470m), the second highest peak of the range (and of the Iberian peninsula); this is a perfectly feasible day-trip from Granada by bus. For more serious enthusiasts, the renowned trek across the sierra is the **Ruta de los Tres Mil**.

The best **map** of the Sierra Nevada including the lower slopes of the Alpujarras (see p.386) is the one co-produced by the Instituto Geográfico Nacional and the Federación Española de Montañismo (1:50,000), which is generally available in Granada. A 1:40,000 **map and guide set**, *Sierra Nevada and La Alpujarra*, published in English by Editorial Alpina (see "Books", p.1113), is also good. The turismo in Granada can advise on **snow conditions** in the mountains, as can the Sierra Nevada Club (☎958 249 119), or visit ⓦwww.sierranevadaski.com.

Flora and fauna

The Sierra Nevada is particularly rich in **wild flowers**, with fifty varieties unique to these mountains. **Wildlife** abounds away from the roads; one of the most exciting sights is the *Cabra hispanica*, a wild horned goat which (with luck) you'll see standing on pinnacles, silhouetted against the sky. Birdwatching is also superb, with the colourful hoopoe – a bird with a stark, haunting cry – a common sight.

The Veleta ascent

The Sierra Nevada is easily accessible from Granada. Throughout the year, Autocares Bonal (☎958 465 022) runs a single daily bus to the Solynieve resort, southeast of the city and, just above this, to the *Parador de Sierra Nevada* (see p.385). The bus leaves from Granada bus station at 9am, returning from the *parador* at 4.30pm (and passing Solynieve 10 minutes later). Tickets to Solynieve (€5.70 round trip) should be bought in advance at the bus station, although you can pay on board if the bus is not full. If there are passengers, the bus will continue the short distance beyond the *parador* to the *Albergue Universitario* (see p.385). For the winter service (Oct–March) ring the bus company or check with the turismo.

With your own transport, take the Acera del Darro east from the Puerta Real and follow the signs for the Sierra Nevada. At the 22km mark, signposted just off the road, is the **"El Dornajo" Sierra Nevada National Park Visitors' Centre** (daily 10.30am–2.30pm & 4.30–7pm; ☎958 340 625, ⓔalhori@imfe), which sells guidebooks, maps and hats (sun protection is vital at this altitude), and has a permanent exhibition on the park's flora and fauna. They can provide hiking information (English spoken) and rent out horses and mountain bikes. The centre also has a pleasant **cafetería** with a stunning terrace **view**.

Ten kilometres beyond El Dornajo you pass the Solynieve ski resort (see opposite), and 2km further on lies the *Parador Sierra Nevada* where the bus terminates. From the *parador*, the Capileira road (closed to vehicles) continues to climb and actually runs past the **peak of Veleta**; now asphalted, it is perfectly

– and tediously – walkable. With your own transport it's possible to shave a couple of kilometres off the walk to the summit by ignoring the no-entry signs at the car park near to the *Albergue Universitario* and continuing on to a second car park further up the mountain from which point the road is then barred. Although the peak of the mountain looks deceptively close from here, you should allow two to three hours up to the summit and two hours down. There is no water en route so you'd be advised to take some along; the summit makes a great place for a picnic. Weather permitting, the **views** beyond the depressing trappings of the ski resort are fabulous: the Sierra Subbética of Córdoba and the Sierra de Guadix to the north, the Mediterranean and Rif Mountains of Morocco to the south, and nearby to the southeast, the towering mass of **Mulhacén** (3479m), the Spanish mainland's highest peak.

With a great deal of energy you could conceivably walk the mountain route all the way to Capileira, though it's a good 30km, there's nothing along the way and temperatures drop pretty low by late afternoon. An hour beyond Veleta you pass just under Mulhacén, two hours of exposed and windy ridge-crawling from the road.

Solynieve

SOLYNIEVE (aka Pradollano), which lies outside the boundaries of the national park, is a hideous-looking ski resort regarded by serious Alpine skiers as something of a joke, but with snow lingering so late in the year, it does have obvious attractions. For budget **accommodation** try the modern and comfortable *Albergue Juvenil*, c/Peñones 22 (☎958 480 305, ⒺReservas@inturjoven.junta-andalucia.es; ❶; open all year), on the edge of the ski resort, where you can get great-value double (❶) and four-bed rooms, all en suite. They also rent out skis and equipment in season. Other places here are pricey in season (and often closed outside it), with even the cheapest doubles priced at around €60. Should you wish to stay in summer, the Granada tourist offices have accommodation lists.

Three kilometres away in isolated Peñones de San Francisco are a couple more options: the *Albergue Universitario* (☎958 481 003, Ⓕ958 480 122; ❷, half board; open all year), with bunk rooms, doubles and a restaurant, and the bleakly modern *Parador Sierra Nevada* (☎958 480 661, Ⓕ958 480 212; ❸), no longer part of the state *parador* chain, and open only in the ski season. The only **campsite** in this area is at the Ruta del Purche (☎958 340 407; open all year), 15km out of Granada and halfway to Solynieve, with a supermarket and restaurant. The bus will drop you at the road leading to the site, from where it's a good kilometre walk.

Ruta Integral de los Tres Mil (High Peaks Traverse)

The classic **Ruta Integral de los Tres Mil**, a complete traverse of all the sierra's peaks over 3000m high, starts in Jerez del Marquesado on the north side of the Sierra Nevada (due south of Guadix) and finishes in Lanjarón, in the Alpujarras; an exhausting three- to four-day itinerary. Taking four days entails overnight stays near Puntal de Vacares, in the Siete Lagunas valley, at the *Refugio de la Caldera*, and at the Cerro Caballo hut. Slightly shorter, and more practicable, variations involve a start from the Vadillo refuge in the Estrella valley (northwest of Vacares), or from Trevélez in the Alpujarras, and a first overnight at Siete Lagunas.

Whichever way you choose, be aware that the section between Veleta and Elorrieta calls for rope, an ice axe (and crampons before June) and good scrambling skills. There is another difficult section between Peñón Colorado and Cerro de Caballo. If you're not up to this, it is possible to **detour** round the Veleta–Elorrieta section, but you will end up on the ridge flanking the Lanjarón river valley on the east rather than on the west; here there is a single cement hut (the *Refugio Forestal*), well placed for the final day's walk to Lanjarón.

For any major **exploration of the Sierra Nevada**, it is essential to take a tent, proper gear and ample food. It's a serious mountain and you should be prepared for the eventuality of not being able to reach or find the huts (which are marked correctly on the 1:50,000 map) or the weather turning nasty. Inside the park, to report any **emergencies** such as forest fires, stranded hikers or personal injuries there is a coordinated emergency service contactable on ☎112; the park's Guardia Civil unit can be reached on ☎062. **Weather forecasts** (in English) are available on ☎906 365 365.

An easier alternative

The full *Ruta* is probably more than most people would want to attempt. A modified version, starting in **Trevélez** (see p.394) and ending in **Lanjarón** (see p.389; with the detour noted above), is more realistic, though still strenuous.

Ascending Mulhacén from Trevélez is a full six hours up, four hours down – assuming that you do not get lost or rest (both unlikely) and that there is no snowpack on Mulhacén's east face (equally unlikely until July). If you decide to try, be prepared for an overnight stop. Heading out of Trevélez, make sure that you begin on the higher track over the Crestón de Posteros, to link up with *acequias* (irrigation channels) coming down from the top of the Río Culo Perro (Dog's Arse River) valley; if you take the main, tempting trail which goes toward Jerez del Marquesado, and then turn into the mouth of the Río Culo Perro, you face unbelievable quagmires and thorn patches. The standard place to **camp** is in the Siete Lagunas valley below the peak, allowing an early-morning ascent to the summit before the mists come up.

Continuing the traverse, you can drop down the west side of Mulhacén (take care on this awkward descent) to the dirt road coming from Veleta. Follow this toward Veleta, and you can spend a second night at the very basic *Refugio Pillavientos*. Moving on, to the west, plan on a third night spent at either the *Refugio Elorrieta*, Cerro de Caballo or the *Refugio Forestal*, depending on your capabilities.

Las Alpujarras

Beyond the mountains, further south from Granada, lie the great **valleys of the Alpujarras**, first settled in the twelfth century by Berber refugees from Sevilla, and later the Moors' last stronghold in Spain.

The valleys are bounded to the north by the Sierra Nevada, and to the south by the lesser sierras of Lujar, La Contraviesa and Gador. The eternal snows of the high sierras keep the valleys and their seventy or so villages well watered all summer long. Rivers have cut deep gorges in the soft mica and shale of the upper mountains, and over the centuries have deposited silt and fertile soil on the lower hills and in the valleys; here the villages have grown, for the soil is rich and easily worked. The intricate terracing that today preserves these deposits was begun as long as 2000 years ago by Visigoths or Ibero-Celts, whose remains have been found at Capileira.

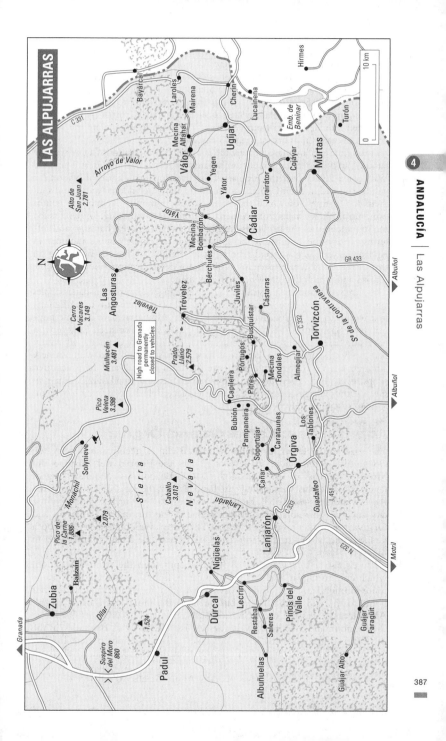

LAS ALPUJARRAS

High road to Granada permanently closed to vehicles

The **Moors** carried on the tradition, and modified the terracing and irrigation in their inimitable way. They transformed the Alpujarras into an earthly paradise, and here they retired to bewail the loss of their beloved lands in *al-Andalus*, resisting a series of royal edicts demanding their forced conversion to Christianity. In 1568 they rose up in a final, short-lived revolt, which led to the expulsion of all Spanish Moors. Even then, however, two Moorish families were required to stay in each village to show the new Christian peasants, who had been marched down from Galicia and Asturias to repopulate the valleys, how to operate the intricate irrigation systems.

Through the following centuries, the land fell into the hands of a few wealthy families, and the general population became impoverished labourers. The Civil War passed lightly over the Alpujarras: the occasional truckload of Nationalist youth trundled in from Granada, rounded up a few bewildered locals, and shot them for "crimes" of which they were wholly ignorant; Republican youths came up in their trucks from Almería and did the same thing. Under Franco the stranglehold of the landlords increased and there was real hardship and suffering. Today, the population has one of the lowest per capita incomes in Andalucía, with – as a recent report put it – "a level of literacy bordering on that of the Third World, alarming problems of desertification, poor communications and a high degree of underemployment".

Ironically, the land itself is still very fertile – oranges, chestnuts, bananas, apples and avocados grow here – while the recent influx of **tourism** is bringing limited wealth to the region. The so-called "High" Alpujarras have become popular with Spanish tourists and also with migrants from northern Europe who have purchased property here; Pampaneira, Bubión and Capileira, all within half an hour's drive from Lanjarón, have been scrubbed and whitewashed. Though a little over-prettified, they're far from spoiled, and have acquired shops, lively bars, good unpretentious restaurants and small, family-run *pensiones*. Other villages, less picturesque, or less accessible, have little employment, and are sustained only by farming.

Approaches: Lanjarón and Órgiva

The road **south from Granada to Motril** climbs steeply after leaving the city, until at 860m above sea level it reaches the **Puerto del Suspiro del Moro** – the Pass of the Sigh of the Moor. Boabdil, last Moorish king of Granada, came this way, having just handed over the keys of his city to the Reyes Católicos (see p.368). From the pass you catch your last glimpse of the city and the Alhambra. Just beyond Béznar is the turning to **Lanjarón** and **Órgiva**, the market town of the region. There are several buses a day from both Granada and Motril to Lanjarón and Órgiva, and one a day from Almería in the east.

There's also a **bus** (currently 8.30am & 6pm from the main bus station) which goes to Ugíjar, in the "Low" Alpujarras, from Granada, via a less scenic route through Lanjarón, Órgiva, Torvizcón, Cadiar, Yegen and Valor; about four hours to the end of the line. A bus direct to the more spectacular **"High" Alpujarras** leaves the main Granada bus station at 10.30am (terminating at Pitres), noon and 5.15pm daily. It goes via Trevélez as far as Bérchules; in the other direction it currently leaves Bérchules at 5am and 5pm, passing Trevélez half an hour later, arriving in Granada at 8.45am and 8.45pm respectively (with a service from Pitres to Granada at 3.30pm). Further information on these services is available from the bus operator Alsina Graells (⊕958 185 480).

Lanjarón

LANJARÓN has been subject to tourism and the influence of the outside world for longer than anywhere else in the Alpujarras, due to the curative powers of its **spa waters**, sold in bottled form throughout Spain. Between March and December the spa baths are open, and the town fills with the aged and infirm. The place itself is little more than a ribbon of buildings, mostly modern, flanking the road through the village, the Avenida Alpujarra, and its continuation, the Avenida Andalucía. Below, marking Lanjarón's medieval status as the gateway to the Alpujarras, is a Moorish castle, now dilapidated and barely visible. A ten-minute stroll reveals its dramatic setting – follow the signs down the hill from the main street and out onto the terraces and meadows below the town.

The countryside and mountains within a day's walk of Lanjarón, however, are beyond compare. Walk up through the backstreets behind the town and you'll come across a track that takes you steeply up to the vast spaces of the **Reserva Nacional de la Sierra Nevada**. For a somewhat easier day's walk out of Lanjarón, go to the bridge over the river just east of town and take the sharply climbing, cobbled track which parallels the **river**. After two to two-and-a-half hours through small farms, with magnificent views and scenery, a downturn to a small stone bridge permits return to Lanjarón on the opposite bank. Allow a minimum of six hours.

Practicalities

Should you wish to try a cure at the **Balneario** on Avenida Alpujarra (☎958 770 137, ⓦwww.aguasdelanjaron.es; open March–Dec), a basic soak will cost about €11, with add-ons for massage, mud baths and all kinds of other alarming-sounding *tracciónes* and *inyecciónes*. Opposite is Lanjarón's semi-official **information kiosk** (9.30am–1.30pm & 5.30–8.30pm; ☎958 770 282), and midway along the same street is the Alsina Graells **bus terminal**. **Internet** access is available at *Cyberplay Lanjaron*, Avda. de Andalucía 30, at the eastern end of the main street to the side of the La Caixa bank (daily except Wed 6pm–midnight).

Largely to cater for the Balneario's clients, there's no shortage of **hotels** and **pensiones** in the town. The grand-looking *Hotel España*, Avda. Alpujarra 42 (☎ & ⓕ958 770 187, ⓔihgalisa@hotmail.com; ❸), next door to the *balneario*, is very friendly and has a pool. Further along the road, a signed turnoff leads downhill to the equally good *Apartamentos Castillo Alcadima*, c/General Rodrigo 3 (☎ & ⓕ958 770 809, ⓦwww.castillo-alcadima.es; ❷), which offer excellent studio apartments with kitchenette and stunning balcony views over the castle below the town, as well as a pool and pleasant terrace restaurant. The proprietor also hires out mountain bikes and offers horse-riding treks and rock-climbing courses. Towards the east end of town and before the church, *Bar Galvez*, c/Real 95 (☎958 770 087; ❶), offers the cheapest rooms in town and does excellent-value meals, while 1km further east – on the road out – the refurbished and revitalized *Venta El Buñuelo* (☎958 770 461; ❶) has economical en-suite rooms with great views, a decent terrace restaurant below and easy parking.

Lanjarón has plenty of **restaurants** and tapas bars too, many attached to the hotels which often offer a good-value *menú*. Apart from these, the *Manolete*, c/San Sebastián 3, is much esteemed by the locals for its tapas, while the more expensive *El Club*, at Avda. de Andalucía 18, specializes in Alpujarran dishes and is reckoned to serve the best food in town. For seafood (also offering some meat and vegetarian dishes and a *menú* for €9) try *Los Mariscos*, Avda. de La

Alpujarra 6, in a small square off the east end of the main street. Not far from here, *Jamones Gustavo Rubio*, Avda. de Andalucía 38, is worth a visit for its excellent tapas bar behind a shop selling the wines, *jamones* and other products of the Alpujarras. Lanjarón even sports a **nightclub**, *Noche Azul*, on the corner of the main square, while a disco-bar, *El Barco*, has opened down a flight of steps opposite.

Órgiva

Eleven kilometres east of Lanjarón is **ÓRGIVA** (also spelled Órjiva), the "capital" of the western Alpujarras. It is closer to the heart of the valley but is still really a starting point; if the bus goes on to Capileira, you may want to stay on it. If you're **driving** it's worth noting that petrol stations become scarcer from this point on.

Órgiva is a lively enough town, though, with a local produce market on Thursdays, and a number of good bars and hotels. On the main street is a sixteenth-century Moorish palace which today houses various shops. A yoga centre, Cortijo Romero, just 1km east of town, is a sign of the times hereabouts; Órgiva, and surrounding farms and villages, are attracting a growing band of expatriate "New Age" Europeans. The **mercado** building in town has wholefood stalls and the occasional juggler, and there's a **tepee village**, "El Beneficio", on the edge of town, where assorted Europeans and their offspring endure freezing winters under canvas.

Practicalities

For budget **accommodation**, one of the nicest places is the pretty *Alma Alpujarreña* (☎958 784 085; ❶), a little beyond the traffic lights at the town's main (and solitary) intersection, with a leafy terrace restaurant. Good rooms with bath are also on offer at *Hostal Mirasol*, Avda. González Robles 3, on the way in from Lanjarón (☎958 785 159; ❶); they also have a more upmarket hotel (❷) next door. Close to here, *Casa Rural El Molino*, Avda. González Robles 12 (☎958 785 745; ❸), has attractive rooms in a refurbished olive-oil mill. Órgiva's **campsite** (☎958 784 307; open all year), with a pool, bar and restaurant, lies 2km south of town, reached by continuing along the road where the bus drops you. It also rents out cabins (❷), bungalows (❸), has its own restaurant and pool and can advise on **walking routes** and renting horses in the nearby Sierra de Lújar.

For **food**, both the *Alma Alpujarreña* and the *Hostal Mirasol* do good tapas and reasonable *menús*. The best tapas, though, are at *Paradise* near the church and *Bar*

Houses in the Alpujarras

Houses in the valleys are built of grey stone, flat-roofed and low; whitewashing them is a recent innovation. The coarse walls are about 75cm thick, for summer coolness and protection from winter storms. Stout beams of chestnut, or ash in the lower valleys, are laid from wall to wall; on top of these is a mat of canes or split chestnut; upon this flat stones are piled, and on the stones is spread a layer of *launa*, the crumbly grey mica found on the tops of the Sierra Nevada. It must – and this maxim is still observed today – be laid during the waning of the moon for the *launa* to settle properly and thus keep rain out. Gerald Brenan wrote in *South from Granada* of a particularly ferocious storm: "As I peered through the darkness of the stormy night, I could make out a dark figure on every roof in the village, dimly lit by an esparto torch, stamping clay into the holes in the roof."

Trekking in the Alpujarras

Half a century ago the Camino Real (Royal Way), a mule track that threaded through all the high villages, was the only access to the Alpujarras. Today the little that's left is quiet, used only by the occasional local mule or foreign walker. At their best, Alpujarran paths follow mountain streams, penetrate thick woods of oak, chestnut and poplar, or cross flower-spangled meadows; in their bad moments they deteriorate to incredibly dusty firebreaks, forestry roads or tractor tracks, or (worse) deadends in impenetrable thickets of bramble and nettle. Progress is slow, grades are sharp and the heat (from mid-June to Sept) is taxing. A reasonable knowledge of Spanish is a big help.

For the determined, the most rewarding sections of treks include:

Pitres to Mecina Fondales: Twenty minutes' trek, and then a good hour-plus from neighbouring Ferreirola to Busquistar.

Busquistar towards Trevélez: One hour's trek, and then two-plus hours of road walking.

Pórtugos towards Trevélez: Two hours' trek, meeting the tarmac a little beyond the end of the Busquistar route.

Trevélez to Berchules: Four hours' trek, but the middle two hours is dirt track.

Trevélez to Juviles: Three hours' trek, including some sections of firebreak.

Semáforo close to the traffic lights at the junction. For good meals at reasonable prices try the quiet, family-run *Mirasierra* at the bottom on the way out of town towards Torvizcón. Incidentally, this is where a certain (now famous, but then unknown) writer wrote most of his work about life on a nearby Alpujarras hill farm; it's a fine, airy place serving up decent tapas and *raciones*.

The High (Western) Alpujarras

The best way to experience the **High Alpujarras** is to walk, and there are a number of paths between Órgiva and Cadiar, at the furthest reaches of the western valleys (see box, above). Equip yourself with a compass and the Instituto Geográfico Nacional/Federación Española de Montañismo 1:50,000 map or the Editorial Alpina map (see p.363), which cover all the territory from Órgiva up to Bérchules (Alpina) and Berja (IGN/FEM) respectively. Alternatively, a bus leaves daily from Lanjarón at 1pm and winds through all the upper Alpujarran villages; hitching, too, is generally good in these rural areas, though cars are few and far between.

Cañar, Soportújar and Carataunas

Heading on from Órgiva, the first settlements you reach, almost directly above the town, are **CAÑAR** and **SOPORTÚJAR**, the latter a maze of sinuous white-walled alleys. Like many of the High Alpujarran villages, they congregate on the neatly terraced mountainside, planted with poplars and laced with irrigation channels. Both have bars where you can get a **meal** and Soportújar can provide excellent-value en-suite **rooms** for the night for around €20; ask at *Bar Correillo* (T958 787 578; ❶) on c/Real (behind the church). Both villages are perched precariously on the steep hillside with a rather sombre view of Órgiva in the valley below, and the mountains of Africa over the ranges to the south. Just below the two villages, the tiny hamlet of **CARATAUNAS** is particularly pretty, and offers a comfortable place to stay at *El Montañero* (T & F958 787 528, Wwww.hotelmontanero.com; ❸), which has a pool and offers a variety of activities, such as mountain-biking, horse-riding and mountain walks. Two kilometres out of Carataunas a turn-off on the left (signed "*Camino Forestal*") beyond the *Los Llanos* restaurant ascends 6km (the last three a rugged unpaved track) to the Buddhist monastery of Osel Ling (see below).

The Poqueira Gorge and up to Capileira

Shortly after Carataunas the road swings to the north, and you have your first view of the **Poqueira Gorge**, a huge, sheer gash into the heights of the Sierra Nevada. Trickling deep in the bed of the cleft is the Río Poqueira, which has its source near the peak of Mulhacén. The steep walls of the gorge are terraced and wooded from top to bottom, and dotted with little stone farmhouses. Much of the surrounding country looks barren from a distance, but close up you'll find that it's rich with flowers, woods, springs and streams.

A trio of villages – three of the most spectacular and popular in the Alpujarras – teeters on the steep edge of the gorge among their terraces. The first is **PAMPANEIRA**, neat, prosperous and pretty. On its leafy main square, Plaza de la Libertad, is Nevadensis, an **information centre** (Tues–Sat 10am–2pm & 5–7pm, Sun & Mon 10am–3pm; ☏958 763 127, ⦿www.nevadensis.com; English spoken) for the Natural and National Parks of the Sierra Nevada; they also sell large-scale topographical maps of the zone, offer horse-riding tours and **guided treks**, including an ascent of Mulhacén. At the entrance to the village, **rooms** are available at a pair of *hostales*: the homely *Hostal Pampaneira* (☏958 763 002; ❶), at c/José Antonio 1, has some en-suite rooms, and just opposite, for a bit more comfort, the *Hostal Ruta del Mulhacén*, Avda. de Alpujarra 6 (☏958 763 010, ⦿rutamul@arrakis.es; ❷), has balcony rooms with bath and central heating. For **food** the *Hostal Pampaneira* has its own good restaurant, and also worth considering is *Casa Julio*, up some steps nearby. On the main square, Plaza de la Libertad, *Casa Diego* is another restaurant possibility, with a terrace, and a *menú* for €8.

Above Pampaneira, on the very peak of the western flank of the Poqueira Gorge, is the **Tibetan Buddhist Monastery of Osel Ling** ("Place of Clear Light"), founded in 1982 by a Tibetan monk on land donated by the communities of Pampaneira and Bubión. Three years later, in 1985, a baby born to Spanish parents in Granada was recognized by the Dalai Lama as the reincarnation of a former head lama – one Yeshé – and the youth is currently undergoing training under the Dalai Lama in the Himalayas. The simple, stone-built monastery complete with stupas and stunning **views** across the Alpujarras welcomes visitors between 3 and 6pm daily; lectures on Buddhism are held regularly and facilities exist for those who want to visit for periods of retreat in cabins dotted around the site (☏958 343 134 for details).

BUBIÓN is the next of the three villages up the hill, backed for much of the year by snowcapped peaks. The village now has a private **museum**, the Casa Alpujarreña, just off Plaza de la Iglesia, the main square (daily except Tues 11am–2pm, Sat & Sun also 5–7pm; €1.80), displaying aspects of the folklore, daily life and architecture of the Alpujarras in a traditional house. For **places to stay**, there's a fancy hotel, *Villa Turística de Bubión* (☏958 763 111, ⦿www.villabubion.com; ❹), with its own restaurant, and a comfortable *pensión*, *Las Terrazas* (☏958 763 034, ⦿www.terrazasalpujarra.com; ❶), which also has some excellent apartments (☏958 763 217; ❷) downhill at c/Parras that come with terrace, kitchen and satellite TV; the proprietors also rent out **mountain bikes**. A decent **restaurant**, *La Artesa*, at c/Carretera 2, turns out *alpujarreño* specialities and has an economical *menú*. In the maze of alleys below *Las Terrazas*, the laid-back *Ciber Monfí Café*, c/Pérez Ramón 2, has leafy terraces with fabulous views, serves tea and coffee and North African cuisine (specials include tagines and cous-cous) and offers **Internet** access. For **horse-rid-ing trips** of one to five days the friendly *Rancho Rafael Belmonte* (☎958 763 135) at the bottom of the village near *Rustic Blue*, or *Cabalgar*, c/Ermita s/n (☎958 763 135, ⓦwww.ridingandalucía.com), are the places to contact. *Rustic Blue* (☎958 763 381, ⓦwww.rusticblue.com; English spoken), on the main road to the right as you enter the village, can also book horse-riding and walk-ing tours and help with accommodation in fully equipped houses across the Alpujarras (minimum two nights' stay; from around €310 per week).

Capileira

Two kilometres north of Bubión, **CAPILEIRA** is the highest of the three villages and the terminus of the road – Europe's highest, but now closed to traf-fic – across the heart of the Sierra Nevada from Granada (see p.365). In addition to the direct daily afternoon **bus** from Granada, continuing to Murtas and Bérchules, anything going to Ugíjar and Berja will come very close to Capileira; the bus out to Granada and Órgiva currently passes by at 6.15am, 3.45pm and 6.15pm. If you're thinking to be doing any walking in this zone, this is probably the best village in which to base yourself.

The **kiosco** at the centre of the village, near where the bus drops you, hands out a **village map**, sells newspapers and large-scale walking maps, and acts as an information office. Just downhill from here lies the village's **museum** (Tues–Sun 11.30am–2.30pm), containing displays of regional dress and handi-crafts, as well as various bits and pieces belonging to, or produced by, Pedro Alarcón, the nineteenth-century Spanish writer who made a trip through the Alpujarras and wrote a (not very good) book about it. There are numerous **places to stay** starting with, as you enter the village to the right, *Hostal Atalaya* (☎958 763 025, ⓦwww.hostalatalaya.com; ❶ incl. breakfast), a newly opened place with en-suite rooms and terrific views from those at the front. Near the bus stop, the friendly *Mesón-Hostal Poqueira* (☎ & ⒻBEL958 763 048; ❶) with en-suite heated rooms is another good place, which also offers a substantial *menú* for around €7 in its terrace restaurant at the rear. Further uphill, *Hostal Paco Lopez* (☎958 763 011; ❶) has comfortable rooms with balconies and views plus a few bargain apartments (❷) nearby. Continuing uphill, the pleasant *Finca Los Llanos* (☎958 763 071, Ⓕ958 763 206; ❸) has apartment-style rooms with kitchenettes and terraces, together with its own pool and a good restaurant.

For **food**, all of the above and many of the other hotels and *hostales* have **restaurants** or tapas and *raciones* bars attached; *Paco Lopez's* restaurant offers quite a few vegetarian options, too. *Restaurante El Tilo*, on the focal Plaza Calvario in the lower village, is a decent place for *platos combinados* or watch-ing-the-world-go-by drinks on its tranquil terrace shaded by a lime tree. Near the museum (see above) the tangerine-tinted dining room of *Ibero Fusion*, c/Parra 1 (open for lunch and dinner weekends, weekdays evenings only), is another good place to find vegetarian dishes among the very tasty cous-cous, Indian and other adventurous concoctions emerging from its kitchen; there's also a *menú* for €10.50.

Capileira is a handy base for easy **day walks** in the Poqueira Gorge. For a not-too-strenuous example, take the northernmost of three paths below the village, each with bridges across the river. This sets off from alongside the *Pueblo Alpujarreño* villa complex. The path winds through the huts and terraced fields of the river valley above Capileira, ending after about an hour and a half at a dirt track within sight of a power plant at the head of the valley. You can either retrace your steps or cross the stream over a bridge to follow a dirt track back to the village. In May and June, the fields are tended laboriously by hand, as the steep slopes dictate. Reasonably clear paths or tracks also lead to **Pampaneira** (2–3hr, follow lower path to the bridge below Capileira), continuing to Carataunas (1hr, mostly road) and Órgiva (45min, easy path), from where you can get a bus back. In the other direction, taking the Sierra Nevada road and then the first major path to the right, by a ruined stone house, you can reach **Pitres** (2hr), Pórtugos (30min more) and Busquistar (45min). Going in the same direction but taking the second decent-sized path (by a sign encouraging you to "conserve and respect nature"), **Trevélez** is some five hours away – you can also get to Pórtugos this way. More fine walking routes in this zone are detailed in *Landscapes of Andalucía* by John and Christine Oldfield, *Walking in Andalucía* by Guy Hunter-Watts and *Holiday Walks in the Alpujarra* by Jeremy Rabjohns (see "Books", p.1112).

Along the High Route to Trevélez

PITRES and **PÓRTUGOS**, 6km east of Pampaneira and the next two villages on the High Route, are perhaps more "authentic" and less polished. You're more likely to find rooms here during the summer months, while all around spreads some of the best Alpujarran walking country. For **accommodation** in Pitres you could try the *Fonda Sierra Nevada* (☎958 766 017; ❶), on the main square for rather overpriced rooms sharing bath; they also rent out apartments nearby with *salón*, kitchen and bathroom (❷). Alternatively, *Hotel San Roque*, c/Cruz 1 on the east side of the village (☎958 857 528; ❸), has pleasant rooms with (on the south side) views. On the village's eastern edge the *Refugio de los Albergues* (☎958 766 004; €7) is an old Civil War hostel with very cheap dormitory beds and cooking facilities. Close by, and on the main road, *El Jardín* is a British-run restaurant with garden terrace, great views and an eclectic vegetarian menu (currently open evenings only). Pitres's **campsite**, *Balcón de Pitres* (☎958 766 111), with restaurant and pool, is located in a stunning position 1km west of the village; it also rents out cabins (❷). A couple of kilometres east, Pórtugos has the *Hostal Mirador* (☎958 766 014; ❶), on the main square, with en-suite rooms and its own decent restaurant.

Down below the main road (GR421) linking Pitres and Pórtugos are the three villages of Mecina Fondales (and its offshoot, Mecinilla), Ferreirola and Busquistar; along with Pitres, these formed a league of villages known as the *Taha* under the Moors. **FERREIROLA** and **BUSQUISTAR** are especially attractive, as is the path between the two, clinging to the north side of the valley of the Río Trevélez. You're out of tourist country here and the villages display their genuine characteristics to better effect. In Busquistar there's an **inn**, the newly renovated *Alcázar de Busquistar* (☎ & ℱ958 857 470, ⓦwww.ugr.es/~jguardia/; ❸), which lies just uphill from the church and has one of the best views in the Alpujarras, a **restaurant** with vegetarian possibilities, and even squeezes in a pool. It's also well sited for a hike up to Trevélez and beyond, and the proprietor, a *montañero* (hill climber), can advise on this and other trekking routes in this zone. **MECINILLA** also has a charming *hostal-restaurante*, *L'Atelier*, c/Alberca, located in the old village bakery (☎ & ℱ958 857 501, ⓦwww.ivu.org/atelier; ❷, breakfast included); it's run by an affable French chef specializing in **vegetarian/vegan** cuisine who, besides supervising the very good restaurant, also offers cookery courses. The establishment has recently added a small art gallery; readers with this guide will receive a ten percent discount on accommodation.

TREVÉLEZ, at the end of an austere ravine carved by the Río Trevélez, is purportedly Spain's highest permanent settlement, with cooler temperatures year-round than its neighbours. In traditional Alpujarran style, it has lower, middle and upper quarters (*barrios bajo*, *medio* and *alto*) overlooking a grassy, poplar-lined valley where the river starts its long descent.

The village is well provided with **hostales**; if you are susceptible to low temperatures, outside July and August you may want a place with efficient heating. In the *barrio medio*, *Hostal Fernando* (☎958 858 565; ❶) is friendly and has heated en-suite rooms, as does the comfortable *Hotel La Fragua*, c/Antonio 4 (☎958 858 626, ✉fragua@navegalia.com; ❷), in the *barrio alto*, which also has an excellent restaurant. Trevélez's **campsite** (☎958 858 735) lies 1km out along the Órgiva road and is officially open all year, although you can expect arctic conditions in midwinter; it also rents out some heated cabins (❸).

Besides the *Fragua*'s restaurant, other **places to eat** include the *Río Grande*, down near the bridge in the *barrio bajo*, which serves good, solid mountain food, and for **tapas** a couple of good bars worth seeking out (especially for sampling *jamón*) are *Bar Rosales* (near *Hostal Fernando*) and *Bar Cerezo*, both in the *barrio medio*. Trevélez's best restaurant is the newly opened *Asador Despensa de la Alpujarra*, c/El Puente s/n (☎958 858 757), just across the bridge (direction Granada) from the Plaza Francisco Abellán in the *barrio bajo*; it specializes in *platos alpujarreños* and there's a great-value *menú* for €7.50. Trevélez's **jamón serrano** is a prized speciality and an obsession throughout eastern Andalucía, and good places to try it include *Mesón del Jamón* above the Plaza de la Iglesia or *Mesón Joaquín* in the lower *barrio*.

Although Capileira is probably the more pleasant base, Trevélez is traditionally the jump-off point for the **high sierra peaks** (to which there is a bona fide path) and for treks across the range (on a lower, more conspicuous track). The latter begins down by the bridge on the eastern side of the village. After skirting the bleak Horcajo de Trevélez (3182m), and negotiating the Puerto de Trevélez (2800m), the path drops gradually down along the north flank of the Sierra Nevada to Jerez del Marquesado (see the "Ruta de los Tres Mil", p.385).

East from Trevélez

Heading east from Trevélez, you come to **JUVILES**, an attractive town straddling the road. At its centre is an unwhitewashed, peanut-brittle-finish church with a clock that's usually running slow (like most things round here). A single all-in-one *fonda-restaurante*-store, *Bar Fernandez* (☎958 769 168; ❶), is simple and very friendly, with great views from the second floor east over the valley to Cadiar. The pricier *Pensión Tino* (☎958 769 174; ❶), a little back along the main street, has rooms with bath and serves *raciones*.

BÉRCHULES, a high village of grassy streams and chestnut woods, famous for its *jamón*, lies only 4km beyond Juviles, but a greater contrast can hardly be imagined. It is a large, abruptly demarcated settlement, three streets wide, on a sharp slope overlooking yet another canyon. For **accommodation** the *Fonda-Restaurante Carayol*, c/Iglesia 18 below the church (aka *Pensión Resu*; ☎958 769 092; ❶), has economical rooms with bath; the more expensive *La Posada* (☎958 852 541, ✉laposadaberchules@wanadoo.es; ❶ including breakfast), on the central Plaza Victoria (aka Plaza Abastos), is another possibility and vegetarian meals are available. On the main road the more upmarket *Hotel Bérchules* (☎ & ☏958 852 530; ❷) has comfortable rooms above its own restaurant. For **food**, *Bar Vaqueras*, also on Plaza Victoria, does decent tapas, and there's an excellent grocery in the village – a godsend if you're planning on doing any walking out of here, since most village shops in the Alpujarras are rather primitive.

Just below Bérchules, **CADIAR**, the central town of the Alpujarras, is more attractive than it seems from a distance, and there are a handful of **hostales** and *camas* if you want to stay. The best deal is at *La Ruta de la Alpujarra* (☎958 768

059, ⓕ958 768 805; ❷), sited near the petrol station as you arrive from Bérchules, where spacious rooms come with fully equipped kitchenette and fridge. The inexpensive *Hostal Montoro*, c/San Isidro 20 (ⓣ958 768 068; ❶), near the central plaza, with en-suite heated rooms, is also good. A tempting out-of-town option with your own transport is the upmarket apartment-hotel *Alquería de Morayma* (ⓣ958 343 303, ⓦwww.alqueriademorayma.com; ❸), sited in a typical Alpujarran *cortijo* in 86 acres of farmland. With its own good restaurant (open to visitors) and mountain biking and horse riding on offer to guests, it lies 2km out of town along the A348 towards Torvizcón. For **food**, the restaurant of *La Ruta de la Alpujarra* (see above) is very good and has an economical *menú*, or there are tapas and *raciones* to be had in its bar or in other bars in and around the main square. There's a colourful **produce market** on the 3rd and 18th of every month, sometimes including livestock, and from October 5 to 9 the **Fuente del Vino** wine and cattle fair takes place, turning the waters of the fountain literally to wine.

Cadiar and Bérchules mark the end of the western Alpujarras, and a striking change in the landscape; the dramatic, severe, but relatively green terrain of the Guadalfeo and Cadiar valleys gives way to open rolling land that's much more arid, a prelude to the deserts of Almería that lie ahead.

Eastern Alpujarras

The villages of the eastern Alpujarras display many of the characteristics of those to the west, but as a rule they are poorer and much less visited by tourists. **Yegen** is one of the most famous these days, due to its connection with the Bloomsbury writer Gerald Brenan, and **Ugíjar** is a busy focal hub for traffic heading north over the mountains to Guadix and south to the coast. There are vineyards on the hills in the south of this region, and the good dry red wine available in most of the Alpujarran villages, west or east, is always worth asking for.

Yegen and Ugíjar

In **YEGEN**, some 7km northeast of Cadiar, there's a plaque on the house (just along from the central fountain) where **Gerald Brenan** lived during his ten or so years of Alpujarran residence. His autobiography of these times, *South from Granada*, is the best account of rural life in Spain between the wars, and describes the visits made here by Virginia Woolf, Bertrand Russell and the arch-complainer Lytton Strachey. Disillusioned with the strictures of middle-class life in England after World War I, Brenan rented a house in Yegen and shipped out a library of 2000 books, from which he was to spend the next eight years educating himself. He later moved to the hills behind Torremolinos, where he died in 1987, a writer better known and respected in Spain (he made an important study of St John of the Cross) than in his native England.

Brenan connections aside, Yegen is still one of the most characteristic Alpujarran villages, with its two distinct quarters, cobbled paths and cold-water springs. It has a **fonda**, *Bar La Fuente* (ⓣ958 851 067; ❶), opposite the fountain in the square, whose proprietor and Brenan aficionado, Eduardo Moreno, is trying to set up a museum dedicated to the author. There are also rooms with bath at the slightly more expensive *El Tinao* (ⓣ958 851 212, ⓔloranne123@hotmail.com; ❶, breakfast included), on the main road. Heading east out of the village, more upmarket accommodation is available at *El Rincón de Yegen* (ⓣ958 851 270; ❷), where heated rooms come with TV and where there are apartments (❸) for longer stays, as well as a pool and good restaurant with an economical *menú*. Other places serving **food** are thin on the ground, but *Bar La Fuente* (see above) does tapas and *raciones*.

UGÍJAR, 12km on from Yegen, is the largest community of this eastern zone, and an unassuming, quiet market town. There are easy and enjoyable walks to the nearest villages (up the valley to Mecina-al-Fahar, for example), and plenty of **places to stay**: try the relatively luxurious *Pensión Pedro*, c/Fabrica, near the church (☎958 767 149; ❶), which has en-suite heated rooms, or the equally good *Hostal Vidaña* (☎958 767 010, ⓕ958 854 004; ❶), nearby on the Almería road, with a terrace **restaurant** below and good-value *menú*. There is a **bus** service on to Almería (3hr).

The southern ranges

The tiny hamlets of the southern Alpujarras have an unrivalled view of the Mediterranean, the convexity of the hills obscuring the awful development that mars the coast. There are few villages of any size, but the hills host the principal **wine-growing district** of the Alpujarras. For a taste of the best of its wine, try the *venta* (wine shop) at Haza del Lino (Plain of Linen), 25km southwest of Cadiar and reached by following the A345 and GR433; the house brew is a full-bodied rosé.

Inland towards Almería

An alternative **route from Granada to Almería** runs via **Guadix**, a crumbling old Moorish town with a vast and extraordinary cave district. East again, one of the finest hilltop castles in Andalucía hoves into view at **La Calahorra**. From here a spectacular but lonely mountain road ascends to the Puerto de la Ragua, Andalucía's highest mountain pass

Guadix

A busy country town 60km east of Granada, Guadix is famous for its troglodyte quarter, the **Barrio Santiago**, which extends over a square mile or so in area and houses some 10,000 people. Consisting of dwellings hollowed out of the hard, compacted clay which is a geological feature of this zone, they are easy to excavate and remain virtually impermeable to rain. Thought to have been founded by seventeenth-century Moors who fled underground to escape religious persecution, cave dwellings soon caught on as a way to get a home on the cheap. The entrance to the Barrio is behind the whitewashed church of Santiago and the lower caves, on the outskirts, are really proper cottages with upper storeys, electricity, television and running water. But as you walk deeper into the suburb, the design quickly becomes simpler – just a whitewashed front, a door, a tiny window and a chimney. Penetrating right to the back, you'll come upon a few caves which are no longer used: too squalid, too unhealthy, their whitewash long-unrepainted. Yet right next door there may be a similar, occupied hovel, with a family sitting outside and other figures following dirt tracks still deeper into the hills. A **Cueva Museo** opposite the church of San Miguel, in Plaza Padre (Mon–Sat 10am–2pm & 5–7pm, Sun 10am–2pm; €1.50), provides an insight into cave culture, with intriguing reconstructions of troglodytic life. In the town's central zone a couple of monuments worth a look are the ruined ninth-century **Alcazaba** (Mon–Fri 9am–2pm & 4–7pm, Sat 9am–2pm; €0.60), entered from an adjoining theological school with fine views from the ramparts over the Barrio Santiago cave district. Nearby lies Guadix's impressive sixteenth-century red-sandstone **cathedral** (Mon–Sat 11am–1pm & 4–6pm; €1.50), built on the site of a former mosque and circled on Saturdays by a lively market. Just across from the cathedral entrance, beyond an arch, stands the elegant Plaza Mayor, an arcaded Renaissance square, which was reconstructed after suffering severe damage in the Civil War.

Practicalities

A map from the **turismo**, Ctra. de Granada just west of the cathedral (Mon–Fri 8am–3pm; ☎958 662 665), will help you find your way around; when this is closed many of the *kioskos* around the centre stock a small fold-out version.

There's little in the way of budget **accommodation**, but you could try the *Hotel Mulhacen* on c/Buenos Aires, the main road into town from the north (☎958 660 750, ℱ958 660 661; ❷). If you can afford the extra, however, you should stay at the *Hotel Comercio*, c/Mira de Amezcua 3, east of the imposing cathedral (☎958 660 500, ℮hotelcomercio@moebius.es; ❸), an elegant and refurbished turn-of-the-twentieth-century hotel. If you've been smitten with the idea of cave life there's a chance to experience it for a night in the cave district at the spotless **cave hostal** *Chez Jean & Julia*, c/Ermita Nueva 67 (☎958 669 191, ⓦwww.altipla.com/jj), where you have a choice of a double room (❷, breakfast included) or your own en-suite cave apartment (❺) with salon, kitchen and washing machine. It's near the cave museum (see p.397); to find it, give the proprietors (English spoken) a ring for directions.

For **food**, the *Hotel Comercio* has an excellent restaurant with a good-value *menú* for around €12. Otherwise try the Plaza de Naranjos, a stone's throw east of the cathedral, where there are plenty of popular eating places, such as *Cafetería Cart Luis* which does **tapas**, **raciones**, hamburgers and a cheap *menú*.

Buses run direct from Granada to Guadix (Empresa Autodia from c/Rector Marín). The bus station in Guadix is a five-minute walk outside the walls, to the southeast of the centre off Medina Olmos. Guadix's **train station**, 2km northeast of the centre along the Murcia road, is served by four daily trains (in each direction) from Granada and Almería.

On from Guadix

En route towards Almería you pass through more of the strange, tufa-pocked landscape from which the Guadix caves are hewn. The main landmark, 16km beyond Guadix, is a magnificent sixteenth-century castle on a hill (a fifteen-minute hike) above the village of **La Calahorra**. One of the finest in Spain, with a remarkable Renaissance patio within, it's open Wednesdays only (10am–1pm & 4–6pm; €3); outside these times visit the guardian's house – avoiding siesta time – at c/de los Claveles 2 (☎958 677 098; Spanish only), and he will open it up for a consideration. From La Calahorra a minor road, the A337, climbs dizzily and scenically to the **Puerto de la Ragua**, at 1993m Andalucía's highest all-weather pass. It's another route into the Alpujarras, and once through the pass the road descends to Ugíjar (see p.397).

Heading east, Guadix–Almería buses normally follow the train line, along the minor N324 over the last section. If you're driving, you might want to keep going straight on the main road, meeting the Almería–Sorbas road at what has become known as **Mini Hollywood** (see p.402), the preserved film set of *A Fistful of Dollars*.

Almería Province

The **province of Almería** is a strange corner of Spain. Inland it has an almost **lunar landscape** of desert, sandstone cones and dried-up riverbeds. The coast to the east of the provincial capital is still largely unspoiled; lack of water and roads frustrated development in the 1960s and 1970s and it is only now beginning to take off. Inland the lack of development allowed the creation in the 1980s of the **Parque Natural de Cabo de Gata**, a haven for flora and fauna. To the west of Almería is another story, though, with a sea of plastic greenhouses spreading for a good 30km across the Campo de Dalías, the source of much of Almería's new-found wealth. A number of **good beaches** are accessible by bus, and in this hottest province of Spain they're worth considering during what would be the off season elsewhere, since Almería's summers start well before Easter and last into November. In midsummer it's incredibly hot (frequently touching 100°F/38°C in the shade), while all year round there's an intense, almost luminous, sunlight. This and the weird scenery have made Almería one of the most popular **film locations** in Europe – much of *Lawrence of Arabia* was shot here, along with scores of spaghetti westerns.

Almería

ALMERÍA is a pleasant, modern city, spread at the foot of a stark grey mountain. At the summit is a tremendous **Alcazaba** (Tues–Sun 9am–8.30pm,

The landscape of Almería

The landscape of Almería, like much of southern Spain, is dominated by mountain chains composed of hard, ancient rocks, separated by lower-lying basins filled with younger, softer rocks. The highest mountains – the Sierra Nevada, Sierra de Gádor, Sierra de Baza and the Sierra de los Filabres, which reach altitudes of over 2000m – were created by the collision of the African and Eurasian tectonic plates which took place at around the same time as the Alps were being formed, ending some ten million years ago. The basins between the mountain ranges were once below sea level and rivers cut into them, leading to the creation of the stunning landscapes that we see today.

Almería is also one of the driest parts of Europe, with an average rainfall of only 250–300mm per year. When rainfall does occur, however, it can be of very high intensity: the storms which swept the region in the winter of 1993 deposited 247mm of rain in just four days, causing flash flooding and severe erosion of hill slopes – something the region is prone to with its semi-arid climate and relatively sparse vegetation cover.

The landscape which most vividly illustrates the interaction between tectonic uplift and erosion is the area of "badlands" to the west of Tabernas, which can be best viewed from the road behind Mini Hollywood leading up to the radio mast on the summit of the Sierra Alhamilla. The badlands have been caused by tributaries of the Tabernas and Gérgal rivers cutting into soft limestone and sandstone deposits between the Sierra Alhamilla and Sierra de los Filabres. As the basin was uplifted, so the rivers cut deeper into the landscape, creating the stunning setting used by numerous Almería-made Westerns.

There are also a number of excellent raised beaches near Mojácar and La Garrucha, which were once at sea level but have been uplifted by tectonic movements to heights of several metres above the present beach. You'll have to be quick to see them, however, as many of the better sites are being progressively bulldozed to make way for villa developments.

Oct–March closes 6.30pm; free with EU passport, otherwise €1.50), probably the best surviving example of Moorish military fortification, with three huge walled enclosures, in the second of which are the remains of a mosque, converted to a chapel by the Reyes Católicos. In the eleventh century, when Almería was an independent kingdom and the wealthiest, most commercially active city of Spain, this citadel contained immense gardens and palaces and some 20,000 people. Its grandeur was reputed to rival the court of Granada but comparisons are impossible since little beyond the walls and towers remains, the last remnants of stuccowork having been sold off by the locals in the eighteenth century.

From the Alcazaba, however, you do get a good view of the coast, of Almería's **cave quarter** – the Barrio de la Chanca on a low hill to the left – and of the city's strange, fortified **Cathedral** (Mon–Fri 10am–4.30pm, Sat 10am–1pm; €2), built in the sixteenth century at a time when the southern Mediterranean was terrorized by the raids of Barbarossa and other Turkish and North African pirate forces; its corner towers once held cannons. There's little else to do in town, and your time is probably best devoted to sampling the cafés, tapas bars and *terrazas* in the streets circling the Puerta de Purchena, the focal junction of the modern town, strolling along the main Paseo de Almería down towards the harbour, and taking day-trips out to the beaches along the coast. The city's own **beach**, southeast of the centre beyond the train lines, is long but dismal.

Practicalities

The **turismo** (Mon–Fri 9am–7pm, Sat & Sun 10am–2pm; ☎950 274 355, ℗950 274 360) is on c/Parque de Nicolás Salmerón facing the commercial harbour. They have a list of most buses out of Almería in all directions, as well as train and boat schedules. For **Internet** access *Cyber Planet*, c/Las Tiendas 20, just south of the focal Puerta de Purchena, is the town's most central Internet café (daily 10.30am–midnight; €1.80 per hr). Almería's gleaming international **airport** is 8km out of town with a connecting bus service (#14, labelled "El Alquián") every half-hour from the junction of the Avenida Federico García Lorca and c/Gregorio Marañon (just above the top right corner of our city map). There is also a **daily boat to Melilla** on the Moroccan coast throughout the summer (less often out of season), a six-hour journey which can pay dividends in both time and money over Algeciras if you're driving. In summer (June–Sept) a high-speed vessel does the trip in four hours. For information and tickets contact the *Compañía Trasmediterránea* (☎950 263 714, ⊛www.trasmediterranea.es), Parque Nicolás Salmerón 19, near the port. The daily six-hour route to Nador in Morocco is operated by *Ferrimaroc* (☎950 274 800, ⊛www.ferrimaroc.com) who have an office at the port.

Rooms are not normally difficult to come by at any time of the year, and a good place to start looking is around the Puerta de Purchena. Just off this intersection, the recently refurbished *Hotel La Perla*, Plaza del Carmen 7 (☎950 238 877, ℗950 275 816; ❸), is Almería's oldest hotel and once played host to big-name stars making westerns at Mini Hollywood (see p.402). Just behind is a cheaper option, *Hostal Nixar*, c/Antonio Vico 24 (☎ & ℗950 237 255; ❷); ask for a high, airy room. On the square itself, the atmospheric *Fonda Universal*, Puerta de Purchena 3 (☎950 235 557; ❶), with a fabulous foyer staircase from its previous incarnation as a minor *casa señorial*, is very basic but clean, while close to the bus station, *Hostal Americano*, Avda. de la Estación 6 (☎950 258 011; ❷), with some rooms en suite, is handily

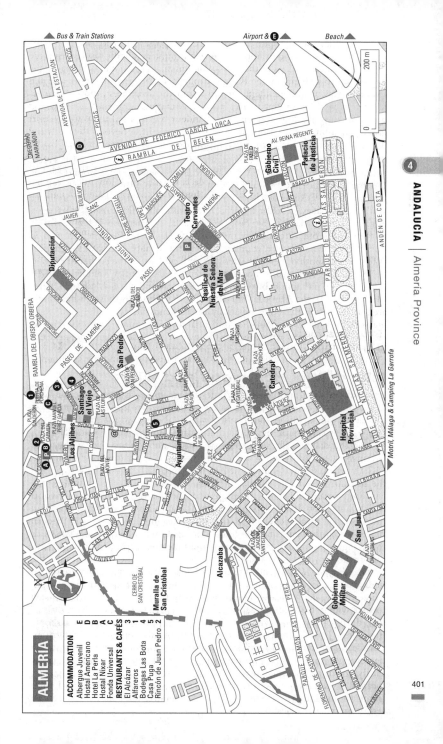

Bus & Train Stations ▲ **Airport &** 🅴 ▲ **Beach** ▲

200 m

0

4

ANDALUCÍA | Almería Province

▼ *Motril, Málaga & Camping La Garrofa*

401

ALMERÍA

ACCOMMODATION
Albergue Juvenil — E
Hostal Americano — D
Hotel La Perla — B
Hostal Nixar — A
Fonda Universal — C

RESTAURANTS & CAFÉS
El Alcázar — 3
Alfareros — 1
Bodegas Las Bota — 4
Casa Puga — 5
Rincón de Juan Pedro — 2

placed if you're arriving on a late bus. The *Albergue Juvenil Almería*, c/Isla de Fuerteventura s/n (℡950 269 788; ❶), is a swish new 150-double-roomed affair on the east side of town next to the Estadio Juventud sports arena; take bus #1 from the junction of Avenida Federico García Lorca and c/Gregorio Marañon. The nearest **campsite**, *La Garrofa* (℡950 235 770; open all year), is on the coast at La Garrofa, some 5km west, easily reached by the buses to Aguadulce and Roquetas de Mar where there is another large site (℡950 343 809; open all year).

When it comes to **eating** and **drinking**, the Puerta de Purchena is a great place to head for, particularly at night. On the north side, in a small street, *Restaurante Alfareros*, c/Marcos 6, has an excellent-value *menú* for around €7.50. On the opposite side of the junction, there's a popular *marisquería*, *Bar El Alcázar*, Paseo de Almería 4, with plenty of tapas possibilities. Just in from here, you'll find an alley, c/Tenor Iribarne, filled with tables from many other tapas establishments and, close by, *Bodegas Las Botas*, c/Fructuoso Perez 3, is well worth seeking out. Alternatively, the *Rincón de Juan Pedro*, Plaza del Carmen, is one of the town's better restaurants, serving top-quality Almerian specialities. A few blocks south of here the atmospheric *Casa Puga*, at the corner of c/Lope de Vega and c/Jovellanos, is the city's outstanding tapas outlet, founded in 1870. For drinking and music **bars**, try the streets around Plaza Masnou, off the southern end of the Alameda, and c/San Pedro slightly northeast of here, both areas bouncing with action especially at weekends. To move the night-time *marcha*, or scene, away from the residential area in summer, the city council erects a line of **disco marquees** at the start of the Paseo Marítimo, near the beach – around 3am these places start to get quite wild.

Inland: Mini Hollywood and Níjar

Travelling inland from the city of Almería gives you a chance to take in some of the dramatic desert landscapes to be found here. Two possible routes leave the city: the A370 heads northwest towards Tabernas, whilst the E15–N344 cuts east, passing Níjar before turning north. Both routes eventually unite beyond the dramatically sited town of Sorbas, and you are then within easy striking distance of the coast and resorts such as Mojácar (see p.405).

The northwest route follows the Andarax riverbed before forking right into the badlands, an area resembling Arizona, which looks as if it should be the backdrop for a Hollywood western. Just beyond the fork, at **Mini Hollywood** (daily: July–Sept 10am–10pm; Oct–June 10am–7pm; €16, kids €9), you discover that someone else had the same idea first. A full-blown Western movie-set, a visit here is hard to resist – especially if you're travelling with kids – although it's probably better value if you time your arrival to coincide with one of the shows (see below for times). Once inside you can walk around the set of *A Fistful of Dollars* and various other spaghetti westerns that were filmed here, and wander down main street into the *Tombstone Gulch* saloon for a drink. Three times a day in season (noon, 5pm & 8pm) the fantasy is carried a step further with acted-out "shows" when actors in full cowboy rig blast off six-guns during a mock bank raid or re-enact the "capture, escape and final shooting of Jesse James". The complex has recently added a somewhat incongruous **zoo**, featuring birds and reptiles as well as lions and other big cats prowling depressingly small cages. Further along the road towards Tabernas, **Texas Hollywood** (same hours; shows at 5.30pm & 7.30pm; €10.50, kids €6.50), location for the shooting of *Once Upon a Time in the West*, and **Western Leone** (similar hours and prices to the above) are a couple of less commercialized film sets in spectacular desert scenery.

Following the eastern route along the E15-N344 for 24km brings you to the turn-off for **NÍJAR**, famed throughout Andalucía for its pottery. A neat, white and typically Almerian town, with narrow streets designed to give maximum shade, it makes a good base from which to explore the coast and the natural park of Cabo de Gata to the south (see below). The town is firmly on the tourist trail due to the inexpensive **handmade pottery** manufactured in workshops and sold in the shops along the broad main street – Avenida García Lorca – and c/Real to the west where many of the potters have their workshops. If you're looking for a souvenir to take home, avoid the more commercial places on the main street – the more authentic potters are located in the **barrio alfarero**, along c/Real running parallel to the main street, where the workshops of Gongora, Granados, El Oficio, and the friendly and cheaper Angel y Loli (at no. 54) are located. The town is also known for its *jarapas*: quilts, curtains and rugs made from rags and widely on sale around the town.

There are a couple of **places to stay** along the main street; try *Montes*, Avda. García Lorca 26 (☎951 360 157; ❶), with en-suite rooms. For **food**, further up the same street at no. 6 *Casa Pedro* is a very good bar-restaurant with a street terrace, and there are more tapas and *raciones* bars in the upper square, Plaza La Glorieta, beyond the church.

Cabo de Gata to Mojácar

Almería's best **beaches** lie on its eastern coast; those to the west of the city, particularly Aguadulce and Roquetas de Mar, have already been exploited, and although they're not quite as bad as many on the Costa del Sol, they're not a lot better either. Either place is an easy day-trip, however, with hourly buses along the coast. The eastern stretch of the Almerian coastline offers some of the most relaxing beaches left in Spain: half-abandoned fishing communities which have only begun to be promoted for tourists relatively recently. Outside the centres of **Mojácar** and **San José** development is low-key, and with a short walk along the coast you should be able to find plenty of relatively secluded spots to lay your towel.

El Cabo de Gata

Heading east, the closest resort with any appeal is the modest **EL CABO DE GATA**, now inside the **Parque Natural de Cabo de Gata**, where there is a long expanse of coarse sand. Five buses a day run between here and Almería, making an intermediate stop at Retamar, a retirement/holiday development. Arriving at El Cabo, you pass a lake, the **Laguna de Rosa**, protected by a conservation society and home to flamingos and other waders throughout the summer. Around the resort are plentiful bars, cafés and shops, plus a fish market. There's little accommodation, though, and for **rooms** you'll need to head inland to the friendly but pricey *Hostal Las Dunas*, c/Barrionuevo 58 (☎950 370 072; ❸), 100m back from the beach, offering air-conditioned, en-suite rooms with TV. On the coast 2km northwest of the village there's a campsite, *Cabo de Gata* (☎950 160 443; open all year), with its own pool and restaurant. The beach gets windy in the afternoons, and it's a deceptively long walk eastwards to **Las Salinas** (The Salt Pans) for a couple of bar-restaurants and a café.

A few kilometres south of here, the **Faro de Cabo de Gata** (lighthouse) marks the cape's southern tip. In the lighthouse car park an **information cabin** (May–Sept daily 10am–2pm & 4.30–8.30pm; Oct–April Sat & Sun 10am–3pm) has maps and information on the natural park. There's also a friendly tapas bar here, *Bar José y María*, serving up tasty, locally caught fried fish, as well as a **mirador** from where you can get a great view of the rock cliffs and – on clearer days – a sight of Morocco's Rif mountains.

San José

Ten kilometres east of the lighthouse lies **SAN JOSÉ**, also reached by bus from Almería. Although it's possible to hike to the resort along a coastal track from the lighthouse, this is now closed to vehicles and to get there by road entails retracing your route to El Cabo de Gata village and following the inland road via the village of El Pozo de los Frailes. When you reach it, San José is an established and popular family resort, set back from a sandy beach in a small cove, with shallow water. More fine **beaches** lie within easy walking distance and one of the best – the Playa de los Genoveses – a kilometre-long golden strand, can be reached by a track to the southwest.

On the main street, c/Correos, near the centre of the village you'll find the official **Centro de Información** for the Natural Park (daily 10.30am–2pm & 5.30–8.30pm; ☎950 380 299) who have lots of information, lead guided walking and horse treks and hire out mountain bikes; they also have a complete list of accommodation and information on apartments to rent. **Internet** access is available at *Tierra Red San José*, Plaza de Genova, on the main junction at the centre of the village (daily 10.30am–2pm & 5–10pm).

Practicalities

Accommodation of any kind can be hard to come by in summer and the cheaper rooms tend to be snapped up quickly. In the centre of town *Hostal Costa Rica*, c/Correos s/n (☎950 380 103, ⊛www.parquenatural.com/costarica; ❸), has air-conditioned en-suite rooms with TV above a restaurant of the same name, and the nearby *Hostal Bahía*, c/Correos (☎950 380 114; ❸), is a comfortable modern *hostal* with en-suite facilities. The more upmarket *Hotel Las Gaviotas* on the way into the village (☎950 380 010, ⊛www.hlasgaviotas.com; ❹) has decent en-suite rooms, and its neighbour, the new *Hostal Agades Agidir* (☎950 380 390, Ⓕ950 380 006; ❹), is a hotel in all but name and has en-suite balcony rooms with air conditioning plus a garden pool, bar and restaurant for only slightly more. On a street running behind these two, *Hostal El Paraiso II* (☎950 380 380; ❶) is a friendly budget option for rooms with and without bath and a few come with their own terrace. San José also has a good beachfront **campsite**, *Camping Tau* (☎950 380 166; April–Oct), and an equally pleasant **Albergue Juvenil** (☎950 380 353; €13.35), both reached by a signed road on the left as you enter the village.

There are numerous **places to eat** among the excellent bars, restaurants and cafés around the beach and harbour zones, plus a couple of well-stocked supermarkets. For fresh fish try the restaurants overlooking the Puerto Deportivo – *La Cueva* is noted for its *salomonetes* (red mullet fried with garlic). Near the main junction, *Bar-Restaurante El Emigrante*, the restaurant of the *Hotel Bahía*, prepares good fish and has a *menú* for €8.

Los Escullos to Las Negras

Next along the coast is the isolated but developing resort of **LOS ESCULLOS**, with a reasonable sandy beach fronted by a formidable eighteenth-century ruined fort, the **Castillo de San Felipe**. There's a **campsite**, *Camping Los Escullos* (☎950 389 811), set back from the sea with limited shade and, closer to the beach, a couple of accommodation possibilities including the slightly overpriced beachfront hotel-restaurant, *Casa Emilio* (☎950 389 761; ❸). Two kilometres further east, **LA ISLETA** is another fishing hamlet, with a sleepy atmosphere, a rather scruffy village beach but a much better one in the next bay to the east – the Playa la Ola. A **hostal** overlooking the harbour, *Hostal Isleta de Moro* (☎951 389 713; ❷), has reasonably priced en-suite rooms with a popular **bar-restaurant** for tapas and good fish meals below.

LAS NEGRAS, 5km further on, is another place with a decidedly Spanish feel, where there's a cove with a pebbly beach and a few bars and restaurants plus an attractive **hostal**, *Arrecife* (☎950 388 140; ❷), close to the village shop, *Estanco Piedra García* (☎ & ℱ 950 388 075, ⓦwww.lasnegras.com). If the *hostal* is full, you can enquire here (English spoken) about a room in a private house or renting an apartment nearby. A **campsite**, *La Caleta* (☎950 525 237), set in a tranquil location with its own bay, is reached via a one-kilometre road just outside the village on the way in.

Agua Amarga

There's no paved road from Las Negras to Agua Amarga (10km north as the crow flies) but a dusty track – passable by car – heads east from the inland village of Fernan Pérez. The track, marked with an improvised sign to "Agua Amarga", leads through a no-man's land for 11km to an asphalt road where you need to turn right to reach Agua Amarga, a couple of kilometres further. For an all-asphalt alternative, keep ahead through Fernan Pérez to reach the N344, then head east, turning off at Venta del Pobre. There is no public transport on either route but Agua Amarga is served by a direct bus service from Almería.

When you reach it **AGUA AMARGA** is a one-time fishing hamlet that has transformed itself into a pleasant and easy-going resort. A fine sand EU blue-flagged beach is the main attraction, and this is backed by a tasteful crop of villas. There are limited **places to stay**, which means booking ahead in high summer if you want to avoid disappointment. Best value is the French-run *Pensión Family* (☎950 138 014, ⓔriovall@teleline.es; ❸), set back from the south end of the beach; you'll need to book well ahead in high season. *Hostal La Palmera* (☎950 138 208, ⓔhrlapalmera@terra.es; ❹), on the beach at the end of town, has small en-suite rooms with balconies. On a rise behind *Pensión Family*, *Hotel El Tío Kiko* (☎950 138 080, ⓦwww.eltiokiko.com; ❼, breakfast included) is one of a clutch of new luxury hotels here, catering for upmarket travellers.

Towards Mojácar

Leaving the Natural Park of Cabo de Gata behind, **CARBONERAS**, 11km north of Agua Amarga, is a fishing port with an average beach somewhat marred by the shadow of a massive cement factory which dominates its bay. Heading north again, the road passes a succession of small, isolated coves, backed by a characteristically arid Almerian landscape of scrub-covered hills and dried up *arroyos*, or water courses. The road then winds perilously through the hills some way inland, ascending the Punta del Santo with fine views along the coast, before descending to the **Playa de Macenas** another pleasant beach with rough-camping possibilities. There are a couple more beaches – the **Costa del Pirulico** is a good one with a beach *chiringuito* – before the urban sprawl of Mojácar takes over.

Mojácar

MOJÁCAR, 22km north of Carboneras, is eastern Almería's main and growing resort, hugely popular with Spaniards and foreign visitors throughout the summer. The coastal strip takes its name from the ancient hill village which lies a couple of kilometres back from the sea – Mojácar Pueblo – a striking agglomeration of white cubist houses wrapped round a harsh outcrop of rock. In the 1960s, when the main Spanish *costas* were being developed, this was virtually a ghost town, its inhabitants having long since taken the only logical step and emigrated. The town's fortunes suddenly revived, however, when the local mayor, using the popularity of other equally barren spots in Spain as an example, offered free land to anyone willing to build within a year. The bid was a modest success, attracting one of the decade's multifarious "artist colonies", now long supplanted by package holiday companies and second-homers. The long and sandy **beach**, down at the development known as Mojácar Playa, is excellent and the waters (like all in Almería) are warm and brilliantly clear.

Mojácar Pueblo

The upper village is linked to the coastal resort 2km below by a road which climbs from a prominent seafront junction called "El Cruce"; half-hourly buses also make the climb from here (summer 9am–11.30pm; €0.60). Arriving in the upper village, the **turismo** (Mon–Fri 10am–2pm & 5–8pm, Sat 10.30am–1.30pm; ☏950 615 025, ⓦwww.mojacarviva.com) is located just below the main square – you'll need their free **map** to negotiate the maze of narrow streets – with the **post office** in the same building and a convenient ATM **cash machine** next door. The village is more about atmosphere than sights and once you've cast an eye over the heavily-restored fifteenth-century church of **Santa María**, the main diversion is to wander the narrow streets with their flower-decked balconies and cascading bougainvillea, and call in at the numerous boutiques and bars.

If you want to stay here there are a handful of small **hostales**; try *Casa Justa*, c/Morote 5 (☏950 478 372; ❷), for pleasant rooms with and without bath, or the basic (and not much cheaper) *La Esquinica* on nearby c/Cano (☏950 475 009; ❷). The more upmarket but good-value *Mamabel's* at c/Embajadores 3 (☏ & ⓕ950 472 448, ⓦwww.mamabels.com; ❺) is the best of the fancier places, with beautiful en-suite rooms, some with stunning views.

For cheap **eats** up here, *Rincón de Embrujo*, on the plazuela fronting the church, does decent *platos combinados*, whilst the good, mid-priced restaurant of *Mamabel's* is worth a meal for its spectacular terrace views alone and has a great-value *menú* for €17 (including wine).

Mojácar Playa

The beach resort of **MOJÁCAR PLAYA** is a refreshingly brash alternative to the village above and caters to a mix of mainly Spanish tourists who fill its four-kilometre-long beach all summer. The busy road behind the strand is lined with hotels, restaurants and bars stretching away north and south of the main junction, *El Cruce*, marked by a large *centro comercial*. Just south of here, **Internet** access is available at *Internet*, Paseo del Mediterráneo 293 (Mon–Fri 9.30am–3pm & 5–11pm, Sat & Sun 11am–2pm & 6–11pm; ☏950 615 156). **Scooters** and **moto-cross bikes** can be rented from the same place.

There are plenty of **places to stay**, including rooms and a good **campsite**, *El Cantal de Mojácar* (☏950 478 204; open all year). Of the hotels, you could try the good-value, one-star *El Puntazo* (☏951 478 229, ⓕ951 478 285; ❸), which also has a pricier three-star extension, to the south of the *centro comercial* on the seafront. Nearby, *Hostal Bahía* (☏951 478 010; ❸) has rooms around a pleasant patio. The modern and rather dull *Parador Reyes Católicos* (☏950 478 250, ⓕ950 478 183; ❻) is set in a palm-tree landscape close to the beach.

Places to eat along the seafront are fairly dismal and standards tend to fall markedly in high season. For a decent no-frills **meal**, head for the *Cafetería Rosa*, facing the south side of the *centro comercial*. A good kilometre south of *El Cruce*, the seafront *Restaurante Bogavante*, Paseo Mediterráneo 85, facing the Playa de las Ventanicas, is a rare exception to the general dross and serves up a tasty *menú* on its terrace for €9. Other places worth a try on the seafront in this zone are the restaurant of *Hotel El Puntazo* (see opposite), and the nearby *Sal Marina*, attached to a hotel of the same name. Other restaurants and fast-food outlets, mostly of indifferent quality, are to be found all along the seafront, where after dark you'll also find plenty of **nightlife** in throbbing beach bars and *discotecas*. The sassiest of the discos is *Pascha*, easily tracked down at the foot of the strobe light it beams into the sky every night, and the beachfront *Goa*, near *El Cruce*, is similar.

La Garrucha

Five kilometres north from Mojácar, **LA GARRUCHA** is a lively, if modest, town and fishing harbour. It is in the process of development, with villas now thick on the ground and many more in the offing, but it does have a life of its own besides tourism. There are several expensive **hostales** – *Hostal-Restaurante Cortés*, Paseo Marítimo 200 (℡950 132 813; ❸), overlooking the promenade and excellent beach, is worth a try – but you're more likely to visit its reasonable beach as a good afternoon's break from Mojácar. There are also some fine fish **restaurants** around the fishing harbour; *El Almejero*, with its terrace actually fronting the quayside, is one of the best – if the fish landed don't meet their high standards, they don't open – and they have an equally excellent tapas bar, too.

Travel details

Trains

Algeciras to: Córdoba (2 daily; 4hr 30min); Granada (2 daily; 4hr–4hr 30min); Madrid (2 daily; 11hr or 6hr with AVE from Sevilla). All Algeciras northbound trains go via Ronda (1hr 45min) and Bobadilla.

Almería to: Granada (4 daily; 2hr 15min); Guadix (4 daily; 1hr 15min); Madrid (2 daily; 6hr 30min–10hr); Sevilla (3 daily; 5hr 30min).

Cádiz to: Córdoba (4 daily; 3hr); Madrid (AVE 2 daily; 5hr); Sevilla (12 daily; 1hr 50min).

Córdoba to: Algeciras (2 daily; 4hr 30min); Cádiz (4 daily; 3hr); Granada (2 daily; 3hr 20min); Jaén (1 daily; 1hr 30min); Madrid (13 daily, 4–6hr; AVE 14 daily, 1hr 45min); Málaga (2 daily; 3hr); Sevilla (6 daily, 1–2hr; AVE 16 daily, 45min).

Granada to: Algeciras (3 daily; 4hr 30min); Almería (4 daily; 2hr 15min); Antequera (7 daily; 1hr 30min); Córdoba (2 daily; 3hr 20min); Guadix (4 daily; 1hr 10min); Linares-Baeza (4 daily; 2hr 30min); Madrid (2 daily; 6–8hr); Málaga (2 daily; 3hr 30min); Ronda (3 daily; 2hr 30min); Sevilla (4 daily; 3hr); Valencia (3 daily; 8–10hr, 1 via Linares-Baeza).

Huelva to: Madrid (AVE 1 daily; 4hr 15min); Sevilla (3 daily; 1hr 30min); Zafra (2 daily; 4hr 30min).

Jaén to: Cádiz (1 daily; 4hr 30min); Córdoba (1 daily; 1hr 30min); Sevilla (1 daily; 2hr 50min).

Málaga to: Algeciras (3 daily; 2hr 30min); Córdoba (9 daily; 3hr 30min); Fuengirola (every 30min;

45min); Granada (1 daily; 2hr 30min); Madrid (5 daily; 6–8hr; AVE 5 daily; 4hr 10min); Ronda (3 daily; 1hr); Sevilla (5 daily; 2hr 15min–3hr 30min); Torremolinos (every 30min; 30min).

Sevilla to: Algeciras (2 daily; 4hr 30min); Badajoz (4 daily; 5–7hr); Cádiz (12 daily; 1hr 30min–2hr); Córdoba (6 daily, 1–2hr; AVE 17 daily, 45min); Granada (4 daily; 3hr); Huelva (3 daily; 1hr 30min); Madrid (at least 14 daily; AVE 2hr 15min or 6–9hr); Málaga (6 daily; 2hr 30min); Mérida (1 daily; 3hr 30min).

Buses

Algeciras to: Cádiz (10 daily; 2hr); La Línea (for Gibraltar; hourly; 30min); Madrid (4 daily; 6–8hr); Sevilla (5 daily; 3hr 15min); Tarifa (10 daily; 30min).

Almería to: Agua Amarga (1 daily; 1hr 15min); Alicante (2 daily; 7hr); Cabo de Gata/San José (10 daily; 30min/45min); Carboneras (3 daily; 1hr 15min); Córdoba (2 daily; 5–6hr); Granada (5 daily; 2hr 15min); Guadix (9 daily; 1hr 15min); Madrid (2 daily; 7hr 30min); Málaga (10 daily; 3hr 15min–4hr); Mojácar (6 daily; 1hr–1hr 45min); Níjar (1 daily; 45min); Sevilla (3 daily; 5–6hr); Tabernas (3 daily; 35min); Ugíjar (2 daily; 1hr 30min).

Cádiz to: Algeciras (10 daily; 2–2hr 30min); Arcos de la Frontera (5 daily; 1hr 30min); Chipiona (7 daily; 1hr 30min); Conil (14 daily; 1hr); Granada (2 daily;

8hr); Jerez de la Frontera (14 daily; 45min); Málaga (3 daily; 5hr); El Puerto de Santa María (15 daily; 40min); Sanlúcar de Barrameda (8 daily; 1hr 15min); Sevilla (12 daily; 1hr 30min); Tarifa (7 daily; 1hr 30min); Vejer de la Frontera (8 daily; 1hr 15min).

Córdoba to: Badajoz (1 daily; 6hr 30min); Écija (5 daily; 1hr 15min); Granada (8 daily; 2hr 30min); Jaén (7 daily; 1hr 30min); Málaga (5 daily; 2hr 30min); Madrid (6 daily; 4hr 30min); Sevilla (10 daily; 2hr 30min).

Granada to: Alicante (5 daily; 4hr 45min–6hr 45min); Almería (10 daily; 2hr 15min); Cádiz (2 daily; 5hr); Cazorla (2 daily; 1hr 30min); Córdoba (8 daily; 2hr 30min); Guadix (12 daily; 1hr 15min); Jaén (12 daily; 2hr); Madrid (9 daily; 5–6hr); Málaga (17 daily; 2hr); Mojácar (2 daily; 3hr 30min); Motril (9 daily; 1hr 30min); Ronda (3 daily; 3hr); Sevilla (9 daily; 3hr 30min–4hr 30min); Sierra Nevada/Alpujarras (5 daily to Lanjarón & Órgiva: 1hr; 2 daily to most of the other villages along most of the routes); Solynieve (2 daily; 45min); Valencia (5 daily; 7hr 30min); Úbeda/Baeza (7 daily; 2hr–3hr).

Huelva to: Aracena (2 daily; 1hr 30min); Ayamonte/Portuguese frontier (10 daily; 1hr); Granada (1 daily; 4hr); Isla Cristina (6 daily; 1hr); Matalascañas (6 daily; 1hr 15min); Moguer/Palos (12 daily; 45min); Punta Umbría (hourly; 30min); Sevilla (14 daily, 6 direct; 1hr 15min–1hr 45min).

Jaén to: Almería (2 daily; 4hr 30min); Baeza/Úbeda (14 daily; 1hr–1hr 30min); Cazorla (2 daily; 2hr); Córdoba (8 daily; 2hr); Granada (14 daily; 1hr 30min–2hr); Madrid (4 daily; 6hr); Málaga (4 daily; 4hr); Sevilla (3 daily; 5hr).

Jerez to: Algeciras (8 daily; 2hr); Arcos de la Frontera (17 daily; 40min); Cádiz (19 daily; 45min); Chipiona (7 daily; 40min); Córdoba (1 daily; 3hr 30min); Málaga (1 daily; 5hr); El Puerto de Santa María (12 daily; 30min); Ronda (4 daily; 2hr 30min–3hr); Sanlúcar de Barrameda (16 daily; 30min); Sevilla (6 daily; 1hr); Vejer de la Frontera (2 daily; 1hr 30min).

Málaga to: Algeciras (12 daily; 2hr 30min); Almería (8 daily; 4hr); Almuñécar (11 daily; 1hr 15min); Cádiz (5 daily; 4–5hr); Córdoba (5 daily;

2hr 30min); Fuengirola (every 40min; 45min); Gibraltar (stops at La Linea border; 4 daily; 2hr 30min); Granada (16 daily; 1hr 30min–2hr); Huelva (1 daily; 5hr); Jaén (3 daily; 4hr); Jerez (1 daily; 3hr); Madrid (7 daily; 6hr); Marbella (every 30min; 45min); Motril (10 daily; 1hr 30min); Nerja (14 daily; 1hr); Ronda (6 daily; 2hr); Salobreña (11 daily; 45min); Sevilla (10 daily; 2hr); Torremolinos (every 15min; 30min); Úbeda-Baeza (1 daily; 4hr).

Ronda to: Arcos de la Frontera (5 daily; 1hr 30min); Cádiz (5 daily; 3hr 30min); Grazalema (2 daily; 35min); Jerez (5 daily; 2hr 30min); Málaga (6 daily; 2hr) Olvera (1 daily; 30min); San Pedro de Alcántara (1hr 30min, continuing to Málaga); Setenil (2 daily; 20min); Sevilla (5 daily; 2hr 30min); Ubrique (2 daily; 45min).

Sevilla to: Albufeira, Portuguese Algarve (via Ayamonte and Faro; 2 daily; 2hr 30min); Algeciras (8 daily; 3hr 30min); Almería (3 daily; 6hr); Aracena (8 daily; 1hr 30min); Badajoz (2 daily via Zafra, 2 daily via Jerez de los Caballeros; 3hr 30min); Cádiz (9 daily; 1hr 30min–2hr 30min); Carmona (34 daily; 45min); Córdoba (12 daily; 1hr 45min–3hr 15min); Écija (11 daily; 1hr 15min); El Rocío (5 daily; 1hr 30min); Granada (10 daily; 3–4hr); Huelva (11 daily; 1hr 30min); Jerez (13 daily; 1hr); Madrid (14 daily; 5–8hr); Málaga (10 daily; 2hr); Matalascañas (5 daily; 2hr); Mérida (12 daily; 3hr 30min); Ronda (5 daily; 2hr 45min).

Ferries

Algeciras to: Ceuta (10 boats daily; 35min); Tangier (18 hourly boats daily; 2hr).

Almería to: Melilla (April–Sept daily; 6hr); Nador (April–Sept daily; 6hr).

Cádiz to: El Puerto de Santa María (4–6 daily; 45min); Las Palmas (every 2 days in season, every 5 out; 48hr); Tenerife (every 2 days in season, otherwise every 5; 36hr).

Gibraltar to: Tangier (1 weekly: Fri only at 6pm; 1hr).

Málaga to: Melilla (daily except Sun; 7hr).

Tarifa to: Tangier (2 daily catamaran ferries; 35min).

Old Castile and León

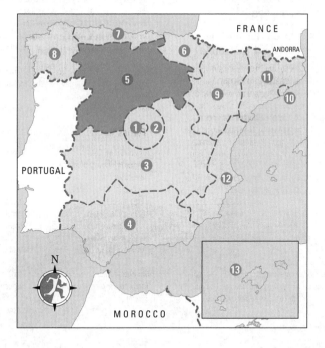

CHAPTER 5

Highlights

* **Salamanca** One of the most graceful and beautiful of Spanish cities. See p.415

* **La Alberca, Sierra Peña de Francia** Delightful village in the midst of the beautiful and rugged mountain range. See p.428

* **Museo Nacional de Escultura, Valladolid** The finest collection of sculpture in Spain. See p.438

* **A Gran Reserva from Ribera del Duero or La Rioja** A must when you are in the country's premier wine-growing area. See p.455

* **Burgos Cathedral** An extraordinary masterpiece of Gothic art. See p.460

* **Santo Domingo de Silos monastery** Mass sung by the monks is a moving and atmospheric experience. See p.463

* **The stained-glass windows in León cathedral** A stunning exhibition of medieval craftsmanship. See p.472

* **Las Médulas** The devastation wreaked by Roman gold mining created an eerily beautiful region. See p.478

△ Burgos Cathedral

Old Castile and León

The foundations of modern Spain were laid in the kingdom of Castile. A land of frontier fortresses – the castillos from which it takes its name – it became the most powerful and centralizing force of the Reconquest, extending its domination through military gains and marriage alliances. By the eleventh century it had merged with and swallowed León; through Isabel's marriage to Fernando in 1469 it encompassed Aragón, Catalunya and eventually the entire peninsula. The monarchs of this triumphant and expansionist age were enthusiastic patrons of the arts, endowing their cities with superlative monuments, above which, quite literally, tower the great Gothic cathedrals of Salamanca, León and Burgos.

Salamanca and **León** are the two outstanding highlights, ranking in interest and beauty alongside the other great cities of Spain, such as Toledo, Sevilla and Santiago. Try to take in some of the lesser towns, too, such as **Ciudad Rodrigo** and **El Burgo de Osma**, or the village of **Covarrubias**. In all of them you'll be struck by a wealth of mansions and churches incongruous with present, or even imagined past, circumstances and status. In the people, too, you may notice something of the classic Castilian *hidalgo* archetype – a certain haughty solemnity of manner and a dignified assumption of past nobility, however straitened present circumstances.

Although the Castilian soil is fertile, the harsh extremes of land and climate don't encourage rural settlement, and the vast central plateau – the 700- to 1000-metre-high *meseta* – is given over almost entirely to grain. Huge areas stretch into the horizon without a single landmark, not even a tree.

Surprisingly, however, the Duero River, which has the most extensive basin in Spain, runs right across the province and into Portugal. And despite being characterized by *meseta* landscape, there are enclaves of varied scenery – in particular, the **valley of Las Batuecas** and the lakeland of the **Sierra de Urbión**, where the Duero begins its course.

The sporadic and depopulated villages, bitterly cold in winter, burning hot in summer, are rarely of interest – travel consists of getting as quickly as you can from one grand town to the next. The problem with many of the smaller places, and even some of the larger ones, is that they have little appeal beyond their monuments: **Burgos** and **Valladolid**, for example, are important historically but the cities are unexciting in themselves. The most impressive of the castles are at **Coca**, **Gormaz** and **Berlanga de Duero**. The other architectural feature of the region is the host of Romanesque churches, monasteries and hermitages, a legacy of the **Camino de Santiago** (pilgrim route) which cuts across the top of the province.

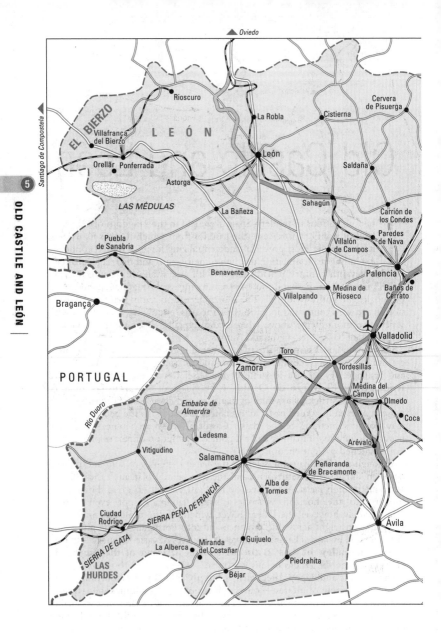

Technically, parts of the **Picos de Europa** lie in León province, and there are good approaches to the region from the south. However, this mountain range – with its superb villages, wildlife and treks – is covered in the chapter "Cantabria and Asturias" (see p.545), where its heartland lies.

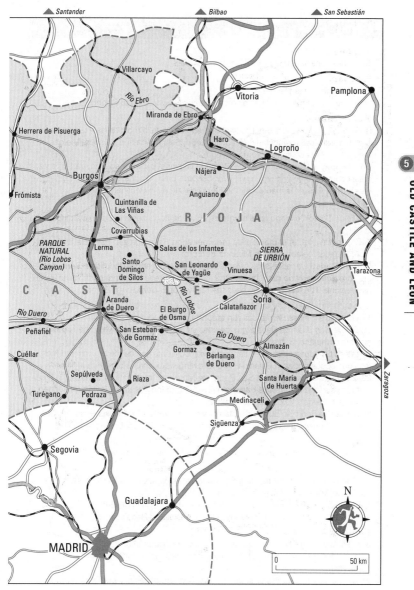

Fiestas

January
30 Processions in Burgos to honour *San Lesmes*.

February
3 *Romería* to Ciudad Rodrigo.
Week before Lent *Carnaval* is also particularly lively in Ciudad Rodrigo.

March/April
Holy Week is even more fanatically observed here than in most areas – processions in all the big cities, particularly Valladolid, León, Salamanca and Zamora. The one at Medina de Rioseco is also worth aiming for.
Good Friday in Bercanos de Aliste (Zamora) is almost chillingly solemn, participants dressed in white gowns which will later become their shrouds.
Week after Easter is marked by the *Fiesta del Ángel* in Peñafiel.

May
12 *Día de Santo Domingo* is celebrated with a traditional fiesta in Santo Domingo de la Calzada.
Pentecost (variable) is marked by the week-long *Feria Chica* in Palencia and with more religious celebrations in Miranda de Ebro.
Corpus Christi (variable) sees celebrations in Palencia and Valladolid; in Benavente the *Toro Enmaromado* runs through the streets in the evening, endangering the lives of everyone. The following day sees the festival of *El Curpillos* in Burgos.

June
11 Logroño's *Fiestas Bernabeas* run around this date.
12 *Día de San Juan de Sahagún* is celebrated in Salamanca (of which he is patron) and his birthplace, Sahagún.
24 *Día de San Juan* sees a secular fiesta with bullfights and dance in León and more religious observances in Palencia. The following week sees a big fiesta in Soria.
23–26 *Fiesta de San Juan* at San Pedro de Manrique (northeast of Soria) – the first night opens with the famous barefoot firewalking of the *Paseo del Fuego*, described in Norman Lewis's *Voices of the Old Sea*.
29 *Día de San Pedro*. In Burgos the start of a two-week-long *feria*; lesser events in León, and in Haro there's the drunken *Batalla del Vino* celebrating local wine production.

July
22 In Anguiano performance of the famous stilt dance – *danza de los zancos*.

August
15 Colourful festivals for the Assumption in La Alberca, Coca and Peñafiel.
16 *Día de San Roque* fiesta in El Burgo de Osma.
Last week *Fiesta de San Agustín* in Toro, with the "fountain of wine" and *encierros*, and in Medinaceli, musical evenings with medieval and Renaissance music.

September
8 A big day everywhere – the first day of Salamanca's major fiesta, beginning the evening before and lasting two weeks, as well as a famous bull running in Tordesillas.
21 *Día de San Mateo*. Major *ferias* in Valladolid and especially Logroño, where the Rioja harvest is celebrated.

October
First Sun *Fiesta de las Cantaderas* in León.
Valladolid's *International Film Week* also falls in October.

November
13 The *Toro Júbilo* runs through the streets of Medinaceli on the night of the nearest Saturday.

Southern Old Castile: Salamanca to Soria

This first part of the chapter follows a route across **Southern Old Castile**, from west to east, starting at Salamanca and covering the provinces of Salamanca, Zamora, Valladolid, Palencia, the northern part of Segovia and Soria. From Zamora on, it follows the path of the **Río Duero** with its plethora of magnificent castles, to the crags and lakes of the wild Sierra de Urbión beyond Soria. Most of this region is well covered by **bus** and **train** routes, with Salamanca, in particular, a nexus of transport with links to all the region's major cities and beyond.

Salamanca and around

SALAMANCA is the most graceful city in Spain. For four centuries it was the seat of one of the most prestigious universities in the world and, despite losing this reputation in the seventeenth century, the atmosphere is still dominated by its seat of learning. It's still a small place, and is given a gorgeous harmony by the golden sandstone from which almost the entire city is constructed.

Two great architectural styles were developed, and see their finest expression, in Salamanca. **Churrigueresque** takes its name from José Churriguera (1665–1723), the dominant member of a prodigiously creative family. Best known for their huge, flamboyant altarpieces, they were particularly active around Salamanca. The style is an especially ornate form of Baroque, long frowned upon by art historians from a north European, Protestant tradition. **Plateresque** came earlier, a decorative technique of shallow relief and intricate detail named for its resemblance to the art of the silversmith (*platero*); Salamanca's native sandstone, soft and easy to carve, played a significant role in its development. Plateresque art cuts across Gothic and Renaissance frontiers – the decorative motifs of the university, for example, are taken from the Italian Renaissance but the facade of the New Cathedral is Gothic in inspiration.

Arrival and information

The compact **old centre** of Salamanca, with the **Plaza Mayor** at its heart, spreads back from the Río Tormes, bounded by a loop of avenues and *paseos*. The **bus and train stations** are on opposite sides of the city, each about fifteen minutes' walk from the centre. From the bus station at Avda. de Filiberto Villalobos 73–83 simply turn right and keep going straight until you find yourself in the Plaza Mayor. If you've arrived by train, go left down the Paseo de la Estación and you'll reach Plaza de España, from where c/Toro leads to the Plaza Mayor; alternatively, take bus #1 from the station to Plaza del Mercado, right next to the Plaza Mayor.

The main city **turismo** (summer Mon–Sat 9am–2pm & 4.30–8pm, Sun 9am–2pm & 4.30–6.30pm, winter closes at 6pm; ☎923 218 342,

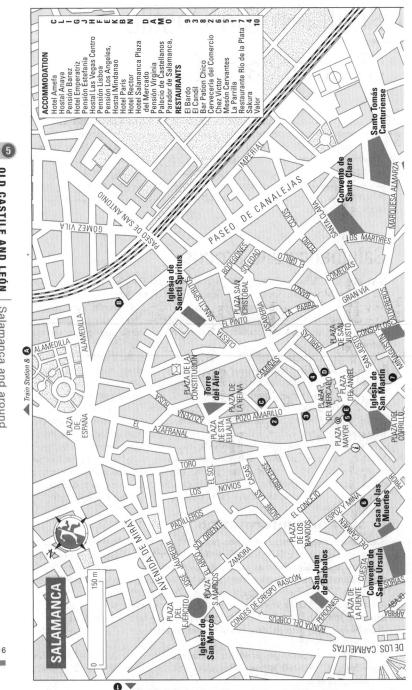

SALAMANCA

0   150 m

ACCOMMODATION
Hotel Amefa	C
Hostal Anaya	L
Pensión Barez	I
Hotel Emperatriz	G
Pensión Estefania	J
Hostal Las Vegas Centro	H
Pensión Lisboa	F
Pensión Los Angeles,	E
Hostal Mindanao	K
Hotel París	B
Hotel Rector	N
Hotel Salamanca Plaza	
del Mercado	D
Pensión Virginia	A
Palacio de Castellanos	M
Parador de Salamanca,	O

RESTAURANTS
El Bardo	9
El Candil	3
Bar Pation Chico	8
Cervecería del Comercio	2
Chez Victor	6
Mesón Cervantes	5
La Parrilla	1
Restaurante Río de la Plata	4
Sakura	7
Valor	10

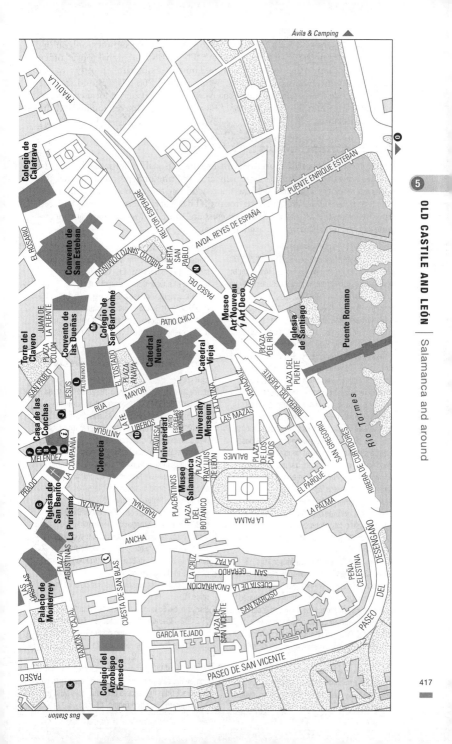

Ávila & Camping ▲

Bus Station ▼

417

Colegio de
Calatrava

Convento de
San Esteban

PUENTE ENRIQUE ESTEBAN

AVDA. REYES DE ESPAÑA

PUERTA
SAN PABLO

Ⓝ

Museo
Art Nouveau
y Art Déco

PLAZA
DEL RIO

Iglesia
de Santiago

Puente Romano

Río Tormes

Torre del
Clavero

PLAZA
COLÓN

Convento
de las Dueñas

Colegio de
San Bartolomé

PATIO CHICO

Catedral
Nueva

Catedral
Vieja

PLAZA
DEL PUENTE

PLAZA
ANAYA

RIBERA DEL PUENTE

SAN GREGORIO

RIBERA DE CURTIDORES

EL ROSARIO

PRADILLA

JUAN DE
LA FUENTE

SAN PABLO

JESÚS

PALOMINOS

RÚA

LA FE

MAYOR

EL TOSTADO

LIBEROS

Casa de las
Conchas

Ⓙ

ⓘ

Ⓕ
Ⓗ
Ⓘ
Ⓘ
Ⓘ
Ⓘ

MELÉNDEZ

Ⓜ

Clerecía

ANTIGUA

TRAVIESA

Universidad

Ⓘ⓪

University
Museum

LAS MAZAS

LA LATINA

VERACRUZ

PLAZA
DE LOS
CAÍDOS

BALMES

EL PARQUE

LA PALMA

PLAZA
FRAY LUIS
DE LEÓN

Museo
Salamanca

PLACENTINOS

RABANAL

CANIZAL

LA COMPAÑÍA

PRADO

Ⓖ

Iglesia de
San Benito
La Purísima

PLAZA
AGUSTINAS

Ⓛ

CUESTA DE SAN BLAS

ANCHA

PLAZA
DEL
BOTÁNICO

LA PALMA

ARROYO SANTO DOMINGO

RECTOR ESPERABE

PASEO DEL

PLAZA
DE SAN VICENTE

GARCÍA TEJADO

PASEO DE SAN VICENTE

CUESTA DE LA ENCARNACIÓN

SAN NARCISO

SAN
GERARDO

LA CRUZ

LA PAZ

PEÑA
CELESTINA

DESENGAÑO

DEL

PASEO

Ⓚ

Colegio del
Arzobispo
Fonseca

Palacio de
Monterrey

LAS
ÚRSULAS

RAMÓN Y CAJAL

PASEO

Ⓞ

▶

ⓦ www.salamanca.es) is on the Plaza Mayor, and there are summer-only information booths at the train and bus stations. There's also a regional tourist office for Salamanca province (summer Mon–Thurs & Sun 9am–8pm, Fri & Sat 9am–9pm; winter daily 9am–2pm & 5–8pm; ☎ 923 268 571) around the side of the Casa de las Conchas, facing Rúa Mayor. Information on local events can be found in a monthly guide, *Ciudad Viva*, free from bars, restaurants and the city tourist office.

Accommodation

Prices for **accommodation** in Salamanca are reasonable, but it can be hard to find a room in high season – especially at fiesta time in September. During the summer months you may well be approached at the train or bus station and offered *casas particulares* (private rooms). These are often the lowest-priced options available as many of the *pensiones* are more or less permanently occupied by students during the academic year.

Budget options

Hostal Anaya c/Jesus 22 ☎ & ⓕ 923 271 773. Mid-range *hostal* excellently located in a quiet but very central side street, with ten neat and airy en-suite rooms. ②

Pensión Barez c/Meléndez 19, 1° ☎ 923 217 495. Cheaper than most of its competitors, this plain but clean *pensión* has singles, doubles and triples with simple wooden furniture. ①

Pensión Estefanía c/Jesús 3–5 ☎ 923 217 372. Brave one of Salamanca's dingiest staircases to reach this cheap and clean *pensión*, centrally located on a relatively quiet side street very close to the Casa de las Conchas. Rooms are a bit gloomy, though most have small balconies. ①

Hostal Las Vegas Centro c/Meléndez 13 ☎ 923 218 749, ⓦ www.lasvegascentro.com. Choose from a range of large, light doubles, triples and quadruples, all with private bathrooms, in this attractive, plant-filled flat on one of the old city's most vibrant streets. ②

Pensión Lisboa c/Meléndez 1, 2° ☎ 923 214 333. Serviceable *pensión* overlooking one of the liveliest squares in the city. Rooms – some en suite – are good value, though those facing the street can be a bit noisy. ②

Pensión Los Angeles Plaza Mayor 10 ☎ & ⓕ 923 218 166. Friendly, no-frills *pensión* with four basic en-suite rooms boasting stunning views over the Plaza Mayor, plus another five shared-bath doubles with good views over the old city. ②

Hostal Mindanao Paseo de San Vicente 2 ☎ & ⓕ 923 263 080. Large, modern *hostal* with comfortable en-suite rooms, situated just outside the old city, a 10min walk from the Plaza Mayor. A decent budget alternative to the old-city *pensiones* if you don't mind the rather uninspiring setting next to a busy main road – try to get an inward-facing room. ①

Hotel París c/Padilla 1–5 ☎ & ⓕ 923 262 970. Thirteen plush a/c rooms in the modern town on the way to the train station – good value, though it's a bit of a walk from the sights. ②

Pensión Virginia Paseo de la Estación 109–115 ☎ 923 241 016. A well-run *pensión*, right in front of the train station – convenient if you've a train to catch, though quite a way from the city centre. ②

Moderate and expensive options

Hotel Amefa c/Pozo Amarillo 18–20 ☎ 923 218 189, ⓕ 923 260 200. Understated, good-quality hotel in an extremely central location, even if it's on one of old Salamanca's least scenic roads. ④

Hotel Emperatriz c/Compañía 44 ☎ 923 219 200, ⓦ www.emperatrizhotel.com. Two-star hotel in a beautiful old mansion on a lovely pedestrianized Salamantine street. Rooms are comfortable enough, and good value, even if they don't quite live up to the historic setting. ③

Palacio de Castellanos c/San Pablo 58–64 ☎ 923 261 818, ⓔ nhpalaciodecastellanos@nh-hotels.com. Opulent, marbled four-star hotel set in a fifteenth-century palace facing the Convento de San Esteban. The entrance area – a glassed-in Renaissance cloister converted into a drawing room – is stunning, as it should be for this price. ⑦

Parador de Salamanca Toso de Feria 2 ☎ 923 192 082, ⓔ salamanca@parador.es. Modern building with swimming pool and great views, situated just across the Puente Romano. ⑦

Hotel Rector Paseo del Rector Esperabé 10 ☎ & ⓕ 923 218 482, ⓦ www.hotelrector.com. The setting by the side of a dusty main road does nothing to detract from this superb boutique hotel with just 14 gorgeously outfitted rooms. ⑥

Hotel Salamanca Plaza del Mercado ☎923 272 250, ⓦwww.salamancaplaza.com. This recently renovated hotel has bright, airy, nicely-furnished rooms (ask for one of the larger ones) with comfy chairs, big windows and spotless bathrooms. ❺

Camping

Camping Regio ☎923 138 888, ⓦwww .campingregio.com. Salamanca's excellent campsite is open all year round, 4km along the Ávila road behind the *Hotel Regio*.

The City

Salamanca boasts a seemingly endless wealth of architectural sights: it has two **cathedrals**, one Gothic and the other Romanesque, which vie for attention with stately Renaissance **palaces** embellished with fabulous Plateresque decoration. It is also home to the most elegant **Plaza Mayor** in Spain, while the surviving university buildings are tremendous throughout. The city's beauty stems in part from the warm golden sandstone, known as Villamayor, with which its finest buildings were constructed.

The Plaza Mayor and around

The grand **Plaza Mayor** is the hub of Salamantine life; its bare central expanse, in which bullfights were staged as late as 1863, is enclosed by a continuous four-storey building, broken only by the grand, three-storey *ayuntamiento* on its northern side. Decorated with iron balconies and medallion portraits, including a much-abused image of General Franco in the northeast corner, the building was the work of Andrea García Quiñones and Alberto Churriguera, younger brother of José, and nowhere is the Churrigueras' inspired variation of Baroque so refined as here.

Leave Plaza Mayor via the southwest corner, past the Romanesque Iglesia de San Martín, and walk straight down c/Meléndez to reach the **Universidad Pontifícia** (Tues–Fri 10.30am–1.30pm & 5–7.30pm, Sat 10am–noon & 2–5pm, Sun 10am–2pm; obligatory Spanish-only guided tours lasting half an hour set off every 50mins; €1.50), founded in 1614, which specializes in journalism, medicine and training for the priesthood. The tour starts at a magnificent stone staircase that seems to hang suspended in the air. The visit also takes in the richly decorated Aula Magna, where ceremonial events take place, and a grandiose Baroque courtyard that looks a little like a miniature version of the Plaza Mayor, around the upper level of which Jesuit priests walked meditational circuits, believing themselves to be physically closer to heaven at such a height. The tour ends in the vast Baroque church of **La Clerecía** next door to the university.

Opposite stands the city's most distinctive (and photographed) building, the early sixteenth-century mansion, **Casa de las Conchas** (House of Shells), named after the rows of carved scallop shells, symbol of the pilgrimage to Santiago, which decorate its facade. It's worth popping into the courtyard (summer Mon–Fri 9am–9pm, Sat 9am–2pm & 5–8pm, Sun 10am–2pm & 4–8pm; winter Mon–Fri 9am–9pm, Sat 9am–2pm & 4–7pm, Sun 10am–2pm & 4–7pm; free), a quaint mishmash of Gothic and Renaissance elements with a good view of La Clerecía from the upper storey.

The University and around

From the Casa de las Conchas, turn right onto Rua Antigua then left along c/de los Libreros to reach the **Universidad Civil** (Mon–Sat 9.30am–1pm & 4–7pm, Sun 9.30am–1pm; €1.80). The ultimate expression of Plateresque, the **facade** is covered with medallions, heraldic emblems and a profusion of floral decorations, amid which lurks a hidden frog said to bring good luck and

The university at Salamanca

Salamanca University was founded by Alfonso IX in the 1220s, and after the union of Castile and León swallowed up the University of Palencia to become the most important in Spain. Its rise to international stature was phenomenal and within thirty years Pope Alexander IV proclaimed it equal to the greatest universities of the day. As at Oxford, Paris and Bologna, theories formulated here were later accepted as fact throughout Europe. It made major contributions to the development of international law, and Columbus sought support for his voyages of discovery from the enlightened faculty of astronomy. The university continued to flourish under the Reyes Católicos, even employing a pioneering woman professor, Beatriz de Galindo, who tutored Queen Isabel in Latin. In the sixteenth century it was powerful enough to resist the orthodoxy of Felipe II's Inquisition but, eventually, freedom of thought was stifled by the extreme clericalism of the seventeenth and eighteenth centuries. Books were banned for being a threat to the Catholic faith, and mathematics and medicine disappeared from the curriculum. Decline was hastened during the Peninsular War when the French demolished 20 of the 25 colleges, and by the end of the nineteenth century there were no more than 300 students.

Today, although socially prestigious, Salamanca University ranks low academically, well behind Madrid, Barcelona and Sevilla. It does, however, run a highly successful language school – nowhere else in Spain will you see so many young Americans.

marriage within the year to anyone who spots it unaided. The centre is occupied by a portrait of Isabel and Fernando, surrounded by a Greek inscription commemorating their devotion to the university; above them is the coat of arms of Carlos V, grandson and successor of Isabel.

Inside, the old **lecture rooms**, surprisingly small for a seat of learning that once boasted over 7000 students, are arranged round a courtyard. The **Aula Fray Luís de León**, on the left side of the ground floor, preserves the rugged original benches and the pulpit where this celebrated professor lectured. In 1573, the Inquisition muscled its way into the room and arrested Fray Luís for alleged subversion of the faith; five years of torture and imprisonment followed, but upon his release he calmly resumed his lecture with the words "*Dicebamus hesterna die...*" ("As we were saying yesterday...").

The remainder of the heavily restored lower floor has surprisingly little to show for its illustrious past. An elegant Plateresque stairway leads to the upper floor, where you'll find a section of fanciful Moorish *techumbre* ceiling and, next to it, the old university **library**, stuffed with thousands of antiquated books on wooden shelves and huge globes of the world, whose faded magnificence gives some idea of Renaissance Salamanca's academic splendour.

Facing the university entrance is the **Patio de las Escuelas**, a tiny square surrounded by further university buildings. At the back of the square, an arch leads through to the pretty Renaissance courtyard of the **Escuelas Menores**, which served as a kind of preparatory school for the university proper. On the far side of this courtyard, the **University Museum** (Mon–Sat noon–2pm & 5.30–8.30pm, Sun noon–2pm; free) has a fine zodiacal ceiling, moved here from the chapel after two-thirds of it was destroyed by tremors from the 1755 Lisbon earthquake.

Just behind the Patio de las Escuelas Menores (walk left down Traviesa then left again to the Plaza del Fray Luís de León), the **Museo Salamanca**, also known as the Museo de Bellas Artes (Tues–Sat 10am–2pm & 5–8pm, Sun 10am–2pm; €1.20), occupies an exquisite fifteenth-century mansion – originally the home of Isabel's personal physician – which is at least as interesting as the mildly diverting collection of Spanish religious paintings and sculpture contained within it.

The cathedrals

The **Catedral Nueva** (daily: April–Sept 9am–8pm; Oct–March 10am–1pm & 4–6pm; free) was begun in 1512 as a declaration of Salamanca's prestige, and was a glorious last-minute assertion of Gothic architecture. It was built within a few yards of the university and acted as a buttress for the Old Cathedral, which was in danger of collapsing. The main Gothic-Plateresque entrance is contemporary with that of the university and equally dazzling in its wealth of ornamental detail, while the doorways on the north side facing Plaza de Anaya are scarcely less fine. For financial reasons, construction spanned two centuries and thus the building incorporates a range of styles, with some Renaissance and Baroque elements and a tower modelled on that of the cathedral at Toledo; stand under the dome to see the transition from Gothic at the bottom to late Baroque at the top. Alberto Churriguera and his brother José both worked here – the former on the choir stalls, the latter on the dome.

The Romanesque **Catedral Vieja** (daily: April–Sept 10am–7.30pm; Oct–March 10am–12.30pm & 4–5.30pm; €3) is dwarfed by its neighbour, through which it's also entered. Its most striking feature is the massive fifteenth-century *retablo* by Nicolás Florentino: 53 paintings of the lives of the Virgin and Christ surmounted by a powerfully apocalyptic portrayal of the Last Judgement. A thirteenth-century fresco on the same theme is hidden away in the **Capilla de San Martín** at the back of the building. Close by is the entrance to the **Torre Mocha** (same opening hours as the cathedral; €2) which you can climb for outstanding views over the city and out to the water meadows of the Río Tormes.

The chapels opening off the cloisters were used as university lecture rooms until the sixteenth century. One, the **Capilla de Obispo Diego de Anaya**, contains the oldest organ in Europe (mid-fourteenth century); the instrument shows Moorish influence and, in the words of Sacheverell Sitwell, "is one of the most romantic, poetical objects imaginable". In the Chapter House there's a small **museum** with a fine collection of works by Fernando Gallego, Salamanca's most famous painter. Active in the late fifteenth century, he was a brilliant and conscious imitator of early northern Renaissance artists such as Rogier van der Weyden.

Outside, the cathedral's most distinctive feature is its *media naranja* dome, known as the **Torre de Gallo** (Cock Tower) on account of its rooster-shaped weathervane. Shaped like the segments of an orange, the dome derives from Byzantine models and is similar to those at Zamora and Toro; there's a good view of it from Patio Chico around the back of the cathedrals.

The Art Nouveau Museum and Puente Romano

Right behind the Old Cathedral stands Salamanca's quirkiest museum, the **Museo Art Nouveau y Art Deco** (April to mid-Oct: Tues–Fri 11am–2pm & 5–9pm, Sat & Sun 11am–9pm; mid-Oct to March: Tues–Sun 11am–2pm & 4–7pm; €2.10). The development of these two, closely linked, movements – Art Nouveau and Art Deco – from the *belle époque* years at the turn of the twentieth century through to the 1930s, is illustrated here by a miscellany of objects including paintings, bronze statues, porcelain figures, lamps, vases, jewellery and furniture. Among the notable exhibits are the glass vases and lamps created by Emile Gallé (Room 5), one of the most eminent Art Nouveau artists; the famous scent bottles René Lalique designed for Guerlain and Worth (Room 4); and Hagenauer's highly stylized and instantly recognizable carved figures (Room 13). The chief attraction, however, is the building itself, the Casa Lis, which was built for an Art Nouveau enthusiast at the turn of the twentieth century and appears to be half-constructed from amazing, vibrantly painted glass.

Just south of the Casa Lis, the Rio Tormes is straddled by the majestic **Puente Romano** (Roman Bridge), some 400m long, from where there's a stunning panoramic view of the old city up on the hill above. The fifteen arches nearest to the city are originals, while the others have been rebuilt over the centuries.

West of the Plaza Mayor

There's another swathe of impressive buildings west of the Plaza Mayor. Following Calle de la Compañía from the Casa de las Conchas takes you past the rather severe Iglesia de San Benito, with some fine Renaissance mansions on the tiny plaza behind, before reaching the Plaza Agustinas. In front is the large **Palacio de Monterrey**, a sixteenth-century construction with end towers, unfortunately not seen to best advantage in the narrow street. Across from it is the seventeenth-century Augustinian monastery usually called **La Purísima**, for which Ribera painted several fine altarpieces, including the main "Immaculate Conception".

Behind the Palacio de Monterrey there's another interesting convent, **Convento de Santa Ursula** (daily 11am–1pm & 4.30–6pm; €2), a tall, plain structure recognizable by its unusual open-topped tower; its church contains the superb marble tomb of Archbishop Alonso Fonseca by Diego de Siloé. Facing the east wall of this church is the impressive Plateresque facade of the **Casa de las Muertes** (House of the Dead), the mansion of leading Salamantine architect Juan de Álava, named after the four skulls at the base of the upper windows.

West from Las Ursulas across a small park, c/de Fonseca leads to the magnificent Plateresque **Colegio del Arzobispo Fonseca** (daily 10am–2pm & 4–7pm; €1, free Mon am), a corporate work by many of the leading figures of Spanish architecture in the early sixteenth century, including Diego de Siloé (who designed the facade, an unusually restrained affair for the period) and Juan de Álava. The two-storey Renaissance cloister is particularly fine, with beautifully carved portrait medallions, each distinctly characterized, while the chapel contains a fine *retablo* with paintings and sculptures by Alonso Berruguete.

San Esteban, Santa Clara and around

Just east of the New Cathedral, the facade of the **Convento de San Esteban** (daily: summer 9.45am–1.30pm & 4–7.30pm; winter 9.30am–1.30pm & 4–6pm; €1.50) is another faultless example of Plateresque art, covered in a tapestry of sculpture, the central panel of which depicts the stoning of its patron saint, St Stephen. The east end of the church is occupied by a huge Baroque *retablo* by José Churriguera, a lavish concoction of columns, statuary and floral decoration. The monastery's cloisters, through which you enter, are magnificent too.

The most beautiful cloisters in the city, however, stand across the road in the **Convento de las Dueñas** (daily: summer 10.30am–1pm & 4.30–7pm, winter closes 5.30pm; €1.20). Built on an irregular pentagonal plan in the Renaissance-Plateresque style of the early sixteenth century, the imaginative upper-storey capitals are wildly carved with human heads and skulls. To supplement their income, the nuns sell boxes of divinely crumbly almond pastries from a booth next to the entrance. On the opposite side of San Esteban stands the **Colegio de Calatrava**, a large and rather sober structure designed by José Churriguera. It's occasionally open for temporary exhibitions.

Just north of here is the thirteenth-century **Convento de Santa Clara** (Mon–Fri 9.30am–1.40pm & 4–6.40pm, Sat & Sun 9am–2.40pm; €1.20), outwardly plain but with a beautiful interior which encompasses virtually every important feature of Spanish architecture and design. In 1976 the walls of the chapel, whitewashed during a long-forgotten cholera epidemic, were found to be decorated with an important series of frescoes from the thirteenth to the eighteenth century, while further probing of the ceiling revealed medallions similar to those in the Plaza Mayor. Romanesque and Gothic columns, and a stunning sixteenth-century polychrome ceiling, were also uncovered in the cloister. But the most incredible discovery was made in the church, where the Baroque ceiling constructed by Joaquín Churriguera was found to be false; rising above this, you can see the original fourteenth-century beams, decorated with heraldic motifs of the kingdoms of Castile and León. The prize-winning restoration is fascinating, and the icing on the cake is perhaps the city's best view of the New Cathedral.

From Santa Clara, head west to reach the **Torre de Clavero**, a fifteenth-century octagonal tower with quaint Gothic pepperpot turrets. Its precise function remains obscure, though it was probably attached to a (now-vanished) mansion.

Eating, drinking and nightlife

Salamanca is a great place for hanging out in bars and cafés. Those in the Plaza Mayor are nearly twice the usual price but worth every euro. Close at hand in the Plaza del Mercado (by the **market**, itself a good source of provisions), there's a row of lively **tapas bars**. Just south of Plaza Mayor, the adjacent c/Meléndez and Rua Mayor are packed with **bars** and **restaurants**, with tables set out in the pedestrianized streets; Plaza Corilla, where the two streets join, is particularly lively.

It is well worth the fifteen-minute walk north from the old city to sample the delights on offer in c/Van Dyck where many of Salamanca's finest tapas bars, each with its own speciality, are located. There is another good, more budget-oriented, selection of places to eat and drink around the university area, particularly along the streets between the Casa de las Conchas and the Museo Salamanca.

El Bardo c/Compañía 8. Good-value restaurant next to the Casa de las Conchas, with a lively bar attached. *Menús* go for around €10, and there's often a vegetarian option.

El Candil c/Ruiz Aguilera 14–16. Sedate old Salamantine restaurant with pricey but excellent Castilian dishes including regional specialities such as roast suckling lamb (*lechazo asado*) and suckling pig (*cochinillo*).

Bar Pation Chico c/Meléndez 13. Buzzing bar-restaurant serving tasty Spanish staples at reasonable prices.

Cervecería del Comercio c/Pozo Amarillo 23. Gorgeous tiled bar decorated with bullfighting photos and Salamanca's largest collection of used beer cans conceals this relaxed restaurant serving moderately priced Castilian meat and fish dishes.

Chez Victor c/Espoz y Mina 26. Upmarket French-influenced restaurant specializing in game. Reckoned to be Salamanca's finest. Closed Sun night, Mon & Aug.

Mesón Cervantes Plaza Mayor 15. Pleasant, rustic upstairs bar-restaurant in a prime position overlooking the Plaza Mayor – it's worth arriving early to get a window seat – with cheap, basic *platos combinados* from around €6 and more sophisticated *raciones*.

La Parrilla c/Van Dyck 55–57. Known for its unbeatable *pincho moruno*, this is one of several excellent tapas bars on this popular street.

Restaurante Río de la Plata Plaza Peso 1. Quality Castilian home cooking with a long menu of meat and fish dishes ranging from *lomo de cerdo* (€8) to *chateaubriand de ternera* (€15), a few vegetarian options plus an enticing wine list. Closed Mon & July.

Sakura Plaza del Mercado 14. Stylish restaurant specializing in Japanese and Chinese cuisine. An abundance of tempura and stir-fried vegetables will delight anyone in search of greens, while sushi and sashimi fans will be in raw fish heaven.

Valor Libreros 14. This Art Deco-style café does wonderful breakfasts with more than a hint of French sophistication. Later in the day indulge in fabulous home-made pastries, ice creams and *Valor*'s speciality – wickedly rich dark chocolate.

Nightlife

The presence of so many local and foreign students and tourists makes Salamanca easily the liveliest city in Old Castile. There's a whole host of student-oriented **bars and clubs** in the rectangle of streets on the southeast edge of the old town formed by Grand Vía, c/Calderos, c/Consuelo and c/Varillos. Those along Gran Vía, such as *El Gran Café Moderno* at no. 75 (with an excellent DJ and live sets), are better established, while those in the other streets tend to be impromptu student hang-outs with dodgy paint jobs and raucous music. Just over Grand Vía at c/San Justo 27, the mainly gay *De Laval Genovés*, popularly known as "Submarino" due to its nautical decor (look for the ships' lanterns outside the discreet entrance), plays good music, has three bars and stays open until 5am. Back in the old town, *Camelot*, near the convent of Las Ursulas on c/Bordadores, is popular with the town's many language students.

There are also many laid-back **cafés** where you can hear live music: try *El Corrillo* in Plaza San Benito for jazz, or *El Callejón*, Gran Vía 68, for folk. Also good for folk is the excellent *Country Bar* at c/Juan de Almeida 5 (round the corner from *El Gran Café Moderno*). There's no sign anywhere, just an unpromising black door, but downstairs you'll find a small, atmospheric tavern covered wall-to-wall in beautiful, swirling mosaics (the owner is a Gaudí fanatic).

Listings

Bookshops Librería Portonaris, Rúa Mayor 35 (Mon–Fri 10am–2pm & 5–8pm, Sat 10am–2pm) has a reasonable selection of English-language books and some titles in other European languages. Alternatively, try Cervantes, Plaza de Santa Eulalia 13 (Mon–Fri 10am–1.30pm & 6.30–8pm, Sat 10am–2pm), not to be confused with the original Cervantes bookshop just round the corner on c/Azafranel, which stocks a meagre range of English-language books.

Bus information ☎923 236 717.

Car rental Major operators include Avis, Paseo de Canalejas 49 ☎923 269 753; Europcar, Paseo de Canalejas 123 ☎923 269 041; Eurodollar-Atesa, Avda. de Comuneros 30 ☎923 249 901; Goyacar, Paseo Dr Torres Villarroel 49 ☎923 233 526; and Hertz, Avda. de Portugal 131 ☎923 243 134.

Internet access *Ciberplace*, Plaza Mayor 10, underneath Pensión Los Angeles (daily 10.30am–2am; €0.75 for 30min, €1.20 for 1hr; prices drop by a third after 9pm).

Language courses Spanish language courses are big business in Salamanca, and the following is only a small selection: Colegio de España, c/Compañía 65 ☎923 214 788, ☏923 218 791; Colegio de Estudios Hispanicos, c/Bordadores 1 ☎923 214 837, ☜www.cehispanic.com; Cursos

Internacionales de la Universidad de Salamanca, Patio de Escuelas Menores ☎923 294 418, ☏923 294 504; ISLA, Plaza de los Basilios, 8 ☎923 210 394, ✉salamanca@academiaisla.com.

Laundry The nearest laundries to the centre are Lavandería Sol at Cuesta del Carmen 10 (Mon–Fri 9am–2pm & 5–8pm, Sat 9am–2pm), which also offers dry cleaning, and Coin Laundry at Pasaje Azafranal 19, off c/ Azafranal (daily: summer 10am–8pm; winter 9.30am–2pm & 4–8pm; a wash costs €3.15 including powder, drying costs the same again). There is an Internet café out the back (€1.50/hour) so you can check your email while you wait.

Post office The main *Correos* is at Gran Vía 25 (Mon–Fri 8.30am–8.30pm, Sat 9.30am–2pm).

Swimming pool To cool down after a hard day's sightseeing head for the enormous open-air Piscina San José, a 20min walk from the centre on the south side of the river next to the Puente Príncipe de Asturias (June–Sept daily 11am–9pm; €2.23). There's a children's pool, café and a grassy sunbathing area.

Taxis There are two 24-hour companies: Radio Tele-Taxi ☎923 250 000 and Radio Taxi ☎923 271 111.

Train information ☎923 120 202.

Around Salamanca

The countryside around Salamanca is an attractive swathe of New Castile, particularly along the Río Tormes, which flows into the Duero to the northwest. The small hillside town of **ALBA DE TORMES**, 20km southeast of Salamanca and connected to it by regular bus (16 daily; 30min), makes an interesting day's excursion. The main attraction here is the **Convento de Carmelitas** (daily 9am–1.30pm & 4–6.30pm, Oct–April closes 7.30pm; free), founded by Santa Teresa in 1571, with an ornate Renaissance facade and a rather dubious reconstruction of the cell in which Teresa died. Alba is a centre for making traditional Castilian **pottery**, and you can watch its manufacture at Bernardo Pérez Correas on c/Matadero near the river. If you want to **stay the night**, the *Hostal América*, across the bridge on c/La Guía (☎923 300 071, ℗923 300 346; ❷), has decent en-suite rooms or, for something more central, the friendly *El Trébol*, on Plaza Santa Teresa (☎923 300 089; ❶), above a bar-restaurant, is a good option.

In the opposite direction, heading northwest from Salamanca, a delightful minor road via Ledesma makes an excellent alternative route to **Zamora**. For most of the way this route trails the beautiful Río Tormes, where there's excellent fishing (for giant carp), herons and storks in the trees, enormous, delicious mushrooms (*setas*) in autumn and a variety of meadow flowers in spring. **LEDESMA** itself – little more than a large village these days – retains its ancient walls, the remains of a Roman bridge and baths, and a couple of attractive churches. If you're staying overnight, the *Fonda Mercado*, c/Mercado 12 (☎923 570 146; ❷), is good. The greenery round here seems atypical of Castile – it's created in large part by the **Embalse de Almendra**, a dam almost at the Portuguese border, whose reservoir stretches all the way back to Ledesma.

Ciudad Rodrigo and the Sierra Peña de Francia

In the far southwest corner of Salamanca province, the unspoiled frontier town of **Ciudad Rodrigo** – astride the road and rail line to Portugal – is worth a detour even if you don't plan to cross the border. East of the town lies the **Sierra Peña de Francia**, with good walking and a stunning village, **La Alberca**, the whole of which has been declared a national monument.

Ciudad Rodrigo

CIUDAD RODRIGO is an endearingly sleepy old place which, despite an orgy of destruction during the Peninsular War, preserves streets full of **Renaissance mansions**. The best way to get an overview of the town is by making a circuit of the impressive **walls** – originally twelfth century, with seventeenth-century additions. En route you'll pass an austere **castle** (now a *parador* – see p.427), which overlooks a Roman bridge on the Río Águeda and commands an enticing view across into Portugal. If you're around over the weekend, the **Centro de Interpretación de la Ruta de las Fortificaciones** (Sat & Sun 10am–2pm & 5–8pm; €1.90), on the northern edge of the old town, has entertaining displays on the history of the walls – ask nicely and they may even let you try on one of their suits of armour.

Inside the walls, Ciudad Rodrigo's empty streets are ideal for aimless

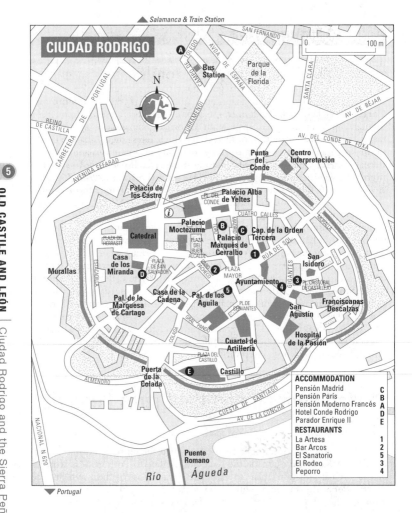

wandering. All roads lead sooner or later to the picture-perfect **Plaza Mayor**, while north of here on Plaza Conde are three of the town's most imposing mansions: the **Palacio de los Castro**, the **Palacio Alba de Yeltes** and the **Palacio de Moctezuma** (now the town's Casa Municipal de la Cultura). Just west of the Plaza Conde is the **Catedral** (daily 10am–1pm & 4–7pm), built in a mixture of styles but originally Transitional Gothic: take a look at the unusual eight-part vaults, dome-like in shape. Other interesting features include the *coro*, with wonderfully grotesque stalls carved by Rodrigo Alemán, who also created those at Toledo and Plasencia; the narthex, with statues of Apostles; and the cloisters (€1.20, free Wed), half of which are fourteenth century and half sixteenth century, with lurid carvings of biblical scenes.

A monument to **General Herrasti** and his men (see box on p.427) stands in the little square beside the cathedral. A plaque in the corner of the walls near

Ciudad Rodrigo in the Peninsular War

Along with Badajoz, Ciudad Rodrigo was a crucial border point in the Peninsular War. No army could cross safely between Spain and Portugal unless these two towns were secured. Ciudad Rodrigo fell to the French in 1810, despite valiant resistance from General Herrasti's Spanish garrison – in admiration for whose bravery, the French permitted them to march away from the devastated city.

Britain's Duke of Wellington retook Ciudad Rodrigo with a devastatingly rapid siege in 1812. Aware that French reinforcements were approaching, Wellington had announced "Ciudad Rodrigo must be stormed this evening" – his soldiers duly did so, embarking on a triumphant rampage of looting and vandalism. When order was restored, the troops paraded out dressed in a ragbag of stolen French finery. A bemused Wellington muttered to his staff, "Who the devil *are* those fellows?"

this marks the site of the Great Breach through which the British entered Ciudad Rodrigo; from outside the walls the position of the hole, later patched up with differently coloured stone, is clearly visible. The British guns were on the two ridges opposite (the lower one with the block of flats, the other higher up beyond the rail line) – you can see the cannonball dents above the doorway on this side of the cathedral.

Practicalities

Ciudad Rodrigo's **bus station** is a five-minute walk north of the town centre; the **train station** is ten minutes' walk along the road to Lumbrales, though there's only one train a day into Portugal leaving at 6am, and another nightly to Irún leaving at 1.15am. The town's **turismo** (Mon–Fri 9am–2pm & 5–7pm, Sat & Sun 10am–2pm & 5–8pm; ☏923 460 561, ⊛www.ciudadrodrigo.net) faces the cathedral at the northern entrance to the town.

For reasonable budget **rooms** try *Pensión Madrid*, c/Madrid 20 (☏923 462 467), which has a couple of doubles (**②**) and three fully equipped apartments with kitchen and bath for two (€30) or three (€42) people. Other budget options include the excellent *Pensión París*, in the centre of the old town at c/Toro 10 (☏923 482 349; **①**), and the impeccably clean *Pensión Moderno Francés*, c/Campo de Toledo 8 (☏923 461 968; **①**), which is rather unatmospherically located opposite the bus station, above the bar of the same name (there's no sign). *Hotel Conde Rodrigo*, Plaza de San Salvador (☏923 461 404, ⊛www.conderodrigo.com; **③**), offers more comfort and is located in an attractive square, while *Parador Enrique II* (☏923 460 150, ⊜ciudadrodrigo@parador.es; **⑥**) has an unrivalled location in the castle. There's a **campsite**, *La Pesquera*, by the river, just off the road to Cáceres (☏923 481 348; April–Sept).

Plaza Mayor is lined with **bars and restaurants** including the pleasant *La Artesa*, by the *ayuntamiento*, which has good *menús* (from €10) and breakfasts (€1.75), while further along the square the cheaper *Bar Arcos* has reasonable-value *platos combinados*. Directly opposite the *Arcos* is the atmospheric little bar-restaurant *El Sanatorio*, its walls covered in bullfighting memorabilia, with cheap snacks (from €2.40) and meat dishes (€4–9). For even cheaper meals, head just east of the Plaza Mayor to c/Gigantes, where several restaurants offer bargain *menús*, among them the pleasantly old-fashioned *El Rodeo* at no. 10, and *Peporro*, which has less ambience but more choice, including a few vegetarian options. For a splurge, the restaurant at the *parador* is the best and most expensive in town.

The Sierra Peña de Francia

The best place to head for in the **Sierra Peña de Francia** is the attractive village of **La Alberca** which makes a good starting point for walks in the surrounding hills. There are daily buses from Salamanca, but only on Sunday does the timetable make a day-trip possible.

La Alberca

LA ALBERCA has an extraordinary collection of houses, constructed from diverse materials: wood, pebbles, stone and rubble built in amongst the rocks. Due to its national monument status, plenty of tidying up is going on, and "local craft" shops have sprung up all over, but the character of a rural community remains: horses still take precedence over cars, the restorers use donkeys instead of vans, and goats, sheep and poultry often block the streets.

The most elegant houses are in the **Plaza Mayor**, which is dominated by a Calvary. Look into the church in the square behind for its elaborate polychromed pulpit. These days most of the houses in the Plaza Mayor seem to serve as cafés for the tourist trade, but there is an air of timelessness to the place. Many age-old traditions, including costumes, have survived, and the local celebration of the Feast of the Assumption on August 15 is considered to be the best in Spain.

Those looking for budget **accommodation** should head to *Pensión Hernandez* off the Plaza Mayor at c/Tablado 3 (☎923 415 039; ❶), which is extremely cheap, although there's no heating. A bit more upmarket is the *Alberca*, at the other end of c/Tablado on Plaza Padre Arsenio (☎923 415 116 & ☎659 390 098; ❷), which has spacious, nicely furnished en-suite rooms with central heating – essential for chilly winter nights. If money's no problem, the luxurious *Hotel Doña Teresa* (☎923 415 308, ⓦwww.gpm.es/hotelteresa; ❺), on the road to Mogarraz, is very chic and well equipped (with Jacuzzi, gym, sauna and sunbeds), while the long-established *Hotel Las Batuecas* (☎923 415 188, ⓦwww.hotelasbatuecas.com; ❸), on the road to Las Batuecas, has a more rustic feel and an excellent restaurant. There is a campsite, the *Al-Bereka* (☎923 415 195; March–Oct), with a pool, on the Salamanca road.

La Peña de Francia

It's a fifteen-kilometre uphill walk along mountain paths to the summit of the **Peña de Francia**, so many visitors choose to drive there. The circuitous road emerges from the trees halfway up to give fine panoramas not only of the mountain itself (marred by a television tower) and the plains below, but also out over the wild hills of Las Hurdes to the south and the Sierra de Gredos to the east. At the top you can have lunch or refreshments at the *hospedería* of the **Monasterio Peña de Francia**, where it's also possible to stay overnight (☎923 164 000, ⓔpdefrancia@verial.es; ❹).

Valle de Las Batuecas

Another excellent trip from La Alberca is south to the **Valle de Las Batuecas**, a national reserve bordering Las Hurdes (see p.223). This makes an impressive day-long walk or a beautiful drive; you'll need to take a picnic, for although fresh water abounds, there isn't a bar, restaurant or even house in sight until you reach the village of Las Mestas, just over the Extremaduran border, some 19km away.

From La Alberca, take the minor road south out of the village. After 2km you'll come to the pass of **El Portillo**, surrounded by solemn, rugged hills. From here, the road dips and loops spectacularly, offering a different vista at every turn. On the valley floor at the 12km point, a short road leads to the gate of the **Carmelite Monastery**, founded at the beginning of the seventeenth century for a reclusive community. One of the first tasks of the monastery was to exorcize the demons and evil spirits which supposedly inhabited the nearby valleys of Las Hurdes. In 1933, the great film-maker **Luis Buñuel** stayed in the monastery – then a hotel – while shooting his early masterpiece, *Land Without Bread*, about the extremely primitive lifestyle of the people of these valleys.

A footpath skirts the outside of the monastery's perimeter wall and follows the course of the river, which forms a gorge with splendid rock formations. There are **caves** with prehistoric rock paintings and carvings here, but unfortunately the most important ones have had to be closed in order to preserve them from deterioration and vandalism.

If you're walking back to La Alberca after exploring the valley, you're faced with a daunting climb; there is little traffic, although the chances of a lift from cars that do pass are good. By car, it makes a good round trip to keep going beyond **Las Mestas**, turning east at the T-junction and crossing back into Salamanca province via **Miranda del Castañar**, with its pretty views and romantic, crumbling castle.

Zamora to Valladolid

Zamora, at just 50km from the Portuguese border, is the quietest of the great Castilian cities, with a population of just 75,000. Its province is pretty low-key, too, though with a cluster of historic names. The road east from Zamora follows the **Río Duero** into the heartland of Old Castile, taking in **Toro**, the site of the battle which established Fernando and Isabel on the Spanish throne in 1476, and **Tordesillas**, where the treaty which ratified the division of lands discovered in the New World was signed between Spain and Portugal in 1494. A detour south from here takes in **Medina del Campo**, home to one of the region's most impressive castles.

Zamora

In medieval romances, **ZAMORA** was known as *la bien cercada* (the well enclosed) on account of its strong fortifications; one siege here lasted seven months. Its old quarters, still walled and medieval in appearance, are spread out along the top of a ridge which slopes down to the banks of the Río Duero. The minor road heading east to Toro along the south bank of the river offers good opportunities for birdwatching and fishing.

Arrival and information

Zamora is very spread out, and arrival can be confusing. The **train station** and the **bus terminal** are close to each other, twenty minutes' walk north from the Plaza Mayor. By foot from the bus station, turn right out of the main entrance then right again around the side of the terminal to reach the main road, the Avenida de las Tres Cruces; turn left along this road to reach the old town. From the train station walk straight out over the roundabout in front to join the Avenida de las Tres Cruces, which veers round to the right. Alternatively, two local buses – #3 and #4 – leave from outside the bus station and pass close by to the Plaza Mayor (ask the driver to let you know when to get off).

The **turismo** (daily: April–Sept 10am–2pm & 4–7pm; Oct–March 10am–2pm & 5–8pm; ℡ & ℻ 980 533 694, ⓦ www.ayto-zamoradipu.org) is at c/Plaza de Arias Gonzalo 6. For **Internet** access, head for *Ciberc@fé* on Plaza Viriato (Tues–Sun 11am–3am).

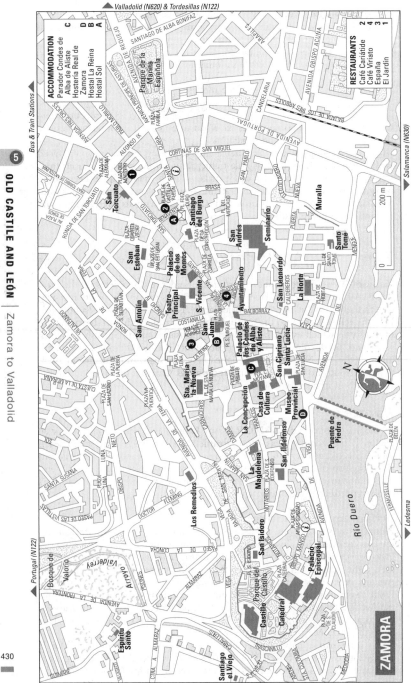

ZAMORA

Valladolid (N620) & Tordesillas (N122)

Bus & Train Stations

Portugal (N122)

Salamanca (N630)

Ledesma

ACCOMMODATION
Parador Condes de
  Alba de Aliste   C
Hostería Real de
  Zamora   D
Hostal La Reina   B
Hostal Sol   A

RESTAURANTS
Café Cariátide   2
Café Viriato   4
España   3
El Jardín   1

Accommodation

Zamora has a reasonable spread of **accommodation**, most of it centred in the old quarter. Except during Easter week few places run out of space, but if you do get stuck the turismo can help you out.

Parador Condes de Alba de Aliste Plaza de Viriato 1 ☎ 980 514 497, ✉ zamora@parador.es. One of Spain's most beautiful *paradores*, situated in a fifteenth-century ducal palace in the heart of town and with a superb restaurant attached. Pop in for a look at the marvellous courtyard even if you're not staying. ❻

Hostería Real de Zamora Cuesta Pizarro 7 ☎ & ℱ 980 534 545, ⓦ www.hosteriasreales.com. Gorgeous and surprisingly affordable hotel set in the 400-year-old Palacio de Inquisidores, complete with tiled staircases, cobbled Renaissance patio and goldfish pond. The larger downstairs rooms with river views are much better value than those upstairs. ❹

Hostal La Reina c/La Reina 1, 1° ☎ 980 533 939. Best budget accommodation in town, with spacious and immaculate rooms (some en suite) overlooking the Plaza Mayor, and a very friendly *dueña*. ❶

Hostal Sol c/Benavente 2, 3° ☎ 980 533 152, ℱ 980 509 190. Modern rooms, a little on the small side, but smart and well equipped (all with bathroom, TV and phone). ❷ It's in the same block as the slightly cheaper *Hostal Luz* ☎ 980 533 152. ❷

The Town

In and around the old centre are a dozen **Romanesque churches** (usually open Tues–Sun: March–Sept 10am–1pm & 5–8pm; Oct–Dec 10am–2pm & 4.30–6.30pm) which, with their unassumingly beautiful architecture and towers populated by colonies of storks, are the city's most distinctive feature. The majority date from the twelfth century and reflect Old Castile's sense of security following the victorious campaigns against the Moors by Alfonso VI and El Cid – notably the recapture of Toledo in 1085. **San Juan de Puerta Nueva**, in Plaza Mayor, and **Santiago del Burgo**, to the northeast along c/Santa Clara, are two of the most rewarding. Attached to Santa María la Nueva, slightly west of Plaza Mayor, the unusual **Museo de la Semana Santa** (Mon–Sat 10am–2pm & 5–8pm, Sun 10am–2pm; €2.70) contains the *pasos* – statues depicting the Passion of Christ – which are paraded through the streets at Easter.

The **Catedral** (same hours as churches), enclosed within the ruined citadel at the far end of town, has little of the discreet charm of the city's churches. Begun in 1151, its mainly Romanesque body is largely hidden behind an overbearing Renaissance facade, above which the building's most striking feature – a Byzantine-inspired dome similar to that of the Old Cathedral at Salamanca – perches in incongruous splendour. Inside, note the carved choir stalls, which depict lusty carryings-on between monks and nuns. The cathedral **museum** (Tues–Sun: April–Sept 11am–2pm & 5–8pm; Oct–March 11am–2pm & 4–6pm; €2) houses the city's celebrated "Black Tapestries". Every inch of these fifteenth-century Flemish masterpieces is woven in stunning detail. The traditional Greek and Roman themes are depicted with contemporary dress and weaponry included, illustrating how nobles in the Middle Ages liked to see themselves as heroes from the past.

Next to the cathedral are the impressive moated remains of the **Castillo**; wander round the back for majestic views over the surrounding countryside and River Duero, along with Zamora's massively burgeoning suburbs.

Eating and drinking

Most of the town's **restaurants and cafés** are around the Plaza Mayor and on the side streets off c/Santa Clara to the east. There's also a lively cluster of no-nonsense **tapas bars** in the alleys between the eastern end of c/Santa Clara and Plaza de Alemania.

Café Cariátide c/Benavente 5. Pleasant and spacious old café-bar with a modest range of *bocadillos* and tapas and a restaurant attached.
Café Viriato c/Viriato. Elegant place to enjoy a quiet drink outside on the pavement by day; by night it attracts a young crowd, staying open until 3am at weekends.
España c/Ramón Álvarez. Wonderfully old-fash-

ioned restaurant with fusty 1950s decor and clientele to match. Choice of *menús* (€8) and cheap à la carte dishes, plus a few vegetarian options – none of them expensive.
El Jardín Plaza del Maestro 5–8. One of the many lively tapas bars in this area; also serves gargantuan *menús* (€8) on the pleasant square outside.

Toro

TORO, 30km east of Zamora, looks dramatic: "an ancient, eroded, red-walled town spread along the top of a huge flat boulder", as Laurie Lee described it in *As I Walked Out One Midsummer Morning*. Its raw, red, hillside site is best contemplated from the rail line several hundred metres below the town in the Duero valley; at closer quarters it turns out to be a pleasant, rather ordinary provincial town, though embellished with one outstanding Romanesque reminder of past glory.

Toro did, however, play a role of vital significance in both Spanish and Portuguese history. The **Battle of Toro** in 1476 effectively ended Portugal's interest in Spanish affairs and laid the basis for the unification of Spain. On the death of Enrique IV in 1474, the Castilian throne was disputed: almost certainly his daughter Juana la Beltraneja was the rightful heiress, but rumours of illegitimacy were stirred up and Enrique's sister Isabel seized the throne. Alfonso V of Portugal saw his opportunity and supported Juana. At Toro the armies clashed in 1476 and the Reyes Católicos – Isabel and her husband Fernando – defeated their rivals to embark upon one of the most glorious periods in Spanish history.

Toro had long been a major military stronghold, and the monument that most strongly bears witness to this former importance is the **Colegiata Santa María la Mayor** (Tues–Sun: April–Sept 10am–1pm & 5–8pm; Oct–March 10am–2pm & 4.30–6.30pm; €1). The West Portal (c.1240) inside the church is one of the best-preserved and most beautiful examples of Romanesque art in the region, its seven recessed arches carved with royal and biblical themes, still retaining much of their colourful original paint. It's worth checking out the *Virgin of the Fly*, a notable fifteenth-century painting hanging in the sacristy – the eponymous insect perches on the Virgin's robes. Outside, there are grand views over the *meseta*, with the River Duero far below.

The Dominican **Monasterio Sancti Spiritus** on the western edge of town (Tues–Sun: guided tours April–Sept 10.30am, 11.15am, noon, 5.30pm, 6.15pm & 7pm; Oct–March 10.30am, 11.15am, noon, 4.30pm, 5.15pm & 6pm; €2.40) is worth a visit, too. It's a rambling fourteenth-century building containing some genuine treasures in amongst the mass of exhibits – chiefly a series of sixteenth-century Flemish tapestries depicting the betrayal and Crucifixion of Christ. In the church is the tomb of Beatriz of Portugal (wife of Juan I of Castile, died 1410), who lived here for various periods after she was widowed at the age of 18.

Practicalities

Trains to Toro are few and far between, and it's a steep 1.5km uphill walk from the station to the town. It's much easier to visit using one of the reasonably frequent Zamora–Valladolid **buses** (Mon–Sat 5–7 daily, Sun 3 daily); these drop passengers on the north side of town – walk through the big arch and straight on for about five minutes (passing directly under the church tower) to reach the *ayuntamiento*, where you'll find the **turismo** (Tues–Sat 10am–2pm &

4–8pm, Sun 10am–2pm, Oct–March closes at 7pm; ☎980 694 747, ⓦwww.toroayto.es). The Colegiata Santa María la Mayor is immediately behind here.

If you want **to stay**, there's a choice between the simple *Hostal Doña Elvira*, Carreterra Tordesillas 38 (☎980 690 062; ❷); the smart *Hostal María de Molina* (☎ & ⓕ980 691 414, ⓔh.molina@helcom.es; ❸) and the upmarket *Hotel Juan II* at Plaza del Espolón 1 (☎980 690 300, ⓦwww.hoteljuanii.com; ❹), right by the Colegiata Santa María la Mayor, which has a terrace bar with fantastic views. If you're coming by train, there's also a *hostal*, *La Estación* (☎980 692 936; ❶), next to the station. For **eating** and **drinking**, try the colourful line of bar-restaurants opposite the *ayuntamiento* or the restaurant at the *Hostal María de Molina*.

Tordesillas

TORDESILLAS, 32km east of Toro, can also boast an important place in Spain's history. It was here, under the eye of the Borgia Pope Alexander VI, that the **Treaty of Tordesillas** (1494) divided "All Lands Discovered, or Hereafter to be Discovered in the West, towards the Indies or the Ocean Seas" between Spain and Portugal, along a line 370 leagues west of the Cape Verde Islands. Brazil, allegedly discovered six years later, went to Portugal – though it was claimed that the Portuguese already knew of its existence but had kept silent to gain better terms. The rest of the New World, including Mexico and Peru, became Spanish.

Further fame was brought to Tordesillas by the unfortunate **Juana la Loca** (Joanna the Mad), who spent 46 years in a windowless cell here. She had ruled Castile jointly with her husband Felipe I from 1504–6 but was devastated by his early death and for three years toured the monasteries of Spain, keeping the coffin perpetually by her side, stopping from time to time to inspect the corpse. In 1509 she reached the Convent of Santa Clara in Tordesillas, where first Fernando (her father) and later Carlos V (her son) declared her insane, imprisoning her for half a century and assuming the throne of Castile for themselves.

Juana's place of confinement could have been worse. The **Real Monasterio de Santa Clara** (April–Sept Tues–Sat 10am–1.30pm & 4–6.30pm, Sun 10.30am–1.30pm & 3.30–5.30pm; Oct–March Tues–Sat closes 5.45pm, Sun 10.30am–1.30pm & 3.30–5.30pm; €3.60 or €4.60 joint entrance with Arab Baths, free Wed on presentation of an EU passport) overlooks the Duero and is known as "The Alhambra of Castile" for its delightful Mudéjar architecture. Built as a royal palace by Alfonso el Sabio (the Wise) in 1340, its prettiest features are the tiny "Arab Patio" with horseshoe arches and Moorish decoration, and the superb *artesonado* ceiling of the main chapel, described by Sacheverell Sitwell as "a ceiling of indescribable splendour, as brilliant in effect as if it had panes or slats of mother-of-pearl in it". The fourteenth-century **Arab Baths** (April–Sept Tues & Thurs–Sat 10am–noon & 4–7pm, Sun 10.30am–noon & 3.30–4pm; Oct–March Tues & Thurs–Sat 10am–noon & 4–4.15pm, Sun 10.30am–noon & 3.30–4pm), comprising a changing room and hot, warm and cold bathing areas, utilized a system developed by the Romans of heating the floors with underground boilers. They are closed during wet weather in order to protect the Mudéjar wall paintings from humidity.

Further places of interest in Tordesillas include the long medieval **bridge** over the Duero, the arcaded **Plaza Mayor** and the church of **San Antolín** (Tues–Sat 10.30am–1.30pm & 4.30–6.30pm, Sun 10.30am–1.30pm; €1.80), now a museum with an impressive collection of sculpture and excellent views from its tower.

Practicalities

The bus station is just outside the centre – you can see the old town walls from the terminal. Inside the walls, all roads lead sooner or later to the Plaza Mayor. From here exit the square beneath the building sporting the clock and flags to reach a bluff overlooking the river. Turn left here to reach the Real Monasterio de Santa Clara or right to reach San Antolín, next door to which there's a small **turismo** (April–Sept Tues–Sat 10am–1.30pm & 5–9.30pm, Sun 10am–2pm; Oct–March Tues–Sat 10am–1.30pm & 4–6.30pm, Sun 10am–2pm; ☎983 771 067, ⓦwww.tordesillas.net).

There's only one place **to stay** in the old town, the brand new, good-value *Hostal San Antolín* at c/San Antolín 8 (☎ & ⓕ983796771, ⓔsanantolin@ telefoncia.net; ❷), which is sparkling clean and done out with smart furniture and vibrant colours. There are plenty of alternatives in the drab modern surrounding areas but they tend to be expensive. One of the best is *Los Toreros*, Avda. de Valladolid 26 (☎983 771 900, ⓦwww.hotellostoreros.com; ❷), which has immaculate rooms and a good restaurant. The modern *parador* (☎983 770 051, ⓔtordesillas@parador.es; ❸) is on the Salamanca road, and there's a well-equipped **campsite** (☎ & ⓕ983 770 953, ⓦwww.campingelastral.com; April–Sept) opposite. Inexpensive **places to eat**, including the busy *Viky*, can be found on the Plaza Mayor and along c/San Anton. For a treat, the restaurant at the *parador* is excellent.

Medina del Campo

MEDINA DEL CAMPO, 24km south of Tordesillas, and the major rail junction before Valladolid, stands below one of the region's great castles. The Moorish design of the brick-built **Castillo La Mota** (April–Sept Mon–Sat 11am–2pm & 4–7pm, Sun 11am–2pm; Oct–March Mon–Sat 11am–2pm & 4–6pm, Sun 11am–2pm; €1.20) is similar to that at Coca further east, but less exotic and more robust. It was intended as another stronghold for the same family, the Fonsecas, but they were thrown out by the townsfolk in 1473. Queen Isabel lived here for several years, after which the castle was reincarnated as a prison, then as a girls' boarding school. You can go inside the castle walls, but there are no rooms to see, and it is the exterior which is impressive.

In the fifteenth and sixteenth centuries, Medina del Campo (Market of the Field) was one of the most important market towns in the whole of Europe, with merchants converging from as far afield as Italy and Germany to attend its fairs. The largest sheep market in Spain is still held here, and the beautifully ramshackle **Plaza Mayor** (also known as Plaza de la Hispanidad), where the townsfolk converge in the evening to eat, drink and gossip, is evocative of the days when its bankers determined the value of European currencies.

There is only one option for **accommodation** in the centre, *Hostal la Plaza* (☎983 811 246; ❷), on the Plaza Mayor. You could also try *Hostal Orensano* at c/Claudio Moyano 20 (☎983 800 341; ❷) or the mid-range *Hotel La Mota* (☎983 800 450; ❸) at c/Fernando el Católico 4, both on the other side of the bridge from the centre. For **meals**, *Restaurante Monaco* on the Plaza Mayor is a splendid place with a bargain *menú*.

Valladolid

VALLADOLID, at the centre of the *meseta*, ought to be exciting. Many of the greatest figures of Spain's Golden Age – Fernando and Isabel, Columbus, Cervantes, Felipe II – lived in the city at some point and for many years it vied with Madrid as the royal capital. In reality its old quarter is today an oppressive labyrinth of dingy streets, and those of its palaces that survive do so in a woeful state of decline. Many of the finest have been swept away on a tide of speculation and official incompetence, to be replaced by a dull sprawl of high-rise concrete. Modern Valladolid may be an expanding industrial city of 400,000 inhabitants but it has lost much that was irreplaceable. The one time you might actively seek to be in Valladolid is **Semana Santa** – Easter week – when it is host to some of the most extravagant and solemn processions in Spain.

Arrival and information

Arrival points are centred around the Campo Grande, a large triangular park to the southwest of the city centre where Napoleon once reviewed his troops: the **train station** is on Paseo de Campo Grande, and the **bus station** is a ten-minute walk west at c/Puente Lodgante 2. There is a small **airport** 7km outside the city serviced by national flights and budget airlines; flights are linked to town with a bus service. The **turismo** is in the city centre at c/Santiago 19 (July to mid-Sept Mon–Thurs & Sun 9am–9pm, Fri & Sat 9am–9pm; mid-Sept to June daily 9am–2pm & 5–8pm; ☏983 344 013, ⓦwww.dip-valladolid .es), and there's an **Internet** café, *Bocattanet*, at Maria de Molina 16, just north of Plaza de Zorilla (Mon–Thurs 8am–5pm, Fri 8am–midnight, Sat 9am–1pm).

Accommodation

Accommodation in Valladolid is plentiful and good value. The main concentration of rooms – in all price ranges – is in the pleasant area around the Plaza Mayor; there are also lots of cheaper options down the east side of Campo Grande on the way to the bus and train stations.

Near Plaza Mayor

Pensión La Cueva c/Correos 4 ☏983 330 072. Slightly frayed but perfectly comfortable en-suite rooms in an excellent location just off the Plaza Mayor. ❶

Hotel Imperial c/del Peso 4 ☏983 330 300, ⓦwww.himperial.com. Swish hotel in a beautiful old-town mansion right by the Plaza Mayor. Worth visiting the bar for a drink among the Renaissance columns even if you're not staying. ❼

Hostal París c/Especería 2 ☏983 370 625, ⓦwww.hostalparis.com. Comfortable and central hotel with good-quality rooms grouped around a superb *modernista*-style staircase. ❸

Hotel Roma c/Héroes del Alcázar de Toledo 6 ☏983 351 833, ⓕ983 355 461. Plush, excellent-value rooms in a great location, with a good restaurant attached and its own parking. ❸

Near Campo Grande

Pensión Dani c/Perú 11, 1º ☏983 300 249. Atmospheric and beautifully maintained old *pensión* with creaky wooden floors and high ceilings, in a quiet side street five minutes south of the city centre. Excellent value. The *Pensión Dos Rosas* upstairs (☏983 207 439) is owned by the same family and is equally good value. ❶

Hotel La Enara Plaza de España 5 ☏983 300 211, ⓕ983 300 311. Reasonable hotel in a central location, with characterful wood-panelled and stained-glass entrance. Rooms are OK, though a little past their best. ❸

The City

Despite the despoliation of many of the city's finest monuments, there are a couple of terrific examples of late-Gothic **architecture**, excellent Oriental

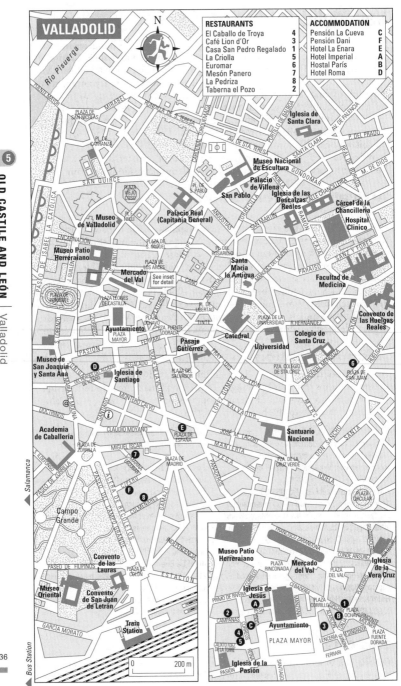

VALLADOLID

N

RESTAURANTS

El Caballo de Troya	4
Café Lion d'Or	3
Casa San Pedro Regalado	1
La Criolla	5
Euromar	6
Mesón Panero	7
La Pedriza	8
Taberna el Pozo	2

ACCOMMODATION

Pensión La Cueva	C
Pensión Dani	F
Hotel La Enara	E
Hotel Imperial	A
Hostal París	B
Hotel Roma	D

Río Pisuerga

PLAZA DE SAN NICOLÁS

MIRABEL

RONDILLA DE TERESA

PLAZA DE CARRANZA

AV DE STA TERESA

AV DE PALENCIA

Iglesia de Santa Clara

P. DEL PRADO

M. DE DIOS

SAN QUIRCE

PLAZA VIEJO COSO

Museo Nacional de Escultura

GONDOMAR

PL. DE S. PABLO

Palacio de Villena

San Pablo

Iglesia de las Descalzas Reales

Cárcel de la Chancillería

Hospital Clínico

Museo de Valladolid

PL.º NIELLI

Palacio Real (Capitanía General)

ENCARNACIÓN

ANGUSTIAS

SANT MARTIN

RAMÓN Y CAJAL

SANZ Y FORES

PARAÍSO

Museo Patio Herreriano

PLAZA DE S. MIGUEL

PLAZA DE LOS ARCES

Mercado del Val

Santa María la Antigua

Facultad de Medicina

PLAZA LEONES DE CASTILLA

See inset for detail

PL. DE LIBERTAD

Convento de las Huelgas Reales

Ayuntamiento

PLAZA MAYOR

PLAZA PUENTE DORADA

PLAZA DE LA UNIVERSIDAD

R HERNÁNDEZ

Catedral

Universidad

Colegio de Santa Cruz

Museo de San Joaquín y Santa Ana

Pasaje Gutiérrez

PLAZA DEL SALVADOR

PZA. COLEGIO DE STA CRUZ

6

PLAZA DE SAN JUAN

Iglesia de Santiago

D

REGALADO

LÓPEZ GÓMEZ

MONTERO CALVO

i

CLAUDIO MOYANO

PLAZA DE ESPAÑA

E

JOSÉ M.ª LACORT

Santuario Nacional

Academia de Caballería

MIGUEL ISCAR

PLAZA DE ZORRILLA

MANTERIA

PZA. DE LA CRUZ VERDE

7

PLAZA DE MADRID

PLAZA CIRCULAR

F

8

Campo Grande

Convento de las Lauras

PLAZA DE COLÓN

ESTACIÓN

Museo Oriental

Convento de San Juan de Letrán

GARCÍA MORATO

Train Station

0   200 m

◄ Salamanca

◄ Bus Station

Museo Patio Herreriano

PLAZA RINCONADA

Mercado del Val

PLAZA DEL VAL

Iglesia de la Vera Cruz

Iglesia de Jesús

A

1

B

Ayuntamiento

2

C

3

PLAZA FUENTE DORADA

4

5

PLAZA MAYOR

Iglesia de la Pasión

FERRARI

SANTIAGO

and modern art **museums** and – above all – the finest collection of **sculpture** assembled anywhere in Spain. Aside from the national museum, almost all of the city's historic churches contain further examples of Valladolid's passionate religious sculpture.

The Plaza Mayor and around

The heart of Valladolid is the spacious **Plaza Mayor**, a broad, pedestrianized expanse surrounded by arcaded buildings painted a striking, uniform red. Originally laid out in the sixteenth century after a fire had devastated the city, it was the first plaza of its kind in the country, becoming the model for countless similar civic centrepieces both in Spain and her South American colonies. Though much rebuilt since, it's still one of the grandest urban spaces in Spain and a pleasant place to watch the world go by, while many of Valladolid's best restaurants can be found in the narrow streets just off its western edge.

A few minutes' walk to the west of the plaza, the **Museo de San Joaquín y Santa Ana** (April–Sept: Mon–Fri 10am–1.30pm & 5–8pm, Sat 10am–2.30pm; Oct–March: Mon–Fri 10am–1.30pm & 5–7pm; free) is filled mostly with religious dust-collectors but has a few good statues, plus three Goya paintings in the chapel. North of the plaza in the restored **Monasterio de San Benito**, the **Museo Patio Herreraiano** (Tues–Sun 11am–8pm; €6), Valladolid's newest museum, is dedicated to contemporary Spanish art dating from 1918 to the present day. The rooms, half of which house permanent exhibitions while the other half present a rotating display of works, are arranged around a Renaissance courtyard of luminous pale gold stone. The collection includes the work of early twentieth-century *vanguardistas* such as Rafael Barrados and Joaquin Torres-García, who were at the forefront of the Spanish Cubism and Surrealism movements; later abstract sculptures and paintings by Julio González, Joan Miró and Ángel Ferrant; and works by more recent luminaries including Juan Muñoz, Antoni Tapiés and Eduardo Chillida. It's an impressive collection exhibited in a sophisticated modern space, but there's not much information or contextualization provided alongside the art. The museum's excellent bookshop is well worth a browse.

Continuing north up c/San Ignacio brings you to the **Museo de Valladolid** (July–Sept: Tues–Sat 10am–2pm & 5–8pm, Sun 10am–2.30pm; Oct–June: Tues–Sat 10am–2pm & 4–7pm, Sun 10am–2pm; €1.20), an old-fashioned archeological museum and art gallery set in a Renaissance mansion.

The cathedral and university

Ten minutes' walk east of the Plaza Mayor, the **Catedral**, which, unless you're attending a service, can only be viewed as part of a visit to its museum, was designed but not completed by Juan de Herrera (architect of El Escorial) and later worked on by Alberto Churriguera. Only half of it was ever built, but the model in the museum (Tues–Fri 10am–1.30pm & 4.30–7pm, Sat & Sun 10am–2pm; €2.50) shows how classically grand the original design was. What stands is a disappointment: the vast dimensions and sweeping arches do have something of Herrera's grandeur, but the overall effect is one of plainness and severity. Inside, the highlight is the *retablo mayor* by Juan de Juni, which was actually made for the Gothic Santa María la Antigua in the large plaza behind.

Just beyond the cathedral, Valladolid's **Universidad** has a portal by Narciso Tomé, the man who built the *Transparente* in Toledo Cathedral – one of his very few surviving works. Further on, part of the university administration is housed in the **Colegio de Santa Cruz**, a late fifteenth-century edifice which signals the introduction of Renaissance architecture to Spain. The beautiful three-storey patio is open to the public during office hours.

San Pablo and the sculpture museum

North of the cathedral, c/de las Angustias leads to Plaza de San Pablo and its unmistakeable church. The exuberant facade of **San Pablo** is a wild mixture of styles: the lower part is a product of the lavish form of late Gothic known as Isabelline, whereas the upper part is a Plateresque confection, similar to the New Cathedral and San Esteban at Salamanca. The facade of the adjacent **Colegio de San Gregorio**, a purer example of the Isabelline style, is adorned with coats of arms, sculpted twigs, naked children clambering in the branches of a tree and several comical, long-haired men carrying maces. It's very much like icing on a cake – Jan Morris, for one, was convinced that the flamboyant facades must be edible.

The San Gregorio usually houses the dynamic **Museo Nacional de Escultura** (Tues–Sat 10am–2pm & 4–6pm, Sun 10am–2pm; €2.40) but this has been temporarily relocated in the sixteenth-century Palacio de Villena, directly opposite, while restoration work takes place. Some of the most brilliant works of the Spanish Renaissance are on display here. Much the most important figures in this movement were Alonso Berruguete, Diego de Siloé and Juan de Juni: all three were active in the sixteenth century and spent several years in Florence where they perfected the realistic depiction of anatomy, fell heavily under the influence of Michelangelo and immersed themselves in the Italian Renaissance. Their genius lies in the adaptation of the classical revival to the religious intensity of the Spanish temperament. The masterpiece of **Alonso Berruguete** (1486–1561) is a massive, dismantled *retablo* which occupies rooms 2–4 of the museum – a remarkable demonstration of his skills in painting, relief sculpture and freestanding statuary. **Diego de Siloé** (1495–1565) was even more versatile. He created a classical building from the Gothic cathedral at Granada and was an equally accomplished sculptor – see his *Sagrada Familia* in Room 10 and the carved choir stalls in Room 11. Works of the Frenchman **Juan de Juni** (1507–77) show an almost theatrical streak and foreshadowed the emotional and naturalistic sculpture of the seventeenth and eighteenth centuries. This later period is best exemplified by the agonizingly realistic work of **Gregorio Fernández** (rooms 5 and 6) and **Alonso de Villabrille** (especially his *Head of San Pablo*, Room 14).

If you visit following the museum's return to the San Gregorio, you should also take in the beautiful **patio** with lace-like tracery, and several Moorish-inspired ceilings taken from other buildings in the city. The chapel also has many interesting exhibits, including another *retablo* by Alonso Berruguete, this time intact.

The Museo Oriental

The delightful **Museo Oriental** (Mon–Sat 4–7pm, Sun 10am–2pm; €3) is on the southern side of the city centre, near the train station. This occupies a dozen rooms in the Colegio de Agustinos, which sent missionaries to China and the Philippines for four centuries until their expulsion in 1952. Among the countless exquisite gems of Chinese art on show are some beautiful nature paintings on rice paper (mainly Sung dynasty; Room 9), three gorgeous porcelain pieces entitled *The Three Happy Chinamen: Fu, Shou and Lou* (Qing epoch; Room 2) and some stunning ivory carvings from the Philippines (Room 14). On the way out you can admire the lavishly decorated interior of the church, a good example of the academic style of Ventura Rodríguez, fashionable in the late eighteenth century. Have a look, too, at the elaborate facade of the **Convento San Juan de Letran** next door.

Eating, drinking and nightlife

The central area is the best place for **eating and drinking**. The Plaza Mayor is a popular place to linger, while c/Correos, just to the west, is packed with smart restaurants. There's a cluster of raucous late-opening **bars** northeast of the cathedral around Santa María la Antigua and up c/Marqués de Duero and c/Paraíso, and there's also **live jazz** in the *Café España* at Plaza Fuente Dorada 8, just east of the Plaza Mayor. For something a little different try the antiquated *El Penicilino* on Plaza de la Libertad, by the cathedral; with an atmosphere more like an apothecary than a bar, its speciality is a lurid (but alcohol-free) range of fluorescent fruit liquors made on the premises.

El Caballo de Troya c/Correos. Upmarket but affordable Castilian cuisine: choose between the award-winning restaurant or the slightly cheaper *taverna*, both with *menús* (€19 in the restaurant; €11.20 in the *taverna*) and pricier à la carte dishes. Alternatively, have a drink and tapas in the tiny gem of a Renaissance courtyard.

Café Lion d'Or Plaza Mayor. Attractive old café on the Plaza Mayor with black marble pillars, gilt mirrors and wrought-iron furniture – somewhere between a Viennese coffee house and a garden centre – plus outside seating on the square; a good place to watch the world go by.

Casa San Pedro Regalado Plaza del Ochavo 1. Nice little bar-restaurant housed in a cave-like twelfth-century synagogue close to Plaza Mayor, with traditional Castilian fare and good-value *menús* (€9).

La Criolla c/Correos. One of many restaurants in town serving the Valladolid speciality, *lechazo asado* (roast suckling lamb). Closed Mon.

Euromar Plaza de San Juan. Popular modern tapas bar on a pleasant tree-shaded square near the university. The *tortilla riojana* (with peppers) is highly recommended.

Mesón Panero c/Marina Escobar 1 ☎ 983 301 673. This smart, cosy basement restaurant, all wood panelling and Spanish tiles, has a changing daily menu and an excellent reputation. Main courses cost €10–15. Closed Sun evening.

La Pedriza c/Colmenares 10. The menu here is extremely simple as the restaurant serves only its speciality, *lechazo asado*, in portions of different sizes. Closed Mon eve.

Taberna el Pozo c/de Campañas 2 (off c/Correos). Moderately priced Castilian specialities, plus a long and varied list of tapas and *raciones*; very popular with locals. Closed Aug.

Palencia

PALENCIA is Castile's least known and least impressive province and its capital city is no exception. Despite a rich past, it has no great sights. There are numerous plazas, usually dominated by Romanesque churches built in a rather gaunt white stone, but while all are pleasant, none is outstanding.

The **Catedral** (mid-May to Sept Mon–Sat 8.45am–1.30pm & 4.30–7.30pm, Sun 11.15am–1pm; Oct to mid-May same hours but Mon–Sat closes at 6.30pm; free), a fourteenth- to fifteenth-century Gothic building, is plain by Spanish standards, except for the two south portals. Inside, most of the decoration is contemporary with, or only slightly later than, the architecture, thanks to the patronage of Bishop Fonseca. Soon after it was completed, Palencia fell into decline, hence the almost complete absence of Baroque trappings. Buy a ticket in the sacristy to see the artistic treasures (accompanied visits Mon–Sat 10.30am, 11.30am, 12.30pm, 4.30pm, 5.30pm & 6.30pm (summer-only); Sun 11.15am); one of the staff will take you to the crypt (part Visigothic, part Romanesque; €1) and the museum (€3) in the cloisters, which includes a very early *San Sebastián* by El Greco and Flemish tapestries. In addition, lights are switched on so you can see the various altars, and the chapel doors opened. The highlight is probably the *retablo mayor*, which contains twelve beautiful little panels, ten of them painted by Juan de Flandes, court painter to Isabel la Católica – it's the best collection of his work anywhere.

Practicalities

Palencia's **bus and train stations** are both located off the Plaza de los Jardinillos to the north of the city. Calle Mayor is over on the far side of the square to your left as you leave either terminal; walk down it for ten minutes, passing the Plaza Mayor en route, to reach the **turismo** (daily: July & Aug 9am–8pm; Sept–June 9am–2pm & 5–8pm; ☎979 740 068, ⓦwww .palencia.com/ayuntamiento or www.dip-palencia.es) at c/Mayor 105, just before the end of the pedestrianized section (there's another kiosk opposite the station (June–Sept daily 10.30am–2pm & 4–8.30pm; Oct–May weekends only). A couple of minutes further on is the friendly *El Salón*, Avda. República Argentina 10 (☎979 726 442; ❶), with thirteen spotless **rooms** in a modern block, or try the smart *Tres de Noviembre* at c/Mancornador 18 (☎979 703 042; ❷). *Hostal Ávila*, at c/Conde Vallellano 5 (☎979 711 910, ⓕ979 711 910; ❸), is more luxurious but still good value; it's tucked away in the backstreets between Plaza Mayor and the turismo – turn left down c/San Bernado. For coffee and cakes, head to the splendid *belle-époque*-style *Café Los Cuatro Cantones*, at c/Mayor 43, which has huge mottled mirrors, sparkly chandeliers and some tables outside. For something more substantial try *La Taberna* in the southeast corner of the Plaza Mayor, or *Casero*, slightly further along c/Mayor, which has a good *menú* and a big selection of tapas and *raciones*. For a bit of a splurge, *Rosario*, La Castilla 3 (☎979 740 936), is the city's top restaurant and quite modestly priced.

Around Palencia

Seven kilometres south of Palencia, at the ugly, modern town of **Venta de Baños**, is an important train junction. If you are changing trains here, it's well worth following the signs to the village of **BAÑOS DE CERRATO**, 2km out of town. This has the oldest church in the peninsula – *Monumento Nacional 1* in the catalogue: a seventh-century basilica (daily: April–Sept 10am–1.30pm & 5–8pm; Oct–March 10.30am–1.30pm & 4–6pm; €1) dedicated to **San Juan** by the Ostrogoth King Recesvinto. It has tiny lattice windows, horseshoe arches and incorporates materials from Roman buildings.

PAREDES DE NAVA, 20km northeast of Palencia and on the train line to León, has another church of interest, **Santa Eulalia** (closed for renovation at the time of writing but due to reopen in 2004; if you wish to visit outside opening hours call ☎979 830 469). The great sculptor Alonso Berruguete was born here, as were many of his lesser-known relatives, and the parish church (with a beautifully tiled Romanesque tower) has been turned into a small museum full of their work. The collection is arranged in every available space, and includes pieces by many of the best-known of Berruguete's contemporaries, gathered from all the churches of this little town. Paredes also has a couple of **pensiones** including *La Venta* on c/General Cabanellas (☎979 830 495; ❷), should you wish to stay.

Located just outside the village of Pedrosa de la Vega, near the town of Saldaña, 60km from Palencia, the **Villa Romana de la Olmeda** (Tues–Sun: April to mid-Oct 10am–1.30pm & 4.30–8pm; mid-Oct to March 10.30am–1.30pm & 4–6pm; closed Jan; €1.80) is among the most important domestic **Roman remains** in Spain. Dating from the fourth century, when the Roman Empire was nearing its end, the villa boasts more than 1000 square metres of well-preserved mosaics remarkably intact *in situ*. In the smaller rooms, red, blue and yellow tiles create geometric and swirling patterns interspersed with beautiful organic leaf and flower designs, while the most important mosaic – a work so fine that viewed from the walkway above it looks like a painting – is in the reception room. Minuscule multicoloured stones make up the central scene in which Ulysses discovers Achilles on the Greek island of Skyros. The frieze border depicts exotic birds along with portraits of the villa's former inhabitants, and below that is a hunting scene in which fearless Romans tackle snarling, savage beasts including leopards and lions. The objects recovered from the site have been transferred to the **Museo de la Villa de la Olmeda** (same hours as villa; ticket includes entry to museum) in the Iglesia de San Pedro in Saldaña. The collection, which includes hunting arrows, tools, coins, glassware, pots, jewellery and other domestic miscellanea, is rather less impressive than the villa itself. If you don't have your own transport, it's an easy three-kilometre walk from Saldaña to the villa. Saldaña can be accessed by bus from Palencia (8am & 1.30pm).

Castles south of the Duero

It is said there were once ten thousand castles in Spain. Of those that are left, some five hundred are in a reasonable state of repair, and Castile has far more than its fair share of them. The area south of Valladolid, and towards Segovia, is especially rich – ringed with a series of fortresses, many of them built in the fifteenth century to protect the royal headquarters.

Coca

Sixty kilometres south of Valladolid and connected with a regular bus (Mon–Sat 1 daily), the village of **COCA** is home to the prettiest **fortress** imaginable (Mon–Fri 10.30am–1pm & 4.30–6.30pm, Sat & Sun 11am–1pm & 4–6.30pm, July–Sept closes 7pm, closed first Tues of each month; €2.25). Less a piece of military architecture than a country house masquerading as one, it's constructed from narrow pinkish bricks, encircled by a deep moat and fantastically decorated with octagonal turrets, merlons and elaborate castellation – an extraordinary design strongly influenced by Moorish architecture. The building dates from about 1400, and was the base of the powerful **Fonseca family**.

The village itself is pretty lifeless, but there are a few bars and if you ask in these you should be able to find a room for the night. While here, try to see the inside of the parish church of **Santa María**, where there are four tombs of the Fonseca family carved in white marble in the Italian Renaissance style. The power of the dynasty is indicated by the fact that they were able to hire Bartolomé Ordóñez, the sculptor of the tombs of the Reyes Católicos in Granada.

Cuéllar, Turégano, Pedraza and Sepúlveda

The route south by road from Valladolid passes another impressive ancient castle at **CUÉLLAR** (Tues, Thurs, Fri 10.30am–2pm & 4.30–7.30pm, Sat & Sun 10.30am–2pm & 4–7.30pm; €2), served by regular buses from Valladolid (Mon–Fri 12 daily, Sat & Sun 7 daily). Dating from the fifteenth century, the castle boasts a wonderful Mudéjar portal and an elegant Renaissance gallery. Even more stunning is the one at **TURÉGANO**, 28km north of Segovia; it's essentially a fifteenth-century structure enclosing an early thirteenth-century church, though it's currently closed for restoration (call ☎921 462 914 for up-to-date information).

East of Turégano, just off the main Segovia–Soria road, there are rewarding diversions to be made to Pedraza and Sepúlveda, both extraordinarily pretty villages. **PEDRAZA** is almost perfectly preserved from the sixteenth century, a homogeneity enhanced by the uniformity of the rich brown stone in which it's constructed. The village is protected on three sides by a steep valley; the only entrance is the single original gateway (which used to be the town prison) from where the narrow lanes spiral gently up towards a large **Plaza Mayor**, still used for a **bullfighting festival** in the first week in September. Pedraza also has a **castle** (privately owned), where the eight-year-old dauphin of France and his younger brother were imprisoned in 1526, given up by their father François I who swapped his freedom for theirs after he was captured at the battle of Pavia.

SEPÚLVEDA is less of a harmonious whole, but has a more dramatic setting, strung out high on a narrow spit of land between the Castilla and Duratón river valleys. Its physical and architectural high point is the distinctive Romanesque church of **El Salvador** below which is a ruined castle out of which the town hall protrudes. To see the church, you'll need to organize a guided visit (€2) at the **turismo**, Plaza del Trigo 6 (July–Sept daily 10am–3pm & 4–6pm; Oct–June: Mon & Thurs–Sun 10am–3pm & 4–6pm, Tues 12–2.30pm; ☎921 540 237). Minimum group sizes vary so it would be better to call in advance outside the high season.

Turégano, Pedraza and Sepúlveda cannot be reached by bus from Valladolid – if you don't have your own transport you'll have to catch the bus to Segovia and then take a local service from there. The villages are best avoided at weekends, when every *madrileño* with a Mercedes seems to descend on them for the local speciality, roast lamb. Sepúlveda is the better bet for **accommodation**, with three *hostales*: *Hernanz*, c/Conde de Sepúlveda 4 (☎921 540 378, ℱ921 540 809; ❸); *Postigo*, a few doors along at no. 22 (☎921 540 172; ❷); and *Villa de Sepúlveda* on Ctra Boceguillas (☎921 500 302; ❷). Pedraza has two hotels, both expensive (and luxurious): *De la Villa*, c/Calzada (☎921 508 651, ⓦwww.elhoteldelavilla.com; ❺), and *La Posada de Don Mariano*, c/Mayor 14 (☎ & ℱ921 509 887; ❹).

The Pantano de Burgomillodo and Riaza

In addition to its castles, this area of Old Castile is rich in **wildlife**. The **Pantano de Burgomillodo**, a reservoir just to the west of Sepúlveda, is a particularly exciting spot for birdwatchers, surrounded by heaths of wild lavender which are the haunt of griffon vultures and other exotic species. From here you can head towards El Burgo de Osma on the road through **RIAZA**, skirting the foothills of the Sierra de Guadarrama. It's a lovely route, and Riaza itself is a pleasant place to stop with several good bars (try *El Museo*) and restaurants, and a couple of places offering rooms. There's also a **station** here on the main line from Madrid to Burgos.

Along the Duero: Valladolid to Soria

The **Duero**, east from Valladolid to Soria, is trailed by a further panoply of castles and old market towns; the river long marked the frontier between Christian and Arab territory. Road (and bus) routes follow the river, allowing leisurely and rewarding small-town stops.

Peñafiel

The reason for stopping at **PEÑAFIEL**, 60km east of Valladolid, is to see its fabulous elongated **castle** (Easter–Sept Tues–Sun 11.30am–2.30pm & 4.30–8.30pm; Oct–Easter Tues–Fri 11.30am–2.30pm & 4.30–7.30pm, Sat & Sun closes at 8.30pm; €2), which bears an astonishing resemblance to a huge ship run aground: it is 210m long but only 23m across, with its central tower playing the role of the ship's bridge. Built in 1466 out of the region's distinctive white stone, the castle was designed around the narrow ridge upon which it stands, a location best appreciated from the top of the tower. There's not much to see inside the castle, part of which has now been turned into a **Museo Provincial del Vino** (combined ticket with castle €5 or €12 with wine-tasting), but it's well worth going up to the battlements for the glorious panoramas over the surrounding countryside, including a tremendous view of Peñafiel from the "prow" of the castle.

In the town itself, the main sight is the extraordinary **Plaza del Coso**. All the buildings on this square are wooden, with several tiers of loggias, and it makes the most spectacular bullring in Spain when bullfights are held here in August. The nearby **San Pablo**, now a college, has a superb brick Gothic-Mudéjar apse, to which a Plateresque chapel was later added; if you want to see inside, ask at the turismo.

Practicalities

There are seven daily **buses** (4 on Sun; 1hr) to and from Valladolid. These drop you on the edge of town – turn right down Travesia de Calvario, walk over the bridge, then turn right again to reach San Pablo and the Plaza del Coso, where you'll find the **turismo** (daily: April–Sept 10am–2.30pm & 5–8.30pm; Oct–March 10am–2.30pm & 4.30–8pm; ☎983 881 526, ⓦwww .turismopenafiel.com). If you need a **place to stay**, the *Hostal Chicopa*, conveniently located next to the *ayuntamiento* in the centre of town, has cheap and tidy rooms (☎983 880 782; ❶) and a reasonable tapas bar downstairs. For something more luxurious, Peñafiel offers one of the region's best hotels, the *Hotel Ribera de Duero*, Avda. Escalona 17 (☎983 873 111, ⓦwww .hotelriberadelduero.com; ❹), set in a grand old building with very stylish rooms, almost all with views of the castle. For **dinner** the *Molino de Palacios*, Avda. de la Constitución 16, serves traditional Castilian dishes in a converted sixteenth-century watermill over the Duratón River, while *Bar Plata*, at c/Franco 22, does good tapas and is a bit of a nightspot.

El Burgo de Osma and around

EL BURGO DE OSMA, the episcopal centre of Soria Province, is a wonderfully picturesque place, with crumbling town walls and ancient colonnaded streets overhung by houses supported on precarious wooden props. In the relaxed village atmosphere of the Plaza de la Catedral, the **Catedral** (Tues–Sun: July–Oct 10am–1pm & 4.30–7.30pm; Oct–June 10.30am–1pm & 4.30–6pm), one of the richest in Spain, seems more than usually over the top. Basically Gothic in style, it has had many embellishments over the years, notably the superb Baroque tower decorated with pinnacles and gables which dominates the town. If you buy a visitor's ticket (€3), you will get a guided tour and lights will be switched on for you to see the theatrical **retablo mayor** by Juan de Juni and his pupils, and a series of dark chapels, one of which contains a powerful Romanesque carving of the Crucifixion; you'll also be shown the cloisters and the museum. Most impressive of all is the thirteenth-century painted stone tomb of San Pedro de Osma – an unusually naturalistic treatment for its age. Just beyond the cathedral there's a small but impressive surviving stretch of the fifteenth-century town walls.

A couple of minutes' walk up the quaintly arcaded c/Mayor is Osma's other main square, the **Plaza Mayor**, flanked on opposite sides by the former Hospital de San Agustín of 1699 and the *ayuntamiento* of 1771 with its over-the-top iron steeples – quaint monuments to provincial self-esteem. Further evidence of Osma's former importance can be found slightly beyond here, at the junction of c/Mayor and c/Universidad, where the Instituto Santa Catalina occupies a fine old sixteenth-century mansion which was once the seat of the town's **university**.

Practicalities

Two daily buses to Soria (1 on Sun) leave from the town's new **bus station**, just northwest of the Plaza Mayor. It's a couple of minutes from here to the **turismo** (Wed–Sun 10am–2pm & 4–8pm; ☎975 360 116, ⓦwww.burgosma.es) at Plaza Mayor 9.

There are several options for **accommodation:** the very basic *Pensión San Roque*, c/Universidad 1 (☎677 431 246; ❷), is somewhat overpriced but the interior is much nicer than the rather grubby exterior would suggest, while the brand new *Hostal Mayor* (☎975 368 024; ❷), at c/Pedro Soto 4, a narrow street of c/Mayor, is better value although a little more expensive. If money is not a problem, the town's best hotel is *Il Virrey* (☎975 341 311, ⓦwww.virreypalafox.com; ❺) on the Plaza Mayor, complete with baronial wooden fittings, and a staircase and chandelier which are virtually tourist attractions in their own right. For **food**, *Cafeteria 2000*, on Plaza Mayor, has reasonable *menús* (€8), or try the tapas bar in the *Hostal Mirador*.

San Esteban de Gormaz and Gormaz

Thirteen kilometres to the west of El Burgo de Osma, **SAN ESTEBAN DE GORMAZ** has a ruined castle and a pair of Romanesque churches. There's also a pleasant **hostal**, *El Moreno*, Avda. Valladolid 1 (☎975 350 217; ❷), and a good hotel, *Rivera del Duero* (☎975 350 059, ⓦwww.hotelrivera.es; ❹), which could be useful if you find everything full in Osma.

GORMAZ, 15km south of El Burgo de Osma, is a particularly intriguing fortification originally built in the caliphate style, of which two Moorish doorways dating from the tenth century have survived. Later captured and modified by Christians, it was one of the largest fortified buildings in the West – there are 28 towers in all, ruined but impressive. The inside is a shell, but there are good panoramas from here, and the wonderful views as you approach make the long walk up less daunting. Gormaz itself is little more than a hamlet, without any accommodation.

Calatañazor

Just off the main El Burgo–Soria road lies **CALATAÑAZOR**, a severely depopulated medieval village with walls and the ruins of a castle, chiefly remarkable for its **houses**, with their distinctive conical chimneys, decorative coats of arms and wooden balconies. The only available **accommodation** is the *Hostal Calatañazor*, c/Real 10 (☎975 183 642 or 975 371 334; ❷), an ancient house on the main village street which also has a **restaurant**, but the place makes a good half-day excursion from either El Burgo de Osma or Soria, 30km east.

Berlanga de Duero and around

BERLANGA DE DUERO, east again along the Duero, stands just off the main road between El Burgo de Osma and Almazán; it can also be reached from Soria by daily **bus**.

Once again, the main attraction is a **castle**, whose massive cylindrical towers and older double curtain wall, reminiscent of Ávila, loom above the town. The way up is through a doorway in a ruined Renaissance palace at the edge of town (watch out for the lethal uncovered hole dropping down to an underground cavern); entrance is free. The other dominant monument is the **Colegiata**, one of the last flowerings of the Gothic style. Its unusually uniform design is a consequence of rapid construction – it was built in just four years. Berlanga also has an old-world **Plaza Mayor** (where markets are held regularly), several fine mansions, arcaded streets, an impressive entrance gateway and the unique **La Picota**, a pillar of justice to which offenders were tied (it's on waste ground outside the old town, where the buses stop).

The only **place to stay** in Berlanga is at the fairly upmarket *Hotel Fray Tomás*, c/Real 16 (☎975 343 033, ☎975 343 169; ❸), which also has a very good restaurant.

Ermita de San Baudelio de Berlanga

Eight kilometres south of Berlanga, the tiny **Ermita de San Baudelio de Berlanga** (June & Aug Wed–Sat 10am–2pm & 5–9pm, Sun 10am–2pm; April–May & Sept–Oct Wed–Sat 10am–2pm & 4–7pm, Sun 10am–2pm; Nov–March Wed–Sat 10am–2pm & 3.30–6pm, Sun 10am–2pm; €0.60) is the best-preserved and (with San Miguel de Escalada, see p.469) most important example of Mozarabic style in Spain. It was even better before the 1920s: five years after being declared a national monument, its marvellous cycle of frescoes was acquired by an international art dealer and exported to the USA. After much fuss, the Spanish government got some of them back on indefinite loan, but they are now kept in the Prado.

In spite of this loss, the hermitage remains a beauty. Its eight-ribbed interior vault springs from a central pillar, while much of the space is taken up by the tribune gallery of horseshoe arches. Some original frescoes do remain, including two bulls from the great sequence of animals and hunting scenes of the nave. You can also see the entrance to the cave below, which the hermit, San Baudelio, made his home.

Almazán

Some 35km due south of Soria lies **ALMAZÁN**, which despite a lot of ugly modern development still possesses complete **medieval walls**, pierced by three gateways. On the Plaza Mayor stands the fine Renaissance **Palacio Hurtado de Mendoza**, with a Gothic loggia at the rear, visible from the road around the walls. The church of **San Miguel**, across from the palace, has a memorable interior, with Romanesque and early Gothic features, and a remarkable dome in the Córdoban style. To gain access, try the parish offices in the adjacent Plaza Santa María, opposite the church of the same name.

Places to stay include *Hostal El Arco*, c/San Andrés 7 (☎975 310 228; ❶), and *Hostal Mateos*, c/San Lázaro 2 (☎975 301 400; ❷), across the river. The latter is also one of the few **places to eat** in town. However, you are not likely to want to stay long, and there are regular **bus** and **train** connections to Soria.

Medinaceli

MEDINACELI, perched in an exhilarating, breezy position above the Río Jalón, is something of a ghost town – steeped in history and highly evocative of its former glory as a Roman and Moorish stronghold. It's 40km south of Almazán and positioned on the main Madrid–Barcelona rail line. If you arrive this way, it's a three-kilometre climb by road up from the station to the village, though you can take a short cut straight up the hill to a distinctive Roman arch. The **Roman arch** – a triple arch in fact – is worn but impressive, and unique in Spain. Its presence is something of a mystery, as such monuments were usually built to commemorate military triumphs, but the cause of celebration at Medinaceli is unknown. Nearby stands the dilapidated Moorish **castle**, now a mere facade sheltering a Christian cemetery.

The quiet streets are full of ancient mansions with proud coats of arms, the grandest of which is the **Palacio de los Duques de Medinaceli** on the dusty and desolate Plaza Mayor. The palace was the seat of the family regarded as rightful heirs to the Castilian throne until, in 1275, Fernando, eldest son of Alfonso el Sabio (the Wise), died before he could assume his inheritance. His two sons were dispossessed by Fernando's brother Sancho el Valiente (the Brave), and their descendants, the dukes of Medinaceli, long continued to lay claim to the throne. Today Medinaceli is a declining village with no more than 900 inhabitants, though its *duquesa* remains the most titled woman in Spain.

There are several **places to stay** by the train station: *Hostal Nicolás* (☎975 326 004; ❷) and *Hotel Duque de Medinaceli* (☎975 326 111, ℻975 326 472; ❶) are both very pleasant, while the *Pensión Anton*, c/Numancia 5 (☎975 326 058; ❶), at the edge of the new village en route to the old, is fairly basic but exceedingly cheap. If you prefer to stay up in the old village there's the *Hostal Medinaceli*, c/del Portillo 1 (☎975 326 102; ❷), next to the Roman arch, and the attractive *La Ceramica*, c/Yedra 1 (☎975 326 381; ❸), which also has a good **restaurant** serving hearty meals.

Southwest of Medinaceli, Sigüenza (see p.201) is just 20km away across the border in New Castile, a couple of stops on any Madrid-bound train.

Soria and around

SORIA is a modest little provincial capital – an attractive place, despite encroaching suburbs. It stands between a ridgeback of hills on the banks of the Duero, with a castle ruin above, a medieval centre dotted with mansions and Romanesque churches, and one of the country's most unusual set of cloisters.

Arrival, information and accommodation

Soria's **train station** is at the extreme southwest of the city; the **bus station** is on Avenida de Valladolid on the western side of the city, a twenty-minute walk from the centre. There's a helpful **turismo** (July to mid-Sept: Sun–Thurs 9am–8pm, Fri & Sat 9am–9pm; mid-Sept to June: daily 9am–2pm & 5–8pm;

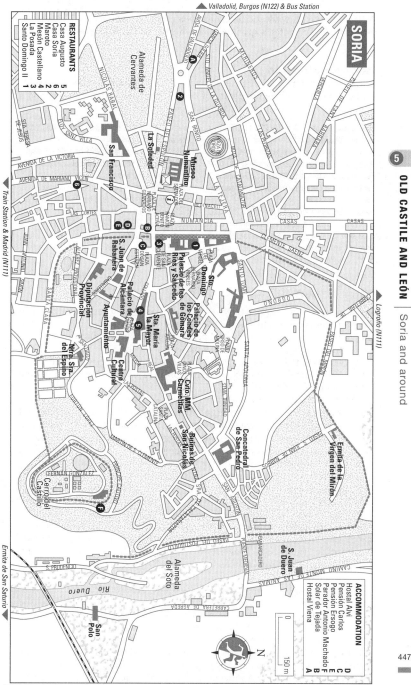

RESTAURANTS
Casa Augusto 5
Casa Soria 6
Maroto 2
Mesón Castellano 4
La Posada 3
Santo Domingo II 1

Alameda de Cervantes

La Soledad

San Francisco

Museo Numantino

AVENIDA DE LA VICTORIA

AVENIDA DE MARIANO VICEN

NUMANCIA

Palacio de los Condes Ríos y Salcedo

Sto. Domingo

Palacio de los Condes de Gómara

Palacio de Alcántara

S. Juan de Rabanera

Diputación Provincial

Ntra. Sra. del Espino

Sta. Maria la Mayor

Ayuntamiento

Centro Cultural

Cristo. MM. Camelitas

Ruinas de San Nicolás

Concatedral de San Pedro

Ermita de la Virgen del Mirón

Fernán González

Cerro del Castillo

Alameda del Soto

S. Juan de Duero

San Polo

Rio Duero

S. Prudencio

ACCOMMODATION
Hostal Alvi D
Pensión Carlos C
Pensión Ersogo E
Parador Antonio Machado F
Solar de Tejada B
Hostal Viena A

N

0   150 m

ⓣ975 212 052, Ⓦwww.sorianitelaimaginas.com) on c/Medinaceli 2, near the Alameda de Cervantes, a spacious park which is one of Soria's most attractive features.

Accommodation

Soria's tourists are rarely in great numbers, so finding a **place to stay** should-n't be a problem. There are plenty of centrally located budget options, and a reasonable choice of mid-range and upmarket hotels.

Hostal Alvi c/Alberca 2 ⓣ975 228 112, Ⓕ975 228 140. Well-equipped en-suite rooms in a central modern block with private parking. ❸

Pensión Carlos Plaza del Olivio 2 ⓣ975 211 555. Ten very cheap but perfectly adequate rooms in the corner of a central but relatively quiet square. ❶

Pensión Ersogo c/Alberca 4, 4º ⓣ975 213 508. Light, airy rooms in a clean, comfortable flat on a quiet side street near Plaza San Esteban. ❶

Parador Antonio Machado Parque del Castillo ⓣ975 240 800, Ⓔsoria@parador.es. Modern and relatively cheap *parador* in a beautiful hilltop location with great views. ❺

Solar de Tejada c/Claustrilla 1 ⓣ & Ⓕ975 230 054, Ⓦhttp://perso.wanadoo.es/solardetejada. With its exposed wood and old stone walls, beautifully decorated rooms all painted in different colours and cosy sitting room, this is hands down the best mid-range option in the city. ❸

Hostal Viena c/García Solier 1 ⓣ975 222 109. Spacious and comfortable rooms in this pleasant, central, reasonably priced *hostal*, with own restaurant attached. ❷

The Town

Over on the eastern edge of the city centre, Soria's cathedral, the **Concatedral de San Pedro**, is a rather stolid Plateresque building whose interior (open only for church services) takes the Spanish penchant for darkness to a ridiculous extreme. To the side are three bays of a superb Romanesque cloister (July–Sept Mon 11am–1pm, Tues–Sat 10am–1pm & 4.30–7.30pm, Sun 10am–1pm; Oct–June Tues–Sun 11am–1pm; €1), which belonged to the cathedral's predecessor.

From the cathedral, follow the main road that skirts the old town to reach the convent church of **Santo Domingo**. A twelfth-century building, its beautiful rose-coloured facade is decorated symmetrically with sixteen blind arches and a wheel window with eight spokes. The recessed arches of the main portal are excellently preserved and magnificently sculpted, with scenes from the life of Christ and a wonderful gallery of heavily bearded musicians who look uncannily like the lost medieval ancestors of ZZ Top – look out in particular for the fetching three-in-a-bed scene.

Also worth a look in the centre of town is **San Juan de Rabanera** (July–Oct Tues–Sun 11am–2pm & 5–7pm; Nov–June open 30 mins before services, daily 9.30am & 7pm), another fine Romanesque church, the massive sixteenth-century **Palacio de los Condes de Gomara** and the **Museo Numantino** (June–Sept Tues–Sat 9am–2pm & 5–8pm, Sun 10am–2pm; Oct–May Tues–Sat 10am–2pm & 4–7pm, Sun 10am–2pm; €1.20), which features excellent displays of the finds from Numancia and Tiermes, another Celto-Iberic and Roman city, south of El Burgo de Osma.

Just across the Duero, some ten minutes' walk from the centre, stand the ruined cloisters of **San Juan de Duero** (April, May, Sept & Oct Tues–Sat 10am–2pm & 4–7pm, Sun 10am–2pm; June–Aug Tues–Sat 10am–2pm & 5–9pm, Sun 10am–2pm; Nov–March Tues–Sat 10am–2pm & 3.30–6pm, Sun 10am–2pm; €0.60), one of the most bizarre medieval monuments in the region. Built in the thirteenth century by Mudéjar masons, each of the four sides of the cloister is in a different style: Romanesque, Transitional Gothic,

Gothic, and finally a totally original section of vaguely Moorish-looking arches. If the cloisters are closed, you can get a partial aerial view from a low hill across the road. The church, converted into a museum, is more orthodox in style, but has two unusual little freestanding temples inside.

From here, there's a good walk south along the banks of the river, passing the former Templar church of **San Polo** (now a private home), and arriving, after 2km, at the **Ermita de San Saturio**, a two-tiered complex including an octagonal chapel with thirteenth-century frescoes (July & Aug Tues–Sat 10am–2pm & 5–9pm, Sun 10.30am–2pm; mid-May to June & Sept to mid-Oct Tues–Sat 10.30am–2pm & 4.30–7.30pm; mid-Oct to mid-May Tues–Sat 10.30am–2pm & 4.30–6.30pm, Sun 10.30am–2pm; free). The landscape here is typical of the province, with its parched, livid, orange earth and the solemn river lined by poplars.

Eating and drinking

The city's **bars and restaurants** are plentiful and lively, most of them serving excellent tapas. You'll find the best selection around Plaza San Clemente, just behind Citibank at the western end of the main drag – c/Collado.

Casa Augusto Plaza Mayor 5. An excellent restaurant in a central location with a friendly owner and a good, six-course *menú* (€19). The cooking is quite creative; specialities include stuffed green peppers and breadcrumbs sautéed with garlic, bacon and grapes. El Mesón de Isabel next door is run by the same people and specializes in food with a Mediterranean twist.

Casa Soria Avda. Mariano Vicén 5. Slightly out of the way, but worth searching out this friendly local eatery for its simple but good-value *menú* (€7). Open from 7am.

Maroto Paseo del Espolón 20. Conservative, swanky and quite pricey, this is where Soria's well-heeled older generation come to dine. Good Castilian food, beautifully presented – there's a *menú* for €14 plus à la carte meat, fish and game

(*caza*) dishes from €10.80. Closed Thurs.

Mesón Castellano Plaza Mayor 2. Specializing in a fairly rich form of Castilian cuisine and located in a smart but cosy building of warm brick and wooden beams, this is one of Soria's best – and priciest – restaurants.

La Posada Plaza San Clemente 6. Downstairs from the *Hostal La Posada*, on Soria's liveliest square and serving some of the best tapas in town.

Santo Domingo II c/Aduana Vieja 15. Upmarket restaurant, just south of Santo Domingo: €23 buys you a six-course *menú*, or choose from mouthwatering à la carte dishes such as oxtail in red wine (*rabo de buey al vino tinto*; €10.80) or kid goat fried with red peppers (*cabrito frito con ajillos*; €11.40).

Río Lobos Canyon and the Sierra de Urbión

Some of Castile's loveliest and least visited countryside lies northwest of Soria, on either side of the N234 to Burgos. South of this road a **Parque Natural** has been created around the canyon of the Río Lobos. To the north rises the **Sierra de Urbión**, a lakeland region much loved by the Sorian-born poet, Antonio Machado. The Cañón Río Lobos can also be approached on minor roads from El Burgo de Osma, to the south.

Río Lobos Canyon

The whole area of the **Parque Natural del Cañón del Río Lobos** is impressive, with fantastically shaped rocks on both sides of the canyon. The most interesting part lies 1km from the park's car park, southeast of San Leonardo de Yagüe. Here, as well as some of the prettiest rock formations, there's a **Romanesque chapel** founded by the Templars (kept locked) and, behind this, a beautiful natural **cave**. From here, the path continues through the Lobos gorge; at times the river is a mere trickle – its tributaries have dried up completely, providing ready-made walking tracks. For this, or more adventurous treks into the high ground, you really need proper walking boots, but any shoes will do on the main paths. The park will appeal to birdwatchers; eagles and vultures are often seen, even though they are not protected here.

SAN LEONARDO DE YAGÜE makes a convenient base, with a good *hostal*, the *Torres*, c/Magdalena 4 (☎975 376 156; ❷). Alternatively, you can camp in the officially designated areas around the entrance to the park (☎975 363 565; mid-March to mid-Oct).

Vinuesa and the Sierra de Urbión

For the **Sierra de Urbión**, the most obvious base is **VINUESA**, situated just north of an enormous man-made reservoir, **Embalse la Cuerda del Pozo**. On a slow country bus route between Soria and Burgos, it's a spaciously laid-out village with many fine old houses and plenty of **accommodation** to choose from down by the bridge: *Visontium* (☎975 378 354, ⓕ975 378 362; ❷), and *Santa Inés* (☎ & ⓕ975 378 126; ❷), both on Carretera Laguna Negra, are two attractive *hostales* owned by brothers; the slightly more expensive *Hostal Urbión* on Avenida Constitución (☎975 378 494; ❷) also has good rooms, and in the middle of the village there's an excellent *pensión*, *Mesón Tito*, c/Reina Sofía 30 (☎975 378 031; ❶). With the exception of the *Santa Inés*, all these places have their own restaurant. There's also a **campsite** 2km along the Montenegro road (☎975 378 331; April to mid-Oct), which has bikes for hire. For information on the area and maps of walking trails, visit the small **turismo** kiosk on the main road (mid-June to mid-Oct Wed–Sun 10am–2pm & 4–7.30pm; mid-Oct to mid-June weekends only; ☎975 378 170, ⓦwww .villa-de-vinuesa.org).

Nineteen kilometres north of Vinuesa lies the most famous of the lakes, the beautiful **Laguna Negra**. There's no public transport to it, but a good road leads through thickly wooded country before climbing steeply up the green mountainside. For the last couple of kilometres, by the side of a ravine, the road is much rougher; from July to mid-September a minibus shuttles to and fro along this section. Finally, a path leads 200 metres to the lagoon. Ice Age in origin, and set in an amphitheatre of mountains from which great boulders have fallen, it presents a primeval picture – Machado was inspired to write some of his most purple verse here. The area remains delightfully unspoiled, though, and the **bar** (July–Sept only) and **picnic area** are out of sight, 3km down the mountain.

Serious hikers can make a tortuous ascent from the Laguna Negra to the **Laguna de Urbión**, just over the border in Logroño Province – a route that takes in a couple of other tiny, glacially formed lakes. A less taxing version of the same excursion is to take the long way round, from the village of **Duruelo de La Sierra**, some 20km west of Vinuesa.

For seaside-style fun head to **Playa Pita**, a long sandy beach on the southwestern shore of the Embalse la Cuerda del Pozo, 11km south of Vinuesa, and 4km from the main Soria–Burgos road. Popular with Spanish families, there are barbecue and picnic areas, restaurants and bars, pedaloes and boats for hire and **camping** in a shady forest (☎975 184 030; June–Sept).

The Camino de Santiago:
from Logroño to León

This part of the chapter is laid out in an east–west direction, following, more or less, the **Camino de Santiago**, the great pilgrim route to the shrine of St James at Compostela (see p.606). The route had many variants but its most popular point of entry to Spain was – and remains – the pass of Roncesvalles in the Pyrenees. From there, the old paths strike south through Navarra to Logroño and then west across Castile through the great cathedral cities of **Burgos** and **León**. These are major architectural sights but each of the smaller towns along the *camino* has some treasure or reminder – a bridge, a Romanesque church, or a statue of the saint. For uncommitted pilgrims, the highlights of the route can be taken in by car, bus, or sometimes train.

Old Castile, in this section, is used in a loose, historical sense, for this region actually takes in two other provinces. In the east is **La Rioja**, Spain's premier wine-producing region, with its capital in **Logroño** and wine trade centre in nearby **Haro**. Over to the west is the old kingdom of **León**, whose northern reaches merge with Asturias in the Picos de Europa mountains (see p.567).

The Camino de Santiago in Old Castile and León

This stretch of the **Camino de Santiago** passes through the wine country of La Rioja before arriving at the *meseta* (plains) of Castile. This is the flattest, driest part of the path, and the lack of shade makes it uncomfortably hot in summer. Time your arrival for spring, when wild flowers edge the wheat fields, or wait for autumn, when La Rioja's grape harvest is in full swing. The walking is generally good, although the route often shadows the main road along a purpose-built gravel track. Still, there are many well-marked detours along isolated tracks crunchy with wild thyme.

Pilgrims are sharply divided about the *meseta*. Fans praise the big, empty skies and the contemplative nature of the unchanging views, while detractors bemoan the bone-chilling wind that blows for nine months of the year and the depressing way that you can see your destination hours before you reach it. The *meseta* certainly isn't all drudgery: the camino brings you to the glorious Gothic cathedrals of Burgos and León (see p.456 & 469) and to the town of Hospital de Órbigo, 36km after León, where legend has it that a Don Suero de Quiñones, a jilted knight, defeated 300 men in a jousting tournament at the town's famous 20-arch medieval bridge.

The *meseta* ends at the lovely town of Astorga (see p.475), about 50km on from León, home to Gaudí's Palacio Episcopal and *cocido Maragato*, the local speciality meatfest. After Astorga, you'll climb the Cordillera Cantábrica to the highest pass of the *camino* (1517m), where mist and fog can descend year-round and snow makes winter travel difficult. Traditionally, pilgrims bring a stone from home to leave on a massive pile at Cruz de Hierro, just before the pass. Things warm up considerably as you descend through beautiful villages and gorgeous scenery to the Bierzo valley, 50km from Astorga, where it's sunny enough to grow grapes. Here, you can visit the Templar Castle of Ponferrada (see p.477) and the charming riverside town of Villafranca del Bierzo (see p.478), an ideal place to rest before heading uphill into Galicia (see chapter 8, p.599). For practicalities on the Camino, see p.618.

Logroño

LOGROÑO is a modern, prosperous city, lacking in great monuments, but pleasant enough with its broad, elegant streets and open squares. It has a lively old section, too, stretching down towards the Río Ebro from the twin-towered cathedral. Whether you stay or not, you're likely to pass through Logroño at some point since it lies on the borders of Old Castile, the Basque provinces and Navarra, a position that has stimulated commerce and light industry. Most importantly, however, this is the very heart of the **Rioja wine region**.

The Town

Before the wine trade and industry brought prosperity to Logroño, it owed its importance for some six centuries to the **Camino de Santiago**. In almost every town on the route you can still find a church dedicated to the saint; in Logroño it stands close to the iron bridge over the Río Ebro – the lofty six-teenth-century Gothic structure of **Santiago el Real**. High on its south side, above the main entrance, is a magnificent eighteenth-century Baroque eques-trian statue of the saint, mounted in full glory in his role of *Matamoros* (Moorslayer), on a stallion which Edwin Mullins, in his fascinating book *The Pilgrimage to Santiago*, describes as "equipped with the most heroic genitals in all Spain, a sight to make any surviving Moor feel inadequate and run for cover".

Other fine Logroño churches include **San Bartolomé**, which has an unre-fined but richly carved Gothic portal, and the **Catedral de Santa María la Redonda** (Mon–Sat 8am–1pm & 6.30–8.45pm, Sun 9am–2pm & 6.30–8.45pm). The latter was originally a late-Gothic hall church with a love-ly sweeping elevation which was extended at both ends in the eighteenth cen-tury – the twin-towered facade is a fine example of the Churrigueresque style.

In addition to the churches, the **Museo de la Rioja** (Tues–Sat 10am–2pm & 4–9pm, Sun 11.30am–2pm; free, with photo ID), is well worth a visit. Located in an eighteenth-century mansion opposite the main post office, its collection is composed of two main groups: religious art taken from abandoned monasteries in the region, and nineteenth-century paintings on permanent loan from the Prado. The most impressive exhibits are on the first floor and include *Las Tablas de San Millán*, a series of beautifully preserved fourteenth-century paintings, and a roomful of remarkable, life-size wooden carvings cre-ated in 1597 by Pedro de Arbulo for the *retablo mayor* of the Monasterio de la Estrella. It's a pleasure to be able to see this kind of sculpture so close up and well lit. On the second floor are the Prado paintings, most of which won medals in the *Exposiciones Nacionales* in the late nineteenth century.

Practicalities

The heart of Logroño, the gardens of the wide **Paseo del Espolón**, is a five-minute walk from both the **bus station** (straight up c/General Vara de Rey) and the **train station** (up Avda. de España to the bus station, then up c/General Vara de Rey). The **turismo** is located in a modern building inside the gardens of the Paseo del Espolón (Mon–Fri 9am–2pm & 5–8pm, Sat 10am–2pm & 5–8pm, Sun 10am–2pm; ☎941 291 260, Ⓦwww.larioja .org/turismo).

The northern side of the Paseo del Espolón marks the start of the old quar-ter, which has the liveliest bars and restaurants and the lowest-priced **accom-modation**. *Residencia Daniel*, c/San Juan 21 (☎941 231 581; ❷), and *Pensión Sebastián* (☎941 242 800; ❷), in the same block, are two excellent budget

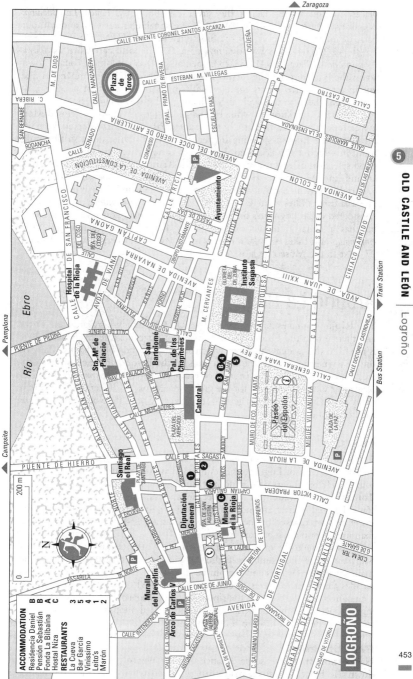

LOGROÑO

▲ Zaragoza

▲ Pamplona

▲ Campsite

Río Ebro

PUENTE DE PIEDRA

PUENTE DE HIERRO

ACCOMMODATION
Residencia Daniel   B
Pensión Sebastián   B
Fonda La Bilbaína   A
Hostal Niza   C
RESTAURANTS
La Cueva   3
Bar García   5
Vinissimo   4
Leito's   1
Marón   2

N

0   200 m

Hospital de la Rioja

Sta. Mª de Palacio

San Bartolomé

Pal. de los Chapiteles

Catedral

Santiago el Real

Diputación General

Museo de la Rioja

Muralla del Revellín

Arco de Carlos V

Plaza de Toros

Ayuntamiento

Instituto Sagasta

Paseo del Espolón

Plaza de la Paz

▼ Train Station

▼ Bus Station

453

places, though rooms facing the street can be noisy. *Fonda La Bilbaína*,
c/Gallarza 10 (℡941 254 226; ❷), also has reasonable rooms with and without
bath, or for more comfort, try the functional modern *Hostal Niza*, c/Gallarza
13 (℡941 206 044, Ⓦwww.hostalniza.com; ❸). The local **campsite**, *La Playa*,
Avenida de la Playa (℡941 252 253; open all year), is a kilometre out of town
across the Río Ebro, and lies beside its own sandy river beach; campers get free
entrance to a nearby sports complex with an enormous outdoor pool.

For **tapas**, head to the lively c/San Juan: good places include *La Cueva* (no.
13) and *Bar García* (no. 28) while best of all is *Vinissimo* at no. 23 (closed Mon
eve & Tues) which has fantastic home-made tapas, a carefully-selected wine list
on which the English-speaking owner is happy to advise, and a small dining
room in which a €9 *menú* and various á la carte options are served. There's a
good selection of **restaurants** along c/San Agustín, c/Laurel and c/del Peso,
around the Museo de la Rioja; other excellent options include *Leito's*,
c/Portales 30, which has a wonderful *menús* for €12, and a small list of elaborate à la carte dishes from €9 (closed Sun & Mon) and *Marón*, c/Portales 49,
considered to be Logroño's finest. It's not cheap – main courses start at €15 –
but has a fantastic reputation for quality. For snacks – including superb
empanadas and cakes – make a detour to *El Paraíso*, a bakery at c/San Agustín
27, next to the Museo de la Rioja.

Around La Rioja

The **Rioja** area takes its name from the Río Oja, which flows into the Tirón
and thence into the Ebro to the northwest of Logroño. Effectively, though, it
is the Ebro that waters the vines, which are cultivated on both banks. Many of
the best vineyards are on the north bank in the Basque province of Alava, an
area known as the *Rioja Alavesa*. Look out above all for wines described as
Reserva or *Gran Reserva*, and for the great vintages of '68, '69 and '70 – though
many say that with controls getting stricter every year, the younger wines are
the better ones.

Haro

The main centre of Rioja production is **HARO**, an attractive, working town,
40km northwest of Logroño. In addition to **wine-tasting** possibilities, it has
some lovely reminders of a grand past, notably the Renaissance church of **San
Tomás** with its wedding-cake tower, an imposing sight on any approach to
town. The old quarter around it is attractive in a low-key, faded kind of way, its
lower margins marked by the **Plaza de la Paz**, a glass-balconied square whose
mansions overlook an archaic bandstand.

The best time to be in Haro is in the last week of June, during the **fiestas** of
San Juan, San Felices and San Pedro. All the *bodegas* bring their wares to the
main square for tastings and bargain buys; there are free outdoor concerts and
parades through the streets of elaborately costumed characters on giant stilts.
The climax of these fiestas is the riotous *batalla del vino* on June 29, when thousands of people climb the Riscos de Bilibio (a small mountain near the town)
to be drenched from head to foot in wine.

Practicalities

Haro's **train station** is some distance out of town; to get to the centre, walk
down the hill to the main road, turn right and when you reach the bridge

Wine is at the very heart of La Rioja's identity, and few people will pass through Haro without wanting to buy a few bottles. It's a good idea to equip yourself with some **vocabulary** so you know what you're buying: *cosecha* (which literally means harvest), when used on its own, refers to young wines in their first or second year, which tend to have a fresh and fruity flavour; *crianzas* are wines which are at least in their third year, having spent at least one year in an oak cask and several months in the bottle; *reservas* are vintages that have been aged for three years with at least one year in the oak; and *gran reservas* have spent at least two years in oak casks and three years in the bottle. **Good years** to look out for include '75,'78,'81,'82,'91,'94, '95 and '01.

The most convenient **place to buy** your wine is at c/Santo Tomás 13 (just off the Plaza de la Paz) which has four excellent wine shops whose dark cellars stock a vast range of wines; another good outlet is El Rincón de Quintín near the bus station. You can expect to buy decent *crianzas* from around €5 and *reservas* from around €10. The town's famous *bodegas* include Bodegas Bilbaínas, CVNE (pronounced Cune), La Rioja Alta and Muga; most are located down by the train station. Many are reluctant to open their doors unless you're with a group, but Muga, in response to the increasing interest in wine tourism in the region, now run fascinating tours of their winery (summer Mon–Fri 11am in English, 12.30pm in Spanish; winter 11am in English, 4.30pm in Spanish, closed first two weeks of Aug; €3). Muga produce wine according to artesanal strictures with much of the work being done by hand; they make their own barrels and use egg whites to clean the wine of impurities – a slow, expensive, traditional method which has been rejected by many modern wineries in favour of a cheaper, quicker gelatine substitute. The tour takes in the entire wine production process including fermenting, ageing and barrelling, and finishes with a tasting session and a visit to the shop. To see other *bodegas*, try asking for help at the turismo who can supply you with telephone numbers or simply hanging around the gates looking interested but not too thirsty. To find out more about wine production, the high-tech **Museo del Vino** (Mon–Sat 10am–2pm & 4–8pm, Sun 10am–2pm; €2, free Wed), in the Estación Erológico on c/Breton de los Herreros, behind the bus station, has detailed and highly complicated displays of the processes involved, but no tastings.

(campsite off to the right), cross it and head straight uphill. **Buses** stop in Plaza Castañares, a ten-minute walk from the centre (follow signs for *centro* straight up c/la Ventilla). The **turismo** is on Plaza M. Florentino Rodríguez (July to mid-Sept daily 10am–2pm & 4.30–7.30pm; mid-Sept to June Tues–Fri & Sun 10am–2pm, Sat 10am–2pm & 4–7pm; ☎ & ℱ941 303 366, ⓦwww .beronia.org).

There's a variety of **accommodation** options in town: the best budget choice is *Pensión la Peña*, Plaza de la Paz 17, 2° (☎941 310 022; ❷), which has spotless rooms, some of them en suite and most with a balcony overlooking the plaza, and there are more modern (though smaller) rooms attached to *Bar-Restaurante Vega*, Plaza Juan García Gatio 1 (☎941 312 205, but you cannot reserve by phone; ❷). The brand-new, mid-range *Hostal Higinia*, in Plaza Virgen de la Vega (☎941 304 344, ℱ941 303 148; ❸), is extremely comfortable and has an attractive garden area shaded by a leafy vine. If it's luxury you're after, head for *Los Agostinos*, c/San Agustín 2 (☎941 311 308, ℮losagustinos@aranzazu -hoteles.com; ❺), a superb hotel in a converted Augustinian monastery. There's also an excellent **campsite** (☎941 312 737; open all year), down by the river below town with a bar and swimming (in the river or pool) nearby.

Even the humblest *menú del día* in town is transformed by a bottle of Rioja, and you'll get more wine – and very cheaply – in the many good **bars** that lie between the *ayuntamiento* and the church of San Tomás. There are plenty of good **restaurants** including the perennially popular *Beethoven I* (closed Wed evening & Thurs) and the more formal *Beethoven II* (closed Mon eve & Tues), opposite each other on c/San Tomás; *Terete* on c/de Lucrecia 26 (closed Sun night & Mon) and *Mesón Atamauri* on Plaza García Gatio.

Nájera

Fifteen kilometres south of Haro, **NÁJERA** is dramatically situated below a pink rock formation, and has an interesting Gothic monastery, **Santa María la Real** (May–Sept Mon–Sat 9.30am–1pm & 4–7pm, Sun 10am–12.30pm & 4–6.30pm; Oct–April Tues–Sat 10am–1pm & 4–5.30pm, Sun 10am–12.30pm & 4–5.30pm; €2). This contains a royal pantheon of ancient monarchs of Castile, León and Navarra – a host of sarcophagi and statues, some of which seem to have been made long after the death of the sitter. Best of all is the cloister of rose-coloured stone and elaborate tracery, closer to the Manueline style of Portugal than anything in Spain. There is nothing more to detain you, but if you want to stay there are several cheap restaurants, a **hotel**, *San Fernando* (☎941 363 700, ✉sanfernando@sanmillan.com; ❹), next to the river, and a *hostal*, *Hispano II* (☎ & ☏941 363 615; ❷).

Burgos

BURGOS was for some five hundred years the capital of Old Castile, and with its dark-stone old town and castle it remains redolent of these years of power and military strength. It has historic associations as the home of El Cid in the eleventh century, and as the base, two centuries later, of Fernando el Santo (Fernando III), the reconqueror of Murcia, Córdoba and Sevilla. It was Fernando who began the city's famous Gothic **cathedral**, one of the greatest in all Spain, though it, too, seems to share in the solemnity and severity of the city's history.

To Spaniards, the city has more modern military connotations. A large military garrison was stationed here for many years following the Civil War, when Franco temporarily installed his fascist government in the city. Burgos also owes much of its modern industry and expansion to Franco's "Industrial Development Plan", a strategy to shift the country's wealth away from Catalunya and the Basque country and into Castile. Even now, such connotations linger.

The most exciting times to be in Burgos are during **El Curpillos**, which takes place the day after the feast of Corpus Christi, and at the end of June for the two-week **Fiesta de San Pedro**, when *gigantillos* parade in the streets, and there are bullfights and all-night parties.

Arrival, orientation and information

Orientation in Burgos could not be simpler, since wherever you are the cathedral makes its presence felt. The Río Arlanzón bisects the city and neatly delimits the old quarters. The main pedestrian bridge is the **Puente de Santa María**, nearest the cathedral and facing the gateway of the same name. The **bus station** is on the "new" (south) side of the river at c/Miranda 4; the **train sta-**

tion is a short walk away at the bottom of Avenida Conde de Guadalhorre. Burgos is well-endowed with **turismos**. The most central, and consequently most busy, office is on Plaza Rey San Fernando, opposite the cathedral (daily: July–Sept 10am–8pm; Oct–June 10am–2pm & 5–8pm; ☎947 288 874, ⓦwww.aytoburgos.es); its counterpart on the Paseo del Espolón (July–Sept Mon–Sat 10am–2pm & 5–8pm, Sun 10am–2pm; Oct–June Mon–Sat 10am–2pm & 4.30–7.30pm, Sun 10am–2pm) is a five-minute walk away and has much shorter queues. The office at Plaza de Alonso Martínez 7 (daily: July–Sept 9am–8pm; Oct–June 9am–2pm & 5–8pm; ☎947 203 125), a five-minute walk northeast of the cathedral, also has information on the province of Castilla-Leon.

Accommodation

Rooms can often be difficult to come by; they're at a premium in late June and July, while during the university year many of the cheaper *pensiones* are brimful of students, so it's worth calling ahead to check. The best place to try for inexpensive accommodation is south of the river around the Plaza de Vega, and any road off towards the bus station as far as c/de San Pablo. There are plenty of smart, upmarket hotels in town, as well as one of the region's most luxurious and memorable places to stay just out of town on the road to Madrid.

The local **campsite**, *Camping Fuentes Blancas* (☎947 486 016; April–Sept), is out by the Cartuja de Miraflores (see p.462 for directions), 45 minutes' walk or a bus ride from the centre (buses hourly between 11am and 9pm, leaving from the Cid statue) – it's a very good site with excellent facilities, including a pool.

North of the river

Hotel Cordón c/Puebla 6 ☎947 265 000, ⓦwww.hotelcordon.com. Burgos's most characterful hotel, with very smart rooms in a beautiful, glass-balconied building. ⓺

Mesón Del Cid Plaza de Santa María 8 ☎947 208 715, ⓦwww.mesondelcid.es. Facing the cathedral, this is the smartest hotel in the old town, in a handsome old building and a modern block opposite, with its own parking (€12 per night). ⓺

Hostal Lar c/Cardenal Benlloch 1 ☎947 209 655, ⓕ947 209 655. Burgos's best mid-range option, despite its location on a busy main road, with big, comfy en-suite rooms and very friendly owners. ⓷

Hostal Manjón c/Gran Teatro 1 ☎947 208 689. Ten clean, comfortable and good-value modern rooms – some en suite – on the edge of the old town, a 10min walk from the cathedral. ⓶

Pensión Peña c/Puebla 18 ☎947 206 323. Easily the top budget option in Burgos, this welcoming and immaculate *pensión* offers outstanding value in a quiet but central location. ⓵

Pensión Victoria c/San Juan 3 ☎947 201 542. Rooms are basic and simply furnished but light and airy. It's more expensive than most *pensiónes* but very central. ⓶

South of the river

Hotel Conde de Miranda c/Miranda 4 ☎947 265 267, ⓕ947 207 770. Smart and comfortable rooms, if not particularly cheap, located (literally) on top of the bus station. ⓷

Pensión Dallás Plaza de Vega 6 ☎947 205 457. Reasonable rooms in this *pensión* on a busy roundabout right on the river front. ⓵

Landa Palace Carretera Madrid–Irún ☎947 257 777, ⓦwww.landapalace.es. A stunning and fabulously expensive hotel in a medieval tower, just out of town on the road to Madrid, complete with antique furnishings and a renowned restaurant. ⓼

The City

Arriving across the Puente de Santa María, you are confronted with the great white bulk of the **Arco de Santa María**. Originally this gateway formed part of the town walls; its facade was castellated with towers and turrets and embellished with statues in 1534–36 in order to appease the wrath of Carlos V after Burgos's involvement in a revolt by Spanish noblemen against their new

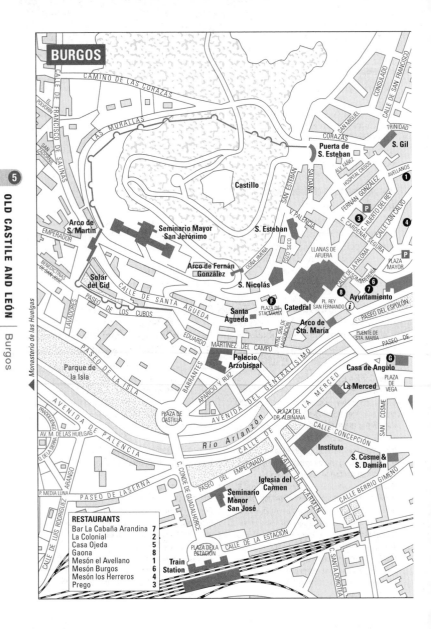

BURGOS

Castillo

Puerta de
S. Esteban

S. Gil

Arco de
S. Martín

Seminario Mayor
San Jerónimo

S. Esteban

Arco de Fernán
González

S. Nicolás

Solár
del Cid

Santa
Agueda

Catedral

Ayuntamiento

Arco de
Sta. María

Palacio
Arzobispal

Casa de Angulo

La Merced

Parque de
la Isla

Río Arlanzón

Instituto

S. Cosme &
S. Damián

Iglesia del
Carmen

Seminario
Menor
San José

Train
Station

RESTAURANTS

Bar La Cabaña Arandina	7
La Colonial	2
Casa Ojeda	5
Gaona	8
Mesón el Avellano	1
Mesón Burgos	6
Mesón los Herreros	4
Prego	3

Belgian-born king. Carlos's statue is glorified here in the context of the greatest Burgalese heroes: Diego Porcelos, founder of the city in the late ninth century; Nuño Rasura and Laín Calvo, two early magistrates; Fernán González, founder of the Countship of Castile in 932; and **El Cid Campeador**, who was surpassed only by Santiago *Matamoros* in his exploits against the Moors. El

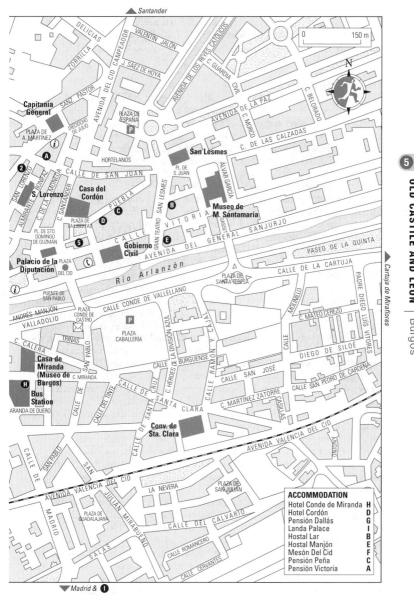

ACCOMMODATION

Hotel Conde de Miranda	H
Hotel Cordón	D
Pensión Dallás	G
Landa Palace	I
Hostal Lar	B
Hostal Manjón	E
Mesón Del Cid	F
Pensión Peña	C
Pensión Victoria	A

Cid was born Rodrigo Díaz in the village of Vivar, just north of Burgos, though his most significant military exploits actually took place around Valencia; *Cid*, incidentally, derives from the Arabic *sidi* (lord), and *Campeador* means "supreme in valour". There's a splendid **equestrian statue** of him – with flying cloak, flowing beard and raised sword – lording over the **Puente**

de San Pablo, the main road bridge to the old town. The statue, one of the city's principal landmarks, stands at the end of the **Paseo del Espolón**, a fashionable tree-lined promenade round which most of the evening life takes place.

The cathedral

The old quarters of Burgos are totally dominated by the **Catedral** (daily 9.30am–1.15pm & 4–7.15pm; €3, includes entrance to the museum), whose florid filigree of spires and pinnacles is among the most extraordinary achievements of Gothic art. The building is such a large complex of varied and opulent sections that it's difficult to appreciate it as a whole; it is the sheer accumulation of masterpieces – both inside and out – that impresses. Burgos has outstanding individual achievements in ironwork, woodcarving and sculpture, and almost every entrance and chapel seems to be of interest. Oddly enough, the most ornate entrance of all, the **Puerta de la Pellejería** at the northeast corner, is in a Renaissance-Platesque style, quite different from the bulk of the exterior. Most of the cathedral has now emerged from a lengthy period of restoration, looking cleaner than it has for a number of centuries, though some parts are still under wraps.

The Chapels

Inside the cathedral you're immediately struck by the size and number of side chapels, the greatest of which, the Capilla del Condestable, is almost a cathedral in itself. The most curious, though, is the **Capilla del Santo Cristo** (first right) which contains the bizarre *Cristo de Burgos*, a cloyingly realistic image of Christ (c. 1300), endowed with real human hair and nails and covered with the withered hide of a water buffalo, still popularly believed to be human skin. Legend has it that the icon was modelled directly from the Crucifixion and that it requires a shave and a manicure every eighth day.

The adjacent **Capilla de la Consolación** has a distinctive, early sixteenth-century star-shaped vault, a form adapted from the Moorish "honeycomb" vaults of Granada. Similar influences can also be seen in the cathedral's central dome (1568), highlighted with gold and blue and supported on four thick piers which fan out into remarkably delicate buttresses – a worthy setting for the **tomb of El Cid**, marked by a simple slab in the floor below.

The sumptuous, octagonal **Capilla del Condestable**, behind the high altar, contains a third superb example of star-vaulting. Here the ceiling is designed to form two eight-pointed stars, one within the other. The chapel, with its profusion of stone tracery, was founded in 1482 by Fernández de Velasco, Constable of Castile, whose marble tomb lies before the altar; the architect was the German Simón de Colonia. Between 1442 and 1458 his father Hans (Hispanicized as Juan) had built the twin openwork spires of the west facade, possibly modelling them on the spires planned for the cathedral in his home city of Cologne. In the third generation, Francisco de Colonia built the central dome and the Puerta de la Pellejería. Another father-and-son combination of artists was that of Gil and Diego de Siloé, the former from Flanders but his son born and raised in Spain. Gil worked on the *retablo* in the Capilla de Santa Ana (second left), while Diego's masterpiece, one of the crowning achievements of the cathedral, is the glorious **Escalera Dorada**, a double stairway in the north transept. Your ticket also admits you to the cloisters, the Diocesan Museum inside them, the Capilla del Condestable and the **Coro** at the heart of the cathedral, which affords the best view into the dome.

San Nicolás and San Esteban

Overlooking the plaza in front of the cathedral stands the fifteenth-century church of **San Nicolás** (June–Sept Mon–Fri 10am–2pm & 4.30–7pm, Sat & Sun 10am–noon; Oct–May on either side of daily services – ask at the turismo for service times; €1). Unassuming from the outside, it has an altarpiece within by Francisco de Colonia which is as rich as anything in the city. At the side of San Nicolás, c/Pozo Seco ascends to the early Gothic church of **San Esteban**, which now houses the mildly interesting **Museo del Retablo** (June–Sept Tues–Sat 10.30am–2pm & 4.30–7pm, Sun 10.30am–2pm; Oct–May Sat & Sun only, same hours; €1.20).

Monasterio de las Huelgas

Inevitably the lesser churches of Burgos tend to be eclipsed by the cathedral, but on the outskirts are two monasteries which are by no means overshadowed. The closer, the Cistercian **Monasterio de las Huelgas** (Tues–Sat 10am–1.15pm & 3.45–5.45pm, Sun 10.30am–2.15pm; €5, free Wed), is remarkable for its wealth of Mudéjar craftsmanship. It lies on the "new side" of the river, a twenty-minute walk from the city centre: cross Puente de Santa María, turn right and follow the signs along the riverbank. Founded in 1187 as the future mausoleum of Alfonso VIII and Eleanor of Aquitaine, wife of Henry II of England, it became one of the most highbrow and powerful convents in Spain. It was popularly observed that "if the pope were to marry, only the abbess of Las Huelgas would be eligible!" The main **church**, with its typically excessive Churrigueresque *retablo*, contains the tombs of no fewer than sixteen Castilian monarchs and nobles. Priceless embroidery, jewellery and weaponry of a suitably regal splendour were discovered inside the tombs and are exhibited in a small museum.

Among the highlights in the rest of the monastery are a set of delicate Romanesque cloisters, **Las Claustrillas**, and the ceiling of the main Gothic cloisters, which is adorned with patches of Mudéjar decoration, including the familiar eight-pointed stars and rare peacock designs – a bird holy to the Moors. The **Capilla de Santiago**, an obvious reminder that Las Huelgas stood on the pilgrim route, also has a fine Mudéjar ceiling and pointed horseshoe archway. Its cult statue of St James has an articulated right arm, which enabled him to dub knights of the Order of Santiago (motto: "The Sword is Red with the Blood of Islam") and on occasion even to crown kings. The convent was also responsible for the nearby Hospital del Rey where food and shelter were provided free for two nights. It now houses the university's faculty of law and it's worth visiting to see the portals.

The Cartuja de Miraflores

The second of the town's two notable monasteries, the **Cartuja de Miraflores** (Mon–Sat 10.15am–3pm & 4–6pm, Sun 11.20am–12.30pm, 1–3pm & 4–6pm; free), is famous for three dazzling masterpieces by Gil de Siloé. The buildings are still in use as a monastery and most are closed; you can, however, visit the **church**, built between 1454 and 1488 by Juan and Simón de Colonia. In accordance with Carthusian practice, it is divided into three sections for the public, the lay brothers and the monks. In front of the high altar lies the star-shaped joint tomb of Juan II and Isabel of Portugal, of such perfection in design and execution that it forced Felipe II and Juan de Herrera to admit "we did not achieve very much with our Escorial". Isabel la Católica, a great patron of the arts, commissioned it from Gil de Siloé in 1489 as a memorial to her parents. The same sculptor carved the magnificent altarpiece, which was plated with the first gold shipped back from America. His third masterpiece is the tomb of the Infante Alfonso, through whose untimely death in 1468 Isabel had succeeded to the throne of Castile.

Miraflores lies in a secluded spot about 4km from the centre: turn left from the Puente de Santa María along c/de Valladolid, from where the monastery is well signposted. There's a good restaurant in the nearby park. A bus runs on Sunday but returns right after the well-attended Mass; there's also a bus to the nearby campsite (see p.457).

Eating, drinking and nightlife

You'll find plenty of **restaurants** in Burgos serving traditional Castilian dishes – *cordero asado* (roast lamb) and *morcilla* (a kind of black pudding with rice) – but there's also a wide choice of other food and, due to the large student population, a lively **bar** scene.

Bar La Cabaña Arandina c/Sombrerería. Looking oddly like a marooned American diner, this fun eatery around the back of Plaza Mayor serves up cheap *platos combinados* and *bocadillos* around a big three-sided bar stuffed with tapas.

La Colonial c/San Lorenzo 35. Bistro-style restaurant, on a lively street, with a generous *menú* that offers a range of options (€9.50) and tables outside where you can sit and watch the world go by.

Casa Ojeda c/Vitoria 5. Huge, ornately decorated bar-deli-patisserie-restaurant complex, with a smart Castilian restaurant upstairs, a less expensive *comedor* downstairs, or tapas at the bar. À la carte dishes in the restaurant start at €15; *platos combinados* at €10.

Gaona c/de la Paloma 41. Formal and upmarket Spanish restaurant, very close to the cathedral, with a huge menu of meat and fish dishes from around €11 and no less than eight *menús* (€10.50–21).

Mesón el Avellano c/Avellanos. Cosy bar with a few tables and a fine array of tapas and *raciones*.

Mesón Burgos c/Sombrerería 8. Small, old-fashioned wooden bar, with a snug restaurant behind serving Castilian meat and fish standards from €7.

Mesón los Herreros c/San Lorenzo 18. Choose from an assortment of tapas at the bar or from a variety of meat and fish dishes in the *comedor* upstairs. One of many restaurants and bars on this vibrant street.

Prego c/Huerto del Rey. Pleasant if not particularly cheap Italian restaurant with a big menu including pasta (from €6), meat dishes (€9) and pizza (from €11).

Nightlife

What **nightlife** there is in staid Burgos is mainly generated by the local students, who hang out in the noisy and (mainly) nasty bars down c/Huerto del Rey and around Llanas de Afuera, just behind the cathedral: *Trastos*, at c/Huerto del Rey 13, is as good a place as any to go deaf in quickly. Alternatively, try the lively bunch of **tapas bars** in c/Avellanos and near the cathedral in c/de la Paloma and c/Sombrerería. After 3am, head for the **clubs** in the new district of Bernardos round c/Las Calzadas and Avenida de la Paz, just to the east of the old city. Most places play loud rock and dated heavy metal; for a more relaxed atmosphere and soothing jazz music, try *Café de España*, at c/Laín Calvo 12, or listen to mellow tunes at *Café de las Artes* at c/Laín Calvo 31, near the Plaza Mayor.

Listings

Bus information ☎947 288 855.
Car rental Operators include Avis, c/Maestro Justo del Río, 2–4 ☎947 220 606; Europcar, c/Santa Clara 32 ☎947 273 745; and Hertz, c/Madrid 2 ☎947 201 675.
Internet access *Ciber-Café*, c/Puebla 21 (June–Sept Mon–Fri 12.30pm–2am, Sat & Sun 5pm–4am; Oct–May Mon–Thurs 4pm–2am, Fri &

Sat 4pm–4am, Sun 5pm–2am; €2 for 30min, €4 for 1hr).
Post office The main office is at Plaza de Conde de Castro, by the Puente San Pablo (Mon–Fri 8.30am–8.30pm, Sat 9.30am–2pm).
Taxis Abutaxi ☎947 277 777 and Radio Taxi ☎947 481 010; both offer a 24-hour service.
Train information ☎947 203 560.

Southeast of Burgos

Southeast of Burgos, off the road to Soria, is a trio of sights: the great monastery of **Santo Domingo de Silos**; the town of **Covarrubias**, a medieval treasure on the Río Arlanza; and **Quintanilla de las Viñas**, a tiny Visigothic church and hermitage. These are easy excursions if you have transport. If you don't, you'll need commitment and time to get the daily early-evening bus from Burgos to Silos via Lerma, staying for two nights (the bus back to Burgos leaves at 8am so there is no time to see the monastery). Pilgrims, of course, used to (and still do) walk the 60km to Silos as a detour from the *camino*.

Santo Domingo de Silos and around

The Benedictine abbey of **SANTO DOMINGO DE SILOS** is one of Spain's greatest Christian monuments. Its main feature is a great double-storey eleventh-century **Romanesque cloister** (Mon & Sun 4.30–6pm, Tues–Sat 10am–1pm & 4.30–6pm; €2.40), whose beautiful sculptural decoration is in many ways unique. The most remarkable features of the cloister are eight almost life-sized **reliefs** on the corner pillars. They include *Christ on the Road to Emmaus*, dressed as a pilgrim to Santiago (complete with scallop shell), in solidarity with those pilgrims that make a detour from the main route to see the tomb of Santo Domingo, the eleventh-century abbot after whom the monastery is named.

The same sculptor was responsible for about half of the **capitals**. Besides a famous bestiary, these include many Moorish motifs, giving rise to speculation that he may even have been a Moor. Whatever the case, it is an early example of the effective mix of Arab and Christian cultures, which was continued in the fourteenth century with the painted Mudéjar vault showing scenes of everyday pastimes. A quite different sculptor carved many of the remaining capitals, including the two that ingeniously tell the stories of the Nativity and the Passion in a very restricted space. A third master was responsible for the pillar with the Annunciation and Tree of Jesse, which is almost Gothic in spirit.

Visits to the monastery also include entry to the eighteenth-century **pharmacy**, which has been reconstructed in a room off the cloister, and the **museum**, which houses the tympanum from the destroyed Romanesque church. The **church** itself is an anticlimax, a rather nondescript construction designed by the eighteenth-century academic Ventura Rodríguez. Its Romanesque predecessor was too dark for the taste of the times; fortunately, the cloister's size and spaciousness saved it from a similar fate. The monks, who released a platinum-selling CD in the 1990s, are considered one of the top three best Gregorian chant choirs in the world; it's particularly worth attending the morning Mass (Mon–Sat 9am) or, even better, vespers (daily, 7pm), while the best singing of all can be heard at noon on Saturdays and Sundays.

Practicalities

Men can **stay** in the monastery itself if they contact the Guest Master (*Padre Hospedería*) in advance (☎947 390 049, ⓦ www.silos.arrakis.es); he prefers people to stay a few days. This is a wonderful bargain, with comfortable single rooms and good food at a ridiculously low cost (€24 per night). There are also some excellent places to stay in the village: the *Hotel Arco de San Juan*, Pradera de San Juan 1 (☎ & ⓕ947 390 074; ❸), very near the cloister entrance, which has a pleasant garden; the new, clean and well-furnished *Hostal Cruces* in the Plaza Mayor (☎947 390 064, ⓔhotsalcruces@terra.es; ❷), which has an

△ La Madre de todo los pueblos

informative, English-speaking manager and serves good-value evening meals; and the *Hotel Tres Coronas de Silos*, Plaza Mayor 6 (T & F 947 390 065; ❹), an imposing stone house which dominates the square.

The Gorges of Yecla

The landscape around Silos is some of the most varied in Castile. A short walk up the hill gives a superb bird's-eye view of the village and the surrounding countryside and nearby are the impressive **gorges of Yecla**.

To reach these, take the road to Aranda de Duero, heading south of Silos. After 3km you pass through two tunnels in quick succession. On exiting the second tunnel, descend a flight of stairs to the left which leads down to a concrete walkway through an incredibly narrow rocky gorge, the **Desfiladero de la Yecla**. It makes a spectacular 15-minute walk, with birds of prey circling high in the thin strip of visible sky. At the other end of the gorge, another flight of stairs takes you back to the road. If you continue 500m south from the gorge rather than heading straight back to Silos, you can climb to the picturesque hilltop village of **Hinojar de Cervera** and descend on the far side, after a couple of kilometres, to the **Cueva de San García**. This is a small cave containing various faded and rudimentary examples of prehistoric art.

Covarrubias

The superbly preserved small town of **COVARRUBIAS** is just under 20km north of Silos, on the C110 between Lerma and the Burgos–Soria road. The town itself is the attraction: many of its white houses are half-timbered, with shady arcades, and remnants of the fortifications are still standing, including a tenth-century tower. The **Colegiata** (Mon & Wed–Sat 10.30am–2pm & 4–7pm, Sun 10.30am–noon & 4–7pm; €2) looks plain from the outside, but a visit to the interior is a must. Inside you'll find a late-Gothic hall church crammed with tombs, giving an idea of the grandeur of the town in earlier times. The organ is an amazing seventeenth-century instrument still in good working order, though you'll probably have to be content with hearing a recording. There are several good paintings in the museum, but the chief attraction is a triptych whose central section, a polychromed carving of the *Adoration of the Magi*, is attributed to Gil de Siloé.

Public **transport** is limited: there's no bus service between Covarrubias and Silos, although it is just possible to see both towns in a day on foot; the alternative is to come direct on one of the two daily buses from Burgos (leaving 1pm & 6.30pm). If you plan **to stay** in Covarrubias, there are three excellent options: the mid-range *Hotel Arlanza*, Plaza Mayor 11 (T 947 406 441, W www.hotelarlanza.com; ❸), is great value for money, as is the equally attractive *Hotel Rey Chindasvinto*, Plaza del Rey Chindasvinto 5 (T 947 406 560, E hotelchindas@wanadoo.es; ❸), right next to the Colegiata. The only budget accommodation is above the restaurant *Casa Galín* (T 947 406 552, F 947 406 552; ❶), which is also the best place to **eat** in the village.

Quintanilla

An equally important monument, this time a rare Visigothic survival, is to be found at **QUINTANILLA DE LAS VIÑAS**, which lies 4km north of Mazanriegos on the main Burgos–Soria road, about 40km southeast of Burgos. Signs labelled *Turismo* lead to a house where the caretaker of the **Ermita de Santa María** (April–Sept Wed–Sun 9.30am–2pm & 4–7pm, Oct–March Wed–Sun 10am–5pm, closed last weekend in each month) lives; if he isn't there, he'll probably be at the hermitage itself, 1km further north (or you can call him on ☎626 496 215). It's a simple building, of which only the transept and the chancel survive. Dating from about 700, it's remarkable for its unique series of sculptures: the outside bears delicately carved friezes, and inside there's a triumphal arch with capitals representing the sun and moon, and a block which is believed to be the earliest representation of Christ in Spanish art.

Burgos to León

The pilgrim route west from Burgos to León is one of the most rewarding sections in terms of art and architecture. The N120 between the two cities passes through **Carrión de los Condes** and **Sahagún**, and the other stops on the *camino*, along with some impressive **Roman remains** near the town of Saldaña, are only a short detour off the main road.

Frómista

FRÓMISTA was the next important pilgrimage stop after Burgos. The present-day town is much decayed, with a fraction of the population it once had. There's only one sight of any note – the extremely beautiful, deconsecrated church of **San Martín**, which was originally part of an abbey which no longer exists (daily: summer 10am–2pm & 4.30–8pm; winter 10am–2pm & 3–6.30pm; €1, free Wed). Carved representations of monsters, human figures and animals run right around the church, which was built in 1066 in a Romanesque style unusually pure for Spain, with no traces of later additions. In fact, what you can see now is a result of an early twentieth-century restoration which was perhaps rather too thorough, although it is pleasing to the eye. Its beauty is enhanced by being completely devoid of furnishings; there's nothing to detract from the architecture, and the only colour is provided by twin wooden statues of San Martín and Santiago. The other church associated with the pilgrimage, **Santa María**, is near the train station, but it is also redundant and is kept locked.

If you want to **stay** there are three comfortable places: *Pensión Camino de Santiago*, c/Francesca 26 (☎979 810 053, ⓦwww.caminofromista.com; ❶), on the square with the children's playground on the road north to Santander, *Pensión Marisa* (☎979 810 023; ❶), behind San Martín, and the slightly more upmarket *Hotel San Martín*, Plaza San Martín 7 (☎ & ⓕ979 810 000; ❷), which also does a very popular lunchtime *menú*. The *Hostería de Los Palmeros*, Plaza San Telmo (☎988 810 067), is a former medieval pilgrims' *hostal* now converted into an excellent restaurant. The **turismo** (summer daily 9.30am–2pm & 4.30–8pm; winter Sat & Sun only; ☎979 810 113) is at the crossroads in the centre of town where the tour buses stop. Frómista is connected with Burgos by a daily bus, although it's reached more easily from Palencia since it lies on the Palencia–Santander rail line.

Villalcázar de Sirga

Thirteen kilometres from Frómista lies **VILLALCÁZAR DE SIRGA**, notable for a **church** built by the Knights Templar: from a distance it seems to crush the little village by its sheer mass, and originally its fortified aspect was even more marked. The Gothic style here begins to assert itself over the Romanesque, as witnessed by the figure sculpture on the two portals and the elegant pointed arches inside. The **Capilla de Santiago** has three polychromed tombs, among the finest of their kind and contemporary with the building. If the church is closed, as it usually is, take the street to the left in front of it and turn left at the corner; the sexton's house is the brick building with scallop shell motif tiles on the facade.

If you want **to stay**, the brand new, extremely comfortable and tastefully furnished *Hostal Doña Leonor* (℡979 888 015, ℻979 888 164, ❷) has a range of en-suite rooms on offer. In the square itself are a few medieval houses, one of which has been converted into the excellent **restaurant**, *El Mesón de Villasirga*. For more information on Villalcázar see ⓦwww.villalcazardesirga.org.

Carrión de los Condes

The dusty, quiet atmosphere of **CARRIÓN DE LOS CONDES** belies its sensational past. It's reputed to be the place where, before the Reconquest, Christians had to surrender one hundred virgins annually to the Moorish overlords – a scene depicted on the portal of **Santa María** (situated at the edge of town, where the buses stop). For finer sculpture, however, look at the doorway of **Santiago**'s own church in the centre of town, overlooking the Plaza Mayor. Time has not treated this kindly; burned out during the last century, the church was rebuilt but now stands disused and neglected. Look out for the extraordinarily delicate covings above the door, which depict the trades and professions of the Middle Ages. The town's third main monument is the Plateresque cloister of the **Monasterio de San Zoilo** (May to mid-Oct daily 10.30am–2pm & 4.30–8pm; mid-Oct to April Mon–Fri 10.30am–2pm, Sat & Sun 10.30am–2pm & 4–6.30pm; €1.50), located over the sixteenth-century bridge; a side room off the cloister contains the tombs of the counts of Carrión, from whom the town's name comes. The nuns of the **Real Convento de las Clarisas** have opened a small **museum** (Tues–Sun April to mid-Oct 10.30am–1.30pm & 4.30–7.30pm; mid-Oct to March 11am–1pm & 4.30–7pm; €2) with a moderately interesting collection, including one of Spain's oldest organs and their main work of art, the theatrical *Piedad* by Gregorio Fernández.

For **accommodation**, there are two budget options: the extremely cheap *El Resablón* at c/Fernan Gomez 19 (℡979 880 433; ❶) or the more upmarket, *Hostal La Corte*, at c/Santa María 34 (℡ & ℻979 880 138; ❶). For more comfort and style try the *Hostal Santiago*, at Plaza de los Regents (℡979 881 052, ℻979 880 272; ❷), which has large, spotlessly clean, thoughtfully furnished en-suite rooms, while by far the most atmospheric place to stay is the splendid *Hotel Real Monasterio San Zoilo* (℡979 880 049, ⓦwww.sanzoilo.com; ❹), recently converted from part of the monastery. The hotel is also the best place **to eat** in town; alternatives include the excellent, cheap restaurant at *Hostal La Corte*, or the cosy *Cervecería JM* at Plaza Marques de Santillana which serves up hearty *menús* (€7) and a varied á la carte selection. There's plenty of room for unofficial **camping** down by the river, or in the shady and modern official campsite, *El Edén* (℡979 881 152), also by the river and back from the main road. Carrión is linked by **bus** to both Burgos and Palencia.

Sahagún and San Miguel de Escalada

From Carrión the direct route west continues to **Sahagún**. No other town so clearly illustrates the effect of the decline from the heyday of the pilgrimage. Once the seat of the most powerful monastery in all Spain, it's now a largely modern town, above which the towers of the remaining old buildings rear up like dinosaurs in a zoo. The nearby monastery at **San Miguel de Escalada** has similarly slipped into insignificance.

Sahagún

SAHAGÚN is generally thought to be the birthplace of Spain's Mudéjar brick churches which were built by Moorish craftsmen who stayed on to work for the Christians after the Reconquest. Unfortunately, its great Benedictine **monastery** is these days little more than a largely ruined shell whose main surviving sections – the gateway and belfry – date from a period of reconstruction in the seventeenth century. Right beside these is the most delicate of Sahagún's Mudéjar churches, the twelfth-century **San Tirso** (July–Sept Tues–Sat 10am–1.30pm & 5–8pm, Sun 10am–1.30pm; Oct–June Tues–Sat 10am–2pm & 4–7pm, Sun 10am–2pm), now beautifully restored and looking almost unnaturally pristine in comparison to the monastery remains scattered around it. Just to the other side of San Tirso is the plain building of the **Monasterio Santa Cruz**, whose museum (Tues–Sat 9.45am–12.30pm & 4–6.30pm, Sun 10am–12.30pm; €1.50) houses the great *custodia* made by Enrique de Arfe, founder of a dynasty of silversmiths. Its big sister is the famous one at Toledo; like that one, the only airing it gets is during the Corpus Christi celebrations. The nuns prefer only to open up to groups, but try anyway if you're on your own – many pilgrims pass by here to get the official stamp for their *Camino de Santiago* card.

Walking across town you'll see the grand brick towers of further Mudéjar edifices rising incongruously above Sahagún's otherwise dull and modern skyline. The most imposing is the church of **San Lorenzo** (July–Sept Wed–Sun 10am–2pm & 4–8pm; Oct–June irregular hours), just off the Plaza Mayor up the unnamed road behind the Banco Herrero, which has a very grand exterior. It contains a small **Museo de Semana Santa** – a fairly gory collection of life-sized, blood-spattered Christs either being led to the cross or crucified upon it. It's also worth hunting out **La Peregrina**, on the edge of town five minutes' walk beyond San Tirso, a thirteenth-century monastery now crumbling into atmospheric rubble, though there's a beautiful little restored chapel inside (ask at San Tirso about visiting), with fine stuccowork.

Practicalities

There's a small **turismo** at c/El Arco 87, in a converted church (daily: July–Sept 10am–10pm; Oct–June 10am–2pm & 4.30–7pm; ☎987 782 117), which can supply local information. **Buses** leave from the Plaza Mayor but are very infrequent; it's much easier to come by **train** from León or Palencia (13 daily in each direction). Turn right out of the train station down Avenida Constitución to reach Plaza Mayor, a ten-minute walk. En route you'll pass several of the town's **accommodation** options: the good-value *Pensión La Asturiana* on Plaza Lesmes Franco, next to San Tirso (☎987 780 073; ❶), which has clean, functional rooms with shared bathrooms; the slightly pricier *La Cordoniz* (☎987 780 276, ☎987 780 186; ❷); and, just off on a side street to the left, the good-value *Alfonso VI* (☎987 781 144, ☎987 781 258; ❷). There's a nice faux-medieval **restaurant** at *La Codorniz* with a *menú* for €9, while bar-restaurant *Luís* on Plaza Mayor and the *Cafetería Caracas* just up the hill on Avenida Constitución are both good places for a drink or snack.

San Miguel de Escalada

Although León is just a short distance further on from Sahagún, the medieval pilgrim would probably first have made a slight detour to see the monastery of **SAN MIGUEL DE ESCALADA**, a precious Mozarabic survival from the tenth century. Founded by refugee monks from Córdoba, it's a touching little building, with a simple interior of horseshoe arches, and a later portico, again Moorish in style. You'll need your own transport to visit: although there are two buses a day to and from León, one turns back thirty minutes after it arrives, while the other requires spending the night – and there's nowhere to stay.

León

Even if they stood alone, the stained glass in the cathedral of **LEÓN** and the Romanesque wall paintings in its Royal Pantheon would merit a very considerable journey, but there's much more to the city than this. León is as attractive – and enjoyable – in its modern quarters as it is in those parts that remain from its heyday; it's a prosperous provincial capital and lively university town.

Arrival, orientation and information

León's modern sectors have been imaginatively laid out with wide, straight streets radiating like spokes from three focal plazas. The first of these is the **Glorieta de Guzmán el Bueno** near the river and the **train station**. Just south of here is the **bus station** on Paseo Ingeniero Miera.

From the Glorieta you can see straight down the Avenida de Ordoño II and across the **Plaza de Santo Domingo** to the towers of the cathedral. Just off the Plaza de Santo Domingo stands the **Casa de Botines**, an uncharacteristically restrained work by Antoni Gaudí. The third key square is the **Plaza de la Inmaculada**, connected to the Glorieta by the Avenida de Roma. Head straight up from Plaza de Santo Domingo to the cathedral and you'll arrive in the Plaza Regia; here, directly opposite the cathedral's great west facade, stands the main **turismo** (July & Aug Mon–Thurs & Sun 9am–8pm, Fri & Sat 9am–9pm; Sept–June daily 9am–2pm & 5–7pm; ☎987 237 082, ⓦwww.aytoleon.com). León's old quarter lies to the south of the cathedral, occupying the streets around the Plaza Mayor and Plaza San Martin and juxtaposing old Spain with the new. While the modern part of town is spacious and smart, the old part is a tangle of narrow streets that feel shabby and worn. Despite that, the ramshackle buildings in faded ochre and rose pink give the old *barrio* a charm all of its own. It bursts into life at night when the streets throng and the bars are packed out.

Accommodation

There's a cluster of budget **accommodation** scattered around c/del Carmen in the downtown area just east of the river. Alternatively, there are lots of cheap rooms round the Plaza Mayor which is a much more atmospheric area: they're generally less expensive but a little dingy, and those close to the bars and restaurants can be very noisy at night. Some mid-range options in the old town offer good value for money.

Old town

Boccalino Plaza de San Isidoro 9 ☎987 223 060, ⓕ987 227 878. Nicely furnished hotel with attractive furniture and wooden floors in a honey-coloured building above the restaurant of the same name, on this lovely square overlooking the church. ❹

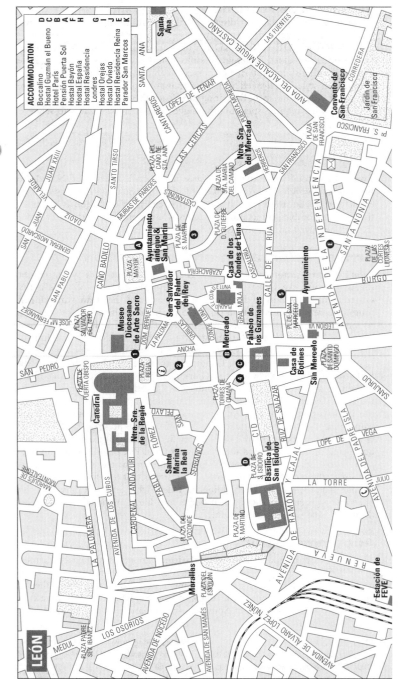

LEÓN

Asturias ▲

ACCOMMODATION

Boccalino	D
Hostal Guzmán el Bueno	C
Hotel París	B
Pensión Puerta Sol	A
Hostal Bayón	F
Hostal España	H
Hostal Residencia	
Londres	G
Hostal Orejas	I
Hostal Oviedo	J
Hostal Residencia Reina	E
Parador San Marcos	K

Santa Ana

Convento de San Francisco

Jardín de San Francisco

Ntra. Sra. del Mercado

Ayuntamiento antiguo & San Martín

Casa de los Condes de Luna

San Salvador del Palat del Rey

Museo Diocesano de Arte Sacro

Palacio de los Guzmanes

Ayuntamiento

Mercado

Casa de Botines

San Marcelo

Catedral

Ntra. Sra. de la Regla

Santa Marina la Real

Basílica de San Isidoro

Murallas

Estación de FEVE

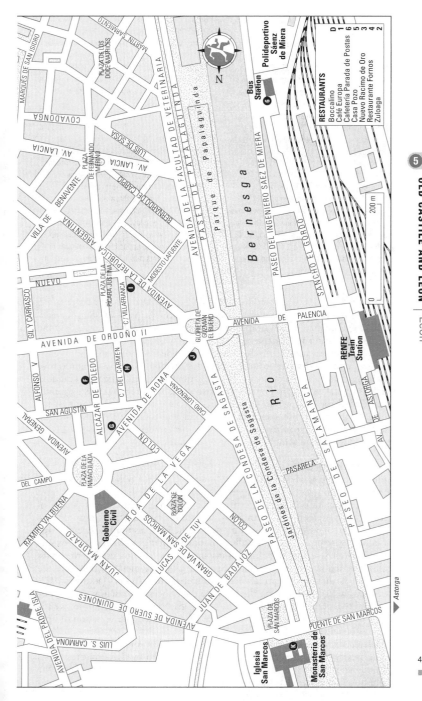

OLD CASTILE AND LEÓN | León

471

RESTAURANTS

	D
Boccalino	1
Café Europa	6
Cafetería Parada de Postas	5
Casa Pozo	3
Nuevo Racimo de Oro	4
Restaurante Fornos	2
Zuloaga	

N

Polideportivo Sáenz de Miera

Bus Station

Parque de Papalaguinda

Paseo de Papalaguinda

Bernesga

Paseo del Ingeniero Sáez de Miera

AVENIDA DE LA FACULTAD DE VETERINARIA

MARTÍN SARMIENTO

PLAZA DE LOS DOCE MÁRTIRES

MARQUÉS DE SAN ISIDRO

COVADONGA

AV. LANCIA

PLAZA DE FERNANDO MERINO

LUIS DE SOSA

AV. LANCIA

BERNARDO DEL CARPIO

BENAVENTE

VILLA DE

ARGENTINA

PLAZA DE LA PÍCARA JUSTINA

ANSELMO OLISÓN

NUEVO

GIL Y CARRASCO

AVENIDA DE LA REPÚBLICA

C/ VILLAFRANCA

I

AVENIDA DE ORDOÑO II

GLORIETA DE GUZMÁN EL BUENO

AVENIDA DE PALENCIA

ALFONSO V

SAN AGUSTÍN

ALCÁZAR DE TOLEDO

F

C/ DEL CARMEN

H

AVENIDA DE ROMA

CARD. LORENZANA

J

AVENIDA GENERAL

AVENIDA DE ORDOÑO II

G

COLÓN

PASEO DE LA CONDESA DE SAGASTA

Río

SANCHO EL GORDO

RENFE Train Station

DE ASTORGA

AV.

DE SALAMANCA

PASEO

DEL CAMPO

PLAZA DE LA INMACULADA

RAMIRO VALBUENA

JUAN MADRAZO

ROA DE LA VEGA

LUCAS DE TUY

GRAN VÍA DE SAN MARCOS

Gobierno Civil

PLAZA DE COLÓN

COLÓN

ZOTRAL DE BADAJOZ

PASARELA

Jardines de la Condesa de Sagasta

LUIS S. CARMONA

AVENIDA DEL PADRE ISLA

AVENIDA DE SUERO DE QUIÑONES

JUAN DE BADAJOZ

PLAZA DE SAN MARCOS

Iglesia San Marcos

Monasterio de San Marcos

PUENTE DE SAN MARCOS

Astorga

0   200 m

Hostal Guzmán el Bueno c/López Castrillón 6 ☎ & ⓕ987 236 412. Well-equipped rooms in a handy central location near Palacio de los Guzmanes. ❷

Hotel París c/Ancha 18 ☎987 238 600, ⓦwww.hotelparisleon.com. Luxurious modern rooms in a former palace close to the cathedral. ❹

Pensión Puerta Sol c/Puerta del Sol 1 ☎987 211 966. Reasonable rooms in an excellent location overlooking the attractive Plaza Mayor; one of the few *pensiones* here not permanently occupied by students. ❶

New town

Hostal Bayón c/Alcázar de Toledo 6 ☎987 231 446. Best budget accommodation in town: stripped-pine floors, high ceilings, large windows, quiet rooms and firm beds throughout. There are only five rooms though, so best book ahead. ❶

Hostal España c/del Carmen 3 ☎987 236 014. Good-value, clean *hostal* with charming owners located in a quiet side street. ❶

Hostal Residencia Londres Avda. de Roma 1 ☎987 222 274. Spotless rooms, all with bathroom, TV and phone, with nice views; good value. ❷

Hostal Orejas c/Villafranca 8 ☎ & ⓕ987 252 909. Comfortable, if somewhat nondescript, rooms with bath, TV and pale wooden furniture in a 1950s building. ❸

Hostal Oviedo Avda. de Roma 26 ☎987 222 236. Slightly worn but perfectly comfortable rooms near the train station. ❶

Hostal Residencia Reina Puerto de la Reina 2 ☎987 205 212. Neat, modern little eleven-room *hostal*, quite centrally located, with pleasant and excellent-value rooms, some en suite. ❶

Parador San Marcos Plaza San Marcos 7 ☎987 237 300, ⓔleon@parador.es. Once described as the best hotel in the world, this sensational *parador* in one of León's most historic buildings (see opposite), with antiques in the rooms, seems reasonably priced at €135 a night. ❼

The City

In 914, as the Reconquest edged its way south from Asturias, Ordoño II transferred the Christian capital from Oviedo to León. Despite being sacked by the dreaded al-Mansur in 996, the new capital rapidly eclipsed the old – a scenario that was to repeat itself as the Reconquest unfolded. As more and more territory came under the control of León, it was divided into new administrative groupings: in 1035 the county of Castile matured into a fully fledged kingdom with its capital at Burgos. For the next two centuries León and Castile jointly spearheaded the war against the Moors – as often as not under joint rule – until, by the thirteenth century, Castile had come finally to dominate her mother kingdom. These two centuries were nevertheless the period of León's greatest power, from which date most of her finest monuments.

The cathedral

León's Gothic **Catedral** (July–Sept: Mon–Sat 8.30am–1.30pm & 4–8pm, Sun 8.30am–2.30pm & 5–8pm; Oct–June same hours but closes at 7pm; ⓦwww.catedraldeleon.org) dates from the final years of the city's period of greatness. Its stained-glass **windows** (thirteenth century and onwards) are equal to the masterpieces in any European cathedral – a stunning kaleidoscope of light streaming in through walls of multicoloured glass. While such extensive use of glass is purely French in inspiration, the colours used here – reds, golds and yellows – are essentially Spanish. Other elements which take the cathedral further away from its French model are the cloisters (admission €1, but they are also included on the ticket to the Diocesan Museum – see opposite) and the later addition of the *coro*, whose glass screen, added in the twentieth century to give a clear view up to the altar, enhances the sensation of light with its bewildering refractions.

Outside, the magnificent **west façade**, dominated by a massive rose window, comprises two towers and a detached nave supported by flying buttresses – a pattern repeated at the south angle. The inscription *locus appelationis* on the main porch indicates that the Royal Court of Appeal was held here, and amid the statuary a king ponders his verdict, seated on a throne of lions. Above the **central doorway** a more sublime trial – the Last Judgement – is in full swing. The sculpture on this triple portal of the facade is some of the finest on the Pilgrim Route, although later in date than most. The doorways of the south transept and the polychromed door to the north transept (shielded from the elements by the cloister) are other attractions. The cloister houses the rather eclectic **Diocesan Museum** (June Mon–Sat 9.30am–1.30pm & 4–7pm; July–Sept Mon–Fri 9.30am–1.30pm & 4–7.30pm, Sat 9.30am–2pm & 4–7pm; Oct–May Mon–Fri 9.30am–1.30pm & 4–7pm, Sat 9.30pm–1.30pm; €3.50).

The Pantéon

From the Plaza de Santo Domingo, Avenida de Ramón y Cajal leads to the Basilica of San Isidoro (open all day) and the Royal Pantheon of the early kings of León and Castile. Fernando I, who united the two kingdoms in 1037, commissioned the complex as a shrine for the bones of San Isidoro and a mausoleum for himself and his successors. The church dates mainly from the mid-twelfth century and shows Moorish influence in the horseshoe arch at the west end of the nave and the fanciful arches in the transepts. The bones of the patron saint lie in a reliquary on the high altar.

The **Pantéon** (July & Aug Mon–Sat 9am–8pm, Sun 9am–2pm; Sept–June Mon–Sat 10am–1.30pm & 4–6.30pm, Sun 10am–1.30pm; €3, free Thurs pm), reached through the door to the left of the main entrance and comprising two surprisingly small crypt-like chambers, was constructed between 1054 and 1063 as a narthex or portico preceding the west facade of the church. It's one of the earliest Romanesque buildings in Spain, and the carvings on the portal which links the Pantéon and church herald the introduction of figure sculpture into the peninsula. In contrast, the capitals of the side piers and the two squat columns in the middle of the Pantéon are carved with thick foliage which is still rooted in Visigothic tradition. Towards the end of the twelfth century, the extraordinarily well-preserved vaults were vividly covered in some of the most significant, imaginative and impressive paintings of Romanesque art. The central dome is occupied by Christ Pantocrator surrounded by the four Evangelists depicted with animal heads – allegorical portraits which stem from the apocalyptic visions in the Bible's Book of Revelation. One of the arches bordering the dome is decorated with quaint rustic scenes which represent the months of the year. Eleven kings and twelve queens were laid to rest here, but the chapel was desecrated during the Peninsular War and the remaining tombs command little attention in such a marvellous setting.

You can also visit the treasury and library; the former contains magnificent reliquaries, caskets and chalices from the early Middle Ages, but only reproductions of the manuscripts are on view.

San Marcos

If the Pantéon is a perfect illustration of the way Romanesque art worked its way into Spain along the Pilgrim Route from France, the opulent **Monasterio de San Marcos** (reached from the Plaza de la Inmaculada via Gran Vía de San Marcos) stands as a more direct reminder that León was a station on this route. Here, on presentation of the relevant documents, pilgrims were allowed to regain their strength before the gruelling Bierzo mountains west of León. The original monastery was built in 1168 for the Knights of Santiago, one of several chivalric orders founded in the twelfth century to protect pilgrims and lead the Reconquest. Eventually these powerful, ambitious and semi-autonomous knights posed a political threat to the authority of the

Spanish throne, until in 1493 Isabel la Católica subtly tackled the problem by "suggesting" that her husband Fernando be "elected" Grand Master. Thus the wealth and power of this order was assimilated to that of the throne.

In time, the order degenerated to little more than a men's club – Velázquez, for instance, depicts himself in its robes in *Las Meninas* – and in the sixteenth century the monastery was rebuilt as a kind of palatial headquarters. Its massive facade is lavishly embellished with Plateresque appliqué designs: over the main entrance Santiago is once again depicted in his battling role of *Matamoros*; more pertinently, the arms of Carlos V, who inherited the grand mastership from Fernando in 1516, protrude above the ornate balustrade of the roofline. The monastery is now a *parador* (see p.472), and is officially off-limits to non-residents beyond its foyer and (modern) bar and restaurant, though you may be able to sneak in for a discreet look at the fine cloisters and the *coro alto* of the church (access only from the hotel), which has a fine set of stalls by Juan de Juni.

Adjacent to the main facade stands the **Iglesia San Marcos**, vigorously speckled with the scallop shell motif of the pilgrimage. Its sacristy houses a small **museum** (July–Sept Tues–Sat 10am–2pm & 5–8pm, Sun 10am–2pm; Oct–April Tues–Sat 10am–2pm & 4–7pm, Sun 10am–2pm; €1.20), whose most beautiful and priceless exhibits include a thirteenth-century processional cross made of rock crystal and an eleventh-century ivory crucifix.

Eating, drinking and nightlife

Along with Salamanca, León is the best place to eat and drink in Old Castile. The liveliest **bars and restaurants** are those in and around the small square of San Martín – an area known as the **Barrio Húmedo** (the Wet Quarter) for the amount of liquid sloshing around. All the bars here will give you a *pincho* with every drink, so you can eat pretty well if you drink enough, especially hopping from bar to bar ordering *cortos* – small tumblers of beer for about €0.70. The garlic-smothered potatoes dished up in *El Rincón del Gaucho* are particularly delicious.

Things really take off during **Semana Santa**, and for the **fiestas** of San Juan and San Pedro in the last week of June. The celebrations, concentrated around the Plaza Mayor, get pretty riotous, with an enjoyable blend of medieval pageantry and buffoonery.

Boccalino Plaza de San Isidoro 9. Beautifully located restaurant, with outdoor seating on the square facing San Isidoro and (given the setting) surprisingly cheap pizza and pasta (from €7), plus slightly more expensive Castilian fare.

Café Europa Plaza Regla 9. This cosy café is a top spot for coffee (with or without a multitude of liqueurs), gazing up at the cathedral while you drink.

Cafetería Parada de Postas Vast restaurant in the unlikely setting of the bus terminal, serving one of the best lunchtime *menús* (€7.10) in northern Spain.

Casa Pozo Plaza San Marcelo 15 ☎987 223 039. Excellent *bodega* for traditional Leónese dishes, behind the *ayuntamiento*, with *menús* from €9 and à la carte dishes from €12. Closed Sun in July, Aug & Sept.

Restaurante Fornos c/Cid 8. Down-to-earth restaurant with good atmosphere serving cheap, basic fill-you-up dishes like roast chicken (€4.50) and more expensive concoctions like clams with French beans (*alubias con almejas*; €9.50). Closed Sun night & Mon.

Nuevo Racimo de Oro Plaza San Martín 8. Slightly formal restaurant offering an oasis of restraint on the corner of León's liveliest square. À la carte dishes (from €9) are expensive, but worth it. Closed Wed in winter.

Zuloaga c/Sierra Pambley 3 ☎987 237 814. This sophisticated, stylish restaurant, with its romantic candlelit garden terrace brimming with plants and trees, produces Leónese cuisine with an unusual amount of flair and imagination. Main courses start at €14.

Listings

Astorga and beyond

For the fittest of the pilgrims it was one day's walk 29 miles southwest of León to the next major stop at Astorga. On the way – at **Puente de Orbigo** – you pass the most ancient of the bridges along the route (probably the oldest in all Spain), now bypassed by the new road and offering a delightful and popular spot for a riverside stroll or picnic. As you get closer to Galicia, the terrain becomes mountainous and offers spectacular views. Beyond the valley town of **Ponferrada**, weary pilgrims confronted the mountains of **El Bierzo**, a region linked historically with León though distinct in more than just geography; in remoter villages you'll hear *gallego* spoken and see rather hopeful graffiti demanding independence for the area.

Astorga

ASTORGA resembles many of the smaller cities along the *camino*: originally settled by the Romans, it was sacked by the Moors in the eleventh century, then rebuilt and endowed with the usual hospices and monasteries, but as the pilgrimage lost popularity in the late Middle Ages the place fell into decline. It's now a small but lively provincial capital with a smattering of museums, an incongruously grand cathedral and the bizarre Modernista **Palacio Episcopal** – commissioned by a Catalan bishop from his countryman Antoni Gaudí. Surrounded by a moat and built of light grey granite, the palace resembles some horror-movie Gothic castle from the mountains of Transylvania with an equally striking, remarkably spacious interior. For half a century it stood empty and was considered a scandalous and expensive white elephant, but nowadays it houses the excellent **Museo de los Caminos** (Tues–Sat 10am–2pm & 4–8pm, Sun 10am–2pm; €2.50, €4 joint ticket with Museo Catedralicio). A host of knick-knacks throws interesting sidelights on the story of the pilgrimage: hanging on the wall are examples of the documents issued at Santiago to certify that pilgrims had "travelled, confessed and obtained absolution", and there are photographs of the myriad villages and buildings along the way, and charts to show the precise roads taken through the towns.

Opposite – though stylistically worlds apart – stands the florid **Catedral** (daily 9am–noon & 5–6.30pm; free). Built between 1471 and 1693, it combines numerous architectural styles, but still manages to be totally upstaged by the palace. The **Museo Catedralicio** (daily 10am–2pm & 4–8pm; €2.50, €4 joint ticket with Museo de los Caminos; entrance to the left of the main facade) is interesting, however, especially for its beautiful twelfth-century wooden tomb painted with scenes from the lives of Christ and the Apostles.

While you're here, you could also take in the **Museo del Chocolate**, c/José María Goy (Tues–Sat 10.30am–2pm & 4.30–8pm, Sun 10.30am–2pm; €1),

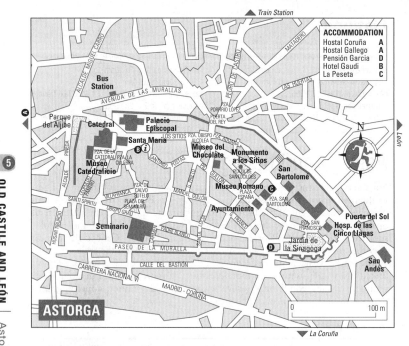

Train Station

ACCOMMODATION
Hostal Coruña   A
Hostal Gallego   A
Pensión Garcia   D
Hotel Gaudi   B
La Peseta   C

ASTORGA

0   100 m

La Coruña

which charts the growth of Astorga's flourishing chocolate industry during the eighteenth and nineteenth centuries. There are also 75-minute guided walks departing from the turismo (around 12 daily; €1.20) along the **Ruta Romana**, which take you through Astorga's Roman remains, while the **Museo Romano** (Tues–Sat 10.30am–2pm & 4.30–8pm, Sun 10.30am–2pm; €1.50) displays various bits of Roman stonework recovered from the area by archeologists.

Practicalities

Astorga is connected with León by train, but as the **train station** is a long way from the centre of town it makes far more sense to arrive and depart by **bus**, as the bus station is very conveniently placed opposite the Palacio Episcopal. The **turismo** (Tues–Sun: July–Sept 10am–2pm & 4–7.30pm; Oct–June 10am–1.30pm & 4–7pm; ☏987 618 222, ⓦwww.ayuntamientodeastorga.com) is located opposite the Palacio Episcopal at c/Eduardo de Castro 5 and offers Spanish-only guided tours of the town (July–Sept Tues–Sun noon & 5pm; Oct–June Sat & Sun noon & 5pm; €1.50).

Several of Astorga's better **restaurants** are attached to accommodation: the homely little *comedor* in the *Pensión García* has a good *menú* for €9.60, or try the slightly more upmarket restaurant in the *Peseta*, where award-winning Castilian dishes start at a reasonable €8.40. For a splurge, the restaurant in the *Hotel Gaudí* is the best in town. **Accommodation** is limited, and what there is isn't particularly good value, so you might prefer to visit on a day-trip from León. If you do want to stay, it's worth booking ahead.

The Maragatos

Astorga is the traditional market town of the **Maragatos**, a mysterious race of people, possibly descended from the Berbers of North Africa, who crossed into Spain with the first Moorish incursions of the early eighth century. For several centuries they dominated the Spanish carrying trade with their mule trains. Marrying only among themselves, they maintained their traditions and individuality well into recent decades. Along with the Maragato *cocido*, a typically hearty stew made with meat, chickpeas and cabbage, their only obvious legacy to the town is a pair of colourful clockwork figures dressed in traditional costume who jerk into action to strike the hour on the town-hall clock in Plaza de España.

Hostal Coruña Avda. Ponferrada 72 ☎ & ℱ 987 615 009. Decent *hostal*, though unattractively located on a dreary road a 10min walk from the cathedral. ❷

Hostal Gallego Avda. de Ponferrada 78 ☎ 987 615 013, ℱ 987 615 450. Bigger and more expensive than the almost adjacent *Coruña*, and in a similarly uninspiring setting, though the rooms themselves are perfectly OK. ❸

Pensión García c/Bajada del Postigo 3 ☎ 987 616 046. Just inside the old town, with basic but clean rooms and a good *comedor*. ❷

Hotel Gaudí c/Eduardo de Castro 6 ☎ 987 615 654, ℱ 987 615 040. Astorga's top hotel, with classy rooms looking directly onto Gaudí's palace. The restaurant and wood-panelled bar are rather fine, too. ❼

La Peseta Plaza de San Bartolomé ☎ 987 617 275, ℱ 987 615 300. Smart but overpriced *hostal* above an excellent restaurant. ❸

Ponferrada

At first sight the heavily industrialized, bowl-shaped valley, centred on the large town of **PONFERRADA**, seems to have little to offer, but the mountainous terrain around has scenery as picturesque as any in Spain. The town of Ponferrada itself sums up this dichotomy, dominated by a huge slag heap and spreading suburbs, yet with a quiet, unspoiled old quarter. The two are separated by a river blackened by coal mining and spanned by the iron bridge that has given Ponferrada its name. Above the sharp valley the fancy twelfth-century turrets and battlements of the **Castillo de los Templarios** (June & July Tues–Sat 10.30am–2pm & 5.30–9pm, Sun 10.30am–2pm; Aug: same hours but open daily; Sept–May Tues–Sat 10.30am–2pm & 5–9pm, Sun 11am–2pm; €2, free on Sun) may look like gingerbread, but they were built to protect pilgrims against the very real threat of the Moors, and the arcaded streets and overhanging houses of the old quarter grew up in their protective shadow. A quaint Puerta del Reloj (Clock Gateway) leads into the **main square**, Plaza del Ayuntamiento, with a late seventeenth-century town hall, similar in design to its contemporary counterpart at Astorga. The **Museo del Bierzo** (Tues–Sat: May–Sept 11am–2pm & 5–8.30pm; Oct–April 11am–2pm & 4–7pm; Sun 11am–2pm; €2, free on Sun), situated in an old prison just off the Plaza near the clocktower, has a well-presented collection of local archeological and cultural miscellanea spanning 4000 years from prehistoric times to the present day.

There are several churches in the town, but the most important is a short walk away in the northeast outskirts: **Santo Tomás de las Ollas** (irregular opening hours but the lady next door has the keys), a small Mozarabic church dating from the tenth century, with nine round Moorish horseshoe arches and Visigothic elements.

Practicalities

Bus and train stations, and most accommodation, are in the new part of town, which can be quite difficult to find your way around. From the **bus station**, head across the open space outside to the far left-hand corner to pick up c/General Gomez Nuñez (subsequently Avenida Perez Colino) and walk straight down it for ten to fifteen minutes to reach the river, from where you'll see the castle up on your left. The **train station** is more centrally located, right on the edge of the town centre. The **turismo** (June–Aug Mon–Fri 10am–2pm & 4.30–8.30pm, Sat 10.30am–1.30pm & 5–7pm, Sun 10.30am–1.30pm; Sept–May Mon–Fri 10am–2pm & 3–7pm, Sat 10.30am–1.30pm & 5–7pm, Sun 10.30am–1.30pm; ℡987 424 236, ℮turismo@ayuntamiento ponferrada.org) is next to the castle.

The best low-price **place to stay** is the nice *Hostal Santa Cruz*, c/Marcelo Macías 4 (℡ & ℉987 428 351, ℮hsantacruz@wanadoo.es; ❶). For something plusher, try the *Hotel Madrid*, Avda. de la Puebla 44 (℡987 411 550, ℉987 411 861; ❸), or the more central *Hotel Bierzo Plazo* (℡987 409 001, ⓦwww.hotel-bierzoplaza.com; ❹) on the Plaza del Ayuntamiento which boasts lots of smart, characterful rooms whose big windows overlook the city. If you're after four-star luxury, head for the *Hotel del Temple*, on Avenida de Portugal (℡987 410 058, ℮comercial@hotelestemple.com; ❹). There's a good, if pricey, **restaurant** in the *Hotel Madrid*, or try the *Taberna Los Arcos* in the *Hotel Bierzo Plaza* where a sumptuous *menú* (€8.20) is served up in an airy, subterranean cavern.

Las Médulas

Twenty kilometres southwest of Ponferrada lies **LAS MÉDULAS**, the jagged remains of Roman strip mining for gold. Nine hundred thousand tonnes of the precious metal were ripped from the hillsides using specially constructed canals, leaving an eerie scene reminiscent of Arizona, peppered with caves and needles of red rock. From **Carucedo**, a road leads for 4km up to the village of Las Médulas; from here you can walk right through the zone. It's a good idea to make for the ridge overlooking the whole desolation; the quarry visible in the background from here is a reminder of how nature can turn man's devastation into beauty given a few thousand years. Opposite the *mirador* on the ridge a **tunnel**, used by the Romans to transport water, cuts through a hill to emerge in a cave which offers another, though more limited, view; you can hire a hard hat and a torch to walk through (€1.50). Another road leads from here back down to Carucedo; the round trip takes about four or five hours. If you want to drive to the viewpoint, follow signs to the village of Orellán.

Villafranca del Bierzo

The last halt before the climb into Galicia, **VILLAFRANCA DEL BIER-ZO**, was where pilgrims on their last legs could chicken out of the final trudge. Those who arrived at the Puerta del Perdón (Door of Forgiveness) at the church of **Santiago** (June–Sept daily 10.30am–1.30pm & 4.30–8pm; Oct–May Sat & Sun 10.30am–2pm & 3.30–7pm; same hours apply to all churches) could receive the same benefits of exemption of years in Purgatory as in Santiago de Compostela itself. The simple Romanesque church is of little interest, and the impressive castle opposite is in private hands and unvisitable, but the town itself is quietly enchanting, with slate-roofed houses, cool mountain air and the clear Burbia River providing a setting reminiscent of the English Lake District. Of the other churches, the most rewarding is **San**

Francisco just off the Plaza Mayor; it has a beautiful Mudéjar ceiling, a *retablo* so warped that it makes you dizzy to contemplate it, and an unusual well. The **turismo** at Avda. B. Díez Ovelar 10, just off the Plaza Mayor (May–Sept daily 10am–2pm & 4–8.30pm; Oct–April closes at 7pm; ℡987 540 028, Ⓦwww.ayto-villafranca.com), offers guided tours of the town at 11.30am and 5.30pm during the summer months and noon and 4pm during the winter (minimum 5 people; €3).

Regular half-hourly **buses** from Ponferrada stop near the *parador*. **Places to stay** include the modern *Parador de Villafranca del Bierzo*, Avenida Calvo Sotelo (℡987 540 175, Ⓔvillafranca@parador.es; ❺), and the *Hostal Comercio*, Puente Nuevo 2 (℡987 540 008; ❶), an atmospheric fifteenth-century house whose spacious rooms are a real bargain. *Don Nacho*, in a little alley off the Plaza Mayor, is a good place to **eat**, serving tapas, *menús* and fish specialities.

Travel details

Trains

Burgos to: Ávila (6 daily; 2hr 30min); Barcelona (4 daily; 8hr); Bilbao (4 daily; 3hr 15min); Irún (5 daily; 4hr); León (4 daily; 2hr); Logroño (4 daily; 2hr); Lugo (2 daily; 6hr); Madrid (5 daily; 4–5hr); Palencia (9 daily; 45min–1hr); Valladolid (10 daily; 1hr 20min); Vitoria (11 daily; 1hr 30min); Zaragoza (4 daily; 4hr).

León to: Ávila (7 daily; 2hr 45min); Barcelona (3 daily; 10–12hr); Bilbao (1 daily; 5hr); Burgos (4 daily; 2hr); A Coruña (2 daily; 7hr); Logroño (2 daily; 4hr); Lugo (2 daily; 4hr 30min); Madrid (7 daily; 4hr 30min); Medina del Campo (7 daily; 2hr); Ourense (4 daily; 4hr); Oviedo (7 daily; 2hr); Ponferrada (8 daily; 2hr) Santiago de Compostela (1 daily; 6hr); Valladolid (10 daily; 1hr 30min); Vigo (4 daily; 6hr 30min); Vitoria (2 daily; 3hr); Zaragoza (3 daily; 5hr 30min).

Logroño to: Barcelona (3 daily; 6–7hr); Bilbao (2 daily; 3hr–3hr 30min); Burgos (4 daily; 2hr); León (2 daily; 4hr); Madrid (1 daily; 5hr); Valladolid (2 daily; 3hr 30min); Vitoria (1 daily; 1hr 30min); Zaragoza (7 daily; 2hr).

Medina del Campo to: Barcelona (1 daily; 10hr); Bilbao (2 daily; 5hr); León (7 daily; 2hr); Lugo (1 daily except Sat; 6hr); Madrid (14–18 daily; 2hr 15min); Ourense (2 daily; 4hr); Oviedo (3 daily; 3hr 45min); Valladolid (hourly; 20min); Vigo (2 daily; 6hr 30min); Zamora (3 daily; 1hr); Zaragoza (1 daily; 5hr 30min).

Salamanca to: Ávila (7 daily; 1hr 15min); Burgos (3 daily; 2hr 30min); Madrid (6 daily; 2hr 30min); Valladolid (6 daily; 1hr 30min).

Valladolid to: Ávila (15 daily; 1hr); Barcelona (1 daily; 10hr); Bilbao (2 daily; 5hr); Burgos (10 daily; 1hr 20min); León (10 daily; 1–2hr); Lisbon (1 daily; 7hr 40min); Logroño (2 daily; 3hr 30min); Madrid (15 daily; 2hr 30min–4hr); Medina del Campo (hourly; 20min); Palencia (hourly; 30min); Salamanca (6 daily; 1hr 30min); San Sebastián (4 daily; 4–5hr); Zamora (1 daily; 1hr 30min); Zaragoza (1 daily; 5hr 45min).

Zamora to: Ávila (2 daily; 2hr); A Coruña (2 daily; 5hr 20min–7hr); Madrid (2 daily; 3hr–3hr 45min); Medina del Campo (3 daily; 1hr); Santiago de Compostela (2 daily; 4hr 20min–5hr 30min); Valladolid (1 daily; 1hr 30min); Vigo (2 daily; 5hr–5hr 30min).

Buses

Burgos to: Bilbao (8 daily; 2hr); Carrión de los Condes (1 daily; 1hr 30min); Ciudad Rodrigo (1 daily; 6hr); Covarrubias (2 daily; 1hr); Frómista (1 daily; 1hr); León (1 daily; 3 hr 30min); Logroño (8 daily; 2hr); Madrid (10 daily; 2hr 45min); Palencia (1 daily; 1hr 15min); Pamplona (4 daily; 3hr 30min); Sahagún (1 daily; 2hr); Salamanca (3 daily; 4hr); San Sebastián (7 daily; 3hr 30min); Santander (3 daily; 3hr); Santo Domingo de la Calzada (6 daily; 1hr); Soria (3 daily; 2hr–2hr 30min); Valladolid (3 daily; 2hr 30min); Vinuesa (2 daily; 2hr 15min); Zamora (1 daily; 3hr 30min); Zaragoza (4 daily; 4hr 30min).

León to: Astorga (hourly; 30min–1hr); Bilbao (2 daily; 5hr 45min); Burgos (1 daily; 3hr 30min–4hr); Logroño (3 daily; 5hr); Lugo (2 daily; 3hr 30min); Madrid (12 daily; 4hr); Oviedo (9 daily; 1hr 30min); Palencia (1 daily; 2hr); Ponferrada (13 daily; 2hr); Salamanca (2 daily; 2hr 30min); Santander (2 daily; 5hr); Valladolid (8 daily; 2hr); Villafranca del Bierzo (3 daily; 3hr 30min); Zamora (5 daily; 1hr 40min).

Logroño to: Barcelona (3 daily; 6hr); Bilbao (5 daily; 2hr 30min); Burgos (7 daily; 2hr); Haro (5 daily; 1hr); León (2 daily; 4hr); Pamplona (5 daily; 2hr); Santander (1 daily; 3hr 30min); Santo Domingo de la Calzada (9 daily; 45min); Soria (5 daily; 1hr 30min); Vitoria (6 daily; 1hr); Zamora (3 daily; 4hr 30min); Zaragoza (6 daily; 2–3hr).

Palencia to: Burgos (3 daily; 1hr); Carrión de los Condes (3 daily; 45min); A Coruña (3 daily; 6hr); León (1 daily; 2hr); Lugo (5 daily; 5hr 30min); Madrid (6 daily; 3hr); Salamanca (3 daily; 2hr 30min); Valladolid (9 daily; 1hr); Zamora (2 daily; 2hr 30min); Zaragoza (2 daily; 5hr).

Salamanca to: Ávila (8 daily; 1hr 30min); Badajoz (3 daily; 4hr 30min); Barcelona (2 daily; 11hr); Burgos (5 daily; 3hr 30min); Cáceres (8 daily; 3hr 45min); Ciudad Rodrigo (hourly; 1hr); Madrid (hourly; 2hr 30min); Palencia (7 daily; 2hr 30min); Santander (4 daily; 5hr 30min); Sevilla (6 daily; 8hr); Soria (2 daily; 5hr); Valladolid (15 daily; 1hr 30min); Zamora (hourly; 1hr).

Soria to: Almazán (4 daily; 45min); Barcelona (2 daily; 6hr); Berlanga de Duero (1 daily; 1hr); Burgos (4 daily; 3hr–3hr 30min); El Burgo de Osma (2 daily; 1hr); Logroño (5 daily; 1hr 30min); Madrid (8 daily; 2hr 30min); Medinaceli (2 daily; 1hr); Pamplona (5 daily; 2hr); Peñafiel (2 daily; 2hr 15min); Salamanca (2 daily; 4hr 30min); Valladolid (3 daily; 3hr); Vinuesa (2 daily; 45min); Zaragoza (9 daily; 2hr).

Valladolid to: Burgos (5 daily; 2hr); León (8 daily; 2hr); Madrid (15 daily; 2hr 15min); Palencia (hourly; 1hr); Peñafiel (7 daily; 1hr); Salamanca (6 daily; 1hr 30min); Segovia (12 daily; 2hr); Zamora (14 daily; 1hr 30min); Zaragoza (3 daily; 5hr 30min).

Zamora to: Burgos (1 daily; 4hr 20min); León (4–6 daily; 2hr 30min); Logroño (2 daily; 5hr); Madrid (6 daily; 3hr 15min); Palencia (2 daily; 2hr 15min); Salamanca (hourly; 1hr); Valladolid (14 daily, 6 on Sun; 1hr 15min).

Euskal Herria

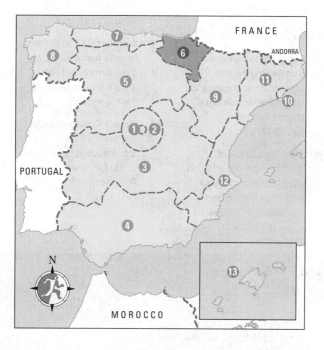

FRANCE

ANDORRA

PORTUGAL

MOROCCO

N

CHAPTER 6 # Highlights

✳ **Euskara – Bat, bi, hiru...** The Basque language has survived 3000 years of isolation. Impress locals by learning some. See p.488

✳ **Pintxos** Basque gourmet bar snacks are the way to dine in the *cascos viejos* throughout the region. See p.487

✳ **Paseo de la Concha, San Sebastián** The *belle-époque* elegance of one of the world's great urban beaches. See p.497

✳ **Mundaka Estuary** Sublime scenery and world-class surfing, an enchanted forest and Gernika, the Basque spiritual capital. See p.508

✳ **Guggenheim Museum, Bilbao** The giant titanium sculpture that has become the symbol of the regenerated city. See p.515

✳ **Zalduondo** Catch the traditional *carnaval* parade in this tiny Alavan village. See p.524

✳ **San Fermin** Pamplona's famous fiesta. Rowdy, dirty, lunatic, but for once the bulls get a fair shot. See p.528

✳ **Otsagi-Ochagavia** This riverbank village of old stone houses is the pride of the Navarran Pyrenees. See p.541

△ La Concha, San Sebastián

6

Euskal Herria: the País Vasco & Navarra

uskal Herria is the name the Basque people give to their own land, an area that covers the three Basque provinces – **Gipuzkoa**, **Bizkaia**, and **Alava**, known collectively as the País Vasco (Euskadi) – together with **Navarra**, and part of southwestern France. It's an immensely beautiful region – mountainous, green and thickly forested. It rains often, and much of the time the countryside is shrouded in a fine mist. But the summers – if you don't mind the occasional shower – are a glorious escape from the unrelenting heat of the south.

Despite some of the heaviest industrialization on the peninsula, Euskal Herria is remarkably unspoiled – neat and quiet inland, rugged and wild along the coast – and transport everywhere is easy and efficient. **San Sebastián** is the big draw on the coast, a major resort with superb but crowded beaches, but there are any number of lesser-known, equally attractive villages along the coast all the way to **Bilbao**, home to the magnificent **Guggenheim Museum**. Inland there's **Pamplona**, with its exuberant **Fiestas de San Fermín**, as well as many other destinations with charms of their own, from the drama of the **Pyrenees** to the laid-back elegance of **Vitoria**.

The Basques

The origin of **the Basques** is something of a mystery. They are a distinct people, generally with a different build from the French and Spanish and a different blood group distribution from the rest of Europe. Their language, the complex *Euskara*, is unrelated to any other, and was already spoken here when Indo-European languages such as Celtic and Latin began to arrive from the east some 3000 years ago. Written records were scarce until the first books in *Euskara* were published in the mid-sixteenth century; language and culture

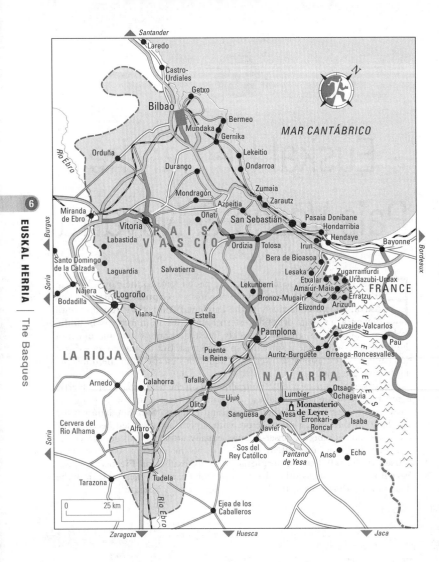

were maintained instead through oral traditions, including that of the *bertsolar-iak*, popular poets specializing in improvised verse, a tradition still alive today.

Archeological and genetic evidence suggests that the Basque people may be the last surviving representatives of Europe's aboriginal population. Skull fragments of late Cro-Magnon man believed to date from the Paleolithic era, around 9000 BC, have been shown to be identical to present-day Basque cranial formation. Much anthropological work, above all by the revered José Miguel de Barandiarán (who died in December 1991, aged 101), lends itself to the view that the Basques have continuously inhabited the western Pyrenees for thousands of years.

January
19–20 *Festividad de San Sebastián*, 24 hours of festivities, including *tamborrada* (a march with pipes and drums).

February
Weekend before Ash Wednesday *Carnaval* throughout, but especially Bilbao, San Sebastián and Tolosa; traditional parade in Zalduondo.

March
4–12 A series of pilgrimages to the castle at Javier, birthplace of San Francisco Javier.

April
Extensive Easter celebrations in Vitoria and Balmaseda, also Segura.
28 *Fiesta de San Prudencio* is celebrated with *tamborradas*, and a re-enactment of the retreat is staged in Vitoria.

June
Mid-June Getxo International Blues Festival.
Mid-June Village festival in Segura.
24 *Fiestas de San Juan* in Lekeitio, Laguardia-Biasteri and Tolosa.
Last week *Fiesta de San Pedro* in Mundaka, with Basque dancing.

July
First week sees the great fiesta at Zumaia with dancing, Basque sports and an *encierro* on the beach. Also Getxo International Jazz Festival.
7–14 *Fiestas de San Fermín* in Pamplona, featuring running with the bulls.
Third week International Jazz Festival in Vitoria.
22 *Fiesta de la Magdalena* in Bermeo, with torch-lit processions of fishing boats and the usual races and Basque sports.
24–28 *Encierro* in Tudela.
25 *Santiago Apóstol*, International Paella Competition in Getxo.
Mid- to late-July Jazz Festival in San Sebastián.
31 *Día de San Ignacio Loyola*, celebrated throughout, but above all in Loyola and Getxo where there are fireworks, jazz and a cycling competition.

August
First weekend Patron saint's celebration in Estella.
4–9 *Fiesta de la Virgen Blanca* in Vitoria, with bullfights, fireworks and *gigantones*.
14–17 *Fiestas de Andra Mari* in Ondarroa.
15 *Semana Grande* witnesses an explosion of celebration, notably in Bilbao, with Basque games and races; Zarautz with rowing regattas; Gernika and Tafalla with an *encierro* and San Sebastián where the highlight is an International Fireworks Competition.

September
First week *Euskal Jaiak* (Basque games) in San Sebastián.
4 *Fiesta de San Antolín* in Lekeitio, where the local youth attempt to knock the head off a goose.
9 *Euskal Jaiak* (Basque games) in Zarautz and *Día del Pescador* in Bermeo.
12 Sangüesa holds its own *encierros*.
14 Patron saint's day in Olite, with yet more bulls.
Last two weeks International Film Festival in San Sebastián.

December
Christmas Celebrations are particularly exuberant in Pamplona. At midnight on Christmas Eve there's an open-air Mass by firelight in Labastida (Alava).

EUSKAL HERRIA | The Basques

485

At the time of the **Roman invasion**, large areas of southwestern Gaul and parts of northern Iberia were inhabited by an ethnic group called the *Aquitani*, who spoke an ancestral version of Basque. Most of the *Aquitani* were defeated and Romanized, but the invaders, for once, saw little to gain from subjugating the *Vascones*, wild tribes living in the infertile mountains of Euskal Herria. In exchange for allowing the Romans trading rights and free passage through their territory, the *Vascones* were allowed to retain their tribal customs, language, and independence.

After the fall of Rome, the new rulers were not so accommodating. Successive **Visigoth** kings attempted to eradicate the Basques, but the Basques gave as good as they got. The **Moors**, as they stormed through Spain, conquered the lowlands of Alava and Navarra as far north as Pamplona, but never really had a firm grip on the mountainous north. This new enemy, however, forced the Basques, hitherto a collection of more or less allied tribes, to unite, and in 818 one Basque leader, Iñigo Iñiguez, was proclaimed the first ruler of the **Kingdom of Navarre**. Inevitably, in the context of the holy wars sweeping Europe, the Basques at last embraced Christianity, while maintaining many of their ancestral beliefs and customs. Chief among these customs were the ancient laws by which the Basques governed themselves, maintained by oral tradition until the twelfth century, when they were first written down (in Spanish) and known as **fueros**.

Once the Reconquest was complete and Spain was being welded into a single kingdom, Navarre (by now ruled by French monarchs) was one of the missing pieces. The Reyes Católicos persuaded the Bizkaians, Gipuzkoans and Alavans to split away from Navarre and join Castile. In return, their ancient laws and privileges, the *fueros*, including exemption from customs duty, conscription and central taxation, would be respected. Under duress, the Navarrese agreed to the same deal, and by 1512 all four territories were subject to rule from Madrid.

Having given up their political independence in return for the right to self-government, the Basques would jealously defend this right for the next four centuries. It was not until 1876 and the final defeat of the **Carlists**, whom most Basques supported as upholding their traditional rights, that the victorious Liberals finally abolished the *fueros* altogether. However, this only served to inflame the Basque desire for self-government, and the late nineteenth and early twentieth centuries saw the beginnings of Basque nationalism as an ideology. The conservative **Basque Nationalist Party** (PNV) was founded in 1895 by Sabino Arana, the son of a Carlist shipbuilder.

At the start of the Civil War, the Nationalists quickly seized control of predominantly rural, conservative Navarra and Alava. Bizkaia and Gipuzkoa, dominated by left-leaning industrial cities, supported the Republic, in return for promises of autonomy. Irún was quickly captured by Navarrese troops (in September 1936), cutting off the northern Republican zone from France. San Sebastián was quickly surrendered to spare its avenues from bombardment. An autonomous Basque government, in practice limited to Bizkaia, was declared with José Antonio Aguirre as *lehendakari* (president); it was to last only nine months. After failing to capture Madrid, Franco turned on the Basques, who were finally conquered in June 1937, after a vicious campaign that included the infamous German bombing of **Gernika**.

After the war Franco's boot went in hard, and as many as 21,000 people died in his attempts to tame the Basques. Public use of the language was forbidden and central control was asserted with the gun. But state violence succeeded only in nurturing a new resistance, **ETA** (*Euskadi ta Askatasuna* – "Basque Homeland and Freedom"), whose most spectacular success was the assassination in Madrid of Franco's right-hand man and probable successor, Admiral Carrero Blanco. In contrast to the PNV, ETA became increasingly identified with the radical left.

Things changed following the **transition to democracy**. The new constitution granted the Basques limited autonomy, with their own parliament and tax collection. Today, there's a regional police force, the *ertzaintza* (distinguished by its red berets) much in evidence in the streets, and the Basque **language** is taught in schools and universities. The Basque flag (*ikurriña*), banned under Franco, flies everywhere. Basque demands for independence have not ended, however, and nor has the **violence**. ETA's attacks have continued against a diversity of targets, from members of the Spanish police and armed forces to Basque businessmen and politicians, academics, journalists, the tourist industry and random civilians. The total number of deaths caused by ETA exceeds 800. Meanwhile, human rights organizations continue to denounce not only ETA's activities, but also police brutality and alleged torture, and the dispersal of ETA prisoners to jails around Spain.

The **ceasefire** declared in September 1998 was heralded as a major breakthrough. But talks between Basque nationalists and the governing PP (Popular Party) broke down over the perennial issue of constitutionality: the Spanish constitution, whose validity many Basque nationalists deny, is founded on the indivisible unity of the nation.

With the talks in ruins, ETA returned to violence. Since January 2000 more than forty people, including journalists and PP representatives in the País Vasco, have been killed. Each death has been met with enormous popular demonstrations, but there remains a small but solid nucleus of support for ETA and Batasuna (the latest denomination of the political party allied with ETA, formerly known as Herri Batasuna, then Euskal Herritarok).

In the context of the global "war on terror", the PP raised the stakes in August 2002 by banning Batasuna and closing down its offices. This was followed in February 2003 by the closure of *Egunkaria*, the only remaining Basque-language newspaper, for alleged support of ETA, and the detention of ten journalists. Both moves were met by considerable popular protest. To what extent these events will alter the Basque political landscape remains unclear. The PNV retained power in the May 2003 regional elections, and have continued to press for a referendum on "self-determination" for the Basque country. The vast majority of Basques continue to show their opposition to violence at home and abroad. ETA activity has not stopped, but fortunately visitors to Euskal Herria aren't in any danger. Despite the presence of threatening graffiti, you're extremely unlikely to meet with any type of violence here.

Food

Basque cuisine is accepted as Spain's finest, and the people here are compulsive eaters: try *bacalao* (cod) *a la vizcaina* or *al pil-pil*, *merluza* (hake) *a la vasca*, *txipirones en su tinta* (squid cooked in its ink) or *txangurro* (spider crab), which you'll find in very reasonably priced roadside *caseríos* (*baserri* in Basque), on the outskirts of towns throughout the region. For an earthier experience, try the cider-houses *(sidrerías* or *sagardotegiak)* where slabs of beef, bacalao and chorizo are washed down with all the cider you can drink, served straight from the barrel (see box on p.498). You'll also come across traditional Basque food in the form of tapas (known in the Basque country as **pintxos**) in virtually every bar, freshly cooked and usually excellent.

Almost everywhere in the province, street and road signs are in both Basque and Castilian, but the latter is often painted over. Many town halls have officially chosen to use the Basque names and this is reflected on new tourist brochures and maps. We have, therefore, used the Basque name for towns, giving the Castilian in brackets. Some towns, however, including Pamplona and Bilbao, are still generally referred to by their Castilian names and in these cases we have supplied the Basque name in brackets.

It is worth noting a couple of key letter changes which may help to decipher initially confusing words on, for example, menus and signs: notably, the Castilian *ch* becomes *tx* (*txipirones* as opposed to *chipirones*), *v* becomes *b* and *y* becomes *i* (*Bizkaia* as opposed to *Vizcaya*). Above all, *Euskara* features a proliferation of *k*s, as this letter replaces the Castilian *c* (*Gipuzkoa* instead of *Guipúzcoa*) and *qu* (*Lekeitio* instead of *Lequeitio*) and is also used to form the plural and the possessive (eg *Bilboko* means "of Bilbao").

Castilian name	Basque name		
Bilbao	Bilbo	Bai	Yes
San Sebastián	Donostia	Ez	No
Vitoria	Gasteiz	Eta	And
Pamplona	Iruña/ Iruñea	Baina	But
Fuenterrabía	Hondarribia	Bat	1
Motrico	Mutriku	Bi	2
Oñate	Oñati	Hiru	3
Guernica	Gernika	Lau	4
Pasajes	Pasaia Donibane	Bost	5
Roncesvalles	Orreaga	Zenbat da?	How much is it?
Zumaya	Zumaia	Ni John naiz	I am John
		Ni Londres-en bizi naiz	I live in London
Some common phrases		Zurito	Glass of beer
Kaixo	Hello	Kafe(-sne)	Coffee (with milk)
Agur	Goodbye	Aparkalekua	Car park
Gabon	Goodnight	Hondartza	Beach
Egun on	Good morning	Jatetxea	Restaurant
Ongi etorri	Welcome	Turismo Bulegoa	Tourist office
Mesedez	Please	Udaletxea	Town hall
Eskerrik asko	Thank you very much	Ertzantza	Basque police
		Udaltzaingoa	Municipal police

The tradition of **gastronomic societies** (*txokos*), unique to the Basque country, deserves special mention: first founded in the mid-nineteenth century, they came about originally as socializing places for different craftsmen. Controversy has surrounded them due to the traditional barring of women (although this is changing); all cooking is done by men who pay a token membership fee for the facilities. Members prepare elaborate dishes to perfection as a hobby and it could be said that true Basque cookery has largely retreated to these societies. The so-called *Nueva Cocina Vasca* (New Basque Cookery), heavily influenced by French cuisine, is increasingly evident on menus throughout the country.

Sport

The **Basque sport** of *pelota* (a version of which is known as *jai alai*, Basque for "happy party") is played all over Spain, but in Euskal Herria even the smallest village has a *pelota* court or *fronton*, and betting on the sport is rife. Rowing is another Basque obsession, and regattas are held every weekend in summer. Other unique Basque sports include *aizkolaritza* (log-chopping), *harri-jasotzea* (stone-lifting), *soka-tira* (tug-of-war) and *segalaritza* (grass-cutting). The finest exponents of the first two in particular are popular local heroes (the world champion stone-lifter Iñaki Perurena's visit to Japan resulted in the sport being introduced there – he remains the only lifter to surpass the legendary 315-kilo barrier). All Basque sports form an important part of the many local fiestas.

Accommodation

The main drawback to travelling in the region is that prices (except for food) are higher than in much of Spain, particularly for **accommodation**, although it's cheaper inland (with the exception of Pamplona). Choice, quiet accommodation in rural spots abounds, thanks to the Basque government's **nekazal-turismoa** (*agroturismo* or homestay) programme, which offers the opportunity to stay in traditional Basque farmhouses and private homes, usually in areas of outstanding beauty, at very reasonable cost. In Navarra, as in much of the country, these are known as **casas rurales** or *landa exteak*. In Gipuzkoa, Bizkaia and Alava, properties participating in the programme are identified by a rectangular green sign with white lettering, or a sun-and-sea-scape in a circular plaque. Lists showing facilities and prices may be obtained from regional tourist offices (who also handle bookings); alternatively, look at Ⓦwww.nekatur.net or www.ecoturismorural.com. Except in very small villages, there is usually a *fonda* or *hostal*; alternatively, entering any bar and asking for a room will generally produce results.

Irún and around

The Basque province of Gipuzkoa abuts the French frontier, and its border town, **Irún**, is one of the major road and rail entry points into Spain. There are fast, regular onward connections to San Sebastián, although if you're travelling more slowly, the fishing ports of **Hondarribia** and **Pasaia Donibane** (Pasajes San Juan) are worth a stop. The main route to the south crosses quickly into Navarra and leads initially via the beautiful **Valle de Bidasoa** to Pamplona (Iruña).

Irún

Like most border towns, sprawling, graceless and largely modern **IRÚN**'s chief concern is how to make a quick buck from passing travellers. The main point in its favour is the ease with which you can leave; there are trains to **Hendaia** (Hendaye) in France and to San Sebastián throughout the day, with regular long-distance and international connections. If arriving by train from Paris (or elsewhere in France) at Hendaia, note that the quickest way to cross the border is to take the *topo* (mole train, so-called because of all the tunnels it goes through) from the separate platform on the right outside Hendaia's main station; it runs every thirty minutes to Irún station, at Avda. de Colón 52, then on to San Sebastián. Of the town's few attractions, the **Ermita de Ama Xantalen** (alias de Santa Elena; open Tues & Thurs 3–5pm, Sat/Sun 10am–noon; free), an eleventh-century chapel serving as a museum with Roman remains discovered here in 1969, is worth a visit. To get there, head up c/Prudéncia Arbide next to the *ayuntamiento*, bear left at the first major intersection, and then right at c/Santa Elena.

Practicalities

In the vicinity of Irún's main train station are several small, reasonably priced **hostales** and **restaurants** specializing in good local food. If you do need to spend the night, there are plenty of bars and places to eat, and prices are markedly lower than in France, Hondarribia or San Sebastián. *Pensión Bidasoa*, c/Estación 14 (℡943 619 913; ❷), and *Bar Pensión los Fronterizos*, c/Estación 7 (℡943 619 205; ❷), have some of the least expensive rooms; for more comfort try the nearby *Hostal Matxinbenta*, Paseo Colón 21 (℡943 621 384; ❸). There is also one reasonable **casa rural** nearby: the *Mendiola*, Barrio Ventas, Landexte (℡943 629 763; ❷), 2km west of town on the N1 road.

Hondarribia

The fishing port of **HONDARRIBIA** (Fuenterrabía), 6km north of Irún and looking over the Bidasoa river mouth to Hendaia, is a far more attractive prospect, though the waterfront itself is disappointingly modern, enlivened with just a few cafés. The lower town's real appeal lies in the main streets running parallel to the front, and the backstreets further inland, where traditional, wood-beamed Basque houses are interspersed with bars offering some of the best seafood and *pintxos* around. During the summer, the fine **beaches** immediately north of the town are an alternative to the ultracrowded San Sebastián.

Hondarribia has a picturesque, walled old town entered through the fifteenth-century **Puerta de Santa María**. Calle Mayor, leading up to the Plaza de Armas, has further fine examples of half-timbered houses with painted balconies and studded doors, some displaying family coats of arms above doorways. The square itself is dominated by the **Palacio de Carlos Quinto** (now the *parador*), started originally in the tenth century by Sancho the Strong of Navarra and subsequently extended by Carlos V in the sixteenth. Slightly uphill and southwest, the smaller, arcaded Plaza Gipuzkoa with its wrought-iron railings is also worth seeking out.

Practicalities

The helpful **turismo** is on Javier Ugarte 6, at the base of the road up to the old town (July–Aug Mon–Sat 9am–8pm, Sun 10am–2pm; Sept–June Mon–Fri 9am–1.30pm & 4–6.30pm, Sat 10am–2pm; ℡943 645 458). There's no train service; buses for San Sebastián leave frequently from a stop on c/San Pedro.

There's a fair amount of characterful, if rather pricey, **accommodation** in Hondarribia. On the budget side, try the *Hotel San Nikolas* on Plaza de Armas 6 (℡943 644 278; ❹) with en-suite rooms, or the *Txoko-Goxoa* on c/Marrua 22 near the Puerta de Santa María (no phone; ❸). Pick of the plusher establishments is the two-star *Hotel Obispo*, offering modern rooms with balconies in an old stone manor on Plaza del Obispo (℡943 645 400, ℻943 642 386; ❻), or the *Parador Nacional El Emperador Carlos V*, in a fortified *palacio* on Plaza de Armas 14 (℡943 645 500, ✉hondarribia@parador.es; sometimes closed Nov–Feb; ❻). If you have your own transport, some excellent **casas rurales** just outside town offer better value, though they're very popular and need to be reserved well in advance. The closest, uphill from the airport in Barrio Arkoll-Santiago, is *Iketxe* (℡ & ℻943 644 391; ❸), built in 1988 in traditional style, with a variety of huge wood-ceilinged rooms with balconies. Alternatively, 3km from town in Jaizubia hamlet, *Arotzenea* (℡ & ℻943 642 319; ❷), in a half-timbered medieval farmhouse, offers particularly good breakfasts. Two others are found on the Jaizkibel uplands, accessed from the roundabout outside the old town walls: the overmodernized *Postigu* (℡943 643 270; ❷), 3km from the centre near the shrine of Guadalupe, and the remoter (2km more) *Artzu* (☎943 640 530; ❷), a converted farmhouse (most rooms with shared bathrooms) near the top of a sea cliff at the end of the road. For the impecunious, the **youth hostel**, *Juan Sebastián Elkano*, is on Higer Bidea 7, the shore road north of town (☎943 641 550; open all year; €10 per bunk), though it's often packed out in summer with school groups. The closest **campsite**, *Camping Jaizkibel* (☎943 641 679; open all year), is 2km west of town along Carretera Guadalupe towards Pasaia Donibane (Pasajes San Juan); there's no public transport.

A dozen or so **restaurants** and **bars** along parallel c/Santiago and c/San Pedro, a couple of short blocks inland from the water, are the best hunting ground for **food** and **drink**. For something special, try the classic *Hermandad de Pescadores* (reservations on ☎943 642 738; closed Sun pm & Mon) at c/Zuloaga 12, parallel to the waterfront. The €13 *menú* is rather dull, and you'd do better choosing from the *a la carta* menu (approx €30 a head). Otherwise, in the upper town, tucked away in a narrow, cobbled alley two streets behind c/Mayor, the *Mamutzar* (closed Tues) serves a good-value *menú*, as does the *Danontzat* at c/Las Tiendas 6, near the church (*menú* €15, *a la carta* €29).

Pasaia Donibane

The other place you might consider stopping for any length of time en route between Irún and San Sebastián is the port of Pasaia, 16km from Hondarribia via a scenic road through the Jaizkibel uplands. While much of the town is highly industrialized – cranes steadily pick through heaps of scrap metal on the south side of the bay – the old town, **PASAIA DONIBANE** (Pasajes San Juan), has retained its charm. The narrow cobbled c/San Juan (Victor Hugo once lived at no. 65) leads to Plaza de Santiago lined with colourful houses. Pasaia Donibane is famous for its waterside **fish restaurants**, which are rather less expensive than those in San Sebastián's old quarter. Two to try are *Casa Camara*, c/San Juan 79, for shellfish (closed Sun pm & Mon low season; allow €35 per head), and *Ziaboga*, at no. 91, for fish (from €30). A launch (*txalupa*) runs throughout the day and evening across the harbour to Pasaia San Pedro, from where frequent **buses** depart to San Sebastián's Alameda del Boulevard.

Towards Pamplona

If you're heading straight down to Pamplona, you'll pass through the **Bidasoa valley** with its succession of beautifully preserved towns just off the N121a, the best of which are **Bera-Vera de Bidasoa**, **Lesaka** and **Etxalar** – all just over the border in Navarra. At Oieregi, just under halfway to Pamplona, there's a junction left for the Valle de Baztán, where the Navarran Pyrenees really start (see p.538). Both valleys are on direct bus routes from San Sebastián/Irún and Pamplona respectively.

Bera (Vera) de Bidasoa
BERA (VERA) DE BIDASOA offers some of the finest examples of old wood-beamed and traditional stone houses in the region: the brightly painted buildings along c/Altzarte and the main square are particularly attractive. About a hundred metres off the square, just past the old customs house, is the former home (no. 24) of the Basque writer Pío Baroja; at the time of writing the museum here is closed indefinitely, but you can check the latest situation with the turismo in Pamplona (see p.526).

Options for **staying** include the comfortable *Hostal Euskalduna* at the noisy central junction (☎948 630 392; ❷); the plainer *Hostal Zalain* (☎948 631 106;

$\bullet$), beyond the industrial-warehouse district in the remote Barrio de Zalain; and a *casa rural* in a converted farmhouse, *Casa Alkeberea* ($\textcircled{T}$948 630 540; $\bullet$), 2km out on the Lizuniago road, with secure car and bike parking.

Six kilometres northeast of Bera, straddling the French border, **Monte Larroun** (900m) is an easy climb: from the summit you'll get spectacular views across the Pyrenees and the French Basque coast. There's a bar-restaurant at the top of the rack-railway up from the French side.

Lesaka

Some 4km south of Bera along the Bidasoa valley, a right turn leads to **LESA-KA**. Despite the large, eyesore factory and lumber depots on the outskirts of town, it's an attractive place dominated by the hilltop parish church in which the pews bear family names of the local farms and mansions. On the banks of the irrigation channel which flows through town is one of the best remaining examples of a *casa torre* (fortified private house) of a design peculiar to the Basque country, dating back to the days when north Navarra was in the hands of a few powerful and constantly feuding families.

Places to **stay** include the restaurant-less *Hostal Ekaitza* at central Plaza Berria 13 ($\textcircled{T}$948 627 547; $\bullet$), and the more upmarket *Hotel Bereau* ($\textcircled{T}$948 627 509, $\textcircled{F}$948 627 647; $\bullet$), somewhat noisily situated by the main highway, 2km east of Lesaka proper, but with its own restaurant – independent eating options in Lesaka are few.

Etxalar

ETXALAR is a small, bucolic place, 4km above the Bidasoa valley on the way up to a minor border crossing at the Lizarrieta pass, but it is perhaps the best-preserved village of the valley, famous for an impressive array of Basque funerary stelae in the churchyard. Among numerous **casas rurales** here, two good ones with rooms available for short stays are the central *Casa Domekenea* ($\textcircled{T}$948 635 031; $\bullet$) and the *Casa Herri-Gain* ($\textcircled{T}$948 635 208; $\bullet$), the latter perched on a steep hill with fantastic views of the surrounding area. There are also a couple of restaurants and bars near the giant church.

San Sebastián (Donostia)

The undisputed queen of the Basque resorts, **SAN SEBASTIÁN (DONOS-TIA**) is a picturesque – and expensive – seaside town with good beaches. Along with Santander, it has always been a fashionable place to escape the heat of the southern summers, and in July and August it's packed. Although it tries hard to be chic, San Sebastián is too much of a family resort to compete in those terms with the South of France, which is all to its benefit. Set around the deep, still bay of La Concha and enclosed by rolling low hills, the town is beautifully situated; the old quarter sits on the eastern promontory, its back to the wooded slopes of Monte Urgull, while newer development has spread along the banks of the Urumea, around the edge of the bay to the foot of Monte Igeldo and onto the hills overlooking the bay.

Arrival and information

Most **buses** arrive at Plaza Pío XII, fifteen minutes' walk along the river from the centre of town (the ticket office for these companies is around the corner next to the river on Paseo de Bizkaia). Buses from Pasaia and Astigarraga arrive on the Alameda del Boulevard, and from Hondarribia on Plaza de Gipuzkoa. RENFE's main-line **Estación del Norte** is across the Río Urumea on Paseo de Francia, although local lines of the *Eusko Tren* from Hendaia, or Bilbao via Zarautz and Zumaia (neither line accepts InterRail passes), have their terminus on Plaza Easo at the **Estación de Amara**. The small **airport** serving domestic flights from Madrid is 22km from the city centre, just outside Hondarribia; an airport bus plies back and forth as necessary.

San Sebastián's helpful **turismo** is on c/Regina Regente (June–Sept Mon–Sat 8am–8pm, Sun 10am–2pm; Oct–May Mon–Sat 9am–1.30pm & 3.30–7pm, Sun 10am–2pm; ☎943 481 166, ⓦ www.sansebastianturismo.com), by the Puente de Zurriola, and produces *Donostiaisia*, a very useful free monthly guide to what's on.

San Sebastián is something of a travel hub for the region. Viajes TIVE, c/Tomás Gros 3 (☎943 276 934), is a youth/student **travel agency** that sells tickets for international buses and discount plane tickets. Another good general travel agency is Viajes Aran, c/Elkano 1 (☎943 429 009). For travel books and maps (both local and elsewhere), and for books on all things related to the Basque country, head for Graphos on the corner of Alameda del Boulevard and c/Nagusia. Also recommended is Bilintx, c/Fermín Calbetón 21, with CDs of local music. The most central **Internet cafés** are *Donosti-NET*, with two premises at c/Embeltrán 2 and c/San Jerónimo 8 (daily 9am–11pm).

Accommodation

Places to stay, though plentiful, can be pricey and hard to come by in season – if you arrive between mid-July and the end of August, or during the film festival in September, you'll have to start looking early in the day if you haven't booked ahead. There is no great difference in rates between the cheapest places in the *parte vieja* (old quarter) and elsewhere, although *hostales* along the Alameda del Boulevard tend to be slightly pricier. There is often more chance of finding space in the *zona romántica* district around c/Easo, c/San Martín, c/Hondarribia and c/San Bartolomé, or on one or other bank of the river, either in Gros (east of the *zona romántica*) or in the new part of town, Amara Nuevo, on the way to the Anoeta sports complex. If you're driving and have a bit of cash to spare, you might well consider basing yourself on Monte Igeldo, west of the beaches, and take a bus into town rather than pit yourself against the nightmarish parking situation.

Parte Vieja

Pensión Amaiur c/Treinta y Uno de Agosto 44, 2º ☎943 429 654. Pleasant, friendly *pensión* with carpeted doubles and a few triples, all with shared bath. ❷

Pensión Anne c/Esterlines 15, 2º ☎943 421 438, ⓔ pensionanne@euskalnet.net. Recently-opened

pensión with friendly, English-speaking staff. 10 percent discount for Rough Guide users. ❸

Pensión Arsuaga c/Narrika 3, 3º ☎943 420 681. Very friendly *pensión* with simple, spacious doubles. Has its own restaurant and offers full-board deals. ❷

Hostal La Estrella Plaza de Sarriegi 1 ☎943 420 997. Attractive old *hostal*, offering old-fashioned

Street renaming in Euskal Herria

Following autonomy, there has been a massive campaign of **street renaming** throughout the Basque country – something to be aware of if given an older city plan. Sometimes the difference is merely spelling (eg: Narrika versus Narrica) but equally often it can be something completely different (eg, Nagusia for Mayor). *Kalea*, incidentally, is Euskera for "Street", and follows the proper name.

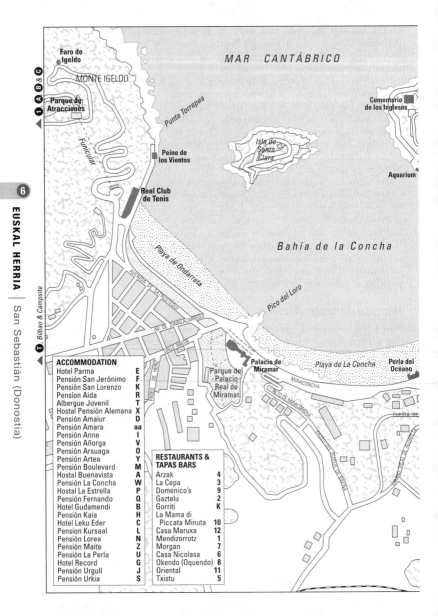

MAR CANTÁBRICO

Faro de Igeldo

MONTE IGELDO

Parque de Atracciones

Punta Torrepea

Cementerio de los Ingleses

Peine de los Vientos

Isla de Santa Clara

Aquarium

Real Club de Tenis

Bahía de la Concha

Playa de Ondarreta

Pico del Loro

Playa de La Concha

Perla del Océano

Palacio de Miramar

Parque del Palacio Real de Miramar

MIRACONCHA

ALTO DE MIRACONCHA

CUESTA DE

AVENIDA DE SATRUSTEGUI

AV. DE ZUMALACARREGUI

CALLE MATIA

PASEO DE HERIZ

ACCOMMODATION

Hotel Parma	E
Pensión San Jerónimo	F
Pensión San Lorenzo	K
Pensión Aida	R
Albergue Juvenil	T
Hostal Pensión Alemana	X
Pensión Amaiur	D
Pensión Amara	aa
Pensión Anne	I
Pensión Añorga	V
Pensión Arsuaga	O
Pensión Artea	Y
Pensión Boulevard	M
Hostal Buenavista	A
Pensión La Concha	W
Hostal La Estrella	P
Pensión Fernando	Q
Hotel Gudamendi	B
Pensión Kaia	H
Hotel Leku Eder	C
Pension Kursaal	L
Pensión Lorea	N
Pensión Maite	Z
Pensión La Perla	U
Hotel Record	G
Pensión Urgull	J
Pensión Urkia	S

RESTAURANTS & TAPAS BARS

Arzak	4
La Cepa	3
Domenico's	9
Gaztelu	2
Gorriti	K
La Mama di Piccata Minuta	10
Casa Maruxa	12
Mendizorrotz	1
Morgan	7
Casa Nicolasa	6
Okendo (Oquendo)	8
Oriental	11
Txistu	5

Bilbao & Campsite

494

but clean rooms – some en suite – either over-looking the plaza or Alameda del Boulevard. **③** **Pensión Kaia** c/Puerto 12, 2º ☎ 943 431 342. Pleasant, modern rooms with bath. Prices fall by a third out of season. **④**

Hotel Parma c/General Jauregi Gudalburuaren 11 ☎ 943 428 893, ⓦ www.hotelparma.com. Nicely located between the *parte vieja* and Paseo Nuevo, this rather characterless modern building offers comfortable rooms with all amenities, the best

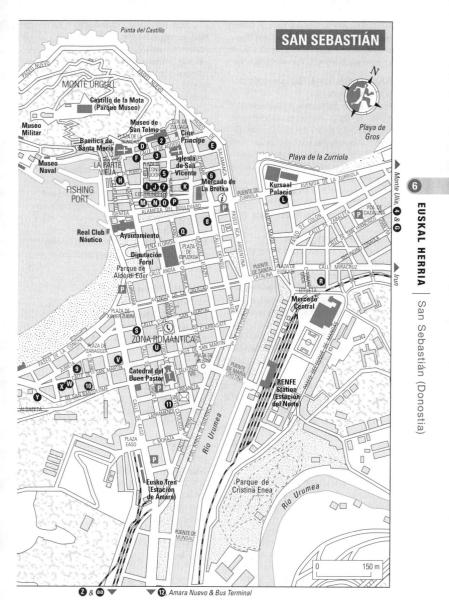

ones overlooking the sea. **⑤**

Pensión San Jerónimo c/San Jerónimo 25, 2º
☏ 943 420 830. Adequate *pensión*, though the
rooms are spartan and the hallway and stairs
somewhat the worse for wear. **②**

Pensión San Lorenzo c/San Lorenzo 2, 1º ☏ 943

425 516. Backpackers' cheapo haven with just six
shared-bath rooms, Internet access and a self-
catering kitchen; usually full, and does not accept
advance reservations, so contact them the evening
or morning before your intended stay. **②**

Pensión Urgull c/Esterlines 10, 3º ☏ 943 430

047. Just five airy, spotless and tastefully furnished rooms – the English-speaking owner won't take reservations far in advance, so arrive early or book the same day. Some noise from nearby bars. ❷

Alameda del Boulevard and around

Pensión Boulevard Alameda del Boulevard 24 1º ☎943 429 405. Comfortable, modernized rooms in an older building, Only one en-suite room. ❷
Pensión Fernando Plaza de Gipuzkoa 2, 1º ☎943 425 575. Fair-sized, relatively quiet rooms with shared showers at this friendly *pensión* overlooking a leafy square. ❷
Pensión Lorea Alameda del Boulevard 16 ☎943 427 258. The best en-suite option at this address, with heating and TV in the en-suite rooms. ❸

Zona Romántica

Hostal Pensión Alemana c/San Martín 53, 1º ☎943 462 544, ✉halemana@adegi.es. Perfectly located just behind La Concha, this fine *belle-époque* two-star offers affordable splendour in its large en-suite rooms with all mod cons, plus off-street parking. Reservations required year-round. ❹
Pensión Añorga c/Easo 12, 1º ☎943 467 945. Large, fairly plain one-star *pensión* on two floors, but the rooms are clean and some have a bath. ❷
Pensión Artea c/San Bartolomé 33 ☎943 455 100. Recently renovated *pensión* offering en-suite rooms in a good location near La Concha; rates drop by a third out of season. ❸
Pensión La Concha c/San Martín 51 ☎943 450 389, ✉hostallaconcha@telefonica.net. Excellent value en-suite rooms in a salubrious neighbourhood just a few steps from La Concha. ❸
Pensión La Perla c/Inazio Loiola 10 ☎943 428 123. Excellent-value *pensión*, near Buen Pastor cathedral and the food market, offering spotless heated en-suite rooms with TV; a firm favourite with readers. ❷
Pensión Urkia c/Urbieta 12, 3º ☎943 424 436. Run by the sister of the owner of *La Perla*, this *pensión* has equally good en-suite rooms, though there is some street noise. When full, there's another relative in waiting at *Casa Elisa* ☎943 453 950. ❷

On the river banks

Pensión Aida Iztueta 9, 1º, Gros ☎943 327 800, ✇www.pensionesconencanto.com. Relatively new *pensión* with cheerful, pastel decor and en-suite rooms. ❹
Pensión Amara Isabel II 2, 1º, Amara ☎943 468

472. Clean, comfortable accommodation in this highly recommended *pensión*. ❸
Pensión Kursaal c/Peña y Goñi 2, 1º, Gros ☎943 292 666, ✇www.pensionesconencanto.com. Co-managed with the similar *Aida*, this is in a superb location just a few steps from Zurriola and the Kursaal itself. Great value and even better out of season when prices lower. ❹
Pensión Maite Avda. de Madrid 19, 1º B, Amara ☎943 470 715, ☏943 454 826. Good-value rooms with shower and TV; handy for the bus station, Astoria cinema and Anoeta football stadium. The owners also run the *Bar Maite* opposite. ❷
Hotel Record Calzada Vieja de Ategorrieta 35, Gros ☎943 271 255, ☏943 278 521. At the east end of this district and a pleasant alternative to the bustle of the *parte vieja* and *zona romántica*; well connected by bus, or a 15min walk from the centre, with plenty of parking. All rooms with shower or bath (though the cheapest lack toilet); the larger have terraces. ❸–❹

Monte Igeldo

Hostal Buenavista Barrio de Igeldo ☎943 210 600. Stone-clad, mock-trad Basque chalet on the main road to Monte Igeldo, featuring sweeping sea views and a good restaurant. Good value for the area. ❹
Hotel Gudamendi Paseo de Gudamendi, Monte Igeldo ☎943 214 000, ☏943 215 108. In a peaceful, park-like cul-de-sac near the top of the mountain, this rambling, converted hunting lodge scores for its pleasant pool and common areas. There are usually vacancies even in summer because it's somewhat overpriced. Rooms were completely rebuilt in 2003, so expect rates to inch up in the future. ❻
Hotel Leku Eder Barrio de Igeldo ☎943 210 964, ☏943 210 107. Just a few hundred metres below the *Buenavista*, this is a rather sterile concrete block but many rooms have great views towards the lighthouse. ❹

Youth hostel and camping

Albergue Juvenil Paseo de Igeldo ☎943 310 268, ☏943 214 090. San Sebastián's youth hostel, known as *La Sirena*, is just a few minutes' walk from the end of Ondarreta beach (or take bus #5 or #16). En-suite 6-bunk rooms €9.50 per person. Open all year.
Igeldo Paseo Padre Orkolaga 69, Barrio de Igeldo ☎943 214 502, ☏943 280 411. San Sebastián's campsite is excellent but it's 5km from the centre on the landward side of Monte Igeldo (up a steep hill), reached by bus #16 from the Alameda del Boulevard. Open all year.

The Town

The **parte vieja** (old quarter) at the base of Monte Urgull is the town's highlight – cramped and lively streets where the crowds congregate in the evenings to wander among the many small bars and shops or sample the shellfish from the street traders down by the fishing port. Much of it was destroyed by a fire in 1813 and carefully restored, though the old medieval wall was swept away to allow expansion later the same century – the Alameda del Boulevard marks its former course.

The *parte vieja* contains San Sebastián's chief sights: the elaborate Baroque facade of the eighteenth-century church of **Santa María**, and the more elegantly restrained sixteenth-century Gothic church of **San Vicente**. The centre of the old quarter is **La Plaza de la Constitución** (known by the locals simply as *La Consti*) – the numbers on the balconies around the square date from the days when it was used as a bullring. Situated just off c/Treinta y Uno de Agosto (the only street to survive the great fire of August 31, 1813), behind San Vicente, is the excellent **Museo de San Telmo** (July–Aug Tues–Sat 10.30am–8.30pm, Sun 10.30am–2pm; rest of year Tues–Sat 10.30am–1.30pm & 4–7.30pm, Sun 10.30am–2pm). Its displays – around the cloisters of a former convent – include a fine Basque ethnographic exhibition and the largest collection of keyhole-shaped funerary stelae in the País Vasco. The convent chapel is decorated with a series of frescoes depicting scenes from Basque life by José Sert.

A stairway off the plaza flanking the museum rises to **Monte Urgull**, crisscrossed by winding paths. From the mammoth figure of Christ on its summit, a 45-minute climb, there are great views out to sea and back across the bay to the town. On the way down you can stop at the **Aquarium** (mid-June to mid-Sept daily 10am–9pm; mid-Sept to mid-June Mon–Fri 10am–7pm, Sat–Sun 11am–8pm; €9, kids under 12 €5) on the harbour; it contains the skeleton of a whale caught in the last century and an extensive history of Basque navigation. Although there are not a great deal of fish, you can walk through the middle of a giant aquarium in a perspex tube. Close by, at Paseo de Muelle 24, is the **Museo Naval** (Tues–Sat 10am–1.30pm & 4–7.30pm, Sun 11am–2pm; €1.50), with video facilities and exhibits tracing the tradition and history of Basque fishing.

Still better views can be had around the bay from the top of **Monte Igeldo**: take the #16 bus marked *Igeldo* from the Boulevard or walk round the bay to its base near Real Club de Tennis, from where a **funicular** (daily: summer 10am–8pm; winter 11am–6pm; every 15min; €1 round trip) will carry you to the summit. Continuing along the *paseo* past the tennis club, you end up at Eduardo Chillida's striking iron **sculpture**, *El Peine de los Vientos* (The Comb of the Winds), looking as if it is trying to grasp the waves in its powerful rusting arms. More of Chillida's work is on display at the Chillida-Leku museum in Hernani (see p.500).

Beaches

There are **four beaches** in San Sebastián: Playa de la Concha, Playa de Ondarreta, Playa de la Zurriola and Playa de Gros. **La Concha** is the most central and the most celebrated, a wide crescent of yellow sand stretching around the bay from the old town. Despite the almost impenetrable mass of flesh here during much of the summer, this is the best (if most regimented) of the beaches, enlivened by sellers of peeled prawns and cold drinks and with great swimming out to the diving platforms moored in the bay. Out in La Concha bay is a small island, **Isla de Santa Clara**, which makes a good spot for picnics; a boat leaves from the port every half hour in the summer (daily 10am–8pm; €1.50 round trip).

La Concha and Ondarreta are the best beaches for swimming – the latter is a continuation of the same strand beyond the rocky outcrop which supports the Palacio de Miramar, once a summer home of Spain's royal family. Set back from Ondarreta beach are large villas, some of the most expensive properties in Spain, and mostly owned by wealthy families from Madrid who holiday here – the area used to be known as La Diplomática for this reason and has a reputation for being rather more staid than the central area, although the lively district of El Antiguo with its many bars is only a few minutes' walk beyond.

Far less crowded, and popular with surfers, Playa de la Zurriola and the adjacent Playa de Gros were re-graded during the 1990s and breakwaters added to shield them from dangerous currents and river pollution. A recent addition to the elegant promenade is the giant beached glass blocks of Rafael Moneo's Kursaal. In addition to an auditorium and art gallery, the building houses a pleasant café-restaurant with an outside terrace in summer. One of the best views of the whole town and bay may be had by climbing up the steps to the cider house on the side of Monte Ulia from the far end of the beach. This walk can easily be extended for about 5km along the coast to the lighthouse overlooking the entrance to Pasaia harbour.

Eating and drinking

San Sebastián is a great place for a gastronomic treat, with some of the best restaurants in Spain, as well as plenty of lively bars. Most are in the *parte vieja* but there are also a few in the *zona romántica*; note that the majority close for some of Sunday and all of Monday. Prices in the old quarter tend to reflect the area's popularity, but lunchtime *menús del día* are generally good value, and the *pintxos* and *raciones* set out in all but the fanciest bars are a great way to eat reasonably. For those on a budget, there are a few worthy Italian and Asian eateries, while the Mercado de la Bretxa, a former *pescadería*, is a newly refurbished mall housing some affordable snack bars. One of the best establishments here, in the Zinekale section, is *Padang*, a fruit-juice bar serving every conceivable variety of fresh-whipped *zumos* and *batidos*.

Sidrerías

If you're in San Sebastián between late January and early May, a visit to one of the many sidrerías (*sagardotegiak* in Basque, or cider houses) in the area around Astigarraga, about 6km from town, is a must – take the red Hernani-bound bus from the Alameda del Boulevard or a taxi for about €6.

Cider production is one of the oldest traditions in the Basque country – until the Civil War and the subsequent move towards industrialization, practically every farmhouse in Gipuzkoa and to a lesser extent the other provinces produced cider, which was a valuable commodity used for barter. Barter remained the main form of exchange in rural communities here until comparatively recently, and the farms were practically open houses where local people drank cider and socialized – the *bertsolariak* tradition of oral poetry originated in these places.

Since the 1980s, cider houses are again flourishing, and for €9–18 you can feast on delicious food, drink unlimited quantities of cider and in general enjoy the raucous atmosphere. Of the seventy or so *sidrerías*, some of the most accessible include *Petritegi* and *Gartziategi*, just a few kilometres out of town in Astigarraga, while many of the more rustic and authentic ones, such as *Sarasola* and *Oiarbide*, are on the *ruta de las sidrerías* (cider trail) just beyond Astigarraga. Check in the *turismo* for a full list with phone numbers.

Arzak Alto de Miracruz 21, Monte Ulia ☏ 943 278 465. A shrine of Basque cuisine, with three Michelin rosettes and a superb *menú* for around €50 a head without wine.

La Cepa c/Treinta y Uno de Agosto 7. Inexpensive *raciones* served amidst decor of bullfighting kitsch and dangling hams; also a pricier *comedor*. Closed Wed.

Domenico's c/Zubieta 3 ☏ 943 471 537. Smart but affordable Italian restaurant with an emphasis on pasta; budget for €18–24 or choose the €10 weekday *menú*. Very popular, so reservations essential.

Gaztelu c/Treinta y uno de Agosto 22. Bland decor in the rear *comedor*, where sustaining fare with no airs or graces forms the cheapest (€7.50) *menú* in the *parte vieja*; more exciting *a la carta* runs to €18, or good *raciones* available in the front bar. Closed Wed.

Gorriti c/San Juan, corner c/Lorenzio. One of the town's best counter-top collections of fresh, seafood-strong tapas, *bocadillos* and *pintxos* to be found at this hole-in-the-wall.

La Mama di Piccata Minuta c/San Bartolomé 18, corner c/Triunfo. Good, relatively inexpensive Italian restaurant serving vegetarian dishes and pizzas. Allow about €18, without drink.

Casa Maruxa Paseo de Bizkaia 14. Specializes in food from Galicia and attracts the crowd on their way to the Astoria cinema complex just around the corner.

Mendizorrotz Barrio Igeldo, at the central plaza two stops before end of #16 bus line ☏ 943 212 023. Brief but superbly executed choice of dishes with specialities like *pimientos de padrón* (grilled green peppers) and *pudding de txangurro* (spider-crab mousse). Reckon on €22–30 including local cider and dessert in the tiny *comedor* or have the cheap *menú* (Mon–Fri) at the bar tables. Open daily.

Morgan c/Narrika 7. Bohemian clientele and a jazz soundtrack set the tone for this spot specializing in the "new Basque" school of cookery, emphasizing lighter, first courses – stuffed eggplant, venison carpaccio – and creative desserts, rather than the traditional hearty main courses. The bill can quickly mount to €30 *a la carta*, though there is a €12 lunch *menú*.

Casa Nicolasa c/Aldamar 4, 1º ☏ 943 421 762. Classic – and expensive – Basque cookery featuring seafood, game and meat; there's a €46 *menú*, but otherwise the bill can climb to €75. Closed Sun & Mon eve.

Okendo (Oquendo) c/Okendo 8. A decor of cinema-festival posters and delicacies such as crab cannelloni, venison and pigeon help justify the *menú*'s €30 price tag; *a la carta* isn't much more.

Oriental c/Reyes Católicos 6. Extremely friendly Chinese restaurant that's the best in terms of quality of food and value – allow €16 *a la carta*; eat in or take away. Open daily.

Txistu Plaza de la Constitución 14. Vast range of tapas inside, plus much-sought-after table service outside; the usual Basque suspects including mushrooms, kidneys, cuttlefish on skewers. Closed Tues.

Entertainment

In the evenings, you'll find no shortage of action, with clubs and bars everywhere. The two main areas are the **parte vieja**, especially along Fermín Calbetón, Puerto and Juan de Bilbao and in the **Zona Romántica** around the intersection of c/Reyes Católicos and c/Larramendi, where a large number of the city's more expensive music pubs and cafés are located. For **jazz**, try *Altxerri* at c/Reina Regente 2 (closed Mon), or *Etxekalte* (no sign) at c/Mari 11 at the fishing port. Once the pubs close around 2am, the action moves on to various **clubs** until dawn: try the handful along Fermín Calbetón. **Film** venues include the ten-plex Cine Principe, on the Plaza de Zuloaga by San Telmo in the *parte vieja*, and the Cine Trueba at Secundino Esnaola 2, across the Santa Catalina bridge in Gros, which often shows art and *versión original* movies.

Festivals

Throughout the summer there are constant **fiestas**, many involving Basque sports including the annual rowing (*trainera*) races between the villages along the coast, which culminate in a final regatta on September 9. The **Jazz Festival** (☏ 943 440 034, ⓦ www.jazzaldia.com), held at different locations throughout the town for six days during the latter half of July, invariably attracts top performers as well as hordes of people on their way home from the fiesta in

Pamplona. The week around August 15 – known as **Semana Grande** or Aste Nagusia (ⓦ www.paisvasco.com/donostia/ingles/indexi.htm) – sees numerous concerts, special events and fireworks laid on. There is also the **Film Festival** (ⓦ www.sansebastianfestival.ya.com) during the second half of September and frequent theatrical and musical performances throughout the year at the Auditorio del Kursaal or the Teatro Principal.

Inland from San Sebastián: a circuit through Gipuzkoa

In many ways **Gipuzkoa** is the heartland of Basque language and culture. Medieval towns like **Tolosa** with its traditional *carnaval* and **Orduña**, famous for its ancient university, and well-preserved villages like **Segura** are set in spectacular mountain scenery, with excellent walking in the Sierra de Aralar near the market town of **Ordizia**. In the nearby Sierra de Urkilla, the **Monasterio de Arantzazu** is a prime pilgrimage destination for Basques. A visit to the open-air museum in **Hernani**, dedicated to Basque sculptor Eduardo Chillida, is another way to sample the essence of this area.

Gipuzkoa is the smallest province in Spain and public transport is good, meaning that most places of interest can be visited comfortably as a day-trip from San Sebastián. Alternatively, the circuit set out below can act as a stepping stone to Vitoria and places further south.

Hernani

The reason for a visit to Hernani, 7km south of San Sebastián, is **Chillida-leku** (April–Oct 15, Mon, Wed–Sat 11am–6pm, Sun 11am–4pm; Oct 16–March, Mon, Wed–Sat 11am–4pm; €7.20; ⓦ www.eduardo-chillida.com), the open-air museum dedicated to the life and work of the internationally renowned sculptor Eduardo Chillida, whose massive works can be seen all over the Basque country and further afield, including San Sebastián (see p.497), Gernika (see p.507) and Gijón (see p.586). Buses leave every half hour from c/Okendo in San Sebastián, near the main tourist office.

The sculptures, housed in a beautifully refurbished 16th-century farmhouse and the surrounding field (which can be muddy), present an elemental solidity that almost seems to capture the essence of Basqueness. There's also an impressive video about Chillida's life.

Tolosa and Ordizia

Twenty-four kilometres south of San Sebastián is **TOLOSA**, famous for its **carnival** in February, celebrated here with fervour and considered by Basques to be superior to San Sebastián's (it was the only one whose tradition was maintained throughout the Franco era). Although fairly industrialized, Tolosa has an extensive old quarter with an impressive old town square and makes a lively place for a weekend night out. Make sure you sample a plate of *alubias* (kidney beans) in one of the many eating places – they're considered the best in Euskal Herria. If you want to **stay**, try the *Albergue Municipal Zuloaga Txiki*, about 20 minutes' walk out of town along the Careterra Tolosa-Anoeta s.n. (ⓣ & ⓕ 943 650 036; ❶), with its own restaurant that serves a good *menú* for €9. In the old town, try *Hostal Oyarbide*, Plaza Gorriti 1 (ⓣ & ⓕ 943 670 017; ❷), or the more upmarket *Hotel Oria*, c/de Oria 2 (☎943 654 688, ℱ943 653 612; ❹), which has its own restaurant and *sidrería* with a €20 *menú*. There are two good **restaurants** in Plaza Euskalerria near the *Oyarbide: Agustin Enea* at no. 6 (☎943 650 986) with a good-value *menú* for €9, and, two doors down at no. 8, the pricier *Astelena* (☎943 650 996).

A further 20km south, on the main railway line to Vitoria, is **ORDIZIA**, a prosperous town with a well-preserved historical centre. If your visit coincides with a Wednesday, don't miss the weekly **market** of farm products when farmers from the region converge on the town to buy and sell livestock, cheese and the like. Ordizia is backed by the impressive peak of **Txindoki**, rising above the town like a mini-Matterhorn. You can climb it in about three hours from Larraitz, the highest village, and the whole thing can be done as a day-trip from San Sebastián or Tolosa. Another good walking destination stretching beyond Txindoki is the **Sierra de Aralar** (see p. 530); one option is to walk across the plateau from Larraitz to the Sanctuario de San Miguel in Excelsis (7–8hrs in all; see p.531).

Segura and the monastery of Arantzazu

One of the most attractive inland villages in Gipuzkoa is **SEGURA**, about 5km southeast of Ordizia. Originally a seigneurial village from where the powerful Guevara family wielded power, there are various old mansions proudly displaying their coat of arms lining the long, winding main street. Today, it's a sleepy backwater which comes alive during the **Easter processions** (not otherwise much celebrated in Euskal Herria) and which hosts one of the best village fiestas in the region in mid-June.

Segura and Zegama, further south, were important stops on one of the branches of the ancient **Pilgrim Route** to Santiago, which joined up with the main route in Santo Domingo de la Calzada (La Rioja). The old Roman way the pilgrims once followed is still partly in evidence and you can walk a section of it as an easy day-trip, even without your own transport (although you should double-check all transport details before setting out). Take an early Vitoria-bound train from San Sebastián to **OTZAURTE**, a small halt south of Zegama. From here it's an hour's walk to the refuge of **San Adrián** (summer daily; rest of year Sat & Sun only; meals available). The best-preserved section of Roman road on the mountain is just beyond the natural tunnel of San Adrián above the refuge, from where it's downhill (2hr) to **Araia**, the first town in Araba just off the Vitoria–Pamplona road; from here, a bus departs at 3.15pm for Vitoria and trains leave from the station 2km beyond town.

Alternatively, head west across the plateau or along the spectacular ridge of Aitzkorri to the refuge of **Urbia** (same hours as San Adrián) and the monastery of **Arantzazu** (3–4hr). This is the prime place of pilgrimage for Basques – **Our Lady of Arantzazu** is the patron saint of Gipuzkoa – and is located in a spectacular setting, clinging to the mountainside above a gorge. Although a monastery on this site dates back to the fifteenth century, the present spiky building was built in 1950 and features contemporary work by the sculptors Chillida (the doors) and Sáenz de Oteiza (part of the facade). It's frankly hideous, but worth looking inside for the soaring stained-glass windows. It gets packed out on Sundays when worshippers come from all over the province and elsewhere. There are several *hostales* and hotels here, the best value of which are the *Hospedería de Arantzazu* (☎943 781 313, ℮ostatua@euskalnet.net; ❷), which is basic but popular with hiking groups and pilgrims, and the newer *Sindica* (☎943 781 303; ❷) next door, with better views and its own swimming pool; both places offer meals.

Oñati

OÑATI, 8km below Arantzazu, is without doubt the most interesting inland town in Gipuzkoa, with some fine examples of Baroque architecture among its many historic buildings; indeed the Basque painter Zuloaga described it as the "Basque Toledo".

The old **university** (Mon–Fri 9am–5pm, Sat–Sun 11am–2pm; free) dominates the town, built in 1548 and the only functioning university in Euskal Herria for hundreds of years. The facade, with its four pilasters adorned with figures, and the serene courtyard, are particularly impressive. The Baroque town hall and parish church of **San Miguel** (Sun 10am–2pm, otherwise enquire at tourist office) are at opposite ends of the arcaded Plaza de los Fueros. In the church crypt are buried all the Counts of Oñati from 988 to 1890; the cloister is unusual in that it is actually built over the river. Other fine buildings around the town include various *casas torres* of the type also found in northern Navarra, private family mansions and the Plateresque-style monastery of **Bidaurreta** (Mon–Fri 10am–noon & 3.30–8.30pm, Sat 3.30–8.30pm; free).

You'll find a very helpful **turismo** at Foru Enparantza 11 (Mon–Fri 10.30am–1pm & 4–7.30pm, Sat 10am–1pm & 4–6.30pm, Sun 11am–2pm & 4.30–6.30pm; winter closed Sat & Sun pm; ☏ 943 783 453), which can arrange visits to the university and parish church, and provide a free map of the town, as well as plenty of leaflets detailing local walking and motoring routes.

The *Bar-Restaurante Echeverria*, R.M. Zuazola 15 (☏ 943 780 460; ❶), is the best value **hostal** in the town centre; the **restaurant** below also offers a reasonable *menú del día*. If you'd prefer to stay in an **agroturismo**, try *Arregi*, Garagaltza 19 (☏ & ℻ 943 780 824; ❷), run by a very friendly family who offer evening meals on request (€9), or the attractive *Etxe Aundi* (☏ 943 781 956, ⊛ www.exteaundi.com; ❸), in a sixteenth-century tower 2km from town on the Mondragón road, with its own restaurant offering a *menú* for €10.

There are two daily **buses** from Oñati to Bilbao, and several to Vitoria, changing at Mondragón – an otherwise unappealing town famous as the cradle of the Basque cooperative movement.

The Costa Vasca

Heading west from San Sebastián, both road and rail run inland, following the Río Oria, towards the coast at Zarautz. Along the way, the pretty fishing village of **Orio** on the estuary makes an enjoyable break in the journey. From **Zarautz** onwards, the coastline of the **Costa Vasca** is glorious – rocky and wild, with long stretches of road hugging the edge of the cliffs – all the way to Bilbao. There are buses that take the motorway along this route, but even if you're not planning to stop (and there are plenty of picturesque villages to tempt you to do so) it's worth taking the old road for the scenery. The further you go, the less developed the resorts are.

Zarautz

ZARAUTZ is a fashionable overspill of San Sebastián with a splendid seaside walk and an attractive old town. The town and surrounding area (and, to a lesser extent, towns further along the coast towards Bizkaia) are famous for the production of *txakoli*, a strong, dry white wine – the vineyards cling to hillsides along the coast from here to Getaria. The week beginning September 9, Zarautz hosts "Basque Week", when you can watch traditional dances and hear *bertsolaris* performing improvised poetry in Basque.

The well-stocked **turismo** (Mon–Sat 9am–1pm & 3.30–7pm, Sun 10am–2pm; ☎943 830 990, Ⓦwww.turismozarautz.com) is on Avda. Navarra, the busy main road through town; staff here can advise on **accommodation**. There are several pricey hotels in town, including the *Zarautz* at Avda. Navarra 26 (☎943 830 200, Ⓦwww.hotelzarauz.com; ❺), and some cheaper *pensiones*, such as *Lagunak* at c/San Francisco 10 (☎943 833 701, Ⓕ943 134 656; ❸). One of the best places to stay, however, is a large *agroturismo*, *Agerre-Goikoa* (☎943 833 248; ❷), just off the main road to San Sebastián, with views of the old town and the mountains. The nearby *restaurante-asador Zubiondo*, Avda. Navarra 47 (☎943 830 267), has a tasty *menú* for €10. The **youth hostel** *Igerain* on c/San Inazio (☎ & Ⓕ943 132 910, Ⓔjuv.zarautz@gazteria.gipuzkoa.net; ❷), on the Meagas road out of town, is open all year, offering double rooms and meals for €6. Zarautz has two **campsites**: *Gran Camping Zarauz* (☎943 831 238, Ⓕ943 132 486; open all year), on the cliff tops overlooking the beach, reached from town on the old San Sebastián road, with a marked turning on the left up the hill; and the cheaper *Talai-Mendi* (☎943 830 042) at the edge of town on the San Sebastián road, 250m from the beach but open only from late-June to mid-September.

While in Zarautz you should try the local speciality, *chipirones a lo Pelayo* (cuttlefish with onion). One of the best places to do so is *Restaurante Kuliska*, Bixkondu 1 (☎943 134 604), overlooking the beach.

Getaria

Five kilometres on is **GETARIA**, a tiny fishing port sheltered by the humpbacked islet of **El Ratón** (The Mouse). It's a historic little place, one of the earliest towns on the coast, preserving the magnificent fourteenth-century church of San Salvador, whose altar is raised theatrically above the heads of the congregation. The first man to sail around the world, Juan Sebastián Elcano, was born here around 1487. His ship was the only one of Magellan's fleet to make it back home. Every four years on August 6, during the village's **fiestas**, Elcano's landing is re-enacted on the beach; the next will be in 2007. There's a small but interesting **art gallery**, next to the church at c/Katrapuna 2, with oil reliefs by local painter Elorza.

Getaria has a small, summer-only **turismo** at Aldamar Parkea 2 (Easter to mid-Sept Mon 3–9pm, Wed 11.15am–1.15pm & 3–9pm, Thurs–Sun 10.15am–2.15pm & 3–9pm; ☎943 140 957); when it's closed, the turismo in Zarautz has some information. **Accommodation** options include the comfortable *Pensión Iribar*, near the church at Kale Nagusia 34 (☎943 140 406; ❷), with attractive views, and *Pensión Getariano*, near the main road at c/Herrerieta 3 (☎943 140 567; ❸). There are also three cheaper *agroturismos* a few kilometres up the hillside on the way to Meagas, including the *Casa Rural Itsas-Lore* (☎943 140 619, Ⓦwww.itsaslore.com; ❷), with lovely views of the sea and the mountains. Check the prices at the tempting fish **restaurants** in the old town and port before you eat, as they can be pricey. If you're feeling flush, though, the *Elkano*, at c/Herrerieta 2 (☎943 140 614), does truly excellent fresh fish and seafood meals for around €60 a head. Alternatively, *The Mayflower bar* overlooking the harbour, has excellent sardines and the daily *menú* is a bargain at €10.

Zumaia, Azpeitia and around

The coast becomes still more rugged on the way to **ZUMAIA** – an industrial-looking place at first sight, but with an attractive centre and pleasant waterfront along the estuary of the Río Urola. Zumaia's local **fiesta** in the first days of July is one of the region's most exuberant, with Basque sports, dancing and bullocks let loose on the beach to test the mettle of the local youth.

Zumaia has two very different **beaches** – one of these, over the hill behind the town, is a large splash of grey sand enclosed by extraordinary sheer cliffs of layered slate-like rock which channel the waves in to produce some of the best surfing on the coast. There are spectacular walks along the cliff tops to the west. The other beach, across the river from the port, is yellow and flat, sheltered by a little pine forest. On the road behind this you'll find the **Villa Zuloaga** (Wed–Sun 4–8pm; €3), former home of the nineteenth-century-born Basque painter Ignacio Zuloaga, and now a small art museum displaying his work and that of other Basque artists, together with a rather bizarre exhibition of bull-fighting memorabilia.

There's a very helpful **turismo** on the main square (Mon–Sat 10am–2pm & 4–8pm; ☎943 143 396, ⓦwww.zumaia.net). Good-value **accommodation** can be found at the central *Pensión Goiko*, Erribera 9 (☎943 861 391; ❷), or the quiet, friendly *Agroturismo Jesuskoa*, Oikia Auzoa (☎943 861 736; ❷), with a well-renowned restaurant specializing in grilled lamb, 3km from the centre along the Meagas road. There are also a couple of hotels: the *Zumaia* at c/Alai 13 (☎943 143 441, ⓕ943 860 764; ❸), in-between the train station and the centre; and the pricier *Zelai*, Larretzo 16 (☎943 865 100, ⓦwww.talasozelai.com; ❻), above the *Playa de Itzurun*, with a sea-water therapy centre. Recommended places to **eat** include *Algorri*, near the marina at c/Puerto Deportivo s/n (☎943 865 617), with a *menú del día* for €9 or *menú de sidrería* from €18. Try the traditional Basque dessert of *queso con membrillo y nueces* (cheese with quince jelly and walnuts) if you get the chance.

Inland from Zumaia, 1km from the town of **AZPEITIA**, is the imposing eighteenth-century Baroque **Basilica of Loyola** (daily 8.30am–2pm & 3–9pm), built in honour of local son San Ignacio de Loyola, the founder of the Society of Jesus or Jesuits, with an impressive rotunda and marble decor – this is a major pilgrimage spot. On the way from Zumaia to Azpeitia you pass through the town of **ZESTOA**, which has a rich supply of thermal and mineral waters. The luxurious *Gran Hotel Balneario Cestona* (☎943 147 140, ⓦwww.balneariocestona.com; ❺) lies just off the main road and offers a wide range of spa treatments including thermal showers.

Mutriku

MUTRIKU, 10km west of Zumaia, despite some ugly recent construction above the town, has some attractive narrow streets leading steeply down to the fishing harbour. It's the centre of another *txakoli*-producing area. Admiral Churruca, the "Hero of Trafalgar" to locals, was born here; his imposing statue faces the incongruous church of Nuestra Señora de Asunción, built along the lines of a Greek temple, with a painting attributed to Zurbarán inside. Mutriku has a **turismo** on Xemein Etorbidea 13 (mid–June to mid–Sept 10.30am–2pm & 4.30–8pm; ☎943 603 378, ⓦwww.mutriku.net) and no fewer than four **campsites** around several small beaches. There is also a hotel beside the port, *Kofradi Zaharra*, Moila 1 (☎943 603 954; ❸), and a choice of **agroturismos**: *Casa Matzuri* (☎943 603 001; ❷), 1km beyond town on the road to Ondarroa with lovely sea and mountain views, and the self-catering *Koostei* (☎943 583 008; ❷), perched high up in the hills several kilometres from the main road, which offers horse-riding. Beyond Mutriku, the road temporarily turns inland until it reaches the coast 2km further on at the beach of **Saturrarán**, which is very popular and crowded in summer, when there's a **campsite** (☎943 603 847; June–Sept) and a restaurant, *Mijoa*, which does *menús* for €10.

Ondarroa

Around the headland from Saturrarán, **ONDARROA**, the first coastal town in Bizkaia, presents a very different aspect from the other small resorts further east. Here, the usual town beach and attractive tree-lined *rambla* end at a nononsense **fishing port** filled with an eclectic set of trawlers. In the early morning, an endless succession of trucks files in from the coastal road to fill up with fish – the traffic is so great that a large bridge has been built across the bay to channel the fishing trucks directly to the port. Ondarroa is an interesting place to stop over, particularly in mid-August when the town hosts its **fiestas**. The *casco viejo* was razed to the ground by French troops in 1794, but the late-Gothic church of Santa Maria, in the town centre, survived; its extremely ornate facade includes flower and animal motifs and a "court" of twelve figures including a king, queen, pilgrims, crossbowmen, a minstrel and a wet nurse.

Ondarroa's **turismo** is nearby on the port at Kofradia Zaharra Erribera 9 (☎946 831 951 or 946 844 017). If you want to **stay**, head for the *Hostal Arrigorri*, c/Arrigorri 3 (☎946 134 045, ⓦwww.arrigorri.net; ❶), on the Mutriku road, with magnificent harbour views from the better rooms; the **restaurant** serves a good €9 *menú* of the catch of the day. There's also the excellent and inexpensive *Pensión Patxi*, c/Aria-Bide 21 (☎609 986 446; ❶). The nearby *Restaurante Ametza*, Artabide 24 (☎946 830 608), specializes in *bacalao*. The **bars** at the harbour stay open late (some 24hr) as deckhands come and go, and, stuffed with a tempting array of seafood *pintxos*, they're accommodating enough to keep the promenading locals and occasional stray tourist happy.

Markina and Bolibar

Ten kilometres south of Ondarroa, the attractive town of **MARKINA** is famous for producing many of the finest *pelota* players – the *frontón* here is known as *La Universidad de la Pelota*. The village is also worth a look for its remarkable collection of fortified tower-houses, although these can't be visited. If you want **to stay**, try the comfortable *Hostal Vega* in the main square beside the Torre Antxia (☎946 866 015; ❷), which has a good restaurant, *Niko* (☎946 167 528), with *menú* for €10. From Markina you can visit the tiny village of **BOLIBAR**, ancestral home of the South American liberator, where there is a small museum depicting the great man's feats (Tues–Fri 10am–1pm, Sat & Sun noon–2pm; July & Aug also daily 5–7pm; free). From the village a short, restored stretch of a branch of the Camino de Santiago leads up to the **Colegiata de Zenarruza** (Mon–Sat 10.15am–1.30pm & 4–7pm; Mass Sun 12pm), a former pilgrims' *hostal* and hospital containing a beautiful sixteenth-century cloister and Romanesque church.

Lekeitio

LEKEITIO, 10km further west, is another good bet along this stretch of the coast. Still an active fishing port, it has two fine **beaches** – one beside the harbour, the other, much better, across the river to the east of town. It's worth stopping in at the **church** of Santa Maria, in the town centre, with its magnificent sixteenth-century Flemish Gothic altarpiece, the third largest in the peninsula after those of the cathedrals of Sevilla and Toledo. The **tourist office**, Plaza de la Independencia s/n (☎946 844 016, ⓦwww.learjai.com; Mon–Sat 10am–2pm, 4–7pm, Sun 10.30am–2pm; closed Mon in winter), can help with information about accommodation. The best of the **hotel** options is the *Hotel Emperatriz Zita*, c/Santa Elena s/n (☎946 842 655, ☏946 243 500;

❹), with excellent sea views from the better rooms; it also has a restaurant and sea-water therapy centre. Another excellent place to say is the elegant *Hotel Zubieta*, Portal de Atea s/n (☏946 843 030, ℻946 841 099, closed Christmas; ❹), set in the gardens of an old palace at the edge of town. Otherwise try the cheaper *Hostal Piñupe*, Avda. Pascual Abaroa 10 (☏946 842 984, ℻946 840 772; ❸), in the town cente. A **campsite**, *Endai* (☏946 842 469; open mid-June to mid-Sept), can be found on the main road to Ondarroa; alternatively, head for *Leagi* (☏946 842 352, ⓦwww.campingleagi.com), in the village of Mendexa, 3km inland between Ondarroa and Lekeitio, which is open all year. There is also a summer-only **agroturismo**, *Itxas-ertx*, Barrio Likona (☏946 243 177; ❷ with bath), 1km from town on the Mendexa road. Horse-riding, mountain biking and kayaking are all available nearby. Lekeitio is literally teeming with **bars**, many offering food, and there are also several good seafood **restaurants** including *Kaia* at Txatxo Kaia 5 (☏946 840 204), with various *menús* for between €8 and €20; *Legaña*, at Antiguako-Amak 2 (☏946 840 103; €7.50–22); and *Goitiko*, near the tourist office in Plaza de la Independencia (☏946 843 103; €7–18). Out on the edge of town near the *Hotel Zubieta* is the welcoming *Meson Arropain* (☏946 840 313), again specializing in fish and seafood.

Elantxobe

The road turns inland from Lekeitio, but the well-preserved fishing village of **ELANTXOBE**, 10km further west, is worth a detour back to the coast. Perched high above a small harbour, the village is connected to it by an incredibly steep cobbled street lined with attractive fishermen's houses. The calle Mayor continues 2km up to the cemetery from where a signposted track leads to **Mount Ogoño** – at 280m the highest cliff on the Basque coast.

Elantxobe has a couple of small **restaurants** including the recommended *Makues*, c/Bide 1 (☏946 276 513), and one central *pensión*, *Itsasmin Ostatua*, at c/Nagusia 32 (☏946 276 174, ℻946 276 293; ❸). Alternatively, you can stay at one of the two *agroturismos* located in Ibarrangelu, 1km from the crossroads in the direction of Gernika: *Caserio Arboliz*, at c/Arboliz 12 (☏946 276 283; ❸ with bath), or the slightly cheaper *Etxetxu* (☏946 276 337; ❷) next door. Direct **buses** run between Elantxobe and Gernika (twice daily) or, from Lekeitio, take the Gernika bus to Ibarrangelu and walk 1km down to the village.

Gernika and around

Immortalized by Picasso's nightmare picture (finally brought home to Spain after the death of Franco, and now exhibited in the Centro de Arte Reina Sofía, Madrid (see p.106), **GERNIKA**, inland and west of Lekeitio, is the traditional heart of Basque nationalism. It was here that the Basque parliament used to meet, and here, under the **Tree of Gernika** (the *Gernikako Arbola*), that their rights were reconfirmed by successive rulers. It was more for its symbolic importance than the presence of a small-arms factory that Gernika was chosen during the Civil War as the target for one of the first ever saturation bombing raids on a civilian centre. In just four hours on April 27, 1937, planes from the Condor Legion (lent to Franco by Hitler) destroyed the town centre and killed more than 1600 people, many of them attending the weekly market (still held every Monday in the Plaza de Gernika). The nearby town of Durango had in fact been bombed a few days earlier, but because there were no foreign observers, the reports were simply not believed.

The parliament building, the **Casa de las Juntas** (daily 10am–2pm, 4pm–7pm; closes at 6pm in winter; ☎946 251 138, ⓔgernikako .batzar.etxea@bizkaia.org; free), is well worth a visit for the stained-glass window depicting the tree and important scenes and monuments from the region. The adjacent church of Santa María la Antigua, adorned with portraits of the various nobles of Bizkaia who pledged allegiance to the *fueros*, traditionally served as a meeting house (although in fine weather, assemblies were held under the tree). The parliament, church and tree remained miraculously unscathed by the bombing, but the rest of the town was destroyed and has been rebuilt and is now rather nondescript, apart from the arcaded main street. Here you'll find the **Gernika Peace Museum** (Sept to mid-June Mon–Sat 10am–2pm & 4–7pm, Sun 10am–2pm; mid-June to Aug Mon–Sat 10am–7pm, Sun 10am–2pm; free guided tours in Spanish & Basque only, noon & 5pm; ☎946 270 213, ⓔmuseoa@gernika-lumo.net; €4), with a stirring display on the bombing, and a collection of Picasso's sketches for *Guernica*. For a Basque, at least, a visit to Gernika is more pilgrimage than tourist trip. A walk through Europa Park, with its ornamental gardens, fast-flowing stream and peace sculptures by Henry Moore and Eduardo Chillida, captures something of the elegiac atmosphere.

Housed in the Palacio Udetxea next to the park is the headquarters of the **Urdaibai Biosphere Reserve** (Mon–Thurs 9am–1.30pm & 3–5pm, Fri 9am–2.30pm; free), which often holds exhibitions on environmental and cultural themes. The reserve itself, which encompasses the watershed of the Mundaka estuary, was declared by UNESCO in 1984 as an area of world cultural and natural heritage; it includes the most diverse range of habitats in Euskal Herria and is the resting place for hosts of migrating birds.

Practicalities

There's a helpful **turismo** at c/Artekale 8 (Mon–Sat 10am–2pm & 4–8pm, Sun 10am–2pm; ☎946 255 892, ⓦwww.gernika-lumo.net) in the arcaded main street, with one of the best selections of pamphlets in English on all areas of Euskal Herria and details of **places to stay**. Otherwise, head for the cheap and central *Pensión Akelarre Ostatua*, Barrenkale 5 (☎946 270 197, ⓦwww.ake-larre.euskalnet.net; ❷), the *Hotel-Restaurante Boliña*, Barrenkale 3 (☎946 250 300), next door, with good fish and meat dishes, or, for more luxury, *Gernika*, Carlos Gangoiti 17 (☎946 254 948, ⓦwww.hotelgernika.com; ❹). If you have your own transport, the turismo can make bookings at any one of four **agro-turismos** within a ten-kilometre radius of town. Places **to eat** include *Julen*, c/Industria 14 (☎946 254 927), or *Gernika*, next door at c/Industria 12 (☎946 250 778), specializing in salads and ham.

Hourly **buses** run via Zornotza to Bilbao starting at 7.10am. There is also a regular service to Bermeo (12 daily).

The Cueva de Santimamiñe and Bosque Encantado de Oma

Five kilometres from Gernika, off the Lekeitio road, lies the **Cueva de Santimamiñe** (guided tours Mon–Fri at 10am, 11.15am, 12.30pm, 4.30pm & 6pm; free, but tipping customary). Inside are extraordinary rock formations and some Paleolithic cave paintings of bison – which are now, unfortunately, off limits due to deterioration brought about by rising temperatures.

Without your own transport, it may be worth coming on an organized tour (details from tourist offices in Gernika or Bilbao), as there is no public transport to the cave. You can, however, get a taxi from Gernika for about €7, or the thrice-daily Gernika–Lekeitio bus can drop you at Kortezubi from where it's a two-kilometre signposted walk. It's a steep climb up to the entrance and you may have to wait as numbers are limited to fifteen at one time – a good **bar-restaurant** in the car park helps pass the time. If you do have to wait, or wish to spend longer, the area is very scenic and walking trails from the cave are well signposted. For accommodation, try *Morgota* (T946 252 772; ➋), a peaceful *agroturismo*, in sleepy Kortezubi.

From the *Lezika* restaurant on the Santimarniñe road, a single-track road leads to the lovely village of **OMA**, 5km away, tucked in a lush green valley. Here, veteran Basque artist Augustin Ibarrola has transformed a pine plantation into the **Bosque Encantado de Oma** (Enchanted Wood of Oma), by painting tree trunks in such a way that from certain points in the wood, where the trees line up correctly, pictures are formed – of rainbows, strange beasts and other fabulous images. The effect is impressively eerie, and although the wood was vandalized by ETA supporters in April 2000, it's still well worth the trip. As well as the road, there is a dirt track to the wood (also starting from the *Lezika*) that allows access with a reasonably sturdy vehicle, and also enables you to see the wood as part of a ten-kilometre circular walk (allow 4hr in total, including time in the wood). If you want to stay in Oma, there's an *agroturismo*, *Bizketxe* (T946 254 906; ➋) – you can book at the Gernika turismo.

Mundaka and Bermeo

Continuing the route west, the Río Mundaka flows from Gernika into a broad estuary fringed by hilly pine woods and dotted with islets. There's a succession of sandy coves to swim in, but the best spots are at Sukarrieta (Pedernales) and especially **MUNDAKA**, where there's a **campsite**, *Portuondo* (T & F946 877 701, Wwww.campingportuondo.com; open all year), high above the water with steps leading down to a rocky beach. There is magnificent surfing to be had here, including the longest left break in the world; championships often take place, and on any windy day the plaza next to the church makes a good spot to watch the surfers battle the waves. A passenger ferry plies across the river (June–Sept 10am–8pm; every 20min; €1.20) to the **Playa de Laída**, an enormous area of white sand, which at low tide stretches across the mouth of the bay in an unbroken crescent. Places to **stay** in Mundaka include the attractive and clean *Hotel Mundaka*, Florentino Larriñaga 9 (T946 876 700, Wwww.hotelmundaka.com; ➍), and the friendly *Hotel el Puerto*, c/Portu 1 (T946 876 625, F946 177 064; ➍), right on the fishing port. Note that the town gets very crowded in summer, so book ahead.

The local *EuskoTren* train line from Bilbao and Gernika gives good access to the estuary beaches and continues beyond Mundaka for 3km to **BERMEO**, whose fishing fleet is the largest remaining in these waters, a riot of red, green and blue boats in the harbour. Worth checking out while you're here is the **Museo del Pescador** near the harbour (Tues–Sat 10am–1.30pm & 4–7.30pm, Sun 10am–1.30pm; free), which is full of local interest and more general maritime displays. Apart from a stroll through the narrow, cobbled streets, there's not much else to see, and no beach worth the name – but while you're here you should try some of the fish in the restaurants around the port: the local standards – *merluza* (hake) and *bacalao* (cod) – are particularly good. Bermeo's **turismo** (daily 10am–1pm & 5–8pm; T946 179 154), just opposite the train station at Askatasun Bidea 2, has a good pamphlet detailing a walk through the town and can put you in touch with the several *agroturismos* in the area. At the lower end of the scale of **hotel** options there is an attractive and inexpensive *pensión*, *Torre Ercilla*, at Talaranzko 14 (T946 187 598, Ebarrota@piramidal.com; ❷), and the centrally located *hostal*, *Aldatxeta*, c/Erremedio 24 (☎946 187 703; ❸), in a renovated building with bath and TV in all rooms. The *Hotel Txaraka*, Almike Bidea (☎946 885 558, ℻946 885 764; ❹), in a quiet area on the edge of town with easy parking, is a slightly more upmarket possibility.

Eight kilometres west of Bermeo, on the way to the sleepy resort town of **BAKIO**, the hermitage of **San Juan de Gaztelugatxe** stands on a rocky peninsula, connected to the shore by a long and winding flight of 231 steps at one of the most rugged parts of the Bizkaian coast. If you're travelling by bus, ask the driver to let you off at the cliff-top crossroads and walk down.

Bakio itself backs directly onto a good **beach** and there are walking and mountain-bike trails in the quiet surrounding hills. If you fancy a bit of luxury, try the colonial-style *Hotel Joshe Mari*, c/Bentalde 31 (☎946 194 005, ℻946 195 703; ❹), with excellent views and its own restaurant with a €25 *menú*.

After Bakio, the coast road passes **Lemóniz**, infamous for the government's attempt to build a nuclear power station and the Basques' fierce resistance to it. The project was shelved after one of its engineers was kidnapped and assassinated by ETA. The abandoned, half-finished power station, enclosed in a narrow valley, is a striking, if rather sinister, sight.

Bilbao

Stretching for some 14km along the narrow valley of the heavily polluted Río Nervión, **BILBAO** (Bilbo) is a large city that rarely feels like one, its urban sprawl having gradually engulfed a series of once-separate communities. Even in the city centre you can always see the green slopes of the surrounding mountains beyond the high-rise buildings. A prosperous, modern city with a busy and attractive centre, surrounded by grim, graffiti-covered slums and smoke-belching factories, Bilbao is in the process of reinventing itself after the collapse of its traditional industrial base in the 1980s and 1990s. Steel mills and shipyards have been transformed into conference centres and luxury flats, and the famous Guggenheim Museum, which opened in 1997, has sparked a tourism boom. A new metro and airport have opened and celebrations of Bilbao's 700th anniversary, in 2000, brought new impetus to the redevelopment programme. The city also has some of the best places to eat and drink in the whole of the region, and very open, friendly inhabitants with an abundance of civic pride.

Arrival

Most long-distance and international **bus** companies use the **Termibús station** (☎944 395 077; ⓂSan Mamés), which fills an entire block between Luis Briñas and Gurtubay in the new part of town. Many provincial buses depart from the **Bizkaiabus station** on c/Sendeja, next to the main turismo in the Parque del Arenal; the turismo has information on timetables. The bus from Bilbao's spanking new **airport**, 15km from town (☎905 505 505 or 902 222 265), arrives at the Plaza Moyua in the centre of the new town and takes 40 minutes (daily 6am–10.30pm, every 30min; €1). A cab would cost about €20.

The main RENFE train station is the **Estación de Abando** (☎902 240 202) on Plaza Circular, but local services to San Sebastián, Gernika, Bermeo and Durango use the **Estación Atxuri** (☎944 019 900), on the other side of the river, to the south of the *casco viejo*. FEVE services, along the coast to

▲ Tunnel to Airport

▼ Vitoria, San Sebastián & Madrid

Santander and beyond, stop at the highly decorative **Estación de Santander** (☎944 250 615) on the riverbank right below the Estación de Abando.

The **P&O ferry** from Portsmouth in the UK docks at **Santurtzi**, across the river from Getxo (Las Arenas), to the north of the city centre. Regular buses and trains run from the docks to the centre of town. An unusual way to cross the Río Nervión is by the hundred-year-old *puente colgante* (hanging bridge) in Portugalete, some 3km south of the ferry terminal; either take the gondola across at street level (24hrs/day, €0.20) or else get the lift up to the 43m-high viewing platform (10am–7pm; €2.40) and walk across.

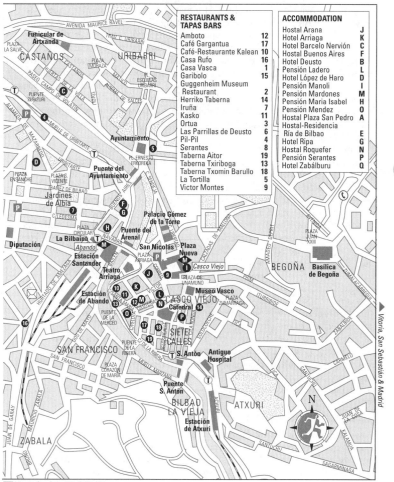

RESTAURANTS & TAPAS BARS

Amboto	12
Café Gargantua	17
Café-Restaurante Kalean	10
Casa Rufo	16
Casa Vasca	1
Garibolo	15
Guggenheim Museum Restaurant	2
Herriko Taberna	14
Iruña	7
Kasko	11
Ortua	3
Las Parrillas de Deusto	6
Pil-Pil	4
Serantes	8
Taberna Aitor	19
Taberna Txiriboga	13
Taberna Txomin Barullo	18
La Tortilla	5
Victor Montes	9

ACCOMMODATION

Hostal Arana	J
Hotel Arriaga	K
Hotel Barcelo Nervión	C
Hostal Buenos Aires	F
Hotel Deusto	B
Pensión Ladero	L
Hotel López de Haro	D
Pensión Manoli	I
Guggenheim Museum	M
Pensión Mardones	H
Pensión Maria Isabel	O
Pensión Mendez	A
Hostal Plaza San Pedro	
Hostal-Residencia Ría de Bilbao	E
Hotel Ripa	G
Hostal Roquefer	N
Pensión Serantes	P
Hotel Zabálburu	Q

▼ Vitoria, San Sebastián & Madrid

Information and orientation

The well-stocked main **turismo** (Mon–Fri 9am–2pm & 4–7.30pm, Sat 9am–2pm, Sun 10am–2pm; ☎944 795 760, ⓦwww.bilbao.net; Ⓜ Moyua, take "Diputación" exit) is temporarily located at c/Rodriguez Arias 3, near the centre of town; its permanent home has yet to be decided. There's a more convenient turismo outside the Guggenheim Museum (July–Aug Mon–Fri 11am–2pm & 4–6pm, Sat 11am–2pm & 5–7pm, Sun 11am–2pm; rest of year closed Mon), a booth at the airport (Mon–Fri 7.30am–11pm, Sat & Sun 8.30am–11pm, ☎944 710 301) and a helpful turismo on Getxo's beachfront at Muelle de Ereaga (daily 10am–8pm; ☎944 910 800).

The new town (or "Ensanche") is situated in a broad loop of the Río Nervión, with the main radial avenues affording direct views of the mountains from the bustling streets. On the opposite (right) bank of the river, there's the *casco viejo* to the south, and Deusto, famous for its university, to the north.

Most facilities are along the city's main thoroughfare, the **Gran Vía Don Diego López de Haro**, where you'll find all the major **banks**, public buildings, expensive shops and the department store, El Corte Inglés. The Gran Vía goes straight through the heart of the modern city, from the Plaza Circular by the RENFE station, to the Plaza Sagrado Corazón, situated between the new **Euskalduna Palace** and the huge stadium of **San Mames**, the "cathedral of football" as *bilbainos* would have it.

Transport around the city was revolutionized by the completion of a spanking new **metro** system, designed by Lord Norman Foster; the distinctive tube-like entrances are popularly known as *fosteritos*. An easy, efficient service runs every four minutes along the "right bank" from Plentzia (to the northeast of Getxo) to Bouleta, south of the city centre; a recently completed second line covers parts of the industrial "left bank". Free metro maps are available from the tourist offices. The 32 stops are divided into three zones, but all journeys in the city centre (including the *casco viejo*) are within one zone (€1.20). For parts the metro doesn't reach, there are red municipal **buses** (€0.90) with route maps at the green bus shelters, or for longer journeys (including to the airport) the blue and yellow *Bizkaibuses*. The green **trams** (€0.60) run along a single line, opened in 2002, linking the *casco viejo* and the Guggenheim Museum with San Mames and the bus station. The Bilbao transport system has won a European award – despite which, traffic is awful and parking a nightmare, especially in the city centre.

If you're staying a few days, it's a good idea to get a *Creditrans* **travelcard**, available in kiosks, newsagents and metro stations in denominations of €5, €10 and €20. This smart card works for all Bilbao's various modes of transport – the metro, tram, municipal and provincial buses, the Artxanda funicular and the *ascensores* at Puente la Salve and elsewhere – and cuts fares by almost fifty percent.

Accommodation

Now that Bilbao is firmly on the tourist map, accommodation is frequently booked out, so it's well worth planning ahead. The best **places to stay** are in the *casco viejo* – especially along **c/Bidebarrieta**, which leads from Plaza Arriaga to the cathedral, and in the streets around it: c/Lotería, c/Santa María and c/Barrencalle Barrena. Calle Barrencalle is best avoided if you value your sleep – the bars get very noisy at night. Rock-bottom options (rather grim *fondas* and *casas de huéspedes*) are on the east bank around the Estación de Abando, particularly round the back on c/San Francisco. The parallel c/de las Cortes is the red-light district, and not for the nervous; avoid it if you can. Another decent area for rooms is in the streets leading down from Plaza Circular around c/Buenos Aires (Ⓜ Abando). Staying in **Deusto** is a good alternative, handy for the art galleries and main shopping districts and boasting its own crop of restaurants and bars. **Getxo** is another viable option, since with the metro it's easy to reach anywhere on the east bank in minutes; you can book accommodation in the Getxo turismo.

The nearest **campsites** are to the northeast, on the beaches at Sopelana, *Sopelana* (☎946 762 120; bus towards Plentzia or Ⓜ Sopelana), and Gorliz, *Arrien* (☎946 771 911; just beyond Plentzia); both campsites are open all year.

Budget options

Pensión Ladero c/Lotería 1, 4° ☎944 150 932, Ⓜ Casco Viejo. Friendly management and clean, good-value rooms with modern furnishings but no baths. There is also a fifth-floor annexe reached by a narrow spiral staircase. ❷

Pensión Manoli c/Libertad-Askatasuna 2 ☎944 155 636, Ⓜ Casco Viejo. Spacious, clean rooms off Plaza Nueva. ❶ There's an annexe just down the street at c/Gordóniz 66. ❷

Pensión Mardones c/Jardines 4 ☎944 153 105, Ⓜ Casco Viejo. Entrance at the side of a newspaper kiosk, there are smart, clean rooms here – with or without bath. Preferable to the annexe on the second floor. ❸

Pensión Maria Isabel c/Amistad 5, 1° ☎944 248 566, Ⓜ Abando. Basic, but clean and well-run *pensión*, that's handy for the station. ❶

Pensión Mendez c/Santa María 13 ☎944 160 364, Ⓜ Casco Viejo. In the *casco viejo* near the Stock Exchange; clean and convenient. ❶

Hostal Roquefer c/Lotería 2 ☎944 150 755, Ⓜ Casco Viejo. On the second and fourth floors of a dark and musty building. The best (and lightest) rooms overlook the cathedral square. ❷

Pensión Serantes c/Somera 14 ☎944 151 557, Ⓜ Casco Viejo. This is the cheapest place in town. Rather down-at-heel but with friendly young staff. ❶

Moderate and expensive options

Hostal Arana c/Bidebarrieta 2 ☎944 156 411, Ⓦ www.hthotels.com, Ⓜ Casco Viejo. Friendly, very quiet and conveniently located *hostal* in the *casco viejo*. ❸

Hotel Arriaga c/Ribera 3 ☎944 790 001, ☏944 790 516, Ⓜ Casco Viejo. Best of the medium-range hotels, near the Teatro, by the river; modern, comfortable rooms with bath and TV; garage available. ❹

Hotel Barcelo Nervión Campo Volantín 11 ☎944 454 700, Ⓦ www.bchoteles.com. Plush new hotel overlooking the Zubizuri bridge. Weekend reductions. ❹–❼

Hostal Buenos Aires Plaza Venezuela 1, 3° ☎944 240 765, ✉joseiro21@hotmail.com, Ⓜ Abando. Comfortable and well-run *hostal* with a pleasant lounge and small bar. ❹

Hotel Deusto c/Francisco Macia 9 ☎944 760 006, Ⓦ www.nh-hoteles.es, Ⓜ Deusto. Business hotel near the University of Deusto, with substantial weekend reductions. ❹–❼

Hotel Igeretxe Playa Ereaga, Getxo ☎944 607 000, ☏944 608 599. Upmarket hotel right on the seafront with a bar where you can watch the ships coming in to port. ❻

Hotel López de Haro Obispo Orueta 2 ☎944 235 500, Ⓦ www.hotellopezdeharo.com, Ⓜ Moyua. Luxury five-star hotel near the Jardines de Albia. ❽

Hotel Neguri Avda. Algorta 14, Getxo ☎944 910 509, ☏944 911 943, Ⓜ Algorta. Good-value place with decent rooms and plenty of facilities. ❺

Hostal Plaza San Pedro c/Luzarra 7 ☎944 763 126, ☏944 763 895, Ⓜ Deusto. Across the river in Deusto in a slightly grim-looking street, this little place has very comfortable en-suite rooms with TV. ❸

Hostal-Residencia Ría de Bilbao Ribera de Deusto 32 ☎944 765 060, Ⓦ www.riabilbao.com; Ⓜ Deusto. Nice quiet place overlooking the river, a 10min walk from the Palacio Euskalduna. Garden and cooking facilities. Highly recommended. ❷

Hotel Ripa c/Ripa 3 ☎944 239 677, ☏944 231 816, Ⓜ Abando. Just over Puente del Arenal from the *casco viejo*, on the street by the waterfront; good-value rooms with bath and TV. ❸

Hotel Zabálburu Pedro Martínez Artola 8 ☎944 437 100, ☏944 100 073. Good, clean doubles in a hotel handy for the train stations. ❹

The City

Bilbao's **casco viejo**, the old quarter on the east bank of the river, holds many of the city's sights: the beautiful **Teatro Arriaga**, the elegantly arcaded **Plaza Nueva** (or *de los Mártires*), the Gothic **Catedral de Santiago** and the **Museo Arqueológico, Etnográfico e Histórico Vasco** at c/Cruz 4 (Tues–Sat 11am–7pm, Sun 11am–2pm; €3, free Thurs). The museum is housed in the former Colegio de San Andrés with its beautiful cloister and large selection of coats of arms of the former Bizkaian nobility – a lovely retreat from the city bustle. It has an intriguing and eclectic collection, from an enormous, obsessively detailed three-dimensional map of Bizkaia on the top floor, to an exhibition on Basque emigrants to the Americas. The museum is deceptively extensive and it's best to start at the top and work your way down. It's in the

△ Guggenheim Museum, Bilbao

old town, too, that the best **bars and restaurants** are situated among the narrow streets and antiquated shops contained in the *siete calles* (seven streets) area bordered by c/de la Ronda and c/Pelota.

From the *casco viejo* it's a pleasant ramble along the river through the Parque del Arenal and past the **ayuntamiento** – a favourite *paseo* for Bilbainos, although the smell of the River Nervión can be overpowering in hot weather. For some fresh air, leave the river at the Zubizuri bridge and head three blocks north to the Plaza Funicular, where the **Artxanda funicular** (€1) sweeps you up the mountain for a panoramic vista of the city; you can also see over into the next valley, with views of the new Calatrava-designed airport. The top station is a nice spot for a picnic, and you can stroll down the hill again (about 45min) through the lush suburbs of the *Ciudad Jardín* (Garden City).

Guggenheim Museum

The biggest attraction in Bilbao, however, is undoubtedly Frank O. Gehry's astounding **Guggenheim Museum** (Tues–Sun 10am–8pm; July & Aug also Mon; €8, special exhibits €10; under-12s free), which dominates the quayside opposite the University of Deusto. You can cross the delicate arch of the Zubizuri footbridge to approach the museum from below along the west bank, or take in the full panorama from across the river before crossing the new Pedro Arrupe footbridge in front of the University of Deusto; alternatively, for an aerial view, take the *ascensor* (or seven flights of steps) up to the Puente de la Salve. Described by architect Philip Johnson as "the greatest building of our time", the Guggenheim is the keystone of the Basque government's plans to revitalize the city; it has been developed in cooperation with the Solomon R. Guggenheim Foundation, and provides a European showcase for the Foundation's unparalleled collection of twentieth-century art. The permanent collection, which rotates between Bilbao and the Foundation's other museums in New York and Venice, includes works by all the major modern and contemporary figures, including Kandinsky, Klee, Mondrian, Picasso, Cézanne, Chagall, Warhol, Calder and Rauschenberg, to name a few; the museum also hosts various top-flight temporary exhibitions. One painting, though, is conspicuous by its absence: Picasso's *Guernica* – in the Reina Sofía, Madrid (see p.106) – whose "return" the Basques have been demanding for years (indeed, some say they built the Guggenheim specially).

The art, however, takes a back seat to the **building** itself: a gargantuan sculpture whose sensual titanium curves glimmer like running water in the sun. The main entrance, on the city side, is home to *Puppy*, Jeff Koons' kitschy flower sculpture, which was originally installed as a temporary exhibit for the opening ceremony but became a permanent feature after Bilbainos clamoured for it to stay. It is now an inseparable part of the museum and has probably paid for itself many times over in *Puppy* key rings and soft toys.

Inside the museum, galleries and walkways lead off a vast, light-filled atrium. Your ticket is valid for the whole day, so it's worth arriving early and taking a break for lunch – perhaps at the museum's classy, yet inexpensive, **restaurant** (see "Restaurants and tapas bars"). Free guided tours (in English) start at 11am, 12.30pm, 4pm and 6.30pm. Major exhibitions are held in the 130m-long "Fish Gallery"; films, talks and other events are also organized regularly. To find out what's on, visit the museum's website ⓦwww.guggenheim-bilbao.es or call ☎944 359 000.

West of the Guggenheim

The area of former docks and rail depots to the west (downriver) of the Guggenheim, known as **Abandoibarra**, is under construction, with parks, luxury high-rise apartments and a giant shopping centre taking shape. The *paseo* along the river to the Palacio Euskalduna (see below) is now complete, but for the moment, you have to follow Alameda de Mazarredo – a conduit for heavy traffic from Puente la Salve – west from the Guggenheim's main entrance in order to get to the **Museo de Bellas Artes** (Tues–Sat 10am–8pm, Sun 10am–2pm; €4.50, free Wed, combined ticket €11), in the Parque de Doña Casilda de Iturriza. Although overshadowed by its world-famous neighbour, this houses a diverse, well-displayed collection, including works by El Greco, Goya and Van Dyck; Basque artists, of course, are also well represented.

Continuing through the park you come to the rusty iron bulk of the **Palacio Euskalduna**, backed by the curved Euskalduna bridge. Built on the ruins of the city's last shipyard, which closed in the 1980s, the Palacio hosts conferences and classical performances (see "Bars and entertainment"). It's a beautiful building to look around – particularly the tiled floors inside – but staff are rather snooty to the casual visitor. However, there are one-hour guided tours (depart noon on Sat; €2), starting from door 4 on street level – call ☎944 035 000 or just turn up fifteen minutes early to get your ticket. At quayside level, just past the Palacio Euskalduna, is the latest piece in Bilbao's urban jigsaw, the **Ria de Bilbao Maritime Museum** (winter Tues–Thurs 10am–6pm, Fri–Sun 10am–8pm; summer Tues–Thurs 10am–8pm, Fri–Sun 10am–10pm; ⓦwww.meseomaritim-bilbao.org; €7, ⓂSan Mames), with an impressive collection.

For a behind-the-scenes glimpse of pre-facelift Bilbao, cross the Euskalduna Bridge and stroll downriver along the 2km-long **Zorrozaurre peninsula** (ⓦwww.zorrozaurre.org) – a post-industrial wilderness of fine old buildings with grass-grown roofs, tumbledown houses, jungly vacant lots and working factories, including one that makes the world's biggest anchor chains. The future of the peninsula is now a political hot potato, with speculators salivating at the thought of marinas and luxury apartments, and the area's 400-odd residents holding out for decent services, a clean environment and affordable housing.

Beaches

The city is well served with **beaches** along the mouth of the estuary and around both headlands. The metro means it's easier to reach the beaches on the east bank, such as those at **Sopelana** (ⓂLarrabasterra), including the nudist Playa de Arrietara. **Getxo** (ⓂAlgorta) has a pretty old quarter with white houses and green-painted doors, and an impressive waterfront promenade fringed with private mansions belonging to Bilbao's millionaire set. At the end of Metro Line 1, 15km north of the city, **Plentzia** (ⓂPlentzia) is generally cleaner and not quite so crowded as the beaches closer to town.

Eating, drinking and nightlife

Bilbao is definitely one of those cities where the most enjoyable way to eat is to move from bar to bar, snacking on *pintxos*. The city can be very lively at night – and totally wild during the August **fiesta**, with scores of open-air bars, live music and impromptu dancing everywhere, and a truly festive atmosphere. The *casco viejo* has most of the interesting places to **eat and drink**, with almost wall-to-wall places on c/Santa María and c/Barrencalle Barrena.

If you want to get together something of your own, the attractive Art Nouveau **Mercado de la Ribera**, on c/de la Ribera towards the Estación Atxuri, offers a dazzling array of fresh produce, particularly seafood.

Amboto c/Jardines 2; ⓂCasco Viejo. Classic Basque cuisine, with *bacalao* a speciality. Meals for about €30 per head.

Café Gargantua c/Barrencalle Barrena; ⓂCasco Viejo. Simple café serving sandwiches, and a selection of different priced *menús* and *platos combinados*.

Café-Restaurante Kalean c/Santa María; ⓂCasco Viejo. Very popular, offering excellent economical *nueva cocina vasca*. After midnight, there's a resident pianist and great atmosphere.

Casa Rufo c/Hurtado de Amézaga 5; ⓂAbando or Moyua. The best of traditional Basque cuisine. T-bone steak a speciality. Evening meals for about €30.

Casa Vasca Avda. Lehendakari Aguirre 13–15; ⓂDeusto. Traditional Basque restaurant in Deusto, across the bridge from the Museo de Bellas Artes; does great breakfasts (the hot chocolate is the best in town).

Garibolo c/Fernandez del Campo 7; ⓂMoyua. Good if unsurprising vegetarian restaurant does lunch Mon–Sat, dinner Fri & Sat.

Guggenheim Museum Restaurant ☎944 239 333. A surprisingly inexpensive lunch *menú* (€10) from the *nueva cocina vasca* school. Be sure to book by 1pm for lunch.

Herriko Taberna c/de la Ronda 20; ⓂCasco Viejo. Excellent place for a straightforward, inexpensive meal; a strong Basque nationalist atmosphere and a great *menú*.

Iruña Jardines de Albia; ⓂAbando. The spicy lamb *pintxos morunos* in this popular bar are indispensable to build your strength for a night out.

Kasko c/Santa María; ⓂCasco Viejo. Trendy café offering *nueva cocina vasca* with a delightful evening *menú* for €15.

Ortua Alameda Mazarredo 18. Vegetarian restaurant doing an excellent *menú* for €8 (lunch only). Convenient for a break from the Guggenheim.

Las Parrillas de Deusto Travesía de los Espinos 6; ⓂDeusto. You can't get more authentic than this locals' *cerveceria* a 5min walk from the Euskalduna bridge. Good *menús* from €9 up – the *langostinos a la plancha* are great.

Pil-Pil Muelle de Uribitarte, ☎944 650 065. A rather pricey 4hr boat trip with dinner and live music, for €47. Leaves from near the Zubizuri bridge, 9.30pm Fri & Sat. There's also a 1hr tour (no meal) for €10, leaving at noon, 1pm, 5pm and 6pm Fri & Sat.

Serantes Licenciado Poza 16; ⓂMoyua or Indautxu. Top-notch *marisquería* where a meal comes to about €42 per head. Watch for specials on *langostino* and other crustacean delights.

Taberna Aitor c/Barrencalle Barrena; ⓂCasco Viejo. Excellent tapas bar and one for football fans, with the bonus of a beautiful wooden interior.

Taberna Txiriboga c/Santa María; ⓂCasco Viejo. Lively tapas bar in the heart of the *casco viejo*, with a wide selection of *pintxos*.

Taberna Txomin Barullo c/Barrencalle; ⓂCasco Viejo. Great café-bar with nationalist murals, specializing in more experimental *nueva cocina vasca* (lunch *menú* only Thurs–Sun) at reasonable prices.

La Tortilla Plaza Ernesto Erkoreka; ⓂCasco Viejo. Opposite the *Ayuntamiento*, this bar offers *mejillones* of mythical quality.

Victor Montes Plaza Nueva 8; ⓂCasco Viejo. Outstanding baked neck of *merluza* (bass) for around €34.

Bars and entertainment

Bars can be found all through the **casco viejo**, with the traditional approach to drinking – *poteo* – consisting of a high-speed bar crawl, spending less than ten minutes in each place. If (as Bilbainos hold to be self-evident) Bilbao is the centre of the universe, then the *siete calles* on a Saturday night are the whirling hub of it all, with the heart of the madness centred on c/Barrenkale. For the more leisurely, *Lamiak* on c/Pelota is a café-bar full of students, with good music and a noticeboard worth checking for events, women's groups, work, flatshares and the like. *Txokolanda* is a **gay** bar, upstairs from *Solokuetxe*, reached via steps from c/de la Ronda and, along with the *Lasaí* bar on c/de la Ronda itself, is one of the last places to close. For a relaxed drink in the early evening, head for the outdoor tables in the beautiful Plaza Nueva, which are not as pricey as you might expect. Bilbao's **historic cafés** include the gorgeous Art Nouveau *Boulevard* on c/Ribera near the Teatro Arriaga (which has free tango lessons upstairs at 9pm on the first Saturday of each month), and the spacious, elegant *Granja* in Plaza Circular.

In the **new town**, lively areas with a slightly smarter atmosphere are near the Plaza Circular, between the Alameda de Mazarredo and c/de Buenos Aires, especially on c/Ledesma, a street teeming with bars and especially popular during early evening. *Bar Iruña*, on Colón de Larreategui, opposite the Jardines de Albia, is marvellously atmospheric. Bilbao is also full of **Irish** pubs; one of the best is the *Wicklow Arms*, c/Rodriguez Arias 30, which allegedly serves the most pints of Guinness per square metre of any bar in Spain.

Farther east, south of the Gran Vía, around the junction of c/de Licenciado Poza and Gregorio de Revilla, an area known as **Pozas** (Ⓜ️Indautxu) is highly popular before lunch and in the early evening; *Ziripot* is a bar worth trying here. For action well into the night, one of the in-places is the cluster of bars known as the **Ripa** on the modern city side of the riverbank between Puentes del Arenal and the ayuntamiento, with a mixed crowd ranging from Basque yuppies to rockabillies.

Live music abounds in Bilbao; check the listings in the local newspaper *El Correo*. *Café Antxokia* on c/San Vicente is a theatre-turned-nightclub with an emphasis on world music, folk- and punk-influenced groups. *La Merced-Bilborock*, across the Puente La Merced from the *casco viejo*, is the place for rock and alternative music, while *Palladium*, on c/Iparraguirre two blocks from the Guggenheim, has jazz on Fridays. Teatro Arriaga (☏944 163 333), in the *casco viejo*, hosts dance and music events as well as theatre, and the Palacio Euskalduna (☏944 035 000, ⓦwww.euskalduna.net) offers opera and classical music, plus the odd wrinkly rocker, with ticket prices ranging from €6 to €60; you can pick up a bimonthly programme from the box office (downstairs on the river level; Mon–Fri 9am–2pm & 4–7pm.) *El Correo* also has **cinema** listings; few films are screened in English, but two venues that do show films in their original language are the Filmoteca at the Museo de Bellas Artes – films generally start around 6pm and 8pm – and (less often) Multicines at José Maria Escuza 13.

Listings

Bookshops TinTas, c/General Concha 10 (Ⓜ️Indautxu) is a large travel bookshop with a wide range of maps and guides; Borda, c/Somera 45 (Ⓜ️Casco Viejo), also specializes in maps and guidebooks, including English-language publications, and sells hiking/travel gear. The best place to buy English and other foreign newspapers (one day late) is Librería Cámara on c/Euskalduna 6, four streets up on the right from Plaza Circular along Hurtado de Amézaga (Ⓜ️Abando). Librería Urretxindorra, c/Iparraguirre26 (Ⓜ️Moyua), has a large selection of local books and music.

Car rental Avis, Alameda Dr Areilza 34 ☏944 275 760; Europcar, Licenciado Poza 56 ☏944 422 849; Budget, Dr Nicolás Achúcarro 8 ☏944 150 870; all Ⓜ️Indautxu. There are several booths at the airport as well, but watch out for the airport surcharge.

Consulates The British consulate is at Alameda Urquijo 2 ☏944 157 600, and the Irish at Amann 2, Getxo ☏944 912 575.

Hospital Hospital de Basurto, Avda. de Montevideo 18 ☏944 418 700 (Ⓜ️San Mames), or take the

tram to the last stop. Call ambulances on ☏944 410 081 or 944 100 000 (24hr).

Internet access *Antxi*, Luis Briñas 13 (ⓦwww.cybercafe-antxi.com; €2.40/hr; Ⓜ️Moyua); *El Señor de la Red*, Rodriguez Arias 69; Ⓜ️Moyua or Avda. Lehendakari Aguirre, next to Deusto University (ⓦwww.elsenordelared.com; €2.10/hr; Ⓜ️Deusto; with free coffee).

Post office The main *Correos* is at Alameda Urquijo 19 (Mon–Fri 8am–9pm, Sat 9am–2pm; Ⓜ️Abando or Moyua). There is another post office near the Guggenheim main entrance, Alameda Mazarredo 13 (same hours).

Taxi TeleTaxi (☏944 102 121) or Radio Taxi Bilbao (☏944 448 888).

Telephones There is a *telefónica* at c/Baroeta Aldamar 7, close to the Plaza Circular (Ⓜ️Abando).

Travel agents Barcelo Viajes, Rodríguez Arias 8 ☏944 200 400; TIVE, Iparraguirre 3 ☏944 231 862, specializes in student/youth travel and international buses, as does USIT at Plaza Moyúa 6 ☏944 240 218. All Ⓜ️Moyua.

Inland routes from Bilbao

Inland Bizkaia is well off the beaten track yet has much to offer, with spectacular walking and climbing country, particularly around **Durango**, and remarkable limestone caves in the **Encartaciones** area, accessible as a day-trip from Bilbao.

Around Durango

The otherwise uninspiring factory town of **DURANGO**, 30km southeast of Bilbao (easily accessible by train from Atxuri station) is the gateway to the impressive **Duranguesado Massif**. To explore this area of rocky peaks, the best access point is the Urkiola Pass (on the Durango–Vitoria road and bus route) from where it's about three hours to the highest peak, **Amboto**. This summit is a favourite with Basque walkers and climbers – the final scramble to the top can be a bit vertigo-inducing. Alternatively, head for the beautiful Atxondo valley off the Durango–Elorrio road, where there are more walking possibilities. If you don't have your own transport, take the hourly buses as far as the signposted crossroads and then walk 2.5km to the village of **Axpe-Marzana**, nestling at the base of Amboto – a good base for a couple of days' walking. There is a good **agroturismo**, *Imitte-Etxebarria* (☎946 231 659; ❷), 500m before the village.

West to the limestone caves

The little-known area of **ENCARTACIONES**, stretching for some 30km west of Bilbao, makes another rewarding day-trip, with places to stay if you want to extend your visit. Head for the village of **Carranza** on the Bilbao–Ramales road (or one hour by train on the Santander line out of Abando station; no public transport onwards to the caves). On the way, you pass through the small village of **SOPUERTA**, where there's a new **museum** dedicated to the area (summer Tues–Sat 10am–2pm & 5–7pm, Sun 10am–2pm; winter Tues–Sat 10am–2pm & 4–6pm, Sun 10am–2pm; free). Four kilometres west of Carranza on the main road, just past a curious thermal spa resort run by German monks at **MOLINAR** – where you can stay and eat (☎946 806 002; ❷) – a road heads 3km up the mountain to the tiny village of **Ranero** and the **Cuevas de Pozalagua** (Sat & Sun 11am–2pm & 4–7pm; €4; groups must ring ahead – ☎946 806 012). The caves are remarkable for their coral-like stalactites, although some of the formations have unfortunately been damaged by dynamiting in local quarries. The area abounds with other caves, including the **Torca del Carlista**, one of the world's largest cave chambers.

A few kilometres north of Carranza, in the *barrio* of Biañez, the **Parque Ecologico Bizkaia** (Sat & Sun 11am–7pm; €2) is an unusual wildlife sanctuary that treats injured animals, before, if possible, releasing them into the wild. It's a good place to see the native fauna, including brown bears from the Picos de Europa.

Vitoria and around

VITORIA (Gasteiz), the capital of Alava, crowns a slight rise in the heart of a fertile plain. Founded by Sancho el Sabio, King of Navarre, it was already a prosperous place by the time of its capture by the Castilian Alfonso VIII in 1200. Later, as the centre of a flourishing wool and iron trade, Vitoria became

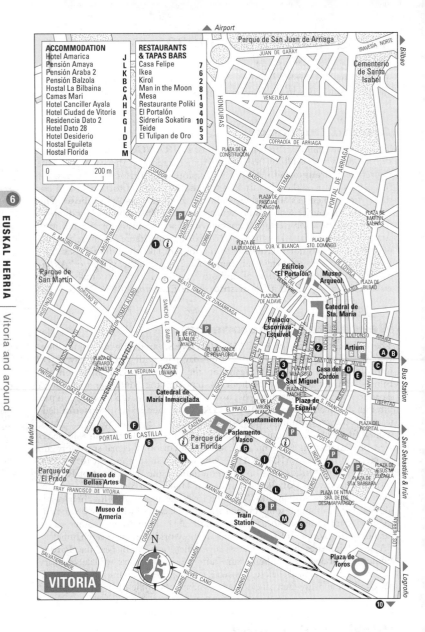

ACCOMMODATION
Hotel Amarica — J
Pensión Amaya — L
Pensión Araba 2 — K
Pensión Balzola — B
Hostal La Bilbaina — C
Camas Mari — A
Hotel Canciller Ayala — H
Hotel Ciudad de Vitoria — F
Residencia Dato 2 — G
Hotel Dato 28 — I
Hotel Desiderio — D
Hostal Eguileta — E
Hostal Florida — M

RESTAURANTS
& TAPAS BARS
Casa Felipe — 7
Ikea — 6
Kirol — 2
Man in the Moon — 8
Mesa — 1
Restaurante Poliki — 9
El Portalón — 4
Sidreria Sokatira — 10
Teide — 5
El Tulipan de Oro — 3

VITORIA

seriously rich, and the town still boasts an unusual concentration of
Renaissance palaces and fine churches.

It's off the tourist circuit but by no means dull. There's a relaxed, easy-going
attitude to life in comparison with the other Basque provinces, summed up in
Euskara as *lasai* – perhaps best translated as "chill out". The old town is full of

rowdy bars and *tabernas*, not to mention an abundance of excellent Basque restaurants, making it as pleasant a place as you'll find to pass a few days away from the crowds.

Arrival and information

The **bus station** (℡945 258 400) is on c/los Herran, a two-minute walk up the cobbled Cantón de San Francisco Javier from the old town. The RENFE **train station** is south of the town centre at c/Dato 46 (℡902 240 202 or 945 141 207, ℱ945 143 333). The town's useful **turismo** (Mon–Sat 9am–1pm & 4–8pm, Sun 10am–2pm; ℡945 161 598, ℰturismo@vitoria-gasteiz.org) is at c/Dato 11 (corner of c/General Alava), in the city centre straight up from the train station, with lots of colourful brochures and a good free map. The Alava regional turismo is at c/Ramón y Cajal (in the corner of Parque de la Florida; ℡943 131 321, ℴwww.alava.net) a bit further away from the centre. There's a second branch on the corner of Avenida de Gasteiz and c/de Chile (Mon–Sat 10am–7pm, Sun 11am–2pm). The **post office**, c/de Postes, and most other services, including **banks**, are located in the central area around the Plaza de la Virgen Blanca.

Accommodation

The only time you might have trouble locating a room is during Vitoria's annual **jazz festival** in the third week of July, or during the town's summer **Virgen Blanca festival** (August 4–9). There are several budget **places to stay** near the train station, around the junction of c/de los Fueros and Ortiz de Zarate and near the bus station, but it's far nicer, if noisier, to stay in the old quarter near the action.

Hotel Amarica c/Florida 11 ℡945 130 506. Popular modern hotel, offering two singles and eight doubles with bath and satellite TV. ❹

Pensión Amaya c/La Paz 15 ℡945 255 497. Centrally located with a few single rooms and plenty of doubles with bath. ❷

Pensión Araba 2 c/Florida 25 ℡945 232 588. Centrally located *pensión*, offering four clean rooms with or without bath. ❷

Pensión Balzola c/Prudencio María de Verástegui 6, 2° ℡945 256 279. Simple but clean *pensión*, with doubles and singles; ring bell beside CH sign. ❶

Hostal La Bilbaina c/Prudencio María de Verástegui 2 ℡945 254 400, ℱ945 279 757. Comfortable rooms above a large *cafetería*, all with cable TV. ❸

Hotel Canciller Ayala c/Ramón y Cajal 5 ℡945 130 000, ℱ945 133 505. One of Vitoria's top hotels, situated on the edge of the Parque de la Florida. Newly refurbished and very comfortable. ❼

Hotel Ciudad de Vitoria Portal de Castilla 8 ℡945 141 100, ℱ945 143 616. Comfortable, upmarket accommodation in a stylish Art Deco building. ❼

Camas Mari c/Prudencio María de Verástegui ℡945 277 303. Clean rooms near the bus station with shared bath. ❷

Residencia Dato 2 c/San Antoni 17 ℡945 130 400, ℱ945 232 320. Bizarre decor – including a pair of plaster stags fighting in the lobby – but the rooms are very comfortable and spacious. ❷

Hotel Dato 28 c/Dato 28 ℡945 147 230, ℴwww.hoteldato.com. Excellent-value hotel on the main pedestrian mall down from the station. There's a different colour scheme in every room, and colourful batik bedspreads. All rooms with bath and some have an enclosed balcony. ❷

Hotel Desiderio Colegio San Prudencio 2 ℡945 251 700, ℱ945 521 722. Spacious rooms with bath and TV in the centre of the old town. Breakfasts for €2.20. ❷

Hostal Eguileta c/Nueva Fuera 32 ℡945 251 700, ℱ945 251 722. Cheaper annexe of the *Hotel Desiderio* opposite, offering reasonable doubles with washbasin. ❶

Hostal Florida c/Manuel Iradier 33 ℡945 260 675. Comfortable, well-furnished rooms on the first street down from the station towards the bullring. Has more expensive rooms with bath. ❶

The Town

The streets of the Gothic old town spread out like a spider's web down the sides of the hill, surrounded on level ground by a neater grid of later development. You'll get the feel of Vitoria simply by wandering through this old quarter. Although parts of it can be rather shabby, it is on the whole a harmonious place, the graceful mansions and churches all built from the same greyish/gold stone. The porticoed **Plaza de España**, especially, is a gem, a popular location for early-evening strolling and drinking.

The heart of the old town is the old cathedral of **Santa María**, which is under serious reconstruction. Guided tours (April–Oct daily, 10am–2pm & 5–8pm; €2; ℡945 255 135; booking essential) take you through the different periods of construction, beginning in the thirteenth-century when the cathedral was an integral part of the town's defences, and explain how Renaissance attempts to remodel the heavy Gothic structure resulted in serious structural defects – one look at the severely twisted arches that hold the whole thing up may send you running for the exit. The fourteenth-century west doorway is superb, intricately and lovingly carved; seen from the level of the scaffolding, the faces of the saints appear distorted, since they were carved to be viewed from ground level.

Take time also to visit the fine medieval church of **San Miguel** (Mon–Sat 11am–noon & 6.30–8pm, Sun 10.30am–2.30pm), just above the Plaza de España, which marks the southern end of the old town. Outside its door stands the fourteenth-century stone image of the Virgen Blanca, revered patron of the city. The streets below hold any number of interesting buildings, one of the finest being the **Escoriaza-Esquivel Palace** with its sixteenth-century Plateresque portal, on c/Fray Zacarías.

Behind the cathedral, down the hill on the left, the **Portalón** is the most impressive of the surviving trading houses of Renaissance Vitoria, its dusty red brick and wooden beams and balconies in marked contrast to the golden stone of the rest of the town. Today it is an extremely good, but expensive, restaurant (see opposite). Over the road you'll find the province's **Museo Arqueológico** at c/Correria 116 (Tues–Fri 11am–2pm & 4–6pm, Sat 10am–2pm, Sun 11am–2pm; free). An annexe of this museum houses the unusual **Museo de Naipes** (same opening times; free), with over 6000 exhibits of playing cards from all corners of the globe. Also near the centre, at c/Francia 24, is the **Artium** (Tues–Fri 11am–8pm, Sat, Sun & holidays 10.30am–8pm; €3, free Wed), Vitoria's attractive new museum of modern art, where a comprehensive collection of 1600 exhibits focuses on Basque and Spanish artists whose work is organized loosely in conceptual themes. The light-flooded foyer houses the gigantic stained-glass *A piece of crystallized sky* by Javier Pérez.

Fiesta de la Virgen Blanca

To experience Vitoria's annual festivities (August 4–9) is to see the good-natured Vitorians at their finest. On the first day of the festival you need to be in the Plaza de la Virgen Blanca with a blue and white festival scarf, a bottle of champagne, a cigar and wearing old clothes. At 6pm the umbrella-toting figure of Celedón appears from the church tower and flies through the air over the plaza. This is the signal to spray champagne everywhere (hence the old clothes), light the cigar and put on your scarf – which the real hard core don't take off until midnight on the 9th, when Celedón returns to his tower, signalling the end of the fiesta. In-between, the town is engulfed in a continuous party.

Southwest of the centre, on the attractive, pedestrianized, tree-lined Paseo de Fray Francisco de Vitoria, is the **Museo de Bellas Artes** (Tues–Fri 11am–2pm & 4–6pm, Sat 10am–2pm, Sun 11am–2pm; free), with a fine collection of paintings centred on the period from 1700 to 1950; highlights include Euskal Herria's best collection of *costumbrista* paintings, depicting Basque cultural and folk practices. Nearby, the **Museo de Armería**, Paseo de Fray Francisco 3 (same opening times; free), features imaginative displays of medieval weapons and suits of armour.

Eating and drinking

The streets of the **old town** – particularly c/Cuchillería, c/Pintorería, c/Hurrería and c/Zapatería – are lined with lively **bars**, **tabernas** and **bodegas**, differentiated only by music and perhaps decor. Each, however, manages to spill onto the narrow pavements at night. For a good selection of restaurants and tapas bars head for the **casco histórico** to sample a selection of Basque dishes. Further down, on the pedestrianized section of c/Dato, you'll find a variety of bars and cafés with charming terraces which offer a quieter ambience. Equally pleasant are the outdoor cafés of Plaza de España and those on the other pedestrian thoroughfares in the lower section of the new town.

Casa Felipe c/Fueros 28 ☎945 134 554. Reasonably priced restaurant specializing in local dishes – try the *pimientos rellenos* and *chorizo a la sidra*. Closed Mon.

Ikea Portal de Castilla 27 ☎945 144 747. Expensive, fashionable spot serving good Basque food; €50 for a tasting platter. The liver pâté in port wine and the fried artichoke with asparagus are both highly recommended. Closed Sun night & Mon.

Kirol c/Cuchillería. This café-bar has an amazing selection of *raciones*, including – for the brave – deep-fried pig's ear.

Man in the Moon c/Manuel Iradier. Desperately craving real ale in Vitoria? Very good English brew-pub with live jazz on Thurs.

Mesa c/Chile 1 ☎945 228 494. Classic, simple place with Basque specialities for around €25 a head and a good-value *menú* for €12. Try the

merluza con setas y almejas. Closed Wed.

Restaurante Poliki c/Manuel Iradier. Modern Basque restaurant with a good-value *menú del día* for €8.

El Portalón c/Correría 15 ☎945 142 755. Expensive restaurant specializing in traditional Basque cooking, set in beautiful 16th-century surroundings. *Menú* for €20. Closed Sun.

Sidreria Sokatira c/Las Trianas 15 ☎945 140 440. The most authentic *sidrería* in town with a great party atmosphere at weekends. Often booked up. Closed Sun night & Mon.

Teide Avda. de Gasteiz 61 ☎945 221 023. Solid Basque cuisine at moderate prices in a classic atmosphere. Lunch *menú* for €12. Closed Tues.

El Tulipan de Oro c/Correría, two doors down from El Portalón. Serves *chorizo* flambéed at the bar over pig-shaped alcohol burners.

Around Vitoria

Attractive though the town is, a significant part of Vitoria's charm is the beauty of the surrounding **countryside**. Almost every hamlet of this once-rich farming territory has something of interest: an old stone mansion proudly displaying the family coat of arms, a lavishly decorated church, or a farmhouse raised on stilts.

A few kilometres to the west of Vitoria, a popular day-trip is to the village of **MENDOZA**, dominated by a fortified tower-house now established as the **Museo de Heraldica** (summer Tues–Fri 11am–2pm & 4–7.30pm, Sat & Sun 10am–2.30pm; winter Tues–Sun 11am–2.30pm; free), which contains a fascinating collection of coats of arms of the Basque nobility through the ages and an exhibition of the history of the principal clans and their often bloody feuds.

The **Embalse de Ulibarri**, 10km to the northeast of Vitoria, is a large scenic reservoir very popular with the locals; the waterside villages of Gamboa-Ullibarri and Landa (both served by three buses daily) make a pleasant retreat on a hot summer's day.

Zalduondo

To the east, on the **Llanada Alavesa** (Plain of Alava) are some of the best-preserved villages of inland Euskal Herria, all served by a twice-daily bus from
Vitoria. With your own transport, take the A3012 off the main N1 *autovía*
towards the village of Narvaja. From here, the road continues to **ZAL-
DUONDO**, one of the highlights of the area, with a very good **museum** of
local ethnography (Sat 5.30–7pm, Sun noon–2pm), which is housed in the sixteenth-century Palacio de los Lazárragas; look out for the heraldic crest over
the main door, one of the most elaborate in the País Vasco. Zalduondo,
although tiny, is famous for its traditional **carnaval** celebrations, where a Guy
Fawkes-like figure, "Markitos", is ritually tried and then burned as a scapegoat
for the misfortunes of the past year. From Zalduondo it's a pleasant three-
kilometre walk to **ARAÍA**, from where a branch of the Camino de Santiago
leads to the San Adrián tunnel and its refuge (see p.501).

Salvatierra

The main town on the plain, **SALVATIERRA**, situated on the
Vitoria–Pamplona rail line, makes a good base for exploration. The old walled
quarter rises above the countryside offering splendid views, and the Gothic
church of Santa María is visible for miles around. At the other end of town, in
the Plaza de San Juan, there's an extremely helpful **turismo** (℡945 312 535,
Ⓦwww.jet.es/touragurain), opposite which is a *fonda* attached to the *Bar
Merino* (℡945 300 052; ❶); the town's other *fonda*, *Hostal Jose Mari*, is at
c/Mayor 53 (℡945 300 042, ❶). The town also has a convent whose nuns
make and sell their own pastry.

Laguardia and the Rioja Alavesa

South of Vitoria lies the wine-growing district of **Rioja Alavesa** and its town
of **LAGUARDIA**, which is served by regular buses from Vitoria (3 or 4 daily;
1hr). If you're driving, don't miss stopping at the *Balcon de la Rioja*, a viewpoint
35km south of Vitoria, with magnificent views over the plain. Laguardia has a
useful **turismo**, c/Sancho Abarca (Mon–Fri 10am–2pm & 4–6.30pm, Sat
10am–2pm, Sun 10.45am–2pm; ℡945 600 845, Ⓦwww.laguardia-alava.com),
with a free map of the town as well as information on the many **bodegas** in
the area – visits usually require a phone call beforehand. *Bodegas Palacio*, just
out of town on the A3210 to Elciego, however, has scheduled tours (11.30am
and 1.30pm Mon to Fri; just turn up).

   Laguardia itself is an interesting old walled town of cobbled streets and historic buildings, entered through the Puerta de San Juan. The turismo has keys
to the church of Santa María de los Reyes with its ornately carved Gothic
doorway, and offers guided tours for €2. One of the best places to **stay** is
Larretxori, c/Portal de Páganos (℡ & Ⓕ945 600 763; ❷), a small *agroturismo* in
the old town. You can also stay at one of the two *hostales* on the main road: the
good-value *Pachico Martínez*, c/Sancho Abarca 20 (℡945 600 009, Ⓕ945 600
005; ❸), and the more elegant *Marixa*, c/Sancho Abarca (℡945 600 165,
Ⓔhotelmarixa@terra.es; ❹), or the new *Hotel Villa de Laguardia*, outside the
town wall at Paseo San Raimundo 15 (℡945 600 560; ❺), with a good restaurant. Otherwise, if you're looking for a place to **eat**, *La Muralla*, Paganos 42,
serves a good *menú del día* for under €8, specializing in meat dishes.

   The whole **RIOJA ALAVESA** area is great to explore (with your own
transport): rolling countryside with sleepy villages like Elciego, Samaniego and
Labastida, *bodegas* and farmhouses. Ask at the turismo in Laguardia for more
information or check out the websites Ⓦwww.laguardia-alava.com and
Ⓦwww.alavaturismo.com.

Pamplona and around

PAMPLONA (Iruña) has been the capital of Navarra since the ninth century, and long before that was a powerful fortress town defending the northern approaches to Spain at the foothills of the Pyrenees. Even now it has something of the appearance of a garrison city, with its hefty walls and elaborate pentagonal citadel. With a long history as capital of an often semi-autonomous state, Pamplona has plenty to offer around its old centre, the *casco antiguo* – enticing

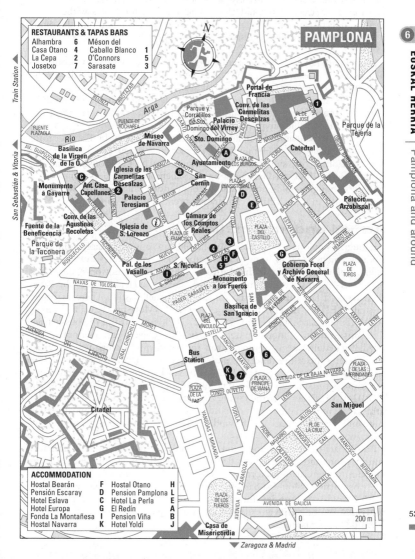

RESTAURANTS & TAPAS BARS

Alhambra	6	Méson del	
Casa Otano	4	Caballo Blanco	1
La Cepa	2	O'Connors	5
Josetxo	7	Sarasate	3

PAMPLONA

ACCOMMODATION

Hostal Bearán	F	Hostal Otano	H
Pensión Escaray	D	Pension Pamplona	L
Hotel Eslava	C	Hotel La Perla	E
Hotel Europa	G	El Redín	A
Fonda La Montañesa	I	Pension Viña	B
Hostal Navarra	K	Hotel Yoldi	J

0   200 m

▼ Zaragoza & Madrid

churches, a beautiful park, the massive citadel – and it's an enjoyable place to be throughout the year. But for anyone who has been here during the thrilling week of the **Fiestas de San Fermín**, a visit at any other time can only be an anticlimax; indeed it could be said that Pamplona makes up for its one week of manic excitement by being incredibly stolid the rest of the year.

San Fermín

From midday on July 6 until midnight on July 14 the city gives itself up entirely to riotous nonstop celebration. The centre of the festivities is the **encierro**, or the running of the bulls, which draws tourists from all over the world, but this is just one aspect of a massive fair along with bands, parades and 24-hour dancing in the streets. You could have a great time here for a week without ever seeing a bull, but even if you are vehemently opposed to bullfighting, the *encierro* – in which the animals decisively have the upper hand – is a spectacle not to miss.

Six bulls are released each morning at eight (traditionally it was an hour earlier, so that the festival started on the seventh hour of the seventh day of the seventh month) to run from their corral near the Plaza Santo Domingo to the bullring. In front, around, and occasionally under them run the hundreds of locals and tourists who are foolish or drunk enough to test their daring against the horns. It was Hemingway's *The Sun Also Rises* that really put "Los San Fermines" on the map to foreigners, and the area in front of the Plaza de Toros has been renamed Plaza Hemingway by a grateful council. His description of it as "a damned fine show" still attracts Americans by the thousands and the running of the bulls has become a bit of a cliché for people. No amount of outsiders, though, could outdo the locals in their determination to have a good time, and it's an indescribably exhilarating event in which to take part.

Arrival and information

Although Pamplona is a sizeable city, the old centre is remarkably compact – nothing you're likely to want to see is more than ten minutes from the main **Plaza del Castillo**. The **train station** is a little further out on Avenida San Jorge; bus #9 runs every ten minutes from here to the citadel end of the Paseo de Sarasate, a few minutes' walk from the Plaza del Castillo. There's a handy central RENFE ticket office at c/Estella 8 (Mon–Fri 9.30am–2pm & 4.30–7.30pm, Sat 9.30am–1pm; ☎948 227 282), just north of the bus station. The **bus station** is more central, on c/Conde Oliveto just in front of the citadel: schedules are confusing, given the number of companies operating from here – check the timetable posted at the station, or pick up one at the helpful **turismo** (summer daily 9am–8pm; San Fermín daily 8am–8pm; winter Mon–Sat 10am–2pm & 4–7pm, Sun 10am–2pm; ☎948 206 540, ℉948 207 034) at c/Eslava 1, at the corner of Plaza San Francisco. The staff will also arrange accommodation, including advance bookings if you intend to strike out into the Pyrenees. Daily updates on the festivities are posted on ⓦwww.sanfermin.com.

Banks are scattered throughout the central area, with much-restricted, morning-only hours during the fiesta – one that also opens in the afternoons (4–6pm) is the Caja de Ahorros de Navarra in c/Roncesvalles. There's a central **post office** (Mon–Fri 8am–9pm, Sat 9am–7pm) on c/Estella, next to the RENFE office. A **laundry** (in case your clothes have borne the brunt of the festivities) can be found at c/de Descalzos, a couple of minutes' walk from the Plaza de San Francisco.

Accommodation

Most of the budget **fondas** and **hostales** are in c/San Nicolás and c/San Gregorio, off the Plaza del Castillo. Even outside San Fermín, when prices can double or triple, rooms fill up quickly in summer, and it might be easier to accept that you'll have to pay a little more to avoid the hassle of trudging around. If you want to continue looking, the streets around the cathedral, across the Plaza del Castillo, yield other possibilities. Further away from the Plaza del Castillo and the old town, there are several *hostales* in the more modern, yet not so interesting, central area.

Budget options

Pensión Escaray c/Nueva 24, 1 ☎948 227 825. Next to the upmarket *Hotel Maisonnave*, offering well-furnished doubles and singles. ❷

Fonda La Montañesa c/San Gregorio 2 ☎948 224 380. Doubles and singles without bath; cheap, but otherwise nothing very special. ❶

Hostal Navarra c/Tudela 9, 2º ☎948 225 164, ℱ948 223 426. Well-established *hostal* going back more than 40 years, near the bus station; all rooms have en-suite facilities. ❸

Pensión Pamplona c/Tudela 5, 1º ☎948 229 963. Clean, new *pensión*, also near the bus station. ❷

Pensión Viña c/Jarauta 24, 1º ☎948 227 825. Central new *pensión* with private bathrooms. ❷

Moderate and expensive options

Hostal Bearán c/San Nicolás 25 ☎ & ℱ948 223 428. Comfortable, clean *hostal* offering rooms with TV. ❸

Hotel Eslava Plaza Virgen de la O 7 ☎948 222 270, ℱ948 225 157. Cosy, comfortable hotel run by the Eslava family in a quiet corner of the old city – views from balconies overlooking the plaza. Singles and doubles, with a bar in the basement. ❸

Hotel Europa c/Espoz y Mina 11 ☎948 221 800, ⓦwww.hreuropa.com. Just off Plaza del Castillo; a good three-star hotel with a fine restaurant. ❺

Hostal Otano c/San Nicolás 5 ☎948 227 036, ℱ948 212 012. Well-run *hostal* above bar and restaurant which have been in the same family since 1929. The restaurant serves a popular *menú del día* for €11. ❷

Hotel La Perla Plaza del Castillo 1 ☎948 227 706, ℱ948 221 519. Luxury hotel with great character and historical associations; a few rooms have balconies overlooking the plaza (prices triple during San Fermín). Ernest Hemingway stayed in Room 217. ❻

Bar-Restaurante El Redín c/Mercado 5 ☎948 222 182. Nicely located in the street by the market, within a stone's throw of the start of the *encierro*. Mostly double rooms, with a bar-restaurant downstairs; full board available. ❹

Hotel Yoldi Avda. de San Ignacio 11 ☎948 224 800, ⓦwww.hotelyoldi.com. This is where the bullfighters and VIPs from the *taurino* world stay during San Fermín. Garage parking. ❻

The Town

The **Plaza del Castillo**, ringed with fashionable cafés, is the centre of the town and sees much of its activity. The narrow streets of the former *Judería* fill the area to the south and west, towards the city walls by the cathedral; this is virtually the only trace of a large Jewish community that thrived here before the persecutions and expulsions of the Inquisition. From the opposite side of the square, c/San Nicolás runs down towards the citadel and the more modern area of the city to the east. It's in c/San Nicolás and its continuation, c/San Gregorio, that you'll find most of the *hostales* and *fondas*, a number of excellent small restaurants and loads of raucous little bars.

The **Catedral de Santa María** (Mon–Fri 10.30am–6pm, Sat 10.30am–1.30pm, mid-Sept to mid-July closed 1.30–4pm; €3) is basically Gothic, built over a period of 130 years from the late fourteenth to the early sixteenth century but with an unattractive facade added in the eighteenth. It doesn't look promising, but the interior, containing the tomb of Carlos III and Eleanor in the centre of the nave, and the ancient *Virgen de los Reyes* above the high altar, is fine, and the cloister is magnificent: don't miss the many sculpted

Accommodation and security

Don't expect to find **accommodation** during the fiesta unless you have booked well in advance – the town is packed to the gills, and most rooms double in price. However, the turismo opposite the bullring fills with women willing to let **rooms** for the night at exorbitant prices. If you have no luck, accept that you're going to sleep on the ramparts, in the park or plaza (along with hundreds of others), and deposit your valuables and luggage at the bus station on c/Conde Oliveto – it's inexpensive, and you can have daily access (this fills early in the week, too – hang around and be insistent). There are also showers here.

Probably the **best plan**, though, is not to stay here at all: find a room somewhere else (Vitoria or Estella, for instance), get plenty of sleep, leave your luggage there, and arrive in Pamplona by bus, staying as long as you can survive on naps in the park before escaping for some rest and a clean-up. You can always come back again. The first few days are best – by the end the place is getting pretty filthy.

Alternatively, there's a **campsite**, *Ezcaba* (☎948 330 315 or 948 331 665), 7km out of town on the road to France. You have to be there a couple of days before the fiesta to get a place. Facilities include good toilets and showers but they can't really handle the numbers during San Fermín – be prepared for long queues, and bear in mind that the shop is only really well stocked in the drinks department. The main bonus is that security is tight – admission is by pass only and there's a guard who patrols all night. For the period of the fiesta there is a **free campsite**, by the river just below *Ezcaba*; security is doubtful, however. The bus service, which goes to all the campsites, is poor (approx 4 daily, first at 6am, last at 1am), but it's easy to hitch or, more expensively, get a lift on one of the tour buses that stay at the official campsite (they leave in time to see the *encierro*).

Wherever you sleep, keep an eye on everything you have with you – there's a very high rate of **petty crime** during the festival; cars and vans are broken into with alarming frequency and people are often robbed as they sleep, occasionally with violence. Several **banks** and a **post office** are open mornings during the festival, so changing travellers' cheques is no problem. Note that everything is closed over the weekend.

El Encierro

To watch the *encierro* it's essential to arrive early (about 6am) – crowds have already formed an hour before it starts. The best **vantage points** are near the starting point around the Plaza Santo Domingo or on the wall leading to the bullring. If possible, get a spot on the outer of the two barriers – don't worry when the one in front fills up and blocks your view, as all these people will be moved on by the police before the run. The event divides into two parts: firstly there's the actual running of the bulls, when the object is to run with the bull or whack it with a rolled-up newspaper. It can be difficult to see the bulls amid all the runners but you'll sense the sheer terror and excitement down on the ground; just occasionally this spreads to the watching crowd if a bull manages to breach the wooden safety barriers. Then there's a separate event after the bulls have been through the streets, when bullocks with padded horns are let loose on the crowd in the bullring. If you watch the actual running, you won't be able to get into the bullring (too many people), so go on two separate mornings to see both things. For the bullring you have to arrive at about 6am to get the free lower seats. If you want to pay for a seat higher up, buy from the ticket office outside, not from the touts inside, who will rip you off. On Sunday you have to pay.

We advise against it, but if you do decide to **run**, remember that although it's probably less dangerous than it looks, at least one person gets seriously injured (sometimes killed) every year. Find someone who knows the ropes to guide you through the first time, and don't try any heroics; bulls are weighed in tonnes and have very sharp horns. Don't get trapped hiding in a doorway and don't get between a scared bull and the rest of the pack. Traditionally, women don't take part, though more and more are doing so; if you do, it's probably best to avoid any officials, who may try to remove you. A glass of *pacharán*, the powerful local liqueur, is ideal for a dose of courage.

The only official way in is at the starting point, Plaza Santo Domingo, entered via Plaza San Saturnino; shortly before the start the rest of the course is cleared, and then at a few minutes before eight you're allowed to make your way along the course to your own preferred starting point (you should walk the course beforehand to get familiar with it). To mark the start, two rockets are fired, one when the bulls are released, a second when they are all out (it's best if these are close together, since the bulls are far safer if they're running as a herd rather than getting scared individually). As soon as the first goes you can start to run, though if you do this you'll probably arrive in the ring well before the bulls and be booed for your trouble; if you wait a while you're more likely to get close to the bulls. Although there are plenty of escape points, these are only for use in emergency – if you try to get out prematurely you'll be shoved back.

Other events

There are plenty of other hazardous things to do in Pamplona, especially once the atmosphere has got the better of a few people's judgement. Many people (especially tourists) have fun hurling themselves from the fountain in the centre of town and from surrounding buildings (notably *La Mesillonera* – the mussel bar), hoping their friends will catch them below. Needless to say, several people each year are not caught by their drunken pals.

Other events include **music** from local bands nightly from midnight in the bars and at Plaza del Castillo, continuing until about 4am in the fairground on the Avda. de Bayona, which is where local political groupings and other organizations have their stands. There are **fireworks** every evening in the citadel (about 11pm), and a **funfair** on the open ground beside it. Competing **bands** stagger through the streets all day playing to anyone who'll listen. If things calm down a bit you can sunbathe, take a shower, catch up on sleep and even swim at the public **swimming pool** outside the walls below the Portal de Zumalacárregui.

Bullfights take place daily at 6.30pm, with the bulls that ran that morning. Tickets are expensive (about €12–72), and if you have no choice but to buy from the touts, wait until the bullfight has begun, when you can insist on paying less (the price drops with each successive killing). You can also buy tickets the day before from the ticket office in Plaza de Toros (opens 8am), but be prepared to queue. At the end of the week (midnight, July 14) there's a mournful candlelit procession, the **Pobre De**, at which the festivities are officially wound up for another year.

If you're hooked on danger, many **other Basque towns** have fiestas which involve some form of *encierro*. Among the best are Tudela (July 24–28), Estella (first weekend in August, and one of the few that has no official ban on women participants), Tafalla (mid-Aug) and Ampuero in Cantabria (Sept 7–8).

doorways, particularly the *Puerta de la Preciosa*, and the chapel with a lovely star vault, built by a fourteenth-century bishop to house his own tomb. You enter the cathedral from c/Dormitaleria, via the **Museo Diocesano**, a notable collection of Navarran sacred art housed in two superb buildings, the refectory and the kitchen – both worth seeing in their own right.

Behind the cathedral is one of the oldest parts of the city, an area known as **La Navarrería**. Here you'll find the best section of the remaining **city walls** with the Baluarte de Redín and Portal de Zumalacárregui (or de Francia) looking down over a loop of the Río Arga. If you head out through the gate, paths lead down to the river from where you get the full force of the impregnability of these defences. Follow the inside of the walls and you'll come to the impressive **Museo de Navarra** (Tues–Sat 10am–2pm & 5–7pm, Sun & holidays 11am–2pm; €2.50) in the magnificent old hospital building on c/Santo Domingo. Inside is displayed material on the archeology and history of the old kingdom of Navarra, along with some good mosaics and an art collection that includes a portrait of the Marqués de San Adrián by Goya. Heading back to the plaza via c/Santo Domingo and the Plaza Consistorial you'll pass the **market** and the fine Baroque **ayuntamiento**.

There's much more to be seen within the old town, with ancient churches and elegant buildings on almost every street. In particular, though, take time to wander around the parks and gardens on Avenida Ejército that surround and include the ruinous **Citadel**, with its views over the new town, and a gallery (Tues–Sat 11.30am–1.30pm & 6–8pm, Sun 11am–2pm; free). From here you can follow the line of the old walls through the **Parque de la Taconera** and down to the river by an alternative route.

Eating and drinking

For good, inexpensive **menús**, and a wide range of **tapas** and *bocadillos*, head for the streets around c/Major, in particular c/San Lorenzo. The elegant *Café Iruña*, on Plaza del Castillo, is the place to sit over a leisurely coffee and take in the action, or try the more modern yet equally enjoyable *Café Niza* opposite the turismo on c/Duque de Ahumada. For **breakfast** in peaceful surroundings and a chance to read the paper, there's no better place than *Café Alt Wien*, known to the locals as *El Vienés*, in the Jardines de la Taconera – it can get crowded with families in the afternoon.

Alhambra c/Bergamín 7 ☏948 243 007. Prestigious restaurant serving good local dishes, especially the stuffed lamb. Dinner from €40. Closed Sun.

Casa Otano c/San Nicolás. Popular *menú del día* for €21 at this restaurant which excels in *cocina Navarra*. Evening meals from €42. Closed Sun night.

La Cepa c/San Lorenzo 2. Fine selection of tapas and *bocadillos*.

Josetxo Plaza Príncipe de Viana ☏948 222 097. One of the best restaurants in town, specializing in

meat dishes like *rabo de buey*. Dinners from €42. Closed Sun.

Méson del Caballo Blanco c/Redín. Lots of character at this surprisingly inexpensive restaurant serving up *raciones* and traditional local cooking. Evenings only.

O'Connors Paseo Sarasate 22. A pub serving a strange but excellent mixture of Irish and Spanish tapas – baked potatoes with *jamón serrano* for example. Very popular with locals.

Sarasate c/San Nicolás 19. ☏948 225 727. Very decent vegetarian restaurant with a *menú* for €10.

Around Pamplona: the Sierra de Aralar

Some 30km to the northwest of Pamplona, the **Sierra de Aralar**, a 200-square-kilometre plateau dominated by beech woods, is an area rich in legends of mythological creatures, dragons and demons. It makes a good hiking destination, with paths of all grades, mostly well marked, criss-crossing the sierra past prehistoric dolmens, waterfalls and caves. The sierra is also home to Navarra's oldest and most spectacularly situated church: the Sanctuario de San Miguel in Excelsis.

The village of **LEKUNBERRI**, 25km from Pamplona on the A5 Pamplona–San Sebastián motorway, is the best place to go for maps and information about the area. Its old railway station at c/Plazaola 21 has been converted into a helpful **turismo** (Mon–Sat 10am–2pm & 4–7pm, Sun 10am–2pm; ☏948 507 204, Ⓔoit.lekunberri@cfnavarra.es). From the doorstep you can set off along the former train tracks, now transformed into the picturesque Via Verde de Plazaola ("**green way**") leading south to Pamplona and north into Gipuzkoa. The route is over 90km in all, mostly in poor condition, following the tracks all the way; the first 5km north from Lekunberri, however, are excellent, after which the track enters the 2.7km tunnel of Uitzi. Bring a torch (or follow the alternative path) to continue to the larger mountain village of Leitza, 8km further north, which has an impressive assortment of Basque *caserios* (houses).

Sanctuario de San Miguel in Excelsis

From Lekunberri, a road heads 17km up the mountainside through the beech and birch forest to the **Sanctuario de San Miguel in Excelsis**, passing on its way after 12km the *Casa Forestal (Guardetxea)*, a popular starting point for hikers, which offers hearty home-cooked meals (lunch from €7.20). At the top (1237m), above a massive car park and a rather ugly bar, is the small, squat church of San Miguel (daily 9.30am–8pm), built mainly between 783 and 940, with some later additions. Although unimpressive from the outside, San Miguel's interior is beautifully simple and austere. The only ornamentation is in the shape of eight carved capitals, six of them in the tiny twelfth-century central chapel. The church houses two wonderful medieval enamel works: the shrine of the archangel in the central chapel, and the stunning twelfth-century gilt copper *retablo*, depicting a rosily smiling Madonna and Child flanked by Evangelists and Apostles. Not surprisingly, the sanctuary is an extremely popular pilgrimage destination – half the villages in Navarra have an annual *romeria* to San Miguel, many centring around the saint's day of September 29.

Another route up to the church starts at the tiny village of **Arakil**, on the main train and bus routes between Vitoria and Pamplona. The single-track road is a tough but exhilarating climb whether on foot or by car, with breathtaking views across the valley and vultures circling overhead and below.

Practicalities

The Lekunberri area is not strong on **accommodation**: your best bet is the *Hostal Ayestarán*, in the centre at c/Aralar 22 (☏& Ⓕ948 504 127; ❸), which also has a good-value restaurant with a *menú* for €12, specializing in *alubias rojas*. In nearby Aldatz, 2km away, there's an excellent *casa rural*, *Uhaldeko Borda* (☏948 396 013; ❷). Most of the other villages around have at least one *casa rural*, all of which can be booked from the turismo in Lekunberri. In Leitza, 8km north, the new *Hostal Musunzar*, c/Elbarren 14 (☏948 510 607; ❷), has clean and spacious en-suite rooms with TV.

Buses to Lekunberri from Pamplona are operated by Roncalesa (☏948 222 079), Muguiroarra (☏948 227 172) and Leizaran-Mariaezcurrena (☏948 224 015); the last of these companies runs services via Lekunberri and Leitza to Santesteban on the Pamplona–Irún highway.

Southern Navarra

South of Pamplona, the country changes rapidly; the mountains are left behind and the monotonous plains so characteristic of central Spain begin to open out. The people are different, too – more akin to their southern neighbours than to the Basques of the north. There are regular bus and train services south to **Tudela**, the second city of Navarra, passing through **Tafalla** and **Olite**, once known as the "Flowers of Navarra", though little remains of their former glory. Many attractive smaller towns and villages dot the area, most looking as if not much has happened in them for the last five hundred years.

Tafalla

TAFALLA, 35km south of Pamplona, is a shabby provincial town apparently left behind by modern Spain. If you find yourself here, it's worth going to the parish church of **Santa María**, where there's a huge *retablo*, one of the finest in Spain. It was carved by Juan de Ancheta, among the most recognized of the Basque country's artists. The *retablo* was started in 1853 and completed after the artist's death in 1858 by his disciple Pedro Gonzalez de San Pedro.

There are a few rather overpriced places to **stay**: *Pensión Arotza*, in the centre at Plaza de Navarra 3 (☎948 700 716; ❷; reception in *Bar Tubal*, which also does a good *menú* for €12), the nearby, more elegant, *Hotel Ciudad de Tafalla*, Escuelas Pias 7 (☎948 704 046, ℱ948 703 918; ❹), with a restaurant specializing in charcoal-grilled lamb and beef, and *Hostal Tafalla* (☎948 700 300, ℱ948 703 052; ❸), 1km out of town on the main Pamplona–Zaragoza road, next to the service station.

Olite

OLITE is a more attractive proposition. Now hardly more than a village, it boasts a magnificent **castle** (daily 10am–2pm & 4–7pm; Oct–March closes at 6pm; July & Aug closes 8pm; €2.70), which was once the residence of the kings of Navarra. A ramble of turrets, keeps and dungeons straight out of Walt Disney, part of the building houses a *parador*. There are also two gorgeous old churches, Romanesque **San Pedro** and Gothic **Santa María**, the latter with a superb carved *retablo*.

Olite's central square, Plaza Carlos III, sits atop a series of impressive **medieval galleries** (Mon–Fri 10am–2pm & 4–7pm, Sat & Sun 10am–2pm; ☎948 741 885 for guided visits; €1.50), whose existence was a local legend for centuries before they were unearthed in the 1980s. Their original purpose is still a mystery, although it is thought they could have been a market or crypt, or even part of a secret tunnel linking Olite with Tafalla. Today they house a somewhat random display on the town's history.

Olite has its own *encierro* during the exuberant Fiesta del Patronales, 13–19 September, and there's a medieval festival during the week leading up to the saint's day of Olite's patron, the "Virgin of the Cholera" on August 26, which commemorates the town's salvation from the cholera epidemic of 1885.

The **turismo** is near the central square on Rua Mayor 1 (daily 10am–2pm & 4–7pm) ☎948 741 703, ⓦwww.animsa.es/navarra/olite). **Accommodation** in Olite is generally expensive. Apart from the *Parador Príncipe de Viana*, Plaza de los Teobaldos 2 (☎948 740 000, ℱ948 740 201; ❻), there are a couple of other pricey hotels: *Casa Zanito*, Rúa Mayor 16 (☎948 740 002, ℱ948 712 087; ❹), among the old streets, is the more atmospheric, but frequently full during the summer, while *Hotel Carlos III el Noble*, Plaza Carlos III (☎948 740 644, ℱ948

740 557; **❹**), has amazing stained-glass *miradores* and also offers a good *menú* for €12. If you want to camp, head for *Camping Ciudad de Olite* 2km out of town on the Tafalla–Peralta Road (☎948 741 014; open all year).

Ujué

East of Tafalla and Olite in the direction of Sangüesa, a winding road branches off to the right at San Martín de Unx (a good place to stock up on wine from the local *bodega*), to the hilltop village of **UJUÉ** – one of the real jewels of Navarra. It's a perfect medieval defensive village perched up on the terraced hillside above the harsh, arid landscape and dominated by the thirteenth-century Romanesque church of **Santa María** (daily 10am–8pm), where the heart of King Carlos II of Navarra is supposedly preserved inside the altar. The church has Gothic additions dating from the fourteenth century and, from its balconied exterior, the view extends over the whole southern Navarra region of La Ribera. The main doorway contains some intricate sculptures depicting the Last Supper and the Three Kings. Ujué is the destination of one of Navarra's most notable **romerías** (pilgrimages), held on the first Sunday after St Mark's (April 25), when half the populace of Tafalla, among others, walk through the night to celebrate Mass here in commemoration of their town's reconquest from the Moors in 1043.

From the main square, a couple of pedestrianized cobbled streets plunge down to another beautiful little square and a **casa rural**, *Casa Isolina Jurio* (☎948 739 037; **❶**); there are two others in the village, *El Chófer I* and *II* (☎948 739 011; **❷**), both comfortable places in a rustic style. To **eat**, try the *Meson Las Torres*, c/Santa Maria s/n (☎948 739 052) which has a variety of *menus* (€12–24), featuring the local speciality of *migas de pan* – fried breadcrumbs with *txistorro* sausage. There are at least ten *casa rurales* in the area, which can be booked through the turismo in Olite; ask here also about a guide and transport to the village from San Martín de Unx, as there is no public transport.

Tudela

The route south continues to **TUDELA** on the banks of the Ebro. On arrival, it seems as ugly a town as you could ever come across, but don't despair – a short walk down the main street takes you into the old town and an entirely different atmosphere. Around the richly decorated **Plaza de los Fueros** are a jumble of narrow lanes apparently little changed since the Moorish occupation of the city was ended by Alfonso I of Aragón in 1114. The twelfth-century **Colegiata de Santa Ana** is a fine, strong, Gothic construction. It has a rose window above the intricately carved alabaster west doorway which portrays a chilling vision of the Last Judgement. Inside there's an unusual *retablo* and some beautiful old tombs, while the Romanesque cloister has some deft primitive carvings, many badly damaged. The bizarre thirteenth-century **bridge** over the Ebro looks as if it could never have carried the weight of an ox cart, let alone seven centuries of traffic on the main road to Zaragoza.

There is a **turismo** on Plaza Vieja 1 (Mon–Sat 9am–3pm & 4–6pm, Sun 10am–2pm; ☎948 848 058), and a couple of pricey **hostales** on the main street through the new part of town: best value is *Hostal Remigio*, just off Plaza de los Fueros, at c/Gaztambide 4 (☎948 820 850, ℗948 824 123; **❷**), which also has more expensive rooms with bath; *Delta*, Avda. Zaragoza 29 (☎948 821 400, ✉nhdelta@nh_hoteles.es; **❻**), has rooms with TV and video; or try *La Estrella*, at c/Carniceras 13 (☎948 821 039; **❶**), above the *Restaurante La Estrella* in the old town. You'll find many other places to **eat and drink** around the Plaza de los Fueros; *Bar Arbella* is good for fresh *calamares fritos*. Tudela has no less than three cybercafés, all in the old town, so **Internet** access is never a problem: *Café Ciberpraga*, Avda. Santa Ana 10; *Pleey*, c/Herrerías 32; and *Tu-Ciber*, c/Zurradores 4.

The Pilgrim Route

The ancient pilgrimage route of the **Camino de Santiago** passes through Aragón (see p.659) and into Navarra just before Leyre, travelling through the province via **Sangüesa**, **Puente la Reina** (where it met an alternative route crossing the Pyrenees at Roncesvalles) and **Estella**, before crossing into Old Castile at Logroño. For more on the Camino, see below.

Yesa and the Monasterio de Leyre

The first stop for the pilgrims in Navarra is the **Monasterio de San Salvador de Leyre** (daily 10am–9pm), which stands amid mountainous country 4km

---

The Camino de Santiago in Navarra

The **Camino de Santiago** crosses into Navarra from France via the foothills of the Pyrenees, descending steeply to the historic abbey at Roncesvalles (or Orreaga-Roncesvalles; see p.539). As the mountains peter out, the path passes alongside trout-filled rivers lined with beech trees and through traditional whitewashed Basque villages graced with Romanesque churches.

Navarra has invested considerably in this section of the route and its twenty or so *albergues* – all with comfortable, if basic, facilities – are some of the best along the *camino*. The path mainly follows dirt farm tracks, although some stretches have been recently paved, which makes the walking less messy but leaves pilgrims prone to blisters.

Traces of Charlemagne's tenth-century foray into Spain are everywhere in Navarra, from the pass before Roncesvalles by which he entered the country to a stone monument some 20km further on that depicts the massive stride of Roland, his favourite knight. The region also contains some of Hemingway's favourite haunts, and the camino passes through his trout-fishing base at Auritz-Burguete (see p.539), just 3km from Roncesvalles, and the lively town of Pamplona (see p.525), another 40km into the walk.

There are a couple of stiff climbs, notably the 300m up to the Alto de Perdón, just outside Pamplona. Here, legend tells of an exhausted medieval pilgrim who stood firm against the Devil's offer of water in exchange for a renunciation of his Christian faith. The pilgrim was rewarded with the appearance of Santiago himself, who led him to a secret fountain.

Navarra boasts some of the finest Romanesque architecture in Spain, including the octagonal church at Eunate, 20km from Pamplona, thought to be the work of the Knights Templar, and the graceful bridge that gave its name to Puente la Reina (see p.536), 4km further on. The architectural highlight is undoubtedly the small town of Estella (see p.536), where it's worth spending an afternoon exploring the Palacio de los Reyes de Navarra and the many lovely churches. The route from Estella is lined with vineyards, and the free Bodegas de Irache wine fountain just outside town is said to fortify pilgrims for the journey on through the Rioja region (see p.454) to Santiago de Compostela. For practicalities on the Camino, see p.617.

from Yesa, on the main Pamplona–Jaca road, connected with both places by a daily **bus** in either direction. **YESA** has a couple of *hostales* and *habitaciones*, but much the best local accommodation is at the monastery itself.

From the village a good road leads up to Leyre, arriving at the east end of the monastery. Although the convent buildings are sixteenth to eighteenth century, the church is largely Romanesque; its tall, severe apses and belfry perched on the south apsidal roof are particularly impressive. After languishing in ruins for over a century, it was restored and reoccupied by the Benedictines in the 1950s and is now in immaculate condition. The crypt, with its sturdy little columns, is the highlight of the guided tour (Mon–Fri 10.15am–2pm & 3.30–7pm, Sat, Sun & holidays 10.15am–2pm & 4–7pm; Spanish-only guided tours, minimum 15 people, every 45min, €1.80); otherwise, you can access the church only by coinciding with Mass (5 daily 6am–9.10pm all year). This is well worth doing, since twenty or so white-habited monks employ Gregorian chant (except for matins) – albeit in Spanish, not Latin.

The former hospice now works as a two-star **hotel**, the *Hospedería de Leyre* (☎948 884 100, ⓦwww.monasteriodeleyre.com; ❹), which has particularly good-value single rates. Even if you don't stay, the restaurant is well worth visiting for its carefully prepared three-course *menú* (€16).

Javier

From Yesa it's only a few kilometres south to **JAVIER**, birthplace of San Francisco Xavier – one of the first Jesuits – and home to a fine **castle** (daily 10am–1pm & 4–7pm; free). Javier had nothing to do with the Pilgrim Route, but it is something of a place of pilgrimage in its own right, with a **museum** of the saint's life in the restored keep. Look out for the set of extraordinary demonic murals – recently discovered – depicting the Dance of Death. There's also an interesting display about Jesuit missionaries in Asia and South America.

It's a popular picnic spot and there's a tranquil, traditional **hotel** in the grounds, *Hotel Xavier* (☎948 884 006, Ⓕ948 884 078; ❸), which has a good restaurant – the speciality is *pimientos de Tudela*. Alternatively, try the cheaper *El Mesón*, Plaza de Javier (☎948 884 035, Ⓕ948 884 226; ❶). Javier and Pamplona are connected by one daily **bus**.

Sangüesa

The Pilgrim Route proper next stops 3km away at **SANGÜESA**, a delightful little town preserving many outstanding monuments, including several churches from the fourteenth century and earlier. See above all the south facade of the church of **Santa María Real** (at the far end of town beside the river), which has a richly carved doorway and sculpted buttresses: God, the Virgin and the Apostles are depicted amid a chaotic company of warriors, musicians, craftsmen, wrestlers and animals. Sangüesa is an enjoyable place simply to wander around. Many of its streets have changed little in centuries, and aside from the churches – Romanesque Santiago is also lovely – there are some handsome mansions, the remains of a royal palace and a medieval hospital, as well as the *ayuntamiento*, housed in the seventeenth-century Palacio de Vallesantoro.

Sangüesa's helpful **turismo** is at c/Mayor 2 (Mon–Fri 10am–2pm & 4–7pm, weekends & holidays 10am–2pm; ☎948 871 411, Ⓔoit.sanguesa@ cfnavarra.es). Unfortunately, there's not much in the way of **accommodation**:

the *Pensión Las Navas*, c/Alfonso el Batallador 7 (☎948 870 077; ❷), opposite the main bus stop, is the only convenient place to stay, though there's also a fairly fancy hotel, *Yamaguchi* (☎948 870 127, ℱ948 870 700, ℮yamaguchi@ interbook.net; ❹), on the road to Javier. If you want to **camp**, *Camping Cantolagua* (☎948 430 352, ℮camping.sanguesa@alva.net) is just outside town by the river, and has a great swimming pool. Three **buses** daily run to and from Pamplona and one (leaving Sangüesa very early) goes to the Aragonese town of Sos del Rey Católico, 12km away.

Puente La Reina

Perhaps no town is more perfectly evocative of the days of the medieval pilgrimage than **PUENTE LA REINA**, 20km southwest of Pamplona. This is the meeting place of the two main Spanish routes: the Navarrese trail, via Roncesvalles and Pamplona, and the Aragonese one, via Jaca, Leyre and Sangüesa. From here onwards, all the pilgrims followed the same path to Santiago.

At the eastern edge of town, the **Iglesia del Crucifijo** (open for services only) was originally a twelfth-century foundation of the Knights Templar, its porch decorated with scallop shells (the badge of the Santiago pilgrims). To one side is the former pilgrims' hospice, later in date, but still one of the oldest extant. In town, the tall buildings along c/Mayor display their original coats of arms, and there's another pilgrim church, Santiago (daily 9am–1pm & 5–8pm), whose Romanesque portal is sadly worn, but which has a notable statue of St James inside. The **bridge** at the end of the street gives the town its name. The finest medieval bridge in Spain, it was built at the end of the eleventh century by royal command and is still used by pedestrians and animals only – an ugly modern bridge has been constructed for vehicular traffic.

Accommodation in town is limited to *Hostal Puente*, Paseo de los Fueros (☎948 340 146; ❺), which is friendly, clean and serves good food, though it can be noisy. *Mesón del Peregrino* (☎948 340 075, ℱ948 341 190; ❾), an ancient building with a modern pool, just out of town on the main road towards Pamplona, offers more luxury, or try next door at the *Hotel Jakue* (☎948 341 017, ℱ948 341 120; ❹) for decent rooms. There's a good **campsite**, *El Molino* (☎948 340 604, ℗www.campingelmolino.com; open all year), at **Mendigorria**, 5km south, with a large swimming pool. There are several places to **eat**, most near the main road which, thankfully, skirts the town. *La Conrada*, Plaza de los Fueros s/n (near *Hostal Puente*; ☎948 340 052, closed Tues & Wed evening), has an excellent set menu for €10, while *Sidrería Ilzarbe*, on c/Irundibea, offers delicious cider and tapas.

Estella

Twenty kilometres west lies **ESTELLA**, a town rich in monuments but surrounded by unattractive sprawl. During the civil wars of the nineteenth century this was the headquarters of the Carlists, and each May there is still a pilgrimage up a nearby mountain to honour the dead.

The centre of town, around **Plaza de los Fueros**, sits in a loop of the river Ega, but most of the interesting buildings are situated across the river in Barrio San Martín. Here on c/San Nicolás you'll find the twelfth-century **Palacio de los Reyes de Navarra**, Navarra's only large-scale Romanesque civil edifice, now open as an art gallery (Tues–Sat 11am–1pm & 5–7pm, Sun & holidays 11am–1pm; free) devoted to the Navarrese painter Gustave de Maeztu.

Estella has a wealth of churches, the interiors of which may only be visited just before or just after Mass (times vary, but normally Mon–Fri 7–8pm, Sun 11am–1pm), unless you're with a tour guide. Most are best seen from the outside, in any case. Particularly striking is the fortified pilgrimage church of **San Pedro de la Rúa**, just up the hill from the turismo, whose main doorway shows unmistakeable Moorish influence. From the former *ayuntamiento*, an elegant sixteenth-century building just opposite the Palacio, c/de la Rúa leads past many old merchants' mansions. Further along, past a stud farm, you reach the abandoned church of Santo Sepulcro with a carved fourteenth-century Gothic doorway. Cross the hump-backed bridge, take the first left, then right uphill, and you come to the church of **San Miguel**: not a terribly inspiring building in itself, but with a north doorway that is one of the gems of the Pilgrim Route. Its delicate capitals are marvellous, as are the modelled reliefs of the *Three Marys at the Sepulchre* and *St Michael Fighting the Dragon*.

Practicalities

Estella's well-stocked **turismo** is next door to the Palacio de los Reyes de Navarra at c/San Nicolás 1 (April–Aug Mon–Sat 9am–8pm, Sun 10am–2pm; Sept Mon–Sat 10am–2pm & 4–7pm; Oct–March Mon–Sat 10am–5pm, Sun 10am–2pm; ☎ & ☏948 556 301, ✉oit.estella@cfnavarra.es); you can arrange to join a guided tour in English of the main monuments here (€3.60 per person, minimum 4 people) or else pick up a free street map and follow your own route.

If you want to **stay**, many of the budget places are located round the Plaza de los Fueros. *Pensión San Andrés*, c/Mayor 1 (☎948 554 158; ❹), is a good choice, while in the streets nearby several cheaper options include *El Volante*, c/Merkatondoa 2 (☎948 554 309; ❸), and *Fonda Izarra*, c/Calderería (☎948 550 678; ❸; closed Sept), which has a comfortable bar. For more comfort, head for *Hostal Cristina*, Baja Navarra 1 (☎948 550 450, ☏948 550 772; ❺) which can be a bit noisy in the mornings, or the clean and modern *Hotel Yerri*, Avda. Yerri 35 (☎948 546 034, ☏948 555 081; ❺). There's also a **casa rural**, *Casa Laguao* (☎948 520 203; ❸), with two double rooms and a single, 8km north in the village of Abarzuza, and a **campsite**, *Camping Lizarra* (☎948 551 733, ⓦwww.navarra.net/lizarra).

Estella has plenty of **bars**, many serving good-value *platos combinados*. If you're on the lookout for local cuisine, try the *Casanova* at c/Fray Wenceslao de Oñate 7, which has a good weekday *menú* for €8, or the slightly pricier *Asador Astarriaga*, Plaza de los Fueros 12. Alternatively, *La Navarra*, just outside the old town at Gustavo de Maetzu 16 (☎948 550 040; closed Sun eve & Mon), serves an excellent *menú* for €16.80 including wine; specialities include *gorrin* (pork).

Buses operate to Pamplona (11 daily), Logroño (7 daily) and San Sebastián (4 daily).

Estella to Logroño

From Estella, the Pilgrim Route follows the main road to Logroño and there are a number of interesting stops. At **IRACHE**, near the village of Ayegui, there's a **Cistercian monastery** (Tues 9.30am–1.30pm, Wed–Fri 9.30am–1.30pm & 5–7pm, Sat & Sun 8.30am–1.30pm & 4–7pm), which boasts an ornate Plateresque cloister. Beside the adjacent **Museo de Vino** (Sat & Sun 10am–2pm & 4–8pm), principally a showroom for Bodega Irache, are two taps in the wall, ostensibly for use by pilgrims – out of one comes water and from the other, red wine. Seventeen kilometres further on is **LOS ARCOS**, whose handsome church of **Santa María** has a Gothic cloister which is open just before and just after Mass (Mon–Sat 8pm, Sun noon &

6pm). If you decide to **stay**, *Hostal Ezequiel* (T948 640 296, F948 640 278; **❸**) is clean and comfortable, and has a special pilgrim rate; alternatively, *Hotel Monaco*, Plaza del Coso 22 (T948 640 000; **❺**), is a good bet, with en-suite rooms.

Of greater interest is **TORRES DEL RÍO**, 7km further still. This unpretentious village is built round the church of the **Holy Sepulchre**, a little octagonal building whose function is uncertain – it may have been a Knights Templar foundation or a funeral chapel. The names of the local women who look after the monument are posted on the wall of the church, and any one of them may be found to show visitors around (access at any reasonable time; €0.60). Inside it's a surprise to find that the dome is of Moorish inspiration.

VIANA, the last stop before the border and the place where Cesare Borgia died, is an attractive place with many beautiful Renaissance and Baroque palatial houses, in addition to the Gothic church of Santa María with its outstanding Renaissance carved porch. Logroño is only 10km away, but Viana's **pensión**, *La Granja*, c/Navarro Villoslada 19 (T948 645 078; **❺**), has comfortable rooms with bath. Viana also has a useful **turismo** on Plaza de los Fueros (Mon–Fri 10am–2pm & 4.45–8pm, Sat 10.15am–2pm; T948 446 302, Wwww.animsa.es/navarra/viana).

The Navarran Pyrenees

The Navarran Pyrenees may not be as high as their neighbours to the east, but they're every bit as dramatic and far less developed. There's not – yet – a single ski lift in the province, though a busy Nordic skiing centre does function at Belagoa. The historic **pass of Roncesvalles** provides the major route northeast through the mountains from Pamplona, as it has done for centuries – celebrated in the *Song of Roland* and, more recently, by Jan Morris who called it "one of the classic passes of Europe and a properly sombre gateway into Spain". This was the route taken by countless pilgrims throughout the Middle Ages; Charlemagne's retreating army was decimated here by Basque guerrillas avenging the sacking of Pamplona; Napoleon's defeated armies fought a running battle along the pass as they fled Spain; and thousands of refugees from the Civil War made their escape into France along this narrow corridor.

Beautiful foothill valleys, particularly the **Valle de Baztán** due north of Pamplona, and the **Valle de Salazar** to the east, make a perfect place to relax, with the largest concentration of good-value **casas rurales** in the province. The Pyrenees really start to get serious at the top of the **Valle de Roncal**, where there's a large mountain refuge (the westernmost in the Spanish Pyrenees) and challenging hiking up to and along the karst ridges nearby.

Auritz-Burguete and Orreaga-Roncesvalles to France

Northeast of Pamplona, the N135 winds upwards and across two valleys until it reaches the neighbouring villages of **Auritz-Burguete** and **Orreaga-Roncesvalles**, about half an hour's walk apart. The surrounding rolling country is superb for gentle riverside strolls, or simply to sit back and admire. Beyond these villages, the road continues into France via the border settlement of **Luzaide-Valcarlos**.

Auritz-Burguete

AURITZ-BURGUETE, a typical Navarran Basque village straggling for a kilometre or so along its single street, has a pleasant atmosphere despite the through traffic, and if you've come on the daily bus from Pamplona you've little choice but to stay here, as it doesn't arrive until about 8pm. The best choice amongst conventional **accommodation** is the *Hostal Burguete*, at the north end of the main street (☎948 760 005; ❸), with its three echoing storeys of huge, spotless, squeaky-wood-floored rooms, most en suite. Hemingway stayed here in the early 1920s, and immortalized it in *Fiesta*; the room he favoured (no. 25, formerly no. 18), is still preserved much as he described it, save for discreetly placed photos of the great man. The four rooms of the *Hostal Juandeaburre* (☎948 760 078; ❶) at the south end of the high street are rather more basic, while directly opposite stands the modern, anonymous *Hotel Loizu* (☎948 760 008; ☎948 790 444; ❹). Failing these, try one of the *casas rurales*, all on or just off the through road, for a more traditional feel: *Casa Pedroarena* (☎948 760 164; ❷), in a nondescript mock-trad building, has en-suite rooms; the cozier *Casa Loperena* (☎948 760 068; closed Dec–Easter; ❶), above the **bank** (next-to-last one before the frontier); or *Casa Vergara* (☎948 760 044; ❷) with six en-suite rooms and a communal lounge. A **campsite**, *Urrobi* (☎948 760 200; April–Oct), lies 3km south of the village at Auritzberri-Espinal. For **eating** out, the *Loizu* has the best restaurant in town, with *menús* for about €13, and game and regional specialities costing around €22 à la carte); otherwise, there's little to distinguish the cheaper, sustaining fare at the *Burguete's comedor* from the *Txikipolit* across the way.

Orreaga-Roncesvalles

The few buildings at **ORREAGA-RONCESVALLES**, 2.5km north of Auritz-Burgete, cluster around the Augustinian **Colegiata**, its echoing church and beautiful Gothic cloister somewhat spoiled by the abbey's oxidized-zinc roofs and the construction cranes overhead engaged in renovations. The *Sala Capitular* to one side of the cloister houses a prostrate statue of Sancho VII el Fuerte (the Strong) atop his tomb; measuring 2.25m long, it is supposedly life-size. Here also is a fragment of the chains that Sancho broke in 1212 at the battle of Navas de Tolosa against the Moors – a motif which found its way into the Navarrese coat of arms. Admission to the cloister (€2, crypt €1 extra) includes entry to a small ecclesiastical **museum** next to the monastery (April–Oct daily 10am–2pm & 3.30–7pm; Nov, Dec, Feb & March closes 5.30pm; Jan daily except Wed 1.30am–2.30pm). A beautiful half-hour walk from behind the monastery (on the marked GR65 path, the Camino de Santiago) will bring you up to the **Puerto de Ibañeta**, said to be the very pass used by Charlemagne.

There is a fair choice of **accommodation**: head for the small *Hostal Casa Sabina*, right next to the monastery (☎948 760 012; ❷), or the much larger *La Posada* (☎948 760 225; ❷), run by the monastery itself. Bona fide pilgrims following the Camino de Santiago can use the hostel at the monastery (token donation requested). There is a small, not particularly useful **turismo** (☎948 760 301) housed in an eighteenth-century millhouse behind *Casa Sabina*.

Luzaide-Valcarlos

If you're continuing into France you'll come to the border village, **LUZAIDE–VALCARLOS**, 18km on. There's no bus service beyond Auritz-Burguete, but it's a pleasant walk along the GR65. Luzaide-Valcarlos is a typical border town full of tatty souvenirs and booze – though the views are better than usual – with the en-suite *Hostal Maitena* (☎948 790 210; ❷) conveniently situated on the main road, should you need to **stay**. On the Franceward side of the village, the excellent *Casa Etxezuria* (☎948 790 011; ❶) has two beautifully furnished shared-bath rooms offering luxury at a bargain price – it's a big hit with pilgrims following the Camino de Santiago, so phone ahead if possible. There are four other **casas rurales**, including the remoter, thirteenth-century *Casa Navarlaz* (☎948 790 042; ❷).

Valle de Baztán

Due north of Pamplona, the heavily travelled N121a climbs over the Belate-Velate pass before descending to the village of **ORONOZ-MUGAIRI** and the **Parque Señorio de Bértiz** (daily 10am–2pm & 4–7pm; €1.50), a combined botanical garden and recreational forest. Immediately beyond, at Oieregi, the N121a forks left to head up the scenic Valle de Bidasoa (see p.491) towards Irún and San Sebastián. Continuing along the right fork and the N121, you enter the **Valle de Baztán** with its succession of villages, beautiful landscapes and cave formations.

Elizondo

The "capital" of this most strongly Basque of Navarran valleys is **ELIZONDO**. What's visible from the through road leaves a poor impression, but, further in, the town is full of typical Basque Pyrenean architecture, especially alongside the river. Three **buses** run daily from both Pamplona and San Sebastián, but there is no public transport to the smaller villages beyond.

There are several places to **stay** in and around Elizondo, which make it a potential base for exploring the beautiful surrounding villages and countryside. An inexpensive option is the central *Pensión Eskisaroi*, c/Jaime Urrutia 40 (☎948 580 013; ❶), offering en-suite rooms above a recommended restaurant. There are also two pricier places: the modern, three-star *Hotel Baztán* (☎948 580 050, ☎948 452 323; ❹) on the Pamplona road south of town, complete with garden and pool, and, back in town, *Hostal Saskaitz*, 200m east of the through road at c/María Azpilikueta 10 (☎948 580 488, ☎948 580 615; ❸), a modern two-star hotel.

Of the handful of **restaurants**, the *Txokoto*, c/Braulio Iriarte 25 (closed Wed), has been in the same family for three generations, and its cosy, water-view *comedor* does a good line in seafood and meat. Alternatively, there's the *Eskisaroi*, which is justly popular (*menú* €9), with long waits for tables after 2.30pm, or the similarly priced *Galarza*, at the very northern town limits by the Río Baztan, which is strong on seafood (reckon on at least €19 per head).

Around Elizondo

Some 3.5km north at **ARIZKUN**, beside the minor road to the Izepegui Pass and the French border, the seventeenth-century **convent** of Nuestra Señora de los Angeles flaunts its striking Baroque facade. Just beyond the village, there's a typical example of a fortified house (very common in the valley) where Pedro de Ursua, the leader of the Marañones expedition up the Amazon in 1560 in search of El Dorado, was born. You can **stay** in Arizkun at the friendly, well-run *Pensión Etxeberría*, near the west edge of town at c/Txuputo 43 (☎948 453 013; ❶), which does additional duty as a bar, general store and reasonable, if basic, restaurant. For slightly more comfort try *Casa Gontxea* (☎948 453 433; ❶).

Some 4km northeast and the last Spanish village before France, **ERRATZU** is another architectural gem. There are a few well-preserved **casas rurales**: *Casa Etxebeltzea* (☎948 453 157; ❷), a fourteenth-century seigneurial manor at the south edge of the medieval core; the more affordable *Casa Kordoa* (☎948 453 222; ❷); and, most economical of all, *Casa Indatxipia* (☎948 453 121; ❶).

AMAIUR-MAIA, 6km north of Arizkun just off the N121, and scene of the last unsuccessful battle to preserve the independence of Navarra, is another unspoilt village worth a stop. The gateway to its single street displays the village shield depicting a red bell – most houses still proudly emblazon their door lintels with this coat of arms. There are several **casas rurales** here, too, including the *Casa Goiz-Argi* (☎948 453 234; ❷) with en-suite rooms and the *Casa Miguelenea* (☎948 453 224; ❷).

Urdazubi-Urdax and Zugarramurdi

Northwest of Amaiur-Maia, the N121 climbs over the **Otxondo Pass** to the villages of Urdazubi-Urdax and Zugarramurdi, reached by separate side roads 16km and 20km respectively from Amaiur-Maia. Both are potential stopovers between Pamplona and the French Basque coastal towns of Biarritz and Bayonne, but the only public transport on this stretch is the noon postbus from Elizondo – check in town to confirm departure.

URDAZUBI-URDAX, ringed by hills and guarded by a tiny castle overlooking the Río Olavidea, has three *hostales* and *pensiones*, the most upmarket and central of which is the *Hostal Irigoiena* (☎948 599 267, ✉hoirigoienea@jet.es; ❸), in a renovated farmhouse. If your budget won't stretch to that, try the more modest *Pensión Beotxea* on the Zugarramurdi road (☎948 599 114; ❷), or the only *casa rural* not let by the week, *Dutaria* (☎948 599 237; ❷). For **eating**, the *Bar Restaurante Indianoa-Baita* opposite the church has reasonable *menús*.

ZUGARRAMURDI is famous for its caves, the **Cueva de las Brujas** (allow 45 minutes for the walk-through tour), whose highlight is the giant natural arch through which the *regata de infierno* (Hell's stream) flows. The cavern was a major centre for witchcraft in the Middle Ages and consequently the area bore the brunt of persecution at the time of the Inquisition. Underneath the arch, *akelarres* or witches' sabbaths allegedly took place up to the seventeenth century, and have passed into Basque legend – and into the content of the local **fiesta** – the "Witches' Festival" in July. The appealing village itself makes a good base for excursions into the surrounding countryside; one possibility is to walk 3km along the track beyond the caves into France to another set of caves, the **Grottes de Sare**. Zugarramurdi has three **casas rurales** letting rooms, but be warned that they are heavily subscribed at weekends: the relatively basic *Casa Iparrea Bajo* (☎948 599 225) and *Casa Teltxeguia* (☎948 599 167; ❶), or the larger, en-suite *Casa Sueldeguía* (☎948 599 088; ❷), all in the village centre.

Valle de Salazar

East of Pamplona, 13km before Yesa, the N178 road leads northeast from the town of Lumbier into the beautiful valley of the Río Salazar. One kilometre from Lumbier looms the entrance to the **Foz de Lumbier**, a major nesting place for **eagles** which can usually be spotted high up in the sides of this canyon or circling overhead. But the most spectacular part of the lower valley is the **Foz de Arbaiun-Arbayún**, a deep, six-kilometre-long gorge which may be descended by the intrepid, but is also visible from a viewing platform by the road. Numerous **griffon vultures** scythe the skies above.

Some 40km further on you reach the showcase Pyrenean village of **OTSA-GI-OCHAGAVÍA**, served by one daily bus from Pamplona (except Sun). Cobbled lanes wander off from the tree-lined quays on each side of the river, crossed by a series of low stone bridges. If you're looking for somewhere **to**

stay, the *Hostal Orialde* (☎948 890 027; ❷–❸), on the east bank, has antique-furnished rooms – some en suite – that are better value than those of the *Hostal Auñamendi* on Plaza Gúrpide (☎948 890 189; ❸), though the latter has a decent **comedor**. More than a dozen **casas rurales** offer rooms in the traditional stone houses for which the town is famous; two worth singling out are *Casa Nabarro* (☎948 890 355; ❶), with some en-suite rooms, and *Casa Osaba* (☎948 890 011; ❶), both on the west bank.

The **forest of Irati** to the north is one of the most extensive pine and beech forests in Europe, and **Pico de Ori** (Orhy), the westernmost summit of over 2000m in the Pyrenees, offers excellent walking and climbing options with views every bit as spectacular as the highest peaks. For those relying on public transport, the forest is inaccessible, but there are some good walks in the hills surrounding Ochagavía. Ask for details at Ochagavía's **turismo** (☎948 890 641), on the opposite side of the river to the bus stop, and/or lay hands on the Editorial Alpina 1:40,000 map-booklet *Roncesvalles/Irati*.

Valle de Roncal – and the Parque Natural Pirenaico

If you're really serious about exploring alpine mountains, the **Valle de Roncal**, the next major valley to the east, is considerably more rewarding, although it is very popular in July and August. The bus route from Pamplona ventures briefly into Aragón by the huge Embalse de Yesa (whose recently approved enlargement is set to drown three villages and 20km of the Camino de Santiago), before heading north up the valley of the Esca and back into Navarra. It's a lovely route, criss-crossing the river all the way up through Burgui and Erronkari-Roncal to Isaba. There's a helpful regional **turismo** (Mon–Sat 10am–2pm & 4.30–7.30pm, Sun 10am–2pm; ☎948 475 256) in **ERRONKARI-RONCAL**, "capital" of the valley. As well as a *hostal*, the *Zaltua* (☎948 475 008; ❷), on the through road, there are also three *casas rurales*, the best of which is *Casa Villa Pepita* (☎948 475 133; ❷), serving *table d'hôte* meals at a very reasonable price.

Isaba and around

ISABA (Izaba), with its network of streets looping around a giant fortified church, presents a more imposing prospect than Erronkari-Roncal 7km south, with the small, sterile modern district at the south end of the village (home to a small **turismo** and a **bank** with an ATM) easily ignored.

There are no fewer than eight **casas rurales** (all ❶–❷) in the village, though expect to have to try several places at weekends, since the area is a major touring centre for the western Pyrenees, as well as a Nordic ski base in winter. The largest and most comfortable of the options are *Casa Francsco Mayo* (☎948 893 166; ❷) and *Casa Garatxandi* (☎948 893 261; ❷). The pick of the other **accommodation** is the sleek and clean *Hostal Lola* (☎ & ℉948 893 012, ⓔhostallola@jet.es; ❸), east of the busy through road on narrow c/Mendigatxa, with a few precious parking spots and the best restaurant in town (allow €21–24 a *la carta*). Alternatively, *Pensión Txiki* (☎948 893 118; ❷), at the junction of c/Mendigatxa, is above the eponymous bar-restaurant, which serves a good fish soup (*menú* €10). In peak season you could also try the quiet *Pensión Txabalkua*, west of the through road at c/Izarjentea 16 (☎948 893 083; ❶). The *Albergue Oxanea* (☎948 893 153; €9 per person) on c/Bormapéa west of the main street is an unusually salubrious private **youth hostel**, which also offers meals, while Isaba's **campsite**, *Asolaze* (☎948 893 034; closed Nov &

Dec), with bungalows for rent, is 6km upstream towards the border.

For magnificent scenery and the best walking, continue 19km up the valley of the Río Belagoa to the *Refugio Angel Olorón de Belagoa* (☎ & ℱ948 394 002; €10), almost at the border but just inside the **Parque Natural**. It stands in grand isolation, overlooking pastures and the high limestone peaks to the east, with the river gleaming between forested slopes below to the south. As there's no longer a bus service beyond Isaba, those without their own transport will have to get a lift up here (easily done). The inconsistently managed refuge offers a complete programme of sports, both summer and winter (several Nordic ski-ing pistes begin at the door), as well as economical meals (€7 *menú*), though the most characterful local **restaurant**, the popular *Venta de Juan Pito*, is a couple of kilometres below, at the base of the road's hairpins. There are many **walks** you can undertake from here – the most obvious treks to peaks on the frontier ridge – but to do them in safety (the landscape abounds in deep sinkholes) you'll need a proper **map** (Editorial Alpina's 1:40,000 *Ansó-Echo* covers the park), a compass and good conditions. Take advice from the refuge wardens.

Travel details

Trains

Bilbao Estación de Abando to: Alicante (5 daily; 16hr); Barcelona (2 daily; 10–12hr); Logroño (6 daily; 2hr 30min); Madrid (1 daily; 8hr); Orduña (hourly; 1hr); Salamanca (1 daily; 9hr).
Bilbao Estación Atxuri to: Durango (10–12 daily; 40min); Bermeo via Gernika (15–25 daily; 1hr 15min); San Sebastián (9 daily; 2hr 30min–3hr).
Bilbao Estación de Santander to: Karranza (3 daily; 1hr); Santander (3 daily; 2hr 25min); Balmaseda (15–30 daily; 50min).
Irún to: Hendaye, France (every 30min 7.30am–9.30pm; 5min); Paris (2 daily; 8hr); San Sebastián (every 30min 5am–11pm; 30min).
Pamplona to: Madrid (2 daily; 6hr); San Sebastián (1 daily; 2hr 30min); Tudela (1 daily; 1hr 15min); Vitoria (2 daily; 1hr); Zaragoza (7 daily; 2hr 30min).
San Sebastián to: Bilbao (9 daily; 2hr 30min–3hr); Burgos (12 daily; 4hr); Irún (every 30min; 30min); Madrid (4 daily; 6hr 30min–8hr 30min); Ordizia (every 30min; 50min); Pamplona (6 daily; 2–3hr); Salamanca (2 daily; 9hr); Valencia (1 daily; 12hr); Vitoria (7 daily; 1hr 50min); Zaragoza (4 daily; 4–5hr).
Vitoria to: Miranda del Ebro (1 daily; 1hr 25min); Pamplona (1 daily; 1hr); San Sebastián (7 daily; 1hr 50min).

Buses

Bilbao to: Barcelona (4 daily; 8hr); Bayonne (2 daily, 2hr 50min); Burgos (4 daily; 2hr); Durango (5 daily; 30min); Elantxobe (3 daily; 1hr 30min); Gernika (25 daily; 40min); Lekeitio (5 daily; 1hr 30min); León (2 daily; 7hr); Logroño (5 daily; 2hr 15min); Madrid (15

daily; 5hr 30min); Oñati (2 daily; 1hr 15min); Ondarroa via Markina (4 daily; 1hr 30min); Pamplona (6 daily; 4hr); San Sebastián (2 hourly; 1hr 10min); Santander (30 daily; 1hr 30min); Vitoria (30 daily; 1hr); Zaragoza (10 daily; 4hr).
Irún to: Pamplona (3 daily; 2hr); San Sebastián (constantly; 30min).
Pamplona to: Bilbao (3 daily; 4hr); Burguete (1 daily; 1hr 30min); Castro (2 daily, 2hr 40min); Elizondo (4 daily; 2hr); Estella (11 daily; 1hr); Irún (3 daily; 2hr); Isaba (1 daily; 2hr); Jaca (July–Aug 2 daily, rest of year 1 except Fri & Sun 2; 1hr 45min); Ochagavía (1 daily, except Sun; 2hr); Roncal (1 daily; 1hr 45min); San Sebastián (6 daily; 1–3hr); Yesa (July–Aug 2 daily, rest of year 1 except Fri & Sun 2; 1hr); Zaragoza (2–3 daily; 4hr).
San Sebastián to: Bilbao (2 hourly; 1hr 15min); Elizondo (3 daily; 2hr); Hondarribia (every 20min; 30min); Irún (constantly; 30min); Lekeitio (3–5 daily; 2hr); Lesaka (2 daily; 1hr 15min); Pamplona (6 daily; *Autovía* 1hr; others 3hr); Bera-Vera de Bidasoa (2 daily; 1hr); Vitoria (7 daily; 2hr 30min); Zarautz (hourly; 30–40min); Zumaia (4 daily; 1hr).
Vitoria to: Araía (via villages of Llanada Alavesa; 2 daily; 1hr); Bilbao (30 daily; 1hr); Durango (4 daily; 1hr); Estella (4 daily; 1hr 15min); Laguardia (4 daily; 1hr 45 min); Logroño (8 daily; 1hr); Pamplona (10 daily, fewer Sunday; 1hr 30min); Pantanos de Zadorra (3 daily; 30min); Santander via Castro Urdiales (7 daily; 2hr 15min).

Ferries

Bilbao to: Portsmouth (departs Bilbao Thurs & Mon, departs Portsmouth Tues & Sat; 35hr).

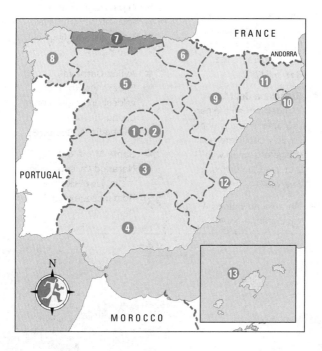

Cantabria and Asturias

CHAPTER 7 # Highlights

✳ **Playas** From el Sardinero to el Tostadero, los Biquinis to los Locos – with 202 beaches to choose from, you needn't worry about finding space for your towel.

✳ **Sidra** Asturias' national drink must be poured from a great height to attain optimum fizz. See p.547

✳ **Santillana del Mar** Wander around the narrow streets of this unbelievably chocolate-box village crammed with picturesque houses. See p.561

✳ **Naranjo de Bulnes** A vast, orange-tinted megalith is the icon of the Picos de Europa. See p.574

✳ **Ruta del Cares** A horizontal walk through the vertical world of the Cares Gorge. See p.574

✳ **Gijón** Hard-working and -playing city with a laid-back, unpretentious feel. See p.584

✳ **Avilés Carnaval** Experience Spain at its wildest and most vibrant during the *mardi gras* celebrations. See p.585

✳ **Santa Maria del Naranco** Oviedo's enigmatic, jewel-like pre-Romanesque church. See p.591

△ Picos de Europa

Cantabria and Asturias

The northern provinces of Cantabria and Asturias are popular holiday terrain for Spaniards and the French, but hardly touched by the mass tourism of the Mediterranean coast, mostly because of the somewhat unreliable weather. But the sea is warm enough for swimming through the summer months, and the sun does shine, if not every day; it is the warm, moist climate too that gives rise to the wealth of forests and rich vegetation that give the region its name, *Costa Verde*, or the Green Coast. The provinces also boast old and elegant seaside towns, and a landscape that becomes more dramatic the further west you travel, with tiny, isolated coves along the coast and, inland, the fabulous Picos de Europa, with peaks, sheer gorges, and some of Europe's most spectacular montane wildlife.

Cantabria, centred on the city of Santander, was formerly part of Old Castile, and was long a conservative bastion amid the separatist leanings of its coastal neighbours. **Santander**, the modern capital, is an elegant, if highly conventional, resort, with one of Spain's two ferry links with Britain – to Plymouth. Either side lie attractive, lower-key resorts, crowded and expensive in the holiday season – August especially – but quieter during the rest of the year. The best are **Castro Urdiales**, to the east, and **Comillas** and **San Vicente de la Barquera** to the west. Perhaps the pick of the province's towns, though, is the beautiful **Santillana del Mar**, overloaded with honey-coloured mansions and, at times, with tourists too. Inland is a series of **prehistoric caves**, one of which can be seen at **Puente Viesgo**, near Santander, though the most famous, **Altamira**, is no longer open to the public.

To the west are the harsh peaks and rugged coves of mountain-locked **Asturias**, a land with its own idiosyncratic traditions, which include status as a principality (the heir to the Spanish throne is known as the *Príncipe de Asturias*), and a distinctive culture that includes bagpipes and cider (*sidra* – served from above head height to add fizz). Asturias has a base of heavy industry, especially mining and steelworks, and a long-time radical and maverick workforce. Having conducted wildcat strikes during the early days of the Republic, Asturian miners were among the staunchest defenders of the Republic against Franco.

For the most part, the coastline is a delight, with wide, rolling meadows leading down to the sea. Tourism here is largely local, with a succession of old-fashioned and very enjoyable **seaside towns** such as **Ribadesella**, **Llanes** and **Luarca**. Inland, everything is dominated by the **Picos de Europa**, though a

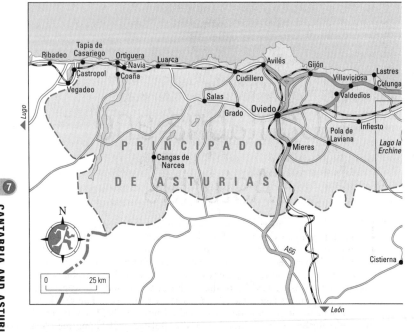

Fiestas

January

First Sunday Local fiesta with people dressed as sheep and in other bizarre costumes, in Iguña.

22 Saint's day fiesta at San Vicente de la Barquera.

February/March

Start of Lent Week-long *carnaval* festivities in Avilés, Gijón, Oviedo, Mieres, Santoña – fireworks, fancy dress and live music.

March/April

Good Friday Over-the-top re-enactment of the Passion at Castro-Urdiales.

Easter Sunday and Monday *Bollo* (cake) festival at Avilés.

First weekend after Easter *La Folia*, torch-lit maritime procession at San Vicente de la Barquera.

June

29 Cudillero enacts *La Amuravela* – an ironic review of the year – and then proceeds to obliterate memories.

July

First Friday *Coso Blanco* nocturnal parade at Castro Urdiales.

10 Fiesta at Aliva.

15 Traditional festival at Comillas with greased-pole climbs, goose chases and other such events.

16, 17 & 18 Fiestas in Tapia de Casariego.

25 Festival of St James at Cangas de Onis.

Last Sunday *Fiesta de los Vaqueros* – cowboys – at La Brana de Aristebano near Luarca.

Through July Weekly fiestas in Llanes, with Asturian dancers balancing pine trees

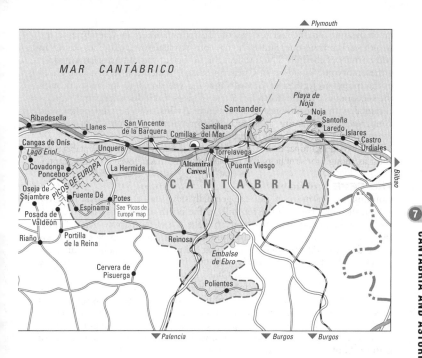

on their shoulders and swerving through the streets. Also, tightrope walking and live bands down at the harbour.

August

First or second weekend Mass canoe races from Arriondas to Ribadesella down the Río Sella, with fairs and festivities in both towns.

First Sunday Asturias Day, celebrated above all at Gijón.

12 Fiesta at Llanes.

15 *El Rosario* at Luarca – the fishermen's fiesta when the Virgin is taken to the sea.

31 Battle of the Flowers at Laredo.

Last week Fairly riotous festivities for San Timoteo at Luarca: best on the final weekend of the month, with fireworks over the sea, people being thrown into the river, and a Sunday *romería*.

Through August Music and cultural festival at Santander. This being one of the wealthiest cities of the north, you can usually depend on the festival featuring some prestigious acts.

September

7–8 Running of the bulls at Ampuero (Santander).

14 Bull running by the sea at Carreñón (Oviedo).

16 Llanes folklore festival, strong on dancing.

19 Americas Day in Asturias, celebrating the thousands of local emigrants in Latin America; at Oviedo there are floats, bands and groups representing every Latin American country. The exact date for this can vary.

21 *Fiesta de San Mateo* at Oviedo, usually a continuation of the above festival.

Last Sunday *Campoo Day* at Reinosa, featuring a parade in traditional dress.

29 San Miguel *romería* at Puente Viesgo.

November

First or second weekend Orujo (local liquor) festival in Potes.

30 Small regatta for San Andrés day at Castro Urdiales.

quiet pleasure on the peripheries of the mountains, as in Cantabria, is the wealth of Romanesque, and even rare pre-Romanesque, churches found in odd corners of the hills. These reflect the history of the old Asturian kingdom – the embryonic kingdom of Christian Spain – which had its first stronghold in the mountain fortress of **Covadonga**, and was slowly to spread south with the Reconquest. To the north lies a trio of cities: **Oviedo** a delightful regional capital, with a recently restored old centre, **Avilés**, at its best during the wild Lent *carnaval* celebrations, and nearby **Gijón**, which makes up for its aesthetic shortcomings with a vibrant nightlife and cultural scene.

The Picos de Europa, in fact, take in parts of León, as well as Cantabria and Asturias, though for simplicity the whole National Park is covered in this chapter.

The FEVE railway

Communications in this region are generally slow, with the one main road following the coast through the foothills to the north of the Picos de Europa. If you're not in a hurry, you may want to make use of the narrow-gauge **FEVE rail line** (ⓦwww.feve.es), which is unmarked on many maps and independent of the main RENFE system; note that rail passes are not valid on this service. The FEVE line can be broadly split into three routes, Bilbao in the Basque country to Santander; Santander to Oviedo (where local services serve the triangle of Gijón, Avilés and Oviedo); and Oviedo to Ferrol in Galicia. The route is, on the whole, breathtakingly beautiful, skirting beaches, crossing *rías* and snaking through a succession of limestone gorges, but you will need several days to see it in its entirety. An expensive "train hotel" runs at night, but with the scenery the main attraction of the route it's not the most practical way of getting about.

Santander

Long a favourite summer haunt of *madrileños*, **SANTANDER** is an elegant, refined resort – much in the same vein as Biarritz and San Sebastián – though away from the beaches, the modern city is rather unattractive. Some people find Santander a clean and restful base – indeed it's a popular centre for summer Spanish language courses – while others (especially younger Spaniards) will tell you it's dull and pretentious. On a brief visit, the balance is probably tipped in its favour by its variety of excellent beaches and the sheer style of its setting, though the town itself has a lack of any real sights. The narrow Bahía de Santander is dramatic, with the city and port on one side in clear view of open countryside and high mountains on the other – a great first view of Spain if you're arriving on the ferry from Plymouth.

In the summer, the city holds an **international university**, augmented by a **music and cultural festival** throughout August. You'll need to book accommodation well ahead if you plan to stay at these times.

Information and orientation

The **centre** of Santander is a compact grid of streets, set between the city's two ports, the **Puerto Grande** (where the ferries arrive) and the **Puerto Chico** (which serves pleasure boats). The main square is **Plaza de Pombo**, filled with the tables of swish cafés in summer, though the ornamental gardens of the **Paseo Pereda** are likely to capture your attention first. It is here that you'll find the informative municipal **turismo** (summer daily 9am–2pm & 4–9pm;

winter Mon–Fri 9.30am–1.30pm & 4–7pm, Sat 9.30am–1.30pm; ☎942 203 000, Ⓦwww.santanderciudadviva.com). If you are only planning a short stay, ask for their excellent *Turismo Urbano City Break* booklet. One block north of the Paseo along c/Trafalgar Zabaleta, the **Cantabrian Regional Turismo** (daily 9.30am–1.30pm & 4–7pm; ☎942 310 708, Ⓦwww.turismo .cantabria.org) is housed in the brand new Mercado del Este, an upmarket Cantabrian culture centre with gift shops and a bar. Around the waterfront to the east, **La Magdalena**, a wooded headland, shelters **Playa Magdalena**, on its near side and, beyond, the two-kilometre-long sands of **El Sardinero**, with its beachside suburb.

The **RENFE** and **FEVE** train stations are side by side on the Plaza Estaciónes, just back from the waterside, under an escarpment which hides the main roads. A largely subterranean **bus station** faces them directly across the square. The **Aeropuerto de Santander** (☎942 202 100) is 4km out of town at Parayas on the Bilbao road – an inexpensive taxi ride (€4) away; there is no public transport link. **City buses** #1, #3, #4, #7 and #E shuttle daily between the centre and El Sardinero.

Accommodation

July and August aside, Santander usually has enough **accommodation** to go round, and prices can fall dramatically outside peak months. There is a choice of locations between the **centre** and **El Sardinero**, though many of the *pensiones* and *hostales* in the latter area don't open until July.

In the centre

Hostal Carlos III Avda. Reina Victoria 135 ☎ & Ⓕ942 271 616. Well-run *hostal* in a wonderful old mansion overlooking the Magdalena beach. ❺

Pensión La Corza c/Hernán Cortés 25 ☎942 212 950. Attractive, centrally-located *pensión* with surprisingly modern, bright rooms, all with TV. ❷

Pensión Gómez c/Vargas 57A ☎942 376 622. Small, friendly base not far from the station. It's on the sixth floor, though so it's worth waiting for the lift. ❸

Hostal Liébana c/Nicolás Salmerón 9 ☎942 223 250, Ⓕ942 229 910. Pleasant, quiet *hostal* in the centre of town, with en-suite rooms with TV and telephone. There's also a bar and parking service. ❸

Pensión Plaza c/Cadiz 13 ☎942 212 967, Ⓦwww.pension-plaza.com. Modern, good value and conveniently located for travel connections. Rooms with TV. ❸

Pensión La Porticada c/Méndez Núñez 6 ☎942 227 817. Spotless, friendly and right next to the bus and train stations. Arguably the best of the central budget options. ❷

Hotel Real Paseo Pérez Galdós 28 ☎942 272 550, Ⓕ942 274 573. Elegant, upmarket hotel, near the Playa de la Magdalena, with good sea views. ❽

El Sardinero

Pensión Coloma Avda. Maura 23 ☎942 270 636. Clean, airy and right next to the Sardinero beach.

Just about the best budget option in Sardinero. ❷

Hotel Hoyuela Avda. de los Hoteles 7 ☎942 282 628, Ⓕ942 280 040. Traditional, upmarket and expensive hotel, perfect for the beach. Weekend price offers are much more affordable, but should be booked well in advance, especially in summer. ❽

Hostal Paris Avda. de los Hoteles 6 ☎942 272 350, Ⓕ942 271 744. Upmarket *hostal* ageing gracefully with large, bright rooms, some with stylish balconies. Well placed just off Plaza Italia. ❺

Hotel Sardinero Plaza de Italia 1 ☎942 271 100, Ⓕ942 271 698. Smart beachside hotel with style and character. ❼

Hostal La Torre Avda. de los Castros 53 ☎942 275 071. A good 10min walk from the beach, but one of the few Sardinero *hostales* that stays open all year round. ❸

Camping

Camping Bellavista ☎942 391 530, Ⓕ942 391 536; open all year & **Camping Cabo Mayor** ☎&Ⓕ942 391 542; open all year. Two well-equipped sites, 2km north of the Casino on a bluff known as Cabo Mayor, not far from the Sardinero beach and right next to a smaller, less-frequented one, the Playa de Matalañas. Take bus #9 to Cueto from opposite the *ayuntamiento*.

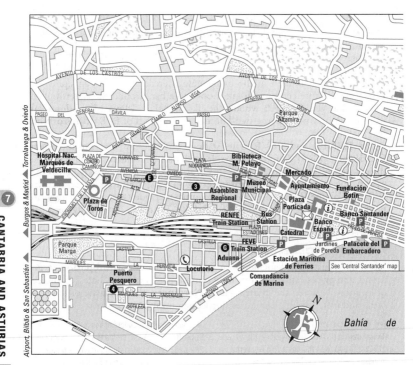

The Town

Santander was severely damaged by fire in 1941, when it lost most of its former pretensions, along with its medieval buildings. What was left of the old city was reconstructed on the grid around the cathedral, but, while the avenues are pleasant enough, and some of the shops have their appeal, there is little of interest beyond a couple of museums. The appeal of the town lies firmly in its beaches.

Santander's **Catedral** (Mon–Fri 10am–1pm & 4–7.30pm, weekends & holidays 10am–1pm & 4.30–8.45pm) is a dull building, almost uniquely bereft of treasures, save for its Gothic-Romanesque **crypt** (separate entrance; daily 8am–1pm & 4–8pm). The **Museo Municipal de Bellas Artes** (June–Sept Mon–Fri 11.15am–1pm & 5.30–9pm, Sat 10.30am–1pm; Oct–May Mon–Fri 10.15am–1pm & 5.30–9pm, Sat 10am–1pm; free), nearby, houses an eclectic mix of past and present, from Goya portraits to modern-day mosaics and sculptures, including a reproduction of a cereal box by Gomez-Bueno. Near the port, the expensive but excellent **Museo Marítimo** (Tues–Sat 11am–1pm & 4–7pm, Sun 11am–2pm; €6), near the port, has exhibits ranging from pickled two-headed sardines to entire whale skeletons, plus a real-life aquarium. If you're planning to visit the caves at Puente Viesgo (see p.562), you might look in at the **Museo Provincial de Prehistória**, c/Juan de la Costa 1 (Tues–Sat 10am–1pm & 4–7pm, Sun 11am–2pm; free), a well-arranged display of reconstructed finds from the province's numerous prehistorically inhabited caves.

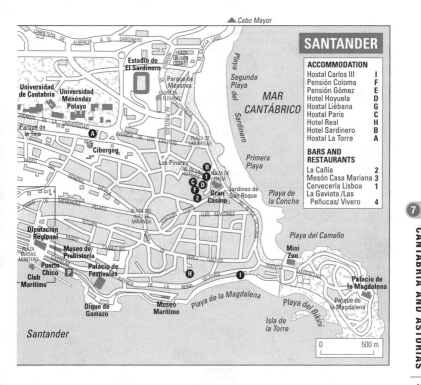

Cabo Mayor

SANTANDER

MAR CANTÁBRICO

ACCOMMODATION

Hostal Carlos III	I
Pensión Coloma	F
Pensión Gómez	E
Hotel Hoyuela	D
Hostal Liébana	G
Hostal Paris	C
Hotel Real	H
Hotel Sardinero	B
Hostal La Torre	A

BARS AND RESTAURANTS

La Cañía	2
Mesón Casa Mariana	3
Cervecería Lisboa	1
La Gaviota /Las Peñucas/ Vivero	4

0 — 500 m

Santander

Peninsula de la Magdalena and the beaches

Perched on a wooded headland east of the centre, the **Palacio de la Magdalena** (bus #1 from Pereda) affords magnificent views along the golden coastline. Built at the end of the nineteenth century by Alfonso XIII, whose residence was largely responsible for the town's fashionability, the grounds are now a popular retreat for families keen to escape the crowded beaches. A small, rather sad **zoo** now houses only a few penguins and some sea lions, but the real attraction is strolling around the gardens themselves. Should you find the hills hard work, a tourist train (€1.80) departs regularly from the park gates.

The first of Santander's beaches, **Playa de la Magdalena**, begins on the southern side of the headland. A beautiful yellow strand, sheltered by cliffs and flanked by a summer **windsurfing** school, it is deservedly popular. So, too, is **El Sardinero** itself: a further 2km of beach, round the headland to the north. If you find both beaches too crowded, there are long stretches of dunes and excellent views across the bay at **Somo** (which has boards to rent and a summer **campsite**) and **Pedreña**; to get to them, jump on the taxi-ferry which leaves every fifteen minutes from the central Puerto Chico (€2.95 return).

Eating, drinking and nightlife

There is a huge choice of **cafés**, **bars** and **restaurants** in the centre, around the **Puerto Pesquero** (the fishing port), and at **El Sardinero**, while if you want to picnic or cook for yourself, there's a good food market behind the *ayuntamiento*.

7

CANTABRIA AND ASTURIAS | Santander

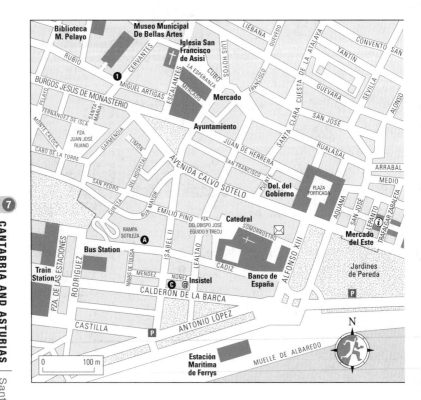

Being a university town and a pretty flash resort, Santander also has plenty of **nightlife**, at its liveliest from Thursday to Saturday in summer. **Calle Río de la Pila** is the heart of the scene – a whole street of bars, with people spilling out into the small hours; a slightly older crowd is to be found 300m uphill (and left out of c/Río de la Pila) in **Plaza Cañadio** and out towards the **Puerto Chico** around Hernán Cortés and General Mola. The nearby small towns of **Renedo** (on Saturday nights) and **Solares** (on Sundays), connected by RENFE and FEVE trains respectively, are quieter nightlife alternatives, should you wish to escape the city crowds.

Tapas bars and restaurants

Bar Cantabria c/Río de la Pila 12. Traditional tapas bar with a ceiling adorned with hanging Cantabrian hams. Wonderful *empanadas* and *pinchos*, with a little dining room at the back, should the popular bar be a little claustrophobic.

Bodega Cigaleña c/Daoiz y Velaverde. Atmospheric bar/museum decorated with old bottles. Closed Sun, last week in May and Nov, and first week in June and Dec.

Bar El Solórzano c/Peña Herbosa 17. Great neighbourhood bar with traditional music, *vermut* on tap, and an array of Cantabrian seafood including *Albondigas de Bonito*.

Bodega Bringas and **Bodega Mazon** c/Hernán Cortés 47 and Peña Herbosa. These *bodegas* serve tasty local food, wine and *sidra*, amidst vast wine vats. *Bringas* is reputed for its *anchoas* and *pimientos*; *Mazon* is good for *chipirones* and *tortilla*. Closed Sun.

Bodega del Riojano c/Río de la Pila 5. Traditional *bodega* with stacks of casks and good tapas. Popular with the thirty-something crowd. Closed

CENTRAL SANTANDER

ACCOMMODATION

Pensión La Corza	B
Pensión La Porticada	C
Pensión Plaza	A

RESTAURANTS & TAPAS BARS

Bodega Bringas	8
Bodega Cigaleña	6
Bodega Mazon	9
Bodega del Riojano	3
Bar Cantabria	2
Restaurante/Bar Cañadio	5
La Conveniente	4
El Limonar de Soano	1
Bar El Solórzano	7

CANTABRIA AND ASTURIAS | Santander

Sun night & Mon.

El Limonar de Soano c/Rubio 3. Rustic and stylish restaurant and *bodega* with a varied and unusual menu including partridge hamburgers. Expect to pay around €11 per dish. Closed Sun.

La Cañía c/Joaquín Costa 45, Sardinero. Unpretentious restaurant with excellent seafood and a good *menú*.

Cervecería Lisboa Plaza Italia, Sardinero.The best of a clutch of restaurants in front of the casino, all with summer terrazas.

La Conveniente c/Gómez Oreña 19. Nineteenth-century *bodega* with live music, fried fish and other delicious, but pricey, snacks. Open evenings only & closed Sun.

La Gaviota, Las Peñucas and **Vivero** c/Marqués de la Ensenada, Barrio de Puerto Pesquero. Three popular and unpretentious seafood restaurants down by the fishing port, featuring street barbecues of spectacular, freshly-caught seafood. You can spend anything, from a few euro for a *menú del día* or plate of sardines, to a small fortune for

fishy exotica.

Mesón Casa Mariana c/Vargas 23. Hugely popular *menú del día* (€7.20) virtually guarantees you will have to wait for a table.

Restaurante Cañadio and **Bar Cañadio** Plaza Cañadio ☎942 314 149. The *Cañadio* is the city's most famous restaurant, known far and wide for the sublime fish and regional cooking of its chef, Paco Quirós. Prices are surprisingly reasonable and there is a good daily *menú* for €12, otherwise just join the foodies snacking on a fabulous spread of canapés at the much more modest bar.

Bars and clubs

Agua de Valencia c/Perines. Popular place to start the evening, with a killer house cocktail at €6 a jug. Closed Sun.

Bar del Puerto c/Hernán Cortés. Swish bar and restaurant popular with the sailing crowd. Closed Sun night & Mon.

Blues Plaza Cañadio. Blues and jazz music bar, with an expensive connecting restaurant. Closed

555

Sun & Mon.

Canela and **Ventilador** Plaza Cañadio. Popular bars, always full at the start of the evening in a thronging plaza.

Castelar–5 c/Castelar 5. Pleasant music bar with a summer terraza.

La Casa del Indiano Mercado del Este, Trafalgar Zabaleta. South American-style sit-down bar with something of a nautical theme.

The Celtic's Tavern c/Gándara 3 esq c/General Mola. Live folk music, imported beers and English-speaking staff.

Cerveceria Cruz Blanca c/Hernán Cortés 16. Another popular place to begin the evening, with a

huge variety of international beers.

Dolce Vita c/General Mola 45. Biggest club in town, with two floors (dance/latino) and a quieter bar area. €6 men entrance fee, women free. Thurs–Sat only.

Escena Plaza Rubén Darío, at the north end of Sardinero. Old-time dance club still frequented for *rumbas* and *sevillanas*.

Molly Doolan´s Irish Tavern and **Indian's** both on c/Casmiro Sainz and open for dancing till dawn.

Rocambole c/Hernán Cortés 35. Late-night club attracting a young and trendy crowd from 3am; Motown music and expensive drinks. Thurs–Sat only.

⑦

Listings

American Express c/o Viajes Altair, c/Calderón de la Barca 11 ☎942 311 700.

Car rental Alcar, Estación de FEVE ☎942 218 307; Atesa, c/Marcelino Sanz de Santuola 2 ☎942 222 926; Budget, c/San Luis 8 ☎942 238 485; Europcar, c/Rodríguez 9 ☎942 214 706.

Consulates British Consulate, Paseo Pereda 27 ☎942 220 000.

Ferry tickets Tickets for the Brittany Ferries crossing to Plymouth are sold by Modesto Piñeiro at their office at the ferry dock (☎942 214 500, ⓦwww .brittany-ferries.com). Advance reservations are essential in summer, both for cars and passengers.

Hospital Santander's General Hospital is on Avda. Valdecilla ☎942 202 520.

Internet Santander's burgeoning crop of *ciber-cafés* includes *Ciber Lugano*, c/Hernán Cortés 55 ☎942 224 280, attached to a stylish café-cum-heladería; access is €3 per hour including a free drink. *Insistel* (c/Méndez Núñez) is conveniently

located a few hundred yards from the bus and train stations (Mon–Fri 10am–1.30pm & 5–8.30pm, Sat 10am–1.30pm; €2.80 per hour). There is a cluster of Internet bars in the streets around Mendez Pelayo y Sta Lucia, including *El Sol* on Pasadizo Zorilla. In Sardinero, *Cibergeg* (c/Honduras 3) is very cheap at €2 per hour.

Laundry *Natural Sec*, c/Trafalgar Zabaleta, around €10 per kilo; *Lavatu*, Avda. de los Castros 29 in Sardinero.

Post office The city's main *Correos* is on Avda. Alfonso XIII (Mon–Fri 8am–9pm, Sat 9am–2pm).

Telephones In the centre there are *locutorios* on Cuesta del Hospital, off Avda. Calvo Sotelo, and near the Puerto Pesquero on c/Marqués de la Hermida; in Sardinero there is a *locutorio* beside the casino.

Trekking Federación Cantabria de Montaña, c/Rubio 2 (☎942 373 378), provides information and organizes treks in the Picos de Europa.

East along the coast to Castro Urdiales

The coast east of Santander has been heavily developed, with villas and apartment complexes swamping most of the coves. **Noja**, until recently remarkable only for the strange-shaped rocks along its shore, now has seven campsites, while **Laredo** has become one of the north's major holiday resorts. Things improve as you move east, however, to the beaches at **Islares** and **Oriñon**, or the fishing ports of **Santona** and **Castro Urdiales**.

Laredo and around

An increasing stream of tourists means that the sleepy atmosphere of **LARE-DO** is changing rapidly. In summer the beaches and profusion of pubs, clubs and discos attract a young crowd keen to party, while there is enough of interest during the rest of the year to ensure that most of the hotels and restaurants remain open. For a spell in the nineteenth century it was Cantabria's provincial capital, and the village-like core of the old town, the **Puebla Vieja**, rambles back from the harbour, with occasional traces of its former walls and gates, climbing up towards a splendid thirteenth-century parish church, **Santa María de la Asunción** (daily 10am–1pm & 4–7.30pm). Beyond the church you can climb quickly out of town to the cliffs and to grand open countryside, while below lies the best **beach** this side of San Sebastián, a gently shelving crescent of sand, 5km long and well protected from the wind.

Practicalities

All **buses** arrive and depart from the new terminal on the eastern approach to town at Avenida Duque de Ahumada. A new and well-stocked **turismo** (daily 9am–2pm & 5–7pm; ☎942 611 096) stands on a fork in the road between c/Comandante Villar and c/Lopéz Seña just around the corner from the terminal. There isn't much in the way of budget **accommodation** in Laredo but there are no less than four **campsites** close to the beach: *Laredo* (☎942 605 035; June–Sept), *Costa Esmeralda* (☎942 603 250; June–Sept), *Playa de Regatón* (☎942 606 995; April–Sept) and *Carlos V* (☎942 605 593; open all year). The cheapest places you'll find are *Pensión Cantabria* on c/Menéndez Pelayo 7 (☎942 605 073; ❶) and *Pensión Esmeralda* on c/Fuente Fresnedo 6 (☎942 605 219; ❷), both simple but perfectly acceptable, and the latter handy for the town's nightlife. Otherwise, head for *Hotel Montecristo*, c/Calvo Sotelo 2 (☎942 605 700; ❹), with its pleasant garden terrace, and *Hotel El Cortijo*, c/González Gallego 3 (☎942 605 600, ☏942 605 591; ❹), with a good restaurant; both have en-suite rooms with TV and are located near the beach. If money is no object, *Hotel El Risco*, Blvd Arenosa 2 (☎942 605 030, ☏942 605 055; ❺), perched on top of a hill with great views out to sea, is the best bet; alternatively, head for the elegant *Hotel El Ancla*, c/González Gallego 10 (☎942 605 500, ☏942 611 602; ❻).

You'll find bars and *cafeterías* on the beach, while in the old town Rúa de San Marcial has a good selection of **restaurants**. If you want the town's best, it is the *Mesón del Marinero* (☎942 606 008), on c/Zamanillo a little way west of the turismo off c/Lopéz Seña, a creative, though pricey, shellfish specialist; *El Pescador*, on the seafront, is another good option – their catch of the day is always excellent.

For those interested in **scuba diving**, Laredo is the base of *Mundo Submarino* (☎942 611 861, ⓦ www.ayaba.es/mundosubmarino), who run PADI affiliated courses across the Cantabrian Sea.

Santoña

Just across the bay from the west end of Playa de Laredo lies the resort of **SANTOÑA**. Ferries run across the water to the small beach, or it's thirty minutes from Laredo by hourly bus. Santoña is, remarkably, still a working fishing port; you can watch the catch being unloaded and sample it in the tiny bars grouped around the streets leading up from the port, particularly c/General Salinas. There are grand views across the bay to Laredo from the hilltop castle of **Fuente de San Martín**. Should you wish **to stay**, the three-star *Hotel Castilla* (☎942 662 261, ⓦ www.hotelcastilla.com; ❸) at c/Manzanedo 29, with modern, comfortable rooms and a good bar, is probably the best bet in town.

Islares and Oriñon

If you're looking for somewhere more peaceful, the villages of **ISLARES** and **ORIÑON**, 8km east from Laredo on opposite sides of the Río Agüera, are pleasant and as yet little developed. Islares, on the east side of the river, is little more than a conglomeration of farming plots clustered around a tiny port and secluded beach, though the ambience is somewhat affected by the coastal highway roaring past on the hillside above. Oriñon, down in the valley beside the main beach, sheltered by the mountains on either side, is a better bet. Another, much wilder beach is located 2km away around the headland below the village of Sonabia. From here you can see the strange rock formation known as the *ojos del diablo* (devil's eyes) on the mountainside above.

Oddly enough for such small villages, there is no shortage of **places to stay**. In Islares, *Hosteria Lantarón* (formerly *El Langostero*) (℡942 871 212, ℻942 862 212; ❸) boasts large, clean, modern rooms, many with beach terrazas, as well as an excellent restaurant. Closer to the main road, *Pensión Playamonte* (℡942 862 696; ❷) is a cheaper, but noisier, option. *Hostal Areníllas* (℡942 870 900; ❷), which has its own campsite, is Islares's original *hostal*, though it can be very crowded in July and August. In Oriñon, *El Conde* (℡942 878 624; ❷; Easter & June–Sept) is a basic *pensión* with shared bathrooms, and there is also a **campsite** (℡942 863 152). There are several bars that serve food in both villages, although *Restaurante Lantarón* in Islares, with its tanks of live lobsters, is the best bet in the area.

Castro Urdiales

Twenty kilometres or so east of Laredo, **CASTRO URDIALES** is a congenial and good-looking resort, less developed than Laredo, although it's not far behind these days. Rooms and space on the beaches are at a premium in high season and at weekends, when crowds descend from Santander and Bilbao. At such times, the main "town beach", **Playa del Brazomar**, a small strip of sand hemmed in by a cement esplanade used for sunbathing, and bordered by two large hotels, can be very busy. However, the crowds can be left behind by heading further east to more secluded coves, or west to **Playa Ostende**, with its rough, dark sand. From this latter beach, there's an unusual walk back to town along the cliffs, with the sea pounding the rocks beneath you. Along the route is a tiny bay where the sea comes in under a spectacular overhang.

As well as its tourist functions, the town retains a considerable fishing fleet, gathered around a beautiful natural harbour. Above this looms a massively buttressed Gothic church, **Santa María**, and a lighthouse, built within the shell of a Knights Templar castle. These are linked to the remains of an old hermitage by a dramatic reconstructed **bridge**, medieval in age, but known locally as the Puente Romano, under which the sea roars at high tide. The old quarter, the **Mediavilla**, is relatively well preserved, with arcaded streets and tall, glass-balconied houses.

Practicalities

The **turismo** (Mon–Sat 9am–2pm & 5–7pm; ℡942 871 512) is found at the top end of Paseo Maritimo, alongside an open-air fish grill, *Asador Perla*, which serves fresh sardines and tuna in summer. **Internet** access, at *Cibercafé Linkin* on c/de Los Jardines near the port, costs €2 per hour.

Accommodation

The town's best budget **accommodation** is scattered throughout the narrow, pedestrianized streets of the old town. For modern and expensive hotels, head towards the beach and the newer part of town. There is a **campsite** in Barrio Campijo near the beach – *Castro*, Camino Allende Laguna (℡942 870 300, ℻942 870 306).

△ Castro Urdiales

Pensión Alberto Avda. República Argentina 2
☎ 942 862 757. Comfortable rooms without bath, but very central location. July–Sept only. ❶
Pensión Catamaran c/Victorina Gainza ☎ 942 860 066. Modern, value-for-money rooms with TV and en-suite bathroom. Conveniently located for both the beach and the town centre. ❷
Pensión El Cordobes c/Ardigales 15 ☎ 942 860 089. Quaint and faintly eccentric *pensión* with a good choice of clean, spacious rooms with or without bath, and a bar. ❸
Pensión La Mar c/La Mar 27 ☎ 942 870 524, ℉ 942 862 828. Smart, refurbished *pensión* in the old town, with spacious rooms. Well located for bars and restaurants. ❷

Hotel Miramar Avda. de la Playa 1 ☎ & ℉ 942 860 204. Rather ugly exterior gives way to a pleasant, modern interior. Right on the beach with panoramic views of the port. ❺
Hotel Las Rocas Avda. de la Playa ☎ 942 860 400, ℉ 942 861 382. Expensive but classy hotel close to the beach but some distance from the centre, located in a quiet residential area. All the quality of service that you'd expect from a hotel in this category. ❼
Pensión La Rosa c/Ardigales 4 ☎ 635 742 421. Small, clean *pensión* in the heart of the action. ❷
Pensión La Sota c/La Correría 1 ☎ 942 871 188, ℉ 942 871 284. Just behind the *ayuntamiento*, an excellent base for exploring the harbour and castle and close to the bars beneath the arches.

Eating and drinking

Castro Urdiales has no shortage of places to **eat**, and in the old town especially, the choice of restaurants and bars can be daunting. If you're on a budget, head for the less expensive places under the arches around the *ayuntamiento* at the castle end of the harbour, where there are some excellent fish/seafood bars around the square and on c/El Carrerias. Alternatively, a huge number of seaside restaurants of varying price and quality line the Paseo del Mar. The lively c/Ardigales is packed with *mesónes* and *tabernas*, and is also the centre of the **nightlife** scene, with two discos, *Mambo* at no. 12 and *Safari* at no. 26. Fashionable disco-pubs and late-night bars continue on down the same street into c/La Rua.

Restaurante Biritxi c/Ardigales 38. Hugely popular fish restaurant with tank containing the best of the day's catch. Expect to pay around €12 for a main course. Closed Mon.
Bar El Funi c/La Mar 27. Upmarket café-bar next to *Pensión La Mar*, a great place to relax with an afternoon coffee.
El Marichu c/Ardigales. No-frills stand-up bar, favoured by locals for its great selection of *pinchos*.
Mesón Marinero c/Correría 23 ☎ 942 860 005. Castro's renowned fish restaurant, in an unmiss-

able building opposite the *ayuntamiento*. Can be pricey, with main courses around €15, but if you sit at the bar and choose from the wide selection of *raciónes* you can eat very well and relatively cheaply.
Restaurante Baracaldo c/Matilde de la Torre 11 ☎ 942 862 012. Highly recommended restaurant with good seafood *menú*.
Sidrería Marcelo c/Ardigales 10. Traditional *sidrería* next to Mambo Discoteca, a great place for one last drink before dancing the night away.

Moving on

The new **bus terminal** is in the far east of town on c/Leonardo Rucabado, a good half-hour walk from the centre. There are through services to towns between Irún and Gijón from here. If you don't fancy the walk, local (blue) buses make the journey into town for €0.75. Buses to **Bilbao** and local buses back to the terminal leave from in front of the *Café-Bar Ronda* on Paseo Menendez Pelayo.

Santillana and the prehistoric caves

If you see a postcard depicting a village of gorgeous sandstone churches and mansions, it is more than likely **Santillana del Mar**, an outrageously picturesque place, 26km west of Santander, prettified beyond belief for tourism. It remains beautiful, by the skin of its teeth, but in season it's a major tourist spot, and can be a nightmare to visit. The crowds would be even worse, were the famous prehistoric cave paintings at **Altamira**, on the edge of the village, still open to visitors, but a less impressive though still very extensive set of Altamira-epoch paintings is preserved in another set of caves at **Punte Viesgo**.

Santillana

Jean-Paul Sartre (in *Nausea*) describes **SANTILLANA DEL MAR** as "*le plus joli village d'Espagne*" – an unlikely source, but none the less accurate for that. The town's unusual name derives from a bastardization of Santa Juliana, whose remains were brought to the village by its monastic founders 1200 years ago. Juliana was put to death by her husband for her refusal to renounce her virginity. Referring to its literal translation, the locals jokily call it the "town of the three lies" – as it's neither very holy (*santí*) nor particularly flat (*llana*), and despite the *del Mar* actually stands some three or four kilometres back from the sea. Today Santillana has become something of a tourist trap, busloads of visitors arriving to peruse the seemingly endless rows of souvenir shops, but, despite the crowds, the town is not without charm. Many fine ochre-coloured stone mansions belie the rural origins of the village, while seeing the sights is extraordinarily simple, thanks to a single pedestrianized street, with one loop and two plazas – Mayor and Las Arenas. The street saunters back from the access road towards a wonderful Romanesque collegiate church and then stops abruptly amidst farms and fields.

Santillana's fifteenth- to eighteenth-century **mansions**, mainly located in the streets around the Plaza Mayor, vie with each other in the extravagance of their coats of arms, and are as splendid as they are anomalous. One of the best is the **Casa de los Hombrones**, on c/Cantón one block from the Plaza Mayor, named after two moustached figures, flanking its grandly sculpted escutcheon. Although many of the mansions still belong to the original families, their noble owners have rarely visited in the last couple of centuries; indeed, up until the 1970s, villagers kept their cattle in some of the less-used mansions.

Just down from the Casa de los Hombrones is the **Museo de la Tortura** (daily 10am–9pm; €3.60) which displays a macabre amd disturbing collection of torture instruments, with historical notes in English. The village church, **La Colegiata** (daily 10am–1.30pm & 4–7.30pm), on Plaza Las Arenas, is dedicated to Santa Juliana, whose tomb it contains; she is legendarily supposed to have captured the Devil and is depicted with him in tow in various scenes around the building. Its most outstanding feature, however, is the twelfth-century **Romanesque cloister** (€2.50), one of the best preserved in the whole country, with its squat, paired columns and lively capitals carved with animals and hunting scenes.

Also worth a look is the seventeenth-century **Convento de Regina Coeli** (same hours and tickets as the Colegiata cloisters), on the main road just across from the entrance to the village. This houses an exceptional museum of painted wooden figures and other religious art: pieces brilliantly restored by the nuns and displayed with great imagination to show the stylistic development of certain images, particularly of San Roque, a healing saint always depicted with his companion, a dog who licks the wound in his thigh. There is supposedly a resident ghost, too, on the first floor.

A kilometre outside of town on the road to Torrelavega is a small but well-presented **zoo** (daily 9.30am–dusk; €5), with the unusual attraction of almost daily butterfly births, though you'll have to be there before 11am to see them.

Practicalities

There are several direct **buses** daily to Santillana from Santander, run by Autobuses La Cantabria from the main station (July–Aug first bus 8.30am); you are dropped outside the convent with the town straight ahead across the main road. Buses on to Comillas and San Vicente de la Barquera leave from the same place approximately every two hours in summer, although the service is reduced at weekends. You can also get to the village by regular buses from Torrelavega, which is on the FEVE railway line. You'll find a **turismo** (daily 9.30am–1.30pm & 4.30–7.30pm; ☎942 818 251; ⊛www.santillana delmar.com) at c/Jesús Otero 20, at the beginning of the main loop road into town.

Santillana is an attractive **overnight stop** if you are travelling out of season, and it has rooms to suit most budgets, though they fill quickly in summer. Least expensive are the *casas de huéspedes* (guest houses), just off Plaza de Ramón Pelayo, and the *habitaciónes* advertised by many of the bars in high season. Alternatively, *Casa Fernando* (☎942 818 018; ❶), a little way out towards Altamira, is a good-value budget option. For more comfort, head for *Casa La Solana*, at the top of c/Los Hornos 12 (☎942 818 106, ⊛www .posadasolana.com; ❸), a beautifully restored country house, perched above the hustle and bustle of the village. *Posada del Organista*, on the same street (☎942 840 452, ✉lacasadelorganista@hotmail.com; ❺), is another beautiful eighteenth-century house and does great breakfasts. *Posada Santa Juliana*, c/Carrera 19 (☎942 840 106, ✉santajuliana@santillanadelmar.com; ❸), is one of the cheaper *posadas*, but maintains high standards. The grand old *Hotel Altamira*, Cantón 1 (☎942 818 025, ℻942 840 136; ❺), is a good choice if you can afford to splash out, and also does a very good *menú* for €12; but Santillana's choicest accommodation is the *Parador Gil Blas*, housed in one of the town's finest mansions in the heart of the village (☎942 028 028; ❼). There is also a large campsite, *Camping Santillana* (☎942 818 250; all year), 1km out along the Altamira road with a pool and good facilities.

Restaurants in Santillana are abundant but largely expensive and unexceptional. *La Viga*, c/de la Carrera 2, one block from the Plaza Mayor, has a lovely courtyard restaurant and is also one of the few bars that stay open late. *Bar El Jardín*, on the same street as *Hotel Altamira*, is an attractive place with a secluded, shady garden behind. *Café Concana*, on c/Hornos just off the Plaza Mayor, boasts a pleasant *terraza* on which to enjoy a quiet drink.

The prehistoric caves

The prehistoric **Caves of Altamira** lie 2km west of Santillana. Dating from around 12,000 BC, they consist of an extraordinary series of caverns, covered in paintings of bulls, bison, boars and other animals etched in red and black with a few confident and impressionistic strokes. When discovered in the 1870s, they were in near-perfect condition, with striking and vigorous colours, but in the 1950s and 1960s the state of the murals seriously deteriorated, and they are now **closed** to prevent the build-up of surplus moisture (from breathing) in the cavern's atmosphere. Visitors with a serious academic interest can apply in writing (at least three years in advance) to the Museo Altamira (39330 Santillana de Mar, Cantabria, ☎ & ℻942 818 102). For less serious visitors there is only a **museum** (summer Mon–Sat 9.30am–7.30pm, Sun 9.30am–5pm; winter daily 9.30am–5pm; €2.40) situated next to the caves, which contains a faithful replica of the drawings.

A more rewarding trip is to **PUENTE VIESGO**, 24km from Santander on the N623 road to Burgos (SA Continental bus from the main station in

Santander). Set in a river gorge amid magnificent forested escarpments, the village itself is worth the trip, but most people are drawn initially by the set of **prehistoric caves**. A winding mountain road leads up 1.5km from beside the bus stop to an informative visitor centre from where guided tours (in Spanish only) depart. Two of the four caves are open to the public, **Las Monedas** and the slightly better **El Castillo** (April–Oct daily 10am–1pm & 4–7.30pm; Nov–March Wed–Sun 9.30am–4pm; ☎942 598 425; €3, children €1.50); but places are limited and in summer it's best to book at least 24 hours in advance. The caves are magnificent, with stalactites and stalagmites in the weirdest shapes, and bizarre organ-like lithophones, natural features used by paleolithic man to produce primitive music, in addition to the remarkable paintings – clear precursors to the later developments at Altamira. Should you be unable to find a place on a tour, the visitor centre has an excellent interactive exhibit enabling 360-degree views and tours of all four caves from the comfort of a computer terminal.

If you want **to stay**, the village has a luxurious four-star hotel on c/Manuel Pérez Mazo, the *Gran Hotel Balneario* (☎942 598 061, ⓦwww.balneario puentesviesgo.com; ❼), with its own health club, set in a glorious river valley. More affordable are the basic *La Tropical* (☎942 598 117; ❶), and the rather better *Hostal La Terraza* (☎942 598 102; ❷; open July–Sept), both with simple rooms and shared bath, located either side of the bus stop. There's also an excellent new *posada*, *La Anjana* (☎942 598 526; ❹), with spacious, well-equipped rooms, where the price includes breakfast in the excellent restaurant. Several other places also open up for the summer season.

South of Santander: Reinosa and the Ebro

South of Santander lies a large area of quiet Cantabrian countryside, dominated by the extensive Pantano del Ebro. The N611 to Palencia brushes the shores of this reservoir and passes through **Reinosa**, a transport hub for the region and a pleasant old town if you want to break your journey. To the west, the high Sierra de Peña Labra has **skiing** opportunities, with a small resort at **Alto Campoo**, 24km from Reinosa. To the east, the **Río Ebro** trails a lovely valley, past a succession of unspoilt villages, Romanesque architecture and cave churches.

Reinosa

REINOSA is a pretty, characteristically Cantabrian town with glass-fronted balconies and *casonas* – seventeenth-century town houses – displaying the coat of arms of their original owners. The **turismo** (summer Mon–Fri 9.30am–2pm & 4–7pm, Sat & Sun 10am–2pm; winter Mon–Fri 9.30am–2pm & 4–7pm; ☎942 755 215, ⓦwww.ayto-reinosa.es) occupies one of these, midway down the main street, Avenida Puente Carlos III, near the distinctive Baroque church of **San Sebastián**.

The last Sunday in September is known as "**Campoo Day**", when the people of the Alto Campoo region, of which Reinosa is the capital, celebrate their unique folklore and traditions. There is a parade of people dressed in the distinctive alpine-style costume of the region – complete with the unusual stilted clogs known as *albarcas* – as well as displays of traditional dance, typical foods and the usual late-night festivities.

The best of the budget **accommodation** is in the area around c/Julióbriga just off the main Avenida. These include *Hostal San Cristóbal*, c/Julióbriga 1 (☎942 751 768; **❶**), and *Hostal Residencia Sema* (☎942 750 047; **❷**), opposite at c/Julióbriga 14, which is near the train station and has a good restaurant. For a bit more comfort, head for the very reasonable *Hotel Rubén*, c/Abrego 12 (☎ & ℱ942 754 914; **❷**), where rooms include TV and bathroom, or the stylish *Posada San Roque*, in the east of town at Avda. de Cantabria 3 (☎942 754 788; **❸**).

For a small town, Reinosa has a surprising range of traditional **bodegas** and **mesónes**. On the main street, *Pepe de los Vinos* is a good place for a glass of wine and a snack, while the restaurants *Avenida* and *Los Peñas* offer more substantial meals. For a late drink try *Los Ángeles* nearby along the same road. While you're here, don't miss the tasty *pantortillas* (sweet, crumbly pastries), which can be bought from most bakeries.

If you are pressing on deeper into the countryside, two local **buses** daily (Mon–Fri) run south to Polientes, while Empresa Muñoz run a further two services east around the reservoir (Mon–Fri 11am & 6.30pm) to **Cabañas**. The RENFE station just behind the bus station connects Reinosa with all destinations between Valladolid and Santander (3 daily trains in either direction).

Skiing: Alto Campoo

Twenty-four kilometres to the west of Reinosa lies the ski resort of **ALTO CAMPOO**, served by regular buses in the skiing season. It's a tiny resort, with a ski school, 20km of pistes and a three-star **hotel**, *La Corza Blanca* (☎ & ℱ942 779 250; **❼**).

Along the Ebro: Polientes

Southeast of Reinosa, a network of tiny, winding roads trails the Ebro river, passing through villages of no more than a few houses. The largest of these, 45km or so away, is **POLIENTES**, a lovely place, totally rural, though with a couple of places to stay: *Pensión Demetrio* (☎942 776 018; **❷**) by the bus stop, and a *hostal* just down the road, *Sampatiel* (☎942 776 053, ℱ942 776 136; **❷**) – in season, be sure to ring before you arrive. The café-bar in the main square serves good **food** and the *hostal* does a good value *menú*, too.

East of Polientes, you'll need your own transport to continue along the valley and on to the Santander–Burgos road. Twelve kilometres from Polientes is the village of **San Martín de Elines**, with a twelfth-century Romanesque **Colegiata** containing medieval sarcophagi, and a church set into rock. At nearby **Cadalso**, you'll find another smaller rock church.

The coast: Comillas to Unquera

The coast west of Santillana, as far as **Unquera** on the border with Asturias, is dotted with a succession of small, low-key resorts. The main towns, **Comillas** and **San Vicente de la Barquera**, are stunning and well worth a visit, having retained a traditional, earthy feel long since abandoned elsewhere in a flood of high-rise hotels and apartments. The **FEVE line** runs inland along this stretch, but the towns are linked by regular bus services. Between Santillana and Comillas lies the small town of **CÓBRECES**. Above it on a hillside, and visible from the road, is a powder-blue abbey, adjacent to a pastel-pink parochial church. The abbey is famous for its cheese-making monks who conduct Masses consisting entirely of Gregorian chants. There's an **albergue** in the monastery (☎942 725 259; **❷**), should you wish to stay, where you can also buy the cheese.

Comillas

COMILLAS, the first resort west of Santillana del Mar, is a curious rural town with pretty cobbled streets and squares, and an inland feel, despite being only just set back from the sea. It has a pair of superb beaches: **Playa de Comillas**, the closest, has a little anchorage for pleasure boats and a few beach cafés, while the longer and less developed **Playa de Oyambre** is 4km west out of town towards the cape.

Oddly out of place in the otherwise provincial town is a trio of mansions, including a Gaudí-designed villa, **El Capricho**, a short (and signposted) walk from the centre. This is now an excellent but expensive restaurant, but its gardens are open to visitors, and it's certainly worth a look even if you're not staying in Comillas. With its whimsical tower, playful miniaturizations and futuristic use of colour, it has the incongruous air of a Hansel and Gretel gingerbread house.

Next door to El Capricho is another nineteenth-century *modernista* flourish, the **Palácio de Sobrellano** (summer daily 10.30am–2pm & 4–7.30pm; winter same hours Wed–Sun only; visit by guided tour only, €3), designed by Gaudí's associate, Juan Martorell, and the former residence of the Marqués de Comillas whose statue stands Rio-style on a hillside overlooking the beach. The Marqués, an industrialist friend of Alfonso XII, also commissioned the gargantuan **Universidad Pontífica**, on the hillside above, from Domenech y Montaner, another of the Barcelona *modernista* group; the gardens are open to the public.

Practicalities

Comillas is actually skirted by the FEVE line, though it has good **bus** connections with San Vicente de la Barquera to the west and Santillana and Santander to the east. Buses arrive at and leave from c/Marqués de Comillas, the continuation of Paseo de Solatorre, the main road at the bottom of the town. There is a Friday market here. **Accommodation** is better priced than surrounding resorts, but in season you will need to book ahead, or arrange a private room through the **turismo** (summer Mon–Sat 9am–9pm, Sun 11am–1pm & 5–8pm; winter Mon–Sat 11am–1pm & 4.30–7pm, Sun 11am–1pm; ☎942 720 768), centrally located at c/La Aldea 2.

The cheapest and best budget **rooms** are at *Pensión Bolingas*, c/Gonzalo de la Torre (☎942 720 841; ❶), which is clean, friendly and just off the main square, Plaza Primo de Rivera. Also good is *Pensión La Aldea*, c/La Aldea (☎942 721 046; ❶), which has a superb restaurant downstairs. *Pensión Villa*, Cuesta Carlos Diaz de la Campa 21 (☎942 720 217; ❶), has two buildings, one modern and comfortable above the main square and another more characterful house just off the Plaza de Ibañez. *Fuente Real*, c/Sobrellano 19 (☎942 720 155; ❶), right beside El Capricho, is cheap, though some rooms are better than others. More upmarket choices include *Hotel Josein*, c/Manuel Noriega 27 (☎942 720 225; ✉hoteljosein@ceoecant.es; ❹), with excellent coastal views, and *Hostal Esmeralda*, c/Antonio López 7 (☎942 720 097, ℻942 722 558; ❹), a beautifully furnished place at the top of the town. There are **campsites** at both beaches, with the *Comillas* (☎942 720 074; June–Sept) on the east side of town significantly better than *El Rodero* at Oyambre (☎942 722 040; all year).

Comillas has good **food** to offer. At the bottom end of the scale, *Picoteo*, off Plaza Generalísimo Franco, does generous meals at rock-bottom prices, while good, cheap tapas are available at *Bar Filipinas* at the crossroads next to the bus stop. The main square is packed with outdoor tables and café-restaurants, most specializing in *barcas* (huge platters) of seafood. *Gurea*, at c/Ignacio Fernandez de Castro 12 (☎942 722 446), is an outstanding Basque restaurant where a traditional three-course meal plus wine will cost around €21–24; try their tasty

Merluza Pil Pi if you get a chance. If you really want to splash out, credit cards can pay for Gaudí decor and Spanish *nouvelle cuisine* at *El Capricho* (☎942 720 365), where main courses start from around €16.

Given its size, Comillas has a surprisingly lively nightlife, with a clutch of **disco-pubs** on c/Pérez de la Riva, above the sloping Plaza Generalísimo, including the excellent *Don Porfirio*, with gardens and a small dance floor, and *Pub Chinin* opposite.

San Vicente de la Barquera

Twelve kilometres west of Comillas, the approach to **SAN VICENTE DE LA BARQUERA** is dramatic, with the town marooned on both sides by the sea and entered across a long causeway, the Puente de la Maza. Local lore maintains that if you manage to hold your breath all the way across the bridge, your wish will come true. Inland, dark green, forested hills rise towards the Picos de Europa, dramatically silhouetted as the sun goes down. Looking down from the hill which looms over the centre of town are an impressive Renaissance **ducal palace** (Tues–Sun 11am–2pm & 5–8pm; €1.20) and a Romanesque-Gothic church, **Santa María de los Ángeles**, the latter with restored, gilded altarpieces and a famous reclining statue of the Inquisitor Corro, born here in 1472. Attached to the church are the ruins of a fourteenth-century pilgrims' hospital. The town itself, a thriving fishing port with a string of locally famed but expensive seafood restaurants, has had its old core encroached upon, and is split by the main coast road with its thundering lorries, but it still makes a good overnight stop. The seafront is more dedicated to work than tourism, but if you're looking for a **beach**, there's a good sweep of sand flanked by a small forest fifteen minutes across the causeway.

Practicalities

The local **turismo** (summer only Mon–Fri 9.30am–2pm & 4–8.30pm, Sat & Sun 10am–1.30pm & 4.30–7.30pm; ☎942 710 797) is on the main road, at Avda. Generalísimo 20. **Accommodation** is easy enough to find, with a good range of options to fit most budgets. At the bottom end of the price scale, the central *Pensión Hostería La Paz*, c/Mercado 2 (☎942 710 180; ❷), is clean and spacious, with the homely *Hospedaje del Corro* (☎942 712 613; ❷) on the steps leading from the back of the main square. More expensive options include the modern *Hotel Boga Boga*, Plaza José Antonio 9 (☎942 710 135, ⓕ942 710 151; ❹), and, on the main road, the rather more refined *Hotel Luzón*, Avda. Miramar 1 (☎ & ⓕ942 710 050; ❸). There is also a pleasant **campsite**, *El Rosal* (☎942 710 165; all year), across the causeway from the town, situated in the woods beside the beach.

For **food**, a cluster of good seafood restaurants is found on Avenida Generalísimo near the turismo, including *Maruja*, *El Puerto*, *El Marinero*, and *El Pescador*, the latter a good place to try *sorropotòn*, the local speciality tuna stew. The waterfront Avenida Miramar, the continuation of Avenida Generalísimo, is awash with bars and cafés, should you need refreshment. Don't forget to try the local sweet pastries, *pejinas* – crumbly, sugared pastries with a sickly-sweet filling – available in bakeries.

Using public transport, San Vicente is best left or approached by **bus** (Alsa serves the coast and Palomera or Cantabrica cover inland routes), as the FEVE station is about 4km south at **La Alcebasa**. Buses arrive and depart from the new bus station at the bottom end of Avenida Miramar, from where it is a short walk along the coast road into town.

Unquera

The last town in Cantabria is **UNQUERA**, 9km west of San Vicente. Here buses for the Picos de Europa turn south towards **Potes** (2–3 daily). *Bar La Granja*, on the main street opposite the FEVE station, serves as the local bus stop. Unquera itself is fairly dire, its only bright spot being the restaurant *La Asturiana* near the bridge, which does a fabulous *sopa de pescado*. The town is famous for its *anis*-flavoured *corbatas* (pastries), which are sold in many of the bars and bakeries along the main street. The **turismo** (daily June–Sept 10am–2pm & 4–7pm; Oct–May 10am–3pm & 4–6pm; ☎942 719 680) is well-stocked with leaflets but almost a kilometre outside town, near the roundabout on the road to Pesues.

The Picos de Europa

The **PICOS DE EUROPA**, although not the highest mountains in Spain, are the favourite of many walkers, trekkers and climbers. The range is a miniature masterpiece: a mere forty kilometres across in either direction, shoehorned in between three great **river gorges**, and straddling the provinces of Asturias, León and Cantabria. The whole area was made a National Park in 1995, although there remain problems in coordinating the activities of the three provinces. Asturians see the mountains as a symbol of their national identity, and celebrate a cave-shrine at **Covadonga**, in the west of the range, as the birthplace of Christian Spain.

Walks in the Picos de Europa are amazingly diverse, considering the size of the region, and they include trails for all levels of activity – from a casual morning's walk to two- and three-day treks. The most spectacular and popular walks are along the twelve-kilometre Cares Gorge – a route you can take in whole or part – and around the high peaks reached from a cable car (*teleférico*) at Fuente Dé. But there are dozens of other paths and trails, both along the river valleys and in woodlands, and up in the mountains. Take care if you go off the marked trails: the Picos are one of Europe's most challenging mountain ranges, with unstable weather and treacherous, unforgiving terrain, and what appears from a distance to be a slowly undulating plateau can too easily turn out to be a series of chasms and gorges. If you do leave the trails, be sure to have adequate equipment and preparation (see box on p.570).

In addition to the walking, the Picos **wildlife** is a major attraction. In the Cares Gorge you're likely to see griffon vultures, black redstarts and ravens, though birdwatchers will be keeping a special eye out for the red-winged, butterfly-like flight of the diminutive wallcreeper, so named because of the mouse-like way it creeps along the vertical cliff faces. Wild and domestic goats abound, with some unbelievably inaccessible high mountain pastures. Wolves are easy to imagine in the grey boulders of the passes, but bears, despite local gossip and their picturesque appearances on the tourist board maps, are not a likely sight. An inbred population of about sixty specimens of *Ursus arctos pyrenaicus* remains in the southern Picos, most of them tagged with radio transmitters; another isolated group survives in western Asturias.

The Picos have long been on the map for trekkers and, as road access has opened up the gorges and peaks, have been brought increasingly into the mainstream of tourism. The most popular areas can get very crowded in July and August, as can the narrow roads, and the *teleférico* at Fuente Dé. If you have the choice, and are content with lower-level walks, spring is best, when the

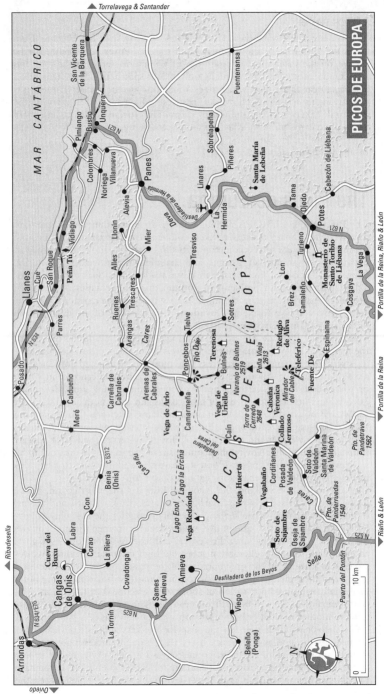

MAR CANTÁBRICO

▲ Torrelavega & Santander

San Vicente
de la Barquera

Unquera

Bustio

Pimiango

Colombres

Noriega

Villanueva

Alevia

Llonin

Mier

Panes

Linares

Sobrelapeña

Piñeres

Santa María
de Lebeña

Cabezón de Liébana

N 129

Desfiladero de la Hermida

La
Hermida

Deva

Tama

Ojedo

Potes

N 621

Tresviso

P I C O S   D E   E U R O P A

Turieno

Lon

Brez

Camaleño

Monasterio de
Santo Toribio
de Liébana

La Vega

Cosgaya

Espinama

Refugio
de Aliva

Sotres

Tielve

Poncebos

Terenosa

Bulnes

Peña Vieja
2613

Teleférico

Fuente Dé

Portilla de la Reina, Riaño & León

Portilla de la Reina

Riaño & León

Naranjo de Bulnes

Río Duje

Torre de
Cerredo
2648

Cabaña
Veronica

Mirador
del Cable

Vega de
Urriello

Camarmeña

Vega de Ario

Cares

Arenas de
Cabrales

Arangas

Trescares

Ruenes

Alles

Carreña de
Cabrales

Caldueño

Parres

Posada

N 634

Llanes

Cué

San Roque

Peña Tú

Vidiago

Colombres

Peña Tú

Meré

Labra

Con

Benia
(Onis)

La Riera

Corao

Cueva del
Buxu

Cangas
de Onis

Covadonga

N 634/E70

La Tornín

Arriondas

N 625

Sames
(Amieva)

Amieva

Viego

Beleño
(Ponga)

Desfiladero de los Beyos

Sella

Oseja de
Sajambre

Soto de
Sajambre

Vega Huerta

Vegabaño

Cordiñanes

Posada
de Valdeón

Soto de
Valdeón

Santa Marina
de Valdeón

Collado
Jermoso

Cain

Desfiladero
del Cares

Casañu

Lago Enol

Lago la Ercina

Vega
Redonda

Cares

Pto. de
Panderruedas
1540

Pto. de
Pandetrave
1562

Puerto del Pontón

Ribadesella

Oviedo

Puerto del Pontón

N 625

Puentenansa

▲ Ribadesella

7

CANTABRIA AND ASTURIAS | The Picos de Europa

568

10 km

N

0

valleys are gorgeous and the peaks still snowcapped, although the changing colours of the beech forests in autumn give some competition.

You can **approach** – and leave – the Picos along half a dozen roads: from León, to the south; Santander and the coast, to the northeast; Oviedo and Cangas de Onis, to the northwest. Public transport now serves much of the park, but services are generally infrequent, even in summer, and often run at inconvenient times.

From the coast to Potes

The N621 heads inland from the coast at Unquera, right on the Cantabria–Asturias border. From there, it follows the twisting course of the Río Deva, past **PANES**, where the C6312 forks west, along the upper reaches of the Río Cares to Arenas de Cabrales (see p.577) and Cangas de Onis (p.578). There is a very good **information kiosk** (Mon, Tues & Thurs–Sat 10am–2pm & 5–8pm; ☎985 414 297) in Panes, opposite the Caja de Asturias, where you can arrange walks and horse-riding.

Panes to Potes: the Deva Gorge

Continuing from Panes towards Potes, you enter the eerily impressive gorge of the Río Deva, the **Desfiladero de La Hermida**, whose sheer sides are so high that they deny the village of **LA HERMIDA** any sunlight from November to April. There are a few **places to stay** here if you want to break your journey, including the clean and modern *Pensión Marisa* (☎ & ⓕ942 733 545; ❷), on the road out towards Potes, the homely *Fonda de La Hermida* (☎ & ⓕ942 733 531; ❸), also on the main road, and the externally garish, but comfortable, *Posada Campo* (☎942 733 510, ⓦwww.posadacampo.com; ❷). The popular **bar-restaurant** *Pagnín*, beneath *Pensión Marisa*, serves up fine traditional cooking. From nearby **Urdón**, a path leads west to Sotres (see p.573); it's a pleasant walk of a few hours, with mountains looming up around you.

Around 10km beyond La Hermida, the village of **LEBEÑA** lies just east of the main road. It is worth a detour to see the church of **Santa María**, built in the early tenth century by "Arabized" Christian craftsmen and considered the supreme example of Mozarabic architecture. It makes an interesting visit with its thoroughly Islamic geometric motifs and repetition of abstract forms, and is set in beautiful countryside – the Hermida gorge having by now opened out into sheltered vineyards and orchards.

Potes and around

POTES is the main base on the east side of the Picos, still not all that high above sea level at 500m but beautifully situated in the shadow of tall white peaks. It is a small town and market centre (there's an open-air **flea market** on Monday mornings), with winding alleys and plenty of small shops, though largely devoted to tourism these days. Look out for the Torre del Infanto, which dates back to the thirteenth century and is now the *ayuntamiento*.

This is a useful town to stock up in, with the last banks before the mountains and **trekking maps** sold in several shops in the main square, Plaza Jesús del Monasterio. You can also rent **mountain bikes**, and arrange paragliding and canyoning at Picos Aventura next to the bridge.

Six kilometres south of Potes is the church of **Santa María Piasca**. This is pure Romanesque in style, beautifully proportioned, and with some terrific exterior sculpture. Like Santo Toribio de Liébana (see p.572), it was once a Cluniac monastery, and is flanked by the ruins of monastic and convent buildings.

Picos practicalities

Accommodation *Albergues, pensiones* and *hostales* have proliferated in recent years in the more popular villages, but whenever you can it is worth phoning ahead to book a room – especially in summer or at weekends, when whole towns can be booked solid. Up in the mountains there are a number of alpine *refugios*, which range from organized hostels to free, unstaffed huts where you'll need to bring your own food and sleeping bag. Rather more comfortable are *Casas Rurales*, dotted around the national park and often surprisingly reasonably priced. Camping beside the *refugios* is accepted, and there are about half a dozen campsites, too, scattered around the villages. Camping outside these sites is officially prohibited below 1600m, and subject to on-the-spot fines, but unofficially you won't be disturbed once away from populated areas.

Banks with ATMs are located on the periphery of the region: at Panes, Potes, Arenas de Cabrales, Riaño and Cangas de Onis.

Climate There are good days for walking in the valleys even in the depths of winter, but at high altitudes the walking season is from late June to September, varying according to the amount of snowfall the previous winter. All year round, the weather is unstable, with brilliant sunshine rapidly turning to clouds, cold rain or dense mist; in summer, cloud often descends on the valleys, while higher up it is bright and clear. Rain gear and a compass are therefore highly advisable.

Equipment Most trails in the Picos are stony, rugged and steep; walking boots are needed on all but the easiest routes. Safe, reliable water sources are sporadic and you'll need to carry a bottle. The routes given in this guide, unless mentioned otherwise, are straightforward and well marked; for walks at high altitude or off the marked trails, proper equipment and experience are essential, especially if you attempt any actual rock climbing.

Guided walks From July to September the National Park service runs free daily guided walks of easy to moderate standard, leaving from various points around the park's perimeter. They are an excellent way for novice walkers to get to know the

Practicalities

You'll find a useful **turismo** in the new bus station at the top end of town towards Fuente Dé (daily 10am–2pm & 4–8pm; ☎942 730 787). **Internet** access is available at *Ciber Plaza* or in the Galería next door at *Locutorio Liebana* on c/Dr Encinos, both €2 per hour.

Potes has a good range of **accommodation**. If you want to be in town, *Casa Cayo*, c/Cántabra 6 (☎942 730 150; ❷), is very friendly and welcoming, with a lively bar and excellent restaurant downstairs. Facing it across the river, *Lombraña*, on c/El Sol (☎942 730 519; ❶), is one of the better-value options with large rooms, although bathrooms are shared. For a bit more comfort, head for the modern *Picos de Europa*, San Roque 6 (☎942 730 005, ⓕ942 732 060; ❸), the first hotel on the left coming into town from Panes, with a range of rooms with and without bath, or the *Rubio* (☎942 730 015, ⓕ942 730 405; ❸) next door, which has its own garage.

If you're unsure just how to tackle the Picos and don't speak much Spanish, the English-owned *Casa Gustavo Guesthouse* (☎942 732 010; ❶) is ideal, although 3km away in Aliezo. **Skiing** and **canoeing trips** for residents (and all-comers) are on offer here. Also good for arranging activities is *Albergue El Portalón*, 6km south of Potes at Vega de Liébana (☎ & ⓕ942 736 048, ⓦwww.albergue-el-portalon.com; €10). This is a private hostel, with dormitory rooms, and an "Escuela del aire libre" (Outdoor Activity Centre) offering **paragliding**, mountain-biking, climbing and trekking.

Picos, although guides won't necessarily speak any English. Call or visit the park offices for details. The National Park offices also have lists of guiding companies operating in each province; contact are details given below.

Maps Best are the Adrados editions, in two 1:25,000 sheets, one covering the western massif, the other the central and eastern massifs. Adrados also publish good walking and climbing guides. The Topografico Nacional de España 1:25,000 series, in four sheets, is neither as accurate nor as useful. Maps are available in Cangas de Onis, Cain, Potes, Sotres, Bulnes and Arenas de Cabrales.

Mountain federations You can get further information on trekking and climbing in the Picos from these organizations: Federación Asturiana de Montaña, c/Melquiades Álvarez 16, Oviedo ☏985 252 362 (Mon–Thurs 5–8pm) and Federacíon Cantabrica, c/Rubio 2, Santander ☏942 373 378.

National Park offices The main park office is at c/Arquitecto Reguera 13 (☏985 241 412, ✉picos@mma.es) in Oviedo. There are three provincial offices, providing information on routes, activities and wildlife within the park, although you may find each one short of information on the other two regions: Casa Dago, Cangas de Onis, Asturias (☏985 848 614); Camaleño, Cantabria (☏942 730 555, ⓦwww.conc ejodeonis.com/turismo/parque.htm); Posada de Valdeón, León (☏987 740 549, ⓦwww.liebanaypicosdeeuropa.com/visita/picos.htm). Seasonal information centres operate in the summer months in Poncebos, Fuente Dé, Panes, Potes and Valdéon.

Potholing federations For details on potholing in the area, contact Apt. de Correos 540, Oviedo ☏985 211 790 (Fri 7–9pm), Apt. de Correos 51, Santander, or c/Alfonso X el Sabio 1, Burgos (☏947 222 427). Permits are required from the National Park offices.

Transport There are no motorable roads which cross the Picos (except the 4WD track from Espinama to Sotres), and circuits by road are long and slow; if you plan to trek across the range, make sure you allow sufficient time to get back to your starting point. There are bus services along the main roads but they're limited to one or two a day, often at unsociable hours, and are very sketchy out of season. Bike rental in Potes and other main towns is another option.

For **food** you could do a lot worse than the hotel restaurant at *Casa Cayo* where prices are reasonable and portions healthy. A series of bars along c/Cantabra do good, cheap *raciónes*, including *Café Llorente* and, opposite, *Casa Susy*. For **nightlife** Plaza la Serna is the place to be, home to *Pub Albert* and the town's only disco, *Uvas*.

In summer there are three Palomera (☏942 880 611) **buses** daily from Potes to Fuente Dé (8am, 1pm and 8pm; returning at 8.45am, 5pm & 8.45pm). Services also run to Unquera and on to Santander three times a day (7am, 9.30am & 5.45pm), with two on Sunday (10.30am & 5.45pm).

Potes to Espinama and Fuente Dé

The road from **Potes** to **Espinama** and **Fuente Dé** runs below a grand sierra of peaks – the Macizo Oriental – and past a handful of villages, built on the slopes. In summer, and at weekends, the road to the *teleférico* at Fuente Dé can be busy, but the villages en route are good bases for woodland walks, and from Espinama you can cut across the range to Sotres.

Turieno and Liébana

TURIENO, 3km west of Potes along the road to Espinama, is a quiet village where you will be as likely to share the road with a donkey as with a car. Well placed for acclimatizing to the mountains, a series of narrow mule tracks runs short distances to nearby villages which scarcely see a tourist from one year to the next. The walk to the hamlets of **Lon** and **Brez** is especially worthwhile, through a profusion of wild flowers and butterflies. Turieno has two good rural **hotel**s, *Posada Javier* (T & F 942 732 122; ❷) and *Posada Laura* (T 942 730 854; ❹), both in idyllic settings amongst forested fields, as well as the more functional but equally charming *Hospedería Floranes* (T 942 732 104; ❷) at the opposite end of town. There's also an attractive **campsite**, *La Isla* (T 942 730 896; April–Oct), situated behind an orchard, with a swimming pool and **pony-trekking** on offer. If it's full, the *San Pelayo* campsite in Baró (T 942 733 087; Easter–Oct), a little further up the road towards Espinama, is also good. Also in Baró is the excellent *Albergue Valdebaró* (T & F 942 733 092, W www .valdebaro.com; ❷), located in an attractive nineteenth-century farmhouse.

Close by Turieno, but off the main road from Potes, is the eighth-century **Monasterio de Santo Toribio de Liébana** (daily 10am–2pm & 4–8pm; free), one of the earliest and most influential of medieval Spain. Although much reconstructed, it preserves fine Romanesque and Gothic details, the largest claimed piece of the True Cross, and some extraordinary Mozarabic paintings of the Visions of the Apocalypse (now replaced by reproductions). When the saint's day, April 16, falls on a Sunday (next due in 2006), the Puerto del Perdon (Door of Pardon) is opened, indicating the start of a Jubilee Year, during which the monastery is accorded the same pilgrimage status as Santiago de Compostela, Rome and Jerusalem – meaning a huge increase in the number of pilgrims and tourists.

Cosgaya

COSGAYA, midway between Potes and Espinama, is a quiet village well located to be an attractive base for exploring the surroundings. If you feel like a little luxury before or after trekking, the Alpine-looking *Hotel del Oso* (T 942 733 018, F 942 733 336, E hoteldeloso@mundivia.es; ❸), on the main road, is the place, set in neat paddocks beside a tiny stream, and with a swimming pool in summer. The *Posada de la Casona* (T 942 733 077; ❸), a seventeenth-century farmhouse hidden away in the woods off the side of the road, is equally relaxing. Inexpensive rooms are provided by the *Mesón de Cosgaya* (T 942 733 047; ❶), which also does excellent meals.

Espinama

Twenty kilometres from Potes, **ESPINAMA** is really into the mountains. Like Cosgaya, its position and one-time isolation are marred by the road running through, but there are plenty of walks in the nearby woods and meadows for those seeking rural tranquillity.

You'll find comfortable accommodation at any of the four **hostales**: *Hospedaje Sobrevilla* (T 942 736 669; ❸) is excellent, more like a *posada* than a *hospedaje*, with friendly service, and just off the main road; *Remoña* (T & F 942 736 605; ❷) and the *Puente Deva* (T 942 736 658; ❷) both boast en-suite rooms, good restaurants and represent good value. *Apartamentos Nevandi* (T & F 942 736 608, W www.apartamentosnevandi.com; ❸) is a slightly more upmarket, self-catering option with spacious, rustic rooms, some with terraces offering great views of the mountains. All of these serve **meals**; the *menú* at the *Remoña* is particularly good value at €8.60, but the *Vicente Campo* (*Puente Deva*'s restaurant) probably has the edge, if only for its feel of a wayfarers' inn, and a crackling fire in winter. The village also has a grocery store which provides for picnics and trekking snacks.

Fuente Dé and the teleférico

The road comes to a halt 4km past Espinama, in a steep-sided cul-de-sac of rock. This is the source of the Río Deva; debate as to whether its name should be Fuente de Deva or Fuente de Eva has left it called simply **FUENTE DÉ**. Here you can stay at the modern, eponymous **parador**, next to the cable car (☎942 736 651, ✉Fuentede@parador,es; ❾), or the attractive *Hotel Rebeco* (☎942 736 601 ℱ942 736 600; ❸), nearby. There's also a **campsite**, *El Redondo* (☎942 736 699, June–Sept), with a basic dormitory (€6).

The **teleférico** (cable car) lurches alarmingly up 900m of sheer cliff. It's an extremely popular excursion throughout the year, and in summer a long wait to ascend is by no means uncommon, especially in the middle of the day (€10 return, €6 one-way). Remember that you may well have to queue again before coming down, which, at 1900m above sea level, is not nearly so congenial in the mountain chill.

At the top is an extraordinary mountainscape, where on warm days Spanish day-trippers wander around in bathing suits. However, within a few minutes' walk there is hardly a soul. If you are in the mood for a walk, you can follow a bulldozer track 4km to the **Refugio de Aliva** (☎942 730 999; ❷), which has hotel-like rooms and prices, a restaurant, and its own *fiesta* on July 2. From there, you can wend your way back down to Espinama a further 7km along another rough track.

Espinama to Sotres – and beyond

The **trek from Espinama to Sotres** is a superb route along a dirt track, practicable by 4WD, or around five hours on foot. If you are walking, set out north from the *Peña Vieja* bar in Espinama, under an arching balcony, and on to the twisting track behind. This path, climbing stiffly, winds past hand-cut hay fields and through groups of barns, until tall cliffs on either side rise to form a natural gateway. Through this you enter a different landscape of rocky summer pasture and small streams. As you near the highest point the track divides at a small barn. Ignore the left-hand path which leads up to the Refugio de Aliva (see above) and the top of the cable car, and take the track ahead past a chapel (visible from the junction) up to the ridge forming the pass.

Over the divide the scenery changes again, into a mass of crumbling limestone. In spring or winter, the downhill stretch of track here is slippery and treacherous to all but goats – and perhaps 4WDs. The hamlet of **Vegas de Sotres**, at the bottom of the hill, has a seasonal bar selling drinks; from there you need to climb again slightly to reach Sotres, which, when it appears, has a grim, almost fortified feel, clinging to a cliff edge above a stark green valley.

Sotres

SOTRES is an established walkers' base – it is a trailhead for some superb treks – and has three fairly basic **places to stay**. The *Pensión Casa Cipriano* (☎985 945 024; ❷) has good rooms but disappointing meals in a *comedor* with a €7.50 *menú*. It also has a basic *albergue* (❶). The better-equipped *albergue*, however, is the *Peña Castil* (☎985 945 080; ❶). The bar at the north end of the village has good food and an excellent atmosphere. The village **store** does good meals, and sells tasty cured sheep's and cow's milk cheeses.

East to Tresviso

Until the late 1980s, only a mule path led east from Sotres to **TRESVISO**. This is now a paved road, though still a beautiful route. If you prefer your walking a bit rougher, you can cut down a footpath from this road, 5km out of

Sotres, which leads through the **Valle de Sobra** down to **La Hermida**; the final stretch is a spectacular switchback. In Tresviso, the local bar has clean, modern **rooms** (☎942 744 444; ❶) and a restaurant.

West to Bulnes

Most walkers head west from **Sotres to Bulnes**, heading up to the broad, windy pass of **Pandébano** using the dirt road. This is officially closed to private traffic, although it is navigable by car, with care, and many do still drive up. At the top are high meadows still used for summer pasture by villagers from Bulnes, who live in simple stone dwellings there during the summer months. An old, steep cobbled path leads down to Bulnes.

Previously, the only access to the pretty village of **BULNES** was by donkey track (see p.576), but this changed with the opening in 2001 of a **funicular railway** (€15 return 10am–8pm) from Poncebos (see p.576). It runs every half hour, although occasional journeys are restricted for residents' use only.

For now, at least, Bulnes remains a sleepy village, in two parts: Castillos and La Villa. There are two **albergues**, both also offering breakfast and evening meals: the *Bar/Albergue Bulnes* (☎985 845 943; ❶), and the *Albergue Peñamain* (☎985 845 939; ❶). Camping is also tolerated.

The Naranjo de Bulnes – and across the massif

From the pass at Pandébano and from Bulnes village there are well-used paths up to the **Vega de Urriello**, the high pasture at the base of the **Naranjo de Bulnes**, the Picos' trademark peak – an immense slab of orange-tinted rock standing aloof from the jagged grey sierras around it. The approach from Pandébano is easier, a two- to three-hour hike along a track passing the small *refugio* of Terenosa. The direct path up from Bulnes is heavy-going, and can take up to six hours in bad conditions, with a slippery scree surface which can prove very difficult and dangerous when wet. Once up on the plateau, you'll find another *refugio*, the Vega de Urriello (altitude 1953m), and a permanent spring, as well as large numbers of campers and rock climbers, for whom the Naranjo is a popular target.

Experienced trekkers can stay the night in the Vega de Urriello *refugio* and then continue across the central massif, through a roller-coaster landscape unforgiving of mistakes, to the **Cabaña Veronica** *refugio*. Cabaña Veronica only has three bunks, so don't plan on sleeping; it's an easy descent from here to the top of the **Fuente Dé** cable car. Alternatively, you can continue west through further challenging terrain to another *refugio* at **Collado Jermoso** before a descent down the ravine of Asotín takes you finally to Cordiñanes at the top of the **Cares Gorge**. If you're planning this trek, make sure you go in a group with proper maps and gear.

The Cares Gorge

The classic walk in the Picos – and deservedly so – is the **Cares Gorge**, which separates the central massif from the western one of Cornión. The most enclosed section **between Caín and Poncebos** – a massive cleft more than 1000m deep and some 12km long – bores through some awesome terrain along an amazing footpath hacked out of the cliff face. It's maintained in excellent condition by the water authorities (it was built to service a hydroelectric scheme) and is perfectly safe. With reasonable energy you can walk it both ways in well under a day – or you could, like many Spanish day-trippers, get a taste of it by walking just a section from Caín. Such is the popularity of this route that in August it can seem to be a stream of hikers – unless you're an early riser.

The usual **starting point** is from the southern trailheads, **Posada de Valdeón** and **Caín**, which can be reached from Potes via Portilla de la Reina, from Cangas de Onis via Oseja de Sajambre, or from León via Riaño. There is a single daily bus to Posada de Valdeón from León via **Portilla de la Reina**, an odd little hamlet at the bottom of a lichen-covered chasm of limestone; Portilla itself is on the León–Potes bus line. On foot, you can reach Posada de Valdeón from Fuente Dé in about four hours, over a mix of dirt tracks and footpaths; the occasional Land Rover makes the trip in summer.

Access from the north is, if anything, easier, with a Land Rover bus connecting **Poncebos**, the northern trailhead, with Arenas de Cabrales – which has a regular bus service to Cangas de Onis, Llanes and Panes. Poncebos can also be reached on foot from Bulnes – see p.576.

Posada de Valdeón, Cordiñanes and Caín

POSADA DE VALDEÓN is very much on the tourist trail, though nothing can detract from the views of the huge mountains that hem in the valley to the south and shorten the days. There is little to the village itself, although the **National Park office** (Mon–Sat 9am–2pm & 4–6.30pm, Sun 9am–3pm; ☎987 740 549) can be a valuable source of information on the area. Its main value is as a base for further exploration, with a series of excellent walks, including the famous Cares Gorge, in the vicinity. There is also one **ATM** machine in town, tucked away near the entrance to *Hostal Casa Abascal*, otherwise it's a long way back to Cangas de Onis (one daily bus at noon) or León (one daily bus at 3.15pm).

The most characterful **accommodation** is at the old *Pensión Begoña* (☎987 740 516; ❶, no bathroom), while en-suite rooms are available next door at *Hostal Campo* (☎987 740 502 or *Begoña* number; ❷), under the same ownership. The sign for the *Hostal Casa Abascal* (☎987 740 507; ❷) is unmissable, dominating the village skyline, and rooms including TV and bathroom are good value. Slightly pricier is *Cumbrés Valdeón* (☎987 742 701; ❸), which also has a smart restaurant. If you are on a tight budget, you can get a dormitory bed at the *Albergue Cuesta-Valdeón* (☎987 740 560; €6) on the northern edge of the village. There is also a **campsite**, *El Valdeón* (☎987 742 605), 3km east of the village, at the hamlet of Soto de Valdeón. For **meals**, *Pensión Begoña* does a good set menu of cheap, basic but filling food for residents, while *Cumbrés Valdeón* is perhaps the better bet if you are looking for something rather more interesting.

The **Río Cares** runs through Posada, and its gorge begins just north of the village. Over this first section – to Caín – it is relatively wide and is trailed by a road. However, it's still pretty delightful, with odd pockets of brilliant green meadows at the base of the cliffs. It's possible to bypass some of the tarmac by taking a dirt track from the lower end of Posada to the **Mirador del Tombo**, just past the village of Cordiñanes; from there to Caín it's around 6km, along a downhill road. If you're pushed for time (or energy) there is a **Land Rover** service (☎987 742 619; €27 per carload) from Posada to the trailhead.

CORDIÑANES makes for a pleasant night's stop – a quieter base than Posada or Caín – and has a couple of small **pensiones**: *El Tombo* (☎987 740 526; ❷) and *El Rojo* (☎987 740 523; ❷). In summer, **CAÍN** itself is quite a honeypot, full of cars, coaches, day-trippers and trekkers. It has a handful of bars and a supermarket. There is a single **hostal**, *La Ruta* (☎987 742 702; ❷; March–Oct), right at the opening of the gorge path, although the *Casa Cuevas* (☎987 740 500; ❷ with bath, ❶ without) also offers beds, and the nearby hotel, *La Posada del Montañero* (☎985 849 021; ❷), is reasonable value, with a large restaurant and terrace. Alternatively, you can **camp** in the meadow nearby for the princely sum of €2 (no amenities whatsoever). For **food**, *Casa Chevas* and *Bar La Senda* are reliable and convenient, while *La Ruta* has decent food and a pleasant covered terrace.

Into the gorge

Just beyond Caín the motorable road ends, the valley briefly opens out, then, following the river downstream, suddenly seems to disappear as a solid mountain wall blocks all but a thin vertical cleft. This is where the **gorge** really begins, the path along its course dramatically tunnelled within the rock in the early stages before emerging onto a broad, well-constructed and well-maintained footpath.

The path owes its existence to a long-established hydroelectric scheme, for which a canal was constructed (often buried inside the mountain) all the way from Caín to Poncebos, and into which the river can be diverted in varying quantities. The path is still used for maintenance and each morning a power-plant worker walks the entire length, checking water volume in the canal and waking up those who have elected to spend a night out in the mountains. If you feel like camping, but with more privacy, there is a side valley leading off to the east about 1km into the gorge.

The first stretch of the path is more of an engineering spectacle than anything else and in midsummer or at weekends is thronged with day-trippers strolling through the dripping tunnels and walkways. Once you get 4km or so from Caín, you're down to more committed walkers, and the mountains, freed of most waterworks paraphernalia, command your total attention. They rise pale and jagged on either side, with griffon vultures and other birds of prey circling the crags. The river drops steeply, some 150m below you at the first bridge but closer to 300m down by the end.

A little over halfway along, the canyon bends to the right and gradually widens along the **descent to Poncebos**. At about 7km and 9km into the gorge some enterprising individuals have cornered the summer market with makeshift refreshments stands, handy as there are no springs. For the final 3km of the gorge, the main route climbs a dry, exposed hillside; an alternative riverside path can be reached by a steep side trail that zigzags down the precipice. Just before Poncebos another side path leads up to the cliffside village of **CAMARMEÑA**, where *La Fuentina* (☎985 846 625; ❶) has a bar, *camas* and tremendous perspectives on the Naranjo de Bulnes peak.

Poncebos – and a trail to Bulnes

At **PONCEBOS** you'll find **places to stay**, including the *Hotel El Garganta del Cares* (☎985 846 463; ❸) and, a bit further down past the bridge (coming from Caín), next to the power plant, the modern *Hostal Poncebos* (☎985 846 447; ❷), and the large *Mirador de Cabrales* (☎985 846 673; ☎985 846 685; ❹), which has a rather ugly self-service restaurant. Any of these might be welcome facilities at the end of a long day, but they're a bit institutional and somewhat gloomy due to blocked sunlight. They are, incidentally, the only buildings at Poncebos – in no sense is the place a village. If daylight permits and the funicular doesn't appeal, you might prefer to make the superb, but steep, hour-and-a-half trek up the gorge of the Tejo stream to **Bulnes** (see p.574) and stay overnight there. The path begins over the photogenic medieval bridge of Jaya, located just to the right (south) at the end of the marked Cares path – there's no need to descend to the hotels.

Arenas de Cabrales

The foothill area to the north of the Picos is known as **Cabrales**. The C6312 runs through the valley; there are buses (Mon–Fri 4 daily, 2 daily at weekends) between Cangas de Onis and Arenas de Cabrales, two of which run through to Panes and on to the coast. If you're driving, the minor roads to the coast are pleasant, allowing you to bypass traffic on the Cangas road.

ARENAS DE CABRALES (Las Arenas on some maps) is the main village of this region, famed for the exceptionally strong Cabrales cheese that is produced here and in nearby villages. Gastronomes will want to check out the **Cueva del Cares** (summer daily 10.15am–2pm & 4.15–8pm; winter Sat & Sun only same hours; €2.50, guided tour in Spanish), a cheese-making museum complete with its own natural cave of fermenting cheese. The last Sunday in August is the **Asturian Cheese Festival**, an excuse for plenty of dancing and music but, oddly enough, not all that much cheese.

Practicalities

A helpful **turismo** booth on the main street near the bridge (summer only Tues–Sun 10am–2pm & 4–8pm; ☎985 846 484, ⓦturismo.cabrales .org/2/index.htm) can fill you in on walking routes or transport schedules. Three daily buses run towards Cangas and Oviedo (7.25am, 8.35am & 5.50pm daily, with an extra service at 4pm Mon–Fri). **Buses** arrive and depart from outside the turismo. A single **Internet** terminal is located at the unmarked *La Curuxa* bar down near the bridge.

Accommodation

Arenas is well blessed with **accommodation** options, including a number of charming *pensiones* that represent excellent value. Pricier options are all of a high standard, with little to choose between them. There's a **campsite**, *Camping Naranjo de Bulnes* (☎985 846 578), 1km to the east. Alternatively, there are three further *hostales* 3km down the road in Carreña de Cabrales, the best of which is *Hotel Cabrales* (☎985 845 006; ❷).

Fermín ☎985 846 566. Welcoming and homely rooms with shared bathroom, but modern and comfortable, and all have TV. Conveniently located opposite the turismo. ❶

El Castaneu ☎985 846 573. On the street behind *Fermín*, this is another excellent-value option with a warm welcome and comfortable rooms. ❶

Casaño ☎985 846 798. Rustic yet well-equipped, this new *hostal* has a quieter setting just across the bridge, a short walk from the town. Recommended. ❶

Picos de Europa ☎985 846 491. The premier hotel in town, offering en-suite rooms with TV, mini-bar and telephone. There is also a pleasant communal terraza with views of the mountains. ❺

Villa de Cabrales ☎985 846 719. An elegant hotel, with prices slashed considerably out of season. En-suite rooms, a good bar and a garden terrace with mountain views. ❹

Naranjo de Bulnes ☎985 846 519. Less traditional than the other hotels in the same price range, but equally good, with en-suite rooms. ❹

Apartments Montecaoru ☎693 001 691. Self-catering *agroturismo* on the main road, should you wish to prepare your own meals. ❸

Restaurants and bars

For something **to eat**, the *Mesón Castañeu* has outstanding à la carte food at *menú* prices, while *Restaurante Cares* next to the post office is excellent if a little pricey. *Bar Palma*, a little further on, is a lively spot for an evening's drinking – they serve *queimadas* (hot Galician punch) if you're in a large enough group. *La Jueya* above the BBVA bank is a good *sidrería* with a decent *menú*, opposite *Restaurante La Panera* with a terrace garden providing nice views of the surroundings.

Over to the west: the Sella valley and Riaño

The road running along the western end of the Picos, the N625 between Cangas de Onis and Riaño, is arguably as spectacular as the Cares Gorge. Mountains rear to all sides and for much of the way the road traces the gorge of the **Río Sella**. The central section of this, the **Desfiladero de los Beyos**, is said to be the narrowest motorable gorge in Europe – a feat of engineering rivalling anything in the Alps and remarkable for the 1930s.

In summer there is one daily EASA **bus** in each direction between Cangas and Posada de Valdeón via Oseja de Sajambre.

The Sajambre villages

Coming from Posada de Valdeón, you turn onto the N625 right by the frequently foggy 1290m **Puerto del Pontón**. Heading north, the road passes through **OSEJA DE SAJAMBRE**, a very pretty village, high on the steep slope of a broad and twisting valley. Comfortable **rooms** and good **meals** are available at *Hostal de Pontón* (☎987 740 348; ❷).

Six kilometres above Oseja, to the east of the road, is **SOTO DE SAJAMBRE**, an excellent base for walkers, with a lovely **hostal**, the *Peña Santa* (☎987 740 395; ❷), which also has dormitory beds (€24 in summer; €16.50 in winter) and a restaurant. This is a possible starting point for a south-to-north traverse of the western Picos massif to the Lakes of Covadonga, as well as for treks in the valley of the Río Dobra. There is a refuge, *Vegabaño*, one hour above the village.

Cangas de Onis, Covadonga and the lakes

The main routes between the Picos and central Asturias meet at **Cangas de Onis**, a busy market town, and a bit of a traffic bottleneck, especially in summer and at weekends. It's an excellent base for a visit to **Covadonga** (4 daily buses all year), with its pilgrim shrine and **mountain lakes** beyond, or for taking a **canoe trip** down the Río Sella (€22 for 3 hours). There are no direct buses from Cangas de Onis to the lakes, although there are connections from Covadonga (4 daily in summer only), staggered with the Cangas-Covadonga buses to allow time to visit both on a day-trip.

Cangas de Onis

The distant peaks around **CANGAS DE ONIS** provide a magnificent backdrop to its big sight – the so-called **Roman bridge**, which you'll see splashed across the front of many Asturian tourist brochures. The bridge has been rebuilt many times, most recently in the twentieth century, but, festooned with ivy, it retains a certain charm. The town's other attraction, less photogenic but perhaps more curious, is the **Capilla de Santa Cruz**, a fifteenth-century rebuilding of an eighth-century chapel founded over a Celtic dolmen stone. This, like the Liébana monastery at Potes, is among the earliest Christian sites in Spain, and Cangas, as an early residence of the fugitive Asturian-Visigothic kings, lays claim to the title of "First Capital of Christian Spain". Today, however, it belies such history: a functional town, specializing in activity tourism, though good for a comfortable night and a solid meal after a spell in the mountains.

Practicalities

Most facilities lie within a few hundred metres of the **bus station** (in front of the *ayuntamiento*). The **turismo** (July–Sept daily 10am–10pm; Oct–June Mon–Sat 10am–2pm & 4–7pm; ☎985 848 005) is on Plaza Ayuntamiento right next to the bus stop. More comprehensive information for trekkers and mountaineers is available from Casa Dago, a **National Park headquarters** (☎985 848 614), just up the road from the turismo. A shop opposite sells excellent **maps** of the area. **Internet** access is available at the *TeleCentro* (daily 4–8pm; €2 per hour) next to the turismo. Adventure tour operators are dotted throughout town, with prices fairly consistent; one of the largest, *Cangas Aventura*, is particularly recommended, its office unmissable on the main street.

The best of the budget **accommodation** is near the bridge along Avenida de Castilla: *Pensión Labra* (☎985 849 047; ❷) at no. 1, which includes TV and bathroom, and the friendly *Hostal Covadonga* (☎985 848 135, ℱ985 947 054; ❸) at no. 38. Budget places tend to book out quickly in summer, so it's best to book in advance. More upmarket is the *Hotel Puente Romano*, across the bridge at Puente Romano 8 (☎985 849 339, ℱ985 947 284; ❹), and *Hotel Santa Cruz*, next to the *capilla* at Avda. Constantino González 11 (☎985 849 417; ❹). Two kilometres down the road to Arriondas there's the *Parador de Cangas de Onís* (☎985 849 402; ❻) in the sumptuously restored monastery of La Vega, and a youth hostel, *La Posada del Monasterio* (☎985 848 553; €14; March–Dec), a useful fallback when everywhere's full in town. If you want to camp, there is a **campsite** in Soto de Cangas: *Covadonga* (☎985 940 097; Easter & June–Sept).

Freshwater fish and *sidra* are the specialities in the **restaurants** here. The *Sidrería/Mesón Puente Romano* by the bridge has a grand outdoor setting under the plane trees, with good-value *menús*, while *El Molín de la Pedrera* between the Plaza Ayuntamiento and c/Bernabé Pendás has a less romantic setting but excellent cooking. For **nightlife** the bars along c/Bernabé Pendás near the plaza are a good starting point for a night out, especially *Tribunal* which is popular with a younger crowd. In summer almost everybody heads towards *Farmacia de Guardia* on Avenida de Castilla, its river terraza providing the perfect end to the evening.

Covadonga and the lakes

The **Reconquista** is said to have begun at **COVADONGA**, 11km southeast of Cangas in a northerly sierra of the Picos. Here in 718 the Visigothic King Pelayo and a small group of followers repulsed the Moorish armies – at odds, according to Christian chronicles, of 31 to 400,000. The reality was slightly less dramatic, the Moors being little more than a weary and isolated expeditionary force, but the symbolism of the event is at the heart of Asturian and Spanish, national history, and the defeat allowed the Visigoths to regroup, slowly expanding Christian influence over the northern mountains of Spain and Portugal.

Certainly, Covadonga is a serious religious shrine, with signs proclaiming it as a place of prayer, and daily Masses in the **cave** (9am–6pm; free), which is the focus of the pilgrimage. This shrine, said to have been used by Pelayo and containing his sarcophagus, is now a chapel, sited impressively on the side of a mountain above a waterfall and plunge pool. Across the road is a grandiose nineteenth-century pink basilica, more impressive from the outside than in, and, nearby, the **Museo de Covadonga** (daily except Tues 10.30am–2pm & 4–7pm; €2), displaying various religious treasures. A small **turismo** kiosk (Tues–Sun 10am–2pm & 4–7pm) has useful English-language leaflets about the site.

There is one inexpensive **fonda** on the road into town, the *Hospedería del Peregrino* (℡985 846 047, Ⓕ985 846 051; ❸), which has an excellent restaurant, specializing in *fabada asturiana*. There is also a *casa rural*, *Casa Priena* (℡985 846 070; ❷), with bath, TV and telephone. For more upmarket accommodation, you'll find the *Auseva* nearby (℡985 846 023, Ⓕ985 846 151; ❹), and *Hotel Pelayo* right next to the caves (℡985 846 061, Ⓕ985 846 054; ❺).

Lakes Enol and Ercina

Beyond Covadonga the road begins to climb sharply, and after 12km you reach the **mountain lakes** of **Enol** and **Ercina**. These are connected to Covadonga by four daily buses (June 15 to September 15 only), but it's not difficult to hitch if you miss one. The **Mirador de la Reina**, a short way before the lakes, gives an inspiring view of the assembled peaks.

The **lakes** themselves are placid, but subject to quirky weather. Even if it's misty at Cangas or Covadonga, you may find that the cloud cover disperses abruptly just before the lakes. There is a **campsite** at the southwest corner of Lake Enol, and a bar-restaurant beside Ercina.

The Cornión Massif

From the higher Lake Ercina a good path leads east-southeast within three hours to the **Vega de Ario**, where there's a **refugio** (℡639 812 069), camping on the meadow, and unsurpassed **views** across the Cares Gorge to the highest peaks in the central Picos. Unless you have serious hiking experience for the steep descent to the Cares, this is something of a dead end, since to cross the bulk of the western peaks you'll need to backtrack at least to Lake Ercina to resume progress south.

Most walkers, however, trek south from the lakes to the **Vegarredonda refugio** (℡985 922 952). This popular route initially follows a dirt track but later becomes an actual path through a curious landscape of stunted oaks and turf. Vegarredonda, about three hours' walk, overlooks the very last patches of green on the Asturias side of the Cornión massif. From here the path continues west for another hour up to the viewing point, the **Mirador de Ordiales**.

Beyond the **Vegarredonda refugio**, walks are in a different category of difficulty altogether. Nerve and skill are required to cross the barren land to **Llago Huerta**, the next feasible overnight spot – and like Redonda popular with potholers who disappear down various chasms in the area. From Llago Huerta it's possible to descend to Cordiñanes, Santa Marina de Valdeón or Oseja de Sajambre.

The coast: Llanes to Gijón

Once you get into Asturias, the coast becomes wilder and more rugged. You can never forget the presence of the **Picos de Europa** – just 20km inland from **Llanes**, the first major resort along the coast, and a good base for exploring the mountains. The **FEVE line** hugs the coast as far as **Ribadesella**, an attractive little fishing port, before turning inland in the direction of Oviedo. West of Ribadesella, the coast deteriorates towards Gijón, although there are some attractive spots such as the fishing villages of **Lastres** and **Villaviciosa**.

7

Llanes

The delightful seaside town of **LLANES** is Asturias's easternmost resort – and one of its most attractive, crammed between the foothills of the Picos and a particularly dramatic stretch of the coast. To the east and west stretch sheer cliffs, little-known beaches and a series of beautiful coves, yours for the walking. The three town beaches are small, but pleasant, while the excellent **Playa Ballota** is only 3km to the east, with its own supply of spring water down on the sand (and a nudist stretch). A long *rambla*, the **Paseo de San Pedro**, runs along the top of the dramatic cliffs above the western town beach, the Playa del Sablón.

In the centre, a tidal stream lined with cafés and seafood restaurants runs down into a small harbour. On the west bank of the stream you'll find the **Aula del Mar** (Tues–Fri 5–9pm, Sat 11am–2pm & 5–9pm, Sun 11am–2pm; €1.20), an interesting new museum exploring the maritime heritage of the village, with special emphasis on whaling. Behind it lies the old town where tall medieval walls shelter a number of impressive buildings in various stages of restoration or decay. These include a **medieval tower** housing the turismo, the semi-ruined and overgrown Renaissance palaces of the **Duques de Estrada** and the **Casa del Cercau** (both closed to the public), and the **Basilica**, built in the plain Gothic style imported from southern France, although the sculpted east door is preserved from an earlier Romanesque building.

Llanes makes an excellent base (or rest cure) for the Picos, with good transport connections via nearby Unquera. Those with their own transport could also visit a curious Bronze Age monolith 10km east along the coast road at **Peña Tu**.

Practicalities

There's a useful **turismo**, open year-round, in the Torre Medieval (summer Mon–Sat 10am–2pm & 5–9pm, Sun 10am–3pm; winter Mon–Fri 10am–2pm & 4–6.30pm, Sat 10.30am–1.30pm; ☎985 400 164), and in summer a **turismo kiosk** opens on the bridge (daily noon–2pm & 5–8pm). **Buses** arrive and depart from the new bus terminal at the bottom end of c/Pidal, a short walk east of the centre. **Accommodation** is rather pricey and the only real budget option is the characterful *Pensión Puerto de Llanes* (☎985 400 883; ❶), above a lively *sidrería* overlooking the river. Other cheaper options are the old-fashioned and spacious *Hospedaje Casa del Río*, Avda. de San Pedro 3 (☎985 401 191; ❸), and the smart, central *Pensión La Guía*, Plaza Parres Sobrino 1 (☎ & ℱ985 402 577; ❸). For more comfort, *Sablon's Hotel* (☎985 400 787, ℱ985 401 988; ❹) overlooks the Playa del Sablón, but is a fair walk from the centre. A classier option is the beautiful, central *Posada del Rey*, c/Mayor 11 (☎985 401 332, ⓦlaposadadelrey.iespana.es; ❻), frequented in 1517 by Carlos, first king of the united Spain. A wide selection of **casas rurales** in this area includes *La Torre 1* (☎985 417 207; ❺), 5km away in Andrín, and the nearby, but more expensive, *La Torre 2* (☎985 417 207; ❼). There is a large **campsite**, *Las Baracenas* (☎985 402 887; June–Sept), 2km east of town, although the slightly smaller *Entre Playas* (☎985 400 888; Easter & June–Oct), on the headland between the two town beaches to the east, is better situated.

For good **seafood** – and Asturian *sidra* – head for *La Marina*, a restaurant shaped like a boat at the end of the harbour, where you can sit outside and tuck into swordfish steaks and sardines. Alternatively the simple open-air **café-restaurants** by the river just inland from the bridge serve up above-average seafood *raciones* for between €3.60 and €12 a dish; *Mesón del Riveru* is particularly good. *El Bodegón*, hidden in the tree-shaded Plaza de Siete Puertas, is good for *sidra* and Asturian *raciones*, while for more formal meals and *menús*, try the restaurants on c/Manuel Cué including *El Pescador* and *La Covadonga*. *Café Pitin* opposite the casino on the main road is a great place to enjoy a coffee with the locals.

For **nightlife** there is a small disco, *Kamba*, and a terraza-pub, *El Brezzo*, adjacent to each other on the inland side of the stream. Opposite is *Aventura Bar Rumbo de Picos* (☎985 403 787) which organizes all manner of adventure activities from canoeing and white-water rafting to hiking and horse-riding. *Ciber Travelling* is a lively bar on the small pedestrian street off c/Nemesio Sabrino, with **Internet** access for €2 per hour.

Villahormes and Nueva

Following the coast (and FEVE line), the next tempting stop to the west of Llanes is **VILLAHORMES**. This is an unprepossessing-looking place: no more than a train station, a handful of houses, a café-bar and a very shabby-looking *hostal*. Follow the rusty signpost to **Playa de la Huelga**, however, and, after 1500m of driveable track, you reach one of the best swimming coves imaginable, with a rock arch in the bay and an enclosed sea pool for kids to splash around in safety. It is flanked by a pleasant bar-restaurant. The **Playa de Gulpiyuri**, 1km to the northeast, is an unusual beach set back from the shoreline but fed by an underground channel of seawater.

A thirty-minute walk west of Villahormes, or five minutes more on the train, will get you to another hamlet, **NUEVA**, tucked into a fold of the hills, and 3km inland from another gorgeous little cove. If you decide to **stay**, head for the *Ereba* (☎985 410 139; ❷) at c/Triana 137, a pleasant *casa rural*. There is also a good *pensión*, *San Jorge* (☎985 410 285; ❸), and a **campsite**, *Palacio de Garaña* (☎985 410 075; mid-June to mid-Sept).

Ribadesella

RIBADESELLA, 18km west of Llanes, is an unaffected old port, split into two by the Sella River, and bridged by a long causeway. On the east side is the old town, with dozens of great little bars and *comedores* on the streets parallel to the **fishing harbour**. Freshly caught fish is still unloaded after midnight at the *lonja* and, although the catch is increasingly small, it's fun to hang out in the bars and watch it being hauled in. In the seafood joints lining the harbour you can sample delicacies such as *centollas* (spider crabs) and *lubina* (sea bass). To the west, the new town contains the more upmarket accommodation, the excellent town **beach** *Playa Santa María*, and the **Cueva Tito Bustillo** (April to mid-Sept Wed–Sun 10am–4.15pm; €2.10, free Wed for a 25min guided tour in Spanish; ☎902 190 508,), an Altamira-style cave more impressive for its stalactites than its paintings, though it has a museum of prehistoric finds from the area. Only 375 visitors are allowed into the caves each day, so in summer you'll need a reservation to get in.

Practicalities

Arriving by train, you'll emerge at the **FEVE station**, at the top end of the old town, on Carretera Santander; the **bus station** is on the main road at the entrance to the old town. There is a **turismo** (summer daily 10am–10pm; winter Tues–Sat 10am–1pm & 4–8pm, Sun 11am–2pm; ☎985 860 038) in the old town just by the causeway at the entrance to the port.

Accommodation is a bit pricier than usual, although the impecunious may be able to find *camas*. There's a **youth hostel** on c/Ricardo Cangas (☎985 861

105; €11) in an old house on the east side of the estuary, but it is often booked out by groups. There is only one *hostal*, *El Pilar* (☎985 860 446; ❸), 200m from the beach in the new town on c/Puente del Pilar, which has a restaurant serving traditional Asturian food. The most reasonable hotel is *Covadonga* (☎985 860 222; ❹), above a *sidrería* with a boat-shaped bar, at c/Manuel Caso de Villa 9, while the *casa rural*, *La Llosona* (☎985 860 607; ❸), 1km south of the new town in Granda-Ardines, is good value with great views of the surrounding area. At the top end of the market, Ribadesella's best hotel, the old-fashioned *Gran Hotel del Sella* (☎985 860 150; ℱ985 857 449; ❼), fronts the beach and the promenade. If your budget doesn't quite stretch that far, there are also two **campsites**: *Los Sauces*, near the beach on Carretera San Pedro la Playa (☎985 861 312; Easter & mid-June to Sept), and *Ribadesella* (☎985 858 293; Easter & July–Sept), just south of Puente del Pilar, at Sebreño.

For **meals**, the *Rompeolas* on c/Manuel Fernandez Juncos is a classic if slightly pricey *marisquería* in the old town, with piles of seafood lining its long wooden counter; alternatively, there's *Casa Basilio* on c/Manuel Caso de la Villa, which serves great tapas, or *Sidrería El Mesón* for a wide variety of *raciónes* on the same street. Nearer the bridge, *Restaurante Náutico* and *Bar del Puerto* are both good. **Internet** access is at *Sella System* opposite *Rompeolas* for €2 per hour.

Lastres, Colunga and Villaviciosa

Beyond Ribadesella the railway turns inland, as do most tourists, heading for Cangas de Onis and the western flanks of the Picos de Europa. The route into the mountains – the N634 and N625 – is a superb one, following the valley and gorge of the Río Sella. The coast around Gijón, Asturias's main industrial port, isn't pretty, though there are a few last highlights, including the town of **Colunga**, noted for its seafood and cider, and the fishing villages of **Lastres** and **Villaviciosa**. Colunga has a useful **turismo**, located in an original *hórreo* in the town park (summer only Tues–Sat 10am–2pm & 5–8pm, Sun 10am–3pm; ☎985 852 200).

Lastres

LASTRES, a couple of kilometres north of Colunga off the Santander–Gijón highway, is a tiny fishing village built dramatically on a steep cliffside with a new harbour and a couple of good beaches on its outskirts. It has escaped much tourist attention so far and if you've just come from a few strenuous days' trekking in the Picos, this would be as good a spot as any to recuperate. **Buses** run from Gijón via Ribadesella every two hours in summer.

Two neighbouring **restaurants** on the road down to the port, *Sidrería El Escanu* and *Bar Bitacora*, serve good seafood, with terrace views. There is only a handful of **hotels**, but *Casa Eutimio* (☎985 850 012; ❹), near the port in Plaza San Antonio and with its own seafood restaurant, is a good bet. If you have money to spare, the nearby *Miramar*, Bajada al Puerto (☎985 850 120; ❼, though much cheaper outside of July & August), has some rooms with great seaviews, and the luxury *Palacio de los Vallados*, Pedro Villarta (☎985 850 444, ℱ985 850 517; ❺), will also fit the bill. There are two *casas rurales*: *Pipo*, in the tiny village of Sales, 4km away (☎985 856 590; ❷), and *Pernús* (☎985 928 819; ❷) in Pernús, the next village along. The excellent beach, Playa la Griega, 2km to the east, has a **campsite**, *Costa Verde* (☎985 856 373; Easter & June–Sept).

Villaviciosa and around

VILLAVICIOSA, 30km from Gijón (daily buses on the hour 7am–9pm), is set in beautiful Asturian countryside, on the shores of the Río Villaviciosa, with green rolling hills behind. There's a market on Wednesday and an atmospheric old town where you'll find the thirteenth-century **Iglesia de Santa María**. The town is famed as the "apple capital" of Spain, and visits to the **cider factory**, *El Gaitero*, reveal how the country's most famous cider is manufactured (May–Sept Mon–Fri 10am–1.30pm & 4–6.30pm, Sat 10am–1.30pm; half-hour guided tours in Spanish, free). The factory is 1.5km outside town on the Santander road. Nearby there's a good **beach** for swimming – Playa Rodiles, visible from the main road.

Buses arrive at the terminal on c/Marqués de Villaviciosa, from where it is a short walk into town to the **turismo** (summer only Mon 10am–2pm & 5–8pm, Tues–Sat 10am–2pm & 4–7pm, Sun 10am–2pm; ☎985 891 759) on Parque Ballina. You'll find the cheapest **rooms** at the friendly *Pensión Sol*, c/Sol 27 (☎985 891 130; ❶), which is basic but good. A hundred yards from the turismo is *Hotel La Ría* (☎985 891 555; ❸), on c/Marqués de Villaviciosa, offering free Internet access to residents in the *ciber* below (€3 per hour for non-residents). On Plaza Carlos I, *Hotel Carlos I* (☎985 890 121, ℻985 890 051; ❸) and *Hotel Casa España* (☎985 892 030, ℻985 892 682; ❸) are more upmarket, but they offer deals out of season when prices fall dramatically. For **food**, the a clutch of bar-restaurants around Parque Ballina offers a good choice.

Nine kilometres southwest of Villaviciosa, tucked away in the beautiful Puelles valley, lies the Cistercian monastery of **Valdediós** (Tues–Sun: May–Oct 11am–1pm & 4.30–6.30pm; Nov–April 11am–1pm; €1 per church). Abandoned for many years, the buildings are now being restored and a small community of monks returned in 1992. It's worth a look around the grounds and impressive thirteenth-century monastery church, where you can attend one of the five offices sung daily, but the main sight is the wonderful **Iglesia de San Salvador**, built in the ninth century in the unique style known as Asturian, or pre-Romanesque; look out for the columns borrowed from a nearby Roman ruin and the beautiful geometric motifs in the stone windows. There are seven buses daily between Oviedo and Villaviciosa which stop at San Pedro de Ambas. From here, it's a 1.5km walk downhill to the monastery, where it's sometimes possible to stay in the **hospedería** (☎985 892 324).

Gijón and Avilés

On departing the tranquil Llanes coast or the isolation of the Picos, the industrial outskirts of **Gijón** and **Avilés** can initially come as something of a shock. Long the heart of the Asturian steel and mining ventures, the smoking factory chimneys and scarred hillsides are not pretty, but the cities have more than enough going for them to warrant an extended stay: Gijón has a big-city "feel", surprisingly good beaches and legendary nightlife, while Avilés boasts a well-preserved old centre. In addition, both cities know how to party, especially during **Carnaval** (see box, opposite) and during **Semana Santa**, when Avilés hosts some of the country's most spectacular parades.

Gijón

GIJÓN, the largest city in Asturias, was completely rebuilt after its destruction in the Civil War. It was the scene of one of the most intensive bombardments of the war, when, in August 1936, miners armed with sticks of dynamite stormed the barracks of the Nationalist-declared army. The beleaguered colonel asked ships from his own side, anchored offshore, to bomb his men rather than let them be captured. The city itself hosts a number of museums and other sights, and has a reputation for lively nightlife and wild weekends.

Carnaval in Asturias

Carnaval, the *mardi gras* week of drinking, dancing and excess, takes place over late February and early March. In Spain, the celebrations are reckoned to be at their wildest in Tenerife, Cadiz and Asturias – and, in particular, **Avilés**.

Events begin in **Avilés** on the **Saturday** before Ash Wednesday, when virtually the entire city dons fancy dress and takes to the streets. Many costumes are bizarre works of art ranging from toothbrushes to mattresses and packets of sweets. By nightfall, anyone without a costume is likely to be drenched in some form of liquid, as gangs of nuns, Red Indians and pirates roam the streets. Calle Galiana is central to the action, and the local fire brigade traditionally hoses down the street, and any passing revellers, with foam. A parade of floats also makes its way down this street, amid the frenzy.

The festivities, which include live music, fireworks and fancy-dress competitions, last till dawn. It's virtually impossible to find accommodation, but the celebrations continue throughout Asturias during the following week, so after a full night of revelling you can just head on to the next venue. The first buses leave town at 6.45am. Sunday is, in fact, a rest day before *Carnaval* continues in **Gijón** on the **Monday** night. Much the same ensues and fancy dress is again essential; La Ruta is the place to be for the start of the night, with people and events shifting between Plaza Mayor and the harbour area till dawn. On **Tuesday** night, the scene shifts to **Oviedo**: the crowds are smaller here and events are less frantic, but a fair part of the city again dons costume. There's a parade along Calle Uria, a midnight fireworks display in the Plaza Escandelera, and live bands in the Plaza Mayor.

Finally, on the Friday after Ash Wednesday, **Mieres**, a mining town, just southeast of Oviedo, plays host to *Carnaval*. Events take place in an area known as Calle del Vicio, which locals claim contains the highest concentration of bars in the province.

Arrival, orientation and information

The city **centre** is a fairly small area, just south of the old town and headland. Its three main squares, separated by a couple of blocks each, are, from south to north, Plaza El Humedal, Plaza El Carmen and Plaza El Marqués (flanked by the Palacio de Revillagigedo). The **train station** (FEVE and RENFE local services) is on Plaza El Humedal, and the **bus station** (a wonderful piece of Art Deco) just off it between c/Ribadesella and c/Llanes. Long-distance RENFE services use a third train station on Avenida de Juan Carlos I, west of the centre.

The **turismo** (Mon–Fri 9am–2pm & 4.30–6.30pm; ☎985 346 046) is on c/Marqués de San Esteban, off the Plaza del Marqués near the port. **Internet cafés** are dotted all over the place. Good value and open until the early hours of the morning are *Cafeteria San Siro* (€2 per hour) on c/Rufo Rendueles, behind Playa de San Lorenzo, and *El Café del Chat* on c/Ezcurdia 114 (€1.80 per hour or €1.25 per 30min, including a drink) a few blocks away. *Café Connexion* next to the bus station has an offer of €3 for any length of connection between 6.30am and 4pm (€2.10 per hour otherwise).

Accommodation

Finding a **place to stay** is rarely a problem, with a broad range of places to cater for all budgets. Most of the accommodation is concentrated at the lower end of town, beyond the Playa de San Lorenzo; good streets to head for include c/San Bernardo, c/Santa Lucía and c/Pedro Duro. The pleasant municipal **campsite** is 1.5km east along the coast at Las Cascrias (☎ & ☎985 365 755; Easter & June–Sept).

Hotel Asturias Plaza Mayor 11 ☏985 350 600, ⓔhotelasturias@fade.es. Friendly but pricey hotel on the atmospheric main square between the beach and port. ❻

Hostal Brasas c/San Antonio 12 ☏985 356 331. Large, modern rooms with TV and bathroom, well-located above a very reasonable *parrilla*, just around the corner from the turismo. ❸

Pensión Gonzalez c/San Bernardo 30 ☏985 355 863 Good *pensión* with large, airy rooms in a well-furnished old mansion house. **Pensión Argentina** ☏985 344 481 upstairs is slightly cheaper but very similar and also a good bet. Respectively ❷ & ❶

Hostal Manjón Plaza del Marqués 1 ☏985 352 378. Nicely located and reasonably-priced *hostal*; ask for a room overlooking the harbour. ❷

Pensión El Atillo c/Capua 17 ☏985 349 222. A good choice for the beach and nightlife, located just behind Playa de San Lorenzo and not far from *El Náutico*. ❸

Parador Molino Viejo Parque de Isabel la Católica ☏985 370 511, ⓕ985 370 233. Luxury accommodation, set in an attractive park at the east end of the beach. ❼

Hotel Pathos c/Santa Elena 6 ☏985 176 400, ⓌWww.celuisma.com. Upmarket business hotel offering Internet access in the rooms. ❻

The City

Visitors willing to spend a little time to get to know Gijón will be pleasantly surprised. Once past the industrial outskirts, the city has quite a breezy, open feel about it, with a grid of streets backing onto the sands of the **Playa de San Lorenzo**, a lengthy golden beach reminiscent of the one at San Sebastian. In winter, you'll find the occasional hardy surfer out here, while in the summer the whole city seems to descend for the afternoons and weekends, as well as the evening *paseo*.

The old part of town, **Cimadevilla**, occupies a headland northwest of the beach. Its chief monument is the eighteenth-century **Palacio de Revillagigedo** (summer Tues–Sat 11am–1.30pm & 4–9pm, Sun noon–2.30pm; winter Tues–Sat 10.30am–1.30pm & 4–8pm, Sun noon–2.30pm; free), built in a splendid mix of neo-Baroque and neo-Renaissance styles; it now houses a gallery of twentieth-century art, and hosts music, theatre and other cultural events. Facing the palace, in the centre of the square, is a statue of Pelayo, the seventh-century king who began the Reconquest. Nearby is the **Torre del Reloj**, c/Recoletas 5 (March–June & Sept Tues–Sat 10am–1pm & 5–8pm, Sun 11am–2pm; July & Aug Tues–Sat 11am–1.30pm & 5–9pm, Sun 11am–2pm; Oct–Feb Tues–Sat 10am–1pm & 5–7pm, Sun 11am–2pm; free), a modern tower built on the ruins of a sixteenth-century one, housing an interesting display about Gijón's history, but mainly worth climbing for the view across the city. At the end of the headland is the grassy **Parque La Atalaya**, with great views of the Cantabrian Sea framed by Eduardo Chillida's sculpture *Eulogy to the Horizon*.

West from Cimadevilla is the pretty **Puerto Deportivo**, the harbour area and main departure point for the city's evening and weekend *paseo*, which continues on through the Plaza Mayor and down along the beach promenade to the tranquil **Parque Isabel La Catolíca**. There are a few scattered museums here, the most unusual being the **Museo del Pueblo de Asturias**, c/La Guelga off Paseo Dr Fleming (summer Tues–Sat 11am–1.30pm & 5–9pm, Sun 11am–2pm; winter Tues–Sat 10am–1pm & 5–8pm, Sun 11am–2pm; free), which incorporates a bagpipe museum, housing an amazing array of instruments from all over the Celtic world and beyond.

Eating and drinking

The streets around the seafront and immediately behind contain a mass of little **café-restaurants**, all reasonably priced and most with a *menú*.

La Botica Indiana c/San Bernardo 2. Typical *sidrería* (cider house) under the arches on the Plaza Mayor.

Heladería Islandia c/San Antonio 4. Inventive ice-cream joint offering (among others) *sidra*, *fabada* and *cabrales* cheese flavours.

Casa Justo Avda. del Hermanos Felgueroso 50. Superb *sidrería* with a good restaurant behind it, specializing in seafood. Closed Thurs, first half of May and second half of Sept.

La Marina c/Trinidad 9. Fine *sidra* and tapas and the ideal place to assimilate yourself into the Asturian way of life. Closed Tues.

La Pondala Avda. Dionisio Cifuentes 58, Somio ☎985 361 160. Upmarket restaurant, a little way east of centre, famous for its seafood and rice. Closed Thurs & Nov.

El Puerto Puerto Deportivo. Posh and pricey, but the seafood menu is interesting, even if your budget doesn't stretch to €60 for a taste of caviar.

Closed Sun night.

El Retiro c/Begoña 26, La Ruta. Asturian cooking with an excellent-value three-course €6 *menú*.

Pizzería Vesuvio c/Muelle de Oriente. Good-size pizzas and Italian food at a price that won't break the bank. Closed Wed.

Sol Naciente c/Rufo Rendueles 4 ☎985 341 731. Standard Chinese fare but the best-value *menú* in town if you're on a budget. Three courses, plus drink, dessert, prawn crackers and liqueur for €5.50.

Torremar c/Ezcurdía 120. Wonderful place for *sidra* and *parrillas* (grills), and the place to be for carnivores.

Nightlife

Gijón's **nightlife** scene centres around the area known as **La Ruta**, a grid enclosed by c/Santa Lucía, c/Buen Suceso and c/Santa Rosa, a few hundred yards east of Plaza El Carmen. Especially popular are *La Gasolinera*, on c/Santa Rosa, and *La Noviera* nearby. There are all manner of **bars** along c/Rufo Rendueles and its extensions along the beach, including the stylish *Gavanna Playa* and the exceptionally loud *Zapping*, but the main **club and disco** area is focused around **El Náutico** further north. *Náutico* and *Otto*, in an unmissable building on El Náutico itself, are always full, especially after a long day on the beach, but you should also wander along the streets nearby, where c/Jacobo Olañeta and c/San Agustín are also lively.

In early July the city hosts Semana Negra, officially an arts festival, but fast turning into another excuse for the locals to party. The hub of the action is around Gijón's El Moliñon football stadium in Parque Isabel La Catolíca, and while there are a host of poetry recitals, art displays and culture groups dotted around, these days you are just as likely to see loud music, candyfloss and fairground rides.

Avilés

AVILÉS, 23km inland from Gijón, was once ranked among the most polluted cities in Europe. Ringed by line upon line of grim factories, even the hardiest of travellers may be put off by the approach, but the city has worked hard to clean up its act and its image, and those who press on to the arcaded centre of the old town will not be disappointed.

Arrival, information and accommodation

Avilés is a good transport junction and you may well find yourself here changing buses or trains. The **FEVE**, **RENFE** and **bus stations** are all sited in the same terminus on Avenida Telares just down from Parque Muelle and the old town. The city's excellent **turismo** (Mon–Fri 9.30am–2pm; ☎985 544 325) is off Plaza de España, at c/Ruíz Gómez 21, and the main **post office** is on c/La Ferrería a block or two behind. **Internet** access at *PC3*, c/Palacio Valdés, just around the corner from the turismo, costs €2 per hour, and there is also a clutch of cybercafés on c/Rivero that are open late, including *B@ngo* at no. 25, which closes when the last person leaves.

Staying in Avilés is surprisingly tricky as **accommodation** is scarce, and the reasonably priced *hostales* fill quickly. A good place to start looking is c/Fruta off Plaza España. *Hotel Don Pedro* (☎985 512 288; ④) at no. 22 has well-equipped rooms with beautiful stone walls, as well as its own *pensión* opposite – *La Fruta* (same number; ❸), which has a choice of rooms with or without bath. *Hotel Luzana*, c/Fruta 9 (☎985 565 840, ℻985 564 912; ❹), is more expensive and has rather less character, although its restaurant is good. At the bottom end of the scale, *Pensión El Norte*, c/La Estación 57 (☎985 564 803; ❶), opposite the station is as cheap as it is basic. Rather better is *Pensión Puente Azud*, c/El Acero 5 (☎985 550 177; ❷), though it is some way east of the centre near to the bridge.

The City

From the bus and train stations, c/La Estación heads directly into the heart of the old town. Halfway down the street is a statue of the diminutive Eugenia Martinez Vallejo, court jester to Carlos II, whose short, fat frame and pug-like features earned her the nickname "La Monstruosa". Strewn with fourteenth- and fifteenth-century churches and palaces, the **old district** is extremely pleasant, and most of the shops, bars and places to stay are here too, as well as the pretty, walled **Parque de Ferrera**. Among several churches worth a closer look are the Romanesque church **San Nicolás de Bari**, on c/San Francisco, and the thirteenth-century **Santo Tomás**. La Iglesia de los Padres Franciscanos contains the tomb of the erstwhile governor of Florida, Don Pedro Menéndez de Avilés. There are also some superb palaces, especially the Baroque **Camposagrado**, in Plaza Camposagrado, built in 1663, and the seventeenth-century **Palacio de Marqués de Ferrera** in Plaza de España, now an expensive hotel (☎985 129 080; ❽, ❻ at weekends). Around the corner on c/San Francisco is the city's most distinctive monument, the seventeenth-century **Fuente de los Caños** with its six grotesque heads spouting water.

Eating, drinking and nightlife

The area on and around Plazas de España, Domingo Acebal and Carbayedo is full of promising **bars and restaurants**, especially along c/del Ferrería and c/Rivero. *Casa Lin*, Avda. Telares 3, near the train station is a fine *sidrería* with excellent seafood. *Casa Tataguyo*, Plaza Carbayedo 6, a beautiful 1840s *mesón* (the oldest in town), and *La Fragata* near the church on Plaza Domingo Acebal serve Asturian specialities; all are moderately priced. If you're waiting for a bus or train, the bars along c/de la Estación diagonally across from the RENFE station offer excellent lunchtime *menús* for around €6, especially *Tasca El Matú* at no. 17, with its secluded rear patio. The **nightlife** scene changes rapidly and it is always best to seek local advice if you are planning a serious night on the tiles. The Sabugo district in the northwest of town continues to be a popular destination, and *Florida* and *Paradis* on c/Cámara are always busy. A younger crowd heads towards *Discoteca 4* on c/Demetrio Suárez in the old port area near the river.

Oviedo

OVIEDO's bourgeois culture and pretentious attitude are in stark contrast to the working-class ethos of its neighbours. As the Asturian capital, it has long been fairly wealthy, a history which can be traced through its plethora of grand administrative and religious buildings, lovingly restored and rendering the city one of the most attractive in the north. The old quarter, all the better for being completely pedestrianized, is a knot of squares and narrow streets built in warm yellow stone, while the newer part is redeemed by a huge public park right in

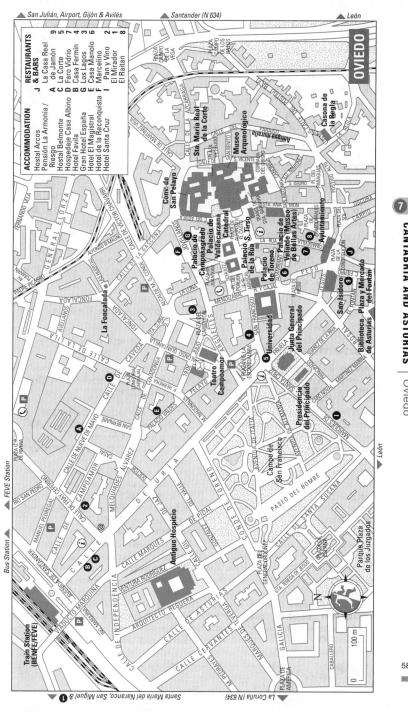

ACCOMMODATION
Hostal Arcos
Pensión La Armonia /
Riesgo
Hostal Belmonte
Hospedaje Casa Albino
Hotel Favila
Gran Hotel España
Hotel El Magistral
Hotel de la Reconquista
Hotel Santa Cruz

**RESTAURANTS
& BARS**
J La Casa Real
   de Jamón   9
A La Corte   5
D Faro Vidrio   7
B Casa Fermín   4
G Los Lagos   3
C Casa Manolo   6
   Marcelino
F El Mirador   2
I Pan y Vino   1
   El Raitan   8

Plaza
de Campo
de la Vega

Plaza
Campo
de los
Reyes

Casona de
la Regla

Museo
Arqueológico

Sta. María Real
de la Corte

Conv. de
San Pelayo

Antigua muralla

Palacio de
Camposagrado

Palacio de
Valdecarzana

Catedral

Palacio de
la Rúa

Palacio de
Toreno

S. Tirso

Velarde (Museo de
Bellas Artes)

Ayuntamiento

San Isidoro

Plaza y Mercado
del Fontán

Biblioteca
de Asturias

La Foncalada

Teatro
Campoamor

Universidad

Junta General
del Principado

Presidencia
del Principado

Campo de
San Francisco

Antiguo Hospicio

Parque Plaza
de los Juzgados

Train Station
(RENFE/FEVE)

FEVE Station

Bus Station

100 m

589

the centre. Throughout the city are excellent bars and restaurants, many aimed at the lively student population. The principal cultural reason for visiting the city, however, is to see three small **churches**. They are among the most remarkable in Spain, built in a style unique to Asturias which emerged in the wake of the Visigoths and before the Romanesque style had spread south from France. All of them date from the first half of the ninth century, a period of almost total isolation for the Asturian kingdom, which was then just 65km by 50km in area and the only part of Spain under Christian rule. Oviedo became the centre of this outpost in 810 with the residence of King Alfonso II, son of the victorious Pelayo (see p.579).

Arrival, information and orientation

Oviedo's transport connections are all conveniently located to the northeast of the city centre; the **RENFE** (⊕902 240 202) and **FEVE** (⊕902 100 818) **train stations** are in the same building on Avenida de Santander, and the **bus terminal** (⊕985 222 422) is just down the road to the northeast.

Central Oviedo is enclosed by a loop of roads. At its heart is the extensive **Parque de San Francisco**; the **Catedral** is a couple of blocks to the east of this, with the **Plaza de la Constitución** and **ayuntamiento** to its south. The city **turismo** (Mon–Fri 9am–2pm & 4.30–6.30pm, Sat–Sun 10am–2pm & 4.30–7.30pm; ⊕985 213 385, ⑤985 228 459), which also covers the whole of Asturias, is at c/Uría 64 near the train station; there's also a summer booth at Marqués de Santa Cruz 1 (Mon–Fri 10.30am–2pm & 4.30–7.30pm, Sat & Sun 11am–2pm; ⊕985 227 586).

Accommodation

Oviedo has a good supply of **accommodation**, with a concentration of cheaper *hostales* on c/Uría, opposite the RENFE train station and along c/Nueve de Mayo and its continuation, c/de Caveda.

Hostal Arcos c/Magdalena 3 ⊕985 214 773. Rather basic, but great location in the heart of old Oviedo, just off Plaza Mayor. ❷

Hostal Arias c/Palacio Valdés 12 ⊕985 215 097. Large, well-furnished en-suite rooms with TV. The best rooms have *terrazas* at no extra cost. The only drawback is that it is on the fifth floor, though there is a lift. ❸

Pensión La Armonia and **Pensión Riesgo** c/Nueve de Mayo 14 and 16 ⊕985 220 301. A pair of small, family-run *pensiones*. Both good value and not too far from the bus station. ❶

Hostal Belmonte c/Uría 31 ⊕985 241 020, ⑥calogon@teleline.es. Pleasant and modern, some with clean but slightly makeshift bathrooms. ❷

Hospedaje Casa Albino c/Gascona 2 ⊕985 210 445. Cheap and functional in the heart of the *sidrería* district near the cathedral. Opposite a restaurant of the same name which does an excellent *menú* for €6. ❷

Hotel El Magistral c/Jovellanos 3 ⊕985 215 116, ⑩www.elmagistral.com. Comfortable, ultra-modern hotel, behind the cathedral. ❺

Hotel Favila c/Uría 37 ⊕985 253 877. Pleasant business hotel with half-board and full-board options. En-suite rooms with TV and telephone. ❸

Gran Hotel España c/Jovellanos 2 ⊕985 220 596, ⑤985 222 140. Grand hotel, more than a century old, close by the cathedral. Expensive, but reduced weekend rates. ❻

Hotel de la Reconquista Gil de Jaz 16 ⊕985 241 100, ⑩www.hoteldelareconquista.com. Luxurious and seriously decadent accommodation with a price tag to match, in a seventeenth-century palace near Parque de San Francisco. ❼

Hotel Santa Cruz c/Marqués de Santa Cruz 6 ⊕985 223 711. Cheerful and friendly with a great location overlooking Parque de San Francisco. Rooms with TV and bathroom. Recommended. ❸

The Town

Around the cathedral, enclosed by scattered sections of the medieval town walls, is a compact, attractive quarter, the remains of **Old Oviedo**. As at Gijón, much was destroyed in the Civil War when Republican Asturian miners laid siege to the Nationalist garrison; the defenders were relieved by a *gallego* detachment when on the brink of surrender. The centre nevertheless preserves a number of medieval churches and squares, and some fine government buildings and town houses built on the industrial wealth of the area, although most of these cannot be visited.

The cathedral and around

In the ninth century, King Alfonso II built a chapel, the Cámara Santa (Holy Chamber), to house the holy relics rescued from Toledo when it fell to the Moors. Remodelled in the twelfth century, this now forms the inner sanctuary of Oviedo's **Catedral** (Mon–Fri: March to mid-May & Oct 10am–1pm & 4–7pm; mid-May to June 10am–1pm & 4–8pm; July–Sept 10am–8pm; Nov–Feb 10am–1pm & 4–6pm; €2.40 including Cámara Santa & Diocesan museum), an unusually uncluttered Gothic structure at the heart of the modern city. The **Cámara Santa** is in fact a pair of interconnecting chapels. The innermost, with its primitive capitals, is thought to be Alfonso's original building. The antechapel, rebuilt in 1109, is a quiet little triumph of Spanish Romanesque; each of the six columns supporting the vault is sculpted with a pair of superbly humanized Apostles. Built around the attractive Gothic cloister, itself built on pre-Romanesque foundations, the **Diocesan museum** has a higher-quality collection of devotional art and artefacts than is typical.

Around the cathedral, some of the city's ancient **palaces** – not least the archbishop's, next door – are worth a look, though most are in government use and none is open to visitors. Of interest, too, is the **Museo Arqueológico** (Tues–Sat 10am–1.30pm & 4–6pm, Sun 11am–1pm; free), immediately behind the cathedral in the former convent of San Vicente. This displays various pieces of sculpture from the "Asturian-Visigoth" churches.

The nearest of these churches, **San Julian de los Prados**, or **Santullano** (Tues–Fri: May–Sept 10am–1pm & 4–6pm, Sat 9.30–11.30am & 3.30–5.30pm, Mon 10am–1pm; Nov–April noon–1pm & 4–5pm; €1.20 including guided tour in Spanish), is ten minutes' walk to the northeast along the c/de Gijón, and by some unfortunate quirk of local city planning stands right next to a highway. However, it's well worth seeing. Built around 830, it is considerably larger and more spacious than the other Asturian churches, with an unusual "secret chamber" built into the outer wall. There are original frescoes inside, executed in similar style to those of Roman villas.

Santa María del Naranco

The greatest of the Asturian churches, indeed the architectural gem of the principality, is **Santa María del Naranco** (May to mid-Oct Tues–Sat 9.30am–1.30pm & 3.30–7.30pm, Sun 9.30am–1.30pm; mid-Oct to April Tues–Sat 10am–1pm & 3–5pm; closed Mon; €2.20 guided tour in Spanish), majestically located on a wooded slope 3km above the city. It's a 45 minutes' walk from the station through the quiet suburb of Ciudad Naranco, slowly climbing the slopes of the eponymously named Monte. If you lack the energy for the walk, there is a bus (#3). You should get off at La Cruce, from where a pedestrian track leads up to the church.

The initial glimpses of the warm stone and simple bold outline, in perfect harmony with its surroundings, led Jan Morris to describe it as "formidable beyond its scale", but while it retains the ability to impress, the effect is somewhat lessened by the huge tour groups that descend upon it in summer. The present structure was originally designed as a palatial hunting lodge for Ramiro I (842–852) Alfonso's successor, being converted into a church at the end of the ninth century. Architecturally, the open porticoes at both ends are most interesting – an innovation developed much later in Byzantine churches – as well as the thirty or so decorative medallions that skirt the roof. The crypt bears a notable resemblance to the Cámara Santa back in town.

A couple of hundred metres beyond Santa María is King Ramiro's palace chapel, **San Miguel de Lillo** (same hours and ticket as Santa María), built with soft golden sandstone and red tiles. This is generally assumed to be by the same architect as Santa María, Tiodo (whom some scholars also credit with the Cámara Santa and San Julian de los Prados), though its design is quite different. In fact, less than half of the original ninth-century church remains, the rest having been swept away by a landslide and rebuilt in the thirteenth century. Much of its interior sculpture has been removed to the archeological museum, but look for the window grilles carved from single slabs of limestone, and the superb Byzantine-style carved door frames depicting, incongruously enough, the investiture of a Roman consul, complete with circus-style festivities.

Further up from the two little churches is a Rio-style **figure of Christ** that looks out over the city and is spectacularly illuminated at night. It was built by Republican prisoners of war, and, although ugly close up (it's constructed from concrete blocks), it affords wonderful views of the city below.

Eating, drinking and nightlife

Head to the area around the cathedral for the best **eating and drinking**. You can't help but notice the *sidrerías*, spit-and-sawdust places with a lot of people pouring a lot of drink from a great height. This may baffle the newcomer, but just order a bottle (about €2), and you'll soon pick up the right drinking method. Most of the best, including *Asturias* and *La Pumarada*, are along c/Gascona, down from the cathedral. There are plenty of cafés and bars, too, most with remarkable-value *menús* – anything over €7 is expensive – as well as more pricey traditional *mesónes* serving *fabada* and other Asturian fare.

La Casa Real de Jamon c/Covadonga 20. A carnivore's dream, with meats hanging from the ceiling, adorning the walls and accompanying just about every dish. Specializes in *jamónes* and *quesos*.

La Corte Esq c/Fruela y c/San Francisco. Chic café-bar metamorphosing into a stylish restaurant at night. Try the tasty *salmon a la naranja*.

Faro Vidrio c/Cimadevilla 19. Upmarket *sidrería-mariquería* with attractive garden. Large and varied tapas menu in addition to main menu.

Casa Fermín c/San Francisco 8 ☎985 216 497. A classic, much-written-about restaurant, serving imaginatively recreated Asturian dishes. Very pricey, you'll get little for under €18, but worth it for a special occasion. Closed Sun.

Los Lagos Plaza del Carbayón 3. Excellent *sidrería* filled with the heady smell of strong Asturian foods, cider and sawdust. Another branch on c/Cervantes 7.

Casa Manolo c/Altamirano 9 ☎985 212 561. Superior and pricey *sidrería*, known for its game and tapas.

Marcelino Pan y Vino c/Campoamor 17. Bustling, characterful, sawdust-floored *sidrería*, jam-packed with locals taking advantage of the generous portions. Closed Sun.

El Mirador On the road to Naranco. One of several decent restaurants with terraces that look out over the whole city and the mountains beyond.

El Raitán Plaza Trascorrales 6 ☎985 214 218. Superb, atmospheric restaurant in a delightful square off Plaza Mayor. There is a selection of *menús*, ranging from €14 to the huge *menú degustación de cocina Asturiana* for €26. Closed Sun night.

Nightlife and entertainment

Oviedo can be quiet in summer when the student population is away and the local youth tends to flock to the nearby resorts of Salinas and Pola de Siero, but during the rest of the year there's a huge scene. Irish pubs have taken hold in a big way, particularly along c/Jovellanos, and you'll also find loud Irish music playing at the popular *Ca Beleño* and *Antigua Estación* on c/Martínez Vigil. Calle Mon is the place to go for the thriving **disco-pub** scene, with music to cater for most tastes. The *Diario Roma* is loud and crowded with a great atmosphere, while *Maná* next door and the retro *Twentieth Century Bar* opposite are also popular. *Flamin*, on the nearby Plaza de Sol, plays pop and rock, and on the tiny c/Carta Puebla, off c/Postigo Alto, *Planeta Tierra* hosts a more dance-oriented scene. *Gotíco* at no. 2 has a harder rock edge.

Places on c/Altamirano stay open a bit later – *El Hispania* has a good selection of music, *La Botica* more of a dance feel and *Tamara* a mixed crowd. Two big popular clubs are *Tribeca* on c/del Peso, off Plaza Mayor, and *La Real* on c/Cervantes, good for house and with a mixed gay/straight crowd.

For **classical music**, watch out for Oviedo's Orquestra de Asturias, who are based here and perform mainly in the Teatro Campoamor (☎985 207 590). There are usually a couple of concerts each week, and summer performances in the university and cathedral cloisters.

Listings

Airport Aeropuerto de Asturias (☎985 127 500) is 13km away in Ranon, just off the N632. Regular flights to Madrid, Barcelona, Canary Islands, Balearics, London Gatwick and Paris.

American Express c/o Viajes Cafranga, c/Uría 26 ☎985 225 217.

Books Librería Cervantes, c/Dr Casal 3/9, has a good stock, including walking and wildlife guides to Asturias, and English-language novels.

Car rental Avis, c/Ventura Rodríguez 12 ☎985 241 383; Europcar, c/Uría, in RENFE station ☎985 245 712; National Atesa, c/Asturias 41 ☎985 229 940.

Internet access *Workcenter*, c/Fray Ceferino y c/Uría, is open 24 hours (€3 per hour). *Ciberexpres@* on the second floor of the train station is cheaper (€2.40 per hour) but closed Sun & Sat afternoon.

Laundry *Wash n Dry* (daily 9am–9pm; €4.50 per load, drying €2), though self-service only on Sundays.

Post office The *Correos Principal* is at c/Alonso Quintanilla 1 (Mon–Fri 8.30am–8.30pm, Sat 9.30am–2pm).

Taxis Radio Taxi Oviedo (☎985 250 000); Radio Taxi Principado (☎985 252 500).

Telephones There is a *locutorio* just off Plaza Primo de Rivera on Avenida General Elorza for international phone calls and Internet access.

Trekking The Federacíon Asturiana de Montaña, Avda. Julian Clavería (☎985 252 362), provides information and organizes treks in the Picos. The student agency, TIVE, c/Calvo Sotelo 5 (☎985 231 112), also offers good-value trekking trips.

West to Galicia

The **coast west of Avilés**, as far as the Río Navia, is pretty rugged, with scarcely more than a handful of resorts carved out from the cliffs. The most attractive by far is the old port and resort of **Luarca**, but there are other pretty ports here too, notably **Cudillero**. West again from the Río Navia, the coast becomes marshy and, save for an honorary mention of the attractive fishing village of **Tapia de Casariego**, unexceptional. Again, the FEVE line trails the coast, with some spectacular sections, though some of the stations (including Cudillero and Luarca) are inconveniently sited some way out of town.

Inland from Oviedo, the N634 and C630 offer a winding approach over the hills to Lugo in Galicia. The old town of **Salas**, with its castle, is of passing interest, but the main appeal of the route is the mountainous wildness of this area, which hardly sees a tourist from one year to the next.

Cudillero

CUDILLERO is a small, active and picturesque fishing port, with brightly coloured arcaded houses rising one upon another over a steep horseshoe of cliffs around the port. Despite rapidly encroaching tourism, the town nonetheless manages to retain its charm. As there's no beach as such here – the nearest is **Playa Aguilar**, 3km to the east – the most obvious attractions are the **fish tavernas** in its cobbled, seaside plaza; at weekends these are packed out, with prices geared to tourist rather than local trade. *Mariño*, on c/Concha de Artedo, is renowned for its traditional Asturian fish dishes and has a terrace with views along the beach.

Practicalities

Cudillero can be reached by **FEVE trains** from Avilés or Oviedo; the station is at the top of town, a fifteen-minute walk from the centre. The **bus station** is midway between here and the town centre, with thirteen daily buses to Avilés and a sporadic service to Oviedo and Gijón, although you can walk 3km to **El Pito** on the main road to pick up the full coastal service. In summer, there's a **turismo** (Mon–Fri 10am–9pm, Sat & Sun 3–8pm; ☎985 591 377) on Plaza de la Marina, near the harbour.

The village is reasonably well supplied with **accommodation**, though it tends to be pricey. Hotels include the well-equipped *San Pablo*, c/Suárez Inclán 38 (☎985 591 155; ❸), where rooms have TV and telephone, and the excellent *La Casona de Pio*, c/Riofrio 3 (☎985 591 512; ❸), with en-suite rooms and room service. At the lower end of the scale and on the road out of town towards El Pito is the very clean and modern *Pensión Álvaro* (☎985 590 204; ❷). The best of the town's **campsites** is *Camping Cudillero* (☎985 590 663; Easter & June to mid-Sept), off the same road above Playa Aguilar.

Luarca

The coast west of Cudillero is rugged and the main highway, the N632, leaps over viaducts spanning deep, pine-wooded gorges. About 50km west of Cudillero is the port of **LUARCA**, accessed from the N632 by a road that dips down steeply to the coast. This is one of the most attractive towns along the whole northern coastline, a mellow place, built around an S-shaped cove surrounded by sheer cliffs. Down below, the town is bisected by a small, winding river, and knitted together by numerous narrow bridges.

Luarca is a seaside resort in a very modest sort of way. In contrast to Cudillero, it has defiantly retained its traditional character, including a few *chigres* – old-fashioned Asturian taverns – where you can be initiated into the art of *sidra* drinking. The town **beach** is divided in two. The closer strip is narrower but more protected, the broader one beyond the jetty is subject to seaweed litter. From the turismo, c/de la Carril leads up to the cliffs overlooking the port where you will find a decorative **cemetery** considered by many the most attractive in Asturias, a hermitage chapel and a lighthouse. Nearby, the excellent **Aula del Mar** (summer daily 11am–1pm & 4–9pm; winter same hours weekends only; €3), a marine zoology museum, contains the largest collection of giant squid in Europe. The fishing harbour area is the heartbeat of the town: cross the bridge from the plaza, and follow the river. You can watch the small fishing boats returning at around midnight and see the catch auctioned off at the *lonja* at around 3pm the following afternoon.

Practicalities

Luarca has good **bus** connections to Oviedo, Gijón, Avilés and into Galicia; you'll find the bus station just off c/del Crucero on the river. The FEVE station is 2km out of town. The **turismo** (April–Sept Mon–Fri 11am–2pm & 4–8pm, Sat–Sun 11am–2pm & 5–8pm; ☎985 640 083), at c/Olavarrieta 27, provides lists of private rooms and apartments. There is also a summer kiosk on Plaza Alfonso X (daily 11am–3pm & 4–8pm). **Internet** access at *Ciber C@lifornia* (Mon–Fri 10am–2pm & 4.30–10.30pm, Sat 10am–2pm) on c/Ramón Asenjo costs €2.40 per hour.

On the way into town, there are some good **places to stay**, including *El Redondel* (☎985 640 733; ❷), on the main highway, 3km from the centre, in Almuña. In town there are two good *hostales* near the bus station – *Oria*, c/Crucero 7 (☎ 985 640 385; ❸), with a garden terrace and TVs in the rooms, and, almost next door, *Oviedo* (☎985 640 906; ❸) with ten comfortable rooms, half of which are doubles. Just around the corner on the river is the more upmarket *Hotel Gayoso*, Paseo Gómez 4 (☎985 640 054, ℉985 470 271; ❺), reputedly the oldest hotel in Spain (founded 1856), which has a cheaper annexe (❹) on Plaza Alfonso. *Hotel Rico* (☎985 470 585; ❸) at Plaza Alfonso 6 is also good value, with clean, modern rooms with TV, and Internet access in the café below. *Hotel Baltico* (☎985 640 991; ❸) has nice views over the harbour and a good restaurant. A YHA Hostel (☎985 640 676; €30 non-members, €17 members) on Plaza Ramón Losada, next to the Aula del Mar, has full- and half-board options, but is some way from the centre and fills quickly with groups in summer. Facing the lighthouse across a rocky cove is a **campsite**, *Los Cantiles* (☎985 640 938; open all year), with facilities to match its superb setting.

You'll find an excellent **restaurant**, *Casa Consuelo*, on the main road, Carreterra San Sebastián, which attracts people from miles around; try the *merluza con anguilas* (hake with eels). In town, the gourmet choice is the excellent *Villablanca*, at Avda. de Galicia 27. In the port area you can pretty much take your pick of a number of good seafood restaurants, endowed daily with the pick of the day's catch. *El Barometro* and *Mesón de la Mar* are both good, while portions at *Mesón El Ancre* are always large. For cheaper but still high-quality cuisine, try *La Estrella*, Ramón Asenjo 26, also in the port area.

Luarca to Ribadeo

Fifteen kilometres west from Luarca, **NAVIA** is a pleasant little port, though it lacks some of the style and life of its neighbour. On approach, crossing the wide Río Navia gives a foretaste of Galicia´s *rías* or estuaries. If you have transport, the inland route from here to Lugo is fascinating. If you want **to stay**, the *Palacio Arias*, Avda. de los Emigrantes 11 (☎985 473 671, ℉985 473 683; ❸–❺), is quite luxurious, even in the less expensive modern annexe, while cheaper options include *La Barca*, c/Manuel Suárez 19 (☎985 473 477; ❸), and *Hostal La Marina*, c/Salazar 61 (☎985 630 602; ❷). At **COAÑA**, 5km south of Navia and connected by local buses, there's a *castro*, or Celtic settlement (Tues–Sun 11am–2.30pm & 4–7.30pm; free), and beyond that the road winds above the reservoirs of the Navia River before twisting into Galicia and the remote mountainous region around Fonsagrada.

The best beach along this stretch is almost the last in Asturias, the **Playa de Los Campos**, which flanks the fishing village of **TAPIA DE CASARIEGO**. This is a lively place, with an entertaining "alternative" Teatro Popular, and a very helpful **turismo** (mid-June to mid-Sept Mon–Sat 10.30am–2pm & 5–8.30pm; ☎985 472 968) in a small kiosk in the plaza. There are several reasonably priced **hotels**, including *La Ruta* (☎985 628 138; ❸), on Avenida Primo de Rivera, and *Puente de los Santos* (☎985 628 155, ℉985 628 437; ❸), just opposite. Buses stop right outside. Just outside town are two **campsites**, about 1km towards Ribadeo: *Playa de Tapia* (☎985 472 721; June to mid-Sept) and *El Carbayín* (☎ & ℉985 623 709; open all year). Downhill from the main plaza, the port area is again the place to eat and drink, though many of the bars only open evenings and at weekends. *Palermo* on c/Bonifacio Amago 13 is an upmarket choice specializing in regional Asturian cuisine. For dessert, try the *helado de queso*.

CASTROPOL, set back from the coast on the Río Eo – the border with Galicia – is a tiny, pretty place with a few places to stay. *Peña Mar* (☎985 635 149; ❸) is the best option, but you're better off staying across the border in Ribadeo (see p.623). There's a **turismo** (Tues–Sat 10am–2pm & 5–8pm, Sun 10am–3pm; ☎608 380 386) on the main highway, if you're entering from Galicia and want pamphlets and information on Asturias.

Salas

Standing in the shadow of forested mountainsides, the winding, decorative stone streets of **SALAS**, 35km west of Oviedo, represent the last worthwhile stopover in Asturias. The town was once the home of the Marqués de Valdés-Salas, founder of Oviedo University and one of the prime movers of the Inquisition, and is chock-full of period buildings bearing the coats of arms of local noble families. The town **castle** is actually the Marqués's old palace; you can climb an adjoining tower from the **turismo** on Plaza de la Campa (Mon–Sat: summer 11am–2pm & 4–8pm; winter 9am–2pm & 4–7pm; ☎985 830 988) for fine views of the town and surrounding countryside. Among the other monuments are a sixteenth-century **Colegiata** and, in the main square, the tenth-century church of **San Martín**.

If you want to **stay**, there are two good options: the *Hotel Castillo de Valdés Salas* (☎985 830 173, ℉985 830 183; ❹), in the castle, with an out-of-the-ordinary restaurant; and the cheaper *Casa Soto*, c/Arzobispo Valdés 9 (☎985 830 037; ❷), which has big, clean rooms. **Buses** to Oviedo leave on the hour from outside the *Café Berlin*.

Travel details

Trains

RENFE

Oviedo to: Barcelona (2 daily; 12hr–13hr 15min); León (7 daily; 2hr–2hr 30min); Madrid (3 daily; 5hr 50min–8hr 35min).

Santander to: Madrid (3 daily; 6hr 10min–8hr 35min), change at Palencia for east–west routes including León.

FEVE

This delightful independent service (🕸 www.feve.es) runs along the north coast between Bilbao, Santander, Oviedo and Ferrol. The narrow-gauge railway has recently been modernized, and the line is punctual and scenic, though still slow for longer trips; the full journey from Ferrol to Bilbao can't be done in one day. Timetables can be picked up at any main station, but these can be confusing. In practical terms it is best to think of the service divided between through trains that cover the longer distances between the big cities, and local trains, which run more frequently between the smaller towns. There are also a few *cercanías*, or local branch lines, most of which are centred around Gijón.

Through trains: Bilbao to Santander (3 daily; 2hr 30min); Santander to Oviedo (2 daily; 4hr 25min); Oviedo to Ferrol (2 daily; 6hr 30min).

Local trains: Orejo to Santander (18 daily; 25min); Santander to Puente de San Miguel (every 30min; 25min); Puente de San Miguel to Cabezon de la Sal (hourly; 20min); Cabezon to Llanes (2 daily; 1hr); Llanes to Ribadesella-Infiesto (3 daily in winter, 5 in summer; 35min); Ribadesella to Nava (7 daily; 1hr 8min); Nava to Oviedo (24 daily; 45min); Oviedo to Pravia (21 daily; 1hr); Pravia to Cudillero (18 daily; 20–30min); Cudillero to Navia (3 daily; 1hr 20min); Navia to Ribadeo (2 daily; 50min); Ribadeo to Ferrol (4 daily; 3hr).

Branch lines: Gijón to Avilés (30 daily; 40min); Gijón to Pravia (for main line to Ferrol; 15 daily; 30min).

Buses

The majority of buses along the coast, and all those covering longer distances, are run by the Alsa bus company (ⓦwww.alsa.es). Some of these buses covering shorter distances are also labelled EASA or Turytrans, but the livery is the same distinctive blue-grey and all buses carry the Alsa logo. A number of smaller companies operate more local services between coastal resorts and inland destinations, but you should note that these buses often have reduced services outside July and August.

Castro Urdiales to: Bilbao (10 daily; 1hr); Santander (13–18 daily; 1hr–1hr 50min); Vitoria (3 daily; 1hr 15min–1hr 50min).

Comillas to: San Vicente (3 daily; 30min); Santander (7 daily; 45min); Santillana (4 daily; 35min).

Gijón to: Bilbao via Oviedo (3 daily; 4–5hr); León via Oviedo (10–11 daily; 2hr 30min); Madrid via Oviedo (11–13 daily; 5hr 30min–6hr); Oviedo (every 15min; 1hr); Ribadeo via Luarca, Navia, Castropol and Vegadeo (4 daily; 3hr–3hr 30min); Salamanca (5 daily; 4hr 30min–5hr); Sevilla (3 daily; 12hr–12hr 45min); Villaviciosa (14–15 daily; 45min).

Llanes to: Madrid via Cangas and Oseja (1 daily; 8hr); Oviedo via Ribadesella (7–9 daily; 1hr 30min–2hr 30min); San Vicente (6 daily; 30min); Santander (7 daily; 1hr 30min–2hr); Unquera (4 daily; 20min).

Oviedo to: Avilés (every 30min; 1hr); Cangas de Onis (10–14 daily; 1hr–1hr 30min); A Coruña via Betanzos (3 daily; 3hr 45min–5hr 45min); Covadonga (5 daily; 1hr 20min–1hr 45min); Cudillero (1–2 daily; 1hr 10min); Gijón (hourly; 1hr); León (10–11 daily, 1hr 30min–2hr); Lugo (3 daily; 4hr 15min–5hr); Madrid (12 daily; 5hr 30min); Pontevedra (2 daily; 7hr 30min); Ribadeo via Luarca (6 daily; 3hr–3hr 30min); Ribadesella (8–11 daily; 1hr 20min–2hr); Santander (2–5 daily; 2hr 15min–3hr 15min); Santiago (3 daily; 4hr 30min–6hr 45min); Sevilla (3 daily; 11hr 30min–12hr 15min); Valladolid (5 daily; 3hr 15min–4hr); Vigo (2 daily; 6hr 45min–8hr); Villaviciosa via San Pedro de Ambas (7 daily; 1hr).

Picos buses Arenas de Cabrales–Cangas de Onis (4 daily; 45min); Bustio–Arenas via Panes (2 daily; 50min); Cangas de Onis–Covadonga (9 daily; 45min); Cangas de Onis–Posada de Valdeón via Sajambre (1 daily in summer; 2hr 15min); Llanes–Madrid via Cangas, Sajambre and Riaño (1 daily in summer; 3 weekly in winter; 6hr 15min); León–Posada de Valdeón via Riaño and Portilla de la Reina (1 daily; 3hr); Potes–Espinama–Fuente Dé (3 daily; 45min). Also Land Rover service between Valdeón and Caín.

Ribadesella to: Lastres (7 daily; 35min); Llanes (8–10 daily; 40min); Oviedo via Arriondas (change at Arriondas for Cangas; 6–9 daily; 1hr–2hr); San Vicente (1 daily; 1hr 10min); Villaviciosa (7 daily; 1hr).

San Vicente to: Llanes (5 daily; 35min); Ribadesella (1 daily; 1hr); Santander (1–4 daily; 1hr–1hr 35min).

Santander to: Barcelona (3 daily; 9hr); Bilbao (28 daily, 10 of which continue to French border; 1hr 30min–2hr); Castro Urdiales (9–13 daily; 1hr); Comillas (7 daily; 45min; more by changing in Torrelavega); Laredo (18–23 daily; 40min); León (1–3 daily, 1 via Potes; 3hr 30min–5hr); Llanes (7 daily; 1hr 15min); Logroño (1–2 daily, 3hr 20min–4hr 35min); Oviedo (6 daily; 2hr 15min–3hr 15min); Potes via San Vicente and Unquera (3 daily; 3hr); Puente Viesgo (5 daily; 40min); Santiago (2 daily; 11hr); Santillana (7 daily, 4 daily in winter; 45min); San Vicente la Barquera (2 daily; 1hr); Vitoria via Castro Urdiales (5 daily; 2hr 15min); Zaragoza (2–3 daily, 4hr 30min).

Ferries

Car/passenger ferry from Santander to Plymouth (Mon & Thurs), 24hr; to Poole (Feb to early March weekly; 28hr).

Galicia

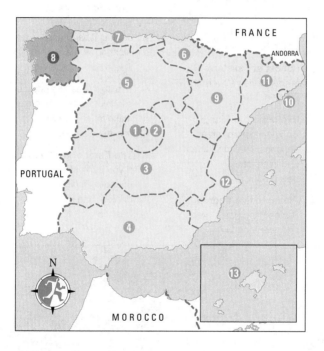

CHAPTER 8

Highlights

* **Santiago de Compostela** With the magnificent cathedral at its centre, this is one of the most beautiful cities in Spain. See p.605

* **A Coruña** Perched on the rugged northwestern coast, this Atlantic port is one of the most underrated cities in Spain. See p.627

* **Sunset at Finisterre** For fantastic views over the Atlantic. See p.634

* **Exploring the Rias Baixas** Hosts of great beaches, fishing villages and lively bars. See p.635

* **Pimientos de Padrón** Randomly piquant green peppers fried in hot oil and sea salt. See p.638

* **Pontevedra** Pontevedra's sleepy *zona monumental* metamorphoses into a lively party zone after dark. See p.644

* **A mariscada and some white wine** Galicia is renowned for its delicious seafood and unique *Ribeiro* and *Albariño* wines. See p.654

* **The Illas Cíes** The pristine sands of these three islets make for an irresistible day-trip. See p.650

* **The Parador at Baiona** If you can't stretch to spending a night, try a drink at one of Spain's best hotels. See p.651

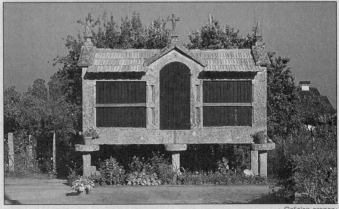

△ Galician granary

Galicia

emote, rural, and battered by the Atlantic, Galicia is a far cry from the popular image of Spain. It not only looks like Ireland; there are further parallels in the climate, culture and music, as well as the ever-visible traces of its Celtic past. Above all, despite its green and fertile

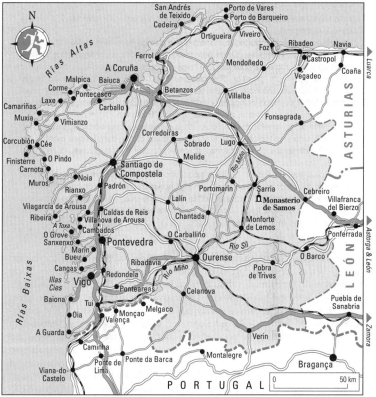

Gallego food and drink

Gallegans boast that their **seafood** is the best in the world, and although the residents of Newfoundland may have a thing or two to say about it, there is no doubting the quality and sheer diversity of what is available. Local wonders to look out for include *vieiras* (the scallops whose shells became the symbol of St James), *mejillones* (the rich orange mussels from the *rías*), *cigallas* (Dublin Bay prawns, though often inadequately translated as shrimp), *anguilas* (little eels from the River Minho), *navajas* (razor shells), *percebes* (barnacles), *nécoras* (shore crabs) and *centollas* (spider crabs). *Pulpo* (octopus) is so much a part of *gallego* eating that there are special *pulperías* cooking it in the traditional copper pots, and it is a mainstay of local country fiestas. In the province of Pontevedra alone, Vilanova de Arousa has its own octopus festival, Arcade has one devoted to oysters, and O Grove goes all the way, with a generalized seafood fiesta. When eaten as *tapas* or *raciónes* seafood is not overly expensive, although there are a few exceptions. Tantalizing tanks full of a variety of crabs and lobsters are always on display at restaurants, but demand is so high that many of these specialities have to be imported from abroad and prices are correspondingly elevated.

Throughout Galicia there are superb **markets**; the coastal towns have their rows of seafront stalls with supremely fresh fish, while cities such as Santiago have grand old arcaded market halls, piled high with farm produce from the surrounding countryside. Most enjoyable of all are ports like Cambados, with *lonjas* open to the public, where you can wait for the fishing boats to come home (usually around midnight, but more like 6am in A Coruña) and watch the auctioning of their catch – much of which will have left Galicia well before dawn for the restaurants of Madrid, on the special nightly train.

Another speciality, imported from the second *gallego* homeland of Argentina, is the **churrasquería** (grill house). Often unmarked and needing local assistance to find, these serve up immense *churrascos* – huge portions of boned steaks cooked on a traditional open grill (*parrilla*). The *gallegos* don't normally like their food highly spiced, but *churrascos* are usually served with a devastating garlic-based *salsa picante*. Other common dishes are *caldo gallego*, a thick stew of cabbage and potatoes in a meat-based broth, *caldeirada*, a filling fish soup, *lacon con grelos*, ham boiled with turnip greens, and the ubiquitous *empanada*, a light-crusted pasty, often filled with tuna and tomato. Should you be around during the summer months, be sure to try *pimientos de Padrón*, sweet green peppers fried in oil, served as a kind of lucky dip with a few memorable spicy ones in each serving.

The local beer is Estrella Galicia, good and strong. **Liqueurs** tend to be fiery, based on the clear *aguardiente* (elsewhere known as *eau de vie* or *aquavit*), nowadays often flavoured with herbs or coffee liquor; one much-loved *gallego* custom is the *queimada*, when a large bowl of *aguardiente* with fruit, sugar and coffee-grains is set alight and then drunk hot.

appearance, Galicia has a similar history of famine and poverty, with a decline in population owing to forced emigration which is only now slowly being reversed with government subsidies for returning emigrants of *gallego* ancestry.

Galicia is lush and heavily wooded in native oaks and pines, although subsidized plantations of imported eucalyptus are becoming dominant. The **coastline** is shaped by fjord-like inlets, source of some of the best **seafood** in Europe. In the north these *rías* shelter unspoiled old villages and fine beaches, while the sunnier southern coast is becoming increasingly built up with new resorts and roads. As you enter Galicia from the east, the rolling meadows of Asturias are replaced by a patchwork of tiny fields, with terraces of vines supported on granite props and allotments full of turnip-tops and cabbages growing on stalks. Archaic inheritance laws have meant a constant division and redivision of the land into little plots too small for machinery and worked with primitive agricultural methods; ox carts with solid wooden wheels are still seen on the backroads. Everywhere you see *hórreos*, granaries made here of granite rather than wood, with saints and sculpted air vents, standing on mushroom-shaped pillars to protect the contents from rodents.

While it is a poor part of the country, a wave of road improvements, motorways and new building in the last decades is rapidly changing the character of the region. Food is plentiful, most people being involved in its production, and there's a strength and solidity in the culture, run, uniquely for Spain, by the women. In the countryside, women and children traditionally work the land while the men work at sea, whether as merchant seamen or fishermen, catching octopus and lobster from rowing boats, and minding the *mejilloneiras* (the mussel rafts anchored in the *rías*). Others, undoubtedly, are engaged in the old standby of smuggling – which, these days, means drugs as well as more traditional contraband. For centuries men have also sought their fortunes abroad, traditionally in Argentina (there are said to be more *gallegos* in Buenos Aires than in Galicia), though more often these days as migrant labourers in northern Europe.

Gallego

The **gallego language** sounds like a fusion of Castilian and Portuguese, but has existed every bit as long as either, and is still spoken by an estimated 85 percent of the population. It is definitely a living language, taught in schools and with its own literary heroes such as the twentieth-century poet Rosalia de Castro and the essayist and caricaturist Castelao. Road signs and maps these days tend to be in *gallego* (though the Castilian version is often given as well). We have therefore used the *gallego* name for towns, supplying the Castilian version in parentheses where it varies significantly, or is helpful. The most obvious characteristic of *gallego* is the large number of *X*s, which in Castilian might be *G*s, *J*s or *S*s; these are pronounced as a soft *sh*. You will also find that the Castilian *la* becomes *a* (as in A Coruña), *el* is *o* (as in O Grove), *de la* is *da* and *del* is *do*.

Below is a glossary of common words that you are likely to come across and that differ significantly from the Castilian.

One	*Un*	Right	*Dereita*
Two	*Dous*	Near	*Cerca*
Three	*Tres*	Far	*Lonxe*
Four	*Catro*	Plaza	*Praza*
Five	*Cinco*	Beach	*Praia*
Six	*Seis*		
Seven	*Sete*	Monday	*Luns*
Eight	*Oito*	Tuesday	*Martes*
Nine	*Nove*	Wednesday	*Mercores*
Ten	*Dez*	Thursday	*Xoves*
		Friday	*Venres*
Good morning	*Bos Dias*	Saturday	*Sabado*
Good afternoon	*Boas Tardes*	Sunday	*Domingo*
Good night	*Boas Noites*	Open	*Aberto*
		Closed	*Pechado*
More	*Mais*	Today	*Hoxe*
A lot	*Moito*	Yesterday	*Onte*
A little	*Pouco*	Tomorrow	*Mañá*
Left	*Esquerda*		

Fiestas

January
1 Livestock fair at Betanzos.
6 Horseback procession of *Los Reyes* (the Three Kings) in Baiona.
15 *San Mauro* – fireworks at Vilanova de Arousa.

March
1 Celanova's big festival, of *San Rosendo*, at the monastery above town.
Pre-Lenten *carnavales* throughout the region, along with the *Lazaro* festival, a gathering of both *gallego* and Portuguese folk groups, at Verín.

April
Palm Sunday Stations of the Cross at Monte San Tecla, near A Guarda.
Holy Week Celebrations include a symbolic *descendimiento* (descent from the Cross) at Viveiro on Good Friday and a Resurrection procession at Finisterre.
Sunday after Easter *Angula* (elver) festival at Tui.
Second Monday after Easter *San Telmo* festival at Tui.
25 *San Marcos* observance at Noia.
Late April–early May (dates vary from year to year) Festival at Ribadavia celebrating and promoting Ribeiro wines.

May
1 *Romería* at Pontevedra.
22 *Santa Rita* at Vilagarcía de Arousa.
Last week Vino de la Ribeira Sacra festival at Monforte de Lemos.

June
Corpus Christi Flower festival, with flower "carpets" in the streets, in Ponteareas.

July
First Saturday *Percebes* (barnacle) festival at Corme.
First weekend *Rapa das Bestas* – capture and breaking in of wild mountain horses – at Viveiro and San Lourenzo de Sabucedo (Pontevedra). At the latter the horses are raced before being let loose.
11 *San Benito* fiesta at Pontevedra, with river processions, and folk groups, and a smaller *romería* at Cambados.
16 *Virgen del Carmen*. Sea processions at Muros and Corcubión.
24–25 Two days of celebration for *San Juan* in many places, with processions of big-

Galicia has always been deeply conservative and since 1875 has provided Spain with a gallery of prominent right-wing leaders; it was the birthplace of General Franco, and is today dominated by the right-wing Partido Popular, whose founder, Manuel Fraga, is another local boy. Nonetheless, there is a strong and proud *gallego* nationalist movement, which capitalized on the wave of public protest in the wake of the Prestige oil disaster (see p.631 & p.1043). The nationalists have formed links with Celtic groups in Brittany and Ireland and encouraged the revival of the long-banned local language. Though they do not reach the intensity of the Catalan or Basque movements, many *Gallegos* feel that they are demanding too much too soon.

The obvious highlight of Galicia is the splendid regional capital of **Santiago de Compostela**, the end of the road for pilgrims following the various routes of the Camino de Santiago since medieval times. The spectacular cathedral and the granite colonnades and mossy facades of the city make Santiago quite unforgettable, but there are smaller and equally charming old stone towns throughout the region. Some, such as **Pontevedra** and **Betanzos**, make an

heads and *gigantones* on the 24th and spectacular parades with fireworks and bands through the following evening.

July
25 *St James*. Galicia's major fiesta, at its height in Santiago de Compostela. The evening before, there's a fireworks display and symbolic burning of a cardboard effigy of the mosque at Córdoba. The festival – also designated *Galicia Day* – has become a nationalist event with traditional separatist marches and an extensive programme of political and cultural events for about a week on either side.

August
First Sunday Albariño wine festival at Cambados; bagpipe festival at Ribadeo; *Virgen de la Roca* observances outside Baiona; Viking *romería* in Catoira (Pontevedra); Pimiento festival at Padrón; *Navaja* (razor shell) festival at Finisterre; *Mejillón* (mussel) festival at Vilanova de Arousa.
Second Sunday *Fiesta del Pulpo* in O Carballiño (Ourense).
16 *San Roque* festivals at all churches that bear his name: at Betanzos there's a Battle of the Flowers on the river and the launching of the *Fiesta del Globo*; at Sada (10km east of A Coruña) there are boat races and feasts.
24 Fiesta (and bullfights) at Noia.
25 *San Ginés* at Sanxenxo.
28 *Romería del Naseiro* outside Viveiro.
Last Sunday *Romería* sets out from Sanxenxo to the Praia de La Lanzada.

September
6–10 *Fiestas del Portal* at Ribadavia.
8 *San Andreu* at Cervo (20km east of Viveiro).
First Sunday after 8th *Romería* at Muxia.
14 Seafood festival at O Grove; *romería* with bigheads at Viveiro.

October
13 *Fiesta de la Exaltación del Marisco* at O Grove – literally "a celebration in praise of shellfish".

November
11 *Fiesta de San Martín* at Bueu; *Magosto castaña* (a type of chestnut) festival at Ourense.

December
Last week *O Feitoman*. Crafts fair at Vigo.

GALICIA

8

enjoyable base for exploring the region. Alternatively, the route west from the Roman walls of **Lugo** takes in numerous monasteries and churches that once provided refreshment for pilgrims along the Camino de Santiago.

The coastal countryside is always spectacular: the **Rías Altas** of the far north providing a gentle introduction to the distinctive appearance of the region, but the most definitively Galician environment of all is found amongst the tiny, picturesque fishing ports of the **Costa do Morte**, where the traditional *gallego* lifestyle of smallholdings and small-scale fishing still survives. Further south, the best and safest swimming beaches are along the picturesque **Rías Baixas** towards Portugal, with O Grove and Baiona two of the most popular resorts. Far fewer visitors come here than to the Mediterranean, and while the sea is never as warm, the pine-fringed coves are delightful. Inland, Galicia can be bleak and empty; the most rewarding route is along the **Rio Minho** south via **Ribadavia** through the lush valleys of the Ribeiro wine-producing region to the Portuguese border.

Santiago de Compostela and the Camino

No trip to Galicia is complete without a visit to **Santiago de Compostela**, an ancient pilgrimage centre and one of the most visually stunning cities in Spain. Warrens of honey-coloured streets wind their way past a succession of beautiful churches, culminating in the approach to the immense Praza do Obradoiro, flanked by the magnificent Cathedral, the supposed resting place of the remains of St James.

The **Camino de Santiago**, the pilgrims' route, is the longest-established "tourist" route in Europe, and its final section through Galicia gives a glimpse of the medieval pilgrimage to the thousands who walk it every year, armed with the traditional staff and the scallop shell emblem of St James. Hundreds more cycle the route, and it's possible to drive, too, although this is the least satisfying way of making the journey, offering tantalizing glimpses of ancient footpaths winding through woods as the road and footpath intertwine and then separate. Both routes are well signposted with yellow scallop-shell symbols, and local buses cover much of the road route, a boon to the footsore. Basic hostels for pilgrims are set up along the way, with priority given to walkers. Walking or cycling, the *camino* is a tough but unforgettable experience.

Santiago de Compostela

Built in a warm golden granite, **SANTIAGO DE COMPOSTELA** is one of the most beautiful of all Spanish cities. The medieval city has been declared in its entirety to be both a national monument and a UNESCO World Heritage site, and remains a remarkably integrated whole, all the better for being almost completely pedestrianized. The buildings and the squares, the long stone arcades and the statues, are hewn from the same granite blocks and blend imperceptibly one into the other.

The **pilgrimage** to Santiago captured the imagination of Christian Europe on an unprecedented scale. At the height of its popularity, in the eleventh and twelfth centuries, the city was receiving over half a million pilgrims each year. People of all classes came to visit the supposed shrine of St James the Apostle (Santiago to the Spanish, Saint Jacques to the French), making this the third holiest site in Christendom, after Jerusalem and Rome.

The place is now as busy as it must have been in the days of the first pilgrims, though these days tourists are as likely to be attracted by Santiago's art and history as by religion. Not that the function of pilgrimage here is dead; it fell into decline with the Reformation – or as the local chronicler Molina reported, "the damned doctrines of the accursed Luther diminished the number of Germans and *wealthy* English" – but fortunes have revived of late and more than enough visitors still sport a *vieira* (scallop shell) symbol of the pilgrim. Each year at the **Festival of St James** (see p.605) on July 25, there is a ceremony dedicating the country and government to the saint at his shrine. Years in which the saint's day falls on a Sunday are designated "Holy Years", and the activity becomes even more intense. After 2004 the next one isn't until 2010.

With its large population of students, most of whom live in the less appealing modern city slightly downhill, Santiago is always a lively place to visit, far more than a mere historical curiosity. Uniquely, it's also a city that's at its best in the rain; in fact it's situated in the wettest fold of the *gallego* hills, and suffers brief but frequent showers. Water glistens on the facades, gushes from the innumerable gargoyles, and flows down the streets. As a result, vegetation sprouts everywhere, with the cathedral coated in orange and yellow lichens, and grass poking up between the tiles and cobbles. It's also a manageable size – you can wander fifteen minutes out of town and reach wide-open countryside.

Arrival, orientation and information

Arriving at the **bus station**, you are 1km or so east of the town centre; bus #10 (€0.70) will take you to Praza de Galicia on the outskirts of the pedestrianized old town. If you're walking, go straight ahead down the road in front of the terminal to the roundabout at Praza da Paz. From here, Campo de Pastoriza and its continuations run past the Convento de Santa Clara into town. The **train station** is more centrally located: head straight out of the station up Rúa do Horreo to Praza de Galicia, a ten-minute walk. Labacolla **airport** (☏981 547 501) is some 13km east of town on the road to Lugo. Frequent buses run between the airport and bus station (1–2 hourly); there are also less frequent services from opposite the Iberia office at Rúa Xeneral Pardiñas 24. The **turismo**, at Rúa do Vilar 43 (summer daily 9am–9pm; winter daily 10am–3pm & 5–8pm; ☏981 584 081, Ⓦwww.santiagoturismo.com), has details of the €12 *Tarjeta Turística* which gives large discounts over a 48-hour period if you intend to do and see everything. There is also a small office at the bus station (daily 10am–2pm & 4–8pm).

Accommodation

You should have no difficulty finding an inexpensive **room** in Santiago. The biggest concentration of places is on the three parallel streets leading south from the cathedral: Rúa Nova, Rúa do Vilar, and Rúa do Franco (this last named after the French pilgrims, rather than the late dictator). Even during the July festival, there's rarely a problem, with half the bars in the city renting out rooms, and landladies dragging you off from the bus and train stations on arrival.

Budget options

Hostal Alameda Rúa do San Clemente 32 ☏981 588 100, Ⓕ981 588 689. Smart, stylish rooms – some en suite – with polished floors, large windows and TV. Pleasantly located by the Alameda. ❷
Hostal Barbantes Rúa do Franco 1 ☏981 576 520. Clean and light en-suite rooms, some with balconies overlooking a little square. There's a good bar and restaurant below. ❷
Hostal La Estela Avda. Rajoy 1 ☏981 582 796. Good-value *hostal* on a pretty street just off the Praza do Obradoiro, with both en-suite and shared-bath rooms. A little close to the Cathedral, though, if you are sensitive to noise. ❷
Hostal Mapoula Rúa do Entremurallas 10 ☏981 580 124, Ⓕ981 584 089. Cheap, friendly *hostal* with spacious, en-suite rooms, all with TV and phone, though located on a rather dingy backstreet. ❷

Hostal Paz de Agra Rúa Caldeireria 37 ☏981 583 517. Cheap and cheerful. Reception rather oddly located one block away in the *Restaurante Zingara* on Praza de Mazarelos. ❷
Hostal Suso Rúa do Vilar 65 ☏981 586 611. Neat, comfortable *hostal*, with a good bar-restaurant downstairs, located in a lively street, a few doors along from the turismo. ❷

Moderate options

La Artes Travesa Dúas Portas 2 ☏981 555 254. A small hotel with lots of character. Rooms are named rather than numbered, each decorated in a distinctive but traditional style. All rooms en suite with TV. ❺

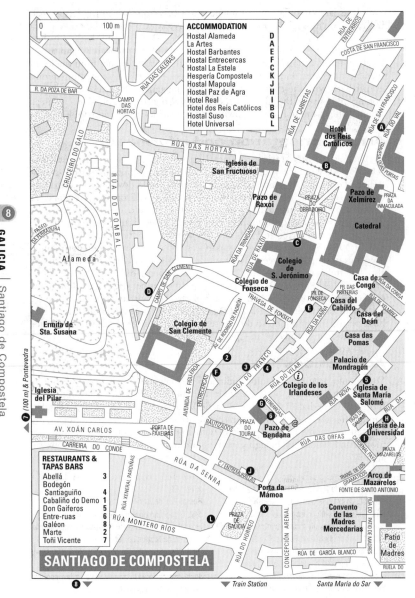

ACCOMMODATION

Hostal Alameda	D
La Artes	A
Hostal Barbantes	E
Hostal Entrecercas	F
Hostal La Estela	C
Hesperia Compostela	K
Hostal Mapoula	J
Hostal Paz de Agra	H
Hotel Real	I
Hotel dos Reis Católicos	B
Hostal Suso	G
Hotel Universal	L

RESTAURANTS & TAPAS BARS

Abellá	3
Bodegón Santiaguiño	4
Cabaliño do Demo	1
Don Gaiferos	5
Entre-ruas	6
Galéon	8
Marte	2
Toñi Vicente	7

SANTIAGO DE COMPOSTELA

▼ Train Station   Santa María do Sar ▼

Hostal Entrecercas Entrecercas 11 ☎981 571 151. Modern, bright and stylish, yet retaining a traditional feel. Rooms well-equipped with TV and bathroom. ④

Hotel Real Rúa Caldeirería 49 ☎981 569 290.

Comfortable and functional, centrally located on a wide (by Santiago standards) but quiet street. En-suite roms with TV. ④

Hotel Universal Praza Galicia 2 ☎981 585 800. Located near the bus stop just outside the old

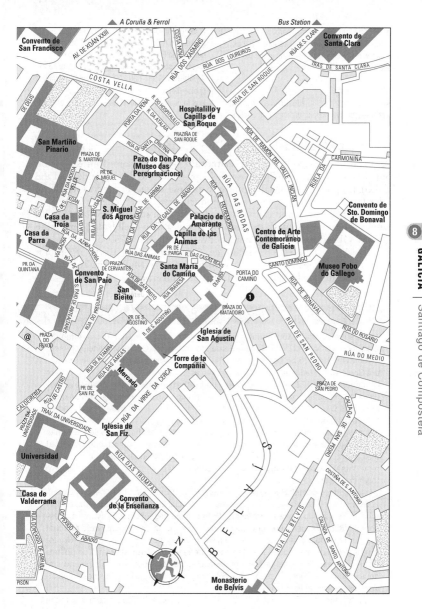

Convento de San Francisco

AV. DE XOAN XXIII

Convento de Santa Clara

RÚA DOS YÁSMINS

RÚA DE S. CLARA

RÚA DOS LOUREIROS

COSTA NOVA

TRAS DE SANTA CLARA

COSTA VELLA

DE DEUS

RÚA DE SAN ROQUE

PORTA DA PENA

R. DO HOSPITALILLO

R. DA ATALAIA

Hospitalillo y Capilla de San Roque

PRAZIÑA DE SAN ROQUE

RÚA DE RAMON DEL VALLE - INCLAN

CARMONIÑA

RUELA DA

RÚA DE SANTA CRISTINA

San Martiño Pinario

PRAZA DE S. MARTIÑO

Pazo de Don Pedro (Museo das Peregrinacions)

PR. DE S. MIGUEL

RÚA DAS RODAS

Convento de Sto. Domingo de Bonaval

RÚA DA MOEDA VELLA

RÚA DA TRONA

CES XOAN

Casa da Troia

VÍA SACRA

RÚA DA AZABACHERÍA

RÚA DE XELMÍREZ

RÚA DA ALGALIA DE ARRIBA

S. Miguel dos Agros

RÚA DE ENTREMUROS

RÚA DA ALGALIA DE ABAIXO

Palacio de Amarante

Capilla de las Ánimas

PR. DE S. PARGA

R. DAS CASAS REAIS

Centro de Arte Contemporáneo de Galicia

SANTO DOMINGO

Museo Pobo do Gallego

Casa da Parra

PR. DA QUINTANA

@

PRAZA DO FEIXOO

PRAZA DE CERVANTES

Convento de San Paio

RÚA DE SAN BIEITO

RÚA DAS ÁNIMAS

Santa María do Camiño

RÚA TRAVESA

PORTA DO CAMIÑO

San Bieito

RÚA DE PAIO DE ANTEALTARES

RÚA DO PREGUNTOIRO

PR. DE S. AGOSTIÑO

RÚA DE BONAVAL

RÚA DO ROSARIO

PRAZA DO MATADOIRO

❶

RÚA DE SAN PEDRO

RÚA DO MEDIO

RÚA DE S. AGOSTIÑO

Iglesia de San Agustín

RÚA DE ALTAMIRA

RÚA DAS AMEAS

Mercado

Torre de la Compáñia

RÚA DA VIRXE DA CERCA

CALZADA DE SAN PEDRO

PRAZA DE SAN PEDRO

PR. DE SAN FIZ

Iglesia de San Fiz

RÚA DAS TROMPAS

CALDEIRERIA

RÚA DO CASTRO

PRAZA DA UNIVERSIDADE

TRAV. DA UNIVERSIDADE

Universidad

Casa de Valderrama

RÚA DO POZIGO DE ABAIXO

Convento de la Enseñanza

B E L V Í S

COSTIÑA DE S. ANTONIO

RÚA DE BELVIS

CALZADA DE SANTO ANTONIO

N

PISON

RÚA DO POZIGO DE ARRIBA

B E L V Í S

Monasterio de Belvís

town in a rather ugly building, though rooms are comfortable and spacious. ❸

Expensive options

Hesperia Compostela Rúa Hórreo 1 ☎ 981 585

700. Housed in a castle-like building just off Praza de Galicia, this is a swish option with all mod cons including satellite TV, room service and banquet halls. ❼

Hostal dos Reis Católicos Praza do Obradoiro 1

℡ 981 582 200, ✉ santiago@parador.es. A modest €189 buys you a night in Spain's most famous *parador*, reputedly the oldest hotel in the world – see also p.614. ⑥

Camping

As Cancelas ℡ 981 580 266. Open all year and within reasonable walking distance of the town

(2.5km northeast of the cathedral). Reached via the road to A Coruña, branching off at the Avda. del Camino Francés; the route is also served by regular buses to the airport and the city bus #9.
As Sirenas ℡ 981 698 722. Reasonable second choice 6km out on the Santa Comba road, with less frequent connecting buses. Also open all year.

The cathedral

All roads to Santiago lead to the **Catedral** (Mon–Sat 11am–1pm & 4–6pm, Sun 10am–1.30pm & 4–7pm). You first appreciate the sheer grandeur of the cathedral upon venturing into the vast expanse of the Praza do Obradoiro. Directly ahead stands a fantastic Baroque pyramid of granite, flanked by immense bell towers and everywhere adorned with statues of St James in his familiar pilgrim guise with staff, broad hat and scallop-shell badge. This is the famous **Obradoiro facade**, built between 1738 and 1750 by an obscure Santiago-born architect, Fernando de Casas. No other work of Spanish Baroque can compare with it, nor with what Edwin Mullins (in *The Road to Compostela*) sublimely calls its "hat-in-the-air exuberance".

The history of the pilgrimage to Santiago

The great **pilgrimage to Santiago** was the first exercise in mass tourism. Although the shrine was visited by the great – Fernando and Isabel, Carlos V, Francis of Assisi – you didn't have to be rich to come. The various roads through France and northern Spain which led here, collectively known as El Camino de Santiago (The Way of St James, or the Pilgrim Route), were lined with monasteries and charitable hospices for the benefit of the pilgrims. Villages sprang up along the route, and an order of knights was founded for the pilgrims' protection. There was even a guidebook – the world's first – written by a French monk called Aymery Picaud, which recorded, along with water sources and places to stay, such facts as the bizarre sexual habits of the Navarrese Basques (who exposed themselves when excited, and protected their mules from their neighbours with chastity belts). All in all it was an extraordinary phenomenon in an age when most people never ventured beyond their own town or village.

Why did they come? Some, like Chaucer's Wife of Bath, who had "been in Galicia at Seynt Jame", had their own private reasons: social fashion, adventure, the opportunities for marriage or even for crime. But for most pilgrims, it was simply a question of faith. They believed in the miraculous power of St James, and were told that the journey would guarantee them a remission of half their time in purgatory. Not for a moment did they doubt that the tomb beneath the high altar at Compostela Cathedral held the mortal remains of James, son of Zebedee and Salome and first cousin of Jesus Christ. It seems scarcely credible that the whole business was an immense ecclesiastical fraud.

Yet the legend, at each point of its development, bears this out. It begins with the claim, unsubstantiated by the Bible, that St James came to Spain, at some point after the Crucifixion, to spread the gospel. He is said, for example, to have had a vision of the Virgin in Zaragoza. He then returned to Jerusalem, where he was undoubtedly beheaded by Herod Agrippa. His body should, by all rights and reason, be buried somewhere in the Nile delta. But the legend records that two of James's disciples removed his corpse to Jaffa, where a boat appeared, without sails or crew, and carried them to Padrón, twenty kilometres downstream from Santiago. The voy-

The main body of the cathedral is Romanesque, rebuilt in the eleventh and twelfth centuries after a devastating raid by the Muslim vizier of Córdoba, al-Mansur, in 977. He failed to find the body of the saint (perhaps not surprisingly), but forced the citizens to carry the bells of the tower to the mosque at Córdoba – a coup which was later dramatically reversed (see p.350). The building's highlight – indeed one of the great triumphs of medieval art – is the **Pórtico de Gloria**, the original west front, which now stands inside the cathedral behind the Obradoiro. Completed in 1188 under the supervision of Maestro Mateo (his signature is on the right lintel of the central arch), this was both the culmination of all Romanesque sculpture and a precursor of the new Gothic realism, each of its host of figures being strikingly relaxed and quietly humanized. They were originally painted, and still bear traces of a seventeenth-century renovation.

The real mastery, however, is in the assured marshalling of the ensemble. Above the side doors are representations of Purgatory and the Last Judgement, while over the main door Christ presides in glory, flanked by his Apostles (Matthew with an angel, Luke with a winged bull, John with an eagle and Mark with a lion), and surrounded by the 24 Elders of the Apocalypse playing celestial music. St James sits on the central column, beneath Christ and just above eye level in the classic symbolic position of intercessor, since it was

age took just seven days, at once proving the miracle since, as Richard Ford wrote in 1845, "the Oriental Steam Company can do nothing like it".

At this stage the body was buried, lost and forgotten for the next 750 years. It was rediscovered at Compostela in 813, at a time of great significance for the Spanish Church. Over the preceding century, the Moors had swept across the Iberian peninsula, gaining control over all but the northern mountain kingdom of Asturias, and in their campaigns they had introduced a concept entirely new to the West: *jihad*, or holy war. They also drew great strength from the inspiration of their champion, the Prophet Muhammad, whose death (in 632) was still within popular memory and a bone from whose body was preserved in the Great Mosque of Córdoba. Thus the discovery of the bones of St James, under a buried altar on a site traditionally linked with his name, was singularly opportune. It occurred after a hermit was attracted to a particular spot on a hillside by visions of stars, and the hill was known thereafter as Compostela, from the Latin *campus stellae*, meaning "field of stars". Alfonso II, king of Asturias, came to pay his respects, built a chapel, and the saint was adopted as the champion of Christian Spain against the infidel.

Within decades the saint had appeared on the battlefield. Ramiro I, Alfonso's successor, swore that he had fought alongside him at the Battle of Clavijo (844), and that the saint had personally slaughtered 60,000 Moors. Over the next six centuries *Santiago Matamoros* (Moor-killer) manifested himself at some forty battles, even assisting in the massacre of American Indians in the New World. It may seem an odd role for the fisherman-evangelist, but presented no problems to the Christian propagandists who portrayed him most frequently as a knight on horseback in the act of dispatching whole clutches of swarthy, bearded Arabs with a single thrust of his long sword. (With consummate irony, when Franco brought his expert Moroccan troops to Compostela to dedicate themselves to the overthrow of the Spanish Republic, all such statues were discreetly hidden under sheets.)

The cult of Santiago was strongest during the age of the First Crusade (1085) and the Reconquest; people wanted to believe, and so it gained a kind of truth. In any case, as Ford acidly observed, "If people can once believe that Santiago ever came to Spain at all, all the rest is plain sailing."

For practicalities on the Camino de Santiago, see p.618.

△ Detail of the cathedral Santiago de Compostela

through him that pilgrims could gain assurance of their destiny. To either side are the Prophets of the Old Testament, most famously Daniel, apparently smiling seraphically across at Esther on the other side of the portico. The pilgrims would give thanks at journey's end by praying with the fingers of one hand pressed into the roots of the Tree of Jesse below the saint. So many millions have performed this act of supplication that five deep and shiny holes have been worn into the solid marble. Finally, for wisdom, they would lower their heads to touch the brow of Maestro Mateo, the humble squatting figure on the other side.

The spiritual climax of the pilgrimage, however, is the approach to the **High Altar**. You climb steps behind the altar, embrace the Most Sacred Image of Santiago, kiss his bejewelled cape, and pilgrims that have travelled over 100km are handed, by way of certification, a document in Latin called a *Compostela*. The altar is a riotous creation of eighteenth-century Churrigueresque, but the statue has stood there for seven centuries and the procedure is quite unchanged. The pilgrims would then make confession and attend a High Mass.

You'll notice an elaborate pulley system in front of the altar. This is for moving the immense "**Botafumeiro**" (incense burner), which, operated by eight priests (*tiraboleiros*), is swung in a vast 30-metre ceiling-to-ceiling arc across the transept. The Botafumeiro is now used ceremonially only at certain services (ask around to see if there's one during your visit), though its original purpose was to fumigate the bedraggled pilgrims in an attempt to prevent the spread of disease. The saint's bones are kept in a **crypt** beneath the altar. They were lost for a second time in 1700, having been hidden before an English invasion, but were rediscovered during building work in 1879. In fact they found three skeletons, which were naturally held to be those of St James and his two disciples. The only problem was identifying which one was the Apostle. This was fortuitously resolved as a church in Tuscany possessed a piece of Santiago's skull which exactly fitted a gap in one of those here. Its identity was confirmed in 1884 by Pope Leo XIII, and John Paul II's visit in 1982 presumably reaffirmed official sanction.

The cathedral is full of collecting boxes; there are two on either side if you wish to kneel before the bones. But to visit the **Treasury**, **Cloisters**, **Buchería** (Archeological Museum), Pazo de Xelmírez (see p.614) and Mateo's beautiful **Crypt of the Portico**, you need to buy a collective ticket (summer Mon–Sat 10am–2pm & 4–8pm; winter Mon–Sat 10am–1.30pm & 4–6.30pm, Pazo de Xelmírez different hours see p.614; €5). The late Gothic cloisters in particular are well worth seeing; from the plain, mosque-like courtyard you get a wonderful view of the riotous mixture of the exterior, crawling with pagodas, pawns, domes, obelisks, battlements, scallop shells and cornucopias. Underneath the cloister, in the Buchería, is Mateo's original stone choir and the remains of the thirteenth-century cloister. The crypt lies directly under the Portico de Gloria, accessed from beneath the main entry staircase; the museum and cloister entrance is just to the right on the cathedral square.

The rest of the city

The whole city, with its flagstone streets and arcades, is enchanting, but if you want to add direction to your wanderings, perhaps the best plan is first to examine the buildings around the cathedral – the Pazo de Xelmírez and Hostal dos Reis Católicos – and then head for some of the other monasteries and convents. Finally, to get an overall impression of the whole architectural ensemble of Santiago, take a walk along the promenade of the **Paseo da Ferradura** (Paseo de la Herradura), in the spacious **Alameda** just southwest of the old part, at the end of Rúa do Franco.

Around the cathedral

The **Pazo de Xelmírez** (Palacio Arzobispal Gelmírez; Tues–Sun 10am–1.30pm & 4–7.30pm; €5 same ticket as Catedral treasury and cloisters) occupies the building to the north side of the cathedral, balancing the cloister, with its entrance just to the left of the main stairs. Archbishop Xelmírez was one of the seminal figures in Santiago's development. He rebuilt the cathedral in the twelfth century, raised the see to an archbishopric, and "discovered" a ninth-century deed which gave annual dues to St James's shrine of one bushel of corn from each acre of Spain reconquered from the Moors – a decree which was repealed only in 1834. In his suitably luxuriant palace are a vaulted twelfth-century kitchen and a thirteenth-century synodal hall featuring scenes of a medieval banquet.

As late as the thirteenth century the cathedral was used to accommodate pilgrims, but slowly its place was taken by convents founded around the city. Fernando and Isabel, in gratitude for their conquest of Granada, added to these facilities by building a hostel for the poor and sick. This, the elegant Renaissance **Hostal dos Reis Católicos** (Hostal de los Reyes Católicos), fills the northern side of the Praza do Obradoiro in front of the cathedral. It is now a *parador*, which means that unless you're staying here, it's not all that easy to get in to see the four superb patios, the chapel with magnificent Gothic stone carving, and the vaulted crypt-bar (where the bodies of the dead were once stored).

You could easily spend half an afternoon exploring the squares around the cathedral. The largest is the **Praza da Quintana**, where a flight of broad steps joins the back of the cathedral to the high walls of a convent. The "Porta Santa" doorway in this square is only opened during those Holy Years in which the Feast of Santiago falls on a Sunday. To the south is the **Praza das Praterías**, the silversmiths' square, centred on an ornate fountain of four horses with webbed feet, and featuring the 70-metre-high *Berenguela* or **clock tower**. On the west side is the extraordinarily narrow **Casa del Cabildo**, built in 1758 to fill the remaining gap and ornamentally complete the square. North of the cathedral is the **Praza da Inmaculada**, dominated by the grand Baroque facade of San Martiño Pinario (see below), at 20,000 square metres one of the largest religious buildings in Spain.

Central churches and museums

From Praza da Inmaculada, walk round the side of the Benedictine monastery of **San Martiño Pinario** (Tues–Sun 10am–2pm & 4–6pm; €2), and down one of a series of twisting staircases to reach the entrance to the monastery church on Praza de San Martiño. Inside, the vast altarpiece ("a fricassee of gilt gingerbread", according to Ford) depicts its patron riding alongside St James. In the monasterio itself is an atmospheric *comedor* that serves reasonable set **meals** for €8.40.

East of San Martiño, the fascinating museum of pilgrimage, the **Museo das Peregrinaciónes** (Tues–Fri 10am–8pm, Sat 10.30am–1.30pm & 5–8pm, Sun 10.30am–1.30pm; free), lies just off Praza de San Miguel in a sixteenth-century mansion, the Pazo de Don Pedro, also known as the Gothic House. It traces the history of the *camino*, the city and cathedral, using excellent models and displays, and there is a comprehensive (and free) guide in English. The real jewel of the museum is the original copy of the twelfth-century *Codex Calixtinus*, a travel guide for pilgrims, which recommended routes and lodgings and pointed out the various dangers of the *camino*, such as the "malicious, swarthy, ugly, depraved, perverse, despicable, disloyal and corrupt" Navarrese.

Just outside to the east of the city, lies the old convent and church of **Santo Domingo**, featuring a magnificent seventeenth-century triple stairway, each spiral leading to different storeys of a single tower. Inside the convent buildings, the fascinating **Museo do Pobo Gallego** (Tues–Sat 10am–2pm & 4–8pm, Sun 11am–2pm; Ⓦwww.museodopobo.es; free) features a diverse overview of *gallego* crafts and traditions. Many aspects of the way of life displayed haven't yet entirely disappeared, though you're today unlikely to see *corozas*, straw suits worn into the last century by mountain shepherds. The convent gardens and orchards on the hillside behind are a wonderful spot for a little solace and a break from sightseeing. **The Centro de Arte Contemporáneo de Galicia** (Tues–Sun 11am–8pm; free) opposite, a beautiful addition to Santiago's architectural heritage by the Portuguese architect Álvaro Siza, houses interesting temporary exhibitions of contemporary art and sculpture.

Santa María do Sar

Outside the main circuit of the city, the one really worthwhile visit is to the curious Romanesque church of **Santa María do Sar**. This lies about a kilometre down the Rúa de Sar, which begins at the Patio das Madres on the southern edge of the old city. The remarkable fifteen-degree slant of its pillars is its most notable feature, attributed to deficient foundations by some and to the mastery of its designers by the faithful. It also has a wonderfully sculpted cloister, reputedly the work of Maestro Mateo.

Eating, drinking and nightlife

Gallego food is plentiful and excellent in Santiago, with a plethora of good, solid **places to eat**, particularly on Rúa do Franco, which is lined with seafood restaurants. If you're shopping for your own food, don't miss the large covered **market** held daily until 3pm in the old halls of the Praza de Abastos, on the southeast edge of the old city. Thursday is the main market day, when it is bustling. There are also a number of tiny delicatessens thoughout the town which sell the traditional breast-shaped **cheese**, the rich *queso de tetilla*.

The presence of so many students in Santiago guarantees that the city has a healthy animation to go with its past. In term time the main **bar** scene is down in the new town, particularly on and around Rúa Nova de Abaixo. The slightly more expensive old town is lively throughout the year, particularly if you're lucky enough to witness (or foolhardy enough to attempt) the legendary **Paris–Dakar race**: participants must start at *Bar Paris* at the top of end of Rúa do Franco and have one drink at each of the 48 bars on the way down to *Bar Dakar* on Rúa da Raiña, finishing by midnight. It's on these two streets that you'll find the best **tapas bars**, although after midnight people tend to move on to the pubs scattered around the city.

Santiago is also the best place in Galicia to hear the local Celtic **music**, played on *gaitas* (bagpipes), often by student groups known as *tunas*. In summer there are nightly performances in the Praza do Obradoiro from 10pm onwards.

Restaurants

Abellà Rúa do Franco 30. One of this street's many seafood places, with generous portions and good service – try the *caldo gallego* (€2.10).

Bodegón Santiaguiño Rúa do Franco 29. Lobster is a speciality here and there's also the luxury of quiet outdoor seating, almost unheard of on Rúa do Franco.

Cabaliño do Demo Porta do Camiño 7. Reasonable vegetarian restaurant, with a €7.25 *menú* and an imaginative range of à la carte dishes, many of them with an Asian twist.

Don Gaiferos Rúa Nova. Superb – but expensive – seafood in attractive cellar-like surroundings, with fish dishes from €16.

Entre-Rúas Callejon de Entre Rúas 2. Excellent

seafood *raciónes* at this small, unpretentious bar-restaurant, shoehorned into a tiny square up an even tinier alley between *rúas* Nova and Vilar.

Galeón Rúa de Alfredo Brañas 35. Inventive selection of burgers, platos and sandwiches, hugely popular with students attracted by the lively atmosphere, healthy portions and the fact that almost everything on the menu costs less than €2.60.

Marte Avda. Rodrigo de Padrón 11. Popular restaurant and café with outdoor seating in a pleasant location not far from the main drag. Excellent €8 *menú* contains several dishes that are elsewhere rather expensive.

Toñi Vicente Avda. Rosalía de Castro 24. Very expensive *nouvelle cuisine* with *gallego* elements; winner of the 1998 prize for Spanish cuisine – main courses start at €18.

Bars

O Beiro Rúa da Raiña 3. Pleasant *bodega* stocking a range of Spanish wines vast enough to suit even the most exacting vinophile.

Casa das Crechas Via Sacra 5. Just behind the Praza da Quintana, a well-known folk bar, often with live *gallego*, Celtic or international folk music. Hanging *brujas* and a first-rate draught Kilkenny complete the effect.

Fonte Sequelo Rúa Xelmírez. Worth checking out just to try traditional Galician *queimada* served in pottery bowls.

O Gato Negro Rúa da Raiña 17. Unprepossessing but unmissable old *tasca* that's permanently packed solid with vociferous locals.

Klausura Rúa San Pelayo 20. One of a cluster of brash, unatmospheric but popular summer-night pubs on a tiny square.

Bar Chocolatería Metate Travesa de San Paio Antealteres. A must for chocolate fans, with a large menu of hot and cold alcohol- and non-alcohol-based chocolate drinks in addition to the usual choice of beverages.

Momo Virxen da Cerca 23. Popular hang-out with wide-ranging appeal, though full of students during term time. Fantastic and varied decor includes a Paris street complete with mini café-bars, free popcorn, an outdoor terrace and a jungle dance-floor.

Listings

Airlines Labacolla airport is served by a number of airlines, including: Iberia ☎981 597 550; Air Europa ☎981 594 950; and Spanair ☎902 567 022.

Bookshops Variable secondhand selection, including foreign-language titles and book-exchange, from Librería Vetusta, Rúa Nova 31 (daily 5–9pm). Huge choice of new titles at Librería Follas Novas, Rúa Montero Ríos 37, in the new town.

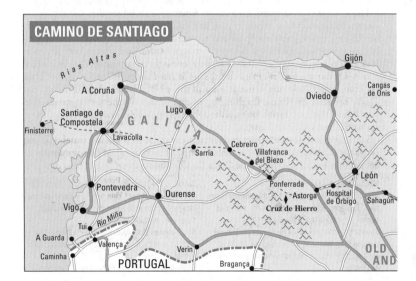

Bus information ☎ 981 587 700.
Car rental Operators include: Autos Brea, Rúa Xral Pardiñas 21 ☎ 981 565 056; Avis, Rúa República de El Salvador 10 ☎ 981 573 718; Europcar, Avda. Lugo ☎ 981 597 476.
Internet cafés *Ciber Nova50* at the top end of Rúa Nova is very central (€1.20 per hour). *Mundonet*, Rúa Xelmírez 19, just off Plaza Praterias (€1.38 per hour).

Laundry Lavandería la Económica is a self-service launderette at Rúa Ramón Cabanillas 1 (off Praza Roxa, a few blocks west of Praza de Galicia).
Post office The main office is on the corner of Travesía de Fonseca and Rúa do Franco.
Trains RENFE information ☎ 981 520 202 (long-distance reservations ☎ 981 153 338); information and booking also available from many of the travel agents in town.

The Camino de Santiago

The Pilgrim Route branches off the main Ponferrada–Lugo road at the **Pedrafita do Cebreiro** pass which marks the *gallego* frontier. This is a desolate spot, where hundreds of English soldiers froze or starved to death during Sir John Moore's retreat towards A Coruña in 1809. In such a forbidding landscape, you can only be impressed by the sheer scale of work that medieval builders put into providing spiritual and material amenities for the pilgrims. Crumbling castles, convents and humble inns line the road, and it's not hard to imagine what a welcome sight each must have been.

For more on the Camino de Santiago see the box on p.618.

Cebreiro and Monasteiro de Samos

The village of **CEBREIRO** is quite appallingly situated to catch the worst of the *gallego* wind and snow – although on one of the rare fine days of summer you would hardly realize. It's highly picturesque, an undulating settlement of thatched stone huts (*pallozas*) surrounding a stark, ninth-century church. No one actually lives in the *pallozas* any more, which are maintained as a national monument, with a guide on site to answer visitors' questions. In high season

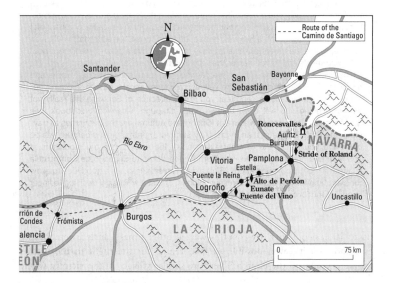

Today's pilgrims rarely make the complete journey from their homes to Santiago de Compostela and back; most follow one of the half a dozen or so standard pilgrimage routes through Spain and France. The most popular by far is the 750km **camino francés**, which heads westward from the Pyrenees across northern Spain. Many people begin their pilgrimage in Roncesvalles (or Orreaga-Roncesvalles in Basque) but you need only walk the final 100km, or cycle the last 200km, to earn your *compostela* (certificate of pilgrimage). For some pilgrims, the journey to Santiago is a lifelong dream borne of religious faith, others want to immerse themselves in Spanish history and culture, while many enjoy it as a relaxed holiday, returning year after year to complete a different section. Whatever the reason for the journey, the *Camino*'s popularity has exploded in recent decades; while only a handful of people walked to Santiago in the 1960s, the route now attracts about 70,000 pilgrims a year. In Holy Years, such as 2004 and 2010, when St James' feast day (July 25) falls on a Sunday, the number of pilgrims more than doubles. The appeal for some is no doubt the entitlement to bypass Purgatory entirely, while those arriving in Santiago in other years only get half their time off. It is not necessary to be Christian, however, or even religious, to follow the route.

To prove your pilgrim status at the *albergues*, you'll need a **credencial** (pilgrim passport); it's best to get one in advance from your local pilgrim association (see opposite), although you can also pick one up at the *albergue* in Roncesvalles. Along the way, you'll collect *sellos* (stamps as proof of your pilgrimage) from *albergues*, churches and even some enterprising cafés, then at the end of your journey in Santiago, you'll show your stamped *credencial* in order to get a *compostela*. If your motives are other than spiritual and you want more than sore feet and memories to commemorate your endeavour, apply for a *certificado* rather than a *compostela*.

Daily costs along the camino can be as low as €20 a day, although you'll spend a little more if you want to allow yourself some treats along the way. Most people stay in pilgrim hostels, called *albergues* or *refugios*, conveniently spaced anywhere from 10km to 20km apart. These provide simple accommodation in dormitories, are usually equipped with hot showers, sometimes provide kitchen facilities and charge either a nominal fee of a few euros or ask for a donation. *Albergues* can get crowded in the summer months, and pilgrims sometimes have to sleep on mattresses on the floor. For those who crave a little more comfort, there are plenty of more upmarket choices, and pilgrims often treat themselves to a night in a *parador* or other hotel when the snoring at the *albergues* gets a little too much. As a pilgrim, you'll also receive special treatment at restaurants – most will have a pilgrim *menú* for about €7 – and meals are served earlier than the Spanish norm, at about 8pm.

It's difficult to lose your way on the camino. The route sticks to good tracks and minor roads, is clearly marked with yellow arrows and mostly passes through populated areas where locals can steer you in the direction of Santiago. It's really not worth weighing yourself down with a map, although a *camino* guidebook (see p.1111) would be a good investment. Spring and autumn are the best times to travel, as the route is quieter than in the busy summer months, most *albergues* will be open and you'll miss the weather extremes of the *meseta* and the mountains. If you're fit and healthy, you can walk from Roncesvalles to Santiago de Compostela in about a month, covering about 25km a day. Nevertheless, it's a good idea to allow for extra time for rest days, unforeseen injuries, or just a whimsical decision to linger in one of the lovely towns on the way.

up to 1000 people per day pass this way; at other times it feels as remote as it ever did, and it's even possible to take refuge for the night in the former monastery next to the church. There are similar villages in the vicinity, where

Pilgrim associations

Confraternity of St. James ☏020 7928 9988, ⓦwww.csj.org.uk. The UK-based Confraternity is the most established and respected English-language pilgrims' association. It promotes research into the *camino*, publishes a newsletter, maintains a library and organizes meetings.

Irish Society of the Friends of St James ⓦwww.saintjamesirl.com. This website provides a discussion board and useful information for Irish pilgrims.

Friends of the Road to Santiago ⓦwww.geocities.com/friends_usa_santiago. A US group that publishes a newsletter and produces a popular bulletin board.

Little Company of Pilgrims ⓦwww.santiago.ca. Canadian organization that publishes a newsletter and offers helpful advice.

The Camino de Santiago in Galicia

The **Camino de Santiago** in Galicia passes few tourist sights, meandering instead through hundreds of tiny villages strung out along the way. Pilgrims work a little harder on this last leg as the route clambers up and down steep hills and valleys, but the scenery is gorgeous compensation: green with oak forests and patchworked fields. Galicia is green for a reason, however; the region gets a lot of rain, and you can get caught in a storm even in summer.

The Galician government has made a huge effort to promote the camino. To mark the 1993 Holy Year, they *placed* concrete bollards marking the distance left to Santiago every 500m, and built a clutch of *albergues*, all with kitchens. Although some are already the worse for wear, with broken cookers and cold-water showers, you'll rarely travel more than 10km without finding alternative accommodation. The route begins with the fiercest climb of the Camino, a steep hike up cobbled paths often slick with mud and dung to the mountain village of O Cebreiro (see p.617), 30km uphill from Villafranca del Bierzo (see p.478). There can be snow here in winter, and fog often obscures the spectacular views, but it's one of the most magical places along the route, with round, thatched-roof *pallozas* (stone huts) and intricate *horréos* (granaries).

The camino is more crowded in Galicia, with the volume of pilgrims reaching a crescendo at Sarría (see p.622), 115km from Santiago and the last major town where you can begin your walk and still earn a *compostela*. The closer you get to Santiago, the more pilgrim rituals you'll encounter. At Lavacolla, just 10km outside the city, medieval pilgrims washed themselves in the river to prepare for their arrival at the cathedral. As part of this ritual cleansing – for many the first bath since leaving home – pilgrims would pay extra-special attention to their private parts – *lavacolla* is said to mean scrotum-washing. From Lavacolla, pilgrims are supposed to race to Monte de Gozo (Mount of Joy), 5km away, where the winner is declared the king of the group. Here pilgrims were once rewarded with their first view of Santiago de Compostela's cathedral spires, although it's impossible to see the spires these days through the buildings of suburban Santiago.

Although most people end their pilgrimage at Santiago de Compostela, after the rituals in the cathedral (see p.610) some continue walking on to Finisterre, a Celtic route towards the setting sun that predates the medieval pilgrimage by at least a millennium. It's another 75km along a quiet, well-marked, rural route to Cabo Finisterre, the westernmost point of mainland Europe and as far west as you can go without getting your feet wet. Below the lighthouse, at a small bronze sculpture of a pair of walking boots, pilgrims traditionally burn their clothes after a dip in the sea to celebrate the end of the journey.

a few farmers still choose to live in the ancient dwellings; their children, however, seem to be unanimous in the desire to move away in pursuit of creature comforts, and the old way of life must surely be coming to an end.

Many of the ancient buildings along the Pilgrim Route are now little more than ruins, but some survive. For example, the **Monasterio de Samos** (daily 10.30am–1pm & 4.30–7pm), 40km west of Cebreiro, famous for its library in the Middle Ages, and badly damaged by fire in 1951, has been restored, and its *hospedería* reopened for pilgrims. Its moss-covered exterior, pierced only by two small barred windows, leads to two sunny and peaceful cloisters.

Lugo and around

Despite an apparently advantageous location on the route and already being an ancient city a thousand years ago, the Camino de Santiago bypassed **LUGO**. Built on a Celtic site above the Minho (and named after the Celtic sun god Lug), it is the only Spanish town to remain completely enclosed within superb **Roman walls**. These are ten to fifteen metres high, with 85 circular towers along a circuit of almost 3km, and are broad enough to provide a pleasant thoroughfare for walks around the city. Sadly, insensitive building and a busy loop road make it impossible to appreciate the walls from any distance outside, but the road does at least keep the traffic out of the centre, which maintains an enjoyable if slightly neglected medley of medieval and eighteenth-century buildings.

Lugo is an excellent base for visiting some of the sights along the Camino, including the glorious monastery at **Sobrado de Monxes** or the impressive castle at **Portomarín**.

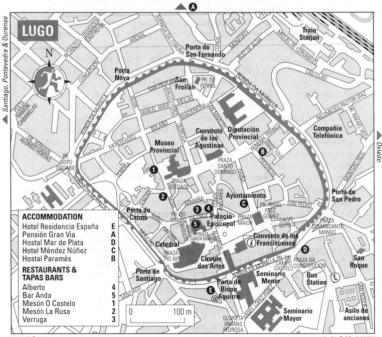

The Town

Lugo may be short on great sights, but it's a fine place to wander around, savouring the many granite staircases, narrow arcades and relaxed open spaces. The largest and best of the city's gardens, the **Parque Rosalía de Castro**, has a fine little café and weekend performances by the local brass band. It's a popular destination for the evening *paseo*, positioned a little way out of the Porta de Santiago, with good views over the Minho valley.

The large mossy **Catedral** (daily 8am–8.30pm, museum Mon–Sat: July & Aug 11am–1pm & 4–6pm; Sept–June 11am–noon; free), flanked by three distinctive towers, was, like so many *gallego* churches, modelled after the one at Santiago de Compostela. Inside, choir stalls cramp the central space, forcing you around a ring of chapels, in one of which an imperial soldier in cherubic posture tramples a dying Moor. Walk down Rúa Nova and you'll come to Lugo's excellent **Museo Provincial** (July & Aug: Mon–Fri 11am–2pm & 5–8pm, Sat 10am–2pm, Sun 11am–2pm; Sept–June: Mon–Sat 10.30am–2pm & 4.30–8.30pm, Sat closes at 8pm; free), partly housed in the old Convento de San Francisco. This is a well-displayed collection of *gallego* art, contemporary Spanish work swiped from the Prado and an early collection of Galicia's Sargadelos china, alongside the more predictable Roman remains and ecclesiastical clutter.

Though the **Praza Maior**, one block east of the Catedral, is gracefully colonnaded, it is worth passing through the nearby, and otherwise less inviting, **Praza Santo Domingo** where a statue of a Roman imperial eagle commemorates the bimillennial anniversary of Caesar Augustus's entry into the city. Outside the walls, things are rather less appealing, though those with an interest in Roman history may wish to make their way down to the banks of the nearby Río Minho. Here a much reconstructed **Roman bridge** spans the waters, while the nearby **spa** predates the walls by over 250 years (entry by appointment ℡982 221 228, ℻982 221 659).

Practicalities

The **train station** (to the north) and **bus terminal** (to the east) are immediately outside the walls, a fair distance apart. If you enter the town through the southwest **Porta de Santiago**, the best of its old gates, you can then climb up onto the most impressive stretch of wall, leading past the cathedral. Lugo's **turismo** (July–Aug daily 10am–2pm & 4–8pm; Sept–June Mon–Fri 9.30am–2pm & 4–6.30pm; ℡982 231 361) is hidden away in a small shopping arcade off the south side of the Praza Maior. For **Internet** access, *Futura*, on Villalba 4, is open daily until 4am (€2.40 per hour).

Most of the budget **hostales** are outside the walls, around the train and bus stations. Outside Porta Bispo Aguirre, *Hotel Residencia España*, Rúa Villalba 2 (℡982 231 540; ❷), is well run, while the new *Pensión Gran Via*, Rúa Fraga 3 (℡982 229 263; ❶), near the train station, is exceptionally cheap. The pleasant *Hostal Mar de Plata*, Ronda de Muralla 5 (℡982 228 910; ❶), is one of a clutch of cheap options right next to the bus station. There are limited options within the walls: *Hostal Paramés*, Rúa do Progreso 28 (℡982 226 251; ❸), offers comfortable, good-value rooms, while *Hotel Méndez Núñez*, Rúa Raiña 1 (℡982 230 711, ℻982 229 738; ❸), is more upmarket.

The best **restaurants** are on Rúa da Cruz. At no. 12 the swanky *Verruga* has top-notch seafood, as does the equally posh *Alberto* a few doors down at no. 4. Rather cheaper but still good is *Bar Anda* at no. 7. The best place to look for **bars** and **tapas** is the long, straight Rúa Nova nearby. *Méson O Castelo*, Rúa Nova 23, has a good, cheap *menú* for €7.20, or try the *bodega*-cum-*pulpería*, *Mesón La Rusa*, a little further along at no. 13. For a quick coffee, the abundance of cafés on the Praza Maior have outdoor seating.

West from Lugo: Sobrado dos Monxes and Portomarín

The once-great monastery of **Sobrado dos Monxes** (daily 10.15am–1.30pm & 4.15–6.45pm), midway between Lugo, Santiago and Betanzos, was also allowed to decay for a long time, but thanks to restoration work carried out by the provincial government, with your own transport it remains a highly worthwhile detour. After the empty approach road, the huge cathedral church with its strong west towers comes as a dramatic shock. The range of the abbey buildings proclaims past royal patronage, their scale emphasised by the tiny village below. The church itself sprouts flowers and foliage from every niche and crevice, its honey-coloured stone blossoming with lichens and mosses. Within, all is immensely grand – long, uncluttered vistas, mannerist Baroque, and romantic gloom; there are superb, worm-endangered choir stalls (once in Santiago cathedral) and, through a small arch in the north transept, a small, ruined Romanesque chapel. These are the highlights, but take time to explore the outbuildings, too, including a magnificent thirteenth-century kitchen with a massive chimney flue. A small community of monks maintains the monastery and operates a small shop.

The town of **PORTOMARÍN**, 26km south of Lugo, was flooded by the damming of the Minho, but its Templar castle and church were carried stone by stone to a new site further up the hillside. There's an expensive but well-equipped *pousada* here on Avenida de Sarría (☎982 545 200; ❺) and a much cheaper hotel, *Villajardín* (☎982 545 252; ❷), at Rúa do Miño 14.

South from Lugo: Sarría and Monforte de Lemos

Equipped with a handful of *hostales* and cafés, **SARRÍA**, 31km south of Lugo, makes a logical stopover on this part of the *camino*; try the *Londres*, Calvo Sotelo (☎982 532 456, ☎982 533 006; ❷), or the nearby *Roma* at no. 2 (☎982 532 211; ❷), which are both good value. The lower part of town is unimpressive, but old Sarría straggles gloriously uphill, topped by a (privately owned) castle.

On the plain 66km south of Lugo along the C546, **MONFORTE DE LEMOS** is a major rail junction. The station is some way from the town centre, but Monforte is a satisfyingly unspoilt and ancient place. Its **Torre de Lemos** looks out across a featureless expanse from the top of a hill full of tumbledown old houses, and there's a strikingly elegant Renaissance **Colegio** lower down. If you want **to stay**, *Hostal Puente Romano* (☎982 411 168; ❶) on Praza Dr Goyanes 6 is a good, cheap bet, as is *Hostal Riosol* (☎982 400 319; ❶), nearer the station at Rúa Estación 5.

The North Coast

The fishing villages of the **Rías Altas** are a gentle introduction to the rest of coastal Galicia. The elegant port of **Viveiro** is the main draw along the north coast, though a succession of smaller and quieter fishing villages such as **Porto de Vares** and **Ortigueira** are rewarding day-trips. Further south, the historic maritime city of **A Coruña** is a lively base for visiting the Roman town of

Betanzos and for exploring the infamous **Costa da Morte**. **Malpica** and **Corme** are timeless fishing villages easily accessible from A Coruña, while to the Romans the isolated outpost of **Finisterre** represented the "end of the world". With transport links slow and infrequent, the Costa da Morte sees barely a handful of tourists from year to year, yet there is ample reward waiting for anybody willing to make the effort to investigate the endless coves and bays of the region.

The Rías Altas

The savagery of the ocean has etched Galicia's north coast with a series of dramatic bays and estuaries known as the **Rías Altas** (High Estuaries). Approaching from Asturias, the coastline becomes noticeably more desolate, the road twisting around rocky inlets flanked by villages clinging to the shore as they are battered by the frequent high winds. It's not nearly as difficult as it once was to get around – roads, which until relatively recently were poorly surfaced and barely frequented, are now reliable and safe, and the facilities for visitors have improved – but travel remains slow, and even if you have a car you should allow plenty of time to get from one place to the next.

If you have the time to enjoy it, the closing stretch of the **FEVE railway** from Luarca to Ferrol is perhaps the most picturesque of the entire route. It clings to every nuance of the coastline, looping around a succession of *rías* and rambling through the eucalyptus forests and wild-looking hills which buffer the villages from the harsh Atlantic. Settlements are concentrated at the sides of the estuaries, with the occasional beach tacked beside or below them, but unless you are planning an extended stay it's advisable to choose just a couple of targets – the pretty port of **Viveiro**, for example, or the ancient town of **Betanzos**. **Ferrol**, this section's major city, is deep in the throes of industrial decay, and it may be better to push on towards A Coruña if you are looking for an aesthetically-pleasing base.

Ribadeo and around

RIBADEO, the first *gallego* town and *ría* if you're coming from the east, makes a poor introduction to the region, although it does have a certain crumbling charm. Most of its best architecture is located around the Plaza España, site of the new **turismo** (summer Mon–Fri 8am–3pm & 4–8pm, Sat–Sun 10am–2pm & 4–8pm; winter afternoon only; ℡982 128 689). The **Palacio del Marqués de Sargadelos**, opposite, with its unusual decorative tower, is the town's main monument. There are a few places **to stay** – such as the good-value and friendly *Galicia*, Rúa Virgen del Camino 1 (℡982 128 777; ❷), and the *parador* on Rúa Amador Fernández 7 (℡982 128 825, ✉ribadeo@parador.es; ❻) – but overall it's drab. The nearest **beach**, the Praia do Castro, is a few kilometres further west, with **campsites** at Benquerencia (℡982 124 450; all year) and Reinante (℡982 134 005; June–Sept), but by now you're getting a bit too close to the ugly port of Foz. **MONDOÑEDO**, 20km up the valley of the Río Masma, is an attractive old riverside town, while 15km further on, at **CERVO**, a road turns south to the tiny village of **SARGADELOS**, home since the nineteenth century to a working ceramics factory that today allows visits (Mon–Fri 9am–12.30pm & 2.30–5.30pm; free).

Viveiro

Once a remote, elegant port, the area around **VIVEIRO** has seen an influx of summer visitors over the last decade, changing the character of the large *ría* with a rash of holiday homes spreading up the hillsides. The old town, however, is protected by a circuit of Renaissance walls, and its narrow streets are largely closed to traffic and lined with glass-fronted houses in delicate white wooden frames.

The bay shelters several peaceful **beaches**, particularly the Praia de Faro up towards the open sea. The large town beach, the Praia de Covas, is a good ten minutes' walk from town across a causeway.

Practicalities

The **bus station** is on the waterfront Avenida de la Marina: turn right out of the station, and after 100m go left through a stone arch to reach the Praza Maior. The **FEVE station** (3–4 trains daily in each direction to Ribadeo and Ferrol) is a ten-minute walk from the town centre: bear left out of the station to reach the main road, then turn left under the bridge and walk straight on to reach the bus station. The **turismo** (mid-June to mid-Sept daily 10.30am–1.30pm & 5–8pm; ☎982 560 879) is in a wooden hut opposite the bus station. **Internet** access is available at *Fox Ciber* on c/Montenegro for €2.40 per hour.

Inside the walls there are a couple of good, inexpensive **places to stay**: *Nuevo Mundo*, Rúa María Teodoro de Quirós 14 (☎982 560 025; ❶), has attractive balconied rooms, although those at the front are within ear-splitting distance of the bells of Santa María church opposite. More upmarket but still excellent value is *Hostal Vila*, Rúa Nicolás Montenegro 57 (☎982 561 331, ℱ982 563 112; ❷), in a rather drab street just outside the walls at the Porta del Vallado at the top end of town. Most luxurious of all, though, is *Hotel Orfeo*, Rúa García Navia Castrillón 2 (☎982 562 101, ℱ982 560 453; ❹), with private parking and rooms overlooking the bay. There's a **campsite**, *Vivero* (☎982 560 004; June–Sept), behind the Praia de Covas.

Places **to eat** are fairly thin on the ground. The *Nuevo Mundo* has a good restaurant upstairs – €6 for a four-course feast for guests only, but there's no choice of dishes. *Restaurante O Muro*, near the bus station on Avenida Cervantes, is a *pulpería* and grill with a wide menu of fish and meats. Three blocks southwest of the square at Rua Melitòn Cortiñas 15 is *O Asador*, an excellent and reasonably-priced option, while opposite, at no. 26, *Laurel* has a range of seafood-based *menús* for €7.25. On the other side of the Praza Maior, just above San Francisco church at Rúa Antonio Bas 2, *Restaurante Serra* serves decent seafood and *menús* for €7.80.

Porto do Barqueiro, Ortigueira and Porto de Vares

The next two *ría* villages (and FEVE stops) are **PORTO DO BARQUEIRO**, 16km west of Viveiro, a tiny and very picturesque fishing port of slate-roofed houses near Spain's northernmost point, and the larger **ORTIGUEIRA**, 14km further on, set amid a dark mass of pines. The former has three places **to stay** dotted around its tiny harbour: *Estrellas del Mar* (☎981 414 105; ❷), with great sea views; *La Marina* (☎981 414 098; ❷), a little smarter and pricier but with only two sea-facing rooms; and the stylish and very comfortable *Bodegón O Forno* (☎981 414 124; ❷), also looking onto the sea. Ortigueira, too, has a couple of decent *hostales*, including the *Monterrey*, at Avda. Franco 105 (☎981 400 135, ℱ981 400 417; ❷).

If you have your own transport, you should take the opportunity to head the 7km north of Barqueiro up to the headland, through pine and eucalyptus forest, to straggly Vila de Vares. Two kilometres beyond, **PORTO DE VARES** is a highly attractive clump of fishermen's houses overlooking the bay, flanked to the south by a superb, wide, sandy beach, where you can camp. In the hamlet, there's a single *hostal*, *Porto Mar* (☎981 418 676; ❷), with smart rooms and beautiful sea views. There's also a terrific seafood **restaurant**, *Marina*, with outdoor tables and window seats overlooking both bay and beach. Fresh seafood meals – including great octopus – start from €9.60 a head, though the *paella especial* will set you back considerably more.

San Andrés de Teixido and around

The FEVE heads inland after Ortigueira, but drivers or the very determined could make a side-trip to the hermitage at **SAN ANDRÉS DE TEIXIDO**, the so-called "Mecca of the Gallegos". Like so many of Galicia's sanctuaries, it is based on a pre-Christian religious site, but although a monastery was already in place by the twelfth century, the first reference to it as a *santuario* was not until 1391. It is a dramatic spot, with the nearby cliffs at **Vixia de Herbeira** claiming the title of the highest in Europe at over 600m. There are a couple of places to stay in **CEDEIRA**, a port with a long sweep of beach set in an attractive *ría*, 12km away: try the comfortable *Avenida*, Rúa Cuatro Caminos 6 (☎981 480 998, ℱ981 492 112; ❹), or the basic *Hostal Chelsea*, Plaza Sagrado Corazón 15 (☎981 481 111; ❷), or, slightly better, the *Hostal Paris St Tropez*, at Paseo Castelao 73 (☎981 480 430; July & Aug only; ❶).

Ferrol

The city of **FERROL**, historically one of Spain's principal naval bases and dockyards, is now struggling to survive the collapse of the shipbuilding industry. Unfortunately, the navy and dockyards have usurped the best of the coastline, leaving a provincial centre dominated by a status-conscious, navy-oriented community and a large, paint-spattered statue of El Caudillo (the Chief), Francisco Franco, who was born here in 1892. Although frequently considered a bastion of conservatism, Ferrol was also the birthplace of Pablo Iglesias, founder of the Spanish Socialist Party, whose government initially steered the country through the transitional years after the dictatorship.

Getting out shouldn't be too difficult; the **FEVE** and **RENFE** stations are housed in the same building, and the **bus station** is just outside – exit and make two quick lefts, and you'll see it some 50m ahead of you. If you need **accommodation**, one of the more reasonable places is the spartan *Noray*, on Rúa Venezuela 117 (☎981 310 079; ❶), and there are plenty of other choices along Rúa Pardo Bajo – including the simple *Aloya*, at no. 28 (☎981 351 231, ℱ981 351 231; ❷), which has heated rooms, vital in winter – or Rúa del Sol and Rúa María, all within a few minutes' walk of the station and the central Praza de España. If you're driving, beware of the gridlock out of Ferrol on Friday and in again on Sunday nights, when the entire community heads out of the city for the weekend, blocking local roads solid.

The Ría de Betanzos

Ferrol stands more or less opposite A Coruña, 20km away across the mouth of the **Ría de Betanzos**, but a seventy-kilometre trip by road or rail. The coast between the two cities is surprisingly rural, with the contours of the *ría* speckled with forests and secluded beaches.

Pontedeume, Perbes and Sada

Heading south from Ferrol, you cross the Río Eume either by the vast medieval bridge at **PONTEDEUME** (Puentedeume), or the vaster-still motorway flyover nearby. The stones on either side of the old bridge as you enter town are, in fact, boars from the coat of arms of the once-powerful overlords, the counts of Andrade. Their tower overlooks the river at Pontedeume, and the Castelo de Andrade is perched on a hill over the town. Should you wish to stay, *Hostal Allegue* on Rúa Chafarís 1 (℡ & ℱ981 430 035; ❷) is a decent bet.

Just beyond, *Camping Perbes* (℡981 783 104; June–Sept) is sandwiched between woods and water on the popular **Praia Perbes**, 6km south of Pontedeume. At **SADA**, opposite, you'll find the *Marina Española* **youth hostel** (℡981 620 118; ❶), and there are also several **campsites** in the area, the best of which is *Velo Mar* (℡981 617 076; all year).

Betanzos

The ancient town of **BETANZOS**, 36km southeast of A Coruña, is built on a pre-Roman site so old that what was once a steep seaside hill is now located well inland at the confluence of the Ríos Mendo and Mandeo. The base of the hill is surrounded by fragments of the medieval walls, though these are now largely built over with houses. Above these rises a mass of twisting and tunnelling narrow streets, within which lies the twelfth-century church of **Santa María do Azougue**, reconstructed by the Andrade lords in the fourteenth century. The tomb of Conde Fernán Perez de Andrade "O Boo" (The Good), who commissioned the building of the church, lies inside the Gothic **Igrexa de San Francisco** opposite. Look out for an unusual stone boar with a cross on its back on the roof – an early Christian symbol.

The focus of Betanzos is the large, attractive main square, the **Praza dos Irmáns García Naveira**, named after (and boasting a statue of) the two Betanzos-born brothers who left to make their fortunes in Argentina at the end of the nineteenth century and then returned to endow the town with hospitals, schools and the remarkable O Pasatempo park (see below).

Just behind the square, in Rúa Emilio Romay, the excellent **Museo das Mariñas** (summer Mon–Fri 10am–2pm & 5–8pm, Sat 10.30am–2pm & 5–8pm, Sun 11am–2pm; winter Mon–Fri 10am–1pm & 4–8pm, Sat 10.30am–1pm; €1.20) provides a fascinating insight into the history of Betanzos and neighbouring *mariñas* (sea-facing villages), including a colourful collection of period costumes.

A ten-minute, well-signposted walk away on the edge of town is the remarkable "encyclopedia park", **O Pasatempo** (daily 4–8.30pm; free), rescued from almost total dereliction and restored to something resembling its original splendour. Founded by Juan García Naveira in 1893, the park's sculptures and murals were intended to give the folk of provincial Betanzos a picture in stone of all that was then the newest or strangest in the world – a biplane, a deep-sea diver, the Panama Canal – along with more purely whimsical elements like the strange grotto with Gaudí-esque pillars and a bank of granite clocks showing times around the world (it's always midday in Betanzos), all of it looking as quaintly old-fashioned now as it might have seemed thrillingly modern at the time.

Practicalities

Half-hourly **buses** (hourly at weekends) from A Coruña (a 45-minute journey) pull up right opposite the Museo de Mariñas on Rúa de Emilio Romay just behind the main square Plaza García Naviera. Buses from Ferrol arrive at the Betanzos Ciudad RENFE **train station**, itself used only for the four daily trains to and from Ferrol and A Coruña; it's a ten-minute walk into town, across the park and over the bridge to the town walls. Other trains use the Betanzos Infesta station, 2.5km away at the top of a steep climb – you're better off coming by bus. The new **turismo** (summer Mon–Fri 10am–2pm & 5–8pm, Sat 10.30am–2pm & 5–8pm, Sun 11am–2pm; winter Mon–Fri 10am–1pm & 4–8pm, Sat 10.30am–1pm; ☎981 770 100, ⓦwww.betanzos .net) is conveniently located on Plaza García Naviera. Limited **accommodation** options mean that most people prefer to make the day-trip from A Coruña, but if you need a place to stay, the very basic *Hospedaje Universal*, Avda. Linares Rivas 18 (☎981 770 055; ❶), is a cheap fallback just around the corner from the main square; and on the far side of the plaza, *Hotel Los Ángeles*, Rúa dos Ánxeles 11 (☎981 771 213, ⓕ981 776 459; ❸), is professionally run, if a bit anonymous.

Eating and drinking venues centre around the row of bars on the main square and the two tiny alleys running either side of it. The popular *O Pote* on the first alley, the *Travesía do Progreso*, has a wide range of good tapas, while at Rùa do Rollo 6, directly behind the statue of the García brothers, the wood-panelled *Mesón Os Arcos* serves an excellent-value *menú del día* (€6.60) and great grills. If you're in Betanzos on August 16, don't miss the *Fiesta del Globo*, the highlight of which is the midnight launch from the Torre de Santo Domingo in the main square of the world's largest paper balloon, daubed with political slogans. There is also a medieval **festival** in the second weekend of July, when the town is transported back to the times of the Andrade lords.

A Coruña

Despite its long history, the port of **A CORUÑA** is surprisingly modern, focused more on the office blocks and apartments of its rising middle class than on its past. However, its position is impressive, crammed onto a peninsula with one side looking across the *rías* to Ferrol, the other exposed to the Atlantic, and its medieval quarter remains fairly extensive. It's also a major transport nexus, with a good beach right in the centre, some of the best tapas bars in Galicia and a vibrant nightlife that ends with 5am *chocolate con churros*.

Arrival, information and accommodation

The **bus** and **train** stations are close to each other either side of Plaza de Madrid, a good twenty-minute walk south of the city centre. From here take bus #1 or #1a to their termini, the Praza de María Pita (all city buses €0.80). The **regional turismo** is at the Dársena de la Marina (Mon–Fri 10am–2pm & 4–7pm, Sat 11am–2pm & 5–7pm, Sun 11am–2pm; ☎981 221 822, ⓦwww.turgalicia.es). The **city turismo** is nearby at Avda. de la Marina 18 (Mon–Sat 10am–2pm & 4–8pm; ☎981 184 344, ⓦwww.turismocoruna.com), with a wealth of information in English. If you are thinking of spending a while in the city and visiting all of the attractions, the *Coruña Card*, available from the turismo, may be worth the investment. It gives 48 hours, unlimited access to the museums and aquarium, shopping discounts and forty percent off car hire (€12, €25 family card).

Accommodation

Alborán Rúa Riego de Agua 14 ☎ & ℱ981 222 562. Excellent location on a pedestrianized street very close to Praza María Pita with 30 comfortable rooms, all with bath and TV, and some with balconies overlooking the street. ❹

Hotel Finisterre Paseo del Parrote 2 ☎981 205 400, ⓦwww.latojahoteles.com. The top option in town, this vast orange waterfront palace comes complete with tennis courts, Olympic-size swimming pool and all mod cons. ❼

Hostal La Perla Rúa Torreiro11 ☎981 226 700. Friendly, spacious rooms with TV and bathroom, a short distance from Plaza María Pita and the best of the city's tapas bars. ❸

Hostal Las Rías Rúa San Andrés 141 ☎981 226 879. Spotless modern en-suite hotel-style rooms at *pensión* prices. All rooms with TV and telephone. ❷

Hostal Roma Rúa Nueva 3 ☎981 228 075. Good-value clean, modern rooms with TV and bathroom, plus Internet access. ❸

Hostal El Sol Rúa Sol 10 ☎981 210 362. Unprepossessing exterior, complete with bordello-style flashing sign, though inside rooms are stylish and comfortable. ❹

The City

Departure point of the doomed 1588 Armada, and veteran of the Peninsular Wars, A Coruña has a lengthy history of naval combat. At the heart of the town is the huge, colonnaded **Praza de María Pita**, named after (and featuring a statue of) the spear-waving María Pita, a redoubtable local heroine who helped repel an English siege in 1589. Some of the best of A Coruña's distinctive glassed-in balconies – a practical innovation against wind and showers – are on Rúa Riego de Agua, directly west of here, and on the nearby waterfront Dársena, from where the **Paseo Marítimo** walkway edges the city's extensive coastline, bending around the port and marina.

East of the plaza are the narrow and atmospheric streets of the medieval town, which wind around the Romanesque churches of **Santiago** and **Santa María del Campo** and are shielded from the sea by a high wall, much of which still remains, notably some fine sixteenth- and seventeenth-century gates. On the far eastern side of the old town is the walled **Jardín de San Carlos** and, inside, the **tomb of Sir John Moore**, killed in 1809 during the British retreat from the French in the Peninsular Wars, and immortalized in the jingoistic rhythms of Reverend Charles Wolfe ("Not a drum was heard, not a funeral note..."), which you will find here inscribed. Directly across the road, the **Museo Militar** (daily 10am–2pm & 4–7pm, closed Sun pm; free) has a huge collection of guns, ordnance, uniforms and toy soldiers from the Peninsular to Bosnian wars.

Beyond here, on a spit of land poking out into the sea, the restored Castelo San Antón was once a garrison and, until the 1960s, a military and political prison. Today it houses the **Museo Arqueolóxico e Histórico** (Tues–Sat 10am–7.30pm, July & Aug closes 9pm, Sun 10am–2.30pm; €2), worth the entrance fee if only for the view across the bay from the top and the medieval stone carvings at the back.

The city's much-trumpeted lighthouse, the **Torre de Hercules** (daily April–June & Sept 10am–7pm; July & Aug 10am–9pm, open till midnight on Fri and Sat; Oct–March 10am–6pm; €2), symbol of A Coruña, lies on a rocky outcrop north of the centre (bus #3 or #3a from the turismo or #4 from the bus station). It has been warning ships off the treacherous Costa da Morte since Roman times, and somewhat dubiously claims the title of the oldest functioning lighthouse in the world, although no trace of the original ancient stonework remains to be seen. The city's brilliant, state-of-the-art **Aquarium** (daily 10am–10pm; €6) is built on the headland just below the Torre de Hercules. Far more than just a series of fish tanks, it offers a vast array of inter-

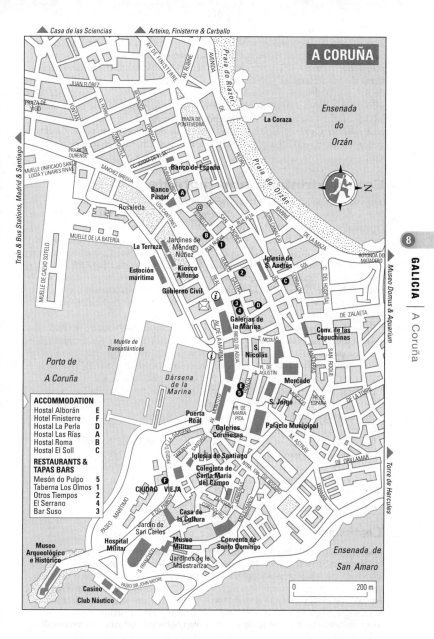

ACCOMMODATION

Hostal Alborán	E
Hotel Finisterre	F
Hostal La Perla	D
Hostal Las Rías	A
Hostal Roma	B
Hostal El Soll	C

RESTAURANTS & TAPAS BARS

Mesón do Pulpo	5
Taberna Los Olmos	1
Otros Tiempos	2
El Serrano	4
Bar Suso	3

active displays that will delight adults and children alike, as well as the 4.5-million-litre *Nautilus* tank which submerges you into a world filled with the marine life of the Atlantic coast.

Following the Paseo Maritimo around, you reach the superbly designed **Museo Domus** (Museum of Mankind; daily: summer 11am–9pm; winter

10am–7pm; Ⓦ www.casaciencias.org; €1.80), which takes you on an educational trip around the workings of the human body via a series of fascinating interactive exhibits. The joint entry ticket also gets you into the less interesting **Casa de las Sciencias** (same hours), an interactive science museum in Parque de Santa Margarita, out towards the bus station, or a €7 *bono ticket* will get you into the aquarium as well. South of here, and on the opposite side of the headland from the Dársena, lies the sweeping golden arc of the city's main beaches, **Praia do Orzán** and the contiguous **Praia de Riazor**. Surprisingly clean and unpolluted, you'll have to get there early in summer to guarantee a prime spot.

Eating, drinking and nightlife

The chain of small streets leading west from Praza de María Pita, from Rúa de la Franja, through to Rúa La Galera, Rúa Los Olmos and Rúa Estrella, are crowded with bars that offer some of Spain's finest seafood. There's a cluster of *marisquerías* immediately west of Praza María Pita on Rúa de la Franja, including the popular *Mesón do Pulpo* at no. 9. Beyond here there's a big selection of seafood tapas bars – try *Bar Suso* at Rúa Galera 31 or *Taberna Los Olmos* at Rúa Los Olmos 22 – and several good *jamonerías*, such as *Otros Tiempos* at Galera 56 and *El Serrano* at no. 23. The crowd of waterfront **restaurants** along the Avenida de la Marina competes neither in quality nor atmosphere, although *O Piote* at no.10 is the best.

In summer the waterfront **bars** around the adjacent beaches of Praia de Riazor and Praia do Orzán do a roaring trade, especially *Bar Egeo*, *Trataplán* and *Cazuza*, while *Montesol* often boasts several drink offers. Another good place to start the evening is Rúa Orillamar, where bars such as *Patachín*, *Galeón* and *Nectar* are always full at weekends. For **late-night** action, *Corralón* on Rúa Panaderas has live music, while *Punto 3*, nearby in the Mercado San Agustín, doesn't even get started until 5am. Further inland, *Terraza*, on Rúa Juan Florez, plays a blend of soft rock and pop, while the perennial *Pirámide* on the same street is a nightclub with a Latin dance theme.

Five kilometres out of town, the bars and clubs at **Praia Santa Cristina**, a lovely wooded spit of sand further up the *ría*, are lively throughout the summer. Check out *Brothers* and *Chevalier* for the best of the late-night action. You can pick up a bus from the main station until 10pm, or a boat from the Dársena de la Marina until 8pm, but once there you'll either have to stay the course until the following morning or get a taxi back to town.

Listings

Bookshops Librería Colón, Rúa Riego de Agua 24, has possibly Galicia's best selection of English-language books, plus a wide range of foreign newspapers.

Football Estadio del Riazor, just north of the Plaza do Riazor, is home to Deportivo, consistently amongst Spain's top three sides over the last decade. There is a stadium shop, and matches usually take place on a Sunday evening (tickets from €10).

Internet Internet, fax and photocopying service at Comunicopy, Rúa Angel 19, near the Museo de Bellas Artes (€1.20 per hour; daily 10am–11pm). Open later is Estrella Park in an amusement arcade at Rúa Estrella 12, with coin-operated machines (€1.40 per hour).

Laundry Clean and Clean laundries are located on Avda. Conchiñas, Avda. Finisterre and at Rúa Juan Florez 63. Self-service at Glu-Glu, Rúa Alcalde Marchese 4, near the bus station.

Post Office Main post office is located opposite the city turismo on Avda. de la Marina.

Telephones International calls, fax and Internet at the *telefónica* on a tiny side street between Rúa La Galera and Rúa del Real, though clearly signposted from the former (Mon–Fri 10am–2pm & 4–10pm, Sat 10am–2pm).

The Prestige disaster

During an Atlantic storm on November 13 2002 the **oil tanker Prestige**, carrying 77,000 tonnes of crude oil, ran into difficulties just off the Galician coast. Six days of inaction later, on November 19, the ship broke in two and sank to a depth of 3600 metres, carrying with it most of its cargo. One hundred and twenty-five tonnes of oil seeped daily from its fractured hull, with disastrous consequences for marine life, as well as the Galician fishing and tourist industries. Over 16,000 fishermen and 6500 fishing boats were grounded for months after the disaster, and 662 of Spain's 1064 beaches (437 in Galicia alone) were affected by oil, which travelled as far east as southwestern France. The authorities concentrated their efforts on stemming the flow of oil from the vessel, Prime Minister Aznar personally taking charge of the proceedings, but they failed to win public confidence after a series of false assurances about the scale of the disaster, including the claim that the oil would surely congeal in the freezing temperatures of the seabed. Local Galician newspapers penned headlines like "a shipwreck of confidence" and "a tide of discontent", and the people began to take matters into their own hands under the political slogan "Nunca Mais" (Never Again). Tens of thousands of volunteers and thousands of troops were involved in the clean-up operation, a remarkable display of people power that minimized the effects of the disaster more than could ever have been hoped. Just twelve months later there was barely a trace of oil on most beaches, but the clean-up operation continues, albeit at a smaller scale, with officials in protective clothing still scouring the tourist beaches to pick up remnants. As a direct result of the *Prestige* disaster, and in an attempt to prevent a repeat, all single-hulled oil tankers were banned from European waters.

The Costa da Morte

Wild, windy and occasionally desolate, the infamous **Costa da Morte**, or Coast of Death, west of A Coruña is often passed over by tourists as they head south to the beaches of the Rías Baixas. But while the Costa da Morte has neither the climate nor the infrastructure to cope with large-scale tourism, it boasts equally beautiful coves, tiny fishing villages huddled against the headlands and forested mountain slopes aplenty, making it well worth the diversion. Yet it is this very sense of seclusion that is the single biggest attraction of the area. For the Romans this was the edge of the world, for the Celts a place of legend, and for the sailors buffeted by the Atlantic waves a place to fear. Hundreds of shipwrecks litter the seabed, a testimony to the dangers of the rocks hidden beneath the waves and the origins of the name of the region.

Should the challenge appeal to you, make sure that you allow plenty of time for getting around. Though things have improved, progress is still slow, and, with no train lines, buses are the only **public transport** option. Transport Finisterre buses connect all the places mentioned below, while the south is better served by frequent Castromíl buses, at least in summer. If you have your own car, or you're prepared to hitch, it's well worth following the length of the coastal road from A Coruña down to **Finisterre** and around to **Muros** and **Noia**. Celtic dolmens and *castros* (forts) abound, but you'll need a good map and plenty of patience to find most of them.

You should also be warned that even where the isolated coves do shelter fine beaches, you will rarely find resort facilities. While the beaches may look splendid, braving the water is recommended only to the strongest of swimmers, and the climate is significantly wetter and windier here than it is a mere 100km or so further south.

Malpica to Traba

There are few potential stopping points immediately west of A Coruña; your best bet is to get on a Transportes Finisterre bus and stay on it until you're well past Carballo (a busy inland road junction), after which the bus takes you to a succession of tiny seaside harbours. The first of these is **MALPICA**, crammed onto the neck of a narrow peninsula, with a harbour on one side and a marvellous – though exposed – beach hardly 100m away on the other. Out to sea are three desolate islands which make up a seabird sanctuary; access is possible only if you come to some informal arrangement with a fisherman. If you want a **place to stay**, *Hostal Panchito*, Praza Villar Amigo 6 (℡981 720 307; ❷), has smart rooms with private bath, while *Hostal JB* (℡981 721 906; ❷) is right on the beach. The best seafood **restaurants** here are *San Francisco*, Rúa Eduardo Pondal, where you can choose your dinner from a tankful of live sea creatures, and *O Burato*, overlooking the port off the square.

Unlike its neighbours, **CORME**, 10km from Malpica, is hardly visited by tourists, which can be a relief in the high season. Across the headland from Malpica, it is set back above a deep, round bay, with three beaches just to the east: two in small rocky inlets and a larger one backed by sand dunes a walkable distance around the bay. The town itself has few bars or restaurants, only a couple of cramped streets leading to a minute *praza*. Even by the standards of local villages whose social structures are still clan-based, Corme is fiercely insular. In the 1940s and 1950s, it was the stamping ground of *gallego* guerrillas, who swooped down from the hills to beat up the Civil Guard. There are **beds** available at *O Cabazo*, Rúa Arnela 23 (℡981 738 077; ❷), if you want to stay. The view across the harbour from the back of *Bar O Biscoiteiro*, on Avenida Remedios, is lovely, and the **food**'s good, too, or alternatively try the *Café-bar Méndez* on the main road.

Midway between Malpica and Corme, young Spaniards set up tents around small fires on the sheltered **Praia de Niñóns**. Follow the signposts from Corme and turn left at the granite cross – then follow the road between fields of maize to the sea. There's a *fuente* (fountain) beneath the granite church that overlooks the beach, and a solitary bar that closes at night so you'll need to bring your own supplies. Another great, though illegal, campsite is at **Praia de Balarés**, below Corme and approaching Ponteceso – a lovely, sheltered inlet with a couple of high-season bars, and relatively safe swimming.

An ancient bridge crosses the River Anllóns at **PONTECESO**, 6km southeast of Corme, just beyond the stone mansion that was the home of the nineteenth-century *gallego* poet, Eduardo Pondal – you'll see roads named after him all over Galicia. There's a single *pensión* here, *Teyma* at Avda. Bergantiños 28 (℡981 715 404; ❷), should you wish to stay, but it's not particularly good value. Ten kilometres further around the bay, a long sweep of fine, clean sand is backed by café-lined streets at **LAXE** (pronounced *lashay*), which offers the area's safest swimming, thanks to a formidable seawall protecting a small harbour. *Bar Mirador*, off the square, is owned by the descendant of a family of photographers who began work here in the 1870s – there's a pictorial history of the area up on the bar walls. The most reasonable **place to stay** here is the pleasant *Hostal Beiramar*, Rúa Rosalía de Castro 30 (℡ & ℻981 728 109; ❷). Basic rooms are also available at the *Restaurante Sardiñeira*, Rúa Rosalía de Castro 51 (℡981 728 029; ❶). Close by are two beaches, the deserted **Praia de Soesto**, which, though exposed, more than rivals the town beach, and a perfect cove, the **Praia de Arnado**. **TRABA**, 6km south, has its own massively long beach, the **Praia de Traba**, remote as anything, and backed by sand dunes and a jigsaw of mini-fields.

Camariñas to Finisterre

The stretch of coast from **Camariñas** to **Finisterre** is the most exposed and westerly part of Spain. Ever since a Roman expedition under Lucius Florus Brutus was brought short by what seemed to them an endless sea, it has been known as *finis terrae* (the end of the world), and it is not hard to see why. The savagery of the currents and weather are notorious, though the surrounding seas are rich in marine life. This is prime territory for hunting *percebes* (barnacles), which have to be scooped up from the very waterline, and collectors are commonly swept away by the dreaded "seventh wave", which can appear out of nowhere from a calm sea. *Percebes* are one of Galicia's most popular delicacies, with high prices reflecting the dangers involved in their collection.

Camariñas

Picturesque **CAMARIÑAS** is back on the bus route: if you're planning a night's stay it has a definite edge over Finisterre. Curled around an attractive harbour containing a fishing fleet and the yachts of well-heeled visitors, Camariñas' buildings have white-painted, glassed-in balconies, while the town sports a tradition in lacemaking – you'll see old women with lacemaking pillows in markets, strategically placed to corner tourists.

Accommodation prices are surprisingly low. *La Marina* (☎981 736 030, ℻981 736 030; ❷), Rúa Miguel Freijó 3, at the beginning of the harbour wall, has clean rooms, great views and a good restaurant. There's also *Hostal Plaza* in the old market square (☎981 736 103; ❶; April to mid-Sept only), and, about 1km out of town at Area de Vilá (by the sandy beach), the more expensive *Triñanes II* (☎981 736 108; ❷).

From Camariñas to **Cabo Vilán** a five-kilometre trek leads to a lighthouse on a rocky outcrop guarding the treacherous shore; climb the adjacent rocks for a stunning sea view. Winds whip viciously around the cape, making it the ideal place to locate the experimental wind farm which stands next to the lighthouse. Huge, sci-fi propellers spin eerily in the wind, lit by the searchlight beam of the lighthouse once darkness falls.

Muxía

On the tip of a rocky promontory across the *ría* from Camariñas, the small port of **MUXÍA** itself is nothing special. Make your way up to the Romanesque church on the hill above, though, and there's a fabulous view to either side of the headland. From here a footpath leads down to the eighteenth-century **Santuario de la Virgen de la Barca**, once the second most important site of Galicia's pre-Christian animist cult after San Andrés de Teixido (see p.625). The cult was centred around the strangely shaped granite rocks at the furthest point of the headland, some of which are precariously balanced and said to make wonderful sounds when struck correctly; others are supposed to have healing power. In later times, the rocks were reinterpreted as being the remains of the stone ship which brought the Virgin to the aid of Santiago, an obvious echo of the saint's own landing at Padrón.

The best **place to stay** is the delightful *Casa Isolina* (☎981 742 367; ❷), a beautiful old house one block back from the seafront, with a vine-terraced garden behind. There's also a reasonable *pensión* at *Plaza* on Rúa Quintàns 194 (☎981 750 452; ❶). For great **seafood**, visit the tiny, tumbledown *Casa Marujita*, up left from the far end of the seafront road.

On to Finisterre

The inland road (C552) from A Coruña to Finisterre is surprisingly good, a result of the unprecedented burst of road building over the past two decades that is changing Galicia forever.

Heading west, past the industrialized port of Cée, **CORCUBIÓN**, 14km northeast of Finisterre, retains some elegance, though ribbon-strip development has now joined it with its uglier neighbour. For a cheap room, try the small *La Sirena*, Rúa Antonio Porrua 15 (℡981 745 036; **❶**), above the bar of the same name just off the square, or, if you're after luxury, *El Hórreo* on the seafront (℡981 745 500, ℻981 745 563; **❺**). Halfway between Corcubión and Finisterre, a fine white-sand beach nestles in a small cove at **ESTORDE**, 1km short of the larger village of **Sardiñeiro**. Overlooking the beach is a pleasant **hostal**, the *Praia de Estorde* (℡981 745 585; **❸**), and just across the road, a small wooded **campsite**, *Ruta de Finisterre* (℡ & ℻981 746 302; June to mid-Sept).

Finisterre

The town of **FINISTERRE** (Fisterra) still feels as if it's ready to drop off the end of the world, but, other than for its symbolic significance, there's no great reason to stay. It's no more than a grey clump of houses wedged into the rocks on the side of a headland away from the open ocean, but it does have a number of inexpensive **hostales**, the cheapest of which is the *Casa Velay* (℡981 740 127; **❶**), overlooking the tiny bay just beyond the long harbour wall. *Hospedaje Lopéz* (℡981 740 449; **❷**) on the north side of the harbour has some rooms with balconies and views; the *Rivas*, Carreterra de Faro (℡981 740 027; **❶**), is excellent value; and the *Cabo Finisterre*, Rúa Santa Catalina 1 (℡981 740 000; **❷**), is good, too. For **food**, bypass the fancier restaurants with giant lobster tanks and head for the south side of the harbour where you'll find a cluster of places with *sardiñadas* (open-air sardine grills) and fresh *mariscos*.

The actual tip of the **headland** is a four-kilometre walk beyond, along a heathered mountainside, then through a pine forest plantation. On the way out of town, stop at **Santa María das Areas**, a small but atmospheric church with Romanesque and Gothic elements and a beautiful carved altar, which, like the strange weathered tombs to the left of the main door, is considerably older than the rest of the building. At the cape, a lighthouse perches high above the waves, and when, as so often, the whole place is shrouded in thick mist and the mournful foghorn wails across the sea, it's an eerie spot. Traditionally, this is the spot where pilgrims would come to burn their clothes, signalling the end of the pilgrimage, and also collect their scallop shell; the wearing of a scallop throughout the journey is a relatively recent phenomenon. When the sun shines, you're better steering clear of the ice-cream kiosks and shell-necklace sellers, and turning right up the zigzag road that climbs to the **Vista Monte do Facho**, high above the lighthouse, for stupendous views.

Ezaro, O Pindo and Carnota

Around **EZARO**, where the Río Xallas meets the sea, the scenery is marvellous. The rocks of the sheer escarpments above the road are so rich in minerals that they are multicoloured, and glisten beneath innumerable tiny waterfalls. Upstream there are warm, natural lagoons and more cascades. In Ezaro itself, the *hostal* above the *Bar Stop* (℡981 7125 777; **❷**) has inexpensive en-suite **rooms**, or you could continue another couple of kilometres to the little port of **O PINDO**. Beneath a stony but thickly wooded hill dotted with old houses,

there's a small beach here and two **places to stay**, *A Revolta* (☎981 764 927;
❷), with a recommended *marisquería*, and *Pensión Sol E Mar* (☎981 760 298;
❷).

Towards **CARNOTA** the series of short beaches finally joins together into
a long, unbroken line of dunes, swept by the Atlantic winds. The village of
Carnota is 1km from the shore, but its palm trees and old church are still
thoroughly caked in salt. Set in fields just outside town, *Casa Fandiño*, Rúa
Calvo Sotelo 23 (☎981 857 020; ❶), is an excellent choice, with spotless,
quiet rooms, while *Hostal Miramar*, Praza de Generalísimo 2 (☎981 857 016;
❸), is nice but a little pricey.

The Rías Baixas

The **Rías Baixas** (Rías Bajas) are where most Galicians choose to spend their
summers. Here the rías are wider, more like large bays, filled with floating mussel rafts and pleasure boats, and lined with strands of golden sand. Tourism is an
industry here, exploiting the milder climate and natural beauty of the region,
as well as the historic and strategic importance of cities such as **Pontevedra**
and **Vigo**.

The most northerly of the **Rías Baixas**, the **Ría de Muros e Noia** is largely underdeveloped, and in climate and appearance perhaps more reminiscent of
the Costa da Morte. If you are looking for creature comforts, though, you
should head for the three lowest Rías – **Arousa**, **Pontevedra** and **Vigo**. Here
the summer sun is fairly dependable and the climate mild, avoiding the worst
of the Atlantic storms, which tend just to brush the northwest corner. Each of
these three inlets is sheltered by islands and sandbanks offshore. They are deep
and calm beneath mountains of dark pines, busy with bright fishing boats and
mussel rafts, and fringed with little towns of whitewashed houses and safe
bathing beaches. Most visitors are Spanish or Portuguese, and although there is
none of the overexploitation of the Mediterranean resorts, the coastline is
becoming increasingly built up along the new roads, particularly around Vigo
and Vilagarcía.

The region is also famous for its **wines** (see box on p.654), although they are
less well known outside Spain than the ubiquitous Rioja. The area between
Vilagarcía and Sanxenxo is particularly heavily cultivated, most famously with
the pale Albariño grape.

Ría de Muros e Noia

The first of the Rías Baixas, the Ría de Muros e Noia lacks much of the charm
of those further south; however, there are some highlights. Some of the best
traditional *gallego* architecture outside Pontevedra can be found in the old town
of **MUROS**, enhanced by a marvellous natural setting at the widest point of
the Ría de Muros just before it meets the sea. The town rises in tiers of narrow streets from the curve of the seafront to the Romanesque Iglesia de San

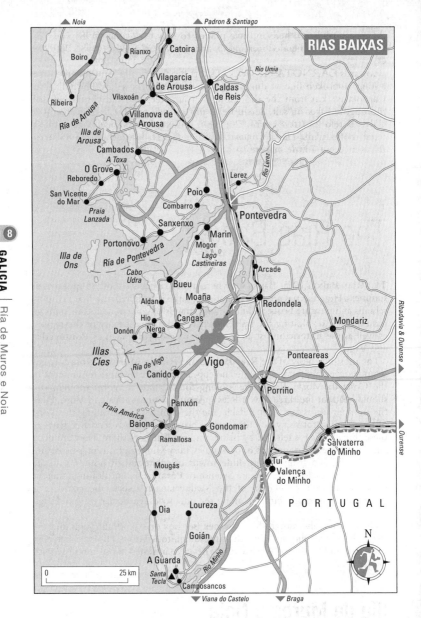

Pedro. Everywhere you look are squat granite columns and arches, flights of wide steps, and benches and stone porches built into the house fronts. There's also a nice – though small – **beach** on the edge of town next to the road to Finisterre.

A seasonal **turismo** (summer only Mon–Fri 10.30am–2.30pm & 5.30–6.30pm, Sat 11.30am–2pm; ☎981 256 050) is located in the *ayuntamiento* at a bend in the coast road. Any of the half-dozen **hostales** along the seafront Avenida Calvo Sotelo (later called Avenida de la Marina) would make for a pleasant stay, although you'll have to book ahead to get a sea-facing room: *Hostal Ría de Muros* (☎981 826 056; ❷), at Avda. de Calvo Sotelo 53, has spacious double rooms with balconies and views, while *A Muradana* (☎981 826 885; ❸), at Avda. de la Marina 107, is also recommended. There's a **campsite**, *A Bouga* (☎981 826 025; open all year), beside the beach 3km out at Louro. There's no shortage of **places to eat**. *Pulpería Pachanga*, at Avda. Calvo Sotelo 29, has a stone-vaulted interior, fresh seafood and grilled meats, while the *Dársena*, just down the road at no. 11, serves huge, cheap pizzas. One block back from the seafront immediately behind the *Hostal Ría de Muros*, the Praza da Pescadería has several good café-restaurants under the arches. Castromíl **bus** services stop at the office below the *Ría de Muros*; Transportes Finisterre buses terminate 100m back down the seafront near the *A Muradana*.

The larger town of **NOIA** (Noya), 25km away around the bay, near the head of the first of the Rías Baixas is, according to a legend fanciful even by *gallego* standards, named after Noah, whose Ark is supposed to have struck land nearby. Scarcely less absurd is Noia's claim to be a "Little Florence", principally on the strength of a couple of nice churches and an arcaded street. If you do want **to stay**, the *Hostal Sol y Mar*, a dreary concrete box down by the small bridge on Avenida de San Lázaro (☎981 820 900; ❷), has lovely views over the river. Smarter and pricier – with some rooms en suite – is *Ceboleiro I*, Rúa Galicia 15 (☎ & ⓕ981 824 497; ❷–❸), opposite the grand *ayuntamiento*. From Noia the AC301 heads inland through deep, lush gorges towards Padrón, avoiding the long, winding coastal route (C550) which becomes increasingly bleak as it heads towards the Ría de Arousa.

The southern side of the Ría da Noia, which is sometimes called the "Cockle Coast", is dauntingly exposed, although in good weather the dunes serve as excellent beaches. At **BAROÑA** (Basonas), a rocky outcrop juts from the sand into the sea, and built on top of it you can still see the ruins of an impregnable pre-Roman settlement, with round stone huts enclosed behind a fortified wall.

Ría de Arousa

The Ría de Arousa is less developed than places further south, but it does have some resorts popular with Galician families. The main rail route south from Santiago swings inland at **Vilagarcía**, without reaching **O Grove**, the main resort of this first *ría*. The island of **A Toxa**, just offshore, attracts a more wealthy crowd, while the town of **Cambados** is renowned for its beautiful main plaza. Inland, gastronomic purists will want to try authentic *pimientos* in the village of Padrón.

Padrón and the north shore

According to legend, the corpse of St James arrived in Galicia by sailing up the Ría de Arousa as far as **PADRÓN**, where his miraculous voyage ended. The modern town along the highway has surprisingly little to show for the years of pilgrimage, except an imposing seventeenth-century church of Santiago in which the *padrón* (mooring post) to which the vessel was tied supposedly resides under the high altar. Padrón is no longer on the sea – the silt of the Río Ulla has stranded it a dozen kilometres inland.

The poet **Rosalía de Castro** (1837–1885), revered as one of the great champions of the *gallego* language, lived in Padrón, and her former house has been converted into a **museum** (summer Tues–Sat 10am–2pm & 4–8pm, Sun 10am–1.30pm; winter Tues–Sat 10am–1.30pm & 4–7pm, Sun 10am–1.30pm; €1.40). Unless you're already acquainted with her life and work, the random jumble of texts, photographs and bric-a-brac on display here won't make a great deal of sense, but the low-ceilinged rooms furnished in period style have character and the gardens are pleasant. The house is a ten-minute walk from the centre of Padrón, opposite the RENFE station – cross the railway line and turn left.

Perhaps the main reason for visiting Padrón is to sample authentic *pimientos de Padrón*. Available throughout Galicia in the summer months only, they are small, shallow-fried green peppers served whole, dripping in oil and liberally sprinkled with sea salt. Though the majority are sweet, one in ten in each serving is memorably hot, unusual in *gallego* cooking where piquancy is generally frowned upon.

If you want **to stay** (though there's no very compelling reason to do so), the best-value place is the *Hostal Jardín*, Rúa Salgado Araújo 3 (℡981 810 950; ❷), a beautiful eighteenth-century house overlooking a shady park. *La Ponderosa*, Calvo Sotelo 2, near the bus station (℡981 811 511; ❶), is cheaper but not as good. There's a small **turismo** kiosk (June–Sept Mon–Sat 10am–1.30pm & 4–8pm; Oct–May Mon–Fri 10am–1.30pm & 4–8pm; ℡627 210 777) on the main road close by, and a top-quality octopus **restaurant**, the *Pulpería Rial*, on Plazuela de Traviesa. For peppers try *O Pementeiro* at Praza do Castro 3, just off the main road.

The north side of the *ría* is quite underpopulated, with only Rianxo (Rianjo), Boiro and **RIBEIRA** large enough to support *hostales*. Ribeira (also known as Santa Eugenia, or Santa Uxia in *gallego*) is a thriving fishing port, which has good restaurants alongside a lot of modern apartment buildings. On either side of the town there are long beaches; the small *Coroso* **campsite** (℡981 838 002; April–Sept) on the Praia de Coroso, next to the C550 road, provides an escape from staying centrally.

On from Padrón

The N550 runs inland and halfway between Padrón and Pontevedra passes the thermal spa town of **CALDAS DE REIS**, where there's a Roman fountain, the waters of which guarantee you will be married within a year, should you be so foolhardy as to drink them.

As the road continues towards Pontevedra there is a turn-off on the left-hand side to the tiny but charming **Parque Natural de Ría Barosa**. Here a series of old mills perches precariously on the side of a gentle waterfall that gives way to a delightfully bridged brook. There are a couple of unexceptional cafés here if you are in need of refreshment.

Vilagarcía and Isla de Arousa

Sprawling **VILAGARCÍA**, 23km from Padrón, is the unofficial capital of Galicia's drug-smuggling industry, its otherwise attractive beach (Praia da Concha) being ruined by the shadow of an ugly swathe of docks. Behind these, the main road, Avenida de la Mariña, is lined with modern mansions and chic cafés, while at its southern end is a seasonal **turismo** (June–Oct Mon–Fri 10am–2pm & 5–9pm, Sat & Sun 11am–2pm & 5–8pm; ℡600 370 275) opposite the fish market. The best **places to eat** are around here, including *Mesón da Mariña* under the plane

Smugglers

Smuggling is a long-established tradition in Galicia. Not all the boats you see sailing into the picturesque fishing harbours are carrying fish; not all the lobster pots sunk offshore are used for holding crustaceans; not all those huts on the mussel rafts are occupied by shellfish-growers. All along the coast you'll find beaches known locally as the "Praia de *Winston*", notorious for the late-night arrivals of shipments of foreign cigarettes.

Recently, however, it has become more difficult to laugh off the smugglers as latter-day Robin Hoods. Taking advantage of the infrastructure developed over the years by small-time tobacco smugglers, and of the endlessly corrugated coastline frequented by innumerable small boats, the big boys have moved in. At first, there were stories of large consignments of hashish brought in at night; now heroin abuse has become a major concern. At some point, the Medellín cartel of Colombia began to use Galicia as the European entrance point for large consignments of cocaine. Several major police crackdowns, particularly on the Isla de Arousa where certain segments of the population seemed all of a sudden to have become inexplicably rich, have yet to reverse the trend that has locals worrying that Galicia is heading towards becoming "another Sicily".

---

trees at no. 58. **Accommodation** is pricey, although *Hostal Cantabria* (☎986 503 859; ❷), Avda. da Mariña 110, and *Hostal Martis* (☎986 505 410; ❶), just inland at Praza Martín Gómez Abel 2, are reasonable value.

The nearby beach at **Vilaxoán** (Villajuán) is superior to the town beach. Buses leave from outside the fish market. On the road towards Vilaxoán lies Galicia's most famous **restaurant**, *Chocolate* (☎986 501 199, ⓦ www.restaurantechocolatehotel.com; closed Sun). The walls are festooned with letters of praise from eminent guests such as former Argentine president Juan Perón, and former British Prime Minister Edward Heath. The flamboyant owner personally serves clients with two-pound steaks impaled on pitchforks, and the fish is superb – though the prices are predictably high, starting at around €15 per dish.

The best of the nearby beaches are on the wooded **ISLA DE AROUSA**, out in the *ría* but accessible from the mainland by a short road bridge. Easiest to get to is the **Praia de Vao**, just to the right of the bridge as you cross over onto the island. There's a **campsite**, *Salinas* (☎986 527 444; June–Sept), at the nearby Praia de Xastelas, and a *hostal* in the main village, *Benalua*, Rúa Méndez Núñez (☎986 551 335; ❷), which offers comfortable but simple en-suite double rooms.

Cambados

CAMBADOS, further south again, has a remarkable paved stone square, the **Praza de Fefiñanes**, with beautiful buildings on all sides, including a seventeenth-century church and a *bodega* where you can sample the excellent local Albarino wines; otherwise, it's a fairly sleepy town with an unremarkable seafront. The helpful **turismo** (summer daily 10am–2pm & 4.30–8.30pm, Sun 11am–1.30pm & 5–9.30pm; winter daily 10am–2pm & 4.30–7.30pm) is housed in a small booth on the Praza do Concello at the junction of the main roads. If you can't afford to stay at the **parador** – the *Albariño*, on Paseo Cervantes (☎986 542 250, ☞986 542 068; ❻) – try the rather more basic *El Duende*, Rúa Ourense 10 (☎986 543 075, ☞986 542 900; ❷), just off the seafront and Praza do Concello.

O Grove and A Toxa

O GROVE, at the northern tip of the peninsula and across the bay from Cambados, exists primarily as a family resort. It is packed with places to stay, while inexpensive bars and restaurants compete for the attention of the summer influx of visitors. Across the bridge the pine-covered islet of **A TOXA** (La Toja) caters for a completely different clientele. Playground of the wealthy, expensive hotels and luxury holiday homes lie in the forest clearings, while a nine-hole golf course ensures that guests can practise their swing. Press on to the less developed side of the island, though, and things are very different. Quiet, peaceful and relatively untouched by the residents, you can begin to imagine that you are many miles from civilization, although there is no guarantee that this will remain the case for long.

Practicalities

Regular **buses** from Pontevedra (10 daily) and Santiago (8 daily) pull in to O Grove right by the port, where there's a small seasonal **turismo** (June–Nov daily 10am–9pm; ☎986 731 415) in a kiosk. There are dozens of **places to stay** along the waterfront Rúa Teniente Dominguez (facing the bridge leading over to A Toxa) and its continuation, Avenida Castelao, including the *Hotel Molusco* (☎986 730 761; ❹) facing the bridge. Rather cheaper are *Hotel Isolino* at Rúa Castelao 30 (☎986 730 236, ⓕ986 730 287; ❷), or *Casa Campaña*, on the same street at no. 60 (☎986 730 919, ⓕ986 732 277; ❸). The most luxurious accommodation is on A Toxa, with *Gran Hotel de La Toja* (☎986 730 025; ❾) costing a small fortune, although facilities are outstanding. For **eating**, the waterfront by the port is solid with the inevitable *marisquerías*; for something without tentacles, head for the *Amalfi*, also on the waterfront by the port, which has pizza and pasta from €5.

West to San Vicente do Mar

Regular buses run across the peninsula from O Grove west to San Vicente do Mar, via the village of **REBOREDO**. Just prior to here is a fine aquarium, the **Acquariumgalicia** (daily: June–Oct 10am–9pm; Nov–May 10am–7pm; €6), a 45-minute walk west across the headland from O Grove. One of the largest in Spain, it has a huge selection of Atlantic marine life and arranges ninety-minute trips on the *ría* in glass-bottomed boats (July–Sept every half hour 10.30am–7.30pm; June–Oct 4 daily; €12), a worthwhile excursion if you're interested in looking at Galicia's sea creatures rather than eating them. Any number of **campsites** are associated with the numerous beaches along the 7km stretch of coast to San Vicente, one of the best being *Moreiras* (☎986 731 691; all year) at km3.

Charming pine-forested hillsides provide a stunning backdrop to the pretty village of **SAN VICENTE DO MAR**. The forest conceals several delightful sandy coves, most of which remain deserted even at the height of summer. In the bay fishing boats are anchored between mussel rafts and the town retains a tranquil feel that has long since deserted its neighbours. There are limited places **to stay** here; *Casa O Casal*, on Rúa Cacheiras (☎986 738 308; ❷), is open in July and August only, but there's also an excellent campsite, *Paisaxe II* (☎986 738 331; mid-June to mid-Sept), just outside town at Rúa Iglesia 11. The town's largest **beach**, *Area Grande*, is close to a small pre-Roman and Roman burial site.

Ría de Pontevedra

Of all the Rías Baixas, the long, narrow **Ría de Pontevedra** is the archetype, closely resembling a Scandinavian fjord with its steep and forested sides. **Pontevedra** itself is a lovely old city, now set slightly back from the sea at the point where the Río Lérez begins to widen out into the bay. It's a good base for expeditions along either shore of its *ría* – such expeditions made necessary by the fact that the town itself doesn't have a beach. The **north coast** of the *ría* is the more popular with tourists and **Sanxenxo** (Sanjenjo) is the best-known resort, often full of British and German visitors as well as wealthy Pontevedrans. If you want to avoid the crowds, head for the **south coast**, which stretches out past lovely beaches towards the rugged headland, ideal for camping in privacy.

Praia La Lanzada and the beaches of the north shore

East of San Vicente the peninsula reaches a bottleneck adorned by the region's largest and most famous beach, the vast golden arc of **PRAIA LA LANZADA**. Packed with sun worshippers in summer and a favourite of windsurfers in winter, it has a tiny chapel at its southern end. According to local legend, women wishing to become pregnant would visit the chapel priest who would bathe them in the waters, only for them to be miraculously with child weeks later. With time – and presumably to divert suspicion from the priest – the legend changed, and today it is said that bathing seven times under a full moon is the best way to guarantee the patter of tiny feet. In the summer there are temporary enclaves of cafés and restaurants, and **campsites** such as the recommended *Muiñeira* (☎986 738 404; all year), or *O Espiño* (☎986 738 048; all year).

To the east are several more excellent **beaches**, often far less crowded than La Lanzada and most with a nearby campsite, should you wish to stay. Praia Montalvo is backed by pines and has great views of the Illas Cíes and Ons (camping ☎986 724 087; June–Oct), and Praia Canelas, adjacent to the village of the same name, is also good (camping ☎986 691 025; April to mid-Oct).

Sanxenxo and Portonovo

Characterless **SANXENXO** (Sanjenjo), 10km south along the coast from La Lanzada, is the main venue for a serious summer **nightlife**. From 10pm until 8am the next morning the seafront bars and cafés are packed with revellers, the discos playing Eurodance music to a lively and largely inebriated crowd. You can judge the scale of things by the fact that there are around a hundred largely seasonal hotels between here and the similar resort of **PORTONOVO**, 3km to the west, but unless you intend to dance and drink until you drop you may wish to pass straight through. **Accommodation** prices are high and you'd be lucky to find anything under €40 in summer, but if you're on a budget try *Hostal San Roque* (☎986 724 082; March–Oct; ❷) at Rúa Anebados 6 in Portonovo, or *Hostal Venezuela* (☎986 720 086; ❷; June–Sept) in Sanxenxo itself at Rúa Carlos Casas 6. On the main road between the two, the **discoteca** *Zoo* is a popular place to end the evening. If you are driving, be aware that this stretch of coast is lethal after dark, with several accidents caused by inebriated Pontevedrans chancing the journey to and from the city in their cars.

Isla de Ons

In the ocean at the mouth of the Ría de Pontevedra lies the beautiful **ISLA DE ONS**, wilder and more windswept than the nearby Illas Cíes (see p.650), and home to a community of fishermen and some interesting birdlife. There are good walking tracks here with terrific views of coast and sea, and you can hike round the entire island in about three hours. Of the **beaches**, Praia Melide, a gorgeous stretch of white sand a couple of kilometres north of the jetty, is perhaps the best. If you want to stay, you can **camp** for free in the specified "camping zone" (*zona de acampada*). Eight daily ferries (June 28–Sept 21; €10 return) run from Sanxenxo and Portonovo, and three daily ferries also run from the nearby naval base at **Marín** (July 5–Sept 7; same price). The last departure from the islands is at 7.30pm.

Combarro

The coastal village of **COMBARRO**, 7km west of Pontevedra, is justly famed for the largest collection of **hórreos** in Galicia, lining the waterfront and looking out across the Ría to Marín. A path cut into the rocks leads from the main square behind the *hórreos*, littered with souvenir shops and poky but atmospheric bars. A typical fishing village, it hosts a **sardine festival** on June 23, the fish being grilled in the open air on the shore. Inland, the tight streets are lined with little houses, each with Baroque stone balconies and galleries, winding claustrophobically towards the Chapel of San Roque at the heart of the town. One block away is the **turismo** at Correiro do Campo (June–Sept Mon–Sat 10.30am–noon & 5.30–9pm, Sun 6.30–9pm; ☎986 833 204). A great place to eat and try the local Albariño wine is the classy *Taberna de Albariños*, while a cluster of bars on the Peirao da Rúa serve outdoor tapas and drinks at the water's edge. For details of various ferry cruises in the Ría, contact *Nautilus* (☎986 746 609). Free **guided walks** around the town depart from the turismo in July and August (Mon–Fri noon & 8pm).

Monasterio de Poio

Two kilometres east of Combarro lies the seventeenth-century Benedictine **MONASTERIO DE POIO**. Turn off from the main road to Pontevedra above the modern town of Poio. Behind lies reputedly the largest *hórreo* in Galicia, while the monastery itself contains a wonderful *hospedaría* (☎986 770 000; ❷), modern and efficient despite the age and beauty of its setting. It's an excellent base for visiting Combarro, but if you decide to move on it's only a further 5km south around the Ría to Pontevedra.

Pontevedra

Thanks in part to a policy of urban regeneration by Galician Nationalist mayor Miguel Lores, **PONTEVEDRA** is now the definitive old *gallego* town. A compact maze of pedestrianized flagstoned alleyways, colonnaded squares with granite crosses and squat stone houses with floral balconies, it is today one of Galicia's most tourist-friendly towns. A lively place, it's perfect for a night out, with the local food and drink both at their best in the attractive *zona monumental*, lying hard against the Río Lérez within the sweeping crescent of the main boulevards.

Arrival and information

Both the **bus** and **train** stations are about 1km southeast of the centre, side by side, and connected to the Praza de España in the centre by half-hourly buses

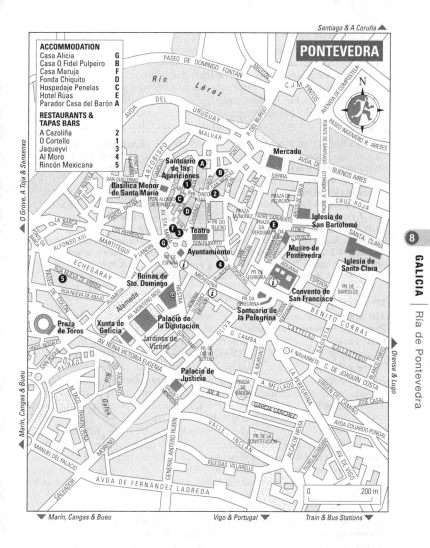

PONTEVEDRA

ACCOMMODATION
Casa Alicia	G
Casa O Fidel Pulpeiro	B
Casa Maruja	F
Fonda Chiquito	D
Hospedaje Penelas	C
Hotel Rúas	E
Parador Casa del Barón	A

RESTAURANTS & TAPAS BARS
A Cazoliña	2
O Cortello	1
Jaqueyvi	3
Al Moro	4
Rincón Mexicana	5

(from platform 14 of the bus station; €0.85). If you're coming in on foot, head out of the bus station and follow Rúa Calvo Sotelo as it bears round to the left; walk to the roundabout then straight over onto Avenida de Vigo and follow this all the way to the Praza da Peregrina on the edge of the old town. The main **turismo** is nearby at Calle Xeneral Gutierrez Mellado 3 (Mon–Fri 9.30am–2pm & 4.30–6.30pm, Sat 10am–12.30pm; ☎986 850 814), but a pair of seasonal kiosks (July–Sept Mon–Sat 10am–2pm & 5–9pm) are better located on Praza de España and Praza Ourense. **Internet** access is at *Ciber Ruinas* (daily until early hours of the morning; €1.50 per hour) on Rúa Riestra next to the ruins of Santo Domingo church.

Accommodation

Finding a **place to stay** in Pontevedra should be straightforward. The best-value places are in the winding streets of the **zona monumental**; the widest choice is among budget places, but there are a couple of good upmarket options here, too. The new town offers a number of hotels on and around **Avenida de Vigo**, but these are mostly characterless and overpriced. *Albergue Peregrino* next to the bus station offers one night's free basic accommodation to **pilgrims**, but don't get confused with the *Hostal* of the same name opposite.

Casa Alicia Avda. de Santa María 5 ☎986 857 079. Good-value, spotless rooms, all en suite, in a pleasant house on the edge of the old quarter. ❶
Fonda Chiquito Rúa Charino 23 ☎986 862 192. The cheapest place in town, but perfectly adequate. ❶
Casa O Fidel Pulpeiro Rúa San Nicolás 7 ☎986 851 234. Pleasant, well-kept rooms above a friendly bar with great *pulpo*. ❶
Casa Maruja Rúa Alta ☎986 854 901. Immaculate en-suite rooms in this comfortable modern *pension*, opposite *Casa Alicia*. ❷
Parador Casa del Barón Rúa del Barón 19 ☎986

855 800, ⓔpontevedra@parador.es. Housed in a historic stone mansion in the heart of the old quarter, this is the best – and most expensive – place to stay in Pontevedra. ❻
Hospedaje Penelas Rúa Alta 17 ☎986 855 705. Atmospherically located *hospedaje* in the old quarter, with simple, but spotlessly clean, rooms with wafer-thin walls. ❷
Hotel Rúas Rúa Padre Sarmiento 20 ☎986 846 416, ⓕ986 846 411. Handsome old hotel in an excellent location, next to the Museo de Pontevedra. ❹

The Town

The boundary between Pontevedra's old and new quarters is marked by the **Praza da Peregrina** – site of a pilgrim chapel, the **Santuario de la Peregrina**, a tall, eye-catching Baroque structure with a floor plan in the shape of a scallop shell – and the **Praza da Ferrería** (known simply as the "Ferrería"), a paved square lined by arcades on one side and rose trees on the other. To the east is the town's main church, **San Francisco**, best admired from outside. Amid the surrounding fountains, gardens, and open-air cafés, all the daily rituals of life in a small town take place, especially during the Sunday *paseo* when the entire population hits the streets.

A selection of narrow lanes leads north from the Ferrería into the **zona monumental**, Rúa Figueroa leading down to the elegant and well-conceived **Museo de Pontevedra** (June–Sept Tues–Sat 10am–2.15pm & 5–8.45pm, Sun 11am–2pm; Oct–May Tues–Sat 10am–1.30pm & 4.30–8pm, Sun 11am–2pm; free, though you'll need to show a passport or driving licence). Five separate sites now make up the museum. Four are in beautiful mansion houses clustered around the small and shaded **Praza de Leña**, a typical *gallego* square with granite columns and a calvary, while the fifth is the ruins of the **Igrexa Santo Domingo**, off Praza de España. Highlight of the **Castro Monteagudo building**, on the Praza de Leña, is a large collection of pre-Roman gold and silver and a selection of works from Spanish masters including Ribera, Zubarán and Murillo. The main draw, though, is the adjacent **García Florez building** with exhibits of jet jewellery from Santiago (the city held a monopoly on the stone in the Middle Ages) and a floor dedicated to twentieth-century artist, caricaturist and writer Alfonso Castelao, author of *Sempre en Galizia*, the bible of *gallego* nationalists and now a set text for the region's schools. His drawings, at their most moving when depicting prewar poverty and the horror of the Civil War, celebrate the strength and resilience of the *gallego* people and their culture. The **Fernández López building** houses a library, while the **Sarmiento building** is used more for temporary exhibitions of Galician art.

Leading down from Praza de España towards the sea, the **Alameda** is a grand promenade watched over by magnificent buildings and dotted with monuments commemorating largely naval achievements. Slightly off the Alameda stands a one-armed **statue** of Galicia's favourite Genoese, **Christopher Columbus**, who is said to have sailed from the town. There are even those who insist that Columbus, along with just about anybody else of note, was born a *gallego*.

Eating and drinking

The twisting streets of the *zona* are packed with tiny **bars** and **restaurants** and at weekends jammed late into the night with revellers. Though most bars serve an excellent array of tapas, *Jaqueyvi* (abbreviation of *Jamón, queso y vino*) in front of the Teátro Municipal on Rúa Dona Tareixa is the place to go for traditional Galician hams and cheeses. *Al Moro*, at the top end of Rúa Villaverde, does a filling, home-cooked *menú* for €6, while *A Cazoliña* on Praza da Cinco Rúas is a good place to sample *zamboriñas* (mini scallops in a delicious garlic sauce). Pick of the bunch, though, is the rustic *O Cortello*, on Rúa Isabel II just behind the Santa Maria church, a wonderful and remarkably cheap tapas bar that couldn't be further removed from its *gallego* name – which means pigsty. Outside the old town, *Rincón Mexicano* on Rúa Nova de Arriba, just off the Alameda, is the most authentic Mexican restaurant in Galicia.

The **nightlife** scene is changing rapidly as the *zona* develops, with most people starting the evening in the numerous bars that take over Prazas Verdura and Méndez Nuñez once night falls. *Bar Maristas*, on Praza da Vedura, is sought after for the astonishing liqueur **Tumba Dios** ("God falls down"), an esoteric but fearsome blend of *aguardiente* (firewater) and *vino de pasas* (raisin wine), laced with sundry secret herbs and spices. A little way west, Praza da Cinco Rúas marks a central point from where five streets lined with bars run spoke-like in all directions; just follow the crowds. *Highlander*, at Isabel II 24, is a slightly bizarre Scottish-themed bar, popular with whisky drinkers, while Rúa Charino is packed with **disco-bars**. *Camarú* and *Nonno*, both on Praza de Teucro, attract a good mix of people and are excellent places to end the evening. A younger crowd aims for *Carabás*, on Rúa Cobián Rofignac (near the junction with Rúa Benito Corbal), which is always packed – mainly with teenagers.

The southern shore

Though the first stretch of the southern side of the Ría de Pontevedra is extremely ugly, those who press on beyond the military town of Marín, 7km southwest of Pontevedra, will be amply rewarded with a series of gorgeous and largely deserted little bays. **Buses** run roughly every twenty minutes from Pontevedra (departing from Praza de Galicia, not the main bus station), travelling right around the headland and along the southern shore of the Ría.

Mogor, Bueu and beyond

Beyond Marín the bay broadens into a whole series of breathtaking sandy coves. A narrow side road drops away from the main coast road immediately beyond the naval academy outside Marín, leading to three beaches. The second of these, the **Praia de Mogor** (on the bus route from Pontevedra), is perfect, with fields of green corn as the backdrop to a crescent of fine, clean sand, one end of which is shielded by a thick headland of dark green pines. There are a couple of bars overgrown with vines, and the villagers' rowing boats are pulled up in the shade of the trees.

BUEU (pronounced *bwayo*) is a quiet market town and port about 19km beyond Pontevedra, and offers pleasant strips of **beach** stretching away from its rambling waterfront; the quieter spots are round the headland to the west. **Accommodation** here is mostly expensive; you'll get little for less than €40 in the summer, although the unmarked *Hostal Fazanes*, Rúa Eduardo Vincenti 29 (☎986 320 046; ❶), has cheap, basic rooms in the town centre. Other affordable options include the *Incamar*, Rúa Montero Ríos 147 (☎986 390 026, ℉986 390 607; ❸), or, to the east, *A Centoleira*, Praia de Beluso (☎986 320 896; ❷).

A smaller road turns away from the sea at Bueu, towards Cangas, and is served by half-hourly buses in summer, but if you make your way along the coast, towards the village of **ALDÁN** and the cape of **Hío**, you'll find an unspoiled expanse of pine trees and empty beaches – an ideal place to go **camping** if you stock up in advance. There's also an official campsite (☎ & ℉986 329 468), but it's only open June to September. Particularly worth following is the unpaved road to the huge boulders at **Cabo Udra**, where the waves come crashing down in deserted coves and wild horses roam the hillside. For those without transport, it may be easier to access the more southerly areas via Cangas (see below).

Ría de Vigo

Following the main road south from Bueu, you cross the steep ridge of the Morrazo peninsula to astonishing views on the far side over the **RÍA DE VIGO**, one of the most sublime natural harbours in the world. This region was once a hotbed of witchcraft, although *gallegos* are careful to distinguish between *brujas* (malevolent witches) and *meigas* (wise herbalists with healing powers). Tradition tells of a local woman who was accused of consorting with the devil by the Inquisition in the seventeenth century. She won her claim to be a *meiga*, and was sentenced to stand outside Cangas church in her oldest clothes every Sunday for six months – presumably she caught the Holy Inquisition in one of its more lenient moods. Even today, you'll find charms against witches (in the shape of a clasped hand) on sale everywhere in Galicia, often next to crucifixes.

The *ría's* narrowest point is spanned by a vast suspension bridge which carries the Vigo-Pontevedra highway; you'll see its twin towers from all around the bay. On the inland side is what amounts to a saltwater lake, the inlet of **San Simón**. The road and railway from Pontevedra run beside it to **Redondela**, separated from the sea by just a thin strip of green fields, and pass close to the tiny San Martín islands, once a leper colony and used during the Civil War as an internment centre for Republicans. Beneath these waters lies a fleet of Spanish bullion galleons, sunk by a combined Anglo-Dutch force at the Battle of Rande in 1703.

The city of **Vigo** looks very appealing, spread along the waterfront, but although it is a good base for visiting the surroundings, it has very few attractions of its own. The obvious trip is to get a **ferry** across to the little resort of **Cangas**; another would be to take a bus out to **Baiona**, at the edge of the ocean, but the pick of the bunch is the boat trip out to the wonderful **Illas Cíes**.

Cangas and Moaña

CANGAS is today a burgeoning resort, at its most lively during the Friday **market**, when the seafront gardens are filled with stalls. It's worth visiting simply for the superb, twenty-minute **ferry** trip across the *ría* from Vigo (every 30min 6.30am–10.30pm, hourly at weekends; €3.30 return, €2.10 if the outbound trip is before 9am), but there's an excellent beach, too. The **Praia de Rodeira** is a beautiful 500-metre stretch of sand with majestic views across the water – alight from the ferry, turn left and walk along the seafront for ten minutes to reach it.

The **bus** station is right next to where ferries dock, and there's a **turismo** booth here, too (July–Oct & Easter daily 10am–2pm & 5–9pm). Free guided tours of the old town leave in July and August (Mon–Fri 11am), and ferry services to the Illas Cíes (July–Aug 4–5 daily) also depart from here when weather permits. The cheapest **rooms** in town are at *Hostal Belén*, tucked away in a hard-to-find backstreet, behind the town gardens, on Rúa Antonio Nores (☎986 300 015; ❷), and the *Playa*, Avda. Ourense 78 (☎986 303 674, ☎986 301 363; ❸), at the beginning of the Praia de Rodeira. More expensive is the modern *Hotel Airiños*, at Rúa Eugenio Sequeiros 30 (☎986 304 000; ❸), where rooms at the front have sea views. Accommodation fills rapidly in summer, though prices fall sharply outside high season.

The main cluster of **bars and restaurants** is around the port. Up some steps, slightly to the left of the jetty as you face the town, is the *Bar Celta*, looking out over the bay at Rúa Alfredo Saralegui 28, an excellent old-fashioned tapas bar whose *comedor* serves budget meals. *Casa Macillos*, next door, is similar and also good. En route to the Praia de Rodeira, *Taberna O Arco*, on Praza do Arco, and *O Porrón*, on Eugenio Sequeiros (just beyond the fish market), are two very good bars specializing in seafood. For a more upmarket meal try *El Velero*, on Rúa Vicenti, behind the Alameda.

West of Cangas, the beaches and hills are stunning and all but deserted. In summer, hourly buses take you from Cangas to **Nerga**, from where it's a short walk to the huge sandy strip extending from the Praia de Nerga to the nudist Praia de Barra. There is also a 2pm bus (returning at 7.30pm) to **Donón**, from where it's a two-kilometre walk to the Praia de Melide on the tip of the peninsula, an isolated cove backed by woods and a lighthouse, with superb walks along the cape.

Hourly boats from Vigo (same hours and prices as to Cangas) also leave for **MOAÑA**, 5km along the coast from Cangas, and similar to it in feel. Again, much of the appeal of a trip here is the ferry ride, which takes you right alongside the local *mejilloneiras* – ramshackle rafts, perched on the river like water-spiders and sometimes topped by little wooden huts, which are used for cultivating mussels. Moaña itself boasts a fine, long **beach**, but relatively few facilities for visitors. Places **to stay** include *Hostal Prado Viejo*, Rúa Ramón Cabanillas 16 (☎986 311 634; ❷), with en-suite rooms and private parking, and *Hostal Antonio*, Rúa Méndez Núñez 2 (☎986 313 684; ❶), which has rooms both with and without bath. A little further up the street, the no-frills *La Paz* (☎986 314 254; ❶) is the only other option in town.

Vigo

VIGO is a large and superbly situated city, dominating the broad expanse of its *ría*. Seen from a ship entering the harbour, it is magnificent, though once ashore it fails to live up to its initial promise. Well sheltered from the Atlantic, the wharves and quays which make it Spain's chief fishing port stretch along the shore for nearly 5km, but for the visitor the city will be more useful as a comfortable base from which to explore the surroundings, as well as an excellent place to sample the local *mariscos*.

Arrival and information

Vigo's **turismo** is opposite the port on Avda. Cánovas del Castillo 22 (July & Aug Mon–Fri 9.30am–2pm & 4.30–7.30pm, Sat & Sun 10am–2pm & 5–6.30pm; Sept–June Mon–Fri 9.30am–2pm & 4.30–6.30pm, Sat 10.30am–12.30pm; ☎986 430 577, ⓦwww.turismodevigo.org). The **RENFE station**, on the edge of the city centre, has direct services to Santiago,

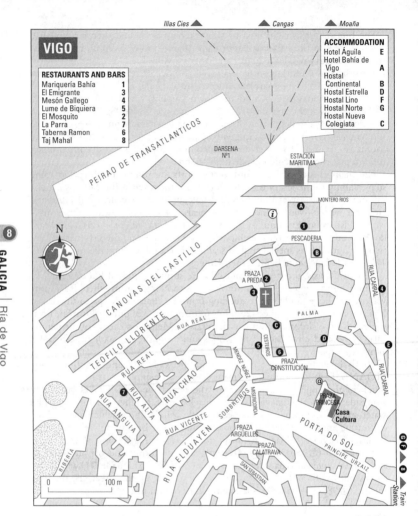

Illas Cíes ▲   ▲ Cangas   ▲ Moaña

VIGO

ACCOMMODATION
Hotel Águila	E
Hotel Bahía de Vigo	A
Hostal Continental	B
Hostal Estrella	D
Hostal Lino	F
Hostal Norte	G
Hostal Nueva Colegiata	C

RESTAURANTS AND BARS
Mariquería Bahía	1
El Emigrante	3
Mesón Gallego	4
Lume de Biquiera	5
El Mosquito	2
La Parra	7
Taberna Ramon	6
Taj Mahal	8

Barcelona and Madrid, and down into Portugal. The **bus station** is further out, around 1.5km from the centre. Half-hourly buses to the old town run from the stop just outside the bus station entrance (#12 and #12B), and from Platform 1 inside the station (Vitrasa bus #C4C), and cost €0.87. Both buses run past the train station, on the way to the central Porta do Sol, marked by a bizarre half-man/half-fish statue. **Internet** access at *Ciberstation* on the Porta do Sol costs €1.80 per hour.

Accommodation

Places to stay tend to be reasonably priced and are concentrated in two main areas: up by the train station, and in the old town down by the port. The latter is more atmospheric and is also where you'll find the best restaurants and bars.

Hotel Águila Rúa Victoria 6 ☎986 431 398, ⓦwww.hotelaguila.com. Old-fashioned but well-equipped hotel with bags of charm. All rooms are en suite with cable TV, though some are a bit small. ❸

Hotel Bahía de Vigo Rúa Canovas del Castillo 24 ☎986 226 700. Adjacent to the turismo, this is the city's real luxury option. Its café is decorated like an ocean liner, while the restaurant, *Marisquería Bahía*, is huge. ❼

Hostal Continental Baixada a Fonte 3 ☎986 220 764. Good en-suite rooms in a great location just off Rúa de Pescadería back from the waterfront. ❷

Hostal Estrella Rúa Joaquín Yánez 1 ☎986 226 363. An unpromising entrance through a shop gives way to a pleasant enough *hostal*. If you'e on a tight budget you're unlikely to find anywhere cheaper. ❶

Hostal Lino Rúa Lepanto 26 ☎986 439 311, ⓕ986 449 663. Close to the train station, with a range of rooms (some smart and modern; some older and cheaper), all en-suite and with TV and breakfast included. ❹

Hostal Norte Rúa Alfonso XIII 29 ☎986 223 805, ⓕ986 437 007. Conveniently located next to the train station; most rooms have bath, TV and phone, and there are some cheaper ones without. ❷

Hostal Nueva Colegiata Praza da Igrexa 3 ☎986 220 952. Well-kept and good-value *hostal* on a lovely central square; all rooms en-suite. ❶

The City

Today Vigo's passenger port may be declining, but it has kept the prime spot in the middle of this stretch of shore. Here, generations of *gallego* emigrants have embarked for and returned from the Americas, and Caribbean immigrants have had their first glimpse of Europe. Although, these days, the only people arriving at the **Estación Marítima de Ría** are tourists who have come on the ferry from Cangas and Moaña, the steep, winding streets of the old city remain crammed with tiny shops and bars catering for the still-plentiful sailors.

The cobbled streets around the **Rúa Real**, once the main street, remain a focal point for visitors. Along the seafront early in the morning, kiosks revive fishermen with strong coffee, while there and in the nearby **market** their catch is sold. From early morning to mid-afternoon women stand at granite tables rooted in **Rúa da Pescadería**, with plates of fresh oysters (€6 per dozen) set out for passers-by. On **Rúa Carral** shops sell kitsch marine souvenirs, and in the evening the myriad bars on all the tiny streets come alive.

The Beaches

For the most part, the **beaches** adjacent to Vigo are crowded and not nearly as appealing as those further along, or across the *ría* – and certainly not a patch on the Illas Cíes (see p.650). Heading south, however, the beach at **Samil** (bus #C15B and #C15C from Rúa Colón, late-night return #LN hourly until 3am) is better, and very popular for late Saturday-night revels. A little further on, the beaches at **Vao** (bus #L11 from Rúa Colón) and **Canido** (same bus), 10km out from Vigo, are also quite reasonable, and equipped with campsites – including *Canido* (☎ & ⓕ986 462 072; all year).

Eating and drinking

Rúa da Pescadería is the most lively place for **lunch**, at an outdoor table amongst the oyster sellers. Most of one side of the street is taken up by the *Marisquería Bahía*, allegedly the largest seafood restaurant in Spain, decorated with an odd mixture of underwater scenes and the heads of African antelopes. The seafood is predictably excellent here and prices are not too steep, starting at around €10. Climbing the nearby stairs to Praza A Pedra, you'll find the understated *El Emigrante*, one of the cheapest and best places for *raciónes*. If you're prepared to pay extra for service, *El Mosquito* nearby is a classy option, while *Mesón Gallego* on Rúa Carral does a good set *menú* for €5.50. Virtually all of the **bars** in the old streets serve great tapas, the local delicacy being *anguilas*, the baby eels which come swimming up the Río Minho, ready to be eaten: Rúa dos Cesteiros, off the Praza de Constitución, shelters some of the best. The no-frills *Taberna Ramón* (for cuttlefish) and the rustic *Lume de Biqueira* (for *langostinos*) stand out, while *La Parra* on Rúa Alta does great octopus. If you find yourself craving a curry, *Taj Mahal*, at Rúa Vazquez Varela 45, further out near the railway station, is Galicia's only Indian restaurant and reasonably priced.

The Illas Cíes

The most irresistible sands of the Ría de Vigo must be those of the **Illas Cíes**. These three islands protect the entrance to the *ría*, and can be reached by boat from Vigo, and (less regularly) from Baiona and Cangas. The islands were once a refuge used by Sir Francis Drake when conducting pirate raids on Spanish shipping, and are now a nature reserve. The most southerly, **Illa de San Martiño**, is an off-limits bird sanctuary; the other two, **Illa do Monte Ayudo** and **Illa do Faro**, are joined by a narrow causeway of sand, forming a beach open on one side to the Atlantic and on the other to a placid lagoon. Between mid-June and the end of August ferries ply the forty-minute journey, dropping you off at the beach. Most visitors stay on the sands, with their sprinkling of bars and a campsite in the trees, so if you want to escape the crowds it's easy to find a deserted spot – particularly on the Atlantic side of the islands. From the beach, a long climb up a winding rocky path across desolate country leads to a lighthouse with a commanding ocean view.

The **campsite** (☎986 687 630; June–Sept) is the only legal accommodation on the islands, so if you want to stay in mid-season, book ahead to make sure there's space. There is a small shop, as well as a couple of decent restaurants, but as they're free to charge what they choose, if you're on a budget you might prefer to take your own supplies. In season there are nine **ferries** per day **from Vigo**'s Estación Marítima (daily 9am–7pm, though note that some services may not run in bad weather; €14.50 return), the last one back leaving the islands at 8pm. In addition, there are boats **from Baiona** and **from Cangas** (4–5 daily) – you can call Vigo's Estación Marítima on ☎986 225 272 to confirm the timetables, although you may need to speak some Spanish. Only a certain number of visitors are allowed to go to the Cíes on any one day, so aim for an early boat to make sure.

Baiona and around

BAIONA (Bayona), 21km south of Vigo, is situated just before the open sea at the head of a miniature *ría*, the last and the smallest in Galicia. This small and colourful port was the first place in Europe to hear of the discovery of the New World, when Columbus's *Pinta* appeared on March 1, 1493, an event commemorated by numerous sculptures scattered around the town. An exact replica of the *Pinta* sits in the harbour, which nowadays contains more pleasure yachts than fishing boats.

The **medieval walls**, surrounding the wooded promontory which is Baiona's most prominent feature, enclose an idyllic *parador* (see opposite). It's definitely worth paying the €1 fee to walk around the parapet, with an unobstructed view across the *ría* to the chain of rocky islets which leads to the Illas Cíes. There's a footpath beneath the walls at sea level, barely used, which gives access to several diminutive beaches. These are not visible from the town proper, which has only a small patch of sand despite its fine esplanade.

There are two good **beaches** next to the road from Vigo a couple of kilometres before Baiona. The first is the **Praia de América** – take the hourly

Vigo–Baiona bus via Panxón (Panjón) – a superb, long curve of clean sand backed by rows of vacation villas. This has its own **campsite**, *Playa América* (☎986 365 404; mid-March to mid-Oct); however, the *Bayona Playa* (☎986 350 035; all year) is nearer the town (and accessible on both bus routes) on the shorter and scruffier **Praia Ladeira**, about a kilometre east of the centre of Baiona. The inlet here is popular with **windsurfers**.

Practicalities

Buses (roughly every 30min from Vigo; 3 daily from A Guarda) stop by Praza Pedro de Castro on the esplanade right in the middle of town; the land-side stop is for buses to Vigo and the local beaches, the sea-side stop for buses to A Guarda. There's a seasonal **turismo** (June–Oct Mon–Fri 10am–3pm & 4–9pm; ☎986 687 067, ⓦwww.baiona.org) by the entrance to the *parador*. Out of season, CAT (Mon–Fri 9am–2pm), a private tourist office and travel agent, on the corner of Rúas José Antonio and Ventura Misa, can provide information, though hours are limited. **Internet** access is available at Rúa Ventura Misa 12 (daily 10am–2pm & 4.30pm–12.30am; €2 per hour).

Most **accommodation** is along either the seafront esplanade or Rúa Ventura Misa, the narrow pedestrianized street that runs just behind it. Cheapest is the cramped but well-located *Hospedaje Kin*, Rúa Ventura Misa 27 (☎986 355 695; ❶–❷). For a step up in comfort take a short walk out to the *Mesón del Burgo* (☎986 355 309; ❸) by the Praia Santa Marta (next to the Campsa petrol station, a ten-minute walk from the centre towards Vigo), which has sunny, spacious rooms looking out to sea. The *Hotel Tres Carabelas* (☎986 355 441, ⓦwww.hoteltrescarabelas.com; ❸), Rúa Ventura Misa 61, is a smart mid-range option, as is *Hotel Pinzon* (☎986 356 046; ❹), Rúa Elduayen 21, which has a good bar downstairs and rooms with coastal views. If you've got the money it's hard to resist the gorgeous *Parador Conde de Gondomar* (☎986 355 000, ⒺBaiona@parador.es; ❼), which boasts a reputation as one of Spain's best hotels. It has a couple of bars, both open to non-residents, including a nice one standing alone in the grounds.

There's an abundance of **seafood restaurants** around Praza Pedro de Castro and along Rúa Ventura Misa, most with tanks stuffed full of doomed marine creatures. Amongst the best are *El Túnel*, at no. 21, and *Plaza*, a little further along, both of which have outdoor seating on a pleasant, sheltered square. Those on the seafront have nice views of the port, but lack the bustling atmosphere, although *Pedro Madruga*, near the turismo, does a good paella. Rúa Ventura Misa is also the hub of the town's **nightlife**, with several bars and pubs open late. Check out *Blues* and, just around the corner on Rúa Xogo da Bola, *Aquarium*, which provide the main focus of youthful late-night revelry.

Baiona to the Portuguese border

The C550 continues south from **Baiona**, tracing the coastline to the port of A Guarda (see p.655) 3km north of the **Portuguese border**. Only three daily buses make this route, once a deserted and windswept wilderness, but now scattered with *hostales* and hotels.

Two kilometres west of Baiona is the **Virgen de la Roca**, a massive granite image overlooking the sea; on appropriately solemn religious occasions it is customary to climb up inside it and onto the boat she holds in her right hand. Halfway between Baiona and A Guarda is the town of **OIA**, no more than a very tight bend in the coast road, beneath which nestles a remarkable Baroque **monastery**, with its sheer stone facade surviving the constant battering of the ocean. A small **turismo** (daily 10am–2pm & 4.30–7pm) is open in July and

August if you need more information about the monastery.

There are no beaches on this stretch of coast, but the sight of the ocean foaming through the rocks is mightily impressive. If you're looking for a beach, it's best to press on and take a ferry across the river where miles of dunes stretch along the Portuguese coast to Viana do Castelo. Regular car and passenger ferries cross the river mouth frontier between Spanish A Guarda and Portuguese Caminha and, a few miles upstream, between Goian (Goyan) in Spain and the delightful Portuguese walled village of Vila Nova da Cerveira.

Along the Minho

Stunningly wide and beautiful for much of its course, the **Río Minho** (Río Míño) is at its most spectacular upstream, arriving at the town of **Ourense**, having flowed south from Lugo through the harsh landscape traversed by the Camino de Santiago. It continues south through the **Ribeiro wine region**, via its capital **Ribadavia**, and on via some of the province's most spectacularly beautiful countryside. Around here the river has been tamed by a series of dams, before it turns abruptly west to form the frontier with Portugal. Surprisingly narrow at its mouth – no more than 100 metres of mainly sandbank – it separates Spain from its neighbour.

Ourense

At first sight, **OURENSE** (Orense) is disappointing: a vast clutter of anonymous modern apartment and office blocks which are made to look even drearier by their splendid natural setting, but buried inside the city's bland outer shell is a personable old quarter. It's a small but attractive tangle of stepped streets, patrician mansions with escutcheoned doorways and grand little churches squeezed into miniature arcaded squares. The whole area has been lovingly restored, and with its pedestrianized streets and outdoor cafés is one of urban Galicia's more pleasurable city centres. At its centre is the dark **Catedral**, an imitation of Compostela's, with a painted (but greatly inferior) copy of the Pórtico de Gloria, and a museum of religious clutter (Tues–Sat 10am–2pm & 4–6pm, Sun 10am–2pm; €0.90) in the cloisters. Directly south of here, the recently restored **Claustro de San Francisco** (same hours), in a fascinating fourteenth-century Gothic convent, is the city's most important monument. Other specific sights are few on the ground, though it's worth dropping into the **Museo Arqueolóxico** (Tues–Sun 9.30am–2.30pm & 4–9.30pm, closed Mon & Sun pm; €2.40) near the cathedral. Housed in the former Palacio Episcopal, parts of which date back to the twelfth century, it's an interesting display of sculptures, ceramics and other finds from the province.

Ourense's location on a bend in the expansive River Minho has led to it being crossed here by a bewildering number of bridges. The oldest is the thirteenth-century **Ponte Romana**, but perhaps more visually stunning is the brand new **Ponte Milenio**, a futuristic road bridge with an undulating pedestrian loop providing great views of the surroundings. A kilometre or so west of here, the **Termas Chavasqueira** (Tues–Thurs 10am–3pm & 5–11pm, Fri 10am–3pm &

5pm–3am, Sat 10am–3am, Sun 10am–11pm; €3) boast indoor and outdoor spa pools and are a great way to wind down after a hard day on the road.

Practicalities

It's a twenty-minute walk into town from the **train station** on the opposite side of the river: cross the road in front of the station and bear right down the road signposted to the Ponte Romana, cross the bridge then turn left up Rúa do Concello to reach the Parque San Lázaro, the new town's main square. The **bus station** is five minutes further out past the train station (fairly frequent buses run from both terminals into town). To get back to the bus station take bus #6 or #12 from the main street Rúa do Progreso. The **turismo** (summer daily 9am–2pm & 4–8pm; winter Mon–Fri 9am–2pm & 4.30–6.30pm; ☎988 372 020) is on the city end of the Ponte Romana.

There are several *fondas* scattered around the area facing the train station, though you'll do better to head for the pleasant little enclave of **hostales** on the quiet Rúa San Miguel, near the cathedral: the *San Miguel II* at no. 14 (☎988 239 203, ℱ988 242 749; ❶) is a good cheapie, or there's the more upmarket *Hotel Zarampallo* at no. 9 (☎988 220 053; ❸). Not far from the turismo on Rúa Ervedelo are a couple of mid-range options – *Hotel Corderi* (☎988 221 293; ❷) and *Hotel Altiana* (☎988 370 952; ❷), the latter of which has a bar below. Most luxurious of all, though, is *Gran Hotel San Martín* (☎988 371 811; ❼), overlooking Parque San Lázaro, at Rúa Curras Enriquez 1. There are several good **restaurants** in the area around the Catedral. On Rúa San Miguel try *Carroleiro* at no. 10 or *Pingallo* next door but one, which both serve up good regional dishes.

Ribadavia

Following the N120 highway or the train line parallel to the Minho takes you through the heart of the *Ribeiro* wine-producing region. The best base for exploring the surroundings is undoubtedly **RIBADAVIA**, the trip south by train to Tui making a lovely riverside journey, although the valley of the Minho does tend to fill up with mist until midday or so. The town stands among woods and vineyards above the river, looking grander than its size would promise, with several fine churches and a sprawling **Dominican monastery** which was once the residence of the kings of Galicia. There's also an interesting **Barrio Xudeo** (Barrio Judío, or Jewish quarter), dating from the eleventh century when Ribadavia received its first Jewish immigrants; by the fourteenth century these had become half the town's population, and formed one of the most important and prosperous Jewish communities in Spain, although many were forced to convert to Catholicism during the Inquisition. Head for the tiny square behind the Iglesia de la Magdalena for a wonderful view of the hillside terraces. Look out, too, for the remains of the small but quaint **Castillo de los Condes de Ribadavia**, immediately above the Praza Maior.

Practicalities

Buses stop by the river, from where it's a five-minute walk uphill to the Praza Maior; the **train** station is a little further out along the same road. A new bus terminal opposite the train station has been complete for some time but is still not operational. The town's **turismo** is on the Praza Maior (July–Sept: Mon–Sat 10am–3pm & 5–8pm, Sun 10.30am–3pm; Oct–June Mon–Sat 9.30am–2.30pm & 4–6.30pm, Sun 10.30am–3pm; ☎988 471 275, ⓦwww.ribadavia.com) in a Baroque palace which was once home to the Dukes of Ribadavia. **Internet** access (€2 per hour) is in an unmarked building on Praza San Xoán, 20m from the Igrexa San Xoán.

Galician white wines

The cool, fresh Galician climate is reflected in the light, clean flavour of the region's **white wines**. Long the most widely drunk white wines in Spain, it is only recently that they have come to the attention of the world market. The two main grape varieties are the *Ribeiro* which produces a crisp, dry wine reminiscent of Portuguese Vinho Verdes, and the intense, aromatic *Albariño*, considered superior in body and character, and fetching a higher price in the marketplace. Neither wine is heavy in alcohol and they perfectly compliment the region's limitless supply of seafood.

The centre of the Ribeiro wine-producing region (⊛www.do-ribeiro.com) is Ribadavia, and several of the local wine producers allow visits to their *bodegas* by appointment. Near to Ribadavia, *Vitivinícola do Ribeiro* (☎988 477 210) is one of the larger producers, but much more quaint are the private *bodegas*, including *Viña de Martín* (☎608 989 752) a little way south near the pueblo of Arnoia. All visits are currently free, though the turismo in Ribadavia organizes five-hour guided tours of the region for €12.

Albariño cultivation (⊛www.doriasbaixas.com) centres around the Rías Baixas. The English-owned *Bodega Castro Martin* (☎986 710 202) in Barrantes, just outside Pontevedra, will accept visitors, but you should phone in advance as you will not be admitted without an appointment. To get there, follow the Via Rapida (VR4-G) from Pontevedra and take the Cambados exit. Barrantes is about 2km from the junction and is well signposted.

You'll also find the only **hostal** in the old town on the Praza Maior, the *Hostal Plaza* (☎988 470 576; ❶), which has good en-suite rooms. Alternatively, *Hostal Evencio*, Avda. Rodriguez Valcarcel 30 (☎988 471 045; ❸), is rather soulless but has spacious, well-equipped rooms with great views. Several pleasant **bars** around town serve the region's excellent *Ribeiro* wine (see box above). For **food** there are several bar-restaurants on the Praza Maior, including *Latina* and the restaurant below the *Hostal Plaza*, while *Celta*, on Rúa Fonte de Prata 6, has an excellent *menú* for €7.50.

Celanova

The first hydroelectric dam blocks the Minho about 30km below Ribadavia, and it's from then on up that the flooding of the valley makes the river so broad and smooth-flowing, with forests right to the water's edge. The high and winding road along the south bank through Cortegada to the border at São Gregorio makes a good excursion, and can also be used as part of the route to **CELANOVA**, 35km east of Ribadavia. This is hardly more than a village, dominated by a vast and palatial **Benedictine monastery**. It was here that Felipe V retired into monastic life, having spent much of his reign securing the throne in the War of the Spanish Succession (1701–13). The monastery is now a school, but you can explore its two superb cloisters – one Renaissance, the other Baroque – and the cathedral-sized church. Most beautiful of all is the tiny Mozarabic chapel of **San Miguel** in the garden of the monastery. This dates from the tenth century, and is the work of "Arabicized" Christian refugees from *al-Andalus*. **Buses** also come in from Ourense (8 daily). If you wish to stay, the **hotel** *Betanzos* on Castor Elices 12 (☎988 451 036; ❷) is excellent value for money, with some en-suite rooms.

Tui

TUI (Tuy, pronounced *twee*), 64km southwest of Ribadavia, is the main *gallego* frontier town on the Minho, staring across to the neat ramparts of Portuguese Valença do Minho. The old town stands back from the river, tiered amid trees and stretches of ancient walls above the fertile riverbank. Sloping lanes, paved with huge slabs of granite, climb to the imposing fortress-like **Catedral** dedicated to San Telmo, patron saint of fishermen; its military aspect is a distinctive mark of Tui, scene of sporadic skirmishes with the Portuguese throughout the Middle Ages. There are other churches of interest in the old town, too, such as the Romanesque San Telmo on Rúa San Telmo, or the Gothic Santo Domingo with its ivy-shrouded cloisters on Rúa Antero Rubin. Most memorable, though, is the lovely rambling quality of the place, coupled with a pair of enticing little river beaches on the far side of the old town from the main street.

Practicalities

Frequent **buses** from Vigo and A Guarda stop opposite the *Hostal La Generosa* on old Tui's main street, the acacia-lined Paseo Calvo Sotelo. If you're arriving by rail from Ribadavia and Ourense, it's much quicker to catch your **train** to Guillarei station, 3km east of town, than to wait for a connection in Tui itself. The **city turismo** is in front of the Palacio de Justicia (June–Sept daily 10am–8pm; no phone) a short walk from the bus stop. A **regional turismo** (summer Mon–Fri 10am–2pm & 5–7.30pm, Sat & Sun 10am–2pm & 5–6.30pm; winter Mon–Fri 9.30am–1.30pm & 4.30–6.30pm, Sat 10am–noon; ☏986 601 789) is located in a huge church-like building on Rúa Colón and is open all year. The room next door is an office giving information about the Camino de Santiago (same hours), a fork of which passes through the town.

If you want **to stay**, the *Hostal La Generosa* (☏986 600 055; ❶), at Paseo Calvo Sotelo 37, is ageing gracefully and excellent value. Other more expensive options include the *Hostal San Telmo 91*, Avda. de la Concordia 88 (☏986 603 011; ❷), outside town opposite the train station, and *Hotel Colón* (☏986 600 223; ❹), Rúa Colón 11, with large comfortable rooms, a pool and views of Portugal. Best of the lot, though, if your budget will stretch, is the *Parador San Telmo* (☏986 600 300, ✉tui@parador.es; ❻) out near the border.

Tui's best **restaurants** are located in the old town. *O Nuevo Cabalo Furado*, on Praza de Generalísimo next to the cathedral, is expensive but excellent, while on the street below its sister bar, *O Vello Cabalo Furado*, is equally good and much more affordable.

Crossing the border

It's a fifteen-minute walk to the Portuguese border, across an iron bridge designed by Eiffel; the little town of **VALENÇA DO MINHO**, dwarfed behind its mighty ramparts, lies a similar distance beyond. There's no border control at the bridge: just stroll (or drive) across and head up the hill to the centre.

A Guarda

At the mouth of the great Río Minho stands the workaday port of **A GUARDA** (La Guardia), largely the modern creation of emigrants returned from Puerto Rico. The main attraction here is the extensive remains of a **celta** (pre-Roman fortified hill settlement), just above the town in the thick woods of Monte Santa Tecla. The ruins are about two-thirds of the way up the mountain, a stiff thirty-minute climb – follow the signs from the Tui side of the town centre. There's also a tarmac road up to the summit, but no bus.

The *celta* was probably occupied between around 600 and 200 BC, and abandoned when the Romans established control over the north – such settlements were common in this part of Galicia, and even more so in northern Portugal. The site consists of the foundations of well over a hundred circular dwellings, crammed tightly inside an encircling wall. A couple of them have been restored as full-size thatched huts; most are excavated to a metre or so, though some are still buried. Set in a thick pine grove on the bleak, seaward hillside, the ancient village forms a striking contrast to the humdrum roofscape of the modern town below. On the north slope of the mountain there is also a large **cromlech**, or stone circle, while continuing upwards you pass along an avenue of much more recent construction, lined with the Stations of the Cross, and best seen looming out of a mountain mist. Five minutes further on, at the top, are a church, a small **archeological museum** (March–Nov daily 9.30am–11pm; €0.80) of Celtic finds from the mountain, and a hotel (see below).

A Guarda itself has a couple of small **beaches**, but there's a better stretch of sand at the village of **Camposancos** about 4km south, facing Portugal and a small islet capped by the ruins of a fortified Franciscan monastery. A **ferry** (daily every 30min summer 9.30am–10.30pm, winter until 7.30pm; pedestrians €0.60, car & driver €2.49 one way) links Camposancos with Caminha in Portugal.

Practicalities

A seasonal **turismo** (daily June–Sept 9am–3pm & 7–9pm) behind the fisherman's monument, at Rúa do Porto 48, is well-equipped with English-language leaflets. ATSA **buses** (every 30min from Tui; 3 daily from Baiona) arrive at the small Praza Avelino Vicente. From here, follow Rúa Concepción Arenal downhill to Rúa do Porto (at the end of which lies the seaport), where there's a string of low-key but excellent **seafood restaurants**. Try *Alborada* at no. 34 for good-value meals and *O Paseo* at no. 32 for tapas straight out of the sea.

If you want **to stay**, try the *Hostal Martirrey*, at Rúa José Antonio 8, a short walk uphill from the bus stop 8 (☎986 610 349; ❶); the *Hostal Fidel Mar* (☎986 614 550; ❶), a fifteen-minute walk from the centre out on the Praia Arena Grande, is very cheap with wonderful sea views (follow the main Baiona road until you see signs for the *praia*). For real comfort, there's the beautiful *Hotel Convento de San Benito*, right by the port, at Praza San Benito (☎986 611 166, ℱ986 611 517; ❹), housed in an old Benedictine convent. Alternatively, the one-star *Hotel Pazo Santa Tecla* (☎986 610 002, ℱ986 611 072; June–Sept; ❸), above the *celta* at the top of Monte Santa Tecla, boasts glorious views along the coast and the Río Minho. There's **camping** out towards the river at *Camping Santa Tecla* (☎986 613 011; open all year), a kilometre or so from town.

Travel details

Trains

As well as the FEVE line (see p.623) which journeys along the north coast from Asturias to Ferrol, there are two main lines into and out of Galicia: one from Madrid via Avila, Medina del Campo and Zamora to Ourense; the other from León to Monforte, the junction between Lugo and Ourense. Many of these trains continue to Santiago and A Coruña, but you can usually get about more easily using the *regionales*. Galicia has two regional lines: the first runs from A Coruña to Vigo via Santiago; the second from Vigo to Ourense and on to Monforte. Two further minor lines connect Ferrol with A Coruña, and A Coruña with Lugo and Monforte.

A Coruña to: Barcelona (2 daily; 15hr 45min); Betanzos (3 daily; 30min); Bilbao (1 daily; 12hr); Burgos (3 daily; 8–9hr); Ferrol (4 daily; 1hr–1hr 20min); León (3 daily; 5–6hr); Lugo (4 daily; 2hr);

Madrid (3 daily; 8hr 30min–10hr 30min); Ourense (4 daily; 2hr 15min–3hr); Santiago de Compostela (17 daily; 1hr–1hr 30min); Vigo (16 daily; 2hr–3hr 30min); Zamora (3 daily; 5hr 20min); Zaragoza (2 daily; 12hr 30min).

Ourense to: A Coruña (4 daily; 2hr 30min–3hr 30min); Burgos (3 daily; 4–6hr); León (4 daily; 4hr); Madrid (3 daily; 7–8hr); Medina del Campo (3 daily; 3hr 30min–4hr 30min); Monforte (5 daily; 45min); Ponferrada (5 daily; 2hr 30min); Pontevedra (3 daily; 2hr 45min); Ribadavia (6 daily; 25min); Santiago de Compostela (5–7 daily; 1hr 20min–2hr); Vigo (8 daily; 2hr); Zamora (2 daily; 3hr).

Santiago de Compostela to: A Coruña (18–24 daily; 1hr); Ávila (2 daily; 6hr); Bilbao (1 daily; 10hr 45min); Burgos (1 daily; 8hr); Irún (1 daily; 11hr 30min); León (1 daily; 6hr); Madrid (2 daily; 8–10hr); Medina del Campo (2 daily; 5hr 20min); Ourense (6 daily; 1hr 20min–2hr); Palencia (1 daily; 7hr); Vigo (15–18 daily; 1hr 15min–1hr 45min); Zamora (2 daily; 5hr 30min–6hr 30min).

Vigo to: A Coruña (15–18 daily; 2hr–3hr 30min); Ávila (2 daily; 6hr 30min–8hr 30min); Barcelona (1–2 daily; 15hr–16hr 30min); Burgos (2–3 daily; 8hr); Irún (1 daily; 11hr 30min); León (3–4 daily; 6hr); Madrid (2 daily; 8–10hr); Medina del Campo (2 daily; 6hr 30min); Ourense (7–8 daily; 2hr); Ponferrada (4–5 daily; 4–5hr); Pontevedra (15–18 daily; 30min); Ribadavia (4 daily; 1hr 30min); Santiago de Compostela (15–18 daily; 1hr 15min–1hr 45min); Tui (3 daily; 45min); Zamora (2 daily; 5–6hr); Zaragoza (1–2 daily; 9–12hr).

Buses

A Coruña to: Betanzos (every 30min, hourly at weekends; 45min); Camariñas (3–5 daily; 1hr 45min); Carnota (1–2 daily; 2hr 40min); Cee (2–7 daily; 2hr 15min); Corme (2–7 daily; 1hr 30min); Ferrol (hourly; 1hr); Finisterre (2–7 daily; 2hr 30min); Laxe (2–6 daily; 1hr); Lugo (8–14 daily; 2hr); Madrid (8 daily; 7hr); Malpica (5–7 daily; 1hr 15min); Ourense (6 daily; 3hr 30min); Oviedo (4 daily; 3hr 45min–6hr); Pontevedra (10 daily; 1hr 45min); Santiago de Compostela (hourly; 1hr

30min); Ribadeo (5 daily; 4hr); Vigo (9 daily; 2hr 15min); Viveiro (6 daily; 3hr 30min).

Costa da Morte to: Camariñas–Muxia–Cee (3 daily; 30min/1hr 30min); Finisterre–Corcubión–Muxia–Camariñas (3 daily; 15min/1hr 15min/2hr); Finisterre–Muros (3 daily; 1hr); Laxe–Muxia (1 daily; 1hr 30min); Muros–Cee (9 daily; 1hr); Muxia–Camariñas (3 daily; 30min).

Lugo to: A Coruña (hourly; 2hr); Foz (5 daily; 2hr); Ourense (5 daily; 2hr); Pontevedra (5 daily; 2hr); Santiago de Compostela (9 daily; 2hr); Vigo (5 daily; 3hr); Viveiro (4 daily; 2–3hr).

Ourense to: Celanova (8 daily; 1hr 30min); A Coruña (6 daily; 3hr 30min); Lugo (5 daily; 2hr); Santiago de Compostela (6 daily; 2hr 30min); Vigo (12 daily; 2hr).

Pontevedra to: Bueu (15 daily; 30min); Cambados (11 daily; 1hr); Cangas (15 daily; 1hr); A Coruña (9 daily; 2hr); O Grove (10 daily; 1hr); Isla de Arousa (5 daily; 1hr 30min); Lugo (5 daily; 3hr); Noia (1 daily; 1hr 30min); Ourense (7 daily; 2hr); Padrón (14 daily; 1hr); Santiago de Compostela (every 30min; 1hr); Tui (4 daily; 1hr); Vigo (every 30min; 30min–1hr); Vilagarcía (15 daily; 45min).

Santiago de Compostela to: Betanzos (7 daily; 1hr 30min); Camariñas (4 daily; 3hr); Cambados (5 daily; 2hr); Cee (3–7 daily; 2hr); A Coruña (hourly; 1hr 30min); Ferrol (6–8 daily; 2hr 30min); Finisterre (3–7 daily; 2hr 30min); Lugo (9 daily; 2hr); Madrid (3–6 daily; 9hr 30min); Malpica (3 daily; 2hr); Muros (hourly; 2hr 30min); Noia (hourly; 1hr 30min); Ourense (9 daily; 2hr 30min); Padrón (every 30min; 45min); Pontevedra (every 30min; 1hr); Vigo (hourly; 1hr 30min–2hr); Vilagarcía (9 daily; 1hr).

Vigo to: Baiona (every 15min; 1hr); Barcelona (1 or 2 daily; 14hr); Cangas (1–3 daily; 1hr); A Coruña (7–9 daily; 3hr); O Grove (2 daily; 1hr 15min); Lugo (5–6 daily; 3hr); Madrid (3 daily; 8hr); Noia (1 daily; 3hr); Oporto and Lisbon (3 weekly; 3hr 30min/6hr); Ourense (13 daily; 2hr); Oviedo (1 daily; 6hr 15min); Padrón (12 daily; 2hr); Pontevedra (every 30min; 30min–1hr); Ribadavia (13 daily; 1hr 30min); Santiago de Compostela (every 30min; 2hr 30min); Tui (every 30min; 45min).

Aragón

CHAPTER 9

Highlights

* **Basilica de Nuestra Señora del Pilar, Zaragoza** The majestically set, monumental shrine of the patron saint of Spain. See p.668

* **Aljafería, Zaragoza** The most spectacular Moorish monument outside Andalucía. See p.670

* **El Maestrazgo** Head off the beaten track to explore atmospheric medieval villages in this wild, mountainous region. See p.683

* **Teruel** The old town of this historic provincial capital has superb Mudéjar architecture. See p.677

* **Albarracín** Wander through this picturesque medieval town. See p.680

* **Castillo de Loarre** A fairytale castle in the Pyrenean foothills, with sweeping views. See p.690

* **Parque Nacional de Ordesa** A dramatic, canyon-slashed landscape for fine high-altitude hiking. See p.702

△ Parque Nacional de Ordesa

Aragón

Politically and historically Aragón has close links with Catalunya, with which it formed a powerful alliance in medieval times, exerting influence over the Mediterranean as far away as Athens. It is a Castilian rather than Catalan-speaking area, though, and, locked in on all sides by mountains, has always had its own identity, with traditional *fueros* like the Basques. The modern *autonomía* – containing the provinces of Zaragoza, Teruel and Huesca – is well out of the Spanish political mainstream, especially in the rural south, where Teruel is the least populated region in Spain. Coming from Catalunya or the Basque country, you'll find the Aragonese pace, in general, noticeably slower.

It is the **Pyrenees** that draw most visitors to Aragón, with their sculpted valleys, stone-built farming villages, and trekking. The mountains are remarkably unspoilt – still less commercialized than across the border in France – and they have a stunning focus in the **Parque Nacional de Ordesa**, with its panoply of canyons, waterfalls and peaks. Aragón's Pyrenean towns are also renowned for their sacred architecture; **Jaca** has the country's oldest **Romanesque** cathedral.

The most interesting monuments of central and southern Aragón are, by contrast, **Mudéjar**: a series of churches, towers and mansions built by Muslim workers in the early decades of Christian rule. **Zaragoza**, the Aragonese capital, and the only place of any real size, sets the tone with its remarkable **Aljafería Palace**, the most spectacular Moorish monument outside Andalucía. Other examples are to be found in a string of smaller towns, in particular **Tarazona**, **Calatayud** and – above all – the southern provincial capital of **Teruel**.

In southern Aragón, two mountainous regions are also of interest. West of Teruel, the Montes Universales, a frontier with Cuenca province, offer some gorgeous routes and walking, especially around the massively walled village of **Albarracín**. To the east is the isolated region encompassing the **Sierra de Gúdar** and **El Maestrazgo**, a wild countryside stamped with dark peaks and gorges, whose villages feel extraordinarily remote.

This chapter is arranged in two sections: **Zaragoza, Teruel and southern Aragón** (covering Zaragoza and Teruel provinces); and **The Aragonese Pyrenees** (covering Huesca province).

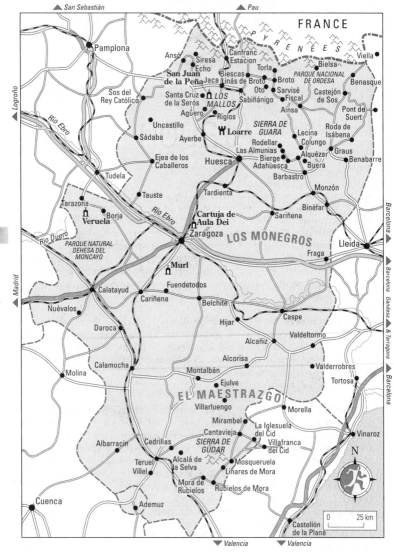

San Sebastián   Pau

FRANCE

P Y R E N E E S

Viella

Pamplona

Ansó   Siresa   Canfranc
Echo   Estación
San Juan   Biescas   Torla   Bielsa
de la Peña   Jaca   Linás de Broto   Broto   PARQUE NACIONAL   Benasque
Sos del   Santa Cruz   Oto   DE ORDESA
Rey Católico   de la Serós   Sabiñánigo   Sarvisé   Castejón
LOS   Fiscal   de Sos
Agüero   MALLOS   Ainsa   Pont de
Riglos   Suert
Uncastillo   SIERRA DE   Roda de
Loarre   GUARA   Lecina   Isábena
Sádaba   Ayerbe   Rodellar   Colungo   Graus
Las Almunias   Alquézar   Benabarre
Ejea de los   Bierge   Buera
Caballeros   Huesca   Adahüesca
Barbastro

Logroño   Tudela   Monzón

Río Ebro   Tauste   Tardienta   Binéfar
Tarazona   Barcelona
Borja   Río Ebro   Cartuja de   Sariñena
Veruela   Aula Dei   Lleida
Río Duero   Zarágoza   LOS MONEGROS
PARQUE NATURAL
DEHESA DEL   Fraga   Barcelona
MONCAYO

Madrid   Murl   Barcelona   Gandesa & Tarragona   Barcelona
Calatayud   Fuendetodos
Cariñena   Belchite
Nuévalos   Caspe
Híjar
Daroca   Valdeltormo
Alcañiz
Calamocha   Alcorisa
Molina   Montalbán   Valderrobres
Ejulve   Tortosa
EL MAESTRAZGO
Villarluengo   Morella
Mirambel   La Iglesuela
Cantavieja   del Cid   Vinaroz
Albarracín   Cedrillas   SIERRA DE   Villafranca
GÚDAR   del Cid
Teruel   Alcalá de   Mosqueruela
Villel   la Selva   Linares de Mora
Mora de   Rubielos de Mora
Rubielos
Cuenca   Ademuz   N

Castellón   0   25 km
de la Plana

Valencia   Valencia

ARAGÓN

Zaragoza, Teruel and Southern Aragón

Zaragoza houses nearly half of Aragón's 1.5 million population, and most of its industry. It's a big but enjoyable city, with a lively zone of bars and restaurants tucked in among remarkable monuments, and it's a handy transport nexus too, both for Aragón and beyond. Its province includes the Mudéjar towns of **Tarazona, Calatayud** and **Daroca**, and, along the border with Navarra, the old **Cinco Villas**, really just ennobled villages, of which the most interesting is **Sos del Rey Católico**. Wine enthusiasts may also want to follow the **Ruta de los Vinos**, south from Zaragoza through Cariñena to Daroca.

Teruel province is a lot more remote, and even the capital doesn't see too many passing visitors. It is unjustly neglected, considering its superb Mudéjar monuments, and if you have transport of your own there are some wonderful rural routes to explore: especially east, through **Albarracín** to Cuenca, or south through to Valencia. The valleys and villages of the **Sierra de Gúdar** and **El Maestrazgo**, which borders Valencia province, are the most remote of the lot: a region completely untouched by tourism, foreign or Spanish, and where transport of your own is a big help.

Zaragoza

ZARAGOZA is an interesting and inviting place, having managed to absorb its rapid growth with a rare grace, and its centre, at least, reflects an air of prosperity in its wide, modern boulevards, stylish shops and bars. In addition, the city preserves the spectacular Moorish **Aljafería**, and an awesome basilica, devoted to one of Spain's most famous icons, **Nuestra Señora del Pilar**.

The city's **fiestas** in honour of Nuestra Señora del Pilar – which take place throughout the second week of October – are well worth planning a trip around, so long as you can find accommodation. In addition to the religious processions (which focus on the 12th), the local council lays on a brilliant programme of cultural events, featuring top rock, jazz and folk bands, floats, bullfights and traditional *jota* dancing. It's a pretty lively town for the rest of the year too, and if you're anywhere nearby at the weekend, it's well worth spending an evening here just to experience the atmosphere around the old quarter.

Orientation and information

The **old centre** of Zaragoza is bordered to the north by the **Río Ebro**, and on the other sides by a loop of broad *paseos*; bisecting it is the **Avenida de César Augusto**, leading in from the old city gate, Puerta del Carmen. With the exception of the **Aljafería**, most other points of interest are within this loop. Backing onto the river are the two cathedrals, **La Seo** and the **Basílica de Nuestra Señora del Pilar**, flanked on their south side by **Plaza del Pilar**, a huge stone square which is in every sense the heart of the city. Just south of

April

8–9 Pilgrimage to the Santuario de Nuestra Señora de la Alegría in Monzón, the journey made in decorated carriages.

Holy Week Small-scale but emotional celebrations at Calatayud and elsewhere. On Maundy Thursday/Good Friday there's the festival of *La Tamborrada* in Calanda, near Alcañiz.

May

First Friday Jaca commemorates the Battle of Vitoria against the Moors with processions and folkloric events.

25 More of the same at Jaca for the *Fiesta de Santa Orosia*.

Monday of Pentecost *Romería Nuestra Señora de Calentuñana* at Sos del Rey Católico.

June

Nearest Sunday to the 19th Cantavieja celebrates the *Fiesta de los Mozos*: a serious religious event but with dancing and the usual fairground activities.

30 *Ball de Benas*: small festival at Benasque.

July

First Sunday *Romería del Quililay*, pilgrimage and picnic up the mountain above Tarazona.

First and second week Teruel bursts into ten days of festivities for the *Vaquilla del Ángel*, one of Aragón's major festivals.

Late July/early August International Folklore Festival of the Pyrenees alternates between France and Spain: it's at Jaca in odd-numbered years, accompanied by a very full programme of traditional music and dance.

Last two weeks *Pireneos Sur* world music festival at Sallent de Gallego, with performances by international artists on a floating stage in Lanuza reservoir.

August

Early August Fiesta at Huesca in honour of San Lorenzo.

14–15 *Fiestas del Barrio* in Jaca – street markets and mass parties.

16 Patron saint's festival at Biescas – "bigheads" and eats.

27–28 *Encierros* – crazy local bull-running – at Cantavieja.

September

Early September Teruel fair.

4–8 Fiesta at Barbastro includes *jota* dancing, bullfights and sports competitions (such as pigeon-shooting contests).

8 Virgin's birthday signals fairs at Alcañiz, Hecho, Calatayud, Alcalá de la Selva and Villel.

12–15 Three days of patron saint festivities at Graus, including stylized traditional dances and "dawn songs". *Romería* at L'Iglesuela del Cid, with the "Mojiganga", a socially satiric procession, held on the Sunday closest to the 14th.

8–14 Bull-running and general celebrations at Albarracín.

October

Second week Aragón's most important festival in honour of the *Virgen del Pilar*. Much of the province closes down around the 12th and at Zaragoza there are floats, bullfights and *jota* dancing.

---

the square, between c/de Alfonso and c/de Don Jaime, is a zone known as **El Tubo**, the hub of Zaragoza's bar and nightlife scene. This leads to the **Plaza de España**, a central terminus for local city buses.

Points of arrival are scattered around the town. **Trains** use the brand new

Estación Delicias, two miles from the centre. From here, catch the bus #51 right outside the station to the Paseo Constitución, a 10-minute walk from El Tubo, or the bus #25 on Avenida Navarra which will take you to Avenida César Augusto, just west of Plaza del Pilar. If you decide to walk, a small **turismo** booth (daily 10am–8pm) at the station can supply you with a map. By **bus**, you could arrive at various terminals. The principal one is at Paseo María Agustín 7, near the Puerta del Carmen; Agreda services for Madrid, Catalunya and several destinations in Old Castile, and La Oscense/Agreda services to Huesca and Jaca, operate from here. Services south to Daroca, Cariñena and Muel, and some other local destinations, use a terminal across the railway tracks at Avda. Valencia 20. Viajes Viaca buses to many northern destinations leave from outside their offices at c/Pignatelli 120, just opposite the bullring.

Leaving for elsewhere, it's best to check with the **turismo** opposite the basilica on Plaza del Pilar (daily 10am–8pm; ☎976 201 200, Ⓦwww .turismozaragoza.com). This caters for the city and province of Zaragoza, and also has pamphlets and maps on destinations and routes throughout Aragón. They offer a series of themed **guided walks** of the city (info ☎902 201 212 or 976 201 200; €3.05 plus entrances), which set off at 11am at weekends and last a couple of hours. From July to October you'll also find up to twenty tourist information officers – dressed in yellow jackets – at various points around the centre.

Accommodation

There are only two **places to stay** close to the train station, a fairly functional area of shops and offices. There's much more atmosphere in **El Tubo**, where you'll find upwards of a dozen *pensiones* located in airy mansion blocks; c/Méndez Núñez and the smaller streets off it, such as c/Estabañes, are good locations, although they can be noisy at night. Alternatively, there are a number of decent options dotted around to the east of the Plaza de España.

In the centre

Albergue Juvenil Baltázar Gracián c/Franco y López 4, off Avda. de Valencia ☎976 306 692. Zaragoza's youth hostel is on the fifth street on the right as you walk down Avda. de Valencia from Avda. Francisco de Goya. The rooms are basic but clean and sleep 2, 4 or 8 people on bunk beds with bedding and breakfast included. Check-in is from noon–5pm or until 9pm with a prior reservation, and there's a midnight curfew. €8.60 for under 26s, €9.80 for over 26s.
Posada de las Almas c/San Pablo 22 ☎976 439 700, Ⓕ976 439 143. Soak up the faded grandeur in this well-located old hotel, with its own restaurant and garage (€6 per day for a car). ➋
Descanso San Lorenzo 2 ☎976 291 741. Light, clean, exceedingly cheap rooms next to a pleasant, tree-shaded square. ➊
Hostal Milmarcos c/Madre Sacramento 40 ☎ &

Ⓕ976 284 618. Modern, comfortable rooms with TV and bath. Tends not to get too busy so worth trying to negotiate a cheap deal. ➋
Fonda La Peña c/de Cinegio 3, 1º ☎976 299 089. Comfortable, clean and inexpensive rooms at this family-run *fonda*. Recommended. ➊
Hostal Plaza Plaza del Pilar 14 ☎976 294 830, Ⓕ976 399 406. The rooms are decent, if a little past their prime, but the location is unbeatable. Parking available for €9 per day. ➋
Hotel Sauce Espoz y Mina 33 ☎976 205 050, Ⓦwww.hotelsauce.com. Along with its great name, this hotel boasts attractively furnished, a/c rooms. Recommended. ➌
Hotel Las Torres Plaza del Pilar 11 ☎976 394 250, Ⓔtorres@able.es. Comfortable, reasonably priced, en-suite rooms in an excellent position, looking directly onto the basilica. ➌
Hotel Vía Romana c/Don Jaime I 54 ☎976 398 215, Ⓔviaromana@husa.es. Smart hotel just off the Plaza del Pilar; cheaper at weekends. ➎

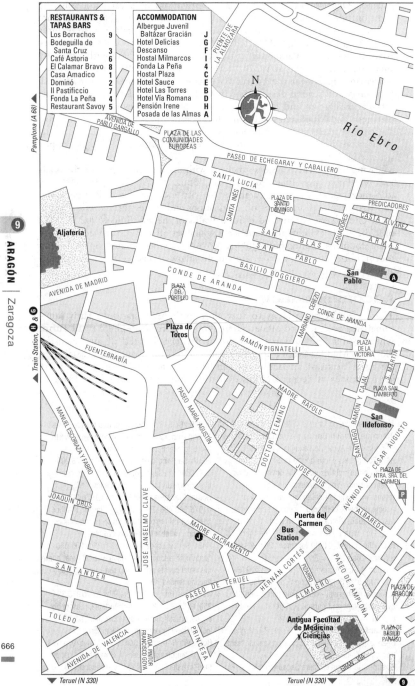

RESTAURANTS & TAPAS BARS

Los Borrachos	9
Bodeguilla de Santa Cruz	3
Café Astoria	6
El Calamar Bravo	8
Casa Amadico	1
Dominó	2
Il Pastificcio	7
Fonda La Peña	4
Restaurant Savoy	5

ACCOMMODATION

Albergue Juvenil Baltázar Gracián	J
Hotel Delicias	G
Descanso	F
Hostal Milmarcos	I
Fonda La Peña	4
Hostal Plaza	C
Hotel Sauce	E
Hotel Las Torres	B
Hotel Vía Romana	D
Pensión Irene	H
Posada de las Almas	A

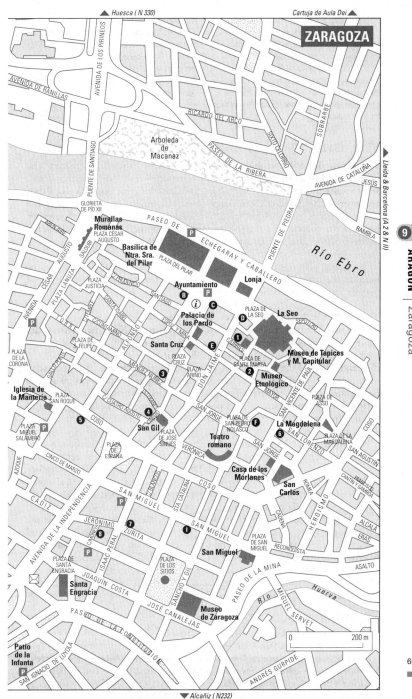

▲ Huesca (N 330)

Cartuja de Aula Dei ▲

▶ Lleida & Barcelona (A 2 & N II)

AVENIDA DE RANILLAS

AVENIDA DE LOS PIRINEOS

RICARDO DEL ARCO

SOBRARBE

SIXTO CELORRIO

Arboleda de Macanaz

PASEO DE LA RIBERA

AVENIDA DE CATALUÑA

JESÚS

RAMBLA

PUENTE DE SANTIAGO

GLORIETA DE PÍO XII

PLAZA CÉSAR AUGUSTO

SALDUBA

PASEO DE

ECHEGARAY Y CABALLERO

PUENTE DE PIEDRA

Río Ebro

Murallas Romanas

Basílica de Ntra. Sra. del Pilar

PLAZA DEL PILAR

P

Ayuntamiento

B

i

C

Lonja

PLAZA DE LA SEO

La Seo

SEPULCRO

Palacio de los Pardo

D

Santa Cruz

E

1

Museo de Tapices y M. Capitular

CURRIES

PLAZA DE SANTA MARTA

Museo Etnológico

2

MAYOR

PLAZA DE ASSO

SAN VICENTE DE PAÚL

ARRIANDA

AVENIDA

CÉSAR AUGUSTO

AUGUSTO

PLAZA JUSTICIA

FRIGENCIO

SANTIAGO

SANTA ISABEL

PTCANTAMINO

ALFONSO I

ESPOZ Y MINA

PLAZA CRUZ

PLAZA ARIÑO

DON JAIME I

SAN JORGE

PLAZA DE S. FELIPE

PLAZA DE LA CORONA

GALICETA

MÉNDEZ NÚÑEZ

3

Iglesia de la Manteria

PLAZA SAN ROQUE

C. CUATRO AGOSTO

4

San Gil

PLAZA DE JOSÉ SINUÉS

PLAZA DE SAN PEDRO NOLASCO

F

La Magdalena

6

PLAZA DE LA MAGDALENA

SAN LORENZO

SAN AGUSTÍN

COSO

PLAZA MIGUEL SALAMERO

5

COSO

CINCO DE MARZO

PLAZA DE ESPAÑA

VERÓNICA

Teatro romano

SAN JORGE

San Carlos

CANTÍN Y GAMBOA

FRANCISCO

ALCALÁ

ERAS

AZOQUE

CADIZ

SAN MIGUEL

FRANCIS

STA CATALINA

COSO

Casa de los Morlanes

CADENA

ROMEA

HEROÍSMO

RECONQUISTA

ASALTO

JERÓNIMO

ZURITA

7

8

ISAAC PERAL

CAMONES

PLAZA DE SANTA ENGRACIA

SAN MIGUEL

I

San Miguel

PLAZA DE SAN MIGUEL

PASEO DE LA MINA

Río HUERVA

Santa Engracia

JOAQUÍN COSTA

PLAZA DE LOS SITIOS

SANCHO Y GIL

Museo de Zaragoza

JOSÉ CANALEJAS

PASEO DE LA CONSTITUCIÓN

Río MIGUEL SERVET

Patio de la Infanta

SAN IGNACIO DE LOYOLA

ANDRÉS GURPIDE

▼ Alcañiz (N232)

0   200 m

Near the train station

Camping

The City

The **Plaza del Pilar** is the obvious point to start exploring Zaragoza. The square, paved in a brilliant, pale stone, was remodelled in 1991, creating a vast, airy expanse from the old cathedral, **La Seo**, past the great **Basilica del Pilar**, and over to the Avenida César Augusto. A look around the square spans the whole extent of the city's history: at one end a patch of Roman wall remains; between the churches is a Renaissance exchange house, **La Lonja**; while at the centre is some modern statuary and a waterfall shaped like a map of South America.

Even if you plan only to change trains or buses in Zaragoza, it is worth coming into the centre to see the square and basilica, and making your way west over to **La Aljafería**, either on foot (around 20min) or by taxi.

The Basilica de Nuestra Señora del Pilar

Majestically fronting the Río Ebro, the **Basilica de Nuestra Señora del Pilar** (daily: summer 5.45–9.30pm; winter 5.45–8.30pm) is one of Spain's greatest and most revered religious buildings. It takes its name from a pillar – the centrepiece of the church – on which the Virgin is said to have descended from heaven in an apparition before St James the Apostle. The structure around this shrine is truly monumental, with great corner towers and a central dome surrounded by ten brightly tiled cupolas; it was designed in the late seventeenth century by Francisco Herrera el Mozo and built by Ventura Rodríguez in the 1750s and 1760s.

The **pillar**, topped by a diminutive image of the Virgin, is constantly surrounded by pilgrims, who line up to touch an exposed (and thoroughly worn) section, encased in a marble surround. The main artistic treasure of the cathedral is a magnificent alabaster *reredos* on the high altar, a masterpiece sculpted by Damián Forment in the first decades of the sixteenth century.

Off the north aisle is the **Museo Pilarista** (Tues–Sun 9am–2pm & 4–6pm; €1.50), where you can inspect at close quarters the original sketches for the decoration of the domes by Francisco de Goya, González Velázquez, and Francisco and Ramón Bayeu. Your ticket also admits you to the **Sacristía Mayor**, off the opposite aisle, with a collection of religious paintings and tapestries. You'll have to pay extra, however, if you want to enjoy the panoramic views from the **Torre**, the tower at the northwest corner of the church (Sat–Thurs 9.30am–2pm & 4–7pm; €1.50).

Around the square

The old cathedral, **La Seo** (summer Tues–Fri 10am–2pm & 4–7pm, Sat 10am–1pm & 4–7pm, Sun 10am–noon & 4–7pm; winter Tues–Fri 10am–2pm & 4–6pm, Sat 10am–1pm & 4–6pm, Sun 10am–noon & 4–6pm; free), recently reopened after extensive restoration work, stands at the far end of the Plaza del Pilar. The now gleaming exterior is essentially Gothic-Mudéjar, with minor

△ Nuestra Señora del Pilar, Zaragoza

Baroque and Plateresque additions, while to the left of the main entrance is a Mudéjar wall with elaborate geometric patterns. Inside, the superb *retablo mayor* contains some recognizably Teutonic figures executed by the German Renaissance sculptor, Hans of Swabia.

Midway between the two cathedrals stands the sixteenth-century **Lonja**, the old exchange building, a Florentine-influenced structure, with an interior of elegant Ionic columns, open periodically for art exhibitions. Over to the other side of the basilica is the **Torreón de la Zuda**, part of Zaragoza's medieval fortifications, and the remains of **Roman walls**, insignificant ruins but a reminder of the city's Roman past. Zaragoza's name derives from that of Caesar Augustus (César Augusto in the Spanish form).

South of the Plaza del Pilar

A block south of the square, in the impeccably restored Palacio de los Pardo at c/Espoz y Mina 23, the **Museo Camón Aznar** (Tues–Fri 9am–2.15pm & 6–9pm, Sat 10am–2pm & 6–9pm, Sun 11am–2pm; €1) houses the private collections of José Camón Aznar, one of the most distinguished scholars of Spanish art. Highlights include a permanent display of most of Goya's prints (the artist was born at nearby Fuendetodos, see p.672). At the far end of the street, which becomes c/Mayor, the church of **La Magdalena** has the finest of Zaragoza's several Mudéjar towers.

You can see more works by Goya at the **Museo de Zaragoza** (Tues–Sat 10am–2pm & 5–8pm, Sun 10am–2pm; free), in the Plaza de los Sitios. Other exhibits span the city's Iberian, Roman and Moorish past. Close by the museum is a pair of interesting churches: **San Miguel**, with a minor *retablo* by Forment and a Mudéjar tower, and **Santa Engracia**, with a splendid Plateresque portal and paleo-Christian sarcophagi in its crypt. Two further Mudéjar towers are to be seen at **San Pablo** (daily guided tours at 10am, 11am & noon; €1), over to the west of Plaza del Pilar, with another *retablo* by Damián Forment, and **San Gil**, near the Plaza de España.

The Aljafería

Moorish Spain was never very unified, and from the tenth to the eleventh century Zaragoza was the centre of an independent dynasty, the Beni Kasim. Their palace, the **Aljafería** (mid-April to mid-Oct Sat–Wed 10am–2pm & 4.30–8pm, Fri 4.30–8pm; mid-Oct to mid-April Sat, Mon–Wed 10am–2pm & 4–6.30pm, Fri 4–6.30pm, Sun 10am–2pm; €3), was built in the heyday of their rule in the mid-eleventh century, and as such predates the Alhambra in Granada and Sevilla's Alcázar. Much, however, was added later, under twelfth- to fifteenth-century Christian rule, when the palace was adapted and used by the *reconquista* kings of Aragón. Since 1987, the Aragonese parliament has met here.

From the original design the foremost relic is a tiny and beautiful **mosque**, adjacent to the entrance. Further on is an original and intricately decorated court, the **Patio de Santa Isabella**. Crossing from here, the **Grand Staircase** (added in 1492) leads to a succession of mainly fourteenth-century rooms, remarkable for their carved *artesonado* ceilings; the most beautiful is in the Throne Room.

Eating, drinking and nightlife

Zaragoza's **bars** are neatly concentrated in the old quarter, along with many of the best-value **restaurants** – no-nonsense *comedores*, often incorporated into the *fondas* and *pensiones*. As you'd expect in a place of this size, there are some very good, more upmarket restaurants, too, scattered all over the city. The old quarter also has a *zona* of **music bars** and **nightclubs** around c/Cantamina and c/Temple, which get unbelievably lively at the weekends, and another, more alternative, *zona* right behind El Corte Inglés at the bottom of Avenida de la Independencia.

Tapas bars and restaurants

Los Borrachos Paseo Sagasta 64 ℡976 275 036. A classic Zaragoza restaurant, just south of the Plaza de Aragón, whose specialities are mostly game dishes. The *a la carta* options are expensive; reckon on €35 and up for a meal with wine, but the tasting menu is much better value at just €14 per person (minimum 2 people).

Bodeguilla de Santa Cruz c/Santa Cruz 3. Characterful bar that looks like a cross between Aladdin's cave and an old apothecary, serving a creative selection of beautifully presented tapas and *raciones*.

Café Astoria c/San Vicente de Paúl 20. Stylish eatery with modern art on the walls, a great salad selection and an unusual variety of reasonably priced, French-influenced dishes.

El Calamar Bravo c/Moneva 5. Hugely popular and inexpensive stand-up seafood tapas bar with outstanding *calamares* sandwiches. Closed Mon.

Casa Amadico c/Jordán de Urriés 3. A popular *cervecería* with a large range of tapas, especially seafood. Closed Mon & mid-July to early Sept.

Dominó Plaza Santa Marta. Situated on a lively little square full of bars and outdoor tables in summer. Tapas include a fine selection of local cheeses, hams and *chorizo*, and there's a good range of Aragonese wines to accompany them.

Il Pastificcio c/Zurita 15. Cosy, bistro-style Italian restaurant serving up sumptuous pizzas and fresh pasta in a bewildering variety of shapes and sizes.

Fonda La Peña c/de Cinegio 3. The *comedor* here, open to all, dishes up particularly vast quantities of simple home cooking with its €6 *menú*.

Restaurant Savoy Coso 42, facing c/Alfonso. The best place to treat yourself without splashing out. High-class international cuisine and a decent house wine make the €9 *menú* a bargain.

Music bars and nightlife

Bar Azul c/Pizarro 10. The perfect place to get your finger on the pulse of Zaragoza, with art on the walls and up-to-date DJs: big-beats, drum'n'bass, funk, acid jazz and pop all feature, while Sunday features an ambient and trip-hop chill-out.

La Campana de los Perdidos c/Prudencio 7. There's a great atmosphere and regular comedy acts and folk music (Thurs, Fri & Sun nights) in the cellar of this bar.

Chastón c/Plaza Ariño 4. Pleasant city-centre bar with jazz and blues sounds, a mellow, woody interior with lots of comfy cushions and a summer *terraza*. Starts getting busy after 11pm.

Oasis c/Boggiero 28. Grand old concert hall transformed into a glitzy disco. Open Fri & Sat only.

Sala Morrisey Gran Via 33. Irish pub with bogus olde-worlde interior but great alternative DJs Thurs–Sun plus occasional live music.

Listings

Bikes You can rent mountain bikes from the Parque Primo de Rivera, at the south end of Gran Vía (bus #30 or #40 from Plaza de España). From the park, paths lead out into forest land on the edge of the city.

Buses Main station on Paseo María Agustín ℡976 229 343; terminal at Avda. de Valencia 20 ℡976 554 588. Eurolines Julia ℡976 306 858, have the most extensive international services and also operate from the terminal at Avda. de Valencia 20.

Car rental Atesa is at Avda. Valencia 6 ℡976 350 408; Avis c/Santa Orosia 21 ℡976 489 236; Hertz c/Santa Orosia 7 ℡976 320 400.

Cinema The Filmoteca, Plaza de San Carlos, has an arts programme, including original-language movies.

Emergencies For an ambulance call ℡976 222 222.

Hospital Miguel Servet, Plaza Isabel la Católica 1 ℡976 765 500.

Internet Locutorio San Lorenzo, c/San Lorenzo 26 (daily 10am–midnight; €1.20 per hour).

Flea market *El Rastro* takes place near the football stadium, La Romadera, every Sun and Wed morning for clothes, accessories and household objects. The more eclectic *Mercadillo* is held on Sun mornings outside the bullring.

Laundry The most central self-service launderette is at c/San Vicente de Paúl 27.

Post office The *Correos Central* is at Paseo de la Independencia 33 (Mon–Fri 8.30am–8.30pm, Sat 8.30am–2pm).

Shops The big shopping street is Paseo de la Independencia, south of Plaza de España, lined with chain shops including a branch of El Corte Inglés. The newsstands outside carry foreign newspapers and magazines.

Skiing If you plan to go skiing in the Pyrenees you are probably better off buying a package deal from a travel agent in Zaragoza than turning up and going your own way. One of the best agents to try is the Marsans chain; there is a branch on Avda. de la Independencia 18 ☎976 236 965, ⓦwww.marsans.es; there are others on Paseo

María Agustín.

Swimming pools There's a pleasant open-air pool in the Parque Primo de Rivera, at the south end of Gran Vía (bus #30 or #40 from Plaza de España; June to mid-Sept daily 10.30am–9pm).

Taxis Radio-Taxi Aragón ☎976 383 838; Radio-Taxi Cooperativi ☎976 751 515; Radio-Taxi Zaragoza ☎976 424 242.

Around Zaragoza

Few tourists spend much time exploring the sights and towns around Zaragoza, and with the Pyrenees just a step to the north, it is perhaps no wonder. However, wine buffs heading south might want to follow the **Ruta de los Vinos** south through **Cariñena**, and for Goya enthusiasts there are murals at the monastery of **Aula Dei** and at **Muel**.

Further afield, northwest of the capital, the **Cinco Villas** stretch for some 90km along the border with Navarra. These are really little more than villages, set in delightful, scarcely visited countryside; their title is owed to Felipe V, who awarded it for their services in the War of the Succession (1701–13). The most interesting of the five is the northernmost "town", **Sos del Rey Católico**, on the C127 to Pamplona.

The Cartuja de Aula Dei

At the **Cartuja de Aula Dei**, 12km north of Zaragoza, Goya painted a series of eleven murals depicting the lives of Christ and the Virgin in 1774. They suffered badly after the Napoleonic suppression, when the buildings were more or less abandoned, but subsequent repainting and restoration have revealed enough to show the cycle to be one of the artist's early masterpieces. Today the monastery is a strict Carthusian community and visits are currently only possible on the last Saturday of the month by prior arrangement (☎976 714 934). However, this situation may change in the future and it's worth phoning to check, or ask at the turismo in Zaragoza.

To reach Aula Dei, take the Montañana road out of the city, along the east bank of the Río Gallego. The Agreda bus to San Mateo de Gallego runs past the monastery.

The wine route and Goya trail

There are vineyards dotted all over Aragón, but the best wines – strong, throaty reds and good whites – come from the region to the south of Zaragoza, whose towns and villages are accessible from both the road and rail line down to Teruel. The tourist authorities have marked out a **Ruta del Vino** through the area; an alternative route could take you on a brief **Goya trail**, to see further frescoes and his birthplace.

Muel and Fuendetodos

MUEL marks the northernmost point of the region and was once a renowned pottery centre. It has seen much better days, however, and few trains stop here any more. The town's interest lies in a Roman fountain and a hermitage, **La Ermita de Nuestra Señora del Fuente**, which has some early (1771) frescoes of saints by Goya. The artist, who became court painter to Carlos IV, was in fact born at the village of **FUENDETODOS**, 24km southeast, where a little **Casa Museo** has been done up with period furnishings (Tues–Sun 11am–2pm & 4–7pm; €1.80).

Cariñena

Continuing south from Muel, **CARIÑENA** is a larger, rather ramshackle old town, with a clutch of **wine bodegas**. There's a small **Museo del Vino**, at Camino de la Platero 1 (Tues–Fri 10am–2pm & 4–7pm, Sat 11am–2pm & 5–8pm, Sun 11am–2pm; €1.50), that can supply information about the local *bodegas*. To taste and buy wine, a good place to head is the *tienda* at the Grandes Vinos y Viñedos *bodega* (daily 10.30am–1.30pm & 4.30–7.30pm). To get there, follow the main road north towards Zaragoza and after 2km turn left at the sign for Santuario de Ntra. Sra. De Lagunas.

If you want **to stay** – and Cariñena, with its open-air swimming pool (June to mid-Sept daily 11am–8pm; €3), is a quiet alternative to Zaragoza – you'll find good rooms at the reasonable *Hostal Iliturgis* on the Plaza Ramón, near the church (℡976 620 492; ❶), and the busy *Hotel Cariñena* (℡976 620 112; ❷), on the main Zaragoza road near the wine *bodegas*, which also has a restaurant. The town has a small **flea market** on Saturdays.

Sos del Rey Católico and the Cinco Villas

Moving north from Zaragoza, the **Cinco Villas** comprise **Tauste**, **Ejea de los Caballeros**, **Sádaba**, **Uncastillo** and **Sos del Rey Católico**. Sos, the most interesting of the five, attracts the most visitors while remote, tranquil Uncastillo and Sádaba, with its handsome castle, are also very rewarding. The area is not well served by public transport; only one **bus** a day makes it up from Zaragoza to Sos and you'll need your own transport if you want to explore further. For those en route to the Pyrenees (the road past Sos continues to Roncal in Navarra), or Pamplona, the Cinco Villas make a pleasant stop-off.

Zaragoza to Sos

TAUSTE, closest of the "towns" to Zaragoza, has an interesting parish church built in the Mudéjar style – and **accommodation** at the central *Hostal Casa Pepe*, c/Santa Clara 7 (℡976 855 832; ❸).

Nearby **EJEA DE LOS CABALLEROS** retains elements of Romanesque architecture in its churches and has a handful of **places to stay**, including *Hostal Aragón*, c/Media Villa 21 (℡976 660 630; ❶), which has simple rooms with shared bathrooms, and the more comfortable *Hostal Cinco Villas*, c/Paseo del Muro 10 (℡ & ℻976 660 300; ❹).

Twenty kilometres northwest, **SÁDABA** boasts an impressive thirteenth-century castle, as well as the remains of an early synagogue, and a good **hotel**, *Hospedería de Sádaba*, c/Mayor 18 (℡976 675 377; ❹). **UNCASTILLO**, on a minor road to Sos, through the Sierra de Santo Domingo, also has a castle, as its name suggests, this time dating from the twelfth century, and the remains of an aqueduct. **Accommodation** is fairly limited but there are some good choices, including the charmingly renovated, excellent-value *Posada la Pastora* (℡976 679 499; ❸) and the attractive but more expensive *Equestre*, c/Mediavilla 50 (℡976 679 481; ❹), which also has a very good – though fairly pricey – restaurant.

Sos del Rey Católico

SOS DEL REY CATÓLICO, 120km from Zaragoza, is the most interesting town of the five and an excellent place to relax, especially if you're on your way to or from Navarra. The town derives its name from Fernando II, El Rey Católico, born here in 1452 and as powerful a local-boy-made-good as any Aragonese town could hope for. The narrow cobbled streets, like so many in Aragón, are packed with marvellously grand mansions, including the **Palacio**

de Sada where Fernando is reputed to have been born, and there's an unusually early parish **church**, with a curious crypt dedicated to the Virgen del Pilar. These are the real attractions of the place, but you could wander up, too, towards the **Castillo de la Peña Fernando** for lovely views over the village's terracotta rooftops and surrounding countryside, and into the **ayuntamiento**, which displays – as ever – interesting titbits of information about local government in a town whose population scarcely tops a thousand.

There are three **places to stay**: the *Fonda Fernandina*, c/Emilio Alfaro (℡948 888 120; ❶), which is great value and serves inexpensive meals; the modern *Hostal Las Coronas*, opposite the *ayuntamiento* (℡948 888 408, ℻948 888 471; ❸); and the superb *parador* (℡948 888 011, ✉sos@parador.es; ❻), whose rooms give sweeping panoramic views across the hills.

Tarazona and around

The Aragonese plains are dotted with reminders of the Moorish occupation, and nowhere more so than **TARAZONA**, which the local tourist authorities promote as "La Ciudad Mudéjar" and even "the Aragonese Toledo". The latter is a bit of an overstatement, but Tarazona is a fine-looking place, and if you're en route to Soria or Burgos, it makes a good place to break the journey. Don't miss out, either, on the superb Cistercian monastery of **Veruela**, 15km southeast, off the N122 to Zaragoza.

Tarazona

It is the **Barrios Altos**, the old "upper quarters" of Tarazona, that are the main attraction here. They stand on a hilly site, overlooking the river, with medieval houses and mansions lining the *callejas* and *pasadizos* – the lanes and alleyways.

At the heart of the quarter, as ever, is a Plaza de España, which is flanked by a truly magnificent **ayuntamiento**, a sixteenth-century town hall, with a facade of coats of arms, sculpted heads and figures in high relief. A 30cm-high frieze, representing the triumphal procession of Carlos V after his coronation as Emperor in Bologna, runs the length of the building, while the large figures underneath represent Hercules and other classical heroes performing feats of mythological proportions. From here, a *ruta turística* directs you up to the church of **Santa Magdalena**, whose Mudéjar tower dominates the town. The *mirador* (viewpoint) gives a good view of the town, and especially the eighteenth-century **Plaza de Toros** – a circular terrace of houses, with balconies (now filled in) from which spectators could view the *corrida*. Further uphill lies another church, **La Concepción**, again with a slender brick tower.

In the lower town, the main sight is the **Catedral**, built mainly in the fourteenth and fifteenth centuries. It is a typical example of the decorative use of brick in the Gothic-Mudéjar style, with a dome built to the same design as that of the old cathedral in Zaragoza. Unfortunately, the interior, with its Mudéjar cloisters, has been closed for restoration for the last couple of decades.

If you are around for the **fiesta** on August 27, watch out for "El Cipotegato", a luckless character dressed in jester-like red, green and yellow stripy pyjamas who runs through the streets while everyone pelts him with tomatoes. He kicks off the town's annual week-long festivities, during which there are street parties, live music events and bullfights.

Practicalities

The **turismo** is on Plaza de San Francisco, the main square below the cathedral (Mon–Fri 9am–1.30pm & 4.30–7pm, Sat & Sun 10am–1.30pm & 4.30–7pm; ☎976 640 074, Ⓦwww.tarazona.org). If they are closed, take a look at the **town plan** outside the office, showing the principal sights.

There are three **accommodation** choices in the centre of town: *Hostal Palacete de los Arcedianos*, Plaza Arcedianos 1 (☎976 642 303; ❷), near the *ayuntamiento*, and the homely *Meson O'Cubillar*, at Plaza de Nuestra Señora (☎976 641 192; ❷). Both offer decent en-suite rooms, although the charming, stylish and pricey *Hostal Santa Agueda*, c/ Visconti 26 (☎976 640 054, Ⓦwww.santaagueda.com; ❹), just off the Plaza San Francisco, is easily the most attractive option. *Hotel Brujas de Becquer*, Ctra de Zaragoza (☎976 640 404, Ⓦwww.lanzadera.com/hotelbrujas; ❸), just out of town on the Zaragoza road, is large, modern and convenient for drivers who wish to avoid the tangle of narrow lanes in the old town.

The *Galeón*, in the lower town at Avda. La Paz 1, is a mid-priced **restaurant**, with good traditional food, while the restaurant below, the *Meson O'Cubillar*, has a good *menú* for €7.20.

Veruela

El Monasterio de Veruela (Tues–Sun: April–Sept 10am–2pm & 4–7pm; Oct–March 10am–1pm & 3–6pm; €1.80), isolated in a fold of the hills and standing within a massively fortified perimeter, is one of Spain's greatest religious houses. Fifteen kilometres to the southeast of Tarazona, it makes an easy excursion or a break in the journey to Zaragoza: if you are travelling by bus, you need to get off at **Vera de Moncayo** and then walk uphill for 3km. The monastery is uninhabited now, but the great church, built in the severe twelfth-century transitional style of the Carthusians, is kept open. The monastery admission ticket also gives access to the fourteenth-century cloisters and convent buildings, as well as a small and not terribly interesting **Museo del Vino** that sits rather uneasily in the monastic grounds.

Calatayud, Piedra and Daroca

Like Tarazona, **Calatayud** is a town of Moorish foundation, with some stunning Mudéjar towers, and again it offers access to a Cistercian monastery, **Piedra**, set in lush parkland. The town itself, however, is an uninviting, impoverished place, where you wouldn't choose to be stranded, especially with the delightful old town of **Daroca** so close, on the train line and main road southeast to Teruel.

Calatayud

If you are passing, it's worth climbing up to the old upper town of **CALATAYUD**, where amid a maze of alleys are the churches of **San Andrés** and **Santa María**, both of which have ornate Mudéjar towers, reminiscent of Moroccan minarets. Santa María, the collegiate church, also has a beautifully decorative Plateresque doorway, while **San Juan**, towards the river, has frescoes attributed to the young Goya.

Ruins of the Moorish **castle** survive, too, on high ground at the opposite end of town from the train station. The views from here are outstanding, though for a closer view of the towers you'd do best to climb the hill to the hermitage in the centre of the old town.

If you have to **stay** in Calatayud, there are a couple of *fondas* immediately across the square from the train station, the most salubrious being *Fonda Los Ángeles* (☎976 881 133; ❶). In the centre the best budget option is the *Fonda El Comercio* on c/Dato 33 (☎976 881 115; ❶), although you would be considerably more comfortable at *Mesón de los Dolores* at Plaza Mesones 4 (☎976 889 055, ⓦwww.mesonladolores.com; ❸), which occupies a beautiful old *palacio* and has a good restaurant. Check out the website ⓦwww.calatayud.org for more **information** on the town.

El Monasterio de Piedra

El Monasterio de Piedra – "The Stone Monastery" – lies 20km south of Calatayud, 4km from the village of **NUÉVALOS**. The monastic buildings, once part of a grand Cistercian complex, are a ruin, but they stand amid park-like gardens (daily: summer 9am–8pm; winter 9am–6pm; €9), which seem all the more verdant in this otherwise harsh, dry landscape.

The whopping entrance fee includes a guided tour of the monastery's cloisters, church, wine cellar, refectory and kitchens. Red arrows mark out a **route** through the park and take you past a series of romantically labelled waterfalls, grottoes and lakes. If there are crowds, it will be easy enough to escape them, though be warned that you're not allowed to take food into the park.

There are two **places to stay** up here; the luxurious *Hotel Monasterio de Piedra*, near the park entrance (☎976 849 011, ⓦwww.monasteriopiedra.com; ❻), and, a little further down the road, the well-equipped and reasonably priced *Hotel Las Truchas* (☎976 849 040, ⓕ976 849 137, ⓦwww.hotellastruchas.com; ❸), with its own pool, tennis courts and gym. Down in the village, the *Hotel Río Piedra*, at the foot of the road up to the monastery (☎976 849 007, ⓕ976 849 087; ❷), has a range of rooms, some with bath. Alternatively, there is a very well-equipped **campsite**, *Lago Park Camping* (☎976 849 038; April–Sept), 1km from Nuévalos (in the other direction from the monastery) on a promontory by a reservoir. There are good fishing opportunities here, too, if you're an enthusiast, but you would need a licence from the police station in Calatayud.

Just one **bus** daily runs from Zaragoza (from c/Almagro 18) to Nuévalos, leaving at 9am and returning at 5pm; note that from October to June, the bus only runs on Tuesdays and Thursdays and at weekends. If you have your own transport, the **roads south** to Cuenca or Albarracín (see p.680) are enjoyable routes.

Daroca

DAROCA, 38km southeast of Calatayud, is a lovely old place, set within an impressive run of **walls** that comprise no fewer than 114 towers and enclose an area far greater than that needed by the present population of 2200. The last major restoration of the walls was in the fifteenth century, but today, though largely in ruins, they are still magnificent.

You enter the town through its original gates, the **Puerta Alta** or stout **Puerta Baja**, the latter endowed with a gallery of arches and decorated with the coat of arms of Carlos I. Within, the Calle Mayor runs between the two gates, past ancient streets dotted with Romanesque, Gothic and Mudéjar churches. The principal church, the **Colegiata de Santa María**, is sixteenth-century Renaissance and has a small museum of religious artefacts including robes, silverwork, *retablos* and paintings. But the appeal of Daroca lies more in the whole ensemble rather than any specific monuments. The small **turismo** in front of the Colegiata (Mon 10am–2pm, Tues–Sun 10am–2pm & 4–7.30pm, ☎976 800 129) has pamphlets describing a walking tour in a number of languages.

There are two choices of **accommodation** in the old town. *Pensión El Ruejo*, c/Mayor 88, near the Puente Baja (℡976 800 962; ❶), has serviceable rooms with some en suite, but by far the nicest place to stay is *La Posada del Almudí*, c/Grajera 5, just off the Plaza Santiago (℡976 800 606, Ⓦwww.staragon .com/posadadelalmudi; ❸), which has 13 gorgeously furnished rooms in an artfully restored mansion house, plus a bar and restaurant which, with its excellent-value *menú* (€8.40), is also the best place **to eat**. There are two further accommodation options close together on the outskirts of town on the Carretera Sagunto-Burgos, near the Puerta Alta: the rather basic *Hostal-Residencia Agiria* (℡967 800 731; ❶), and the friendly *Hostal Legido* (℡976 800 190, Ⓕ976 802 048; ❷), which has a lively tapas bar patronized by locals. Daroca is connected to Calatayud, Teruel and Cariñena/Zaragoza by a couple of daily **bus** services; buses pull in on the c/Mayor close to the Puerta Baja.

Teruel

The little provincial capital of **TERUEL** is basically a market town, catering for its remote and sparsely populated rural hinterlands. It is hard to overestimate how much of a backwater this corner of Aragón is: a survey not so long ago found that it was the only part of Spain where deaths outnumbered births. The land is very harsh, and very high, with the coldest winters in the country. If you like back-of-beyond villages, with medieval sights that haven't been prettified, it is a region that merits a fair bit of exploring.

Arrival and information

Teruel doesn't feel quite like a city, despite its capital status, and the separation of the old town from the new reinforces this by making it feel small and provincial. Nonetheless, it has most facilities you might need, **trains** from Zaragoza and Valencia, and **buses** from most destinations in the province. The train and bus stations are both close to the city centre: from the former, cross the ring road and walk north up c/Nueva, and from the latter walk north a short way up the ring road, taking the first left to Plaza Judería. There are no fewer than thirteen bus companies in Teruel, many serving the same destinations, so check the timetables in the windows before buying a ticket on departure, as some buses are considerably slower than others.

The city's focal point is Plaza del Torico (shown as Plaza Carlos Castel on some maps); just east of here, at c/Tomás Nogués 1, is the **turismo** (July–Sept Mon–Sat 9am–2pm & 5–8pm, Sun 10am–2pm & 5–8pm; Oct–June same hours but closes at 7.30pm, ℡ & Ⓕ978 602 279, Ⓦwww.teruel.org or Ⓦwww .teruel.net). To connect to the **Internet**, head to *Mister Phone*, c/San Andrés 19 (Mon–Sat noon–2pm & 5.30–10.30pm, Sun 5.30–10.30pm; €2 per hour).

Accommodation

Accommodation is rarely a problem, though be warned that if you're here for the raucous **Fiesta Vaquilla del Ángel** (at the beginning of July) every place in town will be booked solid, and you may have to join other exhausted revellers sleeping in the park down by the train station.

Hostal Alcazaba c/Joaquin Costa 34 ℡978 617 813. Immaculate rooms, with a restaurant below, on a pedestrian street lined with grocery stores

and tapas bars. ❷
Hostal Aragón c/Santa María 4 ℡978 611 877. Small but comfortable rooms, with some triples and

quadruples available, close to the cathedral.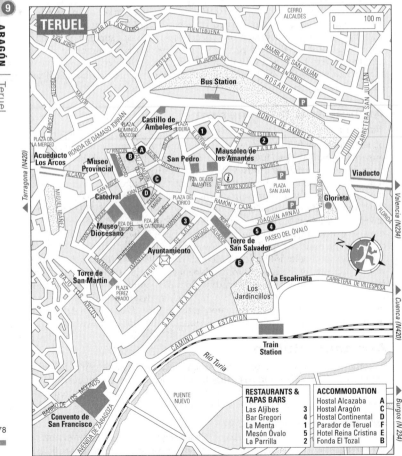

Hostal Continental c/Juan Pérez 9 ☎978 602
317. If *Hostal Aragón* is full, this is just around the
corner, with similar rooms. ●

Parador de Teruel 2km out on the Zaragoza road
☎978 601 800, ✉teruel@parador.es. This modern building, in an inspired position on a wooded
hillside overlooking the town and towers, has a
swimming pool and tennis courts but not much in

the way of character. ●

Hotel Reina Cristina Paseo del Óvalo 1 ☎978
606 860, ⓕ978 605 363. Attractive, traditional
hotel with an excellent restaurant, located by the
Torre del Salvador. ●

Fonda El Tozal c/Rincón 5 ☎978 601 022. A
characterful *hostal* in an ancient building, but be
warned that it can get extremely chilly in winter. ●

The Town

Teruel is a likeable and impressively monumental place, with some of the finest
Mudéjar work to be found. Like Zaragoza, it was an important Moorish city
and retained significant Muslim and Jewish communities after its Reconquest

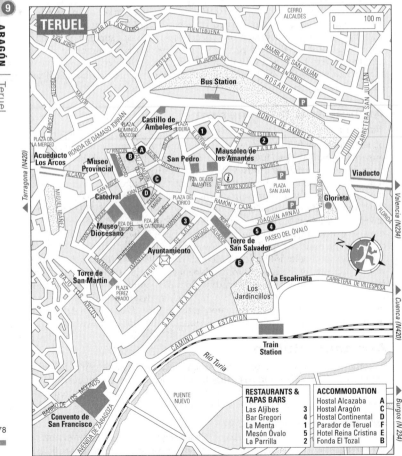

by Alfonso II in 1171. Approaching the town, the Mudéjar towers, built by Moorish craftsmen over the next three centuries, are immediately apparent. These – and the fabulous Mudéjar ceiling in the cathedral – should not be missed. The old town, or **casco histórico**, on a hill above the Río Turia, has a confusing layout, enclosed by the odd patch of wall, and with a viaduct linking it to the modern quarter to the south. Leading off to the north is a sixteenth-century aqueduct, **Los Arcos**, a slender and elegant piece of monumental engineering.

If you arrive by train, you will see straight ahead of you **La Escalinata**, a flight of steps decorated with bricks, tiles and turrets that is pure civic Mudéjar in style. From the top of the steps c/El Salvador leads to the **Torre de San Salvador** (daily 11am–2pm & 5–8pm; €1.50), the finest of the town's four Mudéjar towers, and the only one you can go up. It's covered with intricately patterned and proportioned coloured tiles, to stunning effect, echoed closely in its more modest sister tower, **San Martín**, best reached via c/de los Amantes. A common feature of all the towers is that they stand separate from the main body of the church, a design most probably influenced by the freestanding minarets of the Muslim world.

The **Catedral** (daily 11am–2pm & 4–8pm; €1.80), built in the twelfth century, but gracefully adapted over subsequent years, boasts another fine Mudéjar tower, incorporating Romanesque windows, and a lantern that combines Renaissance and Mudéjar features. The interior follows a more standard Gothic-Mudéjar pattern and at first sight seems unremarkable, save for its brilliant Renaissance *retablo*. Climb the stairs by the door, however, and put money in the illuminations box, and the fabulous **artesonado ceiling** is revealed. This was completed between 1260 and 1314 by Moorish craftsmen, in a gorgeous and fascinating mix of geometric Islamic motifs and medieval painting of courtly life.

Standing next to the cathedral, the sixteenth-century Palacio Episcopal houses the **Museo Diocesano** (Mon–Sat 10am–2pm & 4–8pm; €1.20). Inside, look out for *Calvario*, a beautiful woodcarving of Jesus (whose arms are missing), St John and the Virgin Mary, carved in the fifteenth century but for many years hidden behind a wall in a church in Sarrón, where it was discovered in 1946. Another highlight is the *Arbol de la Vida*, a striking seventeenth-century ivory carving of Christ.

A couple of blocks from the museum is Plaza del Torico (aka Plaza Carlos Castell), the centre of the old quarter, which is flanked by a trio of *modernista* houses. Just beyond here, in another attractive square, is the church of **San Pedro**, once again endowed with a Mudéjar tower. Its fame, however, relates to the adjacent **Mausoleo de los Amantes** (daily 10am–2pm & 5–7.30pm; €0.60), a chapel containing the alabaster tomb of the *Lovers of Teruel*, Isabel de Segura and Juan Diego Martínez de Marcilla. This pair's thirteenth-century tale of thwarted love is a legend throughout Spain. The story goes that Diego, ordered by his lover's family to go away and prove himself worthy, left Teruel for five years, returning only to find that Isabel was to be married that same day. He asked for a last kiss, was refused, and expired, heartbroken; Isabel, not to be outdone, arranged his funeral at San Pedro, kissed the corpse, and died in its arms. The lovers' (reputed) bodies were exhumed in 1955 and now lie illuminated for all to see; it is a macabre and popular pilgrimage for newly-weds.

Lastly, if you intend heading out to the Teruel countryside, a visit to the **Museo Provincial** (Tues–Fri 10am–2pm & 4–7pm, Sat & Sun 10am–2pm; free), close by the cathedral, could be worthwhile. Its range of exhibits includes objects of local folklore and traditional rural life.

El Rincón de Ademuz, due south of Teruel, is a strange little region: a Valencian province enclosed within Aragonese territory. It is a very remote corner of Spain, with a bleak kind of grandeur, and scarcely a tourist from one year to the next.

The place to head for – and if you are bussing it, the only realistic place to get to from Teruel – is **ADEMUZ** itself, without doubt Spain's tiniest and least significant provincial capital. Strung along a craggy hill at the confluence of two long rivers, this could make a beautiful base for walking, and there's a fascination just in wandering the streets with their dark stone cottages and occasional Baroque towers. If you want to stay, there's a single, smart *hostal*, Casa Domingo (☏978 782 030, ℻978 782 056; ❷), which also serves a €9.60 *menú*.

For energetic trekking, Torre Baja lies to the north along the Río Turia, and beyond it the beautiful village of Castielfabib. The most interesting of these little Ademuz hamlets, Puebla de San Miguel, lies to the east, in the Sierra Tortajada, most easily accessible by road from Valencia, but also from a small route just out of Ademuz in the Teruel direction, east over the Río Turia bridge and signposted to Sabina, Sesga and Mas del Olmo.

Eating and drinking

The main area for **food and drink** in Teruel is at the eastern side of the old quarter, principally Plaza Judería, c/Bartolomé Esteban, c/Abadía and c/San Esteban (the first street into the old town from the bus station). The area east of the Mausoleo de los Amantes has a few **bars**, but don't expect much. One laid-back place is *Lennon*, c/San Andres 23, which has occasional live music.

Las Aljibes c/Yagüe de Salas 3. Smart, buzzy restaurant specializing in regional cuisine with a wonderful salad selection, well-stocked tapas counter and an extensive wine list featuring local vintages. Closed Sun in Aug & Sept plus the last 2 weeks of July.

Bar Gregori Paseo Ovalo 6. This friendly tapas bar is the locals' choice, complete with pigs' ears on the menu. Outside tables, good wine, and sangria for €5.75 a litre all make it a pleasant place to pass the evening. The *Gregori Plus* next door is a little more upmarket and just as popular. Open daily.

La Menta c/Bartolomé Esteban 10 – behind the Mausoleo de los Amantes. The city's top restaurant – pricey, with dishes for €10 and up, but a good choice for a splurge in southern Aragón. Closed Mon, Sun & middle two weeks of Jan & July.

Mesón Óvalo Paseo del Óvalo 2. Very popular *mesón* with quality cooking (the trout dishes are excellent) and a pretty good-value €12 *menú*. Closed Mon & Jan.

La Parrilla c/San Esteban 2. Good-value grill restaurant, with traditional interior, where the meat is flame-grilled on a wood fire. Closed Sun eve.

Albarracín

ALBARRACÍN, 37km west of Teruel, is one of the more accessible targets in rural southern Aragón – and one of the most picturesque towns in the province, poised above the Río Guadalaviar and retaining, virtually intact, its medieval streets and tall, balconied houses. There's a historical curiosity here, too, in that from 1165 to 1333 the town formed the centre of a small independent state, the kingdom of the Azagras.

Over the last few years a small trickle of tourism has begun, and some of the houses have been prettified a bit too much. But Albarracín's dark, enclosed lanes and those buildings that remain unrestored, with their splendid coats of arms, still make for an intriguing wander – reminders of lost and now inexplicably prosperous eras. Approaching from Teruel, you may imagine that you're about to come upon a large town, for the **medieval walls** swoop back over the hillside – protecting, with the loop of the river, a far greater area than the extent of the town, past or present.

The town follows the line of a ridge, above the river, and breaks into two main parts. On the Teruel side, you enter through a gate known as El Túnel, and shortly reach the **Plaza Mayor** and **ayuntamiento**. Follow the c/de Santiago, up towards the walls, and you reach Santiago church and a gateway, the Portal del Molina. If instead you take c/de la Catedral, a quiet rural lane, you reach a small square (cars can access this from the other side) with the **Catedral** – a medieval building remodelled in the sixteenth and eighteenth centuries – and the Palacio Episcopal.

Practicalities

If you want to stay – and you'll have to if you arrive on the daily bus from Teruel – there is a cluster of **hostales and hotels** at the foot of the hill, where the buses stop, which are all pleasant and housed in converted mansions. Choices include the basic but clean *Hotel El Gallo* (☎978 710 032; ➋), the *Hostal Olimpia* (☎978 710 083; ➋), which has attractive en-suite rooms, and the good-value *Hostal los Palacios* (☎978 700 327, ⓕ978 700 358; ➊), whose terrace bar affords lovely views. There's also a good **youth hostel**, the *Albergue Juventud Rosa Bríos* (☎976 714 797; ➊), in a lovely medieval mansion just past the cathedral at c/Santa María 5, but it's only open when there's sufficient business, so call in advance (9am–2pm) to make a reservation. The local **fiesta** takes place from September 8 to 17.

Moving on from Albarracín, if you have transport, there's a fabulous route west to Cuenca through beautiful country, by way of **Frías de Albarracín** and the **source of the Río Tajo** (see p.207).

Sierra de Gúdar and El Maestrazgo

The mountains of the **Sierra de Gúdar** and **El Maestrazgo**, to the east and northeast of Teruel, are an area of great variety and striking, often wild, beauty, with their severe peaks, deep gorges and lush meadows. One hundred years ago, this now impoverished region had four times the number of inhabitants that it does today. Defeated in their attempts to make a living from agriculture, many left to seek their fortunes in the cities, leaving behind the crumbling remains of once grand, honey-hued farmhouses that dot the landscape and stone-walled terraces etched into the steep-sided hills.

Tourism isn't a presence here, though you will find at least one simple *fonda* in most of the tiny, scattered villages. The places below are just a small selection and are geared to the more accessible; armed with a decent map, your own transport, or the will to do some walking, the choice is very much your own.

Inevitably, **buses** are infrequent (often their main purpose is to deliver the mail) but most villages are connected with each other, and/or Teruel, once a day; an alarm clock is useful since they have a nasty habit of leaving before dawn. A daily bus leaves Teruel at 2.30pm for Mora de Rubielos and Rubielos de Mora – from here local buses connect to Linares de Mora and Mosqueruela, both of which can also be reached directly from Teruel. The main approaches to El Maestrazgo are also from Teruel (daily bus to Cantavieja and Villafranca del Cid), or from Morellá in the province of Castellón (see "Valencia" chapter on p.936).

For more **information** on the Maestrazgo check out ⓦwww.elmaestrazgo.com.

Sierra de Gúdar

A landscape of sharp, rocky crags, the **Sierra de Gúdar** is easy to access by following the N234 southeast from Teruel and then heading northeast into the mountains along the A232. This will bring you to the lovely medieval village of **Mora de Rubielos**, 42km from Teruel, and then onto its even more stunning twin, **Rubielos de Mora**. Heading north from here brings you to **Linares de Mora**, turn-off point for the Valdelinares ski resort, and Mosqueruela, another charming and remote mountain village.

Mora de Rubielos and Rubielos de Mora

These confusingly-named villages, with their fine collections of medieval houses whose small, wrought-iron balconies are often bedecked with flowers, are a good introduction to the region. For such a small place, **Mora de Rubielos** has an extremely grand **castle** (July to mid-Sept 10.30am–1.30pm & 4.30–8.30pm daily; mid-Sept to June 10.30am–1.30pm & 4.30–6.30pm Sat & Sun; €1.30), built in a luminous pinky gold stone which, during the Middle Ages, served as both defensive fort and noble residence, and was the heart of the town's life. Inside, several fairly nondescript rooms squeezed between the castle's outer and inner walls are set around a courtyard of pointed arches. One room hosts a small *Museo Etnográfico* – a motley collection of rustic antiquities. It's worth having a peek inside the bulky, Gothic **church** below the castle if it's open.

There's a small **turismo** on c/Diputación next to Plaza de la Villa (July–Aug 11am–1pm & 5–7pm daily; Sept–June same hours, Sat & Sun only; ☎978 806 132). There's no budget **accommodation**, but the attractive and recently restored *Hotel Jaime I*, in an old mansion on Plaza de la Villa near the *ayuntamiento* (☎978 800 092, ℱ978 800 067; ❹), is a good place to stay and has a decent restaurant.

Rubielos de Mora is a gem of a village and a great place to while away a couple of hours wandering round the narrow streets, admiring the handsome *palacios* with their finely-carved wooden eaves and soaking up the mellow atmosphere. The **church**, Colegiata de Santa María, on the Plaza de Marques de Tosos, has an ostentatious tiered bell tower. If you want to see inside, ask at the **turismo** in the *ayuntamiento* on Plaza de Hispano América (July–Sept 10am–2pm & 5–8pm daily; Oct–June irregular opening hours; ☎978 804 001, ℮rubimora@teleline.es). The only **hotel**, *Los Leones* (☎978 804 477, ℮hotelleones@gudar.com; ❹), on Plaza Igual y Gil, a beautifully restored seventeenth-century palace complete with antique bedsteads, beamed ceilings and heavy wooden doors, also has a good **restaurant**.

Northeastern Sierra

As the A1701 climbs north from Rubielos de Mora to **Linares de Mora**, the vegetation becomes scrubbier and the views more dramatic. A couple of kilometres before the village, a superbly positioned *mirador* affords hair-raising views down an almost vertical slope to the village below. Linares, the turn-off point for the ski resort of Valdelinares, is a beguiling place, with houses piled higgledy-piggledy up the mountainside and glorious views. Its ruined castle is situated, rather precariously, on a jutting rock above the village, while another promontory hosts a church.

There are two good options for **accommodation**: *El Portalico* (☎978 802 110; ❷), in an old mansion house, has attractive en-suite rooms with TV, while the good-value *La Venta* (☎978 802 018; ❶), by the church, also has a restaurant.

Continuing northeast along the A1701, you'll come to **Mosqueruela**. With its ramshackle streets and back-of-beyond charm, this sleepy village feels as if it hasn't changed much since its foundation in 1262, and it's not uncommon to see flocks of sheep being herded through the centre. The village boasts an attractive, porticoed Plaza Mayor and a couple of pretty churches, but there's not much more to detain you. If you want to stay, there's a good modern **hotel**, the *Montenieve* (T & F 978 805 123; ❷), with comfortable if rather plain rooms, a five-minute walk from the Plaza Mayor.

Southern Maestrazgo

Approaching the Maestrazgo from Teruel, on the newly-constructed A226, you pass nearby **Cedrillas** with its conspicuous, ridge-top castle ruin. From here the road starts climbing into the hills, scaling high mountain passes and affording spectacular sweeping views of the valleys. The first village of any size is **Cantavieja**.

If you're approaching the area from the Sierra de Gúdar, you can continue along the A1701 to La Iglesuela del Cid or take the small road directly north from Mosqueruela to Cantavieja.

Cantavieja and El Cid country

CANTAVIEJA, dramatically situated by the edge of an escarpment, at an altitude of 1300m, is a little livelier and larger than most Maestrazgo villages, though its population is still under a thousand. The beautiful, porticoed **Plaza Mayor** here is typical of the region, and the escutcheoned *ayuntamiento* bears a Latin inscription with suitably lofty sentiments: "This House hates wrongdoing, loves peace, punishes crimes, upholds the laws and honours the upright." It is a useful base for exploring – or walking in – the region, with a **turismo** (mid-July to mid-Oct daily 10am–1.30pm & 4–7pm; rest of the year weekends only; T 964 185 243), an exceptionally good-value **hotel**, the *Balfagón Alto Maestrazgo* (T 964 185 076, W www.maestrazgo.org/balfagon.htm; ❸) near the municipal swimming pool, and a reasonable *fonda*, the *Julián* (T 964 185 005; ❶). There's also an unexpectedly stylish and pricey **restaurant**, *Buj* (lunchtimes only; closed Feb), run by a woman and her two daughters and specializing in refined Aragonese cuisine. The food at the *Balfagón* is also good, and there is a €10.50 *menú*. The area is famous for its truffles which, unusually, are rooted out by dogs rather than pigs.

MIRAMBEL, 15km northeast of Cantavieja and walkable in about four hours, has a population of a mere 145 and preserves a very ancient atmosphere, with its walls, gateways and stone houses. The village was temporarily thrown into a whirl of excitement when Ken Loach and his team filmed *Land and Freedom* here some years ago, but these days it's back to its usual, sleepy self. There are a couple of *casas rurales* offering **rooms**; the one at c/Eras 12 (T 964 178 211; ❶), next door to the main **bar**, *Tasca las Tejas*, is simple but homely with rustic wooden furniture. There is also an excellent little *fonda*, the *Guimera* (T & F 964 178 269; ❶), on the main street, c/Agustín Pastor, with en-suite rooms at bargain rates and a good-quality, popular **restaurant** with a cheap and delicious *menú*.

A similar distance to the southeast of Cantavieja, and another fine walk along a rough country road, is **LA IGLESUELA DEL CID**. The village's name bears witness to the exploits of El Cid Campeador, who came charging through the Maestrazgo in his fight against the infidel. Its ochre-red, dry-stone walls, ubiquitous coats of arms and stream flowing right through the centre are striking enough in this remote countryside, though these features aside, it's a shabby sort of place. The central, compact Plaza de la Iglesia is enclosed by the old *ayuntamiento*, an attractive church and a restored eighteenth-century *palacio*, now home to a stunning luxury **hotel**, *Hospedería La Iglesuela del Cid* (☎964 443 476, ✉hospederiaiglesuela@husa.es; ❻), which has an expensive restaurant. There is also a characterful **fonda**, *Casa Amada* (☎ & ℱ964 443 373; ❷), at c/Fuente Nueva 10, which offers good, substantial country cooking.

Continuing east for 10km brings you to **VILLAFRANCA DEL CID**, often referred to by its Valencian name Vilafranca, across the border in Castellón Province – and at the end of the bus route from either Teruel or Morella. Straddling the hillside, this is a lively, attractive village, and with a population of 2600 it's larger than most places around here. The only **place to stay** in the centre is the *Hostal Prismark*, c/Sagrado Corazón de Jesús (☎964 441 110; ❷), which has good-value en-suite rooms, although *Hotel Los Arcos* (☎964 441 442; ❷), 2km out of town towards Castellón, is more comfortable. Alternatively, there's a well-equipped campsite (☎964 441 409, mid-June to mid-Oct) 1.5km outside town on the Paseo de Losar. If you decide to return to Teruel from here, the **bus** departs at 5.55am (Mon–Fri only), passing through La Iglesuela del Cid at 6.10am, or there's a bus to Castellón (Mon–Sat) which leaves at 6am.

Northwest from Cantavieja

Another dramatic, almost Alpine, route is in store if you head northwest from Cantavieja, past Cañada de Benatanduz, to **VILLARLUENGO**, a beautiful village of ancient houses stacked on a terraced hillside. Just beyond here, you cross a pass, and the Río Pitarque, with a side valley leading to a hamlet of the same name. Here, by the riverside, in isolated and magnificent countryside, is the stylish *Hostal de la Trucha* (☎978 773 008, ℱ978 773 100; ❹), with a **restaurant** which serves trout caught a few yards away. Back in Villarluengo, the friendly *Fonda Villarluengo*, on Plaza Carlos Castell (☎978 773 014; ❶), with centrally heated, en-suite double rooms above a bar and *comedor*, and *Pensión Josefina*, on c/La Fuente (☎978 773 151; ❶), with three en-suite rooms painted in restful pastels, are rather more affordable.

Over another higher pass, the Puerto de Majalinos (1450m), the road drops down to the small village of Ejulve, and just a few more kilometres north you reach the N420 between Montalbán and Alcañiz. The **bus** runs this way once a day from Cantavieja (Mon–Fri only), taking three hours to cover the ninety-kilometre journey to **Alcorisa** on the N420.

Northern Maestrazgo: Alcañiz and Valderrobres

The northern limits of the Maestrazgo edge into Tarragona Province in Catalunya, and can be approached from Tarragona/Gandesa, or from Zaragoza through **Alcañiz**, situated at the end of the N420 east of Alcorisa. Alacañiz itself does not have great appeal or outstanding sights but it's a useful hub for local transport and gives access to the lovely town of **Valderrobres** with its superb **castle** and elegant Gothic **church**.

Alcañiz

The castle-topped town of **ALCAÑIZ** is an impressive sight from a distance, though close up it's a bit of a disappointment. The **Castillo** has been unsympathetically modernized as the *Parador de Alcañiz* (☎978 830 400, ✉alcañiz@parador.es; ❻), and the best thing about the place is the panorama from its heights. These allow a grand bird's-eye view of the huge Baroque church of **Santa María** which dominates the town below.

The town (and this is a big place in comparison to the Maestrazgo villages, with a population of around 12,500) gives access by bus to Valderrobres (see below), Zaragoza to the east and west to the coast at Tortosa or Viñaros via Morella. You probably won't need or want **to stay** but – in addition to the *parador* – there are several cheapish options; try the comfortable *Guadalope* (☎978 830 750, ℻978 833 233; ❷), on Plaza España near the *castillo*, or, for those on a tight budget, the basic *Hostal Alcañiz* on Plaza Santo Domingo (☎978 870 155; ❶).

Valderrobres

VALDERROBRES is one of the Maestrazgo's most accessible and attractive towns. It stands 36km from Alcañiz, near the border with Catalunya and astride the Río Matarrana, whose crystal waters, flanked by lush valleys, teem with trout. The old quarter is crowned by a **castle-palace** (July–Sept Tues–Sun 11am–1pm & 5–8pm; Oct–June Sat & Sun 11am–1pm & 4–6pm; €0.90), once occupied by the kings of Aragón, and a Gothic parish church – **Santa María** – which has a fine rose window. In the Plaza Mayor, the unassuming seventeenth-century **ayuntamiento** was considered so characteristic of the region that it was reproduced in Barcelona's *Poble Espanyol* (see p.751) in 1929.

There are a number of good **places to stay**, including the central *Posada La Plaza* (☎978 850 106, ⓦwww.posadalaplaza.com; ❷), opposite the *ayuntamiento*, which has attractive, en-suite rooms. The cheapest option is *Fonda Albesa*, Avda. Hispanidad 46 (☎978 850 063; ❶), in the new town close to the more upmarket *Hostal Querol* (☎978 850 192, ⓦwww.sermat.net/hquerol; ❷), at Avda. Hispanidad 14, which has an excellent *comedor*. If all else fails, the **turismo**, at Avda. Cortes de Aragón 7, near the iron bridge (July & Aug Mon–Tues 10am–2pm & 5–7pm, Wed–Sun 10am–2pm & 5–9pm; Sept–June Mon–Sat 10am–2pm & 5–7pm, Sun 10am–2pm; ☎978 890 886, ⓦwww.matarranya.org), can supply you with a list of alternatives.

The Aragonese Pyrenees

Aragón has the highest and best stretch of the **Pyrenees** on the Spanish side: a fabulous region offering everything from casual day-walks in the high valleys to long-distance treks across the mountains. There are numerous trails, marked by the Aragón mountain club as either **GR** (*grande recorrido* – long-haul, red-and-white blazes) or **PR** (*pequeño recorrido* – short-haul, blue-and-white or yellow-and-white) trails.

The most popular jumping-off point for the mountains is **Jaca**, an attractive town in its own right, with an important cathedral. From here, most walkers head northeast to the spectacular alpine landscape of **Parque Nacional de Ordesa**, with its canyons and waterfall valleys. Northwest of Jaca, the valleys of **Ansó** and **Echo** offer less rigorous hiking, while southeast of the park, **Aínsa**, with its picturesque old town, makes another pleasant gateway to the moun-

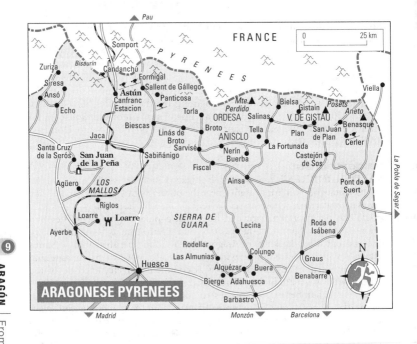

tains. Still further east, **Benasque** offers access to the two loftiest Pyrenean peaks, Aneto (3404m) and Posets (3371m), as well as to the bluff-top cathedral-village of **Roda de Isábena**. In winter there's affordable **skiing** at the well-equipped resorts of Candanchú, Astún, Formigal, Panticosa and Cerler.

There are a variety of possible **routes into the region**. For Jaca and Ordesa, the most obvious way is via **Huesca**, the provincial capital, which is no great shakes in itself but convenient for visiting the great castle of **Loarre**, **Los Mallos** sugarloaf mountains or the increasingly popular sub-range of the **Sierra de Guara**, with its labyrinthine gorges. If you're coming from Catalunya (and aiming for Benasque or Aínsa), you could follow a route via **Fraga** and **Barbastro**.

You can **travel by rail** through Huesca, Jaca and up to the Spanish border at Canfranc – though there, sadly, the trains stop. Rail-buses, however, continue **into France** through the **Somport tunnel**, while drivers can also cross over the **Puerto del Portalet** to the east or, east of Ordesa, go through the **Bielsa tunnel**. All of these are open year-round, except during periods of exceptionally heavy snow.

From the east: Fraga, Monzón and Barbastro

If you're coming to the Pyrenees from Catalunya, you're likely to approach via Lleida, especially by public transport. If you have your own transport, you could follow the little-used minor route along the Río Cinca valley from

Fraga, a pleasant medieval town. Most travellers will reach either Huesca or Benasque via **Monzón** and **Barbastro**; both have regular bus connections with Lleida (Lérida), though their appeal lies strictly in a handful of sights.

Fraga

It's worth spending a morning wandering around **FRAGA**, 25km from Lleida, and just off the *autopista* to Zaragoza. An array of fine brick buildings helps maintain the medieval air of the old town, perched high over the Río Cinca. If you've arrived by bus, cross back over the river from the bus station and strike uphill through the steep and convoluted streets of the old town. The originally twelfth-century (but much altered) tower of **San Pedro** keeps disappearing and reappearing until you reach a tiny square, dominated entirely by the **church**. If you want to stay, there are central **rooms** at *Hostal Flavia*, Paseo Barrón 13 (T974 471 540; ❷), and the more comfortable *Hostal Trébol*, Avda. de Aragón 9 (T974 471 533; ❷).

North of Fraga, a tiny road, unserved by public transport, follows the east bank of the Río Cinca to Monzón, starting out immediately below Fraga's old town. En route, great steppes fall away to the west beyond the river, while coarse vegetation and red clay cliffs flank the road. For those without their own vehicle, Fraga has **bus** connections with Lleida (4 daily) and Huesca (leaving Mon–Sat at 6.45am).

Monzón

MONZÓN, 50km from Fraga, stands in a triangle between the rivers Cinca and Sosa (the latter usually dry), a strategic position that explains its **Templar castle**, on the crumbling rock above. Originally a ninth-century Moorish fort, it was later endowed to the Templars by Ramón Berenguer IV and was the residence of Jaime I (king of Aragon 1213–76) in his youth. The ruins (winter Tues–Fri 11.30am–1pm & 3–5pm, Sat 5–7pm, Sun 10am–2pm; summer Tues–Fri 11am–1pm & 5–8pm, Sat 5–7pm, Sun 10am–2pm) include a tenth-century Moorish tower and a group of Romanesque buildings.

The substantial modern town below is among the grimmest in Aragón, and few will want to linger. The **bus station** is northwest of the castle, between the old and new towns. If you're stuck, most budget **accommodation** stands opposite the **train station**, though none is especially recommendable. A more comfortable option lies not much further southwest on the northerly ring road: two-star *Hotel Vianetto*, Avda. Lérida 25 (T974 401 900, Wwww.mlonzon.net/vianetto; ❸), with a secure garage and expensive restaurant. You'd do better just stopping in Monzón for a meal; good choices include *Jairo*, south of the Río Sosa at c/Santa Barbara 10 (closed Mon), and *Piscis*, close to the bus station at Plaza de Aragón 1; despite the fishy name, the latter's a good allrounder with a *menú* for under €12.

Barbastro

BARBASTRO, 20km from Monzón, straddling the Río Vero before it joins the Cinca, is a historic town of no small importance. The union of Aragón and Catalunya was declared here in 1137, sealed by the marriage of the daughter of Ramiro of Aragón to Ramón Berenguer IV, lord of Barcelona. Although it's now just a slightly shabby provincial market town, Barbastro retains an air of past dignity in its *casco viejo*, or old quarter. Topping a rise just south of the river, the Gothic **Catedral** (Mon–Sat 10am–1.30pm & 4–7.30pm, Sun 10am–noon;

€2), on a site once occupied by a mosque, has a high altar whose construction was under the authority of Damián Forment. When he died in 1540 only part of the alabaster relief had been completed, and the remainder was finished by his pupils. Just northeast of the cathedral on the Plaza de la Constitución, the facade of the restored fifteenth-century **ayuntamiento**, designed by the Moorish chief architect to Fernando el Católico, is also worth a look. Elsewhere, narrow, pedestrianized shopping streets are lined by faded-pastel houses piled up with their backs towards the river, while the central, tree-lined **Paseo del Coso** at the southwest edge of the old quarter is home to outdoor tables for many of the town's bars and cafés.

Nowadays, Babastro is best known for its **wine**, and the town lies at the centre of the Somontano *denominación de origen* vintage district, the most important in Aragón, and one of the most prominent in Spain. Visits can be organized to three of the biggest wineries – Bodega Pirineos, Viñas del Vero and Enate (details from the turismo, see below). Both Hemingway and Orwell tippled in Barbastro during the 1920s and 1930s; unfortunately, their favourite watering hole, the *Fonda San Ramón*, shut in 2000 (though the sign is still visible outside).

Practicalities

The **bus station** is at the southwest end of the *paseo*; there are regular departures from here for Huesca and Lleida (daily), and Benasque (Mon–Sat). The helpful English-speaking **turismo** (July & Aug daily 10am–2pm & 4.30–8pm; Sept–June Tues–Sat 10am–2pm & 4.30–8pm; ☎974 308 350, ⊛www.barbastro-ayto.es) is 200m uphill and south from the station, inside the restored Conjunto de San Julián y Santa Lucía.

Since the demise of the *Fonda San Ramón*, appealing budget accommodation is scarce; as basic as you'd want to be is the *Hostal Goya* (☎974 311 747; ➊), at c/Argensola 13, a slightly sleazy street just south of the river. More comfort is available at two establishments on c/Corona de Aragón, running parallel to the river at the northeast edge of the *casco viejo*: *Hostal Roxi* at no. 21 (☎974 311 064, ℻974 312 462; ➋), and the *Hotel Clemente* at no. 5 (☎974 310 186; ➌). Several decent **restaurants** have sprung up to take advantage of the wine trade. The most central is *Cenador de San Julián* (closed Sun pm & Mon), just beside the turismo in a round, brick-walled *comedor*, considered one of the town's best, though its €18 *menú* includes surprisingly average wine. Further afield in the new quarter, within walking distance of the centre via the Avenida Pirineos bridge, are two more possibilities: *Flor* at c/Goya 3 and *Cocina Vasca* adjacent at no. 5 – *menús* at both go for around €13.

Huesca and around

HUESCA is the least memorable of the three Aragonese provincial capitals, and if you're heading for the mountains you could bypass it altogether, staying on the train to Jaca or beyond. However, it does provide a base for exploring the striking **Los Mallos** pinnacles and the castle at **Loarre** to the northwest of the town, as well as the **Sierra de Guara** to the northeast.

Huesca

Dead centre of Husca's **Casco Viejo**, tucked into a loop of *paseos* and the Río Isuela, stands a late-Gothic **Catedral**, whose unusual facade combines the thirteenth-century portal of an earlier church with a brick Mudéjar gallery, and a

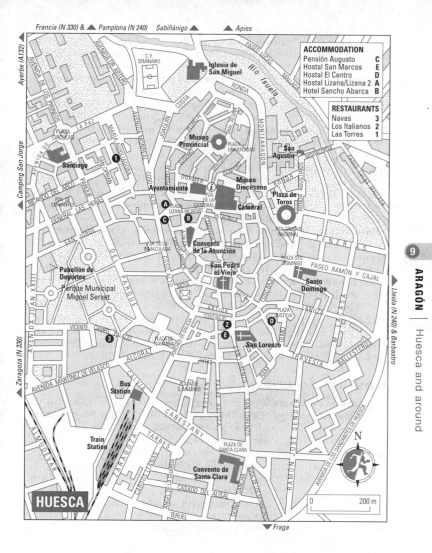

ACCOMMODATION

Pensión Augusto	C
Hostal San Marcos	E
Hostal El Centro	D
Hostal Lizana/Lizana 2	A
Hotel Sancho Abarca	B

RESTAURANTS

Navas	3
Los Italianos	2
Las Torres	1

C. F. SEMINARIO

Iglesia de San Miguel

Río Isuela

PASEO LUCAS MALLADA

RONDA

Averbe (A132)

Camping San Jorge

Zaragoza (N 330)

Lleida (N 240) & Barbastro

PLAZA CIRCULAR

Santiago

Museo Provincial

PLAZA UNIVERSIDAD

San Agustín

Ayuntamiento

Museo Diocesano

Plaza de Toros

PZA. DE LA CATEDRAL

Catedral

PLAZA LIZANA BILAFORT

PZA. DE LA INMACULADA

Convento de la Asunción

San Pedro el Viejo

PLAZA STO. DOMINGO

PASEO RAMÓN Y CAJAL

Santo Domingo

Pabellón de Deportes

Parque Municipal Miguel Servet

PLAZA JUSTICIA

San Lorenzo

PLAZA DE NAVARRAS

Bus Station

Train Station

PLAZA DE SANTA CLARA

Convento de Santa Clara

HUESCA

N

0   200 m

Fraga

ARAGÓN | Huesca and around

9

---

pinnacled uppermost section that's Isabelline in style. The great treasure inside
is the *retablo* by Damián Forment, a Renaissance masterpiece depicting the
Crucifixion and the Deposition. Next door, the **Museo Diocesano** (Mon–Sat
10am–1.30pm & 4–6pm, Sat 10am–1.30pm; €2) contains a rather mixed collection, gathered from churches in the surrounding countryside. These apart,
there's little to detain you. The liveliest time to visit is during Huesca's big **fiesta** in honour of San Lorenzo, held over the week of August 10.

Practicalities

Finding your way around Huesca shouldn't be a problem. The **train station** is
at the south end of c/Zaragoza, a main thoroughfare, and the **bus station** is

just in front. The **turismo** (daily 9am–2pm & 4–8pm; ☎974 292 100, ⓦwww.huescaturismo.com) is opposite the cathedral inside the Renaissance *ayuntamiento*, and stocks various pamphlets on the Aragonese mountains.

    Accommodation can be hard to find, and during summer, when trekkers are passing through, it is well worth booking ahead. At the budget end of things, there's the *Pensión Augusto*, c/Aínsa 16 (☎974 220 079; ❶), with tidy rooms above a bar; the *Hostal San Marcos*, c/San Orencio 10 (☎974 222 931; ❸), a good mid-range option with en-suite rooms; and *Hostal El Centro*, c/Sancho Ramírez 3 (☎974 226 823, ⓕ974 225 112; ❷), in a grand old building with large, well-renovated en-suite rooms, many with a balcony. More comfortable choices on the central Plaza Lizana, just downhill from the cathedral, include the *Hostal Lizana/Lizana 2* (☎974 220 776; ❷–❸), and the adjacent three-star *Hotel Sancho Abarca* at no. 13 (☎974 220 650, ⓕ974 225 169; ❺), where most rooms have balconies or air conditioning. The **campsite**, *San Jorge* (☎974 227 416), is at the end of c/Ricardo del Arco.

    Restaurants are plentiful enough, typically offering solid mountain fare, including lamb and freshwater fish specialities. *Restaurante Marisquería Navas*, at c/Vicente Campo Palacio 3 (late June & late Oct closed Sun pm & Mon), is considered Huesca's top restaurant by virtue of its delicious fish and game dishes and home-made desserts; the chef's full works will cost you around €32 plus wine, but there's also a €18 *menú*. Its only serious rival is *Restaurante Las Torres*, at c/María Auxiliadora 3 (closed Sun & Aug 20–Sept 3) – a fancy place offering *nouvelle* Aragonese cuisine (try the *menú gastronómico* at €40). For excellent **tapas bars** and **nightlife** head for the *zona* around c/San Lorenzo and c/Padre Huesca, between the Coso Bajo and the Plaza de Santa Clara, while for *horchata* and real *gelato*, there's *Los Italianos* at Coso Bajo 18.

Castillo de Loarre

The **Castillo de Loarre** (April–Sept 10.30am–1.30pm & 4–7pm; Oct–March 11am–2pm & 4–5.30pm; closed Mon except in Aug; free) is Aragón's most spectacular fortress – indeed, there are few that can rival it anywhere in Spain. As you approach, the castle seems to blend into the hillside, but up close assumes a breathtaking grandeur: compact but intricate, its south ramparts rooted in a sheer palisade, commanding the landscape for miles around.

    Its builder was Sancho Ramírez, king of Navarra (1000–35), who used it as a base for his resistance to the Moorish occupation. Inside the curtain walls is a delicately proportioned Romanesque church, with 84 individually carved capitals. Of the towers, the Torre de la Reina has ornate windows, while the taller Torre del Homenaje – climbable to the penultimate storey – is dominated by a massive hooded fireplace.

    The castle stands some 30km northwest of Huesca, and 4km beyond the village of **LOARRE**. By **public transport**, it's an awkward journey, as bus timetables in particular conspire against a day-trip. Loarre village has three buses daily from Huesca, all in the afternoon, but there's adequate **accommodation** in both Loarre and **AYERBE**, 5km southwest, with the nearest train station, if you decide to stay the night. Closest choice to the castle is the three-star *Hospedaria de Loarre*, a restored seventeenth-century mansion on the central plaza in Loarre (☎974 382 706, ⓕ974 382 713; ❸), with rather bland rooms and no air conditioning, though the **restaurant** is well respected (€15 *menú* or about €25 *a la carta*; closed Sun). Failing this, Loarre has one *casa rural*, and Ayerbe a further four, the most characterful being the *Antigua Posada del Pilar* at Plaza Aragón 38 (☎974 380 052; ❶), with good suppers offered – though the proprietress will sit and watch you eat every bite. There's also a quiet **campsite**, 1500m out of Ayerbe on the road to Loarre, *La Banera* (☎974 380 242; open all year). **Restaurant** options in Ayerbe include the sustaining *Floresta*, at the start of the Loarre road (*menús* €9–12), and the fancier *Rincón del Palacio*, next to a medieval manor house on the plaza, where the €19 *menú* gives you access to most of the *carta*.

Los Mallos

The train line from Huesca to Jaca and the N240 road from Huesca to Pamplona give views not only of Loarre but of the fantastic, pink-tinged sugarloaf mountains known as **Los Mallos** – "the ninepins", beloved of abseilers and divided into two separate formations at Riglos and Agüero. Their majesty, however, may not serve to protect them from partial inundation by a proposed new dam at Biscuarés on the Río Gállego.

If you're travelling by train and want a closer look at the mountains, get off at **Concilio** station (you must ask the conductor to stop) and walk along a side road for around 2km to **RIGLOS** village, tucked high up underneath the most impressive stretch of the peaks. At Riglos there's another (unstaffed) station, below the village, from where you can resume your journey; alternatively, **stay** the night above the *Bar Restaurante El Puro* at *Casa Toni* (☎974 383 176; ❷).

More *mallos* loom behind **AGÜERO**, an isolated village 5km off the main Huesca–Pamplona road at Murillo de Gállego or a seven-kilometre walk from Concilio station. Agüero itself is characterful and unspoiled, graced by two Romanesque **churches**: the central San Salvador, and the remote Santiago, both with superb portal carvings by the Master of San Juan de la Peña (see p.698). You may wish to **stay** at *Hostal La Costera* at the top of the village (☎974 380 330; ❷), with basic, prefab rooms but lovely grounds, a pool and restaurant.

Sierra de Guara

North of the N240 road linking Huesca and Barbastro sprawls the **Sierra de Guara**, a thinly inhabited region protected as a *parque natural* since 1990. The sierra has no dramatic peaks – the highest point is 2078-metre Puntón de Guara – and the vegetation often looks distinctly scrubby, but its allure lies lower down, in an unrivalled array of sculpted gorges, painted prehistoric caves and appealing villages. This is the main centre for **canyoning** in Spain, and indeed Europe; it's been known to the French for decades, and French cars match or outnumber local number plates in the popular centres. Many of the adventure outfitters, too, are French-run – there's at least one in every village – though the Spanish are clawing back some of the trade. Walking opportunities are relatively limited, with poor trail marking, and hiking is best in spring or autumn, when the weather is cooler.

The eastern half of the Guara is much more popular, and covered by the Alpina 1:40,000 **map** *Sierra de Guara II*, a must for touring. Due to massive depopulation, there's **no public transport** anywhere in the region; similarly, the only petrol and bank (with an ATM) is at Alquézar.

Alquézar and around

At the far southeastern corner of the range and *parque*, 22km from Barbastro, **ALQUÉZAR** ("Alquezra" in Aragonese) is the Guara's main gateway and most developed tourist centre. Lying on the west bank of the Río Vero, it's an atmospheric village, though packed to the gills most weekends and all summer. Arcaded lanes culminate in the eighth-century Moorish **citadel** on a pinnacle overlooking the river; the Christians took it in 1064, and by the start of the twelfth century had built the **Colegiata de Santa Maria la Mayor** (daily: summer 11am–1pm & 4.30–7.30pm; winter Wed–Mon 11am–1pm & 4–6pm; €2, guided visits only) within its fortifications. Only the cloister, its column capitals carved with biblical scenes, remains from the Romanesque era; the Gothic-Renaissance church itself dates from the sixteenth and seventeenth centuries. It's crammed with a miscellany of Baroque art, mostly polychrome wood except for an unpainted pine organ, and a masterly thirteenth-century wooden Crucifixion in the side chapel. From near the citadel a path leads for 45 minutes down to the river and the **Puente de Villacantal**, one of several ancient bridges in the *sierra*.

There's a **turismo** at the edge of town on c/Arrabal (Easter & July–Sept Tues–Sun 10.30am–1.30pm & 4–9pm; Oct–June weekends only, same hours), which sells the recommended Alpina map. **Accommodation** is fairly abundant but still needs advance booking at busy times. Among several *albergues*, two worth noting are *Tintorero* (☎974 318 354; 6-bunk rooms; €10; April–Sept) in the heart of town at c/San Gregório 18, and *La Marmita de Guara*, on c/Pilaseras, above the main car park (☎974 318 956; 6-bunk rooms; €10; April–Sept). There are also two campsites close by: *Alquézar*, 1km downhill by the petrol pump (☎974 318 300, ⓦwww.alquezar.com; open all year), and the slightly lower-standard *Río Vero* (☎974 318 350; April–Oct), down by the river. Representative of six *casas rurales* are the friendly *Casa Jabonero* on c/Pedro Arnal 8 (☎974 318 908; ❶), and *Casa Espartero*, at San Lucas 20 (☎974 318 07; ❶). The more helpful and reliably open of the two bona fide hotels is *Villa de Alquézar* on c/Pedro Arnal 12 (☎ & Ⓕ974 318 416; ❸), whose large doubles have castle-view balconies; rates include a generous breakfast.

The **bars and restaurants** lining Plaza Nueva at the southwest edge of the village are generally pretty poor, and pricey to boot; much better options include *Casa Gervasio* in the centre and the eatery attached to *La Marmita de Guara*. With your own transport, head 5km southwest for slightly precious but imaginative nouvelle Spanish cuisine at *El Puntillo* (€24 *menú*), in **ADAHUESCA**. Finally, the village of **BUERA**, 6km southeast across the river, has another lodging and eating option in the *Posada de Lalola* (☎974 318 347, ❹), which offers exquisite designer rooms opening onto a garden and serves respectable table d'hôte fare (reservations necessary; €24).

North: the road to Lecina

The HU340 district road from below Alquézar heads northeast to the village of **COLUNGO**, 5km away – attractive in a low-key way with its arched doorways and massive buttressed church. The sole accommodation option is the friendly *Hostal Mesón de Colungo* (☎974 318 195; ❷), and you can sample the locally made *aguardiente de anís* at *A'Olla* bar-restaurant opposite.

The road continues, in and out of the minor Fornocal gorge, passing two of the four prehistoric **painted caves** of the Vero valley, which can only be visited on escorted tours (Easter week & mid-July to mid-Sept daily; Easter to early July & mid-Sept to early Oct weekends only; otherwise make arrangements through the Barbastro turismo, see p.688). For visits during peak season, just show up at the signposted lay-bys at 10am or 6pm for the **Covacho de Arpan**, or at 12.15pm or 4.30pm for the **Tozal de Mallata**; for the **Covacho de Barfaluy**, assemble at the turismo in Lecina (see opposite) at 10am or 5pm. The 4.30pm visits to the remote **Abrigo de Chimiachas** must always be booked through the Alquézar turismo (see above), as a long 4WD journey is involved.

LECINA itself, some 16km from Colungo, has some imposing houses – it was one of the wealthier Guara villages – and good views northeast to the high peaks. There's a superb place to **stay** and **eat** here: *La Choca* (☎ & ℱ974 343 070 or ☎659 633 636; ❷), a restored mansion opposite the church with some of the best food in the Guara (supper only except weekends, Easter, & July–Aug; *menú* for around €13). There's also a **campsite** down by the river, *Lecina* (☎974 318 386; May–Sept), which doubles as the local canyoning outfitter.

The area around Lecina is one of the few places where **walkers** are actively catered for. The local municipality has waymarked sixteen PR trails, indicated on a sketch map available from the tiny turismo in Lecina or from *La Choca*; a good outing is the three-hour loop to Lecina via Almazorre and Betorz.

Northwest: the road to Rodellar

West from Alquézar and Adahuesca, the next significant village is **BIERGE**, with a couple of good **places to stay** including the *Casa Rufas*, a restored inn in the centre at c/La Cruz 2 (☎974 318 373; ❷). *Casa Barbara* (☎974 318 060; €10 per person, but half board at €32 per person encouraged), is a welcoming *albergue* on the outskirts aimed at canyoners who don't mind being packed nine to a dorm; the food is excellent – including own-baked breads and fruit turnovers – served out in the garden.

North along the ridgetop HU341, the scenery gets grander after about 5km, with canyons yawning to either side. Beyond Km11, you descend through woods to *Expediciones*, the most pleasant **campsite** of three in the Alcanadre river valley (☎974 343 008, ⓦwww.expediciones.sc.es; open June–Sept); they're also about the most switched-on canyoning operator hereabouts. **LAS ALMUNIAS**, 2km further, is the first pleasant village, offering the *Hostal Casa Tejedor* (☎ & ℱ974 343 015; ❷; March–Oct), with a restaurant, plus the *Albergue Las Almunias* across the road (☎974 343 218; 6-bunk rooms; €9).

RODELLAR, some 4km further and 18km from Bierge at the end of the road, looks achingly photogenic draped along a ridge above the Río Mascún, though the reality close up in peak season is likely to be cars parked nose-to-tail and overstretched **accommodation**. This comprises *Casa Arilla* (☎974 318 343; ❷; April–Oct) and *Casa Ortas* (☎974 318 364; ❷), while the *Bar-Restaurante Florentino*, opposite *Casa Arilla*, is the only spot to eat or drink. Two **campsites**, *Mascún* at the edge of the village (☎974 318 367, ⓦwww .guara-mascun.com; April–Oct), and *El Puente*, 1500m south by the river and the medieval Pedruel bridge (☎974 318 312; April–Oct), also act as canyoning guide centres. If you're not interested in plumbing the deep gorges hereabouts, the most popular activity is the two-and-a-half-hour (one-way) **hike** north to the abandoned hamlet of **Otín**, though path-marking is terrible. It's sobering to reflect that before the current canyoning boom began when French aficionados bought houses in the 1960s, just two families lived at Rodellar full time.

Jaca and around

Jaca is approached through featureless, traffic-choked suburbs: an unpromising introduction to this early capital and stronghold of Aragón – and the base from which the kingdom was recaptured from the Moors. The old centre, however, is a lot more characterful, overlooked by a huge star-shaped citadel, and endowed with a cathedral that is one of the high points of Romanesque architecture. This, and the monastery of **San Juan de la Peña**, 20km southeast, are the major local sights, though in winter there is a bonus in the proximity of **Candanchu-Astún**, Aragón's most challenging ski resort. Rail (and, in winter, ski) enthusiasts may be tempted by the trip to **Canfranc**, almost at the French border.

Jaca

After a spell in the mountains, **JACA**'s relatively "big town" feel and facilities may well be an equal attraction to its ancient monuments. It's enlivened by conscripts at the large military academy and a summer English-language university, and hosts a terrific week-long **fiesta** (last week of June) with live bands in the main square, lots of traditional costume, and partying in the streets.

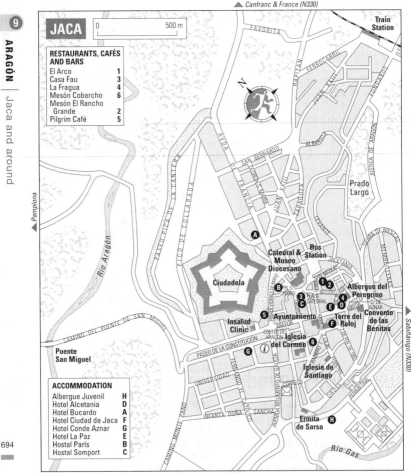

Arrival, orientation and information

Central Jaca's old quarter has two aspects. The northeast side, beyond the cathedral and south of the bus station, is a little dingy, and shelters all of the budget accommodation and rowdier bars; the southwest quarter, abutting either side of Avenida Regimiento de Galicia, is smarter, with sidewalk cafés, smarter restaurants and banks.

The **train station** (ticket office open 10am–noon & 5–7pm) is a fair walk from the centre, so look out for the shuttle bus (€0.50), which runs to and from the **bus station** on Avenida Jacetania, around the back of the cathedral. Useful bus services include those for Pamplona, Biescas via Sabiñánigo, and Echo/Anso, as well as even more frequent services to Zaragoza and Huesca. Although the timetables don't say so, hardly any buses run on Sundays. **Drivers** will find parking easiest in the roomier southwestern quarter, especially around the far end of the Paseo de la Constitución, though look out for pay-and-display zones.

If you're heading for the mountains, it's worth stopping in at the helpful **turismo**, Avda. Regimiento de Galicia (summer Mon–Fri 9am–2pm & 4.30–8pm, Sat 9am–1.30pm & 5–8pm, Sun 10am–1.30pm; winter Mon–Fri 9am–1.30pm & 4.30–7pm, Sat 10am–1pm & 5–7pm; ☎974 360 098, Ⓦwww.aytojaca.es), which has a range of leaflets on trekking, skiing, mountain biking, horse-riding and festival programmes.

Accommodation

As Jaca is a gateway to the peaks, the **accommodation** facilities are almost always stretched, so advance booking is prudent.

Hotels and hostales

Albergue Juvenil Avda. Perimetral s/n ☎974 360 536. This YHA-affiliated youth hostel, in the south of town by the ice rink, has doubles, triples and five-bedded rooms. €11 adult, €5 under-29s; ❶
Hotel Alcetania c/Mayor 45 ☎974 356 100, Ⓕ974 356 200. Former *hostal* refurbished as a hotel in 1995; avoid the slightly sleazy ground-floor bar by using the alternative entry from c/Conde Aznar. ❸
Hotel Bucardo Avda. de Francia 13 ☎974 362 485, Ⓕ974 362 828. Plain, functional en-suite rooms with twin beds only and TV; most face a quiet side street, where there's free parking. ❷
Hotel Ciudad de Jaca c/Siete de Febrero 8 ☎974 364 311, Ⓕ974 364 395. Centrally located but quiet place with good en-suite rooms. ❷
Hotel Conde Aznar Paseo de la Constitución 3 ☎974 361 050, Ⓕ974 360 797. An attractive old family-run hotel, with well-renovated rooms and fairly abundant (if metered) street parking. ❹

Hotel La Paz c/Mayor 41 ☎974 360 700, Ⓕ974 360 400. Large, somewhat airless en-suite rooms with heating in winter. ❸
Hostal París Plaza de San Pedro 5 ☎974 361 020. Best budget *hostal* in town, across from the cathedral, offering clean, spacious rooms with washbasin, currently overlooking an archeological dig. ❶
Hostal Somport c/Echegaray 11 ☎ & Ⓕ 974 363 410. Jaca's most affordable en-suite digs, in another renovated old building; salubrious ground-floor bar-restaurant. ❷

Camping

Camping Peña Oroel 3km east on the Sabiñánigo road ☎974 360 215. An attractive campsite, set amid woods, with excellent facilities. Open Easter week and mid-June to mid-Sept.
Camping Victoria 1500m out of town on the Pamplona road ☎974 360 323. An equally shady if cheaper and rather basic site, near the Río Aragón. Open all year.

The Town

Jaca is an ancient town, founded by the Romans and occupied continuously since. It had a very brief period of Moorish rule, after being captured around 716, but in 760 the Christians reconquered the town and held it, save for a few years, from then on. The battle of **Las Tiendas** in 795, when Moorish armies were repulsed in large part by women, is still commemorated on the first

Friday in May, in a mock all-women battle between Christians and Muslims. The town's greatest period, however, came after 1035, when **Ramiro I**, son of Sancho of Navarre, established a court here. It was during this era that the first parliament on record took place, and that the cathedral was rebuilt.

The cathedral

Just east of the Ciudadela, the **Catedral** (daily 8am–2pm & 4–8pm; free) is the main legacy of Jaca's years as the seat of the young Aragonese kingdom, and ranks as one of Spain's most architecturally important monuments. Rebuilt on old foundations part way through the eleventh century, it was the first Spanish cathedral to adopt the French Romanesque style of architecture and, as such, exerted considerable stylistic influence on other churches along the Camino de Santiago.

Ramiro's endowment of the cathedral was undoubtedly intended to confirm Jaca's role as a Christian capital, in what was still an overwhelmingly Moorish Iberian peninsula. Its design saw the introduction of the classic three-aisled basilica, though unhappily the original Romanesque simplicity has been much obscured by florid decoration over the centuries. It retains some of the original sculpture, however, including realistic carving on the capitals and doorway – a sixteenth-century statue of Santiago looks down from the portal. Inside, the main treasure is the silver shrine of Santa Orosía, Jaca's patron saint; a Czech noble, married into the Aragonese royal family, Orosía was martyred by the Moors for refusing to renounce her faith.

Installed in the dark cathedral cloisters is an unusually good **Museo Diocesano** (June–Sept daily 10am–2pm & 4–8pm; Easter–May daily 10am–1.30pm & 4–7pm; winter Tues–Sun 11am–1.30pm & 4–7pm; may shut for works 2004; €2), which features frescoes and wooden religious sculpture gathered from village churches in the area and from higher up in the Pyrenees. Highlights include an eerily modern Pantocrator fresco from a church in Ruesta, a walnut crucified Christ, and the *Flight into Egypt* and *Adoration of the Magi* from Navasa, all from the twelfth century. The Renaissance work is more variable, but features some splendid *retablos*.

The Ciudadela and Puente San Miguel

The **Ciudadela**, a redoubtable sixteenth-century fort, built in the French stellar plan then prevalent, is still part-occupied by the military. You can visit a part of the interior (daily: April–June & Sept–Oct 11am–noon & 5–6pm; July–Aug 11am–noon & 6–8pm; Nov–March 11am–noon & 4–5pm; €4) by guided tour only. Its walls offer good views of the surrounding peaks, and of the wooded countryside around.

Below the citadel, reached along a steep, rutted road from the end of the Paseo de la Constitución, is a remarkable medieval bridge, the **Puente San Miguel**. It was across this bridge, over the Río Aragón, that pilgrims on the Camino Aragonés – a branch of the **Camino de Santiago** (see p.451) – entered Jaca. It must have been a welcome sight, marking the end of the arduous Pyrenean stage for pilgrims following the route from Provence into Spain over the Puerto de Somport. From Jaca, the pilgrims headed on westwards, through Puente la Reina de Jaca, towards Navarra, where they joined up with the more popular route from Roncesvalles. This Aragón section of the Camino de Santiago – like other branches of the route – has experienced quite a revival since the early 1990s, though it's constantly threatened with either inundation by dams or covering over by building projects. In town, there's an **Albergue del Peregrino** (pilgrims' hostel) in the medieval hospital on c/Conde Aznar (daily 9–10am & 3–10pm), while route maps and pilgrimage-related souvenirs are widely available.

Eating and drinking

Jaca has a lively and inviting selection of **restaurants** and **bars** with fairly reasonable prices, especially during the summer months.

El Arco c/San Nicolás 4. That rare Spanish breed: a vegetarian, no-smoking restaurant. Fresh, filling, international dishes and inexpensive *menús* at €10–12. Closed Sun in winter.

Casa Fau Plaza de la Catedral 4. Jaca's classic tapas bar, with a few tables under the arches, more inside, and reliably rude staff. All the usual platters, plus *ciervo* (venison) sausage, *boletus* (wild mushrooms), quiche; €4–6 for three tapas and a *caña*.

El Conde Aznar Paseo de la Constitución 3. The *comedor* of the eponymous hotel is reckoned to be one of the best eateries in town. There is a choice of unusually interesting *menús* for about €13, while *a la carta* won't much exceed €18 (booze extra in either case).

La Fragua c/Gil Berges 4. Generous, reasonably priced grills without any airs or graces; no *menú*, budget €20 *a la carta*. Closed Wed.

Mesón Cobarcho c/Ramiro Primero 2. Don't let the decor – part Gaudí, part Flintstones – distract you from the excellent cooking; the €12 *menú* features both seafood and meat, though *a la carta* is pricey at €25–30.

Mesón El Rancho Grande c/del Arco 2. Impressive Aragonese cooking, using fish, meat and vegetables equally well; skip the dull €11.50 *menú* in favour of the *carta* (allow €25).

Pilgrim Café Avda. Primer Viernes de Mayo 7. Inevitably a bit touristy but occupies a fine old industrial, wood-floored building with outdoor tables facing the Ciudadela's lawn. Serves a variety of breakfasts (including bacon and eggs) as well as snacks.

Listings

Adventure activities Jaca Adventura, Avda. Francia 1 (℡974 363 521), Mountain Travel on Avda. Regimiento Galicia (℡974 355 770), and Alcorce-Adventura, opposite the turismo at Avda. Regimiento Galicia 1 (℡974 356 781) organize a variety of expeditions; all these companies have English-speaking staff.

Hospital Besides the main one on c/Rapitan, off the map beyond the train station, there's the very central, public Insalud clinic on Paseo de la Constitución, good for minor ailments.

Laundry There's a self-service *lavandería* next to the supermarket, Superpirineos, on c/Astún.

Maps La Unión at c/Mayor 34 and El Siglo at c/Mayor 17 sell all the maps and guides required for the region.

Outdoor gear In the centre, Charli at Avda. Regimiento de Galicia 3, and Intersport-Piedrafita, at Avda. de Francia 4, have a limited stock; for much the widest selection, go to Sportland, in a shopping mall at the far northeast edge of town. It's a bit tricky to reach; you have to go under the N330 via two tunnels near the RENFE station.

South to San Juan de la Peña and Santa Cruz de la Serós

San Juan de la Peña, up in the hills to the southwest of Jaca, is the best-known monastery in Aragón. In medieval times San Juan was an important detour on the pilgrim route from Jaca to Pamplona, as it was reputed to hold the Holy Grail – a Roman-era chalice which later turned up in Valencia cathedral. These days, most tourists (and there are many – including school parties) visit for the views and Romanesque cloister.

The most direct **route to the monastery** begins from the Jaca–Pamplona (N240) highway. A side road, 11km west of Jaca, leads south 4km to the village of **Santa Cruz de la Serós**, and from here it's a further 7km by road up to San Juan. There is no public transport, although you could take a Puente la Reina/Pamplona bus from Jaca and walk from there – assuming an overnight stay in Santa Cruz.

Santa Cruz de la Serós

The picturesque village of **SANTA CRUZ DE LA SERÓS**, which comes to life in summer, is dominated by its thick-set but nonetheless stylish Romanesque **church** (daily 10am–2pm & 4–7pm; €1), once part of a large Benedictine monastery which flourished until the sixteenth century. There are a couple of places to **eat** and **drink** in the village: the *Casa d'Ojalatero* in the centre, with plain fare including good house wine, *trigueros con gambas* and grills (*menú* €9.50, or €16–20 *a la carta*), and the *Hostal Santa Cruz* (similar prices), also housing the village bar. The latter also has high-standard, recently built **rooms** (☎974 361 975, ⓦwww.santacruzdelaseros.com; ❸), four with balconies.

From Santa Cruz, walkers can take the **old path** up to San Juan in about an hour. The path is waymarked as Variant 2 of the GR65.3.2 and is signposted from near the church (where there is also a map-placard). The road takes a more circuitous route around the mountainside, giving wonderful views of the Pyrenean peaks to the north and the distinctive Peña de Oroel to the east.

San Juan de la Peña

SAN JUAN DE LA PEÑA actually comprises two monasteries, 2km apart. Coming from Santa Cruz, you reach the lower (and older) one first.

Built into a hollow under a rocky escarpment, from which various springs seep, the **Lower Monastery** (summer Tues–Sun 10am–2pm & 3.30–8pm; spring & autumn Tues–Sun 10am–2pm & 4–7pm; winter Wed–Sun 11am–2pm; €3) is an unusual and evocative complex, even in its partial state of survival. It was here, in 1071, that the Latin Mass was introduced to the Iberian peninsula by Cluniac monks, and here also that the Aragonese maintained a stronghold in the early years of the Reconquest. Entering, you pass into the Sala de Concilios – once the refectory – and the adjacent, double-naved, ninth-century Mozarabic chapel. These two chambers were adapted as the crypt of the main Romanesque **church**, built two centuries later, and both retain fragments of Romanesque frescoes. Upstairs, alongside the main church, is a **pantheon** for Aragonese and Navarrese nobles; reliefs on the Gothic nobles' tombs depict events from the early history of Aragón. An adjacent pantheon for the kings of Aragón was remodelled in a cold, Neoclassical style during the eighteenth century and later sacked by Napoleon's troops.

All this is just to whet your appetite, however, for the twelfth-century Romanesque **cloisters**. Only two of the bays are complete – another is in a fragmentary state – but the surviving capitals rank among the greatest examples of Romanesque carving in Spain. They were the artistry of an anonymous, idiosyncratic craftsman who made his mark on a number of churches in the region. He is now known as the Master of San Juan de la Peña, his work easily recognizable by the unnaturally large eyes on the figures.

The seventeenth-century **Upper Monastery**, a sizeable complex with a flamboyant Baroque facade, can be seen from the outside only. Facing the monastery is a popular picnic ground in a huge, forest-enclosed meadow; if you arrive by car, this is where you must park most of the year – a shuttle bus will take you down to the older monastery.

Canfranc-Estación

Since the French railways discontinued their part of the local trans-Pyrenean line, the enormous, badly vandalized train station at **CANFRANC-ESTACIÓN**, 30km north of Jaca, has become a white elephant, with tall

There are five **ski resorts in the Aragonese Pyrenees** and most of them – following Jaca's unsuccessful bid to host the 2010 Winter Olympics – are well equipped. As in Catalunya, you may find that package deals, bought from any travel agent in northern Spain, work out cheapest, but there are also often mini-packages arranged by the turismos and hotels of each valley. Wherever possible you should take advantage of slow, midweek periods and thus avoid the busiest weekends and major holidays when all accommodation is booked a month in advance.

About the most advanced runs are at the adjacent centres of **CANDANCHÚ** and **ASTÚN**, north of Canfranc (buses from Jaca). The resorts – smaller Astún dating from 1975, and bigger, slightly higher Candanchú, the first established in these mountains – are just 4km apart, but do not (yet) have a link or shared lift passes. Treeless Astún has five chairlifts, prone to closure from high winds; also, liaisons between the sectors can be obscure, and you really need to be of intermediate ability to enjoy this resort (beginners are probably better off at Candanchú). There's just one single, monolithic chalet-style hotel at Astún, the *Europa* (☎974 373 312; ❸), while three rather pricier hotels are available at Candanchú. The most economical of these is the *Candanchú* (☎974 373 025, ⓦwww.candanchu.com; ❹), though there's also an *albergue*, *El Águila* (☎974 373 291; 4-bed en-suite rooms, €16 per person; 6-bed dorms, €11; open ski season & July–Aug). With a car, you may prefer to stay in Canfranc (see p.698). Skiers – and in summer, GR11 trekkers – congregate at friendly *Cafeteria Cristiania*, which, despite the name, does full meals.

Among the other ski centres, **FORMIGAL** (closest reasonable lodgings at Sallent de Gallego, of which the *Balaitus* – ☎974 488 959; ❸ – is characterful and clean) and **PANTICOSA** (try the *Vicente*, ☎974 487 022; ❸, just above the eponymous village) are both served by daily buses from Sabiñanigo via Biescas. Formigal nearly rivals Candanchú/Astún for interest and challenge on the piste, but Panticosa – despite massive investment – remains too low and too limited in its piste plan for expert skiers, though families love it. The remotest and highest Aragonese resort is **CERLER**, close to Benasque; it, too, has undergone a massive facelift, with new snow cannons, well-coordinated chairlifts and runs finishing through forest, making it an excellent intermediate centre. Much the best accommodation choice here is *Casa Cornel* in the old village (☎974 551 102, ⓦwww.casacornel.com; *hostal* wing ❸, hotel wing ❺).

weeds now growing in the tracks. It's a sad fate for an elegant spot which saw heads of state attend its inauguration in 1928, and served as a location for the film *Doctor Zhivago*. Spanish undercutting of French ski-resort prices prompted the closure of the line in the first place in 1973 (ironically, the Spanish slopes are now pricier), though the last straw was the collapse of a critical bridge, left unrepaired to this day. However, following the opening of the Somport car tunnel in 2002, EU funding for the rehabilitation of the rail line between Oloron-Ste-Marie and Canfranc has been approved.

The village, such as it is, exists primarily to catch the passing tourist trade (mostly French), with a few gift shops and lodgings. It's just about worth the day's trip from Jaca, even if you don't continue into France, for the train ride up the valley. **Accommodation**, all on or just off the through highway, includes the high-quality *Albergue Pepito Grillo* (☎974 373 123; 5-bunk rooms; €10; open all year), and the friendly *Hotel Villa Anayet*, Plaza de Aragón (☎974 373 146; ❷). There are also two adjacent *casas rurales* next to the *Villa Anayet*: *Casa Marieta* (☎974 373 365; ❷) and *La Tuca* (☎974 373 104; ❷), as well as a campsite (☎608 731 604; April to mid-Sept) 5km north on the road towards Candanchú. For **meals**, the *comedor* at the *Hotel Villa Anayet* offers the best value.

Though there's no proper train (yet), you can travel on into France several times daily on **buses** run by the French SNCF. Consult Canfranc's **turismo** (July–Sept Mon–Sat 9am–1.30pm & 4.30–8pm; Oct–June Tues–Sat 9am–1.30pm & 3.30–7pm, closed Nov 1–15; ☎974 373 141, Ⓦwww.canfranc.com), opposite the station, for current information on trains and skiing.

Echo and Ansó

Echo and **Ansó** are two of the most attractive valleys in Aragón, their rivers – Aragón Subordan and Veral – joining the Río Aragón west of Jaca. Until the 1960s, both valleys felt extremely remote, with villagers wearing traditional dress and speaking a dialect, *Cheso*, descended from medieval Aragonese. These days, they're very much on the map for Spanish weekenders and foreign visitors, and the last rural activity seriously engaged in is timber-cutting.

There is only one daily **bus** (Mon–Sat), which calls first at Echo and continues on to Ansó; it leaves Jaca at 6.30pm, arriving in Anso at 8.10pm, and begins the journey back from Ansó at 6am, passing Echo 45 minutes later. For **trekking in the region**, the 1:40,000 Editorial Alpina booklet *Valles de Ansó y Echo* is useful.

Valle de Echo

ECHO is a splendid old village, where whitewash outlines the windows and doors of the massive stone houses. It figures in Aragonese history as the seat of the embryonic Aragonese kingdom under Conde Aznar Galíndez in the ninth century, and as the birthplace of the "warrior king" Alfonso I. Although it seems ancient, Echo as you see it is less than two centuries old – like so many villages in these hills, it was burnt and sacked during the Napoleonic Wars.

An annual arts festival, which ran from 1975 to 1984, has left a permanent legacy in the open-air **gallery of sculpture** on the hillside west of the village. Created by a group of artists under Pedro Tramullas, the 46 pieces are not individually stunning but, taken as a whole, quite compelling. Local resistance to the expansion of the venture has been overcome, but unfortunately funds are now lacking to take the project further. Near the enormous central church, there's a more conventional museum, the **Museo Etnológico** (Easter & July–Aug daily 11am–2pm & 6–9pm; €1), with interesting collections on Pyrenean rural life and folklore.

The **turismo** is in the *ayuntamiento* (daily June–Sept 10am–2pm & 5–7pm; ☎974 375 329); if it's shut, ask upstairs and they may open it for you. In summer or at weekends you'd be well advised to book ahead for one of Echo's several **places to stay**. The clear first choices are *Casa Blasquico*, barely marked at Plaza Palacio de la Fuente 1 (☎974 375 007; ❷), with five tastefully converted en-suite rooms, and the *Danubio*, on the hillside opposite (☎974 375 033; ❷), with appealing, newly decorated en-suite rooms above a bar. Fallbacks, in descending order of preference, are the *Hostal de la Val* (☎974 375 028; ❸) and *Lo Foratón* (☎974 375 247), the latter comprising a somewhat shabby *hostal* (❶) and a slightly better hotel (❷), all towards the north end of the village. A **campsite**, *Valle de Echo* (☎974 375 361; all year), lies just south of the village, though *Borda Basáltico* (☎974 375 388), 5km north, is of a much higher standard, offering dorm beds in an *albergue* (€9) as well.

For **meals**, don't miss a chance to eat at *Casa Blasquico* (seatings at 1.30pm & 8.30pm – reservations mandatory ☎974 375 007; closed part of Sept), where the emphasis is on game, duck and decadent sweets and definitely worth a €30 splurge *a la carta* – if money's tight, ask about the cheaper *menú*. Owner-chef Gaby Coarasa was among the first stars of Pyrenean *nouvelle cuisine*, and the walls of the tiny *comedor* are lined with awards to prove it. If you can't get in, the *Restaurante Cantaré* nearby is nearly as good, while the friendly *Bar Subordán*, next door to *Casa Blasquico*, will feed you with superb, inexpensive *raciones* of *pimientos de piquillo, longaniza* and *chipirrones*.

Siresa and beyond

Two kilometres north of Echo stands the small, quiet village of **SIRESA**. Keeping watch over riverside pastures is a remarkable ninth-century monastic church, the massive, austere **San Pedro** (daily 11am–1pm & 5–8pm; €1.50). The owners of the pleasant local **hotel**, the *Castillo d'Acher* (☎974 375 313; ❷), also operate an annexe *fonda* (❶) over the village bar, and a reasonable **restaurant**. For the truly impecunious, Siresa offers the YHA-affiliated *Albergue Siresa* in the old school (☎974 375 385; 6-bunk dorms €10.50).

Walkers may be tempted to continue up the valley from Siresa, along the GR65.3.3, a minor variant of the Camino de Santiago; much of the paved road can be missed out by following the "Via Romana", not Roman but certainly early medieval, signposted 3km above Siresa. Once through the **Boca de Infierno** narrows, you emerge at **Selva de Oza**, where there is a pleasant bar. Selva is the jump-off point for climbing **Castillo de Acher** (2390m); the other limestone peaks, including **Bisaurín** (2669m) and **Agüerri** (2449m), are best tackled from the excellent *Refugio de Gabardito* (☎974 375 387 or 676 850 843; 60 bunks; €11; open all year), further down the valley at the end of the track serving the *Borda Basáltico* campsite. The *refugio* is run by the Compañia de Guías Valle de Echo, the people to see about either summer climbing or wintertime Nordic skiing.

North of Selva de Oza, the paved road ends near **La Mina**, trailhead for the two-hour hike up to the **Acherito lake**, one of the local beauty spots. **Laraille/Laraya** peak (2147m) just overhead is another popular target, as is the nearby frontier peak of **Lariste** (2168m). The GR11 long-distance footpath also passes through La Mina, on its way west from Canfranc, heading towards Zuriza in the Ansó valley, a short day's hike distant; at **Zuriza** there's the well-equipped *Camping Zuriza* (☎974 370 196; all year), with an *albergue* (6- or 8-bunk rooms, €8–22 depending on en-suite arrangements), *hostal* (❷) and restaurant.

On to Ansó

The daily **bus** from Jaca to Echo continues west along 12km of narrow, twisting road, climbing over the Sierra de Vedao before dropping into the **Valle de Ansó**; the final approaches are guarded by two strangely shaped rocks known locally as "the Monk and the Nun", just above a tunnel.

Non-drivers should use the very enjoyable two-and-a-half-hour hiking **trail** from **Siresa to Ansó**, waymarked as the PR18 and signposted as "Fuen d'a Cruz" by the stream below Siresa.

Valle de Ansó

Once a prosperous, large village, **ANSÓ** fell upon hard times during the 1950s depopulation of rural Aragón. Today, however, there are signs of revival, with Jaca and Pamplona professionals keeping second residences here, and a growing traffic of tourists. It's certainly an attractive weekend base, with a little river beach down by the Río Veral. There are few specific sights, though there's a **Museo Etnológico** (summer daily 10.30am–1.30pm & 3.30–8pm; €1.50), housed in an ancient church.

Ansó's growing popularity is reflected in several **places to stay**, most filling quickly in summer. Best is the *Posada Magoria* (☎974 370 049; ❸), in palatial quarters by the church, with a garden and views; they serve communal vegetarian meals (preference given to guests). Worthy alternatives include the *Hostal Kimboa* (☎974 370 184, ⓕ974 370 130; open all year by arrangement; ❷), with double-glazed, comfortable rooms, and *Hostal Estanés* (☎974 370 146; summer only; ❷), both at the north end of the village. A new **campsite** began operating during 2003 beside the municipal swimming pool, at the south end of the village.

Among the few **restaurant** options, *Kimboa* is easily the best, their own reared meat featuring in €12 *menús*, served under the terrace canopy in summer (lunch only out of season). There's more choice in **bars**, the liveliest being the friendly *Zuriza* on the main street.

Parque Nacional de Ordesa

The **PARQUE NACIONAL DE ORDESA Y MONTE PERDIDO** was one of Spain's first protected national parks, and is perhaps the most dramatic, with beech and poplar forests, mountain streams, dozens of spring-to-early-summer waterfalls, and a startling backdrop of limestone palisades. The **wildlife**, too, is impressive, including golden eagles, lammergeiers, griffon and Egyptian vultures, and Pyrenean chamois – the latter so numerous that at certain times hunters are allowed to cull the surplus. The park is an enduringly popular destination for walkers, and its foothill villages are becoming increasingly commercialized each year. In midsummer, you'll need to book accommodation well in advance, even if you plan to camp. Nevertheless, this is the Aragonese Pyrenees at its most spectacular, and well worth a few days of anyone's time.

The route to Ordesa

Heading for Ordesa from the lowlands, the place to make for is the gateway village of **Torla**, from where the GR15.2 leads into the park. A daily **bus** service from Sabiñánigo to Aínsa stops at Torla and all villages on the way, including Biescas, Linás de Broto, Broto, Sarvisé and Fiscal. If you're coming **from the southwest**, this leaves Sabiñánigo at 11am, reaches Biescas fifteen minutes later, and gets to Torla at noon. In July and August there's an additional work-day service between Sabiñánigo and Sarvisé, leaving the former at 6.30pm; this departure runs reliably Friday and Sunday most of the year. Sabiñánigo receives at least two daily buses from Jaca, the 10.15am and 6.15pm departures connecting directly with the onward services cited above.

Coming **from the southeast**, a bus service leaves Aínsa at 2.30pm, arriving in Torla at 3.30pm; the evening service noted above leaves Sarvisé at 7.45pm, calling at Torla about fifteen minutes later. For the valleys on the east side of the park, there's currently just a single daily bus (July–Aug Mon–Sat; rest of year 3 weekly) at 8.45pm, as far as Bielsa. Aínsa itself is served by a 7.45pm bus from Barbastro from Monday to Saturday, with an extra late-morning departure during July and August.

Sabiñánigo, Biescas and Linás de Broto

There's not much joy in industrial **SABIÑÁNIGO** and you'll probably want to push straight on; it is, however, an almost unavoidable transport hub, especially coming from Huesca – the **bus terminal** is right outside the **train sta-**

tion. Should you need to stop over, there are a dozen mostly overpriced **places to stay**, on the through road, Avenida de Serrablo. A reasonable choice, near the transport terminals, is *Hostal Laguarta* (T974 480 004; ❷) at no. 21, above the *Bar Lara*.

If you miss the daily through service to Torla, take the late-afternoon Sallent de Gállego service which passes **BIESCAS**, 17km north, from where you could try your luck hitching the remaining 25km to Torla (or pick up the Torla bus the following morning). If you get stuck, which is likely, Biescas is quite pleasant, with several **places to stay**: *Pensión Las Herras* (T974 485 027; ❷) offers en-suite rooms in an old stone house in a quiet cul-de-sac across the river from the *ayuntamiento*, while *Casa Ruba*, just off the Plaza del Ayuntamiento (T974 485 001; F974 485 001; ❸), has been in the same family since 1884 and offers a lively bar and a respected *comedor*. There's also a central campsite, *Edelweiss* (T974 485 084; mid-June to mid-Sept), and a **turismo** (most of year 10am–1.30pm & 5–8.30pm) next to the bridge. The tiny stone hamlet of **LINÁS DE BROTO**, 17km east on the way to Torla, with four lodgings along the through road and a fine position, also makes a reasonable base: the *Hostal Jal* (T & F974 486 106; ❷), with a restaurant, has links to a reputable local adventure company.

Torla

The old stone village of **TORLA**, just 8km short of Ordesa, is well encased in ranks of modern hotels, and awash with souvenir stalls. It exists very much as a walkers' base and almost everything is geared to park visitors. The **bus** from Sabiñánigo and Aínsa stops at the southern edge of town, by the large car park where all visitors to the park must leave their vehicles (€6 per day). The central **turismo** (late June to mid-Sept Mon–Fri 10am–1pm & 6–8pm, Sat & Sun 9.30am–1.30pm & 5–8.30pm; T974 229 804) offers free sketch maps showing the main paths in the park, though you'll need a proper contour map. The village also has a bank (with ATM) and shops stocking basic foods and mountain gear.

During July and August, you'll need to book **accommodation** in Torla at least a week ahead; at other times it's rarely a problem, although from October to Easter most establishments shut from Monday to Thursday. Top mid-range choices are the *Hostal Alto Aragón* (T & F974 486 172; ❷), with en-suite rooms, and the co-managed *Hotel Ballarín* opposite (T & F974 486 155; ❸); the *Ballarin's comedor* is a fine source of sustaining *menús* (€13). Among several fancier hotels, the *Villa de Torla* (T974 486 156; F974 486 365; ❹) on the village square is professionally run, with a pool and a decent restaurant; the top-floor rooms are best. For budget lodgings, try *Casa Borruel* (T974 486 067; ❶) and *Casa Laly* (T974 486 168; ❶), both on c/Fatás, next to the turismo, or one of two *albergues*: the friendly, high-standard *Refugio Lucien Bret* (T974 486 221; 3- to- 6-bunk rooms; €7–15), with most rooms en suite, self-catering facilities and an excellent restaurant (*Bar Brecha*), or the snootier, cramped *L'Atalaya* (T974 486 022; Easter–Dec; 8-bunk rooms €7), also with a basement restaurant. Additionally, there are three **campsites** along the road out to Ordesa; closest is the riverside *Río Ara* (T974 486 248), 2km from Torla on the far side of the stream.

Broto, Oto, Sarvisé, Fiscal and Aínsa

If you find Torla full or just too commercialized, you may prefer to stop in one of the villages to the southeast, along the road to Aínsa. **BROTO**, 4km south of Torla, is a noisy, teeming place, its old quarter hemmed by traffic and new construction. Upriver, just beside the village's collapsed Romanesque bridge, is the quietest place to stay, and one of the last to fill, *Tabierna O Puente* (☎974 486 072; ❷); you could also try the *Hostal Español* (☎974 486 007, ⓕ974 486 423; ❷), nearby on the through road. The **turismo** (June–Sept Tues–Sun 10am–2pm & 4.30–8.30pm; ☎974 486 002) can advise on vacancies in high season. If you're walking, you can follow a well-trodden *camino* to Torla in 45 minutes; part of the GR15.2, it begins near the ruined bridge.

OTO, 2km southwest, is more attractive, with traditional architecture and a pair of medieval towers. It has two somewhat bland **casas rurales** – *Herrero* (☎974 486 093; ❷) and *Pueyo* (☎974 486 371; ❷) – and a large if basic **campsite** (☎974 486 075; April to mid-Oct). A further 4km from Broto is **SARVISÉ**, the lowest village of the Valle de Broto, but with the highest-quality **accommodation**. Top two picks are the secluded *Casa Puyuelo* (☎974 486 140; ❷), with small but comfortable rooms, or – arguably the best in the Aragonese Pyrenees – *Hotel Casa Frauca* (☎974 486 182, ⓕ974 486 353; closed Jan 6–March; ❹) on the main road, with cosy, wood-floored rooms. Their famous ground-floor *comedor* draws crowds from near and far (€13 *menú*, €23 *a la carta*; reservations required).

Below Sarvisé, the Ara river valley turns east and widens markedly, with evidence of large-scale depopulation; villages just off the road are largely deserted, their fields gone to seed. Aragón in general has the highest proportion of abandoned settlements in Spain, but here the impetus was a never-executed dam at Jánovas. In 1959 local property was expropriated for a pittance by the hydro company, and by 1964 many villagers had been forced to move, their houses dynamited by the Guardia Civil to get the point across.

One village that's found a new lease of life through tourism is **FISCAL**, its older houses scattered agreeably on the far bank of the river from the highway. There's a range of **places to stay**: *Saltamontes* (☎974 503 113; 6- to- 8-bunk rooms; €7.50), an *albergue* opposite the church; *Casa del Arco* (☎ & ⓕ974 503 042, ⓦwww.pireneo.com/casadelarco; ❷), in an eighteenth-century building with antique-furnished rooms and engaging management; and the luxurious *Hostal Casa Cadena*, near the top of the village (☎ & ⓕ974 503 077; ❸), with an equally smart restaurant (€12 *menú* or €30 *a la carta*). There are also two all-year **campsites**, the cosier *El Jabalí Blanco* (☎974 503 074) – also with bungalows – having the edge.

The next place of any size is **AÍNSA**, which has been prettified since 1994 with stone walkways and boutiques in an attempt to cash in on some of the cross-border trade pouring over through the Bielsa tunnel to the north. Its hilltop **old quarter** remains attractive, centred on an exceptional Romanesque church with a primitive crypt and a climbable belfry, plus a vast, arcaded Plaza Mayor. Limited **accommodation** in the medieval quarter includes *Casa El Hospital* (☎974 500 750; ❷), an old stone house right next to the church, or for a splurge, the two-star *Posada Royal* at Plaza Mayor 6 (☎974 500 977; ❹); most other choices are down in the noisy new town. Old-town **eating** options are more plentiful, if expensive; *Bar Restaurante Fes* at c/Mayor 22 offers reasonable value, while *Bar Bodega L'Alfil*, c/Travesera s/n, is the place for tapas and cider.

The Ordesa Canyon and central park treks

An asphalt road from Torla leads 4km to the **visitors' centre** (Centro de Visitantes; July–Oct 10am–1pm & 4–8.30pm) just past the Puente de los Navarros, and from here continues another 4km to the entrance to the **Ordesa Canyon**. During summer all private cars are banned beyond Puente de los Navarros; unless you hike in from Torla, you must use the regular **shuttle bus** (€3 one-way or return) from the car park at the village outskirts. The well-marked GR15.2 **path** starts beside the *Hotel Bella Vista* in Torla, crossing to the east bank of the river; at Puente de la Ereta it links up with the GR11 – the left fork leads to the information office, while the right fork takes you directly to **Pradera de Ordesa**, some 2hr out of Torla and the start of most of the hikes set out below.

At the information office you can buy a range of **maps** of the park; the clearest is the 1:50,000 IGN sheet (which also covers Gavarnie, across the French border), though cheaper ones are perfectly adequate if you're going to stick to the popular, signed paths. All maps mark the park's network of very basic stone **refugios**, where you will need to stay on longer treks, as camping is prohibited in the park (except when the *refugios* are full in the summer months, when you're allowed to camp alongside them). There are no shops beyond Torla, so come prepared.

Treks in the park

Most day-trippers to Ordesa aim no further than a loop to the *mirador* (viewing point) at the **Cascada del Abánico**, six easy and well-waymarked kilometres from the Pradera de Ordesa, with a return path on the opposite bank of the Río Arazas. However, there are dozens of other trails, encompassing most levels of enthusiasm and expertise. The following is just a selection.

Circo de Soasco

This is one of the most popular and rewarding, but not too difficult, short-distance treks. A steep, 7.5-kilometre walk along a signposted path brings you out at the **Cola de Caballo** (Horsetail Waterfall) in three to four hours (reckon on 6–7hr round trip). The trail begins through beech forest and then climbs past a *mirador*, to emerge at the upper reaches of a startling gorge.

For more solitude in summer, an alternative approach involves climbing the steep **Senda de los Cazadores** (the Hunters' Path) which emerges at the Mirador de Calcilarruego; from here the path levels out along the Faja de Pelay, which merges with the Circo de Soaso.

Cotatuero Falls and beyond

A shorter walk visits the impressive **Cotatuero Falls**. Starting from Pradera de Ordesa, the Cotatuero route takes you steeply but easily through the woods to a vantage point below the waterfall. An exciting onward route beckons here, if you have a head for heights. With the help of iron pegs, you can climb above the falls to reach the Brecha de Rolando and trek onwards to Gavarnie (see p.706) – an all-day undertaking.

Carriata Falls and beyond

From both La Pradera and the information office, another waterfall route is signposted towards the **Carriata Falls**. You head into the trees and then leave the contour trail to begin a steep zigzag up to the cascade, most impressive in late spring when melted snow keeps it flowing.

If you want to continue, the left-hand route (at a fork on the open mountainside) ascends to the top of the gorge wall via a series of thirteen iron pegs, not so intimidating as those on the Cotatuero route and feasible for any reasonably fit walker. The right-hand fork contours spectacularly along the canyon's north wall to meet up with the path up to Cotatuero.

Refugio Góriz and Monte Perdido

A path climbs up from the top of Circo de Soaso to the **Refugio Góriz** (2169m; 99 places; ☎974 341 201; open all year), about an hour's walk away.

More elaborate than many refuges, it is equipped with beds, sheets and an over-priced restaurant; during July and August, it's packed to the gills, but you can camp alongside provided you dismount your tent each morning.

For most walkers, the refuge is a starting point for the ascent of **Monte Perdido** (3355m). This is a scramble rather than a climb but a serious expedition nonetheless, for which you should be properly prepared. It takes around five hours to get to the summit, which is reached via an almost permanently frozen lake, Lago Helado.

Torla to Gavarnie

The Ordesa park adjoins the French **Parc National des Pyrénées** and it is possible to trek across to the French alpine town of **Gavarnie**. This is a fair haul – best spread over two days – and most easily done from Torla; routes out of the Ordesa park proper are longer and harder.

Leaving Torla, you follow the GR15.2 as far as the indicated left fork for the Puente de los Navarros (just under 1hr), then climb down to the river and follow the GR11 markers up the valley. There's a **campsite**, *Camping Valle Bujaruelo* (☎974 486 348; mid-April to mid-Oct), after another 4km, and, 3km further, the ruined shrine and medieval bridge of San Nicolás. Here the 2002-refurbished *Mesón de Bujaruelo* (☎974 486 412, ⓦwww.meson debujaruelo.com; mostly 4-bunk rooms, €11) is an **albergue** geared to activity groups, though they also manage a campsite outside and offer lunch to all comers. From the old bridge the path heads over the mountains and down to Gavarnie – six to eight hours' walk, partly on broad track.

The southeastern canyons: Escuaín and Añisclo

In the southeast corner of the Ordesa park yawn a pair of **canyons** – the *gargantas* of **Escuaín** and **Añisclo** – every bit the equal of the Ordesa gorge but with far fewer visitors. The lack of transport to the trailheads, and limited accommodation, contribute to this, but the extra effort is amply rewarded.

The Añisclo canyon

The **Garganta de Añisclo** is the more spectacular of the two canyons, and more frequently visited. If you have your own transport, you can reach it on a minor but paved road from Sarvisé to Escalona (10km north of Aínsa) – though a one-way system forces you to park 1km above the canyon. Westbound traffic from Escalona runs through a narrow gorge, the **Desfiladero de las Cambras**, at the western end of which knots of parked cars announce the mouth of the canyon – though it's planned to close the *desfiladero* to private traffic in future and institute bus shuttles.

From here, two broad paths – each as good as the other – lead north into this marvellous, wild gorge; it's five hours' round trip through the most spectacular section to La Ripareta. Long-haul trekkers also use the canyon as an alternative approach to the Góriz *refugio* (see p.705), exiting the main gorge via the Fon Blanca ravine.

If you're doing a day walk, good places to stay locally include **NERÍN**, 45 minutes' walk west of the canyon along the GR15 trail, via the deserted hamlet of Sercué. Nerín has a fine Romanesque **church** – typical of these settlements – and an *albergue* (☎974 489 008; 5-bunk rooms; €7.50), which serves meals to residents. Alternatively there's the *Pensión El Turista* (☎974 489 016; ❷) and the plush, chalet-style *Hotel Palazio* (☎974 489 002, ⓕ974 489 026;

❸), also with a restaurant. Attractive **BUERBA**, just south of the canyon, is the closest habitation and offers the relaxed, en-suite *Casa Marina* (☎608 714 450, Ⓦwww.integridad-total.com/marina.htm; ❷), with young, English-speaking management and home-cooked meals (vegetarian on request).

The Escuaín canyon

The **Garganta de Escuaín**, more properly the valley of the Río Yaga, is reached most easily from **LAFORTUNADA**, 17km northeast of Aínsa and the most convenient overnight base. *Hotel Badain* (☎974 504 006, Ⓕ974 405 048; ❷) has one of the best restaurants in these valleys (*menú* €12.50, with wine). From Lafortunada, the quickest way into the canyon country if you don't have transport is along the **GR15** trail; it's a two-hour climb along this to the picturesque village of **TELLA**, with a clutch of Romanesque churches and a park **information office** (daily late June–Oct 9am–2pm & 3–9pm). Beyond, the trail drops to the river at Estaroniello hamlet before climbing through thick woods to **Escuaín**, an abandoned settlement taken over in summer by enthusiasts exploring **the gorge**, which lies just upstream. There's another park information office here (same hours) but no other amenities, so bring enough food to sustain you further into the water-sculpted ravine. The GR15 continues west, then south to handsome Bestué village, the only habitation en route to Nerín or Buerba (all 4–5hr distant) – the *albergue* here has closed, so take all you need for a traverse.

Day-hikers, however, should cross the gorge east on a non-GR trail to **Revilla**, a similarly desolate hamlet on the opposite bank. From there you can backtrack to Tella or follow the lovely and little-trodden **PR3** path through Estaroniello to Hospital de Tella, 3km west of Lafortunada. You can complete this figure-of-eight itinerary in a single, long summer's day, taking in the best this limestone Shangri-La has to offer.

The Valle de Gistau

The **Valle de Gistau**, long beloved of Spaniards but still attracting few foreign guests, is the next valley up from Escuaín, draining east to west. A secluded area which should appeal to those wanting to get away from the busier Pyrenean valleys, it's also the easiest jump-off point for the Viadós refuge (see p.709) and thence to the peak of Posets. A web of PR and GR trails links several villages here – just as well, since bus services are down to just three weekly.

PLAN is the valley's "capital", with shops and **accommodation**, including the comfortable *Hotel Mediodía* (☎974 506 006; ❹); the best **restaurant** is *Casa Ruche*, on the bypass road. **SAN JUAN DE PLAN**, 2km north, has more character as a village, offering the best-value **place to stay and eat** in the valley: *Hostal Casa la Plaza* (☎ & Ⓕ974 506 052; ❷), with wood-decor rooms and an excellent, mountain-style *menú* (€10) downstairs. *Casa Sanches* nearby, also with a *comedor*, is a worthy fallback (☎974 506 050; ❷). *Casas rurales* are the norm for local accommodation, and there are many more in **GISTAÍN** just west, including the inexpensive, ebulliently friendly *Casa Zueras* (☎974 506 038; ❶), huge breakfasts extra, or the nearby *Casa Palacín* (☎974 506 295; ❷), with en-suite rooms and meals available.

Heading west from Gistaín, the GR19 trail leads through Sin en route to **SALINAS** – where *Caserío San Marcial* (☎974 504 010) on the west side of the highway has basic rooms (❶), a studio (❷) and **camping** terraces – and eventually Lafortunada (see above). The GR19.1 variant peels off at Sin to reach Bielsa, the northeasterly gateway to the Ordesa country, with daily evening bus service from Aínsa.

Bielsa

BIELSA, 8km north of Salinas, was heavily damaged during the Civil War – it was one of the last Republican strongholds – and today its character is further distorted by the needs of Spanish and (especially) French day-trippers. That said, it becomes more congenial after dark, with good-value **accommodation** near the Plaza Mayor including the *Hostal Pirineos Meliz* (☎974 501 015; ❷), old-fashioned but en suite and with a ground-floor restaurant, or the *Hostal Vidaller* (☎974 501 004; ❶–❷), with some en-suite rooms. **Eat** at the *Pineta* on the square, or out at the *Hostal Pañart's comedor*, on the main highway. A **museum** (July–Sept Tues–Sun 5–9pm; €3) in the *ayuntamiento* tells the story both of Bielsa's wartime experience, and its outrageous winter **carnival**.

Benasque and around

Serious climbers and trekkers gravitate to **Benasque** in the Ésera river valley, for overhead, just out of sight, loom the two highest peaks in the Pyrenees: **Aneto** (3404m) and **Posets** (3371m). The town can be reached most easily from Huesca or Barbastro on the one or two daily buses. Southeast of Benasque, near the border with Catalunya, the cathedral village of **Roda de Isábena** stands in glorious isolation on its bluff.

Benasque town

Though now surrounded by apartment blocks, **BENASQUE** remains an agreeable place occupying a wide stretch of river valley, good for a rest before or after the rigours of trekking. It combines modern amenities with old stone houses, some of them built by the Aragonese nobility in the seventeenth century.

The rather world-weary turismo at the southeast edge of town (daily: winter 10am–2pm & 5–9pm; summer 9am–2pm & 4–9pm; ⓦwww.turismo benasque.com) also has coin-op **Internet** access. Budget **accommodation** is limited to *Casa Gabás-Pichuán*, on quiet c/El Castillo (☎974 551 275; ❷), offering both en-suite rooms and self-catering units, and the somewhat shabby *Fonda Vescelia*, c/Mayor 3 (☎974 551 654; ❶), a mountaineer's hang-out with a cheap *comedor*. For more comfort, try the *Hotel Aragüells* (☎974 551 619, ⓕ974 551 664; ❸) at Avda. de los Tilos 1, the main commercial street; the *Hotel Avenida* next door at no. 3 (☎974 551 126, ⓕ974 551 515; ❹), with good half-board deals; or the more institutional *Hotel Aneto* on Ctra. de Anciles (☎974 551 061, ⓦwww.hoteles-valero.com; ❸), which has a pool, tennis courts, gym, sauna and parking facilities.

Competition for custom means that reasonable *menús* abound at the **bars and restaurants**. The *comedor* at *Bar Bardanca* does a sustaining one for €8, while *Bar Sayó* at c/Mayor 13 includes quails and sardines in its *menú* (€11.50). Snackier options include *La Pizzeria*, just off pedestrianized Plaza Mayor, and the tapas at *Bar Ñam-Ñam*, behind Avenida de los Tilos. For a splurge, *La Parilla* on Ctra. Francia (the bypass road) purveys *nouvelle* Aragonese cooking for €28 and upwards, *a la carta* only. *Asador Itxarso*, near the turismo, is more reasonable at €21 *carta*.

Climbs and walks from Benasque

Benasque attracts committed climbers and trekkers, and if you already count yourself among their number you'll be intent on bagging the **peaks of Aneto and Posets**. These ascents require crampons, ice axe and a rope, and a helmet to guard against falling rocks; if you're not experienced, go with one of the three local group outfitters.

For casual walkers, however, there are plenty of possibilities. The Aragón mountain club has marked out a number of **pequeño recorrido** (PR) paths, documented in a locally available guide prepared by the club. The trails, to surrounding villages and also to all three local refuges, are routed so that you avoid roads as much as possible.

Benasque is a major halt on the **GR11** trail and its variants, hereabouts at their most spectacular. The easiest and most popular **traverse** is northwest, just upstream from town, along the Estós valley and over the Puerto de Gistaín to the *Refugio de Viadós* (℡974 506 082; open Easter & July–Sept), an eight- to nine- hour hike. Seasoned trekkers may prefer the path which heads northwest up the Eriste valley, 4km southwest of Benasque, and then over the high Collado de Eriste on the shoulder of Posets peak, before dropping down to Viadós. This longer route is best broken partway at the *Refugio Ángel Órus* (℡974 344 044; open most of year).

Heading east past Maladeta, use the public **shuttle bus** (5 daily) up the Vallivierna, which cuts out a lot of dreary track-tramping; from the unstaffed Coronas hut here at the top of the valley, the GR11 climbs, then descends east through lonely, lake-spangled country to the *Hospitau Refugi Sant Nicolau* on the Viella road – the better part of two days' hiking from Coronas, with a tent advised.

Another bus (6 daily) brings you to **La Besurta**, near the top of the Ésera valley and just below the *Refugio Renclusa* (℡974 552 106; open Easter & July–Sept). From here the HRP heads southeast over the high Molières pass (crampons always required), giving eye-to-eye views of Aneto, before dropping down another empty valley to the Sant Nicolau refuge – again, tents are suggested.

Roda de Isábena

Attractive hill villages are in seemingly endless supply in Aragón, but **RODA DE ISÁBENA**, in the middle of nowhere on a minor road between El Pont de Suert and Graus (just 80km from Benasque by paved if narrow roads), is unique for its superb Romanesque **cathedral** at the heart of town. Originally a monastic church, it's a three-aisled affair with Lombard apses and an eighteenth-century octagonal belfry notable from afar, but there ends any conformity to pattern. The ornate entrance portal, with six series of columns inside a Renaissance portico, breaches the south wall, because the west end of the nave is occupied by a carved choir and a fine organ, claimed to be one of the best in Europe. Mass is celebrated on the purported sarcophagus of San Ramón, squirming with twelfth-century carvings showing the Nativity and the Flight into Egypt. Immediately below the raised altar area is a vast triple crypt, the central section with worn column capitals but the northerly one graced by brilliant Romanesque frescoes, thought to be painted by the unknown Master of Taüll. Admission is only by guided visit (daily every 45min 11.15am–1.30pm & 4.30–7.15pm; €2), though you can see the cloister and its colonnade (eroded like the crypt's) by patronizing the excellent restaurant (see p.710) installed in the former refectory. When you have finished admiring the cathedral, it's enjoyable just to wander the attractive streets and gawp at the views, literally 360-degree from the *mirador*, which explain why the medieval counts of Ribagorça chose Roda as a stronghold.

A single daily Graus–El Pont de Suert **bus** passes along the valley-floor road 1500m below, but most people come with their own transport. It has become a popular weekend retreat, so you need to book **accommodation** year-round. Top choices include the excellent-value *Hospedaría de Roda*, right on the terraced central plaza (T974 544 554, F974 544 500; ❷), for rooms with a view and all mod cons, and the friendly, English-speaking *Casa Simón* (T974 544 528 or enquire at *Bar Mesón de Roda*), with both en-suite rooms (❷) and 4-bed apartments. For food, the *Mesón de Roda* does decent meals and breakfasts with a ringside seat on the plaza, but the best **restaurant** here is the *Hospedería La Catedral* (reserve on T974 544 545) with *a la carta* so reasonable (€15–18) that there's little point in taking the €11 *menú*.

Travel details

Trains

Huesca to: Canfranc (2 daily; 2hr 40min); Jaca (2 daily; 2hr); Sabiñánigo (2 daily; 1hr 40min); Zaragoza (4 daily; 1hr).
Zaragoza to: Barcelona (14 daily; 4–5hr); Bilbao (4 daily; 5hr); Burgos (5 daily; 4hr); Cáceres (1 daily; 7hr); Cádiz (1 daily; 9hr); Córdoba (2 daily; 6–8hr); Gijón (2 daily; 9hr); Girona (1 daily; 6hr 30min); Huesca (1 daily except Sat; 1hr); Jaca (1 daily except Sat; 3hr 20min); Irún (4 daily; 4hr–5hr 30min); León (3 daily; 6hr); Lleida (10–12 daily; 1hr 40min); Logroño (9 daily; 2hr); Lugo (2 daily; 8–9hr); Madrid (12 daily; 3hr); Málaga (1 daily; 11hr); Medina del Campo (1–3 daily; 3hr 30min–6hr); Orense (2 daily; 10hr); Oviedo (2 daily; 8hr); Palencia (3 daily; 4–5hr); Pamplona (7 daily; 2–3hr); Sabiñánigo (1 daily; 3hr); Salamanca (3 daily; 4hr 30min–8hr); San Sebastián (4 daily; 4hr); Sevilla (1 daily; 7hr); Tarragona (8 daily; 3hr); Teruel (3 daily; 3hr); Valladolid (3 daily; 5–6hr); Vigo (2 daily; 11hr); Vitoria (1 daily; 3hr).

Buses

Aínsa to: Bielsa (daily at 8.45pm, returns 6am next day; 40min); Plan (July–Aug Mon–Sat, otherwise Mon, Wed & Fri only at 8.45pm, returns 5.45am next day; 1hr); Sabiñánigo (1 daily; 2hr).
Barbastro to: Benasque (daily 11am, plus Mon–Sat 5.30pm; 2hr); Boltaña via Aínsa (Mon–Sat at 7.45pm, returns next day 6.45am; July 15–Aug 31 also 11am, returning 3pm; Huesca–Barbastro 10am/6.30pm services link with this); Lleida (6 daily; 1hr 15min).

Huesca to: Barbastro (4–7 daily; 50min); Barcelona (2–4 daily; 4hr 20min); Fraga (1 daily; 2hr 15min); Jaca (4–5 daily; 1hr); Lleida (6 daily; 2hr); Loarre (3 daily; 45min); Monzón (4 daily; 1hr 10min); Pamplona (3 daily; 2hr 50min); Sabiñánigo (4–5 Mon–Sat, 3–4 Sun & hols; 55min); Zaragoza (18 Mon–Fri, 10 Sat, Sun & hols; 1hr).
Jaca to: Ansó via Echo (1 daily; 1hr 40min); Astún/Candanchú (5 daily; 45min); Biescas (1–2 daily; 50min); Canfranc-Estación (5 daily; 30min); Huesca (4–5 daily; 1hr); Pamplona (1–2 daily; 1hr 35min); Sabiñánigo (2 daily; 20min); Zaragoza (3–5 daily; 2hr 15min).
Roda de Isábena to: El Pont de Suert (1 daily Mon–Fri at 4.37pm, returns next day at 6.15am; 1 hr); Graus (1 daily at 7.18am, returns at 4pm; 40min).
Teruel to: Albarracín (1 daily; 2hr); Barcelona (1 daily; 5hr); Cantavieja/La Iglesuela del Cid (1 daily; 2hr 30min/3hr); Cuenca (1 daily; 2hr 30min); Valencia (5 daily; 2hr); Zaragoza (7 daily; 2hr). All services reduce dramatically on Sun.
Zaragoza to: Astorga (1 daily; 7hr 30min); Barcelona (hourly; 3hr 45min); Bilbao (9 daily; 4hr); Burgos (3 daily; 4hr 15min); Cariñena (2 daily; 45min); A Coruña (1 daily; 12hr); Huesca (every half hour; 1hr); Jaca (6 daily; 2hr 15min); León (3 daily; 7hr); Lleida (3 daily; 2hr 30min); Logroño (3 daily; 2hr 15min); Lugo (2 daily; 11hr); Madrid (hourly; 3hr 45min); Palencia (1 daily; 5hr 45 min); Ponferrada (2 daily; 9hr); Salamanca (2 daily; 7hr); Santiago de Compostela (1 daily; 13hr); Soria (2 daily; 3hr); Sos del Rey Católico (1 daily; 2hr 15min); Tarragona (7 daily; 2hr 45min); Valladolid (5 daily; 5hr); Zamora (2 daily; 7hr).

Barcelona

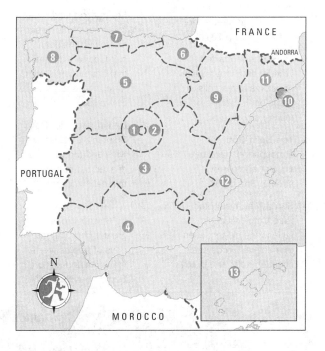

* **Modernisme** The spectacular *modernista* creations dotted around the city by the architect genius Antoni Gaudí and his contemporaries. See p.754

* **The Ramblas** The city's famous thoroughfare, bustling with buskers, vendors and street-performers. See p.731

* **La Boqueria market** Wander among a festival of colours and smells in Barcelona's most famous market city. See p.734

* **The Barri Gòtic** An atmospheric maze of ancient and narrow streets. See p.737

* **Santa Maria del Mar** Pure Catalan-Gothic style in the elegant lines of medieval Barcelona's finest church. See p.744

* **MNAC** Visit the outstanding collection of Romanesque murals housed on the slopes of Montjuïc. See p.750

* **Parc Güell** If you visit only one park, make it this one – an extraordinary flight of fancy. See p.759

* **Montserrat** Catch the cable car or mountain railway up the soaring cliff face to a monastery that has drawn pilgrims for a thousand years. See p.763

* **La Viñatería del Call** Sample typical Catalan wine and tapas in the relaxed surroundings of this neighbourhood bar. See p.767

* **La Mercè** The city's greatest festival, three days of free concerts, fireworks and folklore in September. See p.716

△ Gaudí's Casa Batló

Barcelona

Barcelona, the self-confident and progressive capital of Catalunya, vibrates with life. A thriving port and prosperous commercial centre, the city is almost impossible to exhaust, and even in a lengthy visit you will likely only scrape the surface: it boasts some superb **museums** – including the world-class Museu d'Art de Catalunya, and individual art museums dedicated to Picasso, Joan Miró and Antoni Tàpies – as well as outstanding Gothic and *modernista* (Art Nouveau) **architecture**, most perfectly and eccentrically expressed in the work of Antoni Gaudí. From midday to long after midnight the city's avenues, from the world-famous **Ramblas** to the broad boulevards of the new town, are choked with people strolling, browsing, listening to buskers or watching street performers. On sunny afternoons, the city's **beaches** and promenade beckon thousands of sunbathers and swimmers, cyclists and diners. The energy of Barcelona is boundless, channelled into its industry and business, art and music, political protest and merrymaking. The city is a pleasure at any time of year, but to see it at its best, come during one of the main **festivals** (*festes* in Catalan), listed in the box on p.716. Barcelona has long had the reputation of being the avant-garde capital of Spain, especially in design and architecture, though in the 1980s much of the intellectual impetus passed to Madrid. Hosting the 1992 **Olympics** was an important boost: the enormous popular support for sports in Barcelona (especially for football, the chief focus of the incessant rivalry with Madrid) helped win the nomination in the first place, and the legacy of the games was an outstanding set of new facilities on the hill of Montjuïc and a spruced-up city centre. The **Olympic port and village** development emerged from the disintegrating industrial area of Poble Nou, while the harbour area at the foot of the Ramblas was completely overhauled as part of the revitalized **Port Vell** area. Meanwhile, more change is underway in the **Raval** neighbourhood, around MACBA, the striking modern art museum, where new bars, galleries and restaurants infiltrate the once rundown back streets.

Despite the constant drive for improvement and the high-tech edge to much of recent development, parts of the old town can be disconcertingly dirty and neglected – there is still a great deal of poverty here and drug use is evident. **Petty crime** is rife and it's not unusual for tourists to feel threatened around the seedier areas flanking the Ramblas, particularly at night; see p.56 for common scams. It's best to keep passports and tickets locked up in your hotel, and leave bags under tables with your feet on them in outdoor cafés. Don't be unduly paranoid, however. Although incidents of pickpocketing and bagsnatching are high, Barcelona is rarely any more dangerous than any other big

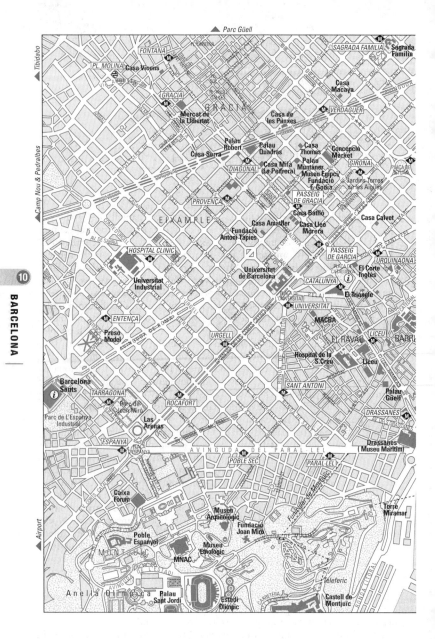
▲ Parc Güell

city and it would be a shame to stick solely to the tourist boulevards, since you'll miss so much. Tapas bars hidden down alleys little changed for a century or two, designer boutiques in gentrified old-town quarters, bargain lunches in workers' taverns, unmarked gourmet restaurants, craft outlets and work-

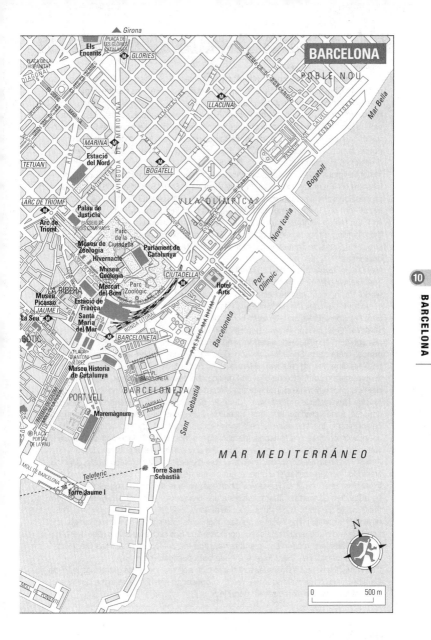

shops, *fin de siècle* cafés, restored medieval palaces, neighbourhood markets and specialist galleries – all are just as much Barcelona as the Ramblas or Gaudí's Sagrada Família.

January
The *Cavalcada de Reis*, on the afternoon of January 5, is when the Three Kings (who distribute Christmas gifts to Spanish children) ride into town. The parade begins at the port at about 5pm; the next day is a public holiday.

February/March *Festes de Santa Eulàlia* (Feb 12; ⓦwww.bcn.es/santa-eulalia) sees a week's worth of music, dances, children's processions, *castellars* and fireworks in honour of one of Barcelona's patron saints. Barcelona's *Festes de Carnaval* (Feb/March) are not as famous as those in Sitges, but there are colourful parades and nearly everyone dresses up in costume.

Easter Religious celebrations and services at churches throughout the city. Special services are on Thursday and Friday in Holy Week at 7–8pm, Saturday at 10pm; there's a procession from the church of Sant Agustí on c/de l'Hospital (El Raval) to La Seu, starting at 4pm on Good Friday. Public holidays on Good Friday and Easter Monday.

April On *Dia de Sant Jordi* (April 23), celebrated as a nationalist holiday in Catalunya, the city fills with roses and books and sweethearts exchange them as gifts. The stalls set up on Plaça de Sant Jaume and the Ramblas to sell them are mobbed all day with customers.

May *Dia del Treball* (May Day/Labour Day; May 1) is a public holiday, with union parades. The *Festival de Música Antiga* attracts medieval and Baroque groups from around the world. Paying concerts are held in larger venues, but free shows can be seen outdoors in old town squares. *Dia de Sant Ponç* (May 11) is celebrated by a market running along c/de l'Hospital (El Raval) with fresh herbs, flowers, cakes, aromatic oils and sweets.

June The *Grec* season (ⓦwww.bcn.es/grec) starts in the last week (and runs throughout July and into August), a performing arts festival incorporating theatre, music and dance. There's also *Sónar* (ⓦwww.sonar.es), a three-day cutting-edge electronic music and multimedia art festival; *Marató de l'Espectacle* (Entertainment Marathon; ⓦwww.marato.com), two days' worth of local theatre, dance, cabaret, music and children's shows which takes place at the Mercat de les Flors theatre; and the *Festa de la Musica* (ⓦwww.fusic.org/fm), when June 21 sees scores of concerts taking place in squares, parks, civic centres and museums all over the city. The city's wildest annual celebration is the *Verbena/Dia de Sant Joan* (June 23/24), the eve and day of Saint John, with bonfires and fireworks (particularly on Montjuïc), drinking and dancing, and watching the sun come up on the beach. The day (24) itself is a public holiday.

August The *Festa Major de Gràcia* (ⓦwww.festamajordegracia.org) sees music, dancing, fireworks, human castles and other events in the neighbourhood's streets and squares.

September *Festa de la Mercè* (ⓦwww.bcn.es/merce) is the city's biggest festival. The parades, free concerts of international stature, fireworks and general mayhem last from the 22nd to the 25th. The 24th is a public holiday.

November/December The *Festival de Jazz* highlights visiting big-name solo artists and bands in the clubs, and hosts street concerts. The *Fira de Santa Llúcia* (Dec 1–22) is a special Christmas market and crafts fair outside the cathedral. Christmas Day (*Nadal*) and St Stephen's Day (*Sant Esteve*; 26) are both public holidays.

Cap d'Any (New Year's Eve) sees street and club parties, and mass gatherings in Pl. de Catalunya and other main squares. You're supposed to eat 12 grapes in the last 12 seconds of the year for 12 months of good luck.

Orientation

Despite a population of over three million, Barcelona is a surprisingly easy place to find your way around. The famous **Ramblas** – a kilometre-long tree-lined avenue mostly given over to pedestrians, pavement cafés and performance artists – splits the old town in two: the medieval **Barri Gòtic** (Gothic Quarter) lies on the eastern side of the avenue, with the traditional *barri* of **Sant Pere** and the nightlife quarter of **La Ribera** beyond; while over on the western side is the edgier, artier neighbourhood of **El Raval**. At the bottom of the Ramblas is the harbour area known as **Port Vell**; walking east from here takes you past the marina, through the old fishing and restaurant quarter of **Barceloneta**, past the **Parc de la Ciutadella** and out along the promenade to the **Port Olímpic** and **Vila Olímpica**. At the top of the Ramblas, **Plaça de Catalunya** marks the start of the nineteenth-century extension of the city – the **Eixample** – a modern, gridded expanse holding most of Barcelona's most celebrated architectural wonders.

Much of what you'll want to see in the city centre – Gothic cathedral, Picasso museum, markets, Gaudí buildings, history museums and art galleries – can all be reached on foot in under twenty minutes from Plaça de Catalunya. A fast metro system takes you directly to more peripheral attractions, like Gaudí's amazing church, the **Sagrada Família**, to the museums, gardens and galleries of **Montjuïc**, or the attractive suburb of **Gràcia** and nearby **Parc Güell**. Out of the city limits, the one day-trip everyone should make is to the mountain-top monastery of **Montserrat**, 40km northwest, not least for the extraordinary ride up to the monastic eyrie by cable car or mountain railway.

Arrival

Barcelona's **airport** is 12km southwest of the city at El Prat de Llobregat and linked to the city by regular train or bus services. The city's **train stations** – Barcelona Sants and Estació de França – **ferry terminal** and the Estació del Nord **bus station** are all more central, with convenient metro stations for onward travel. In most cases, you can be off the plane, train, bus or ferry and in your hotel room within the hour. **Driving** into Barcelona is also reasonably straightforward, with traffic only slow in the morning and evening rush hours (Mon–Fri 7.30–9.30am & 6–8.30pm). Parking, however, is a different matter altogether – rarely easy and not cheap. If your trip is just to the city and its sur-roundings, our advice is not to bother with a car at all.

By air

Barcelona's **airport** (general information ☎932 983 838, flight information ☎902 400 550) has three adjacent terminals (A, B and C) with taxis and airport buses found immediately outside each terminal and the airport train station a short distance away along the overhead walkway. There's an information office in each terminal, as well as ATMs, exchange facilities and car rental office.

The airport **train** (daily 6.13am–10.43pm; journey time 18min; €2.20; ☎902 240 202) runs every thirty minutes to Barcelona Sants and – more usefully if you're staying in the Barri Gòtic – continues to the station at Plaça de Catalunya. There's also a very useful **Aerobus** service (Mon–Fri 5.30am–11pm, Sat & Sun 6am–11.30pm; €3.30), which leaves every twelve minutes, stopping at Plaça d'Espanya, Gran Via de les Corts Catalanes (at c/Comte d'Urgell), Plaça Universitat, Plaça de Catalunya (in front of El Corte Inglés) and Passeig de Gràcia (at c/la Diputació). The bus takes around thirty minutes to reach Plaça de Catalunya, though allow longer in the rush hour. At night, local bus #106 takes over, leaving the airport at 10.15pm, 11.35pm, 12.50am, 2.05am and 3.20am and ending its run at Plaça d'Espanya (south of Barcelona Sants). A **taxi** from the air-port to the centre costs roughly €20–25, including the airport surcharge.

By train

The main station for national and some international arrivals is **Barcelona Sants** (ⓂSants-Estació), 3km west of the centre, which has a train and advanced booking office (daily 6.30am–10.30pm), tourist information, exchange and car rental offices. From Sants, metro line 3 runs direct to Liceu for the Ramblas and Catalunya for Plaça de Catalunya.

Estació de França (ⓂBarceloneta), next to Parc de la Ciutadella, east of the centre, handles many of the long-distance arrivals and departures: essentially, this means Talgo services from Madrid, Sevilla and Málaga, Intercity services from other major Spanish cities, and international trains from Paris, Zurich, Milan and Geneva. Many trains stop at both Sants and França – check the timetable first. From França either take metro line 4 from nearby Barceloneta, or simply walk for five minutes up into the Barri Gòtic.

Other possible arrival points by regional and commuter trains are the stations at: **Plaça de Catalunya**, at the top of the Ramblas (for trains from coastal towns north of the city, the airport, and towns on the Puigcerdà–Vic line); **Plaça d'Espanya** (from Montserrat); and **Passeig de Gràcia** (from Lleida, Tarragona, Port Bou, Figueres and Girona).

By bus and ferry

The main bus terminal, used by most international, long-distance and provincial buses, is the **Estació del Nord** on Avinguda Vilanova (main entrance on c/Ali-Bei; ☎932 656 508; ⓂArc de Triomf), three blocks north of Parc de la Ciutadella. There's a bus information desk on the ground floor (daily 7am–9pm), with the ticket offices above at street level (advanced booking advised). Intercity and international departures also leave from the smaller station just behind Estació Sants at Plaça Joan Peiró (ⓂSants-Estació/Plaça de Sants).

Ferries from the Balearics dock at the **Estació Marítima**, Moll de Barcelona, Port Vell, located at the bottom of Avinguda Paral.lel (ⓂDrassanes), not far from the Ramblas. There are ticket offices inside the terminal. Services are on regular ferries or the quicker, and more expensive, high-speed ferries or catamarans. For onward journeys, buy tickets inside the terminal from: Trasmediterranea ☎902 454 645, Ⓦwww.trasmediterranea.com, to Palma de Mallorca, Mahón and Ibiza; Iscomar Ferry ☎902 119 128, Ⓦwww.iscomar.com, to Palma de Mallorca; or Umifasa ☎902 454 645, Ⓦwww.umifasa.com, to Ibiza. Navi Grandi Veloci (☎934 439 898, Ⓦwww1.gnv.it) has a year-round service to Genoa, Italy. The ferries get very crowded in July and August – book ahead.

By car

Driving into Barcelona along any one of the *autopistes*, head for the Ronda Littoral, the southern half of the city's ring road, and follow signs for "Port Vell", the main exit for the old town. There are many indoor **car parks** in the city centre, linked to display boards that indicate where there are free spaces. Although convenient, these can be expensive (usually €17.50–20 for 24 hours). With the exception of the blue meter-zones in the central section of the Eixample, **street parking** is free, but it is not permitted in most of the old town, and it can be tough to find spaces, particularly in areas like Gràcia. Don't be tempted to double-park or leave your car in loading zones – the cost of being towed can exceed €120, and no mercy is shown to foreign-plated vehicles.

Information and maps

The main tourist office is under the southeast corner of **Plaça de Catalunya**, down the steps (daily 9am–9pm; ☎906 301 282 if calling from within Spain, ☎+34 933 698 730 from abroad, ☻www.barcelonaturisme.com). There are also tourist offices at both **airport** terminals (daily 9am–9pm); at **Barcelona Sants** (April–Sept daily 8am–8pm, otherwise Mon–Fri 8am–8pm, Sat, Sun & holidays 8am–2pm); and at **Plaça de Sant Jaume**, entrance at c/Ciutat 2 (Mon–Fri 9am–8pm, Sat 10am–8pm, Sun & holidays 10am–2pm). There is also a summer information **kiosk** (July–Sept) in front of the Sagrada Família and wandering **tourist information officers** in red jackets in most touristed areas. You can pick up a free large-scale **map** of the city and a public transport map from any of the above offices, plus brochures and tour information. *Barcelona: The Rough Guide Map* is also a good investment.

For information about travelling in Catalunya go to **Palau Robert**, Pg. de Gràcia 107 (Mon–Sat 10am–7.30pm, Sun & hols 10am–2.30pm, ☎932 384 000). The **Institut de Cultura**, Palau de la Virreina, Ramblas 99 (Mon–Sat 10am–8pm, Sun 11am–3pm, ☎933 017 775), provides fliers and advance information on everything that's happening in the city as well as ticket sales. The *ajuntament* has a website with an English-language version (☻www.bcn.es) for tracking down everything from sports centres to festival dates. There is also the city's **Informació Metropolitana** line (Mon–Sat 8am–10pm; ☎010; some English spoken), which can help with information about transport and other public services.

City transport and tours

The best way to get around Barcelona is on foot, using the city's excellent transport system as needed. The system comprises the metro, buses, local trains

---

Discount cards

If you're going to be in the city more than a day or two, and want to make the most of your sightseeing, consider buying one of the following cards:

The city tourist offices sell the **Barcelona Card** (1 day, €16.25; 2 days, €19.25; 3 days, €22.25; 4 days, €24; or 5 days, €26), which gives free travel on public transport, discounts on the airport Aerobus and the Montjuïc cable car, and big reductions on museum entry and in some shops and restaurants.

The **Articket** (€15; valid three months) provides half-price admission into six major art centres and galleries (MNAC, MACBA, CCCB, Fundació Antoni Tàpies, Fundació Joan Miró, and Centre Cultural Caixa Catalunya at La Pedrera) – available at participating centres and galleries, and at Plaça de Catalunya and Barcelona Sants tourist offices.

The **Ruta del Modernisme** (€3; valid one month), a map and guide to the city's *modernista* sites, also gets you fifty-percent discounts at four specific attractions (saving you around €9). Currently, the discounted attractions are the tour of the Palau de la Música Catalana and entry to the Fundació Antoni Tàpies, the Museu de Zoologia and the Museu d'Art Modern (though as this last collection will relocate to the Museu Nacional d'Art de Catalunya at Montjuïc in 2004, it's unclear if it will continue to be included in the *Ruta*). In addition, you can join a free English-language tour of the facades at the Mansana de la Discòrdia. The card is available at the Centre del Modernisme in the Casa Amatller, Pg. de Gràcia 41 (see p.755).

BARCELONA TRANSPORT

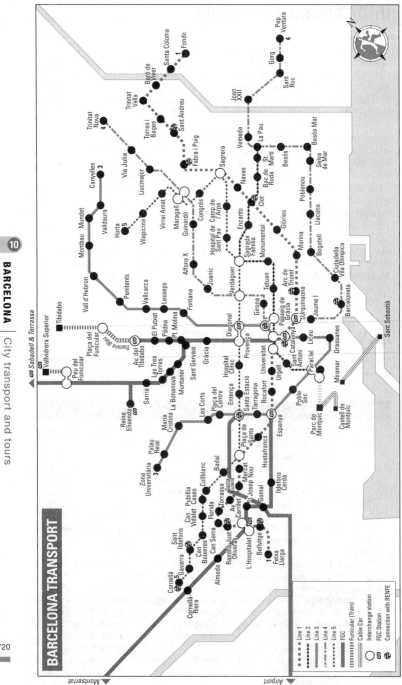

Line 1
Line 2
Line 3
Line 4
Line 5
FGC
Funicular (Tram)
Cable Car
Interchange station
FGC Station
Connection with RENFE

◂ Montserrat

◂ Airport

◂ Sabadell & Terrassa

and a network of funicular railways and cable cars. There's an invaluable free public transport map (*Guia d'Autobusos Urbans de Barcelona*), usually available at any city tourist office and also at the Transports Metropolitans de Barcelona (TMB) customer services centres at Sants train station, and Diagonal, Sagrada Família and Universitat metro stations. The map and ticket information is also posted at major bus stops and all metro stations. Detailed information is available by telephone (℡010) and on the Internet (ⓦwww.tmb.net).

There's a **flat fare** on both metro and buses of €1.05 per journey, but it works out cheaper to buy a **targeta** (ticket-strip) from metro station ticket offices. The **T-10** ("tay day-oo" in Catalan) gives you ten journeys for €5.80, and can be used by more than one person at a time – just feed it through the barrier for each person travelling. It covers the metro, buses (including night buses), funiculars and regional train lines within the city (passes are also available for outlying zones). Changing trains or buses within 75 minutes counts as one journey with the T-10 (you'll have to re-punch the ticket but it only registers once). There's also a single-person, one-day **T-Dia** ("tay dee-ah") for €4.40 for unlimited travel within Zone 1. Anyone caught without a valid ticket is liable to an **on-the-spot fine** of €40.

The metro and buses

The quickest way of getting around Barcelona is by the modern and efficient **metro**, which runs on five lines; entrances are marked with a red diamond sign. Its hours of operation are Monday to Thursday 5am to midnight; Friday, Saturday and the day before a public holiday 5am to 2am; Sunday and public holidays 6am to midnight.

Bus routes are easy to master if you get hold of a copy of the transport map and remember that the routes are colour-coded: **city-centre buses** are red and always stop at one of three central squares (Catalunya, Universitat or Urquinaona); **cross-city buses** are yellow; green buses run on all the **peripheral routes** outside the city centre; and **night buses** are blue (and always stop near or in Plaça de Catalunya). In addition, the route is marked at each bus stop, along with a timetable – useful bus routes are detailed in the text. Most buses operate daily, roughly from 4/5am until 10.30pm, though some lines stop earlier and some run on until after midnight. The night buses fill in the gaps on all the main routes, with services every twenty to sixty minutes from around 10pm to 4am.

Trains, funiculars and cable cars

The city has a commuter **train line** run by the Ferrocarrils de la Generalitat de Catalunya (FGC; ℡932 051 515, ⓦwww.fgc.es), with its main stations at Plaça de Catalunya and Plaça d'Espanya. You'll need this going to Montserrat and Tibidabo.

A train-trolley, the **Tren Turístic de Montjuïc**, trundles around the Montjuïc area during the summer months, while several **funicular railways** still operate in the city, most notably to Montjuïc (see p.748) and Tibidabo (p.762). Weekend visits to Tibidabo also combine a funicular trip with a ride on the antique **tram**, the Tramvia Blau. There are also two **cable-car** (*telefèric*) rides you can make: from Barceloneta across the harbour to Montjuïc (p.746), and then from the top station of the Montjuïc funicular right the way up to the castle (p.753). Both aerial rides are worth doing for the views alone.

Taxis

Black-and-yellow **taxis** (with a green roof light on when available for hire) are inexpensive and plentiful. There's a minimum charge of €1.80 and then it's around €0.75 per kilometre. Taxis won't take more than four people and charge extra for baggage and on public holidays, for trips to the airport, and for a multitude of other things, but they have meters so prices are generally transparent; ask for a receipt (*rebut*) if you wish to ensure that the price is fair. Cabs can be called on the following numbers (though English is unlikely to be spoken): ☎933 577 755; ☎933 001 100; ☎932 250 000; ☎933 033 033; ☎933 300 300; ☎934 208 088.

City tours

Although you can find your way around the city easily enough with a map and a guidebook, taking a tour is a good way to orientate yourself on arrival. The Bus Turístic (tour bus) can drop you outside virtually every attraction in the city. Alternatively, Barcelona has some particularly good walking tours, showing you parts of the old town you might not find otherwise, while bike tours and sightseeing boats offer a different view of the city.

Barcelona Walking Tours ☎906 301 282, ⓦwww.barcelonaturisme.com. Advance booking advised (at Pl. de Catalunya tourist office, ⓂCatalunya) for the historical walking tour of the Barri Gòtic (Sat & Sun all year, in English at 10am; plus April–Sept Thurs & Fri at 10am; €7.50); tour lasts 90min. Also "Picasso Tours" (Sat & Sun all year, in English at 10.30am; €10, includes entry to Picasso Museum).

Bus Turístic Year-round, hop-on-and-off sightseeing service (daily 9am–7pm; departures every 6–30min), starting at Plaça de Catalunya and linking all the main sights and tourist destinations; a full circuit takes 2hr. Tickets cost €15 for one day, €19 for two days, and also give discounts at various sights and on the tram to Tibidabo; buy on board the bus or at the Pl. de Catalunya, Barcelona Sants or Pl. de Sant Jaume tourist offices.

Catamaran Orsom ☎932 258 260, ⓦwww.barcelona-orsom.com. Barcelona from the sea: three daily departures (€12) from the quayside opposite the Columbus statue, at the bottom of the Ramblas (ⓂDrassanes) – there's a ticket kiosk there, or phone the day before. Also summer evening jazz cruises (June, July & Aug; €12).

Mike's Bike Tours ☎933 013 612, ⓔinfo@mikesbiketoursbarcelona.com. Four-hour city bike tours (March to mid-Dec 1–2 daily; €22, bike included) through the old town, port area, beach and to the Sagrada Família, meeting at the Columbus monument at the bottom of the Ramblas (ⓂDrassanes).

My Favourite Things ☎933 295 351 or 637 265 405, ⓦwww.myft.net. Highly individual tours, whether it's bohemian Barcelona, furniture and fashion, or where and what the locals eat. Tours (in English) cost €25 per person and last 4hr. Departures are flexible, so contact them for information.

Travel Bar c/Boqueria 27, Barri Gòtic ☎933 425 252, ⓦwww.travelbar.com; ⓂLiceu. The travellers' bar organizes a variety of youth-oriented tours, including an old-town walking tour (€12), evening bar crawl (€23, includes some drinks), tapas bar tour (€18, includes some food), bike tour (€20) and kayaking on the harbour (June–Sept only; €23).

Accommodation

Hotel rooms in Barcelona are among the most expensive in Spain and finding a vacancy can be very difficult, especially at Easter, in summer and around the time of any festivals or trade fairs. You're advised to book in advance – several weeks at peak times – especially if you want to stay at a particular place. The absolute cheapest double rooms in a simple family-run **pension**, sharing an outside shower, cost around €30, though for anything bearable (and certainly for anything with an en-suite shower) you'll really need to budget on a minimum of €40–50 a night. If you want air conditioning, a TV, soundproofing and an elevator to your room, there's a fair amount of choice around the €60–90 mark, while up to €150 gets you the run of decent **hotels** in most city areas. For Barcelona's most fashionable and exclusive hotels, room rates are set at European capital norms – from €250–400 a night. Right at the other end of the scale is the burgeoning number of city **youth hostels**, where a dorm bed goes for between €15 and €20.

Barcelona's tourist offices can supply accommodation lists, though these don't usually include the very cheapest places. You can also book accommodation (no commission) at the tourist offices, but only in person on the day – they do not make advance reservations, nor do they have a telephone reservation service. However, you can **book online** through the tourist office website (ⓦwww.barcelonaturisme.com), or with Barcelona On-Line (ⓦwww .barcelona-online.es; also phone reservations on ☎902 887 017). Or contact My Favourite Things (see "City tours" opposite), who arrange quality *pensión* and bed-and-breakfast city accommodation.

Hotels and hostales

Most of the budget accommodation in Barcelona is to be found in the **Barri Gòtic**, though what may be atmospheric by day can seem plain threatening after dark. As a general rule, anything right on the **Ramblas** itself or north of **the cathedral**, on the east side, should be reliable and safe – though if you hanker after a Ramblas view in particular, you're going to pay heavily for the privilege. The best hunting ground for out-and-out budget accommodation is between the Ramblas and **Plaça de Sant Jaume**, in the area bordered by c/Escudellers and c/Boqueria, where there are loads of options, from basic *pensiones* to three-star hotels. Further east, in **La Ribera**, are a number of safely sited budget and mid-range options, handy for the Born nightlife area. The other main area for budget accommodation is on the west side of the Ramblas in **El Raval**, which still has its rough edges but is changing fast. Look on c/de Sant Pau, c/de l'Hospital, and c/Junta del Comerç for a mix of bargains and restored mansions. The top end of the Ramblas, around **Plaça de Catalunya**, is a safe and central place to stay – with the added advantage of being reached directly from the airport by train or bus. North of here, you're in the **Eixample** – the gridded modern city – whose central spine, **Passeig de Gràcia** – has some of the city's most luxurious hotels, often housed in converted palaces and mansions. There are more possibilities in the **Gràcia** district, which – though further out – is easily reached by metro.

BARCELONA | Accommodation

The Ramblas

The further up the Ramblas you go, towards Plaça de Catalunya, the quieter, more pleasant and more expensive the places become. Alternatively, there are several places on Plaça Reial, halfway down the Ramblas, a nineteenth-century square dotted with palm trees and arcaded walks. Although perfectly fine during the day, the square can have a slight edge after dark – be careful with money and valuables, particularly in the streets to the south of here.

Benidorm Ramblas 37 ☎933 022 054; Ⓜ️Drassanes. Refurbished *hostal* rooms opposite Plaça Reial that offer real value for money. Rooms available for one to five people, with bathtubs, showers and a Ramblas view if you're lucky. ❷

Lloret Ramblas 125 ☎933 173 366, ☎933 019 283; Ⓜ️Catalunya. A grand building whose large air-conditioned rooms are better value than most in this category – lots have Ramblas views. Continental breakfast costs €3. ❹

Mare Nostrum Ramblas 67, entrance on c/Sant Pau ☎933 185 340, ☎934 123 069; Ⓜ️Liceu. Cheery two-star *hostal* whose English-speaking management offers comfortable double or triple/family rooms with satellite TV, a/c, some with balconies. Breakfast included. ❹

Marítima Ramblas 4, entrance on Ptge. de la Banca ☎933 023 152; Ⓜ️Drassanes. Thirteen threadbare rooms, some with shower cubicles plonked in the corner, plus self-service laundry (€5) and luggage storage service (€2). No credit cards. ❶

Noya Ramblas 133, 1° ☎933 014 831; Ⓜ️Catalunya. A popular stop for young travellers, above a café-restaurant. Simple *pensión* rooms – hot in summer, chilly in winter – all share a bathroom. ❷

Oriente Ramblas 45 ☎933 022 558, ☎www.husa.es; Ⓜ️Liceu. If you're looking for somewhere traditional but comfortable on the Ramblas, this historic three-star hotel is your best bet. ❼

Roma Reial Pl. Reial 11 ☎933 020 366, ☎www.todobarcelona.com/romareial; Ⓜ️Liceu. Always busy, though sometimes with noisy groups. Bare-walled rooms all have smartish bathrooms, heating and a/c, and some can sleep up to four. Breakfast available, but best not to bother. ❹

Carrer de Ferran and Carrer de la Boqueria

These two streets, and the alleys that run between them, are a good place to start for budget possibilities back from the Ramblas.

California c/Rauric 14 ☎933 177 766, ☎www.seker.es/hotel_california; Ⓜ️Liceu. Tucked down a side street crossing c/de Ferran, this friendly hotel is popular with gay travellers. Rooms are nicely colour-coordinated, and have a/c and full bathrooms; breakfast included. ❺

Dalí c/Boqueria 12 ☎ & ☎933 185 580, Ⓔpensiondali@wanadoo.es; Ⓜ️Liceu. The terracotta-tiled facade, sculpted doorway and stained glass suggest a grandeur long lost. However, the rooms themselves are perfectly serviceable; some have en-suite bathrooms, and there's a common room and Internet access. ❷

Fernando c/Ferran 31 ☎933 017 993, ☎www.barcelona-on-line.es/fernando; Ⓜ️Liceu. Light, modern rooms with sinks and TV, with or without en-suite shower. Dorm accommodation also available (€19) in four- to eight-bed rooms; some have attached bathroom, and all have lockers. ❷

Palermo c/Boqueria 21 ☎ & ☎933 024 002; Ⓜ️Liceu. Friendly, fairly spacious *pensión* with clean, high-ceilinged rooms with or without bath. It's a bit overpriced in July and August, but outside these months rates come down by up to 25 percent. ❹

Around Plaça de Sant Miquel and Plaça de Sant Jaume

The streets between and around the Barri Gòtic's two central squares are rather more attractive than most in the area and contain several decent budget hotels.

Avinyó c/d'Avinyó 42 ☎933 187 945, ☎www.hostalavinyo.com; Ⓜ️Jaume I. Rooms are lighter than you'd expect on this street, either freshly painted or tiled and with a ceiling fan; some have little sofas. Rooms with private bath available. Street-side rooms are noisy at weekends. No credit cards. ❷

Canadiense Bxda. de Sant Miquel 1, 1° ☎933 017 461; Ⓜ️Jaume I. A friendly couple (no English spoken) oversees a decidedly old-school *hostal*. Everything has seen better days, but the clean rooms all have sinks, showers and a washing line strung at each window. One cheap single available. No credit cards. ❸

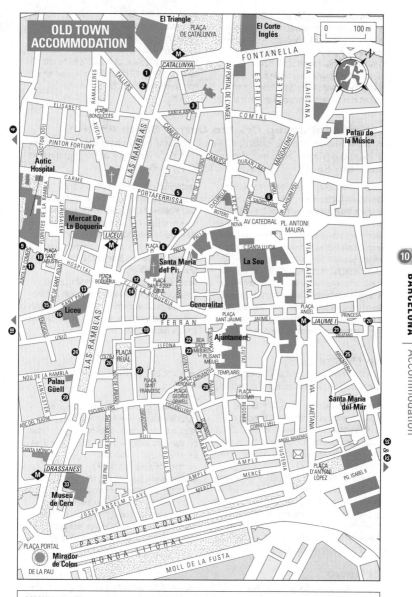

ACCOMMODATION

Avinyó	30	España	16	Lloret	2	Oriente	24
Banys Orientals	25	Fernando	17	Lourdes	20	Orleans	32
Barcelona Mar	18	Gat Raval	4	Malda	7	Palermo	12
Benidorm	29	Gothic Point	21	Mare Nostrum	13	Peninsular	15
California	19	Itaca	6	Mari-Luz	28	Rembrandt	5
Canadiense	22	Jardí	8	Marítima	33	Roma Reial	27
Center Ramblas	9	Kabul	26	Noya	1	Sant Agustí	10
Dalí	14	Levante	23	Nuevo Colón	31	Santa Anna	3
						Terrassa	11

Levante Bxda. de Sant Miquel 2 ☎933 179 565, ⊛www.hostallevante.com; ⓜJaume I. A backpackers' favourite with fifty rooms – singles, doubles, twins, triples – on two rambling floors. Communal bathrooms get pretty busy, staff can be scatty, and the rather noisy comings and goings aren't to everyone's liking. Six apartments with kitchen also available, sleeping 5 to 7 people (€30

per person a day). ❸
Mari-Luz c/de la Palau 4, 2° ☎ & ☏933 173 463, ⓔpensionmariluz@menta.net; ⓜJaume I. Six inexpensive doubles with shared bathrooms set in a secluded old palace. As it's also a hostel with 35 dorm beds (€13–16 depending on season) it's a tight squeeze when full. ❷

Plaça Sant Josep Oriol to Carrer Santa Anna

Around and beyond the cathedral, from Plaça Sant Josep Oriol northwards, the price and quality of accommodation take a general step up. Carrer Portaferrissa and Carrer Santa Anna, in particular, have several decent choices.

Jardí Pl. Sant Josep Oriol 1 ☎933 015 900, ⓔhoteljardi@retemail.es; ⓜLiceu. The location sells this small hotel – overlooking the very attractive Pl. del Pi – which explains the steep prices for rooms that, though smart and modern, can be a bit bare and poky. Breakfast costs €5; advance reservations essential. ❺
Malda c/del Pi 5 ☎933 173 002; ⓜLiceu. One of the cheapest deals in the centre (enter through the arcade), where rooms in a rambling, old-fashioned *hostal* share communal bathrooms. There's a stuffed fox in the lounge and some very questionable paintings – family heirlooms all. No credit cards. ❶

Rembrandt c/Portaferrissa 23 ☎ & ☏933 181 011; ⓜLiceu. Rooms (with and without bathroom) have a balcony or little patio, while larger ones are more versatile – one has a gallery with single bed above the double, while a rather Victorian-looking "suite" (two rooms split by hanging net curtain) can sleep two or four. Breakfast (€3), beer and fans available. ❸
Santa Anna c/Santa Anna 23 ☎933 012 246; ⓜCatalunya. Attractive little rooms (with and without private shower room) on two floors, many with a small balcony onto the street or the rear. Singles are box-like but cheap. ❷

La Ribera

Accommodation in **La Ribera** varies in quality, but if you want to be close to the Born nightlife there's no better place to stay.

Banys Orientals c/Argenteria 37 ☎932 688 460, ⊛www.hotelbanysorientals.com; ⓜJaume I. Funky boutique hotel with stylish rooms at decent prices. Hardwood floors, crisp white sheets, urban chic decor. Advance reservations essential; breakfast (€9) not included. ❺
Lourdes c/Princesa 14 ☎933 193 372; ⓜJaume I. Absolutely basic backpackers' choice – "habitaciones confortables" is pushing it a bit – but cheap as chips, especially for rooms without a bath. No credit cards. ❷
Nuevo Colón Avgda. Marquès de l'Argentera 19, 1° ☎933 195 077, ⊛www.hostalnuevocolom.com;

ⓜBarceloneta. A really pleasant *hostal*, in the hands of the same friendly family for over 70 years, offering spacious, hotel-quality rooms kitted out with good beds and double-glazing. Also three self-catering apartments available (€150 per night), which sleep up to six. ❸
Orleans Avgda. Marquès de l'Argentera 13, 1° ☎933 197 382, ⊛www.hostalorleans.com; ⓜBarceloneta. Spick-and-span rooms on two floors of a tranquil, homely family-run *hostal*. Front rooms with balconies face França station and the busy main road, so you'll get some noise. ❸

El Raval

There are lots of places to stay in El Raval, though the surviving red-light district doesn't make it the most enticing part of Barcelona. However, the places listed below are all reliable and mostly only a minute or two's walk off the Ramblas.

España c/de Sant Pau 9–11 ☎933 181 758, ⊛www.hotelespanya.com; ⓜLiceu. Designed by Domènech i Montaner; the highlight of this elegant hotel is the splendid *modernista* dining room.

Rooms are hardly in the same league, but some give onto a delightful internal patio-garden. Breakfast included. ❺
Gat Raval c/Joaquín Costa 44, 2° ☎934 816 670,

@www.gataccommodation.com; ⓂUniversitat. At
the boutique end of the budget market, with a
lime-green theme, each room sports folding chair,
sink, TV, fan/heating, and signature back-lit street
photographs/artwork. Only 6 of the 24 rooms have
en-suite showers, but communal facilities are
good. At the similar nearby sister hotel, *Gat Xino*,
c/Hospital 149–155, all the rooms are en suite. ❹
Peninsular c/de Sant Pau 34 ☎933 023 138,
☎934 123 699; ⓂLiceu. An interesting old building originally belonging to a priestly order, which
explains the slightly cell-like quality of the hotel
rooms (with and without private bathroom). There's
an attractive inner courtyard, while breakfast is
served in the arcaded dining room. ❸

Sant Agustí Pl. Sant Agusti 3 ☎933 181 658,
@www.hotelsa.com; ⓂLiceu. Barcelona's oldest
hotel is housed in a seventeenth-century building,
with balconies overlooking the vast bulk of the
namesake church. Reservations essential.
Breakfast included. ❼
La Terrassa c/Junta del Comerç 11 ☎933 025
174, ☎933 012 188; ⓂLiceu. Clean and friendly
backpackers' favourite, with plain rooms with a
partition shower-toilet – though the owners are
putting in proper little bathrooms, and adding big
closets and double-glazed windows. Prices are a
bargain, especially for the new rooms. ❷

Plaça Universitat and around

On the northern borders of El Raval, this is a useful location – not quite old
town, not quite Eixample, but easy to reach from either.

Australia Ronda Universitat 11, 4º ☎933 174 177,
@www.residenciaustralia.com; ⓂUniversitat.
Always busy – try at least a fortnight in advance in
summer. It's a bit old-fashioned, though rooms will
take a third person for an extra €12, and they also
offer a roomier one-bed suite with lounge, fridge
and coffee-making machine. ❸, suite ❹
Cèntric c/Casanova 13 ☎934 267 573 or 902 014
881, @www.hostalcentric.com; ⓂUniversitat.
Hotel-quality rooms for *pensión* prices; it's near
c/de Floridabianca. All rooms feature new furniture,
decent beds and plenty of light. There's a sunny
terrace at the rear, and Internet access. ❹
Gravina c/Gravina 12 ☎933 016 868,

@www.hotelh10gravina.com; ⓂUniversitat. The
old-style facade deceives, for this is a contemporary update with high comfort levels – toiletries,
robes and hairdriers in the bathrooms, prints and
artwork in the sharply styled public areas, and a
good buffet breakfast included. ❽
Meson Castilla c/Valldonzella 5 ☎933 182 182 or
☎902 100 710, @www.husa.es; ⓂUniversitat.
Contemporary Barcelona outside, Fifties rural Spain
inside, with large, airy rooms (some with terraces)
filled with country furniture, a vast rustic dining
room (buffet breakfast included) and lovely tiled
rear patio. ❼

Around Plaça de Catalunya and Plaça Urquinaona

Here, near the top of the Ramblas, prices tend to be higher than in the old town,
but it's less frenetic and with a safer feel. Plus you're within easy walking distance
of either old-town bars and restaurants or Eixample architecture and galleries.

Duques de Bergara c/Bergara 11 ☎933 015
151, @www.hoteles-catalonia.es; ⓂCatalunya.
Bright rooms with parquet floors, brown marble
bathrooms and little sitting areas – upgrade to a
junior suite and you get jet-black marble and a
Jacuzzi bath, lounge area and huge TV. Buffet
breakfast is €12. ❽, suites ❾
Ginebra Rambla de Catalunya 1, 3º ☎933 171
063, @hotelginebra@telefonica.net; ⓂCatalunya.
Good-sized rooms with nice old furniture, bathrooms you can turn round in for a change, pot
plants, cappuccino machine and a small bar. Ask
for one of the four rooms with a balcony. ❹
Girona c/Girona 24 ☎932 650 259,
@www.hostalgirona.com; ⓂUrquinaona. Rug-laid
corridors, polished wooden doors, paintings and

restored furniture announce a family *pensión* kept
with care. A fair choice of rooms, either with shower and loo or (for €8 less) just shower, and some
bathroom-less singles, too. ❸
Goya c/de Pau Claris 74 ☎933 022 565;
ⓂUrquinaona. A dozen older-style *hostal* rooms,
not all en suite, and seven more on the "boutique
hotel" floor below, fitted with laminate flooring, a/c,
stylish bed linen and modern bathrooms. Hostal
❸, hotel ❹
Ribagorza c/Trafalgar 39/Méndez Núñez 17, 1º
☎933 191 968, ☎933 191 247; ⓂUrquinaona or
Arc de Triomf. Mixed bag of *hostal* rooms overseen
by an enthusiastic owner. Most have mosaic-tile
floors and sinks, and though the very cheapest are
internal, others have balconies and en-suite bath-

rooms. **②**

Rondas c/Girona 4, 3° ☎932 325 102;
Ⓜ︎Urquinaona. About as cheap as you'll find in the
Eixample. Good for lone travellers as there are four
singles; otherwise the choice is between six
cramped doubles, some of which are en suite. No
credit cards. **②**

San Remo c/del Bruc 20, 2° ☎933 021 989,
☎933 010 774; Ⓜ︎Urquinaona. The doubles aren't

a bad size for the money and the small, tiled bathrooms are pretty nice for this price range. **③**

Pensió 2000 c/Sant Pere Més Alt 6, 1° ☎933 107
466. Ⓜ︎Urquinaona. Six huge rooms in a mansion
apartment strewn with books, plants and pictures.
A third person could easily share most rooms
(€18 supplement), while breakfast (€3) is served
in your room or on the patio. **③**

Eixample

Some of the city's best hotels are found in the Eixample. But if you know
where to look you can still score a bargain – and not necessarily sacrifice any
character or atmosphere.

Claris c/Pau Claris 150 ☎934 876 262, ☻www
.derbyhotels.es; Ⓜ︎Passeig de Gràcia. Very select,
very palatial five-star hotel, from the incense-scent-
ed marble lobby complete with authentic Roman
mosaics, to the appealing rooms ranged around a
soaring atrium. Prices are on the ludicrous side (at
least €260) though they soften at weekends. **⑨**

Condes de Barcelona Pg. de Gràcia 73–75 ☎934
674 780, ☻www.condesdebarcelona.com;
Ⓜ︎Passeig de Gràcia. Straddling two sides of
c/Mallorca, the *Condes* is fashioned from two former palaces – rooms are classily styled, some with
Jacuzzi and balcony, and some with views of
Gaudí's La Pedrera. Also a pretty roof terrace and
plunge pool, bar and restaurant. **⑨**

Eden c/Balmes 55 ☎934 526 620; Ⓜ︎Passeig de
Gràcia. Eager-to-please staff and a wide choice of
simply furnished rooms, but overpriced given its
student-dorm atmosphere and occasional rough
edges. Plenty of facilities, though, including TV/DVD

lounge, free Internet access, 24-hr reception, laundry and coffee machine. **③**

Neutral Rambla de Catalunya 42 ☎934 8763 90,
☎934 876 848; Ⓜ︎Passeig de Gràcia. Fixtures and
fittings are a bit on the tired side, but you can't
fault the price. Front rooms with avenue views are
noisy, but they have TV, shower or bath, and are
available for two to four people. **③**

Oliva Pg. de Gràcia 32, 4° ☎934 881 789 or ☎934
880 162; Ⓜ︎Passeig de Gràcia. Ride the antique lift
to the top floor for an Eixample bargain – marble
floors, high ceilings and plenty of light. Be warned
that the street noise permeates, even at these rari-
fied levels. No credit cards. **③**

Windsor Rambla de Catalunya 84 ☎932 151 198;
Ⓜ︎Passeig de Gràcia. Small, genteel *hostal* set in a
lovingly furnished building on the Eixample's nicest
avenue. Fifteen rooms, all with en-suite shower
and toilet, all often booked days in advance. No
credit cards. **④**

Gràcia

Staying in Gràcia, you're further away from the sights but the trade-off is the
pleasant local neighbourhood atmosphere and the proximity to some excellent
bars, restaurants and clubs.

Norma c/Gran de Gràcia 87, 2° ☎932 374 478;
Ⓜ︎Fontana. The narrow, down-at-heel stairway
leads to something better – half a dozen little
rooms giving on to the internal patio (the quietest
choice) or the street. **②**

San Medín c/Gran de Gràcia 125 ☎932 173 068,
☎934 154 410; Ⓜ︎Fontana. Better looking inside
than out, this friendly and well-located *pensión* has
twelve rooms, some with shower. **③**

Valls c/Laforja 82, 2° ☎932 096 967; Ⓜ︎Fontana.
Just west of Gràcia (past c/d'Aribau) and kept

spick-and-span, this family-run place makes a
clean, quiet base in a residential neighbourhood
(5min from Via Augusta). English is spoken and
breakfast included. **③**

Via Augusta Via Augusta 63 ☎932 179 250;
Ⓜ︎Fontana. Decently priced two-star hotel. Rooms
at the front are potentially noisy, but there's a
breakfast salon on the third floor (continental €4,
buffet €8) and you're handily poised for the neighbourhood's sights and attractions. **⑤**

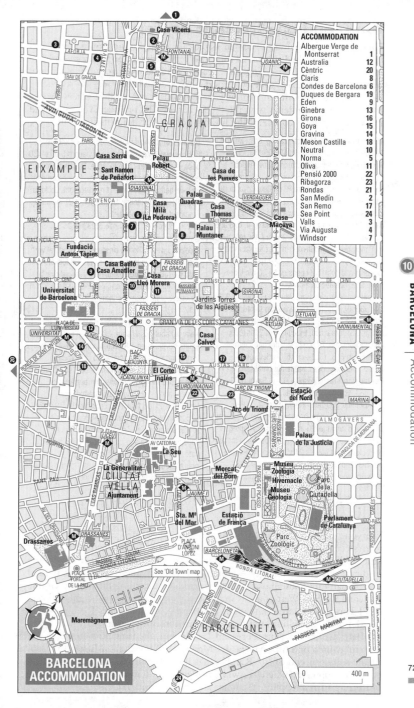

ACCOMMODATION

Albergue Verge de Montserrat	1
Australia	12
Cèntric	20
Claris	8
Condes de Barcelona	6
Duques de Bergara	19
Eden	9
Ginebra	13
Girona	16
Goya	15
Gravina	14
Meson Castilla	18
Neutral	10
Norma	5
Oliva	11
Pensió 2000	22
Ribagorza	23
Rondas	21
San Medín	2
San Remo	17
Sea Point	24
Valls	3
Via Augusta	4
Windsor	7

BARCELONA ACCOMMODATION

0   400 m

Youth and backpacker hostels

There are lots of central hostels in Barcelona, though you should always call ahead to reserve a bed as most of them are very popular. You won't save a huge amount of money over taking the cheapest available *pensión* room, but hostel facilities are usually pretty good, with Internet access, kitchens, common/games rooms and laundry as standard. Rates at most places drop a few euros in the winter. Always use the lockers or safes provided. You only need an IYHF card for a couple of the hostels, but you can join on check-in.

Albergue Verge de Montserrat Pg. de la Mare de Déu del Coll 41–51, Horta ☎932 105 151, ⓦwww.tujuca.com; ⓂVallcarca (follow Avgda. República d'Argentina, c/Viaducte de Vallcarca and then signs) or bus #28 from Pl. de Catalunya stops just across the street. Stunning converted mansion with gardens, terrace and city views – a long way out, but close to Parc Güell. Dorms sleep 4, 6, 8 and 12, plus lockers, left-luggage, laundry and Internet. IYHF membership required; 5-night maximum stay; reception open 8am–3pm & 4.30–11pm; main door closes at midnight, but opens every 30min thereafter. €23 includes breakfast.

Barcelona Mar c/de Sant Pau 80, El Raval ☎933 248 530; ⓂParal.lel/Drassanes. On the fringe of the Rambla de Raval, so slightly edgy around here at night. Secure place, though, with 24hr reception, lockers, a/c, TV room, laundry and Internet. Dorms – in 6, 8, 10, 14 or 16-bedded rooms – are mixed. Price includes continental breakfast. €21

Center Ramblas c/Hospital 63, El Raval ☎934 124 069, ⓦwww.center-ramblas.com; ⓂLiceu. Very popular 200-bed hostel, 100m from the Ramblas, with lounge, bar, laundry, Internet, travel library and luggage storage. Dorms – sleeping from three to ten – have flagged floors and individual lockers, and there's 24hr access. IYHF membership required. No credit cards. Under 26s €15.50, over 26s €20, includes breakfast.

Gothic Point c/Vigatans 5, La Ribera ☎932 687 808, ⓦwww.gothicpoint.com; ⓂJaume I. Over 130 beds in a great old-town location. Rooms have 14 bunks and attached bathrooms, and each bed gets its own bedside cabinet and reading light. Lockers and left-luggage facility. Open 24hr. €21 includes breakfast and free Internet.

Itaca c/Ripoll 21, Barri Gòtic ☎933 019 751, ⓦwww.itacahostel.com; ⓂJaume I. Bright and breezy converted house close to the cathedral with spacious dorms (sleeping 8 or 12) with lockers and balconies. Dorms are mixed, though there is a 6-bed women-only dorm; no TV lounge, but a kitchen for guests, and choice of three €2 breakfasts. €17.

Kabul Pl. Reial 17, Barri Gòtic ☎933 185 190, ⓦwww.kabul-hostel.com; ⓂLiceu. A budget travellers' haven, open 24hr a day, with a good noticeboard and weekly pub crawls to help you get acquainted. Dorms are a bit cramped, but it's a safe hostel with a common room/bar, kitchen, laundry and TV. €15 including breakfast.

Sea Point Pl. del Mar 1–4, Barceloneta ☎932 247 075, ⓦwww.seapointhostel.com. Neat little bunk rooms sleeping six or seven, with an integral shower-bathroom and big lockers. The attached café, where you have breakfast, looks right out onto the boardwalk and palm trees. Open 24hr. €21 includes breakfast and free Internet.

The City

Everyone starts with the **Ramblas**, no bad thing since it helps fix the old town's central spine in your mind from the offset. You'll spend a lot of your time strolling up and down here, before diving off into the **Barri Gòtic**, the medieval nucleus of the city – around 500 square metres of narrow, twisted streets, mansions, museums and historic buildings including the mighty Gothic cathedral, **La Seu**. West of the Ramblas is the rapidly changing neighbourhood of **El Raval** (sometimes known as the Barri Xines, or China Town), focused on **MACBA**, Barcelona's contemporary art museum. On the east side – past the Barri Gòtic – is **Sant Pere** and **La Ribera**, the latter *barri* home to the graceful church of **Santa María del Mar** and the celebrated **Museu Picasso**. At the southern end of the Ramblas lies the harbour and the **Port Vell** (old port) development, where a swing bridge skips across the harbour to the **Maremàgnum** shopping, restaurant and cinema complex.

Outside these old town areas parks characterize the city, notably the **Parc de la Ciutadella**, just beyond La Ribera, and the fortress-topped hill of **Montjuïc**, southwest of El Raval. The latter houses some of the city's best museums, galleries and gardens, as well as the main Olympic stadium, while a cable car connects Montjuïc with **Barceloneta**, the old fishing district east of the harbour, below the Parc de la Ciutadella. Northeast along the coast from Barceloneta, the old industrial suburb of Poble Nou has been transformed in recent years, with the **Port Olímpic** and **Vila Olímpica** marking the start of a five-kilometre promenade of landscaped beaches.

Beyond Plaça de Catalunya at the top of the Ramblas stretches the modern city and commercial centre known as the **Eixample**. Its simple nineteenth-century grid plan is split by two huge avenues that lead out of the city; the **Gran Vía de les Corts Catalanes** (or simply "Gran Vía") and the **Avinguda Diagonal** ("La Diagonal"). It's in the Eixample that some of Europe's most extraordinary architecture – including Gaudí's **Sagrada Família** – is located. Beyond the Eixample lie the suburbs, the nearest, and the one you're most likely to visit, being trendy **Gràcia**, with its small squares and lively bars. Gaudí left his mark here, too, in the nearby **Parc Güell**, while other suburban trips might include a ride out to the **Camp Nou** football stadium (home of Barcelona FC) or to **Pedralbes** for its applied art museums and stunning Gothic monastery. Finally, if you're saving yourself for just one aerial view of Barcelona, wait for a clear day and head for **Tibidabo**, way to the northwest; a mountain with an amusement park and a couple of bars with the best views in the city.

The Ramblas and around

It is a telling comment on Barcelona's character that one can recommend a single street – **the Ramblas** – as a highlight. No day in the city seems complete without a stroll down at least part of what, for Lorca, was "the only street in the world which I wish would never end". Littered with cafés, shops, restaurants and newspaper stalls, it's at the heart of Barcelona's life and self-image – a focal point for locals every bit as much as for tourists, and one to which you'll return again and again. The name, derived from the Arabic *ramla* (or "sand"), refers to the bed of the seasonal stream which once flowed here. In the dry season, the channel created by the water was used as a road, and by the fourteenth century this had been paved over in recognition of its use as a link between the harbour and the old town. In the nineteenth century, benches and decorative trees were added, overlooked by stately, balconied buildings, and today – in a city choked with traffic – this wide swathe is still given over to pedestrians, with cars forced up the narrow strip of road on either side.

For the visitor, the first eccentricity is that the tree-lined Ramblas is (or rather, are) **five separate streets** strung head to tail – from north to south, Rambla Canaletes, Estudis, Sant Josep, Caputxins and Santa Mònica – though this plurality of names doesn't amount to much more than a subtle change in what's being sold from the kiosks as you head down the street. Here, under the plane trees, you'll find pet canaries, rabbits, tropical fish, flowers, plants, postcards and books. You can buy jewellery and contraband cigarettes, have your palm read and your portrait painted, or just listen to the buskers and watch the human statues and performance artists. If you're around when Barça (FC Barcelona) wins an important match you'll catch the Ramblas at its best: the street erupts with instant and infectious excitement, fans driving up and down with their hands on the horn, cars bedecked with Catalan flags, pedestrians waving champagne bottles.

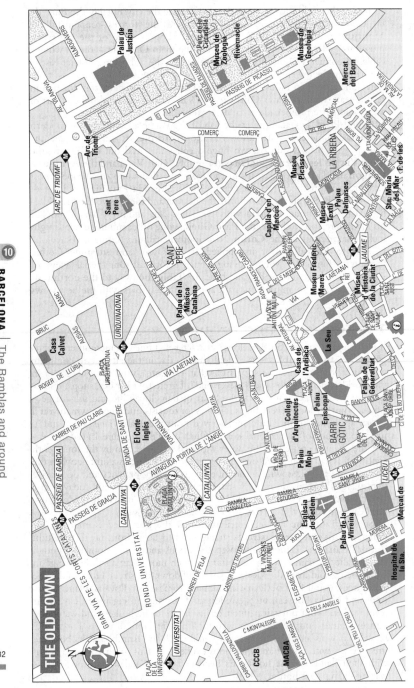

THE OLD TOWN

N

Palau de Justícia

Parc de la Ciutadella

Museu de Zoologia

Hivernacle

Museu de Geologia

Mercat del Born

ALMOGÀVERS

AV. VILANOVA

PASSEIG DE PUJADES

PASSEIG DE PICASSO

Arc de Triomf

ARC DE TRIOMF

COMERÇ   COMERÇ

PL. COMERCIAL

DEL REL

LA RIBERA

AV. M. DE L'ARGENTERA

Sant Pere

Museu Picasso

Palau Dalmases

Sta. Maria del Mar

PASSEIG DE SANT PERE ALT

SANT PERE

Capella d'en Marcús

Museu Tèxtil

MONTCADA

L'ARGENTERIA

CARDERS

CC. ASCÀNOI DURIS

Palau de la Música Catalana

URQUINAONA

PR. RAMON BERENGUER III

Museu Frederic Marès

Museu d'Història de la Ciutat

JAUME I

C. DEL SOTS

C. DE

BRUC

MARC

AUSIÀS

ROGER DE LLÚRIA

Casa Calvet

PLAÇA URQUINAONA

VÍA LAIETANA

VIA

LAIETANA

La Seu

Casa de l'Ardiaca

Palau de la Generalitat

PLAÇA DE SANT JAUME

PASSEIG DE GRÀCIA

PASSEIG DE GRÀCIA

CARRER DE PAU CLARIS

RONDA DE SANT PERE

El Corte Inglés

Collegi d'Arquitectes

Palau Episcopal

BARRI GÒTIC

GRAN VIA DE LES CORTS CATALANES

CATALUNYA

PLAÇA CATALUNYA

Palau Moja

Palau de la Virreina

Església de Betlem

LICEU

Mercat de

Hospital de la Sta.

RONDA UNIVERSITAT

UNIVERSITAT

PLAÇA DE LA UNIVERSITAT

CARRER DE PELAI

CCCB

MACBA

C MONTALEGRE

C DELS ÀNGELS

RAMBLA CANALETES

RAMBLA ESTUDIOS

RAMBLA SANT JOSEP

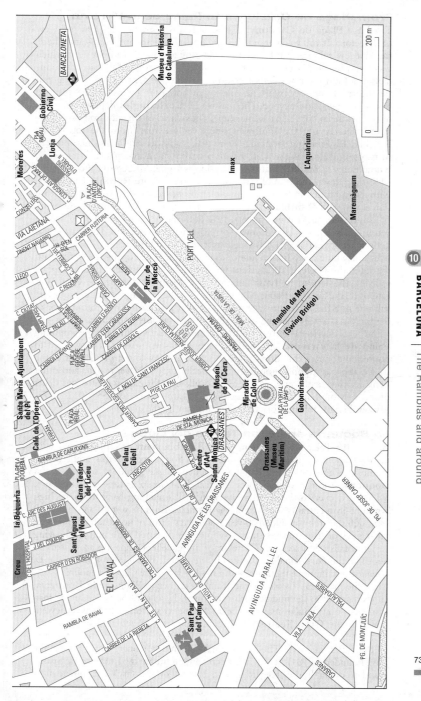

10

733

0   200 m

BARCELONETA

Gobierno Civil

PLAU

Llotja

Moreres

Santa Maria del Pi

VIA LAIETANA

Museu d'Història de Catalunya

Imax

L'Aquàrium

Maremàgnum

PORT VELL

Rambla de Mar (Swing Bridge)

Parr. de la Mercè

MOLL DE LA FUSTA

PASSEIG COLOM

Ajuntament

Cafè de l'Òpera

Gran Teatre del Liceu

la Boqueria

Palau Güell

Centre d'Art Santa Mònica

RAMBLA DE STA. MÒNICA

Museu de la Cera

Mirador de Colon

Golondrinas

PLAÇA PORTAL DE LA PAU

Sant Agustí el Nou

Creu

Sant Pau del Camp

RAMBLA DE RAVAL

EL RAVAL

RAMBLA DE CAPUTXINS

Drassanes (Museu Marítim)

AVINGUDA DE LES DRASSANES

AVINGUDA PARAL·LEL

PG. DE JOSEP CARNER

PG. DE MONTJUÏC

The huge **Plaça de Catalunya** (Ⓜ Catalunya) is many people's first real view of Barcelona. If you've emerged blinking from the metro and train station here, the first few minutes can be a bit bewildering as you try to figure out which way to go for the Ramblas. The square, with its central gardens, seats and fountains, is a focal point for demonstrations, buskers and festivals, and lies right at the heart of the city, with the old town and port below it, the planned Eixample above and beyond. The massive **El Corte Inglés** department store, in the northern corner, has some stupendous views of the city from its ninth-floor cafeteria. On the southwest side, over the road from the top of the Ramblas, **El Triangle** shopping centre makes another landmark. Incorporated in its ground floor is the *Café Zurich*, a traditional Barcelona meeting place, whose ranks of outdoor seats are a day-long magnet for beggars and buskers.

Heading down the Ramblas, the first two stretches are **Rambla Canaletes**, with its iron fountain (a drink from which supposedly means you'll never leave Barcelona), and **Rambla Estudis**, named after the city's medieval university (L'Estudi General) that was situated here until the beginning of the eighteenth century, when it was closed down for pro-Catalan subversion. This part is also known locally as Rambla dels Ocells as it contains a bird market, the little captives squawking away from a line of cages on either side of the street. Over on the right, the **Església de Betlem** was begun in 1681, built in heavy Baroque style by the Jesuits; its lavish interior was destroyed during the Civil War. Opposite, the arcaded **Palau Moja** dates from the late eighteenth century and still retains a fine exterior staircase and elegant great hall. The ground floor of the building, restored by the Generalitat, is now an arts bookshop.

Further along the Ramblas, on the corner of c/del Carme, sits the imposing **Palau de la Virreina** (Ⓜ Liceu), an eighteenth-century palace now used to house temporary exhibitions of art and photography. The ground floor of the palace also has a good shop featuring locally produced *objets d'art* and other items relating to the city, and there is a walk-in information centre and ticket office (Mon–Sat 10am–8pm, Sun 11am–3pm; ☎933 017 775, Ⓦ www.bcn.es/cultura) for cultural events run by the *ajuntament*.

La Boqueria and Gran Teatre del Liceu

Beyond the Palau de la Virreina starts **Rambla Sant Josep**, the switch in names marked by the sudden profusion of flower stalls at this point of the Ramblas. The city's most famous produce market, known locally as **La Boqueria**, though officially the Mercat Sant Josep (Mon–Sat 6am–8pm; Ⓜ Liceu), is over to the right, a cavernous hall stretching back from the high wrought-iron entrance arch facing the Ramblas. Built between 1836 and 1840 – though the arch was added 30 years later – it's a riot of noise and colour, with great piles of fruit and vegetables, whole legs of cured ham and an amazing variety of fish and seafood. There are some excellent stand-up snack bars in here, like the *Bar Central La Boqueria* in the central aisle (closes 4pm), while *La Garduña* restaurant at the back of the market is a great place for lunch.

Past the market is the part of the Ramblas known as **Plaça de la Boqueria**, and is marked (in the middle of the pavement) by a large round mosaic by Joan Miró. By now you've reached the Liceu metro station, a little way beyond which is the **Gran Teatre del Liceu**, Barcelona's celebrated opera house, which burned down for the third time in 1994 but has been rebuilt in its former neo-Baroque style. The building has had an unfortunate history, to say the least. Founded in 1847, it was first rebuilt after a fire in 1861 to become Spain's grandest opera house. Regarded as a bastion of the city's late nineteenth-

△ La Boqueria market

century commercial and intellectual classes, tragedy struck again in 1893 when an anarchist threw two bombs into the stalls during a production of *William Tell*. The latest restoration added a rather large and unsightly extension, the Espai Liceu, which runs south along the Ramblas. It's from here that you embark on **tours of the opera house** (daily 10am, 11am, noon & 1pm; €5; Ⓦwww.liceubarcelona.com), which show you the lavishly decorated auditorium. Across the way, at Ramblas 74, is the famous **Café de l'Opera**, traditional favourite of opera performers and *cognoscenti* for over a century and one of the best places in Barcelona to enjoy a coffee or drink (it stays open until 3am).

Plaça Reial to Mirador de Colón

A hundred metres or so further down the Ramblas, now the **Rambla de Caputxins**, the elegant nineteenth-century **Plaça Reial** (ⓂLiceu) is another good place to call a halt – it's hidden behind an archway on the left and is easy to miss. Laid out in around 1850, the Italianate square is studded with tall palm trees and decorated iron lamps (by the young Gaudí), bordered by arcaded buildings, and centred on a fountain depicting the Three Graces. The square was once a haven of drug addicts and vagabonds, but it's been cleaned up and its terraces now make an ideal spot for a drink while enjoying the jugglers and fire-breathers (though you should still take care late at night). Sunday's **coin and stamp market** (10am–2pm) draws many serious dealers, but its lighter-weight exhibits and frenetic bargaining make it entertaining.

Off the Ramblas at the southern end of the square, **Carrer dels Escudellers** was once a thriving red-light street but it has gradually hauled itself up by its bootlaces and teeters on the edge of respectability. Bars and restaurants around here attract a youthful crowd on the whole, nowhere more so than those flanking **Plaça George Orwell**, at the eastern end of c/dels Escudellers. The wedge-shaped square was created by levelling an old-town block – a favoured tactic in Barcelona to let in a bit of light – and it's quickly become a hangout for the grunge crowd.

There's little else to see until you reach the bottom of the Ramblas, though at the weekend there's an afternoon street market selling jewellery, ornaments and clothes. On the right-hand side, amidst one of the last and toughest knots of Barcelona's surviving red-light district, sits the plain facade of a former convent church, now the **Centre d'Art Santa Mònica** for temporary art exhibitions (Tues–Sat 11am–8pm, Sun 11am–3pm; free). The city's wax museum, the **Museu de Cera** (July–Sept daily 10am–10pm; Oct–June Mon–Fri 10am–1.30pm & 4–7.30pm, Sat & Sun 11am–2pm & 4.30–8.30pm; €6.65; Ⓦwww.museo cerabcn.com), is located on the opposite side of the Ramblas, at nos. 4–6, in an impressive nineteenth-century bank building; the entrance is along Ptge. de Banca. It's of little relevance to Barcelona, or even Spain, being the usual trawl through the internationally famous and infamous, plus dated film characters, and underwater and space capsule simulations. However, it is worth poking your head into the museum's extraordinary bar, the *Bosc de les Fades* (see p.773), while for true kitsch value there are "night visits" every Saturday (€12, drink included; Spanish only) with actors and special effects ratcheting up the atmosphere.

The Ramblas ends at **Plaça Portal de la Pau** (ⓂDrassanes), coming up hard against the teeming traffic that runs along the harbourside road. In the centre stands Columbus, pointing out to sea at the top of a tall and slender iron column built for the Universal Exhibition in 1888: the **Mirador de Colón**. You can get inside (June–Sept daily 9am–8.30pm; Oct–March Mon–Fri 10am–1.30pm & 3.30–6.30pm, Sat & Sun 10am–6.30pm; April & May Mon–Fri 10am–1.30pm & 3.30–7.30pm, Sat & Sun 10am–7.30pm; €2) and take the lift 52m up to his head for aerial views of the city.

The Drassanes: Museu Marítim

Opposite Columbus, set back from the road on the western side of the Ramblas, are the **Drassanes**, medieval shipyards dating from the thirteenth century. Originally used as a dry dock to fit and arm Catalunya's war fleet in the days when the Catalan-Aragonese crown was vying with Venice and Genoa for control of the Mediterranean, the shipyards – long, parallel halls facing the sea – were in continuous use until well into the eighteenth century. Nowadays the huge, stone-vaulted buildings make a fitting home for an excellent **Museu Marítim** (daily 10am–7pm; €5.40; ⓦwww.diba.es/mmaritim), whose centrepiece is a copy of the sixteenth-century Royal Galley (*Galeria Reial*), a red-and-gold barge rowed by enormous oars. It's surrounded by smaller models, fishing skiffs, sailing boats, old maps and charts, and other nautical bits and pieces – none of which, worthy though they are, can really compete with the soaring building itself. There's also a permanent exhibition about the dangers of the sea, in which you can take a virtual-reality trip in a submarine.

The Barri Gòtic

The **Barri Gòtic**, or Gothic Quarter (ⓜJaume I), forms the very heart of the old town, spreading out from the east side of the Ramblas. It's a remarkable concentration of beautiful medieval buildings principally dating from the fourteenth and fifteenth centuries when Barcelona reached the height of her commercial prosperity before being absorbed into the burgeoning kingdom of Castile. It will take the best part of a day to see everything here, with the cathedral – **La Seu** – a particular highlight, and you certainly won't want to miss the archeological remains at the **Museu d'Història de la Ciutat** or the eclectic collections of the **Museu Frederic Marès**. That said, sauntering through the medieval alleys and hogging a café table in one of the lovely squares is just as much an attraction.

The picture-postcard images of the Barri Gòtic are largely based on the streets north of c/de Ferran and c/de Jaume I, where tourists throng the boutiques, bars, restaurants, museums and galleries. South of here – from Plaça Reial and c/d'Avinyo to the harbour – the Barri Gotic is rather more traditional (or sometimes just plain seedy). There are no specific sights or museums in this section, though there are plenty of great tapas bars and restaurants – just take care at night.

Plaça de Sant Jaume

The quarter is centred on the **Plaça de Sant Jaume**, a spacious square at the end of the main c/de Ferran. Once the site of Barcelona's Roman forum and marketplace, it's now one venue for the weekly dancing by local people of the Catalan folk dance, the *sardana*, and is also the traditional site of demonstrations and gatherings.

On the south side stands the town hall, the **Ajuntament**, parts of which date from as early as 1373, though the Neoclassical facade is nineteenth century, added when the square was laid out. You get a much better idea of the grandeur of the original structure by nipping around the corner, down c/de la Ciutat, for a view of the former main entrance. Entering the building from Plaça de Sant Jaume, you can take a look at the lovely wall paintings, the work of contemporary Catalan artist Albert Rafols Casamada. On Sundays (10am–2pm; free) the restored fourteenth-century council chamber, the **Saló de Cent**, on the first floor, is open to the public.

Right across the square rises the **Palau de la Generalitat**, traditional home of the Catalan government, from where the short-lived Catalan Republic was proclaimed in April 1931. Begun in 1418, this presents its best – or at least its oldest – aspect around the side on c/del Bisbe, where the early fifteenth-century facade by Marc Safont contains a spirited medallion portraying Saint George and the Dragon. Through the Renaissance main entrance, facing the square, there's a beautiful cloister on the first floor with superb coffered ceilings, while opening off this gallery are two fine rooms – the chapel and salon of **Sant Jordi** (Saint George, patron saint of Catalunya as well as England), also by Safont – and other chambers of the former law courts. You can visit the interior on a **guided tour** (frequently in English; every 20min; 10am–2pm; free) on the second and fourth Sunday of each month. The Generalitat is also traditionally open to the public on April 23 (expect a 2hr wait) – **Dia de Sant Jordi** – when the whole square is festooned with book stalls and rose sellers.

La Seu and around

La Seu (daily 8am–1.30pm & 4–7.30pm, at weekends it opens an hour later in the afternoon; free), Barcelona's cathedral, is one of the great Gothic buildings of Spain. Located just behind the Generalitat, on a site previously occupied by a Roman temple, it was begun in 1298 on the foundations of an earlier church and finished in 1448, with one notable exception commented on by Richard Ford in 1845: "The principal facade is unfinished, with a bold front poorly painted in stucco, although the rich chapter have for three centuries received a fee on every marriage for this very purpose of completing it." Perhaps goaded into action, the authorities set to and completed the facade within a ten-year period in the 1880s.

Artificial lighting has transformed the **interior**, replacing the dank mystery with a soaring airiness to echo the grandeur of the exterior. The cathedral is dedicated to Santa Eulàlia, martyred by the Romans for daring to prefer Christianity, and her tomb rests in a crypt beneath the high altar; if you put money in the slot the whole thing lights up to show off its exemplary Catholic kitsch. Look out, too, for the rich altarpieces, the carved tombs of the 29 side chapels and the painted wooden coffins of Ramon Berenguer I (Count of Barcelona from 1018 to 1025), and his wife Almodis, hanging on the wall just to the left of the exit to the cloister. However, the most unique part of the cathedral is its magnificent fourteenth-century **cloister** (daily 8.45am–1.15pm & 4–7pm; free), which looks over a lush garden complete with soaring palm trees and – more unusually – honking white geese. The geese have lived in the cloister's pond for the last five centuries, though no one can recall their origin.

Outside La Seu is the **Museu Diocesà-La Pia Almonia** (Tues–Sat 10am–2pm & 5–8pm, Sun 11am–2pm; €2), a small but impressive collection of religious art and artefacts from around Barcelona, housed in a renovated fourth-century Roman tower. Highlights include the frescoes of the Apocalypse from a church in Polinyà, and some great *retablos*, including one of St Bartholomew being skinned. The large **Plaça Nova**, facing the cathedral, marks one of the medieval entrances to the old town – beyond it, you're fast entering the wider streets and more regular contours of the modern city. Even if you're sticking with the Barri Gòtic for now, walk over to study the frieze surmounting the modern **Collegi d'Arquitectes** (College of Architects) building on the other side of the square. Designed in 1960 by Picasso, it has a crude, almost graffiti-like quality at odds with the more stately buildings to the side. The square itself is at its best during the weekly **antique market** (Thurs 10am–4pm) and the massive **Christmas market**, the *Fira de Santa Llúcia* (Dec 1–22).

Plaça del Rei and around

The cathedral and its associated buildings aside, the most concentrated batch of historic monuments in the Barri Gòtic is the grouping around the neat **Plaça del Rei**, behind the cathedral apse. The square was once the courtyard of the Palau Reial Major, the palace of the counts of Barcelona, and stairs climb to the great fourteenth-century **Saló del Tinell**, the palace's main hall and a fine, spacious example of secular Gothic architecture. At one time the Spanish Inquisition met here, taking full advantage of the popular belief that the walls would move if a lie was spoken. Nowadays it hosts various exhibitions, while concerts are occasionally held in the hall or outside in the square.

The palace buildings also include the romantic Renaissance **Torre del Rei Martí** (currently closed for restoration), which rises above one corner of the square, as well as the beautiful fourteenth-century **Capella de Santa Agata**, with its tall single nave and fine Gothic retable. All can be seen more closely during a visit to the **Museu d'Història de la Ciutat** (June–Sept Tues–Sat 10am–8pm, Sun 10am–3pm; Oct–May Tues–Sat 10am–2pm & 4–8pm, Sun 10am–2pm; €4, free 1st Sat of the month; Ⓦ www.museuhistoria.bcn.es), housed in the building that closes off the rest of Plaça del Rei – the entrance is on c/del Veguer. The museum's crucial draw is its underground archeological section – nothing less than the extensive remains of the Roman city of Barcino, stretching under Plaça del Rei and the surrounding streets as far as the cathedral. The remains date from the first to the sixth centuries AD and reflect the transition from Roman to Visigothic rule – at the end of the sixth century, a church was erected on top of the old Roman salt fish factory, preserved down here almost in its entirety. Not much survives above chest height, but explanatory diagrams show the extent of the streets, walls and buildings, while models, mosaics, murals and displays of excavated goods help flesh out the reality of daily life in Barcino.

Another extraordinary display greets visitors in the **Museu Frederic Marès** (Tues–Sat 10am–7pm, Sun 10am–3pm; €3, free Wed afternoon & first Sun of month; Ⓦ www.museumares.bcn.es), which occupies a further wing of the old royal palace, behind Plaça del Rei; the entrance is through Plaça de Sant Iu, off c/dels Comtes. Frederic Marès (1893–1991) was a sculptor, artist and restorer who more or less singlehandedly restored Catalunya's decaying medieval treasures in the early twentieth century. The ground and basement floors of the museum consist of his personal collection of medieval sculpture, including a notable series of wooden crucifixes showing the stylistic development of this form from the twelfth to the fifteenth century. However, it's the upper two floors, housing Marès' personal collectibles, which tend to make jaws drop. These present an incredible retrospective jumble gathered during fifty years of travel, with entire rooms devoted to keys and locks, cigarette cards and snuff boxes, fans, gloves and brooches, playing cards, walking sticks, dolls' houses, toy theatres and archaic bicycles, to name just a sample of what's on show.

Santa María del Pi and around

With the cathedral area and Plaça del Rei sucking in every old-town visitor at some point during the day, the other focus of attraction is to the west, around the church of Santa María del Pi – five minutes' walk from the cathedral or just two minutes from Ⓜ Liceu on the Ramblas.

The fourteenth-century **Església de Santa María del Pi** stands at the heart of three delightful little squares. Burned out in 1936, and restored in the 1960s, the church boasts a Romanesque door but is mainly Catalan-Gothic in style, with just a single nave with chapels between the buttresses. The rather plain interior only serves to set off some marvellous stained glass, the most impressive of which is contained within a huge rose window, often claimed (rather boldly) as the largest in the world. The church stands on the middle square, **Plaça Sant Josep Oriol**, the prettiest of the three, overhung with balconies and scattered with seats from the *Bar del Pi*. This whole area becomes an **artists' market** at the weekend (Sat 11am–8pm, Sun 11am–2pm), while buskers and street performers often appear here, too. The squares on either side – Plaça del Pi and Placeta del Pi – are named, like the church, for the pine tree that once stood here.

El Raval

The old-town area west of the Ramblas is known as **El Raval** (from the Arabic word for suburb). In medieval times, it was the site of hospitals, churches and monasteries and, later, of trades and industries that had no place in the Gothic quarter. Many of the street names still tell the story, like c/de l'Hospital or c/dels Tallers (named for the district's slaughterhouses). By the twentieth century the area south of c/de l'Hospital had acquired a more sinister reputation as the city's main red-light area, known to all as the Barrio Chino, or Barri Xinès in Catalan – China Town. Even today in the backstreets around c/de Sant Pau and c/Nou de la Rambla are found pockets of sleaze, loitering hookers and listless drug addicts. However, El Raval is changing rapidly. North of c/de l'Hospital the main engine of change was the building of the contemporary art museum, MACBA, designed by American architect Richard Meier, around which entire city blocks were demolished, open spaces created and old buildings cleaned up. To the south, between c/de l'Hospital and c/de Sant Pau, a new boulevard – the Rambla del Raval – has been gouged through the former tenements and alleys, providing a huge new pedestrianized area. Bars, restaurants, galleries and boutiques have followed in the wake of this development, although you'd still hesitate to call El Raval gentrified, as it clearly still has its rough edges. You needn't be unduly concerned during the day as you make your way around, but it's as well to keep your wits about you at night, particularly in the southernmost streets.

Museu d'Art Contemporani de Barcelona and around

Reached along c/del Bonsuccés and c/d'Elisabets from the Ramblas is the huge, white, almost luminous **Museu d'Art Contemporani de Barcelona** or **MACBA** in Plaça dels Àngels (June–Sept Mon & Wed–Sat 10am–8pm, Sun 10am–3pm; Oct–May Mon & Wed–Fri 11am–7.30pm, Sat 10am–8pm, Sun 10am–3pm; general entrance €7, Wed €3, special exhibitions €4; Ⓦwww.macba.es; ⓂCatalunya/Universitat). Once inside, you go from the ground to the fourth floor up a series of swooping ramps which afford continuous views of the plaça below – usually full of careering skateboarders – and the sixteenth-century Convent dels Àngels. The collection represents the main movements in contemporary art since 1945, mainly in Catalunya and Spain but with a good smattering of foreign artists as well. The pieces are shown in rotating exhibitions so you may catch works by Joan Miró, Antoni Tàpies, Eduardo Chillida, Alexander Calder, Robert Rauschenberg or Paul Klee. Joan Brossa, leading light of the Catalan *Dau al Set* group, has work here too, as do Catalan conceptual artists like the Grup de Treball, Muntadas and Francesc Torres.

While you're in the vicinity, it's worth looking around the small private galleries or having a drink in one of the fashionable new bars that have sprung up in the wake of MACBA, especially on c/del Pintor Fortuny, c/de Ferlandina, c/dels Àngels and c/del Dr Joaquim Dou. For a sit-down in one of Barcelona's nicest traffic-free squares, head back along c/d'Elisabets to the arcaded **Plaça de Vicenç Martorell**, where *Kasparo*'s tables overlook a popular children's playground.

Adjoining the MACBA building, up c/Montalegre, is the **Centre de Cultura Contemporània de Barcelona** or **CCCB** (Tues, Thurs & Fri 11am–2pm & 4–8pm, Wed & Sat 11am–8pm, Sun 11am–7pm; €4 or €5.50 depending on number of exhibitions you see; Ⓦwww.cccb.org), which hosts temporary art and city-related exhibitions. The building is another example of the juxtaposition of old and new; built as the Casa de la Caritat in 1714 on the site of a fourteenth-century Augustine convent, and added to in the late eighteenth and nineteenth centuries, it was for hundreds of years an infamous workhouse and lunatic asylum. At the back of the building there is a nice **café** (Mon–Fri 9am–7pm, Sat & Sun 11am–6pm) with a *terrassa* on the modern square joining the CCCB to the MACBA.

Hospital de la Santa Creu

On the northern fringes of the Barri Xines the **Hospital de la Santa Creu** is the district's most substantial relic. The attractive complex of Gothic buildings, reached down c/de Hospital, was founded as the city's main hospital in 1402, a role that it retained until 1930. Today the complex has been converted to cultural and educational use, and its spacious courtyard, punctuated by orange trees, provides airy respite from the Raval's dark streets. Just inside the entrance are some superb seventeenth-century *azulejos* of various religious scenes. The grand staircase on the left side leads up to the Biblioteca de Catalunya (National Library of Catalunya; see "Listings", p.786), housed in the spacious fifteenth-century hospital wards. **La Capella** (Tues–Sat noon–2pm & 4–8pm, Sun 11am–2pm; free), which is entered separately from c/de L'Hospital, is a former chapel, now used as an exhibition space featuring a changing programme of works by young Barcelona artists.

Walking west along c/de l'Hospital, it's 100m or so to the bottom of **c/de la Riera Baixa**, a narrow street that's at the centre of the city's secondhand/vintage clothing scene. The **Rambla de Raval** is then just a few steps beyond, where you can pull up a chair at a pavement café and consider the merits of the latest boulevard to be driven through the old town.

Sant Pau del Camp

Three blocks south from here on c/de Sant Pau, which runs through the heart of the Raval, is the church of **Sant Pau del Camp** (St Paul of the Field; Mon & Wed–Sun 11.30am–1pm & 6–7.30pm, Tues 11.30am–12.30pm; free), its name a reminder that it once stood in open fields beyond the city walls. The oldest church in Barcelona, Sant Pau is laid out in the cruciform Greek style, with a main entrance decorated with faded Romanesque carvings of fish, birds and faces, and a tranquil thirteenth-century cloister.

Palau Güell

Much of Antoni Gaudí's early career was spent constructing elaborate follies for wealthy patrons. The most important was Eusebio Güell, industrialist and aristocrat, who in 1885 commissioned the **Palau Güell**, at c/Nou de la Rambla 3, just off the Ramblas (Mon–Sat 10am–1pm & 4–7pm; €3). Here, Gaudí's feel for different materials is remarkable. At a time when architects sought to conceal the iron supports within buildings, Gaudí turned them to his advantage, displaying them as attractive decorative features. The roof terrace, too, makes a virtue of its functionalism, since the chimneys and other outlets are decorated with glazed tiles, while inside, columns, arches and ceilings are all shaped and twisted in an elaborate style that was to become the hallmark of Gaudí's later works. To visit the building you'll have to join one of the frequent, mandatory, guided tours (in English), and queues form early – having waited in line, you might well be given a later time slot, as visitor numbers are limited.

Sant Pere and La Ribera

The Barri Gòtic is bordered on its eastern side by Via Laietana, which was cut through the old town at the beginning of the twentieth century. Across it to the east stretches the quiet neighbourhood of **Sant Pere**, named after its medieval monastic church, Sant Pere de les Puelles. In the very centre of the neighbourhood, work has continued to spruce up the streets and squares around the restored mid-nineteenth-century **Mercat Santa Caterina** (ⓂJaume I), another of Barcelona's attractive central market buildings. The discovery of the foundations of a major medieval convent held up its renovation for a while, but it's expected to be open again to the public during 2004. Market aside, visits to the *barri* tend to concentrate on its one remarkable building, the Palau de la Música Catalana, just off the northern end of Via Laietana, but the neighbourhood rewards a slow stroll through on your way to the richer tourist area of **La Ribera**. Bordered by Via Laietana to the west, c/de la Princesa to the north and Parc de la Ciutadella to the east, La Ribera is one of the most visited city neighbourhoods, as it is home to the Museu Picasso, Barcelona's biggest single tourist attraction. Over the last decade it's also become the location of choice for designers, artists and craftspeople whose boutiques and workshops lend the neighbourhood an air of creativity. The *barri* is at its most hip, and most enjoyable, in the area around the **Passeig del Born**, the elongated square leading from Santa María church to the old Born market. This – widely known as the Born – is one of the city's premier nightlife centres.

Palau de la Música Catalana

Domènech i Montaner's stupendous **Palau de la Música Catalana** (ⓂUrquinaona) doesn't seem to have enough breathing space in the tiny c/Sant Pere Més Alt. Built in 1908 for the Orfeó Català choral group, its bare brick structure is lined with tiles and mosaics, the highly elaborate facade resting on three great columns, like elephant's legs; the corner sculpture, by Miquel Blay, represents Catalan popular song. The dramatic tiled lobby provides a taster of the stunning interior, which incorporates a bulbous stained-glass skylight capping the second-storey auditorium – and which contemporary critics claimed to be an engineering impossibility.

Fifty-minute-long **guided tours** (daily 10am–5pm, in English hourly on the hr; €7; Ⓦ www.palaumusica.org) are offered of the interior, but as only 55 people at a time are taken you'll almost certainly have to book in advance, which you can do at the box office or at the nearby gift shop, Les Muses del Palau, c/Sant Pere Mes Alt 1. The best way to see the building, however, is to get a ticket for one of the many fine concerts.

Museu Picasso

The **Museu Picasso**, c/de Montcada 15–19 (Tues–Sat & holidays 10am–8pm, Sun 10am–3pm; €5, free first Sun of month; Ⓦ www.museupicasso.bcn.es), is housed in a series of striking medieval palaces converted specifically for the museum. It's one of the most important collections of Picasso's work in the world, but even so, some visitors are disappointed: the museum contains none of his best-known works, and few in the Cubist style. But what is here provides a

Although born in Málaga, **Pablo Picasso** (1881–1973) spent much of his youth – from the age of 14 to 23 – in Barcelona. He maintained close links with Barcelona and his Catalan friends even when he left for Paris in 1904, and is said to have always thought of himself as Catalan rather than Andaluz. The time Picasso spent in Barcelona spanned the whole of his "Blue Period" (1901–04) and many of the formative influences on his art.

Apart from the Museu Picasso, there are echoes of the great artist at various sites throughout the old town. Not too far from the museum, you can still see many of the buildings in which Picasso lived and worked, notably the **Escola de Belles Arts de Llotja** (c/Consolat del Mar, near Estació de França), where his father taught drawing and where Picasso himself absorbed an academic training. The apartments where the family lived when they first arrived in Barcelona – Pg. d'Isabel II 4 and c/Cristina 3, both opposite the Escola – can also be seen, though only from the outside. His first public exhibition was in 1901 at **Els Quatre Gats** (c/Montsió 3). Less tangible is to take a walk down c/d'Avinyó, which cuts south from c/de Ferran to c/Ample. Large houses along here were converted into brothels at the turn of the twentieth century, and Picasso used to haunt the street sketching what he saw; women at one of the brothels inspired his seminal Cubist work, **Les Demoiselles d'Avignon**.

unique opportunity to trace Picasso's development from his early paintings as a young boy to the major works of later years.

The museum opened in 1963 with a collection based largely on the donations of Jaume Sabartés, friend and former secretary to the artist. The **early drawings** in which Picasso – still signing with his full name, Pablo Ruíz Picasso – attempted to copy the nature paintings in which his father specialized, and the many studies from his art school days, are fascinating. Indeed, it's the early periods that are the best represented: some works in the style of Toulouse-Lautrec, such as the menu Picasso did for *Els Quatre Gats* restaurant in 1900, reflect his interest in Parisian art at the turn of the twentieth century; other selected works show graphically Picasso's development of his own style – there are paintings here from the famous **Blue Period** (1901–04), the Pink Period (1904–06), and from his Cubist (1907–20) and Neoclassical (1920–25) stages.

The large gaps in the main collection (for example, nothing from 1905 until the celebrated *Harlequin* of 1917) only underline Picasso's extraordinary changes of style and mood. This is best illustrated by the large jump after 1917 – to 1957, a year represented by two rooms on the first floor which contain the fascinating works Picasso himself donated to the museum, his fifty-odd interpretations of Velázquez's masterpiece *Las Meninas*.

Along Carrer de Montcada

The street that the Museu Picasso is on – **Carrer de Montcada** – is one of the best looking in the city. Laid out in the fourteenth century, until the Eixample was planned almost 500 years later it was home to most of the city's leading citizens who occupied spacious mansions built around central courtyards, from which external staircases climbed to the living rooms on the first floor.

Almost opposite the Picasso Museum, at no. 12, the fourteenth-century Palau de Lió and its next-door neighbour contain the extensive collections of the **Museu Textil i d'Indumentaria** (Tues–Sat 10am–6pm, Sun 10am–3pm; €3.50, free first Sun of month; Ⓦ www.museutextil.bcn.es) – 4000 items altogether, including textiles from the fourth century onwards and costumes from the sixteenth, dolls, shoes, fans and other accessories. A joint ticket system also allows you entry to the ceramics and decorative art museum at Pedralbes (see p.761) or to the adjacent **Museu Barbier-Mueller** on c/de Montcada (Tues–Sat 10am–6pm, Sun 10am–3pm; €3, free first Sun of month), a collection of Pre-Columbian art housed in the renovated sixteenth-century Palau Nadal.

If you want to get a feel of more of the architecture on the street, pop into the private gallery at no. 25, the **Galeria Maeght** (Tues–Sat 10am–2pm & 4–8pm; free), spread across two floors of the former Palau dels Cervelló, while at no. 20, the Gothic **Palau Dalmases** has been opened as an upmarket bar.

Santa María del Mar and the Born

At the bottom of c/de Montcada sits the glorious church of **Santa María del Mar** (daily 9am–1.30pm & 4.30–8pm; Sun choral Mass at 1pm), begun under orders of King Jaume II in 1324, and built in only five years. Situated on what was then the seashore, at the entrance to the trading district (c/Argentería, named after the silversmiths who worked there, still runs from the church square to the city walls of the Barri Gòtic), the church symbolized the maritime supremacy of the medieval Crown of Aragon, of which Barcelona was capital. The church, with its soaring lines, is an exquisite example of Catalan-Gothic architecture.

Fronting the church is the fashionable **Passeig del Born**. Once the site of medieval fairs and tournaments, it is now lined with classy boutiques, bars and cafés, and capped at the far end by the hulking iron skeleton of the **Mercat del Born**, the city's main market from the late 1800s to the 1960s – now under renovation as a public library.

Parc de la Ciutadella

East of La Ribera, across Passeig de Picasso, the **Parc de la Ciutadella** is the largest green space in the city centre, home to a splendid fountain, large lake, plant houses, two museums and the city zoo. It's also the meeting place of the Catalan parliament, which occupies part of a fortress-like structure right at the centre of the park, the surviving portion of the star-shaped Bourbon citadel from which the park takes its name. In 1888, the park was chosen as the site of the **Universal Exhibition** and the city's *modernista* architects, including the young Gaudí, left their mark here in a series of eye-catching buildings and monuments. The park's main gates are found on Passeig de Picasso (ⓂBarceloneta), and there's also an entrance on Passeig de Pujades (ⓂArc de Triomf); only use ⓂCiutadella-Vila Olímpica if you're going directly to the zoo, as there's no access to the park itself from that side.

Perhaps the most notable of the park's sights is the **Cascada**, the Baroque fountain in the northeast corner. Designed by Josep Fontseré, the architect chosen to oversee the conversion of the former citadel grounds into a park, this was the first of the major projects undertaken here. Fontseré's assistant in the work was the young Antoni Gaudí, then a student, who was also thought to have had a hand in the design of the Ciutadella's iron park gates, at the entrance on Avinguda Marqués de l'Argentera. Just inside the main entrance, Domènech i Montaner designed a castle-like building intended for use as the exhibition's café-restaurant. Dubbed the Castell dels Tres Dragons, it became a centre for *modernista* arts and crafts, and is now the **Museu de Zoologia** (Tues, Wed & Fri–Sun 10am–2pm, Thurs 10am–6.30pm; €3, free first Sun of month), whose decorated red-brick exterior out-dazzles the rather more mundane interior. Beyond the museum you pass the attractive late nineteenth-century **Hivernacle** (conservatory) – which houses a pleasant café-bar – and **Umbracle** (palmhouse), between which sits the park's other museum, the

Museu de Geologia (same hours and price as Museu de Zoologia). The geology museum offers an educational tour past a collection of geological and paleontological bits and pieces, including 120-million-year-old fossils.

Ciutadella's most popular attraction by far is the city's zoo, the **Parc Zoològic** (daily: July & Aug 9.30am–7.30pm; Sept–June 10am–5pm; €11.50; Ⓦwww.zoobarcelona.com), taking up most of the southeast of the park. There's an entrance on c/de Wellington, as well as one inside the park. The zoo's days in its current form are numbered – the powers that be perhaps having finally appreciated the irony of its juxtaposition next to the Parlement, and grown weary of explaining to visiting dignitaries the source of the strong smell pervading the area. There are advanced plans to move the marine animals to a new coastal zoo and wetlands area (by 2008) being laid out at the new Diagonal Mar seashore at Besós.

Port Vell, Barceloneta, the Port Olímpic and Poble Nou

Perhaps the greatest transformation in the city has been along the waterfront, where harbour and Mediterranean have once again been placed at the heart of Barcelona. At the inner harbour, known as **Port Vell**, the old wharves and warehouses have been replaced by an entertainment zone that encompasses the Maremàgnum shopping and nightlife centre, the city's high-profile aquarium and IMAX screens and, across the marina, the impressive Museu d'Història de Catalunya. The wedge of land backing the marina is **Barceloneta**, an eighteenth-century fishermen's quarter that's the most popular place to come and sample the dishes of which Barcelona is most proud – fresh and grilled seafood, fish stews, paella and *fideuà*. From Barceloneta, six interlinked **beaches** stretch up the coast, backed by an attractive promenade. The main development is around the **Port Olímpic**, filled with places to eat, drink and shop, and though fewer tourists keep on as far as the old working-class neighbourhood of **Poble Nou**, its beaches, historic cemetery and pretty *rambla* make for an interesting diversion.

You can reach all the areas covered below by metro, though there's a fair amount of walking required between neighbourhoods – nothing too off-putting, though from the bottom of the Ramblas to Poble Nou would take an hour. There are also daily **sightseeing boat** departures with *Las Golondrinas* (Ⓣ934 423 106, Ⓦwww.lasgolondrinas.com; ⓂDrassanes) from Plaça Portal de la Pau, behind the Columbus monument: either around the port (35min; €3.50), or port and coast including the Port Olímpic (1hr 30min; €8.50). Departures are at least hourly June to September, less frequently October to May.

Port Vell

The city's old timber wharf, the **Moll de la Fusta** (ⓂDrassanes), was among the first to be prettified, backed by sedate nineteenth-century buildings along the Passeig de Colom. From the Columbus-statue end of the wharf, the wooden **Rambla de Mar** swing bridge strides across the harbour to **Maremàgnum** (daily 11am–11pm; Ⓦwww.maremagnum.es), a typically bold piece of Catalan design, inside which are two floors of gift shops and boutiques, plus a range of bars and restaurants with harbourside seating and high prices. It's a fun place to come at night, though no self-respecting local would rate the food as anything but ordinary.

Next door, **L'Aquàrium** (daily; July & Aug 9.30am–11pm; Sept–June 9.30am–9pm, until 9.30pm at weekends; €11.50; Ⓦwww.aquariumbcn.com)

drags in families and school parties to see fish and sea creatures in 21 themed tanks representing underwater caves, tidal areas, tropical reefs, the planet's oceans and other maritime habitats. It's vastly overpriced, and despite the claims of excellence it offers few new experiences, save perhaps the eighty-metre-long walk-through underwater tunnel, which brings you face to face with rays and sharks. **IMAX Port Vell** next to the aquarium has three screens showing films in 3D or in giant format (☎932 251 111, ⓦwww .imaxportvell.com; €7–10, depending on the film).

The only surviving warehouse on the harbourside is known as the Palau de Mar, home to the **Museu d'Història de Catalunya** (Tues & Thurs–Sat 10am–7pm, Wed 10am–8pm, Sun 10am–2.30pm; €3, free first Sun of month & public holidays; Ⓜ Barceloneta), which traces the history of Catalunya from the Stone Age to the twentieth century. A lift takes you to the permanent displays on the upper floors: second floor for year dot to the Industrial Revolution, and third for periods and events up to 1980 (though later coverage is planned). On the fourth floor, the café-bar boasts a glorious view from its huge terrace.

Barceloneta

Barceloneta (Ⓜ Barceloneta) was laid out in 1755 – a classic eighteenth-century grid of streets where previously there had been mudflats – to replace part of La Ribera that was destroyed to make way for the Ciutadella fortress to the north. The long, narrow streets are still very much as they were planned, broken at intervals by small squares and lined with multiwindowed houses. These days, it's the neighbourhood's many fish and seafood restaurants that are its *raison d'être*, found scattered right across the tight grid of streets but most characteristically lined along the harbourside **Passeig Joan de Borbó** (see p.771 for reviews).

Recent development has been most marked on the seaward side of Barceloneta. The beachside snack bars and simple restaurants – *xiringuitos* – that used to line this stretch disappeared in the Olympic clean-up and, in their place, Barceloneta acquired a beach, furnished with boardwalks, showers, benches, climbing frames, water fountains and public art. **Platja de Sant Sebastià** is the first in a series of beaches that stretches north along the coast as far as the River Besòs. A double row of palms backs the **Passeig Marítim**, a sweeping stone esplanade which runs as far as the Port Olímpic, a fifteen-minute walk away.

The cross-harbour cable car

The most thrilling ride in the city centre is across the inner harbour on the **cable car**, which sweeps from the **Torre de Sant Sebastià**, at the foot of Barceloneta, to Montjuïc, with a stop in the middle at **Torre de Jaume I**. The views are stunning, approaching either Montjuïc or Barceloneta, and you can pick out with ease the towers of the cathedral and Sagrada Família, while the trees lining the Ramblas look like the forked tongue of a serpent.

Departures are every fifteen minutes (daily 10.45am–7pm), though in summer and at weekends you may have to wait for a while at the top of the towers for a ride, as the cars only carry about twenty people at a time. **Tickets** cost €7.50 one way or €9 return for the whole journey, or €7.50 one way/return if you join at the middle station, Torre de Jaume I.

Barcelona is hosting the **Universal Forum of Cultures** (⊛www.barcelona2004.org) from May 9 to September 26, 2004. The closing ceremony will coincide with the traditional end of the annual Mercè festival. Best described as a peace, cultural diversity and sustainability Expo, the Forum is being held in the Poble Nou area of the city, with twenty weeks of activities, exhibitions, workshops, festivals, debates, games, markets, installations, concerts and other performances. Most of these events are being held in the new plaza, buildings and conference centre at the site, though the city's museums and cultural institutions will play a role, too.

Admission fees will be charged for entry to the main Forum site, and to other related events and activities, with **tickets** costing €21 (one day), €42 (three days) or €169 (season pass); there are discounts for senior citizens and children under 16; under 7s get in free. Tickets are available in advance from Plaça de Catalunya tourist office, the cultural information office at Palau Virreina, Ramblas 99, and at the Generalitat's information office at Palau Robert, or you can buy them on the gate after the Forum opening. There's more information on the website, including a full programme of events.

Vila Olímpica, Port Olímpic and Poble Nou

From any point along the Passeig Marítim, the soaring twin towers of the 1992 Olympic village and port impose themselves upon the skyline. The **Vila Olímpica** (Olympic Village) housed the 15,000 competitors and support staff, with the apartment buildings and residential complexes converted into permanent housing after the Games. It was a controversial plan, not least because the local population from the old industrial neighbourhood of Poble Nou – part of which was destroyed in the process – was excluded as property prices here later soared. Generally agreed to have been more beneficial is the **Port Olímpic** (ⓂCiutadella-Vila Olímpica), site of the Olympic marina and many of the watersports events. Backed by the city's two tallest buildings – the **Torre Mapfre** and the steel-framed **Hotel Arts Barcelona** – the port area has filled up with restaurants, bars, shops and nightspots, and is a major target for visitors and city dwellers at weekends and on summer nights.

Beyond here, on the far side of the port, **Nova Icària** and **Bogatell** beaches – each with a beachside café, play facilities, showers and loungers – stretch up to the **Poble Nou** neighbourhood, now also in the throes of major development. The neighbourhood is hosting the Universal Forum of Cultures (May–Sept 2004, see box above), a sort of cultural and environmental Expo, which is bringing new amenities built by some top names in the architectural world in its wake – convention centre, marina, green zones, new beaches, housing, university campus, metro links and even an improved site for part of the city's zoo.

It's fifteen minutes' walk from the Port Olímpic to the end of Bogatell beach, while crossing the main highway backing the beach puts you at the bottom of the pretty, traffic-free, tree-lined **Rambla Poble Nou**. This runs inland through the most attractive part of nineteenth-century Poble Nou and is entirely local in character – no card sharps or human statues here. Poble Nou metro (yellow line 4) is at the top of the *rambla* and a block over to the right, and will take you back to Ciutadella, Barceloneta or the city centre.

Montjuïc

Rising over the city to the southwest, the steep hill of **Montjuïc** took its name from the Jewish community that once settled on its slopes, and there's been a castle on the heights since the mid-seventeenth century, which says much about the hill's obvious historical defensive role. Since the erection of buildings for the International Exhibition of 1929, however, Montjuïc's prime role has been cultural, and you could easily spend a full day at its varied attractions, which include five museums and galleries, various gardens and the famous "Spanish Village", quite apart from the buildings and stadiums associated with the 1992 Olympics, which was centred on Montjuïc. For those short on time, the Museu Nacional d'Arte de Catalunya is undoubtedly the highlight, though fans of Miró will not want to miss the Fundació Joan Miró, and architectural pilgrims come from far and wide to visit the Pavelló Mies van der Rohe. Above all, perhaps, there are the views to savour from this most favoured of Barcelona's hills: from the steps in front of the Palau Nacional, from the castle ramparts, from the Olympic terraces, or from the cable cars which zigzag up the steepest slopes of Montjuïc.

The hill covers a wide area so it's wise to plan your visit carefully around the various opening times.

Montjuïc transport

Getting there

• Arriving by **metro** (ⓂEspanya) deposits you at the foot of Avinguda de la Reina Maria Cristina, for easy access to Caixa Forum, Poble Espanyol and the Museu Nacional d'Art. The Olympic area can then be reached by escalators behind the Museu Nacional d'Art.

• The **Funicular de Montjuïc** (daily 9am–10pm, every 10min; city transport tickets and passes apply) departs from inside the station at ⓂParal.lel. At the upper station on Avinguda de Miramar you can switch to the Montjuïc cable car (see "Getting around" below), or you're only a few minutes' walk from the Fundació Joan Miró.

• The **cross-harbour cable car** (see p.746) from Barceloneta drops you outside the Jardins de Miramar, on the far southeastern slopes. From here, it's a ten-minute walk to the Montjuïc cable car and funicular stations.

Getting around

• **Buses.** From Plaça d'Espanya (Avgda. de la Reina Maria Cristina), bus #13 for Caixa Forum and the Poble Espanyol; bus #50 for Caixa Forum, Poble Espanyol, Olympic area, funicular and cable car stations; or bus #PM (Parc de Montjuïc; weekends only) for the same route plus the castle. The Bus Turístic (see p.722) also stops at the main Montjuïc attractions.

• **Tren Turístic de Montjuïc.** The train-trolley leaves from Plaça d'Espanya (mid-June to mid-Sept daily; otherwise April–Oct Sat & Sun only, 10am–8.30pm; every 30min; €3) and runs to all the major sights on Montjuïc, including the castle. The round trip lasts about an hour and your ticket allows you to complete the full circuit once, getting on and off where you like.

• **Telefèric de Montjuïc.** The Montjuïc cable car (June to mid-Sept daily 11am–9pm, mid-Sept to Oct, April & May daily 11am–7pm; rest of the year weekends only 11am–7pm; €3.40 one way, €4.80 return), from Avinguda de Miramar, whisks you up to the castle and back in little, four-person gondolas.

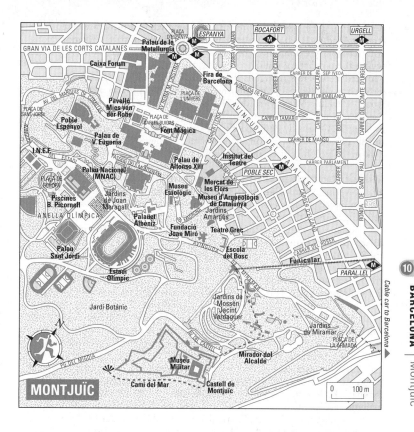

MONTJUÏC

0   100 m

Plaça d'Espanya and around

From the **Plaça d'Espanya**, past the square's 47-metre-high twin towers and up the imposing Avinguda de la Reina Maria Cristina, you can either make the stiff climb on foot, or take the long outdoor escalators. On either side of the avenue and terraces (laid out by Puig i Cadafalch) are various exhibition buildings from 1929, still in use as venues for the city's trade fairs, while the central position in front of the Palau Nacional is given over to the illuminated fountains, the **Font Màgica**, which form part of a spectacular sound and light show (May–Sept Thurs–Sun 8pm–midnight, music starts 9.30pm; Oct–April Fri & Sat only at 7pm & 8pm; free).

To the right of the fountain (before climbing the steps/escalators), and hidden from view until you turn the corner around Avinguda del Marquès de Comillas, is **Caixa Forum** (Tues–Sun 10am–8pm; free; Ⓦ www.fundacio.lacaixa.es), an arts and cultural centre set within the old Casamarona textile factory (1911). The factory shut down in 1920 and lay abandoned until pressed into service as a police building after the Civil War. The subsequent renovation under the auspices of the Fundacío La Caixa has produced a remarkable building, entered beneath twin iron-and-glass canopies representing spreading trees. The centre houses the foundation's celebrated contemporary art collection, focusing on the period from the 1980s to the present, with hundreds of artists represented, from Antoni Abad to Rachel Whiteread. Works are shown in partial rotation, along with temporary exhibitions. The café is a nice spot in an airy converted space within the old factory walls.

Immediately across Avinguda del Marquès de Comillas from Caixa Forum, set back from the road, the 1986 reconstruction by Catalan architects of the iconic **Pavelló Mies van der Rohe** (daily 10am–8pm; €3.40; Ⓦwww .miesbcn.com) recalls part of the German contribution to the 1929 Exhibition. Originally designed by Mies van der Rohe, the pavilion has a startlingly beautiful conjunction of hard straight lines with watery surfaces, its dark-green polished onyx alternating with shining glass.

Museu Nacional d'Art de Catalunya (MNAC)

The towering **Palau Nacional**, set back at the top of the flight of steps, was the centrepiece of Barcelona's 1929 International Exhibition; it was due to be demolished once the exhibition was over but gained a reprieve and five years later became home to one of Spain's great museums, the **Museu Nacional d'Art de Catalunya** (MNAC; Tues–Sat 10am–7pm, Sun 10am–2.30pm; €4.80, first Thurs of the month free; Ⓦwww.mnac.es). This is by far the best art museum in Barcelona, with a splendid collection of medieval paintings combined with MNAC's impressive holdings of European Renaissance and Baroque art, as well as the collection of nineteenth- and twentieth-century Catalan art (until the 1940s) formerly housed in the Parc de la Ciutadella – everything from the 1950s and later is covered by the MACBA (see p.740). There are also usually one or two temporary exhibits on the lower level (separate entry, €4.20, joint admission with main museum €6), which turn over every two to four months.

The **Romanesque** collection is superb, without a doubt the best of its kind in the world. From the eleventh century, the Catalan villagers of the high Pyrenees built sturdy stone churches which were then lavishly painted in vibrantly coloured frescoes depicting Christ in majesty, angels and Apostles, martyrs and mythical animals. To save them from robbery and degradation, these were painstakingly removed early in the twentieth century and remounted in mock church interiors within the museum. The collection is laid out chronologically, starting with stone sculptures from the sixth to the tenth century, but the bulk of the work dates from the thirteenth century. The frescoes, still luminescent after eight hundred years, have a vibrant, raw quality, best exemplified by those taken from churches in the Boí valley (see p.881) in the Catalan Pyrenees – like the work of the anonymous "Master of Taüll" on the churches of Sant Climent and Santa Maria; look out for details such as the leper, to the left of the Sant Climent altar, patiently suffering a dog to lick his sores.

The **Gothic** collection is also extensive, ranging over the whole of Spain – particularly good on Catalunya, Valencia and Aragón – and again, laid out chronologically, from the thirteenth to the fifteenth century. The evolution from the Romanesque to the Gothic period was marked by a move from mural painting to painting on wood, and by the depiction of more naturalistic figures

Modern art collection

The modern art collection of nineteenth- and twentieth-century Catalan art will be transferred to MNAC in the second half of 2004, with the gallery inauguration expected in December 2004.

showing the lives (and rather gruesome deaths) of the saints and, later, portraits of kings and patrons of the arts.

In the **Renaissance** and **Baroque** sections, major European artists from the fifteenth to eighteenth centuries are represented, and though there are no real masterpieces, you will find works by Lucas Cranach, Quentin Massys, Peter Paul Rubens, Giovanni Battista Tiepolo, Jean Honoré Fragonard, Francisco de Goya and others. These act as a taster for the **modern Catalan art** collection, which, as you might expect, is particularly good on *modernista* and *noucentista* painting and sculpture, the two dominant schools of the nineteenth and early twentieth centuries. The collection starts with works by Marià Fortuny who – though he died young in 1874 – is often regarded as the earliest *modernista* artist; he was certainly the first Catalan painter known widely abroad. *Noucentisme* was a style at once more classical and less consciously flamboyant than *modernisme* – perhaps the best known *noucentista* artist, Joaquim Sunyer, is among those displayed, though there are works by a host of others, including Xavier Nogués and the sculptor Pau Gargallo.

Museu Etnològic and Museu Arqueològic

Downhill from the Palau Nacional, just to the east, are a couple more collections to find time for – the city's excellent ethnological and archeological museums. The **Museu Etnològic** (Tues–Sun 10am–2pm; €3, first Sun of the month free, Ⓦ www.museuetnologic.bcn.es) boasts extensive cultural collections from Central and South America, Asia, Africa, Australia and the Middle East, housed in a series of glass hexagons.

More compelling, or at least more relevant to Catalunya, is the important **Museu d'Arqueologia de Catalunya** (Tues–Sat 9.30am–7pm, Sun 10am–2.30pm; €2.40; Ⓦ www.mac.es), lower down the hill. Mostly devoted to the Roman period, the museum also has Carthaginian relics (especially from the Balearics), Etruscan bits and pieces and lots of prehistoric objects; it's of particular interest if you're planning to visit Empúries on the Costa Brava (see p.809), since most of the important finds from that impressive coastal site, and some good maps and photographs, are housed here. Among the more unusual exhibits in the museum is a reconstructed Roman funeral chamber whose walls are divided into small niches for funeral urns – a type of burial known as *columbaria* (literally pigeon-holes), which may be seen *in situ* in the south of Spain, at Carmona in Andalucía (see p.342).

Poble Espanyol

A short walk over to the western side of the Palau Nacional brings you to the **Poble Espanyol** or "Spanish Village" (Mon 9am–8pm, Tues–Thurs 9am–2am, Fri & Sat 9am–4am, Sun 9am–midnight; €7; Ⓦ www.poble-espanyol.com). This was designed for the International Exhibition and its streets and squares consist of famous or characteristic buildings from all over the country. "Get to know Spain in one hour" is what's promised and it's nowhere near as cheesy as you might think. As a crash-course introduction to Spanish architecture it's not at all bad – everything is well labelled and at least reasonably accurate. The echoing main square is lined with cafés, while the streets, alleys and buildings off here contain around forty workshops where you can see engraving, weaving, pottery and other crafts.

The village has become a vibrant and exciting centre of Barcelona nightlife. Two of Barcelona's hippest designers, Alfredo Arribas and Xavier Mariscal, installed a club, the *Torres de Avila*, in the Ávila gate in the early 1990s. Other fashionable venues followed and, this being Barcelona, the whole complex now stays open until the small hours.

The Olympics on Montjuïc

From the Poble Espanyol, the main road through Montjuïc climbs around the hill and up to the city's principal **Olympic area**, passing on its way Ricardo Bofill's **Sports University** (the Institut Nacional d'Educació Física de Catalunya), the **Complex Esportiu Bernat Picornell** (swimming pools and sports complex), and the low-slung, Japanese-designed, steel-and-glass **Palau Sant Jordi**, a sports and concert hall seating 17,000 people.

Overhead looms the **Estadi Olímpic**, a marvellously spacious arena, which comfortably holds 65,000. Built originally for the 1929 Exhibition, the stadium was completely refitted by Catalan architects to accommodate the 1992 opening and closing ceremonies. Remarkably, the only part not touched in the rebuilding was the original Neoclassical facade – everything else is new. The **Galeria Olímpica** (Mon–Fri 10am–1pm & 4–6pm; €2.40) exhibits items from the opening and closing ceremonies, and displays videos of the Games themselves, while between the stadium and the Palau Sant Jordi a vast *terrassa* provides one of the finest vantage points in the city.

The 1992 Olympics were the second planned for Montjuïc's stadium. The first, in 1936 – the so-called "People's Olympics" – were organized as an alternative to the Nazis' infamous Berlin games of that year, but the day before the official opening Franco's army revolt triggered the Civil War and scuppered the Barcelona games. Some of the 25,000 athletes and spectators who had turned up stayed on to join the Republican forces.

Fundació Joan Miró

Continuing down the main Avinguda l'Estadi, heading towards the cable-car station, you pass what is possibly Barcelona's most adventurous museum, the **Fundació Joan Miró** (Tues–Sat 10am–7pm, Thurs until 9.30pm, Sun 10am–2.30pm; €7.20, exhibitions €3.60; Ⓦwww.bcn.fjmiro.es), an impressive white structure, opened in 1975 and set among gardens overlooking the city. Joan Miró (1893–1983) was one of the greatest of Catalan artists, establishing an international reputation whilst never severing his links with his homeland. He had his first exhibition in 1918 and after that spent his summers in Catalunya (and the rest of the time in France) before moving to Mallorca in 1956, where he died. His friend, the architect Josep-Luís Sert, designed the beautiful building that now houses the museum, a permanent collection of paintings, graphics, tapestries and sculptures donated by Miró himself and covering the period from 1914 to 1978.

The paintings and drawings, regarded as one of the chief links between Surrealism and abstract art, are instantly recognizable. Perhaps the most affecting pieces in the museum are those of the *Barcelona Series* (1939–44), a set of fifty black-and-white lithographs executed in the immediate post-Civil War period. Other exhibits include his enormous bright tapestries (he donated nine to the museum), pencil drawings and sculpture outside in the gardens.

As well as the permanent exhibits, excellent temporary exhibitions are a regular feature. There is work by other artists, too, on permanent display, including pieces conceived in homage to Miró by the likes of Henri Matisse, Henry Moore, Robert Motherwell and Eduardo Chillida. The single most compelling exhibit, however, has to be Alexander Calder's **Mercury Fountain**, which he built for the Republican pavilion at the Paris Universal Exhibition of 1936 – the same exhibition for which Picasso painted *Guernica* (see p.106). It is housed in a corridor on the ground floor.

Castell de Montjuïc

A few minutes' walk east of the Fundació Joan Miró, the Teleferic de Montjuïc tacks up the hillside, offering magnificent views on the way, before depositing you within the walls of the eighteenth-century **Castell de Montjuïc**. The fort's outer defences are constructed as a series of angular concentric perimeters, designed for artillery deflection, but the inner part is startlingly medieval in appearance, with its straight walls and square shape. The fort served as a military base and prison for many years after the Civil War and it was here that the last president of the pre-war Generalitat, Lluís Companys, was executed on Franco's orders on October 15, 1940.

You are free to take a walk along the ramparts, taking photographs from the various viewpoints, and there's a little outdoor café within the walls. You have to pay to go inside the inner keep, where you'll find Barcelona's **Museu Militar** (mid-March to mid-Nov Tues–Sun 9.30am–8pm; mid-Nov to mid-March Tues–Sun 9.30am–5pm; €2.50), containing models of the most famous Catalan castles and an excellent collection of swords and guns, medals, uniforms, maps and photographs. Below the castle walls, a panoramic pathway – the **Camí del Mar** – has been cut from the cliff edge, providing scintillating views, first across to Port Olímpic and the northern beaches and then southwest as the path swings around the castle. The path is just over 1km long and ends at the back of the castle battlements near the **Mirador del Migdia**, where a small house (weekends only) sells drinks and rents out bikes for use on the surrounding wooded trails.

The Eixample

As Barcelona grew more prosperous throughout the nineteenth century, the Barri Gòtic was filled to bursting with an energetic, commercial population. By the 1850s it was clear that the city had to expand beyond the Plaça de Catalunya. A contest was held by the *ajuntament* and the winning plan was that of the engineer Ildefons Cerdà i Sunyer, who drew up a grid-shaped new town marching off to the north, intersected by long, straight streets and cut by broad, angled avenues. Work started in 1859 on what became known as the *Ensanche* in Spanish – in Catalan, the **EIXAMPLE**, or "Extension". It immediately became the fashionable area in which to live, and the moneyed classes moved from their cramped quarters by the old port to spacious and luxurious apartments along the wide new avenues. As the money in the city moved north, so did a new class of *modernista* architects who, commissioned by the status-conscious bourgeoisie, began to pepper the Eixample with ever more striking examples of their work. The buildings – most notably the work of **Antoni Gaudí**, **Lluís Domènech i Montaner** and **Josep Puig i Cadafalch**, but others, too (see box on p.754) – are still often in private hands, restricting your viewing to the outside, but turning the Eixample into a huge urban museum around which it's a pleasure to wander.

The Eixample is still the city's main shopping and business district, spreading out on either side of the two principal (and parallel) thoroughfares, **Passeig de Gràcia** and **Rambla de Catalunya**, both of which cut northwest from the Plaça de Catalunya. The best-known *modernista* buildings are those in the famous block known as the **Mansana de la Discòrdia** and Gaudí's **La Pedrera** apartment building, found on Passeig de Gràcia. Almost everything else you're likely to want to see is found to the east of here in the area known as **Dreta de l'Eixample** (the right-hand side), including Gaudí's extraordinary **Sagrada Família** church – the one building in the city to which a visit is virtually obligatory. Other **museums** in the *Dreta* are devoted to Egyptian

Modernisme, the Catalan offshoot of Art Nouveau, was the expression of a renewed upsurge in Catalan nationalism in the 1870s. The early nineteenth-century economic recovery in Catalunya had provided the initial impetus, and the ensuing cultural renaissance in the region – the *Renaixença* – led to the fresh stirrings of a new Catalan awareness and identity after the dark years of Bourbon rule.

Lluís Domènech i Montaner (1850–1923) – perhaps the greatest *modernista* architect – was responsible for giving Catalan aspirations a definite direction with his appeal, in 1878, for a national style of architecture, drawing particularly on the rich Catalan Romanesque and Gothic traditions. The timing was perfect, since Barcelona was undergoing a huge expansion: the medieval walls had been pulled down and the gridded Eixample was giving the city a new shape, with a rather French feel to it, and plenty of new space to work in. By 1874 **Antoni Gaudí i Cornet** (1852–1926) had begun his architectural career. He was born in Reus (near Tarragona) to a family of artisans, and his work was never strictly Modernist in style (it was never strictly anything in style), but the imaginative impetus he gave the movement was incalculable. Fourteen years later the young **Josep Puig i Cadafalch** (1867–1957) would be inspired to become an architect (and later a reforming politician) as he watched the spectacularly rapid round-the-clock construction of Domènech's *Grand Hotel* on the Passeig de Colom. It was in another building by Domènech (the café-restaurant of the Parc de la Ciutadella) that a craft workshop was set up after the Exhibition of 1888, giving Barcelona's *modernista* architects the opportunity to experiment with traditional crafts like ceramic tiles, ironwork, stained glass and decorative stone carving. This combination of traditional crafts with modern technology was to become the hallmark of *modernisme* – a combination which produced some of the most fantastic and exciting architecture to be found anywhere in the world.

Most attention is usually focused on the three protagonists mentioned above; certainly they provide the bulk of the most extraordinary buildings that Barcelona has to offer. But keep an eye out for lesser-known architects who also worked in the Eixample; **Josep María Jujol i Gilbert** (1879–1949), renowned as Gaudí's collaborator on several of his most famous projects (including the mosaics at Parc Güell), can also boast a few complete constructions of his own, or there's the hard-working **Jeroni Granell i Barrera** (1867–1931), and **Josep Vilaseca i Casanoves** (1848–1910), who was responsible for the brick Arc de Triomf outside the Ciutadella park.

It's Antoni Gaudí, though, of whom most have heard – by training a metalworker, by inclination a fervent Catalan nationalist and devout Catholic. His buildings are the most daring creations of all Art Nouveau, apparently lunatic flights of fantasy which, at the same time, are perfectly functional. His architectural influences were Moorish and Gothic, while he embellished his work with elements from the natural world. Yet Gaudí rarely wrote a word about the theory of his art, preferring its products to speak for themselves. Although he worked throughout Spain, Gaudí has become a symbol of Barcelona and Catalunya; in early 2000 he was proposed to the Vatican for beatification, and he may become the first Catalan saint of the twenty-first century.

antiquities, and Catalan art and ceramics, with a special draw provided by the gallery devoted to the works of Catalan artist **Antoni Tàpies**. There's less to get excited about on the west side of Rambla de Catalunya – the so-called **Esquerra de l'Eixample** – which housed many of the public buildings contained within Cerdà's nineteenth-century plan.

Mansana de la Discòrdia

The most famous grouping of buildings, the so-called **Mansana de la Discòrdia** or "Block of Discord", is just four blocks up from Plaça de Catalunya (ⓂPasseig de Gràcia). It gets its name because the adjacent buildings – built by three different architects – are completely different in style and feel.

On the corner of c/de Consell de Cent, at Pg. de Gràcia 35, the privately owned six-storey **Casa Lleó Morera**, completed by Domènech i Montaner in 1906, is perhaps the least appealing of the buildings in the block; it has the least extravagant exterior and has suffered more than the others from "improvements" wrought by subsequent owners, which included removing the ground-floor arches and sculptures.

A few doors up at no. 41, Puig i Cadafalch's **Casa Amatller** is more striking. The facade rises in steps to a point, studded with coloured ceramic decoration and with heraldic sculptures over the doors and windows. Step inside the hallway for a peek: the ceramic tiles continue along the walls and there are twisted stone columns, fine stained-glass domes and an interior glass roof. The ground floor contains the **Centre del Modernisme** (Mon–Sat 10am–7pm, Sun 10am–2pm; free), where you'll find temporary exhibitions on the buildings and personalities of the *modernista* period, as well as an excellent selection of postcards for sale. You can also buy the *Ruta del Modernisme* ticket here (see p.719).

Perhaps the most extraordinary creation on the Block of Discord is next door, at no. 43, where Gaudí's **Casa Batlló** (Mon–Sat 9am–2pm, Sun 9am–8pm; €10; ☎932 160 306) – designed for the industrialist Josep Batlló – was similarly wrought from an apartment building already in place but considered dull by contemporaries. Gaudí was hired to give it a facelift and contrived to create a facade that Dalí later compared to "the tranquil waters of a lake". There's an animal aspect at work here, too: the stone facade hangs in folds like skin, and, from below, the twisted balcony railings resemble malevolent eyes. The interior resembles the insides of some great organism, and tours visit the main floor, patio and rear facade – it's best to reserve in advance (by phone or in person) as this is a very popular attraction.

Fundació Antoni Tàpies

Turn the corner onto c/d'Aragó and at no. 255 (just past Rambla de Catalunya) you'll find Domènech i Montaner's first important building, the Casa Montaner i Simon, finished in 1880. The building originally served the publishing firm after which it was named, but, as the enormous aluminium tubular structure on the roof now announces, it's been converted to house the **Fundació Antoni Tàpies** (Tues–Sun 10am–8pm; €4.20; ⓦwww .fundaciotapies.org; ⓂPasseig de Gràcia).

Tàpies was born in the city in 1923. His first major paintings date from 1945, at which time Tàpies was interested in collage (using newspaper, cardboard, silver wrapping, string and wire) and engraving techniques. Later, coming into contact with Miró among others, he underwent a brief Surrealist period (the fruits of which are displayed in the basement). After a stay in Paris he found his feet with an abstract style that matured during the 1950s, during which time he held his first major exhibitions, including a show in New York. His work became increasingly political during the 1960s and 1970s: the harsh colours of *In Memory of Salvador Puig Antich* commemorate a Catalan anarchist executed by Franco's regime. Temporary exhibitions focus on selections of Tàpies' work, and the foundation also includes a library and a collection of works by other contemporary artists.

Museu Egipci and Fundacío Francisco Godia

Half a block east of Passeig de Gràcia, the **Museu Egipci de Barcelona** at c/de València 284 (Mon–Sat 10am–8pm, Sun 10am–2pm; €5.40; Ⓦwww.fundclos.com; ⓂPasseig de Gràcia) is a high-quality collection of artefacts from ancient Egypt, ranging from the earliest kingdoms to the era of Cleopatra. The emphasis is on the shape and character of Egyptian society, and a serendipitous wander is a real pleasure, turning up items like a wood-and-leather bed of the First and Second Dynasties (2920–2649 BC), some examples of cat mummies of the Late Period (715–332 BC) or a rare figurine of a spoonbill (ibis) representing an Egyptian god (though archeologists aren't yet sure which). If you'd like to know more, an egyptologist leads **guided tours** every Saturday at 11am and 5pm (included in the entry price).

The building next door houses the private art collection of the **Fundacío Francisco Godia** (daily except Tues 10am–8pm; €4.50, joint admission with Museu Egipci €8.50; Ⓦwww.fundacionfgodia.org). Specializing in medieval art, ceramics and modern Catalan art, in many ways it serves as a taster for the huge collections at Montjuïc in MNAC, and its small, select size makes it immediately more accessible. Various Romanesque carvings and Gothic paintings give way to the *modernista* and *noucentista* paintings of Isidre Nonell, Santiago Rusiñol and Ramon Casas, among others. There's a varied selection of ceramics on show, too, from most of the historically important production centres in Spain. For a guided tour of the exhibits, visit on Saturday or Sunday at noon.

La Pedrera and Vinçon

Gaudí's apartment block, the Casa Milà, at Pg. de Gràcia 92 (ⓂDiagonal) is another building not to be missed. Constructed between 1905 and 1911, the rippling facade, which curves around the street corner in one smooth sweep, is said to have been inspired by the mountain of Montserrat, and the apartments themselves, whose balconies of tangled metal drip over the facade, resemble eroded cave dwellings. The building is more popularly known as **La Pedrera**, the "rock pile" or "stone quarry". The building is still split into private apartments and is administered by the Fundació Caixa de Catalunya. Through the main entrance you can access the Fundació's first-floor **exhibition hall** (daily 10am–8pm; free; guided visits Mon–Fri at 6pm), which hosts temporary art shows of works by international artists. The side entrance on c/Provença – you can't miss the queues – is where you go in to **visit La Pedrera** itself (daily 10am–8pm; €7). This includes a trip up to the roof, as well as an exhibition about Gaudí's work in the *golfes* (or top rooms) of the building; El Pis ("the apartment") is a recreation of a *modernista*-era bourgeois apartment, with period furniture and decoration. Perhaps the best way to see the building is buying a ticket for **La Pedrera de Nit**, when you can enjoy the rooftop and night-time cityscape with complimentary *cava* and music (July–Sept, weekends at 9pm; €9) – advance booking at the ticket office essential.

Right next to La Pedrera, in the same block, the **Casa Casas** dates from 1899, a huge building designed for the artist Ramon Casas who maintained a home here. In 1941, the **Vinçon** store was established in the building, which emerged in the 1960s as the country's pre-eminent purveyor of design and furniture, a position today's department store (Mon–Sat 10am–2pm & 4.30–8.30pm) still maintains; there are entrances at Pg. de Gràcia 96, c/de Provença 273 and c/Pau Claris 175.

Dreta de l'Eixample: between Passeig de Gràcia and Avinguda Diagonal

The buildings along Passeig de Gràcia are perhaps the best known in the Eixample, but the blocks contained within the triangle to the east, formed by the Passeig and **Avinguda Diagonal**, sport their own important, often extraordinary, structures. Several are by the two hardest working architects in the Eixample, Domènech i Montaner and Puig i Cadafalch, while Gaudí's first apartment building, the Casa Calvet, is also here. Apart from the Casa Calvet, all the buildings are within a few blocks of each other between the Passeig de Gràcia and Diagonal metro stops.

Just a few blocks from the Plaça de Catalunya, Gaudí's **Casa Calvet** (c/de Casp 48) dates from 1899. This was his first apartment block and, though fairly conventional in style, the Baroque inspiration on display in the main facade was to surface again in his later, more elaborate buildings on the main Passeig de Gràcia. There's now a fancy Catalan restaurant inside the building. If you need another target, aim for the church and market of **La Concepció**, in-between c/de Valencia and c/d'Aragó. The early fifteenth-century Gothic church and cloister once stood in the old town, part of a convent abandoned in the early nineteenth century and then transferred here brick by brick in the 1870s by Jeroni Granell. The market was added in 1888. One block north, the neo-Gothic **Casa Thomas** at c/de Mallorca 291, with its understated pale ceramic tiles, has a ground floor that welcomes visitors into its furniture design showroom.

From here you can head up to Avinguda Diagonal, and the soaring Casa Terrades at nos. 416–420. More usually known as the **Casa de les Punxes** (House of Spikes) because of its red-tiled turrets and steep gables, it is Puig i Cadafalch's largest work. Further along Avinguda Diagonal, on the other side of the road at no. 373, Puig's almost Gothic **Palau Quadras** from 1904 is typically intricate, with sculpted figures and emblems by Eusebi Arnau and a top row of windows which resemble miniature Swiss chalets. Down the Diagonal, at Pg. de Sant Joan 108, Puig i Cadafalch's palatial **Casa Macaya** is another superbly ornamental building, with a Gothic-inspired courtyard and canopied staircase from which griffins spring.

Sagrada Família

The Eixample's most famous monument is, without question, Antoni Gaudí's great **Temple Expiatori de la Sagrada Família** (daily: April–Sept 9am–8pm; Oct–March 9am–6pm; €8, €11 including guided tour; Ⓦwww.sagradafamilia.org; ⓂSagrada Família). It's an essential stop on any visit to Barcelona, for more than any building in the Barri Gòtic it speaks volumes about the Catalan urge to glorify uniqueness and endeavour.

Begun in 1882 by public subscription, the Sagrada Família was originally conceived by its progenitor, the Catalan publisher Josep Bocabella, as an expiatory building that would atone for the city's increasingly revolutionary ideas. Bocabella appointed the architect Francesc de Paula Villar to the work, and his plan was for a modest church in an orthodox neo-Gothic style. After arguments between the two men, Gaudí took charge two years later and changed the direction and scale of the project almost immediately, seeing in the Sagrada Família an opportunity to reflect his own deepening spiritual and nationalist feelings. Indeed, after he finished the Parc Güell in 1911, Gaudí vowed never to work again on secular art, but to devote himself solely to the Sagrada Família (where, by now, he lived in a workshop on site), and he was adapting the plans ceaselessly right up to his death. (He was run over by a tram on the Gran Vía in June 1926 and died in hospital two days later – initially unrecognized, for he had become a virtual recluse, rarely leaving his small studio. His death was treated as a Catalan national disaster, and all of Barcelona turned out for his funeral procession.)

Work restarted in the late 1950s amid great controversy. Although the church building survived the Civil War, Gaudí's plans and models were destroyed in 1936 by the anarchists, who regarded Gaudí and his church as conservative religious relics that the new Barcelona could do without. Since no one now knows what Gaudí intended, the arguments continue: some maintain that the Sagrada Família should be left incomplete as a memorial to Gaudí's untimely death, others that he intended it to be the work of several generations, each continuing in their own style. The current work has attracted criticism for infringing Gaudí's original spirit, not least the work on the Passion facade by sculptor Josep María Subirach, which has been going on since 1987. Certainly, contemporary methods and materials are being used – including computers and high-tech construction techniques – but on balance it's probably safe enough to assume that Gaudí saw the struggle to finish the building as at least as important as the method and style. Construction of the vaults over the side aisles began in 1995 and for the first time a recognizable church interior is starting to take shape. In early 2001 the roof over the central nave was finished, and the whole church is due to be roofed in due course. There's still an awfully long way to go though, and engineering paraphernalia will continue to dominate the church for years to come – the latest mooted completion date is around 2020.

The size alone is startling. Eight **spires** rise to over one hundred metres. They have been likened to everything from perforated cigars to celestial billiard cues, but for Gaudí they symbolized the twelve Apostles; he planned to build four more above the main facade and to add a 180-metre tower topped with a lamb (representing Jesus) over the transept, itself to be surrounded by four smaller towers symbolizing the Evangelists. A precise **symbolism** also pervades the facades, each of which is divided into three porches devoted to Faith, Hope and Charity. The east facade further represents the Nativity and the Mysteries of Joy; the west (currently the main entrance and nearing completion) depicts the Passion and the Mysteries of Affliction.

Use the **lift** (€2), which runs up one of the towers around the rose window, or face the long, steep climb to the top (a vertiginous 400 steps). Either route will reward you with partial views of the city through an extraordinary jumble of latticed stonework, ceramic decoration, carved buttresses and sculpture. You're free to climb still further around the walls and into the other towers, a dizzy experience to say the least. Your entrance ticket also gives you access to the crypt, where a small **museum** (times as for the church) traces the career of the architect and the history of the church.

Esquerra de l'Eixample: Plaça de Catalunya to Barcelona Sants

The long streets west of the Passeig de Gràcia – making up the **Esquerra de l'Eixample** – are no competition when it comes to planning a route around the Eixample, and most visitors only ever travel this part of the city underground, on their way into the centre by metro. This was the part of the Eixample meant by Cerdà for public buildings, and many of these still stand: the grand **Universitat** (1902) building, at Plaça de la Universitat; the local **Hospital Clinic** (1904); the **Universitat Industrial** (1908), a converted textile complex; the prison – the **Preso Model** (1902) – with its star-shaped cell blocks; and **Les Arenes** bullring, a beautiful structure from 1900 with fine Moorish decoration.

For more of an offbeat walk, take the metro out to the **Parc Joan Miró** (Ⓜ Tarragona), built on the site of the nineteenth-century municipal slaughterhouse. It's a raised piazza whose main feature is Miró's gigantic phallic sculpture *Dona i Ocell* (Woman and Bird), towering above a small lake. It's a familiar symbol if you've studied Miró's other works, and was originally entitled "The Cock", until the city authorities suggested otherwise. Even more controversial are the open park areas created around Barcelona Sants station, just up the road. Directly in front of the station, the **Plaça dels Països Catalans** features a series of walls, raised meshed roofs and coverings designed by Helio Piñon – a rather comfortless "park" in most people's eyes. It's easier to see the attraction of Basque architect Luís Peña Ganchegui's **Parc de l'Espanya Industrial**, two minutes' walk away around the side of the station. Built on an old textile factory site, it has a line of red-and-yellow-striped lighthouses at the top of glaring white steps, with an incongruously classical Neptune in the water below.

Gràcia

Gràcia is the most satisfying of Barcelona's peripheral districts, and, given its concentration of bars, clubs and restaurants, the one you're most likely to visit. Beginning at the top of the Passeig de Gràcia, and bordered roughly by c/de Balmes to the west and the streets above the Sagrada Família to the east, it has been a fully fledged suburb of the city since the late nineteenth century. Traditionally the home of a Romany (gypsy) community, it was colonized in the 1970s by arty and political types, students and the intelligentsia, and today still supports a core local population which lends Gràcia an attractive, no-frills, small-town atmosphere. **Getting there** by public transport means taking the FGC railway from Plaça de Catalunya to Gràcia station; bus #22 or #24 from Plaça de Catalunya up c/Gran de Gràcia; or taking the metro to either Diagonal, to the south, or Fontana, to the north.

Gaudí's first major private commission, the **Casa Vicens** (which he finished in 1885), is at c/de les Carolines 24 (Ⓜ Fontana). Here he took inspiration from the Mudéjar style, covering the facade in linear green-and-white tiles with a flower motif. From Casa Vicens, it's a five-minute walk east along c/Santa Agata, c/de la Providencia and then south into pretty **Plaça de la Virreina**, backed by its much-restored parish church of Sant Joan. This is one of Gràcia's favourite squares, with the *Virreina Bar* and others providing drinks and a place to rest. Another five minutes to the southwest, **Plaça del Sol** is the beating heart of much of the district's nightlife, though it's not quite so appealing during the day. It was redesigned rather soullessly in the 1980s, losing much of its attraction for older locals at least. Far more in keeping with Gràcia's overall tenor is **Plaça Rius i Taulet**, a couple of minutes to the south across Travessera de Gràcia. The thirty-metre-high clock tower was a rallying point for nineteenth-century radicals – whose twenty-first-century counterparts prefer to meet for brunch at the popular café *terrassas*, like the friendly and inexpensive *El Nou Candanchu*. Also, don't miss the market, the **Mercat de la Libertat**, Plaça de la Libertat, a block west of c/Gran de Gràcia, its food stalls sheltered by a *modernista* wrought-iron roof.

Parc Güell

From 1900 to 1914 Gaudí worked for Eusebio Güell – patron of his Palau Güell, off the Ramblas (see p.741) – on the **Parc Güell** (daily: May–Aug 10am–9pm; Sept & April 10am–8pm; Oct & March 10am–7pm; Nov–Feb

10am–6pm; free), on the outskirts of Gràcia. This was Gaudí's most ambitious project after the Sagrada Família, commissioned as a private housing estate of sixty dwellings and furnished with paths, recreational areas and decorative monuments. In the end, only two houses were actually built, and the park was opened to the public instead in 1922.

Laid out on a hill, which provides fabulous views back across the city, the park is an almost hallucinatory expression of the imagination. Pavilions of contorted stone, giant decorative lizards, a vast Hall of Columns (intended to be the estate's market), the meanderings of a huge ceramic bench – all combine in one manic swirl of ideas and excesses. The mosaics and decorations (many made from broken crockery) found throughout the park were mostly executed by J.M. Jujol, who assisted on several of Gaudí's projects, while one of Gaudí's other collaborators, Francesc Berenguer, designed and built a house in the park in 1904, in which Gaudí was persuaded to live until he left to camp out at the Sagrada Família for good. The house is now the **Casa Museu Gaudí** (daily: April–Sept 10am–8pm; Oct–March 10am–6pm; €3), a small but diverting collection of some of the furniture he designed for other projects as well as plans and objects related to the park and to Gaudí's life.

To get to the park, take **bus** #24 from Plaça de Catalunya right to the side gate by the car park, or the **metro** to Vallcarca, from where you walk down Avinguda de l'Hospital until you see the mechanical escalators on your left, then follow the path right to the park entrance. Be warned, however, that the escalators are often not working and the climb up on foot is a particularly stiff one. **Walking from Gràcia**, head straight up the main c/Gran de Gràcia and you'll pass Lesseps metro station, where you should turn right on to the Travessera de Dalt and follow the signs.

Camp Nou: the Museu del Barça

Northwest of the centre, within the city's Diagonal area, the magnificent **Camp Nou** football stadium of FC Barcelona (ⓂCollblanc/María Cristina) will be high on the visiting list of any sports fan. Built in 1957, and enlarged to accommodate the 1982 World Cup semi-final, the comfortable stadium seats a staggering 120,000 people in steep tiers that provide one of the best football-watching experiences in the world – on a par with the famous Maracaña stadium in Brazil. The club is historically one of Spain's most successful teams, although in recent years it has suffered on the field at the hands of arch-rival Real Madrid who added insult to injury by poaching star player Figo from the team in 2000. But it's more than just a football club to most people in Barcelona. During the Franco era, it stood as a Catalan symbol, around which people could rally, and perhaps as a consequence FC Barcelona has the world's largest football club membership.

If you can't get to a game, a visit to the stadium's **Museu del Barça** (Mon–Sat 10am–6.30pm, Sun 10am–2pm; €5, guided tours €9; Ⓦwww.fcbarcelona.com) is hardly second best, since it's a splendid celebration of Spain's national sport. There's an excellent English-language photo-history, an audiovisual display of goals galore, team and match photos dating back to 1901, and a gallery of the celebrated foreign players who have graced Barça's books. You can also see an exhibition of football memorabilia, paintings and sculpture, and there's a souvenir shop and café at the ground.

Palau Reial de Pedralbes and the Finca Güell

On the other side of Avinguda Diagonal, the **Palau Reial de Pedralbes** (ⓂPalau Reial) is an Italianate palace set in pleasant, formal grounds. Since 1990 the city has used its rooms to show off some of its applied art collections. There are plans to shift the displays to a new purpose-built museum, but for the foreseeable future the palace contains separate **museums of ceramics and decorative arts** (Tues–Sat 10am–6pm, Sun 10am–3pm; €3.50; free on first Sun of the month), both accessible on one ticket – which you can also use within one month to get into the Museu Textil i d'Indumentària in La Ribera (see p.743).

The bulk of the exhibits at the **Museu de la Ceràmica** range from the thirteenth to the nineteenth century, and include fine Mudéjar-influenced tiles and plates from the Aragonese town of Teruel, as well as whole rooms of Catalan water spouts (some from the seventeenth century), jars, dishes and bowls. In the modern section, Picasso, Miró and the *modernista* Antoni Serra i Fiter are all represented. Across the corridor, the rooms of the **Museu de les Arts Decoratives** are arranged around the upper gallery of the palace's former throne room, presenting a collection of household objects and industrial design from the Middle Ages to the modern day.

From the palace, it's a walk of fifteen minutes or so up Avinguda Pedralbes to the monastery. Just a couple of minutes along the way, you'll pass Gaudí's **Finca Güell** on your left. Built as a stables and riding school for the family of Gaudí's old patron, Eusebio Güell, and now a private residence, you can see no further than its extraordinary metal dragon gateway, with razor teeth snarling at the passers-by.

Monestir de Pedralbes

At the end of Avinguda Pedralbes, the Gothic **Monestir de Santa María de Pedralbes** (Tues–Sun 10am–2pm; monastery €4, art collection €3.50, both €5.50, free on first Sun of the month) is reached up a cobbled street that passes through a small archway set back from the road. It's a twenty-minute walk from Palau Reial metro station, or you can get there directly by bus from the city centre (30min): the #22 from Plaça de Catalunya and Passeig de Gràcia stops outside, while the #64 from Ronda Sant Antoni and c/Aribau ends its run at the monastery.

Founded in 1326 for the nuns of the Order of St Clare, this is in effect a self-contained religious community, preserved on the outskirts of the city. Access is allowed to the historic parts of the complex, particularly the harmonious **cloisters**, which are built on three levels and adorned by the slenderest of columns. The preserved rooms opening off here give the clearest impression of early monastic life you're likely to see in Catalunya: there's a large refectory, a fully equipped kitchen, an infirmary (complete with beds and water jugs), a separate infirmary kitchen, and windows overlooking a well-tended kitchen garden. The adjacent **church**, a simple, single-naved structure which retains some of its original stained glass, is also well worth looking in on. In the chancel, to the right of the altar, the foundation's sponsor, Elisenda de Montcada, wife of Jaume II, lies in a superb, carved marble tomb.

The immense private art collection of Baron Heinrich Thyssen-Bornemisza came to Spain in 1989, and the bulk of it is displayed in Madrid's Villahermosa palace (see p.104), but the promptings of the baron's Catalan wife ensured a cache of paintings found its way to Barcelona. This now forms the **Col.lecció Thyssen-Bornemisza**, on permanent view in one of the monastery's capacious old dormitories, which has been given a black marble floor and soaring oak-beamed ceiling. It's a small but superb body of work, including priceless pieces from five major movements in European art from the fourteenth to the eighteenth centuries, displayed more or less chronologically. The collection begins with a series of medieval Italian religious paintings, of which the undoubted highlight is the sublime *Madonna of Humility* by Fra Angelico, painted in 1433. Subsequent works range far and wide – a Canaletto here, a Rubens there – but there are more pieces of genuine quality, including Titian's sensuous *Madonna and Child* and a famous Velázquez portrait of the bulbous-nosed Maria Anna of Austria.

Tibidabo

If the views from the Castell de Montjuïc are good, those from the 550-metre heights of **Mount Tibidabo** – which forms the northwestern boundary of the city – are legendary. On one of those mythical clear days you can see across to Montserrat and the Pyrenees. The very name is based on this view, taken from the Temptations of Christ in the wilderness, when Satan led him to a high place and offered him everything which could be seen: *Haec omnia tibi dabo si cadens adoraberis me* ("All these things will I give thee, if thou wilt fall down and worship me").

At the summit there's a modern **church** topped with a huge statue of Christ, and – immediately adjacent – a wonderful **Parc d'Atraccions** (mid-June to mid-Sept daily noon–10pm, until 1am at weekends; mid-Sept to mid-June Sat & Sun only noon–6pm; hours sometimes vary, call ☎932 117 942 for exact times; €10 or €20), founded in 1901. The amusements are scattered around several levels of the mountain-top, connected by landscaped paths and gardens, and comprise a good mix of traditional rides and high-tech attractions, at all of which large queues form at peak times. The most expensive entrance ticket allows unlimited access to everything, otherwise you're limited to a selection of the best rides and attractions, including the **Museu d'Autòmates**, a collection of coin-operated antique fairground machines in working order. If you want a real thrill, try the aeroplane ride, a Barcelona icon; it's been spinning since 1928.

To get there, first take the FGC **train** (Tibidabo line) from the station at Plaça de Catalunya to Avinguda Tibidabo (the last stop). An antique **tram** service (the *Tramvia Blau*; weekends and holidays 10am–5.45pm, every 15–30min; €2 one way, €2.90 return) then runs you up the hill to Plaça Doctor Andreu; there's a bus service instead (Mon–Fri 7.45am–8.40pm, every 20min) during the rest of the week. Near the tram and bus stop on Plaça Doctor Andreu there are several café-bars and restaurants and a **funicular station**. When the Parc d'Atraccions is open, this has regular connections to Tibidabo at the top (€2, one way, €3 return). If the funicular isn't running, you could take a taxi from Avinguda Tibidabo instead, which will cost about €8 to Tibidabo. Alternatively, the special **Tibibus** runs direct to Tibidabo from Plaça de Catalunya, outside El Corte Inglés (weekends & holidays year round, every 30min; plus weekdays in summer, hourly; €2).

Out of the city: Montserrat

The **mountain of Montserrat**, with its strangely shaped crags of rock, its monastery and ruined hermitage caves, stands just 40km northwest of Barcelona, off the road to Lleida. It is one of the most spectacular of all Spain's natural sights, a sawtoothed outcrop left exposed to erosion when the inland sea that covered this area around 25 million years ago was drained by progressive uplifts of the earth's crust. Legends hang easily upon it. Fifty years after the birth of Christ, St Peter is said to have deposited an image of the Virgin carved by St Luke in one of the mountain caves, and another tale makes this the spot in which the knight Parsifal discovered the Holy Grail. Inevitably, the monastery and mountain are no longer remote; in fact they're ruthlessly exploited as a tourist trip from the Costa Brava, while the main **pilgrimages** to Montserrat take place on April 27 and September 8. But don't be put off – the place itself is still magical and you can avoid the crowds by striking out onto the mountainside, along well-signposted paths, to potent and deserted hermitages. You could also stay the night, though the hotels and restaurants within the complex are overpriced, and the campsite and mountain refuges often very busy.

The monastery and mountain

It is the "Black Virgin" (*La Moreneta*), the icon supposedly brought here by Saint Peter (but curiously reflecting the style of sixth-century Byzantine carving), which is responsible for the existence of the **monastery of Montserrat**. The legend is loosely wrought, but it appears the icon was lost in the early eighth century after being hidden during the Muslim invasion. It reappeared in 880, accompanied by the customary visions and celestial music and, in the first of its miracles, would not budge when the bishop of Vic attempted to remove it. A chapel was built to house it, and in 976 this was superseded by a Benedictine monastery, set about three-quarters of the way up the mountain at an altitude of nearly 1000m. Miracles abounded and the Virgin of Montserrat soon became the chief cult image of Catalunya and a pilgrimage centre second in Spain only to Santiago de Compostela. For centuries, the monastery enjoyed outrageous prosperity, having its own flag and a form of extraterritorial independence along the lines of the Vatican City. Its fortunes declined only in the nineteenth century; in 1835 the monastery was suppressed for supporting the wrong side in the civil war (the First Carlist War) – monks were allowed to return nine years later, but by 1882 their numbers had fallen to nineteen. Later, when the Catalan language was suppressed by Franco, the monastery acted to preserve native literature and as a focus of clandestine nationalism. In recent decades Montserrat's popularity has again become established; today there are over 300 brothers and, in addition to the tourists, tens of thousands of newly married couples come here to seek *La Moreneta*'s blessing on their union.

The monastery itself is of no particular architectural interest, save perhaps in its monstrous bulk. Only the Renaissance **Basilica** (daily 8–10.30am & noon–6.30pm; free) is open to the public. **La Moreneta**, blackened by the smoke of countless candles, stands above the high altar – reached from behind, by way of an entrance to the right of the basilica's main entrance. The best time to be here is at the chanting of Ave Maria, around 1pm (noon on Sun), when Montserrat's world-famous **boys' choir** sings. Near the entrance to the basilica, the **Museu de Montserrat** (Mon–Fri 10am–6.45pm, Sat & Sun

9.30am–7.45pm; €5.50) presents a few archeological finds as well as an art collection that boasts paintings by Caravaggio, El Greco, Tiepolo, Degas, Monet, Picasso and others. The joint ticket also gets you in the **Espai Audiovisual** (daily 9am–6pm), near the tourist office, a multimedia exhibition which tells you something of the life of a Benedictine community.

After you've poked around the monastery grounds, it's the **mountain walks** that are the real attraction. Following the tracks to various caves and the thirteen different hermitages, you can contemplate what Goethe wrote in 1816: "Nowhere but in his own Montserrat will a man find happiness and peace." Two separate **funiculars** run from points close to the cable-car station, with departures every 20 minutes (daily 10am–6pm; weekends only in winter). One drops to the path for **Santa Cova** (€2.50 return), a seventeenth-century chapel built where the icon is said to have been found originally. It's an easy walk there and back that takes less than an hour. The other funicular rises steeply to the hermitage of **Sant Joan** (€6.10 return), from where it's a tougher 45 minutes' walk to the **Sant Jeroni** hermitage, and another 15 minutes to the Sant Jeroni summit at 1236m. A joint ticket (€6.90) covers return journeys on both funiculars.

Practicalities

FGC **trains** (line R5, direction Manresa; ⓦ www.fgc.net) leave from beneath Plaça d'Espanya daily from 8.36am at hourly intervals; get off at Montserrat Aeri (52min). From here, the connecting **cable car** (*Aeri*; every 15min, daily 9.25am–1.45pm & 2.20–6.45pm) completes the journey, a five-minute swoop up the sheer mountainside to a terrace just below the monastery – probably the most exhilarating ride in Catalunya. The alternative approach is by the *cremallera*, or cog-wheel **mountain railway** (ⓦ www.cremalleradementserrat.com), which departs from Monistrol de Montserrat (the next stop 4min after Montserrat Aeri); this leaves every twenty to sixty minutes (depending on season), connecting with train arrivals from Barcelona, and takes twenty minutes to climb to the monastery. **Returning to Barcelona**, the return trains depart hourly from Monistrol de Montserrat (9.33am–11.33pm) and Montserrat Aeri (9.37am–11.37pm). **Drivers** should take the A2 motorway as far as Martorell, and then follow the N11 and C1411 before zigzagging up to the monastery.

A **return ticket** from Plaça d'Espanya costs €11.80 (train and cable car/train and *cremallera*), and there are also two combined tickets: the **Transmontserrat** (€20.50 return), which includes the metro, train, cable car/*cremallera* and unlimited use of the two mountain funiculars; and the **Totmontserrat** (€34.50), which includes the same plus museum/audiovisual entry and a self-service cafeteria lunch. The combined tickets are also available from any city FGC station. There is also a daily morning **bus service** (€7.40 return, weekends €8.40) from Barcelona to the monastery and full bus tour (€38), both with *Julia Tours* (information from any tourist office), but these can't compete for thrills with the public transport rides.

Information and food

There's a tourist office at Montserrat, just up from the *cremallera* station, marked **Informació** (daily 9am–5.45pm, July–Sept until 7pm; ☏ 938 777 701, ⓦ www.abadiamontserrat.net), where you can pick up maps of the complex and mountain. There are plenty of places to eat, but all are relatively pricey and none particularly inspiring. Best views are from the *Restaurant de Montserrat* (with *menús* at €12.60 and €19.80), in the cliff-edge building near the car park, though here and in the **self-service cafeteria** (*menú* €9.40), one floor up, there's no *à la carte* choice – ie, you have to have the full meal – and the food is produced in industrial quantities. The latter is where you eat with the all-inclusive Totmontserrat ticket. There's a cheaper self-service cafeteria near the upper cable-car station, a **bar** in the square further up, plus a patisserie and a **supermarket**, and there's a lot to be said for taking your own picnic and striking off up the mountainside.

Eating

There is a great variety of food available in Barcelona and even low-budget travellers can do well for themselves, either by using the excellent markets and filling up on snacks, or eating cheaply from the set menus. Nearly all cafés and restaurants offer a three-course *menú del día* at lunchtime, with the cheapest starting at about €7, rising to €10–12 in fancier places.

Pizza, burger, felafel/kebab and **cappuccino** joints are ubiquitous, especially on the Ramblas and on the main streets in the Eixample. **Local and Spanish chains** include: *Pans & Company* and *Bocatta*, for hot and cold baguette-based sandwiches and salads; *Fresh and Ready* for deli, sandwich and juice offerings; *Il Caffè di Roma,* serving coffee and other hot drinks, pastries and ice creams; the classier *Aroma* cafés; and the warehouse-style *Café di Francesco* for coffee, tea and croissants.

Good tapas bars and **restaurants** are easily found all over the city, though you'll probably do most of your eating where you do most of your sightseeing, in the old town. However, if you step no further than the Ramblas, or the streets around the cathedral, you are not going to experience the best of the city's cuisine – in the main tourist areas food and service can be indifferent and prices high. You need to be a bit more adventurous, and explore the backstreets of **La Ribera** and **El Raval** where you'll find excellent restaurants, some little more than hole-in-the-wall cafés or traditional taverns, others surprisingly funky (and surprisingly expensive). In the **Eixample** prices tend to be higher, though you'll find plenty of lunchtime bargains around; **Gràcia**, further out, is a nice place to spend the evening, with plenty of good mid-range restaurants. For the food which Barcelona is really proud of – elaborate *sarsuelas* (fish stews), *paellas*, and all kinds of fish and seafood – you're best off in **Barceloneta**, down by the harbour, or in the **Port Olímpic**.

All the places below are marked on the **maps** on p.714 and p.715.

Cafés and snacks

You can get coffee and bread or croissants almost anywhere, but a few cafés and specialist places – *granjas* and *orxaterias* (milk bars) especially – are worth looking out for. Snacks and sandwiches abound, too, and you'll be tempted by *ensaimadas* (pastry spirals), pizza slices and cakes at any bakery or pastry shop.

Antiga Casa Figueres Ramblas 83; ⓂLiceu. Wonderful *modernista* pastry shop with a few tables outside. Mon–Sat 9am–3pm & 5–8.30pm.
Bagel Shop c/Canuda 25; ⓂCatalunya. The café that introduced the bagel to Barcelona – there's cream cheese and smoked salmon and many others, including one rubbed with tomato, garlic, olive oil and salt for the local crowd. Mon–Sat

9.30am–9.30pm, Sun 11am–4pm.
Café d'Estiu Pl. de Sant Iu 5–6; ⓂJaume I. A summer-only café housed on the delightful interior terrace of the Museu Marès. April–Oct Tues–Sun 10am–10pm.
Café del Sol Pl. del Sol 16, Gràcia; ⓂFontana. Popular, split-level neighbourhood café-bar, with seats outside in the square attracting the local

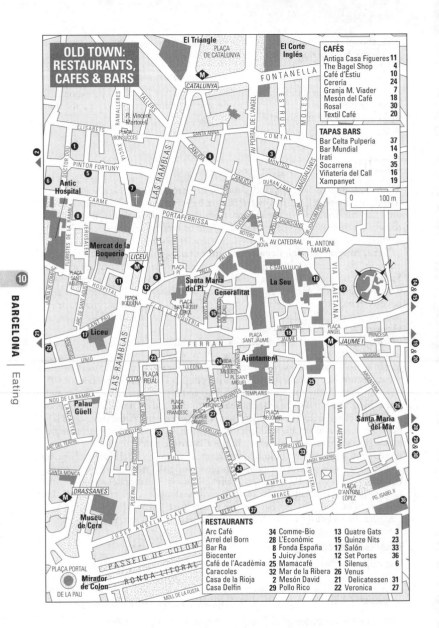

OLD TOWN: RESTAURANTS, CAFES & BARS

CAFÉS

Antiga Casa Figueres	11
The Bagel Shop	4
Café d'Estiu	10
Cerería	24
Granja M. Viader	7
Mesón del Café	18
Rosal	30
Textil Café	20

TAPAS BARS

Bar Celta Pulpería	37
Bar Mundial	14
Irati	9
Socarrena	35
Viñatería del Call	16
Xampanyet	19

0   100 m

RESTAURANTS

Arc Café	34	Comme-Bio	13	Quatre Gats	3
Arrel del Born	28	L'Econòmic	15	Quinze Nits	23
Bar Ra	8	Fonda España	33	Salón	33
Biocenter	5	Juicy Jones	12	Set Portes	36
Café de l'Acadèmia	25	Mamacafé	1	Silenus	6
Caracoles	32	Mar de la Ribera	26	Venus	
Casa de la Rioja	2	Mesón David	21	Delicatessen	31
Casa Delfín	29	Pollo Rico	22	Veronica	27

poseurs. Daily except Mon 1pm–3am.

Cerería Bxda. de Sant Miquel 3–5; ⓂJaume I. Amiably hip café that attracts its fair share of literary types and pseudo-intellectuals. Food is breakfast- and veggie-friendly, with great-looking cakes

and a changing roster of *platos del día*. Daily 10am–10pm.

Granja M. Viader c/Xuclà 4–6; ⓂLiceu. Delicious snacks including home-made *flans*, cakes and hot chocolate with cream, in a traditional Raval *granja* bar, tucked away down a narrow alley just off c/del Carmé. Tues–Sat 9am–1.45pm & 5–8.45pm.

Laie Llibreria Café c/Pau Claris 85; Ⓜ️Urquinaona. Bookshop café where the choice is between the bar and mezzanine seating or the roomier salon at the back under bamboo matting. The buffet breakfast spread is popular. Mon–Fri 9am–1am, Sat 10am–1am.

Mesón del Café c/Llibreteria 16; Ⓜ️Jaume I. Tiny, offbeat bar where you'll probably have to stand to sample the pastries and the excellent coffee,

including a cappuccino laden with fresh cream. Mon–Sat 7am–11pm.

Rosal Pg. del Born 27; Ⓜ️Jaume I. The *terrassa* at the end of the Born gets the sun all day, making it a popular meeting place, though it's also packed on summer nights. Daily 9am–2am.

Textil Café c/de Montcada 12–14; Ⓜ️Jaume I. Set inside the shady, cobbled medieval courtyard of the Museu Textil i d'Indumentaria. Serves hummous, tzatziki, quiche, salads, chilli, lasagne and big sandwiches. Tues–Sun 10am–midnight.

Tapas bars

Tapas are not a particularly Catalan phenomenon, with most **tapas bars** in the city run by people from other parts of Spain, especially Galicia and the Basque Country. That's not to say the tapas bars aren't any good, far from it. The most famous concentration in the Barri Gòtic is down by the port, between the Columbus monument and the post office – along c/Ample, c/de la Mercè, c/del Regomir and their offshoots. Jumping from bar to bar, with a bite to eat in each, is as good a way as any to fill up on some of the best food that the city has to offer. Done this way, your evening needn't cost more than a meal in a medium-priced restaurant – say €15–20 a head. More Catalan in execution are the city's **llesqueries**. A *llesca* is a thick slice of country bread which is toasted, rubbed with garlic and tomato, and sprinkled with olive oil, better known as *pa amb tomàquet* (bread with tomato). This is served in more upmarket bars, along with cured ham or cold cuts, cheeses or *escalivada* (roasted pepper, onion and aubergine).

Barri Gòtic

Bar Celta Pulpería c/de la Mercè 16; Ⓜ️Drassanes. Excellent, no-nonsense Galician tapas bar, specializing in octopus, fried pimientos and heady Galician wine. Out-of-towners should double-check the bill. Mon–Sat 10am–1am, Sun 10am–midnight.

Irati c/Cardenal Casañas 17; Ⓜ️Liceu. Locals think favourably of the Basque *pintxos* featuring country sausage to smoked salmon. Careful, though – the price soon mounts up. Tues–Sun noon–midnight; *pintxos* served noon–3pm & 7–11pm.

La Socarrena c/de la Mercè 21; Ⓜ️Drassanes. Asturian bar serving goat's cheese, cured meats and cider (*sidra*). Check out the waiter's contortionist, but traditional, pouring technique (over the back of his head), designed to aerate the cider. Daily 1.30–3pm & 6pm–3am.

La Viñatería del Call c/Sant Domènec del Call 9; Ⓜ️Liceu/Jaume I. A typical Catalan *llesquería: pa amb tomàquet* with cheese, ham, *escalivada*, fish, fried peppers and much more, plus a wide range of wines. Mon–Sat 6pm–1am.

La Ribera and Barceloneta

Jai-Ca c/Ginebra 13; Ⓜ️Barceloneta. Don't let the gruff interior fool you, this is one of the best tapas

finds in Barceloneta. In summertime, take your food out onto the tiny street-corner patio. Daily 10am–11pm.

Bar Mundial Pl. de Sant Agusti el Vell 1; Ⓜ️Jaume I. Simple 70-year-old neighbourhood bar, famous for its seafood tapas and meals, washed down with cold white wine. Mon & Wed–Sat 10am–11pm, Sun 10am–4pm; closed two weeks in Aug.

Xampanyet c/de Montcada 22; Ⓜ️Jaume I. Terrific, bustling, blue-tiled bar with fine seafood tapas, sweet sparkling wine by the glass or bottle, and local *sidra*. As is often the way, the drinks are cheap and the tapas rather pricey, but there's always a good atmosphere. Tues–Sat noon–4pm & 6.30–11pm, Sun noon–4pm; closed Aug.

Eixample

ba-ba-reeba Pg. de Gràcia 28; Ⓜ️Passeig de Gràcia. Catering for all needs from breakfast to suppertime and beyond. A good range of tapas, from all corners of Spain, spreads along a twenty-metre bar. Daily 7.30am–1.30am.

La Bodegueta Rambla Catalunya 100; Ⓜ️Diagonal. Long-established basement *bodega* with *cava* by the glass, a serious range of other wines, and good ham, cheese, anchovies and *pa amb tomàquet* to soak it

As a rough guide, you'll be able to get a three-course meal with drinks in Barcelona for:
Inexpensive: Under €15
Moderate: €15–30
Expensive: €30–45
Very expensive: Over €45
But bear in mind that the lunchtime *menú del día* often allows you to eat for much less than the à la carte price category might lead you to expect; check the listings for details.

all up. Daily 8am–2am; closed mornings in Aug.
Ciudad Condal Rambla de Catalunya 18; ⓂPasseig de Gràcia. Describes itself as a *cerveceria* (and indeed has twenty beers available), but that's only half the story in this cavernous city pitstop. Breakfast sees the bar groan under the weight of a dozen types of crispy baguette sandwich, while the tapas selection ranges far and wide. Daily 7.30am–1.30am.

Sarrià

Bar Tomás c/Major de Sarrià 49; FGC Sarrià. It requires a special trip to the 'burbs (12min on the train from Pl. Catalunya FGC station) to taste the *patatas bravas* of the Gods – a dish of spicy fried potatoes with garlic mayo and *salsa picante* for €1.55. They fry between noon and 3pm and 6pm and closing, so if it's only *bravas* you want, note the hours. Daily except Wed 8am–10pm.

Restaurants

The most common restaurants in Barcelona are those serving **Catalan** food, though more mainstream Spanish dishes are generally available, too. There are several **regional Spanish and colonial Spanish** restaurants as well, which are nearly always worth investigating, while traditionally the fancier restaurants have tended towards a refined Catalan-French style of dining. This has been superseded recently by so-called "fusion" cuisine (basically Mediterranean flavours with exotic touches). The range of **international cuisine** is not as wide as in other European cities, but if you've been in Spain for any length of time, you may be grateful that there's a choice at all – pizzas, Chinese and Indian/Pakistani food provide the main choices, though the cuisines of Mexico, North Africa, the Middle East and Japan are represented, too.

Restaurants are generally **open** approximately 1 to 4pm and 8 to 11pm. A lot of restaurants **close on Sundays, on public holidays and throughout August** – check the listings for specific details but expect changes since many places imaginatively interpret their own posted opening days and times.

Barri Gòtic

ⓂLiceu/Jaume I
Arc Café c/Carabassa 19 ☎933 025 204. One of the best of the new brasserie-bars in the old town, popular with students, foreigners and arty types. Breakfasts served until 1pm, otherwise a €7.50 *menú* and a changing à la carte choice. Mon–Thurs 9am–1am, Fri 9am–3am, Sat 11am–3am, Sun 11am–1am. Inexpensive.
Café de l'Acadèmia c/Lledó 1 ☎933 198 253. Creative Catalan cooking in a romantic, stone-flagged old-town restaurant. The prices are very reasonable and it's always busy, so reservations are essential. Mon–Fri 1.30–4pm & 8.45–11.30pm; closed 2 weeks in Aug. Moderate.

Los Caracoles c/Escudellers 14 ☎933 023 185. A cavernous Barcelona landmark with spit-roast chickens turning on grills outside and an open kitchen straight out of Mervyn Peake's *Gormenghast*. The restaurant name means "snails", a house speciality, and the chicken's good too, but there's a full Catalan/Spanish menu in a multitude of languages. Daily 1pm–midnight. Expensive.
Els Quatre Gats c/Montsió 3 ☎933 024 140. The *modernista*-designed haunt of Picasso and his contemporaries – the lofty interior has rich furnishings and paintings, and was the setting for Picasso's first public exhibition. Now a pricey Catalan restaurant-and-bar (lunchtime *menú* is

Vegetarians will find themselves pleasantly surprised by the choice available in Barcelona if they've spent any time in other areas of Spain. The restaurants listed below are the pick of the specifically vegetarian places in the city, but you'll also be able to do pretty well for yourself in regular tapas bars and modern Catalan brasseries and restaurants. Otherwise, there are a fair few pizza places and Indian/Pakistani restaurants – you certainly shouldn't starve.

Arco Iris c/Roger de Flor 216 ☏934 5822 83; Ⓜ Verdaguer. Simple café serving a low-cost, four-course lunchtime veggie *menú del día* for €8.20 (drinks extra). Mon–Sat 1–4pm; closed Aug. Inexpensive.

L'Atzavara c/Muntaner 109 ☏934 545 925; Ⓜ Provença. Lunch-only spot for fresh-tasting vegetarian dining on proper tablecloths. It's a bit more gourmet than many similar places: you pay €8.10 and choose from half a dozen starters and soups, three mains and four puds. Mon–Sat 1–4pm. Inexpensive.

Biocenter c/Pintor Fortuny 25 ☏933 014 583; Ⓜ Liceu. The €7.75 *menú* starts serving at 1pm, with a trawl through the salad bar the best option for a first course, followed by market-fresh mains. Mon–Sat 9am–5pm. Inexpensive.

Comme-Bio Via Laietana 28 ☏933 198 968; Ⓜ Jaume I. Restaurant, juice and sandwich bar within a big store selling organic fruit and vegetables, health foods and related items. The buffet lunch spread (Mon–Sat 1–3.45pm, Sun 1.15–4pm; €8.45) is the big attraction. Mon–Sat 8am–11.30pm, Sun noon–11.30pm. Moderate.

Illa de Gràcia c/Sant Domènec 19 ☏932 380 229; Ⓜ Diagonal. Sleek Gràcia vegetarian dining room where the food is a cut above – think grilled tofu, stuffed aubergine gratin or wholewheat spaghetti *carbonara*. Tues–Fri 1–4pm & 9pm–midnight, Sat & Sun 2pm–midnight; closed mid-Aug to mid-Sept. Inexpensive.

Juicy Jones c/Cardenal Casañas 7 ☏933 024 330; Ⓜ Liceu. Veggie-vegan restaurant/juice bar with a €7 *menú del día* that touches all corners of the world – cashew, carrot and coriander soup could be followed by pumpkin-stuffed *gnocchi*. Juices squeezed and soy milkshakes whizzed at the front bar. Daily 10am–midnight. Inexpensive.

€10) though some find the food disappointing. Mon–Sat 11am–2am, Sun 5pm–2am. Expensive.

Les Quinze Nits Pl. Reial 6 ☏933 173 075. Approaching institution status, this elegant brasserie on Barcelona's most touristy square delivers on its one big promise – price. Get there early and join the queue as reservations aren't accepted. Daily 1–3.45pm & 8.30–11.30pm. Moderate.

El Salón c/L'Hostal d'en Sol 6–8 ☏933 152 159. Renovated old building with a Gothic feel, serving imaginative dishes in a relaxed atmosphere – rabbit with a *mole* sauce and tacos or curried vegetables with a yoghurt and coconut sauce. Mon–Sat 1.30–4.30pm & 8.30pm–midnight. Expensive.

La Veronica c/d'Avinyo 30 ☏934 121 122. Crispy pizzas (all bar one vegetarian), inventive salads and tables outside on funky Plaça George Orwell. Daily noon–1am; closed 2 weeks in Aug. Moderate.

Venus Delicatessen c/Avinyó 25 ☏933 011 585. The Med-bistro cuisine is good for vegetarians, with things like lasagne, couscous, moussaka and

salads, and there's a weekday lunchtime *menú* for €8. Mon–Sat noon–midnight. Inexpensive.

La Ribera

Ⓜ Jaume I/Barceloneta

Arrel del Born c/Fusina 5 ☏933 199 299. Lovely, light-filled contemporary restaurant with a roomy warehouse-style interior, opposite the old Born market. Fish is the speciality here, exquisitely cooked – the *menú del día* is €15, weekends €21. Mon–Sat 1–4pm & 8.30pm–midnight, Sun 1–4pm. Expensive.

Casa Delfin Pg. del Born 36 ☏933 195 088. Old-school paper-tablecloth bar-restaurant that packs in the locals for a cheap and cheerful *menú del día*. Mon–Sat 8am–5pm; closed Aug. Inexpensive.

Mar de la Ribera c/Sombrerers 7 ☏933 151 336. A friendly little place around the back of Santa Maria del Mar serving up the best *gallego* seafood at prices that encourage large and leisurely meals. Mon 8–11.30pm, Tues–Sat 1–4pm & 8–11.30pm. Moderate.

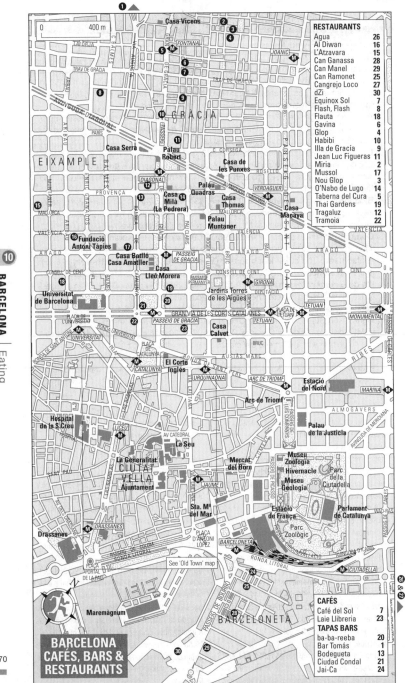

RESTAURANTS

Agua	26
Al Diwan	16
L'Atzavara	15
Can Ganassa	28
Can Manel	29
Can Ramonet	25
Cangrejo Loco	27
dZi	30
Equinox Sol	7
Flash, Flash	8
Flauta	18
Gavina	6
Glop	4
Habibi	10
Illa de Gràcia	9
Jean Luc Figueras	11
Miria	17
Mussol	17
Nou Glop	3
O'Nabo de Lugo	14
Taberna del Cura	5
Thai Gardens	19
Tragaluz	12
Tramoia	22

CAFÉS

Café del Sol	7
Laie Llibreria	23

TAPAS BARS

ba-ba-reeba	20
Bar Tomás	1
Bodegueta	13
Ciudad Condal	21
Jai-Ca	24

BARCELONA CAFÉS, BARS & RESTAURANTS

Set Portes Pg. d'Isabel II 14 ☎933 192 950. The decor in the "Seven Doors" has barely changed in 150 years, and, while very elegant, it's not exclusive – book ahead, though, as the queues can be enormous. The seafood is excellent, particularly the *arroz* dishes, of which there are several fairly reasonably priced (€11–16) variations. Daily 1pm–1am. Expensive.

El Raval

Ⓜ Liceu

Bar Ra Pl. de la Garduña ☎934 231 878. Extremely hip restaurant/bar behind the Boqueria market, serving up eclectic world cuisine for lunch and dinner on a sunny patio. Mon–Sat 9am–2am. Moderate.

Casa de la Rioja c/Peu de la Creu 8–10 ☎934 433 363. Introducing Barcelona to the regional food of La Rioja with dishes like *jurel* (a grilled white fish smothered in anchovy paste). The lunchtime *menú del día* (€8.50) is an absolute bargain, with three courses, coffee and a bottle of – what else – Rioja. Mon–Sat 1–4pm & 8–11pm. Moderate.

Fonda España c/de Sant Pau 9–11 ☎933 181 758. Eat Catalan food in *modernista* splendour in the lavishly tiled dining room of a building designed by Domènech i Montaner. The decor is generally more memorable than the dishes served, though the *menú* is good value at €7.90 (a few euros more at night). Daily 1–4pm & 8.30pm–midnight. Moderate.

Mamacafé c/del Dr Joaquim Dou 10 ☎933 012 940. Mains cover everything from a house hamburger to salmon with Indonesian-style rice, and though prices are on the highish side, ingredients are fresh and carefully judged. A good-value *menú del día* is €8. Mon–Sat 1pm–1am; Aug, open evenings only. Moderate.

Mesón David c/de les Carretes 63 ☎934 415 934. Down-to-earth Gallego-owned bar-restaurant where the €6 *menú* is a steal – maybe some lentil broth followed by grilled trout and home-made *flan*. There's a bang on the clog-gong for anyone who tips. It's down c/de Sant Pau, near Sant Paul del Camp. Daily except Wed 1–4pm & 8pm–midnight. Inexpensive.

Pollo Rico c/de Sant Pau 31 ☎934 413 184. It's been here for ever and, while it's not to everyone's taste, if you're in the market for spit-roast chicken, fries and a beer, served quick-smart at the bar, this is the place. Daily 10am–midnight. Inexpensive.

Silenus c/dels Àngels 8 ☎933 022 680. Arty place near MACBA presenting some unique dishes – like fillets of that well-known Catalan marsupial, the kangaroo. Come for lunch and you can eat from the *menú del día* for a shade over €10. Mon 1–4pm, Tues–Sat 1–4pm & 8.30–11.30pm. Expensive.

Barceloneta and Port Olímpic

Ⓜ Barceloneta or Ⓜ Ciutadella-Vila Olímpica

Agua Pg. Marítim 30 ☎932 251 272. Depending on the weather, you can choose between the sleek, split-level dining room or seafront boardwalk garden in this Vila Olímpica favourite. It's a contemporary Mediterranean menu but there's a short selection of tapas, pastas and salads. Daily 1.30–4pm & 8.30pm–midnight, Fri & Sat 1am. Moderate.

Can Ganassa Pl. de Barceloneta 4–6 ☎932 216 739. Extensive range of tapas, snacks and *torradas* on Barceloneta's central square. There's a cheap and filling €6.90 *menú del día* at lunchtime, and more expensive seafood dinners if you want. Daily except Wed 9am–11pm; closed Nov. Inexpensive.

El Cangrejo Loco Moll de Gregal 29–30 ☎932 210 533. The large outdoor terrace or huge picture windows at the "Crazy Crab" offer panoramas of the local coast and Olympic marina, and the fish and shellfish are first-rate. Daily 1pm–1am. Expensive.

Can Manel Pg. Joan de Borbó 60 ☎932 215 013. An institution since 1870 and fills very quickly, inside and out, because the food is both good and reasonably priced – not always the case down here. There's a weekday lunchtime *menú* at €8.25, although there's usually not much fish or seafood choice on this. Daily 1–4pm & 8pm–midnight. Moderate.

Can Ramonet c/Maquinista 17 ☎933 193 064. Reputedly the oldest restaurant in the port area. Full seafood meals are pricey, but you can always hunker down in the front bar where the tapas is piled high on wooden barrels. Daily 10am–4pm & 8pm–midnight; closed Sun dinner & Aug. Expensive.

dZi Pg. Joan de Borbó 76 ☎932 212 182. It's pronounced "zhee", which is a Tibetan sacred stone, but the lovely fresh-tasting food is Southeast Asian, mainly Chinese, Malaysian and Japanese, either served in the small, serene dining room or outside on the shady *terrassa*. A weekday lunch *menú* costs €8.85. Daily 1–4pm & 8pm–midnight. Moderate.

Eixample

Al Diwan c/València 218 ☎934 540 712; Ⓜ Universitat. Traditional Lebanese cuisine with all of the usual tabbouleh, hummus and *kofta* dishes.

Things liven up in the evening with traditional belly-dancing (Thurs, Fri & Sat), Mon–Fri 1–4pm & 8.30–11pm. Sat 8.30–11pm. Moderate.

La Flauta c/d'Aribau 23 ☎933 237 038; ⓂUniversitat. A real local favourite for the excellent-value €8.50 lunchtime *menú del día*, but also a good pit stop at any time for a stuffed *flauta* – a thin, crispy baguette sandwich – or a range of tapas. Mon–Sat 8am–1am. Inexpensive.

Fresc Co branches at c/València 263 ☎934 881 049, ⓂPasseig de Gràcia; Ronda Universitat 29 ☎933 016 837, ⓂPasseig de Gràcia. Packed-out self-service diners with an enormous salad bar, plus pizzas, pastas and desserts. Pile your plate high for €6.90 at lunch (Mon–Fri) or €8.80 evenings and weekends. Daily 1–5pm & 8pm–1am. Inexpensive.

El Mussol c/Aragó 261 ☎934 876 151; ⓂPasseig de Gràcia. Big rustic diner of the type that's all the rage in the city, known for its meat and vegetables *a la brasa*, most of which run between €4 and €8. Daily 1pm–1am. Inexpensive.

O'Nabo de Lugo c/de Pau Claris 169 ☎932 153 047; ⓂDiagonal. À la carte meals in this renowned Galician seafood restaurant can easily top €40, but the budget-conscious can snack on the excellent tapas or arrive at lunch when a mere €9 (only €7.60 if you eat in the bar) buys you the three-course *menú del día*, drink included. Mon–Sat 1–4pm & 8.30pm–midnight. Very expensive.

Thai Gardens c/Diputació 273 ☎934 879 898; ⓂPasseig de Gràcia. Barcelona's favourite Thai restaurant. Enjoy an excellent lunch menu for under €12 (Mon–Fri only), or an all-out *menú degustación* for €25. Daily 1.30–4pm & 8.30pm–midnight, until 1am at weekends. Expensive.

Tragaluz Ptge. de la Concepció 5 ☎934 870 621; ⓂDiagonal. Designer space, where the classy Mediterranean-with-knobs-on cooking doesn't disappoint. Cheaper eats come courtesy of the *Tragarapid* menu for those fresh off the *modernista* trail (La Pedrera is just across the way). Daily 1.30–4pm & 8.30pm–midnight, until 1pm Thurs–Sat. Very expensive.

La Tramoia Rambla de Catalunya 15 ☎934 123 634; ⓂCatalunya/Passeig de Gràcia. Fashionable multi-space eatery for anything from a coffee and croissant to a filling meal. Snack downstairs on tapas and *torrades* or head upstairs for Catalan brasserie food, including meat, fish and seasonal vegetables straight from the grill. Daily 7.30am–1.30am. Moderate.

Gràcia

Equinox Sol Pl. del Sol 14 ☎934 157 976; and *Equinox Verdi* c/Verdi 21–23 ☎932 373 270; ⓂFontana. Supreme falafels and *shawarma*, available wrapped in pitta for under €3 or as a "plat" (€4.50–5.25). The Plaça del Sol branch has outside tables. Mon–Thurs 6pm–2.30am, Fri–Sun noon–3.30am; closed Tues. Inexpensive.

Flash, Flash c/de la Granada del Penedès 25 ☎932 370 990; ⓂDiagonal. Tortillas (most under €5) served any way you like, from plain and simple to elaborately stuffed or doused in *salsa*, with sweet ones for dessert. Daily 1pm–1.30am, bar open 11am–2am. Inexpensive.

La Gavina c/Ros de Olano 17 ☎934 157 450; ⓂFontana. This wacky pizzeria, known locally as "Els Angels" – due to the fact that the only sign is a series of *putti* pasted over the door – is a Gràcia legend. Arrive after 8pm and you will have a long wait, but no reservations are accepted. Tues–Sun noon–1am. Inexpensive.

Habibi c/Gran de Gràcia 7 ☎932 179 545; ⓂDiagonal. Bright and breezy North African dining. The *Plat Habibi* (€5.50) gives you a taste of all the house specials – from a minty *tabouleh* to lamb and chicken *shawarma* – but there's plenty of choice for grazers and vegetarians alike. Mon–Fri 1pm–1am, Sat 2–4.30pm & 8pm–1am. Inexpensive.

El Glop c/Sant Lluís 24 ☎932 137 058; **El Nou Glop** c/Montmany 49 ☎932 197 059; ⓂJoanic. Authentic tavernas within a few paces of each other, serving honest Catalan portions and specializing in items from the grill. The €6.45 lunch *menú* is one of the city's best deals; otherwise around €15 a head. Tues–Sun 1–4pm & 8pm–1am. Moderate.

Jean Luc Figueras c/Santa Teresa 10 ☎934 152 877; ⓂDiagonal. Franco-Catalan cooking of the highest calibre, at the highest prices – reckon on at least €80 a head. It's a very sophisticated place, with a seasonally changing menu. Mon–Fri 1.30–3.30pm & 8.30–11.30pm, Sat 8.30–11.30pm; closed Aug. Very expensive.

Miria Pl. Rius i Taulet 11 ☎932 185 198; ⓂDiagonal. The sunny *terrassa* on the square is half the attraction, but it's nice inside, too – simple but stylish, in a modern Catalan kind of way, with mellow sounds to accompany the well-priced food. Daily 1–4pm & 7–11pm. Moderate.

Taberna del Cura c/Gran de Gràcia 83 ☎932 181 799; ⓂFontana. Quality tapas and grills in tavern-style surroundings. Prices soon edge up if you're going to tackle a fillet steak or shoulder of lamb, but there's a good-value lunchtime *menú degustación*. Daily 1pm–1am. Expensive.

Drinking and nightlife

There's often little difference between a **bar** and café (indeed, many places incorporate both words in their name), but some of the other names you'll see do actually mean something – a *bodega* specializes in wine; a *cervesería* in beer; and a *xampanyería* in champagne and *cava*. Barcelona also has a range of **designer bars** – *bars moderns* or *bars musicals* – geared towards late-night drinking, and there's a club **nightlife** that is one of Europe's most enjoyable. It's worth noting, that – unlike restaurants – most bars stay open throughout August.

Bars

Generally, the bars in the old town are a mixture of traditional tourist haunts, local drinking places or fashionista hangouts. **La Ribera** is still one of the hottest destinations, with Passeig del Born (the square at the end of c/de Montcada behind Santa María del Mar) the main focus. In the **Barri Gòtic**, it's the streets around c/d'Avinyó and c/Escudellers that have their share of the action; over in the upper **Raval**, the most fashionable places are opening up near MACBA. The **Port Olímpic** and the **Port Vell** Maremàgnum complex have become more mainstream summer night-time playgrounds for locals and tourists alike. The hi-tech, music-filled *bars moderns* or *bars musicals* tend to be concentrated mainly in the **Eixample** and the streets in the western part of **Gràcia** around **Plaça Molina** (like c/Santaló and c/Marià Cubí). The "in" places change rapidly, with new ones opening up all the time; the decor is often astounding, the drinks always expensive. Local bars are usually licensed to stay open till 11pm, although some keep going till 3am. Music bars usually go till 2 or 3am, after which you'll have to resort to a club.

Barri Gòtic

Ⓜ Catalunya/Liceu/Jaume I

L'Ascensor c/Bellafila 3 (bottom of c/de la Ciutat). Old lift doors and control panel signal the entrance to this popular local bar. Untouristy, and with a comfortable feel. Daily 6.30pm–3am.

El Bosc de les Fades Ramblas 6. Tucked away in an alley beside the entrance to the wax museum, the "Forest of the Fairies" is sculpted with gnarled plaster tree trunks and populated by plastic gnomes. Sun–Thurs 10.30am–1am, Fri & Sat 10.30am–3am.

Glaciar Pl. Reial 3. Traditional Barcelona meeting point and the first and best of the *terrassas* on Pl. Reial. Packs out at weekends. Mon–Thurs 4pm–2am, Fri & Sat 4pm–3am, Sun 9am–2am.

Leticia c/Codols 21. Cosy bar tucked away in one of the less attractive streets of Barri Gòtic. Relaxed atmosphere, eclectic interior, ideal for a chat on the sofa at the back. Daily except Tues 7pm–3am.

Margarita Blue c/Josep Anselm Clavé 6. A bustling place, with live music and DJs a couple of times a week. Sit at the lengthy bar and sip a cocktail or eat Tex-Mex food if you want (though both are pretty average quality), but it's more about the atmosphere. Mon–Wed 11am–2am, Thurs–Sun 7pm–3am.

Parnasse c/Gignás 21. Laid-back and friendly atmosphere in this hip bar, where you can listen to jazz over a single-malt whisky or the legendary *absinthe à la française*. Tues–Sat 6pm–3am.

Pipa Club Pl. Reial 3. Very popular late-night bar with an olde-worlde, jazzy atmosphere. To get in, ring the bell and make your way up the stairs. Daily 11pm–3am.

Schilling c/Ferran 23. Fashionable café-bar packed all day with a mixture of locals and tourists; shout for your drink over the music and be prepared to wait for it. Daily 10am–2.30pm.

Soda c/d'Avinyó 24. Once the designer rags are locked away in this boutique, the place turns into a wicked bar with comfy armchairs, tasty cocktails and electronic tunes. DJ at the weekend. Daily 9pm–2.30am.

Travel Bar c/Boqueria 27. Backpacking Catalans have brought their experiences home to provide a bar where travellers can hang out and meet like-minded souls, sign up for walking/biking/drinking tours, practise their Spanish and generally chill out. Sun–Thurs 9am–2am, Fri & Sat 9am–3am.

Zoo c/Escudellers 33. Animals (obviously) provide the central theme, the subject of the decoration (miniatures and pictures galore) and the inspiration for the names of the sandwiches and salads. Very wide music selection – world to electronica. Daily 7pm–2am.

La Ribera

Ⓜ Jaume I/Barceloneta

Borneo c/Rec 49. Downmarket hipness in this popular drinking hole, just off the main drag of the Born. Tues–Sat 7pm–3am.

Café del Born Pl. Comercial 10. Relaxed gay-friendly bar with pavement tables in summer, which is a popular meeting place. Daily 8.30am–3.30am.

Espai Barroc c/de Montcada 8. Expensive and slightly snooty, the renovated interior of the fifteenth-century Palau Dalmasses looks like it may have served as a Peter Greenaway film set. On Thurs (11pm) there's live Baroque and chamber music (€18, drink included). Tues–Sat 8pm–2am, Sun 6–10pm.

Pas del Born c/Calders 8. A tiny and wacky haunt of musicians, artists and acrobats. Often hosts frenetic and interactive flamenco shows, as well as circus trapeze acts (check the listings on the bar's window). Wed–Sun 6pm–3am.

La Rosa de Foc c/del Rec 69. Multicultural space with exhibitions and live music twice a week, plus presentations of books, poetry, etc. Daily 6pm–2.30am.

Suborn c/Ribera 18. A tapas place by day and a restaurant/music bar by night. A nightly rotation of DJs spin just about everything while you dine on imaginative Mediterranean cuisine, or just have a drink. Mon–Thurs 10am–5pm & 7.30pm–2.30am, Fri 10am–2.30am, Sat noon–3am, Sun noon–2.30am.

La Vinya del Senyor Pl. Santa Maria 5. Nook-and-cranny wine bar with tables right outside the lovely church of Santa Maria del Mar. Mon–Thurs noon–1am, Fri & Sat noon–2am, Sun noon–midnight.

El Raval

Ⓜ Catalunya/Liceu/Universitat

Almirall Joaquim Costa 33. Dating from 1860, Barcelona's oldest bar – a venerated leftist hang-out – is a great place to chat or to kick off an evening of more intense bar hopping. Live music some nights. Daily 7pm–3am.

Bar Pastis c/Santa Mònica 4 (just behind Centre d'Art Santa Mònica). Tiny, dark bar, right in the red-light district, awash with artistic and theatrical memorabilia, and soothed by wheezy French music. Daily except Tues 7.30pm–2.30am, Fri & Sat until 3.30am.

La Confitería c/de Sant Pau 128. Old sweet shop in *modernista* style (amazing carved wood bar and murals, beautiful chandeliers), now a popular meeting point. Friendly, relaxing atmosphere. Daily 6pm–3am.

Kentucky c/Arc del Teatre 11. A kitschy dive where peculiar locals and *guiris* (foreigners) mingle. Making your way through the narrow aisle might take you a while, but it's quite an experience. Tues–Thurs 10pm–3am, Fri & Sat till 5am.

London Bar c/Nou de la Rambla 34. Opened in 1910, this well-known *modernista* bar today attracts a mainly tourist clientele, and puts on live music most nights, mainly jazz, swing, blues and funk. Wed–Sun 5pm–4am.

Marsella c/de Sant Pau 65. Late nineteenth-century bar now frequented by a spirited mix of local characters and young trendies downing absinthe. Occasional live music and performances. Mon–Thurs & Sun 9am–2.30am, Fri & Sat 6pm–3.30am.

Muebles Navarro c/Riera Alta 4–6. Big, airy café-bar in a converted furniture store (hence the name), which is a friendly, comfortable place to have a drink or a snack. Mon–Sat 11am–midnight, Sun 5pm–midnight.

Port Vell and Port Olímpic

Café Café Moll de Mestral 30; Ⓜ Ciutadella-Vila Olímpica. One of the Port Olímpic's more relaxed and better-decorated bars, serving lots more besides coffee. Daily noon–3am, 5am at weekends.

Luz de Gas In front of Palau de Mar; Ⓜ Barceloneta. Sip a drink on the moored boat for some great marina and harbour views. It's especially nice at night. March–Oct daily noon–3am.

Mojito Bar Maremàgnum; Ⓜ Drassanes. Typically Maremàgnum in style is this themed Caribbean playhouse, with tropical decor, cocktails and free daily salsa classes. Live music with the Cuban big band on Sun. Daily 5pm–5am.

Eixample

L'Arquer Gran Vía 454; Ⓜ Universitat. Bar with good tapas and – believe it or not – an archery range where you can have a go under the careful supervision of someone more sober than you. Daily 6pm–2.30am, weekends till 3.30am.

Dry Martini c/Aribau 166; Ⓜ Hospital Clínic. Legendary Barcelona cocktail bar, with a rich dark wood and brass interior. Business types dominate in the early evening, while a younger set moves in on weekend nights. Daily 6.30pm–2.30am, Fri & Sat to 3am.

La Fira c/Provença 171; Ⓜ Provença. One of the city's most bizarre – and fun – bars, complete with fairground rides, and decorated with circus paraphernalia. Tues–Thurs 10pm–3am, Fri & Sat 7pm–4.30am, Sun 6pm–1am.

Gay and lesbian Barcelona

There's a vibrant local gay and lesbian crowd in Barcelona, not to mention the lure of Sitges, forty minutes south by train and mainland Spain's biggest gay resort (see p.884). The expression for the scene is *el ambiente*, which simply means "the atmosphere" – it's the name of the useful section in the weekly listings magazine *Guía del Ocio*, which lists gay and lesbian bars, clubs, restaurants and other services. There's a particular concentration of bars, restaurants and clubs in the so-called **Gaixample**, the "Gay Eixample", an area of a few square blocks just northwest of the main university in the Esquerra de l'Eixample. The city's annual **lesbian and gay pride march** is on the nearest Saturday to June 28, starting in the evening at Plaça Universitat.

There's a **lesbian and gay city telephone hotline** on ☎900 601 601 (Mon–Fri 6–10pm only) run by the *ajuntament*. Cómplices, c/Cervantes 2 (Ⓜ Liceu; ☎934 127 283), and Antinous, c/Josep Anselm Clavé 6 (Ⓜ Drassanes; ☎933 019 070), are **gay bookshops** with useful contacts and information – the latter has a café at the back. For a **map** of gay Barcelona, detailing bars, clubs, hotels and restaurants, contact the sex shops *Sestienda*, c/Rauric 11 (Ⓜ Liceu; ☎933 188 676), or *Zeus*, c/Riera Alta 20 (Ⓜ Sant Antoni; ☎934 429 795). Look out also for a free magazine called *Nois* (Ⓦ www.revistanois.com), which carries an up-to-date list of the scene.

Gay bars and discotecas

Aire Sala Diana c/Valencia 236, Eixample; Ⓜ Passeig de Gràcia. The hottest, most stylish lesbian bar in town. Thurs–Sat 11.30pm–3am, Sun 6–10pm.

Arena Madre c/Balmes 32, Eixample Ⓦ www.arenadisco.com; Ⓜ Passeig de Gràcia. The "mother" club sits at the helm of the Arena empire, all in the same block, which includes the high disco antics of *Arena Classic* (c/de la Diputació 233; Fri & Sat 12.30–5am) and more of the same plus house and garage at the more mixed *Arena VIP* (Gran Via de les Corts Catalanes 593; Fri & Sat 12.30–6am). Arena Madre open Tues–Sat 12.30–5am, Sun 7pm–5am.

Café Dietrich c/Consell de Cent 255, Eixample; Ⓜ Universitat. This well-known music-bar hangout serves food until midnight, with drag shows punctuating the DJ sets. Daily 6pm–2.30am.

Ironic Café c/Consell de Cent 245, Eixample; Ⓜ Urgell/Univertsitat. High-concept cocktail bar with smooth sounds and temporary art shows – Sunday night is Spanish music night. Tues–Sun 7pm–2.30am.

Metro c/Sepúlveda 158, Eixample Ⓦ www.metrodiscobcn.com; Ⓜ Universitat/Urgell. This gay institution gets extremely crowded at weekends in its two rooms playing either current dance and techno or retro disco. Sun–Thurs midnight–5am, Fri & Sat midnight–6am.

Oui Café c/Consell de Cent 247, Eixample; Ⓜ Urgell/Univertsitat. A meet-and-greet destination, with a popular summer *terrassa*. Sun–Thurs 5pm–2am, Fri & Sat 5pm–3am.

Punto BCN c/Muntaner 63–65, Eixample; Ⓜ Universitat. A Gaixample classic that attracts an uptown crowd for drinks, chat and music. Daily 6pm–2am.

Salvation Ronda de Sant Pere 19–21 Ⓦ www.matineegroup.com; Ⓜ Urquinaona. Huge Ibiza-scene gay club playing the best in European house. Fri–Sun midnight–5am.

Zeltas c/Casanova 75 Ⓦ www.zeltas.net; Ⓜ Urgell. Pumped-up house music bar for the pre-club crowd. Wed–Sun 11pm–3am.

Les Gens Que J'aime c/Valencia 286; Ⓜ Passeig de Gràcia. Stylish, brothel-like interior – red velvet, dimmed light, atmospheric music – frequented by middle-class locals. Daily 7pm–2.30am.

Santecafé c/del Comte d'Urgell 171; Ⓜ Hospital Clinic. One of the more interesting bars in the Eixample, with a live DJ at weekends. Daily 8pm–3am.

El Velòdrom c/Muntaner 213; Ⓜ Diagonal. Old-style bar and pool hall, with an Art Deco interior dating to before the Civil War. A great spot to relax and kick back. Mon–Sat 6pm–1.30am; closed Aug.

Gràcia

El Canigó Plaça de la Revolucio 10; ⓂFontana/Joanic. Family-run neighbourhood bar now entering its third generation. Weekend evenings it packs out with a young, hip and largely local crowd. Tues–Sun 11am–midnight.

Casa Quimet Rambla del Prat; ⓂFontana. Very picturesque bar where you have to supply the music yourself. Numerous guitars are hanging from the ceiling: pick out your favourite one and pluck away. Tues–Sun 6.30pm–2am.

La Cerveseria Artesana c/Sant Agustí 14; ⓂDiagonal. The recipes at this Catalan attempt at a brewpub may need a bit of refinement, but fortunately a good range of imported English beer is available, too. Wed–Sun 6pm–2.30am.

El Galpon Sur c/Guilleries 16; ⓂFontana. A refuge for homesick Andalucians, the *Galpon* is popular both for drinks and for southern Spanish food. Tues–Sun 4pm–1am.

Mi Bar c/Guilleries 6; ⓂFontana. Tiny neighbourhood bar for Gràcia's alternative music set. The DJ spins a mix of everything from punk to flamenco. Tues–Sat 11pm–3am.

Mond Bar Pl. del Sol 21; ⓂDiagonal. Every night a different DJ plays the newest beats in the bar where "pop will make us free". Daily 8.30pm–3am.

Virreina Pl. de la Virreina 1; ⓂFontana. Popular bar with seats outside in one of Gràcia's loveliest squares. A great place to enjoy hard-to-find Trappist beers from Belgium. Daily except Wed noon–2am.

Around Plaça Molina

Mas i Mas c/Marià Cubí 199; FGC Muntaner. One of the bars that started it all and, in their own words "a cross between a cocktail bar and a dancehall". The music policy is blues, acid jazz, hip hop, house and funk, and the crowd young and equally funky. Sun–Thurs 7pm–2.30am, Fri & Sat 7pm–3am.

Universal c/Marià Cubí 184; FGC Pl. Molina. A classic designer bar that's been at the cutting edge of Barcelona style since 1985. Be warned, they operate a strict door policy here and if your face doesn't fit you won't get in. Daily 11pm–4.30am.

Zig Zag c/de Plató 13; FGC Muntaner. All the minimalist designer accoutrements – chrome and video – but more varied music than usual (predominantly acid jazz, funk and hip hop), and a young, rich clientele. Daily 10pm–3am.

Tibidabo

Mirablau Pl. del Dr Andrea, Avgda. Tibidabo; FGC Avgda. del Tibidabo & Tramvia Blau/taxi. Unbelievable city views from a chic, expensive bar, that fills to bursting at busy times. Daily 11pm–5am.

Clubs

The main city-centre **neighbourhoods** for clubbing are the Barri Gòtic, Raval, Eixample and Gràcia, though it's actually the peripheral areas where you'll find the bulk of the big-name warehouse and designer venues. Poble Nou, for example, might not attract you during the day, but will be high on the list of any seasoned clubber, as will the otherwise tourist fantasy village of Poble Espanyol in Montjuïc. **Admission prices** are difficult to predict: some places are free before a certain time, others charge a few euros entry, a few only charge if there's live music, while in several entry depends on what you look like rather than how much is in your pocket. Those that do charge tend to fall into the €10–18 range, though this usually includes your first beer or soft drink (look for the word *consumició*). If there is free entry, don't be surprised to find that there's a minimum drinks charge of anything up to €10 – you'll be given a card as you go in which is punched at the bar; if you don't spend enough you will have to pay the difference when you leave. Also note that the distinction between a music-bar and a disco is between a closing time of 2 or 3am and 5am – with a corresponding price rise.

Barri Gòtic

Café Royale c/Nou de Zurbano 3, off Pl. Reial; ⓂLiceu. Glamorous lounge bar where all the beautiful people get together. At weekends, it's heaving with blonde divas and Greek Gods, showing off their best moves to Latin Jazz and funky tunes. Daily 7pm–3am.

Dot c/Nou de Sant Francesc 7; ⓂDrassanes. From the bar at the front you can walk through the time-machine cell right onto the dance floor, where the music changes nightly – electronica, Brazilian, funky fusions, whatever. Daily 10pm–3am.

Karma Pl. Reial 10; ⓜLiceu. A studenty basement place which can get claustrophobic at times, with Indie, Britpop and US college sounds, and a lively local crowd milling around the square outside. Tues–Sun 11.30pm–5am.

El Raval

Dos Trece c/Carme 40; ⓜLiceu. Under the restaurant there's a smallish club where musicians and DJs take care of the ambience. Young and groovy crowd, every night is different. Daily 11.30pm–4am.

Moog Arc del Teatre 3; ⓜDrassanes. Lively disco playing techno and house to a fashionable crowd. Daily 11pm–5am.

La Paloma c/Tigre 27; ⓜUniversitat. Fabulous *modernista* ballroom where old and young alike are put through their rumba and cha cha cha steps from 6pm to 9.30pm. Then, after 11.30pm, the projections are turned on, dancers climb onto the stage, and DJs take their positions. Mainly techno and house, though Saturday's Eighties night is a blast. Thurs–Sat 6pm–5am.

Poble Nou

The Loft c/Pamplona 88; ⓜBogatell. Two dance floors located in an old warehouse, with gigs and international DJs offering a wide range of sounds. Fri & Sat 1–6am.

Oven c/Ramon Turró 126; ⓜPoble Nou. An old factory converted into a fabulously designed restaurant/bar/club. Lounge room at the front, restaurant at the back, with a stunning open kitchen. After midnight the place turns into a club, with DJs until 3am. Mon–Fri 1.30pm–2am, Sat 6pm–3am.

Montjuïc

Discothèque Avgda. Marquès de Comillas, Poble Espanyol; ⓜEspanya. The winter season destination for dedicated hedonists. Almost two thousand cram in here for house, garage, big-name DJs and a whole lot of style on the main dance floor. Oct–May Fri & Sat midnight–7am.

Firestiu Pl. Univers y Palau 4 de la Fira; ⓜEspanya. Multispace entertainment in a series of tents and awnings in the exhibition centre zone. Inside are dozens of bars set up by well-known city venues, as well as dance floors, fairground rides, minigolf and even bungee-jumping.

June–Aug Thurs–Sat 10pm–5am.

La Terrazza Avgda. Marquès de Comillas s/n, behind Poble Espanyol; ⓜEspanya. Nonstop techno, and the place to be in summer, though don't get there until at least 4am. Fri & Sat midnight–7am.

Torres de Ávila Avgda. Marqués de Comillas, Poble Espanyol; ⓜEspanya. Located inside the mock twelfth-century gateway in the "Spanish Village", this is a stunning fantasy, with a fabulous panoramic terrace. Beware that the dress code is strict (no sports shoes) and drinks are very expensive. Thurs–Sat 10pm–5am.

Eixample

Antilla Barcelona c/Aragó 141–143; ⓜHospital Clinic. Caribbean tunes galore: salsa, merengue, mambo, you name it. There are live bands, and dance classes from Mon–Thurs at 10.30pm. Daily 10.30pm–5am, weekends until 6am.

Bikini c/Deu i Mata 105, off Avgda. Diagonal; ⓜMaria Cristina. This traditional landmark of Barcelona nightlife offers regular live music and a popular disco, specializing in salsa and tangos on Sun. Tues–Sun 11pm–5am.

Carpe Diem Avgda. Dr Gregorio Marañón 17; ⓜPalau Reial. Near the university campus and Camp Nou stadium, *Carpe Diem* is a huge tent containing various bars, restaurants and dance floors. Open all year, but best and most packed in summer. Daily 6pm–5am.

Velvet c/Balmes 161; ⓜDiagonal. The creation of designer Alfredo Arribas, this club was inspired by the velveteen excesses of film-maker David Lynch. Daily 10.30pm–4.30am.

Gràcia

Mond Club Sala Cibeles, c/Corsega 363 ☎933 177 994, ⓦwww.mondclub.com; ⓜDiagonal. Old ballroom converted into stylish Friday-night club, with a bit of everything thrown into the mix – punk, glam, electronica and guest DJs. Fri 12.30–6am.

Otto Zutz c/de Lincoln 15; FGC Pl. Molina. Still one of the most fashionable places in the city, this three-storey former textile factory has a dance floor, three bars, VIP lounge and a shed-load of pretensions. With the right clothes and face you're in; the serious dancing is 2–5.30am. Tues–Sat midnight–5.30am.

Music and the arts

Quite apart from the city's countless bars, restaurants and clubs, there's a full cultural life worth sampling. Barcelona hosts a wide range of **live music** events throughout the year and **film** and **theatre** are also well represented, as you'd expect in a city this size. Even if you don't speak Catalan or Spanish there's no need to miss out, since several cinemas show films in their original language. Catalan performers have always steered away from the classics and gone for the innovative, and so the city also boasts a long tradition of **street and performance art**. Best of the annual arts events is the Generalitat's summer **Grec** season, when theatre, music and dance can be seen at various venues around the city, including the Teatre Grec at Montjuïc.

The most important ticket office is in the **Palau de la Virreina**, Ramblas 99 (Mon–Sat 10am–8pm, Sun 11am–3pm; ☎933 017 775, ⓦwww.bcn.es /cultura; ⓂLiceu), which dispenses programmes, advance information and tickets for all the *ajuntament*-sponsored productions, performances and exhibitions, including the summer *Grec* season events. With a credit card you can use the **ServiCaixa** (☎902 332 211, ⓦwww.servicaixa.com) automatic dispensing machines in branches of La Caixa to obtain tickets for many events; you can also order tickets by phone or online. Theatre, concert, cinema and exhibition tickets can also be bought over the phone or online through **Tel-Entrada** (☎902 101 212, ⓦwww.telendtrada.com). There's also a concert ticket desk in the FNAC store, El Triangle, Plaça Catalunya, while the music shops along c/dels Tallers (ⓂCatalunya), just off the Ramblas, carry tickets, too.

For **listings** of almost anything you could want in the way of culture and entertainment, buy a copy of the weekly *Guía del Ocio* (ⓦwww .guiadelociobcn.com) from any newspaper stand. This has full details of film, theatre and musical events (free and otherwise), as well as extensive sections on festivals, bars, restaurants and nightlife. It's in Spanish but easy enough to decipher. There are similar listings in *El País*, and there's also a free monthly guide published by the *ajuntament*, available from tourist offices.

Celebrating Catalan-style

Catalunya's national **folk dance**, the *sardana*, can be seen for free at several places in the city, including in front of the cathedral (Feb–July & Sept–Nov Sat 6.30pm & Sun noon; ⓂJaume I), and in Plaça Sant Jaume (Sun 6.30pm; ⓂJaume I). Mocked in the rest of Spain, the Catalans claim theirs is a very democratic dance. Participants (there's no limit on numbers) all hold hands in a circle, each puts something in the middle as a sign of community and sharing, and since it is not overly energetic (hence the jibes), old and young can join in equally.

The main event in a traditional Catalan festival (see list on p.716) is usually a **parade**, either promenading behind a revered holy image (as at Easter) or a more celebratory costumed affair that's the centrepiece of a neighbourhood festival. It's at the latter that you'll come across the **gegants**, grotesque giant figures with papier-mâché heads, which run down the streets terrorizing children. Also typically Catalan is the **correfoc** ("fire-running"), where brigades of drummers, dragons and devils with spark-shooting flares fitted to pitchforks cavort in the streets. Perhaps most peculiar of all are the **castellers**, the red-shirted human tower-builders who draw crowds at every traditional festival, piling person upon person, feet on shoulders, to see who can construct the highest, most aesthetically pleasing tower (ten human storeys is the record).

Live music

Many major **rock and pop** bands include Barcelona on their tours at a variety of pricey stadium venues. However, lots of the city's smaller clubs regularly feature bands, while the city's **jazz** clubs are pretty relaxed, too. The more reliable places are listed below, and entrance to these is usually reasonably priced and often includes a complimentary drink. Most of Barcelona's **classical music** concerts take place in Domènech i Montaner's Palau de la Música Catalana (see p.742) or at the purpose-built, contemporary L'Auditori, while **opera** is performed at its traditional home, the Gran Teatre del Liceu on the Ramblas (p.731). Many of the city's churches, including the cathedral and Santa Maria del Mar, host concerts and recitals, while other interesting venues to watch out for include the Barri Gòtic's Saló del Tinell, FNAC at El Triangle (the shopping centre) at Plaça de Catalunya, and the Fundació Joan Miró (particularly for contemporary music). The Teatre Grec on Montjuïc is an open-air summer venue for concerts and recitals, used extensively during the **Grec festival** season. There are also free or cheap experimental music concerts sponsored year-round by the Gràcia collective, **Gràcia Territori Sonor** (Ⓦwww.gracia-territori.com), while the Centre Artesà Tradicionàrius (see below) hosts the annual **Tradicionàrius** international folk and traditional dance festival (Jan to April). For details of Barcelona's other live music festivals, see the festival calendar on p.716.

Rock, pop and folk

Centre Artesà Tradicionàrius (CAT) Trav. de Sant Antoni 6–8, Gràcia ☎932 184 485, Ⓦwww.tradicionarius.com; ⓂFontana. Folk recitals by Catalan and visiting performers, usually on Fri around 10pm (though the bar is open nightly).

The Clansman c/Vigatans 13, La Ribera ☎933 197 169; ⓂJaume 1. Scottish pub hosting Celtic music every Fri & Sun. Daily 5pm–3am.

Luz de Gas c/Muntaner 246, Eixample ☎932 097 711; ⓂDiagonal. Smart venue popular with a slightly older crowd, with live music (local blues, rock, jazz and covers) every night around midnight.

Razzmatazz c/dels Almogavers 122 ☎933 208 200; ⓂBogatell/Marina. Huge former warehouse where major gigs are held (Fri & Sat). *Razz Club* (indie, pop, rock, electro and retro) takes over after 1am.

Sala Apolo c/Nou de la Rambla 113 ☎934 414 001; ⓂParal.lel. Regular live gigs with the occasional big name in an old-time ballroom setting. The techno/electronica *Nitsaclub* kicks off at weekends after midnight (until 5am).

Sidecar c/Heures 4–6, at Pl. Reial Barri Gòtic ☎933 021 586; ⓂLiceu. Hip bar – pronounced "See-day-car" – with a pool table, downstairs concert space and nightly gigs and DJs. Daily 10pm–3am.

Jazz and flamenco

La Boite Avgda. Diagonal 477, Eixample ☎933 191 789, Ⓦwww.masimas.com; ⓂDiagonal. Regular jazz and blues sessions, plus funk, soul and salsa, with gigs Mon–Sat from around midnight. Tickets €9, rising to €22 for big names.

La Cova del Drac c/Vallmajor 33, Gràcia ☎933 191 789, Ⓦwww.masimas.com; FGC Muntaner. One of Barcelona's best jazz clubs serves up live music Tues–Sat from 11pm. Cover charge €9–20 depending on the act. Closed Aug.

Harlem Jazz Club c/Comtessa de Sobradiel 8, Barri Gòtic ☎933 100 755; ⓂJaume I. Small, central and usually jam-packed venue for mixed jazz styles, from African and Gypsy to flamenco and fusion; live music nightly at 10.30pm and midnight (weekends 11.30pm and 1am). Cover charge up to €5. Closed Aug.

Jamboree Pl. Reial 17, Barri Gòtic ☎933 191 789, Ⓦwww.masimas.com; ⓂLiceu. Jazz gigs nightly at 11pm and 12.30am, and then you stay on for the club, playing funk, swing, hip-hop and R&B. Admission €6–9.

Soniquete c/Milans 5, Barri Gòtic ☎639 382 354; ⓂDrassanes. Cosy candlelit, authentic flamenco bar, one of the very few in town (or indeed Catalunya). No cover. Thurs–Sun 9pm–3am.

Tarantos Pl. Reial 17, Barri Gòtic ☎933 191 789, Ⓦwww.masimas.com; ⓂLiceu. Barcelona's oldest *tablao flamenco*, with daily performances at 10pm (from around €25), followed by Latin and world music sounds until 5am with the resident DJ.

Classical music and opera

L'Auditori c/Lepant 150, Eixample ☎932 479 300, Ⓦwww.auditori.org; ⓂMarina/Monumental. Concerts by the Orquestra Simfònica de Barcelona i Nacional de Catalunya (OBC), whose season runs Sept to May, plus other concerts and recitals. Under 26s with ID get fifty-percent discount on all tickets 1hr before performance.

La Casa Elizalde c/València 302, Eixample ℡934 880 590; ⓂPasseig de Gràcia. Regular small-scale classical concerts, usually with low-cost or free entry.

L'Espai de Dansa i Música Trav. de Gràcia 63, Gràcia ℡934 143 133; ⓂDiagonal. Performances by a variety of soloists and groups, especially good for dance.

Gran Teatre de Liceu Ramblas 51–59 ℡934 859 900, ⓦwww.liceubarcelona.com; ⓂLiceu. Full programme of opera and recitals, plus late-night concerts (*sessions golfes*). Check the website and make bookings well in advance.

Palau de la Música Catalana c/Sant Francesc de Paula 2, off c/Sant Pere Més Alt ℡932 957 200, ⓦwww.palaumusica.org; ⓂUrquinaona. Home of the Orfeó Català choral group, and venue for concerts by the Orquestra Ciutat de Barcelona among others. Concert season runs Oct–June.

Theatre and cabaret

The **Teatre Nacional** (National Theatre) was specifically conceived as a venue to promote Catalan productions, and features a repertory programme of translated classics (such as Shakespeare in Catalan), original works and productions by guest companies from elsewhere in Europe. The other big local theatrical project is the **Ciutat del Teatre** (Theatre City) on Montjuïc, which incorporates the fringe-style Mercat de les Flors, a second stage for Gràcia's Teatre Lliure and the Insitut del Teatre theatre and dance school. The centre for commercial theatre is Avinguda. Paral.lel and the nearby streets. Some theatres draw on the city's strong **cabaret** tradition – more music-hall entertainment than stand-up comedy, and thus a little more accessible to non-Catalan/Spanish speakers. Tickets are available from the usual outlets (see main introduction on p.719), but for advance tickets for the Mercat de les Flors productions, you have to go to the Palau de la Virreina (Ramblas 99), or try at the theatre itself one hour before the performance.

Llantiol c/Riereta 7 ℡933 299 009, ⓦwww.llantiol.com; ⓂParal.lel. Cabaret-café featuring curious bits of mime, song, clowns, magic and dance. Shows normally begin at 9pm & 11pm. Closed Mon.

Mercat de les Flors c/de Lleida 59, Poble Sec ℡934 261 875, ⓦwww.mercatflors.com; ⓂPoble Sec. Hosts visiting fringe theatre and dance companies in a splendid nineteenth-century building.

Teatre Lliure Pl. Margarida Xirgu, Poble Sec ℡932 289 747; ⓂPoble Sec; and c/Montseny 47, Gràcia ℡932 189 25; ⓂFontana; ⓦwww .teatrelliure.com. The "Free Theatre" – a progressive Catalan company – performs its own work and hosts visiting dance companies, concerts and recitals at two different venues.

Teatre Nacional de Catalunya (TNC) Pl. de les Arts 1 ℡933 065 700, ⓦwww.tnc.es; ⓂGlòries. Intended to foster Catalan works, this theatre – built as a modern emulation of an ancient Greek temple – features Spanish, Catalan and European companies.

Teatre Romea c/Hospital 51, El Raval ℡933 015 504; ⓂLiceu. The Centre Dramàtic de la Generalitat de Catalunya, based here, has an emphasis on Catalan-language productions (and occasional English-language productions with simultaneous Catalan translation).

Film

All the latest films reach Barcelona fairly quickly, though at most of the larger cinemas and multiplexes (including the Maremàgnum screens at Port Vell) they're usually shown dubbed into Spanish or Catalan. However, several cinemas do show mostly **original-language** ("V.O.") foreign films; the best are listed below. Tickets cost €5.50–6, and most cinemas have one night (usually Mon or Wed) – *el día del espectador* – when entry is **discounted**, usually to around €4. Many cinemas also feature **late-night** screenings (*madrugadas*) on Friday and Saturday nights, which begin at 12.30 or 1am.

Filmoteca Avgda. de Sarrià 33, Eixample ☎9341
07 590; Ⓜ️Hospital Clínic. Run by the *Generalitat*,
the Filmoteca has an excellent programme, showing three or four different films (often foreign, and
usually in V.O.) every night; €2.70 per film, or buy
a discounted pass allowing entry to ten films.
Icaria-Yelmo c/de Salvador Espriu 61, Vila
Olímpica ☎932 217 585; Ⓜ️Ciutadella. No fewer
than fifteen screens showing V.O. movies at a
comfortable multiplex. Late-night screenings on Fri
and Sat; discount night Mon.

Maldá c/Pi 5, Les Galeries Maldá, Barri Gòtic
☎933 178 529; Ⓜ️Liceu. Repertory cinema fea-
turing two different shows per day (usually English
V.O.). Late-night sessions on Fri & Sat, matinees
Sat & Sun; reduced price Wed.
Verdi c/Verdi 32, and **Verdi Park** c/Torrijos 49,
Gràcia ☎932 387 990; Ⓜ️Fontana. Sister cinemas
in adjacent streets showing quality V.O. movies.
Late-night films at *Verdi* on Fri & Sat; discount
night at both on Mon.

Shopping

While not on a par with Paris or the world's other style capitals, Barcelona still
leads the way in Spain when it comes to **shopping**. It's the country's fashion
and publishing capital, and there's a long tradition of innovative design, which
is perhaps expressed best in the city's fabulous architecture but which is also
revealed in a series of shops and malls selling the very latest in designer clothes
and household accoutrements. The **annual sales** (*rebaixes*, *rebajas* in Castilian)
follow the main fashion seasons – mid-January until the end of February, and
throughout July and August. Shop **opening hours** are typically
Monday–Friday 10am–1.30/2pm and 4.30–7.30/8pm, Saturday
10am–1.30/2pm, although various markets, department stores and shopping
centres open right through lunch. Main department stores and shopping malls
stay open until 10pm.

Antiques, arts and crafts

There are lots of antiques stores in the old town; perhaps the best area for
browsing is around c/de Palla, between the cathedral and Plaça del Pí.

Art Escudellers c/Escudellers 23–25; Ⓜ️Liceu. An
enormous shop selling ceramics from different
regions of Spain. Not cheap, but a good selection.
El Bulevard dels Antiquarius Pg. de Gràcia
55–57; Ⓜ️Passeig de Gràcia. Over seventy shops
full of (overpriced) antiques of all kinds.
La Caixa de Fang c/Freneria 1 Ⓜ️Jaume I. Off
Bxda. de la Llibretaria, behind the cathedral, this
has very good-value ceramics and recycled glass.
Cereria Subirà Bxda. Llibreteria 7; Ⓜ️Jaume I.

Barcelona's oldest shop (since 1760), selling hand-
crafted candles.
Espai Vidre c/dels Angels 8; Ⓜ️Liceu. Famous
gallery selling artistic items of glass and crystal by
different designers.
La Manual Alpargatera c/Avinyó 7; Ⓜ️Liceu.
Workshop making and selling *alpargatas* (espadrilles)
to order, as well as other straw and rope work.
1748 Pl. de Montcada 2; Ⓜ️Jaume I. Good ceramic
shop with one of the widest selections.

Books

You'll find English-language books, newspapers and magazines at the stalls
along the Ramblas, and a good selection of English-language books (novels and
general, unless otherwise stated) at the following shops:

Altair Gran Via de les Corts Catalanes 616;
Ⓜ️Universitat. Travel books, guides, maps and
world music.
Casa del Llibre Pg. de Gràcia 62, Eixample;
Ⓜ️Passeig de Gràcia. Barcelona's biggest book
emporium, strong on literature and humanities
with lots of English titles.

Crisol Rambla de Catalunya 81, Eixample;
Ⓜ️Passeig de Gràcia. Magazines, books and music
– open until 1am.
Elephant c/Creu dels Molers 12, Poble Sec;
Ⓜ️Poble Sec. Only stocks English-language books
with cheap prices for current novels, classics, children's books and secondhand.

Happy Books c/Pelai 32 and Pg. de Gràcia 77, Eixample; ⓂUniversitat/Catalunya, Passeig de Gràcia. Good travel and dictionary sections, as well as some other English-language titles. Generally the best prices and some very good sales.

Laie Pau Claris 85; ⓂPasseig de Gràcia. Bookstore with excellent selection of humanities and literature and lots of English-language titles. Café/restaurant upstairs.

Llibreria Pròleg c/Dagueria 13; ⓂJaume I. A women's/feminist bookshop, though with most works in Spanish/Catalan. Closed Aug.

Llibreria Quera c/Petritxol 2; ⓂLiceu. Maps and trekking guides in a cramped little Barri Gòtic store. Closed Sat in Aug.

Ras c/Doctor Joaquim Dou 10; ⓂLiceu. Specializes in books and magazines on graphic design, architecture and photography. Temporary exhibitions at the back.

Clothes, shoes and accessories

New **designers** can be found in the streets of La Ribera, around Passeig del Born, where recently a series of funky shops has opened up. For **secondhand and vintage clothing**, stores line the whole of c/de la Riera Baixa (El Raval), with others nearby on c/del Carme and c/de l'Hospital, and on Saturdays there's a street market here.

Antonio Miró c/Consell de Cent 348; ⓂPasseig de Gràcia; plus Groc Rambla de Catalunya 100 ⓂDiagonal, and c/Muntaner 385 ⓂPasseig de Gràcia. The showcases for Barcelona's most innovative designer, Antonio Miró, especially good for men's suits, with Miró clothes and shoes for men and women plus other labels at the Groc outlets.

Camper El Triangle, Pl. de Catalunya; ⓂCatalunya; also in Eixample at c/Muntaner 248; ⓂDiagonal; c/València 249; ⓂPasseig de Gràcia; and Avgda. Pau Casals 5; ⓂDiagonal; Spain's most stylish, value-for-money shoe-shop chain.

Custo Barcelona Pl. de les Olles 7; ⓂBarceloneta; and c/Ferran 40 ⓂLiceu. Colourful designer T-shirts, tops and sweaters of all kinds for men and women.

Giménez & Zuazo c/Elisabets 20; ⓂCatalunya; and c/del Rec 42; ⓂJaume I. Cutting-edge women's fashion, funky and informal.

Jean-Pierre Bua Avgda. Diagonal 469; ⓂDiagonal. The city's temple for fashion victims: a postmodern shrine for Yamamoto, Gaultier, Miyake, Westwood, Miró and other international stars.

Joaquín Berao c/Roselló 277; ⓂDiagonal. Avant-garde jewellery in a stunningly designed shop.

Lailo c/Riera Baixa 20; ⓂLiceu. Secondhand and vintage Raval clothes shop that's usually worth a look, with a massively wide-ranging stock. Theatre costumes for rent at the back.

Mango Avgda. Portal de l'Ángel 7; ⓂCatalunya; Pg. de Gràcia 65; ⓂDiagonal; La Maquinista; ⓂSant Andreu; l'Illa; ⓂMaría Cristina; plus others. Barcelona is where Mango began (and the prices here are cheaper than in North America and other European countries).

Muxaert c/Rosselló 230; ⓂDiagonal; and Rambla Catalunya 47; ⓂCatalunya. Barcelona's top-class shoe designer, pricey gems for men and women.

Rafa Teja Atelier c/Santa Maria 18; ⓂJaume I. Gorgeous silk scarves, mohair wraps and Chinese-style silk jackets and dresses.

Recicle Recicle c/Riera Baixa 13; ⓂLiceu. Secondhand and vintage fashion, from the Fifties onwards, with a rapid turnover.

Stockland c/Comtal 22; ⓂUrquinaona. Bargain-hunter's dream. Top-name haute couture at 30- to 60-percent discounts.

Zara Avgda. Portal de l'Ángel 7; ⓂCatalunya; Avgda. Diagonal 584; ⓂDiagonal; c/Pelai 58; ⓂUniversitat; Rambla de Catalunya 67; ⓂPasseig de Gràcia; La Maquinista; ⓂSant Andreu; plus others. Trendy but cheap seasonal fashion. Their Bershka outlets (on c/Pelai and Avgda. Portal de l'Ángel) sell funky stuff for teenagers.

Department stores and malls

The Tomb Bus shopping line service connects Plaça de Catalunya with the Diagonal (Pl. Pius XII), an easy way to reach the uptown L'Illa and El Corte Inglés stores. Departures are every 7min (Mon–Fri 7am–9.38pm, Sat 9.10am–9.20pm); tickets (available on the bus) are €1.25 one way, €5 for one day's unlimited travel, or €8 for seven trips.

Centre Comercial Barcelona Glòries Pl. de les Glòries Catalanes 1; ⓂGlòries. Big mall with all the national high-street names as well as bars, restaurants and a cinema complex. Mon–Sat 9.30am–10pm.

El Corte Inglés Pl. de Catalunya 14; ⓂCatalunya;

10

Avgda. del Portal de l'Ángel 19–21; ⓂCatalunya; Avgda. Diagonal 471 & 617; ⓂMaría Cristina. The city's biggest department store – top-floor café in the Pl. de Catalunya branch, music, books, computers and sports gear at Portal de l'Ángel. Mon–Sat 10am–9.30pm.

L'Illa Avgda. Diagonal 555–559; ⓂMaría Cristina. Uptown shopping mall with national and international shops, including a FNAC which is good for music and books. Mon–Sat 10am–10pm.

Maremàgnum Moll d'Espanya, Port Vell; ⓂDrassanes. Souvenir, leisure and sportswear shops – including an official FC Barcelona store –

alongside restaurants, fast-food joints and a multi-screen cinema. Daily 11am–11pm.

El Mercadillo c/Portaferrissa 17; ⓂLiceu. Double-decker complex of shops selling skate-, club- and beach-wear and shoes – look out for the camel marking the entrance. There's a bar upstairs with a nice patio garden. Mon–Sat 11am–9pm.

El Triangle Pl. de Catalunya 4; ⓂCatalunya. Shopping centre dominated by the flagship FNAC store, which specializes in books (good travel and English selections), music CDs and computer software. Mon–Sat 10am–10pm.

Design and decorative art

BD Ediciones de Diseño c/Mallorca 291; ⓂDiagonal. The building is by Domènech i Montaner, the interior filled with the very latest in furniture and household design.

D. Barcelona Avgda. Diagonal 367; ⓂDiagonal. Contemporary, imaginative household and personal items.

Dom Pg. de Gràcia 76; ⓂPasseig de Gràcia.

Original, amusing household and personal items at accessible prices.

Vinçon Pg. de Gràcia 96; ⓂPasseig de Gràcia. This palace of design houses stylish and original items, pioneered since the 1960s by Fernando Amat, and with logo and carrier bags by Mariscal and other top designers. Temporary art and design exhibitions are held here, too.

Food

Casa Gispert c/Sombrerers 23; ⓂJaume I. Roasters of nuts, coffee and spices for over 150 years – a truly delectable store.

Colmado Quílez Rambla de Catalunya 63; ⓂPasseig de Gràcia. Classic Catalan grocery, piled high with tins, preserves, wines and chocolates, plus a groaning *xarcuteria* counter.

Formatgeria La Seu c/Daguería 16; ⓂJaume I. The best farmhouse cheeses from all over Spain. Catherine, who's Scottish, will introduce you into the world of cheese with Saturday cheese tastings.

Origens 99,9% c/Vidrería 6-8; ⓂJaume I. Catalan delicatessen extraordinaire: pâtés, special sauces, olive oils, *turron* and more.

Markets

Barcelona's **daily food markets**, all in covered halls, are open Monday–Saturday 8am–3pm and 5–8pm, though the most famous, La Boqueria on the Ramblas, opens right through the day. Other **specialist markets** are open only on certain days. Good ones to try include:

Antiques Avgda. de la Catedral, Barri Gòtic; ⓂJaume I. Every Thurs (not Aug) from 9am. Better for bargains is the market on the Port Vell harbour-side (ⓂBarceloneta) at weekends from 11am.

Christmas Avgda. de la Catedral, and surrounding streets, Barri Gòtic; ⓂJaume I. The *Fira de Santa Llúcia*, daily from Dec 1–22, 10am–9pm.

Coins, books and postcards Mercat Sant Antoni, Ronda de Sant Pau; ⓂSant Antoni. Every Sun from 9am to 2pm. Finish off with a *vermouth negre* in the *Tres Tombs* bar.

Flea market Els Encants, northwest side of Pl. de les Glòries Catalanes, Eixample; ⓂGlòries. Every Mon, Wed, Fri and Sat 8am–1.30pm, for clothes, jewellery, junk and furniture.

Music

Independent **music** and CD stores are concentrated on and around c/dels Tallers (El Raval), just off the top of the Ramblas.

La Casa Pl. Sant Vinçenç Martorell 4; ⓂCatalunya. Barcelona's best for hip-hop, acid jazz, house and techno.

Discos Castelló c/Tallers 3 & 7; ⓂCatalunya. Large vinyl and CD selections with a separate store for classical (no. 3). A good place to pick up

△ Antigua Casa Figueras, Las Ramblas

concert tickets.
Etnomusic c/del Bonsuccés 6; ⓂCatalunya. World music specialist, especially good for all types of South American music.
Planet Music c/Mallorca 214; ⓂPasseig de Gràcia. Big selection, particularly good on flamen-co, classical and world music.
Revolver c/Tallers 11 & 13; ⓂCatalunya. Barcelona's most famous specialist store for rock and pop music. Also one of the most important ticket outlets in Barcelona.

Listings

Airlines Air Europa ☎934 784 713; Air France ☎901 112 666; Alitalia ☎902 1003 23; British Airways ☎902 111 333; Easyjet ☎902 299 992; Iberia ☎902 400 550; KLM ☎902 222 747; Lufthansa ☎902 220 101; Spanair ☎902 131 415; Swissair ☎901 116 706; TAP ☎901 116 718.

Banks and exchange Main bank branches are in Pl. de Catalunya and along Pg. de Gràcia, and there are ATMs all over the city, including on arrival at the airport, Barcelona Sants station and Estació del Nord bus station. Exchange offices include: airport (daily 7.30am–10.45pm); Barcelona Sants (daily 8am–10pm); El Corte Inglés, Pl. de Catalunya (Mon–Sat 10am–9.30pm); Postal Transfer, Pl. Urquinaona at c/Roger de Lluria (Mon–Fri 10am–11pm, Sat 11am–midnight, Sun noon–11pm); tourist office, Pl. de Catalunya 17 (daily 9am–9pm).

Bike rental Half-day rental costs around €15, full-day €25, with the following companies: Biciclot, c/Sant Joan de Malta 1 ☎933 077 475; Bicitram, Avgda. Marquès de l'Argentera 15 ☎607 226 069 or 636 401 997 (weekends and hols only); Decathlon, Pl. Villa de Madrid 1–3 ☎933 426 161; Scenic, c/Marina 22 ☎932 211 666; Un Coxte Menys, c/Esparteria 3 ☎932 682 105.

Consulates Most foreign consulates in Barcelona are open to the public for enquiries Mon–Fri only, usually 9am–1pm and 3–5pm, though the morning shift is the most reliable. Australia, Gran Via Carles III 98 ☎934 909 013; Canada, c/Elisenda de Pinós 10 ☎932 042 700; Ireland, Gran Via Carles III 94 ☎934 915 021; New Zealand, Trav. de Gràcia 64 ☎932 090 399; UK, Avgda. Diagonal 477 ☎933 666 200; USA, Pg. de la Reina Elisenda 23 ☎932 802 227.

Cultural institutes The British Council, c/Amigó 83, FGC Muntaner ☎932 419 700, has an English-language library, lists of language schools and a good noticeboard advertising lessons and accommodation. The North American Institute, Via Augusta 123, FGC Plaça Molina ☎932 405 110, has newspapers, magazines and a reference library.

Emergency services ☎112 for ambulance, police and fire services.

Hospitals For emergency hospital treatment, go to one of the following central hospitals, which have 24hr accident and emergency services: Centre Perecamps, Avgda. Drassanes 13–15, El Raval ⓂDrassanes ☎934 410 600; Hospital Clínic i Provincial, c/Villaroel 170 ⓂHospital Clínic ☎932 275 400; Hospital del Mar, Pg. Marítim 25–29 ⓂCiutadella-Vila Olímpica ☎932 489 011; Hospital de la Santa Creu i Sant Pau, c/Sant Antoni Maria Claret ⓂHospital de Sant Pau ☎932 919 000.

Internet access Competition has driven prices down to around €1 an hour, sometimes a bit more, sometimes a bit less. A stroll down the Ramblas, through the Barri Gòtic, La Ribera, El Raval and Gràcia will reveal a host of possibilities, but major Internet centres include: Ciberopcion, Gran Via de les Corts Catalanes 602 ⓂUniversitat (Mon–Sat 9am–1am, Sun 11am–1am); Cibermundo Bergara, c/Bergara 3 ⓂUniversitat (daily 9am–1am); Cibermundo Balmes, c/Balmes 8 ⓂUniversitat (Mon–Fri 10am–11pm, Sat noon–11pm, Sun 1–11pm); Easy Internet, Ronda Universitat 35 ⓂUniversitat (daily 8am–1am), and Ramblas 31 ⓂLiceu (daily 24hr); and Insòlit, Maremàgnum, Port Vell ⓂDrassanes (daily 12.30pm–midnight).

Language schools The cheapest Spanish or Catalan classes in Barcelona are at the Escola Oficial d'Idiomes, Avgda. Drassanes ⓂDrassanes ☎933 292 458, Ⓦwwwwww.eoibd.es – expect big queues when you sign on. Or try International House, c/Trafalgar 14 ⓂUrquinaona ☎932 68 4 511, Ⓦwww.ihes.com/bcn. The Generalitat offers low-cost Catalan classes to Spaniards and foreigners through the Centre per a la Normalització Linguística; call ☎010 for information. Language courses are also offered at most Spanish universities; contact Barcelona University at Gran Via de les Corts Catalanes 585 ⓂUniversitat ☎934 035 519, Ⓦwww.ub.es. The Pl. de Catalunya tourist office has a list of all other language schools in Barcelona.

Laundries Lavomatic, a self-service launderette, has two old-town branches, both open Mon–Sat 9am–9pm: at Pl. Joaquim Xirau 1 ☎933 425 119, off the Ramblas south of c/Escudellers; and in La Ribera at c/Consolat del Mar 43–45 ☎932 684 768, at Pl. del Palau. It costs €3.75 per 7kg of laundry plus €0.75 per 5min for drying. Self

-service laundry too at Bugaderia Roca, c/Joaquín Costa 16, El Raval ☎934 425 982 (Mon–Fri 8.30am–7.30pm, Sat 8am–2pm); Wash 'N' Dry, c/Nou de la Rambla 19, El Raval ☎934 121 953 (daily 7am–11pm); and Aribau, c/Aribau 29, Eixample ☎934 538 933 (Mon–Fri 9am–1.30pm & 4–8pm, Sat 9am–1.30pm. A law, much ignored in the old city, forbids you from leaving laundry hanging out of windows over a street, and some *hostales* can get shirty if you're found doing excessive washing in your bedroom sink. A dry-cleaner is a *tintorería*.

Left-luggage At Barcelona Sants the *consigna* is open daily from 5.30am–11pm and costs €3–4.50 a day. There are lockers at the Estació de França, Passeig de Gràcia station and the Estació del Nord (all 6am–11.30pm; €3–4.50).

Libraries Biblioteca de Catalunya, c/de l'Hospital 56, El Raval ☎932 702 300, ⒲www.gencat.net/bc (Mon–Fri 9am–8pm, Sat 9am–2pm) – you will only be able to enter this with a letter of academic reference, though there is the Biblioteca Popular Sant Pau (a public library) in the same building (Tues, Thurs & Sat 10am–2pm, Mon–Fri 3.30am–8pm). The Biblioteca de l'Universitat de Barcelona, Gran Via de Corts Catalanes 585 ☎934 035 315, ⒲www.ub.es (Mon–Fri 8am–8.30pm; Oct–June also Sat 9am–2pm), is open to the public.

Lost property Best bet is the main lost property office (*objectes perduts*), round the corner from the *ajuntament* at c/de la Ciutat 9 Ⓜ Jaume I (Mon–Fri 9.30am–1.30pm; ☎934 023 161). You could also try the transport office at Universitat metro station, or call the Institut Metropolità del Taxi ☎932 235 151, which hangs on to anything left in a taxi.

Newspapers and magazines You can buy foreign newspapers at the stalls down the Ramblas, on Pg. de Gràcia, on Rambla de Catalunya, around Pl. de Catalunya and at Barcelona Sants, as well as at major bookstores and in larger hotels. The same stalls also sell an impressive array of international magazines and trade papers. If you can't find what you're looking for there, try Llibreria Mallorca, Rambla de Catalunya 86 (Ⓜ Passeig de Gràcia), which stocks a big selection of British and American newspapers and magazines.

Pharmacies For minor health complaints look for the green cross of a *farmàcia*. Usual hours are Mon–Sat 9am–1pm & 4–8pm. At least one in each neighbourhood is open 24hr (and marked as such), or phone ☎010 for information on those open out of hours. A list of out-of-hours pharmacies can also be found in the window of each pharmacy store.

Police The easiest place to report a crime is at the Guàrdia Urbana (city police) station at Ramblas 43,

opposite Pl. Reial (Ⓜ Liceu; open 24hr; English spoken). If you've had something stolen, you need to go to Policía Nacional office at c/Nou de la Rambla 80, El Raval (Ⓜ Paral.lel) – you need the report from here for your insurance claim (take your passport, provided that wasn't stolen, of course). Otherwise, contact the police on the following numbers: Policía Nacional ☎091, Guàrdia Urbana ☎092.

Post offices The main post office (*Correus*) in Barcelona is at Pl. d'Antoni López, facing the harbour at the end of Pg. de Colom (Ⓜ Barceloneta/Jaume I; Mon–Sat 8.30am–9.30pm, Sun 8.30am–2.30pm; entrance from Via Laietana on Sun). There's a poste restante/general delivery service here (*llista de correus*), plus express post, fax service and phone card sales. Postal Transfer, Pl. Urquinaona at c/Roger de Lluria (Ⓜ Urquinaonoa; Mon–Fri 10am–11pm, Sat 11am–midnight, Sun noon–11pm), offers after-hours postal services, plus money exchange, fax/photocopying, phone card sales, etc. Other central post office branches are at Ronda Universitat 23 and c/Aragó 282, both in Eixample (both Mon–Fri 8.30am–8.30pm, Sat 9.30am–1am). Each city neighbourhood also has its own post office, though these have far less comprehensive opening hours and services.

Swimming pools The city beaches are usually fine for swimming, though if you'd prefer a pool, try the summer-only open-air pools at Piscina Municipal de Montjuïc, Avgda. Miramar 31, Montjuïc (end July to mid-Sept daily 11am–6pm; €4); the indoor and outdoor beachside pools at Club Natació Atlètic Barceloneta, Pl. del Mar, Barceloneta (Mon–Fri 6.30am–11pm, Sat 7am–11pm, Sun 8am–5pm, summer Sun until 8pm; €8); or the Olympic-rated Piscines Bernat Picornell, Avgda. de l'Estadi 30–40, Montjuïc (Mon–Fri 7am–midnight, Sat 7am–9pm, Sun 7.30am–4pm; €8).

Telephone offices For international calls, you can use any of the street cabins, paying with coins, phone card or credit card. However, the cheapest way to make an international call is to go to one of the ubiquitous phone centres, or *locutorios*, which specialize in discounted overseas connections – you'll find them scattered through the old city, particularly in the Raval and Ribera. If the rates to the country that you want to call are not posted, just ask. You'll then be assigned a cabin to make your calls, and afterwards you pay in cash.

Travel agencies General travel agencies are found on the Gran Vía de les Corts Catalanes, Pg. de Gràcia, Vía Laietana and the Ramblas. For city tours, Catalunya holidays and local trips, contact

Julia Tours, Ronda Universitat 5 ☎ 933 176 454 or 933 176 209. For youth/student travel there are: Asatej, Ramblas 140, 5th floor ☎ 934 126 338 and

Abando, Ramblas 88–94 ☎ 933 182 593. The American Express office, Pg. de Gràcia 101 ☎ 932 550 000, also has a travel agency.

Travel details

Trains

See p.31 for contact details for RENFE.
Barcelona to: Cerbère, France (18 daily; 2hr 55min); Figueres (hourly; 1hr 40min); Girona (at least hourly; 1hr 15min); Lleida (9 daily; 2hr 30min–3hr); Madrid (8 daily; 12hr); Paris (7 daily; 11–15hr); Portbou (hourly; 2hr 20min); Puigcerdà (7 daily; 3hr 20min); Ripoll (hourly; 2hr); Sitges (every 30min; 25–40min); Tarragona (every 15–30min; 1hr); Valencia (16 daily; 4–5hr); Vic (hourly; 1hr 15min); Zaragoza (14 daily; 4hr 30min–6hr 30min).

Buses

See p.7180 for bus station details.
Barcelona to: Alicante (4 daily; 9hr); Andorra (2 daily; 4hr 30min); Banyoles (2–3 daily; 1hr 30min); Besalú (2–3 daily; 1hr 45min); Cadaqués (2–5

daily; 2hr 20min); Girona (Mon–Sat 6–9 daily, Sun 3 daily; 1hr 30min); Lleida (12 daily, Sun 4 daily; 2hr 15min); Lloret de Mar (July to mid-Sept 10 daily; 1hr 15min); Madrid (12 daily; 8hr); Olot (2–3 daily; 2hr 10min); Palafrugell (8 daily; 2hr); Perpignan, France (2 daily; 4hr); La Pobla de Segur (1 daily; 3hr 30min); La Seu d'Urgell (2 daily; 4hr); Tarragona (18 daily; 1hr 30min); Torroella (3 daily; 4hr 30min); Tossa de Mar (July to mid-Sept 12 daily; 1hr 35min); Valencia (10 daily; 5hr 30min); Vall d'Aran (1 daily; 7hr); Viella (June–Nov 1 daily; 7hr); Zaragoza (11 daily; 4hr 30min).

Ferries

See p.718 for ferry details.
Barcelona to: Genova, Italy (3 weekly; 18hr); Palma, Mallorca (June–Sept up to 4 daily, less frequent in winter; 4–9hr); Ibiza (June–Sept 1 daily, rest of the year 2–4 weekly; 9hr); Mahón (1 daily; 7hr 30min).

⑩

BARCELONA | Travel details

Catalunya

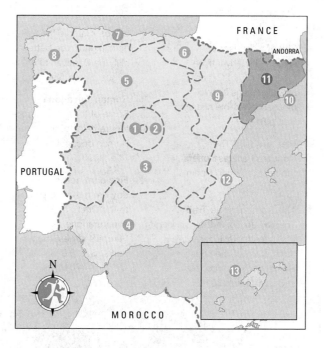

CHAPTER 11

Highlights

* **Get Surreal!** The Dalí Triangle affords a glimpse into the life and work of the artist. See p.813, p.814, p.825 & p.830

* **Cremat at midnight** Savour the traditional sailors' drink on the seafront at Llafranc, Calella or Tamariu. See p.805

* **City of a thousand sieges** The labyrinthine medieval city of Girona proudly retains its two-thousand-year-old history. See p.817

* **Wet and wild** The Noguera Pallaresa offers the best rafting in Spain. See p.867

* **The Romanesque Trail** The Vall de Boí in the Pyrenees foothills features many of the finest Romanesque churches in Spain. See p.881

* **Zip up to Núria** Ride the "zip" train to the mountain sanctuary of Núria. See p.849

* **Classic traverses** Follow paths between staffed refuges in the mountains of the Aigüestortes National Park. See p.875

* **Sitges** Sample the frenetic nightlife or, better still, the Carnival, of chic Sitges. See p.884

* **Roman Tarragona** Some of the most important remains of the Roman occupation. See p.893

* **Five continents in one day** From the Far West to the Orient at Port Aventura, one of Europe's largest theme parks. See p.898

△ Costa Brava

Catalunya

Y ou can't think of visiting Barcelona without seeing something of its surroundings. Although the city is fast becoming international, the wider area of **Catalunya** (Cataluña in Castilian Spanish, traditionally Catalonia in English) retains a distinct regional identity that borrows little from the rest of Spain, let alone from the world at large. Out of the city – and especially in rural areas – you'll hear Catalan spoken more often and be confronted with better Catalan food, which is often highly specialized, varying even from village to village. Towns and villages are surprisingly prosperous, a relic of the early industrial era, when Catalunya developed far more rapidly than most of Spain, and the people are enterprising and open, celebrating a unique range of festivals (see p.796) in almost obsessive fashion. There's a confidence in being Catalan that dates right back to the fourteenth-century Golden Age, when what was then a kingdom ruled the Balearics, Valencia, the French border regions, Sardinia, and even parts of Greece and Corsica. Today, Catalunya is officially a semi-autonomous province, but it can still feel like a separate country – cross the borders into Valencia or Aragón and you soon sense the difference.

Catalunya is also a very satisfying region to tour, since two or three hours in any direction puts you in the midst of varying landscapes of great beauty, from rocky coastlines to long, flat beaches, from the mountains to the plain, and from marshlands to forest. There are some considerable distances to cover, especially in the interior, but on the whole everything is easily reached from Barcelona, which is linked to most main centres by excellent bus and train services. The easiest targets are the **coasts** north and south of the city, and the various **provincial capitals** – Girona, Tarragona and Lleida – all destinations that make a series of day-trips or can be linked together in a loop.

The best of the beach towns lie on the famous **Costa Brava**, which runs up to the French border. This was one of the first stretches of Spanish coast to be developed for mass tourism, and though that's no great recommendation, the large, brash resorts are tempered by some more isolated beaches and lower-key holiday and fishing villages, such as **Cadaqués**. Just inland from the coast, the small town of **Figueres** contains the Museu Dalí, Catalunya's biggest tourist attraction. South of Barcelona, the **Costa Daurada** is less enticing, though it has at least one fine beach at **Sitges** and the attractive coastal town of **Tarragona**; inland, the romantic monastery of **Poblet** figures as one approach to the enjoyable provincial capital of **Lleida**.

Travels in inland Catalunya depend on the time available, but even on a short trip you can take in the medieval city of **Girona** and the surrounding area, which includes the isolated **Montseny hills** and the extraordinary volcanic

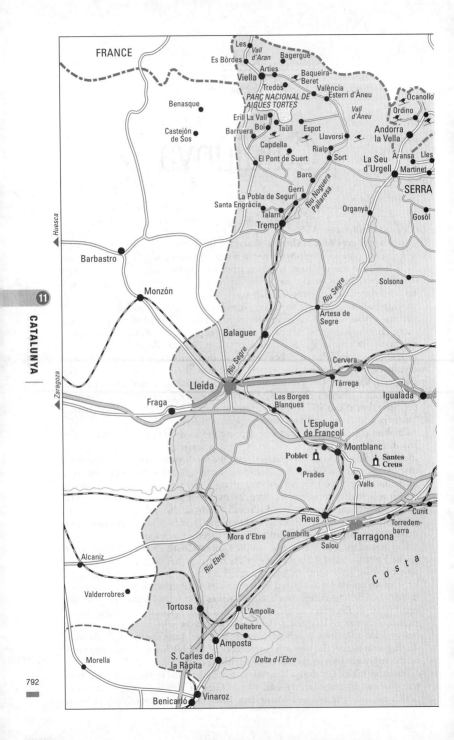

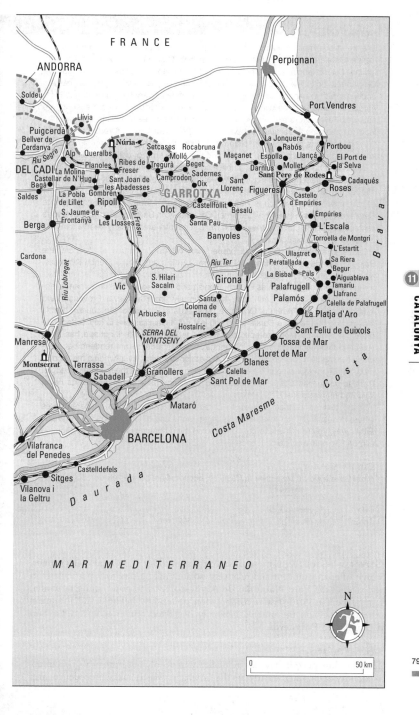

Català

The traveller's main problem throughout the province is likely to be **language** – *Català* (Catalan) has more or less taken over from Castilian and you might not realize that *Dilluns tancat*, for example, is the same as *cerrado Lunes* (closed Monday). On paper it looks like a cross between French and Spanish and is generally easy to understand if you know those two but, spoken, it has a very harsh sound and is far harder to come to grips with, especially away from Barcelona, where accents are stronger. Few visitors realize how ingrained and widespread *Català* is, and this can lead to resentment because people won't "speak Spanish" for you. Increasingly, though, *Català* is replacing Castilian rather than cohabiting with it, a phenomenon known as the *venganza* (revenge). Never commit the error of calling it a dialect!

When Franco came to power, publishing houses, bookshops and libraries were raided and *Català* books destroyed. While this was followed by a let-up in the mid-1940s, the language was still banned from the radio, TV, daily press and, most importantly, schools, which is why many older people today cannot read or write *Català* (even if they speak it all the time). Conversely, in Barcelona virtually everyone *can* speak Castilian, even if they don't, while in country areas, many people can only understand, not speak it.

Català is spoken in Catalunya proper, part of Aragón, much of Valencia, the Balearic islands, the Principality of Andorra, and in parts of the French Pyrenees, albeit with variations of dialect (it is thus much more widely spoken than several better-known languages such as Danish, Finnish and Norwegian). It is a Romance language, stemming from Latin and, more directly, from medieval Provençal and *lemosi*, the literary French of Occitania. Spaniards in the rest of the country belittle it by saying that to get a *Català* word you just cut a Castilian one in half. In fact, the grammar is much more complicated than Castilian, and the language has eight vowel sounds (including three diphthongs). There is a deliberate tendency at present in the media to dig up old words not used for centuries, even when a more common, Castilian-sounding one exists. In Barcelona, because of the mixture of people, there is much bad *Català* and much bad Castilian spoken, mongrel words being invented unconsciously.

In the text we've tried to keep to *Català* names (with Castilian in parentheses where necessary) – not least because street signs and turisme maps are in *Català*. Either way, you're unlikely to get confused as the difference is usually only slight: ie Girona (Gerona) and Lleida (Lérida).

Català glossary

Most **Català** words are similar to Castilian, but some are completely unrecognizable.

One	*Un(a)*		Four	*Quatre*
Two	*Dos (dues)*		Five	*Cinc*
Three	*Tres*		Six	*Sis*

Garrotxa region. With more time you can head for the **Catalan Pyrenees**, which offer magnificent and relatively isolated hiking territory, particularly in and around the **Parc Nacional de Aigüestortes**, and good skiing in winter. East of here is **Andorra**, a combination of tax-free hellhole and mountain retreat set beyond the quieter, generally neglected border towns of **La Seu d'Urgell** and **Puigcerdà**.

Some history

The **Catalan people** have an individual and deeply felt historical and cultural identity, seen most clearly in the language, which takes precedence over

English	Catalan	English	Catalan
Seven	Set	None, some, any, towards	Cap
Eight	Vuit	In	Dins
Nine	Nou	With	Amb
Ten	Deu	Still/yet/even	Encara
Eleven	Onze	A lot, very	Força
Twelve	Dotze	A little	Una mica
		Near	(a) Prop
Monday	Dilluns	Far	Lluny
Tuesday	Dimarts	(Six) years ago	Fa (sis) anys
Wednesday	Dimecres	Self/same	Mateix
Thursday	Dijous	Half/middle	Mig/mitja
Friday	Divendres	Stop, enough!	Prou!
Saturday	Dissabte	Too much/too many	Massa
Sunday	Diumenge		
Day before yesterday	Abans d'ahir	To work	Treballar
Yesterday	Ahir	To go	Anar
Today	Avui	To call, phone	Trucar
Tomorrow	Demà	To have dinner (evening)	Sopar
Day after tomorrow	Demà passat	To eat	Menjar
Left, Right	Esquerre(a), Dret(a)		
Ladies, Gents (WC)	Dones, Homes (Serveis)	Girl	Una noia
Open, Closed	Obert(a), Tancat	Boy	Un noi
Good morning/Hello	Bon dia	Child/term of affection	Nen(a)
Good evening	Bona nit	Dog	Gos
Goodbye	Adéu		
Very well	Molt bé	Place	Lloc
Bad	Malament	Comedor	Menjador
Got a light?	Tens foc?	Drinking glass	Got
I like	M'agrada	Table	Taula
Well, then	Sisplau	Milk	Llet
What do you want?	Que vols?	Egg	Ou
Where is?	On és?	Strawberry	Maduixa
Sometimes	A vegades	Orange	Taronge
Never, ever	Mai	Carrot	Pastanaga
More	Més	Lettuce	Enciam
Nothing	Res	Salad	Amanida
		Apple	Poma

Castilian on street names and signs. Despite being banned for over thirty years during the Franco dictatorship, Catalan survived behind closed doors and has staged a dramatic comeback since the Generalísimo's death. As in the Basque country, though, regionalism goes back much further than this. On the expulsion of the Moors in 874, Guifré el Pelós (Wilfred the Hairy) established himself as the first independent **Count of Barcelona**; his kingdom flourished and the region became famous for its seafaring, mercantile and commercial skills, characteristics which to some extent still set the region apart. In the twelfth century came union with Aragón, though the Catalans kept many of their traditional, hard-won rights (*usatges*). From then until the fourteenth century

In some cases, dates may vary slightly from year to year.

January

20–22 Traditional pilgrimage in Tossa de Mar, the *Pelegri de Tossa*, followed by a lively fiesta. Annual festival at Llança.

February/March

Carnaval Sitges has Catalunya's best celebrations (see p.888). Celebrations also at Solsona, Sort, Rialp and La Molina.

Easter

The *Patum* festival in Berga (see p.850) is the biggest and best Easter festival in Catalunya. Holy Week celebrations at Besalú, Girona and La Pobla de Segur.

April

23 *Semana Medieval de Sant Jordi* in Montblanc – a week of exhibitions, games, dances and medieval music to celebrate the legend of St George.

May

11–12 Annual festival in Lleida, and the annual wool fair, *Festa de la Lana*, in Ripoll. *Festa de Corpus Christi* in Sitges – big processions and streets decorated with flowers. **Third week** *Fires i Festes de la Santa Creu* in Figueres; processions and music.

June

21–23 Festival in Camprodon.
24 *Día de Sant Joan* celebrated everywhere; watch out for things shutting down for a day on either side.
29 Annual festival at Tossa de Mar.
Last week The *Raiers* (rafters) festival and river racing in Sort.

July

First Sunday Annual festival at Puigcerdà.
10 Sant Cristófol festival in Olot, with traditional dances and processions.
Third week *Festa de Santa Cristina* at Lloret de Mar. Annual festival at Palafrugell.
25 Festival at Portbou in honour of Santiago (Sant Jaume, St James).
26 Annual festival at Blanes.

August

First week *Festa Major* at Andorra la Vella; annual festival at Sant Feliu de Guixols.
10–12 Annual festival at Castelló d'Empúries.
15 Festival at La Bisbal and Palafrugell.
19 Festa de Sant Magi in Tarragona.
Last week *Festa Major* in Sitges, to honour the town's patron saint, Sant Bartolomeu.

September

First week Festival at Cadaqués and at L'Escala.
8 Religious celebrations in Cadaqués, Núria and Queralbs. Processions of *gigantes* at Solsona. Festivals at Sort and Esterri d'Àneu.
22 Annual festival at Espot.
23 *Festa de Santa Tecla* in Tarragona, with processions of *gigantes* and human castles.
24 Annual festival at Besalú.

October

8 Annual fair at Viella.
Last week *Fires i Festes de Sant Narcis* in Girona; *Festa de Sant Martirià* in Banyoles.

November

1 *Sant Ermengol* celebrations in La Seu d'Urgell.

December

18 Festival at Cadaqués.

marked Catalunya's **Golden Age**: by the end of that time the kingdom ruled the Balearic islands, the city and region of Valencia, Sardinia, Corsica and much of present-day Greece. In 1359 the Catalan Generalitat – Europe's first parliamentary government – was established.

In 1469, through the marriage of Fernando V (of Aragón) to Isabel I (of Castile), the region was added on to the rest of the emergent Spanish state. Throughout the following centuries the Catalans made various attempts to secede from the stifling grasp of central bureaucracy, which saw Catalan enterprise as merely another means of filling the state coffers. Early industrialization, which was centred here and in the Basque country, only intensified political disaffection, and in the 1920s and 1930s anarchist, communist and socialist parties all established major power bases in Catalunya. In 1931, after the fall of the dictator General Primo de Rivera, a **Catalan Republic** was proclaimed and its autonomous powers guaranteed by the new Republican government. Any incipient separatism collapsed, however, with the outbreak of the Civil War, during which Catalunya was a bastion of the Republican cause, Barcelona holding out until January 1939.

In return, Franco pursued a policy of harsh suppression, attempting to wipe out all evidence of Catalan cultural and economic primacy and finally to establish the dominance of Madrid. Among his more subtle methods – employed also in Euskal Herria – was the encouragement of immigration from other parts of Spain in order to dilute regional identity. Even so, Catalunya remained obstinate, the scene of protests and demonstrations throughout the dictatorship. After Franco's death there was massive and immediate pressure – not long in paying dividends – for the reinstatement of a **Catalan government**. This, the semi-autonomous Generalitat, enjoys a very high profile, whatever the complaints about its lack of real power. It controls education, health and social security, with a budget based on taxes collected by central government and then returned proportionally. Since autonomy was granted, the region has consistently elected centre-right governments, which may be difficult to understand in view of the recent past, but which might be explained by the fact that such regimes are seen to be better able to protect Catalan business interests.

The Costa Brava

Stretching from Blanes, 60km north of Barcelona, to the French border, the unfairly maligned **Costa Brava** (Rugged Coast) boasts wooded coves, high cliffs, pretty beaches and deep blue water. Struggling under its image as the first developed package-tour coast in Spain, it is very determinedly rediscovering itself by revitalizing its local essence and shifting away from mass tourism. It is undeniable that the unharnessed tourist boom wreaked damage in some areas, but thankfully the old sangria-and-chips image, which was never as widespread as its press would suggest, is giving way to greater prominence for the area's undoubted natural beauty and fascinating cultural heritage.

Broadly, the coast is split into three areas: **La Selva** at the southern tip, clustered around brash Lloret de Mar, which most closely resembles the area's

Driving is the easiest way to get around, though you can expect the smaller coastal roads to be very busy in summer and parking to be tricky in the major towns. **Buses** in the region are almost all operated by SARFA, with an office in every town, which offers an efficient service along the length of the coast; consider using Girona or Figueres as a base for lateral trips to the coast; both are big bus termini and within an hour of the beach. To visit the smaller, and subsequently lovelier, coves, though, a car or bike would make life easier, or you could be prepared to walk the fabulous **camí de ronda** necklace of footpaths running along almost all of the coastline. The **train** from Barcelona to Portbou and the French border runs inland most of the time, serving Blanes, Girona and Figueres, but emerging on the coast itself only at Llançà. There are also daily **boat services** (*creuers/cruceros*) which operate along the coast between Easter and September. Fares vary depending on the type of boat, but by way of example a trip from Blanes to Sant Feliu de Guíxols – nine stops and three main towns away – costs €14 return.

once-popular image, and the medieval walled town of Tossa de Mar; the stylish central area of **Baix Empordà** between Sant Feliu de Guíxols and Pals, popular with the chic Barcelona crowd, which boasts some wondefully scenic stretches of roiling coastline around Palamós and the beaches and villages of inland Palafrugell and hilltop Begur; and the more rugged **Alt Empordà** in the north, marked by the broad sweep of the Golf de Roses, site of a nature reserve, the Parc Natural dels Aiguamolls de l'Empordá, and the alluring peace of the ancient Greek and Roman settlement of Empúries, before giving way to the spectacular Cap de Creus headland and park, home to the bohemian **Cadaqués**, which attracts an arty crowd paying tribute to Salvador Dalí, who lived most of his life in the labyrinthine warren of converted fishermen's huts in a neighbouring cove – now a fabulous museum.

There's more **accommodation** along the Costa Brava than anywhere else in Catalunya, ranging from campsites of all prices and sizes, through self-catering apartments to luxurious, spectacularly located hotels. A recent development is a network of *turisme rural* houses, an imaginative alternative to more traditional forms of self-catering. A lot of hotels in the more popular resorts are block-booked by agencies, so even though it is possible to turn up and find a room in July and August, it's always advisable to book in advance; despite this block-booking, there are still plenty of options for independent travellers. One word of caution is that many of the cheaper hotels on the coast are closed outside the summer months. Online reservations for local hotels, apartments and *turisme rural* houses can be made through Eoland (Ⓦ www.eoland.com). There are dozens of campsites, ranging from tiny, family-run affairs to mini-villages; the ones inland tend to be some distance from the nearest town or village, while on the coast there are plenty near the beaches or walking distance from the town centres. For hostels, the Catalan regional government offers a centralized information and reservation service (Ⓦ www.tujuca.com).

La Selva

The area of the Costa Brava that was most distorted by the tourist boom, **La Selva** and its three major towns nonetheless have something to offer most visitors, even if it's just a few hours pottering about the still-beautiful coves or peaceful gardens. To the south, **Blanes** is a microcosm of the coast, divided as it is into a high-rise hotel district and a charming old town with a working port. Neighbouring **Lloret de Mar** has become synonymous with tourist excess, well suited to those who like their holdiays loud, late and libidinous – but it does also boast an absorbing history and some tranquil scenery. Surrounded by quiet coves, Catalunya's only walled coastal town, **Tossa de Mar**, escaped the worst of development fever.

Blanes

Just over an hour from Barcelona, **BLANES** is the first town of the Costa Brava. With its beach split in two by the small Sa Palomera headland, the town is divided into the high-rise, touristy S'Abanell to the southeast, which boasts a long, sandy **beach**, and the more pleasing old town on the northwest side with its small beach and fishing port. Above the harbour stands the clifftop **Mar i Murtra botanical gardens** at Pg. Karl Faust 9 (April–Oct daily 9am–6pm; Nov–March Mon–Fri 10am–5pm, Sat–Sun 10am–2pm; €2.70), well worth the visit for the coastal views and for the amazing variety of plants and trees from all over the world. Blanes' finest beach is **Cala Sant Francesc**, fifteen minutes' walk from the botanical gardens.

There are dozens of **hotels and hostales** in S'Abanell – the best bargains are back from the seafront – and no fewer than twelve local **campsites**. The **turisme** in Plaça de Catalunya (June–Sept Mon–Sat 9am–8pm, July & Aug also Sun 9am–2pm; May & Oct Mon–Fri 9am–2pm & 4–7pm; Nov–April Mon–Fri 9am–3pm; ℡972 330 348, Ⓦwww.blanes.net) can help you find a room. Best places to **eat** are in the old town and port, most notably the down-to-earth and very cheap *Marisqueria El Port* (Port Pesquer), while *Casa Oliveras* at Pg. Cortils i Vieta 12 serves an imaginative blend of Catalan and Latin American dishes for around €20 a head. The trendiest **nightlife** is to be found around c/Vila de Paris, tucked amid the tourist spots of S'Abanell.

The **train** station is inland, a little way out of town; there's a half-hourly service to Barcelona and several trains daily to Girona and Figueres. Regular buses run from the station to the beach, and **buses** also connect Blanes with Lloret every twenty minutes until 9.35pm.

Lloret de Mar

Six kilometres northeast of Blanes, tourist central **LLORET DE MAR** is everything you've ever heard about it and a lot more besides. Yet underneath its undeniably brash commercialism and gaudy nightlife is a centuries-old town trying to make itself known; the result is one of Europe's highest concentrations of clubs clustered around a delightful fifteenth-century church, high-rise monstrosities alongside genteel mansions and a packed main beach that belies some of the splendid rocky coves tucked away to the north and south of the town.

Any sightseeing in Lloret is centred around the warren of streets in the **old town**, amid the sometimes overwhelming hustle of clubbing clothes shops and tourist paraphernalia, where the colourful late-Gothic **Església Parroquial** holds court. Originally fortified, its brick walls and bright tiles influenced later Modernist architects; inside, the elaborately gilded sixteenth-century altarpieces are worth seeing. Where the old town emerges on to the promenade opposite the turisme, the marvellously eclectic **Centre Cultural Verdaguer** (June–Sept daily 10am–1pm; Oct–May Tues–Sat 10am–2pm & 4–6pm, Sun 10am–2pm; free) lies at Pg. Camprodón i Arrieta 1, in a nineteenth-century mansion built by a returning émigré. It offers a surprising insight into how the town must have looked in its pre-tourism heyday, including some rooms with their original decor.

Lloret's main **beach** and neighbouring Fenals beach, where many of the hotels are grouped, get packed and noisy; the south end of Fenals, backed by a pine wood, is much less crowded. Further afield are a number of tiny **coves** favoured by local bathers. Of the more accessible by road and public transport, Cala Santa Cristina and the adjacent Cala Treumal are the best, while the lovely Cala Boadella is a favourite for nude bathing; all are off the Blanes road. On a headland above the last beach is the surprising tranquillity of the **Jardins de Santa Clotilde** (Tues–Sun 10am–1pm & 4–8pm; €3.60), ornamental gardens laid out in Modernist style in the early twentieth century, which offer fabulous views over the Mediterranean; visitor numbers are limited to fifty at a time, but you're most likely to find yourself alone, even in August.

Practicalities

Cruceros and other coastal **boats** dock at the beach, which is where the ticket offices are, too; in the summer there are around a dozen daily services up and down the coast. The **bus station** is north of the town centre, on Carretera de Blanes. As well as regular services from nearby Blanes and Tossa, there are several daily buses from Barcelona and Girona. There's a very good **turisme** in the centre close to the seafront at Plaça de la Vila 1 (June–Sept Mon–Sat 9am–9pm, Sun 9.30am–2pm; March–May & Oct Mon–Sat 9.30am–1pm & 4–8pm; ☎972 364 735, ✉lloretpmt@versin.com), and another smaller one at the bus station (May–Oct Mon–Sat 9.30am–1pm & 4–8pm; Nov–April closes 7pm; ☎972 365 788).

Accommodation

Most **hotels** in Lloret are block-booked by agents, so it's highly advisable to book in advance, especially in the summer. As you'd expect, there are a lot of high-rise hotels, but there are also some very good places in the old part of town not far from the beach or on the outskirts.

Hotel Guitart Rosa c/St Pere 67 ☎972 365 100, ⓦwww.guitarthotels.com. Sheer indulgence at a reasonable price in this colonial mansion in the heart of the old town. ❻

Hostal La Habana c/Les Taronges 11 ☎972 367 707, ⓕ972 372 074. Smart, family-run *pensió* with a good restaurant on a narrow street leading from the beach to the old town. ❹

Pensió Reina Isabel c/Vall de Venecia 12 ☎972 364 121, ⓕ972 369 978. Very quirky and friendly *pensió* in the heart of the old town just one block

from the beach. March–Oct. ❹

Hostal Santa Cristina Ermita de Santa Cristina ☎972 364 934. An antiquated and charming *hostal* next to the Church of Santa Cristina perched on a headland between the beaches at Santa Cristina and Cala Treumal. March–Oct. ❸

Hotel Vila del Mar c/de la Vila 55 ☎972 349 292, ⓕ972 371 168, ⓦwww.hotelviladelmar.com. A small and stylish hotel whose comfortable rooms are surprisingly quiet in the midst of the old town's bustle. Feb–Nov. ❽

Eating and drinking

Although you're never going to be far from a fast-food joint, there's still a reasonably good choice of places to **eat** in the old town. All types and qualities of cuisine abound, including Italian, Greek and Mexican, while the best Catalan choices are *Can Tarrades* at Plaça d'Espanya 7, where you'll pay around €25, and *La Lonja* at c/St Cristòfol 2, which has a good *menú del día* for €8.80 and a great range of tapas. **Clubs** are mainly centred around Avgda. Just Marlés, the main road into town running perpendicular to the seafront, while the most atmospheric **bars** are to be found in the streets around Plaça d'Espanya c/del Carme.

Tossa de Mar

Arriving by boat at **TOSSA DE MAR**, 13km north of Lloret, is one of La Selva's highlights, the medieval walls and turrets of the Vila Vella rising pale and shimmering on the hill above the modern town. Caught on the brink of becoming a full-blown tourist trap, Tossa is still very attractive and makes a much more restful base than Lloret.

Founded originally by the Romans, Tossa has twelfth-century walls surrounding an old quarter, the **Vila Vella**, a maze of cobbled streets, whitewashed houses and flower boxes, slowly climbing the headland and offering terrific views over beach and bay. Within the quarter you'll eventually happen upon the **Museu de la Vila Vella** at Plaça Roig i Soler 1 (Tues–Sun June–Sept 10am–10pm; Oct–May 10am–1pm & 3–6pm; €2.70), which features some Chagall paintings, a Roman mosaic and remnants from a nearby excavated Roman villa. Several parts of the ramparts are accessible, while the whole of the Vila Vella, topped by a squat nineteenth-century lighthouse, is crisscrossed with paths and narrow streets. Above the remains of the town's original medieval church and overlooking the beach stands a **statue of Ava Gardner**, who made the town famous in the 1950 film, *Pandora and the Flying Dutchman*.

Tossa's best **beach** (there are four) is the Mar Menuda, around the headland away from the old town, and is very popular with divers; look for a natural pink cross in the granite, supposedly marking where Sant Ramon de Penyafort gave a dying man his absolution in 1235. The main central beach, though pleasant, gets crowded; if you have your own transport, the tiny coves north and south of the town are much more rewarding. Booths on the main beach sell tickets for **boat trips** around the surrounding coastline; especially good is the trip to Sant Feliu.

Practicalities

There are plenty of day-trippers in Tossa, which is linked to Lloret by half-hourly **buses**. *Crucero* **boats** (see the box on p.798) stop right at the centre of the beach, with the ticket offices nearby. If you're going to stay, pick up a free map and accommodation lists from the efficient **turisme** (Easter–Sept Mon–Sat 9am–8pm, Sun 10am–2pm; Oct–March Mon–Sat 10am–1pm & 4–7pm, Sun 10am–2pm; ☎972 340 108, ⓦwww.tossademar.com), located next to the bus station at Avgda.del Pelegrí 25. To reach the centre, and the beaches, head straight down the road opposite the bus station.

Accommodation

There is plenty of **accommodation** to be had in the warren of tiny streets around the church and below the old city walls; in summer, the more obscure streets away from the front are the ones to check. There are five local **campsites**, all within 2 to 4km of the centre: best are *Cala Llevadó* (☎972 340 314, ⓦcalallevado.com; May–Sept), 3km out, off the road to Lloret, and the plush *Pola* (☎972 341 050; May–Oct), in a pretty cove 4km north off the corniche road.

Pensió Can Tort Trav. del Portal 1 ☎972 341 185. Simple and friendly option; breakfast included. April–Oct. ❷

Pensió Cap d'Or Pg. del Mar 1 ☎972 340 081. Very friendly seafront *pensió* nestling under the walls of the old town. April–Oct. ❹

Hotel Capri Pg. del Mar 17 ☎972 340 358, ⓦwww.tossa.com/capri. Good-value, comfortable hotel on the seafront. April–Oct. ❺

Hotel Diana Plaça d'Espanya 6 ☎972 341 886, ☎972 341 103. Nicely located hotel in a *modernista* mansion in an attractive square. Prices drop dramatically outside summer. Late March to mid-Nov. ❼

Hotel Mar Blau Avgda. de la Costa Brava 16 ☎972 340 282. Pleasant hotel on the edge of the old town where the weekly market is held. June–Sept. ❹
Gran Hotel Reymar Platja de Mar Menuda s/n ☎972 340 312, ⓕ972 341 504. Sumptuous beachfront hotel across the bay from the Vila Vella. April–Oct. ❾
Hotel Tonet Plaça de l'Església 1 ☎972 340 237, ⓕ972 343 096. Pleasantly located family-run hotel with comfortable, good-value rooms. One of the few places in town open all year. ❸

Eating

Most of Tossa's **restaurants** offer an oddly eclectic variety to cater for all tastes, with varying degrees of quality. The better ones include *Bahía*, Passeig del Mar (☎972 340 322), whose swish interior is the setting for tasty seafood meals, *Es Molí*, c/Tarull 3 (☎972 341 414; closed Tues & Oct–April), expensive but with a garden patio and fine local cooking, and *Castell Vell*, c/Pintor Roig i Soler s/n (☎972 341 030; closed Nov–Feb), also expensive but serving excellent fish and seafood on a shaded terrace. A less exclusive place, *Roqueta Mar*, c/de la Roqueta 2, serves a filling *menú del día* and has a lovely setting, with a creeper-shaded terrace in a rambling corner of the old town. For tapas, the atmospheric *La Lluna* at c/Abad Oliva s/n has an excellent selection for around €15 a head.

⑪ Baix Empordà

North from La Selva, while there are still one or two touristy places, the feel of the **Baix Empordà** marks a change from one of package holiday hot spots to a more stylish type of town with a greater local flavour. Known as the Triangle d'Or (Golden Triangle), as the rising property prices and burgeoning number of four- and five-star hotels will bear out, it is much favoured by chic Catalans and foreign visitors seeking less mass tourism-oriented delights. The first part includes a smarter version of Lloret in **Platja d'Aro** and the more family feel of Sant Antoni de Calonge, bookended by the working fishing ports of **Sant Feliu de Guíxols** and **Palamós**, both of which remain largely aloof to their boisterous neighbours. Moving north, the area around the market town of **Palafrugell** boasts some fabulous cove towns, while hilltop **Begur** stands over a string of lovely little coves. **Inland**, it's striking how quickly the scenery changes to give way to the medieval towns of Pals and Peratallada, atmospheric Iberian ruins at Ullastret and the bustling pottery industry of La Bisbal.

Sant Feliu de Guíxols and around

Separated from Tossa by 22km and, reputedly, 365 curves of stunning corniche, **SANT FELIU DE GUÍXOLS** retains an air of gentility and old money. With a striking blend of colonial and Moorish-style architecture, the town owes its handsome buildings and prosperity to the nineteenth-century cork industry which was based here, but its origins go back as far as the tenth century, when a town grew up around the Benedictine **monastery**, whose ruins still stand in Plaça Monestir. The squat round tower and tenth-century arched gateway, the Porta Ferrada, sit back from the square, and if you want to look inside, the complex is usually open from 8am Mass until noon, and again at 8pm Mass. Inside the monastery, the **Museu de la Vila** (June–Sept Tues–Sun 11am–2pm & 6–9pm; Oct–May Tues–Sun 11am–2pm & 5–8pm; €4) has an interesting exhibition of the various eras in the town's past.

Sant Feliu's old-world style is at its most apparent in the mansions lining the wide **Passeig del Mar**, the most ornate of which are the Modernist Casa

Patxot, on the corner of Rambla Portalet, now home to a bank, and the curious Moorish-style Casino dels Nois; built in 1899, with brightly coloured swooping arches, the casino is a great place for an afternoon coffee. The avenue follows the sweep of the coarse sand **beach** and yachting marina, while the streets back from the sea are great for a stroll past the shops and bars and the eighteenth-century **Plaça del Mercat**, with its lively daily market.

Cruceros **boats** dock on the main beach, where you'll also find the various ticket offices. Teisa **bus** services to and from Girona stop opposite the monastery, next to which is the **turisme**, at Plaça Monestir (June–Sept Mon–Sat 10am–2pm & 4–8pm, Sun 10am–2pm; Oct–May Mon–Sat 10am–1pm & 4–7pm, Sun 10am–2pm; ☎972 820 051, ✆otsfg@ddgi.es); the SARFA bus station (for buses to and from Palafrugell, Girona and Barcelona) is five minutes' walk north of the centre on the main Carretera de Girona, at the junction with c/Llibertat.

A score of family-run **pensiones and hotels** can be found in the old town streets, all within a five-minute walk of each other and the sea. Opposite the turisme at Avgda. Juli Garreta 43–45, just off Plaça Monestir, is the *Hostal Zürich* (☎972 321 054; ❹), while a favourite budget choice is the central *Hostal Buxó*, c/Major 29 (☎972 320 187; ❸). Set back from the seafront in the market square is the friendly, family-run *Hotel Plaça*, Plaça Mercat 22 (☎972 325 155, ⊛www.hotelplaza.org; ❺), while the very laid-back *Hotel Tulipán*, c/Joan Maragall 28 (☎972 323 251, ⊛www.hotel.tulipan.com; ❻), offers good value for money.

The town is famous locally for its fish **restaurants**, with the ensuing high prices, although most serve a reasonable *menú del día*. Probably the best-value *menú del día*, at €8.60, is at *Can Claver*, c/Joan Maragall 18, while the atmospheric *Cau del Pescador*, c/St Domènec 11, is a snip at €12. Otherwise, try the Art-Deco *El Dorado Petit*, at Rambla Vidal 23, or the more traditional *Bahia* at Pg. del Mar 17–18; both are expensive of you go *à la carte* but their *menús* are great value. For tapas and a more eclectic range, try the quirky and inexpensive *La Cava* at c/Joan Maragall 11.

S'Agaró

On a headland north of Sant Feliu is the curious village of **S'Agaró**, created in the 1920s, where every house was built in the Modernist style by Rafael Masó, a student of Antoni Gaudí; the short Camí de Ronda leading to the fabulous **Cala Sa Conca** beach is the best way to explore and take in a swim. Also in S'Agaró is the understated luxury of the Costa Brava's first five-star hotel, *Hostal de La Gavina* (☎972 321 000, ✆gavina@iponet.es; ❾).

Platja d'Aro, Calonge and around

A few kilometres to the north, **PLATJA D'ARO** is a neon strip of bars and shops running parallel to, but hidden from, a long sandy beach. By no means picturesque, what it does offer is excellent **nightlife** far removed from the excesses of Lloret, a great **beach** and some stylish **shopping**. The best **restaurants** are the inexpensive and very imaginative *Els Cinc Pebres* at c/Església 64, and the more expensive *Big Rock*, 3km northeast at Avinguda Fanals s/n, serving traditional Catalan fare in a luxurious farmhouse.

Beyond Platja d'Aro, the road leads to the more family-oriented but not terribly pretty **SANT ANTONI DE CALONGE**; more enticing are the **coves** and beaches strung out between the two towns, all of which can be reached by the serpentine and sometimes tricky **Camí de Ronda** or by a number of footpaths descending from the main road. Two kilometres inland, the parent town of Calonge merits an hour or so to visit the closely packed medieval centre with a church and castle.

Eleven kilometres west of Calonge, along a minor road (no public transport), the ancient, megalithic stone of **Cova d'en Daina**, 1km from the hamlet of **ROMANYÀ DE LA SELVA**, is one of the very few surviving examples in Catalunya. If you're driving, the diversion is warranted, especially if you follow it with lunch at one of a pair of very good restaurants in Romanyà.

Palamós and around

Immediately northeast of Sant Antoni de Calonge, **PALAMÓS** hides what remains of its original medieval harbour behind the buildings of the new town. Originally founded in 1277 and sacked by Barbarossa in 1543, the old quarter is set apart from the new on a promontory at the eastern end of the bay. The working fishing port is also home to the curious **Museu de la Pesca** (June–Sept Tues–Sun 11am–9pm; Oct–May Tues–Sat 10am–1.30pm & 3–9pm, Sun 10am–2pm & 4–7pm; €3), chronicling the town's fishing and maritime history; it also organizes a variety of trips on the *Rafael* sailing boat, built in 1915. Even if the museum doesn't grab you, the old town is simply a great place for an afternoon's wandering and an evening at one of the many extremely good **restaurants**, especially the locally famous *Maria de Cadaquéss*, c/Tauler i Servià 6, founded in 1936 as a fishermen's tavern, or the innovative *Flor de Sal* at c/Pagès Ortiz 53. The **nightlife** makes no concessions to foreign tastes, and is consequently a much more fun and spontaneous affair; the best places are between the old town and the port in the La Planassa area, most notably *La Plata*, in a ruined building with a lively downstairs bar and leafy terrace upstairs, while later revellers decamp to the string of lively bars at the marina, about ten minutes' walk east.

Accessible from Palamós by road or along the Camí de Ronda are two fabulous **beaches**. The first, the idyllic **Cala S'Alguer**, is framed by nineteenth-century fishermen's huts, while the larger **Platja de Castell** was rescued from the clutches of property developers, thanks to a local referendum. Perched on the headland at the northern tip of Platja de Castell are the tranquil ruins of an Iberian settlement, visited by surprisingly few people.

Palafrugell and around

The small town of **PALAFRUGELL**, 4km inland from a delightful coastline, has managed somehow to remain almost oblivious to its tourist-dominated surroundings. An old town at its liveliest during the morning market, Palafrugell maintains a cluster of old streets and shops around its sixteenth-century church that aren't entirely devoted to foreigners. It's a pleasant place to visit, and also a convenient place to base yourself if you're aiming for the nearby coastline – and considerably less expensive than staying at the beach.

The coast, too, takes on a more relaxed air. With no true coastal road, this stretch boasts quiet, pine-covered slopes backing three of the loveliest villages on the Costa Brava – Calella, Llafranc and Tamariu – each with a distinct character and all with scintillatingly turquoise waters. The beach development here has been generally mild – low-rise, whitewashed apartments and hotels – and although a fair number of foreign visitors come in season, it's also where many of the better-off Barcelonans have a villa for weekend and August escapes. All this makes for one of the nicest (though hardly undiscovered) stretches of the Costa Brava. Between June and September, buses run from Palafrugell to Calella and then on to Llafranc (8am–9pm: July and Aug every 30min, June &

Sept roughly hourly); a less frequent service runs to the more distant beach at Tamariu (June–Sept 3–4 daily). These services are drastically reduced outside the summer.

Practicalities

Buses arrive at Palafrugell's SARFA **bus terminal** at c/Torres Jonama 67, a ten-minute walk from the town centre. The main **turisme** is in a small lane next to the church on Plaça Església (April–Sept Mon–Sat 10am–1pm & 5–8pm, Sun 10am–1pm; Oct–March Mon–Sat 10am–1pm & 4–7pm, Sun 10am–1pm; ☎972 611 820, ⓦwww.palafrugell.net). A smaller information office is at c/Carrilet 2 (same hours year-round, except July & Aug Mon–Sat 9am–9pm, Sun 10am–1pm; ☎972 300 228). There are a few pay **car parks** on the edge of the centre.

Places to stay can be found at any of the nearby beaches, though rooms here are expensive and zealously sought after. It's easier and cheaper to stay in Palafrugell itself and get the bus to the beach: in summer it's wise to try and book ahead. The best budget choice is *Fonda L'Estrella*, c/de les Quatre Cases 13 (☎972 300 005; ❷), on a little street near the main Plaça Nova. The rooms are simple and cool, arranged around a cloistered courtyard with tables and potted plants. On the other side of the square but not nearly so charming is *Pensió Familiar*, c/Sant Sebastià 29 (mobile ☎972 300 043; ❷), which has clean rooms with separate baths and showers. Further down the same street, the *Hostal Plaja* at c/Sant Sebastià 34 (☎972 610 828, ⓕ972 300 526; ❸) is slightly pricier and more comfortable, and has a secure garage.

If you stay in Palafrugell, you'll have to **eat** there as well since the last bus back from the beaches is at around 8.30pm. There's not a great deal of choice, but what there is is generally good value. The friendly *La Taverna*, just off c/de la Verge Maria on the narrow c/de Giralt i Subirós, has a decent €8 *menú del día*, and substantial *platos del día* for much less. Up a few steps from Plaça Nova, *Restaurant l'Arc* is recommended for inexpensive pizzas and other main dishes. Pricier are *La Xicra*, c/de Sant Antoni 17, a very pleasant Catalan restaurant where a meal will run to €25 a head, and the similarly priced and highly praised *Mas Oliver*, on Avinguda d'Espanya. The town **market** runs daily (not Mon) from 7am till 1pm; it's on c/Pi i Margall, leading north from Plaça Nova.

Calella

One of the most enjoyable towns on the Costa Brava, **CALELLA** possesses a gloriously rocky coastline punctuated by several tiny sand and rocky **beaches** strung out along a backdrop of whitewashed arches and fin-de-siècle villas. From the thoroughly charming area around the minuscule main beaches, the town stretches southwards along a winding Camí de Ronda to the hidden **El Golfet** beach. Above this cove, the Cap Roig headland is home to the **Castell i Jardins de Cap Roig** (daily: June–Sept 8am–8pm; Oct–May 9am–6pm; €2.50), a cliff-top botanical garden and castle begun in 1927 by an exiled colonel from the Tsar's army and his aristocrat English wife; the grounds also host open-air jazz concerts in July and August.

Accommodation is not cheap here but is well recommended; the best bets are the *Hotel Sant Roc* at Plaça Atlàntic 2 (☎972 614 250, ⓦwww.santroc.com; ❻), a plush hotel with superb views over the coves, and the friendly *Hotel Port-Bo*, c/August Pi i Sunyer 6 (☎972 614 962, ⓕ972 614 065; ❺), set a few streets back from the beach. There are several good **eating** places; ones worth seeking out are *La Gavina*, c/Gravina 7, where you can enjoy excellent traditional Catalan cooking and a different selection of fish and seafood every day for around €24, or a modern take on local cuisine at the similarly-priced *El Tragamar*, Pg. Canadell s/n, in a lovely setting below the promenade at beach level. While you're in Calella or neighbouring Llafranc, try *cremat*, a typical drink of the fishing villages in this region, reputedly brought over by sailors from the Antilles. The concoction contains rum, sugar, lemon peel, coffee grounds and sometimes a cinnamon stick; it will be brought out in an earthenware bowl and you have to set fire to it, occasionally stirring until (after a few minutes) it's ready to drink.

Llafranc

A gentle, hilly, twenty-minute walk high above the rocks along the Camí de Ronda brings you to **LLAFRANC**, tucked into the next bay, with a good, if packed, stretch of **beach** and a glittering **marina**. A little more upmarket than Calella, it's a self-consciously opulent place with expensive beachside restaurants and hillside villas glinting in the sun. Steps lead up from the port for the winding climb through residential streets to the **Far de Sant Sebastia** lighthouse, where you'll be rewarded with some terrific views and a swanky hotel and restaurant.

Llafranc has some attractive **hotels**, most with very good restaurants. Perched halfway up a flight of steps, the *Hotel Casamar*, c/del Nero 3 (☎972 300 104, ☏972 610 651; ❺), is worth it for the view of the bay from the hotel's balconies. On the seafront, the *Hotel Terramar*, Pg. Cipsela 5 (☎972 300 200, ☒www.hterramar.com; ❻), is friendly with rooms overlooking the beach, while the sumptuous *El Far*, Platja Llafranc (☎972 301 639, ☏972 304 328; ❼), next to the lighthouse, is sheer tranquil luxury. For a **meal** try *Llevant*, c/Francesc Blanes 5, famed for its seafood but not cheap, or *La Txata*, c/Carudo 12–14, for moderately priced Basque nouvelle cuisine; *La Llagosta* at c/Francesc Blanes 24 serves a good *menú del día* for around €10.

Tamariu

TAMARIU, 4km north of Llafranc, is quieter still and a great favourite with well-heeled Catalan families. Everything is focused on the small seafront, and the **promenade** – lined with tamarind trees, the source of the town's name – has a hushed allure, with small shops, pavement restaurants and elderly people sitting on their front porches. Geared more towards second-homers, the town boasts few **hotels**, but most are good: the seafront *Tamariu*, Pg. del Mar 2 (☎972 620 031, ☒www.tamariu.com; ❻), originally a fishermen's tavern in the 1920s, has comfortable rooms, while a more basic option set back from the sea is the quiet *Sol d'Or*, c/Riera 18 (☎972 620 172; ❸). **Eating** places abound on the promenade, although there is little to set them apart from one another.

Begur and around

In the lee of a ruined hilltop castle, chic **BEGUR**, about 8km from Palafrugell and slightly inland, stands at the centre of a web of winding roads leading down to its tranquil and equally stylish beaches. In the town itself, narrow streets lead to the simple exterior and surprisingly ornate Gothic interior of the **Església Parroquial de Sant Pere**; most remarkable is the odd contrast between statuary and architecture, especially the simplicity of the alabaster Madonna and Child compared with the busy altarpiece. Watching over it all, the thrice destroyed **Castell de Begur** offers fabulous perspectives of the rocky coves to the south and the curving swathe of the Golf de Roses to the north.

Summer bus services lead down hourly to the town's various enticing **beaches**; these include the tiny and exclusive coves of **Aiguafreda** and

Fornells, the first of which also has some excellent beachside restaurants and a stunning parador (see below), and the pretty hamlets of **SA TUNA** and **SA RIERA**. There are a few fairly expensive places to **stay** at the beaches, the flagship being the modern *Parador d'Aiguablava*, Platja d'Aiguablava 9 (☎972 622 162, ⓦwww.parador.es; ❼), on a craggy headland jutting out into the sea; a cheaper and still very comfortable option is in Begur itself at the excellent-value *Hotel Rosa*, c/Pi i Ralló 11 (☎972 623 015, ⓔinfo@hotel-rosa.com; ❺). For a **meal** or a **drink**, besides the beachside spots, your best bet is to head into Begur, where you'll find some great places around the main square; worth trying for traditional Catalan fare is the moderately-priced *Can Torrades* at c/Pi i Tató 5.

Inland: La Bisbal to Torroella

Inland from Palafrugell there are several towns and villages that are worth visiting either as an afternoon's escape from the beach or even as more peaceful bases from which to explore the region.

La Bisbal and around

LA BISBAL, 12km northwest of Palafrugell and on the main road to Girona, is a medieval market town in an attractive river setting. Since the seventeenth century, La Bisbal has specialized in the production of **ceramics**, and pottery shops line the main road through town, great for browsing and picking up some terrific local pieces; if the industry grabs you, the **Museu Terracota** at c/Sis d'Octubre 99 (May–Sept Mon–Sat 10am–1pm & 5–9pm, Sun 10am–1pm; €3.25) makes for an interesting diversion. Ceramics apart, La Bisbal makes a pleasant stop anyway, as its handsome old centre retains many impressive mansions, the architectural remnants of a once thriving Jewish quarter and the fortified medieval **Castell Palau** (Easter–Oct Tues–Sat 10.30am–1.30pm & 4.30–8.30pm, Sun 10.30am–1.30pm; Nov–March Mon–Fri 5–8pm, Sat 11am–2pm & 5–8pm, Sun 11am–2pm. €2.20), built for the bishops of Girona.

If you fancy a luxurious **stay** or **meal** locally, *Hotel Castell d'Empordà* (☎972 646 254, ⓦwww.castelldemporda.com; ❽), perched atop a hill 3km north of the town in an 800-year-old castle that once belonged to one of Columbus's captains, is a most rewarding detour. Equally opulent bases are at *Arcs de Monells*, 3km northwest at c/Vilanova 1 in Monells (☎972 630 304, ⓦwww.hotelarcsmonells.com; ❽), a lovely hotel in a fourteenth-century hospital, and *Mas Torrent*, a secluded five-star hotel 9km east in Torrent (☎972 303 292, ⓦwww.mastorrent.com; ❾).

Pals

The journey north to L'Escala from Palafrugell can be broken 8km north at **PALS.** This fortified medieval village was long neglected until it was painstakingly restored by a local doctor after the Civil War, which has earned it the rather unfortunate side effect of being invaded by scores of day-trippers. Even so, its fourteenth-century streets and hilltop setting make it an enjoyable place for a stroll amid the golden-brown buildings clustering around a stark tower, all that remains of the town's Romanesque castle; below is the beautifully vaulted Gothic parish church. You could also look into the **Museu-Casa de Cultura Ca La Pruna**, c/La Mina (Mon–Sat 10am–2pm & 5–9pm, Sun 10am–2pm; €3.50); exhibits here include a facsimile of an eighteenth-century pharmacy and odds and ends retrieved from an English warship sunk in the siege of Roses in the 1808 War of Independence. There's a good **turisme** on the edge of the new town at c/Aniceta Figueres 6 (June–Sept Mon–Sat 9am–9pm, Sun 10am–2pm & 4–8pm; Oct–May Mon–Fri 9am–2pm, Sat & Sun 10am–2pm; ☎972 667 857).

Peratallada and Ullastret

West of Pals, the medieval walled town of **PERATALLADA** has rapidly stolen the former's fire by preserving its rustic feel while still injecting a vitality into its tiny streets and squares that is missing in Pals. An influx of small hotels and restaurants has proved to be surprisingly in keeping with their thirteenth-century Romanesque setting, making it both an alluring place for a meal and a stroll or a fabulous base away from the beach. Focal point is the **Castell de Peratallada** – now a hotel – whose origins have been dated back to pre-Roman times; the ruined five-storey Torre d'Homenatge dels Cavallers is open to the public (€6). If you fancy **staying**, the *Hostal La Riera*, Pl de les Voltes 3 (☎972 634 142, ℻972 635 040; ❺), in a seventeenth-century building, is the most economical option; more expensive are the tiny *Hostal Miralluna*, Pl de l'Oli 2 (☎ & ℻972 634 304; ❼), in an eighteenth-century house set back from the street, and the bougainvillea-gardened *El Pati*, c/Hospital 13 (☎972 634 069, ⓦwww.hotelelpati.net; ❼). There are numerous very good places for a **meal**.

Six kilometres northwest is the medieval village of **ULLASTRET**, enjoyable for a short visit but most famous for the nearby **Poblat Ibéric d'Ullastret** (Tues–Sun: Easter & June–Sept 10am–8pm; Oct–May 10am–6pm. €2.20), a tremendously peaceful ruined Iberian settlement with a fascinating museum.

Torroella de Montgrí and L'Estartit

TORROELLA DE MONTGRÍ, 9km beyond Pals on the Ter River, was once an important medieval port but today has been left high and dry by a receding Mediterranean. It now stands 5km inland, beneath the shell of a huge, battlemented thirteenth-century castle (a stiff thirty-minute walk away), and remains distinctly medieval in appearance with its narrow streets, fine mansions and fourteenth-century parish church. If you decide to **stay**, the *Fonda Mitja*, at c/d'Església 10 (☎972 758 003; ❸), just off the arcaded Plaça de la Vila, is excellent value, or for a more luxurious option there's the fabulous ninth-century *Palau Lo Mirador*, Passeig de l'Església 1 (☎972 758 063, ⓦwww .palaumirador.com; ❾), once the royal palace of Jaume I. In the summer, a **turisme** stand (June–Sept Mon 10am–2pm, Tues–Sat 10am–1pm & 5–8pm) is in the free car park on the L'Estartit road. The town is probably best known for its annual **classical music festival**, held over July and August in the main square and church. Advance bookings can be made from early June at the Festival Internacional de Música, Apt 70, Codina 28 (☎972 760 605, ⓦwww.ddgi.es/tdm/fimtdm).

The nearest beach is 6km to the east at **L'ESTARTIT**, curiously divided between the rather scruffy entrance, where you'll find all-day breakfast joints, and the instantly more stylish **port** area, lined with very good restaurants and bars. There's a wide, though not particularly stunning, beach, and boat services to the nearby **Illes Medes**, Catalunya's only offshore islands. These form a protected nature reserve, hosting the most important colony of herring gulls in the Mediterranean, numbering some 8000 pairs. There are hourly **buses** from Torroella to L'Estartit.

CATALUNYA | Baix Empordà

11

Alt Empordà

Beyond Torroella de Montgrí, the scenery changes quite suddenly as you move into the fertile plains and wetlands of the southern part of the **Alt Empordà**, dominated by the broad swathe of the Golf de Roses. Coves give way to long stretches of sand as far north as **Roses**, which nestles in its own closed-in bay. On the way, the landscape passes through low-key developments such as the pleasant old fishing port of **L'Escala**, made more remarkable by the presence of **Empúries**, a ruined Greek and Roman settlement and one of Spain's most important archeological sites. Beyond Roses, the familiar crashing rocks and deeply indented coves return with a vengeance in the wild Cap de Creus headland. The jewel in the crown here is **Cadaqués**, eternally linked to **Salvador Dalí**, who lived for years in the neighbouring fishermen's village of **Portlligat**, now home to an absorbing museum in his former bizarre residence. For the final run to the French border the road swoops along the coast through quieter villages of the likes of whitewashed **Port de la Selva** and the busy fishing port of **Llançà**, before reaching the time-warp frontier crossing of **Portbou**.

L'Escala and Empúries

At the southernmost end of the sweeping billhook of the Golf de Roses, **L'ESCALA** is split between its very picturesque **old town**, favoured by local holidaymakers, and the more commercial **Riells** quarter, the haunt of foreign visitors. Infinitely more appealing, the narrow pedestrianized streets of the old town huddle around the ancient port, where you'll find medieval mooring posts and a cannonball embedded in the wall of the house at c/Joan Massanet 2, fired from a ship in May 1809. A further enticement is L'Escala's proximity to the archeological site of **Empúries**, which lies just a couple of kilometres out of town. One of Spain's most interesting sites, Empúries's fascination derives from its distinct Greek and Roman quarters as one culture steadily usurped the other. You can see the ruins in a leisurely afternoon, spending the rest of your time either on the crowded little sandy **beach** in L'Escala or on the more pleasant duned stretch in front of the ruins. The wooded shores around here hide a series of lovely cove beaches with terrific, shallow water and soft sand. L'Escala is also widely known for its canning factories where Catalunya's best **anchovies** are packaged. You can sample them in any bar or restaurant, or buy small jars to take home from shops around town.

Practicalities

Buses all stop on Avinguda Girona, just down the road from the **turisme** at Plaça de las Escoles 1 (daily 9am–9.30pm; ☎972 770 603, ⓦwww.lescala.org). **Parking** is tricky, although there are a number of small car parks around the centre or meters along the promenade between the old port and Riells.

The best **hotels** are around the old town, although with little or no mid-price options, the choice is between pricey three-star places and variable-quality one-star establishments. Best on offer are the self-catering *Avenida Zodiac*, Avgda.Ave Maria 37–39, Apartado 281 (☎972 770 110; closed Nov–March; minimum stay one week; ❸), a well-equipped apartment complex, *Hostal Garbi*, c/Sta. Maxima 7 (☎ & ⓕ972 770 165; ❺), a very friendly *hostal* with renovated rooms in a lovely old building, and *Hotel Voramar*, Pg. Lluis Albert 2 (☎972 770 108, ⓕ972 770 377; ❺), with a saltwater pool and bar above the waves. There's also a very good **hostel** next to the beach near Empúries at

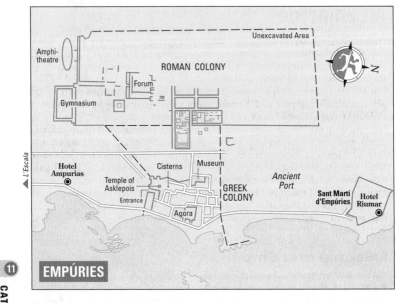

EMPÚRIES

c/Les Coves 41 (☎972 771 200, ☏972 771 572; €17 dorm bed).

Freshly-caught fish and seafood are the speciality of the town's **restaurants**, where you'll find a good choice lining the port and straggling through the old streets; for tapas, try *La Cava del Port* at c/del Port 33. For a **drink**, you're also better staying in the old part, where you'll find a range from fishermen's taverns to trendy bars.

Empúries: the site

Empúries was the ancient Greek *Emporion* (literally "Trading Station"), founded in 550 BC by merchants who, for three centuries, conducted a vigorous trade throughout the Mediterranean. In the early third century BC, their settlement was taken by Scipio, and a Roman city – more splendid than the Greek, with an amphitheatre, fine villas and a broad marketplace – grew up above the old Greek town. The Romans were replaced in turn by the Visigoths, who built several basilicas, and *Emporion* disappears from the records only in the ninth century when, it is assumed, it was wrecked by either Saracen or Norman pirates.

The **site** (daily: Easter & June–Sept 10am–8pm; rest of year 10am–6pm; €2.60) lies behind a sandy bay about 2km north of L'Escala. The remains of the original **Greek colony**, destroyed by a Frankish raid in the third century AD – at which stage all moved to the Roman city – occupy the lower part of the site. Among the ruins of several temples, to the left on raised ground is one dedicated to Asklepios, the Greek healing god whose cult was centred on Epidavros and the island of Kos. The temple is marked by a replica of a fine third-century BC statue of the god, the original of which (along with many finds from the site) is in the Museu Arqueològic in Barcelona. Nearby are several large cisterns: *Emporion* had no aqueduct so water was stored here, to be filtered and purified and then supplied to the town by means of long pipes, one of which has been reconstructed. Remains of the town gate, the **agora** (or central marketplace) and several streets can easily be made out, along with a mass of house foundations, some with mosaics, and the ruins of Visigoth basilicas. A small **museum** (€1.80) stands above, with helpful models and diagrams of the excavations as well as some of the lesser finds, and an excellent audiovisual display giving a brief history of the settlement. Beyond this stretches the vast but only partially excavated **Roman town**. Here, two luxurious villas have been uncovered, and you can see their entrance halls, porticoed gardens and magnificent mosaic floors. Further on are the remains of the **forum**, **amphitheatre** and outer walls.

Sant Marti d'Empúries

A short walk along the shore from the site brings you to the tiny walled hamlet of **SANT MARTI D'EMPÚRIES**. What was once a lovely, decaying place has been entirely taken over by visiting tourists who descend upon the shaded bar-restaurants in the square for lengthy lunches. Though it's still undeniably pretty, there are usually too many people around for comfort; generally, it's less oppressive in the evenings, when Sant Marti can still be perfect for a drink amid the light-strung trees. From the walls outside the village you can see the whole of the Golf de Roses, with kilometre after kilometre of beach stretching right the way round to Roses itself, glinting in the distance. The best place to stay is *Hotel Riomar* (T & F 972 770 362; May–Sept; ❹), next to the beach.

The Golf de Roses

The **Golf de Roses** stretches between L'Escala and Roses, a wide bay backed for the most part by flat, rural land, well watered by the Muga and Fluvià rivers. Left to its own quiet devices for centuries, this coast is distinct from the otherwise rocky and touristy Costa Brava, and has really only suffered the attention of the developers in towns at either end of the bay, most notably in the few kilometres between the marina-cum-resort of Ampuriabrava and Roses.

Parc Natural dels Aiguamolls de l'Empordà

Halfway around the bay in two parcels of land on either side of the Ampuriabrava is one of Spain's more accessible nature reserves, the **PARC NATURAL DELS AIGUAMOLLS DE L'EMPORDÀ** (open daily; free), an important wetland reserve created by the Catalan government in 1983 to save what remained of the Empordà marshland, which once covered the entire plain here, but has gradually disappeared over the centuries as a result of agricultural developments and cattle-raising. Relying heavily on the natural history students of Barcelona University and volunteers, the park attracts a wonderful selection of birds to both its coastal terrain and the paddy fields typical of the area. There are two main paths around lagoons and marshes: the first will take around two hours, while a second five-hour trek takes in more open land and can be cycled. Hides have been created along the way: morning and early evening are the best times for birdwatching in the marshes and you'll see the largest number of species during the migration periods (March–May & Aug–Oct). You'll almost certainly see marsh harriers and various waterfowl, and might spot bee-eaters, kingfishers and the rare glossy ibis.

Without your own transport, access is by one of the numerous daily **buses** of the SARFA company plying the Figueres–Roses road; get off the bus at Castelló d'Empúries and take the turning south in the direction of Sant Pere

Pescador. After about 4km, you'll see a sign on the left pointing the way to the visitors' centre at El Cortalet (daily: April–Sept 9.30am–2pm & 4.30–7pm; Oct–March 9.30am–2pm & 3.30–6pm; ☎972 454 222, ⓦwww.aiguamolls.org), where you can pick up a brochure marking the recommended routes and rent binoculars for €2.20 for the day. The visitors' centre also provides free **parking**. Best **campsites** for the park are the massive *Nàutic Almatà* (☎972 454 477, ⓦwww.campingparks.com; mid-May to Sept), or the smaller *La Laguna* (☎972 450 553, ⓦwww.campinglaguna.com; April–Oct).

Sant Pere Pescador

The nearest village to the park is **SANT PERE PESCADOR**, 3km south of the information centre. The village is easily reached by bus from Figueres and there are also services from Palafrugell, L'Escala and Girona. Largely passed by in the tourist boom, it's frequented mainly by local fruit-growers and the occasional tourist: there are half a dozen *hostales* and hotels (most open only June–Sept), and several bars and restaurants, including the exceptional *Can Ceret*, c/Mar 1 (☎ & ⓕ972 530 433; ❺), originally an eighteenth-century farmhouse, where you can get comfortable rooms and an excellent meal.

Castelló d'Empúries

The delightful small town of **CASTELLÓ D'EMPÚRIES**, halfway between Roses and Figueres, makes a much more attractive base for the park – and indeed is worth a stop in passing anyway. A five-minute walk from the outskirts where the bus halts (and where cars should be parked) transports you into a little medieval conglomeration that's lost little of its genteel charm. Formerly the capital of the counts of Empúries, the town's narrow alleys and streets conceal some fine preserved buildings, a medieval bridge, and a towering thirteenth-century church, **Santa María**, whose ornate doorway and alabaster altarpiece alone are reward enough for the trip; known as the Cathedral of the Empordà, it was intended to be the centre of an Episcopal see, but opposition from the bishopric of Girona meant this was never to be, so bequeathing Castelló with a church out of proportion to the town. The town's medieval **prison** (daily 9.30am–1pm & 4–8pm; €2.20) on c/Presó, has a curiosity value in the graffiti scratched by prisoners on the walls.

The nature reserve lies around 5km south, reached on the minor road to Sant Pere Pescador, and the beach at Roses is also close by – only fifteen minutes away by bus. Best **places to stay** include the *Hotel Canet* (☎972 250 340, ⓦwww.hotelcanet.com; ❸), which enjoys a fine position at Plaça Joc de la Pilota 2 and has a good terrace restaurant, or the same owners' lavish new place in a seventeenth-century mansion at *Hotel de la Moneda*, Pl. Moneda 8–10 (☎972 158 602, ⓦwww.hoteldelamoneda.com; ❻).

Finally, there are a couple of **cases rurales** in the area worth considering. *La Caputxeta* is just across the river from Castelló (☎972 250 310 or 972 250 646; ❸); there's also a self-catering kitchen. The other, in the remoter village of **SIURANA D'EMPORDÀ** between Figueres and Sant Pere Pescador, is *El Molí* (☎972 525 139, ⓦwww.turismerural.com/elmoli; ❸), an award-winning premises set amongst vast gardens.

Roses

ROSES itself enjoys a brilliant situation, beneath medieval fortress walls at the head of the grand, sweeping bay. It's a site that's been inhabited for over three thousand years – the Greeks called the place *Rhoda*, when they set up a trading colony around the excellent natural harbour in the ninth century BC – but apart from the castle, the extensive ruined citadel and the surviving sections of the city wall, there's little in present-day Roses to hint at its long history. Instead, Roses is a full-blown package resort, which trades exclusively on its 4km of sandy beach, which have fostered a large and popular water-sports industry. If you're staying, worthwhile escapes include the bus ride over the hill to more attractive Cadaqués (see below), which gives superb views back over the town and bay, or the **boat excursions** around the cape to Cadaqués or out to the Illes Medes.

Buses stop at the corner of c/Gran Vía Pau Casals and c/Riera Ginjolas, where a station is scheduled for completion in 2004. If you feel like staying, the **turisme** (daily: June–Sept 9am–9pm; Oct–May 9am–1pm & 4–8pm; ☎972 257 331, ⓦwww.rosesnet.com), on the seafront promenade, has an extensive **accommodation** list.

Cadaqués and around

CADAQUÉS is by far the most pleasant place to stay on the northern Costa Brava, reached only by the winding road over the hills from either Roses or Port de la Selva and consequently retaining an air of isolation. With white-washed and bougainvillea-festooned houses lining narrow, hilly streets, a tree-lined promenade and craggy headlands on either side of a harbour that is still a working fishing port, it's genuinely picturesque. Already by the 1920s and 1930s the place had begun to attract the likes of Picasso, Man Ray, Lorca, Buñuel, Thomas Mann and Einstein, but Cadaqués really "arrived" as an **artis-tic-literary colony** after World War II when Surrealist painter **Salvador Dalí** and his wife Gala settled at nearby Port Lligat, attracting for some years a floating bohemian community. Today, a seafront statue of Dalí haughtily gazing on the artists, well-heeled Barcelonans and art-seeking foreigners who have rolled up in his wake provides the town's physical and spiritual focal point.

Local **beaches** are all tiny and pebbly, but there are some enjoyable walks around the harbour and nearby coves, while the town itself makes for an inter-esting stroll, clambering around the streets below the church amidst art gal-leries and studios, smart restaurants and trendy clothes shops. At the top of the hill, the church itself, the austere-looking sixteenth-century **Església de Santa Maria**, opens up to reveal an ornate eighteenth-century altarpiece and a side chapel on the left painted by Dalí. Below the church, the **Museu Municipal d'Art** on c/Monturiol 15 (opening hours and prices vary) features temporary exhibitions by local artists and intriguing displays relating to aspects of Dalí's work.

Practicalities

Buses arrive at the little SARFA bus office on c/Sant Vicens, on the edge of town, next to a large pay **car park**. From here, you can walk along c/Unió and c/Vigilant to the seafront or go past the car park to climb up through the old streets to reach it. Just back from Plaça Frederic Rahola on the seafront, the **turisme** is at c/des Cotxe 2 (Mon–Sat 10am–1pm & 4–8pm; Easter–Oct also Sun 10am–1pm; ☎972 258 315).

Accommodation

Finding **rooms** is likely to be a big problem unless you're here outside peak season: a town plan posted at the bus stop marks all the possibilities. There's a noisy though well-equipped **campsite** (☎972 258 126, ⓕ972 159 383; April–Sept) on the road to Port Lligat, 1km out of town.

Llané Petit c/Dr Bartomeus 37 ☎972 258 050, ⓔllanepetit@ctv.es. Friendly, relaxing hotel at the southern end of the town. Most rooms have sea views. ❻

Hostal Marina c/Riera 3 ☎972 159 091, ⓕ972 258 199. Closed Jan & Feb. Well-located verandah-fronted hotel a short distance from the beach. ❹

Misty Ctra Portlligat ☎972 258 962, ⓕ972 159 090. Closed Jan & Feb. Hacienda-style hotel grouped around a garden and swimming pool on the road to Portlligat. ❹

Playa Sol Pianc 3 ☎972 258 100, ⓦwww .playasol.com. Closed Oct–Dec. Set in a curve of the seafront, this quiet hotel offers rooms with great views of the town or over tranquil gardens. ❺

Hostal Vehí c/Església 6 ☎972 258 470. Closed Nov–Feb. Friendly, excellent-value *hostal* in a lovely central location near the church. ❷

Eating and drinking

Along the seafront is a string of moderately priced seafood **restaurants**, any of which is worth trying, while dotted about the old town and along c/Miquel Rosset are places to suit a wide range of tastes and budgets: an institution in the town is the traditional Catalan fare of *Casa Anita*, c/Miquel Rosset 16, although you should be prepared to queue, while part of the same family has opened *Can Tito* at c/Vigilant s/n, specializing in progressive local cuisine. *La Sirena*, hidden away in c/Es Call, serves some of the best seafood in town, while *Rincón de Marta*, below the church at c/Curós 10, offers a new take on pasta, meat and fish dishes. **Nightlife** is a pleasurable blend of laid-back idling at the beachside terraces and stylish hobnobbing around the bars and restaurants on c/Miguel Rosset: one must-see is Dalí's favourite haunt, *L'Hostal*, at Pg. del Mar 8, which still retains a slightly surreal air.

Around Cadaqués: the Casa-Museu Salvador Dalí and Cap de Creus

A well-signposted twenty-minute walk north of Cadaqués is the tiny harbour of **PORTLLIGAT**, former home of Salvador Dalí. The artist had spent much of his childhood and youth in Cadaqués, and later, with his wife and muse, Gala, he converted a series of waterside fishermen's cottages in Portlligat into a sumptuous home that has all the quirks you would expect of the couple, such as speckled rooftop eggs and a giant fish painted on the ground outside. The house is now open to the public as the **Casa-Museu Salvador Dalí** (mid-June to mid-Sept daily 10.30am–9pm; rest of year Tues–Sun 10.30am–6pm; closed Jan & Feb; last entry 50min before closing; ☎972 251 015, ⓦwww .dali-estate.org; €8), and although there's not much in the way of artworks, it's worth the visit to see first-hand how the bizarre couple lived until Gala's death in 1982, after which Dalí moved to Figueres. Visitor numbers are strictly controlled and you have to book a visit by ringing the museum beforehand.

Tours take in most of the house, and include Dalí's studio, the exotically draped model's room, the couple's master bedroom and bathroom and, perhaps best of all, the oval-shaped sitting room that Dalí designed for Gala, which, apparently by accident, boasts stunning acoustics. Upstairs you can see the garden and swimming pool where the couple entertained guests – they didn't like too many strangers trooping through their living quarters. The phallic swimming pool and its various decorative features, including a giant snake and a stuffed lion, are a treat.

A winding road snakes past glimpses of inviting wave-plundered coves to the wind-buffeted **Cap de Creus** headland, the most easterly tip of the Iberian peninsula, which provides breathtaking views of the coast. A false lighthouse in front of the real 1853 one was built for the 1971 film, *The Light at the End of the World*. Standing on the clifftop is the *Cap de Creus* bar and **restaurant** (Mon–Thurs noon–8pm, Fri–Sun 11am–midnight), which has a slightly hippie feel and a great terrace.

Port de la Selva to Portbou

From Cap de Creus, the coastline winds past a series of low-key towns and villages favoured by local tourists and dominated by the hilltop monastery of Sant Pere de Rodes until the border crossing at Portbou. Regular **buses** ply the route along the coast and inland to Figueres, while the main **trains** from Barcelona and Figueres meet the sea at Llançà, stopping at the towns en route to the French border.

Port de la Selva

Thirteen kilometres northwest of Cadaqués, **PORT DE LA SELVA** has a rather engaging faded charm and not one single high-rise block. Strung out in a thin line along the water's edge, the town centres on its fishing and pleasure **ports**, while either side is a ribbon of lovely **coves** with some of the cleanest water in the Mediterranean: those to the north are far more rugged and reached on foot or by sea, while the ones to the west are easier to get to and, therefore, more popular. By no means a lively place, it's a calming base for exploring Cap de Creus and, especially, Sant Pere de Rodes, the most important monastery in the region.

The few places to **stay** are generally of a high standard: the *Pensió Sol y Sombra*, c/Nou 5 (T972 387 060, F972 387 527; ❹); the *Hostal La Tina*, c/St Baldiri 16 (T972 126 444; ❸), is comfortable and central; or there's the more expensive *Hotel Porto Cristo*, c/Major 59 (T972 387 062, F972 387 529; ❺), with sumptuously decorated rooms. Choice of **restaurants** is limited basically to the above hotels and *pensiones*. There are also a few **campsites** within 2km of the beach, the best being *Port de la Vall*, Ctra. de Llanca km 6 (T972 387 186, Wwww.campingportdelavall; Easter–Sept).

Sant Pere de Rodes

Just below the 670-metre-high summit of the Serra de Roda stands the Benedictine monastery of **Sant Pere de Rodes** (Tues–Sun June–Sept 10am–8pm; Oct–May 10am–2pm & 3–5.30pm; €3.60, plus €1.20 per car; Tues free). It's 8km up the paved **road** from Port de la Selva, via Selva de Mar; approaching **by foot**, use the marked trail (90min) through the Vall de Santa Creu, which begins at Molí de la Vall.

The monastery was one of the many religious institutions founded in this area after the departure of the Moors. The first written record dates back to 879, and in 934 the monastery became independent, answerable only to Rome: in these early years, and thanks especially to the Roman connection, the monks became tremendously rich and powerful. As the monastery was enlarged it was also fortified against attack, starting a period of splendour that lasted four hundred years before terminal decline set in. Many fine treasures were looted when it was finally abandoned in 1789, and it was also pillaged by the French during the Peninsular War; some of the rescued silver can be seen in Girona's Museu d'Art.

Once one of the most romantic ruins in all of Catalunya, its central church universally recognized to be the precursor of the Catalan Romanesque style, overzealous restoration is robbing it of a great deal of its charm. No original columns or capitals remain in the cloister and some of the work looks too clinical. The redeeming feature, apart from the view, is the **cathedral**, which retains its original stonework from the tenth to fourteenth centuries, including eleventh-century column capitals carved with wolves' and dogs' heads.

Nearby is the peaceful pre-Romanesque church of **Santa Elena**, all that remains of the small rural community that grew up around the monastery. Above the monastery (and contemporary with it) stands the much more atmospheric ruined **Castell de Sant Salvador**, a twenty-minute scramble up a steep, narrow path. This provided the perfect lookout site for the frequent invasions (French or Moorish), which normally came from the sea; in the event of attack, fires were lit on the hill to warn the whole surrounding area.

Llançà

Like many towns on the coast, **LLANÇÀ**, 7km northwest of Port de la Selva, is divided between the **Vila**, built inland to escape the attentions of pirates, and the **Port**, which grew up out of the old town. In the Vila, a tiny café-ringed **Plaça Major** houses an outsize fifteenth-century episcopal palace attached to a later parish church, as well as the renovated remains of the fourteenth-century defensive **Torre de la Plaça**, which houses an exhibition (Mon–Fri 5.30–9pm; Sat 6.30–9pm) of photographs of bygone Llança.

The road down to the **port**, where there's a clothes market every Wednesday morning, is lined with restaurants, souvenir shops and miniature golf courses. At the end you'll find a coarse sandy beach backed by a concrete esplanade. For better, more secluded **beaches**, you'll need to head 2–3km north to **Cap Ras**, a promontory covered by a forested nature reserve crisscrossed by trails: north-facing **Borró** is the main sandy bay here, near the parking area. Beyond Borró, accessible by path only, lie more protected coves popular with nudists.

Six **buses** a day from Figueres and two from Portbou stop in the port, while the **train station** lies 1km northeast of the town. The **turisme** (July & Aug Mon–Sat 9.30am–9pm; Sept–June Mon–Fri 9.30am–2pm & 4.30–8pm, Sat 10am–1pm & 5–7pm; ☎972 380 855, ⓦwww.llanca.net) is halfway along the seafront at Avgda. de Europa 37. For **accommodation**, there are some cheap *hostales* in the old Vila, or you can stay down at the Port. Try the pleasant *Hotel La Goleta* (☎972 380 125, ⓕ972 120 686; ❹), 50m from the beach; or the beach-side *Hotel Berna*, Pg. Marítim 13 (☎972 380 150, ⓕ972 121 509; ❹), or the near-by *Pensió Miramar*, Pg. Marítim 7 (☎972 380 132; ❹), which has a good restaurant. A couple of recommended **restaurants** are the pricey *La Brasa*, Plaça Catalunya 6 (open March–Nov), which specializes in grilled meat and fish, and a seafood restaurant, *Can Narra*, c/Castellar 37, which is slightly cheaper.

Colera

One of the smallest villages on this coast, **COLERA**, 7km north of Llançà, is a rather shabby, down-at-heel place, dominated by a huge railway bridge passing overhead, with the redeeming feature being its rugged, pebbly beaches. If you want to **stay**, *Pensió Mont Mercè*, by the sea at c/Mar 107 (☎972 389 126; ❸), is an adequate place to sleep and eat, while the well-kept *Hostal La Gambina* (☎972 389 172; ❹) also has a good restaurant. A couple of pricey **restaurants** overlook the water, or there are some more reasonable, equally congenial, alternatives inland on the village square, Plaça Pi i Margall.

For cheaper lodging – and a better beach, albeit rather crowded – head 2km south to **Platja de Garbet**, where the *Pensió Garbet* (☎972 389 001, ⓕ972 128 059; ❸) offers comfortable rooms and the added bonus of its locally prestigious seafood restaurant.

Portbou

PORTBOU, 7km further north, and only 3km from the French border, is a fine place to approach by road, over the hill and around the bay. It's even worth walking from Colera (it takes around two-and-a-half hours) and suffering the initial steep climb to enjoy the view down over the green hills, deep blue water and small, pebbled **beach**. Once a haven for fishermen in stormy seas, it was transformed in 1872 with the construction of a huge railway station, to which the town's fate became irrevocably linked. Still oddly charming, with a pleasant seafront, it seems a throwback to the days when it made its fortune from the border crossing and customs agent trade, both now defunct, and today exudes an air of a town hopefully trying to redefine itself as a holiday location. It's in an attractive position, surrounded as it is by relatively uncrowded coves reached on footpaths scratched out of the rocks. A short walk above the town is the moving **Walter Benjamin Memorial**, a stark metal monument to the German philosopher, who committed suicide in the town in 1940 rather than be handed over to the Gestapo; he's buried in the adjacent cemetery.

There's a friendly **turisme** (May–Sept daily 9am–8pm; ☎972 390 284) right at the harbour on Passeig Lluis Companys, which has a map and list of hotels to give away. There's a reasonable range of **places to stay**, including the delightful *Hotel Comodoro*, c/Mendez Nuñez 1 (☎972 390 187; ❺), near the harbour, *La Masia*, Pg. Sardana 1 (☎972 390 372; ❹), with large balconies giving onto the beach, or the good-value *Hostal Juventus*, Avgda. Barcelona 3 (☎972 390 241; ❸).

Most of the **restaurants** along the seafront promenade are very overpriced; the best bet here is *L'Ancora*, which serves a fabulous seafood paella, and also has a €10 *menú del día*. The *Hostal Juventus* serves appetizing snacks and pizzas, or the *Art in Café*, at c/Mercat 11, makes good crêpes and salads.

Girona and around

Just an hour inland from the coast, the city of **Girona** with its medieval core provides a startling and likeable break from sand and sea. It's easy to make the day-trip here from the coast, or from Barcelona (to which it's connected by regular trains and buses), but it really warrants more time than that – two or three nights in Girona would show you the best of the city and let you enjoy some of the striking surrounding countryside. The quickest trip is to the lakeside town of **Banyoles**, only half an hour from Girona, and it's not much further on to beautiful **Besalú**, one of the oldest and most attractive of Catalan towns. Standing between the city and France, the otherwise quiet **Figueres** receives well-deserved attention for the fact that it holds one of the most visited museums in Spain: the **Teatre-Museu Dalí**, created by Salvador Dalí, an enthralling glimpse of the artist's outrageous genius.

To see more of the province of which Girona is capital you have to head for **Olot**, an hour and a half west of the city, at the heart of the **Garrotxa** region. Much of this is an ancient volcanic area, now established as the **Parc Natural de la Zona Volcanica**, whose rolling, fertile countryside is pitted with spent craters. Some of these are within the town boundaries of Olot itself, but the best of the scenery is around the village of **Santa Pau**, just to the east. North of here, and also close to Olot, **Castellfollit de la Roca** is the starting point for several good excursions which take you into the foothills of the nearby Pyrenees.

In the other direction, south towards Barcelona, those with a little more time can veer off into the mountainous **Serra del Montseny**, whose spa towns make for a restful diversion – though one you'll find easiest to see if you have your own transport, since buses are infrequent.

Girona

The ancient, walled city of **GIRONA** stands on a fortified hill, high above the Riu Onyar. It's been fought over in almost every century since it was the Roman fortress of *Gerunda* on the Vía Augusta and, perhaps more than any other place in Catalunya, it retains the distinct flavour of its erstwhile inhabitants. Following the Moorish conquest of Spain, Girona was an Arab town for over two hundred years, a fact apparent in the maze of narrow streets in the centre, and there was also a continuous Jewish presence here for six hundred years. By the eighteenth century, Girona had been besieged on 21 occasions, and in the nineteenth it earned itself the nickname "Immortal" by surviving five attacks, of which the longest was a seven-month assault by the French in 1809. Not surprisingly, all this attention has left Girona a hotchpotch of architectural styles, from Roman classicism to *modernisme*, yet the overall impression for the visitor is of an overwhelmingly beautiful medieval city, whose attraction is heightened by its river setting.

In the past, most visitors to Girona chose rainy days and market days to stroll around the old town as a break from the beach. However, the city's growing profile as a local capital and the fact that its airport is now on the budget flight route are slowly leading to greater numbers making the effort to explore the sights. It's an alluring place, which has undergone enormous changes in recent years, but which has been able to do so while still maintaining its tremendous historical and cultural heritage intact. There are a number of excellent museums and a cathedral that's the equal of anything in the region. Even if these leave you unmoved it's hard to resist the lure of simply wandering the superbly preserved medieval streets, fetching up now and again at the river, above which high blocks of pastel-coloured houses lean precipitously over the banks.

Arrival and information

Traditionally used mainly by Costa Brava package charters, whose clientele are transferred to their resorts by special buses, Girona's **airport** (☎972 186 600), 13km south of the city, is steadily upgrading, thanks largely to its now being served by budget airlines from the UK. A bus service runs between the airport and Girona (€1.65), while a taxi will cost you around €15–18. The **train station** is at Plaça d'Espanya, across the river in the new part of the city; from here, it's a twenty-minute walk into the old centre, where you're most likely to want to stay. The **bus station** is around the back of the train station. If you **drive** in, be aware that the old town is a controlled-access zone for residents only; use the car park at Plaça Catalunya or the underground car park at Plaça Constitució. Girona's old town area is compact and easily explored on foot. Buses cover the greater city, but you're more likely to use a **taxi** for short hops – there are ranks at the train station, Plaça Catalunya and Plaça Independencia.

There's a **turisme** inside the train station (July to mid-Sept Mon–Sat 9am–2pm & 4–8pm), while the main office is at Rambla de la Llibertat 1 (April–Sept Mon–Sat 9am–8pm, Sun 9am–2pm; Oct–March Mon–Sat 9am–5pm, Sun 9am–2pm; ☎972 226 575, ⓦwww.girona-net.com), right on the river at the southern end of the old town. Both offices have well-informed English-speaking staff who can supply you with useful maps and accommodation lists, as well as bus and train timetables for all onward services. A third office, the Punt de Benvinguda, at c/Berenguer Carnicer 3 (☎972 211 678), will reserve hotels and restaurants and has Internet access at €1.80/30min.

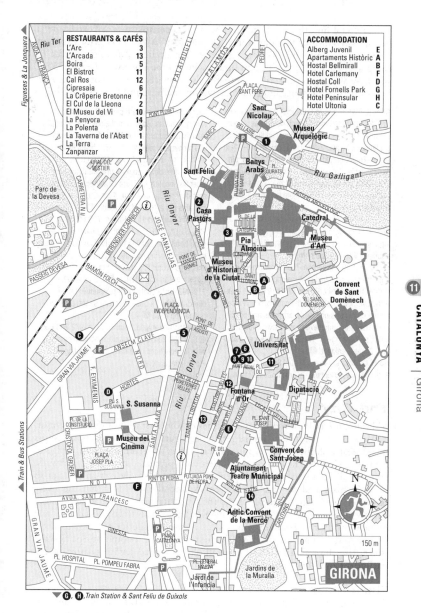

RESTAURANTS & CAFÉS

L'Arc	3
L'Arcada	13
Boira	5
El Bistrot	11
Cal Ros	12
Cipresaia	6
La Crêperie Bretonne	7
El Cul de la Lleona	2
El Museu del Vi	10
La Penyora	14
La Polenta	9
La Taverna de l'Abat	1
La Terra	4
Zanpanzar	8

ACCOMMODATION

Alberg Juvenil	E
Apartaments Històric	A
Hostal Bellmirall	B
Hotel Carlemany	F
Hostal Coll	D
Hotel Fornells Park	G
Hotel Peninsular	H
Hotel Ultonia	C

GIRONA

11

CATALUNYA | Girona

Accommodation

There are plenty of **places to stay** in Girona, including one or two *hostales* near the train station, though if you arrive at any reasonable time during the day it's much better to look for a place in or near the old town, which is also

819

where you'll find the youth hostel. The nearest **campsite** is at Fornells de la Selva, 8km south of town and open all year (☎972 476 117), with excellent amenities and an English-speaking proprietor, though you might prefer to camp at livelier Banyoles, half an hour by bus to the northwest (see p.825). If you have your own transport, you might also consider a couple of *turisme rural* houses between Girona and Banyoles, within easy reach of both (see p.826).

Alberg Juvenil c/dels Ciutadans 9, off Plaça del Vi ☎972 218 003. Girona's youth hostel has a good old-town location and smart new facilities, including laundry, TV and video; reception open 8–11am and 6–10pm; breakfast included in the price, dinner available. But note that it's hardly any better value than the very cheapest of the *hostales*, and if you're over 25 it's actually more expensive. Open July–Sept only. **②**

Apartaments Històric c/Bellmirall 4/A ☎972 223 583, ℮historic@navigalia.com. In a restored building, these superb 2-, 4- or 6-person flats with fully equipped kitchens are currently the best value in Girona at €30 per person. The management is voluble, friendly and English-speaking.

Hostal Bellmirall c/Bellmirall 3 ☎972 204 009. Attractive *pensió*, close to the cathedral and nicely turned out, with stone walls, artefacts and paintings. There are only seven rooms (two without bath), so book ahead. The price includes an excellent, filling breakfast. **③**

Hotel Carlemany Plaça Miquel Santaló ☎972 211 212, ⊛www.carlemany.es. Luxurious rooms in a

new hotel in the modern part of the city about twenty minutes' walk from the old town. A locally famous restaurant in the hotel offers traditional and innovative cooking at €36 a head. **⑦**

Hostal Coll c/Hortes 24 ☎972 203 086. Inexpensive, clean rooms, some with balconies, in a central location by Plaça Constitució. Enquire next door at *Bar Coll* (daily 7am–10pm), where you can also get a €6 midday *menú*. **②**

Hotel Fornells Park CN-II, km 719 ☎972 476 125, ℱ972 476 579. Bright, airy rooms in a rambling hotel 3km outside the city – an ideal, relaxing base for a touring holiday. A very good restaurant and large swimming pool add to its attraction. **⑦**

Hotel Peninsular c/Nou 3 ☎972 203 800, ℱ972 210 492. Well-located and pleasant (if rather bland) hotel on a busy shopping street, near the bridge and river. **④**

Hotel Ultonia Avgda. Jaume I 22 ☎972 203 850, ℱ972 203 334. Comfortable, modern rooms in a very friendly hotel on a busy street leading into Plaça Independencia. **⑥**

The City

Although the bulk of modern Girona lies on the west side of the Riu Onyar, bordered to the north by the large riverside Parc de la Devesa, most visitors spend nearly all their time in the **old city**, over the river. This thin wedge of land, tucked under the hillside and still partially protected by its medieval walls, contains all the sights and monuments, and as it takes only half an hour or so to walk from end to end it's easy to explore thoroughly. From the lively **Rambla**, lined with terrace cafés and the favourite place for the evening stroll, narrow lanes lead off into a zone of high walls, stepped streets, closed gates and hidden courtyards. Teeming with exclusive shops, galleries and restaurants – Girona and its province have the highest per capita income in Spain – the streets rise through **El Call**, the beautifully preserved Jewish quarter, to the **cathedral**, presiding over the city.

The cathedral

The centrepiece of the old city is Girona's **Catedral** (summer Tues–Sat 10am–8pm, Sun 10am–2pm; winter Tues–Sat 10am–2pm & 4–7pm, Sun

Girona's **Museum Pass** (multi-entrada Girona Museus) covers entry to all of the city's museums (apart from the Museu del Cinema) for €6. It can be bought at the Punt de Benvinguda or at any of the participating museums.

10am–2pm), a mighty Gothic structure built onto the hillside and approached by a magnificent flight of seventeenth-century Baroque steps. This area has been a place of worship since Roman times, and a Moorish mosque stood on the site before the foundation of the cathedral in 1038. Much of the present building dates from the fourteenth and fifteenth centuries, though parts are four hundred years older, notably the five-storey Torre de Carlemany, and the Romanesque cloisters with their exquisite sculpted capitals.

The main facade, remodelled in the eighteenth century, bursts with exuberant decoration: faces, bodies, coats of arms, and with saints Peter and Paul flanking the door. Inside, the cathedral is awesome – there are no aisles, just one tremendous single-naved Gothic vault with a span of 22m, the largest in the world. Contemporary sceptics declared the vault to be unsafe, and building went ahead only after an appeal by its designer, Guillermo Bofill, to a panel of architects. The huge sweep of stone rises to bright stained glass, the only thing obstructing the grand sense of space being the enormous organ, installed late in the nineteenth century.

You can visit the cloisters by buying a ticket to the **Museu Capitular** (same times as cathedral; €3.50) inside the cathedral, which in this case is certainly a good idea. The museum is rich in religious art, including a perfect *Beatus* illuminated by Mozarabic miniaturists in 975, and the famous eleventh- to twelfth-century *Creation Tapestry* in the end room – the best piece of Romanesque textile in existence, depicting in strong colours the months and seasons, and elements of the earth. The irregularly shaped twelfth-century **cloisters** themselves boast minutely carved figures and scenes on double columns, while steps lead up to a chamber above, full of ecclesiastical garb and adornments.

The Museu d'Art

On the eastern side of the cathedral in the restored Episcopal Palace, the large **Museu d'Art** (March–Sept Tues–Sat 10am–7pm, Sun 10am–2pm; Oct–Feb Tues–Sat closes 6pm; €2.20) is well worth a visit. Early wings highlight Romanesque art, particularly rare manuscripts such as an eleventh-century copy of Bede and an amazing *Book of Martyrs* from the Monastery of Poblet, and impressive *Majestats* (wooden images of Christ garbed in a tunic) rescued from the province's country churches. Of these, the most impressive are the tenth-century portable altar from Sant Pere de Rodes, one of the very few still preserved in Europe, and an intricately detailed twelfth-century crossbeam from the church in Cruïlles. You then progress through Renaissance works – including a room full of fifteenth-century *retablos* – to the collection of nineteenth- and twentieth-century Catalan art on the top two floors. Here you'll find some fine nineteenth-century Realist works, as well as pieces by the so-called Olot School of artists, and examples of local *modernista* and *noucentista* art.

Around Sant Feliu

Climb back down the cathedral steps for a view of one of Girona's best-known landmarks, the blunt tower of the large church of **Sant Feliu**, whose huge bulk backs onto the narrow main street. Shortened by a lightning strike in 1581 and never rebuilt, the belfry tops a hemmed-in church that happily combines Romanesque, Gothic and Baroque styles. The most notable pieces inside the church are found either side of the high altar: eight second- to fourth-century sarcophagi, thought to date from the Roman necropolis originally on this site.

At the foot of steps in front of the church is **El Cul de la Lleona** (The Lioness's Rear), a copy of a twelfth-century statue of a lioness climbing a pillar.

The Banys Arabs

Close to Sant Feliu, through the twin-towered Portal de Sobreportes below the cathedral, are Girona's so-called **Banys Arabs** (April–Sept Mon–Sat 10am–7pm, Sun 10am–2pm; Oct–March Tues–Sun 10am–2pm; €2.40, audio-guide €2.75 extra), probably designed by Moorish craftsmen in the thirteenth century, a couple of hundred years after the Moors' occupation of Girona had ended. They are the best-preserved baths in Spain after those at Granada and show a curious mixture of Arab and Romanesque styles. Closed down in the fifteenth century, supposedly to protect morals, the building was taken over by a Capuchin convent in 1617. Left for years to decay, the baths were restored by local *modernista* architects, Rafael Masó and Emili Blanc, in 1929, and subsequently opened to the public as a museum. The layout, a series of three principal rooms for different temperatures, with an underfloor heating system, is influenced ultimately by the Romans. The cooling room (the *frigidarium*) is the most interesting; niches (for your clothes) and a stone bench provide seats for relaxation after the steam bath, while the room is lit, most unusually, by a central skylight vault supported by octagonally arranged columns.

The Museu Arqueològic and the city walls

From the cathedral square, the main street, Pujada Rei Marti, leads downhill to the Riu Galligants, a small tributary of the Onyar. The **Museu Arqueològic** (summer Tues–Sat 10.30am–1.30pm & 4–7pm, Sun 10am–2pm; winter Tues–Sat 10am–2pm & 4–6pm, Sun 10am–2pm; €2.20) stands on the far bank in the former church of Sant Pere de Galligans, a harmonious setting for the varied exhibits. The museum has few English notes, so you may want to splash out €1.80 for the English guidebook. In the museum you'll find exhibits from the Paleolithic era to Roman times, including many items from the Greek and Roman settlements at Empúries. Most striking is a largely intact Roman mosaic depicting a chariot race, discovered in 1876 in a villa in the outskirts of Girona, and a collection donated by the estate of an amateur nineteenth-century archeologist, including an elaborate fourth-century sarcophagus from Empúries.

The Passeig Arqueològic

From the museum you can gain access to the **Passeig Arqueològic**, where steps and landscaped grounds lead up to the walls of the old city; the walls can also be accessed through an archway between the cathedral and the Museu d'Art. Once onto the **ramparts** (daily 8am–10pm), there are fine views out over the rooftops and the cathedral, and endless little diversions into old watchtowers, down blind dead ends and around crumpled sections of masonry. The walls and the little paths lead right around the perimeter of the city, with several other points of access along the way. One or two detours are worth taking, especially the steps down to the shaded gardens of the **Jardins dels Alemanys**, the remains of seventeenth-century barracks where German mercenaries were billeted. Further on is the rubble-strewn site of the **Torre Gironella**, where Jewish citizens were locked up for their protection during anti-Semitic riots in 1391 and which was finally destroyed by Napoleon's troops in the 1809 siege. Some of the best views over the city and surrounding countryside are to be had by climbing the spiral staircase of the Torre del Telègraf o del Llamp or the less vertiginous steps of Torre de Sant Domènec and Porta de la Reina Joana.

Carrer de la Força and the Call

Quite apart from its Roman remains and Arab influences, Girona also contains the best-preserved **Jewish quarter** in western Europe. There is evidence that

Jews settled in Girona before the Moorish invasion, although the first mention of a real settlement – based in the streets around the cathedral – dates from the end of the ninth century. Gradually, the settlement spread, having as its main street the **c/de la Força**, which in turn followed the course of the old Roman road, Vía Augusta. The area was known as the **Call** and at its height was home to almost a thousand people who formed a sort of independent town within Girona, protected by the king in return for payment. From the eleventh century onwards, however, the Jewish community suffered systematic persecution, with attacks on them and their homes by local people: in 1391 a mob killed forty of the Call's residents, while the rest were locked up, for their own protection, in the now ruined Torre Gironella tower until the fury had subsided. For the next hundred years, until the expulsion of the Jews from Spain in 1492, the Call was effectively a ghetto, its residents restricted to its limits, forced to wear distinguishing clothing if they did leave, and prevented from having doors or windows opening onto c/de la Força.

For an idea of the layout of this sector of tall, narrow houses and maze-like interconnecting passages, visit the **Centre Bonastruc Ça Porta** (May–Oct Mon–Sat 10am–8pm, Sun 10am–3pm; Nov–April Tues–Sat 10am–6pm, Sun 10am–3pm; €1.20), which is signposted (to "Call Jeu") up the skinniest of stepped streets off c/de la Força. Opened to the public in 1975, the complex of rooms, staircases, a courtyard and adjoining buildings off c/de Sant Llorenç was the site of the synagogue, the butcher's shop and the community baths. The complex also houses a museum, an information office, a café and a small library (Mon–Fri 10am–3pm & 5–8pm, Sun 10am–2pm) if you want to find out more (books in English available).

The Museu d'Historia de la Ciutat

A little way back up c/de la Força, at no. 27, the **Museu d'Historia de la Ciutat** (Tues–Sat 10am–2pm & 5–7pm, Sun 10am–2pm; €2) completes Girona's set of museums in the old city. For casual browsing it's the most rewarding of all, housed in an eighteenth-century convent. Remains of the convent's cemetery are visible as you enter, with niches reserved for the preserved bodies of the inhabitants. The rest of the collection is fascinating, less for the insights into how Girona developed as a city – though this is explained efficiently through text, exhibits and photos – than for the strange, miscellaneous bits and pieces displayed. A circuit of the rooms shows you old radios from the 1930s, a 1925 Olivetti typewriter, a 1970 IBM computer, a printing press, cameras, machine tools, engines and a dozen other mechanical and electrical delights. On the upper floors you'll find a history of the various sieges of the city, with scale layouts, and an interesting depiction of the story of the city walls.

Museu del Cinema

Tucked away in a side street near the Plaça Independencia at c/Sequia 1, the **Museu del Cinema** (Tues–Sat 10am–8pm, Sun 11am–3pm; €3.40) is a fascinating and fun interactive museum detailing the history of the cinema from the first moving images to the present day. Based on a private collection belonging to Tomás Mallol, an award-winning local director, the museum has exactly the right mix of hands-on exhibits and informative displays to please kids and adults. Most interesting are the attempts by the most diverse cultures at creating animated images and some surprisingly sophisticated examples of early experiments in recording pictures. A shop on the ground floor is full of cinema memorabilia, ranging from posters and models to experiment packs for children.

Eating and drinking

Girona's chic **bars** and **restaurants** are grouped on c/de la Força, on and around the riverside Rambla Llibertat and on the parallel Plaça del Vi; the last two places are also where you'll find the best daytime cafés with outdoor seating. Another little enclave of restaurants with good *menús* is over the river in Plaça de la Independencia. A five-minute taxi ride from the centre will take you to the Pedret area on the road out to Palamós north of the river, where you'll find a wide variety of eateries and late-night bars.

Nightlife in Girona has undergone a transformation in recent years, with a number of very lively and fashionable bars opening in and around Plaça Independencia and in Pedret, while the old city is gradually re-emerging as a late-night venue. During the summer there are also some pricey open-air bars – collectively known as *Les Carpes* – in the Parc de la Devesa, which have live music or dancing from Wednesday to Saturday.

Restaurants

Boira Plaça de la Independencia 17. The best food on the square, very popular with locals and visitors alike. €10 buys a very Catalan *menú*.

El Bistrot Pujada de Sant Domènec. An imaginative take on traditional Catalan cooking, with a good range of crêpes (many of them vegetarian) and meat and fish dishes, in jazzy surroundings.

Cal Ros Cort Reial 9. Old-fashioned restaurant serving lovely traditional Catalan fare and specializing in cod and rice dishes. Closed Sun eve & Mon.

Cipresaia c/General Fournàs 2. Superb creative Catalan cuisine, specializing in fish dishes, in plush surroundings. Expect to pay around €30. Closed Mon.

La Crêperie Bretonne Cort Reial 14. A piece of France in Girona. Delicious savoury crêpes for €4.50–5, excellent salads and while you wait for your food you can use the crayons provided to draw on the tablecloths. Closed Mon & Wed lunchtime in winter.

El Cul de la Lleona Calderers 8. An imaginative fusion of Catalan and Moroccan cuisine in a tiny restaurant near the Sant Feliu church. The €12 *menú* is very reasonable but eating *a la carta* can get expensive. Closed Mon.

El Museu del Vi Cort Reial 14. Conspicuously Catalan bar-restaurant serving up typical dishes in its pebble-dashed *comedor*. Plenty of filling *plats combinats* for around €4.80, plus a €8.80 *menú* and excellent *torrades* (toasts). Closed Mon.

La Penyora c/Nou del Teatre 3. Staunchly Catalan restaurant hidden away and worth seeking out. There are two €12 *menús del día* – one vegetarian and one non-vegetarian – and a reasonable, if limited, *a la carta* choice. Closed Sun eve & Tues.

La Polenta c/Cort Reial 16. This tiny vegetarian restaurant serves delicious organic grub – the *menú* is €8.80 – and is always busy. Open lunchtimes only; closed Sat, Sun and Aug.

Bars and cafés

Aleshores Plaça Independencia 4. House music in a long, narrow bar with a dance floor at the far end – if you can get to it. Open daily until 3am.

L'Arc Plaça Catedral 9. Recently reopened after building refurbishment, this laid-back bar is something of an institution in the city. Open during the day as a café and in the evening as a bar.

L'Arcada Rambla Llibertat 38. Bar-restaurant situated underneath the arcade, serving good breakfast pastries and outstanding pizzas. Outdoor tables are a nice place to relax in summer – though you'll pay for the privilege.

La Taverna de l'Abat Galligants. Atmospheric bar in the sixteenth-century guest rooms of the Bishop's House, opposite the Museu Arqueològic, where you can also get good light snacks. Live music plus tango and jazz nights. Closed Mon.

Nummulit c/Nord 7. Very lively bar near Plaça Independencia, where half Girona's young seems to fetch up after midnight. Open daily till 3am.

Sala del Cel c/Pedret 118. Enormous club built on various levels in an old mansion, playing mainly house music from resident and visiting DJs, but with some quieter areas and terraces. Open 11pm–6am.

La Terra c/Ballesteries 23. Colourful tiled-wall bar with window seats overlooking the river, ideal for a relaxing early-evening snack or late-evening drink. Open daily from 6pm to 2am.

Zanpanzar c/Cort Reial. Best of Girona's tapas bars serving delicious and reasonably priced Basque *pinos*.

Listings

Banks and exchange There's an exchange office at the train station, and you'll find banks and ATMs along the Rambla Llibertat.

Books English-language books available at the friendly and reasonably well-stocked Girona Books, c/Rutlla 22 ☎972 224 612.

Buses From the bus station (☎972 212 319), there are Rafael Mas services (☎972 213 227) to Lloret de Mar; SARFA (☎972 201 796) to places all along the Costa Brava; Teisa (☎972 200 275) to Olot; and Barcelona Bus (☎972 202 432) express services to Barcelona and Figueres. International bus services are run by Eurolines, Via and Julia (all on ☎972 211 654).

Car rental Most agencies are close to the train station on c/Barcelona: Avis ☎972 206 933 and Hertz ☎972 210 108. Local companies such as Cabeza, c/Barcelona 30 (☎972 218 208), are much cheaper, though all cars have to be returned to Girona.

Emergencies Dial ☎092 or contact the Cruz Roja on ☎972 222 222.

Hospital Doctor Trueta, Avgda. França 60 ☎972 202 700.

Internet access *Frangipane*, c/Bastiments 7 (€6 per hour); *Ciberxuxes*, c/Carme 55 (€6 per hour).

Newspapers British and American newspapers available at the kiosks in Plaça de la Independencia and Plaça de Catalunya.

Police Policia Municipal at c/Bacià 4 ☎972 419 090 or 972 419 092; Mossos d'Esquadra (Catalan police: ☎972 213 450).

Post office At Avgda. Ramón Folch 2; Mon–Fri 8.30am–8.30pm, Sat 8.30am–2pm.

Around Girona: Púbol

If you're interested in Salvador Dalí, you might want to make the effort to travel the 22km to the tiny village of **PÚBOL**, site of the medieval castle Dalí bought – and decorated – for his wife Gala in 1970. The castle has now been opened to the public as the **Casa-Museu Castell Gala Dalí** (mid-March to mid-June & mid-Sept to Nov Tues–Sun 10.30am–6pm; mid-June to mid-Sept daily 10.30am–8pm; €5.50) and, as at Portlligat (see p.814), it gives a fascinating glimpse of the painter's lifestyle. Contained within are a host of artworks Dalí gave his wife to decorate the house, as well as various pieces of furniture and other bizarre objects the couple bought. Particularly interesting are the elephant sculptures and Richard Wagner swimming pool in the garden, and Gala's collection of *haute couture* dresses. Dalí lived permanently at the castle after his wife's death in 1982 (Gala is buried in the grounds), writing extensively and painting his last authenticated work (*Kite's Tale and Guitar*) until a fire broke out in 1984, injuring Dalí and causing him to move to Figueres.

Getting to Púbol is tricky without your own transport; you're best off catching the train (every 90min; 30min) from Girona to Flaçà (also on the C255 to La Bisbal), and then taking a taxi for the remaining 5km (around €5). There's not much else in the village, and unless you've already organized a taxi on the way out, you'll have to ask to phone for one (☎972 488 107) from the village bar, as there's no phone box.

Banyoles and around

For an escape into the countryside around Girona, take a bus to **BANYOLES**, half an hour (18km) north of the city. Here, the Pyrenees are on the horizon and the town basks around its greatest attraction – the **lake**, famed for its enormous carp. The venue of the 1992 Olympic rowing events, it's a pleasant place for messing about in the water or, with more time, walking the perimeter. Fifteen minutes' walk east of the lake, the town is surprisingly dull, worth the visit really only for the porticoed Plaça Major. North of Banyoles, the **Coves de Serinyà** archeological site makes an interesting detour.

The Town

Banyoles grew up around a monastery originally founded by Benedictines in 812. This, the **Monestir de Sant Esteve** at the eastern end of town, is still easily the biggest structure in old Banyoles, and though it's usually locked, you might try asking around for the key holder who lives nearby. If you do get in, don't miss the magnificent fifteenth-century *retablo* by Joan Antigo. The medieval streets which lead back into town from here are full of other ancient buildings, including an almshouse and a dye market. In the end, all streets lead to the central **Plaça Major**, a lovely tree-lined, arcaded space with several café-bars and a Wednesday market that has been held here since the thirteenth century.

From the square, signs point the way to the **Museu Arqueològic Comarcal** (July & Aug Tues–Sat 11am–1.30pm & 4–8pm, Sun 10.30am–2pm; Sept–June Tues–Sat 10.30am–1.30pm & 4–6.30pm, Sun 10.30am–2pm; €1.80), installed in a fourteenth-century poorhouse in Plaça de la Font. The museum used to contain the famous jawbone of a pre-Neanderthal man found in the nearby Serinya caves, but nowadays you have to make do with a replica; authentic specimens include Paleolithic tools, and bison, elephant and lion bones, all found locally.

The lake itself – the **Estany de Banyoles** – is a fifteen-minute walk from Plaça Major. It's long been used for water sports, so the Olympic choice wasn't surprising, and although there's little that's distinctive or attractive about the area nearest the centre, a clearly signposted thirty-minute walk through the woods around the southern edge takes you to the tiny hamlet of **PORQUERES**, where the water is at its deepest (63m). Here the elegant Romanesque church of **Santa María** was consecrated in 1182 and has a barrel-vaulted interior, and unusual capitals with plant and animal designs. Carrying on from here you complete the circuit of the lake in about another hour, unless you take in the signed detour to the **Mirador**, a 500m rewarded by fabulous views. The lake itself boasts a whole series of **boating** options, including cruises, rowing boats and pedaloes, and there are designated swimming areas.

Practicalities

Buses all stop on Passeig de l'Indústria at the entrance to the town. The **turisme** is on the same road at no. 25 (June–Aug Mon–Sat 10am–2pm & 5–7pm, Sun 10am–1pm; Sept–May Mon–Fri 10am–2pm & 5–7pm, Sat 10am–1pm; ☎972 575 573, ⓦwww.plaestany.org).

With Girona so close, there is no advantage in staying in Banyoles, whose **hotels** are expensive anyway. If you do want to stay, the best place is on the lake. *Hotel Mirallac*, Pg. Darder 50 (☎972 571 045; ❻), has large rooms with lake views; less expensive due to its being not on the lakeside is *Fonda La Paz*, Ponent 18 (☎972 570 432; ❷), which also has a good restaurant. In town, a smart *Alberg de Joventut*, c/Migdia 10 (☎972 575 454, ⓕ972 576 747), just to the south of Plaça Major, has comfortable dorms for €17 a bed. **Camping** is a popular proposition here; there's a large site, *El Llac* (☎972 570 305, ⓔe.llac@retemail.es), just before the church in Porqueres. Alternatively, if you've a car or bike, there are two good local **turismes rurales**: *Can Ribes*, 6km south of Banyoles beyond the hamlet of Camós (☎972 573 211, ⓔcan.ribes@retemail.es; ❸), has simple, tiled-floor rooms, some en suite, and a roof terrace; even better if you're staying for a minimum of a week is *Can Fabrica* (☎ & ⓕ972 594 629; closed Jan 7–Easter; ❸), a restored seventeenth-century farmhouse 1km beyond the hamlet of Santa Llogaia del Terri.

There are a few places to **eat and drink** in the old town. *La Cisterna*, c/Alvarez de Castro 36 (closed Mon), serves good Catalan cuisine, while the slightly cheaper *El Capitell*, Pl Major 14 (closed Mon), specializes in cod and grilled meats. Eating in the hotel-restaurants overlooking the lake is more expensive unless you go for the *menú del día*; of these, the popular *La Masia*, a huge place with a pleasant terrace, offers a very reasonable *menú* at €9 but is otherwise extortionate. One of the best options is the *Fonda la Paz*, c/Ponent 18 (closed Sun), whose chef has made quite a name for himself locally in recent years. The best place for an evening drink is Plaça Major, whose café-bars spill under the medieval arcades, or on the lakeside near the *Hotel Mirallac*.

Coves de Serinyà

Three kilometres north of Banyoles on the Olot road are the Paleolithic caves of the **Coves de Serinyà** (July–Sept daily 11am–7pm; March–June Tues–Fri 10am–4pm, Sat & Sun 11am–6pm; Oct–Feb Tues–Fri 10am–3pm, Sat & Sun 11am–5pm; €1.80). Laid out around a peaceful footpath through oaks and silver birches, the site allows access to two caves where excavation has turned up evidence of human habitation alongside remains of lions, panthers, hyenas and elephants. Finds date back between 100,000 and 15,000 years, and include worked flint and funeral urns. A 200,000-year-old tooth, the oldest human remain in Catalonia and now on display in Barcelona, was found at the foot of a third cave.

Besalú

From the road, the imposing eleventh-century bridge by the confluence of the Fluvià and Capellada rivers is the only sign that there is anything remarkable about **BESALÚ**, 14km north of Banyoles (and connected by regular daily buses). But walk a couple of minutes into the town and you enter a medieval settlement that provides one of the most interesting half-day outings from Girona. Steep narrow streets, sunbaked squares and cave-like arcaded shops bear silent witness to an illustrious history out of proportion to its current humble status. Besalú was an important town before the medieval period – Roman, Visigothic, Frankish and Moorish rulers came and went – but all the surviving monuments date from the eleventh century and after, when it briefly became the seat of a small, independent principality. Despite having a total population of just eight hundred, it prospered and remained a place of importance well into the fourteenth century.

The Town

The most striking reminder of Besalú's grandeur is the splendid eleventh-century **Pont Fortificat** – fortified bridge – over the river Fluvià. In the middle stands a fortified gatehouse complete with portcullis. Down to the left beyond the bridge the **Miqwé**, or Jewish bathhouse (ask at tourist office for accompanied visit; €1), was originally attached to a synagogue positioned in the old Jewish quarter in the heart of the lower town, along the riverbank.

Plaça Llibertat, in the centre of Besalú, is entirely enclosed by medieval buildings, including the elegant thirteenth-century Casa de la Vila, which now houses the *ajuntament* and the turisme. There's a weekly **market** in the square each Tuesday. The majestically porticoed c/Tallaferro leads up from here to the ruined shell of **Santa María** (you can't get inside), which for just two years (1018–20) was designated Cathedral of the Bishopric of Besalú; union with Barcelona meant the end of its short-lived episcopal independence.

Further west, the twelfth-century monastery church of **Sant Pere** is the sole remnant of the town's Benedictine community, which was founded in 977. It stands in its own square, El Prat de Sant Pere, from where the most eye-catching feature is the window in the otherwise severe main facade, flanked by a pair of grotesque stone lions. Elsewhere in the web of cobbled streets radiating from Plaça Llibertat, you'll come across other attractive buildings – many sporting elaborate stone embellishments, ornate windows and columns. Finally, you can work your way around to the delightful little church of **Sant Vicenç**, close to the main Olot–Banyoles road in a plant-decked square with a café-restaurant and outdoor seating. The simple and lovely Catalan Romanesque facade of the church is strangely dissonant with an ornate thirteenth-century rose window and the elaborate carvings of a Gothic side door. A Moorish rock-crystal vase, now in Girona's Museu d'Art, was uncovered when the church was set alight in the Spanish Civil War.

Practicalities

The **bus** stop is on the main Olot–Banyoles road, from where it's a short walk south to the central Plaça de la Llibertat. Here you'll find the **turisme** (daily 10am–2pm & 4–7pm; ☎972 591 240), where you can pick up a map and plan your tour.

The town has a good range of **places to stay**. The *Hotel Siqués* (☎972 590 110, ✉siques@agtat.es; ❹) is at Avgda. Lluís Companys 6, on the main road just down from the bus stop. In the old town itself, the *Hotel Comte Tallaferro* (☎972 591 609; ❺), c/Ganganell 2, is in an ideal setting next to the church of Sant Pere, while the atmospheric *Residencia María* (☎972 590 106; ❷) is also well positioned, right on Plaça Llibertat; the best budget choice is the spick-and-span *Fonda Venència*, c/Major 6 (☎972 591 257; ❷). Possibly the best location goes to the ten-roomed *Els Jardins de la Martana* (☎972 590 009, ⓦwww.lamartana.com; ❻), c/Pont 2, set in lovely gardens at the foot of the old bridge. The nearest **campsite** is *Can Masia Coromines* (☎972 591 108; closed Nov–Feb) in Maià de Montcal, 4km towards Figueres, which has a pool, bar and restaurant.

For **meals**, the *Hotel Siqués* has an enormous *menú del día* for around €10 (closed Mon Nov–Easter), while at the *Curia Reial* (closed Tues and Feb), you can sit on the outdoor terrace next to the square, or on the beautiful patio at the rear overlooking the bridge. Eating at both places can lead to rather large bills if you don't have the *menú*. *Pont Vell*, c/Pont Vell 28, is much more expensive (around €30 a head), but beautifully situated, with outdoor tables more or less under the bridge, while if you really want to splash out, *Els Fogons de Can Llaudes*, on Prat de San Pere, serves the best food in town for around €36 per person. There are a few places for a snack around Plaça Llibertat and El Prat de Sant Pere.

Figueres and around

Forming a triangle with Girona and Besalú and lying some 37km from the first and 27km from the second, **FIGUERES** is irrevocably linked to Salvador Dalí. Home to the **Museu Dalí**, installed by the artist in a building as surreal as the exhibits within, the town is all but overshadowed by the museum, the only reason most people come here. Stay longer, though, and you'll find a pleasing town with a lively central *rambla* and one or two other sights that warrant a visit. It's also a decent starting point for excursions into the little-visited **Serra d'Albera mountains** to the north, which form part of the border with France.

Arrival and information

Arriving at the **train station**, you reach the centre of town by simply following the "Museu Dalí" signs. The **bus station** is just a couple of minutes' walk up on the left, at the top of Plaça Estació above the train station, and underground **parking** is available at Plaça Catalunya. There's a small **tourist information booth** just outside the bus station (July–Sept Mon–Sat 9.30am–1pm & 4–7pm), while the main **turisme** is at the other end of town, on Plaça del Sol, in front of the post office (July & Aug daily 9am–9pm; rest of year Mon–Sat 9.30am–1pm & 4–7pm, Sun 9.30am–1pm; Ⓦwww.figueresciutat.com).

Accommodation

There's a good choice of **places to stay**, ranging from the most basic to the more upmarket, though many of the better hotels and *hostales* lie on the main roads out of town. The best-value budget accommodation is *Pensió Bartis*, c/Méndez Núñez 2 (Ⓣ972 501 473; ❷), not far from the train and bus stations; if you want to be more central, *Hotel Los Angeles*, c/Barceloneta 10 (Ⓣ972 510 661, Ⓦwww.hotelangeles.com; ❸), is handy for the museums. For more comfort, try the old-style *Hotel Duran*, c/Lasauca 5 (Ⓣ972 501 250, Ⓦwww.hotelduran.com; ❺), just off La Rambla, or the plush *Hotel Empordà*, CN-II s/n (Ⓣ972 500 562, Ⓦwww.hotelemporda.com; ❼), on the main road out of town, which is famous locally for its excellent restaurant. There's a good

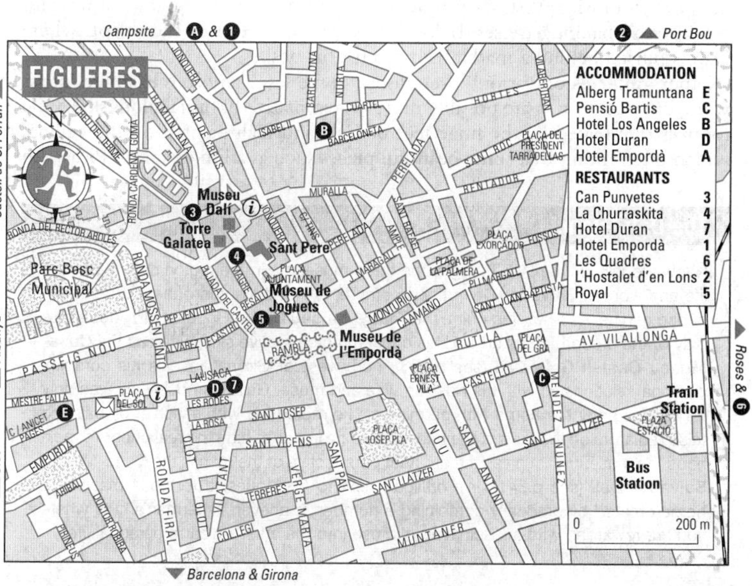
Campsite A & 1
2 Port Bou
FIGUERES
ACCOMMODATION
Alberg Tramuntana E
Pensió Bartis C
Hotel Los Angeles B
Hotel Duran D
Hotel Empordà A
RESTAURANTS
Can Punyetes 3
La Churraskita 4
Hotel Duran 7
Hotel Empordà 1
Les Quadres 6
L'Hostalet d'en Lons 2
Royal 5
Museu Dalí
Torre Galatea
Sant Pere
Parc Bosc Municipal
Museu de Joguets
Museu de l'Empordà
RAMBLA
AV. VILALLONGA
Train Station
Bus Station
PLAÇA ESTACIÓ
PLAÇA JOSEP PLA
PLAÇA DEL SOL
PASSEIG NOU
RONDA FIRAL
0 200 m
Castell de S. Ferran
Albanyà
Olot
Roses & 6
Barcelona & Girona

youth hostel off the Plaça del Sol, *Alberg Tramuntana*, c/Anicet Pagès 2 (☏972 501 213; closed Sept; €19 for a dorm bed), and a clean, good-value **campsite**, *Pous* (☏972 675 496; open April–Oct), 2km out on the road to France.

The Museu Dalí

The **Teatre-Museu Dalí** (July–Sept daily 9am–7.45pm; Oct–June Tues–Sun 10.30am–5.45pm; €9; ⓦ www.dali-estate.org), the most visited museum in Spain after the Prado and Bilbao's Guggenheim, is a real treat. Dalí was born in Figueres in 1904 and gave his first exhibition here when he was just fourteen. In 1974, in a reconstruction of the town's old municipal theatre, the artist inaugurated his Museu Dalí, which he then set about fashioning into an inspired repository for some of his most bizarre works.

Having moved back to Figueres at the end of his life, Dalí died here on January 23, 1989; his body now lies behind a simple granite slab inside the museum. Although it does contain paintings (some by other artists) and sculpture, the thematically arranged display is not a collection of Dalí's "greatest hits" – those are scattered far and wide. Nonetheless, what you do get is a tantalizing taste of his skill and art which is not to be missed.

The very **building** (signposted from just about everywhere, on Plaça Gala i Salvador Dalí, a couple of minutes' walk off the *rambla*) is an exhibit in itself. Topped by a huge metallic dome and decorated with luminous egg shapes, it gets even crazier inside. In the **courtyard**, the walls of the circular central well are adorned with faceless mannequins preparing to dive from the heights, while in the centre a buxom Queen of Persia rises above a Cadillac – inside which rain falls onto two vine-strewn figures. Towering above this is a soaring totem pole of car tyres topped with Gala's rowing boat and an umbrella.

Beyond this is the **dome room**, which features an extraordinary trompe l'oeil painting, at first glance resembling a pixillated jumble with a portrait of Gala until you view it through the inverted telescope placed in front when it reveals the face of Abraham Lincoln. A room next to this contains an unnerving portrait of Mae West, viewed by peering through a mirror at giant nostrils, red lips and hanging tresses. Below the stage, stairs lead to the **crypt**, where Dalí is buried behind a marble slab, against his wishes.

Other **galleries** on various levels display some less clamorous examples of his work, but ones which are possibly more representative of his fabulous skill. One room is dominated by the huge feet of Gala and Dalí painted on the ceiling, which often means that some beautiful pieces such as a lithograph of Picasso in

The Dalí Triangle

Known locally as the Dalí Triangle, the three museums in the region devoted to the life and work of **Salvador Dalí** offer a comprehensive insight into the artist's bewildering genius. As a starting point, the **Teatre-Museu Dalí** in Figueres provides a display of the breadth of his art and his consummate creative skill, whereas the **Casa-Museu Castell Gala Dalí** (see p.825), northwest of Girona, reveals his complex personal relationship with his Russian wife and muse, Gala. Famously, he was only allowed to enter her home with permission; he repaid her with mischief by painting false radiators on the covers she had insisted he install to hide the real ones. Yet perhaps the museum that gives the greatest perspective of the man is the **Casa-Museu Salvador Dalí** (see p.841), in Portlligat, next to Cadaqués, a tortuous maze of a home created by gradually combining a number of uneven fishermen's huts where you are rewarded with a fascinating glimpse into the artist's bizarre personal life.

emperor's laurels or a haunting self-portrait by Dalí can go unnoticed. Higher floors also house paintings by other artists, the most notable being those by Antoni Pitxot, in which moss-covered stones portray various classical figures.

The rest of town

After the museum, the main sight in town is the huge eighteenth-century **Castell de Sant Ferran** (daily: July–Sept 10.30am–7pm; Oct–June 10.30am–2pm; €5.50), 1km northwest of the centre – follow Pujada del Castell from just beyond the Dalí museum, going straight on at the roundabout along c/Al Castell de Sant Ferran. Originally built as a defence against the French in 1753, in its first action it fell without a shot being fired. During the Civil War, it was used as a barracks for newly arrived members of the International Brigade before they moved on to Barcelona and the front, and also housed the last government of the Spanish Republic in 1939, before its leaders fled into exile. More recently, it was used as a prison for Colonel Tejero after his failed coup attempt in 1981. Converted into a museum, it makes for an interesting walk around the impressive perimeter walls and into the old living and working quarters.

Back in the centre, pavement cafés line the *rambla*, and you can browse around the art galleries and gift shops in the streets and squares surrounding the church of Sant Pere. There are two more museums, too. The **Museu de l'Empordà** at Rambla 2 (Tues–Sat 11am–7pm, Sun 10am–2pm; €1.80), has some local Roman finds and an outstanding art collection, bolstered by some works on loan from Madrid's Prado, including sombre paintings by the Olot School and the more vibrant works of Sorolla. The **Museu de Joguets** (June–Sept Mon–Sat 10am–1pm & 4–7pm, Sun 11am–1.30pm & 5–7.30pm; Oct–May closed Mon & Sun pm; €3.90), further up the *rambla* on the same side, is a toy museum with over 3000 exhibits from all over Catalunya. The statue at the bottom of the *rambla* is a monument to Narcis Monturiol, a local who distinguished himself by inventing the submarine.

Eating and drinking

A gaggle of tourist **restaurants** cram into the narrow streets around the Dalí museum, particularly along c/Jonquera. More stylish, but still reasonably priced, is *Can Punyetes*, 300m west of the Dalí museum, which serves excellent Catalan food, and *La Churraskita* at c/Magre 5, serving imaginative Argentinian and Italian dishes for about €20 a head. If money's no object, head for the *Hotel Duran*, which serves generous regional dishes with a modern touch, or the even pricier *Hotel Empordà*. Outside town, *Les Quadres*, a five-hundred-year-old tied cottage in the hamlet of El Far d'Empordà, 1km southeast, specializes in duck, while in Vilabertran, 2km northeast, *L'Hostalet d'en Lons*, c/Concha 6 (closed Mon), serves equally good Catalan fare for around €20. Both the *rambla* and the area around Plaça de l'Ajuntament and Plaça Pius XII have several popular pavement **cafés**; *Royal* at Rambla 28 is one of the best bets. Eating aside, Figueres used to be generally fairly comatose **at night**, but a string of bars of all shapes and sizes on Plaça del Sol opposite the turisme is doing much to change that.

North of Figueres: the Serra d'Albera mountains

The most interesting inland outings **west from Figueres** visit large villages to either side of the forest-fringed **Pantà (Reservoir) de Boadella**, a focus for local water-sports enthusiasts. During World War II the region **north of Figueres** was so deserted that there were no Guardia Civil stationed between the Castell de Requesens and Portbou, which made the eastern Serra d'Albera a favoured escape route from France. Of late, numbers of foreigners – mainly Dutch and German – have moved in to convert the crumbling farms to second homes, and Catalan trippers scour the countryside at weekends, replenishing their cellars at the many wineries that dot the area.

Sant Llorenç de la Muga

There's a single midday bus from Figueres to **SANT LLORENÇ DE LA MUGA**; driving yourself, follow signs out of town for the N11 to La Jonquera, and then keep an eye out for the poorly marked turning for Llers, and thence to Sant Llorenç itself, about 17km west of the town. This large, fortified village, nestled in greenery along the Riu Muga (spanned here by a fourteenth-century bridge), makes an excellent excursion; it's linked to Maçanet de Cabrenys (see below) by a marked but rough track (hikers or 4WD only) skirting wetlands on the reservoir's west shore. The sole **eatery** is *Sa Muga* on the central *rambla*, or you can have a drink at either *El Lluro* on Plaça Baixa or the *Societat La Fraternitat* on the *rambla*. As yet, there's nowhere to **stay** in the old quarter, though you'll find a **campsite**, *La Fradera* (☎972 542 054), 1.5km west of the village, and a **casa rural**, *Can Carreras* (☎972 569 199; ❸), 5km west overlooking the river – though it's also a working hog farm.

Darnius and Maçanet de Cabrenys

North of the Pantà de Boadella – accessible from the Muga valley by a good road below the dam, or directly off the N11 – lies **DARNIUS**, which has bus links (Mon–Sat) to Figueres. It's not exactly a thriving place, with only one really commendable **place to stay**: *Can Massot*, a massive, vaulted medieval *casa rural* at the south edge of town (☎972 535 193; ❸). A preferable and more rural alternative nearby is *La Central* (☎972 535 053, ⓦwww.hlacentral.com; ❹–❻), set in idyllic surroundings 6km southwest of Darnius along a well-marked track. Occupying a *modernista* chalet, this low-key spa resort also has an excellent in-house **restaurant** (open to all), renowned for its seafood; count on €25 per head, plus drinks.

Culture buffs may prefer to stay on the same bus or point their car or bicycle towards livelier and more atmospheric **MAÇANET (MASSANET) DE CABRENYS**, 26km from Figueres. The **bus** stops a few paces south of this densely packed, oval-shaped medieval ensemble, next to a summer-only **turisme** – cars can proceed with care into the old quarter. Of two places to **stay** and **eat**, *Hostal La Quadra* at the northwest edge of town (☎972 544 032, ⓦwww.laquadra.com; open most of year; ❸) has the edge, with recently refurbished rooms and a popular vaulted cellar restaurant serving regional specialities.

The Espolla region

Northeast of Figueres, a daily bus heads for **ESPOLLA**, which boasts at least ten prehistoric sites nearby. Easiest to find is the **Dolmen de la Cabana Arqueta**, nearly five thousand years old; from Espolla take the **Sant Climent** road, and at the rising bend 1km beyond the village turn down the farm track to the right – the dolmen is ten minutes' walk from the main road. The most important, however, is the **Dolmen del Barranc**, the only carved tomb yet found in the area; it lies 3km from the village off the track leading north to the Col de Banyuls.

Espolla itself is a typical village of Alt Empordà county, its shuttered houses crammed into a labyrinth of streets that come to life each year with the flurry of the grape harvest. At present there are no reliable tourist facilities in the village other than the Centre d'Informació (May–Oct daily, Nov–April Sat & Sun only; ☎972 545 039) for the recently established *parc natural* protecting the fragile habitats of the Serra d'Albera. The closest restaurant lies 4km south in the centre of **MOLLET DE PERALADA**, where the big, barn-like *Ca La Maria* (closed Mon evenings, and all day Tues Oct–April) serves hearty country fare – it's an Alt Empordà institution and highly recommended.

Some 4km east of Espolla, the *plaça* at **RABÓS D'EMPORDÀ** is home to a more modest eatery (*Can Tomàs*, closed Weds), but mostly serves as the gateway for the derelict Benedictine monastic church of **Sant Quirze de Colera**, 6km north by dirt track, at the head of a secluded valley below the frontier ridge. The adjacent, well-priced *Restaurant Corral de Sant Quirze* (open for lunch all year, and also evenings June–Sept; closed Wed) makes an equally worthwhile target.

Alta Garrotxa

The **Alta Garrotxa** stretches north from the main Besalú–Olot road as far as the peaks along the French border. With more than a hundred catalogued caves, the region is a speleologist's dream, and it's a fabulous area for walkers as well; the Editorial Alpina *Garrotxa* map is a useful aid.

Castellfollit de la Roca

Fourteen kilometres west of Besalú, just off the N260, **CASTELLFOLLIT DE LA ROCA** still hasn't recovered from being on the main road for so long, despite the opening of a new four-lane bypass. The village presents its best aspect as you climb up from the main road, being built on the edge of a precipice that falls sheerly 60m to the Fluvià river, with the church crowded by houses onto the very rim of the cliff. It's an impressive sight from a distance (even more so at night, when spotlights play on the natural basalt columns), but close to it's another story, with grubby and ordinary brown buildings. It is, however, worth a stop to take in the **view** from the top of the village over the edge of the cliff – head south from the prominent clocktower to the church and the viewing platform behind. On the through road, 100m downhill from the clocktower, Castellfollit's **Museum of Sausages** (Mon–Sat 9.30am–1.30pm & 4–8pm, Sun 9.30am–2pm & 4.30–8pm; free), run by the Sala family to celebrate over a century and a half in the skin-stuffing business, is almost certainly unique, as claimed.

Castellfollit is the starting point for some of the region's best excursions, heading north and northeast through the Alta Garrotxa. You could easily **stay** in Olot, but if you want an early start then the *Ca la Paula* (☎972 294 032; ❷), in the centre of Castellfollit at Plaça de Sant Roc 3, is surprisingly comfortable, with a decent restaurant and bar attached.

North to France

It's 8km from Castellfollit up the **Llierca valley** past Montagut de Fluvià to **SADERNES** (minor road all the way), taking in en route the photogenic **Pont de Llierca**, a Romanesque bridge which today carries the GR1 on its way to Besalú (3hr distant). Sadernes is barely a hamlet, but it does boast the popular *Hostal de Sadernes* (July–Sept daily except Wed; Oct–June Fri–Sun only), which serves up hearty **meals** (€17 for three courses, drinks extra) on the arcaded ground floor of an old farmhouse. Vehicle entry upstream from

Sadernes is restricted during summer, but you can continue on foot to the *Refugi de Santa Aniol*, right on the northern edge of the Garrotxa. From here, the **Col de Massanes** (1126m) border crossing can be reached by continuing north on the footpath from the refuge, spending the next night at Coustouges or Saint-Laurent-de-Cerdans, both French villages in the Tech valley.

Oix, Beget and Rocabruna

Staying in Spain, a more populated route heads **northwest** into the Ripoll region. From Castellfollit de la Roca, take the paved but narrow road 9km northwest to the attractive village of **OIX**, flanked by a small medieval bridge. You can **stay** at the *Hostal de la Rovira* (☎ & ⑤972 294 347; ❹), a well-restored mansion with keen new management and a ground-floor **restaurant**; it's right opposite the Romanesque church of Sant Llorenç on Plaça Major. Alternatively, there are two **campsites** 1km west, on opposite sides of the valley; *Els Alous* (☎972 294 173; April–Oct) is the more likely to be open of the two.

Eighteen kilometres northwest, a wide paved road leads to the showcase village of **BEGET**, done up by lowlanders as a weekend retreat and now veering perilously close to tweeness. The graceful twelfth-century church of **Sant Cristòfor**, standing at the entrance to the village, is celebrated for its particularly solemn and serene *Majestat*. All but a dozen or so of these Catalan wooden images of a fully dressed Christ were destroyed in 1936; this example is one of the very few that can be seen in its intended context (keys are available from house no. 7 when the church is closed). Beget has three **restaurants**, two with **accommodation**: *Can Joanic*, by the church (☎972 741 241; ❷), and the pricier *El Forn* (☎972 741 230; half-board only, ❺) near the top of the village. The GR11 passes through here; these are the only places to stay on this stretch of the trail.

Some 7km west on either the GR11 or the again-narrow road, **ROCABRUNA** stands just below the watershed dividing the Garrotxa from El Ripollès, the county of Ripoll (though the official border is at Beget), and boasts a ruined castle and a handsome Romanesque church. The only place to **stay**, 2km west on the main road and then 1km down a dirt track, right astride the GR11, is the friendly, English-speaking *Casa Exalde* (☎972 130 317, ⓔetxalde@wanadoo.es; ❸); self-catering kitchens make it ideal for trekkers and cyclists; half-board is also available. Surprisingly for such a tiny place, Rocabruna itself has two good **restaurants** which draw crowds on weekend nights from far afield. *Can Po* is the more ambitious – reckon on €21–35, and mandatory reservations (☎972 741 045); *Can Pluja* offers good, honest mountain food for about €25.

Baixa Garrotxa: along the C524

Most of the **Baixa Garrotxa** region – accessible on the minor C524 which runs between Banyoles and Olot – is volcanic in origin, and has been within the **Parc Natural de la Zona Volcanica de la Garrotxa**, which covers almost 120 square kilometres, since 1985. It's one of the most interesting such areas in Europe, the road passing through a beautiful wooded landscape, climbing and dipping around the craters, offering some lovely valley views. It's not, however, a zone of belching steam and boiling mud; the last eruption was almost 12,000 years ago, during which time the ash and lava have weathered into a fertile soil whose luxuriant vegetation masks the contours of the dormant volcanoes. There are thirty cones in all in the area, the largest of them some 160m high and 1500m across the base.

An excellent way to get acquainted with the Baixa Garrotxa is to take a **loop walk** out of Olot which almost totally avoids paved roads and can easily be completed by any reasonably fit person in a single day. If you're not up for the full 28-kilometre distance, you could arrange to be fetched at Santa Pau, roughly halfway.

Begin in Olot by following the multiple signposts directing you across the Riu Fluvià, from where it's an hour south along surfaced country lanes, equally suited to horse-riding or mountain-biking (as is most of this circuit), to the **Fageda d'en Jordà**. Although much reduced, this beech forest is still a treat in the autumn when the leaves are turning; it takes about half an hour more to emerge on the far side of the spooky, maze-like groves, deserted except for the tourist *carruatges* (horsecarts) visiting from Santa Pau.

Turn left when you meet the helpfully marked **GR2** long-distance trail, then right twice in succession when you encounter the track to Sa Cot. Follow the signposts to stay on the GR2, which soon becomes a proper path as it heads east for thirty minutes to the medieval chapel of **Sant Miquel de Sa Cot**, a popular weekend picnic spot. The **Volcà Santa Margarida** is visible just behind and, within forty minutes more, you should be up on its rim and then down into its grassy caldera, where another tiny chapel sits at the bottom. From the turn-off to the cone – just fifteen minutes from Sant Miquel – you descend to the **Font de Can Roure**, source of the only water en route, before skirting Roca Negra with its disused quarry, then entering Santa Pau 45 minutes from the shoulder of Santa Margarida, and some three hours from Olot (not counting the detour to the caldera).

From Santa Pau the GR2 continues north towards the scenic **Serra de Sant Julià del Mont**, just east of which are two superb places to stay in the tranquil **La Miana** hamlet (also reachable by a signposted, six-kilometre track from the Besalú–Olot road): the English-run *Can Jou* (☎972 190 263, ✉canjou@turismerural.net; ❷), which also organizes horse-riding; and the amazing *Rectoria de la Miana* (☎972 190 190 or 972 223 059; ❷), a medieval manor complete with crumbling twelfth-century Romanesque chapel. However, for day-trekkers, this would inconveniently lengthen the circuit, so you're best advised to bear west at **Can Masnou** and approach **Volcà Croscat** via the *Lava* campsite (see "Santa Pau" below). You skirt the northeast flank of Croscat, badly scarred by quarrying, and from the campsite it's another hour, along a progressively narrowing track unsigned except for "BATET" painted on hunting-zone signs, to the high (720m) plateau of **Batet de la Serra**, scattered with handsome farms. Here you meet a marked path and track coming west from the Serra de Sant Julià, turning west yourself to follow the road briefly before adopting the well-marked *camí* – beautiful and partly cobbled in basalt – which passes the hamlet of Santa María de Batet on its way down to Olot. It takes just under another hour of downhill progress, or a total of something less than seven hours, to emerge at the top of c/Sant Cristòfor, which runs right down to the main boulevard through Olot.

If you don't have your own transport, you'll find **access** a little problematic, since the only bus is the three-times-weekly Olot–Santa Pau–Banyoles service (Mon, Wed & Sat) to Santa Pau, the central village of the volcanic zone. Alternatively, you might consider **staying in Olot** (see p.836) and walking to Santa Pau from there – it's three hours by track and trail, with the added bonus of passing through the beautiful Fageda d'en Jordà beech forest.

Santa Pau

The central village of the volcanic zone, medieval **SANTA PAU**, 9km southeast of Olot, makes a great base for some gentle local walking. To the outside world it presents a defensive perimeter of continuous and almost windowless house walls; inside the village, balconies overflow with flowers, steps and walls are tufted with grass and huge potted plants line the pavement arcades. Further off the tourist trail than Besalú, it's even more atmospheric. The cobbled alleys converge on the thirteenth-century arcaded Plaça Major, with its dark Romanesque church of Santa María and an **information centre** (Mon & Wed–Sat noon–5pm, Sun noon–3pm) that's good for trekking information. The more adventurous can book a hot-air balloon ride over the volcanoes setting off from Santa Pau (℡972 680 255, ⓦwww.garrotxa.com/voldecoloms), with *cava* and a hearty breakfast thrown in, for around €120.

In the square adjacent to Plaça Major, Plaçeta dels Balls, you'll find pricey but tasty **meals** at *Cal Sastre* (open Fri–Sat only in winter, closed Sun night & Mon year-round); they also offer **accommodation** in a renovated old building with beamed ceilings and antique furnishings at the edge of town, at c/de les Cases Noves 1 (℡972 680 049, Ⓔsastre@agtat.es; ⑤). Better still is the atmospheric Can Menció (℡972 680 014; ❸), on Plaça Major, which acts as village shop, bar (serving huge sandwiches) and *pensión*. For **self-catering**, *Can Marfany* (℡972 680 578; ❸ minimum two nights), Plaça Major 4, offers three small but comfortable apartments. Three kilometres outside town, *Lava* (℡972 680 358; open all year) is a large, well-positioned **campsite** in the shadow of two volcanic cones.

Olot

OLOT, the main town of the Garrotxa, makes a good base for the region, with frequent bus connections and a fair choice of food and accommodation. It's a far nicer place than first impressions suggest – as you penetrate towards the centre, the industrial outskirts and snarling through roads give way to a series of narrow, old-town streets and a pleasant *rambla*. The centre is largely made up of attractive eighteenth- and nineteenth-century buildings, evidence of the destructive geological forces that surround the town: successive fifteenth-century earthquakes levelled the medieval town, and – thankfully dormant but easily accessible – three small volcanoes can be seen just to the north, reminders of the volcanic zone beyond.

Arrival and information

The **bus station** is on c/Bisbe Lorenzana, the main road through town. The **turisme** is located inside the Museu Comarcal de la Garrotxa at c/Hospici 8 (Mon–Fri 9am–2pm & 3–7pm, Sat 10am–2pm & 5–7pm, Sun 11am–2pm; ℡972 260 141, ⓦwww.olotweb.info), which has English-speaking staff and contains a good stock of local brochures, maps and timetables, as well as accommodation lists.

Accommodation

Olot has a reasonable range of **places to stay**, and if you've got transport there are also a few good *turismes rurals* in neighbouring hamlets. The closest **campsite** is La Fageda (℡ & Ⓕ972 271 239; open all year), 4km out on the minor road to Santa Pau (no bus).

Alberg Torre Malagrida Passeig de Barcelona 15 ℡972 264 200. Youth hostel in a 1920s mansion southwest of the centre overlooking the river, about halfway to the Casal dels Volcans. €19 for a dorm bed.

Mas La Garganta La Pinya hamlet (follow signs west out of Olot toward Riudaura) ℡972 271 289, Ⓔgarganta@agtat.es. *Casa de pagès* set in a rambling farmhouse looking southwest over the fertile Vall d'en Bas towards the Collsecabra volcano.

Rooms are tasteful and en suite, and breakfast is served on a balcony. The cooking draws on the family's *charcuterie* shop in town, though vegetarian options are available, plus a kitchen for self-catering. Half board ⑤
Mas El Guitart Above Sant Andreu de Socarrats village ☎972 292 140, ✉guitart@agtat.es. Perched just above the Romanesque *ermita* of Santa Margarida, this *casa de pagès* has mock-antique-furnished wood-floor rooms; there are also self-catering apartments available. A minimum stay of two days is required. ③

Hostal Sant Bernat Ctra. de les Feixes 31 ☎972 261 919, ✉bernat@agtat.es. Although it's a bit out of the way towards the northeast end of town, this *hostal* is quiet and friendly, and its garage makes it the best choice if you've got a car or a bike. Some rooms have bath. ②
La Torra de Santa Margarida Above Sant Andreu de Socarrats village ☎972 291 321. More old-fashioned and homely than *Mas El Guitart*, set on a working cattle farm where roaring fires heat common areas during colder months (vital on this north-facing slope). Half board ⑤

The Town

If you arrived by bus on the busy main through road, the older streets nearby – between Plaça Major and Sant Esteve church – are a revelation. Filled with fashionable shops, art galleries and smart patisseries, they tell of a continuing wealth, historically based on textiles and the production of religious statuary. **Sant Esteve** lies right at the heart of town, built high above the streets on a platform, its tower a useful landmark. Beyond the church, the central **rambla**, Passeig d'en Blay, is lined with pavement cafés and benches, and adorned by the delightful nineteenth-century Teatre Principal. Between 6 and 8pm, this whole area teems with life as the well-dressed *passeig* swings into action.

Museu Comarcal de la Garrotxa

The substantial cotton industry that flourished here in the eighteenth century led indirectly to the emergence of Olot as an artistic centre: the finished cotton fabrics were printed with coloured drawings, a process that provided the impetus for the foundation of a Public School of Drawing in 1783. Joaquim Vayreda i Vila (1843–94), one of the founders of the so-called **Olot School** of painters, was a pupil of the school, but it was his trip to Paris in 1871 that was the true formative experience. There he came under the spell of Millet's paintings of rural life and scenery, and must have been aware of the work of the Impressionists. From these twin influences, and the strange Garrotxa scenery, evolved the distinctive and eclectic style of the Olot artists.

Some of the best pieces produced by the Olot School can be seen in the town's excellent museum, the **Museu Comarcal de la Garrotxa** (11am–2pm & 4–7pm, closed Sun afternoon & Tues; €1.80), which occupies the third floor of a converted eighteenth-century hospital at c/Hospici 8, a side street off c/Mulleras. The first part of the museum traces the development of Olot through photos and models of its industries. The bulk of the collection, though, is work by local artists and sculptors, and it's an interesting and diverse set of paintings and figures. There's characteristic work by Ramón Amadeu, whose sculpted rural figures are particularly touching; Miquel Blay's work is more monumental, powerfully influenced by Rodin, while Joaquim Vayreda's *Les Falgueres* is typical of the paintings in its recreation of the Garrotxa light. By way of contrast – and indicative of a continuing artistic tradition in the town – there's also a room of modern ironwork sculpture and a few striking postwar paintings.

Jardí Botànic and the Casal dels Volcans

A twenty-minute walk from the centre are the town's landscaped botanical gardens, the **Jardí Botànic** (daily: April–Sept 9am–9pm, Oct–March 9am–7pm; free); follow the signs for Casal dels Volcans. They're worth walking out to, not least because they contain the fascinating **Casal dels Volcans** itself (July–Sept 10am–2pm & 5–7pm; Oct–June 10am–2pm & 4–6pm; closed Tues & Sun pm; €1.80 or free with Museu Comarcal ticket), a small museum devoted to the local volcanic region and housed in a Palladian building. Even if you don't speak Catalan or Castilian, you'll get a pretty good idea of the displays: there are photos and maps of the local craters, rock chunks and a seismograph, and even a floor-shaking simulation of an earthquake. The building also houses an information centre on activities in the Garrotxa volcanic zone.

Eating, drinking and nightlife

Olot's attractive historical centre boasts numerous lively **bars** and **restaurants**, where you'll find Catalan fare and the even more local *cuina volcànica* cuisine, based around eleven ingredients from truffles and boar to beans and potatoes.

Can Guix c/Mulleras 3. Cheerful bar-restaurant where queues form for large servings. Eat heartily for €9 – the local wine is served in a *porrón*, but you get a glass to decant it into if you chicken out. Closed Sun.

Il Retrovo della Dolce Vita Passeig de Barcelona 2. Smart and trendy pizzeria serving the best pizza in town for around €10 a head.

Font de l'Àngel Plaça Móra 3. Snack bar/café with garden seating and inexpensive *menús* and

platos combinados. Closes Sundays after characteristically lively Saturday nights.

Ramón Plaça Clara 11. Bar serving mid-priced Catalan tapas and *platos combinados* – also a good vantage point if you just want a drink.

La Terra c/Bonaire 22 ☎972 274 151. Macrobiotic veggie restaurant that serves a very tasty lunchtime *menú* for €8.80. Closed evenings and weekends, though will open by prior arrangement for groups of six or more.

Nightlife

More than a dozen **bars and cafés** are scattered between the bullring and Plaça Carmé at the eastern end of the Barri Antic. Aside from some obvious ones on the Passeig d'en Blay (itself the best place for an outdoor drink), try the genteel *Cocodrilo* on c/Sant Roc, the slightly hippyish *Bruixes i Maduixes*, c/Bonaire 11, or the Senegalese-run *Bar-Restaurant Malem*, c/Pare Antoni Soler 6, a spacious converted clothing factory decorated with original artworks. For more youthful venues, try *Bar 6T7* at c/dels Sastres 35, and *Vanil*, on the same street at no. 10. For something a little alternative, there's also the raucous *Bar del Carme*, Plaça del Carme 3, which plays all sorts of music and hosts impromptu jam sessions.

The Montseny and around

South of Girona, the train line and main road to Barcelona both give a wide berth to the province's other great natural attraction, the **Serra del Montseny**, a chain of mountains that rises in parts to 1700m. It's a well-forested region, and from it comes the bulk of Catalunya's mineral water, which is bottled in small spa villages. You can approach from either Girona or Barcelona, though if you're using public transport you'll have to be prepared to stay the night in whichever village you aim for, since the infrequent services rarely allow for day-trips. The company which operates most of the routes below is La Hispano Hilariense, whose buses leave from the bus station in Girona or from Barcelona's Pla de Palau. On the westward side of the mountains, the road swoops down through wooded slopes to the pleasant market and university town of **Vic**, standing at the crossroads of the Girona-Lleida and Barcelona-Pyrenees roads.

Breda and Riells

The bus route from Girona into the region passes through **HOSTALRIC**, an old walled village in the heart of a cork-oak growing district, but **BREDA**, about 6km further on, is a better place to call a halt – known for its ceramic shops, and adorned by a Gothic church with an eleventh-century tower.

There's a fork at Breda, with a minor road (and occasional local bus) running the 7km up to **RIELLS**, which provides your first real glimpse of the hills. There's not much to Riells, and little to do except stroll around the pretty surroundings, but there is a good **place to stay** just before the village: *Hostal Marlet* (☎972 870 903; ❷), with a garden and restaurant. It's open July and August, and weekends throughout the year, and you have to take full board.

Sant Hilari Sacalm

The main bus route continues up the other road, past Arbúcies, with the views getting ever more impressive as you approach **SANT HILARI SACALM** (1hr 20min from Girona, 2hr from Barcelona). Perched at around 850m above sea level, Sant Hilari is a pleasant spa town that could make an enjoyable base for a couple of days. It's famous for its *Via Crucis Vivent*, or Easter-time Passion stagings, the most full-blown of several such in Catalunya. Many of its hotels and **hostales** cater for people taking the curative local waters, and consequently open only during the summer (July–Sept); one option that seems to stay open most of the year is the central *Hostal Torras*, Plaça del Dr Gravalosa 13 (☎972 868 096; closed Jan; ❸), which also serves good food. A **turisme** (July–Sept Mon–Sat 10am–2pm & 4–8pm, Sun 11am–2pm; ☎972 868 826), at the junction of the main roads through town, has details of all bus connections in the area.

Viladrau

If you're driving, it's a splendid, winding seventeen-kilometre ride southwest to **VILADRAU**, another mountain spa town, though not as large as Sant Hilari. By public transport, you have to approach from the other side of the range, by taking the train from Barcelona to Balenyá (on the line to Vic) and connecting with the local bus from there for a twenty-kilometre journey to Viladrau. Even this is not easy, as there are currently only two services a week from Balenyá; check first in Barcelona.

Being more difficult to reach, Viladrau manages to preserve a very tranquil feel within its old streets and attractive surrounding countryside. There are plenty of local wooded walks – ask at the sporadically functioning turisme on the Plaça Major – and a handful of places to stay, should the area appeal to you: the *Hotel La Coromina*, Ctra. Vic (☎938 849 264; ❺), is a romantic hideaway among the trees, or there's the *Hostal Bofill* at c/Sant Marçal 2 (☎938 849 012; ❸), a vast *belle époque* period piece with a reasonable restaurant attached.

Vic

The quickest approach to the mountains from Barcelona is to take the train north to Ripoll. About an hour out of the city, the route passes through the handsome town of **VIC**, whose few well-preserved relics are just about worth stopping to see. Capital of an ancient Iberian tribe, Vic was later a Roman settlement (part of a second-century temple survives in town) and then a wealthy medieval market centre. The **market** continues to thrive here, taking place twice weekly (Tues and Sat) in the enormous arcaded main square. Vic is also renowned for its excellent sausages, which you'll see on sale in the market and throughout the town.

The old quarter of town is dominated by a rather dull, Neoclassical **Catedral**, containing some impressive wall paintings by Josep María Sert. Next door in Plaça del Bisbe Oliba is the more interesting **Museu Episcopal** (April–Sept Tues–Sat 10am–7pm, Sun 10am–2pm; Oct–March Tues–Fri 10am–1pm & 3–6pm, Sat 10am–7pm, Sun 10am–2pm; €2.50), which houses a wealth of eleventh- and twelfth-century frescoes and wooden sculptures rescued from local Pyrenean churches – the second most important collection of Romanesque art outside Barcelona's Museu d'Art de Catalunya. As with the Barcelona collection, you don't need to be a specialist to appreciate the craft that went into these objects, and the work here is likely to set you off on the trail of other similar pieces scattered throughout the region.

All this said, however, the best reason to come to Vic is for one of its two annual **music festivals**: the *Mercat de Música Viva* (Live Music Market), four days of live events in mid-September spanning genres from jazz to rock by way of Catalan *cançó*; and the mid-March *Festival de Jazz*, mostly centred on the club *Vic Bang Jazz Cava* on Rambla dels Moncada.

Practicalities

From the **train station**, walk east straight along the road opposite to reach the main market square, Plaça Major. **Drivers** will need to park in the outskirts, as traffic is highly restricted (and parking virtually impossible) in the centre. The **turisme** (Mon–Fri 9am–8pm, Sat 9am–2pm & 4–7pm, Sun 10am–1pm; ℡938 862 091, ⓦwww.victurisme.com) is based here, along with a handful of small **hotels**; the best option is *Balmes Vic*, at c/Francesc Pla el Vigatà 6 (℡938 891 272, ℱ938 892 915; ➎). A good place for **lunch** or dinner is the renowned *La Taula*, Plaça Don Miquel de Clariana 4 (℡938 863 229; closed Sun night, Mon & Feb), a restaurant in an old mansion, with fine local food at around €30 a head.

If you have transport (and plenty of cash), you might be tempted to drive the 14km north to the Embassament de Sau reservoir, overlooking which is the grand **Parador Nacional de Vic** (℡938 122 323, ⓦwww.parador.es; ➎). This converted country house has all the upmarket facilities you'd expect, including a good Catalan restaurant.

The Catalan Pyrenees

You don't have to travel very far from the coast and Catalunya's three largest cities before you reach the foothills of the **Catalan Pyrenees**, the easternmost stretch of the mountain chain that divides Spain and France. From Barcelona, you can reach **Ripoll** by train in just a couple of hours (though allow an extra hour for typical delays). The area north of here has been extensively developed with a number of **skiing stations**: during summer it's also increasingly busy, particularly in the valleys leading to **Camprodon**. Following the Freser valley north from Ripoll brings you to **Ribes de Freser**, start of the private train line up to **Núria** (a combination of shrine and ski centre), one of the most stunning rides in Catalunya. Further north, by the French border, **Puigcerdà** has the only surviving train link with France over the Pyrenees, while the peculiar Spanish enclave of **Llívia** lies wholly enclosed within France.

For serious Pyrenean walking – and a wider range of scenery, flora and fauna – you need to head further west, beyond **La Seu d'Urgell** and the adjacent duty-free principality of **Andorra**, which approximately mark the middle of the Catalan Pyrenees. Although more interfered with (by hydroelectric projects in particular) than, say, the Aragonese peaks to the west, the mountains here offer some of the best trekking in the whole range. The **Noguera Pallaresa** valley, the **Vall d'Aran** and the superbly scenic **Parc Nacional d'Aigüestortes i Estany de Sant Maurici** are all reasonably accessible,

---

Skiing in the Catalan Pyrenees

If you want to go **skiing** in the Catalan Pyrenees, it's usually cheapest to buy an inclusive **package** – prices are similar to those in the French Pyrenees, but up to a third less than in the Alps. The main destination promoted overseas is Andorra, though some agents and websites offer Núria and Baqueira-Beret in Spain, too. If you're already in Spain you'll get most choice if you go through a travel agency in Barcelona or any of the larger Catalan towns, though an increasing number of resorts are offering on-the-spot "mini-packages". The local tourist office usually has information about valley hotels offering all-in deals of half board and lift pass, which save a good 25 percent compared to doing it "à la carte", even more if you show up on weekdays. Full kit (skis, boots, poles) typically costs about €14 per day, less for multi-day periods, whilst lift passes bought on their own cost €18–24 daily (again, less for longer periods), depending on day of the week and complexity and quality of the lift.

The best Spanish Catalan **downhill** resorts for beginners or families are Núria, Port-Ainé, above the Noguera Pallaresa, and Super Espot at the east edge of the Parc Nacional de Aigüestortes i Estany de Sant Maurici; intermediate and advanced skiers might prefer La Masella at the south edge of the Cerdanya, Boí-Taüll at the west edge of Aigüestortes, and Baqueira-Beret at the head of the Vall d'Aran. For **cross-country skiing**, the north margin of the Cerdanya (p.854) and much of the Cadí (p.850) are covered with trails, with a handful of developed centres north of the La Seu–Puigcerdà road.

Pyrenean skiing tends to cost less because the range lacks international cachet and (until recently) convenient airports; Barcelona and Toulouse are the busiest choices, but Perpignan and Girona also have year-round flights. The **clientele** is family-oriented and almost totally Spanish, with a smattering of French. There's none of the snootiness or nocturnal excess often met with in the Alps, and as a foreigner you'll be the object of benign curiosity or outright friendliness – though you may have trouble finding English-speaking instruction. **Infrastructure** is adequate – certainly better than in Romania or Bulgaria – and improving as large sums are periodically spent on snow cannons or new lifts. The downside is that, cannons or not, snow can be thin and/or mushy, since Catalunya gets its weather from the Mediterranean rather than the damper Atlantic; don't set out specially for a week's holiday without checking conditions first.

The system for **rating pistes** used in local ski literature is based on a universal colour code: green for beginners, blue for easy, red for intermediate and black for difficult. It's not a completely dependable system – a red run in one resort might rate only as blue in another – but it does give a fair idea of what to expect.

offering hikes for novices, as well as more specialist routes. A further lure is the **Vall de Boí** on the western edge of the national park, which has a magnificent concentration of **Romanesque churches**.

One complication for anyone intent upon seeing more than a small part of the Catalan Pyrenees in one go, even with their own transport, is the geographical layout of the region. The Vall d'Aran, in the northwestern corner of Catalunya, has an east–west orientation, as do the Cerdanya uplands, but most of the other valleys run north–south, with few lateral roads, which means that connecting between them on two or four wheels is not always easy. Determined hikers can follow various passes between the valleys; otherwise, you'll have to backtrack a bit out of the mountains before venturing up a new valley.

This section is arranged accordingly, starting in the east, closest to Barcelona, and moving west; it details the easiest approaches by public transport, as well as useful, time-saving side roads and tunnels for those with a bike or car.

Ripoll

RIPOLL occupies so prominent a place in Catalunya's history that it's impossible not to be initially disappointed by this rather shabby place, buzzing with traffic and divided by the manifestly polluted Riu Ter. The inhabitants seem to agree, resigned to working here but deserting it in droves on Saturday afternoons, when Ripoll assumes the air of a ghost town until Monday. But just ten minutes' walk from the southeast corner of town – where trains and buses stop – lies one of the most remarkable monuments in the Catalan Pyrenees, the **Monestir de Santa María**, founded in 888 by Guifré el Pelós (Wilfred the Hairy) to spur Christian resettlement of the surrounding valleys following the expulsion of the Moors. Sadly, the old Benedictine monastery was destroyed in a fire in 1835; today's barrel-vaulted **nave** (daily 8am–1pm & 3–7pm) is a copy of the original structure erected over Guifré's tomb by Abbot Oliba, a cousin of the counts of Besalú, in the early eleventh century. The magnificent Romanesque **west portal**, however, survived the fire, and is now protected against the elements by a glass conservatory. Erected in the twelfth century, and now the main entrance, this portal squirms with carvings of religious and astrological subjects: the Apocalypse (across the top), the Book of Kings (to the left), Exodus (to the right), scenes from the lives of David, St Peter and St Paul (at the bottom), and the months of the year (around the inner side of the pillars).

The adjacent, twin-columned **cloister** (daily 10am–1pm & 3–7pm; €1) was far less damaged in the succession of earthquakes, sackings and fires visited on the monastery, and is particularly beautiful. The **capitals** of the lower colonnade, dating from the twelfth-century Romanesque "Golden Age", portray monks and nuns, beasts mundane and mythical, plus secular characters of the period. They completely overshadow the nominal **Museu Lapidari** here, which displays assorted stonework, sarcophagi and funerary art along the walls. Next door to Santa María, and entered from it, the fourteenth-century church of **Sant Pere** houses the **Museu Etnogràfic** (hours variable; €2.50), which has supplanted the Museu dels Pireneus. You're now only able to get into this church when it serves as a venue for Ripoll's **music festival**, staged on successive weekends during July and August.

Besides the monastery and museums there's little to detain you, though it's worth climbing around the back of Sant Pere to a **terrace**, from where you can look down on Santa María. Down in the modern district, two *modernista* specimens may claim your attention: the spouting stone flourishes and battlements of **Can Bonada**, c/del Progrés 14, on the way to the bus and train stations, and the tiny church of **Sant Miquel de la Roqueta** (1912), a couple of blocks up the hill, looking like a pixie's house with a witch's cap on top – and designed by Antoni Gaudí's contemporary Joan Rubió.

Practicalities

The **train and bus stations** stand within sight of each other, a ten-minute walk from the heart of town, over the Pont d'Olot to the Plaça de l'Ajuntament. The **turisme** (Aug daily 10am–2pm & 4–8pm; June, July & Sept daily 9.30am–1.30pm & 4–7pm; Oct–May Mon–Sat 9.30am–1.30pm & 4–7pm, Sun 10am–2pm; ☎972 702 351), on the adjacent Plaça d'Abat Oliba, near the monastery and Sant Pere, stocks plenty of maps, pamphlets and local transport timetables. Aside from this helpful spot, conventional tourism in Ripoll marches resolutely backwards: accommodation tends to be overpriced, noisy and uninspiring, and there are very few places for a sit-down meal. Taken together, these factors make it highly advisable to base yourself somewhere nearby (such as Ribes de Freser, see p.847) and make a flying visit.

If you do decide **to stay**, the least expensive option is the *Habitacions Paula*, Plaça de l'Abat Arnulf 6 (☎972 700 011; ❷), 70m west of the tourist office. *Hostal del Ripollès*, on Plaça Nova (☎972 700 215; ❷), entered through its ground-floor pizzeria, is of similar standard. The overpriced *Pensió La Trobada*, across the river at Passeig Honorat Vilamanyà 4 (☎972 714 353; ❸), is your only other option. There's also a large **campsite**, the *Solana de Ter* (☎972 701 062; April–Oct), 2km south of town on the Barcelona road.

If you have transport, it's worth foregoing all of the above in favour of *La Riba* (☎972 198 092; B&B ❸), a **casa de pagès** in the hamlet of **LES LLOSSES**, 18km away on the road to Berga, then 6km further on its own dirt track. En-suite doubles and triples occupy a rambling, sixteenth-century manor with ample common areas; in such a remote locale, it's best to take half-board.

Eating and drinking options in Ripoll are far from plentiful. *Restaurant Perla*, Plaça Gran 4, features rather expensive *a la carta* food along with humdrum *menús*, though the *Pizzeria Piazzetta* on the ground floor of the *Hostal del Ripollès* is more reasonable and appetizing, as is *Canaules* next door. These are the only full-service restaurants in the centre; for tapas and crêpes, head for *Bar El Punt* at Plaça de l'Ajuntament 10, which has tables both outside and in the air-conditioned premises.

Northeast: the Ter Valley

From Ripoll, the valley of the Riu Ter, dotted with beautiful Romanesque churches and monasteries, leads northeast into the mountains. To follow the whole route by public transport you'll have to be prepared to wait (sometimes overnight) for buses, which get scarcer the further north you go. The first two towns, **Sant Joan de les Abadesses** and **Camprodon**, are easy to reach on day-trips from Ripoll or Olot (see p.836). The other, more distant villages take more time and effort but are correspondingly less developed, except in the vicinity of the Vallter 2000 **ski resort**.

Sant Joan de les Abadesses

The small town of **SANT JOAN DE LES ABADESSES**, 11km northeast of Ripoll, owes its existence to the eponymous **monastery** (daily: March–April & Oct 10am–2pm & 4–6pm; May, June & Sept 10am–2pm &

4–7pm; July & Aug 10am–7pm; Nov–Feb 10am–2pm, also 4–6pm weekends; €2) founded in 887 by Guifré el Pelós, apparently for the benefit of his daughter Emma, the first abbess. However, the institution was closed temporarily in 1017 by Pope Benedict III as a result of politically motivated accusations of immorality by Count Bernat Tallaferro, to whom devolved – not coincidentally – all the feudal privileges of the convent. The present church, consecrated in 1150, is a single-nave structure of impressive austerity, built to a Latin-cross plan with five apses, and housing a curious thirteenth-century wooden sculpture depicting Christ's Deposition, the *Santíssim Misteri*, in its main chapel. According to the printed handouts, the figure of Christ retains on his forehead "a piece of Holy Bread . . . preserved untouched for seven hundred years". Admission to the monastery also includes entry to the Gothic **cloisters** and the **Museu del Monestir**, whose well-presented exhibits include ornate chalices, curiosities such as a crucifix in rock crystal, and a fine series of late-medieval altarpieces.

Other than the monastery, there are few specific sights in Sant Joan, but the old quarter boasts a fair-sized grid of ancient houses along streets almost shorter than their names, all leading to a small but appealingly arcaded Plaça Major. The slender twelfth-century bridge down in the well-tilled valley was only restored in 1976, after being destroyed in fierce fighting during February 1939, during the final Republican retreat of the Civil War.

Practicalities

Buses arrive at a shelter behind the monastery church apse; the well-stocked **turisme** (Mon–Sat 10am–2pm & 4–7pm, Sun 10am–2pm; ☎972 720 599) occupies the cloistered, fifteenth-century Palau de Abadia, just fifty paces left from the Museu del Monestir's entrance.

In theory, Sant Joan would make a far more pleasant base than Ripoll, with frequent bus links in each direction; in practice, however, finding somewhere **to stay** may prove difficult. The sole options are both in the newer district near the bus stop: *Pensió Ca La Nati* at c/Pere Rovira 3 (☎972 720 114; **❷**), with large shared-bath rooms; and *Pensió Can Janpere*, around the corner at c/del Mestre Josep Andreu 3 (☎972 720 077; **❷**), which offers comfortable en-suite rooms with heating and TV. Preferable to either, if you have a car, is the **turisme rural** property *Mas Mitjavila* (☎972 722 020, **✉**masmitjavila@tiscali.es; **❸**), 10.5km northwest of Sant Joan in the hamlet of **SANT MARTÍ D'OGASSA**. From the north side of the new bridge, follow the asphalt road 4.2km to the ex-mining village of Ogassa Surroca, then continue the remaining distance on a cement driveway. Along with the adjacent tenth-century church of Sant Martí, *Mas Mitjavila* was once a dependency of the monastery of Sant Joan; it enjoys a superb eyrie-like setting 1350m up, overlooking the valleys of Ripoll. The large, rustic rooms comfortably accommodate four, and have all mod cons, plus kitchens. Meals are available in the supper-only restaurant, in the old sheep barn.

Back in town, far and away the best **restaurant** is *Can Janpere*, with a €13.50 *menú* and a more adventurous *carta* featuring mushrooms in various guises, roast goat and duck in orange sauce (allow €25, including drinks). Otherwise, you can sit outside at the pleasant cafés on Passeig Comte Guifré, the main *rambla*.

Camprodon

Climbing gradually along the lively Riu Ter from Ripoll and Sant Joan, the first place with the character of a real mountain town is **CAMPRODON** (950m), a fact exploited in the nineteenth century by the Catalan gentry who arrived by a (now defunct) rail line to spend summer in the hills – the tracks' former course is now a marked cycling route, La Ruta del Ferro. The town, 14km from Sant Joan, still retains the prosperous air of those times, with shops full of leather goods, outdoor gear, cheese and sausages. Ornate villas front a *rambla* clogged with towering trees, and other town houses are occasionally embellished with *modernista* flourishes.

Like Ripoll, Camprodon straddles the confluence of two rivers, here the Ter and the Ritort, and is knit together by little bridges. The principal one, the sixteenth-century **Pont Nou**, still has a defensive tower. From here you can follow the narrow main commercial street to the restored Romanesque monastic church of **Sant Pere** (consecrated in 904), near the northeast end of town next to the larger parish church of Santa María. There is also a small castle overhead, most easily reached by crossing the Pont Nou and then climbing the narrow lanes on the far side.

Camprodon was the birthplace of the composer **Isaac Albéniz** (1860–1909), a fact which neither the town nor the region made much of until recently – probably because there is little that is distinctively Catalan in the music he produced during his wanderings through Spain. However, the great man now has a street, and a **café** on c/València (recommended for croissants and coffee), named for him, a bust near Sant Pere, an eponymous **music festival** held at Sant Pere in July, and a less worthwhile **museum** (daily 11am–2pm & 4–7pm; €2.50) near the bridge, commemorating his life and times.

Practicalities

Buses from Ripoll stop 300m south of the main Plaça d'Espanya, where you'll find the **turisme** (July–Sept Tues–Sat 10am–2pm & 4–7pm, Sun 10am–2pm; Oct–June Tues–Sat 10am–2pm & 4–7pm, Sun 10am–2pm; ☎972 740 010) in the *ajuntament* building. **Accommodation** tends to be expensive, given the town's role as a minor ski resort, and advance reservations are advisable much of the year. On often noisy c/Josep Morer there's *Can Ganansi* at no. 9 (☎972 740 134; ❷) and *Hostal Sayola* at no. 4 (☎972 740 142; ❸), both with en-suite rooms. The overpriced *Hotel Sant Roc* (☎972 740 119; ❹) and the better-value *Pensió La Placeta* (☎972 740 807; ❸) overlook Plaça del Carmé, just east of c/Josep Morer and the first square you reach as you come into town from Sant Joan. For a splurge, try the *Hotel de Camprodon* on Plaça Dr. Robert 3 (☎972 740 013, ℱ972 740 716; ❸), in a *modernista* building with elegant common areas. The best local **campsite** is *Vall de Camprodon*, 2km or so down the road towards Ripoll (☎972 740 507; open all year).

Can Ganansi's **restaurant** offers at least two different *menús* plus local dishes such as duck and trout, while *Pensió La Placeta* also has an attached diner (dinner only). Alternatively, *Bar-Restaurant Núria*, at Plaça d'Espanya 11, is a characterful place and features a good-value lunch *menú* (at night it's *a la carta* only, including such delights as "prog legs"). *El Pont 9* has views to the river bridge and a *menú* priced similarly to Núria's. Local specialities, besides the ubiquitous *ànec amb peres* (duck with pears), include *pinyes*, extremely rich and dense pine-nut sweets, which you can find on sale at bakeries throughout the town.

Beyond Camprodon: the Ter and Ritort valleys

Beyond Camprodon you're increasingly dependent on your own transport and ultimately your own legs. The majority of people who venture this way are either hikers, or skiers driving northwest up the **Ter valley** to the runs of

Vallter 2000, with comparatively little traffic moving northeast up the **Ritort** that isn't bound for France. The construction of holiday flats for lowlanders, and of more short-term tourist facilities, now reigns supreme, but you still catch a glimpse of the area's former agricultural economy in the herds of grazing horses, and cattle ambling home at dusk.

The first settlement that might tempt you to stop is rather ordinary **VILAL-LONGA DE TER**, 5km from Camprodon. Opposite the standard-issue Romanesque church of **Sant Martí** on the main *plaça* are two **accommodation** possibilities: *Hostal Pastoret* (☎972 740 319; ❸), at Constitució 9, and the unstaffed *Hostal Cal Mestre* around the corner at c/del Pou 1 (information at c/Major 3; ☎972 740 407; ❸). There's also an all-year **campsite**, *Conca de Ter* (☎972 740 629), in the outskirts, pitched mainly at well-anchored caravanners. Just one bus daily from Camprodon passes through here on its way to Setcases (see below).

Alternatively, bear left 1km past Vilallonga for the steep detour to **TREGURÀ**, 5km from the main road. Perched on a sunny hillside at 1400m, with sweeping views east over the valley, the upper part of this double village has a church dating from about 980. There are also two places to **stay**: the welcoming *Fonda Rigà* (☎972 136 000; ❸, half board ❹), with its vastly popular **restaurant**, and the rather more institutional *Hotel El Serrat* (☎972 136 019; half board only ❹).

From Tregurà, it's possible to hike west in a day to **Queralbs**, where you can pick up the rack-and-pinion railway down to Ribes or up to Núria. This route provides a lower-altitude, more scenic alternative to the GR11 long-distance trail, which crosses the Ter valley much higher up. Using the lower path, you can break the journey after three hours or so at the friendly **Refugi Coma de Vaca** (1995m; 42 places; ☎972 198 082; staffed Easter & mid-June to mid-Sept, or by arrangement on ☎936 824 237) at the top of the Gorges del Freser. It's packed to the gills on summer weekends, but fairly quite midweek. Another path, the GR11.7, connects Coma de Vaca with the **Refugi Ulldeter** (2220m; 52 places; ☎972 192 004; open Easter and mid-June to mid-Sept and weekends all year) on the slopes of the Vallter ski resort.

Setcases and Vallter 2000

SETCASES, 6km northwest of Vilallonga in the Ter valley, has been completely gentrified since the 1980s. Once an important agricultural village, it was almost totally abandoned until the nearby ski station began to attract hoteliers, chalet developers and second-home owners. The ski trade ensures that short-term beds and food are relatively pricey; if you need to **stay**, the most affordable accommodation is next to the riverside road: the *Hostal Ter* (☎972 136 096; ❸) or the *Nueva Can Tiranda* (☎972 136 037; ❷), though you may be required to take half board – as you definitely are in the village centre at *Hostal El Molí* (☎972 136 049; ❹ half board). At those rates, the relative luxury of *Hotel La Coma* (☎972 136 073; B&B ❹), at the entrance to the village, might be worth considering. Local trippers flock here to eat at weekends, most notably at the independent restaurant *Can Jepet* (reserve on ☎972 136 104; closed Thurs Oct–June). The food – well-presented salads, grilled quail with artichoke and roast peppers, home-made *flan* – is excellent value at under €22 a head.

Situated at the head of the valley, below the frontier summits of Bastiments (2874m) and Pic de la Dona (2702m), compact **VALLTER 2000** (no public transport) is the most easterly downhill ski resort in the Pyrenees. While south-facing, the glacial bowl here has a chilly microclimate that lets snow linger into April most years – though the runs remain heavily dependent on cannons. The range of *pistes* is enough to keep you interested for a weekend, when Barcelonans flood the place.

The Ritort valley

From Camprodon, the road up to the **Col d'Ares** (1513m) and down into France initially follows the relatively treeless **Ritort valley**. The main – though slight – attraction at **MOLLÓ**, 8km from Camprodon, is the Romanesque church of **Santa Cecília**, with its four-storey bell tower; one bus daily (except Sun) makes the trip from Camprodon. The best place to **stay** in the village is *Hotel Restaurant Calitxó*, a modern structure at the outskirts (☎972 740 386, ⓕ972 740 746; ⑤); the rooms are good-standard, with balconies, wood trim everywhere and tubs in the baths, but it's rather overpriced except in low season (④). The alternative is a **casa de pagès**, *Can Illa* (☎972 740 512; ②), 3km north in Ginestosa district. This working cattle ranch has sweeping views, mostly en-suite rooms, a self-catering kitchen, a common room with wood stove, and a refuge-type dorm for groups. Your final chance of food and a place to stay before the border is the *Habitacions El Quintà* (☎972 741 374; ③) at the base of the attractive hillside hamlet of **ESPINAVELL**, 2.7km northeast of the main road (and 4.2km in total from Molló; turn off before Ginestosa); half board is also available through the affiliated *Restaurant Les Planes* next door.

Another option, a bit east of the Ritort valley, just off the start of the road up to Rocabruna, is *Mas Tubert* (☎972 130 327, ⓔtubert@abaforum.es; half board only, ⑤), a *casa de pagès* which will be enjoyed by connoisseurs of the middle of nowhere. It's 7km by rough track from the *urbanizació* of Font Rubí, itself about 6km from either Camprodon or Molló. Rooms are medium-sized if rustic; the cooking nouvelle verging on the precious (miniature frozen liver lollies, and so on).

The Upper Freser valley and Núria

From Ripoll, the **Freser valley** rises to Ribes de Freser (912m) and then climbs steeply to Queralbs, where it swings eastwards through a gorge of awesome beauty. Just above Queralbs, to the north, the Riu Núria has scoured out a second gorge, beyond which lie the ski station and valley sanctuary of Núria. You can take the **train** all the way from Barcelona on this route, one of Catalunya's most extraordinary rides. The first stretch is by RENFE to Ribes de Freser, nominally a two-and-a-half-hour ride (or just twenty minutes from Ripoll). From there, the *Cremallera* (Zipper) rack-and-pinion railway takes over; the small carriages of this private line take another 45 minutes to reach Núria.

Ribes de Freser

Generally bypassed in the rush up to Núria, dull but unobjectionable **RIBES DE FRESER** offers little to the traveller except hotels – more plentiful and better value than anything in Ripoll – and, out of season, its integrity as a real town. Local shops sell sacks of grain, seeds, oils and other agricultural and domestic paraphernalia, and there's a much-used *petanca* (boules) court in the centre, as well as a lively weekly market and an annual sheepdog contest every September.

Regular **trains** on the Barcelona–Puigcerdà line serve Ribes in either direction. Alight at "Ribes de Freser-RENFE" for the ten-minute walk into town, or just cross the platform to "Ribes-Enllaç" and take the *Cremallera* train (see box on p.849), which makes a stop in the centre of town (Ribes-Vila) to pick up more passengers, before scooting off into the mountains.

Practicalities

If the idea of staying appeals, the pick of the town's **accommodation** is *Mas Ventaiola* (booking essential on ☎972 727 948), a *casa de pagès* 1km from the centre, reached via the cemetery track taking off from the Pardines road. Perched on the hillside and recently refurbished, this offers both en-suite rooms (❷) and several four-bed apartments. Otherwise, in the town itself, very close to the *Cremallera* station, quietest choices are *Hotel Caçadors*, c/Balandrau 24–26 (☎972 727 006, ℱ972 728 001; ❷–❹), which has a range of en-suite rooms in two separate premises, or the plainer rooms of *Hostal Porta de Núria* just around the corner at c/de N. S. de Gràcia 3 (☎972 727 137; ❷). If you're still stuck, there's a helpful **turisme** at Plaça de l'Ajuntament 3 (Tues–Sat 10am–2pm & 5–8pm, Sun 11am–1pm; ☎972 727 728), or repair to the *Vall de Ribes* campsite, less than 1km from Ribes-Vila station on the Pardines road (☎972 728 820; open all year; ❶); it's basic but pleasant, with tent pitches on the lower terraces, plus bungalows. **Eating** out, the restaurant at the *Caçadors* is pleasant if slightly overpriced; count on €23 for three courses *a la carta*; a *menú* is available at weekday lunchtimes.

Along the Cremallera Line

The *Cremallera* makes a fabulous introduction to the mountains. After a leisurely start through the lower valley, the tiny, blue-and-white, two-car train lurches up into the mountains, following the river between great crags before starting to climb high above both river and forests. Occasionally it slows down, leaving you poised between a sheer drop into the valley and an equally precipitous rock face soaring overhead.

Queralbs and Fustanyà

The only intermediate stop on the *Cremallera* (you'll occasionally have to change trains here) is at **QUERALBS** (1220m), an attractive stone-built village, though it's now being dwarfed by apartment complexes on its outskirts, and also suffers from the attentions of too many tourists in peak season. Near the highest point, beside the GR11 trail, which passes through the village, stands the tenth-century church of **Sant Jaume**, adorned with a fine colonnaded porch. Reasonable en-suite **accommodation** is provided by *Hostal L'Avet*, on the main street (☎972 727 377; open daily 24 June to mid-Oct, weekends only at other times; half board only ❹); rooms are small but wood-trimmed, and there's a cosy lounge on the ground floor. The *table d'hôte* fare at the attached *Ca La Mary* restaurant is very good (allow €16).

For year-round board and lodging, head 3km out of Queralbs to the well-signposted *Mas La Casanova* on the opposite side of the valley (☎972 198 077; B&B ❸), in **FUSTANYÀ** hamlet. This good-value **casa de pagès** is set in a superbly restored farmhouse, where the outgoing proprietress provides reasonable *table d'hôte* evening meals, and there are also large family suites available; the only drawback is that the wood architecture amplifies any sound.

Núria

Beyond Queralbs, the *Cremallera* hauls itself up the precipitous valley to **NÚRIA**, twenty minutes further on. Once the train passes the entrance to the Gorges del Freser, seen tantalizingly to the right, and enters the Gorges de Núria, the views are dramatic. Having passed through a final tunnel, you emerge into a south-facing bowl, with a small lake at the bottom and – at the far end – the hideously monolithic, *café au lait*-coloured **Santuari de Nostra Senyora de Núria** (1964m), founded in the eleventh century on the spot where an image of the Virgin was said to have been found. The Virgin of Núria is believed to bestow fertility on female pilgrims, and many Catalan girls – presumably the result of successful supernatural intervention – are named after her.

The sanctuary combines a dull church, tourist office (which posts weather reports), bar, restaurants, ski centre and **hotel** all in one. Rates at the *Hotel Vall de Núria* (☎972 732 000, ⓕ972 732 001; half board only ❻–❼) vary by season – winter is cheaper – and its **restaurant**, open for lunch and dinner, is also pricey. The only indoor budget lodging is the youth hostel *Pic de L'Àliga* (☎972 732 048; €11), marvellously poised at the top of the ski centre's cablecar line (though this often doesn't run in summer). **Camping** is permitted only at a designated site behind the sanctuary complex.

Besides the hotel, **eating** options include *La Cabana dels Pastors*, behind the complex, sporadically offering expensive bistro fare at lunchtime only; the *Bar Finestrelles*, downstairs in the sanctuary building, with typical bar snacks; and, best value of all, the lunchtime-only *Autoservei* self-service restaurant in the west wing, where you can eat reasonably well for €12–16.

Summertime activities in the valley include an archery range, pony riding (high summer only) and boating on the lake. The entire resort has a dedicated **website** at ⓦwww.valldenuria.com.

Walking and skiing

Despite the day-trippers and hordes of kids, solitude is easily found amidst the bleak, treeless scenery. Serious **climbers** can move on from Núria to the summit of **Puigmal** (2909m), a four-to-five-hour hike: the 1:25,000 *Puigmal-Núria* Editorial Alpina contoured map/guide booklet is recommended. Most people, however, aren't this committed, so the **return to Queralbs** on foot along the river gorge (2hr 30min) ranks as the most popular hike out of Núria. The GR11 threads the gorge on a high-quality, well-marked path, but you'll still want good shoes and a water bottle. With an early start, you can make the long day's walk through the **Gorges de Freser**, following the GR11.7 (the "Camí del Enginyers") to the *Refugi Coma de Vaca* (see p.846), then doubling back on another marked trail down the other side of the gorge to just below Queralbs.

Downhill **skiing** at Núria – best for beginners and weak intermediates – is surprisingly popular, given that the piste plan is very limited, the chair lift only reaches 2262m, and the maximum altitude difference is a paltry 288m. Lift passes are accordingly cheap by Pyrenean standards, though equipment hire is much the same as elsewhere.

⑪

CATALUNYA | The Upper Freser valley and Núria

Berguedà

An alternative approach to this eastern section of the Catalan Pyrenees is to aim initially for the *comarca* (county) of **Berguedà**, west of Ripoll. It's easiest with your own transport: from Barcelona, the fast, improved C1411 road runs through Manresa and then heads due north to Puigcerdà, via the **Túnel del Cadí**, Spain's longest (and most expensive, at €7 per car) toll-tunnel. You can come this way by bus, too – heading first for **Berga**, the region's main town, from Barcelona – though this approach is slower than the train trip to Puigcerdà via Ripoll.

There's nothing as immediately spectacular in this region as the Núria train journey, though northeast of Berga, villages and hamlets like **Gombrèn**, **Sant Jaume de Frontanyà** and **Castellar de N'Hug** lend architectural interest. To the northwest, the vast Serra del Cadí offers the best local walking, including treks around (and a possible ascent of) the twin peaks of that most recognizable of Catalan mountains, **Pedraforca**.

Berga

The Pyrenees seem to arrive with a startling abruptness at **BERGA**, the capital of the Berguedà *comarca*. The town itself is fairly dull, bearing ample traces of its long history as an industrial centre, but it does have a ruined castle, a well-preserved medieval core and onward connections to higher settlements in the county, provided by the ATSA bus company at the top of Passeig de la Pau. It's also served by twice-daily buses from Barcelona (2hr).

The other main reason to come to Berga is during Corpus Christi when the town hosts the **Festa de la Patum**, one of the most famous of Catalunya's festivals. For three days, huge figures of giants and dwarfs process to hornpipe music along streets packed with red-hatted Catalans intent on a good time. A dragon attacks onlookers in the course of a symbolic battle between good and evil, firecrackers blazing from its mouth, while the climax comes on the Saturday night, with a dance performed by masked men covered in grass.

Not surprisingly, **accommodation** is impossible to find during the festival unless you've booked weeks in advance; at other times you should have few problems. Try the small but well-appointed *Hotel Passasserres*, c/La Valldan (☎938 210 645; ❸), with sauna, gym and off-street parking; *Pensió Passeig*, Passeig de la Pau 12 (☎938 210 415; ❷); or the very central two-star *Hotel Queralt*, Plaça de la Creu 4 (☎938 210 611; ❸), whose en-suite rooms have all mod cons. There's also a **campsite**, out of town on the C1411 (☎938 211 250; open all year). The **turisme** is just behind it (June–Sept daily 9am–1pm & 4–8pm; Oct–May reduced hours; ☎938 221 500). The best **restaurant** in town is the *Sala* at Passeig de la Pau 27 (closed Sun evening and Mon) – count on about €35 a head for a full gourmet meal, less if you opt for the *menú*. If your budget doesn't stretch to that, the *menjador* of the *Hostal Guiu*, Ctra de Queralt, offers regional specialities.

Northwest of Berga: the Serra del Cadí

For fully equipped and experienced trekkers, the **Serra del Cadí** range to the northwest of Berga offers three or four days' trekking through wild, lonely areas. A number of paths and tracks cross the range, though the favourite excursion remains the ascent of Pedraforca. As in other limestone massifs, finding fresh water can be problematic, and that – combined with intense summer heat at this relatively low altitude – means the peak visitors' season is during

May–June and September. In recognition of its unique landscape, the Cadí was declared a natural reserve some years ago, and it maintains several fairly well-placed, staffed refuges, accessible from a number of foothill villages which are themselves served poorly, or not at all, by bus, so you may have to drive, walk or hitch to them from the larger towns down-valley. For extended explorations of this region, you'll need the Editorial Alpina 1:25,000 *Serra del Cadí/Pedraforca* and *Moixeró* maps and guide, or the Catalunya IGN *Mapa Excursionista* for the same area.

From the Llobregat valley extending north of Berga there are two major routes west into the Cadí. **From Bagà**, a partly paved road follows the Riu Bastareny to the hamlet of Gisclareny. A much busier paved road highway beginning just south of **Guardiola de Berguedà** runs parallel to the Saldes river valley to Gòsol village, via Saldes village, the closest habitation to Pedraforca.

Bagà and Gisclareny

BAGÀ, the second town in the *comarca* after Berga, has something going for it in the form of a tiny old quarter with an arcaded *plaça* and several **accommodation** options. Choose between *Hotel La Pineda*, c/Raval 50 (☎938 244 515; ❸), at the eastern end of the main shopping street, and the *Hostal Ca L'Amagat* (☎938 244 032; ❷), quietly placed in the heart of the old town. On the southeast edge of town, *Hostal Cal Batista* (☎938 244 126; ❷) occupies two unexciting modern buildings, but staying here does solve parking problems, and they also have a well-regarded **restaurant** with a nice line in local trout and rabbit *all-i-olli*. The *Bastareny* **campsite** (☎938 244 420; open all year), 1km west of town by the river, caters mostly for caravans.

The fourteen-kilometre road up the **Bastareny valley** begins at the campsite, climbing steeply through dense forest before emerging via the **Coll de l'Escriga** (1360m) onto the south side of the mountain. **GISCLARENY**, 3km beyond the pass, is merely a handful of spread-out farms and two **campsites**, one of which – *Cal Tasconet* (☎608 493 317), 1500m west of the hamlet centre – also operates a **refuge**. Beyond Gisclareny, trails or tracks give handy access to the heart of the Cadí within a few hours. Arriving on foot, it's possible to skip the Bastareny valley-floor track in favour of the direct Bagà–Gisclareny **path**, shown more or less correctly on the Editorial Alpina *Moixeró* map. A more exciting option is to thread the Gorges dels Empredats northwest from Bagà to reach the **Refugi Sant Jordi** at Font del Faig on the Cadí ridge (1640m; 48 places; ☎933 322 381; open Easter & June 27 to Sept 11), even better placed for traverses of the range.

Guardiola de Berguedà, Saldes and Gòsol

Strung out grimly along the old course of the C1411 (a new bypass avoids the town), **GUARDIOLA DE BERGUEDÀ** is on the bus routes from Berga (21km south) and Ripoll, and is only 1.5km north of the turning for Saldes and Gòsol (see p.852). The sole **accommodation** option is the *Pensió Guardiola* (☎938 227 048; ❶), on the main street at the south end of town, which also does meals. There's just one daily (5.35pm) bus to Saldes and Gòsol – note that it doesn't enter town, but turns at the junction 1.5km south.

The first significant habitation, after 18km, is the small village of **SALDES**, set dramatically at the foot of Pedraforca and the usual starting point for explorations of the peak. Here you'll find two stores with trekking provisions, plus two inexpensive **inns**: the *Fonda Carinyena* (☎938 258 025; ❷) near the church, and the pricier *Cal Manuel* (☎938 258 041; ❸), on Plaça Pedraforca (where cars park), serving meals. Reservations are virtually mandatory in season at both. Better value than either of these, however, is *Cal Xic* (☎938 258 081; ❸), a *casa de pagès* 1.5km west of the village in Cardina hamlet, at the start of the road up towards Pedraforca. Although a somewhat sterile building, the en-suite rooms are heated, clean and cheerful, and asking for a *desayuno salado* gets you ham, sausages, cheese and a *porrón* to wash it all down with.

The old stone village of **GÒSOL**, 10km beyond Saldes, is an altogether more substantial place, spilling appealingly off a castellated hill. Pablo Picasso came here from Paris during the summer of 1906 and stayed for several weeks in fairly primitive conditions, inspired to paint by the striking countryside; one of the streets off the Plaça Major is named after him. Gòsol makes a good alternative base to Saldes for explorations of the entire Cadí, with well-trodden trails up towards the less spectacular backside of Pedraforca. There are two **hostals**, both with decent attached restaurants: *Cal Franciscó*, on the little roundabout as you come into town (☎ & ℻973 370 075; ❷, half board ❹), and the smaller, central *Can Triuet*, Plaça Major 4 (☎973 370 072; ❷). There's also a **campsite**, *Cadí de Gòsol* (☎973 370 134; open all year), southwest of the village, reached by dirt road from beside *Cal Franciscó*, plus three *casas rurales*.

Up Pedraforca and beyond

Most people tackle **Pedraforca** (the "stone pitchfork") from Saldes: a good ninety-minute path short-cuts the road up, which passes fifteen minutes' walk below the **Refugi Lluís Estasen** (1640m; 100 places; advance booking recommended on ☎938 220 079; open all year). The ascent of the 2491-metre peak is a popular outing from here, steep but not technically demanding if you approach clockwise via the scree-clogged *couloir* heading up the "fork"; at the divide between the two summits you'll meet a proper path coming up from Gòsol. The **anticlockwise climb** from the refuge via the Canal de Verdet is harder, and the descent that way is almost impossible. However you do it, count on a round trip of five to six hours.

From the *Estasen* refuge, a day's walk separates you from either the *Refugi Sant Jordi* to the east, or the Segre valley to the north. The easiest traverse route north, on a mixture of 4WD tracks and paths, goes through the **Pas dels Gosolans**, a notch in the imposing, steeply dropping north face of the Cadí watershed. An hour's steep descent below, the *Refugi Cesar Torres* at **PRAT D'AGUILÓ** (2037m; 30 places; ☎973 250 135; open all year, staffed in summer) is well situated near one of the few springs in these mountains. From the refuge it's best to arrange a ride along the 15km of track north via Montellà to Martinet, on the main valley road linking La Seu d'Urgell with Puigcerdà.

Northeast of Berga

From Berga a daily bus heads northeast to **LA POBLA DE LILLET**, an hour away; you can also get here by the afternoon bus from Ripoll, 28km to the east, via Gombrèn (see opposite) Here two ancient bridges arch over the infant Llobregat river, with a well-stocked **turisme** (daily summer and Easter 10am–2pm & 5–8pm) beside the smaller one; the old districts to either side of the stream make for a pleasant half-hour stroll, but there's little else to see. **Accommodation** and **eating** are both overpriced and restricted to the central *Hostal Can Pericas*, c/Furrioles Altes 3 (☎938 236 162; ❸), and the slightly shabbier *Hostal Cerdanya* at Plaça del Fort 5 (☎938 236 083; ❸). With your own transport, you'll do much better for food and lodging heading north or east.

From La Pobla there's a steady eleven-kilometre ascent northeast towards Castellar de N'Hug and, since you can leave the road only for a short section at the beginning and at the end, without transport you miss little by hitching – or waiting for the evening **bus** (daily except Sun) up from Berga via La Pobla. Three kilometres out of La Pobla on the left stands **El Clot de Moro**, a flamboyant *modernista* building designed by Rafael Guastavino in 1901 as a cement factory; it's now a museum (July to mid-Sept daily 10am–2pm & 4–7pm; mid-Sept to June Sat & Sun 10am–3pm). Approaching Castellar, you'll come to the **Fonts del Llobregat**, source of the river that divides Catalunya in two. Every year hundreds of Catalans come here as if on a pilgrimage – summer droughts cause many local rivers to dwindle to nothing, so there's great pride in any durable water source, and this one has never stopped in living memory, even during the driest year.

North to Castellar de N'Hug
Heaped up against the ridge of the Serra de Montgrony at an altitude of 1400m, **CASTELLAR DE N'HUG** makes a good if slightly touristy base for the Moixeró section of the natural reserve, or (in winter) for snow sports at Alp 2500 (see p.854). High seasons here are September and October – when people come mushroom-hunting in the surrounding forests – and the skiing season of January and February. There's a fair amount of inexpensive **accommodation**: first choices are the friendly *Hostal Fonda La Muntanya* (☎938 257 065; half board only, ❹) at Plaça Major 4, with excellent, copious dinners, and the *Pensió Fanxicó* (☎938 257 015; half board ❹) across the way, which is popular at lunchtime. Avoid the unwelcoming, overpriced *Pensió Peremiquel*. Somewhat plainer, if potentially quieter, is the *Hostal Alt Llobregat* (☎938 257 074; B&B ❸, half board ❹), at the southeast edge of the village on the road down towards the **Santuari de Montgrony**, 11km distant, which is magnificently perched on a cliff face and incorporates a *hostal* (☎972 198 022; half board only ❹; closed Tues Oct–June).

North from Castellar, the bleakly scenic BV4031 road, sporadically snowploughed during winter, continues over the range to La Molina and the Collada de Toses via the 1880-metre **Coll de la Creueta**. There are paths in this direction as well, but they're not marked; it's best to ask advice in the village for the five-hour walks to Toses or Planoles and equip yourself with the Editorial Alpina map *Montgrony/Fonts del Llobregat*.

East to Sant Jaume de Frontanyà and Gombrèn
The eleventh-century church at **SANT JAUME DE FRONTANYÀ**, unquestionably the finest Romanesque church in the region, lies 12km southeast of La Pobla de Lillet, easily accessible by a recently paved road not yet shown on many commercial or tourist office maps; the turning south from the B402, 2km east of La Pobla, is well marked. Set at the foot of a naturally terraced cliff, the church is built in the shape of a Latin cross with three apses and a twelve-sided lantern. Keys are kept by both of the hamlet's two excellent, characterful **restaurants**: "*Hostal*" *Sant Jaume* and *Fonda Cal Marxandó*; the latter also has inexpensive, shared-bath **rooms** (☎938 239 002; ❷) above its beam-ceilinged *menjador*.

From the Santuari de Montgrony (see above) it's a six-kilometre drive south to **GOMBRÈN**; from La Pobla, a twistier sixteen-kilometre ordeal east over the Coll de Merolla. Either way, the bright spot of this little village is *La Fonda Xesc* (☎972 730 404, ✉xesc@cconline.es; B&B ❸), whose **restaurant** (Oct–June closed Mon & Tues all day, Wed & Sun eve) draws crowds from afar for the sake of its elegant new-wave cuisine. The en-suite rooms are on the spartan side, but all common areas were overhauled in 2003.

To the French border: the Cerdanya

The train from Barcelona, via Ripoll and Ribes de Freser, ends its run on the Spanish side of the border at Puigcerdà, having cut through the Spanish portion of the **Cerdanya**. This wide agricultural plain, flanked by mountains to the north and south, shares a past and a culture with French Cerdagne over the border. The division of the area followed the 1659 Treaty of the Pyrenees, which also gave France control of neighbouring Roussillon, but left Llívia as a Spanish enclave just inside France. Spanish Cerdanya remains marginally more rural and traditional than the French side, though it began to be a popular summer holiday area for wealthy Barcelonans during the nineteenth century. Since the early 1990s this trend has accelerated, with blocks of second-home flats dwarfing nearly every village. Besides skiing – the main impetus for all this construction – golf, horse riding, glider-piloting and even hot-air ballooning are growing in popularity, with the gently rolling countryside ideal for such activities.

A **train service** (with a change of trains) continues over the border into France via Puigcerdà. This is the only surviving trans-Pyrenean rail route and provides a good alternative method of leaving or entering Spain. Note that if you're heading to France by train, it's wise to reserve a seat in advance in Barcelona, or you may find yourself turfed out at La Tour de Carol, the first French station, to fight for space with holidaymakers on their way back to Toulouse and Paris.

Ripoll to Puigcerdà

All routes **from Ripoll** initially follow the Freser river north to Ribes de Freser (p.847), and then veer west, climbing steadily up the Rigart river valley. The train line to Puigcerdà sticks to the bottom of the valley, while the N152 road takes a higher course, allowing a good look south over the Serra Montgrony. Beyond the Collada de Toses, technically in the Cerdanya, the ski resort of **Alp 2500** is one of the more serious winter-sports areas in the Catalan Pyrenees.

Planoles, Fornells and Toses

PLANOLES, 7km from Ribes, is nothing extraordinary as a village but makes a good base for the ski slopes to the west. There's an outstanding **casa de pagès**, *Mas Cal Sadurní* (☏972 736 135; half board only ❹), set in a superbly restored farmhouse on a natural terrace just uphill from the train station. This is packed out most weekends and offers a mix of doubles and family-size quads, most en suite, plus an eight-bunk "refuge" for groups. The in-house restaurant closes Tuesday and Wednesday, when your best local **eating** option is the widely acclaimed *Restaurant-Casino* (lunch only; menú available; closed Mon) behind the church. The nearby hamlet of **FORNELLS DE LA MUNTANYA**, 8.5km beyond Planoles, also has a popular restaurant, *Can Casanova* (closed Mon eve & Tues; ☏972 736 075), with large if basically presented portions of hearty mountain cuisine from a limited menu. It's good value at under €20 per person, including a strong house wine; lunch is served until 4.30pm, and reservations are advised. You can stay at the comparatively ordinary *Can Pastor* just uphill (☏972 736 163; ❷).

TOSES, 3.5km beyond Fornells, is the last village in the Rigart valley and, at 1450m altitude, is one of the highest permanently inhabited villages in Spain. The only **accommodation**, 100m from the train station, is the welcoming, good-value *Cal Santpare* (☎972 736 226; B&B ❸, half board ❹), with a decent restaurant (closed Wed) and comfortable en-suite rooms. The glory of Toses is its tenth-to-twelfth-century church of **San Cristófol**, at the highest, southeast end of the village, with a simple barrel-vaulted nave and a so-called "Lombard" belfry, rectangular and gable-roofed. The ancient key (obtain from *Cal Pep* on the square) allows you inside to see the **frescoes** (skilful copies of the originals are in the Museu d'Art de Catalunya in Barcelona). The main theme, Christ's Ascension, is half-obliterated, but there's a well-preserved image around the lancet window of a lad hefting a sheep – highly apt for this pastoral community.

Beyond Toses, road and train enter Cerdanya respectively over and under the Collada de Toses – the railway by the amazing **Cargol tunnel**, where the line executes a complete spiral to gain altitude. The pass affords excellent views west, the bare rolling mountains of the Montgrony range relieved by swathes of deep green forest.

Alp 2500 and Alp village

The broad meadows of Tosa d'Alp (2537m) and Puigllançada (2406m) form the pistes of **LA MOLINA** and **MASELLA**, adjacent ski resorts linked via lifts and runs and marketed together as "**ALP 2500**", claimed to be the largest ski area in the Spanish Pyrenees. Both have their own websites – ⓦwww.lamolina .com and ⓦwww.masella.com respectively – and by Spanish Pyrenean standards the skiing is impressive. Publicly run La Molina is probably more suitable for beginners; larger, private Masella is better managed, with more scenic runs.

Getting to the slopes, it's really best to have your own car, though during winter an infrequent "Bus Blanc" is provided, with one early-morning departure up from the Cerdanya flatlands, and two returns in the afternoon. With the exception of the wood-and-stone chalet *Niu dels Falcons*, c/Font Moreu 10, at La Molina (☎972 892 073; ⓦwww.niudelsfalcons-xalet.com; half board only ❺), **accommodation** at the foot of the slopes is overpriced and sterile; you're far better off staying in the villages of the Cerdanya to the north (see "Villages around Puigcerdà", p.857). Closest of these is **ALP**, 6km northwest, where the friendliest of the three lodgings is the *Aero Hotel Cerdanya*, Passeig Agnès Fabra 4 (☎972 890 033, ⒻFAX972 890 862; ❷–❸), which also has a competitively priced gourmet **restaurant**, *Ca l'Eudald*, in the basement (*menú* from €10, *a la carta* €25).

Puigcerdà

Although it was founded by King Alfonso I of Aragón in 1177 as a new capital for then-unified Cerdanya, **PUIGCERDÀ** (pronounced "Poocherdah") retains no compelling medieval monuments, partly owing to heavy bombing during the Civil War. The church of Santa María was one of these wartime casualties, but its forty-metre-high **belltower** still stands in the namesake *plaça*. The east end of town, down the pleasant, tree-lined Passeig Deu d'Abril, escaped more lightly; here, you can see medieval murals in the gloomy parish church of **Sant Domènec**. Dwelling morbidly on the saint's martyrdom, surviving fragments show Dominic's head being cloven in two by a sabre. The town's greatest attraction, however, is its atmosphere – if you've just arrived from France, the attractive streets and squares, with their busy pavement cafés and well-stocked shops, present a marked contrast to moribund Bourg-Madame just over the border. Allow at least enough time for a meal or an evening in a bar; enjoyable outdoor cafés crowd the merged *plaças* of Santa María and dels Herois. Between drinks, you can explore the older quarter between Plaça de l'Ajuntament and Passeig Deu d'Abril, or amble up to the small recreational lake, five minutes' walk to the north.

Arrival, information and accommodation

From the **train station** (outside which buses stop) in Plaça de l'Estació, wearyingly steep steps lead ten minutes up to Plaça de l'Ajuntament in the heart of town, with reviving views far west over the Cerdanya. At the top of the steps, to the right, stands the newish Casa de la Vila, with the central **turisme** alongside at c/Querol 1 (June to mid-Sept daily 9am–2pm & 3–8pm; mid-Sept to May Mon 9am–1pm, Tues–Sat 10am–1pm & 4–7pm; ☎972 880 542). The giant **regional branch**, 1.5km southwest of town near the *Puigcerdà Park Hotel* (May to mid-Sept same hours daily 9am–2pm & 3–8pm; mid-Sept to May Mon–Sat 9am–1pm & 4–7pm, Sun 10am–2pm; ☎972 140 665), is particularly well stocked with leaflets and more convenient with your own transport.

There's not a great selection of **accommodation** in Puigcerdà, and you might consider staying in one of the nearby villages instead (see opposite). Acceptable budget options in town include the very central, friendly *Hostal Alfonso*, c/d'Espanya 5 (☎972 880 246; ❷) – the upper-storey rooms are far superior; or the *Hostal Residència Rita Belvedere* at c/Carmelites 6–8 (☎972 880 356; ❷–❸), which offers excellent views and a choice of old-style or modern rooms; the main drawback is its restricted opening (daily July 25 to Sept 30; Christmas to Easter Fri & Sat; and public holidays). For a mild splurge, you can't do better than the *Hotel del Lago*, Avinguda Dr Piguillém (☎972 881 000, Ⓦwww.hotellago.com; ❹), set in a garden just off Plaça Barcelona towards the lake.

Eating and drinking

Passing French tourists are responsible for the relatively high prices and bland menus in Puigcerdà, but there are still a number of reasonable places to **eat**. At the budget end of the scale, *Sant Remo* at c/Ramon Cosp 9 has a pleasant upstairs *menjador* offering large *menús* at €7.50 and €9.50; the *Carmen*, on Plaça de Santa María off c/Major, with an upstairs *menjador*, is similar. For a jump in standards (and prices) in the same area, head for the fancier *La Cachimba* at c/Beates 12. The best wood-oven pizzas (around €12 each) in town are at *Pizzeria del Reg*, on Plaça del Reg, at the top end of c/Major.

The **bars** with outdoor seating on Plaça dels Herois and the adjoining Plaça de Santa María – in particular, the adjacent *Kennedy* and *Miami Dos* – are usually busy, and while their full-on food service is tourist pap, they're okay for a drink and tapas. Just round the corner on Rambla Josep Martí, *Bar Arenas* is quieter, considerably cheaper and also has outdoor seating. The atmospheric *Bodega*, at c/Miguel Bernades 4, has a clientele of locals and French tourists and the wine is served and sold from the barrels that line the walls: sample a glass or two in its intimate interior or bring your own bottle and fill it up to take away. The *Cerveseria Claude*, on arcaded Plaça Cabrinetty, specializes in international beers: you can sit indoors or out, tippling your way around the world's breweries.

Moving on to Andorra and France

If you're heading **west towards Andorra** on public transport, you may have to spend the night in Puigcerdà as there are only three buses a day to La Seu d'Urgell, via Bellver de Cerdanya (see p.858). Heading **into France**, three trains daily cross the border, bearing northwest to Latour-de-Carol, six minutes away, with quick connections for Toulouse (2hr 30min–3hr). If you're driving, you enter France via the small town of Bourg-Madame, 2km from the centre of Puigcerdà; it's also a simple matter to walk there across the border, which is open 24 hours, year-round; controls are nonexistent.

Villages around Puigcerdà

You'll find better-value accommodation, and often food, in the hamlets and villages immediately south of Puigcerdà, which are home to some of the more distinguished members of Girona province's *turisme rural* scheme. Top billing goes to the superb *Residència Sant Marc*, 1.5km south of the edge of town on the road to **LES PERERES** hamlet (T972 880 007, Wwww.santmarc .galeon.com; half board only ❺). Set on a 150-hectare stud farm, this elegant *belle époque* mansion has huge, varied common areas, wood-floored rooms with antique furniture, and is managed by friendly Latin Americans; reservations are recommended in summer. Two kilometres east of Puigcerdà in **AGE**, the *Cal Marrufès/Hipica Age* (T972 141 174, Wwww.calmarrufes.com; B&B ❸) is a tasteful restoration of an old stone-built farm in the village centre; it also has four-person suites.

In sleepy **URTX**, 5km south of Puigcerdà, the friendly *Cal Mateu* (T972 890 495; ❸ B&B) is part of a working dairy farm; the good-value en-suite rooms are bland modern rather than rustic and the breakfasts are nothing special, but self-catering is available; booking is advised for summer and over Christmas/New Year. Urtx hasn't any other facilities; the closest good **eats** are 1.5km downhill inside the converted but still-functioning Queixans RENFE station, where *L'Estació* (closed Wed) has two cheap lunch *menús* or *a la carta* at €15–20 per head.

Finally, in resolutely rural **SANAVASTRE**, *Can Simó* (T972 890 240; ❷, half board ❹), at the edge of the village, is another engagingly rustic cow farm which hasn't been overly restored, though most units are en suite; despite map appearances, Sanavastre is accessible *only* from Alp (not from the main highway to La Seu).

Llívia

The Spanish town of **LLÍVIA**, 6km from Puigcerdà but totally surrounded by French territory, is a curious place indeed, worth visiting not least so you can say you've been there. There are several **buses** daily from Puigcerdà (the Alsina Graells bus stops in front of the train station and again in Plaça Barcelona), but the ninety-minute walk out isn't too strenuous: bear left at the junction 1km outside town, just before the border at Bourg-Madame, and keep to the main road.

French **history** books claim that Llívia's anomalous position is the result of an oversight. According to the traditional version of events, in the exchanges that followed the Treaty of the Pyrenees the French delegates insisted on possession of the 33 Cerdan villages between the Ariège and newly acquired Roussillon. The Spanish agreed, and then pointed out that Llívia was technically a town rather than a village, and was thus excluded from the terms of the handover. Llívia had in fact been capital of the valley until the foundation of Puigcerdà, and Spain had every intention of retaining it at the negotiations, which were held in Llívia itself.

There's a strong medieval feel to the centre of town, not least in the fifteenth-century fortified **church** (June–Sept daily 10am–1pm & 3–7pm; Oct–May Tues–Sun 10am–1pm & 3–6pm), which boasts fine carved-wood sacred art in the north side chapels. Since 1982, an increasingly popular **music festival** has been held in and around the church on August weekends. Opposite the church, the unusual **Museu Municipal** (April–June Tues–Sat 10am–6pm, Sun 10am–2pm; July–Sept daily 10am–7pm, closed Mon in Sept; Oct–March Tues–Sat 10am–4.30pm, Sun 10am–2pm; €2) contains the interior of the oldest pharmacy in Europe, in business in Llívia from 1594 until 1918. Displays feature apothecarial pots and hand-painted boxes of herbs, as well as local Bronze Age relics, old maps and even the eighteenth-century bell mechanism from the church. The entry ticket may also get you into the fifteenth-century **Tour Bernat de So**, adjoining the church.

Practicalities

Most visitors just stay long enough for a **meal** – not a bad idea given the limited choice of accommodation. In the main Plaça Major at no. 1, there's the attractive *Can Ventura* restaurant (closed Mon evening & Tues), with flower-filled balconies; their Cerdanyan cuisine with the freshest ingredients weighs in at an extravagant €30 (there's no *menú*). *Cal Cofa* nearby at c/Frederic Bernades 1 is a cheaper (€24) alternative for country fare. Still further up the slope near the church, the good-value *Can Francesc* at c/dels Forns 7–15 has courtyard dining in summer and a three-course €11 *menú*.

The few places to **stay** tend to fill quickly, and budget options are unreliable since *Can Marcel-li* (☎972 146 096; ❷) at c/Frederic Bernades 7 closed in July 2003, perhaps permanently. The better value of the pair of hotels on the busy main road is the *Llívia* (☎972 146 000, ✉llivia@grn.es; ❺), a monstrous structure but with a pool, tennis courts and private parking.

Bellver de Cerdanya and Martinet

The second largest village in the Cerdanya – it's almost a town – and a possible halting point on the road between Puigcerdà and La Seu d'Urgell, **BELLVER DE CERDANYA** stands on a low hill on the left bank of the trout-laden Segre, 18km west of Puigcerdà. Its semi-fortified hilltop old town, with an arcaded Plaça Major and a massive church at the summit, is visually polluted by a hideous telecoms antenna, but still merits a stop. The Romanesque church of **Santa María de Talló** lies 2km southeast of the town. Known locally as the "Cathedral of Cerdanya", this is a rather plain building, but has a few nice decorative touches in the nave and apse, and retains a wooden statue of the Virgin that's as old as the building itself.

The **turisme** occupies an old chapel at Plaça Sant Roc 9 (☎973 510 229; Christmas, Easter & mid-June to mid-Sept Mon–Sat 11am–1pm & 6–8pm, Sun 11am–1pm; rest of year unreliable). The best place by far to **stay** is the *Fonda Biayna*, c/Sant Roc 11 (☎973 510 475, ☏973 510 853; half board only ❺), an atmospheric, rambling old mansion of creaky wood-floored rooms with small bathrooms and antique furnishings. It also has a lively downstairs bar, while the adjacent *menjador* is the best restaurant in town, with €14 *menús* including house wine. During summer, the *fonda*'s terraces serve as a venue for Saturday-night events like film screenings and live music. Bellver also has a pleasant **campsite** on the outskirts, *Solana del Segre* (☎973 510 310; open all year).

Continuing downstream along the Riu Segre towards La Seu d'Urgell on the N260, the next place you're likely to stop is **MARTINET**; the road from the refuge at Prat d'Aguilo, in the Cadí foothills to the south, also emerges here. Martinet is mostly strung uninspiringly along the through road, c/El Segre, but there is at least one good place to **stay**: *Fonda Miravet*, north of the highway on c/de les Arenes 2 (☎973 515 016; ❸), with views across a little stream. Unless the *Fonda Pluvinet*, at c/El Segre 13, reopens, there is currently no recommendable restaurant in Martinet. For meals, with your own wheels, you'll have to head north from the edge of Martinet, either 9km to **LLES** village, where there's **accommodation** and a **restaurant** at *Ca L'Abel* (☎973 515 048; ❷), or (forking left just below Lles) 12km to **ARANSA**, where you can choose between *Hostal Pas de la Pera* (☎973 515 001; ❸) or the adjacent *Cal Sandic* (☎973 515 193; half board only ❹), both of which have **restaurants** open to all. Both villages are the usual bases for their respective nordic ski centres, a few kilometres beyond.

The road to Andorra

The semi-autonomous principality of Andorra (p.862) is not much of a summertime goal in itself, and you'll get immeasurably better trekking (if that's what you're after) in the Pyrenees to either side. However, if you're curious – or in transit back towards France – the route there is a reasonably interesting one, covered regularly by buses **from Barcelona**. These end their run in La Seu d'Urgell, the last Spanish town before Andorra. You can also approach Andorra **from Puigcerdà**, by taking the bus west along the N260 to La Seu d'Urgell.

The bus service from Barcelona to La Seu d'Urgell is run by the Alsina Graells company (Ronda Universitat 4), and takes four to four-and-a-half hours. Whether travelling by public transport or driving yourself, the most interesting route is via Cardona and Solsona (see below) on the C26; this eventually joins the C14 for the final run up the Segre valley to La Seu. This route is the quickest if you're driving towards Andorra or the western Pyrenees, though less attractive than the roads further east.

Cardona

CARDONA lies about halfway between Barcelona and Andorra, and is dominated by a medieval hillside castle, whose eleventh-century chapel contains the tombs of the counts of Cardona. The castle has been converted into a *parador* (☎938 691 275, ⓦwww.parador.es; ❻), which would be hard to beat as a luxurious overnight stop, particularly since it also contains an excellent Catalan restaurant, where dinner runs to around €35 a head. Perhaps the most remarkable thing about Cardona, however, is its salt "mountain", the *Salina*, close to the river – a massive saline deposit which has been in existence since ancient times.

Solsona

Twenty kilometres further on, **SOLSONA** is a smallish, ramshackle town of considerable charm, with medieval walls and gates, and a ruined castle. The **Catedral** here is gloomy and mysterious, in the best traditions of Catalan Gothic, and has fine stained glass and a diminutive twelfth-century image of the Virgin, reminiscent of the Montserrat icon. Inside the adjacent seventeenth-century Bishop's Palace is the **Museu Diocesà** (May–Sept Tues–Sat 10am–1pm & 4.30–7pm, Sun 10am–2pm; Oct–April Tues–Sat 10am–1pm & 4–6pm, Sun 10am–2pm; €1.20), a collection of Romanesque frescoes, altar panels and sculpture taken from local churches.

If you want to break the journey to Andorra without splashing out on Cardona's *parador*, Solsona is probably the best place. The most central **accommodation** is the *Pensió Pilar* near the cathedral square (☎973 480 156; ❷), with a *comedor* attached, and the *Pensió Sant Roc*, Plaça de Sant Roc 2 (☎973 480 827, ⓕ973 480 006; ❸), just off the road to La Seu opposite the *Bar San Fermín* (where most buses stop).

The Segre valley and Organyà

Once you've left Solsona, and joined the main highway from Lleida (the C14), the drama begins. Amid tremendous mountain vistas the road plunges through the impressive gorge of Tresponts, lined with terraces of rock jutting out above. This journey upstream through the Segre valley alone makes the trip worthwhile, and Andorra starts to seem an alluring prospect by the time you reach La Seu d'Urgell.

Only one spot – **ORGANYÀ** – merits a brief stop en route. A small, round building (summer Mon–Sat 10am–2pm & 6–9pm, Sun 10am–2pm; winter Mon–Sat 11am–2pm & 5–7pm, Sun 11am–2pm) on the main road contains both the local **turisme** (☏973 382 002) and what is possibly the oldest document in the Catalan language, the twelfth-century *Homilies d'Organyà* – annotations to some Latin sermons, discovered in a local presbytery at the beginning of the twentieth century. If you get stranded here, there's *La Cabana* (☏973 383 000; ❷) **hostal** almost opposite, with a restaurant.

La Seu d'Urgell

The capital of Alt Urgell *comarca*, **LA SEU D'URGELL** lies beside the Riu Segre 23km upstream from Organyà. For years a rather sleepy place with a neglected medieval core, La Seu has undergone a mild transformation since the 1992 Olympic canoeing competitions were held nearby. There are two or three fancy new hotels, as well as the purpose-built canoe facilities by the Segre, but as most new development has fallen outside the old quarter, you should still be able to enjoy a fairly relaxed stay before sampling the excesses of Andorra.

The Town

Named after the imposing cathedral at the end of c/Major, La Seu has always had a dual function as episcopal seat and commercial centre – there's still a street farmers' market each Tuesday and Saturday, attracting vendors from throughout the *comarca*. A bishopric was established here as early as 820, and it was squabbling between the bishops of La Seu d'Urgell and the counts of Foix over local land rights that led directly to the independence of Andorra in the thirteenth century.

The original **cathedral** and city, on the hill where Castellciutat (see opposite) now stands, was destroyed in the eighth century by Moorish invaders. The present cathedral (June–Sept Mon–Sat 10am–1pm & 4–7pm, Sun 10am–1pm; Oct–May Mon–Fri noon–1pm, Sat & Sun 11am–1pm) was consecrated in 839 but completely rebuilt in 1175, and restored several times since. Nonetheless, it retains some graceful interior decoration and fine cloisters with droll capitals, which you can see by buying an inclusive ticket around the back of the church – €2.50 gets you into the cloisters, the adjacent eleventh-century church of Sant Miquel and the **Museu Diocesà** (same hours as the cathedral), containing a brilliantly coloured tenth-century Mozarabic manuscript with miniatures, the *Beatus*. To see only the cloister and church costs €1.

Other than these few sights, time is most agreeably spent strolling the dark, cobbled and arcaded streets west of the cathedral, where you'll find many of La Seu's better bars and restaurants. A strong medieval feel is accentuated by the fine buildings lining c/dels Canonges (parallel to c/Major); the town's fourteenth-century stone corn measures still stand under the arcade on c/Major.

Castellciutat

Fine views of the Segre valley can be enjoyed from the village of **CASTELL-CIUTAT**, just 1km west of town, and its nearby ruined castle (now a luxury hotel). Follow c/Sant Ermengol, cross the river and climb up to the village; there's a *pensió* on this road and another on Castellciutat's square (see "Accommodation", below) – either makes a nice retreat from La Seu. From Castellciutat, follow a path around the base of the castle and cross the main road for the nearby **Torre Solsona**; the scanty remains of the old fortifications are crumbling away here, assisted by quarrying below – take care near the edges. You can vary your route to Castellciutat or back by following the walkways through the pleasant, post-Olympic riverside **Valira** park: from La Seu, head west from Avinguda de Pau Claris (north of c/Sant Ot) to intercept it.

Practicalities

The **bus station** is on c/Joan Garriga Massó, just north of the old town; local services include the thrice-daily Alsina Graells buses to Puigcerdà and much more frequent La Hispano-Andorrana departures to Andorra (for details of which, see p.863). The **turisme** (Mon–Sat 10am–2pm & 5–8pm; ☎973 351 511) is on Avinguda de les Valls d'Andorra, the main road into town from the north. Drivers should use the handy free **parking** area signposted east of the cathedral.

Accommodation

In the wake of the Olympic facelift, almost no decent **budget accommodation** remains in La Seu. The standard seems set by *Pensió Palomares*, c/dels Canonges 38–40 (☎973 352 178; ❶), a warren of windowless chipboard closets, tolerable only if you can obtain one of the multi-bedded front rooms with balcony. Otherwise, there's only *La Valira* **youth hostel** (☎973 353 897; closed Sept), at the western end of c/Joaquim Viola la Fuerza beyond the *petanca* court, by the Valira park. The colossal **campsite**, *En Valira* (☎973 351 035; open all year), is 300m northeast of the hostel, at Avgda. del Valira 10.

Under the circumstances, you're probably better off at one of the **hotels** on the main roads through town. Best placed of these is the *Andría*, Passeig Joan Brudieu 24 (☎973 350 300; ❸–❹), an elegant if faded establishment with a range of rooms offering all mod cons. Less attractive, but friendly and adequate, is the *Pensió Cadí* (☎973 350 150; ❸) at c/Josep de Zulueta 4, close to Plaça de Catalunya. Top of the heap is the exclusive *El Castell de Ciutat* (☎973 350 704; ❾), now reinvented as a "wellness and anti-stress" spa, incorporated within the castle, as the name implies. The *parador* by the cathedral is shut indefinitely for refurbishment, so runner-up in the plushness sweepstakes is *Hostal La Glorieta* (☎973 351 045; ✉glorietavalirasl@tiscali.es; ❺), also in Castellciutat, with a pool and restaurant, and an eyeful of the valley, perched above the river on the road up to the village.

Eating and drinking

Traditional **tapas bars** are dying out in La Seu's old town: *Bar Eugenio* at c/Major 20 is the most reliable survivor, flanked by the sort of modern bar-cafés – *Café dels Escoberts* at no. 24, and *Cafetó* at no. 6 – which have displaced its rivals. For good-value **restaurant** meals, *Cal Pacho*, in a quiet corner on c/la Font (at the southern end of c/Major, then east), has a lunch *menú* and *a la carta* dishes in the evening – cod-stuffed peppers and roast goat will set you back around €18, dessert and drink extra.

Outside of the old quarter there's more choice. *Les Tres Portes* at c/Joan Garriga Massó 7 (closed Tues & Wed) offers nouvelle *a la carta* fare (allow €30) in a quaint chalet-style house with a summer patio. The *menjador* of the *Hotel Andria* also has gourmet *a la carta* dishes at similar prices, featuring home-reared chicken and mushrooms in season. Moving towards the snackier end of things, there's the *Bambola Pizzeria-Creperia* at c/Andreu Capella 4, just east of the main *passeig*.

Andorra

After seven hundred years of feudalism, modernity has finally forced itself upon the **PRINCIPALITY OF ANDORRA**, 450 square kilometres of mountainous land between France and Spain. A referendum held on March 14, 1993 (henceforth the big national holiday) produced an overwhelming vote in favour of a democratic constitution, replacing a system in effect since 1278, when the Spanish bishops of La Seu d'Urgell and the French counts of Foix settled a long-standing quarrel by granting Andorra semi-autonomous status under joint sovereignty.

Despite a certain devolution of powers – the counts' sovereignty passed successively to the French king and then the French president – the principality largely managed to maintain its independence over the centuries. The Spanish and French co-seigneurs appointed regents who took little interest in the day-to-day life of the principality. The country was run instead by the Consell General de les Valls (General Council of the Valleys), made up of appointed representatives from Andorra's seven valley communes, who ensured that the principality remained well out of the European mainstream – it even managed to remain neutral during the Spanish Civil War and World War II.

It was during these conflicts that Andorra began its meteoric economic rise, as locals first smuggled goods from France into Spain during the Civil War and, a few years later, goods from Spain into France under German occupation. After World War II, this trade was largely replaced by legitimate duty-free business in alcohol, tobacco and electronics, and by the huge demand for winter skiing. Much of the principality became little more than an unsightly, drive-in megastore, with the main road through the country clogged with French and Spanish visitors. Seasoned Spain-watcher John Hooper has called Andorra "a kind of cross between Shangri-La and Heathrow Duty-Free", while the Spanish daily broadsheet *El Pais* once dismissed it as a "high-altitude Kuwait".

Ironically, though, this **tax-free status** held the seeds of Andorra's belated conversion to democracy. Although the inhabitants enjoyed one of Europe's highest standards of living, twelve million visitors a year began to cause serious logistical problems: the country's infrastructure was sorely stretched and the valleys increasingly blighted by speculators' building sites, while the budget deficit grew alarmingly since little entrepreneurial wealth went towards the public sector. Spanish entry to the EU in 1986 only exacerbated the situation, diminishing the difference in price of imported goods between Spain and Andorra (which now typically measures about twenty percent). However, the damage has long since been done; Andorra's cancerous commercial growth has killed off any significant trade in the nearest French or Spanish towns.

The 1993 referendum was an attempt to come to terms with the economic realities of twentieth-century Europe. Or rather, some of the economic realities, since none of the parties involved in the negotiations and arguments seriously suggested that the solution would be to introduce direct taxation: there

Andorra practicalities

Getting there

From Spain, there are four daily buses direct from Barcelona (6am, 7am, 2.30pm & 7pm; 4hr 30min), and hourly services with La Hispano Andorrana from **La Seu d'Urgell** (Mon–Sat hourly 7am–8pm; Sun 5 daily between 7.45am and 6.30pm), taking forty minutes to reach Andorra la Vella, and another five to Escaldes.

From France, daily buses co-run by La Hispano Andorrana and Pujol Huguet leave **L'Hospitalet** at 7.35am and 7.45am, arriving at Pas de la Casa 25 minutes later; from **La Tour de Carol** there are departures at 10.45am and 1.15pm, taking 45 minutes to reach Pas de la Casa. During July and August only there is an additional service from **Ax-les-Thermes** at 4.20pm. From Pas de la Casa the onward bus journey to Andorra la Vella takes an hour.

Even if you're **driving**, consider leaving the car behind and taking the bus – in high season (summer or winter) the traffic is so bad that the bus isn't much slower, and parking in Andorra la Vella is an ordeal. On the plus side, **petrol** is famously cheap – about 12–15 percent less than in Spain – so fill up before leaving.

Leaving Andorra

Buses back to **La Seu d'Urgell** (Mon–Sat 14 daily between 8.05am and 9.05pm; Sun 5 daily between 8.20am and 7.20pm) leave from Plaça Guillemó in Andorra la Vella, parallel to the main road; buses actually originate in Escaldes. **To France**, La Hispano-Andorrana and Pujol Huguet run at least two buses daily from Andorra la Vella to Pas de la Casa (1hr) at 5.45am and 5pm, with services at 7.30am and 10.30am to La Tour de Carol. During July and August there's an additional departure at 1.30pm to Ax-les-Thermes.

Getting around

Internal **bus services** are cheap and frequent. The following routes run between about 7.30am and 9pm: Andorra la Vella–Sant Julià de Lòria, Andorra la Vella–Encamp–Canillo, and Andorra la Vella–La Massana–Ordino. Buses leave from Plaça Guillemó.

Currency, mail and phones

Andorra never had **money** of its own – both pesetas and French francs were accepted, and the euro is now the common currency. There's a shared, "foreign" postal system, with both a French and Spanish **post office** in Andorra la Vella and Canillo, for example. Andorra has its own **phone system** and phone code – ☎376 – applicable to the whole republic. A single mobile network, MobileAnd/STA, provides surprisingly good coverage even in the deepest valleys.

Language

Catalan is the official **language**, but Spanish and, to a slightly lesser extent, French are widely understood.

is still no income tax in Andorra, and barely any indirect taxes either. Instead, the strategy has been to transform Andorra into a kind of "offshore" banking centre, to rival the likes of Gibraltar, Liechtenstein and the Caymans, with the slight whiff of unsavouriness attached to such places.

Following the referendum, the state's first **constitutional election** was held in December 1993. Only the ten thousand native Andorrans were entitled to vote (out of a then total population of sixty thousand) and an eighty-percent turnout gave Oscar Ribas Reig, outgoing head of the Consell General, the biggest share of the vote. His Agrupament Nacional Democratic took eight seats in the new 28-seat parliament – also dubbed the **Consell General** – and formed a coalition with other right-wing parties to usher in the new democratic era. Since then, Andorran citizens (those born there, or who have lived there for over twenty years) can vote freely, and join trade unions or political parties, while their government now has the right to run its own foreign policy and establish its own judicial system; Andorra is a full member of the United Nations and the Council of Europe.

Given all this, it's useful to remember that as recently as 1950 Andorra was virtually cut off from the rest of the world – an archaic region which, romantically, happened also to be a separate country. There are still no planes and no trains, but the rest of the development has been all-encompassing: it can take an hour in bumper-to-bumper traffic to drive the few kilometres from La Seu d'Urgell to Andorra la Vella, the main town, while the large-scale ski resorts have already monopolized the most attractive corners of the state, with enlargements of existing ones mooted and a new resort planned for the beautiful Prat Primer upland. If you're curious, it can be worth a day or so for the cheap shopping, and it's worth getting at least a little way out of the capital to see some of the scenery that attracted early visitors. Don't expect to find an unspoiled spot anywhere, though, unless you're prepared to strike off up the mountains on foot – and if you are, there are much more rewarding places on either side of Andorra where you could shoulder a rucksack.

Andorra la Vella

Set at an altitude of over 1000m, **ANDORRA LA VELLA** – with its stone church, river and enclosing hills – must once have been an attractive little town. Today the main street is a seething mass of tourist restaurants (specializing in six-language menus), tacky discos and brightly lit shops crammed with everything from electricals, perfumes and watches to cars and kitchenware. There's partial respite in the old quarter, the **Barri Antic**, which lies on the heights above the river Valira, to the south of the main through road, Avinguda Princep Benlloch. But even here, the sole monument is the sixteenth-century stone **Casa de la Vall** in c/de la Vall (free guided tours Mon–Fri 10am–1pm & 3–7pm), which houses the Sala de Sessions of Andorra's parliament, and a small museum on the top floor.

Practicalities

Buses leave passengers on Avenguda Princep Benlloch, very near the church of Sant Esteve. There are about half a dozen public **car parks** scattered around town, should you bring your own vehicle; the huge covered car park at Planta de la Creu in the centre usually has spaces. The **turisme**, on c/Dr Vilanova (summer Mon–Sat 10am–1pm & 3–7pm, Sun 10am–1pm; winter Mon–Sat 10am–1.30pm & 3–7pm; ☎376 820 214), east of the Barri Antic, has lists of local accommodation, restaurants and bus timetables. There are several reasonable places to **stay**: the friendly, basic *Hostal del Sol*, at Plaça Guillemó 3 (☎376 823 701; ❶); the relatively comfortable *Hotel Florida* (☎376 820 105; ❹) with balconied rooms nearby at c/La Llacuna 15; and the *Hotel Racó d'en Joan*, in the old quarter at c/de la Vall 20 (☎376 820 811; ❷), which also has an attached restaurant.

A better plan, perhaps, is to linger just long enough for something to **eat**, since the intense competition fosters low prices. Best value in the Barri Antic is *Minim's* (*Casa Leon*; closed Wed Oct–June), tucked away in the tiny Placeta de la Consorcia, a small, stylish place with three *menús* of French cuisine. Another fairly central and characterful place is the basic and cheap *Restaurant Macary*, c/Mossèn Tremosa 6, just northeast of the Plaça Princep Benlloch, which does Spanish rather than Catalan dishes. The favourite spot for a cake and a drink is the *Granja Pastisseria del Barri*, opposite the church of Sant Esteve

If you do stay the night, there are two **cinemas** (at Avgda Meritxell 26 and Avgda Meritxell 44) and a live jazz **club**, *Àngel Blau*, in c/de la Borda.

Up the Valira d'Ordino

It's hard to convince yourself that not all of Andorra is like the capital (sadly, much of it is), but with a bit of effort you can effect a partial escape by heading up the **Valira d'Ordino**. At **LA MASSANA**, 7km out of Andorra la Vella, the road splits, the left-hand fork climbing up to the ski resorts of **ARINSAL** and **PAL**. The former is the most developed – with five daily buses from Andorra la Vella, 23 runs and a lively nightlife – while the latter is a pretty, stone-built village with a fine belfried Romanesque church (the ski centre is 5km beyond the village).

A right fork at La Massana leads to **ORDINO**, a quiet, agreeable place with a handful of old stone edifices amongst the new chalets and apartment buildings. Right opposite the free central car park, *Topic* is a combination restaurant-café-pizzeria-bar, serving supper until 10.30pm; continuing along the main street towards the church brings you to an alternative bar-restaurant, *Babi*. The *Hotel Santa Barbara* on the *plaça* (☎376 837 100, ℱ376 837 092; ❸) is an affordably priced place to **stay** here. Alternatively, 2km beyond Ordino there's a pleasant riverside campsite, the *Borda d'Ansalonga* (☎376 850 374, ℱ376 850 445; closed May & Oct), at Sornàs. Just before the campsite, there's another late-opening **eatery**, *La Farga/Les Gargues*, a good-value grill where the *menú*, including grilled rabbit and house wine, runs to under €20.

You'll generally have more choice of food and lodgings in the little villages of the valley proper, along the 8km or so north of Ordino; the landscape becomes more appealing here, with fewer tower-cranes and high-rises. There's also the partly Romanesque church of **Sant Martí de Cortinada** (daily 10am–1pm & 3–7pm) in La Cortinada to visit, with original frescoes. Reasonable **accommodation** en route includes the *Hotel Sucarà* (☎376 850 151; ❸) in La Cortinada, 2.5km north of Ordino; the well-worn but spacious *Hotel Arans* (☎376 850 111; ❷) in Arans hamlet, 500m beyond, near the GR11; and *Pensió Vilaró* (☎376 850 225; ❶; rooms with shared bath only), slightly isolated just below the village of **LLORTS**, some 5km from Ordino. Llorts also offers one of the better rural **restaurants** in Andorra, *L'Era del Jaume* (closed Sun eve; ☎376 850 667), which specializes in grills (€27 *a la carta*, plus a lunchtime *menú*).

El Serrat and Ordino-Arcalis

Eighteen kilometres (and three daily bus departures) from Andorra la Vella, **EL SERRAT** stands at the head of the valley, graced by some tumbling waterfalls. Here you'll find the last **accommodation** before the ski centre of Ordino-Arcalis, including the *Hotel Bringué* (☎376/850 300, ℱ376/850 773; ❹), and the *Hostal del Serrat* (☎376/735 735, ℱ376/735 740; ❹), which also has a well-regarded restaurant.

From El Serrat the road climbs steeply 5km more to the ski resort of **ORDINO-ARCALIS**, which retains snow well into April and is probably the most pleasant place to ski at intermediate level in Andorra, with a mostly Spanish, French and local clientele, and appealing views north over the Tristaina lakes and border ridge beyond. In summer, the area around the base of **La Coma** lift sees steady traffic for the sake of the half-hour walk north to the cirque containing the Tristaina lakes; after your exertions, the **restaurant** complex here is worth a visit (around €15 at the self-service, €25 upstairs at the full-service; open for lunch year-round except May and Nov).

The road to France: the Valira del Orient

It's around 35km from Andorra la Vella to the French border at Pas de la Casa, a route served as far as Soldeu by hourly buses from the capital. You're unlikely to be tempted to get off anywhere for casual touring, though there are a few possibilities.

Just 2km northeast of Andorra la Vella, **LES ESCALDES**, is little more than a continuation of the capital – cars, coaches, hotels and restaurants – though it does have an excellent spa complex to unwind at. On a shelf of land just to the north is **Sant Miquel d'Engolasters** (daily 10am–1pm & 3–7pm), one of Andorra's most attractive Romanesque churches, though its frescoes, like those of many Andorran churches, have been taken to the Museu d'Art de Catalunya in Barcelona. To get there, take the road that climbs to the dammed lake of Engolasters, passing the church after 4km.

Canillo

CANILLO, 14km from Andorra, makes one of the best compromise bases: along the main road (and bus route) between Andorra la Vella and the nearby ski resort of Soldeu-El Tarter, but far enough away from both to retain some dignity and character. On the eastern fringe of the town, most of the belfried Romanesque church of **Sant Joan de Caselles** (daily 10am–1pm & 3–7pm) is originally eleventh century, with a unique stucco-relief Crucifixion complete with sun, moon and lance-wielding Romans. Back in the centre, a warren of old streets north of the highway leads to **Sant Sadurní**, nearly as ancient. When snow levels are sufficient, a bubble-lift rises south up to **El Forn**, part of El Tarter ski centre (see above).

Hotels line c/General, the main through road, with a couple of budget choices: the rock-bottom *Comerç* (☎376 851 020; ❶) and the more comfortable *Canigó* (☎376 851 024; ❸–❹), just west. Among several local **campsites**, best is the tree-shaded *Camping Santa Creu* (☎376 851 462; mid-June to Sept) near the centre, on the south bank of the river. The restaurant at the *Comerç* offers French-style *table d'hôte*; alternatively, try the *Molí del Peano* (closed mid-May to mid-June & mid-Oct to mid-Nov), where €24 will get you grilled duck, goat's cheese salad, home-made mousse and a beer or two (they also have *menús* for €12.50–15.50).

Soldeu and Pas de la Casa

Development at **SOLDEU** village, 3km on, is surprisingly restrained considering that the adjacent ski centre is the largest in Andorra, with ample skiing for all ability levels amongst 47 pistes – it's the best place in Andorra for beginners, a fact appreciated by the British and Spanish families who seem to make up the main clientele. Once over the **Port d'Envalira** (though a tunnel is being prepared), the road tumbles down to the ghastly high-rise **PAS DE LA CASA**, a combination of duty-free bazaar and winter sports station and of not more than passing interest.

The Noguera Pallaresa valley

The **Noguera Pallaresa**, the most powerful river in the Pyrenees, was once used to float logs down from the mountains to the sawmills at La Pobla de Segur, a job now done by truck. These days, the river is known for its river-rafting opportunities, while the valley also provides an efficient way of getting

The main **rafting season** on the Noguera Pallaresa lasts from April until September, though some organizations offer programmes from March to October if snowmelt (and the power company) are amenable. The original rafts – used for the journey downstream to the sawmills of La Pobla de Segur – were logs lashed together ten-wide. Today's water-sport versions are reinforced **inflatables**, up to six and a half metres long. If you sign up for a trip – which guarantees a soaking and about as much excitement as any well-balanced person would want – you'll usually share a boat with seven others, including your guide/pilot, who sits in the rear.

The 14km between Llavorsí and Rialp is the easiest and thus most commonly rafted sector of the river, while the 18km from Sort to Desfiladero de Collegats is advanced and even more scenic. Daily **departures** are typically at 11am and noon; in the former case you'll be in the water by 11.20am, and clambering into the return-shuttle van at Rialp by 12.40pm. **Prices** start at about €29 for a two-hour rafting trip, either Llavorsi to Rialp or Sort to Collegats, or €50 for the entire 35-kilometre distance (a full afternoon's outing; packed lunch €13 extra).

into the high Pyrenees, particularly to the Vall d'Aran and the east flank of the Parc Nacional d'Aigüestortes i Estany de Sant Maurici. Access to the valley is easiest through La Pobla de Segur (see below), which can be reached directly from Barcelona or Lleida. Approaching from the east, there's a road (2 buses daily) from La Seu d'Urgell to Sort, in the middle of the valley (see p.868), through 53km of gorgeous scenery. Alsina Graells buses leave Barcelona (from Plaça de la Universitat) for La Pobla de Segur, a three-and-a-half-hour ride via dismal Artesa de Segre. It's better to take the regular **train** from Lleida to La Pobla – a spectacular ride behind a steam locomotive, with glimpses of cliff and water between spells in the many tunnels.

Tremp, Talarn and Santa Engràcia

However you approach, the first major halt in the Noguera Pallaresa valley itself is at **TREMP**, poised between two hydroelectric dams that supply much of Catalunya's power. There's accommodation here, a pleasant central square, and even a tourist office, but if you're going to be overnighting locally, there are far better spots to stay and eat – with or without your own transport – just outside of town.

Two kilometres northwest is the large, fortified hill town of **TALARN**, where the *Casa Lola*, c/Soldevila 2, shines as a beacon of country cuisine (meals €20 *a la carta*, plus drink), attracting clientele from near and far; proprietress "Lola" (Florita) is a character, giving free *pa amb tomàquet*-making lessons to the uninitiated. She also has several state-of-the-art, self-catering studios (☎973 650 814; ❸). Alternatively, if you have your own transport, you can head out from just below Talarn along a narrow but paved ten-kilometre road west to **SANTA ENGRÀCIA**, one of the most spectacularly located villages in Catalunya, tumbling off the south flank of a rock monolith. Here, the *Casa Guilla* (☎973 252 080, ⓦwww.casaguilla.com; closed Dec–Feb; half board only ❺), a restored rambling farmhouse with sweeping views, offers rustic, en-suite rooms – including a family quad – plus a mineral-water pool, restaurant and bar; reservations are advised.

La Pobla de Segur

Thirteen kilometres north of Tremp, **LA POBLA DE SEGUR** is a lively enough town if you want to break your journey, although most people only come here for onward connections. La Pobla is served by a twice-daily Alsina Graells **bus** from Barcelona (departures at 7.30am and 2.30pm from Plaça de la Universitat, labelled *Pont de Rei*), and by three daily **trains** from Lleida which terminate here. The bus from Barcelona continues up the Noguera Pallaresa through Sort and Llavorsí, passing within 7km of Espot, a major entry point to the Aigüestortes national park (see p.875). Arriving from Lleida, morning train and bus services should connect with this bus, which departs La Pobla at 11.40am; there's another service at 2.20pm. From June to mid-November, the first of these two bus services continues over the pass into the Vall d'Aran. As well as these buses along the Noguera Pallaresa, local services also journey west to El Pont de Suert, Boí and Capdella for the western margins of the Aigüestortes region, and to Viella through its namesake tunnel for the Vall d'Aran.

Trains arrive in the new town, from where you walk up the road, cross the bridge and head along the main street 200m towards the kiosk-shelter which is the terminal for the Alsina Graells bus company. Don't get stranded: there is nowhere to stay in La Pobla. There's a not especially welcoming but well-stocked **turisme** at the north end of town (Mon–Sat 9am–2pm).

Gerri de la Sal and around

From La Pobla de Segur the C13 road threads through the **Desfiladero de Collegats**, an impressive gorge hewn by the Noguera Pallaresa through 300-metre-high cliffs. Unfortunately, since a series of tunnels was blasted through much of the defile, drivers see little of the spectacular valley, though the narrow, abandoned old road is still open to cyclists and pedestrians. The Catalan intelligentsia have been coming here to admire the scenery since the 1880s, and the portion of the canyon labelled as **L'Argenteria**, with its sculpted, papi-er-mâché-like rockface streaked with rivulets, was apparently the natural inspiration for Antoni Gaudí's La Pedrera apartment building in Barcelona.

As the gorge opens out, you emerge at the rickety village of **GERRI DE LA SAL** – "de la Sal" because of the local salt-making industry. You'll see still-functioning saltpans by the riverside as you pass by, but the most obvious land-mark is the Benedictine monastery of **Santa María** (daily: Easter & June–Sept 11am–1pm & 4.30–7.30pm; rest of year by appointment on ☎973 662 068; €1.50), which faces the village on the far side of a beautiful old bridge. The monastery was originally founded in 807, though the present structure, with its huge and dilapidated bell-wall, dates from the twelfth century.

If you have a vehicle this is a good place for a short break, though Gerri only has a few rooms to let above the **restaurant-bar** on the through road. There are more facilities 4km north at the tiny village of **BARO**, including rooms and food at the *Bar Restaurant Cal Mariano* (☎973 662 077; ❷), plus a large riverbank **campsite**, the *Pallars Sobirà* (☎973 662 033; open all year), and a supermarket.

Sort, Rialp and Port-Ainé

SORT, 30km north of La Pobla, retains an old centre of tall, narrow houses, though it's now hemmed in by apartment buildings. This rapid development is owed mainly to the fact that Sort and neighbouring villages have suddenly found themselves among the premier **river-running spots** in Europe (see box on p.857). Every year during late June or early July, the communities of the valley stage the festival of the *Raiers* (Rafters), re-enacting the exploits of the old-time timber pilots who could still put the slick new daredevils to shame.

Because of the upmarket sports clientele it attracts, Sort has priced itself out of any casual trade, and in any case it's not a place to linger unless you're here for the action. Its main street is almost exclusively devoted to rafting and adventure shops – among these, *Rubber River* (☎973 620 220, ⓦwww.rubber-river.com) is reputable, and maintains its own hotel, the *Florido* (☎973 620 237; ❺).There's nowhere really inexpensive to stay or eat, though there is a **turisme** (summer Mon–Fri 9am–2pm & 5–9pm, Sat 10am–1pm & 5–8pm; ☎973 621 002) on the main street.The bus stops at an obvious shelter on Plaça Catalina Albert, at the north end of town where the two through roads join up.

RIALP, 3km north, is a marginally more appealing mix of old houses and new boutiques; the bus stop and ticket office here is the bar under the *Hotel Victor* (☎973 620 379; ❸), the most reasonable – if somewhat unexciting – place to stay. Fourteen kilometres northeast, the ski station at **PORT-AINÉ** offers some of the best beginners' and intermediates' skiing in the Catalan Pyrenees on its 28 longish runs.

Llavorsí

Probably the most attractive base along this stretch of the valley is **LLA-VORSÍ**, 10km above Rialp at the meeting of the Noguera Pallaresa and the Cardós rivers. Despite extensive renovation, a rash of new bars and restaurants, rafting outfitters on the main road and a mammoth power substation across the way, this tight huddle of stone-built houses and slate roofs still retains much of its character. There are two good riverside **campsites**, both with pools and bars: the *Aigües Braves* 1km north of town (☎973 622 153; March–Sept), and the smaller and basic but tent-friendly *Riberies* just east of the centre (☎973 622 151; mid-June to mid-Sept) – plus ample **accommodation** catering for the river trade (though in rafting season, it's best to reserve in advance).Try the *Hotel Lamoga* (☎973 622 006, ⓔlamoga@muntanyesdelpirineu.com; B&B ❹, half board preferred ❺) on the riverfront; the quieter, adjacent *Hostal de Rey* (☎973 622 011, ⓔmcaste@mixmail.com; B&B ❸); or the *Hotel Noguera* (☎973 622 012; ❷) on the opposite bank.The *Lamoga* also has the best **restaurant** in town, though the *a la carta* (€15–20) is much better value than the *menú*.The *Noguera*'s restaurant has river-view seating and a reasonable if rather limited *menú*.

Local **sports/adventure operators** offering rafting, canyoning, hydrospeed, mountain biking and rock climbing include *Yeti Emotions* (☎973 622 201, ⓦwww.yetiemotions.com), some 500m south of Llavorsí, on the west bank of the river opposite a road tunnel, and the central, friendly *Rafting Llavorsi* (☎973 622 158, ⓦwww.raftingllavorsi.com).

The Vall d'Àneu

From Llavorsí the road continues upstream along the Noguera Pallaresa, past the turning for Espot (see p.879) and the placid, artificial lake of Pantà de la Torrasa, to **LA GUINGUETA D'ÀNEU** at the head of the reservoir. This is the first of three villages incorporating the name of the local valley, the **Vall d'Àneu**.

ESTERRI D'ÀNEU, 4km further beyond the lake and – from late November to May, the end of the line for the bus from Barcelona – was transformed virtually overnight during the early 1990s from somnolent farming community to chic resort. Parts of town still form as graceful an ensemble as you'll see in the Catalan Pyrenees – the few huddled houses between the road and the river, an arched bridge and slender-towered Sant Vicenç church – but the new apartment buildings and fancy hotels to the south are another matter. For the moment Esterri's growth has stalled, tied to the overflow of the Super Espot ski clientele (see p.879) for its trade, but the just-begun expansion of the closer Baqueira-Beret resort (see p.871) could set off another spasm of construction.

Nonetheless, there are worse places to end up in the evening. The best-value place to **stay** and **eat** is still the delightful *Fonda Agustí* (T973 626 034; half board only ❹), in a quiet location behind the church at Plaça de l'Església 6, with an old-fashioned, popular *menjador*. Alternatively, try *Pensió Costa 2* (T973 626 401; ❸), or *Pensió La Creu* at c/Major 3 (T973 626 437, Wwww .pensiolacreu.com; ❸–❹), some of its rooms with river view. The closest **campsite**, *La Presalla* (T973 626 263; April–Sept), is 1.5km south of the village and has chalet huts available to rent.

València d'Àneu and the Port de la Bonaigua

Three kilometres further up the main road, now the C28, **VALÈNCIA D'ÀNEU**'s traditional stone houses and small Romanesque church are beginning to be overshadowed by modern development at the outskirts, as the long-mooted expansion of Baqueira-Beret shifts into gear. València was much more important at one time than its current sleepy profile suggests; an ongoing archeological dig on the outskirts has brought to light the remains of a tenth-century **castle**, apparently the power base of counts who ruled over many of the surrounding valleys. When the volunteer excavators are present in summer, visitors are welcome to have a look around.

The best choice for **accommodation** here – don't be put off by the odd Spanish coach tour – is the exceptionally good-value *Hotel La Morera* (T973 626 124, Wwww.hotel-lamorera.com; closed Nov, Feb & March; B&B ❹), with variable balconied rooms, a valley-side pool and wonderful breakfasts; supper is also excellent as long as you dine *a la carta* and shun the dull half-board *table d'hôte*. Honourable mention goes to the smaller, rustic-decor *Hotel Lo Paller* (T973 626 129; B&B ❸) on c/Major, in the village centre off the highway, with a pleasant rear garden. Another worthwhile spot to eat, a few paces down from *Lo Paller*, is *Felip*, with a €10 *menú* or an ample *carta*.

Beyond València, the road quits the Noguera Pallaresa as it climbs above the quilt of green and brown fields around Esterri; the Riu de la Bonaigua takes over as the roadside stream, lined by forests of silver birch, pine and fir. The views get ever more impressive as you approach the treeline, above which is perched the **restaurant-bar** of *Mare de Déu de les Ares* (daily 9am–6pm), next to the eponymous *ermita*; count on around €15 for lunch. Near the top of the bleak **Port de la Bonaigua** (2072m; usually closed in winter), snow patches persist year-round, half-wild horses graze and you get simultaneous panoramas of the valleys you've just left and the Vall d'Aran to come. There's a fine if somewhat strenuous full-day hiking circuit south from here via Estany Gerber through the Circ de Saborèdo, with its half-dozen lakes and staffed **refuge** (2310m; 18 places; T973 253 015), then back to the pass; drive or arrange a ride to or from the starting point, as bus timings are unhelpful.

The Vall d'Aran

The **Vall d'Aran**, with its luxuriantly alpine feel, is completely encircled by the main Pyrenean watershed and its various spur-ridges. Although it has belonged to Aragón or Catalunya – and later unified Spain – since 1192, the valley, with the Garona river cleaving down the middle, eventually opens to the north, and is actually much more accessible from France. Like Andorra, it was virtually independent for much of its history, and for centuries was sealed off from the rest of Spain by snow for seven months of the year, but in 1948 the Viella tunnel was finally finished (through slave labour provided by Republican POWs) to provide a year-round link with the provincial capital of Lleida along the N230 highway.

Since the early 1980s, life in the valley has changed beyond recognition. The old scythe-wielding hay-reapers of summer have been replaced by Massey Ferguson balers, overlooked by holiday chalets for city folk, which have sprouted at the edge of each and every village. Although the development is undeniably sympathetic – the new Aranese-style stone buildings fit closely with the originals – the vast numbers of chi-chi restaurants and sports shops sit incongruously with the little medieval villages they surround. By getting off the perennially congested main road through the valley it's still possible to get some idea of the region as it was fifty years ago, but even there don't expect virgin rural expanses. Aran is best regarded as a comfortable overnight or two en route to more spectacular destinations, and overall the valley is one of the most expensive, overdeveloped and (unless you're skiing) overrated corners of alpine Catalunya.

The valley's legendary greenness derives from the streams that drain into it – mostly from the lakes of Aigüestortes on the south slope – rather than particularly high rainfall. When the weather is wet, black and yellow fire salamanders move with unconcerned slowness on the damp footpaths; before and after the rain, equally brilliant butterflies, for which the Vall d'Aran and the Aigüestortes park are both famous, flutter about.

Among themselves the inhabitants speak Aranés, a **language** (not a dialect, as a glance at the bizarre road signs will tell you) based on elements of medieval Gascon and Catalan, with a generous sprinkling of Basque vocabulary. *Aran*, in this language, means "valley": Nautaran (High Valley) is the most scenic eastern portion. The Aranese spelling of local place names is given in parentheses below.

Baqueira-Beret

The ride down from Port de la Bonaigua isn't for the acrophobic or those with dodgy brakes, with its hairpins and sharp drop into the Ruda valley on one side. The first place you encounter coming down from the pass is **BAQUEIRA-BERET**, a mammoth skiing development that has served as the biggest engine of change in the region. The resort core itself is modern, posey (the Spanish royal family and government ministers frequent it), and has little to offer other than four- or five-star hotels, but it's no trouble to stay nearby at Salardú or Tredòs (see p.873) and show up for the skiing, some of the best in these mountains – at least until March, when the snow can get mushy. Day lift passes are among the priciest in the Pyrenees at about €28, but you are being pampered with a preponderance of chair lifts and an interlinked domain of 47 runs, with more in train on the east side of Bonaigua – the full story is at Ⓦ www.baqueira.es.

Salardú

SALARDÚ, a few kilometres further west, is in effect the capital of **Nautaran**, the highest of the three divisions of the Vall d'Aran. It's also the most logical base for explorations: large enough to offer a reasonable choice of accommodation and food, but small enough to feel pleasantly isolated (except in August, or peak ski season). With steeply pitched roofs clustered around the church, it retains some traditional character, though the main attraction in staying is to explore the surrounding villages, all centred on beautiful Romanesque churches.

Salardú's is the roomy, thirteenth-century church of **Sant Andreu**, set in its own pleasant grounds. The doors are flanked by the most ornate portal in the valley, whose carved column capitals feature birds feeding their young and four eerie little human faces peeping out; once inside, you can enjoy some fine sixteenth-century fresco patches, restored in 1994, including Christ Enthroned, the Assumption, various saints and smudged panels of the Four Virtues personified.

Practicalities

There's a wooden **turisme** hut (June–Sept daily 10am–1.30pm & 4.30–8pm) just off the main road at the turning for Bagergue. The one **bank** in the village has an ATM; there's also a **swimming pool** (mid-June to Aug daily 11am–7pm) if you fancy a dip. Even at the height of the summer you should be able to find a **bed** (if not a room) easily enough in Salardú. Dependable options aimed at trekkers are the *Refugi Rosti*, Plaça Major 1, in a 300-year-old building on the main square (☎973 645 308, Ⓕ973 645 814; closed May, June, Oct & Nov; ❹ half board in non-en-suite doubles; or €17 per person in six-bunk dorms); and the *Refugi Juli Soler Santaló* (☎973 645 016; €16 per person in four- or five-bunk rooms), 200m east of the tourist booth next to the pool. For conventional accommodation, try the *Pensió Casat* at c/Major 6 (☎973 645 056; B&B ❷), or *Residència Aiguamòg* at c/Sant Andreu 12 (☎973 645 996; B&B ❸). More upmarket choices include the *Hotel deth Pais* in Plaça dera Pica (☎973 645 836, Ⓕ973 644 500; closed May & Nov; B&B ❹), with underfloor heating and a few balconies; and, top of the heap for Salardú, the *Hotel Colomers* near the bank (☎973 644 556, Ⓕ973 644 170; B&B ❺), with designer rooms and a family suite.

Most of the places to stay in the village serve good-value **meals**: non-guests can eat excellent *menús* at the *Refugi Juli Soler Santaló* or *a la carta* dishes (about €25) at *Prat Aloy*, an across-the-river affiliate of the *Hotel deth Pais*. Alternatives are scarce, and the handful of village restaurants are overpriced. While the restaurant at the *Refugi Rosti* is decent enough, its main appeal is the nicest **bar** in town: *Delicatesen*.

Villages around Salardú

The bus from La Pobla de Segur gets into Salardú at around 2pm, leaving plenty of time to find accommodation and then strike off into the surrounding villages. Houses here are traditionally built of stone, with slate roofs, and there's surprisingly little to distinguish a 400-year-old home from a four-year-old one. Many display dates on the lintels – not of the same vintage as the churches but respectable enough, with some going back as far as the sixteenth century.

UNYA (Unha), 700m up the hill into the Unyola valley, boasts a shrine of the same age as the church in Salardú, though you're more likely to be interested in the half-dozen **restaurants** here, the most economical of which are *Es de Don Joan* and *Casa Restaurante Perez*. **BAGERGUE**, 2km higher up the road (or reached via the marked GR211 path from Unya), remains the most countrified of the Nautaran settlements, and offers yet another handsome church – plus several more **restaurants**. The most famous of these is *Casa Perú* (evenings only; closed May, June, Oct & Nov; reserve on ☎973 645 437), which deserves the plaudits adorning its entrance, thanks to offerings including an *olha aranesa* (hotpot) to die for, venison meatballs in wild mushroom sauce, wild-fruit flan with meringue, plus good house wine, all for €26 – far less than more pretentious equivalents in Salardú or Arties. Bagergue also has excellent-value **accommodation** at the *Residencia Seixes* (℡973 645 406, ⓦwww.aranweb.com/seixes; B&B ❸), whose wood-trimmed rooms fill quickly at weekends; it's at the entrance to the village, with relatively easy parking.

Across the river from Salardú, and about twenty minutes' walk upstream along the country lane signposted as the *Camin Reaiu* (King's Road), **TREDÒS** was once the prettiest of the Nautaran villages but has had its old core – including a massive church with free-standing belfry – overwhelmed by a rash of new ski chalets. In the centre, the *Restaurante Saburedo* is a find, with a hearty four-course *menú* for about €20. They also have en-suite and shared-bath **rooms** (℡973 645 089; ❷–❸) if you want **to stay**, as does the *Casa Micalot* (℡973 645 326; ❸) on the same lane. Much the smartest place here, though, is the *Hotel de Tredòs*, on the outskirts of the village (℡973 644014, ⓦwww.hoteldetredos.com; B&B ❹–❻), with a small pool and chalet-style rooms.

Arties

ARTIES, 3km west of Salardú, features the usual complement of recent holiday homes, with more under construction. Nevertheless, if you're driving, and Salardú is full up, it has considerable appeal, particularly in its old village core straddling the Garona, and its two **churches**: Santa María, with Templar fortifications, and deconsecrated Sant Joan on the main road, now home to a small **museum** of changing exhibits (Tues–Fri 5–8pm, Sat 10am–1pm & 5–8pm, Sun 10am–1pm; €1.50). Arties is also known for its high-quality food and lodging (see below), and for its **hot springs**, long shut down but recently sold and undergoing renovation. The *camí* leading past them (marked as the GR211.1) cuts out 3km of the busy main highway, rejoining it at Casarilh village, a boon if you're cycling.

The best budget **accommodation** is at the quiet *Pensió Barrie*, alias *Casa Portolá* (℡973 640 828; ❷), at c/Mayor 21 – three floors of wood-and-tile en-suite rooms. For more comfort, try either the stylish *Hotel Besiberri*, by the stream at c/Deth Fòrt 4 (℡973 640 829, ⓕ973 642 696; closed Nov; B&B ❹), with smallish but well-appointed rooms and lovely common areas; or the top-end *Hotel Valarties* at c/Major 3 (℡973 644 364; closed May to mid-June & mid-Oct to Nov; ❺), which should emerge from a year-long refurbishment in 2004. There's also a **campsite**, *Era Yerla d'Arties* (℡973 641 602; open all year), just below the village on the main road to Viella, considered the best in the valley.

Arties' seven or eight **restaurants** are also better value for money than those in Salardú, though many hike up their prices during ski season. Tried and tested options include *Montagut* (closed Tues all day and Wed lunch) up on the highway, with three *menús* (€10–23), the mid-range one featuring French pâté, carrots in mustard, duck *confit* and dessert; and the friendly, Zimbabwean-run *El Pollo Loco* (open Dec–April only), in the same building as *Montagut*, which offers four *menús* (including a vegetarian one) featuring local pâtés, duck, game and, of course, the chicken of the name, all washed down by organic cider. For something slightly more upmarket, try *Sidreria Iñaki* across the road for Basque-style grills, dishes and tapas like *alubias de Tolosa* and *bacalao*; or *Restaurant Urtau*, on the eponymous plaça, which has *a la carta* only for about €27. The same *plaça* is home to three **bar-clubs**, at least one of which should be going summer or winter.

Viella

From Nautaran, you move west into **Mijaran** (Mid-Aran), whose major town is **VIELLA** (Vielha), administrative centre for the whole valley and end of the line for the bus from Barcelona and La Pobla de Segur in summer. This arrives at 2.30pm, with the daily service in the opposite direction leaving at about 11.45am. You may also reach Viella from Lleida, via El Pont de Suert, a spectacular route in its final stages that culminates in the awesome **Túnel de Viella**, nearly 6km long and currently being widened to two lanes in each direction.

In truth, the ride to Viella from either direction is more attractive than the town itself, and there's little reason to stay, particularly if you have your own wheels or can make a bus connection onwards. Viella has become intensely developed and smartened up since 1990, a trend aggravated by the French customers of the numerous supermarkets, boutiques and restaurants. If you have time to kill, pop into the parish church of **Sant Miquèu**, right in the centre on the east bank of the Riu Nere; its twelfth-century wooden bust, the *Cristo de Mijaran* – probably part of a *Descent from the Cross* – is reckoned the finest specimen of Romanesque art in this part of the Pyrenees. The **Museu dera Val d'Aran** (Tues–Sat 10am–1pm & 5–8pm, Sun 11am–2pm; €1.50), at c/Major 26, west of the church and across the Nere, is also worth a look for its coverage of Aranese history and folklore. The only other potential diversion is the mammoth **Palai de Gèu** (Ice Palace) across the Garona, a combination swimming pool, ice rink, sauna and gymnasium (€11.60 admission to all facilities including skate hire).

Practicalities

Buses stop just downhill from the major roundabout at the west end of town. The **turisme** (theoretically open 9am–9pm all year; ☎973 640 110), is near the post office at c/Sarriulera 6, just off the church square, and offers maps and complete valley accommodation lists. As you might expect, there's no shortage of **accommodation** in Viella, but most of it is aimed at ski clientele, with little of outstanding value. Coming from the church, you'll find the best of the inexpensive places by turning left along the main street and then right down the lane just across the bridge towards a car park. Just off to the left, at Plaça Sant Orenç 3, there's the *Hotel El Ciervo* (☎973 640 165, ℱ973 642 072; ❸); the often full *Pensió Puig*, c/Camin Reiau 4 (☎973 640 031; ❷); and – most comfortable of all – the *Hotel Turrul* at no. 7 (☎973 640 058; ❸).

Least expensive and most central of Viella's **restaurants** is the *Basteret*, c/Major 6b, with a €12 *menú* or a more adventurous *carta* including ham-stuffed trout and blueberry cheesecake (€22 with house wine). For something a bit more upmarket, try *Eth Cornèr* on Passeig dera Llibertat 7, with *a la carta* fare, or consider the two-kilometre detour east to Escunhau hamlet, where *Casa Turnay* in the centre (closed May to mid-July & Sun eve; open weekends only mid-Sept to Nov) features Aranese-style game, fish and elaborate vegetable dishes (allow €25 per person).

Baixaran

You can continue from Viella by bus, car or bike through **ARRÒS** (6km) and **ES BÒRDES** (Era Bordeta; 9km), two places that play a key role in Aranese domestic architecture. Es Bòrdes supplies the granite for the walls and Arròs the slates for the slightly concave roofs that are generally demanded in Nautaran and Mijaran. Arròs itself, though, is almost in the lower **Baixaran** (Low Aran) region, and the balconied houses here, around the octagonal bell tower, have rendered white walls and red-tiled roofs. There are two mammoth **campsites** at Arròs – the *Artigané* (☎973 640 189; June–Sept) and the *Verneda* (☎973 641 024; June–Sept) – plus two smaller ones just past Es Bòrdes.

The focus of Baixaran is the large village of **BOSSÒST**, 16km from Viella, where the houses are strung out along the main road, alternating with tacky shops. There's no real reason to stop: it's only 4km to **LES**, with a spa and less expensive accommodation; 9km to the **French border** at Eth Pònt de Rei, and 20km to the first significant French town, Saint-Béat.

Parc Nacional d'Aigüestortes i Estany de Sant Maurici

Deservedly the most popular target for trekkers in the Catalan Pyrenees is the **Parc Nacional d'Aigüestortes i Estany de Sant Maurici**, a vast and beautiful mountainous area constituting Catalunya's only national park (albeit not recognized as such by international bodies, owing to its intrusive hydroelectric works). Established in 1955, and considerably enlarged between 1986 and 1996 to over 140 square kilometres, it's a rock- and forest-strewn landscape of harsh beauty, including spectacular snow-spotted peaks of up to 3000m, nearly four hundred lakes and dramatic V-shaped valleys. For the less adventurous, there are any number of mid-altitude rambles to be made through some lovely scenery. The Sant Nicolau valley and its tributaries (in the west) have many glacially formed lakes and cirques, as well as the water meadows of Aigüestortes (Twisted Waters) themselves. In the eastern sector, highlights include the Circ de Saborèdo and the Peguera valley, as well as the Estany de Sant Maurici, at the head of the Escrita valley. Just outside the park, in the so-called "peripheral zone of protection" of 270 square kilometres, are even more lake-spangled cirques.

The most common **trees** are fir and Scotch pine, along with silver birch and beech, especially on north-facing slopes. There's also an abundance of flowers in spring and early summer. As for the **fauna**, wild boar, fox and hare roam here and at the very least you should see *isards* (chamois); otters are considerably more elusive. **Birds** you might spot include the golden eagle, kestrel, ptarmigan and black woodpecker.

Which **approach** to the park you use rather depends upon which zone you intend to explore and how strenuous you want your walking to be. Access to the Sant Maurici zone is via the village of **Espot**, just beyond the eastern fringes of the park and within 7km of the main highway from La Pobla de Segur to València d'Aneu. The quickest access to the high and remote peaks is via **Capdella**, south of the park at the head of the Flamisell river – this is the next valley west from Noguera Pallaresa, served by sporadic bus from La Pobla de Segur. For the western Aigüestortes zone, the usual entrance is from **Boí**, approached via **El Pont de Suert**, which has regular bus service from La Pobla de Segur and Viella. Finally, from the Vall d'Aran, narrow roads, then tracks, and finally trails lead up from **Arties** and **Tredòs** to the Restanca and Colomers refuges respectively, on the north flank of the peripheral zone. It's somewhat boring hiking up to these, but at least you're not at the mercy of sparse bus schedules.

If you can afford only a day or two, and are strictly reliant on public transport, then Boí is probably the best place for which to aim. It's easy to reach, just off the bus line to Caldes de Boí, and though the village itself lies some 7km from the park entrance, the public bus past the La Farga trailhead or a 4WD-taxi up to Aigüestortes will solve this problem. All the approaches – and details of how to move on into the park – are dealt with fully below, while for **practical details** about the park itself check the box on p.878.

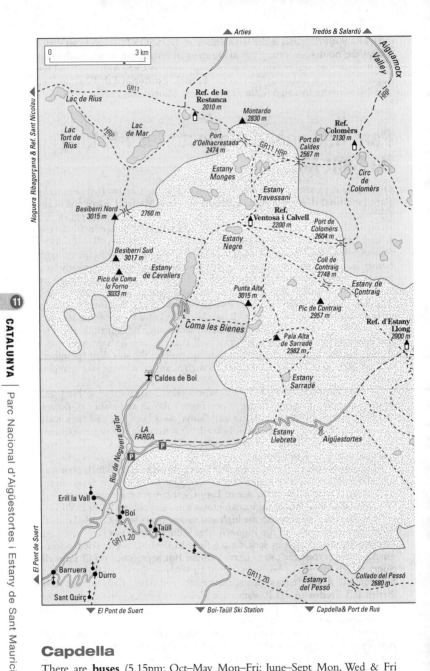

Capdella

There are **buses** (5.15pm; Oct–May Mon–Fri; June–Sept Mon, Wed & Fri only) operated by Alsina Graells from La Pobla de Segur to **CAPDELLA**, 30km upstream. The village, the highest of half a dozen in the little-known Vall Fosca, is in two quite distinct parts: the upper part has no facilities, while the lower,

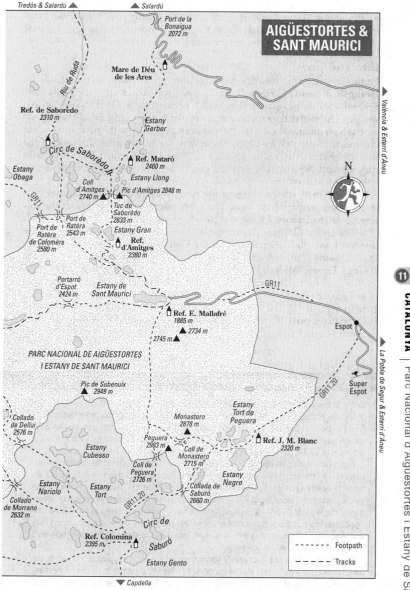

Tredòs & Salardú ▲

▲ Salardú

Port de la Bonaigua 2072 m

Mare de Déu de les Ares

Riu de Ruda

Ref. de Saborèdo 2310 m

Estany Gerber

Circ de Saborèdo

Estany Obaga

▲ Ref. Mataró 2460 m

Estany Llong

GR11

Coll d'Amitges 2740 m ▲

Pic d'Amitges 2848 m

Tuc de Saborèdo 2833 m

Port de Ratèra 2543 m

Estany Gran

Port de Ratèra de Colomèrs 2580 m

Ref. d'Amitges 2380 m

Portarró d'Espot 2424 m

Estany de Sant Maurici

GR11

Espot

Ref. E. Mallafré 1885 m

▲ 2734 m

2745 m ▲ ▲

PARC NACIONAL DE AIGÜESTORTES I ESTANY DE SANT MAURICI

GR11.20

Super Espot

Pic de Subenuix 2949 m

Collada de Dellui 2576 m

Monastero 2878 m ▲

Estany Tort de Peguera

Peguera 2983 m ▲

Coll de Monastero 2715 m

☐ Ref. J. M. Blanc 2320 m

Estany Cubesso

Coll de Peguera 2726 m

Estany Negre

Estany Neriolo

Estany Tort

GR11.20

Collada de Saburó 2660 m

Collado de Morrano 2632 m

Circ de

Ref. Colomina 2395 m

Saburó

- - - - - Footpath

- - - - Tracks

Estany Gento

▼ Capdella

2km below – where the bus stops – is based around the Central (de Energia), the oldest hydroelectric power plant in these parts, dating back to 1914. For **accommodation**, *Hostal Leo* (☎973 663 157; half board only ❹), originally built to host the power company workers, is fairly elegant if not especially welcoming; the friendlier *Hotel Monseny* (☎973 663 079; half board only ❹), 800m south and officially in Espui village, is newer but equally good value. Both lodgings are currently open only from Easter to November, although this may change if a planned ski resort for the area becomes a reality.

Into the park

From Capdella it's a half-day trek, past the Sallente dam, to the wonderful **Refugi Colomina** (2395m; 40 places; open year-round, but staffed only early Feb, mid-March to mid-April & mid-June to Sept; ☏973 252 000), an old wooden chalet ceded to mountaineers by the power company and set among superb high mountain lakes on the southern perimeter of the park. You can cut out much of the trek by taking the *teléferic* (cable car) from the back of the Sallente reservoir to within 45 minutes' walk of the refuge (July–Sept only, daily upward departures at 9am & 3pm, down at 1pm & 6pm; €6 one-way, €9.60 same-day return).

The immediate surroundings of the refuge have several short outings suitable for any remaining daylight. The more adventurous will set out the following day to **Estany Llong** and its refuge, via Estany Tort and the Collada (Pass) de Dellui (2576m). Alternatively, there's the classic (if difficult) traverse due north into the national park via the Coll (Pass) de Peguera (2726m), taking six hours. You end up near the base of the Sant Maurici dam at the **Refugi Ernest Mallafré** (1885m; 24 places; mid-June to Sept; ☏973 250 118), poised for further walks. If it's full, the comfortable **Refugi d'Amitges** is just ninety minutes away (2380m; 66 places; open late Feb, Easter & mid-June to Sept; ☏973 250 109). If you enter the park this way, there's a seasonal **information post** (Easter & July–Sept daily 9.30am–2pm & 4–6.30pm) by the Sant Maurici dam.

Park rules and practicalities

Entry to the park is free, but private cars are completely prohibited. The only means of vehicle access is via the reasonably priced 4WD-taxis which ply from designated ranks in both Espot and Boí. Driving yourself, the closest you can get are the 200-vehicle-capacity car parks 4km west of Espot, at the east boundary, or the smaller car park at La Farga north of Boí in the west, by the edge of the peripheral zone.

Accommodation in the park is limited to five mountain refuges (staffed with wardens during the summer – you'll need sleeping bags at all of them), but there are six more in nearly as impressive alpine areas just outside the park boundaries. Each refuge has bunk beds (about €8 per head), a meal service and a telephone or emergency transmitter. FEEC-managed places allow you to self-cater inside; CEC-managed ones do not. Be warned that most of the refuges are booked solid during July and August, and on most weekends from late June to early September, so you'll need to reserve weeks in advance.

Camping in the park is officially forbidden, and technically restricted within the peripheral zone – for which you're supposed to secure a permit from the nearest village – but as long as you pitch your tent well away from refuges and paths, nobody will bother you. There are managed campsites at Taüll in the west, and at Espot in the east. All the approach villages have *hostales*, *cases de pagès* and hotels.

The region is covered by several Editorial Alpina **map-booklets**: the two you'll need for walking any of the routes described below are *Sant Maurici* for the east, and *Montardo/Vall de Boí* for the west, both 1:25,000 and available in Boí, Espot and good bookshops throughout the Pyrenees and in Barcelona. You can also buy the two-for-the-price-of-one *Parc Nacional d'Aigüestortes I Estany de Sant Maurici*,

Espot and Super Espot

The approach from Espot is less strenuous, though purists (and people with heavy backpacks) will object to the possible necessity of road walking both the very steep 7km up from the turning on the main road where the Barcelona–Viella bus drops you, and the similar distance beyond the village to the usual park entrance. Wait for a 4WD-taxi at the turn-off and save your legs for later; it costs €4 per person for the short run up to Espot.

ESPOT (1320m) itself is still relatively unspoiled, despite decades of exploitation as a tourist centre. Two kilometres above the village is the ski centre of **SUPER ESPOT** (Ⓦ www.espotesqui.com) which, despite a northeast orientation, hasn't got a snow record to match most neighbouring resorts; many runs may be closed by March, and the whole place can shut for the day at 3pm.

The **park information office** (April–Oct daily 9am–1pm & 3.30–6.45pm; Nov–March Mon–Sat 9am–2pm & 3.30–6pm, Sun 9am–2pm; ☎973 624 036), at the edge of Espot, has **maps** of the park and information about trekking conditions. The best-value **accommodation** in Espot village is at *Casa Felip* (☎973 624 093; ❷), simple but very clean with most rooms en suite, plus laundry service and a small front garden. Other possibilities include the *Pensió La Palmira* (☎973 624 072; ❷) and the plush *Hotel Roya*, next to *Casa Felip* (☎973 624 040, ☏973 624 041; B&B ❹). There are three **campsites** close by: the smallish *Sol i Neu* (☎973 624 001; Easter & June–Sept), just a few hundred metres from the village, has excellent facilities, including a pool; *De La Mola* (☎973 624 024; Easter & July–Sept), 2km further down the hill, also has a pool; while at the far (upstream) edge of Espot, beyond the old bridge, is the tiny *Solau* (☎973 624 068), in the *barrio* of that name, which also rents out rooms at *Casa Peret de Peretó* (❷) – a good fallback if the village centre is full.

without the booklet. If you intend to approach from the north, you'll need the 1:40,000 *Vall d'Aran* Alpina map; a decent and accurate alternative is the Catalunya IGN 1:50,000 *Mapa Excursionista*. Sketched handouts available at the various park information offices are insufficient for route-finding – get a proper commercial map if you intend to leave the most popular paths.

Be aware of, and prepared for, **bad weather**, which, as everywhere in the Pyrenees, can arrive rapidly and without warning. In midsummer many rivers are passable which are otherwise not so, but temperature contrasts between day and night are still very marked. Local climatic patterns in recent years have alternated between daily rain showers throughout July and August, or prolonged drought, with a general trend (*pace* global warming) towards hotter, drier summers. The best times to see the wonderful colour contrasts here are autumn and early summer. Many passes, even those mapped with a bona fide trail over them, will be difficult or impossible without special equipment after a harsh winter, owing to lingering snow. If you're going to do a less common traverse, tell the warden of the refuge you'll be leaving, who should be able to give current **route pointers** and, if there's any cause for concern, phone or radio ahead to your destination to give an estimated time of arrival – and perhaps make you a reservation.

In **winter**, the park is excellent for cross-country and high-mountain **skiing**, though there are as yet no marked routes. The refuges usually open around Christmas and Easter, as well as on selected weekends and school holidays in between. There are currently two ski resorts on the fringes of the park: Boí-Taüll in the west and Super Espot in the east – with another planned for the slopes of the Pic de Llena southwest of Capdella.

Classic traverses

One of the classic hikes – accessible to anyone in reasonable shape – is right across the park from east to west, starting at the Sant Maurici reservoir and climbing over the Portarró d'Espot (2429m). To reach the jeep-taxi terminus at Aigüestortes it's about six hours' walking; if you have to hoof it all the way to Boí, allow ten hours. The **Refugi d'Estany Llong** (2000m; 36 places; open late Feb, Easter, June to mid-Oct; satellite phone ☎0088 21650 100090) is at **Estany Llong**, four hours along this wide track; there are some excellent day-treks from the refuge.

Committed and well-equipped trekkers will find better traverses from the east side of the park. Heading northeast from Sant Maurici on the GR11 path, you can reach the **Refugi de Colomèrs** (2130m; 40 places; open weekends Feb & March, daily Easter & mid-June to late Sept; ☎973 253 008), at the base of its lake-swollen cirque, within five to six hours via the westerly Port de Ratèra de Colomèrs (2580m). From the Colomèrs hut, most hikers continue along the GR11 for an easy but scenic day, partly in the park, to the **Refugi de la Restanca** (2010m; open weekends most of the year, plus daily Easter week and mid-June to late Sept; ☎608 036 559), a 1990s construction perched near its namesake reservoir; from here the **Hospitau Refugi Sant Nicolau** (1630m; open most of the year; ☎973 697 052), right by the main Viella-bound road at the southern mouth of the tunnel, is another four hours away along the GR11.

The fifth of the refuges within park boundaries, **Refugi Josep Mariá Blanc** (2380m; 40 places; staffed mid-June to Sept; ☎973 250 108), in the Peguera valley, is reached by a direct trail from Espot in around three and a half hours. You can continue to the Colomina refuge in another three and a half to four hours from here: this is a well-travelled route, marked as the GR11.20 variant trail. From Colomina the same trail continues generally west on a very long day to Taüll.

Quality **eating** opportunities are limited to the vine-shrouded *Ju Quim* in the centre, which gets jammed at lunch thanks to its €14 *menú*; and the *menjador* of the *Pensió La Palmira*. A cluster of "pubs" near the *Hotel Roya* provide some semblance of **nightlife**. There are also two well-stocked **supermarkets** and another shop selling maps, camping gas cartridges, and the like.

Into the park

From Espot, another road leads 3.5km to the park boundary and from there a further 3.5km to the end of the tarmac at the **Estany de Sant Maurici**. The GR11 trail avoids most of the road, or alternatively take a 4WD taxi – at €4 per passenger they're not a terribly expensive way to miss out some fairly dull road walking. Once at the lake, the classic postcard view is south, dominated by the 2700-metre-plus spires of **Els Encatats** ("The Enchanted Ones"), in legend two hunters and their dog, who snuck off to go hunting instead of to church on the day of the patron saint's festival, were lured heavenward by a spectral stag, and then forthwith turned to stone by a divine lightning bolt.

El Pont de Suert and the route to Boí

The route into the western area of the Aigüestortes park begins just past **EL PONT DE SUERT**, a small town 41km northwest of La Pobla de Segur: currently, there's an Alsina Graells **bus** daily in summer at 9.30am from La Pobla, as well as two daily services in each direction from Viella and Lleida; all buses stop at a terminal by the southeast edge of town.

The centre is dominated by an unmissably hideous modern church, erected in 1955 as a sort of perverse homage to the real Romanesque churches further up the valley. Otherwise, El Pont de Suert is pleasant enough if you have to spend the night before catching the bus north to Boí the next day (11.15am, daily June–Sept only), though you shouldn't need to, as the morning buses from Viella, Lleida and La Pobla are all designed to dovetail with the Boí service. The only **accommodation** in the old town is the *Hotel Mestre* at Plaça Major 8 (☎973 690 306; ❸), with a pleasant river-view **restaurant**, or the *Pensió Cotori* nearby on the post-office *plaça* (☎973 690 096; ❷).

Up the Vall de Boí

Some 2km northwest of El Pont de Suert, a good side road turns off to thread north along the **Vall de Boí**, following the Noguera de Tor towards Caldes de Boí, and passing the turn-offs for several villages on the way. It's an area crammed with **Romanesque churches**, the finest such specimens in Catalunya. The main disappointments are that most of their frescoes are reproductions, the originals having long since been whisked away to the Museu d'Art de Catalunya in Barcelona, and that the remoter churches open only for Mass, or guided tours offered by the local tourist office. Unless otherwise stated, the most-visited churches all have the same admission price (€1) and opening hours (summer daily 10am–2pm & 4–8pm; winter Mon–Sat 10.30am–2pm & 4–7pm, Sun 10.30am–2pm).

After about 8km there's a turn-off left to the village of **CÓLL**, up on the hillside, with its twelfth-century **Santa María de l'Assumpció**; the church's west portal and masonry are particularly fine, but the grounds are usually locked. Cóll is also where you'll find the family-run *Hotel Casa Peyró* (☎973 297 002; ❹, half board ❺), with one of the best **restaurants** in the area. It isn't cheap, but the food is worth it, especially the *entrantes*.

BARRUERA, 5km further on and much larger, has several places to **stay**, the least expensive being *Casa Coll* (☎973 694 005; ❶), an echoing old mansion near the top of c/Major in the old town. For more comfort, repair to *Hotel Farré d'Avall* (☎973 694 029, ℻973 694 096; ❸), also in the old quarter. Barruera supports the valley's main, well-stocked **turisme** (Mon–Sat 9am–2pm & 5–7pm, Sun 10am–2pm; ☎973 694 000), right opposite the petrol station. Just opposite the cramped **campsite** stands Barruera's Romanesque church, the riverside **Sant Feliu**, with its engaging thirteenth-century portal and creaking interior. There's another church 3km away in relatively unspoilt **DURRO**: **La Nativitat de la Mare de Déu**, with a massive bell tower and Lombard brickwork. You can eat here at *Casa Xoquín*, which does a reasonable *menú*, or tapas in the bar.

Further on, just before the turn-off for Boí, a one-kilometre side road leads west to **ERILL LA VALL**, whose twelfth-century church of **Santa Eulàlia** sports an unusual arcaded porch, and a six-storey belfry which rivals Sant Climent's in Taüll (see p.883); the interior is now done up as a gallery of sacred art, with a replica of a carved-wood twelfth-century *Deposition* given pride of place. In high season Erill is a relatively quiet base, more likely to have a vacancy than either Boí or Taüll, and thus far blessedly free of chalets at the outskirts. The top **accommodation** choices are next to one another in the centre: the recently refurbished *Hostal La Plaça* opposite the belfry (☎973 696 026, ℻973 696 128; B&B ❸), with a few family suites; and the plainer but serviceable *Hostal L'Aüt* (☎973 696 048, ℻973 696 126; half board only ❺), with a popular restaurant serving simple, but abundant, good-value food – go *a la carta*.

Boí

BOÍ stands 1km above the main road, which continues up to Caldes de Boí; buses usually take you up into the centre. On arrival, the village may prove something of an anticlimax: a minuscule medieval core swamped by a mess of car parks, modern buildings, and old houses defaced with new brick repairs. The twelfth-century church of **Sant Joan** has been extensively renovated, the only original parts being the squat belfry and part of the apse; the reproduction frescoes on the spandrels of the north aisle feature vivid animals symbolic of the Christian virtues, such as the camel of submission and humility.

One compensation for being based in Boí is that you're well poised to visit other local villages and their churches **on foot**. The non-GR path to Erill la Vall from Boí, across the valley, takes half an hour; the hiking route to Durro is the well-signposted GR11.20 path which you can pick up behind Boí village – it starts just over the little bridge at the back of the village and takes around an hour to follow. In the other direction, the well-signposted GR11.20 up to Taüll takes about forty minutes, greatly shortcutting the steep three-kilometre road.

Practicalities

Although Boí is the least prepossessing of local villages, you may want or need to **stay** at the beginning of (or conclusion to) a visit to the park. Despite being out of the way, one good choice is the *Hostal Pascual*, down by the junction and bridge, equidistant from Erill (℡973 696 014; ❷ with shared bath, ❸ en suite), with helpful owners and pleasant terrace seating for the *menjador*. In the village itself, the central *Hotel Pey* (℡973 696 036; ❹) is more comfortable. There are also some clean, modern **rooms** in a *casa de pagès* just through the stone archway in the old quarter – look for the *habitacions* sign.

Eating out, you'll not do better than at the *Casa Higinio*, 200m up the road to Taüll, above the village centre. Its wood-fired range produces excellent grilled meat dishes, or try the fine *escudella* (minestrone soup) and trout – a big meal accompanied by the local wine will come to about €13. None of the other restaurants attached to the various central lodgings is anywhere near as good value.

The **national park office** (April–Oct daily 9am–1pm & 3.30–6.45pm; ℡973 696 189) is tucked under an archway in the old quarter; you can buy maps here at a slight mark-up. The 4WD-taxis have a rank on the central Plaça Treio (book space on ℡973 696 314). The **bank** behind the supermarket has an ATM.

Into the park

It's 3.5km from Boí to the national **park entrance**, and another 3.5km to the scenic waterfalls of **Aigüestortes**, tumbling from their eponymous water meadows to feed the Estany Llebreta. A final kilometre above the falls – passed closely by both road and trail (see below) – there's another park **information booth** (July–Sept daily 9.30am–2pm & 4–7pm), next to which is a map-placard with various suggested **day hikes**; the most popular leads east to Estany Llong (1hr one-way).

4WD-taxis from Boí's square make the trip as far as the information booth; as in Espot, this costs €4 one-way, €8 round trip. Vehicles wait to depart until they're full; the last downhill return from Aigüestortes is at 7pm in midsummer, 6pm in spring and autumn. The closest you can get to the park boundary in your **own vehicle** is the car park at La Farga, or another, much smaller one 1.5km east right at the boundary. If you leave your car at either, and arrange for a 4WD-taxi to meet you and take you further uphill, at day's end you can follow the trail from the information booth (signposted for "Aparcament") which shortcuts the road by a good 45 minutes.

Alternatively, you can flag down the one midday bus from the junction of the Boí side road up to the spa complex of **Caldes de Boí**, 5km upstream, where the bus line ends. Nearby, the conspicuously high dam at the south end of Estany de Cavallers marks the trailhead for walks towards the beautiful natural lakes northwest of the park, just below Besiberri and Montarto peaks; the closest refuge is **Joan Ventosa i Calvell**, at Estany Negre (2220m; 80 places open mid-June to late Sept & some winter weekends; ☎973 297 090), just over an hour away and itself within easy reach of the Colomers or Restanca huts.

Taüll and Boí-Taüll

The character of **TAÜLL** has been altered considerably by the ski resort of Boí-Taüll, established on the mountainside a few kilometres to the southeast. There's an enormous holiday complex 1500m beyond the village at Pla de l'Ermita, en route to the ski station, and even in summer Taüll is a target for tour coaches and family cars seeking out panoramic picnic spots. But once away from the peripheral ski chalets, the village centre retains considerable character, and is certainly preferable to Boí as a long-term base.

Moreover, two of the best local Romanesque churches stand in the village. **Sant Climent de Taüll** is the more immediately impressive by virtue of its famous six-storey belfry and original triple apse. Inside, some original fresco fragments survive along with a respectable collection of religious art. Your admission ticket entitles you to climb the rickety wooden steps to the top of the bell tower for sweeping views through the delicately arched windows. At the heart of the village, **Santa María** (daily 10am–8pm; free) is very similar in design, though after a millennium of subsidence, there's not one right angle remaining in the building, with the four-storey belfry in particular at an engaging list.

Some 11km southeast of Taüll, the ski centre at **BOÍ-TAÜLL** (inaugurated in 1990) is the newest in the Catalan Pyrenees and the only rival to Baqueira-Beret for really serious skiing, with 41 pistes, more than half of them red-rated; accordingly it's not the best resort for beginners or weak intermediates. For more information, visit ⓦwww.boitaullresort.es.

Practicalities

Budget **accommodation** options, some part of the *cases de pagès* programme, include the en-suite *Pensió Sant Climent* (☎973 696 052; ❷), at the village entrance, which has limited parking (a problem in Boí) and four-person apartments; the upper-storey rooms are quieter. The *Casa Plano Minguero* (☎973 696 117; ❷) is well located in the upper part of the village, and again has its own parking. *Ca de Corral* (☎973 696 176; ❸), run by the sister of the *Bar Mallador* management (see below), offers en-suite rooms in an old house well situated in the lower part of the village. For something smarter, try *Pensió Santa María* (☎973 696 170; ✉santamaria@taull.com), a lovingly restored old house with garden studios (❸) and tastefully rustic upstairs rooms (B&B ❺), or the welcoming *El Xalet de Taüll* (☎973 696 095; B&B ❹–❺), whose big strength is the attic breakfast room and library with panoramic windows. A **campsite** (☎973 696 082; open all year), also offering bungalows, spreads attractively on the slope below Sant Climent.

Sant Climent's **restaurant** is justly popular for filling, no-nonsense feeds (*menú* under €10). *El Caliu*, at the top of Taüll, is well regarded for more careful cooking, and is still affordable at €13 for the *menú* or around €20 *a la carta*. Last but not least, just beside Sant Climent church, *Mallador* (closed May to early June & mid-Oct to Nov) is run by nice folk with good taste in music, and combines the virtues of being the most popular village **bar** (garden seating in summer), with elaborate snacks that make a meal, **Internet** access and a Romanesque-theme gift shop upstairs.

The South

The great triangle of land **south** of Barcelona is not the first place most people think of going when they visit Catalunya. It's made up of the province of Tarragona and part of the province of Lleida (the rest of which takes in the western Pyrenees) and, with the exception of the obvious attractions of the coast and a trinity of medieval monasteries, almost all the interest lies in the provincial capitals themselves.

Just forty minutes south of Barcelona, the vibrant **Sitges** is one of the few exceptions, boasting some fine Modernist architecture and bolstered by its reputation as a major gay summer destination. Beyond this is the **Costa Daurada** – the coastline that stretches from just north of Tarragona to the Delta de l'Ebre – which suffered less exploitation than the Costa Brava, and it's easy enough to see why it was so neglected. All too often the shoreline is drab, with beaches that are narrow and characterless, backed by sparse villages overwhelmed by pockets of villas. There are exceptions, though, and if all you want to do is relax by a beach for a while, there are several down-to-earth and perfectly functional possibilities, ranging from tiny **Cunit** to the region's biggest holiday resorts at **Salou** and **Cambrils**.

The Costa Daurada really begins to pay dividends, however, if you can forget about the beaches temporarily and plan to spend a couple of days in **Tarragona**, the provincial capital. It's a city with a solid Roman past – reflected in an array of impressive ruins and monuments – and it makes a handy springboard for trips inland into Lleida province. South of Tarragona, Catalunya peters out in the lagoons and marshes of the **Delta de l'Ebre**, a riverine wetland that's rich in bird life – perfect for slow boat trips, fishing and sampling the local seafood.

Inland attractions are fewer, and many travelling this way are inclined to head on out of Catalunya altogether, not stopping until they reach Zaragoza. It's true that much of the region is flat, rural and dull, but nonetheless it would be a mistake to miss the outstanding monastery at **Poblet**, only an hour or so inland from Tarragona. A couple of other nearby towns and monasteries – notably medieval **Montblanc** and **Santa Creus** – add a bit more interest to the region, while by the time you've rattled across the huge plain that encircles the provincial capital of **Lleida** you've earned a night's rest. Pretty much off the tourist trail, Lleida makes a very pleasant overnight stop: from here, it's only two and a half hours to Zaragoza, or you're at the start of dramatic road and train routes into the western foothills of the Catalan Pyrenees.

Sitges

SITGES, 40km from Barcelona, is definitely the highlight of the coast south of Barcelona. Established in the 1960s as a holiday town whose loose attitudes openly challenged the rigidity of Franco's Spain, it has now become the great weekend escape for young Barcelonans, who have created a resort very much in their own image. It's also a noted **gay** holiday destination, with a nightlife to match: indeed, if you don't like vigorous action of all kinds, you'd be wise to avoid Sitges in the summer – staid it isn't. As well as a certain style, the Barcelona trippers have brought with them the high prices from the Catalan

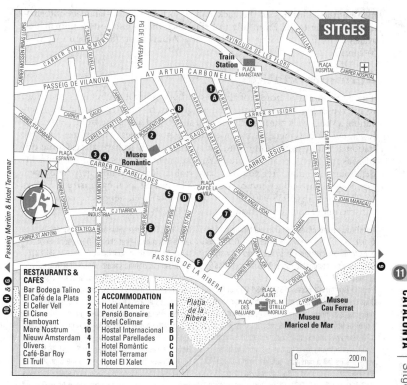

SITGES

RESTAURANTS & CAFÉS

Bar Bodega Talino	3
El Café de la Plata	9
El Celler Vell	2
El Cisne	5
Flamboyant	8
Mare Nostrum	10
Nieuw Amsterdam	4
Olivers	1
Café-Bar Roy	6
El Trull	7

ACCOMMODATION

Hotel Antemare	**H**
Pensió Bonaire	**E**
Hotel Celimar	**F**
Hostal Internacional	**B**
Hostal Parellades	**D**
Hotel Romàntic	**C**
Hotel Terramar	**G**
Hotel El Xalet	**A**

capital – the bars, particularly, can empty the deepest wallets – while finding anywhere to stay (at any price) can be a problem unless you arrive early in the day or book well in advance. None of this deters the varied and generally well-heeled visitors, however, and nor should it, since Sitges as a sort of Barcelona-on-Sea is definitely worth experiencing for at least one night.

The town itself is reasonably attractive – a former fishing village whose pleasing houses and narrow streets have attracted artists and opted-out intellectuals for a century or so. The beaches, though crowded, are far from oppressive, and the town has a smattering of cultural interest.

Arrival and information

Trains to Sitges leave Barcelona-Sants every ten to twenty minutes throughout the day; the station is about ten minutes' walk from the town centre and seafront. **Buses** stop in front of the train station, except those to and from Barcelona which stop outside the main turisme. If you're driving, it's probably best to pay for a **car park** rather than leave your vehicle on the street: car parks are marked on the map.

On arrival, the **turisme** (July to mid-Sept daily 9am–9pm; mid-Sept to June Mon–Fri 9am–2pm & 4–6.30pm, Sat 10am–1pm; ☏938 945 004 or 938 944 251, ⓦwww.sitgestur.com), at c/Sínia Morera 1, is worth a visit for the useful map with local listings on the back, and all sorts of English-language information about the town. From July to September, there's also tourist information available from a building on Plaça de l'Ajuntament (daily 10am–1pm & 5–9pm).

Accommodation

There are dozens of **hotels** of all types and prices in Sitges, but it's a good idea to reserve in high season as they fill up quickly. If you arrive without a reservation, a short walk through the central streets and along the front (particularly Passeig de la Ribera) reveals most of the possibilities – the places near the station are not exactly glamorous, but are more likely to have space. Come **out of season** (after Oct and before May) and the high prices tend to soften a little, though in midwinter you may have real difficulty finding anywhere open, especially at the budget end of the scale. The nearest local **campsite** is *El Rocà* (☎938 940 150, ℱ938 940 150; late March–Oct), well signposted north of the turisme under the railway bridge.

Hotel Antemare c/Mare de Déu del Montserrat 50 ☎938 947 000, ⓦwww.antemare.com. One street back from the sea, this classy hotel has very stylish rooms at reasonable rates. Also offers thalassotherapy. ❼

Pensió Bonaire c/Bonaire 31 ☎938 945 326. Just back from the sea, this tiny *pensió* is one of the least expensive around. Open April–Sept. ❸

Hotel Celimar Passeig de la Ribera 20 ☎938 110 170, ⓦwww.hotelcelimar.com. Pleasant seafront hotel, worth trying for a balconied room with a view. Prices fall a category outside high season. ❼

Hostal Internacional c/Sant Francesc 52 ☎938 942 690, ℱ938 947 331. Clean and simple place where the family owners have made a bit of effort with the decor, the rooms are light and crisp. Nearer the station than the beach, but not massively inconvenient. Open all year. ❸

Hostal Parellades c/de les Parellades 11 ☎938

940 891. The large, airy rooms and decent location make this a good first choice. Open April–Sept. ❷

Hotel Romàntic c/Sant Isidre 33 ☎938 948 375, ⓔromantic@hotelromantic.com. Attractive, old converted nineteenth-century villa in the quiet streets away from the front, not far from the train station. It's a favourite with gay visitors. Many rooms have a terrace overlooking the gardens; those with showers are in the next category. Open April to mid-Oct. ❺

Hotel Terramar Passeig Marítim 80 ☎938 940 050, ⓦwww.hotelterramar.com. Superb position at the end of the long promenade, and splendid views from its large, balconied rooms. Open April–Dec. ❼

Hotel El Xalet c/Illa de Cuba 33–35 ☎938 110 070, ℱ938 945 579. Charming, discreet hotel in a beautiful *modernista* house near the train station. There are only ten rooms – booking ahead is a necessity in summer. Price includes breakfast. ❺

The Town

It's the **beach** that brings most people to Sitges, and it's not hard to find, with two strands right in town, to the west of the church. From here, a succession of beaches of varying quality and crowdedness stretches west as far as the *Hotel Terramar*, a couple of kilometres down the coast. A long seafront promenade, the **Passeig Marítim**, runs all the way there, and all along there are beach bars, restaurants, showers and watersports facilities. Beyond the hotel, following the train line, you eventually reach the more notorious nudist beaches, a couple of which are exclusively gay.

Back in town, it's worth climbing up the knoll overlooking the beaches, topped by the Baroque parish church – known as *La Punta* – and a street of old whitewashed mansions, known locally as the Corner of Calm. One contains the **Museu Cau Ferrat**, an art gallery for want of a better description. Home and workshop to the artist and writer Santiago Rusiñol (1861–1931), its two floors contain a massive jumble of his own paintings, as well as sculpture, painted tiles, drawings and various collected odds and ends, such as the

All **museums** in Sitges have the same opening hours and prices: mid-June to mid-Oct daily 9am–9pm; mid-Oct to mid-June Tues–Fri 10am–1.30pm & 4–9pm, Sat 10am–7pm, Sun 10am–3pm; €3 each (free first Wed of month) or €4.80 for a **combined ticket** for all the museums, valid for a month.

decorative ironwork Rusiñol brought back in bulk from the Pyrenees. Two of his better buys were the minor El Grecos at the top of the stairs on either side of a crucifix. The museum also contains works by the artist's friends (including Picasso) who used to meet in the *Els Quatre Gats* bar in Barcelona.

Two other museums are worth giving a whirl on a rainy day. The **Museu Maricel de Mar**, next door to the Museu Cau Ferrat, has more minor art-works, medieval to modern, and maintains an impressive collection of Catalan ceramics and sculpture. More entertaining is the **Museu Romàntic** (guided tour every hour), which aims to show the lifestyle of a rich Sitges family in the eighteenth and nineteenth centuries by displaying some of their furniture and possessions. It's full of nineteenth-century knick-knacks, including a set of working music boxes and a collection of antique dolls. The museum is right in the centre of town, at c/Sant Gaudenci 1, off c/Bonaire.

A date worth noting in your diary is the **International Film Festival**, held in a number of venues around the town, which runs for about ten days between October and November (exact dates change, information and venues from the turisme) every year. Originally a horror and fantasy film extravaganza, it has grown to embrace a wide range of genres and attracts some big-name actors and directors.

Restaurants

International tourism has left its mark on Sitges: multilingual and "international" menus, a euphemism for burgers, are everywhere. Fortunately there are also some good **restaurants** here, with a fairly wide range of cuisines and quality, and some reasonable *menús del día*. Good general areas to explore are the side streets around the church, and the beachfront for more expensive seafood restaurants. For picnic supplies, the town's **market** – the Mercat Nou – is very close to the train station, on Avinguda Artur Carbonell. **Ice-cream** fiends should check out *Dino's*, on Passeig de la Ribera, *Italiana*, c/Jesús, or *Heladería* and *Il Gelatieri*, both on c/Parellades.

El Celler Vell c/Sant Bonaventura 21. Very good Catalan food served in rural-chic surroundings. Around €22 a head or there's a very good-value €8.80 *menú*.

El Cisne c/Sant Pere 4 (junction with c/de les Parellades). Nothing adventurous here, but you'll get well-cooked food in a dining room at the back of the bar – around €12 for the *menú del día*.

Flamboyant c/Pau Barrabeig, off c/Carreta. Rather expensive, but with a beautiful garden setting. Around €25–32 a head unless you go for the €18 *menú*. Open daily from 8.30pm.

Mare Nostrum Passeig de Ribeira 60. Long-established fish restaurant situated on the seafront, with a menu that changes according to the catch and season. Around €25 a head, unless you stick to the *platos del día*.

Nieuw Amsterdam c/de les Parellades 70. Medium-priced Indonesian and Dutch specialities.

Olivers c/Illa de Cuba 39. A mid-priced Spanish, rather than Catalan, restaurant, but the menu has some interesting flourishes that make the food memorable. Meals from around €24 a head. Open daily from 8.30pm.

El Trull c/Mossèn Félix Clarà 3, off c/Major. Fairly pricey French-style restaurant in the old town, though with careful selection you could get away with around €15 for a meal.

Bars and nightlife

The main part of the action in Sitges is concentrated in a block of streets just back from the sea in the centre of town. Late-opening bars started to spring up here in the late-1950s: today, **c/1er (Primer) de Maig** (marked as c/Dos de Mayo on some old maps) and its continuation, **c/Marqués de Montroig**, are fully pedestrianized, while c/de les Parellades and c/Bonaire complete the block – not somewhere to come if you're looking for a quiet drink. This is basically one long run of disco-bars, pumping music out into the late evening, interspersed with the odd restaurant or fancier cocktail bar, all with outdoor tables vying for your custom. The bars are all loud and their clientele predominantly young, and you can choose from just about any style you care to imagine. More **genteel bars** are not so easy to come by, though the places right on the seafront are generally quieter.

Afrika c/1er de Maig 7. One of the best of the music bars despite an unprepossessing entrance, it's popular with a house crowd.

Atlántida Sector Terramar, 3km out of town. The town's favourite club, the cliff-top *Atlántida* can be reached on regular buses which run there and back all night from the bottom of c/1er de Maig.

Bar Bodega Talino c/de les Parellades 72. A good, traditional tapas bar.

Café-Bar Roy c/de les Parellades 9. An old-fashioned café with dressed-up waiters and marble tables. It's good for breakfast, or for a glass of *cava* and a fancy snack.

El Café de la Plata Pg. d'Aiguadolç 47. Upmarket tapas bar with a small but interesting menu.

Otto Zutz Port d'Aiguadolç. One of Barcelona's most stylish clubs transposed onto Sitges with terrific views of the beach.

Parrots Pub Plaça de la Industria. Stylish bar at the top of c/1er de Maig that's a required stop at some point of the day; it's just one place you can pick up the free gay map of Sitges (see below).

The gay scene

The **gay scene** in Sitges is frenetic and ever-changing, but chronicled on a gay map of town available from *Parrots Pub* in Plaça Indústria, as well as from several other bars and clubs. Most of the bars and clubs are centred around Plaça Indústria and in the triangle made up by c/Espalter, c/Sant Francesc and c/Parellades.

During the day, a favourite hang-out is the *Picnic Bar* on Passeig de la Ribera, popular for its sandwiches. By early **evening**, everyone's moved on to *Parrots Pub* for cocktails and then to *Bar Seven*, at c/Nou 7, before moving on to **later venues** and clubs. Currently popular bars include *Piano Bar*, c/Sant Bonaventura 37, and *B Side* at c/Sant Gaudenci 7; while *Bourbons*, c/Sant Buenaventura 9, and *Bar Azul* (at no. 10), where gay women are welcome, remain favourites. On c/Joan Tarrida, a bar and club has opened for gay women at *Marypili*. The best gay clubs are *Trailer* at c/Àngel Vidal 14, and *Organic* at c/Bonaire 5.

Carnaval

Carnaval in Sitges (Feb/March) is outrageous, thanks largely to the gay populace. The official programme of parades and masked balls is complemented by an unwritten but widely recognized schedule of events. The climax is the Tuesday late-night parade, in which exquisitely dressed drag queens swan about the streets in high heels, twirling lacy parasols and coyly fanning themselves. Bar doors stand wide open, bands play, and processions and celebrations go on until four in the morning; *Bar Seven* has photos of parades from days gone by if you miss the action.

Listings

Banks Banco Español de Credito, Plaça Cap de Vila 9; Banco de Sabadell, Plaça Cap de Vila 7; La Caixa, c/de les Parellades 16.

Cinema Casino Prado, c/Francesc Gumà 4, and El Retiro, c/Àngel Vidal 13.

Hospital Hospital Sant Camil, c/de Puigmolte ☎938 960 025; in emergencies, call Ambulancis Urgències ☎904 100 904.

Pharmacist Two central *farmacias* are Ferret de Querol, c/de les Parellades 1, and Planas, c/Artur Carbonell 30.

Police Plaça de l'Ajuntament ☎938 117 625.

Post office Plaça Espanya (Mon–Fri 8am–2.30pm, Sat 9.30am–1pm).

Taxis There's a rank outside the train station (☎938 941 329), and you should find someone prepared to take you to/from Barcelona airport, which is 30km away.

Train information Call ☎934 900 202.

Vilanova i la Geltrú

Eight kilometres south down the coast is the large fishing port of **VILANOVA I LA GELTRÚ**. Sitges gets most of its fish from here, but Vilanova borrows little in return – this is a real working port, whose quayside is lined with huge trucks waiting to load the catches from the hundreds of boats moored alongside. Although the town itself is nothing special, it's fascinating to wander along the docks through the scattered fishing nets, and when you tire of this there's a tourist side to Vilanova which is a pleasant contrast to the excesses of Sitges. There are two **beaches**: one beyond the port, the second – better – at the end of the seafront promenade.

You might be tempted by Vilanova's fair smattering of **museums**, two of which are found right next to the train station: one of Spain's few railway museums is to the right on Plaça Eduard Maristany (July–Sept Tues–Fri 11am–2pm & 5–8pm; Sept–June Tues–Fri 10.30am–2.30pm, Sat 10.30am–2.30pm & 4–6.30pm; €2.20), which is diverting enough to tempt even non-enthusiasts, and the **Biblioteca Museu Balaguer** (June–Sept Tues–Sat 10am–1.30pm & 4.30–7pm, Sun 10am–1.30pm, Wed closes 8.30pm; Oct–May Tues–Sat 10am–1.30pm & 4–6.30pm, Sun 10am–1.30pm, Wed closes 8.30pm; €2.20) to the left, founded by a local nineteenth-century politician. This is actually a quite rewarding stop, featuring archeological finds up to the Roman era alongside a hoard of Catalan nineteenth- and twentieth-century paintings. Best of all, though, is the town's **Museu Romàntic Can Papiol**, on c/Major 32, behind the church at the very top of the Rambla Principal (Tues–Sat 10am–1pm & 4–6pm, Sun 10am–2pm; €2.20). It's the sister museum to the one in Sitges, and the entrance fee includes a guided tour around the lavishly furnished eighteenth-century town house in which the collection is housed.

Practicalities

Trains and **buses** run about every twenty to thirty minutes from Sitges, and there are daily bus connections between Vilanova and Vilafranca del Penedés if you want to take an inland loop back to Barcelona; the main **bus** stop is in front of the train station. The port is on the left, while to the right is the Passeig Marítim where you'll find the **turisme** (July & Aug Mon–Sat 10am–8pm, Sun 10am–2pm; Sept–July Mon–Sat 10am–2pm & 5–8pm, Sun 10am–2pm; ☎938 154 517, ⓔturismevng@readysoft.es) on Pg. del Carme.

For somewhere to **stay**, the best choices are *Hotel Ceferino* (☎938 151 719, ⓕ938 158 931; ⓺), overlooking the beach at Pg. Ribes Roges 2–3, or the more economical *Hotel Ricard* (☎938 157 100, ⓕ938 159 957; ⓸), with views over the port. Vilanova also has three **campsites**, including the friendly beach-based *Platja Vilanova* (℡ & Ⓕ 938 950 767; June–Sept). There are a dozen or so **restaurants** along the seafront *passeig*, which on the whole are better value than the equivalents in Sitges. All have outdoor seating, and while the views may not be quite so special as further up the coast, the atmosphere is a lot more down to earth. Good choices are the *Daviana*, at no. 104, which offers a hearty *menú del día* for around €12 or a terrific paella for the same price, and *La Platja*, at no. 39, which has a relaxing terrace and serves good seafood, paella and *fideuà*.

Cunit, Puerta Romana and Torredembarra

If the beaches so far seem too crowded and frenetic – a distinct possibility in high season – there are a couple of other possible stops before Tarragona. Travelling by train, make sure you catch a local and not an express which will run straight through.

CUNIT, about 15km south of Sitges, is the first stop inside Tarragona province. Rather soulless – more a collection of villas than a village – nonetheless it has a good, long beach. There's a **campsite**, *Mar de Cunit* (℡ 977 674 058; June–Sept), behind the beach and a few good places **to stay**: *Hostal La Diligencia* at Plaça Major 4 (℡ 977 674 081, Ⓕ 977 675 235; ❹), opposite the church in the centre, or *Los Hunos* (℡ 977 161 280, Ⓕ 977 164 240; ❻), on the seafront at Avgda. Mediterrani 6. Both have reasonable restaurants.

Again little more than a few streets of villas, the hamlet of **PUERTA ROMANA**, 15km before Tarragona, has perhaps the best swimming and sunbathing on this stretch of coast, with clean sand and clear water. It's not on the map or signposted from the main road, and the nearest train station is at the small resort of **TORREDEMBARRA**, 4km south, which also has a good beach in the dunes of Platja Muntanyans. Torredembarra itself makes a reasonable stop for a wander about the old town, with its 400-year-old castle, twelfth-century tower and a pair of gateways left standing from the original medieval walls. If you feel like **staying**, *Hotel Morros* at c/Pérez Galdós 15 (℡ 977 640 225, Ⓦ www.morros.es; ❺) is a comfortable if down-to-earth option, while *Costa Fina* (℡ 977 640 075, Ⓕ 977 640 559; ❹), Avgda. Montserrat 33, offers good value for money. For campers, the simple *Gavina* (℡ 977 801 503; April–Oct) is right on the beach at Puerta Romana.

Tarragona

Sited on a rocky hill, sheer above the sea, **TARRAGONA** is an ancient place. Settled originally by Iberians and then Carthaginians, it was later used as the base for the Roman conquest of the peninsula, which began in 218 BC with Scipio's march south against Hannibal. The fortified city became an imperial resort and, under Augustus, *Tarraco* became capital of Rome's eastern Iberian province – the most elegant and cultured city of Roman Spain, boasting at its peak a quarter of a million inhabitants. Temples and monuments were built in and around the city and, despite a history of seemingly constant sacking and looting since Roman times, it's this distinguished past which still asserts itself throughout modern Tarragona.

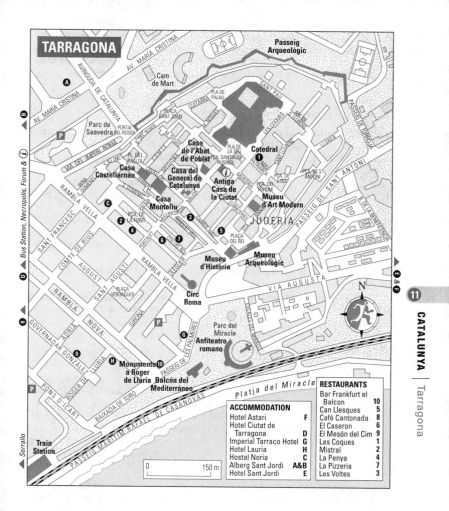

TARRAGONA

Passeig Arqueològic

AV. MARIA CRISTINA

AVINGUDA DE CATALUNYA

Cam de Mart

SANT PAU

PLA DE PALAU

PLAÇA SANT JOAN

GUITARRA

LES COQUES

Parc de Saavedra

PORTAL DEL ROSER

VIA DEL IMPERI ROMA

Casa de l'Abat de Poblet

PLA DE LA SEU

PÇA. SANTIAGO RUSIÑOL

Catedral

RAMBLA VELLA

Casa Castellárnau

Casa del General de Catalunya

Antiga Casa de la Ciutat

PÇA. DEL FORUM

Museu d'Art Modern

Casa Montoliu

PÇA. DE LA FONT

JUDERIA

PLAÇA DEL REI

Museu d'Història

Museu Arqueològic

SANT FRANCESC

COMTE DE RIUS

AUGUST

SANT AGUSTI

RAMBLA VELLA

OLEGUER

Circ Roma

VIA AUGUSTA

N

RAMBLA NOVA

PLAÇA VERDAGUER

GIRONA

Parc del Miracle

Anfiteatro romano

GOVERNADOR

ADRIA

LLURIA

ROGER DE LLURIA

PASSEIG DE LES PALMERES

Monumento a Roger de Lluria

PASSEIG DE

Balcón del Mediterráneo

PONS D'ICART

BAIXADA DE TORO

BAIXADA DE CASANOVAS

platja del Miracle

RESTAURANTS

Bar Frankfurt el Balcon | 10

Serrallo

Train Station

PASSEIG MARITIM RAFAEL DE CASÁNOVAS

ACCOMMODATION

Hotel Astari | F
Hotel Ciutat de Tarragona | D
Imperial Tarraco Hotel | G
Hotel Lauria | H
Hostal Noria | C
Alberg Sant Jordi | A&B
Hotel Sant Jordi | E

Can Llesques | 5
Café Cantonada | 8
El Caseron | 6
El Mesón del Cim | 9
Les Coques | 1
Mistral | 2
La Penya | 4
La Pizzeria | 7
Les Voltes | 3

0   150 m

◄ Bus Station, Necropolis, Forum & ⓘ

CATALUNYA | Tarragona

Time spent in the handsome upper town quickly shows what attracted the emperors to the city: strategically – and beautifully – placed, it's a fine setting for some splendid Roman remains and a few excellent museums. There's an attractive medieval part, too, while the rocky coastline below conceals a couple of reasonable beaches. If there's a downside, it's that Tarragona is today the second largest port in Catalunya, so the views aren't always unencumbered – though the fish in the Serrallo fishing quarter is always good and fresh. Also, the city's ugly outskirts to the south have been steadily degraded by new industries which do little for Tarragona's character as a resort: chemical and oil refineries, and a nuclear power station.

The city divides clearly into two parts, on two levels: a predominantly medieval, walled upper town (where you'll spend most time), and a prosperous modern extension below. Heart of the upper town is the sweeping **Rambla**

Nova, a sturdy provincial rival to Barcelona's, lined with fashionable cafés and restaurants. Parallel, and to the east, lies the **Rambla Vella**, marking – as its name suggests – the start of the old town. To either side of the *rambles* are scattered a profusion of relics from Tarragona's Roman past, including various temples, and parts of the forum, theatre and amphitheatre.

Arrival and information

The **train station** is in the lower town: when you arrive, turn right and climb the steps ahead of you and you'll emerge at the top of the Rambla Nova, from where everything is a short walk away. The **bus terminal** is at the other end of the Rambla Nova, at Plaça Imperial Tarraco. The **turisme** is at c/Major 39 (July–Sept Mon–Fri 9.30am–8.30pm, Sat 9.30am–2pm & 4–8.30pm, Sun 10am–2pm; Oct–June Mon–Fri 10am–2pm & 4.30–7pm, Sat 10am–2pm, Sun 10am–2pm; ☎977 245 064, ⓦwww.fut.es/~turisme), and there is also a seasonal information booth (July–Sept same hours) at Plaça Imperial Tarraco. If you're travelling further afield the regional tourist office is near Rambla Nova at c/Fortuny 4 (Mon–Fri 9am–2pm & 4–6.30pm, Sat 9am–2pm; ☎977 233 415, ⓦwww.gencat.es/turisme).

You're unlikely to use the city's **local bus** network, other than for trips out to the campsite or to the aqueduct (details are given below), but the turisme can let you know the routes if you're interested. They can also provide you with the excellent *Guia d'Accessibilitat*, which lists all **wheelchair-accessible** buildings in the city.

Accommodation

Tarragona makes a great stopover, and is certainly less exhausting than Sitges. The nicest **rooms** in town, or at least the ones in the best location, are in the pedestrianized Plaça de la Font, just in the old town off Rambla Vella. If these are full, there are a couple of less desirable places near the train station. The cheapest lodgings are at the *Alberg Sant Jordi* (see below), while down towards the beach, Platja Arrabassada, a few kilometres out of town, are some more small hotels and **campsites**: to get to *Camping Tarraco* (☎977 239 989; April–Sept) take bus #1, #3 or #9 (every twenty minutes) from Plaça de Corsini, near the market and local forum.

Hotel Astari Via Augusta 95 ☎977 236 900, ⓔastari@tinet.fut.es. Friendly three-star hotel on the road to the beaches, with decent swimming pool. ❺

Hotel Ciutat de Tarragona Plaça Imperial Tarraco 5 ☎977 250 999, ⓦwww.sbhotels.es. Impersonal but very comfortable hotel on the main roundabout at the entrance to Rambla Nova. ❻

Imperial Tarraco Hotel Rambla Vella 2 ☎977 233 040, ⓔimperial@tinet.fut.es. The city's best and most expensive hotel, modern but beautifully positioned, sitting on top of the cliff and facing out to sea. ❼

Hotel Lauria Rambla Nova 20 ☎977 236 712, ⓦwww.hlauria.es. Well-located three-star hotel on the main *rambla*. Outside July and Aug, room prices become eminently reasonable. ❺

Hostal Noria Plaça de la Font 53 ☎977 238 717. Smarter and more upmarket than most around the *plaça*, but good value out of season. Ask inside the bar/cafetería. ❷

Alberg Sant Jordi Avgda. President Companys 5 ☎977 240 195, ⓕ977 243 134. An IYHF hostel with four- or six-bedded rooms (over-26s pay fifty percent more) and sports facilities; breakfast included in the price. Reception open 7–10am & 2–8pm; reservations advised in July & Aug; closed Sept. €19 for dorm bed.

Hotel Sant Jordi Vía Augusta 185 ☎977 207 515, ⓔhsjordi@tinet.fut.es. Old-time favourite, moved from its previous berth in Plaça de la Font into these more roomy premises on the way to the beaches. Well run and friendly; all rooms have bath. ❹

The City

Much of the attraction of Tarragona lies in the **Roman remains** dotted around the city. Some of the most impressive monuments are a fair way out (see "Out of the centre" on p.895), but there's enough within walking distance to occupy a good day's sightseeing and to provide a vivid impression of life in Tarragona in imperial Roman times. It's worth noting in advance that all Tarragona's sights and museums except for the cathedral are **closed on Mondays**, and, unless otherwise stated, cost €1.90.

Passeig Arqueològic

For an overview of the city and its history, start at the **Passeig Arqueològic** (Oct–March Tues–Sat 10am–1.30pm & 3.30–5pm, Sun 10am–2pm; April–Sept Tues–Sat 9am–9pm, Sun 9am–3pm; free entry with Port Aventura pass), a promenade which encircles the northernmost half of the old town. From the entrance at the Portal del Roser, a path runs between **Roman walls** of the third century BC and the sloping, **outer fortifications** erected by the British in 1707 to secure the city during the War of the Spanish Succession. Megalithic walls built by the Iberians are excellently preserved in places, too, particularly two awesome gateways; the huge blocks used in their construction are quite distinct from the more refined Roman additions. Vantage points (and occasional telescopes) give views across the plain behind the city and around to the sea, while various objects are displayed within the Passeig – several Roman columns, a fine bronze statue of Augustus, and eighteenth-century cannons still defending the city's heights.

Roman Tarragona: the Necropolis, Forum and Amphitheatre

The most interesting remains in town are those of the ancient Necropolis, a twenty-minute walk out of the centre down Avinguda Ramón i Cajal, which runs west off Rambla Nova. Here, both pagan and Christian tombs have been uncovered, spanning a period from the third to the sixth century AD. They're now contained within the fascinating **Museu i Necropolis Paleocristians**, at c/Ramon i Cajal 80 (June–Sept Tues–Sat 10am–1pm & 4.30–8pm, Sun 10am–2pm; Oct–May Tues–Sat 10am–1.30pm & 4–7pm, Sun 10am–2pm), whose entrance is on Passeig de la Independencia. The museum is lined with sarcophagi and displays a few fragmented mosaics and photographs of the site, but it's outside in the covered trenches and stone foundations that you get most sense of Tarragona's erstwhile importance. Scattered about are amphorae, inscribed tablets and plinths, rare examples of later Visigothic sculpture, and even the sketchy remains of a mausoleum. Most of the relics attest to Tarragona's enthusiastically Christian status: St Paul preached here, and the city became an important Visigothic bishopric after the break-up of Roman power. Back in the centre, the Roman forum has survived, too. Or rather forums, since – as provincial capital – Tarragona sustained both a ceremonial **provincial forum** (the scant remnants of which are close to the cathedral) and a **local forum**, on c/Lleida, whose more substantial remains are on the western side of Rambla Nova, near the market hall and square. Located on the flat land near the port, this was the commercial centre of imperial *Tarraco* and the main meeting place for locals for three centuries. The site (April & May Tues–Sat 10am–1.30pm & 3.30–6.30pm, Sun 10am–2pm; June–Sept Tues–Sat 9am–9pm, Sun 10am–2pm; Oct–March Tues–Sat 10am–1.30pm & 3.30–5.30pm, Sun 10am–2pm), which contained temples and small shops ranged around a porticoed square, has been split by a main road: a footbridge now connects the two halves where you can see a water cistern, house foundations, fragments of stone inscriptions and four elegant columns.

Tarragona's other tangible Roman remains lie close to each other at the seaward end of the Rambla Vella. Most rewarding is the **Amfiteatre** (March–Sept Tues–Sat 9am–9pm, Sun 9am–3pm; Oct–Feb Tues–Sat 9am–5pm, Sun 10am–3pm; free entry with Port Aventura pass), built into the green slopes of the hill beneath the *Imperial Tarraco* hotel. The tiered seats backing onto the sea are original, and from the top you can look north, up the coast, to the headland; the rest of the seating was reconstructed in 1969–70, along with the surviving tunnels and structural buildings.

Above here, on the Rambla Vella itself, are the visible remains of the Roman Circus, the **Circ Roma**, also known as Les Voltes del Circ, whose vaults disappear back from the street into the gloom and under many of the surrounding buildings. If you want a closer look, the Circ now forms part of the **Museu de la Romanitat**, on Plaça del Rei (June–Sept Tues–Sat 9am–9pm, Sun 9am–3pm; Oct–May Tues–Sat 10am–1.30pm & 4–7pm, Sun 10am–2pm). Built at the end of the first century AD to hold chariot races, the Circ has been restored and presented to spectacular effect. The rest of the museum contains computer-generated pictures of Roman Tarragona's buildings, and a lift cuts right through the building and onto the roof for the best views in Tarragona.

The old town

For all its individual Roman monuments, the heart of Tarragona is still the steep and intricate streets of the medieval **old town** which spreads east of the Rambla Vella. Here and there the towering mansions in the side streets incorporate Roman fragments, while the central c/Major climbs to the quarter's focal point, the **Catedral** (mid-March to June Mon–Sat 10am–12.30pm & 4–7pm; July to mid-Oct Mon–Sat 10am–7pm; mid-Oct to mid-Nov Mon–Sat 10am–12.30pm & 3–5pm; mid-Nov to mid-March Mon–Sat 10am–2pm; €2.40), which sits at the top of a broad flight of steps. This, quite apart from its own grand beauty, is a perfect example of the transition from Romanesque to Gothic forms. You'll see the change highlighted in the main facade, where a soaring Gothic portal is framed by Romanesque doors, surmounted by a cross and an elaborate rose window. Except for services, entrance to the cathedral is through the **cloisters** (*claustre*; signposted up a street to the left of the facade), themselves superbly executed with pointed Gothic arches softened by smaller round divisions. The cloister also has several oddly sculpted capitals, one of which represents a cat's funeral being directed by rats. The ticket lets you proceed into the cathedral, and into its chapterhouse and sacristy, which together make up the **Museu Diocesa**, piled high with ecclesiastical treasures.

Strolling the old town's streets will also enable you to track down Tarragona's excellent clutch of museums. The least obvious – but worth seeing for the setting inside one of the city's finest medieval mansions – is the **Casa Museu de Castellarnau** on c/Cavallers 14 (June–Sept Tues–Sat 9am–8pm, Sun 10am–2pm; Oct–May Tues–Sat 10am–1pm & 4–7pm, Sun 9am–3pm). The interior courtyard alone rewards a visit, with its arches and stone coats of arms built over Roman vaults. Otherwise, the small-scale collections are largely archeological and historical (coins and jars), rescued from banality by some rich eighteenth-century Catalan furniture and furnishings.

Museums of archeology and history

The most stimulating exhibitions in town are in adjacent buildings off Plaça del Rei at the edge of the old town. The splendid **Museu Nacional**

Arqueològic (June–Sept Tues–Sat 10am–8pm, Sun 10am–2pm; Oct–May Tues–Sat 10am–1.30pm & 4–7pm, Sun 10am–2pm; €2.40; discount with Port Aventura pass) is a marvellous reflection of the richness of imperial *Tarraco*. Its huge collection is admirably laid out, starting in the basement with a section of the old Roman wall preserved *in situ*. On other floors are thematic displays on the various remains and buildings around the city, accompanied by pictures, text and relics, as well as whole rooms devoted to inscriptions, sculpture, ceramics, jewellery – even a series of anchors retrieved from the sea. More importantly, there's an unusually complete collection of mosaics, exemplifying the stages of development from the plain black-and-white patterns of the first century AD to the elaborate polychrome pictures of the second and third centuries.

Out of the centre

Tarragona is compact enough not only to be able to walk everywhere in the city, but to reach most of the outlying districts on foot, too. It's less than half an hour to either the port area of **Serrallo** or, across town, to the best local beach at **Arrabassada**. The Roman **Aqueduct**, 4km inland, is best reached by bus, but for most of the other Roman remains dotted around the surrounding countryside you'll need transport of your own.

Other Roman remains

Perhaps the most remarkable (and least visited) of Tarragona's monuments stands outside the original city walls. This is the **Roman Aqueduct**, which brought water from the Riu Gayo, some 32km distant. The most impressive extant section, nearly 220m long and 26m high, lies in an overgrown valley, off the main road in the middle of nowhere: take bus #5, marked "Sant Salvador" (every twenty minutes from the stop outside Avgda. Prat de la Riba 11, off Avinguda Ramón i Cajal; last bus back at around 10.45pm) – a ten-minute ride. The trip is undoubtedly worthwhile; the utilitarian beauty of the aqueduct is surpassed only by those at Segovia and the Pont du Gard, in the south of France. Popularly, it is known as El Pont del Diable (Devil's Bridge) because, remarked Richard Ford, of the Spanish habit of "giving all praise to 'the Devil', as Pontifex Maximus".

Other local Roman monuments of similar grandeur are more difficult to reach: in fact, without your own transport, almost impossible. If you're determined, keep an eye out for signs, and expect to have to ask directions from time to time. The square, three-storeyed **Torre dels Escipions**, a funerary monument built in the second century AD and nearly 10m high, stands just off the main Barcelona road, the N340, 6km northeast up the coast. A couple of kilometres further north, the **Pedrera del Medol** is the excavated quarry that provided much of the stone used in Tarragona's constructions, while 20km from the city, after the turn-off for Altafulla, is the triumphal **Arc de Bera**, built over the great Via Maxima in the second century AD.

Serrallo and the beaches

A fifteen-minute walk west along the industrial harbour front from the train station (or the same distance south from the Necropolis) takes you right into the working port of **SERRALLO**, Tarragona's so-called "fishermen's quarter". Built a century ago, the harbour here is authentic enough – fishing smacks tied up, nets laid out on the ground for mending – but the real interest for visitors is the line of **fish and seafood restaurants** which fronts the main Moll dels Pescadors (see p.896).

North of the Serrallo district, the closest beach to town is the long **Platja del Miracle**, over the rail lines below the amphitheatre. The nicest, though, is a couple of kilometres further up the coast, reached by taking Vía Augusta (off the end of Rambla Vella) and turning right at the *Hotel Astari*. Don't be put off upon the way: the main road and railway bridge eventually give way to a road which winds around the headland and down to **Platja Arrabassada**, an ultimately pleasant twenty-minute walk with gradually unfolding views of the beach. There are regular buses in summer (#1, #3 or #9) from various points throughout town.

Arrabassada is nothing special, though it's spacious enough and has a few other diversions that make it worthwhile. Top of the list is the *Brasilmos* beach **bar-restaurant**, at the far end by the headland, which features seafood tapas, Latin American sounds, a pool table and occasional live music on summer evenings. There are a couple of other beach bars, too, and under the railway line, by *Brasilmos*, tiny **ARRABASSADA** village itself, which boasts two or three restaurants, a couple of hotels and *hostales*, a supermarket and two **campsites**, including *Camping Tarraco* (see p.892). A bit further along the coast at **Platja Llarga**, a cluster of restaurants offer good food at low prices and stay open late. There's also a very lively Cuban **disco**, the *Corason*, where you'll find local families – including grandparents – dancing the night away, fuelled by potent cocktails. Entrance is free, but you'll be expected to buy at least one drink.

Eating and drinking

There are plenty of good **restaurants** in the centre of Tarragona; many – particularly in and around Plaça de la Font – have outdoor seating in the summer. Alternatively, you might try the fish and seafood places down in Serrallo; not cheap, but the food is as fresh as can be and you can find some *menús del día* for around €15 in the narrow street behind the main Moll dels Pescadors. *Pescado romesco* (fish with *romesco* sauce) is the regional **speciality** and you'll find it on several *menús del día* around town: *romesco* sauce has a base of dry pepper, almonds and/or hazelnuts, olive oil, garlic and a glass of Priorato wine. Beyond this there are many variations, as cooks tend to add their own secret ingredients. The best **bars** are to be found around the cathedral and in the streets between the train station and Rambla Nova.

Restaurants

Can Llesques c/Natzaret 6, on Plaça del Rei. Cramped, atmospheric restaurant with low stone arches serving endless variations of *Pa amb tomaquet*, accompanied by drinks in ceramic pitchers. It's amazingly popular, thanks to its reasonable prices; go early or prepare to hang around for a table. Sitting outside attracts a ten-percent surcharge.

El Caseron c/de Cos del Bou 9. Small restaurant just off Plaça de la Font, with a decent menu of staples – rabbit, paella, grills and fries – and a very good-value *menú del día*. Closed Mon after 5pm, Sat & Sun.

Les Coques c/Nou del Patriarca 2. Fine dining in an upmarket Catalan restaurant, just off Plaça de la Seu near the cathedral. Upwards of €18 a head. Closed Sun.

El Mesón del Cim c/Governador González 15. Good selection of tapas and wines in a friendly bar.

Mistral Plaça de la Font 19. Pizzas for around €5–7, plus the usual *menú* for €9.50, including pricey *pescado romesco*. Tables on the square in summer are its main attraction, though.

La Pizzeria c/Cos del Bou 8. There are cheaper pizzerias, but this family-run place has a relaxed and friendly atmosphere. Closed Mon lunch & Sun.

La Puda Moll dels Pescadors 25. In the Serrallo quarter, this smart fish restaurant has tables overlooking the harbour inside and out. There's a short selection of seafood tapas, and a main *menú* that doesn't come cheap at €48 but is very good.

Les Voltes c/Trinquet Vell 12. One of the best restaurants in the cathedral area, recommended for its hearty *pa amb tomàquet* meals and grilled meats. Around €12. Closed Sun.

Bars and cafés

Bar Frankfurt el Balcon Rambla Nova 3. Outdoor tables in the best spot on the *rambla*, on the balcony overlooking the sea next to the statue of Roger de Lluria. Sandwiches and tapas.

Bar Musical El Cau c/Trinquet Vell 2. Situated in an underground Roman vault in the old town, this dark venue has live indie-pop or rock every Saturday night. Open daily 10pm–4am.

Café L'Antiquari c/Santa Anna 3. Laid-back café-bar with funk and rock sounds and a liberal use of borrowed religious artefacts and statues, including a confessional box converted into a telephone cabin. A noticeboard at the entrance has details of events around town.

Café Cantonada c/Fortuny 21. Civilized café-bar whose roomy interior and pool table encourage extended visits. Good tapas and Internet access at €5/hour; closed Mon.

El Candil Plaça de la Font 13. Fashionable, friendly bar with tapas, a wide selection of herbal teas and coffees as well as alcohol. Open late at weekends.

Cucudrulus c/del Protectorat. Popular with an international crowd, this bar is good for live music.

Frankfurt c/Canyelles (off Rambla Nova, on the left before the fountain). A bar with good hot and cold sandwiches prepared in front of you – a wide selection for €23 a go.

La Geladeria Plaça del Rei 6. Popular ice-cream parlour outside the archeological museum.

Moto Club Tarragona Rambla Nova 53. Busy and ever-popular *rambla* bar. Open daily from 7am to midnight for drinks and snacks.

La Penya Plaça de la Font 35. Friendly, hippyish bar offering hearty Catalan cuisine, with generous shots of *vermouth de la casa*.

Poetes c/Sant Llorenç 15. A short walk from the cathedral, this lively bar often has live music in the cellar.

Listings

Airlines Iberia, Rambla Nova 116 ☏977 240 751.

Banks and exchange Many banks have offices along Rambla Nova. Outside banking hours you can exchange money and travellers' cheques at Viajes Eurojet, Rambla Nova 42 (Mon–Fri 9am–1.30pm & 4.30–8.30pm, Sat 9am–1pm). This agency also handles American Express matters, and will exchange cheques and hold mail.

Bus information Local bus information is available from the tourist offices or the cabin on c/Cristòfor Colom ☏977 549 480. Bus station information on ☏977 229 126.

Car rental Atesa, at Viatgens Marsans, c/Lleida 11 ☏977 219 867; Racc, Rambla Nova 114 ☏977 211 962; Avis, c/Pinisoler 10 ☏977 219 156; Hertz, Vía Augusta 91 ☏977 384 137.

Cinemas Movies are shown at Oscars, c/Ramón i Cajal 15; Lauren Multicines, c/Vidal I Barraquer 15–17; and Catalunya, Rambla Vella 9. Listings from the tourist offices or in the local newspaper.

Emergencies Call ☏092 or ☏977 222 222 for an ambulance.

Hospitals Hospital de Sant Pau i Santa Tecla, Rambla Vella 14 ☏977 259 900.

Internet access Bar Cantonada (see above); *Aquari*, c/Roger de Llúria, opposite side entrance of Hotel Lauria (€5/hour).

Markets Daily food market (not Sun) on and around Plaça Cosini, near the provincial forum; indoor food market at Plaça de Corsini (Mon–Fri 9am–1pm & 4–8pm, Sat 9am–1pm). On Sundays, there's an antiques market at the top of the cathedral steps, with jewellery, bric-a-brac, ornaments and antiques spilling over into the arcades along c/Mercería.

Post office At Plaça de Corsini (Mon–Fri 8am–8.30pm, Sat 8am–2pm).

Taxis There are ranks on Rambla Nova (at the Moto Club), in Plaça del Font, and at the bus and train stations. Or call ☏977 221 414, 977 236 064 or 977 215 656.

Train information RENFE has an office on Passeig d'Espanya for tickets and enquiries (Mon–Fri 9am–1pm & 4–7pm; ☏977 240 202).

Travel agencies For local tours, train and bus information, and tickets, contact Viajes Eurojet, Rambla Nova 42; Viatgens Marsans, c/Comte de Rius 26; Vibus, Rambla Nova 125; or Wagon Lits, c/Cristòfor Colom 8.

Costa Daurada

The coast south of Tarragona is an uninspiring prospect. The occasional beaches are not easily reached by public transport, and few of them have anything to encourage a stop – long, thin strips of sand, they are almost universally backed by gargantuan caravan-camping grounds, packed full and miles from anywhere.

This part of the Costa Daurada also boasts one of Catalunya's biggest tourist developments, the extended coastal stretch that is the resort of **Salou**, which merges into the prettier **Cambrils**. Beyond here, a fairly featureless expanse runs as far as the reasonably pleasant towns of **L'Ametlla de Mar** and **L'Ampolla**, before the coast fans out into the Delta d'Ebre.

Salou

Neither the ten-minute train ride nor the drive through the outskirts from Tarragona to **SALOU** make a promising start, passing through a mesh of petrochemical pipes and tanks before rounding on the resort itself – an almost entirely unrelieved gash of apartment blocks and hotels spilling down towards the sea. There are three or four separate beaches here, ringed around a sweeping bay and backed by a promenade studded with palms. From the seafront it's quite an attractive prospect, but the town is resolutely downmarket and stuffed to the gills in summer, the streets back from the sea teeming with "English pubs" and poor restaurants serving overpriced food and beer. Just outside town lies **Port Aventura** (daily: mid-June to mid-Sept 10am–midnight; mid-Sept to mid-June 10am–8pm; information ☎902 202 220; various price offers). This massive theme park, with its own RENFE station, boasts five themed "lands" including China and the Wild West, each offering death-defying rides, garish restaurants and live entertainment. If it's your bag, you might want to buy a three-day pass (€59) and stay in Salou, which is packed with hotels and *pensiones*. Otherwise, you're much better off heading for Cambrils, 7km south. Buses regularly ply the coastal road between the two, or it's one more stop on the train.

Cambrils

Smaller **CAMBRILS** is nicer in every way, the town set back from a large harbour which still has working boats and fishing nets interspersed among the restaurants and hotels. In summer it's as full as anywhere along the Catalan coast, and Cambrils is probably better seen as a day-trip from Tarragona, only fifteen minutes to the north. Out of season, though, it's more relaxed, and while inexpensive accommodation isn't easy to come by, it might be worth persevering for a night to eat in the good fish restaurants and amble around the harbour and nearby beaches. There's a **market** in town every Wednesday. Worth a visit if only for the views is the **Museu Torre del Port**, at Pg. Miramar 31 (Tues–Sat 11am–2pm & 6–9pm, Sun 11am–2pm; €1), a seventeenth-century circular watchtower in the harbour, which has been converted into a maritime museum.

Practicalities

Arriving by bus from Tarragona, you'll pass through Salou and can ask to be dropped in Cambrils on the harbour front. By **train**, you're faced with a fifteen-minute walk from the inland part of town down to Cambrils-Port and the harbour: from the station, turn right and then right again at the main road, heading for the sea. Across the bridge on your left is the main **turisme** (daily 10am–1pm & 5–8pm; ☎977 792 307, ✉ptur.cambrils@altanet.org), at Pg. de les Palmeres 1, which has free maps, local bus and train timetables posted on the door, and may be able to help find a room. From here, Cambrils-Port is straight ahead, down any of the roads in front of you.

There are plenty of **hotels** in town, but as with all places on the coast, you'll need to reserve in high season, especially if you want to be in the harbour. One street in from the sea is *Hotel Princep*, at c/Narcís Monturiol 2 (☎977 361 127, ⓦwww.hotelprincep.com; ④), which is not very pretty from the outside but is comfortable and good value; the *Hotel-Restaurant Miramar*, Passeig Miramar 30 (☎977 360 063; ⑤), is more expensive, but nicely positioned overlooking the sea. There are also nine **campsites** in and around Cambrils, and the turisme has a free map showing where they all are. Closest to the centre is *Don Camilo* (☎977 361 490, ⓕ977 364 988; March–Oct), at Avgda, Diputació 42; the others are spread up and down the coast in both directions.

For a meal, there's plenty of choice and some splendid fish **restaurants** along the harbour if you're prepared to dust off your wallet. Expect to pay around €12 for a good *menú del día*, though *a la carta* seafood at one of the harbourfront restaurants comes in at considerably more than that. Less expensive meals are found at several places along c/Pau Casals, or go for the modestly priced *platos combinados* at *Cafetería La Sirena*, c/Sant Pere 2 (entrance on c/Roger de Llúria; closed Thurs). The bar opposite the train station has seafood tapas and the usual *comedor* standbys.

L'Ametlla de Mar and L'Ampolla

Thirty kilometres down the coast from Cambrils, the rather shabby outskirts of **L'AMETLLA DE MAR** belie a pretty harbour area, where low buildings and terrace restaurants cluster around the busy enclosed fishing port. Adjacent to the working area is a second beach with an uncluttered promenade backed by a few hotels and shopping streets. If you have your own transport, bumpy roads lead to some picturesque rough and ready beaches to the north of the town, which rarely get overwhelmingly packed. If you decide to stay, the *Hotel del Port*, at c/Major 11 (☎977 457 043, ⓔhotelport@navegalia.com; ③), in the fishing harbour, is good value, or you could try the *Hotel L'Alguer*, at c/Mar 20 (☎977 493 372, ⓕ977 493 375; ④), in front of the neighbouring blue-flag beach. For a **meal or drink**, there are plenty of terrace bars and restaurants in the port; *Mare Nostrum*, next to the Hotel del Port, serves good seafood, while *Llesquería La Masia*, next door again, has a broader range of meat, fish and salads.

A further 4km southwest from L'Ametlla de Mar, **L'AMPOLLA** is a smaller and quieter version, with low-key cafés and restaurants backing a blue-flag beach and pleasing small fishing port; either side of the town are some equally good stretches of sandy shore. The *Casa Llambrich* **restaurant**, on the seafront at c/Mig 8, is popular with locals and serves a decent *menú del día* for €9; under the name *Ampolla Sol* (☎977 460 008, ⓔhotelampollasol @turinet.net; ④), it also doubles up as a comfortable **hotel** if you want to linger.

Tortosa

The only town of any size in Catalunya's deep south is **TORTOSA**, slightly inland astride the Riu Ebre. In the Civil War the front was outside Tortosa for several months until the Nationalists eventually took the town in April 1938. The battle cost 35,000 lives, and is commemorated by a gaunt metal monument standing on a huge stone plinth in the middle of the river in town. The fighting took its toll in other ways, too: there's little left of the medieval quarter in the few old streets around the **cathedral**, though the building itself is worth a look. Founded originally in the twelfth century on the site of an earlier mosque, it was rebuilt in the fourteenth century, and its Gothic interior and quiet cloister – although much worn – are very fine. Several *modernista* houses around town (marked on the turisme map) also add a bit of interest.

Tortosa's brightest point is also its highest. **La Suda**, the old castle, sits perched above the cathedral, glowering from behind its battlements at the Ebre valley below and the mountains beyond. Like so many in Spain, the castle has been converted into a luxury *parador* (see below), but there's nothing to stop you climbing up for a magnificent view from the walls, or from going into the plush bar and having a drink. From the cathedral, c/de la Suda takes you straight there. On the other side of La Suda, a garden beneath the castle houses a collection of **sculptures** (April to mid-Sept Tues–Sat 10am–1pm & 4.30–7.30pm, Sun 10am–2pm; mid-Sept to March Tues–Sat 10am–1pm & 3.30–5.30pm, Sun 10am–2pm; €3) of the human figure by Santiago de Santiago.

Practicalities

Tortosa is the main transport terminus for the region: in particular, regular buses run from here out to the principal towns and villages of the Delta de l'Ebre (see below). This, really, is the main reason to come, since the town is otherwise hardly an inspirational stopover, unless you stay at the *parador*. **Moving on** from Catalunya, regular **buses** run from Tortosa to Vinaròs (in Castellón province to the south), from where you can reach the wonderful inland mountain town of Morella; and less regularly west to Alcañiz (in Aragón). **Trains** head south, passing through Vinaròs, on their way to Valencia.

The main **turisme** (Mon–Fri 10am–1pm & 4–7pm, Sat 10am–1pm; ☎977 510 822, ✉aj.tortosa@altanet.org) is in the Plaça del Bimil.lenari, to the south of the town, and there's a more central summer turisme (April–Sept Tues–Sat 10am–1pm & 4–8pm, Sun 10am–1pm) on the main road into town, Avinguda de la Generalitat, in the park on the left-hand side. To get there from the bus or train stations, follow the train tracks towards the river and turn left – away from the centre – under the bridge. Further out of town along here is the *Pensió Virginia*, at no. 139 (☎977 444 186; ❷), a good place to stay if your budget doesn't run to the **parador** (☎977 444 450, ℻977 444 458; ❻) at La Suda. If you do stay at the *parador* you should eat there as well, since it has the best **restaurant** in town, open to non-guests. The *Virginia* also has a decent restaurant, but other good places to eat are thin on the ground in Tortosa.

The Delta de l'Ebre

In the bottom corner of Catalunya is the **Delta de l'Ebre** (Ebro Delta), 320 square kilometres of sandy delta constituting the biggest wetland in Catalunya and one of the most important aquatic habitats in the western Mediterranean. Designated a natural park, its brackish lagoons, marshes, dunes and reed beds are home to thousands of wintering birds and provide excellent fishing; around fifteen percent of the total Catalan catch comes from this area. The scenery is unique in Catalunya, with low roads running through field after field of rice paddies, punctuated by solitary houses and small villages, before emerging onto dune-lined beaches.

Since much of the area of the **Parc Natural de Delta de l'Ebre** is a protected zone, access is limited. It's also difficult to visit without your own transport, though the effort of doing so is rewarded by tranquillity and space. If you're relying on buses, aim for one of the three main towns – Amposta, Sant Carles de la Ràpita or Deltebre – where you'll find accommodation and boat services on into the delta. The nearest **turisme** is in Amposta at Sant Jaume 1 (April to mid-Sept Mon–Sat 10am–1pm & 4–7pm, Sun 10am–2pm; mid-Sept to March Mon–Fri 11am–1pm; ☎977 703 453, ✉otur.amposta@altanet.org), which can advise you about accommodation and the possibility of renting a boat to take you down to the river mouth.

Deltebre, Sant Jaume d'Enveja and around

The best place to head to first to get an idea of the area is **DELTEBRE**, at the centre of the delta: road and river run here from Amposta (buses from Tortosa). The **park information office** here, on the edge of town on Plaça Vint de Maig and well signposted (Mon–Fri 10am–2pm & 3–6pm, Sat 10am–1pm & 3.30–6pm, Sun 10am–1pm; ☎977 489 679), can provide you with a map of the delta, and has information about tours and local walks. At the same place there's an interesting **Ecomuseum** (Tues–Sun 9am–1pm; €1), which has an aquarium displaying species from the delta, and also maintains hides for bird-watchers which overlook a pond. There are three or four places to stay in Deltebre, all reasonably priced, as well as a **youth hostel** (☎977 480 136, ℻977 481 284; €17 for a dorm bed) at Avinguda de les Goles del Ebre, and a ferry across to **SANT JAUME D'ENVEJA** on the opposite shore. The local restaurants serve wonderful fish dishes, the speciality being *arròs a banda*, similar to paella except that the rice is brought before the seafood itself.

On the north bank of the river, the road leads out to **Riumar**, where you'll find good, if windy, bathing on sandy beaches, connected to the road by duckboards winding through the dunes. Excursion boats cross from near the popular *Casa Nuri* restaurant to the **Illa de Buda**, the largest of the islands in the delta and covered in rice paddies; it can also be reached by excursion boats from Deltebre or by scheduled ferry from Sant Jaume. The road which runs along the south bank of the river leads to the so-called Eucaliptus **beach**, where there's a campsite, *Mediterrani Blau* (☎977 479 046; April–Sept). If you do camp, bring plenty of mosquito repellent, as they are a pest, especially in the evening.

Sant Carles de la Ràpita

SANT CARLES DE LA RÀPITA, to the south, is a more inviting place, with regular daily buses from Tortosa – though few at the weekend – and a **turisme** (June–Sept Mon–Fri 9am–2pm & 4–6pm, Sat & Sun 11am–1pm & 5–7pm; Oct–May Mon–Sat morning only, closed Sun; ☎977 740 100, ✉turisme@larapita.com) in the *ajuntament* on Plaça Carles III. It's quite a busy town in summer, drawing families to the several campsites stretching away down the coast and to the dozens of restaurants which are said to serve the best prawns in the Mediterranean. Unless you've access to a car, though, you'll be able to explore only the immediate surroundings.

For **rooms** in town, try the large *Hotel Rocamar*, Avgda. Constitucío 8 (☎977 740 458; ❷), whose rooms without bath are fine, or the more comfortable *Llansola*, c/Sant Isidre 98 (☎977 740 403; ❹). An excellent **restaurant**, much frequented by locals, is the *Can Victor*, signposted from all over town, whose position right beneath the market guarantees the freshest of produce.

Inland: the route to Lleida

The train line from Barcelona forks at Tarragona, and the choice is either south towards Tortosa or **inland** for the fairly monotonous three-hour ride northwest across the flat lands to Lleida. The Tarragona–Lleida bus is a slightly more attractive proposition than the train, if only because it climbs the odd bluff and ridge on the way for good views over the plain. The bus also takes you directly to the region's only major attraction, the monastery of Poblet, which you could see in half a day and then move on to Lleida. Access to the monastery by train is possible, but means walking some of the way along a signposted footpath through farmland – a pleasant experience if the weather's fine, since the surroundings are lovely.

Montblanc

The walled medieval town of **MONTBLANC**, 8km before the turning to the monastery at Poblet, is also on the train line to Lleida, so it's easy enough to see both on the same trip. It's a surprisingly beautiful place to discover in the middle of nowhere, and astonishingly lively during the evening *passeig* around the picturesque Plaça Major. There are many fine little Romanesque and Gothic monuments contained within a tight circle of old streets; all are marked on a map attached to the town's medieval gateway, the **Portal de Boue**, which is just a hundred metres or so up from the train station.

The grand Gothic parish church of **Santa María**, just above the central square, is perhaps the first thing to look out for: its elaborate facade has lions' faces on either side of the main doorway and cherubs swarming up the pillars. There's a fine view from the once-fortified mound that rises behind the church – over the rooftops, defensive towers and walls, and away across the plain. A couple of other churches to track down are Romanesque Sant Miquel (usually locked) and Sant Marcel, on the other side of the mound, which contains the **Museu Marès** (June–Sept Tues–Sat 10am–2pm & 4–8pm, Sun 10am–2pm; Oct–May Sat & Sun only; guided tours €2.25). Like the one in Barcelona, it's an eclectic collection of religious sculpture and art. Montblanc also has a fine local history museum, the **Museu Comarcal de la Conca de Barberà** (June–Sept Tues–Sat 10am–2pm & 5–8pm, Sun 10am–2pm; Oct–May Tues–Sat 10am–1pm & 4–7pm, Sun 10am–2pm; €2.40), just off Plaça Major below the church, which is bright and informative, although all annotated in Catalan.

Practicalities

There's a very helpful **turisme** (opening hours vary; ☎977 861 733) in the Antiga Església de Sant Francesc, where you can pick up a free map. If you're driving, Montblanc would make a fine base for visiting Poblet – even on foot, it's only 8km to the monastery. The friendliest place to stay is the *Fonda Cal Blasi*, c/Alenyà 11–13 (☎977 861 336, ⓦwww./fondacalblasi.com; ❺), a restored nineteenth-century farmhouse a short distance from the bus station; it also serves meals.

The Monestir de Poblet

There are few ruins more stirring than the **MONESTIR DE POBLET**. It lies in glorious open country, vast and sprawling within massive battlemented walls and towered gateways. Once *the* great monastery of Catalunya, it was in effect a complete manorial village and enjoyed scarcely credible rights, powers and wealth. Founded in 1151 by Ramón Berenguer IV, who united the king-doms of Catalunya and Aragón, it was planned from the beginning on an immensely grand scale. The kings of Aragón-Catalunya chose to be buried in its chapel and for three centuries diverted huge sums for its endowment, a munificence that was inevitably corrupting. By the late Middle Ages Poblet had become a byword for decadence – there are lewder stories about this than any other Cistercian monastery – and so it continued, hated by the local peas-antry, until the Carlist revolution of 1835 when a mob burned and tore it apart.

The monastery was repopulated by Italian Cistercians in 1940 and over the decades since then a superb job of restoration has been undertaken. Much remains delightfully ruined, but, inside the main gates, you are now proudly escorted around the principal complex of buildings. As so often, the **cloisters**, focus of monastic life, are the most evocative and beautiful part. Late Romanesque, and sporting a pavilion and fountain, they open onto a series of rooms: a splendid Gothic **chapterhouse** (with the former abbots' tombs set in the floor), wine cellars, a parlour, a **kitchen** equipped with ranges and copper pots, and a sombre, wood-panelled **refectory**.

Beyond, you enter the **chapel** in which the twelfth- and thirteenth-century tombs of the kings of Aragón have been meticulously restored by Frederico Marès, the manic collector of Barcelona. They lie in marble sarcophagi on either side of the nave, focusing attention on the central sixteenth-century altarpiece. You'll also be shown the vast old **dormitory**, to which there's direct access from the chapel choir, a poignant reminder of Cistercian discipline. From the dormi-tory (half of which is sealed off since it's still in use), a door leads out onto the cloister roof for views down into the cloister itself and up the chapel towers.

Entry to the monastery costs €4.80, and it's open daily from 10am to 12.30pm and from 3 to 6pm (closing half an hour earlier in the winter). Officially, it can be toured only by members of a **guided group**. The tours take an hour and depart roughly every half-hour (every fifteen minutes Sunday and holidays). However, the porter may let you in to walk around alone if there aren't enough people within a reasonable period of time. There's a **turisme** at Passeig Abat Conill 9 (daily 10am–1.30pm & 3–5.30pm; ☎977 871 247).

Getting there by bus

Three **buses** a day (Mon–Sat only) run to Poblet from Tarragona or Lleida, passing right by the monastery. It's an easy day-trip from either city, or can be seen on the way between the two – the gap between buses is roughly three hours, which is enough time to get around the complex. You could also **stay overnight** at Poblet, an even more attractive proposition if you have your own transport, since there are several pleasant excursion targets in the surrounding countryside (see below). The solitary *Hostal Fonoll* outside the main gate of the monastery (☎977 870 333, ✉mifove@terra.es; ❷) has a decent restaurant and bar, functional standard rooms and more expensive rooms with bath; while 1km up the road, around the walls, the hamlet of **LES MASIES** has a couple more hotels and restaurants, including the *Villa Engràcia* (☎977 870 308, ℗977 870 326; ❸), which has a pool, tennis courts and parking facilities.

Getting there by train: L'Espluga de Francolí

The approach by **train** is much more atmospheric. You get off at the ruined sta-tion of **L'ESPLUGA DE FRANCOLÍ**, from where it's a beautiful three-kilo-metre walk to the monastery, much of it along a signposted country track. L'Espluga itself is a bit of a one-horse town, but there are a couple of places **to stay**, including the *Fonda Les Disset Fonts* (☎977 870 302; ❸), near the train station.

You can of course vary your approach to the monastery, taking the bus one way and choosing to walk to or from L'Espluga (3km), Montblanc (8km) or even Vimbodi (5km), at all of which the Tarragona–Lleida train stops.

Around Poblet: excursions

If you have time and transport, a couple of excursions into the countryside surrounding Poblet are well worth making. The red-stone walled village of **PRADES**, in the Serra de Prades, 20km from the monastery, is a beautifully sited and tranquil place that needs no other excuse for a visit. The *Hotel Espasa*, c/Sant Roc 1 (T977 868 023; ❸), offers simple accommodation if you decide you like it enough to stay on. Prades is also the place to be during the second weekend of July, when they replace the water in the fountain with *cava*, and for a mere €9 you can join in and help yourself.

The other option is to take in two more twelfth-century Cistercian monasteries. **Santes Creus** (summer daily 10am–1.30pm & 3–7pm; winter Tues–Sun 10am–1.30pm & 3–6pm; €3.60, Tues free) is the easier to reach, northeast of **VALLS** on the other side of the Tarragona–Lleida highway. It's built in Transitional style, with a grand Gothic cloister and some Romanesque traces, and you can explore the dormitory, chapterhouse and royal palace. There's a once-daily bus from Tarragona to Valls, which connects with a local service to Santa Creus, but check on return times because you don't want to get stranded in these parts. Trickier to find, though worth the drive, is the monastery of **Vallbona de les Monges** (summer Mon–Sat 10.30am–1.30pm & 4.30–6.45pm, Sun noon–1.30pm & 4.30–6.45pm; winter daily closes 5.45pm; free), north of Poblet, reached up the C240 from Montblanc. This has been occupied continuously for over 800 years, and the church is particularly fine.

Lleida

LLEIDA (Lérida), at the heart of a fertile plain near the Aragonese border, has a rich history. First a *municipium* under the Roman empire and later the centre of a small Arab kingdom, it was reconquered by the Catalans and became the seat of a bishopric in 1149. Little of those periods survives in today's pleasant city but there is one building of outstanding interest, the old cathedral, which is sufficient justification in itself to find the time for a visit. If you have to spend the night in Lleida – and you will if you're heading north to the Pyrenees by train or bus – there are a couple of museums and a steep set of old-town streets to occupy any remaining time. Rooms are easy to come by, and the students at the local university fill the streets and bars on weekend evenings in good-natured throngs.

Arrival and information

Plaça de Sant Joan is a fifteen- to twenty-minute walk east of the **train station**, with the **bus station** a similar distance in the other direction, down Avinguda de Blondel. The very informative **turisme** (Mon–Sat 11am–8pm, Sun 11am–1.30pm; T902 250 050, Wwww.paeria.es/turisme) is at Plaça Espanya 1 and includes a shop and free hotel and restaurant reservation service. There's also a provincial/national office (June–Sept Mon–Fri 9am–8pm, Sat 9am–2pm; Oct–May Mon–Fri 9am–7pm, Sat 9am–2pm; T973 270 997) at Avgda. Madrid 36, overlooking the river. You can connect to the **Internet** at *Cafetó d'Internet*, c/Bonaire 8 (Mon–Sat 9am–2pm & 3.30pm–2am, Sun 7pm–midnight; €4.50 per hour).

Accommodation

There are a couple of **places to stay** right outside the train station, and more along the road straight ahead – Rambla Ferrán – which leads into the centre. Otherwise, press on to the central Plaça Sant Joan, around which there are several possibilities. There's a **campsite**, *Les Basses* (Ⓣ973 235 954; mid-May to Sept), a couple of kilometres out of town on the Huesca road. Take the bus labelled "BS" or "Les Basses" (every 45min from Rambla Ferrán).

Alberg Sant Anastasi Rambla d'Aragó 11 Ⓣ973 266 099. Lleida's youth hostel, smartly renovated and centrally located but only open in July and Sept. €19 for a dorm bed.

Pensió Alex c/Tallada 33 Ⓣ973 275 629. Good, family-run *pensió* on a quiet street near the market. ❷

Hotel Principal Plaça de la Paeria 7 Ⓣ973 230 800, Ⓔinfo@hotelprincipal.net. One of the more comfortable options around Plaça de Sant Joan. ❸

Hotel Sansi Park c/Alcade Porqueras Ⓣ973 244 000, Ⓦwww.ows.es/sansihoteks. The most characterful of the mid-priced options in the centre. ❻

Hotel Ramon Berenguer IV Plaça Ramon Berenguer IV 3 Ⓣ973 237 345, Ⓕ973 239 541. Good value for money and well-equipped rooms in a renovated building near the train station. ❹

The City

The **Seu Vella** (Tues–Sat 10am–1.30pm & 4–7.30pm, closes 5.30pm in winter, Sun 9.30am–1.30pm; €2.40), or old cathedral, is entirely enclosed within the walls of the ruined castle (La Suda), high above the Riu Segre, a twenty-minute climb from the centre of town – or you can take the lift from Plaça de Sant Joan (same hours; €0.40). It's a peculiar fortified building, which in 1707 was deconsecrated and taken over by the military, remaining in military hands until 1940. Enormous damage was inflicted over the years (documented by photos in a side chapel) but the church remains a notable example of the Transitional style, similar in many respects to the cathedral of Tarragona. Once again the Gothic cloisters are masterly, each walk comprising arches different in size and shape but sharing delicate stone tracery. They served the military as a canteen and kitchen. Outside, the views from the walls, away over the plain, are stupendous.

You can climb back down towards the river by way of the aforementioned new cathedral, the **Seu Nova**, a grimy eighteenth-century building only enlivened inside by a series of minuscule, high stained-glass windows. Nearby, halfway up the steep c/Cavallers at no. 15, is the **Museu de Arte Jaume Morera** (June–Sept Tues–Sat 10am–1pm & 6–9pm, Sun 10am–2pm; Oct–May Tues–Sat 11am–1pm & 5–8pm, Sun 11am–2pm; free), a permanent display of contemporary art by local artists, housed on the second floor of an old monastery building. On the other side of the cathedral, on Avinguda de Blondel, the **Museu Arqueològic** (June–Sept Tues–Fri 11am–2pm & 6–9pm, Sat 11am–2pm & 7–9pm; Oct–May Tues–Fri noon–2pm & 5.30–8.30pm, Sat noon–2pm & 5.30–8.30pm; free) is a fairly negligible collection, but again is housed in an interesting building, this time the fifteenth-century Santa María hospital.

Once you've seen the cathedral and museums, you've just about seen the lot that Lleida has to offer, though its central pedestrianized shopping streets are good for a browse, and you can wind up in the newly renovated **Plaça de Sant Joan** for a drink in one of the outdoor cafés.

Eating and drinking

There are plenty of places to **eat** or **drink** in both the old and new parts of town, although Sunday can be a problem when many places are closed

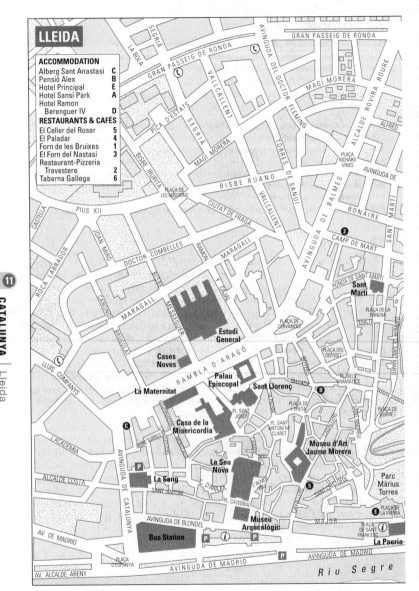

(including most of those detailed below). In the old town, *El Celler del Roser*, at c/Cavallers 24, set in an old cellar, has good local dishes, especially cod and snails, while the rustic and welcoming *El Paladar*, c/Anselm Clavé 10, special-izes in hearty platters of cheese and cold cuts and grilled meats. The modern *La Forn de les Bruixes*, at Avgda. Prat de la Riba 35, has a good range of beers

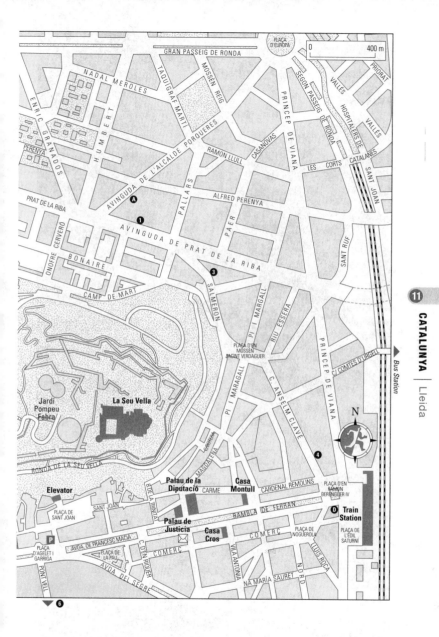

and serves imaginative Catalan fare. For a more expensive option, *El Forn del Nastasi*, at c/Salmerón 10, is a good exponent of modern Lleida cuisine for around €27 per head and is open for Sunday lunch.

If you're looking for more variety and better restaurants, head for the block of streets north of the church of Sant Marti. The university is close by, and this

△ Sant Climent de Taüll

is where the students come to eat and hang out, in the restaurants and loud **music-bars** along the block formed by c/Sant Marti, c/Camp de Marti, c/Balmes and Avinguda Prat de la Riba. As well as a couple of budget Catalan places, there are several pricier pizzerias here, including the popular *Restaurant-Pizzeria Travestere*, c/Camp de Mart 27. Finally, the *Taberna Gallega,* south of the river at Avgda. Garrigues 52, has a strong seafood tapas menu. For **nightlife**, there's only one club, *Brownie's,* on c/Comtes d'Urgell, near the station, but it doesn't start kicking until after 3am. If you fancy something a little mellower, try *Antares Jazz*, c/Ballesters 15, which is open daily, has live music on Fridays and has a wide selection of alcoholic drinks as well as herbal teas.

Travel details

For services from Barcelona to destinations in Catalunya, see p.787.

Trains

Blanes to: Figueres (2 daily; 1hr 30min); Girona (10 daily; 45min).
Figueres to: Barcelona (27 daily; 1hr 30min–2hr); Blanes (2 daily; 1hr 30min); Colera (9 daily; 25min); Girona (27 daily; 25–35min); Llançà (16 daily; 20min); Portbou (12 daily; 30min).
Girona to: Barcelona (29 daily; 1hr 10min–1hr 30min); Blanes (10 daily; 45min); Figueres (27 daily; 35min); Portbou (14 daily; 1hr 10min).
Lleida to: Barcelona via Valls or Reus/Tarragona (23 daily; 2hr–4hr 15min); La Pobla de Segur (3 daily; 2hr 10min); Tarragona (11 daily; 1hr 30min–2hr); Zaragoza (20 daily; 1hr 50min).
Puigcerdà to: La Tour de Carol (6 daily; 5min).
Ribes de Freser to: Núria (9–13 daily in summer; 45min); Queralbs (9–13 daily; 25min).
Ripoll to: Barcelona (12 daily; 2hr 20min–2hr 40min); Puigcerdà (5–6 daily; 1hr 10min–1hr 30min; 4 continue to the first French station, Latour-de-Carol).
Sitges to: Barcelona (every 30min; 25–40min); Cunit (12 daily; 15min); Tarragona (every 30min; 1hr); Vilanova (every 10–20min; 10min).
Tarragona to Barcelona (every 30min; 1hr 30min); Cambrils (12 daily; 20min); Cunit (10 daily; 50min); Lleida (12 daily; 2hr); Salou (11 daily; 10min); Sitges (direct every 30min; 1hr); Tortosa (13 daily; 1hr); Valencia (16 daily; 4hr); Vilanova i la Geltrú (20 daily; 50min); Zaragoza (12 daily; 3hr 30min).

Buses

Banyoles to: Besalú (Mon–Sat 8 daily, Sun 4; 15min); Girona (Mon–Sat 11–16 daily, Sun 6; 30min); Olot (Mon–Sat 8 daily, Sun 4; 50min).
Cadaqués to: Barcelona (2 daily; 2hr 20min); Castelló d'Empúries (4 daily; 1hr); Figueres (3 daily; 1hr 5min); Roses (4 daily; 30min).

Camprodon to: Molló (Mon–Sat 1 daily; 15min); Setcases (Mon–Sat 1 daily; 30min).
L'Escala to: Barcelona (July–Sept 3 daily; 2hr 40min); Figueres (4 daily; 45min); Girona (2 daily; 1hr); Palafrugell (4 daily; 45min); Pals (4 daily; 35min); Sant Pere Pescador (4 daily; 20min); Torroella de Montgrí (4 daily; 20min).
Figueres to: Barcelona (3–8 daily; 1hr 30min); Cadaqués (3 daily; 1hr 5min); Castelló d'Empúries (5 daily; 15min); El Port de la Selva (2 daily; 40min); L'Escala (4 daily; 45min); Espolla (1 daily; 35min); Girona (Mon–Sat 4–8 daily, Sun 3; 1hr); Llançà (4 daily; 25min); Olot (2–3 daily; 1hr 30min); Palafrugell (5 daily; 1hr 30min); Pals (3 daily; 1hr 20min); Roses (5 daily; 30min); Sant Pere Pescador (4 daily; 35min); Torroella de Montgrí (3 daily; 1hr 10min).
Girona to: Banyoles (Mon–Sat 11–16 daily, Sun 6; 30min); Barcelona (Mon–Fri 7 daily, Sat & Sun 3; 1hr 30min); Besalú (Mon–Sat 8 daily, Sun 4; 50min); L'Escala (Mon–Sat 2 daily; 1hr); Figueres (Mon–Sat 8 daily, Sun 3; 1hr); Olot (Mon–Sat 14 daily, Sun 9; 1hr 15min); Palafrugell (hourly; 1hr 15min); Palamós (23 daily; 1hr); Platja d'Oro (23 daily; 45min); Sant Feliu (Mon–Sat 13 daily, Sun 5; 45min); Sant Hilari Sacalm (Mon–Fri 3 daily, Sat 1; 1hr 15min); Tossa de Mar (July–Sept 2 daily; 1hr).
Lleida to: Artesa de Segre (3 daily; 1hr); Barcelona (Mon–Sat 9 daily, Sun 4; 2hr 15min); Huesca (5 daily; 2hr 30min); La Seu d'Urgell (2 daily; 3hr 30min); Montblanc (6 daily; 1hr 30min); Pobla de Segur (1 daily; 2hr); Poblet (Mon–Fri 3 daily; 1hr 15min); Tarragona (3 daily; 2hr); Viella, via Túnel de Viella (2 daily; 3hr); Zaragoza (Mon–Sat 4 daily, Sun 1; 2hr 30min).
Lloret de Mar to: Barcelona (July to mid-Sept 10 daily; 1hr 15min); Blanes (every 15min; 15min); Girona (5 daily; 1hr 20min); Palafrugell (2 daily; 1hr 30min); Palamós (2–4 daily; 1hr); Platja d'Oro (2–4 daily; 50min); Sant Feliu (2–4 daily; 40min); Tossa

de Mar (every 30min; 15min).

Olot to: Banyoles (Mon–Sat 8 daily, Sun 5; 50min); Barcelona (Mon–Sat 7–8 daily, Sun 4; 2hr 15min); Besalú (Mon–Sat 8 daily, Sun 6; 30min); Camprodon (1–2 daily; 45min); Figueres (2–3 daily; 1hr); Girona (11 daily Mon–Sat, Sun 4; 1hr 15min); Ripoll (5 daily; 50min–1hr); Santa Pau (Wed & Sat am, plus Mon 2; 15min); Sant Joan de les Abadesses (2–3 daily; 50min).

Palafrugell to: Barcelona (8 daily; 2hr); L'Escala (4 daily; 35min); Figueres (5 daily; 1hr 30min); Girona (19 daily; 1hr); Lloret de Mar (2 daily; 1hr 30min); Palamos (20 daily; 15min); Pals (4 daily; 10min); Sant Feliu (17 daily; 45min); Sant Pere Pescador (3 daily; 1hr); Torroella de Montgrí (4 daily; 25min).

La Pobla de Segur to: Barcelona (1 daily; 3hr 45min); Capdella (Sept–May Mon–Fri 1 daily, June–Aug 3 weekly; 1hr); Esterri d'Aneu (2 daily Mon–Sat; 1hr 15min); Lleida (1 daily; 2hr); El Pont de Suert (Mon–Sat 1 daily; 1hr 30min); Viella (May–Nov Mon–Sat 1 daily; 3hr).

El Port de la Selva to: Figueres (4 daily; 40min); Llançà (July to mid-Sept 9 daily, rest of the year 2–4 daily; 25min).

Puigcerdà to: Alp (2 daily; 10min); Bagà/Berga (2 daily; 35min–1hr); Llívia (2 daily; 20min); La Molina (1 daily; 30min); La Seu d'Urgell (3 daily; 1hr).

Ripoll to: Camprodon (6–8 daily; 45min); Gombrèn (Mon–Fri 1 daily; 20min); Guardiola de Berguedà (Mon–Fri 1 daily; 2hr); La Pobla de Lillet (Mon–Fri 1 daily; 1hr 45min); Olot (3–4 daily; 50min); Sant Joan de les Abadesses (6–8 daily; 20min).

Sant Feliu to: Barcelona (8 daily; 1hr 30min); Girona (July–Sept 11 daily; 2hr); Lloret de Mar (July & Aug 2 daily; 40min); Palafrugell (16 daily; 45min); Palamós (19 daily; 30min); Platja d'Oro (19 daily; 15min).

La Seu d'Urgell to: Andorra la Vella (Mon–Sat 14 daily, 5 on Sun; 40min); Barcelona (4 daily; 3hr 40min); Lleida (2 daily; 2hr 30min); Puigcerdà (3 daily; 1hr); Sort (2 daily; 1hr 15min).

Tarragona to: Andorra (1–2 daily; 4hr 30min); Barcelona (18 daily; 1hr 30min); Berga (July & Aug 1 daily, rest of the year Sat & Sun only; 3hr 10min); L'Espluga (3 daily; 1hr); La Pobla de Lillet (July & Aug 1 daily, rest of the year Sat & Sun only; 4hr 15min); La Seu d'Urgell (daily at 8am; 3hr 45min); Lleida (3 daily; 2hr); Montblanc (3 daily; 50min); Poblet (3 daily; 1hr 5min); Salou-Cambrils (every 30min; 20min); Tortosa (Mon–Fri 1 daily; 1hr 30min); Valencia (7 daily; 3hr 30min); Zaragoza (4 daily; 4hr).

Tortosa to: Deltebre (Mon–Fri 5 daily, Sat 2; 1hr); Sant Carles de la Ràpita (Mon–Sat 5 daily, Sun 1; 40min); Tarragona (Mon–Fri 1 daily; 1hr 30min).

Tossa de Mar to: Barcelona (July–Sept 12 daily; 1hr 35min); Girona (July–Sept 2 daily, Oct–June 1; 1hr); Lloret de Mar (every 30min; 15min).

Viella to: Lleida (2 daily; 3hr); La Pobla de Segur (May–Nov –1 daily; 3hr); Salardú (1 daily; 20min).

Cruceros boats

Blanes to: Lloret de Mar/Tossa de Mar (June–Sept 5 daily; 20min/45min).

Tossa de Mar to: Sant Feliu (June–Sept 5 daily; 45min); Platja d'Aro/Sant Antoni de Calonge/Palamós (June–Sept 4 daily; 1hr 15min/1hr 25min/1hr 45min).

Valencia and Murcia

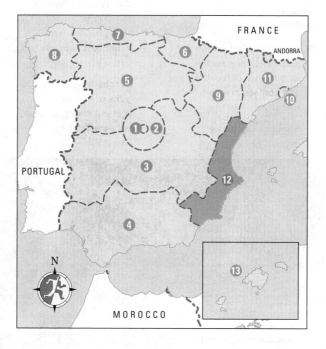

△ La Ciudad de las Artes y Ciencias, Valencia

Valencia and Murcia

The area known as the **Levante** (the East), combining the provinces of Valencia and Murcia, is an incongruous mix of the ancient and modern, of beauty and beastliness. The rich *huerta* of **Valencia** is one of the most fertile regions of Europe: crowded with orange and lemon groves, date palm plantations, and rice fields still irrigated by systems devised by the Moors. Evidence of the lengthy Moorish occupation can be seen throughout the province, in the castles, irrigation systems, crops and place names – Benidorm, Alicante, Alcoy are all derived from Arabic. The growing self-assurance of the region is evident in the increasing presence of *Valenciano* – a dialect of Catalan – which challenges Castilian as the main language of education and broadcasting in the area. There's even an extreme nationalist group that denies the dialect's Catalan origins, but it hasn't managed to convince anyone else.

Murcia is quite distinct, a *comunidad autónoma* in its own right, and there could hardly be a more severe contrast with the richness of the Valencian *huerta*. This southeastern corner of Spain is virtually a desert and is some of the driest territory in Europe. It was fought over for centuries by Phoenicians, Greeks, Carthaginians and Romans, but there survives almost no physical evidence of their presence – or of five hundred years of Moorish rule, beyond an Arabic feel to some of the small towns and the odd date palm here and there.

Much of the region's **coast** is marred by heavy overdevelopment, with concrete apartment blocks and sprawling holiday complexes looming over many of the best beaches. However, away from the big resorts, particularly around **Denia** and **Xàbia** (Jávea) in Valencia, there are some attractive isolated coves, while the historic hilltop settlements of **Altea** and **Peñíscola** are undeniably picturesque, if touristy. In Murcia, the resorts of the **Mar Menor** are reasonably attractive, but very popular with Spanish families in high season; the best beaches are in the extreme south, around **Águilas** where you'll find some dazzling unspoilt coves. The increasingly vibrant cities of **Valencia** and **Alicante** are the major urban centres, and there are several delightful historic small towns and villages a short way inland, such as **Morella**, **Xàtiva** and **Lorca**.

Getting around by public transport is relatively straightforward with frequent train and bus services, though you'll need your own transport to really explore the region. If you do have your own wheels, the motorway network is excellent, but tolls are quite pricey.

There's no shortage of **culinary pleasures** in the region. Gourmets tend to agree that the best paellas are to be found around (but not *in*) Valencia, the city where the dish originated. It should be prepared fresh, and cooked over wood (*leña*), not scooped from some vast, sticky vat; most places will make it for a

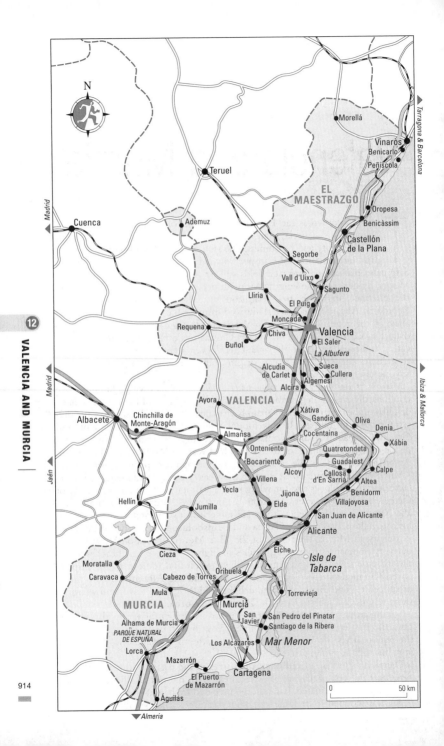

N

Morellá

Vinarós
Benicarló
Peñíscola

EL
MAESTRAZGO

Oropesa

Benicàssim

Teruel

Cuenca

Ademuz

Castellón
de la Plana

Segorbe

Vall d'Uixo
Sagunto

Lliria
El Puig

Moncada
Requena
Chiva
Valencia
Buñol
El Saler
La Albufera

Alcudia
de Carlet
Sueca
Cullera

Algemesi
Alcira

Ayora VALENCIA

Albacete
Chinchilla de
Monte-Aragón

Xàtiva
Gandia
Oliva
Denia

Almansa
Cocentaina
Xàbia

Onteniente
Quatretondeta

Bocariente
Guadalest

Alcoy
Callosa
d'En Sarriá
Calpe
Altea

Villena
Benidorm
Villajoyosa

Yecla
Jijona

Hellín
Elda
San Juan de Alicante

Jumilla
Alicante

Cieza
Elche
Isle de
Tabarca

Moratalla
Caravaca
Cabezo de Torres
Orihuela

Mula
Torrevieja

MURCIA Murcia

Alhama de Murcia
San
Javier
San Pedro del Pinatar
PARQUE NATURAL
DE ESPUÑA
Santiago de la Ribera

Los Alcázares Mar Menor
Lorca

Mazarrón

El Puerto
de Mazarrón
Cartagena

Águilas

0   50 km

minimum of two people, with advance notice. Of the region's other rice-based dishes, the most famous is *arròs a banda*, which is served in two stages: first the rice, then the fish. Another speciality is eels served with piquant *all i pebre* (garlic and pepper) sauce. The sweet-toothed should try *turrón*; made of nuts and honey, it traditionally comes in a soft, flaky variety or very hard like a nougat (the *turrón* from Jijona is the finest). You could follow it with an *horchata* (or *orxata*), a rich drink made from tiger nuts (*chufas*) or almonds (*almendras*).

The Valencia area has a powerful tradition of **fiestas** and there are a couple of elements unique to this part of the country. Above all, throughout the year and more or less wherever you go, there are mock battles between Muslims and Christians (*Moros y Cristianos*). Recalling the Christian Reconquest of the country – whether through symbolic processions or recreations of specific battles – they're some of the most elaborate and colourful festivities to be seen anywhere, above all in Alcoy (see box on p.948). The other recurring feature is the *fallas* (bonfires) in which giant carnival floats and figures are paraded through the streets before being ceremoniously burned.

Valencia

Valencia is emerging as one of the nation's most progressive cities. Spain's third largest, it may not yet be able to approach the cosmopolitan vitality of Barcelona or the cultural variety of Madrid, but the city is shaking off a slightly provincial reputation and reinventing itself at a heady pace. In the last few years a vast, iconic new cultural complex – **La Ciudad de las Artes y Ciencias** – has emerged, a state-of-the-art metro has opened, the city beaches has been revitalized, while dozens of hip new bars, restaurants and boutiques have injected new life into the historic centre. Even Valencia's Club de Fútbol have chipped in and put the city on the map, winning La Liga in 2002 and reaching two European Cup finals. Nevertheless, despite its size, Valencia retains an unpretentious air, and there are few tourists outside *Fallas* time.

Always an important city, Valencia was fought over for the agricultural wealth of its surrounding *huerta*. After Romans and Visigoths, it was occupied by the Moors for over four centuries with only a brief interruption (1094–1101) when El Cid recaptured it. He died here in 1099 but his body, propped on a horse and led out through the gates, was still enough to cause the Moorish armies – previously encouraged by news of his death – to flee in terror. It wasn't until 1238 that Jaime I of Aragón permanently wrested Valencia back. It has remained one of Spain's largest and richest cities ever since.

The city has long boasted some of the best **nightlife** to be found in mainland Spain. *Vivir Sin Dormir* (Live Without Sleep) is the name of one of its bars, and it could be taken as a Valencian mantra. The city is alive with noise and colour throughout the year, with explosions of gunpowder, fireworks and festivities punctuating the calendar. Valencia's **fiestas** are some of the most riotous in Spain and the best is *Las Fallas*, March 12–19 (see box on p.921), which culminates in a massive bonfire where all the processional floats are burned. In July the city celebrates the *Feria de Julio* with bullfights, concerts, the "Battle of the Flowers" and fireworks, while in September there's a spectacular fireworks competition held in the riverbed park.

February

2–5 Moors and Christians battle for the castle in Bocariente, with wild firework displays at night.

Week before Lent *Carnaval* in Águilas is one of the wildest in the country. Good carnival celebrations also in Cabezo de Torres and Vinaròs.

March

12–19 *Las Fallas de San José* in Valencia is by far the biggest of the bonfire festivals, and indeed one of the most important fiestas in all Spain. The whole thing costs as much as €1,200,000, most of which goes up in smoke (literally) on the final *Nit de Foc* when the grotesque caricatures, fashioned from papier-mâché and wood, are burned. Throughout, there are bullfights, music and stupendous fireworks; see p.921.

The middle of the month, especially around the **19th** (*San José*), also sees smaller *fallas* festivals in Xàtiva, Benidorm and Denia.

Third Sun of Lent *Fiesta de la Magdalena* in Castellón de la Plana celebrates the end of Moorish rule with pilgrimages and processions of huge floats.

April

Holy Week is celebrated everywhere. In Elche there are, naturally, big Palm Sunday celebrations making use of the local palms, while throughout the week there are also religious processions in Cartagena, Lorca, Orihuela, Moncada and Valencia. The **Easter processions** in Murcia are particularly famous, and they continue into the following week with, on the Tuesday, the *Bando de la Huerta*, a huge parade of floats celebrating local agriculture, and, on the Saturday evening, the riotous "Burial of the Sardine" which marks the end of these spring festivals.

22–24 Riotous *Moros y Cristianos* fiesta in Alcoy. After a colourful procession, a huge battle commences between the two sides in the main square.

25 Morella holds the traditional fiesta of *Las Primes*.

May

1–5 *Fiestas de los Mayos* in Alhama de Murcia, and *Moros y Cristianos* in Caravaca de la Cruz.

Second Sun *La Virgen de los Desamparados* in Valencia. The climax of this celebration is when the statue of the Virgin is transferred from her basilica to the cathedral.

Third Sun Moors and Christians battle it out in Altea.

June

23–24 *Noche de San Juan*. Magnificent *hogueras* festival in Alicante (and San Juan de Alicante) with processions and fireworks, culminating as huge effigies and bonfires are burnt in the streets at midnight. Celebrated on a smaller scale on the beaches of Valencia (Malvarossa, Cabanyal and Aloboraya) with bonfire-jumping. Altea also celebrates with a popular tree-bearing procession, and a bonfire in the old town.

Arrival and information

Arriving by train at Valencia's beautifully tiled **Estación del Nord**, you're very close to the town centre; walk north along Avenida Marqués de Sotelo to the Plaza del Ayuntamiento, the central square. The **bus station** is some way out on the north side of the river; take local bus #8, the metro to Turia, or allow 25 minutes if you decide to walk. The **Balearic ferry terminal** connects with the central square via bus #4 and with the train station via the #19.

July

Early July *Fiestas de la Santísima Sangre* in Denia with dancing in the streets, music and mock battles.

15–20 *Moros y Cristianos* in Orihuela.

16 In San Pedro del Pinatar a maritime *Romería* in which an image of the Virgin is carried in procession around the Mar Menor.

Second week *Feria de Julio* in Valencia with music, bullfights, and above all fireworks, ending with the Battle of the Flowers in the Alameda. Festival of music in Valencia throughout the month, featuring open-air concerts in Viveros park, plus electronic music events at the IVAM museum.

25–31 *Moros y Cristianos* battle in Villajoyosa by both land and sea.

August

4 Festival in El Palmar with processions by boat into the lake.

First week Local fiesta in Segorbe.

First weekend Benicàssim's international music festival, a massive party bringing together the major names in alternative and electronic music.

14–15 Elche presents a mystery play, based on a drama dating back to medieval times.

14–20 *Feria de Agosto* in Xàtiva has a very extensive cultural dimension including concerts, plays and exhibitions, plus bullfights and barrages of fireworks.

15 Local festivities in Denia, Jumilla, and Requena.

21–23 Local festivities in Jijona.

Last week *La Tomatina*, a riotous free-for-all of tomato-throwing, takes place in Buñol usually on the last Wednesday of the month (see the box on p.930). Morella hosts a music festival.

Last Wed Local fiesta in Sagunto and at the same time the great Moors and Christians festival and a mystery play in Elche.

September

4–9 *Moros y Cristianos* in Villena.

8 *Mare de Deu de la Salut* – colourful folkloric processions in Algemesi.

Second week Bull running through Segorbe's streets at 2pm daily.

8–9 *Les Danses* in Peñíscola's old quarter includes human tower construction.

10–13 International Mediterranean Folk Festival in Murcia.

13 Rice festival in Sueca includes a national paella contest.

22 Fiesta of *Santo Tomás* in Benicàssim with bands and a "blazing bull".

October

Second Sun *La Virgen de Suffrage* Benidorm celebrates its patron saint's day.

18–22 Moors and Christians in Calpe.

November

1 *Fiesta de Todos los Santos*; All Saints' festival in Cocentaina.

December

6–8 *La Fiesta de la Virgen* in Yecla when the effigy of Mary is carried down from the sanctuary on top of the hill amid much partying.

14 The weekend after this date sees four days of Moors and Christians in Petrel.

Most of Valencia's sights are centrally located and can be reached by foot, while there are efficient **public transport** links to the outlying sights (including the Ciudad de las Artes y Ciencias) and the beaches. Buses and trams cost €0.90 per journey, the metro €1.10. If you really want to explore the city, consider buying a **Valencia Card** (one day €6; three days €12) which gives you unlimited access to the entire transport system and discounted entry to many museums – you can buy one at any metro station or newspaper kiosk.

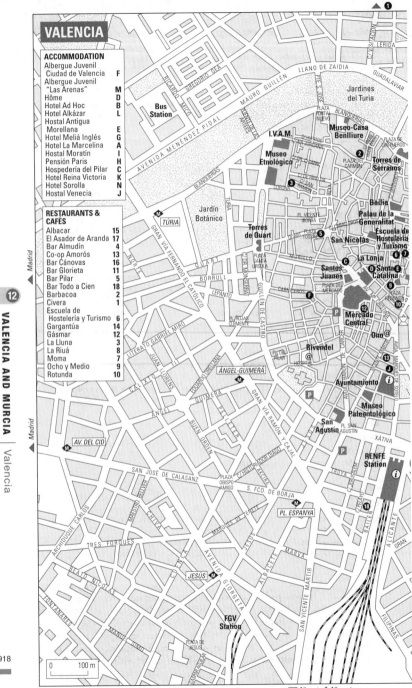

VALENCIA

ACCOMMODATION
Albergue Juvenil
Ciudad de Valencia   **F**
Albergue Juvenil
"Las Arenas"   **M**
Hôme   **D**
Hotel Ad Hoc   **B**
Hotel Alkázar   **L**
Hostal Antigua
Morellana   **E**
Hotel Meliá Inglés   **G**
Hotel La Marcelina   **A**
Hostal Moratín   **I**
Pensión Paris   **H**
Hospedería del Pilar   **C**
Hotel Reina Victoria   **K**
Hotel Sorolla   **N**
Hostal Venecia   **J**

RESTAURANTS &
CAFÉS
Albacar   15
El Asador de Aranda   17
Bar Almudín   4
Co-op Amorós   13
Bar Cánovas   16
Bar Glorieta   11
Bar Pilar   5
Bar Todo a Cien   18
Barbacoa   2
Civera   1
Escuela de
Hostelería y Turismo   6
Gargantúa   14
Gásmar   12
La Lluna   3
La Riuá   8
Moma   7
Ocho y Medio   9
Rotunda   10

0   100 m

▼ Alicante & Albacete

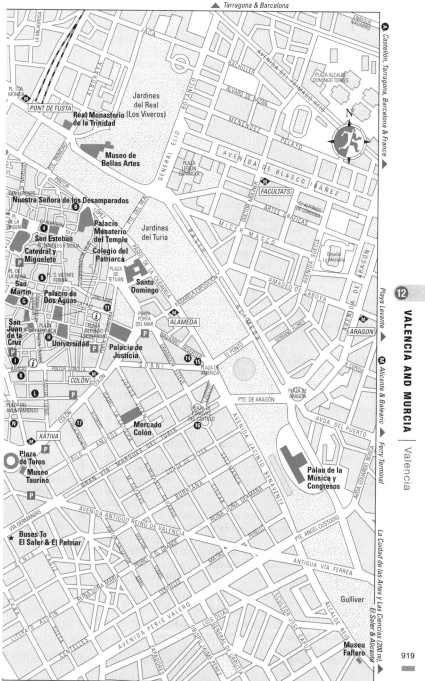

Ⓐ Castellón, Tarragona, Barcelona & France ▶

ENRIQUE NAVARRO

LA MILAGROSA

JACA

PL. STA MONICA

PONT DE FUSTA

Jardines del Real (Los Viveros)

Real Monasterio de la Trinidad

PLAZA ALCALDE DOMINGO TORRES

ALVARO DE BAZAN

BACHILLER

AVENIDA DEL PRIMADO REIG

MENENDEZ PELAYO

N

Museo de Bellas Artes

PLAZA LEGION ESPAÑOLA

AVENIDA DE BLASCO IBÁÑEZ

SAN LORENZO

Nuestra Señora de los Desamparados Ⓑ

EL ALFONSO DE CÓRDOBA

Ⓜ FACULTATS

ARTES GRÁFICAS

Playa Levante ▶

Palacio Monasterio del Temple

Jardines del Turia

MICER MASCO

Estadio La Mestalla

AVENIDA SUECA

ARAGÓN

San Esteban

Catedral y Miguelete

Colegio del Patriarca

PLAZA DE TETUÁN

AMADEO DE SABOYA

AVENIDA DE

Ⓜ Alicante & Balearic ▶

Ⓐ

San Martín

Santo Domingo

PLAZA PORTA DEL MAR

SERRANO FLORES

Ⓜ ARAGON

Palacio de Dos Aguas

Ⓜ ALAMEDA

San Juan de la Cruz

PLAZA DEL AYUNTAMIENTO

Universidad

Palacio de Justicia

PLAZA DE AMÉRICA

PLAZA DE ARAGÓN

COLÓN

XÀTIVA

Mercado Colón

PLAZA DE CÁNOVAS DEL CASTILLO

PTE. DE ARAGÓN

AVDA. DEL PUERTO

Ferry Terminal ▶

Plaza de Toros

Museo Taurino

GRAN VÍA MARQUÉS DEL TURIA

RUAR IANA

Palau de la Música y Congresos

PTE. ANGEL CUSTODIO

VÍA GERMANÍAS

Buses To El Saler & El Palmar

AVENIDA ANTIGUO REINO DE VALENCIA

REINA DOÑA GERMANA

ANTIGUA VÍA FERREA

La Ciudad de las Artes y Las Ciencias (200 m), El Saler & Alicante ▶

Gulliver

AVENIDA PERIS VALERO

Museu Fallero

The city's main **turismo**, at c/de la Paz 48 (Mon–Sat 9am–6.30pm; ☎963 986 422, Ⓦwww.comunitat-valenciana.com), has helpful English-speaking staff and an excellent stock of information. Other branches are located at the Plaza del Ayuntamiento (Mon–Fri 9am–2.15pm), the train station (Mon–Fri 9am–6.30pm), c/Poeta y Querol, and there's also a kiosk in the Plaza de la Reina.

Accommodation

Most of Valencia's hotels are situated in the central area, between the train station and Río Turia. Upmarket hotels drop their prices by as much as thirty percent at weekends when there's less demand from business clientele. There are **campsites** all along the coast, but none less than 18km from the city.

Hotel Ad Hoc c/Boix 4 ☎963 919 140, Ⓦwww.adhochoteles.com. Valencia's first boutique hotel is suitably comfortable and stylish, with exposed brick walls and textile wall hangings, in a building with plenty of period character. ❻

Hotel Alkázar c/Mosén Femades 11 ☎963 529 575, Ⓕ963 512 568. Dependable and well-cared-for town-centre hotel, near the post office. All rooms with private shower. ❹

Hostal Antigua Morellana c/d'En Bou 2 ☎ & Ⓕ963 915 773, Ⓦhttp://inicia.es/de/hostalam/. Tastefully renovated hotel close to the Barrio del Carmen with excellent-value rooms, all with a/c. Book ahead. ❸

Hotel Meliá Inglés Marqués de Dos Aguas 6 ☎963 516 426, Ⓔmelia.ingles@solmedia.com. Recently refurbished hotel, very conveniently situated near the Palacio de Dos Aguas. ❻

Hotel La Marcelina Paseo de Neptuno 72, near the sea ☎963 725 135. Pleasant place offering comfortable rooms with baths. ❸

Hostal Moratín c/Moratín 15 ☎963 521 220. Good-value, central *hostal* with clean and comfortable rooms. ❷

Pensión Paris c/Salvá 12 ☎963 526 766. Excellent, family-owned: the pleasant rooms have pine furniture and some have private shower. ❶

Hospedería del Pilar Plaza Mercado 19 ☎963 916 600. Well-located *hostal* with large, airy, light rooms, some with private shower. No credit cards. ❶ or with bath ❷

Hotel Reina Victoria c/Barcas 4 ☎963 520 487, Ⓔhreinavictoriavalencia@husa.es. Upmarket, centrally located hotel near the Plaza del Ayuntamiento, with off-season and weekend discounts. ❻

Hotel Sorolla Convento Santa Clara 5 ☎ 963 523 392, Ⓦwww.hotelsorolla.com. Very comfortable, slightly Japanese-influenced rooms (all with a/c and some with sun terraces) and a good location on a pedestrianized street makes this one of the best three-star hotels in town. Price includes breakfast. ❺

Hostal Venecia c/en Llop 5 ☎963 524 267, Ⓦwww.hotel-venecia.com. Modernized *hostal* with a selection of comfortable a/c rooms; some with views over the Plaza del Ayuntamiento. ❹

Hostels

Albergue Juvenil Ciudad de Valencia c/Balmes 17 ☎963 925 100, Ⓦwww.alberguedevalencia.com. Attractive new youth hostel, situated close to the Mercado Central that's been refurbished to a high standard. €8 up to age 25, €11 over 25s.

Albergue Juvenil "Las Arenas" c/Egenia Viñes 24 ☎963 564 288, Ⓔalberguelasarenas @infonegocio.com. Grubby but character-rich hostel, situated right by the southern end of Malvarossa beach at the end of bus route #32. Very sociable place with kitchen facilities, a laundry, gym and no curfew. Phone ahead to see if it's still open for business, as the owners have had licensing problems. €8 up to age 25, €11; RG readers receive fifty-percent discount.

Hôme c/La Lonja 4 & second branch at c/Cadires 11 ☎963 916 229, Ⓦwww.likeathome.net. The best budget options in the city. These two stylish backpacker hostels are located in the heart of the historic quarter and boast retro-chic furnishings and very clean dorms plus private rooms. Full kitchen, laundry and Internet facilities, bike rental and a friendly atmosphere. The c/Cadires branch is slightly more spacious and attractive. €14pp in dorm, doubles ❷

Camping

Devesa Gardens Nazaret-Oliva ☎961 611 136, Ⓔcampingdevesagardens@ctv.es. Eighteen kilometres out, near El Saler beach and La Albufera; take the hourly bus from the junction of Gran Vía and c/Sueca to El Saler-Perelló. Open all year.

The City

The most atmospheric area to explore is undoubtedly the maze-like streets of the **Barrio del Carmen**, roughly the area north of the Mercado Central to the Río Turia, extending up to the Torres de Serranos and west to the Torres de Quart. This long neglected quarter of the city is experiencing a period of lengthy regeneration, as buildings are renovated and stylish cafés open up next to crumbling town houses, but for now it retains a slightly edgy, alternative appeal. There's a wealth of detail to admire: in c/de Caballeros, look for the old door knockers placed high up for the convenience of the horse-borne gentlemen residents (hence the name of the street). The **city walls**, which, judging from the two surviving gates, must have been magnificent, were pulled down in 1871 to make way for a ring road, and the beautiful church of **Santo Domingo**, in Plaza de Tétuan, has been converted into a barracks – the very barracks from which General Milans del Bosch ordered his tanks onto the streets during the abortive coup of 1981. This incident, however, isn't representative of the city's political inclination, which has traditionally been to the left – Valencia was the seat of the Republican government during the Civil War after it fled Madrid, and was the last city to fall to Franco.

The oldest part of the city is almost entirely encircled by a great loop of the **Río Turia**, which is now a landscaped **riverbed park**. In 1956, after serious flooding damaged much of the old town, the river was diverted. The ancient stone bridges remain, but the riverbed now houses cycle paths and footpaths,

Las Fallas

From March 12 to 19, around the saint's day of San José, Valencia erupts in a blaze of colour and noise for the **Fiesta de las Fallas**. During the year, each *barrio* or neighbourhood builds a satirical caricature or **falla**. These begin to appear in the plazas of each *barrio* at the beginning of March and are judged and awarded prizes before being set alight at midnight on March 19, the *Nit de Foc*. The festival takes its name from the Valencian word for torch. Traditionally, carpenters celebrated the day of San José and the beginning of spring with a ritual burning of spare wood. They would decorate the torches used over the winter and add them to the bonfire. This simple rite of spring has become an international tourist attraction, and it's an extraordinary sight to watch these painstakingly constructed models, some as tall as buildings, some big enough to walk inside, be strung with firecrackers and literally go up in smoke. The *fallas* are ignited in succession; the last to go up are the prizewinners. Each *falla* has a small model or **ninot** beside it, usually created by the children of the *barrio*. The *ninots* are exhibited in La Lonja before the fiesta begins, and the best is added to the Museu Faller; the rest are burnt with the *fallas*. Finally, around one o'clock, the *falla* of the Plaza del Ayuntamiento goes up in flames, set off by a string of firecrackers, followed by the last thunderous firework display of the fiesta.

During the fiesta, processions of *falleros*, dressed in traditional costume and accompanied by bands, carry flowers to the Plaza de la Virgen, where the flowers are massed to create the skirt of a huge statue of La Virgen. The daily **Las Mascaletas** firecracker display takes place at 2pm in the Plaza del Ayuntamiento – for a reputedly unpunctual race, the Valencians observe the timing of this celebration religiously. Traffic comes to a standstill, streets are blocked and the whole city races to the central square for a ten-minute series of body-shuddering explosions. There are nightly fireworks, bullfights, paella contests in the streets and *chocolate y buñuelos* stalls selling fresh doughnuts. On March 20, Valencia returns to normality – the streets are cleaned overnight, and the planning begins for the next year's *Fallas*.

football pitches and also the astonishing architecture of **Ciudad de las Artes y Ciencias**, Europe's largest cultural complex and the most ambitious construction project the city has ever undertaken.

Around the Plaza del Ayuntamiento

Within the **Plaza del Ayuntamiento** is a central square lined with flower stalls, and an impressive floodlit fountain. The *ayuntamiento* houses the **Museo Histórico Municipal** (Mon–Fri 9am–2.30pm; free) whose library has an impressive eighteenth-century map of Valencia showing the city walls intact.

The distinctive feature of Valencian architecture is its wealth of elaborate Baroque facades – you'll see them on almost every old building in town, but none so extraordinary or rich as the **Palacio del Marqués de Dos Aguas**. Hipólito Rovira, who designed its amazing alabaster doorway, died insane in 1740, which should come as no surprise to anyone who's seen it. Inside is the **Museo Nacional de Cerámica** (Tues–Sat 10am–2pm & 4–8pm, Sun 10am–2pm; €2.40, free Sat pm & Sun), with a vast collection of ceramics from all over Spain. Valencia itself was a major ceramics centre, largely owing to the size of its *morisco* population. Apart from an impressive display of *azulejos*, the collection contains some stunning plates with gold and copper varnishes (*reflejos*), and a trio of evocatively ornate eighteenth-century carriages. In the same decorative vein as the *palacio* is the church of **San Juan de la Cruz** (or San Andrés) next door, whose facade is currently being restored.

Nearby to the northeast, in the Plaza Patriarca, is the Neoclassical former **Universidad** with lovely cloisters where free classical concerts are held throughout July, and the beautiful Renaissance **Colegio del Patriarca**, where the small **art museum** (daily 11am–1.30pm; €1.20) includes excellent works by El Greco, Morales and Ribalta. Another Ribalta, *The Last Supper*, hangs above the altar in the college's **chapel**; in the middle of the *Miserere* service at 10am on Friday mornings it's whisked aside to reveal a series of curtains. The last of these, drawn at the climactic moment, conceals a giant illuminated crucifix. The whole performance is amazingly dramatic, and typical of the aura of miracle and mystery which the Spanish Church still cultivates. The university **library** contains the first book printed in Spain, *Les Trobes*, in 1474.

The cathedral and around

Northwest from the university is the café-rich **Plaza de la Reina**, which is overlooked by the florid spire of the church of Santa Catalina and octagonal tower of Valencia's **Catedral** (daily 7.30am–1pm & 4.30–8.30pm). The cathedral, founded in the thirteenth century, embraces an eclectic combination of architectural styles, with the lavishly ornate Baroque main entrance leading to a largely Gothic-built interior. It's an exhausting climb up the cathedral tower, known as the **Miguelete** (Mon–Sat 10am–12.30pm & 4.30–7.30pm, Sun 10am–1pm & 5–7pm; €1.20) but the spectacular views of the city and its many blue-domed churches more than compensate.

The cathedral's most celebrated religious icon is a gold and agate chalice (the Santo Cáliz), said to be the one used by Christ at the Last Supper – the Holy Grail itself. It's certainly old and, hidden away throughout the Dark Ages in a monastery in northern Aragón, it really did inspire many of the legends associated with the Grail. Other treasures include the two Goya paintings of the San Francisco chapel, one of which depicts an exorcism (the corpse was originally naked, but after Goya's death a sheet was painted over it). The cathedral's **museum** contains more paintings and also a 2300-kilo tabernacle made from gold, silver and jewels donated by the Valencian people. Above the structure's crossing, the cathedral's fourteenth-century lantern is another fine feature, as are its soaring windows glazed with thin sheets of alabaster to let in the Valencian light.

Leaving the cathedral through the Puerta de los Apóstoles, you enter the Plaza de la Virgen. Here, close to the doorway, the Tribunal de las Aguas, the black-clad regulatory body of Valencia's water users, meets at noon every Thursday to judge grievances about the water irrigation system of the *huertas*. The practice dates back to Moorish times, and Blasco Ibáñez (1867–1928) describes their workings in detail in his novel *La Barraca*, which is about peasant life in the Valencian *huerta* and remains the best guide to the life of the region at that time.

Two footbridges allow the clergy (only) to go straight from the cathedral into the Archbishop's Palace and on to the domed basilica of **Nuestra Señora de los Desamparados** (currently closed for restoration), also on the Plaza de la Virgen, where thousands of candles constantly burn in front of the image of the Virgin, patron of Valencia.

From the plaza, c/Caballeros leads to the **Palau de la Generalitat**, which dates from the fifteenth century and today is the seat of the Valencian autonomous government. The courtyard can be visited on weekdays (9am–6pm; free), but to see inside you need to make an appointment (☎963 866 100; English-speaking guide available). It's worth the effort to see the beautifully painted ceilings and frescoes depicting a meeting of the assembly (1592) in the Salón Dorado and the tiled Salón de Cortes.

Silk exchange and markets

If you tire of Baroque excesses, the wonderfully sombre interior of the Gothic **La Lonja** (also known as Lonja de la Seda, or the Silk Exchange; Tues–Sat 9.30am–2pm & 5–9pm, Sun 9.30am–2pm; free) is in the Plaza del Mercado. The main focus of this UNESCO-listed building is its superb main hall, with an elegant rib-vaulted ceiling supported by slender, spiralling columns; the wooden trading tables are now used on Sundays by coin and stamp collectors.

Opposite is the enormous **Mercado Central**, a Modernist iron, girder and glass structure built in 1928, embellished with a collage of tiles and mosaics, and crowned with swordfish and parrot weathervanes. It's one of the biggest markets in Europe – fitting for *huerta* country – with almost a thousand stalls selling fruit and vegetables, meat and seafood, hard-to-find herbs and health foods. It winds down by around 2pm, and is closed all day on Sundays.

About a kilometre to the southeast, Valencia's other market, the recently-renovated **Mercado Colón** on c/Cirilo Amoros, is an even more impressive Modernista building. Its open-sided rectangular design loosely resembles a church, with slim wrought-iron columns supporting a steep pitched roof, and monumental arched facades at either end. However, it's the building's detail that's really outstanding, combining two-tone brickwork with broken tile mosaic chimneys, features that reveal the influence of Antoni Gaudí (see p.1054) – indeed, the market's architect Francisco Mora was a close personal friend of the Catalan genius. The Mercado Colón now houses a couple of upmarket cafés, a restaurant, some flower stalls and a bookstore.

Museums and galleries

The **Museu de Belles Artes** (Tues–Sun 10am–8pm; free), on the far side of the river, has one of the best general collections in Spain, with works by Bosch, El Greco, Goya, Velázquez, Ribera and Ribalta, as well as quantities of modern Valencian art. Outside is the largest of Valencia's parks – the **Jardines del Real** (also called the Viveros) – in the centre of which is a small **zoo** (daily 10am–9pm; €3.80). The gardens host various events during the summer: a book fair in May and a music fair in July with open-air concerts.

As you head back into town don't miss the fourteenth-century **Torres Serranos** (Tues–Sat 9am–1.45pm & 4.30–7.45pm, Sun 9am–1.45pm; free), an impressive gateway defending the entrance to the town across the Río Turia, with panoramic views from the top. The other gateway, guarding the western approach, is the **Torres de Quart**, a simpler structure but equally awesome in scale, that was once a women's prison.

A couple of minutes' walk east of here is IVAM, the **Instituto Valenciano de Arte Moderno** (Tues–Sun 10am–8pm; €2.10, free Sun), whose main gallery at c/Guillém de Castro 118 has a permanent display of works by sculptor Julio González as well as many excellent temporary exhibitions by mainly Spanish contemporary artists. It also has a smaller gallery near Plaza del Carmen at c/Museu 2 (Tues–Sat 10am–2.15pm & 4–7.30pm, Sun 10am–7.30pm; free), currently devoted to temporary shows.

To gain insight into Valencia's *Fiesta de las Fallas* (see box on p.921, head for the **Museu Fallero**, Plaza de Monteolivete (Tues–Sat 9.15am–2pm & 5.30–9pm, Sun 9.15am–2pm; €2), near the riverbed park (bus #13 from Plaza del Ayuntamiento). Here you'll find a fascinating array of *ninots* which have been voted the best of their year, and consequently saved from the flames. For a more hands-on experience, the **Museo del Artista Fallero** (same hours; €2), at c/del Ninot 24 (bus #27 from behind the *ayuntamiento*), reveals exactly how the *fallas* are made.

La Ciudad de las Artes y las Ciencias

More than any other project, the breathtaking **Ciudad de las Artes y las Ciencias** (City of Arts and Sciences; ⓦ www.cac.es), still rising from the riverbed in the south of the city, symbolizes the city government's vision for Valencia and quest to establish the city as a prime tourist destination. A giant complex consisting of four futuristic edifices, designed mainly by Valencian architect Santiago Calatrava, it will rank as Europe's largest cultural centre when the final building, the iconic pistachio nut-shaped **Palacio de las Artes**, is completed in 2004.

The architecture itself is simply stunning. Even if you only have a day or two in the city, it's well worth the effort getting here to take in the eye-catching buildings surrounded by huge, shallow pools. Calatrava's designs adopt an organic form, his technical and engineering brilliance providing the basis for his pioneering concrete, steel and glass creations. However, despite near universal acclaim

△ Hemisfèric

for the architecture of the Ciudad, the complex has not completely escaped criticism. Some on the political left feel that the vast cost of constructing the complex should have been used to tackle the city's pressing social issues, while other critics have been less than overwhelmed by some of the content inside the Ciudad's startling structures. To decide for yourself, you'll find there are several discounted ticket options – a combined **entrance** to all three attractions is €25.85. You'll need a full day to see everything, and there are cafés and restaurants inside all the buildings. The only transport link to the Ciudad is by **bus**; take #35 from Avenida Marqués de Sotelo, just south of the Plaza del Ayuntamiento; the journey takes about twenty minutes.

The **Hemisfèric** (daily June–Sept 10am–10pm; Oct–May 10am–9pm; €6.60) is arguably the most astonishing of the lot: a striking eye-shaped concrete structure – complete with lashes, and an eyeball that forms a huge concave screen used to project IMAX movies. Unfortunately, the documentary films are pretty disappointing, and spoiled by gimmicky laser effects. Next door, the colossal **Museo de las Ciencias** (Science Museum; daily June–Sept 10am–10pm; Oct–May 10am–9pm; €6), whose protruding supports make the building resemble a giant sun-bleached carcass, is crammed with interactive exhibits about science, sport and the human body that are sure to appeal to children. Parallel to these two buildings, it's well worth a stroll along the elegant roof of the complex car park, L'Umbracle, which is planted with palm trees and Mediterranean scrubs.

Some 500m to the south, the **Parque Oceanográfico**, designed by Félix Candela (Jan to mid-March & mid-Oct to Dec Mon–Fri 10am–6pm, Sat & Sun 10am–8pm; mid-March to June & Sept to mid-Oct Mon–Fri 10am–8pm, Sat & Sun 10am–10pm; July & Aug daily 10am–midnight; €19.80), is one of the world's largest aquariums. Divided into ten zones, there are beluga whales in the Arctic area, Japanese spider crabs in the Temperate zone and a kaleidoscopic collection of reef fish, sharks and turtles in the 70-metre tunnel that forms the Tropical zone. Controversially, in what's supposed to be a scientific institution, the Oceanográfico also includes dolphin shows.

Eating

Although it's the home of **paella**, the city of Valencia doesn't offer the best opportunities for sampling this most Spanish of dishes. The finest places to eat it are, in fact, out of town in Perellonet or El Palmar (see p.931), or along the

---

Horchata

Valencia is also known for its **horchata** – a drink made from *chufas* (tiger nuts) served either liquid or *granizada* (slightly frozen). It is accompanied by *fartóns* (long, thin cakes). Legend has it that the name "horchata" was coined by Jaume I, shortly after he conquered Valencia. He was admiring the *huerta* one hot afternoon, and an Arab girl offered him a drink so refreshing that he exclaimed, "*Aixó es or, xata*" (this is gold, girl).

You can get *horchata* all over the city, but the best traditionally comes from **Alboraya**, formerly a village in the Valencian suburbs, now absorbed into the city. The oldest *horchatería* in town is the *Santa Catalina* on the southwest corner of Plaza de la Reina. The various *horchaterías* and *heladerías* on Plaza San Lorenzo, just in from the Torres de Serranos, are excellent and very good value. To get to Alboraya, take bus #70 or metro line #3 to Metro Alboraya from Estación Pont de Fusta (across the river from Torres de Serranos). The most renowned *horchatería* is *Daniel*, Avda. de la Horchata 41, where you can sit on the terrace and escape from the summer heat of the city.

Valencian cuisine

Gastronomy is of great cultural importance to the Valencians. Rice is the dominant ingredient in dishes of the region, grown locally in paddy fields still irrigated by the Moorish canal system (*acequias*). The genuine **Paella Valenciana** doesn't mix fish and meat. It typically contains chicken, rabbit, green beans, *garrofón* (large butter beans), snails, artichokes and saffron. Shellfish are eaten as a starter.

Rice dishes vary around the region: *arroz negro* is rice cooked with squid complete with ink which gives the dish its colour, and served with *all i oli*, a powerful garlic mayonnaise. *Arroz al horno* is drier, baked with chickpeas. *Fideuá* is seafood and noodles cooked paella-style. You'll find *arroz a banda* further south on the coast around Denia – it's rice cooked with seafood, served as two separate dishes: soup, then rice. Around Alicante you can try *arroz con costra*, which is a meat-based paella topped with a baked egg crust. Apart from rice, vegetables (best *a la plancha*, brushed with olive oil and garlic) are always fresh and plentiful.

city beach, **Playa Levante** – Paseo Neptuno is lined with small hotels, all with their own paella and *marisco* restaurants. For tapas and budget eating, you're best off heading to the area around the Mercado Central, where there are plenty of places offering set meals for under €10.

Albacar c/Sorní 35 ☎963 951 005. Stylish restaurant near Plaza de la América serving modish and fairly expensive Mediterranean cuisine. Closed Sat lunchtime, Sun & Aug 7–Sept 7.

El Asador de Aranda c/Félix Pizcheta 9 ☎963 529 791. Fine Aragonese delicacies, including *lechazo asado*. Closed Sun eve during July & Aug.

Bar Almudín c/Almudín 14. Busy place located just behind the cathedral and renowned for its excellent seafood tapas.

Coop Amorós c/en Llop 3, just off Plaza del Ayuntamiento. Atmospheric, inexpensive tapas bar which has specialized in seafood tapas for over seventy years. Closed Sun and mid-Aug.

Bar Cánovas Plaza Cánovas Castillo. One of the city's best tapas bars, which also serves full meals including a €6 *menú*.

Bar Glorieta Plaza Alfonso Magnánimo. Large old bar serving tapas and excellent coffee (closes about 9pm). Closed Sun & Easter.

Bar Pilar on the corner of c/Moro Zeit, just off Plaza del Esparto. Traditional place for *mejillones* (mussels) – they serve them in a piquant sauce and you throw the shells into buckets under the bar. Closed Wed.

Bar Todo a Cien c/Bailen 42. Great budget eats beside the train station; many tapas cost under a euro, and they also serve a €5.60 *menú* during the week. Closed Sun.

Barbacoa Plaza del Carmen 6 ☎963 922 448. Serves a wonderful *menú del día* including barbecued meat for €11.40. Although recently expanded, reservation is recommended at weekends as it's popular.

Civera c/Lérida 11 & 13 ☎963 475 917. Valencia's best seafood restaurant, situated across the river from the Torres de Serranos, with mains from €11.

Escuela de Hostelería y Turismo c/Correjería 28 ☎963 155 250. Set in a beautiful seventeenth-century mansion, enjoy excellent food and service at moderate prices from Valencia's future restaurateurs and *maitres d'*. Closed Sun & July–Aug.

Gargantúa c/Navarro Reverter 18 ☎963 346 849. Good Valencian restaurant serving regional specialities. Closed Sat lunchtime, Sun, late Aug & Easter.

Gásmar c/Palafox 9. Tapas bar with tables overlooking the market, plus a delicious set *menú* for €9.

La Lluna c/San Ramón 23 ☎963 922 146. Inexpensive vegetarian restaurant right in the heart of the Barrio del Carmen with a bargain-priced *menú del día*. Closed Sun, Aug & Easter.

La Riuà c/del Mar 27. Pleasingly no-frills place that's famous for seafood, home-made paella and *fideuá*. Main dishes start at €9.

Moma c/Correjeria 12 ☎963 926 462. Close to the Plaza de la Reina, this fashionable restaurant offers creative, modern Spanish cuisine at affordable prices. Closed Sun.

Ocho y Medio Plaza Lope de Vega 5 ☎963 922 022. Very stylish place, with terrace seating and an elegant dining room, serving an inventive and delicious European *menú*. Expect to pay around €30 per person.

Rotunda Plaza Redonda. Moderately priced restaurant, with a good selection of local dishes situated on Valencia's distinctive round mini plaza. Open for lunch only.

Bars and nightlife

Valencia takes its **nightlife** very seriously and has one of the liveliest bar scenes in mainland Spain. However, the action is widely dispersed, with many locations across the Turia, and if you don't know where to go, the city can seem dead at night. If you do decide to jump from one zone to another, taxis are inexpensive; you'll rarely have to pay more than €6. To get a grip on what's going on, *24–7 Valencia* is an excellent free monthly English-language listings guide – you can pick up copies in places where foreigners get together, including *Finnegan's* pub on Plaza de la Reina.

Barrio del Carmen

In town, the **Barrio del Carmen** (in Valenciano "de Carmé") is one of the liveliest areas at night, especially around c/Cabelleros, with scores of small cafés, music-bars and restaurants. The whole area between Plaza de la Reina, Plaza Santa Ursula and Plaza Portal Nueva is heaving at the weekend. It's a peculiar mix of the *pijo* (posh) and *grunge* (grungy), and more or less everything shuts at 3 or 4am. The bars of Plaza del Negrito are sociable and atmospheric, with *Café del Negrito* and *Cava del Negret* both drawing an artistic crowd, and *Ghecko*, which has outside seating, a more well-heeled clientele. Of the many bars on the main drag, c/Cabelleros, *Sant Jaume* at no. 52 (which has a great terrace) is always popular, while close by, *Radio City*, at c/Santa Terera 19, is always lively and hosts poetry, films and live music, with genuine flamenco on Tuesdays. For a reggae vibe, head to *Juanito's* at c/Lepanto 8, close to the Torres de Quart. One of the best *pijo* clubs in the area is *Calcutta*, in a converted old house in c/Reloj Viejo off c/Cabelleros; it's open until 8am. You'll find plenty of other lively options along c/Serranos, c/Alta (where *Circus* has electronica nights) and c/Baja (where *Jimmy Glass* hosts live jazz).

Across the Río Turia

On the other side of the river most of the "in" places are close to the new **university** region. Some of the best bar-clubs are around c/Blasco Ibáñez – try *Warhol* at no. 111 for alternative rock and electronica. Close by, *Woodstock* at Poly y Peyrolón 37 has a student vibe and plays indy and rock music, or *Black Note*, on the same street, has live soul and jazz-influenced music. *Wah Wah* at Campoamor 52 has a bohemian ambience and live bands.

Combinados Valencianos

The *valencianos* really seem to like *combinados*, or **cocktails**, which don't necessarily have the upmarket connotation they have elsewhere. *Agua de Valencia* – made with orange juice, Cava and vodka – is *the* classic cocktail, and is served by the jug. Head to the *Cervecería de Madrid*, a popular old-fashioned bar just below Plaza de la Reina, at c/de la Abadía de San Martín 10, for a taste; or in Barrio del Carmen *Cava del Negret* on Plaza del Negrito is another legendary venue to sample the city's cocktail of choice. *Café Malvarrosa*, c/Ruíz de Lihoro, off c/de la Paz, has its own *Agua de Malvarrosa*, made with lemon instead of orange. The *Rincón Latino*, c/Gobernador Viejo 10, off c/Conde Montornes, near Plaza San Vicente Ferrer, is a smoky cellar where the speciality is inexpensive Nicaraguan drinks – order a rum and pineapple cocktail and you'll get a tiny glass of each, the idea being to toss back all the rum in one go, quickly followed by the juice.

Malvarrosa beach

In **summer**, the bars lining the **Malvarrosa beach** are the places to be, especially *Genaro*, *Tropical* and *Akuarela* on c/Eugenio Vines (the beach road). To get there, take bus #19 from Plaza del Ayuntamiento or the tram from the north side of the Pont de Fusta bridge; night bus #1 or an €8 cab ride will get you back to the centre of town. There are also several bars between Paseo Neptuno and the Paseo Marítimo next to the port which are less rowdy; *Vivir Sin Dormir* is popular with travellers, while the open-air *La Floridita* serves up Latin sounds to an older crowd.

Plaza Cánovas del Castillo

The fashionable area in and around **Plaza Cánovas del Castillo**, just west of the Puente de Aragón, is full of *pubs* (music bars) where people go to see and be seen. The bars along c/Serrano Morales (especially *Champán*) and c/Grabador Esteve are yuppie haunts (the cars outside are a good indicator), but those on the south side of the plaza, down c/Salamanca, c/Conde de Altea and c/Burriana, are more mixed. In both cases, each bar has its own particular age group and style – there's something for everyone, from salsa to flamenco to *bacalao* (see below). In many of the bars around Plaza Cánovas you can ask the waiters for discount/free entrance cards for clubs.

Clubs

Valencia has had a vibrant clubbing scene since the late 1980s, though the commercial **bacalao** or *makina* (machine) rave music that developed in the city is now waning in popularity. Check out the free *A Little Beat* magazine for the latest events. Most clubs play vocal-rich house, but techno, drum'n'bass and other genres also have their aficionados. The unpretentious *Latex Community*, located 200m south of the train station on Gran Vía Germanias 31, is recommended, with two levels: electronica on the ground floor and leading house DJs upstairs. Further from the centre, *Le Club*, at c/Fuente en Corts, is the premiere house club, with three floors, a fashionable crowd and a great sound system and visuals. **Salsa** and Latin music lovers tend to congregate around the c/Juan Llorens area where you'll find *Havana* at no. 41, *Brisa de Cayo* at no. 48 at *Cayo Largo* at no. 3.

Gay scene

Valencia has a thriving **gay scene**, and there are scores of bars and clubs, many close to the Mercado Central and along c/Quart. *Venial* at c/Quart no. 26 is young, trendy, open at midnight and you pay to get in only at weekends (€8), *La Goulue*, almost next door at no. 32, is a popular club-bar, and *La Guerra* at no. 47 is a large club spread over several floors. Full listings of gay Valencian venues are produced by the Collectiu Lambada de Gais i Lesbianes, available free at most venues or from their offices at c/Salvador Giner 9 (Mon–Sat 5–10pm, ☎963 802 211).

Listings

Airlines Iberia c/de la Paz 14 ☎963 520 677, or their telephone information line ☎902 400 500; British Airways Plaza Rodrigo Botet 6 ☎ 953 512 284.

Airport Manises, 9km away (☎961 598 515); bus #105 from bus station (daily 5am–11.40pm; every 15min, except Sun every 30min).

Banks Main branches of most banks are around the Plaza del Ayuntamiento or along c/Las Barcas. Outside banking hours, there's a branch of the Caja de Ahorros at c/Játiva 14, to the left as you come out of the train station (Mon–Sat 9am–8pm).

Beaches Malvarrosa is pretty clean for a city beach and has an elegant promenade. Catch the tram from Pont de Fusta, or bus #32 runs from the Plaza del Ayuntamiento, supplemented during the summer by buses #20, #21, #22 and #23 which go from various points in the centre (9am–8.30pm; every 10–15mins). El Salér is a more pleasant beach: a long, wide stretch of sand with pine trees behind, with a nudist area at its northern end. A bus leaves from the corner of Gran Vía Marqués del Turia and c/Sueca (May–Sept every 30min; Oct–April hourly; 30mins).

Bookstores English books are available from the ABC International Bookshop on c/Ruzafa, the English Book Centre on c/Pascual y Genis 16, and Crisol, c/Antic Regne de Valencia.

Bus information Main station is at Avda. Menéndez Pidal 3, across the Turia (☎963 497 222; Ⓜ Turia).

Car rental Best value is probably Cuñauto, c/Burriana 51 ☎963 748 561. Otherwise, there's Avis at the airport and at c/Isabel la Católica 17 ☎963 510 734, Hertz at the airport and c/Segorbe 7 ☎963 415 036, Atesa at the airport and c/Joaquín Costa 57 ☎963 953 605.

Cinema Original-language films are shown regularly at the subsidized municipal Filmoteca, Plaza del Ayuntamiento, and are sometimes also shown at Albatros Mini-Cines, Plaza Fray Luís Colomer, and Babel, c/Vincente Sancho Tello 10.

Consulates UK c/Colón, 22 5-H ☎963 520 710; USA, c/Dr Romagosa 1 2-J ☎963 516 973.

Cycling Valencia is not well set up for cyclists, but there a few cycle paths (marked in green) running through the city; watch out for straying pedestrians. Cicloturismo, c/Na Jordana 44 ☎963 910 777, rents bicycles for €10 a day, and organizes tours.

Ferries Information and tickets from Trasmediterránea, Avda. Manuel Soto 15 (☎902 454 645, ⓦwww.trasmediterranea.es), or from any of the half-dozen travel agents on Plaza del Ayuntamiento. Note that if you are going to the Balearics outside of the summer months, it's cheaper and quicker to go from Denia.

Hospital Hospital General, Avda. del Cid, at the Tres Cruces junction, ☎963 862 900; Ⓜ Avda. del Cid.

Internet access *ONO* c/San Vicente Mártir 22 (Mon–Fri 9am–1am, Sat & Sun 11am–1am; €1.80–3.60 per hour; *Rivendel*, c/Hospital 18 (Mon–Fri 8.30am–10pm, Sat 10.30am–10pm, Sun 10.30am–2.30pm; €1 per hour mornings, €1.90 after).

Laundry El Mercat, Plaza Mercado 12.

Left luggage Self-store lockers at RENFE; 24hr access, €1.80–3.60 a day.

Markets Check out the crowded Sunday flea market, next to the football stadium on c/Sucia. Otherwise, there are markets selling clothes and general goods in a different location daily – ask at the tourist office for details. For food, the Mercado Central is a treat.

Police Headquarters are on Gran Vía Ramón y Cajal 40 ☎963 539 539.

Post office The main *correos* on the Plaza del Ayuntamiento is closed for renovation. There's a branch close by at c/San Vicente Mártir 23 (Mon–Fri 8.30am–8.30pm, Sat 9.30am–2pm); the *poste restante* is on the first floor.

Telephones Pasaje Rex 7, just off Avda. Marques de Sotelo, close to Plaza del Ayuntamiento (Mon–Fri 9am–3pm & 4–9pm, Sat 9am–2pm) or inside the RENFE station (daily 10am–10pm).

Taxis Radio Taxi ☎963 703 333, Auto Taxis ☎963 959 560, Tele Taxi ☎963 571 313.

Train information RENFE is on c/Játiva 24 ☎902 240 202. Several trains depart daily for Barcelona, Alicante, Madrid and Málaga. For destinations around Valencia, there's the FGV (metro) from Plaza España (lines 1 & 2) and Puente de Madera (line 3).

Trekking Treks through various mountain areas in the region are organized year-round. You can either join a guided group or, if you want to go it alone, they'll provide route maps and info. Details from Centro Excursionista de Valencia, Plaza Tabernes de Valldigna 4 ☎963 911 643.

Around Valencia

There are a number of good **day-trips** to be made from Valencia, including a visit to the monastery at El Puig or a meal at some of the region's very best paella restaurants at El Palmar, El Perelló and Perellonet.

Real Monasterio del Puig de Santa María

Eighteen kilometres north of Valencia on the road to Sagunto is the small town of **EL PUIG** (pronounced "pooch") where it's well worth spending a couple of hours visiting the impressive **Real Monasterio del Puig de Santa María** (Tues–Sun 10am–1pm & 4–7.30pm, 3–5.30pm in winter; €2.40), a huge fort-like structure flanked by four towers, which dominates the town and

All pulped out: la Tomatina

La Tomatina – the tomato-throwing festival of Buñol – is about as wild and exces-sive as Spanish fiestas get. Picture this: 30,000 people descend on a small provin-cial town, at the same time as a fleet of municipal trucks, carrying 120,000 tonnes of tomatoes. Tension builds. 'To-ma-te, to-ma-te' yell the crowds. And then the truckers let them have it, hurling the ripe, pulpy fruit at everyone present. And every-one goes crazy, hurling the pulp back at the trucks, at each other, in the air... for an hour. It is a fantasy battle made flesh: exhausting, not pretty, and not to everyone's taste. But it is Buñol's contribution to fiesta culture, and most participants will tell you that it is just about as much fun as it is possible to have with your clothes on. Not that you should wear a great deal.

The Tomatina has been going since 1944, but it has got a lot bigger in recent years, following a string of articles in the press in Spain and abroad. The novelist Louis de Bernières was one of the first foreign writers to cover the event: he wrote a superb account that is reprinted in *Spain: Travelers Tales*, and concluded that, if he planned his life well and kept his health, he could attend another 19 tomatinas, before he would be too enfeebled for the occasion.

If the idea of a tomato fight appeals, then you will need to visit Buñol on the last Wednesday of August (but call the Valencia Tourist Office just to check, as some years it takes place a week early). You can get there by train or bus in around an hour, but try to arrive early, with a spare set of clothing that you should leave at a bar – as Buñol has no hotel. The tomato trucks appear on the central Plaza del Ayuntamiento at midday and battle commences on the dot: this is no spectator sport – everyone is considered fair game. At 1pm an explosion signals the end of the battle and nobody hurls another speck of tomato for the next twelve months. Instead, the local fire brigade arrive, hose down the combatants, buildings and streets, and a lull comes over the town. And then, miraculously, within the hour, everyone arrives back on the street, perfectly turned out, to enjoy the rest of the fies-ta, which, oddly enough, includes such refined pursuits as orchestral concerts in the town's open-air auditorium.

As Buñol has no accommodation options – and indeed no reason to visit outside Tomatina time – most people take in the fiesta as a day-trip from Valencia.

---

surrounding countryside. The Orden de la Merced – the order which acts as guardians of the sanctuary – was founded by Pedro Nalaso in 1237 after he'd seen a vision of the Virgin Mary on the nearby hill. It is a favourite pilgrimage for Valencians and royalty alike, from Jaime I to the present monarchs Juan Carlos I and Doña Sofia, although in Franco's time, it was put to a rather dif-ferent use – as a prison.

In the lower cloister, the **Museum of Print and Graphics** (one of the most important in Europe) contains a wealth of artefacts, including the smallest book in the world – the size of a thumbnail. Looking at it through a magnify-ing glass reveals the Padre Nuestro (Lord's Prayer) in half a dozen languages. Other star exhibits include a copy of the Gutenberg Bible and a wonderful pic-torial atlas of natural history, both from the sixteenth century. In the upper cloister, the ceramics room houses various Roman pieces, but its real treasures are the fourteenth-century plates, bowls and jars recovered from the seabed close to El Puig. Keep an eye out, too, throughout the monastery for the neck manacles which the monks use as candle holders.

There's a good beach 2km east of the monastery, though the sands are over-looked by apartment complexes. El Puig is served by **train** (15 daily; 20min) and **bus** (every 30min; 30min) from Valencia.

La Albufera and the paella villages

La Albufera, just 12km south from Valencia, is a vast lagoon separated from the sea by a sandbank and surrounded by rice fields. Being one of the largest bodies of freshwater in Spain, it constitutes an important wetland, and attracts tens of thousands of migratory birds – a throng composed of 250 species, of which ninety breed here regularly. In the Middle Ages it was ten times its present size but the surrounding paddies have gradually reduced it. After growing contamination by industrial waste, domestic sewage and insecticide, the area was turned into a natural park. Whether you're into birdwatching or not, the lagoon area makes a relaxing change from the city. By far the easiest way to explore La Albufera is to jump aboard a *bus turistic* (3–4 daily; ☏963 414 400, Ⓦ www.valenciabusturistic.com); they leave from the Plaza de la Reina in Valencia and the trip includes a boat trip on the lake and a guided tour. It's possible to "hop on, hop off" this service, and tuck into some **paella**, or eels with *all i pebre* (piquant sauce) for lunch in the lakeside village of **EL PALMAR,** which is packed with restaurants. One of the better restaurants is *Mateu*, on the main street, c/Vincente Baldovi, at no. 17 (☏961 620 270). On August 4 El Palmar celebrates its **fiesta**; the image of Christ on the Cross is taken out onto the lake in a procession of boats to the *illuent*, or centre, of the lake, where hymns are sung.

Another 2km further along the road to El Perelló is the small – and otherwise unexceptional – village of **PERELLONET,** where you can eat some of the best paella around. Try *Blayet*, Avda. Gariotas 17 – which is also a **hostal** (☏961 777 454, Ⓕ961 177 366; ❸) – or *Gaviotas*, next door (☏961 777 575; booking required), which also does good *mariscos* and *all i pebre*. Also worth a visit is *Vert i Blau*, further down Avda. Gariotas at no. 72, for *patatas Amparín* – a potato *tapa* with a kick. The nearest **campsite** is *Devesa Gardens* (☏961 611 136; open all year), 2km out on the Carretera El Saler, near the golf course of the same name. Regular hourly **buses** run from the Gran Vía Germanías in Valencia via El Saler and on to the lagoon, El Palmar and El Perelló.

North of Valencia – the Costa del Alzahar

Most of the Costa del Alzahar north of Valencia is dotted with **beach resorts,** with some of the best sands around **Benicàssim,** north of the provincial capital, **Castellón de la Plana.** Further north still, the historic walled city of **Peñíscola** commands a spectacular clifftop location, while **Vinaròs** is more port than resort. Apart from the appeal of the coastline, there are fine Roman ruins at **Sagunto,** sweeping mountain scenery and good hiking around **Segorbe** and **Montanejos,** while the fortified town of **Morella** is definitely worth a visit for its castle and Gothic architecture.

Sagunto and around

Twenty-four kilometres north of Valencia are the fine Roman remains of **SAGUNTO** (Sagunt). This town passed into Spanish legend when, in 219 BC, it was attacked by Hannibal in one of the first acts of the war waged by Carthage on the Roman Empire. Its citizens withstood a nine-month siege before burning the city and themselves rather than surrendering. When belated help from Rome arrived, the city was recaptured and rebuilding eventually got under way. Chief among the ruins is the second-century Roman amphitheatre, the **Teatro Romano** (May–Sept Tues–Sat 10am–8pm, Sun 10am–2pm; Oct–April Tues–Sat 10am–6pm, Sun 10am–2pm; contact the tourist office for programme information), the basic shape of which survives intact. Debate continues about its recent restoration: it's now functional and plays are performed here during the summer, but for many people it has lost its authenticity. However, the views from its seats are wonderful, taking in a vast span of history – Roman stones all around, a ramshackle Moorish castle on the hill behind, medieval churches in the town below and, across the plain towards the sea, the black smoke of modern industry. Further Roman remains are being excavated within the walls of the huge **acropolis-castle** (same hours). Also worth a look is Sagunto's well-preserved Jewish quarter, where you'll find medieval houses among the cobbled alleyways.

Twenty-eight kilometres north of Sagunto, at **VALL D'UIXO**, is the underground river of San José, featuring caves with wonderful stalactites – you can tour the river by boat with Río Subterraneo de San José, based on the road leading to the caves (Wwww.riosubterraneo.com; daily 11am–1.15pm & 3.30–5pm in winter; 3.30–6.30pm in spring and autumn and 3.30–8pm in summer; €6.50). Twelve daily buses from Sagunto pass through Vall d'Uixo.

Practicalities

The theatre and castle complex is a twenty-minute walk from the train station. The route is signposted and passes the **tourist office** (T962 662 213) and the Jewish quarter.

There are hourly **trains** and very frequent buses to Sagunto from Valencia. If you want to **stay** near Sagunto, the leisure complex *La Pinada* (T962 660 850, Wwww.serbit.com/lapinada; ❸), which has swimming pools and saunas, is very good value; it's 3km out of town on the CN234, the road to Teruel. Alternatively, *Hostal Carlos*, near the station on the busy Avda. País Valencia at no. 43 (T962 660 902; ❸), is slightly more expensive but conveniently located.

Segorbe and Montanejos

About 30km inland from Sagunto is **SEGORBE**, the Roman Segóbriga, which is worth a visit more for its tranquillity and surrounding scenery than its sights, though part of the old city wall remains. It lies in the valley of the Río Palancia, among medlar and lemon orchards.

Segorbe's **cathedral** was begun in the thirteenth century, but suffered in the Neoclassical reforms, and only the cloister is original. Its **museum** (May–Sept Tues–Sun 10am–2pm & 6–8pm; Oct–April Sat & Sun 10am–2pm; €2.40) contains a few pieces of Gothic Valencian art, with a *retablo* by Vicente Maçip. One kilometre outside town on the road to Jérica, you'll find the "fountain of the provinces" which has fifty spouts, one for each province of Spain, each labelled with the coat of arms.

There are four daily **trains** and eight daily **buses** between Valencia and Segorbe. If you want **to stay**, the renovated *Tasca el Palen* (T964 710 740, ✉lpalen@info-bit.es; ❹), at c/Franco Ricart 9, set in a historic building in the centre of town, is very comfortable. Segorbe has its **fiestas** at the beginning of September, when *La Entrada* takes place, and bulls are run through the town by horses.

From Segorbe, it's 38km to **MONTANEJOS** (not to be mistaken for Montan, the village just before). Turn off at Jérica for the road to Montanejos, or catch the bus in Segorbe. This tiny village is popular with visitors for the hot springs, **Fuente de Baños**, where the water emerges at 25°C and has medicinal properties. Walks around the village join up with the nationwide network of paths, the *Gran Recorrido*. If you want to **stay** here, the *Refugio de Escaladores* (℡964 131 317) is an excellent budget place with camping, dorms (€8 per person) and wood cabins (❷); *Hostal Gíl*, at Avda. Fuente de Baños 25 (℡964 131 063; ❷), is also inexpensive, or there's the upmarket *Hotel Rosaleda del Mijares*, Carretera de Tales 28 (℡964 131 079, ⓦwww.hotelesrosaleda.com; ❹), right next to the spa.

Castellón de la Plana

Continuing north along the coast, **CASTELLÓN DE LA PLANA** is the main city in the north of the Valencia region, and a provincial capital. It's a prosperous enough place, with a sight or two, but there's no real reason to linger long here, except perhaps for the nearby **beaches**. In the centre of town, there's a fine seventeenth-century **ayuntamiento** (Mon–Fri 8am–1.15pm), with a collection of works by local artists and a painting of San Roque attributed to Francisco Ribalta. Nearby is the sixteenth-century bell tower **El Fadrí** and the striking, neo-Gothic **Concatedral de Santa María** (daily 8.30am–1pm & 5–9pm; free) – the original eleventh-century building was destroyed in the Civil War. Crossing the square, the **Convento de Capuchinas** (daily 5–8pm; free) has some valuable works by Francisco Zurbarán. The striking contemporary premises of the **Museo de Bellas Artes** on c/Caballeros 25, about 400m southwest of the Plaza Mayor (Tues–Sat 10am–8pm, Sun 10am–2pm; €2.30), are also worth a visit, with displays of ceramics, pictures and sculptures by local artists and new rooms devoted to the region's archeology and ethnology.

There are beaches at Castellón's *grau* (port), 5km east of the centre, but you'll find the best stretches along the coastal road north to Benicàssim. **Buses** for the former leave regularly from Plaza Borrull, while for the latter departures are from the nearby Plaza Farrell.

Practicalities

Arriving by **bus** or **train**, you'll find yourself at the combined station on Avenida Pintor Oliet. To get to the centre either walk the twenty minutes or so down Paseo Morella, or catch the frequent bus #9, which also stops at Plaza María Agustina. Here there is a helpful **turismo** (July & Aug Mon–Fri 9am–7pm, Sat 10am–2pm; Sept–June Mon–Fri 9am–2pm & 4–7pm, Sat 10am–2pm; ℡964 358 688, ⓦwww.culturalcas.com), which has a wealth of information about the city and the whole province. If you do decide to **stay the night**, the *Hostal La Esperanza*, c/Trinidad 37 (℡964 222 031; ❷), has immaculate rooms, but none with private bathrooms, but it does have a good restaurant, with a *menú* for €5.60. Alternatively, if you want a beachside base, *Pensión Los Herreros*, Avda. del Puerto 28 (℡964 284 264; ❸), is a good bet.

There are plenty of **places to eat**, especially in the streets just south of the Plaza Santa Cruz: try *Tasca la Nécora* at c/Barraques or *Mesón La Cuerva*, at c/Isaac Peral 7, for tapas. By the Grau, *Club Náutico*, Escollera de Poniente, serves good *arroz* and *pescado al horno*, while *Casa Juanito*, Paseo Buenavista 11, offers an excellent selection of seafood.

For **nightlife**, many locals start off with a few tapas around Plaza Santa Cruz before heading off to the bars around c/Lagasca and c/Tenerías. For **clubs**, there are two *zonas* that come to life at about 3am: Polígono "Los Cipréses", way out on the main Valencia road, which has something for everyone, and the north of the town around c/Cuadra de Borriolenc, which attracts a younger, alternative crowd. To get to either, you'll need to take a taxi from the centre. During the **summer**, everyone heads to the beach to party, with Plaza del Mar the starting point, moving on later to the many bars and clubs on the beach going up towards Benicàssim.

⑫

Villafamés

VILLAFAMÉS, 24km inland from Castellón, is an attractive hill town which successfully mixes the medieval, Renaissance and modern. In the highest part of the town there's an ancient ruined castle, conquered by Jaime I in 1233. The fifteenth-century Palau del Batle houses the **Museo de Arte Contemporáneo** (summer Tues–Sat 10.30am–1.30pm & 5–8pm, Sun 10.30am–1.30pm; winter Tues–Sat 10.30am–1.30pm & 4–7pm, Sun 10.30am–1.30pm; €2), a collection of over five hundred sculptures and paintings including works by Miró, Lozano and Mompó. There are good **rooms** at *El Rullo*, c/de la Fuente 2 (℡964 329 384; ❷), which also has a restaurant.

Benicàssim and around

BENICÀSSIM, a few kilometres north of Castellón, is famed for its Moscatel wine, and was once well known as a wine-producing area, although today very few vineyards remain and the town is better known as a tourist resort. Wine-tasting visits are on offer at *Bodegas Carmelito* on Avenida Castellón (summer 10am–8pm; winter 10am–5pm; free).

Benicàssim is heavily developed for package tourism and budget accommodation is quite scarce – the **turismo**, c/Santo Tomás 74–76 (summer Mon–Sat 9am–3pm & 5–8.30pm, Sun 10am–3pm; winter Mon–Sat 9am–2pm & 5–7pm; ℡964 300 102, ⓦwww.benicassim.org), has a list of **hostales** and will provide a free map. Most of the better-value places are close to the train station: *Garamar*, at c/Leopoldo Querol 3 (℡964 300 011; ❷), is a good bet, or *Buenavista*, c/San Antonio 13 (℡964 300 905; ❸; closed Oct–March), is inexpensive for large rooms with bath. More upmarket is the *Hotel Montreal*, by Terrers beach at c/Les Barracas 5 (℡964 300 681, ⓦwww.hmontreal.com; ❹), which has lots of facilities including a swimming pool. There's also a year-round **youth hostel**, *Argentina*, at Avda. de Ferrandis Salvador 40 (℡964 300 949; €11 including breakfast), and at least seven **campsites** in the area; *Camping Florida*, Sigalero 34 (℡964 392 385; April–Sept), is close to the beach, with a pool and tennis courts. In the centre of town you'll find plenty of **restaurants** along c/Santo Tomás, including great tapas and grilled meats in the Argentinian-owned *Divino* at no. 98.

Six kilometres inland from Benicàssim is the **Desierto de las Palmas**, a Carmelite monastery in an idyllic setting dating from 1694. The Carmelites run meditation courses here (℡964 300 950) and there is also a museum of religious history (daily 10am–12.30pm & 4.30–7pm; free, but entry only as part of a group of ten, so you may have to wait a while).

There is a regular **bus** service from Benicàssim to Castellón: buses leave from c/Santo Tomàs every 15 minutes in summer, every 30 minutes in winter.

FIB

The annual **Benicàssim** international festival (ⓦwww.fiberfib.com) on the first weekend of August (Thurs to Sun) draws tens of thousands to hear the world's biggest names in alternative pop and rock. In addition to the music there are chill-out zones, club tents and the ubiquitous festival carnival of henna tattooists, trinket sellers and jugglers. There's a massive campsite, and a festival ticket entitles you to free camping for nine days around the event.

Peñíscola

There's not much else along the stretch of coast north of Benicàssim until you reach **PEÑÍSCOLA** 60km away. The town occupies a heavily fortified promontory jutting out into the Mediterranean. Though undeniably touristy today, the medieval walled city is still richly atmospheric (particularly outside high season) and there's a warren of alleys and lanes to explore. There was once a Phoenician settlement here, and later it saw Greek, Carthaginian, Roman and Moorish rulers, but the present castle was built by the Knights Templar with alterations by Pedro de la Luna. Pope Benedict XIII (Papa Luna) lived here for six years after he had been deposed from the papacy during the fifteenth-century Church schisms. The **castle** today (daily: summer 9.30am–2.30pm & 4.30–9.30pm; winter 9.30am–1pm & 3.15–6pm; €2), where part of *El Cid* was filmed, is well worth a visit to admire the colossal vaulted guards' quarters, basilica and the views from its roof. The resort's slender **beach** has recently been beefed up with several thousand tonnes of Saharan sand; the further north you get from the castle the quieter it becomes. There's also a smaller cove beach, Playa Sur, 200m west of the old town.

Practicalities

You'll find a **turismo** on Paseo Marítimo (summer Mon–Sat 9am–8pm, Sun 10am–1pm; winter Mon–Fri 9.30am–1pm & 4–7pm; ☎964 480 208, Ⓦwww.peniscola.org), and a kiosk just below the entrance to the walled city – both will provide a decent map that marks all the town's **accommodation**, the eleven campsites, and an informative leaflet about the castle. Peñíscola is very crowded in high season, but inside the walled city there are attractive rooms, some with private showers, above the *Chiki Bar* at Calle Mayor 3 (☎964 480 284, ❷). Just below the walls there are two more good places: *Simó*, Porteta 5 (☎ & Ⓕ964 480 620, Ⓦwww.restaurantesimo.com; ❸), where some rooms have sea views, and *Pensión El Torcio*, c/José Antonio 18 (☎964 480 202; ❷), just 100m from the sea. For more comfort try the beachside *Hostería del Mar* on Avda. Papa Luna 18 (☎964 480 745; ❺). The area just below the old town is thick with **restaurants**, many serving local dishes such as *susquet de peix* (fish stew), and *all i pebre de polpet* (small octopus with garlic and pepper sauce). **Buses** run down the coast from Vinaròs every half-hour between 7am and 10pm.

Vinaròs

The **beaches** of the scruffy port-cum-resort **VINARÒS**, next along the coast, are small but rarely packed, and in town there's an elaborate Baroque church, with an excellent local produce market nearby. Right on the seafront, the **turismo** (summer Mon–Fri 10am–2pm & 5–8pm, Sat 11am–1.30pm, Sun 6–8pm; winter Mon–Sat 10am–2pm & 4–6pm, ☎964 453 334) has a decent map and will help to locate **accommodation**: *Habitaciones Vinaròs* at c/Pintor Puig Roda 8 (☎964 452 475; ❶) is clean and cheap, while rooms at the *Hostal Miramar* (☎964 451 400; ❸), right on the seafront at c/Paseo de Blasco Ibáñez 12, are all en suite.

In the early evenings it's worth going down to the dockside market to watch the day's catch being auctioned and packed off to restaurants all over the region. Locally caught **fish** is excellent, with the *langostinos* reputedly the best in Spain. Almost overlooking the portside action *Bar Puerto* and the neighbouring *Bar Folet*, both on c/Costa y Borràs, are good for a bite to eat or a drink. There's one **bus** on to Morella (weekdays only at 8am), leaving Plaza San Esteban. The town's **train station**, over 2km west of the centre, has eight daily services to Valencia (via Castellón) and Barcelona (via Tarrogona).

Morella

MORELLA, 62km inland on the road from the coast to Zaragoza, is the most attractive town in the province of Castellón and one of the most remarkable in the area. A medieval fortress town, it rises from the plain around a small hill crowned by a tall, rocky spur and a virtually impregnable **castle** which dominates the countryside for miles around. A perfectly preserved ring of ancient walls defends its lower reaches. The city was recovered from the Moors in the thirteenth century by the steward of Jaime I. He was reluctant to hand it over to the crown, and it is said that the king came to blows with him over the possession of the city.

Chief among the monuments is the church of **Santa María la Mayor** (*Iglesia Arciprestal*; summer daily 11am–2pm & 4–7pm; winter daily 11am–2pm & 4–6pm), a fourteenth-century Gothic construction with beautifully carved doorways and an unusual raised *coro* reached by a marble spiral stairway. A few minutes' walk to the left, at the foot of the castle, is the restored **Monasterio de San Francisco** (daily: summer 10.30am–7.30pm; winter 11am–2pm & 4–6pm), worth visiting for its elegant Gothic cloister and chapterhouse. The **fortress** itself (daily: May–Sept 10.30am–7.30pm; Oct–April 10.30am –6.30pm; €2) is in ruins, but still impressive. It's a tiring climb but there are tremendous views in every direction from the crumbling courtyard at the top – down over the monastery, bullring and town walls to the plains. In the distance are the remains of the peculiar Gothic **aqueduct** which once supplied the town's water.

Not far from the monastery is the curious **Museo Tiempo de los Dinosaurios** (Tues–Sun 11am–2pm & 4–7pm; Oct–April closes 6pm; €1.80), containing fossils of dinosaurs found in the area. Also of interest is the house on c/de la Virgen de Villavana where San Vicente Ferrer performed the prodigious miracle of resurrecting a child who had been chopped up and stewed by its mother – she could find nothing else fit for a saint to eat. Annually in the last week of August Morella hosts a **festival of classical music**.

Practicalities

Be prepared for lower temperatures in Morella than elsewhere in the province, and for snow in winter. The **turismo** (daily 10am–2pm & 4–7pm, closes at 6pm in winter; ☎964 173 032, ⓦ www.morella.net) is a five-minute walk from the bus station, in Plaza de San Miguel, and has useful maps and leaflets on town sights.

Inexpensive **accommodation** can be found at *La Muralla*, c/Muralla 12 (☎964 160 243; ❷), and at *Hostal El Cid*, Puerta San Mateo 2 (☎964 160 125; ❷), right by the bus stop and town gate, with views of the hills from its balconied rooms (but it can be noisy). Otherwise, *Hotel Cardenal Ram* (☎964 173 085, ⓔ hotelcardenalram@ctu.es; ❸), in a converted medieval cardinal's palace, is an amazing place to stay, and has a good restaurant. During fiestas and national holidays, you should book rooms in advance, as Morella is very popular with Spanish holidaymakers. If you are stuck without accommodation, the neighbouring village of **FORCALL** has an excellent *hostal*, *Alguilar*, at Avda. III Centenario 1 (☎964 171 106; ❷), as well as a comfortable hotel, *Palau dels Osset*, Playa Major 16 (☎964 177 524, ⓕ964 177 556; ❺).

Morella's main porticoed street, **Els Porxos**, bisected by steep steps leading down to the lower walls, is the place to focus on for **food**, with its bars, bakeries and cafés – *Vinatea* and *Rourera* are both excellent for tapas. Below the monastery are a couple of small plazas where you can sit at outdoor cafés – especially pleasant in the evening.

Morella is one possible approach to the Maestrazgo region of southern Aragón. **Buses** leave for Alcañiz (3–5 weekly at 10am) and Cantavieja/Villafranca del Cid (1 daily Mon–Fri), as well as to Vinaròs (1 daily Mon–Fri) and Castellón (1 daily Mon–Fri).

The Costa Blanca

South of Valencia stretches a long strip with some of the **best beaches** on this coast, especially between Gandía and Benidorm. Much of it, though, suffers from the worst excesses of **package tourism**, with concrete building projects looming over much of the coast, and more on the way. It pays to book ahead in summer, particularly in August when most hotels are fully booked. Campers have it somewhat easier – there are hundreds of campsites – but driving can be a nightmare unless you stick to the toll roads.

If you're taking the inland route as far as **Gandía**, you'll get the opportunity to see the historic town of **Xàtiva**.

Xàtiva and around

The ancient town of **XÀTIVA** (Játiva), 50km south of Valencia, was probably founded by the Phoenicians and certainly inhabited by the Romans. Today it's a scenic, tranquil place and makes a good day-trip. Medieval Xàtiva was the birthplace of Alfonso de Borja, who became Pope Calixtus III, and his nephew Rodrigo, father of the infamous Lucrezia and Cesare Borgia. When Rodrigo became Pope Alexander VI, the family moved to Italy.

Xàtiva has a fine collection of mansions scattered around town, but most are private and cannot be entered. Many of the churches have been recently renovated, and the **old town** is a pleasant place to wander.

From the old town, it's a long and tiring walk up a steep hill to the plain but sturdy **castle** (Tues–Sun 10am–7pm; Nov–Feb till 6pm; €2) – follow signposts from the main square, the Plaza del Españoleto, or take a taxi from outside the turismo. On the way, you'll pass the thirteenth-century **Iglesia de San Feliu** (April–Sept Tues–Sat 10am–1pm & 4–7pm, Sun 10am–1pm; Oct–March Tues–Sat 10am–1pm & 3–6pm, Sun 10am–1pm), a hermitage built in transitional Romanesque-Gothic style; ancient pillars, fine capitals and a magnificent Gothic *retablo* are the chief attractions of the interior.

Back in the centre of town, the **Museo del Almudín** (Tues–Fri 10am–2.30pm & 4–6pm, Sat & Sun 10am–2pm; €2.20) consists of two separate sections, one an archeological collection, the other an art museum. The latter includes several pictures by José Ribera (who was born here in 1591) and engravings by Goya – *Caprichos* and *Los Proverbios*. A portrait of Felipe V is hung upside down in retribution for his having set fire to the city in the War of Succession and for changing its name (temporarily) to San Felipe.

Fiestas are held during Holy Week and in the second half of August when the *Feria de Agosto* is celebrated with bullfights and livestock fairs.

Practicalities

Arriving by **train**, follow c/Baixada Estación up towards the central tree-lined c/Alameda Jaume I, where you'll find the **turismo** at no. 50 (Mon–Sat 10am–2pm & 4–6pm, Sun 10.30am–2pm; ☎962 273 346, ⓔTouristinfo .xativa@turisme.m400.gva.es). If you're enjoying Xàtiva's peace and quiet and want to **stay**, the best budget place for price and location is the *Hostal*

Margallonero, Plaça del Mercat 42 (☎962 276 677; ❶); they also serve food. The comfortable *Hotel Murta* at c/Ángel Lacalle s/n (☎962 276 611; ❸) is a step up in quality, but if you can afford it, head for the wonderful *Hostería de Mont Sant* (☎962 275 081, ⓦwww.seridex.com/montsant; ❻), on the way up to the castle, which has stunning gardens and a pool. For stays of a week or more, *Calixto III* (☎902 120 691; closed winter), at Plaza Calixte III 8, offers spotlessly clean en-suite rooms with TV and kitchenette, and with a day's notice they will knock you up a meal of paella and pumpkin pie. Prices for a three-bed room apartment are around €300 a week.

Keep an eye open for **arnadí** in the bakeries – it's a local speciality of Moorish origin, a rich (and expensive) sweet made with pumpkin, cinnamon, almonds, eggs, sugar and pine nuts. For a good **restaurant** head for the mid-priced *Casa La Abuela*, c/Reina 17 (☎962 281 085; closed mid-June to mid-Aug); many Valencians drive out here to savour its traditional fare. For something less expensive, there is a host of *cafeterías* with cheap *menús* around the train station, or *Don Pepe*, Avda. de Selgas 12 (the continuation of c/Alameda Jaume I), has great tapas and pleasant outdoor seating.

Xàtiva is served by **buses** and **trains** from Valencia; the train (1hr) is cheaper, and leaves every half-hour. There are also connections to Gandía by bus and to Alicante by train.

Gandía

There's not much along the coast until you get to **GANDÍA**, 65km south of Valencia and the first of the main resorts, which attracts mainly Spanish visitors. A few kilometres inland from the modern seafront development, the old town is quiet and provincial, with one sight that's well worth seeing, and some good, inexpensive accommodation.

Gandía was once important enough to have its own university, but the only real testimony to its heyday is the **Palacio Ducal de los Borja**, built in the fourteenth century but with Renaissance and Baroque additions and modifications. There are regular guided tours throughout the year (Tues–Sun 10am–2pm & 5–7pm; €2.70). Tours are in Spanish, but photocopied translations are available at the reception. The lifetime of Duke Francisco de Borja is much responsible for the golden age of the town (late fifteenth to early sixteenth century) in terms of urban and cultural development. Learned and pious, the duke opened colleges all over Spain and Europe, and was eventually canonized. The palace contains his paintings, tapestries and books, but parts of the building itself are of equal interest, such as the *artesonado* ceilings and the pine window shutters, so perfectly preserved by prolonged burial in soil and manure that resin still oozes from them when the hot sun beats down. There are also several beautiful sets of *azulejos*, but these are outshone by the fourteenth-century Arabesque wall tiles, whose brilliant lustre is unreproducible as it was derived from pigments of plants that became extinct soon after the Muslims left.

Practicalities

Both **buses** and **trains** arrive on Avenida Marqués de Campo. The **turismo** (Mon–Fri 9.30am–1.30pm & 4.30–7.30pm, Sat 10am–1.30pm; ☎962 877 788, ⓔtouristinfo.gandia@turisme.m4000.gva.es) occupies a brown hut, cleverly camouflaged behind some trees opposite the station. For **Internet access**, head to *Intern@aut@* at c/Magistrado Catalá 5 (Mon–Sat 10–11pm, Sun 4–10.30pm; €2.60 per hour). There is a handful of **places to stay** in town; good bets include *Hotel Los Naranjos*, c/Avda. del Grau 57 (☎962 873 143, ⓕ962 873 144; ❸), and

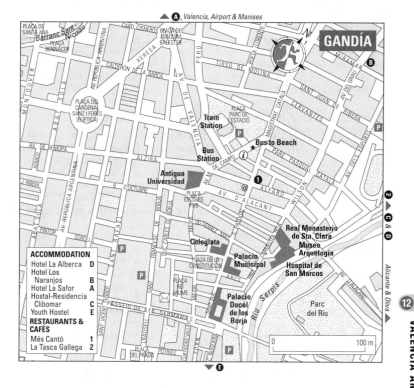

GANDÍA

ACCOMMODATION
Hotel La Alberca **D**
Hotel Los
  Naranjos **B**
Hotel La Safor **A**
Hostal-Residencia
  Clibomar **C**
Youth Hostel **E**

RESTAURANTS & CAFÉS
Més Cantó **1**
La Tasca Gallega **2**

the *Hotel La Safor*, Avda. de Valencia 40 (☎962 864 011, ℻962 864 179; ❹), with phone, TV and air conditioning in all rooms. For a base close to the beach, there's the *Hostal-Residencia Clibomar* (☎962 840 237, ✉h-rclibomar@ctv.es; closed Nov–Easter; ❸) at c/Alcoy 24 by the Playa de Gandía, or the slightly cheaper *Hotel La Alberca*, at c/Culera 8 (☎962 845 087; ℻962 845 163; ❸). The exceptionally pleasant **youth hostel** (☎962 831 748; €9.70 per bed; closed Christmas–Feb) is on the beachfront at **Playa de Piles**, 5km down the coast, and there are nine daily buses there from outside the train station.

In the town centre, *Més Cantó* at c/Magistrat Català 8 has good, inexpensive tapas and a *menú* for €7, while there are plenty of decent **restaurants** at the beach, along with most of the **bars**. One recommended place – that isn't overly expensive – is the popular *La Tasca Gallega*, on Avenida de la Paz, which serves well-cooked Galician fare.

Gandía beach

Buses run every fifteen to twenty minutes (6am–11.30pm) from the turismo down to the enormous **beach**, Gandía Playa, 4km to the east. The beach is packed in summer and lined with apartment blocks, where remarkably good-value rooms are available out of season. You'll find the town's second **turismo** here at Paseo Neptuno 45 (mid-March to mid-Oct Mon–Sat 10am–2pm & 5–8pm, Sun 10am–1.30pm). The beach zone is a good place for **seafood** and paellas; don't miss *fideuà*, a local speciality with a strong seafood flavour, cooked with vermicelli instead of rice, and freshly made *cocques* (similar to pizzas) from

Taro bakery on Passeig de los Germaines. *La Gamba* (☎962 841 310; lunch only), on Carretera Nazaret-Oliva, a few blocks back from the beach, is one of the best – and most expensive – places to eat seafood. Most of Gandía's **clubs** are located in the beach area: *Bacarrá* has house DJs, *CocoLoco* mainly salsa and Latin sounds, while at *Fakata* music varies night by night, and includes techno, house and hip hop.

Gandía to Altea – around the cape

A string of attractive little towns and beaches stretches from **Gandía** to **Altea** before you reach the developments of Benidorm and Alicante, but your own transport is essential to enjoy the best of them and accommodation can be pricey. The most inexpensive option along this coast is to camp. There are scores of decent **campsites**, and a useful booklet listing them is available from local turismos. Try *La Merced*, 12km northwest of Altea in Calpe, Urb La Merced 1a (☎965 830 097; open all year), or *El Naranjal*, 1.5km out of Xàbia on the Carreterra de Cabo (☎965 792 989; March–Sept only).

Oliva

OLIVA, 8km south beyond Gandía, is a much lower-key development. Again the town is set back from the coast and, although the main road, the N332, charges through its centre, it's relatively unspoiled and there are a couple of **places to stay**. In town, just off the N332 at c/Ausias March 16, *Hostal Azahar* (☎962 838 607; ❷, closed Jan), has clean functional rooms, all with air conditioning and bath; while for a beachside base *Hotel Pau–Pi*, at c/Roger de Lauria 2 (☎962 851 202, ⓔhotelpaupi@oliva.infoville.net; ❸ including breakfast), is a good choice. There's a **turismo** on Passeig Luís Vives (Sept–June Mon–Sat 10am–1.30pm & 4.30–6.30pm; July & Aug Mon–Sat 10am–2pm & 5–7.30pm, Sun 10am–1pm; ☎962 855 528), which can provide you with a map of the town. Oliva's **beach** is served by frequent buses until 10pm. The sandy shoreline continues a long way to the south, almost as far as Denia, so if you're prepared to walk, or better still if you've got transport, you can easily escape the crowds altogether. Playa de Oliva itself has hundreds of villas and apartments (booked up throughout July and Aug) but is refreshingly free of concrete and tackiness. A good **place to eat** is *La Rústica*, where they have an inexpensive *menú*, near the *Más y Más* supermarket on the N332 highway; and for a **drink** try *Dr. Watson's*, a friendly English pub at Gómez Ferrer 2.

Denia

DENIA, at the foot of the Montgó Natural Park, is a far bigger place, a sizeable, sprawling town even without its summer visitors. There is a combined train and bus service to Alicante airport throughout the day, and a rattling narrow-gauge railway runs down the coast from Denia to Alicante, with seven daily FGV trains. There are also daily **ferry services** to Mallorca and Ibiza: for information contact Baleària (☎902 191 068, ⓦwww.balearia.com); Trasmediterránea (☎902 454 645, ⓦwww.trasmediterranea.es); or Iscomar (☎902 119 108, ⓦwww.iscomarferrys.com), which has the cheapest fares. Beneath the wooded capes beyond, bypassed by the main road, stretch probably the most beautiful **beaches** on this coastline – but you'll need a car to get to most of them, and there's limited inexpensive accommodation. If you want to **stay** in town *Hostal Residencia Cristina*, Avda. del Cid 5 (☎966 423 158; ❷), has excellent-value rooms, all with TV and some with private bath; while *Hostal Residenica Loreto*, c/Loreto 12 (☎966 435 419; ⓦwww.hostalloreto.com, ❸), has plenty of character for the price. The *Hotel Costa Blanca*, Pintor Llorens 3 (☎965 780 336, ⓦwww.hotelcostablanca.com; ❺), is more upmarket and handy for the train station and port.

Xàbia

At the heart of this area, very near the easternmost Cabo de la Nao, is **XÀBIA** (Jávea), an attractive, prosperous town surrounded by hillside villas, with a fine beach and a very pleasant old town. In summer both Denia and Xàbia are live-ly in the evenings, especially at weekends, as they're popular with Valencianos. Two of Xàbia's best-value places **to stay** are *Pensión La Favorita*, c/Magellanes 4 (☎965 790 477; ❷), and *Hostal Residencia Portichol*, Partida Portichol 157 (☎966 461 050; ❸). There is also the modern *Parador de Jávea* (☎965 790 200, ⓦwww.paradores-spain.com/spain/pjavea.html; ❼) on Avenida del Mediterráneo, which has low-season rates at fifty percent off the full price. **Nightlife** is centred round the beach; good bars include *Cafémar*, which has chillout sessions, and *Terra*. Later in the evening, the crowds move to the out-of-town clubs on the road to Cabo de San Antonio or *Molí Blanc* in the port area on the road to Cabo de la Nao.

There are plenty of idyllic cove beaches close to Xàbia; one of the best is **Cala Portitxol** (also known as Playa la Barraca), a wonderful sand-and-peb-ble bay, backed by high cliffs, 5km east of the main beach, where you'll find a tremendous seafood restaurant, *La Barraca* (☎965 770 919), that's renowned for its paella; book well ahead on Sundays.

Altea and around

Heading southeast, you pass the dramatic rocky outcrop known as the **Peñón de Ifach**, its natural beauty now irretrievably besmirched by the encroaching concrete towers of the neighbouring package resort of **Calpe** (Calp) – there's no reason to linger at all. But just 11km to the south, **ALTEA** is a much more attractive proposition: a small resort set below a historic hilltop village, with views overlooking the whole stretch of coastline. Restrained tourist develop-ment is centred on the seafront, where there's a pebble beach and attractive promenade of low-rise apartment buildings interspersed with tottering old fishermen's houses. There are plenty of cafés and restaurants along the seafront, as well as the **turismo** (Mon–Sat 10am–2pm & 5–7pm, in summer Sun 10am–1pm too; ☎965 844 114).

The old village, or *poble antic*, up the hill is even more picturesque with its steep lanes, white houses, blue-domed church and profuse blossoms. In sum-mer the entire quarter is packed with pavement diners and boutique browsers. **Accommodation** can be tricky in high season, but *Hostal Fornet*, c/Beniards 1 (☎965 843 005; ❸ with bath), high up on the northern edge of the old vil-lage, is a good choice, or on Calle San Pedro, which is the seafront strip, *Hotel San Miguel* (☎965 840 800; ❸) at no. 7 has plenty of character, and the mod-ern *Hotel Altaya* (☎965 840 800; ❹) at no. 28 is also good. *Hostal Paco* on Avenida Jaime I (☎965 840 541, ⓔatfrpega@altea.infoville.net; ❸) is over-priced but often has space. As for **restaurants**, it's a treat to eat in the old town, where there's something of an epidemic of pizza restaurants, all charging very similar prices. By the sea, *Avant 03* scores highly for budget-priced *bocadillos* and snacks, while *L'Obrador*, at c/Concepción 8, serves some of the best pasta in the area. The best places to **drink** are to be found around the main square of the old village: *Tribú* on Plaza Tónico Ferrer is a hip bar with great electro, funk and lounge sounds.

Benidorm

Hugely high-rise, vaguely Vegas and definitely dodgy, **BENIDORM** is the king when it comes to package tourism. Just over forty years ago Rose Macaulay could still describe Benidorm as a small village "crowded very

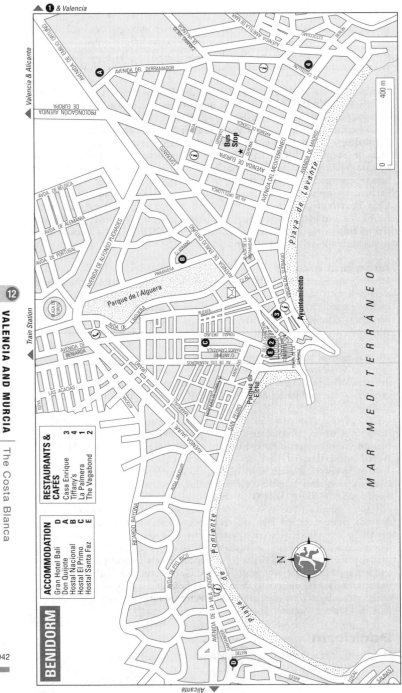

BENIDORM

ACCOMMODATION
Gran Hotel Bali — D
Don Quijote — A
Hostal Nacional — B
Hostal El Primo — C
Hostal Santa Faz — E

RESTAURANTS & CAFES
Casa Enrique — 3
Tiffany's — 4
La Palmera — 1
The Vagabond — 2

MAR MEDITERRÁNEO

Playa de Levante

Playa de Poniente

Parque de l'Alguera

Ayuntamiento

Bus Stop

Valencia & Alicante

Train Station

Alicante

beautifully round its domed and tiled church on a rocky peninsula". The old part's still here, but it's so overshadowed by the miles of towering concrete that you'll be hard-pressed to find it. If you want hordes of British and Scandinavian sunseekers, scores of "English" pubs, almost two hundred discos and club-bars, and bacon and eggs for breakfast, then this is the place to come. The **Playa de la Levante**, Benidorm's biggest highlight, with its 2km of golden sand, is undeniably pleasant when you can see it through the hordes of roasting corpses. A little further from the centre is the slightly more relaxed and less exposed **Playa de Ponienete**, which has slightly more Spanish flavour.

Practicalities

Trains arrive at the top of town, off Avenida de Beniarda, while the main **bus stop** is at the junction of Avenida de Europa and c/Gerona, with the ticket offices in the shopping centre there. You'll find Benidorm's helpful **turismo** in the old town, at Avda. Martínez Alejos 16 (July–Sept Mon–Fri 9am–9pm, Sat 10am–1.30pm & 5–9pm; Oct–June Mon–Sat 10am–1.30pm & 4.30–8pm; ℡965 851 311, ⓦwww.benidorm.org), which provides a useful list of accommodation and a free map – sponsored by none other than the British newspaper *The Sun*. Other turismos can be found on Avenida de Europa and on Avenida del Derramoor. Getting to Alicante, you can either take the **bus** or the **train** – both leave every half-hour and are similarly priced, but the bus is much quicker and more convenient. There's also a night train, the *Trensnochador*, that runs along the coast to Alicante in July and August. For Valencia, there are no trains, but a regular bus service.

Accommodation

With over 40,000 hotel beds and hundreds of apartments, finding a **place to stay** isn't a problem (except perhaps in August). Budget places are clustered around the old town and out of season many of the giant hotels slash their prices drastically, making Benidorm a cheap base from which to explore the surrounding area. One of the best *hostales* in town is the comfortable *Hostal Santa Faz*, c/Santa Faz 18 (℡965 854 063, Ⓔhotelsantafaz@ctv.es; ❹), while *Hostal El Primo*, c/Antonio Ramos Carratalá 1 (℡965 866 943; ❸), is basic but clean, and not far from the beach. For more comfort, and a swimming pool, head for the very central *Hostal Nacional*, c/Verano 9 (℡ & ℻965 850 432; ❺); or for a real splurge check in to Europe's highest hotel, the 52-storey, 776-room *Gran Hotel Bali*, c/Luís Prendes (℡966 815 200, ⓦwww.grupobali.com; ❽), where prices plummet in low season to €89 a double. Benidorm has no fewer than nine **campsites**, the closest – and least expensive – being the basic *Don Quijote* (℡965 855 065), at the end of c/Esperanto.

Eating

Fish and chips dominate, and if you're after a fry-up, you'll be spoilt for choice. For authentic **Spanish food**, head for the pleasant and reasonably priced *Casa Enrique*, near the main turismo on Carrer de Ricardo, with its set *menú* for €8.90, or *La Palmera*, on Avenida Severo Ochoa, which specializes in rice dishes – allow €18 per person. *Tiffany's*, at Avda. Mediterráneo 51, offers great, if pricey, international cuisine, while *The Vagabond*, hidden away in the old town at c/Retiro 4, is a less expensive English-run restaurant that serves Greek and Indian specialities and always has **vegetarian** dishes.

Inland from Benidorm

In total contrast to the coastal strip, the remote mountainous terrain inland from Benidorm harbours some of the most traditional and isolated villages in the Valencia region – tourist-swamped Guadalest excepted. Better roads and local government grants (which encourage the conversion of rural properties into guesthouses) are slowly opening up this area to tourism, but for now the austere *pueblos* retain an untouched character, Castilian is very much a second language, and the main visitors are hikers. The area is rich in bird life, with golden eagles, and, in autumn, griffon vultures, often spotted soaring over the limestone ridges. There's no bus or train service, other than links to Alcoy and Guadalest, so you'll need your own wheels to get around.

Heading west from Benidorm an excellent new highway heads 21km to **GUADALEST**, justifiably one of the most popular tourist attractions in Valencia. The sixteenth-century Moorish castle town is built into the surrounding rock and you enter the town through a gateway tunnelled into the mountain. If you can put up with the hordes of tourists and gift shops, it's worth visiting for the view down to the reservoir (which is accessible via the village of Beniarda just to the west) and across the valley. In the main street you'll find the **Casa Típica**, an eighteenth-century house-museum (Mon–Fri & Sun 10am–9pm; €1.80), with exhibitions of antique tools and agricultural methods. The modern **turismo**, c/Avenida de Alicante (daily: April–Sept 10am–6pm; Oct–March 11am–2pm & 4–6pm; ☏965 885 298), is very helpful and has maps of the town.

If the scenery around Guadalest appeals, the wonderfully scenic CV70 road continues on westwards up the valley, passing the village of **CONFRIDES** after 10km, where *El Pirieno* (☏965 885 858; ❷) has pleasant rooms with great views, and then follows a serpentine route towards the town of Alcoy (see box on p.948). The best base for exploring the villages of this region and the craggy peaks of the Serra d'Aitana is the hamlet of **QUATRETONDETA**, 4km northeast of the village of Gorga. Here you'll find the welcoming, British-run *Hotel Els Frares* (☏965 511 234, ⓦwww.inn-spain.com; ❸), with pleasant en-suite rooms and good food. The owners lead walking tours around the region and will pick up guests from Alicante airport.

All the villages in the area are well signposted, and most, including Quatretondeta, have wonderful municipal **swimming pools** (July & Aug only). At **Balones**, 10km west of Quatretondeta, the bar–café *El Mirador* offers friendly service and great valley views; while **Benimassot**, 8km further east, has an excellent restaurant – *La Cassola de Test* (Sat & Sun only). Tiny **Facheca**, 7km east of Balones, also has a good bar-restaurant and a beautiful pool. It's possible to loop back to the coast from here via a beautiful route that passes through **CASTELL DE CASTELLS**, an isolated village 10km to the east, where there are two good places to stay: *Casa Pilar* (☏965 518 157, ⓦwww.casapilar.com; ❷), a very friendly small guesthouse with attractive rooms and fine home-cooking, and *Hotel Serrella* (☏965 518 138, ⓦwww.hotelserrella.com; ❷), on the main road, which is less attractive, but comfortable enough, plus a couple of bars.

Continuing eastwards from Castell de Castells, it's another 15km to the village of **Tàrbena**, and then a further 12km to **CALLOSA D'EN SARRIÀ**, where *Pensión Avenida*, on Ctra d'Alacant 9 (☏965 880 053; ❸), is a good place to stop – just 3km away from here you'll find the **Fuentes del Algar**, a series of very pretty waterfalls in a secluded spot, which makes a perfect place for a dip. From here it's just 15km to Benidorm, or the coastal highway south to Alicante.

Alicante (Alacant)

There is little to see anywhere along the coast south of Benidorm before you reach **ALICANTE (ALACANT)**. This thoroughly Spanish city has a decidedly Mediterranean air: its wide esplanades, such as the Rambla Méndez Núñez, and its seafront *paseos*, full of terrace cafés, are perfect for people-watching. Founded by the Romans, who named it "Lucentum" (City of Light), and dominated by the Arabs in the second half of the eighth century, the city was finally reconquered by Alfonso X in 1246 for the Castilian crown. In 1308 Jaime III incorporated Alicante in the kingdom of Valencia.

Today Alicante is Valencia's second largest city, and receives millions of visitors through its airport each year. With its long sandy beaches, mild and pleasant climate, recently renovated old town and lively nocturnal offerings, this is definitely a city to spend at least one night in. The main **fiesta**, *Las Hogueras*, is at the end of June, and ignites a series of cracking celebrations second only to the *Fallas* in Valencia.

Arrival and information

The main **train station**, Estación de Madrid, on Avenida Salamanca, has direct connections to Madrid, Albacete, Murcia and Valencia; but trains on the FGV line to Benidorm and Denia leave from the far end of the Playa del Postiguet – you can catch a **tram** there from the Plaza del Mar. The **bus station** for local and long-distance services is on c/Portugal. Arriving by air, the **airport** is 12km south from the centre of Alicante, in El Altet. Airport buses into town operate between 6.30am and 11.30pm (every 30min; €1.30) and stop outside the bus station and on the central Rambla Méndez Núñez.

Alicante's enormous regional **turismo** is at Avda. Rambla Méndez Núñez 23 (summer Mon–Sat 10am–8pm; winter Mon–Fri 10am–7pm, Sat 10am–2pm & 3–7pm; ☎965 200 000, ⓦ www.alicanteturismo.com). There are also municipal branches on the Playa del Postiguet and at both the bus and train stations.

Accommodation

Except in late July and August, you should have little problem finding a **room**, with the bulk of the possibilities concentrated at the lower end of the old town, above the Explanada de España (an attractively tiled seafront walk seen on all local postcards), on c/San Fernando and c/San Francisco. Among several **campsites** along the coast, *El Molino* on the Playa de San Juan (☎965 652 480) is the closest and is accessible by bus #21. Otherwise, *Internacional La Marina* (☎965 419 051), 29km out on the Ctra Alicante–Cartagena and served by Costa Azul buses, is pleasantly located in some woods, near a good beach. Both are open all year.

Sol Rambla Méndez Núñez 3 ☎965 203 000, ⓔ gransol@trypnet.com. Very central, renovated town residence where the comfortable rooms all have TV and a/c, and some have sea views. ❼

Hotel Mediterranea Plaza Plaza del Ayuntamiento 6 ☎965 210 188, ⓕ965 206 750. Tasteful four-star hotel, with large rooms, all mod cons and a location in the heart of town. ❻

Hostal Les Monges c/San Agustín 4 ☎965 215 046, ⓕ965 147 189. Attractive, popular *hostal*, with refurbished rooms, all en suite. ❹

Habitaciones La Orensana c/San Fernando 10 ☎965 207 820. Simple rooms with shared bath beside *Café Bolero*. Useful for old town and nightlife. ❷

Hostal Residencia Portugal c/Portugal 26 ☎965 929 244. Light, airy rooms near the bus station in this clean and convenient *hostal*. ❷

Hotel Rambla Rambla Méndez Núñez 9 ☎965 144 580, ⓦ www.hotelrambla.com. Refurbished hotel with pleasant modern rooms – all with TV and a/c. ❹

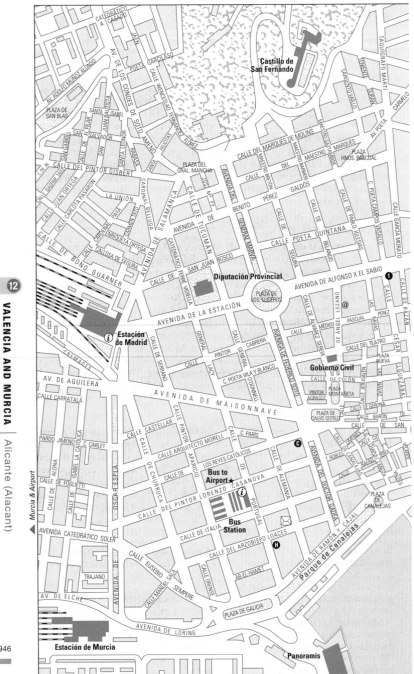

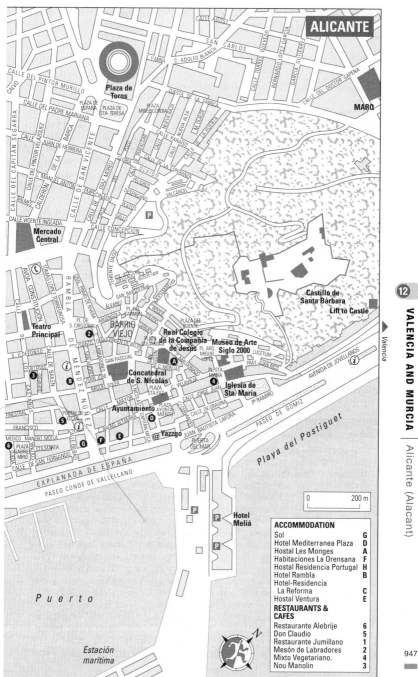

ALICANTE

CALLE AGOST
SAN CARLOS
CALLE DEL PINTOR MURILLO
Plaza de Toros
CALLE DEL PADRE MARIANA
Mercado Central
Teatro Principal
BARRIO VIEJO
Real Colegio de la Compañía de Jesús
Museo de Arte Siglo 2000
Concatedral de S. Nicolás
Iglesia de Sta. María
Ayuntamiento
Yazzgo
Castillo de Santa Bárbara
Lift to Castle
AVENIDA DE JOVELLANOS
PASEO DE GOMIZ
Playa del Postiguet
EXPLANADA DE ESPAÑA
PASEO CONDE DE VALLELLANO
Hotel Meliá
Puerto
Estación marítima

MARO

0   200 m

ACCOMMODATION

Sol	**G**
Hotel Mediterranea Plaza	**D**
Hostal Les Monges	**A**
Habitaciones La Orensana	**F**
Hostal Residencia Portugal	**H**
Hotel Rambla	**B**
Hotel-Residencia La Reforma	**C**
Hostal Ventura	**E**

RESTAURANTS & CAFÉS

Restaurante Alebrije	**6**
Don Claudio	**5**
Restaurante Jumillano	**1**
Mesón de Labradores	**2**
Mixto Vegetariano.	**4**
Nou Manolin	**3**

Hotel-Residencia La Reforma c/Reyes Católicos 7 ☎965 928 147, Ⓕ965 923 950. Clean functional rooms with a/c, TV and phone. ❹

Hostal Ventura c/San Fernando 10 ☎ & Ⓕ965 208 337. Simple double rooms with bath and TV, in a family-owned *hostal*. ❷

The Town

The rambling **Castillo de Santa Bárbara** (daily: April–Sept 9.30am–8pm; Oct–March 9am–6.30pm; free), an imposing medieval fortress located on the bare rocky hill above the town beach, is Alicante's main historical sight. It's best approached from the seaward side where a 205-metre shaft has been cut straight up through the hill to get you to the top; the lift (€2.50 in coins only) entrance is on Avenida de Jovellanos. Almost opposite are the Iberian and Roman remains that have been found on the site, but most of the present layout dates from the sixteenth century. The castle grounds, or **Parque de la Ereta**, are attractively landscaped, with olive groves, pathways, a café and tremendous views of the city.

One of Alicante's other main attractions, the **Museo de Arte Siglo 2000**, just north of the impressive *ayuntamiento*, is currently closed, but it's well worth checking to see if it's reopened, as it houses a remarkably good collection of works by Picasso, Tàpies, Miró and Dalí. Otherwise, you could do a lot worse than visit the impressive, very stylish **archeological museum**, or MARQ (Ⓦwww.marqalicante.com; June–Sept Tues–Sat 10am–8pm, Sun 10am–2pm; Oct–May Tues–Sat 10am–2pm & 4–8pm, Sun 10am–2pm; €6), on Plaza Dr Gómez Ulla, featuring locally found relics from the Iberian to medieval periods; bus #2 from Rambla Méndez Núñez will get you there.

Beaches

The city's beach – **Playa del Postiguet** – gets very crowded in summer, and the beaches at **San Juan de Alicante**, about 6km out, are very built up, but reached either by bus #21 or #22 from the Plaza del Mar or via the FEVE Alicante–Denia railway. **Playa Arenales**, backed by sand dunes, is more pleasant;

Fiestas de Moros y Cristianos

One of the most important fiestas in the region and the most important of its kind is the three-day **Fiesta de Moros y Cristianos** in **Alcoy**, about 60km from Alicante. It happens the three days around St George's Day (*San Jorge*, April 23), but the date varies slightly according to when Easter falls. Magnificent processions and mock battles for the castle culminate in the decisive intervention of St George himself – a legend that originated in the Battle of Alcoy (1276) when the town was attacked by a Muslim army. New costumes are made each year and prizes are awarded for the best, which then go into the local museum, Museu de la Festa Casal de Sant Jordi, at c/San Miguel 60 (Mon–Fri 11am–1pm & 5.30–7.30pm, Sat & Sun 10.30am–2pm; free).

On day one the Christians make their entrance in the morning, the Moors in the afternoon; day two is dedicated to St George, with several religious processions; day three sees a gunpowder battle, leading to the saint's appearance on the battlements. Access from Alicante is easy, with five buses a day. You may have to commute, since reasonably priced accommodation in Alcoy is not plentiful; though try *Hostal Savoy*, c/Casablanca 5 (☎965 547 272; ❹ during fiestas), *Hotel Reconquista*, Puente San Jorge 1 (☎965 330 900, Ⓦwww.hotelodon.com; ❸, ❻ during fiestas), or the rural *Hotel Els Frares* (see p.944) in Quatretondeta, 18km away. After Alcoy's fiesta, the *Moros y Cristianos* fiestas in **Villena** (beginning of Sept) and **Elche** (August) are two of the best.

it's 12km south of the city and reachable by the hourly Baile bus from the main bus station. You can also take a day-trip to the **island of Tabarca** (a marine reserve), to the south – boats leave, weather permitting, from the Explanada de España (June–Sept 4 daily; Oct–May Sat & Sun 1 daily; €12.80 return; 30min) – but the rock tends to get very cramped and crowded during the summer.

Eating, drinking and nightlife

There are dozens of **restaurants** clustered around the *ayuntamiento* – including a couple of places on c/Miquel Saler where you can eat couscous, and a couple of decent *churrerías*. Over on the other side of town, c/San Francisco, leading off a square near the bottom end of the *rambla*, has a group of restaurant/*tabernas* with seats outside and *menús* for under €9 – *Don Claudio* has the cheapest. In Plaza Santa María, opposite the Baroque facade of the church, you'll find a good **vegetarian** restaurant, *Mixto Vegetariano*. To sample the best of Alicante's culinary delights, at about €30 a head, head for one of the following: the smart *mesón*-style *Restaurante Jumillano*, c/César Elguezábal 64 (☎965 212 964), serves a mean *perdices escabechadas* (pickled partridge); *Nou Manolín*, c/Villegas 3 (☎965 200 368), is more *moderno*, with a tapas bar downstairs and a €14 lunchtime *menú*; or try the critically acclaimed and very stylish *Restaurante Alebrije*, Plaza Gabriel Miró (☎965 216 814). For **tapas** head to the atmospheric *Mesón de Labradores*, c/Labradores 19, and sample their *montaditos* (tiny bread rolls) or seafood specialities – if you can't squeeze in here, there's another smaller branch at c/San Pasuel 3.

If you want to buy your own food, visit the enormous **Mercado Central**, housed in a wonderful old *modernista* building on Avenida Alfonso X el Sabio. Near here there are plenty of good places to buy Alicante's famous nougat-like **turrón**, with many shops on c/Capital Serralla, and in the centre on c/Mayor – Turrón 1880 is the best. Another market (a major outdoor event) is held by the Plaza de Toros on Thursdays and Saturdays (9am–2pm).

Bars and nightlife

For **drinking** and the best **nightlife** the city is divided between three main zones. In the old town, or Barrio Santa Cruz (around the cathedral and Plaza del Carmen), the small, smoky bars have a 4am curfew. In El Barrio, as it's known, an excellent starting point is *Desdén*, c/Labradores 22, which plays jazz in the afternoon and house, dance and funk through the night. Both the *Armstrong* bar, c/Carmen 3, and *Desafinado*, Santo Tomás 6, have great jazz, while *Celestial Copas* on c/San Pascual draws an arty crowd. Over towards the west end of c/San Fernando there are more bars including lively *Byblos* and *Fitty*, and *Cha Cha* which has live DJs; while close by is the club *Z* at Plaza Gabriel Miró. The third area, El Puerto, tends to draw a smarter crowd, and the bars stay open until 7am at weekends: try *Café di Roma*, *Compañía Haddocks* and *Samoa*, which all play salsa and Latin music.

Listings

Airlines Iberia's offices are at Avda. Dr Gadea 12 (☎965 217 982) and British Airways' at the airport (☎966 919 472).
Airport Located in El Altet, 12km from Alicante city centre (☎966 919 100 or 966 919 400).
Banks Along Avda. Rambla Méndez Núñez, and the Explanada – where you'll also find *bureaux de change* offices.

Bus information ☎965 130 700.
Cinema Cine Astoria, Plaza del Carmen sometimes has original-language films; or the Panoramis complex in the port for Hollywood movies.
Consulates British Consulate, Plaza Calvo Sotelo 1–2 ☎965 216 022.
Doctor Centro de Salud, c/Gerona 24 ☎965 143 587.

Internet *Yazzgo Internet*, Explanada de España 3;
Up Internet, c/Ángel Lozano 3.
Police The *Commisaría* is at c/Médico Pascual
Pérez ☎965 148 888.
Post office Near the bus station at the junction of
c/Alemania with c/Arzobispo Loaces (Mon–Fri
8am–8.30pm).

Telephones There are *locutorios* throughout the
centre, especially along c/San Francisco and c/San
Fernando. Telefónica has an office inside the bus
station (Mon–Fri 10am–2pm & 5–9pm).
Train information Estación de Madrid ☎902 240
202. For FGV trains call ☎965 262 233.

Inland – Elche and Orihuela

ELCHE (ELX), 20km inland and south from Alicante, is famed throughout
Spain for its exotic **palm forest** and for the ancient stone bust known as La
Dama de Elche discovered here in 1897 (and now in the Museo Arqueológico
in Madrid, see p.1114). The palm trees, originally planted by the Moors, are still
the town's chief industry – not only do they attract tourists, but the female trees
produce dates, and the fronds from the males are in demand all over the country for use in Palm Sunday processions and as charms against lightning. You can
see the forest, unique in Europe, almost anywhere around the outskirts of the
city; the finest trees are those in the specially cultivated **Huerto del Cura** on
c/Federico García Sánchez.

Elche is also the home of a remarkable **fiesta** in the first two weeks of August
which culminates in a centuries-old mystery play – *Misteri*, held in the eighteenth-century **Basilica Menor de Santa María** over August 14–15.
Additional celebrations include one of the best examples of the mock battles
between Christians and Muslims. Over several days the elaborately costumed
warriors fight it out before the Moors are eventually driven from the city and
the Christian king enters in triumph.

There are **buses** more or less hourly from Alicante to Elche. Outside fiesta
time you should have no problem finding somewhere to **stay**, though there are
limited options: try *Pensión Juan*, c/Pont dels Ortissos 15 (☎965 458 609; ❷),
for basic but clean rooms with shared bathroom. Elche's smartest place is
undoubtedly *Hotel Huerto del Cura*, located just south of the gardens of the
Huerto del Cura at Porta de la Morera 14 (☎966 610 011, ⓦwww
.hotelhuertodelcura.com; ❼, ❺ at weekends), which has stunning gardens and
a pool. The *Bar Águila*, on c/Dr Coro 31, is highly recommended for convivial
drinking and good **tapas**, while the restaurant in the park, *Parque Municipal*,
serves delicious *arroz con costra*, the local rice dish. For a taste of the best local
cuisine, however, head to the more pricey *El Granaino*, 300m west of the
Punete d'Altamira at c/José María Buck 40 (closed Sun & mid-Aug).

Orihuela

Just over 50km southwest of Alicante lies the capital of the Vega Baja district,
ORIHUELA, where in 1488 los Reyes Católicos held court. The town's aristocratic past is reflected in the restored old quarter, and the impressive renovation of the **Teatro Circo**. Despite its proximity to the coast, Orihuela retains
its provincial charm and is worth a wander. Orihuela also has a natural attraction in **El Palmeral**, the second largest palm forest in Spain – walk out beyond
Colegio de Santo Domingo or take the Alicante bus (from the centre) and ask
to be dropped off. Many of the town's seventeenth- and eighteenth-century
mansions are closed to the public; however, you can roam around the one
occupied by the turismo (see "Practicalities" opposite) and parts of the Palacío
Marqués de Arneva, which now houses the *ayuntamiento*.

Opposite the turismo is the **Iglesia de Santiago** (Mon–Fri 10am–1pm & 4–7pm, Sat 10am–1pm), one of the town's three medieval churches – all of which are Catalan Gothic (subsequently altered), a style you won't find any further south. The oldest part of the church is the front portal, the Puerta de Santiago, a spectacular example of late fifteenth-century Isabelline style. Inside, the furniture is Baroque, and there is a *retablo* by Francisco Salzillo. Heading back down towards the town centre, just past the *ayuntamiento*, you'll see the second medieval church, the **Iglesia de Santas Justa y Rufina** – its tower is the oldest construction in the parish and has excellent gargoyle sculptures.

Just round the corner, on c/Salesas Marques Arneva, is one of Orihuela's hidden treasures, the Baroque **Monestario de la Visitación Salesas** (Tues only 10am–2pm, 4–5.30pm & 6.30–7pm; €0.60), whose cloisters contain several paintings by the nineteenth-century artist Vincente López – a monk will show you around.

Right in the centre of the old town is the medieval **Catedral** (Mon–Fri 10am–1.30pm & 5–7.30pm, Sat 10am–1.30pm), no bigger than the average parish church, built with spiralling, twisted pillars and vaulting. A painting by Velázquez, *The Temptation of St Thomas*, hangs in a small museum in the nave – and don't overlook the Mudéjar-influenced, fourteenth-century Puerta de las Cadenas. The **Museo Diocesano de Arte Sacro** (same hours as cathedral; €0.60), above the cloister, contains an unexpectedly rich collection of art and religious treasures (including a painting by Ribera), many of which are brought out during *Semana Santa*, the town's most important fiesta.

Orihuela's other main sight is the Baroque **Colegio de Santo Domingo** (Tues–Fri 10am–2pm & 5–8pm; reduced hours in winter; free), out towards the palm forest. Originally a Dominican monastery, it was converted into a university in 1569 by Pope Pío V, then closed down by Fernando VII in 1824. The two cloisters are well worth seeing, along with the fine eighteenth-century Valencian tiles in the refectory. For a view of the town and surrounding plains, walk up to the seminary on top of the hill. From Plaza Caturla in the centre of town, take the road leading up on the right; not far from the top, there are a couple of steeper short cuts to the right.

Practicalities

Arriving by **bus** or **train**, you'll find yourself at the combined station at the bottom of Avenida de Teodomiro, where there's a helpful tourist information desk. Otherwise, the main **turismo** is located in the impressive Palacio Rubalcara, c/Francisco Die 25 (Mon–Sat 9am–2pm & 5–7.30pm, Sun 10am–2pm; ☎965 302 747). For **accommodation**, *Hostal Rey Teodomiro* at Avda. Teodomiro 10 (☎966 743 348; ❸) has good rooms, all with bath; otherwise, the refurbished four-star *Hotel Palacio de Tudemir* (☎966 738 010, ℉966 738 070; ❻) is very comfortable indeed, and has an excellent restaurant.

If you cross over the road from the *Hostal Rey Teodomiro* and take the first right, you'll come to the best **place to eat** in town, *Mesón Don Pepe* at c/Valencia 3, which has tapas and a good weekday lunch *menú*, including local speciality *arroz con costra* (literally "rice and crust", made with rice, eggs, *embutidos*, chicken and rabbit). Alternatively, try *Mesón Ramón*, just off Avenida Duque de Tamamas on c/Luís Bacala, for cheaper food.

Murcia

MURCIA, according to the nineteenth-century writer Augustus Hare, would "from the stagnation of its long existence, be the only place Adam would recognize if he returned to Earth". Things have certainly changed – today the city of over 350,000 boasts a modern, spruced-up centre and a healthy cultural life. Founded in the ninth century on the banks of the Río Segura (no more than a trickle now) by the Moors, the city soon became an important trading centre and, four centuries later, the regional capital. It was extensively rebuilt in the eighteenth century, and the buildings in the old quarter are still mostly of this era.

Today it's the commercial centre of the region and most of the industry is connected with the surrounding agriculture. Though there are very few tourists, a substantial student population ensures that there's a lively bar and club scene.

Arrival, information and accommodation

Both bus and train stations are on the edge of town. If you're arriving by **bus**, either walk southeast via the plazas Pedro Pou and San Pedro towards the cathedral, or buses #5 or #17 will take you there. The **train station** is across the river at the southern edge of town – take bus #9, #11 or #17 to the centre. The town's **airport** is 45km away in San Javier (see p.955). Murcia's huge regional **turismo** is at Plaza Julián Romea (Mon–Fri 9.30am–2pm & 5–7pm, Sat 10am–1pm; ☎902 101 070, ⓦwww.murcia-turismo.com). Two other **municipal offices** can be found by the theatre on c/Santa Clara and close to the cathedral on Plaza Cardenal Belluga.

Accommodation

Albergue Juvenil Albergue del Valle ☎968 607 185. Beautiful youth hostel in a *parque natural* in La Alberca, 5km outside Murcia. Catch bus #29 from the Jardín de Floridablanca over the bridge on the south side of town. The YH is signposted about 1km beyond the last stop. ❶

Pensión Avenida c/Canalejas 10 ☎968 215 294. Basic budget *pensión* on the other side of the river across Puente Viejo, offering rooms without baths. ❷

Pensión Desvío-Rincón de Paco c/Cortés 27 ☎968 218 436. Very basic, but acceptable budget choice, conveniently located for the bus station. ❶

Pensión Hispano I c/Trapería 8 ☎968 216 152, ⓕ968 216 859. Conveniently located in a pedestrianized zone, with rooms either with or without private bath. ❷

Hotel Hispano II c/Radio Murcia 3 ☎968 216 152, ⓦwww.hotelhispano.net Good mid-range hotel, with a decent restaurant and parking. ❹

Hotel Rincón de Pepe c/Apósteles 34 ☎968 212 239, ⓔnhrincondepepe@nh-hotels.com. One of the best hotels in Murcia, with a famous restaurant downstairs. Heavily discounted weekend rates. ❼

The City

The **Catedral** (daily 10am–1pm & 5–7pm) towers over the mansions and plazas of the centre. Begun in the fourteenth century and finally completed in the eighteenth, it's a strange mix of styles, dubbed "Mediterranean Gothic". The outside is more interesting architecturally, particularly the west side with its Baroque facade, and the tower rising on the north, which you can climb for great views of the city. Inside, the most remarkable aspect is the florid Plateresque decoration of the chapels – particularly the **Capilla de los Vélez** (1491–1505). Originally designed as a funeral area, but never completed, it's one of the finest examples of medieval art in Murcia and one of the most interesting pieces of Hispanic Gothic; an urn in the niche of the main altar contains the heart of Alfonso the Wise. The **museum** (closed for restoration at the time of writing) has some fine primitive sculptures and, above all, a giant processional monstrance – 600 kilos of gold and silver twirling like a musical box on its revolving stand.

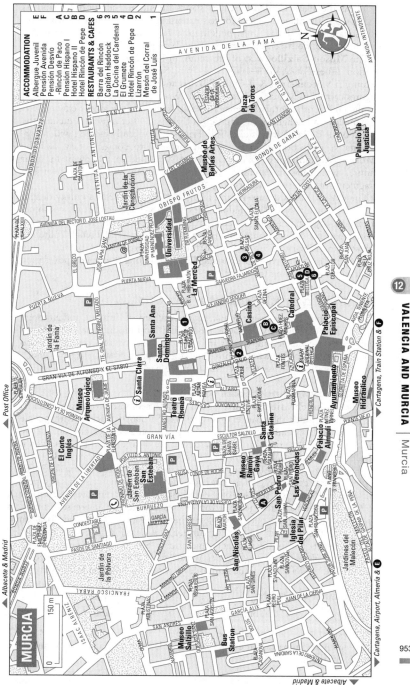

MURCIA

0 — 150 m

ACCOMMODATION
Albergue Juvenil   E
Pensión Avenida   F
Pensión Desvío   A
-Rincón de Paco   C
Pensión Hispano I   B
Hotel Hispano II   D
Hotel Rincón de Pepe   D

RESTAURANTS & CAFES
Barra del Rincón   6
Capitán Haddock   3
La Cocina del Cardenal   5
El Grumete   4
Hotel Rincón de Pepe   D
Lizarrán   2
Mesón del Corral
de José Luis   1

Across the Plaza Cardenal Belluga stands the newest addition to Murcia's architectural heritage. Rafael Moneo's extension to the **ayuntamiento** closes the square with a strict regular building that faces the cathedral facade with a rhythmic twentieth-century version of the Baroque *retablo*.

The **Museo Salzillo**, west of the centre in Plaza San Agustín, near the bus station (Tues–Sat 9.30am–1pm & 4–7pm, Sun 11am–1pm; July and Aug Mon–Fri 9.30am–1pm & 4–7pm; €3), has an extraordinary collection of the figures carried in Murcia's renowned Holy Week procession. They were carved in the eighteenth century by Francisco Salzillo and display all the cloying sentimentality and delight in the "rustic" of that age. Other museums include the **Museo de Bellas Artes** at c/Obispo Frutos 12 (currently closed), with a representative collection of local art from medieval to contemporary; and the **Museo Arqueológico**, Gran Vía Alfonso X 5 (due to reopen in the near future), which has an extensive collection of ceramic and potsherds (broken fragments of pottery) collection.

The **Casino** (daily 10am–9pm; €1.20), at c/Trapería 22, is a quirky delight and well worth a visit. The building dates from 1847 and eclectically combines an Arabic-style patio and vestibule, an English-style library reading room, a Pompeiian patio with Ionic columns, a billiard room and French ballroom. Most extraordinary of all, perhaps, is the neo-Baroque ladies' powder room (open to all) whose ceiling depicts angelic ladies among the clouds, powdering their noses and tidying their hair.

Eating, drinking and nightlife

Murcia is known as *la huerta de Europa* (the orchard of Europe), and although this might be a slight exaggeration, you'll find local produce on most restaurant menus: vegetable soups, grills and paellas are the main specialities. It's also an important rice-growing region, and the local variety, *Calasparra*, which ripens very slowly, is the variety used to make paella.

Restaurants and tapas bars

Just before **lunchtime** the whole of the Gran Vía Alfonso X and the Plaza de las Flores (towards the river end of Gran Vía Salzillo) is packed with people drinking aperitifs and picking at tapas. If you're on a budget, any one of the *mesones* in the Plaza de Julián Romea (beside the theatre) and Plaza San Juan is a safe bet. For an excellent *menú del día* for €10.20, head for *Mesón del Corral de José Luís*, Plaza de Santo Domingo 23. You'll find great **tapas** at *Barra del Rincón* (which shares the same chef as *Hotel Rincón de Pepe*), which also has a superb *menú* for €10 and is easily one of the liveliest places to eat in town; *Lizarrón* at c/Polo de Medina is also good. If you fancy **seafood**, *El Grumete* serves tasty, fresh *mariscos* by weight, and has two branches at c/Vara de Rey 6 and Plaza San Nicolas 3 (both closed Mon). For **dinner**, *La Cocina del Cardenal* in Plaza Belluga excels, but for the ultimate – and pricey – gastronomic experience, visit the famous *Hotel Rincón de Pepe*, at c/Apósteles 34 (☎968 212 239) – expect to pay around €50 a head and be sure to leave room for *leche frita* for dessert.

Bars and nightlife

As a university town, Murcia has a good **nightlife** during term time – to get a grip of what's hot, pick up a copy of free listings magazines *Sample* or *Murcia Anderground*. One of the liveliest areas is around the university, near the Museo de Bellas Artes, in particular c/Dr Fleming, c/de Saavedra Fajardo and the side streets off them.

A good place to start the evening is by the university on Plaza Beato A. Hibermón in the intimate bar *Icaro*, or on the terrace of *El Refugio* on the nearby Plaza de Bolsas, which is more or less at the centre of the action. Most bars offer the same mix of happy Spanish pop and mainstream techno tunes, though there are exceptions: *B12*, c/Trinidade 17, plays excellent funk, hip hop and reggae; *Boca de Lobo*, on c/Luisa Aledo, is the best for rock and metal; *El Perro Azul* (of the *pensión* of the same name) is a bit more relaxed, with rock and pop. Murcia-based English speakers gather at *Fitzpatrick's* on Plaza Cetina near the cathedral. At 3am the action disperses to the clubs, which are located all over the city: *Mundaka*, at Ctra. Catalina 26, and *On*, located on the road to Benianhan (km4), play house and techno. For midnight munchies, *Capitán Haddock*, c/Vara del Rey 17, makes excellent toasted sandwiches and serves drinks till the small hours.

For **jazz**, *La Puerta Falsa*, on the other side of the university at c/San Martin de Porres 5, is an outstanding bar with live music every night; while for **salsa** and Latin grooves, *Código*, on Gran Vía Alfonso X, and *Cha Cha Cha*, just round the corner, are your best bets and stay open till late. There is also a sizeable **gay** scene in Murcia: *Piscis*, Plaza Santo Domingo 6, and *Maricoco*, on c/Vitorio, are popular bars, with the crowd moving on to the *Metropol* club, off Ctra. Puente Tocinos.

Listings

Airlines Iberia, Avda. Alfonso X el Sabio 11 ☎968 240 050. Most of the others are represented by travel agencies.

Airport Located 45km away at San Javier on the Mar Menor (☎968 172 000). Ryanair, and some charters, fly to the UK, and there are limited internal flights to Almería, Barcelona and Madrid. To get to the airport, bus #70 goes to San Javier, from where it's a 3km walk or taxi ride.

Banks All the big ones, with foreign exchange desks, are on both the Gran Vías.

Bookshops Antaño, on c/Puerta Nueva, sells a good selection of English books.

Bus information The bus station is on c/Sierra de la Pila ☎968 292 211.

Car rental Hertz, next to the train station on Plaza Condestable ☎968 299 015; Europcar, Avda. Miguel de Cervantes 9 ☎968 283 086; Sol Mar, Avda. Juan de Borbón 36 ☎968 239 387; and Atessa, Juan Carlos I 2 ☎902 100 101.

Hospitals While the General Hospital is being rebuilt, the main centre is Hospital José Maria Morales Meseguer (☎968 360 900) near Plaza Circular at Avda. Marqués de los Vélez 22; Red Cross ☎968 222 222.

Internet L@ Red, c/Antonio Puig 1, just north of the university (Mon–Sat 10.30am–10pm; €2.45 per hour).

Market The Mercado Municipal, c/Verónicas, has stacks of wonderful local produce including kiwi fruit, dates, bananas and, of course, citrus fruit.

Police Avda. San Juan de la Cruz ☎968 266 600.

Post office The *Correos* is at Plaza Circular (Mon–Fri 9am–2pm & 5–8pm, Sat 9am–2pm).

Shopping El Corte Inglés has two buildings either side of Gran Vía Salzillo. The main shopping area is around the Gran Vías.

Train information RENFE, Plaza de la Industria ☎968 252 154.

Telephones *Telefónica* is on c/Jerónimo de Roda, off Gran Vía Salzillo.

The coast south of Torrevieja

The stretch of coast around the south of **Torrevieja** has been developed at an alarming rate, and is now home to a mix of Europeans, Russians and Spaniards. Just to the south is a series of pleasant beaches, known collectively as **Las Playas de Orihuela** (as they come within Orihuela's provincial boundary). Both Playa La Zenía and Playa Cabo Roig are good, clean options with car parks and cafés (the restaurant at Cabo Roig is also exceptionally good and enjoys wide views over the harbour).

The Murcian Costa Cálida starts at the **Mar Menor** (Lesser Sea), a broad lagoon whose shallow waters (ideal for kids) warm up early in the year, making this a good out-of-season destination. With its high-rise hotels, the "sleeve" (*la manga*) looks like a diminutive Benidorm; the resorts of **San Pedro del Pinatar** and **Santiago de la Ribera** on the land side of the lagoon are more appealing, and they do have a few *hostales*. Book your accommodation ahead in high season.

Santiago de la Ribera

The neighbouring resort on the Mar Menor, **SANTIAGO DE LA RIBERA**, is a more enticing place to spend a day or two by the coast, and is popular with *murciaños*. There's a good sandy beach, an attractive promenade, and an important sailing club here – the calm sea is perfect for novices. The **turismo** (Mon–Fri 10am–1.45pm & 6–8.15pm, Sat & Sun 10am–1.30pm; ☎968 571 704, ⓦwww.marmenor.net) is located 300m back from the seafront on c/Padre Juan. You'll find the best **accommodation** in the streets just behind the seafront, including the family-owned *Pensión K-Hito*, c/Maestre 9 (☎968 570 002, ❷; May–Oct), which has small but attractive rooms with bath, and *Manida*, at c/Muñoz 11 (☎ & ⓕ968 570 011; ❷), which has a range of rooms and good full-board deals. The newly built *Hotel Albohera* (☎968 335 910, ⓦwww.hotelalbohera.com; ❸) is very good value, with large modern rooms. If you're looking for seafood, you'll get the best in town at *Mesón El Pescador* on Explanada Barnuevo. There are two **campsites** in the area, both open all year: *Alcázares* (☎968 575 100) in Los Alcázares, with a pool, and *Mar Menor* (☎968 570 133) on the Alicante–Cartagena road.

The nearest **train station** for this area is Balsicas (connected with San Pedro and Santiago by 4–5 buses daily in summer). Trains run direct from here to Barcelona, Valencia and Madrid.

Cartagena

Whether you're approaching **CARTAGENA** from one of the numerous resorts along Mar Menor, inland from Murcia, or from Almería to the south, it's not a pretty sight. Scrub and semi-desert give way to a ring of hills littered with disued factories and mines, eventually merging into the newer suburbs. It's only when you reach the old part of town down by the port, with its narrow medieval streets, packed with bars and restaurants, that the city's real character emerges.

Cartagena was Hannibal's capital city on the Iberian peninsula, named after his Carthage in North Africa, and a strategic port and administrative centre for the Romans. International Nautical Week is celebrated here in June, in July the Mar de Músicas festival (ⓦwww.lamardemusicas.org) presents some of the best in world music, and in November the city hosts an International Festival of Nautical Cinema. The **fiestas** of *Semana Santa* are some of the most elaborate in Spain, with processions leaving from the church of Santa María de Gracia in the early hours of Good Friday morning.

Arrival, information and accommodation

Cartagena's **bus station** is on c/Trovero Marín, with the FEVE **train station** (trains running to Los Nietos on the Mar Menor) almost next door and the RENFE station nearby at the end of Avenida América. The city's **turismo** is on Plaza del Almirante Basterreche (summer Mon–Fri 10am–2pm & 5–7pm, Sat 10am–1pm; winter Mon–Fri 10am–2pm & 4–6pm, Sat 10am–1pm; ☎968 506 483, ⓦwww.ayto-cartagena.es).

Places to stay are quite thin on the ground. For good value and a central location, head for *Hotel Peninsular*, c/Cuatro Santos 3 (☎ & ⓕ968 500 033; ❸), just off c/Mayor. *Pensión Isabelita*, Plaza María José Artes 7 (☎968 507 735; ❷), adjacent to Plaza del Ayuntamiento, is clean and fairly decent, while *Hostal Cartagenera*, at c/Jara 32 (☎968 502 500; ❸), is also good. The *Hotel Los Habaneros*, c/San Diego 60 (☎968 505 250, ⓦwww.hotelhabaneros.com; ❹), is more upmarket and has a good-quality, but pricey, restaurant.

The City

Cartagena does not have an excess of sights and much of what it does have is in ruins. The vast military **Arsenal** that dominates the old part of the city dates from the mid-eighteenth century and, like the Captaincy General building, is still in use, heavily guarded and not open to the public. However, you can visit the **Naval Museum**, c/Menéndez Pelayo 6 (Tues–Sun 10am–1.30pm; free), set in the walls of the Arsenal, and the **National Museum for Underwater Archeology** (summer Tues–Sat 9.30am–2pm, Sun 10am–2pm; winter Tues–Sat 9.30am–3pm & Sun 10am–3pm; free), which is a long walk round the outer walls of the Arsenal on the way to the lighthouse, and has a reconstructed Roman galley and a lot of interesting exhibits salvaged from shipwrecks. The **Museo Archeológico**, c/Ramón y Cajal 45 (Tues–Fri 10am–2pm & 5–8pm, Sat & Sun 11am–2pm; free), in the new part of town, is built on a Roman burial ground and has an excellent collection of Roman artefacts and a good introduction to the ancient history of the city.

The best of Cartagena's churches is **Santa María de Gracia**, on c/San Miguel, which contains various works by Salzillo, including the figures on the high altar. There are more works by Salzillo and a fine art collection in the Neoclassical church **La Caridad** on c/la Caridad. You'll see a large number of *modernista* buildings around the city. Most of these are the work of former Cartagenian and disciple of Gaudí, Victor Beltri (1865–1935). In particular, have a look at Casa Maestre in Plaza San Francisco, Casa Cervantes, c/Mayor 15, and the old *Hotel Zapata*, Plaza de España.

To get a feel of the city's distinguished past, wander along the sea wall towards the old military hospital. It's a huge, empty, but evocative building, now falling into disrepair, and no one will mind you having a poke around. From the lighthouse there are great views of the harbour and city, but perhaps the best **city views** are from Torres Park, reached along c/Gisbert. Past the ruins of the old cathedral, the road winds down back into Plaza del Ayuntamiento.

Eating, drinking and nightlife

There are plenty of local **bars** and **restaurants** in the old town with Spanish-only menus and uninflated prices. The best places to look for food are the Plaza del Ayuntamiento and Plaza María José Artes – including the good-value *Casa Pedrero* on the corner of Plaza María José Artes, with very low-priced *platos combinados* and a €6 *menú del día*. *Mesón Artes*, opposite, has a vast range of tapas, while *El Mejillonería*, c/Mayor 4, just off Plaza del Ayuntamiento, is ever popular. The side streets around the squares also contain plenty of options: on c/Escorial, *El Bahía* is a tiny seafood restaurant with meals cooked straight from its tanks of live fish, and the more expensive *Mare Nostrum*, down by the port, also offers excellent seafood dishes as well as tapas.

In the evening, try *El Macho*, on the corner of c/Aire and c/del Cañon, which specializes in *pulpo* and *patatas bravas*; *La Uva Jumillana*, on c/Jara, which serves extremely strong wines from the barrel; or the more modern *Cervecaría-Restaurante Principal*, c/Príncipe de Vergara 2, which serves fine tapas and has art exhibitions and notice boards detailing cultural events. You'll find Cartagena's **clubs** and late-night bars on c/del Cañon, on the streets of Plaza de San Agustín and along c/Jiménez de la Espada.

The Golfo de Mazarrón

South of Cartagena, much of the scenic coastline south to the border with Andalucía is undeveloped, with a succession of fine coves lying beneath a backdrop of arid, serrated hills. The region's main resorts, **Puerto de Mazarrón** and **Águilas**, are both fairly small scale and easy-going, mainly attracting Spanish families. Public transport is pretty limited, however, so you'll need your own transport to get to the better beaches.

Mazarrón and around

The inland village of **MAZARRÓN**, 39km from Cartagena, is small and peaceful with an attractive plaza and a few **places to stay**; both *Pensión Calventus II*, Avda. de la Constitución 60 (☎968 590 094; ②), and the fancier *Guillermo II*, c/Carmen 3 (☎968 590 436, ⍟www.mazarron.com/holidays/Guillermo; ③), are worth trying. Puerto de Mazarrón resort is 6km away, served by three daily buses from Cartagena.

Despite a fair amount of development, **PUERTO DE MAZARRÓN** is pretty quiet even in season, but most of the **accommodation** is in expensive resort hotels. If you're looking for something a little less pricey, *Pensión Delfín*, by the beach at Caudillo 13 (☎968 594 639; ②), and *La Línea*, c/San Isidro (☎968 594 350; ②), are both clean and reasonable. For more comfort, head for *Hotel Bahía*, Playa de la Reya (☎968 594 000, ℻968 154 023; ④), or the beachside *Hotel Playa Grande*, Avda. Castellar 19 (☎968 594 684, ⍟www.hotel-playagrande.com; ⑥). The website ⍟www.mazarrononline.com has more information on short-term villa and apartment rentals. The massive **campsite**, *Garoa Playa de Mazarrón* (☎968 150 660), on Crta. Bolnuevo, is open year round. You'll find a useful **turismo** at c/Doctor Meca 20 (summer Mon–Sat 9.30am–2pm & 5–9pm, Sun 10am–1pm; winter Mon–Sat 9am–2pm; ☎968 594 426).

There are great **beaches** within easy reach of Puerto de Mazarrón. Heading along the coast to the southwest, there are bus services to Bolnuevo (6km away) where there's a superb stretch of sand. Continuing west of Bolnuevo, the route becomes a dirt track, with access to several coves popular with nudists, until you reach the headland of Punta Calnegre, 15km from Puerto de Mazarrón, where there are more good stretches of sand. Alternatively, if you head northeast from Puerto de Mazarrón the best beaches are around Cabo Tiñoso, 13km away. If you get tired of sunbathing, the nature reserve at **La Rambla de Moreras**, 2km north of Bolnuevo, has a lagoon which attracts a variety of migratory birds.

For **food** the best place to head for is *Virgen del Mar* on Paseo de la Sal, which serves excellent *arroz con bogavante* (rice with lobster). Slightly cheaper is the seafood restaurant *Beldemar*, Avenida Costa Cálida, where you buy fresh fish and have it cooked for you on the spot, while *Los Cazadores*, 5km along the road to Águilas (☎968 158 943), serves great barbecued meats and has a *menú del día* for €7.85. In summer, the **nightlife** is centred along Vía Axial.

Águilas

ÁGUILAS, 47km from Mazarrón, and almost on the border with Andalucía, is surrounded by plastic-sheeted fields of tomatoes – one of the few things that can grow in this arid region – and hemmed in by the parched hills of the Sierra del Contar. Along with the cultivation of tomatoes, fishing is the mainstay of the economy here, and a fish auction is held at around 5pm every day in the port's large warehouse. **Carnaval** is especially wild in Águilas, and for three days and nights in February the entire population lets its hair down with processions, floats and general fancy-dress mayhem.

Arrival and information

You'll find the **turismo** (summer Mon–Sat 9am–1.30pm & 5–9pm, Sun 11am–2pm; winter Mon–Fri 9am–2pm & 5–7pm; ☎968 493 285, ⓦ www.aguilas.org) on Plaza de Antonio Cortijos, near the port. **Buses** stop at the *Bar Peña Aguileña*, with services to Almería, Cartagena, Murcia (all 5 or 6 daily) and Lorca (Mon–Fri 16, Sat & Sun 6). There are also three **trains** daily to both Murcia and Lorca. If you plan on exploring the surrounding beaches, hiring a car or bike is a good idea; **car rental** is available from Auriga, c/Iberia 65 (☎968 447 046), and **mountain bikes** can be found along c/Julián Hernández Zaragoza for around €9 a day.

Accommodation

In the centre of town, the very basic *Pensión Águileña*, at c/Isabel la Católica 8 (☎968 410 303; ❶ without bath), is run by a friendly family from Ecuador, and guests have access to a kitchen. *Pensión Rodríguez*, Ramón y Cajal 3 (☎968 410 615; ❷), and *Hotel Madrid*, Plaza de Robles Vives (☎968 411 109, ⓦ www.hotel-madrid.co.uk; ❸), are more comfortable, while *Hotel Carlos III* at c/Rey Carlos III 22 (☎968 411 650, ⓦ www.hotelcarlosiii.com; ❸) has 1970s-style rooms with air conditioning, TV and bath. The *Albergue Juvenil* (☎968 413 029; €8.30 per bed under 25) is 4km out of town at Calarreona along the Carretera Almería, but there is no bus out this way. There are two **campsites** in the area, both open all year: *Águilas* (☎968 419 205) is 2km from the beach, and *Bellavista* (☎968 449 151) is on the Vera–Almería road in a quiet green spot. Most accommodation is fully booked between late July and late August.

The town and its beaches

Águilas is a popular spot as the beaches are plentiful (some served by public transport) and the area has a superb year-round climate. The town itself has managed to escape the worst excesses of tourism, and retains much of its rural charm and character.

You'll find fine **beaches**, and over thirty small *calas* (coves) in the vicinity – those to the north are rockier and more often backed by low cliffs, while the best are the wonderful, undeveloped **cuatro calas** south of town. You'll need your own wheels to reach these beaches, which get better the further you get away from Águilas, but all are signposted. The first two, **Calarreona** and **La Higuérica** have fine sands and are backed by dunes and the odd villa, but 6km south of Águilas where the coast is completely wild, the ravishing back-to-back sandy coves of **Cala Carolina** and **Cala Cocedores** are simply superb.

If you don't have your own transport, there are a chain of beaches north of Águilas served by regular buses (mid-July to end Aug only). Playa Hornillo is a nice beach with a couple of bars, Playa Amarillo is decent but in a built-up area, then there's *playas* Arroz, La Cola and finally Calabardina (7km from town), where the bus service ends. If you feel energetic you could head across Cabo Cope to yet another chain of beaches beginning at Ruinas Torre Cope.

Eating and drinking

For a fine selection of fresh fish and *arroz a la piedra* (a tasty rice dish with fish, shrimps and tomato), head for *El Puerto*, right by the port on Plaza Robles 18 (✆968 447 065; closed Wed), which specializes in *pulpo* (octopus) and has *menús del día* for €8 and €11. Very close by, behind the turismo, *Submarino* at c/Isaac Peral 3 (✆968 447 257) is excellent value for money, with inexpensive but very tasty tapas and good *frituras de pescado*. There's also a good covered **market**, three blocks inland from the port, with plenty of locally grown fresh fruit and vegetables: the *churros* stall here does a roaring trade in the mornings, as does the neighbouring *El Lorita* café on c/Isabel la Católica.

Inland to Lorca

Many of the historic villages of inland Murcia are accessible only with your own transport, but one place you can reach easily is **Lorca**, an attractive former frontier town.

Lorca

Though surrounded by sprawling modern suburbs, once you reach its historic centre, **LORCA** still has a distinct aura of the past. For a time it was part of the Córdoba caliphate, but it was retaken by the Christians in 1243, after which Muslim raids were a feature of life until the fall of Granada, the last Muslim stronghold. Most of the town's notable buildings – churches and ancestral homes – date from the sixteenth century onwards.

Lorca is famed for its **Semana Santa** celebrations which out-do those of Murcia and Cartagena, the next best in the region. There's a distinctly operatic splendour about the dramatization of the triumph of Christianity, with characters such as Cleopatra, Julius Caesar and the royalty of Persia and Babylon attired in embroidered costumes of velvet and silk. The high point is the afternoon and evening of Good Friday.

Arrival, information and accommodation

Arriving by **train**, get off at Lorca Sutullera; **buses** will also drop you at the station, but the bus stop before is closer to town. The **turismo**, on c/Lópe Gisbert (daily: Mon–Fri 9.30am–1.30pm & 5.30–7.30pm, Sat 11am–2pm; winter Mon–Fri 9.30am–1.30pm & 5.30–6.30pm, Sat 11am–1.30pm; ✆968 466 157, ⓦwww.ayuntalorca.es), can provide a good map, an excellent hour-long guided architectural walk around the town and plenty of glossy material. Both trains and buses connect Lorca with Murcia, although the train is cheaper and a little quicker. Heading south to Granada there are three daily buses.

Even though it really only takes an hour or two to look around Lorca, it's still a good place to stop overnight, with inexpensive **rooms** all along the highway. *Pensión del Carmen*, c/Rincón de los Valientes 3 (✆968 466 459; ❷), and *Casa Juan*, c/Guerra 10 (✆968 468 006; ❸), are decent and reasonably priced, while *Hotel Félix*, Avda. Fuerzas Armadas 146 (✆968 467 654, Ⓕ968 467 650; ❷), is old-fashioned but good value. The large *Hotel Alameda* (✆968 406 600; ⓦwww.hotel-alameda.com; ❸), in the centre of town at c/Musso Valiente 8, is a small step up in quality, offering large rooms with air conditioning. If you're coming for Semana Santa or Holy Week you'll have to book at least a month in advance, or stay in Murcia or Águilas.

The Town

Before heading up to the old town it's worth popping into the **Centro de Artesanía**, next door to the turismo, which displays and sells work combining traditional crafts with avant-garde design (Mon–Fri 10am–2pm & 5–7.30pm; free).

The old part of town lies up the hill from c/López Gisbert. The **Casa de los Guevara** (Tues–Sat 10.30am–2pm & 5–7.30pm; €2), next to the turismo, is an excellent example of civic eighteenth-century Baroque architecture and is the best mansion in town. On the corner of Plaza San Vicente and c/Corredera, the main shopping artery, is the **Columna Milenaria**, a Roman column dating from around 10 BC: it marked the distance between Lorca and Cartagena on the *Vía Heraclea*, the Roman road from the Pyrenees to Cádiz. The Gothic **Porche de San Antonio**, the only gate remaining from the old city walls, lies at the far end of the Corredera. On Plaza de España, the focal point of the town, and seemingly out of proportion with the rest, you'll find the imposing **Colegiata de San Patricio** (Mon–Fri 11am–1pm & 4.30–6.30pm, Sat & Sun 11am–1pm; free), with its enormous proto-Baroque facade, built between the sixteenth and eighteenth centuries – there's a marked contrast between the outside and the sober, refined interior, which is largely Renaissance. Nearby is the **ayuntamiento**, with its seventeenth- to eighteenth-century facade. An equally impressive front is presented by the sixteenth-century **Posito**, down a nearby side street – originally an old grain storehouse, it's now the municipal archive.

Unfortunately, some bright spark in the tourism department has decided to transform the brooding thirteenth- to fourteenth-century **Castillo** (April–Oct 10.30am–8pm; reduced hours in winter; adults €12) overlooking the town into an expensive, medieval-themed tourist attraction. Your ticket does include entrance to a flashy visitor centre in the lower town, and a toy-town train-bus ride up to the castle, but it's perfectly possible to walk (or drive) up via the impoverished *barrio antiguo* above the Colegiata de San Patricio under your own steam, too. To be fair, the castle complex is still being renovated and developed, and there are some well-presented exhibits about its history, plus re-enacted scenes of warfare using wooden stone-throwers and knights – but it all seems a bit contrived nonetheless.

Eating and drinking

There are places around Plaza España, including *Don Jamón* on c/Musso Valiente 2, which does great tapas. Alternatively, *Restaurante Barcas Casa Cándido*, c/Santo Domingo 13, has very good *menús*, or, up the road from here in c/Tintes, on the corner of Est. Cava, is a great, seedy **bodega**, where they serve powerful shots of port-like *vino tinto* for next to nothing.

Caravaca de la Cruz and Moratalla

CARAVACA DE LA CRUZ, 60km from Lorca and an important border town, is best approached from Murcia (hourly buses; 1hr 30min), though there is one daily service from Lorca. The town is dominated by the **Castillo**, which contains a beautiful marble and sandstone church, **El Santuario de Vera Cruz**. The church houses the cross used in the Easter celebrations, and on May 3 the cross is "bathed" in the temple at the bottom of town to commemorate the apparition of a cross to the Moorish king of Valencia, Zayd Abu Zayd, in 1231. Just outside the church, cloisters lead to the **museum** (guided visit: Aug daily every hour 10am–1pm & 5–8pm, otherwise Tues–Sun 11am–1pm & 5–7pm; €2.60), which concentrates on religious art and history. The churches that tower over the rest of the town, **La Iglesia del Salvador** and **La Iglesia**

de la Concepción, are also worth a visit; the latter contains some excellent examples of carved Mudéjar wood. **Accommodation** is limited, but if Caravaca's provincial charm appeals, good bets include *Pensión Victoria*, c/María Girón 1 (T968 708 624; ❷), *Pensión Patio Andaluz*, Gran Vía 28 (T968 707 682; ❷), and *Hotel Central*, Gran Vía 18 (T968 707 055, F968 707 369; ❸), which also has a decent restaurant.

Moratalla

Fourteen kilometres on is **MORATALLA**, a pretty village spread around the foot of a fortress. The steep, winding streets of the old town lead up to the **castle** from where there are stunning views of the surrounding countryside and its vast forests.

Moratalla is a lovely place to **stay** if you want to relax: *Pensión Levante*, Carretera del Canal 21 (T968 730 454; ❷), although slightly out of town, has comfortable rooms and modern bathrooms, while *Pensión Reyes*, c/Tomas el Cura 7 (T968 730 377; ❷), is simple but clean. There is a **campsite** 8km out of town in La Puerta (T968 730 008, Elapuerta@forodigital.es; open all year). If you're driving, you might head out to *Hotel Cenajo* (T968 721 011, F968 720 645; ❹), hidden away in the hills (but signposted), overlooking a beautiful reservoir. Moratalla is full of little **bars**; the *Alhameda* is one of the best for food. For **tapas**, head for *Bar Luquillas*, c/Ctra San Juan 34, which serves delicious ham-filled *croquetas*. There are several daily **buses** between Moratalla and Caravaca de la Cruz.

Travel details

Trains

Alicante to: Albacete (10 daily; 1hr 30min); Benidorm (hourly; 1hr 10min); Denia (7 daily; 2hr 15min); Madrid (8 daily; 3hr 45min); Murcia (5 daily; 1hr 15min); Valencia (9 daily; 1hr 30min–2hr 15min); Xàtiva (8 daily; 1hr 20min).
Murcia to: Águilas (4 daily, 1 Sun; 2hr); Barcelona (2 daily; 7hr); Cartagena (8 daily; 1hr); Granada (2 daily; 8hr); Lorca (10–16 daily; 1hr); Madrid (4 daily; 4hr 30min).
Valencia to: Alicante (9 daily; 1hr 30min–2hr 15min); Barcelona (14 daily; 2hr 50min–4hr 45min); Benicàssim (7 daily; 1hr 10min); Castellón (17 daily; 45min–1hr); Gandía (every 30min; 50min); Madrid (8 daily; 3hr 30min–4hr 30min); Málaga (2 daily; 9hr); Murcia (5 daily; 3hr 25min); Orihuela (5 daily; 3hr); Peñíscola (8 daily; 1hr 30min); El Puig (every 20min; 20min); Sagunto (10 daily; 30min); Segorbe (4 daily; 1hr); Xàtiva (17 daily; 1hr); Zaragoza (3 daily; 5hr–6hr 45min).

20min); San Pedro del Pinatar (11 daily; 1hr 15min); Torrevieja (10 daily; 1hr).
Murcia to: Águilas (6 daily; 2hr); Albacete (2–6 daily; 2hr 30min); Alicante (10 daily; 1hr 45min); Almería (6 daily; 3hr 30min); Barcelona (5–7 daily; 8hr); Cartagena (hourly; 1hr); Granada (5 daily; 6hr); Lorca (12 daily; 1hr 15min); Madrid (9 daily; 6hr 30min); Málaga (5 daily; 7hr); Mazarrón (3–4 daily; 1hr 30min); Orihuela (7 daily; 1hr); Valencia (5–7 daily; 4hr 45min).
Valencia to: Alicante (13–15 daily; 2hr 30min–3hr 30min); Barcelona (17–19 daily; 4hr 15min–5hr); Benidorm (11 daily; 2hr 30min); Bilbao (3 daily; 9hr); Castellón (8–10 daily; 1hr 30min–2hr); Cuenca (3 daily; 4hr); Denia (8 daily; 1hr 45min); Gandía (8 daily, 12 in summer; 1hr); Madrid (13 daily; 4hr); Murcia (5–7 daily, 10 in summer; 4hr 45min); Oliva (8 daily, 12 in summer; 1hr 30min); Orihuela (2 daily; 3hr); El Puig (14 daily; 30min); Sagunto (25 daily; 45min); Segorbe (8 daily; 1hr 15min); Sevilla (4 daily; 11hr).

Buses

Alicante to: Albacete (2 daily; 2hr 30min); Almería (2 daily; 5hr 30min); Barcelona (6 daily; 8hr); Cartagena (10 daily; 2hr); Granada (5 daily; 5hr); Madrid (5 daily; 6hr); Málaga (6 daily; 8hr); Murcia (10 daily; 1hr 45min); Orihuela (10 daily; 1hr

Balearic connections

From Alicante Air Nostrum/Iberia 1–2 daily flights to Ibiza.
From Denia Baleària ferry service to Sant Antoni, Ibiza (2 daily; 2hr 15min & 4hr) and to Palma (daily 5hr, 1 weekly on Sun 3hr 30min). Iscomar also sail

Denia–Ibiza Town (daily, 4hr 30min) and the boat continues on to Palma (10hr 30min).

From Valencia Trasmediterránea sail to: Palma de Mallorca (June–Sept 2 daily; 5hr 45min & 7hr 15min; Oct–May 1 weekly; 9hr); Ibiza (June–Sept 1 daily; 2hr 45min; Oct–May 1 weekly; 4hr 45min); Mao, Menorca (June–Sept 1 weekly on Sat, 14hr). At least 5 flights daily with Air Europa and Air Berlin to Palma (40min), at least 2 daily to Ibiza (30min).

The Balearic Islands

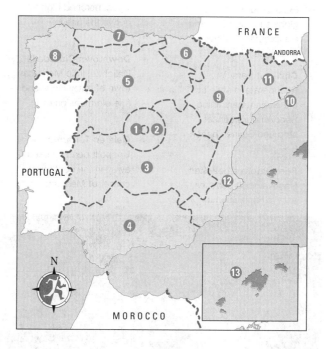

CHAPTER 13

Highlights

* **Dalt Vila** Explore Ibiza Town's souk-like walled city, a UNESCO World Heritage site. See p.975

* **Ibiza's calas** Dozens of exquisite bite-shaped cove beaches including Benirràs and Cala Mastella. See p.979

* **Ibiza's clubs** The globe's leading DJs and a supremely hedonistic ambience. See p.977

* **Chill-out bars** Recuperate in style at the elegant bars lining Sant Antoni's sunset strip and Salines beach. See p.980

* **Formentera's beaches** Undeveloped beaches, with expansive white powder sands and crystalline waters. See p.985

* **Palma's old town** Charming Renaissance mansions cluster this delightful part of town. See p.992

* **Deià, Mallorca** One of Mallorca's prettiest villages, perched high above the ocean. See p.1001

* **Downtown Ciutadella** Delightful little Menorcan town of mazy lanes and fine old mansions. See p.1019

* **Cala en Turqueta** Unspoilt beach tucked away in the southwest corner of Menorca. See p.1024

△ Palma Cathedral, Mallorca

The Balearic Islands

East of the Spanish mainland, the four chief Balearic islands – Ibiza, Formentera, Mallorca and Menorca – maintain a character distinct from the rest of Spain and from each other. **Ibiza**, firmly established among Europe's trendiest resorts, is wholly unique, with an intense, outrageous street life and a floating summer population that seems to include every club-going Spaniard from Sevilla to Barcelona. It can be fun, if this sounds like your idea of a good time, and above all if you're gay – Ibiza is a very tolerant place. **Formentera**, small and a little desolate, is something of a beach-annexe to Ibiza, though it struggles to present its own alternative image of reclusive artists and "in the know" tourists. **Mallorca**, the largest and best-known Balearic, also battles with its image, popularly reckoned as little more than sun, booze and high-rise hotels. In reality you'll find all the clichés, most of them crammed into the mega-resorts of the Bay of Palma and the east coast, but there's lots more besides: mountains, lovely old towns, some beautiful coves and the Balearics' one real city, Palma. Mallorca is in fact the one island in the group you might come to other than for beaches and nightlife, with scope to explore, walk and travel about. And finally, to the east, there's **Menorca** – more subdued in its clientele, and here, at least, the grim modern resorts are kept at a safe distance from the two main towns, the capital Maó, and the highly scenic, pocket-sized port of Ciutadella.

Access to the islands is easy from Britain, with charter **flights** and complete package deals, often at absurdly low prices out of season or if you book at the last minute. There are also charters from mainland Spain, though bizarrely these can often cost as much as or even more than those from the UK. **Ferries** – from Barcelona, Valencia and Dénia – are slightly less expensive: the single passenger fare from Barcelona to Ibiza, for example, will set you back around €48, with vehicle rates starting at around €127 one-way. **Catamarans**, which run from the same mainland ports from mid-June to mid-September, are even more expensive – Valencia to Ibiza, for instance, costs €65, while Valencia to Palma is €115. Rates for **inter-island** ferries are also high, and for journeys such as Ibiza–Mallorca or even Mallorca–Menorca it can sometimes be better value to fly. The catch here is availability: in the high season tickets are snapped up fast, so it's a good idea to book ahead – a few days beforehand is usually sufficient. For fuller details on **routes**, see "Travel details" on p.1024.

Expense and **over-demand** can be crippling in other areas, too. As "holiday islands", each with a buoyant international tourist trade, the Balearics charge considerably above mainland prices for **rooms** – which from mid-June to mid-September can double in cost, and are in very short supply. If you go at these times, it's sensible to try to fix up some kind of reservation in advance,

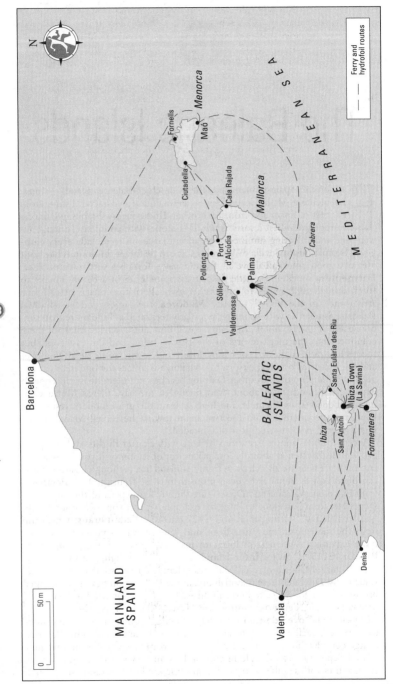

THE BALEARIC ISLANDS

N

MAINLAND
SPAIN

Barcelona

Valencia

Denia

0   50 m

*BALEARIC
ISLANDS*

Ibiza

Sant Antoni

Ibiza Town
(La Savina)

Santa Eulària des Riu

Formentera

Mallorca

Palma

Valldemossa

Sóller

Pollença

Port
d'Alcúdia

Cala Rajada

Ciutadella

Fornells

Maó

Menorca

Cabrera

M E D I T E R R A N E A N   S E A

—— Ferry and
hydrofoil routes

or at least get a bag of small change and phone round before tramping the streets (though many places accept only agency bookings). If you plan to rent a **car**, note that these can also be in short supply in season. **Mopeds, scooters and bicycles** are a good option on the islands, but be sure to check your insurance policy: it should definitely include theft as well as accident. To avoid the latter, store most of your baggage somewhere before setting out – riding with a pack is both exhausting and dangerous. Without your own transport, the **bus** network is reasonably comprehensive – and services are detailed in "Travel details" as well as the text for the specific islands.

As elsewhere in Spain, the Balearics have revived their own **dialects** since the death of Franco. A dialect of **Catalan** is spoken throughout the islands, though each of the three main islands has a different sub-dialect – indeed, many inhabitants object to their language being called Catalan at all. Generally the islanders speak their native language and Castilian (Spanish) with equal fluency. For the visitor, confusion arises from the difference between the islands' road signs and street names – which are almost exclusively in Catalan – and many of the maps on sale, which are in Castilian. In particular, note that Menorca now calls its capital Maó rather than Mahón, while both the island and town of Ibiza are usually referred to as Eivissa. The influx of tourists also means that you'll find no shortage of people with fluent English, German or sometimes French. In this chapter we give the Catalan name for towns, beaches and streets, with the Castilian name in brackets where helpful, except for Ibiza and Ibiza Town which are not widely known by their Catalan names outside Spain.

Ibiza

IBIZA – or **Eivissa** in Catalan – is an island of excess. Beautiful, and blessed with scores of stunning cove beaches, towering cliffs and dense pine forests, it's nevertheless the islanders (*ibicencos*) and their visitors who make it special. However outrageous you may want to be (and outrageousness is the norm here) the locals have seen it all before – and remain determinedly blasé about the mullet-haired fashionistas and euroslackers preening themselves on the beaches during the day, in preparation for the mother of all sessions in the bars and clubs.

For years Ibiza was *the* European hippie escape, but nowadays it's the extraordinary clubbing scene that most people come here to experience. Home to some of the most famous venues in Europe, the island can lay a strong claim to be the globe's clubbing capital, with virtually all of the world's top house DJs, and many more minor players, performing during the summer season. Visit the island between October and May, however, and you'll find a very different and much more peaceful island – just one club (*Pacha*) and a few funky bars remain open through the winter months. **Ibiza Town**, the capital, is the obvious place to base yourself: only a short bus ride from two great beaches – **Ses Salines** and **Es Cavallet** – and crammed with bars, restaurants and boutiques. **Sant Antoni de Portmany**, a large, high-rise resort on the western coast, is far less cosmopolitan in character – largely catering to young British clubbers

January

16 *Revetla de Sant Antoni Abat* (Eve of St Antony's Day) is celebrated by the lighting of bonfires (*foguerons*) in Palma and several of Mallorca's villages – especially Sa Pobla and Muro, where the inhabitants move from fire to fire, dancing round in fancy dress. Also observed in Sant Antoni (Ibiza).

17 *Beneides de Sant Antoni* (Blessing of St Antony). St Antony's feast day is marked by processions in many of the Balearics' country towns, notably Sa Pobla and Artà on Mallorca.

17 *Processó d'els Tres Tocs* (Procession of the Three Knocks). Held in Ciutadella, Menorca, this procession commemorates the victory of Alfonso III over the Muslims here on January 17, 1287.

19 *Revetla de Sant Sebastià.* Palma, Mallorca, has bonfires, singing and dancing for St Sebastian.

20 *Festa de Sant Sebastià.* Celebrated in Pollença, Mallorca, with a religious procession accompanied by *cavallets* (literally "merry-go-rounds"), two young dancers each wearing a cardboard horse and imitating the animal's walk. Of medieval origin, you'll see *cavallets* at many of the islands' festivals.

21 *Festa de Santa Agnès de Corona*, Ibiza. Traditional dances, live music and fireworks.

February

Carnaval Towns and villages throughout the islands live it up during the week before Lent with marches and fancy-dress parades.

March/April

Semana Santa (Holy Week) is as widely observed here as everywhere else in Spain. On Maundy Thursday in Palma, Mallorca, there's a religious procession through the streets. There are also Good Friday (*Divendres Sant*) processions in many towns and villages, especially in Palma, Sineu (Mallorca) and Maó. Most holy of all, however, is the Good Friday *Davallament* (the Lowering), the culmination of Holy Week in Pollença, Mallorca.

March

19 *Festa de Sant Josep* in Ibiza features live classical music followed by a firework display.

April

5 *Festa de Sant Vicent*, Ibiza. Tiny village fiesta.

23 *Festa de Sant Jordi*, Ibiza. Traditional dances (*ball pagès*) in Sant Jordi, and book-giving throughout the Balearics.

– but can almost match Ibiza Town in the hedonism stakes, its wide bay and "sunset strip" lined with groovy chill-out bars. North of Ibiza Town, **Santa Eulària des Riu** is the island's only other real town – a rather mundane little place that's popular with holidaying families, though it's fairly featureless except for a pretty hilltop church. Around the entire shoreline of the island, you'll find dozens of exquisite **cove beaches** (*calas*), many all but deserted even in high season, though you'll need your own transport to reach the best spots. **Inland**, the scenery is hilly and thickly wooded, dotted by a series of tiny hamlets, each boasting a stunning whitewashed village church, and an atmospheric local bar or two.

Salt attracted the Greeks, and after them the Phoenicians and **Carthaginians**, who made the island a regular stop on their Mediterranean cruises – to such an extent that Ibiza has hundreds of Punic burial sites. Under

May

Mid-May *Festa de Nostra Senyora de la Victòria* in Port de Sóller, Mallorca, features mock battles between Christians and infidels in commemoration of the thrashing of Turkish pirates here in 1561. Lots of booze and firing of antique rifles (in the air).
30 *Festa de Sant Ferran* in Sant Ferran, Formentera.

June

23–25 In Ciutadella, Menorca, the midsummer *Festa de Sant Joan* features jousting competitions, folk music, dancing, and processions. Also wildly celebrated in Sant Joan, Ibiza, with bonfires and fireworks.

July

15–16 *Día de Virgen de Carmen*. The patron saint of seafarers and fishermen is honoured with parades and the blessing of boats, especially in Ibiza Town and La Savina, Formentera.

August

2 *Mare de Déu dels Àngels*. Moors and Christians battle it out in Pollença, Mallorca.
8 *Sant Ciriac*. Small ceremony in Dalt Vila, Ibiza, to commemorate the Reconquest of 1235, plus a mass watermelon fight in Es Soto below the walls, and a huge firework display in the harbour.
Second weekend *Festa de Sant Llorenç*, in Alaior, Menorca; high jinks on horseback through the streets of the town. Also a small fiesta in Sant Llorenç, Ibiza.
20 *Cavallet*. Week-long festival in Felanitx, Mallorca.
24 *Día de Sant Bartomeu*. Concerts, cultural events and a large firework display in the harbour area of Sant Antoni de Portmany, Ibiza.
Throughout August International Festival at Pollença, Mallorca, including art and sculpture exhibitions and chamber music.

September

Second week *Nativitat de Nostra Senyora* (Nativity of the Virgin) in Alaró, Mallorca, with a pilgrimage to a hilltop shrine near the Castell d'Alaró.

November

16 *Festa de Santa Gertrudis*, Ibiza. Folk dancing and live music in the village square.

December

3 *Día de Sant Francesc* celebrated in Sant Francesc Xavier, Formentera, with fireworks, dancing and bonfires.
Christmas (*Nadal*) is especially picturesque in Palma, Mallorca, where there are Nativity plays in the days leading up to the 25th.

Roman rule the island continued to prosper until dropping into the familiar pattern of Spanish history, occupied successively by Vandals and Moors before being liberated by the Catalans early in the thirteenth century. Thereafter decline set in and, despite occasional imperialist incursions, Ibiza was effectively an abandoned and impoverished backwater until the middle of the twentieth century, when it began to acquire status as the most chic of the Balearics.

Ibiza practicalities

Getting around the island is relatively easy. There is a good **bus service** between Ibiza Town, Sant Antoni, Santa Eulària, Portinatx, the airport and a few of the larger beaches, and local **boats** from the three main towns serve various destinations along the coast; however, renting some form of **vehicle** (see p.969 & p.978) will widen your options no end. The main problem – and

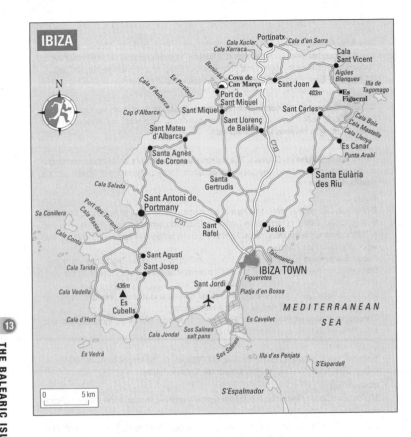

expense – on the island is **accommodation**, which is difficult, sometimes impossible, to find in high season; Ibiza Town is generally your best bet. The excellent Ⓦ www.ibiza-spotlight.com is by far the most informative website devoted to the island.

Ibiza Town

IBIZA TOWN (Ciutat d'Eivissa) is easily the most attractive settlement on the island. Approach by sea and you'll get the full-frontal effect, with the old medieval walls rising like a natural extension of the rocky cliffs which protect the harbour. Within the walls, the ancient quarter is topped by a sturdy cathedral, whose illuminated clock shines out across the harbour throughout the night.

Daylight hours are usually spent on the **beaches** at Ses Salines and Es Cavellet or the nearer (but not so nice) Figueretes or Talamanca. In summer, the streets are packed with people exploring the whitewashed, warren-like port area, where many of the fashionable boutiques stay open until 2am, and stalls line the pavements, selling everything from jewellery and sarongs to Ibiza-mix CDs. **Bars** stay open until 3.30am or later, and afterwards the action moves to the **clubs** until daylight, and for the serious hedonists, there are yet more after-hours bar-clubs. As a break from the stress of sunbathing and the simple pleasures of wandering the streets, there are a couple of modest museums and fancy modern art galleries with prices that will amaze you even if the displays don't.

Arrival, information and orientation

Ibiza's international **airport** is situated 6km southwest of Ibiza Town. The efficient **turisme** (May–Sept daily 10am–midnight) here can provide maps and lists of the island's accommodation, and several car rental firms have desks in the Arrivals lounge (see "Listings", p.978). From the airport you can take a bus (hourly 7.30am–10.30pm; €1.20) or a taxi (€11) into Ibiza Town. Ibiza Town has two **ferry terminals**: one near the foot of Avinguda Sta Eulària for local boats along the Ibiza coast and to Formentera, and the other on Passeig des Moll for the Spanish mainland and Mallorca.

The waterfront is just a stone's throw from the **lower town** – the old port area – which divides into two quarters, La Marina and Sa Penya. From here, it's a brief walk straight ahead to the walls of **Dalt Vila**, literally "High Town". The unattractive, sprawling **new town** lies to the west, beyond the Passeig Vara de Rey. The **bus station** is located in the new town on Avinguda Isidor Macabich. Ibiza's main **turisme** is on the harbour front on Passeig des Moll (June–Sept Mon–Fri 8.30am–2.30pm & 5–7pm, Sat 9.30am–1.30pm; Oct–May Mon–Fri 8.30am–2.30pm; ☎971 301 900).

Accommodation

Most of the **budget accommodation** is situated in the lower town within easy striking distance of the waterfront, and half a dozen establishments are clustered in the side streets around the Passeig de Vara de Rey. Even if you stay to the west of the centre in Figueretes, you're not that far removed from the action. The turisme has a comprehensive list of hotel accommodation, as well as **apartments** for stays of a week or more, but remember that in the height of the season last-minute vacancies are *very* hard to come by. If you haven't booked ahead, you may well be reduced to one of the island's four **campsites**: two are in the vicinity of Santa Eulària des Riu, and two are close to Sant Antoni de Portmany.

Hostal Bimbi c/Ramón Muntaner 55, Figueretes ☎971 305 396, ⊕971 305 396. Comfortable family-run *hostal*, just above Figueretes beach and a 10min walk from the centre of town. Popular with backpackers, the nineteen rooms – singles, doubles and triples – are all tastefully decorated and kept spotlessly clean. Open Easter–Oct only. ❷
Hostal Residencia Juanito & Hostal Residencia Las Nieves c/Joan d'Austria 18 ☎971 315 822. A couple of blocks north of the Passeig de Vara de Rey, these two *hostales* have plain, clean rooms, some en suite. Same management and prices for both. ❷
Hotel Lux Isla c/Josep Pla 1, Talamanca ☎971 313 469, ⓦwww.luxisla.com. Small hotel with bright, comfortable rooms located a stone's throw from Talamanca beach and 1km from Ibiza Town's marina. ❺
Hostal La Marina c/Barcelona 7 ☎971 310 172, ⓦwww.ibiza-spotlight.com/hostal-lamarina. Historic portside hotel with a choice of stylish rooms, some overlooking the harbour, divided between three neighbouring locations. ❹–❻
Ocean Drive Port d'Eivissa ☎971 661 738, ⓦwww.oceandrive.de. Art Deco-inspired hotel commanding a fine position overlooking the marina, and a short stumble from Talamanca beach and the *Pacha* and *El Divino* clubs. The rooms (all a/c) are surprisingly reasonable in low season, when double room rates fall as low as €90. ❽

RESTAURANTS & TAPAS BARS

Bon Profit	8
La Brasa	7
C'an Alfredo	6
C'an Costa	3
Macao	4
La Marina	2
Los Pasajeros	5
La Plaza	10
Sa Torreta	9
La Victoria	1

ACCOMMODATION

Hostal Bimbi	L
Hostal Residencia Juanito	C
Hostal Residencia Las Nieves	E
Hotel Lux Isla	A
Hostal La Marina	D
Ocean Drive	B
Hostal Residencia Parque	H
Apartamentos Roselló	K
Hostal Residencia Sol y Brisa	F
La Torre del Canónigo	J
Casa de Huéspedes Vara de Rey	G
Hostal Residencia La Ventana	I

IBIZA TOWN

Hostal Residencia Parque Caieta Soler s/n
℡971 301 358. Excellent modern *hostal* overlooking a pleasant, leafy square. Very good-value single rooms, and though the doubles are quite small, they're spotless and come with a/c. ❹

Apartamentos Roselló c/General Juli Cirer i Vela, Puig des Molins ℡ & ℻971 302 790. Excellently located apartments, positioned right above the Mediterranean just five minutes' walk from Figueretes beach and Ibiza Town. The apartments are very tranquil and comfortable, with simply decorated living areas – most also have wonderful sun terraces. Tricky to find, but best reached through the tunnel (*el túnel*) behind Dalt Vila. ❹

Hostal Residencia Sol y Brisa Avgda Bartomeu Vicente Ramón 15 ℡971 310 818. Family-run *hostal* with small, very clean and fairly comfortable rooms close to the port area, though it can be a little noisy at night. Shared bathrooms. ❷

La Torre del Canónigo c/Major 8, Dalt Vila ℡ 971 303 884, ⓦwww.elcanonigo.com. Wonderful apartment-hotel, magnificently located in Dalt Vila, though it's a hike down to the port area. The suite-size rooms are all much more spacious than most luxury hotels in Ibiza Town, and also the best appointed, with a/c, satellite TV and private Jacuzzi, and either harbour or city views. Good value, considering the quality of accommodation, and with a wonderful pool, too. Open April–Nov & New Year. ❽

Casa de Huéspedes Vara de Rey Passeig de Vara de Rey 7 ℡971 301 376, ⓦwww.ibiza-spotlight.com/huespedes. Set on the third floor of an old building in a good, central location, this clean and friendly guesthouse offers reasonably priced rooms with fans, some decorated with original driftwood sculptures. ❸

Hostal Residencia La Ventana Sa Carrossa 13 ℡971 390 857, ⓕ971 390 145. High-quality accommodation, located just inside the walls of Dalt Vila. Rooms are tasteful, though smallish for the price, and come with four-poster beds. There's also a stylish restaurant and a great roof terrace. ❽

The Town

The city's stone walls reach a dramatic climax at the imposing main entrance, the **Portal de ses Taules**, a triple gateway designed to withstand the heaviest artillery barrage. Inside this monumental entrance lies the historic enclave of **Dalt Vila**, declared a UNESCO World Heritage Site in December 1999. Just beyond the main gate, **Plaça de Vila** is packed with restaurants and cafés, while above the arch of the Portal de ses Taules is the **Museu d'Art Contemporani** (May–Sept Tues–Fri 10am–1.30pm & 5–8pm, Sat 10am–1.30pm; Oct–April Tues–Fri 10am–1pm & 4–6pm, Sat 10am–1.30pm; €2.60), whose large stone premises house good contemporary art exhibitions and cultural events.

Heading east uphill along Sa Carrossa, you'll pass a strip of fine restaurants, and have easy access to the top of the colossal walls, which provide great views down over the town. At the end of Sa Carrossa is c/General Balanzat, where the sixteenth-century church of **Sant Domingo** (also known as the Església de Sant Pere) stands next to its former monastery, converted in 1838 into the *ajuntament*, which overlooks the pretty, palm-lined Plaça d'Espanya. Continuing uphill along c/Santa Maria you'll soon get to Plaça de la Catedral. Some 90m above sea level, the site of the cathedral has been a place of worship for over two thousand years, originally occupied by a Carthaginian temple, then a Roman replacement, dedicated to Mercury, and later a mosque. Today's thirteenth-century **Catedral** (Tues–Sun: June–Sept 9am–4pm; Oct–May 10am–2pm; free) is pleasingly austere, its sombre, sturdy Gothic lines supported by giant buttresses. Inside, the decor is far less attractive: whitewashed throughout, with somewhat trite Baroque embellishments. A plaque commemorates the massacre of over a hundred churchmen, soldiers and islanders at the hands of anarchists during the Civil War. The cathedral's **Diocesan museum** (Tues–Sat 10am–2pm, €1.20) exhibits medieval Catalan art and displays of ecclesiastical regalia: bishops' mitres, sandals, gloves, cloaks and so on.

Across the square is the **Museu Arqueològic d'Eivissa i Formentera** (April–Sept Tues–Sat 10am–2pm & 5–8pm, Sun 10am–2pm; Oct–March Tues–Sat 10am–1pm & 4–6pm, Sun 10am–2pm; €2), with a collection of local archeological finds. The majority of the objects on display are from Phoenician and Carthaginian (Punic) sites, but there are also some bones from Formentera that date back to 1600 BC, and various Arab and Roman curiosities.

Outside the walls

Not quite as grand, nor as ancient, as Dalt Vila, the **Sa Penya** quarter of the lower town snuggles between the harbour and the ramparts, a maze of raked passages and narrow streets crimped by balconied, whitewashed houses. Here, especially along the waterside promenade and c/d'Enmig, the evening *passeig* reaches its exuberant peak and everyone – local and visitor alike – gravitates towards the bars and restaurants. This is where many of the shops are, too, occupying almost every doorway that isn't a bar.

Further to the west, the **new town** is generally of less interest, but there's activity here as well, centred on the boulevard-like Passeig de Vara de Rey and the leafy, pedestrianized Plaça des Parc just to the south. Both places have scores of cafés and restaurants and are popular meeting places.

Set on a rocky hillside 300m west of Dalt Vila are the remains of a huge **Punic necropolis** (Tues–Sat 10am–2pm & 6–8pm, Sun 10am–2pm; free); the entrance is on Via Romana. There's not that much to see today – though you can descend into some of the tombs – but thousands of terracotta pieces, clay figurines, amphorae and amulets depicting Egyptian gods have been uncovered here. Ibiza, the sacred island of the goddess Tanit, functioned as an A-list burial site, with wealthy Carthaginians paying by special minted currency for the shipment of their bodies to the island upon death, in anticipation of a fast-track passage to heaven. The site's museum is closed.

Eating

Ibiza Town has a glut of **cafés** and **restaurants** to cater for the crowds. Many of the pricier places are up in Dalt Vila – mostly on Plaça de Vila and Sa Carrossa – or down by the waterfront, while less expensive establishments are dotted round the lower town in between. Opening hours are fairly elastic, with many places staying open from the morning until very late at night. For an **early breakfast**, head for *Madagascar*, on Plaça des Parc, or the *Croissant Show* on Plaça de sa Constitució.

If you plan to prepare your own meal, or want to gather ingredients for a picnic, be warned that the covered **market** in Plaça de sa Constitució sells vastly overpriced fruit and vegetables, so you're better heading to the Supermercado Spar, on the east side of Plaça des Parc, or the SYP store at the southern end of Avinguda d'Ignasi Wallis.

Restaurants

Bon Profit Plaça des Parc 5. Very stylish canteen-style place, with shared tables and a bargain-priced menu. No reservations, and be prepared to queue.

La Brasa c/Pere Sala 3 ☎971 301 202. Elegant Mediterranean restaurant with a delightful garden terrace and a simple, but pretty pricey, fish and meat-based menu. Service manages to be relaxed but efficient.

C'an Alfredo Passeig de Vara de Rey ☎971 311 274. Classy restaurant catering for any wallet, with main courses from €6 to €16. International dishes set the tone, but there are Balearic specialities too, and the seafood is outstanding.

C'an Costa c/Crue 19 ☎971 310 866. Smoky, moderately priced restaurant in the lower town serving good, fresh Spanish dishes, plus plenty of hearty Ibizan specials. Closed Sun.

Macao Passeig des Moll s/n ☎971 314 707. Set at the extreme eastern end of the port, this smart Italian restaurant is very popular with the celebrity crowd and offers a surprisingly reasonably priced menu with fine fresh pasta.

La Marina c/Barcelona 7 ☎971 310 172. Formal top-notch seafood restaurant down by the harbour. On the pricey side, but a good place for a splurge.

Los Pasajeros c/Vicent Soler s/n. First-floor restaurant that's one of the hippest places to dine in town, with unpretentious, plain decor and a tasty Spanish *menú* and cheap wine. Open until 2am.

La Plaza Plaça de Vila 18 ☎971 307 617. Elegant restaurant with a great pavement terrace; the menu mainly concentrates on meat and fish dishes, though there's also reasonably priced pasta.

Sa Torreta Plaça de Vila s/n. ☎971 300 411. Excellent, expensive French-inspired menu and sublime, atmospheric setting inside the walled city. Closed Nov–March.

La Victoria c/Riambau 1 ☎971 310 622. Popular and well-established Ibizan restaurant in the lower town, offering generous portions of inexpensive but tasty local specialities – excellent value.

Drinking and nightlife

However good the restaurant scene in Ibiza Town, it's something of a sideshow compared with the bars and clubs which have made the island internationally famous – you come to Ibiza to party. In summer the island buzzes with action pretty much 24 hours a day, and with money, mobility and stamina the night is yours, never mind the morning. The town's **bars** throng the streets of the lower town, where unsuspecting visitors are herded into terrace bars around Plaça de sa Tertulia by teams of hustlers and fleeced as much as €7 for a beer. Better to start the night in Plaça des Parc in *Sunset* or *Madagascar*, where prices are more reasonable, and then head for the stylish bars of Sa Penya – *Bar Zuka* on c/de la Verge, *Base Bar* and *Rock Bar* at the eastern end of c/Garijo – all attract a seriously funky, clubby clientele. In winter there's far less choice, but try *Can Pou Bar* on c/Lluís Tur i Palau, *La Tierra* on Passatge Trinitat 4, or the hip *Warhol* on the corner of c/Joan Xico and c/Ramón Muntaner.

The **gay scene** is centred on c/de la Verge, perhaps the wildest street in the western Mediterranean, where dozens of bars and myriad shops cater for an almost exclusively (male) gay crowd; *Caprichio* and *Bar JJ* are both fashionable spots, but the *Dôme* bar close by at c/d'Alfonso XII is the really *über*-hip gay destination bar. Meanwhile, some of the globe's most spectacular **clubs** are spread across the southern half of the island: in Sant Antoni, Sant Rafel, Platja d'en Bossa, and in Ibiza Town itself. It's actually quite easy to hop from one club to the other courtesy of the *Disco Bus* (nightly 0.30–6.30am; €1.80 per journey). Neither is there much difficulty in finding out what's happening: each club employs PR people, who descend on Ibiza Town to parade through the streets in a competitive frenzy of night hype. Processions of stilt-walkers, silver- and gold-painted angels, devils and dwarfs strut through the streets bearing club banners to drum up custom. Many of the happening bars also hand out free club entry tickets to drinkers, which represent a significant saving. None of the clubs opens until midnight, but there again they do carry on until at least 7am. Most have a policy of a free drink with the admission price and the majority accept credit cards.

For **live music**, the prime spot is *Teatro Pereira*, c/Comte de Rosselló 3, housed in the old municipal theatre near the Passeig de Vara de Rey. This splendid old building has a great atmosphere and showcases live acts each night – blues, R&B, reggae, rock and jazz. It's open 8pm to 5am all year, and admission is free, although the drinks are expensive.

Clubs

Amnesia Ibiza Town–Sant Antoni road, km6 ℡971 198 041, ⊛www.amnesia-ibiza.com. Cavernous club with a capacity of five thousand, historically the island's most innovative venue, where resident DJs helped kickstart the acid house revolution. Today the club is split in two halves: a dark, moody club ideal for trance and hard house and an airy, verdant atrium-topped terrace ideal for Balearic tunes. Booked by Cream and gay promoters La Troya Asesina in the summer, and also features foam parties. Open daily June–Sept. Admission €30–45; drinks from €6.

Anfora c/Sant Carles 7, Dalt Vila ℡971 302 893, ⊛www.anforna-disco.com. Gay club built into a natural cave in the old quarter of Dalt Vila. Attracts a very international, mixed-age crowd with a combination of tribal house and camp anthems. Open daily May to early Oct. Admission €7 before 2am, €12 after.

DC10 On the Sant Jordi–Salines road at km1. This unpretentious club, located at the end of the airport runway, is *the* success story of the last few years. There's a large open terrace where the atmosphere can be electric, and a scruffy interior. Hosts day and night events – the Monday slot, promoted by the Anglo-Italian *Circo Loco* ensemble, is one not to miss. Open Mon from 9am, occasional evenings June–Sept. Admission €15–25, drinks from €5.

El Divino Port d'Eivissa ℡971 190 176, ⊛www.eldivino-ibiza.com. Across the bay from *La Marina*, jutting into the harbour waters with superb views of Dalt Vila from its luxuriant outdoor terrace. Comparatively small – with a capacity of 1000 – *El Divino* attracts an older, moneyed crowd with soulful house mixes. Open daily mid-June to late-Sept. Admission €30–45; drinks from €6.

Pacha Avgda 8 d'Agost ℡971 313 600, ⊛www.pacha.com. On the edge of Ibiza Town, just north of the marina. The *grand dame* of the Ibizan club scene, superbly set in a converted white farmhouse. There's house music in the main room, alternative sounds in the Global Zone, plus a funky room and salsa salon. The beautiful terrace overlooks the city, and there's also a fine restaurant and a sushi bar. Used by the UK Ministry of Sound club in the summer season. Open daily April–Sept; Oct–March weekends only. Admission €35–50; drinks from €9.

Pin-Up Platja d'en Bossa Ⓦ www.pinupibiza.com. New club venue, with a great beachside terrace and stylish interior. Got off to a slow start in 2002, but if the right promoters are secured the party potential is superb. Open June–Sept. Admission €15–25; drinks from €5.

Privilege Just off the Ibiza Town–Sant Antoni road at km7 Ⓣ 971 198 160, Ⓦ www.privilege -ibiza.com. Formerly known as Ku, this club is located high up in the hills; a vast glass-sided and -roofed building with terrific views over the interior. Inside, the club (which has a capacity of around 10,000) resembles a movie set, with a swimming pool in the centre of the vast main room, fourteen bars, an outdoor terrace garden, a chill-out dome, and a café. Home to the legendary Manumission (Ⓦ www.manumission.com). Open daily June–Sept. Admission €30–50; drinks from €7.

Space Platja d'en Bossa Ⓣ 971 396 793, Ⓦ www.space-ibiza.com. This club on the beach is essentially a day venue (opening its doors around 9am), though it also now has some night-time dance sessions. Split into two distinct parts: a shadowy interior with pounding techno and trance, and a delightful open-air terrace where DJs play funky house and Balearic mixes. The most cosmopolitan clubbing crowd in Ibiza gathers for the legendary Sunday session, extended in recent years into a 22-hour carry-on-clubbing marathon. Only for the hardcore. Admission €30–48.

Listings

Airport information Ⓣ 971 809 000.
Airlines Iberia, Passeig de Vara de Rey 15 Ⓣ 971 300 614 (outside office hours call Ⓣ 902 400 500).
Car rental There are branches of Avis (Ⓣ 971 809 176) and Hertz (Ⓣ 971 809 178) at the airport; alternatively, try Isla Blanca at c/Felipe II in Ibiza Town, Ⓣ 971 315 407.
Consulates UK, Avgda d'Isidor Macabich 45 Ⓣ 971 301 818 (Mon–Fri 9am–3pm).
Ferries There are sailings to the mainland and Mallorca with Trasmediterránea (Ⓣ 971 315 050, Ⓦ www.trasmediterranea.es), Baleària (Ⓣ 971 314 005, Ⓦ www.balearia.com) and Iscomar (Ⓣ 902 119 128, Ⓦ www.iscomar.com). Boats to Formentera are operated by several companies, including Transmapi (Ⓣ 971 310 711) and Umafisa (Ⓣ 971 314 513).
Hospital Hospital Can Misses, on the way to the airport Ⓣ 971 397 000.
Internet access There are several places to go online in Ibiza Town, with two on Avgda d'Ignasi Wallis alone, but the best is *Chill*, at Via Púnica 49 (Mon–Sat 10am–midnight, Sun 5pm–midnight), where you'll also find delicious, healthy snacks like bagels and salads.
Laundry The best place is Wash & Dry, Avgda d'Espanya 53, where you can surf the web while waiting for your wash. Otherwise Masterclean, c/Felip II, is efficient.
Moped rental Motos Valentín, Bartomeu Vicent Ramón 19 Ⓣ 971 310 822; Motosud, Avgda d'Espanya s/n Ⓣ 971 302 442 – a 1km walk west of the centre.
Post office The main *Correu* (Mon–Fri 8.30am–2pm) is 1km from the centre of town at the eastern end of Avgda d'Isidor Macabich.

Around Ibiza Town: the beaches

There's sea and sand close to Ibiza Town at **Figueretes**, **Platja d'en Bossa** and **Talamanca**, but the first two of these are built-up continuations of the capital with over-exploited beaches, and only at the third is there any peace and quiet. All are accessible by short and inexpensive ferry rides from the terminal near the foot of Avinguda Santa Eulària.

Ses Salines and Es Cavallet

To the **south of Ibiza Town**, stretching from the airport to the sea, are thousands of acres of **salt flats**. Ibiza's history, and its powerful presence on ancient trade routes, was based on these salt fields (*salines*), a trade that was vital, above all, to the ancient Carthaginians. Indeed, salt remained an important economic resource until comparatively recently; the island's only rail line ran from the middle of the marshes to **La Canal**, a dock where an enormous container ship would arrive weekly to be loaded with the bright, pinky-white sea salt. Even now, though tourism brings in far more money and the rail line has been torn up, salt production continues.

There are two beaches around here, and buses from Ibiza Town leave regularly for the more westerly, **SES SALINES**, whose fine white sand arcs around a bay, the crystal-clear waters fringed by pines and dunes. The beach also has a handful of beach bars, with cool chill-out sounds at *Sa Trinxa* at the southern end of the sands. From Ses Salines, it's a brief walk around the rocks or along the paths that maze the sand dunes to **ES CAVALLET**, a quieter if broadly similar beach that's long been a favourite of gay visitors – the dunes behind the beach are a well-known cruising area. The southern ends of both beaches are reserved for nude sunbathing.

The east coast

Heading northeast from Ibiza Town, it's just 15km to **SANTA EULÀRIA DES RIU**, a slightly mundane little town pushed tight against the seashore and situated beside the only river in the Balearics. It does boast an attractive hilltop **church**, however, a fortified whitewashed sixteenth-century construction with a beautifully shady, arched entrance porch. Set in an ancient farmhouse just below the church is a little **ethnological museum** (May–Oct Mon–Sat 10am–1pm & 5–8pm; Nov–April Mon–Sat 10am–1pm & 4–6pm; €2), with a not wildly exciting collection of old tools, ploughs and an olive press. There's nothing else to see in Santa Eulària, so it's best to press on to **SANT CARLES**, 7km to the north, an agreeable one-horse village. Here you can refuel at *Las Dalias* bar-café, just before you reach the village, where there's a "hippie market" every Saturday, or at the legendary *Anita's* bar, opposite the whitewashed church, which attracts islanders and resident bohemians in roughly equal proportion.

East of Sant Carles the road passes through burnt-red fields of olive, almond and carob trees to several almost untouched beaches. **CALA LLENYA**, 4km from Sant Carles, a 200-metre-wide sandy cove, with sparkling waters, a snack bar and shade and sunbeds for hire, is the nearest, and is popular with families. Tiny **CALA MASTELLA**, 2km further north, is a supremely peaceful spot, with a diminutive sandy beach, crystal-clear sheltered water and two simple fish restaurants, *Sa Seni* and *El Bigotes*, some 50m around the shoreline (both summer only). Just 1km to the north of Cala Mastella, **CALA BOIX** is another stunning sandy cove, a little larger and more exposed, where you'll find fine, moderately priced seafood at the *Restaurant La Noria* (℡971 335 397; open all year) and spacious, excellent-value rooms at the *Hostal Cala Boix* (℡971 335 224; ❷) on the cliffs above the shore. North of Cala Boix, the coastal road follows an exhilarating, serpentine route above the shore, through thick pine forests, via the lonely nudist beach of **AIGÜES BLANQUES** to **CALA DE SANT VICENT** where the developers have dumped huge concrete hotels on a once-breathtaking beach.

The north

From Cala de Sant Vicent, it's a tortuous ascent up over the spine of the Serra de la Mala Costa to the pretty hilltop village of **SANT JOAN**, home to a typically minimalist, whitewashed Ibizan village church, the *Eco Centre* Internet café, and cheap, clean rooms at the *hostal Can Pla Roig* (T & F971 333 012; ❷). There are more stunning beaches north of Sant Joan, especially remote **CALA D'EN SERRA**, a tiny, exquisite sandy cove, with turquoise waters perfect for snorkelling and a decent *chiringuito* bar-café. From Sant Joan a road also wriggles through a beautiful, fertile valley, past olive terraces down to **PORTINATX**, an inoffensive but somewhat banal resort, which sprawls around three pretty bays, where you'll find the two-star *Hostal Cas Mallorqui* (T971 333 082, F971 333 159; ❺), whose comfortable rooms overlook the resort's Es Port beach.

Three kilometres west of Sant Joan along the Sant Miguel road there's a turn-off for **BENIRRÀS**, another beautiful cove, backed by high, wooded cliffs and all but untouched except for a few unobtrusive villas and three beachside café-restaurants. Benirràs is Ibiza's premier hippie-centric beach – dozens gather here to burn herbs and pound drums to the setting sun, especially on Sundays. There's also an excellent **yoga** retreat here – visit Wwww.ibizayoga.com for more information. The next village to the west is **SANT MIQUEL**, where there's another fine hilltop church, and a number of simple tapas bars – try *Es Pi Ver* or *Bar March* for a simple, inexpensive feed. The once astonishingly beautiful, almost fjord-like inlet at **PORT DE SANT MIQUEL**, 3km north of the village, has also been badly mauled by the developers, – unenticing surroundings for the modest cave complex **Cova de Can Marçà** (daily 11am–1.30pm & 3–5.30pm, guided tours every half-hour; €4.50), which is well signposted on the twisting road above the bay. The cave features some spectacular lighting effects, including a very kitsch artificial waterfall that cascades over fossil-rich rocks to a soundtrack of 1970s band Tangerine Dream. There's also an excellent **view** of the coastline from outside.

The west coast: Sant Antoni de Portmany

For years unchallenged at the top of Europe's *costa hooligania* league table, **SANT ANTONI DE PORTMANY** is trying hard to shake off its tarnished, boozing 'n' brawling image. The untidy, high-rise skyline remains as unappealing as ever, the nauseous pubs of the West End district haven't changed, but an attractive "sunset strip" of funky new chill-out bars, spread around the north end of the bay, now provides a tranquil environment for a drink and a meal. Virtually everyone in Sant Antoni is here on a package tour, with beds very hard to come by in high season, but try the helpful **turisme** (Mon–Fri 9.30am–8.30pm, Sat & Sun 9.30am–1pm; T971 343 363), at the beginning of the waterfront Passeig de ses Fonts, for information on **places to stay**. Reasonably priced, downtown options include the recently renovated *Hostal Residencia Roig*, c/Progres 44 (T971 340 483; ❸), where all the rooms have good-sized bathrooms and pleasant pine furniture; and *Hotel Residencia Salada*, c/Soletat 7 (T971 341 130; Easter–Oct; ❷), a spotless place on a quiet street. Alternatively, there's a pricier-than-average **campsite**, *Camping San Antonio*

THE BALEARIC ISLANDS | The north

13

△ Benirràs Bay, Ibiza

(☎617 835 845; April–Oct), just outside town beside the main road to Ibiza Town. The palm-shaded grounds boast a swimming pool and bar, and there's also a laundry. Pitches cost €4.50, plus €4.40 per person, and there are also bungalows (❷–❸).

There are plenty of **cafés** and restaurants to choose from. You'll find good global grub at the northern end of the sunset strip at the *Kasbah* (☎971 348 364), in Caló des Moro, and tasty Spanish food at *Rias Baixes* (☎971 340 480), at c/d'Ignasi Riquer 4 in the centre of the town. There are now a dozen or so "sunset" bars, all offering prime views, but the best are still the original chill-out bar, *Café del Mar*, at the west end of c/Vara de Rey, and *Mambo*, next door. A little further north from here, the spectacular new *Coastline* bar-restaurant is a striking new addition to the scene, with three pools and a huge sun terrace. San An has two huge **clubs**: *Es Paradis* (🌐www.esparadis.com), topped by a huge glass pyramid, and *Eden* (🌐www.edenibiza.com), which looks like a psychedelic mosque, complete with electric blue domes and minarets. They're both just off Avinguda Dr. Fleming in the centre of town and are open May to October, with entrance typically costing €25–38. Both book big-name DJs like Judge Jules and Ibiza's own DJ Gee.

Car rental is available from Avis, down by the harbour on Passeig de la Mar (☎971 342 715), and from Betacar, just behind the waterfront on c/General Balanzat (☎971 345 068). **Bicycle rental** outlets include Autos Reco, c/Ramón i Cajal (☎971 340 388), a few minutes' walk from the harbour front on the east side of the town centre. Sant Antoni offers a wide range of **boat trips**, from glass-bottomed tours of the harbour and a shuttle service west across the bay to the undeveloped, but busy, broad sandy beach of Cala Bassa, through to trips to Formentera. **Buses** leave for Ibiza Town every half-hour and four times daily to Santa Eulària. There are also frequent departures to the southwest *calas* Vedella, Conta and Tarida between May and October. **Timetables** are available at the turisme, and all buses leave from the Passeig de la Mar.

Around Sant Antoni

There's another attractive beach and glorious countryside within easy striking distance **north** of Sant Antoni. From here the road climbs steeply through thick aromatic pine forests, passing a turn-off, 3km from Sant Antoni, to the small cove of **CALA SALADA**, where the beach is of fine sand and the sea excellent for swimming. There's a small and cheerful restaurant here, a beach bar and epic sunsets. Further north, and inland, the sleepy hamlet of **SANTA AGNÉS DE CORONA** drapes over a hillside surrounded by picturesque fields dotted with hundreds of almond and fruit trees. The village has a wonderful whitewashed church, and a superb village bar, *Can Cosmi*, which serves excellent tapas and the finest tortilla in Ibiza. From the village, a rough but paved country road continues east across the hilly interior of the island via diminutive Sant Mateu to Sant Miquel (see p.980).

South of Sant Antoni is the ugly, sprawling package ghetto zone known as "San An Bay", which stretches to the small resort of Port des Torrent, but travel a few kilometres further and there are several exquisite coves. Of the first two beaches, sheltered **CALA BASSA** gets packed with holidaying families in high season, but it does have a campsite (☎971 344 599), while the more exposed, blue-flag beach of **CALA CONTA** is less crowded, with three simple fish restaurants above the shore and pole position for sunsets over the ocean. The most beguiling beach in the Balearics, **CALA D'HORT**, is in the extreme southwest of the island, with a lovely quiet sand-and-pebble shoreline plus three good, moderately priced seafood restaurants. What really sets the beach apart, however, are the mesmeric vistas of **Es Vedrà**, a canine tooth of rock stabbing through the bay just offshore. This jagged, 378-metre-high islet is revered by islanders and island hippies alike and is the subject of various myths and legends – including a claim to be Homer's island of the sirens.

Sant Antoni to Ibiza Town

It's just 15km from Sant Antoni to Ibiza Town east along the main road, but you can detour taking the southern, more scenic route via **SANT JOSEP**, a pretty village with a magnificently minimalist village church and a selection of good places to stop for a drink or a snack: *El Destino* (☏971 800 341), opposite the church, serves superb healthy dishes, with plenty of choice for vegetarians. Some 5km further east from Sant Josep, a side road turns south through fields of melons and grapes to **CALA JONDAL**, a popular pebble beach where you can get delicious juices at *Tropicana*, superb seafood at *Yemanjá* or chill out to choice tunes at the *Particular* bar.

Formentera

Just eleven nautical miles south of Ibiza Town, **FORMENTERA** (population 6120) is the smallest of the four main Balearic islands, measuring just 20km from east to west (it's actually two small islets joined together by a narrow, sandy isthmus). Formentera's history more or less parallels that of Ibiza, though for nearly three hundred years – from the early fifteenth century to the end of the seventeenth – it was left uninhabited for lack of water and fear of Turkish pirate raids. The island is still very arid, and mainly covered in rosemary, which grows wild everywhere; it also crawls with thousands of brilliant-green **Ibiza wall lizards** (*Podarcis pityusensis*), which flourish in parched scrubland. Modern income is derived from tourism (especially German, Italian and British), taking advantage of some of Spain's longest, whitest and least-crowded beaches. The shortage of fresh water keeps development within acceptable limits – there are only around forty *hostales* and hotels on the whole island – and for the most part visitors come here seeking escape rather than sophistication. Nevertheless, Formentera has become increasingly popular with day-trippers from neighbouring Ibiza, and is certainly not the "unspoilt paradise" it once was, especially in high season. Nude sunbathing is the norm just about everywhere.

Arrival, information and accommodation

Plenty of **ferries**, operated by rival companies, make the crossing from Ibiza; return fares are about €15, or €24 by hydrofoil. There is a basic **bus** service from the port of arrival, **La Savina**, but buses connect only the settlements along the main island road, plus a few of the larger resorts, leaving you long, hot walks to any of the more isolated beaches. Getting about by **bicycle** is a

very popular option, since apart from the hill of La Mola, the island is extremely flat. There's a line of bike rental places at La Savina by the ferry dock, and in Es Pujols. A day's hire will set you back €6–10, depending on the bike. **Renting a car** costs from €30 per day (see box on p.985), or scooters start at €12. **Taxis** are also fairly cheap; you'll find ranks at La Savina, Sant Francesc and Es Pujols (see box on p.985). Fares are about €7.40 for 5km, but as the distances involved are small, the cost is never extortionate. In August, it's best to book a taxi the day before you need it.

The island's only **turisme** (Mon–Fri 10am–2pm & 5–7pm, Sat 10am–2pm; ☎971 322 057) is at the ferry port in La Savina; staff can provide decent maps and information on all aspects of the island. There's also a private **accommodation agency** (☎971 323 224, ⓦwww.formenterareservations.com) next door to the turisme if you're looking for an apartment or a villa to rent.

Accommodation

Most visitors treat Formentera as a **day-trip** from Ibiza, and if you want to be one of the few who **stay** you'd be well advised to make an advance reservation, particularly in August – the bulk of the island's limited supply of beds is snapped up early. Bear in mind also that most hotels close down between November and April. There's no campsite in Formentera, and although people do doss down behind the beaches, it's not encouraged and has, in the past, damaged the delicate ecology of the dunes.

Pensión Bon Sol Sant Ferran ☎971 328 882. Eight simple but clean and fairly spacious rooms, with shared bathrooms. Just about the cheapest accommodation in Formentera. ❷

Hostal Residencia Illes Pitiüses Sant Ferran ☎971 328 189, ⓦwww.ibizaformentera hotels.com/illespitiuses. Twenty-six very comfortable, tasteful rooms, all equipped with satellite TV and a/c. It's on the main road, and there's a café-restaurant downstairs. Open all year. ❸

Hostal Residencia Mar Blau Caló de Sant Agustí ☎ & ⓕ971 327 030. Small and attractive hotel next to a tiny fishing harbour, a short stroll from Ses Platgetes beach. The bright, modern rooms all have panoramic sea views, and there are also good apartments next door run by the same owners. Open April–Oct. ❹

Hostal Residencia Mayans Es Pujols ☎ & ⓕ971 328 724. Pleasant, good-value *hostal*, 100m from the beach, in a quiet spot away from the main resort area. The 23 modern, attractive rooms come either with sea or island views, and all have private bathrooms. There's a swimming pool, and the terrace café serves an excellent buffet breakfast. Open April–Oct. ❹

Hostal La Savina La Savina ☎971 322 279, ⓔhostallasavina@terra.es. Large, well-run *hostal*, located on the edge of town on the main road to Sant Francesc. The cheerful, comfortable rooms all have a/c and pleasant bathrooms, and there's a beach below. Open mid-April to Oct. ❺

Around the island

Sailing out of Ibiza Town harbour, there's a stupendous view of the citadel astride its cliff, and soon the sand-fringed islets which herald Formentera hove into view – one of the tiniest being the Illa d'es Penjats ("Hanged Men's Island"), once the last stop for Ibiza's criminals. Ferries and hydrofoils then proceed to Formentera's one and only ferry dock at **LA SAVINA**. There's nothing much to the place, apart from a taxi rank and rows of rental cars, bicycles and mopeds, all racked up for a quick getaway, and a few places to stay. The island capital, **SANT FRANCESC XAVIER**, is 4km inland from the port and is easily reached by bike, bus or taxi. The town is something of a crossroads and serves as the island's commercial and shopping centre, with restaurants, cafés, bars, banks, supermarkets, a health-food shop, a pharmacist and open-air markets – but it's an insignificant place all the same, its only real sight being the mighty fortified **church**, now stripped of its defensive cannons, sitting in a large square at the top of the town.

Heading east from the capital, it's just 3km along the main island road to tiny **SANT FERRAN**, the island's second town and home to *Pepe*, c/Major, a long-established and laid-back bohemian bar-cum-restaurant, which is something of an island institution. You can also stay here, though most rooms are block booked by tour operators in high season.

Formentera: useful numbers

Car rental Autos Ca Marí ☎971 322 921; Isla Blanca ☎971 322 559; Hertz ☎971 322 242.

Emergencies For the police, fire brigade or an ambulance call ☎112.

Ferries Umafisa ☎971 323 007; Transmapi ☎971 322 703; Trasmediterrànea ☎971 315 050.

Post office Plaça de sa Constitució 1, Sant Francesc.

Taxis Taxis La Savina ☎971 328 016; Taxis Sant Francesc ☎971 322 243; Taxis Es Pujols ☎971 322 016.

From Sant Ferran, a side road leads to the north coast at **ES PUJOLS**, Formentera's largest resort development – though it's still tiny, and tame by mainland (and Mallorcan) standards. Originally a fishing village, the resort centres on two fine sandy beaches which nestle between a small craggy outcrop. The islet-studded bay is very pretty, the sand is bright white and the sea is clear and shallow. If you do hang around, there's windsurfing and other water sports, plenty of good seafood restaurants and some late-night bars.

Northwest of Es Pujols, the **Es Trucadors peninsula** pokes a flat and sandy finger out towards Ibiza. There are more long and slender beaches here – notably the spectacular sands of **Platja de Ses Illetes** on the west shore – and at the peninsula's end, across a narrow channel, lies the uninhabited island of **Espalmador**, where there's another great beach, and water turquoise enough to trump any Caribbean brochure. It's possible to wade across most of the year, or you can get to Espalmador using one of the regular boats (May–Oct only, €10 return) from La Savina.

Back in Sant Ferran, the main island road travels east, passing the rough, dirt turnings which twist south through arable farmland and acres of sand dunes to the middle portion of the **Platja de Migjorn**, whose white sands and crystalline waters extend for some 5km. There's some development at either end of the beach – in the west at **Es Ca Mari** and to the east around the equally unenticing **Mar i Land** – but the centre remains largely untouched and it's here in the dunes you'll find the superb *Blue Bar*, one of the finest beach cafés in the Balearics, with languid, chill-out tunes and tasty snacks.

Beyond the Mar i Land turning, the main road leaves the flatlands to snake up through pine forests as it skirts the northern flanks of **La Mola**, at 192m the island's highest point. En route you'll pass the first-rate *El Mirador* restaurant (☎971 327 037), with exceptional views of Formentera, before reaching the drowsy little town of **El Pilar**. Beyond here, the road straightens for the final two-kilometre dash to the **Far de La Mola** (lighthouse), which stands on the cliffs high above the blue ocean. It was here that Jules Verne was inspired to write his *Journey Round the Solar System* as he gazed into the clear night sky – hence the large stone block with the bronze plaque. Before you head back, you can soak up the scene at the tiny bar-café, *Es Puig*, next to the lighthouse, where they serve up tremendous plates of cheese and ham.

Eating and drinking

Es Pujols, the principal resort, has a plethora of seafront **bars and restaurants**, with menus to suit most wallets, and excellent seafood on offer. Good options include the busy little *Bar Pupit*; *Can Vent*, which serves great seafood; and *Rigatoni*, which does Italian food in stylish surrounds – all are on, or just off, the seafront. For breakfast, try the café at *Hostal Residencia Mayans*. Es Pujols is also where you'll find the island's **nightlife**, with a strip of late bars, including the trendy *Moon Bar*, and a small club, *Flower Power*.

Elsewhere on the island, you'll find the best pizza at the Italian-owned *Es Pla* (☎971 322 903), by the turning for Cala Saona, while *Restaurant Rafalet* (☎971 327 077), in Caló de Sant Agustí, boasts a lovely seafront setting for delicious fish and seafood. Sant Ferran has several good bars around its plaza, including the atmospheric *Fonda Plate*, where you can enjoy a languid drink. Most of Formentera's *hostales* serve meals, or you can get your own supplies from the SYP supermarket in Sant Francesc.

Mallorca

Few Mediterranean holiday spots are as often and as unfairly maligned as **MALLORCA**. The island is commonly perceived as little more than sun, sex, booze and high-rise hotels – so much so that there's a long-standing Spanish joke about a mythical fifth Balearic island called *Majorca* (the English spelling), inhabited by an estimated eight million tourists a year. However, this image, spawned by the helter-skelter development of the 1960s, takes no account of Mallorca's beguiling diversity. It's true that there are sections of coast where high-rise hotels and shopping centres are continuous, wedged beside and upon one another and broken only by a dual carriageway to more of the same. But the spread of development, even after fifty years, is surprisingly limited, essentially confined to the Badia de Palma (Bay of Palma), a thirty-kilometre strip flanking the island capital, and a handful of mega-resorts notching the east coast.

Elsewhere, things are very different. **Palma** itself, the Balearics' one real city, is a bustling, historic place whose grand mansions and magnificent Gothic cathedral defy the expectations of many visitors. And so does the northwest coast, where the rearing peaks of the rugged **Serra de Tramuntana** harbour

beautiful cove beaches, a pair of intriguing monasteries at Valldemossa and Lluc, and a string of delightful old towns – Deià, Sóller and Pollença – as well as the picturesque villages of Biniaraix and Fornalutx. There's a startling variety and physical beauty to the land, too, which, along with the mildness of the climate, has drawn tourists to visit and well-heeled expatriates to settle here since the nineteenth century, including artists and writers of many descriptions, from Robert Graves to Roger McGough.

Mallorca practicalities

Palma lies at the hub of an extensive **public transport** system, with bus services linking the capital to all Mallorca's principal settlements and even a couple of train lines – one, a beautiful ride up through the mountains to Sóller (see p.999), is an attraction in itself. And with your own transport, Palma is within three hours' drive of anywhere on the island. The main constraint for travellers is **accommodation**. From mid-June to mid-September rooms are in short supply and, if you do go at this time, you're well advised to make a reservation several months in advance or to book a package. Out of season, things ease up and you can idle round, staying pretty much where you want. Bear in mind also that five of Mallorca's **monasteries** rent out renovated cells at exceptionally inexpensive rates – reckon on €18–30 per double room per night. The Monastir de Nostra Senyora at Lluc (see p.1004) and the Ermita de Nostra Senyora del Puig outside Pollença (see p.1005) are both reachable via public transport, while those with their own transport could also try the Ermita de Sant Salvador at Felanitx (☎971 827 282), the very basic Ermita de Nostra Sra. de Bonany at Petra (☎971 561 101), and the rather more comfortable Ermita de Nostra Sra. de Cura in Algaida Randa (☎971 120 260).

Palma

In 1983, **PALMA** became the capital of the newly established Balearic Islands autonomous region, since when it's shed the dusty provincialism of yesteryear, developing into a go-ahead and cosmopolitan commercial hub of over 300,000 people. The new self-confidence is plain to see in the city centre, a vibrant and urbane place which is akin to the big cities of the Spanish mainland – and a world away from the heaving tourist enclaves of the surrounding bay. There's still a long way to go – much of suburban Palma remains obdurately dull and somewhat dilapidated – but the centre now presents a splendid ensemble of lively shopping areas, mazy lanes and refurbished old buildings, all enclosed by what remains of the old city walls and their replacement boulevards.

This geography encourages downtown Palma to look into itself and away from the sea, even though its **harbour** – now quarantined by the main highway – has always been the city's economic lifeline. Indeed, arriving here by sea, Palma is still beautiful and impressive, with the grand bulk of the cathedral towering above the old town and the remnants of the medieval walls. In these are encapsulated much of the city's and island's history: Moorish control from the ninth to the thirteenth century, reconquest by Jaume I of Aragón and a meteoric rise to wealth and prominence in the fifteenth century as the main port of call between Europe and Africa.

Arrival and information

Mallorca's gleaming international **airport** is 11km east of Palma, immediately behind the resort of Ca'n Pastilla. It has one enormous terminal, which handles both scheduled and charter flights, with separate floors for arrivals (below) and departures (above). On the arrivals floor, a flotilla of **car rental** outlets jostle for position by the luggage carousels. Beyond here, the main arrivals hall has 24-hour **ATMs** and **currency exchange** facilities, as well as a **provincial tourist office** (Mon–Sat 9am–10pm, Sun 9am–2pm), where you can pick up public transport timetables, taxi rates, maps and accommodation lists. If the tourist office is closed, try the helpful staff at the **airport information office**, centrally located on the arrivals (lower) level and open 24 hours. If you need help finding **accommodation**, try the helpful Prima Travel (ⓦ www.prima-travel.com) in the main arrivals hall, which has English-speaking staff and a good selection of hotels, apartments and villas.

The airport is linked to the city and the Bay of Palma resorts by a busy highway (*autopista*) which shadows the shoreline from S'Arenal in the east to Magaluf in the west. The least expensive way to reach Palma from the airport is by **bus** #1 (5.40am–2.30am; €1.80), which leaves every fifteen minutes from the main entrance of the terminal building, just behind the taxi rank, and goes to Plaça Espanya, on the north side of the city centre. A **taxi** from the airport to the city centre will set you back about €15; taxi rates are controlled and a list of island-wide fares is available from – or displayed in the window of – the provincial tourist office in the arrivals hall.

The Palma **ferry terminal** is about 4km west of the city centre. Trasmediterranea ferries arrive at Terminal 2, Balearia ferries at Terminal 3, about 150m away. **Bus** #1 (5.40am–2.30am; €1.80) leaves every fifteen minutes from outside Terminal 2 to the Plaça Espanya. There are also **taxi** ranks outside both terminal buildings; the fare to the city centre is about €10.

The **provincial turisme** (Mon–Fri 9am–8pm, Sat 9am–2.30pm; ☎971 712 216) is just off the Passeig d'es Born at Plaça de la Reina 2, while the main **municipal office** (Mon–Fri 9am–8pm, Sat 9am–1.30pm; ☎971 724 090) is at c/Sant Domingo 11, in the subway at the end of c/Conquistador. Both provide island-wide information, dispensing free maps, accommodation lists, bus and ferry schedules, lists of car rental firms, boat trip details and all sorts of special-interest leaflets. A second municipal tourist office (Mon–Fri 9am–8pm, Sat 9am–1pm; ☎971 754 329), located a few metres from the Inca train station on the northeast edge of Plaça Espanya, offers a similar service.

Accommodation

There are around twenty *hostales* and thirty-plus hotels dotted around Palma, and if you haven't got a reservation, your first move in the summer should be to pick up the official list from the tourist office. The bulk of Palma's **accommodation** is dotted around the city centre – fortunately enough, this is by far the most engaging part of the city; the immediate suburbs are quite unprepossessing. Note that in high season some places insist on a minimum stay of two or three nights.

Budget

Hostal Apuntadors c/Apuntadors 8 ☎971 713 491, ⓔ apuntadors@jet.es. Appealingly laid-back *hostal* in an old house off the Passeig d'es Born. Rooms are simple but adequate, and there's a café downstairs. ❷

Hostal Brondo c/Ca'n Brondo 1 ☎& ⓕ 971 719 043. Stylish little place, in a central but quiet location, with Mallorcan antiques and newly done-up rooms. ❸

Hostal Residencia Bonany c/Almirall Cervera 5 ☎971 737 924. A newly done-up one-star *hostal*

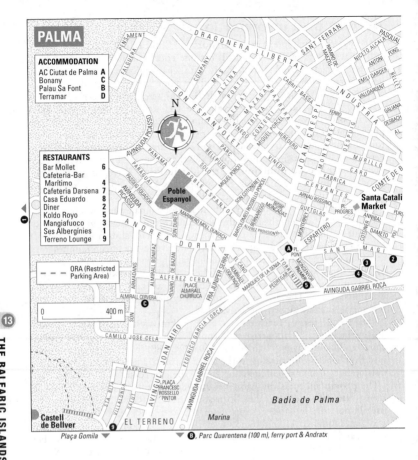

PALMA

ACCOMMODATION

AC Ciutat de Palma	A
Bonany	C
Palau Sa Font	B
Terramar	D

RESTAURANTS

Bar Mollet	6
Cafeteria-Bar Marítimo	4
Cafeteria Darsena	7
Casa Eduardo	8
Diner	2
Koldo Royo	5
Mangiafuoco	3
Ses Alberginies	1
Terreno Lounge	9

– – – ORA (Restricted Parking Area)

0   400 m

Poble Espanyol

Santa Catali Market

Castell de Bellver

Badia de Palma

Marina

EL TERRENO

Plaça Gomila ▼   ▼ **B**, *Parc Quarentena (100 m), ferry port & Andratx*

on a quiet residential street about 2km west of the city centre, close to Castell de Bellver. There's a small pool out back and all rooms are en suite. Take bus #6 from Plaça de la Reina and get off at c/Marquès de la Sènia, just before the start of Avgda Joan Miró. April–Oct. ❷

Hostal Residencia Cuba c/Sant Magí 1 ☎971 738 159, ☎971 403 131. Pleasant, functional rooms in an attractively refurbished stone house, complete with its own tower and balustrade and overlooking the bottom of busy Avgda Argentina. ❷

Hostal Residencia Pons c/Vi 8 ☎971 722 658. Simple rooms in a lovely old house with a court-yard and house plants. In the old part of town, near the Passeig d'es Born. ❷

Hostal Ritzi c/Apuntadors 6 ☎971 714 610. Basic, one-star rooms in an ancient, five-storey house off the Passeig d'es Born; can get noisy at night. ❸

Hostal Residencia Terminus c/Eusebi Estada 2 ☎971 750 014, ✉terminus@mail.cinet.es. Decent hotel next to the train station, with a quirkily old-fashioned foyer and fairly large bedrooms. ❷

Hostal Terramar Plaza Mediterraneo 8, El Terreno ☎971 739 931, ⊕www.palma-hostales.com. Newly refurbished comfortable, modern rooms convenient to all the nightlife on this side of town, as well as to the Castell de Bellver, which some rooms look out onto. Guests have free use of the kitchen. ❷

Moderate and expensive

AC Ciutat de Palma Plaza Puente 3 ☎971 222 300, ⊕www.ac-hotels.com. One kilometre west of the city centre, this gleaming new hotel is modern, comfortable and friendly, with lots of welcoming touches including a free coffee and snack lounge for guests. ❻

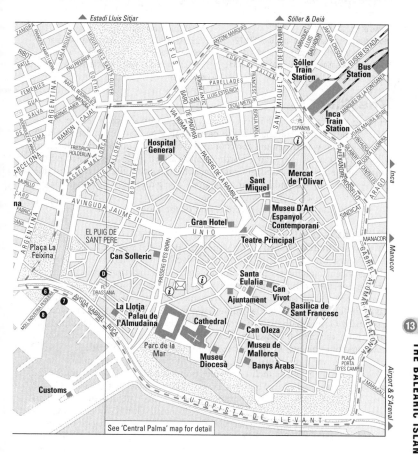

See 'Central Palma' map for detail

Hotel Almudaina Avgda Jaume III 9 ☎971 727 340, ✉almudaina@bitel.es. Smart, modern rooms above a noisy street right in the centre. ❺

Hostal Born c/Sant Jaume 3 ☎971 712 942, ✉hborn@bitel.es. Comfortable and justifiably popular *hostal* in an excellent downtown location. Set in an old, refurbished mansion with its own courtyard café. ❹

Hotel Convent de la Missió c/de la Missió 7A, ☎971 227 347, ⓦwww.conventdelamissio.com. Stunning new hotel with cool and serene decor and strategically placed artworks. There's also an excellent in-house restaurant. ❼

Hotel Dalt Murada c/Almudaina 6 ☎971 425 300, ⓦwww.daltmurada.com. Set in a magnificent sixteenth-century mansion with period architecture but all modern comforts and conveniences. ❼

Hotel Residencia Palacio Ca Sa Galesa c/Miramar 8 ☎971 715 400, ⓦwww.palacio

casagalesa.com. Charmingly renovated seventeenth-century mansion set amongst the narrow alleys of the old town, with just a dozen luxurious – and very expensive – rooms and suites. There's a small indoor pool, and a wonderful rooftop terrace with fine views of the city. ❾

Hotel Palau Sa Font c/Apuntadores 38 ☎971 712 277, ⓦwww.palausafont.com. Cool new designer hotel, serenely decorated in earthy Italian colours. There's a small pool on the roof terrace and wonderful views from many of the rooms. ❼

Hotel Residencia Palladium Passeig Mallorca 40 ☎971 713 945, ⓕ971 714 665. Clean, trim and tidy rooms in a modern high-rise. ❺

Hotel Portixol Calle Sirena 27 ☎971 271 800, ⓦwww.portixol.com. On the Badía de Palma, 2km east of the city centre, this top-notch hotel and its first-rate Mediterranean restaurant are located on their own tiny bay, with a large pool and stirring

views of the cathedral. **8**
Hotel Saratoga Passeig Mallorca 6 ☎971 727 240, ⓦwww.hotelsaratoga.es. Excellent modern hotel with swimming pool. Most rooms have balconies overlooking the boulevard. **7**

Hotel Sol Jaime III Passeig Mallorca 14 ☎971 725 943, ⓕ971 725 946. Agreeable three-star hotel with spacious, modern twin-bed rooms, most with balconies. Discounts possible outside high season. **4**

The City

Finding your way around Palma is fairly straightforward once you're in the centre. The obvious landmark is the **cathedral** – *Sa Seu* in Catalan – which dominates the waterfront and backs onto the oldest part of the city, a cluster of alleys and narrow lanes whose northern and eastern limits are marked by the zigzag of avenues built beside – or in place of – the city walls. On the west side of the cathedral, Avinguda d'Antoni Maura/Passeig d'es Born cuts up from the seafront to intersect with Avinguda Jaume III/Unio at Plaça Rei Joan Carles. These busy thoroughfares form the centre of the modern town.

The cathedral

Palma's **cathedral** (April–Oct Mon–Fri 10am–6.15pm, Sat 10am–2pm; Nov–March Mon–Sat 10am–3pm; €3.50), five hundred years in the making, is a magnificent building – the equal of almost any on the mainland – and a surprising one, too, with *modernista* interior features designed by Antoni Gaudí. The original foundation came with the Christian Reconquest of the city, and the site taken, in fulfilment of a vow by Jaume I, was that of the Moorish Great Mosque. Essentially Gothic, with massive exterior buttresses to take the weight off the pillars within, the church derives its effect through its sheer height, impressive from any angle but startling when glimpsed from the waterside esplanade.

In the central nave, fourteen beautifully aligned, pencil-thin pillars rise to 21m before their ribs branch out – like fronded palm trees – to support the single-span, vaulted roof. The nave, at 44m high, is one of the tallest Gothic structures in Europe and its length – 121m – is of matching grandeur. This open, hangar-like construction, typical of Catalan Gothic architecture, was designed to make the high altar visible to the entire congregation, and to express the mystery of the Christian faith, with kaleidoscopic floods of light filtering in through the **stained-glass windows**. For once the light isn't trapped by the central *coro* (choir) that normally blocks the centre of Spanish cathedrals. The innovative sidelining of the *coro*, and the fantastic forms of the lighting system above the altar, were Gaudí's work, undertaken between 1904 and 1914. At the time, these measures were deeply controversial; no *coro* had ever before been removed in Spain. The artistic success of the project, however, was undeniable, and it was immediately popular. Compared with Gaudí's designs in Barcelona (see p.757), everything here is simple and restrained but there are touches of his characteristic flamboyance, notably in the wrought-iron baldachin above the altar that symbolizes the Crown of Thorns.

On the way into the church, you pass through the three rooms of assorted ecclesiastical bric-a-brac that comprise the **Museu de la Catedral**. The first room's most valuable exhibit, in the glass case in the middle, is a gilded silver monstrance of extraordinary delicacy, its fairy-tale decoration dating from the late sixteenth century. On display around the walls are assorted chalices and reliquaries and a real curiosity, the portable altar of Jaume I, a wood and silver chessboard with each square containing a bag of relics. The second room is mainly devoted to the Gothic works of the **Mallorcan Primitives**, a school of painters who flourished on the island in the fourteenth and fifteenth centuries, producing strikingly naive devotional works of bold colours and cartoon-like detail.

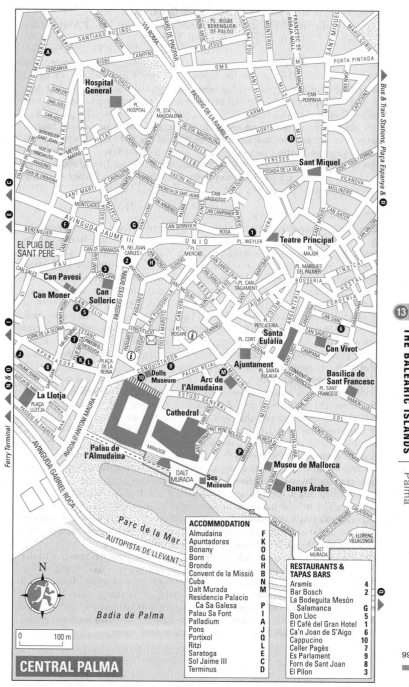

ACCOMMODATION

Almudaina	F
Apuntadores	K
Bonany	O
Born	G
Brondo	H
Convent de la Missió	B
Cuba	N
Dalt Murada	M
Residencia Palacio	
Ca Sa Galesa	P
Palau Sa Font	I
Palladium	A
Pons	J
Portixol	Q
Ritzi	L
Saratoga	E
Sol Jaime III	C
Terminus	D

RESTAURANTS & TAPAS BARS

Aramís	4
Bar Bosch	2
La Bodeguita Mesón	
Salamanca	G
Bon Lloc	5
El Café del Gran Hotel	1
Ca'n Joan de S'Aigo	6
Cappucino	10
Celler Pagès	7
Es Parlament	9
Forn de Sant Joan	8
El Pilon	3

CENTRAL PALMA

0 ——— 100 m

The Palau de l'Almudaina and Sa Llotja

Opposite the cathedral entrance stands the **Palau de l'Almudaina** (April–Sept Mon–Fri 10am–6.30pm, Sat 10am–2pm; Oct–March Mon–Fri 10am–2pm & 4–6pm, Sat 10am–2pm; €3; free on Wed to EU citizens with passport), originally the palace of the Moorish *walis* (governors) and later of the Mallorcan kings. The interior has been painstakingly restored, but its rabbit warren of rooms and corridors has been left comparatively bare, the only decorative highlight being a handful of admirable Flemish tapestries, each devoted to classical themes.

A steep flight of steps leads down from the Palau de l'Almudaina through some pleasant gardens and a restored section of the old city walls to the fifteenth-century **Llotja** (Tues–Sat 11am–2pm & 5–9pm, Sun 11am–2pm; free), the city's former stock exchange. This carefully composed building, with its octagonal turrets and tall windows, now hosts frequent and often excellent exhibitions.

The rest of the city

Even more engaging is the medina-like maze of streets at the back of the cathedral, and here, at c/Can Serra 7, you'll come upon the **Banys Àrabs** (daily: April–Nov 9.30am–8pm; Dec–March 9.30am–7pm; €1.50). One of the few genuine reminders of the Moorish presence, this small brick *hammam* (bath-house) contains an elegant, horseshoe-arched and domed chamber, though if you've been to the ones in Girona or Granada, the impact can be anticlimactic; the garden outside, with picnic tables, is perhaps nicer. Nearby, at c/Portella 5, the **Museu de Mallorca** (Tues–Sat 10am–7pm, Sun 10am–2pm; €2.40), occupying one of the many fifteenth- and sixteenth-century patrician mansions that dot this part of town, has extensive local archeology exhibits and some exceptionally fine medieval religious paintings, including further examples of the work of the Mallorcan Primitives.

A five-minute walk away along Pont i Vich and Pare Nadal, and occupying, oddly enough, the site of the old Moorish soap factory, the **Basílica de Sant Francesc** (Mon–Sat 9.30am–12.30pm & 3.30–6pm, Sun 9.30am–12.30pm; €0.60) is the finest among the city's host of worthy medieval churches. A substantial building founded towards the end of the thirteenth century, the church's main facade displays a stunning severity of style, with a great sheet of dressed sandstone stretching up to an arcaded balcony and pierced by a gigantic rose window. Entered via a very fine trapezoidal Gothic cloister and a grassy quadrant, the cavernous interior is a little disappointing, but you can't miss the monumental **high altar**, a gaudy, gold leaf affair illustrative of the High Baroque. The strange statue outside the church – of a Franciscan monk and a loin-clothed native American – celebrates the missionary work of **Junípero Serra**, a Mallorcan priest dispatched to California in 1768, who subsequently founded San Diego, Los Angeles and San Francisco.

From the basilica, it's a couple of minutes' walk west to **Santa Eulàlia** (Mon–Fri 7am–12.30pm & 5.45–8.30pm, Sat 7am–1pm & 4.30–8.45pm, Sun 8am–1pm & 6.30–8.30pm; free), the first church to be built after Jaume's arrival, a typically Gothic construction with a yawning nave originally designed – as in the cathedral – to give the entire congregation a view of the high altar. Close by, the **ajuntament** (town hall) is a debonair example of the late-Renaissance style, with a grand and self-assured foyer.

Eating

Eating in Palma is less pricey – or can be – than anywhere else in the Balearics. Inexpensive **cafés** and **tapas bars** are liberally distributed around the city centre, with a particular concentration in the side streets off the Passeig d'es Born and Avinguda Antoni Maura. In central Palma, especially along the harbour front and around Plaça Llotja, many **restaurants** are unashamedly geared to the tourist trade, with menus in a babble of Euro-tongues. Most serve perfectly reasonable food, mainly grilled meats and fish, but away from these enclaves you'll find that prices are a little lower and menus more exclusively Catalan and Spanish. At all but the most expensive of places, €18 will cover the cost of a starter, main course, and half a bottle of wine.

Cafés and tapas bars

Bar Bosch Plaça Rei Joan Carles I. One of the most popular and inexpensive tapas bars in town, the traditional haunt of intellectuals and usually humming with conversation. At peak times you'll need to be assertive to get served.

Bar Mollet c/Contramuelle Mollet 2 ☎971 719 871. Located just across from the fish market, and with the freshest fish in town. The fine *menú del día* (Mon–Fri; €8.75) includes wine, water and dessert. Lunchtimes only; closed Sun.

La Bodeguita Mesón Salamanca c/Sant Jaume 3. Delicious tapas and wine bar on the ground floor of a tastefully refurbished, warren-like mansion off Avgda Jaume III – but avoid the overpriced, stuffy restaurant upstairs.

Bon Lloc c/Sant Feliu 7. One of the few vegetarian café-restaurants on the island, centrally situated off the Passeig d'es Born, with an informal atmosphere and good food at low prices. Open Mon–Sat 1–4pm and the odd evening, usually Fri, till 9pm.

El Café del Gran Hotel Plaza Weyler 3. A good place for a tasty lunch, with tables inside and out on a pleasant square. The *menú del día* is excellent value at €13.90.

Cafeteria Darsena Darsena de Sant Matgi, 1896 (Paseo Marítimo) ☎971 180 504. Fresh fish, seafood tapas and full meals, including salads, right on the marina, just opposite the Royal Nautical Club.

Cafeteria-Bar Marítimo c/Jardines de Santo Domingo de la Calzada s/n (Paseo Marítimo) ☎971 738 192. Tranquil and appealing garden setting, right under the walls and overlooked by old windmills – an ideal spot to take a break halfway between the city centre and the port. Good *menú del día* for €8.90.

Ca'n Joan de S'Aigo c/Can Sanç 10. In a tiny alley near Plaça Santa Eulàlia, this long-established coffee house has wonderful, freshly baked *ensaimadas* (cinnamon-flavoured spiral pastry buns) for just €0.70 and fruit-flavoured mousses to die for. Charmingly formal, period-piece decor. Closed Tues.

Cappuccino c/Conqustador, Palau March. Fabulous new terrace café set in a beautiful palace with gardens and views across the historic centre. Serves inventive salads and sandwiches, as well as various coffee combinations.

Diner c/Sant Magi 23, Santa Catalina ☎971 736 222. A little slice of Americana, serving hamburgers, milkshakes, hash browns, pancakes, BLTs and Dixie fried chicken – all homemade and using only the best ingredients. Open seven days a week, 24 hours a day. Phone for take-away.

Restaurants

Aramis c/Montenegro 1 ☎971 725 232. Set in an old stone mansion on a side street off Passeig d'es Born, though the decor inside is smart and very nouveau. The menu is imaginative and international, and there's an unbeatable *menú del día* (€12.50). Reservations always recommended. Closed Sun and Mon.

Casa Eduardo Moll Industria Pesquera 4 ☎971 721 182. Spick-and-span restaurant located upstairs in one of the plain modern buildings beside the fish dock. There's an enjoyable view of the harbour, but the real treat is the fresh fish – a wonderful range, all simply prepared – grilled is best. It's about five minutes' walk west along the harbourfront from Avgda d'Antoni Maura; the fish dock is just before Avgda Argentina. Closed Sun and Mon.

Celler Pagès Off c/Apuntadors at c/Felip Bauza 2 ☎971 726 036. Tiny, inexpensive restaurant with an easy-going family atmosphere serving traditional Mallorcan food. Reserve at weekends. Closed Sun.

Es Parlament c/Conquistador 11 ☎971 726 026. All gilt-wood mirrors and chandeliers, this old and polished restaurant specializes in paella. The tasty and reasonably priced *menú del día* is recommended too. A favourite hang-out of local politicians and lawyers.

Forn de Sant Joan c/Sant Joan 4 ☎971 728 422. Set in an old bakery, this smart and extremely popular family-run Catalan restaurant does a range of fine fish dishes (€15–20) and *tapas* (from €6). **Koldo Royo** Paseo Marítimo (Avgda Gabriel Roca) 3 ☏971 732 435. Pricey, but well worth it to experience the creations of the Michelin-starred Basque chef. Closed Sun. Reservations a must. **Mangiafuoco** Plaza Vapor 4, Santa Catalina ☏971 451 072. Tuscan-owned restaurant-cum-wine bar offering top-notch Italian food and specializing in dishes featuring truffles, which are flown in weekly from Tuscany. Best to reserve. **El Pilon** c/Can Cifre 4, off the north end of Passeig d'es Born. Vibrant, cramped and crowded tapas bar serving all manner of Spanish and Mallorcan dishes at very reasonable prices.

Ses Albergínies c/Rector Vives 2, where it crosses Na Burguesa in Gènova ☏971 404 779. Top-notch gourmet cuisine, featuring original takes on traditional Mallorcan and Mediterranean dishes. Well worth a special trip for lunch or dinner, perhaps combined with a visit to the Fundació Miró (see p.998). Bus #4 provides frequent access to Gènova from Palma. Phone for reservations. **Terreno Lounge** c/Bellver 8 ☏971 454 787. Lush and luxurious place with patio, pool, cool hangings and tropical plants – a romantic place for a candlelit dinner of elegant Mediterranean food. Count on around €40 a head; reservations recommended.

Drinking and nightlife

There's a cluster of lively **late-night bars** – mostly with music as the backdrop rather than the main event – amongst the narrow side streets backing onto Plaça Llotja. A second concentration of slightly more upmarket bars embellishes the bayside modernity of Avinguda Gabriel Roca, about 3km west of the city centre. The grimy suburb of El Terreno, also west of the centre, once accommodated Palma's best late-night bars. The district has gone downhill, and now features topless "entertainment" and porn shops, but it's here you'll find the occasional offbeat bar, as well as several gay bars.

The **club scene** in Palma is small but improving, with more and more leading European DJs visiting the city. The city's clubs are never worth investigating until around midnight; entry charges cost anything between €6 and €24, depending on the night and what's happening.

Late-night bars

Abaco Just off c/Apuntadors at c/Sant Joan 1. Set in a charming Renaissance mansion, this is easily Palma's most unusual bar, with an interior straight out of a Busby Berkeley musical: fruits cascading down its stairway, caged birds hidden amid patio foliage, elegant music and a daily flower bill you could live on for a month. Drinks, as you might imagine, are extremely expensive (beers €6, cocktails from €12) but you're never hurried into buying one. The clientele is less than hip but it's a good place to start an evening out.
Barcelona Jazz Café Club c/Apuntadors 9. Groovy little spot on one of the busiest streets in town. Jazz, blues and Latin sounds. Metres from the corner of c/Sant Joan.
BED c/Jaume Ferrer 14. Wine bar and chill-out lounge which is popular with twenty- and thirty-something tourists from about 10pm till 11am before they head off to other nightspots.
La Bóveda c/Boteria 3, off Plaça Llotja. Classy, bustling bar – one of several on this short alley – with long, wide windows and wine stacked high along the back wall. Be prepared to queue to get in, or come early.

Box Office Avgda Gabriel Roca 31. Hip and popular bar near the Jardins La Quarentena, about 3km west of the centre along the waterfront.
Escape Plaza Drassana 13. Friendly little place, and always lively, set just off a square that gets busier and prettier every year.
Gotic Plaça Llotja 4. Cramped bar redeemed by its stylish, often candle-lit patio, and pavement tables which nudge out across the piazza.
Latitud c/Felip Bauza 8, off c/Apuntadors. Tiny, upbeat bar, playing jazz, blues and sometimes classical music.
La Lonja opposite Sa Llotja. Gregarious, vaguely pub-like haunt, with revolving doors, chessboard-tiled floors and darkwood panelling and furnishings. Good mix of locals, backpackers and tourists. Reasonable prices.
Made in Brazil Avgda Gabriel Roca (Paseo Marítimo) 27. Great Brazilian sounds and cocktails (including the inevitable *caipirinhas*) in a pocket-sized club-cum-bar with alarming tropical decor.
Parc de la Mar Across the lagoon in front of the cathedral. This bar stays busy until at least midnight and stages frequent musical performances and movies.

Clubs

In addition to the two places listed below, the **Santa Barbara** area, just south of *Pacha*, is currently known for its chill-out and house music clubs such as *113* and *Garito*, though the names and exact musical styles change from season to season.

Pacha Avgda Gabriel Roca 42 ☎971 455 908. Raucous club and garden bar with guest DJs from Ibiza, the mainland and the UK playing funky house, plus a little trance and R&B. It's some 3.5km west of the centre along the waterfront.
Tito's Plaça Gomila 3 ☎971 730 017. With its stainless steel and glass exterior, this long-estab-

lished nightspot looks a bit like something from a sci-fi film set. Outdoor lifts carry you up from the back entrance on the waterfront Avgda Gabriel Roca to the dance floor, which pulls in huge crowds from many countries with its mainstream house and garage mixes. It's about 2.5km west of the centre.

Listings

Banks There are many banks on and around the Passeig d'es Born and Avgda Jaume III as well as 24-hour ATMs dotted round the city.
Bookshops The biggest department store in town, El Corte Inglés, at Avgda Jaume III 15 (Mon–Sat 10am–10pm), sells a small and rather eccentric assortment of English-language books – from Ken Follett to Anne Frank – and also has a modest selection of Mallorca guidebooks and maps. Libreria Fondevila, near the Teatre Principal at Costa de Sa Pols 18 (Mon–Fri 9.45am–1.30pm & 4.30–8pm, Sat 9.45am–1.30pm; ☎971 725 616), doesn't do much better when it comes to novels and guidebooks, but does have a fairly good selection of general maps of Mallorca, plus a reasonably comprehensive selection of IGN hiking maps. Also see "Maps" below.
Car rental There are heaps of car rental companies at the airport and in the city, where there's a concentration – including many small concerns – along Avgda Gabriel Roca. Big companies include Atesa-National, Avgda Gabriel Roca 25 ☎971 456 762 (airport ☎971 789 896); Avis, Avgda Gabriel Roca 16 ☎971 730 720 (airport ☎971 789 187); Betacar-Europcar, Avgda Gabriel Roca 20 ☎971 455 200 (airport ☎971 789 135); Hertz, Avgda Gabriel Roca 13 ☎971 734 737 (airport ☎971 789 670). You can also try easyCar, Avgda Comte Sallent (☎906 292 827) or local companies such as Serra, c/Vaixell, s/n (☎971 269 411); Ca'n Pastilla; Sixt, Airport (☎971 789 351); Centauro, Airport (☎902 104 103) or Camí Son Fangos, s/n, Ca'n Pastilla (☎971 266 564); Hasso, Camí de Ca'n Pastilla 100 (☎971 789 376); Hiper Rent a Car, Camino de Ca'n Pastilla (☎971 261 799), s/n; and Tui-Ultramar Express, Airport or Riu Center, c/Maravillas, Local D (Arenal) (☎971 789 760). The tourist office will supply a complete list of rental companies.
Consulates Ireland, c/Sant Miquel 68A ☎971 719

244; United Kingdom, Plaça Major 3 ☎971 712 445; USA, Avgda Jaume III 26 ☎971 725 051.
Emergencies General emergency number ☎112.
Ferries Palma's tourist offices have ferry schedules and tariffs. Tickets can be purchased at travel agents or direct from the offices of the two ferry lines down at the ferry port, about 3.5km west of the city centre along Avgda Gabriel Roca. Trasmediterranea (☎902 454 645) ferries to Maó on Menorca, Ibiza, Barcelona and Valencia leave from Terminal 2. Balearia (☎902 160 180) services to Valencia, Ibiza and Dénia depart from Terminal 3, a couple of minutes' walk away. For details of routes see "Travel details" on p.1024.
Hospital Policlínica Miramar, Camino de La Vileta 30 ☎ 971 767 500; Clínica Juaneda, C/Company 20 ☎ 971 222 222; Hospital General, Plaça Hospital 3 ☎971 212 000.
Internet access *La Red* cybercafé, c/Concepció 5, just off Avgda Jaume III (Mon–Fri 11am–1am, Sat & Sun 4pm–midnight; €3–4 per hour) has fifteen PCs plus fax machines, scanners and snacks and drinks. *Cyber Central*, c/Soledad 4, in the heart of the old city (daily 9am–10pm, €2.50 per hour), is also excellent.
Laundry There's a downtown self-service laundry, Lavandería Self Press, at c/Annibal 14, off Avgda Argentina ☎971 730 643.
Maps Palma has one specialist map shop, the Casa del Mapa, c/Sant Domingo 11 ☎971 225 945 (Mon–Fri 9am–2pm), with a fairly comprehensive selection of IGN hiking maps as well as various maps of the island and Palma. See also "Bookshops", above.
Mopeds RTR Rental, Avgda Joan Miró 340 ☎971 702 775.
Post office The central *correu* is at c/Constitució 5 (Mon–Fri 8.30am–8.30pm, Sat 9.30am–2pm).
Taxis Taxi ranks can be found outside major hotels. Alternatively, telephone Taxi Palma (☎971

401 414), Taxi Telefono (☏971 744 050), Fono Taxi (☏971 728 081) or Radio Taxi (☏971 755 440). Trains The tourist office has train timetable details, or you can phone direct on ☏971 752 245 (Palma to Inca and beyond) or ☏971 752 051 (Palma to Sóller).

Around Palma

Anywhere in the west or centre of the island is readily accessible as a **day-trip** from Palma. If you're after a quick **swim** the most convenient option is to stick to the resorts strung along the neighbouring **Badia de Palma** (Bay of Palma). Locals tend to go east on the #15 bus (every 10min; 30min) from Plaça Espanya to the *balneario* (beach bar) sections of **S'Arenal**, where there's an enormously long, if crowded, sandy beach.

Alternatively, you might be tempted by the **Castell de Bellver** (April–Sept Mon–Sat 8am–8pm, Sun 10am–7pm; Oct–March Mon–Sat 8am–7pm, Sun 10am–5pm; €3; free on Sun, when the castle museum is closed), a strikingly well-preserved fortress of canny circular design built for Jaume II at the beginning of the fourteenth century. The castle perches on a wooded hill top some 3km west of the city centre and offers superb views of Palma and its harbour. Also worth a visit is the **Fundació Pilar i Joan Miró**, at c/Joan de Saridakis 29, 4km southwest of the town centre (Tues–Sat 10am–7pm, Sun 10am–3pm; mid-Sept to mid-May closes 6pm; €4), which displays examples of Joan Miró's work drawn from its prodigious collection of more than six thousand pieces by the renowned Catalan Surrealist.

Andratx, Sant Elm and Illa Dragonera

Inland from Palma bay, you could spend an afternoon by hopping on a bus to **ANDRATX**, a small, undeveloped town huddled among the hills to the west. From here, it's another short bus ride through a pretty, orchard-covered landscape to the dishevelled, low-key resort of **SANT ELM**. There are plans to expand the resort, but at present it's a relatively quiet spot where there's a reasonable chance of a **room** in high season, either at the conspicuous *Hotel Aquamarín* (☏971 239 105, ℱ971 239 125; May–Oct; ❸) or, preferably, at the *Hostal Dragonera* (☏971 239 086, ℱ971 239 013; March–Oct; ❸), a simple, modern building with clean and neat rooms, most of which offer sea views. For such a small place, there's also a surprisingly wide choice of **cafés and restaurants**, one of the best being *Vista Mar*, at c/Jaime I 46, which specializes in seafood and has a charming terrace and ocean views – reckon on €36 for a complete meal, including house wine.

Occasional **buses** ply between Sant Elm and Andratx (May–Oct 4–6 daily; Nov–March 1 daily). With more time to spare, **boats** shuttle across from Sant Elm's minuscule harbour to the austere offshore islet of **Illa Dragonera**, an uninhabited chunk of rock some 4km long and 700m wide, with an imposing ridge of sea cliffs dominating its northwestern shore.

Northern Mallorca

Mallorca is at its scenic best in the gnarled ridge of the **Serra de Tramuntana**, the imposing mountain range which stretches the length of the island's western shore, its rearing peaks and plunging sea cliffs intermittently intercepted by valleys of olive and citrus groves and dotted with some of the island's most beguiling towns and villages. There are several possible routes through the

Easily the best way to get to the Serra de Tramuntana is to take the train from Palma to Sóller, a 28-kilometre journey that takes about one hour and twenty minutes on antique rolling stock that seems to have come straight out of an Agatha Christie novel. The rail line, constructed on the profits of the nineteenth-century orange and lemon trade, dips and twists through the mountains and across fertile valleys, offering magnificent views. There are five departures daily from Palma throughout the year (sometimes six from Sóller); a return costs €4.94 (€2.47 one-way), though the two *Turist* trains (10.50am & 12.15pm) – with air-conditioning and a brief photo-stop in the mountains – will set you back €8.47 return (€6 one-way).

region, but perhaps the most straightforward if you're reliant on public transport is to travel up from Palma to **Sóller**, in the middle of the coast, and use this town as a base, making selected forays along the coastal road, the C710; not far away to the **southwest** lie the mountain village of **Deià** and the monastery of **Valldemossa**, while within easy striking distance to the **northeast** are the monastery of **Lluc**, the quaint town of **Pollença** and the relaxing resort of **Port de Pollença**.

The Serra de Tramuntana also provides the best walking on Mallorca, with scores of **hiking trails** latticing the mountains. Generally speaking, paths are well marked, though apt to be clogged with thorn bushes. There are trails to suit all levels of fitness, from the easiest of strolls to the most gruelling of long-distance treks, but in all cases you should come properly equipped – certainly with an appropriate hiking map (available in Sóller and Palma), and, for the more difficult routes, with a compass. Also available locally is a variety of **hiking books**, the best of which are those by Herbert Heinrich (*12 Classic Hikes through Majorca*), while the *Rough Guide to Mallorca* details several of the island's most famous hiking routes, too. Spring and autumn are the best times to embark on the longer trails; in midsummer the heat can be enervating and water is scarce. Bear in mind also that the mountains are prone to mists, though they usually lift at some point in the day. For obvious safety reasons, lone mountain walking is not recommended.

As far as **beaches** are concerned, most of the region's coastal villages have a tiny, shingly strip, and only around the bays of Pollença and Alcúdia are there more substantial offerings. The resorts edging these bays have the greatest number of hotel and *hostal* rooms, but from June to early September, and sometimes beyond, vacancies are extremely thin on the ground. Indeed, **accommodation** – especially if you have a tight itinerary and are travelling in the summertime – requires some forethought, though there's a reasonable chance of getting a room on spec in Sóller, and in the monasteries at Lluc and just outside Pollença. To compensate, distances are small, the roads are good and the **bus** network is perfectly adequate for most destinations. One of the most useful buses is the service along the C710 from Port de Sóller to Port de Pollença and on to Port d'Alcúdia (May–Oct Mon–Fri 2 daily). **Taxis** can work out a reasonable deal too, if you're travelling in a group – the fare for the thirty-kilometre trip from Palma to Sóller is about €30, for instance.

Sóller

Arriving by train at **SÓLLER**, the obvious option is to continue by **tram** (7am–9pm every 30min–1hr; 15min; €1) down to the seashore at **Port de**

Sóller (see below), a rumbling, five-kilometre journey. If you pass straight through, however, you'll miss one of the most laid-back and enjoyable towns on Mallorca. Rather than any specific sight, it's the general flavour that appeals, the town's narrow, sloping lanes cramped by eighteenth- and nineteenth-century stone houses, whose fancy grilles and big wooden doors once hid the region's rich fruit merchants. All streets lead to the main square, **Plaça Constitució**, an informal, pint-sized affair of crowded cafés just down the hill from the train station. The square is dominated by the hulking mass of the church of **Sant Bartomeu**, a crude neo-Gothic remodelling of the medieval original, its only saving grace the enormous rose window cut high in the main facade. Inside, the cavernous nave is suitably dark and gloomy, the penitential home of a string of gaudy Baroque altarpieces.

Although the options are very limited, there's a good chance of finding a vacant **room** in Sóller during the high season. Options include the *Hotel El Guía*, c/Castanyer 2 (☎971 630 227, ℻971 632 634; April–Oct; ❹), a lovely old-fashioned one-star (head down the steps from the train station platform and turn right); *Casa de Huéspedes Margarita Trías Vives*, c/Reial 3 (☎971 634 214; April–Oct; ❶), in an attractive old terraced house also close to the train station; and *Hostal Residencia Nadal*, c/Romaguera 27 (☎ & ℻971 631 180; ❷), a simple, central two-star, in a neatly decorated and well-kept house about five minutes' walk north of Plaça Constitució. The best place to **eat** is at the *Hotel El Guía* (closed Mon, and limited opening hours Nov–March) – it may be a little formal for some, but the prices are reasonable enough, with a delicious *menú del día* for around €18. Alternatively, *Café Soller*, at Plaça Constitució 14, is a great spot for tapas and *raciòns*, starting at €4 and €5 respectively.

Port de Sóller

PORT DE SÓLLER is one of the most popular resorts on the west coast, and its horseshoe-shaped bay must be the most photographed spot on the island after the package resorts around Palma – although the high jinks of the Badia de Palma are about the last thing imaginable down here at this relatively staid, family-oriented town. The best **swimming** is around the bay away from the road, along the pedestrianized area, where the water is clear and the beach clean, broad and long. Also good fun is the fifty-minute stroll out to the **lighthouse**, which guards the cliffs above the entrance to Port de Sóller's inlet. From here, the views out over the wild and rocky coast are spectacular, especially at sunset. Directions couldn't be easier as there's a tarmac road all the way: from the centre of the resort, walk round the southern side of the bay past the beach and keep going along the seashore.

Trams from Sóller clank to a halt beside the waterfront, bang in the centre of town and a couple of minutes' walk from the **turisme** (March–Oct Mon–Fri 9am–12.50pm & 2.40–4.50pm, Sat 10am–12.50pm; also March–June Sun 10am–12.50pm; ☎971 633 042), which is located beside the church on c/Canonge Oliver and can provide a full list of local hotels and *hostales*. Outside peak season there's a chance of a reasonably priced room at the *Hotel Brisas*, Camino del Faro 15 (☎971 631 352, ℻971 632 146; ❷), a modest family-run establishment on the far shore, or at the resort-like *Hotel Es Port*, c/Antonio Montis (☎971 631 650, ⓦwww.hotelesport.com; ❸), which has lovely gardens and pools. The string of one- and two-star hotels and *hostales* behind the Platja den Repic on the south side of the bay is worth considering, too: the pleasant *Los Geranios*, Passeig sa Platja 15 (☎971 631 440, ℻971 631 651; ❺), has more atmosphere than the rest.

Port de Sóller heaves with **cafés** and **restaurants**, but standards are very variable: some serve up mediocre food with the package tourist in mind, others are more authentically *Mallorquín* – or at least Spanish. The majority are dotted along the waterfront, with a cluster of better restaurants on c/Santa Caterina d'Alexandria, a short side street that cuts up from the waterfront close to the naval base. One appealingly simple option is *S'Ancora*, c/Santa Catalina 2, an unassuming neighbourhood spot where the food is inexpensive and the emphasis is on traditional Mallorcan dishes; or try *Restaurant Embat*, c/Església 8 (☎971 634 971), which has first-rate cooking done with a French flair. Consider also the pricey *Es Faro* (☎971 633 752), which perches high up on the cliffs at the entrance to the harbour, offering spectacular views and great food – reservations are recommended.

Deià

It's a dramatic ten-kilometre journey southwest from Sóller along the C710 to the beautiful village of **DEIÀ**. The mighty Puig des Teix meets the coast here and although its lower slopes are now gentrified by the villas of the well-to-do, the mountain retains a formidable, almost mysterious presence. Doubling as the coastal highway, Deià's main street skirts the base of the Teix, showing off most of the village's hotels and restaurants. At times, this main street is too congested to be much fun, but the tiny heart of the village, tumbling over a high and narrow ridge on the seaward side of the road, still preserves a surprising tranquillity. Labyrinthine alleys of old peasant houses curl up to a pretty country **church**, in the precincts of which stands the grave of **Robert Graves**, the village's most famous resident – marked simply "Robert Graves: Poeta, E.P.D." (*En Paz Descanse*: "Rest In Peace"). From the graveyard, the views out over the coast are truly memorable.

Graves put Deià on the international map, and nowadays the village is the haunt of long-term expatriates. These inhabitants congregate at the **Cala de Deià**, the nearest thing the village has to a beach – some 200m of shingle at the back of a handsome rocky cove of jagged cliffs, boulders and white-crested surf. It's a great place for a swim, the water is clean, deep and cool, and there's a ramshackle beach bar, but in summer the cove often gets crowded, especially when the day-trippers arrive by boat from Port de Sóller. It takes about twenty minutes to walk from the village to the *cala*, a delightful stroll down a wooded ravine; from the bus stop, walk in the Palma direction to a sharp right bend in the main road, then turn right down the shallow steps and continue downhill, taking a right fork after a few minutes. When the lane ends a signposted footpath continues in the same direction; after about five minutes turn right by a white painted sign and follow the path until it joins a surfaced road about 500m from the cove. Alternatively, driving there takes about ten minutes: head north along the main road out of Deià and watch for the sign.

Practicalities

The Palma–Port de Sóller **bus** scoots through Deià five times daily in each direction (Nov–March reduced service on Sun). For tourist information, head to the town hall office or *ajuntament*, just up from the bus stop (☎971 639 077; Mon–Fri 10am–2pm, Sat 10am–noon); alternatively, the village's hotels and *hostales* will gladly provide local advice on walks and weather, and can fix you up with a **taxi** – or do it yourself on ☎971 630 571. Of the two places where there's a good chance of a reasonably priced **room** in high season, the *Pensión Villa Verde*, c/Ramón Llull 19 (☎971 639 037; ☎971 639 485; ❸), has lovely premises near the village church, while the *Hotel d'es Puig* (☎971 639 409,

Ⓦwww.hoteldespuig.com; Feb–Dec; ❹) occupies a tastefully converted old stone house close by. Deià also possesses two of the finest hotels on Mallorca, both overlooking the main road: *Es Moli* (☏971 639 000, Ⓦwww.esmoli.com; April–Oct; ❾) and *La Residencia* (☏971 639 011, Ⓦwww .hotel-laresidencia.com; ❾), each of which occupies a gracious and beautifully maintained mansion.

As for **eating** in Deià, you're spoiled for choice. There's a concentration of cafés and restaurants along the main street towards the west end of the village. These include *Bar Sa Fàbrica*, which offers reasonably priced tapas, *bocadillos* and the traditional *pa amb oli* (bread rubbed with olive oil), and the *Restaurante Deià*, where you'll pay a little more for a light meal, but with the compensation of a terrace overlooking the valley. Moving up the price scale, the *Restaurant Jaime* (☏971 639 029), also at the west end of the village, offers mouthwatering Mallorcan cuisine.

Valldemossa

Some 10km **southwest of Deià** along the C710 is the ancient and intriguing hill town of **VALLDEMOSSA**, set in a lovely valley whose tiered and terraced fields ascend to the town, a sloping jumble of rusticated houses and monastic buildings backclothed by the mountains. The origins of Valldemossa date to the early fourteenth century, when the asthmatic King Sancho built a royal palace here in the hills where the air was easier to breathe. Later, in 1399, the palace was given to Carthusian monks from Tarragona, who converted and extended the original buildings into a **monastery**, now the island's most visited building after Palma cathedral.

Remodelled on several occasions, most of the present complex – the **Real Cartuja de Jesús de Nazaret** (Mon–Sat 9.30am–6pm, Sun 10am–1.30pm; Nov–Feb Mon–Sat closes 4.30pm; €8), as it's formally named – is of seventeenth- and eighteenth-century construction, its square and heavy church leading to the shadowy corridors of the cloisters beyond. The monastery owes its present fame almost entirely to the novelist and republican polemicist **George Sand**, who, with her companion, the composer **Frédéric Chopin**, lived here for four months during 1838–39 in a commodious set of vacant cells – the last monks had been evicted during the liberal-inspired suppression of the monasteries three years earlier. Their stay is commemorated in Sand's *A Winter in Majorca*, a stodgy, self-important book that is considerably overplayed hereabouts, being available in just about every European language.

A visit begins in the gloomy, aisleless **church**, which is distinguished by its fanciful bishop's throne, though the lines of the nave are spoiled by the clumsy wooden stalls of the choir. In the adjoining cloisters, the first port of call is the **pharmacy**, which survived the expulsion of the monks to serve the town's medicinal needs well into the twentieth century. Its shelves are crammed with a host of beautifully decorated majolica jars, antique glass receptacles and painted wood boxes, each carefully inscribed with the name of the potion or drug. The nearby **prior's cell** is, despite its name, a comfortable suite of bright, sizeable rooms with splendid views down the valley. It's also, together with the adjoining library and audience room, the proud possessor of a wide assortment of religious *objets d'art*. Further along the corridor, **cell no. 2** exhibits miscellaneous curios relating to Chopin and Sand, from portraits and a lock of hair to musical scores and letters (it was in this cell that the composer wrote the "Raindrop" Prelude). There's more of the same next door in **cell no. 4**, plus Chopin's piano, which arrived only after three months of unbelievable complications – and just three weeks before the couple left for Paris. Considering the hype, these incidental mementoes are something of an anticlimax, but persevere: upstairs, there's a small but outstanding collection of **modern art**, including work by Miró, Picasso, Francis Bacon and Henry Moore. And be sure also to take the doorway beside the prior's cell, which leads outside the cloisters to the enjoyable **Palace of King Sancho**. It's not the original palace at all – that disappeared long ago – but it is the oldest part of the complex and its fortified walls, mostly dating from the sixteenth century, accommodate a string of handsome period rooms.

Practicalities

Valldemossa is easily reached by **bus** from Deià, Sóller and Palma; there's also a bus four days a week from Andratx and points west along the coast. Buses stop at the west end of town beside one of the several car parks that edge the bypass; from the bus stops, it's just a couple of minutes' walk to the monastery – cross the bypass and keep going straight on.

For **accommodation**, there's the *Ca'n Mario*, c/Uetam 8 (☎971 612 122, ⓔhostalcanmario@eresmas.com; ❸), an attractive *hostal* with an elegant, curio-cluttered foyer and comfortably old-fashioned rooms; it's situated just a couple of minutes' walk from the monastery – from the pedestrianized area between the church and the palace, go downhill and take the first turning on the right. Alternatively, the upmarket *Valldemossa*, Ctra Vieja de Valldemossa s/n (☎971 612 626, ⓦwww.valdemossahotelrural.com; ❾), is a brand-new luxury property that commands the best views in town, and is also home to an excellent restaurant.

The centre of Valldemossa is packed with **restaurants and cafés**, mostly geared up for day-trippers – and many offer dire fast food at inflated prices. Nonetheless, there are one or two quality places amongst the dross, in particular *Costa Nord*, Avgda Palma 6 (☎971 612 425), owned by local residents Michael Douglas and Catherine Zeta-Jones and featuring Mediterranean-style cuisine.

Northeast from Sóller to Lluc

Beyond doubt, the most interesting approach to the northernmost tip of the island is the continuation of the **C710** northeast from Sóller, slipping through the highest and harshest section of the **Serra de Tramuntana**. For the most part, the mountains drop straight into the sea, precipitous and largely unapproachable cliffs with barely a cove in sight. The accessible exceptions are the basic beach at **Cala Tuent** and the horribly commercial hamlet of **Sa Calobra** next door. But easily the best place to break your journey is at **LLUC**, tucked away in a remote mountain valley about 35km from Sóller. Mallorca's most important place of pilgrimage since the middle of the thirteenth century, supposedly after a shepherd boy named Lluc (Luke) stumbled across a tiny, brightly painted statue here in the woods, Lluc is dominated by the austere, high-sided dormitories of the **Monestir de Nostra Senyora** (daily 10am–11pm; free). At the centre of the monastery is the main shrine and architectural highlight, the **Basílica de la Mare de Déu de Lluc**, a dark and gaudily decorated church dominated by heavy jasper columns, whose stolidness is relieved by a dome over the crossing. On either side of the nave, stone steps extend the aisles round the back of the Baroque high altar to a modest chapel. This is the holy of holies, built to display the much-venerated statue of the Virgin, commonly known as **La Moreneta** ("the Little Dark-Skinned One") ever since the original paintwork peeled off in the fifteenth century to reveal brown stone underneath.

From the information desk close to the basilica, a stairway climbs up one floor to the enjoyable **Museu de Lluc** (daily 10am–1.30pm & 2.30–5.15pm; €2). After a modest section devoted to archeological finds from the Talayotic and Roman periods come cabinets of intricate old vestments, medieval religious paintings, and an intriguing assortment of votive offerings – folkloric bits and bobs brought here to honour La Moreneta. The museum also boasts an extensive collection of **majolica**, tin-glazed earthenware whose characteristic shapes are two-handled drug jars and show dishes or plates, of which some two or three hundred are on display. Allow time, too, for a stroll along the **Camí dels Misteris del Rosari** (Way of the Mysteries of the Rosary), a broad pilgrims' footpath that winds its way up the rocky hillside behind the monastery.

Practicalities

Buses to Lluc, which is situated 700m off the C710, stop right outside the monastery. In addition to the Port de Sóller–Port de Pollença–Port d'Alcúdia service, buses run to Lluc at least twice a day from Palma via Inca. **Accommodation** at the monastery (℡971 871 525, @www.lluc.net, reductions for stays longer than one or two nights) is either in simple double rooms with private bath (€30) or in much nicer 4-bed apartments (€35.50); rooms (but not apartments) are subject to an 11pm curfew. In summer phone ahead if you want to be sure of space; at other times simply book at the monastery's information office on arrival. For **food**, there are two restaurants beside the car park, plus a café-bar and a small general store. Far preferable, even though it's a little pricey, is the elegant *Sa Fonda*, the monks' former dining room, where you can get traditional Spanish food – the meat dishes are much better than the fish.

Pollença

Northeast of Lluc, the C710 twists through the mountains to travel the 20km to **POLLENÇA**, a tranquil and ancient little town which nestles among a trio of hillocks where the Serra de Tramuntana fades into the coastal flatlands.

Following standard Mallorcan practice, the town was established a few kilometres from the seashore to militate against sudden pirate attack, with its harbour, Port de Pollença (see p.1006), left an unprotected outpost. For once the stratagem worked. Unlike most of Mallorca's old towns, Pollença avoided destruction, but nevertheless little of the medieval town survives today, and the austere stone houses that cramp the twisting lanes of the centre mostly date from the eighteenth century. In the middle, **Plaça Major**, the main square, accommodates a cluster of laid-back cafés and the dour facade of the church of **Nostra Senyora dels Àngels**, a sheer cliff-face of sun-bleached stone pierced by a rose window. Pollença's pride and joy is, however, its **Via Crucis** (Way of the Cross), a long, steep and beautiful stone stairway, graced by ancient cypress trees, which ascends **El Calvari** (Calvary hill) directly north of the principal square. At the top, a much-revered statue of the **Mare de Déu del Peu de la Creu** (Mother of God at the Foot of the Cross) is lodged in a simple, courtyarded **Oratori** (chapel), whose whitewashed walls sport some of the worst religious paintings imaginable. However, the views out over coast and town are sumptuous. On Good Friday, a figure of Jesus is slowly carried by torchlight down from the Oratori to the church of Nostra Senyora dels Àngels, in the **Davallament** (Lowering), one of the most moving religious celebrations on the island.

There are further magnificent views from the **Ermita de Nostra Senyora del Puig**, a rambling, mostly eighteenth-century monastery which occupies a serene and beautiful spot on top of the Puig de Maria, a 320-metre-high hump facing the south end of town. The monastic complex, with its fortified walls, courtyard, chapel, refectory and cells, has had a chequered history, alternately abandoned and restored by both monks and nuns. The Benedictines now own the place, but the monks are gone and today a custodian supplements the order's income by renting out cells to tourists (see below). To get to the monastery, take the signposted turning left off the main Pollença–Inca road just south of town, then head up this steep, 1.5-kilometre lane until it fizzles out, to be replaced by a cobbled footpath which winds up to the monastery entrance. It's possible to drive to the top of the lane, but unless you've got nerves of steel, you're better off leaving your vehicle by the turning near the foot of the hill. Allow just over an hour each way if you're walking from the centre of town.

Practicalities

Regular **buses** from Palma, Lluc and Port de Pollença halt immediately to the south of Pollença's Plaça Major and across the street from the **turisme** (Tues–Sat 9am–1pm & 5–8pm, Sun 9am–1pm; ☎971 535 077). The most central place to **stay** is the excellent *Hotel Juma*, Plaça Major 9 (☎971 535 002, ⓦwww.hoteljuma.com; March–Oct; ❺), a medium-sized hotel with comfortable, air-conditioned modern bedrooms. Nearby, at c/Marquès Desbrull 7, is the newly opened and very welcoming *Desbrull* (☎971 535 055, ⓦwww .desbrull.com; ❺). There are also much cheaper lodgings at the Ermita de Nostra Senyora del Puig (☎971 184 132; €6 per person) – see above for directions – where the original monks' cells have been renovated to provide simple accommodation. Be warned, though, that it can get cold and windy at night, and the refectory food is mediocre.

Pollença does well for **cafés** and **restaurants**. On Plaça Major, the *Café Espanyol* offers snacks and a good strong cup of coffee, the *Juma* serves up first-rate tapas and the *Restaurante Il Giardino* provides superb Italian-style cuisine. On c/Montisión, in between the main square and El Calvari, you'll also find the upbeat and fashionable *Restaurante Cantonet* (dinner only), where the seafood is delicious.

Port de Pollença

Over at **PORT DE POLLENÇA** things are a little more touristy, though still pleasantly low-key. With the mountains as a backcloth, the resort arches through the flatlands behind the Badia de Pollença, a deeply indented bay whose sheltered waters are ideal for swimming. The **beach** is the focus of attention, a narrow, elongated sliver of sand that's easily long enough to accommodate the crowds, though as a general rule you'll have more space the further southeast (towards Alcúdia) you walk. A rash of apartment buildings and hotels blights the edge of town, and the noisy main road to Alcúdia runs close to most of the seashore, but all in all the place is very appealing, especially in the centre behind the marina, where old narrow streets hint at the resort's origins as a small port and fishing harbour.

For a change of scene, **water taxis** shuttle between the marina and the Platja de Formentor (April–Oct 5 daily; 30min; €7.30 return), one of Mallorca's most attractive beaches, while **boat trips** cruise the bay (June to mid-Oct Mon–Sat 1 daily; 2hr 30min; €16) or work their way along to Cap de Formentor (Mon–Wed & Fri; 1 daily; 1hr; €17).

There's also a delightful three-kilometre (each way) **hike** across the neck of the Península de Formentor to **Cala Boquer**. On the seafront north of the marina, take a left up **Avinguda Bocchoris**. Proceed over the Formentor road and keep straight along a wide footpath fringed with pine trees and tamarisk. Beyond the end of the footpath is an untidy area, whose tarmac marks the layout of a proposed housing development. Ahead, at a sign saying "Predio Bóquer Propriedad Privada Camin Particular", take the wide path north with the ridge of Serra del Cavall Bernat straight ahead and you'll soon reach an iron gate, beyond which is Bóquer farmhouse. The trail leads on through the mountain-sheltered **Vall de Boquer** (Boquer Valley), a favourite of ornithologists, especially for its migrant birds, and of botanists for its wild flowers and shrubs. After about 45 minutes' walking you reach a small, shingly **beach** offering good swimming in clean water (though the shore is sometimes rubbish-strewn).

Practicalities

Buses to Port de Pollença from Palma, Alcúdia, Port d'Alcúdia and Port de Sóller stop by the marina right in the town centre. The **turisme** is just a couple of minutes' walk away inland at c/Monges 9 (June–Sept Mon–Fri 9am–1.30pm & 4–7pm, Sat 9am–1pm; Oct–May Mon–Fri 8am–3.30pm, Sat 9am–1pm; ☎971 865 467). The flatlands edging the Badia de Pollença and stretching as far as Alcúdia and Pollença make for easy, scenic cycling. **Mountain bikes** can be rented for €8 a day from a shop called March at c/Joan XXIII 89 (☎971 864 784), as can **mopeds** and **motorcycles**. The walking holiday specialist Globespan has a waterfront office at the *Sis Pins* hotel, Passeig Anglada Camarasa 77 (☎971 867 050, ⓦwww.globespan.com), where you can pay to join one of their day-long guided walks (€10–25 per person); you should book a minimum of 24 hours beforehand.

There are several reasonably priced and convenient **accommodation** options, though getting a room in season may be difficult. Just steps from the beach stands the serviceable *Hostal Residencia La Goleta*, Passeig Saralegui 118 (☎971 865 902, ⓦwww.puertopollensa.com; ❸), with comfortable and spacious rooms. On the pedestrian-only promenade, the *Hotel Miramar*, Passeig Anglada Camarasa 39 (☎971 866 400, ⓦwww.pollensanet.com/miramar; April–Oct; ❻), is an attractive three-star hotel, with balconied rooms set behind

THE BALEARIC ISLANDS | Northern Mallorca

a grand facade; also by the water is the friendly and unpretentious *Hostal Bahia*, Passeig Voramar 27 (T971 865 984, F971 865 630; ❹), which also has an excellent fish restaurant.

Among a plethora of **restaurants**, the most obvious choice is the *Restaurant Stay* (T971 864 013), out on the marina's Moll Vell jetty, a chic place which features the freshest of seafood; it's a popular (and romantic) spot, so reservations are advised; count on around €45 for a full à la carte meal. Other possibilities include the *La Balada del Agua del Mar*, Passeig Voramar 5 (T971 864 276), one of the prettiest choices along the promenade, with main courses averaging €15; and the attractive *Restaurante Ivy Garden*, c/Llevant 14 (T971 866 271), which features an inventive modern menu, with full meals costing about €45.

The Península de Formentor

Heading northeast out of Port de Pollença, the road clears the military zone at the far end of the resort before weaving up into the craggy hills of the twenty-kilometre-long **Península de Formentor**, the final spur of the Serra de Tramuntana. At first, the road (which suffers a surfeit of tourists from mid-morning to mid-afternoon) travels inland, out of sight of the true grandeur of the scenery, but after about 4km the **Mirador de Mal Pas** rectifies matters with a string of lookout points perched on the edge of plunging, north-facing sea cliffs. From here, it's another couple of kilometres to the woods backing onto the **Platja de Formentor**, a pine-clad beach of golden sand in a pretty cove. It's a beautiful spot, with views over to the mountains on the far side of the bay. From May to October there are **buses** here from Port de Pollença (Mon–Sat 4 daily) and Palma (1 daily). At the end of the cove, opposite a tiny islet, stands the *Hotel Formentor* (T971 899 100, W www.hotelformentor.net; ❾). Opened in 1930, this grand hotel – the island's first and at one time its best – lies low against the forested hillside, its hacienda-style architecture enhanced by Neoclassical and Art Deco features and exquisite terraced gardens. Beyond the turn-off for the beach, the main peninsula road runs along a wooded ridge, before tunnelling through Mont Fumat to emerge on the rocky mass of **Cap de Formentor**, a tapered promontory of bleak seacliffs and scrub-covered hills which offers spectacular views.

Alcúdia

Moving south from Port de Pollença, it's just 10km round the bay to the pint-sized town of **ALCÚDIA**, whose main claim to fame is its impeccably restored medieval walls, although some people find the whole place overly spick and span. Situated on a neck of land separating two large, sheltered bays, the site's strategic value was first recognized by the Phoenicians, and later by the Romans, who built their island capital, Pollentia, here in the first century AD, on top of the earlier settlement. In 426, the place was destroyed by the Vandals and lay neglected until the Moors built a fortress in about 800, naming it *Al Kudia* (On the Hill). After the Reconquest, Alcúdia prospered as a major trading centre, a role it performed well into the nineteenth century, when the town slipped into a long and gentle decline – until tourism refloated its economy.

It only takes an hour or so to walk around the antique lanes of Alcúdia's compact centre, and to explore the town walls and their fortified gates. This pleasant stroll can be extended by a visit to the meagre remains of Roman **Pollentia**, whose broken pillars and rubble lie just outside the walls (April–Sept Tues–Fri 10am–1.30pm & 5–7pm, Sat & Sun 10.30am–1pm; Oct–March Tues–Fri 10am–1.30pm & 3.30–5.30pm, Sat & Sun

10.30am–1pm; €2). The entrance ticket includes admission to the small but excellent **Museu Monogràfic** across from Sant Jaume Church, just inside the walls. A fairly well preserved **Roman theatre** (entrance free) lies a further one kilometre to the south.

Buses to Alcúdia halt beside the town walls on Plaça Carles V; there's no tourist office. For **food**, there are several good cafés on Plaça Constitució, but it's hard to beat the cosy café-bar of *Ca's Capella*, just east of the church of Sant Jaume along c/Rectoria.

Port d'Alcúdia

PORT D'ALCÚDIA, 2km south of Alcúdia, is easily the biggest and busiest of the resorts on the Badia d'Alcúdia, its clutch of restaurants and café-bars attracting crowds from a seemingly interminable string of high-rise hotels and apartment buildings. The tower blocks are, however, relatively well distributed and the streets neat and tidy. Predictably, the daytime focus is the **beach**, a superb arc of pine-studded golden sand, which stretches south for 10km from the combined marina and fishing harbour.

Port d'Alcúdia acts as northern Mallorca's summertime transport hub, with frequent **bus** services to and from Palma, Port de Sóller, Port de Pollença, Pollença and Artà, as well as other neighbouring towns and resorts. Most local and long-distance bus services travel the length of **Carretera d'Artà**, the main drag, which slices right through the resort, running broadly parallel to the bay and punctuated by a series of clearly signed bus stops (there is no bus station). The main **turisme** (Easter to Oct Mon–Sat 9am–7pm; ☎971 892 615) is situated on Carretera d'Artà, about 2km south round the bay from the marina, while there's a second office on the Passeig Marítim (☎971 547 257). Both can supply all sorts of information, most usefully free maps marked with all the resort's hotels and apartments, but bear in mind that in season vacant rooms are few and far between, and in winter almost everywhere is closed. In addition, there's a superabundance of **car, moped and bicycle rental** companies strung out along Carretera d'Artà. Mountain bikes cost around €8 per day, or about €20 for three days.

Parc Natural de S'Albufera

Heading south around the bay from Port d'Alcúdia on the C712, it's about 6km to the **Parc Natural de S'Albufera** (daily: April–Sept 9am–7pm; Oct–March 9am–6pm; free), an eight-square-kilometre segment of pristine wetland, all that remains of the marshes that once extended round most of the bay. The signposted entrance to the park is on the C712, but access is only on foot or cycle – so if you're driving you'll need to park up on the main road. About 1km from the entrance, you come to the park's **reception centre**, from where footpaths radiate out into the reedy, watery tract beyond. It's a superb habitat, with ten well-appointed hides allowing excellent **birdwatching**. Over two hundred species have been spotted: resident wetland-loving birds, autumn and/or springtime migrants, and wintering species and birds of prey in their scores. There's no problem getting here by public transport – **buses** from Port d'Alcúdia to Ca'n Picafort stop beside the entrance.

Southeastern Mallorca

Mallorca's **southeast coast**, stretching for about 60km north from Cala Figuera to Cala Rajada, is fretted by narrow **coves**, the remnants of prehistoric river valleys created when the level of the Mediterranean was much lower. Of great natural beauty, all but the least accessible of these coves has, however, been engulfed by a tide of development and, frankly, you're better off staying away, especially if you haven't got your own transport. That said, if you do decide to pass this way, there are one or two incidental attractions, not least the attractive minor road which links the resorts, running, for the most part, a few kilometres inland along the edge of the **Serres de Llevant**, a slim and benign band of grassy hills which rises to over 500m at its two extremities, south outside Felanitx and north around Artà.

Porto Cristo

Halfway up the east coast, **PORTO CRISTO** is the largest town hereabouts, a busy and slightly old-fashioned place near the two sets of caves that are the area's most popular tourist attractions. These are the **Coves des Hams** (daily: April–Oct 10am–6pm; Nov–March 10.30am–5pm; €9) and the **Coves del Drac** (daily: April–Oct 10am–5pm; Nov–March 10.30am–3.30pm; €7.50), each of which can only be visited on a guided tour. The cave complexes are very similar – and both feature classical musicians sailing around on a subterranean lake – so you'd hardly want to visit them both; opt for the Drac (Dragon) caverns, which are located about fifteen minutes' walk from the centre of Porto Cristo.

Artà and around

Heading north from Porto Cristo, it's about 20km to **ARTÀ**, an ancient hill town of sun-bleached roofs clustered beneath a castellated chapel-shrine, with the bunching peaks of the Serres de Llevant providing a dramatic backdrop. It's a delightful scene, though at close quarters the town is something of an anticlimax – the cobweb of cramped and twisted alleys doesn't quite match the setting. Nonetheless, the ten-minute trek to the **Santuari de Sant Salvador**, the shrine at the top of Artà, is a must for the views out over eastern Mallorca. Also make time to visit the substantial remains of the prehistoric settlement of **Ses Paisses** (April–Sept daily 9am–1pm & 3–7pm; Oct–March Mon–Fri 9am–1pm & 2.30–5pm, Sat 9am–1pm; €2), tucked away in a grove of olive, carob and holm oak trees about 1km to the south of the town.

Buses to Artà stop on the edge of the town centre, beside the C715. From the bus stop, it's a couple of hundred metres west to the short main street, c/Ciutat, where there are several **cafés**. The best is *Café Parisien*, at no. 18, a trendy little place with an outside terrace and tasty tapas and salads at reasonable prices. The *Ca'n Balague*, at no. 19, is a more traditional café-bar also serving light meals.

Artà is a major crossroads: to the **east**, the main road cuts through the village of **CAPDEPERA** – a dusty, elongated village, crouched below a fine crenellated castle – before descending to the coast at the massive resort of **CALA RAJADA**, whose excellent beaches are a favourite haunt of German package tourists. Twice-daily, passenger-only **catamarans** connect the resort with Ciutadella in Menorca (see p.1019) throughout the year. To the **west**, the C712 weaves through the hills to Ca'n Picafort and the Badia d'Alcúdia (see p.1008).

Menorca

The second largest of the Balearic Islands, boomerang-shaped **Menorca** is often and unfairly maligned as an overdeveloped, package-tourist ghetto. Contrary to its reputation, however, Menorca remains the least developed of the Balearics, an essentially rural island with rolling fields, wooded ravines and humpy hills filling out the interior in between its two main – but still small – towns of **Maó** and **Ciutadella**. Much of this landscape looks pretty much as it did at the turn of the twentieth century, and only around the edges of the island, and then only in parts, have its rocky coves been colonized by sprawling villa complexes. Neither is the development likely to spread: the resorts have been kept at a discreet distance from the two main towns, and this is how the Menorcans like it. Furthermore, determined to protect their island from the worst excesses of the tourist industry, the Menorcans have clearly demarcated development areas and are meanwhile pushing ahead with a variety of environmental schemes – the island was declared a UNESCO Biosphere Reserve in 1993, and over forty percent of the island now enjoys official protection.

Menorca is also littered with prehistoric monuments, weatherworn stone remains that are evidence of a sophisticated culture. Little is known for sure of the island's prehistory, but the monuments are thought to be linked to those of Sardinia and are classified as part of the second-millennium BC **Talayot culture**. *Talayots* are the rock mounds found all over the island – popular belief has it that they functioned as watchtowers, but it's a theory few experts accept. They have no interior stairway, and only a few are found on the coast. Even so, no one has come up with a much more convincing explanation. The megalithic *taulas* – huge stones topped with another to form a T, around 4m high and unique to Menorca – are even more puzzling. They have no obvious function, and they are almost always found alongside a *talayot*. Some of the best-preserved *talayot* and *taula* remains are on the edge of Maó at the **Trepucó** site. Then there are *navetas* (dating from 1400 to 800 BC), stone-slab constructions shaped like an inverted bread tin. Many have false ceilings, and although you can stand up inside they were clearly not living spaces – communal pantries, perhaps, or more probably tombs.

In more recent history, the long and slender, deep-water channel of the port of Maó promoted Menorca to an important position in European affairs. The British saw its potential as a naval base during the War of the Spanish Succession and achieved their aim by having the island ceded to them through the Treaty of Utrecht (1713). Spain regained possession in 1783, but with the threat of Napoleon in the Mediterranean, a new British base was temporarily established under admirals Nelson and Collingwood. The British influence is still considerable, especially in architecture: the sash windows so popular in Georgian design are still sometimes referred to as *winderes*, locals often part with a fond *bye-bye*, and there's a substantial expatriate community. The British also moved the capital from Ciutadella to Maó and constructed the main island road. More importantly, they introduced the art of distilling juniper berries: Menorcan **gin** (Xoriguer, Beltran and Nelson) is renowned.

Before much of it was killed off by tourism, Menorcan **agriculture** had become highly advanced. A dry stone wall protected every field from the *tramóntana* (the vicious north wind), which ripped away the topsoil, and even

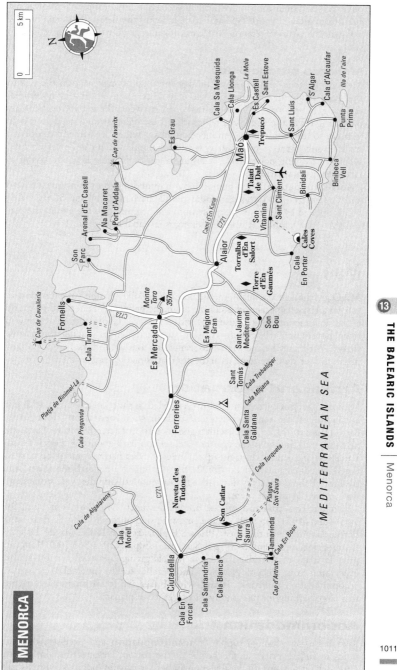

MENORCA

MEDITERRANEAN SEA

N

0 5 km

Cala Sa Mesquida
Cala Llonga
La Mola
Es Castell
Sant Esteve
S'Algar
Cala d'Alcaufar
Illa de l'aire
Punta Prima
Binibeca Vell
Binidali
Sant Lluís
Es Grau
Maó
Trepucó
Talatí de Dalt
Cap de Favàritx
Cales Coves
Son Vitamina
Sant Climent
Cala En Porter
Alaior
Torralba d'En Salort
Torre d'En Gaumés
Camí d'En Kane
C721
Arenal d'En Castell
Na Macaret
Port d'Addaia
Son Parc
Monte Toro
357m
Es Migjorn Gran
Sant Jaume Mediterrani
Son Bou
Fornells
C723
Cala Tirant
Cap de Cavalleria
Es Mercadal
Sant Tomás
Cala Trebalúger
Cala Mitjana
Cala Santa Galdana
Platja de Binimel·là
Cala Pregonda
Ferreries
Cala Turqueta
Naveta d'es Tudons
C721
Son Catlar
Torre Saura
Platges Son Saura
Tamarinda
Cala En Bosc
Cap d'Artrutx
Cala de Algaiarens
Cala Morell
Ciutadella
Cala En Forcat
Cala Santandria
Cala Blanca

olive trees had their roots individually protected in little stone wells. Nowadays, apart from a few acres of rape and corn, many of the fields are barren, but the walls survive. Any vegetation that dares to emerge above their safety is soon swept away by the gusts.

Menorca practicalities

Menorca stretches from the enormous natural harbour of Maó in the east to the smaller port of Ciutadella in the west. **Bus** routes are distinctly limited, adhering mostly to the main central road between these two, occasionally branching off to the larger coastal resorts. Consequently, you'll need your own **vehicle** to reach any of the emptier **beaches** – which are sometimes down a track fit only for four-wheel-drive – and the wind, which can be very helpful when it's blowing behind you, is distinctly uncomfortable if you're trying to ride into it on a **moped**.

Accommodation is at a premium, with quite limited options outside Maó and Ciutadella – and you can count on all the beds in all the resorts being block-booked by the tour operators from the beginning to the end of the season (May to October). Advance booking is essential in August.

Maó

MAÓ (Mahón in Castilian), the island capital, is likely to be your first port of call. It's a respectable, almost dull little town, the people restrained and polite. So is the architecture – an unusual hybrid of classical Georgian sash-windowed town houses and tall, gloomy Spanish apartment blocks shading the narrow streets. Port it may be, but there's no seamy side to Maó, and the harbour is now home to a string of restaurants and cafés that attract tourists in their droves.

Arrival and information

Menorca's **airport**, just 5km southwest of Maó, is short on amenities, with just a handful of car rental outlets and a **tourist information desk** (daily 8am–11pm; ☎971 157 115) with a good selection of free literature. There are no buses into the town; the taxi fare will set you back about €8. **Ferries** from Barcelona and Palma sail right up the inlet to Maó harbour, mooring next to the Trasmediterránea offices (☎902 454 645) directly beneath the town centre. From behind the ferry dock, it's a five-minute walk up the wide stone stairway to the old part of town.

Maó has two **turisme** offices, one at the port (Mon–Fri 8am–9pm, Sat 9am–1pm; ☎971 355 952), on the landward side of the Edificio de Autoridad Portuaria, and the other near Plaça S'Esplanada at c/Rovellada de Dalt 24 (Mon–Fri 9am–1.30pm & 5–7pm, Sat 9am–1.30pm; ☎971 363 790). Both can provide maps of the island and free leaflets giving the lowdown on almost everything from archeological sites and beaches to bus timetables, car rental, accommodation and banks. **Island-wide buses** and **local buses** all converge in a large parking lot just southwest of Plaça S'Esplanada.

Accommodation

Maó has a very limited supply of **accommodation** and excessive demand tends to inflate prices at the height of the season. Despite this, along with Ciutadella it remains the best Menorcan bet for bargain lodgings, with a small

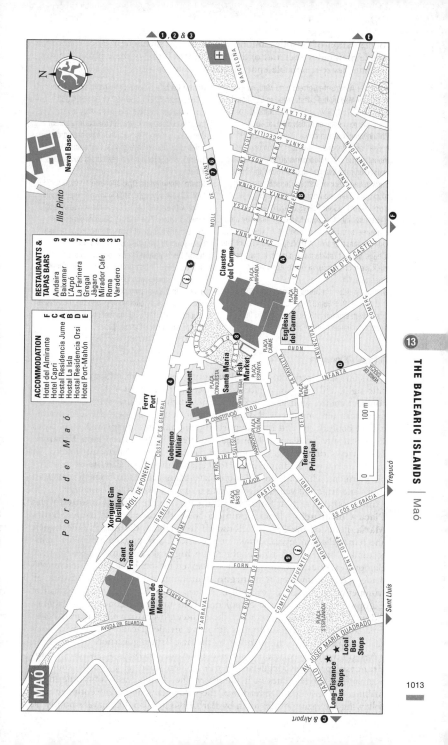

MAÓ

ACCOMMODATION
Hotel del Almirante   F
Hotel Capri   C
Hostal Residencia Jume   A
Hostal La Isla   B
Hostal Residencia Orsi   D
Hotel Port-Mahón   E

RESTAURANTS &
TAPAS BARS
Andaira   9
Baixamar   4
L'Arpó   6
La Farinera   7
Gregal   1
Jàgaro   2
Mirador Café   8
Roma   3
Varadero   5

Port de Maó

Illa Pinto

Naval Base

Xoriguer Gin
Distillery

Sant
Francesc

Museu de Menorca

Ferry
Port

Gobierno
Militar

Ajuntament

Santa Maria

Fish
Market

Claustre
del Carme

Església
del Carme

Teatre
Principal

Long-Distance
Bus Stops

Local
Bus Stops

▲ ⓐ & Airport

◀ Sant Lluís

◀ Sant Lluís

◀ Trepucó

concentration of **hostales** among the workaday streets near Plaça Princep, a couple of minutes' walk east of the town centre. None of these places is inspiring, but they're reasonable enough, and convenient.

Hotel del Almirante Carretera de Maó, nearly 2km from Maó by the coastal road to Es Castell ☎971 362 700, ⓦwww.hoteldelalmirante.com. Once the residence of British admiral Lord Collingwood, this maroon and cream Georgian house has a delightful, antique-crammed interior, though some of the bedrooms are modern affairs overlooking the swimming pool round the back. The package-tour operators Thomson use the place, but there are often vacancies. ❺

Hotel Capri c/Sant Esteve 8 ☎971 361 400, ⓔcapri@rtmhotels.com. Large, proficiently modern three-star hotel in the centre of Maó, popular with business people. A rooftop spa and pool and a huge buffet breakfast are pluses. It's a brief walk west of the tourist office along Avgda Quadrado. ❹

Hostal Residencia Jume c/Concepció 6 ☎971 363 266, ⓕ971 364 878. Efficiently run modern *hostal* with spartan, but well maintained furnishings; a convenient choice near the town centre. ❷

Hostal La Isla c/Santa Caterina 4, at the corner of c/Concepció ☎971 366 492 or 971 364 358. Excellent, comfortable one-star run by a very friendly couple, who also run the bar/restaurant downstairs. The 25 attractive rooms are on the small side, but all have private baths and TV. There's a popular bar and restaurant downstairs. ❷

Hostal Residencia Orsi c/Infanta 19 ☎ & ⓕ971 364 751. The nicest *hostal* in town. Frugal rooms, most with shared bath, have large windows and green shutters. The friendly Scottish-American owners are a mine of local information. A simple help-yourself breakfast is included. ❷

Hotel Port-Mahón Avgda Fort de l'Eau s/n ☎971 362 600, ⓕ971 351 050. Elegant colonial-style hotel in a superb location overlooking the Maó inlet, with a swimming pool and all mod cons. Room prices vary enormously, with the top whack a hefty €192. It's a 20min walk east of the town centre along via c/Carme. ❹

The Town

Maó's fine setting and crowded old mansions are its charm, rather than any specific sight, and you can explore the place thoroughly in a day – the town's compact centre, with its deep streets rising high above the water's edge, is no more than ten minutes' walk from top to bottom. From near the ferry terminal, set beneath the cliff that supports the remains of the city wall, a generous stone stairway leads up to four small squares. The first, the **Plaça Espanya**, offers views right across the port and bay and houses Maó's fish market, in operation since 1927. Immediately to the left is the **Plaça Carme**, with a simple Carmelite church whose cloisters have been adapted to house a variety of shops and fruit and vegetable stalls, plus a supermarket in the basement.

In the other direction from Plaça d'Espanya lie the **Plaça Conquesta** and **Plaça Constitució**. Plaça Constitució boasts the town's main church, **Santa María**. Founded in 1287 by Alfonso III to celebrate the island's Reconquest and remodelled on several subsequent occasions, the church is a pleasing architectural hybrid. Inside, a highlight is the **high altar**, whose larger-than-life Baroque excesses shoot up to the roof flanked by spiral columns. The church's pride and joy, however, is its **organ**, a monumental piece of woodwork, all trumpeting angels and pipes, built in Austria in 1810 and lugged across half of Europe at the height of the Napoleonic Wars under the concerned charge of Admiral Collingwood. Next door, the eighteenth-century **ajuntament** benefited from British largesse too, its attractive arcaded facade graced by a clock that was presented to the islanders by the first British governor.

A short walk away, at the end of c/Isabel II, the Baroque facade of **Sant Francesc** appears as a cliff-face of pale golden stone set above the rounded, Romanesque-style arches of its doorway. The church was a long time in the making, its construction spread over the seventeenth and eighteenth centuries following the razing of the town by Barbarossa in 1535. The nave is poorly lit, but it's still possible to pick out the pinkish tint in much of the stone and the unusual spiral decoration of the pillars. In contrast, the **Chapel of the Immaculate Conception**, tucked away off the north side of the nave, is flooded with light – an octagonal wonderland of garlanded vines and roses which offers an exquisite example of the Churrigueresque style. The chapel is attributed to Francesc Herrara, who trained in Rome and worked in both Menorca and Mallorca.

The adjacent monastic buildings now house the **Museu de Menorca** (Tues–Sat 10am–2pm & 4–8.30pm, Sun 10am–2pm; €2.40), easily the island's biggest and best museum. Entry to the collection is through the **cloister** of Sant Francesc, whose sturdy pillars and vaulted aisles represent the high point of Menorcan Baroque. Beyond, up the stairs, the museum's **first floor** holds a wide sample of prehistoric artefacts, beginning with bits and pieces left by the Neolithic pastoralists who settled here about 4000 BC; there's also an extensive range of material from the Talayotic period. Most of the exhibits carry multilingual labels.

From the museum, it's a brisk five-minute walk up through the town to the flowerbeds and fountains of the undistinguished main square, the **Plaça S'Esplanada**. Back near the ferry terminal, the **Xoriguer gin distillery** (June–Aug Mon–Fri 8am–7pm, Sat 9am–1pm; Sept–May Mon–Fri 9am–1pm & 4–7pm; free) dishes out free samples of gin, various liqueurs and other spirits. From here, you can stroll the entire length of the **quayside** to the southeast edge of town, a half-hour walk that will take you past a long string of restaurants, bars and cafés, as well as the town's bulging marinas. By day, this makes a relaxing stroll; at night it's slightly more animated, particularly after midnight, when a few clubs get going.

Trepucó

South from Plaça S'Esplanada, it's a thirty-minute walk to the prehistoric remains of **Trepucó** (open access; free). To get there, follow c/Moreres from the northeast corner of the square, take the first right down c/Cós de Gràcia and then go straight on down c/Verge de Gràcia to the ring road. Here, go straight over the traffic island and follow the twisting lane dead ahead, past the cemetery. Thereafter the route is not, at present, clearly signed. After 200m, go straight at the fork, and then – 500m later – veer left at the fork and, after a further 100m, turn right.

Surrounded by olive trees and dry-stone walls, the tiny site's focal point is a 4.2-metre-high and 2.75-metre-wide **taula**, one of the largest and best preserved of these T-shaped monoliths on the island. The *taula* stands inside a circular compound which is edged by the remains of several broadly circular buildings. These were thoroughly excavated by a team of archeologists from Cambridge University in the late 1920s, but even they couldn't work out how the complex was structured. There are two cone-shaped **talayots** close by, the larger one accessible, the other not. The shape of the larger *talayot* is, however, not entirely authentic, as the French increased its width to mount their guns during the invasion of 1781.

Eating, drinking and nightlife

Maó has a place in culinary history as the eighteenth-century birthplace of **mayonnaise** (*mahonesa*). Various legends, all of them involving the French, claim to identify its inventor: take your pick from the chef of the French commander besieging Maó; a peasant woman dressing a salad for another French general; or a housekeeper disguising rancid meat from the taste buds of a

French officer. The French also changed the way the Menorcans bake their bread, while the British started the dairy industry and encouraged the roasting of meat. Unfortunately, traditional Balearic food is not very much in evidence these days, as most of Maó's **restaurants** specialize in Spanish, Catalan or Italian dishes. These tourist-oriented establishments are mainly spread out along the harbourside – the Moll de Ponent west of the main stairway, the Moll de Llevant to the east. There's also a smattering of cheaper restaurants and **coffee bars** in the centre of town, though surprisingly few **tapas bars**.

Nightlife is not Maó's forte, though there are some fairly lively **bars** along the harbourfront which stay open until around 2am on summer weekends, as well as a few **clubs**, which get going around midnight.

Cafés and tapas bars

Café Baixamar Moll de Ponent 17. Attractively decorated little café-bar, with old-fashioned mirrors and soft-hued paintwork, serving tasty traditional Menorcan snacks and tapas – island cheese and sausage, for example, costs just €3.

Café-bar La Farinera Moll de Llevant 84. Spruce and modern café-bar offering tasty snacks near the ferry port. Usually open from 6am. Also has a selection of interesting photographs of old Menorca stuck on the walls.

Mirador Café Plaça Espanya s/n. Tasty snacks and great views over the harbour from this little café-bar with a terrace. Footsteps from the fish market, at the top of the main stairway leading from the harbour to the town centre. Jazz is the favoured background music.

Varadero Moll de Llevant 4. Close to the ferry terminal, this smart, modern place has a restaurant on one side and a café-bar on the other. The café-bar is the place to aim for – a stylish spot to nurse a drink and sample a small range of tapas. Very popular with tourists in summer.

Restaurants

Andaira c/Forn 62 ☎971 484 285. Intimate and cosy family-run place featuring traditional Menorcan cuisine, with main courses from around

€12. It's near Plaça S'Esplanada: leave the square along c/Pi, a short pedestrianized alley on its north side, take the first right and then the first left. Dinner only. Closed Mon, sometimes Sun too.

L'Arpó Moll de Llevant 124 ☎971 369 844. Cosy and intimate restaurant featuring a superb selection of fish dishes from €11. Try the paella.

Gregal Moll de Llevant 306 ☎971 366 606. The decor is uninspired – just run-of-the-mill modern and comfortable – but the food is outstanding, with mouthwatering seafood dishes prepared in all sorts of delicious (and often traditional) ways. Try, for instance, the John Dory in leek sauce (€27), or the sea anemone fritters (€10). Near the east end of the harbour front.

Jàgaro Moll de Llevant 334 ☎971 362 390. Ambitious restaurant with a smart, traditional interior and a terrace packed with greenery. The menu is perhaps a little too wide-ranging for its own good, featuring everything from hamburgers to paella. Stick to the fish at €12–18 per main course. It's at the east end of the waterfront.

Roma Moll de Llevant 295. Popular place with fast service specializing in well-prepared Italian food at bargain prices, with pasta and pizzas from €5.50. The decor is a tad old-fashioned, but that seems to suit the clientele. Closed in winter.

Bars and nightclubs

Maó's **nightclubs** are all down by the port – head up Costa d'es General, the ramped lane across from the ferry terminal, to find *Tse-Tse*, at no.14, and nearby, *Berri* and *Terminal*, all of which come to life after midnight.

Bar Akelarre Moll de Ponent 41. Down on the waterfront near the ferry terminal, this is probably the best – and certainly the most fashionable – bar in town, occupying an attractively renovated ground-floor vault with stone walls and a miniature garden-cum-terrace at the back, right at the foot of the old city walls. Jazz and smooth modern sounds form the backcloth, with occasional live acts.

Nou Bar c/Nou 1. The ground-floor café here, with its dumpy armchairs (reserved for members) and gloomy lighting, is a dog-eared old place much favoured by locals. On the corner of Costa de Sa Plaça.

Si Discoteca c/Verge de Gràcia 16. Low-key, late-night locals' joint south of Plaça Reial. Usually open from 11.30pm to around 3am.

Listings

Banks Banco de Credito Balear, Plaça S'Esplanada 2; Banca March, c/Sa Ravaleta 7; Banco de Santander, c/Moreres 46 and 69.

Bicycle rental VRB, c/S'Arraval 52 (℡971 353 798), rents ordinary and mountain bikes at reasonable rates. Advance booking recommended.

Bookshops Llibrería Fundació, facing Plaça Colón at Costa de Sa Plaça 14 (Mon–Fri 9.30am–1.30pm & 5–8pm, Sat 9.30am–1.30pm; ℡971 363 543), has a fair selection of English-language guidebooks and is strong on birdwatching guides. It also has general maps of Menorca – including the pick of the bunch, the Distrimapas Telstar (1:75,000) – plus a reasonable, though far from exhaustive, assortment of IGN walking maps.

Car rental Amongst several companies, both Avis (℡971 361 576) and Atesa (℡971 366 213) have branches at the airport, while downtown there's another Avis outlet at Plaça S'Esplanada 53 (℡971

364 778), plus many smaller concerns – the tourist office has an exhaustive list.

Emergencies General emergency number (fire, police and ambulance) ℡112. Local police ℡092.

Ferries Schedules, tariffs and tickets are available direct from the ferry line, Trasmediterránea (℡902 454 645), next to the ferry port.

Internet access *Webera*, opposite the Església de Santa Maria at c/ Església 1B (Mon–Fri 10am–2pm & 4–9pm, Sat 6–10pm; €3/hr; ℡971 356 873).

Maps See "Bookshops" above.

Mopeds Motos Gelabert, Avgda J. A. Clavé 12 ℡971 360 614.

Post office The central *correu* is at c/Bon Aire 11–13, near Plaça Bastió (Mon–Fri 9am–5pm, Sat 9am–1pm).

Taxis There's a taxi rank on Plaça S'Esplanada. Alternatively, telephone Radio Taxis ℡971 367 111. Fares between any two towns on the island are fixed by law at about €1 per kilometre.

Northwest to Fornells

Northwest of Maó, the road to Fornells runs through some of Menorca's finest scenery – the fields are cultivated and protected by great stands of trees, and the land rises as the road approaches Monte Toro (see p.1019) and skirts round it to the north. At the end of the road, just 25km from the capital, **FORNELLS** is a low-rise, classically pretty fishing village at the mouth of a long and chubby bay. Despite the lack of a decent beach, it has been popular with tourists for years, above all for its **seafood restaurants**, whose speciality, *caldereta de llagosta* (*langosta* in Castilian), is a fabulously tasty – and wincingly expensive – lobster stew. Nevertheless, there's been little development, just a slim trail of holiday homes extending north from the village in a suitably unobtrusive style.

The wild and rocky coastline west of Fornells boasts several **cove beaches** of outstanding beauty. Getting to them, however, can be a problem: this portion of the island has barely been touched by the developers, so the coast is often poorly signposted and the access roads are of very variable quality – some are just dirt tracks. These access roads branch off from the narrow, asphalted country lanes which crisscross the lovely pastoral hinterland. One excellent beach to head for is **Cala Pregonda**, though it's a bit of a hike. Public transport around here is, as you might expect, nonexistent, and the nearest car rental is back in Maó (see above).

As regards **food**, Fornells boasts several fine waterfront **restaurants** to either side of the minuscule main square, Plaça S'Algaret. Such is their reputation that King Juan Carlos regularly drops by on his yacht, and many people phone up days in advance with their orders. The royal favourite is the harbourside *Es Pla* (℡971 376 655), which offers a superb paella for two for €60, as well as the traditional lobster stew for €70. More relaxed alternatives include *Sibaris*, Plaça S'Algaret 1 (℡971 376 619), which concentrates on a magnificent *caldereta de llagosta* (€42) – as does the *Es Port*, nearby at c/Riera 5 (℡971 376 403), where it goes for €54. As a general rule, reckon on about €15–20 for a seafood main course, three times that for paella or lobster stew.

Fornells has three reasonably priced, comfortable **hostales**. The two-star *S'Algaret*, Plaça S'Algaret 7, is a neat little place, with a pool and plain but cheerful rooms (May–Oct; ☎971 376 674, ℗971 376 666; ❹); the nearby *Hostal Residencia La Palma*, Plaça S'Algaret 3 (April–Oct; ☎971 376 634; ❹), is similar, though more quaintly decorated. The *Hostal Fornells*, c/Major 17 (☎971 376 676, ℮fornells@chi.es; ❺), is a slightly smarter, sprucely modern three-star with a particularly nice swimming pool.

Across the island

The road from Maó to Ciutadella, the **C721**, forms the backbone of Menorca, and what little industry the island enjoys – a few shoe factories and places making the island's famous cheeses – is concentrated along it.

Alaior

Just 4km out of Maó, you pass the short and clearly signposted country lane leading to **Talatí de Dalt**, another illuminating Talayotic remnant. Much larger than Trepucó, the site is enclosed by a Cyclopean wall and features an imposing *taula*, which is adjacent to the heaped stones of the main *talayot*. All around are the scant remains of prehistoric dwellings. The exact functions of these are not known, but there's no doubt that the *taula* was the village centrepiece, and probably the focus of religious ceremonies. The rustic setting is charming – olive and carob trees abound and a tribe of boar roots around the undergrowth.

Cheese is a good reason to stop at **ALAIOR**, 12km from Maó, an old market town which has long been the nucleus of the island's dairy industry. There are two major companies, both of which have factory shops near to – and clearly signposted from – the old main road as it cuts across the southern periphery of the town centre: come off the new bypass at the most easterly of the three Alaior exits and follow the signs. Approaching from Maó, the first shop is owned by **La Payesa** (Mon–Fri 9am–1pm & 4–7pm), while the second is the bigger and better outlet of **COINGA** (Mon–Fri 9am–1pm & 5–8pm). Both companies sell a similar product, known generically as *queso Mahon*, after the port from which it was traditionally exported. It's a richly textured, white, semi-fat cheese made from pasteurized cow's milk with a touch of ewe's milk added for extra flavour. The cheese is sold at four different stages of maturity, either *tierno* (young), *semi-curado* (semi-mature), *curado* (mature) or *añejo* (very mature). Both shops have the full range and, although quite expensive, their prices are the best you'll see.

On the hill above the cheese shops, the old centre of Alaior is a tangle of narrow streets and bright white houses set beneath the imposing church of **Santa Eulàlia**. Apart, however, from a quick gambol up and down the hill, there's not much reason to hang around – unless you happen to be here the second weekend of August when Alaior lets loose during the **Festa de Sant Llorenç**.

Es Mercadal and Monte Toro

Nine kilometres northwest of Alaior, **ES MERCADAL** squats amongst the hills at the very centre of the island. Another old market town, it's an amiable little place of whitewashed houses and trim allotments whose antique centre straddles a quaint watercourse. The town also boasts a top-notch **restaurant**, the *Can*

Aguedet, at c/Lepanto 30 (☎971 375 391), which serves up traditional Menorcan cuisine, and a simple, one-star **hostal residencia**, the spick-and-span *Jeni*, in a modern building at c/Miranda del Toro 81 (☎971 375 059, ⓦwww .hotel-jeni.de; ❸). To get there, leave the main square – Sa Plaça – along c/Nou and take the first left and then the first right. **Buses** from Maó and Ciutadella stop just off the C721 on Avinguda Metge Camps, which leads on to c/Nou.

From Es Mercadal you can set off on the ascent of **Monte Toro**, a steep 3.2-kilometre climb along a serpentine road. At 357m, the summit is the island's highest point and offers wonderful vistas: on a good day you can see almost the whole island, on a bad one you still see to Fornells, at least. From this lofty vantage point, Menorca's geological division becomes apparent: to the north, Devonian rock (mostly reddish sandstone) supports a rolling, sparsely populated landscape edged by a ragged coastline; to the south, limestone predominates in a rippling plain that boasts both the island's best farmland and, as it approaches the south coast, its deepest valleys.

Monte Toro has been a place of pilgrimage since medieval times, and the Augustinians plonked a monastery on the summit in the seventeenth century. Bits of the original construction survive in the **convent**, which shares the site today with an army outpost and a monumentally ugly statue of Christ. Much of the convent is out of bounds, but the public part, approached across a handsome courtyard, encompasses a couple of gift shops, a delightful terrace café and a cosy church.

Ferreries

The next town along the C721 is **FERRERIES**, an appealing little place, no more than a village really. There's little to detain you here, though one definite plus is the *Vimpi* bar on the plaza at the entrance to town, which serves some of the tastiest tapas on the island. Heading on from Ferreries, you'll find one of the best examples of a *naveta* – the **Naveta d'es Tudons** – beside the main road some 6km short of Ciutadella. Seven metres high and fourteen long, the structure is made of massive stone blocks slotted together in a sophisticated dry-stone technique. The narrow entrance leads into a small antechamber, which was once sealed off by a stone slab; beyond lies the main chamber where the bones of the dead were stashed away after the flesh had been removed. Folkloric memories of the *navetas*' original purpose survived into modern times, for the Menorcans were loathe to go near these odd-looking and solitary monuments well into the eighteenth century.

Ciutadella and around

Like Maó, **CIUTADELLA** sits high above its harbour, though navigation is far more difficult here, up a narrow channel too slender for any but the smallest of cargo ships. Despite this nautical inconvenience, Ciutadella has been the island's capital for most of its history. The Romans chose it, the Moors adopted it as *Medina Minurka*, and the Catalans of *La Reconquista* flattened the place and began all over again. In 1558, the Catalan-built town was, in its turn, razed by Turkish corsairs. Several thousand captives were carted off to the slave markets of Istanbul, but the survivors determinedly rebuilt Ciutadella in grand style, its compact, fortified centre brimming with the mansions of the rich. To the colonial powers of the eighteenth century, however, Ciutadella's feeble port had no appeal when compared with Maó's magnificent inlet. In 1722 the

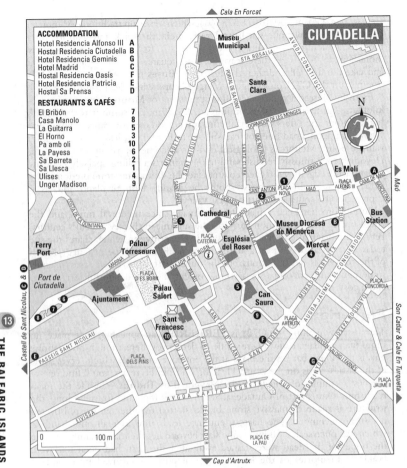

British moved the capital to Maó, which has flourished as a trading centre ever since, and Ciutadella stagnated – a long-lasting economic hiatus that has, fortunately, preserved its old and beautiful centre as if in aspic. The bulk of the Menorcan aristocracy remained in Ciutadella, where the colonial powers pretty much left them to stew – an increasingly redundant, landowning class far from the wheels of mercantile power. Consequently, there's very little British or French influence in Ciutadella's **architecture**; instead, the narrow, cobbled streets boast fine old palaces, hidden away behind high walls, and a set of Baroque and Gothic churches very much in the Spanish tradition.

Essentially, it's the whole architectural ensemble that gives Ciutadella its appeal rather than any specific sight, and that, together with some excellent restaurants and an adequate supply of *hostales* and hotels, makes this a lovely place to stay. Allow at least a couple of days, more if you seek out one of the beguiling cove beaches within easy striking distance of town: **Cala en Turqueta** is the pick of the bunch.

Arrival and information

Ciutadella's compact centre could hardly be more convenient. **Buses** from Maó and points east arrive at the station on c/Barcelona, just south off the end of the Camí de Maó, an extension of the main island highway, the C721. **Local buses** shuttle up and down the west coast from Plaça dels Pins, on the west side of the town centre next to the main square, Plaça d'es Born. **Catamarans** from Cala Rajada and **car ferries** from Port d'Alcúdia, both on Mallorca, dock in the harbour below the Plaça d'es Born.

The **turisme** (Mon–Fri 9.30am–8.30pm, Sat 9am–1pm, Sun 5–8pm; ☎971 382 693) has buckets of information on Menorca as a whole and Ciutadella in particular. It's opposite the cathedral on Plaça Catedral, bang in the middle of the old town.

Accommodation

There's hardly a plethora of **accommodation** in Ciutadella, but the town does have two quality hotels that aren't booked up by package-tour operators and a handful of fairly comfortable and reasonably priced *hostales* dotted in and around the centre, with a concentration in the vicinity of Plaça Alfons III and Plaça Artrutx.

Hotel Residencia Alfonso III Camí de Maó 53 ☎971 380 150, ✉halfonso@supersonik.com. Brashly modern but fairly well-maintained hotel with fifty simple one-star rooms. Located beside the main road from Maó, a couple of minutes' walk from the ring road; try to get a room at the back away from the noisy road. Breakfast included. ❸

Hostal Residencia Ciutadella c/Sant Eloi 10 ☎ & ☎971 383 462. Unassuming yet comfortable two-star, in an old terraced house down a narrow side street off Plaça Alfons III. Breakfast included. ❸

Hotel Residencia Geminis c/Josepa Rossinyol 4 ☎971 384 644, ☎971 383 683. Well-tended, central and comfortable one-star with comfortable rooms decorated in bright modern style. Closed Jan. ❹

Hotel Madrid c/Madrid 60 ☎971 380 328, ☎971 482 158. Fourteen quite comfortable rooms in a villa-style building with its own ground-floor café-bar. Located near the sea a 15min walk west of the town centre, halfway along c/Madrid: follow Passeig Sant Nicolau from the Plaça dels Pins, take the third turning on the left (c/Saragossa) and

you'll hit c/Madrid just east of the hotel at the first major intersection. ❸

Hostal Residencia Oasis c/Sant Isidre 33, footsteps away from Plaça Artrutx ☎971 382 197. Attractive one-star with nine simple rooms set around a courtyard-restaurant. Breakfast included. ❷

Hotel Residencia Patricia Passeig Sant Nicolau 90 ☎971 385 511, ⊛www.hoteles-hesperia.es. The best hotel in town, popular with business folk and handy for the centre. The extremely comfortable, ultramodern rooms come with all facilities, the only down point being the lack of a sea view – though the best rooms have rooftop balconies with panoramic vistas. ❺

Hostal Sa Prensa Plaça Madrid s/n ☎971 382 698. Villa-like, one-star *hostal* with six spartan rooms above a café-bar. It's a 15min walk west of the centre, close to the rocky seashore at the end of c/Madrid. To get there, follow Passeig Sant Nicolau from the Plaça dels Pins, take the fifth turning on the left (c/Joan Ramis i Ramis) and you'll hit c/Madrid just beside the *hostal*. ❸

The Town

Ciutadella's compact centre crowds around the fortified cliff face shadowing the south side of the harbour. The main *plazas* and points of interest are within a few strides of each other, on and around the main square, **Plaça d'es Born**, in the middle of which is a soaring **obelisk** commemorating the futile defence against the Turks in 1558. On the western side of the square stands the **ajuntament**, whose nineteenth-century arches and crenellations mimic Moorish style, purposely recalling the time when the site was occupied by the wali's Alcázar (palace). In the square's northeast corner, the massive **Palau**

Torresaura, built in the nineteenth century but looking far older, is the grandest of several aristocratic mansions edging the plaza. Embellished by self-important loggias, its frontage proclaims the family coat of arms above a large wooden door giving onto an expansive courtyard. The antique interior, however, is off limits, as the house is still owner-occupied – like most of its neighbours.

From Palau Torresaura, c/Major d'es Born leads to the **Cathedral** (Mon–Sat 8am–1pm & 6.30–9pm; free), built by Alfonso III at the end of the thirteenth century on the site of the town's chief mosque. Constructed soon after the Reconquest, its construction is fortress-like, with windows set high above the ground – though the effect is somewhat disturbed by the flashy columns of the Neoclassical west doorway, the principal entrance. Inside, light from the narrow, lofty windows bathes the high altar in an ethereal glow, the hallmark of the Gothic style. There's also a wonderfully kitschy, pointed altar arch, and a sequence of glitzily Baroque side chapels.

Cutting down c/Roser from the cathedral, you'll pass the tiny **Església del Roser**, whose striking Churrigueresque facade, dating from the seventeenth century, boasts a quartet of pillars engulfed by intricate tracery. The church was the subject of bitter controversy when the British commandeered it for Church of England services – not at all to the liking of the Dominican friars who owned the place. At the end of c/Roser, turn left past the palatial, seventeenth-century mansion of **Can Saura**, which is distinguished by its elegant stonework, and then left again for c/Seminari and the **Museu Diocesà de Menorca** (Tues–Sat 10.30am–1.30pm; €2), housed in an old and dignified convent. Inside, the convent buildings surround an immaculately preserved Baroque cloister, whose vaulted aisles sport coats of arms and religious motifs. The museum's collection is distributed chronologically; the first three rooms hold the most interesting pieces – a hotchpotch of Talayotic and early Classical archeological finds, notably a superbly crafted, miniature bull and a similarly exquisite little mermaid, both Greek bronzes dating from the fifth century BC.

Behind the museum lies the **mercat** (market), on Plaça Llibertat, another delightful corner of the old town, where fresh fruit, vegetable and fish stalls mingle with lively and inexpensive cafés selling the freshest of *ensaimadas*. Alternatively, c/Seminari proceeds north to intersect with the narrow, pedestrianized main street that runs through the old town – here **c/J.M. Quadrado**, though it goes under various names along its route. To the east of this intersection is a parade of whitewashed, vaulted arches, **Ses Voltes**, distinctly Moorish in inspiration and a suitable setting for several attractive shops and busy cafés. Carrer J.M. Quadrado then leads into **Plaça Nova**, a minuscule square edged by some of the most popular pavement cafés in town. Continuing east along c/Maó, you leave the cramped alleys of the old town at Plaça Alfons III.

Retracing your steps along c/J. M. Quadrado, turn north down c/Santa Clara for the five-minute walk to the **Museu Municipal** (Tues–Sat 10am–2pm; €2), inhabiting part of the old city fortifications at the end of c/Portal de Sa Font. Inside the museum, a long vaulted chamber is given over to a wide range of archeological finds, amongst which there's a substantial collection of Talayotic remains, featuring artefacts garnered from all over the island and covering the several phases of Talayotic civilization. A leaflet detailing the exhibits in English is available free at reception.

Eating and drinking

For an early **breakfast** make your way to the market on Plaça Llibertat, where a couple of simple cafés serve coffee and fresh pastries. Later in the day, round **lunchtime**, aim for c/J. M. Quadrado, Plaça Nova and Plaça Alfons III, which together hold a good selection of inexpensive café-bars, offering tapas and light meals. In the **evening**, more ambitious and expensive food is available at a string of excellent restaurants down by the harbourside, or at a couple of good places tucked away near Plaça d'es Born. Almost all the harbourside places have the advantage of an outside terrace, but note that – unlike those restaurants near the Plaça d'es Born – they usually close down in winter.

Cafés and café-bars

Pa amb oli c/Nou de Julio 4. Kitted out in vaguely rustic style, this excellent café-bar specializes in all things *menorquín*, with bowls of peppers and olives liberally distributed along the counter and smoked sausages hanging from the ceiling. The food is filling, delicious and traditional – and inexpensive, too. Just off Plaça d'es Born. Highly recommended.

Sa Barreta c/J. M. Quadrado 16. In the vaulted arches – Ses Voltes – bang in the middle of the old town, this unassuming family-run café is great for fresh *pa amb oli* and other traditional Menorcan snacks – sausage and so forth.

Sa Llesca Plaça Nova 4. One of several pleasant, and largely indistinguishable, café-bars on this tiny square. The ground-floor terrace café is one of the more popular spots in the old town and there's a first-floor dining room inside, too.

Ulises Plaça Llibertat. Next to the market, this amenable, low-key café-bar is a locals' favourite. Their *ensaimadas* are probably the best in town, and a snip at €1.20.

Unger Madison c/Sant Joan 8, near Plaça Artrutx. The most chic bar in town, with angular wooden tables, soft lighting, modern paintings and a first-rate selection of domestic and imported wines. Open Mon–Fri from 6pm till early in the morning, Sat from 8pm; closed Sun.

Restaurants

El Bribón c/Marina 107 ☎971 385 050. Superb harbourside restaurant specializing in seafood, often prepared in traditional Menorcan style. Reckon on around €13 for the *menú del día*, €12–15 for a main course. Next door to *Casa Manolo*.

Casa Manolo c/Marina 117 ☎971 380 003. Fabulous seafood, with main courses averaging around €15. At the end of the long line of restaurants flanking the south side of the harbour.

La Guitarra c/Dolors 1 ☎971 381 355. Arguably the best restaurant in town, this superb spot features the very best of Menorcan cuisine with main courses – anything from seafood to lamb – averaging a very reasonable €9. The restaurant occupies an old cellar, whose stone walls sport a scattering of agricultural antiques. It's located a short walk from the cathedral. Open Mon–Sat 12.30–3.30pm & 7.30–11pm; closed Sun. Highly recommended.

El Horno c/Forn 12 ☎971 380 767. French-style basement restaurant, with good and reasonably priced food. Near the northeast corner of Plaça d'es Born. Evenings only.

La Payesa c/Marina 65 ☎971 380 021. Popular tourist restaurant with a wide-ranging menu, featuring everything from pizzas through omelettes to seafood. Very child-friendly.

Listings

Banks Banca March, Plaça d'es Born 10 and Plaça Alfons III 5; Sa Nostra, c/Maó 2, on Plaça Nova.

Bicycle and moped rental Bicicletas Salord, c/Sant Isidre 32, off Plaça Artrutx ☎971 381 576.

Car rental Ciutadella has half a dozen car rental companies including Betacar, on the ring road at Avgda Jaume I El Conqueridor 59 (☎971 382 998), and Avis c/Sabaters 1, Poligono Industrial (☎971 381 174).

Catamarans and ferries Two ferry companies link Ciutadella and Mallorca. The first, Cape Balear de Cruceros (☎902 100 444, ⓦwww.capebalear.com), operates a passenger-only catamaran service from Cala Rajada twice daily (75min; €90 return, €45 single). The second is Iscomar (☎902 119 128, ⓦwww.iscomar.com), whose car ferries run from Port d'Alcúdia once or twice daily in two and a half hours. The single fare is €31 and vehicles up to 4.5m in length cost an additional €51. Remember, however, that car hire firms on the Balearics do not allow their vehicles off their home island. In Ciutadella, the tourist office has information on sailings – as does

Menorca's daily newspaper, the *Menorca – Diario Insular*. Both ferry companies have a kiosk down on the harbourside, but these are only open around departure times. You can buy tickets at the kiosk, or (if they aren't open) on the boat.

Internet access Café Internet, Plaça dels Pins 37 (€1.20/hr).

Emergencies General emergency number (fire, police and ambulance) ☎ 112. Local police ☎ 092.

Maps and books Both Punt i Apart, c/Roser 14, and Libreria Pau, c/Nou de Juliol 23, have a rea-sonably good selection of travel books, general maps and Menorcan walking maps from the IGN series.

Post office The main *correu* is handily located at Plaça d'es Born 8 (Mon–Fri 8.30am–2.30pm, Sat 9.30am–1pm).

Taxis There are taxi ranks on Plaça dels Pins and Avgda Constitució, round the corner from Plaça Alfons III. Fares between any two towns on the island are fixed by law at about €1 per kilometre.

Southeast of Ciutadella: Cala en Turqueta

Beginning at the traffic island on c/Alfons V, the cross-country **Camí de Sant Joan de Missa** runs southeast from Ciutadella to the remote coves of the south coast. The one to head for is **Cala en Turqueta**, a lovely cove flanked by wooded limestone cliffs. About 3km from town, you reach the clearly marked farmhouse of **Son Vivó**, where the road branches into two with the more easterly (signposted) road leading to the **Ermita de St Joan de Missa**, a squat, brightly whitewashed church with a dinky little bell tower. There's a fork here too, but the signs are easy to follow and you keep straight with the road slicing across the countryside before swerving round the **Marjal Vella farmhouse**. Shortly afterwards, about 4.3km from the church, you reach the start of the one-kilometre-long, private lane that leads down to the little dell behind **Cala en Turqueta**. The beach, a sheltered horseshoe of white sand, slopes gently into the sea and is ideal for swimming – and because there are no facilities it's most unusual to find a crowd. Admission costs €5 per person.

Travel details

Ibiza

Buses

Ibiza Town to: Figueretes (every 30min; 5min); Platja d'en Bossa (every 30min; 10min); airport (hourly, 20min); Portinatx (2–3 daily; 45min); Sant Antoni (every 15–30min; 30min); Ses Salines (hourly; 20min); Santa Eulària des Riu (hourly; 25min); Sant Joan (2–6 daily; 35min); Sant Miquel (2–4 daily; 30min); Sant Josep (5 daily, 20min).

Boats

Ibiza Town to: Es Canar (7 daily; 1hr 10min); Platja d'en Bossa (6 daily; 20min); Santa Eulària des Riu (7 daily; 50min), Talamanca (every 20min, 10min).

Mallorca

Buses

Palma to: Alcúdia (May–Oct Mon–Sat hourly, 5 on Sun; Nov–April 3–5 daily; 1hr); Andratx (hourly; 45min); Artà (Mon–Sat 4 daily, 1 on Sun; 1hr 25min); Coves del Drac (May–Oct Mon–Sat 4 daily, 2 on Sun; Nov–April 1 daily; 1hr); Deià (Mon–Fri 5 daily, 2 on Sat & Sun; 45min); Platja de Formentor (May–Oct Mon–Sat 1 daily; 1hr 15min); Pollença (Mon–Sat 8 daily, 2 on Sun; 1hr); Port d'Alcúdia (May–Oct Mon–Sat hourly, 5 on Sun; Nov–April Mon–Sat 3–5 daily; 1hr 10min); Port de Pollença (Mon–Sat 8 daily, 2 on Sun; 1hr 10min); Port de Sóller (via the tunnel: Mon–Fri 14 daily, 3 on Sat & Sun, 35min; via Valldemossa: 5 daily; 55min); Sóller (via the tunnel: Mon–Fri hourly, 6 on Sat, 3 on Sun; 30min; via Valldemossa: Mon–Fri 5 daily, 2 on Sat & Sun; 50min); Valldemossa (Mon–Fri 5 daily, 2 on Sat & Sun; 30min).

Port d'Alcúdia to: Alcúdia (May–Oct every 15min; Nov–April 11 daily; 5min); Cala Rajada (May–Oct Mon–Sat 2 daily; 40min); Ca'n Picafort (May–Oct every 15min; Nov–April 11 daily; 20min); Lluc (May–Oct Mon–Sat 2 daily; 1hr 15min); Palma (May–Oct Mon–Sat hourly, 5 on Sun; Nov–April 3–5 daily; 1hr 10min); Platja de Formentor (May–Oct 2 daily; 25min); Pollença (May–Oct every 15min, Nov–April 11 daily; 20min); Port de

Pollença (May–Oct every 15min; Nov–April 11 daily; 20min); Port de Sóller (May–Oct Mon–Sat 2 daily; 2hr).

Port de Pollença to: Alcúdia (May–Oct every 15min; Nov–April 11 daily; 20min); Ca'n Picafort (May–Oct every 15min; Nov–April 11 daily; 1hr); Palma (3–5 daily; 1hr 10min); Platja de Formentor (May–Oct 2 daily; 20min); Pollença (14–20 daily; 10min); Port d'Alcúdia (May–Oct every 15min; Nov–April 11 daily; 20min); Port de Sóller (May–Oct Mon–Sat 2 daily; 1hr 50min); Sóller (May–Oct Mon–Sat 2 daily; 2hr).

Port de Sóller to: Deià (2–5 daily; 20min); Palma (via the tunnel: Mon–Fri 14 daily, 3 on Sat, 2 on Sun, 35min; via Valldemossa: 5 daily, 55min); Pollença (May–Oct Mon–Sat 2 daily; 1hr 45min); Port d'Alcúdia (May–Oct Mon–Sat 2 daily; 2hr); Port de Pollença (May–Oct Mon–Sat 2 daily; 1hr 50min); Sóller (5 daily; 5min); Valldemossa (5 daily; 30min).

Porto Cristo to: Ca'n Picafort (May–Oct Mon–Sat 3 daily; 1hr); Port d'Alcúdia (May–Oct Mon–Sat 3 daily; 1hr).

Valldemossa to: Andratx (Mon–Sat 1 daily; 1hr); Deià (5 daily; 15min); Palma (5 daily; 30min).

Menorca

Buses

Ciutadella to: Alaior (6–7 daily; 40min); Es Mercadal (6–7 daily; 30min); Ferreries (6–7 daily; 20min); Maó (6–7 daily; 1hr).

Ferreries to: Alaior (6–7 daily; 20min); Ciutadella (6–7 daily; 20min); Es Mercadal (6–7 daily; 10min); Maó (6–7 daily; 40min).

Fornells to: Es Mercadal (May–Oct 1–2 daily except on Sun; Nov–April 4 weekly; 15min); Maó (May–Oct 5 daily except on Sun; Nov–April 4 weekly; 35min).

Maó to: Alaior (Mon–Sat 12 daily, 6 on Sun; 20min); Ciutadella (6–7 daily; 1hr); Es Mercadal (6–7 daily; 30min); Ferreries (6–7 daily; 40min); Fornells (May–Oct 5 daily except on Sun; Nov–April 4 weekly; 35min).

Inter-island flights, ferries and hydrofoils

Flights are operated by Iberia (℡902 400 500, Ⓦwww.iberia.com) and Air Europa (℡902 401 501, Ⓦwww.aireuropa.com). Inter-island ferries and hydrofoils are operated by Trasmediterránea (℡902 454 645, Ⓦwww.trasmediterranea.es), Baleària (℡902 191 068, Ⓦwww.balearia.com), Iscomar (℡902 119 128, Ⓦwww.iscomar.com), and Cape Balear (℡902 100 444, Ⓦwww.capebalear.com).

Formentera to: Ibiza (10 ferries daily in summer, 5 in winter; 1hr; 15 passenger-only hydrofoils daily in summer, 7 daily in winter; 35min).

Ibiza to: Palma (11 daily flights; 30min; 2 daily ferries; 5hr; and 2 daily summer-only hydrofoils; 2hr 30min).

Palma to: Maó (8 flights daily, 30min; 1–2 Trasmediterránea car ferries weekly, 6hr).

Cala Rajada to: Ciutadella (2 Cape Balear catamarans daily; 1hr 15min).

Port d'Alcúdia to: Ciutadella (1–2 Iscomar car ferries daily; 2hr 30min).

Car ferries from the mainland

Car ferries to the Balearics from the Spanish mainland are operated by Trasmediterránea (℡902 454 645, Ⓦwww.trasmediterranea.es), Balearia (℡902 160 180, Ⓦwww.balearia.com) and Iscomar (℡902 119 128, Ⓦwww.iscomar.com).

Barcelona to: Ibiza (2–5 weekly with Trasmediterránea; 9hr); Maó (3–8 weekly with Trasmediterránea; 10hr); Palma (1 daily with Trasmediterránea; 8hr).

Dénia to: Ibiza (6 weekly; 4hr 30min); Palma via Sant Antoni with Balearia (1 daily; 7hr).

Valencia to: Ibiza (daily in summer, 2 weekly in winter; 8hr); Maó with Trasmediterránea (1 weekly; 12hr); Palma with Trasmediterránea (6 weekly; 9hr); Palma with Balearia (1 daily; 8hr).

Catamarans from the mainland

Catamaran services to the Balearics from the Spanish mainland are operated by Trasmediterránea (℡902 454 645, Ⓦwww.trasmediterranea.es) and Balearia (℡902 160 180, Ⓦwww.balearia.net).

Barcelona to: Palma with Trasmediterránea (mid-June to mid-Sept 2 daily; 4hr 30min).

Valencia to: Ibiza with Trasmediterránea (mid-June to mid-Sept 1 daily; 2hr 45min); Palma with Trasmediterránea (mid-June to mid-Sept 1 daily; 6hr 15min).

Contexts

Contexts

History

The first Europeans of whom we have knowledge lived in southern Spain. A recent series of spectacular discoveries at **Orce**, seventy miles east of Granada, rocked the archeological world as the date for the **arrival of early humans in Europe** was pushed back from c.700,000 years ago to perhaps a million years before this, making Orce – if the findings are scientifically confirmed – the earliest known site of human occupation in Europe by a long way. Other finds of early human remains around 800,000 years old in the Sierra de Atapuerca to the east of Burgos are further confirmation of early activity on the peninsula. Evidence of occupation by Stone Age societies stretching back some 400,000 years was already known about from discoveries at Venta Micena, close to Orce, where early inhabitants hunted elephant and rhino and left behind tools and camp fires. Some of the earliest **human fossils** found on the Iberian Peninsula were unearthed inside the **Gibraltar** caves with evidence of **Neanderthals** dating from around 100,000 BC. In the Paleolithic period, the first **homo sapiens** arrived on the Iberian peninsula from southern France, settling around the Bay of Biscay as well as in the south. They were cave dwellers and hunter-gatherers and at **Altamira** in the Cantabrian mountains near Santander and the Pileta and Nerja caves near Málaga have left behind remarkable **cave paintings** and deftly stylized cave murals depicting the animals that they hunted. The finest examples (created about 12,000 BC) are at Altamira – now closed for general visits, though you can see similar paintings at Puente Viesgo nearby. During the later Neolithic phase, a sophisticated material culture developed in southern Spain attested to by the finds of esparto sandals and baskets as well as jewellery in the **Cueva de los Murcilélagos** in Granada. This period also saw the construction of **megalithic tombs** (dolmens) along the perimeter of the Iberian peninsula such as the superbly preserved examples at Romanya de la Selva in Catalunya and **Antequera**, near Málaga.

Subsequent prehistory is more complex and confused. There does not appear to have been any great development in the cave cultures of the north. Instead the focus shifts south to Almería, which was settled around 5000–4000 BC by the "Iberians", **Neolithic** colonists from North Africa. They had already assimilated into their culture many of the changes that had developed in Egypt and the Near East. Settling in villages, they introduced pastoral and agricultural ways of life and exploited the plentiful supply of copper. Around 1500 BC, with the onset of the **Bronze Age**, they began to spread outwards into fortified villages on the central Meseta, the high plateau of modern Castile. At the turn of the millennium they were joined by numerous waves of **Celtic** and **Germanic** peoples. Here, Spain's divisive physical make-up – with its network of mountain ranges – determined its social nature. The incoming tribes formed distinct and isolated groups, conquering and sometimes absorbing each other but only on a very limited and local scale. Hence the Celtic "urnfield people" established themselves in Catalunya, the **Vascones** in the Basque country and, near them along the Atlantic coast, the **Astures**. Pockets of earlier cultures survived, too, particularly in Galicia with its *citanias* of beehive huts.

First colonies

The Spanish coast meanwhile attracted colonists from different regions of the Mediterranean. The **Phoenicians** founded the port of Gadir (Cádiz) around 1100 BC and traded intensively in the metals of the Guadalquivir valley. Their wealth and success gave rise to a Spanish "Atlantis" myth, based on the lost kingdom of Tartessus, mentioned in the Bible and probably sited near Huelva; the sophisticated jewellery it produced is on display in Sevilla's archeological museum. Market rivalry later brought the **Greeks**, who established their trading colonies along the eastern coast – the modern Costa Brava. There's a fine surviving site at Empúries, near Barcelona.

More significant, however, was the arrival of the **Carthaginians** in the third century BC. Expelled from Sicily by the Romans, they saw in Spain a new base for their empire, from which to regain strength and strike back at their rivals. Although making little impact inland, they occupied most of Andalucía and expanded along the Mediterranean seaboard to establish a new capital at Cartagena. Under Hannibal they prepared to invade Italy and in 219 BC attacked Saguntum, a strategic outpost of the Roman Empire. It was a disastrous move, precipitating the **Second Punic War**; by 210 BC only Cádiz remained in their control and they were forced to accept terms. A new and very different age had begun.

Romans and Visigoths

The **Roman colonization** of the peninsula was far more intense than anything previously experienced and met with great resistance from the Celtiberian tribes of the north and centre. It was almost two centuries before the conquest was complete and indeed the Basques, although defeated, were never fully Romanized.

Nonetheless, Spain became the most important centre of the Roman Empire after Italy itself, producing no fewer than three emperors, along with the writers Seneca, Lucan, Martial and Quintilian. Again, geography dictated an uneven spread of influence, at its strongest in Andalucía, southern Portugal and on the Catalan coast around Tarragona. In the first two centuries AD the Spanish mines and the granaries of Andalucía brought unprecedented wealth and Roman Spain enjoyed a brief "**Golden Age**". The finest monuments were built in the great provincial capitals – Córdoba, Mérida (which boasts the most impressive remains) and Tarragona – but across the country more practical construction was undertaken: roads, bridges and aqueducts. Many were still used well into recent centuries – perhaps the most remarkable being the aqueducts of Segovia and Tarragona – and quite a few bridges remain in use even today.

Towards the third century, however, the Roman political framework began to show signs of decadence and corruption. Although it didn't totally collapse until the Muslim invasions of the early eighth century, it became increasingly vulnerable to **barbarian invasions** from northern Europe. The Franks and the Suevi (Swabians) swept across the Pyrenees between 264 and 276, leaving devastation in their wake. They were followed two centuries later by further waves of Suevi, Alans and Vandals. Internal strife was heightened by the arrival of the **Visigoths** from Gaul, allies of Rome and already Romanized to a large degree. The triumph of Visigothic strength in the fifth century resulted in a period of spurious unity, based upon an exclusive military rule from their capital at Toledo, but their numbers were never great and their order was often fragmentary and nominal, with the bulk of the subject people kept in a state of disconsolate servility, and the military elite divided by constant plots and factions – exacerbated by the Visigothic system of elected monarchy and by their adherence to the heretical Arian philosophy. In 589 **King Recared** converted to Catholicism but religious strife was only multiplied: forced conversions, especially within the Jewish enclaves, maintained a constant simmering of discontent.

Moorish Spain

In contrast to the long-drawn-out Roman campaigns, **Moorish conquest** of the peninsula was effected with extraordinary speed. This was a characteristic phenomenon of the spread of Islam – Muhammad left Mecca in 622 and by 705 his followers had established control over all of North Africa. Spain, with its political instability, its wealth and its fertile climate, was an inevitable extension of their aims. In 711 Tariq, governor of Tangier, led a force of 7000 Berbers across the straits and routed the Visigoth army of King Roderic; two years later the Visigoths made a last desperate stand at Mérida and within a decade the Moors had conquered all but the wild mountains of Asturias. The land under their authority was dubbed "**al-Andalus**", a fluid term which expanded and shrunk with the intermittent gains and losses of the Reconquest. According to region, the Moors were to remain in control for the next three to eight centuries.

It was not simply a military conquest. The Moors (a collective term for the numerous waves of Arab and Berber settlers from North Africa) were often content to grant a limited autonomy in exchange for payment of tribute; their administrative system was tolerant and easily absorbed both Jews and Christians, those who retained their religion being known as "Mozarabs". And al-Andalus was a distinctly Spanish state of Islam. Though at first politically subject to the Eastern Caliphate (or empire) of Baghdad, it was soon virtually independent. In the tenth century, at the peak of its power and expansion, Abd ar-Rahman III asserted total independence, proclaiming himself caliph of a new **Western Islamic Empire**. Its capital was Córdoba – the largest, most prosperous and most civilized city in Europe. This was the great age of Muslim Spain: its scholarship, philosophy, architecture and craftsmanship were without rival and there was an unparalleled growth in urban life, in trade, and in agriculture aided by magnificent irrigation projects. These and other engineering feats were not, on the whole, instigated by the Moors, who instead took basic Roman models and adapted them to a new level of sophistication. In **architecture** and the **decorative arts**, however, their contribution was original and unique – as may be seen in the fabulous monuments of Sevilla, Córdoba and Granada.

The Córdoban caliphate for a while created a remarkable degree of unity. But its rulers were to become decadent and out of touch, prompting the brilliant but dictatorial **al-Mansur** to usurp control. Under this extraordinary ruler Moorish power actually reached new heights, pushing the Christian kingdom of Asturias-León back into the Cantabrian mountains and sacking its most holy shrine, Santiago de Compostela. However, after his death the caliphate quickly lost its authority and in 1031 disintegrated into a series of small independent kingdoms or *taifas*, the strongest of which was Sevilla.

Internal divisions amongst the *taifas* weakened their resistance to the

Christian kingdoms which were rallying in the north, and twice North Africa had to be turned to for reinforcement. This resulted in two distinct new waves of Moorish invasion – first by the fanatically Islamic **Almoravids** (1086) and later by the **Almohads** (1147), who restored effective Muslim authority until their defeat at the battle of Las Navas de Tolosa in 1212.

The Christian Reconquest

The **reconquest** of land and influence from the Moors was a slow and intermittent process. It began with a symbolic victory by a small force of Christians at Covadonga in the Asturias (727) and was not completed until 1492 with the conquest of Granada by Fernando and Isabel.

Covadonga resulted in the formation of the tiny Christian **Kingdom of the Asturias**. Initially just 65 by 50km in area, it had by 914 reclaimed León and most of Galicia and northern Portugal. At this point, progress was temporarily halted by the devastating campaigns of al-Mansur. However, with the fall of the Córdoban caliphate and the divine aid of Spain's Moor-slaying patron, St James the Apostle (see "Santiago de Compostela"), the Reconquest moved into a new and powerful phase.

The frontier castles built against Arab attack gave name to **Castile**, founded in the tenth century as a county of León-Asturias. Under Fernando I (1037–65) it achieved the status of a kingdom and became the main thrust and focus of the Reconquest. Other kingdoms were being defined in the north at the same time: the Basques founded Navarra (Navarre), while dynastic marriage merged Catalunya with Aragón. In 1085 this period of confident Christian expansion reached its zenith with the capture of the great Moorish city of Toledo. The following year, however, the Almoravids arrived on invitation from Sevilla, and military activity was effectively frozen – except, that is, for the exploits of the legendary **El Cid**, a Castilian nobleman who won considerable lands around Valencia in 1095.

The next concerted phase of the Reconquest really began as a response to the threat imposed by the Almohads. The kings of León, Castile, Aragón and Navarra united in a general crusade which resulted in the great victory at **Las Navas de Tolosa** (1212). Thereafter Muslim power was effectively paralyzed and the Christian armies moved on to take most of al-Andalus. Fernando III ("El Santo", the saint) led Castilian soldiers into Córdoba in 1236 and twelve years later into Sevilla. Meanwhile, the kingdom of Portugal had expanded to more or less its present size, while Jaime I of Aragón was to conquer Valencia, Alicante, Murcia and the Balearic Islands. By the end of the thirteenth century only the kingdom of Granada remained under Muslim authority and for much of the following two centuries it was forced to pay tribute to the monarchs of Castile.

Two factors should be stressed regarding the Reconquest. First, its unifying religious nature – the **spirit of crusade**, intensified by the religious zeal of the Almoravids and Almohads, and by the wider European climate (which in 1085 gave rise to the First Crusade). This powerful religious motivation is well illustrated by the subsequent canonization of Fernando III, and found solid expression in the part played by the military orders of Christian knights, the most important of which were the **Knights Templar** and the Order of Santiago. At the same time the Reconquest was a movement of **recolonization**. The fact that the country had been in arms for so long meant that the nobility had a major and clearly visible social role, a trend perpetuated by the redistribution of captured land in huge packages, or *latifundia*. Heirs to this tradition still remain as landlords of the great estates, most conspicuously in Andalucía. Men from the ranks were also awarded land, forming a lower, larger stratum of nobility, the *hidalgos*. It was their particular social code that provided the material for Cervantes in *Don Quixote*.

Any spirit of mutual cooperation that had temporarily united the Christian kingdoms disintegrated during the fourteenth century, and independent lines of development were once again pursued. Attempts to merge **Portugal** with Castile foundered at the battle of Aljubarrota (1385), and Portuguese attention turned away from Spain towards the Atlantic. Aragón experienced a similar pull towards the markets of the Mediterranean, although pre-eminence in this area was soon passed to the Genoese. It was **Castile** that emerged the strongest over this period: self-sufficiency in agriculture and a flourishing wool trade with the Netherlands enabled the state to build upon the prominent military role played under Fernando III. Politically, Castilian history was a tale of dynastic conflict until the accession of the Catholic monarchs.

Los Reyes Católicos

Los Reyes Católicos – the **Catholic Monarchs** – was the joint title given to **Fernando V of Aragón and Isabel I of Castile**, whose marriage in 1479 united the two largest kingdoms in Spain. Unity was in practice more symbolic than real: Castile had underlined its rights in the marriage vows and Aragón retained its old administrative structure. So, in the beginning at least, the growth of any national unity or Spanish – as opposed to local – sentiment was very much dependent on the head of state. Nevertheless, from this time on it begins to be realistic to consider Spain as a single political entity.

At the heart of Fernando and Isabel's popular appeal lay a **religious bigotry** that they shared with most of their Christian subjects. The **Inquisition** was instituted in Castile in 1480 and in Aragón seven years later. Aiming to establish the purity of the Catholic faith by rooting out heresy, it was directed mainly at Jews – resented for their enterprise in commerce and influence in high places, as well as for their faith. Expression had already been given to these feelings in a pogrom in 1391; it was reinforced by an edict issued in 1492 which forced up to 400,000 Jews to flee the country. A similar spirit was embodied in the reconquest of the **Kingdom of Granada**, also in 1492. As the last stronghold of Muslim authority, the religious rights of its citizens were guaranteed under the treaty of surrender. Within a decade, though, those Muslims under Christian rule had been given the choice between conversion or expulsion.

The year 1492 was symbolic of a fresh start in another way: it was in this year that Columbus discovered America, and the papal bull that followed, entrusting Spain with the conversion of the American Indians, further entrenched Spain's sense of a mission to bring the world to the "True Faith". The next ten years saw the systematic conquest, colonization and exploitation of the **New World** as it was discovered, with new territory stretching from Labrador to Brazil, and new-found wealth pouring into the royal coffers. Important as this was for Fernando and Isabel, and especially for their prestige, priorities remained in Europe and strategic marriage alliances were made with Portugal, England and the Holy Roman Empire. It was not until the accession of the Habsburg dynasty that Spain could look to the activities of Cortés, Magellan and Pizarro and claim to be the world's leading power.

Habsburg Spain

Carlos I, a Habsburg, came to the throne in 1516 as a beneficiary of the marriage alliances of the Catholic monarchs. Five years later, he was elected emperor of the Holy Roman Empire as Carlos V (**Charles V**), inheriting not only Castile and Aragón, but Flanders, the Netherlands, Artois, the Franche-Comté and all the American colonies to boot. With such responsibilities it was inevitable that attention would be diverted from Spain, whose chief function became to sustain the Holy Roman Empire with gold and silver from the Americas. It was only with the accession of **Felipe II** in 1556 that Spanish politics became more centralized. The notion of an absentee king was reversed. Felipe lived in the centre of Castile near Madrid, creating a monument to the values of medieval Spain in his palace, El Escorial.

Two main themes run through his reign: the preservation of his own inheritance, and the revival of the crusade in the name of the Catholic Church. In pursuit of the former, Felipe successfully claimed the Portuguese throne (through the marriage of his mother), gaining access to the additional wealth of its empire. Plots were also woven in support of Mary Queen of Scots' claim to the throne of England, and to that end the ill-fated Armada sailed in 1588, its sinking a triumph for English naval strength and for Protestantism.

This was a period of unusual religious intensity: the **Inquisition** was enforced with renewed vigour, and a rising of *Moriscos* (subject Moors) in the Alpujarras was fiercely suppressed. Felipe III later ordered the expulsion of half the total number of *Moriscos* in Spain – allowing only two families to remain in each village in order to maintain irrigation techniques. The **exodus** of both Muslim and Jew created a large gulf in the labour force and in the higher echelons of commercial life – and in trying to uphold the Catholic cause, an enormous strain was put upon resources without any clear-cut victory.

By the middle of the seventeenth century, Spain was losing international credibility. Domestically, the disparity between the wealth surrounding Crown and Court and the poverty and suffering of the mass of the population was a source of perpetual tension. Discontent fuelled regional revolts in Catalunya and Portugal in 1640, and the latter had finally to be acknowledged as an independent state in 1668.

Bourbons and the Peninsular War

The **Bourbon dynasty** succeeded to the Spanish throne in the person of **Felipe V** (1700); with him began the War of the Spanish Succession against the rival claim of Archduke Charles of Austria, assisted by British forces. As a result of the Treaty of Utrecht which ended the war (1713), Spain was stripped of all territory in Belgium, Luxembourg, Italy and Sardinia, but Felipe V was recognized as king. Gibraltar was seized by the British in the course of the war. For the rest of the century Spain fell very much under the French sphere of influence, an influence that was given political definition by an alliance with the French Bourbons in 1762.

Contact with France made involvement in the **Napoleonic Wars** inevitable and led eventually to the defeat of the Spanish fleet at Trafalgar in 1805. Popular outrage was such that the powerful prime minister, Godoy, was overthrown and King Carlos IV forced to abdicate (1808). Napoleon seized the opportunity to install his brother, Joseph, on the throne.

Fierce local resistance was eventually backed by the muscle of a British army, first under Sir John Moore, later under the Duke of Wellington, and the French were at last driven out in the course of the Peninsular War. Meanwhile, however, the **American colonies** had been successfully asserting their independence from a preoccupied centre and with them went Spain's last real claim of significance on the world stage. The entire nineteenth century was dominated by the struggle between an often reactionary monarchy and the aspirations of liberal constitutional reformers.

Seeds of civil war

Between 1810 and 1813 an ad hoc Cortes (parliament) had set up a **liberal constitution** with ministers responsible to a democratically elected chamber. The first act of Fernando VII on being returned to the throne was to abolish this, and until his death in 1833 he continued to stamp out the least hint of liberalism. On his death, the right of succession was contested between his brother, Don Carlos, backed by the Church, conservatives and Basques, and his infant daughter, Isabel, who had the support of the liberals and the army. So began the **First Carlist War**, a civil war that lasted six years. Isabel II was eventually declared of age in 1843, her reign a long record of scandal, political crisis and constitutional compromise. Liberal army generals under the leadership of General Prim effected a coup in 1868 and the queen was forced to abdicate, but attempts to maintain a republican government foundered. The Cortes was again dissolved and the throne returned to Isabel's son, Alfonso XII. A new constitution was declared in 1876, limiting the power of the Crown through the institution of bicameral government, but again progress was halted by the lack of any tradition on which to base the constitutional theory.

The years preceding World War I merely heightened the discontent, which found expression in the growing **political movements** of the working class. The Socialist Workers' Party was founded in Madrid after the restoration of Alfonso XII, and spawned its own trade union, the UGT (1888), successful predominantly in areas of high industrial concentration such as the Basque region and Asturias. Its anarchist counterpart, the CNT, was founded in 1911, gaining substantial support among the peasantry of Andalucía.

The loss of **Cuba** in 1898 emphasized the growing isolation of Spain in international affairs and added to economic problems with the return of soldiers seeking employment where there was none. A call-up for army reserves to fight in **Morocco** in 1909 provoked a general strike and the "Tragic Week" of rioting in Barcelona. Between 1914 and 1918, Spain was outwardly neutral but inwardly turbulent; inflated prices made the postwar recession harder to bear.

The general disillusionment with parliamentary government, together with the fears of employers and businessmen for their own security, gave **General Primo de Rivera** sufficient support for a military coup in 1923 in which the king, Alfonso XIII, was pushed into the background. Dictatorship did result in an increase in material prosperity, but the death of the dictator in 1930 revealed the apparent stability as a facade. New political factions were taking shape: the

Liberal Republican Right was founded by Alcalá Zamora, while the Socialist Party was given definition under the leadership of Largo Caballero. The victory of antimonarchist parties in the 1931 municipal elections forced the abdication of the king, who went into exile, and the **Second Republic** was declared.

The Second Republic

Catalunya declared itself a republic independent of the central government and was conceded control of internal affairs by a statute of 1932. **Separatist movements** were powerful, too, in the Basque provinces and Galicia, each with their own demands for autonomy. Meanwhile, the government, set up on a tidal wave of hope, was hopelessly divided internally and too scared of right-wing reaction to carry out the massive tax and agrarian reforms that the left demanded, and that might have provided the resources for thoroughgoing regeneration of the economy.

The result was the increasing polarization of Spanish politics. **Anarchism**, in particular, was gaining strength among the frustrated middle classes as well as among the workers and peasantry. The **Communist Party** and left-wing **Socialists**, driven into alliance by their mutual distrust of the "moderate" socialists in government, were also forming a growing bloc. On the right the **Falangists**, basically a youth party founded in 1923 by **José Antonio Primo de Rivera** (son of the dictator), made uneasy bedfellows with conservative traditionalists and dissident elements in the army upset by modernizing reforms.

In an atmosphere of growing confusion, the left-wing Popular Front alliance won the general election of **February 1936** by a narrow margin. Normal life, though, became increasingly impossible: the economy was crippled by strikes, peasants took agrarian reform into their own hands, and the government failed to exert its authority over anyone. Finally, on July 17, 1936, the military garrison in Morocco rebelled under **General Franco**'s leadership, to be followed by risings at military garrisons throughout the country. It was the culmination of years of scheming in the army, but in the event far from the overnight success its leaders almost certainly expected. The south and west quickly fell into Nationalist hands, but Madrid and the industrialized north and east remained loyal to the Republican government.

Civil War

The ensuing **Civil War** was undoubtedly one of the most bitter and bloody the world has seen. Violent reprisals were taken on their enemies by both sides – the Republicans shooting priests and local landowners wholesale, the Nationalists carrying out mass slaughter of the population of almost every town they took. Contradictions were legion in the way the Spanish populations found themselves divided from each other. Perhaps the greatest irony was that Franco's troops, on their "holy" mission to ensure a Catholic Spain, comprised a core of Moroccan troops from Spain's North African colony.

It was, too, the first modern war – Franco's German allies demonstrated their ability to wipe out entire civilian populations with their bombing raids on Gernika and Durango, and radio proved an important weapon, as Nationalist propagandists offered the starving Republicans "the white bread of Franco".

Despite sporadic help from Russia and thousands of volunteers in the International Brigade, the Republic could never compete with the professional armies and the massive assistance from Fascist Italy and Nazi Germany enjoyed by the Nationalists. In addition, the left was torn by internal divisions which at times led almost to civil war within its own ranks. Nevertheless, the Republicans held out in slowly dwindling territories for nearly three years, with **Catalunya** falling in January 1939 and armed resistance in **Madrid** – which never formally surrendered – petering out over the following few months. As hundreds of thousands of refugees flooded into France, General Francisco Franco, who had long before proclaimed himself head of state, took up the reins of power.

Franco's Spain

The early reprisals taken by the victors were on a massive and terrifying scale. Executions were commonplace and upwards of two million people were put in concentration camps until "order" had been established by authoritarian means. Only one party, the Falange, was permitted, and censorship was rigidly enforced. By the end of World War II, during which Spain was too weak to be anything but neutral, **Franco** was the only fascist head of state left in Europe, one responsible for sanctioning more deaths than any other in Spanish history. Spain was economically and politically isolated and, bereft of markets, suffered – almost half the population were still tilling the soil for little or no return. When General Eisenhower visited Madrid in 1953 with the offer of huge loans, it came as water to the desert, and the price, the establishment of American nuclear bases, was one Franco was more than willing to pay. However belated, economic development was incredibly rapid, with Spain enjoying a growth rate second only to that of Japan for much of the 1960s, a boom fuelled by the tourist industry and the remittances of Spanish workers abroad.

Increased **prosperity**, however, only underlined the political bankruptcy of Franco's regime and its inability to cope with popular demands. Higher incomes, the need for better education and a creeping invasion of Western culture made the anachronism of Franco ever clearer. His only reaction was to attempt to withdraw what few signs of increased liberalism had crept through, and his last years mirrored the repression of the postwar period. Trade unions remained outlawed, and the rampant inflation of the early 1970s saw striking workers across Spain hauled out of occupied mines and factories and imprisoned, or even shot in the streets. Attempts to report these events by the liberal press resulted in suspensions, fines and censorship. **Basque nationalists**, whose assassination of Admiral Carrero Blanco had effectively destroyed Franco's last hope of a like-minded successor, were singled out for particularly harsh treatment. Hundreds of so-called terrorists were tortured, and the Burgos trials of 1970, together with the executions of August 1975, provoked worldwide protest.

Franco finally died in November 1975, nominating **King Juan Carlos** as his successor. Groomed for the job and very much in with the army – of which he remains official commander in chief – the king's initial moves were cautious in the extreme, appointing a government dominated by loyal Francoists who had little sympathy for the growing opposition demands for "democracy without adjectives". In the summer of 1976 demonstrations in Madrid ended in violence, with the police upholding the old authoritarian ways.

The return of democracy

The violent events leading up to and following his mentor's death seem to have persuaded Juan Carlos that some real break with the past and a move towards **democratization** was now urgent and inevitable. Using the almost dictatorial powers he had inherited, he ousted Franco's reactionary prime minister, Carlos Arias Navarro, and replaced him with **Adolfo Suárez**, an ambitious lawyer and former head of Spanish TV. In 1976 Suárez pushed a **Law of Political Reform** through the Cortes, reforming the legislature into two chambers elected by universal suffrage – a move massively endorsed by the Spanish people in a referendum. Suárez also passed legislation allowing the setting up of free trade unions, as well as legitimizing the Socialist Party (PSOE) and, controversially, the Communists. Several cabinet ministers resigned in protest and an outraged military began planning their *coup d'état*.

Autonomy and separatism

Autonomy – the granting of substantial self-rule in the 1978 Constitution to the seventeen *autonomías* into which Spain is now divided – has created as many problems as it has solved. In Franco's time even speaking the regional languages such as Catalan or Basque was banned, and the backlash against this has turned all Spaniards into potential separatists. Although each of the autonomous regions now has its own president, parliament and civil service – all at enormous and spiralling cost – the main beneficiaries of the new arrangement have been the Basques and Catalans in the north, who throughout the 1990s held the balance of power in the Madrid parliament. Spain's chronic economic problems in the late 1980s enabled these two to drive hard bargains with the ailing PSOE administration. Jordi Pujol, a veteran of Franco's jails and supremely canny regional president of the Catalans for an uninterrupted 23 years until his retirement in 2003, once said that whilst Catalunya had long been the economic locomotive pulling the rest of Spain, it had never been the driver, and that this would change. As good as his word, he managed to secure a concession from the central government which allows the Catalan Regional Government to collect and spend thirty percent of its income tax. The other autonomies demanded equal treatment and the law was applied to them, too, with unforeseeable long-term repercussions for the national economy.

Predictably, having won one victory over Madrid and with Catalan regional elections on the horizon, late in 1998 Pujol attempted to use his support for the Aznar government as a bargaining chip to up the fiscal figure to one hundred percent. The prime minister retorted that he would sooner call a general election than be blackmailed, but it was an ominous sign for the future. When the *autonomías* do get hold of the cash they tend to spend it not on fostering an entrepreneurial spirit or investment for the long term, but subsidizing benefit payouts to the poor in order to buy votes. Similarly, and to justify their existence, the regional leaders (many of whom earn salaries higher than the Spanish prime minister) have ploughed vast resources into grandiose schemes such as the Sevilla Expo '92, which often leave behind staggering debt mountains. At the same time, the *autonomías* have become fiefdoms used by the victorious party to reward its members and supporters with jobs in the regional government pyramid, ranging from senior civil service posts, all the way down the social scale to school inspectors and refuse collectors, often with a blind eye turned to lack of qualifications. Being *enchufado* ("plugged in" or well connected) is just as important a part of the Spain of the Aznar era as it was during the PSOE's time in power.

When elections were held in June 1977, Suárez's own hastily formed centre-right party, the Unión del Centro Democrático (UCD), was rewarded with a 34 percent share of the vote, the Socialists coming in second with 28 percent, and the Communists and Francoist **Alianza Popular** marginalized at 9 percent and 8 percent respectively. Despite the overwhelming victories in Catalunya and the Basque Country of parties appealing to regional sentiment, this was almost certainly a vote for democratic stability rather than for ideology, something reflected in the course of the parliament, with Suárez governing through "consensus politics", negotiating settlements on all important issues with the major parties.

The first parliament of the "New Spain" now embarked on the formidable task of drawing up a **constitution**, whilst the Suárez government applied for membership of the then EEC. On December 6, 1978, the new constitution was overwhelmingly endorsed in a national referendum and, remarkably, only three years after the death of Franco, Spain had become a full democracy.

Elections in March 1979 almost exactly duplicated the 1977 result, but when

José María Aznar's outright victory in the general election of 2000 applied a temporary brake to the ability of the regional parties to dictate terms to the government in Madrid, but the genie of nationalism remains out of the bottle. In fact, the Basques and Catalans continue spearheading demands for ever more powers – in 2003 the Basque Nationalist Party (PNV) demanded a referendum on the creation of a Basque "state", whilst the ruling CiU party in Catalunya declared that the region would achieve self-government before their northern neighbours – the opposite is more likely. The weaknesses of the *autonomía* system are evident, including the fact that there is no forum in which the leaders of the *autonomías* can meet to co-ordinate policies – the only time they ever gather together in the same place is for a royal wedding. Some regional leaders have suggested that the moribund Spanish Senate should be reformed to resemble Germany's Bundesrat, or upper house, where the German Länder (the equivalent of Spain's autonomous regions) are represented.

The violence by the Basque terrorist group ETA remains a threat, and although it has claimed over 800 lives since 1968 there are signs that support both for its methods and its political wing, Euskal Herritarok, is waning, as more Basques openly condemn the violence and voice their protests at frequent demonstrations. However, a substantial number of Basques (perhaps as many as 60 percent) support the aims, if not always the actions, of ETA and this has made a solution hard to come by. Influenced by the peace process in Northern Ireland (ETA and the IRA have long had close links), in the summer of 1998 ETA announced an **indefinite ceasefire**, somewhat catching the hardline Aznar administration on the hop. Aznar's subsequent inflexibility, when he categorically refused to allow the referendum on "self-determination" demanded by the Basque nationalists, and delayed any talks with the terrorists until they permanently renounced violence, resulted in a stagnant deadlock. Apparently convinced that Aznar would never agree to serious negotiations, in November 1999 ETA **called off its ceasefire** and a series of car bombs and assassinations of Partido Popular and non-nationalist politicians throughout the Basque country followed. Recent murders of police officers as well as journalists and newspaper executives who have voiced criticism of ETA's strategy have plunged both the nation and the Basque country back into the darkest days of the 1980s with little apparent hope of any solution in the foreseeable future. In 2002 the Aznar government pushed a law through the Cortés **banning Batasuna** (ETA's political wing) from taking any future part in the electoral process. However, there seems little chance that this will influence the terrorist group's strategy of bombings and assassinations, and any peace breakthrough is almost certain to depend on a new initiative emerging from Madrid.

the UCD, a fractious coalition of moderates and extremists, started to crack at the seams, Suárez resigned in January 1981. This provided the trigger for a **military coup**, launched by a contingent of Civil Guards loyal to Franco's memory and commanded by the tragi-comic, moustachioed Colonel Antonio Tejero. They stormed into the Cortes with Tejero brandishing a revolver, and sub-machine-gunned the ceiling as *diputados* (MPs) dived for cover. The crisis, for a while, was real; tanks were brought out onto the streets of Valencia, and only three of the army's ten regional commanders remained unreservedly loyal to the government. But as it became clear that the king would not support the plotters, most of the rest then affirmed their support. Juan Carlos had taken the decision of his life and emerged with immensely enhanced prestige in the eyes of most Spaniards.

The González era

On October 28, 1982, the Socialist PSOE, led by charismatic **Felipe González**, was elected with the biggest landslide victory in Spanish electoral history to rule a country that had been firmly in the hands of the right for 43 years. The Socialists captured the imagination and the votes of nearly ten million Spaniards with the simplest of appeals: "for change".

Once in power, however, the Socialist Party chose the path of pragmatism, and a relentless drift to the right followed. Four successive election victories kept the party in power for fourteen years and by the mid-1990s the PSOE government's policies had become indistinguishable from the conservative administrations of Britain or Germany.

González himself, meanwhile, had been equally transformed, from a radical young labour lawyer into a careworn elder statesman. Control of inflation had become a more urgent target than reducing unemployment, whilst loss-making heavy industries (steel and shipbuilding especially) were ruthlessly overhauled and other industries privatized. European Community (now **European Union**) membership came in 1986, and the pride which most Spanish people felt at this tangible proof of their acceptance by the rest of Europe bought the Socialists more valuable time.

The issue of **NATO** (or OTAN, as the Spaniards know it), perhaps more than any other, demonstrated how much González had sacrificed to pragmatism. During the 1982 election campaign he had made an impassioned speech at a rally against Spain remaining a member of NATO, which the dying UCD administration had rushed into joining at the behest of the military. When the promised referendum was finally held four years later – which surprisingly turned out marginally in favour of staying in – his was one of the main voices in favour of continued membership. González finally buried the question of NATO as a political issue for the mainstream left when in 1995 he agreed to and supported the elevation of his foreign secretary and close colleague, Javier Solana, to the post of secretary general of the organization he had spent most of his political life reviling.

After long years of being hopelessly divided, in the late 1980s the **Spanish right** realigned itself when former prime minister Adolfo Suárez's UCD Christian Democrats merged with the Alianza Popular to form the new right-of-centre **Partido Popular** (PP) which came a respectable second in the 1989 elections; a new far-left coalition, **Izquierda Unida** (United Left), composed of the Communists and smaller leftist parties, came third, albeit with the same number of seats (18) in the Congress of Deputies as the Catalan Nationalists, barely a tenth of the PSOE's representation.

The nation's progressive disillusionment with Felipe González's government in the early 1990s saw the rise to prominence of **José María Aznar** as leader of the PP. A former tax inspector and devoid of charisma, Aznar was dogged in his criticism of government incompetence in dealing with its own sleaze and the growing economic crisis. This debilitated the PSOE's position still further in the build-up to the **1993 elections**. However, the PSOE confounded the pundits and the opinion polls to hang on to power by the skin of its teeth, albeit with the help of a coalition with Pujol's Catalan Nationalists. But González's victory was a poisoned chalice, for he had no new ideas to deal with urgent economic problems, whilst his past now began to catch up with him. As illegal financing of the PSOE and corruption and commission-taking on government projects by party officials and ministers were being exposed, the director of the Guardia Civil (appointed by González) jumped the country with millions of dollars of secret service funds, and the governor of the Bank of Spain was caught out making a private (and illegal) fortune. But the most serious of all the scandals to beset González was the **GAL affair** (Grupo Antiterrorista de Liberación), when it was discovered that a semi-autonomous antiterrorist unit had been carrying out a dirty war against the ETA terrorists in the 1980s, which included kidnapping and wholesale assassinations of suspected ETA members. The press – and a later judicial investigation – exposed police participation in these crimes and a clear chain of command reaching up to the highest echelons of the PSOE government. González's attempts to muzzle journalists' investigations only poisoned further relations between the government and the media, and feeling grew that the truth would never come out. However, in the summer of 1998, the legal system confounded the cynics by convicting two senior ex-ministers of sponsoring kidnapping and misappropriating public funds whilst coordinating GAL activities. They were each sentenced to ten years' imprisonment (later rescinded on appeal) for covering up the plot, and stiff prison terms were given to chiefs in the Guardia Civil, as well as several officers.

Contemporary politics

The PSOE administration limped on towards what looked likely to be a crushing defeat in the **1996 elections**. The surprise result, however, was another **hung parliament**, making everyone a loser. Aznar, the narrow victor, was denied the "absolute majority" he had believed to be his throughout the campaign, which meant that he would be forced to do a deal with the nationalist parties (whom he had described as "greedy parasites" on the hustings) to have a workable parliamentary majority. Meanwhile, the PSOE's avoidance of the expected overwhelming defeat was proclaimed as a vindication by González, who hastily dismissed ideas of retirement. This merely delayed the inevitable and, unable to make any significant impact on changing public opinion, and with the PSOE still in turmoil, early in 1998 **González** finally **resigned** the leadership of the party he had dominated for 23 years.

The reasons for Aznar's failure to win an outright majority are equally significant. When Felipe González told the king after the PSOE's first election victory in 1982 that his party's success had completed the transition from dictatorship to democracy, the monarch sagely advised him that the end of the transition would be when the Socialists lost an election to the right. The long and repressive Franco period still casts a heavy shadow across the Spanish political scene, and many voters seemed to have become nervous at the prospect of a right-wing party with a big majority curtailing their new-found liberties and dismantling the social security system – a vital lifeline in poorer regions such as Extremadura and Andalucía. Thus it was that **Andalucía**, one of the largest *autonomías*, performed its traditional role as the *sartenilla* or frying pan of Spanish politics – traditionally frying the votes of the right-leaning north – by confounding the opinion polls and turning out to vote for the discredited government, effectively denying Aznar a majority.

Elected on a centre-right platform, during his first term in office following his narrow 1996 victory, Aznar progressively moved his party to the centre, shifting aside the government's remaining hardliners in the hope of gaining the electorate's confidence and a working majority not dependent on alliances with the northern nationalists. In tandem with this realignment, he frequently declared his admiration for the ideas of British Prime Minister Tony Blair.

Following the resignation of Felipe González in 1998, a PSOE leadership election replaced him with his former transport minister **José Borrell** – who soon resigned when his name was linked with a financial scandal – and then the distinctly uncharismatic **Joaquín Almunia**. Paunchy, whiskered and balding, Almunia cut little ice with the Spanish electorate, not helped by his refusal to criticize the record of his mentor González. With a general election now on the horizon and the PSOE still trailing in the polls, Almunia set up an electoral pact with the ex-communist Izquierda Unida (United Left), thinking that their combined votes could overturn a likely Aznar victory.

The outcome of the March 2000 **general election** was a stunning **triumph for Aznar** and the PP, and for the first time since the death of Franco the right was in power with an overall majority. Naturally, this was a disaster for the left: apparently the electorate had been unconvinced by the "shotgun marriage" between the PSOE and the IU (bitter enemies since the Civil War), which smacked more of political opportunism than a government in waiting. Moreover, large numbers of voters seemed unwilling to risk the undoubted economic gains of Aznar's period in office, while many of the left's traditional supporters didn't bother to vote at all. On election night, when the scale of the PSOE/IU defeat became clear, Joaquín Almunia **resigned** from the leadership of the PSOE. At the party convention which followed, the old guard and its candidates were swept aside and delegates elected a relatively unknown young politician, **José Luis Rodríguez Zapatero** – a member of the moderate socialist "Nueva Vía" (new way) group within the PSOE – as their **new leader**.

After an unpromising start in which he struggled to get to grips with both Aznar and the party's powerful regional "barons", Zapatero pursued a policy of admitting the PSOE's past mistakes, stating emphatically that any government led by him would be radically different. This seemed to go down well with the electorate and the opinion polls began to move in the PSOE's favour. However, what should have been a tonic victory for the socialists in the **local elections of May 2003** against an Aznar government on the ropes because of its immensely unpopular support of the USA and Britain in the **Iraq war** and the mishandling of the *Prestige* disaster (see opposite), turned out to be a public relations debacle for the PSOE. Not only did Aznar's PP hold on to most of its municipal strongholds – including the city of Madrid which Zapatero had turned into a trial of strength – but just as the socialists were celebrating a narrow victory in the Comunidad de Madrid (the autonomous region surrounding the capital) two of its newly elected candidates resigned from the party, denying the PSOE its overall majority and plunging the region into chaos. In a rerun of the election later the same year the PSOE suffered an ignominious defeat and it remains to be seen whether Zapatero can forge the party into a force capable of wresting power from the PP in the general election of 2004.

In 2001 José María Aznar – always a puzzle to those around him – announced that he would not be leading the PP into the next general election and that it must seek a new leader. In the autumn of 2003 he nominated **Mariano Rajoy**, his deputy prime minister, to succeed him and his choice was quickly rubber-stamped by the party's ruling council. Although more affable and less prickly than his boss, Rajoy is even more of an unknown entity than was Aznar himself when he first came to public attention, and one political commentator described the leader-designate's core political beliefs as "a mystery wrapped in an enigma". Aznar said his reasons for choosing Rajoy were his "bravery" and "because he is rigorous", which did not enlighten anyone. The reasons for Aznar's retirement – he will be only 52 at the time of the next general election in 2004 – are unclear, but what is certain is that some of the gloss had started to wear off the Aznar government. Despite impressive economic growth figures throughout his administration's period in office, Spain still has the highest level of **unemployment** in the EU, and many experts point to the lack of investment in education and training as the reason why the economy is now starting to show signs of a downturn. Labour law and social security reforms slashing benefits were intended to make the labour market more flexible and cut government spending, but incurred the wrath of workers and trade unions which brought about a **general strike** in June 2002.

In November 2002 the sinking of the oil tanker **Prestige** (see p.631) off the coast of Galicia seemed to encapsulate the government's lack of organization and direction. When the tanker went down, the PP leader of Galicia's autonomous government and the Madrid government's environment minister were away on a joint shooting holiday and – as the ecological disaster unfolded into one of Europe's worst ever – saw no reason to return to their posts. The lack of equipment and government preparedness to deal with this crisis saw images of polluted beaches and fishing grounds and furious ruined fishermen filling the TV screens for weeks. When Aznar belatedly announced that he intended to visit the region he was advised by police chiefs that public anger with the government meant that they would not be able to guarantee his safety.

The problems in the **Basque country** (see box on p.1038) which have dogged the PP government since it came to power are also no nearer resolution, and Aznar must have had a feeling of *déjà vu* in the summer of 2003 when he held a crisis summit with the leader of the Basque regional government Juan José Ibarretxe, whose PNV party had won a comprehensive victory in the May local elections. The meeting was called by Aznar to attempt to persuade Ibarretxe (whom in the past he has described as an ETA apologist) to adopt a firmer line against terrorism; the quid pro quo demanded by Ibarretxe for control of the Basque social security system and the transfer of Basque prisoners (many of them ETA terrorists) to the region's prisons from the rest of Spain was regarded as a price too high by Aznar, and the talks broke up in acrimony. When Ibarretxe then announced a plan to revise the País Vasco's *autonomía* status in favour of a greater degree of self-rule and vowed to put this to a referendum in the Basque lands, more alarm bells began to sound in Madrid. Equally worryingly for the central government, **Catalan regional elections** in the autumn of 2003 saw the number of seats won by the main separatist party double, and – because the other major parties will need its help to gain a working majority – the resulting administration is certain to have a more nationalist agenda. All this will have a significant impact on the **general election** to be held in 2004 as leaders of both major parties have warned that giving any further ground to the Basque and Catalan nationalists will lead to the break-up of the Spanish state.

Geoff Garvey

Architecture

Spain's architectural legacy is a highly distinctive one, made up of a mixture of styles quite unlike anything else in Europe. The country was usually slow to pick up on the main currents of European architecture, and when a new style was adopted it was often in an extreme or stylized form. There are French, Dutch, German and Italian currents, but all were synthesized into something uniquely Spanish. Centuries of Moorish occupation have left an indelible mark, too, manifested both in the handful of wonderful buildings which represent the high point of Moorish civilization in Andalucía, and in a powerful influence on Christian and secular architecture, including the layout of entire towns.

There has been less of the wanton destruction of old buildings in Spain than in most other countries, and in general the architecture here is astonishingly well preserved. There's perhaps less purity of form than elsewhere in Europe – additions over the years have left many buildings with a medley of different styles – but no other country can boast quite as many old churches, castles and unspoiled towns and villages.

At the risk of making generalizations, it's possible to identify a number of **trends** in the buildings of Spain. As a rule, there is an emphasis on the longitudinal, and on solidity of construction. A heavy use of surface ornament is often popular, with elaborate doorways and rich decoration. Because of the warm climate there is an interest in outdoor living and a need for cool and open space, which accounts for the prevalence of patios in civic buildings and cloisters in religious edifices, including those which were not monastic. There is also a tendency to break up long vistas by various means, creating a variety of compartments within a large space.

The Roman period

Although fragments of earlier civilizations do exist, Spain's architectural history (in terms of surviving buildings) begins in the **Roman** period, from which there remain a number of remarkable structures. These have no particular Spanish flavour, nor were they to prove as influential on subsequent developments as in some other countries, but nonetheless the aqueduct at **Segovia**, the bridge at **Alcántara** (the highest in the Roman world and still in use), and the theatre and associated remains at **Mérida** belong among the first rank of Roman survivals anywhere. There's another fine group in and around **Tarragona**, with walls, a necropolis, an arena, a forum and a praetorium in the city itself, and more notably an aqueduct, the Centcelles Mausoleum, the Arco de Bar and the Torre de Scipio all within a radius of a few kilometres.

Other Roman monuments worthy of special note include the walls of Lugo, the amphitheatre and castle at Sagunto, and the three-span triumphal arch at Medinaceli. Excavations of complete towns can be seen at Empúries, Itálica, Numancia and Bilbilis.

Visigothic and Asturian periods

The **Visigothic** period, which succeeded the Roman, bequeathed a small number of buildings of uncertain date. Visigothic buildings have simple exteriors, and were the first in Spain to adopt the horseshoe arch (later to be altered and used widely by the Moors). They also developed elements from Roman buildings, the most refined example of which is at **Quintanilla de las Viñas** in Old Castile, a church whose exterior is enlivened by delicately carved stone friezes set in bands; inside there's a triumphal arch over the apse, carved with the earliest surviving representation of Christ in Spain. Other remnants of the era survive at the modern industrial town of **Tarrasa** in Catalunya, formerly Egara, in the shape of three churches, one of which – the Baptistry of San Miguel – dates from the fifth or sixth century; the other two have apses that are probably of ninth-century construction. Other Visigothic buildings include part of the crypt of Palencia Cathedral, and the nearby basilica of San Juan at Baños de Cerrato, documented as seventh century.

Hard on the heels of the Visigothic epoch was the **Asturian** period, named after the small kingdom on the northern coast, which developed its own style during the ninth century. This retained Visigothic elements alongside technical developments that anticipated the general European trends still to come. A little group of buildings centred around **Oviedo** – the Cámara Santa, the church of Santulano in the city itself, San Miguel de Lillo and Santa María de Naranco on the slopes of Monte Naranco nearby – are, unusually in Spanish history, clearly superior to and more highly developed than any contemporaneous work in Europe. The last represents the pinnacle of the style, a perfectly proportioned little building with barrel vaulting and arches supported on pilasters, as well as delicate decoration using Roman and Byzantine elements. The isolated surrounding countryside holds a few similar buildings from the succeeding century, but the Asturian style was soon to be swallowed up by the new Romanesque movement which swept across the north of Spain from France and Italy.

The Moorish period

By this time most of Spain was under Muslim domination. It remained so, at least in part, until the final defeat of the Moors in 1492. During this period Moorish architecture did not develop in the way we understand the word, and it is best to consider the different epochs of building separately.

The first real style was the **Caliphate**, centred around Córdoba, whose great surviving monument – the **Mezquita** – was built and added to over a period from the eighth to the tenth century. The Caliphate style demonstrates most of the vocabulary used by Moorish builders over the years – horseshoe, cusped and multifoil arches, the contrasting use of courses of stone and brick, the use of interlacing as a particular feature of design, doors surmounted by blind arcades, stuccowork, and the ornamental use of calligraphy along with geometric and plant motifs. Various technical innovations, too, were introduced in the construction of the Mezquita, from the original solution of two-tiered arches to give greater height, to the ribbed dome vaults in front of the *mihrab* (prayer-niche).

Another example of the Caliphate style, the (now ruined) palace-city of **Medina Azahara**, just outside Córdoba, was no less splendid than the Mezquita. Many of its buildings were produced according to the descriptions of Solomon's temple. In **Toledo**, El Cristo de la Luz is a small-scale Caliphate mosque, and the old Bisagra Gate was part of the fortifications of that time. As the Reconquest progressed, other fortifications went up. Gormaz was begun in around 965. Only part of the original Moorish building has survived, including two gateways. Calatayud, in the north, holds more fortifications of the period, probably of an even earlier date.

With the fall of the caliphate at the end of the eleventh century, Moorish Spain was divided into independent kingdoms or **taifas**, giving rise to the *alcazabas* or castles at Granada, Málaga, Guadix, Almería, Tarifa and Carmona. The Aljafería palace in Zaragoza also dates from this period, much altered over the years but preserving its mosque and a tower. The strongest *taifa* was at Sevilla, where later the **Almohad** dynasty created an art of refined brickwork and left behind the Patio de Yeso in the Alcázar, the Torre del Oro, which originally formed part of the city's fortifications, and the Giralda – former minaret of the mosque and arguably the finest tower ever built in the Arab world.

The apotheosis of pure Muslim art came, however, with the **Nasrid** dynasty in Granada, the last city to fall to the Christians. The gorgeously opulent palace of the **Alhambra** went up between the thirteenth and fifteenth centuries. Built on a hill against the romantic backdrop of the Sierra Nevada, this structure provided the necessary partner in the union between art and nature sought by the Moorish architects, especially in the lush gardens of the more modest Generalife section. As for the palace itself, the buildings are structurally very poor, with no exterior features of note; yet the interior, around the two great courtyards, is one of the most intoxicating creations in the world, the culminating ideal of Moorish civilization, built when it was already in irreversible decline.

Mozarabic and Mudéjar

The Moorish occupation had an indelible influence on the architecture of Spain, and led directly to two hybrid architectural styles unique to the country – **Mozarabic** and Mudéjar. The former was the style of Christians subjugated by the Moors who retained their old religion but built in the Arabic style. Their churches are mostly in isolated situations – San Miguel de Escalada east of León, Santa María de Lebena near the Picos de Europa and San Baudelio near Berlanga de Duero in Soria Province are the finest examples.

Mudéjar is far more common, the style of the Arabs who stayed on after their homelands had been conquered, or who had migrated to the Christian kingdoms. Often they proved to be both the most skilful builders and the cheapest workforce, and they left their mark on almost all of the country over a period of several centuries. They continued to build predominantly in brick, mainly working on the construction of parish churches, resulting in an odd – though unmistakeably Moorish – Christian-Islamic hybrid that some claim is barely a distinct architectural style at all. There are details of Mudéjar buildings under the relevant European headings below, although a number deserve inclusion here as being more firmly within the Arab tradition. Among these are the palaces of Tordesillas and the Alcázar in Sevilla; various secular buildings in Toledo; the Chapel of the Assumption of Santiago at Las Huelgas; and the synagogues of Toledo and Córdoba.

The Romanesque

Back in the mainstream of European architecture, the **Romanesque** style in Spain is most associated with the churches, bridges and hospices built along the **pilgrim road** to Santiago de Compostela. None of the hospices has survived, but the Puente la Reina in Navarra is the most famous of a number of Romanesque-era bridges. The churches come in various shapes and forms, but all include beautiful sculpture. The cathedral of Jaca, the monasteries of Santa Cruz de la Seros, San Juan de la Peña and Leyre, and the churches of Santa María la Real at Sanguesa, San Miguel at Estella, San Martín at Fromista and San Isidoro at León are the most notable examples, but the climax, of the style as of the pilgrimage, came with the great **Cathedral of Santiago** itself. This is now almost entirely encased by Baroque additions, but preserves the original shape of the interior. Begun around 1070, it was built to allow as much space as possible for the pilgrims to circulate – hence the large triforium gallery, and the ambulatory with radiating chapels. Santiago's cathedral also served as a model for many contemporary derivations, particularly the nearby cathedrals of Lugo, Orense and Tuy.

Elsewhere, the influence of the great Burgundian abbey of Cluny, which so influenced the development of the pilgrimage, can be seen most clearly at **San Vicente** in Ávila. Another building closely related to the pilgrimage churches is the monastery of **Santo Domingo de Silos**, where the architecture and superb bas-reliefs of the cloisters, the only surviving part of the original building, are clearly derived from French models. There's an additional ingredient, too: most of the capitals here show an unmistakeable Moorish influence – a very early example of the mix of East and West to be found in Spain.

Other Romanesque buildings tend towards regional variants. In **Catalunya**, whose architectural history so often diverges from that of the rest of Spain, the influence was more from Lombardy than France, with tall, square bell towers, prominent apses, blind arcading and little sculptural detail – although this last was later to become important, for example in the cloisters of the cathedral and San Pedro in Girona.

Belfries were a dominant feature in **Segovia**, where the main innovation was the construction of covered arcades in the manner of cloisters built against the sides of the building, making the parish churches of this city amongst the most distinctive in Spain. **Soria**'s churches, particularly San Domingo, recall those of Poitiers, although the fantastic cloister of San Juan de Duero defies classification in its combination of the round-headed Romanesque, early pointed Gothic, and Moorish horseshoe and intersecting arches in one extraordinarily capricious composition. **Zamora** was unusual in having a Byzantine influence; also its portals tended to lack tympana, but had richly carved archivolts. Finally, there are a number of churches in a crossover **Mudéjar**/Romanesque style in such places as Toledo, Sahagún, Cúellar and Arévalo.

Military architecture of this period is dominated by the complete walls of Ávila, the best preserved in Europe, and by the castle at Loarre, the most spectacular of the early Christian castles built to defend the conquered lands. Survivors of civil buildings are few and far between, but there are precious examples in the form of the palaces of Estella and Huesca.

The Transitional style

With the advent of the Cistercian reforms, the **Transitional** style was intro-duced to Spain in the middle of the twelfth century, first in a series of monas-teries – La Oliva, Veruela, Poblet, Santes Creus, Las Huelgas and Santa María la Huerta – that are notable for massiveness of construction combined with the introduction of such Gothic characteristics as the pointed arch and the ribbed vault.

In some ways, **La Oliva** can claim to be the first Gothic building in Spain, although in both its solidity and ground plan it is still Romanesque in spirit. The severe, unadorned style of the Cistercians was to have a great impact at a time when the rest of Europe was moving towards an appreciation of the struc-tural advantages of Gothic, not quickly realized in Spain. The late twelfth and early thirteenth centuries saw the construction of a number of cathedrals in the Transitional style – Siguenza, Ávila, Santo Domingo de la Calzada, Tarragona and Lleida – all of which had fortress-like features and were indeed at times used for defensive purposes. Similar is the Collegiate church at Tudela, although the sculpture here, in direct contravention of Cistercian rules, is among the richest in Spain.

A few buildings of the same period show clear **Byzantine** influence – the Old Cathedral of Salamanca, Zamora Cathedral and the Colegiata at Toro – each with a distinctive central dome, although their design otherwise shows normal Transitional elements. Closely related are the cathedral of Ciudad Rodrigo and the often octagonally shaped buildings associated with the Knights Templar: La Vera Cruz in Segovia, and two mysterious buildings on the Pilgrim Route whose exact nature is uncertain – Eunate and Torres de Río.

The Gothic style

Examples of the early **Gothic** style in Spain are rare, and those that there are seem to derive from French and English sources. The refectory of Santa María la Huerta is as pure and elegant as the best in France; Cuenca Cathedral, begun about 1200, seems to derive from a Norman or English model. Later, buildings began to develop a more specifically Spanish style, eschewing any notions of purity of form.

Three great cathedrals commenced in the 1220s best exemplify the increas-ingly Spanish features of the churches of the time. Of these, the overall plans and building of **Burgos** and **Toledo** are obviously indebted to French mod-els, but they are far from the grace and lightness of the great French Gothic cathedrals. The windows are much smaller – partly, perhaps, to cut down on excessive sunlight, partly to preserve a greater sense of mystery than their French equivalents did. Both were also given the rich interior decoration that soon became the norm for Spanish cathedrals, most characteristic of which was the *coro*, an elaborate set of choir stalls often enclosed by a *trascoro* or retrochoir, situated in the nave – a feature that looks odd to those used to the chancel-based choirs of northern Europe. The reasons for this are unclear, but it seems it was associated with the predominance of the choir services of the clergy, which meant that the construction of the *coro* made the best use of the space; it may also have been felt that the chancel should be reserved solely for the

Holy Sacrament, and not downgraded for any other purpose.

Equally typical are the giant *retablos*, the most important of which are situated over the high altar, again masking the architecture. Generally these were carved and multicoloured, and contained a series of scenes from the life of Christ and of the Virgin, perhaps along with statues of saints. Basically their function was similar to that of stained-glass windows in the cathedrals of France, providing pictorial representation of the Bible to an illiterate population. Smaller *retablos*, either painted or carved, were placed over smaller altars. In addition, tombs of monarchs, aristocratic families, bishops and saints were often placed in specially built chapels, and sometimes enclosed by iron gates or grilles (*rejas*) which were often of a highly elaborate workmanship and would enclose the entrances to the *coro* and the chancel, too. The overall effect of all this decoration can appear oversumptuous to the modern eye, but it gives a better impression of a medieval cathedral than anything that can be found in northern Europe, where reformation, revolution, war and restoration have combined to leave buildings that are architecturally far purer but spiritually far less authentic.

The third great cathedral of the 1200s, **León**, was the only one to adopt the normal French system of triple portal, prominent flying buttresses and large windows filled with brilliantly coloured stained glass. Even here, however, there were Spanish touches, such as the cloister and its dependencies, and the later construction of a *coro*.

All the other cathedrals followed the model of Burgos and Toledo. **El Burgo de Osma** is in a way a miniature version of them, although it's purer Gothic in form. **Palencia**, built in the fourteenth and fifteenth centuries, is unusual in that most of its decoration is roughly contemporary with the architecture, with very few later additions. At **Pamplona** and **Huesca**, the architects built in the knowledge that there would be a *coro* in the nave – though ironically these were removed relatively recently by restorers. Pamplona's cloister, the earliest part of the building, is perhaps the most beautiful Gothic cloister in Spain. It has several fine doorways and a chapel with an exquisite star vault, a feature that was to be Spain's main contribution to the vocabulary of Gothic architecture, as characteristic as fan vaulting in England, although far more common – and with an obvious debt to Moorish models. There are other, equally grand, examples of the national Gothic style: **Murcia** and **Oviedo** are two, **Sevilla** a more spectacular one, its vast size determined by the ground plan of the mosque that preceded it.

Regional styles

Regional forms of Gothic are found in Catalunya and Aragón. In **Catalunya**, churches were built with huge arcades, omitting the triforium and including only a small clerestory. Long spans were also common; aisles, if there were any, were very nearly the same height as the nave; buttresses were internalized by the construction of tall, straight-walled chapels built between them, lending a rather sober appearance to the outside. Barcelona's **Cathedral of Santa María del Mar** is a good example of all these features, as is **Palma Cathedral**, although the most spectacular of the Catalan cathedrals is **Girona** – so daring structurally as to be admired more for its engineering than its aesthetic appeal.

In **Aragón** there was strong Mudéjar influence, which extended even to the cathedrals of **Zaragoza**, **Tarazona** and **Teruel**. The towers of these cities, and of **Calatayud**, tend to be either square in shape and decorated with ceramic tiles that glisten in the sun, or else octagonal and of brick only. Both show a virtuoso skill in decoration with what appear to be very basic and unpromising materials. Each of the cathedrals has a central cupola, while Tarazona has an amazing cloister filled with Mudéjar ornament. There's another unusual cloister far away in Guadalupe, while more orthodox Mudéjar Gothic churches are all over, though there's a fine concentration in **Toledo**.

Military architecture

Turning to **military architecture**, a number of fortified towns from the Gothic period still survive. Toledo has several gateways and two bridges of the era, and there are fine examples of walls at Albarracín, Daroca, Morella, Berlanga de Duero, Madrigal de las Altes Torres and Montblanch. Spain's castles of this period are without parallel in Europe. However, those that had a genuine function in the Reconquest are as a rule in the poorest condition, while those that look most impressive today often had little if any defensive purpose. It should be remembered that there is no Spanish equivalent at any time to the English or French country house. Where great houses were built by the nobility in Spain, they often resembled castles, even if they were never used for military purposes.

Perhaps the finest fourteenth-century castle is that of **Bellver** near Palma, a circular structure built as a summer residence by the kings of Mallorca. The great fifteenth-century castle at **Olite** is a palace in the pastiche form on a grand scale. For all the monumentality of its towers, many are wholly ornamental and would have been quite useless in time of war. Unfortunately, what you see today gives little hint of the richness of the former interior decoration.

Along the banks of the Duero are castles which were genuinely in action at the time of the Reconquest. **Gormaz** is particularly interesting, showing how an originally Moorish building was adapted by the Christians after its capture. **Peñafiel**'s fifteenth-century castle is actually the successor to the one that was built as protection against the Moors; apart from its own severe beauty, it clearly shows the importance of a strong strategic location. The many brick castles in the **area of Segovia and Valladolid** should be thought of more as expressions of the wealth and power of the nobility than as genuine military constructions of the time. These often incorporated Mudéjar features, and their construction was often in reality rather delicate: **Coca** is the best example of this.

Civil buildings and Late Gothic

The legacy of **Gothic civil architecture** is also impressive. Large numbers of towns preserve their medieval character in layout and design, even if many of the houses are not, strictly speaking, original. Important town mansions survive all over the country, often characterized by the carving of a coat of arms on the facade. **Cáceres**, in Extremadura, is probably the richest place for seigneurial houses, although most of the other towns in this province are also notable for vernacular architecture of this, and later, dates. Elsewhere, the shipyards of **Barcelona** constitute a unique survival from the Gothic period, as do parts of the Barri Gòtic, which contains a number of original municipal buildings. Barcelona also has the earliest *lonja*, or exchange – later and more exotic examples of which can be found in Valencia, Palma and Zaragoza.

Spanish **late-Gothic** architecture is particularly spectacular, the increasing ornamentation partly the result of the mid-fifteenth-century influx of artists from Germany and the Netherlands to Spain. **Burgos** and **Toledo** were the centre of the developing style. Juan de Colonia built the superb openwork spires of Burgos Cathedral, modelled on those of his native Cologne – which themselves, ironically, existed only on paper until the nineteenth century. His son, Simon, was responsible for other work on the same building, particularly the Capilla del Condestable at the east end, and worked with his father on the Cartuja de Miraflores. At the same time, Anequin de Egas from Brussels began a series of additions to Toledo Cathedral.

A little later the focus shifted to **Valladolid** and became increasingly florid – the **Isabelline** style – reaching its most extreme in the facades of San Pablo and the Colegio San Gregorio. It's not known who was responsible for these, or for the equally ornate facade of Santa María in Aranda de Duero, though a variety of people have been suggested, not least Juan Guas, who is known to have built San Juan de los Reyes in Toledo, the gallery of the castle at **Manzanares el Real** and perhaps the Palacio del Infantado in **Guadalajara**. The Isabelline style, at its best, combined the Moorish penchant for hanging decoration with standard European motifs, and has been seen by some commentators as the one chance Spain had to create its own special, unified architectural style. However, Isabelline had a very short life. The queen after whom it was named became more enchanted by the Italians before long, and encouraged the adoption of the Renaissance in Spain.

There was also a countermovement towards a purer Gothic form. The New Cathedral of **Salamanca** and the cathedral of **Segovia** were both begun in the sixteenth century in what was then a wholly archaic language by Juan Gil de Ontañón, and continued by his son Rodrigo. Juan de Álava also built a number of monuments in this style – San Esteban in Salamanca, part of the cathedral at Plasencia, and the cloisters at Santiago. **Segovia Cathedral**, too – unusually for Spain – displays a remarkable unity of form, using the traditional Gothic elements rejected by earlier builders.

The Renaissance

Oddly enough, the **Renaissance** was introduced to Spain with the **Collegio Santa Cruz** in Valladolid, just a few hundred metres from the simultaneous construction of two Isabelline facades. The architect, Lorenzo Vázquez, for all his historical importance, remains a rather shadowy figure. (Later, he was to build an Italian Renaissance palace at La Calahorra in Andalucía.) Enrique de Egas, who built the hospitals at Toledo (Santa Cruz), Granada and Santiago, and who also worked in a late-Gothic style, as witnessed by his Capilla Real in Granada and his design for the adjoining cathedral, is much better documented.

Much early Spanish Renaissance architecture is termed **Plateresque**, from the profusion of carving which allegedly resembled the work of silversmiths. The term is now applied rather loosely, but it is most associated with **Salamanca**, which is built of an extremely delicate rose-coloured sandstone. The supreme masterpiece of the style is the facade of the **University** here, where, instead of the wild and irregular carvings of Valladolid, a generation before, all is order and symmetry, while equally ornate. The motifs used in Plateresque carving are wholly Italianate – figures in medallions, *putti*, candelabra, grotesques, garlands of flowers and fruit, scrollwork and coats of arms. No convincing attribution has been made for the university facade, but one Plateresque architect whose work can be traced is **Alonso de Covarrubias**. He built the Capilla de los Reyes Nuevos in Toledo Cathedral, part of the Alcázar and probably the Hospital de Tavera in the same city, and worked on Sigüenza Cathedral, particularly the amazing sacristy. The facade of the University of Alcalá de Henares is a more severe Plateresque masterpiece by Rodrigo Gil de Ontañón; other important works are San Marcos in León by Juan de Badajoz, and the Hospital del Rey near Burgos.

The **High Renaissance**, by contrast, centred around **Andalucía**, the part of the country that was most lacking in Christian architecture following its liberation from the Muslim powers. The real masterpiece of the style is the **Palace of Carlos V** in Granada – incongruously located in the Alhambra, but a superbly pure piece of architecture. It is rare in being based on a round courtyard, and is the only surviving building by Pedro Machuca. As for churches, the leading architect of the Andalucian Renaissance in this field was Diego de Siloé, who began his career as a sculptor in Burgos under his father, Gil, and built the marvellous Plateresque Escalera Dorada in the cathedral there. Following study in Italy, he worked as an architect, devising an ingenious east end for the cathedral at Granada, and designing Guadix Cathedral and El Salvador at Úbeda. The last-named was actually built by his pupil, Andrés de Vandelvira, whose own main work is the monumental cathedral of Jaén. All these buildings show a strongly classical influence.

The severest, purest and greatest Spanish Renaissance architect was **Juan de Herrera**, who succeeded Juan Bautista de Toledo as architect of **El Escorial**, to which he devoted much of his working life. To many, this vast building is excessively sober, particularly in a country where ornamentation has so often reigned supreme. However, it does have a unique grandeur, and illustrates the Spanish penchant for taking any style to its extremes. Herrera's other main building is the **Cathedral of Valladolid**, though sadly only half of this was ever built, and some of that well after Herrera. In this truncated form it can appear rather cold and sombre, although the model for the complete building shows what a well-proportioned, harmonious and majestic edifice it might have become.

The Baroque

For a time, Herrera's style was to spawn a number of imitations, and early **Baroque** architecture was remarkably restrained – Madrid's early seventeenth-century **Plaza Mayor** by Juan Gomez de Mora being a case in point. In the east, Neapolitan influence was paramount, and led to the building of a large number of dignified churches.

Before long, however, this early phase gave way to an exuberant, playful and confident style that is perhaps Spain's most singular contribution to European architecture, the **Churrigueresque** – taken from the name of the family of architects, the Churrigueras, with whom the style was most associated. Ironically, their own work in architecture was far less ornate than that of many of their successors, although they also designed **retablos**, which are as embellished as anything that followed, so large as to seem almost pieces of architecture in themselves. These were typically of carved wood, painted and gilded, with twisted columns populated by saints in visionary or ecstatic mood and swirling processions of angels. *Retablos* of this type were soon to be found in churches all over Spain. Often the work of far cruder imitators, they raised the ire of visiting Protestant travellers, who used the term "Churrigueresque" to signify all that was basest in art. It's still a pejorative term, although the Churrigueras did actually create a number of masterpieces.

José, the eldest brother, created a complete planned town in **Nuevo Baztán**, not far from Madrid. Alberto, the youngest and most talented, laid out the **Plaza Mayor** in Salamanca in collaboration with Andrés García de Quiñones – a superb and harmonious piece of town planning, integrated wonderfully with the town's older buildings, and with the plain sides enlivened by carvings deriving from Plateresque work, and the rhythmic facade of the *ayuntamiento* providing a central focus on the north side.

The Churrigueras' contemporaries were more profusely ornate, often imitating the form of the *retablos* in their portals, perhaps the finest example of which is the **Hospicio San Fernando** in Madrid by Pedro de Ribera. Another new architectural feature was the *transparente*, in which a lavish altarpiece is lit from above by a window cut in the vault, giving a highly theatrical effect. The most famous example is that in **Toledo Cathedral** by Narciso Tomé, a brilliant piece of illusionism when the sun shines through, though in an utterly incongruous setting.

The Baroque style was also, of course, used when making additions to existing buildings, something you see all over Spain. Sometimes the merging of Baroque and medieval was triumphantly successful, as in the mid-eighteenth-century Obradoiro facade of **Santiago Cathedral** by Fernando Casas y Novoa, the climax of about a century's work, encasing the old Romanesque building in a lively Baroque exterior. While the loss of the Romanesque exterior is regrettable, particularly as some of the Baroque building is mediocre, the facade ranks as one of the most joyous creations in all architecture, and the ultimate triumph of Spanish Baroque. Other notably successful Baroque additions are the towers of the cathedrals of El Burgo de Osma, Santo Domingo de la Calzada and Murcia, which all harmonize surprisingly well with the existing structures, and give them a dimension they previously lacked. Many other additions, however, were far less fortunate: much of the time Baroque builders paid insufficient attention to the scale, style and materials of the existing work, and even when each is a competent piece of work in its own right, old and new scream at each other in horror.

Because of the trend towards enlivening old buildings, only one complete Baroque cathedral was built in Spain, at **Cádiz**. Nor are there many notable Baroque monasteries, although a number of charterhouses (*cartujas*) were built, not least at **Granada**, which became more and more extreme as construction progressed, culminating in the outrageous *sagrario* (sacristy) by Francesco Hurtado Izquiero. However, Spanish Baroque never found favour at court, where Italian and French models were preferred, and architects and decorators were imported from these countries, producing the Bourbon palaces of Aranjuez, La Granja de San Ildefonso and Madrid, which stand apart from Spanish buildings of the period. Filippo Juvara, the famous architect of Turin, was summoned to Spain in the penultimate year of his life to design the garden front of La Granja and the overall plan for Madrid, although both were executed by his pupil, Giovanni Battista Sachetti.

Neoclassicism

In time, the court taste changed to **Neoclassical**, enforced by the mid-century establishment of academies, and the presiding architectural style became heavy and monumental in scale. The dominant figure was **Ventura Rodríguez**, a technically competent architect who built a lavish Augustinian church in **Valladolid** and completed the **Basílica del Pilar** in Zaragoza – a colossal building with elements drawn from a variety of styles that is more notable for its grandiose outline than for any other feature. But Rodríguez's talents were not put to their best use: his facade for **Pamplona Cathedral** would look fine on a bank but is wholly incongruous for a church, and a serious distraction in what is otherwise a fine building; and his plain, rather nondescript church at **Santo Domingo de Silos** is a similarly poor partner for the great cloister there. Another leading Neoclassical architect was **Juan de Villanueva**, who built the **Prado** (actually as a natural history museum) and the two **Casitas** at El Escorial.

Spain's subsequent provincial history is mirrored in the paucity of buildings of much consequence. The slow process of industrial and social change meant that there were few of the self-confident expressions of prosperity found all over northern Europe. There were a host of imitative styles, but it is really only on the small scale that they give much pleasure. **Neo-Gothic**, also, was nowhere near as vital or as prevalent as elsewhere: the cathedrals built in this style, at **San Sebastián** and **Vitoria**, are not especially notable, and the most satisfying work was probably the completion of **Barcelona Cathedral**, which was actually accomplished according to a fifteenth-century plan.

The twentieth century

Spain's architecture in the twentieth century was characterized by four distinct epochs: the tail end of the Modernisme movement in Catalunya, which flourished between 1880 and 1910; the early modernism of the Second Republic in the 1930s; the imperialism of the fascist years; and the resurgent contemporary architecture of the socialist era at the end of the twentieth century.

Modernisme

The Catalan **Modernisme** (or *modernista*) movement – characterized by organic form, structural daring and sculptural expression – sprang up in Barcelona at the end of the nineteenth century, fuelled by the city's economic prosperity and its subsequent radical growth (developed within the strict grid of the Eixample, planned by Ildefons Cerdà in 1859). At the forefront of the movement was **Antoni Gaudí**, one of the most distinctive voices of the age. His main architectural influences were Moorish and Gothic, which he considered the greatest European styles. From the former he took towers, *trompe l'oeil* effects, repeated elements, ceramics, cornices, dragons and the use of water, all employed, like his Gothic influences, in a free and fantastic way. He was also influenced by the natural world – trees, rocks, embankments, animals, birds, eroded and organic forms – and captivated by the potential of industrial technologies. He combined all these elements in an amazing – and distinctive – architectural vocabulary.

Some of his projects were almost impossibly ambitious. He worked for over forty years on the **Sagrada Familia**, yet only built a small portion. The **Parc Güell** was another vast project for a complete garden city, a commercial failure that has become a successful public park. Still, many less grandiose plans in a variety of forms were completed in Barcelona, and his work can also be seen in Astorga, León and Comillas.

Although Gaudi stands out amongst his **contemporaries**, a number of other architects of the time were instrumental in the *modernista* movement and produced schemes of great significance, both in terms of their visual impact on the city and in the influence they exert on Catalan architects today. Buildings worthy of particular note are Francesc Berenguer's Garraf Wine Cellar (1890); Josep Puig i Cadafalch's Casa Macaya (1901); Lluís Domènech i Montaner's sumptuous Palau de la Musica Catalana (1908, brilliantly refurbished by Oscar Tusquets in 1990); and J.M. Jujol's Casa Planells (1923) on the Avenida Diagonal.

Modernism

The advent of **modernism** (the International Style) in Spain is inextricably linked to the rise of socialism. In 1929 the International Exposition in Barcelona saw the construction of one of the twentieth century's masterpieces, the **German Pavilion**, designed by Mies van der Rohe (and rebuilt in 1986). Its rigorous geometry, pared down yet luxurious palette of materials and sensitive exploitation of natural light precede the very best of the world's contemporary architecture, and its impact on the young modernists of Spain was instrumental in the formation of **GATEPAC** (Grupo de Arquitectos y Tecnicos Españoles para una Arquitectura Contemporanea) in 1930 – a movement which promoted the adoption of new technologies and functional design. The group's best buildings were constructed in Barcelona; key amongst these was Sert, Torres and Subirana's Dispensario Antituberculoso (1934–38), which managed to be both modern in expression and traditional in planning, and thus paved the way for Spain's contemporary fusion of modernism with traditional idioms.

Imperialism

The outbreak of civil war in 1936 brought a sudden end to socialist ideals and dramatically ushered in the **iconoclastic** and **imperial style** of the **fascists**. The early years of the Falange regime were characterized by cultural introversion, centralization and retrogressive pastiche. Overscaled buildings blighted city centres, none worse than the vast, overbearing Air Ministry at Moncloa in Madrid (1957). The majority of Spain, however, was saved from total desecration by a severe shortage of cash preventing any significant building programme. The period even threw up one or two individual gems which have proved influential to the modern day: Cabrero and Aburto's brick-clad gridded Casa Sindical (1949; now the Ministry of Work and Social Affairs), opposite the Prado in Madrid, acted as a precursor to much of the city's rationalist social housing of the 1980s, while in Barcelona, Coderch's Casa de la Marina, with its inflected facades and fragmented plan, stands as a key reference to influential contemporary Catalan architects such as MBMP, Garces and Sorria, and Torres Martínez-Lapeña.

By the end of the 1950s introverted politics had brought Spain close to bankruptcy and the fascists were forced to turn to America for economic salvation. The country opened its doors to the **internationalism** which was spreading through the rest of the developed world. In contrast with its more prosperous neighbours, Spain's construction had limited technical capacity, and the majority of new buildings from this era were built in brick with concrete floors, softening the lines of the tough reinforced concrete, steel and glass buildings mushrooming all over northern Europe. Nonetheless, the advent of international intervention did bring with it some catastrophic development which, with little thought to urban planning, marred much of Spain's coastline and cities. Amongst this unchecked destruction, three architects stand out for high quality and hugely influential work: Alejandro de la Sota (architect of the Maravillas Gymnasium in Madrid, 1962), Javier Sáenz de Oiza (architect of the Torres Blancas in Madrid, 1968) and Oriel Bohigas (architect of the Thau School in Barcelona, 1970). Each, through their emblematic buildings and teaching, heralded the dramatic architectural change of the late twentieth century.

Contemporary architecture

With the death of Franco in 1975, the socialists swept into power on a wave of optimism – proclaiming change and using architecture to prove it. Planning legislation was reformed to save the nation's heritage and encourage considered building. Investment poured in, and throughout the country there was a massive construction programme of social housing, schools, libraries, medical centres and small urban spaces. These projects, geared towards **community regeneration**, were intended to foster public confidence in the new regime. Representative of this regeneration are the vast number of new housing projects in Vallecas in Madrid and the numerous public spaces instigated by Oriel Bohigas in Barcelona.

The massive building programme culminated in the **1992 Barcelona Olympics** and **Sevilla World Expo**. These events acted as major catalysts of urban regeneration in each city, and opened the world's eyes to Spain's emergent modern architecture – and Spain's doors to the world's best architects. In **Barcelona** vast arrays of redundant warehousing were ripped down to make way for the Olympic Village and Port, master-planned by Martorell, Bohigas, Mackay, Puigdomenec (MBMP), with buildings by the best of Catalunya's new wave of young architects, including Viaplana and Piñon, Bach and Mora, Torres Martínez-Lapeña, Enric Miralles, Garces and Sorria. The hill top of Montjuic was taken over for the sporting arenas. To facilitate the developments a whole new infrastructure was required; fast dual carriageways were constructed and the airport was doubled in size by Ricardo Bofill. Architects from around the world designed complementary monuments, eminent among them Norman Foster's Torre de Collserola communications tower and Arato Isozaki's Palau Saint Jordi indoor stadium on Montjuic. The impact of the Expo on **Sevilla** was less significant, although Santiago Calatrava's Alamillo bridge over the Guadalquivir and MBMP's Pabellon de Exposiciones stand out as structural *tours de force*. More significant was the construction of the AVE high-speed train link between two of Europe's most elegant modern stations – Rafael Moneo's Atocha in Madrid and Cruz and Ortiz's Santa Justa in Sevilla.

The recession which enveloped the rest of the world left Spain with a particularly harsh hangover after the euphoria of 1992, though it also enabled a younger generation to explore new ideas and technologies. As the recession passed, Spain's regional authorities returned to architecture to express optimism in the future, this time recruiting **international architects** to add glamour and prestige to the projects. After Frank O. Gehry's spectacular titanium-clad **Guggenheim** reinvented Bilbao, the frontiers have been thrown open to construction on all scales from Peter Eisenmann's mammoth City of Galician Culture in Santiago de Compostela, through Jean Nouvel's expansion of the Reina Sofía Museum in Madrid to Herzog & de Meuron's Barcelona Forum 2004 Building. Simultaneously, Spain's own architects have increasingly won significant commissions around the world. Notable projects by **Spanish architects abroad** include Rafael Moneo's cathedral in Los Angeles; Navarro Baldeweg's work in Princetown; and the late Enric Miralles' polemical Scottish Parliament in Edinburgh.

Alongside its flagship schemes, Spain continues to invest in both public and private projects, creating modern architecture that is amongst the best in the world. Such buildings include Mansilla & Tuñon's Fine Arts Museum in Castellón, Rojo, Verdasco, Fernández-Shaw's theatre in Guadalajara and Ábalos & Herreros's gymnasium pavilion in the Retiro in Madrid. Allied with a healthy respect for the conservation of its historical inheritance, this new wave of construction places Spain at the forefront of European architecture and makes it one of the most exciting architectural destinations in the world.

Gordon McLachlan and Hugh Broughton

Art

rom the Middle Ages to the present day, the history of Spanish painting is one of fits and starts, a process of development marked on one hand by extreme originality and on the other by near-fatal injections of foreign influence. Nevertheless, the high points are high, from Catalan Romanesque art and the monastic manuscript tradition through giants such as El Greco, Velázquez, Goya, Picasso and Dalí. Spanish art is at its best when its roots are deepest in Iberian soil: from the ecstatic agony of Castile and Andulucía in Zurbarán, or the darkness and satire of Aragonese Goya, to the irreverent subversiveness of Catalan Surrealism.

Early examples of this strength of expression can be found in the **illuminated manuscripts** and **mural paintings** of the eleventh and twelfth centuries. Dominant among the manuscripts are the many versions of Beatus's *Commentaries on the Apocalypse*, the original text of which, written by an eighth-century Spanish monk, inspired a whole series of versions illuminating the text with brilliantly coloured miniatures. These books have found their way into libraries all over the world, but many still remain in Spain, with those in Girona, El Burgo de Osma and La Seu d'Urgell particularly worthy of note.

The great decorated interiors of village churches are also characteristic of the period, especially in Catalunya, though for the most part these are no longer *in situ*; many were saved just in time to prevent them from deteriorating irrevocably, and have been removed to museums, of which Barcelona's have by far the finest collection. The most imposing example of this style is by the so-called **Master of Taüll**, whose decoration of the apse of the church of Sant Climent combines a Byzantine hierarchical composition with the vibrant colours and strong outlines of the manuscript illuminators. His overall rawness and monumentality seem strangely anticipatory of much of the best modern art.

Amazingly, two other highly talented painters also worked in the village of Taüll in the 1120s: art historians have christened them the **Master of Maderuelo** and the **Master of the Last Judgement**. Another notable artist of the period is the **Master of Pedret**, who incorporated scenes of everyday and natural life into his paintings.

Catalan studios also produced painted wooden altar frontals, often based on a central figure of a saint, surrounded by scenes from his life. In time, this grew in scale into the large *retablo* over the high altar – a key feature of Spanish churches for centuries. The most remarkable frescoes outside Catalunya are those of the Panteón de los Reyes in San Isidoro in León. These date from the second half of the twelfth century, and show a softer, more courtly style, perhaps influenced by French models.

The Catalan school

In the Gothic period, Catalunya's predominance continued, rivalled only by Valencia. The leader of the school was **Ferrer Bassa** (c. 1285–1348), court painter to Pedro IV (king of Aragón and count of Barcelona) and a manuscript illuminator. Unfortunately, his only certain surviving work comes from late in his long career – a series of murals in the Convent of Pedralbes in Barcelona.

These are charming, notable for their colouring and descriptive qualities, along with a sense of movement and skilled draughtsmanship, and are clearly influenced by the paintings of the Sienese school, though they're freer and less refined. Bassa may also have been influenced by the rounder qualities of Giotto and the Florentine school – Italian currents that are also found in the work of the artist's followers, along with various French trends.

The most notable names of this school were **Jaume Serra** (d. 1395), his brother, **Pere Serra** (d. 1408), **Ramon Destorrents** (1346–91), **Lluís Borrassa** (d. 1424) and **Ramon de Mur** (d. 1435). **Bernat Martorell** (d. 1452) is perhaps the most appealing of the group, a notable draughtsman who worked very carefully and deliberately, striving to give character to faces in his paintings. **Lluís Daimau** (d. 1460) came strongly under the influence of contemporary Flemish painting, in particular that of Jan van Eyck, and no other foreign currents are discernible in his work. **Jaume Huguet** (c. 1414–92) applied this new realism to the traditional forms of the Catalan school, and can thus be seen as a representative of the International Gothic style of painting.

The Valencian school

The Valencian school tended towards a more purely Italian influence, although one of its main painters, **Andrés Marzal de Sax** (d. 1410), may have been German. Other notable names are **Pedro Nicolau** (d. 1410), **Jaime Baco** ("Jacomart") (d. 1461), **Juan Rexach** (1431–92), and **Rodrigo de Osona** (d. 1510), the last of whom was influenced by the Renaissance. The greatest of all the Spanish Primitives, however, was **Bartolomé Bermejo** (d. 1495/8), originally from Córdoba, who worked in both Valencia and Barcelona. He seems to have had a fairly long career, but only a few works, of a consistently high quality, survive. His earlier paintings, of which the Prado's *Santo Domingo de Silos* is a good example, are sumptuous; the later works, particularly the *Pietà* in Barcelona Cathedral, are altogether more complex, with a haunting sense of mystery and a Flemish and French influence that marks the introduction of oil painting to Spain.

The Castilian school

In Castile, artists of foreign origin predominated – **Deillo Delli** ("Nicolas Florentino"; d. 1470) in Salamanca, **Nicolás Francés** (1425–68) in León, **Jorge Inglés** (dates unknown) in Valladolid, and **Juan de Flandes** (d. 1514) in Salamanca and Valencia. The last became court painter to Isabel la Católica and introduced a Renaissance sense of space along with the beautiful modelling and colouring typical of the Flemish school. There was a rustic local school active in Ávila, however, and towards the end of the century native artists came increasingly to the fore. Particularly notable is **Fernando Gallego** (c. 1440–1507), who worked in Zamora and Extremadura. Superficially, his paintings seem strongly reminiscent of Flemish types, but his exaggerated sense of drama – manifested in distorted expressions, strange postures and movements frozen in mid-course – is far removed from these models. Nonetheless, the garments are realistically drawn, and landscape is often a feature of the backgrounds.

Pedro Berruguete (c. 1450–1504) was originally trained in the Flemish style, but spent an extended period in Italy at the court of Urbino. His productions from this period are so close to those of the Fleming Justus van Gent that art historians have frequently been unable to distinguish between them. On his return to Spain in 1482, Berruguete worked in a hybrid style: although his drawing was precise and he introduced chiaroscuro to Spanish art, he persisted in using the traditional gold backgrounds – an anachronistic mixture that is surprisingly satisfying. Berruguete was never a slavish imitator of Italian models, like too many of his successors, and his most impressive works are those with crowd scenes, where the differentiation of types and attitudes is remarkable. **Alonso Berruguete** (1486–1561), his son, also went to Italy, and his paintings are heavily Mannerist in style, with strong drawing and harsh colours. His work as a sculptor is more significant: uneven in quality but sometimes truly inspired, with many powerful and intensely personal images. Certainly, he was the most distinctive and arguably the greatest native Spanish artist of the Renaissance.

The late Renaissance

Too often the quality of Italian art was diluted in Spain: neither nudes nor mythological subjects – both of crucial importance in Italy – had any attraction here, and there is barely an example of either. Instead, there was a sweetening and sentimentalization of religious models. In Valencia, **Fernando Yáñez** (d. 1531) and his collaborator **Fernando de los Llanos** (dates unknown) adopted this facet of the art of Leonardo da Vinci, while **Juan Vicente Masip** (c. 1475–1550) and his son of the same name, usually referred to as **Juan de Juanes** (1523–79), drew more from Raphael, becoming ever more saccharine as time went on.

Sevilla also had a school of painters, beginning with **Alejo Fernández** (d. 1543), but although less slavishly imitative of Italian models than the Valencian, it also failed to produce an artist of the very first rank. The Extremaduran **Luís Morales** (c. 1509–86) is more notable; he was revered by the common people, who referred to him as "El Divino", but he never found favour with authority, and much of his work is still in village churches. He is at his best with such small-scale subjects as the Madonna and Child, which he repeated many times with slight variations. Strongly Mannerist in outlook, his drawing is rather stiff and his colours often cold, but he has a genuine religious feeling.

Ironically enough, it took a foreigner, Domenico Theotocopoulos (1540–1614), universally known as **El Greco**, to forge a truly great and quintessentially Spanish art in the late-Renaissance period. He arrived in Toledo in 1575, having come from his native Crete via Italy. Presumably he hoped to find favour at court, particularly in the decoration of El Escorial, but was soon disappointed, and spent the rest of his life painting portraits of the nobility, along with a host of religious works for the many churches and monasteries of Spain's ecclesiastical capital. Having shown himself adept at both the Byzantine and Venetian styles of painting, he drew from both to create a highly idiosyncratic art that was ideally suited to the mood of Spain at the time. Distinguished features of his style include elongated faces and bodies, together with a sense of spiritual ecstasy that gives a strong feeling of the union of the terrestrial and the celestial. El Greco's gift for portraiture, too, is shown not only in his paintings of real-life sitters, but also in those of historical subjects, most notably in the several series of Apostles he was required to produce. His greatest work, *The Burial of the Count of Orgaz*, in Santo Tomás in Toledo, displays all the facets of his genius in a single canvas. Later, El Greco's style became increasingly abstract, with a freeing of his brushwork that anticipates many subsequent developments in the history of art. Sadly, although he maintained a flourishing studio which produced many replicas, none of El Greco's followers picked up much of his master's style. Most talented was **Luís Tristán** (1586–1624), whose own output was very uneven.

At court, a school of portraiture was founded by a Dutchman, **Antonio Moro** (1517–76), who emphasized the dignity of his sitters in their facial expressions and by giving prominence to clothes and jewellery – a style that was followed by two native artists, **Alonso Sánchez Coello** (1531–88) and **Juan Pantoja de la Cruz** (1553–1608). At El Escorial, minor Italian Mannerists were imported in preference to native artists. An exception was the deaf-mute **Juan Navarret** (1526–79).

In Valencia, **Francisco Ribalta** (1565–1628) began working in a similar Mannerist style, but soon came under the influence of Caravaggio and introduced naturalism and the sharp contrasts of light associated with tenebrism into Spain. He was followed by a yet more significant painter, **Jusepe (José) de Ribera** (1591–1652). Ribera spent nearly all his career in Naples under the protection of the Spanish viceroys, who sent many of his works back to his native land. He had two distinctive periods: early on in his career he used heavy chiaroscuro and small, thick brushstrokes; later he brightened his palette considerably. Above all, he was interested in the dignity of human beings, and whether he painted ancient philosophers in contemplation, saints in solace, or martyrs resigned to their fate, his art is a concentrated one, with the spotlight very much on the main subject. His subjects at times can appear gruesome, but they are very much of their period in that respect, and the treatment is never mere sensationalism. For a long time out of critical favour, Ribera now appears as one of the most accomplished artists of European Baroque.

The seventeenth century

In the early seventeenth century, Sevilla and Madrid replaced Valencia and Toledo as the main artistic centres of Spain. **Francisco Pacheco** (1564–1654) was the father figure of the Sevillan school, although nowadays his work as a theorist is considered more significant than his paintings. He adopted a naturalistic approach as a reaction against Mannerism, and was followed in this by **Francisco Herrera** (c. 1590–1656) and his son of the same name (1622–85), who painted in an increasingly bombastic and theatrical manner.

Towering high above these, Pacheco's son-in-law, **Diego Velázquez** (1599–1660), is probably the artist the Spanish people take most pride in. Velázquez was a stunning technician. His genre scenes of Sevillan life, painted while he was still in his teens, have a naturalistic quality that is almost photographic. In contrast with many of his fellow countrymen, Velázquez was a slow and meticulous worker: he probably painted fewer than 200 works in his entire career, some 120 of which survive, almost half of them in the Prado.

In 1623 Velázquez went to Madrid to work for the court, a position he retained for the rest of his life. As well as the many royal portraits, he portrayed the jesters and dwarfs of the palace, giving them a Spanish sense of dignity. In *The Surrender of Breda* he revolutionized history painting, ridding it of supernatural overtones. His greatest masterpieces, *Las Hilanderas* and *Las Meninas*, date from near the end of his life, and are remarkable for the way they immortalize fleeting moments, as well as for their absolute technical mastery, particularly of aerial perspective.

Juan Bautista del Marzo (c. 1615–67), son-in-law and assistant to Velázquez, was so adept at imitating his style that it is often difficult to determine which works are the originals and which are copies. His independent work, however, is altogether of inferior quality. **Juan Carreno de Miranda** (1614–85) also followed Velázquez's portrait style closely, and was very active as a painter of religious subjects, a field largely abandoned by Velázquez in his maturity.

In Sevilla, the greatest painter was **Francisco de Zurbarán** (1598–1664), who is best known as an illustrator of monastic life of the times. He painted mainly for the more austere orders, such as Carthusians and Hieronymites, and many of his portraits of saints are modelled on real-life monks, some of them single figures of an almost sculptural quality. Zurbarán's palette was a bright one, his lighting effects are subtle rather than dramatic, and he ranks as one of the supreme masters of still lifes, which have a frequent presence in his larger paintings as well as in a few independent compositions. A complete example of one of his decorative schemes is still extant at Guadalupe, but sadly his later work sometimes shows a fall-off in quality: to pay off his debts he was forced to produce a large number of works for export to religious foundations in Latin America.

Zurbarán also sentimentalized his style in order to meet the competition of his highly successful younger contemporary, **Bartolomé Esteban Murillo** (1618–82), who spent his entire career in Sevilla. Murillo's light, airy style was in perfect accord with the mood of the Counter-Reformation, and he was to have an important impact on Catholic imagery. His versions of subjects such as the Immaculate Conception, Madonna and Child, and the Good Shepherd, became the norm in terms of the portrayal of traditional dogma. His genre scenes of street urchins and portraits in the manner of van Dyck made him popular in northern Europe, too, and for a long time he was considered one of the greatest artists of all time. His reputation slumped considerably in the nineteenth century, and it is only in the last few years that critical opinion has turned again in his favour. Certainly his subject matter can seem cloying to modern tastes, but Murillo nearly always painted beautifully, and he was a marvellous storyteller. His later works were particularly successful, employing the *vaporoso* technique of delicate brushwork and diffuse forms, and there's no doubt that he was a substantial influence on much subsequent eighteenth- and nineteenth-century painting in Spain, France and England.

In complete contrast to Murillo, **Juan Valdés Leal** (1622–90) preferred the violent and macabre side of the Baroque. His work was very uneven in quality; the paintings in the Hospital de la Caridad in Sevilla are the most celebrated. **Alonso Cano** (1601–67) was the leading painter of Granada and also active as an architect and sculptor. He led a rather dissolute life, and changed his working style abruptly several times. Perhaps the most successful of his paintings are the mature, pale-coloured religious works, which reveal debts to van Dyck and Velázquez.

A large number of artists can be grouped together under the **Madrid school**. One of the earliest was the Florentine-born **Vicente Carducho** (1576–1638), who painted large-scale works in sombre colours for the Carthusians and other orders. **Fra Juan Rizi** (1600–81) illustrated contemporary monastic life in a different and less mystical way than Zurbarán. His brother, **Francisco Rizi** (1614–85), favoured full-blown canvases of Baroque pomp. **Fra Juan Bautista Maino** (1578–1649) was more influenced by the classical aspects of seventeenth-century art; he painted some notable religious and historical canvases with strong colouring, but with little interest in lighting effects. **Juan de Arellano** (1614–76) and **Bartolomé Pérez** (1634–93) worked mainly with landscape and historical religious works, while **José Antolínez** (1635–75) was particularly renowned for his versions of the Immaculate Conception. **Mateo Cerezo** (1626–66) painted fluid religious canvases under the influence of the works by Titian and van Dyck in the royal collections. The last major figure was probably also the most accomplished: **Claudio Coello** (1642–93), who was a master of the large-scale decorative style, using techniques of spatial illusion and very complicated arrangements of figures. His work at El Escorial shows his style at its best.

The eighteenth and nineteenth centuries

The late seventeenth century and the first half of the eighteenth century was a very thin time in the history of Spanish painting: even the French and Italian artists imported by the Bourbon court were seldom of great merit. One native artist worthy of mention, however, is **Luís Meléndez** (1716–80), a master of still-life subjects. **Anton Raphael Mengs** (1728–79) came to Spain from Bohemia in 1761 as court painter, and in this capacity was a virtual dictator of style for a while, spearheading the adoption of an academic, Neoclassical tone, particularly in portraiture. His assistant, **Francisco Bayeu** (1734–95), was a prolific fresco painter for both royal and religious patrons, and was also in charge of the cartoons for the Royal Tapestry Factory. His brother, **Ramón Bayeu** (1746–93), worked on similar projects but was far less accomplished.

It was the Bayeus' brother-in-law, however, **Francisco Goya** (1746–1828), who was the overwhelmingly dominant personality of the period. Goya's output was prolific and his range of subject matter and style so immense that it is hard to believe one man was responsible for so much. Interestingly, he was no prodigy. In his twenties he became a highly competent painter of religious murals, his work at Zaragoza and Aula Dei already surpassing that of his contemporaries. After moving to Madrid, he worked for many years on tapestry cartoons (preparatory drawings), which in their graceful handling and skilful grouping made the most of their rather frivolous subject matter and gave Goya an entry into court circles, after which he became a fashionable portrait painter. It was in this role that his originality began to show through: his portraits eschew any attempt at flattery, and it's clear that he was less than impressed by his sitters. A serious illness in the early 1790s left him deaf and led to a more bitter and sarcastic art; his increasingly fantastic style may have emerged from his developing interest in witchcraft, which resulted in many paintings and two series of etchings: *Los Caprichos* and, later, *Los Disparates*. The marvellous frescoes in San Antonio de la Florida in Madrid are the exception here, among his most beautiful creations ever and containing a remarkable representation of the various social types of the day. But the Peninsular War further darkened Goya's mood, as shown by *The Second of May* and especially *The Third of May*, and by the engravings *The Disasters of War*. The last paintings are probably his most remarkable, especially those of bullfights, in which he showed an extraordinary visual perception, the exactness of which was proved only with the development of the slow-motion camera. Finally, there were the despairing "black paintings" made on the walls of his own house, the Quinta del Sordo, now detached and hung in the Prado.

Of Goya's contemporaries, the most interesting are **Luís Paret y Alcázar** (1746–99), who painted Rococo scenes under French and Italian influence, and **Vicente López** (1772–1850), an academic portrait painter in the manner of Mengs whose severe portrait of Goya hangs in the Prado. The nearest artist to Goya in style was **Eugenio Lucas** (1824–70), who followed his interest in bullfighting and Inquisition scenes, but made little stylistic advance. Indeed, most of the nineteenth century was extremely barren in terms of Spanish art, a period of imitation, largely of French models, at least twenty years late. The most gifted painter was perhaps **Mariano Fortuny** (1838–74), who specialized in small, very highly finished canvases, often of exotic subjects. Other artists worthy of mention are **Dario de Regoyos y Valdés** (1857–1913), the nearest thing to an Impressionist working in Spain at the time; **Joaquín Sorolla** (1863–1923), who was noted for his beach scenes; and **Ignacio Zuloaga** (1870–1945), who painted portraits against landscape backgrounds.

The twentieth century

As with architecture, it was Catalunya that took the lead in painting towards the end of the nineteenth century. **Isidoro Nonell** (1873–1911) was best known as a naturalistic painter of the poor. In contrast, **José María Sert** (1874–1945) was at his best in large-scale mural decorations, particularly in the powerful sepia and grey frescoes he produced for Vic Cathedral, replacements for two earlier sets.

Although born in Málaga, **Pablo Picasso** (1881–1973), the overwhelmingly dominant figure in twentieth-century art, spent many of his formative years in Barcelona. In 1900 he first visited Paris, where the influence of Toulouse-Lautrec made itself felt in the "blue period" of 1901–4, during which he depicted many of society's victims in Paris and Barcelona, following the lead of Nonell. The "rose period" of 1904–6 was perhaps Picasso's most Spanish phase (although by now he was living in Paris). Actors, clowns and models featured among his subjects, and his interest turned to the work of El Greco and ancient Iberian sculpture. The following "negro period" of 1907–9 marked the break with traditional forms, as manifested in the key work, *Les Demoiselles d'Avignon*. After this Picasso returned to representational painting only for a short time in the 1920s, and from 1910 onwards developed Cubism in association with Frenchman Georges Braque.

The movement's first phase, analytical Cubism, was largely concerned with form, with being able to depict objects as if seen from different angles at the same time. This was followed by synthetic Cubism, which showed a revival of interest in colour and handling. For a time in the 1920s and 1930s, Picasso combined Cubism with Surrealism, inventing a new anatomy for the human form, and eventually becoming noted as a painter of protest, most markedly in *Guernica*, a cry of despair about the Civil War in his native land (which he had by then left for good). Until his death, Picasso worked in a variety of styles,

In the wake of Franco's demise, Spain shed its mantle of political pariah and its reputation as a cultural wasteland. Nowhere is this more apparent than in the plastic arts which have seen an exponential revival in recent decades. By the mid-1990s Spanish sculpture boasted a rich variety of accomplished artists including some of the nation's first internationally lauded female artists.

Considered to be one of the most important sculptors in Spain today, **Susana Solano**'s (b.1946) metal constructions have received considerable critical acclaim. With her penchant for working in iron, Barcelona-based Solano is formally linked to Picasso and the Rebel Tradition of Spanish sculpture in the 1920s. In 1988 she was accorded the distinction of being one of only two artists representing Spain in the Venice Biennale.

Cristina Iglesias (b.1956) is celebrated for her architectural use of space and the often organic textures created with a variety of industrial materials. Her international profile was secured when she became one of the youngest artists to be given a solo exhibition at the Guggenheim Museum, New York in 1997, since when she has consolidated her reputation with exhibitions across the world.

Her husband, **Juan Muñoz** (1953–2001), dominated the international contemporary art scene for over two decades. At a time when most sculptors were exploring the realm of abstract or conceptual art, Muñoz was respected as one of the most intelligent and innovative figurative sculptors of his generation. His signature work, which occupied him for much of the 1990s, was *Conversation pieces* – anonymous resin-coated grey diminutive human figures in grey suits. Aged just 48, he died at the height of his career, at a time when his massive, audacious installation *Double Bind* was on show at the Tate Modern in London. Enjoyed by a daily audience of 10,000 people, it was a fitting bequest, given that throughout his life he had been a great advocate of public sculpture, famously saying "the great unfinished assignment for artists of the twentieth century is public sculpture. In this sense, sculptors have thoroughly failed".

active in sculpture and ceramics as well. He was prolific to an almost unimaginable degree – in 1969 alone he produced almost as many canvases as Velázquez did in his lifetime, among the most notable of which were variations on well-known paintings such as *Las Meninas*.

One of the most faithful Cubists was **Juan Gris** (1887–1927), who favoured stronger colours and softer forms than others in the group. In **Surrealism**, two Catalans were among the leading figures: **Joan Miró** (1893–1983) and **Salvador Dalí** (1904–89). Miró created the most poetic and whimsical works of the movement, showing a childlike delight in colours and shapes, and developing a highly personal language that was freer in form and more highly decorative than that of the other Surrealists. One of his favourite techniques during the 1930s was to spill paint on the canvas and move his brush around in it. He was also active in a variety of artistic media besides paint and canvas: collage, murals, book illustrations, sculpture and ceramics. Aside from an early period as a Futurist and Cubist, Dalí was more concerned with creating his own vision of a dream world. He was particularly interested in infantile obsessions and in paranoia, and his works often showed wholly unrelated objects grouped together, the distortion of solid forms, and unrealistic perspectives. He also worked on book illustrations, some of them his own texts, and on films. In later years he looked for other stimuli and painted a number of religious subjects. Few other artists in history have shown such talent for self-publicity. There are few artists, either, who have been so easily forged: in his later years

Dalí reputedly made millions by signing thousands of blank pieces of paper.

Artists of the same generation include **Óscar Domínguez** (1906–57), who used both the Cubist and Surrealist idioms, at times combining the two in a wholly individualistic way. Another isolated figure of note was **José Gutiérrez Solana** (1885–1945), whose impoverished background led him to seek out his subjects amongst the lowlife of Madrid he knew so well, adopting a realist approach with strong use of colour.

Spanish art of the late twentieth century was dominated by the "abstract generation", many of whom are still living, and who run a museum at Cuenca devoted solely to their works. By far the most individual figure of the group was **Antonio Saura** (1930–1999), whose violently expressive canvases, the earlier of which are painted in black and white only, are overtly political in tone, showing Man oppressed but unbowed. He used religious themes in a deliberately humanist or even blasphemous way in his triptychs of crowd scenes, and transformation of the Crucifixion into a parable of secular oppression. The Catalans **Joan Brossa** (b. 1919) and **Antoni Tàpies** (b. 1923) are abstractionists in the tradition of the Dada movement. Brossa, primarily a sculptor, is also famous as a dramatist and poet; while Tàpies, who is better known, began by making collages out of newspaper, cardboard, silver wrapping, string and wire. For a period he turned to graffiti-type work with deformed letters, before returning to experiments with unusual materials, particularly oil paint mixed with crushed marble.

For those who despair of the theoretical and iconoclastic side of the modern movement, **Antonio López García** (b. 1936) comes as a refreshing change – a hyperrealist painter of landscapes, cityscapes, and sculptor of still lifes and nudes with an unsettling photographic clarity to his work. **Eduardo Arroyo** (b. 1937) is a follower of the Pop Art movement, with its emphasis on large-scale depictions of familiar everyday faces and objects.

The political changes of the 1970s injected a frenetic optimism into Spanish art, and the end of censorship provoked a brash and sensational reaction featuring much concept art – a rejection of painting itself by the generation of this period, which the Mallorcan **Miquel Barceló** (b. 1957), whose "Action Painting" follows the tradition of Pollock and Tàpies, characterized as having produced more junkies than artists. The 1980s saw the pendulum swing back towards traditional Spanish painting before the "Post-Enthusiast" 90s, which neither rejected nor glorified painting, but incorporated it with other media, including sculpture, photography and video. Spanish art is now globalizing, and is ever more susceptible to foreign currents and trends. Typical of the tendency to cross-media are young artists like **Pedro G. Romero** (b. 1961) who is an artist and rock musician, or **Rogelio Lopez Cuenca** (b. 1959) whose pop art and video are heavily influenced by the Russian avant-garde. Other new lights include the Duchamp-influenced **Federico Guzmán** (b. 1964), **José Espaliu** (b. 1955) and **Fermín García** (b. 1961), a self-taught painter whose city- and landscapes blend realism with impressionistic touches.

With some justification, **Santiago Sierra** (b. 1966), born in Spain but now working in Mexico, is often described as the *enfant terrible* of the contemporary Spanish art. His controversial video work and installations raise questions of the nature of a capitalist system: he ignited an art gallery with petrol on its opening night for one piece and paid impoverished immigrants paltry wages to move heavy concrete blocks round an exhibition room, for another. He provided Spain's contribution in the 2003 Venice Biennale, with a rough breeze-block wall which obstructed the entrance to the Spanish Pavilion and a passport control at the back of the building that restricted entrance to an empty building to Spanish nationals. His critics, who are as vocal as his admirers, argue that his work is repetitive, simplistic and that it exploits the human dignity of the participants. But they are opposed by a strong following who admire his readiness to confront the harsh reality of the global economy. Both camps agree, however, that Sierra is extending the limits of art and forcing it into the political arena.

Gordon McLachlan
With contributions by Holly Pelham

Wildlife

Despite its reputation as the land of the package holiday, you can't beat Spain for sheer diversity of landscape and wildlife. When the Pyrenees were squeezed from the earth's crust they created an almost impenetrable barrier stretching from the Bay of Biscay to the Mediterranean Sea. Those animals and plants already present in Spain were cut off from the rest of Europe, and have been evolving independently ever since. In the same way, the breach of the land bridge at what is now the Strait of Gibraltar, and the subsequent reflooding of the Mediterranean basin, stranded typical African species on the peninsula. The outcome was an assortment of wildlife originating from two continents, resulting in modern-day Iberia's unique flora and fauna.

Spain is the second most **mountainous** country in Europe after Switzerland. The central plateau – the Meseta – averages 600–700m in elevation, slopes gently westwards and is surrounded and traversed by imposing sierras and *cordilleras*. To the north, the plateau is divided from the coast by the extensive ranges of the Cordillera Cantábrica, and in the south the towering Sierra Nevada and several lesser ranges run along the Mediterranean shores. Where these southern sierras continue across the Mediterranean basin, the unsubmerged peaks today form the Balearic Islands. The Pyrenean chain marks the border with France, and even along Spain's eastern shores the narrow coastal plain soon rises into the foothills of the Sierras of Montseny, Espuña and los Filabres, among others. The ancient Sierras de Guadarrama and Gredos cross the Meseta just north of Madrid, and the Sierra Morena and the Montes de Toledo rise out of the dusty southern plains. With such an uneven topography it is not surprising to find an alpine element in the flora and fauna, with the most strictly montane species showing adaptations to high levels of ultraviolet light and prolonged winter snow cover.

The centre of Spain lies many kilometres from the coast, with a **climate** almost continental in character. The summers can be scorching and the winters bitter, and what rain there is tends to fall only in spring and autumn. To the east, the Mediterranean Sea moderates this weather pattern, blessing the coastal lands with mild winters and summers which become progressively hotter as you move south towards Africa. With the Costas representing the popular perception of the country, first-time visitors are often surprised by the contrast between the almost subtropical south and the cool, wet, temperate north. Depressions coming in from the Atlantic Ocean bring high rainfall, persistent mists and a landscape akin to the West of Ireland. Appropriately named the Costa Verde (Green Coast), temperatures are mild even in summer, and when the sun does shine the high humidity can sometimes make it feel uncomfortable.

These climatic variations have produced a corresponding diversity in Spanish wildlife. The wet, humid north is populated by species typical of northern Europe, whilst the southern foothills of the Sierra Nevada have more in common vegetation-wise with the Atlas Mountains of Morocco. The continental weather pattern of much of the **interior** has given rise to a community of drought-resistant shrubs, together with annual herbs which flower and set seed in the brief spring and autumn rains, or more long-lived plants which possess underground bulbs or tubers to withstand the prolonged summer drought and winter cold.

Landscape

Like most of Europe, the Iberian peninsula was once heavily forested. Today though, following centuries of deforestation, only about ten percent of the original **woodland** remains, mostly in the north. Historically, much of the Meseta was covered with evergreen oaks and associated shrubs such as laurustinus and strawberry tree (*madroño* – the tree in the symbol of Madrid), but the clearance of land for arable and pastoral purposes has taken its toll, as have the ravages of war. Today tracts of Mediterranean woodland persist only in the sierras and some parts of Extremadura. When it was realized that much of the plateau was unsuitable for permanent agricultural use, the land was abandoned, and is now covered with low-growing, aromatic scrub vegetation, known as *matorral* (maquis). An endangered habitat, the maquis is a haven for many rare and distinctive plant and animal species, some found nowhere else in Europe. The southeastern corner of the Meseta is the only part of Spain which probably never supported woodland; here the arid steppe **grasslands** – *calvero* – remain basically untouched by man. In northern Spain, where vast areas are still forested, the typical tree species are more familiar: oak, beech, ash and lime on the lower slopes, grading into pine and fir at higher levels – and the appearance is distinctly northern European.

Much of the Meseta is predominantly flat, arid and brown. Indeed, in Almería, Europe's only true **desert** is to be found, such is the lack of rainfall. But the presence of subterranean water supplies gives rise to occasional **oases** teeming with wildlife. The numerous tree-lined **watercourses** of the peninsula also attract birds and animals from the surrounding dusty plains. The great Ebro and Duero rivers of the north, and the Tajo and Guadiana in the south, have been dammed at intervals, creating **reservoirs** which attract wildfowl in winter.

The Spanish **coastline** has a little of everything: dune systems, shingle banks, rocky cliffs, salt marshes and sweeping sandy beaches. In Galicia, submerged river valleys, or *rías*, are reminiscent of the Norwegian fjords, and the offshore islands are home to noisy sea-bird colonies; the north Atlantic coast is characterized by limestone promontories and tiny, sandy coves; the Mediterranean coast, despite its reputation for wall-to-wall hotels, still boasts many undeveloped lagoons and marshes; and southwest of Sevilla lies perhaps the greatest of all coastal wetlands: the Coto Doñana.

While the rest of Europe strives for agricultural supremacy, in Spain much of the land is still **farmed** by traditional methods, and the landscape has changed little since the initial disappearance of the forests. The olive groves of the south, the extensive livestock-rearing lands of the north and even the cereal-growing and wine-producing regions of the plains, exist in harmony with the indigenous wildlife of the country. It is only since Spain joined the European Community that artificial pesticides and huge machines have made much impact. Even so, compared to its neighbours, Spain is still essentially a wild country. Apart from a few industrial areas in the northeast and around Madrid, the landscape reflects the absence of modern technology, and the low population density means that less demand is made on the wilderness areas that remain.

Flowers

With such a broad range of habitats, Spain's **flora** is nothing less than superb. Excluding the Canary Islands, about 8000 species occur on Spanish soil, approximately ten percent of which are found nowhere else in the world. The plethora of high **mountains** allows an alpine flora to persist in Spain well beyond its normal north European distribution, and because of the relative geographical isolation of the mountain ranges, plants have evolved which are specific to each. In fact there are about 180 plants which occur only in the Pyrenees, and over forty species endemic to the Sierra Nevada.

This effect is clearly illustrated by the **buttercup** family. In the Pyrenees, endemic species include the pheasant's-eye *Adonis pyrenaica* and the meadow-rue *Thalictrum macrocarpum*; the Sierra Nevada has *Delphinium nevadense* and the monkshood *Aconitum nevadense*, and of the columbines *Aquilegia nevadensis* occurs here alone. *A. discolor* is endemic to the Picos de Europa, *A. cazorlensis* is found only in the Sierra de Cazorla and *A. pyrenaica* is unique to the Pyrenees. Other handsome montane members of this family include alpine pasque flowers, hepatica, hellebores, clematis and a host of more obvious buttercups.

The dry Mediterranean grasslands of Spain are excellent hunting grounds for **orchids**. In spring, in the meadows of the Cordillera Cantábrica, early purple, elder-flowered, woodcock, pink butterfly, green-winged, lizard and tongue orchids are ten a penny, and a little searching will turn up sombre bee, sawfly and Provence orchids. Further into the Mediterranean zone, exotic species to look for include Bertoloni's bee, bumblebee and mirror orchids. Lax-flowered orchids are common on the Costa Brava and high limestone areas will reveal black vanilla orchids, frog orchids and summer lady's tresses a bit later in the year.

The Mediterranean **maquis** is a delight to the eye and nose in early summer, as the cistus bushes and heaths come into flower, with wild rosemary, thyme, clary and French lavender adding to the profusion of colour. The *dehesa* grasslands of southwest Spain are carpeted with the flowers of *Dipcadi serotinum* (resembling brown bluebells), pink gladioli and twenty or so different trefoils in May. In the shade of the ancient evergreen oaks grow birthworts, with their pitcher-shaped flowers, bladder senna and a species of lupin known locally as "devil's chickpea".

Even a trip across the **northern Meseta**, although reputedly through endless cereal fields, is by no means a dull experience. Arable weeds such as cornflowers, poppies, corncockle, chicory and shrubby pimpernel add a touch of colour and are sometimes more abundant than the crops themselves. Where the coastal **sand dunes** have escaped the ravages of the tourist industry you can find sea daffodils, sea holly, sea bindweed, sea squill and the large violet flowers of *Romulea clusiana*.

Mammals

The great mammalian fauna that roamed Europe in the Middle Ages today survives only as a relict population in the wildest areas of Spain. Forced to seek refuge from hunters and encroaching civilization, it is perhaps surprising that the only species to have succumbed to extinction is the little known European Beaver. Unfortunately, with elusiveness the key to their survival, the mammal species that remain can be almost impossible to see. Endangered, but common in the mountains of the north, the **wolf** (*lobo*) avoids contact with humans as much as possible. Persecuted for centuries in response to the exaggerated threat portrayed in folk tales, they are still today regarded as a major threat to livestock in some quarters, despite their dwindling numbers. Although afforded official protection, many farmers would not think twice about shooting on sight. Similarly, the omnivorous **brown bear** (*oso pardo*) shows none of the inquisitive boldness exhibited by its American cousins, and with numbers as low as 100 in Spain, anybody catching a glimpse of one should consider themselves exceptionally fortunate.

In the **northern mountains** – the Pyrenees and the Cordillera Cantábrica – you should get at least a glimpse of chamois, roe and red deer, and possibly **wild boar** (*jabalí*), which can be seen at dusk during the winter conducting nightly raids on village potato patches. The **Spanish ibex** (*cabra montés*), the scimitar-horned wild goat, had represented the main quarry of locals since prehistoric times. However, whilst it was able to sustain low levels of predation, its agility was no match for modern hunters and it almost disappeared in the early years of the twentieth century. Thanks to effective conservation measures, its numbers are slowly beginning to recover and it is becoming an increasingly common sight in the Sierras de Cazorla, Grazalema (both Andalucía), and Gredos (Castilla-León). Europe's answer to prairie dogs, **marmots** (*marmotas*) can occasionally be seen in the Pyrenees, where they graze in alpine meadows, while the surrounding pine forests support large numbers of their arboreal relatives – the red squirrel. Less well-known, and considerably more difficult to see, is the bizarre **Pyrenean Desman**, a large, shrew-like creature closely related to moles, which inhabits the mountain streams of the Pyrenees and the Cordillera Cantábrica.

The typical mammals of **southern Spain** have more in common with Africa than Europe, the separation of the two continents leaving several species stranded to evolve in isolation. Specialities of African origin include the sleek, cat-like **spotted genet**, and the adaptable, intelligent **Egyptian mongoose**, both of which are active mainly at night but can be glimpsed during the day. The undoubted jewel of the south, though, is the **Iberian lynx** (*lince ibérico*), paler, more heavily spotted and less heavily built than the northern European species, in adaptation to the subtropical climate. Highly endangered, and now almost completely confined to the Coto Doñana national park, its haunting cries on spring nights are sadly becoming more and more infrequent.

In the **air**, no fewer than 27 species of **bat** occupy caves and woodlands throughout Spain. Highly visible and often attracted to artificial light sources by the clouds of insects, they are amongst the easiest of wild mammals to see, although identification to species level is best left to experts. Most interesting are the four types of horseshoe bat and Europe's largest bat, the rare **Greater Noctule**, which, with a wingspan of 45cm, even feeds on small birds.

The most spectacular **aquatic mammals** are the twenty or so species of **whale** and **dolphin**, whose presence has encouraged the appearance of numerous boating companies to run trips out to see them. **Pilot whales** and **sperm whales** are common in the Straits of Gibraltar, and **dolphins** will often choose to accompany boat trips in all areas. Isolated and protected coves on the Mediterranean shores shelter some of the last breeding colonies of the **Mediterranean monk seal**, a severely threatened species perhaps doomed to extinction. **Fresh water** also supports a number of mammal species, perhaps the best known being the playful **European otter** which is still fairly numerous in the north.

Birds

If any country in Europe qualifies as a paradise for **birdwatching** then it must surely be Spain. Most twitchers head straight for the world-famous Coto Doñana National Park where over half of all European bird species have been recorded, but other parts of the country are just as rewarding, even if you have to work a little harder to get a matching list.

Birds of prey are particularly visible, and as many as 25 species of raptor breed here, but it is during the spring and autumn migrations that you will see the most dramatic numbers. Clouds of honey buzzards, black kites and Egyptian vultures funnel across the Straits of Gibraltar, aided by warm currents, followed by less numerous but equally dramatic species such as short-toed and booted eagles. Resident species include the widespread griffon vulture, the surprisingly common red kite and the dramatic Bonelli's eagle. Twitchers, though, are likely to have their sights set on four attention-grabbing species: the Eurasian black vulture fighting against extinction in Extremadura; the bone-breaking bearded vulture of the Pyrenees; the diminutive but distinctive black-winged kite of the southern plains; and the endangered, endemic Spanish imperial eagle. The latter is most easily seen in the Coto Doñana, where guides take great delight in pointing out this emblematic hunter.

There is no less variety in other types of birds. Woodpeckers are most abundant in the extensive forests of the **northern mountain ranges**. While white-backed woodpeckers are confined to the Pyrenees, other such rarities as black and middle-spotted woodpeckers may also be seen in the Cordillera Cantábrica, and the well-camouflaged wryneck breeds in the north and winters in the south of the country. Other typical breeding birds of these northern mountains are the turkey-like capercaillie, pied flycatchers, blue rock thrushes, alpine accentors, citril and snow finches, and that most sought-after of all montane birds, the unique, butterfly-like wallcreeper.

In the open **grasslands** and cereal fields of the Meseta, larks are particularly common. Look out for the calandra lark, easily identified by its chunky bill and the trailing white edge to the wing. More rewarding are great and little bustards – majestic at any time of year, but especially when the males fan out their plumage during the springtime courtship display. In a tiny area of the Mediterranean coast, strange nocturnal mooing calls from low-growing scrub betray the presence of the secretive **Andalucian buttonquail**, a tiny, quail-like bird, strangely enough more closely related to the bustards than the quails. Look out also for the exotically patterned pin-tailed sandgrouse, one of only two European members of a family of **desert-dwelling birds**, as well as stone curlews and red-necked nightjars, the latter seen (and heard) mainly at dusk.

Olive groves are an ornithological treasure trove playing host to a colourful assemblage of birds – hoopoes, azure-winged magpies, golden orioles, southern grey and woodchat shrikes, bee-eaters, rollers, great spotted cuckoos and black-eared wheatears. On a sunny summer's day, these birds are active and often easy to spot if you are patient.

Fluctuating water levels, particularly in the south, mean that there is no shortage of seasonally-flooding freshwater habitats positively teeming with bird life. In reedbeds you may come across the vividly-coloured purple gallinule, the high-stepping Bailon's crake, the thrush-sized great reed warbler or localized colonies of sociable bearded reedlings. In winter large flocks of migrant waterfowl may gather, but it is the resident species that bring more reward: the exotic red-crested pochard; the rare ferruginous duck; the delicate marbled teal and the threatened white-headed duck being among the highlights.

Coastal wetlands and **river deltas** are a must for any serious birdwatcher, with common summer occupants including black-winged stilts, avocets, greater flamingos and all but one of the European representatives of the heron family: cattle and little egrets, purple, grey, squacco and night herons, bitterns and little bitterns. In the right conditions and at the right time of year, almost all the species can be seen breeding together in vast and noisy heronries – an unforgettable sight. Wintering waders are not outstandingly distinctive, though wherever you go, even on the Atlantic coast, you should look for spoonbills. Grey phalaropes visit the northwest corner, as do whimbrel, godwits, skuas and ruff, taking a break from their northern breeding grounds. For **sea birds**, the Islas Cíes, off the Galician coast, are unbeatable, providing breeding grounds for shags, the rare Iberian race of guillemot and the world's southernmost colony of lesser black-backed gulls.

Even towns have their fair share of notable species. The **white stork** (*cigüeña blanca*) is a summer visitor that has endeared itself to Andalucía and south central Spain, and few conurbations are without the unkempt nest atop a bell tower, electricity pylon or war monument. Finches such as serin and goldfinch are numerous, and the airspace above any town is usually occupied by hundreds of swifts, martins and swallows; you may be able to pick out alpine, pallid and white-rumped swifts, and red-rumped swallows if you are in the southern half of the country, as well as crag martins in the north.

The **Balearic Islands** can provide you with a few more unusual cliff-nesting species, such as Eleanora's falcon, while deserted islets are ideal for hole-nesting sea birds such as Cory's shearwater and storm petrels.

Reptiles and amphibians

Around sixty species of reptiles and amphibians occur in Spain, including some of Europe's largest and most impressive. Four species of salamander inhabit the peninsula. The brightly-coloured **fire salamander**, an attractive patchwork of black and yellow, is perhaps the most well known. Named for its habit of seeking solace in woodpiles and later emerging when the fire was lit, the legend grew that the salamanders were somehow born out of the flames. The foot-long **sharp-ribbed salamander** of the southwest is Europe's largest, and bizarrely pierces its own skin with its ribs when attacked. The two remaining species, the drab, misnamed **golden-striped salamander** and the **Pyrenean brook salamander**, are confined to the cool, wet, mountainous north.

Closely related to the salamanders are the **newts**, of which there are only four species in Spain. If you take a trip into the high mountain pastures of the Cordillera Cantábrica, where water is present in small, peaty ponds all year round, you should see the brightly-coloured **alpine newt**, while the aptly-named **marbled newt** can be seen round the edges of many of Spain's inland lakes and reservoirs. Searches through tall waterside vegetation frequently turn up the tiny, lurid-green **tree frog**: striped in the north and west, but stripeless along the Mediterranean coast.

Two species of **tortoise** occur in Spain; **spur-thighed tortoises** can still be found along the southern coast and on the Balearic Islands, the latter the only Spanish locality for the other species – **Hermann's tortoise**. European **pond terrapins** and **stripe-necked terrapins** are more widely distributed, but only in freshwater habitats. Beware of confusion between these native species and the introduced North American **red-eared terrapin**, the result of the release of unwanted pets following the decline of the Teenage Mutant Ninja Turtle craze. **Marine turtles** are uncommon visitors to the Mediterranean and Atlantic coasts. Perhaps the most frequently encountered is the protected **green turtle**, especially in the waters around Gibraltar, but **loggerhead** and **leathery turtles** are very occasionally reported.

The most exotic reptilian species to occur in Spain is the **chameleon**, although again this swivel-eyed creature is confined to the extreme southern shores where its camouflage skills render it difficult to find. **Lizards** are numerous, with the most handsome species being the large **ocellated lizard** – green with blue spots along the flank. Some species are very restricted in their range, such as Ibizan and Lilford's wall lizards, which live only in the Balearic Islands. In the south, the most noticeable lizards are **Moorish geckos**, large-eyed nocturnal creatures usually seen on the walls of buildings both inside and out. Adhesive pads on their feet enable them to cling perilously to vertical surfaces as they search for their insect prey.

Similarly, **snakes** are common, although few are venomous and even fewer are ever likely to bite. When faced with humans, evasive action is the snake's preferred option, and in most cases a snake will be long gone before the intruder even knew it was there. The **grass snake** will even play dead rather than bite, if cornered. **Asps** and **western whip snakes** occur in the Pyrenees, while the commonest species in the south is the harmless **horseshoe whip snake**, the distinctive horseshoe mark on the back of its head giving it the common name.

The most unusual Spanish reptile is undoubtedly the **amphisbaenian**, sometimes misleadingly called the blind snake. Adapted to a subterranean existence, this rarely encountered and harmless creature can sometimes be found by searching through rotten leaves and mulch in forested environments and gardens of the south.

Insects

Almost 100,000 insects have been named and described in Europe and an untold number await discovery. In a country with areas where no one knows for sure how many bears there are, the insects have barely even begun to be explored.

From early spring to late autumn, as long as the sun is shining, you will see **butterflies**: there are few European species which do not occur in Spain, but by contrast there are many Spanish butterflies which are not found north of the Pyrenees. These seem to be named mostly after obscure entomologists: Lorquin's blue, Carswell's little blue, Forster's furry blue, Oberthur's anomalous blue, Lefèbvre's ringlet, Zapater's ringlet, Chapman's ringlet, Zeller's skipper, and many others. You need to be an expert to identify most of these, but the more exciting butterflies are in any case better-known ones: the Camberwell beauty, almost black and bordered with gold and blue; swallowtails, yellow and black or striped like zebras, depending on the species, but always with the distinctive "tails"; the lovely two-tailed pasha, which is often seen feeding on the ripe fruit of the strawberry tree; and the apollo (papery white wings with distinctive red and black eyespots), of which there are almost as many varieties as there are mountains in Spain. Other favourites include the small, bejewelled blues, coppers, fritillaries and hairstreaks that inhabit the hay meadows.

Aside from the butterflies, keep an eye open for the largest **moth** in Europe, the giant peacock, which flies by night but is often attracted to outside lights, or the rare, green-tinted Spanish moon moth, a close relative of tropical silk moths. During the day, take a closer look at that hovering bumble bee, as it may be a hummingbird hawkmoth, or a broad-bordered bee-hawk, flying effortlessly from flower to flower. Oleander and elephant hawkmoths (resplendent in their pink and green livery) are often seen around flowering honeysuckle bushes at dusk. Despite the often nondescript appearance of the adult forms, many moths have bizarre caterpillars, for example the lobster moth, which feeds on beech, or the pussmoth, found on willows and poplars.

Grasslands and arid scrub areas are usually good hunting grounds for **grasshoppers and crickets**, which can be located by their calls. Mole crickets and field crickets live in burrows they have excavated themselves, but look to the trees for the most colourful species, like the enormous great green bush cricket, about 7–8cm long. French lavender bushes in the maquis are a favourite haunt of the green mantis *Empusa pennata*, identified by a large crest on the back of the head and the familiar "praying" posture. **Stick insects** are harder to spot, as they tend to sit parallel with the stems of grasses, where they are well camouflaged.

Members of the *Arachnidae* (**spiders**) to be found include two species of **scorpion** in the dry lands of southern Spain. Look out also for long-legged *Gyas*, the largest harvest-spider in Europe, with a pea-sized body suspended by ridiculous gangly legs and a diameter of about 10cm. Spanish **centipedes** can grow to quite a size, too. *Scutigera coleopatra*, for example, which often lives indoors, has fifteen pairs of incredibly long, striped legs, which create a wonderful rippling effect when they move across walls. The daddy of them all, though, is the massive *Scolopendra cingulatus*, up to 15cm long and with a vicious venomous bite when molested.

Where and when to go

Virtually anywhere in Spain, outside the cities and most popular tourist resorts, rewards scrutiny in terms of wildlife. Perhaps the best thing about this country is that so much wilderness remains to be discovered on your own, without guidebooks to tell you where to go.

The following suggestions are largely limited to those which are easily accessible by public transport. Inevitably this means that other people will be there, too: you'll have to head off into the hills on foot in order to experience the best of Spanish wildlife.

Southern Spain is a good choice for any **time of year**, since even in the depths of winter the climate is mild and many plants will be in full bloom. If you decide on the **northern mountain ranges**, spring and early summer are best. The weather can be temperamental, but for the combination of snowy peaks and flower-filled meadows, it's worth taking the risk. The **interior** of Spain is freezing in winter and almost too hot to bear in midsummer, so spring or autumn – to coincide with the occasional rains and the flowering of the maquis and steppe grasslands – are best. Again, if your real interest is the **coastal bird life** of Spain, visit in spring or autumn, not only to catch the phenomenal migrations of birds between Africa and northern Europe, but also because accommodation in the resorts can be incredibly low-priced outside the tourist season.

The Pyrenees

Known by the Moors as El Hadjiz – the barricade – this imposing range of mountains effectively isolates Iberia from the rest of Europe. The Spanish slopes of the Pyrenees are somewhat warmer and drier than their northern counterparts, resulting in a more scrubby vegetation type, but where forested areas do occur they are astoundingly beautiful and the high passes are snow-bound for several months in the winter.

If you avoid the ski resorts there are still many unspoiled valleys to explore, with their colourful alpine meadows studded with Pyrenean hyacinths and horned pansy, and some of the highest forests in Europe, extending up to 2500m in places. The **Vall d'Aran**, close to Pico de Aneto (the highest point of the chain, at 3408m), is a botanical paradise at any time of year. Go in spring and you will find alpine pasque flowers, trumpet gentians and sheets of daffodils, among them pale Lent lilies and pheasant's-eye narcissi. A little later in the year sees the flowering of Turks'-cap lilies, dusky cranesbill and Pyrenean fritillaries, sheltering among the low-growing shrubs on the hillsides; while in autumn, following the annual haymaking, the denuded meadows shimmer with a pink-purple haze of merendera and autumn crocuses.

In the Aragonese Pyrenees of the west, Spain's oldest national park, the **Parque Nacional de Ordesa y Monte Perdido**, boasts valleys clothed in primeval pine, fir and beech forests, and is home to 32 species of mammal including pine martens, wildcats, genets, red squirrels, polecats and wild boar. One of the last remaining Pyrenean glaciers can be seen at Monte Perdido (the lost mountain), whilst the forest is broken up by sheer cliffs, spectacular waterfalls and towering rock formations. Here the sprightly chamois thrives, skipping effortlessly along vertical rock faces with astonishing agility, while in the air the determined birdwatcher will hope to be rewarded with a glimpse of the rare bearded vulture. Its Spanish name – *quebrantahuesos* – means "bone-break-er" and refers to the rarely observed habit of dropping animal bones from great heights to smash on the rocks below, exposing the tender marrow.

The second national park in the Spanish Pyrenees is that of **Aigüestortes**, centred on the glacial hanging valleys and impressive cirques of northern Catalunya. Its Catalunyan name means "winding waters", a reference to the profusion of freshwater lakes, streams and waterfalls that distinguish the park. Complemented by flowering meadows, rugged forests and jaw-droppingly picturesque snowcapped peaks, the park has been referred to as "The Jewel of the Pyrenees". **Lake Sant Maurici** in particular is renowned for its beauty, a shimmering, cut-glass surface mirroring the surrounding forests and mountain peaks. The extensive coniferous forests of Scots pine and common silver fir are populated by capercaillie and black woodpeckers. Just above the timberline, early purple orchids and alpine and southern gentians flourish in the superb alpine meadows, and the rocky screes conceal pale, delicate edelweiss and yellow mountain saxifrage. Otters frolic in the fast-flowing mountain rivers and the secretive Pyrenean desman, a type of aquatic mole, is native to the area.

Cordillera Cantábrica

The Cordillera Cantábrica mountain chain traces a rugged and at times breathtakingly beautiful course parallel to the north coast, from the Portuguese border eastwards into the Basque country. Despite recent transport improvements, harsh winter weather still renders large sections impassable and the mountains continue to act as a natural barrier separating the cool, wet north from the warmer, drier interior of the country. The vegetation is clearly affected by the rain-laden clouds which constantly sweep in from the Atlantic, as can be seen by the extensive oak and beech forests that shroud the slopes. Extensive beef and dairy farming is the traditional way of life, and the majority of the flower-filled meadows have never been subjected to artificial fertilizers and pesticides. One of the most fascinating aspects is the abundance of meadow flowers fast disappearing in northern Europe: lizard orchids, heath lobelia, greater yellow rattle, moon carrot, Cambridge milk-parsley, galingal and the delicate white flowers of summer lady's-tresses.

The high point of the Cordillera Cantábrica is the **Parque Nacional Picos de Europa**, at nearly 65,000ha the largest national park in Western Europe. The craggy limestone peaks are visible from miles offshore in the Bay of Biscay and provide welcome refuge for over sixty species of mammal. From the tiny snow voles, denizens of the high peaks, to the last of the brown bears it is almost a snapshot of medieval Europe, when such diversity was much more widespread across the continent. Red squirrels, roe deer and chamois are easy to see, but many of the mammals which haunt these mountains, such as genets, beech martens and wildcats, are secretive nocturnal beasts.

Perhaps the most outstanding landscape feature of the Picos de Europa is the famous **Cares gorge**, where the river bed lies almost 2000m below the peaks on either side. The sheltered depths of the gorge are home to a number of shrubs more typical of Mediterranean Spain – figs, strawberry trees, wild jasmine and barberry – and the sheer rock faces are home to the exotic wall-creeper, a small ash-grey bird with splashes of crimson on the wings, the sight of which is highly coveted by birdwatchers. Hard-core birders will also be delighted by the sight of the comparatively drab, but equally impressive, snow finch or alpine accentor.

The western massif around **Covadonga** has as its focal point the glacial lakes of Enol and Ercina. In spring the verdant pastures which surround the lakes are studded with pale yellow hoop-petticoat daffodils and tiny dog's-tooth violets, but a visit later in the year will be amply rewarded by the discovery of hundreds of purple spikes of monkshood and the steel-blue flowers of Pyrenean eryngo. Alpine choughs scavenge among the litter bins in the café car park, while entomologists will be excited by the presence of almost a third of Europe's butterfly species occurring within the park boundaries.

For those who prefer more gentle scenery, **Galicia**, with its green rolling hills and constant mists, is hard to beat. Few people live in the countryside, which as a consequence is teeming with wildlife. The oak and beech woods of Ancares provide shelter for deer and wild boar, although the chamois were hunted to extinction for food during the Civil War. The meadows benefit from the frequent rains and you can find all manner of damp-loving plants, such as large-flowered butterwort, bog pimpernel, globe flowers, marsh helleborines, whorled caraway and early marsh orchids.

The interior

Despite its reputation as a flat, barren plain covered with mile after mile of bleached cornfields, inland Spain has more than its fair share of wildlife – if you know where to look.

A good place to start is the **central sierras**. Just to the north of Madrid, almost bisecting the vast plain of the Meseta, run several contiguous mountain ranges which are well worth a visit. They may not have the rugged grandeur of the Pyrenees but there is plenty of wildlife to be found on the rocky, scrub-covered slopes. The extensive pine forests of the **Sierra de Guadarrama** are a great place to look for Spanish bluebells and the unmistakeable toadflax, *Linaria triornithophora*, which has large, tailed snapdragon-like flowers of pink or white. Birds of prey are abundant, and, with practice, not too difficult to tell apart. Both red and black kites can be seen, easily distinguished from other raptors by their distinctly forked tails (the red kite has clear white patches under its wings), booted eagles are identified by the black trailing edge to their wings, and the short-toed eagle, here known as *águila culebrera*, the "snake eagle", is almost pure white below, with a broad, dark head.

Further west the granite bulk of the **Sierra de Gredos** boasts some of the highest peaks in Spain after the Sierra Nevada and the Pyrenees. Scots and maritime pines occur at the higher levels, sweet chestnut and Pyrenean and cork oaks on the southern slopes. The springtime flora is superb, including lily-of-the-valley, conspicuous St Bernard's and martagon lilies, and several species of brightly coloured peonies. On some of the drier slopes, where the trees have been cleared, the aromatic gum cistus forms a dense layer up to 2m high. There is no need to fight your way through their sticky branches to discover the delights of the flora here: even the edges of the shepherds' tracks are ablaze with asphodels, French lavender, a strange-looking plant called the tassel hyacinth and the closely related grape hyacinth. But best of all in the Gredos are the ibex, easily seen in the pine zones between the cirques of Laguna Grande and Cinco Lagunas. Look out also for Egyptian and griffon vultures, and Bonelli's eagles overhead, while crossbills and firecrests hop around the treetops of the coniferous forests, and rock buntings, identified by their grey-striped heads, are almost everywhere.

Moving away from the mountains towards the plains is **Monfragüe Natural Park**, in Extremadura. Located at the confluence of the Rivers Tajo and Tietar, areas of *Dehesa* and *Cistus* scrub are broken up by mixed oak forest and dramatic rocky outcrops and gorges. Golden orioles, woodchat and southern grey shrikes, hoopoes and bee-eaters are colourful summer inhabitants, while in winter huge flocks of crane descend on the nearby **Embalse de Borbollon**, a reservoir born out of a damming project in the late 1960s.

Monfragüe is perhaps best known for its breeding population of the endangered **Spanish imperial eagle**, the largest in the world outside of the Coto Doñana. The central reserve where this raptor nests is open only to permit holders, but you may see them soaring over the *Dehesa*. The same can be said for the rare **Eurasian black vulture**, of which Monfragüe has the largest known breeding colony (about sixty pairs). Most people head for the huge rock outcrop known as Peñafalcón, where black storks, now extremely rare as a breeding bird in Spain, can be seen perched up on the cliff face, and the sky is constantly filled with griffon vultures coming and going. Look out, too, for a smallish, light-coloured hovering bird – it might be a rare black-winged kite, which you certainly won't see elsewhere in Europe.

Heading in the other direction, towards Zaragoza in the northeastern corner of the plains, you might consider visiting the **Laguna de Gallocanta**. This is Spain's largest natural inland lake, and has a lot to recommend it. Also present are birds more typical of the arid plains – pin-tailed sandgrouse and stone curlews – as well as those usually associated with fresh water. Gallocanta is a national stronghold for red-crested pochard.

Mediterranean coast

Spain's Mediterranean coast conjures up visions of sandy beaches packed with oiled bodies and a concrete wall of hotels stretching from the French border to Gibraltar. Even in the heart of the Costa Brava, though, there's rich wildlife to be found. The **Parc Natural dels Aiguamolls de l'Empordà** in Catalunya is a salt marsh and wetland reserve sandwiched between the A7 motorway and the hotel developments in the Gulf of Roses. It is the nearest thing in Spain to a British nature reserve, with signposted nature trails, a well-equipped information centre and several bird hides. This rather detracts from the wilderness aspect of the site, but it is nevertheless a good place to watch out for the 300 species of birds that have been observed here. Apart from the more typical water birds, look out for little bittern, black-winged stilt, bearded reedling, purple gallinule and purple heron, all of which breed here. Spring is perhaps the best time, when flamingos, glossy ibis and spoonbills pass through on migration.

If you can't stand the mosquitoes from the marshes, try the drier, Mediterranean scrub areas nearby, which are ideal for spotting breeding lesser grey shrikes (the only Spanish locality), stone curlews, great spotted cuckoos and moustached and Marmora's warblers in summer. Marsh and Montagu's harriers are, of course, always present.

Other promising wildlife locations include the fan-like **Delta de l'Ebre** (Ebro Delta), with up to 100,000 wintering birds and a large colony of purple herons. Again isolated from the mainland by the A7 motorway, the lagoons and reed beds here attract squacco and night herons, avocets and red-crested pochard, with isolated islands providing nesting areas for the rare Audouin's and slender-billed gulls. Look out, too, for lesser short-toed larks, and a multitude of tern species, including gull-billed, whiskered, roseate and sandwich.

Further south again lies the **Albufera de Valencia**, one of the most ornithologically important sites in Spain. Despite being so close to the city of Valencia, its combination of wetland, lagoon, marsh and sand-dune habitats create a unique patchwork of landscapes that attracts a plethora of unusual species. Waterfowl are the big attraction, especially in winter when vast flocks of shoveler, pintail, gadwall and teal rub shoulders with smaller numbers of specialities like red-crested pochard, marbled teal and ferruginous duck. Other water birds to look out for are the extremely rare crested coot, as well as cattle and little egrets, night, purple and squacco herons, little bitterns, black-necked grebes and penduline tits.

Southern Spanish sierras

Stretching for miles behind the coastal metropolises of the Costa del Sol, these lofty mountains are a complete contrast from the sun-and-sea image of southern Spain. Perhaps the best known is the **Sierra Nevada** at the eastern end of the range, which was upgraded to **national park** status in 1999. The range's highest peak is Mulhacén (3482m), the highest mountain in mainland Spain and snowcapped for much of the year at the highest levels, but the south-facing foothills are only about 150km from Africa. In a small area the environmental conditions thus range from alpine to almost tropical. Not surprisingly, there is an incredible range of plant and animal life. If you are equipped to visit the high mountains when the snow is starting to melt you should see such attractive endemic plants as glacier eryngo, looking not unlike its Pyrenean counterpart, and Nevada daffodils, saxifrages and crocuses. Later on in the year there is still plenty to see, including the strange, spiny mountain tragacanth, wild tulips, peonies, pinks, alpine gentians, the Nevada monkshood and columbine, and the white-flowered rockrose *Helianthemum apenniunum*.

Owing to the extreme altitude of the Sierra Nevada, birds more commonly found further north – crossbills, alpine accentors and choughs – have a final European outpost here. You should also see many of the smaller birds which favour dry, rocky hillsides. Perhaps the most distinguished of these is the black wheatear, the males identified by their funereal plumage and white rump. Further north, in the limestone **Sierras de Cazorla y Segura**, raptor-watching will be amply rewarded. The endangered bearded vulture once bred in Cazorla in small numbers, and an ongoing reintroduction and captive breeding programme aims to re-establish a viable population from foreign stock. Small numbers of golden and Bonelli's eagles nest in the peaks and goshawks frequent the extensive forests (black, maritime and Aleppo pines at high levels and holly, holm and Lusitanian oaks, with narrow-leaved ash and strawberry trees, on the lower slopes).

These mountain ranges, birthplace of the great Río Guadalquivir, are rather unusual in Spain in that they run approximately north–south rather than east–west. They also have a flora of some 1300 unique species including such handsome rock-dwelling plants as the crimson-flowered Cazorla violet (*Viola cazorlensis*), the columbine *Aquilegia cazorlensis*, a relict carnivorous butterwort (*Pinguicula vallisneriifolia*) and several endemic narcissi.

To the west lie some extraordinary Jurassic limestone ranges, eroded over centuries into formations known collectively as *torcales*. One of the more famous of these is **Grazalema**, renowned for its Spanish fir forest. This tree (*Abies pinsapo*) is a unique pre-Ice Age survivor, now restricted to just a handful of localities in southern Spain, including the **Serranía de Ronda**, and a specialized flora has evolved to cope with the dense shade that the trees cast. You should be able to find the colourful peonies *Paeonia coriacea* and *P. broteri*, as well as paper-white daffodils and the winter-flowering *Iris planifolia*, with a large, solitary flower on a ridiculously short stem. A whole range of typical Mediterranean shrub species grows here, including laurustinus, grey-leaved and poplar-leaved cistus, Spanish barberry, Etruscan honeysuckle, the nettle tree (*Celtis australis*) and *Acer granatense*, a maple species confined to the mountains of southern Spain. Within these woods the powerful **eagle owl** breeds, large enough to prey on mammals the size of roe deer and birds as large as capercaillie.

As a break from the mountains you might consider a visit to **Fuente de Piedra**, the largest inland lagoon in Andalucía (about 15 square kilometres). Partly because the water is never more than 1.5m deep (the level being further reduced by intense evaporation in summer), and also due to the lack of pollution, large numbers of flamingos construct their conical mud nests here every year, with over 8000 pairs present in good years. As one of only two regular sustainable breeding places for greater flamingos in Europe, Fuente de Piedra has been designated a *Reserva Integral*, the most strictly protected type of nature reserve in Spain. Altogether about 120 species of bird, 18 mammals and 21 reptiles and amphibians have been recorded here.

Southern Atlantic coast

The more or less tideless Mediterranean ends at Gibraltar, so the coast stretching westwards up to the Portuguese border is washed by the Atlantic Ocean. Here, the low-lying basin formed by the Río Guadalquivir contains one of Europe's finest wetlands: the **Coto Doñana**, Spain's most famous national park. Because of its fame and the huge volume of visitors that it would otherwise attract, today the only way to view the park is by group tours in unwieldy vehicles not entirely conducive to watching wildlife. However, the main species can usually be seen on these tours and the non-specialist is unlikely to be disappointed.

Here the most sought-after spectacles are the breeding colonies of spoonbills and herons in the cork oaks which border the marshes, but equally impressive are the huge flocks of **waterfowl** which descend on the lagoons during the winter. As for breeding ducks, Doñana is the European stronghold for the marbled teal, a smallish, mottled-brown dabbling duck which rarely breeds in Europe outside Spain. Ruddy shelduck – large, gooselike birds, generally confined to the eastern Mediterranean – are also present throughout the year, but breeding has not yet been proven. White-headed ducks definitely nest and rear their young here, although the more renowned nursery for this is at the Lagunas de Córdoba in central Andalucía. One of Europe's rarest birds is the crested coot, distinguished from the common coot only at close range by two small red knobs on its forehead, or in flight by the absence of a white wing-bar. It breeds in Morocco, migrating northwards into southern Spain for the winter; Doñana is the only Spanish locality where this species is resident all year round, although again no one is quite sure whether it breeds here or not.

Water birds aside, keep an eye out for large flocks of pin-tailed sandgrouse, which perform prodigious aerobatics in perfect time, rather like a shoal of fish; and, at ground level, cattle egrets in the grasslands, usually in the company of some of the renowned black bulls of the region. A smaller bird to watch out for is the Spanish sparrow, which commonly makes its home in the nether regions of the large, untidy nests of the white stork. Doñana also boasts an impressive roll call of birds of prey, including the Spanish imperial eagle and Eurasian black vulture.

Some large **mammals** are relatively easy to see in Doñana: red and fallow deer and wild boar display an inordinate lack of fear when approached by people, despite the fact that this area was a Royal Hunting Reserve until quite recently. The same, unfortunately, cannot be said for Doñana's pardel lynxes, of which there are some 25 pairs, estimated to represent about half the total Spanish population. Egyptian mongooses also frequent the dry, scrubby areas, and genets are occasionally seen by day in the more remote, forested parts of the national park. If you can drag your eyes from the veritable feast of bird life you might spot a curious creature known as Bedriaga's skink. Endemic to Iberia, this small lizard has only rudimentary legs and you are most likely to see it frantically burrowing into the sand in an effort to escape detection.

The nearby **Marismas de Odiel**, which lie within the boundaries of the city of Huelva, a little to the west, are also very worthwhile. Apart from the flamingos, which are increasingly preferring these saline coastal marshes as breeding grounds to the nearby Doñana, you will also be rewarded by the sight of large numbers of spoonbills, purple herons and other typical southern Spanish water birds.

The Balearic Islands

Despite the sun-seeker image of the Balearic Islands, there are many remote spots which have escaped the ravages of the tourist industry. Even on the big ones you can escape easily enough, and the majority of the fifteen islands that make up the Balearics are actually uninhabited.

One of the wilder regions is the **Sierra de Tramuntana**, which runs along the northern coast of Mallorca, dropping abruptly into the sea for much of its length. It is a good place to watch the aerobatics of Eleanora's falcon, a rare coastal species that pursues both insects and birds with incredible speed and agility. Around your feet you can feast your eyes on an array of exotic plants such as *Cyclamen balearicum*, an autumn-flowering crocus (*Crocus cambessedesii*),

Helleborus lividus (a rare member of the buttercup family), the pink-flowered *Senecio rodriguezii*, and many other endemic species of peony, birthwort and hare's ear. Even in January many plants are in flower, but the best time of year to see the blossoming of the islands is from March to May.

Away from the mountains, other wildlife refuges are the low-lying coastal marshes which have to date defied the hotel trade. **S'Albufera**, on Mallorca, is a birdwatcher's paradise. The maze of tamarisk-lined creeks and lagoons is the summer haunt of water rail, spotted crake and little egrets, and a little careful scrutiny may reveal more secretive occupants: Savi's, Cetti's, Sardinian, moustached, fan-tailed and great reed warblers. Also easy to get to are the saltpans known as **C'an Pastilla**, close to the airport at Palma, where whiskered and white-winged black terns, as well as Mediterranean and Audouin's gulls (this latter bird is the rarest breeding gull in Europe) are frequently seen.

The Balearics are also ideal places for watching the endemic races of lizards; they are usually quite undeterred by your presence, and make excellent subjects for portrait photography. If you are keen on marine life, don't forget your flippers and snorkel, as the underwater scenario is superb.

Teresa Farino
Updated by Paul Smith

Music

The Spanish music scene at the beginning of the twenty-first century contrasts sharply with that of the 1960s and 1970s when Spain was starting to emerge from many dark years of dictatorship. Music at the time was either a challenge to the dictatorial regime or a cliché. In the former camp there were singers such as Raímon, Joan Manuel Serrat, Luís Eduardo Aute and Lluís Llach, who dared with the strength of their voices and lyrics, filling many venues and selling thousands of records; in the latter camp there was the easy-listening music about love and romantic passion from Julio Iglesias, Raphael and Camilo Sesto. There was relatively little space for experimentation, and such that there was came from jazz (groups such as Pegasus) and avant-garde rock (groups such as Rock Laieta).

The **1980s** were a time of explosive creativity, with the urban music scene opening up fully to foreign influences, mainly Latin American and Anglo-Saxon, and everyone finally free to experiment: folk musicians incorporated electric sounds and crossed over into other genres; pop and rock musicians looked to the UK's new wave and punk movements; flamenco performers mixed in elements of pop, rock and blues. The beginning of the current scene was taking shape. Pop and rock bands such as El Ultimo de la Fila, Radio Futura, Gabinete Caligari, La Union, Loquillo y los Trogloditas, Los Secretos, Rebeldes, Heroes del Silencio, Nacha Pop and the massive Mecano defined the soundtrack for a new generation.

The 1990s saw a maturing of these styles and the growing self-confidence of the nation was reflected in the music. Spanish musicians were no longer copying foreign styles but were appropriating them, creating their own and exporting it across the world. From the pop star Enrique Iglesias to Mala Rodríguez, an Andalucian female rap artist addressing Spanish social and political problems, home-grown talent is no longer regarded as second best.

Flamenco

Flamenco – one of the most emblematic musics of Spain and its richest musical heritage – has recently enjoyed huge exposure and today is more popular than ever before. Twenty-five years or so ago it looked like a music on the decline, preserved only in the clubs or *peñas* of its *aficionados*, or in travestied castanet-clicking form for tourists. However, prejudice vanished as flamenco went through a tremendous period of innovation in the 1980s and 1990s, incorporating elements of pop, rock, jazz and Latin, and today there's a new respect for the old "pure flamenco" artists and a huge joy in the new.

The initial impetus for flamenco's new-found energy came at the end of the 1960s, with the innovations of guitarist **Paco de Lucía** and, especially, the late, great singer **Camarón de la Isla**. These were musicians who had grown up learning flamenco but whose own musical tastes embraced international rock, jazz and blues.

They have been followed by groups such as **Ketama**, **Raimundo Amador** (ex Pata Negra), **La Barbería del Sur**, **Navajita Plateá** and **Niña Pastori**, who have all reached massive audiences which neither Paco de Lucía nor the great Camarón de la Isla could have dreamt of decades before. At the end of the 1990s there were even successful comebacks from such established artists as **Enrique Morente** and **José Mercé**. Morente – the established king of flamenco – experimentally revisited old styles and combined them with new moves, releasing a spectacular new album, *Omega*, in 1996, with **Lagartija Nick**, one of the most emblematic bands of the Spanish indie rock scene. José Mercé collaborated with **Vicente Amigo** – recognized as the most gifted player of the moment, notably for his sense of syncopation – on *Del Amanecer*. Paco de Lucía acknowledges Amigo as his successor in the innovation of flamenco guitar.

Young flamenco musicians include **Miguel Poveda**, **Duquende** and **Ginesa Ortega** (who all hail from the Catalan–Barcelona flamenco scene), as well as **Juan Manuel Cañizares**.

Origins

Flamenco evolved in southern Spain from many sources: Morocco, Egypt, India, Pakistan, Greece, and other parts of the Near and Far East. Most authorities believe the roots of the music were brought to Spain by gypsies arriving in the fifteenth century. In the following century it was fused with elements of Arab and Jewish music in the Andalucian mountains, where Jews, Muslims and "pagan" gypsies had taken refuge from the forced conversions and clearances effected by the Catholic kings and Church. Important flamenco centres and families are still found today in quarters and towns of *gitano* and refugee origin, such as Alcalá, Jerez, Cádiz, Utrera and the Triana *barrio* of Sevilla. Although flamenco is linked fundamentally to **Andalucía**, emigration from that province has long meant that flamenco thrives not only there but also in Madrid, Extremadura, the Levante and even Barcelona – wherever Andalucian migrants have settled.

Flamenco *aficionados* enjoy heated debate about the purity of their art and whether it is more validly performed by a **gitano** (gypsy) or a **payo** (non-gypsy). Certainly during dark times flamenco was preserved by the oral tradition of the closed *gitano* clans. Its power, too, and the despair which its creation overcomes, seem to have emerged from the vulnerable life of a people surviving for centuries at the margins of society. These days, though, there are as many acclaimed *payo* as *gitano* flamenco artists, and the arrival on the scene of singers from Barcelona like Vicente Amigo – who has no Andalucian blood but grew up in a neighbourhood full of flamenco music – has de-centred the debate.

The concept of dynasty, however, remains fundamental for many. The veteran singer **Fernanda de Utrera**, one of the great voices of "pure flamenco", was born in 1923 into a *gitano* family in Utrera, one of the *cantaora* (flamenco singer) centres. The granddaughter of the legendary singer "Pinini", she and her younger sister Bernarda, also a notable singer, both inherited their flamenco with their genes. This concept of an active inheritance is crucial, and has not been lost in contemporary developments: the members of Ketama, for example, the Madrid-based flamenco-rock group, come from two *gitano* clans – the Sotos and Carmonas.

While flamenco's exact origins are debated, it is generally agreed that its "laws" were established in the nineteenth century. Indeed, from the mid-nineteenth into the early twentieth century flamenco enjoyed a Golden Age, the tail end of which is preserved on some of the earliest 1930s recordings. The musicians found a first home in the **café cantantes**, traditional bars which had their own groups of performers (*cuadros*). One of the most famous was the *Café* *de Chinitas* in Málaga, immortalized by the poet Gabriel Garciá Lorca in his poem *A las cinco de la tarde* (At five in the afternoon), in which he intimates the relationship between flamenco and bullfighting, both sharing root emotions and flashes of erratic genius, and both also being a way to break out of social and economic marginality.

The art of flamenco

Flamenco is played at *tablaos* and fiestas, in bars and at *juergas* (informal, more or less private parties). The fact that the Andalucian public are so knowledgeable and demanding about flamenco means that musicians, singers and dancers found at even a local club or village festival are usually very good indeed.

Flamenco songs often express pain. Generally, the voice closely interacts with improvising guitar, which keeps the *compás* (rhythm), the two inspiring each other, aided by the **jaleo** – the hand-clapping *palmas*, finger-snapping *palillos* and shouts from participants at certain points in the song. *Aficionados* will shout encouragement, most commonly *¡olé!* when an artist is getting deep into a song, but also a variety of other less obvious phrases. A stunning piece of dancing may, for example, be greeted with *¡Viva la maquina escribir!* (long live the typewriter), as the heels of the dancer move so fast they sound like a clicking machine; or the cry may be *¡agua!* (water), for the scarcity of water in Andalucía has given the word a kind of glory.

The encouragement of the audience is essential for an artist, as it lets them know they are reaching deep into the emotional psyche of their listeners. They may achieve the rare quality of **duende** – total communication with their audience, and the mark of great flamenco of any style or generation. Latterly the word *duende* has been used to describe "innovation" which, while it is significant, does not always capture the real depth of the word.

Flamenco songs

There is a classical repertoire of more than sixty flamenco **songs** (*cantes*) and dances (*danzas*) – some solos, some group numbers, some with instrumental accompaniment, others *a cappella*. These different styles (or *palos*) of flamenco singing are grouped in families according to more or less common melodic themes, establishing three basic types of cante flamenco: **cante grande** (comprising songs of the *jondo* type), **cante chico**, and **cante intermedio** between the two. Roughly speaking, the *jondo* and *chico* represent the most and the least difficult *cantes* respectively in terms of their technical and emotional interpretation, although any form, however simple, can be sung with the maximum of complexity and depth. **Cante jondo** (deep song) comprises the oldest and "purest" songs of the flamenco tradition, and is the profound flamenco of the great artists, whose *cantes* are outpourings of the soul, delivered with an intense passion, expressed through elaborate vocal ornamentation. To a large extent, however, such categories are largely arbitrary, and few flamenco musicians talk about flamenco in this way; what matters to them is whether the flamenco is good or bad.

The basic *palos* include **soleares**, **siguiriyas**, **tangos** and **fandangos**, but the variations are endless and often referred to by their place of origin: *malagueñas* (from Málaga), for example, *granaínos* (from Granada), or *fandangos de Huelva*. *Siguiriyas*, which date from the Golden Age, and whose theme is usually death, have been described as cries of despair in the form of a funeral psalm. In contrast, there are many songs and dances such as tangos, *sevillanas, fandangos* and *alegrías* (literally "happinesses") which capture great joy for fiestas. The **sevil-**

lana originated in medieval Sevilla as a spring country dance, with verses improvised and sung to the accompaniment of guitar and castanets (rarely used in other forms of flamenco). In the last few years, dancing *sevillanas* has become popular in bars and clubs throughout Spain, but their great natural habitats are Sevilla's April *Fería* and the annual *romería* or pilgrimage to El Rocio. Each year wonderful new *sevillanas* come onto the market in time for the fiestas.

Another powerful and more seasonal form are the **saetas**. These are songs in honour of the Virgins carried on great floats in the processions of *Semana Santa* (Easter Week), and traditionally they are quite spontaneous – as the float is passing, a singer will launch into a *saeta*, a sung prayer for which silence is necessary and for which the procession will therefore come to a halt while it is sung.

Camarón – or more fully **Camarón de la Isla** – was by far the most popular and commercially successful singer of modern flamenco. Collaborating with the guitarists and brothers Paco de Lucía and Ramón de Algeciras, and latterly, Tomatito, Camarón raised *cante jondo* to a new art. He died in 1992, having almost singlehandedly revitalized flamenco song, inspiring and opening the way for the current generation of flamenco artists.

Flamenco guitar

The guitar used to be simply an accompanying instrument – originally the singers themselves played – but in the early decades of this century it began developing as a solo instrument, absorbing influences from classical and Latin American traditions. The greatest of these early guitarists was **Ramón Montoya**, who revolutionized flamenco guitar with his harmonizations and introduced a whole variety of arpeggios – techniques of right-hand playing adapted from classical guitar playing. Along with Niño Ricardo and Sabicas, he established flamenco guitar as a solo medium, an art extended from the 1960s on by **Manolo Sanlucar**, whom most *aficionados* reckon the most technically accomplished player of his generation. Sanlucar has kept within a "pure flamenco" orbit, and not strayed into jazz or rock, experimenting instead with orchestral backing and composing for ballet.

The best known of all contemporary flamenco guitarists, however, is undoubtedly **Paco de Lucía**, who made the first moves towards "new" or "fusion" flamenco. A *payo*, he won his first flamenco prize at the age of 14, and went on to accompany many of the great singers, including a long partnership with Camarón de la Isla. He started forging new rhythms for flamenco following a trip to Brazil, where he was influenced by *bossa nova*, and in the 1970s established a sextet with electric bass, Latin percussion, flute and saxophone. Over the past twenty years he has worked with jazz-rock guitarists like John McLaughlin and Chick Corea, while his own regular band, featuring his other brother, the singer Pepe de Lucía, remains one of the most original and distinctive sounds on the flamenco scene.

Other modern-day guitarists have equally identifiable sounds and rhythms, and fall broadly into two camps, being known either as accompanists or soloists. The former include **Tomatito** (Camarón's last accompanist), Manolo Franco and Paco Cortés, while among the leading soloists are the brothers Pepe and Juan Habichuela; Rafael Riqueni, an astonishing player who is breaking new ground with classical influences; Enrique de Melchor; Gerardo Nuñez; and Vicente Amigo. Jerónimo Maya was acclaimed by the Spanish press as the "Mozart of Flamenco" when he gave his first solo performance, aged seven, in 1984.

Nuevo flamenco

The **reinvention of flamenco** in the 1980s was initially disliked by purists, but soon gained a completely new young public. Paco de Lucía set the new parameters of innovation and commercial success, and following in his foot-steps came **Lolé y Manuel** and others, updating the flamenco sound with original songs and huge success. **Jorge Pardo**, Paco de Lucía's sax and flute player, originally a jazz musician, has continued to work at the cutting edge. **Enrique Morente** and **Juan Peña El Lebrijano** were two of the first to work with Andalucian orchestras from Morocco, and the Mediterranean sound remains important today, together with influences from southern India.

Paco Peña's 1991 *Missa Flamenca* recording, a setting of the Catholic Mass to flamenco, with the participation of established singers like Rafael Montilla "El Chaparro" from Peña's native Córdoba and a classical academy chorus from London, has stayed a bestseller since its first appearance, remaining a bench-mark for such compositions.

The encounter with rock and blues was pioneered at the end of the 1980s by Ketama and Pata Negra. **Ketama** (named after a Moroccan village famed for its hashish) were hailed by the Spanish press as creators of the music of the "New Spain" after their first album, which fused flamenco with rock and Latin salsa, adding a kind of rock–jazz sensibility, a "flamenco cool" as they put it. They then pushed the frontiers of flamenco still further by recording the two *Songhai* albums in collaboration with Malian kora-player Toumani Diabate and British bassist Danny Thompson. The group **Pata Negra**, a band led by two brothers, Raímundo and Rafael Amador, introduced a more direct rock sound with a bluesy electric guitar lead, giving a radical edge to traditional styles like *bulerías*. Their *Blues de la Frontera* album caused an equal sensation. After split-ting, Raimundo Amador has continued as a solo artist.

Collectively, these young and iconoclastic musicians became known, in the 1990s, as **nuevo flamenco** – a movement associated in particular with the Madrid label Nuevos Medios. They form a challenging, versatile and at times musically incestuous scene in Madrid and Andalucía, with musicians guesting at each other's gigs and on each other's records. Ketama have gone on to have massive hits nationally, bringing flamenco fully into the mainstream.

In the 1980s and '90s, the music became the regular sound of **nightclubs**, through the appeal of young singers like **Aurora** – whose salsa-rumba song *Besos de Caramelo*, written by Antonio Carmona of Ketama, was the first 1980s number to crack the pop charts. Pop singer **Martirio** (Isabel Quiñones Gutierrez) is one of the most flamboyant personalities on the scene, appearing dressed in lace mantilla and shades like a cameo from a Pedro Almodóvar film, recording songs with ironic, contemporary lyrics, full of local slang, about life in the cities. Martirio's producer, **Kiko Veneno**, who wrote Camarón's most popular song, *Volando Voy*, is another key artist who helped open up the scene. A rock musician originally, he has a strongly defined sense of flamenco. **Rosario**, one of Spain's top female singers, has also brought a flamenco sensi-bility to Spanish rock music. In the mid-1990s **Radio Tarifa** emerged as an exciting group, leading the exploration of a flamenco–Mediterranean sound with a mix of Arabic and medieval sounds on a flamenco base. They started out as a trio, later expanding to include African musicians.

Other more identifiably *nuevo flamenco* bands and singers to look out for include La Barbería del Sur (who add a dash of salsa), Wili Gimenez and José El Frances.

Discography

Various *Arte Flamenco: Excerpts from the collection* (Mandala).

Various *Arte Flamenco: Vol. 7 La Nina de los Peines* (Mandala).

Various *Arte Flamenco: Vol. 9 El cante en sevilla* (Mandala).

Various *Concurso de Cante Jondo* (Sonifolk).

Various *Duende: The Passion* and *Dazzling Virtuosity of Flamenco* (Ellipsis Arts; 3 CDs).

Various *Magna Antología del Cante Flamenco* (Hispavox; 10 volumes).

Various *Early Cante Flamenco: Classic Recordings from the 1930s* (Arhoolie).

Various *Fiesta: Flamenco Vivo* (Auvidis).

Various *Flamenco: Grande Figures* (Chant du Monde).

Various *Flamenco: The Rough Guide* (World Music Network).

Various *Noches Gitanas* (EPM; 4 CDs).

Various *Sevillanas*: the soundtrack of Carlos Saura's film (Polydor).

Escudero & Ramos de Almaden *Flamenco de Triana* (Tradition).

Remedios Amaya *Me voy contigo* (Hemisphere).

Bebo & Cigala *Lágrimas Negras* (Calle54 records).

Agustín Carbonell Bola *Carmen* (Messidor).

Duquende *Duquende y la guitarra de Tomatito* (Nuevos Medios).

Federico García Lorca *De granada a la luna* (sombra).

Federico García Lorca & La Argentina *Colección de Canciones Populares Españolas* (Sonifolk).

El Indio Gitano *Nací gitano por la gracia de dios* (Nuevos Medios).

Camarón con tomatito *Paris 1987* (Universal).

Camarón de la Isla *Potro de rabia y miel* (Polygram), *Calle Real* (Polygram) and *Una leyenda flamenca, Vivire and Autorretrato* (Philips).

Carmen Linares *Cantaora* (Riverboat).

Paco de Lucía *Luzía* (Polygram) and *Siroco* (Philips).

Enrique de Melchor *Cuchichi* (Fonodisc).

José Menese *El viente solano* (Nuevos Medios).

José Mercé & Vicente Amigo *Del amanecer* (Virgin).

Moraíto *Morao y oro* (Auvidis).

Enrique Morente *Negra, si tú supieras* (Nuevos Medios) and *Omage* (Karonte).

Niña Pastora *Cañailla* (Aviola/BMG).

Paco Peña *Flamenco Guitar Music of Ramon Montoya and Niño Ricardo* (Nimbus Records).

Ramón el Portugués Gitanos de la Plaza (Nuevos Medios).

Saetas *Cante de la Semana Santa Andaluza* (Auvidis).

Tomatito *Barrío Negro* (Nuevos Medios).

Various *Los Jóvenes Flamencos Vol 1–5* (Nuevos Medios).

Amalgama y Karnataka College of Percussion (Nuba).

La Barbería del Sur (Nuevos Medios).

Chano Domínguez *Chano* (Nuba).

Ray Heredía *Quien no corre, vuela* (Nuevos Medios).

Jazzpaña (Nuevos Medios).

Ketama *Canciones hondas* (Nuevos Medios) and *Ketama* (Hannibal).

Lolé . . . *y Manuel* (Gong Fonomusic).

Paco de Lucía Sextet *Solo quiero caminar* and *Live in America* (Philips), *Live . . . One Summer Night* (Phonogram).

Pata Negra *Blues de la Frontera* (Nuevos Medios/Hannibal).

Radio Tarifa *Rumba Argelina* and *Temporal* (both World Circuit).

Songhai (Ketama/Toumani Diabate/Danny Thompson) *Songhai* and *Songhai 2* (Nuevos Medios/Hannibal).

Juan Peña Lebrijano y Orquestra Andalusi de Tanger *Encuentros* (Ariola/Globestyle).

Folk and regional music

Spain has a centuries-long tradition of folk song and dance. At the beginning of the twentieth century certain dances became emblematic of certain regions and their communities – for example, the *muiñeira* in Galicia, the *zortziko* in the Basque country and the *sardana* for Catalunya. As with many other totalitarian regimes, the Franco dictatorship exploited folklore as a way of promoting nationalism, with the women's section of the Falange party collecting folk songs. As a result, what became known as "folklorism" was somewhat discredited, particularly among those most opposed to the regime.

The inspiration of the 1970s, '80s and '90s was therefore to give new value to folk music and rescue it from patriotic cliché and Francoesque kitsch. While the restoration of democracy was crucial, great impetus also came from the fact that Spain is composed of several different autonomies, each with their own financial support and official nurturing from regional government. Today a new generation of folk musicians has also reclaimed the music and made it its own, creating music with elements drawn from all parts of the country.

The key musicians

Currently, folk and regional music is at its most developed in the northwest, from Galicia to Euskadi – Celtic Spain. The *Fiesta del Mundo Celta* at Ortigueira has played a leading role in this revival, and there is a regular summer scene of local festivals in the Basque country, Asturias and Galicia.

Galician music is in particularly fine fettle, rooted in pipes, bagpipes and drums and now heard all over the country, with groups such as **Milladoiro** regulars on the European festival scene. The music of Galician bagpiper **Carlos Nuñez** exemplifies that of a new generation which has grown up steeped in tradition, with classical training and a passion for many other types of music. Nuñez, who served a kind of touring apprenticeship with Irish group The Chieftains, constantly searches out collaborations which bring out different aspects of Galician music, such as the inspiring *pandereta* (tambourine) group and singers of Cantegueiras Xiradella, from Martezo, near A Coruña, who have learnt traditional spirited work songs and *jotas* from older women in the countryside. Nuñez has also collaborated with North American guitarist Ry Cooder and Cuba's Vieja Trova Santiaguera, while his 1999 project, *Os Amores Libres*, explores the rhythmic connections between Celtic and flamenco music, with contributions from Irish and Scottish musicians. Other Galician musicians who have helped revitalize the scene include Na Lua (who combine saxophone with bagpipe); Doa, Citania, Trisquell, Fía Na Roca and Xorima (all traditional and acoustic); Palla Mallada (hyper-traditional); and Alecrín, Brath and Matto Congrio (electric folk). Emilio Cao switches back and forth between traditional folk and more modern singer-songwriting.

The Basque country, **Euskadi**, is home to a wild accordion music called *trikitrixa* (meaning the devil's bellows). *Trikitrixa* maestro, **Josepa Tapia**, who plays with *pandereta* player Leturia in the Tapia et Leturia band, is one of the stars. **Kepa Junkera** has taken *trikitrixa* further afield, playing with Carlos Núñez. Other key Basque musicians include **Ruper Ordorika**, whose music has a rock edge to it, **Benito Lertxundi**, whose energies generally go into traditional Basque music but who has also recently experimented with the Celtic sounds of the northern coast, and **Oskorri**, a fine, politicized electro-acoustic group, who were instrumental in keeping Basque music publicly alive in the latter years of Franco and who have since gone from strength to strength. Also impressive are Ganbara and Azala. Younger artists include Txomin Artola, his former companion Amaia Zubiría, and Imanol.

A Celtic movement exists in **Asturias**, centring on two festivals in Oviedo (the Oviedo Folk Festival and the *Noche Celta*). Most groups are fairly traditional, particularly Ubiña and Lliberdón, though Llan de Cubel are adventurous and challenging.

Turning to the **Balearics**, Mallorcan **María del Mar Bonet** has brought the rich treasury of her own island to huge acclaim at home and abroad. Starting in the 1960s, Bonet was part of the Catalan singer-composer group Els Setge Jutges, and the movement of *nova cançó* (new song) which incurred the displeasure of Franco's censors by singing in Catalan. Key Bonet songs include Mallorca's unofficial hymn, *La Balanguera*, ballads like *La Mort de la Margalida*, as well as lively dances like *La Jota Marinera* and the apocalyptic medieval *La Sybilla*, sung only on Christmas Eve in certain churches in Mallorca. Other Balearic musicians of interest include the groups Musica Nostra, Sis Som, Calitja and Aliorna, who play traditional styles; Coanegra and Siurell Electric, with a more progressive sound; and Calabruix, an electro-acoustic duo.

In **Catalunya**, María del Mar Bonet's colleague and friend in Els Setge Jutges, **Lluís Llach**, has enjoyed a long career, as has fellow Catalan **Joan Manuel Serrat**. Serrat, one of the big record sellers in Spain, sings both in Catalan and Spanish and enjoys a huge reputation in Latin America. The early songs of Llach (from the period when Franco censored Catalan song), such as *El Bandoler* and *L'Estaca*, are still highly esteemed and sung today. For Llach they resulted in four years' exile in France, when his seminal recording at the Paris Olympia with its classic version of *País Petit* (My Small Country) circulated clandestinely. Returning as Franco died, to great celebration, Llach is now a Spanish superstar, touring with a superb group of musicians, and mixing jazz and rock in his arrangements. Another member of Els Setge Jutges, who celebrated thirty years' singing in 1997, is **Raimon**, composer of many key songs including *Al Vent*, a song about being free in the wind, which conjured up images of liberty during the 1960s and '70s. Other interesting Catalan groups, mostly playing folk music, include La Murga and the newer Tradivarius.

Catalunya also has a number of **orchestras** playing traditional dance music – some closer to salsa, like the Orquesta Platería and the Salseta del Poble Sec, others more traditional, like Tercet Treset and the Orquesta Galana. The emblematic *sardana* dance remains important, too, in every local festival, as does a tradition of popular singing linking Catalunya with Cuba, known as *habanera*, which thrives today in summer festivals on the Costa Brava coast, particularly in Calella de Palafrugell. With maritime connections strong in the nineteenth and twentieth centuries, the music of *ida y vuelta*, coming and going, of greeting and farewell, has endured in fishermen's choirs and small groups, and has now been taken up again by young people.

Andalucía is home not only to flamenco but also to other music: Almadraba from Tarifa explore the highly traditional, while Lombarda from Granada are more revivalist. Andalucía is also where you'll find **Sephardic** (Iberian Jewish) music, often a cross between folk and traditional styles. Rosa Zaragoza and Aurora Moreno are two female singers who have produced interesting work in this field; Moreno is also involved in Mozarabic *jarchas* (Arabic verse set to music). Els Trobadors and Cálamus have both also successfully revived medieval traditions, while the outstanding Luís Delgado works with Sephardic, medieval and Spanish Arabic music.

Other Spanish musicians to take note of include Al Tall, an interesting band from Valencia, whose last major project was a joint effort with Muluk El Hwa; Alimara, a group from Marrakesh who are involved with both music and traditional dance; Salpicao, who have experimented with flamenco-based fusions; and La Vella Banda, an innovative horn band. Joaquín Díaz has for many years dominated the musical life of Castile, as have the prolific Nuevo Mester de Juglaría, a distinguished group who established an alternative roots music to Franco's folkloristic ventures. Manuel Luna and La Musgaña have created fine sounds, as has the singer María Salgado, who has made recordings of the *habanera* tradition found outside Catalunya, and who worked on *La sal de la vida* (The Salt of Life), with two other female musicians, Uxía from Galicia and Rasha from the Sudan – together they explore the similarities and differences, rhythms and cadence, of each other's cultures, including largely unheard-of songs from Galicia and Asturias. Other musicians to listen out for include the Segovian group, Rebolada, who include eight *dulzainas* (flutes) in their line-up, and Habas Verdes from Zamora, who produce spirited, vivid versions of traditional tunes on instruments such as the hurdy-gurdy and the *dulzaina*, as well as the cello, organ and guitar.

Singer-songwriters

In the 1990s the scene of **cantautores**, or singer-songwriters, underwent a revival, with new talent following in the footsteps of the heroes of the 1970s and '80s and gaining a younger audience. **Pedro Guerra** developed his own mellow style, influenced by sounds from the Canary Islands, Brazil and classic Latin American singers and poets. **Ismael Serrano** used his melodies to make open social commitment, while **Javier Alvarez**, with his disc *Tres*, shifted away from the classic voice-guitar structure by diving into drum programming and sampling. **Rosana** brought singer-songwriters to the front covers of newspapers with her soft, melodic style and whispering voice, seducing a million Spanish people with her first album.

The most impact, however, has been made by **Joaquín Sabina**, a man who began in the Franco years and whose cult following has made him the most talked-about artist not only in Spain but in much of South and Central America, too. His recent album, *19 dias y 500 noches*, has been acclaimed worldwide by critics and the public as one of his best works.

Discography

Various *El gusto es nuestro* (Ariola).
Various *Magna Antología del Folklore Musical de España* (Hispavox; 17 LPs).
Various *La sal de la vida* (NubeNegra).
Various *Voice of Spain: Spanish regional music* (Heritage).
Rafael Alberti y Paco Ibañez *A galopar* (PDI).
Javier Alvarez *Tres* (EMI).
Bernardo Atxaga *Nueva Etiopia* (Colleccion Lcd el Europeo).
Luís Eduardo Aute y Silvio Rodríguez *Mano a mano* (Ariola).
María del Mar Bonet *Salmaia* (Ariola) and *El cor del temps* (Picap, Spain, 2 CDs).
Andres Calamaro *Honestidad brutal* (Gaza/DRU).
Carlos Cano *Quedate con la Copla* (CBS).
Charo Centenera *No soy la Piquer* (RNE).
Llan de Cubel *L'otru llaou de la mar* (Fono Astur).
Vainica Doble *1970* (RNE).

Fía na Roca (Arpafolk).
Pedro Guerra *Raíz* (BMG).
Pablo Guerrero *Todo la vida es ahora* (Polygram).
Habas Verdes *En el jardin de la yerba buena* (Gam).
Imanol *Alfonsina, viaje de mar y luna* (Ediciones Cúbicas).
Kepa Junkera *Bilbao 00.00* (Resistencia) and *Trikitixa zoom* (Nuba).
Kepa, Zabaleta & Imanol *Triki Up* (Elkar).
Mikel Laboa *Lau-Bost* (Elkar).
Leilía *Leilía* (Discmedi Blau).
Benito Lertxundi *Hyunkidura kuttunak* (Elkar).
Lluís Llach *Lluís Llach A L'Olympia* (Fonomusic), *Ara 25 anys en directe* (Picap) and *Mon porrera* (Picap).
Manuel Luna *Como hablan las sabinas* (RNE).
Rosana Lunas *Rotas* (Universal).
Luar *Na Cubre Cabo do Mundo* (WEA).
La Musgaña *El Diablo Cojuelo* (Sonifolk).
Mestisay *El cantar viene de lejos* (Manzana).

Milladoiro *Galicia no temp* (Discmedi).
Nuevo Mester De Juglaría *25 Aniversario*
(Polygram).
Aurora Moreno *Aynadamar* (Saga).
Carlos Núñez *A Irmandade das Estrelas*
(Ariola) and *Os Amores Libres* (BMG).
Ruper Ordorika *Ez da posible* (Gasa),
Hiru truku (Nuevos Medios) and
Bilduma Bat (Elkar).
Oskorri *Badok hamahiru* (Elkar).
La Paloma *One Song For All Worlds*
(Indigo).
Albert Pla *No solo de rumba vive el hom-*
bre (Ariola).
Port-Bo *Arrel de tres* and *Canela y ron*
(both Picap).
Radio Tarifa *Rumba Argelina* and
Temporai (both World Circuit).

Raímon *Cancons* (Auvidis).
Marina Rossell *Marina* (PDI).
Bleizi Ruz, Leilía, La Musgaña *Hent Sant*
Jakez (Shamrock Records).
Joaquín Sabina *19 dias u 500 noches*
(BMG).
María Salgado *Mirandote* (NubeNegra).
Salpicão (RNE).
Joan Manuel Serrat *Utopia, Mediteraneo,*
Serrat en directo and *Sombras de la*
China (all Ariola).
Al Tall y Muluk el Hwa *Xarq al-Andalus*
(RNE).
Tapia Eta Leturia *Dultzemeneoa* (Elkar).
Els Trobadors *Et ades sera l'Alba*
(Lyricon).
Uxía *Estou vivindo no ceo* (NubeNegra).

Rock, pop and hip-hop

In the 1970s Anglo-American rock inspired the first rock groups, including
Miguel Ríos and **Los Bravos**, as well as the progressive proto-rock of Los
Canarios, Maquina and Música Dispersa, pioneers of the musical underground.
Madrid was dominated by **heavy rock**, with a series of groups like Burning,
Mermelada and Indiana, whose fans lived in the working-class districts of the
capital and in the dormitory towns of the outskirts. Meanwhile, in Barcelona,
the scene was split between musicians who were producing a very cool **jazz-
rock**, and those into a warmer **Catalan salsa**, or Barcelona's own *gitano* music
– **Catalan rumba**, popularized first by Peret, a Barcelona musician. On the
fringes were the singer-songwriters and the Latin American groups who,
despite Franco, managed to tour Spain.

At the end of the 1970s, a **punk** reaction began to take hold among
teenagers, just as it did in Britain and the US. Some older rockers, like
Ramoncín, attempted to take punk on board, but punk challenged and broke
up the old order, setting the scene for the future, with an explosion of diverse
groups.

Since then, straight **pop** has been the main area of activity, but there have
been various phases in which punks, technos, *garajistas*, *siniestros*, Romantics and
rockabillies have had success, crossing over between genres. Today the goddess
of the Spanish pop scene is **Monica Naranjo**, her success based on her unique
kitsch look, passionate lyrics and extraordinary voice. The current king of
Spanish pop is **Alejandro Sanz**, who became a teenage idol in the early 1990s
and has gone on to prove his brilliance with compositions ranging from flamenco to Latin pop. His groundbreaking album *Más* is already a classic for
Spanish audiences of all ages.

A key figure in Madrid from punk days was **Alaska**, a club owner and one-
time muse of modernity, whose records are less significant than her brilliant live
performances. Female singer **Mecano**, accompanied by two male musicians,
became one of the most successful Spanish pop groups ever, popular in Latin
America, France and Italy, as well as Spain. Established bands today include the
country-influenced Los Secretos; the futuristic Aviador Dro; Miguel Ríos and

Ramoncín, both of whom stick to classic rock; and the heavy-metal groups, Rosendo, Obús and Barón Rojo. A slightly younger generation includes Gabinete Caligari (macho Hispano-pop), Los Coyotes (Latin rockabilly) and La Frontera (cowboy), while Luz, and Rosario, an interesting and original singer from a flamenco dynasty (the daughter of Rosa Flores), have become big stars. Look out, too, for Radio Futura, who brought the Latin and Cuban touch onto the scene in the late 1980s with their album *Semilla negra*; Jarabe de Palo, whose *La Flaca* is a classic of the pop scene; Juan Pero (ex Radio Futura); and Enrique Bunbury (ex Heores del Silencio).

In **Barcelona** one of the most innovative bands has been El Ultimo de la Fila, a duo with engaging lyrics and a sophisticated Mediterranean sound; Manolo Garcia has now gone solo. Equally enjoyable are Los Rebeldes, former rockabilly heroes, who have been exploring new directions.

Euskadi has witnessed a two-part musical scene: radical rock has been represented by Negu Gorriak, Potato, Hertzainak and La Polla Records, who use hot rhythms, reggae and ska as a base for a message with a political conscience. On a more straightforward rock level, 21 Japonesas and La Dama se Esconde have demanded attention.

From **Galicia** (especially Vigo) a surprising number and diversity of bands have emerged, including Siniestro Total and Os Resentidos in the 1980s, with Os Diplomaticos an interesting new arrival of the 1990s. Los Ilegales, powerful rockers with a strong live set, have emerged in **Asturias**, as well as Hevia, an electronic pop bagpiper, while in **Aragón**, Heroes del Silencio have been one of the major chart rock groups in the 1990s.

In **Andalucía**, the *malagueño* combo Danza Invisible have had some unforgettable catchy hits, and the long list of artists from Sevilla includes the astonishing Martirio (who combines pop and traditional songs with a playful, witty sense of challenging Spanish stereotypes), Arrajatabla and Kiko Veneno. Veneno's sporadic albums are clever, literate, utterly Spanish rock songs and come highly recommended.

The **indie scene** proved to be one of the most interesting in the 1990s, with the creation of new record companies allowing the exposure of new talent. Pop rock, hip-hop and electronic music have all been at the forefront. In the late 1990s the powerful guitar sound and clear melodies of **Dover** from Madrid became a massive success with *Devil Came To Me*, while **Los Planetas**, from Granada, mix acid guitars and subtle melodies with lyrics on post-teenage love, pain and drugs.

Electronic music emerged in Spain in the 1970s and 1980s. Barcelona was the vanguard city, with groups such as Macromassa, La Fura dels Baus and Gringos making the most impact. Many labels have emerged since then and electronic music has developed into dance sounds. The Sónar **festival** started up in the 1990s in Barcelona, and has become one of the high points of the calendar for musicians from across the world (see p.716). Some of the top names to look out for are the house DJ Toni Rox, drum'n'bass-leaning Oscar Mulero, from the Ibiza scene, the techno tunes of Angel Molina and the more experimental, conceptual sounds of Sandro Bianchi.

Spanish **hip-hop** emerged towards the end of 1996 and is now an industry in itself, acknowledged as one of the most creative musical scenes, with distribution through its own specialized record labels. An urban street genre, it has flourished among teenagers living in working-class areas of big cities, focusing as it does on key political issues including fascism, racism, drugs, immigration and xenophobia. One of the most popular and respected rappers is **Mala Rodriguez**, from Sevilla, whose flamenco-tinted songs are fronted by feminist lyrics.

Discography

7 Notas 7 Colores *Hecho es simple* (BCA).
Ari *Glancho perfecto* (Zona Bruta).
Arrajatabla *Sevilla blues* (Fonomusic).
Ana Belen, Miguel Rios, Víctor Manuel, Joan Manuel Serrat *El gusto es nuestro* (Ariola).
Ana Belen *Veneno para el corazón* (Ariola).
Camela *Simplemente amor* (EMI).
Celtas Cortos *Cuentame un cuento* and *Tranquilo majete* (both DRO).
Ciudad Jardín *Ojos mas que ojos* (Hispavox).
Corcobado *Tormenta de tormento* (Triquinoise).
Dover *Devil came to me* (Subterfuge).
Estopa *Estopa* (BMG).
Fangoria *Una ola cualquiera en Vulcano* (Gasa).
Manolo Garcia *Arena en los bolsillos* (BMG).
Héroes del Silencio *El espíritu del vino* (Hispavox).
Hevia *Tierra de nadie* (Hispavox).
Illegales *Regreso al sexo químicamente puro* (Hispavox).
Jarabe *De palo la flaca* (Virgin).
Luz *A contraluz* (Hispavox).
Los Planetas *Una semana en el motor de un autobus* (BMG).
Monica Naranjo *Palabra de mujer* (Sony).
Negu Gorriak *Borreroak baditu milaka aurpegi* (Esan Ozanki).
Presuntos Implicados *Alma de blues* (WEA).
Radio Futura *Tierra para bailar* (Ariola).
Los Rebeldes *La rosa y la cruz* (Epic).
Os Resentidos *Están aqui* (Gasa).
Miguel Rios *Así que pasen 30 años* (Polydor).
Los Rodríguez *Sin documentos* (Gasa).
Rosario *De Ley* (Epic).
Alejandro Sanz *Más* (WEA).
Los Secretos *Cambio de planes* (Dro).
Seguridad Social *Furia Latina* (Gasa).
Sólo Los Solo *Retorno al principio* (BCA).
Tam Tam Go! *Vida y color* (Hispavox).
Manolo Tena *Sangre Española* (Epic).
El Ultimo de la Fila *Astronomía razonable* (EMI).
Antonio Vega *El sitio de mi recreo* (Polygram).
Kiko Veneno *La Pequeña Salvaje* (Nuevos Medios) and *Échate un cantecito* (BMG).

Jazz

Jazz in Spain has always had loyal fans tucked away in small clubs, but since the end of the 1970s it has really taken off. Many jazz musicians have become internationally acclaimed not only through their jazz music, but also through their ability to merge jazz with local genres such as flamenco and Mediterranean sounds.

In the 1970s, when the great pianist **Tete Montonliu** was already a figure on the international scene, **Pegasus** started introducing experimental fusion sounds, and guitarist **Joan Bibiloni** a very Mediterranean one. Then in the 1980s, the flamenco-influenced generation – many of whom had played with Paco de Lucía and Camarón, including the bass player **Carlos Benavent**, saxophonists **Jorge Pardo**, **Pedro Iturralde** and **Perico Sambeat**, and pianist **Chano Dominguez** – discovered ways of creating and expressing something that was both local and global in its appeal, reaching audiences all over the world with their innovative flamenco-influenced jazz, which embraced influences from Brazil, Peru and other parts of the world.

Names to watch for today include **Baldo Martínez**, whose recent album *No pais dos ananos* was much acclaimed, and **Angel Blanco**. The **Orquesta Nacional de Jazz de España** – created in 2000 by Chano Dominguez – explores a rich Spanish and Latin repertoire. The country's biggest **jazz festi-**

val is held at San Sebastián in July. Vitoria holds one in the same month, and there are two in Madrid: one in May (*Fiestas de San Isidro*), the other in November. There's also a November festival in Barcelona. Other worthwhile events are the *Fiesta de Jazz* in Murcia and the *Muestra de Jazz* in Ibiza.

Discography

Chano Domiguez *Iman* (Nuba/Karonte).
Fangoria *Una temporada en el infierno* (Diablo).
Alex Martin *Join the band* (Coconar).

**Jan Fairly, David Loscos
and Manuel Dominguez**

Cinema

It has not always been easy for cinema to take root in Spain. The lack of a proper infrastructure, the devastation of the Civil War, and the restrictions of the Franco regime all meant that Spanish film-makers had to struggle to get films made, and then often struggle again to get them released.

The vast majority of Spanish films remain unseen outside Spain. From the 1950s onwards, Spanish films would periodically appear on the film festival circuit and, on occasion, be taken up by an art-house cinema. One director in particular, **Carlos Saura**, achieved international prestige even while working under the restrictions of the Franco regime. From an earlier generation, **Luis Buñuel** has long been accepted as one of the major figures in the history of cinema. But Saura was something of an exception, while Buñuel made almost all of his films in either France or Mexico.

The end of the dictatorship, however, was followed by a remarkable degree of film-making activity, and today the films of Spanish directors, **Pedro Almodóvar** in particular, are capable of filling cinemas within and beyond Spain. The garishly modern Madrid of Almodóvar's *Women on the Edge of a Nervous Breakdown*, the dusty Los Monegros plains of Bigas Luna's *Jamón Jamón*, the magical-realist Basque landscape of Julio Medem's *Vacas* – these have all helped to establish Spain on the world cinema map.

The early decades

The history of Spanish film goes back to the nineteenth century, when Spain produced one of the pioneers of early cinema, **Segundo de Chomón**, a man whose use of trick photography rivalled that of the French director, Georges Méliès. Overall, however, Spanish cinema developed slowly. Spain entered the twentieth century lacking the technology, the capital and the urban audiences that produced a thriving film industry in neighbouring France. "In my own village of Calanda," wrote Luis Buñuel in his autobiography, ". . . the Middle Ages lasted until World War I." Like Buñuel, Segundo de Chomón spent most of his career abroad, and ended up producing special effects for other directors in Italy and France. By the 1920s, a Spanish film industry had been established, but its modest scale and pretensions are indicated in the slogan used to promote one film made in 1925 – "It's so good that it doesn't seem Spanish."

Without a strong production base, cinema in Spain was particularly susceptible to the rapidly developing power of **America**. In the early 1930s "Spanish" films were being produced, but often in Hollywood rather than Madrid, as the major American film companies dealt with the coming of sound (and the threat that an active Spanish film industry might have provided) by producing Spanish versions of their English-language product. In the process they deprived Spain of a number of its film-makers.

However, in 1934, a major production and distribution company, **CIFAS**, was founded in Madrid. With a degree of support from the Republican government, and with the native product proving more popular than subtitled American movies (though dubbing was gradually adopted as a standard practice), the Spanish film industry began to appear relatively healthy. Luis Buñuel returned to Spain from France – where, with fellow Spaniard Salvador Dalí, he had directed a couple of Surrealist classics, *Un Chien Andalou* (1928) and *L'Age d'Or* (1930) – to make *Land Without Bread* (1932). This film, an unremitting documentary about rural poverty, was promptly banned, but Buñuel stayed on, dubbing films for Warner Bros, and working as executive producer (and reputedly occasional director) on four more mainstream projects.

The **Civil War** and the eventual Nationalist victory drove Buñuel into exile. It also ended the brief flowering of popular Spanish cinema that had been exhibited in films such as *Paloma Fair* (1935) and *Clara the Brunette* (1936), the latter featuring the first "star" of Spanish cinema, Imperio Argentina.

During the war, the communists and the anarcho-syndicalists produced numerous short works extolling their cause; there were also appeals for international support for the Republican cause in films such as Joris Ivens' *The Spanish Earth* (1937). Some **propagandist** films were produced by the victorious Nationalist regime, including *Madrid Front* (1939) and *Race* (1941), the latter an adaptation of Franco's own novel. More significant was the establishment of the **Supreme Board of Film Censorship**, inaugurating four decades in which censorship became the strongest force in Spanish cinema.

The Franco years

Under Franco, both scripts and completed films had to be submitted for approval, and films had to be dubbed into the "official" Castilian dialect. No actual code of censorship was laid down until 1963, but this only gave greater freedom to the censors. Film-makers also needed to placate the Catholic Church, which in 1950 established the **National Board of Classification of Spectacles** which made its own "recommendations".

Some efforts were made to support an indigenous Spanish film industry. In 1947 a **film school** was established in Madrid (where students were able to see foreign films banned from public exhibition), and in 1952 state **subsidy** regulations were changed to allow for the award of fifty percent of the costs of films deemed to be of "national interest". In practice this did little to vary the diet of epics, dramas, musicals and comedies which glorified the Spanish past and presented **idealized images** of the state, the Church and the family.

It was against this background that a group of **left-wing film-makers** met in 1955, declaring contemporary Spanish cinema to be "1 – Politically futile. 2 – Socially false. 3 – Intellectually worthless. 4 – Aesthetically valueless. 5 – Industrially paralytic." Inspired by the example of Italian neo-realism, such film-makers were, in fact, already beginning to present a less idealized picture of Spanish society. Films such as Luis Berlanga's *Welcome Mr Marshall* (1952), a satire about the effect of America's Marshall Plan on a Spanish village, and Antonio Bardem's *Death of a Cyclist* (1956), suggested that there was some room for alternative voices in the Spanish film industry.

The restrictions continued (in 1956 Bardem was briefly imprisoned for his political views), but the Spanish government did institute a slightly more flexible policy, if largely to attract international support and investment. While American film companies were being persuaded to use relatively inexpensive **Spanish locations** for films such as *Alexander the Great* (1955), the prestige offered by the international film festival circuit meant that even films offering a critical view of Spanish institutions could be used as a means of "selling" Spain abroad.

The contradictions inherent in this policy were shown up most blatantly when Buñuel was invited back to Spain to make a film for the production company **UNINCI**, which had been formed by a group of film-makers including Bardem, Berlanga and Carlos Saura. The resulting film, *Viridiana* (1961), revealed that the director of *L'Age d'Or* could be as uncompromising as ever. Astonishingly, the film was initially passed by the censor despite scenes including a parody of The Last Supper, acted out by an assortment of drunks and beggars – and was only banned after it had been attacked in the Vatican newspaper. The result was that Buñuel resumed his career in Mexico and France, and the promise and short life of UNINCI was brought to a close. Buñuel returned to Spain to make *Tristana* in 1970 and *That Obscure Object of Desire* in 1977, though both were French-Spanish co-productions rather than exclusively Spanish. *Viridiana* was not publicly shown in Spain until 1977.

In the slightly liberalized but still restrictive atmosphere of the 1960s and 1970s, some directors managed to develop the problem of getting round the censor into something of a fine art. **Carlos Saura**, in particular, who had quickly left behind the naturalism of his earliest films, used the power of suggestion, allegory and symbol to attack Francoist pretensions in films such as *The Hunt* (1965) and *The Garden of Delights* (1970). Working with the actress Geraldine Chaplin and the producer Elías Querejeta, he used his developing international prestige to retain a remarkable degree of control over his own films.

Other directors lacked Saura's prestige, though the loose movement known as the **Barcelona School** attempted to challenge the dominance of Madrid and the lack of adventure in mainstream Spanish cinema. Meanwhile, another side of Spanish cinema was revealed in the developing market for **low-budget horror films**, capitalizing on the fact that violence was less heavily censored than the directly sexual or political.

In the last years of the Franco regime, Saura continued to maintain his independence, exploring the scars of the Civil War in *Cousin Angelica* (1973), and the consequences of repression in *Raise Ravens* (1975). The aftermath of the Civil War also provided the theme for Victor Erice's remarkable debut feature, *The Spirit of the Beehive* (1973), a lyrical film set in a bleak Castilian village.

A more violent picture of rural Spain was presented in Ricardo Franco's *Pascuale Duarte* (1975) and José Luis Borau's *Poachers* (1975). In its story of **disintegrating authority**, the latter film, released shortly before Franco's death, seemed almost to anticipate the demise of the dictatorship: it was shown despite objections from the censor, and drew large crowds at the box office.

After Franco

In 1977 censorship was formally abolished, and though a none too sympathetic portrayal of the Civil Guard in **Pilar Miró**'s *The Cuenca Crime* (1980) initially led to that film being seized by the police, Miró's film also went on to break box-office records. In 1982 Miró herself – whose *Gary Cooper, Who Art in Heaven* (1980) told of the difficulties of a woman working in a male-dominated industry – was appointed Director General of Cinema by the incoming Socialist government. After her appointment, she continued to direct, including *Beltenebros* (1991), a *film-noir* treatment of Franco-era Spain, starring Terence Stamp and Patsy Kensit.

With the death of Franco, and the lifting of censorship, Spanish film-makers were able to engage with politics more directly: *Black Brood* (1977), directed by **Manuel Gutiérrez Aragón**, dealt with right-wing terrorists; *The Truth About the Salvatore Affair* (1978), directed by **Antonio Drove**, returned to history (Barcelona between 1917 and 1923) to examine the economic roots of political change; while **Juan Bardem** mixed thriller and documentary in his *Seven Days in May* (1978).

Liberalization brought its own problems. Under Franco the Spanish film industry had been restricted but also cushioned; now film-makers found themselves competing against an influx of American imports for a share of a declining audience. As Director General of Cinema, Miró set out to halt this trend by reintroducing **protectionist measures** and government subsidies. Efforts were also made to decentralize the film industry, and to move away from Franco's exclusive emphasis on Spain's Castilian heritage. For the first time, films using the Catalan language became possible following the establishment in 1975 of the **Institute of Catalan Film**, while the Basque government also financed a number of projects. National and regional subsidies have continued, although they have been significantly reduced in the last decade.

For directors who had mastered the art of indirect statement under Franco, the end of the dictatorship necessitated a change of direction. For **Carlos Saura** this change bore fruit in the form of *Blood Wedding* (1981), which showed Antonio Gades and his troupe rehearsing and performing a ballet version of the Federico Garcia Lorca play; his collaboration with Gades continued with *Carmen* (1983) and *Love the Magician* (1986). Saura returned to the Civil War with the tragi-comic *Ay, Carmela* (1990), and has continued to explore subjects from dance to neo-fascism in films such as *Flamenco* (1995) and *Taxi* (1996). Saura's latest film *Buñuel and King Solomon's Table* (2001) is a fitting tribute to the great Surrealists of the 1930s.

Since *The Spirit of the Beehive*, **Victor Erice** has directed just two full-length films. In *The South* (1983), he gave a further poetic and unsentimental exploration of a father-daughter relationship under the shadow of the Civil War. *The Quince Tree Sun* (1991) – a slow but ultimately rewarding study of an artist at work – recorded the meticulous preparations made by the Spanish artist Antonio López while he waited to capture the exact light needed for his painting.

Julio Medem, one of a number of Basque directors to emerge in recent years, has carved an individual, sometimes mystifying, but certainly striking path. His first film *Vacas* (1991) – four interrelated stories about a feud between two families as seen through bovine eyes – was followed by *The Red Squirrel* (1993), *Earth* (1996), *Lovers of the Arctic Circle* (1998) and *Lucía and Sex* (2001), which maintains the surreal tone of his earlier work.

Vicente Aranda, who directed his first film in 1964, achieved his international breakthrough with *The Lovers* (1991), a highly charged story of fatal attraction in 1950s Madrid starring **Victoria Abril**, who had made her debut in Aranda's *Change of Sex* (1976). More recently Aranda has had commercial if not critical successes with both *Turkish Passion* (1994) and the big-budget Civil War drama *Libertarians* (1996). The costume drama *Juana la Loca* (2001) was better received, with three Goya awards (Spanish equivalent of Oscars) and twelve nominations.

The past has continued to figure prominently in Spanish films, though most directors have avoided directly confronting the Civil War. Pedro Olea's *The Fencing Master* (1993) returned to nineteenth-century Madrid for its narrative of love, fate and death. **Fernando Trueba**'s *Belle Epoque* (1993), set in a nostalgic recreation of the Republican 1930s, became only the second Spanish film to win the Best Foreign Film Oscar (the first being Jose Luis Garci's *Begin the beguins* in 1982), and his *The Girl of Your Dreams* (1998) was another historical drama that looked at film-making and propaganda in Hitler's Germany. Before her death in 1997, Pilar Miró had a box-office success with *The Dog in the Manger* (1996), an adaptation of Lope de Vega's seventeenth-century comedy.

Other directors who came to prominence after the dictatorship seemed intent on turning their back on history. The cinema of **Pedro Almodóvar**, in particular, represents a break with both the idealized films that toed the Franco line, and the social commitment of directors such as Bardem and Berlanga. "I never speak of Franco," he has stated. "I hardly acknowledge his existence. I start after Franco."

Almodóvar made his feature-film debut in 1980 with the cheap and transgressive *Pepi, Lucy, Bom and a Whole Load of Other Girls*. His prodigious output during the 1980s included *What Have I Done to Deserve This?* (1982), a black comedy about drugs, prostitution and the forging of Hitler's diaries; *Matador* (1986), a dark thriller linking sexual excitement with the violence of the bullfight; *The Law of Desire* (1987), a story involving a gay film director, his transsexual brother/sister, murder and incest; as well as the internationally successful *Women on the Edge of a Nervous Breakdown* (1988). Almodóvar's films have benefited from the performances of actors such as Carmen Maura, Victoria Abril, Rosy de Palma and Antonio Banderas, and over time they have gained in narrative coherence and production values while retaining the capacity to offend – notably with *Tie Me Up, Tie Me Down* (1990). One of the very few directors able to attract audiences across the globe with films in a language other than English, Almodóvar's 1995 *Flower of My Secret* pushed him more into the mainstream, while *All About My Mother* (1999), which marks a return to his trademark obsession with transsexuals, won him an Oscar for Best Foreign Film. *Talk to Her* (2002) was if anything even more successful, and won Almodóvar another Oscar, this time for best screenplay – perhaps marking Spanish cinema's escape from the "foreign films" ghetto.

Bigas Luna is another director capable of simultaneously offending and delighting audiences within and beyond Spain. He achieved notoriety with *Jamón Jamón* (1992), and has continued his relentless preoccupation with sex, food and machismo in films such as *Golden Balls* (1993), *The Tit and the Moon* (1994), and *The Sound of the Sea* (2001). **Alex de la Iglesia** has cut his own gruesome trajectory with films like the schlock-sci-fi *Mutant Action* (1993) which imagined a future in which the disabled wage war on the beautiful; the *Torrente* cop series (tag line: "the dumb arm of the law"); the stylish *La Comunidad* (2000) which hilariously exposes the underbelly of a Madrid apartment building where neighbours are willing to kill over a lottery win; and *800 Bullets* (2003), a tribute to paella westerns. **Juanma Bajo Ulloa**, director of the disturbing psychological thriller, *The Dead Mother* (1993), had a hit at the Spanish box office with *Airbag* (1995), a gleefully tasteless comedy about three men searching for a missing wedding ring through a succession of brothels.

New directors have continued to emerge. **Iciar Bollaín**, after acting roles that included the daughter in Erice's *The South* and a fiery freedom fighter in Ken Loach's Civil War drama, *Land and Freedom* (1995), wrote and directed *Hi, Are You Alone?* (1996), a sympathetic portrait of a pair of young women travelling through Spain with an uncertain destination, and the affecting *Flowers from Another World* (1999) about three single women and their very different relationships with the men of a male-dominated Castilian village. **Alejandro Amenábar** made his directorial debut with *Thesis* (1995), an intelligent thriller about a student researching violence in the media. Amenábar, aged 23 when he made the film, belongs to a generation with barely a memory of Spain under Franco, but this didn't prevent him from making the superb *Butterfly's Tongue* (1999), set in Galicia during the Republic. His most recent release, *The Others* (2001), starring Nicole Kidman, has wowed audiences in the USA and at the Venice Film Festival alike.

Since the late 1990s Spanish **actors** have also gained ground abroad, though some of the country's greatest performers, such as **Fernando Ferran Gómez**, remain little known beyond the Pyrenees. **Antonio Banderas**, once the star of Almodóvar's stable, is now successfully installed in Hollywood as both an actor and director, while **Penelope Cruz** has become an A-list celebrity and respected actress on both sides of the Atlantic. Another Spanish favourite currently being feted internationally is **Javier Bardem,** who won critical acclaim and an Oscar nomination for his portrayal of exiled gay Cuban writer Reinaldo Arenas in *Before Night Falls* (2000) and shone as an unemployed dock worker in *Mondays in the Sun* (2002).

Guy Barefoot
With contributions from Robert Alcock

Books

L
istings below represent a highly selective reading list on Spain and matters Spanish. Most titles are in print, although we've included a few older classics, most of them easy enough to find in secondhand bookshops and libraries (indicated by o/p). We have also included the names and websites of several smaller publishers whose publications are not available on Amazon and other similar websites.

If you have difficulty finding any title, an excellent specialist source for books about Spain – new, used, and out of print – is Keith Harris Books, PO Box 207, Twickenham, TW2 5BQ, UK (☎020/8898 7789, ⓦwww.books-on-spain.com).

Travel and general accounts

The best introductions

★ **John Hooper** *The New Spaniards*. This excellent, authoritative portrait of post-Franco Spain was written by *The Guardian*'s former Spanish correspondent in 1986 and published in a revised edition – now in need of a further update – in 1995. It is still one of the best possible introductions to contemporary Spain.

Lucy McCauley (ed) *Spain: Travelers' Tales*. It would be hard to better this anthology of writing on Spain, which gathers its stories and journalism predominantly from the last fifteen years. Featured authors include Gabriel García Márquez, Colm Tóibín and Louis de Bernières, whose "Seeing Red", on the tomato-throwing festival of Buñol, is worth the purchase price on its own.

Carrie B. Douglass *Bulls, Bullfighting and Spanish Identities*. Anthropologist Douglass delves into the symbolism of the bull in the Spanish national psyche, and then goes on to examine the bullfight's role in some of the thousands of fiestas countrywide that support it.

Nina Epton *Grapes and Granite*

(o/p). One of the few English books on Galicia – full of folklore and rural life in the 1960s – and well worth hunting down in libraries or secondhand bookshops.

David Gilmour *Cities of Spain* (Ivan R Dee, US). A modern cultural portrait of Spain, but very much in the old tradition; it is a little fogeyish at times but excellent, nonetheless, in its evocation of history, especially on the Moorish cities of Andalucía.

Miranda France *Don Quijote's Delusions – Travels in Castilian Spain*. France interlaces the colourful account of her year abroad at Madrid University with an absorbing exploration of Cervantes' idiosyncratic knight. An entertaining and dextrous treatment of Spain past and present.

★ **Robert Hughes** *Barcelona*. This is the best of the 1992 books on the Olympic city: a text that, in the author's stated ambition, "explains the *Zeitgeist* of the place and the connective tissue between the cultural icons".

★ **Michael Jacobs** *The Factory of Light*. Another story of an Englishman setting up home in a Granada hill village; however, this is a well-told tale featuring a host of colourful village characters culminating in the resurrection and reopening of the old village cinema. *Andalucía*, by the same author, is an outstanding introduction to the region.

A.L. Kennedy *On Bullfighting.* Curious book by a Scottish fiction author who starts out – knowing nothing of bullfighting – by comparing the dicing with death of the *matadores* in the ring to her own attempted suicide. She travels to Spain, meets the experts, hears the anecdotes and – despite tortured misgivings – becomes an *aficionada*.

Mark Kurlansky *The Basque History of the World.* A brilliantly entertaining take on this much maligned, misunderstood and misrepresented people. Kurlansky uses history, stories, anecdotes and even recipes to concoct this heady brew.

Peter B. Meyer *A True Story About Doing Business in Spain.* This quirkily written insider's view of Spanish business life features encounters with corrupt bureaucracy, shifty lawyers, crooked business partners and a parade of police and politicos straight out of central casting. Sometimes skewed, but always fascinating.

★ **Cees Nooteboom** *Roads to Santiago: Detours and Riddles in the Land and History of Spain.* This is one of the most literary travel books of recent decades: an almost Shandyesque tale (few of the roads travelled lead anywhere near Santiago), garnished from the notebooks of this quirky, architecture-obsessed Dutch writer.

Paul Richardson *Our Lady of the Sewers.* An articulate and kaleidoscopic series of insights into rural Spain's customs and cultures, fast disappearing.

★ **Chris Stewart** *Driving Over Lemons – An Optimist in Andalucía.* A funny, insightful and very charming account of life on a remote peasant farm in the Alpujarras where Stewart and his family set up home. The sequel, *A Parrot in the Pepper Tree*, has more stories from the farm interspersed with accounts of some of the author's earlier adventures as a sheep shearer in Sweden, drummer with rock band *Genesis*, and greenhorn flamenco guitarist in Sevilla.

Jason Webster *Duende – A Journey in Search of Flamenco.* Author Webster sets off on a Spanish odyssey to learn flamenco guitar, which takes him to Alicante, Madrid and finally Granada, with quite a few emotional encounters and upsets along the way.

Robert White *A River in Spain.* Well-written account of an American's love affair with the Duero valley; strong on towns, history, architecture and local folklore.

★ **James Woodall** *In Search of the Firedance: Spain through Flamenco.* This is a terrific history and exploration of flamenco, and as the subtitle suggests it is never satisfied with "just the music" in getting to the heart of the culture.

Earlier twentieth-century writers

★ **Gerald Brenan** *South From Granada.* An enduring classic. Brenan lived in a small village in the Alpujarras in the 1920s, and records this and the visits of his Bloomsbury contemporaries Virginia Woolf, Lytton Strachey and Bertrand Russell.

Camilo José Cela *Journey to the* *Alcarria.* A Nobel Prize-winner for literature, Cela explored a hidden corner of New Castile in 1946 – a study of a rural world that no longer exists.

★ **Laurie Lee** *As I Walked Out One Midsummer Morning, A Rose For Winter, A Moment of War. One Midsummer Morning* is the irresistibly romantic account of Lee's walk through Spain – from Vigo to Málaga – and his gradual awareness of the forces moving the country towards Civil War. As an autobiographical novel, of living rough and busking his way from the Cotswolds with a violin, it's a delight; as a piece of social observation, painfully sharp. In *A Rose For Winter* he describes his return, twenty years later, to Andalucía, while in *A Moment of War* he looks back again to describe a winter fighting with the International Brigade in the Civil War – by turns moving, comic and tragic.

Alfonso Lowe *Companion Guide to the South of Spain.* A travel classic

from the 1970s. Idiosyncratic account of southern Spain, often recording an Andalucía long gone – packed with fascinating background.

James A. Michener *Iberia.* A best-selling, idiosyncratic and encyclope-dic compendium of interviews and impressions of Spain on the brink – in 1968 – looking forward to the post-Franco years. Fascinating, still.

★ **George Orwell** *Homage to Catalonia.* Stirring account of Orwell's participation in the early exhilaration of revolution in Barcelona, and his growing disillu-sionment with the factional fighting among the Republican forces during the ensuing Civil War.

Older classics

George Borrow *The Bible in Spain* and *The Zincali* (both o/p). On first publication in 1842, Borrow subti-tled *The Bible in Spain* "Journeys, Adventures and Imprisonments of an English-man"; it is one of the most famous books on Spain – slow in places but with some very amusing stories. *The Zincali* is an account of the Spanish gypsies, whom Borrow got to know pretty well.

★ **Richard Ford** *A Handbook for Travellers in Spain and Readers at Home; Gatherings from Spain.* The *Handbook* (1845) must be the best guide ever written to any country. Massively opinionated, it is an extremely witty book in its British, nineteenth-century manner, and worth flicking through for the proverbs alone. *The Gatherings* is a rather timid – but no less entertain-

ing – abridgement of the general pieces, intended for a female audi-ence who wouldn't have the taste for the more cerebral stuff.

Washington Irving *Tales of the Alhambra* (published 1832; abridged editions are on sale in Granada). Half of Irving's book consists of oriental stories, set in the Alhambra; the rest of accounts of local characters and his own residence there. A perfect read *in situ.*

George Sand *A Winter in Majorca.* Sand and Chopin spent their winter at the monastery of Valldemossa. They weren't entirely appreciated by the locals, in which lies much of the book's appeal. Local editions, includ-ing a translation by late Mallorcan resident Robert Graves, are on sale around the island.

Anthologies

Jimmy Burns (ed) *Spain: A Literary Companion.* A good anthology, including nuggets of most authors recommended here, amid a whole host of others.

David Mitchell *Travellers in Spain: An Illustrated Anthology.* A well-told

story of how four centuries of trav-ellers – and most often travel writers – saw Spain. It's interesting to see Ford, Brenan, Laurie Lee and the rest set in context. Also published as *Here in Spain* (Lookout, Spain), widely available at bookshops in tourist areas.

History

General

Justin Wintle *The Rough Guide History of Spain*. A very readable – and pocketable – background history to the country, which spans the Romans to the present and the maturing of democratic Spain.

M. Vincent and R.A. Stradling *Cultural Atlas of Spain and Portugal*. A formidable survey of the Iberian peninsula from ancient to modern times, in coffee-table format, with excellent colour maps and well-chosen photographs.

Prehistoric and Roman Spain

★ James M. Anderson *Spain: 1001 Sights, An Archeological and Historical Guide*. A good guide and gazetteer to 95 percent of Spain's archeological sites, with detailed instructions on how to get there.
María Cruz Fernandez Castro *Iberia in Prehistory*. A major study of the Iberian peninsula prior to the arrival of the Romans which surveys recent archeological evidence relating to the remarkable technical, economic and artistic progress of the early Iberians.
Roger Collins *Spain: An Archeological Guide*. Covering just 130

sites, this book's more detailed coverage makes it a more useful guide to the major sites than Anderson's work (above).
S.J. Keay *Roman Spain* (British Museum Publications; California UP). Definitive survey of a neglected subject, well illustrated and highly readable.
John Richardson *Roman Spain*. This recent assessment of the period, which includes recent discoveries and excavations, is part of a fourteen-volume history of Spain, covering prehistoric times to the present.

Early, medieval and beyond

J.M. Cohen *The Four Voyages of Christopher Columbus*. The man behind the myth; one of the best books on Columbus in English.
Roger Collins *The Arab Conquest of Spain 710–97*. Controversial study which documents the Moorish invasion and the significant influence that the conquered Visigoths had on early Muslim rule. Collins's earlier *Early Medieval Spain 400–1000* (Macmillan, UK) takes a broader overview of the same subject.
John A. Crow *Spain: The Root and the Flower*. Cultural/social history from Roman Spain to the present.
★ J.H. Elliott *Imperial Spain 1469–1716*. The best introduction to the "Golden Age" – academi-

cally respected and a gripping tale.
★ Richard Fletcher *The Quest for El Cid* and *Moorish Spain*. Two of the best studies of their kind – fascinating and highly readable narratives. The latter is a masterly introduction to the story of the Moors in Spain.
L.P. Harvey *Islamic Spain 1250–1500*. Comprehensive account of its period – both the Islamic kingdoms and the Muslims living beyond their protection.
David Howarth *The Voyage of the Armada*. An account from the Spanish perspective of the personalities, from king to sailors, involved in the Armada.

Henry Kamen *The Spanish Inquisition.* Highly respected examination of the Inquisition and the long shadow it cast across Spanish history. *The Spanish Inquisition: An Historical Revision* returns to the subject in the light of more recent evidence, while his *Philip of Spain* is the first full biography of Felipe II, the ruler most associated with the Inquisition. In his latest book *Spain's Road to Empire* Kamen skilfully dissects the conquest of the Americas and Philippines and concludes that the Spanish were ill-suited to the imperial role, displaying both organizational incompetence and little interest in the peoples they subjugated.

Elie Kedourie *Spain and the Jews: the Sephardi Experience, 1492 and After.* A collection of essays on the three million Spanish Jews of the Middle Ages and their expulsion by the Catholic kings.

John Lynch *Spain 1598–1700* and *Bourbon Spain: 1700–1808.* Two further volumes in the Blackwells project, written by the General Editor, dealing with Spain's rise to Empire and the critical Bourbon period.

Colin Smith, Charles Melville and Ahmad Ubaydli *Christians and Moors in Spain.* A fascinating collection of documents by Spanish and Arabic writers from the Muslim conquest to the Christian supremacy, which is intended for the lay reader as well as the academic.

The twentieth century

Gerald Brenan *The Spanish Labyrinth.* First published in 1943, Brenan's account of the background to the Civil War is tinged by personal experience, yet still an impressively rounded account.

Raymond Carr *Modern Spain 1875–1980* and *The Spanish Tragedy: the Civil War in Perspective.* Two of the best books available on modern Spanish history – concise and well-told narratives.

Ronald Fraser *Blood of Spain.* Subtitled "Oral History of the Spanish Civil War" this is an equally impressive piece of research.

Ian Gibson *Federico García Lorca, The Assassination of Federico García Lorca* and *Lorca's Granada.* The biography is a compelling book and *The Assassination* a brilliant reconstruction of the events at the end of his life, with an examination of fascist corruption and the shaping influences on Lorca, twentieth-century Spain and the Civil War. *Granada* contains a series of walking tours around parts of the town familiar to the poet.

Gerald Howson *Arms for Spain: the Untold Story of the Spanish Civil War.* This important book uses Russian and Polish archives to reveal how the Republicans were double-crossed by almost every foreign government they attempted to purchase arms from (including the Nazis) during the war – with their avowed ally Moscow one of the major culprits.

Paul Preston *Franco* and *Concise History of the Spanish Civil War.* A penetrating – and monumental – biography of Franco and his regime, which provides as clear a picture as any of how he won the Civil War and survived in power so long. *Civil War* is a compelling introduction to the subject and more accessible than Thomas's work (below).

Adrian Shubert *A Social History of Spain.* Comprehensive and highly readable analysis of social development in Spain from 1800 to the 1980s.

Hugh Thomas *The Spanish Civil War.* This exhaustive 1000-page study is regarded (both in Spain and abroad) as the definitive history of the Civil War.

Paddy Woodworth *Dirty War, Clean Hands: ETA, the GAL and Spanish Democracy*. This important and impeccably researched work analyzes what happens when a democracy abandons the rule of law and shows how the shocking policies of Gonzalez's government on the Basque Country actually strengthened rather than defeated revolutionary terrorism.

⭐ **Gamel Woolsey** *Malaga Burning*. A long ignored minor classic written in the late 1930s and recently reprinted (and retitled) by a US publisher in which the American poet and wife of Gerald Brenan vividly describes the horrors of the descent of their part of Andalucía into civil war.

Art, architecture, photography, film and design

Marianne Barrucand and Achim Bednoz *Moorish Architecture*. A beautifully illustrated guide to the major Moorish monuments.

Bernard Bevan *History of Spanish Architecture* (o/p). Classic study of Iberian and Ibero-American architecture which includes extensive coverage of the Mudéjar, Plateresque and Baroque periods.

Hugh Broughton *Madrid: A Guide to Recent Architecture*. Modern Spanish architecture is at the cutting edge of world design and this is a fluent and pocketable guide to a hundred of the best examples in Madrid, each with its own photo and directions.

Jerrilyn D. Dodds *Al-Andalus*. An in-depth study of the arts and monuments of Moorish Andalucía, put together as a catalogue for a major exhibition at the Alhambra.

Godfrey Goodwin *Islamic Spain*. Portable architectural guide with descriptions of virtually every significant Islamic building in Spain, and a fair amount of background.

Robert Irwin *The Alhambra*. A detailed tour of the building by art expert Irwin who puts the palace in its Islamic context by attempting to determine how the palace actually functioned as a building. The account concludes with an appraisal of the impact of the Alhambra on modern culture.

⭐ **Michael Jacobs** *Alhambra*. Sumptuously produced volume with outstanding photographs and expert commentary. Authoritatively guides you through the history and architecture of the Alhambra, and concludes with a fascinating essay on the hold the palace has had on later artists, travellers and writers, from Irving and Ford to de Falla and Lorca.

⭐ **Cristina García Rodero** *Festivals and Rituals of Spain* and *España Oculta*. *Festival and Rituals* is a mesmerizing photographic record of the exuberance and colour of Spain's many fiestas by Spain's most astonishing contemporary photographer. *Oculta* is an equally atmospheric collection of black and white pictures celebrating the country's religion and mysticism.

Gabriel Ruiz Cabrero *The Modern in Spain*. This readable book is a clear, comprehensive study of postwar Spanish architecture. The author is an architect and professor in the renowned Faculty of Architecture at Madrid's *Politécnica*.

Meyer Schapiro *Romanesque Art*. An excellent illustrated survey of Spanish Romanesque art and architecture – and its Visigothic and Mozarabic predecessors.

Suzanne Slesin et al *Spanish Style*. A gorgeous photographic compendium of Spanish style, old and new, in everything from its statuary and *azulejo* tilework to modern furniture and interiors.

Fréderic Strauss *Almodóvar on Almodóvar*. Frank conversations between Strauss and the Spanish film director concentrate on the work rather than the hype, punctuated by Almodóvar's contagious humour.

Fiction and poetry

Spanish classics

Pedro de Alarcón *The Three-Cornered Hat*. Ironic nineteenth-century tales of the previous century's corruption, bureaucracy and absolutism.

Leopoldo Alas *La Regenta* (European Schoolbook). Alas's nineteenth-century novel, with its sweeping vision of the disintegrating social fabric of the period, is a kind of Spanish *Madame Bovary* (a book that it was in fact accused of plagiarizing at time of publication).

Ramón Pérez de Ayala *Belarmino and Apolonio* and *Honeymoon, Bittermoon*. A pair of tragi-comic picaresque novels written around the turn of the twentieth century.

Emilia Pardo Bazán *The House of Ulloa*. Bazán was an early feminist intellectual and in this, her best-known book, she charts the decline of the old aristocracy in the time of the Glorious Revolution of 1868.

⭐ **Miguel de Cervantes** *Don Quixote* and *Exemplary Stories*. *Quixote* is of course the classic of Spanish literature and still an excellent read. If you want to try Cervantes in a more modest dose, the *Stories* are a good place to start.

Benito Pérez Galdós *Fortunata and Jacinta*. Galdós wrote in the last decades of the nineteenth century and his novels of life in Madrid combine comic scenes and social realism; he is often characterized as a "Spanish Balzac". Other Galdós novels available in translation include *Misericordia, Nazarín*, and the epic *"I"*.

⭐ **Saint Teresa of Ávila** *The Life of Saint Teresa of Ávila*. Saint Teresa's autobiography is said to be the most widely read Spanish classic after *Don Quixote*. It takes some wading through but it's fascinating in parts. Various translations are available.

Modern fiction

Felipe Alfau *Locos: A Comedy of Gestures*. Though Alfau emigrated to New York and wrote in English (in the 1930s and 1940s), his novels are very Spanish; also well ahead of their time in terms of style, so perhaps not the easiest of reads.

⭐ **Bernardo Atxaga** *Obabakoak*. This challenging novel by a Basque writer won major prizes on its Spanish publication. It is a sequence of tales of life in a Basque village and the narrator's search to give them meaning.

⭐ **Arturo Barea** *The Forging of a Rebel* (o/p). Superb autobiographical trilogy, taking in the Spanish war in Morocco in the 1920s, and Barea's own part in the Civil War. The books have been published in UK paperback editions

under the individual titles *The Forge, The Track* and *The Clash*.

Javier Cercas *Soldiers of Salamis*. Literary-prizewinning "true story" of the Spanish Civil War by up-and-coming Spanish writer Cercas. An often gripping tale about the search for the soldier who spared the life of Falange-founder Sánchez Mazas.

Michel del Castillo *The Disinherited*. Riveting account of Madrid during the Civil War, written in 1959.

Victor Català (Caterina Albert i Paradís) *Solitude* (o/p). This tragic tale of a woman's life and sexual passions in a Catalan mountain village is regarded as the most important pre-Civil War Catalan novel.

Juan Luís Cebrián *Red Doll*. Easy-to-read thriller set in post-Franco years, involving Basque terrorists, the KGB, right-wing backlash and, of course, romance.

★ **Camilo José Cela** *The Family of Pascual Duarte*. Nobel Prize-winner Cela was considered integral to the revival of Spanish literature after the Civil War, though his reputation is compromised by his involvement with Franco's government. *Pascual Duarte*, his first and best-known novel, portrays the brutal story of a peasant murderer from Extremadura, set against the backdrop of the fratricidal Civil War.

★ **Juan Goytisolo** *Marks of Identity, Count Julian, Juan the Landless, Landscapes after the Battle, Quarantine*. Born in Barcelona in 1931, Goytisolo became a bitter enemy of the Franco regime, and has spent most of his life in self-exile, in Paris and in Morocco. He is perhaps the most important modern Spanish novelist, confronting, above all in his great trilogy (comprising the first three titles listed above), the whole ambivalent idea of Spain and Spanishness, as well as being one of the first Spanish writers to deal openly with homosexuality. The more recent *Quarantine* documents a journey into a Dante-esque netherworld in which the torments of hell are set against reportage of the Gulf War. Goytisolo has also written an autobiography, *Forbidden Territory*.

Montserrat Lunati (ed) *Rainy Days: Short Stories by Contemporary Spanish Women Writers*. This impressive collection (with Spanish parallel text) has work by celebrated literary lights such as Rosa Montero and Maruja Torres.

★ **Javier Marias** *Tomorrow in the Battle Think on Me*. There are many who rate Marias as Spain's finest contemporary novelist – and the evidence is here in this searching, psychological thriller, with its study of the human capacity for concealment and confession. Harvill also publishes two other Marias novels, *A Heart So White* and *All Souls*.

Ana María Matute *School of the Sun*. The loss of childhood innocence on a Balearic island, where old enmities are redefined during the Civil War.

★ **Manuel Vázquez Montalban** *Murder in the Central Committee, Southern Seas, An Olympic Death, The Angst Ridden Executive* and *Off Side*. Montalban was, until his death in 2003, one of Spain's most influential writers. A long-time member of the Communist Party, he lived in Barcelona, like his great creation, the gourmand private detective Pepe Carvalho, who stars in all of his wry and racy crime thrillers. The one to begin with – indeed, a bit of a classic – is *Murder in the Central Committee*.

★ **Arturo Pérez Reverte** *The Seville Communion*. Entertaining crime yarn by one of Spain's leading writers played out against the colourfully described backdrop of Sevilla. Pérez Reverte's latest book in Spanish, *La Reina del Sur* (Queen of the South; Alfaguera, Madrid), took the Spanish best-seller lists by storm and relates the story of a woman drug trafficker running narcotics between Morocco and Cádiz.

Julián Ríos *Larva*. Subtitled *Midsummer Night's Babel, Larva* is a large, complex, postmodern novel by a leading Spanish literary figure, published to huge acclaim in Spain.

Javier Tomo *The Coded Letter* and *Dear Monster*. A pair of Kafkaesque tales from one of Spain's leading post-Franco-era novelists.

If you can read **Spanish**, the following modern novelists are also of interest: **Luís Martín Santos** (*Tiempo de Silencio*); **Alfonso Grosso** (*Con Flores a María*); **Mariano Antolín** (*Wham!, Hombre Arañal* – the Spanish William Burroughs); **Montserrat Roig** (best of contemporary feminist writers); **Rafael Sánchez Ferlosio** (*El Jarama, Alfanhuí*); **Pío Baroja** (*El Arbol de la Ciencia*); and **Miguel Delibes** (*El Camino*, or any others).

Plays and poetry

Pedro Calderón de la Barca *Life is a Dream and other Spanish Classics, The Mayor of Zalamea*. Some of the best works of the great dramatist of Spain's "Golden Age".

⊟★ **Federico García Lorca** *Five Plays: Comedies and Tragicomedies*. Andalucía's great pre-Civil War playwright and poet.

Lope de Vega The nation's first important playwright (b. 1562)

wrote literally hundreds of plays, many of which, including *Lo Cierto por lo Dudoso* (A Certainty for a Doubt) and *Fuenteobvejuna* (The Sheep Well), remain standards of classic Spanish theatre.

⊟★ **J.M. Cohen (ed)** *The Penguin Book of Spanish Verse*. Spanish poetry from the twelfth century to the modern age, with (parallel text) translations from all the major names.

Spain in foreign fiction

Harry Chapman *Spanish Drums*. An engaging thriller, telling of an Englishwoman outsider's entry into the life of a family in Teruel – and her discovery of all the terrible baggage of its Civil War past.

Kathryn Harrison *A Thousand Orange Trees*. A complex and intense novel set during the Inquisition in the seventeenth century.

⊟★ **Ernest Hemingway** *The Sun Also Rises* and *For Whom the Bell Tolls*. Hemingway remains a big part of the American myth of Spain – *The Sun Also Rises* contains some lyrically beautiful writing, while the latter is a good deal more laboured. He also published an enthusiastic and not very good account of bullfighting, *Death in the Afternoon*.

Arthur Koestler *Dialogue with Death* (o/p). Koestler was reporting the Civil War in 1937 when he was captured and imprisoned by Franco's troops – this is essentially his prison diary.

⊟★ **Matthew Lewis** *The Monk*. You'd be hard-pressed to find a more gripping holiday read than this thriller, set in a Capuchin monastery in Madrid, with its tale of lustful monks, evil abbesses, rape, incest and murder. And oddly enough it's a

classic novel, the most Gothic of the genre, first published in 1796.

⊟★ **Norman Lewis** *Voices of the Old Sea*. Lewis lived in Catalunya from 1948 to 1952, just as tourism was starting to arrive. This book is an ingenious blend of novel and social record, charting the breakdown of the old ways in the face of the "new revolution". The same author's *The Tenth Year of the Ship* is a superb tale about the devastating impact modernization and speculative investment has on the mythical Spanish island of Vedra after a steamboat link is established.

⊟★ **Amin Malouf** *Leo the African*. A wonderful historical novel, re-creating the life of Leo Africanus, the fifteenth-century Moorish geographer, in the last years of the kingdom of Granada, and on his subsequent exile in Morocco and world travels.

Colm Tóibín *The South*. First novel by the Irish writer, who spent the early 1990s in Barcelona. The city is the setting for his tale of an Irish woman looking for a new life after fleeing her boring, middle-class family for a lover and a new life in Catalunya.

Specialist guidebooks

⊟★ **Phil Ball** *Morbo – The Story of Spanish Football* (When Saturday

Comes Books, UK). Excellent account of the history of Spanish football from its nineteenth-century beginnings with the British workers at the mines of Río Tinto in Huelva to the golden years of Real Madrid and the dark days of Franco, with the ever-present backdrop of the ferocious rivalry or *morbo* – political, historical, regional and linguistic – which has driven the Spanish game since its birth. Essential reading for every football aficionado visiting Spain. *White Storm – 100 years of Real Madrid* (Mainstream, UK) is more than a history of Spain's legendary team, probing the murkier evidence of Real's links with Franco, corrupt Madrid politics, and neo-Nazi supporters, and it also attempts to evaluate the club's place in the modern Spanish psyche.

Bob Carrick *Ventas Within a Short Drive of the Costa del Sol.* Useful guide to some of the best *ventas* – Spain's bargain roadside restaurants – within easy reach of the Málaga coast.

The pilgrim route to Santiago

La Ruta de Plata a Pie y en Bicicleta (El País/Aguilar, Spain). Spanish guide to the alternative (and lesser-known) pilgrim route to Santiago, the Ruta de Plata – from Sevilla via Mérida, Cáceres and Salamanca. Also has detailed itinerary of the same route for cyclists.

Millán Bravo Lozano *A Practical Guide for Pilgrims: The Road to Santiago* (Everest). Colourful, informative guide. Includes separate map pages so you can leave the heavy guide at home.

Bethan Davies and Ben Cole *Walking the Camino de Santiago* (Pili Pala Press). Extensive directions, detailed sketch maps, information about culture, food and drink, flora and fauna.

David M. Gitlitz and Linday Kay Davidson *The Pilgrimage Road to Santiago: The Complete Cultural Handbook* (St Martin's Griffin). Hefty, detailed guide to churches, cathedrals and other cultural sights along the camino.

John Higginson *Le Puy to Santiago – A Cyclist's Guide.* A cyclist's guide to the pilgrim route which follows as closely as possible (on tarmac) the walker's path, visiting all the major sites en route.

★ **Edwin Mullins** *The Pilgrimage to Santiago* (o/p). This is a travelogue rather than a guide, but is by far the best book on the Santiago legend and its fascinating medieval pilgrimage industry.

Alison Raju *The Way of St James: Le Puy to the Pyrenees (vol I)* and *Pyrenees–Santiago-Finisterre (vol II)*. Walking guide to the Pilgrims Route divided between the French and Spanish sections. Written by an experienced Iberian hiker and including maps and background information as well as practical information. In *The Via de Plata* she also covers the lesser-known pilgrim route.

David Wesson *The Camino Francés* (Confraternity of St James). Annually updated basic guide to the camino, with directions and accommodation.

Trekking and cycling

Rodney Ansell *Landscapes of Menorca.* Walking and touring guide with plenty of background detail on the Balearic island's prehistoric sites.

David and Ros Brawn *Thirty-four Alpujarras Walks.* Walking guide to this outstandingly picturesque corner of Andalucía, ranging from half an hour to full-day treks.

Matt Butler *Holiday Walks from the Costa del Sol.* Holiday walks within reach of a Costa del Sol base, covering the coast from Cádiz province in in the west to Granada province in the east. Free Internet updates available.

Robin Collomb *Picos de Europa, Sierra de Gredos* and *Sierra Nevada*, plus others (West Col, UK). Detailed guides aimed primarily at serious trekkers and climbers.

Valerie Crespi-Green *Landscapes of Mallorca*. Aimed at fairly casual walkers and picnickers. Sunflower Books also publish reliable and well-researched walking and trekking guides on the Picos de Europa, the Canary Islands, Menorca, Catalunya and the Costa Blanca.

Harry Dowdell *Cycle Touring in Spain*. Well-researched cycle touring guide which describes eight touring routes of varying difficulty in the north and south of Spain. Plenty of practical information on preparing your bike for the trip, transporting it, plus what to take.

★ **Teresa Farino** *Picos de Europa*. An excellent walking and touring guide which details walks in these zones, giving special emphasis to flora and fauna.

★ **Guy Hunter-Watts** *Walking in Andalucía*. First-rate walking guide to the Natural Parks of Grazalema, Cazorla, Los Alcornocales, Aracena and La Axarquía, as well as the Alpujarras and the Sierra Nevada, with 32 walks of various lengths, each with a colour map.

Paul Jenner and Christine Smith *Landscapes of the Pyrenees*. Trips and hikes by authors resident in the Spanish Pyrenees.

Paul Lucia *Through the Spanish Pyrenees: GR11 Long Distance Footpath*. Updated guide to the GR11, a high-level and recently waymarked trail which crosses the Spanish Pyrenees from coast to coast.

Jacqueline Oglesby *The Mountains of Central Spain*. Walking and scrambling guide to the magnificent Sierras de Gredos and Guadarrama by resident author.

John and Christine Oldfield *Andalucía and the Costa del Sol*. This addition to the popular *Landscapes* walking guide series has 23 clearly described walks (with maps) ranging from 5km to 22km in Las Alpujarras, Sierra Nevada, Axarquía and Grazalema, as well as the areas bordering the Costa del Sol. The same authors have also produced the similar-format *Landscapes of the Costa Blanca* detailing walks and trips along the Valencia-Alicante coast.

June Parker *Walking in Mallorca*. This popular guide is now in its third edition, with many new treks.

Jeremy Rabjohns *Holiday Walks in the Alpujarra*. Excellent small walking guide by Alpujarras resident Rabjohns describing 24 walks between 3 and 22km in length with clear maps (including many village street maps) and background information. Free updates and corrections available on the Internet.

Kev Reynolds *Walks and Climbs in the Pyrenees*. User-friendly guide for trekkers and walkers, though half devoted to the French side of the frontier.

Bob Stansfield *Costa Blanca Mountain Walks*. Two-volume set (sold separately) of walks in this little-known, but spectacular, area near Alicante. Volume 1 covers the western Costa Blanca, Volume 2 the eastern sector.

Peter Stone *Madrid Escapes*. Madrid resident Stone describes twenty journeys (by car or public transport) an hour from the capital to interesting country towns with plenty to see both in and around them. Details a number of walks, as well as places to stay and eat, and provides background info.

Robin Walker *Walks and Climbs in the Picos de Europa*. New guide by experienced resident mountaineer.

Andy Walmsley *Walking in the Sierra Nevada*. Reliable coverage of 45 routes, with details of flora and fauna – from easy short walks in the Alpujarras to ascents of the highest peaks.

Derek Workman *Inland Trips from the Costa Blanca*. Useful car-tour guide to finding your way around the scenic backroads near the Costa Blanca (south and east of Valencia). Describes rural customs, cultures and village fiestas and recommends places to eat, drink and stay en-route.

In Spanish, look out for the excellent series of guides published by Sua Edizioak of Bilbao. These include *Topoguias* and *Rutas y Paseos* covering most of the individual Spanish sierras and mountain regions, and a superb range of regional guides for cyclists, *En Bici*, functionally ring-bound, with detailed maps and route contours. The Barcelona-based map publisher Editorial Alpina (⑩ www.editorialalpina.com) has an equally good range of 1:25,000 to 1:40,000 walking maps and guides covering Andalucía, Catalunya, the Pyrenees, the Picos de Europa and other parts of Spain. The reliable Penthalon guides, available from major bookshops in Spain, detail walks in various regions throughout the country.

Wildlife

Clive Finlayson and David Tomlinson *Birds of Iberia*. Reference work rather than field guide, this new book has superb photos of most of the birds to be seen on the Iberian peninsula with detailed descriptions of species and habitats.

★ Frederic Grunfeld and Teresa Farino *Wild Spain*. A knowledgeable and practical guide to Spain's national parks, ecology and wildlife.

Peterson, Mountfort and Hollom *Collins Field Guide to the Birds of Britain and Europe*. Standard reference book – covers most birds in Spain.

Oleg Polunin and Anthony Huxley *Flowers of the Mediterranean*. Useful if by no means exhaustive field guide.

Oleg Polunin and B. E. Smythies *Flowers of South-West Europe*. Covers all of Spain, Portugal and southwest France; taxonomy is old, but still unsurpassed for its plates, line drawings and keys.

K.J. Stoba *Bird Watching in Mallorca*. Guide listing 282 species and where and when to see them.

Food and wine

Coleman Andrews *Catalan Cuisine*. Best available English-language book dealing with Spain's most adventurous regional cuisine. Nicholas Butcher *The Spanish Kitchen*. A practical and knowledgeable guide to creating Spanish dishes when you get back. Lots of informative detail on tapas, olive oil, *jamón serrano* and herbs.

Penelope Casas *The Foods and Wines of Spain*. Superb Spanish cookbook, covering classic and regional dishes with equal, authoritative aplomb. By the same author is the useful *Tapas: the little dishes of Spain*.

Sam and Sam Clark *Moro*. Cookbook based on the successful fusion of Spanish, Portuguese and North African cuisine in evidence at the much-lauded *Moro* restaurant in London. The recipes take time to prepare, but the results are worth it. Alan Davidson *The Tio Pepe Guide to the Seafood of Spain and Portugal*. An indispensable book that details and illustrates every fish and crustacean you're likely to meet in restaurants and bars along the Spanish costas.

★ Julian Jeffs *Sherry*. The story of sherry – history, production, blending and brands. Rightly a classic and the best introduction to Andalucía's great wine.

Jean Claude Juston *The New Spain – Vegan and Vegetarian Restaurants.* (Imprenta Generalife, Spain; copies available from Apartado Postal 126, 18400 Órjiva, or Ⓦ www.vegetarian-guides.com). Very useful guide to vegetarian and vegan restaurants throughout Spain by the owner/chef of a vegetarian restaurant in Las Alpujarras.

Mark and Kim Millon *Wine Roads of Spain.* Everything you ever wanted to know about Spanish wine

and sherry: when, how and where it's made, with a good array of useful maps.

John Radford *The New Spain.* Lavish coffee-table format disguises this book's serious content – a detailed region-by-region guide to Spanish wine with colour maps, *bodega* and vintage evaluations and fine illustrations.

Jan Read *Guide to the Wines of Spain.* Encyclopedic (yet pocketable) guide to the classic and emerging wines of Spain by a leading authority. Includes maps, vintages and vineyards.

Learning Spanish and living in Spain

Breakthrough Spanish The best of the tape- and book-linked home study courses which aims to give you reasonable fluency within three months. The same series has advanced and business courses.

⭐ **Collins Spanish Dictionary** Recognized as the best single-volume bookshelf dictionary. Regularly revised and updated, so make sure to get the latest edition.

⭐ **Get by in Spanish** (BBC Publications, UK; book and cassette). One of the BBC's excellent crash-course introductions which gets you to survival-level Spanish (bars, restaurants, asking the way, etc) in a couple of weeks.

Jonathon Packer *Live and Work in Spain and Portugal.* Well-researched handbook full of useful information on moving to the peninsula, buying

property, seeking work, starting a business, finding schools and lots more.

⭐ **Learn Spanish Now!** (Transparent Language UK/US; Ⓦ www.transparent.com). CD-rom based interactive course incorporating all kinds of gadgets enabling you to compare your pronunciation with a native speaker, access web-based additional learning resources and play skill-improving interactive games. The same publisher's *Wordace Spanish Translation Dictionary* provides an entertaining way – via games and puzzles – to improve vocabulary and verb skills and gives model pronunciation.

⭐ **Rough Guide Spanish Dictionary** Good pocket-size dictionary which should help with most travel situations.

Català

Digui Digui (published by the Generalitat de Catalunya) is the best way of learning Català with a total immersion course consisting of a series of books and tapes presented entirely in Catalan; you'll need to speak Castilian to take this on. In Britain, the best place to find it is Grant & Cutler, 55 Great

Marlborough St, London W1 (☎ 020/7734 2012). *Teach Yourself Catalan* (Hodder & Stoughton) is less ambitious (and presented in English); while if you're serious you'll also need *Catalan Grammar* (Dolphin Book Company) and *Parla Català* (Pia), the only available English–Catalan phrasebook.

Language

Language

Language

O nce you get into it, Spanish is the easiest language there is. English is spoken, but wherever you are you'll get a far better reception if you at least try communicating with Spaniards in their own tongue. Being understood, of course, is only half the problem – getting the gist of the reply, often rattled out at a furious pace, may prove far more difficult.

The rules of **pronunciation** are straightforward and, once you get to know them, strictly observed. Unless there's an accent, words ending in d, l, r and z are **stressed** on the last syllable, all others on the second last. All **vowels** are pure and short; combinations have predictable results.

A somewhere between the "A" sound of back and that of father.

E as in get.

I as in police.

O as in hot.

U as in rule.

C is lisped before E and I, hard otherwise: *cerca* is pronounced "thairka" (though in Andalucía many natives pronounce the soft "c" as an "s").

G works the same way, a guttural "H" sound (like the ch in loch) before E or I, a hard G elsewhere – *gigante* becomes "higante".

H is always silent.

J the same sound as a guttural G: *jamón* is pronounced "hamon".

LL sounds like an English Y or LY: *tortilla* is pronounced "torteeya/tor-teelya".

N is as in English unless it has a tilde (accent) over it, when it becomes NY: *mañana* sounds like "manyana".

QU is pronounced like an English K.

R is rolled, RR doubly so.

V sounds more like B, *vino* becoming "beano".

X has an S sound before consonants, normal X before vowels. More common in Basque, Gallego or Catalan words where it's sh or zh.

Z is the same as a soft C, so *cerveza* becomes "thairvaitha" (but again much of the south prefers the "s" sound).

The list of a few essential words and phrases overleaf should be enough to get you started, though if you're travelling for any length of time a dictionary or phrasebook is obviously a worthwhile investment. If you're using a **dictionary**, bear in mind that in Spanish CH, LL, and Ñ count as separate letters and are listed after the Cs, Ls and Ns respectively.

Basics

Yes, No, OK	*Sí, No, Vale*	With, Without	*Con, Sin*
Please, Thank you	*Por favor, Gracias*	Good, Bad	*Buen(o)/a, Mal(o)/a*
Where, When	*Dónde, Cuando*	Big, Small	*Gran(de), Pequeño/a*
What, How much	*Qué, Cuánto*	Cheap, Expensive	*Barato, Caro*
Here, There	*Aquí, Allí*	Hot, Cold	*Caliente, Frío*
This, That	*Esto, Eso*	More, Less	*Más, Menos*
Now, Later	*Ahora, Más tarde*	Today, Tomorrow	*Hoy, Mañana*
Open, Closed	*Abierto/a, Cerrado/a*	Yesterday	*Ayer*

Greetings and responses

Hello, Goodbye	*Hola, Adiós*	English?	*inglés?*
Good morning	*Buenos días*	I (don't) speak	*(No) Hablo español*
Good afternoon/	*Buenas tardes/*	Spanish	
night	*noches*	My name is...	*Me llamo. . .*
See you later	*Hasta luego*	What's your	*¿Como se llama*
Sorry	*Lo siento/disculpéme*	name?	*usted?*
Excuse me	*perdón/Con permiso*	I am English/	*Soy inglés(a)/*
How are you?	*¿Como está (usted)?*	Australian/	*australiano(a)/*
I (don't) understand	*(No) Entiendo*	Canadian/	*canadiense(a)/*
Not at all/	*De nada*	American/	*americano(a)/*
You're welcome		Irish	*irlandés(a)*
Do you speak	*¿Habla (usted)*		

Hotels and transport

LANGUAGE

L

I want	*Quiero*	nearby?	*aquí cerca?*
I'd like	*Quisiera*	How do I get to...?	*¿Por donde se*
Do you know...?	*¿Sabe...?*		*va a...?*
I don't know	*No sé*	Left, right,	*Izquierda, derecha,*
There is (is there)?	*(¿)Hay(?)*	straight on	*todo recto*
Give me...	*Deme...(uno así)*	Where is...?	*¿Dónde está....?*
(one like that)		the bus station	*la estación de*
Do you have...?	*¿Tiene...?*		*autobuses*
the time	*la hora*	the train station	*la estación de*
a room	*una habitación*		*station ferro-carril*
...with two beds/	*...con dos camas/*	the nearest bank	*el banco mas cercano*
double bed	*cama matrimonial*	the post office	*el correos/la oficina*
...with shower/bath	*...con ducha/baño*		*de correos*
It's for one person	*Es para una persona*	the toilet	*el baño/aseo/servicio*
(two people)	*(dos personas)*	Where does the	*¿De dónde sale el*
for one night	*para una noche*	bus to...leave	*autobús para...?*
(one week)	*(una semana)*	from?	
It's fine, how	*¿Está bien,*	Is this the train	*¿Es este el tren*
much is it?	*cuánto es?*	for Mérida?	*para Mérida?*
It's too expensive	*Es demasiado caro*	I'd like a (return)	*Quisiera un billete*
Don't you have	*No tiene algo*	ticket to...	*(de ida y vuelta)*
anything cheaper?	*más barato?*		*para...*
Can one...?	*¿Se puede....?*	What time does it	*¿A qué hora sale*
camp (near) here?	*¿...acampar aquí*	leave (arrive in...)?	*(llega a...)?*
	(cerca)?	What is there to	*¿Qué hay para*
Is there a hostel	*¿Hay un hostal*	eat?	*comer?*

| What's that? | ¿Qué es eso? | in Spanish? | este en español? |
| What's this called | ¿Como se llama | | |

Numbers and days

one	un/uno/una	ninety	noventa
two	dos	one hundred	cien(to)
three	tres	one hundred and one	ciento uno
four	cuatro	two hundred	doscientos
five	cinco	two hundred and one	doscientos uno
six	seis	five hundred	quinientos
seven	siete	one thousand	mil
eight	ocho	two thousand	dos mil
nine	nueve	two thousand and one	dos mil un
ten	diez	two thousand and two	dos mil dos
eleven	once	two thousand and three	dos mil tres
twelve	doce	first	primero/a
thirteen	trece	second	segundo/a
fourteen	catorce	third	tercero/a
fifteen	quince	fifth	quinto/a
sixteen	diez y seis	tenth	décimo/a
twenty	veinte	Monday	lunes
twenty-one	veintiuno	Tuesday	martes
thirty	treinta	Wednesday	miércoles
forty	cuarenta	Thursday	jueves
fifty	cincuenta	Friday	viernes
sixty	sesenta	Saturday	sábado
seventy	setenta	Sunday	domingo
eighty	ochenta		

Menu reader

Basics

Aceite	Oil	Miel	Honey
Ajo	Garlic	Pan	Bread
Arroz	Rice	Pimienta	Pepper
Azúcar	Sugar	Sal	Salt
Huevos	Eggs	Vinagre	Vinegar
Mantequilla	Butter		

Meals

Almuerzo/Comida	Lunch	Desayuno	Breakfast
Botella	Bottle	Menú del día	Fixed-price set
Carta	Menu		meal
Cena	Dinner	Mesa	Table
Comedor	Dining room	Platos combinados	Mixed plate
Cuchara	Spoon	Tenedor	Fork
Cuchillo	Knife	Vaso	Glass
La cuenta	The bill		

Soups (*Sopas*) and starters

Caldillo	**Clear fish soup**	*Sopa de cocido*	**Meat soup**
Caldo	**Broth**	*Sopa de gallina*	**Chicken soup**
Caldo verde or	**Thick cabbage-**	*Sopa de mariscos*	**Seafood soup**
gallego	**based broth**	*Sopa de pescado*	**Fish soup**
Ensalada	**(Mixed/green)**	*Sopa de pasta*	**Noodle soup**
(mixta/verde)	**salad**	*(fideos)*	
		Verduras con patatas	**Boiled potatoes**
Pimientos rellenos	**Stuffed peppers**		**with greens**
Sopa de ajo	**Garlic soup**		

Fish (*Pescados*)

Anchoas	**Anchovies (fresh)**	*Merluza*	**Hake**
Anguila/Angulas	**Eel/Elvers**	*Mero*	**Perch**
Atún	**Tuna**	*Pez espada*	**Swordfish**
Bacalao	**Cod (often salt)**	*Rape*	**Monkfish**
Bonito	**Tuna**	*Raya*	**Ray, skate**
Boquerones	**Small, sardine-like**	*Rodaballo*	**Turbot**
	fish	*Salmonete*	**Mullet**
Chanquetes	**Whitebait**	*Sardinas*	**Sardines**
Lenguado	**Sole**	*Trucha*	**Trout**

Seafood (*Mariscos*)

Almejas	**Clams**	*Ostras*	**Oysters**
Arroz con mariscos	**Rice with seafood**	*Paella*	**Classic Valencian**
Calamares	**Squid (in ink)**		**dish with saffron**
(en su tinta)			**rice, chicken,**
Centollo	**Spider-crab**		**seafood, etc**
Cigalas	**King prawns**	*Percebes*	**Goose-barnacles**
Conchas finas	**Large scallops**	*Pulpo*	**Octopus**
Gambas	**Prawns/shrimps**	*Sepia*	**Cuttlefish**
Langosta	**Lobster**	*Vieiras*	**Scallops**
Langostinos	**Crayfish**	*Zarzuela de*	**Seafood casserole**
Mejillones	**Mussels**	*mariscos*	
Nécora	**Sea-crab**		

Some common terms

al ajillo	**in garlic**	*cazuela, cocido*	**stew**
asado	**roast**	*en salsa*	**in (usually tomato)**
a la Navarra	**stuffed with ham**		**sauce**
a la parrilla/plancha	**grilled**	*frito*	**fried**
a la Romana	**fried in batter**	*guisado*	**casserole**
al horno	**baked**	*rehogado*	**sautéed**
alioli	**with garlic**		
	mayonnaise		

Meat (*Carne*) and Poultry (*Aves*)

Callos	Tripe	*Hígado*	Liver
Carne de buey	Beef	*Lacón con grelos*	Gammon with
Cerdo	Pork		turnips
Chuletas	Chops	*Lengua*	Tongue
Cochinillo	Suckling pig	*Lomo*	Loin (of pork)
Codorniz	Quail	*Pato*	Duck
Conejo	Rabbit	*Pavo*	Turkey
Cordero	Lamb	*Perdiz*	Partridge
Escalopa	Escalope	*Pollo*	Chicken
Fabada asturiana/	Hotpot with butter	*Riñones*	Kidneys
Fabes a la catalana	beans, black	*Solomillo*	Sirloin steak
	pudding, etc	*Solomillo de cerdo*	Pork tenderloin
Hamburguesa	Hamburger	*Ternera*	Beef/Veal

Vegetables (*Legumbres*)

Acelga	Chard	*Lechuga*	Lettuce
Alcachofas	Artichokes	*Lentejas*	Lentils
Arroz a la cubana	Rice with fried egg	*Menestra/Panache*	Mixed vegetables
	and tomato sauce	*de verduras*	
Berenjenas	Aubergine/eggplant	*Nabos/Grelos*	Turnips
Cebollas	Onions	*Patatas*	Potatoes
Champiñones/Setas	Mushrooms	*Patatas fritas*	French fries (chips)
Coliflor	Cauliflower	*Pepino*	Cucumber
Espárragos	Asparagus	*Pimientos*	Peppers/capsicums
Espinacas	Spinach	*Pisto manchego*	Ratatouille
Garbanzos	Chickpeas	*Puerros*	Leeks
Habas	Broad/fava beans	*Puré*	Mashed potato
Judías blancas	Haricot beans	*Repollo*	Cabbage
Judías verdes,	Green, red, black	*Tomate*	Tomato
rojas, negras	beans	*Zanahoria*	Carrot

Fruits (*Frutas*)

Albaricoques	Apricots	*Melocotones*	Peaches
Cerezas	Cherries	*Melón*	Melon
Chirimoyas	Custard apples	*Naranjas*	Oranges
Ciruelas	Plums, prunes	*Nectarinas*	Nectarines
Dátiles	Dates	*Peras*	Pears
Fresas	Strawberries	*Piña*	Pineapple
Granada	Pomegranate	*Plátanos*	Bananas
Higos	Figs	*Sandía*	Watermelon
Limón	Lemon	*Toronja/Pomelo*	Grapefruit
Manzanas	Apples	*Uvas*	Grapes

Desserts (*Postres*)

Arroz con leche	Rice pudding	*Helado*	Ice cream
Crema catalana	Catalan crème	*Melocotón en*	Peaches in syrup
	brûlée	*almíbar*	
Cuajada	Cream-based	*Membrillo*	Quince paste
	dessert served	*Nata*	Whipped cream
	with honey	*Natillas*	Custard
Flan	Crème caramel	*Yogur*	Yogurt

Cheese

Cheeses (*quesos*) are on the whole local, though you'll get the hard, salty *queso manchego* everywhere. Mild sheep's cheese (*queso de oveja*) from the León province is widely distributed and worth asking for.

Standard tapas and raciones

Aceitunas	**Olives**	*Garbanzos*	**Chick peas**
Albóndigas	**Meatballs**	*Gambas*	**Prawns**
Anchoas	**Anchovies**	*Habas*	**Broad beans**
Berberechos	**Cockles**	*Habas con jamón*	**Broad beans with**
Boquerones	**Anchovies**		**ham**
Cabrillas	**Large snails with**	*Hígado*	**Liver**
	tomato	*Huevo cocido*	**Hard-boiled egg**
Calamares	**Squid**	*Jamón serrano*	**Dried ham (like**
Callos	**Tripe**		**Parma ham)**
Caracoles	**Snails**	*Mejillones*	**Mussels**
Carne en salsa	**Meat in tomato**	*Navajas*	**Razor clams**
	sauce	*Patatas alioli*	**Potatoes in garlic**
Champiñones	**Mushrooms, usually**		**mayonnaise**
	fried in garlic	*Patatas bravas*	**Spicy fried potatoes**
Chocos	**Deep-fried cuttlefish**	*Pimientos*	**Peppers**
Chorizo	**Spicy sausage**	*Pincho moruno*	**Kebab**
Cocido	**Stew**	*Pisto*	**Ratatouille**
Empanadilla	**Fish/meat pasty**	*Pulpo*	**Octopus**
Ensaladilla rusa	**Russian salad**	*Riñones al Jerez*	**Kidneys in sherry**
	(diced vegetables	*Salchicha*	**Sausage**
	in mayonnaise)	*Sepia*	**Cuttlefish**
Escalibada	**Aubergine (egg**	*Tortilla española*	**Potato omelette**
	plant) and pepper	*Tortilla francesa*	**Plain omelette**
	salad		

Glossary of Spanish and architectural terms

Alameda Park or grassy promenade.

Alcazaba Moorish castle.

Alcázar Moorish fortified palace.

Apse Semicircular recess at the altar (usually eastern) end of a church.

Ayuntamiento/ajuntament Town hall.

Azulejo Glazed ceramic tilework.

Barrio Suburb or quarter.

Bodega Cellar, wine bar or warehouse.

Calle Street.

Capilla Mayor Chapel containing the high altar.

Capilla Real Royal Chapel.

Capital Top of a column.

Cartuja Carthusian monastery.

Castillo Castle.

Chancel Part of a church containing the altar, usually at the east end.

Churrigueresque Extreme form of Baroque art named after José Churriguera (1650–1723) and his extended family, its main exponents.

Colegiata Collegiate (large parish) church.

Convento Monastery or convent.

Coro Central part of church built for the choir.

Coro Alto Raised choir, often above west door of a church.

Correos Post office.

Corrida de Toros Bullfight.

Crypt Burial place in a church, usually under the choir.

Custodia Large receptacle for Eucharist wafers.

Dueño/a Proprietor, landlord/lady.

Ermita Hermitage.

Gitano Gypsy or Romany.

Hórreo Granary.

Iglesia Church.

Isabelline Ornamental form of late Gothic developed during the reign of Isabel and Fernando.

Loggia Covered area on the side of a building, usually arcaded.

Lonja Stock exchange building.

Mercado Market.

Mihrab Prayer niche of Moorish mosque.

Mirador Viewing point.

Modernisme (Modernista) Catalan/Spanish form of Art Nouveau, whose most famous exponent was Antoni Gaudí.

Monasterio Monastery or convent.

Morisco Muslim Spaniard subject to medieval Christian rule – and nominally baptized.

Mozárabe Christian subject to medieval Moorish rule; normally allowed freedom of worship, they built churches in an Arab-influenced manner (Mozarabic).

Mudéjar Muslim Spaniard subject to medieval Christian rule, but retaining Islamic worship; most commonly a term applied to architecture which includes buildings built by Moorish craftsmen for the Christian rulers and later designs influenced by the Moors. The 1890s to 1930s saw a Mudéjar revival, blended with Art Nouveau and Art Deco forms.

Narthex Entrance hall of church.

Nave Central space in a church, usually flanked by aisles.

Palacio Aristocratic mansion.

Parador Luxury hotel, often converted

from minor monument.

Paseo Promenade; also the evening stroll thereon.

Patio Inner courtyard.

Plateresque Elaborately decorative Renaissance style, the sixteenth-century successor of Isabelline forms. Named for its resemblance to silversmiths' work (*platería*).

Plaza Square.

Plaza de Toros Bullring.

Portico Covered entrance to a building.

Posada Old name for an inn.

Puerta Gateway, also mountain pass.

Puerto Port.

Raciones Large plate of tapas for sharing.

Reja Iron screen or grille, often fronting a window.

Reliquary Receptacle for a saint's relics, usually bones. Often highly decorated.

Reredos Wall or screen behind an altar.

Retablo Altarpiece.

Ría River estuary in Galicia.

Río River.

Romería Religious procession to a rural shrine.

Sacristía, Sagrario Sacristy or sanctuary of church – room for sacred vessels and vestments.

Sardana Catalan folk dance.

Seo, Seu, la Se Ancient/regional names for cathedrals.

Sidreria Bar specializing in cider.

Sierra Mountain range.

Sillería Choir stall.

Solar Aristocratic town mansion.

Taifa Small Moorish kingdom, many of which emerged after the disintegration of the Córdoba caliphate.

Telefónica The phone company; also used for its offices in any town.

Transepts The wings of a cruciform church, placed at right angles to the nave and chancel.

Tympanum Area between lintel of a doorway and the arch above it.

Turismo Tourist office.

Vault Arched ceiling.

Political parties and acronyms

CNT Anarchist trade union.

Convergencia I Unio Conservative party in power in Catalunya.

ETA Basque terrorist organization. Its political wing is Euskal Herritarrok.

Falange Franco's old fascist party; now officially defunct.

Fuerza Nueva Descendants of the above, also on the way out.

IU Izquierda Unida, broad-left alliance of communists and others.

MC Movimiento Comunista (Communist Movement), small radical offshoot of the PCE.

MOC Movimiento de Objeción de Conciencia, peace group, concerned with NATO and conscription.

OTAN NATO.

PCE Partido Comunista de España (Spanish Communist Party).

PNV Basque Nationalist Party – in control of the right-wing autonomous government.

PP Partido Popular, the centre-right alliance formed by Alianza Popular and the Christian Democrats. The PP is currently Spain's government, under José María Aznar.

PSOE Partido Socialista Obrero Español, the Spanish Socialist Workers' Party, and the main opposition party, led by José Luis Rodríguez, elected in July 2000.

UGT Unión General de Trabajadores, the Spanish TUC.

Rough Guides

advertiser

Rough Guides travel...

ROUGH GUIDES ADVERTISER

...music & reference

Index

and small print

A Rough Guide to Rough Guides

In the summer of 1981, Mark Ellingham, a recent graduate from Bristol University, was travelling round Greece and couldn't find a guidebook that really met his needs. On the one hand there were the student guides, insistent on saving every last cent, and on the other the heavyweight cultural tomes whose authors seemed to have spent more time in a research library than lounging away the afternoon at a taverna or on the beach.

In a bid to avoid getting a job, Mark and a small group of writers set about creating their own guidebook. It was a guide to Greece that aimed to combine a journalistic approach to description with a thoroughly practical approach to travellers' needs – a guide that would incorporate culture, history and contemporary insights with a critical edge, together with up-to-date, value-for-money listings. Back in London, Mark and the team finished their Rough Guide, as they called it, and talked Routledge into publishing the book.

That first *Rough Guide to Greece*, published in 1982, was a student scheme that became a publishing phenomenon. The immediate success of the book – with numerous reprints and a Thomas Cook prize shortlisting – spawned a series that rapidly covered dozens of destinations. Rough Guides had a ready market among low-budget backpackers, but soon also acquired a much broader and older readership that relished Rough Guides' wit and inquisitiveness as much as their enthusiastic, critical approach. Everyone wants value for money, but not at any price.

Rough Guides soon began supplementing the "rougher" information about hostels and low-budget listings with the kind of detail on restaurants and quality hotels that independent-minded visitors on any budget might expect, whether on business in New York or trekking in Thailand.

These days the guides – distributed worldwide by the Penguin group – offer recommendations from shoestring to luxury and cover more than 200 destinations around the globe, including almost every country in the Americas and Europe, more than half of Africa and most of Asia and Australasia. Our ever-growing team of authors and photographers is spread all over the world, particularly in Europe, the USA and Australia.

In 1994, we published the *Rough Guide to World Music* and *Rough Guide to Classical Music*; and a year later the *Rough Guide to the Internet*. All three books have become benchmark titles in their fields – which encouraged us to expand into other areas of publishing, mainly around popular culture. Rough Guides now publish:

- Travel guides to more than 200 worldwide destinations
- Dictionary phrasebooks to 22 major languages
- History guides ranging from Ireland to Islam
- Maps printed on rip-proof and waterproof Polyart™ paper
- Music guides running the gamut from Opera to Elvis
- Restaurant guides to London, New York and San Francisco
- Reference books on topics as diverse as the Weather and Shakespeare
- Sports guides from Formula 1 to Man Utd
- Pop culture books from *Lord of the Rings* to Cult TV
- World Music CDs in association with World Music Network

Visit **www.roughguides.com** to see our latest publications.

Rough Guide credits

Text editor: Lucy Ratcliffe
Layout: Diana Jarvis
Cartography: Manish Chandra
Picture research: Mark Thomas
Proofreader: Jan Wiltshire
....

Editorial: London Martin Dunford, Kate Berens, Helena Smith, Claire Saunders, Geoff Howard, Ruth Blackmore, Gavin Thomas, Polly Thomas, Richard Lim, Lucy Ratcliffe, Clifton Wilkinson, Alison Murchie, Fran Sandham, Sally Schafer, Alexander Mark Rogers, Karoline Densley, Andy Turner, Ella O'Donnell, Keith Drew, Andrew Lockett, Joe Staines, Duncan Clark, Peter Buckley, Matthew Milton; **New York** Andrew Rosenberg, Richard Koss, Yuki Takagaki, Hunter Slaton, Chris Barsanti, Thomas Kohnstamm, Steven Horak
Design & layout: London Helen Prior, Dan May, Diana Jarvis; **Delhi** Madhulita Mohapatra, Umesh Aggarwal, Ajay Verma

Production: Julia Bovis, John McKay, Sophie Hewat
Cartography: **London** Maxine Repath, Ed Wright, Katie Lloyd-Jones; **Delhi** Manish Chandra, Rajesh Chhibber, Jai Prakash Mishra, Ashutosh Bharti, Rajesh Mishra, Animesh Pathak
Cover art direction: Louise Boulton
Picture research: Sharon Martins, Mark Thomas, Jj Luck
Online: New York Jennifer Gold, Cree Lawson, Suzanne Welles; **Delhi** Manik Chauhan, Amarjyoti Dutta, Narender Kumar
Marketing & publicity: London Richard Trillo, Niki Smith, David Wearn, Chloë Roberts, Demelza Dallow, Kristina Pentland; **New York** Geoff Colquitt, David Wechsler, Megan Kennedy
Finance: Gary Singh
Manager India: Punita Singh
Series editor: Mark Ellingham
PA to Managing director: Julie Sanderson
Managing director: Kevin Fitzgerald

Publishing information

This 11th edition published April 2004 by **Rough Guides Ltd**,
80 Strand, London WC2R 0RL.
345 Hudson St, 4th Floor,
New York, NY 10014, USA.
Distributed by the Penguin Group
Penguin Books Ltd,
80 Strand, London WC2R 0RL
Penguin Putnam, Inc.
375 Hudson Street, NY 10014, USA
Penguin Books Australia Ltd,
487 Maroondah Highway, PO Box 257,
Ringwood, Victoria 3134, Australia
Penguin Books Canada Ltd,
10 Alcorn Avenue, Toronto, Ontario,
Canada M4V 1E4
Penguin Books (NZ) Ltd,
182–190 Wairau Road, Auckland 10,
New Zealand
Typeset in Bembo and Helvetica to an original design by Henry Iles.

Printed in Italy by LegoPrint S.p.A

© 2004

1152pp includes index
A catalogue record for this book is available from the British Library

ISBN 1-84353-261-1

1 3 5 7 9 8 6 4 2

SMALL PRINT

Help us update

We've gone to a lot of effort to ensure that the 11th edition of **The Rough Guide to Spain** is accurate and up to date. However, things change – places get "discovered", opening hours are notoriously fickle, restaurants and rooms raise prices or lower standards. If you feel we've got it wrong or left something out, we'd like to know, and if you can remember the address, the price, the time, the phone number, so much the better.

We'll credit all contributions, and send a copy of the next edition (or any other Rough Guide if you prefer) for the best letters. Everyone who writes to us and isn't already a subscriber will receive a copy of our full-colour thrice-yearly newsletter. Please mark letters: "**Rough Guide Spain Update**" and send to: Rough Guides, 80 Strand, London WC2R 0RL, or Rough Guides, 4th Floor, 345 Hudson St, New York, NY 10014. Or send an email to **mail@roughguides.com**

Have your questions answered and tell others about your trip at **www.roughguides.atinfopop.com**

1139

Acknowledgements

Simon Baskett Special thanks to Trini once again for all her hard work and patience. Thanks, too, go to Clifton, Lucy, Antonio and all those who gave recommendations or advice for this edition.

Marc Dubin thanks Niki Forsyth and Richard Cash in Echo, Michael and Rosi Peters at La Miana, Richard and Sandra Loder at Santa Engràcia, David and Consell Bardaji in Taüll.

J.J. Kennedy Thanks to María Andersson, Emilio Balanzó, Maria Casanovas i Codina, Helmut Clemens, Mirella d'Angelo, Tomeu Deyà, Oriol Galgo, Suzanne Hartley, Carlos Baqués Meler, Britta Ploenzke, Anna Skidmore, Ricarda Söhnlein, Mike Suarez, The Suau Family, Davina, et al.

Sarah Lazarus would like to thank the kind taxi driver in León who prevented her car being towed away, and Neale for being so wonderful and for making the tea.

Chris Lloyd Many thanks to Concepció Bascompte, Isabel Godoy and Anna Suades; Saulo Matute Montessori and David Griffiths; special thanks to Liz as ever.

Iain Stewart Thanks above all to the Home boys (Massimo, Fabio, Sergio, Sacci) and Vivekka for great times, bar crawls and paella hunts. I'll be back. Josep Ferri of Valencia Turisme and Will McCarthy of Valencia 24-7 also helped out considerably, as did tourist offices up and down the Comunitat, and in Murcia. Fee and Louis Yoshi were great company. And Santiago – you're a genius.

Readers' letters

Our continued thanks to everyone who has contributed letters, comments, accounts and suggestions over the years, and especially to this 2004 edition.

In particular: P. & L. Acheson, Palmer Adreson, D. Amis, Luke Andrew, Wendy Ashworth, J. H. Aston, Dr Jenny G. Atton, John Bainbridge, David John Barton, Toni Bauchamp, Tom Bengoechea, Steve Bennett, Rob Bishop, M. Bonnett, Ian Bouncer & John Bowen, Tim Bowles, Mike Braide, Caroline Bragg, Rod Braxton, M Brearley, Andrew Brown, Jeff Brown, Christine Brown, Thomas Brown, A Buckland, Tim Bullick, Stefano Burattini, Chris & Marion, Vivienne Carmichael, Janine Carter, George & Emily Cassedy, Eugenia Caumel, Fiona Clampin, Anthony Claff, Di Clarke, Peter Clinch, Sarah Cockings & Alex Crocker, David Cole, Natale Coleman, Shirin Cooper, Paul Connell & Helen Gill, Damon Crawshaw, David Crompton, Tom Crow, Robert Crouch, Eddy le Couvreur, David Daly, Tom Danson, Thomas Daubney & Julia Huddart, Francis Davey, Colin Davies, Frank Davison, Jean & Robin Dods, Lorna Dudgeon, J.F. Eade, Tina Emmott, Susan Elliott, Harry & Denise Failey, Julian Fenn, Heather Fielding, Hugh Finn, Richard Flint, Imogen Forster, Liz Fosbury, Marion Fraser, Barry & Audrie Gant, Becky Gethin, Alice Goddard, Bren & Rob Golder, Peter Goos & Marijke Van Cotthem, Robert Gossling, Sean Gostage, Alma Gould, Lucy & David Green, Tom Green, Amanda & Adrian Grainger, Pyrs Gruffudd, Andrew Guppy, Caroline Hadley, Nick Halstead, Nicola Hambridge, Sam Hardie, Lee Harris, Susie & Kevin Harris, Terry Harper, Felicity Harvest, Carole Hayward, Stephen Hayward, Mike Hibbs, Marion & Derek Hills, Priscilla Hon, Jane Horton, Steven Graham, Päivi Gröndahl & H. Tormanen, Stephen Hrynczak, John Ireland, Elizabeth Johnson, Jaan Johnson, Philip Livingstone, Manya L. Johnson, Frances Jones, Thomas H. Jones, Agnes Kazmierczak, Paul Keeley, Elizabeth Key, John Knight & Juliet Molteno, Emma Lambourne, Paul Lampard, John Landau, Prof Tim Lang, Barbara Lee, D. Lee, Ingrid H. Legat-Crawley, Brannus Legranus, Nicholas Levinge, Ciel van der Lugt, Frances MacGowan, Family Mahieu, Abe Marrache, Marion Marples, Nancy Martinez, Monica Martinez, Jane Maxwell, Barbara & John May, Jeremy May, Martin Maytarn, Gregg Mccabe, Rachel McGill, Matt McLauchlin, David McManus, Rebecca McQuillan, Lai Mie Wright, Lia Mills, Keith Mitchell, Juliet Molteno, John Montre, Clare & Richard Morgan, Carol Mosby, Marilyn Mowbray, Murray Muraskin, P.J. Newey, Eabhan Ni, Waikeen Ng, Chris & Pete Nichols, Richard Owerr, Juliane Palm, Ian Pearson, Famile Phipps, Alex Pike, Patricia Quaife & Francis Davey, Margaret Ratcliff, Phil Riley & Ann Paslar, Aleksander & Monika Rokicki, Eric & Sally Rowland, Michael Rowlandson, Geraldine Russell, Dermot Ryan, Carol Saddingto, Rocco Salata, The Sandhams, Robert Sandham, Arlene Sandler, Julian Sanders, Mary Saso, Anthony Schlesinger, Pauline Sharma, Sol Shaz, Jan Shepherd, Shuileabhain, R. Sinclair, Pete J.W. Smith, Robert Smith, Brigid Spillane, Mabel Stewart, Julia Stine, Julia Stone, R.T. & J.C. Stuart, Ruth Stuber, Naomi & Laura Sutton, Alastair Tainsh, Kate Tangri, Joyce Taylor, W.H. Thomas, D.J. Thompson, Michael Thompson, Toby, Paul Vandehey, John Waddington, Brian Wallis, Jean Wallace, Janine Wanner, Selina Westbury, Olive Williams, Philip Williams, Adrian Whittaker &

Deena Omar, Peter Wickenden, Annie Wickens, Anna Wike, Steve Williford, David & Irene

Williamson, Avril & Kevin Wincomb, Dr. Barrie Wharton, Debbie & Rex Whitrow

Photo credits

Cover credits

Main front: Alcázar, Segovia © Getty
Small front top: Tiles, Toledo © Getty
Small front lower: Picos de Europa © Robert Harding
Back top: Olive groves © Getty
Back lower: La Mancha © Robert Harding

Colour introduction

Tapas Bar © Heidi Grassle/Axiom
Field of sunflowers © David Ball
Andalucian tiles © Peter Wilson
Aigües Tortes-Sant Maurici © Marc Dubin
Chillies © Chris Coe/Axiom
Pilgrims' shells and staff on the Camino de Santiago © K. Gillham/Robert Harding
Plaza Callao, Madrid © Peter Wilson
Galician coastline © Joel W. Rogers/Corbis
Tapas © Owen Franken/Corbis
La Tomatina festival, Valencia © Roberto Arakaki/Robert Harding

Things not to miss

Guggenheim Museum, Bilbao © Neil Setchfield
Skiers, Sierra Nevada © Skishoot-offshoot
Jamon Serrano © Neil Setchfield
Goya, Saturn Devouring One Of His Sons © theartarchive/Museu del Prado/Dagli Orti
Las Alpujarras © Robert Harding
Picasso, Guernica 1937 © Succession Picasso/DACS 2004 supplied by theartarchive/Renia Sofia Museum, Madrid
Salamanca © Peter Wilson
La Pedrera, Gaudí, Barcelona © Neil Setchfield
Las Fallas © Rob Cousins/Robert Harding
Semana Santa, Málaga © Neil Setchfield
Imperial eagle © J.A. Bailey/Ardea London Ltd
Paella © Neil Setchfield
Port Aventura © Ruth Tomlinson/Robert Harding
Carnival © Peter Wilson
Picos de Europe © N & J Wiseman/Trip
Seafood © John & Lisa Merrill/Corbis
Velázquez, Las Meninas © theartarchive/ Museu del Prado Madrid/Album/Josep Martin
San Fermín, Pamplona © Renzo Frontoni/Axiom
Ibiza & Formentera's beaches © Vicki Couchman/Axiom
Pouring sherry © Trip
Fundació Joan Miró, Barcelona © Jerry Dennis
The Pyrenees © Marc Dubin
Roman aqueduct, Segovia © Neil Setchfield
Clubbing in Ibiza © Leelu Morris/PYMCA
Real Madrid © EMPICS/Alejandro Fernández
Tapas bar sign © Neil Setchfield
Spanish Lynx © Ardea
Rioja vineyard © N. Egerton/Travel Ink
Mini-Hollywood, Almeria © Robert Frerck/Robert Harding

Mies Van der Rohe Pavilion, Barcelona © Jerry Dennis
Mezquita, Cordoba © Peter Wilson
The Rastro, Madrid © Michael Jenner
Feria de Abril, Sevilla © Robert Frerck/Robert Harding
Parador D'Alarcón © Trip
Giralda, Sevilla © Peter Wilson
Dalí Museum, Figueres © Steve Hines/Travel Ink
Alhambra, Granada © Michael Jenner
Flamenco © Francesca Yorke/Axiom
Windsurfing, Tarifa © N & J Wiseman/Trip
Toledo © Neil Setchfield
El Camino de Santiago, Galicia © H. Rogers/Trip

Black & whites

Royal Palace, Madrid © Patrick Ward/Corbis (p.70)
Café con leche, Plaza Santa Ana (p.96)
Tiled tapas bar © Neil Setchfield (p.131)
Avila city walls © Adam Woolfitt/Corbis (p.148)
Manzanares el Real castle © Abilio Lope/Corbis (p.173)
La Mancha windmills © Max Alexande/DK (p.196)
Storks' nests © Adam Woolfitt/Robert Harding (p.218)
Señoritas © Geoff Garvey (p.252)
Casares, Andalucía © Trip (p.276)
Sevilla © Neil Setchfield (p.312)
Burgos cathedral, © Archivo Iconografico S.A./Corbis (p.410)
Santo Domingo de Silos © Sarah Lazarus (p.464)
La Concha, San Sebastián © Marc Dubin (p.482)
Guggenheim Museum, Bilbao © Neil Setchfield (p.514)
Picos de Europa © Marc Dubin (p.546)
Castro Urdiales © DK (p.559)
Granary, Galicia © Max Alexander/DK (p.600)
Santiago de Compostela © Jeremy Philips/Travel Ink (p.612)
Ordesa National Park © Viesti Collection/Trip (p.660)
Nuestra Señora del Pilar, Zaragoza © Peter Wilson (p.669)
Casa Batló, Barcelona © Andrew Brown (p.712)
La Boqueria market, Barcelona © Ian Cumming/Axiom (p.735)
Antigua Casa Figueres, Las Ramblas © Heidi Grassley/DK (p.784)
Costa Brava coastline © Max Alexander/DK (p.790)
Saint Climent de Taüll © Max Alexander/DK (p.908)
La Ciudad de las Artes y Ciencias © Iain Stewart (p.912)
L'Hemisfèric © Iain Stewart (p.924)
Palma cathedral, Mallorca © Paul Miles/Axiom (p.966)
Benirràs Bay, Ibiza © Robert Frerck/Robert Harding (p.981)

Index

Map entries are in colour

A

INDEX

O

1143

N

INDEX

Map symbols

maps are listed in the full index using coloured text

▬▬▬	Motorway	🕌	Mosque
▬▬▬	Tolled motorway	⛪	Monastery
═══	Major road	✡	Synagogue
═══	Minor road	Ⓣ	Tram stop
▬▬▬	Pedestrianized street	Ⓜ	Metro station
⊞⊞⊞⊞	Steps	⊖	Cercanías station
═▬═▬	Railway	★	Bus stop
⋯⋯⋯	Funicular railway	Ⓐ	Campsite
•--•	Cable car	▣	Restaurant
-----	Footpath	◉	Accommodation
— —	Ferry route	⬠	Mountain refuge
▬▬▬	Coastline/river	⸙	Chapel
▰▰▰	Wall	⛪	Monastery
─ ─ ─	Chapter division boundary	⊞	Hospital
▬▬ ··	Provincial border	ⓘ	Tourist office
▬▬ ·─	International boundary	✉	Post office
♦	Point of interest	@	Internet access
▲	Mountain peak	ℂ	Telephone office
⛰	Mountain range	⚲	Skiing
⚘	Viewpoint	⛵	Swimming pool
⸙	Rocks	)(	Bridge
🗼	Lighthouse	▭	Market
✈	Airport	▬	Building
⌂	Cave	⊞	Church
⚱	Waterfall	▦	Park
⚘	Gardens	▦	Beach
⚘	Spa	▱	Saltpan